Worship Planning For Today's Episcopal Church

RitePlanning includes everything you need to plan worship every week with ease and flexibility!

- A comprehensive library of liturgical and music resources
- Fully customizable templates
- Content for special services and celebrations
- Accessible online anywhere, anytime

Learn more about this new and exciting program and start your 14-day free trial at www.riteplanning.com

riteplanning

RitePlanning is a product of Church Publishing Incorporated and is hosted by Augsburg Fortress

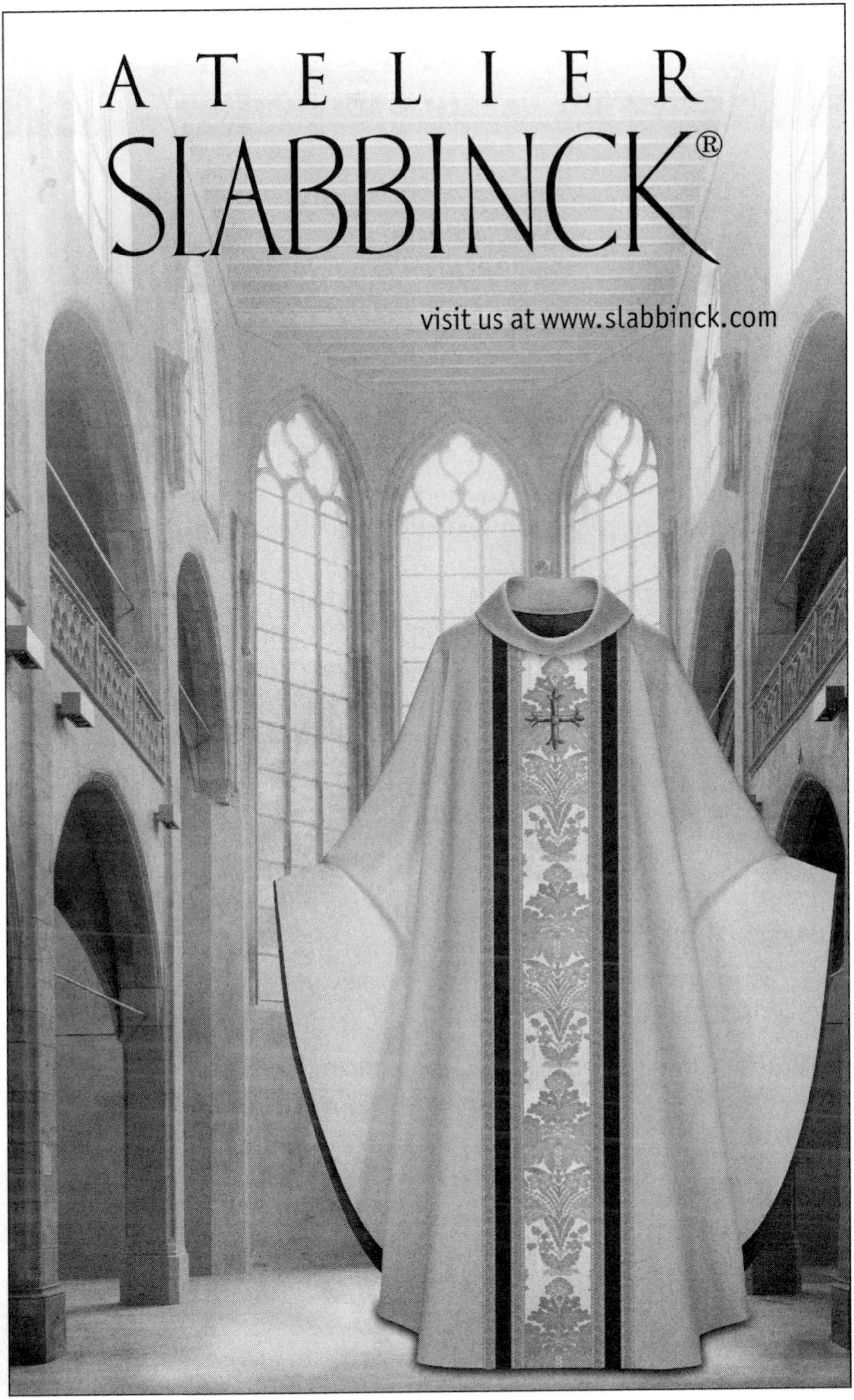
ATELIER
SLABBINCK®
visit us at www.slabbinck.com

The
Episcopal
Church
Annual

2019

General Convention Edition

The Episcopal Church Annual

General Convention Edition

2019

NEW YORK

ISBN-13: 978-1-64065-139-5

9 781640 651395

THE EPISCOPAL CHURCH ANNUAL

Published by

Church Publishing
19 East 34th Street
New York, NY 10016
Fax (212) 779-3392
www.churchpublishing.org

© 2019 by Church Publishing

Information and statistics have been compiled from material supplied by the bishops and secretaries of the dioceses, the Executive Office of the General Convention, The Church Pension Fund, the national, provincial, diocesan, and parochial institutions and organizations of The Episcopal Church and the Anglican Consultative Council. This Annual includes information as of January 1, 2019, which is subject to change.

Although extensive effort was made to assure the accuracy and completeness of the information included in this Annual, Church Publishing Incorporated and its affiliates do not guarantee the accuracy of such information and disclaim any liability associated with this Annual. Please use our website www.theredbook.org or write to the Editor, Episcopal Church Annual, 19 East 34th Street, New York, NY 10016 to report any errors and/or omissions.

Any discrepancy between the clerical status of an individual in this Annual and the official records of The Episcopal Church shall be resolved by reference to such official records. All benefits provided to clergy of The Episcopal Church are governed by the terms of the official plan documents and policies.

ISBN-13: 978-1-64065-139-5

Printed in the United States of America

Contents

SERVING THE EPISCOPAL CHURCH THROUGH THE CENTURIES
TIMELINE OF THE EPISCOPAL CHURCH ANNUAL

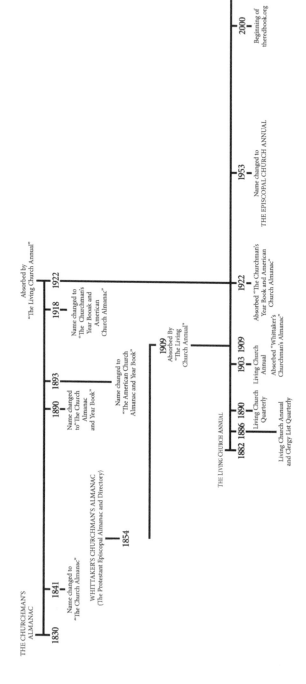

THE CHURCHMAN'S ALMANAC

1830

1841 — Name changed to "The Church Almanac"

WHITTAKER'S CHURCHMAN'S ALMANAC (The Protestant Episcopal Almanac and Directory)

1854

1890 — Name changed to "The Church Almanac and Year Book"

1893 — Name changed to "The American Church Almanac and Year Book"

1918 — Name changed to "The Churchman's Year Boouk and American Church Almanac"

1922 — Absorbed by "The Living Church Annual"

THE LIVING CHURCH ANNUAL

1882 — Living Church Annual and Clergy List Quarterly

1886 — Living Church Annual

1890 — Living Church Quarterly

1903 — Living Church Annual

1909 — Absorbed "Whittaker's Churchman's Almanac"

1909 — Absorbed By "The Living Church Annual"

1922 — Absorbed "The Churchman's Year Book and American Church Almanac"

1953 — Name changed to THE EPISCOPAL CHURCH ANNUAL

2000 — Beginning of theredbook.org

4

DIOCESES WITHIN EACH PROVINCE

Province I
Diocese of Connecticut
Diocese of Maine
Diocese of Massachusetts
Diocese of New Hampshire
Diocese of Rhode Island
Diocese of Vermont
Diocese of Western
  Massachusetts

Province II
Diocese of Albany
Diocese of Central New York
Diocese of Haiti
Diocese of Long Island
Diocese of New Jersey
Diocese of New York
Diocese of Newark
Diocese of Rochester
Diocese of Virgin Islands
Diocese of Western New York
Convocation of American
  Churches in Europe

Province III
Diocese of Bethlehem
Diocese of Central
  Pennsylvania
Diocese of Delaware
Diocese of Easton
Diocese of Maryland
Diocese of Northwestern
  Pennsylvania
Diocese of Pennsylvania
Diocese of Pittsburgh
Diocese of Southern Virginia
Diocese of Southwestern
  Virginia
Diocese of Virginia
Diocese of Washington
Diocese of West Virginia

Province IV
Diocese of Alabama
Diocese of Atlanta
Diocese of Central Florida
Diocese of Central Gulf
  Coast

Diocese of East Carolina
Diocese of East Tennessee
Diocese of Florida
Diocese of Georgia
Diocese of Kentucky
Diocese of Lexington
Diocese of Louisiana
Diocese of Mississippi
Diocese of North Carolina
The Episcopal Church in
  South Carolina
Diocese of Southeast Florida
Diocese of Southwest Florida
Diocese of Tennessee
Diocese of Upper South
  Carolina
Diocese of West Tennessee
Diocese of Western North
  Carolina

Province V
Diocese of Chicago
Diocese of Eastern Michigan
Diocese of Eau Claire
Diocese of Fond du Lac
Diocese of Indianapolis
Diocese of Michigan
Diocese of Milwaukee
Diocese of Missouri
Diocese of Northern Indiana
Diocese of Northern
  Michigan
Diocese of Ohio
Diocese of Southern Ohio
Diocese of Springfield
Diocese of Western Michigan

Province VI
Diocese of Colorado
Diocese of Iowa
Diocese of Minnesota
Diocese of Montana
Diocese of Nebraska
Diocese of North Dakota
Diocese of South Dakota
Diocese of Wyoming
Province VII

Diocese of Arkansas
Diocese of Dallas
Diocese of Fort Worth
Diocese of Kansas
Diocese of Northwest Texas
Diocese of Oklahoma
Diocese of Rio Grande
Diocese of Texas
Diocese of West Missouri
Diocese of West Texas
Diocese of Western Kansas
Diocese of Western Louisiana

Province VIII
Diocese of Alaska
Diocese of Arizona
Diocese of California
Diocese of Eastern Oregon
Diocese of El Camino Real
Diocese of Hawaii
Diocese of Idaho
Diocese of Los Angeles
Diocese of Navajoland
Diocese of Nevada
Diocese of Northern
  California
Diocese of Olympia
Diocese of Oregon
Diocese of San Diego
Diocese of San Joaquin
Diocese of Spokane
Diocese of Taiwan
Diocese of Utah

Province IX
Diocese of Colombia
Diocese of Dominican
  Republic
Diocese of Ecuador Central
Diocese of Ecuador Litoral
Diocese of Honduras
Diocese of Puerto Rico
Diocese of Venezuela

Abbreviations of Dioceses and States

Obvious variants are sometimes used.

A	Albany		**NAM**	Navajoland Area Mission
AK	Alaska		**NB**	Nebraska
AL	Alabama		**NC**	North Carolina
AR	Arkansas		**NCA**	Northern California
At	Atlanta		**ND**	North Dakota
AZ	Arizona		**NH**	New Hampshire
BE	Bethlehem		**NI**	Northern Indiana
C	Chicago		**NJ**	New Jersey
CA	California		**Nk**	Newark
CEcu	Central Ecuador		**NM**	New Mexico (state)
CF	Central Florida		**NMI**	Northern Michigan
CGC	Central Gulf Coast		**NT**	NW Texas
CNY	Central New York		**NV**	Nevada
CO	Colorado		**NWPA**	Northwestern Pennsylvania
Colom	Colombia		**NY**	New York
CPA	Central Pennsylvania		**OH**	Ohio
CT	Connecticut		**OK**	Oklahoma
Dal	Dallas		**OL**	Olympia
DC	District of Columbia		**OR**	Oregon
DE	Delaware		**PA**	Pennsylvania
DomR	Dominican Republic		**Pgh**	Pittsburgh
E	Easton		**PR**	Puerto Rico
EauC	Eau Claire		**quniRG**	Rio Grande
EC	East Carolina		**RI**	Rhode Island
ECR	El Camino Real		**Roch**	Rochester
EcuL	Ecuador Litoral		**SanD**	San Diego
EMI	Eastern Michigan		**SanJ**	San Joaquin
EO	Eastern Oregon		**SC**	South Carolina
Er	Erie		**SD**	South Dakota
ETN	East Tennessee		**SeF**	Southeast Florida
Eur	Europe		**SO**	Southern Ohio
FdL	Fond du Lac		**Sp**	Springfield
FL	Florida		**Spok**	Spokane
FtW	Fort Worth		**SV**	Southern Virginia
GA	Georgia		**SwF**	Southwest Florida
GU	Guam		**SwV**	Southwestern Virginia
Hai	Haiti		**Tai**	Taiwan
HI	Hawaii		**TN**	Tennessee
Hond	Honduras		**TX**	Texas
IA	Iowa		**USC**	Upper South Carolina
ID	Idaho		**UT**	Utah
IL	Illinois		**VA**	Virginia
IN	Indiana		**VEN**	Venezuela
Ind	Indianapolis		**VI**	Virgin Islands
KS	Kansas		**VT**	Vermont
KY	Kentucky		**W**	Washington (dio)
LA	Louisiana		**WA**	Washington (state)
Lex	Lexington		**WI**	Wisconsin
LI	Long Island		**WKS**	Western Kansas
LosA	Los Angeles		**WLA**	Western Louisiana
MA	Massachusetts		**WMI**	Western Michigan
MD	Maryland		**WMA**	Western Massachusetts
ME	Maine		**WMO**	West Missouri
MI	Michigan		**WNC**	Western North Carolina
Mil	Milwaukee		**WNY**	Western New York
MN	Minnesota		**WT**	West Texas
MO	Missouri		**WTN**	West Tennessee
MS	Mississippi		**WV**	West Virginia
MT	Montana		**WY**	Wyoming

Abbreviations Used In The Clergy List
That Differ From The Abbreviations of Dioceses and States List

Ala	Alabama	**NI**	Northern Indiana
Alb	Albany	**NMich**	Northern Michigan
Ark	Arkansas	**Nwk**	Newark
CFla	Central Florida	**NwT**	Northwest Texas
Chi	Chicago	**O**	Ohio
Colo	Colorado	**Okla**	Oklahoma
CP	Central Pennsylvania	**Oly**	Olympia
Del	Delaware	**Ore**	Oregon
DR	Dominican Republic	**SeFla**	Southeast Florida
Eas	Easton	**SJ**	San Joaquin
Eau	Eau Claire	**Spr**	Springfield
Fla	Florida	**SVa**	Southern Virginia
Haw	Hawaii	**SwFla**	Southwest Florida
Ida	Idaho	**SwVa**	Southwestern Virginia
Kan	Kansas	**Tenn**	Tennesseeaa
Los	Los Angeles	**Tex**	Texas
Mass	Massachusetts	**WDC**	Washington
Mich	Michigan	**WK**	Western Kansas
Minn	Minnesota	**WMass**	Western Massachusetts
Miss	Mississippi	**WMich**	Western Michigan
Mont	Montana	**WTenn**	West Tennessee
NCal	Northern California	**WTex**	West Texas
Neb	Nebraska	**WVa**	West Virginia
Nev	Nevada	**Wyo**	Wyoming

Acronyms

AandD	Alcohol and Drugs
AIDS	Acquired Immune Deficiency Syndrome (see also HIV)
BCP	Book of Common Prayer 1979
BSG	Brotherhood of St. Gregory
CA	Church Army Community of the Ascension
CDO	Clergy Deployment Office(r)
CDSP	Church Divinity School of the Pacific
CHC	Church Hymnal Corporation
CPF	Church Pension Fund
COM	Commission on Ministry
CHS	Community of the Holy Spirit
CSJB	Community of St. John the Baptist
CSM	Community of St. Mary
CSSS	Congregation of the Companions of the Holy Savior
DCE	Director/Department of Christian Education
EC	Executive Council
ECL	Executive Council Liaison
ECC	Episcopal Church Center
EDS	Episcopal Divinity School
ECW	Episcopal Church Women
ECS	Episcopal Community Services
ESMA	Episcopal Society for Ministry on Aging
ETSW	Episcopal Theological Seminary of the Southwest
FODC	Franciscan Order of the Divine Compassion
GTS	General Theological Seminary
HIV	Human Immunodeficiency Virus
LAND	Leadership Academy for New Directions
NCC	National Council of Churches
NECAD	National Episcopal Coalition on Alcohol and Drugs
OCP	Order of the Community of the Paraclete
OHC	Order of the Holy Cross
OSA	Order of St. Augustine Order of St. Anne
OSB	Order of St. Benedict
OSH	Order of St. Helena
OSL	Order of St. Luke the Physician
RACA	Recovered Alcoholic Clergy Association
RC	Roman Catholic
SSC	Society of the Holy Cross
SSF	Society of St. Francis
SSJE	Society of St. John the Evangelist
SSM	Society of St. Margaret
SSP	Society of St. Paul
USAF	United States Air Force
USA	United States Army
USN	United States Navy
WCC	World Council of Churches

Partial List of Abbreviations
NAMES

Adv	Advent	M	Martyr
Alb	Alban	Magd	Magdalene
All SS	All Saints	Mer	Merciful
Amb	Ambrose	Med	Mediator
Ancn	Annunciation	Mem	Memorial
Ang	Angels	Mes	Messiah
Ant(h)	Ant(h)ony	Miss	Mission
Apos	Apostle(s), Apostól	Mt	Mount
Arim	Arimathaea	Mths	Matthias
Ben	Benedict	Mthw	Matthew
Beth	Bethany	O	Our
Ble	Bless, Blessed	Pr	Prince
Cbury	Canterbury	Par	Parish
Chap	Chapel	Raph	Raphael
Chrys	Chrysostom	Rdmn	Redemption,
Comf	Comforter		Redemción
Comm	Communion	Rdmr	Redeemer
Cong	Congregation	Recon	Reconciliation
Crux	Crucifixion	Resr	Resurrection,
Cyp	Cyprian		Resurrección
Dun	Dunstan	S	Saint, San
Edm	Edmund		(in parish name)
Edw	Edward	SS	Saints
Emm	Emmanuel	Sac	Sacrament
Evan	Evangelist	Sav	Savior
Faith	Faithful	Shpd	Shepherd
Fell	Fellowship	Sim	Simon, Simeon
Gab	Gabriel	Seb	Sebastian
Gd	Good	Smtn	Samaritan
Geo	George	St	Saint
Geth	Gethsemane		(in other names)
Gr	Grace	Sta	Santa
H	Holy	Ste	Sainte
Heav	Heavenly		(in other names)
Ign	Ignatius	Thad	Thaddeus
Incsn	Intercession	Theo	Theodore
K	King	Trsfg	Transfiguration,
Law(u)	Law(u)rence		Transfiguracción
Lk	Luke	V	Virgin, Virgen

8

Other Abbreviations

accom	accommodations Admin Administrative	Lit	Liturgy, Liturgics
Amb	Ambassador	lm	lay missioner
Angl	Anglican	lr	lay reader
Archdcn	Archdeacon	lt	loc ten (locum tenens)
Bdwy	Broadway	lv	lay vicar
Bp	Bishop	Min	Ministry, Minister
c	curate	Miss	Missioner, Missionary
cap	capacity	Mtn	Mountain
cath	cathedral	N	North
chap	chaplain	NT	New Testament
ch	church	NYC	New York City, New York
Cn	Canon	Ord	Ordinary
Coadj	Coadjutor	OT	Old Testament
Coll	College	par	parish
Chanc	Chancellor	Past	Pastoral
Comm	Communion Committee Commission Community	Pk	Park
		Pkwy	Parkway
Commun	Communication	p-in-c	priest-in-charge
Conf	Conference	prog	program
cont ed	continuing education	prov	province, provincial
		Pt	part time
Cont	Controller, Comptroller	Pt	Port, Point
		ptnshp	partnership
convoc	convocation	r	rector
coord	coordinator	res	residence
ctr	center	ret	retirement
dio	diocese, diocesan	retr	retreat
dir	director	Rt	Route
dcn	deacon	sch	school
Dn	Dean	sem	seminary
d-in-c	deacon-in-charge	So	South
E	East	Spg(s)	Spring(s)
ecum	ecumenical	spir	spiritual/spirituality
em	emeritus	spon	sponsor
Episc	Episcopal	sr	sister
fac	facility	Ste	Suite
fam	family	SR	State Rd/Star Route
grp	group		
Hd	Head (master, mistress)	svc	service
		Theol	Theol, Theologian
Hisp	Hispanic		
Hon	Honorable	trng	training
Hse	House	Twp	Township
indiv	individual	urb	urban
inst	institute	V	Very
int	interim	v	vicar
Inter	Interpretation	W	West
Is	Island	yr-rnd	year-round
Lib	Library, Librarian	yth	youth

Provinces of the Episcopal Church
2016-2018 Triennium

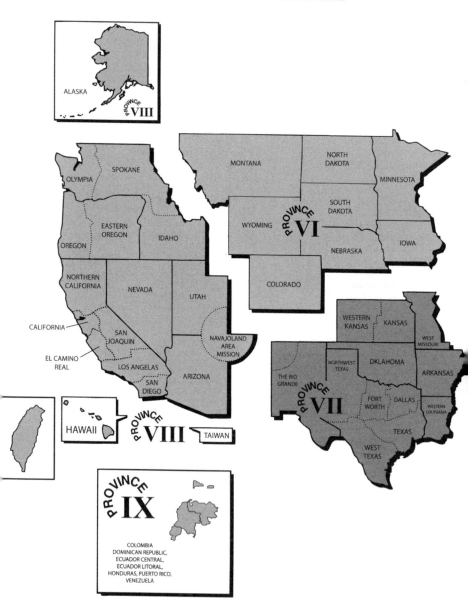

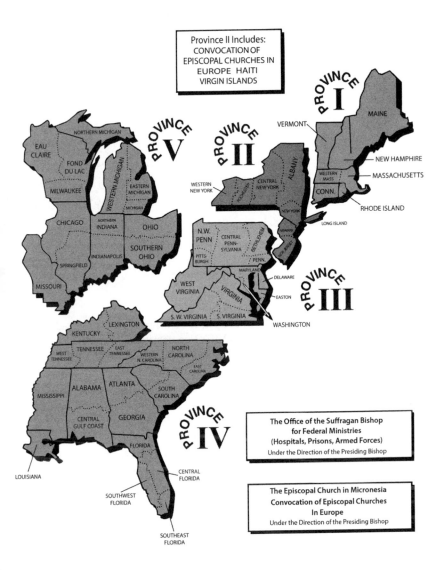

Province II Includes:
CONVOCATION OF
EPISCOPAL CHURCHES IN
EUROPE HAITI
VIRGIN ISLANDS

PROVINCE I

MAINE
VERMONT
NEW HAMPHIRE
MASSACHUSETTS
WESTERN MASS
CONN.
RHODE ISLAND

PROVINCE V

NORTHERN MICHIGAN
EAU CLAIRE
FOND DU LAC
MILWAUKEE
WESTERN MICHIGAN
EASTERN MICHIGAN
MICHIGAN
CHICAGO
NORTHERN INDIANA
OHIO
INDIANAPOLIS
SOUTHERN OHIO
SPRINGFIELD
MISSOURI

PROVINCE II

WESTERN NEW YORK
ROCHESTER
CENTRAL NEW YORK
ALBANY
NEW YORK
LONG ISLAND
NEWARK
NEW JERSEY
N.W. PENN
CENTRAL PENN-SYLVANIA
BETHLEHEM
PITTS-BURGH
PENN.
MARYLAND
DELAWARE
WEST VIRGINIA
VIRGINIA
EASTON
WASHINGTON
S. W. VIRGINIA
S. VIRGINIA

PROVINCE III

LEXINGTON
KENTUCKY
TENNESSEE
EAST TENNESSEE
WESTERN N. CAROLINA
NORTH CAROLINA
WEST TENNESSEE
EAST CAROLINA
ALABAMA
ATLANTA
SOUTH CAROLINA
MISSISSIPPI
CENTRAL GULF COAST
GEORGIA
FLORIDA
LOUISIANA
CENTRAL FLORIDA
SOUTHWEST FLORIDA
SOUTHEAST FLORIDA

PROVINCE IV

The Office of the Suffragan Bishop
for Federal Ministries
(Hospitals, Prisons, Armed Forces)
Under the Direction of the Presiding Bishop

The Episcopal Church in Micronesia
Convocation of Episcopal Churches
In Europe
Under the Direction of the Presiding Bishop

11

SUMMARY OF STATISTICS
as of January 2019

	Reported for 2017	Reported for 2016	Net Change	Percent Change
Parishes and Missions....................................	6,447	6,473	−26	−0.40%
Active Baptized Members.............................	1,712,563	1,745,156	−32,593	−1.87%
Communicants in Good Standing.............	1,368,631	1,399,523	−30,892	−2.21%
Others Active in Congregation...................	174,086	171,526	2,560	1.49%
Average Sunday Attendance........................	556,744	570,453	−13,709	−2.40%
Church School Pupils...................................	147,938	155,614	−7,676	−4.93%
Baptisms..	22,996	25,272	−2,276	−9.01%
Confirmations...	15,638	17,302	−1,664	−9.62%
Received..	5,506	5,813	−307	−5.28%
Marriages..	7,687	8,343	−656	−7.86%
Burials...	27,355	27,461	−106	−0.39%
Clergy (incl. non-parochial).......................	18,398	18,325	73	0.40%

Notes:

1. These figures, except for clergy, are based on 2017 Parochial Reports compiled for the Domestic Dioceses of Provinces I through VIII. Non-domestic figures are not included in the above statistics. For Province IX and other non-domestic Dioceses see the *Table of Statistics of the Episcopal Church.*

2. Average Sunday Attendance is a 52-Sunday average of Sunday worship attendance (which includes attendance on Saturday when Saturday services are considered to be Sunday worship and attendance on a weekday for churches without a Sunday service).

3. Clergy totals include all clergy listed in the clergy list in the *Episcopal Church Annual* including clergy reported as ordained but not yet entered in the clergy list. Source: The Church Pension Group.

Table of Statistics of the Episcopal Church
From 2017 Parochial Reports. Source: The Office of the General Convention as of January 2018

Province	Diocese	Open Parishes & Missions	Active Baptized Members	Commun. in Good Standing	Others Active in Cong.	Average Worship Attendance	Church School Pupils	BAPTISMS Children	BAPTISMS Adults	CONFIRMATIONS Children	CONFIRMATIONS Adults	Received	Marriages	Burials
Province 1	Connecticut	164	48,628	36,040	2,242	12,661	3,788	565	56	238	85	76	176	883
	Maine	60	11,322	9,147	850	3,694	725	97	14	19	47	34	52	240
	Massachusetts	162	55,542	42,568	2,909	14,731	4,996	691	49	204	153	102	220	966
	New Hampshire	48	11,655	8,212	1199	4,173	1,477	127	12	24	48	35	55	241
	Rhode Island	52	17,103	12,117	2,508	4,575	1,009	223	30	39	85	67	95	391
	Vermont	45	5,927	4,772	585	2,029	355	45	5	6	12	23	37	130
	Western Massachusetts	51	14,789	10,706	901	4,110	882	181	21	11	51	28	52	306
	Total	582	164,966	123,562	11,194	45,973	13,232	1,929	187	541	481	365	687	3,157
Province 2	Albany	112	13,868	10,596	1032	5,318	911	170	33	15	29	14	67	302
	Central New York	81	11,416	8,550	753	3,609	836	128	13	23	36	25	67	292
	Churches in Europe	16	2,862	2,330	280	947	222	44	10	13	9	8	34	24
	Haiti	111	87,029	27,805	2,008	13,437	5,710	1,050	639	429	349	135	133	217
	Long Island	131	42,514	32,256	2,363	12,469	2,479	557	132	143	142	35	187	676
	New Jersey	143	37,937	28,840	3,378	11,321	2,904	502	36	220	96	134	183	684
	New York	195	49,880	37,941	4,227	16,357	3,638	640	90	215	121	117	193	647
	Newark	98	24,730	19,205	1,401	7,536	2,162	293	22	108	72	47	122	410
	Rochester	50	7,524	6,136	439	3,362	700	88	15	36	20	27	51	195
	Virgin Islands	14	3,047	2,453	23	1,296	472	54	1	21	0	0	4	106
	Western New York	57	8,063	5,901	647	2,898	690	155	22	27	26	29	53	213
	Total	1,008	288,870	182,013	16,551	78,550	20,724	3,681	1,013	1,250	900	571	1,094	3,766
Province 3	Bethlehem	59	9,654	7,594	582	3,072	688	101	13	26	19	10	68	194
	Central Pennsylvania	63	11,351	8,952	936	3,852	801	113	14	51	48	28	59	203
	Delaware	33	9,372	7,695	627	3,185	753	126	19	48	27	28	51	210
	Easton	38	7,919	5,551	737	2,324	401	93	8	3	16	22	64	152
	Maryland	106	36,943	28,065	2,215	9,507	2,987	453	43	141	64	76	192	568
	Northwestern Pennsylvania	32	3,266	2,623	243	1,342	261	52	7	4	29	27	30	97
	Pennsylvania	133	41,929	33,889	5,170	12,362	3,321	542	73	182	168	164	269	744
	Pittsburgh	36	8,452	7,309	574	2,394	512	120	12	50	23	18	43	113
	Southern Virginia	103	25,134	20,814	3,156	8,806	2,096	244	42	76	142	127	103	419
	Southwestern Virginia	56	10,478	8,545	1,256	3,863	919	100	13	58	64	24	38	143
	Virginia	180	71,495	60,410	10,686	22,285	6,616	845	71	393	316	221	280	829
	Washington	88	38,819	29,030	5,439	12,964	3,273	462	55	156	146	80	162	486
	West Virginia	62	8,016	6,424	404	2,553	607	67	23	12	53	20	37	155
	Total	989	262,828	226,901	32,025	88,509	23,235	3,318	393	1,200	1,115	845	1,396	4,313
Province 4	Alabama	88	31,989	27,684	3,079	9,036	4,343	334	30	177	229	41	120	280
	Atlanta	93	47,866	39,581	7,111	14,244	4,650	616	50	297	367	233	153	516
	Central Florida	86	27,603	22,572	4,267	12,922	2,266	304	64	76	153	126	103	577
	Central Gulf Coast	61	18,054	14,527	1,162	5,686	1,526	176	26	81	127	80	92	254
	East Carolina	67	16,884	14,173	1,631	6,039	1,302	170	24	77	136	115	85	258
	East Tennessee	47	14,605	11,496	1,186	4,944	1,250	149	35	85	144	107	47	207
	Florida	61	26,053	19,631	2,752	8,104	1,855	211	38	118	143	77	85	360
	Georgia	68	14,680	11,334	1,809	5,689	1,359	115	20	85	78	77	71	263
	Kentucky	36	8,093	7,069	559	2,892	1,136	81	10	33	41	28	46	151
	Lexington	34	6,326	5,215	970	2,647	711	83	15	10	49	62	50	104
	Louisiana	46	16,803	13,145	1,650	4,158	1,591	211	10	79	85	54	88	222
4	Mississippi	82	17,918	14,049	1,707	5,861	1,630	173	22	97	148	98	95	250
	North Carolina	109	49,212	40,581	6,540	13,667	7,445	608	42	332	294	174	164	509

13

Province	Diocese	Open Parishes & Missions	Active Baptized Members	Commun. in Good Standing	Others Active in Cong.	Average Worship Attendance	Church School Pupils	BAPTISMS		CONFIRMATIONS		Received	Marriages	Burials
								Children	Adults	Children	Adults			
	South Carolina	31	7,309	6,621	1,012	2,817	1,110	79	7	38	54	44	70	100
	Southeast Florida	76	32,487	25,005	4,662	11,551	2,018	442	54	128	118	107	195	415
	Southwest Florida	77	28,797	23,417	6,305	11,588	1,675	252	33	87	135	135	83	585
	Tennessee	45	16,511	13,553	4,321	5,457	1,902	182	20	80	127	29	72	186
	Upper South Carolina	59	23,395	17,383	1,379	6,755	2,746	216	35	15	236	89	86	285
	West Tennessee	31	8,095	6,381	1,038	2,978	690	94	12	39	48	15	60	106
	Western North Carolina	62	14,838	13,089	1,898	5,916	1,083	99	5	64	83	163	63	295
	Total	1,259	427,518	346,506	55,038	142,951	42,288	4,595	552	1,998	2,795	1,854	1,828	5,923
Province 5	Chicago	122	33,913	28,353	2,496	11,498	3,591	447	36	285	111	110	160	478
	Eastern Michigan	43	4,603	3,917	213	1,857	306	52	18	16	15	7	29	152
	Eau Claire	20	1,770	1,276	161	741	96	18	3	13	8	3	5	42
	Fond Du Lac	34	4,833	3,454	628	1,720	392	44	15	8	24	15	27	120
	Indianapolis	48	8,564	7,426	846	3,538	809	83	31	13	125	48	48	143
	Michigan	75	16,889	14,047	1,647	6,006	1,433	176	41	35	77	53	100	363
	Milwaukee	51	8,053	7,280	643	3,190	764	104	9	13	19	40	54	162
	Missouri	42	10,255	9,262	916	3,444	919	89	11	70	54	30	39	153
	Northern Indiana	36	4,188	3,487	347	1,892	332	62	11	19	36	31	30	94
	Northern Michigan	21	1,314	1,079	89	411	78	3	1	0	0	2	11	31
	Ohio	86	18,007	13,966	1,886	5,678	1,369	129	22	50	70	40	76	402
	Southern Ohio	74	19,250	14,885	1,222	6,440	1,623	183	27	92	108	52	96	294
	Springfield	33	4,087	2,785	328	1,453	225	29	15	3	26	2	10	88
	Western Michigan	56	8,374	7,261	779	3,452	753	77	13	5	23	22	48	198
	Total	741	144,100	118,478	12,201	51,320	12,690	1,496	258	622	696	455	733	2,720
Province 6	Colorado	96	23,710	20,446	4,006	9,186	2,029	364	45	27	117	42	129	408
	Iowa	60	6,824	6,032	448	2,365	646	71	17	28	27	33	41	140
	Minnesota	100	19,388	15,821	1,186	6,054	1,950	244	19	108	86	68	110	315
	Montana	34	4,495	3,787	444	1,380	269	58	5	9	15	7	21	95
	Nebraska	52	7,153	5,425	448	2,582	708	103	7	32	25	25	44	140
	North Dakota	19	2,493	1,807	127	633	286	64	6	18	18	25	12	29
	South Dakota	78	8,631	4,821	343	1,761	500	252	9	11	20	43	29	409
	Wyoming	45	6,454	5,144	758	1,690	599	95	11	21	9	52	64	143
	Total	484	79,148	63,283	7,760	25,651	6,987	1,251	119	254	317	295	450	1,679
Province 7	Arkansas	56	13,638	10,415	1,181	4,572	1,158	152	36	43	185	45	57	190
	Dallas	67	31,235	27,852	3,800	10,912	2,634	453	72	243	200	92	84	367
	Fort Worth	16	4,595	2,496	330	1,374	379	42	4	4	50	15	15	68
	Kansas	44	10,184	8,268	841	3,212	1,004	84	12	30	49	13	33	172
	Northwest Texas	30	5,888	3,922	656	1,705	393	75	3	14	79	25	29	90
	Oklahoma	69	16,374	13,900	1,023	5,314	1,265	159	130	60	160	54	65	240
	Rio Grande	56	10,830	9,065	1,410	3,535	525	98	36	15	63	61	42	180
	Texas	152	75,969	60,524	8,544	23,596	7,504	1,059	118	420	659	293	260	767
	West Missouri	48	9,438	7,528	1,765	3,019	791	101	17	24	41	29	66	149
	West Texas	87	22,011	18,388	2,868	8,464	2,722	304	45	153	173	113	104	350
	Western Kansas	29	1,428	1,257	102	574	126	12	7	8	8	6	14	31
	Western Louisiana	43	8,474	6,728	560	2,765	521	96	15	44	58	35	47	138
	Total	697	210,064	170,343	23,080	69,042	19,022	2,635	495	1,058	1,725	781	816	2,742
Province 8	Alaska	48	6,357	4,949	639	1,193	472	72	9	6	3	4	27	165
	Arizona	58	20,472	17,544	2,831	7,779	1,482	270	128	91	127	93	59	364
	California	78	24,149	19,820	1,822	6,991	2,246	276	30	102	48	14	136	331
	Eastern Oregon	21	2,016	1,450	197	913	92	16	2	1	0	2	11	45

Province	Diocese	Open Parishes & Missions	Active Baptized Members	Commun. in Good Standing	Others Active in Cong.	Average Worship Attendance	Church School Pupils	BAPTISMS Children	BAPTISMS Adults	CONFIRMATIONS Children	CONFIRMATIONS Adults	Received	Marriages	Burials
	El Camino Real	42	10,904	8,872	615	3,485	751	103	9	32	34	22	48	168
	Hawaii	34	6,565	5,322	1,172	2,847	358	100	42	14	43	40	51	139
	Idaho	29	4,795	4,315	338	1,415	466	28	20	4	8	0	14	69
	Los Angeles	128	49,359	37,518	2,755	14,690	3,258	562	96	137	231	81	208	628
	Micronesia	2	261	125	6	99	19	2	0	0	0	0	0	4
	Navajo Missions	10	666	502	4	176	50	6	3	0	8	0	2	23
	Nevada	29	5,669	5,161	1,407	2,648	328	90	35	47	57	27	40	89
	Northern California	67	12,856	11,247	903	4,883	950	121	43	40	92	40	48	248
	Olympia	91	24,292	20,038	1,444	8,629	2,066	190	51	33	106	45	73	383
	Oregon	71	14,566	12,450	1,215	5,510	1,590	145	38	25	56	44	53	248
	San Diego	44	13,370	11,004	2,434	5,235	1,136	183	26	44	72	45	39	260
	San Joaquin	19	2,038	1,905	146	810	179	26	4	1	4	11	13	60
	Spokane	36	4,655	3,679	302	1,645	295	54	6	1	15	2	16	111
	Taiwan	15	1,293	980	134	771	425	31	50	1	62	15	7	19
	Utah	23	5,278	4,357	324	1,579	445	70	18	5	20	13	16	71
	Total	845	209,561	171,238	18,688	71,298	16,608	2,345	610	584	986	498	861	3,425
Province 9	Colombia	29	3,444	1,359	274	1,158	138	170	40	62	97	52	90	14
	Dominican Republic	60	5,524	3,237	658	2,337	1,243	208	56	43	103	34	8	58
	Ecuador, Central	20	1,231	736	177	510	193	58	8	3	22	12	13	24
	Ecuador, Litoral	26	8,627	1,418	457	1,113	442	129	43	309	131	28	5	16
	Honduras	124	39,645	37,282	2,901	5,015	3,874	276	74	31	75	25	35	72
	Puerto Rico	50	4,958	3,974	503	2,063	559	104	29	22	44	98	35	97
	Venezuela	25	1,097	624	83	507	91	74	37	7	13	8	16	15
	Total	334	64,526	48,630	5,053	12,703	6,540	1,019	287	477	485	257	202	296
	Domestic Dioceses	6,447	1,712,563	1,368,631	174,086	556,744	147,938	20,069	2,927	7,043	8,595	5,506	7,687	27,355
	Non-Domestic Dioceses	492	159,018	82,323	7,504	29,253	13,388	2,200	987	941	905	415	380	666
	The Episcopal Church	6,939	1,871,581	1,450,954	181,590	585,997	161,326	22,269	3,914	7,984	9,500	5,921	8,067	28,021

Note: These figures are compiled from 2017 Parochial Reports submitted to the Office of the General Convention, 815 Second Avenue, New York, NY 10017-4564.
For further information about the Parochial Report, contact the research office, DFMS, pr@dfms.org, or phone (800) 334-7626. Figures for Litoral Ecuador are from 2016.
Figures for individual non-reporting congregations are carried over from the previous year.

15

Comparative Statistics of the Episcopal Church, U.S.A.

Year Reported	Parishes and Missions	Clergy	Baptized Members	Communicants Domestic	Communicants Overseas	Communicants Total	Church School Pupils*	Day School Staff	Day School Pupils*	Cand's for Orders	Ordinations Deacons	Ordinations Priests	Baptisms Infant	Baptisms Adult	Baptisms Total	Confirmations (Including Received)	Marriages	Burials	Total Receipts (Gross Receipts) $
1850		1,595				89,359	44,148			175			18,232	2,727	20,959	7,554	2,987	6,226	342,936.49
1855	1,821	1,821				107,560	82,731			236			18,812	3,618	22,430	10,584	6,777	12,542	727,477.00
1860	2,128	2,156				146,588	135,925			292	102	83	26,518	5,247	31,765	14,781	7,356	12,989	1,870,914.98
1865	2,322	2,467				154,118	150,400			220	94	91	24,689	5,297	29,986	15,360	7,487	15,650	2,700,004.08
1870	2,605	2,838				207,762	213,862			361	102	91			—	21,622	9,261	15,802	4,907,872.57
1875		3,187				261,003	235,943			298	110	122			—	22,095	9,690	18,969	6,899,305.94
1880	4,151	3,432		345,433	408	345,841	299,070			431	136	96			—	25,903	12,163	22,518	7,013,762.86
1885	4,565	3,787		397,084	108	397,192	326,203			321	134	108	40,557	8,188	48,745	34,069	14,040	27,893	9,017,155.16
1890	5,330	4,180		504,898	3,394	508,292	393,795			299			46,962	11,227	58,189	40,911	15,819	30,136	12,754,767.53
1895	6,269	4,610		614,136	5,297	619,433	418,674			529			49,777	11,645	61,422	44,627	17,242	34,761	13,449,925.95
1900	6,774	5,011		712,997	6,543	719,540	429,830			506			48,118	10,418	58,536	43,788	19,039	34,138	16,069,580.49
1905	7,480	5,302		817,845	10,548	828,393	450,212			459			50,119	12,899	63,018	51,341	22,527	37,628	16,296,693.95
1910	7,987	5,543		928,780	17,472	946,252	456,275			438			49,981	14,086	64,067	55,020	24,044	45,566	18,382,609.85
1915	8,506	5,800		1,040,896	17,908	1,058,804	483,936			430			53,289	14,537	67,826	61,284	26,231	50,080	20,972,589.78
1920	8,365	5,987		1,075,820	21,075	1,096,895	417,695			310			50,315	10,025	60,340	50,779	28,485	47,788	24,392,091.64
1925	8,397	6,140		1,164,911	28,410	1,193,321	498,814			454	177	157	54,879	12,181	67,060	65,064	29,420	50,336	41,746,055.91
1930	8,253	6,304	1,939,453	1,254,227	33,204	1,287,431	483,413			485	192	193	52,200	11,559	63,759	64,668	30,576	56,163	45,944,896.82
1935	8,098	6,410	2,038,477	1,351,999	37,593	1,389,592	506,400			426	193	162	50,499	12,200	62,699	67,096	25,639	52,611	30,425,500.75
1940	7,995	6,335	2,171,562	1,449,327	40,057	1,489,384	492,554			301	152	149	56,288	13,130	69,418	74,318	28,799	53,446	34,618,420.82
1945	7,818	6,449	2,269,962	1,527,762	40,390	1,568,152	394,456			229	181	209	72,377	14,033	86,410	28,868	31,597	54,650	46,170,035.30
1950	7,784	6,654	2,540,548	1,651,426	37,185	1,688,611	514,754			486	255	240	87,487	16,550	104,037	85,989	28,695	55,354	73,844,880.41
1955	8,053	7,573	3,013,570	1,781,262	84,653	1,865,915	696,028			677	415	354	98,595	20,388	118,983	113,443	24,789	53,114	131,354,945.37
1960	7,657	9,079	3,444,265	2,027,671	95,439	2,123,110	874,550	3,187	44,075	800	424	427	98,312	18,415	116,727	127,861	24,111	57,574	173,013,803.63
1965	7,539	10,309	3,615,643	2,202,607	69,534	2,272,141	880,912	4,590	58,712	710	442	426	91,695	13,627	105,322	128,066	27,728	60,190	223,016,214.03
1970	7,464	11,772	3,475,164	2,238,538	56,017	2,294,555	711,791	6,088	79,962	510	379	311	74,577	8,359	82,936	102,059	37,836	59,504	‡299,426,994.00

Year Reported	Parishes and Missions	Clergy	Baptized Members	Communicants Domestic	Communicants Overseas	Communicants Total	Others Active in Congregations	Church School Staff†	Church School Pupils*	Day School Staff†	Day School Pupils*	Cand's for Orders	Ordinations Deacons	Ordinations Priests	Baptisms Children	Baptisms Adult	Baptisms Total	Confirmations (Including Received)	Marriages	Burials	Total Receipts (Gross Receipts)‡
1975	7,382	12,035	3,039,136	2,051,914	77,337	2,129,251	—	74,574	559,648	8,897	100,465	702	316	271	63,503	5,965	69,468	77,038	36,535	53,473	411,418,722.00
1980	7,591	13,089	3,037,420	1,933,080	85,790	2,018,870	—	69,459	507,448	—	104,839	425	321	314	64,367	8,611	72,978	64,912	39,862	50,070	648,937,788.00
1985	7,858	14,482	2,972,607	1,881,250	82,375	1,963,625	—	70,383	496,930	—	120,259	563	475	330	65,152	7,142	72,294	59,718	36,073	48,277	1,028,818,309.00
1990	7,354	14,878	2,446,050	1,698,240	—	—	—	72,668	495,537	—	100,589	407	379	296	56,862	7,844	64,706	47,270	31,795	43,568	1,379,782,885.00
1991	7,367	14,879	2,474,625	1,615,505	—	—	—	74,350	336,251	—	95,903	405	380	296	55,869	7,714	63,583	46,068	30,557	43,538	1,433,467,803.00
1992	7,391	15,076	2,491,996	1,614,081	—	—	—	72,153	335,297	—	99,366	407	378	290	53,095	7,071	60,166	46,820	28,844	42,226	1,582,457,015.00
1993	7,403	15,004	2,506,047	1,579,444	—	—	—	75,959	327,157	—	101,752	423	378	290	51,643	8,044	59,687	44,509	28,291	43,010	1,613,697,551.00
1994	7,413	14,645	2,517,520	1,577,951	—	—	142,900	72,988	328,512	13,674	102,145	352	399	317	51,049	6,545	57,594	43,234	27,631	42,259	1,311,990,815.00
1995	7,417	15,138	2,411,841	1,584,760	—	—	150,417	71,773	333,645	—	107,203	372	347	265	50,784	7,250	58,034	43,474	27,324	44,239	1,398,179,032.00
1996	7,395	14,295	2,366,054	1,592,693	—	—	159,199	72,874	325,156	20,416	102,042	329	341	296	49,525	6,688	56,213	42,378	25,931	42,244	1,470,455,496.00
1997	7,379	14,428	2,339,113	1,716,977	—	—	168,595	73,940	319,393	†	103,748	326	332	284	49,545	7,433	56,978	42,486	25,989	41,030	1,577,769,316.00
1998	7,384	14,428	2,318,238	1,763,650	—	—	180,253	75,027	309,713	†	†	326	332	284	48,563	7,191	55,754	41,478	23,974	39,735	1,685,701,827.00
1999	7,368	16,891◆	2,296,936	1,812,434	—	—	196,574	†	275,382	†	†	◊	◊	◊	47,519	7,665	55,184	42,579	23,042	45,587	1,864,447,191.00
2000	7,347	16,783 ◆	2,319,844	1,857,843	—	—	187,927	†	300,010	—	†	◊	◊	◊	46,403	7,231	53,634	44,892	22,341	44,762	2,019,266,027.00
2001	7,344	17,336	2,317,515	1,868,960	—	—	199,446	—	297,635	—	—	—	—	—	45,566	6,969	52,535	42,268	19,354	44,199	1,939,281,740.00
2002	7,305	17,443	2,320,221	1,902,525	—	—	209,416	—	303,061	—	—	—	—	—	44,995	6,299	51,294	40,482	18,798	38,154	1,994,893,155.00
2003	7,220	17,174	2,284,233	1,866,157	—	—	208,094	—	287,998	—	—	—	—	—	43,068	6,248	49,316	39,557	18,260	35,840	2,044,377,792.00
2004	7,200	17,209	2,247,819	1,834,530	—	—	200,917	—	275,087	—	—	—	—	—	41,376	5,754	47,130	36,558	17,149	34,744	2,083,916,019.00
2005	7,155	17,817	2,205,376	1,796,017	—	—	203,390	—	266,080	—	—	—	—	—	38,680	5,620	44,300	36,244	16,190	34,372	2,199,993,228.00
2006	7,095	17,922	2,154,572	1,749,073	71,820	1,820,893	191,460	—	253,304	—	—	—	—	—	36,387	4,501	40,888	32,412	14,805	32,564	2,223,317,477.00
2007	7,055	18,019	2,116,749	1,720,477	75,306	1,795,783	189,671	—	242,557	—	—	—	—	—	34,194	4,020	38,214	23,556	13,438	31,457	2,269,075,042.00
2008	6,964	18,002	2,057,292	1,666,202	68,320	1,734,522	181,367	—	227,619	—	—	—	—	—	32,731	3,816	36,547	23,359	12,816	31,212	2,233,075,961.00
2009	6,895	17,868	2,006,343	1,624,025	69,000	1,693,085	183,674	—	216,953	—	—	—	—	—	30,682	3,978	34,660	22,762	11,647	30,853	2,128,331,169.00
2010	6,794	17,975	1,951,907	1,576,721	75,525	1,652,525	180,360	—	203,774	—	—	—	—	—	28,990	3,746	32,736	22,265	10,990	30,109	2,088,030,689.00
2011	6,736	18,112	1,923,046	1,542,072	70,755	1,612,827	179,256	—	197,754	—	—	—	—	—	28,201	3,939	32,140	20,942	10,950	29,813	2,127,489,576.00
2012	6,667	18,040	1,894,181	1,516,117	71,940	1,588,057	179,000	—	190,606	—	—	—	—	—	27,140	3,836	30,976	20,474	10,366	29,442	2,170,806,058.00
2013	6,622	18,170	1,866,758	1,491,423	57,585	1,549,008	184,035	—	184,859	—	—	—	—	—	25,822	3,675	29,497	20,077	9,933	28,960	2,215,042,224.00
2014	6,553	18,198	1,817,004	1,450,472	53,801	1,504,273	179,638	—	173,682	—	—	—	—	—	24,594	3,530	28,124	19,142	10,337	29,011	2,248,977,732.00
2015	6,510	18,345	1,779,335	1,434,461	60,191	1,494,652	179,353	—	163,301	—	—	—	—	—	24,069	3,305	27,374	17,791	9,149	28,571	2,280,563,631.00
2016	6,473	18,325	1,745,156	1,399,523	87,138	1,486,661	171,526	—	155,614	—	—	—	—	—	22,112	3,160	25,272	17,302	8,343	27,461	2,251,792,484.00

*New category or revised in 1992.
◆See notes on clergy on page 15

†Statistics on Day Schools and church school staff are no longer maintained.
‡From 1970 on, excludes all non-income items; includes "other parish funds" (not previously reported.)
◊ Not available

A Table of the General Conventions

No.	Opened	Closed	Place of Meeting	Presiding Bishop	Pres. House of Deputies	Preacher
1	Sept. 27—	Oct. 7, 1785	Philadelphia.	......	Rev. Wm. White, D.D.	Rev. Wm. Smith, D.D.
2	June 20—	June 26, 1786	Philadelphia.	......	Rev. David Griffith.	Rev. Wm. Smith, D.D.
	Oct. 10—	Oct. 11, 1786	Wilmington, Del.	......	Rev. Samuel Provoost, D.D.	Rev. Samuel Megaw, D.D.
3	July 28—	Aug. 8, 1789	Philadelphia.	Bp. William White.	Bishop William White.[1]	Rev. Wm. Smith, D.D.
	Sept. 29—	Oct. 16, 1789	New York.	Bp. Samuel Seabury.	Rev. Wm. Smith, D.D.	......
4	Sept. 11—	Sept. 19, 1792	Philadelphia.	Bp. Samuel Provoost.	Rev. Wm. Smith, D.D.	Bishop Samuel Seabury.
5	Sept. 8—	Sept. 18, 1795	Philadelphia.	Bp. William White.	Rev. Wm. Smith, D.D.	Bishop Samuel Provoost.
6	June 11—	June 19, 1799	Trenton, N.J.	Bp. William White.	Rev. Wm. Smith, D.D.	......
7	Sept. 8—	Sept. 12, 1801	New York.	Bp. William White.	Rev. Abraham Beach, D.D.	Bishop William White.
8	Sept. 11—	Sept. 18, 1804	New York.	Bp. William White.	Rev. Abraham Beach, D.D.	Bishop Benjamin Moore.
9	May 17—	May 26, 1808	Baltimore.	Bp. William White.	Rev. Abraham Beach, D.D.	Bishop William White.
10	May 21—	May 24, 1811	New Haven.	Bp. William White.	Rev. Isaac Wilkins.	Bishop William White.
11	May 17—	May 24, 1814	Philadelphia.	Bp. William White.	Rev. John Croes, D.D.	Bishop John Henry Hobart.
12	May 20—	May 27, 1817	New York.	Bp. William White.	Rev. Isaac Wilkins, D.D.	Bishop Alex. V. Griswold.
13	May 16—	May 24, 1820	Philadelphia.	Bp. William White.	Rev. Wm. H. Wilmer, D.D.	Bishop Richard C. Moore.
I	Oct. 30—	Nov. 3, 1821	Philadelphia.	Bp. William White.	Rev. Wm. H. Wilmer, D.D.	Bishop James Kemp.
14	May 20—	May 26, 1823	Philadelphia.	Bp. William White.	Rev. Wm. H. Wilmer, D.D.	Bishop John Cross.
15	Nov. 7—	Nov. 15, 1826	Philadelphia.	Bp. William White.	Rev. Wm. H. Wilmer, D.D.	Bishop Nathaniel Bowen.
16	Aug. 12—	Aug. 20, 1829	Philadelphia.	Bp. William White.	Rev. Wm. E. Wyatt, D.D.	Bishop Thomas C. Brownell.
17	Oct. 17—	Oct. 31, 1832	New York.	Bp. William White.	Rev. Wm. E. Wyatt, D.D.	Bishop Henry U. Onderdonk.
18	Aug. 19—	Sept. 1, 1835	Philadelphia.	Bp. William White.	Rev. Wm. E. Wyatt, D.D.	Bishop Wm. Murray Stone.
19	Sept. 5—	Sept. 17, 1838	Philadelphia.	Bp. Alexander Viets Griswold.	Rev. Wm. E. Wyatt, D.D.	Bishop Wm. Meade.
20	Oct. 2—	Oct. 19, 1841	New York.	Bp. Alexander Viets Griswold.	Rev. Wm. E. Wyatt, D.D.	Bishop Benj. T. Onderdonk.
21	Oct. 2—	Oct. 22, 1844	Philadelphia.	Bp. Philander Chase.	Rev. Wm. E. Wyatt, D.D.	Bishop Levi S. Ives.
22	Oct. 6—	Oct. 28, 1847	New York.	Bp. Philander Chase.	Rev. Wm. E. Wyatt, D.D.	Bishop John Henry Hopkins.
23	Oct. 2—	Oct. 16, 1850	Cincinnati.	Bp. Philander Chase.	Rev. Wm. E. Wyatt, D.D.	Bishop Benj. B. Smith.
24	Oct. 5—	Oct. 26, 1853	New York.	Bp. Thomas Church Brownell.	Rev. Wm. Creighton, D.D.	Bishop Charles P. McIlvaine.
25	Oct. 1—	Oct. 21, 1856	Philadelphia.	Bp. Thomas Church Brownell.	Rev. Wm. Creighton, D.D.	Bishop Geo. W. Doane.
26	Oct. 5—	Oct. 22, 1859	Richmond, Va.	Bp. Thomas Church Brownell.[2]	Rev. Wm. Creighton, D.D.	Bishop James H. Otey.
A1	July 3—	July 6, 1861[3]	Montgomery, Ala.	Bp. Stephen Elliott.	Met as a single house.	None mentioned.
A2	Oct. 16—	Oct. 24, 1861[3]	Columbia, S.C.	Bp. Stephen Elliott.	Met as a single house.	Bishop William Meade.
27	Oct. 1—	Oct. 17, 1862	New York.	Bp. Thomas Church Brownell.[4]	Rev. James Craik, D.D.	Bishop Sam. A. McCoskry.
A3	Nov. 12—	Nov. 22, 1862[5]	Augusta, Ga.	Bp. Stephen Elliott.	Rev. Christian Hanckel, D.D.	Bishop Henry C. Lay.
28	Oct. 4—	Oct. 24, 1865	Philadelphia.	Bp. John Henry Hopkins.	Rev. James Craik, D.D.	Bishop Fulford of Montreal.
A4	Nov. 8—	Nov. 10, 1865[6]	Augusta, Ga.	Bp. Stephen Elliott.	Rev. C. C. Pinckney, D.D.	None mentioned.
29	Oct. 7—	Oct. 29, 1868	New York.	Bp. Benjamin Bosworth Smith.	Rev. James Craik, D.D.	Bishop Henry W. Lee.
30	Oct. 4—	Oct. 26, 1871	Baltimore.	Bp. Benjamin Bosworth Smith.	Rev. James Craik, D.D.	Bishop John Johns.
31	Oct. 7—	Nov. 3, 1874	New York.	Bp. Benjamin Bosworth Smith.	Rev. James Craik, D.D.	Bishop Selwyn of Lichfield.
32	Oct. 3—	Oct. 25, 1877	Boston.	Bp. Benjamin Bosworth Smith.	Rev. Alex. Burgess, D.D.	Bishop John Williams.
33	Oct. 6—	Oct. 27, 1880	New York.	Bp. Benjamin Bosworth Smith.	Rev. E. E. Beardsley, D.D.	Bishop Wm. I. Kip.
34	Oct. 3—	Oct. 26, 1883	Philadelphia.	Bp. Benjamin Bosworth Smith.[7]	Rev. E. E. Beardsley, D.D.	Bishop Thomas M. Clark.
35	Oct. 6—	Oct. 28, 1886	Chicago.	Bp. Alfred Lee.	Rev. Morgan Dix, D.D.	Bishop Gregory T. Bedell.
36	Oct. 2—	Oct. 24, 1889	New York.	Bp. John Williams.	Rev. Morgan Dix, D.D.	Bishop Henry B. Whipple.
37	Oct. 5—	Oct. 25, 1892	Baltimore.	Bp. John Williams.	Rev. Morgan Dix, D.D.	Bishop Richard H. Wilmer.

No.	Dates	Location	Presiding Bishop	President of the House of Deputies	Preacher
38	Oct. 2—Oct. 22, 1895	Minneapolis.	Bp. John Williams.[8]	Rev. Morgan Dix, D.D.	Bishop Arthur C. Coxe.
39	Oct. 5—Oct. 25, 1898	Washington.	Bp. John Williams.[8]	Rev. Morgan Dix, D.D.	Bishop Daniel S. Tuttle.
40	Oct. 2—Oct. 17, 1901	San Francisco.	Bp. Thomas March Clark.[9]	Rev. J. S. Lindsay, D.D.	Bishop Benj. W. Morris.
41	Oct. 5—Oct. 25, 1904	Boston.	Bp. Daniel Sylvester Tuttle.	Rev. R. H. McKim, D.D.	Bishop Wm. C. Doane.
42	Oct. 2—Oct. 19, 1907	Richmond, Va.	Bp. Daniel Sylvester Tuttle.	Rev. R. H. McKim, D.D.	Bishop Ingram of London.
43	Oct. 5—Oct. 21, 1910	Cincinnati.	Bp. Daniel Sylvester Tuttle.	Rev. R. H. McKim, D.D.	Bp. Wordsworth of Salisbury.
44	Oct. 8—Oct. 25, 1913	New York.	Bp. Daniel Sylvester Tuttle.	Rev. Alex. Mann, D.D.	Bishop William Lawrence.
45	Oct. 11—Oct. 27, 1916	St. Louis.	Bp. Daniel Sylvester Tuttle.	Rev. Alex. Mann, D.D.	Bishop Daniel S. Tuttle.
46	Oct. 8—Oct. 24, 1919	Detroit.	Bp. Daniel Sylvester Tuttle.	Rev. Alex. Mann, D.D.	Bishop Charles H. Brent.
47	Sept. 6—Sept. 23, 1922	Portland, Oreg.	Bp. Ethelbert Talbot.	Rev. Alex. Mann, D.D.	Bishop Edwin S. Lines.
48	Oct. 7—Oct. 24, 1925	New Orleans, La.	Bp. John Gardner Murray.	Rev. Ernest M. Stires, D.D.	Bishop Theo. DuB. Bratton.[10]
49	Oct. 10—Oct. 25, 1928	Washington, D.C.	Bp. James DeWolf Perry.	Rev. ZeB. Phillips, D.D.	Bishop Charles P. Anderson.
50	Sept. 16—Sept. 30, 1931	Denver, Colo.	Bp. James DeWolf Perry.	Rev. ZeB. Phillips, D.D.	Bishop Furse of St. Albans.
51	Oct. 10—Oct. 23, 1934	Atlantic City, N.J.	Bp. James DeWolf Perry.	Rev. ZeB. Phillips, D.D.	Bishop James DeWolf Perry.
52	Oct. 6—Oct. 19, 1937	Cincinnati.	Bp. James DeWolf Perry.	Rev. ZeB. Phillips, D.D.	Bishop Edward L. Parsons.
53	Oct. 9—Oct. 19, 1940	Kansas City, Mo.	Bp. Henry St. George Tucker.	Rev. Phillips E. Osgood, D.D.	Bishop H. St. George Tucker.
54	Oct. 2—Oct. 11, 1943	Cleveland.	Bp. Henry St. George Tucker.	Hon. Owen J. Roberts.	Bishop H. St. George Tucker.
55	Sept. 10—Sept. 20, 1946	Philadelphia.	Bp. Henry St. George Tucker.	V. Rev. Claude W. Sprouse, D.D.	Bishop H. St. George Tucker.
56	Sept. 26—Oct. 7, 1949	San Francisco.	Bp. Henry Knox Sherrill.	V. Rev. C. W. Sprouse, D.D.[11]	Bishop Henry Knox Sherrill.
57	Sept. 8—Sept. 19, 1952	Boston.	Bp. Henry Knox Sherrill.	Rev. T. O. Wedel, Ph.D.	Bishop Henry Knox Sherrill.
58	Sept. 4—Sept. 15, 1955	Honolulu, T.H.	Bp. Henry Knox Sherrill.	Rev. Theodore O. Wedel, Ph.D.	Bishop Henry Knox Sherrill.
59	Oct. 5—Oct. 17, 1958	Miami Beach, Fla.	Bp. Henry Knox Sherrill.	Rev. Theodore O. Wedel, Ph.D.	Bishop Henry Knox Sherrill.
60	Sept. 17—Sept. 29, 1961	Detroit, Mich.	Bp. Arthur Lichtenberger.	Clifford P. Morehouse, LL.D.	Bishop Arthur Lichtenberger.[12]
61	Oct. 11—Oct. 23, 1964	St. Louis, Mo.	Bp. Arthur Lichtenberger.	Clifford P. Morehouse, LL.D.	Bishop Arthur Lichtenberger.
62	Sept. 17—Sept. 27, 1967	Seattle, Wash.	Bp. John Elbridge Hines.	Clifford P. Morehouse, LL.D.	Bishop John Elbridge Hines.
II	Aug. 31—Sept. 5, 1969	South Bend, In.	Bp. John Elbridge Hines.	V. Rev. John B. Coburn.	Bishop John Elbridge Hines.
63	Oct. 11—Oct. 22, 1970	Houston, Tx.	Bp. John Elbridge Hines.	V. Rev. John B. Coburn.	Bishop John Elbridge Hines.
64	Sept. 26—Oct. 22, 1973	Louisville, Ky.	Bp. John Maury Allin.	V. Rev. John B. Coburn.	Bishop John Maury Allin.
65	Sept. 11—Sept. 22, 1976	Minneapolis, Mn.	Bp. John Maury Allin.	V. Rev. John B. Coburn.	Bishop John Maury Allin.
66	Sept. 6—Sept. 20, 1979	Denver, Co.	Bp. John Maury Allin.	Charles R. Lawrence, Ph.D.	Bishop John Maury Allin.
67	Sept. 5—Sept. 15, 1982	New Orleans, LA	Bp. John Maury Allin.	Charles R. Lawrence, Ph.D.	Archbishop Robert A. K. Runcie.
68	Sept. 7—Sept. 14, 1985	Anaheim, CA	Bp. John Maury Allin.	Charles R. Lawrence, Ph.D.	Bishop Edmond Lee Browning.
69	July 2—July 11, 1988	Detroit, MI	Bp. Edmond Lee Browning.	V. Rev. David B. Collins.	Bishop Edmond Lee Browning.
70	July 16—July 25, 1991	Phoenix, AZ	Bp. Edmond Lee Browning.	V. Rev. David B. Collins.	Pamela P. Chinnis.
71	Aug. 24—Sept. 2, 1994	Indianapolis, IN	Bp. Edmond Lee Browning.	Pamela P. Chinnis.	Pamela P. Chinnis.
72	July 16—July 25, 1997	Philadelphia, PA	Bp. Frank T Griswold.	Pamela P. Chinnis.	Archbishop George Leonard Carey.
73	July 5—July 14, 2000	Denver, CO	Bp. Frank T Griswold.	V. Rev. George L. W. Werner.	Bishop Simon Elija Chiwanga.
74	July 30—Aug. 8, 2003	Minneapolis, MN	Bp. Frank T Griswold.	V. Rev. George L. W. Werner.	Archbishop Josiah Idowu-Fearon.
75	June 13—June 21, 2006	Columbus, OH	Bp. Katharine Jefferts Schori.	Bonnie Anderson.	Dr. Jenny Te Paa.
76	July 8—July 17, 2009	Anaheim, CA	Bp. Katharine Jefferts Schori.	Bonnie Anderson.	Bishop Katharine Jefferts Schori.
77	July 5—July 12, 2012	Indianapolis, IN	Bp. Katharine Jefferts Schori.	Rev. Gay Clark Jennings.	Bishop Katharine Jefferts Schori.
78	June 25—July 13, 2015	Salt Lake City, Utah	Bp. Katharine Jefferts Schori.	Rev. Gay Clark Jennings.	Bishop Katharine Jefferts Schori.
79	July 5–July 13, 2018	Austin, Texas	Bp. Michael B. Curry.		

1) From 1785 through the first session of 1789 the General Convention was a single house and Bishop White was president of the Convention at its first session. 2) Absent because of advanced years; Bishop William Meade presided. 3) The First Preliminary meeting of dioceses of the Confederate States was called unofficially. In the Confederate States were officially called by the members of the First Preliminary meeting. In those two meetings there was no official Presiding Bishop, but the oldest bishop in point of consecration, who was present, presided. The dioceses involved had not at that time officially withdrawn from The Protestant Episcopal Church in the United States of America, although in practice they had done so. There was no officially appointed Presiding Bishop until the first meeting of The General Council of The Protestant Episcopal Church in the Confederate States of America. 4) Absent because of advanced years; Bishop John Henry Hopkins presided. 5) First General Council of The Protestant Episcopal Church in the Confederate States of America. 6) Second General Council of The Protestant Episcopal Church in the Confederate States of America. 7) Bishop Smith's advanced years, Bishop Alfred Lee signed the minutes. 8) Absent because of illness; Bishop Wm. C. Doane was Chairman of the House of Bishops and signed the minutes. 9) Absent because of illness; Bishop Thomas U. Dudley of Kentucky was Chairman of the House of Bishops and signed the minutes. 10) Read by Bishop T. F. Gailor because of Bishop Bratton's illness. 11) Died during first day's session. 12) Read by Bishop Ned Cole, at the request of Bishop Lichtenberger.

19

THE CANONICAL STRUCTURE OF THE CHURCH

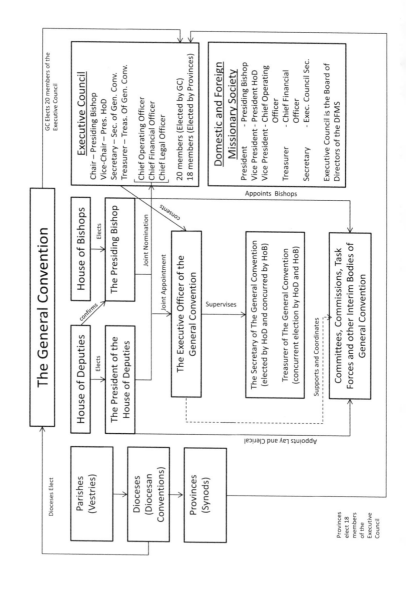

The information listed in this section was generously provided by the Office of the General Convention of The Episcopal Church.

The General Convention of The Episcopal Church
ELECTED OFFICERS OF THE GENERAL CONVENTION

The Most Rev. Michael Bruce Curry, *Presiding Bishop and Primate*; The Rev. Gay Clark Jennings, *President of the House of Deputies*; The Rev. Canon Dr. Michael Barlowe, *Secretary of the General Convention*; Mr. N. Kurt Barnes, *Treasurer*

Most Rev. Michael Curry
Presiding Bishop and Primate

Rev. Gay Clark Jennings
President of the House of Deputies

THE EPISCOPAL CHURCH CENTER

815 Second Avenue, New York, NY 10017 (800) 334-7626 Web: www.episcopalchurch.org Staff members may be reached via e-mail using their first initial with their last name (Ex. jdoe@episcopalchurch.org)

EXECUTIVE OFFICE OF THE GENERAL CONVENTION

(800) 334-7626 Fax: (212) 972-9322 Web: www.generalconvention.org

Rev. Canon Dr. Michael Barlowe, *Executive Officer of the General Convention, Secretary of the General Convention and Registrar*; Rt. Rev. Mary Gray-Reeves, *Vice-Chair House of Bishops*; Wolfe, Dean Elliot, The Rt. Rev. Dean E. Wolfe, *Vice-Chair House of Bishops*; Rushing, Byron, The Hon. Byron Rushing, *Vice President, House of Deputies*; Barnes, N. Kurt, Mr. N. Kurt Barnes, *Treasurer*; Oliver, Juan M.C., The Rev. Dr. Juan M.C. Oliver, *Custodian, Standard Book of Common Prayer*; Duffy, Mark J., Mr. Mark J. Duffy, *Canonical Archivist and Director of Archives*; Mullin, Robert Bruce, Dr. Robert Bruce Mullin, *Historiographer*; Smith, Geoffrey, Rev. Deacon Geoffrey Smith, *Vice President and COO*; Bell, Betsey, Ms. Betsey Bell, *Assistant to the President of the House of Deputies*; Castells-Ortlieb, Laura, Ms. Laura Castells-Ortlieb, *Administrative Assistant for Legislation and Communications*; Conboy, Marian, Ms. Marian Conboy, *Executive Assistant and Deputy for Legislation*; DiLeonardo, Iris J., Ms. Iris J. DiLeonardo, *Research and Data Specialist*; Gonzalez, Jennifer, Ms. Jennifer Gonzalez, *Administrative Assistant*; Haizel, Patrick J. , Mr. Patrick J. Hazel, *Manager for Finance and Meetings*; Ionnitiu, Lori M., Ms. Lori M. Ionnitiu, *Director of Meetings and Convention*; Murray, Brian, Mr. Brian Murray, *Staff Assistant for Meetings*; Rios, Twila, Ms. Twila Rios, *Manager of Digital Information Systems*

THE GENERAL CONVENTION

The 80th General Convention will be held July 5–July 13, 2018 in Austin, Texas [New dates needed.}

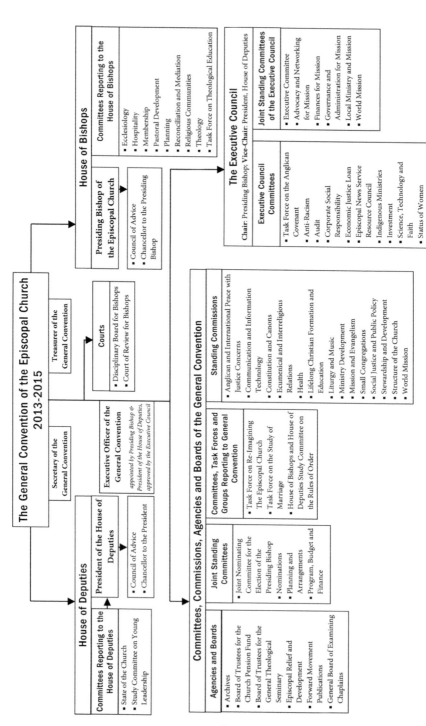

The General Convention of the Episcopal Church 2013-2015

House of Deputies

Committees Reporting to the House of Deputies
- State of the Church
- Study Committee on Young Leadership

President of the House of Deputies
- Council of Advice
- Chancellor to the President

Secretary of the General Convention

Executive Officer of the General Convention
appointed by Presiding Bishop & President of the House of Deputies, approved by the Executive Council

Treasurer of the General Convention

Courts
- Disciplinary Board for Bishops
- Court of Review for Bishops

House of Bishops

Presiding Bishop of the Episcopal Church
- Council of Advice
- Chancellor to the Presiding Bishop

Committees Reporting to the House of Bishops
- Ecclesiology
- Hospitality
- Membership
- Pastoral Development
- Planning
- Reconciliation and Mediation
- Religious Communities
- Theology
- Task Force on Theological Education

The Executive Council

Chair: Presiding Bishop; Vice-Chair: President, House of Deputies

Executive Council Committees
- Task Force on the Anglican Covenant
- Anti-Racism
- Audit
- Corporate Social Responsibility
- Economic Justice Loan
- Episcopal News Service
- Resource Council
- Indigenous Ministries
- Investment
- Science, Technology and Faith
- Status of Women

Joint Standing Committees of the Executive Council
- Executive Committee
- Advocacy and Networking for Mission
- Finances for Mission
- Governance and Administration for Mission
- Local Ministry and Mission
- World Mission

Committees, Commissions, Agencies and Boards of the General Convention

Agencies and Boards
- Archives
- Board of Trustees for the Church Pension Fund
- Board of Trustees for the General Theological Seminary
- Episcopal Relief and Development
- Forward Movement Publications
- General Board of Examining Chaplains

Joint Standing Committees
- Joint Nominating Committee for the Election of the Presiding Bishop
- Nominations
- Planning and Arrangements
- Program, Budget and Finance

Committees, Task Forces and Groups Reporting to General Convention
- Task Force on Re-Imagining The Episcopal Church
- Task Force on the Study of Marriage
- House of Bishops and House of Deputies Study Committee on the Rules of Order

Standing Commissions
- Anglican and International Peace with Justice Concerns
- Communication and Information Technology
- Constitution and Canons
- Ecumenical and Interreligious Relations
- Health
- Lifelong Christian Formation and Education
- Liturgy and Music
- Ministry Development
- Mission and Evangelism
- Small Congregations
- Social Justice and Public Policy
- Stewardship and Development
- Structure of the Church
- World Mission

THE HOUSE OF BISHOPS

Chair: **Curry**, Most Rev Michael Bruce; *Vice-Chair*: **Gray-Reeves**, Rt Rev Mary; *Secretary*: **Bruce**, Rt Rev Diane M Jardine

Committees of the House of Bishops

Presiding Bishop's Council of Advice

(*All terms* 2021) **Curry**, Most Rev Michael Bruce, *Chair*; *Province I*: **Doulas**, Rt Rev Ian; *Province II*: **Duncan-Probe**, Rt Rev Dr DeDe; *Province III*: **Klusmeyer**, Rt Rev William; *Province IV*: **Benhase**, Rt Rev Scott; *Province V*: **Hollingsworth**, Rt Rev Mark; **Ousley**, Rt Rev Todd; *Province VI*: **Prior**, Rt Rev Brian N; *Province VII*: **Benfield**, Rt Rev Larry; *Province VIII*: **Gray-Reeves**, Rt Rev Mary; *Province IX*: **Scantlebury**, Rt Rev Victor; *Staff*: **Hunn**, Rev Cn Michael; **Robertson**, Rev Cn Dr CK; **Spellers**, Rev Cn Stephanie; **Baerga**, Ms Ednice; **Jones**, Ms Sharon; *Ex-Officio*: **Gray-Reeves**, Rt Rev Mary; **Ousley**, Rt Rev Todd

House of Bishops Committee on Pastoral Development

(*All terms* 2021) **Harris**, Rt Rev Gayle E (*Chair*); **Baskerville-Burrows**, Rt Rev Jennifer; **Beauvoir**, Rt Rev Oge; **Daniel**, Rt Rev Clifton; **Goff**, Rt Rev Susan; **Hollerith**, Rt Rev Herman; **Hougland**, Rt Rev Whayne; **Ousley**, Rt Rev Todd; **Owensby**, Rt Rev Jacob W; **Provenzano**, Rt Rev Larry; **Wolfe**, Rt Rev Dean E; *SPG Representative*: **Fisher**, Rev Betsy; *Ex-Officio*: **Curry**, Most Rev Michael Bruce

House of Bishops Planning Committee

(*All terms* 2021) **Prior**, Rt Rev Brian N (*Chair*); **Barker**, Rt Rev Scott; **Budde**, Rt Rev Mariann; **Goff**, Rt Rev Susan; **Hayashi**, Rt Rev Scott B; **Ousley**, Rt Rev Todd; **Quezada Mota**, Rt Rev Moises; **Smylie**, Rt Rev John; *Chaplains*: **Davidson**, Mr Dent; **Greve** OHC, Br Randy; **Howell**, Very Rev Miguelina; *SPG Representative*: **Skirving**, Mrs Sandy; *Ex-Officio*: **Curry**, Most Rev Michael Bruce; **Gray-Reeves**, Rt Rev Mary; **Rowe**, Rt Rev Sean

THE HOUSE OF DEPUTIES

President: **Jennings**, Rev Gay; *Vice President*: **Rushing**, Hon Byron; *Secretary*: **Barlowe**, Rev Cn Dr Michael; *Chancellor to the President*: **Johnson**, Ms Sally A Johnson, Esq

Committees of the House of Deputies

Council of Advice

Jennings, Rev Gay Clark (*Chair*); **Anderson**, Rev Devon; **Barlowe**, Rev Cn Dr Michael; Rev Cn Susan; **Glass**, Michael Glass, Esq; **Johnson**, Sally A Johnson, Esq; **Krislock**, Bryan W Krislock, Esq; **Little**, Thomas A Little, Esq; **MacKenzie**, Lester; **Rowe**, Rt Rev Sean W; **Rushing**, Hon Byron

House of Deputies Committee on the State of the Church

(*All terms* 2021) **Rankin-Williams**, Rev Chris (*Chair*); **McKellaston**, Ms Louisa (*Vice-Chair*); **Sierra**, Jason (*Secretary*); **Akao**, Mr Keane; **Ardry**, Ms Lindsey; **Atkins**, Ms LaClaire; **Canady**, Rev Paul; **de la Torre**, Rev Carlos; **Grandfield**, Dale; **Jimenez**, Ms Erendira; **McCall**, Rev Ramelle; **Preston**, Rev Leigh; **Rowe**, Rt Rev Sean; **Serrano Poveda**, Rev Nelson; **Simon**, Mr James; **Thompson**, Ms Allison; **Wesch**, Rev Kate; *Ex Officio*: **Jennings**, Rev Gay Clark; *Representative of the PHOD*: **Wilson**, Ms Rebecca

THE COURTS

Disciplinary Board for Bishops

Waynick, Rt Rev Catherine M (*Chair, 2021*); **Alarid**, Hon Joseph (*2024*); **Bourlakas**, Rt Rev Mark (*2024*); **Brooke-Davidson**, Rt Rev Jennifer (*2024*); **Gibbs**, Rt Rev Wendell (*2024*); **Harrison**, Rt Rev Dena (*2024*); **Henderson, Jr**, Rt Rev Dorsey F (*2021*); **Hirschfeld**, Rt Rev A Robert (*2024*); **Holding**, Rev Cn Suzann V (*2021*); **Hollerith**, Rt Rev Herman (*2024*); **Knisely**, Rt Rev W Nicholas (*2021*); **Larsen**, Rev Erik (*2021*); **O'Neill**, Rt Rev Robert J (*2021*); **Perrin**, Melissa (*2024*); **Smith**, Mr Marcellus L (*2021*); **So**, Rev Alistair (*2024*); **Stokes**, Ms Deborah J (*2021*); **Tanabe**, Rev Irene (*2024*)

EXECUTIVE COUNCIL

Curry, Most Rev Michael Bruce (*Chair*); **Jennings**, Rev Gay Clark (*Vice-Chair*); *Elected until GC 2021*: **Barlowe**, Rev Cn Dr Michael (*Secretary*); *VII*: **Alexander**, Mr Thomas; *IX*: **Allen**, Rt Rev Lloyd; *VIII*: **Anderson**, Dr Liza; *VI*: **Anderson**, Rev Devon; **Anning**, Douglas; *VII*: **Ayale Harris**, Ms Julia; *IV*: **Ballentine**, Fr Jabriel; *II*: **Barnes**, Mr N Kurt; *VII*: **Butler**, Ms Diane; *V*: **Cisluycis**, Ms Jane; *V*: **Cowden**, Rev Matthew; *II*: **Davis-Wilson**, Rev Lillian; *III*: **Downing**, Rev Patty; *II*: **Duncan**, Cn Noreen; *VIII*: **Eaton**, Re Cn Cornelia; *IX*: **Echeverry**, Sra Blanca; *IV*: **Freeman**, Ms Alice; *VIII*: **Getz**, Ms Pauline; *VIII*: **Glosson**, Mr Louis; *IX*: **Gonzales Polanco**, Ms Mayra Lisbeth; *VI*: **Goodhouse-Mauai**, Rev Angela; *VII*: **Goodman**, Very Rev Mark; *VIII*: **Hayashi**, Rt Rev Scott; *IV*: **Hodges-Copple**, Rt Rev Anne; *III*: **Kitch**, Rt Rev Cn Anne; *I*: **Link**, Ms Alexizendria; *I*: **Lloyd**, Rev Mally Ewing; *IV*: **Logue**, Rev Cn Frank; *IV*: **McKellar**, Mrs Andrea; *VIII*: **Nishibayashi**, Cn Dr Steven; *I*: **Perkins**, Archdeacon Aaron; *II*: **Pollard**, Ms Diane; *IV*: **Powell**, Ms Holli; *III*: **Randall**, Mr Russell; *II*: **Sconiers**, Hon Rose; *I*: **Smith**, Rev Geoffrey; *IV*: **Smith**, Rt Rev Dabney; *III*: **Stonesifer**, Ms Sarah; *IV*: **Wing**, Mr George; *VIII*: **Wong**, Hon Warren J; **Kostel**, Ms Mary (*Chancellor to the PB*); *I*: **Rushing**, Hon Byron (*VP HOD*); *VI*: **Johnson**, Sally A Johnson, Esq (*Chancellor to the PHOD*); *II*: **Conboy**, Ms Marian (*Staff*); **Voss**, Rev William O

STANDING COMMITTEES OF THE EXECUTIVE COUNCIL

Executive Committee of Executive Council

(*All terms* 2021) **Curry**, Most Rev Michael Bruce (*Chair*); **Jennings**, Rev Gay Clark (*Vice-Chair*); **Ayala Harris**, Ms Julia; **Cisluycis**, Ms Jane; **Hayashi**, Rev Scott; **Lloyd**, Rev Mally Ewing; **Logue**, Rev Cn Frank; **Sconiers**, Hon RoseH; **Smith**, Rt Rev Dabney; *Ex Officio*: **Anning**, Douglas; **Barlow**, Rev Cn Dr Michael; **Barnes**, Rev Geoffrey; **Conboy**, Ms Marian (*staff*)

Executive Council Joint Standing Committee on Governance and Operations

(*All terms* 2021) **Cisluycis**, Ms Jane (*Chair*); **Randle**, Mr Russell V (*Vice-Chair*); **Alexander**, Mr Thomas (*Secretary*); **Anderson**, Dr Liza; **Butler**, Ms Diane P; **Getz**, Ms Pauline Getz, Esq; **Glosson**, Mr Louis; **Konieczny**, Rt Rev Dr Edward J; **Perkins** Archdeacon Aaron; *Ex Officio*: **Curry**, Most Rev Michael Bruce; **Jennings**, Rev Gay Clark

Assessment Review Committee

(*All terms* 2021) **Lloyd**, Rev Mally Ewing (*Chair*); **Ballentine**, Cn Rosalie Simmonds; **Downing**, Rev Patty; **Klusmeyer**; Rt Rev William; **Koonce**, Ms Nancy; **Lattime**; Rt Rev Mark; **Rickel**, Rt Rev Gregory; **Taylor**, Rev Dr James; Ex Officio: **Curry**, Most Rev Michael Bruce; **Jennings**, Rev Gay Clark; **Barnes**, Mr N Kurt (*Treasurer*); **Barlowe**, Rev Cn Dr Michael (*staff*)

Executive Council Committee on Anti-Racism & Reconciliation

(*All terms* 2021) **McKim**, Mr. James (*Chair*); **Dannenberg**, Dr. Frances; **Kitagawa**, Rev Cn John; **Martin Fumero**, Rev Emilio; **Mutope-Johnson**, Ms Ayesha; **Romero**, Mr Brian; **Shaefer**, Rev Susie; **Shepherd**, Rev Dr Angela; **Sneve**, Ven Paul; **Thompson**, Jr, Rt Rev Morris K; *Ex Officio*: **Curry**, Most Rev Michael Bruce; **Jennings**, Rev Gay Clark; *Liaison of Executive Council*: **Duncan**, Cn Noreen; **Kim**, Ms Heidi (*staff*)

Executive Council Committee on Corporate and Social Responsibility

(*All terms* 2021) **Fisher**, Rt Rev Douglas (*Chair*); **Watkins**, Grieves, Rev Cn Brian (*Vice-Chair*); **Clark**, Mr Casey; **Goodman**, Very Rev Mark; **Neuhauser**, Mr Paul; **Pollard**, Ms Diane; **Rushing**, Mr Byron; **Snow Spalding**, Rev Kirsten; **Taylor**, Rt Rev John; *Ex Officio*: **Curry**, Most Rev Michael Bruce; **Jennings**, Rev Gay Clark

Executive Council Committee on HBCU

(*All terms* 2021) **Shaw**, Very Rev Dr Martini (*Chair*); **Evenbeck**, Mr Scott (*Vice-Chair*); **Alexander**, Ms Martha Bedell; **Callaway**, Rev Cn James; **Cunningham**, Dr Joel; **Decatur**, Dr Sean; **George**, Dr Anita; **Hagans**, Rev Dr Cn Michele; **Lowe**, Rev Dr Eugene; **Williams Jr**, Rt Rev Arthur B; *Ex Officio*: **Curry**, Most Rev Michael Bruce; **Jennings**, Rev Gay Clark

Executive Council Conant Fund Grant Review Committee

(*All terms* 2021) **Thom**, Rt Rev Brian (*Chair*); **Kitch**, Rev Cn Anne; **Nishibayashi**, Cn Dr Steven; **Smith**, Rt Rev Dabney; *Ex Officio*: **Curry**, Most Rev Michael Bruce; **Jennings**, Rev Gay Clark; **Barnes**, Mr. N. Kurt (*Treasurer*)

Executive Council Constable Grant Review Committee

(*All terms* 2021) **Wing**, Mr George (*Chair*); **Duncan**, Canon Noreen; **Sconiers**, Hon Rose H; *Ex Officio*: **Curry**, Most Rev Michael Bruce; **Jennings**, Rev Gay Clark; **Barnes**, Mr. N. Kurt (*Treasurer*); *Staff*: **Barlowe**, Rev Cn Dr Michael; **Crosnier de Bellaistre**, Ms Margareth; **Mullen**, Rev Melanie

Executive Council Economic Justice Loan Committee

(*All terms* 2021) **Parker**, Ms Lindsey (*Chair*); **Jackson**, Rev Paula (*Vice-Chair*); **Gee**, Mr Timothy; **Hodges-Copple**, Rt Rev Anne; **Mebane**, Rev Will; **Walter**, Rev Andrew; **Wong**, Mr Warren; *Ex Officio*: **Curry**, Most Rev Michael Bruce; **Jennings**, Rev Gay Clark; *Staff*: **Barlowe**, Rev Cn Dr Michael; **Caparulo**, Mrs Nancy; **Crosnier de Bellaistre**, Ms Margareth; **Oconer**, Mr Tanie (*Staff*); **Chaplin**, Christopher; **Daniels**, Ms Keys; **Gritzuk**, Mr Maxwell; **Wright**, Lisa

Executive Council Investment Committee

(*All terms* 2021) **Walter**, The Rev. Andrew (*Chair*); **Talty**, Mr. John (*Vice-Chair*); **Akinla**, Mr. Dale; **Austin**, Ms. Marion; **Barnes**, Mr. N. Kurt; **Brown**, Ms. Janet; **Fowler**, Mr. Gordon; **Powell**, Ms. Holli; **Simon**, Mr. James; *Ex Officio*: **Curry**, Most Rev Michael Bruce; **Jennings**, Rev Gay Clark

Executive Council Joint Standing Committee on Finance

(*All terms* 2021) **Lloyd**, The Rev. Mally Ewing (*Chair*); **Pollard**, Ms. Diane (*Vice-Chair*); **Powell**, Ms. Holli (*Vice-Chair*); **Downing**, The Rev. Patty; **Eaton**, The Rev. Canon Cornelia; **Hodges-Copple**, The Rt. Rev. Anne; **Kitch**, The Rev. Canon Anne; **Link**, Ms. Alexizendria; **McKellar**, Mrs. Andrea; *Ex Officio*: **Curry**, Most Rev Michael Bruce; **Jennings**, Rev Gay Clark; *Staff*: **Caparulo**, Mrs. Nancy; *PB&F member*: **Ehmer**, The Rev. Cn. Mike

Executive Council Joint Standing Committee on Governance and Operations

(*All terms* 2021) **Cisluycis**, Ms Jane (*Chair*); **Randle**, Mr Russell V (*Vice-Chair*); **Alexander**, Mr Thomas (*Secretary*); **Anderson**, Dr Liza; **Butler**, Ms Diane P; **Getz**, Ms Pauline Getz, Esq; **Glosson**, Mr Louis; **Konieczny**, Rt Rev Dr Edward J; **Perkins** Archdeacon Aaron; *Ex Officio*: **Curry**, Most Rev Michael Bruce; **Jennings**, Rev Gay Clark

Executive Council Joint Standing Committee on Mission Beyond The Episcopal Church

(*All terms* 2021) **Smith**, The Rt. Rev. Dabney (*Chair*); **Davis-Wilson**, The Rev. Lillian (*Vice-Chair*); **Cowden**, The Rev. Matthew (*Secretary*); **Echeverry**, Sra. Blanca; **Freeman**, Ms. Alice; **Gonzales Polanco**, Ms. Mayra Liseth; **Goodman**, The Very Rev. Mark; **Hayashi**, The Rt. Rev. Scott; **Wong**, Mr. Warren; *Ex Officio*: **Curry**, Most Rev Michael Bruce; **Jennings**, Rev Gay Clark

Executive Council Joint Standing Committee on Mission within the Episcopal Church

(*All terms* 2021) **Logue**, The Rev. Canon Frank (*Chair*); **Sconiers**, The Hon. Rose H. (*Vice-Chair*); **Wing**, Mr. George (*Secretary*); **Allen**, The Rt. Rev. Lloyd; **Anderson**, The Rev. Devon; **Ayala Harris**, Ms. Julia; **Duncan**, Canon Noreen; **Goodhouse-Mauai**, The Rev. Angela; **Nishibayashi**, Canon Dr. Steven; **Stonesifer**, Ms. Sarah; *Ex Officio*: **Curry**, Most Rev Michael Bruce; **Jennings**, Rev Gay Clark

Executive Council Roanridge Trust Grant Review Committee

(*All terms* 2021) **Wing**, Mr. George (*Chair*); **Callaway**, The Rev. Canon James; **Duncan**, Canon Noreen; **Fischer**, The Rev. Evan; **Harrigan**, The Rev. Canon Katherine; **Sconiers**, The Hon. Rose H.; *Ex Officio*: **Curry**, Most Rev Michael Bruce; **Jennings**, Rev Gay Clark; *Treasurer*: **Barnes**, Mr. N. Kurt; *Staff*: **Barlowe**, The Rev. Canon Dr. Michael; **Malm**, Cecilia; **Mullen**, Rev. Melanie

Joint Audit Committee of the Executive Council and the DFMS

(*All terms* 2021) **Krislock**, Mr. Bryan (*Chair*); **Glover**, Dr. Delbert; **Haas**, Mr. G. William; **Hougland**, The Rt. Rev. Whayne; **Judge**, Ms. Tess; **Lloyd**, The Rev. Mally Ewing; *Ex Officio*: **Curry**, Most Rev Michael Bruce; **Jennings**, Rev Gay Clark

Scholarship Grant Committee

(*All terms* 2021) **Stevenson**, The Rev. Canon E. Mark (*Chair*); **Barnes**, Mr. N. Kurt; **Crosnier de Bellaistre**, Ms. Margareth; **Johnson IV**, Mr. John; **Mead**, The Rev. Matthew; **Nishibayashi**, Ms. Kathryn

United Thank Offering Board

(*All terms* 2021) **Dietrich**, Ms Sherri (*Chair*); **Landers**, Ms Joyce (*Vice-Chair*); **Mank**, Ms Kathy (*Financial Secretary*); **Candelario**, Ms Lorraine; **Cromwell**, Rev Peggy; **Daniels**, Rosamond; **Darnell**, Ms Caitlyn; **Donovan**, Gail; **Gabbard**, Diane; **Jacobson**, Sedona; **Jellison**, Ms Jane; **Lammar**, Hilda; **Plantz**, Rev Christine; **Smith**, Ms Vernese; *Ex Officio*: **Curry**, Most Rev Michael Bruce; **Jennings**, Rev Gay Clark; *Liaison of Executive Council*: **Cowden**, Rev Matthew

COMMITTEES OF COUNCIL

Joint Audit Committee of the Executive Council and the DFMS

(*All terms* 2021) **Krislock**, Bryan W Krislock, Esq (*Chair*); **Glover**, Dr Delbert C; **Haas**, G William Haas, Esq; **Hougland**, Rt Rev Whayne; **Judge**, Ms Tess; **Lloyd**, Rev Mally Ewing; *Ex Officio*: **Curry**, Most Rev Michael Bruce; **Jennings**, Rev Gay Clark

Executive Council Investment Committee

(*All terms* 2021) **Walter**, Rev Andrew (*Chair*); **Talty**, Mr John (*Vice-Chair*); **Akinla**, Mr Dale; **Austin**, Ms Marion; **Barnes**, Mr N Kurt; **Brown**, Ms Janet; **Fowler**, Mr Gordon; **Powell**, Ms Holli; **Simon**, Mr James; *Ex Officio*: **Curry**, Most Rev Michael Bruce; **Jennings**, Rev Gay Clark

Executive Council Committee on Anti-Racism & Reconciliation

(*All terms* 2021) **McKim**, Mr James T (*Chair*); **Dannenberg**, Dr Frances; **Kitagawa**, Rev Cn John; **Martin Fumero**, Rev Emilio; **Mutope-Johnson**, Ms Ayesha; **Romero**, Mr Brian; **Shaefer**, Rev Susie; **Shepherd**, Rev Dr Angela; **Sneve**, Ven Paul; **Thompson, Jr**, Rt Rev Morris K; *Ex Officio*: **Curry**, Most Rev Michael Bruce; **Jennings**, Rev Gay Clark; *Liaison of Executive Council*: **Duncan**, Cn Noreen; **Kim**, Ms Heidi (*staff*)

Executive Council Committee on Corporate and Social Responsibility

(*All terms* 2021) **Fisher**, Rt Rev Douglas (*Chair*); **Grieves**, Rev Cn Brian (*Vice-Chair*); **Clark**, Mr Casey; **Goodman**, Very Rev Mark; **Neuhauser**, Mr Paul M; **Pollard**, Ms Diane; **Rushing**, Mr Byron; **Snow Spaulding**, Rev Kirsten; **Taylor**, Rt Rev John; *Ex Officio*: **Curry**, Most Rev Michael Bruce; **Jennings**, Rev Gay Clark

Executive Council Economic Justice Loan Committee

(*All terms* 2021) **Parker**, Ms Lindsey (*Chair*); **Jackson**, Rev Paula (*Vice-Chair*); **Gee**, Mr Timothy; **Hodges-Copple**, Rt Rev Anne; **Mebane**, Rev Will; **Walter**, Rev Andrew; **Wong**, Mr Warren; *Ex Officio*:

Curry, Most Rev Michael Bruce; **Jennings,** Rev Gay Clark; **Barlowe,** The Rev. Canon Dr. Michael; **Barnes,** Mr. N. Kurt; **Caparulo,** Mrs. Nancy; **Crosnier de Bellaistre,** Ms. Margareth; **Oconer,** Mr. Tanie (*Staff*); **Chaplin,** Christopher; **Daniels,** Ms. Keys; **Gritzuk,** Mr. Maxwell; **Wright,** Lisa

JOINT STANDING COMMITTEES

Joint Nominating Committee for the Election of the Presiding Bishop

(*All terms* 2021) **Ahrens,** Rt Rev Laura J; **Ambrogi,** Ms Sarah; **Baker,** Rev Stannard; **Burgess,** Rev Vicki; **Carmiachael,** Rev Cn Anna; **Duque,** Rt Rev Franciso; **Foster,** Mr Brad; **Gaines,** Ms Carolyn; **Glasspool,** Rt Rev Mary; **Goff,** Rt Rev Susan; **Guzman,** El Rvdo. Franciso. **Hougland,** Rt Rev Whanyne; **Hunn,** Rt Rev Michael CB; **Lantigua,** Mr Hector; **Lees,** Rev Everett; **McDaniel,** Mr Joe; **McPhee,** Ms Sandra; **Petrosh,** Ms Andrea; **Prichard,** Rev Dr Robert; **Rehberg,** Rt Rev Gretchen; **Romero,** Mr Brian; **Russell,** Rev Daniel Scott; **Scarfe,** Rt Rev Alan; **Slenski,** Rev Mary; **Wagner,** Rev Meg; **Webley,** Mrs Alice R; **White,** Rt Rev Terry

Joint Standing Committee on Nominations

(*All* terms 2021) **Haight,** Mr Scott (*Chair*); **Miller,** Rt Rev Susan (*Vice-Chair*); **Pomerenk,** Ms Erica (*Secretary*); **Alarid,** Hon Joseph; **Collins,** Rev Cn Dr Lynn A; **Gordon,** Ms Nanci; **Hogg,** Mrs Toni; **Lambert,** Rt Rev W Jay; **Middleton,** Rev Tracie; **Nishibayashi,** Ms Kathryn; **Scantlebury,** Rt Rev Victor; **Smith,** Rt Rev Dabney; **Taber-Hamilton,** Rev Rachel; *Ex Officio:* **Curry,** Most Rev Michael Bruce; **Jennings,** Rev Gay Clark

Joint Standing Committee on Planning and Arrangements

(*All terms* 2021) **Barlowe,** Rev Cn Dr Michael (*Chair*); **Anderson,** Rev Devon; **Barnes,** Mr N Kurt; **Bruce,** Rt Rev Diane M Jardine; **Gibbs,** Rt Rev Wendell N; **Gray-Reeves,** Rt Rev Mary; **Krislock,** Mr Byron; **Kusumoto,** Mr Ryan; **Patterson,** Ms Karen; **Rushing,** Mr Byron; **Slater,** Rev Cn Scott; **Sutton,** Rt Rev Eugene; *Ex Officio:* **Curry,** Most Rev Michael Bruce; **Jennings,** Rev Gay Clark

Joint Standing Committee on Program, Budget and Finance

(*All terms* 2021) **Ehmer,** Rev Cn J Michael (*Convener*); **Fisher,** Rt Rev Jeff W (*Vice-Convener*); **Barker,** Rt Rev J Scott; **Benkelman,** Ms Cynthia; **Bourlakas,** Rt Rev Mark A; **Braxton,** Mr Michael; **Davila,** Ed Rvdo Angel; **Davis-Lawson,** Rev Karen; **Downing,** Rev Patty; **Duque,** Rt Rev Francisco; **Fleener** Jr, Mr William; **Floberg,** Rev John F; **Gee,**

Mr Timothy; **Hincapie,** Rev David; **Hughes,** Rt Rev Carlye; **Humphrey,** Re Nathan; **Huston,** Ms Kate; **Judge,** Ms Tess; **Knisely,** Rt Rev W Nicholas; **Koonce,** Ms Nancy; **Lloyd,** Rev Mally Ewing; **Plummer,** Ms Chrystal; **Quitmeyer,** Mr David; **Ray,** Rt Rev Rayford; **Rickel,** Rt Rev Gregory H; **Sloan,** Rt Rev John McKee; **Wilcox,** Rev Diana; **Barlowe,** Rev Cn Dr Michael (*Secretary of GC*); *Ex Officio:* **Curry,** Most Rev Michael Bruce; **Jennings,** Rev Gay Clark; **Barnes,** Mr N Kurt (*Treasurer*)

STANDING COMMISSIONS

Standing Commission on Liturgy and Music

Fromberg, Rev Dr Paul D (*2021, Chair*); **Johnston,** Mrs Ellen (*2021, Vice-Chair*); **Nelson,** Ms Jessica (*2021, Secretary*); **Baker,** Rev Stannard (*2024*); **Boney,** Dr Michael (*2024*); **Burford,** Ms Martha (*2021*); **Childers,** Cn Mark (*2024*); **DuPree,** Ms Mary Grace (*2024*); **Floberg,** Mr Joshua (*2024*); **Hahn,** Ms Athena (*2021*); **Hino,** Rev Cn Robert (*2024*); **Lee,** Rt Rev Jeffrey D (*2021*); **Montes,** Mr Ellis (*2024*); **Reyes,** Rev J Sierra (*2024*); **Robert,** Mr John (*2021*); **Turrell,** Rev Cn James F Turrell, PhD (*2021*); **Waldo,** Rt Rev Andrew (*2024*); **Whalon,** Rt Rev Pierre (*2024*); **White,** Rt Rev Terry (*2021*); **Wright,** Rt Rev Carl (*2024*); *Ex Officio:* **Curry,** Most Rev Michael Bruce (*2021*); **Jennings,** Rev Gay Clark (*2021*); *Representative of the PHOD:* **Anslow Williams,** Rev Susan (*2021*); *Liaison of Executive Council:* **Logue,** Rev Cn Frank (*2021*); *Custodian of the Book of Common Prayer:* **Oliver,** Rev Dr Juan M C

Standing Commission on Structure, Governance, Constitution and Canons

James, Rev Dr Molly F James, PhD (*2021, Chair*); **Rowe,** Rt Rev Sean (*2024, Vice-Chair*); **Little,** Mr Thomas (*2024, Secretary*); **Alexander,** Rev Sharon (*2021, Assistant Secretary*); **Cohen,** Ms Nancy Mahoney (*2021*); **Balling,** Rev Valerie (*2024*); **Baskerville-Burrows,** Rt Rev Jennifer (*2024*); **Buchanan,** Ms Annette (*2021*); **Figueroa,** Sra Carmen (*2024*); **Gibbs,** Rt Rev Wendell (*2021*); **Glass,** Michael Glass, Esq (*2021*); **Hayes,** Christopher J Hayes, Esq (*2024*); **Klusmeyer,** Rt Rev William Michie (*2021*); **Kusumoto,** Mr Ryan (*2024*); **Montes,** Ms Luz (*2021*); **Owensby,** Rt Rev Jake (*2021*); **Powel,** Mr William (*2024*); **Smith,** Jamal Smith, Esq (*2021*); **Tabizon Thompson,** Rev Marisa (2024); **Trambley,** Rev Dr Adam (*2024*); *Ex Officio:* **Curry,** Most Rev Michael Bruce (*2021*); **Jennings,** Rev Gay Clark (*2021*); *Representative of the Presiding Bishop:* **Stevenson,** Rev Cn E Mark (*2021*); *Representative of the PHOD:* **Johnson,** Sally A Johnson, Esq (*2021*); *Liaison of Executive Council:* **Cisluycis,** Ms Jane (*2021*)

TASK FORCES OF GENERAL CONVENTION

Task Force on Care of Creation & Environmental Racism

(*All terms* 2021) **Johnson**, Rev Stephanie (*Chair*); **Rice**, Rt Rev David (*Vice-Chair*); **Kerr**, Mr Tyler (*Secretary*); **Acosta**, Rev Richard; **Bascom**, Rev Cn Dr Cathleen; **Demientieff**, Bernadette; **Empsall**, Rev Nathan; **Fitzpatrick**, Rt Rev Robert; **Griffin**, Rev P Joshua; **Heck**, DrDelia; **Hirshfeld**, Rt Rev A Robert; **Hodgkins Jones**, Ms Perry; **Lattime**, Rt Rev Mark; **Mackenzie**, Rev Lester; **Mallette Stephens**, Rev Hershey; **Matthews**, Rev Weston; **Munoz**, Rev Cn Dimas; **Nolan**; Ms Sarah; **Powell**, Rev Dcn Lewis; **Richardson**, Very Rev W Mark; **Selleres-Petersen**, Brian; **Thompson**, Dr Andrew; *Ex Officio*: **Curry**, Most Rev Michael Bruce; **Jennings**, Rev Gay Clark; *Staff*: **Mullen**, Rev Melanie

Advisory Council on Disability & Deaf Access

(*All terms* 2021) **Smith**, Rev Twila (*Chair*); **Watkins**, Ms Sarah (*Vice-Chair*); **Bourquin**, Rev Dr Eugene (*Gene*); **Brown**, Ms. Carrie; **Johnston**, Rev Suzanne; **Martensen**, Ms Cass; **Moore**, Mr Gary; **Skirving**, Rt Rev Rob; **Van Koevering**, Rt Rev Mark; *Ex Officio*: **Curry**, Most Rev Michael Bruce; **Jennings**, Rev Gay Clark

Presiding Officers' Advisory Group on Beloved Community Implementation

(*All terms* 2021) **Johnson**, Rev Edwin (*Chair*); **Corcoran**, Mr Rob; **Doll**, Ms Holly; **Lee**, Prof Brant; **Marquez**, Rev Canon Juan I; **Mbuwayesango**, Dr Dora; **Moore**, MrGary; **Rosero-Nordalm**, Rev Ema; **Rushing**, Mr Byron; **Sotelo**, Fabio; **Wagner**, Rev Meg; **Waldo**, Rt Rev Andrew; *Ex Officio*: **Curry**, Most Rev Michael Bruce; **Jennings**, Rev Gay Clark; *Liaison of Executive Council*: **Eaton**, Rev Cn Cornelia; **Spellers**, Rev Cn Stephanie (*staff*); **Kitagawa**, Rev Cn John

Task Force on Church Planting and Congregational Redevelopment

(*All terms* 2021) **Waggoner**, Rev Cn Janet (*Chair*); **Shin**, Rt Rev Allen (*Vice-Chair*); **Finstad**, Ms Natalie (*Secretary*); **Brooke-Davidson**, Rt Rev Jennifer; **Budde**, Rt Rev Mariann; **Evans**, Mr Jason; **Forsyth**, Cn Katie; **Ivey**, Rev Cn Betsey S; **Lopez**, Dr Gandhy; **McCall**, Caroline; **McCreath**, Very Rev Amy; **Metoyer**, Rev Eric; **Morrow**, Rev Cn Dan; **Rehberg**, Rt Rev Gretchen; **Scarfe**, Rt Rev Alan; **Velez-Riveera**, Rev Daniel; **Wong Nagata**, Rev Cn Dr Ada; *Ex Officio*: **Curry**, Most Rev Michael Bruce; **Jennings**, Rev Gay Clark; *Staff*: **Brackett**, Rev Tom; **Michie**, Rev Michael

Working Group on Readmission of Cuba

(*All terms* 2021) **Barlowe**, Rev Cn Dr Michael (*Convener*); **Anning**, Douglas; **Johnson**, Ms Sally Johnson, Esq; **Kostel**, Ms Mary; **Ousley**, Rt Rev Todd; **Robertson**, Rev Cn Dr Charles K; **Rushing**, Mr Byron; *Ex Officio*: **Curry**, Most Rev Michael Bruce; **Jennings**, Rev Gay Clark

Task Force to Develop Model Sexual Harassment Policies & Safe Church Training

(*All terms* 2021) **Andrews**, Ms Judith (*Chair*); **Ahrens**, Rt Rev Laura (*Vice-Chair*); **Camara**, Ms Kemah; **Cantwell**, Ms Cookie; **Cole**, Ms L Zoe; **Cowell**, Rt Rev Mark; **Fry**, Rev Gwen; **Linares**, Rev Kimberly; **McCray-Goldsmith**, Rev Cn Julia; **Miles**, Caren; **Scriven**, Rev Beth; **Spannaus**, Rev Dcn Tim; **Travis**, Mr Eric; *Ex Officio*: **Curry**, Most Rev Michael Bruce; **Jennings**, Rev Gay Clark; *Other*: **Floyd**, Kathy

Task Force on Clergy Formation & Continuing Education

(*All terms* 2021) **Eccles**, Very Rev M E (*Chair*); **Benfield**, Rt Rev Larry (*Vice-Chair*); **Bader-Saye**, Dr Scott; **Bruce**, Rt Rev Diane M Jardine; **Corbin**, Dr Christopher; **Dempesy-Sims**, Rev Cn Catherine; **Good**, Dr Deirdre; **Hollis**, Rev Dr Deacon Robin; **Lowrey**, Rev Lang; **Robbins**, Dr Gregory; **Scantlebury**, Rt Rev Victor; **Smith**, Mr Marcellus; *Ex Officio*: **Curry**, Most Rev Michael Bruce; **Jennings**, Rev Gay Clark

Task Force on Communion across Difference

(*All terms* 2021) **Bauerschmidt**, Rt Rev John (*Convener*); **Russell**, Rev Cn Susan (*Convener*); **Brewer**, Rev Gregory O; **Brokenleg**, Rev Isaiah "Shaneequa"; **Ellis**, Mr Fred; **Ely**, Rt Rev Thomas; **Escobar**, Mr Miguel; **Garno**, Rev Scott; **Gray-Reeves**, Rt Rev Mary; **Haeffner**, Ms Anna; **Hylden**, Rev Cn Jordan; **Quezada Mota**, Rt Rev Moises; **Wallace**, Rev Cn Tanya; **Wells**, Dr Christopher; *Ex Officio*: **Curry**, Most Rev Michael Bruce; **Jennings**, Rev Gay Clark

Task Force on Dialogue with South Sudanese Anglican Diaspora

(*All terms* 2021) **Mathews**, Rev Ranjit (*Chair*); **Scarfe**, Rt Rev Alan (*Vice-Chair*); **Field**, Rt Rev Martin; **Kraus**, Ms Jackie; **Paul**, Rev Michael; **Randle**, Mr Russell; *Ex Officio*: **Curry**, Most Rev Michael Bruce; **Jennings**, Rev Gay Clark

Task Force on Formation & Ministry of the Baptized

(*All terms* 2021) **Kimball**, Dr Lisa (*Chair*); **Kendrick**, Rt Rev J Russell (*Vice-Chair*); **Aparicio**, Rev Paul; **Brown**, Ms Lisa; **Bucklin**, Rev Cn Lydia; **Erickson**, Rev Heather; **Gallagher**, Rt Rev Carol; **Hodapp**, Rev Cn Timothy; **Prentiss**, Ms Demi; **Rau**, Ms Melissa; **Rushing**, Mr Byron; **Wong**, Rev Peter; **Wright**, Rt Rev Robert; *Ex Officio*: **Curry**, Most Rev Michael Bruce; **Jennings**, Rev Gay Clark

Task Force on Liturgical & Prayer Book Revision

(*All terms* 2021) **Alexander**, Rt Rev J Neil (*Chair*); **Ranadive Pooley**, Rev Dr Nina (*Vice-Chair*); **Mead**, Rev Matthew (*Secretary*); **Ardrey-Graves**, Dr Mark; **Braman**, Mr Ron; **Candler**, Very Rev Samuel G; **Cole**, Rt Rev Brian; **Decatur**, Mr. Christopher; **Dressler**, Mr. Craig; **Geiszler-Ludlum**, Ms Joan; **Gibbs**, Rt Rev Wendell; **Glasspool**, Rt Rev Mary; **Gunter**, Rt Rev Matthew A; **Johnson**, Rev Deon; **Linares-Palacios**, Lcdo. Adrián; **McConnell**, Rt Rev Dorsey; **Meyers**, Rev Dr Ruth; **Monterroso**, Rt Rev Hector; **Moore**, Ms Kathleen; **Moroney**, Rev Dr Kevin; **Nyein**, Rev Zack; **Olver**, Rev Dr Matthew S C; **Partridge**, Rev Dr Cameron; **Poisson**, Sister Ellen Francis; **Prior**, Rt Rev Brian N; **Scott**, Mr James; **Smith**, Rt Rev George Wayne; **Thom**, Rt Rev Brian; **Velez Garcia**, Mr. Bryan; **Winner**, Rev Dr Lauren; *Ex Officio*: **Curry**, Most Rev Michael Bruce; **Jennings**, Rev Gay Clark; *SCLM Liaison*: **Fromberg**, Rev Paul

Task Force on Ministry to Individuals with Mental Illness

(*All terms* 2021) **Gortner**, Rev David; (*Chair*); **Tarrant**, Rt Rev John (*Vice-Chair*); **Bailey**, Rt Rev David; **Beck**, Dr Brandon; **Driscoll**, Rev Dr Jeanine; **Henes**, Ms Amanda; **Phillips**, Rev Deacon Susan; **Phillips**, Rev Dr Robert; **Stewart**, Rev John; **Warren**, Ms Evangeline; **Webley**, Mrs Alice R; **Zimbrick-Rogers**, Dr Charles; *Ex Officio*: **Curry**, Most Rev Michael Bruce; **Jennings**, Rev Gay Clark

Task Force on New Funding for Clergy Formation

(*All terms* 2021) **Barnicle**, Rev Brendan (*Chair*); **Breidenthal**, Rt Rev Thomas (*Vice-Chair*); **Cowart**, Dr Courtney V; **Heller**, Mrs Jill; **Henry-McKeever**, Elizabeth Elizabeth; **Hybl**, Rev Andrew; **Jones**, Rev JoAnn; **Kittredge**, Very Rev Cynthia; **Murphy**, Mr James; **Swimmer**, Mr Joseph; **Taylor**, Rt Rev John; *Ex Officio*: **Curry**, Most Rev Michael Bruce; **Jennings**, Rev Gay Clark

Task Force on the Budget Process

(*All terms* 2019) **Little**, Mr Thomas (*Chair*); **Barnes**, Mr N Kurt; **Ehmer**, Rev Cn Mike; **Fisher**, Rt Rev Jeff; **Johnson**, Ms. Sally Johnson, Esq; **Koonce**, Ms Nancy; **Krislock**, Mr Bryan; **Lane**, Rt Rev Stephen; **Lloyd**, Rev Mally Ewing; **Quittmeyer**, Mr David; **Sconiers**, Hon Rose H; *Ex Officio*: **Curry**, Most Rev Michael Bruce; **Jennings**, Rev Gay Clark

Task Force on Theological Education Networking

(*All terms* 2021) **Hagen**, Rev Maureen-Elizabeth (*Chair*); **Reed**, Rt Rev David M (*Vice-Chair*); **Compier**, Very Rev Don; **Cook**, Ms Amy; **Hall**, Rebecca; **Meridith**, Ms Karen; **Stonesifer**, Ms Sarah; **Wang**, Rev Kit; *Ex Officio*: **Curry**, Most Rev Michael Bruce; **Jennings**, Rev Gay Clark

Task Force on Theology of Money

(*All terms* 2021) **Garner**, Rev Evan (*Chair*); **Brown**, Rt Rev Kevin (*Vice-Chair*); **de Leeuw**, Rev Dr Gawain; **Frazer**, Rev Candice; **Harris**, Rt Rev Gayle; **Hayes-Martin**, Rev Gia; **McKeown**, Mr William B; **Provenzano**, Rt Rev Lawrence; **Smith**, Rt Rev Kirk; **Tomlinson**, Dr Steven; **Ventura**, Ms Celeste; **Walker**, Mr Doug; **Weber-Johnson**, Ms Erin; **Wesley Gomez**, Mrs Pamela; *Ex Officio*: **Curry**, Most Rev Michael Bruce; **Jennings**, Rev Gay Clark

Task Force on Theology of Social Justice Advocacy

(*All terms* 2021) **Lawton**, Ms. Sarah (*Chair*); **Singh**, Rt Rev Prince (*Vice-Chair*); **Dietsche**, Rt Rev Andrew; **Frey**, Ms Ruth; **Hodges-Copple**, Rt Rev Anne; **Lee**, Professor Brant; **Leemhuis**, Rev Deacon Guy; **Lloyd**, Ms Lallie; **Mbuwayesango**, Dr Dora; **Rodriguez-Sanjuro**, Rev Jose; **Varghese**, Reuben; **Watson Epting**, Rev Susanne; *Ex Officio*: **Curry**, Most Rev Michael Bruce; **Jennings**, Rev Gay Clark

Task Force on Women, Truth and Reconciliation

(*All terms* 2021) **Link**, Ms. Alexizendria (*Chair*); **Goff**, Rt Rev Susan (*Vice-Chair*); **Lane**, Mr Neel (*Secretary*); **Ayala Harris**, Ms Julia; **Brock**, Rev Laurie; **Brown Douglas**, Rev Dr Kelly; **De Jesus**, Dr Damaris; **Douglas**, Rt Rev Ian; **Duncan-Probe**, Rt Rev Dr DeDe; **Hammeal-Urban**, Ms Robin; **Loya**, Very Rev Craig; **MacVean-Brown**, Rev Dr Shannon; **Murray**, Mr Alan; **Wiesner**, Rev Kurt; **Woodall**, Rev Dcn Carolyn; *Ex Officio*: **Curry**, Most Rev Michael Bruce; **Jennings**, Rev Gay Clark; *Representative of the PHoD*: **Hayes**, Mr. Christopher; **Smith**, Rev. Geoffrey (*Staff*)

Task Force to Assist the Office of Pastoral Development

(*All terms* 2021) **Mathis**, Canon Jill (*Chair*); **Scanlan**, Rt Rev Audrey (*Vice-Chair*); **Ambrogi**, Mr Robert (*Secretary*); **Bates**, Canon Lynn; **Chambers**, Rev Cn Joseph; **Grant**, Rev Percy; **Hitt II**, Mr Lawrence; **Hollingsworth**, Rt Rev Mark; **Jacobs**, Rev Cn Gregory; **Knudsen**, Rt Rev Chilton; **Seage**, Rt Rev Brian; **Smith**, Rev Cn Nora; **Thomason**, Very Rev Dr Steven; **Yeiser**, Ms Mary T; **Zorrilla**, Rev Canon Rafael; *Ex Officio*: **Curry**, Most Rev Michael Bruce; **Jennings**, Rev Gay Clark; *Representative of the PHoD*: **Johnson**, Ms. Sally Johnson, Esq

Task Force to Coordinate Ecumenical & Interreligious Work

(*All terms* 2024, *unless noted*) **Franklin**, Rt Rev R William (*Chair*); **Yarbrough**, Rev Cn Dr C Denise

(*Vice-Chair*); **Alexander,** Rev Sharon (*2021*); **Baer,** Ven Dr Walter; **Bellam,** Ms Kate; **Briceno,** Mr Jaime; **Hayashi,** Rt Rev Scott; **Montes,** Ms Luz (*2021*); **Mosher,** Dr Lucinda; **Simmons,** Rev David; **Sutton,** Rt Rev Eugene; **Tabizon Thompson** (*2021*), Rev Marisa; Ex *Officio*: **Curry,** Most Rev Michael Bruce; **Jennings,** Rev Gay Clark (*2021*)

Task Force to Develop Churchwide Family Leave Policies

(*All terms* 2021) **Anderson,** The Rev. Devon (*Chair*); **Gutiérrez,** The Rt. Rev. Daniel (*Vice-Chair*); **Ambrogi,** Ms. Sarah; **Creed,** Ms. Barbara; **Dyer,** The Rev. Alex; **Funston,** Mrs. Michael; **Glover,** Ms. Kathryn; **Marray,** The Rt. Rev. Santosh; **Pollard,** Ms. Diane Pomerenk, BSG, Br. Scott-Michael; **Schoeck,** The Rev. Lauren; *Ex Officio*: **Curry,** Most Rev Michael Bruce; **Jennings,** Rev Gay Clark

Task Force to Respond to Opioid Epidemic

(*All terms* 2021) **van Klaveren,** Rev Dina (*Chair*); **Kotval,** Ms Amanda (*Vice-Chair*); **Barten,** Dr Donna; **Bennett,** Rev Debra; **Brown,** Rev Jan M; **Cochran,** Ms Amy; **Harrigan,** Rev Cn Katherine; **Klusmeyer,** Rt Rev William; **Nelson,** Rev Dr Benjamin; **Owensby,** Rt Rev Jake; **Rathbone,** Rev Cn Cristina; **So,** Rev Alistair; **Williams,** Mr Merrick; **Wilson,** Ms Twyla; *Ex Officio*: **Curry,** Most Rev Michael Bruce; **Jennings,** Rev Gay Clark

Task Force to Study Church's Pension System

(*All terms* 2019) **Barlowe,** Rev Cn Dr Michael (*Convener*); **Anning,** Douglas; **Bruce,** Rt Rev Diane M. Jardine; **Cisluycis,** Ms Jane; **Crawley,** Rev Clayton; **Hollingsworth,** Rt Mark; **Mallonee,** Rev Cn Anne; **Sanborn,** Ms Nancy; *Ex Officio*: **Curry,** Most Rev Michael Bruce; **Jennings,** Rev Gay Clark

Task Force to Study Sexism in TEC & Develop Anti-Sexism Training

(*All terms* 2021) **Russell,** Ms Laura (*Chair*); **Mayer,** Rt Rev J Scott (*Vice-Chair*); **Svoboda-Barber,** Rev Dr Helen (*Secretary*); **Beckwith,** Rt Rev Mark; **Cato,** Rev Brooks; **Harris,** Dr John; **Hatcher,** Rev Spencer; **Hunn,** Rt Rev Michael C B; **Johnson** Russell, Rev Tracy; **Karr-Cornejo,** Dr Katherine; **Killewald,** Dr Alexandra; **Kim,** Rev Yein; **Kitch-Peck,** Ms Sophia; **Reddall,** Rev Jennifer; **Sherrod,** Ms Katie; *Ex Officio*: **Curry,** Most Rev Michael Bruce; **Jennings,** Rev Gay Clark

ALL OTHER INTERIM BODIES

Provincial Leadership Council

(*All terms* 2021) **Barta,** Rev Heather; **Benfield,** Rt Rev Larry; **Benhase,** Rt Rev Scott; **Bruckner,** Ms Ellen W; **Callard,** Ms Genevieve; **Carroll,** Mr Jerry; **Cochran,** Dr Pamela; **Douglas,** Rt Rev Ian; **Dowell,**

Rev Elizabeth; **Duncan-Probe,** Rt Rev Dr DeDe; **Fox,** Ms Neva Ray; **Gandell,** Rev Dahn; **Goldsack,** Ms Dorothy-Jane; **Gregory,** Ms Judith; **Heard,** Rev Cn Victoria; **Hollingsworth,** Rt Rev Mark; **Judge,** Ms Tess; **Klusmeyer,** Rt Rev William Michie; **Lytle,** Dr Julie; **McCormick,** Cn Kathryn; **McDonald,** Rev Jim; **Morales,** Rvdo. Francisco; **Morales,** Rt Rev Rafael; **Pierce,** Rev Nathaniel; **Plantz,** MrCharles; **Presler,** Rev Dr Titus; **Prior,** Rt Rev Brian N; **Reid,** Ms Courtney; **Rickel,** Rt Rev Gregory H; **Rodriguez** Sanches, Dr Arnoldo; **Scantlebury,** Rt Rev Victor A; **Wang,** Rev Kit; **Weismore,** Betsy; **Willard,** Mr Eugene; **Williams,** Ms Sandra; **Wong,** Mr Warren

Anglican-Roman Catholic Dialogue in the USA

(*All terms* 2021) **Bauerschmidt,** Rt Rev John C (*Chair*); **Cover,** Rev Dr Michael; **Joslyn-Siemiatkoski,** Dr Daniel; **Kiess,** Dr John; **Waynick,** Bishop Catherine; **Yarbrough,** Rev Cn Dr C Denise; *Ex Officio*: **Curry,** Most Rev Michael Bruce; **Jennings,** Rev Gay Clark;

Lutheran Episcopal Coordinating Committee

(*All terms* 2021) **Sparks,** Rt Rev Douglas E (Chair); **Chittenden,** Rev Nils; **Lucas,** Rev T Stewart; **McGrath Green,** Rev Nancy Sargent; **Perry,** Rev Cn Dr David W; *Ex Officio*: **Curry,** Most Rev Michael Bruce; **Jennings,** Rev Gay Clark

Moravian Episcopal Coordinating Committee

(*All terms* 2021) **Tjeltveit,** Rev Maria (*Chair*); **Allen,** Rev T Scott; **Freeman,** Mrs DeDreana; **Nichols,** Rt Rev Kevin; **Rodman,** Rt Rev Samuel; *Ex Officio*: **Curry,** Most Rev Michael Bruce; **Jennings,** Rev Gay Clark

Presbyterian Episcopal Dialogue Committee

(*All terms* 2021) **Sutton,** Rt Rev Eugene T (*Chair*); **Booker,** Dr Michael; **Johnstone,** Rev Cn Elise; **Ring,** Ms Elizabeth; **Wolyniak,** Rev Joseph; *Ex Officio*: **Curry,** Most Rev Michael Bruce; **Jennings,** Rev Gay Clark

United Methodist Episcopal Committee

(*All terms* 2021) **Good,** Dr Deirdre (*Chair*); **Coleman,** Rev Dr Karen; **Ferguson,** Rev Dr Thomas Ferguson, PhD; **Partee Carlsen,** Rev Cn Mariclair; **Rice,** Rt Rev David; *Ex Officio*: **Curry,** Most Rev Michael Bruce; **Jennings,** Rev Gay Clark

House of Bishops Spouse/Partner Planning Group

(*All terms* 2021) **Bruce,** Mr G Stephen (*Co-Chair*); **Provenzano,** Mrs Jeanne (*Co-Chair*); **Shand,** Mrs Lynne (Secretary); **Fisher,** Rev Betsy; **Lane,** Ms Gretchen; **O'Neill,** Mrs Ginger; **Rickel,** Mrs Marti; **Thompson,** Mrs Rebecca; *Ex-Officio*: **Schori,** Mr Richard; *Chaplain*: **Price,** Very Rev Cn Barbara

AGENCIES AND BOARDS

Board of the Archives of the Episcopal Church

Adams-McCaslin, Ms Pan (*2021, Chair*); **Bardol**, Ms Anne E (*2021*); **Baskerville-Burrows**, Rt Rev Jennifer (*2024*); **Calloway**, Dr Heather (*2024*); **Franklin**, Rt Rev R William (*2021*); **Gerbracht Jr**, Dr Frederick W (*2021*); **Hitt II**, Mr Lawrence R Hitt II, Esq (*2024*); **McCoy**, Rev W Keith (*2024*); **Pace**, Rev Dr Robert F (*2021*); **Porter**, Ms Margaret (*2024*); **Rodman**, Rt Rev Samuel (*2021*); **Wilbert**, Rev Dr Brian K (*2021*); *Ex Officio*: **Curry**, Most Rev Michael Bruce; **Duffy**, Mr Mark; **Jennings**, Rev Gay Clark

Board of Trustees for the Church Pension

Alexander, Ms Martha Bedell (*2021*); **Ballentine**, Cn Rosalie Simmonds (*2024*); **Brown**, Rev Thomas J (*2021*); **Bruce**, Rt Rev Diane M Jardine Bruce (*2024*); **Candler**, Very Rev Samuel G (*2024*); **Daniel**, Rt Rev Clifton Daniel, DD (*2024*); **Glover**, Dr Delbert C (*2024*); **Holguin**, Rt Rev Julio (*2024*); **Kusumoto**, Mr Ryan K (*2024*); **Lind**, Very Rev Tracey (*2021*); **Lindahl**, Mr Kevin B (*2021*); **McCormick**, Cn Kathryn (*2024*); **McPhee**, Ms Sandra F (*2021*); **Mitchell**, Rev Dr Timothy (*2021*); **Niles**, Ms Margaret A Niles, Esq (*2021*); **O'Neal**, Ms Yvonne (*2024*); **Owayda**, Mr Sleiman (Solomon) (*2024*); **Prior**, Rt Rev Brian N (*2021*); **Rickel**, Rt Rev Gregory H (*2021*); **Rios**, RevAustin K (*2024*); **Swan**, Ms Sandra (*2021*); **Vickers**, Ms Anne (*2021*); **Watt**, Ms Linda (*2024*); **Wilson**, Rev Cn Dr Sandye A (*2021*); **Wold**, Ms Mary Kate (*2021*)

Board for Transition Ministry

Easton, Rev Cn Elizabeth (*2021, Chair*); **Conrada**, Rev Victor H (*2024, Vice-Chair*); **Obando**, Mrs Denise (*2021, Secretary*); **Butterworth**, Rev Dr Gary (*2024*); **Clark**, Rev Paula (*2021*); **Fisher**, Rt Rev Douglas (*2021*); **Gutierrez**, Rt Rev Daniel (*2024*); **McVey**, Ms Ellen (*2024*); **Schmidt**, Ms Anne (*2024*); **Shin**, Rt Rev Allen (*2021*); *Ex Officio*: **Curry**, Most Rev Michael Bruce (*2018*); **Jennings**, Rev Gay Clark (*2018*); *Staff*: **Froehlich**, Rev Meghan F

Episcopal Relief and Development Board of Directors

Lane, Mr Neel (*2018, Chair*); **Allen**, Ms Shirley Stover (*2020*); **Ballentine**, Cn Rosalie Simmonds (*2024*); **Constantine**, Mr Mark D (*2019*); **Gray-Reeves**, Rt Rev Mary (*2019*); **Hollingsworth**, Ms Sophie (*2018*); **Killeen**, Rev David C (*2018*); **Lee**, Rt Rev Jeffrey D (*2020*); **MacKinnon**, Mr John A (*2018*); **McCouch**, Dr Robert (*2020*); **Muglia**, Ms Laura Ellen (*2018*); **Paulikas**, Rev Steven (*2020*); **Ramos-Orench**, Rt Rev Wilfrido (*2019*); **Razim**, Rev Cn Genevieve T (*2020*); **Salome Mibenge**, Dr Chiseche (*2020*); **Stoever**, Mr Thomas W (*2020*); *Ex Officio*: **Barnes**, Mr N Kurt; **Curry**, Most Rev Michael Bruce; **Radtke**, Dr Robert W; **Smith**, Rev Geoffrey

General Board of Examining Chaplains

Benfield, Rt Rev Larry R Benfield, DD (*2021, Chair*); **LeVeque**, Ms Anne (*2021, Vice-Chair*); **Ahrens**, Rt Rev Laura J (*2021*); **Anderson**, Dr Liza (*2021*); **Bamberger**, Very Rev Cn Michael (*2021*); **Black**, Rev Dr Cn Katharine C (*2021*); **Bojarski**, Beth (*2024*); **Breidenthal**, Rt Rev Thomas (*2024*); **Duncan-Probe**, Rt Rev Dr DeDe (*2024*); **Erdman**, Rachel (*2024*); **Ferguson**, Rev Dr Thomas Ferguson, PhD (*2021*); **Givens**, Dr Norma N (*2021*); **Hassett**, Rev Miranda (*2024*); **Kradel**, Rev Adam (*2021*); **Lane**, Rev Calvin (*2024*); **Mendoza**, Rev Migualla (*2024*); **Page**, Rev Dr Hugh (*2021*); **Powers Roth**, Ms Janet (*2024*); **Robbins**, Dr Gregory (*2024*); **Slade**, Rev Kara (*2024*); **Smith**, Rev Dr Duane Andre (*2021*); **Story**, Rev Mark (*2024*); *Ex Officio*: **Curry**, Most Rev Michael Bruce (*2021*); **Jennings**, Rev Gay Clark (*2021*)

DFMS STAFF

Office of the Presiding Bishop

The Presiding Bishop & Primate The Most Rev Michael B **Curry** *Canon to the Presiding Bishop for Ministry Within the Episcopal Church* The Rev Canon E Mark **Stevenson** *Canon to the Presiding Bishop for Ministry Beyond the Episcopal Church* The Rev Canon Dr Charles K **Robertson** *Canon to the Presiding Bishop for Evangelism, Reconciliation and the Stewardship of Creation* The Rev Canon Stephanie **Spellers** *Executive Coordinator to the Presiding Bishop* Sharon **Jones** *Administrative Associate to the Canons* Ednice **Baerga** *Chief Operating Officer* The Rev Geoffrey T **Smith** *Executive Assistant to the COO & Operations Manager* Su **Hadden** *Chief Legal Officer* Douglas K **Anning** *Chancellor to the Presiding Bishop* Mary **Kostel** *Bishop for the Office of Pastoral Development* The Rt Rev S Todd **Ousley** *Bishop in Charge of the Convocation of American Churches in Europe* The Rt Rev Mark DW **Edington** *Executive Director General Board of Examining Chaplains* Duncan C **Ely** *Bishop for the Armed Forces and Federal Ministries* The Rt Rev Carl W **Wright** *Canon to the Bishop for Armed Forces and Federal Ministries* The Rev Canon Leslie Nuñez **Steffensen**

Armed Forces & Federal Ministries

Washington National Cathedral
3101 Wisconsin Ave NW
Washington, DC 20016
Tel: 202-459-9998
https://www.episcopalfederalchaplains.org/

Operations

Director Human Resources Raphaelle **Sondak** *Senior Human Resources Officer* Patricia E **Holley** *HR Manager for Benefits, Systems & Finance* Michael H **Walsh** *Director of Information Technology* Darvin

D **Darling** *Executive Assistant to the COO &*
Operations Manager Su **Hadden**

Communication

Senior Manager, Creative Services Jeremy **Tackett**
Operations Manager Bernice **David** *Public Affairs*
Officer Nancy **Davidge** *Associate Public Affairs*
Officer & InfoLine Lisa **Webb** *Manager, Multimedia*
Services Michael F **Collins** *Webmaster* Barry **Merer**
Manager, Language Services Vacant*Advertising*
Manager Matthew **Davies** *Creative Services*
Coordinator Melissa **Walker** *Coordinator for Digital*
Evangelism Christopher **Sikkema** *Managing Editor,*
Episcopal News Service Lynette **Wilson** *Senior*
Editor/Writer, Episcopal News Service The Rev Mary
Frances **Schjonberg** *Editor/ Reporter, Episcopal*
News Service David **Paulsen**

Finance

Treasurer and Chief Financial Officer N Kurt
Barnes *Assistant to the Treasurer* June A
Victor*Administrative Assistant to the Treasurer*
Sheila **Golden** *Director of Investment Management*
and Banking Margareth **Crosnier de Bellaistre**
Controller JoAnne **Brockway** *Assistant Controller*
Arlissa **Dean** *Assistant Controller* Tanie **Oconer**
Payroll Manager Jacqueline **Franco** *Travel Loan*
Supervisor (Episcopal Migration Ministries) Lisa
Gandolfo *Grants and Compliance Officer (Episcopal*
Migration Ministries) Florence **Etienne**

Development Office

Development Officer TJ **Houlihan** *Development*
Officer Cecilia **Malm**

Ministries beyond the Episcopal Church

Canon to the Presiding Bishop for Ministry beyond
The Episcopal Church The Rev Canon Dr Charles K
Robertson *Deputy for Ecumenical and Interreligious*
Relations The Rev Margaret R **Rose**

Global Partnerships & Mission Personnel

Director of Global Partnerships and Mission
Personnel The Rev David **Copley** *Mission Personnel*
Officer Elizabeth **Boe** *Officer, Episcopal Church*
Representative to the United Nations Lynnaia **Main**
Middle East Officer The Rev Robert D **Edmunds**
Officer for Asia and the Pacific The Rev Canon
Bruce W **Woodcock** *Officer for Latin America &*
the Caribbean The Rev Glenda **McQueen** *Staff*
Officer for Africa Relations The Rev Canon Dr Isaac
Kawuki Mukasa *Officer for Global Relations &*
Networking Jenny **Grant**

Office of Government Relations (OGR)

110 Maryland Ave NE Suite 309
Washington DC 20002
Tel: (800) 228 0515 or (202) 547 7300

Fax: (202) 547 4457
E-mail: eppn@episcopalchurch.org

Director of Government Relations Rebecca **Blachly**
Refugee & Immigration Policy Analyst Lacy **Broemel**
Domestic and Environmental Policy Advisor John
Cobb *Legislative Representative for International*
Issues (ELCA shared position) Patricia **Kisare**
Communication Coordinator & Office Manager Alan
Yarborough

Episcopal Migration Ministries

Director Episcopal Migration Ministries Vacant
Director of Operations Demetrio **Alvero** *Manager*
for Church Relations and Engagement Allison
Duvall *Communications Manager* Kendall **Martin**
Senior Program Manager, Resettlement Svetlana
Brajdic *Senior Program Manager, Foundational*
Program Unit Laura **Lamb**

Ministries within the Episcopal Church

Canon to the Presiding Bishop for Ministry Within
the Episcopal Church The Rev Canon E Mark
Stevenson

Formation Ministries

Director for Formation, Youth and Young Adults
Bronwyn Clark **Skov** *Officer for Young Adult &*
Campus Ministries The Rev Shannon **Kelly** *Officer*
for Digital Formation and Events Wendy K **Johnson**

Transition Ministries

Director of Transition Ministries The Rev Meghan F
Froehlich *Coordinator* Sabrina **Nealy**

Mission Priorities

Canon to the Presiding Bishop for Evangelism,
Reconciliation and the Stewardship of Creation The
Rev Canon Stephanie **Spellers**

Ethnic Ministries

Director of Ethnic Ministries The Rev Anthony
Guillén *Missioner for Black Ministries* The Rev
Canon Ronald C **Byrd** *Missioner for Indigenous*
Ministries The Rev Dr Bradley S **Hauff** *Missioner for*
Asiamerica Ministries The Rev Dr Winfred B **Vergara**
Associate Missioner for Latino/Hispanic Ministry &
Program Development The Rev Samuel **Borbón**

Church Planting & Redevelopment

Manager of Church Planting & Redevelopment The
Rev Tom **Brackett** *Staff Officer for Church Planting*
Infrastructure The Rev Mike **Michie**

Reconciliation, Justice & Creation Care

Director of Reconciliation, Justice & Creation Care
The Rev Melanie **Mullen** *Staff Officer for Social*

Justice & Advocacy Engagement The Rev Charles A **Wynder, Jr** *Staff Officer for Racial Reconciliation* Heidi **Kim**

United Thank Offering

Staff Officer for the the United Thank Offering The Rev Heather **Melton** *Associate Staff Officer for the United Thank Offering* The Rev Canon Michelle **Walker**

MISSION COMPANIONS OF THE EPISCOPAL CHURCH

Sending agency key: DFMS—Domestic and Foreign Missionary Society.

China

Ms. Elizabeth Grace Bleynat, Mission to Seafarers, Mariners' Club, 11 Middle Road, Tsim Sha Tsui, Kowloon, Hong Kong, SAR China—(DFMS)

Costa Rica

Ms. Alexandria Marie Fields, Diocese of Costa Rica, 200 Metros Norte de Plaza Cemaco, Apartado 2773-1000, Zapote, San Jose, Costa Rica (DFMS)

Mr. Henry Harrison McLeod, Diocese of Costa Rica, 200 Metros Norte de Plaza Cemaco, Apartado 2773-1000, Zapote, San Jose, Costa Rica (DFMS)

Dominican Republic

The Rev. Emilio M Fumero, Episcopal Diocese, Calle Santiago 253, Gascue Santo Domingo, Dominican Republic—(DFMS)

Mr. William Kunkle, Dominican Development Group, P.O. Box 272261, Tampa, FL 33688-2261—(DFMS)

Dr. Thomas Malcolm McGowan, PhD, 5909 Minter Lane, Lincoln, NE 68516—(DFMS)

Mr. Charles Nakash, Episcopal Diocese, Calle Santiago 253, Gascue Santo Domingo, Dominican Republic—(DFMS)

El Salvador

Mr. Noah Bullock, Diocese of El Salvador, Calle Shafik Handal 5441, Colonia Escalon, San Salvador, El Salvador—(DFMS)

England

Ms. Madeline Parker Roberts, 12 Lady Chapel Close, Liverpool Cathedral, Liverpool L1 7BZ, UK—(DFMS)

Haiti

The Rev. Pierre Simpson Gabaud, Seminaire Theologique de l'Eglise Episcopale d'Haiti, 72 Avenue Christophe, Port-au-Prince, Haiti—(DFMS)

Mrs. Janet O'Flynn, Episcopal University of Haiti, c/o Mission Personnel, Episcopal Church Center, 815 Second Avenue, New York, NY 10017—(DFMS)

Honduras

Mr. Robert Canter, c/o Episcopal Diocese of Honduras, IMC SAP, Dept 215, P.O. Box 52-3900, Miami, FL 33152-3900—(DFMS)

The Rev. Matthew Engleby, El Hogar Projects, Apartado Postal 764, Tegucigalpa DC, Honduras—(DFMS)

The Rev. Stephen Robinson & Mrs. Rhonda Robinson, c/o Mission Personnel, Episcopal Church Center, 815 Second Avenue, New York, NY 10017—(DFMS)

Italy

Mr. Stephen Raymond Nagy—Via Napoli 58, 00184 Roma, Italy—(DFMS)

Jerusalem

The Rev. Dr. Donald Drew Binder—65 Nablus Road, P.O. Box 19122, Jerusalem 91191, Via Israel—(DFMS)

The Rev. Mary June Nestler—65 Nablus Road, P.O. Box 19122, Jerusalem 91191, Via Israel—(DFMS)

The Rev. Joseph Tracy Rivers and Mrs. Carolyn Draper Rivers—65 Nablus Road, P.O. Box 19122, Jerusalem 91191, Via Israel—(DFMS)

Mrs. Della Wager Wells—65 Nablus Road, P.O. Box 19122, Jerusalem 91191, Via Israel—(DFMS)

New Zealand

Mr. Zachary Jeffers, The Mission to Seafarers Wellington, P.O. Box 2288, Wellington 6140, New Zealand—(DFMS)

Panama

Dr. Jennifer Eileen Weeks, PhD, c/o Iglesia Episcopal de Panama, Box 0843-01258, Panama, Rep. De Panama—(DFMS)

Mr. Vernon Wilson & Mrs. Francis Wilson, c/o Iglesia Episcopal de Panama, Box 0843-01258, Panama, Rep of Panama—(DFMS)

Philippines

Mr. Henry Mitchel Bibelheimer, c/o The Episcopal Church in the Philippines, P.O. Box 10321, Broadway Centrum, Quezon City 1112, Philippines—(DFMS)

Ms. Kelly Lyman, c/o The Episcopal Church in the Philippines, P.O. Box 10321, Broadway Centrum, Quezon City 1112, Philippines—(DFMS)

Puerto Rico

Ms. Lydia Grace Pendleton—Iglesia Episcopal Puertorriqueña, P.O. Box 902, Saint Just, P.R. 00978-0902—(DFMS)

Qatar

The Ven. Dr. William Schwartz, P.O. Box 3210, Doha, Qatar—(DFMS)

Romania

The Rev. Dorothee Hahn, c/o Episcopia Huşilor—Str. Kogalniceanu, Nr. 19—Municipiul Huşi—6575, jud.—Vaslui—Romania—(DFMS)

South Africa

Mrs. Jennifer McConnachie, RN, Mariya uMama weThemba Monastery, P.O. Box 6013, Grahamstown, South Africa 6141- (DFMS)

The Rev. Dr. Joseph Samuel Pagano, PhD, College of Transfiguration, NPC, P.O. Box 77, Grahamstown 6140, South Africa—(DFMS)

The Rev. Dr. Amy Richter, PhD, College of Transfiguration, NPC, P.O. Box 77, Grahamstown 6140, South Africa—(DFMS)

Tanzania

Dr. Jenny Coley, Ph, MPH, MSc. CLS, St. Augustine Muheza Institute of Health and Allied Science (SAMIHAS)—P.O. Box 5—Muheza—Tanga, Tanzania—(DFMS)

The Rev. Karen Alicia King, Msalato Theological College, P.O. Box 264, Dodoma, Tanzania, East Africa—(DFMS)

Mr. Gregory Morgan Steffensen, Canon Andrea Mwaka School, P.O. Box 228, Dodoma, Tanzania—(DFMS)

USA

The Rev. Paul-Gordon Chandler, P.O. Box 360, Winfield, IL 60190—(DFMS)

PROVINCIAL CONTACTS

Province I New England

Comprises the dioceses of ME NH VT MA WMA RI CT *Pres* The Rev Kit Wang 121 Mill Ln York ME 03909 (207) 475-7198 *E-mail:* kiturgy@yahoo.com; *VP* The Rt Rev Ian Douglas The Commons The Episcopal Church in Connecticut 290 Pratt Street Box 52 Meriden CT 06450 (203) 639-3501 x111 *E-mail:* itdouglas@episcopalct.org; *Treas* The Rev Dr Titus Pressler, PO Box 501, Montgomery, VT 05471-0501 *E-mail:* tituspresler@earthlink.net; *Bookkeeper* Terry Reimer 143 State Street Portland ME 04101 (207) 772-1953 x134 *Exec Dir* Dr Julie Lytle 81 Blueberry Hill Rd Hyannis MA 02601 (617) 669-8411 *E-mail:* executive.director@province1.org *Web:* www.Province1 .org; *Reps Exec Council* Alexizendria Link 734 Pleasant Street, Unit 2, Worcester, MA 0160 (617) 447-8039 *Email:* atl029@ mail.harvard.edu; The Rev Aaron C Perkins, 26 Moulton Ln, York, ME 03909-1407 aaron@dunesonthewaterfront.com; *Cultural Competency and Anti-Racism* James McKim *E-mail:* jtmckim@gmail.com; *Campus Min* The Rev Thea Keith-Lucas *E-mail:* theakl@mit.edu; *Deacons* Aaron Perkins aperkins@episcopalmaine.org; *Daughters of the King, Pres* Mariana Bauman (WMA) *E-mail:* marianab@earthlink.net, marianabauman@

doknational.org; ECW *Web:* https://province1episcopalchurchwomen.wordpress.org; ECW Board—*Pres* Delores Alleyne (CT) *E-mail:* deloresalleyne@aol.com; *VP* Rev Ema Rosero-Nordalm (MA) *E-mail:* erosero@bu.edu; *Sec* Roberta Stockdale (CT*) E-mail:* rls55@cox.net;*Treas* Priscilla D McFarland (ME) *E-mail:* pdmcfarland1@gmail.com; *Prov I Rep to Nat ECW* Margaret (RI) Noel *E-mail:* Margaret_e_noel@hotmail.com; *National ECW Board Web:* https://www.ecwnational.org/executive/; *United Thank Offering (UTO)* Prov 1 Rep Jane Jellison (RI) *E-mail:* JaneEJellison@gmail.com; *Church Periodical Club (CPC)* Prov 1 Rep Sally Morelle North (RI) *E-mail:* semorelle@gmail.com

Province II: The International Atlantic Province

NY LI A CNY Roch WNY Nk NJ Haiti VI and Convoc of Amer Chs in Europe Cuba (in progress). *Web:* www.province2.org. *Pres* Very Rev Dahn Dean Gandell (Roch) (585) 233-3100 *E-mail:* motherdahn@hotmail.com; *VP* Rt Rev DeDe Duncan-Probe (CNY) (315) 882-0511 *E-mail:* cnybishop@gmail.com; *Sec* Cn Paul Ambos Esq (NJ) (732) 572-8795 *E-mail:* pambos@amboslaw.com; *Treas* Cn Phyllis Jones (NJ) (609) 394-5281 ext. 31 *E-mail:* pjones@dioceseofnj.org; *Rep to Prov Coun* Rt Rev William H "Chip" Stokes (NJ) (609) 394-5281 ext. 11 *E-mail:* wstokes@dioceseofnj.org; Very Rev Joell Szachara (CNY) (607) 221-4020 *E-mail:* revjoell@gmail.com; Yvonne O'Neal (NY) (347) 776-8010 *E-mail:* yvonne.oneal@gmail.com; *Exec Coun Lay* Canon Noreen Duncan (646) 932-9515 *E-mail:* noreen.duncan@att.net; *Exec Coun Cler* Rev Deacon Lillian Davis-Wilson (WNY) (716) 553-6200 *E-mail:* ljdwilson1@verizon.net; *Newsletter* InProv2: Jan Paxton (Nk) (201) 851-1428 *E-mail:* jpaxton46@gmail.com; *Chair, Synod Plan Comm* Dorothy-Jane Connolly (518) 588-5419 *E-mail:* djgoldsack.prov2@gmail.com; *Province II Rep to Exec Coun Comm on Anti-Racism* Brian Romero, LMSW, CASAC-T (LI) (347) 975-6552 *E-mail:* bromeromsw@gmail.com.

Province III Mid-Atlantic

Comprises the dioceses of BETH CPA DE EASTON MD NWPA PA PGH SVA SWVA VA WASH WV *Pres* The Rt Rev William "Mike" Klusmeyer *E-mail:* mklusmeyer@wvdiocese.org; *V* Rev Nathaniel W Pierce *E-mail:* nwpierce@verizon.net; *Sec* Robert Kilp *E-mail:* rlkilp@yahoo.com; *Treas* Judith Lane Gregory *E-mail:* jgregory@delaware. church; *Coord* Dr Pamela DH Cochran *E-mail:* p3coordinator@gmail.com; *Exec Coun* Russell Randle *Email:* russell.randle@squirepb.com; *Rev* Patricia Downing *E-mail:* patricia@trinityparishde. org; *Coun Members* Linda Rogers (Beth) *Email:* parogers13@gmail.com; Rev Dr Howell Sasser (CPA) *E-mail:* rectorstpauls@gmail.com; Rev Sheila B Sharpe(DE) *E-mail:* sgsharpe@comcast. net; Joanne Fisher (Easton) *E-mail:* joanne@dioceseofeaston.org; Rev Scott Slater (MD) *E-mail:*

sslater@episcopalmaryland.org; Rev Geoffrey Wild (NWPA) *E-mail:* gcvicar@gmail.com ; Christopher Hart (PA) *E-mail:* chart@lmc.net; Lisa Brown (PGH) *E-mail:* lcbrown15243@gmail.com; Col. Jean Reed (VA) *E-mail:* jeandreed@verizon.net; Joyce E Haines (SVA) *E-mail:* amielonie@aol.com ; Jack Barrow (SVA) *E-mail:* jc.barrow@embarqmail.com; Rt Rev Mariann Budde (Wash) *E-mail:* mebudde@edow. org; Philip Steptoe (WVA) *E-mail:* philtoe@comcast. net; *Altar Guild* Sharon Stewart Nachman (VA) *E-mail:* sharonsnachman@gmail.com; *Anti-Racism* Nancy Travis Bolden *E-mail:* nltbolden@yahoo. com; *Campus Min* open; *Chr Ed* Bill Campbell (VA) *E-mail:* bill@forma.church; *Church Periodical Club* Linda Getts (PGH) *E-mail:* linda.getts@aol.com; *ECW* Beblon Parks (VA) *E-mail:* bebparks@gmail. com; *Justice and Peace* Rev Linda Watkins (CPA) *E-mail:* rector@stmaryswaynesboro.org; *UTO* Rosamond Daniels (WA) *E-mail:* rosamond47@ gmail.com; *Yth Min* Joanne Fisher (Easton) *E-mail:* joanne@dioceseofeaston.org and Kate Riley *Email:* kriley@episcopalmaryland.org; *Sm Church Min* Rev Judy Parish *E-mail:* revgr8hugger@aol.com; *Health Min* Sharon Logsdon (MD) *E-mail:* sll@atlantic. net; *Vocations Min* Rev Patrick Collins (Easton) *E-mail:* Patrick@dioceseofeaston.org; *Ecumenical Ministries* Rev Maria Tjeltveit *Email:* mtjeltveit@ episcopalmediator.org.

Province IV Southeast

Comprises the dioceses of AL NC EC SC CGC GA AT FL LA MS TN WTN ETN KY LEX CF SEF SWF WNC USC *Pres* Kathryn McCormick *E-mail:* kwmccormick@gmail.com; *VP* The Rt Rev Scott A. Benhase, *E-mail:* bishop@gaepiscopal. org; *Treas* Tess Judge *E-mail:* tessjudgeobx@ gmail.com; *Sec* Marcellus (Mark) Smith *E-mail:* msmith5864@aol.com; *Adm* H Eugene (Gene) Willard *E-mail:* p4admin@icloud.com; *Reps to Exec Coun: Cler* Rev Cn Frank Logue *E-mail:* flogue@ gaepiscopal.org; *Lay E-mail:* Alice B. Freeman E-mail alicebfreeman4@gmail.com; *UTO* Diane Gabbard *E-mail* dianegabbard@gmail.com; *ECW Pres* Rebecca (Becky) Taylor E-*mail:* bekatay@ me.com; *Altar Guild* Ann McCormick E-mail ann. mcc413@gmail.com; *Young Adult & Campus Min* Brian Smith *E-mail:* fb@rugehall.org; *Yth* Cookie Cantwell *E-mail:* cookie@stjames.org; *Envir Min* The Rev Dr Jerry Cappel *E-mail:* jjcappel@hotmail. com; *Companion Dios* Martha B Alexander *E-mail:* marthaebalexander@hotmail.com; *Bishops Chap to the Ret and Surv Spouses* The Rt Rev David B Reed *E-mail:* david.reed@ecunet.org;

Province V Midwest

Comprises the dioceses of OH SO NI Ind C Sp MI WMI NMI EMI FdL MIl EauC MO *Pres* Genevieve L Callard *E-mail:* gcallard@edwm.org; *VP* Mark Hollingsworth *E-mail:* MH@dohio.org; *Sec* Alicia Hager *E-mail:* astrawberrypointe@gmail.com; *Treas*

Courtney Reid *E-mail:* creid@episcopalchicago.org; *Coord* Heather Barta *E-mail:* provincevcoordinator@ gmail.com; *Episcopal Church Exec Coun* Matthew Cowden *E-mail:* frmatthewcowden@gmail.com; Jane Cisluycis *E-mail:* jane@upepiscopal.org; C: Fran Holliday *E-mail:* fran@stmarysepiscopalcl.org; EMI: Katie Forsyth *E-mail:* kforsyth@eastmich.org; FdL: David Annis *E-mail:* david.annis@gmail.com; Ind: Joan Amati *E-mail:* jomati81@hotmail.com; MI: Jo Ann Hardy *E-mail:* jhardy@edomi.org; Mil: Gary Manning *E-mail:* tosapriest@yahoo.com; MO: Pat Glen *E-mail:* gfkp@msn.com; NI: Matthew Cowden *E-mail:* frmatthewcowden@gmail.com; NMI: Lydia Kelsey Bucklin *E-mail:* lydia@upepiscopal.org; OH: Aaron Gerlach *E-mail:* RevGerlach@gmail. com; S: Jan Goossens *E-mail:* utospil@sbcglobal. net; SO: Lynn Carter-Edmands *E-mail:* lcarter-edmands@diosohio.org; WMI: Judy Fleener *E-mail:* fleenerj@gmail.com; *Young Adult/Campus Ministry* Stacy Alan *E-mail:* stacyalan@Brenthouse. org; *Church Periodical Club* Maryfran Crist *E-mail:* maryfrancrist64@gmail.com; *ECW* Karen Birr *E-mail:* ksbirr@gmail.com; *ER&D* Juanita Woods *E-mail:* nitagerman@sbcglobal.net; *Health Min* Maryfran Crist *E-mail:* maryfrancrist64@gmail.com; *JPIC* Cindy Nawrocki *E-mail:* rocki@att.net; *UTO* Gail Donovan *E-mail:* gadonov@aol.com; *Yth Min* Chad Sentua *E-mail:* csentua@episcopalchicago.org.

Province VI Land of Mountains Lakes and Plains

Comprises the dioceses of MN IA NE CO MT SD ND WY *Pres* Sandy Williams *E-mail:* mtsandylou@ gmail.com; *VP* Rt Rev Brian N Prior *E-mail:* brian.p@ episcopalmn.org; *Sec* vacant; *Treas* Mr Charles Plantz *E-mail:* jawa175@aolcom; *Chanc* vacant; *Prov Coord* Ellen Bruckner *E-mail:* ellenwb@mchsi. com; *Lay Reps Clergy Reps*; Shelby Benitz *E-mail:* hawkeyenp2012@gmail.com; The Rev Michael Pipkin *E-mail:* Michael.p@ecmn.org; The Rev Joan Grant (MT) *E-mail:* Joangrant33@hotmail.com; The Rev Chris Plantz (NE) *E-mail:* PastorPlantz@ gmail.com; Cindy King *E-mail:* cindylking@junco. com; Bob Poley (CO) *E-mail:* rpoley@comcast.net; Brandon Mauai (ND) *E-mail:* Brandon.mauai@ gmail.com; Julie Gehm (SD) E-mail: Julie.Gehm@ lifescapesd.com; *Min High Ed* Rev Portia Corbin (SD) *E-mail:* youth.diocese@midconetwork.com; *UTO* Elizabeth Campbell *E-mail:* balnamoon@ gmail.com; *Ecum* The Rev Warren Murphy *E-mail:* warrencmurphy@gmail.com; *ECW* Heather Bauer *E-mail:* greenpeacecats121@yahoo.com; *Anti-Racism* Paul Sneve (SD) *E-mail:* pmsneve@gmail. com; *ERD* Barb Hagen *E-mail:* mtbizmgr@qwest. net; *Daughters of the King* Nancy Sevrin *E-mail:* nssfhs@bresnan.net; *Ex Council Reps* George Wing *E-mail:* gwing@winglaw.com; Angela Goodhouse Mauai *Email:* agoodhouse@yahoo.com; *Care of Creation Task Group:* Paul Anton (MN) *E-mail:* paulanton17@yahoo.com.

Province VII Southwest
Comprises the diocese of WMO WLA AR TX DAL KS RG NWTX WT OK WKS FtW *Pres* The Rt Rev Larry Benfield 5124 Stonewall Rd Little Rock AR 72207 (501) 442-5888 *E-mail:* lbenfield@episcoar. org; *VP* Rev Victoria Heard 8932 Club Creek Circle Dallas TX 75238 (214) 957-3832 *E-mail:* vrtheard@ sbcglobal.net; *Sec* Jo Ann Rachele 2268 North St San Angelo TX 796901 (406) 249-6135 *E-mail:* joannrachele@msn.com; *Treas* Rev Jim McDonald 106 S 5th St Batesville AR 72501 (501) 529-3266 *E-mail:* FatherMcDonald@gmail.com; *Coord* Rev Elizabeth Dabney 14019 Wickersham Ln Houston TX 77077 (832) 462-3228 *E-mail:* elizabethrdowell@ gmail.com; *Members at Large* Rev Scot A McComas 1749 Cimarron Tr Grapevine TX 76051 (704) 779-6113 *E-mail:* Scot.mccomas@yahoo.com; Lee Spence 160 VZCR 1920 Fruitvale TX 75127 (903) 312-4437 *E-mail:* fiberphys@aol.com; Andrea Marie Rabalais Petrosh 6022 Rosemead Cir Bossier City LA 71111 (318) 426-6564 *E-mail:* mpetrosh@bellsouth.net; *Exec Council* The Very Rev J Mark Goodman 9131 Mabry Ave Albuquerque NM 87109 (505) 328-6157 *E-mail:* goodmankmark@gmail.com; Thomas Alexander 291 Pleasant Valley Dr Little Rock AR 72212 (501) 940-7941 *E-mail:* AlexanderTM@ hendrix.edu; *ECW* JoAnn Rachele PO Box 62711 San Angelo TX 76906 *Cell:* (406) 249-6135 *E-mail:* joannrachele@msn.com; *Commun/Web Page* Susan Hanson; *Prog Coord* Sally Russell 2 Hyde Park Dr Hutchinson KS 67502 (620) 662-8024 *Cell:* (620) 694-9145 *Email:* sallyruss@sbcglobal.net; *Youth* The Rev Karen Schlabach, 10003 W 70th Tr Merriam KS 66203 (913) 708-5927 *E-mail:* KSchlabach@ episcopal-ks.org; *Higher Ed* The Rev Matthew Wise 3908 Faimes Ct College Station TX 77845 (210) 363-9259 *E-mail:* canterburytamu@gmail. com; *Christian Formation* Sabrina Evans 924 N Robinson Oklahoma City OK 73102 (405) 232-4820 *E-mail:* SEvans@epiok.org; *ER&D* The Rev Virginia Holleman 5518 Merrimac Dr Dallas TX 75206 (214) 450-9652 *E-mail:* vfholleman@sbcglobal.net; *Multi-Cultural; Restorative Justice/Prison* Dr Ed Davis 2003 Ave P Huntsville TX 77340 (936) 662-3842 *E-mail:* edsalpc@yahoo.com; *Min to Senior Min:* Janet Nocher 4408 Foxfire Way Ft Worth TX (817) 975-4863 *E-mail:* janet.nocher@sbcglobal.net; Helen Appelberg *Email:* helenappelberg@gmail.com.

Province VIII West and Pacific Rim
Comprises the dioceses of AK AZ CA ECR EO HI ID LosA Navajoland NCA NV OL OR SanD SanJ Spok Tai UT *Pres* Warren J Wong *E-mail:* wjwstjames@gmail.com; *VP* The Rt Rev Greg Rickel *E-mail:* grickel@ecww.org; *Treas* Betsy Wiesmore *E-mail:* bwiesmore@gmail.com; *Sec* Pauline Getz *E-mail:* paulinegetz@gmail.com; *Chanc* R Miller Adams Esq *E-mail:* rma99977@gmail.com; *Reps Exec Coun* Warren J Wong *E-mail:* wjwstjames@ gmail.com; The Rev Cn Cornelia Eaton *E-mail:*

ceaton.ecn@gmail.com; *Fin Chr* Nancy Koonce *E-mail:* nkoonce@idahocpa.com; *Rep ECCAR* The Rev Canon John Kitagawa *E-mail:* johnkitagawa@ comcast.net; *CDSP Trustee* Barbara Ross *E-mail:* barbaratross@gmail.com; *Cluster One (Education Ministries) Convener* Dr Jennifer Snow *E-mail:* jSnow@cdsp.edu; *Altar Guild* Sarah Chesbro *E-mail:* sarah.chesbro@gmail.com; *Hlth Min* Susan Wahlstrom–*E-mail:* wahlstrom@volcano.net; *Coord of COM* The Rev Holladay Sanderson *E-mail:* revsanderson@gmail.com; *Campus Min/ High Ed* Brad Eubanks *E-mail:* brad.eubanks+prov@gmail. com; *Children, Youth, and Lifelong Formation* The Rev Anne Clarke *E-mail:* anne@norcalepiscopal. org and Caren Miles *E-mail:* carenm@diocal.org; *Cluster Two (Peace & Justice Ministries) Convener* The Rev Eric Metoyer *E-mail:* ericm@diocal.org; *Racial Reconciliation/Anti-Racism:* The Rev Eric Metoyer *E-mail:* ericm@diocal.org; The Rev Monica Whitaker *E-mail:* monicaannewhitaker@gmail.com; *Asian Min* The Rev Debra Low-Skinner *E-mail:* revdeb95008@gmail.com and The Rev Cn Robert "Moki" Hino *E-mail:* mokionthego@gmail.com; *Black/African American/Caribbean* Dawn Conley *E-mail:* drdconley@yahoo.com and Louis Glosson *E-mail:* lwg1946@aol.com; *Care of Creation & Justice:* Peter Sergienko *E-mail:* petersergienko@ gmail.com; *Indigenous Native American/Alaskan/ Hawaiian* Ronald Braman *E-mail:* singingflat4you@ yahoo.com; *Latino:* The Rev Nancy Aide Frausto *E-mail:* reverendanancy@gmail.com, frausto. nancy@gmail.com and The Rev Roberto Maldonado *E-mail:* padreroberto88@hotmail.com; *Peace and Justice* Alan Murray *E-mail:* sfalanmurray@gmail. com; *Cluster Three (Sending and Serving Ministries) Convener* Evita Krislock *E-mail:* evita@krislock.com; *CPC* Louise Aloy *E-mail:* louisealoy63@gmail.com; *UTO* Laura Orcutt *E-mail:* Laura@orcutt.org; *DOK* Ane Deister *E-mail:* ane.deister@yahoo.com; *ECW* Evita Krislock *E-mail:* evita@krislock.com; *Deacons of Prov VIII* The Rev Maureen Hagen *E-mail:* maureenhagen@gmail.com; *Bro St Andrew* Jack Hanstein *E-mail:* jack.hanstein@brothersandrew. net.

Province IX Caribbean/Latin America/ Northern South America
Comprises the dioceses of Colom DomR CEcu EcuL Hond PR Ven *Pres* Rvdmo Victor A Scantlebury *E-mail:* bpvictor864@ aol.com; *VP* The Rvdmo Rafael L Morales *E-mail:* obisporafael@episcopalpr. org; *Canciller* Fausto Chiluisa *E-mail:* fchiluisa@ gmail.com; *Sec* Gina Angulo Zamora *E-mail:* gina197919@hotmail.com; *Treas* Dr Arnaldo Rodríguez *E-mail:* arnaldo.rodriguez@seepr. org; *Coord* Rvdo P Francisco Morales *E-mail:* coordinador@provincia9.org; *Delegados Clerigo I* Rvda Ana Anthony *E-mail:* revangranch2007@ gmail.com; *Delegado Clerigo II* Rvdo. P Bienvenido Lopez *E-mail:* bienvenidol3@gmail.com; *Delegado*

Laico I Sherly García *E-mail:* garciasherly91@yahoo.
com; *Delegado Laico II* Dr Alfonso Morante *E-mail:*
dralfonsomorante53@gmail.com; *Representante
al Consejo Ejecutivo* Blanca Echeverry *E-mail:*
blecherry@gmail.com; *ECW* Rvda Can Consuelo
Sanchez *E-mail* csanchezhn@hotmail.com; *UTO*
Hilda Lamar *E-mail:* Hilmmar47@gmail.com.

PROGRAM SUPPORT SERVICES

United Thank Offering Board
Staff: UTO Staff Officer The Rev Canon Heather L
Melton Episcopal Church Center 815 Second Ave
New York NY 10017 (1-800) 334-7626 *E-mail:*
hmelton@episcopalchurch.org; UTO Associate Staff
Officer The Rev. Canon Michelle Walker Episcopal
Church Center 815 Second Ave New York NY 10017
(1-800) 334-7626 *E-mail:* miwalker@episcopalchurch.
org *Province Representatives: Prov I* Jane Jellison; *Prov
II* Vernese Smith *Prov III* Rosamond Daniels; *Prov IV*
Diane Gabbard; *Prov V* Gail Donovan; *Prov VI* the
Rev. Chris Plantz; *Prov VII* the Rev. Peggy Cromwell;
Prov VIII vacant; *Prov IX* Hilda Lammar; *Pres* Sherri
Dietrich *VPres* Joyce Landers *Young Adult* Caitlyn
Darnell and Sedona Jacobson.

Episcopal Diocesan Ecumenical and Interreligious Officers (EDEIO)
Pres Rev David Simmons *E-mail:* president@
edeio.org *Web* www.edeio.org; *V Pres* Rev Lynne
Bleich Weber; *Fin Off* Rev James Biegler *E-mail:*
edeioexchequer@comcast.net; *Sec* Richard
Mammana; *Prov Coords I* Rev Dr Frederick Moser;
II Rev Can Richard Visconti; *III* Rev Maria Tjeltveit;
IV Rev Clinton M Wilson; *V* Rev Vanessa EB Clark;
VI Rev Valerie Webster; *VII* Rev Dr Wayne Carter;
VIII Rev Eleanor Ellsworth; *IX* vacant; *At large:* Rev
Dr Thomas Ferguson.

CHURCHWIDE AGENCIES AND ORGANIZATIONS

Archives of the Episcopal Church, The
PO Box 2247 Austin TX 78768-2247 (512) 472-6816
Fax: (512) 480-0437 *Website:* http://episcopalarchives.
org *E-mail:* research@episcopalarchives.org. *Dir and
Can Archivist* Mark J Duffy *Archives:* 606 Rathervue Pl
Austin TX 78705. Research center for The Episcopal
Church, including the Domestic and Foreign
Missionary Society, the General Convention, and
related church-wide organizations, also individual
Episcopalians of note. The Archives collects,
preserves, and makes available original source data
to Church leaders, members, and the public.
Maintains online digital archives, digital repository
holdings, and provides consulting services to
dioceses and parishes. *Records Administration:* 815
Second Ave New York NY 10017-4594. Administers
corporate records. *Rights and Permissions Office:* PO
Box 2247 Austin TX 78768-2247. Administers rights
and permissions for non-current DFMS/General
Convention publications.

The Church Pension Fund
19 East 34th St New York NY 10016 (212) 592-1800
or (800) 223-6602. www.cpg.org. The principal
mission of The Church Pension Fund and its
affiliates (the "Church Pension Group") is to provide
comprehensive, cost-effective retirement, health
and life insurance benefits to the Episcopal Church,
its clergy and lay employees. The Church Pension
Group also provides property and casualty insurance
and risk management services and resources for
Episcopal church institutions; and worship materials,
curriculum and Christian education materials,
books, and music for the Episcopal Church. Over
its history, The Church Pension Fund has paid more
than $6.4 billion in benefits. The Church Pension
Group consists of the following core companies: *The
Church Pension Fund* (founded in 1914), *Church Life
Insurance Corporation* (founded 1922), *The Episcopal
Church Medical Trust* (founded 2002), *The Church
Insurance Company* (founded 1929), *The Church
Insurance Agency Corporation* (founded 1930), *The
Church Insurance Company of New York* (founded
2007), *The Church Insurance Company of Vermont*
(founded 1999), and *Church Publishing Incorporated*
(founded 1918). The CEO and President of The
Church Pension Fund is Mary Kate Wold.

Episcopal Church Building Fund
Established in 1880, the ECBF, an autonomous,
self-funding and self-governing agency, provides
non-mortgage loans up to $1 million (larger
mortgage loans also available) for the purchase,
construction, repair, improvement, or refinancing
of properties, churches, rectories, schools, and other
parochial buildings. Provides consultations on the
creative use of church buildings and properties to
support a congregations' financial sustainability
and increase their connection and relevance to the
community. Partners with ecumenical groups to
achieve a common mission. Provides guidance on
the building planning process. Web resources on
accessibility, greening, liturgical design, and full
video presentations from national symposiums.
Interim Pres The Rev Ruth Woodliff-Stanley; *VP*
Sally O'Brien 563 Southlake Blvd, Richmond VA
23236 (804) 893-3436 *E-mail:* buildchurch@ecbf.org
Web: www.ecbf.org.

Forward Movement
The mission of Forward Movement is inspiring
disciples and empowering evangelists. Primary
publications include the devotionals *Forward Day by
Day* and *Adelante Día a Día* as well as pamphlets,
books, and digital resources for study, devotional,
pastoral, and congregational development use.
Executive Director is the Rev Canon Scott Gunn 412
Sycamore St Cincinnati OH 45202 (513) 721-6659
E-Mail: orders@forwardmovement.org *Web:* www.
forwardmovement.org.

Institutions and Organizations

EDUCATIONAL

THEOLOGICAL SEMINARIES

Berkeley Divinity School at Yale

Founded in 1854, since 1971 the Berkeley Divinity School has functioned as an affiliate of Yale University. Berkeley has its own dean, board of trustees, and bylaws. Berkeley and Yale Divinity School share a single admissions process, curriculum and faculty, and Yale degrees are granted to all students, with Berkeley diplomas and certificates in Anglican Studies to those undertaking the Berkeley program. Berkeley Center 363 St Ronan St New Haven CT 06511 *Administrative Offices:* 409 Prospect St New Haven CT 06511 (203) 432-9285 *Fax:* (203) 432-9353 *Web:* berkeleydivinity.yale.edu

Dean and Pres, McFaddin Prof of Anglican Studies—V Rev Andrew B McGowan BA BD MA PhD

Assoc Dean and Dir Form—Rev Cathy George BA MDiv DMin

Dir of Ed Ldrship and Min Prog—Jere Wells BA MA

Bp Percy Goddard Prof of Lit Studies—Rev B Spinks MTh PhD

Prof Hebrew Scriptures—Rev Carolyn Sharp MAR PhD

Noah Porter Prof of Philosophical Theol—John Hare BA PhD

Henry B Wright Prof of Systematic Theol—Miroslav Volf MA DTh

Prof of Religion and Lit—Peter S Hawkins BA MDiv PhD

Assoc Prof of Asian Theol—Chloe Starr MA DPhil

Lecturer in Art History—Felicity Harley McGowan BA PhD

Frederick Marquand Prof Systematic Theol—Kathryn Tanner MA PhD

Asst Prof of Homiletics—Donyelle McCray BA JD MDiv ThD

Dean of Marquand Chapel and Assoc Prof of Theology and Literature—Maggi Dawn BA PhD

Gilbert L Stark Prof of Christian Ethics and Assoc Dean for Acad Affairs, YDS—Jennifer A Herdt BA MA PhD

Bexley Hall Seabury Western Theological Seminary Federation

www.bexleyseabury.edu

Bexley Hall and Seabury Western have inaugurated a new seminary Federation, bringing the two historic institutions together with a single Board, faculty, and mission. There are two locations: in Columbus, Ohio, on the campus of Trinity Lutheran Seminary; and in Chicago, housed at the ELCA Churchwide headquarters. Bexley Seabury is committed to educating lay and ordained leaders for the church in an ecumenical setting. We offer a residential MDiv program primarily in Columbus, and the DMin with specialization in Congregational Development

and preaching. A Diploma in Anglican Studies (for students enrolled at non-Episcopal seminaries) and programs in leadership education are offered at both sites, including courses in non-profit management in partnership with the Kellogg School of Non-Profit Management at Northwestern University and in asset-based community development.

Columbus: 583 Sheridan Ave Columbus, OH 43209-2324 (614) 231-3095

Chicago: 8765 Higgins Road Chicago IL (773) 380-6780 www.bexleyseabury.edu

Pres and Prof Biblical Interpretation and Practice of Ministry—Rev Roger A Ferlo PhD

Academic Dean and Assoc Prof Church Hist—Rev Thomas Ferguson PhD

Prof Theol and Culture—Rev John A Dally, PhD

Assoc Prof of Theol—Rev Jason Fout PhD

Director DMin and Lecturer Practical Theo—Rev Suzann Holding

Director Field Ed and Formation—Rev KyungJa Oh

Lecturer Sacred Music—M Milner Seifert MM

Research Prof Theol and Ethics—Rev Ellen K Wondra PhD

Church Divinity School of the Pacific

2451 Ridge Rd Berkeley CA 94709 (510) 204-0700 *Fax:* (510) 644-0712 *E-mail:* info@cdsp.edu *Web:* www.cdsp.edu.

Pres and Dean—Rev WM Richardson PhD

Dean Acad Aff—Rev R Meyers PhD

Hodges/Hayes Prof Litur—Rev R Meyers PhD

Assist Prof Theol—S MacDougall PhD

Visiting Prof Ch Hist—Rev W Stafford PhD

Assoc Prof Min Dev—Rev S Singer

Prof ChristianEthics—C Moe-Lobeda PhD

Assist Prof OT—J Gonzalez PhD

DMin Dir—Rev S Singer PhD

Faculty Emer—Rev JL Kater PhD, Rev AG Holder PhD, Rev L Weil PhD, Rev LL Clader PhD

Asst Prof Ch Mus/Dir Chapel Mus—G Emblom MM

Dir Operations and Personal Management—Rev B Rybicki

Dean Stud/Dn of Chapel—Rev LA Hallisey

Dir of Ext Learning / Prof Practical Theo—J Snow PhD

Reg—E Rhee

Dir Recruit—A Hybl

Episcopal Divinity School at Union Theological Seminary in the City of New York (EDS at Union)

3041 Broadway New York NY 10027 (212) 280-1567 *E-mail:* edsinfo@uts.columbia.edu *Web:* utsnyc.edu/eds

Visionary and transformative faith leaders who are grounded in God's love and justice are more important now than ever for ministry. Episcopal

Divinity School at Union endeavors to form such leaders with a focus on theological education, spiritual formation, and community transformation. Here, students carry forth the EDS mission of dismantling racism and working for social justice. EDS, formerly located in Cambridge, MA, affiliated with Union Theological Seminary in 2017. EDS was founded in 1974 with the merger of the Episcopal Theological School (ETS) and the Philadelphia Divinity School (PDS).

Dean, Episcopal Divinity School at Union—The Very Rev Dr Kelly Brown Douglas

Dir, Anglican Studies—Miguel Escobar

Office Manager—Douglas Berger

General Theological Seminary of the Protestant Episcopal Church in the United States

Established by the General Convention, May 27, General Theological Seminary of the Protestant Episcopal Church in the United States Established by the General Convention, May 27, 1817. Constitution adopted by General Convention, 1822. Incorporated April 5 1822. 440 West 21st St NY NY 10011-2981 (212) 243-5150 *Fax:* (212) 727- 3907 *Web:* www.gts.edu.

Pres and Dean - The Very Rev. Kurt H. Dunkle

Prof Ch Mus and Organist—David J Hurd MusD

Prof of NT—Deirdre J Good ThD

Prof of Preaching—Rev Mitties M DeChamplain PhD

Prof of OT—Rev Robert J Owens PhD

Assoc Prof in H Boone Porter Chair of Liturgics—Rev Patrick Malloy PhD

Asst Prof of Pastoral Theology—Rev Amy Lamborn PhD

Assoc Prof of Ascetical Theology—Rev Clair McPherson PhD

Asst Prof of New Testament - Andrew Irving ThD

Controller - Robert Elliot

VP of Advancement—Donna Ashley

VP of Operations - Anthony Khani

Dir of HR and Financial Aid- Trecia O'Sullivan

Dir of Keller Library—Rev Andrew G Kadel MLS

Registrar—Emily Beekman

Exec Dir Preschool and Daycare—Susan Stein

Exec Asst to Dean—Kim Robey

Dir of Commun—Chad Rancourt

Herbert Thompson Prof of Church and Soc, Dir of the Desmond Tutu Center—The Rev Dr Michael Battle

Asst Prof of NT—The Rev Dr Todd HW Brewer

Adj Prof of Church and Soc and Dir of Mission and Reconciliation—The Rev Canon Stephanie Spellers

Affiliate Prof of Sys Theo—Dr Alina N Feld

Affiliate Prof of Liturgics—The Rev Dr Kevin Moroney

Affiliate Profof Church Music and Chapel Organist—The Rev Dr Shane Scott-Hamblen

Nashotah House

2777 Mission Rd Nashotah WI 53058-9793 (262) 646-6500 *Fax:* (262) 646-6504 *E-mail:* mjohnson@nashotah.edu *Web:* www.nashotah.edu

Provost and President—Garwood Anderson PhD

Instructor Ch Mus, Dir of Music and Worship—Rev Alexander Pryor, BMus, MDiv

Prof Hist and Syst Theol—Rev Thomas Holtzen PhD

Dir Library and Assoc Prof of Ascetical Theology—David Sherwood DMin

Assoc Prof Church History/Dir of Residential Life—Rev Thomas Buchan III PhD

Asst Prof OT and Hebrew—Rev Travis Bott, PhD

Asst Prof of Liturgics and Pastoral Theology—Rev Matthew Olver, PhD

Assoc Provost—Dcn Esther Kramer, PhD

Dir of Field Education—Rev Scott Leannah MDiv

Program Dir Doctor of Min and Affiliate Prof of Pastoral Theology—David L. Jones ThD

COO—William Montei

Protestant Episcopal Theological Seminary In Virginia, The

Seminary Post Office 3737 Seminary Rd Alexandria VA 22304 (703) 370-6600 *Fax:* (703) 370-6234 *Web:* www.vts.edu.

Dean and Pres—V Rev Ian Markham PhD

Assoc Dean for Acad Affrs—TF Sedgwick MA PhD

Assoc Dean of Students—A Dyer PhD

Exec Dir Ctr for Ang Comm Studies/Prof Pastoral Theo—Rev JB Hawkins IV MDiv PhD

Dir Field Ed—Rev Allison St Louis MDiv PhD

Doc of Min Prog and Prof of Evan and Cong Ldrshp—Rev David Gortner MA MDiv PhD

Prof NT—Rev LA Lewis MDiv MA MPhil PhD

Prof NT—Rev K Grieb MDiv JD PhD

Prof NT—J Yieh MA MDiv PhD

Prof Ch Hist—Rev RW Prichard MDiv PhD

Asst Prof Ch Hist—Jonathan Gray MA PhD

Prof Theol—Rev K Sonderegger MDiv STM PhD

Asst Prof Hom—Rev R Hooke MAR MA MPhil PhD

Assoc Prof OT—Rev Judy Fentress-Williams MDiv PhD

Prof OT Language and Lit—Stephen L Cook MA MDiv MPhil PhD

Prof of Practical Theol—Rev J Mercer MDiv DMin PhD

Prof of Ch Music—William B Robert MCM DMA

V Pres Admin and Fin—H Zdancewicz MBA

V Pres Inst Advancement—Rev JB Hawkins IV MDiv PhD

Librarian/Prof—M Jarrett-Budde MA MLib DMin

Dir of CMT and Chrs Form and Cong Ldrshp
Elizabeth M Kimball MEd PhD

Assoc Prof of Theo and Liturgy—The Rev James W
Farwell, PhD

The School of Theology, University of the South, Sewanee, Tenn.

335 Tennessee Ave Sewanee TN 37383-0001 (800)
722-1974 *Fax:* (931) 598-1852 *E-mail:* theology@
sewanee.edu *Web:* http://theology.sewanee.edu.

Seminary

*Dean/ Prof of Liturgy, Charles Todd Quintard Prof of
Theol*—The Rt Rev J Neil Alexander ThD

*Assoc Prof of Liturgy/Norma & Olan Mills Prof of
Divinity/Assoc Dean of Academic Affairs/Sub-
Dean of the Chapel of the Apostles*—The Rev
Canon James F Turrell PhD

*Assoc Dean for Community Life, Recruitment, and
Admission*—The Rev Dr Deborah Jackson

Prof of New Testament—The Rev Dr William F
Brosend II

CK Benedict Prof of Old Testament—The Rev Dr
Rebecca Abts Wright

Prof of Christian Ethics and Theology—Dr Cynthia
S W Crysdale

Bishop Frank A. Juhan Prof of Pastoral Theol—The
Rev Dr Julia Gatta

*Assoc Prof of Church History and Dir of the
Advanced Degrees Prog*—The Rev Dr Benjamin
John King

Assoc Prof of Theol—The Rev Dr Robert MacSwain

*Asst Prof of Church Music/Organist/Choir Master for
the Chapel of the Apostles*—Dr Kenneth Miller

Theological Librarian—Dr Romulus Stefanut

Dist Visiting Prof of Global Anglicanism—The Rt Rev
James Tengatenga PhD

*Visiting Asst Prof of Theol Ethics and Dir of
the Alternative Clergy Training at Sewanee
Program*—Dr Andrew R H Thompson

Instr in Homiletics—David Stark

*Acting Dir of Contextual Education and Lect in
Contextual Theol*—The Rev David Cobb

Visiting Asst Prof of World Religions—The Rev Dr
Donna S Mote

*Instr in Pastoral Spanish and Latino/Hispanic
Ministry*—The Rev Leigh Preston

Visiting Lect in Contextual Education—The Rev Dr
Amy Lamborne

Visiting Instr in Christian Education—Hilary Ward

Visiting Asst Prof in Greek—Dr Kyle Sanders

Visiting Asst Prof of Old Testament—Dr Collin
Cornell

*Dir of Publications, Marketing, and
Communications, The School of Theology*—Mary
Ann Patterson

Assoc Dir for Alumni and Advancement—Sukey
Byerly

Dir of Financial Aid—Connie Patton

*CK Benedict Prof of New Testament Emer/Ed of
Sewanee Theological Review*—The Rev Dr
Christopher Bryan

The Beecken Center of the School of Theology

*Exec Dir of the Beecken Center/Assoc Dean of the
School of Theology*—Dr Sheri Kling

*Asst Dir of the Beecken Center/Exec Dir of Education
for Ministry*—Karen Meridith

Asst Dir for Training, Education for Ministry—Elsa
Swift Bakkum

Asst Dir of Education for Ministry—Joshua Booher

Dir, SUMMA Theological Debate Society—The Rev
Dr Christoph Keller

Assoc Dir, SUMMA Theological Debate Society—The
Rev Cindy Fribourgh

Dir of Marketing and Communications, Beecken
Center—Paul Schutz

Dir of Invite Welcome Connect—Mary Parmer

Seminary of the Southwest (Episcopal Theological Seminary of the Southwest)

501 E 32nd St Austin TX 78705 (512) 472-4133 *Fax:*
(512) 472-3098 *E-mail:* info@ssw.edu *Web:* www.
ssw.edu.

Dean & Pres and Prof NT—Very Rev Cynthia Briggs
Kittredge ThD

Exec VPres—Frederick Clement

*Acad Dean and Prof Christian Ethics & Moral
Theology*—Scott Bader-Saye PhD

Prof Theol—Anthony Baker PhD

Dir Library—Alison Poage MLS

Assistant Prof of NT—Rev Jane Patterson PhD

Assistant Prof of Counselor Education—Gena
Minnix PhD

Assistant Prof of Counselor Education—Stephanie
Ramirez PhD

Assistant Prof of Counselor Education—Awa
Jangha PhD

Assoc Prof Church History—Daniel Joslyn-
Siemiatkoski PhD

Associate Prof Lit and Ang Studies—Rev Nathan
Jennings PhD

Dir of Comprehensive Wellness—Steven Tomlinson

Associate Prof OT—Steven Bishop PhD

Interim Dir Hisp Ch Stu—vacant

Interim Dir Formational Outreach—Rev John
Lewis DPhil

Interim VPres Inst Adv—Wally Moore

*Dir Loise Henderson Wessendorff Ctr for Chr Min
and Voc*—Rev Dave Scheider DMin

*Assistant Prof Pastoral Theology and Dir of Field
Ed*—Rev Danielle Tumminio PhD

Registrar and Dir of Assessment—Madelyn
    Snodgrass
Dir Information Tech —Erik Morrow
Dir Enrollment Management and Admissions—Rev
    Hope Benko
Dir Commun—Eric Scott

Trinity School for Ministry

311 Eleventh St., Ambridge PA 15003 (724) 266-3838
Fax: (724) 266-4617 *E-mail:* info@tsm.edu *Web:*
www.tsm.edu. Trinity offers the Master of Divinity,
Master of Arts in Religion (now available entirely
online), Master of Sacred Theology, and the Doctor
of Ministry degrees. Also offered are five diploma
programs (Diploma in Anglican Studies, Diploma
in Christian Ministry, Diploma in Lutheran Studies,
and the Spanish Language Post-Graduate Diplomas
in Anglican Studies and Christian Ministry) and
four certificate programs (Certificate in Christian
Ministry, Certificate of Diaconal Studies, Certificate
of Evangelism—Church Army USA, and Certificate
of Lutheran Studies). In addition to our regular on-
campus and online courses, Trinity offers week-long
Intensive courses in January and June.

Dean and Pres/Assoc Prof Liturgy—The Very Rev
    Henry L Thompson DMin
Dean of Advancement – The Rev Aidan Smith
Acad Dean/Prof Old Testament and Hebrew—Erika
    Moore PhD
Dean of Students—The Rev Deacon Geoffrey
    Mackey
Dean of Administration—Karen Getz
Prof Systematic Theology—David Yeago PhD
Assoc Prof Old Testament—The Rev Don Collett
    PhD
Assoc Prof Practical Theology/Dir DMin Program—
    The Rev Jack Gabig PhD
Assoc Prof New Testament—Wesley Hill PhD
*Assoc Prof Mission and Evang/Dir Stanway
    Institute*—The Rev Cn John Macdonald DMiss
*Assoc Prof Liturgy and Homiletics/Pres North
    American Lutheran Seminary (NALS)*—The Rev
    Amy Schifrin PhD
Assoc Prof Systematic Theol—William Witt,PhD
*Asst Prof Homiletics and Greek/Dir Presbyterian
    Studies*—The Rev Rich Herbster DMin
Asst Prof Church History—The Rev David Ney, hD
*Asst Prof Systematic Theol/Dir Robert E Webber
    Center*—The Rev Joel Scandrett PhD
Dir of Recruitment—Cliff Cartwright
Dir of Library—Susanah Hanson MLIS
Dir of Communications—Mary Lou Harju MS
Dir of Online Education—Russell Warren STM
Registrar/Dir Student Services—Stacey Williard
    MBA MA

SCHOOLS OF THEOLOGY

Bloy House, the Episcopal Theological School at Claremont

1325 N College Ave Claremont CA 91711-3199 (909)
621-2419 *E-mail:* bloyhouse@cst.edu *Web:*www.
bloyhouse.org. A weekend commuter seminary
on the campus of Claremont School of Theology
offering lay, diaconal, and priestly ministry formation
programs including accredited M. Div. coursework
that can be taken through the joint Bloy House/
CST program or the Bloy House partnership with
Church Divinity School of the Pacific. Certificates
for Anglican Studies, Diaconal Studies, and Lay
Leadership are also offered.

Dean and Pres—Very Rev Sylvia Sweeney PhD
Prof OT—Canon James A Sanders PhD
Prof NT—James Dunkly PhD
Prof Greek— James Dunkly PhD
Prof Liturgics—Very Rev Sylvia Sweeney PhD
Prof Ang Studies—Rev Sheryl Kujawa-Holbrook
    PhD
Prof Theo and Ethics—Michael J McGrath PhD
Prof Church Leadership—Rev Robert Honeychurch
    DMin
Prof Church History— Rev Pat Ash PhD
Prof Spiritual Care and Counseling—Rev Karri
    Backer PhD
Prof of Latino Spiritualities—Rev Nancy Frausto &
    Rev Jennifer Hughes PhD

George Mercer Jr Memorial School of Theology

65 Fourth St Garden City NY 11530 (516) 248-4800
x140 *Fax:* (516) 248-4883 *E-mail:* merceroffice@
dioceseli.org *Web:* www.mercerschool.org.
Director of Operations—Diane G Muscarella
Director of Academic Programs—Dr Ted Gerbracht
    PhD
Lib—Charles Egleston

POST-ORDINATION AND TRAINING INSTITUTIONS

Ecumenical Theological Seminary

DMin MDiv MA in Pas Min and Urban Min
Diploma progs. Only ecum Theology sem in SE
Mich; accredited by ATS. *Pres* Kenneth E Harris
2930 Woodward Ave Detroit MI 48201. (313) 831-
5200. *Fax:* (313) 831-1353. *E-mail:* info@etseminary.
edu. *Web:* www.etseminary.edu.

New Directions Ministries, Inc

Provides developmental trng prog for laity and
clergy in small congs with emphasis on mins of all
persons, regional and cluster ministries. Leadership
Academy for New Directions (LAND) is available for
national, regional, dio levels (urban as well as rural).
Ecumenical. *Pres* LaDonna Wind 4434 Buttonbush

Glen Dr Louisville KY 40241-4189 (502) 412-0196 *E-mail:* vanzoelen05@gmail.com; *VPres* The Rev John T Harris PO Box 1291 Gridley CA 95948 (530) 846-4257 *E-mail:* +john1@sbcglobal.net; The Rev Warren Frelund 1029 West State St Mason City IA 50401 (641) 423-1138 *E-mail:* wfrelund@q.com.

School of Theology University South

DMin and STM Program 3-week summer session at Sewanee. Write to Advanced Degrees Program 335 Tennessee Ave School of Theology Sewanee TN 37383-0001 (931) 598-1478 *Fax:* (931) 598-1852. *E-mail:* advdeg@sewanee.edu *Web:* http://theology.sewanee.edu.

Trinity Institute

Trinity Institute equips clergy and lay persons in the Episcopal Church for imaginative and catalytic leadership. Outreach of Trinity Parish in NYC. 120 Broadway, New York, NY, 10271 (212) 602-0800 *Fax:* (212) 602-0722 *Web:* https://trinityinstitute.org.

CHURCH COLLEGES AND UNIVERSITIES

Colleges & Universities of the Anglican Communion (CUAC)—Association of Episcopal Colleges (AEC)

815 Second Avenue, New York, NY 10017 (212) 716-6149 *e-Mail:* office@cuac.org *Web:* www.cuac.org. *General Secretary:* Rev Cn James G. Callaway, DD, *Chair:* The Rev Dr Robert Derrenbacker, Dean, Trinity College Theological School, Melbourne, Australia; *Treasurer:* The Rt Rev Prince Singh, Bishop of Rochester. The Episcopal colleges are autonomous institutions participating in the overall ministry of the Episcopal Church in areas related to their particular contexts and fields. Included are the ten colleges listed below. The AEC develops programs to support Christian values on and off campus and provides the means for distributing gifts or bequests equitably among some or all members. Colleges & Universities of the Anglican Communion is a worldwide network of Anglican colleges and universities which exists for the mutual flourishing of its members through engaging with each other, their churches, and their society as they seek to enable their students, staff, and faculties to become active and responsive citizens in God's world. Founded in 1962, AEC was instrumental in the 1993 founding of CUAC, a worldwide association of 150 Anglican institutions of higher education on five continents, and continues as the American chapter to serve as its headquarters and staff support. CUAC is a "network" of the Anglican Communion.

Bard College

PO Box 5000 Annandale-on-Hudson NY 12504-5000 (845) 758-6822. Coed 1860. Liberal arts, sciences, and fine arts offering a four-year B.A. and a five-year B.S./B.A. degree in economics and finance. M.A. in curatorial studies, and M.S. in environmental policy and climate science and policy at the Annandale campus; M.F.A. and M.A.T. at multiple campuses; and M.A., M.Phil., and Ph.D. in the decorative arts at the Bard Graduate Center in Manhattan. Internationally, Bard confers dual B.A. degrees at the Faculty of Liberal Arts and Sciences, St Petersburg State University, Russia (Smolny College), and American University of Central Asia in Kyrgyzstan; and dual B.A. and M.A.T. degrees at Al-Quds University in East Jerusalem. *Pres* Leon Botstein PhD, *Chap* Rev Mary Grace Williams. *E-mail:* admission@bard.edu *Web:* www.bard.edu

Cuttington University

Box 10-0277 1000 Monrovia 10 Liberia West Africa 011-231-227-413. 1889. Reopened in fall 1998. Emphasis on trad liberal arts, research, and community partnerships in the context of Christian service. *Pres* Rev Dr Herman B Browne, *Chap* Rev James Tamba. Inquiries may also be addressed to CUAC. *E-mail:* cuttingtonuniversity@yahoo.com *Web:* www.cuttington.org.

Hobart and William Smith Colleges

Geneva NY 14456 (315) 789-5500. 1822. Oldest Coll continuously associated with Epis Church in US. William Smith College (for women) and Hobart share faculty, library, and labs. *Interim Pres* Dr. Patrick A. McGuire *Chap* Rev Dr. Maurice Charles. *E-mail:* admissions@hws.edu *Web:* www.hws.edu.

Kenyon College

Gambier OH 43022 (740) 427-5000. Coed 1824. Fine Arts, Humanities, Natural Sciences, and Social Sciences. Publisher of *Kenyon Review* and *Psychological Record.* New Olin Library. *Pres* Sean M Decatur PhD, *Chap* Rev Dr. Rachel Kessler. *E-mail:* admissions@kenyon.edu *Web:* www.kenyon.edu.

St. Augustine College

1333-1345 W Argyle St Chicago IL 60640-3594 (773) 878-8756. Coed 1980 bilingual: Spanish/English. 3-4 yr technological and vocational prog; fully accredited. Main campus, plus four satellite facilities in areas of high concentration of Hispanic residents. *Pres* Reyes González. *Web:* www.staugustine.edu.

Saint Augustine's University

1315 Oakwood Ave Raleigh NC 27610 (919) 516-4000. Coed 1867. Historically Black. Liberal Arts differential curriculum with an academic focus in STEM, Mass Communication and Journalism, Public Health and Criminal Justice. *Pres* Dr Everett B Ward, *Chap* Rev. Nita Johnson Byrd. *E-mail:* admissions@st-aug.edu *Web:* www.st-aug.edu.

The University of the South

735 University Ave Sewanee TN 37383 (931) 598-1000. Coed 1857. Coll of Arts and Sciences and School of Theology. Publ *Sewanee Review,* oldest lit-crit quarterly in US and *Sewanee Theological Review. Chanc* Rt Rev Samuel Johnson Howard, DD, *Vice-Chanc and Pres* JohnM.McCardell Jr PhD, *Chap* Very Rev Thomas E Macfie Jr. *E-mail:* admiss@sewanee.edu *Web:* www.sewanee.edu.

Trinity University of Asia
Cathedral Heights 275 E Rodriguez Sr Ave Quezon City Philippines 1100 011-63-2-702-2882. Coed 1963. Episc Cathedral complex includes pre-school through college with 3,600 students at coll and grad level. Lib Arts, Bus Adm, Ed, Nursing, Med Tech. MA in Educ. *Pres* Dr Wilfred Tiu, *Chap* Chap Rev Edwin J. Ayabo. *Web*: www.tua.edu.ph.

Université Episcopale d'Haiti
14 rue Légitime, Champ de Mars, B.P. Box 2730, Port-au-Prince, Haiti. 509 22 27 7963. Coed 1994. Francophone. Programs in agronomy, education, theology, accounting, management. Affiliated with FSIL Nursing School (Léogâne), Bishop Tharp Business & Technology Institute (Les Cayes), St. Barnabas Agricultural School (Terrier Rouge), Episcopal Theology Seminary (Port-au-Prince). *Pres* Dr Lucien Jean Bernard. *E-mail* unephhaiti@hotmail.com *Web* www.uneph.org.

Voorhees College
Denmark SC 29042 (803) 708-1234. Coed 1897. Historically Black. 4-yr Liberal Arts Coll with 4 acad divisions: Business and Economics, Education and Humanities, Natural Sciences and Mathematics, Social Sciences. Offers 2-yr degree in Secretarial Science and Criminal Justice. Collaborative arrangement with Denmark Technical School and SC State Coll. *Pres* Dr W Franklin Evans, *Chap* Rev Dr James T Yarsiah. *E-mail:* admissions@ voorhees. edu *Web:* www.voorhees.edu.

EPISCOPAL SCHOOLS

National Assoc of Episcopal Schools, Inc. (NAES)
Gov Board Pres: Rev Edmund K Sherrill II, Exton PA. *Office:* 815 Second Ave New York NY 10017. (212) 716-6134, (800) 334-7626 x6134. *Fax:* (212) 286-9366. *E-mail:* info@episcopalschools.org. *Web:* www.episcopalschools.org *Executive Director:* Rev Daniel R Heischman DD *Associate Director:* Ann Mellow *Director of Operations:* Linda A Burnett *Advancement Manager:* Sarah E Tielemans CAE *Communications Manager:* Jonathan F Cooper *Member Services & Events Coordinator:* Heather E Zrubek

The National Association of Episcopal Schools (NAES) is an independent 501(c)(3), voluntary membership organization that supports, serves, and advocates for the vital work and ministry of those who serve nearly 1,200 Episcopal schools, early childhood education programs, and school establishment efforts throughout The Episcopal Church. Chartered in 1965, with historic roots dating to the 1930s, NAES is the only pre-collegiate educational association that is both national in scope and Episcopal in character. The association advances Episcopal education and strengthens Episcopal schools through essential services, resources, conferences, and networking opportunities on Episcopal school identity,

leadership, and governance, and on the spiritual and professional development of school leaders.

Church and Church-Related Schools
Episcopal schools and ECE programs vary in size, scope and educational philosophy. They are parish, cathedral, diocesan, seminary, religious order and independent schools; Montessori and military schools; day and boarding schools; co-educational and single-sex schools. Parishes and cathedrals with schools and ECE programs are identified in the Diocesan Lists with the symbol §. These programs may or may not be NAES members. The following list comprises diocesan, seminary, religious order, and church-related independent schools listed in the NAES database. NAES members, as of January 31, 2019, are identified with the • symbol. The schools are listed alphabetically by diocese and then by name. The individual listed as contact is in most cases the head of school or director. For a searchable database of current NAES member schools, ECE programs and school establishment efforts, visit www.episcopalschools.org/find-a-school.

Alabama *Holy Cross Episcopal School* 4400 Bell Road Montgomery AL 36116 *Grades:* Elementary School *Contact:* Ms Kathy Taylor *Chaplain(s):* Rev David H Peeples
Albany *Doane Stuart School* • 199 Washington Avenue Rensselaer NY 12144 *Grades:* Comprehensive School (P-12) *Contact:* Mrs Sharon M Duker *Chaplain(s):* Ms Sandi Miller, Mrs Patricia Hodgkinson
Albany *Hoosac School* • PO Box 9 Hoosick NY 12089 *Grades:* Secondary School *Contact:* Mr Dean S Foster
Arizona *Imago Dei Middle School* • 55 N Sixth Avenue Tucson AZ 85701 *Grades:* Middle School *Contact:* Mr Cameron Taylor *Chaplain(s):* Rev Donna McNiel
Atlanta *Saint George's Episcopal School* • 103 Birch Street Milner GA 30257 *Grades:* Elementary School *Contact:* Mr Larry Collins
Atlanta *The Ansley School* • 435 Peachtree Street Atlanta GA 30308 *Grades:* Elementary School *Contact:* Katherine Kennedy
Central Florida *All Saints' Academy* • 5001 State Road 540 West Winter Haven FL 33880 *Grades:* Comprehensive School (P-12) *Contact:* Mrs Carolyn Baldwin *Chaplain(s):* Rev Richard H Gomer Jr
Central Florida *Holy Trinity Episcopal Academy* • 5625 Holy Trinity Drive Melbourne FL 32940 *Grades:* Comprehensive School (P-12) *Contact:* Katherine M Cobb JD *Chaplain(s):* Ms Garcia Barnswell-Schmidt, Mr Jared Jones
Central Florida *Saint Edward's School* • 1895 Saint Edward's Drive Vero Beach FL 32963 *Grades:* Comprehensive School (P-12) *Contact:* Mr Michael Mersky *Chaplain(s):* Deacon Jason Murbarger, Rev William T Matthews
Central Florida *Trinity Preparatory School of Florida* • 5700 Trinity Prep Lane Winter Park FL

32792 *Grades:* Secondary School *Contact:* Mr Byron M Lawson Jr *Chaplain(s):* Rev Kenneth N Vinal, Rev Sonia T Sullivan-Clifton, Rev Richard A Towers

Central Gulf Coast *Holy Nativity Episcopal School* • 205 Hamilton Avenue Panama City FL 32401 *Grades:* Elementary School *Contact:* Mrs Judy Hughes *Chaplain(s):* Rev Steven B Bates

Central Gulf Coast *St Paul's Episcopal School* • 161 Dogwood Lane Mobile AL 36608 *Grades:* Comprehensive School (P-12) *Contact:* Mr N Blair Fisher

Chicago *Rose Hall Montessori Preschool* 1140 Wilmette Avenue Wilmette IL 60091 *Grades:* ECE Program (P-K only) *Contact:* Ms Elizabeth Friedman

Colorado *St Anne's Episcopal School* • 2701 S York Street Denver CO 80210-6098 *Grades:* Elementary School *Contact:* Mr Alan Smiley *Chaplain(s):* Rev Alfred Franklin Miller

Colorado *St Elizabeth's School* • 2350 Gaylord Street Denver CO 80205 *Grades:* Elementary School *Contact:* Mr Ramsay C Stabler *Chaplain(s):* Rev Alwen Bledsoe

Connecticut *Kent School* • 1 Macedonia Road Kent CT 6757 *Grades:* Secondary School *Contact:* Rev Richardson W Schell *Chaplain(s):* Rev Kate E Kelderman

Connecticut *Pomfret School* 398 Pomfret St Pomfret CT 6258 *Grades:* Secondary School *Contact:* Mr J Timothy Richards *Chaplain(s):* Rev Bradley Davis, Mr Bobby Fisher

Connecticut *The Rectory School* 528 Pomfret Pomfret CT 6258 *Grades:* Middle School *Contact:* Mr Frederick W Williams *Chaplain(s):* Mr True Bryant

Connecticut *Salisbury School* 251 Canaan Road Salisbury CT 6068 *Grades:* Secondary School *Contact:* Mr Chisholm S Chandler *Chaplain(s):* Rev Kirk Hall, Ms Sarah Mulrooney

Connecticut *South Kent School* • 40 Bull's Bridge Road South Kent CT 06785-9747 *Grades:* Secondary School *Contact:* Mr Lawrence Smith *Chaplain(s):* Rev Stephen B Klots

Connecticut *Wooster School* • 91 Miry Brook Road Danbury CT 6810 *Grades:* Comprehensive School (P-12) *Contact:* Mr Matthew Byrnes *Chaplain(s):* Rev Stephen Tickner

Dallas *The Canterbury Episcopal School* 1708 N Westmoreland Road DeSoto TX 75115 *Grades:* Comprehensive School (P-12) *Contact:* Ms Misty Stern *Chaplain(s):* Rev Michael G Wallens

Dallas *The Episcopal School of Dallas* • 4100 Merrell Road Dallas TX 75229 *Grades:* Comprehensive School (P-12) *Contact:* Mr David L Baad *Chaplain(s):* Rev Amy G Heller, Rev Canon K Michael Harmuth

Dallas *Holy Family School* 500 Throckmorton McKinney TX 75069 *Grades:* ECE Program (P-K only) *Contact:* Ms Betsy Boyd *Chaplain(s):* Rev Michael W Michie

Dallas *St Philip's School & Community Center* 1600 Pennsylvania Avenue Dallas TX 75215 *Grades:* Elementary School *Contact:* Terry J Flowers PhD

Delaware *Saint Andrew's School* • 350 Noxontown Road Middletown DE 19709-1605 *Grades:* Secondary School *Contact:* Mr Daniel T Roach Jr *Chaplain(s):* Rev John F Hutchinson Jr, Rev David P Desalvo

Delaware *St Anne's Episcopal School* • 211 Silver Lake Road Middletown DE 19709 *Grades:* Elementary School *Contact:* Mr Peter C Thayer *Chaplain(s):* Ms Kathy Hanna

Delaware *St Michael's School and Nursery, Inc* 305 E 7th Street Wilmington DE 19801 *Grades:* ECE Program (P-K only) *Contact:* Ms Johanna Seda

East Tennessee *All Saints' Episcopal School* 3275 Maple Valley Road Morristown TN 37813 *Grades:* Elementary School *Contact:* Rev Virginia G Sharp *Chaplain(s):* Rev J Mark Holland

East Tennessee *The Episcopal School of Knoxville* • 950 Episcopal School Way Knoxville TN 37932 *Grades:* Elementary School *Contact:* Jack Talmadge EdD *Chaplain(s):* Rev Matthew Farr

East Tennessee *St Nicholas School* • 7525 Min-Tom Drive Chattanooga TN 37421-1835 *Grades:* Elementary School *Contact:* Mr Mark J Fallo *Chaplain(s):* Rev Janice Robbins, Ms Katherine Cantelou

Ecuador Central *Canterbury School* Box 17-11-6165 Quito Ecuador *Grades:* Comprehensive School (P-12)

Ecuador Central *Escuela Episcopal Chimbacalle* Box 17-11-6165 Quito Ecuador *Grades:* Elementary School *Contact:* Sra Ana Armijos

El Camino Real *York School* 9501 York Road Monterey CA 93940 *Grades:* Secondary School *Contact:* Mr Chuck Harmon *Chaplain(s):* Mr Murray Walker

Florida *Episcopal Children's Services, Inc* 8443 Baymeadows Road #1 Jacksonville FL 32256 *Grades:* ECE Program (P-K only) *Contact:* Ms Connie Stophel

Haiti *Holy Trinity School* Box 1309 Port-au-Prince 1309 OU Haiti *Grades:* Comprehensive School (P-12) *Contact:* Rev Gerard David Cesar

Hawaii *Iolani School* • 563 Kamoku Street Honolulu HI 96826 *Grades:* Comprehensive School (P-12) *Contact:* Timothy R Cottrell PhD *Chaplain(s):* Rev Heather L Patton-Graham, Rev David H Smith DMin

Hawaii *Seabury Hall* • 480 Olinda Road Makawao HI 96768 *Grades:* Secondary School *Contact:* Mr Paul Wenninger *Chaplain(s):* Rev Dr Sara Shisler Goff

Hawaii *St Andrew's Schools* • 224 Queen Emma Square Honolulu HI 96813 *Grades:* Comprehensive School (P-12) *Contact:* Ruth R Fletcher PhD *Chaplain(s):* Rev Annalise Castro Pasalo

Honduras *El Buen Pastor Episcopal School* • 23 Avenida C 21 Calle SO Colonia Trejo San Pedro Sula Cortés Honduras *Grades:* Comprehensive School (P-12) *Contact:* Ms Claudia Chicas

Honduras *Holy Spirit Episcopal School* • Tela Atlantida Honduras *Grades:* Comprehensive School

(P-12) *Contact:* Rev Olga Abelda Barrera

Honduras *Holy Trinity Episcopal School* • Avenida Morazan 48 Bario Dantoni La Ceiba Atlantida Honduras *Grades:* Comprehensive School (P-12) *Contact:* Ms Veronica Flowers

Honduras *St John's Episcopal School* • Bo, El Centro, 6 Calle, 4 Avenida Puerto Cortés 504 Cortés Honduras *Grades:* Comprehensive School (P-12) *Contact:* Mr Alex Segura

Honduras *St John's Episcopal School* • Siguatepeque Comayagua Honduras *Grades:* Comprehensive School (P-12) *Contact:* Ms Sandra Lucia Villatoro

Honduras *St Mary's Episcopal School* • Colonia Florencia Norte 1a Entrada, Boulevard Suyapa Tegucigalpa MDC Honduras *Grades:* Comprehensive School (P-12) *Contact:* Mr Ricardo A Salinas *Chaplain(s):* Very Rev Gerardo A Alonzo Martinez

Kansas *Bishop Seabury Academy* • 4120 Clinton Parkway Lawrence KS 66047 *Grades:* Secondary School *Contact:* Donald Schawang PhD *Chaplain(s):* Rev Stephanie R Jenkins

Los Angeles *Campbell Hall (Episcopal)* • 4533 Laurel Canyon Boulevard North Hollywood CA 91607 *Grades:* Comprehensive School (P-12) *Contact:* Rev Canon Julian P Bull *Chaplain(s):* Rev Canon Norman S Hull, Rev Joseph Courtney

Los Angeles *The Episcopal School of Los Angeles* • 6325 Santa Monica Boulevard Los Angeles CA 90038 *Grades:* Secondary School *Contact:* Mr Peter McCormack *Chaplain(s):* Mr Patrick Hecker, Mr Walter Joseph Thorne

Los Angeles *The Gooden School* • 192 N Baldwin Avenue Sierra Madre CA 91024 *Grades:* Elementary School *Contact:* Ms Jo-Anne Woolner *Chaplain(s):* Rev Michael E Cooper, Rev Francisco Garcia

Los Angeles *Harvard-Westlake School* Upper School Campus 3700 Coldwater Canyon Avenue North Hollywood CA 91604 *Grades:* Secondary School *Contact:* Mr Richard B Commons *Chaplain(s):* Rabbi Emily Feigenson

Los Angeles *St Margaret's Episcopal School* • 31641 La Novia Avenue San Juan Capistrano CA 92675 *Grades:* Comprehensive School (P-12) *Contact:* Mr William N Moseley *Chaplain(s):* Rev Canon Robert D Edwards, Rev Earl Gibson, Rev James Livingston, Rev Linda W Ahron

Louisiana *Episcopal School of Baton Rouge* • 3200 Woodland Ridge Boulevard Baton Rouge LA 70816 *Grades:* Comprehensive School (P-12) *Contact:* Mr Hugh McIntosh *Chaplain(s):* Rev Kirkland W Knight

Louisiana *St Martin's Episcopal School* • 225 Green Acres Road Metairie LA 70003-2484 *Grades:* Comprehensive School (P-12) *Contact:* Mrs Merry Sorrells *Chaplain(s):* Rev Ford Jefferson Millican Jr, Rev Michael C Kuhn DMin, Rev Deborah W Scalia

Maryland *Brown Memorial Weekday School* • 232 St Thomas' Lane Owings Mills MD 21117 *Grades:* ECE Program (P-K only) *Contact:* Rev Malcolm A Ellis DMin

Maryland *St Anne's School of Annapolis* • 3112 Arundel-on-the-Bay Road Annapolis MD 21403-

4605 *Grades:* Elementary School *Contact:* Ms Lisa Nagel *Chaplain(s):* Rev Diana E Carroll

Maryland *St James School* • 17641 College Road Hagerstown MD 21740 *Grades:* Secondary School *Contact:* Rev D Stuart Dunnan DPhil

Maryland *St Timothy's School* 8400 Greenspring Avenue Stevenson MD 21153 *Grades:* Secondary School *Contact:* Mr Randy S Stevens

Maryland *The Wilkes School at Grace and St Peter's* 707 Park Avenue Baltimore MD 21201 *Grades:* Elementary School *Contact:* Mrs Sandra G Shull *Chaplain(s):* Rev Frederick S Thomas

Massachusetts *Brooks School* • 1160 Great Pond Road North Andover MA 01845-1298 *Grades:* Secondary School *Contact:* Mr John R Packard *Chaplain(s):* Rev James D Chapman

Massachusetts *Epiphany School* • 154 Centre Street Dorchester MA 2124 *Grades:* Middle School *Contact:* Rev John H Finley IV

Massachusetts *Esperanza Academy* • 198 Garden Street Lawrence MA 1840 *Grades:* Middle School *Contact:* Mr Jadihel Taveras *Chaplain(s):* Rev Kathleen Lonergan

Massachusetts *Groton School* • 282 Farmers Row Groton MA 01450-1848 *Grades:* Secondary School *Contact:* Mr Temba T Maqubela *Chaplain(s):* Rev Christopher W Whiteman

Massachusetts *St Mark's School* • 25 Marlborough Road Southborough MA 1772 *Grades:* Secondary School *Contact:* Mr John Warren *Chaplain(s):* Rev Barbara Talcott, Rev Loris N Adams

Milwaukee *St John's Northwestern Military Academy* • 1101 Genesee Street Delafield WI 53018 *Grades:* Secondary School *Contact:* Mr Jack H Albert Jr

Minnesota *Breck School* • 123 Ottawa Avenue North Minneapolis MN 55422 *Grades:* Comprehensive School (P-12) *Contact:* Dr Natalia Rico Hernández *Chaplain(s):* Rev John E Bellaimey, Ms Nan Zosel, Ms Alexis Kent

Minnesota *Shattuck-St Mary's School* • 1000 Shumway Avenue Faribault MN 55021 *Grades:* Secondary School *Contact:* Mr Matthew Cavellier *Chaplain(s):* Rev Colin S Maltbie

Mississippi *Coast Episcopal School* • 5065 Espy Avenue Long Beach MS 39560 *Grades:* Elementary School *Contact:* Mr Daren Houck *Chaplain(s):* Ms Kirby Barkley, Rev Clelie McCandless

New Hampshire *Heronfield Academy* • 356 Exeter Road Hampton Falls NH 3844 *Grades:* Elementary School *Contact:* Ms Betsy Kelly

New Hampshire *Holderness School* • 33 Chapel Lane Holderness NH 3245 *Grades:* Secondary School *Contact:* Mr R Phillip Peck *Chaplain(s):* Rev Richard C Weymouth, Rev Canon Randolph Dales, Rev Joshua Ashton Hill

New Hampshire *St Paul's School* • 325 Pleasant Street Concord NH 03301-2591 *Grades:* Secondary School *Contact:* Ms Amy C Richards *Chaplain(s):* Rev Richard E Greenleaf, Rev Alice H Courtright, Terry J Dumansky PhD

New Hampshire *The White Mountain School* • 371 West Farm Road Bethlehem NH 3574 *Grades:*

Secondary School *Contact:* Mr Thomas J Reid *Chaplain(s):* Rev Paul H Higginson

New Jersey *Doane Academy* 350 Riverbank Burlington NJ 8016 *Grades:* Comprehensive School (P-12) *Contact:* Mr George B Sanderson *Chaplain(s):* Rev Paul R Briggs

New York *Children's Garden at The General Theological Seminary* 440 West 21st Street New York NY 10011 *Grades:* ECE Program (P-K only) *Contact:* Ms Brooke Savitsky

New York *The Episcopal School in the City of New York* • 35 E 69th Street New York NY 10021 *Grades:* ECE Program (P-K only) *Contact:* Mrs Susan A Sheahan

New York *Grace Church School* 254 Hicks Street Brooklyn NY 11201 *Grades:* ECE Program (P-K only) *Contact:* Ms Amy Morgano

New York *St Hilda's & St Hugh's School* • 619 W 114th Street New York NY 10025 *Grades:* Elementary School *Contact:* Ms Virginia Connor *Chaplain(s):* Rev Arden Strasser

New York *Trinity School* • 139 W 91st Street New York NY 10024 *Grades:* Comprehensive School (P-12) *Contact:* Mr John C Allman *Chaplain(s):* Rev Timothy L Morehouse, Ms Melissa Lamkin

New York *Trinity-Pawling School* • 700 Route 22 Pawling NY 12564 *Grades:* Secondary School *Contact:* Mr William W Taylor *Chaplain(s):* Rev Michael E Robinson

North Carolina *Canterbury School* • 5400 Old Lake Jeanette Road Greensboro NC 27455-1322 *Grades:* Elementary School *Contact:* Mr Philip E Spears *Chaplain(s):* Rev Hunter Pearson Silides

North Carolina *Palisades Episcopal School* • 13120 Grand Palisades Parkway Charlotte NC 28278 *Grades:* Elementary School *Contact:* Ms Kerin S Hughes

North Carolina *Preschool at the Chapel of the Cross* 304 East Franklin Street Chapel Hill NC 27514-3619 *Grades:* ECE Program (P-K only) *Contact:* Ms Laura Gelblum

North Carolina *St David's School* 3400 White Oak Road Raleigh NC 27609 *Grades:* Comprehensive School (P-12) *Contact:* Mr Jonathan Yonan *Chaplain(s):* Rev Todd von Helms DMin

North Carolina *Saint Mary's School* • 900 Hillsborough Street Raleigh NC 27603 *Grades:* Secondary School *Contact:* Mr Brendan J O'Shea *Chaplain(s):* Rev Ann P Bonner-Stewart

North Carolina *Trinity Episcopal School* • 750 E 9th Street Charlotte NC 28202-3102 *Grades:* Elementary School *Contact:* Mr Thomas J Franz *Chaplain(s):* Ms Emily Phillips, Mr de'Angelo Dia, Rev Lindsey Wells Peery, Rev David Jackson

Northwest Texas *All Saints Episcopal School* • 3222 103rd Street Lubbock TX 79423 *Grades:* Elementary School *Contact:* Mr Bruce Latta *Chaplain(s):* Rev Deacon Paige McKay

Northwest Texas *Trinity School of Midland* 3500 W Wadley Avenue Midland TX 79707 *Grades:* Comprehensive School (P-12) *Contact:* Mrs Shelby Hammer

Oklahoma *Casady School* • 9500 N Pennsylvania Avenue Oklahoma City OK 73120 *Grades:* Comprehensive School (P-12) *Contact:* Mr Nathan L Sheldon *Chaplain(s):* Rev Charles F Blizzard, Mr TimSean Youmans

Oklahoma *Holland Hall School* • 5666 E 81st Street Tulsa OK 74137-2099 *Grades:* Comprehensive School (P-12) *Contact:* Mr Jared P Culley *Chaplain(s):* Rev Arthur P Scrutchins, Rev Justin Boyd

Oklahoma *Oak Hall Episcopal School* • 2815 N Mount Washington Road Ardmore OK 73401 *Grades:* Elementary School *Contact:* Mr Kenneth R Willy *Chaplain(s):* Rev Stephen R Bilsbury

Olympia *Annie Wright Schools* • 827 N Tacoma Avenue Tacoma WA 98403 *Grades:* Comprehensive School (P-12) *Contact:* Mr Christian Sullivan

Olympia *Charles Wright Academy* 7723 Chambers Creek Road West Tacoma WA 98467 *Grades:* Comprehensive School (P-12) *Contact:* Mr Matthew Culberson *Chaplain(s):* Mr Michael Moffitt

Oregon *Oregon Episcopal School* • 6300 SW Nicol Road Portland OR 97223 *Grades:* Comprehensive School (P-12) *Contact:* Ms Mo Copeland *Chaplain(s):* Rev C Phillip Craig Jr, Rev Jennifer B Cleveland, Ms Melissa Robinson

Oregon *St James Santiago School* • 2490 NE Hwy 101 North Lincoln City OR 97367 *Grades: Contact:* Mrs Julie Fiedler

Pennsylvania *The Church Farm School* • 1001 E Lincoln Highway Exton PA 19341 *Grades:* Secondary School *Contact:* Rev Edmund K Sherrill II *Chaplain(s):* Rev John D Daniels

Pennsylvania *The Episcopal Academy* • 1785 Bishop White Drive Newtown Square PA 19073 *Grades:* Comprehensive School (P-12) *Contact:* Thomas J Locke EdD *Chaplain(s):* Rev Albert E R Zug Sr, Rev Timothy P Gavin III, Ms Michelle Bullock

Pennsylvania *Saint James School* • 3217 West Clearfield Street Philadelphia PA 19132 *Grades:* Middle School *Contact:* Mr David J Kasievich *Chaplain(s):* Rev Andrew L Kellner

Rhode Island *St Andrew's School* 63 Federal Road Barrington RI 02806-2407 *Grades:* Secondary School *Contact:* Mr David Tinagero *Chaplain(s):* Mr David Bourk

Rhode Island *St George's School* • PO Box 1910 Newport RI 02840-0190 *Grades:* Secondary School *Contact:* Alexandra Callen EdD *Chaplain(s):* Rev Dr Jaquelyn Kirby

San Diego *The Bishop's School* • 7607 La Jolla Boulevard La Jolla CA 92037 *Grades:* Secondary School *Contact:* Mrs Carol Barry *Chaplain(s):* Rev Nicole M Simopoulos, Rev Nicole M Simopoulos

South Carolina *Porter-Gaud School* • 300 Albemarle Road Charleston SC 29407 *Grades:* Comprehensive School (P-12) *Contact:* Mr D DuBose Egleston Jr *Chaplain(s):* Rev Jill Williams, Rev Charles L Echols PhD, Ms Henrietta Rivers

South Carolina *Trinity-Byrnes Collegiate School* 5001 Hoffmeyer Road Darlington SC 29532 *Grades:* Secondary School *Contact:* Mr Ed Hoffman *Chaplain(s):* Rev Charles D Cooper

Southeast Florida *Palmer Trinity School* • 7900 SW 176 Street Palmetto Bay FL 33157 *Grades:* Secondary School *Contact:* Mr Patrick H F Roberts *Chaplain(s):* Rev Mary Ellen Cassini DMin

Southeast Florida *St Andrew's School* • 3900 Jog Road Boca Raton FL 33434-4498 *Grades:* Comprehensive School (P-12) *Contact:* Mr Ethan Shapiro *Chaplain(s):* The Ven Faye Somers, Rev David Taylor, Rev Charles A Browning II

Southeast Florida *St Stephen's Episcopal Day School* • 3439 Main Highway Coconut Grove FL 33133 *Grades:* Elementary School *Contact:* Ms Silvia Larrauri *Chaplain(s):* Rev Wilifred S N Allen-Faiella, Rev Jorge Sayago-Gonzalez

Southern Ohio *Bethany School* • 555 Albion Avenue Cincinnati OH 45246 *Grades:* Elementary School *Contact:* Mr David Gould *Chaplain(s):* Mr Joseph Snavely

Southern Virginia *Chatham Hall* • 800 Chatham Hall Circle Chatham VA 24531 *Grades:* Secondary School *Contact:* Mrs Suzanne Walker Buck *Chaplain(s):* Rev Ned W Edwards Jr, DMin, Rev Dr Regina Christianson, Rev Becky Crites

Southern Virginia *Good Shepherd Episcopal School* 4207 Forest Hill Avenue Richmond VA 23225 *Grades:* Elementary School *Contact:* Mr Ken Seward *Chaplain(s):* Rev Ross M Wright PhD

Southern Virginia *Trinity Episcopal School* 3850 Pittaway Drive Richmond VA 23235 *Grades:* Secondary School *Contact:* Mr Robert Short *Chaplain(s):* Mr Brian Griffen

Southwest Florida *Berkeley Preparatory School* • 4811 Kelly Road Tampa FL 33615-0009 *Grades:* Comprehensive School (P-12) *Contact:* Mr Joseph W Seivold *Chaplain(s):* Rev Brandon B Peete

Southwest Florida *The Canterbury School of Florida* 990 62nd Avenue NE St Petersburg FL 33702 *Grades:* Comprehensive School (P-12) *Contact:* Mr Mac H Hall *Chaplain(s):* Rev John C Suhar

Southwest Florida *Saint Paul's School* • 1600 St Paul's Drive Clearwater FL 33764 *Grades:* Elementary School *Contact:* Mrs Samantha Campbell

Southwest Florida *Saint Stephen's Episcopal School* • 315 41st Street West Bradenton FL 34209 *Grades:* Comprehensive School (P-12) *Contact:* Janet S Pullen EdD *Chaplain(s):* Rev Richard Clark

Southwestern Virginia *Boys Home of Virginia* 414 Boys' Home Road Covington VA 24426 *Grades:* Secondary School *Contact:* Mr Donnie E Wheatley *Chaplain(s):* Rev Connie Wolfe Gilman, Rev Anne Fletcher Grizzle

Southwestern Virginia *Stuart Hall School* • Middle and Upper School Campus 235 W Frederick Street Staunton VA 24402 *Grades:* Secondary School *Contact:* Mr Mark H Eastham *Chaplain(s):* Mr John Dull, Rev Canon Connor Brindley Gwin

Southwestern Virginia *Virginia Episcopal School* 400 VES Road Lynchburg VA 24503-1146 *Grades:* Secondary School *Contact:* Mr G Thomas Battle Jr *Chaplain(s):* Mr Chad Hanning, Rev Adam White

Tennessee *Episcopal School of Nashville* • 413 Woodland Street Nashville TN 37206 *Grades:* Elementary School *Contact:* Mr Harrison Stuart *Chaplain(s):* Rev Melissa Smith, Mrs Kelsey Davis, Ms Lara Wiggins

Tennessee *St Andrew's-Sewanee School* • 290 Quintard Road Sewanee TN 37375-3000 *Grades:* Secondary School *Contact:* Mr Karl J Sjolund *Chaplain(s):* Rev Molly Short

Texas *All Saints Episcopal School* • 2695 South Southwest Loop 323 Tyler TX 75701 *Grades:* Comprehensive School (P-12) *Contact:* Mr D Michael Cobb Jr *Chaplain(s):* Rev Keith Pozzuto, Rev Kevin E Wittmayer

Texas *All Saints Episcopal School* 4108 Delaware Street Beaumont TX 77706 *Grades:* Elementary School *Contact:* Ms Catherine Clark

Texas *Archway Academy* 6221 Main Street Houston TX 77030 *Grades:* Secondary School *Contact:* Ms Sasha McLean

Texas *Episcopal High School* • 4650 Bissonnet Bellaire TX 77401 *Grades:* Secondary School *Contact:* Mr C Edward Smith *Chaplain(s):* Rev Elizabeth Holden

Texas *Holy Trinity Episcopal School* • 11810 Lockwood Houston TX 77044-5392 *Grades:* Comprehensive School (P-12) *Contact:* Troy Roddy PhD

Texas *St Andrew's Episcopal School* • 1112 W 31st Street Austin TX 78705 *Grades:* Comprehensive School (P-12) *Contact:* Mr Sean Murphy *Chaplain(s):* Ms Ashley Brandon, Rev Whitney B Kirby

Texas *Saint Michael's Episcopal School* 2500 S College Avenue Bryan TX 77801 *Grades:* Comprehensive School (P-12) *Contact:* Ms Jenny Morris

Texas *St Stephen's Episcopal School* • 6500 St Stephen's Drive Austin TX 78746-1727 *Grades:* Secondary School *Contact:* Mr Christopher L Gunnin *Chaplain(s):* Mr Jim Crosby, Rev Todd R FitzGerald, Ms Morgan Stokes, Rev Adam Varner

Texas *Trinity Episcopal School of Austin* • 3901 Bee Cave Road Austin TX 78746-6403 *Grades:* Elementary School *Contact:* Ms Marie H Kidd *Chaplain(s):* Mr Craig L Cannon, Rev Kenneth A Malcolm

Upper South Carolina *Christ Church Episcopal School* • 245 Cavalier Drive Greenville SC 29607 *Grades:* Comprehensive School (P-12) *Contact:* Leonard R Kupersmith PhD *Chaplain(s):* Ms Valerie M Riddle Ms Betsy Burton, Rev D Wallace Adams-Riley, Mr John Mark Elliott

Upper South Carolina *Heathwood Hall Episcopal School* • 3000 South Beltline Boulevard Columbia SC 29201-5199 *Grades:* Comprehensive School (P-12) *Contact:* Mr Christopher P Hinchey *Chaplain(s):* Mrs Raven G Tarpley

Vermont *Rock Point School* 1 Rock Point Road Burlington VT 5408 *Grades:* Secondary School *Contact:* Mr CJ Spirito

Virginia *Anna Julia Cooper Episcopal School* • 2124 N 29th Street Richmond VA 23223 *Grades:* Middle School *Contact:* Mr Michael J Maruca

Virginia *Blue Ridge School* 273 Mayo Drive St George VA 22935 *Grades:* Secondary School *Contact:* Mr William A Darrin III *Chaplain(s):* Rev David B McIlhiney PhD, Rev Anne E K West

Virginia *The Butterfly House* Virginia Theological Seminary 3979 Seminary Road Alexandria VA 22304 *Grades:* ECE Program (P-K only) *Contact:* Mrs Kerry Hual

Virginia *Christchurch School* • 49 Seahorse Lane Christchurch VA 23031-9999 *Grades:* Secondary School *Contact:* Mr John E Byers *Chaplain(s):* Rev Scott D Parnell

Virginia *Episcopal High School* • 1200 N Quaker Lane Alexandria VA 22302 *Grades:* Secondary School *Contact:* Mr Charles M Stillwell *Chaplain(s):* Rev Thomas C Hummel PhD, Rev Elizabeth Carmody Gonzalez, Rev Timothy Seamans

Virginia *St Anne's-Belfield School* 2132 Ivy Road Charlottesville VA 22903 *Grades:* Comprehensive School (P-12) *Contact:* Mr David S Lourie *Chaplain(s):* Mr Robert Clark

Virginia *St Catherine's School* • 6001 Grove Avenue Richmond VA 23226 *Grades:* Comprehensive School (P-12) *Contact:* Terrie Hale Scheckelhoff PhD *Chaplain(s):* Rev Dr Dorothy A White, Ms C Rives Priddy

Virginia *St Christopher's School* • 711 St Christopher's Road Richmond VA 23226 *Grades:* Comprehensive School (P-12) *Contact:* Mr Mason Lecky *Chaplain(s):* Rev Durwood R Steed, Mr Joe Torrence, Rev Whitney Z Edwards

Virginia *St Margaret's School* • 444 Water Lane Tappahannock VA 22560 *Grades:* Secondary School *Contact:* Mrs Catherine M Sgroi *Chaplain(s):* Rev Anita L Braden

Virginia *St Stephen's and St Agnes School* • 1000 St Stephen's Road Alexandria VA 22304 *Grades:* Comprehensive School (P-12) *Contact:* Mrs Kirsten P Adams *Chaplain(s):* Rev Sean H Cavanaugh, Rev Rosemary E Beales DMin, Rev Michael B Hinson, Ms Mary Via

Washington *The Bishop John T Walker School for Boys* • 1801 Mississippi Avenue, SE Washington DC 20020 *Grades:* Elementary School *Contact:* Mr James R Woody *Chaplain(s):* Rev Dr Robert T Phillips

Washington *Rosemount Center* 2000 Rosemount Avenue Washington DC 20010 *Grades:* ECE Program (P-K only) *Contact:* Marsha Boveja EdD

Washington *St Andrew's Episcopal School* • 8804 Postoak Road Potomac MD 20854-3553 *Grades:* Secondary School *Contact:* Mr Robert F Kosasky *Chaplain(s):* Rev Patricia Phaneuf Alexander, Rev Sarah E Slater

Washington *Washington Episcopal School* • 5600 Little Falls Parkway Bethesda MD 20816 *Grades:* Elementary School *Contact:* Mr Daniel Vogelman *Chaplain(s):* Mr Tim Kennedy

West Tennessee *St George's Independent School* • Collierville Campus 1880 Wolf River Boulevard Collierville TN 38017 *Grades:* Comprehensive

School (P-12) *Contact:* Mr J Ross Peters *Chaplain(s):* Rev Jessica Abell, Mr Cedrick Jackson, Ms Kim Finch

West Tennessee *St Mary's Episcopal School* • 60 Perkins Extended Memphis TN 38117 *Grades:* Comprehensive School (P-12) *Contact:* Mr Albert Throckmorton *Chaplain(s):* Ms Susan Whitten, Rev Katherine M Bush, Mrs Rainey Segars

West Texas *St Mark's Episcopal Preschool* 3039 Ranch Road 12 San Marcos TX 78666-2488 *Grades:* ECE Program (P-K only) *Contact:* Ms Bettie Frost

West Texas *Saint Mary's Hall* 9401 Starcrest Drive San Antonio TX 78217 *Grades:* Comprehensive School (P-12) *Contact:* Mr Jonathan Eric Eades *Chaplain(s):* Rev Dr Cameron Delong Gunnin

West Texas *TMI Episcopal* • 20955 West Tejas Trail San Antonio TX 78257-9708 *Grades:* Secondary School *Contact:* Rev Scott J Brown *Chaplain(s):* Rev Nathan L Bostian, Mr Daniel Forman

West Virginia *Greenbrier Episcopal School* 3100 Houfnaggle Road Lewisburg WV 24901 *Grades:* Elementary School *Contact:* Ms Gretchen Graves *Chaplain(s):* Rev C Christopher Thompson

Western Kansas *St John's Military School* 110 West Otis Avenue Salina KS 67401 *Grades:* Secondary School *Contact:* Mr Andy England *Chaplain(s):* Rev Randy E McIntosh

Western Louisiana *Episcopal School of Acadiana* • Cade Campus 1557 Smede Road Broussard LA 70518 *Grades:* Secondary School *Contact:* Paul Baker PhD Andrew D Armond PhD, Dr John M Campbell

Western North Carolina *Christ School* • 500 Christ School Road Arden NC 28704-9914 *Grades:* Secondary School *Contact:* Mr Paul Krieger *Chaplain(s):* Rev David C Brown, Mr Thomas Becker

CAMP, CONFERENCE, AND RETREAT CENTERS

EPISCOPAL CAMPS AND CONFERENCE CENTERS INC (ECCC)

Organization with advocacy role, providing support and educational opportunities; newsletters; annual conference; consultation services. Membership open to Episcopal Church camps, conference and retreat centers. *Dir* Bill Slocumb PO Box 440 Camp Meeker CA 95419 (760) 445-6774 *E-mail:* bill@episcopalccc.org *Web:* www.episcopalccc.org.

ALABAMA

Camp McDowell 105 DeLong Rd Nauvoo AL 35578 (205) 387-1806 *Fax:* (205) 221-3454 *E-mail:* whitney@campmcdowell.com *Web:* www.campmcdowell.com *Contact:* *Exec Dir* Whitney Moore. Total Beds: 600.

ARIZONA

Chapel Rock 1131 Country Club Dr Prescott AZ 86303 (928) 445-3499 *Fax:* (928) 445-0370 *E-mail:* info@chapelrock.net *Web:* www.chapelrock.net *Contact:* *Exec Dir* Kelly Wood. Total Beds: 270.

ARKANSAS

Camp Mitchell 10 Camp Mitchell Rd Morrilton, AR 72110 (501) 727-5451 *Fax:* (501) 727-5761 *E-mail:* director@campmitchell.org *Web:* www.campmitchell.org *Contact: Exec Dirs* Rev. Betsy Baumbargen & Rev. Robert Wetherington. Total Beds: 165

ATLANTA

Camp Mikell Honey Creek 299 Episcopal Conference Center Rd Waverly GA 31565 (912) 265-9218 *Fax:* (912) 267-6907 *E-mail:* office@honeycreek.org *Web:* www.honeycreek.org *Contact: Dir* Dade Brantley. Total Beds: 150.

CALIFORNIA

St Columba Church 12835 Sir Francis Drake Blvd (PO Box 430) Inverness CA 04937 (415) 669-1039. 32 person capacity.

St Dorothy's Rest PO Box B Camp Meeker CA 95419 (707) 874-3319 *Fax:* (707) 874-3349 *E-mail:* sdr@monitor.net *Web:* www.stdorothysrest.org *Contact: Exec Dir* Katie Evenbeck. Total Beds: 120.

The Bishop's Ranch 5297 Westside Rd Healdsburg, CA 95448 (707) 433-2440 *Fax:* (707) 433-3431 *E-mail:* info@bishopsranch.org *Web:* www.bisopsranch.org *Contact: Exec Dir* Sean Swift. Total Beds: 100.

Easton Hall Conference Center—CDSP 2451 Ridge Rd Berkeley CA 94709 (510) 204-0732 *E-mail:* eastonhall@cdsp.edu *Web:* www.cdsp.edu/conference.php. Total Beds: 22.

CENTRAL GULF COAST

Beckwith Camp and Retreat Center (Diocese of Central Gulf Coast) 10400 Beckwith Ln Fairhope AL 36532 (251) 928-7844 *Fax:* (251) 928-7811 *E-mail:* Eleanor@BeckwithAL.com *Web:* www.beckwithal.com. Total Beds: 200.

COLORADO

Cathedral Ridge Retreat & Conference Center, 1364 County Road 75, Woodland Park CO 80863, (719) 687-9038. office@cathedralridge.org.

CONNECTICUT

Incarnation Center PO Box 577 Ivoryton CT 06442 (860) 767-0848 *Fax:* (860) 767-8432 *E-mail:* info@incarnationcenter.org *Web:* www.incarnationcenter.com *Contact: Dir* Nancy Pilon. Total Beds: 217.

Camp Washington Camp and Retreat Ctr 190 Kenyon Rd Lakeside CT 06758 (860) 567-9623 *Fax:* (860) 567-3037 *E-mail:* camp@campwashington.org *Web:* wwwcampwashington.org *Contact: Dir* Bart Geissinger. Total Beds: 160.

DELAWARE

Camp Arrowhead 913 Wilson Road Wilmington DE 19803 (302) 256-0374 *Fax:* (302) 543-8084 *E-mail:* kathymoore@dioceseofdelaware.net *Web:* www.camparrowhead.net *Contact: Dir* Walt Lafontaine. Total Beds: 325.

Memorial House For Contact Information see Camp Arrowhead above. Total Beds: 31.

EASTERN MICHIGAN

Camp Chickagami 111 West Graham Lansing MI 48901 (888) 440-2267 *Fax:* (517) 699-0846 *E-mail:* mbade@eastmich.org *Web:* www.campchickagami.org *Contact:* McKenzie Bade. Total Beds: 130.

EASTON

Camp Wright 400 Camp Wright Ln Stevensville MD 21666 (410)-643-4171 *Fax:* (410) 643-8421 *E-mail:* director@campwright.com *Web:* www.campwright.com Total Beds: 185

FLORIDA

Camp Weed and Cerveny Conference Center 11057 Camp Weed Place Live Oak FL 32060 386-364-5250 *Fax:* 386-362-7557 *E-mail:* kym@campweed.org *Web:* www.campweed.org *Contact: Exec Dir* Kym Hughes. Total Beds: 278.

Camp Wingmann 3404 Wingmann Rd Avon Park FL 33825 866-526-3380 *E-mail:* wingmann@strato.net *Web:* www.campwingmann.org *Contact:* Rev Deke Miller. Total Beds: 147.

Day Spring Conference Center PO Box 661 Ellenton FL 34222 (941) 776-1018 *Fax:* (941) 776-2678 *E-mail:* execdirctor@dayspringfla.org *Web:* www.dayspringfla.org *Contact: Exec Dir* Carla Odell. Total Beds: 315.

Duncan Conference Center 15820 South Military Trail Delray Beach FL 33484 (561) 496-4130 *Fax:* (561) 496-1726 *E-mail:* fremilio@duncancenter.org *Web:* www.duncancenter.org *Contact: Exec Dir* Rev Dr Emilio Rosolen. Total Beds: 79.

Canterbury Retreat and Conference Center 1601 Alafaya Trail (SR 434) Oviedo FL 32765 (407) 365-5571 *Fax:* (407) 365-9758 *E-mail:* jon@canterburyretreat.org *Web:* www.canterburyretreat.org *Contact: Exec Dir* The Rev Jon Davis. Total Beds: 92.

GEORGIA

Camp Mikell Honey Creek Rt 3 Box 3495 Toccoa GA 30577 (706) 886-7515 *Fax:* (706) 886-7580 *E-mail:* mikell@alltel.net *Web:* www.campmikell.com *Contact: Dir* The Rev Kenneth Struble. Total Beds: 236.

HAWAII

Camp Mokuleia 68-729 Farrington Hwy Waialua HI 96791 (808) 637-6241 *Fax:* (808) 637-5505 *E-mail:* reservations@campmokuleia.com *Web:* www.campmokuleia.com Total Beds: 212.

IDAHO

Paradise Point Camp PO Box 936 Boise ID 83701 (208) 345-4522 *Fax:* (208) 345-9735 *E-mail:* mbeck@

idahodiocese.org *Web*: www.paradisepointcamp.org *Contact*: *Dir* Marty Beck. Total Beds: 100.

ILLINOIS
Toddhall Retreat and Conference Center 350 Todd Center Dr Columbia IL 62236 (618) 281-8180 *Fax*: (618) 281-8187 *E-mail*: toddhall@htc.net *Web*: www.toddhallrc.org *Contact*: *Exec Dir* Mark Mann. Total Beds: 92.

INDIANA
Waycross Episcopal Camp and Conference Center 7363 Bear Creek Rd Morgantown IN 46160 (812) 597-4241 *Fax*: (812) 597-4291 *E-mail*: info@waycrosscenter.org *Web*: www. waycrosscenter.org Total Beds: 226.

Wawassee Episcopal Center 7830 E Vawter Park Rd Syracuse IN 46567 (574) 233-6489 *Fax*: (574) 287-7914 *E-mail*: treasurer@edin.org *Web*: www.ednin. org *Contact*: *Dir* Sharon Katona. Total Beds: 26.

KENTUCKY
All Saints Episcopal Center 833 Hickory Grove Rd Leitchfield KY 42754 (270) 259-3514 *Fax*: (270) 259-0526 *E-mail*: bill@allsaintscenter.org *Web*: www. allsaintscenter.org *Contact*: Bill Beam. Total Beds: 114.

The Cathedral Domain 800 Highway 1746 Irvine KY 40336-8701 (606) 464-8254 *Fax*: (606) 464-0759 *E-mail*: asigmon@diolex.org *Web*: www. cathedraldomain.org *Contact*: *Fac Dir* Andy Sigmon. Total Beds: 315.

LOUISIANA
The Solomon Episcopal Conference Center 54296 Highway 445 Loranger LA 70446 (985) 748-6634 *Fax*: (985) 748-2843 *E-mail*: info@solomoncenter. org *Web*: www.solomoncenter.org *Contact*: *Dir* Tanja Wadsworth Total Beds: 88.

MAINE
Camp Bishopswood 143 State St (Winter) Portland ME 04101 (207) 772-1953 x127 *Fax*: (207) 773-0095 *E-mail*: info@bishopwood.org *Web*: www. bishopwood.org *Contact*: *Dir* Michael Douglas *E-mail*: mike@bishopswood.org. Total Beds: 100.

MARYLAND
Bishop Claggett Center PO Box 40 Buckeystown MD 21717 (301) 874-5147 *Fax*: (301) 874-0834 *E-mail*: info@bishopclagget.org *Web*: www.bishopclaggett. org Total Beds: 173.

MASSACHUSETTS
Barbara C Harris Camp and Conference Center PO Box 204 Greenfield NH 03047 (603) 547-3400 *Fax*: (603) 547-3038 *E-mail*: info@bchcenter.org *Web*: www.bchcenter.org. *Contact*: *Exec Dir* John Koch Total Beds: 198.

MICHIGAN
Emrich Retreat Center at Parishfield 7380 Teahen Rd Brighton MI (810) 231-1060 *Web*: www.

discoveremrich.org. Overnight accommodations for 90 on 26 beatutiful, well kept acres.

MISSISSIPPI
Gray Center 1530 Way Rd Canton 39046 (601) 859-1556 *Fax*: (601) 859-1495 *E-mail*: lindac@graycenter. org *Web*: www.graycenter.com *Contact*: *Exec Dir* Grae Dickson. Total Beds: 220.

MONTANA
Camp Marshall 41524 Melita Island Rd Polson MT 59860 (406) 849-5718 *E-mail*: christianformation@ diomontana.com *Web*: www.diomontana.com *Contact*: *Exec Dir*. Rev. Wren Blessing. Total Beds: 150.

NEVADA
Camp Galilee 1776 Highway 50 South PO Box 236 Glenbrook NV 89413 (775) 749-5546 *E-mail*: executivedirector@galileetahoe.org *Web*: www. galileetahoe.org *Contact*: *Exec Dir* Stuart Campbell. Total Beds: 68.

NEW JERSEY
Crossroads Outdoor Ministries 29 Pleasant Grove Rd Port Murray NJ 07865 (908) 832-7264 *Fax*: (908) 832-6593 *E-mail*: www.crossroadsretreat.com *Web*: www.crossroadsretreat.com *Contact*: *Dir* Anthony Briggs. Total Beds: 300.

NEW MEXICO
Bishop Stoney Camp and Conferance Center 7855 Old Santa Fe Trail Santa Fe NM 87505 (505) 983-5610 *Fax*: (505) 983-9150 *E-mail*: info@campstoney. org *Web*: www.campstoney.org. Total Beds: 100.

NEW YORK
Camp DeWolfe PO Box 487 Wading River NY 11792 (631) 929-4325 *Fax*: (631) 929-6553 *E-mail*: office@campdewolfe.org *Web*: www.campdewolfe. org *Contact*: *Dir* Matt Tees. Total Beds: 150.

Christ the King Spiritual Life Center 575 Burton Rd Greenwich NY 12834 (518) 692-9550 *E-mail*: rtodd@ ctkcenter.org *Web*: www.Christ-the-King-Center.org *Contact*: Reuben Todd. Total Beds: 160.

NORTH CAROLINA
Kanuga Confererences PO Box 250 Hendersonville NC 28793-0250 (828) 692-9136 *Fax*: (828) 696-3589 *E-mail*: info@kanuga.org *Web*: www.kanuga.org *Contact*: *Pres* Michael R. Sullivan Total Beds: 750.

Lake Logan Conference Center 154 Suncrest Mill Rd Canton NC 28716 (828) 646-0095 *Fax*: (828) 648-8937 *E-mail*: info@lakelogan.org *Web*: www. lakelogan.org *Contact*: *Exec Dir* Lauri Sojourner. Total Beds: 196.

Trinity Center PO Box 380 Salter Path NC 28575 (888) 874-6287 *Fax*: (252) 247-3290 *E-mail*: penn@ trinityctr.com *Web*: www.trinityctr.com *Contact*: *Exec Dir* Penn Perry. Total Beds: 180.

Valle Crucis Conference Center PO Box 654 Valle Crucis NC 28691 (828) 963-4453 *Fax*: (828) 963-8806 *E-mail*: vccc@highsouth.com *Web*: www.

highsouth.com/vallecrusis *Contact: Exec Dir* Margaret Lumpkin Love. Total Beds: 156.

OHIO

Procter Conference Center 11235 State Rd 38 London OH 43130 (740) 874-3355 *Fax:* (740) 874-3356 *E-mail:* rkimbler@diosohio.org *Web:* www.proctercenter.org *Contact: Exec Dir* Amy Boyd Total Beds: 124.

Sheldon Calvary Camp 4410 Lake Rd Conneaut OH 44030 (440) 593-4381 *Fax:* (440) 593-6250 *E-mail:* executivedirector@calvarycamp.org *Web:* www.calvarycamp.org *Contact: Dir* Tim Green. Total Beds: 250.

Transfiguration Spirituality Center 495 Albion Ave Cincinnati OH 45246 (513) 771-5291 *E-mail:* ctretreats@gmail.com *Contact: Exec Dir* Anne Reed. Total Beds: 50.

OKLAHOMA

St Crispin's Conference Center Rt 2 Box 381 Wewoka OK 74884 (405) 382-1619 *Fax:* (405) 382-1631 *E-mail:* info@stcrispins.org *Web:* www.episcopaloklahoma.org *Contact: Dirs* Joanne & Mike Roberts. Total Beds: 180.

OREGON

Ascension School PO Box 278 Cove OR 97824 (541) 568-4514 *E-mail:* kim@coveascensionschool.com *Web:* www.coveascensionschool.com *Contact: Exec Dir* Kim McClain. Total Beds: 130.

PITTSBURGH

Sheldon Calvary Camp 4411 Lake Rd Conneaut, OH 44030 (440) 593-4381 *Exec Dir* Tim Green *E-mail:* executivedirector@calvarycamp.org *Web:* www.calvarycamp.org.

RHODE ISLAND

Episcopal Conference Center 872 Reservoir Rd Pascoag RI 02859 (401) 568-4055 *Fax:* (401) 568-7805 *E-mail:* director@eccri.org *Web:* www.eccri.org *Contact: Dir* Rev Meaghan Kelly Brower. Total Beds: 225.

RIO GRANDE

Bishop Stoney Camp and Conference Center 7855 Old Santa Fe Trail Santa Fe NM 87505 (505) 983-5610 *Fax:* (505) 983-9150 *E-mail:* info@campstoney.org *Web:* www.campstoney.org. Total Beds: 100.

Bosque Center, The 6400 Coors Boulevard NW Albuquerque NM 87120 (505) 881-0636 *Fax:* (505) 883-9048 *E-mail:* psoukup@dioceserg.org *Web:* www.bosquecenter.org; Total Beds: 39.

SOUTH DAKOTA

Thunderhead Episcopal Center PO Box 890 Lead SD 57754 605-584-2233 (summer) *Fax:* 605-582-2242 *E-mail:* camp.diocese@midconetwork.com *Contact:* Camp Dir. Portia Corbin Total Beds: 106.

TENNESSEE

DuBose Conference Center PO Box 339 Monteagle TN 37356 (931) 924-2353 *Fax:* (931) 924-2291 *E-mail:* David@DuboseConferenceCenter.org *Web:* www.duboseconf.org *Contact:* David Ramsey. Total Beds: 240.

Grace Point Camp and Retreat Center 300 Chamberlain Cove Rd Kingston TN 37763 (865) 567-1159 *E-mail:* gracepoint@etdiocese.net *Web:* www.etdiocese.net. *Contact: Exec Dir* Rev Brad Jones Total Beds: 46.

St Columba Episcopal Conference Center 4577 Billy Maher Rd Memphis TN 38135 (901) 377-9284 *Fax:* (901) 371-0700 *Web:* www.saintcolumbamemphis.org. *Dir* Brad Thompson. Total Beds: 100.

St Mary's Sewanee PO Box 188 Sewanee TN 37375 (931) 598-5342 *Fax:* (931) 598-5884 *E-mail:* reservations@stmaryssewanee.org *Web:* www.stmaryssewanee.org *Contact: Exec Dir* Rev Andy Anderson. Total Beds: 100.

TEXAS

All Saints Camp and Conference Center 418 Stanton Way Pottsboro TX 75076 (903) 786-3148 *Fax:* (903) 786-7535 *E-mail:* info@allsaintsexoma.org *Web:* www.allsaintsexoma.org *Contact: Exec Dir* David Campbell. Total Beds: 176.

Camp Allen 18800 FM 362 Navasota TX 77868 (936) 825-7175 *Fax:* (936) 825-8495 *E-mail:* frontdesk@campallen.org *Web:* www.campallen.org *Contact: Pres* George Dehan. Total Beds: 600.

Camp Capers PO Box 9 Waring TX 78074 (830) 995-3966 *Fax:* (830) 995-2393 *E-mail:* capers@hctc.net *Web:* www.campcapers.org *Contact:* Rob Watson. Total Beds: 220.

Camp Crucis 2875 Camp Crucis Court Granbury TX 76048 (817) 573-3343 *Fax:* (817) 279-7974 *E-mail:* info@campcrucis.org *Web:* www.campcrucis.org Total Beds: 340.

Mustang Island Conference Center PO Box 130 Port Arkansas TX 78373 (361) 749-1800 *Fax:* (361) 749-1802 *E-mail:* lynn.corby@dwtx.org *Web:* www.mustangisland.org *Contact: Oper Mgr* Lynn Corby. *Dir* Kevin Spaeth. Total Beds: 55.

UTAH

Camp Tuttle 80 South 300 East Salt Lake City UT 84110 (801) 322-4131 *Fax:* (801) 322-5096 *E-mail:* mlees@episcopal-ut.org *Web:* www.camptuttle.org *Contact:* Melanie Lees. Total Beds: 165.

VERMONT

Bishop Booth Conference Center 20 Rock Point Circle Burlington VT 05401 (802) 658-6233 *Fax:* (802) 658-8836 *E-mail:* bishopbooth@dioceseofvermont.org *Web:* www.dioceseofvermont.org *Contact:* Tony Drapelick. Total Beds: 110.

VIRGINIA

Virginia Diocesan Center at Roslyn 8727 River Rd Richmond VA 23229 (804)288-6045 *Fax:* (804) 285-3430 *E-mail:* info@roslyncenter.org *Web:* www.roslyncenter.org *Contact:* Katherine Lawrence. Total Beds: 96.

Shrine Mont 221 Shrine Mont Circle Orkney Springs VA 22845 (540) 856-2141 *Fax:* (540) 856-8520 *E-mail:* shrine@shentel.net *Web:* www.shrinemont.com *Contact: Exec Dir* Kevin Moomaw. Total Beds: 550.

WASHINGTON
Camp Cross 245 E 13th Ave Spokane WA 99202 (509) 624-3191 *Fax:* (509) 747-0049 *E-mail:* campcross@spokanediocese.org *Web:* www.campcross.org *Contact:* Colin Haffner. Total Beds: 110.

Huston Camp and Conference Center PO Box 140 Gold Bar WA 98251 (360) 793-0441 *Fax:* (360) 793-3822 *E-mail:* info@huston.org *Web:* www.huston.org *Contact: Dir* Bill Tubbs. Total Beds: 237.

WEST VIRGINIA
Peterkin Camp and Conference Center 286 Clubhouse Rd Romney WV 26757-7521 (304) 822-4519 Fax: (304) 822-7771 *E-mail:* daisymcb1@hotmail.com *Web:* www.peterkin.org *Contact:* Daisy McBride. Total Beds: 150.

Sandcrest Conference and Retreat Center 143 Sandcrest Dr Wheeling WV 26003 (304) 277-3022 *Fax:* (304) 277-3840 *E-mail:* sandcrest@1stnet *Web:* www.sandscrest.com *Contact: Exec Dir* Sarah Lydick. Total Beds: 35.

WESTERN MICHIGAN
Saugatuck Retreat House WMI Diocese PO Box 189 Saugatuck MI 49453 (269) 857-5201. Total 14 rooms. Five bedroom house for overnight and longer retreats run by All Saints Episcopal Church.

WISCONSIN
DeKoven Center 600 21st St Rancine WI 53403 (262) 633-6401 *E-mail:* info@dekovencenter.org *Web:* www.dekovencenter.pair.com *Contact: Dir* Max Dershem. Total Beds: 60.

WYOMING
Wyoming Wilderness Camp 123 S Durbin Casper WY 82601 (307) 265-5200 *Fax:* (307) 577-9939 *E-mail:* jessica@wyomingdiocese.org *Web:* www.wyomingdiocese.org. Total Beds: 30.

NATIONAL ALTAR GUILD ASSOCIATION
Formed in 1921. www.nationalaltarguildassociation.org

Pres Dianne Walters *E-Mail:* dirdh68@gmail.com; *1VP* Albe Larsen *E-mail:* amlarsen@coastside.net; *2VP* Donna Anderson: *E-mail:* Anglican312@msn.com; *Sec* Sandy Wilson *E-mail:* slwilson@att.net *Treas* Marcia Himes *E-mail:* rthimes@wyoming.com. Meets every 3 years at Gen Conv with program and election of officers. Natl Assn mbrshp is $35/year for individuals;$50/year parish; $100/year for diocese. Member incl quarterly issues of newsletter, *Epistle*.

Provincial Presidents
Province I: Diane Grondin *E-mail:* dmgrondin@comcast.net

Province II: Jane Mercer *E-mail:* jpmercer@comcast.net

Province III: Sharon Nachman *E-mail:* sharonsnachman@gmail.com

Province IV: Ann McCormick *E-mail:* Ann.mcc413@gmail.com

Province V: David Hawley-Lowry *E-mail:* Davidh@stmarksgr.org

Province VI: Marcia Himes *E-mail:* rthimes@wyoming.com

Province VII: William Kennard *E-mail:* williamkennard@hotmail.com

Province VIII: Sara Chesebro *E-mail:* sarachesebro@gmail.com

Altar Guild Diocesan Presidents
AL M E Spencer 516 Bennet Dr Alabaster AL 35007 spencermedr@gmail.com

AT Diocesan Altar Guild 2744 Peachtree Rd Atlanta GA 30305

AZ Constance Castillo 10106 West Signal Butte Circle Sun City AZ 85373

CA Jane Phillips 2211 Latham St. #302 Mountain View CA 94040

CFL Judy Henderson 1978 Red Bud Circle NW Palm Bay FL 32907 jem2415@earthlink.com

CHICAGO Beth C. Petti c/o Dioc. Of Chicago 65 E Huron St. Chicago IL60611

CT Jean Kelsey 21 Fairview St. Manchester CT 06040

DAL Anna Houston AYhouston@prodigy.net (214) 232-3089

E Barry Passano PO Box 27 Oxford MD 21654

ECR

ETN Joyce Collom 393 Deep Draw Dr Crossville TN 38555

FL Janet Robinson 2150 Spencer Rd Orange Park FL 32073

FTW Dabney Shires dishires@ sbcglobal.net

HI Rosella Newell 229 Queen Emma Sq Honolulu HI 96813

IA Dioc of Iowa 225 37th St. Des Moines IA 50312

LA Carolyn Douglas Box 991 St Francisville LA 70775

LI Jane Ames 21 Melanie Lane Syosset NY 11791 jacamel@juno.com

LOSA Bea Floyd Box 512164 Los Angeles CA 90051-0164 (213) 482-2040

MA Diane Grondin 18 Hilldale Rd. Weymouth MA 02190

ME Vicki Wiederkehr 143 State St Portland ME 04101

MI Novie Duffy PO Box 430357 Pontiac MI 48343

MIL Micki Hoffmn c/o Dioc.of MIL Altar Guild 804 East Juneau Ave Milwaukee WI 53202

MS Ann Mileted 133 Perry St. Gulfport MS eamlstd@yahoo.com

NC Dioc of NC 200 W. Morgan St. Suite 300 Raleigh NC 27601

NE Diocesan Altar Guild 109 18th St Omaha NE 68102 Heather Bauer greenpeacecats121@yahoo.com

NH Sue Ingram PO Box 185 North Hampton NH 03862

NJ Jane Mercer 31 Baileys Mill Rd. Basking Ridge NJ 07920 jpmercer@comcast.net

NK Sr Suzanne Elizabeth CSJB Box 240 Mendham NJ 07945 srse@csjb.org

NT Nancy McReynolds (806) 928-7734

NWPA Mary Blaine Prince 522 W Corydon St Bradford PA 16701

NWTX Paula Howbert 3803 Stanolind Dr Midland TX 79707

NY Molly B. Jones The NY Altar Guild PO Box 881 Millbrook NY 12545

OK Mary Lu Jarvis 3820 S Hiwassee St Choctaw OK 73020

OL Sherry Garman PO Box 12126 Seattle WA 98102

OR Donna Anderson P.O. Box 1576 Roseburg OR 97470

PA Dioc of PA 5421 Germantown Ave Philadelphia PA 19144

PGH Priscilla Castner 165 Summerlawn Dr Sewickley PA 15143

PI Dioc of Pittsburg/ Shelley Snyder 602 Danbury St. Pittsburg PA 15214

RG Diocesan Altar Guild 4304 Carlisle Blvd NE Albuquerque NM 87107

RI Liz Crawley 275 N Main St. Providence RI 02903

SAND Diocesan Altar Guild 840 Echo Park Ave Los Angeles CA 90026

SANJ Susan Ohanneson 41 Cedarwood Lane Bakersfield CA 93308

SD Vicki Sweet sweetmom@rushmore.com

SOH Craig Foster c/o Altar Guild Dioc. Of SOH 412 Sycamore St. Cincinnati OH 45202

SWF/NORTH Sarah Hill 1906 Carolina Ave NE St Petersburg FL 33703 sarahhill.fl@gmail.com

SWF/SOUTH Sarah Hill 1906 Carolina Ave NE St Petersburg FL 33703 sarahhill.fl@gmail.com

TN Sue Hays 408 N Cameron Ct Hermitage TN 37076

TX Mary Ann Conkel 1015 Herrera Ct Hutto, TX 78634

USC Valerie Riley 81 Cannonade Court Irmo SC 29063

VA Sharon Nachman 866 Vine Street Herndon VA 20170 P3NAGA@gmail.com

VT Sarah Maynard 79 Green St St Johnsbury VT 05819

WKS Sally Russell Grace Episcopal Church sallyruss@sbcglobal.net (620) 662-2946

WLA Ginger Norvell 120 Harolyn Park Dr. Lafayette LA 70503

WMA MA Worton 7 Leland Hill Rd South Graft on MA 01560

WMI David Hawley-Lowry 10312 Riley St. Zeeland MI 49464

WMO Grace and Holy Trinity Cathedral (816) 474-8260

WNC Lois Lynn 468 Vision Rd Canton NC 28716

WNY Janice Beam 134 Bridle Path Williamsville NY 14221

WTN Ann McCormick 3071 Dumbarton Rd Memphis TN 38128

WTX Dee Whiteside 234 Five Oaks Dr. San Antonio TX 78209 dwhiteside@satx.rr.com

WVA Holly Mitchell 5119 Brookside Dr Cross Lakes W VA 25313

EPISCOPAL CHURCH WOMEN

Board Officers
Website for national ECW: www.ecwnational.org; *Pres* Karen O Patterson *E-mail:* president@ecwnational.org; *1st VP* Patricia Wellnitz *E-mail:* firstvp@ecwnational.org; *2nd VP* The Rev Georgene (Gigi) Conner *E-mail:* secondvp@ecwnational.org; *Sec* Samar Fay *E-mail:* secretary@ecwnational.org; *Treas* Jeanne Plecenik *E-mail:* treasurer@ecwnational.org.

Board Members-at-Large
Social Justice The Rev Dcn Ema Rosero Nordalm *E-mail:* socialjustice@ecwnational.org.

Board Provincial Representatives
I—Margaret Noel *E-mail:* province1@ecwnational.org; *II*—The Rev Jennifer Kenna *E-mail:* province2@ecwnational.org; *III*—Cindy Mohr *E-mail:* province3@ecwnational.org; *IV*—Mary Beth Welch *E-mail:* province4@ecwnational.org; *V*—Jan Goossens *E-mail:* province5@ecwnational.org; *VI*—Lynn Fitzgibbon *E-mail:* province6@ecwnational.org; *VII*—Lisa Bortner *E-mail:* province7@ecwnational.org; *VIII*—Canon Martha K Estes *E-mail:* province8@ecwnational.org; *IX*—The Rev Consuelo (Connie) Sanchez Navarro *E-mail:* province9@ecwnational.org.

Provincial Presidents
I—Susan Howland *E-Mail:* howlands@charter.net; *II*—Carolyn Belvin *E-mail:* cjb613@hotmail.com *III*—Beblon G. Parks *E-mail:* bebparks@gmail.com; *IV*—Becky Taylor Scott *E-Mail:* bekatay@me.com *V*—Karen Birr *E-mail:* ksbirr@charter.net; *VI*—Heather Bauer *E-Mail:* greenpeacecats121@yahoo.com; *VII*—The Rev Fran Wheeler *E-Mail:* frances.

wheeler11@gmail.com; *VIII*—Evita Krislock *E-Mail:* evita@krislock.com *IX*—The Rev Consuelo (Connie) Sanchez Navarro *E-Mail:* province9@ecwnational.org

Diocesan Presidents/Contacts: Province I

Connecticut (CT)—Elizabeth Silva *Pres E-mail:* betty.silva@att.net

Maine (ME)—Barbi Tinder *Contact E-mail:* B5tinder@gmail.com

Massachusetts (MA)—Elizabeth Murray *Contact E-mail:* Eg.murray102@gmail.com

New Hampshire (NH)—no contact

Rhode Island (RI)—Linda Guest *Pres E-mail:* lindaeguest@verizon.net

Vermont (VT)—Wendy Grace—Contact *E-mail:* duchs8@gmail.com

Western Massachusetts (WMA)—Susan Howland *Pres E-mail:* howlands@charter.net

Diocesan Presidents/Contacts: Province II

Albany (A)—Mary Young *Contact E-mail:* mar049@yahoo.com

Central New York (CNY)—Jennifer Kenna *Contact E-mail:* province2@ecwnational.org

Europe (EUR)—no contact

Haiti (Hai)—Gloria Orelien *Pres E-mail:* gloriaorelien@hotmail.com

Long Island (LI)—Lois Johnson-Rodney *Pres E-mail:* loisjohsonrodney1@gmail.com

New Jersey (NJ)—Donna L. Freidel *Pres E-mail:* dlfesq@gmail.com

New York (NY)—Dianne Roberts *Pres E-mail:* drobertslaw@gmail.com

Newark (NK)—no contact

Rochester (ROCH)—no contact

Virgin Islands (VI)—Edith Haynes-Lake *Pres E-mail:* hayneslake@yahoo.com

Western New York (WNY)—no contact

Diocesan Presidents/Contacts: Province III

Bethlehem—Dorothy Shaw *Pres E-mail:* flamingo10@frontier.com

Central Pennsylvania (CPA)—Cindy Mohr *Pres E-mail:* province3@ecwnational.org

Delaware (DE)—Beth Fitzpatrick *Pres E-mail:* gr8art@outlook.com

Easton (E)-Ramona Eller *Pres E-mail:* eller1214@netzero.net

Maryland (MD)—Dorothy (Dottie) Arthur *Pres E-mail:* reparthur@gmail.com

Northwestern Pennsylvania (NWPA)—Enid Bishop *Pres E-mail:* tgreene@psu.edu

Pennsylvania (PA)—Shirley Smith *Presider E-mail:* granny7sm@gmail.com

Pittsburgh (PGH)—Betty Duckstein *Pres E-mail:* Bette520@msn.com

Southern Virginia (SV)—Helen Sharpe-Williams *Pres E-mail:* helen.sharpe-williams@earthlink.net

Southwestern Virginia (SWV)—Jackallen (Jackie) Arthur *Pres E-mail:* jackallena@aol.com

Virginia (VA)—Cindy D Helton *Pres E-mail:* cindyhelton505@gmail.com

Washington (W)—Deanne R Samuels *Pres E-mail:* deanne005@yahoo.com

West Virginia (WV)—Becki Krzywdik *Covener E-mail:* bkrzywdik@msn.com

Diocesan Presidents/Contacts: Province IV

Alabama (AL)—Pearl Slay *Pres E-mail:* pslay88@gmail.com

Atlanta (AT)—Gwen Hyman *Pres E-mail:* ghyman@bellsmith.net

Central Florida (CF)—Elizabeth Herrick *Pres E-mail:* ECWofctrll@outlook.com

Central Gulf Coast (CGC)—no contact

East Carolina (EC)—Annie Jacobs *Pres E-mail:* aj34528@aol.com

East Tennessee (ETN)—Lynn Spires *Pres E-mail:* lspires49@aol.com

Florida (FL)—Andrea Geiger *Pres E-mail:* tandageiger@comcast.net

Georgia (GA)—Beth Mithen *Pres E-mail:* bethmithen@gmail.com

Kentucky (KY)—no contact

Lexington (Lex)—Lisa Edwards *Pres E-mail:* lisaedwards102@gmail.com

Louisiana (LA)—Anne M Ball *Pres E-mail:* aball45@yahoo.com

Mississippi (MS)—Laura Griffin *Pres E-mail:* lauragriffin1976@gmail.com

North Carolina (NC)—Mary B Gordon *Pres E-mail:* president@ecw-nc.org

Episcopal Church in South Carolina—Jackie Robe *E-mail:* jrobe18413@aol.com

Southeast Florida (SEF)—Mona Jackson *Pres E-mail:* mebjackson@att.net

Southwest Florida (SwF)—Leila Mizer *Pres E-mail:* ljmizer@yahoo.com

Tennessee (TN)—Diann Schneider *Pres E-mail:* diannb1948@gmail.com

Upper South Carolina (USC)—Kathy Siegel *Pres E-mail:* upperscecwpresident@gmail.com

West Tennessee (WTN)—Jean Arehart *Pres E-mail:* jeanarehart@gmail.com

Western North Carolina (WNC)—Mary Ann Ransom *Pres E-mail:* mransom1@bellsouth.net

Diocesan Presidents/Contacts: Province V
Chicago (C)—Beth C Petti *Pres E-mail:* bcpetti@wideopenwest.com

Eastern Michigan (EMI)—Kate Forsyth *Contact E-mail:* kforsyth@eastmich.org

Eau Claire (EAUC)-The Rev Canon Aaron Zook *Contact E-mail:* administrator@dioec.net

Fond du Lac (FDL)-Lisa Baltes *Contact E-mail:* lbaltes@diofdl.org

Indianapolis (IND)—Amy Paget *Co-Pres E-mail:* amyjpaget@gmail.com; Burnie Wilkins *Co-Pres E-mail:* burnie.wilkins@gmail.com

Michigan (MI)—Darlene Williams *Co-Chair E-mail:* darwills1@aol.com; Ged Youngman *Co-Chair E-mail:* amyged@wowway.com

Milwaukee (MIL)—Connie Ott *Pres E-mail:* cott@chorus.net

Missouri (MO)—Deborah Caby *Pres E-mail:* debbiecaby@yahoo.com

Northern Indiana (NI)—Bishop Sparks *Contact E-mail:* bishopsparks@edmin.org

Northern Michigan (NMI)—Teena Maki *Co-Contact E-mail:* makifarm@up.net; Coralie Hambleton Voce *Co-Contact E-mail:* cvhamblet@hotmail.com

Ohio (OH)-Barbara Jones *Pres E-mail:* shadowoak2199@zoominternet.net

Southern Ohio (SO)—Kathy Mank *Pres E-mail:* kathymank@gmail.com

Springfield (SP)—Cheri King *Pres E-mail:* cheriking@yahoo.com

Western Michigan (WMI)—Pam Chapman *Contact E-mail:* pamchapman811@gmail.com

Diocesan Presidents/Contacts: Province VI
Colorado—Samar Fay *Contact E-mail:* samarfay@gmail.com

Iowa—no contact

Minnesota—Susan Tribenbach *Contact E-mail:* sue9966@gmail.com

Montana—no contact

Nebraska—Rebecca Smith *Co-Convener E-mail:* rsmith1956@msn.com; Beth Agar *Co-Convener E-mail:* bethagar@live.com

North Dakota—no contact

South Dakota—Diana Regan *Pres E-mail:* gmaregan@gmail.com

Wyoming—Melissa Hyde *Pres E-mail:* mhyde1973@gmail.com

Diocesan Presidents/Contacts: Province VII
Arkansas—Terri Crawford *Pres E-mail:* terripcrawford@gmail.com

Dallas— no contact

Fort Worth—Sandy Shockley *Pres E-mail:* dshock9510@aol.com

Kansas—Frances Wheeler *Pres E-mail:* frances.wheeler11@gmail.com

Northwest Texas—Nancy McReynolds *Pres E-mail:* nmcreynolds@suddenlink.net

Oklahoma—Deborah Butcher *Pres E-mail:* geraldbutcher@sbcglobal.net

Rio Grande—no contact

Texas—Trish Johnston *Pres E-mail:* edot.ecw.pres@gmail.com

West Missouri—Judy Turner *Pres E-mail:* jannet@cableone.net

West Texas—Linda Hollingsworth *Pres E-mail:* linda1352@hotmail.com

Western Kansas—no contact

Western Louisiana—Shetwan Roberison *Pres E-mail:* sroberison@gmail.com

Diocesan Presidents/Contacts: Province VIII
Alaska—Pearl Chanar *Contact E-mail:* pdchanar@gci.net

Arizona—Winifred Follett *Contact E-mail:* winnieandcj@gmail.com

California—no contact

Eastern Oregon—c/o Episcopal Diocese of Eastern Oregon *E-mail:* diocese@episdioeo.org.

El Camino Real—Diane Lovelace *Pres E-mail:* dilovelace@aol.com

Hawaii—Louise Aloy *Pres E-mail:*louisealoy63@gmail.com

Idaho—Kirsten Nielson *Diocesan Coordinator Diocesan Phone:* 208-345-4440

Los Angeles—Christine Budzowski *Pres E-mail:* Christine@Trinitywebconsulting.com

Micronesia—Archdeacon Irene Egmalis Maliaman *Diocesan Phone:* O: 1-671-649-0690

Navajoland—Nadine Johnson *Co-Pres E-mail:* Nadinjohnson@frontiernet.net; Margaret Benally *Co-Pres E-Mail:* margaret.benally52@gmail.com cc: (all correspondence) Madelinesampson15@gmail.com

Nevada—Rosemary Kinale *Pres E-mail:* rmkinale1@gmail.com

Northern California—Sophie Carrick *Communications Coordinator E-mail:* Sophie@norcalepiscopal.org

Olympia—Daryl Storey *Contact E-mail:* daryl@isomedia.com

Oregon-Jo Martin *Pres E-mail:* jimjo47@msn.com

San Diego—Sandy Bedard *Contact E-Mail:* sandybedard@yahoo.com

San Joaquin—Elisabeth Ray *Communications Dir Phone:* 209-576-0104

Spokane—Evita Krislock *Convener E-mail:* evita@krislock.com

Taiwan—Pai-Hui Hsu *Contact E-mail:* hph100@yahoo.com.tw

Utah—Linda Garner *Contact E-mail:* mydietcoke@comcast.net

Diocesan Presidents/Contacts: Province IX
Diocesis en la Nueva Provincia
Diocesis de Colombia—no contact

Diocesis de Ecuador Central—no contact

Diocesis de Ecuador Litoral—Elizabeth Calderón *Pres E-mail:* elicalsa_24@hotmail.com

Diocesis de Honduras—The Rev Consuelo (Connie) Sanchez Navarro *Contact E-mail* province9@ecwnational.org

Diocesis de Puerto Rico— Melva Irizarry *Pres E-mail:* melvacats@yahoo.com

Diocesis de la Republica Dominicana—Amanda De la Cruz *Pres E-mail:* amandacruzy@gmail.com

Diocesis de Venezuela—Coromoto Jimenez *Pres E-mail:* pragcjimenez04@gmail.com.

CLERGY INCREASE

Church Scholarship Society, The
Aids candidates for Holy Orders who are accountable to Bp of CT. *Pres* Rt Rev Ian T Douglas The Episcopal Church in CT 290 Pratt Street Box 52 Meriden CT 06450.

Society for the Increase of the Ministry (SIM)
A national organization which has, since 1857, provided financial aid to Postulants and Candidates for Holy Orders. Inquiries to: Trinity Church 120 Sigourney Street Hartford CT 06105 (860) 233-1732. *Exec Dir* Thomas Moore III *E-mail:* info@simministry.org *Web:* www.simministry.org *Facebook:* https://www.facebook.com/SocietyfortheIncreaseoftheMinistry/.

SUPPORT SYSTEMS FOR DEACONS
Association for Episcopal Deacons
Provides resources and advocacy for the diakonia of all believers; offers technical assistance for dioceses who need help with their diaconal programs; promotes and supports the Episcopal diaconate. For information: Dn Lorraine (Lori) Mills-Curran AED *E-mail:* lori@episcopaldeacons.org *Web:* www.episcopaldeacons.org.

Fund for the Diaconate, The
Provides monthly or one time grants for deacons in financial need. *Grant Appl:* Rev Wm Jones *E-mail:* deaconbill1989@verizon.net *Web* www.fundfordiaconate.org

DEVOTIONAL ORGANIZATIONS
Anglican Fellowship of Prayer
International prayer ministry founded in 1958. Our mission: To serve the church by encouraging, facilitating, and promoting the understanding and discipline of prayer in the Anglican Communion. We especially emphasize the value of small group prayer and the parish as a center of prayer. See our website www.afp.org. *Pres* The Rev Dr John R Throop *E-mail:* frjohn@stpetersfalls.org *Web:* www.afp.org.

Brotherhood of St. Andrew
Established in 1883, the Brotherhood of St. Andrew is the official Men's Ministry of the Episcopal Church and Anglican communities. Through their tenants of prayer, study and service their outreach is to men and youth in the church via seven ministries: Scouting, restorative justice (prison reform), veterans affairs, discipleship/mentoring, racial reconciliation, human trafficking and recovery (alcohol, pornography and drugs). Organizational material, newsletters and ministry information is found at www.brothersandrew.net. *Exec Dir* Tom Welch *Office:* 620 South Third Street Louisville KY 40202 *E-mail:* tom.welch@brothersandrew.net *Phone:* 502-540-5640.

Contemplative Outreach, Ltd
An ecumenical spiritual network committed to renewing the contemplative dimension of the Gospel through the practice of Centering Prayer. *Admin* Denis Sheehan. *E-mail:* office@coutreach.org. *Web:* www.contemplativeoutreach.org.

The Episcopal Community
We are a community of Episcopal women committed to living out our Baptismal Covenant as we nurture and support each other's spiritual journeys. Using the Rule of Benedict as our guide, we develop and

follow a personal Rule of Life. While supporting our clergy, our parishes, and The Episcopal Church with our prayers and service, we also provide instruction and mentoring in spiritual disciplines that foster spiritual growth and transformation. *National Pres* Nancy Young *National Office* Box 242, Sewanee TN 37375 *E-mail:* covenant@theepiscopalcomminity. org *Web:* www.theepiscopalcommunity.org.

Evelyn Underhill Association, Ltd
Established in the US in 1990 to honor the legacy of Anglican spiritual writer Evelyn Underhill, offering an online newsletter and Annual Quiet Day in June at Washington National Cathedral. *Contact:* Kathleen Henderson Staudt 9407 Spruce Tree Circle Bethesda MD 20814 *E-mail:* evelynunderhill@gmail. com *Web:* www.evelynunderhill.org.

Fellowship of Contemplative Prayer
Founded in 1949 in England. Members follow a simple Rule stressing daily contemplation of the Word of God and an annual retreat. Clergy and laity. Milo G Coerper 7315 Brookville Rd Chevy Chase MD 20815 (301) 652-8635 *E-mail:* wmcoerp@ verizon.net.

Guild of All Souls
The Guild of All Souls is a prayer guild of people who promise to pray for the sick and departed by name, prayer and an annual Requiem Mass being our only work. Contact: Canon Barry Swain, rector@ resurrectionnyc.org, Website: guildofallsouls.net

Guild of the Living Rosary
Guild of intercessors who use the traditional rosary. The Rev Cn David M Baumann SSC PO Box 303 Salem IL 62881 *E-mail:* guildlivingrosary@gmail. com *Web:* www.guildlivingrosary.org. *Facebook:* facebook.com/guildlivingrosary.

The Order of the Daughters of the King®
An order for lay or ordained women who commit to a lifelong program of prayer, service, and evangelism, dedicated to strengthening the spiritual life of her parish and spreading Christ's Kingdom. *Pres* Krisita Jackson *E-mail:* krisitajackson@doknational.org; *Comm Coord* Mandy Wheeler (x25) *Natl Off:* 101 Weatherstone Dr #870 Woodstock GA 30188-7007 (770) 517-8552 *E-mail:* DOK1885@doknational.org *Mag: Royal Cross, Cross+Links Web:* www.doknational.org.

Order of the Thousandfold
Develops Christian spiritual resources by encouraging daily use of The Thousandfold Prayer. Prayer and tracts in 22 languages. *Dir* Rev DA Puckett PO Box 276 Graniteville SC 29829 *E-mail:* dap@gforcecable.com.

Society of King Charles the Martyr (SKCM)
Promotes devotion to King Charles I and his martyrdom in defense of the Catholic faith in the Church of England and encourages commemorations of the anniversary of his martyrdom and other Caroline observances; open to all Christians. *Contact: Pres*

The Rev Dr Steven Rice; *Epis Patron* The Rt Rev Keith Ackerman *E-mail:* membership@skcm-usa. org *Web:* www.skcm-usa.org.

Society of Mary
A devotional society within the Anglican Communion promoting the honor due the Blessed Virgin Mary. *Sup* The Rev John D Alexander *Sec* Dr Paul Cooper 415 Pennington-Titusville Rd Titusville, NJ 08560-2012 *Membership Adm* Lynne V Walker PO Box 930 Lorton VA 22079 *Web:* www. somamerica.org.

Society of the Companions of the Holy Cross, The
Intentional community of women devoted to intercession, thanksgiving, and simplicity and spiritual growth, offering monthly local gatherings and summer conferences and retreats at Adelynrood retreat center. *Web:* www.Adelynrood.org. Generalmanager@adelynrood.org *Contact: Companion-in-Charge* Alinda Stanley.

Society of the Holy Cross
Better known by its Latin initials, the SSC is the oldest Catholic Society in Anglican Communion; it is open by invitation to priests and bishops for the sanctification of priestly life by rule, the unification of its members in special bond of charity, faith, and discipline, and for the extension of Catholic principles. *Master of the Americas* Rev. Michael Godderz, SSC *E-mail:* rector@allsaints.net *Web:* www.sscamericas.org.

PRAYER BOOK SOCIETIES
Bible and Common PB Soc of Episc Ch
Society for donation of Bibles, PB's, and Hymnals on request with bishop's endorsement. *Pres* Rt Rev Rodney R Michel *Sec* Rev Warren E Haynes *Mgr* Rev Dr David G Henritzy 815 Second Ave NY NY 10017 (212) 716-6131 *E-mail:* biblesandprayerbooks@ episcopalchurch.org.

Bishop White PB Society
Donates Prayer Books and Hymnals on Bishop's endorsement. *Sec* Rev Mark J Ainsworth c/o All Hallows Church 262 Bent Rd Wyncote PA 19095 (215) 885-1641 *E-mail:* mainsworth@allhallowswyncote.org.

Margaret Coffin PB Society
Provides free Prayer Books and Hymnals on request with Bishop's endorsement. Given to parishes, missions, and institutions at home and abroad, unable to purchase them. Rev Marshall W Hunt PO Box 1205 E Harwich MA 02645 (508) 432-2612.

GENERAL ORGANIZATIONS
African American Episcopal Historical Collection (AAEHC)
A joint project of Virginia Theological Seminary and the Historical Society of the Episcopal Church, the

AAEHC gathers and preserves letters, journals, records, photographs, minutes, family histories, sermons, personal writing, conference materials, resumes, oral histories, and similar materials from African American individuals and organizations, and others working with African Americans, in the Episcopal Church. *Web:* vts.edu/aaehc *AAEHC Processing Archivist* Ebonee Davis *E-mail:* edavis@vts.edu.

Alcuin Club

Promotes study of liturgy and worship of the Christian Church by publishing works of scholarship. Members receive two "Liturgical Studies" and a major book *Collection* annually for their dues (US $44 with optional air mail surcharge of US $10)—with occasional disc on other books. For information and membership contact John Collins 5 Saffron St Royston Herts SG8 9TR UK +44 (0) 1763-248676 *E-mail:* alcuinclub@gmail.com *Web:* www.alcuinclub.org.uk.

American Anglican Council

The American Anglican Council is a network of individuals (laity, deacons, priests and bishops), parishes and specialized ministries who affirm biblical authority and Christian orthodoxy within the Anglican Communion and who are working to build up and defend Great Commission Anglican churches in North America and worldwide. *Chairman of the Board* The Rt Rev David C Anderson; *Pres/CEO* The Rev Cn Phil Ashey; *Dir of Human Res* Mary Orr; *Dir of Comm* Robert Lundy; *Admin Asst* Nina Brown-Perry PO Box 2868 Loganville GA 30052 (800) 914-2000 *Fax:* (770) 414-1518 *E-mail:* info@americananglican.org *Web:* www.americananglican.org.

American Bible Society

American Bible Society Distributes the Holy Scriptures without doctrinal note or comment. For catalog of Am Bible Soc or publication *The Record* write to Autumn Black 1865 Broadway NY NY 10023 (212) 408-1215 *Web:* www.americanbible.org.

American Friends of the Episcopal Diocese of Jerusalem, The

AFEDJ transforms lives of the vulnerable and displaced in the Middle East through support of the schools, hospitals and centers for children with disabilities that are owned and operated by the Episcopal Diocese of Jerusalem. These institutions are in Palestine, Israel, Jordan, Lebanon and Syria. AFEDJ is an independent, non-political non-profit. Executive Director: John Lent. Email: jlent@afedj.org. Web: www.afedj.org.

Anglican Frontier Missions

Partnering with members of the worldwide Anglican Communion and other Christians who live near or among unreached peoples, the vision of AFM is to plant biblically-based, indigenous churches where the church is not, among the 6,000+ unreached people groups still waiting to hear the Gospel. *Dir* The Rev Christopher Royer *E-mail:* info@afm-us.org *Web:* www.anglicanfrontiers.com.

Anglican Musicians, Association of

For church musicians and clergy serving Episcopal and Anglican churches. Seeks to promote excellence in church music, working with clergy, commissions on liturgy and music, composers and other artists, and seminaries. Endows the Gerre Hancock Fellowship for organ scholars. Annual conference. Monthly professional journal. *Pres* Paul M Ellison PhD PO Box 7530 Little Rock AR 72217 *Voice/Fax:* (501) 661-9925 *E-mail:* office@anglicanmusicians.org *Web:* www.anglicanmusicians.org.

Anglican Society

To promote and maintain Catholic faith and practice in accordance with the principles of the BCP, to explore and affirm Anglican identity and self-understanding. Rev JR Wright 177 9th Ave Apt 2-H NY NY 10011-4977 *E-mail:* wright@gts.edu *Web:* www.anglicansociety.org.

Anglican Women's Empowerment (AWE)

AWE seeks to be an effective and empowered voice for Anglican Women at the United Nations and throughout the Anglican Communion, with particular focus on the UN Commission on the Status of Women committed to worldwide reconciliation, right relationships and shared work for peace and justice through empowerment and education around global issues through the Beijing Platform for Action, the Millennium Development Goals, and working as appropriate for equal representation of women in the Anglican Consultative Council. *Web:* anglicanwomensempowerment.org.

Anglicans for Life

AFL is the only global Anglican/Episcopal ministry that educates, equips, and engages the Church in fulfilling Scripture's mandate to honor, protect, defend and celebrate every human life, through local Life Chapters and published resources for ministry including adult education DVD curriculums; Project Life & Embrace the Journey. *Pres* The Rev Georgette Forney *E-mail:* info@anglicansforlife.org *Web:* www.anglicansforlife.org.

Associated Parishes for Liturgy and Mission (APLM)

Network of Anglicans in North America who promote renewal of liturgy and mission in Episcopal Church and Anglican Church of Canada through education and formation, advocacy, development of resources and cooperation with renewal efforts in other churches. *Mail* 3405 Alman Dr Durham NC 27705 *E-mail:* info@associatedparishes.org *Web:* www.associatedparishes.org.

Bible Reading Fellowship

Produces and distributes daily Bible reading materials and various other resources for church growth. *Pres* Trip Tucker Box 380 Winter Park FL 32790-0380 (407) 628-4330 *E-mail:* brf@biblereading.org *Web:* www.biblereading.org.

Bishops' Executive Secretaries Together—BEST

B+E+S+T empowers our members through networking and education to value our ministry and to support the ministry of our bishops and the wider church. Meets annually. *Pres* Michele King *Email:* michele.king@edfw.org.

Companions in Mission for Publishing and Communication

Granting agency for miss-related publication projects of the Church. *Pres* Rt Rev Ian T Douglas *E-mail:* CMPC@schrull.us.

Church Periodical Club

Founded in 1888, CPC gives grants for paper and electronic books, periodicals, audio and videotapes, and computer software throughout the Anglican Communion, enabling ministries with limited resources at all levels of the church. *Web:* www.churchperiodical.com.

CODE

The Conference of Diocesan Executives was founded in 1963. Membership is open to lay and ordained people who report to Diocesan Bishops while serving on a Bishop's staff. Key is building relationships and sharing experiences. Facilitates collegiality, confidence, and support. Helps members to find healthy solutions to challenges and to build up the body of Christ. Holds annual conference offering best in speakers, seminars and workshops on a wide ranging variety of topics. Fun is an integral part of CODE Conference experience. *Pres* Rev Cn Lucy Amerman *E-mail:* lucya@diopa.org *VP* Rev Cn Michael Pipkin *E-mail:* michael.p@episcopalmn.org *Treas* David Ramkey *E-mail:* dramkey@wvdiocese.org *Sec* Rev Neysa Ellgren *E-mail:* neysae@diocese-oregon.org *Comm* Tammy Mazure *E-mail:* tmazure@edwm.org *Web Worker:* Rev Cn Bruce Gray *E-mail:* gray@indydio.org. *Web:* http://codeepiscopal.org/ *Facebook:* https://www.facebook.com/groups/625497357532880/.

Conference of Anglican Religious Orders in the Americas

Association of officially recognized religious orders who live in community under vows; coordinates interest and experience of members, provides opportunities for mutual support, and presents a coherent understanding of religious life to the Church. *Gen Sec* The Rev Dr Donald Anderson PO Box 99 Little Britain Ontario K0M 2C0 Canada (705) 786-3330 *E-mail:* dwa1319@gmail.com *Web:* www.caroa.net.

Consortium of Endowed Episcopal Parishes, The

CEEP is a community of Episcopal parishes and seminaries providing a unique opportunity for lay and clergy leadership to make connections with each other. CEEP fills it members with enthusiasm and optimism by sharing food for the mind and tools for action. The tangible solutions shared through CEEP strengthen ministries—lay and clergy. *Exec Dir* Joseph R Swimmer Esq, CEEP PO Box 162734 Austin TX 78716-2734 (202) 905-0103 *E-mail:* jswimmer@endowedparishes.org *Web:* www.endowedparishes.org.

Council of Episcopal Women's Organizations, The (CEWO)

This Council includes women's organizations of the Episcopal Church. Organizational Presidents or their representatives meet annually for networking and organizing in order to increase the effectiveness of women's ministries, to support their different gifts, and to advance the roles of women in God's mission as expressed through the Episcopal Church. *Contact:* The Rev Cynthia Black.

Cursillo

Cursillo is a movement of the Episcopal Church, under the authority of the Presiding and Diocesan Bishops, whose goal is to bring the world to Christ by empowering adult Christian leaders through the use of a specific method that is taught as part of a three-day weekend. The method, a tool for evangelism, equips and encourages Christians to live out their Baptismal covenant to serve Christ. *E-mail:* ECMOffice@EpiscopalCursilloMinistry.org *Web:* http://episcopalcursilloministry.org/.

Educational Center, The

A spiritual resource center for seekers, learners and religious educators. Publishers of BibleWorkbench and TeenText; lectionary based studies, discussion guides and sermon preparation. 3200 Park Rd Charlotte NC 28209 (704) 375-1161 *E-mail:* info@educationalcenter.org *Web:* www.educationalcenter.org.

Episcopal Booksellers Association Inc.

Episcopal Booksellers Association Inc. is a non-profit association of and church-owned book and gift stores serving the Episcopal church and general public. *Exec Dir* William J. Hunter (888) 589-8020 X101 *E-mail:* director@episcopalbooksellers.org. For listing of nationwide member stores and vendors see www.episcopalbooksellers.org / www.episcopalbooksellers.net.

Episcopal Camps and Conference Centers, Inc

A national network within the Episcopal Church, ECCC links diocesan-related camp and conference center facilities together providing educational services, newsletters and professional support. ECCC sponsors an Annual Conference for executive directors, senior staff and board members. Consultative services focusing on executive search, strategic planning, business plans and board development etc. are also available. For information contact *Di-*

rector Bill Slocumb (760) 445-6774 *E-mail:* staff@
episcopalccc.org *Web:* www.episcopalccc.org.

Episcopal Church and Visual Arts (ECVA)

Episcopal Church and Visual Arts (ECVA) is a
virtual organization that curates visual arts exhibi-
tions online and networks artists and organizations
around the country. ECVA assists dioceses and
churches in integrating the visual arts into congregational ministry, liturgy, and mission programs.
Episcopal Church and Visual Arts Inc 815 2nd Ave
New York NY 10017 *E-mail:* ecvaexhibitions@ecva.
org *Web:* www.ecva.org.

Episcopal Church Foundation (ECF), The

ECF partners with congregations, dioceses, and other Episcopal faith communities, empowering them
to engage in strategic visioning and planning, develop effective lay and clergy leadership teams, and raise
financial resources for ministry. ECF's programs,
products, and services help congregations respond
to the changing needs of the Episcopal Church in the
21st century. *Chair* Benjamin Anderson-Ray *Pres*
Donald V Romanik *E-mail:* all@EpiscopalFounda-
tion.org *Web:* www.EpiscopalFoundation.org.

Episcopal Communicators

A self-supporting organization of persons with
communications responsibilities in the Episcopal
Church. The mission of Episcopal Communicators
is to foster community that inspires and supports
excellence in church communications.*Pres* Melodie
Woerman (2017-2020) Diocese of Kansas 835
SW Polk St. Topeka, KS 66612-1688 (785) 224-
5232 *E-mail:* mwoerman@episcopal-ks.org,
episcopalcommunicators@gmail.com *Web:* www.
episcopalcommunicators.org.

Episcopal Community Services in America

Episcopal Community Services in America (ECSA)
is an umbrella 501(c)3 non-profit organization
that seeks to provide a network to build resources,
foster relationships, and encourage advocacy to
the approximately 550 health and human service
agencies associated with the Episcopal Church. *Web:*
episcopalcommunity.org/.

Episcopal Evangelism Society (EES)

Awards grants to Episcopalians in seminaries or
local formation programs, for projects of innovative
evangelism. *Exec Dir* Day Smith Pritchartt *E-mail:*
office@ees1862.org *Web:* www.ees1862.org.

Episcopal Health Ministries

Episcopal Health Ministries (EHM) is a network that
promotes health ministry (including parish nursing)
in Episcopal congregations and provides health
ministry resources to local congs, dioceses and
provinces; collaborates with other faith communities,
institutions and health orgs; offers education for
Episcopal health ministry and parish nursing; and
supports those engaged in cong health min. For

information see www.EpiscopalHealthMinistries.
org 9120 Fredrick Rd Ellicott City MD 21042 *E-mail:*
NEHM@episcopalhealthministries.org.

Episcopal Marriage Encounter

Conducts weekend sessions nationwide, teaching a
positive communication technique for married couples
within God's plan for sacramental marriages. Contact:
Natl Exec Clergy Couple Fr John & Janet Duncan 110
San Benito Ave Aptos CA 95003-4415 (831) 688-1383
E-mail: jnjduncan@yahoo.com *Natl Exec Lay Couple*
Bill & Lee Gill 6 Eames Drive Oxford CT 06478-1183
(203) 888-2043 *E-mail:* bgill96178@aol.com.

Episcopal Media Center

A division of Alliance for Christian Media, which
also incorporates the "Day 1" ecumenical radio
program/podcast, the Episcopal Media Center
offers Episcopal branded and other faith-oriented
merchandise and resources for education and
inspiration. *Pres* Rev Peter Wallace *E-mail:* info@
day1.org *Web:* www.episcopalmarketplace.org .

Episcopal Peace Fellowship

A national membership organization assisting
Episcopalians and others to realize and live out
Christ's call for peace, justice and reconciliation;
promotes prayer, study, education and action;
organizes chapters and action groups around the
country, and provides nonviolence retreats and
training. *Exec Dir* Rev Allison Liles *Chair* Rev Will
Wauters *Vice Chair* Rev Bill Exner *E-mail:* epf@
epfnational.org *Web:* epfnational.org.

Episcopal Preaching Foundation, Inc

The mission and ministry of the Episcopal Preaching
Foundation is to support and enhance preaching in
the Episcopal Church. EPF provides educational
conferences, seminars and programs, including an
annual national conference for seminarians—the
Preaching Excellence Program (PEP) and PEP
II for clergy 3 to five years into their ministry.
Diocesan preaching events are coordinated with
Bishops across the US and Canada. *Chair and
Founder:* Dr A Gary Shilling (973) 467-0070 *E-mail:*
gary@agaryshilling.com; *Phone:* (973) 367-6014
E-mail: preachingfoundation@gmail.com *Web:*
www.preachingfoundation.org.

Episcopal Public Policy Network

A grassroots network of Episcopalians dedicated to
the ministry of public policy advocacy, supported by
the Office of Government Relations, which represents
the policy priorities of the Episcopal Church to the
US government in Washington, DC. *Staff contact:*
Alan Yarborough *E-mail:* eppn@episcopalchurch.
org *Web:* http://advocacy.episcopalchurch.org/
Facebook, Twitter, and Instagram: @TheEPPN.

Episcopal Women's Caucus, The

Episcopal Women's Caucus is a justice organization
of women and men dedicated to the Gospel values of

equality and liberation for all, and committed to the incarnation of God's unconditional love. Founded in 1971 to work for the ordination of women, the Caucus continues to advocate for and support women in leadership and challenge all forms of discrimination with particular attention to matters affecting women. Quarterly journal, local chapters and participation in partnership and coalitions. *Contact:* Christine Mackey-Mason 1103 Magnolia St South Pasadena CA 91030 (626) 201-2363 *E-mail:* mackeychristine@att.net *Web:* www.ewc-ecusa.com/.

Episcopal Women's History Project
Organization to raise awareness in the Church of the roles taken by women, highlighting their valuable contributions to the church and society. Funds support research, grants for scholarly work, use of archives, education for church historians, oral history training, and communication encouraging interest in women's history. Publishes quarterly *The Historiographer* with other Episcopal historical organizations. Conferences with speakers and workshops. *Pres* The Rev Dr Jo Ann Barker *E-mail:* joann.barker@gmail.com *Web:* www.ewhp.org.

Episcopalians on Baptismal Mission (EBM)
A partnership dedicated to the daily ministry of all the baptized, formed in 2006 to advocate within The Episcopal Church for recognizing, affirming, and furthering Monday through Saturday endeavors of baptized persons, grounded in the vows of The Baptismal Covenant; explore common ground and natural alliances with other Episcopal, Anglican, and ecumenical groups; serve as an educational resource, assisting congregations, dioceses, provinces, and seminaries in planning and implementing educational events focused on the calling of all the baptized to their mission in daily life; and provide a communications link among partners through our email list serv and blog, www.livinggodsmission.org

EBM is led by a steering committee of laypersons, priests, and bishops. Membership is open to all. *Contact*: Rev Cn J Fletcher Lowe Jr at *jflowe@aol.com*.

Evangelical Fellowship in the Anglican Communion (EFAC-USA)
EFAC-USA is a gathering of Evangelicals in the Episcopal and Anglican churches for networking, prayer, Bible study, worship, and mutual encouragement in Gospel ministry, both as lay and ordained ministers of the Gospel. Contact Zac Neubauer E-mail: zac@efac-usa.org Web: www.efac-usa.org

Faith Encouragement Ministries
Faith Encouragement Ministries delivers affordable church renewal programs for all churches and missions, regardless of size; and provides tools to the church for follow up after the program in line with the church's goals. *Contact* Nola Schrum (972)

839-3773 *E-mail:* ns0239@yahoo.com *Web:* http://faithencourage.org/.

Forma
The Network for Christian Formation: We celebrate, equip, support and connect leaders who form followers of Jesus. *Eph. 4:11-16.* *Exec Dir* Bill Campbell *E-mail:* bill@forma.church *Web:* www.forma.church.

Forward in Faith, North America (FIFNA)
Formerly Episcopal Synod of America. Association of Episcopal and Anglican congregations, chapters, institutions, laity, religious and clergy who embrace the Gospel of Jesus Christ and uphold the Evangelical faith and Catholic order of the Church. Publication: *Forward in Christ.* Membership open to those who subscribe to the FIFNA Declaration of Common Faith and Purpose. *E-mail:* office@fifna.org *Web:* www.fifna.org.

Friends of Canterbury Cathedral in the US (FOCCUS)
A charitable, not-for-profit corporation whose mission is to provide scholarship funds for seminarians from Third World Countries to attend International Study at Canterbury Cathedral; build relationships between Episcopalians and the Cathedral; encourage involvement with Cathedral's mission; strengthen capacity of the Cathedral as retreat center, support the Cathedral's programs, preservation, and restoration. *Chair* Rt Rev Peter J Lee *V Chairs* Eugene Johnston & Barbara Q Harper 888 17th St NW Ste 608 Washington DC 20006 (202) 822-8994.

Gather the Family Institute for Evangelism and Congregational Development
Provides consultants, training workshops to help congregations and dioceses learn the concepts and skills necessary to develop individualized programs for evangelism and incorporation (assimilation) min. *DMin* Rev GK Sturni PO Box 38447 Germantown TN 38183-0447 (901) 754-7282 *E-mail*: gsturni@gmail.com.

Gathering the Next Generations (GTNG)
Network An online network sustained by lay and ordained Episcopalians of Generation X and following generations (born in or after 1961) to connect and support leadership of the "next generations" in the church and further the mission of Christ. *E-mail:* gtng-owner@yahoogroups.com *Web:* www.gtng.org.

Global Episcopal Mission Network
Founded in 1994 to promote global mission engagement throughout the Episcopal Church, GEMN is an independent network of dioceses, congregations, seminaries, individuals & mission organizations. GEMN offers the Mission Formation Program, convenes the annual Global Mission

Conference, & brings mission activists together for mutual support, inspiration & advocacy. Pres Rev Dr Titus Presler VP Rev Dr Grace Burton-Edwards Contact: Exec Dir Karen Hotte, PO Box 1434 Dublin OH 43017 E-mail: gemn@gemn.org Web www.gemn.org.

Guild of St Ives

Association of Episcopal lawyers and judges who live, work or worship in the Diocese of NY; annually observes Law Day with Choral Evensong between Law Day (May 1) and the Feast of St Ives to recognize public service by members of the legal profession on behalf of the community; presents the Servant of Justice Award in recognition of commitment to the legal profession, public service, and mission of the Church. *Phone:* (212) 316-7400

"Happening—A Christian Experience^{SM}"

A diocesan renewal and evangelism program for High School youth to "Share God's Love Through Community." During a 2-day sequestered weekend, participants experience the wonder and love of God's love as shown through their peers, lay adults and clergy. A Happening National Leadership Conference occurs in the summer of even-numbered years. *Exec Dir* Krisan Lamberti *E-mail:* KrisanLamberti@gmail.com *E-mail:* info@happeningnational.org *Web:* www.happeningnational.org.

Historical Society of the Episcopal Church

Organization for preservation of Episcopal heritage within the Anglican Communion, fostering research, publishing *Anglican & Episcopal History*, as well as *The Historiographer* with other Episcopal historical organizations. *Web:* hsec.us. *Dir of Oper* Matthew P Payne *E-mail:* administration@hsec.us.

Integrity USA

A lesbian, gay, bisexual, and transgender justice ministry in and to the Episcopal Church. There are numerous chapters in 8 provinces. Annual dues start at $25. *Pres* Dr Bruce Garner 770 Massachusetts Ave #390170 Cambridge MA 02139 (617) 952-9971 *E-mail:* info@integrityusa.org *Web:* www.integrityusa.org.

International Order of St Luke the Physican (OSL)

Interdenom Christian fellowship of faith, prayer and service with members from both lay and clergy who believe healing to be an essential part of teaching and practice of Our Lord and who believe that healing ministry of Christ belongs in the church today. *Contact:* North American OSL Ofc *E-mail:* info@orderofstluke.org *Web:* www.orderofstluke.org.

International Order of St Vincent

A fellowship of lay sanctuary ministers of all ages (open to all (men and women, girls and boys) acolytes, lay readers, lectors, lay eucharistic ministers, sacristans, ushers, greeters, vergers, and choristers) serving the One, Holy, Catholic, and Apostolic Church promoting liturgical knowledge, understanding of ritualistic detail and meaning, and encourage intercessory prayer and holy living among our members. Believing that we are also called to serve, we strive to instill reverence, cooperation, responsibility, discipline, mentorship, leadership, humility, quest for excellence, and joy of servanthood by emphasizing a stairway of lay ministry that leads to active adult churchmanship. The OSV is sacramentally centered and encourages living a rule of life (we pray, worship, read, and give). The OSV also publishes a wide range of illustrated liturgical manuals, teaching materials and historical tracts. *Dir Gen* Philip G Dixon, *E-mail:* Director-General@orderstvincent.org *Web:* www.orderstvincent.org.

KEEP (Kiyosato Educational Experiment Project)

American Committee for KEEP (ACK) supports Japanese lay organization since 1950 providing Christian witness of service to others through cross cultural partnerships, international exchange, outreach, and education in the areas of environmental issues, agriculture, youth, and community development. *ACK Pres* Rt Rev Stacy Sauls *E-mail:* ack@ackeep.org.

Living Church Foundation, Inc

Dedicated to providing quality publications for the Episcopal Church and the Anglican Communion. Publishes *The Living Church, Illuminations & Epis Musician's Handbook. Pres* Rt Rev John C Bauerschmidt *Exec Dir* Dr Christopher Wells PO Box 510705 Milwaukee WI 53203-0121 *Web:* livingchurch.org.

National Association of Episcopal Christian Communities, The

NAECC is a coalition of Christian Communities recognized under the canons of the Episcopal Church working with communities-in-formation, dedicated to sharing and communicating the fruits of the Gospel—realized in many forms of community—with the church and the world. *Contact:* Secretary, *E-mail:* naeccsecretary@gmail.com *Web:* www.naecc.net.

National Episcopal Historians and Archivists

Organization of congregational and diocesan historians and archivists to encourage collection, preservation and organization of church records and sharing of church history; publishes quarterly *The Historiographer* with other Episcopal historical organizations. *Pres* Susan Stonesifer *E-mail:* nehahqs@aol.com *Web:* episcopalhistorians.org.

North American Committee of St George's College, Jerusalem

St.George's College Jerusalem is an international community for study and pilgrimage in the Holy Land. It is located in the compound of St George's Cathedral, the seat of the Episcopal Diocese of Jerusalem. The North American Committee links together individuals who have made pilgrimage to Saint George's and works to support the ministry of the College through scholarships, public relations, education and fundraising. *Pres* The Rev James Bimbi *Exec Sec* Nancy Brockway PO Box 12073 (3737 Seminary Rd) Alexandria VA 22304 (404)-386-2924 *E-mail:* nacstgeorges@outlook.com; *Facebook:* www.facebook.com/sgcjerusalem/.

Operation Pass Along

Accepts contributions of new and used books about the church, vestments, clericals and altar fittings and passes them along, without charge, to seminarians, newly ordained priests, and deacons, newly formed parish and mission libraries and others. 805 CR 102 Eureka Springs AR 72632-9705 (800) 572-7929 *E-mail:* OperationPassAlong@anglicandigest.org.

Prayer Book Society of the USA, The

Promotes Anglican doctrine, discipline and worship as expressed in the Common Prayer tradition and Anglican formularies since the first English Prayer Book of 1549, on through the 1928 Book of Common Prayer of the Episcopal Church down to the present day; it advances education in the fullness of what it means to be Episcopalian and Anglican through publications and events, an Annual Conference and Catechetical resources. *Pres* The Revd. Fr. Gavin Dunbar *Web:* www.pbsusa.org and www.anglicanway.org.

Protestant Episcopal Evangelists

Emphasizes inner-city ministries; St Paul's House trains for evangelism. *Exec Dir* Shandra Barahona *Web:* saintpaulshouse.org.

Rock the World Youth Mission Alliance

Engages, equips and empowers young Christians to advance the Kingdom of God. *E-mail:* info@rocktheworld.org *Web:* www.rocktheworld.org.

SAMS—Society of Anglican Missionaries and Senders

Formerly known as the South American Missionary Society, SAMS is a society of missionaries and senders serving in partnership with the Anglican Church globally. SAMS' purpose is to raise up, send, and support Episcopal and other Anglican missionaries to be witnesses and make disciples for Jesus Christ in fellowship with the Anglican Church globally. *Pres & Dir* Stewart Wicker *E-mail:* info@sams-usa.org *Web:* www.sams-usa.org.

Seedlings Inc

Non-profit corp provides Episcopal curriculum for small churches and other unique educational materials. Sunday School lessons over 4-yr cycle, Every Member Uncanvass, Adult Inquirers, and youth confirmation curricula. *Pres* Rev Betty W Fuller (*E-mail:* seedlings@aol.com *Web:* www.seedlingsinc.com.

Society for Promoting Christian Knowledge (SPCK)

The Society for Promoting Christian Knowledge provides resources for Christian knowledge around the world. Patti Joy Posan, Executive Director. *E-mail:* spck@sewanee.edu *Web:* www.spckusa@sewanee.org

Solo Flight: Catch the Vision

A national ministry for single adults in the Episcopal Church providing leadership training, programs, retreats, and specially designed on-site workshops. *Pres* Kay Collier McLaughlin PhD (859) 252-6527 *Fax:* (859) 231-9077 *E-mail:* kcollierm@diolex.org.

SOMA—Sharing of Ministries Abroad

SOMA USA prepares and sends short-term mission teams across national and cultural boundaries. Teams equip and train leaders to minister in the power of the Holy Spirit who renews individuals, empowers the Church, and transforms society. *Natl Dir* Dr Glen Petta SOMA 2501 Ridgmar Plaza #99 Fort Worth TX 76116 (817) 737-SOMA (7662) *E-mail:* office@somausa.org *Web:* www.somausa.org.

SPEAK

Society for Promoting and Encouraging Arts and Knowledge [of the Church]. *Act Chr Bd* The Rev Christopher G Colby.

TENS (The Episcopal Network for Stewardship)

Through online resources, workshops, conferences and consultations, The Episcopal Network for Stewardship works with churches and dioceses to inspire every Episcopalian to transformational generosity in all aspects of their lives. We offer specific programs to help congregations shine the light of Christ more brightly through the mission and ministries of their congregations. TENS is supported through prayer; diocesan, congregational and individual memberships; and generous financial gifts. *E-mail:* tens@tens.org *Web:* www.tens.org.

Union of Black Episcopalians

Organized in 1968 as the Union of Black Clergy and Laity, the Union of Black Episcopalians stands in the continuing tradition of more than 200 years of Black leadership fighting racism in the Episcopal Church. It is the proud inheritor of the work of those people in earlier organizations—the Convocation of Colored Clergy, the Conference of Church Workers Among Colored People—all dedicated to justice and ministry and the inclusion of persons of African descent (Blacks) in the life and leadership of the church. *Natl Pres* Annette L Buchanan; *Immediate Past Pres* John Harris *Natl Off* 701 Oglethorpe St NW Washington DC 20011 (202) 248-3941 *E-mail:* leadership@theube.org *Web:* www.ube.org.

Vergers Guild of the Episcopal Church (VGEC), The

VGEC is an all-volunteer service organization supporting liturgical volunteers and liturgical leaders in the ministry of the verger, a member of the laity who works under the direction of the parish priest, in any size congregation, assisting with the organization and operation of religious services in the Episcopal Church in the US, The Anglican Church of Canada, the Church of England, and the Anglican Communion worldwide. *E-mail:* info@vergers.org *Web:* www.vergers.org.

Vocare International

A Vocare weekend allows young adults to look at God's call and what it means in all areas of life. Primarily in the 19-30 age range, participants share ideas and ways to incorporate Christianity today. Annual Conference in Spring. *Coord* Liz Williams 2007 Belmont Ave Tifton GA 31794 (404) 202-7284 *E-mail:* admin@vocare.org.

Washington National Cathedral

Washington National Cathedral is a church for national purposes called to embody God's love and to welcome people of all faiths and perspectives. A unique blend of the spiritual and the civic, this Episcopal Cathedral is a voice for generous spirited Christianity and a catalyst for reconciliation and interfaith dialogue to promote respect and understanding. We invite all people to share in our commitment to create a more hopeful and just world. Washington National Cathedral 3101 Wisconsin Ave NW (Massachusetts & Wisconsin Aves NW) Washington DC 20016-5098 (202) 537-6200 *Web:* www.nationalcathedral.org.

GENERAL YOUTH ORGANIZATIONS

The Junior Daughters of the King

Baptized young women and girls ages 7-21 who make a promise of daily Prayer and Service, which provides a special opportunity for them to grow in their Christian faith and commitment. *Chair* Anna Stevenson (210) 912-5505 *E-mail:* astevenson@doknational.org *Natl Off Admin* Janice Baker *Natl Off* 101 Weatherstone Dr #870 Woodstock GA 30188-7003 (770) 517-8552 X25 *Fax:* (770) 517-8066 *E-mail:* dok1885@doknational.org *Web:* www.doknational.org.

GFS/USA—Girls' Friendly Society, USA

International, not-for-profit, faith-based organization affiliated with the Episcopal Church for girls and young women 5-21 with a purpose to provide girls and women with a support system aimed at developing the whole person. *E-mail:* deloresalleyne@aol.com or gfspresident@gmail.com *Facebook:* https://www.facebook.com/gfsusa/info *Web:* www.gfsus.org.

RELIGIOUS ORDERS AND COMMUNITIES

Editor's Note: Beginning with the 2002 Edition of *The Episcopal Church Annual,* only those religious orders and communities officially recognized by the Standing Committee on Religious Communities of the House of Bishops are listed in *The Annual.* For information about applying for official status, please contact The Rt Rev Russell E Jacobus *Chair,* House of Bishops Committee on Religious Communities PO Box 155 Townsend WI 54715 (920) 585-7481.

Traditional Orders

FOR MEN

Brothers of Saint John the Evangelist (OSB)

Contemplative semi-monastic religious community within the Order of S Benedict, clergy and lay, living a life of prayer, personal growth, and service to the Church. Emphasis as a monastic community is on the traditional worship, music and arts of the Church Our Fellowship includes Oblates and Associates, with some residing at the Monastery and others as Externs. *Superior* Br Richard Tussey EFSJ *Prior & Oblate Director* Br David McClellan EFSJ Tanglewood Hill Monastery PO Box 782 Freeland WA 98249 *E-mail:* efsj@whidbey.com *Web:* www.brothersofsaintjohn.org.

Order of St Benedict, The

Comm of monks in Episcopal Church living Benedictine rule. *Abbot* Rt Rev A Marr OSB S Gregory's Abbey 56500 Abbey Rd Three Rivers MI 49093-9595 (269) 244-5893 *E-mail:* abbot@saintgregorysthreerivers.org *Web:* www.saintgregorysthreerivers.org.

Order of the Holy Cross, The

A Benedictine monastic community for clergy and laymen. *Superior* Br Robert James Magliula, OHC. Holy Cross Monastery Box 99 West Park NY 12493 (845) 384-6660 x3006 Fax: (845) 384-6031. *E-mail:* superior@hcmnet.org. Mt Calvary Monastery Box 1296 Santa Barbara CA 93102 (805) 682-4117. Holy Cross Priory 204 High Park Ave Toronto M6P 2S6 Ontario CANADA (416) 767-9081. Mariya uMama weThemba Monastery Box 6013 Grahamstown 6141 S AFRICA (011) 27-46-622-6465. *Web:* www.holycrossmonastery.com

Society of St Francis

Community of men (lay and ordained) living under the vows of poverty, chastity, and obedience. After the example of Francis of Assisi, the brothers engage in urban ministry, retreats, prayer, and study. Min Prov Br Jude SSF Prov Headquarters, S Damiano Friary 573 Dolores San Francisco CA 94110 (415) 861-1372 *E-mail:* judehillssf@aol.com. *Web:* www.societyofstfrancis.org.

Society of St John the Evangelist

A Monastic Community of brothers, lay and ordained, who live under a contemporary Rule of Life and take vows of poverty, celibacy and obedience. Oldest Anglican religious community for men, founded by Richard Meux Benson at Oxford, England in 1866. Arrived in the US in 1870. Superior Br James Koester SSJE Monastery of St Mary and St John and the Guesthouse 980 Memorial Dr Cambridge MA 02138-5717 (617) 876-3037. *Brs E-mail:* monastery@ssje.org *Guesthouse E-mail:* guesthouse@ssje.org *Vocational info:* Br Jim Woodrum *E-mail:* vocations@ssje.org. Emery House 21 Emery Ln West Newbury MA 01985 (617) 876-3037 *Web:* www.ssje.org.

Society of St Paul

Celebrating a life of prayer, personal growth, and service to others. *Rector* Cn Barnabas Hunt SSP The Society of St Paul 2567 Second Ave Unit 504 San Diego CA 92103 (619) 794-2095.

FOR MEN AND WOMEN

Order of Julian of Norwich, The

Monastic, enclosed, contemplative community for men and women following the spirituality of Dame Julian. Associate and Oblate affiliations for laity and clergy. *Guardian* Mthr Hilary OJN Our Lady of the Northwoods Monastery W704 Alft Road White Lake WI 54491-9715, (262) 349-3283 *E-mail:* ojn@orderofjulian.org *Web:* www.orderofjulian.org.

FOR WOMEN

Community of the Holy Spirit

Monastic observance of the Divine Offices, biodynamic farming, spiritual direction and social justice ministries underscore the creative charism of the Community of the Holy Spirit — a community of life professed sisters, resident companions and associates. Limited guest facilities. *Leadership: Community Council.* St Hilda's House 454 Convent Ave New York NY 10031 212-666-8249 ext 205. Bluestone Farm and Living Arts Center at Melrose Convent 116 Federal Hill Rd Brewster NY 10509 *E-mail:* chssisters@chssisters.org *Web:* www. chssisters.org.

Community of St Francis, The

Franciscan Sisters living a life in community of prayer, study, and ministry with special concern for urban poor and deprived. Associates program and residential Companions in Franciscan Spirituality programs available. *Min Prov* Sr Sister Pamela Clare St Francis House 3743 Cesar Chavez St San Francisco CA 94110 (415) 824-0288 *E-mail:* csfsfo@aol.com *Web:* www.communitystfrancis.org

Community of St John Baptist

A Community of prayer and service, reaching out to God's people. Retreats, conferences, lay and ordained ministry, outreach to the needy, spiritual direction and other ministries Assoc, Oblate and Alongsider affiliations for lay and clergy. Outreach to addicted youth at residential center on property. Mission to orphans in Cameroon. St Marguerite's Retreat House open to groups. Convent of St John Baptist Box 240 82 W Main St Mendham NJ 07945 (973) 543-4641 *Fax:* (973) 543-0327 *E-mail:* csjb@csjb.org *Web:* www.csjb.org

Community of St Mary (Autonomous Provinces)

Benedictine Communities for women with special dedication to St. Mary offering retreats, conferences, and private guest accommodations.

Eastern Province: Mother Miriam CSM St Marys Convent 242 Cloister Way Greenwich NY 12834-7922 (518) 692-3028 *E-mail:* compunun242@gmail.com. Branch House: St Marys Convent PO Box 20280 Luwinga Mzuzu 2 Malawi. *Web:* www.stmaryseast.net. Facebook page: Community of St. Mary, Eastern Province.

Western Province: Sr Letitia CSM 1840 N Prospect Ave #504 Milwaukee, WI 53202 *E-mail:* srletitia504@gmail.com

Southern Province: Sr Madeleine Mary CSM S Mary's Convent 1100 S Mary's Ln Sewanee TN 37375-2614 (931) 598-0046; *fax* (931)598-9519, *Web:* stmary-conventsewanee.org; Facebook page: Community of St. Mary, Southern Province. St. Mary's Convent Sagada Mtn Province PHILIPPINES.

Community of the Teachers of the Children of God, The

Originally founded in 1934 as a traditionally monastic order for women, now a Community of both women and men, whose mission is to continue to support educational organizations to educate children of all abilities. Consisting of two professed nuns, who continue to the live the religious life, and lay members, the Community is dedicated to the education work of the Episcopal Church and offers through the *Rule of the Associates* the opportunity for religious instruction and spiritual development. *Contact:* Nannette Akins Associate CTCG 5790 E. 14th Street Tucson, AZ 85711 (520) 591-4178. *E-mail:* nannetteak@aol.com.

Community of the Transfiguration

Prayer, worship, hospitality and retreats, educational and recreational ministry with children. Sup Sr Jean Gabriel CT Convent of the Transfiguration 495 Albion Ave Cincinnati OH 45246 *E-mail:* inquire@ctsisters.org *Web:* www.ctsisters.org (513) 771-5291 *Fax:* (513) 771-0839 Local Ministries: Transfiguration Spirituality Ctr *Web:* www.CTRetreats.org. *E-mail:* ctretreats@gmail.com; Bethany Sch: (513) 771-7462 *Web:* www.bethanyschool.org; S Monica's Rec Ctr *E-mail:* mpearl121@gmail.com; Branch Ministries, hospitality and retreats: Tabor Ministry Butler OH 44822 *E-mail:* hilaritas@aol.com.

Episcopal Carmel of Saint Teresa

Semi-enclosed, monastic, contemplative, Carmelite community for women in the tradition of Teresa of Avila and John of the Cross. The community also includes vowed Oblates. Associates are Christian men and women. Life of prayer, silence and solitude lived within community, 123 Little New York Road, Rising Sun, MD. 410-658-6736, STIPerk@gmail.com. http://www.ecst.ang-md.org

Order of St Anne—Bethany

A religious community for women and a ministry of hospitality and community service within the Bethany Convent and Bethany House of Prayer. Sr Ana Clara OSA *Superior* 25 Hillside Ave Arlington MA 02476 (781) 643-0921 *E-mail:* bethanyconvent@aol.com.

Order of St Anne—Chicago

The Order of St Anne's Chicago is a traditional order of Anglican nuns in the Episcopal Church. Since 1921, we have been an active presence in the heart of the city of Chicago. Currently we are called to parish work at the Episcopal Church of the Ascension, and active ministry to the local community. Sr Judith Marie OSA Superior 1125 N LaSalle Blvd Chicago IL 60610 (312) 642-3638 *E-mail:* stannechicago@hotmail.com.

Order of St Helena

A religious community for women dedicated to prayer, community and service. *Leadership Council* The Rev Sr Carol Andrew OSH, Sr Mary Lois OSH, The Rev Sr Ellen Francis OSH. Convent of St Helena 414 Savannah Barony Drive, North Augusta, SC 29841 *E-mail:* sisters@osh.org *Web:* www.osh.org.

Sisterhood of the Holy Nativity

Special dedication to the Incarnation. Religious Order with strong emphasis on life of prayer in community. External ministries are evangelistic in nature and take many forms. Mother House W14164 Plante Dr Ripon WI 54971 (920) 748-5332 *Mother Sup* Sr Abigail *E-mail:* abizac50@hotmail.com *Web*: caroa.net/sites/sisterhoodhn/.

Society of St Margaret

Mission focused Sisters living an ancient tradition with a modern outlook. We were founded in 1855 in East Grinstead, England, by The Rev John Mason Neale. The American House was established in Boston in 1873. Sr Adele Marie SSM *Superior*; St Margaret's Convent PO Box C (50 Harden Hill Rd) Duxbury MA 02331 (781) 934-9477 *E-mail:* sisters@ssmbos.org *Web:* www.ssmbos.org. *Dependencies:* Boston House for Urban Ministry, Dorchester MA; St Margaret's Convent Port-au-Prince HAITI; Sisters of St Margaret Neale House 50 Fulton New York NY 10038.

OTHER CHRISTIAN COMMUNITIES

Anamchara Fellowship

Founded in 2003, Anamchara Fellowship is a dispersed community, open to men and women: single, married and partnered. Dedicated to the Holy Trinity, members use "Celtic Daily Prayer" as part of their daily round of prayer. Members take vows of Simplicity, Fidelity and Obedience and must be approved by their ecclesial authority where they live in order to become part of the Fellowship. Our focus of ministry is pastoral care, catechesis and spiritual direction and we seek to provide these to our parishes and dioceses from which we come. We seek to be guided by our charisms of generosity, hospitality, compassion and love; and the inspiration of the Celtic saints. As a form of the "New Monasticism," Anamchara Fellowship seeks to bridge the gap between the traditional spirit of monastic community and the spirit of the emerging church. For further information view our website: www.anamcharafellowship.org or contact: Sister Barbara Clare at bconroy2207@gmail.com.

Anglican Order of Preachers

The Anglican Order of Preachers (also known as the Dominicans) traces its heritage back to Saint Dominic de Guzman in the thirteenth century. The Order is committed to the proclamation of the Gospel of Jesus Christ, especially through preaching and teaching, as well as other mediums; including, but not limited to scholarship, writing, the arts, and social justice witness. Anglican Dominicans may be celibate or married, lay or ordained, male or female. They take vows of simplicity, purity, and obedience. You can learn more about the Order at http://www.anglicandominicans.com/

Brotherhood of St Gregory

Open to Anglican men, clergy and lay, without regard to marital status, living under a common Rule and serving the Church on parochial, diocesan and national levels. The brothers live individually, in small groups, or with their families, and support the Community's activities from their secular or church-related employment. Inquiries? Please visit our website: www.gregorians.org.

Community of Celebration

Residential community of men/women, lay/clergy, married/single shares common life undergirded by Daily Prayer Book Offices, weekly Eucharist, Taize worship April-October. Members take Benedictine vows of stability, obedience, and conversion of life. Ministry is to be a Christian presence among the poor, to offer hospitality, retreats, sabbaticals, and conferences. Internships and Companion relationships welcome. Bill Farra Guardian Box 309 Aliquippa PA 15001 (724) 375-1510. *E-mail:* mail@communityofcelebration.com *Web:* www.communityofcelebration.com.

Community of the Gospel

We are a non-residential community, open to men and women, single, married and partnered. Dedicated to living the Gospel message through the vows of Daily Prayer, Reflective Study, and

Personal Service, these common roots lead to unique responses to God's love in our lives. Each member develops his or her own Personal Rule of Life based on these vows, and is encouraged to assemble a local spiritual direction network. For more information visit our website at www.communityofthegospel.org or contact Br Daniel-Joseph, Guardian, at N4028 Morgan Dr Waupaca WI 54981 or *E-mail:* brdanjoe@gmail.com

Order of the Community of the Paraclete

Serving since 1971. The Paracletians are men and women, single or married, leading a life of prayer and ministry under a rule and vows. Our work is to bring wholeness to those who need healing in spirit, mind, and body, through the power of the Holy Spirit. Our work is done in three states: AZ, FL, and WA. *Contact:* Min Br Marvin D. Taylor, St Dunstan's Church 722 N 145th St Shoreline WA 98133 *Web:* www.theparacletians.org. *Bishop Visitor:* Bavi Rivera.

Companions of St Luke, OSB

Companions of St Luke OSB is a community founded on the Rule of St Benedict. The Community honors the richness of its tradition, yet knows that each age needs to bring innovation to its history and practice. CSL-OSB is a dispersed community with each member living the Benedictine experience within the context of our parishes and the world. The members of the community live into the Rule of St. Benedict with daily prayer, Lectio Divina, contemplation, study of scripture and the Rule. The Companions of St. Luke, OSB is open to single and partnered persons, lay or ordained. Vocations include Vowed life and Oblation with respective vows and promises made of obedience, conversion of life and stability. For more information visit our website at http://www.csl-osb.org/ or contact us at csl91.membership@gmail.com. *Superior:* Br. Basil Edwards, OSB. *Bishop Visitor:* The Right Reverend R. William Franklin.

Congregation of the Companions of the Holy Saviour

Celibate male bishops, priests, deacons, and cand for H Orders. Founded 1891. Common Rule, but not in community. All attend annual Chapter and retreat. Rule for Priests' Assoc and Lay men and women, monthly area conferences. *Contact:* Fr Justin A Falciani Christ Episcopal Church Box 97 157 Shore Rd Somers Point NJ 08244 (609) 927-6262. *E-mail:* ccsprector@Verizon.net.

The Little Sisters of St. Clare, A Franciscan Women's Community

The Little Sisters of St. Clare is a Community of women who seek to live a contemplative life of prayer, study, and service, in the tradition of St. Clare and St. Francis. As a Community, our beliefs are seen in our actions, in worship, and in our commitment to a common life. We gather monthly, most typically in small chapters located throughout the greater Puget Sound area of Western Washington. We serve a variety of local and global ministries – guiding children and youth, serving the poor, the ill, and the marginalized; nurturing the environment; and healing the other. We have been recognized by The Episcopal Church's House of Bishops since 2002. As individuals, our faith is rooted in our baptismal covenant; we express our response to God's call in a lifestyle which interprets monastic traditions in a contemporary way. We guide our lives by the simple vows of simplicity, fidelity, and purity. We live independently, valuing our proximity to each other, and are single, married and in committed relationships. *Mother Guardian: Brigid Kaufmann, 400* NW Gilman Blvd. #2511 Issaquah, WA 98027. *Email:* lsscmotherguardian@gmail.com *Web:* http://stclarelittlesisters.org

Order of the Ascension

The Order of the Ascension is a dispersed community open to both clergy and laity whose vocations provide opportunities to shape parish life. OA has helped ground and center its members in their daily life and their roles as parish leaders and developers since its founding in 1983. Members take a Promise to seek the presence of Jesus Christ in the people, things and circumstances of life through stability, obedience and conversion of life. The charism of OA is the development of parish churches grounded in Anglican pastoral and ascetical theology, especially Benedictine spirituality. We also draw on the fields of organization development and organizational psychology in our work, which includes published materials to support parish development. New members engage a multi-year formation process after the first taking of the Promise. For more information, visit http://www.orderoftheascension.org/ or contact the *Presiding Sister* directly: Michelle Heyne, OA, michelleheyne@gmail.com. *Episcopal Visitor:* The Rt. Rev. Barry Howe.

Order of Saint Anthony the Great

The intent of the Order is to foster a contemplative spiritual life within the laity and clergy of the Church. We do so through intentional community and weekly classes open to all. We are a community open to men and women, celibate and coupled, in residence and dispersed that live under the vows of stability, constancy, simplicity, and obedience. We currently hold meetings each week in our two Chapter Houses in Atlanta, GA and Houston, TX. We are under the supervision of The Rt. Rev Dorsey Henderson, retired Bishop of Upper South Carolina, Bishop Visitor to the Order. *Abbot* Br. Kenneth Hosley, O.P.C. currently leads our community. You can find out more about the order at www.ordersaintanthony.org, or reach out to Br. Hosley at br.kenneth@gmail.com.

Rivendell Community, The

Rivendell is a Eucharistic community working and praying to hold the vision of the Church as a holy priesthood in and on behalf of the world, loving God "in all things and above all things." The Community's interests include creating and serving houses of prayer and hospitality, participating in ministries of parish leadership, spiritual life, and social justice; and providing priestly ministry for smaller, less affluent churches. Members include women and men, married/partnered and single/celibate, ordained and lay. All follow a common Rule which sustains and nourishes us for contemplative lives in our diverse active ministries. The Rivendell Community PO Box 43 Bolivar MO 65613 (316) 323-3961 *E-mail:* rivendellcommunity.inc@gmail.com *Guardian Barbara Click.*

Sisters of Saint Gregory

A religious community of women in the Episcopal Church who have discerned a call to the religious life. Founded in 1987 as a companion order by the Brotherhood of St Gregory, we became autonomous in 1999. We are clergy and lay, without regard to marital status, living dispersed in the world under a common rule as women of prayer and serving the Church on parochial, diocesan, and national levels. The sisters support the community's activities by their secular or church-related employment. All women eighteen years of age and older who are discerning a vocation to the religious life and who are in good standing with the Episcopal or a sister church are welcome to inquire. *Inquiries:* The Rev. Connie Jo McCarroll, SSG, (937) 698-0004, conniejodo@cs.com. Web: www.sistersofsaintgregory.org.

Society of St Anna the Prophet, The (SSAP)

The SSAP is a dispersed vowed community of women, both lay and ordained, called to Godly aging and to ministry with elders and with children. The vows are simplicity, creativity and balance. The SSAP is open to any woman over 50 years old, confirmed in the Episcopal Church, whose vocation to this prophetic life and ministry is discerned. Vows are taken after a minimum of one provisional year and one novice year. Life vows may be taken after five years. The SSAP includes elders living in care, as well as working and retired elders living independently. Annas are single, married, widowed, and partnered. Founded in the Diocese of Atlanta, the Society is beginning to expand into other areas. Those interested may visit the website at annasisters.org or write the Director of Provisionals and Novices, the Rev. Mary Moore SSAP, Chapter House 1655 Rainier Falls Drive NE Atlanta GA 30329-4107.

Worker Brothers of the Holy Spirit, The

International Covenant Community for Lay Brothers, Lay Workers and Clergy regardless of marital status. Life commitment to common Rule, Benedictine in orientation but not lived in Community. From a Contemplative model of prayer, meditation, worship, the Eucharist and a focus on the Theology concept of being and the Fruit of the Spirit, come the action of miss and ministry in the local parish, church, and world. For contacts, see Worker Sisters of the Holy Spirit, below *Web:* www.workerbrothers.org.

Worker Sisters of the Holy Spirit, The

International Covenant Community for Lay Sisters, Lay Workers, and Clergy regardless of marital status. Life Commitment to common Rule, Benedictine in orientation but not lived in Community. From a Contemplative model of prayer, meditation, worship, the Eucharist, and a focus on the Theology concept of being and the Fruit of Spirit, come the action of miss and ministry in the local parish, church, and world. *Co-Directors* Sr Christine WSHS & Sr Deborah WSHS *US Dir* Sr Christine WSHS 528 First St Windsor CO 80550 *E-mail:* casturges@msn.com *Canada Dir* Sr Deborah WSHS 711 McMurtry Rd Midland Ontario L4R 0B9 CANA DA *E-mail:* strdeborah@hotmail.com *Web:* www.workersisters.org.

PREVIOUS BISHOPS OF THE DIOCESES, DISTRICTS, AND JURISDICTIONS

coadj: coadjutor, const: constituted, dio: diocesan, m: missionary, org: organized, suffr: suffragan

Anking (1910) Daniel T. Huntington 1912-40, Lloyd R Craighill 1940-49. Became Dio of Wan-Gan, H Catholic Church in China 1949.

Asheville Became Dio of WNC 1907.

Boise Became Idaho in 1907.

Central America and Panama Canal Zone (const 1919) Separated into Panama and the Canal Zone, and Central America 1956. See Panama and the Canal Zone.

Central America (const 1956) David E Richards 1957-67. Divided 1967 into 5 districts: CR, ES, Guat, Hond, Nic.

Central Brazil (const 1950) Louis C Melcher 1950-58, Edmund K Sherrill 1959-65. Now part of the Igreja Episcopal do Brasil.

Central Pennsylvania see Bethlehem and Harrisburg.

Central Philippines (const 1901) Chas H Brent 1901-18, Gouveneur F Mosher 1920-40, Robt F Wilner suffr 1936-56, Norman S Binsted 1942-57, Lyman C Ogilby suffr 1953 Bp 1956-67, Ed G Longid suffr 1963-71, CB Manguramas suffr 1969-71, Benito C Cabanban suffr 1957 Bp 1967-78, Manuel C Lumpias coad 1977 Bp 1978-90. Became part of the Province of the Philippines in 1990.

Costa Rica (const 1967) David E Richards 1967-68, Jose Antonio Ramos 1969-76. Became extra-provincial in 1976. Became part of the Province of Central America 1998.

Cuba (const 1901) Albion W Knight 1904-13, Hiram R Hulse 1915-38, Alexander H Blankingship 1939-61, Romualdo Gonzalez 1961-66. Became autonomous dio under metropolitan council in 1966.

Cuernavaca (const 1989) Jose Saucedo 1989-. Became part of the Church of the Province of Mexico 1994.

Dakota Separated into ND and SD in 1883.

Duluth (const 1895) James D Morrison 1897-1922, Granville G Bennett coadj 1920 Bp 1922-23, Benj T Kemerer coadj 1930 Bp 1933-43. Reunited with Minnesota 1944.

Eastern Diocese (org 1810) Alexander V Griswold 1811-43. Incl all of New England except CT. VT separated 1832, NH 1832, RI ME and MA 1843.

Eastern Oklahoma (const 1910) Theodore P Thurston 1911-19. Reunited with Oklahoma 1919.

El Salvador (const w/Bps in charge 1967-1992) Martin Barahona 1992-. Became part of the Province of Central America 1998.

Erie see Northwestern Pennsylvania.

Guatemala (const w/Bps in charge 1967-1981) Armando Guerra 1982-. Became part of the Province of Central America 1998.

Hankow (const 1910) James A Ingle 1902-03, Logan H Roots 1904-37, Alfred A Gilman suffr 1925 Bp 1937-48. Became part of H Catholic Church in China 1948.

Harrisburg (org 1904) James H Darlington 1905-30, Hunter Wyatt-Brown 1931-43, John T Heistand 1943-66, Earl M Honaman suffr 1956-69. *Renamed Central Pennsylvania in 1971.*

Honolulu see Hawaii.

Illinois see Chicago.

Kansas City see West Missouri.

Kearney see Platte.

Kyoto (const 1898) Sidney C Partridge 1900-11, Henry St G Tucker 1912-23, Shirley N Nichols 1926-40. Trans to H Catholic Church in Japan 1941.

Laramie see Platte.

Liberia (const 1851) John Payne 1851-71, John G Auer 1873-74, Chas C Pennick 1877-83, Samuel D Ferguson 1885-1916, Walter H Overs 1919-25, Theophilus M Gardiner suffr 1921-41, Robt E Campbell OHC 1925-36, Leopold Kroll 1936-45, Bravid W Harris 1945-64, Dillard H Brown Jr 1964-69, Geo D Browne 1970-82. Now part of the Province of West Africa.

Marquette see Northern Michigan.

Mexico (est 1879) Sergio Carranza-Gomez 1989. Became part of the Church of the Province of Mexico 1994.

Michigan City see Northern Indiana.

New Mexico and Southwest Texas see Rio Grande.

Nicaragua (const w/Bps in charge 1969-1985) Sturdie Downs 1985-. Became part of the Province of Central America 1998.

Niobrara (1871-83) see South Dakota.

North Central Philippines (const 1989) Artemio M Zabala 1989-90. Became part of the Province of the Philippines in 1990.

69

North Kwanto (org 1893 as No Tokyo, 1938 as No Kwanto) John McKim 1893-1935, Chas S Reifsnyder suff 1924 Bp 1935-41. Became part of the H Catholic Church of Japan.

North Texas Became Dio of Northwest Texas in 1958.

North Tokyo see North Kwanto.

Northern Mexico (const 1973) German Martinez-Marquez 1987-. Became part of the Church of the Province of Mexico 1994.

Northern New Jersey see Newark.

Northern Luzon (const 1986) Richard A Abellon 1986-90. Became part of the Province of the Philippines in 1990.

Northern Philippines (const 1972) Ed G Longid 1972-75, Richard A Abellon 1975-86, Robt LO Longid 1986-90. Became part of the Province of the Philippines in 1990.

Northern Texas see Dallas.

Northwest Diocese Jos C Talbot 1860-65.

Okinawa Edmond L Browning 1968-71. *Transferred to the Nippon Sei Ko Kai 1972.*

Oregon and Washington see Oregon. Washington separated 1880.

Panama (const 1919) James C Morris 1920-30, Harry Beal 1937-44, Reginald H Gooden 1945-72, Lemuel Barnett Shirley 1972-83, Victor Scantlebury suff 1991-94, James H Ottley 1984-95, Clarence Wallace Hayes Dewar 1995-. Became part of the Province of Central America 1998.

Platte, The (const 1889. Name changed to Laramie 1898, Kearney 1908, Western Nebraska 1913) Anson R Graves 1890-1910, Geo A Beecher 1910-43. Reunited with Nebraska 1946.

Puerto Rico (const 1902) James H Van Buren 1902-12, Manuel Ferrando suffr 1923-34, Chas B Colmore 1913-47, Chas F Boynton coadj 1944 Bp 1947-51, A Ervine Swift 1951-65, Francisco Reus-Froylan 1965-79. Became extra-provincial in 1980.

Sacramento see Northern California.

Salina see Western Kansas.

Salt Lake see Utah.

Shanghai Wm J Boone 1844-64, Channing M Williams 1866-74, Samuel IJ Schereschewsky 1877-83, Wm J Boone 1884-91, Fredk R Graves 1893-1937, John W Nichols suffr 1934-38, Wm P Roberts

1937-49. Became Dio of Kiangsu, H Catholic Church in China 1949.

South Florida (const 1892 as Southern Florida, 1922 as South Florida) Wm C Gray 1892-1913, Cameran Mann m 1913 dio 1922-32, John D Wing coadj 1925 Bp 1932-50, Martin J Bramm suffr 1951-56, Wm F Moses suffr 1956-61 Henry I Louttit suffr 1945 coadj 1948 dio 1951-69, James L Duncan suffr 1961-69, Wm L Hargrave suffr 1961-69. *South Florida divided into Central Fla., Southeast Fla. and Southwest Fla. 1969.*

Southern Brazil (est 1890 rec'd into American Church 1907) Lucien L Kinsolving 1907-28, Wm MM Thomas suffr 1925 Bp 1928-49, Louis C Melcher coadj 1948 Bp 1949-50, Athalicio T Pithan suffr 1940 Bp 1950-55, Egmont M Krischke 1955-65. Now part of Igreja Episcopal do Brasil.

Southern Philippines (const 1972) CB Manguramas 1972-84. Narcisco V Ticobay 1986-90. Became part of the Province of the Philippines in 1990.

Southwest Temporary mission jurisdiction 1859-65.

Southwest Texas Included in New Mexico and Southwest Texas since 1895.

Southwestern Brazil Egmont M Krischke 1950-55, Plinio L Simoes 1956-65. Now part of Igreja Episcopal do Brasil.

Southwestern Mexico (const 1989) Claro Huerto-Ramos 1989-. Became part of the Church of the Province of Mexico 1994.

Tohoku (const 1920) Norman S Binsted 1928-41. Transferred to the Holy Catholic Church in Japan 1941.

Washington Territory see Olympia.

Western Colorado (const 1892) Wm M Baker 1894-94, admin by Abiel Leonard 1894-1903, part of Salt Lake 1904-07, recreated 1907, Edward J Knight 1907-08, Benj Brewster 1909-16, Frank H Touret 1917-19. Reunited with Colorado 1919.

Western Mexico (const 1973) Samuel Espinoza 1983-. Became part of the Church of the Province of Mexico 1994.

Western Nebraska see Platte.

Western Texas see West Texas.

Wisconsin see Milwaukee.

Diocesan and Parochial Lists

FOR QUICK REFERENCE, some words have been abbreviated. Please see lists of abbreviations on pages 7, 8, and 9 and at the beginning of some sections.

ADDRESSES OF THE CLERGY may be found in the alphabetical Clergy List in the last section of the *Annual*. Please send Clergy List changes to The Editor of Directories, Church Publishing, 445 Fifth Ave, New York, NY 10016.

CHURCH LISTINGS follow this order:

1 *Official postal name of city*
2 *Name of church*
3 *Type of church (capital letter in bold face):*
   P = parish
   M = mission
   PS = preaching station
   CC = college chapel
   SC = summer chapel
   HC = historical church
   NH = nursing home
   PM = prison ministry
   I = Inactive
   O = Other
4 *Number of communicants in good standing* Actual numbers shown reflect information from the 2008 Parochial Report provided by Congregational Research and the Office of the General Convention, Episcopal Church Center. Information from the 2009 Report will be uploaded to www.theredbook.org in Fall 2010.
5 " **§** " designates a *Parish Day School.*
6 *St Address*
7 *Zip Code*
8 *Alternate mailing address* if applicable
9 *City* (if applicable) and *church*, if city has more than one, of which the church is a mission, or whose clergy serve the mission.
10 *Members of the Clergy.*
11 *Parish Telephone Number*

EXAMPLES

```
     1        2    3  4  5      6
     |        |    |  |  |      |
Westbury  Advent  P (726) § 505 Second St
11590 (PO Box 115) JH Krantz (516) 333-0081
     |          |           |           |
     7          8           10          11
```

Church of the Advent is a parish in the city of Westbury, has 726 communicants and a Parish Day School. It is located at 505 Second St with a mailing address of PO Box 115 11590. Its clergy is the Rev J.H. Krantz, and the phone number is (516) 333-0081.

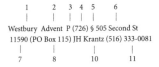

```
     1      2    3   4    6         7       9
     |      |    |   |    |         |       |
Irvington S Paul M (54) 264 E Main St 36544 S Lk Mobile
```

St. Paul's Church is a mission in the city of Irvington, has 54 communicants, and is located at 264 E. Main St. which is also its mailing address. It is either a mission of St. Luke's Church in Mobile, which has more than one church, or is a diocesan mission served by the clergy of St. Luke's.

✠ at beginning of an entry indicates Cathedral or Pro-Cathedral.

PARISH DAY SCHOOLS. Parishes with day schools (above nursery or kindergarten level) are identified by the symbol **§** . For more information, write directly to the parish or to The National Association of Episcopal Schools, 815 2nd Ave New York NY 10017 (800) 334-7626 x6134 for the *Directory of Episcopal Church Schools.*

NON-PAROCHIAL CLERGY. The list includes retired clergy as well as clergy engaged in a variety of ministries. Abbreviations include: ret (retired) dcn (deacon) chap (chaplain) ret Bp (retired Bishop) Dn (Dean) prof (professor) tchr (teacher) dio staff (diocesan staff).

To Make Additions or Corrections

Listings for congregations may be updated using CPG's Employee Roster.

Other corrections to diocesan information, information concerning organizations and the governing structures of the Church come from the dioceses, organizations themselves or from The Executive Council.

Please send Clergy List changes to the Recorder of Ordinations, 19 East 34th St, New York, NY 10016.

STATE OF ALABAMA
Dioceses of Alabama and Central Gulf Coast

DIOCESE OF ALABAMA
(PROVINCE IV)
Comprises northern and central counties in the state of Alabama
DIOCESAN OFFICE 521 N 20th St Birmingham AL 35203
TEL (205) 715-2060   FAX (205) 715-2066
E-MAIL diooffice@dioala.org   WEB www.dioala.org

Previous Bishops—
Nicholas H Cobbs 1844-61, Richard H Wilmer 1862-1900, Henry M Jackson asst 1891-1900, Robt W Barnwell 1900-02, Chas M Beckwith 1902-28, Wm G Mcdowell coadj 1922 Bp 1928-38, Chas CJ Carpenter 1938-68, Randolph R Claiborne Jr suffr 1949-53, Geo M Murray suffr 1953 coadj 1959 Bp 1969-70, Wm A Dimmick asst 1984, Furman C Stough 1971-88, Robt O Miller suffr 1986-88 Bp 1988-98, Henry Nutt Parsley Jr Bp Coad 1996-1998 Bp 1999-2011, Onell A Soto Asst 1999-01, Mark H Andrus suffr 2002-06, J McKee Sloan suffr 2008-12

Bishop—John McKee Sloan (1024) (Dio 7 Jan 12)

Staff Off Fin and Admin Rev RP Morpeth; *Staff Off Cler Trans & Min Dev* S Sartain; *Bookkeeper* J Cook; *Admin Asst to Bp Sloan* J Hall; *Lifelong Form Coord* K Graham; *Spec Events Coord* G Perrine; *Sawyerville Proj Dir* C Jones; *Sawyerville Proj Dev* C Cotton; *Yth Min Coord* B Fetner; *Comm Coord* Rev K Hudlow; *Archdcn* M Holmes

Officers: Sec Rev J Ford; *Treas* P Hall; *Asst Sec-Treas* R Morpeth; *Chanc* R Britton Esq

Stand Comm—Cler: L Shafer C Frazer J Poole A Keyse ; *Lay: Pres* B Edwards J Sanford K White

Council—Cler: D Gafford H Gardner P Pradat A Raulerson K Rengers J Osborne; *Lay:* S Harrison J McCormack M Sexton T Heflin J Boylan L Johnson P Slay R Gauld

PARISHES, MISSIONS, AND CLERGY

Alabaster Church of the Holy Spirit **P** (124) 858 Kent Dairy Road 35007-2027 (Mail to: PO Box 2365 35007-2027) William Blackerby Elton Wright (205) 621-3418

Albertville Christ Episcopal Church **P** (194) 607 E Main St 35950-2447 (Mail to: PO Box 493 35950-0008) (256) 878-3243

Alexander City St James Episcopal Church **P** (263) 347 S Central Ave 35010-2579 (Mail to: 347 S Central Ave 35010-2579) Robert St

Germain-Iler (256) 234-4752

Alpine Trinity Church **P** (26) 6898 Grist Mill Road 35014-0095 (Mail to: PO Box 95 35014-0095) (256) 378-8020

Anniston Grace Episcopal Church **HC** (352) 1000 Leighton Ave 36207-5702 (Mail to: PO Box 1791 36202-1791) (256) 236-4457

Anniston Church of St Michael & All Angels **P** (212) 1000 West 18th St 36201 (Mail to: PO Box 1884 36202-1884) (256) 237-4011

Athens St Timothys Episcopal Church **P** (97) § 207 E Washington St 35611-2651 (Mail to: 207 E Washington St 35611-2651) (256) 232-3541

Auburn Holy Trinity Episcopal Church **P** (925) § 100 Church Dr 36830-5903 (Mail to: 100 Church Dr 36830-5903) Geoffrey Evans Gail Goldsmith Hea Seales Hea Seales (334) 887-9506

Auburn St Dunstan Episcopal Church **CM** (198) 136 E Magnolia Ave 36830-4722 (Mail to: C/O Diocese Of Alabama 521 20th St 35203-2682) Hermon Lowery Norbert Wilson (334) 887-5657

Bessemer Trinity Episcopal Church **P** (61) 2014 Berkley Ave 35020-4236 (Mail to: PO Box 1563 35021-1563) Elton Wright (205) 966-3938

Birmingham All Saints Episcopal Church **P** (1683) § 110 W Hawthorne Rd 35209-3999 (Mail to: 110 W Hawthorne Rd 35209-3999) Glenda Curry Anna Russell Friedman Charles Youngson (205) 879-8651

Birmingham Birmingham Episcopal Campus Ministry **CC** 1170 11th Ave S 35205-5236 (Mail to: 1170 11th Ave S 35205-5236) (205) 320-1500

Birmingham Church of the Ascension **P** (520) § 1912 Canyon Rd 35216-1753 (Mail to: 1912 Canyon Rd 35216-1799) John Alvey (205) 822-3480

Birmingham Grace Episcopal Church **P** (196) 5712 1st Ave 35212-1604 (Mail to: 5712 1st Ave 35212-1604) Robyn Arnold Martha Holmes Joseph Knott Jonathan Waddell (205) 595-4636

Birmingham St Andrews Parish **P** (255) 1024 12th St S 35205-5234 (Mail to: 1024 12th St S 35205-5234) Maurice Goldsmith Tommie Watkins (205) 251-7898

Birmingham St Lukes Episcopal Church **P** (2778) § 3736 Montrose Rd 35213-3832 (Mail to: 3736 Montrose Rd 35213-3832) Rebecca Debow Maurice Goldsmith Maurice Goldsmith Christopher Nations Mary Sullivan Richmond Webster (205) 871-3583

Birmingham St Marks Episcopal Church **P** (58) 228 Dennison Ave Sw 35211-3803 (Mail to: 228 Dennison Ave SW 35211-3803) Jayne Pool (205) 322-8449

Birmingham St Marys on The Highlands Church **P** (1744) § 1910 12th Ave S 35205-3804 (Mail to: 1910 12th Ave S 35205-3804) Harry Gardner Jeremy Carlson Danielle Thompson (205) 933-1140

Birmingham Saint Stephens Episcopal Church **P** (1582) § 3775 Crosshaven Dr 35223-2832 (Mail to: 3775 Crosshaven Dr 35223-2832) John Burruss Maurice Goldsmith James McAdams Joy Phipps (205) 967-8786

Birmingham St Thomas Episcopal Parish **P** (355) 2870 Acton Rd 35243-2502 (Mail to: 2870 Acton Rd 35243-2502) Josiah Rengers (205) 969-2700

Birmingham The Abbey **Ministry** 131a 41st St S 35222-1930 (Mail to: 131a 41st St S 35222-1930) (205) 703-9538

✣ **Birmingham** Cathedral Church of the Advent **O** (3690) § Attn Bryan Helm 2017 6th Ave 35203-2701 (Mail to: C/O Bryan Helm 2017 6th Ave 35203-2701) Deborah Hill Andrew Pearson Matthew Schneider Richard Smalley (205) 251-2324

Boligee Saint Mark's Episcopal Church **P** (5) Rr 1 Box 10 35443-9798 (Mail to: Rr 1 Box 10 35443-9801) (205) 372-4071

Carlowville St Pauls Church Carlowville **P** (24) 310 County Rd 4 36761-3626 (Mail to: PO Box 27 36761-0027) (334) 872-3674

Chelsea St. Catherine's Episcopal Church **P** (99) 4163 County Rd 39 35043-6713 (Mail to: PO Box 577 35043-0577) Eric Mancil (205) 618-8367

Childersburg St Mary Episcopal Church **P** (34) 5th Ave & 5th St 35044 (Mail to: PO Box 303 35044-0303) Frank Young (256) 378-8020

Clanton Trinity Episcopal Church **P** (80) 503 Second Avenue South 35046-2121 (Mail to: PO Box 2121 35046-2121) (205) 755-3339

Cullman Grace Episcopal Church **P** (298) 305 Arnold St Ne 35055-2910 (Mail to: 305 Arnold St NE 35055-2910) James Gardner (256) 734-6212

Decatur Church of the Good Shepherd **P** (98) 3809 Spring Ave Sw 35603-3203 (Mail to: 3809 Spring Ave SW 35603-3203) (256) 351-9955

Decatur St Johns Episcopal Church **P** (606) 202 Gordon Dr Se 35601-2528 (Mail to: 202 Gordon Dr SE 35601-2528) Francis Crittenden John Olson (256) 353-9615

Demopolis Trinity Episcopal Church **HC** (166) 401 Main Ave 36732-2019 (Mail to: PO Box 560 36732-0560) John Barnes (334) 289-3363

Eutaw St Stephens Church **P** (93) 403 Norht Eutaw Ave 35462-0839 (Mail to: PO Box 839 35462-0839) James Vaughn (205) 301-0483

Fairfield Christ Episcopal Church **P** (92) 4912 Richard M Scrushy Pkwy 35064-1456 (Mail to: PO Box 424 35064-0424) (205) 787-2053

Faunsdale St Michael/Holy Cross Episcopal Chur **P** (27) 45 Watkins St 36738 (Mail to: C/O Nancy Terry PO Box 507 36786) (334) 289-3363

Fayette St Michaels Episcopal Church **P** (87) 431 10th St NW 35555-1834 (Mail to: 431 10th St NW 35555-1834) Richelle Thompson (205) 932-6929

Florence Saint Bartholomew's Episcopal Church **P** (86) 1900 Darby Dr 35630-2625 (Mail to: 1900 Darby Dr 35630-2625) Wilbur Eich Danny Whitehead (256) 764-2000

Florence Trinity Episcopal Church **P** (660) 410 Pine St 35630-4655 (Mail to: 410 Pine St 35630-4655) Andrew Keyse Callie Plunket-Brewton (256) 764-6149

Forkland St Johns in the Prairie Episcopal Ch **P** (12) A L Issac Rd 36740-4216 (Mail to: PO Box 839 35462-0839) James Vaughn (205) 289-0399

Fort Payne St Philip's Episcopal Church **P** (78) 2813 Godfrey Ave Ne 35967-3746 (Mail to: 2813 Godfrey Ave NE 35967-3746) William Bender Forrest Ethridge (256) 845-1192

Gadsden Church of the Holy Comforter **P** (417) 156 S 9th St 35901-3646 (Mail to: 156 S 9th St 35901-3646) Carl Saxton (256) 547-5361

Gainesville St Alban's Church **P** (4) 290 Chestnut St 35459 (Mail to: C/O Mr William B Stuart PO Box 844 35470-0844) Richard Losch (205) 652-4210

Greensboro St Pauls Episcopal Church **HC** (81) 905 Church St 36744-1520 (Mail to: 905 Church St 36744-1520) John Kennedy (334) 624-8866

Guntersville Church of the Epiphany **P** (427) 1101 Sunset Dr 35976-1003 (Mail to: PO Box 116 35976-0116) Aaron Raulerson (256) 582-4897

Hartselle St Barnabas Episcopal Church **P** (43) 1450 Sparkman St Nw 35640-4534 (Mail to: PO Box 614 35640-0614) Elvin Basinger (256) 773-4206

Heflin Church of the Messiah **P** (62) Corner Of Lake View & Vaughn 36264 (Mail to: PO Box 596 36264-0596) John Bagby John Bagby (256) 463-2928

Hoover St Albans Episcopal Church **P** (169) 429 Cloudland Dr 35226-1100 (Mail to: 429 Cloudland Dr 35226-1100) Margaret Doyle (205) 822-2330

Hoover Church of the Holy Apostles **P** (350) 424 Emery Dr 35244-4548 (Mail to: 424 Emery Dr 35244-4548) Blake Hutson Mose Stuart (205) 988-8000

Huntsville Church of the Nativity **P** (1786) 208 Eustis Ave Se 35801-4233 (Mail to: 208 Eustis Ave SE 35801-4293) Thomas Goldsmith Virginia Monroe Robert Serio (256) 533-2455

Huntsville Holy Cross-St Christopher's **P** (27) 3740 Meridian St 35811-1116 (Mail to: 3740 Meridian St 35811-1116) (256) 534-7750

Huntsville Saint Stephen's Episcopal Church **P** (359) § 8020 Whitesburg Dr Se 35802-3002 (Mail to: 8020 Whitesburg Dr Se 35802-3002) Jeffrey Evans (256) 881-7223

Huntsville St Thomas Episcopal Church **P** (693) 12200 Bailey Cove Rd Se 35803-2641 (Mail to: 12200 Bailey Cove Rd SE 35803-2641) David Drachlis Katherine Harper Paul Pradat (256) 880-0247

Indian Springs St Francis of Assisi Church **P** (216) 3545 Cahaba Valley Rd 35124-3527 (Mail to: 3545 Cahaba Valley Rd 35124-3527) Corey Jones Donald Owen (205) 715-2060

Jacksonville St Lukes Church **P** (151) 400 Chinabee Ave Se 36265-2810 (Mail to: Attn Penn G Wilson PO Box 55 36265-0055) Robert Fowler (256) 435-9271

Jasper St Marys Church **P** (135) 801 The Trce W 35504-7454 (Mail to: 801 The Trce W 35504-7454) Robin Hinkle (205) 387-7746

Leeds Church of the Epiphany **P** (237) 1338 Montevallo Road 35094-2472 (Mail to: 1338 Montevallo Rd 35094-2472) Monica Carlson (205) 699-2404

Livingston St James Church **P** (25) C/O T Raiford Noland 109 Spring 35470 (Mail to: C/O T Raiford Noland Station Two L U 35470) (205) 652-7462

Lowndesboro St Pauls Episcopal Church **P** (59) § 164 Broad St 36752-3002 (Mail to: PO Box 216 36752-0216) Joseph Knight

Madison St Matthews Episcopal Church **P** (682) 786 Hughes Rd 35758-8972 (Mail to: 786 Hughes Rd 35758-8972) Chris Hartley (250) 864-0788

Marion St Wilfrids Episcopal Church **P** (93) 104 Clements St 36756-1806 (Mail to: PO Box 43 36756-0043) (334) 683-9628

Mentone St Josephs on the Mountain Church **P** (78) 21145 Scenic Hwy 35984 (Mail to: PO Box 161 35984-0161) William Winters (256) 634-4476

Millbrook St Michael and All Angels Church **P** (172) 5941 Robinson Sprin 36054 (Mail to: PO Box 586 36054-0012) Mark Waldo (334) 285-3905

Montevallo St Andrews Episcopal Church **P** (40) 925 Plowman St 35115-3809 (Mail to: 925 Plowman St 35115-3809) Judy Quick Stephen Shanks (205) 665-1667

Montgomery All Saints Episcopal Church **P** (264) 645 Coliseum Blvd 36109-1240 (Mail to: PO Box 3073 36109-0073) David Peeples (334) 272-2591

Montgomery Church of the Ascension **P** (699) § 315 Clanton Ave 36104-5541 (Mail to: 315 Clanton Ave 36104-5541) Candice Frazer Mark Waldo (334) 263-5529

Montgomery Church of the Holy Comforter **P** (251) 2911 Woodley Rd 36111-2842 (Mail to: 2911 Woodley Rd 36111-2898) Jay Croft Rosa Lindahl (334) 281-1337

Montgomery Church of the Good Shepherd **P** (27) 493 S Jackson St 36104-4749 (Mail to: 493 S Jackson St 36104-4749) Elizabeth Powell (334) 834-9280

Montgomery St Johns Episcopal Church **P** (1389) 113 Madison Ave 36104-3623 (Mail to: 113 Madison Ave 36104-3623) Robert Wisnewski Deonna Neal Jamie Osborne (334) 262-1937

✠ **Nauvoo** Chapel of the Ascension **O** 105 Delong Rd 35578 (Mail to: 105 Delong Rd 35578-6550) Mark Johnston (205) 387-1806

Oneonta Calvary Church **P** (38) 1002 Park Ave 35121-0010 (Mail to: PO Box 821 35121-0010) Joan Henrick (205) 274-9444

Opelika Emmanuel Episcopal Church **P** (24) 800 1st AVE 36801-4346 (Mail to: PO Box 2332 36803-2332) (334) 745-2054

Pell City St Simon Peter Church **P** (146) 3702 Mays Bend Rd 35128 (Mail to: PO Box 432 35125-0432) Mollie Roberts (205) 884-0877

Pike Road Grace Episcopal Church **P** (150) 906 Pike Road 36064 (Mail to: PO Box 640096 36064-0096) Martin Bagay Nathaniel Darville (334) 215-1422

Prattville St Marks Episcopal Church **P** (255) 178 E 4th St 36067-3110 (Mail to: 178 E 4th St 36067-3110) Scott Arnold (334) 365-5289

Rainbow City Church of the Resurrection **P** (208) 113 Brown Ave 35906-3122 (Mail to: 113 Brown Ave 35906-3122) Thomas Goldsmith (256) 442-6862

Roanoke St Barnabas Episcopal Church **P** (53) 809 Rock Mills Rd 36274-5347 (Mail to: Attn J Schuessler 266 Guy St 36274-1629) (334) 863-6021

Scottsboro St Lukes Church **P** (275) 402 S Scott St 35768-1935 (Mail to: 402 S Scott St 35768-1935) (256) 574-6216

Seale St Matthews in the Pines **P** (24) 38 Longview Ct 36875-3716 (Mail to: PO Box 221 36875-0221) Donna Gafford (706) 366-6568

Selma St Pauls Episcopal Church **P** (404) 210 Lauderdale St 36701-4521 (Mail to: PO Box 1306 36702-1306) Joseph Knight (334) 874-8421

Sheffield Grace Episcopal Church **P** (293) 103 Darby Ave 35660-1505 (Mail to: PO Box 838 35660-0838) Donald Smith (256) 383-2014

Smiths Station St Stephens Episcopal Church **P** (117) 45 Lee County Road 567 36877-3285 (Mail to: 45 Lee Road 567 36877-3285) (334) 291-0750

Sylacauga St Andrews Episcopal Church **P** (53) § 10 W Walnut St 35150-3312 (Mail to: Atten

Ronald Webster 55 Skyline Dr 35044-1133) Frank Young (256) 249-2411

Talladega St Peters Episcopal Church **P** (189) 208 North St E 35160-2110 (Mail to: PO Box 206 208 E North Street 35161-0206) (256) 362-2505

Tallassee Church of the Epiphany **P** (54) 2602 Gilmer Ave 36078-7212 (Mail to: 2602 Gilmer Ave 36078-7212) (334) 252-8618

Trussville Church of the Holy Cross **P** (224) 90 Parkway Dr 35173-1318 (Mail to: 90 Parkway Dr 35173-1318) Wesley Sharp (205) 655-7668

Tuscaloosa Canterbury Chapel and College Center **P** (447) 812 5th Ave 35401-1206 (Mail to: 812 5th Ave 35401-1206) William Burnette (205) 345-9590

Tuscaloosa Christ Church **P** (1334) 605 Lurleen B Wallace Blvd 35401-1712 (Mail to: 605 Lurleen

B Wallace Blvd 35401-1712) David Meginniss Catherine Collier (205) 758-4252

Tuscaloosa Saint Matthias Episcopal Church **P** (150) 2310 Skyland Blvd E 35405-4327 (Mail to: 2310 Skyland Blvd E 35405-4327) David Hall (205) 553-7282

Tuskegee Institute St Andrews Episcopal Church **P** (75) 701 W Montgomery Rd 36088-1913 (Mail to: PO Box 1213 36087-1213) (334) 727-3210

Uniontown St Michaels/Holy Cross **P** Franklin Street 36786 (Mail to: 515 County Rd 54 36738-3310) (334) 289-3363

Wetumpka Trinity Episcopal Church **P** (272) 5371 US Highway 231 36092-3168 (Mail to: 5375 US Highway 231 36092-3168) Robert Henderson (334) 567-7534

DIOCESE OF ALASKA
(PROVINCE VIII)
Comprises the State of Alaska
DIOCESAN OFFICE 1205 Denali Way Fairbanks AK 99701-4178
TEL (907) 452-3040   FAX (907) 456-6552
WEB www.episcopalak.org

Previous Bishops— Peter T Rowe 1895-1942, John B Bentley suffr 1931 Bp 1943-48, Wm J Gordon Jr 1948-74, David R Cochran 1974-81, George C Harris 1981-91, Steven Charleston 1991-1996, Mark L McDonald 1997-2008, Rustin Kimsey asst

Bishop—Rt Rev Mark Lattime (1050) (Dio 4 Sept 2010)

Bps Sec M Corbett; *Cn for Fin and Adm* S Krull; *Asst Fin and Admin* L Winfrey; *Treas* M Duggar; *Chanc* E Wohlforth; *V Chanc* S Stanley; *Hunger* vacant; *UTO* vacant; *Safe Church* Rev K Hunt

Stand Comm—Cler: *Pres* A Whitney *VPres* C Malseed B Titus M Norton; *Lay:* P Fisher D Hall L Adams M Vent B Coghill

PARISHES, MISSIONS, AND CLERGY

Allakaket St Johns in the Wilderness Episcopal **M** (131) General Delivery 99720-9999 (Mail to: General Delivery 99720-9999) (907) 968-2240

Anchorage All Saints Episcopal Church **P** (252) 545 W 8th Ave 99501-3517 (Mail to: PO Box 100686 99510-0686) David Terwilliger David Terwilliger (907) 279-3924

Anchorage Christ Church Episcopal **P** (89) 5101 O'Malley Rd 99507-6850 (Mail to: PO Box

111963 99511-1963) Katherine Hunt Gail Loken (907) 345-7914

Anchorage St Christophers Church **P** (66) 7208 Duben Ave 99504-1321 (Mail to: PO Box 211896 99521-1896) (907) 333-5010

Anchorage St Marys Episcopal Church **P** (1016) § 2222 E Tudor Rd 99507-1072 (Mail to: 2222 E Tudor Rd 99507-1300) Michael Burke Dawn Allen-Herron Sara Gavit Judith Lethin Gayle Nauska Robert Thwing (907) 563-3341

Anvik Christ Episcopal Church **M** (89) PO Box 138 99558-0138 (Mail to: PO Box 103 99558-0103) (907) 663-6343

Arctic Vlg Bishop Rowe Chapel **M** (141) General Delivery 99722-9999 (Mail to: General Delivery 99722-9999) (907) 587-5320

Beaver St Matthews Episcopal Church **M** (92) C St 99724 (Mail to: PO Box 24009 99724-0009) (907) 628-6114

Chalkyitsik St Timothys Episcopal Church **M** (79) PO Box 54 99788-0054 (Mail to: PO Box 54 99788-0054) (907) 848-8211

Circle Holy Trinity Episcopal Church **M** (82) No Street Identified 99733 (Mail to: 1205 Denali Way 99701-4137) (907) 457-8823

Cordova St Georges Episcopal Church **P** (52) 100 Lake Ave 99574 (Mail to: PO Box 849 99574-0849) Margaret Mickelson (907) 424-5143

Eagle St Johns Episcopal Church **M** (21) PO Box 17 99738-0017 (Mail to: 1205 Denali Way 99701-4137) (907) 547-2226

Eagle River Holy Spirit Episcopal Church **P** (167) 17545 Eagle River Loop Rd 99577 (Mail to: PO Box 773223 99577-3223) Betty Lou Elmer-Anthony (907) 694-8201

Fairbanks Chapel of Alaska Saints **Chapel** 1205 Denali Way 99701-4137 (Mail to: 1205 Denali Way 99701-4137) (907) 452-3040

Fairbanks St Matthews Church **P** (1235) § 1029 First Ave 99701 (Mail to: 1030 2nd Ave 99701-4300) John David Charles Davis Betty Glover Shirley Lee Bella Savino Montie Slusher (907) 456-5235

Fort Yukon St Stephens Episcopal Church **M** (291) No Street Address 99740 (Mail to: PO Box 289 99740-0289) Teresa Thomas (907) 662-7556

Fort Yukon St Peters Episcopal Church **M** (24) PO Box KBC 99740 (Mail to: 1205 Denali Way 99701-4137) (907) 662-2383

Grayling St Pauls Episcopal Church **M** (259) General Delivery 99590-9999 (Mail to: General Delivery 99590-9999) (907) 453-5128

Haines St Michael & All Angels **P** (69) 1.5 Mile Haines Hwy 99827-1236 (Mail to: PO Box 1236 99827-1236) Janice Hotze Janice Hotze (907) 766-3041

Homer St Augustines Episcopal Church **M** (16) 770 E End Rd 99603 (Mail to: PO Box 4274 99603-4274) (907) 235-1225

Hughes St Pauls Episcopal Church **M** (49) Front St 99745 (Mail to: 1205 Denali Way 99701-4137) (907) 889-2255

Huslia Good Shepherd Mission **M** (127) PO Box 78 99746-0078 (Mail to: PO Box 78 99746-0078) (907) 829-2233

Juneau St Brendans Episcopal Church **P** (113) 4207 Mendenhall Loop Rd 99801-9176 (Mail to: 4207 Mendenhall Loop Rd 99801-9176) Caroline Malseed (907) 789-5152

Juneau Church of the Holy Trinity **P** (187) 415 4th St 99801-1003 (Mail to: 415 4th St 99801-1003) Gordon Blue (907) 586-3532

Kenai St Francis by the Sea Church **P** (12) 110 S Spruce St 99611-7937 (Mail to: 110 S Spruce St 99611-7937) Marian Nickelson (907) 283-6040

Ketchikan Saint John's Church **P** (142) 503 Mission St 99901-6423 (Mail to: PO Box 23003 99901-8003) David Yaw Barbara Massenburg (907) 225-3680

Kivalina Kivalina Epiphany Church **M** (374) General Delivery 99750-9999 (Mail to: General Delivery 99750-9999) Jerry Norton (907) 645-2164

Kodiak St James the Fisherman Church **P** (103) 421 Thorsheim St 99615 (Mail to: PO Box 1668 99615-1668) Wallace Mills (907) 486-5276

Kotzebue St Georges in the Arctic **M** (46) 215 3rd Ave 99752-0269 (Mail to: PO Box 269 99752-0269) Kris Lethin (907) 442-2360

Minto St Barnabas Episcopal Church **M** (53) P.O. Box 58064 99758 (Mail to: PO Box 58041 99758-0041) (907) 798-7414

Nenana Saint Mark's Church **M** (129) Front & Market Sts 99760 (Mail to: PO Box 337 99760-0337) (907) 347-4115

Noatak Episcopal Congregation **PS** (10) General Delivery 99761 (Mail to: General Delivery 99761-9999)

North Pole St Judes Episcopal Church **PS** (50) 3408 Laurance Rd 99705-6705 (Mail to: PO Box 55458 99705-0458) John Holz (907) 488-9329

Palmer St Bartholomews Episcopal Church **P** (61) 323 Alaska St 99645-6233 (Mail to: 323 Alaska St 99645-6233) H Dean Mandrell (907) 745-3526

Petersburg St Andrews Episcopal Church **P** (23) PO Box 1815 99833-1815 (Mail to: 301 3rd St 99833-1815) Dawn Allen-Herron (907) 254-0526

Point Hope St Thomas Episcopal Church **M** (270) Natchiq St 99766 (Mail to: 1205 Denali Way 99701-4137) (907) 368-6200

Point Lay St Albans in the Arctic **M** (60) No Street Identified 99759 (Mail to: 1205 Denali Way 99701-4137) (907) 833-2623

Rampart Episcopal Congregation **PS** (53) General Delivery 99761 (Mail to: General Delivery 99767-9999) (907) 485-2144

Seward St Peters Episcopal Church **P** (37) 239 2nd Ave 99664 (Mail to: PO Box 676 99664-0676) Arthur Thomas (907) 224-3975

Shageluk St Lukes Episcopal Church **M** (131) General Delivery 99665-9999 (Mail to: General Delivery 99665-9999) (907) 473-8292

Sitka St Peters by the Sea **P** (226) 611 Lincoln St 99835-7647 (Mail to: PO Box 1130 99835-1130) Julie Platson (907) 747-3977

Skagway St Saviors Congregation **M** (2) No Street Identified 99840 (Mail to: PO Box 617 99840-0617) (907) 983-3868

Stevens Vlg St Andrews Episcopal Church **M** (48) General Delivery 99774-9999 (Mail to: 1205 Denali Way 99701-4137) (907) 478-7127

Talkeetna Denali Church **M** (9) Talkeetna Spur Rd 99676-0038 (Mail to: PO Box 38 99676-0038) (907) 373-0625

Tanacross St Timothys Episcopal Church **M** (93) General Delivery 99776-9999 (Mail to: General Delivery 99776-9999) (907) 883-5576

Tanana St James Episcopal Church **M** (152) 1 Front St 99777 (Mail to: PO Box 52 99777) (907) 366-7251

Valdez Epiphany Lutheran/Episcopal Church **HC** (80) 309 Pioneer Dr 99686-0829 (Mail to: PO Box 829 99686) (907) 835-4541

Venetie Church of the Good Shepherd **M** (208) General Delivery 99781-9999 (Mail to: General Delivery 99781-9999) (907) 849-8129

Wasilla St David's Espicopal Church **P** (97) 2301 Wasilla Fishhook Rd 99654-4011 (Mail to: 2301 Wasilla Fishhook Rd 99654-4011) Ann Whitney (907) 373-0625

Wrangell St Philips Episcopal Church **P** (59) 444 Church St 99929 (Mail to: PO Box 409 99929-0409) David Elsensohn (907) 874-3047

DIOCESE OF ALBANY
(PROVINCE II)
Comprises 19 counties in Northeast NY
DIOCESAN OFFICE 580 Burton Rd Greenwich NY 12834
TEL (518) 692-3350 FAX (518) 692-3352
E-MAIL diocese@albanydiocese.org WEB www.albanyepiscopaldiocese.org

Previous Bishops—
Wm C Doane 1869-1913, Richd H Nelson coadj 1904 Bp 1913-29, Geo A Oldham coadj 1922 Bp 1929-49, Fredk L Barry coadj 1945 Bp 1949-60, David E Richards suffr 1951-57, Allen W Brown suffr 1959 Bp 1961-74, Charles B Per sell Jr suffr 1963-76, Wilbur E Hogg 1974-84, David S Ball coadj 1984 Bp 1984-98, Daniel W Herzog coadj 1997-98, Bp 1998-2007, David J Bena suffr 2000-2007

Bishop—Rt Rev William H Love (1007) (Dio 1 Feb 2007)

Sec Dcn M Sive; *Treas* C Curtis; *Asst Treas* Rev W Tatem; *Lay Cn for Admin* RJ Carroll; *Chanc* Rev W Strickland; *COM* Rev S Waldron; *Deploy* E Strickland; *Cn to Ord* Rev RF Haskell; *Acct Mgr* S Denis; *Comm* Rev J Stellman; *Diaconal Form* Ven H Huth

Stand Comm—Cler: K Alonge-Coons S Garno H Huth B Jones M Neufeld D Ousley E Papazoglakis D Roy; *Lay: Pres* SE Reutsch *Sec* B Beaulac L Gibbs M Haskell E Strickland R Demler

Deans: Metro N McMillan; *N Adirondack* D Ousley; *S Adirondack* D Beaulac; *St Lawrence* C Brown; *U Hudson* D Roy; *Hudson* J Thompson; *Susquehanna* K Hunter; *W Mohawk* N Longe

PARISHES, MISSIONS, AND CLERGY

✤ **Albany** Cathedral of All Saints **O** (393) § 62 S Swan St 12210-2301 (Mail to: 62 S Swan St 12210-2380) Paul Pierson Hugh Wilkes (518) 465-1342

Albany St Andrews Episcopal Church **P** (376) 10 Main Ave 12203-1403 (Mail to: 10 Main Ave 12203-1488) Mary White Keith Scott (518) 489-4747

Albany St Michaels Episcopal Church **P** (177) 49 Killean Park 12205-4035 (Mail to: 49 Killean Park 12205-4087) Daniel Jones (518) 869-6417

Albany Saint Paul's Episcopal Church **P** (153) 21 Hackett Blvd 12208-3407 (Mail to: 21 Hackett Blvd 12208-3496) Edward Dougherty Judith Malionek John McMillan Nancy Rosenblum (518) 463-2257

Albany St Peters Episcopal Church **P** (423) 107 State St 12207-1622 (Mail to: Mr Richard Bolton 107 State St 12207-1683) Paul Hartt Susan Waldron (518) 434-3502

Albany St Francis Mission **P** § 498 Clinton Ave 12206-2705 (Mail to: 498 Clinton Ave 12206-2705) (518) 465-1112

Amsterdam St Anns Episcopal Church **P** (186) 37 Division St 12010-4324 (Mail to: 37 Division St 12010-4398) Neal Longe Alan Hart Mary Hart (518) 842-2362

Au Sable Forks St James Episcopal Church **P** (39) 14216 State Rte 9N 12912 (Mail to: C/o Grace E Bushey PO Box 470 12912-0470) David Ousley (518) 647-5312

Ballston Spa Christ Episcopal Church **P** (577) 15 W High St 12020-1912 (Mail to: 15 W High St 12020-1912) Derik Roy Albert Moser William Pearson (518) 885-1031

Bloomville St Pauls Church **P** (7) 464 River St 13739-1173 (Mail to: PO Box 742 13739-0742) (607) 434 5501

Blue Mountain Lake Church of the Transfiguration **SC** (27) 1 Cedar Ln 12812 (Mail to: C/O B. Pelton Box 567, Hc 2 13436) (240) 442-2152

Bolton Landing Church of St Sacrement **P** (68) 4879 Lake Shore Dr P.O. Box 1185 12814 (Mail to: PO Box 1185 12814-1185) Colin Belton (518) 644-9613

Bovina St James Church **P** (72) 55 Lake Delaware Dr 13753 (Mail to: 8 Rothermel Lane Ext 12106-2110) James Krueger (607) 832-4401

Brant Lake Church of the Good Shepherd **PS** Ny State Route 9 12815 (Mail to: PO Box 119 12815-0119) Michael Webber (518) 494-3314

Brant Lake St Hubert of the Lakes Church **P** (7) Route 8 12108 (Mail to: PO Box 119 12815-0119) (518) 494-3314

Brant Lake St Pauls Church **PS** 6596 State Rte 8 12815 (Mail to: C/O Nancy Torre PO Box 119 12815-0119) Michael Webber (518) 494-3314

Burnt Hills Calvary Episcopal Church **P** (284) 85 Lake Hill Rd 12027-9597 (Mail to: PO Box 41 85 Lakehill Rd 12027-0041) Gabriel Morrow (518) 399-7230

Cairo Calvary Episcopal Church **P** (18) 1 Jerome Ave 12413-3047 (Mail to: PO Box 561 12413-0561) John Miller (518) 622-9172

Cambridge St Lukes Church **P** (68) 4 St Lukes Pl 12816-1111 (Mail to: 4 St Lukes Pl 12816-1111) Mathew Baker (518) 677-2632

Canajoharie The Church of The Good Shepherd **P** (41) 26 Moyer St 13317-0118 (Mail to: PO Box 118 13317-0118) Virginia Ogden (518) 673-3440

Canton Grace Episcopal Church **P** (149) 9 E Main St 13617-1416 (Mail to: 9 E Main St 13617-1471) (315) 386-3714

Castleton St Davids Episcopal Church **P** (215) 2647 Brookview Rd 12033-3709 (Mail to: Attn Gail Neal Treasurer PO Box 475 12061) James Brisbin (518) 477-4536

Catskill St Lukes Church **P** (151) 50 William St 12414-1419 (Mail to: PO Box 643 12414-0643) Leander Harding David Sutcliffe Martin Yost (518) 943-4180

Champlain Christ & St John's Parish **P** (55) 8 Butternut St 12919-5121 (Mail to: PO Box 240 12919-0240) Patricia Beauharnois (518) 298-8543

Chatham St Luke Episcopal Church **P** (25) 12 Woodbridge Ave 12037-1314 (Mail to: 12 Woodbridge Ave 12037-1314) (518) 392-2278

Cherry Valley Grace Church **P** (39) 32 Montgomery St 13320-3562 (Mail to: PO Box 382 13320-0382) Thomas Grennen (607) 264-8303

Clifton Park St Georges Episcopal Church **P** (1023) 912 Route 146 12065-3702 (Mail to: 912 Route 146 12065-3702) Thomas Papazoglakis Katharine Foster Elizabeth Papazoglakis Scott Underhill (518) 371-6351

Cobleskill St Christopher's Episcopal Church **P** (33) 121 St Christopher Pl 12043 (Mail to: PO Box 386 12043-0386) (518) 234-3912

Cohoes St Johns Church **P** (95) § 405 Vliet Blvd 12047-2019 (Mail to: 405 Vliet Blvd 12047-2019) (518) 237-6013

Colton Zion Episcopal Church **P** (77) 91 Main St 13625 (Mail to: C/O Clifton Duval PO Box 9 13625-0009) (315) 262-3106

Cooperstown Christ Church Episcopal **P** (338) 69 Fair St 13326-1309 (Mail to: 69 Fair St 13326-1309) Dane Boston (607) 547-9555

Copake Falls St John in the Wilderness **P** (127) 261 State Route 344 12517-5337 (Mail to: PO Box 180 12517-0180) John Thompson (518) 329-3674

Coxsackie Christ Church **P** (95) 70 Mansion St 12051-1214 (Mail to: PO Box 187 12051-0187) Anne Curtin (518) 731-9883

Delhi St Johns Church **P** (82) 134 1/2 Main St 13753-1213 (Mail to: PO Box 121 13753-0121) Darius Mojallali Nancy Truscott (607) 746-3437

Delmar St Stephens Episcopal Church **P** (326) 16 Elsmere Ave 12054-2118 (Mail to: 16 Elsmere Ave 12054-2100) Scott Garno Justine Guernsey Harvey Huth (518) 439-3265

Deposit Christ Episcopal Church **P** (86) 14 Monument St 13754-1216 (Mail to: 14 Monument St 13754-1216) Linda Servetas (607) 467-3031

Downsville Saint Mary's Church **P** (30) § 15121 Main St 13755 (Mail to: Attn Bruce E Dolph 142 Delaware St 13856) Michael Shank (607) 363-2565

Duanesburg Christ Episcopal Church **P** (102) § 132 Duanesburg Churches Road 12056 (Mail to: PO Box 92 12056-0092) Deborah Beach Alistair Morrison (518) 895-2383

Elizabethtown Church of the Good Shepherd **P** (113) 10 William St 12932 (Mail to: PO Box 146 12932-0146) (518) 873-2509

Essex St Johns Episcopal Church **P** (73) Church St 12936 (Mail to: PO Box 262 12936-0262) Craig Hacker (518) 963-7775

Fort Edward Parish of St James **P** (22) 112 Broadway 12828-1722 (Mail to: 19 Walnut St 12839-1324) (518) 963-7775

Franklin St Pauls Episcopal Church **P** (43) Main And Institute Sts 13775 (Mail to: PO Box 72 13775-0072) (607) 829-6404

Gilbertsville Christ Episcopal Church **P** (107) § 36 Marion Ave 13776 (Mail to: PO Box 345 13776-0345) Donna Steckline (607) 783-2267

Glens Falls Church of the Messiah **P** (477) 296 Glen St 12801-3501 (Mail to: 296 Glen St # 1 12801-3501) Karl Griswold-Kuhn (518) 792-1560

Gouverneur Trinity Episcopal Church **P** (44) § 30 Park St 13642 (Mail to: PO Box 341 13642-0341) Gregory Bailey (315) 287-0755

Granville Trinity Episcopal Church **P** (41) 35 E Main St 12832-1331 (Mail to: Attn Nancy Mc Kenzie 35 E Main St 12832-1331) Arthur Peters (518) 642-2883

Greenville Christ Episcopal Church **P** (125) 11226 State Route 32 12083-3600 (Mail to: PO Box 278 12083-0278) Mark Diebel (518) 966-5713

Greenwich St Pauls Episcopal Church **P** (50) 145 Main St 12834-1214 (Mail to: PO Box 183 12834-0183) William Strickland (518) 692-7492

Guilderland St Boniface Episcopal Church **P** (223) 5148 Western Tpke 12084 (Mail to: PO Box 397 12084-0397) Steven Scherck (518) 355-0134

Herkimer Christ Episcopal Church **P** (78) 300 Main St 13350-1949 (Mail to: 300 Main St 13350-1949) Barbara Stellman (315) 866-0551

Hoosick Falls All Saints Church **P** (81) § 4935 Rt. 7 12090 (Mail to: Attn: Ronald W. Bovie PO Box 211 12089-0211) Gary Strubel (518) 686-9037

Hoosick Falls Church of the Holy Name **P** (46) § 33 Simmons Rd 12090-5000 (Mail to: 33 Simmons Rd 12090-5000) (518) 465-3129

Hoosick Falls St Marks Episcopal Church **P** (50) 70 Main St 12090-2004 (Mail to: PO Box 272 70 Main Street 12090-0272) (518) 686-4982

Hudson Christ Episcopal Church **P** (320) § 431 Union St 12534-2426 (Mail to: PO Box 411 12534-0411) Eileen Weglarz Eileen Weglarz (518) 828-1329

Hudson Falls Zion Episcopal Church **P** (186) 224 Main St 12839-1705 (Mail to: 224 Main St 12839-1705) (518) 747-6514

Ilion St Augustines Church **P** (146) 78 2nd St 13357-2118 (Mail to: 78 2nd St 13357-2118) (315) 894-3775

Johnstown St Johns Episcopal Church **P** (407) § 1 Market St 12095-2139 (Mail to: PO Box 395 12095-0395) Laurie Garramone (518) 762-9210

Keesville St Pauls Church **P** (31) 107 Clinton St 12944-0143 (Mail to: Clinton Street 12944) Blair Biddle (518) 563-6836

Kinderhook St Pauls Episcopal Church **P** (114) 10 Silvester St 12106-2013 (Mail to: PO Box 637 12106-0637) Thomas Malionek Jan Volkmann (518) 758-6271

Lake George St James Episcopal Church **P** (129) 172 Ottawa St 12845-1414 (Mail to: Attn: Michele Molldrem-Hotko 172 Ottawa St 12845-1414) Jean Devaty Barbara Mitchell (518) 668-2001

Lake Luzerne St Marys Episcopal Church **P** (103) 220 Lake Ave PO Box 211 12846 (Mail to: PO Box 211 12846-0211) David Beaulac (518) 696-3030

Lake Placid St Eustace Church **P** (133) 2450 Main Street 12946-3300 (Mail to: 2450 Main St 12946-3300) (518) 523-2564

Latham St Matthews Episcopal Church **P** (275) 129 Old Loudon Rd 12110-4007 (Mail to: 129 Old Loudon Rd 12110-4007) Jacob Evans (518) 785-6029

Little Falls Emmanuel Episcopal Church **P** (339) 588 Albany St 13365-1543 (Mail to: PO Box 592 13365-0592) (315) 823-1323

Malone St Marks Episcopal Church **P** (62) § 34 Elm St 12953-1507 (Mail to: PO Box 331 12953-0331) Elizabeth Papazoglakis Ana Rivera-Georgescu (518) 521-3303

Margaretville St Margarets Church **M** (40) 63 Orchard St 12455 (Mail to: New Academy & Orchard St 12455) Michael Shank (607) 563-9414

Massena St Johns Church **P** (138) 139 Main St 13662-1908 (Mail to: PO Box 15 13662-0015) (315) 769-5203

Mechanicville St Lukes Episcopal Church **P** (253) 40 McBride Road 12118-2325 (Mail to: 40 McBride Rd 12118-3512) David Haig (518) 664-4834

Mohawk Grace Church **P** (66) § 7-9 East Main St 13407 (Mail to: 7 E Main St 13407-1111) William Wheeler (315) 866-4782

Morris All Saints Chapel of Zion Church **Chapel** 1854 State Highway 51 13808 (Mail to: PO Box 156 13808-0156) Robert Witt (607) 263-5783

Morris Zion Church **P** (105) 158 Main Street 13808-0156 (Mail to: PO Box 156 13808-0156) Joseph Norman (607) 263-5927

Morristown Christ Church **P** (45) Main St 13664 (Mail to: PO Box 1297 13669-6296) Edgar LaCombe (315) 375-4497

N Granville All Saints Chapel **SC** State Route 22 12854 (Mail to: Rt 22 Box 166 12854) Jere Berger (518) 743-1740

New Lebanon Church of Our Saviour **P** (90) 14660 Route 22 12125 (Mail to: PO Box 827 12125-0827) Clinton Dugger Randolph Lukas (518) 794-8702

Newcomb St Barbaras Church **PS** 65 Sanford Ln 12852-1709 (Mail to: 30 Marcy Ln 12852-2016) Michael Webber (518) 494-3314

North Creek St Christophers Church **PS** Ridge St 12853 (Mail to: PO Box 119 12815-0019) Michael Webber (518) 494-3314

Norwood St Philips Church **P** (57) PO Box 225 13668-0225 (Mail to: PO Box 225 13668-0225) Kathryn Boswell (315) 353-8833

Ogdensburg St Johns Episcopal Church **P** (217) 500 Caroline St 13669-2604 (Mail to: PO Box 658 500 Caroline St 13669-0658) Michael O'Donnell Arthur Garno (315) 393-5470

Old Forge St Peters Church By-the-Lake **SC** 4800 State Route 28 13420-0111 (Mail to: PO Box 111 13331-0111) (315) 360-6879

Oneonta St James Episcopal Church **P** (290) 305 Main St 13820-2520 (Mail to: 305 Main St 13820-2596) Kenneth Hunter (607) 432-1458

Palenville Gloria Dei Episcopal Church **P** (14) 3393 Route 23a 12463-2318 (Mail to: PO Box 298 12463-0298) (518) 329-4562

Paul Smiths St Johns in the Wilderness **SC** 350 White Pine Rd 12970 (Mail to: PO Box 23 12945-0023) Allen Cooper (518) 891-6746

Philmont St Marks Episcopal Church **P** (27) Main St & Maple Ave 12565 (Mail to: PO Box 628 12565-0628) Mark Mc Darby (518) 672-4062

Plattsburgh Trinity Church **P** (253) 18 Trinity Pl 12901-2933 (Mail to: 18 Trinity Pl 12901-2933) Glen Michaels David Ousley (518) 561-2244

Potsdam Trinity Episcopal Church **P** (216) 8 Maple St Fall Island 13676-1149 (Mail to: 8 Maple St 13676-1181) Christopher Brown Lora Smith Margaret Theodore (315) 265-5754

Pottersville Adirondack Mission **Cluster** (122) 316 Valentine Pond Rd 12860 (Mail to: PO Box 334 12870-0334) Fr Cairns (518) 494-3314

Pottersville Christ Church **P** (16) Nys Route 9 12860 (Mail to: PO Box 119 12815-0119) Michael Webber (518) 494-3314

Rensselaer Church of the Redeemer **P** (55) 1249 3rd St 12144-1821 (Mail to: 1249 3rd St 12144-1821) (518) 326-6722

Rensselaerville Trinity Church Rensselaerville **P** (38) 10 Trinity Ln 12147 (Mail to: PO Box 86 12147-0086) (518) 797-5295

Richfld Spgs St Johns Episcopal Church **P** (40) 98 Main St 13439-2535 (Mail to: PO Box E 13439-1901) Barbara Stellman (315) 858-1121

Round Lake All Saints Church **P** (70) § Simpson Ave 12151 (Mail to: PO Box 35 12151-0035) Scott Evans (518) 899-5510

Salem St Paul's Church **P** (29) E Broadway 12865 (Mail to: PO Box 484 12865-0484) (518) 854-7294

Saranac Lake St Luke the Beloved Physician **P** (306) 102 Main St 12983 (Mail to: 136 Main St 12983-1734) Julianna Caguiat (518) 891-3605

Saratoga Spg Church of Bethesda **P** (454) 41 Washington St 12866-4116 (Mail to: 41 Washington St 12866-4116) Paul Evans Marshall Vang (518) 584-5980

Schenectady Christ Church **P** (308) 970 State St 12307-1520 (Mail to: 970 State St Ste 1 12307-1588) Nelson Jones Lawrence Hubert Peter Schofield Howard Smith (518) 374-3064

Schenectady St Andrews Church **P** (189) 50 Sacandaga Rd 12302-1828 (Mail to: 50 Sacandaga Rd 12302-1894) Michael Neufeld Richard Lehmann (518) 374-8391

Schenectady Saint George's Episcopal Church **P** (243) 30 Ferry St 12305-1609 (Mail to: 30 Ferry St 12305-1697) Matthew Stromberg (518) 374-3163

Schenectady St Pauls Episcopal Church **P** (243) 1911 Fairview Ave 12306-4129 (Mail to: 1911 Fairview Ave 12306-4129) David Culbertson (518) 393-5118

Schenectady St Stephens Church **P** (150) 1229 Baker Ave 12309-5711 (Mail to: 1229 Baker Ave 12309-5711) James Mcdonald Patricia Jones (518) 346-6241

Schenevus Church of the Holy Spirit **P** (25) Arch St 12155 (Mail to: PO Box 354 12155-0354) (607) 432-6835

Schroon Lake St Andrews Church **P** St Rte 9 12870 (Mail to: PO Box 334 12870-0334) Michael Webber (518) 494-3314

Schuylerville St Stephens Episcopal Church **P** (89) § 1 Grove St 12871-1403 (Mail to: 1 Grove St 12871-1403) (518) 695-3918

Sidney St Pauls Church **P** (110) 25 River St 13838-1132 (Mail to: 25 River St 13838-1132) James Shevlin (607) 563-3391

Springfld Ct St Marys Church **P** (40) § 7690 State Hwy 80 13468 (Mail to: C/O Mr. Ed Reiss 153 Reiss Rd 13326-2720) Thomas Grennen (315) 858-4016

Stamford St Peters Church **P** (18) 16155 County Highway 18 12167-1801 (Mail to: 16155 County Highway 18 12167-1801) Darius Mojallali (607) 538-9503

Star Lake Church of the Nativity **SC** (2) 4051 State Highway 3 13690 (Mail to: C/O Mr Richard D Been PO Box 50 13690-0050) (315) 848-3418

Tannersville St Johns Church **SC** Philadelphia Hill 12485 (Mail to: C/O Marjorie Babcock PO Box 224 12485-0224) (518) 589-5412

Ticonderoga The Episcopal Church of the Cross **P** (35) § 129 Champlain Ave 12883-1313 (Mail to: 308 Amherst Ave 12883) (518) 585-4032

Troy St Johns Episcopal Church **P** (376) 146 1st St 12180-4431 (Mail to: Treasurer 146 1st St 12180-4431) Paul Carney Sandra Tatem (518) 274-5884

Troy St Pauls Church **P** (140) 58 3rd St 12180-3906 (Mail to: P O Box 868 12181) Michael Gorchov (518) 273-7351

Troy Trinity Episcopal Church **P** (270) 545 4th Ave 12182-2616 (Mail to: 585 4th Ave 12182-2526) Desmond Francis (518) 235-3873

Tupper Lake Church of St Thomas **P** (51) 8 Brentwood Ave 12986-1513 (Mail to: 8 Brentwood Ave 12986-1513) Allen Cooper (518) 359-8786

Twilight Park Memorial Church of All Angels **SC** 69 Balsam Rd 12485 (Mail to: C/O Malcolm Handte 120 Cabrini Blvd Apt 128 10033-3431) (518) 589-5292

Unadilla St Matthews Church **P** (94) § 240 Main St 13849-2245 (Mail to: PO Box 537 13849-0537) (607) 369-3081

Waddington St Pauls Church **P** (61) 129 Lincoln Ave 13694-3183 (Mail to: PO Box 452 13694) Arthur Garno (315) 388-5680

Walton Christ Church **P** (65) § 41 Gardiner Pl 13856-1320 (Mail to: 41 Gardiner Pl 13856-1320) (607) 865-4698

Warrensburg Church of the Holy Cross **P** (163) § 3764 Main St 12885-1836 (Mail to: 3764 Main St 12885-1897) Thomas Pettigrew (518) 623-3066

Waterford Grace Church **P** (139) 34 3rd St 12188-2538 (Mail to: 34 3rd St 12188-2538) Katherine Alonge-Coons William Strickland (518) 237-7370

Watervliet Trinity Episcopal Church **P** (107) 1336 1st Ave 12189-3317 (Mail to: 1336 1st Ave 12189-3317) Nicolas Hernandez William Tatem (518) 272-0644

West Middleburgh St Paul's Episcopal Church **P** (16) 100 Church Street 12122 (Mail to: C/O Caroline Snyder PO Box 514 12157-0514) (518) 702-5005

Westford St Timothys Episcopal Church **P** (17) 1776 Co Rte 34 13488 (Mail to: PO Box 74 13488-0074) (607) 369-9214

Whitehall Trinity Church **P** (29) 58 Broadway 12887-1201 (Mail to: 58 Broadway 12887-1201) Arthur Peters (518) 480-5833

DIOCESE OF ARIZONA
(PROVINCE VIII)
Comprises the State of Arizona, except for Navajoland,
the Cities of Page and Bullhead City, and Yuma County
DIOCESAN OFFICE 114 W Roosevelt St Phoenix AZ 85003-1406
TEL (602) 254-0976   FAX (602) 495-6603
E-MAIL cathy@azdiocese.org   WEB www.azdiocese.org

Previous Bishops—
Ozi W Whitaker (NV and AZ) 1869-74, Wm-F Adams (NMex and AZ) 1875-76, Geo K Dunlap (NMex and AZ) 1880-88, John M Kendrick (NMex and AZ) 1889-1911, Julius W Atwood 1911-25, Walter Mitchell 1926-45, Arthur B Kinsolving II 1959-62, Joseph M Harte 1962-79, Joseph T Heistand coad 1976-79, Bp 1979-92, Wesley Frensdorff asst 1985-88, Robert R Shahan 1992-2004

Bishop—Rt Rev Kirk Stevan Smith, PhD, DD (996) (Dio 15 Oct 2004)

Cn for Admin and Asst to Bp CC Black; *Cn to Ord Trans and Cong Dev* M Traquair; *Cn for Finance* W Potts; *Cn for Yth and Young Adults* J Villegas; *Cn for Children's Min* J Sundin; *Cn of Comm/Media* N Krug; *Archdcn* S Getts; *Cn for Hisp Min* M Vasquez; *Cn for Native Min* Debbie Royals; *Cn for Stew* Timothy Dombek; *Chanc* C Gregor; *Treas* S Mortenson; *Sec to Conv* S Tuttle; *Dn of Cathedral* T Mendez

Stand Comm—Cler: Pres D Tantimonaco B Garren D Hedges R Hendrickson B Jackson B White; *Lay/Deacon:* C Bro L Derrick P Clark R Hollis C Kunz R Sandwell-Weiss

PARISHES, MISSIONS, AND CLERGY

Benson Saint Raphael In The Valley Episcopal Church **M** (53) 730 S Hwy 80 85602 (Mail to: PO Box 1224 85602-6803) Deborah Royals (520) 586-4335

Bisbee St Johns Sweet Memorial Church **M** (73) 19 Sowle Ave 85603 (Mail to: c/o Diocese of Arizona 114 W Roosevelt St 85003-1406) (520) 432-7006

Casa Grande St Peters Church **P** (197) 704 E McMurray Blvd 85122 (Mail to: 114 W Roosevelt St 85003-1406) David Rickert Jeanne Rasmussen (520) 836-7693

Cave Creek Good Shepherd of the Hills **P** (238) 6502 E Cave Creek Rd 85331 (Mail to: PO Box 110 85327-0110) Nordon Winger John Christopher Glenn Jenks (480) 488-3283

Chandler Saint Matthew's Church **P** (525) 901 W Erie St 85225-4477 (Mail to: PO Box 1959 85244-1959) Michael Halle Dominic Moore David Pettengill Henry Tuell (480) 899-7386

Clarkdale St Thomas of the Valley **M** (79) 889 1st South St 86324 (Mail to: PO Box 1175 86324-1175) (928) 634-8593

Coolidge Saint Michael's Church **M** (100) 800 W Vah Ki Inn Rd 85228-9312 (Mail to: PO Box 547 85128-0010) (520) 723-3845

Douglas St Stephens Episcopal Church **M** (22) 749 E 11th St 85607-2240 (Mail to: 114 W Roosevelt St 85003-1406) (520) 364-7971

Flagstaff Church of the Epiphany **P** (630) § 423 Beaver St 86001-4511 (Mail to: 423 Beaver St 86001-4511) Bess Driver Marianna Gronek (928) 774-2911

Glendale St Andrews Church **P** (218) 6300 W Camelback Rd 85301-7305 (Mail to: 6300 W Camelback Rd 85301-7305) Irineo Vasquez Janice Watts (623) 846-8046

Glendale St John the Baptist Church **P** (367) 4102 W Union Hills Dr 85308-1702 (Mail to: 4102 W Union Hills Dr 85308-1702) Bruce Jackson Charles Milhoan (623) 582-5449

Globe St Johns Church **M** (140) 185 E Oak St 85501-2115 (Mail to: PO Box 1051 85502-1051) Byron Mills Byron Mills (928) 425-9300

Green Valley St Francis-in-the-Valley **P** (366) 600 S La Canada Dr 85614-1902 (Mail to: 600 S La Canada Dr 85614-1902) Daniel Messier Pamela Hyde (520) 625-1370

Holbrook St Georges Church **M** (22) 168 W Arizona St 86025-2824 (Mail to: 114 W Roosevelt St 85003-1406) (928) 524-2361

Kingman Trinity Church **M** (75) 425 E Spring St 86402 (Mail to: c/o Diocese of Arizona 114 W Roosevelt St 85003-1406) Philip Shaw (928) 754 5658

Lakeside Church of Our Saviour **P** (135) 5147 Show Low Lake Rd 85929-5218 (Mail to: 5147 Show Low Lake Rd 85929-5218) Kerry Neuhardt (928) 537-7830

Litchfield Park St Peters Episcopal Church **P** (707) 400 S Old Litchfield Rd 85340-4721 (Mail to: 400 S Old Litchfield Rd 85340-4721) (623) 935-3279

Lk Havasu City Grace Church **P** (198) 111 Bunker Dr 86403-6856 (Mail to: 111 Bunker Dr 86403-6856) Lisa Goforth (928) 855-2525

Mesa Church of the Transfiguration **P** (206) 514 S Mountain Rd 85208-5412 (Mail to: 514 S Mountain Rd 85208-5412) Michael Bauschard Robert Saik (480) 986-1145

Mesa St Marks Church **P** (206) 322 Horne 85203-7933 (Mail to: 322 Horne 85203-7933) Gerardo Brambila (480) 964-5820

Morenci SS Philip and James **M** (19) 784 Mountain Ave 85540 (Mail to: c/o Diocese of Arizona 114 W Roosevelt St 850031406) (928) 439-4015

Nogales St Andrew's Episcopal Church **P** (239) § 969 W Country Club Dr 85621-3985 (Mail to: 969 W Country Club Dr 85621-3985) James Fitzsimmons Derwent Suthers (520) 281-1523

Oro Valley Episcopal Church of the Apostles **M** (290) 12111 La Cholla Blvd 85755-9725 (Mail to: PO Box 68435 85737-8435) Debra Asis (520) 544-9660

Paradise Valley Christ Church Of The Ascension **P** (698) § 4015 E Lincoln Dr 85253-3946 (Mail to: Attn: Accountant 4015 E Lincoln Dr 85253-3946) Daniel Richards Timothy Watt (602) 840-8210

Parker St Philips Church **PS** 1209 S Eagle Ave 853445847 (Mail to: PO Box 923 853440923) (928) 770-4589

Payson St Pauls Church **M** (231) 401 E Tyler Pkwy 855413298 (Mail to: 401 E Tyler Pkwy 855413298) Daniel Tantimonaco (928) 474-3834

Phoenix All Saints Church & Day School **P** (1685) § 6300 Central Ave 85012-1109 (Mail to: 6300 Central Ave 85012-1190) James Bade Johanna Baker Emilie Finn Poulson Reed (602) 279-5539

Phoenix Iglesia Episcopal de San Pablo **M** (532) 2801 31st St 85008-1126 (Mail to: 114 W Roosevelt St 85003) Enrique Cadena Sally Durand (602) 255-0602

Phoenix St Lukes at the Mountain Church **M** (389) 848 E Dobbins Rd 85042 (Mail to: c/o Diocese of Arizona 114 W Roosevelt St 85003-1406) (602) 276-7318

Phoenix St Marys Church **P** (151) 6501 39th Ave 85019-1303 (Mail to: 6533 39th Ave 85019-1303) Robert Bustrin (602) 354-7540

Phoenix St Stephens Church **P** (200) 2310 56th St 85008-2611 (Mail to: 2310 56th St 85008-2611) Cathy Clark (602) 840-0437

Phoenix Santa Maria Episcopal Church **M** 6501 39th Ave 85019-1303 (602) 374-4855

Phoenix St Judes Episcopal Church **M** (78) 6531 39th Ave 85019-1303 (Mail to: 6531 39th Ave 85019-1303) (602) 492-1772

Phoenix St Paul the Apostle Sudanese Mission **M** (220) 527 W Pima St 85003-2754 (Mail to: 114 W Roosevelt St 85003-1406) Anderia Lual (602) 253-4094

✤ **Phoenix** Trinity Cathedral **O** (683) 100 W Roosevelt St 85003-1406 (Mail to: 100 W Roosevelt St 85003-1406) Troy Mendez Holly Herring Mark Sutherland (602) 254-7126

Prescott St Lukes Episcopal Church **P** (396) § 2000 Shepard Ln 86301-6143 (Mail to: 2000 Shepherds Ln 86301-6143) Kimball Arnold Pierre-Henry Buisson Denise Muller (928) 778-4499

Safford All Saints Episcopal Church **M** (55) 210 W Main St 85546-2349 (Mail to: 210 W Main St 85546-2349) (928) 348-9430

Scottsdale Episcopal Church of the Nativity **P** (380) 22405 Miller Rd 85255-4939 (Mail to: 22405 Miller Rd Ste 100 85255-4939) Gary Nicolosi Wayne Whitney (480) 307-9216

Scottsdale St Anthony on the Desert **P** (445) 12990 E Shea Blvd 85259-5305 (Mail to: 12990 E Shea Blvd 85259-5305) Dorian Mulvey Susan Cihak Gordon Gilfeather (480) 451-0860

Scottsdale Saint Barnabas On The Desert **P** (1541) 6715 Mockingbird Ln 85253-4344 (Mail to: 6715 Mockingbird Ln 85253-4344) James Clark Robert Berra Elizabeth Roles Erika Von Haaren (480) 948-5560

Sedona St Andrews Episcopal Church **P** (200) 100 Arroyo Pinon Dr 86336-5004 (Mail to: 100 Arroyo Pinon Dr 86336-5004) Monica Whitaker (928) 282-4457

Sierra Vista St Stephen's Church **P** (226) 2750 E Cardinal Dr 85635 (Mail to: 2750 Cardinal Dr 85635-5447) Allison Cornell (520) 458-4432

Sun City All Saints of the Desert Church **P** (222) 9502 W Hutton Dr 85351-1462 (Mail to: 9502 W Hutton Dr 85351-1462) Julie O'Brien (623) 974-8404

Sun City St Christophers Church **P** (209) § 10233 W Peoria Ave 85351-4248 (Mail to: 10233 W Peoria Ave 85351-4248) John Fabre (623) 972-1109

Sun City West Church of the Advent **P** (525) 13150 W Spanish Garden Dr 85375-5052 (Mail to: 13150 W Spanish Garden Dr 85375-5052) Timothy Dombek Janet Gooltz (623) 584-0350

Tempe Church of the Epiphany **P** (866) 2222 S Price Rd 85282-3013 (Mail to: 2222 S Price Rd 85282-3013) Charles Ruffin Lynn Adwell (480) 968-4111

Tempe St Augustines Church **M** (273) 1735 S College Ave 85281-6695 (Mail to: 1735 S College Ave 85281-6695) Sandra Chilese Chad Sundin Rebecca Williamson Vivian Winter Chaser (480) 967-3295

Tempe St James the Apostle Church **M** (202) 975 E Warner Rd 85284-3232 (Mail to: 975 E Warner Rd 85284-3232) Susan Wilmot (480) 345-2686

Tombstone St Pauls Church **M** (39) PO Box 1489 85638-1489 (Mail to: PO Box 1489 85638-1489) (520) 553-3290

Tucson Christ the King Church **P** (275) 2800 W Ina Rd 85741-2502 (Mail to: 2800 W Ina Rd 85741-2502) Anita Slovak (520) 297-2551

Tucson The Episcopal Church of St Matthew **P** (382) 9071 E Old Spanish Trail 85710 (Mail to: PO Box 17116 85731-7116) Richard Wilson Franklyn Bergen Ruth Brown Mary Martin Michael Smith (520) 298-9782

Tucson St Michael and All Angels Episcopal Church **P** (530) § 602 Wilmot Rd 85711-2702

(Mail to: 602 Wilmot Rd 85711-2702) David Hedges (520) 886-7292

Tucson Grace St Pauls Episcopal Church **P** (1172) 2331 E Adams St 85719-4308 (Mail to: 2331 E Adams St 85719-4398) Kathryn Baird Stephen Kelsey Stephen Keplinger Richard Mallory (520) 327-6857

Tucson St Albans Episcopal Church **P** (912) § Sabino Canyon At Old Sabino Canyon Rd 85750 (Mail to: 3738 Old Sabino Canyon Rd 85750-2102) Bruce White (520) 296-0791

Tucson St Andrews Church Epis Church **M** (95) § 545 S 5th Ave 85701-2413 (Mail to: PO Box 1165 85702-1165) David Carlisle (520) 622-8318

Tucson St Philips in the Hills **P** (1765) 4440 Campbell Ave 85718-6504 (Mail to: PO Box 65840 85728-5840) Clifford Blinman Taylor Devine Beverley Edminster David Gillespie Peter Helman Robert Hendrickson Thomas Lindell Norma Rogers Rosa Sandwell-Weiss Mark Schultz (520) 299-6421

Wickenburg St Albans Church **P** (147) 357 W Yavapai St 85390-3211 (Mail to: 357 W Yavapai St 85390-3211) (928) 684-2133

Williams St Johns Episcopal-Lutheran Church **M** (58) 202 W Grant Ave 86046-2535 (Mail to: 114 W Roosevelt St 85003-1406) (928) 635-2781

Winslow St Pauls Church **M** (53) 600 Henderson St 86047-2427 (Mail to: PO Box 1018 86047-1018) (928) 289-3851

DIOCESE OF ARKANSAS

(PROVINCE VII)

Comprises the State of Arkansas

DIOCESAN OFFICE 310 W 17th St Little Rock AR 72206

(MAIL: Box 164668 Little Rock AR 72216-4688)

TEL (501) 372-2168　　FAX (501) 372-2147

E-MAIL dioark@episcopalarkansas.org　　WEB www.episcopalarkansas.org

Previous Bishops— Leonidas Polk 1838-41, Geo W Freeman 1844-58, Henry C Lay 1859-69, Henry N Pierce m 1870 dio 1871-99, Wm M Brown coadj 1898 Bp 1899-1912, James R Winchester coadj 1911 Bp 1912-31, Edwin W Saphore suffr 1917 Bp 1935-37, Edward T Demby suffr 1918-39, Richard B Mitchell 1938-56, Robt R Brown coadj 1955 Bp 56-70, Christoph Keller Jr coadj 1967 Bp 1970-81, Herbert A Donovan Jr coadj 1980 Bp 1981-93, Larry E Maze dio 1994-2006

Bishop—Rt Rev Larry R Benfield (1011) (Dio 6 Jan 07)

Sec of Conv L Jones; *Treas and Fin* T Gammill; *Chanc* J Tisdale; *Reg* B Matthews; *Fin Coord* MJ Hodges; *Deploy* J Alexander; *Cath Affairs* C Keller; *Com* M Vano; *Hist* M McNeely; *ECW* T Crawford; *UTO* P Cromwell; *Yth and YA Coord* R Curtis; *Comm* J Matthews; *Archdcn* S Loudenslager

Stand Comm—Cler: D Campbell R Leacock; *Lay: Pres* M McNeely B Ware J Crews

PARISHES, MISSIONS, AND CLERGY

Batesville St Pauls Episcopal Church **P** (219) 482 E Main St 72501-5628 (Mail to: PO Box 2255 72503-2255) James Mcdonald (870) 793-2203

Bella Vista St Theodores Episcopal Church **P** (355) 1001 Kingsland Rd 72714-5105 (Mail to: 1001 Kingsland Rd 72714-5105) William Lowry (479) 855-2715

Benton St Matthews Episcopal Church **M** (137) 1112 Alcoa Rd 72015-3502 (Mail to: 1112 Alcoa Rd 72015-3502) Lorraine Slaymaker Gwenneth Fry (501) 776-4176

Bentonville All Saints Church **P** (461) 807 SE 14th St 72712-6716 (Mail to: PO Box 528 72712-0528) Guillermo Castillo Sara Milford (479) 426-1561

Blytheville St Stephens Episcopal Church **M** (30) 1512 Willow St 72315-2361 (Mail to: PO Box 597 72316-0597) (870) 763-8646

Camden St Johns Episcopal Church **M** (30) Corner Of Harrison & Vanburen 71701 (Mail to: PO Box 694 71711-0694) (870) 836-2658

Conway St Peters Episcopal Church **P** (385) 925 Mitchell St 72034-5147 (Mail to: 925 Mitchell St 72034-5147) Peggy Cromwell Nelda McDermott Gregory Warren (501) 329-8174

Crossett St Marks Episcopal Church **M** (45) 909 Hickory St 71635-3513 (Mail to: 909 Hickory St 71635-3513) Robert Allen Robert Allen Amber Carswell (870) 364-2664

Devalls Bluff St Peters Episcopal Church **M** (194) Rr 1 Box 110a 72041-9748 (Mail to: 1002 Highway 86 E 72041-9635) (870) 255-3190

El Dorado St Marys Episcopal Church **P** (305) 512 Champagnolle Rd 71730-4732 (Mail to: 512 Champagnolle Rd 71730-4732) Robert Wetherington (870) 863-7064

Eureka Spgs St James Episcopal Church **M** (150) 28 Prospect Ave 72632-3039 (Mail to:

28 Prospect Ave 72632-3039) David Angus Elizabeth Porter (479) 253-8610

Fayetteville St Martins University Center **CM** 814 W Maple St 72701-3233 (Mail to: PO Box 1190 72702-1190) (479) 443-4791

Fayetteville St Pauls Episcopal Church **P** (1994) 224 East Ave 72701-5225 (Mail to: PO Box 1190 72702-1190) Evan Garner Emily Bost Alice Spellman Suzanne Stoner Charles Walling Lora Walsh (479) 442-7373

Foreman Saint Barnabas Church **M** (43) Bell St & 2nd Ave 71836 (Mail to: PO Box 9 71836-0009) (870) 542-6880

Forrest City Christ Episcopal Church **M** (44) 1120 Ophelia St 72335-4624 (Mail to: PO Box 1077 72336-1077) Belinda Snyder (870) 633-6118

Forrest City Church of the Good Shepherd **P** (42) 400 Hill Ave 72335-3218 (Mail to: 400 Hill St 72335-3218) Travis Frank (870) 633-3093

Fort Smith St Augustines Episcopal Church **M** (11) 1400 9th St 72901-1341 (Mail to: PO Box 8283 72902-8283) (479) 785-1140

Fort Smith St Bartholomews Episcopal Church **P** (215) 2701 Old Greenwood Rd 72903-3317 (Mail to: 2701 Old Greenwood Rd 72903-3399) Michael Briggs (479) 783-2101

Fort Smith Saint John's Episcopal Church **P** (337) 215 6th St 72901-2105 (Mail to: 214 6th St 72901-2106) Michael Lager (479) 782-9912

Harrison St Johns Episcopal Church **P** (167) § 707 West Central Ave. 72601-4901 (Mail to: 707 W Central Ave 72601-4901) Greg Hoover (870) 741-5638

Heber Springs St Francis in the Pines Episcopal Ch **M** (97) 20 Woodland Cove Dr 72543-7688 (Mail to: 20 Woodland Cove Dr 72543-7688) Mary Dalby (501) 362-3311

Helena St Johns Episcopal Church **P** (117) 625 Pecan 72342-3201 (Mail to: P O Box 770 72342) Walter Brown (870) 338-8115

Hope St Marks Episcopal Church **M** (26) 301 S Elm St 71801-5219 (Mail to: PO Box 285 71802-0285) (870) 777-3297

Horseshoe Bnd St Stephens Episcopal Church **M** (12) 1005 Third St 72512-3724 (Mail to: 1005 3rd St 72512-3724) (870) 670-5214

Hot Springs Holy Trinity Episcopal Church **P** (203) 199 Barcelona Rd 71909-3801 (Mail to: 199 Barcelona Rd 71909-3801) Neil Kaminski (501) 922-0299

Hot Springs St Lukes Episcopal Church **P** (696) § 228 Spring St 71901-4151 (Mail to: PO Box 1117 71902-1117) (501) 623-1653

Jacksonville St Stephens Episcopal Church **M** (81) 2413 Northeastern Ave 72076-2969 (Mail to: 2413 Northeastern Ave 72076-2969) James Dalton Bruce Limozaine (501) 982-8701

Jonesboro St Marks Episcopal Church **P** (318) 531 W College Ave 72401-4984 (Mail to: 531 W College Ave 72401-4984) Joshua Daniel (870) 932-2124

Lake Village Emmanuel Episcopal Church **M** (35) 422 North Lakeshore Dr 71653 (Mail to: PO Box 389 71653-0389) (870) 265-2230

Little Rock Christ Episcopal Church **P** (475) 509 Scott St 72201-3807 (Mail to: 509 Scott St 72201-3891) Kathryn Alexander Hannah Hooker Ragan Sutterfield (501) 375-2342

Little Rock Church of the Good Shepherd **M** (60) 2701 S Elm St 72204-6339 (Mail to: PO Box 23668 72221-3668) Michael Courtney (501) 663-8908

Little Rock St Francis House **Chapel** 2701 S Elm St 722046339 (Mail to: 2701 E Elm St 722046339) (501) 664-5036

Little Rock St Margarets Episcopal Church **P** (308) 20900 Chenal Pkwy 72223-9556 (Mail to: 20900 Chenal Pkwy 72223-9556) Mary Vano Stephanie Fox Ragan Sutterfield (501) 821-1311

Little Rock St Marks Episcopal Church **P** (1305) § 1000 Mississippi St 72207-5982 (Mail to: 1000 Mississippi St 72207-5900) Daniel Schieffler Cynthia Fribourgh William Griffin Patricia Matthews Michael Mccain Phillip Plunkett (501) 225-4203

Little Rock St Michaels Episcopal Church **P** (343) 12415 Cantrell Rd 72223-1727 (Mail to: 12415 Cantrell Rd 72223-1727) Claudia Heath Edwin Wills (501) 224-1442

✣ **Little Rock** Trinity Episcopal Cathedral **O** (1475) § 310 W 17th St 72206-1461 (Mail to: 310 W 17th St 72206-1461) Lisa Corry Christoph Keller James Snapp (501) 372-0294

Magnolia St James Episcopal Church **M** (29) 901 Highland Cir 71753-2540 (Mail to: PO Box 846 71754-0846) (870) 234-6944

Marianna St Andrews Episcopal Church **P** (33) 49 S Carolina St 72360-2228 (Mail to: P O Box 241 72360-0241) Marion Miller (870) 295-2534

Maumelle St Nicholas Church **M** PO Box 13677 72113-0677 (Mail to: PO Box 13677 72113-0677) Marna Franson (501) 291-6262

Mc Gehee St Pauls Episcopal Church **M** (6) 100 3rd St 71654-2218 (Mail to: PO Box 246 71654-0246) (870) 222-6519

Mena Christ Episcopal Church **M** (26) 311 8th St 71953-3023 (Mail to: 311 8th St 71953-3023) (479) 216-2645

Monticello St Marys Episcopal Church **M** (26) 836 Hyatt St 71655-4036 (Mail to: PO Box 193 71657-0193) Walter Windsor (870) 536-5493

✣ **Morrilton** Camp Mitchell Episcopal Church **O** 10 Camp Mitchell Rd 72110 (Mail to: C/O Diocese Of Arkansas PO Box 164668 72216-4668) (501) 727-5451

Mountain Home St Andrews Episcopal Church **M** (123) 1050 S Church St 72653-4734 (Mail to: 511 Coley Dr 72653-2503) Kevin Gore (870) 425-3560

N Little Rock Saint Luke's Episcopal Church **P** (300) 4106 John F Kennedy Blvd 72116-8250

(Mail to: C/O Rev.Carey D. Stone 4106 John F Kennedy Blvd 72116-8250) Carey Stone (501) 753-4281

Newport St Pauls Church **P** (121) 301 Hazel St 72112-3825 (Mail to: PO Box 367 72112-0367) (870) 523-2896

Osceola Calvary Episcopal Church **M** (29) 101 Ash St 72370-2648 (Mail to: PO Box 292 72370-0292) (870) 563-2416

Paragould All Saints Episcopal Church **M** (30) 10th & Main Sts 72450 (Mail to: PO Box 212 72451-0212) Evelyn Hornaday (870) 236-2367

Pine Bluff Grace Episcopal Church **P** (77) 4101 S Hazel St 71603-6832 (Mail to: 4101 S Hazel St 71603-6832) Lorraine Slaymaker (870) 535-3852

Pine Bluff Trinity Episcopal Church **P** (392) § 703 W 3rd Ave 71601-4009 (Mail to: PO Box 8069 71611-8069) (870) 534-3832

Rogers St Andrews Episcopal Church **P** (94) Corner Of 9th & Oak Sts 72757 (Mail to: PO Box 339 72757-0339) Craig Gavin (479) 636-4042

Russellville All Saints Episcopal Church **P** (382) 501 S Phoenix Ave 72801-7607 (Mail to: 501 S Phoenix Ave 72801-7607) Teresa Daily Michaelene Miller (479) 968-3622

Searcy Trinity Episcopal Church **P** (142) 200 Elm St 72143-5271 (Mail to: 200 Elm St 72143-5271) Mark Harris Thomas Momberg (501) 268-5270

Siloam Springs Grace Episcopal Church **P** (150) 617 Mt Olive St 72761 (Mail to: PO Box 767 72761-0767) Stanley McKinnon (479) 524-8782

Springdale St Thomas Episcopal Church **P** (329) 2898 S 48th St 72762-5844 (Mail to: 2898 S 48th St 72762-5844) Pamela Morgan (479) 751-9184

Stuttgart St Albans Episcopal Church **P** (99) 1201 S Main St 72160-5307 (Mail to: PO Box 726 72160-0726) (870) 673-2848

Van Buren Trinity Episcopal Church **M** (155) 918 9th St 72956-2720 (Mail to: PO Box 382 72957-0382) Michael Robinson (479) 474-3144

West Memphis Church of the Holy Cross **P** (53) 209 Park Dr 72301-3055 (Mail to: Church Office 209 Park Dr 72301-3055) Andrew Macbeth (870) 735-4517

DIOCESE OF ATLANTA

(PROVINCE IV)

Comprises middle and north GA

DIOCESAN OFFICE 2744 Peachtree Rd Atlanta GA 30305

TEL (404) 601-5320   FAX (404) 601-5330   WATS 800-537-6743

E-MAIL communications@episcopalatlanta.org   WEB www.episcopalatlanta.org

Cleland K Nelson 1907-17, Henry J Mikell 1917-42, John M Walker 1942-51, John B Walthour 1952-52, Randolph R Claiborne Jr 1953-72, Milton L Wood suffr 1967-74, Bennett J Sims 1972-83, C Judson Child Jr 1983-88, Frank Kellogg Allan 1989-2000 J Neil Alexander (2001-2012)

Stand Comm—Cler: N Matthis S Higgenbotham L Holder *Lay:* M Sutton M Cravens T Jenkins

Deans of Convoc—GA Mountains L Schellingerhoudt; *Oconee* D Brown; *Chattahoochee Valley* G Burton-Edwards; *Mid-Atlanta* M Mainwaring; *Marietta* K Oglesby; *N Atlanta* L Affer; *NE Metro:* R Game; *SW Atlanta* B Duke; *E Atlanta* C Vaughn; *Middle GA* D Probst; *NW GA* M Erickson

Bishop—Rt Rev Robert C Wright (1069) (Dio 13 Oct 12)

Assisting Bishop—Rt Rev Don Wimberly (789) (dio 1984)

Cn to Ord A Shuster Weltner *Treas* B King 2744 Peachtree Rd 30305; *Chanc* R Perry 2744 Peachtree Rd 30305; *V Chanc* T Christopher; *Sec of Council* Rev R Game; *Min* J Thompson-Quartey; *COM* Rev K Swanson; *Comm* Rev C Vaughn; *Educ Co-Chair* C Drewry, *Rev J Weston* ; *Stew* T Pallot; *Church Archtr & Constr* Rev T Norris; *Mikell Conf Center* Rev K Struble; *Liturg* ; *Annual Council* J Patterson; *Dir ECF* L Hardegree; *Dir Fin Cn* B Burgess; *Youth Miss* E Davis; *Hispanic Miss* Rev Cn I Rodriguez *Dismantling Racism* C Meeks

PARISHES, MISSIONS, AND CLERGY

Acworth St Teresas Episcopal Church **P** (529) 5725 Fords Rd Nw 30101-4674 (Mail to: 5725 Fords Rd NW 30101-4674) Debora Adinolfi (770) 590-9040

Athens Emmanuel Episcopal Church **P** (1040) § 498 Prince Ave 30601-2449 (Mail to: 498 Prince Ave 30601-2467) Robert Salamone Samuel Porras (706) 543-1294

Athens St Gregory the Great Epis Church **P** (386) 3195 Barnett Shoals Rd 30605-4327 (Mail to: Attn: Kendall Kookogey 3195 Barnett Shoals Rd 30605-4327) Thelma Mathis (706) 546-7553

Athens Episcopal Center at UGA **CC** 980 S Lumpkin St 30605-5119 (Mail to: 980 S Lumpkin St 30605-5119) (706) 353-2330

Atlanta Absalom Jones Student Center **CC** C/O The Rev Frank M Ross 634 W Peachtree St Sw 30308-1925 (Mail to: C/O The Rev Frank M Ross 634 Peachtree Street Sw 30308) (404) 521-1602

Atlanta All Saints Episcopal Church **P** (3051) § 634 W Peachtree St Nw 30308-1925 (Mail to: 634 W Peachtree St NW 30308-1981) Simon Mainwaring Timothy Black William Clarkson Margaret Crammer James Donald Kimberly Jackson Charles May Judson Mull Zachary Nyein Walter Smith (404) 881-0835

✢ **Atlanta** Cathedral of St Philip **O** (6284) § 2744 Peachtree Rd Nw 30305-2937 (Mail to: 2744 Peachtree Rd NW 30305-2920) Samuel Candler George Maxwell J William Harkins Lauren Holder Juan Sandoval Carolynne Williams Cathy Zappa (404) 365-1000

Atlanta Church of the Epiphany **P** (1020) 2089 Ponce De Leon Ave NE 30307 (Mail to: 2089 Ponce De Leon Ave NE 30307-1345) Sharon Hiers Benno Pattison (404) 373-8338

Atlanta Church of the Holy Comforter **P** (87) 737 Woodland Ave Se 30316-2454 (Mail to: 737 Woodland Ave SE 30316-2454) Katharine Hilliard-Yntema Bert Smith (404) 627-6510

Atlanta Church of the Incarnation **P** (143) 2407 Cascade Rd Sw 30311-3225 (Mail to: 2407 Cascade Rd Sw 30311-3286) Lynne Washington (404) 755-6654

Atlanta Emmaus House **P** (119) 1017 Hank Aaron Dr Sw 30315-1705 (Mail to: Finance Department 2744 Peachtree Rd NW 30305-2937) Kenya Thompson Lynne Washington (404) 525-5948

Atlanta The Episcopal Church at Emory **Chaplaincy** 1660 Decatur Rd NE Rm 211 Emory University 30307-1010 (Mail to: Emory University Drawer A 30322-0001) (404) 377-0680

Atlanta Georgia Tech/Georgia State Epis Ctr **CC** 2744 Peachtree Rd. NW 30305 (Mail to: 2744 Peachtree Rd Nw 30305-2937) (404) 881-0835

Atlanta Holy Innocents Episcopal Church **P** (2188) § 805 Mount Vernon Hwy 30327-4338 (Mail to: 805 Mount Vernon Rd NW 30327-4396) William Murray Lisa Zaina Grady Crawford (404) 303-2150

Atlanta Saint Anne's Episcopal Church **P** (1268) § 3098 Saint Annes Ln 30327-1638 (Mail to: 3098 Saint Annes Ln NW 30327-1638) Licia Affer Kent Christopher Lemley Timothy Meyers (404) 237-5589

Atlanta St Bartholomews Episcopal Church **P** (890) 1790 Lavista Rd Ne 30329-3604 (Mail to: 1790 Lavista Rd NE 30329-3604) Beverley Elliott Angela Shepherd (404) 634-3336

Atlanta St Bedes Episcopal Church **P** (1191) § 2601 Henderson Mill Rd Ne 30345-2134 (Mail to: 2601 Henderson Mill Rd NE 30345-2199) Steven Vaughn Caroline Branch Lynnsay Buehler (770) 938-9797

Atlanta St Dunstan's Episcopal Church **P** (116) 4393 Garmon Rd Nw 30327-3831 (Mail to: 4393 Garmon Rd NW 30327-3831) Patricia Templeton Margaret Harney (404) 266-1018

Atlanta St Johns Episcopal Church **P** (164) § 3480 Main St 30337-2064 (Mail to: 3480 Main St 30337-2099) Sandra Brice (404) 761-8402

Atlanta St Luke's Episcopal Church **P** (2008) 435 Peachtree St Ne 30308-3228 (Mail to: 435 Peachtree St NE 30308-3228) Daniel Matthews James Bacon Horace Griffin Elizabeth Shows Caffey (404) 873-7600

Atlanta St Martin in the Fields Episcopal Ch **P** (1458) § 3110 Ashford Dunwoody Rd NE 30319-2751 (Mail to: 3110 Ashford Dunwoody Rd NE 30319-2972) Amy Dills-Moore Joseph Sandlin (404) 261-4292

Atlanta St Patricks Episcopal Church **P** (404) 4755 Peachtree Rd 30338-5812 (Mail to: 4755 Peachtree Rd 30338-5803) Paul Game Julia Rusling (770) 455-6523

Atlanta St Pauls Episcopal Church **P** (973) 294 Peyton Rd Sw 30311-2152 (Mail to: 294 Peyton Rd SW 306 Peyton Rd SW 30311-2152) (404) 696-3620

Atlanta Iglesia Episcopal de Santa Maria **P** (233) 845 Glenway Dr 30344-6703 (Mail to: 845 Glenway Dr 30344-6703) (404) 707-1217

Atlanta Church of Our Saviour **P** (72) § 1068 Highland Ave Ne 30306-3551 (Mail to: 985 Los Angeles Ave NE 30306-3673) Christopher Miller Carole Maddux (404) 872-4169

Austell Church of the Good Shepherd **P** (154) § 6216 Love St 30168-4714 (Mail to: PO Box 682 30168-1050) (678) 851-2006

Blairsville St Clares Episcopal Church **P** (116) 1272 Ledford Rd 30512-3107 (Mail to: 777 Ledford Rd 30512-3110) Elizabeth Schellingerhoudt (706) 745-0607

Buford St Mary & St Martha of Bethany **P** (200) 4346 Ridge Rd 30519-1853 (Mail to: 4346 Ridge Rd 30519-1853) Timothy Watts George Mustard Daniel Shoemake (770) 271-4067

Calhoun St Timothys Episcopal Church **P** (175) PO Box 701 30703-0701 (Mail to: 224 Trammell St 30701-2218) (706) 629-1056

Canton Saint Clement's Episcopal Church **P** (315) 2795 Ridge Rd 30114-9501 (Mail to: PO Box 4156 30114-0010) James Stutler (770) 345-6722

Carrollton St Margarets Episcopal Church **P** (648) 606 Newnan St 30117-3429 (Mail to: 602 Newnan St 30117-3429) Jeffery Jackson (770) 832-3931

Cartersville Church of the Ascension **P** (239) 205 W Cherokee Ave 30120-3003 (Mail to: 205 W Cherokee Ave 30120-3003) Mary Erickson (770) 382-2626

Cedartown Saint James Church **P** (53) § 302 West Ave 30125-3422 (Mail to: PO Box 85 30125-0085) Paul Anderson (770) 748-2894

Clarkesville Grace Calvary Church **P** (314) 260 E Green St 30523 (Mail to: PO Box 490 30523-0009) Samuel Buice (706) 754-2451

Clayton St James Episcopal Church **P** (179) 206 Warwoman Rd 30525-5100 (Mail to: PO Box 69 30525-0002) Mary Demmler Anthony Sgro (706) 782-6179

Columbus St Mary Magdalene Episcopal Church **P** (45) § 4244 Saint Marys Rd 31907-6243 (Mail to: 4244 St Mary Road 31907) (706) 689-2790

Columbus Saint Thomas Episcopal Church **P** (466) § 2100 Hilton Ave 31906-1500 (Mail to: 2100 Hilton Ave 31906-1500) Lydia Burton-Edwards (706) 324-4264

Columbus Trinity Episcopal Church **HC** (575) 1130 First Avenue 31901 (Mail to: PO Box 1146 31901) Timothy Graham Ruth Pattison (706) 322-5569

Conyers St Simons Episcopal Church **P** (196) 1522 Highway 138 Ne 30013-1266 (Mail to: PO Box 102 30012-0102) Jane Weston (770) 483-3242

Covington Church of the Good Shepherd **P** (320) 4140 Clark St SW 30014-2713 (Mail to: 4140 Clark St SW 30014-2713) Maurice Beckham (770) 786-3278

Cumming Church of the Holy Spirit **P** (385) § PO Box 1010 30028-1010 (Mail to: Attn The Rev Keith Oglesby PO Box 1010 30028-1010) (770) 887-8190

Dahlonega St Elizabeths Episcopal Church **P** (143) 1188 Hamp Mill Rd 30533-4872 (Mail to: 1188 Hamp Mill Rd 30533-4872) John Hamilton Paul Roberts (706) 864-5423

Dalton St Marks Episcopal Church **P** (359) § 901 W Emery St 30720-2330 (Mail to: 901 W Emery St 30720-2330) Susan Butler (706) 278-8857

Decatur Church of the Holy Cross **P** (705) 2005 S Columbia Pl 30032-5945 (Mail to: 2005 S Columbia Pl 30032-5945) Dennis Patterson (404) 284-1211

Decatur Holy Trinity Parish **P** (555) 515 E Ponce De Leon Ave 30030-1941 (Mail to: 515 E Ponce De Leon Ave 30030-1992) Jimmy Tallant Joseph Pearson Ellen Purdum Jenna Strizak (404) 377-2622

Decatur St Timothys Episcopal Church **P** (95) 2833 Flat Shoals Rd 30034-1040 (Mail to: 2833 Flat Shoals Rd 30034-1040) Ricardo Bailey (404) 241-7711

Douglasville St Julians Episcopal Church **P** (118) 5400 Stewart Mill Rd 30135-2545 (Mail to: 5400 Stewart Mill Rd 30135-2545) James Duke (770) 949-9949

Eatonton All Angels Episcopal Church **P** (27) PO Box 4695 31024-4695 (Mail to: PO Box 4695 31024-4695) (478) 718-9189

Elberton St Albans Episcopal Church **P** (28) 109 Brookside Dr 30635-2503 (Mail to: PO Box 733 30635-0733) (706) 376-1489

Fayetteville Church of the Nativity **P** (185) 130 Antioch Rd 30215-5701 (Mail to: 130 Antioch Rd 30215-5701) Rita Henault (770) 460-6390

Fort Valley St Andrews Episcopal Church **P** (25) PO Box 308 31030-0308 (Mail to: 309 Central Ave 31030-3740) (478) 987-8291

Fort Valley St Lukes Episcopal Church **P** (113) PO Box 770 31030-0770 (Mail to: PO Box 770 31030-0770) Brian Davy (706) 975-3264

Gainesville Grace Episcopal Church **P** (825) § 431 Washington St SE 30501-3612 (Mail to: 422 Brenau Ave 30501-3612) Stuart Higginbotham Michael McCann Cynthia Park (770) 536-0126

Greensboro Episcopal Church of the Redeemer **P** (183) 303 Main St 30642-1137 (Mail to: PO Box 93 30642-0093) William Combs (706) 453-7171

Griffin St George's Episcopal Church **P** (469) § 132 10th St 30223-2841 (Mail to: 132 10th St 30223-2841) (770) 227-4453

Hamilton St Nicholas Episcopal Church **P** (79) 69 Mobley Rd 31811 (Mail to: PO Box 752 31811-0752) (706) 628-7272

Hartwell St Andrews Episcopal Church **P** (103) § 579 Fairview Ave 30643-2166 (Mail to: 579 Fairview Ave 30643-2166) (706) 376-4986

Jasper Church of the Holy Family **P** (293) § 100 Griffith Rd 30143-4422 (Mail to: 202 Griffith Rd 30143-4422) George Yandell Charles Hackett Byron Tindall (770) 893-4525

Kennesaw Christ Episcopal Church **P** (363) § 1210 Wooten Lake Rd Nw 30144-1347 (Mail to: 1210 Wooten Lake Rd NW 30144-1347) Marshall Day (770) 422-9114

Lagrange St Marks Episcopal Church **P** (396) § 207 Greenwood St 30240-2603 (Mail to: 207 Greenwood St 30240-2603) Robert Pruitt (706) 884-8911

Lawrenceville St Edwards Episcopal Church **P** (557) 737 Moon Rd 30045-6109 (Mail to: 737 Moon Rd 30046-6109) (770) 963-6128

Lilburn Christ the King Episcopal Church **P** (92) 4805 Lawrenceville Hwy NW Suite 403 30047-3845 (Mail to: 4805 Lawrenceville Hwy NW 30047-3859) (770) 309-8589

Macon Christ Episcopal Church **P** (739) 538 Walnut St 31201-2709 (Mail to: 538 Walnut St 31201-2709) Cynthia Knapp Zachary Neubauer Arthur Villarreal (478) 745-0427

Macon St Francis Episcopal Church **P** (447) § 432 Forest Hill Rd 31210-4824 (Mail to: 432 Forest Hill Rd 31210-4824) Ben Wells Joseph Shippen Ben Wells (478) 477-4616

Macon St Pauls Episcopal Church **P** (314) 753 College St 31201-1720 (Mail to: 753 College St 31201-1720) Bryan Hinson Pamela Lightsey (478) 743-4623

Madison Church of the Advent **P** (195) 338 Academy St 30650-1545 (Mail to: 338 Academy St 30650-1545) Daniel Brown (706) 342-4787

Marietta Church of the Annunciation **P** (333) 1673 Jamerson Rd 30066-1213 (Mail to: 1673

Jamerson Rd 30066-1213) Paul McCabe (770) 928-7916

Marietta St Catherines Episcopal Church **P** (982) § 571 Holt Rd Ne 30068-3039 (Mail to: 571 Holt Rd NE 30068-3039) Sarah Fisher (770) 971-2839

Marietta St James Episcopal Church **P** (1327) § 161 Church St Ne 30060-1629 (Mail to: 161 Church St NE 30060-1693) Roger Allen Daron Vroon (770) 428-5841

Marietta St Judes Episcopal Church **P** (162) § 220 Windy Hill Rd Sw 30060-5547 (Mail to: 220 Windy Hill Rd SW 30060-5547) William Austin Scott Harding (770) 435-0936

Marietta Church of St Peter & St Paul **P** (1314) § 1795 Johnson Ferry Rd 30062-6400 (Mail to: 1795 Johnson Ferry Rd 30062-6400) Louis Faucette Elisa Harres Ashley Lytle Thomas Pumphrey (770) 977-7473

Mcdonough St Josephs Episcopal Church **P** (325) 1865 Highway 20 W 30253-7316 (Mail to: 1865 Highway 20 E 30252-2264) Denise Guinta (770) 957-7517

Milledgeville St Stephens Episcopal Church **P** (259) § 220 W Wayne St 31061-3442 (Mail to: PO Box 309 31059-0309) David Probst (478) 452-2710

Milton Saint Aidan's Episcopal Church **P** (498) § 13560 Cogburn Rd 30004-3648 (Mail to: 13560 Cogburn Rd 30004-3648) Warren Simmons (770) 521-0207

Monroe St Albans Episcopal Church **P** (69) 210 Broad St 30655-1844 (Mail to: C/O Parish Treasurer PO Box 655 30655-0655) Patricia Merchant (855) 398-4597

Montezuma St Marys Episcopal Church **P** (11) 608 Rawls St 31063-1332 (Mail to: 608 Rawls St 31063-1332) (478) 472-8758

Morrow St Augustine of Canterbury **P** (334) 1221 Morrow Rd 30260-1624 (Mail to: 1221 Morrow Rd PO Box 169 30260-1624) (770) 961-9353

Newnan St Pauls Episcopal Church **P** (733) 576 Roscoe Rd 30263-4782 (Mail to: 576 Roscoe Rd 30263-4782) Hazel Glover Kyle Mackey (770) 253-4264

Norcross Christ Episcopal Church **P** (628) 400 Holcomb Bridge Rd 30071-2040 (Mail to: 400 Holcomb Bridge Rd 30071-2040) Cecilia Duke Andrew Frearson Irma Guerra (770) 447-1166

Oakwood St Gabriels Episcopal Church **P** (225) 2920 Landrum Education Dr 30566-3405 (Mail to: 2920 Landrum Education Dr 30566-3405) (770) 503-7555

Peachtree City St Andrews in the Pines Epis Church **P** (514) 316 Peachtree Pkwy 30269-1360 (Mail to: 316 Peachtree Pkwy 30269-1360) Amanda Musterman (770) 487-8415

Perry St Christophers at the Crossroads **P** (117) 1207 Macon Rd 31069-2612 (Mail to: 1207 Macon Rd 31069-2612) Lorna Erixson (478) 987-2190

Rome Church of the Transfiguration **P** (69) 304 Coker Dr Sw 30165-3416 (Mail to: 304 Coker Dr SW 30165-3416) Linda Pineo (706) 234-0197

Rome Saint Peter's Church **P** (206) 101 E 4th Ave 30161-3119 (Mail to: 101 E 4th Ave 30161-3119) John Herring (706) 291-9111

Roswell St Davids Episcopal Church **P** (1902) 1015 Old Roswell Rd 30076-1607 (Mail to: 1015 Old Roswell Rd 30076-1607) Kenneth Swanson Antonio Brito Michelle Ortiz Richard Sanders Anne Swiedler (770) 993-6084

Sandy Springs Highpoint Episcopal Community **P** (447) 4945 High Point Rd NE 30342 (Mail to: 4945 High Point Rd 30342-2310) Ruth Pattison (404) 252-3324

Sautee Nacoochee Episcopal Church of the Resurrection **Communion** (120) § 1755 Duncan Bridge Rd 30571-3611 (Mail to: 1755 Duncan Bridge Rd 30571-3611) Scott Kidd (706) 865-9680

Smyrna St Benedicts Episcopal Church **P** (1014) § 2160 Cooper Lake Rd SE 30080-6328 (Mail to: 2160 Cooper Lake Rd SE 30080-6328) Lesley-Ann Drake Ashley Lytle (678) 279-4300

Snellville The Church of St Matthew **P** (660) § 1520 Oak Rd 30078-2230 (Mail to: 1520 Oak Rd 30078-2230) Elizabeth Hendrick (770) 979-4210

Stone Mountain Saint Michael And All Angels Church **P** (506) 6780 James B Rivers Dr 30083-2249 (Mail to: 6780 James B Rivers Dr 30083-2249) Richard Arthur (770) 469-8551

Suwanee St Columbas Episcopal Church **P** (1249) 5400 Laurel Springs Pkwy Ste 1 30024-6056 (Mail to: 939 James Burgess Rd 30024-1128) Paul Norris Robert Millott (770) 888-4464

Thomaston St Thomas of Canterbury Epis Church **M** (14) 400 Georgia Ave 30286-3518 (Mail to: 610 Avalon Rd 30286-4002) Brian Davy (706) 646-3364

Toccoa St Matthias Episcopal Church **P** (208) 995 E Tugalo St 30577-1930 (Mail to: 995 E Tugalo St 30577-1938) (706) 886-4413

Trion St Barnabas Episcopal Church **P** (74) 100 Central Ave 30753-1125 (Mail to: PO Box 685 30753-0685) (706) 734-3098

Warner Robins All Saints Episcopal Church **P** (240) 1708 Watson Blvd 31093-3632 (Mail to: 1708 Watson Blvd 31093-3632) Bonnie Underwood (478) 923-1791

Washington Church of the Mediator **P** (80) PO Box 716 30673 (Mail to: PO Box 716 30673-0716) (706) 678-7226

West Point St Johns Episcopal Church **P** (25) § 501 Avenue C 31833-2037 (Mail to: 502 Avenue C 31833-2026) (706) 645-2156

Winder St Anthonys Episcopal Church **P** (59) 174 Saint Anthonys Dr 30680-1587 (Mail to: 174 Saint Anthonys Dr 30680-1587) (770) 867-5633

AUSTRIA; BELGIUM

See Europe

DIOCESE OF BETHLEHEM

(PROVINCE III)
Comprises 14 counties of Northeastern PA
DIOCESAN OFFICE 333 Wyandotte St Bethlehem PA 18015
TEL (610) 691-5655   FAX (610) 691-1682
E-MAIL office@diobeth.org   WEB www.diobeth.org

Previous Bishops—
Mark AD Howe 1871-95, Nelson S Rulison coadj 1884 Bp 1895-97, Ethelbert Talbot 1898-1928, Frank W Sterrett coadj 1923 Bp 1928-54, Fred J Warnecke coadj 1953 Bp 1954-71, Lloyd E Gressle coadj 1970 Bp 1971-83, Mark Dyer coadj 1982 Bp 1983-95, Paul V Marshall Bp, 1996-2013, Sean Rowe prov 2014-18

Bishop Provisional—Rt Rev Kevin D. Nichols (September 15, 2018)

Cn to Ord Rev Cn AE Kitch; *Sec* Rev JD Moyer; *Treas* EH House ; *Chanc* L Henry; *Int Comp* C Dougan; *Asst for Admin* P Lapinski

Stand Comm—Cler: Pres JD Moyer E Trygar J Bender V Bankston; *Lay:* R Arcario L Holzinger C McMullen L Graham

PARISHES, MISSIONS, AND CLERGY

Allentown Grace Episcopal Church **P** (68) 108 5th St 18102-4108 (Mail to: 108 5th St 18102-4161) Rodney Conn (610) 435-0782

Allentown Saint Andrew's Episcopal Church **P** (176) 1901 Pennsylvania Ave 18109-3111 (Mail to: C/O Treasurer 1900 Pennsylvania Ave 18109-3187) Thomas Allen (610) 865-3603

Allentown Church of the Mediator **P** (233) 1620 W Turner St 18102-3637 (Mail to: 1620 W Turner St 18102-3637) Maria Tjeltveit Twila Smith (610) 434-0155

✣ **Ashland** Memorial Church of St John **O** 106 12th St 17921 (Mail to: C/O North Parish PO Box 82 17921) (570) 874-4532

Athens Trinity Episcopal Church **P** (86) 701 S Main St 18810-1009 (Mail to: 701 S Main St 18810-1009) Benjamin Lentz (570) 888-5715

✣ **Bethlehem** Cathedral Church of the Nativity **O** (981) 321 Wyandotte St 18015-1527 (Mail to: 321 Wyandotte St 18015-1592) Anthony Pompa John Board (610) 865-0727

Bethlehem Trinity Church **P** (520) 44 E Market St 18018-5926 (Mail to: 44 E Market St 18018-

5926) Pamela Payne Richard Ditterline Elizabeth Miller Elizabeth Miller (610) 867-4741

Carbondale Trinity Episcopal Church **P** (121) 58 River St 18407-2306 (Mail to: 58 River St 18407-2306) (570) 282-3620

Clarks Summit The Church of the Epiphany **P** (567) 25 Church HL Dalton 18414-7739 (Mail to: PO Box 189 18411-0189) Mary Lou Divis (570) 563-1564

Dallas Church of the Prince of Peace **P** (164) 420 Main St 18612-1807 (Mail to: 420 Main St 18612-1807) Joseph Rafferty Christine Sutton (570) 675-1723

Douglassville St Gabriels Episcopal Church **P** (301) § 1188 Ben Franklin Hwy E 19518-1803 (Mail to: PO Box 396 19518-0396) Sarah Bosler (610) 385-3144

Drifton St James Church **P** (51) Rt. 940, Main St 18221 (Mail to: PO Box 217 18221-0217) (570) 636-3967

Easton Trinity Episcopal Church **P** (511) 234 Spring Garden St 18042-3657 (Mail to: 234 Spring Garden St 18042-3657) Andrew Gerns Ellen Barrett (610) 253-0792

Emmaus St Margarets Church **P** (139) 150 Elm St 18049-2622 (Mail to: 150 Elm St 18049-2622) (610) 967-1450

Forest City Christ Church **P** (73) 700 Delaware St 18421-1002 (Mail to: 700 Delaware St 18421-1002) (570) 282-3620

Hamlin St Johns Episcopal Church **P** (169) 564 Easton Turnpike 18427 (Mail to: PO Box 118 18427-0118) (570) 689-9260

Hazleton St Peters Episcopal Church **P** (140) 46 S Laurel St 18201-6311 (Mail to: 46 S Laurel St 18201-6399) (570) 454-6543

Hellertown St Georges Episcopal Church **P** (133) 735 Delaware Ave 18055-1819 (Mail to: 735 Delaware Ave 18055-1899) Harold Mayo (610) 838-9355

Honesdale Christ Church **P** (35) 432 W Park St 18431 (Mail to: 210 9th St 18431-1913) (570) 253-3144

Honesdale Grace Episcopal Church **P** (117) 827 Church St 18431-1824 (Mail to: 827 Church St

18431-1824) Edward Erb (570) 253-2760

Jermyn Saint James-Saint George Episcopal Church **P** (166) 398 Washington Ave 18433-1342 (Mail to: 398 Washington Ave 18433-1342) Frank Cliff (570) 876-4896

Jim Thorpe St Marks and St Johns Episcopal Church **P** (223) 21 Race St 18229-2003 (Mail to: 21 Race St 18229-2003) Rebecca Parsons-Cancelliere (570) 325-2241

Kingston Grace Episcopal Church **P** (158) 30 Butler St 18704 (Mail to: 30 Butler St 18704-4706) John Hartman (570) 287-8440

Kutztown St Barnabas Episcopal Church **P** (34) 234 E Main St 19530 (Mail to: 234 E Main St PO Box 236 19530-1517) (610) 683-7787

Lebanon St Lukes Church Episcopal **P** (477) 22 S 6th St 17042-5338 (Mail to: 22 S 6th St 17042-5338) David Zwifka (717) 272-8251

Lehighton All Saints Episcopal Church **P** (230) 301 2nd St 18235-1418 (Mail to: PO Box 147 18235-0147) (610) 377-2675

Milford Good Shepherd & St Johns Church **P** (127) 110 W Catherine St 18337-1418 (Mail to: 110 W Catherine St 18337-1418) Van Bankston Van Bankston (570) 296-8123

Montrose St Pauls Church **P** (78) 276 Church St 18801-1271 (Mail to: 276 Church St 18801-1271) (570) 278-2954

Morgantown St Thomas Church **P** (78) 6251 Morgantown Rd (Rr 10) 19543 (Mail to: PO Box 97 19543-0097) Megan Dembi Donald Howells (610) 286-9547

Moscow St Marks Episcopal Church **P** (118) 1109 Church St 18444-0678 (Mail to: PO Box 678 1109 Church St 18444-0678) Earl Trygar (570) 842-7231

Mount Pocono Trinity Episcopal Church **P** (115) Hcr # Box 1 18344 (Mail to: 137 Trinity Hill Rd 18344-7162) (570) 839-9376

Mountain Top St Martins Church **P** (103) 3085 Church Rd 18707-9035 (Mail to: 3085 Church Rd 18707-9035) Daniel Fitzsimmons (570) 868-5358

Nanticoke Saint Andrew's Church **P** (38) 12 East Kirmar Avenue 18634-3608 (Mail to: "c/o Susan Maza, Sr. Warden" 127 W Union St 18634-3608) Charles Warwick (570) 825-0547

Nazareth St Brigids Church **P** (149) 310 Madison Ave 18064-2613 (Mail to: 310 Madison Ave 18064-2613) William Martin (610) 746-3910

New Milford St Marks Episcopal Church **P** (26) 1148 Main St 18834-2011 (Mail to: PO Box 406 1148 Main Street 18834-0406) (570) 465-3896

Palmerton St Johns Episcopal Church **P** (105) 365 Lafayette Ave 18071-1617 (Mail to: 365 Lafayette Ave 18071-1617) (610) 826-2611

Pen Argyl Saint Joseph's Church **P** (28) 1440 Verona Ave 18072-1350 (Mail to: 1440 Verona Ave 18072-1350) (610) 759-0973

Pittston Trinity Episcopal Church **P** (154) 200 Montgomery Ave 18643-2137 (Mail to: 220 Montgomery Ave 18643-2137) John Major (570) 654-3261

Pottsville Trinity Episcopal Church **P** (246) 200 S 2nd St 17901-3520 (Mail to: 200 S 2nd St 17901-3520) Timothy Albright (570) 622-8720

Reading Christ Church **P** (624) 5th & Court St 19603 (Mail to: PO Box 1094 19603-1094) John Francis (610) 374-8269

Reading St Albans Episcopal Church **P** (363) 2848 Saint Albans Dr 19608-1028 (Mail to: 2848 Saint Albans Dr 19608-1028) Dennis Reid Jeffrey Funk Walter Krieger Nancy Packard (610) 678-7001

Reading St Marys Church **P** (37) 100 W Windsor St 19601-2033 (Mail to: PO Box 13685 19612-3685) (610) 374-7914

Sayre Church of the Redeemer **P** (180) 201 S Wilbur Ave 18840-1605 (Mail to: 201 S Wilbur Ave 18840-1605) Melinda Artman (570) 888-2270

Scranton Church of the Good Shepherd **P** (50) 2425 Washington Ave 18509-1422 (Mail to: 1780 Washington Ave 18509-1959) Howard Stringfellow (570) 347-1760

Scranton St Lukes Episcopal Church **P** (171) 232 Wyoming Ave 18503-1437 (Mail to: 232 Wyoming Ave 18503-1437) Rebecca Barnes (570) 342-7654

Shuykl Haven St James Episcopal Church **P** (64) 100 Dock St 17972-1208 (Mail to: 100 Dock St 17972-1208) (570) 385-0737

✛ **St Clair** Holy Apostles Episcopal Church **O** Nicholas and Hancock Sts 17970 (Mail to: 106 12th St. 17921) James Smith (570) 429-2771

St. Clair North Parish Episcopal Church **P** (176) 307 E. Hancock St. 17970 (Mail to: PO Box 487 17931-0487) Timothy Albright James Smith (570) 429-7107

Stroudsburg Christ Episcopal Church **P** (222) 205 7th St 18360-2113 (Mail to: 205 7th St 18360-2113) James Moyer Michele Causton (570) 421-7481

Susquehanna Christ Episcopal Church **P** (17) 302 W Main St 18847 (Mail to: PO Box 222 18847-0222) (570) 853-9003

Tamaqua Calvary Episcopal Church **P** (33) 300 W Broad St 18252-1821 (Mail to: C/O Miss Georgine P Feel 309 W Broad St 18252-1820) Robert Gildersleeve (610) 377-0874

Towanda Christ Episcopal Church **P** (161) One Main St 18848-1900 (Mail to: 1 Main St 18848-1900) Maureen Hipple Joseph Holman (570) 265-5035

Trexlertown St Anne's Episcopal Church **P** (453) PO Box 368 18087-0368 (Mail to: PO Box 368 18087-0368) Donald Schaible (610) 398-3321

Troy St Pauls Episcopal Church **P** (67) 195 Elmira St 16947-1201 (Mail to: 130 Elmira St 16947-1202) Arie Van den Blink (570) 297-4864

Tunkhannock St Peters Episcopal Church **P** (32) PO Box 459 18657-0459 (Mail to: PO Box 459 18657-0459) Mary Lou Divis (570) 836-2233

Whitehall St Stephens Episcopal Church **P** (135) § 3900 Mechanicsville Rd 18052-3324 (Mail to: 3900 Mechanicsville Rd 18052-3347) Harold Mayo Harold Mayo (610) 435-3901

Wilkes Barre Holy Cross Episcopal Church **P** (160) 373 Main St 18702-4409 (Mail to: 373 Main St 18702-4409) Timothy Alleman John Leo (570) 823-2600

✤ **Wilkes Barre** St Stephens Pro-Cathedral **O** (420) 35 S Franklin St 18701-1202 (Mail to: 35 S Franklin St 18701-1299) Timothy Alleman Brian Pavlac Brian Pavlac (570) 825-6653

Wilkes Barre St Clement and St Peters Church **P** (105) 70 Lockhart St 18702-3604 (Mail to: 70 Lockhart St 18702-3604) Charles Warwick (570) 822-8043

Wind Gap St Marys Episcopal Church **P** (105) 340 S Lehigh Ave, 18091-0365 (Mail to: C/O Parish Of The Holy Family PO Box 36 18072-0036) (610) 863-8007

STATE OF CALIFORNIA

Dioceses of California (CA), El Camino Real (ECR), Los Angeles (LA), Northern California (NCA), San Diego (SD) and San Joaquin (SanJ).

Alameda—CA
Albany—CA
Alhambra—LA
Alpine—SD
Altadena—LA
Alturas—NCA
Anaheim—LA
Anderson—NCA
Antelope—NCA
Antioch—CA
Apple Valley—LA
Aptos—ECR
Arcadia—LA
Arcata—NCA
Arroyo Grande—ECR
Atascadero—ECR
Atwater—SanJ
Auburn—NCA
Avery—SanJ
Bakersfield—SanJ
Barstow—LA
Beaumont—LA
Belmont—CA
Belvedere Tiburon—CA
Benicia—NCA
Ben Lomond—ECR
Berkeley—CA
Beverly Hills—LA
Big Bear Lake—LA
Bolinas—CA
Bonita—SD
Borrego Spgs—SD
Brawley—SD
Brentwood—CA
Buena Pk—LA
Burbank—LA
Burlingame—CA
Calistoga—NCA
Camarillo—LA
Cambria—ECR
Cameron Pk—NCA
Carlsbad—SD

Carmel by the Sea—ECR
Carmel Valley—ECR
Carmichael—NCA
Castro Valley—CA
Chico—NCA
Chula Vista—SD
Claremont—LA
Clayton—CA
Cloverdale—NCA
Colusa—NCA
Compton—LA
Concord—CA
Corning—NCA
Corona—LA
Corona Del Mar—LA
Coronado—SD
Corte Madera—CA
Costa Mesa—LA
Covina—LA
Crescent City—NCA
Crockett—CA
Cupertino—ECR
Daly City—CA
Danville—CA
Davis—NCA
Del Mar—SD
Desert Hot Spgs—SD
Desert Shores—SD
Downey—LA
El Cajon—SD
El Centro—SD
El Monte—LA
El Segundo—LA
Encinitas—SD
Encino—LA
Escondido—SD
Eureka—NCA
Fair Oaks—NCA
Fairfield—NCA
Fallbrook—SD
Ferndale—NCA
Fillmore—LA

Folsom—NCA
Ft Bragg—NCA
Fortuna—NCA
Foster City—CA
Fremont—CA
Fresno—SanJ
Fullerton—LA
Galt—NCA
Garden Grove—LA
Gardena—LA
Gilroy—ECR
Glendale—LA
Glendora—LA
Goleta—LA
Granada Hills—LA
Grass Valley—NCA
Gridley—NCA
Gualala—NCA
Hacienda Hts—LA
Half Moon Bay—CA
Hanford—SanJ
Hawthorne—LA
Healdsburg—NCA
Hemet—SD
Hermosa Bch—LA
Hesperia—LA
Hollister—ECR
Huntington Bch—LA
Huntington Pk—LA
Idyllwild—SD
Indio—SD
Inglewood—LA
Inverness—CA
Irvine—LA
Isla Vista—LA
Jolon—ECR
Kenwood—NCA
Kernville—SanJ
King City—ECR
La Canada—LA
La Crescenta—LA
LaFayette—CA
La Jolla—SD

La Mesa—SD
La Verne—LA
Laguna Bch—LA
Laguna Hills—LA
Laguna Niguel—LA
Lake Almanor—NCA
Lake Elsinore—SD
Lakeport—NCA
Lancaster—LA
Lemon Grove—SD
Lincoln—NCA
Livermore—CA
Lodi—SanJ
Lompoc—LA
Long Bch—LA
Los Altos—CA
Los Angeles—LA
Los Gatos—ECR
Los Olivos—LA
Los Osos—ECR
Madera—SanJ
Malibu—LA
Marina—ECR
Martinez—CA
Marysville—NCA
Menifee—SD
Menlo Pk—CA
Mill Valley—CA
Milpitas—ECR
Modesto—SanJ
Monrovia—LA
Monterey—ECR
Monterey Pk—LA
Monte Rio—NCA
Moraga—CA
Moreno Valley—LA
Morgan Hill—ECR
Morro Bay—ECR
Mt Shasta—NCA
Mtn View—ECR
Napa—NCA
National City—SD
Needles—LA

Nevada City—NCA
Norwalk—LA
Novato—CA
Oakland—CA
Oakhurst—SanJ
Oak Park—LA
Oceanside—SD
Ojai—LA
Ontario—LA
Orange—LA
Orinda—CA
Oroville—NCA
Oxnard—LA
Pacific Grove—ECR
Pacific Palisades—LA
Pacifica—CA
Palm Desert—SD
Palm Spgs—SD
Palo Alto—CA & ECR
Palos Verdes Est—LA
Paradise—NCA
Pasadena—LA
Paso Robles—ECR
Pauma Valley—SD
Petaluma—NCA
Pico Rivera—LA
Pinole—CA
Placentia—LA
Placerville—NCA
Pleasant Hill—CA
Pleasanton—CA
Pomona—LA
Portola Valley—CA
Poway—SD

Quincy—NCA
Ramona—SD
Rancho Cordova—NCA
Rancho Sta Marg—LA
Red Bluff—NCA
Redding—NCA
Redlands—LA
Redondo Bch—LA
Redwood City—CA
Rialto—LA
Richmond—CA
Ridgecrest—SanJ
Rio Vista—NCA
Riverbank—SanJ
Riverside—LA
Rocklin—NCA
Roseville—NCA
Ross—CA
Sacramento—NCA
St Helena—NCA
Salinas—ECR
San Andreas—SanJ
San Ardo—ECR
San Bernardino—LA
San Bruno—CA
San Carlos—CA
San Clemente—LA
San Diego—SD
San Fernando—LA
San Francisco—CA
San Gabriel—LA
San Jose—ECR
San Juan Capistrano—LA

San Leandro—CA
San Luis Obispo—ECR
San Marino—LA
San Marcos—SD
San Mateo—CA
San Pedro—LA
San Rafael—CA
Santa Ana—LA
Santa Barbara—LA
Santa Clara—ECR
Santa Cruz—ECR
Santa Maria—LA
Santa Monica—LA
Santa Paula—LA
Santa Rosa—NCA
Santee—SD
Saratoga—ECR
Sausalito—CA
Scotts Valley—ECR
Seal Bch—LA
Seaside—ECR
Sebastopol—NCA
Sierra Madre—LA
Simi Valley—LA
Skyforest—LA
Sonoma—NCA
Sonora—SanJ
So Gate—LA
So Pasadena—LA
So San Francisco—CA
Stockton—SanJ
Studio City—LA
Susanville—NCA

Sutter Creek—NCA
Taft—SanJ
Tahoe City—NCA
Temecula—SD
Thousand Oaks—LA
Torrance—LA
Tulare—SanJ
Turlock—SanJ
Tustin—LA
Twentynine Palms—LA
Ukiah—NCA
Upland—LA
Vacaville—NCA
Valencia—LA
Vallejo—NCA
Van Nuys—LA
Ventura—LA
Visalia—SanJ
Vista—SD
Walnut Creek—CA
Watsonville—ECR
Wheatland—NCA
Whittier—LA
Willits—NCA
Willows—NCA
Wilmington—LA
Winnetka—LA
Woodland Hills—LA
Woodland—NCA
Yuba City—NCA
Yucaipa—LA
Yucca Valley—LA
Yuma—SD

DIOCESE OF CALIFORNIA
(PROVINCE VIII)
Comprises 5 counties in west-central CA
DIOCESAN OFFICE 1055 Taylor St San Francisco CA 94108
TEL (415) 673-0606   FAX (415) 673-1510
E-MAIL bishopmarc@diocal.org   WEB www.diocal.org

Previous Bishops—
Wm I Kip m 1853 dio 1857-93, Wm F Nichols coadj 1890 Bp 1893-1924, Edward L Parsons coadj 1919 Bp 1924-40, Karl M Block coadj 1938 Bp 1941-58, Henry H Shires suffr 1950-58, James A Pike coadj 1958 Bp 1958-66, G Richard Millard suffr 1960-78, C Kilmer Myers 1966-79, William E Swing 1979-2006

Bishop—Rt Rev Marc Handley Andrus (974)
(Dio 22 Jul 2006)

CFO T Ferguson; *Chanc* C Hayes; *V Chanc* PS Boone

Jr Esq; *Can to Ord* A Bailey (415) 869-7806; *Comm Off* S Martin Taylor (415) 869- 7820; *Faith Form Coord* A Cook (415) 869-7826; *Camps & Conf* J Dowling (707) 433-2440; *Gift Planning* A Kiernan Martin; *Com* M Ridlon; *Treas* R McCaskill; *Conv Sec* D Frangquist

Stand Comm—Cler: M Arase-Barham J Honodel P Jester D White; *Lay* N Huey A Larsen, A Lee, D Randall-Tsuruta

Exec Coun—Cler: Pres M Chan Ong D Low-Skinner J Stratford M Trezevant; *Lay* R Amos P Anderson B Barber S Buckingham M Bustos R Johnson T LaFrance S MacKenzie C Mader D Miller L Ringlee J Wiant

PARISHES, MISSIONS, AND CLERGY

Alameda Christ Episcopal Church **P** (386) 1700 Santa Clara Ave 94501-2515 (Mail to: 1700 Santa Clara Ave 94501-2515) Stephen Mchale Laureen Moyer (510) 523-7200

Albany St Albans Episcopal Church **P** (191) 1501 Washington Ave 947061856 (Mail to: 1501 Washington Ave 94706-1856) Julia Wakelee-Lynch Duane Sisson Kathleen Van Sickle (510) 5251716

Antioch St Georges Episcopal Church **M** (168) 301 E 13th St 94509-1997 (Mail to: 301 E 13th St 94509-1997) Jill Honodel (925) 757-4934

Belmont Good Shepherd Episcopal Church **M** (31) 1300 Fifth Ave 94002-3831 (Mail to: 1300 Fifth Ave 94002-3831) Michael Barham (650) 593-4844

Belvedere St Stephens Episcopal Church **P** (650) 3 Bayview Ave 94920 (Mail to: PO Box 97 94920-0097) Alberta Buller Phillip Ellsworth (415) 435-4501

Berkeley All Souls Parish **P** (527) 2220 Cedar St 94709-1519 (Mail to: 2220 Cedar St 94709-1586) Philip Brochard Donald Brown Joseph Delgado Horace Griffin Marguerite Judson Michael Lemaire Ruth Meyers Paula Nesbitt Daniel Prechtel David Stone (510) 848-1755

Berkeley St Clements Episcopal Church **P** (734) 2837 Claremont Blvd 94705-1446 (Mail to: 2837 Claremont Blvd 94705-1446) Bruce O'Neill (510) 843-2678

Berkeley St Marks Episcopal Church **P** (459) 2300 Bancroft Way 94704-1604 (Mail to: 2300 Bancroft Way 94704-1604) Lizette Larson-Miller Blake Sawicky (510) 848-5107

Berkeley Good Shepherd Episcopal Church **M** (79) 1823 9th St 94710-2102 (Mail to: 1823 9th St 94710-2102) Este Gardner Louis Countryman Ellen Ekstrom Jay Johnson Bonnie Ring (510) 549-1433

Bolinas St Aidans Episcopal Church **M** (37) 30 Brighton Ave 94924 . (Mail to: PO Box 629 94924-0629) (415) 868-1852

Brentwood St Albans Episcopal Church **M** (120) 508 2nd St 94513-1349 (Mail to: PO Box 101 94513-0101) Kathleen Bradford Max Nye (925) 634-1893

Burlingame St Pauls Episcopal Church **P** (468) 415 El Camino Real 94010-5122 (Mail to: 415 El Camino Real 94010-5197) Thomas Skillings Julie Graham (650) 348-4811

Castro Valley Holy Cross Episcopal Church **P** (452) 19179 Center St 94546-3616 (Mail to: 19179 Center St 94546-3616) Mark Spaulding Martha Kuhlmann Patricia Pearson (510) 889-7233

Clayton St Johns Episcopal Church **M** (189) 5555 Clayton Rd 94517-1013 (Mail to: 5555 Clayton Rd 94517-1013) Nancy Eswein John Mcdermott (925) 672-8855

Concord St Michael and All Angels Episcopal **M** (191) 2925 Bonifacio St 94519-2511 (Mail to: 2925 Bonifacio St 94519-2511) Laina Casillas Amanda May (925) 685-8859

Corte Madera Holy Innocents Episcopal Church **P** (113) 2 Tamalpais Dr 94925 (Mail to: PO Box 5 94976-0005) Palmer Wilkins (415) 924-4393

Crockett St Marks Episcopal Church **P** (90) 800 Pomona St 94525-1400 (Mail to: PO Box 515 94525-0515) (510) 787-2989

Daly City Holy Child and St Martins Episcopal Church **M** (220) 777 Southgate Ave 94015-3665 (Mail to: 777 Southgate Ave 94015-3665) Leonard Oakes Lynn Bowdish (650) 991-1560

Danville St Timothys Episcopal Church **P** (664) § 1550 Diablo Rd 94526-1952 (Mail to: 1550 Diablo Rd 94526-1952) Todd Bryant Susan Geissler-O'Neil (925) 837-4993

Foster City St Ambrose Episcopal Church **P** (246) § 900 Edgewater Blvd 94404-3709 (Mail to: 900 Edgewater Blvd 94404-3709) David Ota (650) 574-1369

Fremont St Annes Episcopal Church **P** (141) 2791 Driscoll Rd 94539-4449 (Mail to: 2791 Driscoll Rd 94539-4449) Beth Foote Robert Partanen (510) 490-0553

Fremont St James Episcopal Church **P** (368) 37051 Cabrillo Dr 94536-5709 (Mail to: PO Box 457 94537-0457) Lori Walton Anna Horen (510) 797-1492

Half Moon Bay Church Of The Holy Family **M** (59) § 1590 Cabrillo Hwy S 94019-2245 (Mail to: 1590 Cabrillo Hwy S 94019-2245) Michael Barham

Inverness Saint Columba's Church **P** (54) 12835 Sir Francis Drake Blvd 94937 Vincent Pizzuto (415) 669-1039

Lafayette St Anselms Episcopal Church **P** (335) 682 Michael Ln 94549-5360 (Mail to: 682 Michael Ln 94549-5399) John Sutton Naomi Chamberlain-Harris Ting Yao (925) 284-7420

Livermore St Bartholomews Episcopal Church **P** (175) 678 Enos Way 94551-5917 (Mail to: 678 Enos Way 94551-5917) Andrew Lobban (925) 447-3289

Los Altos Christ Episcopal Church **P** (370) § 1040 Border Rd 94024-4724 (Mail to: 1040 Border Rd 94024-4724) Claire Ranna John Buenz (650) 948-2151

Martinez Grace Episcopal Church **P** (198) 130 Muir Station Rd 94553-4420 (Mail to: 130 Muir Station Rd 94553-4420) Deborah White (925) 228-6574

Menlo Park St Bedes Episcopal Church **P** (340) 2650 Sand Hill Rd 94025-7018 (Mail to: 2650 Sand Hill Rd 94025-7018) Gianetta Hayes-Martin John Oda-Burns David Sheetz (650) 854-6555

Menlo Park Holy Trinity Church **P** (874) 330 Ravenswood Ave 94025-3420 (Mail to: 330 Ravenswood Ave 94025-3420) Matthew Dutton-Gillett (650) 326-2083

Mill Valley The Episcopal Church of Our Saviour **HC** (366) 10 Old Mill St 94941-1813 (Mail to:

10 Old Mill St 94941-1894) Richard Helmer Annette Rankin (415) 388-1907

Novato St Francis of Assisi Epis Church **P** (199) 967 5th St 94945-3105 (Mail to: 967 5th St 94945-3105) Kathleen Crary Stacey Grossman (415) 892-1609

Oakland Episcopal Church of Our Saviour **P** (133) 1011 Harrison St 94607-4426 (Mail to: 1013 Harrison St Ste 202 946074457) Merry Ong (510) 834-6447

Oakland St Augustines Episcopal Church **P** (170) 525 29th St 94609-3512 (Mail to: 525 29th St 94609-3512) (510) 832-6462

Oakland St Cuthberts Episcopal Church **M** (56) 7932 Mountain Blvd 94605-3708 (Mail to: 7932 Mountain Blvd 94605-3799) Izabella Sempari (510) 686-3146

Oakland St James the Apostle Church **P** (70) 1540 12th Ave 94606-3803 (Mail to: 1540 12th Ave 94606-3803) Izabella Sempari (510) 533-2136

Oakland St Johns Episcopal Church **P** (490) 1707 Gouldin Rd 94611-2120 (Mail to: 1707 Gouldin Rd 94611-2120) Scott Denman Franklin Sterling Fran Toy (510) 339-2200

Oakland St Pauls Episcopal Church **P** (204) § 114 Montecito Ave 94610-4556 (Mail to: 114 Montecito Ave 94610-4599) Mauricio Wilson Carolyn Bolton (510) 834-4314

Orinda Saint Stephen's Episcopal Church **P** (1237) § 66 Saint Stephens Dr 94563-1949 (Mail to: 66 Saint Stephens Dr Attn: Treasurer 94563-1949) Stephen Hassett Jane Stratford (925) 254-3770

Pacifica St Edmunds Episcopal Church **M** (105) 1500 Perez Drive 94044 (Mail to: PO Box 688 94044-0688) Kathleen Crary (650) 359-3364

Palo Alto Saint Mark's Episcopal Church **P** (637) 600 Colorado Ave 94306-2510 (Mail to: 600 Colorado Ave 94306-2599) Matthew Mcdermott Ricardo Avila Linda Bunch (650) 326-3800

Pinole Episcopal Church of Christ the Lord **M** (90) 592 Tennent Ave 94564-1629 (Mail to: Atten: Susan Linnell 592A Tennent Ave 94564-1629) Susan Champion (510) 724-9141

Pleasant Hil Episcopal Church of the Resurrection **P** (513) § 399 Gregory Ln 94523-2837 (Mail to: 399 Gregory Ln 94523-2837) Barbara Dawson Stephanie Tramel Kathleen Trapani (925) 685-2288

Pleasanton St Clares Episcopal Church **P** (414) § 3350 Hopyard Rd 94588-5105 (Mail to: 3350 Hopyard Rd 94588-5105) Ronald Culmer Carol Cook (925) 462-4802

Portola Valley Christ Episcopal Church **P** (318) 815 Portola Rd 94028-7206 (Mail to: 815 Portola Rd 94028-7206) Dorothy Jamison Joseph Peters-Mathews Elizabeth Phillips David Sheetz (650) 851-0224

Redwood City El Buen Pastor Iglesia Episcopal **M** (127) 1835 Valota Rd. 94061 (Mail to: 600 Colorado Avenue 90234) (650) 245-7759

Redwood City St Peters Episcopal Church **P** (200) 178 Clinton St 94062-1552 (Mail to: Attn Susan D Parsons 178 Clinton St 94062-1583) Charlotte Wilson (650) 367-0777

Richmond Holy Trinity Episcopal Church **M** (163) 555 37th St 94805-2205 (Mail to: 555 37th St 94805-2205) Jose Torres Bayas Mary Hinse Katherine Salinaro (510) 232-7896

Ross New Skellig Celtic Christian Community **M** PO Box 217 94957-0217 (Mail to: PO Box 217 94957-0217)

Ross St Johns Episcopal Church **P** (1303) 14 Lagunitas Rd 94957 (Mail to: PO Box 217 94957-0217) Chris Rankin-Williams Charlton Fotch William Rankin Virginia Strickland Jan West (415) 456-1102

S San Fran St Elizabeths Episcopal Church **M** (50) 280 Country Club Dr 94080-5743 (Mail to: Attn: Mrs Ellen Jones 280 Country Club 94080-5743) Deborah Hawkins (650) 583-6678

San Bruno St Andrews Episcopal Church **M** (78) § 1600 Santa Lucia Ave 94066-4736 (Mail to: 1600 Santa Lucia Ave C/O Deborah Hawkins 94066-4798) (650) 583-6678

San Carlos Episcopal Church of the Epiphany **P** (526) 1839 Arroyo Ave 94070-3810 (Mail to: 1839 Arroyo Ave 94070-3899) Melanie Donahoe Hailey Delmas Alan Gates (650) 591-0328

San Francisco All Saints Episcopal Church **P** (168) 1350 Waller St 94117-2986 (Mail to: 1350 Waller St 94117-2986) Thomas Traylor (415) 621-1862

San Francisco Christ Episcopal Church Sei Ko Kai **M** (42) 2140 Pierce St 94115-2214 (Mail to: 2140 Pierce St 94115-2214) Debra Low-Skinner (415) 921-6395

San Francisco The Advent of Christ the King **P** (188) 261 Fell St 94102-5147 (Mail to: 162 Hickory St 94102-5908) Paul Allick Graham Hill Gregory Martin Roderick Thompson (415) 431-0454

San Francisco Holy Innocents Episcopal Church **M** (187) 455 Fair Oaks St 94110-3618 (Mail to: 455 Fair Oaks St 94110-3618) John Ayers Jane Mcdougle Kathleen Sylvester (415) 824-5142

San Francisco Episcopal Church of the Incarnation **P** (58) 1750 29th Ave 94122-4223 (Mail to: 1750 29th Ave 94122-4223) Darren Miner Lynn Bowdish Franco Kwan Christopher Webber (415) 564-2324

✠ **San Francisco** Grace Cathedral **O** (2216) § 1100 California St 94108-2206 (Mail to: 1100 California St 94108-2244) Malcolm Young Ellen Clark-King Mary Greene Jude Harmon Raymond Hoche-Mong Kenneth Parris Nina Pickerrell Kristin Saylor (415) 749-6300

San Francisco Iglesia Del Buen Samaritano **M** (70) 1661 15th St 94103-3511 (Mail to: 1661 15th St 94103-3511) (415) 869-7810

San Francisco Saint Aidan's Church **P** (171) 101 Gold Mine Dr 94131-2538 (Mail to: 101 Gold Mine Dr 94131-2538) Donald Fox Angela Guida Mark Henderson Cameron Partridge David Stickley (415) 285-9540

San Francisco St Cyprians Episcopal Church **M** (94) 2097 Turk Blvd 94115-4326 (Mail to: 2097 Turk Blvd 94115-4326) William Scott Thomas Jackson Eric Metoyer (415) 567-1855

San Francisco St Francis Episcopal Church **P** (417) 399 San Fernando Way 94127-1913 (Mail to: 399 San Fernando Way 94127-1913) Clarence Davis George Robert Kossler Christine Trainor (415) 334-1590

San Francisco St Gregory of Nyssa Episcopal Church **P** (391) 500 De Haro St 94107-2306 (Mail to: 500 De Haro St 94107-2306) Paul Fromberg Paul Fromberg Kerri Meyer (415) 255-8100

San Francisco St James Episcopal Church **P** (250) 4620 California St 94118-1225 (Mail to: 4620 California St 94118-1225) John Kirkley Gwen Buehrens Ronnie Willis (415) 751-1198

San Francisco St Lukes Episcopal Church **P** (260) 1755 Clay St 94109-3612 (Mail to: 1755 Clay St 94109-3682) Audrey Miskelley (415) 673-7327

San Francisco St Peters Episcopal Church **P** (48) 420 29th Ave 94121-1726 (Mail to: 430 29th Ave 94121) Ronald Mcbride (415) 751-4942

San Francisco St John the Evangelist Epis Church **P** (96) 1661 15th St 94103 (Mail to: 1661 15th St 94103-3511) Jacqueline Cherry Jeremy Clark-King Albert Pearson Richard Smith (415) 861-1436

San Francisco Church of St Mary the Virgin **P** (1291) 2325 Union St 94123-3905 (Mail to: 2325 Union St 94123-3905) Nancy Bryan David Erickson Mary Jizmagian Marguerite Judson Hollinshead Knight (415) 921-3665

San Francisco Trinity Church **M** (121) 1668 Bush St 94109-5308 (Mail to: 1620 Gough St 94109-4418) Patricia Cunningham (415) 775-1117

San Francisco True Sunshine Episcopal Church **P** (183) 1430 Mason St 94133-4222 (Mail to: 1430 Mason St 94133-4222) Thomas Chesterman Chan-Foo Ng Merry Ong (415) 956-2160

San Leandro All Saints Episcopal Church **P** (192) 911 Dowling Blvd 94577-2125 (Mail to: 911 Dowling Blvd 94577-2190) Justin Cannon Pamela Jester (510) 569-7020

San Mateo Episcopal Church of St Matthew **P** (912) § 1 S El Camino Real 94401-3800 (Mail to: 1 S El Camino Real 94401-3800) Eric Hinds (650) 342-1481

San Mateo Transfiguration Episcopal Church **P** (323) 3900 Alameda De Las Pulgas 94403-4110 (Mail to: 3900 Alameda De Las Pulgas 94403-4110) Matthew Woodward Jureck Fernandez (650) 341-8206

San Rafael Episcopal Church of the Nativity **P** (183) 333 Ellen Dr 94903-1666 (Mail to: 333 Ellen Dr 94903-1666) David Hammond Rebecca Morehouse Kirsten Spalding (415) 479-7023

San Rafael Episcopal Church of the Redeemer **M** (71) 123 Knight Dr 94901-1427 (Mail to: 123 Knight Dr 94901-1427) (415) 456-0508

San Rafael St Pauls Episcopal Church **P** (232) 1123 Court St 94901-2909 (Mail to: 1123 Court St 94901-2909) Christopher Martin (415) 456-4842

Sausalito Christ Episcopal Church **P** (203) 70 Santa Rosa Ave 94965-2041 (Mail to: PO Box 5 94966-0005) Sloane Larrimore Alberta Buller (415) 332-1539

Walnut Creek St Lukes Episcopal Church **P** (69) 1944 Tice Valley Blvd 94595 (Mail to: PO Box 2088 94595-0088) (925) 937-4820

Walnut Creek St Pauls Episcopal Church **P** (500) 1924 Trinity Ave 94596-4037 (Mail to: PO Box 4608 94596-0608) Donald Adolphson Laina Casillas Jeffrey Dodge Krista Fregoso (925) 934-2324

DIOCESE OF CENTRAL FLORIDA
(PROVINCE IV)
Comprises Central Florida
DIOCESAN OFFICE 1017 E Robinson St Orlando FL 32801
Tel (407) 423-3567   FAX (407) 872-0006
WEB www.cfdiocese.org

Previous Bishops —
Wm C Gray 1892-1913, Cameron Mann m 1913 dio 1922-32, John D Wing coadj 1925 Bp 1932-50, Martin J Bram suffr 1951-56, Wm F Moses suffr 1956-61, Henry I Louttit suffr 1945 coadj 1948 Bp 1951-69, James L Duncan suffr 1961-69, Wm L Hargrave suffr 1961-69, Wm H Folwell 1970-89, John W Howe 1989-2012

Bishop—Rt Rev Gregory O Brewer (1063) (Dio 24 March 2012)

Cn to Ord T Nunez; *Sec* S Caprani; *Treas* B Bauder 1417 E Concord St Orlando 32803; *Chanc* C Wooten Jr 236 S Lucerne Ave Orlando 32801-4490; *COM* O Kimbrough; *Ecum* Rt Rev H Pina-Lopez

[For Corrections, see p. 71

Stand Comm—Cler: J Davis A Petiprin E Turner W Garrison; Lay: P Tew S Shannon S Glynn

PARISHES, MISSIONS, AND CLERGY

Apopka Church Of The Holy Spirit **P** (383) 601 S Highland Ave 32703-5343 (Mail to: 601 S Highland Ave 32703-5343) Leonard Bartle John Pallard Gerald Steidl (407) 886-1740

Auburndale St Alban's Episcopal Church **P** (52) 202 Pontotoc Plaza 33823-3408 (Mail to: PO Box 1125 33823-1125) John Gullett (863) 967-2130

Avon Park Church of the Redeemer **M** (49) 910 W Martin Road 33825 (Mail to: PO Box 368 33826-0368) (863) 453-5664

Bartow Holy Trinity Episcopal Church **P** (85) 500 W Stuart St 33830-6200 (Mail to: PO Box 197 33831-0197) Patrice Behnstedt Rebecca Toalster (863) 533-3581

Belleview St Marys Episcopal Church **P** (325) 5750 Se 115th St 34420-4336 (Mail to: PO Box 2373 34421-2373) Carolyn Quinnell Robert Quinnell Lisa Wimmer (352) 347-6422

Bushnell St Francis of Assisi Church **M** (89) 313 Grace St 33513 (Mail to: PO Box 566 33513-0030) Karen House (352) 793-3187

Clermont St Matthias Episcopal Church **P** (286) 574 W Montrose St 34711-2261 (Mail to: 574 W Montrose St 34711-2285) James Dorn (352) 394-3855

Cocoa St Marks Episcopal Church **P** (470) § 4 Church St 32922-7912 (Mail to: 4 Church St 32922-7999) Gary Jackson (321) 636-3781

Cocoa Beach Church Of Saint David's By The Sea **P** (264) 600 S 4th St 32931-2612 (Mail to: 600 S 4th St 32931-2612) Scott Holcombe (321) 783-2554

Crystal River St Annes Episcopal Church **P** (378) 9870 W Fort Island Trl 34429-5383 (Mail to: 9870 W Fort Island Trl 34429-5383) Cheryl Bakker Cheryl Bakker Henry Brown Richard Chandler Gilbert Larsen (352) 795-2176

Daytona Beach St Marys Episcopal Church **P** (309) 216 Orange Ave 32114-4312 (Mail to: 216 Orange Ave 32114-4357) Jason Murbarger (386) 255-3669

Daytona Beach St Timothys Episcopal Church **M** (111) C/O Ms Gertrude Sheppard PO Box 10176 32120-0176 (Mail to: C/O Ms Gertrude Sheppard PO Box 10176 32120-0176) (386) 255-2077

Deland St Barnabas Episcopal Church **P** (457) § 319 W Wisconsin Ave 32720-4132 (Mail to: 319 W Wisconsin Ave 32720-4132) William Garrison (386) 734-1814

Deland The Church of the Holy Presence **M** (29) 355 Kepler Rd 32724-4713 (Mail to: 355 Kepler Rd 32724-4713) Carol McDonald (386) 734-5228

Dunnellon Church of the Advent **P** (151) 11251 Sw Highway 484 34432-6415 (Mail to: 11251 SW Highway 484 34432-6415) (352) 465-7272

Dunnellon Holy Faith Church **P** (108) 19924 W Blue Cove Dr 34432-5811 (Mail to: 19924 W Blue Cove Dr 34432-5811) John Gerhart (352) 489-2685

Enterprise All Saints Episcopal Church **P** (326) 155 Clark St 32725-8188 (Mail to: 155 Clark St 32725-8188) Linda Kromhout Robin Morical Gerald Raschke (386) 668-4108

Eustis Church of St Thomas **P** (396) 317 S Mary St 32726-4201 (Mail to: 317 S Mary St 32726-4201) Janet Clarke Richard Labud (352) 357-4358

Fort Meade Christ Episcopal Church **M** (15) 1 Cleveland Ave 33841-3017 (Mail to: 1 Cleveland Ave 33841-3017) (863) 368-1465

Fort Pierce Church of St Simon the Cyrenian **P** (60) 1700 Avenue E 34950-7953 (Mail to: PO Box 1147 34954-1147) (772) 461-2519

Fort Pierce St Andrews Episcopal Church **P** (490) § 210 S Indian River Dr 34950-4337 (Mail to: 210 S Indian River Dr 34950-4385) Michael Cannon Reid McCormick Lisa Wimmer (772) 461-5009

Fruitland Pk Holy Trinity Episcopal Church **P** (172) § 2201 Spring Lake Rd 34731-5256 (Mail to: 2201 Spring Lake Rd 34731-5256) Gerald Steidl Gregory Wilde (352) 787-1500

Haines City St Marks Episcopal Church **P** (260) 102 9th St 33844-4314 (Mail to: 102 9th St 33844-4314) (863) 422-1416

Inverness St Margarets Episcopal Church **P** (226) 114 Osceola Ave 34450-4121 (Mail to: 114 Osceola Ave 34450-4121) Eugene Reuman Barbara Pemberton (352) 726-3153

Kissimmee St Johns Episcopal Church **P** (585) 1709 John Young Pkwy 34741-3218 (Mail to: 1709 John Young Pkwy 34741-3200) Luis De la Cruz (407) 847-2009

Lake Mary St Peters Episcopal Church **P** (756) 700 Rinehart Rd 32746-4875 (Mail to: 700 Rinehart Rd 32746-4875) Jeremy Bergstrom Dane Wren (407) 444-5673

Lake Placid St Francis of Assisi Epis Church **P** (212) 43 Lake June Rd 33852-8910 (Mail to: 43 Lake June Rd 33852-8910) Elizabeth Nelson (863) 465-0051

Lake Wales The Church of the Good Shepherd **P** (536) 221 S 4th St 33853-3856 (Mail to: 221 4th St S 33853-3856) Timothy Nunez John Motis Suzanne Mulkin (863) 676-8578

Lakeland All Saints Episcopal Church **P** (1103) 202 S Massachusetts Ave 33801-5012 (Mail to: 209 S Iowa Ave 33801-5018) Larry Hensarling Kathy Hulin (863) 688-4502

Lakeland Christ the King Episcopal Church **P** (99) 6400 Socrum Loop Rd 33809-4141 (Mail to: 6400 Socrum Loop Rd 33809-4141) Carolyn Biggs Robert Dinnerville (863) 858-1948

Lakeland St Davids Episcopal Church **P** (561) 145 E Edgewood Dr 33803-4014 (Mail to: 145 E Edgewood Dr 33803-4014) Robert Moses

Robert Moses Raymond Perica Joan Verret (863) 686-4143

Lakeland St Stephens Church **P** (458) 1820 E County Road 540a 33813-3737 (Mail to: 1820 E County Road 540A 33813-3737) David Peoples Douglas Jump Robert Moses (863) 646-6115

Lecanto Shepherd Of The Hills Episcopal Church **P** (400) 2540 W Norvell Bryant Hwy 34461-9422 (Mail to: 2540 W Norvell Bryant Hwy 34461-9422) George Conger Michael Hall Linda Liebert-Hall (352) 527-0052

Leesburg St James Episcopal Church **P** (660) 204 Lee St 34748-4915 (Mail to: 204 Lee St 34748-4915) William Boyer Thomas Trees (352) 787-1981

Longwood Christ Episcopal Church **P** (60) 151 W Church Ave 32750-4105 (Mail to: C/O Heather Kirby 151 W Church Ave 32750-4105) Michelle Roach (407) 339-6812

Longwood Church of the Resurrection **P** (739) § 251 E Lake Brantley Dr 32779-4808 (Mail to: 251 E Lake Brantley Dr 32779-4808) Stephen Clifton John Garland (407) 788-3704

Maitland Church of the Good Shepherd **P** (225) 331 Lake Ave 32751-6331 (Mail to: 331 Lake Ave 32751-6331) Richard Costin Cameron Macmillan (407) 644-5350

Melbourne Holy Trinity Episcopal Church **P** (672) 50 W Strawbridge Ave 32901-4438 (Mail to: 1830 S Babcock St 32901-4443) Victoria Collins Pamela Easterday Stephen Easterday Meghan Farr Stacey Westphal (321) 723-5272

Melbourne Hope Episcopal Church **P** (191) 190 Interlachen Rd 32940-1979 (Mail to: 190 Interlachen Rd 32940-1979) Deborah Vann (321) 259-5810

Melbourne St Johns Episcopal Church **P** (167) 610 Young St 32935-7059 (Mail to: 610 Young St 32935-7059) Eric Turner (321) 254-3365

Melbourne Bch St Sebastians by the Sea **P** (187) 2010 Oak St 32951-2713 (Mail to: 2010 Oak St 32951-2713) John Edwards (321) 723-3015

Merritt Island St Lukes Episcopal Church **P** (293) 5555 Tropical Trl 32953-7202 (Mail to: PO Box 541025 32954-1025) Peter Roberts (321) 452-5260

Mount Dora St Edward the Confessor **P** (251) 460 Grandview St 32757-5676 (Mail to: 460 Grandview St 32757-5676) John Crandall Mark Lafler (352) 383-2832

Mulberry St Luke the Evangelist Church **M** (29) 505 Ne 1st Ave 33860-2434 (Mail to: 505 NE 1st Ave 33860-2434) (863) 425-2472

New Smyrna St Peter the Fisherman Church **P** (271) 4220 Saxon Dr 32169-3923 (Mail to: 4220 Saxon Dr 32169-3923) James Spencer (386) 428-7383

New Smyrna Beach Saint Paul's Episcopal Church **P** (195) 1650 Live Oak St 32168-7771 (Mail to: 1650 Live Oak St 32168-7771) Rodney Roehner David Hoag (386) 428-8733

Ocala Grace Episcopal Church **P** (395) 503 Se Broadway St 34471-2250 (Mail to: 510 SE Broadway St Ste 100 34471-2256) Jonathan French Mary Delancey Chester Trow (352) 622-7881

Ocala St Stephens Episcopal Church **M** (65) 55 Palm Rd 34472-2418 (Mail to: PO Box 831933 34483-1933) Margaret Silk-Wright (352) 687-2400

Okahumpka Corpus Christi Episcopal Church **M** (95) 3430 Country Road 470 34762 (Mail to: PO Box 68 34762-0068) Amanda Bordenkircher (352) 787-8430

Okeechobee Church of Our Saviour **P** (188) 200 Nw 3rd St 34972-4125 (Mail to: 200 NW 3rd St 34972-4125) James Shevlin Edward Weiss Kay Mueller (863) 763-4843

Orange City St Judes Episcopal Church **P** (193) 815 E Graves Ave 32763-5307 (Mail to: 815 E Graves Ave 32763-5307) Phyllis Bartle (386) 775-6200

✣ **Orlando** Cathedral Church of St Luke **O** (1163) Attn Anne Clarke PO Box 2328 32802-2328 (Mail to: 130 Magnolia Ave Ste 200 32801-2300) Joshua Bales Reggie Kidd Clint Matheny Nancy Oliver (407) 849-0680

Orlando Christ the King Episcopal Church **P** (221) 26 Willow Dr 32807-3220 (Mail to: 26 Willow Dr 32807-3298) Charles Rambo (407) 277-1151

Orlando Emmanuel Episcopal Church **P** (491) 1603 East Winter Park Rd 32803-2228 (Mail to: 1603 E Winter Park Rd 32803-2296) David Bumsted (407) 894-1641

Orlando Church of the Ascension **P** (532) 4950 S Apopka Vineland Rd 32819-3104 (Mail to: 4950 S Apopka Vineland Rd 32819-3104) James Sorvillo Matthew Ainsley Beth Wagner (407) 876-3480

Orlando Holy Family Episcopal Church **P** (493) 1010 Hiawassee Rd 32818-6711 (Mail to: 1010 Hiawassee Rd 32818-6711) Peter Magill (407) 293-2236

Orlando Iglesia Episcopal Jesus de Nazaret **M** (169) 26 Willow Dr 32807-3220 (Mail to: 26 Willow Dr 32807-3220) Jose Rodriguez-Sanjurjo (407) 222-7995

Orlando Iglesia Episcopal San Cristobal **M** (149) 7500 Forest City Rd 32810-3710 (Mail to: 7500 Forest City Rd 32810-3710) Carlos Marin (407) 293-5653

Orlando St Mary of the Angels Epis Church **P** (247) 6316 Matchett Rd 32809-5150 (Mail to: 6316 Matchett Rd 32809-5196) Kevin Bartle Raul Rubiano-Alvarado (407) 855-1930

Orlando St Matthews Episcopal Church **P** (428) 5873 Dean Rd 32817-3201 (Mail to: 5873 Dean Rd 32817-3201) Sonia Sullivan-Clifton Kenneth Vinal (407) 657-9199

Orlando St Michaels Church **P** (647) 2499 Westmoreland Dr 32804-4934 (Mail to: C/O Tyler Piercy 2499 Westmoreland Dr 32804-

4934) Richard Luoni Gregory Favazza (407) 843-8448

Orlando St John the Baptist Church **P** (199) 1000 Bethune Dr 32805-3404 (Mail to: 1000 Bethune Dr 32805-3404) (407) 295-1923

Ormond Beach Church of the Holy Child **P** (109) 1225 W Granada Blvd 32174-5914 (Mail to: 1225 W Granada Blvd State Road 40 32174-5914) Stephen Pessah (386) 672-4470

Ormond Beach St James Episcopal Church **P** (716) 38 S Halifax Dr 32176-6597 (Mail to: 38 S Halifax Dr 32176-6597) Ernest Bennett Charles Allison Walter Lyon (386) 677-1811

Oviedo Church of the Incarnation **M** (193) 1601 Alafaya Trl 32765-9485 (Mail to: 1601 Alafaya Trl 32765-9485) Thomas Buchan Thomas Phillips (407) 365-5651

Palm Bay Church of Our Savior **P** (227) 1000 Jersey Ln Ne 32905-5519 (Mail to: 1000 Jersey Ln NE 32905-5519) Dee Bright Thomas Williams (321) 723-8032

Palm Bay Episcopal Church of the Blessed Redeemer **M** (99) 1225 Degroodt Rd SW 32908-7102 (Mail to: 1225 Degroodt Rd SW 32908-7102) Brian Turner (321) 725-6881

Port Orange Grace Episcopal Church **P** (305) 4110 S Ridgewood Ave 32127-4519 (Mail to: PO Box 290245 32129-0245) Charles Burhans (386) 767-3583

Port St Lucie Church of the Nativity **P** (364) 1151 Sw Del Rio Blvd 34953-1520 (Mail to: 1151 SW Del Rio Blvd 34953-1520) John Jasper (772) 343-0401

Port St Lucie Holy Faith Episcopal Church **P** (393) 6990 S Us Highway 1 34952-1424 (Mail to: 6990 S US Highway 1 34952-1499) Orlando Addison (772) 446-9619

Saint Cloud Church of St Luke & St Peter **P** (244) 2745 Canoe Creek Rd 34772-6502 (Mail to: 2745 Canoe Creek Rd 34772-6502) Robert Longbottom (407) 892-3227

Sanford Holy Cross Episcopal Church **P** (237) 410 S Magnolia Ave 32771-1918 (Mail to: 410 S Magnolia Ave 32771-1918) Ann Kruger Edward Smith (407) 322-4611

Satellite Bch Church of the Holy Apostles **P** (215) 505 Grant Ave 32937-2921 (Mail to: 505 Grant Ave 32937-2921) Todd Schmidtetter Donald Goodheart (321) 777-0024

Sebastian St Elizabeths Episcopal Church **P** (263) 901 Clearmont St 32958-4978 (Mail to: 901 Clearmont St 32958-4978) David Newhart (772) 589-2770

Sebring Saint Agnes Church **P** (215) 3840 Lakeview Dr 33870-2066 (Mail to: 3840 Lakeview Dr C/O Scott Walker 33870-2066) Scott Walker (863) 385-7649

The Villages St George Episcopal Church **P** (643) 1250 Paige Pl 32159-9315 (Mail to: 1250 Paige Pl 32159-9315) Edward Bartle Francis Kelly (352) 750-1010

Titusville St Gabriels Episcopal Church **P** (310) PO Box 6584 32782-6584 (Mail to: 414 Pine St 32796-3542) Robert Goodridge (321) 267-2545

Vero Beach St Augustine of Canterbury **P** (743) 475 43rd Ave 32968-1836 (Mail to: 475 43rd Ave 32968-1836) Michael Goldberg Denise Hudspeth (772) 770-3494

Vero Beach Trinity Episcopal Church **P** (282) 2365 Pine Ave 32960-0528 (Mail to: Attn: Accounts Payable 2365 Pine Ave 32960-0528) Christopher Rodriguez Joshua Gritter (772) 567-1146

Wauchula St Anns Episcopal Church **M** (25) 204 9th Ave 33873-2616 (Mail to: PO Box 1874 33873-1874) (863) 773-6418

Winter Garden Church of the Messiah **P** (330) 241 Main Street 34787 (Mail to: 241 Main St 34787-2826) Thomas Rutherford Julie Altenbach Tracy Dugger (407) 656-3218

Winter Haven Holy Cross Church **P** (149) 201 Kipling Ln 33884-2316 (Mail to: 201 Kipling Ln 33884-2316) Woodford Miller (863) 324-4021

Winter Haven St Pauls Church **P** (314) 656 Avenue L Nw 33881-4058 (Mail to: 656 Avenue L Nw 33881-4030) Paul Head Susan Hansell (863) 294-8888

Winter Park All Saints Episcopal Church **P** (1748) 338 E Lyman Ave 32789-4415 (Mail to: 338 E Lyman Ave 32789-4494) Franck Shelby Christopher Nations Rose Sapp Russell Wohlever (407) 647-3413

Winter Park St Richards Episcopal Church **P** (437) 5151 Lake Howell Rd 32792-1027 (Mail to: 5151 Lake Howell Rd 32792-1095) Alison Harrity Robert Vanderau (407) 671-4211

DIOCESE OF THE CENTRAL GULF COAST
(PROVINCE IV)
Comprises Southern AL and Northwest FL
DIOCESAN OFFICE 201 N Baylen St Pensacola FL 32502 (MAIL: Box 13330 Pensacola FL 32591-3330)
TEL (850) 434-7337   FAX (850) 434-8577
E-MAIL (staff name)@diocgc.org WEB www.diocgc.org

Previous Bishops—
George Mosley Murray 1971-81,
Charles Farmer Duvall DD 1981-
2001, Philip Menzie Duncan II
2001-15

Bishop—Rt Rev James Russell Kendrick (Dio July 25 2015)

Dio Admin D Babcock; *Chanc (AL)* K Miller Box 290 Mobile AL 36601; *Chanc (FL)* S Remmington Box 13010 Pensacola FL 32591; *Reg & Hist* A Kennington; *Treas* M Nicrosi

Stand Comm—Cler: R Crow M Shephard B Gibson G Hein M McDonald C Howard; *Lay: Pres* K Branch H Hall B Landrum V Currie A Richey L Ferren G Moore J McDaniel B Scott

PARISHES, MISSIONS, AND CLERGY
Alabama

Andalusia St Marys Episcopal Church **P** (119) 1307 E Three Notch St 36420-3403 (Mail to: 1307 E Three Notch St 36420-3403) Cynthia Howard (334) 222-2487

Atmore St Annas Episcopal Church **M** (143) 100 Lynn Mcghee Dr 36502-5057 (Mail to: 100 Lynn McGhee Dr 36502-5057) Teresa Leifur (251) 368-8606

Atmore Trinity Episcopal Church **P** (39) 203 S Carney St 36502-2404 (Mail to: 203 S Carney St 36502-2404) (251) 368-5933

Bay Minette Immanuel Episcopal Church **M** (50) 700 Mcmillan Ave 36507-4425 (Mail to: Attn Claire B Jackson 700 McMillan Ave 36507-4425) Spergeon Kennington (251) 937-7900

Bon Secour St Peters Episcopal Church **P** (168) 6270 Bon Secour Hwy 36511 (Mail to: PO Box 29 36511-0029) Bryan Gentry Susan McKee (251) 949-6254

Brewton St Stephens Episcopal Church **P** (167) 1510 Escambia Ave 36426-1124 (Mail to: PO Box 1261 36427-1261) (251) 867-4545

Citronelle St Thomas Episcopal Church **M** (4) 19030 S Center St 36522-2546 (Mail to: PO Box 813 36522-0813) (251) 866-7003

Coden St Marys by the Sea Episcopal Church **M** (52) 4875 Highway 188 36523-3703 (Mail to: 4875 Highway 188 36523-3703) Sara Phillips Sara Phillips (251) 873-5602

Daphne St Pauls Episcopal Church **P** (871) 28788 Main St 36526-7258 (Mail to: 28788 Main St 36526-7258) Thack Dyson (251) 626-2421

Dauphin Islnd St Francis Episcopal Church **M** (53) 401 Key St 36528 (Mail to: PO Box 407 36528-0407) (251) 861-2300

Dothan Episcopal Church of the Nativity **P** (549) 205 Holly Ln 36301-1438 (Mail to: 205 Holly Ln 36301-1438) Peter Wong Alice Sawyer (334) 793-7616

Enterprise Episcopal Church of the Epiphany **M** (76) § 302 East Grubbs St 36330-2613 (Mail to: 302 E Grubbs St 36330-2613) John Withrock (334) 347-8210

Eufaula St James Episcopal Church **P** (339) 100 Saint James Pl 36027-1551 (Mail to: 100 Saint James Pl 36027-1551) John Coleman (334) 687-3619

Fairhope St James Episcopal Church **P** (1519) § 860 Section St 36532-6376 (Mail to: 860 Section St 36532-6376) Denson Freeman Mary Jayne Ledgerwood (251) 928-2912

Foley St Pauls Episcopal Church **P** (519) 506 Pine St 36535-2039 (Mail to: PO Box 1745 36536-1745) Thomas Talbert (251) 943-2173

Greenville St Thomas Episcopal Church **P** (156) 210 Church St 36037-2606 (Mail to: 210 Church St 36037-2606) Linda Suzanne Borgen (334) 382-8914

Gulf Shores Holy Spirit Episcopal Church **P** (371) 616 W Fort Morgan Rd 36542-4300 (Mail to: PO Box 2346 36547-2346) Jeffery Garner (251) 968-5988

Jackson St Peters Episcopal Church **M** (35) 100 Hospital Dr 36545-2424 (Mail to: PO Box 146 36545-0146) Patrick Dunn (251) 246-8092

Lillian Church of the Advent **M** (79) 12099 County Road 99 36549-5128 (Mail to: 12099 County Road 99 36549-5128) Mark Mcdonald (251) 961-2505

Magnolia Sprgs St Pauls Episcopal Church **P** (140) 14755 Oak Ave 36555 (Mail to: PO Box 2 36555-0002) Dennis Day Susan McKee Eric Zubler (251) 965-7452

Mobile All Saints Episcopal Church **P** (418) 151 S Ann St 36604-2302 (Mail to: 151 S Ann St 36604-2391) James Flowers (251) 438-2492

Mobile Christ Church Cathedral **P** (593) 115 S Conception St 36602-2606 (Mail to: 115 S Conception St 36602-2606) Marshall Craver Beverly Gibson (251) 438-1822

Mobile Church of the Good Shepherd **P** (206) 605 Donald St 36617-3401 (Mail to: 605 Donald St 36617-3401) John George (251) 452-9596

Mobile St Andrews Episcopal Church **M** (48) 1854 Staples Rd 36605-4560 (Mail to: 1854 Staples Rd 36605-4560) (251) 479-0336

Mobile St Johns Episcopal Church **P** (148) 1707 Government St 36604-1103 (Mail to: 1707 Government St 36604-1194) Thomas Heard (251) 479-5474

Mobile St Lukes Episcopal Church **P** (648) § 1050 Azalea Rd 36693-2804 (Mail to: 1050 Azalea Rd 36693-2804) (251) 666-2990

Mobile St Marks For the Deaf **M** (7) 6109 Howells Ferry The Willmer Hall 36618-3147 (Mail to: PO Box 180068 36618-0068) (251) 281-2148

Mobile St Pauls Episcopal Church **P** (2365) § 4051 Old Shell Rd 36608-1337 (Mail to: 4051 Old Shell Rd 36608-1399) John Riggin John Riggin Reuben Rockwell (251) 342-8521

Mobile Episcopal Church of the Redeemer **P** (261) 1100 Cody Rd S 36695-4400 (Mail to: 7125 Hitt Rd 36695-4431) Joy Blaylock (251) 639-1948

Mobile Trinity Episcopal Church **P** (453) 1900 Dauphin St 36606-1414 (Mail to: PO Box 6176 36660-0176) Lynn Norman (251) 473-2779

Monroeville Saint John's Church **P** (104) 200 Whetstone St 36460-2698 (Mail to: PO Box 853 36461-0853) (251) 743-4549

Ozark St Michaels Episcopal Church **M** (74) 427 Camilla Ave 36360-2281 (Mail to: 427 Camilla Ave 36360-2281) (334) 774-2617

Robertsdale St John the Evangelist Epis Church **M** (110) 22764 Us Highway 90 36567-2805 (Mail to: PO Box 1137 36567-1137) George Gilbert (251) 914-6011

Troy St Mark's Episcopal Church **P** (193) 401 W College St 36081-2108 (Mail to: 401 W College St 36081-2196) Jeffrey Byrd Curtis Kennington (334) 566-2619

Florida

Apalachicola Trinity Episcopal Church **P** (158) 79 6th St 32329 (Mail to: PO Box 667 32329-0667) Donnna Gerold (850) 653-9550

Cantonment St Monicas Episcopal Church **P** (118) 699 S Highway 95a 32533-6485 (Mail to: 699 S Highway 95A 32533-6485) Anthony MacWhinnie (850) 937-0001

Chickasaw St Michaels Episcopal Church **M** (65) 300 Grant St 36611-2132 (Mail to: PO Box 11484 36671-0484) (251) 457-6698

Chipley St Matthews Episcopal Church **M** (67) 736 West Blvd 32428-1629 (Mail to: PO Box 345 32428-0345) Michael Dickey (850) 638-7837

Crestview Episcopal Church of the Epiphany **M** (107) PO Box 612 32536-0612 (Mail to: 424 Garden St 32536-1704) (850) 689-1410

Defuniak Spgs St Agathas Episcopal Church **M** (70) 144 Circle Dr 32435-2545 (Mail to: 144 Circle Dr 32435-2545) (850) 892-7254

Destin St Andrew's By-the-Sea Epis Church **P** (92) 307 Harbor Blvd 32541-2383 (Mail to: PO Box 1658 32540-1658) Joseph Hagberg (850) 650-2737

Ft Walton Bch St Simons on-the-Sound Epis Church **P** (376) 28 Miracle Strip Pkwy Sw 32548-6613 (Mail to: 28 Miracle Strip Pkwy SW 32548-6613) James Knight Thomas Sirmon (850) 244-8621

Gulf Breeze St Francis of Assisi Epis Church **P** (287) 1 Saint Francis Dr 32561-4825 (Mail to: 1 Saint Francis Dr 32561-4825) Timothy Backus (850) 932-2861

Marianna St Lukes Episcopal Church **P** (142) 4362 Lafayette St 32446-2916 (Mail to: 4362 Lafayette St 32446-2916) David Green (850) 482-2431

Milton St Marys Episcopal Church **P** (161) 6841 Oak St 32570-6791 (Mail to: 6849 Oak St 32570-6791) Matthew Dollhausen (850) 623-2905

Navarre St Augustine of Canterbury **P** (133) 7810 Navarre Pkwy 32566-7585 (Mail to: PO Box 5425 32566-0425) (850) 939-2261

Niceville St Judes Episcopal Church **P** (278) 200 Partin Dr 32578-1244 (Mail to: 200 Partin Dr 32578-1244) Charles Hein (850) 678-7013

Panama City Holy Nativity Episcopal Church **P** (703) § 222 Bonita Ave 32401-3853 (Mail to: 1011 E 3rd St 32401-3737) Steven Bates Thomas Weller (850) 747-4000

Panama City St Andrews Episcopal Church **P** (251) 1608 Baker Ct 32401-1900 (Mail to: 1608 Baker Ct 32401-1900) Mary Payne-Hardin (850) 763-7636

Panama City St Patricks Episcopal Church **M** (76) 4025 East Fifteenth Street 32404-5862 (Mail to: PO Box 36943 324010061) Julia Phillips (850) 763-7847

Panama City Beach Grace Episcopal Church **P** (124) 9101 Panama City Beach Pkwy 32407-4021 (Mail to: PO Box 9087 32417-9087) (850) 235-4136

Panama City Beach St Thomas by-the-Sea Epis Church **M** (95) 20408 First Ave 32413-8902 (Mail to: PO Box 7359 32413-0359) (850) 234-2919

Pensacola Christ Episcopal Church **P** (2123) § 18 W Wright St 32501 (Mail to: PO Box 12683 32591-2683) Kathryn Gillett Michael Hoffman Betty Brenemen Walter Kindergan James Lord John Phillips (850) 432-5115

Pensacola Holy Cross Episcopal Church **P** (388) 7979 9th Ave 32514-6460 (Mail to: 7979 9th Ave 32514-6460) Robert Dixon Roger Hungerford (850) 477-8596

Pensacola Holy Trinity Episcopal Church **P** (115) 850 Blue Angel Pkwy 32506-6304 (Mail to: PO Box 3068 32516-3068) (850) 434-7337

Pensacola St Christophers Episcopal Church **P** (1118) 3200 12th Ave 32503-4007 (Mail to: 3200 12th Ave 32503-4007) Walter Kindergan Nicholas Phares Susan Sowers (850) 433-0074

Pensacola St Cyprians Episcopal Church **M** (47) 500 N. Reus St. 32501 (Mail to: PO Box 17165 32522-7165) (850) 438-1958

Pensacola St Johns Episcopal Church **P** (108) 401 Live Oak Ave 32507-3431 (Mail to: 401 Live Oak Ave 32507-3431) Christine Hord (850) 453-9076

Port St Joe St James Episcopal Church **P** (108) 800 22nd St 32456-2298 (Mail to: 800 22nd St 32456-2298) Thomas Dwyer (850) 227-1845

Santa Rosa Bch Christ the King Episcopal Church **P** (298) 480 Hwy 393 32459 (Mail to: PO Box 1677 32459-1677) Richard Proctor (850) 267-3332

Wewahitchka St John the Baptist Episcopal Church **M** (52) 4060 Highway 71 PO Box 595 32465-0595 (Mail to: PO Box 595 32465-0595) (850) 639-2280

DIOCESE OF CENTRAL NEW YORK

(PROVINCE II)
Comprises 14 counties in Central NY
DIOCESAN OFFICE 1020 7th North St Ste 200 Liverpool NY 13088
Tel (315) 474-6596   FAX (315) 457-2947
E-mail office@cnyepiscopal.org   WEB www.cnyepiscopal.org

Previous Bishops—
Frederic D Huntington 1869-1904, Chas T Olm stead coadj 1902 Bp 1904-21, Chas Fiske coadj 1915 Bp 1921-36, Edward H Coley suffr 1924 Bp 1936-42, Malcolm E Peabody coadj 1938 Bp 1942-60, Walter M Higley suffr 1948 coadj 1959 Bp 1960-69, Ned Cole coadj 1964 Bp 1969-83, O'Kelley Whitaker coadj 1981 Bp 1983-92, David B Joslin coadj 1991 Bp 1992-99 David Bowman asst Bp 2000-01 Gladstone B Adams III 2001-16

Bishop — Rt Rev Dr DeDe Duncan-Probe (1097) (Dio 03 Dec 16)

Can to Ord Rev J Crosswaite; *Can for Trans & Church Dev* Rev C Schofield-Broadbent; *Comm* MK Sanderson; *Exec Asst* KD McDaniel; *Conv Sec* Rev J Martinichio; *Chanc* PJ Curtin Jr 42 Albany St Cazenovia NY 13035; *Vice Chan* M Berry; *COM* Rev Dr D Cleaver-Bartholomew; *Cursillo* T Weir; *Ecum Off* TBA; *ER&D* Rev P Mouncey & G Lipp; *Lit* TBA; *Stew* Rev C Schofield-Broadbent; *UTO* M Dawson; *Yth* T Blum; *Safe Church* TBA; *Comp Dio* Rev Dcn Dr C Stewart; *Deploy* C Schofield-Broadbent; *Global Miss* Rev Dcn D Pierce

Stand Comm: Cler: Pres C Day B Cato J Kenna J Amaya; *Lay:* F Hallanan S Balduf M Dawson B Hallinan

Dio Bd—Cler: Ch Bp D Duncan-Probe; Rev J Martinichio Rev W Copeland Rev Dr L Mozeliak Rev Dr D Cleaver-Bartholomew Rev J Kenna; *Lay: Ch* PJ Curtin; *Treas* TBD T Weir M Webber A Smith P Currier C Forrester

PARISHES, MISSIONS, AND CLERGY

Adams Emmanuel Episcopal Church **P** (133) 40 E Church St 13605 (Mail to: PO Box 29 13605-0029) (315) 232-2916

Afton St Anns Church **P** (65) 125 E Main St 13730-2264 (Mail to: PO Box 22 13730-0022)

(607) 639-2330

Alexandria Bay Church of St Lawrence **SC** 7 Fuller St 13607 (Mail to: 7 Fuller St 13607-1393) John Andersen

Auburn Epis Church of SS Peter and John **P** (268) 169 Genesee St 13021-3403 (Mail to: 169 Genesee St 13021-3403) Kathlyn Schofield (315) 252-5721

Aurora United Ministry of Aurora **P** (17) Main St 13026 (Mail to: PO Box 91 13026-0091) (315) 364-8543

Bainbridge St Peters Episcopal Church **P** (173) 1 Church St 13733-1237 (Mail to: 1 Church St 13733-1237) Thomas Margrave (607) 967-3441

Baldwinsville Grace Episcopal Church **P** (338) 110 Oswego St 13027-1129 (Mail to: PO Box 6 13027-0006) Catherine Carpenter (315) 635-3214

Barneveld St Davids Episcopal Church **P** (79) 140 Mappa Ave 13304-2422 (Mail to: PO Box 344 13304-0344) Sarah Lewis (315) 896-2595

Berkshire St Johns Episcopal Church **P** (33) 1504 Seventy 6 Rd 13736 (Mail to: C/O The Rev Richard Schaal 877 Mountain Rd 13827-1187) Richard Schaal (607) 687-1425

Binghamton Christ Church Episcopal **P** (255) 187 Washington St 13901-2713 (Mail to: 10 Henry St 13901-2789) Elizabeth Ewing Charles Jones (607) 722-2308

Binghamton St Marks Episcopal Church **P** (306) 728 River Rd 13901-1263 (Mail to: PO Box 458 13745-0458) Mark Giroux (607) 648-4400

Binghamton Trinity Memorial Church **P** (245) 44 Main St 13905-3108 (Mail to: 44 Main St 13905-3181) Kay Drebert (607) 723-3593

Black River St Johns Episcopal Church **P** (63) 145 W Remington St 13612-3124 (Mail to: PO Box 247 13612-0247) Ninon Hutchinson Wayne Storey (315) 788-3738

Boonville Trinity Episcopal Church **P** (74) Schuyler St 13309-1203 (Mail to: PO Box 151 13309-0151) Linda Logan (315) 942-4726

Brownville St Pauls Episcopal Church **P** (68) 210 Washington St 13615 (Mail to: 314 Clay St 13601-3304) (315) 788-3730

Camden Trinity Episcopal Church **P** (53) 98 Main St 13316-1303 (Mail to: PO Box 102 13316-0102) (315) 245-1987

Camillus St Lukes Episcopal Church **P** (284) 5402 W Genesee St 13031-2138 (Mail to: PO Box 91 13031-0091) Jon White (315) 487-1771

Canastota Trinity Episcopal Church **P** (67) 400 S Peterboro St 13032-1416 (Mail to: PO Box 26 13032-0026) James Heidt (315) 697-2953

Candor St Marks Episcopal Church **P** (76) 17 Main St 13743-1617 (Mail to: 112 Logue Hill Rd 13743-2043) (607) 659-7479

Cape Vincent St Johns Church **P** (52) 352 S. Market St 13618 (Mail to: PO Box 561 13618-0561) Lisa Busby (315) 654-3833

Carthage Grace Episcopal Church **P** (71) 421 State St 13619-1413 (Mail to: 421 State St 13619) (315) 493-0382

Cazenovia St Peters Episcopal Church **P** (160) 10 Mill St 13035-1406 (Mail to: PO Box 419 13035-0419) Jeanne Hansknecht (315) 655-9063

Chadwicks St Georges Episcopal Church **P** (110) 9389 Elm St P.O. Box P 13319 (Mail to: 9389 Elm St 13319-3517) Terry Sheldon (315) 737-8124

Chittenango St Pauls Church **P** (218) 204 Genesee St 13037-1705 (Mail to: 204 Genesee St 13037-1705) (315) 687-6304

Clark Mills St Marks Episcopal Church **P** (110) 19 White St 13321 (Mail to: PO Box 363 13321-0363) Terry Sheldon (315) 853-8124

Clayton Christ Episcopal Church **P** (180) 235 John St 13624-1014 (Mail to: 235 John St 13624-1014) Lisa Busby (315) 686-3703

Clinton St James Episcopal Church **P** (362) 9 Williams St 13323-1705 (Mail to: 9 Williams St 13323-1705) Gary Cyr (315) 853-5359

Constableville St Pauls Episcopal Church **P** (10) 27 Church St 13325 (Mail to: PO Box 69 13325-0069) (315) 942-4726

Constantia Trinity Episcopal Church **P** (24) 1492 George Street 13044-0124 (Mail to: PO Box 124 13044-0124) (315) 623-7431

Copenhagen Grace Church **P** (34) 21 Cataract St 13626 (Mail to: Mrs Holly Evans PO Box 6 13626-0006) Holly Evans (315) 688-2867

Cortland Grace and Holy Spirit Church **P** (247) 13 Court St 13045-2603 (Mail to: PO Box 170 13045-0170) Peter Williams (607) 753-3073

East Syracuse Emmanuel Episcopal Church **P** (120) 400 W Yates St 13057-2140 (Mail to: 400 W Yates St 13057-2140) Gerard Beritela (315) 463-4310

Elmira Emmanuel Church **P** (70) 380 Pennsylvania Ave 14904-1759 (Mail to: 380 Pennsylvania Ave 14904-1759) Robert Adkins (607) 733-8219

Elmira Grace Episcopal Church **P** (427) 375 W Church St 14901-2620 (Mail to: Attn: Anne H Ferris 375 W Church St 14901-2695) Howard Whitaker (607) 732-0545

Elmira Trinity Episcopal Church **P** (348) 304 Main St 14901-2710 (Mail to: 304 Main St 14901-2778) Wanda Copeland (607) 732-3241

Endicott St Pauls Episcopal Church **P** (319) 200 Jefferson Ave 13760-5212 (Mail to: 200 Jefferson Ave 13760-5295) John Martinichio (607) 748-8118

Evans Mills St Andrews Church **P** (16) 8520 LeRay St 13637 (Mail to: C/O Barbara Burnup 22925 Duffy Rd 13601-1719) Anne Wichelns (315) 350-4844

Fayetteville St Davids Episcopal Church **P** (200) 14 Jamar Dr 13066-1619 (Mail to: PO Box 261 13214-0261) Kathryn Corley Katherine Day (315) 446-2112

Fayetteville Trinity Episcopal Church **P** (600) 106 Chapel St 13066-2004 (Mail to: 106 Chapel St 13066-2052) Renee Tembeckjian (315) 637-9872

Fulton All Saints Episcopal Church **P** (155) 153 S 1st St 13069-1716 (Mail to: PO Box 542 13069-0542) (315) 592-2102

Geneva Grace Church Willowdale **P** (17) 3874 E Lake Rd 14456-9256 (Mail to: C/O Lloyd D Evans PO Box 135 14456-0135) (315) 585-9852

Greene Zion Episcopal Church **P** (369) 10 Chenango St 13778-1102 (Mail to: PO Box 88 13778-0088) Geoffrey Doolittle David Hanselman (607) 656-9502

Hamilton St Thomas Episcopal Church **P** (129) 12 1 2 Madison St 13346 (Mail to: 12 1/2 Madison St 13346-1106) Brooks Cato (315) 824-1745

Horseheads St Matthews Episcopal Church **P** (174) 408 S Main St 14845-2409 (Mail to: 408 S Main St 14845-2409) Wanda Copeland (607) 739-5226

Ithaca Episcopal Church at Cornell **CC** G3 Anabel Taylor Hall Cornell 548 College Ave 14853-4902 (Mail to: G3 Anabel Taylor Hall Cornell 548 College Ave 14853-4902) Taylor Daynes (607) 255-4219

Ithaca St Johns Episcopal Church **P** (346) 210 Cayuga St 14850-4333 (Mail to: 210 Cayuga St 14850-4385) Megan Castellan (607) 273-6532

Johnson City All Saints Episcopal Church **P** (191) 475 Main St 13790-1906 (Mail to: 475 Main St 13790-1999) Christine Day Geoffrey Doolittle (607) 797-3354

Jordan Christ Episcopal Church **P** (62) 25 Main Street 13080-0571 (Mail to: PO Box 571 13080-0571) Joseph Bergin (315) 689-3141

Liverpool St Matthews Episcopal Church **P** (290) 900 Vine St 13088-4502 (Mail to: 904 Vine Street 13088-4502) Paul Frolick (315) 457-4633

Lowville Trinity Church **P** (119) § 5411 Trinity Ave 13367-1315 (Mail to: 5411 Trinity Ave 13367-1315) (315) 376-3241

Manlius Christ Church **P** (266) 407 E Seneca St 13104-1910 (Mail to: 407 E Seneca St 13104-1910) Dena Cleaver-Bartholomew (315) 682-5795

✥ **Marathon** St Johns Chapel **O** West Main St 13803 (Mail to: PO Box 541 13783-0541) Elizabeth Groskoph (607) 637-4952

Marcellus St Johns Episcopal Church **P** (182) 15 Orange St 13108-1215 (Mail to: 15 Orange St 13108-1215) (315) 673-2500

Mexico Grace Episcopal Church **P** (46) 4381 Church St 13114 (Mail to: C/O Ms Janice H Clark PO Box 539 13114-0539) (315) 297-0254

Moravia St Matthews Church **P** (96) 14 Church St 13118 (Mail to: 14 Church St 13118) Perry Mouncey (315) 497-1171

✥ **Nedrow** Church of the Good Shepherd **O** US Rte 11 13120 (Mail to: PO Box 143 13120-0143) (315) 469-0247

New Berlin St Andrews Episcopal Church **P** (128) South Main St 13411 (Mail to: PO Box 370 40 S Main St 13411-0370) William White (607) 847-6361

New Hartford St Stephens Church **P** (144) 25 Oxford Rd 13413-2638 (Mail to: 25 Oxford Rd 13413-2662) Joell Szachara (315) 732-7462

Norwich Emmanuel Episcopal Church **P** (385) 37 W Main St 13815 (Mail to: PO Box 203 13815-0203) (607) 334-8801

Oneida St Johns Church **P** (232) 341 Main St 13421-2144 (Mail to: 341 Main St 13421-2144) Arthur Smith (315) 363-1940

Oswego Church of the Resurrection **P** (174) 120 W 5th St 13126-2037 (Mail to: C/O Alexander Thompson 120 W 5th St 13126-2037) Anne Wichelns (315) 343-3501

Owego St Pauls Episcopal Church **P** (148) 117 Main St 13827-1587 (Mail to: 117 Main St 13827-1587) Trula Hollywood (607) 687-2830

Oxford St Pauls Church **P** (150) 36 Main St 13830 (Mail to: PO Box 72 13830-0072) David Hanselman (607) 843-7011

Pville St Pauls Chapel **SC** 310 Montgomery St #200 13429 (Mail to: C/O Saint Stephens Route 12 13429) (315) 733-7575

Pierrepont Manor Zion Church **P** (113) 15639 NY State Rt 193 13674 (Mail to: PO Box 782 13674-0782) Charles Henderson John Throop (315) 232-2916

Port Leyden St Marks Episcopal Church **P** (14) 6988 Main St 13433 (Mail to: PO Box 31 13433-0031) (315) 942-4726

Pulaski St James Episcopal Church **P** (150) 24 Lake St 13142-3243 (Mail to: PO Box 433 24 Lake St 13142-0433) (315) 298-2106

Rome Zion Episcopal Church **P** (107) 140 W Liberty St 13440-5718 (Mail to: 140 W Liberty St 13440-5780) James Heidt (315) 336-5170

Sackets Hbr Christ Church **M** 207 E Main St 13685-3158 (Mail to: East Main Street 13685) (315) 646-2217

Seneca Falls Trinity Episcopal Church **P** (105) 27 Fall St 13148-1428 (Mail to: PO Box 507 13148-0507) (315) 568-5145

Sherburne Episcopal Church of the Epiphany **P** (106) 5 Classic Street 13830 (Mail to: PO Box 538 13460-0538) Bruce MacDuffie (607) 674-4312

Sherrill Gethsemane Episcopal Church **P** (98) 320 Park St 13461-1253 (Mail to: 320 Park St 13461-1253) (315) 363-3244

Skaneateles St James Episcopal Church **P** (591) 96 E Genesee St 13152-1328 (Mail to: 96 E Genesee St 13152-1372) Rebecca Coerper Charles Stewart (315) 685-7600

Slaterville Springs St Thomas Episcopal Church **P** (37) 2729 Slaterville Rd (Rte 79) 14881 (Mail to: PO Box 51 14817-0051) Gary Gruberth (607) 227-5118

South New Berlin St Matthews Church **P** (43) State Hwy 8 13843 (Mail to: PO Box 18 13843-0018) (607) 847-6361

Syracuse Church of the Saviour **Chapel** 437 James St 13203-2224 (Mail to: 437 James St 13203-2224) Gerard Beritela (315) 474-3359

Syracuse Ephphatha Parish for the Deaf **P** 310 Montgomery St Ste 250 13202-2010 (Mail to: 310 Montgomery Street Ste 250 13202) Peter Williams Virginia Nagel (315) 471-3736

Syracuse Grace Church **P** (172) 819 Madison St 13210-1736 (Mail to: 819 Madison St 13210-1793) (315) 478-0901

Syracuse St Albans Episcopal Church **P** (79) 1308 Meadowbrook Dr 13224-1718 (Mail to: 1308 Meadowbrook Dr 13224-1718) Julie Calhoun-Bryant (315) 446-3490

Syracuse St Mark the Evangelist **P** (286) 1612 W Genesee St 13204-1950 (Mail to: 1612 W Genesee St 13204-1950) (315) 488-8511

✥ **Syracuse** St Paul's Syracuse **O** (163) 220 E Fayette St 13202-1904 (Mail to: 310 Montgomery St Ste 1 13202-2096) Philip Major (315) 474-6053

Trumansburg Church of the Epiphany **P** (104) 11 Elm St 14886 (Mail to: PO Box 459 14886-0459) (607) 387-6274

Utica Grace Episcopal Church **P** (492) 193 Genesee St. 13501-2263 (Mail to: 6 Elizabeth St 13501-2263) Georgina Hegney (315) 733-7575

Waterloo St Pauls Episcopal Church **P** (168) 101 E Williams St 13165-1412 (Mail to: 101 E Williams St 13165-1458) Jeffrey Haugaard (315) 539-3897

Watertown Trinity Episcopal Church **P** (372) 227 Sherman St 13601-3611 (Mail to: 227 Sherman St 13601-3691) Barbara Grace Schmitz (315) 788-6290

Waverly Grace Episcopal Church **P** (99) 441 Park Ave 14892-1446 (Mail to: 441 Park Ave 14892-1446) Benjamin Lentz (607) 565-2608

Whitesboro St Johns Episcopal Church **P** (92) 135 Main St 13492-1216 (Mail to: 135 Main St 13492-1216) Sara Heiligman (315) 736-2659

Willard Christ Episcopal Church **P** (35) 1393 Main St 14588 (Mail to: PO Box 275 14588-0275) Arlen Strauss (607) 869-9250

Windsor Zion Episcopal Church **P** (94) § 21 Chapel St 13865-4307 (Mail to: PO Box 85 13865-0085) (607) 655-5533

DIOCESE OF CENTRAL PENNSYLVANIA
(PROVINCE III)
Comprises 24 counties in Central Pennsylvania
DIOCESAN OFFICE 101 Pine St Harrisburg PA 17101 (MAIL: Box 11937 Harrisburg PA 17108-1937)
TEL (717) 236-5959 FAX (717) 236-6448
E-MAIL officemailbox@diocesecpa.org WEB www.diocesecpa.org

Previous Bishops—
Central Pennsylvania: Mark AD Howe 1871-95, Nelson S Rulison coadj 1884 Bp 1895-97, Ethelbert Talbot 1898-1928. *Harrisburg:* James H Darlington 1905-30, Hunter Wyatt-Brown 1931-43, John T Heistand 1943-66, Earl M Honaman suffr 1956-69. *Central Pennsylvania:* Dean T Stevenson 1966-82, Charlie F McNutt coadj 1980 Bp 1982-95, Michael W Creighton Bp 1995-2006, Nathan D Baxter Bp 2006-2014, Robert R Gepert Prov Bp 2014-2015

Bishop—Rt Rev Audrey C Scanlan (1089) (Dio 12 September 2015)

Cn for Fin & Opns C Linder; *Archd for Dcns* Ven J Miron; *Sec* T Powell Esq; *Treas* B Chambers; *Treas Emer* CH Fromer; *Reg* D Robelen; *Chanc* C Banks; *V Chanc* B McLemore T Schmidt; *Dean Stevenson Sch for Min* Very Rev R Szoke-Coolidge; *Ecum* Rev J P Peters; *Cn Cong Life & Miss* Rev D Morrow; *Cn Dioc Events and Comm* A Guszick

Stand Comm—Cler: V Pres J Strader-Sasser K Harrigan J Harwood B Hutchinson P Pierce S Weedon *Lay: Pres* C Weaver-Gelzer A Alexander D Dorgan B Johnson S Schwartz J Stevenson A Swiernik S Weedon

PARISHES, MISSIONS, AND CLERGY

Altoona St Luke Episcopal Church **P** (87) 806 13th St 16602-2422 (Mail to: 806 13th St 16602-2486) (814) 942-1372

Bedford St James Episcopal Church **P** (59) 309 S. Richard St 15522-1029 (Mail to: 309 S Richard St 15522-1744) (814) 623-8822

Bellefonte St John's Episcopal Church **P** (249) 120 W Lamb St 16823-1609 (Mail to: 120 W Lamb St 16823-1609) Carlton Kelley (814) 355-0497

Benton St Gabriel Episcopal Church **P** (18) 7 Saint Gabriel's Road 17814 (Mail to: PO Box 347 17814-0347) (570) 752-6205

Berwick Christ Episcopal Church **P** (130) 712 E 16th St 18603-2302 (Mail to: 712 E 16th St 18603-2302) (570) 752-6205

Bloomsburg St Pauls Episcopal Church **P** (136) 101 E Main St 17815-1806 (Mail to: PO Box 764 17815-0764) James Jenkins Howell Sasser (570) 784-3316

Blue Ridge Summit Calvary Chapel **P** (80) 13646 Summit Avenue 17214-0922 (Mail to: C/O Ch Of The Transfiguration PO Box B 17214) John Mcdowell (717) 794-2229

Blue Ridge Summit Church of the Transfiguration **P** (101) 13646 Summit Ave 17214-9758 (Mail to: Dana Burns PO Box B 17214-0922) John Mcdowell (717) 794-2229

Brookland All Saints Episcopal Church **P** (51) 1568 Fox Hill Rd 16948 (Mail to: PO Box 52 16915-0052) Janis Yskamp (814) 274-8391

Camp Hill Mount Calvary Church **P** (539) 125 25th St 17011-3609 (Mail to: 125 25th St 17011-3609) Gregory Welin (717) 737-3764

Carlisle Saint John's Episcopal Church **P** (634) § 1 Hanover St # A 17013-3014 (Mail to: PO Box 612 17013-0612) Melissa Wilcox Adam Kradel (717) 243-4220

Chambersburg Trinity Episcopal Church **P** (234) 58 S 2nd St 17201-2208 (Mail to: 58 S 2nd St 17201-2208) Carenda Baker (717) 264-6351

Columbia Saint Paul's Church **P** (86) 340 Locust St 17512-0096 (Mail to: PO Box 96 17512-0096)

Coudersport Christ Episcopal Church **P** (85) 601 Main St 16915-1703 (Mail to: PO Box 52 16915-0052) Janis Yskamp (814) 274-8391

Danville Christ Memorial Episcopal Church **P** (127) 120 E Market St 17821-1942 (Mail to: PO Box 363 17821-0363) James Strader-Sasser (570) 275-3903

Eagles Mere St Johns Episcopal Church **SC** 50 Jones Ave 17731-0042 (Mail to: C/O Mrs A S Hollinger PO Box 352 17731-0352) (215) 242-2945

Exchange St James Episcopal Church **P** (17) White Hall Rd State Route 44 17772 (Mail to: 1261 White Hall Rd 17772-9103) (570) 546-6470

Gettysburg Christ Episcopal Church **SC** C/O Mrs Jennifer Railing 50 Confederate Dr 17325-8420 (Mail to: PO Box 3005 17325-0005)

Gettysburg Prince of Peace Memorial Church **P** (244) 20 W High St 17325-2118 (Mail to: PO Box 3005 17325-0005) Herbert Sprouse (717) 334-6463

Hanover All Saints Church **P** (215) 890 Mccosh St 17331-1800 (Mail to: 890 McCosh St 17331-1800) (717) 637-5772

✠ **Harrisburg** St Stephens Cathedral **O** (621) § 221 Front St Ste 101 17101-1407 (Mail to: 221 Front St 17101-1437) John Sivley Shayna Watson Amy Welin Alton Williams (717) 236-4059

Harrisburg St Pauls Episcopal Church **P** (252) 248 Seneca St 17110-1840 (Mail to: 248 Seneca St 17110-1840) Katherine Harrigan Harry Knisely (717) 233-2175

Harrisburg St Andrews Episcopal Church **P** (280) 1852 Market St 17103-2523 (Mail to: 4620 Linglestown Rd 17112-9521) Calvin Hoyt (717) 234-8815

Harrisburg St Andrews in the Valley Episcopal **P** 4620 Linglestown Rd 17112 (Mail to: 4620 Linglestown Rd 17112-9521) Nelson Baliira (717) 657-8583

Hawk Run Chapel Of The Good Shepherd **P** (50) Leonard J Coval Sr Warden 270 Whitman St 16840-0023 (Mail to: PO Box 23 16840-0023) Clifford Johnston (814) 345-5576

Hershey All Saints Episcopal Church **P** (426) 310 Elm Ave 17033-1749 (Mail to: 310 Elm Ave 17033-1749) Susan Claytor (717) 533-2454

Hollidaysburg Church of the Holy Trinity **P** (108) Allegheny & Jones St 16648 (Mail to: 315 Jones St 16648-2007) Jeanne Jacobson (814) 695-7751

Huntingdon Saint John's Episcopal Church **P** (89) 212 Penn St 16652-1444 (Mail to: 212 Penn St 16652-1444) Gene Tucker (814) 643-4732

Jersey Shore Trinity Episcopal Church **P** (64) 174 Mount Pleasant Ave 17740-1762 (Mail to: 176 Mount Pleasant Ave 17740-1762) Veronica Chappell (570) 398-4007

Lancaster St Edward Episcopal Church **P** (387) 2453 Harrisburg Pike 17601-1719 (Mail to: 2453 Harrisburg Pike 17601-1719) Harold Morrow (717) 898-6276

Lancaster Saint James Episcopal Church **P** (1133) 119 Duke St 17602-2815 (Mail to: 119 Duke St 17602-2891) David Peck Richard Bauer Robert Schoeck (717) 397-4858

Lancaster St Johns Episcopal Church **P** (423) 321 W Chestnut St 17603-3509 (Mail to: 321 W Chestnut St 17603-3591) (717) 299-1188

Lancaster St Thomas Episcopal Church **P** (317) 301 Saint Thomas Rd 17601-4832 (Mail to: 301 Saint Thomas Rd 17601-4832) Jennifer Mattson (717) 569-3241

Lewisburg St Andrews Episcopal Church **P** (227) 255 S Derr Dr 17837-1722 (Mail to: 255 S Derr Dr 17837-1722) Sarah Weedon (570) 524-2061

Lewistown St Mark's Episcopal Church **P** (150) 21 S Main St 17044-2116 (Mail to: 21 S Main St 17044-2116) (717) 248-8327

Lock Haven Saint Paul's Church **HC** (50) 112 E Main St 17745-1306 (Mail to: PO Box 206 17745-0206) (570) 748-2440

Manheim Hope Episcopal Church **P** (94) 2425 Mountain Rd 17545-8793 (Mail to: 2425 Mountain Rd 17545-8793) Timothy Small (717) 665-6311

Manheim St Pauls Episcopal Church **P** (91) 90 S Charlotte St 17545-1802 (Mail to: 90 S Charlotte St 17545-1802) (717) 665-6584

Mansfield St James Episcopal Church **P** (50) 30 E Wellsboro St 16933-1121 (Mail to: 30 E Wellsboro St 16933-1121) Rowena Gibbons (570) 662-2003

Marietta Saint John's Church **P** (63) 239 E Market St 17547-1533 (Mail to: PO Box 98 17547-0098) Regina Bautista (717) 426-3189

Mechanicsburg St Lukes Episcopal Church **P** (260) 8 E Keller St 17055-3826 (Mail to: 8 E Keller St 17055-3826) Thomas Joyce Robert Schiesler David Ster (717) 766-5182

Milton Christ Episcopal Church **P** (28) 21 Upper Market St 17847-1225 (Mail to: 21 Upper Market St 17847-1225) Robert Van Deusen (570) 742-4153

Montoursville Church of Our Saviour **P** (39) 31 Loyalsock Ave 17754-1703 (Mail to: 31 Loyalsock Ave 17754-1703) (570) 368-1860

Montoursville Church of the Good Shepherd **P** (13) 827 Good Shepherd Rd 17754-7532 (Mail to: Mabel B Karschner Rd #1 Box 360 17754) (570) 433-3823

Mount Carmel The Resurrection Mission **M** 120 W 4th St 17851-2003 (Mail to: PO Box 353 17851-0353)

Mount Joy St Lukes Episcopal Church **P** (163) 209 S Market St 17552-3109 (Mail to: 209 S Market St 17552-3109) Eleanor Hart Garner (717) 653-4977

Muncy St James Episcopal Church **P** (61) 215 S Main St 17756-1505 (Mail to: PO Box 95 17756-0095) (570) 546-6470

Narvon Bangor Episcopal Church **P** (100) 2099 Main St 17555-9521 (Mail to: 2099 Main Street 17555-9521) William Murphey (717) 445-0253

Newport Nativity& St Stephens Episcopal Parish **P** (124) 159 S 2nd St 17074-1407 (Mail to: The Church of the Nativity 159 S 2nd St 17074-1407) Rebecca Myers (717) 567-6514

Northumberlnd St Mark Episcopal Church **P** (32) 187 King St 17857-1653 (Mail to: 187 King St 17857-1653) Robert Van Deusen (570) 473-3220

Philipsburg St Pauls Church **P** (267) 406 E Presqueisle St 16866 (Mail to: PO Box 170 16866-0170) (814) 342-3180

Selinsgrove All Saints Episcopal Church **P** (46) 129 Market St 17870-1905 (Mail to: PO Box 119 17870-0119) Paul Donecker (570) 374-8289

Shippensburg St Andrews Episcopal Church **P** (243) 206 E Burd St 17257-1402 (Mail to: 206

E Burd St 17257-1402) Barbara Hutchinson (717) 532-8089

State College St Andrews Church **P** (707) 208 W Foster Ave 16801-4822 (Mail to: 208 W Foster Ave 16801-4822) Christian Brady Charles Cruikshank Joseph DeLauter Jeffrey Packard (814) 237-7659

Sunbury St Matthews Episcopal Church **P** (265) 32 Front St 17801-2140 (Mail to: 32 Front St 17801-2140) Robin Jarrell (570) 286-7002

Thompsontown St Stephens Episcopal Church **HC** East Main St 17094 (Mail to: E Main St 17094-9752) (717) 567-6514

Tioga St Andrews Episcopal Church **P** (49) Main St 16946 (Mail to: C/O C F La Vancher PO Box 485 16946-0485) Rudolph Van Der Hiel (570) 662-7600

Tyrone Trinity Episcopal Church **P** (99) 830 Washington Ave 16686-1345 (Mail to: 830 Washington Ave 16686-1345) Jack Hoffer (814) 684-3100

Waynesboro St Marys Episcopal Church **P** (138) 112 E 2nd St 17268-1603 (Mail to: 112 E 2nd St 17268-1603) Linda Watkins (717) 762-1930

Wellsboro Saint Paul's Church **HC** (246) 29 Charles St 16901-1401 (Mail to: PO Box 701 16901-0701) (570) 724-4771

Westfield St Johns Church **P** (37) 205 Elm St 16950-1507 (Mail to: 205 Elm St 16950-1507) (814) 367-2245

Williamsport All Saints Memorial Church **P** (68) 1656 Scott St 17701-4459 (Mail to: 1656 Scott St 17701-4459) (570) 326-0191

Williamsport Christ Episcopal Church **P** (117) 426 Mulberry St 17701-6312 (Mail to: 426 Mulberry St 17701-6375) Veronica Chappell (570) 322-8160

Williamsport Trinity Episcopal Church **P** (284) 844 W 4th St 17701-5824 (Mail to: 844 W 4th St 17701-5824) Kenneth Wagner-Pizza (570) 322-0126

York St Andrews Episcopal Church **P** (353) 1502 4th Ave 17403-2623 (Mail to: 1502 4th Ave 17403-2623) David Bateman Charlene Leigh-Koser Frederic Stevenson (717) 843-3868

York St John The Baptist Episcopal Church **P** (460) 140 Beaver St 17403-5324 (Mail to: 140 Beaver St 17401-5396) Janet Brown Douglas Dailey (717) 848-1862

DIOCESE OF CHICAGO
(PROVINCE V)
Comprises Northern and Western Illinois
DIOCESAN OFFICE 65 E Huron St Chicago IL 60611
TEL (312) 751-4200   FAX (312) 787-5872
E-MAIL Bishop@episcopalchicago.org   WEB www.episcopalchicago.org

Previous Bishops—
Philander Chase 1835-52, Henry J White house coadj 1851 Bp 1852-74, Wm E McLaren 1875-1905, Chas P Anderson coadj 1900 Bp 1905-30, Wm E Toll suffr 1911-15, Sheldon M Griswold suffr 1917 Bp 1930-30, Geo C Stewart coadj 1930 Bp 1930-40, Edwin J Randall suffr 1939-47, Wallace E Conkling 1941-53, Chas L St suffr 1949-63, Gerald F Burrill 1954-71, Quintin E Primo Jr suffr 1972-84, James W Montgomery suffr 1962-65 coadj 1965 Bp 1971-87, William W Wiedrich suffr 1990-97, Frank T Griswold coadj 1985-87 Bp 1987-98, HA Donavan prov 1998-99, William D Persell Bp 1999-2008, Victor A Scantlebury asst 2000-11, John C Buchanan asst Bp 2014, C Christopher Epting asst Bp 2012-15

Bishop—Rt Rev Jeffrey D Lee (1026) (Dio 2 Feb 2008)

Dir of Min A Mysen; *Treas* K Kampert; *Yth/Young Adult Min* C Senuta; *Hist* N Smith; *Chanc* M Peregrine; *Sec Conv* E Saldana; *Dir Operations* C Reid; Acting *Dir Networking* C Plummer

Dio Commissions: Anti-Racism: S Soto

Stand Comm—Cler: E Biddy B Seward; *Lay:* K Leson R Smith M Giraldo

Deans—Aurora G Smith; *Chgo-N* P Raymond; *Chgo-S* R Cristobal; *Elgin* ME Eccles; *Evanston* K Goodman; *Joliet* J Shane; *Oak Park* C Pierce; *Peoria* Deanery R Hungerford; *Rockford* P Williams; *Waukegan* C Williams

PARISHES, MISSIONS, AND CLERGY

Antioch St Ignatius of Antioch Church **P** (215) 500 E Depot St 60002-1564 (Mail to: 500 E Depot St 60002-1564) (847) 395-0652

Arlington Hts Saint Simons Church **P** (600) 717 W Kirchhoff Rd 60005-2339 (Mail to: 717 W Kirchhoff Rd 60005-2339) Stephen R Smith (847) 259-2930

Aurora Saint David's Episcopal Church **P** (86) 701 Randall Rd 60506-1923 (Mail to: 701 Randall Rd 60506-1998) Robert Lambert Elizabeth Meade (630) 896-7229

Aurora Trinity Church **P** (85) 218 E Benton St 60505-4250 (Mail to: 218 E Benton St 60505-4250) Denzil Luckritz (630) 897-7283

Barrington St Marks Episcopal Church **P** (328) 337 Ridge Rd 60010-2331 (Mail to: C/O David A Gibbons 337 Ridge Rd 60010-2331) David Gibbons (847) 381-0596

Barrington St Michaels Episcopal Church **P** (880) 647 Dundee Ave 60010-4258 (Mail to: 647 Dundee Ave 60010-4299) Jesse Perkins Lisa Erdeljon Judith Heinrich Laurie Michaels (847) 381-2323

Batavia Calvary Episcopal Church **P** (261) 222 S Batavia Ave 60510-2564 (Mail to: 222 S Batavia Ave 60510-2564) Michael Rasicci (630) 879-3378

Belvidere Church of the Holy Trinity **P** (110) 217 E Hurlbut Ave 61008-3216 (Mail to: 217 E Hurlbut Ave 61008-3216) Randal Wakitsch (815) 544-2635

Berwyn St Michael & All Angels Episcopal Ch **P** (190) 6732 W 34th St 60402 (Mail to: 6732 34th St 60402-3412) Carlos Plazas (708) 788-2197

Bloomingdale Church of the Incarnation **M** (37) 261 W Army Trail Rd 60108-1376 (Mail to: 261 W Army Trail Rd 60108-1376) Maurice Strong Louisett Ness (630) 351-3249

Bloomingdale First Asian Church **P** 261 W Army Trail Rd 60108-1376 (Mail to: 261 W Army Trail Rd 60108-1376) Simon Singh (630) 351-3393

Blue Island Saint Joseph's And Saint Aidan's Church **M** (67) Oak St & Greenwood Ave 60406-0275 (Mail to: 2457 Oak St 60406-2032) Peter Siwek Rebecca Sperry (708) 389-5933

Bolingbrook Episcopal Church of St Benedict **M** (130) 909 Lily Cache Ln 60440-3131 (Mail to: 909 Lily Cache Ln 60440-3131) Barbara Seward (630) 759-5955

Burr Ridge St Helena Episcopal Church **P** (142) 7600 Wolf Rd 60527-8041 (Mail to: 7600 Wolf Rd 60527-8041) Ethan Jewett (630) 323-4900

Chicago All Saints Episcopal Church **P** (665) 4550 Hermitage Ave 60640-5304 (Mail to: 4550 Hermitage Ave 60640-5304) Bonnie Perry (773) 561-0111

✠ **Chicago** Cathedral of St James **O** (647) 65 E Huron St 60611-2728 (Mail to: C/O Lucia Conrado 65 E Huron St 60611-2728) Dominic Barrington Anna Broadbent Lisa Hackney (312) 787-7360

Chicago Church of Our Saviour **P** (627) 530 W Fullerton Pkwy 60614-5919 (Mail to: 530 W Fullerton Pkwy 60614-5919) Brian Hastings Anthony Vaccaro Richard Wendel Anne Wrider (773) 549-3832

Chicago St Pauls & Redeemer Church **P** (600) § 4945 S Dorchester A 60615-2907 (Mail to: 4945 S Dorchester Ave 60615-2907) Peter Lane Julianne Buenting Kyungja Oh John Seymour (773) 624-3185

Chicago Church of St Thomas **P** (170) 3801 S Wabash Ave 60653-1520 (Mail to: 3800 S Michigan Ave 60653-1514) Fulton Porter (773) 268-1900

Chicago Church of the Ascension **P** (208) 1133 La Salle Dr 60610-2601 (Mail to: 1133 La Salle Dr 60610-2601) Patrick Raymond (312) 664-1271

Chicago Church of the Holy Cross **P** (18) 1201 W 111th Pl 60643-4513 (Mail to: PO Box 438739 60643-8739) Tyrone Fowlkes (773) 779-0777

Chicago Church of the Holy Nativity **P** (101) § 9300 S Pleasant Ave 60620-5644 (Mail to: 9300 S Pleasant Ave 60643-6398) Regina Volpe (773) 445-4427

Chicago El Cristo Rey Mission **M** (322) Y814 60646-4217 (Mail to: 5101 W Devon Ave 60646-4217) Alvaro Araica (773) 561-8189

Chicago Church of the Atonement **P** (440) 5749 Kenmore Ave 60660-4541 (Mail to: 5749 Kenmore Ave 60660-4541) Michael Bice Ted Durst Barbara Henry Sterling Minturn Erika Takacs (773) 271-2727

Chicago Grace Episcopal Church **P** (108) 637 S Dearborn St 60605-1839 (Mail to: 637 S Dearborn St Fl 2 60605-1936) Amity Carrubba Sunny Lopez James Mcknight (312) 922-1426

Chicago Nuestra Senora de las America **M** (147) § 2401 W North Ave 60647-6546 (Mail to: c/o Kimball Avenue UCC 3413 West Medill 60647) (872) 206-2631

Chicago Messiah St Bartholomew Episcopal Church **P** (96) 8255 S Dante Ave 60619-4623 (Mail to: 8255 S Dante Ave 60619-4623) Alan James (773) 721-3232

Chicago St Albans Episcopal Church **P** (130) 6240 Avondale Ave 60631-2452 (Mail to: 6240 Avondale Ave 60631-2452) Mary Milano (773) 599-2545

Chicago St Andrews Chaplaincy **PS** (20) 48 Hoyne Ave 60612-2358 (Mail to: 48 Hoyne Ave 60612-2358) (312) 226-7205

Chicago Church of St Chrysostoms **P** (1227) § 1424 Dearborn St 60610-1506 (Mail to: 1424 Dearborn St 60610-1506) Jihan Murray-Smith Walter Smedley (312) 944-1083

Chicago St Edmunds Episcopal Church **P** (512) 6105 S Michigan Ave 60637-2119 (Mail to: 6105 S Michigan Ave 60637-2119) (773) 288-0038

Chicago Sts George & Matthias Church **M** (70) 164 E 111th St 60628-4346 (Mail to: 164 E 111th St 60628-4346) Robert Cristobal Gwendolyn Dillon (773) 468-1148

Chicago St Johns Episcopal Church **P** (225) 3857 Kostner Ave 60641-2851 (Mail to: 3857 Kostner Ave 60641-2851) Kara Wagner Sherer (773) 725-9026

Chicago St Margaret of Scotland **M** (152) 2555 E 73rd St 60649-2616 (Mail to: 2555 E 73rd St 60649-2616) (773) 221-5505

Chicago Saint Martin's Church **M** (80) 5710 W Midway Park 60644-1818 (Mail to: 5700 W Midway Park 60644-1818) Christopher Griffin (773) 378-8111

Chicago Church of St Pauls by-the-Lake **P** (320) 7100 Ashland Blvd 60626-2502 (Mail to: 7100

Ashland Blvd 60626-2502) John Heschle Matthew Kemp (773) 764-6514

Chicago St Peters Episcopal Church **P** (182) 621 W Belmont Ave 60657-4510 (Mail to: 621 W Belmont Ave 60657-4597) Shane Gormley Nancy Meyer Norma Sutton Ellen Wondra (773) 525-0844

Chicago Santa Teresa de Avila **M** (61) 6201 S Saint Louis Ave 60629-3713 (Mail to: 6201 S Saint Louis Ave 60629-3713) Gary Cox (773) 434-9783

Chicago Trinity Church **P** (137) 125 E 26th St 60616-2310 (Mail to: 125 E 26th St 60616-2310) Raymond Massenburg (312) 842-7545

Clarendon Hls Church Of The Holy Nativity **P** (256) 275 S Richmond Ave 60514-2711 (Mail to: 275 S Richmond Ave 60514-2711) Bradley Linboom (630) 323-6820

Crystal Lake St Marys Episcopal Church **P** (265) 210 Mchenry Ave 60014-6009 (Mail to: 210 S McHenry Ave 60014-6009) Frances Holliday Diane Koenig (815) 459-1009

Deerfield St Gregorys Episcopal Church **P** (362) Deerfield & Wilmot Rds 60015 (Mail to: 815 Wilmot Rd 60015-2723) Scott Elliott Anne Jolly Dennis Lietz Meredith Potter (847) 945-1678

Dekalb St Pauls Episcopal Church **P** (118) 900 Normal Rd 60115-1614 (Mail to: 900 Normal Rd 60115-1614) Joyce Beaulieu Edward Bird Heidi Haverkamp Charles Wilson (815) 756-4888

Des Plaines St Martin's Episcopal Church **HC** (208) 1095 E Thacker St 60016-3361 (Mail to: 1095 E Thacker St 60016-3361) M Eccles (847) 824-2043

Dixon St Lukes Episcopal Church **P** (100) 221 W 3rd St 61021-3015 (Mail to: 221 W 3rd St 61021-3015) (815) 288-2151

Downers Grove St Andrews Episcopal Church **P** (773) 1125 Franklin St 60515-3551 (Mail to: 1125 Franklin St 60515-3599) Gregg Morris Thomas Craighead (630) 968-9188

Dundee St James Episcopal Church **P** (174) 516 Washington St 60118-1245 (Mail to: 516 Washington Street 60118-1245) Donald Frye Darby Everhard (847) 426-5612

Elgin Church of the Redeemer **P** (679) 40 Center St 60120-5609 (Mail to: 40 Center St 60120-5609) Amity Carrubba Richard Frontjes Mary Harriss (847) 742-2428

Elgin Church of St Hugh of Lincoln **P** (199) 36w957 Highland Ave 60123-4875 (Mail to: 36W957 Highland Ave 60123-4875) Marion Phipps (847) 695-7695

Elk Grove Vlg St Nicholas Episcopal Church **M** (158) 1072 Ridge Ave 60007-4642 (Mail to: 1072 Ridge Ave 60007-4642) Manuel Borg (847) 439-2067

Elmhurst Church of Our Saviour **P** (176) 116 E Church St 60126-3404 (Mail to: 116 E Church St 60126-3485) Shireen Baker (630) 530-1434

Evanston St Lukes Episcopal Church **P** (896) 939 Hinman Ave 60202-1801 (Mail to: 939 Hinman Ave 60202-1881) Jeannette Defriest John Connelly Jeannette Defriest Gloria Hopewell William Waff (847) 475-3630

Evanston St Marks Episcopal Church **P** (213) 1509 Ridge Ave 60201-4135 (Mail to: 1509 Ridge Ave 60201-4135) Debra Bullock (847) 864-4806

Evanston St Matthews Episcopal Church **P** (416) 2120 Lincoln St 60201-2282 (Mail to: 2120 Lincoln St 60201-2282) Charles De Kay Kevin Goodman (847) 869-4850

Evanston St Andrews Episcopal Church **M** (152) 1928 Darrow Ave 60201-3404 (Mail to: 1928 Darrow Ave 60201-3404) Lee Gaede Chukwuemeka Nwachuku (847) 328-4751

Flossmoor Church of St John the Evangelist **P** (367) 2640 Park Dr 60422-1228 (Mail to: PO Box 25 60422-0025) Jeremy Froyen (708) 798-4150

Freeport Grace Episcopal Church **P** (376) 10 S Cherry Ave 61032-5069 (Mail to: 10 S Cherry Ave 61032-5069) Brian Prall (815) 232-4422

Galena Grace Episcopal Church **P** (125) 107 S. Prospect St. 61036-0228 (Mail to: 107 S. Prospect St. 61036-1803) (815) 777-2590

Galesburg Grace Episcopal Church **HC** (24) 60 Public Square 61401 (Mail to: PO Box 218 61402-0218) (309) 255-5916

Geneva St Marks Episcopal Church **P** (1179) 320 Franklin St 60134-2639 (Mail to: PO Box 126 60134-0126) Mark Tusken David Baughman William Kruse Robert Lowe Claudia Nalven Amy Peeler (630) 232-0133

Glen Ellyn St Barnabas Episcopal Church **P** (206) 22 W 415 Butterfield Rd 60137 (Mail to: 22W415 Butterfield Rd 60137-7164) Natalie Van Kirk Carol Kraft (630) 469-1394

Glen Ellyn St Mark's Episcopal Church **P** (1628) 393 North Main Street 60137-5068 (Mail to: 393 Main St 60137-5098) George Smith Victor Conrado Varela Walter Dunnett Robert Wyatt (630) 858-1020

Glencoe St Elisabeths Episcopal Church **P** (131) 556 Vernon Ave 60022-1647 (Mail to: 556 Vernon Ave 60022-1647) Daphne Cody Larry Handwerk (847) 835-0458

Glenview St Davids Episcopal Church **P** (578) 2410 Glenview Rd 60025-2713 (Mail to: 2410 Glenview Rd 60025-2713) Susan Sommer Thomas Atamian (847) 724-1341

Grayslake St Andrews Episcopal Church **P** (156) 31 Park Ave 60030-2334 (Mail to: 31 Park Ave 60030-2334) (847) 223-2310

Griggsville St James Episcopal Church **M** (20) 409 S Union St 62340 (Mail to: PO Box 463 62340-0463) William Roeger (573) 221-9111

Gurnee Annunciation of Our Lady **P** (270) 5725 Stearns School Rd 60031-4520 (Mail to: 5725 Stearns School Rd 60031-4520) (847) 336-3730

Hanna City Christ Church Limestone **M** 1604 Christ Church Rd 61536-9011 (Mail to: PO Box 431 61536-0431) (309) 685-8682

Hanover Park Church of St Columba of Iona **P** (36) 1800 W Irving Rd 60103-3253 (Mail to: 1800 Irving Park Rd 60133-3253) (630) 289-1574

Harvey St Clements Episcopal Church **P** (125) 15245 Loomis Ave 60426-3117 (Mail to: PO Box 2307 60426-8307) Peter Siwek

Highland Park Trinity Episcopal Church **P** (376) 425 Laurel Ave 60035-2652 (Mail to: 425 Laurel Ave Ste 1 60035-2689) Courtlyn Williams (847) 432-6653

Hinsdale Grace Episcopal Church **P** (630) 120 E 1st St 60521-4202 (Mail to: 120 E 1st St 60521-4291) Donna Ialongo Donna Ialongo Charles Pierce (630) 323-4900

Joliet St Edward and Christ Episcopal Church **P** (183) 206 Midland Ave 60435-6838 (Mail to: 206 Midland Ave 60435-6838) Richard Lundgren (815) 725-6800

Kankakee St Pauls Episcopal Church **P** (167) St. Paul's Episcopal Church 298 S Harrison Ave 60901-4095 (Mail to: 298 S Harrison Ave 60901-4095) Israel Anchan (815) 932-6611

Kenilworth The Church of the Holy Comforter **P** (843) 222 Kenilworth Ave 60043-1243 (Mail to: 222 Kenilworth Ave 60043-1298) Jason Parkin John Hardman Heath Howe (847) 251-6120

Kewanee St Johns Episcopal Church **P** (54) 123 S Chestnut St 61443-2121 (Mail to: PO Box 268 61443-0268) (309) 853-1421

La Grange Emmanuel Episcopal Church **P** (371) 203 S Kensington Ave 60525-2216 (Mail to: 203 S Kensington Ave 60525-2216) Ellen Ekevag David Jackson William Rimkus (708) 352-1275

La Salle St Paul Episcopal Church **M** (51) 344 Joliet St 61301-2128 (Mail to: 344 Joliet St 61301-2128) Mark Geisler (815) 220-0238

Lake Forest Church of the Holy Spirit **P** (2183) § 400 E Westminster 60045-2258 (Mail to: 400 E Westminster 60045-2258) Nathaniel Back Judith Doran (847) 234-7633

Lake Villa Church of the Holy Family **M** (159) 25291 W Lehmann Blvd 60046-9705 (Mail to: 25291 W Lehmann Blvd 60046-9705) Jose Arroyo (847) 356-7222

Lewistown St James Episcopal Church **M** (69) 420 E. MacArthur Ave. 61542-1250 (Mail to: P.O. Box 63 61542-0063) Barbara Sinclair (309) 543-4248

Libertyville St Lawrence Episcopal Church **P** (540) 125 W Church St 60048-2149 (Mail to: 125 W Church St 60048-2149) Patricia Snickenberger Harold Toberman (847) 362-2110

Lockport Saint John The Evangelist **M** (223) 324 E 11th St 60441-3421 (Mail to: 324 E 11th St 60441-3421) Shawn Schreiner Roberta Molony (815) 834-1168

Lombard Calvary Episcopal Church **P** (303) 105 W Maple St 60148-2513 (Mail to: 105 W Maple St 60148-2513) Maureen O'Connor (630) 620-8899

Macomb St George's Episcopal Church **P** (68) 321 1/2 W University Dr 61455-1144 (Mail to: PO Box 294 61455-0294) (309) 421-0142

Mchenry St Paul's Episcopal Church **P** (167) 3706 W Saint Paul Ave 60050-6108 (Mail to: 3706 W Saint Paul Ave 60050-6108) Lori Lowe William Mclemore (815) 385-0390

Moline All Saints Episcopal Church **M** (79) P O Box 482 91265 (Mail to: PO Box 482 61266-0482) Roger Hungerford James Allemeier (309) 797-2515

Momence Church of the Good Shepherd **M** (46) 123 E 2nd St 60954-1501 (Mail to: 123 E 2nd St 60954-1501) (815) 472-4625

Morris St Thomas Episcopal Church **P** (80) 317 Goold Park Dr 60450-1721 (Mail to: 317 Goold Park Dr 60450-1721) Michael Dwyer (815) 942-1380

Morrison St Annes Episcopal Church **P** (68) 401 Cherry St 61270-2606 (Mail to: 401 Cherry St 61270-2606) James Brzezinski (815) 772-2818

Naperville St Johns Episcopal Church **P** (701) 750 Aurora Ave 60540-6276 (Mail to: 750 Aurora Ave 60540-6276) Verna Fair (630) 355-0467

New Lenox Grace Episcopal Church **M** (128) 114 Pine St 60451-1748 (Mail to: 209 Pine St 60451-1765) Gregory Millikin (815) 485-6596

Northbrook St Giles Episcopal Church **P** (113) 3025 Walters Ave 60062-4370 (Mail to: 3025 Walters Ave 60062-4370) Cynthia Hallas Belinda Chandler (847) 272-6622

Northfield St James the Less Episcopal Church **P** (306) 550 Sunset Ridge Rd 60093-1027 (Mail to: 550 Sunset Ridge Rd 60093-1027) Lisa Senuta (847) 446-8430

Oak Park Grace Church **P** (474) 924 Lake St 60301-1204 (Mail to: Attn Douglas Van Houten 924 Lake St 60301-1204) Jonathan Baumgarten Mary Slenski Clayton Thomason (708) 386-8036

Oak Park St Christophers Episcopal Church **P** (338) 545 S East Ave 60304-1321 (Mail to: 545 S East Ave 60304-1321) Eric Biddy (708) 386-5613

Oregon St Bride Episcopal Church **M** (92) 1000 W Il Route 64 61061-9350 (Mail to: PO Box 223 61061-0223) (815) 732-7211

Ottawa Christ Episcopal Church **P** (103) C/O Fran Gibson 926 Columbus St 61350-2103 (Mail to: C/O Jack Kessler 113 E Lafayette St 61350-2114) Mark Geisler (815) 434-0627

Palatine St Philips Episcopal Church **P** (192) 342 E Wood St 60067-5336 (Mail to: 342 E Wood St 60067-5336) James Snyder (847) 358-0615

Palos Park Church of the Transfiguration **P** (280) 12219 S 86th Ave 60464-1263 (Mail to: 12219 S 86th Ave 60464-1263) Annette Mayer John Nachtrieb (708) 448-1200

Park Forest Church of the Holy Family **P** (291) Sauk Trl & Orchard Dr 60466 (Mail to: 102 Marquette St 60466-2016) Elizabeth Lloyd Johnnette Shane (708) 748-1100

Park Ridge St Marys Episcopal Church **P** (703) 306 S Prospect Ave 60068-4039 (Mail to: 306 S Prospect Ave 60068-4086) Joseph Czolgosz Martha Durham David Grauer Michael Kitt Patrick Skutch (847) 823-4126

Peoria St Paul's Episcopal Church **P** (324) 3601 North St 61604-1548 (Mail to: 3601 North St 61604-1548) Jennifer Replogle Jonathan Thomas (309) 688-3436

Pontiac Grace Church **P** (84) 410 E Torrance Ave 61764-2703 (Mail to: 900 S Manlove St 61764-2605) Mark Middleton (815) 842-1743

Prospect Heights One in Christ Episcopal Church **M** (158) 307 W Hintz Rd 60070-1020 (Mail to: 307 W Hintz Rd 60070-1020) Indon Joo Solomon Lee (847) 537-0590

River Forest Christ Episcopal Church **P** (54) 515 Franklin Ave 60305-1719 (Mail to: 515 Franklin Ave 60305-1719) Peter Campbell (708) 366-7730

Riverside St Pauls Episcopal Church **P** (32) 60 Akenside Rd 60546-1809 (Mail to: 60 Akenside Rd 60546-1809) Richard Daly Luke Wetzel (708) 447-1604

Rockford Emmanuel Episcopal Church **P** (262) 412 Church St 61103-6811 (Mail to: 412 Church St 61103-6883) Thomas Rosa (815) 964-5514

Rockford St Anskar Episcopal Church **P** (94) 4801 Spring Creek Rd 61114-6321 (Mail to: 4801 Spring Creek Rd 61114-6321) (815) 877-1226

Savanna Saint Paul's Church **M** (13) 305 Washington St 61074-1945 (Mail to: 304 Washington St 61074) Robert North (815) 273-7672

St. Charles St Charles Church Episcopal **P** (341) 994 5th Ave 60174-1227 (Mail to: 994 5th Ave 60174-1227) Elizabeth Meade Stacy Walker (630) 584-2596

Sterling Grace EpiscopalChurch **P** (108) 707 1st Ave 61081-3622 (Mail to: 707 1st Ave 61081-3622) David Rude Margaret Williams (815) 625-0442

Streator Christ Episcopal Church **P** (28) 132 S Vermillion St 61364-2936 (Mail to: 132 S Vermillion St 61364-2936) (815) 672-2479

Sycamore Saint Peter's Episcopal Church **P** (164) 218 Somonauk St 60178-1845 (Mail to: 218 Somonauk St 60178-1845) Georges Jallouf (815) 895-2227

Warsaw St Pauls Episcopal Church **M** (83) 240 S 4th St 62379-1205 (Mail to: 530 S 10th St 62379-1423) Larry Snyder (217) 256-4558

Wauconda Church of the Holy Apostles **M** (62) 26238 Il Route 59 60084-2332 (Mail to: 26238 Il Route 59 60084-2399) Martha Gillette (847) 526-7148

Waukegan Christ Episcopal Church **P** (410) 410 Grand Ave 60085-4227 (Mail to: 410 Grand Ave 60085-4284) Eileen Shanley-Roberts Cynthia Hallas (847) 662-7081

Waukegan Nuestra Senora De Guadalupe **M** (661) 2415 Butrick St 60087-3048 (Mail to: 2415 Butrick St 60087-3048) Narciso Diaz (847) 599-3051

Western Sprgs All Saints Episcopal Church **P** (141) 4370 Woodland Ave 60558-1458 (Mail to: 4370 Woodland Ave 60558-1458) Katherine Spelman (708) 246-0030

Wheaton Trinity Church **P** (553) 130 West St 60187-5062 (Mail to: 130 West St 60187-5097) Kevin Caruso James Lanning (630) 665-1101

Wilmette St Augustines Episcopal Church **P** (292) 1140 Wilmette Ave 60091-2604 (Mail to: 1140 Wilmette Ave 60091-2670) Sylvia Nebel Andrew Suitter Kristin White (847) 251-6922

Winnetka Christ Church **P** (1494) 784 Sheridan Rd 60093 (Mail to: 470 Maple St 60093-2652) Christopher Powell Nadia Stefko (847) 446-2850

Woodstock St Anns Episcopal Church **P** (258) 503 W Jackson St 60098-3143 (Mail to: 503 W Jackson St 60098-3143) Scott Zaucha (815) 338-0950

DIOCESE OF COLOMBIA

(PROVINCE IX)
Comprises the Republic of COLOMBIA
DIOCESAN OFFICE Cra 6 No 49-85 Piso 2 Bogotá Colombia
(MAIL: Apartado Aéreo 52964, Bogotá)
TEL 011-57-1-288-3167　　FAX 011-571-2883248
E-MAIL gaiser@bc.edu　WEB www.iglesiaepiscopal.org.co

Previous Bishops-
David B Reed 1964-71 Wm A
Franklin 1972-78 Bernardo
Merino Botero 1979-2001

**Bishop—Rt Rev Francisco
José Duque Gomez (969)** (Dio
14 July 2001)

Sec Conv P Ospina (AA 52964 Bogata); *Treas*
G Santos; *Reg* J Infante (Bogota); *Chanc* E Boss
(Medellin); *Medios y Comunicaciones* E Giraldo
(Bogota); *Con Residencia Canónica* T Prichard M
Ferro; *Dir Mission Dev* Rev TJ Gaiser; *Asst to Bp* MG
Monroy; *Accountant* SV Espitia

PARISHES, MISSIONS, AND CLERGY

Armenia Misión Santo Tomas Apostol **P**
Carrera 1S No. 26-19 (Mail to: Carrera 20 No.
9N-1B-B4 Apto. 301) (315) 283-6844

✣ **Bogota** Catedral de San Pablo **O** (100) Carrera
6 No. 49-85 AA 52964 (Mail to: Carrera 6 No.
49-85) (571) 288-3187

Bogota Iglesia Episcopal San Pedro **P** (80) Calle
22 BIS No. 93 AA 52964 (Mail to: Calle 22 BIS
No. 93) (312) 498-4984

Bogota Parroquia Episcopal El Divino
Salvador **M** Calle 58 Sur 14F78 Este (Mail
to: Calle 58 Sur 14F78 Este) Carlos Guevara
Rodriguez Carlos Guevara Rodriguez (571)
371-7377

Bucaramanga Parroquia San Pedro y San Pablo
M Cra 27 # 51-55 (Mail to: Cra 27 #51-55)
6470610618

Bucaramanta Misión Santa Maria Virgen **M**
Calle O # 14-54 (Mail to: Cra 27 # 51-47)
5776718540

Buenos Aires - Zaragoza Parroquia Nuestra
Senora del Carmen **P** (50) Buenos Aires
Palizada Corregimiento AA 52964 (Mail to:
Cra. 9 No. 9A-20) (313) 526-0209

Cali La Trinidad - Cali **P** (80) Calle 7 Oeste No.
3-43 AA 52964 (Mail to: Calle 7 Oeste No.

3-43) (572) 893-5953

Cali Misión la Natividad del Señor **M** CALLE 7
OESTE # 3-43 (Mail to: Calle 53 No 12-05)
5724480013

Cali Misión la Sagrada Familia **M** Cra 8 No. 71-
05 (Mail to: Cra 8 No. 71-05) 5724331828

Cartagena Iglesia Epis Nuestro Salvador **P** (80)
Piepopa Camino Arriba 22-109 AA 52964
(Mail to: Pie Popa Camino Arriba) (575) 674-
0851

Cartagena Parroquia La Santa Cruz **P** B. 7 de
Agosto Av. Colombia No. 71-15 (Mail to: B.
7 de Agosto Av. Colombia No. 71-15) (314)
506-8507

El Bagre Parroquia la Anunciacion **P** CARRERA
49 # 63 A 74/85/89 Sector Las Delicias (Mail to:
CARRERA 49 # 63 A 74/85/89) (571) 837-0201

Facatativa Misión Santa Marta de Betania **M**
Kilometro 4 via el Rosal (Mail to: Vereda
Noruega Prado Alto Cra 3E 9A-85 INT 2
CASA) (301) 371-4508

Ibague Misión San Juan Bautista **M** (50) Cra. 6
No. 16-69-71 AA 52964 (Mail to: Cra. 6 No.
16-69-71) (571) 2883187

Malambo Nuestra Senora Del Monte Carmelo **M**
(50) Cra. 3A Sur # 11A-02 AA 52964 (Mail to:
Cra. 3A, Sur # 11A-02) (575) 3478061

Medellin Iglesia Episcopal San Lucas **P** (70)
Carrera 80 # 53A-78 (Mail to: Cra 80 # 53A-78
52964) (574) 234-3940

Quibbo - Choco Misión de Cristo Rey **M** Calle
22 #17-7 Blogue 2 (Mail to: Calle 22 #17-7 B
Jardin Sector Rosales) (316) 739-5502

Soacha Misión del Espiritu Santo Tomas **M**
Carrera 5 Este 23-73 (Mail to: Carrera 5 Este
23-73) Carlos Guevara Rodriguez Carlos
Guevara Rodriguez (310) 282-9788

INSTITUTIONS

Centro de Estudios Teológico San Bernardo Abad
(CET) Rev Ernesto Boss Cra 80 No 53 A-78 Medellín
Antioquia

DIOCESE OF COLORADO
(PROVINCE VI)
Comprises the State of Colorado
DIOCESAN OFFICE 1300 Washington St Denver CO 80203-2008
TEL (303) 837-1173   WATS (800) 446-3081 FAX   (303) 837-1311
E-MAIL info@episcopalcolorado.org   WEB www. episcopalcolorado.org.org

Previous Bishops—
Geo M Randall (CO and adjacent) 1865-73, John F Spalding m 1873 dio 1887-1902 Chas S Olmstead 1902-18, Irving P Johnson coadj 1917 Bp 1918-38, Fred Ingley coadj 1921 Bp 1938-49, Harold L Bowen coadj 1947 Bp 1949-55, Daniel Corrigan suffr 1958-60, Jos S Minnis coadj 1954 Bp 1955-69, Edwin B Thayer suffr 1960-69 Actg Eccl Auth 1968-69 Bp 1969-73, Wm C Frey coadj 1972 Bp 1973-90, Wm H Wolfrum suffr 1981-91, William J Winterrowd Bp 1991-2004

Bishop — Rt Rev Robert J O'Neill (989) (Dio 01 Jan 2004)

Exec Asst to the Bp M Stern; *Cn to Ord Rev Cn* R Woodliff-Stanley; *Exec Asst to Cn to Ord* D Draper; *Cn Miss* Ms A Fleming; *Cong Dev and Deploy Admin* N McClung; *Comm Dir* M Orr; *Comm Asst* B Beu; *Controller* P Greenfield; *PT Acct Cl* K Ward; *Chanc* L Hitt 5670 Greenwood Plaza Blvd Ste 417 Greenwood Village CO 80111; *Faith Form Coord (Yth & Young Adult Min)* Rev G Foraker; *Steward (Dir of Operations for) Cathedral* Ridge G Dickson; *Treas* C Thompson; *Dir of Epis Serv Corps* Rev R Crummey; *Jubilee Min Off* Rev R Crummey; *Colo Episc Found* vacant 1300 Washington St 80203 (303) 534-6778

Stand Comm—Cler: C Brumbaugh P Floyd N Johnston *V Pres* T McGugan K Seidman; *Lay: Pres* R Morse *Sec* J Wolfe K Rogers J Johnson H Tournay

PARISHES, MISSIONS, AND CLERGY

Alamosa St Thomas the Apostle Epis Church **M** (26) 607 4th St 81101-2522 (Mail to: PO Box 837 81101-0837) (719) 589-6843

Arvada The Church of Christ the King **P** (394) § 6490 Carr St 80004-3338 (Mail to: PO Box 6 80001-0006) Rebecca Brown (303) 424-5288

Aspen Christ Episcopal Church **P** (280) 536 W North St 81611-1253 (Mail to: C/O Cindy Herndon 536 W North St 81611-1253) Jonathan Brice (970) 925-3278

Aurora St Martin in the Fields Church **P** (194) PO Box 460906 80046-0906 (Mail to: PO Box 460906 80046-0906) Michelle Ryan (303) 693-8872

Aurora St Stephens Episcopal Church **P** (256) 1 Del Mar Cir 80011-8225 (Mail to: 1 Del Mar Cir 80011-8225) Marionette Bennett Kathryn Bradsen Edward Morgan (303) 364-3186

Basalt St Peters Episcopal Church **M** (186) 200 Elk Run Dr 81621-9287 (Mail to: 200 Elk Run Dr 81621-9287) William Fisher (970) 927-4235

Battlement Mesa All Saints Episcopal Church **M** (54) 150 Sipprelle Dr 81635-9229 (Mail to: 150 Sipprelle Dr 81635-9229) Nancy Angle (970) 285-7908

Boulder St Aidans Episcopal Church **P** (259) 2425 Colorado Ave 80302-6806 (Mail to: 2425 Colorado Ave 80302-6806) Mary Rejouis (303) 443-2503

Boulder St Ambrose Episcopal Church **P** (290) 7520 S Boulder Rd 80303-4640 (Mail to: 7520 S Boulder Rd 80303-4640) Peter Munson Janice Pearson (303) 499-3041

Boulder St Johns Episcopal Church **P** (1249) 1419 Pine St 80304 (Mail to: 1419 Pine St 80302-4895) Susan Springer Theodore Howard Amy Lythgoe (303) 442-5246

Boulder Saint Mary Magdalene Church **P** (287) 4775 Cambridge St 80301-4140 (Mail to: 4775 Cambridge St 80301-4140) Bruce Swinehart Spencer Carr (303) 530-1421

Breckenridge St John the Baptist Episcopal Church **P** (181) 100 S French St 80424 (Mail to: PO Box 2166 80424-2166) Charles Brumbaugh (970) 453-4264

Brighton St Elizabeths Episcopal Church **M** (56) 76 S 3rd Ave 80601-2008 (Mail to: 76 S 3rd Ave 80601-2008) William Kindel (303) 659-2648

Broomfield Church of the Holy Comforter **P** (416) 1700 W 10th Ave 80020 (Mail to: 1700 W 10th Ave 80020-1716) Kimberly Seidman Linda Brown William Stanton (303) 466-2667

Buena Vista Grace Episcopal Church **P** (57) 203 W Main St 81211-9169 (Mail to: PO Box 1559 81211-1559) Catherine Tran (719) 395-8868

Canon City Christ Episcopal Church **P** (146) 802 Harrison Ave 81212-3350 (Mail to: 816 Harrison Ave 81212-3350) Mark Meyer (719) 275-2028

Castle Rock Christ's Episcopal Church **P** (377) 615 4th St 80104-2553 (Mail to: C/O Patty Kelly 615 4th St 80104-2553) Harold Warren Brian Winter (303) 688-5185

Centennial Good Shepherd Episcopal Church **P** (744) 8545 E Dry Creek Rd 80112-2750 (Mail to: 8545 E Dry Creek Rd 80112-2750) Gary Brower (303) 740-2688

Centennial St Timothys Episcopal Church **P** (661) 1401 E Dry Creek Rd 80122-3087 (Mail to: 1401 E Dry Creek Rd 80122-3087) Nicholas Myers (303) 794-1565

Central City St Pauls Episcopal Church **M** (14) 226 E 1st High St 80427 (Mail to: PO Box 764 80427-0764) (303) 582-0450

Colorado Spg Church of St Michael the Archangel **P** (618) 7400 Tudor Rd 80919-2615 (Mail to: 7400 Tudor Rd 80919-2615) Peter Floyd Judith Sato (719) 598-3244

Colorado Springs Church of Our Saviour **P** (873) 8 4th St 80906-3155 (Mail to: Attn Sarah FitzPatrick 8 4th St 80906-3155) Krista Dias David Dill (719) 633-2667

Colorado Springs Grace and St Stephens Episcopal Church **P** (701) 601 Tejon St 80903-1009 (Mail to: 601 Tejon St 80903-1009) Martin Pearsall Brendan Williams Jeremiah Williamson Sally Ziegler (719) 328-1125

Colorado Springs St Raphael Episcopal Church **P** (142) 802 Leta Dr 80911-1126 (Mail to: 802 Leta Dr 80911-1126) Twyla Zittle Twyla Zittle (719) 392-3563

Conifer St Laurence Episcopal Church **P** (200) 26812 Barkley Rd 80433-9101 (Mail to: PO Box 361 80433-0361) Nancy Malloy (303) 838-2457

Cortez St Barnabas of the Valley **P** (98) 110 W North St 81321-3119 (Mail to: 110 W North St 81321-3119) Cynthia Irvin (970) 565-7865

Craig Saint Mark's Church **M** (20) 657 Green St 81625-3029 (Mail to: PO Box 711 81626-3034) Arthur White Arthur White (970) 824-3470

Creede Saint Augustine's Church **M** (12) 502 S Main 81130 (Mail to: PO Box 803 81130-0803) Robert Pope (719) 658-2394

Crested Butte All Saints Of The Mountain Episcopal Chapel **Chapel** (41) 401 Sopris Ave 81224 (Mail to: PO Box 701 81230-0701) William Waltz (970) 641-0429

Cripple Creek Saint Andrew's Church **P** (69) 373 Carr St 80813-9613 (Mail to: Attn: Karen Muntzert PO Box 458 80813-0458) William Sermon (719) 689-2920

Delta St Lukes Episcopal Church **P** (75) 145 W 5th St 81416-1803 (Mail to: Treasurer PO Box 724 81416-0724) Thomas Seibert (970) 874-9489

Denver Christ Episcopal Church **P** (673) 2950 S University Blvd 80210-6029 (Mail to: 2950 S University Blvd 80210-6029) Terry McGugan (303) 758-3674

Denver Church of St Philip & St James **P** (233) 2797 S Lowell Blvd 80236-2249 (Mail to: 2797 S Lowell Blvd 80236-2249) John Hill (303) 936-3992

Denver Church of the Holy Redeemer **P** (86) 2552 Williams St 80205-5526 (Mail to: 2552 Williams St 80205-5526) Bonnie Spencer (303) 831-8963

Denver Church of the Epiphany **P** (241) 100 Colorado Blvd 80206-5533 (Mail to: 100 Colorado Blvd 80206-5533) Stacey Tafoya (303) 321-0813

Denver St Peters & St Marys Church **P** (42) 126 W 2nd Ave 80223-1434 (Mail to: 126 W 2nd Ave 80223-1434) Rebecca Crummey Rebecca Crummey (303) 722-8781

Denver Our Merciful Savior Episcopal Church **P** (318) 2222 W 32nd Ave 80211-3318 (Mail to: 2222 W 32nd Ave 80211-3318) (303) 477-4555

Denver St Andrews Episcopal Church **P** (303) 2015 Glenarm Pl 80205-3121 (Mail to: 2015 Glenarm Pl 80205-3121) Elizabeth Randall Melissa Adzima (303) 296-1712

Denver St Barnabas Episcopal Church **P** (466) 1280 Vine St 80206-2912 (Mail to: 1280 Vine St 80206-2912) (303) 388-6469

Denver St Bede Episcopal Church **P** 2201 S University Blvd 80210 (Mail to: Iliff School of Theology 80210) (303) 744-1287

✠ **Denver** St Francis Episcopal Chapel **O** (18) 2323 Curtis St 80205-2627 (Mail to: 2323 Curtis St 80205-2627) (303) 244-0766

✠ **Denver** Saint John's Cathedral **O** (2261) 1350 Washington St 80203-2008 (Mail to: 1350 Washington St 80203-2008) Richard Lawson Broderick Greer Katie Pearson (303) 831-7115

Denver St Lukes Episcopal Church **P** (456) 1270 Poplar St 80220-3023 (Mail to: 1270 Poplar St 80220-3023) Julia Reyes (303) 355-2331

Denver St Michael and All Angels' Episcopal Church **P** (399) 1400 S University Blvd 80210-2407 (Mail to: 1400 S University Blvd 80210-2407) Richard Fraser James Johnson Edward Morgan (303) 777-5181

Denver St Thomas Episcopal Church **P** (318) 2201 Dexter St 80207-3756 (Mail to: 2201 Dexter St 80207-3756) Daniel Hopkins Sally Megeath Rebecca Schunior (303) 388-4395

✠ **Denver** Sudanese Community Church **O** 1350 Washington St 80203-2008 (Mail to: 1350 Washington St 80203-2008) (303) 831-7115

Denver Church of the Ascension **P** (346) 600 Gilpin St 80218-3632 (Mail to: 600 Gilpin St 80218-3632) Louise Blanchard Cassandra Strotheide (303) 388-5978

Durango St Marks Episcopal Church **P** (399) 910 E 3rd Ave 81301-5213 (Mail to: 910 E 3rd Ave 81301-5213) Debra Shew (970) 247-1129

Elizabeth Peace in Christ Church **M** (10) 229 Tabor St 80107 (Mail to: PO Box 2098 80107-2098) (303) 646-6528

Englewood St Gabriel the Archangel Episcopal **P** (457) 6190 E Quincy Ave 80111-1002 (Mail to: 6190 E Quincy Ave 80111-1002) Christopher Ditzenberger Marilyn Schneider (303) 771-1063

Estes Park Saint Bartholomew's Church **P** (283) 880 Macgregor Ave 80517-9065 (Mail to: PO Box 1559 80517-1559) Seth Richmond Robert Burger (970) 586-4504

Evergreen Church of the Transfiguration **P** (150) 27640 Highway 74 80439-5820 (Mail to: PO Box 1630 80437-1630) Michael Mcmanus (303) 674-4904

Fort Collins St Lukes Episcopal Church **P** (792) 2000 Stover St 80525-1545 (Mail to: 2000 Stover St 80525-1545) (970) 493-7512

Fort Collins Saint Paul's Episcopal Church **P** (293) 301 East Stuart St 80525 (Mail to: 301 East Stuart St 80525) Ann Burns Austin Leininger (970) 482-2668

Fort Morgan St Charles the Martyr Epis Church **P** (104) 505 E 8th Ave 80701-3227 (Mail to: 505 E 8th Ave 80701-3227) Steven Hagerman (970) 867-6228

Frederick St Brigit Episcopal Church **M** (102) 110 Johnson St 80530-8022 (Mail to: 110 Johnson St 80530-8022) Felicia SmithGraybeal (720) 208-0280

Georgetown Grace Church **M** (17) 408 Taos St 80444 (Mail to: PO Box 133 80444-0133) (303) 569-2790

Glenwood Spgs St Barnabas Episcopal Church **P** (154) 546 Hyland Park Drive 81601-4276 (Mail to: 546 Hyland Park Dr 81601-4276) Elizabeth Huber (970) 945-6423

Golden Calvary Episcopal Church **P** (852) 1320 Arapahoe St 80401-1815 (Mail to: 1320 Arapahoe St 80401-1815) Scott Campbell Catherine Hitch Timothy Phenna Bethany Thomas (303) 279-2188

Golden Church Of Saint John Chrysostom **P** (171) 13151 W 28th Ave 80401-1601 (Mail to: 13151 W 28th Ave 80401-1601) Timothy Thaden (303) 279-2760

Granby Cranmer Memorial Chapel **Chapel** 75 High Country Dr 80446-0954 (Mail to: PO Box 954 80446-0954) (970) 887-2742

Granby St John the Baptist Episcopal Church **P** (121) 390 Garnet Ave 80446 (Mail to: PO Box 954 80446-0954) Diane Bielski (970) 887-2742

Grand Jct The Church of the Nativity **P** (141) 2175 Broadway 81503-1086 (Mail to: 2175 Broadway 81507-1086) Nature Johnston Teri Shecter (970) 245-9606

Grand Jct St Matthew Episcopal Church **P** (517) 3888 27 1/2 Rd 81506-4186 (Mail to: 3888 27 1/2 Rd 81506-4186) Judith Schneider Hollis Wright (970) 242-3293

Greeley Trinity Episcopal Church **P** (367) 3800 W 20th St 80634-3418 (Mail to: 3800 W 20th St 80634-3418) Jack Stapleton (970) 330-1877

Gunnison Church of the Good Samaritan **P** (136) 307 W Virginia Ave 81230-3038 (Mail to: PO Box 701 81230-0701) (970) 641-0429

Kremmling Trinity Episcopal Church **M** (37) 805 Central Ave 80459 (Mail to: PO Box 996 80459-0996) Karen Smith (970) 724-3626

La Junta St Andrew Holy Cross Lutheran Ch **P** (36) 621 Raton Ave 81050-2425 (Mail to: 621 Raton Ave 81050-2449) Jennifer Shadle (719) 383-3504

Lake City St James Episcopal Chapel **M** (66) 5th St & Hwy 149 81235 (Mail to: PO Box 832 81235-0832) (970) 641-0429

Lakewood St Joseph Episcopal Church **P** (195) 11202 W Jewell Ave 80232-6140 (Mail to: 11202 W Jewell Ave 80232-6140) Michele Quinn (303) 985-7170

Lakewood St Pauls Episcopal Church **P** (288) 9200 W 10th Ave 80215-4701 (Mail to: 9200 W 10th Ave 80215-4701) Allan Cole (303) 233-4991

Lamar St Pauls Episcopal Church **M** (35) 200 E Parmenter St 81052-3241 (Mail to: PO Box 814 81052-0814) (719) 336-4522

Leadville St George Episcopal Church **M** (38) 200 W 4th St 80461-3632 (Mail to: PO Box 243 80461-0243) Alison Lufkin Alison Lufkin (719) 486-3087

Littleton The Episcopal Parish of St Gregory **P** (401) 6653 W Chatfield Ave 80128-5834 (Mail to: 6653 W Chatfield Ave 80128-5834) Lupton Abshire (303) 979-5236

Longmont St Stephens Episcopal Church **P** (650) 1303 S Bross Ln 80501-6803 (Mail to: 1303 S Bross Ln 80501-6803) Lawrence Bradford Dana Solomon (303) 776-1072

Loveland All Saints Episcopal Church **P** (342) 3448 Taft Ave 80538-2556 (Mail to: 3448 Taft Ave 80538-2596) Jean D'Aoust Cynthia Espeseth (970) 667-0303

Mancos St Pauls Church **M** (18) 479 Bauer Ave 81328-9241 (Mail to: PO Box 226 81328-0226) (970) 533-9104

Manitou Springs Saint Andrew's Church **P** (49) 808 Manitou Ave 80829-1730 (Mail to: PO Box 466 80829-0466) Susan Merrin Frances Mutolo (719) 685-9259

Meeker St James Episcopal Church **P** (91) 368 4th St 81641 (Mail to: PO Box 641 81641-0641) Scott Hollenbeck (970) 878-5823

Monte Vista St Stephen the Martyr **M** (26) 729 3rd Ave 81144-1442 (Mail to: PO Box 489 81144-0489) (719) 852-3274

Monument St Matthias Episcopal Church **P** (155) 18320 Furrow Rd 80132-8790 (Mail to: PO Box 1223 80132-1223) Laura Beck (719) 359-9204

New Castle St Johns Episcopal Church **M** (50) First & Main St 81647 (Mail to: C/O St Johns Church PO Box 82 81647-0082) Elizabeth Huber Edmond-Joseph Rivet (970) 984-2780

Ouray St Johns Episcopal Church **P** (94) 329 Fifth Ave 81427 (Mail to: PO Box 563 81427-0563) Lucas Grubbs (970) 325-4655

Pagosa Springs St Patrick Episcopal Church **P** (144) 225 S Pagosa Blvd 81147-8396 (Mail to: 225 S Pagosa Blvd 81147-8396) Douglas Neel (970) 731-5801

Parker Saint Matthew's Episcopal Church **P** (465) 19580 Pilgrims Pl 80138-7354 (Mail to: 19580 Pilgrims Pl 80138-7354) Michael Richardson (303) 841-0121

Pueblo Church of St Peter the Apostle **P** (67) 3939 W Pueblo Blvd 81005-2721 (Mail to: 3939 W Pueblo Blvd 81005-2721) (719) 561-4567

Pueblo Church of the Ascension **P** (426) 420 W 18th St 81003-2625 (Mail to: C/O Janice Bassett 420 W 18th St 81003-2625) Christy Shain-Hendricks Karen Burnham Kenneth Butcher (719) 543-4253

Salida Church of the Ascension **P** (117) 349 E St 81201-2631 (Mail to: PO Box 1540 81201-7540) (719) 539-4562

Salida Little Shepherd of the Hills **M** PO Box 458 81201 (Mail to: 349 E St 81201-2631) (719) 539-4562

Sedalia St Philip in the Field **P** (117) 397 Perry Park Rd 80135-8521 (Mail to: 397 N. Perry Road 80135-8521) Janet Fullmer (303) 688-5444

Steamboat Sprngs St Pauls Episcopal Church **P** (488) 846 Oak St 80477 (Mail to: PO Box 770722 80477-0722) Margaret Greene (970) 879-0925

Sterling Prince of Peace Episcopal Church **M** (34) 201 Phelps St 80751-4044 (Mail to: PO Box 164 80751-0164) (970) 522-0539

Thornton Intercession Episcopal Church **P** (261) 3101 E 100th Ave 80229-2687 (Mail to: 3101 E 100th Ave 80229-2687) (303) 451-8085

Vail Church of the Transfiguration **P** (364) 19 Vail Rd 81657 (Mail to: PO Box 1000 81658-1000)

Stuart Keith Joseph Forinash Emily Lukanich (970) 476-0618

Westcliffe St Lukes Episcopal Mission **M** (49) 201 S 3rd St 81252-9502 (Mail to: PO Box 208 81252-0208) (719) 783-2477

Westminster St Marthas Episcopal Church **P** (91) 4001 W 76th Ave 80030 (Mail to: 4001 W 76th Ave 80030) (303) 429-0495

Wheat Ridge Saint James Episcopal Church **S** (96) 8235 W 44th Ave 80033-4426 (Mail to: 8235 W 44th Ave 80033-4426) Rebecca Jones (303) 424-1118

Windsor St Albans Episcopal Church **P** (279) 525 Walnut St 80550-5145 (Mail to: PO Box 697 80550-0697) William Stanton David Tweedale Janice Windsor (970) 686-9658

Woodland Park St David of the Hills Epis Church **P** (47) 36 Edlowe Rd 80863-8226 (Mail to: 36 Edlowe Rd 80863-8226) (719) 687-9195

THE EPISCOPAL CHURCH IN CONNECTICUT

(PROVINCE I)

Comprises the State of Connecticut

DIOCESAN OFFICE 290 Pratt St Meriden CT 06450

TEL (203) 639-3501   FAX (203) 2035-1008

E-MAIL info@episcopalct.org   WEB www.episcopalct.org

Previous Bishops— Samuel Seabury 1784-96, Abraham Jarvis 1797-1813, Thomas C Brownell 1819-65, John Williams coadj 1851 Bp 1865-99, Chauncey B Brewster coadj 1897 Bp 1899-1928, Edward C Acheson suffr 1915 coadj 1926 Bp 1928-34, Fredk G Budlong coadj 1931 Bp 1934-51, Walter H Gray suffr 1940 coadj 1945 Bp 1951-69, Robert M Hatch suffr 1951-57, John H Esquirol suffr 1958 Bp 1969-71, J Warren Hutchens suffr 1961 Bp 1971-77, Morgan Porteus suffr 1971 coadj 1976 Bp 1977-1981, W Bradford T Hastings suffr 1981-86, Jeffrey W Rowthorn suffr 1987-93, Arthur E Walmsley coad 1979-81 Bp 1981-93, Clarence N Coleridge suffr 1981-93 Bp 1993-99, Andrew D Smith suffr 1996-99 Bp 1999-2010, James E Curry suffr 2000-14

Bishop — Rt Rev Ian T Douglas (1042) (Dio 17 Apr 2010)

Bishop Suffragan — Rt Rev Laura J Ahrens (1018) (Suffr 30 Jun 2007)

Cn for Mission Collaboration Cn T Hodapp; *Cn for Mission Ldrshp* Cn LA Tolzmann; *Cn for Mission Integrity + Training* R Hammeal-Urban; *Cn for Mission Fin + Ops* Cn L Fuertes; *Cn for Comm & Media* K Hamilton; *Bps Exec Sec* A Hollo; *Sec of Dio*

Rev S Cosman; *Sec of Conv* Rev A Yates; *Treas* L Brooks; *Chanc* B Babbitt

Stand Comm—Cler: Pres T Johnson Russell M Hodgkins P Thompson P Walsh M Byers R Kemp; *Lay: Sec* N Staniewicz J Carroll AB Lyons D Gaherty A Atencio T Hagerth

PARISHES, MISSIONS, AND CLERGY

Ansonia Christ Church Episcopal **P** (260) 56 South Cliff St 06401-1910 (Mail to: 56 S Cliff St 06401-1910) (203) 734-2715

Bantam St Pauls Episcopal Church **P** (90) 802 Bantam Rd 06750-1603 (Mail to: PO Box 449 06750-0449) Daniel Mattila Peter Stebinger (860) 567-8838

Bethany Christ Church Episcopal **P** (177) 526 Amity Rd 06524-3015 (Mail to: 526 Amity Rd 06524-3015) Robert Clements (203) 393-3399

Bethel Church of St Thomas **P** (198) 95 Greenwood Ave 06801-2528 (Mail to: 95 Greenwood Ave 06801-2528) Norma Schmidt (203) 743-1494

Bethlehem Christ Episcopal Church **P** (90) Main St 06751 (Mail to: PO Box 520 06751-0520) David Mcintosh Thomas Peters (203) 266-7698

Bloomfield Old St Andrews Episcopal Church **P** (240) 59 Tariffville Rd 06002-1136 (Mail to: 59 Tariffville Rd 06002-1136) Timothy Squier (860) 242-4660

Bloomfield St Stephens Episcopal Church **P** (150) 590 Bloomfield Ave 06002-3044 (Mail to: 590 Bloomfield Ave 06002-3044) Wilborne Austin (860) 242-1152

Bolton St Georges Episcopal Church **P** (58) 1150 BostonTpke 06043-7439 (Mail to: P O Box 158 06040) (860) 643-9203

Branford Trinity Episcopal Church **P** (493) 1109 Main St 06405-3715 (Mail to: 1109 Main St 06405-3770) Sharon Gracen (203) 488-2681

Bridgeport Calvary-St George Episcopal Church **P** (46) 755 Clinton Ave 06604-2302 (Mail to: 755 Clinton Ave 06604-2302) (203) 333-5116

Bridgeport St John's Episcopal Parish **P** (341) 768 Fairfield Ave 06604-3701 (Mail to: 768 Fairfield Ave 06604-3799) Geoffrey Hahneman José Mestre (203) 335-2528

Bridgeport St Lukes-St Pauls Episcopal Church **P** (1208) PO Box 2156 06608-0156 (Mail to: PO Box 2156 06608-0156) (203) 367-7009

Bridgeport St Marks Episcopal Church **P** (328) 401 Newfield Ave 06607-2218 (Mail to: 401 Newfield Ave 06607-2218) (203) 335-5655

Bridgewater St Marks Episcopal Church **P** (49) 5 Main St S 06752-1521 (Mail to: PO Box 143 06752-0143) Daniel Mattila Robert Woodroofe (860) 354-8269

Bristol St Johns Episcopal Church **P** (237) PO Box 2321 06011-2321 (Mail to: PO Box 2321 06011-2321) Diane Caggiano Florencio Ghinaglia Socorro Leonard Hullar (860) 583-5445

Broad Brook Grace Episcopal Church **P** (81) 44 Old Ellington Rd 06016-9735 (Mail to: PO Box 405 06016-0405) (860) 623-1574

Brookfield Saint Paul's Church **P** (340) Attn Chuck Allen 174 Whisconier Road 06804-3307 (Mail to: 174 Whisconier Rd 06804-3307) Joseph Shepley George Crocker William Loring (203) 775-9587

Brooklyn Trinity Episcopal Church **P** (63) 7 Providence Rd 06234-1816 (Mail to: PO Box 276 06234-0276) Jane Hale (860) 774-9352

Cheshire St Peters Episcopal Church **P** (1134) § 59 Main St 06410-2405 (Mail to: 59 Main St 06410-2468) David Stayner Sandra Stayner (203) 272-4041

Clinton Church of the Holy Advent **P** (310) 81 E Main St 06413-2139 (Mail to: PO Box 536 06413-0536) Mary Rogers (860) 669-2232

Collinsville Trinity Church Collinsville **P** (407) 55 River Rd 06022 (Mail to: PO Box 374 55 River Rd 06022-0374) (860) 693-8172

Danbury St James Episcopal Church **P** (556) 25 West St 06810-7824 (Mail to: 25 West St 06810-7877) Lisa Hahneman (203) 748-3561

Danielson St Albans Episcopal Church **P** (62) 254 Broad St 06239-2903 (Mail to: 254 Broad St 06239-2903) (860) 774-8833

Darien Ascension Church For Deaf **M** (6) 1882 Post Rd 06820-5802 (Mail to: 199 Eastgate Dr 06410-2236) (203) 272-9958

Darien St Luke Episcopal Church **P** (2852) § 1864 Post Rd 06820-5802 (Mail to: 1864 Post Rd 06820-5802) Daniel Lennox Dawn Stegelmann Donald Thompson Susan Wyper (203) 655-1456

Darien St Pauls Episcopal Church **P** (335) 471 Mansfield Ave 06820-2116 (Mail to: 471 Mansfield Ave 06820-2198) Novella Lawrence (203) 655-8773

Derby Immanuel St James Parish **P** (85) 105 Minerva St 06418-1896 (Mail to: 105 Minerva St 06418-1896) George Brower (203) 734-4149

Durham Church of the Epiphany **P** (226) 196 Main St 06422-2106 (Mail to: PO Box 337 06422-0337) Anthony Dinoto (860) 349-9644

East Berlin St Gabriels Church **P** (122) 68 Main St 06023-1130 (Mail to: PO Box 275 06023-0275) Audrey Scanlan Robert Watson (860) 828-3735

East Haddam St Stephens Episcopal Church **P** (417) 29 Main St 06423-1305 (Mail to: PO Box 464 06423-0464) Adam Yates (860) 873-9547

East Hartford All Saints Episcopal Church **P** (51) 444 Hills St 06118-2922 (Mail to: 444 Hills St 06118-2998) Michelle Hansen (860) 568-6175

✣ **East Hartford** Greater Hartford Regional Ministry **O** 12 Rector St 06108-2261 (Mail to: 12 Rector St 06108-2261) (860) 528-1474

East Haven Christ and the Epiphany Church **P** (54) 39 Park Pl 06512-2517 (Mail to: 39 Park Pl 06512-2517) Charles Kamano Andrew Osmun (203) 467-2310

East Windsor St Johns Episcopal Church **P** (187) 92 Main St 06088-9651 (Mail to: 92 Main St 06088-9651) (860) 623-3273

Easton Christ Church **P** (317) 59 Church Rd 06612-1411 (Mail to: Attn: Treasurer 59 Church Rd 06612-1411) Ellen Huber (203) 268-3569

Enfield Holy Trinity Episcopal Church **P** (299) 383 Hazard Ave 06082-4718 (Mail to: 383 Hazard Ave 06082-4718) Peter Vaughn (860) 749-2722

Essex St John's Episcopal Church **P** (425) 25 Main St 06426-1134 (Mail to: PO Box 422 06426-0422) Jonathan Folts Benjamin Straley (860) 767-8095

Fairfield St Pauls Episcopal Church **P** (982) 661 Old Post Rd 06824-6648 (Mail to: 661 Old Post Rd 06824-6648) Curtis Farr (203) 259-3013

Fairfield St Timothys Church **P** (245) 4670 Congress St 06824-1721 (Mail to: 4670 Congress St 06824-1721) Kevin Olds (203) 255-2740

Fairfield Trinity-St Michaels Church **P** (44) 554 Tunxis Hill Rd 06825-4412 (Mail to: 554 Tunxis Hill Rd 06825-4412) David Norris (203) 368-3225

Farmington St James Episcopal Church **P** (293) 3 Mountain Rd 06032-2339 (Mail to: 3 Mountain Rd 06032-2339) George Roberts (860) 677-1564

Gales Ferry St Davids Episcopal Church **P** (282) 284 Stoddards Wharf Rd 06335-1130 (Mail to: 284 Stoddards Wharf Rd 06335-1130) (860) 464-6516

Glastonbury St James Episcopal Church **P** (540) 2584 Main St 06033-4220 (Mail to: PO Box 206 06033-0206) Denise Cabana (860) 633-8333

Greenwich Christ Church Greenwich **P** (1981) § 254 E Putnam Ave 06830-4801 (Mail to: 254 E Putnam Ave 06830-4871) Andrew Kryzak Marek Zabriskie (203) 869-6600

Greenwich St Barnabas Episcopal Church **P** (416) 954 Lake Ave 06831-3032 (Mail to: 954 Lake Ave 06831-3099) Edward Pardoe Margaret Finnerud Sanford Key (203) 661-5526

Guilford Christ Church **P** (453) 11 Park St 06437-2629 (Mail to: PO Box 574 06437-0574) Randolph West (203) 453-2279

Guilford St Johns Episcopal Church **P** (95) 129 Ledge Hill Rd 06437-1024 (Mail to: 129 Ledge Hill Rd 06437-1024) Maureen Lederman (203) 457-1094

Hamden Grace And Saint Peter's Episcopal Church **P** (147) 2927 Dixwell Ave 06518-3135 (Mail to: PO Box 5065 06518-0065) Robert Bergner (203) 248-4338

✣ **Hartford** Christ Church Cathedral **O** (458) 45 Church St 06103-1202 (Mail to: 45 Church St 06103-1202) Richard Mansfield Robert Carroon Miguelina Howell Jorge Pallares Arellano Jervis Zimmerman (860) 527-7231

Hartford Good Shepherd El Buen Pastor **P** (149) 155 Wyllys St 06106-1957 (Mail to: 155 Wyllys St 06106-1957) (860) 525-4289

Hartford Grace Episcopal Church **P** (102) 55 New Park Ave 06106-2123 (Mail to: 55 New Park Ave 06106-2123) Robert Carroon Rowena Kemp John Mitman Wayne Pokorny (860) 233-0825

Hartford Saint Martin's Church **M** (209) 290 Cornwall St 06112-1427 (Mail to: 290 Cornwall St 06112-1427) (860) 242-0318

Hartford Saint Monica's Church **P** (250) 3575 Main Street 06120-2326 (Mail to: 3575 Main St 06120-1115) Tracy Johnson Russell (860) 522-7761

Hartford Trinity College Chapel **CC** 300 Summit St 06106-3100 (Mail to: C/O Rev Allison Read 300 Summit St 06106-3100) Allison Read (860) 297-2013

Hartford Trinity Episcopal Church **HC** (588) § 120 Sigourney St 06105-2755 (Mail to: 120 Sigourney St 06105-2796) Donald Hamer Benjamin Wyatt (860) 527-8133

Hebron Saint Peter's Episcopal Church **P** (398) 30 Church St 06248-1427 (Mail to: PO Box 513 06248-0513) Ronald Kolanowski (860) 228-3244

Higganum Middlesex Area Cluster Ministry **P** PO Box 829 06441-0829 (Mail to: PO Box 829 06441-0829) Stephen McCarthy Evelyn Wheeler (860) 345-0058

Higganum St James Episcopal Church **P** (78) 498 Killingworth Rd 06441-4310 (Mail to: PO Box 574 06441-0574) (860) 345-0058

Ivoryton All Saints Episcopal Church **P** (119) 129 Main St 06442-1103 (Mail to: PO Box 576 06442-0576) Brendan Mccormick Brendan Mccormick (860) 767-1698

Kent St Andrews Church **P** (381) 1 Main St 06757-1512 (Mail to: PO Box 309 06757-0309) Roger White Amy Reichman (860) 927-3486

Killingworth Emmanuel Episcopal Church **P** (48) PO Box 686 06419-0686 (Mail to: 50 Emanuel Church Rd 06419-1019) (860) 663-1800

Lakeville Trinity Church Lime Rock **P** (144) 484 Lime Rock Rd 06039-2404 (Mail to: 484 Lime Rock Rd 06039-2404) Heidi Truax (860) 435-2627

Litchfield St Michaels Church Episcopal **P** (420) 25 South St 06759-4005 (Mail to: PO Box 248 06759-0248) E Bevan Stanley (860) 567-9465

Madison St Andrews Church **P** (397) 232 Durham Rd 06443-2451 (Mail to: 232 Durham Rd 06443-2451) Niranjani Molegoda (203) 245-2584

Manchester St Marys Episcopal Church **P** (1154) 41 Park St 06040-5913 (Mail to: 41 Park St 06040-5913) Karen Fedorchak Ann Johnson Perry Mullins Marjorie Roccoberton (860) 649-4583

Marble Dale St Andrews Episcopal Church **P** (133) 247 New Milford Tpke 06777-0007 (Mail to: PO Box 2007 06777-0007) (860) 868-2275

Meriden All Saints Church **P** (65) 201 W Main St 06450 (Mail to: 164 Hanover St 06451-5439) Michael Carroll (203) 235-9596

Meriden St Andrews Episcopal Church **P** (459) 20 Catlin St 06450-4204 (Mail to: 20 Catlin St 06450-4294) Mark Byers (203) 237-7451

Middle Haddam Christ Episcopal Church **P** (118) 60 Middle Haddam Rd 06456 (Mail to: PO Box 81 06456-0081) (860) 267-0287

Middlebury St George Episcopal Church **P** (161) Tucker Hill Rd 06762-2517 (Mail to: PO Box 162 06762-0162) Andrew Zeman (203) 758-9864

Middletown Holy Trinity Church **P** (277) 381 Main St 06457-3309 (Mail to: 381 Main St 06457-3309) Dana Campbell (860) 347-2591

Milford Saint Andrew's Church **P** (93) 283 Bridgeport Avenue 06460-5431 (Mail to: PO Box 2454 06460-0877) Patricia Leonard-Pasley (203) 874-2701

Milford St Peters Church **P** (327) 71 River St 06460-3315 (Mail to: 71 River St 06460-3315) Matthew Lindeman Angela Rowley (203) 874-8562

Monroe St Peters on the Green **P** (270) 175 Old Tannery Rd 06468-1932 (Mail to: 175 Old Tannery Rd 06468-1932) Kurt Huber Christopher Holms (203) 268-4265

Mystic St Marks Episcopal Church **P** (485) 15 Pearl St 06355-2513 (Mail to: 15 Pearl St 06355-2599) Stacey Kohl Adam Thomas (860) 572-9549

N Branford Zion Episcopal Church **P** (248) 326 Notch Hill Rd 06471-1858 (Mail to: 326 Notch Hill Rd 06471-1858) Lucy Larocca (203) 488-7395

Naugatuck St Michaels Episcopal Parish **P** (277) 210 Church St 06770-4120 (Mail to: 210 Church St 06770-4197) Juliusz Jodko (203) 729-8249

New Britain St Marks Episcopal Church **P** (452) 147 W Main St 06052-1316 (Mail to: 147 W Main St 06052-1316) William Eakins Shaw Mudge Joseph Pace (860) 225-7634

New Canaan St Marks Episcopal Church **P** (1250) § 111 Oenoke Rdg Ste 1 06840-4199 (Mail to: 111 Oenoke Rdg 06840-4105) Peter Walsh Justin Crisp Elizabeth Garnsey (203) 966-4515

New Haven Christ Episcopal Church **P** (237) 84 Broadway 06511-3412 (Mail to: 84 Broadway 06511-3499) Stephen Holton Carlos De La Torre Kent Smith (203) 865-6354

New Haven Episcopal Church at Yale **CC** PO Box 201955 06520-1955 (Mail to: PO Box 201955 06511-6612) (203) 432-5401

New Haven St Andrews Episcopal Church **P** (82) 266 Shelton Ave 06511-1847 (Mail to: 262 Shelton Ave 06511-1871) (203) 562-1080

New Haven St Johns Church **P** (149) 400 Humphrey St 06511-3711 (Mail to: 400 Humphrey St 06511-3711) (203) 562-1487

New Haven St Lukes Episcopal Church **P** (224) 111 Whalley Ave 06511-3220 (Mail to: 111 Whalley Ave 06511-3293) Lynne Grifo Paul Jacobson (203) 865-0141

New Haven St Paul - St James Episcopal Church **P** (182) 57 Olive St 06511-5739 (Mail to: 57 Olive St 06511-5739) Kim Litsey (203) 562-2143

New Haven Church of St Thomas **P** (225) § 830 Whitney Ave 06511-1316 (Mail to: 830 Whitney Ave 06511-1398) Keri Aubert Maureen Lederman William Loutrel (203) 777-7623

New Haven Trinity Church on the Green **P** (835) 950 Chapel Street, 2nd Floor 06510-2515 (Mail to: 950 Chapel St # 2 06510-2515) Luk De Volder Elise Hanley (203) 624-3101

New London St James Episcopal Church **P** (313) 76 Federal St 06320-6601 (Mail to: Attn Treasurer 76 Federal St 06320-6601) Ranjit Mathews (860) 443-4989

New Milford Saint John's Church **P** (236) 7 Whittlesey Ave 06776-3023 (Mail to: 7 Whittlesey Ave 06776-3023) John Gilpin Amy Reichman (860) 354-5583

Newington Grace Episcopal Church **P** (226) 124 Maple Hill Ave 06111-2719 (Mail to: 124 Maple Hill Ave 06111-2719) Robert Stocksdale (860) 666-3331

Newtown Trinity Church Episcopal **P** (741) Attn Ellsworth Stringer 36 Main St 06470-2106 (Mail to: 36 Main St 06470-2181) Carrie Combs Carrie Combs Jennifer Montgomery (203) 426-9070

Niantic St Johns Episcopal Church **P** (414) 400 Main St 06357 (Mail to: PO Box 810 06357-0810) Anthony Dinoto Dianne Warley (860) 739-2324

North Haven St Johns Episcopal Church **P** (331) 3 Trumbull Pl 06473-2522 (Mail to: 3 Trumbull Pl 06473-2522) (203) 239-0156

Northford St Andrew Episcopal Church **P** (63) Middletown Ave 06472 (Mail to: Middletown Ave PO Box 96 06472) (203) 484-0895

Norwalk Christ Episcopal Church **P** (174) 2 Emerson St 06855-1330 (Mail to: 2 Emerson St 06855-1330) Patricia Coller (203) 866-7442

Norwalk Iglesia Betania Episcopal **P** (83) 1 Union Park 06850-3316 (Mail to: 1 Trinity Pl 06854-2114) Eddie Lopez (203) 853-6767

Norwalk St Paul's on the Green **P** (621) 60 East Ave Ste 1 06851-4891 (Mail to: 60 East Ave 06851-4909) Nicholas Lang Holley Slauson Peter Thompson (203) 847-2806

Norwich Christ Episcopal Church **P** (192) 78 Washington St 06360-5039 (Mail to: 78 Washington St 06360-5039) John Hugh James (860) 887-4249

Oakville All Saints Episcopal Church **P** (280) 262 Main St 06779-1742 (Mail to: PO Box 33 06779-0033) (860) 274-2352

Old Greenwich St Saviours Church **P** (209) 350 Sound Beach Ave 06870-1930 (Mail to: 350 Sound Beach Ave 06870-1930) Margaret Finnerud (203) 637-2262

Old Lyme St Anns Episcopal Church **P** (213) 82 Shore Rd 06371-1726 (Mail to: 82 Shore Rd 06371-1726) (860) 434-1621

Old Saybrook Grace Episcopal Church **P** (311) 336 Main St 06475-2350 (Mail to: 336 Main St 06475-2350) Charles Hamill (860) 388-0895

Orange Church of the Good Shepherd **P** (252) 680 Racebrook Rd 06477-1931 (Mail to: 680 Racebrook Rd 06477-1931) (203) 795-6577

Oxford Christ Church Quaker Farms **P** (249) 470 Quaker Farms Rd 06478-1307 (Mail to: 470 Quaker Farms Rd 06478-1398) John Donnelly (203) 888-4936

Oxford St Peters Episcopal Church **P** (65) 421 Oxford Rd 06478-1692 (Mail to: 421 Oxford Rd 06478-1236) (203) 888-5279

Pine Meadow St Johns Episcopal Church **P** (242) 51 Church St 06061 (Mail to: PO Box 27 06061-0027) Sandra Cosman (860) 379-3062

Plainfield St Pauls Episcopal Church **P** (111) 27 Babcock Ave 06374-1222 (Mail to: 27 Babcock Ave 06374-1222) Victoria Baldwin (860) 564-3560

Plainville Church of Our Saviour **P** (148) 115 W Main St 06062-1905 (Mail to: 115 W Main St 06062-1905) Leonard Hullar (860) 747-3109

Pomfret Christ Church Episcopal **P** (452) 521 Pomfret St 06258 (Mail to: PO Box 21 06258-0021) David Carter Virginia Army (860) 315-7780

Portland Trinity Church **P** (285) 345 Main St 06480-1561 (Mail to: 345 Main St 06480-1561) Philip Bjornberg (860) 342-0458

Preston St James Church **P** (157) 95 Route 2a 06365-8538 (Mail to: 95 Rte. 2-A 06365) Kim Litsey (860) 889-0150

Putnam St Philip Episcopal Parish **P** (24) 63 Grove St 06260-2109 (Mail to: 63 Grove St 06260-2109) (860) 928-3510

Redding Christ Church Parish **P** (336) 184 Cross Hwy 06896-2101 (Mail to: PO Box 54 06876-0054) Nicki Kimes K Alon White (203) 938-2872

Ridgefield St Stephens Church **P** (658) 351 Main St 06877-4601 (Mail to: 351 Main St 06877-4601) Whitney Altopp Leslie Hughs (203) 438-3789

Riverside St Pauls Church **P** (545) § 200 Riverside Ave 06878-2210 (Mail to: 200 Riverside Ave 06878-2206) Stephanie Johnson (203) 637-2447

Rocky Hill St Andrew the Apostle **P** (503) 331 Orchard St 06067-2022 (Mail to: 331 Orchard St 06067-2022) William Veinot John Rogers (860) 529-7622

Roxbury Christ Church **P** (162) 1 Church St 06783-1702 (Mail to: PO Box 4 06783-0004) (860) 355-3695

Salisbury St Johns Episcopal Church **P** (198) 12 Main St 06068-1800 (Mail to: PO Box 391 06068-0391) Lance Beizer David Sellery (860) 435-9290

Seymour Trinity Episcopal Church **P** (153) 91 Church St 06483-2611 (Mail to: 91 Church St 06483-2611) Patricia Leonard-Pasley (203) 888-6596

Sharon Christ Episcopal Church **P** (72) 9 S Main St 06069-1778 (Mail to: PO Box 1778 06069-1778) Carl Widing Martha Tucker (860) 364-5260

Shelton Church of the Good Shepherd **P** (190) 182 Coram Ave 06484-3347 (Mail to: 182 Coram Ave 06484-3347) (203) 924-8050

Shelton St Pauls Episcopal Church **P** (293) 25 Church St 06484-5802 (Mail to: 25 Church St 06484-5897) Knute Hansen Amjad Samuel (203) 929-1722

Simsbury St Albans Episcopal Church **P** (211) 197 Bushy Hill Rd 06070-2604 (Mail to: 197 Bushy Hill Rd 06070-2699) Rebekah Hatch (860) 658-0406

South Glastonbury St Lukes Episcopal Church **P** (284) PO Box 155 06073-0155 (Mail to: PO Box 155 06073-0155) Deborah Meister (860) 633-7175

South Windsor St Peters Episcopal Church **P** (185) 99 Sand Hill Rd 06074-2023 (Mail to: 99 Sand Hill Rd 06074-2023) Anne Fraley (860) 644-8548

Southbury Church of the Epiphany **P** (78) 262 Main St 06488-1808 (Mail to: 262 Main St 06488-1808) Marston Price (203) 264-8150

Southington St Pauls Episcopal Church **P** (339) 145 Main St 06489-2505 (Mail to: 145 Main St 06489-2590) Suzannah Rohman (860) 628-8486

Southport Trinity Episcopal Church **P** (898) PO Box 400 06890-0400 (Mail to: PO Box 400 06890-0400) Margaret Hodgkins (203) 255-0454

Stafford Springs Grace Church Parish Episcopal **P** (85) 7 Spring St 06076-1504 (Mail to: PO Box 65 06076-0065) Bennett Brockman (860) 684-2824

Stamford Church of Christ the Healer **P** (103) 20 Brookdale Rd 06903-4117 (Mail to: 20 Brookdale Rd 06903-4117) (203) 322-6991

Stamford Eglise De L'Epiphanie **M** (91) 628 Main St 06901-2011 (Mail to: C/O St John's Church 628 Main St 06901-2094) (203) 964-1517

Stamford St Andrews Church **P** (120) 1231 Washington Blvd 06901 (Mail to: 1231 Washington Blvd 06902-2402) Bartlett Gage (203) 325-4359

Stamford St Francis Church **P** (350) 2810 Long Ridge Road 06903-1110 (Mail to: 503 Old Long Ridge Rd 06903-1110) Mark Lingle Mark Lingle Debra Slade (203) 322-2949

Stamford St Johns Church **P** (991) 628 Main St 06901-2011 (Mail to: C/O S Defilippis 628 Main St 06901-2011) Sanford Key Elizabeth Skaleski (203) 348-2619

Stonington Calvary Church **P** (589) 33 Church St 06378-1344 (Mail to: 27 Church St 06378-1344) Douglass Lind Imlijungla Sojwal (860) 535-1181

Storrs St Marks Chapel **P** (158) 42 Eagleville Rd 06268-1710 (Mail to: 42 Eagleville Rd 06268-1710) Brian Blayer (860) 429-2647

Stratford Christ Episcopal Church **P** (359) 2000 Main St 06615-6340 (Mail to: 2000 Main St 06615-6397) Laura Queen (203) 378-1445

Tariffville Trinity Episcopal Church **P** (643) 11 Church St 06081-9624 (Mail to: c/o Ellen Corriveau 11 Church St 06081-9624) J Taylor Albright (860) 651-0201

Thomaston St Peters Trinity Church **Chapel** (233) 160 Main St 06787-1720 (Mail to: 160 Main St 06787-1720) (203) 268-2809

Torrington Trinity Episcopal Church **P** (332) 220 Prospect St 06790-5314 (Mail to: 220 Prospect St 06790-5314) Nikolaus Combs Amy Reichman (860) 482-6027

Trumbull Christ Episcopal Church Tashua **P** (99) 5170 Madison Ave 06611-1110 (Mail to: 5170 Madison Ave 06611-1110) Jane Jeuland (203) 268-5566

Trumbull Grace Episcopal Church **P** (91) 5958 Main St 06611-2413 (Mail to: 5958 Main St 06611-2497) Paul Jacobson (203) 268-2809

Trumbull Trinity Episcopal Church **P** (127) 1734 Huntington Tpk 06611-5114 (Mail to: 1734 Huntington Tpke 06611-5114) Alan Murchie (203) 375-1503

Vernon Rockville St John's Church **P** (357) 523 Hartford Tpke 06066-4900 (Mail to: 523 Hartford Tpke 06066-4900) Virginia Army (860) 872-0517

Wallingford St Pauls Episcopal Church **P** (860) 65 Main St 06492-3709 (Mail to: 65 Main St 06492-3795) Debra Dodd (203) 269-5050

Washington St Johns Church **P** (354) 78 Green Hill Rd 06793-1217 (Mail to: PO Box 1278 06793-0278) Susan Mccone (860) 868-2527

Waterbury Christ Church **P** (70) 2030 E Main St 06705-2607 (Mail to: 2030 E Main St 06705-2607) (203) 753-6921

Waterbury St Johns Episcopal Church **P** (420) 16 Church St 06702-2103 (Mail to: 16 Church St 06702-2103) Michael Carroll (203) 754-3116

Watertown Christ Church Parish Episcopal **P** 25 The Grn 06795-2117 (Mail to: PO Box 241 06795-0241) Mary Gates (860) 274-1910

West Hartford St James Church Episcopal **P** (1062) 1018 Farmington Ave 06107-2105 (Mail to: 19 Walden St 06107-1822) Robert Hooper Charlotte Laforest Molly Louden (860) 521-9620

West Hartford St Johns Church Episcopal **P** (874) 679 Farmington Ave 06119-1895 (Mail to: 679 Farmington Ave 06119-1895) Hope Eakins Susan Pinkerton (860) 523-5201

West Hartford St Pauls Mission of the Deaf **M** (6) c/o St. Johns Church 679 Farmington Ave 06119-1811 (Mail to: 679 Farmington Ave 06119) (860) 756-5601

West Haven Church of the Holy Spirit **P** (216) 28 Church St 06516-4927 (Mail to: 28 Church St 06516-4927) (203) 934-3437

Westbrook St Pauls Episcopal Church **P** (70) 53 S Main St 06498-1902 (Mail to: PO Box 598 06498-0598) (860) 669-7681

Weston Emmanuel Episcopal Church **P** (193) 285 Lyons Plain Rd 06883-2401 (Mail to: 285 Lyons Plain Rd 06883-2441) Katharine Herron-Piazza (203) 227-8565

Westport Christ and Holy Trinity Church **P** (1187) 75 Church Lane 06880-3510 (Mail to: 55 Myrtle Ave 06880-3510) John Betit Marcella Gillis Peter Powell (203) 227-0827

Wethersfield Trinity Episcopal Church **P** (380) 300 Main St 06109-1826 (Mail to: 300 Main St 06109-1892) (860) 529-6825

Willimantic Saint Paul's Episcopal Church **P** (105) 220 Valley St 06226-2332 (Mail to: P.O. Box 63 06226-) Jaclyn Sheldon (860) 423-8455

Wilton St Matthews Episcopal Church **P** (1230) 36 New Canaan Rd 06897-3310 (Mail to: 36 New Canaan Rd 06897-3310) Marissa Rohrbach Richard Mayberry (203) 762-7400

Windham St Pauls Church **P** (110) 26 Plains Rd 06280-1324 (Mail to: PO Box 82 06280-0082) John Burton (860) 423-9653

Windsor Grace Church Episcopal **P** (299) 311 Broad St 06095-2906 (Mail to: 311 Broad St 06095-2906) Harry Elliott Denise Adessa (860) 688-1232

Winsted St James Episcopal Church **P** (133) 160 Main St 06098-1735 (Mail to: 160 Main St 06098-1735) (860) 379-5657

Wolcott All Saints Episcopal Church **P** (168) 282 Bound Line Rd 06716-2508 (Mail to: 282 Bound Line Road 06716-2508) Susan Davidson Sonnie Fish (203) 879-2800

Woodbury St Pauls Episcopal Church **P** (353) 249 Main St S 06798-3408 (Mail to: PO Box 5002 06798-5002) Tuesday Rupp (203) 263-3541

Yalesville St John Evangelist Episcopal **P** (123) 360 Church St 06492-2200 (Mail to: 360 Church St 06492-2283) Peter Quinn (203) 269-9526

Yantic Grace Episcopal Church **P** (56) PO Box 126 06389-0126 (Mail to: 4 Chapel Hill Rd 06389-0126) Kim Litsey Scott Stevens (860) 887-2082

DIOCESE OF DALLAS

(PROVINCE VII)

Comprises 25 counties in Northeast Texas

DIOCESAN OFFICE 1630 N Garrett Ave Dallas TX 75206

TEL (214) 826-8310   FAX (214) 826-5968

E-MAIL info@edod.org   WEB www.edod.org

Previous Bishops—
Alexander C Garrett 1874-1924, Harry T Moore coadj 1917 Bp 1924-46, Chas A Mason coadj 1945 Bp 1946-70, Gerald F Burrill suffr 1950-54, John JM Harte suffr 1954-62, Theology H McCrea suffr 1962-75, William Paul Barnds suffr 1966-73, A Donald Davies 1970-82, Robt E Terwilliger suffr 1975-86, Donis D Patterson 1983-92, David Bruce MacPherson suffr 1999-02, James Monte Stanton 1993-2014, Paul Emil Lambert suffr 2008-16

Bishop — Rt Rev George Robinson Sumner (1090) (Dio 14 Nov 2015)

Treas M Sonom; *Chanc* D Parsons; *Comm* K Durnan; *Misn/ChrEd* J Hylden; *Sec Conv* R D'Antoni; *Dio Serv* SL Mills; *Evang* C Headington; *Budg & Fin* T Young; *Archdcn* R Trei

Stand Comm—Cler: Pres T Reisner M Mills A Van Kirk; *Lay:* J LaCour L Spence L Valenta

PARISHES, MISSIONS, AND CLERGY

Allen Church of the Savior **P** 110 S Alma Dr 75013-3045 (Mail to: 110 S Alma Dr 75013-3045) Donald Griffin (972) 649-4032

Athens Church of St Matthias **P** (35) Attn Charlene Tucker 205 Willowbrook Dr 75751-3537 (Mail to: Attn Treasurer 205 Willowbrook Dr 75751-3537) Matthew Frick (903) 675-3210

Atlanta All Saints Episcopal Church **M** (22) 404 Louise St 75551-2240 (Mail to: PO Box 513 75551-0513) (903) 796-7200

Bonham Church of the Holy Trinity **M** (15) 617 Star St 75418-3630 (Mail to: PO Box 81 75418-0081) (903) 375-3859

Canton St Justin Martyr **PS** (61) 977 W Highway 243 75103-2021 (Mail to: PO Box 87 75103-0087) Ronald Studenny (903) 567-4959

Cedar Hill Church of the Good Shepherd **P** (235) 915 Straus Rd 75104-5317 (Mail to: PO Box 429 75106-0429) Marc Dobson (972) 291-4528

Coppell Church of the Apostles **P** (438) 322 S Macarthur Blvd 75019-3605 (Mail to: 322 S Macarthur Blvd 75019-3605) Timothy Cherry (972) 462-0234

Corsicana St Johns Episcopal Church **P** (333) 101 14th St 75110-5110 (Mail to: 101 14th St 75110-5110) Edward Monk (903) 874-5425

Dallas Christ Episcopal Church **P** (461) 534 West 10th Street 75208-4720 (Mail to: 534 W 10th St 75208-4720) Fabian Villalobos (214) 941-0339

Dallas Episcopal Church of Our Saviour **M** (67) 1616 Jim Miller Rd 75217-1320 (Mail to: 1616 Jim Miller Rd 75217-1320) (214) 391-2824

Dallas Good Samaritan Episcopal Church **M** (55) 1522 Highland Rd 75218-4420 (Mail to: 1522 Highland Rd 75218-4420) Joel Hatfield (214) 328-3883

Dallas Church Of The Good Shepherd **P** (1348) 11122 Midway Rd 75229-4118 (Mail to: 11122 Midway Rd 75229-4199) Michael Mills Matthew Burdette Thomas Hotchkiss Melody Shobe Christopher Steele (214) 351-6468

Dallas Episcopal Church of the Holy Cross **P** (46) 4052 Herschel Ave 75219-2930 (Mail to: 4052 Herschel Ave 75219-2930) George Brown (214) 528-3855

Dallas Church of the Incarnation **P** (4674) 3966 Mckinney Ave 75204-8230 (Mail to: 3966 Mckinney Ave 75204-2099) Anthony Burton James Lee Dorothy Budd Samuel Kincaid Matthew Larsen John Sundara David Thompson (214) 521-5101

Dallas Emmanuel Anglican **PS** C/O St Luke's Episcopal Church 5923 Royal Ln 75230-3841

(Mail to: C/O St Luke's Episcopal Church 5923 Royal Ln 75230-3841) (214) 368-6304

Dallas Episcopal Church of Ascension **P** (533) 8787 Greenville Ave 75243-7140 (Mail to: 8787 Greenville Ave 75243-7197) Paul Klitzke Marci Pounders Sue Ross Andrew Van Kirk (214) 340-4196

Dallas Holy Faith **PS** Trinity Episcopal 12727 Hillcrest Rd 75230-2007 (Mail to: C/O Trinity Episcopal 12727 Hillcrest Rd 75230-2007)

Dallas San Francisco de Asis **P** 11540 Ferguson Rd 75228-1825 (Mail to: 11540 Ferguson Rd 75228-1825) Aquilino Lara Juana Lara Debra Vela (972) 279-6501

Dallas St Albans Canterbury House at SMU **CC** 3308 Daniel Ave 75205-1440 (Mail to: 3308 Daniel Ave 75205-1440) (214) 363-2911

Dallas St Andrews Episcopal Church **P** (220) 2783 Valwood Pkwy 75234-3529 (Mail to: 2783 Valwood Pkwy 75234-3529) Alexander Graham (972) 247-7702

Dallas St Christophers Episcopal Church **P** (93) 7900 Lovers Ln 75225-8200 (Mail to: 7900 Lovers Ln 75225-8200) (214) 363-2792

Dallas St James Episcopal Church **P** (387) 9845 Mccree Rd 75238-3444 (Mail to: 9845 McCree Rd 75238-3444) Michael Hurst Oliver Butler Joel Hatfield (214) 348-1345

Dallas St Johns Episcopal Church **P** (503) 848 Harter Rd 75218-2751 (Mail to: 848 Harter Rd 75218-2792) David Houk Herbert DeWees Andrew Johnson John Thorpe (214) 321-6451

Dallas Saint Luke's Episcopal Church **P** (313) 5923 Royal Ln 75230-3812 (Mail to: 5923 Royal Ln 75230-3841) Mark Anderson (214) 368-6304

✠ **Dallas** Cathedral Church of St Matthew **O** (920) 5100 Ross Ave 75206-7709 (Mail to: 5100 Ross Ave 75206-7798) Robert Price Mark Hall Diana Luck Bonnie Morrill David Petrash (214) 823-8134

Dallas Saint Michael and All Angels Church **P** (6926) § 8011 Douglas Avenue 75225-0385 (Mail to: C/O Keith Quarterman 8011 Douglas Ave 75225-6502) Christopher Girata Robert Johnston Mary Lessmann Eric Liles Lisa Musser Gregory Pickens (214) 363-5471

Dallas St Augustine of Hippo Episcopal Ch **P** (103) 1302 W Kiest Blvd 75224-3235 (Mail to: 1302 W Kiest Blvd 75224-3235) Emily Hylden Jordan Hylden (214) 371-3441

Dallas St Thomas the Apostle Church **P** (405) 6525 Inwood Rd 75209-5314 (Mail to: 6525 Inwood Rd 75209-5399) Joy Daley Leo Loyola (214) 352-0410

Dallas The Episcopal Church Of The Transfiguration **P** (1783) 14115 Hillcrest Rd 75254-8622 (Mail to: C/O Sophie Lawrance 14115 Hillcrest Rd 75254-8622) James Barber Robert Shobe Rebecca Tankersley (972) 233-1898

Dallas Trinity Episcopal Church **P** (41) 12727 Hillcrest Rd 75230-2007 (Mail to: 12727 Hillcrest Rd 75230-2007) Robin Smith Philip Snyder (972) 991-3601

Denison St Lukes Church **P** (178) 427 W Woodard St 75020 (Mail to: 427 W Woodard St 75020-3138) Donald Perschall (903) 465-2630

Denton St Barnabas Episcopal Church **P** (337) 1200 Elm St 76201-2941 (Mail to: 1200 Elm St 76201-2941) Donald Johnson (940) 382-2748

Denton St Davids Church **P** (416) 623 Ector St 76201-2423 (Mail to: 623 Ector St 76201-2423) Paul Nesta (940) 387-2622

Desoto St Anne Episcopal Church **P** (441) 1700 Westmoreland Rd 75115-2272 (Mail to: 1700 Westmoreland Rd 75115-2272) James Harris George Udell (972) 709-0691

Ennis St Thomas Episcopal Church **M** (93) 901 Park St 75119-1607 (Mail to: PO Box 475 75120-0475) (972) 875-2423

Flower Mound Saint Nicholas Church **P** (637) 4800 Wichita Trl 75022-5121 (Mail to: C/O Faith Epley 4800 Wichita Trl 75022-5121) Mark Wright (972) 318-7070

Frisco St Philips Church **P** (1430) § 6400 Stonebrook Parkway 75034 (Mail to: 6400 Stonebrook Pkwy 75034-5711) Thomas Methvin Clayton Elder (214) 619-5806

Garland Holy Trinity Episcopal Church **P** (236) 3217 Guthrie Rd 75043-6121 (Mail to: 3217 Guthrie Rd 75043-6121) John Brown (972) 226-1283

Garland St Barnabas Episcopal Church **P** (276) 1200 Shiloh Rd 75042-5724 (Mail to: 1200 Shiloh Rd 75042-5724) Maria Barrios Antonio Munoz Alyce Schrimsher Alfredo Williams (972) 494-6600

Garland St Davids Church **P** (91) 2022 Saturn Rd 75041-1640 (Mail to: 2022 Saturn Rd 75041-1640)

Greenville St Pauls Episcopal Church **P** (302) 8320 Jack Finney Blvd 75402-3004 (Mail to: 8320 Jack Finney Blvd 75402-3004) Nicholas Funk (903) 455-5030

Irving Episcopal Church of the Redeemer **P** (258) 2700 Warren Cir 75062-9242 (Mail to: 2700 Warren Cir 75062-5799) Victoria Heard (972) 255-4171

Irving St Marks Episcopal Church **P** (144) 516 S O Connor Rd 75060-4059 (Mail to: 516 S O Connor Rd 75060-4059) Robert Corley (972) 253-7124

Irving St Marys Episcopal Church **P** (957) 635 Story Rd 75061-6732 (Mail to: 635 Story Rd 75061-6728) Richard Crownover Luz Elliott (972) 790-4644

Kaufman Church of Our Merciful Saviour **M** (90) 500 S Jackson St 75142-2330 (Mail to: PO Box 520 75142-0520) (972) 932-4646

Kemp St James on the Lake **P** (119) 10707 County Road 4022 75143-4217 (Mail to: 10707 Cr 4022 75143) Mark Melton (903) 498-8080

Lewisville Church of the Annunciation **P** (709) § 602 Old Orchard Ln 75077-2869 (Mail to: PO Box 292365 75029-2365) Catherine Thompson

Ralph Masters Ames Swartsfager (972) 221-3531

Mc Kinney Church of the Holy Family **M** (275) 406 Lincoln St 75069-4263 (Mail to: PO Box 1039 75070-8147) (972) 542-5799

Mc Kinney St Peters Episcopal Church **P** (492) 400 S College St 75069 (Mail to: 511 Foote St 75069-2707) Elizabeth Breyfogle Katherine Heitmann Perry Mullins (972) 562-1166

McKinney St Andrews Episcopal Church **M** (550) 6400 McKinney Ranch Pkwy 75070-9601 (Mail to: 6400 McKinney Ranch Pkwy 75070-9601) Andrew Van Kirk (972) 548-7990

Mineola St Dunstan Episcopal Church **P** (158) 800 Johnson St 75773-1816 (Mail to: PO Box 81 75773-0081) Archibald Young (903) 569-2478

Mt Pleasant St Marks Episcopal Church **P** (93) 205 E Pecan St 75455-5403 (Mail to: PO Box 1837 75456-1837) Ethel Channon (903) 572-3211

Paris Church of the Holy Cross **P** (268) § 322 S Church St 75460-5853 (Mail to: 400 S Church St 75460-5844) Craig Reed (903) 784-6194

Pittsburg St William Laud Epis Church **P** (64) 601 Lafayette St 75686-3057 (Mail to: PO Box 1057 75686-3057) Mary Matthews (903) 856-2675

Plano Iglesia de la Santa Natividad **P** 2200 18th St 75074-4920 (Mail to: 2200 18th St 75074-4920) Noe Mendez

Plano Resurrection Episcopal Church **M** 4500 Quincy Ln 75024-3849 (Mail to: 3609 Steven Dr 75023-3837) Leslie Stewart

Plano Church of the Holy Nativity **P** (309) C/O Dk Andersen 2200 18th St 75074-4920 (Mail to: C/O D K Andersen 2200 18th St 75074-4920) Garrin Dickinson James Evans John Kline (972) 424-4574

Pottsboro St John the Apostle Episcopal Church **M** (157) PO Box 972 75076-0972 (Mail to: PO Box 972 75076-0972) Nancy Powers (903) 786-4339

Prosper St Pauls Episcopal Church **M** (194) 420 S Coit Rd 75078-2907 (Mail to: 420 S Coit Rd 75078-2907) John Schmidt Thomas Smith (972) 347-9700

Richardson Church of the Epiphany **P** (612) 421 Custer Rd 75080-5628 (Mail to: PO Box 830218 75083-0218) Brenda Kroll Anne Randall (972) 690-0095

Rockwall Holy Trinity Episcopal Church **P** (339) 1524 Smirl Dr 75032-7638 (Mail to: Treasurer, John Curtis 1524 Smirl Dr 75032-7638) Norman Turbeville James Detrich (972) 771-8242

Sherman St Stephens Episcopal Church **P** (154) 401 S Crockett St 75090-7171 (Mail to: 401 S Crockett St 75090-7171) James Evans (903) 892-6610

Sulphur Spgs St Philips Episcopal Church **P** (66) 1206 College St 75482-3018 (Mail to: PO Box 636 75483-0636) Barbara Kelton

Terrell Church Of The Good Shepherd **P** (106) 200 W College St 75160-2625 (Mail to: 200 W College St 75160-2625) David Faulkner (972) 563-2412

Texarkana St James Episcopal Church **P** (491) § 413 Olive St 75501-5510 (Mail to: 413 Olive St 75501-5510) Douglas Anderson (903) 794-9224

Waxahachie Saint Paul's Episcopal Church **M** (421) 624 Ovilla Rd 75167-4801 (Mail to: 624 Ovilla Rd 75167-4801) Terry Reisner (972) 938-2126

Winnsboro St Francis Episcopal Church **M** (21) 103 W Sage St 75494-2541 (Mail to: PO Box 1082 75494-1082) (903) 342-7240

THE EPISCOPAL CHURCH IN DELAWARE
(PROVINCE III)
Comprises State of Delaware
DIOCESAN OFFICE 913 Wilson Road, Wilmington, DE 19803
Tel (302) 256-0374   FAX (302) 543-8084
E-MAIL kmoore@delaware.church   WEB www.delaware.church

Previous Bishops— Alfred Lee 1841-87, Leighton Coleman 1888-1907, Frederick J Kinsman 1908-19, Philip Cook 1920-38, Arthur R McKinstry 1939-54, J Brooke Mosley 1955-68, Wm H Mead 1968-74, Wm H Clark 1975-85, Q Primo *Int* 1985-86, C Cabell Tennis 1986-97, Wayne P Wright 1998-2017

Bishop—Rt Rev Kevin S Brown (1107) (Dio 9 December 2017)

Cn to Ord Rev G Rowe; *Bus Mgr* J Gregory; *Asst to Bp* K Moore; *Chanc* A Foster Box 551 Wilmington DE 19899

Stand Comm—Cler: K Athey K Capwell DJ Kiessling S Nelson; *Lay: Pres* J Rania C Maguire T Quinn Gray S Taber

PARISHES, MISSIONS, AND CLERGY

Bethany Beach St Martha's Episcopal Church **P** (174) PO Box 1478 19930-1478 (Mail to: PO Box 1478 19930-1478) Mary Allen (302) 539-7444

Bridgeville St Marys Episcopal Church **P** (41) 114 Delaware Ave 19933-1141 (Mail to: PO Box 21 19933-0021) (302) 337-8981

Camden Wyoming St Pauls Episcopal Church **P** (105) Old North Rd At West St 19934 (Mail to: PO Box 157 19934-0157) John Desaulniers (302) 697-7904

Claymont The Church of the Ascension **P** (279) 3717 Philadelphia Pike 19703-3413 (Mail to: 3717 Philadelphia Pike 19703-3413) (302) 798-6683

Delaware City Christ Church Delaware City **P** (73) 222 Third And Clint 19706 (Mail to: Attn Dan Saunders Treasurer PO Box 523 19706-0523) (302) 834-3328

Delmar All Saints Church Delmar **P** (60) 10th St 19940 (Mail to: PO Box 88 19940-0088) Kenneth Athey (302) 846-9889

Dover Christ Church Dover **P** (396) S State & Water Sts 19903 (Mail to: PO Box 1374 19903-1374) Charles Weiss Ronald Gerber Patricia Malcolm (302) 734-5731

Georgetown St Pauls Church Georgetown **P** (182) 122 East Pine Street 19947 (Mail to: C/O Vicki Reinsfelder P.O. Box 602 19947-0602) (302) 856-2894

Harrington St Stephens Church **P** (74) 190 Raughley Hill Rd 19952-3152 (Mail to: Attn Judith A Viar 2020 Tatnall St 19802-4821) (302) 398-8846

Laurel St Philips Episcopal Church **P** (270) 600 S Central Ave 19956-1410 (Mail to: 600 S Central Ave 19956-1410) Howard Backus (302) 875-3644

Lewes St Georges Chapel **SC** Beaver Dam Rd & Chapel Branch 19958 (Mail to: 18 Olive Ave 19971-2806) Max Wolf (302) 227-7202

Lewes St Peters Church Lewes **P** (540) 211 Mulberry Street PO Box 464 19958-0464 (Mail to: PO Box 464 19958-0464) Jeffrey Ross Jule Gill Mark Harris Larry Hofer (302) 645-8479

Middletown St Andrews School Chapel **School** 350 Noxontown Rd 19709-1621 (Mail to: 350 Noxontown Rd 19709-1605) John Hutchinson (302) 378-9511

Middletown St Annes Episcopal Church **P** (433) 15 E Green St PO Box 421 19709-0421 (Mail to: 19 E Cochran St 19709-1410) Charles Bohner (302) 378-2401

Milford Christ Episcopal Church Milford **P** (283) 200 Church Ave 19963-1123 (Mail to: PO Box 191 19963-0191) Teresa Terry (302) 422-8466

Millsboro St Marks Church **P** (128) 50 Ellis St 19966-0422 (Mail to: PO Box 422 19966-0422) (302) 934-9464

Milton St John The Baptist **P** (144) 307 Federal St 19968-1606 (Mail to: PO Box 441 19968-0441) (302) 856-6844

New Castle Church of the Nativity **P** (51) 206 Sykes Rd 19720-1814 (Mail to: PO Box 662 19720-0662) Margaret Pumphrey Margaret Pumphrey (302) 328-3445

New Castle Immanuel Church On The Green **P** (230) 50 Market St 19720 (Mail to: 100 Harmony Street 19720-4847) Christopher Keene (302) 328-2413

Newark St Nicholas Episcopal Church **P** (93) 10 Old Newark Rd 19713-3944 (Mail to: 10 Old Newark Rd 19713-3944) (302) 368-4655

Newark St Thomas Parish **P** (605) 276 S College Ave 19711-5235 (Mail to: 276 S College Ave 19711-5235) (302) 368-4644

Newport St James Church Newport **P** (110) 2 S Augustine St 19804-2504 (Mail to: 2 S Augustine St 19804-2504) Sarah Nelson (302) 994-2029

Rehoboth Bch All Saints and St Georges Church **P** (766) 18 Olive Ave 19971-2806 (Mail to: 18 Olive Ave 19971-2899) Mariann Babnis Eunice Dunlap Elizabeth Kaeton (302) 227-7202

Seaford St Lukes Episcopal Church **P** (43) 202 North St 19973-2728 (Mail to: 202 North St 19973-2728) Marianne Ell (302) 629-7979

Selbyville St Martins in the Field Church **P** (77) PO Box 697 19975-0697 (Mail to: PO Box 697 19975-0697) (302) 436-8921

Smyrna St Peters Church **P** (80) § 22 Union St 19977-1147 (Mail to: 22 Union St 19977-1147) Donna Jean Kiessling (302) 653-9691

Wilmington Calvary Church Hillcrest **P** (94) 304 Lore Ave 19809-3134 (Mail to: 304 Lore Ave 19809-3134) (302) 764-2027

Wilmington Christ Church Christiana Hundred **HC** (1850) § 505 E Buck Rd 19807-2167 (Mail to: PO Box 3510 19807-0510) Ruth Beresford Stephen Setzer Ann Urinoski (302) 655-3379

Wilmington Church of St Andrews St Matthews **P** (346) 719 Shipley St 19801-1711 (Mail to: 719 Shipley St 19801-1727) David Andrews (302) 656-6628

Wilmington Grace Church Brandywine Hundred **P** (313) 4900 Concord Pike 19803-1412 (Mail to: 4906 Concord Pike 19803-1412) (302) 478-9533

Wilmington Immanuel Church Highlands **P** (203) 2400 W 17th St 19806-1343 (Mail to: 2400 W 17th St Ste A 19806-1346) Kathleen Benson Sheila Sharpe (302) 658-7326

Wilmington St Barnabas Episcopal Church **P** (459) 2800 Duncan Rd 19808-2306 (Mail to: 2800 Duncan Rd Side 19808-2312) Martha Kirkpatrick (302) 994-6607

Wilmington St Davids Episcopal Church **P** (334) § 2320 Grubb Rd 19810-2702 (Mail to: 2320 Grubb Rd 19810-2798) Bradley Hinton (302) 475-4688

Wilmington St James Episcopal Church Mill Creek **HC** (409) 2106 Saint James Church Rd 19808-5225 (Mail to: 2106 Saint James Church Rd 19808-5225) James Bimbi (302) 994-1584

Wilmington Trinity Parish & Old Swedes Church **P** (870) 1108 Adams St 19801-1327 Patricia Downing Charles Cowen (302) 652-8605

DISTRICT OF COLUMBIA

Diocese of Washington

DIOCESE OF THE DOMINICAN REPUBLIC
IGLESIA EPISCOPAL DOMINICANA
(PROVINCE IX)
Comprises the Dominican Republic
DIOCESAN OFFICE Calle Santiago No. 114
Gazcue, Santo Domingo, DOMINICAN REPUBLIC
(Mail: Iglesia Episcopal Dominicana DMG (In process), 100 Airport Ave Venice Fl 34285 USA)
Tel (809) 688-6016, (809) 686-7493
Email iglepidom@codetel.net.do / bishopmoisesquezada@gmail.com   Web www.iglepidom.org

Previous Bishops—
James T. Holly (Haiti) in charge
1897-1911 Charles B. Colmore
(Puerto Rico) in charge 1913-
1922 Harry R. Carson (Haiti)
in charge 1923-1948 (dio 1934-
1940) Mis Dist Haiti and Dom
Rep) Charles Alfred Voegeli
(Haiti) Bp Coadjutor 1943-1948
Paul A. Kellogg Bp 1960-1972
Telésforo Isaac Bp 1972-1991 Julio C. Holguin K. Bp
1991- 2017

Bishop Coadjutor—Moisés Quezada (13 Feb
2016- 3 Nov 2017)

Diocesan Bishop-Moisés Quezada (4 Nov 2017)

Exec Off Vicar General Rev Cn JI Márquez; *Treas* ME
Perez; *Fin Admin* P Santana; *Exec Sec to Bp:* Vacant;
Reg A Richardson; *Team Coord* K Carroll; *Asst Team
Coord* P Martin; *Sec* K Calzado *Concierge* N Cabrera

Archdcns: Central Región F Encarnación; *East Región*
V Saint Juste; *North Región* A García; *South Región*
L García

Exec Council: Cler: M Quezada M JE Sheen L Gómez
L García; *Lay:* M Luciano L Reyes JL Suarez Cruz
M Báez

Counselor B Herrera

PARISHES, MISSIONS, AND CLERGY

Andrés Boca Chica Iglesia **San José** Calle El Peso
No.28 (Mail to Calle El Peso No.28, Andrés
Boca Chica) Tel. (809) 523-4869
Azua Iglesia Episcopal **San Jorge** Calle Hernán
Cortez No.24, Azua (Mail to Calle Santiago
No.114, Gazcue apdo. 764 Santo Domingo)
Tel. 809-686-7493
Azua Iglesia Episcopal **Espíritu Santo** Calle La
Cruz de Ocoa, Las Carreras, Azua (Mail to
Hnas. Mirabal No.74, Barrio La Bombita,
Azua) Tel. 809-512-9318
Azua Iglesia Episcopal **La Reconciliacion** Calle
Las Carreras No.124, Barrio La Bombita, Azua
(Mail to Hnas Mirabal No.74, Barrio La Bom-
bita, Azua) Tel. 809-512-9318
Bani Iglesia Episcopal **La Transfiguración** Calle
Las Violetas No.2, Urb. Brisas del Canal, Bani
(Mail to Calle Las Violetas No.2, Urb. Brisas del
Canal, Bani) Tel. 809-522-9957

Bani Iglesia Episcopal **San Antonio de Padua**
Calle Principal No.80, Carretón, Bani (Mail to
C/principal No. 80, Carretón, Bani) Tel. 829-
466-8177
Bani Iglesia Episcopal **San Bernabé** Calle Prin-
cipal Barrio Pizarrete (Mail to Calle Sánchez
No.73, Santana D.M. Nizao) Tel. 829-312-6804
Bani Iglesia Episcopal **San Timoteo** Calle Mella
No.60, Nizao (Mail to Calle Sánchez No.73,
Santana D.M. Nizao Tel. (829) 312-6804
Bani Iglesia Episcopal **San Matías** Calle Sánchez
Vieja No. 73, Santana, Nizao (Mail to Calle
Sánchez Vieja No.73, Santana, Nizao) Tel. 829
312-6804
Bani Iglesia Episcopal **El Santo Nombre** Calle Al-
tos de los Melones, Catalina, Bani (Mail to Las
Violetas No.1, Bani) Tel 829-466-8177
Barahona Iglesia Episcopal **Jesús Peregrino** Calle
Primera Los Blocks, Batey Central (Mail to
Calle Tony Mota Ricart, Esq. Bomba Texaco,
Barahona) Tel. (849) 408-2880
Barahona Iglesia Episcopal **La Redención** Calle
Tony Mota Ricart, Esq. Bomba Texaco, Bara-
hona (Mail to Calle Tony Mota Ricart, Esq.
Bomba Texaco, Barahona) Tel. 849-408-2880
Bonao Iglesia Episcopal **San Juan Bautista** Cal-
le Padre Billini No.116, Bonao (Mail to Las
Orquídeas No.11, Reside. Mónica VI, Bonao)
Tel. (829)497-3145
Bonao Iglesia Episcopal **Jesús Encarnado** en Boca
de Yuboa Calle Carretera Mayobanex Vargas
No. 251, Bonao (Mail to Carretera Mayobanex
Vargas No.251, Bonao) Tel. 809-551-9374
Bonao Iglesia Episcopal **San Nicodemo**, Piedra
Blanca, Bonao (Mail to: Piedra Blanca, Bonao)
Tel. 829-497-3145
Bonao Iglesia Episcopal **Pentecostés** Bonao, (Mail
to: Bonao) Tel. 829-497-3145
Consuelo, Iglesia Episcopal **San Gabriel** Calle
Duarte No.1, Box 70, San Pedro de Macorís
(email to Calle Duarte No.1, Box 70, San Pedro
de Macorís) Tel. 809-526-7004
Consuelo Misión **La Gran Comisión** Calle Hato
Mayor, Batey Doña Lila, Consuelo, San Pedro
de Macorís (Mail to Calle Hato Mayor, Batey
Doña Lila, Consuelo, San P. Macorís) Tel. 829-
343-2366
Dajabon Iglesia Episcopal **Espíritu Consolador**
Calle Capotillo No. 90, Dajabon (Mail to Calle
Capotillo No.90, Dajabon) Tel. 809-664-7643

Gautier Iglesia Episcopal **Santo Tomas** Calle 1era No.7, Gautier (Mail to Calle 1era. No.7, Gautier) Tel. 809-430-1453

Guerra Iglesia Episcopal **Divina Providencia** Calle Marcos de Rosario No.39, San Antonio de Guerra (Mail to Calle Marcos del Rosario No. 39, San Antonio de Guerra) Tel. 809-764-1327

Haina Iglesia Episcopal **San Marcos** Calle Av. Central Rio No. 46, Haina (Mail to Central Rio No.46, Haina) Tel. 849-402-6959

Haina Iglesia Episcopal **San Juan Evangelista** Calle Tercera No.25, Barrio Piedra Blanca, Haina (Mail to Calle Tercera No. 25, Barrio Piedra Blanca, Haina) Tel. 849-402-6959

Hato Mayor Iglesia Episcopal **San Mateo** Batey Jalonga (Mail to: Batey Jalonga, Hato Mayor) Tel. 829-962-0504

Hato Mayor del Rey Iglesia Episcopal **Cristo Libertador** Calle Las Mercedes No. 66, Hato Mayor (Mail to Calle Las Mercedes No.66, Hato Mayor) Tel. 829-962-0504

Jarabacoa Iglesia Episcopal **Monte de la Transfiguración** Calle El Pedregal Abajo, Jarabacoa (Mail to Calle Santiago No.114, Gazcue, Santo Domingo) Tel. 809-686-7493

Jimani Iglesia Episcopal **San Pablo Apóstol** Calle Mella, Barrio 50, Jimani (Mail to Calle Mella No.50, Jimani) Tel.829-785-2229

Jimani Iglesia Episcopal **San Tito** Boca de Cachón, Jimani (Mail to Calle Mella No.50, Jimani) Tel. 829-785-2229

Jimani Iglesia Episcopal **San Ignacio** Calle Segunda Tierra Nueva, Jimani (Mail to Calle Segunda Tierra Nueva, Jimani) Tel. 829-785-2229

La Caleta, Boca Chica Iglesia Episcopal **De la Gracia** Calle Principal, Barrio Paraíso No.25, La Caleta (Mail to Calle Principal, Barrio Paraíso No. 25, La Caleta, Boca Chica) Tel. 809-764-1327

La Romana Iglesia Episcopal **Todos los Santos** Calle Dr. Ferry No.75, La Romana (Mail to Calle Dr. Ferry No.75, Apdo. 215, La Romana) Tel.809-556-2418

La Romana Iglesia Episcopal **La Encarnación** Calle Sector Invi, La Romana, (Mail to Calle Sector Invi, La Romana) Tel. 809-556-2418

La Vega Iglesia Episcopal **Cristo Resucitado** Calle La Riviera No. 2, (Mail to: Calle La Riviera No.2, La Vega) Tel. 809-973-6989

Mao, Valverde Iglesia Episcopal **Santa María Llena de Gracia** Calle Constitución No.1, Mao Valverde (Mail to Calle Constitución No.1, Mao) Tel. 829-443-2488

Nizao Iglesia Episcopal

Puerto Plata Iglesia Episcopal **Cristo Rey** Calle Sánchez No.21, Esq. José del C. Ariza, Puerto Plata (Mail to Calle Sánchez No.21, Esq. José del C. Ariza, Puerto Plata) Tel. 809-973-6989

Puerto Plata Iglesia Episcopal **San Simón Apóstol** Calle Los Rieles No. 1 Barrio San Marcos, Puerto Plata (Mail to Calle Los Rieles No. 1, Barrio San Marcos, Puerto Plata) Tel.809-973-6989

Puerto Plata Iglesia Episcopal **San Francisco de Asís** Calle Las Avispas, Maimón, Puerto Plata (Mail to Las Avispas, Maimón, Puerto Plata) Tel. 809-973-6989

Puerto Plata Iglesia Episcopal **Jesús Mesías** en Imbert, Puerto Plata (Mail to Imbert, Puerto Plata Tel. 809-973-6989

Puerto Plata Iglesia Episcopal **Santa María Virgen** Calle Principal, Barrio Invi-CEA No.36, Monte Llano (Mail to Calle Principal, Barrio Invi-CEA No.36, Monte Llano Tel. 809-545-9280

Puerto Plata Iglesia Episcopal **Divina Gracia** Calle Principal, Mozovi, Puerto Plata (Mail to Calle Principal, Mozovi, Puerto Plata) Tel. 809-545-9280

Puerto Plata Iglesia Episcopal **San Cornelio** Calle Callejón La Colina, Cabarete, Puerto Plata (Mail to Callejón La Colina, Cabarete, Puerto plata Tel. 809-545-9280

San Cristóbal Iglesia Episcopal **San Bartolomé** Calle Segunda No.3, Barrio Las Flores, San Cristóbal (Mail to Calle Segunda No.3, Barrio Las Flores, San Cristóbal) Tel. 809-664-1335

San Cristóbal Iglesia Episcopal **San Miguel** Calle Andrés Bremo, Doña Ana, San Cristóbal (Mail to Calle Andrés Bremo, Doña Ana, San Cristóbal) Tel. 809-664-1335

✠ **San Francisco de Macorís** Iglesia Episcopal **El Buen Samaritano**, Calle Cesar Agosto Sandino No.8, Barrio San Martin de Porres (Mail to: Calle Cesar Agosto Sandino No.8, Barrio San Martin de Porres, San Fco. De Macorís) Tel. 809-330-3464

San Francisco de Macorís Iglesia Episcopal **Jesús Nazareno** Calle La Cruz No.26, Esq. Ing. Guzmán Abreu, (Mail to: Calle La Cruz No.26, San Francisco de Macorís) Tel. 809-330-3464

San Francisco de Macorís Iglesia Episcopal **La Natividad,** Salcedo (Mail to: Salcedo) Tel.809-330-3464

San Pedro de Macorís Iglesia Episcopal **Santa Cruz**, Calle Salvador Ross, Santa Fe (Mail to: Calle Salvador Ross, Santa Fe, San P. de Macorís) Tel. 809-441-0250

San Pedro de Macorís Iglesia Episcopal **Santiago Apóstol** Calle Principal, Ingenio Angelina (Mail to: Calle Principal, Ingenio Angelina, San Pedro de Macorís) Tel. 809-441-0250

San Pedro de Macorís Iglesia Episcopal **El Buen Pastor** Calle Dra. Ana Betances, Barrio Las Flores (Mail to: Calle Dra. Ana Betances, Barrio Las Flores, San P. Macorís) Tel. 809-526-7004

San Pedro de Macorís Iglesia Episcopal **San Esteban** Calle Sánchez No.9, Miramar, Apdo.128 (Mail to: Calle Sánchez No.9, Miramar Apdo.128, San Pedro de Macorís) Tel. 809-529-

3228

San Pedro de Macorís Iglesia Episcopal **San Pedro Apóstol** Los Conucos, Juan Dolio, San P. Macorís (Mail to Los Conucos, Juan Dolio, San Pedro de Macorís) Tel. 809-441-0250

Santiago Iglesia Episcopal **Cristo Salvador** Calle Proyecto No.52, Mirador del Yaquez, La Yaguita del Pastor (Mail to: Calle Proyecto No.52, Mirador del Yaquez, La Yaguita del Pastor, Santiago) Tel. 809-582-8213

Santiago Iglesia Episcopal **Emmanuel** (Herradura, Santiago) (Mail to: Herradura, Santiago) Tel. 809-582-8213

Santiago Iglesia Episcopal **San Lucas** Calle Cuba No.128, (Mail to: Calle Cuba No.128, Santiago) Tel.809-734-0776

Santiago Iglesia Episcopal **La Anunciación** Calle 6 Esq. Calle 3 No.16, Llanos de Gurabo (Mail to: Calle 6 Esq. Calle 3No.16 Llanos de Gurabo, Santiago) Tel. 809-734-0776

Santiago Iglesia Episcopal **Jesús Maestro** Tamboril (Mail to: Tamboril Santiago) Tel. 809-973-6989

Santo Domingo Catedral Iglesia **Episcopal de la Epifanía** calle Av. Independencia No.253, Gazcue (Mail to: Av. Independencia No.253, Gazcue, Santo Domingo) Tel. 809-689-2070

Santo Domingo Iglesia Episcopal **San Andrés** Calle Marcos Ruiz No. 26, Villa Juana (Mail to: Calle Marcos Ruiz No.26, Villa Juana Santo Domingo) Tel. 809-245-1853

Santo Domingo Iglesia Episcopal **San Felipe Apóstol** Manzana C No.1 Invi Sabana Perdida (Mail to: Apdo. 764) Tel. 809-568-0532

Santo Domingo Iglesia Episcopal **San Pedro y San Pablo** Calle Valera No.60 La Barquita Sabana Perdida (Mail to: Apto 764)

Santo Domingo Este Iglesia Episcopal **Santísima Trinidad** Calle Costa Rica No.21, Ensanche Ozama (Mail to: Calle Costa Rica No.21, Ens. Ozama, Santo Domingo Este) Tel. 809-788-2957

Santo Domingo Este Iglesia Episcopal **Sagrada Familia** Calle 4 de Agosto casi Esq. San Vicente de Paul, Los Mina (Mail to: Apdo. 764) Tel. 809-682-8497

Santo Domingo Este Iglesia Episcopal **Santa Margarita** Calle Orlando Martínez y Alonso Pérez Solares del Almirante (Mail to: Apdo. 764) Tel. 809-530-8289

Santo Domingo Este Iglesia Episcopal **Santa Ana** Calle Primera Buenaventura, Barrio Mendoza

---

DIOCESE OF EAST CAROLINA
(PROVINCE IV)
Comprises eastern North Carolina
DIOCESAN OFFICE 705 Doctors Drive Kinston NC 28501 (MAIL: Box 1336, Kinston, NC 28503)
TEL (252) 522-0885   FAX (252) 523-5272
WEB www.diocese-eastcarolina.org

Previous Bishops—
Alfred A Watson 1884-1905, Robert Strange coadj 1904 Bp 1905-14, Thomas C Darst 1915-45, Thomas H Wright 1945-73, Hunley A Elebash 1973-83, B Sidney Sanders 1979-1997 Clifton Daniel coadj 1996 Bp 1997-2013, Peter James Lee Bp Prov (2013-2014)

Bishop—Rt Rev Robert Stuart Skirving (Dio 8 November 2014)

Stand Comm—Cler: P Stringer J Day P Canady *Lay:* D Trivette J Parrott T Holt

PARISHES, MISSIONS, AND CLERGY

Ahoskie Church of St Thomas **P** (139) PO Box 263 27910-0263 (Mail to: PO Box 263 27910-0263) Jeffrey Douglas (252) 332-3263

Bath St Thomas Episcopal Church **P** (117) 101 Craven St 27808-9789 (Mail to: PO Box 257 27808-0257) Diane Tomlinson (252) 923-9141

Beaufort St Pauls Episcopal Church **P** (681) 215 Ann St 28516-2103 (Mail to: 215 Ann St 28516-2103) Tambria Lee Mary Ogus (252) 728-3324

Belhaven St James Episcopal Church **P** (37) 545 E Main St NC 27810-1547 (Mail to: 545 E Main St 27810-1547) August Wiesner (252) 943-6977

Burgaw St Marys Episcopal Church **P** (57) 506 S Mcneil St 28425-5036 (Mail to: PO Box 841 28425) (910) 259-5541

Chocowinity Trinity Episcopal Church **P** (178) 182 NC Highway 33 W 27817 (Mail to: PO Box 332 27817-0332) Stephen Batten Mark Powell (252) 946-9958

Clinton St Pauls Episcopal Church **P** (91) 110 W Main St 28328-4047 (Mail to: 110 W Main St 28328-4047) Daniel Cenci (910) 592-3220

Columbia St Andrews Episcopal Church **P** (24) 106 North Road St 27925 (Mail to: PO Box 615 27925-0615) William Smyth (252) 441-8542

Creswell Christ Episcopal Church **M** (11) 100 S 6th St 27928-8960 (Mail to: Mr. William H. Peal Sixth Street 27928) (252) 482-8581

Creswell Galilee Mission / Lake Phelps **M** (3) 323 Park Rd 27928-9803 (Mail to: Lake Phelps 27928) (252) 441-8542

Currituck St Lukes Episcopal Mission **M** (30) 2864 Caratoke Hwy 27929-9611 Hubert McGee (252) 435-0530

Edenton Saint Paul's Episcopal Church **P** (405) 101 W Gale St 27932-1815 (Mail to: PO Box 548 27932-0548) John Gilliam (252) 482-3522

Elizabeth City Christ Episcopal Church **P** (447) 200 S Mcmorrine St 27909-4831 (Mail to: 200 S McMorrine St 27909-4831) Walter Broadfoot John Horner Edward Mullins (252) 338-1686

Elizabethtown St Christophers Episcopal Church **P** (32) 2606 W Broad St 28337-9031 (Mail to: PO Box 1841 28337-1841) (910) 879-2777

Engelhard St Georges Episcopal Church **P** (142) P.O. Box 101 31655 Hwy 264 27824 (Mail to: PO Box 101 27824-0101) James Lupton (252) 943-6318

Farmville Emmanuel Episcopal Church **P** (27) 3505 S Walnut St 27828-1658 (Mail to: 3505 South Walnut St PO Box 48 27828-1698) (252) 753-3737

Fayetteville Church of the Good Shepherd **P** (26) PO Box 64008 28306-0008 (Mail to: PO Box 64008 28306-0008) (910) 323-1512

Fayetteville Holy Trinity Episcopal Church **P** (606) 1601 Raeford Rd 28305-5031 (Mail to: Attn Financial Secretary 1601 Raeford Rd 28305-5097) Jeffrey Thornberg Joseph Running (910) 484-2134

Fayetteville St Johns Episcopal Church **P** (774) 302 Green St 28301-5028 (Mail to: PO Box 722 28302-0722) Robert Alves (910) 483-7405

Fayetteville St Josephs Episcopal Church **P** (47) 509 Ramsey St 28301-4911 (Mail to: PO Box 694 28302-0694) Ralph Clark (910) 323-0161

Fayetteville St Pauls in the Pines Epis Ch **P** (134) 1800 Saint Paul Ave 28304-5238 (Mail to: 1800 Saint Paul Ave 28304-5238) John Frazier (910) 485-7098

Gatesville St Marys Episcopal Church **P** (24) Attn Edith Bridger PO Box 174 27938-0174 (Mail to: Attn Edith Bridger PO Box 174 27938-0174) (252) 794-3277

Goldsboro St Andrews Episcopal Church **P** (25) 901 Harris St. 27530-6666 (Mail to: PO Box 1333 27533-1333) (919) 734-0550

Goldsboro St Francis Episcopal Church **P** (122) 503 Forest Hill Drive 27534-1824 (Mail to: PO Box 11406 27532-1406) (919) 735-9845

Goldsboro Saint Stephen's Church **P** (323) 200 North James Street 27530-3631 (Mail to: PO Box 984 27533-0984) Raymond Hanna (919) 734-4263

Greenville St Pauls Episcopal Church **P** (1053) 401 E 4th St 27858-1916 (Mail to: 401 E 4th St 27858-1916) Allen Singer Andrew Cannan (252) 752-3482

Greenville St Timothy's Episcopal Church **P** (320) 107 Louis St 27858-8660 (Mail to: 107 Louis St 27858-8660) Timothy Fulop John Porter-Acee John Robertson (252) 355-2125

Grifton St John Episcopal Church **P** (33) 2016 Price Cannon Rd 28530 (Mail to: PO Box 937 28530-0937) James Cooke (252) 524-5860

Hampstead Holy Trinity Episcopal Church **P** (102) 107 Deerfield Dr 28443-2135 (Mail to: 107 Deerfield Dr 28443-2135) Pamela Stringer (910) 270-4221

Havelock St Christopher's Episopal Church **P** (85) 1000 E Main Street 28532-2218 (Mail to: PO Box 626 28532-0626) Mary Ogus (252) 447-3912

Hertford Holy Trinity Episcopal Church **P** (151) 207 S Church St 27944-1113 (Mail to: PO Box 125 27944-0125) Robert Beauchamp (910) 270-4221

Holly Ridge St Philips Episcopal Church **P** (56) 661 Tar Landing Rd 28445-7671 (Mail to: PO Box 155 28445-0155) (910) 329-1514

Jacksonville St Annes Episcopal Church **P** (252) § 711 Henderson Dr 28540-4477 (Mail to: 711 Henderson Dr 28540-4477) Cynthia Duffus (910) 347-3774

Kinston St Augustines Episcopal Church **P** (38) 707 E Lenoir Ave 28502 (Mail to: PO Box 2263 28502-2263) Bonnie Smith (252) 523-4032

Kinston St Marys Episcopal Church **P** (426) 800 Rountree St 28501-3655 (Mail to: 800 Rountree Ave 28501-3655) Thomas Warren (252) 523-6146

Leland All Souls Episcopal Church **P** (35) 5087 Blue Banks Loop Rd NE 28451-4009 (Mail to: PO Box 475 28456-0475) (910) 655-8935

Lewiston Grace Episcopal Church **P** (15) PO Box 537 27849-0537 (Mail to: PO Box 429 27849-0429) (252) 322-1004

Lumberton Trinity Episcopal Church **P** (364) 1202 Chestnut St 28358-4713 (Mail to: 1202 Chestnut St 28358-4713) (910) 739-3717

Morehead City St Andrew's Church **P** (222) 3003 Bridges St 28557-3329 (Mail to: 2005 Arendell St 28557-3999) John Pollock (252) 727-9093

Nags Head Church of St Andrews by the Sea **P** (398) 4212 S Virginia Dare Trl 27959-9284 (Mail to: PO Box 445 27959-0445) (252) 441-5382

New Bern Christ Episcopal Church **P** (1020) 320 Pollock St 28560-4945 (Mail to: PO Box 1246 28563-1246) Hoyt Canady Cortney Dale (252) 633-2109

New Bern St Cyprians Episcopal Church **P** (48) 604 Johnson St 28563 (Mail to: PO Box 809 28563-0809) (252) 633-3816

Newton Grove La Iglesia de la Sagrada Familia **M** (546) 2989 Easy St 28334-7994 (Mail to: 2989 Easy Street 28334) Marilyn Mitchell (919) 658-1819

Oriental St Thomas Episcopal Church **P** (154) 402 Freemason St 28571-9206 (Mail to: PO Box 461 28571-0461) (252) 249-0256

Plymouth Grace Episcopal Church **P** (72) 107 Madison St 27962-1432 (Mail to: 106 Madison St 27962-1432) Henry Burdick (252) 793-3295

Roper St Lukes & St Annes Epis Church **P** (27) 206 S Bank St 27970-9181 (Mail to: PO Box 85 27970-0085) (252) 793-3295

Salter Path St Francis by the Sea **P** (168) 920 Salter Path Rd 28512-5938 (Mail to: 920 Salter Path Rd 28512-5938) Leonard Thomas James Sproul (252) 240-2388

Seven Springs Church of the Holy Innocents **P** (90) 6861 Hwy 55 W 28578-9493 (Mail to: 6861 Hwy 55 W 28578-9493) (252) 569-3011

Shallotte St James the Fisherman Church **P** (334) 4941 Main St 28470-4503 (Mail to: PO Box 68 28459-0068) Farrell Graves Jean Miller Frank Russ (910) 754-9313

Southern Shores All Saints Episcopal Church **P** (416) 40 Pintail Trl 27949-3847 (Mail to: 40 Pintail Trl 27949-3847) (252) 261-6674

Southport St Philips Episcopal Church **P** (670) 205 E Moore St 28461-3927 (Mail to: PO Box 10476 28461-0476) Tyler Tetzlaff Henrietta Williams (910) 457-5643

Sunbury St Peters Episcopal Church **P** (38) 61 Nc Highway 32 27979-9447 (Mail to: PO Box 153 27979-0153) (252) 326-4757

Swansboro St Peters by the Sea Church **P** (246) P.O. Box 337 28584 (Mail to: PO Box 337 28584-0337) (910) 326-4757

Trenton Grace Episcopal Church **P** (12) PO Box 126 28585-0126 (Mail to: PO Box 126 28585-0126) (252) 448-3241

Washington St Peters Episcopal Church **HC** (733) 101 Bonner St 27889-5016 (Mail to: PO Box 985 27889-0985) James Reed (252) 946-8151

Washington Zion Episcopal Church **P** (55) P.O. Box 1329 27889-9802 (Mail to: PO Box 1329 27889-1329) Sarah Saxe (252) 946-3367

Whiteville Grace Episcopal Church **P** (72) 105 S Madison St 28472-4119 (Mail to: 105 S Madison St 28472-4119) (910) 642-4724

Williamston Church of the Advent **P** (137) 124 W Church St 27892-2402 (Mail to: PO Box 463 27892-0463) Ellen Richardson (252) 792-2244

Wilmington Church of the Good Shepherd **P** (53) 515 Queen St 28401-5243 (Mail to: PO Box 928 28402-0928) (910) 763-6080

Wilmington Church Of The Servant **P** (300) 4925 Oriole Dr 28403-1759 (Mail to: Attn: Janet Autry 4925 Oriole Dr 28403-1759) Jody Greenwood (910) 395-0616

Wilmington Holy Cross Episcopal Church **P** (166) 5820 Myrtle Grove Rd 28409-4322 (Mail to: 5820 Myrtle Grove Rd 28409-4322) Chana Tetzlaff (910) 799-6347

Wilmington St Andrews on-the-Sound Church **P** (832) 101 Arlie Road 28403 (Mail to: 101 Arlie Rd 28403-3701) Richard Elliott Sarah Smith (910) 256-3034

Wilmington St James Episcopal Church **P** (1949) 25 S 3rd St 28401-4530 (Mail to: 25 S 3rd St 28401-4595) Ronald Abrams Cheryl Brainard Catherine Davis Timothy Hamby John Sidebotham (910) 763-1628

Wilmington St John Episcopal Church **P** (565) 1219 Forest Hills Dr 28403-2555 (Mail to: 1219 Forest Hills Dr 28403-2555) Eric Moulton (910) 762-5273

Wilmington St Mark Episcopal Church **P** (79) 600 Grace St 28401-4127 (Mail to: 600 Grace St 28401-4127) Victor Frederiksen (910) 763-3858

Wilmington St Pauls Church **P** (271) 16 16th St 28401-4905 (Mail to: 16 16th St 28401-4905) Victor Frederiksen Adam Pierce Dena Whalen (910) 762-4578

Windsor St Thomas Episcopal Church **P** (126) 302 S Queen St 27983-6728 (Mail to: PO Box 400 27983-0400) Bonnie Smith (252) 794-3420

DIOCESE OF EAST TENNESSEE
(PROVINCE IV)
Comprises the eastern third of the State of Tennessee
DIOCESAN OFFICE 814 Episcopal School Way Knoxville TN 37932
TEL (865) 966-2110   FAX (865) 966-2535
E-MAIL editor@dioet.org   WEB http://dioet.org

Previous Bishops— Wm E Sanders 1985-91, Robert G Tharp 1992-99; Charles G von Rosenberg 1999-2011; George D Young III 2011-17

Bishop—Rt Rev Brian L Cole (Dio 02 December 2017)

Cn to Ord Rev M Bolt; *Sec* L Nichols; *Treas* John Hicks; *Asst Treas* M Keyser; *Chanc* SY Sheppeard Esq; *Comm* V Myers; *Yth* J Davis; *Cn for Mission & Lay Min* B Hurley Hill; *Dio Admin* K Purjet; *Com* L Prestion; *Ecum* RJ Powell

Stand Comm—Cler: Pres T Dinsmore L Parsons; *Lay:* E Jones D Sanders Sr MJ Davidson

PARISHES, MISSIONS, AND CLERGY

Athens St Pauls Episcopal Church **P** (376) 123 S Jackson St 37303-4710 (Mail to: C/O Kathy Clark PO Box 326 37371-0326) Michael Bunting (423) 745-2224

Battle Creek St John the Baptist **P** (38) 12757 Ladds Cove Rd 37380 (Mail to: 335 Tennessee Ave 37383-2001) (931) 598-9546

Bristol St Columbas Episcopal Church **P** (121) 607 Greenfield Pl 37620-6124 (Mail to: 607 Greenfield Pl # 17 37620-6124) (423) 764-2251

Chattanooga Christ Episcopal Church **P** (180) 663 Douglas St 37403-2015 (Mail to: 663 Douglas St Ste 1 37403-2000) David Cobb Harry Lawrence (423) 266-4263

Chattanooga Grace Episcopal Church **P** (486) 20 Belvoir Ave 37411-4501 (Mail to: 20 Belvoir Ave 37411-4599) April Berends Zachary Nyein (423) 698-2433

Chattanooga St Martin of Tours Epis Church **P** (549) 7547 E Brainerd Rd 37421-3166 (Mail to: PO Box 21275 37424-0275) James Wallace (423) 892-9131

Chattanooga Saint Paul's Episcopal Church **P** (1927) 305 W 7th St 37402-1717 (Mail to: 305 W 7th St 37402-1787) Alice Brown Bradford Whitaker Joseph Woodfin (423) 266-8195

Chattanooga St Peter's Episcopal Church **P** (467) § 848 Ashland Ter 37415-3538 (Mail to: C/O Parish Administrator 848 Ashland Ter 37415-3538) Fritz Parman (423) 877-2428

Chattanooga St Thaddaeus Episcopal Church **P** (189) 4300 Locksley Ln 37416-2908 (Mail to: PO Box 16305 37416-0305) (423) 892-2377

Chattanooga Thankful Memorial Church **P** (115) 1607 W 43rd St 37409-1344 (Mail to: PO Box 2274 37409-0274) Leyla King (423) 821-3135

Cleveland St Lukes Episcopal Church **P** (543) 320 Broad St Nw 37311-5038 (Mail to: PO Box 5 37364-0005) Joel Huffstetler (423) 476-5541

Copperhill St Marks Episcopal Church **P** (41) 124 West Hill Street 37317-0576 (Mail to: PO Box 579 37317-0579) Erik Broeren (423) 496-4681

Crossville St Raphaels Episcopal Church **P** (204) 1038 Sparta Hwy 38572-5746 (Mail to: 1038 Sparta Hwy 38572-5746) Felicity Peck Thomas Schneider (931) 484-2407

Elizabethton St Thomas Church **P** (59) 815 E 2nd St 37643-2324 (Mail to: 815 North Second Street 37644) (423) 543-3081

Ft Oglethorp Episcopal Church of the Nativity **P** (132) 1201 Cross St 30742-3230 (Mail to: PO Box 2356 30742-2356) Jason Clark Jason Emerson (706) 866-9773

Gatlinburg Trinity Episcopal Church **P** (96) 509 Historic Nature Trail 37738-0055 (Mail to: PO Box 55 37738-0055) Barbara Harper (865) 436-4721

Greeneville St James Episcopal Church **P** (223) 107 W Church St 37745-3803 (Mail to: 107 W Church St 37745-3803) Kenneth Saunders (423) 638-6583

Harriman St Andrews Episcopal Church **P** (79) 190 Circle Dr 37748-7304 (Mail to: 190 Circle Dr 37748-7304) Stephen Jones (865) 882-1272

Hixson St Albans Episcopal Church **P** (106) 7514 Hixson Pike 37343-1721 (Mail to: 7514 Hixson Pike 37343-1721) Robert Hartmans (423) 842-1342

Jefferson City St Barnabas Episcopal-Lutheran Ch **PS** (28) 807 E Ellis St 37760-2526 (Mail to: 807 E Ellis St 37760-2526) (865) 397-3678-9859

Johnson City St Johns Episcopal Church **P** (416) 500 Roan St 37601-4741 (Mail to: 500 Roan St 37601-4717) (423) 926-8141

Jonesborough St Mary the Virgin Episcopal Church **PS** (19) 109 S 2nd Ave 37659-1105 (Mail to: PO Box 273 37659-1105) (423) 753-2350

Kingsport St Christophers Episcopal Church **P** (126) 584 Lebanon Rd 37663-2908 (Mail to: 584 Lebanon Rd 37663-2908) Margaret Zeller Margaret Zeller (423) 239-6751

Kingsport St Pauls Episcopal Church **P** (302) 161 E Ravine Rd 37660-3807 (Mail to: 161 E Ravine Rd 37660-3839) Anna Brawley Christopher Harpster (423) 245-5187

Kingsport St Timothys Episcopal Church **P** (108) 2152 Hawthorne St 37664-3563 (Mail to: PO Box 3248 37664-0248) Richard Shackleford Jonathan Hermes (423) 247-3992

Knoxville Episcopal Church of the Ascension **P** (1299) 800 S Northshore Dr 37919 (Mail to: 800 S Northshore Dr 37919-7592) Christopher Hogin Amy Morehous Patrick Wingo Sara-Scott Wingo (865) 588-0589

Knoxville Church of the Good Samaritan **P** (629) 425 Cedar Bluff Rd 37923-3600 (Mail to: 425 Cedar Bluff Rd 37923-3600) Joseph Calhoun Margaret Farr (865) 693-9591

Knoxville Church of the Good Shepherd **P** (389) 5409 Jacksboro Pike 37918-3330 (Mail to: PO Box 5104 37928-0104) Richard Carter Dorothy Pratt (865) 687-9420

Knoxville St Elizabeths Episcopal Church **P** (327) 110 Sugarwood Dr 37922-4662 (Mail to: 110 Sugarwood Dr 37934-4662) Brett Backus (865) 675-0450

✠ **Knoxville** St Johns Episcopal Cathedral **O** (1090) 413 Cumberland Ave 37902-2302 (Mail to: PO Box 153 37901-0153) John Ross Christopher Hackett Thomas Rasnick (865) 525-7347

Knoxville St Lukes Episcopal Church **P** (90) 600 S Chestnut St 37914-5829 (Mail to: 600 S Chestnut St 37914-5829) Kay Reynolds (865) 522-4244

Knoxville St Thomas Episcopal Church **P** (100) 5401 Tiffany Ln 37912-4736 (Mail to: 5401 Tiffany Ln 37912-4736) Howard Bowlin (865) 688-2741

Knoxville St James Episcopal Church **P** (512) 1101 Broadway St 37917-6528 (Mail to: 1101 Broadway St 37917-6592) John Wiggers Kirk LaFon Robert Powell (865) 523-5687

La Follette St Clare Episcopal Church **P** (18) 1720 Jacksboro Pike 37766-3226 (Mail to: 1720 Jacksboro Pike 37766-3226) (423) 566-6707

Lookout Mtn Church of the Good Shepherd **P** (995) § 211 Franklin Rd 37350-1223 (Mail to: 211 Franklin Rd 37350-1223) Robert Childers Fred Brown Janice Robbins (423) 821-1583

Loudon Episcopal Church of the Resurrection **P** (161) 917 Pond Rd 37774-6401 (Mail to: 917 Pond Rd 37774-6401) Amy Morehous Lee Ragsdale (865) 986-2390

Maryville St Andrews Church **P** (388) 314 W Broadway Ave 37801-4708 (Mail to: 314 W Broadway Ave 37801-4708) John Dukes (865) 983-3512

Morristown All Saints Episcopal Church **P** (436) 601 W Main St 37814-4508 (Mail to: 601 W Main St 37814-4508) John Holland (423) 586-6201

Newport Church of the Annunciation **P** (87) 304 Cosby Hwy 37821-2913 (Mail to: PO Box 337 37822-0337) James Sharp (423) 625-1864

Norris Saint Francis' Church **P** (243) 158 W Norris Rd 37828 (Mail to: PO Box 29 Frances Oates 37828-0029) Harry Minarik Amanda Lippe Harry Minarik (865) 494-7167

Oak Ridge St Stephens Episcopal Church **P** (494) 212 Tulane Ave 37830-6308 (Mail to: 212 Tulane Ave 37830-6308) Gerald Lovett Larry Minter Patricia Reuss Robert Reuss (865) 483-8497

Ooltewah St Francis of Assisi Epis Church **P** (128) 7555 Ooltewah Georgetown Rd 37363-9582 (Mail to: 7555 Ooltewah Georgetown Rd 37363-9582) Martha Tucker-Parsons Spencer Cantrell (423) 238-7708

Rugby Christ Church **P** (48) 1332 Rugby Parkway 37733-0025 (Mail to: PO Box 25 37733-0002) Peter Keese (423) 628-5627

S Pittsburg Christ Episcopal Church **P** (134) 302 3rd St 37380-1318 (Mail to: PO Box 347 37380-0347) Kim Hobby (423) 837-7715

Sevierville St Joseph the Carpenter **P** (142) 345 Hardin Ln 37862-4507 (Mail to: 345 Hardin Ln 37862-4507) Paige Buchholz (865) 453-0943

Seymour St Pauls Episcopal Church **PS** (72) 1028 Boyds Creek Hwy 37865-4532 (Mail to: PO Box 907 37865-0907) (865) 577-1255

Signal Mtn St Timothys Episcopal Church **P** (752) 630 Mississippi Ave 37377-2293 (Mail to: 630 Mississippi Ave 37377-2293) Derrick Hill Taylor Dinsmore (423) 886-2281

DIOCESE OF EASTERN MICHIGAN

(PROVINCE V)

Comprises the eastern portion of the lower peninsula of Michigan

DIOCESAN OFFICE 924 N Niagara St Saginaw MI 48602

TEL (989) 752-6020   FAX (989) 752-6120

E-MAIL diocese@eastmich.org   WEB www.eastmich.org

Previous Bishops— Edwin M Leidel Jr 1996-2006; S Todd Ousley 2006-17

Provisional Bishop—Rt Rev Cate Waynick (2017)

Bps Admin Asst A Krueger; *Admin* M Girard; *Financial Mgr* S Philo; *Treas* M Turnbull; *Chanc* E Henneke; *Cn to Ord* Rev Cn M Spencer; *Cn for Evangelism* K Forsyth; *Camp Dir and Yth and Young Adult* M Bade; *School Dir* Rev Dr V Fargo

Stand Comm—Cler: D Scheid P Seitz S Rich; *Lay:* W Thewalt J Huff-Worvie

PARISHES, MISSIONS, AND CLERGY

Alma St John Episcopal Church **P** (92) PO Box 605 48801-0605 (Mail to: PO Box 605 48801-0605) (989) 752-6020

Alpena Trinity Episcopal Church **P** (384) 124 E Washington Ave 49707-2837 (Mail to: 124 E Washington Ave 49707-2869) William Mcclure (989) 752-6020

Atlanta St Marks Episcopal Mission **P** (45) 11847 M 33 48638 (Mail to: 11847 M-33 49709) (989) 752-6020

Bad Axe St Pauls Episcopal Church **P** (66) 139 W Huron Ave 48413-1102 (Mail to: 139 W Huron Ave 48413-1102) (989) 752-6020

Bay City St Albans Episcopal Church **P** (187) 105 S Erie St 48706-4431 (Mail to: 105 S Erie St 48706-4599) Nancy Mayhew Sharon Voelker (989) 752-6020

Bay City Trinity Episcopal Church **P** (195) 815 Grant St 48708-5006 (Mail to: C/O Patrick Gray 815 Grant St 48708-5006) Susan Rich (989) 892-5813

Cheboygan St James Church **P** (110) 202 S Huron St 49721-1920 (Mail to: PO Box 253 49721-0253) Lewis Crusoe (989) 752-6020

Corunna St Paul Episcopal Church **P** (47) 111 S Shiawassee St 48817-1357 (Mail to: PO Box 87 48817-0087) (989) 752-6020

Davison St Dunstans Episcopal Church **P** (61) 1523 Oak Rd 48423-9101 (Mail to: 1523 Oak Rd 48423-9101) Sue Colavincenzo (989) 752-6020

Dryden St Johns Episcopal Church **P** (55) 4074 S Mill Rd 48428-9233 (Mail to: PO Box 86 48428-0086) Nancy Steele (989) 752-6020

East Tawas Christ Church **P** (93) 202 W Westover St 48730-1238 (Mail to: 202 W Westover St 48730-1238) (989) 752-6020

Fenton St Judes Episcopal Church **P** (266) 106 E Elizabeth St 48430-2322 (Mail to: 106 E Elizabeth St 48430-2322) Tracie Little (810) 629-5681

Flint St Andrews Episcopal Church **P** (291) 1922 Iowa Ave 48506-3539 (Mail to: C/O Patti Gantz 1922 Iowa Ave 48506-3539) Jay Gantz (989) 752-6020

Flint St Pauls Episcopal Church **P** (305) 711 S Saginaw St 48502-1507 (Mail to: 711 S Saginaw St 48502-1589) Daniel Scheid (810) 234-8637

Flushing Trinity Episcopal Church **P** (68) 745 E Main St 48433-2009 (Mail to: 745 E Main St 48433-2009) (989) 752-6020

Gaylord St Andrews Episcopal Church **P** (80) 525 Weiss Rd 49735-1637 (Mail to: PO Box 920 49734-0920) Pamela Lynch (989) 752-6020

Gladwin St Pauls Church **P** (111) 211 E Cedar Ave 48624-2207 (Mail to: 211 E Cedar Ave 48624-2207) Joseph Downs (989) 752-6020

Grand Blanc St Christophers Episcopal Church **P** (552) 9020 S Saginaw Rd 48439-9576 (Mail to: 9020 S Saginaw Rd 48439-9576) Donald Davidson (989) 752-6020

Grayling St Francis Episcopal Church **P** (88) P.O. Box 501 6441 West M-72 Highway 49738-7787 (Mail to: PO Box 501 49738-0501) Elizabeth Chace (989) 348-5850

Harrisville St Andrews by the Lake **P** (32) PO Box 52 48740-0052 (Mail to: PO Box 52 48740-0052) Joe Jenney (989) 752-6020

Harsens Island St Paul Episcopal Church **P** (54) 208 Orchid Blvd 48028-9556 (Mail to: 2908 S Channel Dr 48028-9577) (989) 752-6020

Hillman Calvary Episcopal Church of Hillman **P** (72) 330 State Street 49746-0158 (Mail to: PO Box 158 49746-0158) (989) 752-6020

Indian River Church of the Transfiguration **P** (152) PO Box 460 49749-0460 (Mail to: PO Box 460 49749-0460) Tyler Richards Audrey Bauer (989) 752-6020

Lachine Grace Episcopal Church **P** (87) 13488 Long Rapids Rd 49753-9632 (Mail to: 8528 Long Rapids Rd 49707-9764) John Laycock (989) 752-6020

Lapeer Grace Episcopal Church **P** (96) 735 W Nepessing St 48446-2006 (Mail to: 735 W Nepessing St 48446-2006) Sarah Parks (810) 664-2841

Lexington Trinity Episcopal Church **P** (167) 5646 S Main Street 48450-0315 (Mail to: 5646 Main St 48450-8842) Kay Houck (810) 3598741

Midland Holy Family Episcopal Church **P** (24) 4611 Swede Ave 48642-3861 (Mail to: 4611 Swede Ave 48642-3861) (989) 752-6020

Midland St Johns Episcopal Church **P** (604) 405 Saginaw Rd 48640-6339 (Mail to: 405 Saginaw Rd 48640-6339) Kenneth Hitch James Harrison James Harrison (989) 631-2260

Mio St Bartholomews Episcopal Church **P** (43) PO Box 787 48647-0787 (Mail to: PO Box 787 48647-0787) Allan Feltner (989) 752-6020

Oscoda Hope-St Johns Parish **P** (45) 223 E. Mill Street 48750-0338 (Mail to: 223 E Mill St 48750-1627) (989) 752-6020

Otter Lake Saint John the Baptist **P** (57) 5811 Forest Ave 48464-9790 (Mail to: C/O Doris Sutton, Treasurer 9534 McPherson Rd 48746-9481) (989) 752-6020

Owosso Christ Episcopal Church **P** (115) 120 Goodhue St 48867-2320 (Mail to: 120 Goodhue St 48867-2320) (989) 752-6020

Port Huron Grace Episcopal Church **P** (470) 1213 6th St 48060-5348 (Mail to: 1213 6th St 48060-5348) Linda Crane Lydia Speller (810) 985-9539

Rogers City St Lukes Episcopal Church **P** (23) 120 First St 49779-1602 (Mail to: C/O Ethel Wickersham 278 S Seventh St 49779-2017) (989) 752-6020

Roscommon St Elizabeths Episcopal Church **P** (118) 2936 E Higgins Lake Dr 48653-7622 (Mail to: PO Box 517 48653-0517) Charles Curtis Mary Shortt (989) 752-6020

Saginaw St Johns Episcopal Church **P** (240) 123 Michigan Ave 48602-4235 (Mail to: 123 Michigan Ave 48602-4235) Curtis Norman (989) 793-9575

Saginaw St Matthews Episcopal Church **P** (92) 1501 Center Rd 48638-5556 (Mail to: 1501 Center Rd 48638-5563) Mary Jo Hudson (989) 752-6020

Saginaw St Pauls Episcopal Church **P** (182) 720 Tuscola St 48607-1583 (Mail to: 4444 State St Apt F318 48603-4092) Judith Boli (989) 752-6020

Saint Clair Holy Fam Epis Ch of Blue Water **P** 115 6th St 48079-4829 (Mail to: 115 6th St 48079-4829) David Vickers (810) 329-3821

Sand Point St Johns Episcopal Church **P** (25) 8271 Crescent Beach Rd 48755-9648 (Mail to: PO Box 1882 48725-1882) (989) 752-6020

Sandusky St Johns Church **P** (27) 41 Delaware St 48471-1006 (Mail to: 41 Delaware St 48471-1006) (989) 752-6020

Standish Grace Episcopal Church **P** (25) PO Box 721 48658-0721 (Mail to: PO Box 721 48658-0721) (989) 752-6020

West Branch Trinity Episcopal Church **P** (64) 100 E Houghton Ave 48661-1124 (Mail to: PO Box 83 48661-0083) Brian Chace Robert Finn (989) 752-6020

DIOCESE OF EASTERN OREGON
(PROVINCE VIII)
Comprises Oregon east of the Cascade Mountains and Klickitat County Washington
DIOCESAN OFFICE 1104 Church St (Box 236) Cove OR 97824
TEL (541) 568-4514   FAX (541) 568-5000
E-MAIL diocese@episdioeo.org   WEB www.episdioeo.org

Previous Bishops—
Robert L Paddock 1907-22, Wm P Remington 1922-45, Lane W Barton 1946-68, Wm B Spofford 1967-79, Rustin R Kimsey 1980-2000, Wm O Gregg 2000-2007, Bavi E. Rivera 2009-2016

Bishop—Rt Rev Patrick W. Bell (Dio 2016–)

BP Sec L Boquist; *Sec of Conv* D Harder; *Treas* R Heise; *Exec Dir Asc Camp* vacant; *Dio coun—Cler:* A Bonebrake J Farber C Wells vacant; *Lay:* B Spell A Brown B Mayo K Morgan K Sharp

Stand Comm—Cler: Pres R Green J Holdorph M Lujan *Lay:* J Reynolds G Henton vacant

PARISHES, MISSIONS, AND CLERGY

Baker City St Stephens Episcopal Church **P** (67) 2177 First Street 97814-2606 (Mail to: 2130 Second Street 97814) Aletha Bonebrake (541) 523-4812

Bend All Saints Of The Cascades Episcopal Church **P** (69) 18143 Cottonwood Rd 97707-9317 (Mail to: 18160 Cottonwood Rd PMB 266 977079317) Nancy Sargent Green (541) 593-5991

Bend Trinity Church **P** (499) 469 Nw Wall St 97703-2605 (Mail to: 469 NW Wall St c/o Treas Charles W Brisson 97701-2605) Jedediah Holdorph (541) 382-5542

Bonanza St Barnabas Episcopal Church **P** (54) 12201 W Langell Valley Rd 97623-9781 (Mail to: C/O Beverly J Yancey 4146 Adelaide Ave Apt 8 97603-3738) Martha Hurlburt (541) 545-1705

Burns St Andrews Episcopal Church **P** (18) 393 E A St 97720-1605 (Mail to: PO Box 627 97720-0627) (541) 573-2632

Canyon City St Thomas Episcopal Church **P** (58) 139 S Washington St 97820-6125 (Mail to: PO Box 164 97820-0164) Daniel Gardner (541) 575-2415

Enterprise St Patricks Episcopal Church **P** (19) 100 NE 3rd St 97828 (Mail to: PO Box 301 97828-0301) Rich Attebury (541) 426-3439

Heppner All Saints Memorial Epis Church **P** (97) 460 Gale St 97836 (Mail to: PO Box 246 97836-0246) (541) 676-9970

Hermiston St Johns Episcopal Church **P** (72) 665 E Gladys Ave 97838-1915 (Mail to: 665 E Gladys Ave 97838-1915) Charles Barnes (541) 567-6672

Hood River St Marks Episcopal Church **P** (187) 400 11th Street 97031-1547 (Mail to: 400 11th St 97031-1547) Paul Mahon (541) 386-2077

Klamath Fall St Pauls Episcopal Church **P** (106) 801 Jefferson St 97601-2929 (Mail to: 801 Jefferson St 97601-2929) Martha Hurlburt Thomas Osgood (541) 884-3585

La Grande St Peters Episcopal Church **P** (53) 1001 O Ave 97850-2424 (Mail to: PO Box 1001 97850-1001) (541) 963-3623

Lakeview St Lukes Episcopal Church **P** (14) 614 S F St 97630-1751 (Mail to: Attn Barbara Snider 614 S F St 97630-1751) Richard Landrith (541) 947-2360

✠ **Madras** St Marks Episcopal Church **O** (20) 13 Sw F St 97741-1301 (Mail to: Attn Treasurer PO Box 789 97741-0110) Carol McClelland (541) 546-6250

Milton Frwtr St James Episcopal Church **P** (34) 719 Pierce St 97862-1434 (Mail to: 719 Pierce Street 97862) Rebecca Hendricks (541) 938-7268

Ontario St Matthews Episcopal Church **P** (147) 802 Sw 5th St 97914-3417 (Mail to: PO Box 788 97914-0788) Deborah Graham (541) 889-6943

Pendleton Church of the Redeemer **P** (131) 241 Se 2nd St 97801-2222 (Mail to: 241 SE 2nd St 97801-2222) Charlotte Wells (541) 276-3809

Prineville St Andrews Episcopal Church **P** (49) 807 E 1st St 97754-2007 (Mail to: PO Box 299 97754-0299) Stephen Uffelman Janet Warner (541) 447-5813

Redmond St Albans Episcopal Church **P** (24) 724 Sw 14th St 97756-2619 (Mail to: 724 S.W. 14th St. 97756-2619) Lee Kiefer (541) 548-4212

Sisters Church of the Transfiguration **P** (198) 68825 Brooks Camp Rd 97759 (Mail to: PO Box 130 97759-0130) Joseph Farber (541) 549-7087

The Dalles St Pauls Episcopal Church **P** (210) 1805 Minnesota St 97058-3319 (Mail to: 1805 Minnesota St 97058-3319) Georgia Giacobbe (541) 296-9587

DIOCESE OF EASTON
(PROVINCE III)
Comprises 9 counties on the eastern shore of Maryland
DIOCESAN OFFICE 314 North St Easton MD 21601
TEL (410) 822-1919 E-MAIL diocese@dioceseofeaston.org
WEB www.dioceseofeaston.org

Previous Bishops—
Henry C Lay 1869-85, Wm F Adams 1887-1920, Geo W Davenport 1920-38, Wm McClelland 1939-49, Allen J Miller 1949-66, George A Taylor 1967-75, W Moultrie Moore Jr 1975-83, Elliott L Sorge 1983-93, Martin G Townsend 1993-2001, Charles L Longest asst 2002-03, James J Shand 2003-2014, Henry Nutt Parsley Jr. prov 2014-16

Bishop — Rt Rev Santosh K. Marray, DMin, DD

Cn to Ord P Collins; *Treas* C Bohn; *Chanc* E Cornbrooks; *Sec to Bp* L Anstatt; *Fin Admin* A Kendall; *Dio Youth* J Fisher; *Reg* P Collins; *Stew* vacant; *Hist* A Leiby; *UTO* M Atwood C Meyer; *Deploy* P Collins; *ER&D* K Bainbridge; *COM* M Moyer

Deans—Northern H Sabetti; *Middle* C Osberger; *Southern* F Malcolm

Stand Comm—Cler: D Williams S Klingelhofer M Garner; *Lay:* T Mendenhall A King N Dick

PARISHES, MISSIONS, AND CLERGY

Berlin St Pauls Church **P** (132) 3 Church St 21811-1209 (Mail to: PO Box 429 21811-0429) Michael Moyer (410) 641-4066

Cambridge Christ Church - Great Choptank Paris **P** (452) 601 Church St 21613-1729 (Mail to: 601 Church St 21613-1729) HBW Schroeder HBW Schroeder (410) 228-3161

Cambridge St Johns Chapel **M** (98) 1213 Hudson Rd 21613-3237 (Mail to: 1213 Hudson Rd 21613-3237) Daniel Dunlap Daniel Dunlap (410) 228-5056

Centreville St Pauls Parish **P** (303) 301 S Liberty St 21617-1221 (Mail to: PO Box 278 21617-0278) Mary Garner (410) 758-1553

Chesapeake City Augustine Parish **P** (120) 310 George St 21915-1223 (Mail to: PO Box 487 21915-0487) (410) 885-5375

Chestertown Emmanuel Episcopal Church **P** (290) 101 Cross St 21620-1527 (Mail to: PO Box 875 21620-0875) Florence Williams (410) 778-3477

Chestertown Saint Paul's Parish, Kent **P** (119) 7579 Sandy Bottom Rd 21620-4520 (Mail to: 7579 Sandy Bottom Rd 21620-4520) Frank St Amour (410) 778-1540

Church Creek Old Trinity Church - Dorchester Parish **P** (40) 1716 Taylors Island Rd 21622

(Mail to: PO Box 157 21622-0157) Daniel Dunlap (410) 228-2940

Church Hill St Luke's Parish **P** (104) 105 Church Ln 21623 (Mail to: PO Box 38 21623-0038) Loretta Collins (410) 556-6060

Denton Christ Church **P** (140) 105 Gay St 21629-1019 (Mail to: PO Box 428 21629-0428) (410) 479-0419

Earleville St Stephens Episcopal Church **P** (143) 10 Glebe Rd 21919-2144 (Mail to: 10 Glebe Rd 21919-2144) (410) 275-8785

Easton All Faith Chapel **P** (54) 26281 Tunis Mills Rd 21601-5523 (Mail to: 26281 Tunis Mills Rd 21601-5523) Patrick Collins (410) 822-1464

Easton Christ Church-St Peters Parish **P** (936) § 111 S Harrison St 21601-2907 (Mail to: 111 S Harrison St 21601-2998) William Ortt (410) 822-2677

✤ **Easton** Trinity Cathedral Episcopal **O** (256) 314 Goldsborough St 21601-3669 (Mail to: 314 North St 21601-3665) Gregory Powell (410) 822-1931

Elkton Trinity Episcopal Church **P** (165) 105 Bridge St 21921-5326 (Mail to: 105 Bridge St 21921-5326) Nicholas Sichangi (410) 398-5350

Hebron St Pauls Episcopal Church **P** (24) 8700 Memory Gardens Ln 21830 (Mail to: PO Box 28 21830-0028) (443) 614-5410

Hurlock St Andrews Episcopal Church **M** (77) 303 S Main St 21643 (Mail to: 6442 Suicide Bridge Rd 21643-3232) Bryan Glancey (443) 366-4652

Kennedyville Shrewsbury Parish Church **P** (399) 12824 Shrewsbury Church Rd 21645 (Mail to: PO Box 187 21645-0187) Henry Sabetti Stephan Klingelhofer (410) 348-5944

Massey St Clements **P** (41) 32940 Maryland Line Rd 21650-1703 (Mail to: PO Box 158 32940 Maryland Line Rd 21650-1706) (410) 928-5051

North East St Mary Anne's Episcopal Church **P** (494) 315 S Main St 21901-3915 (Mail to: 315 S Main St 21901-3915) John Schaeffer (410) 287-5522

Ocean City Church of St Pauls By The Sea **P** (123) 302 Baltimore Ave 21842-3923 (Mail to: 302 Baltimore Ave 21842-3923) Matthew D'Amario (410) 289-3453

Ocean City The Church of the Holy Spirit **P** (316) 10001 Coastal Hwy 21842-2649 (Mail to: 10001 Coastal Hwy 21842-2649) Joseph Rushton (410) 723-1973

Oxford Holy Trinity Church **P** (320) 502 S Morris St 21654 (Mail to: PO Box 387 21654-0387) Kevin Cross (410) 226-5134

Perryville St Marks Episcopal Church **P** (123) 175 Saint Marks Church Rd 21903-2519 (Mail to: 175 Saint Marks Church Rd 21903-2519) Patricia Drost (571) 331-2618

Pocomoke City St Mary the Virgin Epis Church **P** (82) PO Box 383 21851-0383 (Mail to: PO Box 383 21851-0383) Christine Mottl (410) 957-1518

Princess Anne St Andrews Episcopal Church **P** (83) 30513 Washington St 21853-1143 (Mail to: 30513 Washington St 21853-1143) Robert Laws (410) 651-2882

Princess Anne St Pauls Episcopal Church **P** (92) 29618 Polks Rd 21853-3228 (Mail to: 26417 Silver Ln 21817-2458) Michael Lokey (410) 651-1507

Quantico St Philips Episcopal Church **P** (43) 6457 Quantico Rd 21856 (Mail to: PO Box 92 21856-0092) (410) 251-8299

Queenstown St Lukes Chapel **P** C/O Wye Parish 7208 Main St 21658-1628 (Mail to: PO Box 98 21679-0098) (410) 827-8488

Saint Michael Christ Church St Michaels Parish **P** (596) 301 S Talbot St 21663 (Mail to: Attn Carol A Osborne PO Box S 21663-0570) Steven Mosher (410) 745-9076

Salisbury St Albans Episcopal Church **HC** (120) 302 Saint Albans Dr 21804-5267 (Mail to: 302 Saint Albans Dr 21804-5267) Frieda Malcolm (410) 742-6595

Salisbury St Peters Church **P** (728) 115 Saint Peters St 21801-4901 (Mail to: 115 Saint Peters St 21801-4901) Adele Hatfield David Michaud George Murray (410) 742-5118

Snow Hill All Hallows Episcopal Church **P** (116) 109 W Market St 21863-1047 (Mail to: 109 W Market St 21863-1047) Charles Hatfield (410) 632-2327

Stevensville Christ Church Parish Kent Island **P** (569) § 830 Romancoke Rd 21666-2790 (Mail to: 830 Romancoke Rd 21666-2790) Mark Delcuze (410) 643-5921

Trappe Saint Paul's Church **P** (61) 3936 Main St 21673 (Mail to: PO Box 141 21673-0141) (410) 476-3048

Tyaskin St Marys - St Bartholomews Episcopal **P** (12) 21865 Nanticoke Rd 21865-2020 (Mail to: PO Box 76 21865-0076) Dennis Morgan (410) 873-2790

Vienna St Pauls Episcopal Church **P** (36) 203 Church St 21869 (Mail to: PO Box 3 21869-0003) Dennis Morgan Dennis Morgan (410) 376-3376

Worton Christ Episcopal Church **P** (38) 25328 Lambs Meadow Rd 21678-1923 (Mail to: PO Box 161 25328 Lambs Meadow Rd 21678-0161) Frank Adams (410) 778-2821

Wye Mills Wye Parish **P** (279) 14084 Old Wye Mills Rd 21679-2004 (Mail to: PO Box 98 21679-0098) Charles Osberger (410) 827-8484

DIOCESE OF EAU CLAIRE
(PROVINCE V)
Comprises the 26 counties of northwestern Wisconsin
DIOCESAN OFFICE 510 S Farwell St Eau Claire WI 54701
TEL (715) 835-3331
E-MAIL administrator@dioec.net   WEB episcopaldioceseofeauclaire.com/

Previous Bishops—
Frank E Wilson 1929-44, Wm W Horstick 1944-69, Stanley Atkins 1969-80, William C Wantland 1980-99, Keith B Whitmore 1999-2008, Edwin M Leidel Jr 2008-2012

Bishop—Rt Rev William Jay Lambert III (Dio 16 March 2013)

Assisting Bishop—James M Adams Jr

Dio Admin Cn A Zook; *Treas* B Weathers; *Chanc* J Pelish Box 31 Rice Lake WI 54868; *Ecum* Cn A Zook 510 S. Farwell St Eau Claire WI 54701

Stand Comm—Cler: Pres G Usher A Hancock Pe Augustine; *Lay:* D Lorenz N Firth J Smalstig

PARISHES, MISSIONS, AND CLERGY

Ashland St Andrews Episcopal Church **M** (28) 620 3rd St W 54806-1518 (Mail to: PO Box 427 54806-0427) Tanya Scheff (715) 682-5067

Bayfield Christ Episcopal Church **SC** (12) 125 3rd St 54814-4872 (Mail to: Attn E Webster PO Box 816 54814-0816) Elsa Harmon (715) 813-0764

Chippewa Falls St Simeons Church **M** (42) 19058 190th St 54729 (Mail to: PO Box 194 54729-0194) Claudia Hogan Aaron Zook (715) 723-0050

Chippewa Fls Christ Episcopal Church **P** (51) 624 Bay St 54729-2425 (Mail to: 624 Bay St 54729-2425) (715) 723-7667

Clear Lake St Barnabas Episcopal Church **M** (28) 365 5th Ave 54005-3738 (Mail to: 944 140th Ave 54001-2706) Robert Lyga (715) 263-3464

Conrath Holy Trinity Church **M** (58) North 1643 County Hwy G 54731 (Mail to: PO Box 152 54731-0152) (715) 748-2280

✠ **Eau Claire** Christ Church Cathedral **O** (489) 510 S Farwell St 54701-4994 (Mail to: 510 S Farwell St Ste 1 54701-4995) Michael Greene (715) 835-3734

Hayward Church of the Ascension **M** (122) 10612 California Ave 54843 (Mail to: PO Box 637 54843-0637) (715) 634-3283

Hudson St Pauls Episcopal Church **P** (170) 502 County Road Uu 54016-7583 (Mail to: 502 County Road Uu 54016-7583) Guy Usher (715) 386-2348

La Crosse Christ Episcopal Church **P** (330) 111 9th St 54601-3485 (Mail to: P.O. Box 2908 54602) Patrick Augustine Peter Augustine Kathleen Charles Joanne Glasser Thomas Winkler (608) 784-0697

Menomonie Grace Episcopal Church **M** (110) 1002 6th St E 54751-2627 (Mail to: Attn C Kell E4357 451st Ave 54751) Jacalyn Broughton (715) 235-7072

New Richmond Church of St Thomas & St John **M** (14) 354 3rd St 54017-1114 (Mail to: C/O Lynne RIddle 354 3rd St 54017-1114) Catherine Kuschel (715) 246-6602

Owen St Katherine Episcopal Church **M** (29)

206 E 3rd St 54460-9763 (Mail to: PO Box 148 54460-0148) (715) 229-2643

Phillips Church of Our Saviour **M** (11) Attn Kenneth Johnson N11211 Rocky Carrie 54555-7234 (Mail to: Attn: Leonard France W 7125 Hwy W. 54555) William Radant (715) 339-4281

Rice Lake Grace Episcopal Church **M** (80) 119 W Humbird St 54868 (Mail to: Mary Ellen Filken Treas 119-123 W Humbird St 54868) Harry Kirby (715) 234-4226

Sparta St Johns Episcopal Church **M** (74) 322 Water St 54656-1741 (Mail to: 322 Water St 54656-1741) Peter Augustine (608) 269-4266

Spooner St Albans Episcopal Church **M** (49) 220 Elm St 54801-1328 (Mail to: PO Box 281 54801-0281) (715) 635-4704

Springbrook St Lukes Church **M** (27) N8571 County Highwa 54875-9404 (Mail to: Attn Lawrence Neste W3399 Highway 63 54875-9409) (715) 635-4707

Superior St Alban the Martyr Episcopal **M** (51) 1510 New York Ave 54880-2082 (Mail to: 1510 New York Ave 54880-2082) Steven Burns (715) 392-2536

Tomah St Mary Episcopal Church **M** (55) 1001 Mclean Ave 54660-1941 (Mail to: 1001 Mclean Ave 54660-1941) Charles Carter Elna McDaniel Mary Rezin (608) 372-5174

DIOCESES OF ECUADOR
Iglesia Episcopal del Ecuador
(PROVINCE IX)

CENTRAL DIOCESE OF ECUADOR

Previous Bishop—
Adrián Cáceres 1971-90, Wilfrido Ramos-Orench 2006-09

Bishop — Rt Rev Luis Fernando Ruiz (1036)(Dio 1 Aug 2009)

PARISHES, MISSIONS, AND CLERGY

Cuenca Iglesia Sagrada Familia **P** (50) No Bartolome de las Casas #534 y Tirso Moliba NO534 (Mail to: Bartolome de las Casas # 534 y Tirso Moliba)

Guaranda Iglesia San Jose **P** Comunidad San Bartolo (Mail to: Comunidad "San Bartolo")

La Hondonada Iglesia Episcopal Resurreccion **P** San Pedro de Echaleche (Mail to: Oficina Central de la Iglesia Episcopal de Ecuador 00017) (593) 245-6948

La Libertad Iglesia de la Santisima Trinidad **P** Avenida 23 entre calle 30-31 (Mail to: Avda 26 y Calle 40 Esquina) Hector Perez Moreira

Pelileo Iglesia Nueva Jerusalem **P** Via La Libertad El Tambo-P. (Mail to: Cascajal de la Libertad)

Pilahuin, Ambato Iglesia San Lucas de Pilahuin **P** Prinicpal San Lucas (Mail to: Oficina Central Iglesia Episcopal del Ecuador 00017) Raul Herrera Chagna (593) 245-6948

Puyo La Ascencion **P** Manabi y Galapagos (Mail to: Manabi y Galapagos)

✠ **Quito** Catedral de El Senor **O** Av. Real Audiencia #63-47 Y Sabanilla (Mail to: Av. Real Audiencia #63-47 Y Sabanilla) Juan Salvatierra Serian (2) 534419

Quito Cristo Liberador (Iasa-Refugio) **P** Jose Enriquez 63-55 y Camilo Echanique (Mail to: Jose Enriquez 63-55 y Camilo Echanique) Raul Guaillas Carangui

Quito Iglesia de la Epifania **P** Herman Cortez N58-2 Y Vaca De Castro (Mail to: Herman Cortez N58-2 Y Vaca De Castro)

Quito Iglesia del Buen Pastor **P** Palemon Morroy S45-75 Y Av. Ecatoriana (Mail to: Palemon Morroy S45-75 Y Av. Ecatoriana) Gladys Vasquez-Vera

Quito Iglesia Episcopal Reconciliacion **P** Guayabamba E2-29 y Quilotoa (Mail to:

Guayabamba E2-29 y Quilotoa)
Quito Misión Emanuel **P** Avenida Simon Bolivar
s/n Guajalo (Mail to: Avenida Simon Bolivar
s/n Guagalo)

Santo Domingo de los Tscahila San Pedro del
Pupusa-Paraiso **P** Coop 15 de Sep. Calle Julio
Jaramillo Pasaje 7 (Mail to: Coop 15 de Sep.
Calle Julio Jaramillo Pasaje 7)

LITORAL DIOCESE OF ECUADOR

Previous Bishops—
Adrián D Cáceres 1971-88, Luis
Caizapanta 1988-91, M García
Montiel 1992-94

**Bishop—Alfredo   Morante
(Dio 12 Oct 94)**

Diocesan Office Calle Amarilis Fuentes 603 entre Av
JV Trujillo y Calle D Barrio Centenario (Mail: Box
0901-5250) Guayaquil, Ecuador. From the US 011
(593-4) 2443050, 2446699 *Fax* 011 (593-4) 2443088
E-mail iglesia_litoral@hotmail.com

Treas Lcda E Calderon; *Chanc* Rvdo C Leon; *Sec
Conv. Rev.* Gina Angulo Z.; *Sec Dio* Sra M Zambrano;
Contadora CPA Srta S Garcia

Comité Permanente: Pres Rvdo. Carlos Villacís Sec
Sra M Barros Rvdo. Francisco Orrala; Sr. Nelsón
Neira Sr. Wilmer Mejillón

Comité de Ministerio: Pres Rvdo Cristóbal León
Rvdo Carlos Mora Rvda. Betty Juárez Sra Piedad
Vega Sec. Roque Mendoza y Sr. Silvio Neira.

Comité de Disciplina: Pres Rvdo. Gerónimo Álava
Sec. Rvda G Angulo Rvdo. Franklín Macías Rvdo
Carlos Mora Rvda. Mariana Loor   Rvdo. Franklín
Macías Sra. Susana Carrión.

Comité de Compañerismo: Rvdo A Morante Rvda M
Loor Rvda B Juarez Rvdo C Leon Rvda G Angulo
Rvdo G Álava

Secretariados: Comun y *Relac Públic* Rvdo Edgar
Giraldo; *Educ Cristiana* Sr C Villacis; *Mujeres Epis-
copales* Sra Edita González ; *UTO* Sra Mitzer Juárez
; *Fondo Desarr Emergente* Sra M Zambrano; *Him-
nología* Rvda B Juarez y Sra. M Juárez; *Ecumenismo*
Franklín Macías; *Justicia y Paz* Rvda M Loor; *Educ
Teológica* Rvdo G Alava; *Estadísticas* Rvdo C Leon
Ministerio Juvenil Rvda G Angulo.

PARISHES, MISSIONS, AND CLERGY

Babahoyo Iglesia de Belen **M** Rcto Pueblo Nuevo
09015250 (Mail to: Rcto Pueblo Nuevo 0901-
5250)

Duran Iglesia de Jesus Obrero de Duran **M**
Cooperativa 12 de Noviembre Pedro Vicente
Maldonado 0901-5250 (Mail to: Box 0901-
5250)

Guayaquil Iglesia de la Resurreccion **P**
Shushufindi y Paján Pascuales 0901-5250

(Mail to: Amarilis Fuertes 603 y Jose V. Trujillo
0901-5250)

Guayaquil Iglesia de la Transfiguracion **M** 33 Ava
y Maldonado 0901-5250 (Mail to: 33 Ava y
Maldonado 0901-5250)

Guayaquil Iglesia Espiritu Santo **M** Letamendi
entre 38 y 39 0901-5250 (Mail to: Box 090-
15250 Amarilis Fuentes 603 y Vicente Trujillo
0901-5250)

Guayaquil Iglesia Jesus El Senor **M** Guasmo
Sur Cooperativa Battalla de Tarqui 09015250
(Mail to: Amarilis Fuente 603 y V. Trujillo/
Postal 09015250 09015250)

Guayaquil Iglesia Jesus Obrero **M** Guasmo
Norte 0901-5250 (Mail to: RitA LecumBerri
y 10 Callejon/ Postal# 09-01-5250 Amarilis
Fuentes 603 y Vicente Trujillo)

Guayaquil Iglesia San Pedro **M** 18 y la N Plan
Piloto/ Postal# 09015250 (Mail to: 18 y la
N Plan Piloto/ Postal# 09015250) Eugenio
Noboa Viteri

Guayaquil Iglesia Santa Maria **M** 12do. Paseo 17
NE, Sauces 3 (Mail to: Amarllis Fuente 603 y
Vicente Trujillo)

Guayaquil Iglesia Santiago de Jerusalem **M** Coop.
Luz del Guayas Km 10 1/2 Via Daule (Mail to:
Coop. Luz del Guayas Km 10 1/2 Via Daule)

Guayaquil Iglesia Todos los Santos **M** 25 y la
"Q" 0901-5250 (Mail to: Amarilis Fuertes 603
y Jose V. Trujillo 0901-5250) Eugenio Noboa
Viteri

Guayaquil Iglesia Virgen Maria **M** Calle 23 Y
Tercer Callejon **P** 0901-5250 (Mail to: Amarilis
Fuentes 603 y Vicente Trujillo 0901-5250)

Guayaquil Mision de Jesus **M** Mapasinguie
(Coop la Esperanza) 0901-5250 (Mail to:
09-01-5250 Amarilis Fuentes 603 y Vicente
Trujillo 0901-5250)

Guayaquil San Mateo **M** Callejon "O" Entre 23
y 24 0901-5250 (Mail to: Callejon "O" entre
Calle 23 y 24 Amarilis Fuentes 603 y Vicente
Trujillo 0901-5250)

Manta San Esteban-Manabi **M** Sector 10 de
Agosto 0901-5250 (Mail to: Parroquia Eloy
Alfara Barrio Santa Ana)

Manta San Jose Obrero-Manabi **M** Ciudadela 15
de Abril Parroquiz E Afaro (Mail to: Ciudadela
15 de Abril Parroquiz E Afaro 0901-5250)

Manta San Pablo **M** (50) § Calle 19 #208 y Ave 10
Barrio Cordova 0901-5250 (Mail to: 19 #208 y
Ave 10 0901-5250)

MonteCristi Igl Santiago el Apostolo **M** Parroquia
La Pila Mexico y Paquisha 0901-5250 (Mail to:
Parroquia la Pila 0901-5250)

Santa Elena Iglesia Virgen Maria Salanguillo **M** 10 de Agosto Comuna de Salanguillo (Mail to: Apdo 0901-5250 Guayaquil) Hector Perez Moreira

Ventanas Iglesia San Eduardo **M** Recinto San Eduardo Canton Ventana Vía Panamericana 0901-5250 (Mail to: AMarilis Fuentes 603 y Jose V. Trujillo 0901-5250)

Ventanas Iglesia San Gerardo **M** Recinto San Gerardo, Canton Ventanas Vía Panamericana 0901-5250 (Mail to: Amarilis Fuentes 603 y Jose Vicente Trujillo 0901-5250)

Ventanas La Gracia de Dios **M** Sixto Escolona y Pablo Palacios 0901-5250 (Mail to: Amarilis Fuertes 603 y Jose V. Trujillo 0901-5250)

INSTITUTIONS

Escuela Jardín Anne Steven, Box. 0901-5250 San Eduardo, Ventanas

Campamento Episcopal en Playas Box 0901-5250 Guayaquil

Centro de Estudios Teologicos San Patricio

IMEL Instituto para el Ministerio Episcopal Laico

DIOCESE OF EL CAMINO REAL
(PROVINCE VIII)

Comprises 5 counties in central coastal CA except St Mark's Palo Alto and Christ Church Los Altos

DIOCESAN OFFICE 154 Central Ave Salinas, CA 93901 (MAIL: Box 689 Salinas CA 93902)

TEL (831) 394-4465   FAX (831) 394-7133

E-MAIL mbpowell@realepiscopal.org   WEB www.realepiscopal.org

Previous Bishops—
Wm I Kip m 1853 dio 1857-93, Wm F Nichols coadj 1890 Bp 1893-1924, Edward L Parsons coadj 1919 Bp 1924-40, Karl M Block coadj 1933 Bp 1941-58, Henry H Shires suffr 1950-58, James A Pike 1958-66, G Richard Millard suffr 1960-76, C Kilmer Myers 1966-79, William E Swing coadj 1979 Bp 1980(California), C Shannon Mallory 1980-90, R Shimpfky 1990-2004; S Romero asst 2004-2007

Bishop—Rt Rev Mary Gray-Reeves (1022) (Dio 10 Nov 2007)

Conv Sec Rev M Hughes; *Treas* J Shreve; *Dio Admin* Rev B Nordwick; *Admin Asst* MB Powell; *Chanc* S Kottmeier; *Archdcn* Ven J Weber; *Cong Growth & Dev* J Reyes

Board of Trustees—Cler: V Pres K Crowe R Ott A Leininger J Wild R Barney; *Lay:* B Raney E Fisher D Mora L Gonzalez MJ Kelly

Stand Comm—Cler: Pres C Smith S Denney K Doar R Fisher; *Lay:* E Rosenthal E Frost J Melvin S Pearson

PARISHES, MISSIONS, AND CLERGY

Aptos Epis Ch of St John the Baptist **P** (233) 125 Canterbury Dr 95003-4367 (Mail to: PO Box 188 95001-0188) Eliza Linley Tracy Wells Miller (831) 708-2278

Arroyo Grande St Barnabas Episcopal Church **P** (232) 301 Trinity Ave 93420-3384 (Mail to: 301 Trinity Ave 93420-3384) Jeremy Bond Robert Keim (805) 489-2990

Atascadero St Lukes Episcopal Church **P** (114) 5318 Palma Ave 93422-3338 (Mail to: 5318 Palma Ave 93422-3338) (805) 466-0379

Ben Lomond St Andrew Episcopal Church **P** (183) 101 Riverside Ave 95005-9509 (Mail to: PO Box 293 95005-0293) Robert Neville (831) 336-5994

Cambria St Paul Episcopal Church **P** (77) 2700 Eton Rd 93428-4106 (Mail to: 2700 Eton Rd 93428-4106) Brian Palmer (805) 927-3239

Carmel All Saints Episcopal Church **P** (867) 100 Lincoln St 93923 (Mail to: PO Box 1296 93921-1296) Amber Sturgess (831) 624-3883

Carmel St Dunstan's Episcopal Church **P** (220) § 28005 Robinson Canyon Rd 93923-8572 (Mail to: 28005 Robinson Canyon Rd 93923-8572) Robert Fisher Marcia Lockwood (831) 624-6646

Cupertino St Jude the Apostle Episcopal **P** (477) 20920 Mcclellan Rd 95014-2967 (Mail to: 20920 McClellan Rd 95014-2967) Wilma Jakobsen Sarah Lapenta-H (408) 252-4166

Gilroy St Stephen Episcopal Church **P** (119) 651 Broadway 95020-4304 (Mail to: 651 Broadway 95020-4398) Clarence Burley (408) 842-4415

Hollister St Lukes Episcopal Church **P** (132) 720 Monterey St 95023-3826 (Mail to: 720 Monterey St 95023-3826) Kenneth Wratten (831) 637-7570

Jolon St Lukes Church Episcopal **M** (50) Jolon Rd & Mission Rd 93928 (Mail to: PO Box 233 93928-0233) Robert Seifert (831) 227-1202

King City St Mark Church **M** (45) 301 Bassett St 93930-2901 (Mail to: 301 Bassett St 93930-2901) (831) 385-5119

Los Gatos St Luke Episcopal Church **P** (567) 20 University Ave 95030-6009 (Mail to: 20 University Ave 95030-6099) Ricardo Avila Richard Emerson (408) 354-2195

Los Osos St Benedict Episcopal Church **P** (88) 2220 Snowy Egret Ln 93402 (Mail to: PO Box 6877 93412-6877) Caroline Hall Donna Ross Carlton Turner (805) 528-0654

Marina Epiphany Lutheran/Episcopal Church **PM** 425 Carmel Ave 93933-3305 (Mail to: 425 Carmel Ave 93933-3305) Jon Perez Patricia Catalano (831) 384-6323

Monterey St James Episcopal Church **P** (92) 381 High St 93940-2161 (Mail to: 381 High St 93940-2199) George Kohn (831) 375-8476

Monterey St John Episcopal Chapel **P** (167) 1490 Mark Thomas Dr 93940-4919 (Mail to: 1490 Mark Thomas Dr 93940-4919) Robert Ott (831) 375-4463

Morgan Hill St John the Divine Epis Church **P** (226) 17740 Peak Ave 95037-4121 (Mail to: 17740 Peak Ave 95037-4121) Philip Cooke (408) 779-9510

Morro Bay St Peters by the Sea Epis Church **P** (84) 545 Shasta Ave 93442-2541 (Mail to: 545 Shasta Ave 93442-2541) Sidney Symington (805) 772-2368

Mountain View Saint Timothy's Episcopal Church **P** (308) 2094 Grant Rd 94040-3802 (Mail to: 2094 Grant Rd 94040-3899) Lisa McIndoo (650) 967-4724

Pacific Grove Church of St Marys by the Sea **P** (362) 146 12th St 93950-2749 (Mail to: 146 12th St 93950-2760) Jeff Lewis (831) 373-4441

Palo Alto All Saints Episcopal Church **P** (223) 555 Waverley St 94301-1721 (Mail to: 555 Waverley St 94301-1721) Terence Gleeson (650) 322-4528

Paso Robles St James Episcopal Church **P** (122) 1335 Oak Street 93446-2262 (Mail to: 514 14th St 93446-2262) Barbara Miller Jacqueline Sebro (805) 238-0819

Salinas Church of the Good Shepherd **P** (200) 301 Corral De Tierra Rd 93908-8917 (Mail to: 301 Corral De Tierra Rd 93908-8917) Linda Campbell Cynthia Montague (831) 484-2153

Salinas St Georges Episcopal Church **P** (177) 98 Kip Dr 93906-2909 (Mail to: 98 Kip Dr 93906-2909) (831) 449-6709

Salinas St Paul's/San Pablo Episcopal Church **P** (215) 1071 Pajaro St 93901-3001 (Mail to: 1071 Pajaro St 93901-3099) Arnold Hedlund (831) 424-7331

San Ardo St Matthews Church **M** (23) Jolon St & Railroad St 93450 (Mail to: C/O Janyce E. Lacoume P.O. Box 114 93450) Susan Allen (805) 740-2024

San Jose Episcopal Church in Almaden **P** (220) 6581 Camden Ave 95120-1908 (Mail to: 6581 Camden Ave 95120-1908) Shelley Denney (408) 268-0243

San Jose Holy Family Episcopal Church **P** 5038 Hyland Ave 95127-2212 (Mail to: 5038 Hyland Ave 95127-2212)

San Jose St Francis Episcopal Church **P** (364) 1205 Pine Ave 95125-3459 (Mail to: 1205 Pine Ave 95125-3400) Mary London Hughes Stephenie Cooper Katherine Doar John Palmer (408) 292-7090

San Jose St Stephens in the Field Epis **P** (167) 7269 Santa Teresa Blvd 95139-1352 (Mail to: 7269 Santa Teresa Blvd 95139-1352) Karen Cuffie Robin Poppoff (408) 629-1836

✠ **San Jose** Trinity Episcopal Cathedral **O** (691) 81 2nd St 95113-1205 (Mail to: 81 2nd St 95113-1205) Lee Barford Lee Barford Lance Beizer Jerry Drino (408) 293-7953

Santa Clara St Mark Episcopal Church **P** (189) 1957 Pruneridge Ave 95050-6515 (Mail to: 1957 Pruneridge Ave 95050-6515) George Mcdonnell Karin White (408) 296-8383

Santa Cruz Calvary Episcopal Church **P** (376) 532 Center St 95060-4313 (Mail to: 532 Center St 95060-4313) Robert Keim Austin Leininger Ann-Lining Smith (831) 423-8787

Saratoga Saint Andrew's Church **P** (1983) § 13601 Saratoga Ave 95070-5055 (Mail to: PO Box 2789 95070-0789) Channing Smith Peggy Bryan Kathleen Crowe Janet Wild (408) 867-3493

Scotts Valley St Philip the Apostle in Scotts Valley **M** (355) 5271 Scotts Valley Dr 95066-3514 (Mail to: 5271 Scotts Valley Dr 95066-3577) Mary Blessing (831) 438-4360

Seaside El Cristo Rey **M** (146) 1092 Noche Buena St 93955-6221 (Mail to: 437 Rogers Ave 95076-3320) (831) 394-4465

✠ **Seaside** La Iglesia De San Pablo **O** (240) 1092 Noche Buena St 93955-6221 (Mail to: 1092 Noche Buena Street 93935) Rachel Bennett Jose Juarez

Sn Luis Obispo St Stephens Episcopal Church **P** (283) 1344 Nipomo St 93401-3935 (Mail to: 1344 Nipomo St 93401-3987) Ian Delinger Anne Wall (805) 543-7212

Sunnyvale St Thomas Episcopal Church **P** (318) 231 Sunset Ave 94086-5969 (Mail to: 231 Sunset Ave 94086-5938) Sheldon Hutchison Michael Ridgway Sally Wong (408) 736-4155

Watsonville All Saints Episcopal Church **P** (141) 437 Rogers Ave 95076-3320 (Mail to: 437 Rogers Ave 95076-3398) Michael Dresbach (831) 724-5338

CONVOCATION OF EPISCOPAL CHURCHES IN EUROPE
(PROVINCE II)
Under the Jurisdiction of the Presiding Bishop
Convocation Office American Cathedral of the Holy Trinity
23 Ave George F-75008 Paris
TEL +33 1 53 23 84 06
E-MAIL office@tec-europe.org WEB www.tec-europe.org

Previous Bishops in Charge—
EL Browning 1971-74, AE Swift 1974-77, R Millard 1979-80, JM Krumm 1980-83, RB Appleyard 1983-86, AD Davies 1986-88, MP Bigliardi 1988-91, JM Krumm int 1992, MP Bigliardi int 1992-93 JM Rowthorn 1994-2001

Bishop—The Presiding Bishop 815 Second Ave New York NY 10017

Bishop in Charge—Rt Rev Pierre W Whalon (973) (18 Nov 2001)

Archdeacon: Ven Dr WJ Baer; *Convocation Adm:* S Plé

Convocation Officers: Treas D Le Moullac (France); *Sec* Rev R Cole Dcn (Geneva); *COMB Chair* Dr L Williams (France); *Chris Ed Chair* J Day-Strehlow (Munich); *Ecumenical Rep* Rev J Dauphin Dcn (Paris); *Mission Com Chair* D Case (Munich)

Council of Advice: Cler: Rev S Hallanan Rev R Cole Dcn Rev C Easthill Rev R Warren; *Lay* G Battrick M Faigle S March A Swardson; *Ex-Off* Rt Rev P Whalon D Le Moullac Ven W Baer S Plé

Youth Commission Chair C Warren (Royat)

PARISHES, MISSIONS, AND CLERGY

Austria

Muhlbach Am Hochkonig Ecumenical Chapel of the Holy Family Mandlwandstrasse 437, 05505 (Mail to: Mandlwandstrasse) +43 664 539 3530 Clair Ullmann

Belgium

Braine-l'Alleud All Saints Episcopal Church **P** (200) Chaussée de Charleroi #2 1420 (Mail to: Chaussée de Charleroi #2 1420) Sunny Hallanan Katie Osweiler +32 2 384-7780
Charleroi Christ Church **M** Boulevard Audent, 20
Mons Mission Station **M**

France

Montpellier Grace Church **M** Rue Leon Blum c/o Eglise Don Bosco 34000 (Mail to: 10 rue Moilere)
✠ **Paris** Cathedral of the Holy Trinity **O** (1068) 23, Avenue George V 75008 (Mail to: 23, Avenue George V) Lucinda Laird Mary Haddad +33 1 5323-8400,
Royat Christ Church Clermont-Ferrand **P** (118) 1 bis, Avenue du Dr. Jean Heitz 63130 (Mail to: 42, avenue Albert et Elizabeth, 63000 Clermont-Ferrand) Robert Warren +33 4 6322 5035

Germany

Frankfurt am Main Church of Christ the King **P** (394) Sebastian-Rinz Strasse 22 (Mail to: Sebastian-Rinz-Straße 22) John Perris +49 69 55 01 84
Munich Church of the Ascension **P** (587) Seybothstrasse 4 81545 (Mail to: Seybothstrasse 4 81545) Steven Smith +49 89 648 185
Nuremberg St James the Less **M** St. Jakob Kirche Jakobsplatz 1 90402 (Mail to: C/O Sonja March Schillerstrasse 17, 90402) Scott Moore +49 176 22387296
Wiesbaden St Augustine of Canterbury **P** (272) Frankfurter Strasse 3, 65189 (Mail to: Frankfurter Strasse 3) Christopher Easthill +49 611 306674
Augsburg St Boniface **M** Garmischer Str. 2a, 86163 Augsburg,
Karlsruhe, St. Columban's **M** Röntgenstraße 1, 76133 Karlsruhe Hanns Engelhardt

Italy

Florence St James Episcopal Church **P** (210) Via Bernardo Rucellai 9, 50123 (Mail to: Via Bernardo Rucellai 9) Mark Dunnam +39 055 294417
Milan Capella del Buon Pastore **M** via Boccaccio, 1 Archdeacon Maria Vittoria Longhitano
Orvieto Church of the Resurrection **M** In care of St Pauls Via Napoli 58 00184 (Mail to: c/o St Pauls Church Via Napoli 58, 00184) Francisco Alberca +39 06 488 3339
Rome St Paul's within the Walls **P** (177) Via Napoli 58 00184 (Mail to: Via Napoli 58 00184) Austin Rios Mercedes Tutasig +39 06 488 3339
Santa Maria a Ferrano Santa Maria Chapel, Santa Maria a Ferrano Retreat Center (Mail to: Via de' Renai 19, 50060 Pelago (Fi)) Thomas Muller +39 055 0456 959

Switzerland

Geneva Emmanuel Episcopal Church **P** (349) 3 Rue de Monthoux 1201 (Mail to: 3, Rue de Monthoux) Michael Rusk Richard Cole +41 22 732-80-78

STATE OF FLORIDA

Dioceses of Central Florida (CF), Central Gulf Coast (CGC), Florida (FL), Southeast Florida (SeF), and Southwest Florida (SwF)

Apalachicola—CGC
Apopka—CF
Arcadia—SwF
Auburndale—CF
Avon Pk—CF
Bartow—CF
Belleview—CF
Big Pine Key—SeF
Biscayne Park—SeF
Boca Grande—SwF
Boca Raton—SeF
Bonita Spgs—SwF
Boynton Bch—SeF
Bradenton—SwF
Brooksville—SwF
Bushnell—CF
Cantonment—CGC
Cape Coral—SwF
Carrabelle—FL
Cedar Key—FL
Chiefland—FL
Chipley—CGC
Clearwater—SwF
Clermont—CF
Clewiston—SeF
Cocoa—CF
Cocoa Bch—CF
Coral Gables—SeF
Crescent City—FL
Crestview—CGC
Crystal River—CF
Dade City—SwF
Daytona Bch—CF
Deerfield Bch—SeF
DeFuniak Spgs—CGC
DeLand—CF
Delray Bch—SeF
Deltona—CF
Destin—CGC
Dunedin—SwF
Dunnellon—CF
E Palatka—FL
Englewood—SwF
Eustis—CF
Fernandina Bch—FL
Ft Lauderdale—SeF
Ft Meade—CF
Ft Myers—SwF

Ft Pierce—CF
Ft Walton Bch—CGC
Fruitland Pk—CF
Gainesville—FL
Green Cove Spgs—FL
Gulf Breeze—CGC
Haines City—CF
Hallandale Beach—SeF
Hawthorne—FL
Hialeah—SeF
High Spgs—FL
Hilliard—FL
Hobe Sound—SeF
Hollywood—SeF
Holmes Bch—SwF
Homestead—SeF
Hudson—SwF
Indian Rocks Bch—
    SwF
Interlachen—FL
Inverness—CF
Islamorada—SeF
Jacksonville—FL
Jacksonville Bch—FL
Jensen Bch—SeF
Key Biscayne—SeF
Key West—SeF
Kissimmee—CF
LaBelle—SwF
Lady Lake—CF
Lake City—FL
Lake Mary—CF
Lake Placid—CF
Lake Wales—CF
Lake Worth—SeF
Lakeland—CF
Largo—SwF
Lecanto—CF
Leesburg—CF
Lehigh Acres—SwF
Live Oak—FL
Longboat Key—SwF
Longwood—CF
Madison—FL
Maitland—CF
Marathon—SeF
Marco Is—SwF
Marianna—CGC

Mayo—FL
Melbourne—CF
Melbourne Bch—CF
Melrose—FL
Merritt Is—CF
Miami—SeF
Miami Bch—SeF
Micanopy—FL
Milton—CGC
Monticello—FL
Mt Dora—CF
Mulberry—CF
Naples—SwF
Navarre—CGC
Newberry—FL
New Pt Richey—SwF
New Smyrna—CF
Niceville—CGC
N Ft Myers—SwF
N Miami Bch—SeF
N Port—SwF
Ocala—CF
Okahumpka—CF
Okeechobee—CF
Opa Locka—SeF
Orange City—CF
Orange Pk—FL
Orlando—CF
Ormond Bch—CF
Osprey—SwF
Oviedo—CF
Palatka—FL
Palm Bay—CF
Palm Bch—SeF
Palm Bch Gdns—SeF
Palm City—SeF
Palm Coast—FL
Palm Hbr—SwF
Palmetto—SwF
Panama City—CGC
Panama City Bch—
    CGC
Pensacola—CGC
Perry—FL
Pinellas Pk—SwF
Plant City—SwF
Pompano Bch—SeF
Ponte Vedra—FL

Pt Charlotte—SwF
Pt Orange—CF
Pt St Joe—CGC
Pt St Lucie—CF
Punta Gorda—SwF
Quincy—FL
Riviera Beach—SeF
Rockledge—CF
Safety Hbr—SwF
St Augustine—FL
St Cloud—CF
St James City—SwF
St Johns—FL
St Petersburg—SwF
Sanford—CF
Sanibel—SwF
Santa Rosa Bch—
    CGC
Sarasota—SwF
Satellite Bch—CF
Sebastian—CF
Sebring—CF
Seminole—SwF
Spring Hill—SwF
Starke—FL
Stuart—SeF
Sun City Ctr—SwF
Tallahassee—FL
Tampa—SwF
Tarpon Spgs—SwF
Temple Terrace—SwF
Tequesta—SeF
The Villages—CF
Titusville—CF
Valrico—SwF
Venice—SwF
Vero Bch—CF
Wauchula—CF
Welaka—FL
W Palm Bch—SeF
Wewahitchka—CGC
Williston—FL
Winter Garden—CF
Winter Haven—CF
Winter Pk—CF
Zephyrhills—SwF

DIOCESE OF FLORIDA
(PROVINCE IV)
Comprises the northern part of the State of Florida
DIOCESAN OFFICE 325 N Market St Jacksonville FL 32202
TEL (904) 356-1328   FAX (904) 355-1934
E-MAIL sengemann@diocesefl.org   WEB www.diocesefl.org

Previous Bishops—
Francis H Rutledge 1851-66, JohnF Young 1867-85, Edwin G Weed 1886-24, Frank A Juhan 1924-56, Ed Hamilton West 1956-74, Frank S Cerveny coadj 1974-75 Bp 1975-92, Stephen H Jecko 1994-2004

Bishop—Rt Rev Samuel J Howard (992) (Dio 1 Nov 03)

Assisting Bishop—Rt Rev Dorsey F. Henderson (902)

Cn to Ord & DDO A DeFoor; *Reg Cns: First Coast East* BW Ammons; *First Coast West* N Suellau; *River* J Wesley and R Goolsby; *Santa Fe* L Horne; *Apalachee* J Smith; *Sec* L Horne; *Treas* G Hinchliffe; *Dn* K Moorehead; *Comp* J Maysonett; *Bp Exec Asst* V Haskew; *Chanc* Hon F Isaac; *Ecum & Outrch* Rev Cn RV Lee III; *Camp & Conf Ctr* T Frazier (interim)

Stand Comm—Cler: Pres S Britt D Cain R Sloan *Lay:* L Gregory L Baker P Anderson

PARISHES, MISSIONS, AND CLERGY

Carrabelle Church of the Ascension **M** (42) 110 Ne 1st St 32322-2172 (Mail to: PO Box 546 32322-0546) (850) 545-2578

Cedar Key Christ Episcopal Church **M** (55) Corner of Hwy 24 & 5th Street 32625-5154 (Mail to: PO Box 210 32625-0210) (352) 543-6407

Chiefland St Alban Episcopal Church **M** (123) 7550 Nw 149th Pl 32626 (Mail to: PO Box 997 32644-0997) Harold Ritchie (352) 493-2770

Crescent City Church of the Holy Comforter **M** (71) 223 Summit St 32112-2301 (Mail to: 223 Summit St 32112-2301) Timothy Thomas (386) 698-1983

East Palatka St Paul Episcopal Church **P** (85) 124 Commercial Ave 32131-4363 (Mail to: PO Box 6 32145-0006) (904) 692-1967

Fernandina Bch St Peter's Episcopal Church **P** (642) 801 Atlantic Ave 32034-3628 (Mail to: 801 Atlantic Ave 32034-3628) Stephen Mazingo Brian Alberti (904) 261-4293

Gainesville Chapel of the Incarnation **CC** (70) 1522 W University Ave 32603-1812 (Mail to: PO Box 15116 32604-5116) Adam Young (352) 372-8506

Gainesville Holy Trinity Episcopal Church **P** (1160) 100 Ne 1st St 32601-5379 (Mail to: 100 NE 1st St 32601-5390) George Holston John Montgomery (352) 372-4721

Gainesville St Michael Episcopal Church **P** (51) 4315 Nw 23rd Ave 32606-6542 (Mail to: 4315 Nw 23rd Ave 32606-6587) (352) 376-8184

Green Cv Spg St Mary Episcopal Church **P** (123) 400 Saint Johns Ave 32043-3051 (Mail to: PO Box 1346 32043-1346) Celeste Tisdelle (904) 284-5434

Hawthorne Church of the Holy Communion **M** (37) 21810 Se 69th Ave 32640-3959 (Mail to: PO Box 655 32640-0655) (352) 481-3600

High Springs St Bartholomews Episcopal Church **M** (115) 105 Nw 2nd St 32643-0004 (Mail to: PO Box 906 32655-0906) (386) 454-9812

Hilliard Bethany Episcopal Church **M** (34) PO Box 1005 15860 CR 108 32046-1005 (Mail to: PO Box 1005 32046-1005) William Smith (904) 845-2304

Interlachen St Andrew's Episcopal Church **M** (152) 111 S. Francis St 32148-7305 (Mail to: P.O. Box 41 107 S Frances Street 32148) Diane Reeves (386) 684-4506

Jacksonville All Saints Episcopal Church **P** (357) 4171 Hendricks Ave 32207-6323 (Mail to: 4171 Hendricks Ave 32207-6398) Donavan Cain Donavan Cain Elizabeth Greenman Christopher Martin Lisa Meirow (904) 737-8488

Jacksonville Church of Our Saviour **P** (1348) 12236 Mandarin Rd 32223-1813 (Mail to: 12236 Mandarin Rd 32223-1877) Joseph Gibbes Trenton Moore (904) 268-9457

Jacksonville The Church of the Good Shepherd **P** (184) 1100 Stockton St 32204-4237 (Mail to: 1100 Stockton St 32204-4237) Nancee Martin (904) 387-5691

Jacksonville Resurrection Episcopal Church **P** (115) 12355 Fort Caroline Rd 32225-1708 (Mail to: 12355 Fort Caroline Rd 32225-1708) Carrie English (904) 641-8177

Jacksonville St Andrew's Episcopal Church **P** (418) 7801 Lone Star Rd 32211-6001 (Mail to: 7801 Lone Star Rd 32211-6095) Mark Atkinson (904) 725-6566

Jacksonville St Catherine Episcopal Church **P** (190) 4758 Shelby Ave 32210-1716 (Mail to: 4758 Shelby Ave 32210-1716) (904) 387-2061

Jacksonville St Elizabeths Episcopal Church **P** (100) 1735 Leonid Rd 32218-4727 (Mail to: 1735 Leonid Rd 32218-4727) (904) 751-2626

Jacksonville St Gabriel Episcopal Church **M** (72) 5235 Moncrief Rd W 32209-1042 (Mail to: PO Box 12252 32209-0252) (904) 765-0964

Jacksonville Saint George Episcopal Church **P** (186) 10560 Fort George Rd 32226-2442 (Mail to: 10560 Fort George Rd 32226-2442) George Henderson George Henderson (904) 251-9272

✠ **Jacksonville** St John Episcopal Cathedral **O** (1466) 256 E Church St 32202-3132 (Mail to: 256 E Church St 32202-3186) Kate Moorehead Jean Dodd (904) 356-5507

Jacksonville St Lukes Episcopal Church **P** (184) 2961 University Boulevard N. 32211-3398 (Mail to: 2961 University Blvd 32211-3398) (904) 744-2133

Jacksonville St Mark Episcopal Church **P** (2018) § 4129 Oxford Ave 32210-4425 (Mail to: 4129 Oxford Ave 32210-4404) Thomas Murray Nancy Suellau (904) 388-2681

Jacksonville St Marys Episcopal Church **M** (127) 1924 Laura St P.O. Box 3243 32206-3633 (Mail to: 325 Market St 32202-2732) (904) 354-5075

Jacksonville St Pauls Episcopal Church **P** (142) 5616 Atlantic Blvd 32207-2204 (Mail to: 5616 Atlantic Blvd 32207-2204) (904) 725-1150

Jacksonville St Peters Episcopal Church **P** (894) 5043 Timuquana Rd 32210-7440 (Mail to: 5042 Timuquana Rd 32210-7475) James Barnhill (904) 778-1434

Jacksonville St Philips Episcopal Church **P** (220) 321 Union St W 32202-4020 (Mail to: 321 Union St W 32202-4020) (904) 354-1053

Jacksonville San Jose Episcopal Church **HC** (467) § 7423 San Jose Blvd 32217-3429 (Mail to: 7423 San Jose Blvd Ste A 32217-3498) Stephen Britt (904) 733-1811

Jacksonville The Church of the Redeemer **P** (244) 7500 Southside Blvd 32256-7095 (Mail to: 7500 Southside Blvd 32256-7095) Benjamin Ammons (904) 642-4575

Jaxville Bch St Pauls by the Sea Episcopal **P** (609) 465 11th Ave 32250-4722 (Mail to: 465 11th Ave 32250-4722) Connie Loch (904) 249-4091

Lake City St James Episcopal Church **P** (204) 2423 Sw Bascom Norris Dr 32025-4912 (Mail to: 2423 SW Bascom Norris Dr 32025-4912) Douglas Hodsdon (386) 752-2218

Live Oak St Luke's Episcopal Church **P** (339) 1391 SW 11th Street 32064 (Mail to: PO Box 1238 32064-1238) George Hinchliffe Phyllis Doty (386) 362-1837

Madison St Mary Episcopal Church **M** (86) 104 Horry Ave 32340 (Mail to: PO Box 611 32341-0611) David Boyles (850) 973-8338

Mayo St Matthew Episcopal Church **M** (7) PO Box 1570 32066-1570 (Mail to: PO Box 1570 32066-1570) (386) 294-1839

Melrose Trinity Episcopal Church **P** (150) 204 State Road 26 32666-3901 (Mail to: PO Box 361 32666-0361) Anthony Powell (352) 475-2177

Micanopy Church of the Mediator **M** (99) P.O. Box 184 32667-4108 (Mail to: PO Box 184 32667-0184) (352) 466-3364

Monticello Christ Church Episcopal **P** (180) 425 Cherry St 32344-2001 (Mail to: 425 Cherry St 32344-2001) James May (850) 997-4116

Newberry St Joseph Episcopal Church **P** (234) 16921 W Newberry Rd 32669-2811 (Mail to: 16921 W Newberry Rd 32669-2811) (352) 472-2951

Orange Park Grace Episcopal Church **P** (425) § 151 Kingsley Ave 32073-5640 (Mail to: 245 Kingsley Ave 32073-5695) Ian Mccarthy Patrick Soule (904) 264-9981

Palatka St Mark's Episcopal Church **P** (196) 211 Main Street 32177-3508 (Mail to: PO Box 370 32178-0370) (386) 328-1474

Palatka St Marys Episcopal Church **M** (18) Mrs Edith Alexander 809 Saint Johns Ave 32177-4647 (Mail to: 312 2nd St 32177-3508) (386) 328-6394

Palm Coast St Thomas Episcopal Church of Flagle **P** (671) 5400 Belle Terre Pkwy 32137-8824 (Mail to: 5400 Belle Terre Pkwy 32137-8824) Robert Goolsby Horace Johnson Alfred Stefanik (386) 446-2300

Perry St James Episcopal Church **P** (79) 1100 W Green St 32347-3107 (Mail to: 1100 W Green St 32347-3107) Aquilla Hanson (850) 584-7636

Ponte Vedra San Francisco del Campo **M** (30) 895 Palm Valley Rd 32081-4315 (Mail to: 895 Palm Valley Rd. 32081-4315) (904) 615-2130

Ponte Vedra St Francis in the Field **P** (394) 895 Palm Valley Rd 32081-4315 (Mail to: 895 Palm Valley Rd 32081-4315) Michael Ellis (904) 615-2130

Ponte Vedra Beach Christ Episcopal Church **M** (6123) § 400 San Juan Dr 32082-2836 (Mail to: PO Box 1558 32004-1558) Tom Reeder Richard Westbury Jessica Babcock Caroline Kramer Tom Reeder Thomas Slone (904) 285-6127

Quincy St Paul Episcopal Church **P** (77) 10 W King St 32351-1702 (Mail to: 10 W King St 32351-1702) (850) 627-6257

Saint Johns St Patricks Episcopal Church **P** (126) 1221 State Road 13 32259-3184 (Mail to: 1221 State Road 13 32259-3184) Rhonda Willerer Sally Brower Gregory McIntyre Thomas Shaver (904) 287-2807

St Augustine St Cyprian Episcopal Church **M** (101) 37 Lovett St 32084-4858 (Mail to: 37 Lovett St 32084-4858) Edwin Voorhees (904) 829-8828

St Augustine Trinity Episcopal Parish **P** (1213) 215 Saint George St 32084-4410 (Mail to: 215 Saint George St 32084-4410) Kenneth Herzog Eddie Jones (904) 824-2876

Starke St Mark Episcopal Church **P** (89) 212 Church St 32091-3414 (Mail to: PO Box 487 32091-0487) Herbert Daly (904) 964-6126

Tallahassee Episcopal Church of the Advent **P** (298) § 815 Piedmont Dr 32312-2422 (Mail to: 815 Piedmont Dr 32312-2400) Richard Effinger (850) 386-5109

Tallahassee Episcopal University Center **University** (1) 655 W Jefferson St 32304-8013 (Mail to: 325 Market St 32202-2732) Brian Smith (850) 296-7843

Tallahassee Grace Mission Church **M** (143) 303 W Brevard St 32301-1117 (Mail to: PO Box 10472 32302-2472) Amanda Nickles Jeanie Beyer Jennifer Liem (850) 224-3817

Tallahassee Church of the Holy Comforter **P** (511) § 2015 Fleischmann Rd 32308 (Mail to: 2015 Fleischmann Rd 32308-0561) Roy Lima Elizabeth Pessah Jerry Smith (850) 877-2712

Tallahassee St John's Episcopal Church **P** (1321)

211 Monroe St 32301-7619 (Mail to: 211 Monroe St 32301-7691) David Killeen Abigail Moon Kathleen Walker (850) 222-2636

Tallahassee St Michael & All Angels Episcopal Ch **P** (143) 1405 Melvin St 32301-4232 (Mail to: 1405 Melvin St 32301-4232) Hugh Chapman (850) 681-0844

Welaka Emmanuel Episcopal Church **M** (31) PO Box 302 672 Third Ave 32193-0302 (Mail to: PO Box 302 32193-0302) (386) 698-1983

Williston St Barnabas Episcopal Church **M** (33) P.O. Box 615 32696-2050 (Mail to: PO Box 615 32696-0615) (352) 528-2593

DIOCESE OF FOND DU LAC

(PROVINCE V)

Comprises the northeast part of Wisconsin

DIOCESAN OFFICE 1051 N Lynndale Dr Ste 1B

Appleton WI 54914-3094

TEL (920) 830-8866   FAX (920) 830-8761

E-MAIL diofdl@diofdl.org   WEB www.diofdl.org

Previous Bishops—
John HH Brown 1875-88, Chas C Grafton 1889-1912, Reginald H Weller coadj 1900 Bp 1912-33, Harwood Sturtevant coadj 1929 Bp 1933-56, William H Brady coadj 1953 Bp 1956-80, William L Stevens 1980-94; Russell E Jacobus 1994-2013

Bishop—Rt Rev Matthew A Gunter (1081) (Dio 26 Apr 2014)

Sec A Webster; *Admin* MP Payne; *Treas* EA Peterson; *Reg* Rev P Twomey; *Chanc* G Stillings; *Cursillo* D Annis; *Trans Min* Rev M Albright; *Dcn Cncl* Ven M Whitford; *Sisterhood of the Hly Nat* Sr Abigail; *Order of Julian* Sr Hilary; *UTO* C Dobrzynski; *Yth Min* E Wolf; ; *Com Min* Rev M Burkert-Brist; *Com Cong Vit* Rev J Johnson; *Abuse Prevention* S Steinhilber; *CPC* K Powers; *Res Ctr* D Murray; *EFM* Rev R Patience; *Trustees* Rev J Throop; *Sum Cmp* E Wolf; *Const & Cns* B Sajna; *Fin Rvw Tm* E A Peterson; *Archivist* MP Payne; *Historiographer* MP Payne; *Chaps Ret Clergy* Rev J & Rev M Trainor; *Intake Ofcr* Rev R Osborne; *Deaneries Chairs: Lake Winnebago* Rev R Osborne; *Green Bay* Rev E Mills; *Wisconsin River* Rev M Albright; *Mosaic Task Force* Rev E Kirby; *Evangelism* L Wallenfang; *Companion Diocese* R Alexander;

Stand Comm—Cler: Pres Rev M Scolare C Arnold W Roane D Murray; *Lay:* D Annis S Rogers M Mims M Sampey

PARISHES, MISSIONS, AND CLERGY

Algoma St Agnes Episcopal Church **M** (27) 806 4th St 54201-1348 (Mail to: 806 4th St 54201-

1348) Robert Hoppe (920) 487-2015

Amherst St Olaf Episcopal Church **M** (21) 277 Main St 54406-9101 (Mail to: PO Box 204 54406-0204) (715) 824-2577

Antigo St Ambrose Episcopal Church **M** (33) 800 6th Ave 54409-1856 (Mail to: PO Box 134 54409-0134) (715) 623-5532

Appleton All Saints Episcopal Church **P** (656) 100 Drew St 54911-5421 (Mail to: 100 Drew St 54911-5421) (920) 734-3656

De Pere St Anne Episcopal Church **P** (534) 347 Libal St 54115-3460 (Mail to: 347 Libal St 54115-3460) Eric Mills Mary Adams Dale Hutjens (920) 336-9571

Eagle River St Francis Episcopal Church **M** (25) 120 Silver Lake Rd 54521-8017 (Mail to: PO Box 1625 54521-1625) (715) 480-4237

Elkhart Lake All Saints Episcopal Chapel **SC** N7902 Hwy P 53020 (Mail to: C/O Grace Church 630 Ontario Avenue 53081-4029) Karl Schaffenburg (920) 452-9659

Fish Creek Church of the Atonement **SC** 9415 Cottage Row Rd 54212 (Mail to: PO Box 241 54212-0241) (920) 498-8831

✠ **Fond Du Lac** Episcopal Cathedral of St Paul **O** (181) 51 W Division St 54935-4028 (Mail to: 51 W Division St 54935-4028) Cecil Perkins Michael Hackbarth (920) 921-3363

Gardner Precious Blood Episcopal Church **M** (14) County Rd C & County Rd 54204 (Mail to: C/O Erma Hartwig 8933 Pine Ln 54204-9789) (920) 487-2015

Green Bay Blessed Sacrament Episcopal Church **P** (163) 825 Webster Ave 54302-1436 (Mail to: 825 Webster Ave 54302-1436) Michael Scolare (920) 432-4688

Manitowoc St James Episcopal Church **P** (137) 434 8th St 54220-4010 (Mail to: 434 8th St 54220-4010) Diane Murray (920) 684-8256

Marinette St Paul Episcopal Church **P** (130) 917 Church St 54143-2408 (Mail to: 917 Church St 54143-2408) Glenn Kanestrom (715) 735-3719

Menasha St Thomas Episcopal Church **P** (804) 226 Washington St 54952-3353 (Mail to: 226 Washington St 54952-3396) Ralph Osborne Aran Walter (920) 725-5601

Merrill Ascension Episcopal Church **M** (73) 218 Pier St 54452-2449 (Mail to: C/O Stephanie Springborn N2395 Gen Dr 54452-9580) Linda Schmidt (715) 539-0857

Minocqua St Matthias Episcopal Church **P** (185) 403 E Chicago Ave 54548-9307 (Mail to: PO Box 936 54548-0936) Erin Kirby (715) 356-6758

Mosinee St James Episcopal Church **M** (22) 409 2nd St 54455-1420 (Mail to: PO Box 24 54455-0024) Amanda Sampey (715) 573-8830

New London St John Episcopal Church **M** (234) 1513 Pinewood Ln 54961-2449 (Mail to: A Center For Inner Peace 1513 Pinewood Ln 54961-2449) (920) 982-0970

Oneida Holy Apostles Episcopal Church **M** (570) 2937 Freedom Rd 54155-8926 (Mail to: 2937 Freedom Rd 54155-8926) Rodger Patience Deborah Heckel (920) 869-2565

Oshkosh Trinity Episcopal Church **P** (327) 203 Algoma Blvd 54901 (Mail to: 311 Division St 54901-4884) Christopher Arnold Nancy Behm Sandra Muinde (920) 231-2420

Plymouth St Paul Episcopal Church **M** (86) 312 E Main St 53073-1817 (Mail to: PO Box 192 53073-0192) (920) 892-4894

Rhinelander St Augustine Episcopal Church **P** (80) 39 S Pelham St 54501-3458 (Mail to: PO Box 771 54501-0771) Meredyth Albright (715) 362-3184

Ripon St Peter Episcopal Church **P** (108) 217 Houston St 54971-1566 (Mail to: 217 Houston St 54971-1566) (920) 748-2422

Shawano St John Episcopal Church **M** (63) 141 S Smalley St 54166-2347 (Mail to: 141 S Smally St 54166-2347) (715) 526-3686

Sheboygan Grace Episcopal Church **P** (217) 1011 7th St 53081-4019 (Mail to: 1011 7th St 53081)

Karl Schaffenburg Michael Burg Michele Whitford (920) 452-9659

Sheboygan Falls St Peter Episcopal Church **P** (123) 104 Elm St 53085-1592 (Mail to: 104 Elm St Attn Jennifer Dewitz 53085-1592) John Throop Gregory Schultz (920) 467-6639

Sister Bay St Luke Episcopal Church **P** (71) 2336 Canterbury 54234 (Mail to: PO Box 559 54234-0559) Barbara Sajna (920) 854-9600

Stevens Point Intercession Episcopal Church **P** (194) 900 Brilowski Rd 54482-8461 (Mail to: 900 Brilowski Rd 54482-8461) Jane Johnson (715) 341-3233

Sturgeon Bay Christ the King Holy Nativity Episcopal Church **M** (133) 512 Michigan St 54235-2220 (Mail to: PO Box 828 54235-0828) (920) 743-3286

Sturgeon Bay Church of the Holy Nativity **M** 3434 County Road Cc 54235-8611 (Mail to: PO Box 215 54235-0215) George Hillman (920) 743-3286

Suamico St Pauls Episcopal Church **M** (120) 2809 Flintville Rd 54173 (Mail to: PO Box 225 54173-0225) (920) 434-2247

Tomahawk St Barnabas Episcopal Church **M** (9) 201 W Merrill Ave 54487-1209 (Mail to: c/o Stephanie Springborn N2395 Gen Dr 54452-9580) (715) 453-1930

Waupaca St Mark Episcopal Church **P** (117) 415 S Main St 54981-1746 (Mail to: PO Box 561 54981-0561) Nigel Bousfield Bruce Mccallum (715) 258-5125

Waupun Holy Trinity Episcopal Church **M** (40) 315 E Jefferson St 53963-2032 (Mail to: PO Box 488 53963-0488) Monica Burkert-Brist (920) 324-5700

Wausau St John Episcopal Church **P** (160) 330 Mcclellan St 54403-4841 (Mail to: 330 McClellan St 54403-4841) (715) 845-6947

Wautoma St Mary Episcopal Chapel **Chapel** Hwy 21 & Bughs Lake Rd 54982 (Mail to: 217 Houston St 54971-1566) (920) 748-2422

Wisconsin Rapids St John Episcopal Church **P** (82) 320 Oak St 54494-4363 (Mail to: 320 Oak St 54494-4363) David Klutterman (715) 423-2332

DIOCESE OF FORT WORTH
(PROVINCE VII)
Comprises 24 North Central counties
DIOCESAN OFFICE 4301 Meadowbrook Dr Fort Worth TX 76103
TEL (817) 534-1900   FAX (817) 534-1904
E-MAIL: contact@edfw.org   WEB www.edfw.org

Previous Bishops—
A Donald Davies 1983-85, Clarence C Pope Jr 1986-94, Jack Leo Iker 1995-2008, Edwin F Gulick Jr 2009 (Provisional), C Wallis Ohl 2009-12 (Provisional), Rayford B High, Jr 2012-2015 (Provisional)

Bishop—Rt Rev J Scott Mayer (1035) (1 Jul 2015) (Provisional)

Trans Min Off & Cn to Ord J Waggoner; *Dio Sec* A Wright; *Treas* D Lowder; *Hist* K Shepherd; *Reg* T Middleton; *Chanc* S Liser; *Adm Asst* M King; *Dir of Comm* K Sherrod

Stand Comm—Cler: K Calafat S McComas C Jambor; *Lay:* J Dennis R Hicks N Snyder

PARISHES, MISSIONS, AND CLERGY

Aledo Episcopal Church of Parker County **M** PO Box 1869 76008-1869 (Mail to: Attn: Michelle King 4301 Meadowbrook Dr 76103) (817) 935-8612

Aledo St Francis Of Assisi Episcopal Church **M** (26) PO Box 1869 76008-1869 (Mail to: PO Box 1869 76008-1869) (817) 637-0846

Arlington St Alban Episcopal Church **P** (177) 316 W Main St 76010-7114 (Mail to: 316 W Main St 76010-7114) Dwayne Bauman Kevin Johnson Sharla Marks Sharla Marks Judith Upham (817) 264-3083

Fort Worth All Saints Episcopal Church **P** (1608) § 5001 Crestline Rd 76107-3663 (Mail to: 5001 Crestline Rd 76107-3699) Melanie Barbarito Christopher Jambor Noy Sparks Lynne Waltman (817) 732-1424

Fort Worth Christ the King Episcopal Church **P** (48) 5910 Black Oak Lane 76114 (Mail to: 5910 Black Oak Ln 76114-2800) Sandra Michels Christopher Thomas (817) 738-0504

Fort Worth St Anne Episcopal Church **PS** 6916 Miramar Circle 76126 (Mail to: 6055 Azle Ave 76135-2698) (817) 738-2658

Fort Worth St Christophers Church **P** (281) § 3550 Sw Loop 820 76133-2197 (Mail to: 3550 SW Loop 820 76133-2198) William Stanford Edwin Barnett (817) 926-8277

Fort Worth St Elisabeths and Christ the King Episcopal Church **M** (89) 5910 Black Oak Ln 76114-2800 (Mail to: 5910 Black Oak Ln 76114-2800) Sandra Michels (817) 738-0504

Fort Worth St Luke-in-the-Meadow Epis Church **P** (185) 4301 Meadowbrook Dr 76103-2710 (Mail to: 4301 Meadowbrook Dr 76103-2798) Karen Calafat (817) 534-4925

Fort Worth St Simon of Cyrene Episcopal Church **PS** 3550 SW Loop 820 76133 (Mail to: PO Box 24106 76124-1106) (817) 926-8277

Fort Worth St Andrew Episcopal Church **M** (30) C/O University Christian Ch 2720 S University Dr 76109-1150 (Mail to: 3550 SW Loop 820 76133) Edwin Barnett Edwin Barnett (817) 926-8277

Fort Worth Trinity Episcopal Church **P** (1056) § 3401 Bellaire Dr S 76109-2133 (Mail to: C/O Jackie Robinson 3401 Bellaire Dr S 76109-2133) Amy Haynie Tracie Middleton Andrew Wright (817) 926-4631

Granbury Church of the Good Shepherd **P** (74) Seventh Day Adventist Church 2116 Acton Hwy 76049 (Mail to: PO Box 232 76048-0232) Karen Robertson (817) 219-5382

Hamilton Saint Mary's Church **M** (33) 1101 S Rice St 76531-9600 (Mail to: PO Box 562 76531-0562) Linda Sutherland (254) 386-4412

Hillsboro Saint Mary's Church **M** (18) 200 Abbott St 76645-3015 (Mail to: C/O David Skelton M.D 109 Corsicana St 76645-2133) (254) 582-2255

Hurst St Stephen Episcopal Church **P** (123) 463 W Harwood Rd 76054-2941 (Mail to: PO Box 54864 76054-4864) Slaven Manning (915) 479-4669

Keller St Martin in-the-Fields Church **P** (719) § 223 S Pearson Ln 76248-5348 (Mail to: 223 S Pearson Ln 76248-5348) Scot Mccomas Christopher Thomas (817) 431-2396

Stephenville Saint Luke's Episcopal Church **P** (235) 595 Mcilhaney St 76401-5625 (Mail to: PO Box 2506 76401-0041) Bradley Dyche (254) 968-6949

Weatherford All Saints Episcopal Church **PS** (20) 121 S Waco St 76086-4327 (Mail to: 125 S Waco St 76086-4327) (817) 637-0846

Wichita Falls All Saints Episcopal Church **P** (36) 5023 Lindale Drive 76310-2551 (Mail to: 2606 Southwest Pkwy 76308-4607) (940) 692-3982

Wichita Falls Church of the Good Shepherd **M** (52) 5023 Lindale 76310-3551 (Mail to: 1007 Burnett St 76301-3288) (940) 692-3982

Wichita Falls The Episcopal Church of Wichita Falls **M** (55) 5023 Lindale Dr 76310-2551 (Mail to: 5023 Lindale Dr 76310-2551) John Payne (940) 692-3982

FRANCE

See Europe

STATE OF GEORGIA

Dioceses of Atlanta and Georgia

DIOCESE OF GEORGIA

(PROVINCE IV)
Comprises South Georgia
DIOCESAN OFFICE 18 E 34th St Savannah GA 31401
TEL (912) 236-4279　FAX (912) 236-2007
E-MAIL gdawson@gaepiscopal.org　WEB www.gaepiscopal.org

Previous Bishops—
Stephen Elliott 1841-66, John W Beckwith 1868-90, Cleland K Nelson 1892-1907, Frederick F Reese 1908-36, Middleton S Barnwell 1936-54, Albert R Stuart 1954-71, Paul Reeves 1972-85, Harry W Shipps 1985-94, Henry I Louttit 1995-2010

Bishop—Rt Rev Scott Benhase (1039) (Dio 23 Jan 2010)

Cn to Ord Rev FS Logue; *Chanc* Rev J Elliott 3016 N Patterson St Valdosta 31402; *Min Com* Rev T Purdy 6329 Frederica Rd St Simons Island GA 31522; *Cong Dev Dio Ofc* Rev Cn FS Logue; *Comm Off & Reg Dio Ofc* MJ Harris; *Const & Can* B Cheatham 2 Sandy Point Savannah 31404; *ECW* C Jordan 7604 Arcola Rd Brooklet GA 30415; *Hist* Rev Cn F Logue; *Treas* B Robinson 366 E 56 St Savannah GA 31405; *Yth Progs* J Varner *E-mail:* jvarner@gaepiscopal.org *Web:* youth. georgiaepiscopal.org *Addiction Rec Dio Off* Rev RK Kelly; *Anti-Racism Dio Off* Dcn Y Owens; *Conf Ctr* B Rowell; *Cursillo* Rev K Brinson; *ER&D* Rev C Todd

Deans: Albany Rev T Drazdowski 408 S First St Cordele GA 31015 Rev B Alford 2321 Lumpkin Rd Augusta 30906 *Central* Rev J Kilian PO Box 2005 Statesboro, GA 30459 *Savannah* W Willoughby III 1802 Abercorn St Savannah GA 31401 *Southeastern* Rev T Clarkson PO Drawer 929 Darien GA 31305 *Southwestern* Rev S White 101 E Central Ave 3rd Floor Valdosta GA 31601

Stand Comm—Cler: Pres D Ronn A Crumpton T Clarkson RK Kelly; *Lay:* B Kitterman M Stevenson S Jennings C Wooten

PARISHES, MISSIONS, AND CLERGY

Albany St Patricks Episcopal Church **P** (237) 4800 Old Dawson Rd 31721 (Mail to: 4800 Old Dawson Rd 31721-9151) Kedron Nicholson Nicholas Roosevelt (229) 432-7964

Albany St Pauls Episcopal Church **P** (512) 212 Jefferson St 31701-2523 (Mail to: 212 Jefferson St 31701-4892) Reed Freeman Dudley Lippitt Hermon Lowery (229) 436-0196

Albany St John and St Marks Epis Church **P** (104) 2425 Cherry Laurel Ln 31705-4507 (Mail to: 2425 Cherry Laurel Ln 31705-4507) Ridenour Lamb Jonathan Tuttle (229) 436-5268

Americus Calvary Episcopal Church **P** (235) 408 Lee St 31709-3918 (Mail to: 408 S Lee St 31709-3918) Dianne Hall Johnny Lane (229) 924-3908

Augusta Christ Church **P** (62) 1904 Greene St 30904-3906 (Mail to: PO Box 2965 30914-2965) Lucius Johnson (706) 736-5165

Augusta Church of Our Savior **P** (275) 4227 Columbia Rd 30907-1466 (Mail to: 4227 Columbia Rd 30907-1466) Alvin Crumpton Saundra Turner (706) 863-1718

Augusta St Albans Episcopal Church **P** (161) 2321 Lumpkin Rd 30906-3014 (Mail to: 2321 Lumpkin Rd 30906-3014) Billy Alford Rosalyn Panton (706) 798-1482

Augusta St Augustine Canterbury Episcopal Ch **P** (315) 3321 Wheeler Rd 30909-3104 (Mail to: 3321 Wheeler Rd 30909-3199) Amy Bradley Elizabeth Forbes James Said John Warner (706) 738-6676

Augusta St Marys Church **M** (55) 1114 12th St 30901-2706 (Mail to: PO Box 2303 30903-2303) James Menger (706) 722-6061

Augusta St Pauls Church **P** (774) 605 Reynolds St 30901-1431 (Mail to: 605 Reynolds St 30901-1431) William Dolen John Jenkins George Muir (706) 724-2485

Augusta Church of the Good Shepherd **P** (1702) 2230 Walton Way 30904-4302 (Mail to: 2230 Walton Way 30904-4302) Robert Fain Lisa Barrowclough Talmadge Bowden Lucius Johnson James Menger Lynn Prather (706) 738-3386

Bainbridge St Johns Episcopal Church **P** (91) 516 E Broughton St 39817-4040 (Mail to: 516 E Broughton St 39817-4040) (229) 246-3554

Baxley St Thomas Aquinas Church **M** (16) 5686 Golden Isle W 31513-7937 (Mail to: PO Box 1283 31515-1283) Phillip Runge (912) 705-0287

Blakely Holy Trinity Episcopal Church **M** (8) PO Box 186 39823-0186 (Mail to: PO Box 186 39823-0186) (229) 723-3971

Brunswick Good Shepherd Church **M** (26) 1601 Macon Ave 31520-6653 (Mail to: 1601 Macon Ave 31520-6653) (912) 265-2663

Brunswick St Athanasius Episcopal Church **P** (171) C/O Mr Charles L Scott PO Box 977 31521-0977 (Mail to: C/O Mr Charles L Scott PO Box 977 31521) (912) 342-8461

Brunswick St Marks Church **P** (468) 900 Gloucester Street 31520 (Mail to: PO Box 1155 31521-1155) Alan Akridge Gary Jackson Edward Williams (912) 265-0600

Cochran Trinity Episcopal Church **M** (82) Corner of 5th & Cherry St 31014 (Mail to: PO Box 294 31014-0294) Joy Fisher George Porter Eschol Wiggins (478) 934-2771

Cordele Christ Episcopal Church **M** (90) 408 S 1st St 31015-1573 (Mail to: PO Box 264 31010-0264) Edna Drazdowski William Stewart (229) 273-2439

Darien St Andrews Episcopal Church **P** (215) PO Box D929 31305-0930 (Mail to: PO Box D929 31305-0930) Ted Clarkson (912) 437-4562

Darien St Cyprian Episcopal Church **M** (67) C/O Drawer Box 929 Fort King George Dr 31305 (Mail to: C/O Drawer Box 929 31305) Ted Clarkson (912) 437-4562

Dawson Church of the Holy Spirit **M** (15) 1170 Georgia Ave SE 39842-2112 (Mail to: Attn Ann O Duskin 398 7th Ave NE 39842-1504) (229) 995-4729

Douglas Saint Andrew's Episcopal Church **P** (23) 204 Coffee Ave S 31533-0006 (Mail to: 204 COFFEE AVE S 31533-0006) Donald Holland (912) 384-1712

Dublin Christ Church **P** (88) PO Box 417 31040-0417 (Mail to: PO Box 417 31040-0417) (478) 272-3003

Fitzgerald St Matthews Episcopal Church **M** (24) 212 W Pine St 31750-5800 (Mail to: 212 W Pine St PO Box 1153 31750-5800) Frank Christian Frank Christian (229) 423-5268

Harlem Trinity Episcopal Church **M** (18) 345 Louisville St 30814-5356 (Mail to: PO Box 275 30814-0275) Kenneth Rowland Raymond Whiting (706) 556-6282

Hawkinsville St Lukes Episcopal Church **P** (136) Dooley At Broad Sts 31036 (Mail to: PO Box 273 31036-0273) Aaron Brewer (478) 892-9373

Hephzibah Church of the Atonement **M** (87) 2616 Tobacco Rd 30815-7015 (Mail to: PO Box 5785 30916-5785) Lawrence Jesion (706) 796-3545

Hinesville St Philips Episcopal Church **P** (153) 302 E General Stewart Way 31313-2640 (Mail to: 302 E General Stewart Way 31313-2640) Denise Ronn (912) 876-2744

Jekyll Island St Richards of Chichester Episcopal Mission **M** (27) PO Box 13007 31527-0007 (Mail to: PO Box 13007 31527-0007) Jesse Yarborough (912) 230-6341

Jesup St Pauls Episcopal Church **M** (279) PO Box 1291 31598-1291 (Mail to: PO Box 1291 31598-1291) Deborah Shaffer (912) 427-3900

Kingsland King of Peace **P** (221) 6230 Laurel Island Pkwy 31548-6056 (Mail to: 6230 Laurel Island Pkwy 31548-6056) Doris Johnson Alvin Crumpton (912) 510-8958

Louisville Epis Church of St Mary Magdalene **M** (30) 321 W 7th St 30434-1307 (Mail to: PO Box 562 30434-0562) Terri Degenhardt (478) 685-7019

Martinez Holy Comforter Church **M** (408) 473 Furys Ferry Rd 30907-8221 (Mail to: 473 Furys Ferry Rd 30907-8221) Lynn Prather Cynthia Taylor (706) 210-1133

Moultrie St Margaret of Scotland Church **M** (40) 1499 S Main St 31768-5811 (Mail to: PO Box 925 112 1st Ave NE 31776-0925) (229) 616-1116

Pooler St Patricks Church **M** (76) PO Box 576 31322-0576 (Mail to: PO Box 576 31322-0576) David Lemburg (912) 748-6016

Quitman St James Episcopal Church **M** (54) 306 Court St 31643-2036 (Mail to: PO Box 864 31643-0864) James Elliott James Elliott Ned Simmons (229) 263-5053

Richmond Hill St Elizabeths Episcopal Church **P** (239) 16491 Ga Highway 144 31324-5367 (Mail to: 16491 Ga Highway 144 31324-5367) Charles Hubbard (912) 727-2650

Rincon St Lukes Episcopal Church **M** (116) 155 Goshen Rd 31326-5546 (Mail to: 155 Goshen Rd 31326-5546) (912) 826-3332

Saint Marys Christ Episcopal Church **P** (127) 305 Wheeler St 31558-8431 (Mail to: 305 Wheeler St 31558-8431) Dedra Bell-Wolski (912) 882-5308

Sandersville Grace Episcopal Church **M** (31) 114 2nd Ave W PO Box 771 31082 (Mail to: PO Box 771 31082-0771) Carlton Shuford Carlton Shuford (478) 552-5295

Savannah Christ Church Episcopal **P** (398) 28 Bull Street 31401 (Mail to: 18 Abercorn St 31401-2712) Michael White Patricia Davis Samantha McKean Helen White Helen White (912) 236-2500

Savannah St Bartholomews Church **HC** C/O Dio Of Georgia 611 E Bay St 31401-1238 (Mail to: C/O Dio Of Georgia 611 E Bay St 31401-1238) William Willoughby (912) 232-0274

Savannah St Francis of Islands Episcopal Ch **P** (257) 590 Walthour Rd 31410-2610 (Mail to: 590 Walthour Rd 31410-2610) Lauren Flowers (912) 897-5725

Savannah St Georges Episcopal Church **P** (256) 15 Willow Rd 31419-2627 (Mail to: PO Box 61297 31420-1297) David Lemburg (912) 925-6517

Savannah St Johns Episcopal Church **P** (1721) 1 W Macon St 31401-4307 (Mail to: 1 W Macon St 31401-4399) Gavin Dunbar Craig O'Brien (912) 232-1251

Savannah Saint Matthew's Church **P** (263) 1401 Martin L King Jr Blvd 31415-7201 (Mail to: 1401 Martin L King Jr Blvd 31415-7201) Guillermo Arboleda (912) 233-5965

Savannah St Michael & All Angels Episcopal Ch **P** (166) 3101 Waters Ave 31404-6259 (Mail to: 3101 Waters Ave 31404-6259) Roger Kelly (912) 354-7230

Savannah St Peters Episcopal Church **P** (635) 3 Westridge Rd 31411-2951 (Mail to: 3 Westridge Rd 31411-2951) William Lea William Priest Kelly Steele (912) 598-7242

Savannah St Thomas Episcopal Church **P** (380) 2 Saint Thomas Ave 31406-7533 (Mail to: 2 Saint Thomas Ave 31406-7533) William Collins Melanie Lemburg (912) 355-3110

✙ **Savannah** The Collegiate Church of St Paul the Apostle **O** (349) 1802 Abercorn St 31401-8122 (Mail to: 1802 Abercorn St 31401-8122) William Willoughby Charles Todd Robert Bagwell James Carter Michael Chaney Susan Gahagan George Salley (912) 232-0274

St Simons Is Christ Church Frederica **P** (897) 6329 Frederica Rd 31522-5812 (Mail to: 6329 Frederica Rd 31522-5812) Thomas Purdy Katherine Knoll Lenon Rebecca Rowell Jan Saltzgaber James Wethern Ashton Williston (912) 638-8683

St Simons Is Church of the Holy Nativity **M** (61) 615 Mallory St 31522-4018 (Mail to: 615 Mallery St 31522-4018) Thomas Townsend (912) 638-3733

Statesboro Trinity Episcopal Church **P** (149) 4401 Country Club Rd 30458-9188 (Mail to: PO Box 2005 30459-2005) Joan Marie Kilian (912) 489-4208

Swainsboro Church of the Good Shepherd **M** (46) 621 W Main St 30401-3108 (Mail to: PO Box 74 30401-0074) Lucius Johnson (478) 237-7122

Thomasville All Saints Episcopal Church **P** (297) 443 S Hansell St 31792-5512 (Mail to: PO Box 2626 31799-2626) George Brown Paul Hancock (229) 228-9242

Thomasville Church of the Good Shepherd **M** (23) 515 Oak St 31792-5046 (Mail to: PO Box 3136 31799-3136) (229) 403-7515

Thomasville St Thomas Episcopal Church **P** (244) § 216 Remington Ave 31792-5521 (Mail to: 216 Remington Ave 31792-5521) Judith Keith Dwayne Varas (229) 226-5145

Thomson Holy Cross Episcopal Church **M** (13) 515 Fluker St 30824-3018 (Mail to: PO Box 211 30824-0211) Erwin Veale Raymond Whiting (706) 595-4342

Tifton St Annes Episcopal Church **P** (493) 2411 Central Ave 31794-2855 (Mail to: C/O Emily Guerry PO Box 889 31793-0889) Thomas Lacy (229) 386-5989

Tybee Island All Saints Episcopal Church **M** (100) 804 Jones Ave 31328-8735 (Mail to: PO Box 727 31328-0727) Edna Adkins (912) 786-5845

Valdosta Christ Episcopal Church **P** (538) 1521 Patterson St 31602-3848 (Mail to: 1521 Patterson St 31602-3848) David Johnson (229) 242-5115

Valdosta Christ the King Episcopal Church **P** (380) 101 E Central Ave Fl 3 31601-5500 (Mail to: 101 E Central Ave Fl 3 31601-5500) Stanley White (229) 247-6859

Valdosta Saint Barnabas Episcopal Church **M** (82) 3565 Bemiss Rd 31605-6074 (Mail to: 3565 Bemiss RD 31605-6074) Stephen Norris (229) 242-5332

Vidalia Church of the Annunciation **P** (134) 1512 Meadows Ln 30474-4425 (Mail to: PO Box 1311 30475-1311) Denise Vaughn (912) 537-3776

Waycross Grace Episcopal Church **P** (152) 401 Pendleton St 31501-3645 (Mail to: 401 Pendleton St 31501-3645) Katherine Brinson (912) 283-8582

Waynesboro St Michaels Episcopal Church **P** (127) 515 S Liberty St 30830-1508 (Mail to: PO Box 50 30830-0050) Erwin Veale (706) 554-3465

Woodbine St Marks Episcopal Church **M** (19) PO Box 626 31569-0626 (Mail to: PO Box 626 31569-0626) (912) 576-5005

St Jean Baptiste **M** (Mail to: PO Box 1309)

Sts Innocents **M** (300) (Mail to: PO Box 46 Haiti)

St Hillaire de Poitiers **M** (Mail to: PO Box 407139 33340-7139)

St Marc **M** (Mail to: Boite Postale 1309 Haiti)

St Matthieu **M** (Mail to: PO Box 407139 33340-7139)

GERMANY

See Europe

DIOCESE OF HAITI

EGLISE EPISCOPALE D'HAITI
(PROVINCE II)
Comprises the Republic of Haiti
DIOCESAN OFFICE BP 1309 Port-au-Prince HAITI
(Mail: c/o Lynx Air PO Box 407139 Ft. Lauderdale, FL 33340)
Tel 011 (509) 257-8116   FAX 011 (509) 257-3412
E-mail epihaiti@hotmail.com; epihaiti@egliseepiscopaledhaiti.org
WEB www.egliseepiscopaledhaiti.org

Previous Bishops—
James Theodore Holly (106A) 1874-1911, Harry R Carson (327) 1923-43, Spence Burton SSJE (417) suffr 1939-42, C Alfred Voegeli (441) 1943-71, Luc Anatole Jacques Garnier (660) 1971-94

Bishop—Jean-Zaché Duracin (881) (Dio 1994)

Bishop Suffragan—Rt Rev Ogé Beauvoir (1064) (Dio 2012)

Marie-Jose Joseph; *Acct* Frantz Antilus; *Jean-Marie Jean Gilles; Dir Off of Dev* Rev Frantz Cole; *Asst Admn* Nedgie Vixamar; *Hist* Rev Jean McDonald; *Chr Ed Off* Rev M Jean; *Prep of Dio Synods* Rev Fritz Desire Marc Leon Nicole Vixamar; *Comm to Examine Chap* Rev McDonald Jean Rev Kesner Ajax Sister Marie Margaret; *COM* RP Valdema Fritz RP Mathieu Brutus Madame Nicole Vixamar M Dubic Osse RP Phanord J Berhol

Coun Advice—Cler Ven Diegue Joseph Tancrel RP Bernier Noe RP Ajax Kesner; *Lay* Soeur M Raphael SSM Neptune Joubert Joseph Emmanuel

PARISHES, MISSIONS, AND CLERGY

Anse-A-Galets St Francois D'Assise **M** (100) Bas Bureau # 20 (Mail to: PO Box 1309)
Arcahaie Christ-Roi (Leger) **M** (100) Leger (Mail to: Leger)
Arcahaie St Jean L'Evangeliste **P** Jean Dumas (Mail to: Jean Dumas)
Arcahaie St Thomas Episcopal Church **M** (200) 131 Jersusalem (Mail to: 464 Jerusalem)
Bainet Ascension **M** #13, Rue St Faustin (Mail to: St Faustin)
Bainet St Cyprien **M** Labiche (Mail to: Labiche)
Bainet St Luc **SC** La Bresilienne (Mail to: La Bresilienne)
Bainet St Matthieu **SC** Begin-Laurent
Cange Bon Sauveur **M** (400) Plateau Central Rte#3

Cap-Haitien Notre Dame, Molas **PS** (200) Molas (Mail to: PO Box 38)
Cap-Haitien Paroisse St-Esprit **M** (700) 12 et 13A 1309 (Mail to: Rues 12-13A 1309)
Carrefour Ascension **M** Thor 67 (Mail to: PO Box 1309)
Carrefour Sainte Croix **M** (100) Taifer (Mail to: PO Box 1309)
Cayes St Jn Baptiste **M** Savanette
Cayes St Sauveur **M** 96 Rue Simon Bolivar et Prospere Faines (Mail to: PO Box 70)
Cayes Ste Croix **M** Ravine-a-L'Anse
Cazale St Andre **M** (700) Route Port Salut
Ganthier St Sacrement **SC** 1 Cite Rurale (Mail to: 1 Cite rurale Fonds parisien)
Ganthier Transfiguration **SC** Gorman (Mail to: 1 Cite rurale Fonds Parisien)
Gde Colline St Barthelemy **M** Nan Mangot (Mail to: PO Box 1309)
Gonaives La Resurrection **M** (200) 135 Stenio Vincent
Gonaives St Barnabas **M** (200) Treille (Mail to: Treille)
Gonaives St Mathieu **SC** Bayonnais (Mail to: Bayonnais)
Gonaives (Gros-Morne) Bon Samaritain **M** L 'Acul Beaudois (Mail to: L Acul)
Grand Goave St Matthias **M** (400) Cherident - Grande Colline (Mail to: PB 1309)
Hinche St Andre **M** (500) 6 Toussaint Louverture (Mail to: Toussaint Louverture)
Il de La Tortue St Aidan **SC** Montry (Mail to: La Tortue)
Jacmel Mission St Joseph Embouchure **SC** Embouchure (Mail to: Boite Postal # 1309)
La Gonave Saint Jacques **M** No address given (Mail to: No Address given)
La Gonave Sainte Croix **M** (300) Nouvelle Cite Anse-a-Galets (Mail to: PO Box 1309)
La Gonave St Innocents **M** Anse-a-Galets (Mail to: PO Box 1309)
La Gonave (Bois Brule) St Jacques **P** Bois Brule Anse-A-Galets (Mail to: PO Box 1309)

Lascahobas Ascension **M** (200) Pouly (Mail to: Pouly)

Lascahobas St Andre **M** (200) Flande (Mail to: Flande)

Lascahobas St Esprit **M** (200) Stenio Vincent # 1 (Mail to: Stenio Vincent# 1)

Leogane Bonne Nouvelle **M** (300) Bigonet (Mail to: PO Box 1309)

Leogane Epiphanie **M** (200) Nationale #2, Km 42 1309 (Mail to: 86 RUE RIGAUD 1309) (509) 872-1906

Leogane Mission Saint Pierre **M** Gros Morne (Mail to: Boite Postale 1309)

Leogane Mission St Andre **M** (200) Citronnier Mithon (Mail to: Boite Postale 1309)

Leogane Mission St Luc **M** (100) L'Azile Citronier (Mail to: Boite Postale 1309)

Leogane Mission St Michel **M** (300) Petit, Orangers (Mail to: Boite Postale 1309)

Leogane Mission St Timothee **M** (300) Chateau Gaillard (Mail to: Boite Postale 1309)

Leogane Paroisse Annonciation **M** (400) Darbonne (Mail to: Boite Postale 1309)

Leogane Sainte Croix **M** (400) 1 Rue La Croix (Mail to: PO Box 1309)

Leogane St Barthelemy **M** (100) Campan (Mail to: Campan)

Leogane St Etienne **M** (400) Route de L'Amitte (Mail to: PO Box 1309)

Leogane St Jean Baptiste **M** (200) Ave. Mathieu (Mail to: JeanJean)

Leogane St Jean L'Evangeliste **M** (400) Durendisse (Mail to: PO Box 1309)

Leogane St Joseph D'Arimathee **SC** Jasmin Morne a Chandelle (Mail to: PO Box 1309)

Leogane St Matthieu **M** (500) Avenue St Mathieu (Mail to: Matthieu)

Leogane St Nicolas **M** Rue Nicolas (Mail to: PO Box 1309)

Leogane Ste Marguerite **M** (200) Latournelle (Mail to: Latournelle)

Maniche St Augustin **M** (200) Maniche

Miragoane St Marc **M** Jeannette/Paillant (Mail to: PO Box 1309)

Mirebalais St Jacques **M** (200) Rte de Boucan Carre Les Bayes (Mail to: Les Bayes)

Mirebalais St Luc **M** (200) Pouille

Mirebalais St Matthias **M** (400) Deslandes (Mail to: Deslandes)

Mirebalais St Paul **M** (100) Gascogne (Mail to: Gascogne)

Mirebalais St Pierre Episcopal Church **M** (500) Grand Rue 68 Boulevard JJ Desaling (Mail to: PO Box 1309)

Petionvile St Jacques Le Juste **M** Angle Lamarre et Moise #2

Petit Trou de Nippes St Paul **SC** Chevalier (Mail to: PO Box 1309)

Plaine Mapou St Jean Baptiste **M** (Mail to: PO Box 1309)

Port-au-Prince Cathedrale Sainte Trinite **M** (2800) Angle des Rues Mgr Guilloux & Pavee (Mail to: PO Box 1309)

Port-au-Prince Notre Dame de L Annonciation **P** (500) 4eme Ave/Bolosse

Port-au-Prince Paroisse Epiphanie **M** (700) Place Carl Brouard (Mail to: Place Carl Brouard)

Port-au-Prince St Alban **M** (100) Crochu (Mail to: 10 Rue Stenio Vincent Croix des Bouquets)

Port-au-Prince St Marc **P** Lilavois 40 (Mail to: 10 Rue Stenio Vincent 1309)

Port-au-Prince St Martin de Tours **M** (400) 83 Route de Delmas (Mail to: PO Box 1309)

Port-au-Prince St Michel & Tous Les Anges **M** Thomazeau (Mail to: Stenio Vincent #10 Croix Des Bouquets)

Port-au-Prince St Paul **M** Rte Nationale # 1 (Mail to: Rte Nationale #1)

Port-au-Prince St Simeon **M** (200) Rue Stenio Vincent #10 (Mail to: 10 Rue Stenio Vincent Croix des Bouquets)

Rosette St Jacques **M** (200) Morne (Mail to: Morne Rosette)

Savanette Mission St Philippe & St Jacques **M** (200) Corosse (Mail to: PO Box 1309)

Thomonde St Patrick **M** (200) Locorbe (Mail to: Locorbe)

Torbeck Incarnation **M** (100) Route Platon (Le Pretre) (Mail to: Route Platon (Le Pretre))

Torbeck St Barthelemy **M** Route Ducis (Dubreuil) (Mail to: c/o St Paul, Paroisse Torbeck)

Torbeck St Hilaire **M** Route de Saint Jean (Mail to: PO Box 1309)

Torbeck St Paul **M** Rue Saint Joseph

Trouin St Marc **M** 10 Rue St Christophe (Mail to: PO Box 1309)

Trouin St Simeon et St Jude **M** Platon Balai Duny, Leogane (Mail to: PO Box 1309)

DIOCESE OF HAWAII
(PROVINCE VIII)
DIOCESAN OFFICE 229 Queen Emma Sq Honolulu HI 96813
Tel (808) 536-7776   FAX (808) 538-7194
E-mail imartikainen@episcopalhawaii.org   WEB www.episcopalhawaii.org

Previous Bishops—
Eng Bps: Thomas N Staley 1862-70, Alfred Willis 1872-1902. US Bps: Henry B Restarick 1902-20, John D La Mothe 1921-28, S Harrington Littell 1930-42, Chas P Gilson suffr 1961-67, Harry S Kennedy 1944-69, E Lani Hanchett 1967-75, Edmond L Browning 1976-85, Donald P Hart 1986-94, Richard SO Chang 1997-2007

Bishop—Rt Rev Robert L Fitzpatrick (1015)
(Dio 10 Mar 2007)

Chanc W Yoshigai; *Treas & Fin Off* P Pereira; *Conv Sec* R Hino; *Reg* R Costa; *Hist* S Ching

Stand Comm—Cler: P Lillie M Beimes D Leatherman R Woo *Lay: Pres* C Spence P Chang S DeGooyer R Smith

PARISHES, MISSIONS, AND CLERGY

Island of Hawaii

Hilo Church of the Holy Apostles **P** (184) 1407 Kapiolani St 96720 (Mail to: 1407 Kapiolani St 96720-4026) Katlin McCallister (808) 935-5545

Kamuela Saint James Episcopal Church **P** (125) 65-1237 Kawaihae Rd 96743 (Mail to: Attn Sheri Mariscal PO Box 278 96743-0278) David Stout (808) 885-4923

Kapaau St Augustines Episcopal Church **M** (153) 54-3801 Akoni Pule Hwy 96755 (Mail to: PO Box 220 96755-0220) Diana Akiyama Heather Mueller (808) 889-5390

Ocean View St Jude Episcopal Mission **M** (53) Paradise Circle Hov 96737 (Mail to: Star Rt Box 6026 96737) (808) 939-7000

Island of Kauai

Eleele Episcopal Church on West Kauai **M** (124) 322 A Mehana Rd 96705 (Mail to: PO Box 247 96705-0247) Maurice Goldsmith (808) 335-5533

Kapaa All Saints Episcopal Church **P** (140) 1065 Kuhio Hwy 96746 (Mail to: PO Box 248 96746-0248) (808) 822-4267

Kilauea Christ Memorial Church **M** (98) 2509 Kolo Street 96754 (Mail to: PO Box 293 96754-0293) Gae Chalker (808) 482-4824

Lihue Saint Michael And All Angels Church **P** (414) 4364 Hardy St 96766-1263 (Mail to: 4364 Hardy St 96766-1263) Andrew Mcmullen (808) 245-3796

Island of Maui

Kihei Trinity Church By The Sea **P** (85) 100 Kulanihakoi St 96753 (Mail to: PO Box 813 96753-0813) Bruce DeGooyer (808) 879-0161

Kula St Johns Episcopal Church **P** (299) 8992 Kula Hwy 96790-7420 (Mail to: 8992 Kula Hwy 96790-7420) Kerith Harding (808) 878-1485

Lahaina Holy Innocents' Episcopal Church **P** (83) 561 Front St 96761 (Mail to: 561 Front St 96761-1116) Amy Crowe (808) 661-4202

Wailuku Church of the Good Shepherd **P** (452) 2140 Main St 96793-1637 (Mail to: 2140 Main St 96793-1695) Linda Decker John Tomoso Craig Vance (808) 244-4656

Island of Molokai

Hoolehua Grace Episcopal Church **M** (37) 2210 Farrington Ave 96729 (Mail to: PO Box 157 96729-0157) (808) 567-6420

Island of Oahu

Aiea St Nicholas Episcopal Church **M** (61) Christ's Gathering Place 98-939 Moanalua Rd 96701-5012 (Mail to: PO Box 700501 96709-0501) (808) 753-7788

Aiea St Timothys Church **P** (197) 98-939 Moanalua Rd 96701-5012 (Mail to: 98-939 Moanalua Rd 96701-5012) Daniel Leatherman (808) 488-5747

Honolulu Church of the Epiphany **P** (187) 1041 10th Ave 96816-2210 (Mail to: 1041 10th Ave 96816-2210) Irene Tanabe (808) 734-5706

Honolulu Church Of The Holy Nativity **P** (192) § 5286 Kalanianaole Hwy 96821-1826 (Mail to: 5286 Kalanianaole Hwy 96821-1883) Christopher Bridges Kathleen Cullinane (808) 373-2131

Honolulu Good Samaritan Episcopal Church **M** (71) 1801 10th Ave 96816-2907 (Mail to: 1801 10th Ave 96816-2907) (808) 735-5944

Honolulu Parish of St Clement **P** (359) 1515 Wilder Ave 96822-4614 (Mail to: 1515 Wilder Ave 96822-4699) Heather Hill (808) 955-7745

✠ **Honolulu** Cathedral Church of St Andrew **O** (781) 229 Queen Emma Sq 96813-2334 (Mail to: 229 Queen Emma Sq 96813-2334) Malcolm Hee Robert Hino (808) 524-2822

Honolulu St Elizabeths Episcopal Church **P** (285) 720 King St 96817-4511 (Mail to: 720 King St 96817-5791) David Gierlach Imelda Padasdao (808) 845-2112

Honolulu St Luke Episcopal Church **M** (24) 45 Judd St 96817-1760 (Mail to: 45 Judd St 96817-1792) Raymond Woo (808) 533-3481

Honolulu St Mark Episcopal Parish **HC** (175) § 539 Kapahulu Ave 96815-3855 (Mail to: 539 Kapahulu Ave 96815-3855) Paul Lillie (808) 732-2333

Honolulu St Mary Episcopal Church **P** (67) § 2062 S King St 96826-2219 (Mail to: 2062 S King St 96826-2293) Gregory Johnson (808) 949-4655

Honolulu St Paul Episcopal Church **M** (640) 229 Queen Emma Sq 96813-2334 (Mail to: 229 Queen Emma Sq 96813-2334) Randolph Albano Randolph Albano Peter Wu (808) 538-3275

Honolulu St Peters Episcopal Church **P** (222) 1317 Queen Emma St 96813-2301 (Mail to: 1317 Queen Emma St 96813-2394) Jasmine Bostock (808) 533-1943

Honolulu St Albans Chapel Iolani School **M** 563 Kamoku St 96826-5245 (Mail to: Mr Glenn Ching 563 Kamoku St 96826-5245) Heather Patton-Graham David Smith (808) 943-2205

Kailua Emmanuel Episcopal Church **M** (98) 780 Keolu Dr 96734-3508 (Mail to: 780 Keolu Dr 96734-3508) (808) 262-4548

Kailua St Christophers Church **P** (237) 93 Kainalu Dr 96734-2331 (Mail to: 93 Kainalu Dr 96734-2331) Giovan King (808) 262-8176

Kaneohe Calvary Episcopal Church **PS** 45-435 Aumoku St 96744 (Mail to: 45-435 Aumoku St 96744-2037) Dustin Berg (808) 247-2733

Kaneohe St John's By-the-Sea Episcopal Church **M** (114) 47-074 Lihikai Dr 96744 (Mail to: Attn Sarah Yee 47-074 Lihikai Dr 96744-4762) Paul Lucas (808) 239-7198

Kealakekua Christ Church Episcopal **P** (148) 81-1004 Konawaena School Rd 96750-8188 (Mail to: PO Box 545 96750-0545) (808) 323-3429

Wahiawa St Stephen's Episcopal Church **P** (61) 1679 California Ave 96786-2511 (Mail to: 1679 California Ave 96786-2511) Baldo Patterson (808) 621-8662

Waianae St John the Baptist Episcopal Ch **M** (50) 87-227 St Johns Rd 96792-3259 (Mail to: 87-227 Saint Johns Rd 96792-3259) Helen Harper Marilyn Watts (808) 696-5772

Waimanalo St Matthew Episcopal Church **M** (59) 41-054 Ehukai St 96795-0070 (Mail to: PO Box 70 41-054 Ehukai 96795-0070) CS Honey Becker (808) 259-8664

DIOCESE OF HONDURAS
IGLESIA EPISCOPAL DE HONDURAS
(PROVINCE IX)
(Comprises the Republic of Honduras)
DIOCESAN OFFICE Colonia Trejo 23 Ave 21 Calle (MAIL: Apdo 586) San Pedro Sula Cortés 21105
TEL: 011 (504) 556-6155   FAX 011 (504) 556-6467
International Mail: IMC-SAP Dept 215 PO Box 523900 Miami FL 33152-3900
E-MAIL: honduras@anglicano.hn   WEB: www.avanzamedia.net/anglicano/

Previous Bishops—
Bishops in Charge: David E Richards 1968, Wm C Frey 1968-72, Albert E Swift 1973, Anselmo Carral 1973-78; Diocesan Bishops: Hugo L Pina 1978-83, Leopold Frade 1984-2000 James H Ottley int 2000-01

Bishop — Rt Rev Lloyd Emmanuel Allen (971)
(Dio 20 Oct 2001)

Cn to Ord Rev Cn A Brooks; *Oficina Pastoral* V Rev Oscar López; *Dn Atlántida e Islas de la Bahía* V Rev Rosa Angélica Gámez-Cordona; *Dn Tegucigalpa* M Consuelo Cartegena de Arevalo; *Dn Comayagua* V Rev H Madrid-Paz; *Dn Copán* V Rev JA Mejia; *Dn El Paraíso* V Rev Dagobert Chacón-Rodríguez; *Dn Omoa y Puerto Cortéz* V Rev F Midence; *Dn San Pedro Sula* V Rev O López; *Dn St Bárbara* V Rev José Luis Mendoza-Barahona-y-Rodríguez; *Treas* C Antunez; *Sec* Rev J Francisco Lone; *ECW* R de Allen; *Com Min* Rev A Brooks; *Social Min* JJ Calerón; *Comm & Pub Rel* Cn E Monzón; *Finances* Dr G

Frazier; *Global Rel* C de Brooks; *Theology Ed* V Rev Pascual Torres; *Faith* V Rev H Madrid-Paz; *Chris Ed* Lic Elizabeth P de Torres; *Exam Chap* RA Gómez-Cordona; *Stew* Rev F Midence-Valdés; *Bd Gov El Hogar Proj* Rev H Madrid; *Cursillo* LP Consuelo de Brenes; *Const and Can* V Rev P Torres; *Ecum* V Rev P Torres; *Yth* Prof W Barret; *Reg* V Madisson de Molina; *Chanc* V Rev P Torres; *Health* EM Galindo MD Jose Arnaldo Mejia

Stand Comm–Cler: Pres Maria Consuelo Cartagena de Arevalo Juan José Dîaz Jose Alejandro Chirinos; *Lay* Claudia Castro Wendy Avila Nativi Jethy Yolanda Portillo Pedro Herrera

To call Honduras from the US, dial (011) 504, then the number.

PARISHES, MISSIONS, AND CLERGY
Deanato Atlantida e Islas de la Bahia

La Ceiba Iglesia Episcopal Santisima Trinidad **M** § Avenida Morazan # 1175 28 (Mail to: Avenida Morazan # 1175 28) Ethelridge Brooks (504) 440-2772

Roatan Iglesia Episcopal San Pedro del Mar **P** Brick Bay (Mail to: Apartado Postal 193) (504) 445-3891

Tela Iglesia Episcopal Espiritu Santo **P** § Carretera a Telamar 6 (Mail to: Carretera A Telamar) (504) 448-2064

Deanato Comayagua

Pozo Azul el Rosario Santo Tomas Apostol **M** § Principal (Mail to: Apartado Postal # 30)

Siguatepeque Igl Epis San Bartolome Apostol **PS** (60) § Calle Principal la Esperanza Barrio Buena Vista (Mail to: Apartado Postal 30 21105) Hector Madrid 5047735660

Siguatepeque Iglesia Epis Santiago Apostol **M** Barrio Zaragoza 2 cuadras al este de la gasolinera uno (Mail to: Barrio Zaragoza) Hector Madrid

Siguatepeque Misión Episcopal San Matias Apostol **M** Aldea La Laguna (Mail to: La Laguna Siguatepeque) Hector Madrid

Deanato Copán

Capan, Florida Misión Brisas del Chamelecon **PS** Las Brisas (Mail to: Apartado Postal 586)

Copan Misión Episcopal San Mateo **PS** § San Jose Miramar (Mail to: San Jose Miramar)

Florida Misión Episcopal en El Encantadito **PS** El Encantadito (Mail to: El Encantadito)

La Entrada Misión Episcopal Suyapa **PS** Barrio Suyapa (Mail to: Barrio Suyapa Copan)

Nueva Arcadia Cristo Salvador **M** § Chalmeca (Mail to: Apartado Postal # 586)

Proteccion Misión Episcopal en El Zarzal **PS** El Zarzal (Mail to: El Zarzal Santa Barbara)

Proteccion Misión Episcopal en Nuevas Delicias **PS** Nuevas Delicias (Mail to: Nuevas Delicias)

Proteccion Misión Episcopal en Nuevo Porvenir **PS** Pueblo Nuevo (Mail to: Pueblo Nuevo)

Proteccion Santo Tomás Cranmer **SC** § Comunidad Los Mayas (Mail to: Apartado 856)

Deanato El Paraiso

Cabanas Misión Episcopal Cristo Rey **PS** El Barbasco (Mail to: El Barbasco)

Cabanas Misión "San Francisco de Asis" **M** San Francisco de Asis (Mail to: San Francisco de Asis)

Danli Iglesia Episcopal Cristo Rey **M** (100) § Barrio El Carmelo (Mail to: El Carmelo)

El Paraiso Misión Episcopal la Resurrección **PS** (100) Barrio San Jose (Mail to: Barrio San Jose)

Jacaleapa Misión Episcopal la Cena del Señor **PS** Barrio El Centro (Mail to: Barrio, El Centro)

Oropoli Misión Episcopal la Anunciación **PS** Melaisipio Oropoli (Mail to: La Anunciacion)

Yuscaran Iglesia Epis San Miguel Arcangel **P**

Aldea Ojo de Agua (Mail to: Oficina del Deanato de El Paraiso)

Yuscaran Iglesia Episcopal San Antonio **M** § Aldea Los Lainez (Mail to: Apdo 56 Danli Lainez)

Yuscaran Iglesia Episcopal San Jose **M** (100) § Aldea Corral Quemado (Mail to: Aldea Corral Quemado)

Yuscaran Misión Episcopal la Ascensión **PS** Aldea Agua Viva (Mail to: Aldea Agua Viva)

Yuscaran Misión Episcopal la Presentación **SC** Barrio San Juan (Mail to: Barrio San Juan)

Yuscaran Misión Episcopal la Santa Cruz **PS** Aldea Chaguite Oriente (Mail to: Aldea Chaguite Oriente)

Yuscaran Misión Episcopal la Transfiguración **PS** Aldea Las Crucitas (Mail to: Aldea Las Crucitas)

Yuscaran Misión Episcopal la Visitación **PS** Aldea del Ocotal (Mail to: El Ocotal)

Yuscaran Santa María Virgen de Las Mercedes **M** § Aldea Rancho del Obispo (Mail to: Aldea Rancho del Obispo)

Deanato Francisco Morazán

Comayaguela, MDC Iglesia Epis Cristo Redentor **P** (200) § Col. America (Mail to: Lomas Miraflores Sur Bloque "D" #4318) (504) 236-7116

Guaimaca Misión Episcopal la Transfiguración **PS** § Barrio Arriba (Mail to: Barrio Arriba)

Miravalle Misión Episcopal Emmanuel **PS** Misión Episcopal Emmanuel (Mail to: Bo Nueva Progreso)

Pueblo Viejo Misión Episcopal San Esteban **PS** § Pueblo Viejo (Mail to: Pueblo Viejo)

Santa Ana Iglesia Episcopal San Isidro **M** § El Cruce 11001 (Mail to: Iglesia Episcopal San Isidro Apdo. Postal 15023)

Soroguara Iglesia Episcopal San Isidro **M** (100) § Santa Cruz Arriba 4063 (Mail to: Col. Florencia 1era Entrada 1era calle 4063)

Talanga Misión Episcopal San Felipe **M** § Calle Agua Blanca Bo Sabanetilla (Mail to: Residencial San Miguel Agua Blanca)

Tegucigalpa Iglesia San Pedro Cerca del Rio **M** § Km 9. Carretera a Salida Talanga El Guanabano (Mail to: Km 9. Carretera a Talanga)

Tegucigalpa Iglesia Santa Maria de los Angeles **P** (200) 1era Entrada, Col. Florencia Norte 1100 (Mail to: Iglesia Episcopal Santa Maria Apartado Postal 15023 11101) (504) 232-0353

Tegucigalpa Misión en Col Villeda Morales **PS** Villeda Morales (Mail to: Villeda Morales)

Tegucigalpa Misión Episcopal "Nueva Esperanza" **PS** § Col Nueva Esperanza Amarateca (Mail to: Catedral Santa Maria de los Angeles)

Tegucigalpa Misión Episcopal Emmanuel **PS** § Las Moritas, Aldea Yaguacire Germania

Carreterra al Sur (Mail to: Germania Carreterra al Sur Las Moritas)

Tegucigalpa Misión Santa María del Valle **PS** § Alpea de Amarateca (Mail to: Alpea de Amarateca)

Tegucigalpa, A.M.D.C. Misión Episcopal San Esteban **SC** § El Mulular, Quiscamote, A.M.D.C. (Mail to: Catedral Santa Maria de los Angeles)

Tegucigalpa, A.M.D.C. Misión Episcopal San Simón **PS** El Jocomico, Nueva Aldea Santa Cruz Arriba (Mail to: Catderal Santa Maria de los Angeles)

Tegucigalpa, M.D.C Iglesia San Juan Evangelista **P** (200) Terminal de buses, Mano derecha 4063 (Mail to: Apartado Postal #4063)

Tegucigalpa, M.D.C. Iglesia Episcopal "La Anunciacion" **M** § Rincon de Dolores A.M.D.C. (Mail to: Catedral "Santa Maria de los Angeles" Aptdo. 15023)

Tegucigalpa, M.D.C. Misión Episcopal Mesías **PS** Caserio Laguna del Pedregal (Mail to: Col. Florencia Norte 1era entrada, 1era calle Boulevard Suyapa)

Tegucigalpa, M.D.C. St Mary of the Angels Episcopal Church **M** 1st St. Col. Florencia N. y Blvd. Suyapa (Mail to: 1st St. Col. Florencia N. y Blvd. Suyapa)

Villa De San Francisco Natividad Nuestro Señor Jesucristo **M** § La Natividad de Nuestra Sr. Jesucristo (Mail to: Bo Nuevo Progreso)

Deanato Maya

Agua Caliente Misión Episcopal San Antonio **PS** San Antonio (Mail to: San Antonio)

Buena Vista Misión Episcopal San Agustín **PS** Misión San Agustin (Mail to: Misión San Agustin)

Carrizalito Misión Episcopal San Juan Bautista **SC** Calle Central San Juan Bautista (Mail to: San Juan Bautista)

Cedral Misión Episcopal San José **SC** Misión San Jose La Union (Mail to: La Union, Cedral)

Copan Ruinas Misión Episcopal San Jorge **SC** § Agua Caliente (Mail to: Agua Caliente)

Copan Ruinas Misión Episcopal San Lucas **PS** Rio Amarillo (Mail to: Rio Amarillo)

Copan Ruinas Misión Episcopal Santa María Virgen **PS** § Santa María Virgen 000000 (Mail to: Santa María Virgen 000000)

Copan Ruinas Misión San Juan Evangelista **SC** Sesemil II Principal (Mail to: Sesemil Segundo)

Copan Ruinas, Copan Misión Epíscopal Santísima Trinidad **PS** § Sesesmil I (Mail to: Sesesmil I)

Corralitos Misión Episcopal San Miguel Arcángel **PS** § San Miguel Arcangel (Mail to: San Miguel Arcangel)

Dona Ana Iglesia Episcopal San Miguel **M** § Andres Bremo (Mail to: Andres Bremo) (809) 420-1867

El Cordoncillo Iglesia Episcopal San Marcos **SC** El Cordoncillo (Mail to: El Cordoncillo)

El Quebracho Misión Episcopal San Nicolas **SC** § El Quebracho (Mail to: El Quebracho)

El Tigre Misión Episcopal San Ignacio **PS** § San Ignacio (Mail to: San Ignacio)

El Zapote Misión Episcopal Santo Tomás **PS** § Santo Tomas (Mail to: Santo Tomas)

La Laguna Misión Episcopal San Felipe **SC** San Felipe La Laguna (Mail to: San Felipe La Laguna)

Naranjal Misión Episcopal la Sagrada Familia **PS** Misión Sagrada Familia (Mail to: Naranjal)

Nueva Esperanza Misión Episcopal Emmanuel **PS** § Misión Episcopal Emmanuel (Mail to: Misión Episcopal Emmanuel)

Nueva Esperanza Misión Episcopal Santa Cruz **SC** § Misión Santa Cruz (Mail to: Misión Santa Cruz)

Pinalito Misión Episcopal San Matías **PS** San Matias (Mail to: San Matias)

Porvenir II San Andres Porvonis II **PS** San Andres Porvenir II (Mail to: San Andres Porvenir II)

Rio Negro Misión Episcopal Pentecostés **PS** § Misión Pentecostes (Mail to: Misión Pentecostes)

San Pedro Sula Iglesia Episcopal Cristo Redentor **M** Vado Ancho (Mail to: Vado Ancho DCPN 06-52)

Santa Rita Misión Episcopal San Juan Apóstol **PS** § Londres (Mail to: Misión San Juan Apostol)

Santa Rita Misión Episcopal Santiago Ápóstol **PS** § La Castellana (Mail to: La Castellana)

Deanato Omoa y Puerto

Omoa Conversion de San Pablo **M** § Principal, Frente al Centro Comunal (Mail to: Principal, Frente al Centro Comunal)

Omoa Iglesia "Santa Margarita de Escocia" **M** (100) Principal Chachahuala (Mail to: Principal, Chachahuala)

Omoa Iglesia Episcopal San Fernando Rey **M** Principal, Frente al Castillo (Mail to: Bo. San Martin 12 Calle 6/7 Ave Puerto C) Antonio Carcel-Martinez 658-9062

Omoa Iglesia Episcopal San Francisco de Asis **SC** § Principal Muchilena 586 (Mail to: Apartado Postal # 35)

Omoa Iglesia Episcopal San Marcos **M** (200) § Principal (Mail to: Principal)

Omoa La Natividad de la Bendita Virgen Maria **M** § Real Asia Guatemala Centsica N-O 35 (Mail to: San Pedro Sula 35)

Omoa Nuestra Señora de Suyapa **SC** § Suyapa Frontera (Mail to: Suyapa Frontera)

Puerto Cortes Iglesia Episcopal "San Juan Bautista **M** 6 Calle 4 Ave Barrio El Centro (Mail to: Bo El Centro 6 Calle 4 Ave) Pascual Torres Fuentes (504) 665-0200

Puerto Cortes Jesús El Salvador **M** 15 Calle, 4ta Avenida, La Curva Barrio Buenos Aires (Mail to: 15 Calle, 4ta Avenida, La Curva Bo. Buenos Aires) 665-5859

Puerto Cortes Misión Nuestra Señora de Suyapa **PS** Col. Episcopal Chameleconcito (Mail to: Col. Episcopal Chameleconcito)

Puerto Cortes Nuestra Senora de los Desamparados **PS** Autopista Region el Chile (Mail to: Colonia Episcopal)

Deanato San Pedro Sula

Choloma Iglesia Episcopal Cristo Rey **M** (100) § Col. Exitos de Anach No. 2 (Mail to: Apartado # 586)

El Progreso Iglesia Episcopal "San Patricio" **M** (100) Barrio San Jose #1, 4 ave. 9 calle N.E. SPS 586 (Mail to: Barrio San Jose #1, 4 ave. 9 calle N.E. SPS 586) 5046474444

✠ **San Pedro Sula** Catedral Episcopal El Buen Pastor **O** (300) § 21 Calle, 23 Ave. "C" S.O. Colonia Trejo Colonia Trejo (Mail to: Apartado 586) John Park (504) 556-7140

San Pedro Sula Igl Epis San Jose de la Montana **M** (60) Calle Principal (Mail to: Col. Nueva Primavera)

San Pedro Sula Iglesia Episcopal "Fe y Alegria" **M** § Calle Principal, Colonia Episcopal El Ocotillo (Mail to: 23 Ave "C" 21 Calle Trejo)

San Pedro Sula Iglesia Episcopal San Andres **M** (200) § 12 Calle, 10-11 Ave, SE Barrio Cabañas (Mail to: Apartado 586) Oscar Lopez (504) 554-2292

San Pedro Sula Iglesia Episcopal San Lucas **M** (200) § Delicias del Norte (Mail to: Col. Trejo 23 Ave "C" Calle 21 Apartado 586) Oscar Lopez

San Pedro Sula Iglesia Episcopal San Pablo Apostol **M** (100) § 3 y 4 Calle, 2nd Ave Col Satelite II Etapa 586 (Mail to: Iglesia Episcopal Hondurena 586) Roberto Martinez Amengual (504) 559-3055

San Pedro Sula Misión Episcopal la Divina Gracia **PS** § Colonia Stibys (Mail to: Apartado 586)

Villanueva Iglesia Episcopal de la Epifania **M** § Barrio El Centro (Mail to: Apartado Postal No. 586) Jose Pena-Regalado 5046705203

Villanueva Santiago de Jerusalén **M** § Santa Ana de Chasnigua (Mail to: Apartado Postal No. 586)

Deanato Santa Bárbara

Atima Iglesia Episcopal "Jesus Nazareno" **M** (200) Barrio de Jesus (Mail to: Apdo. 586) (504) 556-6155

Chinda Misión Santa Maria Magdalena **SC** § El Retiro (Mail to: Apartado Postal #586)

Concepcion del Norte Iglesia Episcopal "Santa Lucia" **M** (200) Proteccion (Aldea) (Mail to: Apartado No. 586) Hector Madrid

Concepcion del Norte Iglesia Episcopal San Mateo **M** El Cerron (Aldea) (Mail to: Apartado No. 586)

Concepcion del Norte Iglesia Episcopal Santa Ana **M** § Apdo 24 Sta Barbara (Mail to: Apdo 24 Sta Barbara)

Concepcion del Norte La Visitacion de la Bendita Virgen Maria **M** Barrio Nuevo (Mail to: Apartado No. 586)

Petoa Iglesia Episcopal "La Santa Cruz" **M** Las Flores (Mail to: Apartado Postal 586)

Petoa Iglesia Episcopal San Joaquin **M** § San Joaquin (Mail to: Apartado 586)

Petoa Iglesia Episcopal San Pedro Apostol **P** Calle Real Principal (Mail to: Apartado Postal 1106)

Petoa La Resurrección **M** § Plan del Portillo (Aldea) (Mail to: Apartado No. 586)

Santa Barbara Iglesia Episcopal "Santa Barbara" **M** (100) § Calle Principal, Barrio Llano del Conejo 22101 (Mail to: Calle Principal, Barrio Llano del Conejo 22101) (504) 643-2754

Santa Barbara, Concepcion Norte Iglesia Episcopal "La Ascension" **PS** § Montanita (Mail to: Apartado 586)

Trinidad Iglesia Episcopal "La Trinidad" **P** (100) § Las Americas (Mail to: Apartado Postal 586)

Trinidad San Miguel Arcángel **M** § Real Principal (Matazanales) (Mail to: Apartado Postal # 586)

STATE OF IDAHO

Dioceses of Idaho and Spokane

DIOCESE OF IDAHO
(PROVINCE VIII)
Comprises Idaho South of the Salmon River
DIOCESAN OFFICE 1858 W Judith Ln Boise ID 83705
TEL (208) 345-4440   FAX (208) 345-9735
E-MAIL sledwich@idahodiocese.org   WEB www.episcopalidaho.org

Previous Bishops—
Daniel S Tuttle 1867-87, Ethelbert Talbot 1887-1898, James B Funsten 1899-1918, Herman Page 1919, Frank H Touret 1919-24, Herbert HH Fox 1925-26, Middleton S Barnwell 1926-35, Fredk B Bartlett 1935-41, Frank A Rhea 1942-57, Norman L Foote 1957-72, Hanford L King Jr 1972-81, David B Birney IV 1982-89, John S Thornton 1990-98, Harry B Bainbridge III 1998-2008

Bishop—Rt Rev Brian Thom (1032) (Dio 11 Oct 2008)

Canon to the Ord L Ashby; *Conv Sec* S Ledwich; *Treas* T Jones; *Chanc* B Alexander; *Dio Coord* S Ledwich; *Camp Dir* M Beck; *Com* K Brannon

Stand Comm—Cler: Pres R Demarest *Sec* M Butler J Herndon *Lay:* J Ashton K Kissell P Rowett-Matlock

PARISHES, MISSIONS, AND CLERGY

Alta St Francis of Tetons Episcopal Ch **P** (126) 20 Alta School Rd 83414-4518 (Mail to: 20 Alta School Rd 83414-4518) Debra Adams (307) 353-8100

American Fls St Johns Episcopal Church **P** (7) 328 Roosevelt St 83211-1219 (Mail to: Ms Nancy Ross 257 Polk St 83211-1421) (208) 226-2646

Arco Church of the Epiphany **M** (9) 448 Yvonne St 83213-8760 (Mail to: PO Box 672 83213-0672) (208) 220-9785

Blackfoot St Pauls Episcopal Church **P** (69) 72 Shilling Ave 83221-2846 (Mail to: 72 Shilling Ave 83221-2846) (208) 785-4474

Boise All Saints Episcopal Church **P** (347) 704 S Latah St 83705-1547 (Mail to: 704 S Latah St 83705-1547) (208) 344-2537

✢ **Boise** St Michaels Episcopal Cathedral **O** (1525) 518 8th St 83702-5515 (Mail to: 518 8th St 83702-5515) Richard Demarest James Brooks Rick Harvey Margaret Kurtz Emily Sieracki Mary Weiner (208) 342-5601

Boise St Phillips Episcopal Church **M** (7) C/O Diocese Of Idaho 510 W Washington St 83702-5953 (Mail to: C/O Diocese Of Idaho PO Box 936 83701-0936) (208) 876-4291

Boise St Stephens Episcopal Church **P** (335) 2206 Cole Rd 83704-7313 (Mail to: 2206 Cole Rd 83704-7313) David Wettstein Scott Ellsworth

Debra Greenleaf James Mahoney Jeffrey Shankles Eileen Yarbrough (208) 375-3862

Buhl Holy Trinity Episcopal Church **P** (33) 229 9th Ave 83316-1216 (Mail to: PO Box 26 83316-0026) Marilyn Butler (208) 543-8496

Caldwell St Davids Episcopal Church **P** (73) Arlington Ave & East Pine 83605 (Mail to: 1800 Arlington Ave 83605-5254) Wallace Lonergan (208) 459-9261

Emmett St Mary's Episcopal Church **P** (108) 219 E 1st St 83617-2903 (Mail to: PO Box 215 83617-0215) Gretchen Downer Gretchen Downer (208) 365-2309

Fort Hall Church of the Good Shepherd **P** (72) PO Box 608 83203 (Mail to: PO Box 608 83203-0608) Daniel Buchin Daniel Buchin (208) 223-7053

Glenns Ferry Grace Episcopal Church **P** (15) 102 E Cleveland Ave 83623-2400 (Mail to: PO Box 786 83623-0786) (208) 366-7425

Gooding Trinity Episcopal Church **P** (25) 125 7th Ave W 83330-1227 (Mail to: 125 7th Ave W 83330-1227) (208) 934-4779

Hailey Emmanuel Episcopal Church **P** (141) 101 S 2nd Ave 83333-8604 (Mail to: C/O Nancy Gurney PO Box 576 83333-0576) Lea Colvill (208) 788-3547

Idaho Falls St Lukes Episcopal Church **P** (351) 270 Placer Ave 83402-4021 (Mail to: 270 Placer Ave 83402-4021) (208) 522-8465

Jerome Calvary Episcopal Church **P** (18) 201 S Adams St 83338-2600 (Mail to: 201 S Adams St 83338-2600) Richard Goetsch Barbara Ward (208) 324-8480

Mccall St Andrews Episcopal Church **P** (74) Forest And Gamble 83638 (Mail to: PO Box 1045 83638-1045) (208) 634-2796

Meridian Church of the Holy Nativity **P** (134) 1021 W 8th St 83642-2003 (Mail to: 828 W Cherry Ln 83642-1619) Paula Egbert (208) 888-4342

Mountain Home St James Episcopal Church **P** (70) 315 3rd E 83647-2736 (Mail to: PO Box 761 83647-0761) Paul Walsh (208) 587-3516

Nampa Grace Episcopal Church **P** (135) 911 4th St S 83651-4104 (Mail to: 411 10th Ave S 83651-4137) Karen Hunter (208) 466-0782

Payette St James Episcopal Church **P** (30) 110 10th St 83661-2625 (Mail to: PO Box 203 83661-0203) Deborah Graham (208) 642-4222

Placerville Emmanuel Epis Church Placerville **P** (12) 123 S Main St 83666-4065 (Mail to: 301 Granite St 83666-4022) (208) 392-9701

Pocatello Trinity Episcopal Church **P** (159) 248 Arthur Ave 83204-3104 (Mail to: PO Box 1214 83204-1214) Diane Paulson Donald Paulson Donald Paulson (208) 233-2640

Rupert St Matthews Episcopal Church **P** (59) 6th & I St 83350 (Mail to: PO Box 324 83350-0324) Randy Fagg Tammy Jones Barbara Ward (208) 436-4904

Salmon Church of the Redeemer **P** (101) 204 Courthouse Dr 83467-3943 (Mail to: 204 Courthouse Dr 83467-3943) Joseph Marek Robert Perry (208) 756-3720

Shoshone Christ Episcopal Church **P** (23) 106 W B St 83352-5365 (Mail to: Attn Kenneth Crothers PO Box 548 83352-0548) Kenneth Crothers (208) 886-2617

Sun Valley St Thomas Episcopal Church **P** (489) 201 Sun Valley Rd 83353 (Mail to: PO Box 1070 83353-1070) Kenneth Brannon (208) 726-5349

Twin Falls Church of the Ascension **P** (305) 371 Eastland Dr 83301-4417 (Mail to: 371 Eastland Dr 83301-4417) Lauren Schoeck Robert Schoeck (208) 733-1248

Weiser St Lukes Episcopal Church **P** (46) 106 E Liberty St 83672-2259 (Mail to: 101 E Liberty St 83672-2258) Deborah Graham (208) 549-1552

STATE OF ILLINOIS
Dioceses of Chicago (C) and Springfield (Sp)

Albion—Sp	Edwardsville—Sp	Lake Forest—C	Pekin—Sp
Alton—Sp	El Paso—C	Lake Villa—C	Peoria—C
Antioch—C	Elgin—C	LaSalle—C	Pontiac—C
Arlington Hts—C	Elk Grove Village—C	Lewistown—C	Preemption—C
Aurora—C	Elkhart—Sp	Libertyville—C	Princeton—C
Barrington—C	Elmhurst—C	Lincoln—Sp	Prospect Heights—C
Batavia—C	Evanston—C	Lockport—C	Quincy—C
Belleville—Sp	Flossmoor—C	Lombard—C	Rantoul—Sp
Belvidere—C	Freeport—C	Loves Pk—C	River Forest—C
Benson—C	Galena—C	Macomb—C	Riverside—C
Berwyn—C	Galesburg—C	Marion—Sp	Robinson—Sp
Bloomingdale—C	Genesco—C	Mattoon—Sp	Rockford—C
Bloomington—Sp	Geneva—C	McHenry—C	Rock Island—C
Blue Is—C	Glen Carbon—Sp	Moline—C	St Charles—C
Bolingbrook—C	Glen Ellyn—C	Momence—C	Salem—Sp
Cairo—Sp	Glencoe—C	Monmouth—C	Savanna—C
Canton—C	Glenview—C	Morris—C	Silvis—C
Carbondale—Sp	Granite City—Sp	Morrison—C	Springfield—Sp
Carlinville—Sp	Grayslake—C	Morton—Sp	St Charles—C
Centralia—Sp	Griggsville—C	Mt Carmel—Sp	Sterling—C
Champaign—Sp	Gurnee—C	Mt Vernon—Sp	Streator—C
Chesterfield—Sp	Hanover Pk—C	Naperville—C	Sycamore—C
Chicago—C	Harrisburg—Sp	New Lenox—C	Warsaw—C
Chillicothe—C	Harvey—C	Normal—Sp	Wauconda—C
Clarendon Hills—C	Havana—Sp	Northbrook—C	Waukegan—C
Crystal Lake—C	Henry—C	Northfield—C	W Frankfort—Sp
Danville—Sp	Highland Pk—C	Oak Pk—C	Western Springs—C
Decatur—Sp	Hinsdale—C	O'Fallon—Sp & C	Wheaton—C
Deerfield—C	Jacksonville—Sp	Oregon—C	Wilmette—C
DeKalb—C	Joliet—C	Ottawa—C	Winnetka—C
Des Plaines—C	Kankakee—C	Palatine—C	Woodstock—C
Dixon—C	Kenilworth—C	Palos Pk—C	
Downers Grove—C	Kewanee—C	Pk Forest—C	
Dundee—C	La Grange—C	Pk Ridge—C	

STATE OF INDIANA

Dioceses of Indianapolis and Northern Indiana

DIOCESE OF INDIANAPOLIS

(PROVINCE V)
Comprises central and southern Indiana
DIOCESAN OFFICE 1100 W 42nd St Indianapolis IN 46208
TEL (317) 926-5454
TOLL FREE (800) 669-5786   FAX (317) 926-5456.
E-MAIL brinkworth@indydio.org   WEB www.indydio.org

Previous Bishops—
Jackson Kemper (MO and IN) 1835-49, Geo Upfold 1849-72, Jos C Talbot coadj 1865 Bp 1872-83, David B Knickerbocker 1883-94, John H White 1895-99, Jos M Francis 1899-1939, Richard A Kirchhoffer coadj 1939 Bp 1939-59, John P Craine coadj 1957 Bp 1959-77, Edward W Jones coadj 1977 Bp 1977-97, Catherine M Waynick coadj 1997 Bp 1997-2017

Bishop — Rt Rev Jennifer Baskerville-Burrows (1100) (Dio 29 April 2017)

Cn to Ord for Admin & Evan Cn B O'Sullivan-Hale; *Cn to Ord for Cong Dev & Ldrshp* Rev Cn K White; *Treas* L Cornell 402 S Rogers St Bloomington IN 47403; *Chanc* G Plews 1346 N Delaware Indianapolis IN 46202; *Sec* S Sullivan; *Coord Yth Min* V Hoppes; *Resource Dev Officer* J Gedrick; *Hist* L Little; *Bps Exec Sec* J Brinkworth; *Admin Sec* K Christopher

Stand Comm—Cler: K Sullivan H Cooke W Smith; *Lay:* G Eastman P Wills S Hardgrove

PARISHES, MISSIONS, AND CLERGY

Anderson Trinity Episcopal Church **P** (161) 1030 Delaware St 46016 (Mail to: 1030 Delaware St 46016) William Smalley (765) 644-2566

Beanblossom St Davids Episcopal Church **P** (86) 11 State Road 45 46160 (Mail to: PO Box 1798 47448-1798) (812) 988-1038

Bedford St Johns Episcopal Church **P** (111) 1219 14th St 47421-3228 (Mail to: 1219 14th St 47421-3228) (812) 275-6620

Bloomington Episcopal Campus Ministry at IU **CM** (18) 719 E 7th St 47408 (Mail to: PO Box 127 47402-0127) (812) 361-7971

Bloomington Trinity Episcopal Church **P** (365) 111 S. Grant Street 47408 (Mail to: Dio Of Indianapolis-Kim Smith 111 S. Grant Street 47408) Charles Dupree Henrietta Grossoehme Connie Peppler (812) 336-4466

Brownsburg Good Samaritan Episcopal Church **M** 725 S Green St 46112-1612 (Mail to: 1100 W 42nd St 46208-3346) Patrick Burke (317) 926-5454

Cannelton St Lukes Episcopal Church **P** (16) 101 S 3rd St 47520-1504 (Mail to: PO Box 7 47520-0007) (812) 988-1038

Carmel St Christophers Episcopal Church **P** (1178) 1402 W Main St 46032-1442 (Mail to: C/O Cindy Short 1402 W Main St 46032-1442) Stephen Applegate Susan McBeath (317) 846-8716

Columbus Saint Paul's Church **P** (170) 2651 California St 47201-3650 (Mail to: 2651 California St 47201-3650) Marcus Vance (812) 372-7869

Crawfordsvlle St Johns Episcopal Church **P** (139) 212 S Green St 47933-2508 (Mail to: PO Box 445 47933-0445) Janet Oller (765) 362-2331

Danville St Augustine Episcopal Church **P** (287) 600 Washington St 46122-1246 (Mail to: PO BOX 141 46122) William Barfield (317) 745-2741

Elwood St Stephens Episcopal Church **P** (13) 11706 State Road 37 46036-8318 (Mail to: PO Box 291 46036-0291) (765) 552-5356

Evansville St Pauls Episcopal Church **P** (237) 301 Se 1st St 47713-1003 (Mail to: 311 SE 1st St 47713-1003) (812) 422-9009

Fishers Holy Family Episcopal Church **M** (90) 11445 Fishers Point Blvd 46038-2997 (Mail to: 11445 Fishers Point Blvd 46038-2997) Bruce Gray (317) 842-4133

Franklin St Thomas Episcopal Church **P** (94) 600 Paul Hand Blvd 46131 (Mail to: C/o Diocese Of Indianapolis 1100 West 42nd Street 46208) Whitney Rice (317) 535-8985

Greencastle St Andrews Episcopal Church **P** (108) 520 E Seminary St 46135-1745 (Mail to: 520 E Seminary St 46135-1745) John Rumple (765) 653-3921

Indianapolis All Saints Episcopal Church **P** (140) 1559 Central Ave 46202-2606 (Mail to: 1559 Central Ave 46202-2698) Tanya Beck Daniel Billman Elizabeth Wille (317) 635-2538

✣ **Indianapolis** Christ Church Cathedral **O** (735) 125 Monument Cir 46204-2921 (Mail to: 125 Monument Cir 46204-2921) Stephen Carlsen Jean Beniste William Curtis Lauren Grubaugh Lauren Grubaugh Fatima Yakubu-Madus (317) 636-4577

Indianapolis Church of the Nativity **P** (303) 7300 Lantern Rd 46256-2118 (Mail to: 7300 Lantern Rd 46256-2118) Susan Smith Catherine Wilson (317) 915-1020

Indianapolis St Albans Episcopal Church **P** (58) 4601 Emerson Ave 46226-2218 (Mail to: 4601 Emerson Ave 46226-2218) Walter Sherman Debra Dehler Michael Scime Jean Smith (317) 546-8037

Indianapolis St Johns Episcopal Church **P** (147) 5625 W 30th St 46224-3013 (Mail to: 5625 W 30th St 46224-3095) Shannon Macvean-Brown (317) 293-0372

Indianapolis Saint Matthew's Church **P** (140) 8320 E 10th St 46219-5331 (Mail to: 8320 E 10th St 46219-5399) Frank Impicciche (317) 898-7807

Indianapolis St Paul's Episcopal Church **HC** (924) 6050 Meridian St 46208-1549 (Mail to: 6050 Meridian St 462081549) John Denson Jeffrey Bower Barbara Kempf (317) 253-1277

Indianapolis St Philips Episcopal Church **P** (71) 720 Dr Martin L King Jr St 46202-3116 (Mail to: 720 Dr Martin L King Jr St 46202-3116) Michelle Roos Jean Smith Karen Sullivan (317) 636-1133

Indianapolis St Timothys Episcopal Church **P** (164) 2601 East Thompson Road 46227-4496 (Mail to: 2601 E Thompson Rd 46227-4496) Rebecca Nickel (317) 784-6925

Indianapolis Trinity Episcopal Church **P** (809) 3243 Meridian St 46208-4645 (Mail to: 3243 Meridian St 46208-4645) Benjamin Anthony Karen King Julia Whitworth (317) 926-1346

Jeffersonvlle St Pauls Episcopal Church **P** (95) 321 E Market St 47130-3309 (Mail to: 321 E Market St 47130-3309) Nancy Woodworth-Hill (812) 282-1108

Lafayette St Johns Episcopal Church **P** (365) 600 Ferry St 47901-1142 (Mail to: 600 Ferry St 47901-1142) Bradley Pace Hilary Cooke Robert L'Homme (765) 742-4079

Lawrenceburg Trinity Episcopal Church **P** (53) 101 W. Center St. 47025-1942 (Mail to: PO Box 3883 Center And Lake Streets 47025-3883) Mary Taflinger (812) 537-2619

Lebanon St Peters Episcopal Church **M** (138) 950 E Washington St 46052-1901 (Mail to: 950 E Washington St 46052-1901) Christopher Beasley Mary Coufal (765) 482-2322

Madison Christ Episcopal Church **P** (200) 506 Mulberry St 47250-3440 (Mail to: C/O Linda Wenning 506 Mulberry St 47250-3440) Evelyn Wheeler (812) 265-2158

Martinsville St Marys Episcopal Church **M** (31) 1109 E Morgan St 46151-1746 (Mail to: 1109 E Morgan St 46151-1746) Mark Van Wassenhove (765) 342-1682

Mount Vernon St Johns Episcopal Church **P** (80) 602 Mulberry Street 47620 (Mail to: PO Box 503 47620-0503) Allen Rutherford (812) 838-5445

Muncie Grace Episcopal Church **P** (128) 300 S Madison St 47305-2464 (Mail to: PO Box 1732 47308-1732) John Conners (765) 289-7931

New Albany St Pauls Episcopal Church **P** (216) 1015 E Main St 47150-5842 (Mail to: 1015 E Main St 47150-5842) Richard Kautz Gordon Anderson (812) 944-0413

New Castle St James Episcopal Church **P** (46) 2020 Bundy Ave 47362-2920 (Mail to: 2020 Bundy Ave 47362-2920) (765) 529-5309

New Harmony St Stephens Episcopal Church **P** (40) 318 Main St 47631 (Mail to: PO Box 173 47631-0173) Elizabeth Macke (812) 682-4604

Noblesville St Michaels Episcopal Church **P** (201) 444 S Harbour Dr 46062-9107 (Mail to: 444 S Harbour Dr 46062-9109) Lee Schaefer (317) 773-6157

Plainfield St Marks Episcopal Church **P** (150) 710 E Buchanan St 46168-1514 (Mail to: 710 E Buchanan St 46168-1514) Kirsteen Wilkinson (317) 839-6730

Richmond St Pauls Episcopal Church **P** (74) 800 A St 47374-3120 (Mail to: 800 A St 47374-3120) (765) 962-6988

Rockport Peace Episcopal Church **M** 223 Cnty. Rd. 350 W. 47635 (Mail to: PO Box 127 47635-0127) (812) 6495500

Shelbyville St Lukes Church **P** (33) 1201 Riley Hwy 46176-9432 (Mail to: 1201 Riley Hwy 46176-9432) (317) 392-1379

Terre Haute St Stephens Episcopal Church **P** (149) 215 7th St 47807-3103 (Mail to: 215 7th St 47807-3193) Andrew Downs (812) 232-5165

Vincennes St James Episcopal Church **HC** (33) 610 Perry St 47591-2130 (Mail to: 610 Perry St 47591-2130) Dennis Latta Mary Becker (812) 882-9640

W Lafayette Church of the Good Shepherd **CM** (125) 610 Meridian St 47906-2656 (Mail to: 610 Meridian St 47906-2656) (765) 743-1347

Washington St Johns Episcopal Church **P** (38) 509 E Walnut St 47501-2766 (Mail to: 805 W Main St 47501-2514) Dennis Latta (812) 726-5333

West Terre Haute Saint George Episcopal Church **M** (60) 1337 Smith Pl 47885-9644 (Mail to: Att: Rick Baldomero 2382 W Highland Ave 47885-9254) (812) 242-4893

Zionsville St Francis in the Fields Epis Church **P** (424) 1525 Mulberry St 46077-1146 (Mail to: 1525 Mulberry St 46077-1146) C Reed Whitney Rice (317) 873-4377

DIOCESE OF IOWA
(PROVINCE VI)
Comprises the State of Iowa
DIOCESAN OFFICE 225 37th St Des Moines IA 50312-4305
TEL (515) 277-6165   FAX (515) 277-0273
E-MAIL diocese@iowaepiscopal.org   WEB http://www.dioiowa.org

Previous Bishops—
Henry W Lee 1854-74, Wm S Perry
1876-98, Theodore N Morrison
1899-1929, Harry S Longley suffr
1912 coadj 1917 Bp 1929-44, Elwood
L Haines 1944-49, Gordon V Smith
1950-71, Walter C Righter 1972-88
C Christopher Epting 1988-2001

Bishop—Rt Rev Alan Scarfe (983) (Dio 5 Apr 2003)

Sec/Conv KS Milligan; *Fin Ofc* A Wagner; *Exec Asst to Bp* J Allaway; *Chanc* W Graham; *Hist* T Colber D Kaiser 1717 Manor Dr Grinnell, IA 50112; *Treas* B Smith; *Ecum Off* J McCarthy; *ER&D* H Scherff; *Prison Min* Rev A Moats Williams; *UTO* R Graves; *Yth* A Mellies; *Young Adult Miss* vacant; *Op Mgr* J Doherty; *Dio Asst* E Adams; *Altar Guild* M Hippee K Trotter; *Trans Off* vacant; *Comm* M Wagner; *Min Dev* E Bruckner

Stand Comm—Cler: E Popplewell E Caldbeck A Moats Williams; *Lay:* A Chang-Matus G Jones K Brooke

PARISHES, MISSIONS, AND CLERGY

Albia Grace Episcopal Church **M** (8) 205 S. Second St. 52531 (Mail to: C/O Mrs Jack Carlson 311 S D St 52531-2325) (641) 932-2560

Algona Church of St Thomas **M** (62) 213 E Call St 50511-2453 (Mail to: PO Box 611 50511-0611) (515) 295-2113

Ames Iowa State University Chaplaincy **CC** 2338 Lincoln Way 50014-7113 (Mail to: 2338 Lincoln Way 50014) (515) 292-6655

Ames St Johns by the Campus **P** 2338 Lincoln Way 50014-7113 (Mail to: 2338 Lincoln Way 50014-7113) Kim Baker (515) 292-6655

Anamosa St Marks Episcopal Church **M** (19) 107 W 1st St 52205-1831 (Mail to: 201 S Garnavillo St 52205-1939) (319) 462-2933

Ankeny St Annes by the Fields **P** (143) 2110 W 1st St 50023-2487 (Mail to: 2110 W 1st St 50023-2487) Vincent Bete Kathleen Tripses (515) 964-5152

Bettendorf St Peters Episcopal Church **P** (287) 2400 Middle Rd 52722-3250 (Mail to: 2400 Middle Rd 52722-3250) Elaine Caldbeck (563) 355-4640

Boone Grace Episcopal Church **M** (40) 707 8th St 50036-2727 (Mail to: 707 8th St 50036-2727) (515) 432-7586

Burlington Christ Episcopal Church **P** (74) 623 Fifth St 52601 (Mail to: 623 5th St 52601-5029) Carl Mann (319) 752-1381

Carroll Trinity Episcopal Church **M** (13) 127 W 9th St 51401-2305 (Mail to: 1700 Pike Ave 51401-1627) Diana Wright (712) 792-2836

Cedar Falls St Luke's Episcopal Church **P** (199) 2410 Melrose Dr 50613-5234 (Mail to: 2410 Melrose Dr 50613-5234) Elizabeth Popplewell Liane Nichols Ruth Ratliff (319) 277-8520

Cedar Rapids Christ Episcopal Church **P** (588) 220 40th St Ne 52402-5616 (Mail to: 220 40th St NE 52402-5616) Hal Hayek Mark Eccles Randall Lyle Melody Rockwell (319) 363-2029

Cedar Rapids Grace Episcopal Church **P** (108) 525 A Ave Ne 52401-1015 (Mail to: 525 A Ave NE 52401-1015) (319) 362-1929

Chariton St Andrews Episcopal Church **M** (16) 1112 7th St 50049-1208 (Mail to: PO Box 838 50049-0838) Frederick Steinbach (641) 774-4911

Charles City Grace Episcopal Church **M** (13) 902 5th Ave 50616-3006 (Mail to: 902 5th Ave 50616-3006) (641) 228-4519

Clermont Church of the Saviour **M** (13) 610 - 702 Mill St 52135 (Mail to: PO Box 301 52135-0301) (563) 423-5508

Clinton Christ Episcopal Church **P** (85) 2100 2nd St 52732-2418 (Mail to: 2100 2nd St PO Box 3052 52732-2418) Jan Horn (563) 242-5740

Coralville New Song Episcopal Church **P** (132) 912 20th Ave 52241-1404 (Mail to: 912 20th Ave 52241-1404) Jennifer Masada (319) 351-3577

Council Blfs St Pauls Episcopal Church **P** (96) 22 Dillman Dr 51503-1641 (Mail to: 22 Dillman Dr 51503-1692) (712) 323-7188

Davenport St Albans Episcopal Church **P** (167) 3510 W Central Park Ave 52804-2753 (Mail to: 3510 W Central Park Ave 52804-2753) Charles Bencken (563) 386-4087

✠ **Davenport** Trinity Cathedral **O** (579) 121 W 12th St 52803-5227 (Mail to: Office Of The Treasurer 121 W 12th St 52803-5227) John Horn Sinclair Ender (563) 323-9989

Decorah Grace Episcopal Church **M** (38) 506 W Broadway St 52101-1704 (Mail to: PO Box 4 52101-0004) (563) 382-4246

Denison Trinity Church **M** (5) 12 S 16th St 51442-2011 (Mail to: c/o Carol Block 801 1st Ave S 51442-2603) (712) 263-9500

Des Moines All Angels Episcopal Church **M** (15) 225 37th Street 50312 (Mail to: 907 5th St 51566-1916) (515) 277-6165

Des Moines St Andrews Episcopal Church **P** (140) 5720 Urbandale Ave 50310-1250 (Mail to: 5720 Urbandale Ave 50310-1295) Steven Godfrey (515) 255-2101

Des Moines St Lukes Episcopal Church **P** (401) 3424 Forest Ave 50311-2615 (Mail to: 3424 Forest Ave 50311-2615) Martha Kester (515) 277-0875

Des Moines St Marks Episcopal Church **P** (138) 3120 E 24th St 50317-3609 (Mail to: 3120 E 24th St 50317-3609) Sheryl Hughes-Empke Kathleen Travis (515) 266-1304

✠ **Des Moines** Cathedral Church of St Paul **O** (669) 815 High St 50309-2714 (Mail to: 815 High St 50309-2733) Troy Beecham John Doherty (515) 288-7297

Dubuque St Johns Episcopal Church **P** (215) 1410 Main St 52001-4740 (Mail to: 1458 Locust St 52001-4714) Kent Anderson Diane Eddy Kevin Goodrich (563) 556-0252

Durant St Pauls Episcopal Church **P** (45) 206 6th St 52747-9742 (Mail to: PO Box 865 52747-0865) Alice Haugen (563) 785-6228

Emmetsburg Trinity Church **M** (24) 2219 Main St 50536-2446 (Mail to: PO Box 332 50536-0332) (712) 852-3809

Fort Dodge St Marks Episcopal Church **P** (71) 1007 1st Ave S 50501-4801 (Mail to: 1007 1st Ave S 50501-4801) (515) 576-2019

Fort Madison St Lukes Episcopal Church **P** (62) 605 Avenue E 52627-4805 (Mail to: 605 Avenue E 52627-4805) Lyle Brown Lyle Brown (319) 372-6409

Glenwood St Johns Episcopal Church **M** (10) 111 Vine St 51534-1516 (Mail to: PO Box 109 51534-0109) (712) 527-2971

Grinnell St Pauls Episcopal Church **P** (78) 1026 State St 50112 (Mail to: 1026 State St 50112) Wendy Abrahamson Kevin Emge Sallie Verrette (515) 236-6254

Harlan St Pauls Episcopal Church **M** (23) 712 Farnam St 51537-1637 (Mail to: PO Box 526 51537-0526) (712) 755-2793

Independence St James Episcopal Church **M** (22) 202 2nd Ave Ne 50644-1905 (Mail to: 202 2nd Ave PO Box 264 50644-0264) Sean Burke Sue Ann Raymond (319) 334-4297

Indianola All Saints Episcopal Church **M** (24) 501 Jefferson Way Ste 300 50125-1762 (Mail to: 501 Jefferson Way Ste 300 50125-1762) Benjamin Webb (319) 2906306

Iowa City Trinity Episcopal Church **P** (509) 320 E College St 52240-1628 (Mail to: 320 E College St 52240-1628) Judith Crossett Lori Erickson Marcus Haack Thomas Hulme Elizabeth Koffron-Eisen Lauren Lyon William Moorhead Catherine Quehl-Engel (319) 337-3333

Iowa City University of Iowa Chaplaincy **CC** 26 E Market St 52245-1742 (Mail to: 26 E Market St 52245-1742) Jan Horn (319) 337-3333

Iowa Falls St Matthews-by-the-Bridge **M** (21) 507 Railroad St 50126-2240 (Mail to: PO Box 206 50126-0206) (641) 648-6779

Keokuk St Johns Episcopal Church **P** (102) 208 4th St 52632-5602 (Mail to: 208 4th St 52632-5602) (319) 524-4672

Le Mars St Georges Episcopal Church **M** (7) 400 1st Ave Se 51031-2045 (Mail to: 401 1st Ave SE 51031-2044) (712) 546-4604

Maquoketa St Marks Episcopal Church **M** (29) 208 W Maple St 52060-2929 (Mail to: 208 W Maple Street 52060-2929) (563) 652-4970

Marshalltown St Pauls Episcopal Church **P** (77) 201 E Church St 50158-2944 (Mail to: 201 E Church St 50158-2944) Kay Beach (641) 753-6317

Mason City St Johns Episcopal Church **P** (158) 120 1st St Ne 50401-3302 (Mail to: 120 1st St NE 50401-3302) Stephen Benitz (641) 424-1300

Mt Pleasant St Michaels Episcopal Church **P** (37) 202 E Washington St 52641-1933 (Mail to: PO Box 624 52641-0624) (319) 385-2633

Muscatine Trinity Episcopal Church **P** (130) 211 Walnut St 52761-4130 (Mail to: 211 Walnut St 52761-4130) Martha Lang Kathleen Milligan (563) 263-2177

Newton St Stephens Episcopal Church **P** (216) 223 E 4th St 50208-3214 (Mail to: 223 E 4th St 50208-3214) Karen Crawford Merle Smith (641) 792-6971

Orange City Church of the Savior **M** (50) 415 Third St NW 51041-1313 (Mail to: 530 Arizona Ave SW 51041-1935) Karen Wacome (712) 737-3930

Oskaloosa St James Episcopal Church **P** (67) 207 S 3rd St 52577-3137 (Mail to: PO Box 545 52577-0545) Terence Kleven (641) 673-4218

Ottumwa Trinity Episcopal Church **M** (45) 204 E 5th St 52501-2626 (Mail to: 204 E 5th St 52501-2626) (641) 682-5624

Perry St Martins Episcopal Church **P** (57) & 10th Iowa Sts 50220 (Mail to: PO Box 486 50220-0486) (515) 465-3468

Shenandoah St Johns Episcopal Church **M** (43) 1371 230th St 51601-4566 (Mail to: C/O Diann Anderson, Treas 1371 230th St 51601-4566) Holly Scherff (712) 246-4790

Sioux City Calvary Episcopal Church **M** (32) 1308 S Cleveland St 51106-1942 (Mail to: 1308 S Cleveland St 51106-1942) (712) 276-3561

Sioux City St Pauls Indian Mission **M** (569) 524 Center St 51103-3648 (Mail to: PO Box 895 51102-0895) (712) 255-5162

Sioux City St Thomas Episcopal Church **P** (197) 406 12th St 51105-1305 (Mail to: 406 12th St 51105-1305) (712) 258-0141

Spirit Lake St Alban's Episcopal Church **P** (97) 2011 23rd & Zenith 51360 (Mail to: PO Box 85 51360-0085) Thomas Early Elizabeth Preston (712) 336-1117

Storm Lake All Saints Episcopal Church **P** (34) 121 W Marina Rd 50588-7473 (Mail to: 121 W Marina Rd 50588-7473) Stacey Gerhart (712) 732-1314

W Des Moines St Timothys Episcopal Church **P** (502) 1020 24th St 50266-2107 (Mail to: 1020 24th St 50266-2107) Mary Cole-Duvall Jean Smith (515) 225-2020

Waterloo Trinity Episcopal Parish **P** (133) 4535 Kimball Ave 50701-9087 (Mail to: 4535 Kimball Ave 50701-9087) Cathi Bencken Stephanie Moncrieff (319) 232-4714

Waverly St Andrews Episcopal Church **M** (38) 717 W Bremer Ave 50677-2926 (Mail to: PO Box 176 50677-0176) (319) 352-1489

Webster City Church of the Good Shepherd **M** (37) 1100 Mary Ln 50595-2746 (Mail to: PO Box 108 50595-0108) (515) 576-2019

ITALY

See Europe

STATE OF KANSAS

Dioceses of Kansas and Western Kansas

DIOCESE OF KANSAS

(PROVINCE VII)
Comprises eastern Kansas
DIOCESAN OFFICE 835 SW Polk Topeka KS 66612-1688
TEL (785) 235-9255   FAX (785) 235-2449
E-MAIL gbartling@episcopal-ks.org   WEB www.episcopal-ks.org

Previous Bishops—
Thomas H Vail 1864-89, Elisha S Thomas coadj 1887 Bp 1889-95, Frank R Millspaugh 1895-1916, James Wise coadj 1916 Bp 1916-39, Goodrich R Fenner coadj 1937 Bp 1939-59, Edward C Turner coadj 1956 Bp 1959-81, Richard F Grein 1981-88, William E Smalley Bp 1989-2003 Dean E Wolfe coadj 2003 Bp 2004-2017

Bishop—Cathleen Bascom (2019-)

Cn to Ord & Deploy Off T Lightcap; *Bp Assist* J Atha; *Comp* J Currie; *Yth and Int Campus Miss* K Schlabach; *Sec Conv* K Clowers; *Comm* M Woerman;; *Chanc* LF Taylor Box 550 Olathe 66051; *VChanc* M Francis 434 SW Topeka Blvd Topeka KS 66603; *V Chanc* K Harper 833 N Waco Wichita KS 67203; *Treas* B Geary 12061 S Troost St Olathe KS 66061; *Hist* M Woerman

Stand Comm—Cler: S Billman S Drury L Lewis R Matney F Mays A O'Connor C Rohleder *Lay:* T Allison E Doll J Dutra T Flynn S Howard S Mann M Winkler

PARISHES, MISSIONS, AND CLERGY

Abilene St Johns Episcopal Church **P** (85) 519 Buckeye Ave 67410-2531 (Mail to: PO Box 461 67410-0461) Jerry Rankin (785) 263-3592

Arkansas City Trinity Episcopal Church **P** (86) 224 A St 67005-2204 (Mail to: PO Box 544 67005-0544) Laurie Lewis (620) 442-1720

Atchison Trinity Episcopal Church **P** (88) 300 S 5th St 66002-2809 (Mail to: 300 S 5th St 66002-2809) Jon Hullinger (913) 367-3171

Blue Rapids St Marks Church **P** (68) 601 Lincoln St 66411-1545 (Mail to: C/O Joe Warders 400 E 4th St 66411-1545) Arthur Rathbun (785) 363-7542

Chanute Grace Episcopal Church **P** (92) 209 S Lincoln Ave 66720-2463 (Mail to: 209 S Lincoln Ave 66720-2463) Joyce Holmes (620) 431-1210

Clay Center St Pauls Episcopal Church **P** (88) 1010 6th St 67432-2506 (Mail to: PO Box 625 67432-0625) Margaret Dagg (785) 632-3200

Coffeyville St Paul's Episcopal Church **P** (96) 613 Elm St 67337-4935 (Mail to: 613 Elm St 67337-4935) (620) 251-4890

Derby St Andrews Episcopal Church **P** (146) 1062 E Chet Smith Ave 67037-2354 (Mail to: PO Box 8 67037-0008) Michael Loyd (316)

788-2595

Edwardsville St Martin in the Fields Church **P** (87) 1501 Edwardsville Dr 66111-1127 (Mail to: PO Box 13012 66113-0012) (913) 422-5879

El Dorado Trinity Episcopal Church **P** (245) 400 W Ash Ave 67042-2803 (Mail to: PO Box 507 67042-0507) Christine Gilson (316) 321-6606

Emporia St Andrew's Episcopal Church **P** (135) 828 Commercial St 66801-2915 (Mail to: 828 Commercial St 66801-2915) Marc McDonald (620) 342-1537

Galena St Marys Episcopal Church **P** (29) 415 S Washington St 66739-1733 (Mail to: 415 S Washington St 66739-1733) Gary Kennedy (620) 783-5075

Holton Church of St Thomas **P** (8) 512 Wisconsin Ave 66436-1645 (Mail to: 512 Wisconsin Ave 66436) (785) 979-8411

Independence Church of the Epiphany **P** (130) 400 E Maple St 67301-3822 (Mail to: PO Box 655 67301-0655) Gerald Eytcheson (620) 331-4794

Iola St Timothys Episcopal Church **P** (33) 202 S Walnut St 66749-3245 (Mail to: 202 S Walnut St 66749-3245) David Kent (620) 365-7306

Junction City Church of the Covenant **P** (194) 314 Adams St 66441-3071 (Mail to: PO Box 366 66441-0366) (785) 238-2897

Kansas City St Pauls Episcopal Church **P** (154) 1300 18th St 66102-2733 (Mail to: 1300 18th St 66102-2798) Dixie Junk Gail Reynolds (913) 321-3535

Lawrence St Margarets Episcopal Church **P** (368) 5700 W 6th St 66049-4829 (Mail to: 5700 W 6th St 66049-4829) (785) 865-5777

Lawrence Trinity Episcopal Church **P** (551) 1011 Vermont St 660442921 (Mail to: 1027 Vermont Stt 660442921) Robert Baldwin (785) 843-6166

Leavenworth St Pauls Episcopal Church **P** (394) 209 7th St 66048-1930 (Mail to: PO Box 233 66048-0233) Machrina Blasdell (913) 682-1033

Manhattan St Pauls Episcopal Church **P** (227) 601 Poyntz Ave 66502-6006 (Mail to: 601 Poyntz Ave 66502-6006) Gregory Doll Aidan Funston Robert Pearce (785) 776-9427

Marysville St Pauls Episcopal Church **P** (20) 306 17th St 66508-1405 (Mail to: 1103 Elm St 66508-1935) (785) 562-5182

Mission St Michael and All Angels Church **P** (2427) 6630 Nall Ave 66202-4325 (Mail to: 6630 Nall Ave 66202-4399) Brenton Carey Samuel Cox Monte Giddings James Robertson Donald Williams (913) 236-8600

Neodesha Church of the Ascension **P** (41) 702 Osage St 66757-1466 (Mail to: 702 Osage St 66757-1466) Gerald Eytcheson (620) 331-4794

Newton St Matthews Episcopal Church **P** (141) 2001 Windsor Dr 67114-1250 (Mail to: PO Box 342 67114-0342) Jimmy Jackson (316) 283-3310

Olathe St Aidans Episcopal Church **P** (169) 14301 S Blackbob Rd 66062-2537 (Mail to: 14301 S Blackbob Rd 66062-2537) Robert Streepy (913) 764-3050

Ottawa Grace Episcopal Church **P** (31) PO Box 601 66067-0601 (Mail to: 315 W 5th St 66067-2842) (785) 242-5390

Overland Park Church of St Thomas the Apostle **P** (715) 12251 Antioch Rd 66213-1517 (Mail to: 12251 Antioch Rd 66213-1517) Gar Demo Kelly Demo Kevin Schmidt (913) 451-0512

Parsons St Johns Episcopal Church **P** (104) 1801 Corning 67357-4265 (Mail to: PO Box 753 67357-0753) Sharon Billman (620) 421-3775

Pittsburg St Peters Episcopal Church **P** (113) 306 W Euclid St 66762-5106 (Mail to: 306 W Euclid St 66762-5106) William Jenkins (620) 231-3790

Sedan Church of the Epiphany **P** (43) 309 W Elm St 67361-1216 (Mail to: PO Box 367 67361-0367) Foster Mays (620) 725-3701

Shawnee St Lukes Episcopal Church **P** (212) 5325 Nieman Rd 66203-1939 (Mail to: 5325 Nieman Rd 66203-1939) Charles Everson Mary Siegmund (913) 631-8597

Stilwell St Francis of Assisi Epis Church **P** (39) 17890 Metcalf Ave 66085-9326 (Mail to: PO Box 118 66085-0118) Doreen Rice (913) 897-2588

✠ **Topeka** Grace Cathedral **O** (747) 701 Sw 8th Ave 66603-3219 (Mail to: 701 SW 8th Ave 66603-3219) Donald Chubb Nicolette Papanek (785) 235-3457

Topeka St Davids Episcopal Church **P** (486) 3916 Sw 17th St 66604-2438 (Mail to: 3916 SW 17th St 66604-2497) Vicki Smith (785) 272-5144

Wamego St Lukes Episcopal Church **P** (99) 700 Lincoln St 66547-1638 (Mail to: PO Box 109 66547-0109) Catherine Rohleder (785) 456-9310

Wellington St Judes Episcopal Church **P** (22) 1323 Jefferson Ave 67152-4356 (Mail to: PO Box 222 67152-0222) Catherine Shield (620) 326-6406

Wichita Good Shepherd Episcopal Church **P** (408) 8021 W 21st St 67205-1743 (Mail to: 8021 W 21st St 67205-1743) Andrew O'Connor Robert Hirst Michael Loyd (316) 721-8096

Wichita St Bartholomews Episcopal Church **P** (32) 2799 S Meridian Ave 67217-1461 (Mail to: 2799 S Meridian Ave 67217-1461) Walter Miescher (316) 941-4744

Wichita Saint James Church **P** (939) 3750 E Douglas Ave 67208-3708 (Mail to: C/O Bookkeeper 3750 E Douglas Ave 67208-3784) Dawn Frankfurt Carthur Criss Sarah Stewart (316) 683-5686

Wichita St Johns Episcopal Church **P** (332) 402 Topeka St 67202-2414 (Mail to: 402 Topeka St 67202-2414) Edward Curtis Elizabeth Montes (316) 262-0897

Wichita St Stephens Episcopal Church **P** (173) 7404 Killarney Pl 67206-1627 (Mail to: 7404 E Killarney Pl 67206-1699) Barbara Gibson Mary Korte (316) 634-2513

Winfield Grace Episcopal Church **P** (173) 715 Millington St 67156-2838 (Mail to: PO Box 490 67156-0490) Laurie Lewis (620) 221-4252

Yates Center Calvary Episcopal Church **P** (36) 200 S Grove St 66783 (Mail to: PO Box 214 66783-0214) (620) 625-2358

STATE OF KENTUCKY
Dioceses of Kentucky and Lexington

DIOCESE OF KENTUCKY
(PROVINCE IV)
Comprises western Kentucky
DIOCESAN OFFICE 425 S 2nd St Ste 200 Louisville KY 40202
TEL (502) 584-7148   FAX (502) 587-8123
WEB www.episcopalky.org

Previous Bishops—
Benj B Smith 1832-84, Geo D Cummins asst 1866-74, Thomas U Dudley coadj 1875 Bp 1884-1904, Chas E Woodcock 1905-35, Chas Clingman 1936-54, CG Marmion 1954-74, DB Reed coadj 1972 Bp 1974-94, Edwin F Gulick Jr Bp 1994-2010

Bishop—Terry Allen White (1051) (Dio 25 Sept 2010)

Cn to Ord Rev AR Coultas *Chanc* W Robinson Beard 400 W Market St Ste 1800 Louisville; *Sec of Dio* KS Wilkinson; *Treas* D Brooks; *Bp's Staff: All Saints Epis Center Compt* B Meyer; *Comm* Brian Kinnaman; *Yth* K Badgett; *Transition* M Linder; *Ecum* Rev A Coultas; *Ch Form* Rev K Doyle; *Fin & Stew* D Brooks 4010 Fox Meadow Way Prospect KY 40059; *Evang & Cong Dev* B Blodgett 57 Ironwood Dr Murray KY 42071; *COM* Rev P Connell 720 Ford Ave Owensboro 42301; *Cn for Cong Vitality* Rev J Lewis

Stand Comm—Cler: Pres A Vouga J Trimble E Markham; *Lay:* C Stone J Donahue

PARISHES, MISSIONS, AND CLERGY

Bardstown Episcopal Church of the Ascension **P** (109) 211 3rd St 40004-1527 (Mail to: 211 3rd St 40004-1527) (502) 348-4317

Bowling Green Christ Episcopal Church **P** (636) 1215 State St 42101-2650 (Mail to: 1215 State St 42101-2650) Rebecca Kello Steven Pankey (270) 843-6563

Brandenburg Holy Trinity Church **M** (95) 319 Oaklawn Dr 40108-1033 (Mail to: PO Box 645 40108-0645) Roger Walker (270) 422-3721

Campbellsvlle St Thomas Church **M** (59) 116 S Columbia Ave 42718-1339 (Mail to: 116 S Columbia Ave 42718-1339) (270) 789-1601

Elizabethtown Christ Episcopal Church **P** (140) 206 W Poplar St 42701-1537 (Mail to: PO Box 1054 42702-1054) (270) 765-5606

Fulton Trinity Church **M** (58) 1104 Vine Street 42041-1758 (Mail to: 1100 Vine Street 40065) (270) 472-1870

Gilbertsville St Peters of the Lakes Epis Church **M** (56) 47 Black River Rd 42044-9053 (Mail to: PO Box 183 42044-0183) Meghan Holland (270) 362-8301

Harrods Creek St Francis in the Fields Epis Church **P** (1606) 6710 Wolf Pen Branch Rd 40027 (Mail to: PO Box 225 40027-0225) Simon Barnes Walter Langley (502) 228-1176

Henderson St Pauls Episcopal Church **P** (191) 5 S Green St 42420-3536 (Mail to: 5 S Green St 42420-3536) Richard Martindale (270) 826-2937

Hickman St Paul Episcopal Church **M** (6) 611 Church St 42050 (Mail to: 511 E Moulton St 42050) Barbara Burgess Ellen Ekevag (270) 236-3619

Hopkinsville Grace Episcopal Church **P** (173) 216 E 6th St 42240-3433 (Mail to: 216 E 6th St 42240-3433) Alice Nichols (270) 885-8757

Louisville Calvary Church **P** (438) 821 S 4th St 40203-2115 (Mail to: 821 S 4th St 40203-2191) (502) 587-6011

✠ **Louisville** Christ Church Cathedral **O** (248) 421 S 2nd St 40202-1417 (Mail to: 421 S 2nd St 40202-1475) Amy Coultas Joan Pritcher (502) 587-1354

Louisville Church of Our Merciful Saviour **P** (48) 473 S 11th St 40203-1875 (Mail to: 473 S 11th St 40203-1875) Harold Price (502) 587-6129

Louisville Church of the Advent **P** (186) 901 Baxter Ave 40204-2046 (Mail to: 901 Baxter Ave 40204-2046) Timothy Mitchell John Fritschner John Fritschner Drusilla Kemp (502) 451-6066

Louisville Messiah Trinity Episcopal Church **P** 8701 Shepherdsville Rd 40219-5037 (Mail to: 8701 Shepherdsville Rd 40219-5037) John Allen (502) 969-1422

Louisville Resurrection Episcopal Church **P** (149) 4100 Southern Pkwy 40214-1648 (Mail to: 4100 Southern Pkwy 40214-1648) Eva Markham (502) 368-1146

Louisville St Albans Episcopal Church **P** (49) 9004 Beulah Church Rd P. O. Box 91152 40291-2789 (Mail to: PO Box 91152 40291-0152) (502) 239-3444

Louisville St Andrews Episcopal Church **P** (350) 2233 Woodbourne Ave 40205-2105 (Mail to: 2233 Woodbourne Ave 40205-2195) William Parker Anne Vouga (502) 452-9581

Louisville St Clement Episcopal Church **M** (30) 4112 Wimpole Rd 40218-2369 (Mail to: 609 W Main St 40202-2951) (502) 491-6085

Louisville St George Episcopal Church **M** (44) PO Box 3652 40201-3652 (Mail to: PO Box 3652 40201-3652) (502) 776-2030

Louisville St Lukes Chapel **NH** (21) C/O Joy Moll 1201 Lyndon Ln 40222-4319 (Mail to: c/o Chris Ward 7504 Westport Rd 40222-4108) John Allen Mary Cherry Mary Cherry Lisa Tolliver (502) 736-7800

Louisville St Lukes Episcopal Church **P** (250) 1206 Maple Ln 40223-2406 (Mail to: PO Box 23336 40223-0336) Michael Delk Arthur Chard (502) 245-8827

Louisville St Marks Episcopal Church **P** (396) 2822 Frankfort Ave 40206-2640 (Mail to: 2822

Frankfort Ave 40206-2692) Candyce Loescher (502) 895-2429

Louisville St Matthew Episcopal Church **P** (1014) 330 Hubbards Ln 40207-2253 (Mail to: 330 Hubbards Ln Frnt 40207-2394) Jerry Cappel Benjamin Hart Helen Jones Kelly Kirby Harvey Roberts (502) 895-3485

Louisville St Pauls Episcopal Church **P** (232) 4700 Lowe Rd 40220-1532 (Mail to: 4700 Lowe Rd 40220-1532) Andrew Shirota (502) 491-7417

Louisville St Peter Episcopal Church **P** (161) 8110 Saint Andrews Church Rd 40258-3832 (Mail to: 8110 Saint Andrews Church Rd 40258-3832) John Hines (502) 937-3613

Louisville St Thomas Episcopal Church **P** (173) § 9616 Westport Rd 40241-2224 (Mail to: 9616 Westport Rd 40241-2224) Ann Doyle (502) 425-3727

Madisonville St Marys Episcopal Church **P** (209) 163 Main St 42431-1952 (Mail to: 163 Main St PO Box 768 42431-1952) (270) 821-3674

Murray Saint John's Church **P** (111) 1620 Main St 42071-2275 (Mail to: 1620 Main St 42071-2275) Rosemarie Bogal-Allbritten Matthew Bradley (270) 753-6908

Owensboro Trinity Church Episcopal **P** (400) 720 Ford Ave 42301-4632 (Mail to: 720 Ford Ave 42301-4632) David Carletta (270) 684-5326

Paducah Grace Episcopal Church **P** (485) 820 Broadway St 42001-6808 (Mail to: 820 Broadway St 42001-6887) Richard Paxton Charles Uhlik (270) 443-1363

Pewee Valley St James Episcopal Church **P** (304) § 401 Lagrange Rd 40056 (Mail to: PO Box 433 40056-0433) Heather Back (502) 241-8136

Russellville Trinity Episcopal Church **M** (47) PO Box 162 42276-0162 (Mail to: PO Box 162 42276-0162) Geoffrey Butcher (270) 726-3481

Shelbyville St James Episcopal Church **P** (124) 230 Main St 40065-1024 (Mail to: PO Box 166 40066-0166) (502) 633-2718

DIOCESE OF LEXINGTON
(PROVINCE IV)
Comprises eastern Kentucky
DIOCESAN OFFICE 203 E Fourth St
(MAIL: Box 610 Lexington KY 40588-0610) Lexington KY 40508-1515
TEL (859) 252-6527   FAX (859) 231-9077
E-MAIL diocese@diolex.org   WEB www.diolex.org

Previous Bishops—
Lewis W Burton 1896- 1928, Henry PA Abbott 1929-45, Wm R Moody 1945-71, Addison Hosea coadj 1970 Bp 1971-85, Don A Wimberly coadj 1984 Bp 1985-99, Rogers S Harris asst 1999-2000, Stacy F Sauls Bp 2000-2011, Chilton R Knudsen asst

2011-2012, W Douglas Hahn Bp 2012-17, Bruce Caldwell Bp prov (2016-18)

Bishop Provisional—Mark Van Koevering (2018-)

Dn of Lex C Wade; *Dio Admin* Ven B Kibler; *Chanc* MT Yeiser; *Cn to Ord* E Johnston; *Fin* R Lawton; *Treas* K Harper; *Hist* M Brinkman; *Admin Asst* M Yankey; *Depts and Comms: Yth* C Sigmon

Stand Comm—Cler: Pres P Ott A Meaux K Thomas: *Lay:* J Brantley C Jones L McMurry

PARISHES, MISSIONS, AND CLERGY

Ashland Calvary Episcopal Church **P** (310) 1337 Winchester Ave 41101-7553 (Mail to: PO Box 109 41105-0109) Antoinette Azar (606) 325-2328

Beattyville St Thomas Episcopal Church **M** (29) 1 Madison St 41311 (Mail to: PO Box 626 41311-0626) (606) 464-9714

Corbin St Johns Episcopal Church **P** (33) 701 Engineer St 40701-1037 (Mail to: 701 Engineer St 40701-1037) (606) 528-1659

Covington Trinity Episcopal Church **P** (348) 16 E 4th St 41011-1510 (Mail to: 16 E 4th St 41011-1510) Peter D'Angio Justin Gabbard Joseph O'Brochta (859) 431-1786

Cynthiana Advent Church **P** (51) 122 Walnut St 41031-1224 (Mail to: PO Box 308 41031-0308) (859) 234-4163

Danville Trinity Episcopal Church **P** (210) 320 W Main St 40422-1814 (Mail to: 320 W Main St 40422-1814) Amy Meaux (859) 236-3374

Flemingsburg Chapel of St Francis of Flemingsburg **M** (35) 444 Fountain Ave 41041-1032 (Mail to: 444 Fountain Ave 41041-1032) Mary Kilbourn-Huey (606) 845-4001

Florence Grace Episcopal Church **HC** (111) 7111 Price Pike 41042-1665 (Mail to: PO Box 6590 41022-6590) (859) 371-5951

Fort Thomas St Andrews Episcopal Church **P** (604) 3 Chalfonte Pl 41075-1927 (Mail to: PO Box 75027 41075-0027) John Pennington Jeffrey Queen (859) 441-1092

Frankfort Episcopal Church of the Ascension **P** (285) 311 Washington St 40601-1823 (Mail to: 311 Washington St 40601-1823) William Neat (502) 223-0557

Georgetown Church Of The Holy Trinity **P** (160) 209 S Broadway St PO Box 1433 40324-6433 (Mail to: PO Box 1433 40324-1340) Karen Booth (502) 863-0505

Harlan Christ Episcopal Church **P** (57) 119 E Central St 40831-2348 (Mail to: PO Box 858 40831-0858) (606) 573-4210

Harrodsburg St Philips Episcopal Church **HC** (109) 118 W Poplar St 40330-1641 (Mail to: 118 W Poplar St 40330-1641) Peter Doddema (859) 734-3569

Hazard St Marks Episcopal Church **M** (31) 317 Walnut St 41701-1853 (Mail to: 317 Walnut St 41701-1853) (606) 273-7826

Irvine St Timothys Church **M** (7) 170 St. Timothy's Rd. 40336 (Mail to: PO Box 656 40336-0656) Bryant Kibler (606) 726-0607

⚓ **Lexington** Christ Church Cathedral **O** (1116) 166 Market St 40507-1139 (Mail to: 166 Market St 40507-1173) Brent Owens Carol Wade (859) 254-4497

Lexington Church Of The Good Shepherd **P** (753) § 533 E Main St 40508-2341 (Mail to: C/O Dale Chapman 533 E Main St 40508-2341) G Harrison Andrew Hege (859) 252-1744

Lexington Church Saint Michael The Archangel **P** (450) § 2025 Bellefonte Dr 40503-2601 (Mail to: 2025 Bellefonte Dr 40503-2601) Laurie Brock (859) 277-7511

Lexington St Andrews Episcopal Church **P** (61) 401 Upper St 40508-1450 (Mail to: 401 Upper St 40508-1450) Marcia Hunter (859) 254-8325

Lexington St Augustine Episcopal Chapel **CM** 472 Rose St 40508-3342 (Mail to: 472 Rose St 40508-3342) (859) 254-3726

Lexington St Huberts Episcopal Church **P** (88) 7559 Grimes Mill Rd 40391 (Mail to: PO Box 21987 40522-1987) Duane Smith Charles Ellestad Duane Smith (859) 527-6440

Lexington St Raphael Episcopal Church **P** (300) 1891 Parkers Mill Rd 40504-2041 (Mail to: 1891 Parkers Mill Rd 40504-2041) Helen Van Koevering (859) 255-4987

Lexington St Marthas Episcopal Church **P** (37) 1870 Armstrong Mill RD 40517 (Mail to: 1870 Armstrong Mill RD 40517) Sandra Stone (859) 271-7641

Maysville Episcopal Church of the Nativity **P** (71) 31 E 3rd St 41056-1149 (Mail to: PO Box 3 41056-0003) Roxanne Ruggles (606) 564-5850

Middlesboro St Marys Episcopal Church **P** (73) 131 Edgewood Rd 40965-2840 (Mail to: PO Box 744 40965-0744) Aelred Dean (606) 248-6450

Morehead St Albans Church **M** (40) 145 E 5th St 40351-1205 (Mail to: 145 E 5th St 40351-1205) Arthur Conaway Keila Thomas (606) 784-6427

Mt Sterling Church of the Ascension **P** (79) 48 W High St 40353-0653 (Mail to: PO Box 653 40353-0653) (859) 498-3730

Newport St Pauls Episcopal Church **P** (121) 7 Court Pl 41071-1005 (Mail to: 7 Court Pl 41071-1098) Stephen Young Thomas Runge (859) 581-7640

Nicholasville Epis Church of the Resurrection **P** (280) 3220 Lexington Rd 40356-9798 (Mail to: 3220 Lexington Rd 40356-9798) Margaret Shanks Margaret Shanks (859) 885-6391

Paris St Peters Episcopal Church **P** (136) 311 High St 40361-2002 (Mail to: PO Box 27 40362-0027) (859) 987-2760

Prestonsburg St James Episcopal Church **P** (14) 562 University Dr 41653-1800 (Mail to: 562 University Dr 41653-1800) (606) 886-8046

Richmond Episcopal Church of Our Saviour **M** (85) 2323 Lexington Rd 40475-9135 (Mail to: 2323 Lexington Rd 40475-9135) Carol Ruthven (859) 623-1226

Somerset St Patricks Episcopal Church **P** (119) 206 West Columbia Street 42501-1674 (Mail to: PO Box 633 42502-0633) Amanda Musterman (606) 678-4262

Versailles St Johns Episcopal Church **P** (411) 210 Main St 40383-1206 (Mail to: 210 Main St 40383-1206) (859) 873-3481

Winchester Emmanuel Episcopal Church **P** (78) 2410 Lexington Rd 40391-9522 (Mail to: 2410 Lexington Rd 40391-9522) James Trimble (859) 744-4889

DIOCESE OF LONG ISLAND
(PROVINCE II)
Comprises the 4 counties of Brooklyn, Queens, Nassau, and Suffolk
DIOCESAN HOUSE 36 Cathedral Ave Garden City NY 11530
TEL (516) 248-4800   FAX (516) 877-1349
E-MAIL communication@dioceseli.org   WEB www.dioceselongisland.org

Previous Bishops—
Abram N Littlejohn 1868-1901, Fredk Burgess 1901-25, Ernest M Stires 1925-42, John I Larned suffr 1929-47, Frank W Creighton suffr 1933-37, James P DeWolfe 1942-66, Jonathan G Sherman suffr 1949-65 Bp 1966-77, Richd B Martin suffr 1967-74, Chas W MacLean suffr 1962-75, C Shannon Mallory asst bp 1979-80, Henry B Hucles III suffr 1981-88, Robert C Witcher coadj 1975 Bp 1977-91, Rodney R Michel suffr 1997-2007, Orris G Walker Jr coadj 1991-2009, Rt Rev James H Ottley Asst Bp 2007-09

Bishop—Rt Rev Lawrence C Provenzano (1037) (Dio 14 Nov 09)

Chanc R Fardella; *Dir of Yth Min* M Garnes; *Sec* Rev KDM Davis-Lawson; *Treas* P Griffith; *Hist Reg* C Egleston

Stand Comm–Cler: Pres S Foster EC Nesmith D Sibley L Womack; *Lay:* M Thorstenn R Murphy A McPartland V Hinkson

PARISHES, MISSIONS, AND CLERGY

Amagansett St Thomas Episcopal Chapel **SC** Rt 27 & Indian Wells Hwy 11930 (Mail to: PO Box 103 11930-0103) (313) 242-7356

Amityville St Marys Episcopal Church **P** (418) 175 Broadway 11701-2703 (Mail to: C/O Kevin C Fowler 175 Broadway 11701-2703) Randolph Geminder (631) 264-0004

Astoria Church of the Redeemer **P** (706) 30-14 Crescent St 11102 (Mail to: 3014 Crescent St 11102-3249) Juan Quevedo-Bosch (718) 278-8093

Astoria St George's Episcopal Church **P** (65) 14-02 27th Ave 11102 (Mail to: 1420 27th Ave 11102-3873) Karen Davis-Lawson (718) 721-5154

Babylon Christ Episcopal Church **P** (244) 12 Prospect St 11702-3407 (Mail to: 12 Prospect St 11702-3407) Elizabeth Nesmith (631) 661-5757

Baldwin All Saints' Episcopal Church **P** (457) 2375 Harrison Ave 11510-3214 (Mail to: 2375 Harrison Ave 11510-3214) (516) 223-3731

Bay Shore St Peters by the Sea Epis Church **P** (429) § 500 S Country Rd 11706-8295 (Mail to: 500 S Country Rd 11706-8295) Johncy Itty (631) 665-0051

Bayside All Saints Church **P** (246) 21435 40th Ave 11361-2145 (Mail to: 21435 40th Ave 11361-2151) Laurence Byrne (718) 229-5631

Bellmore St Matthias Episcopal Church **M** (8) 2856 Jerusalem Ave 11710 (Mail to: PO Box 573 11710-0573) (516) 783-0558

Bellport Christ Episcopal Church **P** (120) 64 S Country Rd 11713-2519 (Mail to: 64 S Country Rd 11713-2519) Terrence Buckley (631) 286-0299

Brentwood Christ Church **M** (169) 155 3rd Ave 11717-5322 (Mail to: 155 3rd Ave 11717-5322) (631) 273-9504

Bridgehampton St Anns Episcopal Church **P** (230) 2463 Main St 11932 (Mail to: PO Box 961 11932-0961) Timothy Lewis (631) 537-1527

Brookhaven St James Episcopal Church **M** (94) 260 Beaver Dam Rd 11719-9756 (Mail to: 260 Beaver Dam Rd 11719-9756) Hickman Alexandre (631) 286-0726

Brooklyn All Saints Church **P** (173) 286-88 7th Ave 11215-3601 (Mail to: 286-88 Seventh Ave 11215-3601) Steven Paulikas (718) 768-1156

Brooklyn Bushwick Abbey **P** 22 Wyckoff Ave 11237-2635 (Mail to: 22 Wyckoff Ave 11237)

Brooklyn Christ Church Cobble Hill **P** (116) § 180 Kane St 11231-3760 (Mail to: Attn: Mr Clifford Harkness 180 Kane St 11231-3760) Ronald Lau Anthony Bowen (718) 624-0083

Brooklyn Christ Church Bay Ridge **P** (179) 7301 Ridge Blvd 11209 (Mail to: C/O Theresa DeStasio 7301 Ridge Blvd 11209-2113) Lawrence De Lion (718) 745-3698

Brooklyn Church of Calvary and St Cyprian **P** (625) 966 Bushwick Ave 11221 (Mail to: 966 Bushwick Ave 11221-3740) Charles Holdbrooke (718) 453-3764

Brooklyn Church of St Thomas **P** (543) 1405 Bushwick Ave 11207-1408 (Mail to: 1405

Bushwick Ave 11207-1408) Sully Guillaume-Sam (718) 452-2332

Brooklyn St Stephen & St Martin Church **P** (241) 809 Jefferson Ave 11221-3504 (Mail to: PO Box 210160 11221-0160) Audley Donaldson (718) 453-0651

Brooklyn Church of the Ascension **P** (161) 127 Kent St 11222 (Mail to: 127 Kent St 11222-2103) John Merz (718) 383-5402

Brooklyn Church Of The Holy Apostles **P** (102) 612 Greenwood Ave 11218-1302 (Mail to: Attn: Treasurer 612 Greenwood Ave 11218-1302) Kimberlee Auletta Sarah Kooperkamp (718) 871-1615

Brooklyn Church of the Holy Spirit **M** (115) 81-17 Bay Pkwy 11214 (Mail to: 8117 Bay Pkwy 11214-2513) (718) 837-0412

Brooklyn Church of the Nativity **M** (214) 121 Amersfort Pl 11210-2321 (Mail to: 1099 Ocean Ave 11230-1905) (718) 859-8654

Brooklyn Emmanuel Episcopal Church **P** (206) 2635 E 23rd St 11235 (Mail to: 2635 E 23rd St 11235-2825) (718) 934-0189

Brooklyn Grace Church **P** (652) § 254 Hicks St 11201-4028 (Mail to: 254 Hicks St 11201-4097) Allen Robinson Erika Meyer (718) 624-1850

Brooklyn Iglesia de la Santa Cruz **M** (20) 172 St Nicholas Ave 11237 (Mail to: 172 St Nicholas Ave 11237) (917) 507-7088

Brooklyn Saint Alban's Church **P** (525) 9408 Farragut Rd 11236-2028 (Mail to: 9408 Farragut Rd 11236-2028) George Bonner (718) 342-5215

Brooklyn St Andrew Episcopal Church **P** (419) 4917 4th Ave 11220-1819 (Mail to: 4917 4th Ave 11220-1819) Francisco Rodriguez-Padron (718) 439-6056

Brooklyn St Ann and the Holy Trinity Church **P** (111) 157 Montague St 11201-3587 (Mail to: 157 Montague St Ste 1 11201-3587) John Denaro Katherine Salisbury Katherine Salisbury (718) 875-6960

Brooklyn St Augustines Episcopal Church **P** (2180) 4301 Ave D 11203 (Mail to: 4301 Avenue D 11203-5723) Lawrence Womack Joseph Diele Howard Williams (718) 629-0930

Brooklyn St Barnabas Episcopal Church **P** (476) 417 Elton St 11208 (Mail to: 417 Elton St 11208-2129) Sylvester Taylor (718) 277-5407

Brooklyn St Bartholomews Church **P** (109) 1227 Pacific St 11216 (Mail to: c/o Nancy Signore 36 Cathedral Avenue 11530) Pierre Damus (718) 467-8750

Brooklyn St Gabriels Episcopal Church **P** (1121) 331 Hawthorne St 11225-5909 (Mail to: 331 Hawthorne St 11225-5909) Edmund Alleyne (718) 774-5248

Brooklyn St Georges Episcopal Church **P** (1174) 800 Marcy Ave 11216-1513 (Mail to: 800 Marcy Ave 11216-1513) Glenworth Miles (718) 789-6036

Brooklyn St Johns Park Slope **P** (200) 139 St Johns Pl 11217-3401 (Mail to: 139 Saint Johns Pl 11217-3401) Shelley Mcdade (718) 783-3928

Brooklyn Church of St Mark **P** (3416) 1417 Union St 11213 (Mail to: 1417 Union St 11213-4337) Kino Vitet (718) 756-6607

Brooklyn St Marys Episcopal Church **P** (91) 230 Classon Ave 11205-1441 (Mail to: 230 Classon Ave 11205-1441) Gerald Keucher (718) 638-2090

Brooklyn St Pauls Episcopal Church **P** (312) 199 Carroll St 11231-4203 (Mail to: 199 Carroll St 11231-4203) Sean Wallace (718) 625-4126

Brooklyn St Pauls Church in the Village **P** (915) 157 St Pauls Pl 11226-2708 (Mail to: 157 Saint Pauls Pl 11226-2708) Sheldon Hamblin Pierre Damus (718) 282-2100

Brooklyn St Philip's Episcopal Church **P** (63) 1072 80th St 11228 (Mail to: 1072 80th St 11228-2620) (718) 745-2505

Brooklyn St Philips Episcopal Church **P** (519) 334 MacDonough St 11233-1704 (Mail to: C/O Ms Wendy Malliet 265 Decatur St 11233-1704) Carver Israel (718) 778-8700

Brooklyn Church of St Luke and St Matthew **P** (439) 520 Clinton Ave 11238-2211 (Mail to: 520 Clinton Ave 11238-2211) Edwin Chase (718) 638-0686

Brooklyn Church The Epiphany & St Simon **P** (147) 2910 Avenue M 11210 (Mail to: 2910 Avenue M 11210-4699) Allen George (718) 258-1166

Cambria Heights St Davids Episcopal Church **P** (462) 117-35 235th St 11411 (Mail to: 117-35 235th St 11411-1821) (718) 528-2095

Carle Place St Marys Episcopal Church **P** (71) 252 Rushmore Ave 11514-1431 (Mail to: 252 Rushmore Ave 11514-1431) Christopher Sigamoney (516) 333-2290

Central Islip Church of the Messiah **M** (217) 53 Carleton Ave 11722-3018 (Mail to: PO Box 161 11722-0161) (631) 234-5161

Cold Spring Harbor St John's Church **P** (885) 1675 Route 25A 11724 (Mail to: PO Box 266 11724-0266) Gideon Pollach Jesse Lebus (516) 692-6368

Ctr Moriches Church of St John the Baptist **P** (195) 33 Railroad Ave 11934 (Mail to: PO Box 602 11934-0602) (631) 878-0022

Deer Park St Patricks Episcopal Church **P** (141) 305 Carlls Path 11729-5415 (Mail to: 305 Carlls Path 11729-5415) William Mahoney (631) 242-7530

Douglaston Zion Episcopal Church **P** (282) 243-01 Northern Blvd 11363 (Mail to: 243 Northern Blvd # 1 11363) Lindsay Lunnum (718) 225-0466

East Elmhurst Epis ch of Grace and Resurrection **P** (451) 10017 32nd Ave 11369-2501 (Mail to: 10017 32nd Ave 11369-2501) Gilberto Hinds (718) 899-5227

East Hampton St Lukes Episcopal Church **P** (552) 18 James Ln 11937 (Mail to: 18 James Ln 11937-2796) Denis Brunelle Leandra Lambert (631) 329-0990

East Hampton St Peter Episcopal Summer Chapel **SC** 463 Old Stone Hwy 11937 (Mail to: 18 James Ln 11937-2710) (631) 329-0990

East Setauke Caroline Church of Brookhaven **P** (697) 1 Dyke Rd 11733-3014 (Mail to: 1 Dyke Rd 11733-3014) Richard Visconti (631) 941-4245

Elmhurst St James Episcopal Church **P** (105) 8407 Broadway 11373-5727 (Mail to: 8407 Broadway 11373-5727) Paul Lai Winfred Vergara (718) 592-2555

✠ **Far Rockaway** Bishop Charles Maclean Nursing Home **O** 1711 Brookhaven Ave 11691-4406 (Mail to: 1711 Brookhaven Ave 11691-4406) (718) 869-8022

Far Rockaway St Joseph Episcopal Chapel **SC** 327 Beach 19th St 11691-4423 (Mail to: 327 Beach 19th St 11691-4423) Cecily Broderick § Guerra Barbara Jean Maxwell (718) 869-7320

Farmingdale St Thomas Episcopal Church **P** (217) 298 Conklin St 11735-2609 (Mail to: 298 Conklin St 11735-2609) Christina van Liew (516) 752-9254

Fishers Island St Johns Episcopal Church **SC** Oriental Ave 06390 (Mail to: PO Box 475 06390-0475) Michael Spencer (631) 788-7497

Floral Park St Elisabeths Episcopal Church **P** (104) 6 Harvard St 11001-2822 (Mail to: 6 Harvard St 11001-2822) T Abigail Murphy (516) 354-6867

Floral Park St Thomas Episcopal Church **P** (132) 6 Commonwealth Blvd 11001-4141 (Mail to: 6 Commonwealth Blvd 11001-4141) T Abigail Murphy (516) 354-6866

Flushing St Georges Episcopal Church **P** (1166) 135-32 38th Ave 11354 (Mail to: 13532 38th Ave 11354-4483) Wilfredo Benitez Songling Xie Songling Xie (718) 359-1171

Flushing St John's Episcopal Church **P** (169) 149-49 Sanford Ave 11355-1038 (Mail to: 14949 Sanford Ave 11355-1092) Dario Palasi (718) 961-1333

Forest Hills St Lukes Episcopal Church **P** (270) 85 Greenway S 11375 (Mail to: 85 Greenway S 11375-5942) Thomas Reese William Doubleday (718) 268-6021

Freeport Church of the Transfiguration **P** (386) Pine St & S Long Beach Ave 11520 (Mail to: 69 South Long Beach Ave 11520) Raymond Wilson (516) 379-1230

✠ **Garden City** Cathedral of the Incarnation **O** (1106) 50 Cathedral Ave 11530-4435 (Mail to: 36 Cathedral Ave 11530-4435) Michael Sniffen Michael Delaney John Greco Bruce Griffith Morgan Mercer Ladd (516) 746-2955

Garden City Christ Episcopal Church **P** (118) 33 Jefferson St 11530-3929 (Mail to: 33 Jefferson St 11530-3929) (516) 775-2626

Garden City Good Shepherd Episcopal Chapel **CC** 65 4th St 11530-4313 (Mail to: 65 4th St 11530-4313) John Mcginty (516) 248-4800

Glen Cove St Pauls Episcopal Church **P** (103) 28 Highland Rd 11542-2630 (Mail to: 28 Highland Rd 11542-2698) Shawn Williams (516) 676-0015

Great Neck All Saints Episcopal Church **P** (110) 855 Middle Neck Rd 11024-1441 (Mail to: 855 Middle Neck Rd 11024-1441) Joseph Pae (516) 482-5392

Great River Emmanuel Episcopal Church **HC** (104) 320 Great River Rd 11739-0571 (Mail to: 320 Great River Rd 11739-3010) Ellis Tommaseo (631) 581-3964

Greenport Church of the Holy Trinity **P** (111) 768 Main St 11944-1446 (Mail to: PO Box 502 11944-0502) (631) 477-0855

Hampton Bays Church of St Marys **P** (425) 165 Ponquogue Ave 11946-0701 (Mail to: PO Box 782 11946-0701) Philip Hubbard (631) 728-0776

Hempstead St Georges Episcopal Church **P** (477) 319 Front St 11550-4024 (Mail to: 319 Front St 11550-4083) Frederic Miller (516) 483-2771

Hewlett Trinity St Johns Epis Church **P** (651) 1142 Broadway 11557 (Mail to: 1142 Broadway 11557-2302) John Ballard (516) 374-1415

Hicksville Holy Trinity Episcopal Church **P** (337) 130 Jerusalem Ave 11801-4918 (Mail to: 130 Jerusalem Ave 118014934) Winfred Vergara (516) 931-1920

Hollis St Gabriels Episcopal Church **P** (313) 196-10 Woodhull Ave 11423 (Mail to: 19610 Woodhull Ave 11423-2984) Charles Nelson (718) 465-2876

Huntington St Johns Episcopal Church **P** (368) 12 Prospect St 11743-3375 (Mail to: 12 Prospect St 11743-3375) Duncan Burns John Morrison (631) 427-1752

Islip St Marks Episcopal Church **P** (1276) 754 Montauk Hwy 11751-3696 (Mail to: 754 Montauk Hwy 11751-3696) Richard Simpson (631) 581-4950

Jackson Heights St Marks Church **P** (120) 33-50 82nd Street 11372-1499 (Mail to: 3350 82nd St 11372-1499) Antonio Checo Jason Moskal Charles Perrin (718) 639-8893

Jamaica Church of St James the Less **P** (640) 107-66 Merrick Blvd 11433 (Mail to: Attn Mrs Kirsten Brannon 10766 Merrick Blvd 11433-2417) Dennison Richards (718) 262-0535

Jamaica Grace Episcopal Church **P** (323) 15524 90th Ave 11432-3825 (Mail to: C/O Deena Alleyne 15524 90th Ave 11432-3825) Darryl James (718) 291-4901

Jamaica St Stephens Episcopal Church **P** (204) 89-26 168th St 11432-4334 (Mail to: 8926 168th St 11432-4334) Donovan Leys Charles Nelson (718) 523-1917

Kew Gardens Church of the Resurrection **P** (156) 85-09 118th St 11415-2907 (Mail to: 8509 118th St 11415-2907) (718) 847-2649

Lindenhurst St Boniface Episcopal Church **P** (180) 100 46th St 11757-2050 (Mail to: 100 46th St Unit 2 11757-2050) Diane Deblasio (631) 957-2666

Locust Valley St John's Church of Lattingtown **P** (515) 325 Lattingtown Rd 11542 (Mail to: 325 Lattingtown Rd 11560-1022) Mark Fitzhugh Stephen Tamke (516) 671-3226

Long Beach St James of Jerusalem Episcopal Church **P** (120) 220 W Penn St 11561-3933 (Mail to: 220 W Penn St 11561-3933) John King (516) 432-1080

Long Island City All Saints' Episcopal Church **P** (158) 4312 46th St 11104-2002 (Mail to: 43-12 46th St 11104-2002) Gabriel Lamazares (718) 784-8031

Lynbrook St John the Evangelist Epis Ch **P** (168) 49 Blake Ave 11563-2505 (Mail to: 49 Blake Ave 11563-2505) Lynn Collins (516) 792-6050

Manhasset Christ Episcopal Church **P** (345) 1351 Northern Blvd 11030-3007 (Mail to: 1351 Northern Blvd 11030-3007) Allison Moore (516) 627-2184

Massapequa Grace Episcopal Church **P** (460) § 23 Cedar Shore Dr 11758 (Mail to: 23 Cedar Shore Dr 11758-7318) Walter Hillebrand (516) 798-1122

Mastic Beach Saint Andrew's Church **M** (30) 250 Neighborhood Rd 11951-3623 (Mail to: PO Box 488 11951-0488) (631) 281-9133

Mattituck Church of the Redeemer **P** (155) 13225 Sound Ave 11952 (Mail to: 13225 Sound Ave PO Box 906 11952) Edward Blatz Roger Joslin (631) 298-4277

Medford St Marks Episcopal Church **P** (60) 208 Jamaica Ave 11763-3290 (Mail to: PO Box 527 11763-0527) Thomas Sramek (631) 475-7406

New Hyde Park St Philip and St James Church **M** (25) 432 Lakeville Rd 11042-1121 (Mail to: 432 Lakeville Rd 11042-1121) Edwin Chase (516) 354-0458

New York St Andrews-by-the-Sea **SC** (35) 300 W End Ave # 8b 10023-8156 (Mail to: Attn Peter M R Kendall 300 W End Ave # 8b 10023-8156) (631) 583-8382

North Bellmore St Francis Episcopal Church **P** 1692 Bellmore Ave 11710-5530 (Mail to: 1692 Bellmore Ave 11710-5530) Mark Genszler

Northport Trinity Episcopal Church **P** (330) 130 Main St 11768-1723 (Mail to: 130 Main St Ste 1 11768-1784) Michael Bartolomeo Michael Bartolomeo (631) 261-7670

Oakdale St Johns Episcopal Church **M** (11) 1 Berard Blvd 11769-1701 (Mail to: One Berard Blvd 11769) (631) 589-0213

Oyster Bay Christ Episcopal Church **P** (444) 55 East Main St 11771-2400 (Mail to: 55 E Main St 11771-2493) Michael Piret (516) 922-6377

Patchogue St Pauls Episcopal Church **P** (114) 31 Rider Ave 11772-3915 (Mail to: 31 Rider Ave 11772-3999) Elisabeth Tunney (631) 475-3078

Plainview St Margarets Church **P** (253) 1000 Washington Ave 11803-1831 (Mail to: 1000 Washington Ave 11803-1831) Isaias Ginson (516) 692-5268

Prt Jefferson Christ Episcopal Church **P** (130) 127 Barnum Ave 11777-1621 (Mail to: 127 Barnum Ave 11777-1621) Anthony Di Lorenzo (631) 473-0273

Prt Washington St Stephens Episcopal Church **P** (452) 9 Carlton Ave 11050-3105 (Mail to: 9 Carlton Ave 11050-3105) Gary Parker (516) 767-0363

Queens Vlg St Josephs Episcopal Church **P** (725) 9910 217th Ln 11429-1214 (Mail to: 9910 217th Ln 11429-1214) Kassinda Ellis (718) 465-4193

Quogue Church of the Atonement **SC** 17 Quogue St 11959 (Mail to: PO Box 928 11959-0928) (631) 653-6798

Riverhead Grace Episcopal Church **P** (177) 573 Roanoke Ave 11901-2760 (Mail to: 573 Roanoke Ave 11901-2760) (631) 727-3900

Rockville Ct The Church of the Ascension **P** (513) 71 Village Ave 11570-4605 (Mail to: 71 Village Ave 11570-4605) Kevin Morris (516) 766-0693

Ronkonkoma St Marys Episcopal Church **P** (696) 315 Lake Shore Rd 11779-3180 (Mail to: 315 Lake Shore Rd 11779-3147) (631) 588-1888

Roosevelt St Pauls Episcopal Church **M** (129) 25 W Centennial Ave 11575-2028 (Mail to: PO Box 514 11575-0514) (516) 546-2754

Rosedale St Peters Episcopal Church **P** (245) 13728 244th St 11422-1828 (Mail to: 13728 244th St 11422-1828) Steve Foster (718) 528-1356

Roslyn Trinity Episcopal Church **P** (148) 1579 Northern Blvd 11576-1103 (Mail to: 1579 Northern Blvd Unit A 11576-1137) Margaret Peckham Clark (516) 621-7925

Sag Harbor Christ Episcopal Church **P** (130) 5 Hampton St 11963-4242 (Mail to: PO Box 570 11963-0012) Karen Campbell (631) 725-0128

Saint Albans St Alban the Martyr Church **P** (229) 11642 Farmers Blvd 11412-3026 (Mail to: 11642 Farmers Blvd 11412-3026) Keith Voets (718) 528-1891

Saint James St James Episcopal Church **P** (458) 490 Route 25a 11780-1953 (Mail to: 490 Route 25A 11780-1953) (631) 584-5560

Sayville Saint Ann's Church **HC** (682) 262 Middle Rd 11782-3242 (Mail to: 262 Middle Rd 11782-3242) Brian Barry John Hugh James (631) 589-6522

Sea Cliff St Lukes Episcopal Church **P** (221) 253 Glen Avenue 11579-1544 (Mail to: 253 Glen Ave 11579-1544) (516) 676-4222

Seaford St Michael & All Angels **P** (46) 2197 Jackson Ave 11783-2607 (Mail to: 2197 Jackson Ave 11783-2607) (516) 785-3762

Selden St Cuthberts Episcopal Church **P** (63) 18 Magnolia Pl 11784-2902 (Mail to: PO Box 1367 11784-0995) (631) 475-4555

Shelter Island St Marys Church **P** (137) 26 St Marys Rd 11964 (Mail to: PO Box 1660 11964-1660) Charles Mccarron (631) 749-0770

Shoreham St Anselms Episcopal Church **P** (506) 4 Woodville Rd 11786-1329 (Mail to: PO Box 606 11786-0606) John Mcginty (631) 744-7730

Smithtown St Thomas of Canterbury Church **P** (641) 29 Brooksite Drive 11787-3495 (Mail to: 90 Edgewater Ave 11787-3467) Judith Carrick John Purchal (631) 265-4520

South Ozone Park Saint John's Church **P** (169) 133-04 109th Ave 11420 (Mail to: 13316 109th Ave 11420-1703) Frederick Opare-Addo Frederick Opare-Addo (718) 529-0366

Southampton St Johns Episcopal Church **P** (481) 100 S Main St 11968-4804 (Mail to: PO Box 5068 11969-5068) William Edwards (631) 283-0549

Sprngfld Gdnd St Johns Episcopal Church **P** (113) 13767 Belknap St 11413-2619 (Mail to: 13767 Belknap St 11413-2619) Pauline Samuel (718) 525-1444

Stony Brook All Souls Episcopal Church **M** (82) 61 Main Street 11790-1816 (Mail to: 10 Mill Pond Rd 11790-1816) (631) 751-0034

Valley Stream Holy Trinity Episcopal Church **P** (85) 87 7th St 11581-1214 (Mail to: 87 7th St 11581-1290) (516) 825-2903

Valley Stream Nursery 87 7th St 11581-1214 (Mail to: 87 7TH ST 11581-1214) (516) 825-2903

Wading River St Lukes Chapel **SC** 408 Side Rd 11792 (Mail to: 1 Side Rd 11792-1112) (631) 929-4325

Wantagh Church of St Jude **P** (626) 3606 Lufberry Ave 11793-3031 (Mail to: 3606 Lufberry Ave 11793-3031) Christopher Hofer Maxine Barnett (516) 221-2505

Westbury Church of the Advent **P** (344) 555 Advent St 11590-1309 (Mail to: 555 Advent St 11590-1309) (516) 333-0081

Westhampton Beach St Marks Episcopal Church **P** (361) § 40 Main St 11978-2673 (Mail to: PO Box 887 11978-0887) Michael Ralph (631) 288-2111

Whitestone Grace Episcopal Church **P** (217) 14-15 Clintonville Street 11357 (Mail to: 1415 Clintonville St 11357-1825) (718) 767-6305

Williston Pk Resurrection **P** (35) 147 Campbell Ave 11596-1606 (Mail to: 147 Campbell Ave 11596-1606) (516) 746-5527

Woodhaven All Saints Episcopal Church **P** (189) 85-45 96th Street 11421 (Mail to: 8545 96th St 11421-1727) Norman Whitmire (718) 849-2352

Woodside St Paul Episcopal Church **M** (39) 39-04 61st St 11377 (Mail to: 3904 61st St 11377-3536) Anandsekar Manuel (718) 672-8565

Yaphank St Andrew Episcopal Church **P** (126) 244 E Main St 11980-9656 (Mail to: PO Box 249 11980-0249) (631) 924-5083

DIOCESE OF LOS ANGELES
(PROVINCE VIII)
Comprises southern California, except San Diego
DIO OFC 840 Echo Pk Ave Los Angeles CA 90026 (MAIL Box 512164 Los Angeles CA 90051-0164)
TEL (213) 482-2040   FAX (213) 482-5304
E-MAIL communications@ladiocese.org   WEB www.ladiocese.org
The Bishop of the Protestant Episcopal Church in the Diocese of Los Angeles, a Corporation Sole

Previous Bishops—
Jos H Johnson 1896-1928, W Bertrand Stevens coadj 1920 Bp 1928-47, Robt B Gooden suffr 1930-47, F Eric Bloy 1948-73, Donald J Campbell suffr 1949-59, Ivol I Curtis suffr 1960-64, C Rusack suffr 1964-73 Bp 1974-86, Oliver B Garver suffr 1985-90, Frederick Houk Borsch 1988-2002, Chester L Talton suffr 1991-2010, Mary D Glasspool suffr 2010-15, J Jon Bruno 2002-17

Bishop—Rt Rev John Harvey Taylor (1101) (Dio 8 Jul 2017)

Bishop Suffragan—Rt Rev Diane Jardine Bruce (1044) (Dio 15 May 2010)

Sec Conv Cn S Nishibayashi; *Treas* Cn A Tomat; *Cn to Ord/Chief of Staff* Cn M McCarthy; *CFO* M Racusin; *Chanc* Cn R Zevnik; *Cn Form/Deploy* Rev Cn J Satorius; *COM* Very Rev Cn M Bamberger & Cn JB White; *Sch* Dr S Beeks; *Missions* C Bangao

Stand Comm—Cler: Pres Cn JD Larsen N Frausto K Sylvester G Hall D Justin *Lay:* A Wohlcke I Gutierrez Cn R Kimmler

PARISHES, MISSIONS, AND CLERGY

Alhambra Holy Trinity St Benedict Church **P** (219) 412 Garfield Ave 91801-2438 (Mail to: 412 Garfield Ave 91801-2498) Brent Quines (626) 282-9118

Altadena St Marks Episcopal Church **P** (623) § 1014 E Altadena Dr 91001-2041 (Mail to: 1014

E Altadena Dr 91001-2041) Carri Grindon Graham Berry Elizabeth Hooper Joseph Lane Sylvia Sweeney (626) 798-6747

Anaheim St Michaels Episcopal Church **M** (983) 311 W South St 92805-4517 (Mail to: 311 W South St 92805-4598) Juan Jimenez (714) 535-4654

Apple Valley St Timothy's Episcopal Church **P** (150) 15757 St Timothy Rd 92307-2554 (Mail to: 15757 Saint Timothy Rd 92307-2590) John Limo (760) 242-2405

Arcadia Church of the Transfiguration **P** (228) 1881 S 1st Ave 91006-4618 (Mail to: 1881 S 1st Ave 91006-4618) Julie Bryant (626) 445-3340

Barstow St Paul's Episcopal Church **M** (91) 512 E Williams St 92311-2941 (Mail to: PO Box 726 92312-0726) (760) 256-1624

Beaumont St Stephens Church Episcopal **M** (173) 225 E 8th St 92223-5903 (Mail to: 225 E 8th St 92223-5903) William Dunn (951) 845-1358

Beverly Hills All Saints Episcopal Parish **P** (1702) 504 Camden Dr 90210-3299 (Mail to: 504 Camden Dr 90210-3299) Andrew Barnett Robert Dannals Nathaniel Katz William Stanley (310) 275-0123

Big Bear City St Columbas Episcopal Church **M** (193) 42324 North Shore Dr 92314 (Mail to: PO Box 1681 92315-1681) Stuart Swann (909) 866-7239

Buena Park St Joseph Episcopal Church **P** (91) 8300 Valley View St 90620-2738 (Mail to: 8300 Valley View St 90620-2738) Matthew Parker (714) 828-8950

Camarillo St Columbas Church **P** (336) 1251 Las Posas Rd 93010-3001 (Mail to: 1251 Las Posas Rd 93010-3001) Gregory Larkin (805) 482-8831

Claremont St Ambrose Episcopal Church **P** (175) 830 W Bonita Ave 91711-4113 (Mail to: 830 W Bonita Ave 91711-4113) Brian Baker (909) 626-7170

Compton St Timothys Episcopal Church **P** (130) § 312 S Oleander Ave 90220 (Mail to: 312 S Oleander Ave 90220-3118) Anthony Miller (310) 638-6319

Corona St John's Church **P** (382) 526 Magnolia Ave 92879-3113 (Mail to: PO Box 152 92878-0152) Patricia Stansfield (951) 737-1363

Corona Del Mar Saint Michael and All Angels Parish **P** (300) 3233 Pacific View Dr 92625-1109 (Mail to: 3233 Pacific View Dr 92625-1197) Michael Seiler (949) 644-0463

Costa Mesa St John The Divine Church **P** (107) 183 E Bay St 92627-2145 (Mail to: 183 E Bay St 92627-2145) George Okusi (949) 548-2237

Covina Holy Trinity Episcopal Church **P** (328) 100 Third Ave 91723 (Mail to: PO Box 4195 91723-0595) Steven De Muth Mark Stuart (626) 967-3939

Downey St Marks Episcopal Church **P** (99) § 10354 Downey Ave 90241-2512 (Mail to: 10354 Downey Ave 90241-2597) (562) 862-3268

El Monte Immanuel Episcopal Church **M** (371) 4366 Santa Anita Ave 91731-1606 (Mail to: 4366 Santa Anita Ave 91731-1606) Hector Limatu (626) 448-1908

El Segundo St Michael the Archangel Parish **P** (141) § 361 Richmond St 90245-3729 (Mail to: 361 Richmond St 90245-3729) Dina Ferguson (310) 322-2589

Encino St Nicholas Episcopal Church **P** (310) 17114 Ventura Blvd 91316-4003 (Mail to: 17114 Ventura Blvd 91316-4003) Michael Cooper (818) 788-4486

Fillmore Trinity Episcopal Church **P** (97) 600 Saratoga St 93015-1444 (Mail to: PO Box 306 93016-0306) Lawrence Brown (805) 524-1910

Fullerton Emmanuel Episcopal Church **P** (703) § 1145 W Valencia Mes 92833-2218 (Mail to: 1145 W Valencia Mesa Dr 92833-2218) Lynda Crow (714) 879-8070

Fullerton St Andrews Episcopal Church **P** (306) 1231 E Chapman Ave 92831-3908 (Mail to: 1231 E Chapman Ave 92831-3987) Beth Arnold (714) 870-4350

Garden Grove St Anselm of Canterbury Episcopal Ch **P** (192) 13091 Galway St 92844-1633 (Mail to: 13091 Galway St 92844-1698) Jeffrey Clawson Thomas Lee (714) 537-0604

Gardena Church of the Holy Communion **M** (80) 1160 W 141st St 90247-2220 (Mail to: 1160 W 141st St 90247-2220) Arthur Toro (310) 324-1441

Glendale Iglesia de la Magdalena **M** (144) 1011 S Verdugo Rd 91205-3831 (Mail to: 1011 S Verdugo Rd 91205-3831) Roberto Martinez-Morales (818) 243-8670

Glendale St Marks Episcopal Church **P** (400) § 1020 Brand Blvd 91202-2907 (Mail to: 1020 Brand Blvd 91202-2983) Mark Weitzel Susie Kenny Andrea Maier (818) 240-3860

Glendora Grace Episcopal Church **P** (302) 555 E Mountain View Ave 91741-2764 (Mail to: 555 E Mountain View Ave 91741-2764) Susan Scranton (626) 335-3171

Granada Hills St Andrew & Charles Episcopal **P** (305) 16651 Rinaldi St 91344-3632 (Mail to: 16651 Rinaldi St 91344-3698) Gregory Frost (818) 366-7542

Hacienda Hgts St Thomas Episcopal Church **M** (287) 15694 Tetley St 91745-4543 (Mail to: 15694 Tetley St 91745-4543) Hsin Fen Chang (626) 330-7649

Hawthorne St Georges Episcopal Church **M** (57) 4679 W El Segundo Blvd 90250-4349 (Mail to: PO Box C 90251-0165) (310) 324-1617

Hermosa Beach St Cross Episcopal Church **P** (1052) 1818 Monterey Blvd 90254-2906 (Mail to: 1818 Monterey Blvd 90254-2906) Rachel Nyback Patrice Angelo Nathan Biornstad Robin Denney (310) 376-8989

Hesperia St Hilarys Episcopal Church **M** (201) 11305 Hesperia Rd 92345-2170 (Mail to: 11305 Hesperia Rd 92345-2170) (760) 244-6444

Huntington Beach St Wilfrid of York Episcopal Church **P** (556) 18631 Chapel Ln 92646-1831 (Mail to: 18631 Chapel Ln 92646-1831) Christopher Montella William Wells (714) 962-7512

Huntington Park St Clement's Church **M** (283) 6909 Rugby Ave 90255-4721 (Mail to: 6909 Rugby Ave 90255-4721) (323) 587-1277

Inglewood Church of the Holy Faith Parish **P** (174) 260 Locust St 90301-1204 (Mail to: 260 Locust St 90301-1298) Kathryn Derose Francisco Garcia Guy Leemhuis (310) 674-7700

Irvine St Andrew Episcopal Church **M** (281) § 4400 Barranca Pkwy 92604-4739 (Mail to: 4400 Barranca Pkwy 92604-4739) Peter Browning Richard Whittaker (949) 559-4699

Isla Vista St Michaels University Epis Church **M** (80) 6586 Picasso Rd 93117-4651 (Mail to: 6586 Picasso Rd 93117-4651) Scott Claassen Toni Stuart (805) 968-2712

La Canada Saint George's Parish **P** (216) § 808 Foothill Blvd 91011-3336 (Mail to: 808 Foothill Blvd 91011-3336) Amy Pringle Anthony Keller (818) 790-3323

La Crescenta St Luke's of the Mountains Church **M** (40) 2563 Foothill Blvd 91214-3508 (Mail to: 2563 Foothill Blvd 91214-3596) Jorge Pallares Arellano (818) 248-3639

La Verne St John's Episcopal Church **M** (240) 4745 Wheeler Ave 91750-1960 (Mail to: 4745 Wheeler Ave 91750-1960) Kelli Kurtz Jana Milhon-Martin Robert Van Buren Robert Van Buren (909) 596-1321

Laguna Beach St Marys Church Episcopal **P** (352) 428 Park Ave 92651-2337 (Mail to: 428 Park Ave 92651-2337) Lester Mackenzie (949) 494-3542

Laguna Hills St Georges Episcopal Church **P** (334) § 23802 Ave De La Carlota 92653-3117 (Mail to: 23802 Avenida De La Carlota 92653-3148) Bonnie Brandon Patricia McCaughan (949) 837-4530

Laguna Niguel Faith Episcopal Church **M** (95) 27802 El Lazo 92677-3915 (Mail to: 27802 El Lazo 92677-3915) Emily Bell Dawn Vukich (949) 448-8114

Lancaster St Pauls Episcopal Church **P** (372) 502 W Avenue K 93534 (Mail to: PO Box 8836 93539) Nancy Brown (661) 945-6704

Lompoc Saint Mary's Parish **P** (347) 2800 Harris Grade Rd 93436-2211 (Mail to: C/O Elizabeth Hatcher 2800 Harris Grade Rd 93436-2211) Michael Cunningham (805) 733-4400

Long Beach St Thomas of Canterbury Church **M** (100) 5306 E Arbor Rd 90808-1109 (Mail to: 5306 E Arbor Rd 90808-1109) Sharon Sheffield (562) 425-4457

Long Beach St Gregorys Episcopal Church **P** (423) 6201 E Willow St 90815-2247 (Mail to: 6201 E Willow St 90815-2296) Michael Fincher John Crean (562) 420-1311

Long Beach St Lukes Episcopal Church **P** (530) 525 E 7th St 90813-4559 (Mail to: PO Box 20038 90801-3038) Steven Alder Holway Farrar Nancy Frausto Jane Gould Beryl Nyre-Thomas (562) 436-4047

Los Angeles All Saints Episcopal Church **P** (850) 5619 Monte Vista St 90042-3425 (Mail to: 5619 Monte Vista St 90042-3425) Kevin Gunn Otto Vasquez (323) 255-6806

✠ **Los Angeles** Cathedral Congregation of St Athanasius **O** (326) 840 Echo Park Ave 90026-4209 (Mail to: 840 Echo Park Ave 90026-4209) (213) 482-2040

Los Angeles Christ the Good Shepherd Church **P** (261) 3303 W Vernon Ave 90008-5229 (Mail to: 3303 W Vernon Ave 90008-5295) Edith Oloimooja (323) 295-4139

Los Angeles Church of the Epiphany **M** (220) 2808 Altura St 90031-2305 (Mail to: 2808 Altura St 90031-2399) Thomas Carey (323) 227-9931

Los Angeles Episcopal Chapel of St Francis **M** (30) 3621 Brunswick Ave 90039-1727 (Mail to: 3621 Brunswick Ave 90039-1727) (323) 663-2063

Los Angeles Episcopal Church of the Advent **P** (308) 4976 W Adams Blvd 90016-2852 (Mail to: 2614 S Longwood Ave 90016-2811) (323) 731-8831

Los Angeles Holy Nativity Church **P** (177) 6700 W 83rd St 90045-2730 (Mail to: 6700 W 83rd St 90045-2730) Peter Rood Margaret Mccauley Sarah Reynolds (310) 670-4777

Los Angeles St Albans Episcopal Church **P** (339) 580 Hilgard Ave 90024-3234 (Mail to: 580 Hilgard Ave 90024-3297) Susan Klein Warner Traynham (310) 208-6516

Los Angeles St Barnabas Episcopal Church **P** (73) 2109 Chickasaw Ave 90041-1904 (Mail to: 2111 Chickasaw Ave 90041-1904) (323) 254-7569

Los Angeles St Bedes Episcopal Church **P** (235) 3590 Grand View Blvd 90066-1904 (Mail to: 3590 Grand View Blvd 90066-1904) James Newman (310) 391-5522

Los Angeles Saint James Parish **P** (890) § 3903 Wilshire Blvd. 99010-3301 (Mail to: 3903 Wilshire Blvd 90010-3301) Katherine Cress John Kim (213) 388-3417

Los Angeles St Marys Episcopal Church **P** (300) 961 S Mariposa Ave 90006-1413 (Mail to: 961 S Mariposa Ave 90006-1413) Anna Olson Richard Van Horn (213) 387-1334

Los Angeles St Philip's Church / Iglesia de San Felipe **P** (100) 801 E 28th St 90011-5506 (Mail to: Attn Ms Ann Young 2800 Stanford Ave 90011) Glenn Libby Glenn Libby (323) 232-3494

Los Angeles St Thomas the Apostle Hollywood **P** (544) 7501 Hollywood Blvd 90046-2813 (Mail to: 7501 Hollywood Blvd 90046-2813) Ian Davies John Crean Ian Davies Walter Johnson Walter Johnson Mark Stuart (323) 876-2102

✣ **Los Angeles** St Johns Pro Cathedral **O** (390) 514 W Adams Blvd 90007-2616 (Mail to: 514 W Adams Blvd 90007-2616) Mark Kowalewski Daniel Ade Joanne Leslie Fernando Valdes (213) 747-6285

Los Angeles St Mary in Palms **P** (158) 3647 Watseka Ave 90034-3914 (Mail to: 3647 Watseka Ave 90034-3914) Vincent Shamo (310) 558-4124

Los Angeles St Stephen's Episcopal Church **P** (171) 6128 Yucca St 90028-5214 (Mail to: 6128 Yucca St 90028-5214) Jaime Edwards-Acton (323) 469-3993

Los Angeles Trinity Episcopal Church **P** (200) 650 Berendo St 90004-2104 (Mail to: 4274 Melrose Ave. 90029) Nancy Frausto (323) 660-1110

Los Olivos Saint Mark's-In-The-Valley Episcopal **P** (521) § 2905 Nojoqui 93441 (Mail to: PO Box 39 93441-0039) Randall Day (805) 688-4454

Malibu St Aidans Episcopal Church **P** (222) 28211 Pacific Coast Hwy 90265-3911 (Mail to: 28211 Pacific Coast Hwy 90265-3999) Joyce Stickney (310) 457-7966

Monrovia St Lukes Episcopal Church **P** (110) 122 S California Ave 91016-2948 (Mail to: 122 S California Ave 91016-2948) Elizabeth Dumolt Neil Tadken (626) 357-7071

Monterey Park St Gabriels Episcopal Church **P** (165) 133 E Graves Ave 91755-3915 (Mail to: 133 E Graves Ave 91755-3915) (626) 571-2714

Moreno Valley Grace Episcopal Church **M** (158) 11349 Perris Blvd 92557-5657 (Mail to: 11349 Perris Blvd 92557-5657) Barbara Barnum Jo Weeks (951) 924-6760

Needles St John the Evangelist Church **M** (35) 2020 J St 92363-2622 (Mail to: PO Box 817 92363-0817) (760) 326-6673

Newport Beach St James Episcopal Church **M** (125) 3209 Via Lido 92663-3973 (Mail to: 3209 Via Lido 92663-3973) Cynthia Voorhees (949) 675-0210

Norwalk St Francis Episcopal Church **M** (111) 12700 Paddison Ave 90650-3059 (Mail to: 12700 Paddison Ave 90650-3059) (562) 863-9212

Oak Park Episcopal Church of Epiphany **M** (832) § 5450 Churchwood Dr 91377-4797 (Mail to: 5450 Churchwood Dr 91377-4797) Gregory Brown (818) 991-4797

Ojai St Andrews Episcopal Church **P** (233) 409 Topa Topa Dr 93023-3233 (Mail to: 409 Topa Topa Dr 93023-3233) Gregory Kimura Mikel Morrison (805) 646-1885

Ontario Christ Church Parish **P** (130) 1127 San Antonio Ave 91762-1803 (Mail to: 1127 San Antonio Ave 91762-1899) Walter Donaldson Gian Luigi Gugliermetto (909) 983-1859

Orange Trinity Episcopal Church **P** (628) 2400 Canal St 92865-3614 (Mail to: 2400 Canal St 92865-3614) Jeannie Martz Ann Calhoun (714) 637-1390

Oxnard All Saints Episcopal Church **P** (111) 144 S C St 93030-5615 (Mail to: 144 S C St 93030-5693) Melissa Campbell-Langdell (805) 483-2347

Pacific Plsds St Matthew's Episcopal Church **P** (887) § Attn Craig Ehlers 1031 Bienveneda Ave 90272-2314 (Mail to: C/o Chief Financial Officer 1031 Bienveneda Ave 90272) Kristin Barberia Bruce Freeman Christine Purcell William Wallace Stefanie Wilson (310) 454-1358

Palos Verdes Estates St Francis Episcopal Church **P** (402) 2200 Via Rosa P.O. Box 772 90274-1075 (Mail to: PO Box 772 90274-0772) Laurel Coote Peter Huang Paula Vukmanic (310) 375-4617

Pasadena All Saints Episcopal Church **P** (7967) 132 Euclid Ave 91101-1722 (Mail to: 132 Euclid Ave 91101-1796) Michael Kinman Frances Crean Antonio Gallardo-Lucena Sally Howard Sally Howard Thomas Hubbard Susan Russell (626) 583-2741

Pasadena Church of the Angels **P** (183) 1100 Avenue 64 91105-2712 (Mail to: 1100 Avenue 64 91105-2712) Robert Gaestel (323) 255-3878

Pasadena St Barnabas Episcopal Church **P** (84) 1062 Fair Oaks Ave 91103-3011 (Mail to: PO Box 93096 91109-3096) Mark Bradshaw Jamesetta Glosson Hammons (626) 798-2996

Pico Rivera St Bartholomews Episcopal Church **M** (285) 7540 Passons Blvd 90660-4233 (Mail to: PO Box 512164 90051-0164) Juan Barragan (562) 949-5228

Placentia Blessed Sacrament Church **P** (250) 1314 Angelina Dr 92870-3442 (Mail to: 1314 Angelina Dr 92870-3442) (714) 528-2995

Pomona St Pauls Episcopal Church **P** (136) 242 E Alvarado St 91767-4634 (Mail to: 242 E Alvarado St 91767-4698) Thomas Hallahan Thomas Hallahan (909) 622-2015

Rcho Sta Marg St John Chrysostom Church and School **M** (680) § 30382 Via Con Dios 92688-1518 (Mail to: 30382 Via Con Dios 92688-1518) Karen Maurer Paul Potter (949) 888-4595

Redlands Trinity Church **P** (917) § 419 S 4th St 92373-5952 (Mail to: 419 S 4th St 92373-5952) Elizabeth McQuitty Paul Price (909) 793-2014

Redondo Beach Christ Episcopal Church **P** (192) 408 S Broadway 90277-3717 (Mail to: 408 S Broadway 90277-3717) Nickolas Griffith Hyangnam Lee Bonnie McNaughton (310) 540-1722

Rialto St Peter's Episcopal Church **P** (72) 777 Acacia Ave 92376-5246 (Mail to: 777 Acacia Ave 92376-5246) Robert Van Buren (909) 875-5689

Riverside All Saints Episcopal Church **P** (436) § 3847 Terracina Dr 92506-0149 (Mail to: 3847 Terracina Dr 92506-0149) Conrad Nordquist Benjamin Orozco (951) 683-8466

Riverside St Georges Episcopal Church **P** (121) 950 Spruce St 92507-2503 (Mail to: 950 Spruce St 92507-2503) Khushnud Azariah Guy Leemhuis (951) 686-9936

San Clemente St Clements by the Sea **P** (147) 202 Avenida Aragon 92672-5015 (Mail to: 202 Avenida Aragon 92672-5098) Patrick Crerar William Wells (949) 492-3401

San Fernando St Simons Episcopal Church **P** (387) 623 Hagar St 91340-2005 (Mail to: 623 Hagar St 91340-2005) (818) 361-3317

San Gabriel Church of Our Saviour **P** (606) § 535 W Roses Rd 91775-2205 (Mail to: 535 W Roses Rd 91775-2205) William Doulos John Honeychurch Huiliang Ni Marilyn Omernick (626) 282-5147

San Juan Capo St Margaret of Scotland Church **P** (926) § 31641 La Novia Ave 92675-2752 (Mail to: C/O Kim Ashby 31641 La Novia Ave 92675-2752) Linda Ahron Linda Ahron Robert Edwards Earl Gibson James Livingston (949) 661-0110

San Marino St Edmunds Episcopal Church **P** (519) § 1175 S San Gabriel Blvd 91108-2226 (Mail to: PO Box 80038 91118-8038) William Doggett (626) 793-9167

San Pedro St Peters Episcopal Church **P** (210) 1648 W 9th St 90732-3404 (Mail to: 1648 W 9th St 90732-3404) Jeanette Repp (310) 831-2361

Santa Ana Church of the Messiah **P** (786) 614 North Bush Street 92701-4157 (Mail to: 614 Bush St 92701-4157) Norma Guerra James Lee Abel Lopez Katharine MacKenzie (714) 543-9389

Santa Barbara Church of All Saints-by-the-Sea **P** (845) § 83 Eucalyptus Ln 93108-2901 (Mail to: 83 Eucalyptus Ln 93108-2901) Aimee Eyer-Delevett Victoria Mouradian (805) 969-4771

Santa Barbara Christ the King Episcopal Church **P** (124) 5073 Hollister Ave 93111-2637 (Mail to: PO Box 6188 93160-6188) Joy Magala (805) 964-9966

Santa Barbara Trinity Episcopal Church **P** (768) 1500 State St 93101-2514 (Mail to: 1500 State St 93101-2514) Elizabeth Molitors Laurel Johnston (805) 965-7419

Santa Maria St Peter Episcopal Church **P** (252) 402 S Lincoln St 93454 (Mail to: P O Box 1868 93456-1868) Faye Hogan Hi-Jae Kang (805) 922-3575

Santa Monica St Augustines by the Sea **P** (278) 1227 4th St 90401-1303 (Mail to: 1227 4th St 90401-1390) Nathan Rugh Katherine Cadigan Kathryn Derose (310) 395-0977

Santa Paula St Pauls Episcopal Church **P** (80) 117 7th St 93060-2615 (Mail to: 117 7th St 93060-2615) Cynthia Jew (805) 525-3811

Seal Beach St Theodore of Canterbury Church **M** (42) 1240 Oakmont Rd Ste 52b 90740-3650 (Mail to: Leisure World 1240 Oakmont Rd Ste 52B 90740-3650) (562) 430-8619

Sierra Madre Church of the Ascension **P** (452) 25 E Laurel Ave 91024-1915 (Mail to: 25 E Laurel Ave 91024-1915) Michael Bamberger Jennifer Beal Edward Sniecienski (626) 355-1133

Simi Valley Church of St Francis of Assisi **M** (353) 280 Royal Ave 93065 (Mail to: PO Box 940516 93094-0516) Sarah Kitch (805) 526-5141

Skyforest St Richards Episcopal Church **M** (82) 28708 Hwy 18 92385 (Mail to: PO Box 1317 92352-1317) Edward Hulbert (909) 337-3889

Sn Bernrdno St Johns Episcopal Church **M** (96) 1407 Arrowhead Ave 92405-4813 (Mail to: 1407 Arrowhead Ave 92405-4813) (909) 889-1195

South Gate St Margaret's Episcopal Church **P** (365) 4704 Tweedy Blvd 90280-5208 (Mail to: 4704 Tweedy Blvd 90280-5208) Eduardo Bresciani (323) 569-9901

South Pasadena St James Episcopal Church **P** (750) § 1325 Monterey Rd 91030-3228 (Mail to: 1325 Monterey Rd 91030-3291) Anne O'Hara-Tumilty Michelle Baker-Wright Gethin Wied (626) 799-9194

Studio City St Michael & All Angels **P** (356) 3646 Coldwater Canyon Ave 91604-4062 (Mail to: 3646 Coldwater Canyon Ave 91604-4099) Daniel Justin (818) 763-9193

Thousand Oaks St Patricks Church & Day School **P** (304) § 1 Church Rd 91362-1809 (Mail to: 1 Church Rd 91362-1809) George Daisa Sarah Kitch Sarah Kitch (805) 495-6441

Torrance St Andrews Church **P** (176) 1432 Engracia Ave 90501-3201 (Mail to: 1432 Engracia Ave 90501-3201) (310) 328-3781

Tustin St Pauls Episcopal Church **P** (407) § 1221 Wass St 92780-2855 (Mail to: 1221 Wass St 92780-2855) Valerie Hart Laura Siriani Kathleen Sylvester (714) 544-3141

Twentynine Palms St Martin in-the-Fields Church **M** (41) 72348 Larrea Ave 92277-2181 (Mail to: 72348 Larrea Ave 92277-2181) (760) 367-7133

Upland St Marks Episcopal Church **P** (239) § 330 E 16th St 91784-2050 (Mail to: 330 E 16th St 91784-2050) Keith Yamamoto Sally Monastiere (909) 920-5565

Valencia St Stephen's Episcopal Church **P** (387) § 24901 Orchard Village Rd 91355-3074 (Mail to: 24901 Orchard Village Rd 91355-3098) (661) 259-7307

Van Nuys St Marks Episcopal Church **P** (460) 14646 Sherman Way 91405-5860 (Mail to: 14646 Sherman Way Ste A 91405-2297) (818) 785-4251

Ventura St Pauls Episcopal Church **P** (328) 3290 Loma Vista Rd 93003-3002 (Mail to: 3290 Loma Vista Rd 93003-3002) Susan Bek Raymond Steever Richard Swanson (805) 643-5033

Whittier St Matthias Episcopal Church **P** (239) 7056 Washington Ave 90602-1415 (Mail to: 7056 Washington Ave 90602-1496) William Garrison Carole Horton-Howe (562) 698-9741

Wilmington St Johns & Holy Child Epis Church
M (378) 1537 Neptune Ave 90744-2003 (Mail
to: PO Box 1716 90748-1716) (310) 835-7870

Winnetka St Martin in-the-Fields **P** (166) § 7136
Winnetka Ave 91306-3647 (Mail to: 7136
Winnetka Ave 91306-3695) Christopher Eade
Gabriel Ferrer Christopher Montella (818)
348-1419

Woodland Hls Church of the Prince of Peace **P**
(973) 5700 Rudnick Ave 91367-6238 (Mail to:

5700 Rudnick Ave 91367-6299) Rand Reasoner
Onesmus Tayebwa Onesmus Tayebwa (818)
346-6968

Yucaipa St Alban's Episcopal Church **M** (112)
12692 5th St 92399-2571 (Mail to: PO Box 695
92399-0695) Elizabeth Williams (909) 797-
3266

Yucca Valley Saint Joseph Of Arimathea Mission
M (44) 56312 Onaga Trl 92284-3636 (Mail to:
56312 Onaga Trl 92284-3636) (760) 365-7133

STATE OF LOUISIANA

Dioceses of Louisiana and Western Louisiana

DIOCESE OF LOUISIANA

(PROVINCE IV)
Comprises all parishes east of the Atchafalaya River and including all of St Mary's Parish
DIOCESAN OFFICE 1623 Seventh St New Orleans LA 70115
TEL (504) 895-6634   FAX (504) 895-6637   WEB www.edola.org

Previous Bishops—
Leonidas Polk 1841-64, Jos PB
Wilmer 1866-78, John N Galleher
1880-91, Davis Sessums coadj
1891 Bp 1891-1929, James C
Morris 1930-39, John L Jackson
1940-48, Girault M Jones 1949-
69, Iveson B Noland suffr 1952-61
coadj 1961 Bp 1969-75, R Heber
Gooden asst 1972-75 acting 1975-76, James B Brown
1976-98, Charles Edward Jenkins III Bp 1998-2010

Bishop—Rt Rev Morris K Thompson Jr (1043)
(Dio May 8 2010)

Cn to Ord Rev Cn S Manning *Sec/Reg* M Wade; *Treas*
A Brackett; *Chanc* CJ Geary 201 St Charles New
Orleans LA 70170-5100; *Hist* A Threefoot; *Com* Rev
P Bailey

Stand Comm—Cler: Pres R Courtney M MacIntire F
Devall J Miller; *Lay:* K Martin J Figuroa J Zitzmann
F McCullogh

PARISHES, MISSIONS, AND CLERGY

Amite Episcopal Church of the Incarnation **M**
(27) 111 E Olive St 70422-2539 (Mail to: PO
Box 722 70422-0722) (985) 748-9706

Angola Transfiguration at Angola State Pris **M**
Angola State Prison 70712 (Mail to: 3112
Green Acres Rd 70003-1820) (225) 387-0396

Baton Rouge St Albans Episcopal Chapel **CM**
(328) Dalrymple & Highland LSU 70808 (Mail
to: 5261 Highland Rd PMB 376 70808-6547)
Andrew Rollins (225) 343-2070

Baton Rouge St Augustines Episcopal Church **M**
(45) 12954 Joor Rd 70837 (Mail to: PO Box
78123 70837-8123) (225) 261-4344

Baton Rouge St James Episcopal Church **P** (1961)
§ 205 4th St 70801-1403 (Mail to: PO Box 126
70821-0126) Christopher Duncan Ralph Howe
(225) 387-5141

Baton Rouge Saint Luke's Church **P** (935) § 8833
Goodwood Blvd 70806-7919 (Mail to: 8833
Goodwood Blvd 70806-7995) Charles Owen
Christopher Golding Reese Wiggins (225) 926-
5343

Baton Rouge St Margaret's Episcopal Church **P**
(164) 12663 Perkins Rd 70810-1909 (Mail to:
12663 Perkins Rd 70810-1909) Tommy Dillon
(225) 766-8314

Baton Rouge St Michael & All Angels **M** (89)
1666 77th Ave 70807-5405 (Mail to: 1620 77th
Ave 70807-5496) Stewart Cage Floyd Knox
(225) 357-8852

Baton Rouge Trinity Episcopal Church **HC**
(1048) § 3552 Morning Glory Ave 70808-2865
(Mail to: 3552 Morning Glory Ave 70808-
2865) Sharon Alexander John Tober (225) 387-
0396

Bogalusa St Matthews Church **P** (81) 208 Georgia
Ave 70427-3824 (Mail to: 208 Georgia Ave
70427-3824) (985) 732-4328

Clinton St Andrews Episcopal Church **M** (96)
1 St Andrew St 70722 (Mail to: PO Box 8259
70722-1259) (225) 683-5498

Covington Christ Episcopal Church **P** (935) § 120
S New Hampshire St 70433 (Mail to: 120 S New
Hampshire St 70433-3545) William Miller

Morgan Macintire Anne Maxwell Winston Rice (985) 892-3177

Denham Spgs St Francis Church **P** (162) 726 Maple St 70726-3026 (Mail to: 726 Maple St 70726-3026) (225) 665-2707

Franklin St Marys Episcopal Church **P** (43) 805 1st St 70538-5415 (Mail to: PO Box 95 70538-0095) Stephen Crawford (337) 828-0918

Hammond Grace Memorial Episcopal Church **P** (497) 100 W Church St 70401-3205 (Mail to: PO Box 1086 70404-1086) Paul Bailey (985) 345-2764

Harvey St Marks Episcopal Church **P** (106) 3245 Manhattan Blvd 70058-5112 (Mail to: 3245 Manhattan Blvd 70058-5112) Percy Bates (504) 366-0123

Houma St Matthew Episcopal Church **P** (325) 239 Barrow St 70360-4403 (Mail to: 243 Barrow St 70360-4403) Craig Dalferes (985) 872-5057

Innis Saint Stephen's Church **P** (124) 9795 Highway 418 70747 (Mail to: PO Box 1020 70747-0888) John Miller (225) 492-2234

Kenner St Johns Episcopal Church **M** (52) 2109 17th St 70062-6351 (Mail to: 2109 17th St 70062-6351) Charmaine Kathmann (504) 469-4535

La Place St Timothys Episcopal Church **M** (45) § 1101 Belle Alliance Dr 70068-3201 (Mail to: 1101 Belle Alliance Dr 70068-3201) (985) 652-2121

Luling St Andrews Episcopal Church **M** Audbon & Early St 70070 (Mail to: PO Box 621 70070-0621) (985) 758-1607

Mandeville St Michael's Episcopal Church **M** (247) § 4499 Sharp Rd 70471-8919 (Mail to: 4499 Sharp Rd 70471-8919) (985) 626-5781

Metairie St Augustines Episcopal Church **P** (750) 3412 Haring Rd 70006-3902 (Mail to: 3412 Haring Rd 70006-3902) William Heine Michael Hackett Robert Price-Hadzor (504) 887-4801

Metairie Saint Martin's Episcopal Church **P** (500) 2216 Metairie Rd 70001-4205 (Mail to: 2216 Metairie Rd 70001-4200) Frederick Devall Ford Millican (504) 835-7357

Morgan City Trinity Episcopal Church **P** (116) PO Box 1776 70381-1776 (Mail to: PO Box 1776 302 Greenwood 70381-1776) (985) 384-7629

Morganza St Marys Episcopal Church **M** (25) 331 W Tircuit St 70759 (Mail to: PO Box 173 70759-0173) Peggy Scott (225) 694-3609

Napoleonville Christ Episcopal Church **PS** 4829 Highway 1 70390-2002 (Mail to: PO Box 27 70390-0027) (985) 369-2106

New Orleans All Saints' Episcopal Church **P** (273) 100 Rex Dr 70123-3531 (Mail to: 100 Rex Dr 70123-3531) John Angerer (504) 737-2421

New Orleans Chapel of the Holy Comforter **CC** (36) 2220 Lakeshore Dr 70122-3502 (Mail to: 2220 Lakeshore Dr 70122-3502) John Craft (504) 282-4593

✣ **New Orleans** Christ Church Cathedral **O** (700) 2919 Saint Charles Ave 70115-4421 (Mail to: 2919 Saint Charles Ave 70115-4498) David Duplantier Steven Roberts Bridget Tierney (504) 895-6602

New Orleans Chapel of the Holy Spirit **CC** (55) 1100 Broadway St 70118-5243 (Mail to: 1100 Broadway St 70118-5243) Watson Lamb (504) 866-7438

New Orleans Grace Episcopal Church **P** 3700 Canal St 70119-6141 (Mail to: 3700 Canal St 70119-6141) (504) 482-5242

New Orleans Mt Olivet Episcopal Church **P** (109) 530 Pelican Ave 70114-1051 (Mail to: 530 Pelican St 70114-1051) (504) 366-4650

New Orleans St Andrew Episcopal Church **P** (376) § 1116 Short St 70118-2712 (Mail to: 1031 S Carrollton Ave 70118-1145) Robert Beazley James Morrison Charles Ziegenfuss (504) 866-0123

New Orleans St Annas Episcopal Church **P** (183) 1313 Esplanade Ave 70116-1836 (Mail to: 1313 Esplanade Ave 70116-1894) William Terry (504) 947-2121

New Orleans St George's Episcopal Church **P** (177) § 4600 Saint Charles Ave 70115-4834 (Mail to: 4600 Saint Charles Ave 70115-4897) Richard Easterling (504) 899-2811

New Orleans St Lukes Episcopal Church **P** (129) 1222 Dorgenois St 70119-3445 (Mail to: 1222 Dorgenois St 70119-3445) Donald Muth (504) 821-0529

New Orleans St Pauls Episcopal Church **P** (232) § 6249 Canal Blvd 70124-3099 (Mail to: 6249 Canal Blvd 70124-3099) Robert Courtney Elizabeth Embler-Beazley (504) 488-3749

New Orleans St Philips Episcopal Church **P** (324) 3643 Aurora Dr 70131-5507 (Mail to: 3643 Aurora Dr 70131-5507) Stephen Craft (504) 394-2408

New Orleans The Church of the Annunciation **P** (112) 4505 S Claiborne Ave 70125-5007 (Mail to: 4505 S Claiborne Ave 70125-5007) Duane Wiggin-Nettles (504) 895-8697

New Orleans Trinity Episcopal Church **P** (2670) § 1329 Jackson Ave 70130-5131 (Mail to: C/o Gabriella Frank 1329 Jackson Ave 70130-5198) Katherine McLean John Pitzer Robert Price-Hadzor Edgar Taylor Andrew Thayer Jane-Allison Wiggin-Nettles (504) 522-0276

New Roads St Pauls Holy Trinity **P** (81) 607 E Main St 70760-3641 (Mail to: PO Box 386 70760-0386) Peggy Scott (225) 638-8433

Plaquemine Church of the Holy Communion **P** (124) 58040 Court St 70764-2704 (Mail to: PO Box 474 70765-0474) Christopher Capaldo (225) 687-2611

Ponchatoula All Saints Episcopal Church **M** (43) 250 West Hickory Street 70454-3218 (Mail to: Attn Diocese Of Louisiana PO Box 5026 70821-5026) (985) 386-8126

Rosedale Church of the Nativity **M** (54) 302 Laurel St 70772 (Mail to: c/o Shirley Best PO Box 195 70772-0195) (225) 241-2556

Slidell Christ Episcopal Church **P** (375) 1534 7th St 70458-2847 (Mail to: 1534 7th St 70458-2897) Richard Almos Harry Jenkins (985) 643-4531

St Francisvlle Grace Church Of West Feliciana **P** (371) 11621 Ferdinand St 70775-4339 (Mail to: Attn Margaret E Kendrick PO Box 28 70775-0028) Roman Roldan (225) 635-4065

Theriot St Andrews Episcopal Church **M** (292) 3027 Bayou Dularge Rd 70397-9743 (Mail to: 3027 Bayou Dularge Rd 70397-9743) (985) 872-2508

Thibodaux St Johns Episcopal Church **P** (93) 718 Jackson St 70301-2732 (Mail to: 718 Jackson St 70301-2732) Stephen Shortess (985) 447-2910

Zachary St Patricks Episcopal Church **P** (243) § 1322 Church St 70791-2743 (Mail to: 1322 Church St 70791-2743) Ashley Freeman (225) 654-4091

DIOCESE OF MAINE

(PROVINCE I)

Comprises the State of Maine

DIOCESAN OFFICE 143 State St Portland ME 04101-3799

TEL (207) 772-1953

E-MAIL info@episcopalmaine.org   WEB www.episcopalmaine.org

Previous Bishops—
Geo Burgess 1847-66, Henry A Neely 1867-99, Robt Codman 1900-15, Benj Brewster 1916-40, Oliver L Loring 1941-68, Fredk B Wolf 1968-86, Edward C Chalfant coadj 1984-86 Bp 1986-1996, Chilton R Knudsen 1998-2008

Bishop — Rt Rev Stephen T Lane (1028) (Dio 13 Sept 2008)

Cn to the Ordinary M Ambler; *Cn Fin & Stew* T Reimer; *Cn for Form & Networks* J Hartwell; *Exec Asst to Bp, Reg & Arch* B Martin; *Camp Dir* M Douglass; *Sec Conv* L Spahr; *Treas* R Rozene; *Chanc* G Gayer 16 Mare's Hollow Ln Cape Elizabeth ME 04107

Stand Comm—Cler: Pres M Hoecker S Gavit T Higgins *Lay:* B Hamilton C Priest D Mayer

PARISHES, MISSIONS, AND CLERGY

Auburn St Michaels Episcopal Church **P** (153) 78 Pleasant St 04210-5940 (Mail to: 78 Pleasant St 04210-5940) Judson Pealer (207) 782-1346

Augusta St Barnabas Church **M** (61) 60 Bangor St 04330 (Mail to: 60 Bangor St 04330-4804) (207) 248-2687

Augusta St Marks Church **P** (90) 9 Summer St 04330-5128 (Mail to: 9 Summer St 04330-5128) (207) 622-2424

Bailey Island All Saints by the Sea Summer Chapel **SC** Washington Ave 04003 (Mail to: 20 Cedar Beach Rd C/O Dana R Baggett 04003-2521) (207) 772-1953

Bangor St Johns Episcopal Church **P** (282) 225 French St 04401-5012 (Mail to: 234 French St 04401-5013) Jonathan Appleyard Marguerite Steadman (207) 947-0156

Bar Harbor St Saviours Church **P** (132) 41 Mount Desert St 04609-1753 (Mail to: 41 Mount Desert St 04609-1753) Timothy Fleck (207) 288-4215

Bath Grace Episcopal Church **P** (425) 1100 Washington St 04530-2762 (Mail to: 1100 Washington St 04530-2762) Ted Gaiser (207) 443-3792

Belfast Saint Margaret's Church **P** (259) 95 Court St 04915-6135 (Mail to: 95 Court St 04915-6135) (207) 338-2412

Biddeford Christ Church **P** (22) 18 1/2 Crescent St 04005-2520 (Mail to: 35 SOUTH ST 040052520) (207) 283-1783

Biddeford Pool St Martins in Field Summer Chpl **SC** St Martins Ln 04006 (Mail to: Martins Lane 04006) Daniel Meck (207) 772-1953

Blue Hill St Francis By The Sea **P** (360) 330 Hinckley Ridge Rd 04614-5816 (Mail to: PO Box 76 04614-0076) Claudia Smith (207) 374-5200

Brewer St Patricks Episcopal Church **P** (81) 21 Holyoke St 04412-1905 (Mail to: 21 Holyoke St 04412-1905) (207) 989-1308

Bridgton St Peters Episcopal Church **P** (148) 42 Sweden Rd 04009-3528 (Mail to: PO Box 134 04009-0134) (207) 647-8549

Brownville St Johns Episcopal Church **M** (40) 26 Henderson St 04414-3735 (Mail to: PO Box 751 04414-0751) Kevin Holsapple (207) 943-5168

Brunswick St Pauls Church Episcopal **P** (635) 27 Pleasant St 04011-2222 (Mail to: PO Box 195 04011-0195) Carolyn Eklund Peggy Schnack (207) 725-5342

Calais St Annes Church **P** (86) 29 Church St 04619-1636 (Mail to: 29 Church St 04619-1669) Sara Gavit (207) 454-8016

Camden Christ Church Dark Harbor **SC** Attn S Russell Schatz Fletcher 87 Elm St Ste 215 04843-1959 (Mail to: PO Box 147 04848-0147) (207) 734-8207

Camden Church of St Thomas **P** (220) PO Box 631 04843-0631 (Mail to: PO Box 631 33 Chesnut street 04843-2209) Lisa Fry (207) 236-3680

Cape Elizabeth St Alban Episcopal Church **P** (800) 885 Shore Rd 04107-1540 (Mail to: 885 Shore Rd 04107-1540) Timothy Boggs Holly Clark (207) 799-4014

Castine Trinity Episcopal Church **P** (73) Perkins And Tarrant 04421 (Mail to: PO Box 433 04421-0433) Richard Armstrong Ian Bockus Emily Stribling Margaret Thomas (207) 326-4180

Damariscotta St Cuthbert Summer Chapel **SC** C/O Jane Kennedy Hc 61 Box 124 04543 (Mail to: C/O Jane Kennedy Hc 61 Box 124 04543) (207) 371-2517

Deer Isle Saint Brendan's Episcopal Church **P** (44) PO Box 305 04627-0305 (Mail to: PO Box 305 04627-0305) (207) 348-6240

Dovr Foxcroft St Augustines Episcopal Church **M** (64) PO Box 504 04426-0504 (Mail to: PO Box 504 04426-0504) Kevin Holsapple (207) 564-7075

East Boothbay St Columbas Episcopal Church **P** (138) 32 Emery Ln 04538-1965 (Mail to: 32 Emery Ln 04538-1965) Maria Hoecker Maria Hoecker (207) 633-6313

Eastport Christ Episcopal Church **P** (54) PO Box 12 04631-0012 (Mail to: PO Box 12 04631-0012) Lynn Rutledge (207) 853-4598

Ellsworth St Dunstans Episcopal Church **P** (99) 134 State Stree 04605-1832 (Mail to: PO Box 711 04605-0711) (207) 667-5495

Falmouth St Mary the Virgin Epis Church **P** (577) 43 Foreside Rd 04105-1708 (Mail to: 43 Foreside Rd 04105-1708) Nathan Ferrell Jack Haney (207) 781-3366

Farmington St Lukes Church **P** (104) High And School Sts 04938 (Mail to: PO Box 249 04938-0249) Suzanne Cole (207) 645-2639

Ft Fairfield St Pauls Episcopal Church **P** (56) 170 Main St 04742-1220 (Mail to: PO Box 389 04742-0389) (207) 492-4211

Gardiner Christ Church Episcopal **P** (151) 2 Dresden Ave 04345-2633 (Mail to: 2 Dresden Ave 04345-2633) Kerry Mansir Stephen Muncie (207) 582-3354

Hallowell St Matthews Episcopal Church **P** (217) 20 Union St 04347-1369 (Mail to: 20 Union St 04347-1369) David Matson (207) 623-3041

Harborside Our Lady of Evrgrns Summer Chpl **SC** 44 Emerson Pt Rd 04642 (Mail to: PO Box 94 04642)

Houlton Church Of The Good Shepherd **P** (115) 116 Main St 04730-2113 (Mail to: PO Box 1672 04730-5672) Jessie Drysdale Jennifer Reece (207) 532-2927

Hulls Cove Church Of Our Father **P** (87) State Hwy #3 3 04644 (Mail to: PO Box 186 04644-0186) John Allison (207) 288-4849

Jefferson St Giles Episcopal Church **P** (84) 72 Gardiner Rd 04348-3973 (Mail to: PO Box 34 04348-0034) Susan Kraus (207) 549-3158

Kennebunk St Davids Episcopal Church **P** (336) 138 York St 04043-7108 (Mail to: 138 York St 04043-7108) Andrew White (207) 985-3073

Kennebunk Beach Trinity Summer Chapel **SC** 3 Woodland Ave 04043 (Mail to: C/O Norman Kellett P.O. Box 1130 04043) (207) 967-3056

Kennebunkport St Anns Episcopal Church **SC** 1 Ocean Ave 04046-6003 (Mail to: PO Box 44 04046-0044) Peter Cheney (207) 967-8043

Lewiston Trinity Episcopal Church **P** (32) 247 Bates St 04240-7331 (Mail to: PO Box 2324 04241-2324) (207) 312-9410

Limestone Church of the Advent **M** (10) 37 Church St 04750 (Mail to: 650 Main St Ste A 04736-4422) (207) 492-4211

Lisbon Falls St Matthews Episcopal Church **P** (147) 496 Lisbon St 04250 (Mail to: PO Box 879 04250-0879) (207) 353-8453

Machias St Aidans Episcopal Church **M** (51) 36 Hill St 04654-1310 (Mail to: PO Box 271 04654-0271) Lynn Rutledge (207) 255-4995

Millinocket St Andrews Episcopal Church **P** (87) 40 Highland Ave 04462-1413 (Mail to: 40 Highland Ave 04462-1413) Robert Landry (207) 723-5893

Newcastle Saint Andrew's Church **P** (343) PO Box 234 04553-3401 (Mail to: PO Box 234 04553-0234) John Nieman (207) 563-3533

North Haven North Haven Summer Services **SC** Church St 04853 (Mail to: P O Box 318 04853) (207) 867-4876

Northeast Harbor The Parish of St Mary & St Jude **P** (233) PO Box 105 04662-0105 (Mail to: PO Box 105 04662-0105) Jane Cornman (207) 276-5588

Norway Christ Episcopal Church **P** (101) 35 Paris St 04268-5630 (Mail to: 35 Paris St 04268-5630) Nancy Moore Elizabeth Wenthe (207) 743-6782

Old Town St James Episcopal Church **P** (69) 149 Center St 04468-1502 (Mail to: PO Box 183 04468-0183) M Jane White-Hassler (207) 827-5013

Orrs Island All Saints Summer Chapel **SC** 9 Cooper Ln 04066-2112 (Mail to: 9 Cooper Ln 04066) (207) 833-7745

Palmyra St Martins Episcopal Church **M** (48) 900 Main St 04965-3408 (Mail to: PO Box 107 04965-0107) Leslie Nesin Laura Peckham (207) 938-3385

Peaks Island Holy Trinity Episcopal Summer Chapel **SC** 69 Knickerbocker Ln 04108-1562 (Mail to: Robin Walden 60 Centennial St 04108-1102) (207) 766-3376

✤ **Portland** Cathedral Church Of Saint Luke **O** (614) 143 State St 04101-3701 (Mail to: 143 State St 04101-0341) Benjamin Shambaugh K Drew Baker Eleanor Prior Suzanne Roberts (207) 772-5434

Portland St Peters Church **P** (283) 10 Alton St 04103-4906 (Mail to: 10 Alton St 04103-4906) Mary Ann Hoy (207) 775-1179

Portland Trinity Episcopal Church **P** (460) 113 Coyle St 04103-4402 (Mail to: 580 Forest Ave 04101-1545) Lawrence Weeks (207) 772-7421

Presque Isle St Johns Episcopal Church **P** (32) 52 2nd St 04769-2636 (Mail to: PO Box 8 04769-0008) Judith Burleigh Stephen Summerson (207) 764-4298

Rangeley Church of the Good Shepherd **P** (99) 2614 Main St 04970-4114 (Mail to: PO Box 156 04970-0156) (207) 864-3381

Rockland Saint Peter's Church **P** (301) White St 4841 (Mail to: 11 White St 04841-2982) Lael Sorensen (207) 594-8191

Rumford Saint Barnabas Church **P** (19) 71 Rumford Ave 04276-1973 (Mail to: PO Box 591 04276-0591) Timothy Parsons (207) 364-2193

Saco Trinity Episcopal Church **P** (252) 403 Main St 04072-1522 (Mail to: 403 Main St 04072-1522) Linda Cappers (207) 284-4852

Sanford St Georges Episcopal Church **P** (209) 1 Emerson St 04073-3903 (Mail to: 3 Emerson St 04073-3903) (207) 324-8119

Scarborough Saint Nicholas Episcopal Church **M** (186) 350 US Route 1 04074-8307 (Mail to: 350 US Route 1 04074-8307) David Heald (207) 883-9437

Skowhegan All Saints Episcopal Church **M** (38) 169 Malbons Mills Rd 04976-4122 (Mail to: PO Box 412 04976-0412) Regina Knox (207) 474-2629

Sorrento Church of the Redeemer Summer Chapel **SC** 62 Bayview Ave 04677 (Mail to: PO Box 123 04677-0123) (207) 422-3955

Southport All Saints by the Sea Summer Chapel **SC** PO Box 377 04576-0377 (Mail to: PO Box 377 04576-0377) (207) 633-7301

Southwest Hbr Sts Andrew & John Episcopal Church **P** (103) 315 Main St 04679-4403 (Mail to: 315 Main St 04679-0767) Kathleen Killian (207) 244-3229

Thomaston Episcopal Church of St John Baptist **P** (212) 200 Main St 04861-3800 (Mail to: 200 Main St 04861-3800) Peter Jenks (207) 354-8734

Waterville St Marks Church **P** (317) 60 Eustis Pkwy 04901-4932 (Mail to: 60 Eustis Pkwy 04901-4932) John Balicki (207) 872-7869

Windham St Anns Episcopal Church **P** (372) 40 Windham Center Rd. 04062 (Mail to: PO Box 911 04062-0911) Timothy Higgins (207) 892-8447

Winn St Thomas Episcopal Church **M** (28) 14 Main Street 04495 (Mail to: P.O. Box 106 04495-0106) (207) 736-2010

Winter Harbor St Christopher Summer Chapel **SC** 9 Clubhouse Rd 04693 (Mail to: C/O Margaret F Bennett 6 Holly Villa Drive 33436) Thomas Van Culin Ralph Warren (207) 963-5554

Winthrop St Andrews Episcopal Church **M** (54) 219 Winthrop Center Rd. 04364 (Mail to: PO Box 66 04364) Susan Taylor (207) 395-2015

Wiscasset St Philips Episcopal Church **P** (97) 12 Hodge St 04578-4021 (Mail to: 12 Hodge St 04578-4021) (207) 882-7184

Yarmouth St Bartholomews Episcopal Church **P** (469) 396 Gilman Rd 04096-5731 (Mail to: 396 Gilman Rd 04096-5731) Nina Pooley (207) 846-9244

York St George's Episcopal Church **P** (543) 407 York St 03909-1060 (Mail to: PO Box 364 407 York St 03911-0364) Aaron Perkins (207) 363-7376

York Harbor Trinity Church **SC** 546 York Street 03911 (Mail to: 546 York St 03911) (207) 363-5095

STATE OF MARYLAND
Dioceses of Easton (E), Maryland (MD), and Washington (W)

Abingdon—MD
Annapolis—MD
Aquasco—W
Avenue—W
Baltimore—MD
Bel Air—MD
Beltsville—W
Berlin—E
Bethesda—W
Boonsboro—MD
Bowie—W

Braddock Hts—MD
Brandywine—W
Brookeville—W
Brownsville—MD
Brunswick—MD
California—W
Cambridge—E
Centreville—E
Chaptico—W
Charlotte Hall—W
Chesapeake City—E

Chestertown—E
Chevy Chase—W
Church Creek—E
Church Hill—E
Churchville—MD
Clear Spg—MD
Clinton—W
Cockeysville—MD
College Pk—W
Columbia—MD
Crownsville—MD

Cumberland—MD
Damascus—W
Darlington—MD
Deale—MD
Denton—E
District Hts—W
Dundalk—MD
Earleville—E
Easton—E
Edgewater—MD
Elkridge—MD

Elkton—E
Ellicott City—MD
Essex—MD
Forest Hill—MD
Ft Washington—W
Frederick—MD
Frostburg—MD
Gaithersburg—W
Germantown—W
Glen Burnie—MD
Glencoe—MD
Glenwood—MD
Glenn Dale—W
Gwynn Oak—MD
Hagerstown—MD
Halethorpe—MD
Hampstead—MD
Hancock—MD
Havre de Grace—MD
Hebron—E
Highland—MD
Hughesville—W
Hurlock—E
Hyattsville—W
Indian Head—W

Joppatowne—MD
Kennedyville—E
Kensington—W
Kingsville—MD
LaPlata—W
Laurel—W
Leonardtown—W
Lexington Pk—W
Linthicum Hts—MD
Lonaconing—MD
Long Green—MD
Lothian—MD
Lusby—MD
Lutherville Timon—
  MD
Massey—E
Mayo—MD
Monkton—MD
Mt Airy—MD
Mt Rainier—W
Mt Savage—MD
Nanjemoy—W
New Market—MD
Newburg—W
North East—E

Oakland—MD
Ocean City—E
Odenton—MD
Olney—W
Owings Mills—MD
Oxford—E
Parkton—MD
Pasadena—MD
Perryville—E
Pikesville—MD
Pocomoke City—E
Pt of Rocks—MD
Poolesville—W
Pt Republic—MD
Potomac—W
Prince Frederick—MD
Princess Anne—E
Quantico—E
Queenstown—E
Reisterstown—MD
Ridge—W
Rockville—W
St Michael—E
Salisbury—E
Severna Pk—MD

Sharpsburg—MD
Silver Spg—W
Smithsburg—MD
Snow Hill—E
Stevensville—E
Street—MD
Sunderland—MD
Sykesville—MD
Temple Hills—W
Thurmont—MD
Towson—MD
Trappe—E
Tyaskin—E
Upper Marlboro—W
Vienna—E
Waldorf—W
Washington—W
W River—MD
Westernport—MD
Westminster—MD
Worton—E
Wye Mills—E

DIOCESE OF MARYLAND
(PROVINCE III)
Comprises western shore of Maryland excluding Charles,
Montgomery, Prince George's & St Mary's Counties
DIOCESAN OFFICE 4 E University Pkwy Baltimore MD 21218
TEL (410) 467-1399, (800) 443-1399   FAX (410) 554-6387
E-MAIL communications@episcopalmaryland.org   WEB www.episcopalmaryland.org

Previous Bishops—
Thomas J Claggett 1792-1816,
James Kemp suffr 1814 Bp
1816-27, Wm M Stone 1830-38,
Wm R Whittingham 1840-79,
Wm Pinkney coadj 1870 Bp
1879-83, Wm Paret 1885-1911,
John G Murray coadj 1909 Bp
1911-29, Edward T Helfenstein
coadj 1926 Bp 1929-44, Noble
C Powell coadj 1941 Bp 1944-63, Harry L Doll
suffr 1955 coadj 1958 Bp 1963-71, William J Cox
suffr 1972-80, David K Leighton Sr coadj 1968 Bp
1972-85, Barry Valentine asst 1986-88, A Theodore
Eastman coadj 1982 Bp 1986-94, Charles L Longest
suffr 1989-97, Robert W Ihloff Bp 1995-2007, John L
Rabb Bp-in-Charge 2007-08 Suffr 1998-2010, Joe G
Burnett asst 2011-2013, Heather E Cook suffr 2014-
15, Chilton R. Knudsen asst 2015-18

Bishop—Rt Rev Eugene Taylor Sutton (1030)
(Dio 28 June 2008)

Assistant Bishop—vacant

Staff: *Cn to the Ord* Rev SG Slater; *Cn for Mission*
Rev CL McCloud; *Cn for Discernment & Cong Vit*
Rev MC Sulerud; *Cn for Transitions and Human
Resources* Rev SW Wright; *Missioner for Yth & Young
Adults* K Riley; *Cn for Latino Min* Rev RM Santana;
Dir of Comms CS Graves; *Archivist* MO Klein

Officers: *Cn for Fin & CFO* KK Stewart; *Treas*
DE Vaughan; *Chanc* JP Ayres c/o Venable 210 W
Pennsylvania Ave Ste 500 Towson MD 21204; *Sec of
Convention* Rev AO Weatherholt

Stand Comm—*Cler*: *Pres* NH Conway MH Gatza TS
Lucas AP Dawson; *Lay*: *VP* M Garcia MH DeKuyper
J Milan DH Boyce

Archdeacons: Ven J O'Leary Ven RA Elder

PARISHES, MISSIONS, AND CLERGY

Abingdon St Marys Episcopal Church **P** (484) 1
Saint Marys Church Rd 21009-1565 (Mail to:
1 Saint Marys Church Rd 21009-1569) (410)
569-0180

Annapolis St Annes Episcopal Parish **P** (2219)
199 Duke Of Gloucester St 21401-2520

(Mail to: 199 Duke Of Gloucester St 21401-2520) Richardson Libby Timothy Mulder Jessica Sexton Katharine Shahinian M Dion Thompson (410) 267-9333

Annapolis St Lukes Church **P** (120) 1101 Bay Ridge Ave 21403-2901 (Mail to: 1101 Bay Ridge Ave 21403-2901) Diana Carroll (410) 263-5419

Annapolis St Margarets Episcopal Church **P** (1242) § 1601 Pleasant Plains Rd 21401-5928 (Mail to: 1601 Pleasant Plains Rd 21409-5928) Peter Mayer Patti Sachs Patti Sachs (410) 974-0200

Annapolis St Philips Episcopal Church **P** (284) 730 Bestgate Rd 21401-2137 (Mail to: 730 Bestgate Rd 21401-2137) Randy Callender (410) 266-9755

✢ **Baltimore** Cathedral of the Incarnation **O** (945) 4 E University Pkwy 21218-2437 (Mail to: 4 E University Pkwy 21218-2490) Robert Boulter Jon Shematek (410) 467-3750

Baltimore St Katherine of Alexandria **P** (233) 2001 Division St 21217-3323 (Mail to: 2019 Division St 21217-3323) Allston Jacobs (410) 523-2207

Baltimore Church of St Mary the Virgin **P** (100) 3121 Walbrook Ave 21216-3031 (Mail to: 3121 Walbrook Ave 21216-3031) Charles Mercer (410) 383-1575

Baltimore Church of the Advent - Federal Hill **P** (172) 1234 Patapsco St Apt 2 21230-4246 (Mail to: 1301 S Charles St 21230-4218) Tobias Haller Timothy Kroh Eric Whitehair (410) 539-7804

Baltimore Church of the Guardian Angel **P** (72) 2629 Huntingdon Ave 21211-3111 (Mail to: 2629 Huntingdon Ave 21211-3111) Alice Bassett-Jellema (443) 879-9453

Baltimore Church of the Holy Covenant **P** (97) 5657 The Alameda 21239-2738 (Mail to: 5657 the Alameda 21239-2738) (410) 435-3707

Baltimore Church of the Holy Nativity **M** (82) 4238 Pimlico Rd 21215-6961 (Mail to: 4238 Pimlico Rd 21215-6961) (410) 542-9554

Baltimore Church of the Holy Trinity **P** (228) 2300 W Lafayette Ave 21216-4816 (Mail to: 2300 W Lafayette Ave 21216-4898) Ramelle McCall (410) 945-0002

Baltimore Church of the Messiah **P** (140) 5801 Harford Rd 21214-1848 (Mail to: 5801 Harford Rd 21214-1848) Timothy Grayson (410) 426-0709

Baltimore Church of the Nativity **P** (120) 419 Cedarcroft Rd 21212-2523 (Mail to: 419 Cedarcroft Rd 21212-2599) Anthony Hollis Thomas Lucas Thomas Lucas (410) 433-4811

Baltimore Church of the Redemption **P** (98) 1401 Towson St 21230-5301 (Mail to: 1401 Towson St 21230-5301) Mary Davisson (410) 539-8270

Baltimore Church of the Resurrection **M** (80) 2900 E Fayette St 21224-1316 (Mail to: 2900 E Fayette St 21224-1316) Lewis Bradford Rosa Santana (443) 631-0115

Baltimore Emmanuel Episcopal Church **P** (569) 811 Cathedral St 21201-5201 (Mail to: 811 Cathedral St 21201-5201) Joseph Wood (410) 685-1130

Baltimore Christ the King Episcopal Church **P** (124) 1930 Brookdale Rd 21244-1704 (Mail to: 1930 Brookdale Rd 21244-1704) Mary Eliot Diane Fadely (410) 944-6683

Baltimore Grace & St Peters Church **P** (411) 707 Park Ave 21201-4703 (Mail to: 707 Park Ave 21201-4799) Christopher Pyles (410) 539-1395

Baltimore Memorial Episcopal Church **P** (474) 1407 Bolton St 21217-4202 (Mail to: 1407 Bolton St 21217-4202) Natalie Conway Grey Maggiano (410) 669-0220

Baltimore St Bartholomews Episcopal Church **P** (411) 4711 Edmondson Ave 21229-2404 (Mail to: 4711 Edmondson Ave 21229-1440) Florence Ledyard Maria Fedock Thelma Smullen (410) 945-7263

Baltimore Saint David's Church **P** (769) § 4700 Roland Ave 21210-2320 (Mail to: C/O Christine Naylor 4700 Roland Ave 21210-2320) Scott Bellows (410) 467-0476

Baltimore St James Episcopal Church **P** (454) 829 Arlington Ave 21217-2534 (Mail to: 1020 W Lafayette Ave 21217-2555) Carole Douglas Melvin Truiett (410) 523-4588

Baltimore St Johns Church **P** (136) 3001 Old York Rd 21218-3544 (Mail to: 3009 Greenmount Ave 21218-3599) (410) 467-4793

Baltimore St Johns Episcopal Church **P** (100) 1702 South Rd 21209-4504 (Mail to: Attn: Assistant Treasurer 1702 South Rd 21209-4504) (410) 367-7287

Baltimore St Lukes Franklin Square **P** (31) 217 Carey St 21223-1836 (Mail to: Attn Mr O Jordan PO Box 20596 21223-0596) John Hayes (410) 523-6272

Baltimore St Matthias Episcopal Church **P** (94) 6400 Belair Rd 21206-1840 (Mail to: 6400 Belair Rd 21206-1899) Joanne Tetrault (410) 426-1002

Baltimore Church of St Michael & All Angels **P** (131) 2013 Saint Paul St 21218-5929 (Mail to: 2013 Saint Paul St 21218-5998) Richard Meadows (410) 685-3128

Baltimore Saint Paul's Parish **P** (330) 309 Cathedral St 21201-4410 (Mail to: 309 Cathedral St 21201-4410) Christopher Dreisbach Mark Stanley Mary Stanley (410) 685-3404

Baltimore Church of the Redeemer **P** (3264) § 5603 Charles St 21210-2006 (Mail to: 5603 Charles St 21210-2097) Maria Cristina Paglinauan Caroline Stewart David Ware (410) 435-7333

Bel Air Emmanuel Episcopal Church **P** (391) Main St & Broadway 21014 (Mail to: PO Box 628 21014-0628) Mark Gatza Joan Kelly William Smith (410) 838-7699

Boonsboro St Marks Episcopal Church **P** (449) 18313 Lappans Rd 21713-1918 (Mail to: 18313 Lappans Rd 21713-1918) Anne Weatherholt (301) 582-0417

Braddock Heights Church of the Transfiguration **P** (151) 6909 Maryland Ave 21714 (Mail to: PO Box 87 21714-0087) Gordon De La Vars (301) 371-7505

Brownsville Saint Luke's Church **M** (33) 2150 Boteler Rd 21715-2008 (Mail to: 2150 Boteler Rd 21758-1002) Thomas Hudson (301) 432-4209

Brunswick Grace Episcopal Church **P** (74) 114 E A St 21716-1406 (Mail to: 114 E A St 21716-1406) (301) 834-8540

Churchville Holy Trinity Church **P** (146) 2929 Level Rd 21028-1820 (Mail to: PO Box 25 21028-0025) (410) 836-2227

Clear Spring St Andrew's Episcopal Church **M** (82) 22 Cumberland St 21722 (Mail to: PO Box 189 21722-0189) Steven Mccarty (301) 842-2433

Cockeysville Sherwood Episcopal Church **P** (75) 5 Sherwood Rd 21030-2323 (Mail to: 5 Sherwood Rd Ste A 21030-2354) Nancy Hennessey (410) 666-2180

Columbia Christ Episcopal Church **P** (1066) 6800 Oakland Mills Rd 21045-4706 (Mail to: 6800 Oakland Mills Rd 21045-4706) Emmanuel Mercer (410) 381-9365

Crownsville St Stephens - Severn Parish **P** (499) § 1112 Saint Stephens Church Rd 21032-1908 (Mail to: 1110 Saint Stephens Church Rd 21032-1908) Victor Hailey (410) 721-2881

Cumberland Emmanuel Episcopal Church **P** (643) 16 Washington St 21502-2924 (Mail to: 16 Washington St 21502-2976) Martha Macgill (301) 777-3364

Darlington Grace Memorial Church **P** (103) 1022 Main St 21034-1434 (Mail to: C/O Cole Nelson PO Box 35 21034-0035) Lisa Bornt (410) 836-3587

✠ **Deale** St Marks Chapel **O** 361 Deale Rd 20779 (Mail to: c/o St. James' 5757 Solomons Island 20711) (410) 867-2838

Dundalk St George & St Matthew Episcopal Ch **P** (308) 2900 Dunleer Rd 21222-5112 (Mail to: 2900 Dunleer Rd 21222-5112) Jansen String (410) 284-6242

Edgewater All Hallows Episcopal Church **P** (289) 3600 Solomons Island Rd 210373620 (Mail to: 3600 Solomons Island Rd 210373620) Jeffrey Hual (410) 798-0808

Elkridge Grace Episcopal Church **P** (570) 6725 Montgomery Rd 21075-5723 (Mail to: 6725 Montgomery Rd 21075-5723) Travis Smith (410) 796-3270

Elkridge Trinity Episcopal Church **P** (157) 7474 Washington Blvd 21075-6330 (Mail to: 7474 Washington Blvd 21075-6330) Frank Bailey Anne MacNabb (410) 220-3628

Ellicott City St Johns Episcopal Church **P** (1798) § 9120 Frederick Rd 21042-3912 (Mail to: 9120 Frederick Rd 21042-3978) Ann Ritonia Katrina Grusell Stephen Hagerty Wanhong Lee Jennifer Ovenstone (410) 461-7793

Ellicott City St Peters Church **P** (278) § 3695 Rogers Ave 21043-4125 (Mail to: 3695 Rogers Ave 21043-4175) Anjel Scarborough (410) 465-2273

Essex Holy Trinity Episcopal Church **P** (234) C/O The Reverend Eric Zile 1131 Mace Ave 21221-3316 (Mail to: C/O The Reverend Eric Zile 1131 Mace Ave 21221-3316) Eric Zile Cynthia Christopher (410) 687-5531

Forest Hill Christ Episcopal Church **P** (398) 2100 Rock Spring Rd 21050-2632 (Mail to: PO Box 215 21050-0215) Kirk Kubicek (410) 838-6606

Frederick All Saints Church **P** (1115) 108 W Church St 21701-5411 (Mail to: 106 W Church St 21701-5411) Adrien Dawson Jessica Holthus (301) 663-5625

Frostburg St Johns Episcopal Church **P** (35) 52 S Broadway 21532-1710 (Mail to: PO Box 229 21532-0229) Karen Crosby (301) 689-6634

Glen Burnie St Albans Episcopal Parish **P** (231) 105 1st Ave 21060-7627 (Mail to: 105 1st Ave SW 21061-3453) Pamela Conrad (410) 766-1455

Glencoe Immanuel Episcopal Church **P** (176) 1509 Glencoe Rd 21152-9439 (Mail to: 1509 Glencoe Rd 21152-9349) Megan Stewart-Sicking

Glenwood St Andrews Episcopal Church **P** (536) Rte 97 At Union Chapel Rd 21738 (Mail to: PO Box 52 21738-0052) Dina Van Klaveren Charles Shaffer (410) 489-4035

Gwynn Oak St Mary Episcopal Church **P** (66) 5610 Dogwood Rd 21207-5906 (Mail to: 5610 Dogwood Rd 21207-5985) Susan Oldfather (410) 944-4236

Hagerstown St Johns Episcopal Church **P** (487) 101 S Prospect St 21740-5409 (Mail to: 101 S Prospect St 21740-5495) Gary Young (301) 733-2560

Halethorpe The Church of the Holy Apostles **P** (133) 4922 Leeds Ave 21227-2412 (Mail to: 4922 Leeds Ave 21227-2412) James Perra (410) 242-5477

Hampstead St Georges Episcopal Church **P** (333) 2434 Cape Horn Rd 21074-1123 (Mail to: 2434 Cape Horn Rd 21074-1172) Mario Conliffe Anthony Warner (410) 374-9748

Hancock St Thomas Church **P** (823) 2 E High St 21750-1216 (Mail to: 2 E High St 21750-1216) Floyd Weatherholt Kirk DeVore (301) 678-6569

Havre De Grace St Johns Episcopal Church **P** (59) 114 Union Ave 21078-3008 (Mail to: 114 Union Ave 21078-3008) Gail Landers (410) 939-2107

Highland St Marks Episcopal Church **P** (438) 12700 Hall Shop Rd 20777-9544 (Mail to:

12700 Hall Shop Rd 20777-9544) Taylor Smith (301) 854-2304

Joppatowne Copley Parish **P** (90) 700 Anchor Dr 21085-0222 (Mail to: PO Box 222 21085-0222) (410) 679-8700

Kingsville St Johns Episcopal Church **P** (189) 11901 Belair Rd 21087-1155 (Mail to: PO Box 187 21087-0187) Elizabeth Anne Sipos (410) 592-8570

Linthicum Hts St Christopher Episcopal Church **P** (73) 116 Marydel Rd 21090-2130 (Mail to: 116 Marydel Rd 21090-2130) Monique Ellison (410) 859-5633

Lonaconing St Peters Episcopal Church **M** (74) 6 Saint Peters Place 21562 (Mail to: 6 Saint Peters Pl 21539-1135) Garrett Carskadon (301) 463-6144

Long Green Trinity Episcopal Church **P** (181) § 12400 Manor Rd 21092 (Mail to: PO Box 4001 12400 Manor Rd 21057-1001) Virginia Stanford Charles Pugh (410) 592-6224

Lothian St James Parish **P** (594) 5757 Solomons Island Rd 20711-9707 (Mail to: 5757 Solomons Island Rd 20711-9792) John Keydel John Verdon (410) 867-2838

Lusby Middleham and St Peters Parish **P** (390) 10210 H G Trueman Rd 20657 (Mail to: PO Box 277 20657-0277) David Showers Sarah Cardwell (410) 326-4948

Luthvle Timon The Church of the Holy Comforter **P** (378) 130 W Seminary Ave 21093-5523 (Mail to: 130 W Seminary Ave 21093-5599) Christopher Tang William Dunning January Hamill Jo Leslie (410) 252-2711

Luthvle Timon Epiphany Church Dulaney Valley **P** (258) 2216 Pot Spring Rd 21093-2724 (Mail to: 2216 Pot Spring Rd 21093-2797) Kristofer Lindh-Payne Amy Myers (410) 252-4465

Mayo St Andrew the Fisherman **P** (123) Central Ave & Carrs Wharf Rd 21106 (Mail to: PO Box 175 21106-0175) Rock Schuler (410) 798-1533

Monkton St James Episcopal Church **P** (1403) § 3100 Monkton Rd 21111-2113 (Mail to: 3100 Monkton Rd 21111-2199) Joseph Cochran Matthew Rogers (410) 771-4466

Mount Airy St James' Episcopal Church **P** (327) 1307 N. Main Street 21771-0416 (Mail to: 1307 Main St 21771-7499) Kristin Krantz (301) 829-0325

Mount Airy St Pauls Episcopal Church **P** (63) 16457 Old Frederick Rd 21771-3331 (Mail to: 16457 Old Frederick Rd 21771-3331) Susan Keller (410) 489-4411

Mount Savage St Georges Episcopal Church **P** (32) 12811 Saint Georges Ln Nw 21545-1001 (Mail to: 12811 Saint Georges Ln NW 21545-1001) (301) 264-3524

New Market Grace Episcopal Church **P** (250) 4 E Main St 21774 (Mail to: PO Box 17 21774-0017) Sharon Watts (301) 865-3270

Oakland Garrett County Episcopal Church **P** 5234 Maryland Hwy 21550-4807 (Mail to: 5234 Maryland Highway 21550)

Oakland Our Fathers House **SC** 109 C St 21550-3507 (Mail to: PO Box 414 21550-4414) William Lee (301) 334-1197

Oakland St Johns Church **M** (135) 5234 Maryland Hwy 21550-4807 (Mail to: PO Box 414 21550-4414) William Lee (301) 334-2510

Oakland St Matthews Church **P** (195) 126 E Liberty St 21550-1202 (Mail to: PO Box 303 21550-0303) Anne Byrne William Lee (301) 334-2510

Odenton Epiphany Episcopal Church **P** (809) PO Box 110 21113-0110 (Mail to: PO Box 110 21113-0110) Phebe McPherson William McPherson (410) 336-8383

Owings Mills St Thomas Episcopal Church **P** (1321) 232 Saint Thomas Ln 21117-3806 (Mail to: 232 Saint Thomas Ln 21117-3800) Malcolm Ellis Nathan Erdman (410) 363-1043

Parkton St James Episcopal Church **P** (258) 19200 York Rd 21120-9207 (Mail to: PO Box 420 21120-0420) William Alford (410) 357-4473

Pasadena St Andrews Episcopal Church **P** (149) 7859 Tick Neck Rd 21122-2264 (Mail to: 7859 Tick Neck Rd 21122-2264) Jason Poling Corby Zeren (410) 255-1070

Pikesville Church Of Saint Marks On The Hill **P** (388) 1620 Reisterstown Rd 21208-2902 (Mail to: 1620 Reisterstown Rd 21208-2900) (410) 486-3016

Port Republic Christ Church **P** (234) 3100 Broomes Island Rd 20676-2101 (Mail to: 3100 Broomes Island Rd 20676-2101) Christopher Garcia (410) 586-0565

Prnc Frederck St Pauls Episcopal Church **P** (185) 25 Church St 20678-4116 (Mail to: PO Box 99 20678-0099) Richard Humm (410) 535-2897

Pt Of Rocks St Pauls Episcopal Church **P** (51) 1914 Ballenger Creek Rd 21777 (Mail to: PO Box 216 21777-0216) (301) 874-2995

Reisterstown All Saints Episcopal Church **P** (461) 203 E Chatsworth Ave 21136-1302 (Mail to: 203 E Chatsworth Ave 21136-1302) Jason Poling (410) 833-0700

Reisterstown St Johns Church **P** (425) 3738 Butler Rd 21136-3830 (Mail to: 3738 Butler Rd 21136-3830) Tracy Bruce Alistair So-Schoos (410) 429-4690

Severna Park St Martins-in-the-Field Episcopal Ch **P** (1261) § 375 Benfield Rd 21146-2794 (Mail to: 375 Benfield Rd 21146-2794) Matthew Hanisian Henrietta Wiley (410) 647-6248

Sharpsburg St Pauls Episcopal Church **P** (113) 209 W Main St 21782-1743 (Mail to: PO Box 364 21782-0364) (301) 432-7098

Smithsburg St Anns Episcopal Church **P** (48) 9 Maple Ave 21783-9702 (Mail to: PO Box 177 21783-0177) Sandra Kline-Mortimer (301) 824-3033

Street Church of the Ascension **P** (60) 3460 Mill Green Rd 21154-1724 (Mail to: C/O Mr Gregory Buckler 3460 Mill Green Rd 21154-1724) (410) 836-3587

Street Holy Cross Episcopal Church **M** (132) 4603 Rocks Rd 21154-1210 (Mail to: PO Box 103 21154-0103) Marta Johnson (410) 452-5502

Sunderland All Saints Parish **P** (243) 100 Lower Marlboro Rd 20689 (Mail to: PO Box 40 20689-0040) Kenneth Phelps Michelle Doran Margaret VanAuker (410) 257-6306

Sykesville St Barnabas Episcopal Church **P** (238) 13135 Forsythe Rd 21784-5818 (Mail to: 13135 Forsythe Rd 21784-5818) Meredith Olsen (410) 489-2800

Thurmont Catoctin Parish Harriet Chapel **P** (120) 12625 Catoctin Furnace Rd 21788-3008 (Mail to: 12625 Catoctin Furnace Rd 21788-3008) Sally Joyner-Giffin (301) 271-4554

Towson Church of the Good Shepherd **P** (866) § 1401 Carrollton Ave 21204-6518 (Mail to: 1401 Carrollton Ave 21204-6518) Arianne Rice Matthew Welsch (410) 823-0122

Towson St Thomas Episcopal Church **P** (304) 1108 Providence Rd 21286-1743 (Mail to: Attn: Treasurer 1108 Providence Rd 21286-1743) Loree Penner (410) 821-5489

Towson Trinity Episcopal Church **P** (471) 120 Allegheny Ave 21204-4019 (Mail to: 120 Allegheny Ave 21204-4095) (410) 823-3588

West River Christ Episcopal Church **P** (294) 220 Owensville Rd 20778-9704 (Mail to: 220 Owensville Rd 20778-9704) Linda Kapurch (410) 867-0346

Westernport St James Episcopal Church **P** (74) 32 Main St 21539 (Mail to: PO Box 279 21562-0279) Garrett Carskadon John Martin (301) 359-6001

Westminster Church of the Ascension **P** (563) 23 Court St 21157-5109 (Mail to: 23 Court St 21157-5352) Samuel Nsengiyumva Barbara Sears (410) 848-3251

STATE OF MASSACHUSETTS

Dioceses of Massachusetts and Western Massachusetts

DIOCESE OF MASSACHUSETTS

(PROVINCE I)
Comprises eastern Massachusetts
DIOCESAN OFFICE 138 Tremont St Boston MA 02111-1318
TEL (617) 482-5800   FAX (617) 451-6446
E-MAIL info@diomass.org   WEB www.diomass.org

Previous Bishops—
Edward Bass 1797-1803, Samuel Parker 1804-04, Alexander V Griswold (Eastern Dio) 1811-43, Manton Eastburn coadj 1842 Bp 1843-72, Benj H Paddock 1873-91, Phillips Brooks 1891-93, Wm Lawrence 1893-1927, Charles L Slattery coadj 1922 Bp 1927-30, Saml G Babcock suffr 1913-38, Henry K Sherrill 1930-47, Raymond A Heron suffr 1938-54, Norman B Nash coadj 1947 Bp 1947-56, Frederic C Lawrence suffr 1956-68, Anson P Stokes Jr coadj 1954 Bp 1956-70, John M Burgess suffr 1962-69 coadj 1969 Bp 1970-75, Morris F Arnold suffr 1972-82, John B Coburn 1976-86, David E Johnson coadj 1985 Bp 1986-1995, Barbara C Harris suffr 1989-2002, Roy F Cederholm Jr suffr 2001-11, M Thomas Shaw III SSJE 1995-2014

Bishop—Rt Rev Alan M. Gates (1082) (Dio 13 Sep 2014)

Bishop Suffragan—Rt Rev Gayle Elizabeth

Harris (981) (Suffr 18 Jan 2003)

Chanc E Notis-McConarty; *Sec* Sr K Frances SSM; *Asst Sec* L Simons; *Treas* S Voysey; *Reg-Hist* L Smith; *AsstTreas* G Sullivan; *Dean* A McCreath; *Cn to Ord* W Parnell; *Bps Exec Asst* L Simons; *Exec Dir Epis City Miss* A Chambliss

Stand Comm—Cler: Pres A Stoessel Elise Feyerherm M Cadwell J Carson; *Lay:* W Boyce J Iredale W Kennard C Perry

PARISHES, MISSIONS, AND CLERGY

Acton The Church of the Good Shepherd **P** (789) 164 Newtown Rd 01720-3114 (Mail to: 164 Newtown Rd 01720-3114) Ruthann Savage-King (978) 263-5782

Amesbury St James Episcopal Church **P** (176) 120 Main St 01913-2809 (Mail to: PO Box 25 01913-0001) John Satula (978) 388-0030

Andover Parish of Christ Church **P** (1444) 25 Central St 01810-3737 (Mail to: 25 Central St 01810-3780) Michael Hodges Jennifer Vath (978) 475-0529

Arlington Church of Our Saviour **P** (80) 21 Marathon St 02474-6940 (Mail to: 21 Marathon St 02474-6940) Malia Crawford Patricia De Beer (781) 648-5962

Arlington St Johns Church **P** (226) 74 Pleasant St 02476-6516 (Mail to: 74 Pleasant St 02476-6516) Diane Wong (781) 648-4819

Attleboro All Saints Episcopal Church **P** (64) 121 Main St 02703-2221 (Mail to: 121 Main St 02703-2221) Meghan Sweeney Ronald Tibbetts (508) 222-2233

Ayer St Andrews Episcopal Church **P** (230) 7 Faulkner St 01432-1611 (Mail to: 7 Faulkner St 01432-1611) Joyce Scherer-Hoock (978) 772-2615

Barnstable St Marys Episcopal Church **P** (608) 3055 Main St 02630-1119 (Mail to: PO Box 395 02630-0395) Elizabeth Gibson (508) 362-3977

Bedford St Pauls Episcopal Church **P** (386) 100 Pine Hill Rd 01730-1641 (Mail to: 100 Pine Hill Rd 01730-1698) Christopher Wendell Rachel Wildman (781) 275-8262

Belmont All Saints Episcopal Church **P** (148) 17 Clark St 02478-2448 (Mail to: 17 Clark St 02478-2448) Cheryl Minor Paul Minor (617) 484-2228

Beverly St Johns Church **P** (1524) 705 Hale St 01915-2118 (Mail to: PO Box 5610 01915-0522) George Stevens Luther Zeigler (978) 927-0229

Beverly St Peters Episcopal Church **P** (408) 4 Ocean St 01915-5220 (Mail to: 4 Ocean St 01915-5299) Manuel Faria (978) 922-3438

Boston Emmanuel Episcopal Church **P** (319) 15 Newbury St 02116-3105 (Mail to: 15 Newbury St 02116-3185) Pamela Werntz Frederick Stecker (617) 536-3355

Boston Grace Federated Church **M** (8) 760 Saratoga St 02128-1513 (Mail to: 760 Saratoga St 02128-1513) (617) 569-5358

Boston Old North Christ Church **P** (262) 193 Salem St 02113-1123 (Mail to: 193 Salem St 02113-1123) Stephen Ayres Eleanor Terry (617) 523-6676

Boston St Augustine and St Martin **P** (121) 29 Lenox St 02118-3201 (Mail to: 31 Lenox St 02118-3201) Evan Thayer (617) 442-6395

Boston St Cyprians Episcopal Church **P** (213) 1073 Tremont St 02120-2163 (Mail to: 1073 Tremont St 02120-2163) Monrelle Williams Julian Fredie (617) 427-6175

Boston St Johns St James Church **P** (65) 149 Roxbury St 02119-1525 (Mail to: 149 Roxbury St 02119-1525) Rospignac Ambroise (617) 445-8843

Boston St Mary Episcopal Church **P** (99) 14 Cushing Ave 02125-2009 (Mail to: 14 Cushing Ave 02125-2009) John Finley Edwin Johnson (617) 282-3181

Boston St Stephen Episcopal Church **M** (264) 419 Shawmut Ave 02118-3822 (Mail to:

419 Shawmut Ave 02118-3825) Elizabeth Steinhauser (617) 262-9070

✠ **Boston** Cathedral Church of St Paul **O** C/O Diocese Of Massachusetts 138 Tremont St 02111-1318 (Mail to: C/O Lynn Clark 138 Tremont St 02111-1318) Amy Mccreath Robert Greiner Cristine Rathbone Tamra Tucker (617) 482-5800

Boston The Church of the Advent **P** (794) 30 Brimmer St 02108-1002 (Mail to: 30 Brimmer St 02108-1098) Allan Warren Thomas Adams Jay James Daphne Noyes (617) 523-2377

Boston Parish of All Saints **P** (365) 209 Ashmont St 02124-3803 (Mail to: 209 Ashmont St 02124-3898) Michael Godderz (617) 436-6370

Boston Trinity Church Episcopal **P** (922) 206 Clarendon St 02116-3722 (Mail to: 206 Clarendon St 02116-3722) Rita Powell William Rich Patrick Ward (617) 536-0944

Braintree Emmanuel Episcopal Church **P** (205) 519 Washington St 02184-4655 (Mail to: 519 Washington St 02184-4655) Thomas Mulvey (781) 843-0170

Bridgewater Trinity Episcopal Church **P** (286) 91 Main Street 02324-1406 (Mail to: 91 Main St 02324-1406) (508) 697-4311

Brookline All Saints Parish **P** (395) 1773 Beacon St 02445-4214 (Mail to: 1773 Beacon St 02445-4299) Richard Burden (617) 738-1810

Brookline Boston Univ Episcopal Chapel **CC** 40 Prescott St 02446-4038 (Mail to: 40 Prescott St 024464038) (617) 277-5523

Brookline Church of Our Saviour **P** (386) 25 Monmouth St 02446-5604 (Mail to: 25 Monmouth St 02446-5604) Joel Ives (617) 277-7334

Brookline St Pauls Episcopal Church **P** (421) 15 Saint Paul St 02446-6501 (Mail to: 15 Saint Paul St 02446-6501) Jeffrey Mello Elise Feyerherm (617) 566-4953

Burlington St Marks Episcopal Church **P** (266) C/O Sherley Estrella 10 St Marks Rd 01803-3622 (Mail to: C/O Sherley Estrella 10 St Marks Rd 01803-3622) John De Beer Bryan Pearson (781) 272-1586

Buzzards Bay Church of St Peters on the Canal **P** (354) PO Box 265 02532-0265 (Mail to: PO Box 265 02532-0265) Susan Lederhouse Robert Sherwood (508) 759-5641

Cambridge Christ Church **P** (1023) 0 Garden St 02138-3631 (Mail to: 0 Garden St 02138-3656) Joseph Robinson Jonathan Eden Patricia Zifcak (617) 876-0200

Cambridge Episcopal Chaplaincy at Harvard **CC** 2 Garden St 02138-3631 (Mail to: 2 Garden St 02138-3631) Margery Kennelly (617) 495-4340

Cambridge Episcopal Chapel at MIT **CC** 77 Massachusetts Ave 02139-4307 (Mail to: MIT W11 77 Massachusetts Ave 02139-4307) (617) 253-2983

Cambridge Saint Bartholomew's Church **P** (177) 239 Harvard St 02139-2640 (Mail to: 239

Harvard St 02139-2640) Leslie Sterling Patricia Zifcak (617) 354-8582

Cambridge St James Episcopal Church **P** (662) 1991 Massachusetts Ave 02140-1306 (Mail to: 1991 Massachusetts Ave 02140-1342) Judith Gay Robert Massie Matthew Stewart (617) 547-4070

Cambridge St Johns Memorial Chapel **CC** 99 Brattle St 02138-3402 (Mail to: 99 Brattle St 02138-3402) (617) 868-3450

Cambridge St Peters Episcopal Church **P** (155) 838 Massachusetts Ave 02139-3004 (Mail to: 15 Sellers St Attn: Pat Drake 02139-3005) Sarah Conner (617) 547-7788

Canton Trinity Church Episcopal **P** (181) 1 Blue Hill River Rd 02021-1001 (Mail to: 1 Blue Hill River Rd 02021-1001) Kathleen McAdams (781) 828-1810

Acton The Church of the Good Shepherd **P** (789) 164 Newtown Rd 01720-3114 (Mail to: 164 Newtown Rd 01720-3114) Ruthann Savage-King (978) 263-5782

Amesbury St James Episcopal Church **P** (176) 120 Main St 01913-2809 (Mail to: PO Box 25 01913-0001) John Satula (978) 388-0030

Andover Parish of Christ Church **P** (1444) 25 Central St 01810-3737 (Mail to: 25 Central St 01810-3780) Michael Hodges Jennifer Vath (978) 475-0529

Arlington Church of Our Saviour **P** (80) 21 Marathon St 02474-6940 (Mail to: 21 Marathon St 02474-6940) Malia Crawford Patricia De Beer (781) 648-5962

Arlington St Johns Church **P** (226) 74 Pleasant St 02476-6516 (Mail to: 74 Pleasant St 02476-6516) Diane Wong (781) 648-4819

Attleboro All Saints Episcopal Church **P** (64) 121 Main St 02703-2221 (Mail to: 121 Main St 02703-2221) Meghan Sweeney Ronald Tibbetts (508) 222-2233

Ayer St Andrews Episcopal Church **P** (230) 7 Faulkner St 01432-1611 (Mail to: 7 Faulkner St 01432-1611) Joyce Scherer-Hoock (978) 772-2615

Barnstable St Marys Episcopal Church **P** (608) 3055 Main St 02630-1119 (Mail to: PO Box 395 02630-0395) Elizabeth Gibson (508) 362-3977

Bedford St Pauls Episcopal Church **P** (386) 100 Pine Hill Rd 01730-1641 (Mail to: 100 Pine Hill Rd 01730-1698) Christopher Wendell Rachel Wildman (781) 275-8262

Belmont All Saints Episcopal Church **P** (148) 17 Clark St 02478-2448 (Mail to: 17 Clark St 02478-2448) Cheryl Minor Paul Minor (617) 484-2228

Beverly St Johns Church **P** (1524) 705 Hale St 01915-2118 (Mail to: PO Box 5610 01915-0522) George Stevens Luther Zeigler (978) 927-0229

Beverly St Peters Episcopal Church **P** (408) 4 Ocean St 01915-5220 (Mail to: 4 Ocean St 01915-5299) Manuel Faria (978) 922-3438

Boston Emmanuel Episcopal Church **P** (319) 15 Newbury St 02116-3105 (Mail to: 15 Newbury St 02116-3185) Pamela Werntz Frederick Stecker (617) 536-3355

Boston Grace Federated Church **M** (8) 760 Saratoga St 02128-1513 (Mail to: 760 Saratoga St 02128-1513) (617) 569-5358

Boston Old North Christ Church **P** (262) 193 Salem St 02113-1123 (Mail to: 193 Salem St 02113-1123) Stephen Ayres Eleanor Terry (617) 523-6676

Boston St Augustine and St Martin **P** (121) 29 Lenox St 02118-3201 (Mail to: 31 Lenox St 02118-3201) Evan Thayer (617) 442-6395

Boston St Cyprians Episcopal Church **P** (213) 1073 Tremont St 02120-2163 (Mail to: 1073 Tremont St 02120-2163) Monrelle Williams Julian Fredie (617) 427-6175

Boston St Johns St James Church **P** (65) 149 Roxbury St 02119-1525 (Mail to: 149 Roxbury St 02119-1525) Rospignac Ambroise (617) 445-8843

Boston St Mary Episcopal Church **P** (99) 14 Cushing Ave 02125-2009 (Mail to: 14 Cushing Ave 02125-2009) John Finley Edwin Johnson (617) 282-3181

Boston St Stephen Episcopal Church **M** (264) 419 Shawmut Ave 02118-3822 (Mail to: 419 Shawmut Ave 02118-3825) Elizabeth Steinhauser (617) 262-9070

✠ **Boston** Cathedral Church of St Paul **O** C/O Diocese Of Massachusetts 138 Tremont St 02111-1318 (Mail to: C/O Lynn Clark 138 Tremont St 02111-1318) Amy Mccreath Robert Greiner Cristine Rathbone Tamra Tucker (617) 482-5800

Boston The Church of the Advent **P** (794) 30 Brimmer St 02108-1002 (Mail to: 30 Brimmer St 02108-1098) Allan Warren Thomas Adams Jay James Daphne Noyes (617) 523-2377

Boston Parish of All Saints **P** (365) 209 Ashmont St 02124-3803 (Mail to: 209 Ashmont St 02124-3898) Michael Godderz (617) 436-6370

Boston Trinity Church Episcopal **P** (922) 206 Clarendon St 02116-3722 (Mail to: 206 Clarendon St 02116-3722) Rita Powell William Rich Patrick Ward (617) 536-0944

Braintree Emmanuel Episcopal Church **P** (205) 519 Washington St 02184-4655 (Mail to: 519 Washington St 02184-4655) Thomas Mulvey (781) 843-0170

Bridgewater Trinity Episcopal Church **P** (286) 91 Main Street 02324-1406 (Mail to: 91 Main St 02324-1406) (508) 697-4311

Brookline All Saints Parish **P** (395) 1773 Beacon St 02445-4214 (Mail to: 1773 Beacon St 02445-4299) Richard Burden (617) 738-1810

Brookline Boston Univ Episcopal Chapel **CC** 40 Prescott St 02446-4038 (Mail to: 40 Prescott St 024464038) (617) 277-5523

Brookline Church of Our Saviour **P** (386) 25 Monmouth St 02446-5604 (Mail to: 25 Monmouth St 02446-5604) Joel Ives (617) 277-7334

Brookline St Pauls Episcopal Church **P** (421) 15 Saint Paul St 02446-6501 (Mail to: 15 Saint Paul St 02446-6501) Jeffrey Mello Elise Feyerherm (617) 566-4953

Burlington St Marks Episcopal Church **P** (266) C/O Sherley Estrella 10 St Marks Rd 01803-3622 (Mail to: C/O Sherley Estrella 10 St Marks Rd 01803-3622) John De Beer Bryan Pearson (781) 272-1586

Buzzards Bay Church of St Peters on the Canal **P** (354) PO Box 265 02532-0265 (Mail to: PO Box 265 02532-0265) Susan Lederhouse Robert Sherwood (508) 759-5641

Cambridge Christ Church **P** (1023) 0 Garden St 02138-3631 (Mail to: 0 Garden St 02138-3656) Joseph Robinson Jonathan Eden Patricia Zifcak (617) 876-0200

Cambridge Episcopal Chaplaincy at Harvard **CC** 2 Garden St 02138-3631 (Mail to: 2 Garden St 02138-3631) Margery Kennelly (617) 495-4340

Cambridge Episcopal Chapel at MIT **CC** 77 Massachusetts Ave 02139-4307 (Mail to: MIT W11 77 Massachusetts Ave 02139-4307) (617) 253-2983

Cambridge Saint Bartholomew's Church **P** (177) 239 Harvard St 02139-2640 (Mail to: 239 Harvard St 02139-2640) Leslie Sterling Patricia Zifcak (617) 354-8582

Cambridge St James Episcopal Church **P** (662) 1991 Massachusetts Ave 02140-1306 (Mail to: 1991 Massachusetts Ave 02140-1342) Judith Gay Robert Massie Matthew Stewart (617) 547-4070

Cambridge St Johns Memorial Chapel **CC** 99 Brattle St 02138-3402 (Mail to: 99 Brattle St 02138-3402) (617) 868-3450

Cambridge St Peters Episcopal Church **P** (155) 838 Massachusetts Ave 02139-3004 (Mail to: 15 Sellers St Attn: Pat Drake 02139-3005) Sarah Conner (617) 547-7788

Canton Trinity Church Episcopal **P** (181) 1 Blue Hill River Rd 02021-1001 (Mail to: 1 Blue Hill River Rd 02021-1001) Kathleen McAdams (781) 828-1810

Charlestown St John's Episcopal Church **P** (95) 27 Devens St 02129-3735 (Mail to: 27 Devens St 02129-3735) Thomas Mousin Lyn Brakeman Richard Simeone (617) 242-1272

Chatham St Christophers Church **P** (812) 625 Main St 02633-2233 (Mail to: Attn Treasurer 625 Main St 02633-2233) Brian Mcgurk John Martiner (508) 945-2832

Chelmsford All Saints Church **P** (645) 10 Billerica Rd 01824-3011 (Mail to: 10 Billerica Rd 01824-3097) William Bradbury (978) 256-5673

Chelsea St Lukes-San Lucas Episcopal Church **M** (153) 201 Washington Ave 02150-3914 (Mail to: 201 Washington Ave 02150-3914) Edgar Gutierrez-Duarte (617) 884-4278

Chestnut Hill Boston College Campus Ministry **CC** 379 Hammond St Episcopal Chaplain-McElroy 105 02467-1224 (Mail to: C/O Church of the Redeemer 02467-1224) James Weiss (617) 285-6577

Chestnut Hill Church of the Redeemer **P** (1127) 379 Hammond St 02467-1224 (Mail to: 379 Hammond St 02467-1224) Michael Dangelo Emily Garcia (617) 566-7679

Cohasset St Stephens Episcopal Church **P** (779) 16 Highland Ave 02025-1819 (Mail to: 16 Highland Ave 02025-1819) Margaret Arnold (781) 383-1083

Concord Trinity Episcopal Church **P** (1334) 81 Elm St 01742-2252 (Mail to: 81 Elm St 01742-2252) Rebecca Gettel Nancy Hagner (978) 369-3715

Danvers All Saints Church North Shore Inc **P** (310) 46 Cherry St 01923-2820 (Mail to: 46 Cherry St 01923-2820) Marya DeCarlen (978) 774-1150

Dartmouth St Peter's Episcopal Church **P** (40) 351 Elm St 02748-3407 (Mail to: 351 Elm St 02748-3407) Scott Ciosek (508) 997-0903

Dedham Church of the Good Shepherd **P** (90) 62 Cedar St 02026-3222 (Mail to: 62 Cedar St 02026-3237) Chitral De Mel (781) 326-3052

Dedham St Pauls Church Episcopal **P** (466) 59 Court St 02026-4301 (Mail to: 59 Court St 02026-4301) Melanie McCarley (781) 326-4553

Dorchester St Marks Episcopal Church **P** (121) 73 Columbia Rd 02121-3347 (Mail to: 73 Columbia Rd 02121-3347) (617) 436-4319

Dover St Dunstans Episcopal Church **P** (348) 18 Springdale Ave 02030-2353 (Mail to: Atten Sandra Uhlig PO Box 515 02030-0515) Sean Leonard (508) 785-0879

Duxbury Church Of Saint John The Evangelist **P** (1066) 410 Washington St 02332-4552 (Mail to: 410 Washington St PO Box 2893 02331-2893) Daniel Dice (781) 934-8911

Edgartown St Andrews Episcopal Church **P** (349) PO Box 1287 02539-1287 (Mail to: PO Box 1287 02539-1287) Cynthia Hubbard Vincent Seadale (508) 627-5330

Everett Grace Episcopal Church **P** (224) 67 Norwood St 02149-2722 (Mail to: PO Box 490285 02149-0004) Joseph Mumita (617) 387-7526

Fairhaven Spirit of Grace/ St. Andrew's Episcopal Church **P** (51) 357 Main St 02719-3405 (Mail to: 169 Belleville Road 02745) Rebecca Blair Victoria Hunt (508) 992-2281

Fall River Church of the Holy Spirit **P** (181) 160 Rock St 02720-3233 (Mail to: 160 Rock St 02720-3283) Jeremi Colvin M Lise Hildebrandt Matthew Stewart (508) 672-5571

Fall River St Luke's Episcopal Church **P** (86) 315 Warren St 02721-3919 (Mail to: 315 Warren St

02721-3919) James Hornsby Susan Lee (508) 678-5118

Falmouth St Barnabas Memorial Church **P** (781) 91 Main St 02540-2652 (Mail to: PO Box 203 02541-0203) Willie Mebane Matthew Potts (508) 548-3863

Foxborough St Marks Episcopal Church **P** (218) 116 South St 02035-1760 (Mail to: 116 South St 02035-1760) Edward Cardoza (508) 543-8191

Framingham Framingham State College Prot Min **CC** 100 State St 01701-9101 (Mail to: 63a Highland St 02119-1536) (508) 626-4610

Framingham St Andrews Episcopal Church **P** (556) 3 Maple St 01702-2915 (Mail to: 3 Maple St 01702-2915) Julie Carson (508) 875-5095

Franklin St Johns Episcopal Church **P** (394) 237 Pleasant St 02038-3620 (Mail to: PO Box 287 02038-0287) Kathleen McAdams Deborah Woodward (508) 528-2387

Gloucester St Johns Episcopal Church **P** (541) 48 Middle St 01930-5716 (Mail to: 48 Middle St 01930-5795) Bret Hays (978) 283-1708

✣ **Groton** St Johns Chapel **O** 282 Farmers Row 01450-1848 (Mail to: Groton School 01450) (978) 448-7257

Groveland St James Episcopal Church **P** (246) 119 Washington St 01834-1535 (Mail to: C/O Mrs Elaine Hatch 119 Washington St 01834-1535) Kathleen Lonergan (978) 373-1270

Hanover St Andrews Church **P** (540) 17 Church St 02339-2315 (Mail to: 17 Church St 02339-2315) Kevin Sparrow (781) 826-2062

Harwich Port Christ Church Episcopal **P** (284) 671 Route 28 02646-1913 (Mail to: 671 Route 28 02646-1913) Katherine Ragsdale (508) 432-1787

Haverhill Trinity Episcopal Church **P** (126) 26 White St 01830-5702 (Mail to: 26 White St 01830-5702) (978) 372-4244

Hingham Parish of St John the Evangelist **P** (1351) 172 Main St 02043-1911 (Mail to: 172 Main St 02043-1999) Timothy Schenck Jacqueline Clark (781) 749-1535

Holbrook St Johns Episcopal Church **P** (140) 322 S Franklin St 02343-1430 (Mail to: 322 S Franklin St 02343-1430) Timothy Rogers (781) 767-4656

Holliston St Michaels Church **P** (276) 1162 Highland St 01746-1602 (Mail to: 1162 Highland St 01746-1602) Sarah Robbins-Cole (508) 429-4248

Hopkinton St Pauls Church Episcopal **P** (70) 61 Wood St 01748 (Mail to: PO Box 165 01748-0165) Michael Billingsley (508) 435-4536

Hudson St Lukes Episcopal Church **P** (217) 5 Washington St 01749-2409 (Mail to: 5 Washington St 01749-2409) T James Kodera (978) 562-2701

Hyannis Port St Andrew by the Sea **SC** Irving Ave 02647 (Mail to: PO Box 386 02647-0386)

Hyde Park Parish of Christ Church **P** (180) PO Box 366202 02136-0022 (Mail to: PO Box 366202 02136-0022) Kapya Kaoma (617) 361-2457

Hyde Park Iglesia de San Juan **M** (40) PO Box 366202 02136-0022 (Mail to: PO Box 366202 02136-0022) (617) 361-3081

Ipswich Ascension Memorial Church **P** (400) 31 County St 01938-2224 (Mail to: PO Box 547 01938-0547) Bradford Clark (978) 356-2560

Jamaica Plain St Johns Episcopal Church **P** (211) 1 Roanoke Ave 02130-2828 (Mail to: PO Box 300230 02130-0031) Cecil Cole (617) 524-2999

Lawrence Grace Episcopal Church **P** (307) 35 Jackson St 01840-1626 (Mail to: PO Box 467 01842-0967) Joel Almono Roque (978) 682-6003

Lexington Church of Our Redeemer **P** (442) 6 Meriam St 02420-5309 (Mail to: C/O Frank A. Kern 6 Meriam St 02420-5309) Katherine Ekrem Andrew Goldhor (781) 862-6408

Lincoln St Annes Church **P** (400) 147 Concord Rd 01773-4108 (Mail to: PO Box 6 01773-0006) Kathryn Elledge David Holroyd Gregory Johnston (781) 259-8834

Lowell Saint Anne's Church **P** (142) 10 Kirk St 01852-1005 (Mail to: 8 Kirk St 01852-1086) Sarah Lewis (978) 452-2150

Lowell St Johns Episcopal Church **P** (78) 82 Luce St 01852-3034 (Mail to: 260 Gorham St 01852-3345) (978) 453-5423

Lynn Saint Stephen's Memorial Church **P** (387) 74 Sagamore St 01902-3436 (Mail to: 74 S Common St 01902-4594) Evan Barrington (781) 599-4220

Lynnfield St Pauls Episcopal Church **P** (311) 127 Summer St 01940-1827 (Mail to: 127 Summer St 01940-1827) Robert Bacon (781) 334-4594

Malden St Pauls Church **P** (125) 26 Washington St 02148-4903 (Mail to: 26 Washington St 02148-8299) (781) 324-9544

Manchester Emmanuel Chapel **SC** PO Box 705 01944-0705 (Mail to: PO Box 705 01944-0705) Luther Zeigler (978) 526-0085

Marblehead St Michaels Church Episcopal **P** (292) 26 Pleasant St 01945-3432 (Mail to: 26 Pleasant St 01945-3432) Andrew Stoessel (781) 631-0657

Marblehead Wyman Memorial Church of St Andrew **P** (420) 135 Lafayette St 01945-0805 (Mail to: 135 Lafayette St 01945-1113) Charles Elledge (781) 631-4951

Marion St Gabriels Episcopal Church **P** (522) 124 Front St 02738-1634 (Mail to: PO Box 545 02738-0010) Geoffrey Piper Catherine Harper (508) 748-1507

Marshfield Trinity Episcopal Church **P** (174) 229 Highland St 02050-6202 (Mail to: PO Box 388 02051-0388) Noble Scheepers (781) 834-8575

Mattapan Church of the Holy Spirit **P** (511) 525 River St 02126-3013 (Mail to: 525 River

St 02126-3096) Zenetta Armstrong Charles Cherisme Harry Jean-Jacques H Mark Smith (617) 298-0577

Mattapoisett St Philip of Bethsaida Summer Chapel **SC** 34 Water St 02739 (Mail to: 40 Water St 02109-3604) (508) 758-1346

Medfield Church of the Advent **P** (253) 28 Pleasant St 02052-2613 (Mail to: 28 Pleasant St 02052-2613) Marc Eames (508) 359-6303

Medford Grace Episcopal Church **P** (434) 160 High St 02155-3818 (Mail to: 160 High St 02155-3818) Daniel Bell Carol Morehead (781) 396-7215

Medford Tufts University Epis Chapel **CC** 520 Boston Ave 02155-5500 (Mail to: Tufts University 02155) (781) 628-5000

Medway Christ Church **P** (175) 14 School St 02053-1306 (Mail to: 14 School St 02053-1306) Margaret Geller (508) 533-7171

Melrose Trinity Episcopal Church **P** (253) 131 W Emerson St 02176-3136 (Mail to: 131 W Emerson St 02176-3136) Elizabeth Forrest (781) 665-3890

Methuen St Andrews Church **P** (244) 90 Broadway 01844-3838 (Mail to: 90 Broadway 01844-3838) Joseph Wilkes (978) 689-0463

Middleboro Church of Our Saviour **P** (262) 120 Centre St 02346-2233 (Mail to: PO Box 89 02346-0089) David Milam (508) 947-1900

Milton Episcopal Church of Our Saviour **P** (53) 453 Adams St 02186-4359 (Mail to: 453 Adams St 02186-4359) Rachael Pettengill-Rasure (617) 698-4757

Milton Saint Michael's Church **P** (635) 112 Randolph Ave 02186-3401 (Mail to: 112 Randolph Ave 02186-3401) Hall Kirkham Jennifer Grumhaus Jennifer McCracken (617) 698-1813

N Attleboro Grace Church **P** (782) 104 Washington St 02760-1633 (Mail to: 104 Washington St 02760-1633) Austin Almon (508) 695-5471

Nantucket St Pauls Episcopal Church **P** (553) 20 Fair St 02554-3705 (Mail to: 20 Fair Street 02554) Max Wolf (508) 228-0916

Natick St Pauls Episcopal Church **P** (462) 39 E Central St 01760-4612 (Mail to: 39 E Central St 01760) (508) 655-5880

Needham Hgts Christ Episcopal **P** (806) 1132 Highland Ave 02494-1131 (Mail to: 1132 Highland Ave 02494-1131) Mary Miller Nicholas Morris-Kliment (781) 444-1469

New Bedford Grace Church **P** (503) 133 School St 02740-5928 (Mail to: 133 School St 02740-5928) Christopher Morck (508) 993-0547

New Bedford St Andrews Church **P** (293) 169 Belleville Rd 02745-5220 (Mail to: St. Andrew's Episcopal 169 Belleville Rd 02745-5220) Rebecca Blair (508) 992-9274

New Bedford Saint Martin's Episcopal Church **P** (111) 136 Rivet St 02744-1814 (Mail to: 136 Rivet St 02744) Scott Ciosek (508) 994-8972

Newburyport St Pauls Episcopal Church **P** (437) 166 High St 01950-3948 (Mail to: 166 High St 01950-3948) Martha Hubbard Margaret Ingalls (978) 465-5351

Newton Grace Episcopal Church **P** (368) 76 Eldredge St 02458-2017 (Mail to: 76 Eldredge St 02458-2098) David Killian Regina Walton (617) 244-3221

Newton Center Trinity Parish of Newton Centre **P** (66) 1097 Centre St 02459-1536 (Mail to: 11 Homer St 02459-1510) Todd Miller (617) 527-2790

Newton Highlands St Pauls Episcopal Church **P** (182) 1135 Walnut St 02161 (Mail to: 1135 Walnut St 02461-1242) Gretchen Grimshaw (617) 527-6642

Newton Lower Falls St Marys Episcopal Church **P** (405) 258 Concord St 02462-1315 (Mail to: 258 Concord St 02462-1315) Gwen Buehrens Paul Kolbet (617) 527-4769

Newtonville St Johns Episcopal Church **P** (108) 297 Lowell Ave 02460-1826 (Mail to: 297 Lowell Ave 02460-1826) Mark Edington (617) 964-2591

✠ **North Andover** Brooks School **O** 1160 Great Pond Rd 01845-1298 (Mail to: 1160 Great Pond Rd 01845-1298) Robert Flanagan (508) 686-6101

North Andover St Pauls Episcopal Church **P** (296) 390 Main St 01845-3952 (Mail to: 390 Main St 01845-3952) Frederick Emrich Sarah Mato (978) 683-0671

North Billerica St Annes Episcopal Church Bookstore (375) 14 Treble Cove Rd 01862-0134 (Mail to: PO Box 134 01862-0134) Lauren Mcleavey (978) 663-4073

North Dartmouth Univ of Mass - Darmouth Chapel **CC** 285 Old Westport Rd 02747-2300 (Mail to: Old Westport Rd 02747) (508) 999-8875

North Easton Bristol Trinity Episcopal Church **P** 143 Lincoln St 02356-1709 (Mail to: 143 Lincoln St 02356-1709)

Norwood Grace Episcopal Church **P** (183) 150 Chapel St 02062-3130 (Mail to: 150 Chapel St 02062-3130) Robert Brockmann (781) 762-0959

Oak Bluffs Trinity Episcopal Church **SC** 5 Ocean Ave 02557 (Mail to: PO Box 2147 02557-2147) (508) 693-3780

Orleans The Church of the Holy Spirit **P** (578) 204 Monument Rd 02653-3512 (Mail to: 204 Monument Rd 02653-3512) Adam Linton (508) 255-0433

Osterville St Peters Church Episcopal **P** (389) 421 Wianno Ave 02655-1918 (Mail to: 421 Wianno Ave 02655-1918) Elizabeth Grundy (508) 428-3561

Plymouth Christ Church Parish **P** (754) 149 Court St 02360-4003 (Mail to: 149 Court St 02360-4003) David Fredrickson (508) 746-4959

Provincetown The Church Of Saint Mary Of The Harbor **P** (164) 517 Commercial St 02657-2412 (Mail to: 517 Commercial St 02657-2412) Terry Pannell (508) 487-2622

Quincy Christ's Church Quincy **P** (152) 12 Quincy Ave 02169-6712 (Mail to: 12 Quincy Ave 02169-6712) Clifford Brown (617) 773-0310

Quincy St Chrysostom's Episcopal Church **P** (137) 1 Linden St 02170-1809 (Mail to: 1 Linden St 02170-1809) Eric Hillegas Eric Litman (617) 472-0737

Randolph Trinity Church **P** (354) 120 North Main St 02368 (Mail to: Attn Mildred Mukasa 120 Main St 02368-4629) Philip Kuhn (781) 963-2366

Reading Church of the Good Shepherd **P** (389) 95 Woburn St 01867-2907 (Mail to: 95 Woburn St 01867-2907) Patrick LaFortune Brian Raiche (781) 944-1572

Rockland Trinity Episcopal Church **P** (115) 3 Goddard Ave 02370-2325 (Mail to: 3 Goddard Ave 02370-2325) Sarah Brockmann (781) 871-0096

Rockport St Marys Episcopal Church **P** (285) 24 Broadway 01966-1537 (Mail to: PO Box 299 01966-0399) Karin Wade (978) 546-3421

S Hamilton Christ Church **P** (316) 149 Asbury St 01982-1813 (Mail to: 149 Asbury St 01982-1813) Patrick Gray (978) 468-4461

S Weymouth Church of the Holy Nativity **P** (547) 8 Nevin Rd 02190-1611 (Mail to: 8 Nevin Rd 02190-1611) Harold Birkenhead (781) 335-2030

S Yarmouth St Davids Church **P** (254) 205 Old Main St 02664-4529 (Mail to: 205 Old Main St 02664-4529) Andrea Taylor (508) 394-4222

Salem Grace Episcopal Church **P** (531) 385 Essex St 01970-3260 (Mail to: 385 Essex St 01970-3292) Deborah Phillips (978) 744-2796

Salem St Peters Episcopal Church **P** (347) 24 Saint Peter St 01970-3820 (Mail to: 24 Saint Peter St 01970-3820) Nathan Ives (978) 745-2291

Sandwich St Johns Episcopal Church **P** (1063) 159 Main St 02563-2283 (Mail to: Attn Jean Johnson 159 Main St 02563-2283) Thomas Ferguson (508) 888-2828

Saugus St Johns Episcopal Church **P** (300) 265 Central St 01906-2142 (Mail to: 8 Prospect St 01906-2155) Sarah Van Gulden (781) 233-1242

Scituate Saint Luke's Episcopal Church **P** (507) 465 First Parish Rd 02066-3334 (Mail to: PO Box 291 02066-0291) Raymond Low Natasha Stewart (781) 545-9482

Sharon St Johns Church **P** (32) 23 High St 02067-1417 (Mail to: 23 High St 02067-1417) Jennifer Beal (781) 784-3400

Shirley Trinity Chapel **P** (123) 188 Center Rd 01464-2115 (Mail to: 188 Center Rd 01464-2115) Marsha Hoecker (978) 425-9041

Somerset Church of Our Saviour **P** (489) 2112 County St 02726-5501 (Mail to: 2112 County St 02726-5501) Virgilio Fortuna Tara Soughers (508) 678-9663

Somerville St James Episcopal Church **P** (74) PO Box 440185 02144-0002 (Mail to: PO Box 440185 02144-0002) Kevin Sparrow (617) 666-1063

South Dartmouth St Aidan's Chapel **SC** 188 Smith Neck Rd 02748-1310 (Mail to: PO Box P183 02748-0310) (508) 996-2008

Southborough St Marks Episcopal Chapel **School** 25 Marlboro Rd 01772-1207 (Mail to: St Marks School 25 Marlboro Rd 01772-1299) (508) 786-6000

Southborough St Marks Church **P** (885) 27 Main St 01772-1508 (Mail to: 27 Main St 01772-1508) Philip Labelle Christine Whittaker-Navez (508) 481-1917

Stoughton Trinity Episcopal Church **P** (109) PO Box 513 02072-0513 (Mail to: 414 Sumner St 02072-3470) Harry Walton (781) 344-4592

Sudbury St Elizabeths Episcopal Church **P** (408) 1 Morse Rd 01776-1746 (Mail to: 1 Morse Rd 01776-1746) Stephanie Bradbury Jacqueline Clark (978) 443-6035

Swampscott The Church of the Holy Name **P** (120) 60 Monument Ave 01907-1968 (Mail to: 40 Hardy Rd 01907-1981) Mark Templeman (781) 595-1674

Swansea Christ Episcopal Church **P** (248) 57 Main St 02777-4624 (Mail to: 57 Main St 02777-4624) Alan Hesse (508) 678-0923

Taunton Episcopal Church of St Thomas **P** (200) 111 High St 02780-3901 (Mail to: Attn Ritch Price PO Box 149 02780-0149) John Beach (508) 824-9595

Topsfield Trinity Church **P** (568) 124 River Rd 01983-2111 (Mail to: PO Box 308 01983-0408) Johanna Barrett (978) 887-5570

Vineyard Haven Grace Episcopal Church **P** (144) § 36 Woodlawn Ave 02568 (Mail to: PO Box 1197 02568-0903) Stephen Harding Gloria Wong (508) 693-0332

Waban Church of the Good Shepherd **P** (420) 1671 Beacon St 02468-1401 (Mail to: 1671 Beacon St 02468-1401) Daniel Bell James Weldon (617) 244-4028

Wakefield Emmanuel Episcopal Church **P** (249) 5 Bryant St 01880-5008 (Mail to: 5 Bryant St 01880-5008) Matthew Cadwell (781) 245-1374

Walpole Epiphany Church **P** (512) 62 Front St 02081-2810 (Mail to: 62 Front St 02081-2810) Christian Beukman Rebecca Black Christen Mills (508) 668-2353

Waltham Christ Church **P** (452) 750 Main St 02451-0603 (Mail to: 750 Main St Ste 1 02451-0697) Rebecca Black (781) 891-6012

Wareham Church of the Good Shepherd **P** (293) 74 High St 02571-2014 (Mail to: 74 High St PO Box 719 02571-2014) Daniel Bernier (508) 295-2840

Watertown Church of the Good Shepherd **P** (156) 9 Russell Ave 02472-3452 (Mail to: 9 Russell Ave 02472-3452) Elizabeth Berman (617) 924-9420

Wellesley St Andrews Episcopal Church **P** (2335) 79 Denton Rd 02482-6404 (Mail to: 79 Denton Rd 02482-6400) Adrian Robbins-Cole Karen Budney Catherine Healy Margaret Schwarzer (781) 235-7310

Wellfleet Chapel of St James the Fisherman **SC** 2317 State Hwy Rte 6 02667 (Mail to: PO Box 1334 02667-1334) (508) 349-2188

West Newbury All Saints Episcopal Church **P** (84) 895 Main St 01985-1302 (Mail to: 928 Main St 01985-1307) (978) 462-4244

West Roxbury Parish of Emmanuel Church **P** (60) 21 Stratford St 02132-2008 (Mail to: 21 Stratford St 02132-2020) (617) 323-1440

Westford Saint Mark's Church **P** (229) 75 Cold Spring Rd 01886-2410 (Mail to: 75 Cold Spring Rd 01886-0010) Suzanne Wade (978) 692-7849

Weston St Peters Church Episcopal **P** (587) 320 Boston Post Rd 02493-1540 (Mail to: 320 Boston Post Rd 02493-1540) Lynn Campbell (781) 891-3200

Westwood St Johns Episcopal Church **P** (307) 95 Deerfield Ave 02090-1612 (Mail to: 95 Deerfield Ave 02090-1612) Jennifer Phillips (781) 329-2442

Whitman All Saints Parish **P** (116) 44 Park Ave 02382-1419 (Mail to: 44 Park Ave 02382-1419) (781) 447-6106

Wilmington St Elizabeths Episcopal Church **P** (146) 4 Forest St 01887-2811 (Mail to: C/O Pat Fregeau PO Box 294 01887-0294) Christopher Fike (978) 657-8178

Winchester Parish of the Epiphany **P** (1013) 70 Church St 01890-2523 (Mail to: 70 Church St 01890-2523) Thomas Brown Roger Nelson (781) 729-1922

Winthrop St Johns Episcopal Church **P** (128) 222 Bowdoin St 02152-3123 (Mail to: 222 Bowdoin St 02152-3123) Walter Connelly (617) 846-2363

Woburn Trinity Episcopal Church **P** (191) 535 Main St 01801-2991 (Mail to: 535 Main St 01801-2991) (781) 935-0219

Woods Hole Church of the Messiah Epis Church **P** (237) 13 Church St 02543-1007 (Mail to: 13 Church St 02543-1007) Deborah Warner Deborah Warner (508) 548-2145

Wrentham Trinity Episcopal Church **P** (280) 47 East St 02093-1369 (Mail to: PO Box 55 02093-0055) (508) 384-3958

STATE OF MICHIGAN

Dioceses of Eastern Michigan (EMI), Michigan (MI), Northern Michigan (NMI), and Western Michigan (WMI)

Adrian—MI
Albion—WMI
Allegan—WMI
Allen Pk—MI
Alma—EMI
Alpena—EMI
Ann Arbor—MI
Atlanta—EMI
Bad Axe—EMI
Battle Creek—WMI
Bay City—EMI
Beaver Is—WMI
Belleville—MI
Belmont—WMI
Benton Hbr—WMI
Beulah—WMI
Big Rapids—WMI
Birmingham—MI
Bloomfield Hills—MI
Bloomfield Township—MI
Boyne City—WMI
Brighton—MI
Brooklyn—MI
Cadillac—WMI
Charlevoix—WMI
Charlotte—WMI
Cheboygan—EMI

Chelsea—MI
Clarkston—MI
Clinton—MI
Coldwater—WMI
Corunna—EMI
Crystal Falls—NMI
Davison—EMI
Dearborn—MI
DeTour Vil—NMI
Detroit—MI
Dewitt—MI
Dexter—MI
Dowagiac—WMI
Dryden—EMI
Eagle Harbor—NMI
E Lansing—MI
E Tawas—EMI
Ecorse—MI
Elk Rapids—WMI
Escanaba—NMI
Farmington Hills—MI
Fenton—EMI
Ferndale—MI
Flint—EMI
Flushing—EMI
Fremont—WMI
Gaylord—EMI
Gladstone—NMI

Gladwin—EMI
Grand Blanc—EMI
Grand Haven—WMI
Grand Ledge—WMI
Grand Rapids—WMI
Grayling—EMI
Greenville—WMI
Grosse Ile—MI
Grosse Pte—MI
Grosse Pte Farms—MI
Gwinn—NMI
Hamburg—MI
Harbert—WMI
Harbor Spgs—WMI
Harrisville—EMI
Harsens Is—EMI
Hastings—WMI
Hillman—EMI
Hillsdale—MI
Holland—WMI
Houghton—NMI
Howell—MI
Indian River—EMI
Inkster—MI
Ionia—WMI
Iron Mtn—NMI
Iron River—NMI
Ironwood—NMI

Ishpeming—NMI
Jackson—MI
Kalamazoo—WMI
Kentwood—WMI
Lachine—EMI
Lake Orion—MI
Lansing—MI and WMI
Lapeer—EMI
Larium—NMI
Leland—WMI
Lexington—EMI
Lincoln Pk—MI
Livonia—MI
Ludington—WMI
Mackinac Is—NMI
Madison Hts—MI
Manistee—WMI
Manistique—NMI
Marine City—EMI
Marquette—NMI
Marshall—WMI
Marysville—EMI
Mason—MI
Menominee—NMI
Michigan Ctr—MI
Midland—EMI
Milford—MI
Mio—EMI

Monroe—MI
Montague—WMI
Mt Clemens—MI
Mt Pleasant—WMI
Munising—NMI
Muskegon—WMI
Negaunee—NMI
Newaygo—WMI
Newberry—NMI
Niles—WMI
Northport—WMI
Norton Shores—WMI
Novi—MI
Onekama—WMI
Ontonagon—NMI
Oscoda—EMI
Otter Lake—EMI

Owosso—EMI
Paw Paw—WMI
Pentwater—WMI
Petoskey—WMI
Plainwell—WMI
Pleasant Lake—MI
Plymouth—MI
Pte Aux Pins—NMI
Pontiac—MI
Pt Huron—EMI
Portage—WMI
Redford Chtr
Twnshp—MI
Richland—WMI
Rochester—MI
Rogers City—EMI
Romeo—MI

Roscommon—EMI
Rose City—EMI
Royal Oak—MI
Saginaw—EMI
St Clair—EMI
St Clair Shores—MI
St Joseph—WMI
Saline—MI
Sand Pt—EMI
Sandusky—EMI
Saugatuck—WMI
Sault Ste Marie—NMI
Shelbyville—WMI
Southfield—MI
Southgate—MI
S Haven—WMI
Standish—EMI

Sturgis—WMI
Taylor—MI
Three Rivers—WMI
Traverse City—WMI
Trenton—MI
Troy—MI
Utica—MI
Walled Lake—MI
Waterford—MI
W Bloomfield—MI
W Branch—EMI
Westland—MI
Williamston—MI
Wyandotte—MI
Wyoming—WMI
Ypsilanti—MI

DIOCESE OF MICHIGAN

(PROVINCE V)

Comprises the southeastern and southcentral portion of Michigan's lower peninsula

DIOCESAN OFFICE 4800 Woodward Ave Detroit MI 48201

TEL (313) 832-4400　TOLL FREE (866) 545-6424　FAX (313) 831-0259

E-MAIL info@edomi.org　WEB www.edomi.org

Previous Bishops—
Samuel A McCoskry 1836-78, Samuel A McCoskry 1836-78, Samuel S Harris 1879-88, Thomas F Davies 1889-1905, Chas D Williams 1906-23, Herman Page 1923-39, Frank W Creighton coadj 1937 Bp 1940-48, Donald B Aldrich coadj 1945-46, Russell S Hubbard suffr 1948-54, Archie H Crowley suffr 1954-72, Richard S Emrich suffr 1946-48 coadj 1948 Bp 1948-73, Robt L DeWitt suffr 1960-64, C Kilmer Myers suffr 1964-66, WJ Gordon Jr asst 1976-86, H Coleman McGehee Jr coadj 1971 Bp 1973-89, H Irving Mayson suffr 1976-92, R Stewart Wood Jr coadj 1989-90 Bp 1990-2000

Bishop—Rt Rev Wendell N Gibbs Jr (950) (Dio 4 Nov 2000)

Cn for Cong Life J Gettel; *Cn Admin* J Hardy; *Dir of Fin* M Miliotto; *Accountant* K Chapman; *Miss for Yth & Young Adults* E Travis; *Bishop's Ex Asst* B Rowley; *Sec for Admin* J Michalak; *Dir of Whitaker Inst* V Hesse; *Min Dev* N McLaughlin; *Dir of Comm* A Schroen; *Chanc* S Ott; *Asst Chanc* M Norris

Stand Comm—Cler: J Matthews P Miller D Johnson C Mader; *Lay: Chair* A Putallaz G Smereck J. Woods, J Holden

PARISHES, MISSIONS, AND CLERGY

Adrian Christ Episcopal Church **P** (35) 720 Riverside Ave 49221-1445 (Mail to: 720 Riverside Ave 49221-1445) (517) 263-1162

Allen Park St Lukes Episcopal Church **P** (45) 15603 Wick Rd 48101-1532 (Mail to: 15603 Wick Rd 48101-1532) William Hale (313) 381-6345

Ann Arbor Church of the Incarnation **M** (124) 3257 Lohr Rd 48108-9515 (Mail to: 3257 Lohr Rd 48108-9515) Joseph Summers Thalia Johnson Joseph Summers (734) 769-7900

Ann Arbor Canterbury House **CM** 721 E Huron St 48104-5903 (Mail to: 721 E Huron St Ste 2 48104-5903) Matthew Lukens (734) 665-0606

Ann Arbor St Aidans Episcopal Church **P** (55) 1679 Broadway St 48105-1811 (Mail to: 1679 Broadway St 48105-1811) Judith Harmon (734) 663-5503

Ann Arbor St Andrews Episcopal Church **HC** (972) 306 Division St 48104-1441 (Mail to: 306 Division St 48104-1497) Alan Gibson Walter LaBatt Lewis Towler Edward Witke (734) 663-0518

Ann Arbor St Clare of Assisi Episcopal Church **P** (402) 2309 Packard St 48104-6321 (Mail to: 2309 Packard St 48104-6321) James Rhodenhiser (734) 662-2449

Belleville Trinity Episcopal Church **P** (266) 11575 Belleville Rd 48111-2401 (Mail to: 11575 Belleville Rd 48111-2401) Richard Boulter Ian Twiss (734) 699-3361

Birmingham St James Episcopal Church **P** (547) 355 W Maple Rd 48009-3347 (Mail to: 355 W Maple Rd 48009-3348) Robert Hart Joshua Hoover (248) 644-0820

Bloomfield Hills Christ Church Cranbrook **P** (2065) 470 Church Rd 48304-3400 (Mail to:

470 Church Rd 48304-3400) William Danaher Anthony Estes Christopher Harris Imogen Rhodenhiser (248) 644-5210

Bloomfield Township Nativity Episcopal Church **P** (47) 21220 W 14 Mile Rd 48301-4000 (Mail to: 21220 W 14 Mile Road Attn: Treasurer 48301-4000) William Bales (248) 646-4100

Brighton St Pauls Episcopal Church **P** (298) 200 W Saint Paul St 48116-1202 (Mail to: 200 W Saint Paul St 48116-1202) Jenny Housner-Ritter Deon Johnson (810) 229-2821

Brooklyn All Saints Episcopal Church **P** (72) 151 Main St 49230-8979 (Mail to: PO Box 367 49230-0367) (517) 592-2244

Brooklyn St Michael and All Angels **P** (44) 11646 Old Monroe Pike 49230-8706 (Mail to: PO Box 287 49265-0287) Winifred Cook Cynthia Corner Mark Hastings Diana Walworth (517) 467-7855

Chelsea St Barnabas Episcopal Church **M** (46) 20500 W Old Us Highway 12 48118-1309 (Mail to: 20500 W Old US Highway 12 48118-1309) David Glaser Ernest Stech (734) 475-8818

Clarkston Church of the Resurrection **P** (41) 6490 Clarkston Rd 48346-1500 (Mail to: 6490 Clarkston Rd 48346-1500) Heather Barta (248) 625-2325

Clinton St Johns Episcopal Church **M** (251) 122 E Church St 49236-9762 (Mail to: PO Box 518 122 E Church St 49236-0518) Susan Shaefer (517) 456-4828

Dearborn Christ Episcopal Church **P** (437) 120 Military St 48124-1035 (Mail to: 120 Military St 48124-1035) Terri Pilarski (313) 565-8450

Detroit All Saints Episcopal Church **P** (82) 3837 West Seven Mile Road 48221-2218 (Mail to: 3837 W 7 Mile Rd 48221-2218) (313) 341-5320

✠ **Detroit** Cathedral Church of St Paul **O** (429) 4800 Woodward Ave 48201-1310 (Mail to: 4800 Woodward Ave 48201-1399) S Scott Hunter Robert Alltop Veronica Dunbar Frederick Nestrock Brian Shaffer (313) 831-5000

Detroit Christ Episcopal Church **P** (465) 960 E Jefferson Ave 48207-3102 (Mail to: Attn: Dawn Esse 960 E Jefferson Ave 48207-3102) Emily Guffey (313) 259-6688

Detroit Church of the Messiah **P** (301) 231 E Grand Blvd 48207-3739 (Mail to: 231 E Grand Blvd 48207-3788) (313) 567-1158

Detroit Grace Episcopal Church **P** (38) 1926 Virginia Park St 48206-2422 (Mail to: 1926 Virginia Park St 48206-2422) (313) 895-6442

Detroit St Cyprians Episcopal Church **P** (56) 6114 28th St 48210-1400 (Mail to: 6114 28th St 48210-1400) Donald Lutas (313) 896-7515

Detroit St Johns Episcopal Church **P** (246) 2326 Woodward Ave 48201-3431 (Mail to: 50 E Fisher Fwy 48201-3405) Steven Kelly (313) 962-7358

Detroit St Matthews and St Josephs Church **P** (156) 8850 Woodward Ave 48202-2137 (Mail

to: 8850 Woodward Ave 48202-2137) (313) 871-4750

Detroit St Peters Episcopal Church **P** (33) 1950 Trumbull St 48216-1529 (Mail to: 1950 Trumbull St 48216-1529) (313) 757-2985

Detroit Trinity Episcopal Church **P** (153) 1519 Martin Luther King Jr Bl 48208-2867 (Mail to: 1519 Martin Luther King Jr Bl 48208) Robert Smith (313) 964-3113

Dewitt Christ United St Annes **M** (38) 1000 W Webb Rd 48820-8396 (Mail to: 1000 W Webb Rd 48820-8396) (517) 669-9308

Dexter St James Episcopal Church **P** (84) 3279 Broad St 48130-1016 (Mail to: 3279 Broad St 48130-1016) Jenny Housner-Ritter Carol Mader (734) 426-8247

East Lansing All Saints Episcopal Church **P** (593) 800 Abbott Rd 48823-3103 (Mail to: 800 Abbot Rd 48823-3103) Katherine Carlson (517) 351-7160

East Lansing Canterbury at Michigan State Univ **CC** (800) Abbott Rd 48823-3103 (Mail to: C/o University Lutheran Church 1020 S Harrison Rd 48823-5198) (517) 351-1885

Ecorse Church of the Resurrection **M** (42) 27085 W Outer Dr 48229-1282 (Mail to: 27085 W Outer Dr 48229-1282) (313) 382-1781

Farmington Trinity Episcopal Church **P** (251) 26880 La Muera St 48334-4614 (Mail to: 26880 La Muera St 48334-4614) Julia Huttar Bailey (248) 474-2860

Ferndale St Lukes Episcopal Church **P** (122) 540 W Lewiston Ave 48220-1204 (Mail to: 540 W Lewiston Ave 48220-1204) Clare Hickman (248) 677-1804

Grosse Ile St James Episcopal Church **P** (372) 25150 E River RD 48138-1789 (Mail to: 25150 E River RD 48138-1789) Philip Dinwiddie (734) 676-1727

Grosse Pointe Saint Michael's Church **P** (601) 20475 Sunningdale Park 48236-1637 (Mail to: 20475 Sunningdale Park Attn: Michael Rothgery 48236-1637) Maryjane Peck (313) 884-4820

Grosse Pointe Farms Christ Church Grosse Pointe **P** (1568) 61 Grosse Pointe Blvd 48236-3712 (Mail to: 61 Grosse Pointe Blvd 48236-3712) Thomas Van Culin Walter Brownridge Paul Spann (313) 885-4841

Hamburg St Stephens Episcopal Church **P** (102) 10585 Hamburg Rd 48139-1214 (Mail to: PO Box 436 48139-0436) James Pashturro (810) 231-3220

Hillsdale St Peters Episcopal Church **P** (42) 3 Broad St 49242-1601 (Mail to: 3 Broad St 49242-1601) (517) 437-2833

Howell St Johns Episcopal Church **P** (126) 504 Prospect St 48843-1440 (Mail to: 504 Prospect St 48843-1440) James Pashturro (517) 546-3660

Inkster St Clements Episcopal Church **P** (79) 4300 Harrison St 48141-2963 (Mail to: Attn

The Treasurer 4300 Harrison St 48141-2963) Ellis Clifton (734) 728-0790

Jackson St Pauls Episcopal Church **P** (353) 309 S Jackson St 49201-2214 (Mail to: Attn Diane Billingsley 309 S Jackson St 49201-2214) Sarah Hurlbert (517) 787-3370

Lake Orion St Marys-in-the-Hills Epis Church **P** (249) 2512 Joslyn Ct 48360-1938 (Mail to: Attn. Treasurer 2512 Joslyn Ct 48360-1938) (248) 391-0663

Lansing St Michael Episcopal Church **P** (183) 6500 Amwood Dr 48911-5955 (Mail to: 6500 Amwood Dr 48911-5955) Nikki Seger Roger Walker (517) 882-9733

Lansing St Paul's Episcopal Church **P** (569) 218 W Ottawa St 48933-1309 (Mail to: 218 W Ottawa St 48933-1374) Linda Carter Karen Lewis Karen Lewis (517) 482-9454

Lincoln Park St Michaels & All Angels Epis Church **P** (197) 1325 Champaign Rd 48146-3302 (Mail to: 1325 Champaign Rd 48146-3302) (313) 382-5525

Livonia St Andrews Episcopal Church **P** (75) 16360 Hubbard St 48154-6100 (Mail to: 16360 Hubbard St 48154-6100) John Lohmann (734) 421-8451

Madison Hts St Patrick's Episcopal Church **P** (97) 1434 E 13 Mile Rd 48071-1515 (Mail to: 1434 E 13 Mile Rd 48071-1515) Linda Ferguson Paul Leclair Judith Marinco Vincent Marinco (248) 585-9591

Mason St Augustine of Canterbury **P** (36) 546 W South St 48854-1914 (Mail to: 546 W South St 48854-1914) (517) 676-2525

Michigan Ctr St Aidans Episcopal Church **P** (38) 361 E Grove Ave 49254-1511 (Mail to: 361 E Grove Ave 49254-1511) (517) 764-2950

Milford St George's Episcopal Church **P** (144) 801 E Commerce St 48381-1727 (Mail to: 801 E Commerce St 48381-1727) Paul Castelli (248) 684-0495

Monroe Trinity Episcopal Church **P** (61) 11 W 3rd St 48161-6536 (Mail to: 11 W 3rd St 48161-2340) (734) 242-3113

Mount Clemens Grace Episcopal Church **P** (308) 115 S Main St 48043-2379 (Mail to: Attn Treasurer 115 S Main St 48043-2379) Steven Domienik (586) 465-4573

Novi Church of the Holy Cross **P** (137) 46200 W 10 Mile Rd 48374-3004 (Mail to: 40700 W 10 Mile Rd 48375-3510) Alexander Babin (248) 427-1175

Pleasant Lake Christ Church **P** (89) 9900 Meridian Rd 49272-9630 (Mail to: 9900 Meridian Rd 49272-9630) (517) 769-2333

Plymouth St Johns Episcopal Church **P** (655) 574 S Sheldon Rd 48170-1565 (Mail to: 574 S Sheldon Rd 48170-1565) Jeanne Hansknecht (734) 453-0190

Pontiac All Saints Episcopal Church **P** (232) 171 W Pike St 48341-1750 (Mail to: PO Box 430357

48343-0357) Christopher Johnson (248) 334-4571

Redford Charter Township St Elizabeths Episcopal Church **P** (28) 26431 W Chicago 48239-1897 (Mail to: 26431 W Chicago 48239-1897) Richard Iwick (313) 937-2880

Rochester St Philips Episcopal Church **P** (244) 100 Romeo St. 48307-1557 (Mail to: 100 Romeo Rd 48307-1557) Eric Williams (248) 651-6188

Romeo St Pauls Episcopal Church **P** (79) 11100 W St Clair St 48065 (Mail to: PO Box 148 48065-0148) Daniel Lawson (586) 752-3212

Royal Oak St Johns Episcopal Church **P** (378) 26998 Woodward Ave 48067-0923 (Mail to: 26998 Woodward Ave 48067-0923) Elizabeth Bingham Robert Hart Jeffernell Howcott Timothy Spannaus Marjorie Taylor (248) 546-1255

Saline Holy Faith Episcopal Church **M** (134) 6299 Saline Ann Arbor Rd 48176-8805 (Mail to: 6299 Saline Ann Arbor Rd 48176-8805) Donald Dersnah Andrea Martin (734) 429-2991

Southfield St Davids Episcopal Church **P** (550) 16200 W 12 Mile Rd 48076-2959 (Mail to: 16200 W 12 Mile Rd 48076-7357) Christopher Yaw (248) 557-5430

Southfield Episcopal Church of the Redeemer **P** (151) 18140 Cornell Rd 48075-4146 (Mail to: 18140 Cornell Rd 48075-4146) (248) 569-4418

Southgate Grace Episcopal Church **P** (122) 15650 Reeck Rd 48195-3237 (Mail to: 15650 Reeck Rd 48195-3237) Lynda Carter (734) 285-0380

St Clair Shrs Trinity Episcopal Church **P** (76) 30205 Jefferson Ave 48082-1787 (Mail to: 30205 Jefferson Ave 48082-1787) (586) 294-0740

Taylor Church of Christ the King **M** (44) 23045 Wick Rd 48180-3504 (Mail to: 23045 Wick Rd 48180-3504) William Hale (313) 291-4570

Trenton St Thomas Episcopal Church **M** (136) 2441 Nichols St 48183-2419 (Mail to: 2441 Nichols St 48183-2419) Shirley McWhorter (734) 676-3122

Troy St Stephens Episcopal Church **P** (507) 5500 North Adams Road 48098-2399 (Mail to: 5500 Adams Rd 48098-2399) Susan Anslow-Williams (248) 641-8080

Utica St Lukes Episcopal Church **P** (278) 7700 22 Mile Rd 48317-2312 (Mail to: 7700 22 Mile Rd 48317-2312) (586) 731-1221

Walled Lake St Anne's Episcopal Church **M** (46) 430 E. Nicolet St 48390-3589 (Mail to: PO Box 267 48390-0267) Rae Lee Baxter William Roberts Janis Stevenson (248) 624-3817

Waterford St Andrews Episcopal Church **P** (180) 5301 Hatchery Rd 48329-3440 (Mail to: 5301 Hatchery Rd 48329-3440) (248) 673-7635

West Bloomfield Spirit of Grace **P** (139) 2399 Figa Avenue 48324-1808 (Mail to: 2399 Figa

Ave 48324-1808) Stephen Bancroft (248) 338-3505

Westland St Johns Episcopal Church **P** (209) 555 S Wayne Rd 48186-4301 (Mail to: 555 S Wayne Rd 48186-4301) Steven Domienik (734) 721-5023

Williamston Saint Katherine's Church **P** (213) 4650 Meridian Rd 48895-9317 (Mail to: 4650 Meridian Rd # Rt 48895-9317) Jessie Gutgsell (517) 349-4120

Wyandotte St Stephens Episcopal Church **P** (169) 2803 1st St 48192-5113 (Mail to: 2803 1st St 48192-5113) Andrea Morrow (734) 284-8777

Ypsilanti Episcopal Chaplaincy at E Michigan **CM** 120 Huron St 48197-2610 (Mail to: C/O St Lukes Church 120 Huron 48197-2610) (734) 483-4253

Ypsilanti St Lukes Episcopal Church **P** (369) 120 North Huron St. 48197-2610 (Mail to: 120 Huron St 48197-2610) JoAnn Slater (734) 483-4253

EPISCOPAL CHURCH IN MICRONESIA
Under the jurisdiction of the Presiding Bishop
BISHOP'S OFFICE The Episcopal Church in Hawaii 229 Queen Emma Square Honolulu HI 96813
TEL (808) 536-7776   FAX (808) 538-7194   WEB www.episcopalhawaii.org; episcopalmicronesia.org/guam/
LOCAL ADMINISTRATIVE OFFICES 911 N Marine Dr Tamuning GU 96913-4302
TEL (671) 649-0690   FAX (671) 649-0690

Previous Bishops—
HS Kennedy 1957-69, L Hanchett 1969, EL Browning 1969-71, L Hanchett 1971-75, EL Browning 1975-78, CL Burgreen 1978-86, JF Ashby 1986-87, DP Hart 1987-94, CL Keyser 1994-99, GE Packard 1999-2009

Bishop-in-charge—Rt Rev RL Fitzpatrick (1015)

Archdcn Ven Irene Egmalis Maliaman

MISSIONS AND CLERGY
Saipan St Pauls Episcopal Church **M** (42) Gualo Rai Middle Rd 96950 (Mail: PO Box 506610 Saipan MP 96950-4339) (670) 233-6081

Tamuning Epis Ch of St John the Divine **M** (60) § 911 N Marine Corps Dr 96913-4302 (Mail: 911 N Marine Corps Dr Tamuning GU 96913-4302) Dcn Lisa Pang Irene Maliaman (671) 646-1708

DIOCESE OF MILWAUKEE
(PROVINCE V)
Comprises Southern Wisconsin
DIOCESAN OFFICE 804 E Juneau Ave Milwaukee WI 53202-2798
TEL (414) 272-3028   FAX (866) 499-1973
E-MAIL info@diomil.org   WEB www.diomil.org

Previous Bishops—
Jackson Kemper 1854-70, Wm E Armitage coadj 1866 Bp 1870-73, Edward R Welles 1874-88, Cyrus F Knight 1889-91, Isaac L Nicholson 1891-1906, Wm W Webb 1906-33, Benj FP Ivins coadj 1925 Bp 1933-53, Donald HV Hallock coadj 1952 Bp 1953-73, Charles T Gaskell coadj 1973 Bp 1974-85, Roger J White coadj 1984 Bp 1984-03

Bishop—Rt Rev Steven A Miller (991) (Dio 18 Oct 2003)

Fin Off M Udovich; *Treas* C Bachand; *Chanc* S Parsons; *Hist* Rev E Payson; *Bp Asst for Cong Dev* P Bean;

Stand Comm—Cler: S Leannah G Manning A Jones E Tester; *Lay:* M Cairo T Prather C Fine S Slocum S Parsons Esq

PARISHES, MISSIONS, AND CLERGY
Baraboo Trinity Episcopal Church **P** (138) 111 6th St 53913-2157 (Mail to: 111 6th St 53913-2177) David Mowers (608) 356-3620

Beaver Dam St Marks Episcopal Church **P** (65) 700 E Mill St 53916-2435 (Mail to: PO Box 126 53916-0126) Oscar Rozo (920) 885-3536

Beloit St Pauls Episcopal Church **P** (106) 212 W Grand Ave 53511-6109 (Mail to: 212 W Grand Ave 53511-6193) Gregg Schneider Helen Tester (608) 362-4312

Burlington Church of St John the Divine **P** (161) 216 E Chandler Blvd 53105-1901 (Mail to: 216 E Chandler Blvd 53105-1901) Kevin Huddleston (262) 763-7482

Delafield St John Chrysostom Church **P** (136) 1111 Genesee St 53018-1411 (Mail to: PO Box 180082 53018-0082) Philip Cunningham (262) 646-2727

Delavan Christ Church **P** (130) 503 E Walworth Ave 53115-1209 (Mail to: PO Box 528 53115-0528) Pedro Lara William Pelnar Marlyne Seymour (262) 728-5292

Dousman Saint Mary's Episcopal Church **P** (250) 36014 Sunset Dr 53118 (Mail to: PO Box 126 53118-0126) Charles Zellermayer (262) 965-3924

Elkhorn St Johns in the Wilderness **P** (52) 13 S Church St 53121-1707 (Mail to: 13 S Church St 53121-1707) (262) 723-4229

Fort Atkinson St Peters Episcopal Church **P** (88) 302 Merchants Ave 53538-2248 (Mail to: 302 Merchants Ave 53538-2248) Andrew Hanyzewski (920) 563-3889

Greendale Saint Thomas Of Canterbury Church **P** (150) 7255 W Grange Ave 53129-1132 (Mail to: PO Box 342 53129-0342) Scott Leannah Margaret Kiss (414) 421-0130

Hartford St Aidans Episcopal Church **SC** (152) 670 E Monroe Ave 53027-2574 (Mail to: Attn Treasurer 670 E Monroe Ave 53027-2574) Lars Skoglund (262) 673-7273

Hartland Saint Anskar's Episcopal Church **P** (75) N48w31340 State Road 83 53029-8500 (Mail to: N48w31340 State Road 83 53029-8500) Thomas Buchan (262) 367-2439

Janesville Trinity Episcopal Church **P** (310) 419 E Court St 53545-4009 (Mail to: 409 E Court St 53545-4009) Kathleen Lutes (608) 754-3402

Kenosha St Andrews Church **P** (51) 6609 26th Ave 53143-4728 (Mail to: 6609 26th Ave 53143-4728) (262) 652-5118

Kenosha Saint Matthew's Church **P** (216) 5900 7th Ave 53140-4133 (Mail to: 5900 7th Ave 53140-4162) Matthew Buterbaugh (262) 605-5526

Lake Geneva Church of the Holy Communion **P** (96) § 320 Broad St 53147-1812 (Mail to: 320 Broad St 53147-1812) (262) 248-3522

Madison Grace Episcopal Church **P** (430) 116 W Washington Ave 53703-2740 (Mail to: Attn Financial Administrator 116 W Washington Ave Ste 1 53703-2740) Dale Grieser Margaret Irwin Carol Smith (608) 255-5147

Madison St Andrews Episcopal Church **P** (387) 1833 Regent St 53726-4119 (Mail to: 1833 Regent St 53726-4198) Andrew Jones (608) 233-3249

Madison St Dunstans Episcopal Church **P** (298) 6205 University Ave 53562 (Mail to: 6205 University Ave 53705-1056) Miranda Hassett (608) 238-2781

Madison St Lukes Church **P** (132) 4011 Major Ave 53716-1133 (Mail to: 4011 Major Ave 53716-1133) Donald Fleischman (608) 222-6921

Madison St Francis House **Chaplaincy** 1011 University Ave 53715-1092 (Mail to: 1011 University Ave 53715-1092) Melissa Wilcox (608) 257-0688

Menomonee Falls St Francis Episcopal Church **P** (81) N84 W16525 Menomonee Ave. 53051 (Mail to: PO Box 194 53052-0194) (262) 251-7420

Mequon St Boniface Episcopal Church **P** (368) 3906 W Mequon Rd 53092-2728 (Mail to: 3906 W Mequon Rd 53092-2799) Kenneth Miller Terrance Garner Thomas Niehaus (262) 242-2994

✠ **Milwaukee** All Saints Cathedral **O** (222) 818 E Juneau Ave 53202-2714 (Mail to: 818 E Juneau Ave 53202-2714) Kevin Carroll Theodore Parks Steven Peay (414) 271-7719

Milwaukee Christ Church Episcopal **P** (668) 5655 Lake Dr 53217-4849 (Mail to: 5655 Lake Dr 53217-4849) Thomas Binder Katherine Byrd Seth Dietrich Edwin Leidel (414) 964-3368

Milwaukee St Christophers Church **P** (365) 7845 River Rd 53217-3025 (Mail to: 7845 River Rd 53217-3025) Geoffrey Ward (414) 352-0380

Milwaukee St Lukes Episcopal Church **P** (63) 3200 S Herman St 53207-2852 (Mail to: 3200 S Herman St 53207-2899) Jason Lavann (414) 744-3736

Milwaukee St Marks Episcopal Church **P** (306) 2618 Hackett Ave 53211-3832 (Mail to: 2618 Hackett Ave 53211-3832) Ian Burch (414) 962-0500

Milwaukee St Pauls Church **P** (351) 914 E Knapp St 53202-2825 (Mail to: 914 E Knapp St 53202-2898) Sheila Scott Warren Toebben (414) 276-6277

Milwaukee St Peters Episcopal Church **P** (103) 7929 W Lincoln Ave 53219-1752 (Mail to: 7929 W Lincoln Ave 53219-1752) Karen Buker Theodore Parks (414) 543-6040

Milwaukee Trinity Church **P** (537) 1717 Church St 53213-2105 (Mail to: 1717 Church St 53213-2199) Gary Manning Kevin Stewart (414) 453-4540

Mineral Point Trinity Church **P** (34) 409 High St 53565-1220 (Mail to: 403 High St 53565-1220) John Hector (608) 987-3019

Monroe St Andrews Episcopal Church **P** (15) 2810 6th St 53566-1901 (Mail to: 2810 6th St 53566-1901) (608) 328-8265

Northlake St Peters Episcopal Church **P** (37) W314N7412 Hwy 83 53064 (Mail to: PO Box 267 53064-0267) (262) 966-7312

Oconomowoc St Pauls Episcopal Church **P** (46) N982 County Road P 53066-9517 (Mail to: N982 County Road P 53066-9517) Thomas Holtzen (920) 474-4797

Oconomowoc Zion Episcopal Church **P** (130) 135 Rockwell St 53066-2854 (Mail to: 135 Rockwell St 53066-2896) Charles Burch Scott Seefeldt (262) 567-7507

Pewaukee St Bartholomews Episcopal Church **P** (385) N27w24000 Paul Ct 53072-6239 (Mail to: N27W24000 Paul Ct 53072-6239) Joel Prather (262) 691-0836

Platteville Trinity Episcopal Church **P** (54) 250 Market St 53818-2543 (Mail to: 250 Market St 53818-2543) (608) 348-6402

Port Washington St Simon the Fisherman Epis Ch **SC** (62) 3448 Green Bay Rd 53074-9765 (Mail to: PO Box 34 53074-0034) Julian Hills Mary Pain (262) 284-0510

Portage St John the Baptist Episcopal Church **P** (50) 211 W Pleasant St 53901-1744 (Mail to: 201 W Pleasant St 53901-1744) (608) 742-6054

Prairie Du Chien Church of the Holy Trinity **P** (31) 220 S Michigan St 53821-1713 (Mail to: PO Box 365 53821-0365) Carson Culver (608) 326-6085

Racine St Lukes Episcopal Church **P** (97) 614 Main St 53403-1210 (Mail to: 614 Main St 53403-1210) (262) 634-5025

Racine St Michaels Episcopal Church **P** (319) 4701 Erie St 53402-2513 (Mail to: 4701 Erie St 53402-2513) Dustin Fecht (262) 639-2507

Richland Ctr St Barnabas Episcopal Church **P** (73) 297 Main St 53581-2240 (Mail to: PO Box

487 53581-0487) Michael Tess (608) 649-6003

S Milwaukee St Marks Church **P** (292) 1314 Rawson Ave 53172-1939 (Mail to: 1314 Rawson Ave 53172-1939) (414) 762-1772

Sun Prairie Church of the Good Shepherd **P** (150) 3416 Swansee Ridge 53590 (Mail to: 3416 Swansee Rdg 53590-9495) Oscar Rozo (608) 837-3308

Sussex St Albans Episcopal Church **P** (60) W239 N5924 Maple Ave 53089 (Mail to: PO Box 202 53089-0202) Stephen Capitelli (262) 246-4430

Watertown St Pauls Episcopal Church **P** (70) 413 S 2nd St 53094-4420 (Mail to: 413 S 2nd St 53094-4420) Elizabeth Tester (920) 261-1150

Waukesha St Matthias Episcopal Church **P** (379) 111 E Main St 53186 (Mail to: Attn: Sandra Krueger PO Box 824 53187-0824) Richard Fox David Simmons (262) 547-4838

West Bend St James Episcopal Church **P** (221) 148 S 8th Ave 53095-3207 (Mail to: 148 S 8th Ave 53095-3207) Richard Craig Cathleen Mccurry Milliken Melinda Valentine Davis (262) 334-4242

Wisconsin Dells Holy Cross Episcopal Church **P** (59) 322 Unity Dr 53965-9761 (Mail to: 322 Unity Dr 53965-9761) Kenneth Foster Albert Majkrzak (608) 254-8623

DIOCESE OF MINNESOTA

(PROVINCE VI)

Comprises the State of Minnesota

DIOCESAN OFFICE 1101 W Broadway, Minneapolis MN 55411

TEL (612) 871-5311; In MN (800) 596-3839   FAX (612) 871-0552

E-MAIL info@episcopalmn.org   WEB www.episcopalmn.org

Previous Bishops— Henry B Whipple 1859-1901, Mahlon N Gilbert coadj 1886 1900, Samuel C Edsall 1901-17, Frank A Mc Elwain suffr 1912 Bp 1917-43, Benj T Kemerer suffr 1944-48, Stephen E Keeler coadj 1931 Bp 1944-56, Hamilton H Kellogg coadj 1952 Bp 1956-70, Philip F McNairy suffr 1958 coadj 1968 Bp 1971-78, Robert M Anderson 1978 93, Sanford ZK Hampton suffr 1989-95, James L Jelinek 1993-2010

Bishop—Rt Rev Brian N Prior (1040) (Dio 13 Feb 2010)

Miss for Missional-Management Rev Cn M Pipkin; *Miss for Min* Cn K Olson; *Miss for Comm Engagement* R Babbitt; *Miss for Indian Work and Multicultural Min* Rev Cn R Two Bulls; *Miss for Children, Yth, and Camp* S Barnett; *Miss for Young Adult and College Min* S Mullaney; *Miss for Form* Rev S Daughtry; *Miss for Admin* L Geno; *Miss for Comm* K Schuster; *Miss for Fin* J Gamberg; *Miss for the Bp* S Cadiz; *Miss for*

Networking A Mwanda

Stand Comm—Cler: T Cook T Gehlson J Chapman S Hustad R Scarpace D Brown; *Lay:* R Simons J Shoulak A Roy L Bathke S Grove C Commers

PARISHES, MISSIONS, AND CLERGY

Aitkin St Johns Church **M** (14) 222 1st St SE 56431-1706 (Mail to: 417 1st Ave SW 56431-1818) (218) 927-6040

Albert Lea Christ Church **P** (64) 204 W Fountain St 56007-2406 (Mail to: 204 W Fountain St 56007-2446) Henry Doyle (507) 373-3188

Alexandria Emmanuel Episcopal Church **P** (48) PO Box 231 56308-0231 (Mail to: PO Box 231 56308-0231) Thomas Sinning (320) 763-3201

Annandale St Marks Church **SC** (9) 10536 108th St NW 55302-2912 (Mail to: 10536 108th St NW 55302-2912) (320) 230-6337

Anoka Trinity Episcopal Church **P** (288) 1415 6th Ave 55303-5250 (Mail to: 1415 6th Ave 55303-5250) (763) 421-1196

Austin Christ Episcopal Church **P** (118) 301 3rd Ave Nw 55912-3023 (Mail to: 301 3rd Ave NW 55912-3023) John Sullivan (507) 433-3782

Bemidji St Bartholomews Episcopal Church **M** (110) 1800 Irvine Ave Nw 56601-2552 (Mail to: 1800 Irvine Ave NW 56601-2552) (218) 444-6831

Brainerd St Pauls Church **P** (56) 408 7th St 56401-3019 (Mail to: 408 7th St 56401-3019) (218) 829-3834

Burnsville Episcopal Church of the Nativity **P** (516) 15601 Maple Island Rd 55306-5541 (Mail to: 15601 Maple Island Rd 55306-5541) Dana Strande (952) 435-8687

Cannon Falls Church Of The Redeemer **P** (39) 123 3rd St 55009-2012 (Mail to: PO Box 122 55009) (507) 263-3469

Cass Lake St Peters Church **M** (101) 301 Cedar Ave NW 56633 (Mail to: PO Box 222 56633-0222) (218) 536-0834

Chatfield St Matthew Episcopal Church **P** (59) 100 Fillmore St Se 55923-1219 (Mail to: 114 Valley St Se 55923-1429) Alice Applequist (507) 867-3707

Cloquet St Andrews Episcopal Church **P** (18) 204 8th St 55720-1811 (Mail to: 204 8th St 55720-1811) (218) 879-6100

Detroit Lakes St Lukes Episcopal Church **M** (100) 1400 Corbett Rd 56501-4508 (Mail to: C/O Treasurer PO Box 868 56502) (218) 847-5858

Duluth St Andrews by the Lake **M** (156) 2802 Minnesota Ave 55802-2526 (Mail to: 2802 Minnesota Ave 55802-2526) Marta Maddy (218) 727-1262

Duluth St Pauls Episcopal Church **P** (560) 1710 E Superior St 55812-2045 (Mail to: 1710 E Superior St 55812-2045) William Van Oss (218) 724-3535

Edina St Albans Episcopal Church **P** (403) 6716 Gleason Rd 55439-1130 (Mail to: 6716 Gleason Rd 55439-1130) John Peters (952) 941-3065

Elk River Holy Trinity Episcopal Church **P** (86) 1326 4th St 55330-1809 (Mail to: PO Box 65 1326 4th Street NW 55330-0065) (763) 441-5482

Ely St Mary's Church **M** (14) 715 S. Central Avenue 55731-0513 (Mail to: PO Box 513 55731-0513) (218) 365-4914

Eveleth St John's Episcopal Church **P** (38) 210 Mckinley Ave 55734-1600 (Mail to: 210 Mckinley Ave 55734-1600) (218) 341-4195

Excelsior Trinity Episcopal Church **P** (382) 221 Center St 55331-1817 (Mail to: 322 2nd St 55331-1893) Devon Anderson (952) 474-5263

Fairmont St Martins Episcopal Church **P** (52) 102 Park St 56031-2822 (Mail to: 102 Park St 56031-2822) Marilla Whitney (507) 238-2686

✠ **Faribault** Cathedral of Our Merciful Saviour **O** (151) 515 2nd Ave NW PO Box 816 55021-4203 (Mail to: PO Box 816 55021-0816) (507) 334-7732

Farmington Church of the Advent **P** (44) 412 Oak St 55024-1326 (Mail to: 412 Oak St 55024-1326) (651) 460-6636

Fergus Falls St James Episcopal Church **P** (60) 321 S Lakeside Dr 56537-2219 (Mail to: 321 S Lakeside Dr 56537-2219) (218) 736-6736

Frontenac Christ Episcopal Church **M** (41) 29036 Westervelt Ave. Way 55026-0058 (Mail to: PO Box 58 55026-0058) (651) 345-5986

Grand Marais Spirit of the Wilderness **M** (78) 121 Maple Hill Dr 55604 (Mail to: PO Box 1115 55604-1115) Mary Ashcroft Carolyn Schmidt (218) 387-1536

Grand Rapids Christ Episcopal Church **P** (122) 520 Pokegama Ave 55744-2646 (Mail to: 520 Pokegama Ave 55744-2646) (218) 326-6279

Hastings St Lukes Episcopal Church **P** (153) 615 Vermillion St 55033-1939 (Mail to: PO Box 155 55033-0155) Elizabeth Herman Robert Langenfeld Mary Rowan Darcy Valentine Franklin Van De Steeg (651) 437-9855

Hastings St Mary's Afton-Basswood Grove **P** (83) § 8435 Saint Croix Trl S 55033-9495 (Mail to: 8435 Saint Croix Trl S 55033-9495) Scott Monson (651) 338-5364

Hermantown Trinity Episcopal Church **M** (108) 4903 Maple Grove Rd 55811-1446 (Mail to: 4903 Maple Grove Rd 55811-1446) Cheryl Harder David Hill (218) 729-7957

Hibbing St James Episcopal Church **P** (75) 2028 7th Ave E 55746-1706 (Mail to: 2028 7th Ave E 55746-1706) Sally Maxwell (218) 263-5764

Hinckley Trinity Episcopal Church **M** (44) 305 1st St Nw 55037-8712 (Mail to: PO Box 204 55037-0204) (320) 245-2575

Intl Falls Holy Trinity Episcopal Church **P** (79) 820 4th St 56649-2213 (Mail to: PO Box 170 56649-0170) (218) 283-8606

Kasson St Peter's Episcopal Church **P** (105) 101 1st St 55944-1419 (Mail to: PO Box 205 55944-0205) (507) 634-6081

Lake City St Marks Episcopal Church **P** (51) 110 S Oak St 55041-1629 (Mail to: 112 S Oak St 55041-1629) (651) 345-2674

Litchfield Trinity Episcopal Church **P** (33) 3 E 4th St 55355-2121 (Mail to: 3 E 4th St 55355-2121) (320) 693-6035

Luverne Church of the Holy Trinity **P** (6) 220 Cedar St 56156-1601 (Mail to: 220 Cedar St 56156-1601) (507) 449-5893

Mankato St Johns Episcopal Church **P** (222) Warren & Broad St 56002 (Mail to: PO Box 1119 56002-1119) Christine Beebe (507) 388-1969

Marshall St James Episcopal Church **P** (50) 101 5th St 56258-1303 (Mail to: 101 5th St 56258-1303) Marilyn Leach (507) 532-6632

Minneapolis All Saints Episcopal Indian Mission **M** (165) 3044 Longfellow Ave 55407-1811 (Mail to: 3044 Longfellow Ave 55407-1811) James Shoulak (612) 722-2342

✣ **Minneapolis** Cathedral Church of St Mark **O** (877) 519 Oak Grove St 55403-3230 (Mail to: 519 Oak Grove St 55403-3270) Paul Lebens Englund Siri Hustad Anne Mallonee Anna Ostenso Moore (612) 870-7800

Minneapolis Church of the Epiphany **P** (373) 4900 Nathan Ln 55442-3156 (Mail to: 4900 Nathan Ln 55442-3156) Alissa Smith (763) 559-3144

Minneapolis Gethsemane Church **M** (76) 905 Fourth Avenue South 55404-1093 (Mail to: 905 4th Ave S 55404-1093) Cynthia Brickson Sandra Obarski (612) 332-5407

Minneapolis Holy Trinity - St Anskars Church **P** (44) 1808 Riverside Ave 55454-1022 (Mail to: 1219 University Ave SE # 309 55414-2038) (612) 331-1544

Minneapolis St Andrews Episcopal Church **P** (197) 1832 James Ave 55411-3164 (Mail to: PO Box 11745 55411-0745) (612) 529-1320

Minneapolis St James on the Parkway **P** (238) 3225 E Minnehaha Pkwy 55417-1431 (Mail to: 3225 E Minnehaha Pkwy 55417-1446) (612) 724-3425

Minneapolis St John the Baptist Episcopal Church **P** (800) 4201 Sheridan Ave S 55410-1618 (Mail to: 4201 Sheridan Ave S 55410-1618) Lisa Wiens Heinsohn (612) 922-0396

Minneapolis Saint Luke's Church **P** (284) 4557 Colfax Ave S 55419-4736 (Mail to: 4557 Colfax Ave S 55419-4736) Warren Domenick (612) 824-2697

Minneapolis St Nicholas Episcopal Church **P** (186) 7227 Penn Ave S 55423-2820 (Mail to: Treasurer 7227 Penn Ave S 55423-2899) Julie Luna (612) 869-7551

Minneapolis St Pauls Episcopal Church **P** (240) 1917 Logan Ave S 55403-2856 (Mail to: 1917 Logan Ave S Ste 1 55403-2899) Marcus Halley (612) 377-1273

Minneapolis St Stephen the Martyr Church **P** (1204) 4439 W 50th St 55424-1327 (Mail to: 4439 W 50th St 55424-1399) Amelia Arthur Thomas Cook (952) 920-0595

Minneapolis St George's Episcopal Church **P** (244) 5224 Minnetonka Blvd 55416-2104 (Mail to: 5224 Minnetonka Blvd 55416-2104) Thomas Gehlsen Diane Mcgowan (952) 926-1646

Minneapolis University Episcopal Center **Chaplaincy** 1219 University Ave SE 55414-2038 (Mail to: 1101 W Broadway Ave 55414-2570) Jennifer Walding (612) 331-3552

Minnetonka The Episcopal Parish of St David **P** (440) 13000 Saint Davids Rd 55305-4119 (Mail to: 13000 Saint Davids Rd 55305-4119) Leonard Freeman Lindsay Freeman Katherine Lewis (952) 935-3336

Minnetonka Beach Church of St Martins by the Lake **P** (575) 2801 Westwood Rd 55391 (Mail to: PO Box 38 55361-0038) David Langille Jason Cutshall (952) 471-8429

Moose Lake St Andrews Episcopal Church **M** (13) 114 Elm Ave 55767-0840 (Mail to: PO Box P 55767) (218) 485-4945

Morton Bishop Whipple Mission **M** (313) 38378 Reservation Highway 101 56270-1272 (Mail to: PO Box 369 56270-0369) David Sams (507) 697-6433

Naytahwaush Samuel Memorial Church **M** (105) 36 Church Street 56566 (Mail to: PO Box 8 56566-0008) (218) 935-2192

New Ulm St Peters Episcopal Church **P** (5) 125 S Broadway St 56073-3114 (Mail to: 125 S Broadway St 56073-3114) (507) 354-3241

Northfield All Saints Episcopal Church **P** (107) 419 Washington St 55057-2028 (Mail to: PO Box 663 550570663) Gayle Marsh (507) 645-7417

Owatonna St Pauls Episcopal Church **P** (278) 222 S Cedar Ave 55060-2915 (Mail to: 220 S Cedar Ave 55060-2915) Steven Judd Michael Tippett (507) 451-5319

Park Rapids Trinity Church **M** (50) 212 Court Avenue 56470-0262 (Mail to: PO Box 262 56470-0262) (218) 732-4393

Paynesville St Stephens Episcopal Church **P** (10) 320 Wendell St 56362-1248 (Mail to: Attn Doris A Dodds 320 Wendell St 56362-1248) (320) 243-2012

Ponsford Breck Memorial Mission **M** (70) PO Box 141 56575-0141 (Mail to: PO Box 8 56566-0008) (218) 255-1535

Red Lake St John in the Wilderness **M** (24) 15341 St Marys Mission Rd 56671 (Mail to: PO Box 54 56671-0054) (218) 679-4330

Red Wing Christ Episcopal Church **P** (267) 321 West Ave 55066-2250 (Mail to: 321 West Ave 55066-2250) Tristan English Barbara Von Haaren (651) 388-0411

Redby St Antipas Episcopal Church **M** (43) 19050 State Highway 1 56670 (Mail to: PO Box 273 56670-0273) (218) 679-3900

Rice Lake St Philips Church **M** (176) 16101 290th St 56621-9503 (Mail to: C/O Rev Lisa White Smith PO Box 8 56566-0008) (218) 358-0723

Rochester Calvary Episcopal Church **P** (721) 111 3rd Ave Sw 55902-3150 (Mail to: 111 3rd Ave SW 55902-3198) Virginia Royalty (507) 282-9429

Rochester St Lukes Episcopal Church **P** (539) 1884 22nd St Nw 55901-0618 (Mail to: 1884 22nd St NW 55901-0618) Justin Chapman (507) 288-2469

Rushford Emmanuel Episcopal Church **P** (49) 217 W Jessie St 55971-9103 (Mail to: PO Box 443 55971-0443) (507) 864-2164

Saint Cloud St Johns Episcopal Church **P** (112) 1111 Cooper Ave S 56301-4829 (Mail to: 1111 Cooper Ave S 56301-4829) Priscilla Gray (320) 251-8524

Saint Paul Christ Church Episcopal Parish **P** (250) 7305 Afton Rd 55125-1501 (Mail to:

7305 Afton Rd 55125-1501) Anna Doherty (651) 735-8790

Saint Paul Church of the Holy Apostles **M** (931) 2200 Minnehaha Ave 55119-3932 (Mail to: 2200 Minnehaha Ave E 55119-3999) M Letha Wilson-Barnard (651) 735-3016

Saint Paul Church of the Epiphany **P** (45) Attn Kenneth Johnson Treasurer 1636 Van Buren Ave 55104-1818 (Mail to: Attn Kenneth Johnson Treasurer 1636 Van Buren Ave 55104-1818) (612) 645-4466

Saint Paul Holy Trinity Episcopal Church **P** 1636 Van Buren Ave 55104-1818 (Mail to: 501 Dale St Ste 201 Suite 201 55103-1914) James Wilson (651) 228-0930

Saint Paul La Mision El Santo Nino Jesus **M** (180) 463 Maria Ave 55106-4428 (Mail to: 463 Maria Ave 55106-4428) Neptali Rodriguez Espinel (651) 295-7481

Saint Paul Messiah Episcopal Church **P** (477) 1631 Ford Pkwy 55116-2130 (Mail to: 1631 Ford Pkwy 55116-2130) (651) 698-2590

Saint Paul St Annes Episcopal Church **P** (285) 2035 Charlton Rd 55118-4704 (Mail to: 2035 Charlton Rd 55118-4704) Jennifer McNally (651) 455-9449

Saint Paul St Christophers Episcopal Church **P** (444) 2300 Hamline Ave 55113-4200 (Mail to: C/O Ruth Thillen 2300 Hamline Ave 55113-4200) Janet MacNally (651) 633-4589

Saint Paul St Clements Episcopal Church **P** (442) 901 Portland Ave 55104-7032 (Mail to: 901 Portland Ave 55104-7032) Joy Caires (651) 228-1164

Saint Paul St John in the Wilderness Episcopal **P** (550) 2175 1st St 55110-3462 (Mail to: 2175 1st St 55110-3488) Arthur Hancock Randy Johnson (651) 429-5351

Saint Paul St John the Evangelist Epis Church **P** (463) 60 Kent St 55102-2232 (Mail to: 60 Kent St 55102-2232) Craig Lemming Jered Weber-Johnson (651) 228-1172

Saint Paul St Mary Episcopal Church **P** (417) 1895 Laurel Ave 55104-5938 (Mail to: 1895 Laurel Ave 55104-5998) Leeanne Watkins (651) 646-6175

Saint Paul St Matthews Episcopal Church **P** (361) 2136 Carter Ave 55108-1708 (Mail to: 2136 Carter Ave 55108-1708) Blair Pogue Dwight Zscheile (651) 645-3058

Saint Paul Sts Martha & Mary Church **M** (125) 4180 Lexington Ave S 55123-1534 (Mail to: 4180 Lexington Ave S 55123-1534) Bruce Henne Alfred Hopwood (651) 681-0219

Saint Peter Church of the Holy Communion **HC** (98) 118 North Minnesota Ave 56082-2412 (Mail to: PO Box 176 56082-0176) Thomas Harries (507) 934-2542

Sauk Centre Church of the Good Samaritan **P** (16) 529 Main St S 56378-1510 (Mail to: PO Box 205 56378-0205) (320) 352-6882

Stillwater Ascension Episcopal Church **P** (450) 214 3rd St 55082-4806 (Mail to: 215 4th St 55082-4806) Marilyn Baldwin Holt Grace (651) 439-2609

Virginia St Pauls Episcopal Church **P** (46) 231 3rd St S 55792-2619 (Mail to: PO Box 376 55792-0376) Richard Swenson (218) 741-1379

Wabasha Grace Memorial Church **P** (119) 936 Gambia Ave 55981-1011 (Mail to: 205 3rd St E 55981-1401) (651) 565-4827

Wadena St Helens Episcopal Church **M** (69) 22 Dayton Ave Sw 56482-1450 (Mail to: PO Box 311 56482-0311) (218) 583-2206

Walker Saint Johns Episcopal Church **M** (104) 8819 Onigum Rd NW PO Box 1192 56484-2673 (Mail to: PO Box 1192 56484-2673) (218) 547-2570

Warroad St Peters Church **M** (37) PO Box 117 56763-0875 (Mail to: PO Box 875 56763-0875) (218) 386-4334

Waterville St Andrews Episcopal Church **P** (27) 210 Lake St W 56096-1320 (Mail to: 208 Lake St W 56096-1320) (507) 720-5251

Wayzata St Edward the Confessor Episcopal Ch **P** (74) 865 Ferndale Road 55391-1011 (Mail to: 865 Ferndale Rd 55391-1011) Jason Lucas (952) 473-2262

Welch Church of the Messiah **M** (92) 1760 Chakya St 55089-9416 (Mail to: 21449 County 18 Blvd 55089-6402) Martin Balfe (612) 388-7531

White Earth Saint Columba **M** (60) 26094 370th Street 56591-0388 (Mail to: PO Box 388 56591-0388) (218) 935-0259

Windom Church of the Good Shepherd **P** (19) 453 10th St 56101-1407 (Mail to: PO Box 69 56101-0069) (507) 831-1797

Winona St Pauls Episcopal Church **P** (119) 265 Lafayette St 55987-3535 (Mail to: 265 Lafayette St 55987-3535) (507) 452-5355

DIOCESE OF MISSISSIPPI
(PROVINCE IV)
Comprises the State of Mississippi
DIOCESAN OFFICE 118 N Congress St PO Box 23107 Jackson 39225-3107
TEL (601) 948-5954   FAX (601) 354-3401
E-MAIL info@dioms.org   WEB www.dioms.org

Previous Bishops—
Wm M Green 1850-87, Hugh M Thompson coadj 1883 Bp 1887-1902, Theodore D Bratton 1903-38, Wm M Green II coadj 1919 Bp 1938-42, Duncan M Gray 1943-66, Jn M Allin coadj 1961 Bp 1966-74, Duncan M Gray Jr coadj 1974 Bp 1974-93, AC Marble Jr coadj 1991 Bp 1993-2003, Duncan M Gray III coadj 2000 Bp 2003-15

Bishop—Rt Rev Brian R. Seage (1085) (Dio 8 Feb 2015)

Cn to Ord Rev P Stephens; *Sec* Rev B Ponder; *Treas* F Page; *Cn Adm & Fin* Rev B Ponder; *Reg* P Jones; *Chanc* G Tate; *V Chanc* R Ireland and L Lawhorn; *Chm Fin* B Howard; *Ecum* Rev J Switzer; *Yth Adv* W Robinson

Stand Comm—Cler: P Gray W Jones J Deaton G Proctor; *Lay:* M Baria A Perry S Stray J Wheeler

PARISHES, MISSIONS, AND CLERGY

Aberdeen St Johns Episcopal Church **M** (109) 402 W Commerce St 39730-2523 (Mail to: PO Box 54 39730-0054) (662) 369-4854

Bay Saint Louis Christ Church **P** (174) 912 S Beach Blvd 39520-4105 (Mail to: 912 S Beach Blvd 39520-4105) Tucker Dawson (228) 467-7757

Belzoni Mission of St Thomas **M** (19) 210 Castleman St 39038-3924 (Mail to: PO Box 401 39038-0401) (662) 746-5082

Biloxi Church of the Redeemer **P** (361) 1904 Popps Ferry Rd 39532-2125 (Mail to: 1904 Popps Ferry Rd 39532-2125) Jennifer Southall (228) 594-2100

✣ **Bolton** St Mary Episcopal Church **O** (1) 209 E Madison St 39041 (Mail to: 900 First North St. 39183-2616) (601) 209-8044

Brandon St Lukes Church **P** (138) 104 College St 39042-3180 (Mail to: PO Box 1899 39043-1899) (601) 825-5839

Brandon St Peters by the Lake **P** (220) 1954 Spillway Rd 39047-6064 (Mail to: 1954 Spillway Rd 39047-5026) Carol Mead Roy Wilson (601) 992-2691

Brookhaven Church of the Redeemer **P** (196) 230 W Monticello St 39601-3204 (Mail to: PO Box 804 39602-0804) Emily Matthews (601) 833-7399

Canton Grace Episcopal Church **P** (106) 161 E Peace St 39046-4519 (Mail to: 161 E Peace St PO Box 252 39046-4519) Elizabeth Foose (601) 859-2680

Carrollton Mission of Grace **M** (20) Washington St 38917 (Mail to: Washington 38917) (601) 445-8432

Clarksdale St Georges Episcopal Church **P** (216) 106 Sharkey Ave 38614-4402 (Mail to: 106 Sharkey Ave 38614-4402) Jason Shelby (662) 627-7875

Cleveland Calvary Episcopal Church **P** (177) 409 S Court St 38732 (Mail to: 107 S Victoria Ave 38732-3231) Julia Moore (662) 843-5964

Clinton Episcopal Church of the Creator **P** (126) 1445 Clinton Raymond Rd 39056-5443 (Mail to: 1445 Clinton Raymond Rd 39056-5443) William Hanna (601) 924-2261

Collins St Elizabeths Mission **M** (23) 1200 S 4th St 39428 (Mail to: PO Box 652 39428-0652) Susan Hrostowski (601) 765-6809

Columbia St Stephens Episcopal Church **M** (55) 1300 Church St 39429-3128 (Mail to: PO Box 761 39429-0761) (601) 736-5496

Columbus St Pauls Episcopal Church **P** (344) 318 College St 39701-5701 (Mail to: 318 College St 39701-5701) Anne Harris (662) 328-6673

Columbus Epis Church of the Good Shepherd **M** (100) 321 Forrest Blvd 39702-5313 (Mail to: PO Box 2023 39704-2023) Sandra Depriest (662) 327-1953

Como Holy Innocents Episcopal Church **M** (58) 311 Main St 38619-7305 (Mail to: PO Box 391 38619-0391) Donald Chancellor (662) 526-5166

Corinth St Pauls Episcopal Church **P** (74) 250 Hwy 2 Ne 38834 (Mail to: PO Box 1225 38835-1225) Ann Fraser (662) 286-2922

Crystal Springs Mission of Holy Trinity **M** (54) 204 W Railroad Ave S 39059-2772 (Mail to: PO Box 812 39059-0812) (601) 892-5142

Diamondhead St Thomas Episcopal Church **P** (196) 5303 Diamondhead Cir 39525-3203 (Mail to: 5303 Diamondhead Cir 39525-3203) Mary Koppel (228) 255-9213

Enterprise Mission of St Mary **M** (17) 106 Saint John St 39330-8909 (Mail to: St John St PO Box 177 39330-0177) (601) 656-2938

Forest Saint Matthew's Episcopal Church **M** (7) Graham St and Highway 80 E 39074 (Mail to: 108 Azalea Dr 39074-3008) (601) 469-4669

Gautier St Pierre Episcopal Church **M** (123) 4412 Gautier Vancleave Rd 39553-4807 (Mail to: 4412 Gautier Vancleave Rd 39553-4807) John Switzer (228) 497-9819

Greenville Church of the Redeemer **M** (18) 632 W Ohea St 38701-3663 (Mail to: PO Box 494 38702-0494) (601) 332-8658

Greenville St James Episcopal Church **P** (234) 1026 S Washington Ave 38701-6307 (Mail to: 1026 S Washington Ave 38701-6307) Brandt Dick (662) 334-4582

Greenwood Church of the Nativity **P** (318) 400 Howard St 38930-4338 (Mail to: PO Box 1006 389351006) Peter Gray (662) 453-7786

Grenada All Saints Episcopal Church **P** (179) 469 S Main St 38901-3816 (Mail to: PO Box 345 38902-0345) Joshua Messick (662) 226-8234

Gulfport St Marks Episcopal Church **P** (672) 11322 West Taylor St 39503 (Mail to: 11322 E Taylor Rd 39503-4097) Stephen Kidd Clelie Mccandless (228) 896-7597

Gulfport St Peters by the Sea **P** (500) 1909 15th St 39501-2117 (Mail to: 1909 St 39501-2117) Patrick Sanders (228) 863-2611

Hattiesburg Episcopal Church of the Ascension **P** (249) 3600 Arlington Loop 39402-1618 (Mail to: 3600 Arlington Loop 39402-1618) Susan Bear (601) 264-6773

Hattiesburg Trinity Episcopal Church **P** (519) 509 W Pine St 39401-3833 (Mail to: PO Box 1483 39403-1483) Marian Fortner Thomas Allain (601) 544-5551

Holly Springs Christ Episcopal Church **P** (145) 100 Randolph St 38635-2411 (Mail to: PO Box 596 38635-0596) Bruce McMillan (662) 252-2435

Indianola St Stephens Episcopal Church **P** (92) PO Box 1004 38751-1004 (Mail to: PO Box 1004 38751-1004) Giulianna Gray (662) 887-4365

Inverness All Saints Episcopal Church **M** (20) Us Hwy 49 W 38753 (Mail to: PO Box 9 387530009) (662) 265-5775

Jackson All Saints Episcopal Church **P** (103) 147 Daniel Lake Blvd 39212-4942 (Mail to: 147 Daniel Lake Blvd 39212-4942) William Ndishabandi (601) 372-5185

Jackson St Alexis Episcopal Church **M** (110) 650 E South St 39201-5307 (Mail to: PO Box 783 39205-0783) Charles Culpepper (601) 944-0415

✠ **Jackson** St Andrews Episcopal Cathedral **O** (1211) § 305 E Capitol St 39201-3414 (Mail to: Business Admin PO Box 1366 39215-1366) Katie Bradshaw Jennifer Deaton Ronald Pogue (601) 354-1535

Jackson St Christophers Church **M** (52) 643 Beasley Rd 39206-3827 (Mail to: 643 Beasley Rd 39206-2826) (601) 366-6768

Jackson St James Episcopal Church **P** (2655) 3921 Oakridge Dr 39216-3412 (Mail to: 3921 Oakridge Dr 39216-3412) James Mcelroy Abram Jones Ann McLemore Seth Walley Seth Walley (601) 982-4880

Jackson St Marks Episcopal Church **P** (130) 903 Dr. Robert Smith, Sr. Pkwy 39203-3036 (Mail

to: PO Box 3191 39207-3191) Charles Ashford Annie Elliott Gates Elliott Robert Spencer (601) 353-0246

Jackson St Philips Episcopal Church **P** (537) 5400 Old Canton Rd 39211-4254 (Mail to: 5400 Old Canton Rd 39211-4277) Calvin Meaders Kyle Seage (601) 956-5788

Kosciusko St Matthews Church **P** (36) 317 St Matthew Street 39090-3455 (Mail to: PO Box 1455 39090-1455) (662) 289-5326

Laurel St Johns Episcopal Church **P** (209) 541 5th Ave 39440-3410 (Mail to: PO Box 1766 39441-1766) Jeffrey Reich (601) 428-7252

Leland St Johns Episcopal Church **M** (47) 405 California Ave 38756-3305 (Mail to: PO Box 267 38756-0267) (662) 686-4260

Leland St Pauls Episcopal Church **M** (19) C/O The Rev R E Sanders PO Box 267 38756-0267 (Mail to: C/O The Rev R E Sanders PO Box 267 38756-0267) (662) 822-4863

Lexington St Mary Episcopal Church **M** (40) 402 Hillside St 39095 (Mail to: PO Box 63 39095-0063) (662) 834-2973

Long Beach St Patricks Episcopal Church **P** (134) 310 Cleveland Ave 39560-4739 (Mail to: 310 Cleveland Ave 39560-4739) (228) 863-7882

Macon Mission of the Nativity **M** (5) 3376 Jefferson St 39341 (Mail to: PO Box 533 39760-0533) (662) 726-4387

Madison The Chapel of the Cross **P** (635) 674 Mannsdale Rd 39110-7991 (Mail to: 674 Mannsdale Rd 39110-7991) William Compton Benjamin Robertson Robert Spencer (601) 856-2593

Mccomb Parish of the Mediator-Redeemer **P** (135) 215 Broadway 39648-3905 (Mail to: 217 Broadway St 39648-3905) Victor McInnis (601) 684-5682

Meridian St Pauls Episcopal Church **P** (244) 1116 23rd Ave 39301-4017 (Mail to: 1116 23rd Ave 39301-4091) Andrew McGehee Betty Melton (601) 693-2502

Meridian Church of the Mediator **P** (404) 3825 35th Ave 39305-3617 (Mail to: PO Box 3400 39303-3400) Charles Floyd Terrell Griffis Joshua Messick Morris Thompson (601) 483-3959

Michigan City Mission of Calvary **M** (24) 43 Fort St 38647-8554 (Mail to: Route 1 38647) (662) 401-3089

Natchez Trinity Episcopal Church **P** (377) PO Box 1323 39121-1323 (Mail to: 305 S Commerce St 39120-3503) Kenneth Ritter (601) 445-8432

Newton Trinity Episcopal Church **M** (5) PO Box 418 39345-0418 (Mail to: PO Box 418 39345-0418)

Ocean Springs St Johns Episcopal Church **P** (615) 705 Rayburn Ave 39564-3762 (Mail to: 705 Rayburn Ave 39564-3762) Charles Hawkins Robert Lenoir John Switzer (228) 875-4454

✠ **Okolona** Mission of St Bernard **O** (8) 400 W Main St 38860-1305 (Mail to: PO Box 150 38860-0150) (662) 447-2752

Olive Branch Holy Cross Episcopal Church **M** (119) 8230 Highway 178 38654-1116 (Mail to: 8230 Highway 178 38654-1116) (662) 895-5029

Oxford St Peters Episcopal Church **P** (749) 113 S 9th St 38655-3916 (Mail to: 113 S 9th St 38655-3916) Joseph Burnett Bruce McMillan Christopher Robinson Penny Sisson Jennifer Southall (662) 234-1269

Pascagoula St Johns Episcopal Church **P** (480) 3507 Pine St 39567-3117 (Mail to: 3507 Pine St 39567-3100) Thomas Fanning (228) 762-1705

Pass Christian Trinity Episcopal Church **P** (365) 125 Church Ave 39571-4302 (Mail to: 125 Church Ave 39571-4302) Kyle Bennett (228) 452-4563

Philadelphia Mission of St Francis of Assisi **M** (35) 10701 Saint Francis Dr 39350-2170 (Mail to: Attn Rae Gordon, Sr Warden 10701 Saint Francis Dr 39350-2170) Charles Deaton (601) 656-2938

Picayune St Pauls Episcopal Church **P** (38) 1421 Goodyear Blvd 39466-3152 (Mail to: 1421 Goodyear Blvd 39466-3152) Arthur Johnson (601) 798-2802

Port Gibson St James Episcopal Church **M** (72) 305 Jackson St 39150-2327 (Mail to: Mrs Rochelle Abraham 1073 Rattlesnake Rdg 39150-2543) (601) 437-4244

Raymond St Marks Church **M** (15) 201 Main St 39154-9712 (Mail to: PO Box 113 39154-0113) Janet Ott (601) 826-2128

Ridgeland St Columbs Episcopal Church **P** (645) 550 Sunnybrook Rd 39157-1810 (Mail to: 550 Sunnybrook Rd 39157-1810) (601) 853-0205

Rolling Fork Chapel of the Cross **P** (77) 35 McLaurin Ave 39159 (Mail to: C/OWillaim Moore PO Box 336 39054) Frederick Proctor Robert Weatherly (662) 873-2226

Rosedale Mission of Grace **M** (13) Main St 38769 (Mail to: Main St 38769) Sylvia Czarnetzky

Southaven St Timothy Episcopal Church **P** (649) 8245 Getwell Rd 38672-6420 (Mail to: PO Box 325 38671-0004) Sandra Kimmelman Elizabeth Wheatley-Jones (662) 393-3100

Starkville Church of the Resurrection **P** (332) 105 Montgomery St 39759-2903 (Mail to: 105 Montgomery St 39759-2903) Walton Jones Lynn Phillips-Gaines Laurence Wainwright-Maks (662) 323-3483

Sumner Episcopal Church of the Advent **P** (89) 224 Monroe St 38957 (Mail to: PO Box 366 38957-0366) Phillip Parker (662) 375-8848

Terry Mission of the Good Shepherd **M** (76) 109 E Claiborne St 39170-7805 (Mail to: PO Box 325 39170-0325) (601) 878-5612

Tunica Church of the Epiphany **P** (70) 1061 Shady Ln 38676-9499 (Mail to: PO Box 224 38676-0224) Holly Burris (662) 363-2393

Tupelo All Saints' Episcopal Church **P** (376) 608 W Jefferson St 38804-3736 (Mail to: 608 W Jefferson St 38804-3736) (662) 842-4386

Vicksburg Christ Episcopal Church **P** (199) 1115 Main St 39183-2527 (Mail to: 1115 Main St 39183-2527) Samuel Godfrey (601) 638-5899

Vicksburg Church of the Holy Trinity **HC** (257) 900 South St 39180-3256 (Mail to: 900 South St 39180-3256) Elizabeth Hunter (601) 636-0542

Vicksburg St Albans Episcopal Church **P** (161) 5930 Warriors Trl 39180-0878 (Mail to: 5930 Warriors Trl 39180-0878) Billie Abraham Josie Williams (601) 636-6687

Vicksburg St Marys Episcopal Church **M** (42) 900 First North St 39183-2616 (Mail to: 900 First North St 39183-2699) Denny Allman (601) 636-4811

West Point Church of the Incarnation **P** (120) 103 W Broad St 39773-2801 (Mail to: PO Box 316 39773-0316) Patricia Cantrell (662) 494-1378

Woodville St Pauls Episcopal Church **P** (118) 259 S Church St 39669 (Mail to: PO Box 207 39669-0207) Mary Anne Heine (601) 888-6704

Yazoo City Trinity Church **P** (53) 323 Main St 39194-4262 (Mail to: PO Box 145 39194-0145) George Woodliff (662) 746-5082

DIOCESE OF MISSOURI

(PROVINCE V)

Comprises eastern Missouri

DIOCESAN OFFICE 1210 Locust St Louis MO 63103

TEL (314) 231-1220   FAX (314) 231-3373

E-MAIL info@diocesemo.org   WEB www.diocesemo.org

Diocese of Missouri
THE EPISCOPAL CHURCH

Previous Bishops— Jackson Kemper 1835-44, Cicero S Hawks 1844-68, Chas F Robertson 1868-86, Daniel S Tuttle 1886-1932, Fredk F Johnson coadj 1912 Bp 1923-32, Wm Scarlett coadj 1930 Bp 1932-52, Arthur Lichtenberger coadj 1951 Bp 1952-59, George L Cadigan 1959-75, WA Jones Jr 1975-93 Hays H Rockwell 1993-2002

Bishop—Rt Rev George Wayne Smith (975) (Dio 6 June 2002)

Cn to Ord JMC Chambers; *Exec Dir Fin/Admin* D Brattin; *Chanc* HR Burroughs 211 N Broadway St

Louis MO 63102; *Treas* T Hedrick; *Sec of Conv* The Rev M Smith; *Comm* B Felice

Stand Comm—Pres DV Mitchell; *Cler:* D Goldfeder K McGrane R Ragland L Scoopmire *Bp* GW Smith J Stratton *Staff* JMC Chambers; *Lay:* B Bowersox M Fowlkes S Goodlow B Forsyth L Fox L Go *Chanc* H Burroughs, *Staff* D Brattin

Diocesan Council—Chair GW Smith; *Vice-Chair* M Rowe; *Cler:* P Glenn, *Staff* JMC Chambers; *Lay:* T Allen W Cramer T Dillon B Kehl-Fairchild S Kekec J Thompson L Yount *Chanc* H Burroughs *Treas* T Hedrick, *Staff* D Brattin

Diocesan Committees and Commissions—Commission on Ministry: Chair The Rev M Angell; *Companion Diocese Committee: Chair* Dcn D Goldfeder *E-mail:* deborah.goldfeder@gmail.com; *Daughters of the King: Pres* M Steiling; *Dismantling Racism Commission: Chair* Dcn C Hines Jr; *Bishop's Deputy for Gun Violence Prevention* The Rev M Smith *E-mail:* cotterboatworks@aol.com; *Jubilee Officer* Dcn B Click *E-mail:* bgclick@gmail.com; *Task Force for the Hungry: Chair* J Mayfield; *UTO: Dio Coord* J King (314) 231-1220 *E-mail:* ECW@diocesemo.org

PARISHES, MISSIONS, AND CLERGY

Cape Girardeau Christ Episcopal Church **P** (163) 101 Fountain St 63701-7338 (Mail to: 38 Fountain St 637017338) Edith Bird (573) 335-2997

Columbia Calvary Episcopal Church **P** (809) 123 S 9th St 65201-4815 (Mail to: 123 S 9th St 65201-4815) Harold Jacobson Janet Schisser (573) 449-3194

De Soto Trinity Episcopal Church **M** (35) PO Box 9 63020-0009 (Mail to: PO Box 9 63020-0009) (636) 586-2542

Ellisville St Martins Episcopal Church **P** (467) 15764 Clayton Rd 63011-2330 (Mail to: 15764 Clayton Rd 63011-2330) Leslie Scoopmire (636) 227-1484

Eolia Saint John's Church Prairieville **P** (9) Hwy H 63344 (Mail to: 515 Main Cross St 63334-1416) (573) 754-6423

Eureka St Francis' Episcopal Church **M** (105) § 602 Rockwood Arbor Dr 63025-1023 (Mail to: 602 Rockwood Arbor Dr 63025-1023) (636) 938-3733

Farmington All Saints Episcopal Church **M** (36) 1151 W. Columbia 63640 (Mail to: PO Box 651 63640-0651) Catherine Hillquist (573) 756-3225

Florissant St Barnabas Episcopal Church **P** (133) 2900 Saint Catherine St 63033-3628 (Mail to: 2900 Saint Catherine St 63033-3628) Renee Fenner (314) 837-7113

Fulton St Albans Episcopal Church **M** (54) 6 W 9th & Nichols St 65251 (Mail to: PO Box 6065 65251-6065) Marshall Crossnoe (573) 291-9886

Hannibal Trinity Church **P** (129) 213 4th St 63401-3508 (Mail to: 213 North 4th Street Attn: Treasurer 63401) Dawn-Victoria Mitchell Michael Kyle (573) 221-0298

Ironton St Pauls Episcopal Church **M** (36) 106 Knob St 63650-1219 (Mail to: PO Box 62 63650-0062) (573) 546-2397

Jefferson City Grace Episcopal Church **P** (411) 217 Adams St 65101-3203 (Mail to: 217 Adams St 65101-3298) Paula Hartsfield Ian Lasch (573) 635-4405

Kirksville Trinity Episcopal Church **M** (81) PO Box 652 63501-0652 (Mail to: PO Box 652 63501-0652) Carrol Davenport Amy Fallon (660) 665-6155

Kirkwood Saint Thomas Church For The Deaf **M** (12) C/O Grace Episcopal Church 514 E Argonne Dr 63122-4526 (Mail to: c/o Grace Episcopal Church 514 E Argonne Dr 63122-4526) Emily Davis (314) 560-6731

Lake Saint Louis Church of the Transfiguration **P** (357) 1860 Lake Saint Louis Blvd 63367-1318 (Mail to: 1860 Lake Saint Louis Blvd 63367-1318) Lu-Anne Conner (636) 561-8951

Louisiana Calvary Church **P** (29) 706 Georgia St 63353-1612 (Mail to: PO Box 528 63353-0528) Patricia Glenn (573) 754-6423

Manchester St Lukes Episcopal Church **P** (246) 1101 Sulphur Spring Rd 63021-7419 (Mail to: 444 Brightfield Trl 63021-7460) Charles Mahan (636) 227-1227

Mexico St Matthews Episcopal Church **P** (41) 1100 S Grove St 65265-2292 (Mail to: 1100 Grove St 65265-2292) Christina Cobb (573) 581-1498

Poplar Bluff Church of the Holy Cross **P** (103) 420 Main St 63901-5108 (Mail to: 420 Main St 63901-5108) Annette Joseph (573) 785-1098

Portland St Marks Episcopal Church **M** (63) 8645 Co. Road 466 65067 (Mail to: PO Box 148 65067-0148) (573) 291-9886

Rolla Christ Episcopal Church **P** (217) 1000 Main St 65401-2865 (Mail to: PO Box 845 65402-0845) Aune Strom (573) 364-1499

Saint Charles Trinity Episcopal Church **P** (366) 318 S Duchesne Dr 63301-1655 (Mail to: 318 S Duchesne Dr 63301-1655) Tamsen Whistler (314) 949-0160

Saint James Trinity Episcopal Church **M** (65) 120 E Scioto St 65559-1718 (Mail to: PO Box 126 65559-0126) (573) 265-7667

✠ **Saint Louis** Christ Church Cathedral **O** (632) 1210 Locust St 63103-2322 (Mail to: 1210 Locust St 63103-2322) Kathleen Adams-Shepherd Robert Franken (314) 231-3454

Saint Louis Church of the Advent **P** (172) 9373 Garber Rd 63126-2849 (Mail to: 9373 Garber Rd 63126-2849) Daniel Handschy (314) 843-0123

Saint Louis Church of the Good Shepherd **P** (130) 1166 S Mason Rd 63131-1039 (Mail to: 1166 S Mason Rd 63131-1039) Maria Evans (314) 576-5502

Saint Louis Church Of The Holy Communion **P** (315) 7401 Delmar Blvd 63130-4035 (Mail to: 7401 Delmar Blvd 63130-4093) Michael Angell Marc Smith (314) 721-7401

Saint Louis Emmanuel Episcopal Church **P** (834) 9 S Bompart Ave 63119-3225 (Mail to: 9 S Bompart Ave 63119-3282) Jennifer Hulen Martha Metzler (314) 961-2393

Saint Louis Epis Ch of All Saints & Ascension **P** (190) 4520 Lucas and Hunt Rd 63121-2737 (Mail to: 4520 Lucas and Hunt Rd 63121-2737) (314) 304-7425

Saint Louis Grace Church **HC** (692) 514 E Argonne Dr 63122-4526 (Mail to: C/O Shari Bonham 514 E Argonne Dr 63122-4526) Todd McDowell (314) 821-1806

Saint Louis St Johns Church **P** (250) 3664 Arsenal St 63116-4801 (Mail to: 3664 Arsenal St 63116-4801) Amy Cortright (314) 772-3970

Saint Louis St Marks Episcopal Church **P** (251) 4714 Clifton Ave 63109-2701 (Mail to: 4714 Clifton Ave 63109-2701) Mark Kozielec Jerre Birdsong (314) 832-3588

Saint Louis St Michael And St George **P** (1471) PO Box 11887 63105-0687 (Mail to: PO Box 11887 63105-0687) Andrew Archie Peter Speropulos (314) 721-1502

Saint Louis St Pauls Episcopal Church **P** (77) 6518 Michigan Ave 63111-2803 (Mail to: 6518 Michigan Avenue 63111-2803) Rebecca Ragland (314) 352-0370

Saint Louis St Peters Episcopal Church **P** (1540) 110 Warson Rd 63124-1327 (Mail to: 110 Warson Rd 63124-1327) Louis Jernagan Kelly Carlson Joseph Wallace-Williams (314) 993-2306

Saint Louis St Stephens Episcopal Church **P** (294) 33 Clay Ave 63135-2418 (Mail to: 33 Clay Ave 63135-2484) Steven Lawler (314) 521-0138

Saint Louis Saint Timothy's Episcopal Church **P** (540) 808 Mason Rd 63141-6306 (Mail to: 808 Mason Rd 63141-6306) Marvin Foltz Suzanne Eastes (341) 434-5909

Saint Louis Trinity Church **HC** (244) 600 Euclid Ave 63108-1606 (Mail to: 600 Euclid Ave 63108-1606) Jonathan Stratton Barbara Click Harry Leip Beverly Van Horne (314) 361-4655

Sikeston St Pauls Episcopal Church **P** (56) 1010 Main St 63801-5044 (Mail to: PO Box 428 63801) Bruce Cheney (573) 471-2680

Ste Genevieve St Vincents-in-the-Vineyard **M** (15) 24345 State Route WW 63670-9022 (Mail to: 23 The Villages at Chaumette 24345 State Rte WW 63670-9022) (314) 397-3050

Sullivan St John and St James Church **M** (15) 463 Church St 63080-1505 (Mail to: 463 Church St 63080-1505) Carol Wesley (573) 468-3753

DIOCESE OF MONTANA
(PROVINCE VI)
Comprises the State of Montana
DIOCESAN OFFICE 515 N Park Ave Helena MT 59601 (MAIL: PO Box 2020 Helena MT 59624)
TEL (800) 247-1391　　FAX (406) 442-2238
E-MAIL admin@diomontana.com　　WEB https://diomontana.com/

Previous Bishops—
Daniel S Tuttle 1866-1880, Leigh R Brewer m 1880 dio 1904-16, Wm F Faber coadj 1914 Bp 1916-34, Herbert HH Fox suffr 1920 coadj 1925 Bp 1934-39, Henry H Daniels coadj 1939 Bp 1939-57, Chandler W Sterling coadj 1956 Bp 1957-68, Jackson E Gilliam 1968-85, Charles I Jones, 1986-2001, Charles L Keyser Bp asst 2001-2003

Bishop—Rt Rev C Franklin Brookhart (987) (Dio 27 Sept 2003 to 31 Oct 2018)

Cn to Ord & Deploy Off Rev Canon JC Roberts; *Dio Adm* B Hagen; *Sec* G Archey; *Treas* S Yurosko; *Chanc* B Foster

Stand Comm—Cler: Pres D Gleaves T Grotzinger J Collins *Lay:* R Harden C. Benkelman M Messina

PARISHES, MISSIONS, AND CLERGY

Absarokee St Pauls of the Stillwater Epis **M** (44) 111 S Woodard Ave 59001-6316 (Mail to: PO Box 350 59001-0350) (406) 328-4163

Anaconda St Marks Episcopal Church **P** (44) 600 Main St 59711-2937 (Mail to: PO Box 916 59711-0916) Theresa Kelley (405) 563-3625

Big Sky All Saints in Big Sky **P** (19) Meadow Village Big 59716 (Mail to: PO Box 161026 59716-1026) (406) 995-7988

Big Timber St Marks Episcopal Church **P** (78) 203 W 4th Ave 59011 (Mail to: PO Box 626 59011-0626) (406) 932-5712

Bigfork St Patricks Episcopal Church **P** (99) 105 S Crane Mountain Rd 59911 (Mail to: PO Box 431 59911-0431) (406) 849-5465

Billings Saint Luke's Church **P** (254) 119 33rd St 59101-2018 (Mail to: 119 33rd St 59101-2018) Melinda St Clair (406) 252-7186

Billings St Stephens Church **P** (335) 1241 Crawford Dr 59102-2442 (Mail to: 1241 Crawford Dr 59102-2442) Gerald Jasmer Joan Yetter (406) 259-5017

Bozeman St James Episcopal Church **P** (598) 5 West Olive St 59715-4624 (Mail to: 5 W Olive St 59715-4624) Clark Sherman Constance Campbell-Pearson David Smith (406) 586-9093

Butte St John's Episcopal Church **P** (50) 15 Idaho St 59701-9229 (Mail to: PO Box 613 59703-0613) (406) 723-4017

Columbia Falls All Saints Episcopal Church **P** (196) 2048 Conn Road 59912 (Mail to: PO Box 1923 59937-1923) Bradley Wirth (406) 862-2863

Deer Lodge St James-Pintler Cluster **P** (37) 307 Cottonwood Ave 59722-1040 (Mail to: 657 Prairie Ln 59722-2365) (406) 563-3625

Dillon St James Episcopal Church **P** (65) 203 E Glendale St 59725-2707 (Mail to: PO Box 1374 59725-1374) (406) 683-2735

Emigrant St Johns Episcopal Church **P** (71) 8 Story Rd 59027 (Mail to: PO Box 176 59027-0176) (406) 222-0222

Ennis Trinity Episcopal Church **P** (86) 93 Jeffers Rd 59729-9026 (Mail to: PO Box 336 59729-0336) (406) 600-1128

Eureka St Michael & All Angels Church **P** (54) PO Box 342 59917-0342 (Mail to: PO Box 342 59917-0342) Pattiann Bennett (406) 297-7233

Forsyth Church of the Ascension **M** (19) 380 15th Ave 59327 (Mail to: PO Box 876 59327-0876) (406) 234-5188

Fort Benton St Paul Episcopal Church **P** (9) 1112 14th 59442 (Mail to: PO Box 217 59442-0217) (406) 265-2638

Great Falls Church of the Incarnation **P** (172) 600 3rd Ave 59401-2426 (Mail to: PO Box 3046 59403-3046) Timothy Ljunggren (406) 453-4167

Hamilton St Pauls Episcopal Church **P** (135) 600 S 3rd St 59840-2730 (Mail to: C/O Carol Shipman PO Box 758 59840-0758) Richard Reynolds (406) 360-2661

Havre St Mark's Episcopal Church **M** (25) 539 3rd Ave 59501-3915 (Mail to: PO Box 950 59501-0950) (406) 265-2161

✠ **Helena** St Peters Cathedral **O** (452) 511 Park Ave 59601-2703 (Mail to: PO Box 819 59624-

0819) Scott Anderson Raymond Brown Donna Gleaves Richard Johnson John Moran (406) 442-5175

Kalispell Christ Church Episcopal **P** (199) 215 3rd Ave E 59901 (Mail to: 215 3rd Ave E 59901-4531) (406) 257-6182

Lewistown St James Episcopal Church **P** (64) 502 W Montana St 59457-2631 (Mail to: PO Box 744 59457-0744) Jean Collins (406) 538-5151

Livingston St Andrews Episcopal Church **P** (183) 310 W Lewis St 59047-3015 (Mail to: PO Box 835 59047-0835) (406) 222-0222

Manhattan Gethsemane Episcopal Church **P** (10) 305 5th Ave 59741 (Mail to: PO Box 85 59741-0085) (406) 282-0049

Miles City Emmanuel Episcopal Church **M** (18) 208 North 11th 59301 (Mail to: PO Box 1526 59301-1526) (406) 234-5188

Missoula Church of the Holy Spirit **P** (842) 130 S 6th St E 59801-4222 (Mail to: 130 S 6th St E 59801-4222) Douglas Anderson Judith Anderson Myrna Chaney Dorcie Dvarishkis Terri Grotzinger Alice Rognas Gretchen Strohmaier Gretchen Strohmaier (406) 542-2167

Philipsburg St Andrews Episcopal Church **P** (19) 101 E Kearney St 59858 (Mail to: PO Box 601 59858-0601) (406) 563-3625

Polson St Andrews Episcopal Church **P** (86) 110 6th Ave E 59860-2728 (Mail to: 110 6th Ave E 59860-2728) Steven Yurosko (406) 883-5524

Red Lodge Calvary Episcopal Church **M** (80) PO Box 348 59068-0348 (Mail to: PO Box 348 59068-0368) Randall Pendergraft (406) 425-0388

Sheridan Christ Episcopal Church **P** (42) 304 S Main St 59749 (Mail to: Attn Jennifer Boucher PO Box 152 59749-0152) (406) 842-7539

Stevensville St Stephens Episcopal Church **M** (19) 203 Main St 59870-2112 (Mail to: Attn: Donald Artley PO Box 35 59870-0035) Richard Reynolds (406) 777-0028

Troy Holy Trinity Episcopal Church **P** (11) 218 E Missoula Ave 59935 (Mail to: C/o Mariel E Cole PO Box 637 59935-0637) Angelique Bolling (406) 297-7233

Virginia City St Paul Episcopal Church **P** (16) 102 E Idaho St 59755 (Mail to: PO Box 206 59755-0206) (406) 600-1128

NAVAJOLAND AREA MISSION
(PROVINCE VIII)
Comprises portions of Navajo Reservation in Arizona, New Mexico, and Utah
OFFICE: 1257 Mission Ave Farmington NM 87499-0720 (MAIL: Box 720 Farmington NM 87499-0720)
TEL (505) 327-7549 FAX (505) 327-6904
E-MAIL ceaton@ec-n.org WEB www.ecofnavajoland.org

Previous Bishops— Frederick W Putnam 1979-83, Wesley Frensdorff int 1983-88, Wm F Wolfrum int 1988-90, Wm C Wantland int 1990-2005 Steven T Plummer 1990-2005, Rustin R Kimsey 2005-06, Mark L MacDonald 2006-2009.

Bishop—Rt Rev David E Bailey (1049) (Dio 7 Aug 2010)

Admin MM Putnam Box 720 Farmington NM 87499; *Sec* C Eaton Box 720 Farmington NM 87499

Dio Coun—Cler: C Anaya C Eaton K Rhode C Plummer CA Plummer; *Lay:* A Fowler S McKinley G Gordy G Buck C Pioche M Brown M Benally; *Deacons:* P Henson L Sampson

Standing Committee—Cler: Pres R Chan Anaya C Eaton M Sells; *Lay:* S McKinley M Brown G Gordy

PARISHES, MISSIONS, AND CLERGY

Bluff St Christophers Church **M** (61) 3315 East Old Mission Rd 1.7 Mile Utah Route 162 84512 (Mail to: PO Box 28 84512-0028) Patricia Cook Katherine Rohde Merrill Stevens (435) 672-9940

Bluff Utah Region **P** St. Christopher Mission PO Box 720 97499 (Mail to: PO Box 720 87499-0720) Merrill Stevens Patricia Cook (435) 672-2296

Farmington All Saints Church **M** (106) 1271 Mission Ave 87401 (Mail to: PO Box 720 87499-0720) Michael Sells Rosella Jim (505) 327-7549

Farmington St Luke in the Desert **M** (46) PO Box 720 87499-0720 (Mail to: PO Box 720 87499-0720) (505) 327-7549

Farmington San Juan/New Mexico Region **M** 1257 Mission Ave 87499 (Mail to: PO Box 720 87499-0720) (505) 327-7549

Fort Defiance Church of the Good Shepherd **M** (187) 618 Kit Carson Drive 86504 (Mail to: Epis Church In Navajoland PO Box 720 87499) (928) 729-2322

Fort Defiance Saint Mark's, Coalmine **M** (77) Coalmine 86504 (Mail to: PO Box 720 87499-0720) (928) 729-2322

Fort Defiance Southeast Region **HC** Kit Carson Dr 86504 (Mail to: PO Box 618 86504-0618) (928) 729-2322

Many Farms St Joseph Church **M** (9) Indian Route 59 86538 (Mail to: PO Box 618 86504-0618) (928) 729-2322

Montezuma Creek Saint John The Baptizer **M** (60) Mile 12.9 Route 162 3599 W Hwy 162 84534 (Mail to: PO Box 720 87499-0720) Patricia Cook Merrill Stevens (435) 444-0484

Oljato St Mary of the Moonlight **M** (39) Rte 6420 - Oljato Wash Road 84536 (Mail to: PO Box 28 84512-0028) Merrill Stevens Patricia Cook (435) 727-0200

Upper Fruitland St Michaels Episcopal Church **M** (75) Highway N36 87416 (Mail to: PO Box 720 87499-0720) (505) 327-7549

DIOCESE OF NEBRASKA
(PROVINCE VI)
Comprises the State of Nebraska
DIOCESAN OFFICE 109 N 18th St Omaha NE 68102
TEL (402) 341-5373 FAX (402) 341-8683
WEB www.episcopal-ne.org

Previous Bishops— Robt H Clarkson 1865-84, George Worthington 1885-1908, Arthur L Williams coadj 1899 Bp 1908-19, Ernest V Shayler 1919-38, Howard R Brinker 1940-62, Russell T Rauscher coadj 1961 Bp 1962-72, Robert P Varley coadj 1971

Bp 1972-75, Jas D Warner 1976-89, James E Krotz, 1990-03, Joe Goodwin-Burnett 2003-2011

Bishop—Rt Rev J Scott Barker (Dio 8 Oct 2011)

Archdcn B Bennett; *Cn to Ord* Rev Cn E Easton; *Chanc* D Bradford III; *Sec Reg* Rev Cn E Easton; *Treas* J Pirruccello; *Dio Admin* L Rowe; *Dir of Fin* B Byrne

Stand Comm—Cler: Pres Rev J Emerson Rev B Bennett,Rev E Medina Rev C Lewis; *Lay:* B Reno ML Martin C Schrader J Wisniewski

Comm on Min—Cler: Rev R Goeke Rev K Watson Rev E Thober Rev N Huston Rev J Long; *Lay:* Chair M Schaefer D Hendricks C Simmons B Agar R Behrens K Ruthledge

PARISHES, MISSIONS, AND CLERGY

Alliance St Matthews Episcopal Church **P** (102) 312 W 16th St 69301-2205 (Mail to: PO Box 430 69301-0430) Robert Mcclure John Adam Cheryl Harris (308) 762-1965

Arapahoe St Pauls Episcopal Church **P** (42) 909 4th St 68922-2776 (Mail to: PO Box 583 68922-0583) (308) 962-7271

Bassett St Marys Episcopal Church **M** (48) 212 Clark St 68714-5503 (Mail to: PO Box 361 68714-0361) Randall Goeke (402) 684-3943

Beatrice Christ Episcopal Church **P** (148) 524 5th St 68310-2903 (Mail to: 524 5th St 68310-2903) (402) 223-5515

Bellevue Church of the Holy Spirit **P** (258) 1305 Thomas Dr 68005-2973 (Mail to: 1305 Thomas Dr 68005-2973) Thomas Jones (402) 291-7732

Blair St Marys Episcopal Church **P** (131) 1743 Grant St 68008-1916 (Mail to: 1734 Grant St 68008-1917) Ruth Jaynes (402) 426-2057

Broken Bow St Johns Episcopal Church **P** (54) 602 10th Ave 68822-1222 (Mail to: 610 10th Ave 68822-1222) Mary Gockley (308) 872-5900

Central City Christ Church **P** (15) 1414 15th St 68826-1416 (Mail to: 1414 15th St 68826-1416) (308) 946-2640

Chadron Grace Episcopal Church **P** (52) 450 Bordeaux St 69337-2607 (Mail to: 450 Bordeaux St 69337-2607) John Adams (308) 432-2229

Columbus Grace Episcopal Church **P** (69) 2053 23rd Ave 68601-3329 (Mail to: PO Box 306 68602-0306) Jan With (402) 564-0116

Cozad St Christophers Church **P** (20) 1520 Avenue B 69130-1645 (Mail to: 1520 Avenue B 69130-1645) (308) 784-2056

Creighton St Marks Church **P** (10) 901 Garfield St 68729-2949 (Mail to: PO Box 653 68729-0653) (402) 358-3295

Crete Trinity Memorial Chruch **P** (18) 14th & Juniper Sts 68333 (Mail to: 660 Franklin Dr 68333-2513) (402) 826-3390

De Witt St Augustines Episcopal Church **P** (24) 108 Quince 68341-5001 (Mail to: PO Box 201 68341-0201) (402) 683-4110

Elkhorn St Augustine of Canterbury **P** (228) 285 S 208th St 68022-1811 (Mail to: 285 S 208th St 68022-1811) Benedict Varnum Patricia Sheldon (402) 289-4058

Falls City St Thomas Episcopal Church **P** (19) 1602 Harlan St 68355-2655 (Mail to: PO Box 117 68355-0117) (402) 245-2868

Fremont St James Episcopal Church **P** (130) 301 E 5th St 68025-5025 (Mail to: PO Box 2421 68026-2421) Sarah Miller (402) 721-3327

Gordon St Marks Episcopal Church **P** (52) Attn Amy Moore 116 E Lariet St 69343-1135 (Mail to: Attn Amy Moore 924 Elm St 69343) (308) 282-1303

Grand Island St Stephens Episcopal Church **P** (311) 422 W 2nd Street 68801 (Mail to: P. O. Box 2317 68802-2317) Robert Lewis (308) 382-4961

Harrisburg Good Shepherd of Plains **P** (17) Maryland Avenue 69345-0025 (Mail to: PO Box 25 69345-0025) (308) 436-4465

Harvard Saint John's Mission **P** (13) 410 North Harvard 68944 (Mail to: 422 Burlington Ave 68901-5059) (402) 462-4126

✠ **Hastings** St Marks Pro Cathedral **O** (175) 422 Burlington Ave 68901-5059 (Mail to: 422 Burlington Ave 68901-5059) Kathleen Hargis (402) 462-4126

Holdrege St Elizabeths Church **P** (78) 512 Tilden St 68949-2245 (Mail to: PO Box 864 68949-0864) (308) 995-4528

Hyannis Calvary Church Hyannis **M** (32) 302 E Highway 2 69350 (Mail to: Attn Kleo Dredla PO Box 80 69350-0080) Robert Mcclure (308) 458-2336

Kearney St Lukes Church **P** (202) 2304 Second Ave 68847-5317 (Mail to: PO Box 2285 68848-2285) Stephanie Swinnea (308) 236-5821

Kimball St Hilda Church **P** (23) 601 S. Chesnut 69145-1423 (Mail to: 509 Adams St 69145-1709) (308) 235-4588

Lexington St Peters in the Valley Church **P** (9) 903 E 13th St 68850-1741 (Mail to: 905 E 13th St 68850-1741) Kay Knudson (308) 324-6199

Lincoln Church of the Holy Trinity **P** (285) 6001 A St 68510-5006 (Mail to: 6001 A St 68510-5098) Susanna DesMarais Daniel Coffman John Long (402) 488-7139

Lincoln St David of Wales Epis Church **P** (127) 8800 Holdrege St 68505-9417 (Mail to: 8800 Holdrege St 68505-9417) (402) 489-2772

Lincoln St Marks on the Campus Church **P** (269) 1309 R St 68508-1219 (Mail to: 1309 R St 68508-1219) Jerrold Thompson Sidnie Crawford (402) 474-1979

Lincoln St Matthews Church **P** (418) 2325 S 24th St 68502-4005 (Mail to: 2325 S 24th St 68502-4099) Amanda Gott Stephen Lahey (402) 435-2226

Mc Cook St Albans Episcopal Church **P** (129) 509 W 1st St 69001-3102 (Mail to: 509 W 1st St 69001-3102) (308) 345-4844

Mitchell Holy Apostles Church **P** (129) 1730 18th St 69357-1138 (Mail to: 1730 18th St 69357-1138) (308) 623-1969

Mullen St Josephs Church **P** (36) 402 Northwest 1st St 69152 (Mail to: Attn Evelyn Elliott PO Box 453 69152-0453) (308) 546-2262

Nebraska City Grace Episcopal Church **P** (4) 1416 1st Corso 68410-2238 (Mail to: 1416 1st Corso 68410-2238) Richard Swenson (402) 335-2331

Nebraska City St Mary Episcopal Churc 116 S 9th St 68410-2403 (Mail to: At Victor 1729 S 70th Rd 68410) (402) 87

Norfolk Trinity Episcopal Church **P** (24 9th St 68701-5166 (Mail to: 111 S 9th S 5166) Sylvia Landers (402) 371-3080

North Platte Church of Our Savior **P** (W 4th St 69101-3916 (Mail to: 203 69101-3916) (308) 532-0515

Ogallala St Pauls Episcopal Church **P** (2 A St 69153-2609 (Mail to: 318 E A S 2609) (308) 203-1141

Omaha All Saints Episcopal Church 9302 Blondo St 68134-6036 (Mail Blondo St 68134-6099) Marisa Th Lynne Bacon Stephanie Ulrich (402) 3

Omaha Church of the Resurrection **P** (2 Belvedere Blvd 68111-1232 (Mail Belvedere Blvd 68111-1232) Mary Juanita Johnson (402) 455-7015

Omaha St Andrews Episcopal Church **P** (S 84th St 68114-5207 (Mail to: 925 S 68114-5207) Otto Schaefer (402) 391-

Omaha St Martin of Tours Church **P** (1 St 68107-1815 (Mail to: 2324 J St 68 Ralph Agar (402) 733-8815

✠ **Omaha** Trinity Cathedral **O** (477) 113 18th St 68102-4903 (Mail to: 113 18th St 68102-4969) Craig Lova Steven King (402) 342-7010

DIOCESE OF NEVADA
(PROVINCE VIII)
Comprises the State of Nevada and 1 church in Arizona
DIOCESAN OFFICE 9480 S Eastern Ave Ste 236 Las Vegas NV 89123-8037
TEL (702) 737-9190 FAX (702) 737-6488
E-MAIL steven@episcopalnevada.org WEB www.episcopalnevada.org

Previous Bishops—
Ozi W Whitaker (NV and AZ) 1869-86, Henry D Robinson 1908-13, Geo C Hunting 1914-24, Thomas Jenkins 1929-42, Wm F Lewis 1942-59, Wm G Wright 1960-72, Wesley Frensdorff 1972-85, Stewart C Zabriskie 1986-99, Katharine Jefferts Schori 2001-06

Bishop—Rt Rev Dan T Edwards (1023) (Dio 5 Jan 2008–31 Dec 2018)

Conv Sec N Janess; *Treas* D Stufflebeam; *Finan Off* D Barsky; *Chanc* K Bliss; *Cn to Ord* RM Nelson Jr; *Cn for Cong Vit* C Gregg

Stand Comm—Cler: Pres B Polley N Janess W Millsap *Sec* M Asson R Smallwood; *Chap:* S Leach; *Treas* R Pereira; *Lay:* L Baca T Mittelstadt C Marks

D Kesner L Negrete

Dio Staff—Admin and Comm Off: S Sims; *Fin Off:* D Barsky; *Cn for Cong Vit* C Gregg

PARISHES, MISSIONS, AND CLERGY

Austin St George Episcopal Church **P** (9) 156 Main St 89310-0181 (Mail to: PO Box 181 89310-0181) (775) 964-1477

Boulder City St Christophers Episcopal Church **P** (118) 812 Arizona St 89005-2604 (Mail to: C/O Nancy MacFarlane 812 Arizona St 89005-2604) James Lyons (702) 293-4275

Bullhead City Church of the Holy Spirit **P** (40) 580 Hancock Rd 86442-4902 (Mail to: 580 Hancock Rd 86442-4902) (928) 763-1881

Carson City St Nicholas Mission **PM** 1721 Snyder Ave 89701-7812 (Mail to: PO Box 7000 89702) (775) 882-9203

Carson City St Peters Episcopal Church **P** (205) 314 S Division St 89703-4172 (Mail to: 305 Minnesota St 89703-4172) Jeffrey Paul Eric Heidecker (775) 882-1534

Elko St Pauls Episcopal Church **P** (95) 777 Sage St 89801-3318 (Mail to: 777 Sage St 89801-3318) Karen Albrethsen David Grube (775) 738-3264

Ely St Bartholomews Church **P** (63) 209 7th St 89301-1583 (Mail to: PO Box 151585 89315-1207) Mary Bianchi Richard Sims (775) 289-6208

Eureka St James Episcopal Church **HC** (4) 101 S Spring St 89316 (Mail to: C/O Arline Depauli PO Box 473 89316-0473) (775) 289-0557

Fallon Holy Trinity Episcopal Church **P** (80) 507 Churchill St 89406-3902 (Mail to: 507 Churchill St 89406-3902) Patrick Leclaire (775) 423-3551

Glenbrook St Johns in the Wilderness Church **P** (57) 1776 Us Highway 50 89413 (Mail to: 1776 US Highway 50 89413-9714) Victoria Warren Eric Heidecker (775) 588-6793

Henderson St Timothys Episcopal Church **P** (160) 43 W Pacific Ave 89015-7351 (Mail to: 43 W Pacific Ave 89015-7351) John Jordan Carol Walton (702) 565-8033

Incline Vlg St Patrick's Episcopal Church **P** (213) 341 Village Blvd 89451-8237 (Mail to: 341 Village Blvd 89451-8237) David Mussatti Sarah Syer (775) 831-1418

Las Vegas All Saints Episcopal Church **P** (551) 4201 W Washington Ave 89107-2005 (Mail to: 4201 W Washington Ave 89107-2005) Michael Engfer Michael Link (702) 878-2373

Las Vegas Christ Episcopal Church **P** (1014) 2000 S Maryland Pkwy 89104-3200 (Mail to: 2000 S Maryland Pkwy # 1 89104-3200) Jorge Hernandez Richard O' Brien James Vaughn (702) 735-7655

Las Vegas Epiphany Episcopal Church **P** (120) 10450 Gilespie St 89183-4112 (Mail to: 10450 Gilespie St 89183-4112) Richard O' Brien (702) 427-9588

Las Vegas Grace in the Desert Episcopal Church **P** (382) 2004 Spring Gate Ln 89134-6246 (Mail to: 2004 Spring Gate Ln 89134-6246) Mary Bredlau Sherman Frederick Clelia Garrity James Hobart Shannon Leach Barbara Lewis Nicholas Neubauer Barbara Preas James Wallis (702) 838-7444

Las Vegas St Lukes Episcopal Church **P** (68) 832 Eastern Ave 89101-2345 (Mail to: 820 H Street 89106) Antonio Lopez (702) 642-4459

Las Vegas St Matthews Episcopal Church **P** (144) 4709 S Nellis Blvd 89121-3113 (Mail to: C/o Johnson Watts 6540 Bourbon Way 89107-

3331) Christie Leavitt Lionel Starkes (702) 451-2483

Las Vegas St Thomas Episcopal Church **P** (85) 5383 E Owens Ave 89110-1624 (Mail to: C/O Ms Marge Tucker Treasurer 111 Lamb Blvd # 279 89110) Timothy Swonger (702) 452-1199

Lovelock Grace - St Francis Episcopal Church **P** (15) 801 Cornell Ave 89419 (Mail to: C/O Charles M Harris PO Box 1043 89419-1043) (775) 273-7720

Minden Coventry Cross Episcopal Church **P** (39) 1631 Esmeralda Ave 89423-4202 (Mail to: Treasurer PO Box 518 89423-0518) Elizabeth Ann Tattersall Elizabeth Ann Tattersall (775) 782-4161

Nixon St Mary the Virgin Episcopal Church **P** (78) 240 Church St 89424 (Mail to: PO Box 217 89424) (775) 574-0280

Pahrump St Martins in the Desert **P** (75) 631 W Irene St 89060-3929 (Mail to: PO Box 1385 89041-1385) Johnny McClatchy Julie Platson (775) 537-1115

Pioche Christ Episcopal Church **P** (30) Cedar St 89043 (Mail to: PO Box 126 89043-0126) (775) 962-5835

Reno St Catherine of Siena **M** (180) 110 Bishop Manogue Dr 89511-4809 (Mail to: P.O. Box 6791 89513-6791) Laurinda Chappelle (775) 771-4168

Reno Trinity Episcopal Church **P** (745) 200 Island ave 89505-2246 (Mail to: PO Box 2246 89505-2246) Mikayla Dunfee William Millsap Patricia Pumphrey William Stomski (775) 329-4279

Sparks St Pauls Episcopal Church **P** (299) 1135 12th St 89431-3607 (Mail to: PO Box 737 89432-0737) Kirk Woodliff William Arnold (775) 358-4474

Tonopah St Marks Episcopal Church **P** (14) 210 University St 89043 (Mail to: PO Box 447 89049-0447) (775) 482-5546

Virginia City Old St Pauls Episcopal Church **P** (16) F & Taylor St 89440 (Mail to: PO Box 13 89440-0013) (775) 847-9700

Wadsworth St Michael & All Angels Church **P** (39) 445 Reservation Rd 89442 (Mail to: PO Box 310 89442-0310) Richard Snyder (775) 835-6440

Wells St Barnabas Episcopal Church **P** 367 4th St 89835 (Mail to: 335 4th Street 89835) (775) 752-3416

Winnemucca St Marys Episcopal Church **P** 350 Melarkey St 89445-3146 (Mail to: C/O Mrs Dorothy Harrison PO Box 2088 89446-2088) (775) 623-3296

Yerington St Albans Episcopal Church **P** (6) Van Ness & West St 89447 (Mail to: PO Box 207 89447-0207) (775) 463-1276

DIOCESE OF NEW HAMPSHIRE

(PROVINCE I)
Comprises the State of New Hampshire
DIOCESAN OFFICE 63 Green St Concord NH 03301
TEL (603) 224-1914 FAX (603) 225-7884
E-MAIL info@nhepiscopal.org WEB www.nhepiscopal.org

Previous Bishops—
Alexander V Griswold 1811-43, Carlton Chase 1844-70, Wm W Niles 1870-1914, Edward M Parker coadj 1906 Bp 1914-25, John T Dallas 1926-48, Chas F Hall 1948-73, Philip A Smith 1973-86, Douglas E Theuner 1986-2004, V Gene Robinson 2004-13

Bishop—Rt Rev A Robert Hirschfeld (1067) (Dio 5 Jan 2013)

Cn for Mission Res B Ambrogi; *Sec* E Rotch; *Treas* C Porter; *Cn for Fin/ESC Prog Man* G Gallant; *Chanc* RA Wells Jr; *Bps Asst* L Eaton; *Off Asst* J Quinn; *Cn for Trans and Comm Eng* G Avery; *Bps Asst for Pastoral Supp* L Howlett; *Cn for Min Dev* T Pickering

Stand Comm—Cler: Pres R Stevens G Collins K Atkinson; *Lay:* M Porter R Cotton J Stevens

PARISHES, MISSIONS, AND CLERGY

Ashland St Marks Episcopal Church **M** (47) 18 Highland St 03217-4337 (Mail to: PO Box 737 03217-0737) (603) 968-7640

Berlin St Barnabas Church **P** (65) 1 Main St 03570-2414 (Mail to: C/O Christine Lindsey PO Box 545 03570-0545) (603) 752-3504

Bretton Woods Church of the Transfiguration **SC** Rt 302 03860-0382 (Mail to: C/O Christ Church PO Box 382 03860-0382) Susan Buchanan (603) 356-2062

Canterbury Church of the Woods **M** 92 Foster Rd 03224-2517 (Mail to: 92 Foster Rd 03224-2517) (603) 731-5013

Claremont Trinity Episcopal Church **P** (149) 120 Broad St 03743-3621 (Mail to: PO Box 172 03743-0172) Charles Davenport Janet Lombardo (603) 542-2103

Claremont Union-St. Luke's Episcopal Church **P** (58) 133 Old Church Rd 03743 (Mail to: PO Box 902 03743-0902) (603) 542-7209

Colebrook St Stephens Episcopal Mission **M** (23) 16 Parsons St 03576 (Mail to: 1935 Us Route 3 03576-6520) Marlyn Neary (603) 237-8229

Concord Chapel of St Peter and Paul **CC** 325 Pleasant St 03301 (Mail to: 325 Pleasant St 03301) (603) 229-4659

Concord Grace Episcopal Church **M** (144) 30 Eastman St 03301-5409 (Mail to: 30 Eastman St 03301-5409) (603) 224-2252

Concord St Pauls Church **P** (489) 21 Centre St 03301-6301 (Mail to: 21 Centre St 03301-6301)

Kate Atkinson Andrew Courtright Charles Leclerc (603) 224-2523

Contoocook St Andrews Episcopal Church **P** (489) 354 Main St 03229-2627 (Mail to: 354 Main St 03229-2627) Reed Loy John McCausland (603) 746-3415

Derry Church of the Transfiguration **P** (110) 1 Hood Rd 03038-2046 (Mail to: 1 Hood Rd 03038-2046) Raymond Bonin (603) 432-2120

Dover Church of St Thomas **P** (300) 5 Hale St 03820-3712 (Mail to: 5 Hale St 03820-3773) Suzanne Poulin (603) 742-3155

Dublin Emmanuel Church **SC** Dublin Rd 03444 (Mail to: PO Box 499 03444-0499) (603) 563-8029

Dunbarton Church of St John the Evangelist **M** (97) 270 Stark Hwy 03046-4714 (Mail to: 270 Stark Hwy 03046-4714) (603) 774-3678

Durham St Georges Episcopal Church **P** (312) 1 Park Ct 03824-2407 (Mail to: 1 Park Ct 03824-2400) Michael Bradley (603) 868-2785

Exeter Christ Church Episcopal **P** (736) 43 Pine St 03833-2720 (Mail to: C/O Lucia Savage 43 Pine St 03833-2720) Mark Pendleton Charles Nichols (603) 772-3332

Goffstown St Matthews Episcopal Church **P** (1204) 7 Mast St 03045-1709 (Mail to: 7 Mast St 03045-1709) Nancy Vogele (603) 497-2003

Hampstead St Christophers Episcopal Church **M** (207) 187 East Rd 03841-5302 (Mail to: c/o Brenda Getchell 187 East Rd 03841-5340) Zachary Harmon (603) 329-4674

Hampton Trinity Episcopal Church **M** (95) 200 High St 03842-2286 (Mail to: 200 High St 03842-2286) (603) 926-5688

Hanover St Thomas Episcopal Church **P** (469) 9 W Wheelock St 03755-1710 (Mail to: 9 W Wheelock St 03755-1710) Guy Collins Jane Hague (603) 643-4155

Holderness Chapel of Holy Cross **M** Holderness School 33 Chapel Lane 03245 (Mail to: Holderness School PO Box 1879 03264-1879) (603) 536-1257

Keene Parish of St James Church **P** (194) 44 West St 03431-3371 (Mail to: 44 West St 03431-3371) Geoffrey Smith Elsa Worth (603) 352-1019

Laconia St James Episcopal Church **P** (75) 2238 Parade Rd 03246-1520 (Mail to: 2238 Parade Rd 03246-1520) William Gannon (603) 524-5800

Lancaster St Pauls Church **P** (97) 113 Main St 03584-3028 (Mail to: 113 Main St 03584-3028) Weldon Brooks (603) 788-4654

Lisbon Church of the Epiphany **M** (12) 90 School St 03585-6514 (Mail to: 90 School St 03585-6514) (603) 838-8961

Littleton All Saints Episcopal Church **P** (181) 35 School St 03561-4820 (Mail to: 35 School St 03561-4820) Paul Higginson Curtis Metzger (603) 444-3414

Londonderry St Peters Episcopal Church **P** (276) 3 Peabody Row 03053-3302 (Mail to: 3 Peabody Row 03053-6609) Colin Chapman (603) 437-8222

Lost Nation St Timothys Chapel **SC** Lost Nation Road 03584 (Mail to: C/O St Pauls Church 113 Main St 03584) (603) 788-4654

Manchester Grace Episcopal Church **P** (303) 106 Lowell St Attn: Treasurer Richard Feren 03101-1625 (Mail to: Attn: Treasurer Richard Feren 106 Lowell St 03101-1625) Marjorie Gerbracht-Stagnaro William Knight Jane Van Zandt Wesley Wasdyke (603) 622-9813

Manchester St Andrews Episcopal Church **P** (94) 102 Main St 03102-4028 (Mail to: 102 Main St Ste 1 03102-4079) Sarah Rockwell Thomas Vanderslice (603) 622-8632

Marlborough St Francis Chapel **SC** Stone Pond 03444 (Mail to: PO Box 368 03455-0368) Anne Webb Richard Webb (603) 876-4407

Meredith Trinity Episcopal Church **P** (85) 93 Route 25 East 03253-0635 (Mail to: PO Box 635 03253-0635) Robin Soller (603) 279-6689

Merrimack Faith Episcopal Church **M** (56) 590 Daniel Webster Hwy 03054-3429 (Mail to: PO Box 422 03054-0422) Patricia Henking (603) 424-6806

Milford Church of Our Saviour **P** (262) 10 Amherst St 03055-4009 (Mail to: PO Box 237 03055-0237) Hays Junkin Hays Junkin (603) 673-3309

Nashua Church of the Good Shepherd **P** (1188) 214 Main St 03060-2939 (Mail to: Laurie Ascani PO Box 412 03061-0412) Katherine Siberine Alanna Van Antwerpen (603) 882-5352

New London St Andrews Church **P** (769) 15 Gould Rd 03257-5533 (Mail to: PO Box 294 03257-0294) John Macleod (603) 526-6344

Newport Church of the Epiphany **P** (58) 55 Cheney St 03773 (Mail to: PO Box 624 03773-0624) (603) 863-1786

North Conway Christ Episcopal Church **P** (225) 16 Pine St 03860-5210 (Mail to: PO Box 382 03860-0382) Richard Belshaw (603) 356-2062

North Woodstock Church of the Messiah **M** (97) School St 03262 (Mail to: PO Box 267 03262-0267) Teresa Gocha (603) 745-3148

Peterborough All Saints Church **P** (225) 51 Concord St 03458-1510 (Mail to: c/o Treasurer 51-53 Concord St 03458-1510) Sandra Albom Jamie Hamilton Louise Howlett (603) 924-3202

Pittsfield St Stephens Episcopal Church **P** (72) 50 main st 03263 (Mail to: C/O Curtis Metzger PO Box 435 03263-0435) Stephen Blackmer (603) 435-7908

Plymouth Church of the Holy Spirit **P** (281) 170 Main St 03264-1526 (Mail to: PO Box 68 03264-0068) Kelly Seaman (603) 536-1321

Portsmouth Christ Church **M** (95) 1035 Lafayette Rd 03801-5468 (Mail to: Attn Treasurer 1035 Lafayette Rd 03801-7416) David Robinson (603) 436-8842

Portsmouth St John's Episcopal Church **P** (1153) 100 Chapel St 03801-3808 (Mail to: C/O Finance Administration 100 Chapel St 03801-3806) Robert Stevens Nathaniel Bourne Anne Williamson (603) 436-8283

Rye Beach St Andrews by the Sea **SC** Church Rd 03871 (Mail to: PO Box 555 03871-0555) (207) 964-8432

Salem St Davids Episcopal Church **P** (79) 231 Main St 03079-3186 (Mail to: Attn: Treasurer 231 Main St 03079-3186) Carolyn Stevenson (603) 893-0342

Sanbornville Church of St John the Baptist **P** (130) 118 High St 03872-4367 (Mail to: ATTN: Treasurer PO Box 249 03872-0249) Janet Lombardo (603) 522-3329

Sugar Hill St Matthews Summer Chapel **SC** Rte 117 03585 (Mail to: 71 Sunset Hill Rd 03586-4235) (603) 823-5667

Sunapee St James Episcopal Church **SC** 378 Lake Avenue 03782-0178 (Mail to: C/O Mr. A.H. Hardt P.O. Box 178 03782) (603) 526-9070

Tamworth Church of St Andrew in Valley **P** (76) 678 Whittier Road 03886-0436 (Mail to: PO Box 436 03886-0436) Caroline Hines (603) 323-8515

Walpole St Johns Episcopal Church **P** (51) Westminister And Elm Sts 03608 (Mail to: PO Box 179 03608-0179) Susan De Puy Kershaw (603) 756-4533

Weare Church of the Holy Cross **M** (77) 118 Center Rd 03281-4605 (Mail to: PO Box 161 03281-0161) David Ferner (603) 529-1042

Whitefield Church of the Transfiguration **SC** 277 Water St 03598 (Mail to: C/O Mr Christopher Smith Water Street 03598) Gordon Owen (603) 837-2098

Wolfeboro All Saints Episcopal Church **P** (291) 359 S Main St 03894-4413 (Mail to: PO Box 359 03894-0359) (603) 569-3453

Woodsville St Lukes Episcopal Church **M** (75) 3 Church St 03785-1259 (Mail to: PO Box 167 03785-0167) (603) 747-2670

STATE OF NEW JERSEY

Dioceses of Newark and New Jersey

DIOCESE OF NEW JERSEY
(PROVINCE II)
Comprises 14 counties in central and southern New Jersey
DIOCESAN OFFICE 808 W State St Trenton NJ 08618-5326
TEL (609) 394-5281   FAX (609) 394-9546   BISHOP'S FAX (609) 394-8015
E-MAIL diocese@dioceseofnj.org   WEB www.dioceseofnj.org

Previous Bishops—
John Croes 1815-32, Geo W Doane 1832-59, Wm H Odenheimer 1859-74, John Scarborough 1875-1914, Paul Matthews 1915-37, Albion W Knight coadj 1923-35, Ralph E Urban suffr 1932-35, Wallace J Gardner 1937-54, Alfred L Banyard suffr 1945-55 Bp 1955-73, Albert W Van Duzer suffr 1966-72 Bp 1973-82, VK Pettit suffr 1983-91, GPM Belshaw suffr 1975-82 coadj 1982 Bp 1983-94, Joe Morris Doss Bp 1995-2001, David B Joslin asst 2000-03, Sylvestre D Romero 2008-10, George E Councell, DD 2003-2013

Bishop—Rt Rev William H. Stokes, D.D. (Dio 2 Nov 2013)

Cn to Ord Rev Dr Cn BA Jemmott; *Trans Off* Rev Dr Cn BA Jemmott; *COO* Cn P Jones; *Sec of Conv* P Ambos; *Treas* K Bonamici; *Chanc* P Ambos; Esq; *COP Co-Chairs:* Rev J Belmont C White; *Interim Dir of Comm* S Welch; *Com Chair* Rev J Belmont; *Cong Dev* Cn R Droste

Stand Comm—Cler: Pres VBalling AM Jeffery JM Santiago J Memba; *Lay:* K Moore W Blackman K Seda A Maddison

PARISHES, MISSIONS, AND CLERGY

Absecon St Marks and All Saints Church **P** (307) 429 S Pitney Rd 08205-9780 (Mail to: 429 S Pitney Rd 08205-9780) Terrence O'Connor (609) 652-6222

Allenhurst Church of St Andrews by the Sea **SC** 150 Norwood Ave 07711 (Mail to: PO BOX 245 07712-0245) (508) 740-2115

Asbury Park St Augustine Episcopal Church **P** (129) Atlantic And Prospect Aves 07712 (Mail to: PO Box 245 07712-0245) Eddie Lillard William Ndishabandi (732) 774-3069

Asbury Park Trinity Church **P** (411) 503 Asbury Ave 07712-6104 (Mail to: 503 Asbury Ave 07712-6189) Michael Way (732) 775-5084

Atlantic City St Augustines Church **P** (147) 1709 Arctic Ave PO Box1657 08401-4304 (Mail to:

PO Box 1657 08404-1657) Ryan Boyce (609) 345-0718

Avalon St Johns by the Sea **SC** 25th & Avalon Ave 08202 (Mail to: C/O Frederick A Bluefield 621 Pancoast Road 08202) (609) 996-7715

Avon By Sea St Johns Episcopal Church **SC** 100 Woodland Ave 07717-1341 (Mail to: 110 Woodland Ave box 375 07717-1341) (732) 988-9577

Barnegat Light St Peters at the Light Church **M** (94) 607 Central Ave 08006 (Mail to: 700 Central Ave 08006) Donald Turner (609) 494-2398

Basking Ridge St Marks Church **P** (292) 140 S Finley Ave 07920-1428 (Mail to: 140 S Finley Ave 07920-1428) Richard Morley Tammy Young (908) 766-9058

Bay Head All Saints Church **P** (359) 500 Lake Ave 08742-5366 (Mail to: 500 Lake Ave 08742-0053) Robert Nagy (732) 892-7478

Beach Haven Holy Innocents Church **P** (478) 1 Marine St 08008-1635 (Mail to: 410 S Atlantic Ave 08008-1699) Charles Arlin Daniel Hinkle Judith Krom Gretchen Zimmerman (609) 492-7571

Bellmawr Church of the Holy Spirit **M** (85) 20 E. Browning Rd 08031 (Mail to: 300 Smith Ln 08078-1346) (856) 931-0990

Berlin Church of the Good Shepherd **P** (136) 108 W Broad St 08009-1438 (Mail to: 108 W Broad St 08009-1438) Frances Clark (856) 767-0160

Bernardsville St John on the Mountain **P** (361) 379 Mount Harmony Rd 07924-1414 (Mail to: 379 Mount Harmony Rd 07924-1414) David Jones (908) 766-2282

Bernardsville St Bernards Episcopal Church **P** (80) 88 Claremont Rd 07924-2210 (Mail to: 88 Claremont Rd 07924-2210) Elizabeth Sciaino (908) 766-0602

Beverly St Stephens Episcopal Church **P** (167) 158 Warren St 08010-1342 (Mail to: 158 Warren St 08010-1342) Frederick Pray Anne Wrede (609) 387-0169

Blackwood St John Episcopal Church **P** (414) 1720 Old Black Horse Pk 08012-5218 (Mail to: 1720 Old Black Horse Pike 08012-5218) (856) 227-1051

Bordentown Christ Church **P** (194) 124 Prince St 08505-1318 (Mail to: 130 Prince St 08505-1318) James Tucker (609) 298-2348

Bound Brook St Pauls Episcopal Church **P** (174) 214 Church St 08805-1934 (Mail to: 214 Church St 08805-1934) Kristen Foley (732) 356-0247

Bradley Beach St James Episcopal Church **P** (305) 605 4th Ave 07720-1250 (Mail to: PO Box 1 07720-0001) (732) 775-5414

Brick St Raphael the Archangel **P** (74) 1520 Route 88 08724-2320 (Mail to: 1520 Route 88 08724-2320) Nancy Hite Speck Maria Sanzo (732) 458-5743

Bridgeton Church of the Resurrection **P** (120) 186 E Commerce St 08302-2606 (Mail to: 186 E Commerce St 08302-2606) Ellen Rutherford (856) 451-3233

Bridgewater St Martins Episcopal Church **P** (412) § 1350 Washington Valley Rd 08807-1418 (Mail to: 1350 Washington Valley Rd 08807-1418) Bruce Montgomery (908) 526-1353

Burlington St Marys Episcopal Church **P** (305) 145 W Broad St 08016-1341 (Mail to: 145 W Broad St 08016-1341) John Haynes (609) 386-0902

Camden Church of St Andrew the Apostle **M** (452) 3050 River Rd 08105-4134 (Mail to: PO Box 1333 08105-0333) Pedro Guzman (856) 365-0111

Camden St Augustine Episcopal Church **P** (160) Broadway & Royden St 08101 (Mail to: PO Box 1925 Broadway & Royden Street 08101-1925) (856) 365-3243

Camden St Pauls Episcopal Church **P** (185) 422 Market St 08102-1526 (Mail to: PO Box 1551 08101-1551) (856) 365-5880

Camden St Wilfreds Church **M** (37) 83 Dudley St 08105-2425 (Mail to: 3012 Westfield Ave 08105-2411) (856) 365-4924

Cape May Church of the Advent **P** (331) Washington & Franklin Sts 08204 (Mail to: PO Box 261 08204-0261) Douglas Halvorsen (609) 884-3065

Cape May Point St Peters by the Sea **SC** 102 Lake Dr 08212-0261 (Mail to: 603 Arctic Ave 08204-1819) (609) 898-4318

Cherry Hill St Bartholomews Episcopal Church **P** (682) 1989 Marlton Pike E 08003-1830 (Mail to: 1989 Marlton Pike E 08003-1830) Anna Noon Lynn Johnson Arthur Knight Colleen Spaeth (856) 424-2229

Clarksboro St Peter's Episcopal Church **P** (68) 304 Kings Hwy 08020-1404 (Mail to: 304 Kings Hwy 08020-1404) Robert Fitzpatrick (856) 423-4116

Clementon St Mary Episcopal Church **M** (85) 33 Berlin Rd 08021-4501 (Mail to: PO Box 219 08021-0222) Douglas Reans (856) 435-2009

Collingswood Holy Trinity Church **P** (247) 839 Haddon Ave 08108-1941 (Mail to: 839 Haddon Ave 08108-1993) Mark Chattin (856) 858-0491

Cranbury St Davids Episcopal Church **P** (396) 90 S Main St 08512-3144 (Mail to: 90 S Main St 08512-3144) Karin Mitchell Henry Bristol (609) 655-4731

Cranford Trinity Church **P** (239) 205 North Avenue East 07016-2040 (Mail to: North Avenue At Forest Avenue 07016) (908) 276-4047

Dunellen St Francis Episcopal Church **P** (167) 400 New Market Rd 08812-1505 (Mail to: 400 New Market Rd 08812-1505) John Zamboni Margaret Forsythe (732) 968-6781

Eatontown St James Memorial Episcopal Church **P** (161) 69 Broad St # O 07724-1528 (Mail to: PO Box 207 07724-0207) Agostino Rivolta (732) 542-0818

Edison Saint James Church **HC** (61) 2136 Woodbridge Ave 08817-4421 (Mail to: PO Box 1286 08818-1286) (732) 985-2023

Absecon St Marks and All Saints Church **P** (307) 429 S Pitney Rd 08205-9780 (Mail to: 429 S Pitney Rd 08205-9780) **Elizabeth** St Elizabeths Church **P** (185) 305 Broad St 07208-3704 (Mail to: PO Box 510 07207-0510) Andy Moore Theodore Moore (908) 289-0681

Elizabeth St Johns Episcopal Church **P** (375) 61 Broad St 07201-2205 (Mail to: 61 Broad St 07201-2205) (908) 352-2220

Elizabeth San Jose Episcopal Church **M** (985) 38 W End Pl 07202-1724 (Mail to: 38 W End Pl 07202-1724) Toribio Rodriguez-Santos (908) 289-7070

Flemington Calvary Episcopal Church **P** (359) 44 Broad St 08822-1404 (Mail to: 44 Broad St 08822-1404) John Hain Ann Holt Nathan Ritter (908) 782-7227

Florence Sts Stephen and Barnabas Epis Ch **M** (62) Second & Spring Sts 08518 (Mail to: PO Box 365 08518-0365) Linda Moeller (609) 499-0998

Freehold St Peters Episcopal Church **P** (258) 33 Throckmorton St 07728-1946 (Mail to: 33 Throckmorton St 07728-1946) Dirk Reinken (732) 431-8383

Gibbsboro St Johns in the Wilderness Church **M** (214) 77 Hilliards Road 08026-0126 (Mail to: PO Box 126 08026-0126) Martha Dooley (856) 783-8480

Gladstone St Lukes Episcopal Church **P** (702) 182 Main St 07934-2063 (Mail to: PO Box 605 07934-0605) Kent Walley (908) 234-0002

Glassboro St Thomas Episcopal Church **P** (287) 212 Main St 08028-1919 (Mail to: Dr Harold Lucius 212 Main St 08028-1919) Todd Foster Louis De Sheplo (856) 881-9144

Gloucester City Church of the Ascension **P** (142) 110 S Sussex St 08030-1942 (Mail to: 110 S Sussex St 08030-1942) (856) 456-4394

Haddon Heights St Marys Episcopal Church **P** (253) 70 White Horse Pike 08035 (Mail to: 501 Green St 08035-1987) Genevieve Bishop (856) 547-3240

Haddonfield Grace Episcopal Church **P** (1073) 19 Kings Hwy E 08033-2001 (Mail to: 19 Kings Hwy E 08033-2097) (856) 429-0007

Keansburg St Marks Episcopal Church **M** (65) 247 Carr Ave 07734-1452 (Mail to: 247 Carr Ave 07734-1452) Kathleen Murray (732) 787-1075

Keyport St Mary the Virgin **M** (20) 10 E Front St 07735-1525 (Mail to: PO Box 2 07735-0002) Walter Leigh (732) 264-5288

Lakewood All Saints Church **P** (267) 213 Madison Ave 08701-3316 (Mail to: 213 Madison Ave 08701-3316) Juan Monge-Santiago (732) 367-0933

Lambertville St Andrews Episcopal Church **P** (235) 50 York St 08530-2024 (Mail to: 50 York St 08530-2024) Daniel Somers (609) 397-2425

Laurel Springs Church of the Atonement **P** (121) 233 Fairmount Ave 08021-2115 (Mail to: PO Box 487 08084-0487) Elizabeth Oasin (856) 784-8666

Lebanon Church of the Holy Spirit **P** (567) 3 Haytown Rd 08833-4009 (Mail to: 3 Haytown Rd 08833-4009) Philip Carr-Jones Johnine Byrer (908) 236-6301

Linden St John the Baptist Episcopal Church **P** (109) 2018 Dewitt Ter 07036-3700 (Mail to: 2018 Dewitt Ter 07036-3700) Terry Blackburn Peter DeFranco (908) 925-1535

Little Silver St John's Episcopal Church **P** (200) 325 Little Silver Point Rd 07739-1757 (Mail to: 325 Little Silver Point Rd 07739-1757) Valerie Redpath (732) 741-7826

Long Branch St James Church **P** (201) 300 Broadway 07740-6930 (Mail to: 300 Broadway 07740-6930) William Noble Robert Sullivan (732) 222-1411

Longport Church of the Redeemer **SC** 108 S 20th Ave 08403-1135 (Mail to: Attn Mr Philip S Demig 1013 W 9th Ave Ste 9e 19406-1208) (609) 822-7222

Lumberton St Martin in the Fields **P** (173) 489 Main St 08048-1101 (Mail to: 489 Main St 08048-1101) Margaret Smyth (609) 261-4882

Magnolia Christ Church **M** (85) 413 Evesham Ave W 08049-1726 (Mail to: PO Box 67 08049-0067) (856) 783-4281

Manchester Twp St Stephens Episcopal Church **P** (270) 180 Route 539 08759-1248 (Mail to: 180 Route 539 08759-1248) Paul Van Sant (732) 350-2121

Maple Shade St Johns Episcopal Church **M** (90) 41 E Linwood Avenue 08052-2535 (Mail to: 41 E Linwood Ave 08052-2535) John Powell (856) 779-0389

Matawan Trinity Episcopal Church **P** (266) 18 Ryers Ln 07747-3417 (Mail to: 18 Ryers Ln 07747-3497) (732) 591-9210

Medford St Peters Episcopal Church **P** (634) 1 Hartford Rd 08055-9051 (Mail to: 1 Hartford Rd 08055-9051) Helen Orlando (609) 654-2963

Merchantville Grace Episcopal Church **P** (334) 7 E Maple Ave 08109-5005 (Mail to: 7 E Maple Ave 08109-5096) (856) 665-4117

Metuchen St Lukes Episcopal Church **P** (272) 17 Oak Ave 08840-1529 (Mail to: 17 Oak Ave 08840-1529) Edmund Zelley (732) 548-4308

Middletown Christ Church **P** (282) 90 Kings Hwy 07748-2025 (Mail to: 90 Kings Hwy 07748-2025) Frances Bickerton (732) 671-2524

Millville Christ Episcopal Church **M** (21) 225 Sassafras Street 08332-3353 (Mail to: PO Box 357 08332-0357) Donald Richey (856) 825-1163

Mnchstr Twp St Elisabeths Chapel by-the-Sea **SC** 2 Stonybrook Ct 08759-2032 (Mail to: 31 Ocean Bay Blvd 08735-1922) (732) 830-0450

Monmouth Jct St Barnabas Episcopal Church **HC** (150) 142 Sand Hills Rd 08852-3103 (Mail to: 142 Sand Hills Rd 08852-3103) Valerie Balling (732) 297-4607

Moorestown Evergreens Chapel **Chapel** 309 Bridgeboro Rd 08057-1419 (Mail to: C/O Acts Retirement Life Communities PO Box 90 19486) Douglas Halvorsen (856) 439-2000

Moorestown Trinity Church Episcopal **P** (669) 207 W Main St 08057-2325 (Mail to: 207 W Main St 08057-2381) Douglas Halvorsen Henrietta Lavengood Leslie Mazzacano Emily Mellott John Salmon (856) 235-0811

Mount Holly St Andrews Church Episcopal **P** (472) 121 High St 08060-1401 (Mail to: 121 High St 08060-1401) David Snyder (609) 267-0225

Mullica Hill Saint Stephen's Church **M** (100) 51 Main St 08062-9414 (Mail to: 51 Main St 08062-9414) (856) 478-6931

Navesink All Saints Memorial Church **P** (196) 202 Navesink Ave 07752-0326 (Mail to: PO Box 326 07752-0326) Rosemarie Broderick Deborah Cook (732) 291-0214

New Brunswick Christ Church **P** (459) 5 Paterson St 08901-1204 (Mail to: 5 Paterson St 08901-1204) Joanna Hollis Peter Cornell (732) 545-6262

New Brunswick St Albans Episcopal Church **M** (189) 148 Lee Ave 08901-2919 (Mail to: 148 Lee Ave 08901-2919) Ricardo Sheppard (732) 247-0808

New Brunswick Church of St John the Evangelist **P** (75) 189 George St 08901-1319 (Mail to: 189 George St 08901-1399) (732) 545-5619

New Brunswick Episcopal Campus Ministry at Rutgers **CC** 5 Mine St 08901-1111 (Mail to: 5 Mine St 08901-1111) (732) 932-1278

New Providence St Andrews Episcopal Church **P** (312) 419 South St 07974-2131 (Mail to: 419 South St 07974-2194) Daniel Gunn Francis Hubbard (908) 464-4875

Ocean City Holy Trinity Episcopal Church **P** (378) 2998 Bay Ave 08226-2361 (Mail to: 2998 Bay Ave 08226-2361) Elizabeth Ohlson (609) 399-1019

Palmyra Christ Church **M** (62) 638 Parry Ave 08065-2502 (Mail to: 638 Parry Ave 08065-2599) (856) 829-1764

Paulsboro St James Episcopal Church **M** (80) 190 E Jefferson St 08066 (Mail to: 349 Lincoln Ave 08066-1132) (856) 845-4878

Pemberton Grace Episcopal Church **P** (126) 43 Elizabeth St 08068-1215 (Mail to: 43 Elizabeth St 08068-1215) Jane Gober (609) 894-8001

Pennington St Matthews Episcopal Church **P** (1320) 300 S Main St 08534-2804 (Mail to: Attn: Bruce Weise 300 S Main St 08534-2804) Barbara Briggs Ophelia Laughlin John Merz (609) 737-0985

Penns Grove Church of Our Merciful Saviour **P** (176) 110 E Maple Ave 08069-2066 (Mail to: 110 E Maple Ave 08069-2097) (856) 299-6038

Pennsville St Georges Church **P** (75) 305 Broadway 08070-1216 (Mail to: 305 Broadway 08070-3010) William Boatwright William Boatwright (856) 678-7979

Perth Amboy Church of the Holy Cross **M** (50) 351-355 Lawrie Street 08861-3342 (Mail to: 351-355 Lawrie St 08861-3342) Francis Cho (732) 738-0862

Perth Amboy St Peters Episcopal Church **P** (486) 183 Rector St 08861-4739 (Mail to: 183 Rector St 08861-4739) Anne-Marie Jeffery Kathleen Dejohn (732) 826-1594

Pitman Church of the Good Shepherd **P** (728) 315 Highland Ter 08071-1550 (Mail to: 315 Highland Ter 08071-1550) Susan Osborne-Mott (856) 589-8209

Pittstown St Thomas Episcopal Church **P** (313) 98 Sky Manor Rd 08867-4032 (Mail to: PO Box 348 08867-0348) Carol Horton Debra Clarke (908) 996-4091

Plainfield Grace Episcopal Church **P** (337) 600 Cleveland Ave 07060-1727 (Mail to: 600 Cleveland Ave 07060-1727) Theodore Moore Joyce Scheyer (908) 756-1520

Plainfield Church of the Holy Cross **P** (210) 40 Mercer Ave 07060-4630 (Mail to: Att Office Admin C Hill 40 Mercer Ave 07060-4630) Kwabena Owusu-Afriyie (908) 756-2438

Plainfield St Marks Episcopal Church **P** (449) 1430 Park Ave 07060-2911 (Mail to: 1430 Park Ave 07060-2911) Angelo Wildgoose (908) 754-9483

Pleasantville St Marys Episcopal Church **M** (90) 118 W Bayview Ave 08232-3106 (Mail to: 118 W Bayview Ave 08232-3106) Joseph Joseph (609) 646-1604

Princeton All Saints Church **P** (318) 16 All Saints Rd 08540-3634 (Mail to: 16 All Saints Rd 08540-3634) Hugh Brown John Frederick Karl Morrison (609) 921-2420

Princeton Episcopal Church at Princeton **CM** (290) C/O Diocese Of New Jersey 808 State Rd 08540-1416 (Mail to: 53 University Pl 08540-5100) (609) 252-9469

Princeton Trinity Episcopal Church **P** (2023) 33 Mercer St 08540-6807 (Mail to: 33 Mercer St 08540-6893) Paul Jeanes Joanne Epply-Schmidt Christopher McNabb Kara Slade (609) 924-2277

Pt Pleas Bch Church Of Saint Mary's By The Sea **P** (480) 804 Bay Ave 08742-3006 (Mail to: 804 Bay Ave 08742-3006) Victoria Pretti (732) 892-9254

Rahway Church of the Good Shepherd **P** (170) 749 Seminary Ave 07065-3413 (Mail to: 749 Seminary Ave 07065-3413) (732) 388-3460

Red Bank St Thomas Episcopal Church **P** (153) 26 East Sunset Ave 07701-1408 (Mail to: PO Box 502 07701-0502) Eddie Lillard Joseluis Memba (732) 747-1039

Red Bank Trinity Episcopal Church **P** (204) 65 W Front St 07701-1621 (Mail to: Attn: Treasurer 65 W Front St 07701-1621) John Lock (732) 741-4581

Riverside Saint Stephen's Church **P** (90) 324 Bridgeboro St 08075-3205 (Mail to: 158 WARREN ST 08010-1342) Sharon Sutton Anne Wrede (856) 461-1037

Riverton Christ Church **P** (494) 500 4th St 08077-1214 (Mail to: 500 4th St 08077-1214) Richard Wrede (856) 829-1634

Rocky Hill Trinity Episcopal Church **M** (165) 1 Crescent Ave 08553 (Mail to: PO Box 265 08553-0265) Johan Johnson (609) 921-8971

Rumson St Georges- by- the- River **P** (1136) Waterman Ave 07760 (Mail to: 7 Lincoln Ave 07760-2051) Ophelia Laughlin James Jones Jeffrey Roy (732) 842-0596

Salem St Johns Church **HC** (110) 76 Market St 08079-1911 (Mail to: 76 Market St 08079-1911) (856) 935-1798

Scotch Plains All Saints Episcopal Church **P** (408) 559 Park Ave 07076-1705 (Mail to: 559 Park Ave 07076-1777) Susanna Cates (908) 322-8047

Sea Girt The Ch of St Uriel the Archangel **P** (402) § 219 Philadelphia Blvd 087502718 (Mail to: 219 Philadelphia Blvd 08750-2718) Russell Griffin (732) 449-6173

Sewaren St Johns Church **M** (156) 7 Woodbridge Ave 07077-1423 (Mail to: 17 Woodbridge Ave 07077-1423) (732) 634-2397

Shrewsbury Christ Episcopal Church **P** (367) 380 Sycamore Ave 07702-4513 (Mail to: 380 Sycamore Ave 07702-4513) Lisa Mitchell Victoria Cuff (732) 741-2220

Somers Point Christ Church Episcopal **P** (230) 157 Shore Rd 08244-2752 (Mail to: PO Box 97 08244-0097) Justin Falciani (609) 927-6262

Somerville St Johns Episcopal Church **P** (727) 158 W High St 08876-1818 (Mail to: 158 W High St 08876-1881) Ronald Pollock William McCoy (908) 722-1250

South Amboy Christ Church **P** (129) 220 Main Street 08879-1304 (Mail to: 257 4th St 08879-1304) Robert Shearer (732) 721-6262

South River Holy Trinity Episcopal Church **P** (217) § 90 Leonardine Ave 08882-2507 (Mail to: C/O Treasurer 90 Leonardine Ave 08882-2507) Gregory Bezilla (732) 254-1734

Spotswood St Peters Episcopal Church **P** (464) 505 Main St 08884-1734 (Mail to: Attn Finance Chair 505 Main St 08884-1734) Marshall Shelly Allison Burns LaGreca (732) 251-2449

Spring Lake Holy Trinity Episcopal Church **SC** 301 Monmouth Ave 07762-1128 (Mail to: PO Box 317 07762-0317) Peter Stimpson (734) 477-4363

Stone Harbor St Marys Episcopal Church **P** (194) 9425 3rd Ave 08247-1926 (Mail to: 9425 3rd Ave 08247-1926) Peter Stube (609) 368-5922

Summit St Simons by the Sea Church **SC** C/O Mr Sandy White 206 Oak Ridge Ave 07901-3237 (Mail to: Attn Jennifer Buck PO Box 532 08738-0532) (860) 236-5321

Swedesboro Trinity Episcopal Old Swedes Church **M** (99) 1208 Kings Hwy 08085-0031 (Mail to: PO Box 31 08085-0031) (856) 467-1227

Toms River Christ Episcopal Church **P** (768) 415 Washington St 08753-6742 (Mail to: 415 Washington St 08753-6742) Jose Cantos Delgado Theodore Foley Emily Holman Lewis McCrum (732) 349-5506

Trenton Christ Church-Cristo Rey **M** (1083) 331 Hamilton Ave 08609-2716 (Mail to: 331 Hamilton Ave 08609-2716) Francisco Pozo (609) 394-8926

Trenton Grace St Pauls Church **P** (252) 3715 E State St Ext 08619-2447 (Mail to: 3715 E State Street Ext 08619-2447) Amy Cornell (609) 586-6004

Trenton Holy Apostles Episcopal Church **P** (237) 1040 Yardville-Allentown Rd 08620 (Mail to: 1040 Yardville Allentown Rd 08620-9711) Arthur Powell Denise Cavaliere (609) 208-0228

Trenton St Luke's Episcopal Church **P** (158) 1620 Prospect St 08638-3031 (Mail to: 1620 Prospect St 08638-3031) Megan Thomas Alexandra Van Kuiken (609) 882-7614

Trenton St Michaels Episcopal Church **M** (93) 140 Warren St 08608-1308 (Mail to: 140 Warren St 08608-1308) (609) 392-8086

Trenton St Peters IGBO Church **M** 1300 Brunswick Ave 08638-3316 (Mail to: 1300 Brunswick Ave 08638-3316) (609) 599-2880

✠ **Trenton** Trinity Cathedral **O** (508) 801 W State St 08618-5325 (Mail to: C/O William Harmer 801 W State St 08618-5325) Rene John Shawn Armington Peter Bridge Christopher Cox Carol Gilbert (609) 392-3805

Tuckerton Church of the Holy Spirit **M** (204) 220 E. Main 08087-2627 (Mail to: PO Box 174 08087-0174) Richard Wisniewski (609) 296-9618

Union St Luke & All Saints Epis Church **P** (73) 398 Chestnut St 07083-9413 (Mail to: 398 Chestnut St 07083-9413) James Kollin (908) 688-7253

Ventnor City Church of the Epiphany **P** (117) 6605 Atlantic Ave 08406-2617 (Mail to: 21 S Troy Ave 08406-2649) (609) 822-0285

Villas St Barnabas by the Bay Church **M** (138) 13 W Bates Ave 08251-2502 (Mail to: 13 W Bates Ave 08251-2502) Lisa Hoffman Susan Cushinotto (609) 886-5960

Vincentown Trinity Episcopal Church **M** (66) 18 Mill St 08088-8824 (Mail to: 18 Mill St 08088-8824) Robert Haller (609) 859-2299

Wall Township St Michaels Episcopal Church **P** (548) 2015 Allenwood Rd 07719-4633 (Mail to: 2015 Allenwood Rd 07719-4633) (732) 681-1863

Waretown St Stephens Episcopal Church **P** (374) 367 Route 9 08758-1702 (Mail to: 367 Route 9 08758-1702) Terry Martin (609) 698-8561

Wenonah Holy Trinity Episcopal Church **P** (396) 11 Monroe Ave 08090-1735 (Mail to: 11 Monroe Ave 08090-1735) Benjamin Maddison (856) 468-0295

Westfield St Pauls Episcopal Church **P** (1427) § 414 E Broad St 07090-2124 (Mail to: 414 E Broad St 07090-2124) Duncan Johnston John Maher (908) 232-8506

Wildwood St Simeons by the Sea Church **P** (126) 2502 Central Ave 08260-5235 (Mail to: 2502 Central Ave 08260-5235) (609) 522-8389

Williamstown St Marks at the Crossing Church **M** (99) 131 W Malaga Rd 08094-3852 (Mail to: 131 W Malaga Rd 08094-3852) (856) 629-8762

Willingboro Church of Christ the King **M** (306) C/O Clint Jackson 40 Charleston Rd 08046-2066 (Mail to: 40 Charleston Rd 08046-2066) (609) 877-2987

Woodbridge Trinity Episcopal Church **P** (425) 650 Rahway Ave 07095-3530 (Mail to: 650 Rahway Ave 07095-3530) Angela Cipolla (732) 634-7422

Woodbury Christ Episcopal Church **P** (816) 62 Delaware St 08096-5912 (Mail to: 62 Delaware St 08096-5989) Brian Burgess (856) 845-0190

Woodstown Saint Luke's Church **M** (76) 37 E Grant St 08098-1401 (Mail to: PO Box 197 37 E Grant St 08098-1401) (856) 769-0760

STATE OF NEW MEXICO

Diocese of Rio Grande (RG)

STATE OF NEW YORK

Dioceses of Albany (A), Central New York (CNY), Long Island (LI), New York (NY), Rochester (Roch),
and Western New York (WNY)

Adams—CNY
Addison—Roch
Afton—CNY
Albany—A
Albion—WNY
Alden—WNY
Alexandria Bay—CNY
Amagansett—LI
Amityville—LI
Amsterdam—A
Angelica—Roch
Angola—WNY
Arden—NY
Ardsley—NY
Armonk—NY
Astoria—LI
Attica—WNY
Auburn—CNY
Aurora—CNY
Au Sable Forks—A
Avon—Roch
Babylon—LI
Bainbridge—CNY
Baldwin—LI
Baldwinsville—CNY
Ballston Spa—A
Barneveld—CNY
Barrytown—NY
Batavia—WNY
Bath—Roch
Bay Shore—LI
Bayside—LI
Beacon—NY
Bedford—NY
Bellmore—LI
Bellmont—Roch
Bellport—LI
Berkshire—CNY
Binghamton—CNY
Black River—CNY
Bloomfield—Roch
Bloomville—A
Blue Mountain
   Lake—A
Bolton Landing—A
Bovina—A
Branchport—Roch
Brant Lake—A
Brentwood—LI
Brewster—NY
Briarcliff Manor—NY
Bridgehampton—LI
Brockport—Roch
Bronx—NY
Bronxville—NY
Brookhaven—LI

Brooklyn—LI
Brownville—CNY
Buffalo—WNY
Burnt Hills—A
Burt—WNY
Cairo—A
Caledonia—Roch
Callicoon—NY
Cambria Hts—LI
Cambridge—A
Camden—CNY
Camillus—CNY
Canajoharie—A
Canandaigua—Roch
Canaseraga—Roch
Canastota—CNY
Candor—CNY
Canton—A
Cape Vincent—CNY
Carle Pl—LI
Carthage—CNY
Castleton—A
Catskill—A
Cazenovia—CNY
Central Islip—LI
Chadwicks—CNY
Champlain—A
Chappaqua—NY
Chatham—A
Chautauqua—WNY
Chelsea—NY
Cherry Valley—A
Chester—NY
Chittenango—CNY
Clark Mills—CNY
Clayton—CNY
Clifton Park—A
Clifton Spgs—Roch
Clinton—CNY
Cobleskill—A
Cohoes—A
Cold Spg—NY
Cold Spg Hbr—LI
Colton—A
Columbiaville—A
Constableville—CNY
Constantia—CNY
Cooperstown—A
Copake Falls—A
Copenhagen—CNY
Corning—Roch
Cornwall—NY
Corona—LI
Cortland—CNY
Coxsackie—A
Croton on Hudson—

NY
Cuba—Roch
Dansville—Roch
Deer Pk—LI
Delhi—A
Delmar—A
Deposit—A
Dobbs Ferry—NY
Douglaston—LI
Dover Plains—NY
Downsville—A
Duanesburg—A
Dunkirk—WNY
Eastchester—NY
E Aurora—WNY
E Elmhurst—LI
E Hampton—LI
E Setauke—LI
E Syracuse—CNY
Elizabethtown—A
Ellenville—NY
Ellicottville—WNY
Elmhurst—LI
Elmira—CNY
Endicott—CNY
Essex—A
Evans Mills—CNY
Fairport—Roch
Far Rockaway—LI
Farmingdale—LI
Fayetteville—CNY
Fishers Is—LI
Fishkill—NY
Floral Pk—LI
Flushing—LI
Forest Hills—LI
Ft Edward—A
Franklin—A
Franklinville—WNY
Fredonia—WNY
Freeport—LI
Fulton—CNY
Garden City—LI
Garnerville—NY
Garrison—NY
Gates—Roch
Geneseo—Roch
Geneva—Roch & CNY
Gilbertsville—A
Glen Cove—LI
Glens Falls—A
Goshen—NY
Gouverneur—A
Gowanda—WNY
Grand Is—WNY
Granite Spgs—NY

Granville—A
Great Neck—LI
Great River—LI
Greene—CNY
Greenport—LI
Greenville—A
Greenwich—A
Greenwood Lake—NY
Guilderland—A
Hamburg—WNY
Hamilton—CNY
Hammondsport—Roch
Hampton Bays—LI
Harrison—NY
Hartsdale—NY
Hastings on Hudson—NY
Hempstead—LI
Henrietta—Roch
Herkimer—A
Hewlett—LI
Hicksville—LI
Highland Falls—NY
Hilton—Roch
Holley—WNY
Hollis—LI
Honeoye Falls—Roch
Hoosick Falls—A
Hopewell Jct—NY
Hornell—Roch
Horseheads—CNY
Hudson—A
Hudson Falls—A
Huntington—LI
Hyde Park—NY
Ilion—A
Irving—WNY
Irvington—NY
Islip—LI
Ithaca—CNY
Jackson Hts—LI
Jamaica—LI
Jamestown—WNY
Johnson City—CNY
Johnstown—A
Jordan—CNY
Katonah—NY
Keeseville—A
Keuka Park—Roch
Kew Gardens—LI
Kinderhook—A
Kingston—NY
Lake George—A
Lake Luzerne—A
Lake Placid—A
Lakeview—WNY
Lancaster—WNY

Larchmont—NY
Latham—A
LeRoy—WNY
Lewiston—WNY
Lindenhurst—LI
Little Falls—A
Liverpool—CNY
Lockport—WNY
Locust Valley—LI
Long Bch—LI
Long Is City—LI
Lowville—CNY
Lyons—Roch
Mahopac—NY
Malone—A
Mamaroneck—NY
Manhasset—LI
Manlius—CNY
Marathon—CNY
Marcellus—CNY
Margaretville—A
Marlboro—NY
Massapequa—LI
Massena—A
Mastic Bch—LI
Mattituck—LI
Mayville—WNY
Mechanicville—A
Medford—LI
Medina—WNY
Mexico—CNY
Middletown—NY
Millbrook—NY
Mohawk—A
Mohegan Lake—NY
Monroe—NY
Montgomery—NY
Monticello—NY
Montour Falls—Roch
Montrose—NY
Moravia—CNY
Morris—A
Morristown—A
Mt Kisco—NY
Mt Vernon—NY
Nedrow—A
Newark—Roch
New Berlin—CNY
New City—NY
New Hamburg—NY
New Hartford—CNY
New Hyde Park—LI
New Lebanon—A
New Paltz—NY
New Rochelle—NY
New Windsor—NY
Newburgh—NY
Newcomb—A
Niagara Falls—WNY

N Belmore—LI
N Creek—A
N Granville—A
N Salem—NY
N Tonawanda—WNY
Northport—LI
Norwich—CNY
Norwood—A
Nyack—NY
Oakdale—LI
Oceanside—LI
Odessa—Roch
Ogdensburg—A
Old Forge—A
Olean—WNY
Oneida—CNY
Oneonta—A
Orchard Pk—WNY
Ossining—NY
Oswego—CNY
Owego—CNY
Oxford—CNY
Oyster Bay—LI
Palenville—A
Palmyra—Roch
Parishville—CNY
Patchogue—LI
Patterson—NY
Paul Smiths—A
Pawling—NY
Pearl River—NY
Peekskill—NY
Pelham—NY
Penfield—Roch
Penn Yan—Roch
Perry—WNY
Philmont—A
Pierrepont Manor—
   CNY
Pine Plains—NY
Pittsford—Roch
Plainview—LI
Plattsburgh—A
Pleasant Valley—NY
Pleasantville—NY
Pt Chester—NY
Pt Jefferson—LI
Pt Jervis—NY
Pt Leyden—CNY
Pt Washington—LI
Potsdam—A
Pottersville—A
Poughkeepsie—NY
Pulaski—CNY
Queens Village—LI
Quogue—LI
Randolph—WNY
Red Hook—NY
Rensselaer—A
Rensselaerville—A

Rhinebeck—NY
Richfield Spgs—A
Riverhead—LI
Rochester—Roch
Rockville Ctr—LI
Rome—CNY
Ronkonkoma—LI
Roosevelt—LI
Roosevelt Is—NY
Rosedale—LI
Roslyn—LI
Round Lake—A
Rye—NY
Sackets Hbr—CNY
Sag Hbr—LI
St Albans—LI
St James—LI
Salamanca—WNY
Salem—A
Saranac Lake—A
Saratoga Spgs—A
Saugerties—NY
Savona—Roch
Sayville—LI
Scarsdale—NY
Schenectady—A
Schenevus—A
Schroon Lake—A
Schuylerville—A
Scottsville—Roch
Sea Cliff—LI
Seaford—LI
Selden—LI
Seneca Falls—CNY
Shelter Is—LI
Sherburne—CNY
Sherrill—CNY
Shoreham—LI
Sidney—A
Silver Creek—WNY
Skaneateles—CNY
Slaterville Spgs—CNY
Smithtown—LI
Sodus—Roch
Somers—NY
So Fallsburgh—NY
Southampton—LI
So New Berlin—CNY
S Ozone Park—LI
So Salem—NY
Sparkill—NY
Spring Valley—NY
Springfield Ctr—A
Springfield Gdns—LI
Springville—WNY
Staatsburg—NY
Stafford—WNY
Stamford—A
Star Lake—A
Staten Is—NY

Stockport—A
Stone Ridge—NY
Stony Brook—LI
Stony Pt—NY
Suffern—NY
Syracuse—CNY
Tannersville—A
Tarrytown—NY
Ticonderoga—A
Tivoli—NY
Tomkins Cove—NY
Tonawanda—WNY
Troy—A
Trumansburg—CNY
Tupper Lake—A
Tuxedo Park—NY
Twilight Park—A
Unadilla—A
Utica—CNY
Valley Cottage—NY
Valley Stream—LI
Waddington—A
Wading River—LI
Walden—NY
Walton—A
Wantagh—LI
Wappingers Falls—NY
Warrensburg—A
Warsaw—WNY
Warwick—NY
Washingtonville—NY
Waterford—A
Waterloo—CNY
Watertown—CNY
Watervliet—A
Watkins Glen—Roch
Waverly—CNY
Webster—Roch
Wellsville—A
W Middleburgh—A
W Park—NY
Westbury—LI
Westfield—WNY
Westford—A
Westhampton Bch—LI
White Plains—NY
Whitehall—A
Whitesboro—CNY
Whitestone—LI
Willard—CNY
Williamsville—WNY
Williston Pk—LI
Wilson—WNY
Windsor—CNY
Woodhaven—LI
Woodside—LI
Woodstock—NY
Yaphank—LI
Yonkers—NY
Youngstown—WNY

DIOCESE OF NEW YORK
(PROVINCE II)
Comprises 10 counties in southern New York
DIOCESAN OFFICE 1047 Amsterdam Ave New York NY 10025
TEL (212) 316-7400   FAX (212) 316-7405
E-MAIL info@dioceseny.org   WEB www.dioceseny.org

Previous Bishops—
Samuel Provoost 1787-1815, Benj Moore asst 1801 Bp 1815-16, John H Hobart asst 1811 Bp 1816-30, Benj T Onderdonk 1830-61, Jonathan M Wainwright provis 1852-54, Horatio Potter provis 1854 Bp 1861-87, Henry C Potter asst 1883 Bp 1887-1908, David H Greer coadj 1904 Bp 1908-19, Chas S Burch suffr 1911 Bp 1919-20, Wm T Manning 1921-46, Arthur S Lloyd suffr 1921-36, Herbert Shipman suffr 1921-30, Chas K Gilbert suffr 1930 Bp 1947-50, Chas F Boynton suffr 1951-69, Horace WB Donegan suffr 1947-50, coadj 1950 Bp 1950-72, Harold L Wright suffr 1974-78, James S Wetmore suffr 1960-87, Paul Moore Jr coadj 1969 Bp 1972-89, Walter D Dennis suffr 1979-1998, Richard F Grein coadj 1989 Bp 1989-2001, Mark S Sisk coadj 1998-2001 Bp 2001-2013, Catherine S Roskam suffr 1996-2012

Bishop—Rt Rev Andrew ML Dietsche (Dio 2 Feb 2013)

Bishop Suffragan—Rt Rev Allen K Shin

Assistant Bishop—Rt Rev Mary D Glasspool

Chanc G Wade; *V-Chanc* R Vandenberg Jr A Yurke; *Treas* Sr F Margaret CHS; *Sec of Conv & Reg* JA Forde Sr; *Asst Sec of Conv* S Saavedra; *Cn to Ord* Rev Cn JD Perris; *Hist* W Kempton *Cn Min* Rev Cn C Simmons; *Cn Trans Min* Rev Cn L Smith; *Cn Pastor* Rev Cn KJ Person; *Cn for Congregational Vitality* Rev Cn A Perez-Bullard; *Liaison for Global Miss* Rev Y Bass-Choate; *Liaison for Campus & Yng Adult Min* Rev M C Young

Stand Comm—Cler: R Cole J Ferguson C Roland Guzman O Thompson; *Lay:* C Greenidge C Williams D Levitt T Pinckney

PARISHES, MISSIONS, AND CLERGY

Amenia St Thomas Church **P** 40 Leedsville Rd 12501-5836 (Mail to: 40 Leedsville Rd 12501-5836) Lois Szost (845) 373-9161

Arden St Johns Church **P** (44) 26 Homestead Dr 10910-0051 (Mail to: General Delivery 10910-9999) (845) 351-4696

Ardsley St Barnabas Church **P** (97) 2 Revolutionary Rd 10502 (Mail to: 2 Revolutionary Rd 10502-1512) (914) 693-3366

Armonk St Stephens Church **P** (233) 50 Bedford Rd 10504-1830 (Mail to: 50 Bedford Rd 10504-1814) Nils Chittenden (914) 273-3812

Beacon St Andrew and St Luke Episcopal Church **P** 850 Wolcott Ave 12508-4081 (Mail to: 15 South Ave 12508-3114)

Bedford St Matthews Church **P** (1522) 382 Cantitoe St 10507 (Mail to: PO Box 293 10506-0293) Richard Pike John Zahl (914) 234-9636

Brewster St Andrews Church **P** (273) 26 Prospect St 10509-1216 (Mail to: 26 Prospect St 10509-1216) (845) 279-4325

Briarcliff All Saints Church **P** (192) 201 Scarborough Rd 10510-2043 (Mail to: 201 Scarborough Rd 10510-2043) Ann Douglas Yejide Peters (914) 941-6955

Briarcliff St Marys Church **P** (65) 669 Albany Post Rd 10510-2428 (Mail to: 669 Albany Post Rd 10510-2428) (914) 941-3030

Bronx Christ Church Riverdale **P** (339) 5030 Henry Hudson Pkwy 10471-3297 (Mail to: 5030 Henry Hudson Pkwy 10471-3297) Andrew Butler (718) 543-1011

Bronx Church of the Atonement **P** (102) 1344-44 Beach Ave 10472-1909 (Mail to: 1344 Beach Ave 10472-1909) (718) 828-6078

Bronx Church of the Good Shepherd **P** (328) 4401 Matilda Ave 10470-1502 (Mail to: 4401 Matilda Ave 10470-1502) Calvin Mcintyre Joanne Izzo (718) 324-2347

Bronx Church of the Holy Nativity **P** (161) 3061 Bainbridge Ave 10467-3904 (Mail to: 3061 Bainbridge Ave 10467-3999) (718) 652-0443

Bronx Church of the Mediator **P** (305) 260 W 231st St 10463-3904 (Mail to: 260 W 231st St 10463-3904) (718) 548-0944

Bronx Grace Church **P** (45) 104 City Island Ave 10464-1660 (Mail to: 116 City Island Ave 10464-0131) John Covington (718) 885-1080

Bronx Grace Church (West Farms) **P** (112) 1909 Vyse Ave 10460-4343 (Mail to: 1909 Vyse Ave 10460-4343) (718) 542-1946

Bronx Haitian Congregation of the Good Samaritan **P** (80) 777 E 222nd St 10467-5105 (Mail to: 777 E 222nd St 10467-5105) (718) 881-3779

Bronx Iglesia de San Juan Bautista **M** (45) 948 E 156th St 10455-1998 (Mail to: 948 E 156th St 10455-1914) Maria Servellon (718) 893-0376

Bronx St Andrews Episcopal Church **P** (346) 781 Castle Hill Ave 10473-1330 (Mail to: Attn Linda Philips 781 Castle Hill Ave 10473-1396) Allen George Yesupatham Duraikannu (718) 863-2244

Bronx St Anns Church **P** (470) 295 St Ann Ave 10454 (Mail to: 295 Saint Anns Ave 10454-2597) Martha Overall (718) 585-5632

Bronx St Davids Church **P** (152) 384 E 160th St # 200 10451-4404 (Mail to: PO Box 200 10451-0200) Bertram Bennett (718) 665-2747

Bronx St Edmunds Church **P** (55) 1905 Morris Ave 10453-5903 (Mail to: 1905 Morris Ave 10453-5903) Udochukwu Nnaji (718) 299-7567

Bronx St James Church, Fordham **P** (697) 2500 Jerome Ave 10468-4300 (Mail to: 2500 Jerome Ave 10468-4300) William Cusano (718) 367-0655

Bronx Saint Joseph's Church **P** (174) 155 Dreiser Loop 10475-2703 (Mail to: Attn: Glynis Bruce 155 Dreiser Loop 10475-2703) Simeon Johnson (718) 320-0844

Bronx Saint Luke's Episcopal Church **P** (780) Attn Mr Bookal 777 E 222nd St 10467-5105 (Mail to: 777 E 222nd St 10467-5105) Pierre-Andre Duvert (718) 882-3060

Bronx St Margarets Church (Longwood) **P** (136) 940 E 156th St 10455-1914 (Mail to: 940 E 156th St 10455-1998) Theodora Brooks (718) 589-4430

Bronx St Marthas Church **P** (45) 1858 Hunt Ave 10462-3623 (Mail to: 1858 Hunt Ave 10462-3623) Eliza Davies-Aryeequaye (718) 792-3681

Bronx St Pauls Church **P** (100) 489 Saint Pauls Pl 10456-1935 (Mail to: PO Box 507 10456-0520) Horton Scott Ralph Smith (347) 269-7604

Bronx St Peters Church **P** (159) 2500 Westchester Ave 10461-3543 (Mail to: 2500 Westchester Ave 10461-4588) Joade Dauer-Cardasis (718) 931-9270

Bronx St Simeons Church **P** (105) 1858 Hunt Ave 10462-3623 (Mail to: C/O St Marthas Church PO Box 950A 10451) (718) 824-9188

Bronx St Stephens Church (Woodlawn) **P** (65) 439 E 238th St 10470-1701 (Mail to: 439 E 238th St 10470-1701) (718) 324-5427

Bronx Trinity Church of Morrisania **P** (181) 698 East 166th Street 10456-5699 (Mail to: 698 E 166th St 10456-5699) Howard Blunt (718) 542-1309

Bronxville Christ Church **P** (550) Att: Katherine Gojkovich 17 Sagamore Rd 10708-1502 (Mail to: Att: Jocelyn Angelone 17 Sagamore Rd 10708-1599) Michael Bird Jennifer Brown (914) 337-3544

Callicoon St James Church **P** (25) Route 17b 12723 (Mail to: P.O. Box 296 12723-0296) Elizabeth Groskoph Ralph Groskoph (845) 887-4742

Chappaqua Church of St Mary the Virgin **P** (373) 191 South Greeley Avenue 10514 (Mail to: PO Box 380 10514-0380) Alan Dennis (914) 238-8751

Chelsea St Marks Church (Chelsea on Hudson) **P** (9) 9 Liberty St 12512 (Mail to: PO Box 252 12512-0252) (845) 838-1886

Chester St Pauls Church **P** (98) 101 Main St 10918-1328 (Mail to: 101 Main St 10918-1328) (845) 469-2616

Cold Spring St Marys Church in the Highlands **P** (234) 1 Chestnut St 10516-2516 (Mail to: 1 Chestnut St 10516-2598) (845) 265-2539

Cornwall St John's Church **P** (210) 66 Clinton St 12518-1558 (Mail to: PO Box 783 12518-0783) Suzanne Toro (845) 534-5475

Croton Hdsn St Augustines Episcopal Church **P** (278) 6 Old Post Rd 10520-2016 (Mail to: 6 Old Post Rd 10520-2016) Jennifer Owen Beth Glover Sharon Manning-Lew (914) 271-3501

Dobbs Ferry Zion Church **P** (98) 55 Cedar St 10522-1711 (Mail to: 55 Cedar St 10522-1711) Mary Grambsch (914) 693-9320

Dover Plains Mision Ep Santiago Apostol **P** (30) 12 Reimer Ave 12522-5136 (Mail to: PO Box 336 12522-0336) (203) 605-0090

Eastchester St Lukes Church **P** (44) 100 Stewart Ave 10709-5799 (Mail to: 98 Stewart Ave 10709-5799) Charles Pridemore (914) 961-3856

Ellenville St Johns Memorial Church **P** (73) 40 Market St 12428-2132 (Mail to: PO Box 262 12428) (845) 647-7084

Fishkill Trinity Church **P** (346) 1200 Main St 12524-1890 (Mail to: PO Box 484 12524-0484) Garrett Mettler (845) 896-9884

Garnerville Trinity Church **P** (113) 28 Chapel St 10923 (Mail to: 28 Chapel St 10923-1209) (845) 947-1090

Garrison St Philips in the Highlands **P** (310) 1101 Route 9d 10524-3638 (Mail to: PO Box 158 10524-0158) Stephen Holton (845) 424-3571

Goshen St James Church **P** (528) 1 Saint James Pl 10924-2013 (Mail to: 1 Saint James Pl 10924-2013) Michael Lunden Thomas Liotta (845) 294-6225

Granite Spgs Church Of The Good Shepherd **P** (214) 39 Granite Springs Rd 10527-1108 (Mail to: 39 Granite Springs Rd 10527-1108) Harry Roark (914) 248-5631

Greenwood Lake Church of the Good Shepherd **P** (31) 62 Windermere Ave 10925-0011 (Mail to: PO Box 11 10925-0011) (845) 477-2191

Harrison All Saints Church **P** (148) 300 Harrison Ave 10528-3328 (Mail to: 300 Harrison Ave 10528-3360) (914) 835-4716

Hartsdale St Andrews Episcopal Church **P** (47) 101 Central Ave 10530-1912 (Mail to: 101 Central Ave 10530-1912) (914) 946-7931

Hastings Hds Grace Episcopal Church **P** (246) 78 Main St 10706-1602 (Mail to: 78 Main St 10706-1602) Martha Korienek (914) 478-1779

Highland Falls Holy Innocents **P** (200) 401 Main St 10928-0116 (Mail to: P.O. Box116 10928-2016) Judith Ferguson (845) 446-2197

Highland Falls Saint Mark's Church **M** 9 St Marks Place Ft. Montgomery 10928 (Mail to: 40 Main St 11978-0887) (631) 288-2111

Hopewell Junction Church of the Resurrection **P** (89) 182 Route 376 12533-6083 (Mail to: 182 Route 376 12533-6083) Janice Kotuby (845) 226-5727

Hyde Park Saint James Church **P** (204) 4526 Albany Post Rd 12538-1564 (Mail to: 4526 Albany Post Rd 12538-1564) Charles Kramer David Bender Gail Ganter-Toback (845) 229-2820

Irvington St Barnabas Church **P** (559) 15 Broadway 10533-1802 (Mail to: 15 Broadway 10533-1898) Allison Moore (914) 591-8194

Katonah St Luke's Episcopal Church **P** (159) 68 Bedford Rd 10536-2117 (Mail to: PO Box 602 10536-0602) (914) 232-5220

Kingston Church of the Holy Cross **P** (265) 30 Pine Grove Ave 12401-5408 (Mail to: 30 Pine Grove Ave 12401-5408) Frank Alagna Maria Servellon (845) 331-6796

Kingston St Johns Episcopal Church **P** (300) 207 Albany Ave 12401-2511 (Mail to: PO Box 1221 12402-1221) Susan Bonsteel Michelle Meech (845) 331-2252

Larchmont St Johns Church **P** (766) 4 Fountain Sq 10538-4106 (Mail to: 4 Fountain Sq 10538-4199) Alissa Anderson Gwyneth Murphy (914) 834-2981

Mahopac Church of the Holy Communion **P** (96) 1055 Route 6 10541-3402 (Mail to: 1055 Route 6 10541-3402) Kathleen Berkowe David Morris (845) 628-6144

Mamaroneck St Thomas Church **P** (224) 168 W Boston Post Rd 10543-3605 (Mail to: 168 W Boston Post Rd 10543-3605) Carol Gadsden Tami Burks (914) 698-0300

Marlboro Christ Church **P** (122) 222 Old Post Rd 12542-6534 (Mail to: PO Box 27 12542-0027) Robert Pierson (845) 220-7478

Middletown Grace Church **P** (385) 58 North St 10940-5011 (Mail to: 12 Depot St 10940-5707) Victor Sarrazin (845) 343-6101

Millbrook Grace Church **P** (547) 3328 Franklin Ave 12545-5969 (Mail to: PO Box 366 12545-0366) Matthew Calkins (845) 677-3064

Millbrook St Peters Church Lithgow **P** (363) 692 Deep Hollow Rd 12545-1502 (Mail to: PO Box 1502 12545-1502) Albert Ogle (845) 677-9286

Mohegan Lake St Marys Church **P** (256) 1836 E Main St 10547 (Mail to: 1836 E Main St 10547-1226) (914) 528-3972

Monroe Grace Episcopal Church **P** (55) 1 Forest Ave 10950-2809 (Mail to: 1 Forest Ave 10950-2809) (845) 782-8535

Montgomery St Francis of Assisi **P** (28) 74 Wallkill Ave 12549 (Mail to: PO Box 708 12586-0708) Margaret Sullivan (845) 457-7545

Monticello St Johns Episcopal Church **P** (91) 15 St John St 12701-2118 (Mail to: 14 Saint John St 12701-2118) (845) 807-3050

Montrose Church of the Divine Love **P** (193) 80 Sunset Rd 10548 (Mail to: 80 Sunset Rd 10548-1334) (484) 737-1080

Mount Kisco St Marks Church **P** (271) 85 E Main St 10549 (Mail to: 85 E Main St 10549-2313) William Doubleday (914) 666-8058

Mount Vernon Sts John Paul & Clement **P** (• 126 S 9th Ave 10550-3019 (Mail to: 126 S • Ave 10550-3019) (914) 668-0551

Mount Vernon Church of the Ascension **P** (1• 104 Park Ave 10550-1410 (Mail to: 104 Pa Ave 10550-1410) (914) 668-4851

Mount Vernon Trinity Church **P** (113) 335 S • Ave 10550-4103 (Mail to: 335 S 4th Ave 105 4103) (914) 667-8409

New City St Johns Church **P** (246) 365 Strawto• Rd 10956-6632 (Mail to: Attn Margaret Gilles 365 Strawtown Rd 10956-6632) (845) 634-36(

New Hamburg St Nicholas on the Hudson (215) 37 Point St 12590-5529 (Mail to: 37 Po• St 12590-5529) Leigh Hall (845) 297-2010

New Paltz St Andrews Episcopal Church **P** (1: 163 Main St 12561-1116 (Mail to: 163 Main 12561-1116) Robin James (845) 255-5098

New Rochelle Church of St Simon the Cyren• **P** (91) 135 Remington Pl 10801 (Mail to: • Remington Pl 10801-3925) Paulette Remp• (914) 632-5911

New Rochelle St Johns Church Wilmot **P** (94) Wilmot Rd 10804-1514 (Mail to: 11 Wilmot 10804-1514) Jennie Talley (914) 636-0047

New Rochelle Trinity St Pauls Episcopal **P** (1• 311 Huguenot St 10801-7208 (Mail to: 3 Huguenot St 10801-7208) Hollis Galga• Hyacinth Lee (914) 632-5368

New Windsor St Thomas Episcopal Church (103) 47 Old Route 9w 12553-5480 (Mail PO Box 4221 12553-0221) (845) 562-4712

New York All Angels Church **P** (456) 251 W 8• St 10024-5743 (Mail to: 251 W 80th St 100: 5798) Christine Lee (212) 362-9300

New York All Saints Church **P** (225) 230 E 6(St 10065 (Mail to: 230 E 60th St 10022-14• Steven Yagerman Andrew Mullins (212) 7: 0447

New York All Souls Church **P** (65) 88 Sa• Nicholas Ave 10026-2926 (Mail to: 88 Sa• Nicholas Ave 10026-2926) Frank Mora• (212) 663-2351

New York Calvary & St George Church **P** (600• 61 Gramercy Park 10010 (Mail to: 61 Gramer Park Apt 501 10010-5406) Benjamin DeH Jacob Smith (646) 723-4178

✠ **New York** Cathedral of St John the Divine **O** 1047 Amsterdam Ave 10025-1747 (Mail C/O Donna-Mari Fieldsa 1047 Amsterda Ave 10025-1747) Steven Lee Kenton Cur Clifton Daniel Patrick Malloy (212) 316-740•

New York Christ & St Stephens Church **P** (5• 120 W 69th St 10023-5194 (Mail to: 120 69th St Ste 1 10023-5194) Linda Liles • Gordon James Hagen (212) 787-2755

New York Church Of Saint Mary The Virgin• (308) 145 W 46th St 10036-8591 (Mail to: 1 W 46th St 10036-8591) Stephen Gerth Jam Pace Peter Powell James Smith Rebecca Weir Tompkins (212) 869-5830

New York Church of the Ascension **P** (177) 12 W 11th St 10011-8602 (Mail to: 12 W 11th St 10011-8695) Edwin Chinery Lisa Krakowsky Lisa Krakowsky Elizabeth Maxwell (212) 254-8620

New York Church of the Crucifixion **P** (144) 459 W 149th St 10031-2704 (Mail to: 459 W 149th St 10031-2704) (212) 281-0900

New York Church of the Good Shepherd **P** (58) 240 E 31st St 10016 (Mail to: 236 E 31st St 100166303) Mary Grambsch (212) 689-1595

New York Church Of The Heavenly Rest **P** (1601) 1085 Fifth Avenue 10128-0114 (Mail to: 1085 Fifth Avenue 10128-0144) Euan Cameron Matthew Heyd Cynthia Stravers Philippa Turner Anne Witchger (212) 289-3400

New York Church of the Holy Apostles **P** (142) 296 9th Ave 10001-5703 (Mail to: C/O Michael Ottley 296 9th Ave 10001-5703) Anna Pearson Peter Carey Susan Hill Robert Jacobs Andrew Kadel (212) 807-6799

New York Church of the Holy Trinity **P** (704) 316 E 88th St 10128-4909 (Mail to: 316 E 88th St 10128-4999) John Beddingfield Paul Feuerstein John Morelli (212) 289-4100

New York Church of the Incarnation **P** (464) 209 Madison Ave 10016-3814 (Mail to: 209 Madison Ave 10016-3814) John Ousley Adrian Dannhauser (212) 689-6350

New York Church of the Intercession **P** (215) 550 W 155th St 10032 (Mail to: 550 W 155th St 10032-7899) (212) 283-6200

New York Church of the Resurrection **P** (148) 119 E 74th St 10021 (Mail to: 119 E 74th St 10021-3299) Barry Swain E Michael Allen James Harkins Horace Hitchcock (212) 879-4320

New York Church Of The Transfiguration **P** (380) 1 E 29th St 10016-7405 (Mail to: Attn Bookkeeper 1 E 29th St 10016-7405) Patrick Cheng David Fleenor Paul Metzler John Van Dooren (212) 684-6770

New York Congregation of St Saviour **P** (847) 1047 Amsterdam Ave 10025-1747 (Mail to: Attn Aaron W. Koch 1047 Amsterdam Ave 10025-1747) (212) 316-7483

New York Episcopal Church of Our Savior **P** (201) 48 Henry St 10002-6901 (Mail to: 48 Henry St 10002-6901) Ada Nagata (212) 233-2899

New York Eglise Du St Esprit **P** (146) 109-111 E 60th St 10022-1113 (Mail to: 111 E 60th St 10022-1113) Nigel Massey (212) 838-5680

New York Grace Church **P** (799) 802 Broadway 10003-4804 (Mail to: 802 Broadway 10003-4831) James Waring Nicholas Danford Julia Offinger (212) 254-2000

New York Holy Trinity Church - Inwood **P** (78) 20 Cumming St 10034-4804 (Mail to: 20 Cumming St 10034-4804) Rebecca Barnes (212) 567-1177

New York Church of the Holyrood **P** (196) 715 W 179th St 10033 (Mail to: 715 W 179th St 10033-6020) James Hagen (212) 923-3770

New York St Ambrose Church **P** (105) 9 W 130th St 10037 (Mail to: C/O Reuben Best 9 W 130th St 10037-3638) Wayne Dodson (212) 283-2175

New York St Andrews Church **P** (149) 2067 5th Ave 10035-1219 (Mail to: 2067 5th Ave 10035-1297) Terry Jackson (212) 534-0896

New York St Ann's Church For the Deaf **M** (12) 209 E 16th St 10003-3702 (Mail to: 209 E 16th St 10003-3702) (347) 458-9571

New York St Augustines Church **P** (342) 290 Henry St 10002 (Mail to: 333 Madison St 10002-5706) Nathanael Saint-Pierre (212) 673-5300

New York St Clements Church **P** (54) 423 W 46th St 10036-3510 (Mail to: 423 W 46th St 10036-3592) Shawn Duncan Jeffrey Hamblin (212) 246-7277

New York St James Church **P** (3148) 865 Madison Ave 10021-4103 (Mail to: 865 Madison Ave 10021-4195) Brenda Husson Ryan Fleenor Ryan Fleenor Eva Suarez Zachary Thompson (212) 774-4240

New York St Johns in Village Church **P** (185) 224 Waverly Pl 10014-2405 (Mail to: 224 Waverly Pl 10014-2405) Denise Lavetty Graeme Napier (212) 243-6192

New York St Lukes Church **P** (53) 435 W 141st St 10031-6401 (Mail to: 435 W 141st St 10031-6401) (212) 926-2713

New York St Marks Church in the Bowery **P** (205) 131 E 10th St 10003-7504 (Mail to: 131 E 10th St 10003-7590) Winnie Varghese Anne Sawyer (212) 674-6377

New York St Martins Church **P** (166) 230 Lenox Avenue 10027-6340 (Mail to: 230 Malcolm X Blvd 10027-6396) Johan Johnson (212) 534-4531

New York St Marys Church (Manhattanville) **P** (195) 521 W 126th St 10027-2496 (Mail to: 521 W 126th St 10027-2496) Patricia Ackerman Douglas Clark Gordon Duggins Mary Foulke Stephanie Shockley (212) 864-4013

New York St Michaels Church **P** (714) 225 W 99th St 10025-5014 (Mail to: 225 W 99th St 10025-5014) Katharine Flexer Leigh Mackintosh David Rider (212) 222-2700

New York St Peters Church **P** (70) 346 W 20th St 10011-3302 (Mail to: 346 W 20th St 10011-3398) Victoria Duncan Stephen Harding (212) 929-2390

New York St Philip's Church **P** (204) 204 W 134 St 10030 (Mail to: 204 W 134th St 10030-3098) Terence Lee Chloe Breyer Fitzroy Edwards (212) 862-4940

New York Saint Thomas Church **P** (1715) § 1 W 53rd St 10019-5401 (Mail to: 1 W 53rd St 10019-5496) Anne Mallonee David McNeeley Matthew Moretz Nathan Ritter Adam Spencer Carl Turner (212) 757-7013

New York St Bartholomews Church **P** (5506) 325 Park Ave 10022-6814 (Mail to: 325 Park Ave

10022-6814) Susan Anderson-Smith Clayton Crawley Kristina Lewis-Theerman Lynn Sanders Dean Wolfe (212) 378-0265

New York Church of St Edward the Martyr **P** (239) 14 E 109th St 10029-3402 (Mail to: 14 E 109th St 10029-3402) William Derby Matthew Buccheri Alejandra Trillos (212) 369-1140

New York The Church of St Ignatius of Antioch **P** (266) 552 W End Ave 10024-2707 (Mail to: 552 W End Ave 10024-2796) Andrew Blume Paul Kahn (212) 580-3326

New York The Church Of Saint Luke In The Fields **P** (857) 487 Hudson St 10014-2851 (Mail to: 487 Hudson St 10014-6397) Caroline Stacey Milton Gatch Gina Gore William Ogburn Bo Reynolds (212) 924-0562

New York Church of St Matthew and St Timothy **P** (100) 26 W 84th St 10024-4702 (Mail to: 26 W 84th St 10024-4702) Carla Roland George Diaz (212) 362-6750

New York The Church of the Epiphany **P** (220) 1393 York Ave 10021-3407 (Mail to: 1393 York Ave 10021-3407) R Anne Auchincloss J Barrington Bates Jennifer Reddall Horace Whyte Joseph Zorawick (212) 737-2720

New York Trinity Parish **P** (970) § 120 Broadway 38th Fl 10271-0002 (Mail to: 120 Broadway 38th Fl 10271-0002) Phillip Jackson Elizabeth Blunt Mark Bozzuti-Jones Clayton Crawley Bruce Jenneker Cece Loua William Lupfer Kristin Miles Benjamin Musoke-Lubega Daniel Simons (212) 602-0800

Newburgh Church of the Good Shepherd **P** (27) 271 Broadway 12550-5452 (Mail to: PO Box 2865 12550-0119) (845) 562-8545

Newburgh Iglesia Del Buen Pastor **M** (42) 270 Broadway & Mill St 12550 (Mail to: PO Box 2865 12550-0119) (845) 562-8545

Newburgh St Georges Episcopal Church **P** (160) 105 Grand St 12550 (Mail to: 105 Grand St 12550-4613) Dustin Trowbridge (845) 561-5355

North Salem St James Church **P** (334) 296 Titicus Road 10560 (Mail to: PO Box 459 10560-0459) Garrett Mettler (914) 669-5563

Nyack Grace Church **P** (803) 130 First Ave 10960 (Mail to: 130 1st Ave 10960-2633) Owen Thompson Anne Ross (845) 358-1297

Ossining St Pauls on the Hill Epis Church **P** (144) 40 Ganung Dr 10562-3936 (Mail to: 40 Ganung Dr 10562-3944) Charles Mayer (914) 941-6627

Ossining Trinity Church **P** (117) 7 South Highland Avenue Post Office Box # 108 10562-4803 (Mail to: PO Box 108 10562-0108) J Cooper Conway (914) 941-0806

Patterson Christ Church **P** (24) 590 Route 11 12563-0569 (Mail to: PO Box 569 12563-0569) (845) 878-8027

Pawling Holy Trinity Church **P** (232) 22 Coulter Ave 12564-1109 (Mail to: 22 Coulter Ave 12564-1109) (845) 855-5276

Pearl River St Stephens Church **P** (356) 84 Ehrhardt Rd 10965-1930 (Mail to: 84 Ehrhardt Rd 10965-1930) (845) 735-8588

Peekskill St Peters Episcopal Church **P** (216) 137 Division St 10566 (Mail to: 137 Division St 10566-2788) Robert Hamlyn Janet Nunley (914) 737-6312

Pelham Parish of Christ the Redeemer **P** (625) 1415 Pelhamdale Ave 10803-3312 (Mail to: 1415 Pelhamdale Ave 10803-3312) Matthew Mead John Zacker (914) 738-5516

Pine Plains Church of the Regeneration **P** (81) 18 Pine St 12567-5209 (Mail to: PO Box 321 12567-0321) (518) 398-5628

Pleasant Valley St Pauls Episcopal Church **P** (119) 808 Traver Rd 12569 (Mail to: PO Box 1449 12569-1449) Megan Sanders (845) 635-2854

Pleasantville Saint John's Church **P** (342) 8 Sunnyside Ave 10570-3125 (Mail to: C/O Treasurer Ken Foley 8 Sunnyside Ave 10570-3125) Mary Gregorius (914) 769-0053

Port Chester St Peters Church **P** (210) Westchester Ave at Pearl St 10573 (Mail to: 19 Smith St 10573-4505) Mario Martinez John Morelli (914) 939-1244

Port Jervis Grace Church **P** (126) 84 Seward Ave 12771 (Mail to: 84 Seward Ave 12771-2006) David Carlson (845) 856-3026

Poughkeepsie Christ Church **P** (288) 20 Carroll St 12601-4314 (Mail to: 20 Carroll St 12601-4396) Arnulfo Arambulo Susan Fortunato (845) 452-8220

Poughkeepsie Iglesia de la Virgen de Guadalupe **M** (159) 20 Carroll St 12601 (Mail to: 20 Carroll St 12601-4314) (845) 452-8225

Poughkeepsie St Andrews Episcopal Church **P** (20) 110 Overlook Rd 12603-6200 (Mail to: 110 Overlook Rd 12603-6200) (845) 452-6832

Poughkeepsie St Pauls Church **P** (179) 161 Mansion St 12601-2524 (Mail to: 161 Mansion St 12601-2524) Bradley Jones (845) 452-8440

Red Hook Christ Church of Red Hook **P** (126) 7423 S Broadway 12571-1747 (Mail to: 7423 S Broadway 12571-1747) (845) 758-1591

Red Hook St John the Evangelist **P** (180) 1114 River Rd 12571-2938 (Mail to: 1114 River Rd 12571-2938) Mary Grace Williams (845) 758-6433

Rhinebeck Church Of The Messiah **P** (625) 6436 Montgomery St 12572 (Mail to: PO Box 248 12572-0248) Richard McKeon (845) 876-3533

Roosevelt Island Good Shepherd Ch Roosevelt Isl **M** (66) 543 Main St 10044 (Mail to: PO Box 361 10044-0207) (917) 843-3338

Rye Christ's Church **P** (2140) 2 Rectory St 10580-3818 (Mail to: C/O Finance Office 2 Rectory St 10580-3818) Michael Kurth Catherine Lawrence Katherine Malin (914) 967-1749

Saugerties Trinity Church **P** (35) 32 Church St 12477-1809 (Mail to: 32 Church St 12477-1809) Michael Phillips (845) 246-6312

Scarsdale Church of St James the Less **P** (443) 10 Church Lane 10583-5604 (Mail to: 10 Church Ln 10583-4216) Astrid Storm (914) 723-6100

Somers Saint Luke's Church **P** (204) 331 Rte 100 10589-3204 (Mail to: Attn: Kay 331 Route 100 10589-3204) Michael Watson (914) 277-3122

South Fallsburg St Andrews Church **M** (10) 5277 State Route 42 12779-5726 (Mail to: PO Box 55 12788-0055) (845) 436-7539

South Salem St Johns Church **P** (205) 82 Spring St 10590-1417 (Mail to: PO Box 394 10590-0394) Joseph Campo (914) 763-8273

Sparkill Christ Church **P** (60) New St 10976-1203 (Mail to: PO Box 177 10976-0177) Karen Lynn Depue (646) 373-6013

Spring Valley St Pauls Church **P** (345) 26 S Madison Ave 10977-5512 (Mail to: 26 S Madison Ave 10977-5512) Cheryl Parris (845) 356-1857

Staatsburg St Margarets Church **P** (83) 68 Old Post Rd 12580 (Mail to: PO Box 395 12580-0395) Charles Ford (845) 889-4181

Staten Island All Saints Church **P** (109) 2329 Victory Blvd 10314-6621 (Mail to: 2329 Victory Blvd 10314-6689) Lewis Marshall (718) 698-1338

Staten Island Christ Church New Brighton **P** (239) 76 Franklin Ave 10301-1239 (Mail to: 76 Franklin Ave 10301-1239) Trevor Babb Geraldine Swanson (718) 727-6100

Staten Island Church of the Ascension **P** (167) 1 Kingsley Ave 10314-2420 (Mail to: 1 Kingsley Ave 10314-2420) (718) 442-4187

Staten Island St Albans Episcopal Church **P** (208) 76 Saint Albans Pl 10312-5131 (Mail to: 76 Saint Albans Pl 10312-5199) John Morgan (718) 984-7756

Staten Island Church of St Andrew **P** (297) 40 Old Mill Rd 10306 (Mail to: 40 Old Mill Rd 10306-1197) Frederick Fausak Aaron Hudson (718) 351-0900

Staten Island St Johns Church **P** (250) 1333 Bay St 10305 (Mail to: 1333 Bay St 10305-3199) Rhoda Treherne-Thomas (718) 447-1605

Staten Island St Mary's Church Castleton **P** (133) 347 Davis Ave 10310 (Mail to: 347 Davis Ave 10310-1557) Horace Free (718) 442-1527

Staten Island St Pauls Church **P** (110) C/O Gwendloyn Simmons 77 Bard Ave 10310-1605 (Mail to: C/O Richard Mingoia 225 Saint Pauls Ave 10304-2246) (718) 273-9572

Staten Island St Simons Church **P** (63) 1055 Richmond Rd 10304-2401 (Mail to: 1055 Richmond Rd 10304-2401) (718) 987-5252

Staten Island St Stephens Church **P** (97) 7516 Amboy Rd 10307-1423 (Mail to: PO Box 50008 10305) William Baker (718) 984-1722

Stone Ridge Christ the King Church **P** (187) 3021 St Rt 213 E 12484-5101 (Mail to: 3021 State Route 213 E 12484-5101) Alison Quin Robin Beveridge Judith Borzumato Janet Vincent (845) 687-9414

Stony Point St Johns in the Wilderness **M** (63) 119 St John's Rd 10980-3624 (Mail to: 16 Johnsontown Road 10980) (845) 578-6036

Suffern Christ Church of Ramapo **P** (174) 65 Washington Ave 10901 (Mail to: 65 Washington Ave 10901-5619) (845) 357-1615

Tarrytown Christ Church **P** (120) 43 S Broadway 10591-4012 (Mail to: 43 S Broadway 10591-4095) Susan Copley (914) 631-2074

Tivoli St Pauls Church **P** (46) 39 Woods Rd 12583-5433 (Mail to: PO Box 68 12583-0068) (845) 757-3131

Tomkins Cove Church of St John the Divine **P** (52) 170 Mott Farm Rd 10986-1411 (Mail to: PO Box 92 10986-0092) (845) 786-5203

Tuxedo Park St Marys Church **P** (490) 10 Fox Hill Rd 10987-4224 (Mail to: PO Box 637 Fox Hill Road 10987-0637) Richard Datos-Robyn (845) 351-5122

Valley Cottage All Saints Episcopal Church **P** (64) 182 Ridge Rd 10989-2351 (Mail to: 182 Ridge Rd 10989-2351) (845) 268-9542

Walden Saint Andrew's Church **P** (140) 15 Walnut St 12586-1709 (Mail to: Attn: Jody Gridley PO Box 708 12586-0708) Margaret Sullivan (845) 778-5310

Wappingers Falls Zion Church **P** (650) 12 Saterlee Pl 12590-2600 (Mail to: 12 Saterlee Pl 12590-2600) Deborah Magdalene (845) 297-9797

Warwick Christ Church **P** (671) 50 South St 10990-1638 (Mail to: 50 South St 10990-1638) James Erwin Deborah Lee Elizabeth Wille (845) 986-3440

Washingtonville St Annes Church **P** (157) 179 E Main St 10992 (Mail to: 175 E Main St 10992-1723) Claire Lofgren (845) 496-3961

West Park Ch of Ascension & Holy Trinity **P** (108) 1585 Rte 9W 12493 (Mail to: PO Box 1512 12528-8512) Jennifer Barrows Teresa Jones Robert Pierson (845) 384-6723

White Plains Grace Church **P** (648) 33 Church St 10601 (Mail to: 33 Church St 10601-1995) Martha-Jane Dunphy Judith Lee Buddelov Adolfo Moronta (914) 949-2874

White Plains St Bartholomews Church **P** (57) 82 Prospect St 10606-3421 (Mail to: 82 Prospect St 10606-3499) Gawain De Leeuw (914) 949-5577

White Plains St Francis & St Marthas Church **P** (74) 575 Tarrytown Rd 10607 (Mail to: 133 Augustine Rd 10603-2039) Audrey Bailey (914) 946-8846

White Plains St Joseph of Arimathea Church **P** (78) 2172 Saw Mill River Rd 10607 (Mail to: 2172 Saw Mill River Rd 10607-2205) (914) 592-7163

Woodstock St Gregorys Episcopal Church **P** (94) 2578 Rte 212 12498 (Mail to: PO Box 66 12498-0066) Matthew Wright (845) 679-6394

Yonkers Church of the Holy Cross **P** (59) 81 Locust Hill Ave 10701 (Mail to: 81 Locust Hill

Ave 10701-2801) (914) 965-4070

Yonkers St Johns Church Gettys Sq **P** (130) 1 Hudson St 10701 (Mail to: 1 Hudson St 10701-3599) Victoria Sirota (914) 963-3033

Yonkers St Johns Church of Tuckahoe **P** (231) 100 Underhill St 10710-3615 (Mail to: 100 Underhill St 10710-3615) (914) 779-7024

Yonkers St Marks Church **P** (27) 1373 Nepperham Ave 10703-1011 (Mail to: 1373 Nepperhan Ave

10703-1011) Maxine Cleghorn (914) 965-3455

Yonkers Saint Paul's Church **P** (18) 636 Palisade Ave 10703-2122 (Mail to: 636 Palisade Ave 10703-2122) (914) 965-4967

Yonkers San Andres Church **P** (258) 22 Post St 10705 (Mail to: 22 Post St 10705-2241) (914) 963-9523

Ch of the Epiphany and Christ Ch **P** (Mail to: 105 Main St 07050-4026) Joseph Harmon

DIOCESE OF NEWARK
(PROVINCE II)
Comprises Northern New Jersey
DIOCESAN OFFICE 31 Mulberry St Newark NJ 07102
TEL (973) 430-9900   FAX (973) 622-3503
E-MAIL jking@dioceseofnewark.org   WEB www.dioceseofnewark.org

Previous Bishops—
Wm H Odenheimer 1874-79, Thomas A Starkey 1880-1903, Edwin S Lines 1903-27, Wilson R Stearly suffr 1915 coadj 1917 Bp 1927-35, Benj M Washburn coadj 1932 Bp 1935-58, Theodore R Ludlow suffr 1936-53, Donald MacAdie suffr 1958-63, Leland Stark coadj 1953 Bp 1958-73, George E Rath suffr 1964 coadj 1970 Bp 1974-78, John S Spong coadj 1976 Bp 1979-2000, Jack M McKelvey suffr 1991-99, John P Croneberger coadj 1998 Bp 2000-2007, Mark M Beckwith Bp 2007-18

Bishop—The Rt Rev Carlye J. Hughes (1109)
(Dio 22 Sep 2018)

Bp Exec Asst K Lark; *Dio Admin Off* JA King; *Cn to Ord* Rev GA Jacobs; *Asst* R Johnson; *CFO* S Reckford; *Chanc* DE Sammons

Stand Comm—Cler: Pres J Harmon C McCloud M Davis J Mennell; *Lay:* J Garde P Henderson N Horsky W Drake-Schneider

PARISHES, MISSIONS, AND CLERGY

Allendale Trinity Episcopal Church of Bergen County **P** (111) 55 George St 07401-1426 (Mail to: 55 George St 07401-1426) E Michael Allen (201) 327-3012

Bayonne Calvary Episcopal Church **P** (37) 956 Avenue C 07002-3022 (Mail to: C/O Sr Warden 956 Avenue C 07002-2413) (201) 339-3112

Bayonne Trinity Church **P** (78) 141 Broadway 07002-2459 (Mail to: 141 Broadway 07002-2459) Gregory Perez (201) 858-4460

Belvidere Epis Ch of St Luke and St Mary **P** 408 3rd St 07823-1834 (Mail to: 408 3rd St 07823-1834) Rosemarie Hassan (908) 818-9661

Bergenfield All Saints Episcopal Korean Church **M** (98) 12 W Central Ave 07621-1302 (Mail

to: 12 W Central Ave 07621-1302) (201) 244-1004

Boonton St Johns Episcopal Church **P** (213) 226 Cornelia St 07005-1712 (Mail to: 226 Cornelia St 07005-1712) Timothy Carr (973) 334-3655

Budd Lake Christ Episcopal Church **P** (98) 369 Sand Shore Rd 07828-2215 (Mail to: 369 Sand Shore Rd 07828-2215) (973) 347-1866

Chatham St Pauls Episcopal Church **P** (471) 200 Main St 07928-2406 (Mail to: 200 Main St 07928-2467) Mary Davis Ellen Kohn-Perry (973) 635-8085

Chester Church of the Messiah **P** (186) 50 State Route 24 07930-2410 (Mail to: 50 State Route 24 07930-2410) Linda Phillips (908) 879-7208

Cliffside Pk Trinity Church **P** (40) 555 Palisade Ave 07010-3035 (Mail to: 555 Palisade Ave 07010-3035) Willie Smith (201) 943-1034

Clifton St Peters Episcopal Church **P** (145) 380 Clifton Ave 07011-2643 (Mail to: 380 Clifton Ave 07011-2643) Kevin Moroney (973) 546-5020

Denville The Church of the Saviour **P** (761) 155 Morris Ave 07834-1736 (Mail to: 155 Morris Ave 07834-1736) George Wong (973) 627-3304

Dover St Johns Episcopal Church **P** (83) 11 S Bergen St 07801-4634 (Mail to: 11 S Bergen St 07801-4634) John Habecker Rodrigo Perez-Vega (973) 366-2772

East Orange St Agnes & St Pauls Church **P** (65) 206 Renshaw Ave 07017-3313 (Mail to: 206 Renshaw Ave 07017-3313) Esar Budhu (973) 678-6716

Englewood St Pauls Episcopal Church **P** (512) 113 Engle St 07631-2508 (Mail to: 113 Engle St 07631-2508) William Allport (201) 568-3276

Essex Fells St Peters Episcopal Church **P** (1010) 271 Roseland Ave 07021-1313 (Mail to: PO Box 96 07021-0096) Michael Muller (973) 226-6500

Fair Lawn Church of the Atonement **P** (55) 1-36 30th St 07410-3946 (Mail to: 1-36 30th St 07410-3946) Kevin Coffey (201) 797-0760

Fort Lee Church of the Good Shepherd **COO** (96) 1576 Palisade Ave 07024-6929 (Mail to: 1576 Palisade Ave 07024-6993) (201) 461-7260

Glen Ridge Christ Episcopal Church **P** (216) 74 Park Ave 07028-2309 (Mail to: 74 Park Ave 07028-2309) Diana Wilcox Robert Solon (973) 743-5911

Glen Rock All Saints Episcopal Church **P** (332) 40 Central Ave 07452-1837 (Mail to: 40 Central Ave 07452-1837) Mark Collins (201) 444-6874

Hackensack Christ Episcopal Church **P** (217) 251 State St 07601-5512 (Mail to: PO Box 1097 07602-1097) (201) 342-2365

Hackensack Church of St Anthony Padua **P** (692) 72 Lodi St 07601-5350 (Mail to: 72 Lodi St 07601-5363) Brian Laffler (201) 489-3286

Hackensack St Cyprians Church **M** (49) 269 1st St 07601-3434 (Mail to: 269 1st St 07601-3434) (201) 342-5560

Hackettstown St James Episcopal Church **P** (330) 214 Washington St 07840-2146 (Mail to: 214 Washington St 07840-2146) (908) 852-3968

Harrington Park St Andrews Episcopal Church **P** (123) Lynn St And La Roche Ave 07640 (Mail to: 31 Lynn Street 07640-0161) Diane Rhodes (201) 768-0819

Harrison Christ Church **M** (52) 100 Frank E Rodgers Blvd 07029-1402 (Mail to: 100 Frank E Rodgers Blvd 07029-1402) (973) 483-1260

Hasbrouck Hts Church of St John the Divine **M** (140) 229 Terrace Ave 07604-1917 (Mail to: 229 Terrace Ave 07604-1917) Alexei Khamin (201) 288-0002

Haworth St Lukes Episcopal Church **P** (69) 43 Massachusetts Ave 07641-1950 (Mail to: 43 Massachusetts Ave 07641-1950) (201) 384-0706

Hawthorne St Clements Episcopal Church **P** (183) 271 Lafayette Ave 07506-1921 (Mail to: 271 Lafayette Ave 07506-1921) (973) 427-8118

Hillsdale Holy Trinity Episcopal Church **P** (315) 326 Hillsdale Ave 07642-2209 (Mail to: 326 Hillsdale Ave 07642-2209) (201) 664-2428

Ho Ho Kus St Bartholomews Episcopal Church **P** (190) 70 Sheridan Ave 07423-1541 (Mail to: 70 Sheridan Ave 07423-1541) Cathleen Studwell (201) 444-5025

Hoboken All Saints Episcopal Parish **P** (568) § 707 Washington St 07030-5001 (Mail to: 707 Washington St 07030-5001) Elaine Thomas John Morgan (201) 792-3563

Jersey City Church of the Incarnation **P** (100) 68 Storms Ave 07306-3316 (Mail to: 68 Storms Ave 07306-3316) (201) 434-4810

Jersey City Grace Van Vorst Church **P** (343) 39 Erie St 07302-2821 (Mail to: 39 Erie St 07302-2821) Laurie Wurm (201) 659-2211

Jersey City St Paul's Episcopal Church **P** (134) 38 Duncan Ave 07304-0176 (Mail to: Attn Susan Faulkner 38 Duncan Ave 07304-0176) Thomas Murphy (201) 433-4922

Kinnelon St Davids Episcopal Church **P** (166) 91 Kinnelon Rd 07405-2335 (Mail to: Mrs Arther 91 Kinnelon Rd 07405-2335) Jon Richardson (973) 838-6696

Leonia All Saints Episcopal Church **P** (98) 150 Park Ave 07605-2012 (Mail to: 150 Park Ave 07605-2091) Dean Weber (201) 947-1233

Little Falls St Agnes Episcopal Church **P** (106) 65 Union Ave 07424-1321 (Mail to: 65 Union Ave 07424-1397) Young Yoon (973) 256-5020

Livingston St Peter's Episcopal Church **P** (108) 94 E Mount Pleasant Ave 07039-3004 (Mail to: 94 E Mount Pleasant Ave 07039-3094) Elizabeth Wigg-Maxwell (973) 992-1932

Lyndhurst St Thomas Episcopal Church **P** (48) 300 Forest Ave P.O. Box 207 07071-2330 (Mail to: 300 Forest Ave 07071-2330) (201) 438-5668

Madison Grace Church **P** (1099) 4 Madison Ave 07940-1433 (Mail to: 4 Madison Ave 07940-1433) Michel Belt Susan Ironside (973) 377-0106

Maplewood St Georges Episcopal Church **P** (425) 550 Ridgewood Rd 07040-2135 (Mail to: 550 Ridgewood Rd 07040-2198) Gary Commins (973) 762-1319

Maywood St Martins Episcopal Church **P** (53) 29 Parkway 07607-1558 (Mail to: Oak Ave & The Parkway 07607) Ruben Jurado (201) 843-5360

✠ **Mendham** St John Baptist Convent **O** 82 W Main St 07945-1230 (Mail to: PO Box 240 07945-0240) (973) 543-4641

Mendham St Marks Church **P** (148) 9 E Main St 07945-1501 (Mail to: 9 E Main St 07945-1501) (973) 543-4471

Millburn St Stephens Church **P** (269) 119 Main St 07041-1115 (Mail to: 119 Main St 07041-1115) Paula Toland (973) 376-0688

Millington All Saints Church **P** (262) 15 Basking Ridge Rd 07946-1407 (Mail to: 15 Basking Ridge Rd 07946-1407) Victoria Mcgrath Victoria Mcgrath (908) 647-0067

Montclair St James Episcopal Church **P** (444) § 581 Valley Rd 07043-1826 (Mail to: 581 Valley Rd 07043-1826) David Casto Charlotte Hall Audrey Hasselbrook (973) 744-0270

Montclair St Johns Episcopal Church **P** (438) 55 Montclair Ave 07042-4109 (Mail to: 55 Montclair Ave 07042-4109) Candace Sandfort (973) 746-2474

Montclair Saint Luke's Episcopal Church **P** (698) 73 S Fullerton Ave 07042-2627 (Mail to: 73 S Fullerton Ave Ste A 07042-2685) John Mennell (973) 744-6220

Montvale Saint Paul's Church **P** (387) 4 Woodland Rd 07645-2134 (Mail to: C/O Mr Chuch Kurtzke 4 Woodland Rd 07645-2134) Edward Hasse (201) 391-3181

Morris Plains Saint Paul's Episcopal Church **P** (180) 29 Hillview Ave 07950-2114 (Mail to: 29 Hillview Ave 07950-2114) Paul Olsson (973) 285-0884

Morristown Church of the Redeemer **P** (347) 36 South St 07960-4136 (Mail to: 36 South St 07960-7260) Cynthia Black (973) 539-0703

Morristown St Peters Episcopal Church **P** (1036) 121 South Street 07960 (Mail to: 70 Maple Ave 07960-5293) Janet Broderick Daniel Gross (973) 538-0555

Mountain Lks St Peters Episcopal Church **P** (350) 215 Boulevard 07046-1209 (Mail to: 215 Boulevard 07046-1209) Lynne Grifo (973) 334-4429

Mt Arlington St Peters Episcopal Church **P** (69) 50 Edgemere Ave 07856-1164 (Mail to: 50 Edgemere Ave PO Box 403 07856-1164) Elizabeth Myers Wayne Sherrer (973) 398-1890

N Arlington St Pauls Church **M** (21) 11 York Rd 07031-5811 (Mail to: 11 York Rd 07031-5811) (201) 199-1725

Newark Grace Episcopal Church **P** (168) 950 Broad St 07102-2614 (Mail to: 950 Broad St 07102-2684) James Bates Marjorie Lindstrom (973) 623-1733

Newark House of Prayer Episcopal Church **M** (93) 407 Broad St 07104-3310 (Mail to: 407 Broad St 07104-3310) Kathleen Ballard Wade Renn (973) 483-8202

Newark St Andrews Episcopal Church **M** (110) 933 S 17th St 07108-1136 (Mail to: 933 S 17th St 07108-1136) Sylvester Ekunwe James Hagler James Hagler (973) 375-3012

✣ **Newark** The Oasis **O** 31 Mulberry St 07102-5202 (Mail to: 31 Mulberry St 07102-5202) (973) 430-9909

✣ **Newark** Trinity & St Philips Cathedral **O** (206) 24 Rector St 07102-4512 (Mail to: 24 Rector St 07102-4588) George Bowen Thomas Pike Wade Renn Sandra Wilson (973) 622-3505

Newton Christ Church **P** (495) 62 Main St 07860-2024 (Mail to: 62 Main St 07860-2024) Robert Griner (973) 383-2245

Norwood Church of the Holy Communion **P** (135) 66 Summit St 07648-1841 (Mail to: 66 Summit St 07648-1841) James Petroccione (201) 768-0634

Nutley Grace Episcopal Church **P** (539) 200 Highfield Ln 07110-2448 (Mail to: 200 Highfield Ln 07110-2499) Pamela Bakal Nancy Read (973) 235-1177

Oak Ridge St Gabriels Episcopal Church **M** (40) 153 Milton Rd 07438-9598 (Mail to: C/O Dorothy Skelton 153 Milton Rd 07438-9598) (973) 697-5688

Oakland St Albans Episcopal Church **P** (162) 1 Church Ln 07436-4036 (Mail to: 1 Church Ln 07436-4036) Kathryn King (201) 337-4909

Oradell The Church of the Annunciation **P** (89) 343 Kinderkamack Rd 07649-2123 (Mail to: 343 Kinderkamack Rd 07649-2151) Archie Palmer (201) 262-7222

Paramus Saint Matthew's Church **M** (153) 167 Spring Valley Rd 07652-5333 (Mail to: 167

Spring Valley Rd Ste 1 07652-5396) (201) 262-5286

Parsippany St Gregorys Episcopal Church **M** (89) 480 S Beverwyck Rd 07054-3328 (Mail to: 480 S Beverwyck Rd 07054-3328) Susan Saucedo Sica (973) 887-5879

Passaic St Johns Episcopal Church **P** (143) 215 Lafayette Ave 07055-4711 (Mail to: 215 Lafayette Ave 07055-4711) William Thiele (973) 779-0966

Paterson St Pauls Episcopal Church **P** (408) 451 Van Houten St 07501-2119 (Mail to: 451 Van Houten St 07501-2119) Beth Glover Juan Reyes Erik Soldwedel (973) 278-7900

Phillipsburg St Luke Episcopal Church **P** (237) 500 Hillcrest Blvd 08865-1407 (Mail to: 500 Hillcrest Blvd 08865-1499) (908) 859-1479

Pompton Lake Christ Episcopal Church **P** (429) 400 Ramapo Ave 07442-1825 (Mail to: 400 Ramapo Ave 07442-1825) Stephen Rozzelle (973) 835-2207

Ramsey St Johns Memorial Episcopal Church **P** (609) 301 E Main St 07446 (Mail to: Attn: Ellen Joyce 301 E Main St 07446) William Cruse (201) 327-0703

Ridgefield St James Episcopal Church **P** (248) 514 Abbott Ave 07657-2413 (Mail to: 514 Abbott Ave 07657-2413) Mariano Gargiulo (201) 945-0079

Ridgewood Christ Episcopal Church **P** (462) 105 Cottage Pl 07450-3213 (Mail to: 105 Cottage Pl 07450-3217) Thomas Mathews (201) 652-2350

Ridgewood St Elizabeths Church **P** (832) 169 Fairmount Rd 07450-1422 (Mail to: 169 Fairmount Rd 07450-1422) Maylin Biggadike Joan Conley Pierce Klemmt Catherine Quinn Susan Schink (201) 444-2299

Ringwood Church of the Good Shepherd **M** (78) 80 Margaret King Ave 07456-1703 (Mail to: PO Box 727 07456-0727) (973) 962-9510

Rutherford Grace Episcopal Church **P** (139) 128 W Passaic Ave 07070-1935 (Mail to: 128 W Passaic Ave 07070-1935) (201) 438-8623

Secaucus Church of Our Saviour **M** (150) 191 Flanagan Way 07094-3435 (Mail to: 191 Flanagan Way 07094-3435) Barbara Lewis (201) 863-1449

Short Hills Christ Episcopal Church **P** (624) 66 Highland Ave 07078-2829 (Mail to: 66 Highland Ave 07078-2829) A Bowie Snodgrass John Stonesifer (973) 379-2898

South Orange St Andrew and Holy Communion Church **P** (649) 160 W South Orange Ave 07079-1731 (Mail to: 160 W South Orange Ave 07079-1731) Anne Bolles-Beaven (973) 763-2355

Sparta St Marys Episcopal Church **P** (299) 85 Conestoga Trl 07871-2537 (Mail to: 85 Conestoga Trl 07871-2537) Debra Brewin Wilson (973) 729-3136

Succasunna St. Dunstan's Church **P** (107) 179 S Hillside Ave 07876-1197 (Mail to: 179 S Hillside Ave 07876-1197) (973) 927-1485

Summit Calvary Church **P** (1339) Attn Dolores Hofmann 31 Woodland Ave 07901-2157 (Mail to: C/O Pamela Kuhn 31 Woodland Ave 07901-2157) Matthew Corkern Elizabeth Geitz Nathan Huddleston (908) 277-1814

✢ **Summit** Interweave **O** 31 Woodland Ave 07901-2157 (Mail to: 31 Woodland Ave 07901-2157) Robert Morris (908) 277-2120

Sussex Church of the Good Shepherd **M** (88) 200 State Rt 23 07461-3100 (Mail to: 200 State Rt 23 07461-3100) Elizabeth Ostuni (973) 875-0919

Teaneck Christ Church **M** (145) 480 Warwick Ave 07666-2926 (Mail to: 480 Warwick Ave 07666-2926) Ramon Aymerich Michelle White (201) 833-4502

Teaneck St Marks Episcopal Church **P** (504) 118 Chadwick Rd 07666-4204 (Mail to: C/O Anne Beemsterboer 118 Chadwick Rd 07666-4204) (201) 836-7275

Tenafly Church of the Atonement **P** (219) 97 Highwood Ave 07670-1834 (Mail to: 97 Highwood Ave 07670-1834) Lynne Weber (201) 568-1763

Towaco Good Shepherd Episcopal Church **P** 9 Two Bridges Rd 07082-1318 (Mail to: 9 Two Bridges Rd 07082-1318) Lesley Hay (973) 334-2882

Union City Grace Episcopal Church **P** (100) 3901 Park Ave 07087-6127 (Mail to: 3901 Park Ave 07087-6127) Arthur Fouts Juan Rosario De La Cruz (201) 863-6334

Verona The Church of the Holy Spirit **P** (141) 36 Gould St 07044-1928 (Mail to: 36 Gould St 07044-1928) Gerard Racioppi (973) 239-2850

Washington St Peters Church **P** (170) 127 Broad St 07882-1801 (Mail to: 127 Broad St 07882-1801) (908) 689-1019

Wayne St Michaels Episcopal Church **P** (120) 1219 Ratzer Rd 07470-2310 (Mail to: 1219 Ratzer Rd 07470-2310) (973) 694-1026

West Orange Church of the Holy Innocents **P** (77) 681 Prospect Ave 07052-3212 (Mail to: 681 Prospect Ave 07052-3212) (973) 731-0259

West Orange Church of the Holy Trinity **M** (45) 315 Main St 07052-5630 (Mail to: 315 Main St 07052-5624) Miguel Hernandez (973) 325-0369

Westwood Grace Episcopal Church **P** (576) 9 Harrington Ave 07675-1801 (Mail to: 9 Harrington Ave 07675-1899) Anthony Puca (201) 664-0407

Wood Ridge Church of St Paul and Resurrection **P** (123) 483 Center St 07075-2311 (Mail to: 483 Center St 07075-2311) Jacob Nanthicattu Charles Nelson (201) 438-8333

STATE OF NORTH CAROLINA

Dioceses of East Carolina (EC), North Carolina (NC), and Western North Carolina (WNC)

Advance—NC	Clayton—NC	Fuquay Varina—NC	Kinston—EC
Ahoskie—EC	Clemmons—NC	Garner—NC	Laurinburg—NC
Albemarle—NC	Cleveland—NC	Gastonia—WNC	Leland—EC
Ansonville—NC	Clinton—EC	Gatesville—EC	Lenoir—WNC
Asheboro—NC	Columbia—EC	Glendale Spgs—WNC	Lewiston—EC
Asheville—WNC	Concord—NC	Goldsboro—EC	Lexington—NC
Bat Cave—WNC	Cooleemee—NC	Greensboro—NC	Lincolnton—WNC
Bath—EC	Creswell—EC	Greenville—EC	Linville—WNC
Battleboro—NC	Cullowhee—WNC	Grifton—EC	Little Switzerland—
Beaufort—EC	Currituck—EC	Hamlet—NC	WNC
Belhaven—EC	Davidson—NC	Hampstead—EC	Littleton—NC
Bessemer City—WNC	Denver—WNC	Havelock—EC	Louisburg—NC
Black Mtn—WNC	Durham—NC	Haw River—NC	Lumberton—EC
Blowing Rock—WNC	Eden—NC	Hayesville—WNC	Marion—WNC
Boone—WNC	Edenton—EC	Henderson—NC	Marshall—WNC
Brevard—WNC	Edneyville—WNC	Hendersonville—WNC	Mars Hill—WNC
Burgaw—EC	Elizabeth City—EC	Hertford—EC	Matthews—NC
Burlington—NC	Elizabethtown—EC	Hickory—WNC	Mayodan—NC
Burnsville—WNC	Elkin—NC	High Pt—NC	Mills River—WNC
Canton—WNC	Engelhard—EC	Highlands—WNC	Monroe—NC
Cary—NC	Erwin—NC	Hillsborough—NC	Mooresville—NC
Cashiers—WNC	Farmville—EC	Holly Ridge—EC	Morehead City—EC
Chapel Hill—NC	Fayetteville—EC	Huntersville—NC	Morganton—WNC
Charlotte—NC	Flat Rock—WNC	Jackson—NC	Mt Airy—NC
Cherokee—WNC	Fletcher—WNC	Jacksonville—EC	Murphy—WNC
Chocowinity—EC	Franklin—WNC	Kernersville—NC	Nags Head—EC

New Bern—EC
Newland—WNC
Newton—WNC
Newton Grove—EC
Oriental—EC
Oxford—NC
Pittsboro—NC
Plymouth—EC
Raleigh—NC
Reidsville—NC
Ridgeway—NC
Roanoke Rapids—NC
Robbinsville—WNC
Rockingham—NC
Rocky Mt—NC

Roper—EC
Roxboro—NC
Rutherfordton—WNC
Salisbury—NC
Salter Path—EC
Saluda—WNC
Sanford—NC
Scotland Neck—NC
Seven Sprs—EC
Shallotte—EC
Shelby—WNC
Smithfield—NC
Southern Pines—NC
Southern Shores—EC
Southport—EC

Sparta—WNC
Speed—NC
Spruce Pine—WNC
Statesville—NC
Sunbury—EC
Swansboro—EC
Sylva—WNC
Tarboro—NC
Trenton—EC
Troy—NC
Tryon—WNC
Valle Crucis—WNC
Vanceboro—EC
Wadesboro—NC
Wake Forest—NC

Walnut Cove—NC
Warrenton—NC
Washington—EC
Waxhaw—NC
Waynesville—WNC
Weldon—NC
Whiteville—EC
Wilkesboro—WNC
Williamston—EC
Wilmington—EC
Wilson—NC
Windsor—EC
Winston-Salem—NC

DIOCESE OF NORTH CAROLINA
(PROVINCE IV)
Comprises central North Carolina
DIOCESAN OFFICE 200 W Morgan St Ste 300 Raleigh NC 27601-1338
Tel (919) 834-7474 FAX (919) 834-7546
GREENSBORO OFFICE (Suffragan location): 301 N Elm St Ste 308-C Greensboro NC 27401
Tel (336) 273 5770   FAX (336) 273 9253
E-Mail communications@episdionc.org   WEB www.episdionc.org

Previous Bishops—
John S Ravenscroft 1823-30, Levi S Ives 1831-53, Thomas Atkinson 1853-81, Theodore B Lyman coadj 1873 Bp 1881-93, Jos B Cheshire coadj 1893 Bp 1893-1932, Henry B DeLny suffr 1918-28, Edwin A Penick coadj 1922 Bp 1932-59, Richard H Baker coadj 1950 Bp 1959-65, W Moultrie Moore Jr suffr 1967-75, Thomas A Fraser coadj 1960 Bp 1965-83, Frank H Vest Jr suffr 1985-89, Robt W Estill coadj 1980 Bp 1983-94, Huntington Williams Jr suffr 1990-96, Robert C Johnson Jr 1994-2000, J Gary Gloster suffr 1996-2004; Michael B Curry (955) (2000-15)

Bishop Diocesan The Rt Rev Samuel Sewall Rodman III (1102) (Dio 15 July 2017)

Bishop Suffragan The Rt Rev Anne E Hodges-Copple (1076) (Dio 15 June 2013)

Cn Admin M Weigert; *Cn for Trans and Pastoral Mins* C Massey; *Cn for Cong Miss* D Sellery *Reg Cn* R Lee *(South)* E Graham *(Northwest)* C Deats *(East)*; *Exec Asst to Bishops* E Dawkins S Kappauf; *Acct* M Gillespie; *Comm Dir* C McTaggart; *Comm Coord* S Walter; *Lead Yth Miss* B Crow; *Yth Miss* L Aycock A Campbell; *Hisp/Lat* Miss D Robayo *Archdcn* J Lamb; *Sec* C Till; *Treas* W Gresham; *Chanc* E Embree; *Hist* B Graebner;*Ecum & Interfaith Off* J Melnyk; *Lit* D Everhardt; *North Carolina Council of Churches Liaison* J Bullard

Stand Comm—Cler: R Black D Frazelle S French F Sintim; *Lay:* M Alexander M McCann R Taylor ▮ Joyner

Diocesan Council—Cler: B Armstrong J Taylor ? Yancy R Yarbrough A Alexis J Pahl *Lay* Freeman Branch J Fussell D Cisney M Friedman S Guptill N Long F Falkson R Rinaldi

Deans of Convoc—Rocky Mt G Greer; *Raleigh* L Frazelle; *Durham* S Woodard; *Sandhills* T Hushion Greensboro M Williams; *Winston-Salem* D Kinser Charlotte S Hollar; *Lay Wardens of Convoc—Rock* Mt L Smith; *Raleigh* M Harvey; *Durham* M Gardner Woods; *Sandhills* L Holden; *Greensboro* S Mercier Winston-Salem B Morphis; *Charlotte* E Bell

PARISHES, MISSIONS, AND CLERGY

Advance Church of the Ascension **M** (67) 18 Fork Bixby Rd 27006-7217 (Mail to: 183 Fork Bixby Rd 27006-7217) Daniel Wall (336) 998 0857

Albemarle Christ Episcopal Church **P** (152) 428 Pee Dee Ave 28001-4934 (Mail to: PO Box 657 28002-0657) (704) 982-1428

Ansonville All Souls Episcopal Church **M** (6) 52 Highway 52 28007-9798 (Mail to: C/O Jennie Thomas 211 Camden Rd 28170-2629) Timothy Hushion (704) 694-3223

Asheboro Episcopal Church of the Good Shepherd **P** (243) 505 Mountain Rd 27205-4219 (Mail to: 505 Mountain Rd 27205-4219) Joe Mitchell (336) 625-5234

Battleboro St Johns Episcopal Church **M** (12) 211 E. Main Street 27809 (Mail to: PO Box 577 27809-0577) (252) 446-8852

Burlington Church of the Holy Comforter **P** (633) 320 East Davis Street 27215 (Mail to: PO Box 1336 27216-1336) George Silides (336) 227-4251

Cary St Pauls Episcopal Church **P** (1065) § 221 Union St 27511-3763 (Mail to: C/O Church Administrator 221 Union St 27511-3763) George Adamik Javier Almendarez Bautista Jule Holland (919) 467-1477

Chapel Hill The Chapel of the Cross **P** (1863) 304 E Franklin St 27514-3619 (Mail to: 304 E Franklin St 27514-3624) Joyce Cunningham Elizabeth Melchionna Noah VanNiel (919) 929-2193

Chapel Hill Church of the Advocate **M** (101) 8410 Merin Road 27516 (Mail to: 8410 Merin Rd 27516-9231) Lisa Fischbeck (919) 933-3221

Chapel Hill Church of the Holy Family **P** (800) 200 Hayes Rd 27517-5633 (Mail to: 200 Hayes Rd 27517-5633) Clarke French Sarah Ball-Damberg (919) 942-3108

Charlotte Chapel of Christ the King **M** (35) 425 E 17th St 28206-3407 (Mail to: 425 E 17th St 28206-3407) Reginald Payne-Wiens (704) 334-3097

Charlotte Christ Episcopal Church **P** (4525) 1412 Providence Rd 28207-2543 (Mail to: 1412 Providence Rd 28207-2543) Henry Edens James Case Matthew Holcombe Ann Rhyne Elizabeth Saunders Jonathan Soyars (704) 333-0378

Charlotte Church of the Holy Comforter **P** (800) § 2701 Park Rd 28209-1311 (Mail to: 2701 Park Rd 28209-1357) Gregory Brown Eugene Humphreys Amanda Robertson (704) 332-4171

Charlotte St Johns Episcopal Church **P** (2896) 1623 Carmel Rd 28226-5015 (Mail to: 1623 Carmel Rd 28226-5097) Peter Floyd Bradford Smith Robert Voyle (704) 366-3034

Charlotte St Martins Episcopal Church **P** (777) 1510 E 7th St 28204-2410 (Mail to: 1510 E 7th St 28204-2410) Joshua Bowron Armand LaVallee (704) 376-8441

Charlotte Church of St Michael & All Angels **M** (59) 750 East 9th Street 28202-3102 (Mail to: PO Box 11318 28220-1318) (704) 399-3151

Charlotte St Peters Episcopal Church **P** (757) 115 W 7th St 28202-2127 (Mail to: 115 W 7th St Ste 300 28202-0401) Jacob Pierce (704) 332-7746

Clayton Grace Episcopal Mission **M** (200) 111 Lee Ct 27520-7927 (Mail to: PO Box 752 27528-0752) John Gibson (919) 553-2810

Clemmons Saint Clement's Episcopal Church **P** (206) 3600 Harper Rd 27012-8681 (Mail to: PO Box 1547 27012-1547) Jamie Edwards (336) 766-4323

Cleveland Christ Episcopal Church **P** (108) 3430 Old Us Highway 27013-9733 (Mail to: PO Box 37 27013-0037) Sarah Blaies-Diamond (704) 278-4652

Concord All Saints Episcopal Church **P** (423) 525 Lake Concord Rd Ne 28025-2925 (Mail to: 525 Lake Concord Rd NE 28025-2925) Nancy Cox Michael Whitnah (704) 782-2024

Cooleemee Church Of The Good Shepherd **P** (10) 141 Church St 27014 (Mail to: P.O. Box 1047 27014) (336) 284-4359

Davidson St Albans Episcopal Church **P** (573) § 301 Caldwell Lane 28036 (Mail to: 301 Caldwell Lane 28036-0970) Carmen Germino Kevin Lloyd (704) 892-0173

✣ **Durham** Duke Episcopal Center **O** 505 Alexander Ave 27705-4707 (Mail to: 505 Alexander Ave 27705-4707) (919) 286-0624

Durham Iglesia El Buen Pastor **M** (358) 1852 Liberty St 27703-2271 (Mail to: C/O NCPAS 2035 S Nc Highway 119 27302-9739) Habacuc Ramos Huerta (919) 682-3301

Durham St Josephs Episcopal Church **M** (47) 1902 W Main St 27705-4838 (Mail to: 1902 W Main St 27705-4838) Karen Barfield (919) 286-1064

Durham St Lukes Church **P** (360) 1737 Hillandale Rd 27705-3045 (Mail to: 1737 Hillandale Rd 27705-3045) Helen Svoboda-Barber James Craven Daniel Laird Helen Svoboda-Barber (919) 286-2273

Durham St Philips Episcopal Church **P** (1464) 403 E Main St 27701-3719 (Mail to: 403 E Main St 27701-3719) Jill Bullard Sally French Michael Kendall (919) 682-5708

Durham St Stephens Church **P** (582) 82 Kimberly Dr 27707-5446 (Mail to: 82 Kimberly Dr 27707-5446) Robert Kaynor Gail Davis William Shows (919) 493-5451

Durham Church of St Titus **P** (263) 400 Moline St 27707-2348 (Mail to: 400 Moline St 27707-2348) Stephanie Yancy (919) 682-5504

Eden Church of the Epiphany **P** (149) 538 Henry St 27288-6103 (Mail to: 538 Henry St 27288-6103) Linda Nye (336) 623-9410

Eden St Lukes Episcopal Church **P** (92) 604 Morgan Rd 27288-2526 (Mail to: 604 Morgan Rd 27288-2526) Wheigar Bright (336) 627-4668

Elkin Galloway Memorial Chapel **M** (42) 310 W Main St 28621-3314 (Mail to: PO Box 747 28621-0747) (336) 526-2172

Erwin St Stephens Episcopal Church **P** (142) 201 Denim Dr 28339 (Mail to: 209 Denim Dr 28339-2125) Charles Teague (910) 897-5291

Fuquay Varina Trinity Episcopal Church **M** (100) 1128 S Main St 27526-9700 (Mail to: PO Box 821 27526-0821) (919) 552-1056

Garner Saint Christopher's Episcopal Church **M** (80) 1101 Vandora Springs Rd 27529-3746 (Mail to: P O Box 505 27529) David Frazelle (919) 772-7125

Greensboro All Saints Church **P** (237) 4211 Wayne Rd 27407-7314 (Mail to: 4211 Wayne Rd 27407-7314) Paula Rachal (336) 299-0705

Greensboro Church of the Holy Spirit **M** (58) 3910 Yanceyville St 27405-3350 (Mail to: 3910 Yanceyville St 27405-3350) Audra Abt (336) 621-7321

Greensboro Church of the Redeemer **P** (184) 901 E Friendly Ave 27401-3103 (Mail to: 901 E Friendly Ave 27401-3103) Alicia Alexis (336) 275-0033

Greensboro Holy Trinity Episcopal Church **P** (2377) § 607 Greene St 27401-2023 (Mail to: 607 Greene St 27401-2023) Timothy Patterson Timothy Patterson Sarah Carver Gregory Farrand Nathan Finnin Timothy Patterson (336) 272-6149

Greensboro St Andrews Episcopal Church **P** (765) 2105 W Market St 27403-1718 (Mail to: Attn: Kimberly Rathburn 2105 W Market St 27403-1799) Robert Hamilton (336) 275-1651

Greensboro St Barnabas Episcopal Church **M** (241) 1300 Jefferson Rd 27410-3529 (Mail to: 1300 Jefferson Rd 27410-3529) Randall Keeney (336) 294-1282

Greensboro St Francis Episcopal Church **P** (669) § 3506 Lawndale Dr 27408-2804 (Mail to: C/O Linda Allgood 3506 Lawndale Dr 27408-2804) Milton Williams Audra Abt Andrew Harmon (336) 288-4721

✠ **Greensboro** St Marys House **O** (26) 930 Walker Ave 27403-2530 (Mail to: 930 Walker Ave 27403-2530) (336) 334-5219

Hamlet All Saints Episcopal Church **M** (63) 217 Henderson St 28345-3311 (Mail to: PO Box 687 28345-0687) (910) 582-0861

Haw River Saint Andrew's Church **M** (65) P O Box 1088 27258 (Mail to: PO Box 1088 Route 70 272581088) Miriam Saxon (336) 578-3623

Henderson St James Church **M** (13) 3415 Cameron Dr 27536-3820 (Mail to: PO Box 245 27544-0245) (252) 257-3542

Henderson St Johns Episcopal Church **M** (28) N Church & Main Sts 27536 (Mail to: PO Box 974 27536-0974) (252) 492-0082

Henderson Church of the Holy Innocents **P** (361) 210 S Chestnut St 27536-4223 (Mail to: 210 S Chestnut St 27536-4223) Donald Lowery Harrel Johnson (252) 492-0904

High Point St Christophers Episcopal Church **P** (192) Corner Of Eastchester & High 27262 (Mail to: 303 Eastchester Dr 27262-7628) Jerry Lasley Niel Lentz (336) 869-5311

High Point St Marys Episcopal Church **P** (794) 108 W Farriss Ave 27262-3008 (Mail to: 108 W Farriss Ave 27262-3099) David Umphlett Amanda Stephenson (336) 886-4756

Hillsborough St Matthews Parish Church **P** (389) 210 St Marys Rd 27278-2518 (Mail to: PO Box 628 27278-0628) Carl Edwards Lisa Frost-Phillips Katherine Johnson Judith Reese Jean Vail (919) 732-9308

Huntersville St Marks Episcopal Church **P** (461) 8600 Mount Holly Hntrsvlle Rd 28078-8475 (Mail to: 8600 Mount Holly Hntrsvlle Rd 28078-8475) Sarah Hollar (704) 399-5193

Jackson The Church of the Saviour **M** (54) Calhoun & Church Sts 27845 (Mail to: C/O Dana Boone PO Box 613 27845-0613) Richard Galloway (919) 534-0911

Kernersville St Matthews Episcopal Church **M** (103) 1110 Salisbury St 27284-3302 (Mail to: PO Box 1173 27285-1173) Edwin Cox Frances Cox (336) 996-4422

Laurinburg St Davids Episcopal Church **Cluster** (50) Covington & Azure 28353 (Mail to: C/O Donald Nisben PO Box 334 28353) (919) 276-1757

Lexington Grace Episcopal Church **P** (280) 419 S Main St 27292-3234 (Mail to: 419 S Main St 27292-3234) Mark Plummer Bonnie Duckworth (336) 249-7211

Littleton St Alban Episcopal Church **M** (40) 300 Mosby Avenue 27850-0955 (Mail to: PO Box 955 27850-0955) (252) 586-4700

Louisburg St Matthias Episcopal Church **M** (10) Attn Miss Mary L Hill Treas 102 Harris St 27549-2722 (Mail to: Attn Miss Mary L Hill Treas 102 Harris St 27549) (919) 853-2278

Louisburg St Pauls Episcopal Church **M** (74) 301 North Church Street 27549-2417 (Mail to: PO Box 247 27549-0247) Lauren Winner (919) 496-4180

Matthews Thompson Child and Family Focus **P** 6800 Saint Peters Ln 28105 (Mail to: 6800 Saint Peters Ln 28105-8458) (704) 536-0375

Mayodan Church of the Messiah **M** (46) 114 S 2nd Ave 27027-2712 (Mail to: 114 S 2nd Ave 27027-2712) (336) 548-2801

Monroe St Pauls Episcopal Church **P** (217) 116 S Church St 28112-5605 (Mail to: PO Box 293 28111-0293) James Croom (704) 289-8434

Mooresville St James Episcopal Church **M** (47) 851 Shinnville Rd 28115-7111 (Mail to: 851 Shinnville Rd 28115-7111) (704) 664-7115

Mooresville Saint Patrick's Episcopal Church **P** (476) § 164 Fairview Rd 28117-9512 (Mail to: PO Box 1491 28115-1491) Gregory McIntyre Sally Brower Rhonda Willerer (704) 663-5659

Mount Airy Trinity Episcopal Church **P** (259) 472 Main St # 1043 27030-3814 (Mail to: PO Box 1043 27030-1043) Sarah Morris (336) 786-6067

Oxford St Cyprians Episcopal Church **M** (98) 408 Granville St 27565-3673 (Mail to: 408 Cranville Street 27565) Henry Tabor William Joyner (919) 693-1351

Oxford St Stephens Episcopal Church **P** (207) 140 College St 27565-2947 (Mail to: 140 College St 27565-2956) James Pahl (919) 693-9740

Pittsboro St Bartholomews Episcopal Church **P** (216) 204 W Salisbury St 27312-9483 (Mail to: Attn Bookkeeper 204 W Salisbury St 27312-9483) Wilberforce Mundia (919) 542-5679

Raleigh Christ Episcopal Church **P** (2957) 120 E Edenton St 27601-1014 (Mail to: 120 E Edenton St 27601-1014) James Adams Jennifer Brown Mary Davila Daniel Reeves (919) 834-6259

Raleigh Church of the Good Shepherd **P** (1485) 121 Hillsborough St 27603-1762 (Mail to: 121 Hillsborough St 27603-1762) Ashley Bullock Patricia Grace Cheryl McFadden Miriam Saxon (919) 831-2000

Raleigh Church of the Nativity **P** (542) 8849 Ray Rd 27613-1232 (Mail to: 8849 Ray Rd 27613-1232) Stephanie Allen Nancy Allison George Clifford (919) 846-8338

Raleigh NC State Campus Ministry **P** 2208 Hope St 27607-7334 (Mail to: 2208 Hope St 27607-7334) (919) 834-2428

Raleigh St Ambrose Episcopal Church **P** (374) 813 Darby St 27610-4017 (Mail to: 813 Darby St 27610-4017) Robert Taylor (919) 833-8055

Raleigh St Augustines Chapel **P** (8) 1315 Oakwood Ave 27610-2247 (Mail to: 1315 Oakwood Ave 27610-2247) (919) 516-4000

Raleigh St Marks Episcopal Church **P** (461) 1725 New Hope Rd 27604-8304 (Mail to: 1725 New Hope Rd 27604-8304) Tyrone Fowlkes John Wall (919) 231-6767

Raleigh St Marys School Chapel **School** 900 Hillsborough St 27603-1610 (Mail to: 900 Hillsborough St 27603-1689) Ann Bonner-Stewart (919) 424-4122

Raleigh St Michaels Episcopal Church **P** (1885) § 1520 Canterbury Rd 27608-1106 (Mail to: C/O Susan Little 1520 Canterbury Rd 27608-1106) Samuel Jones Robert Fruehwirth Holly Gloff (919) 782-0731

Raleigh St Timothys Church **P** (816) 4523 Six Forks Rd 27609-5709 (Mail to: 4523 Six Forks Rd 27609-5709) Vincent Kopp Henry Presler Douglas Remer (919) 787-7590

Reidsville St Thomas Episcopal Church **P** (167) § 315 Lindsey St 27320-3649 (Mail to: PO Box 72 27323-0072) Richard Miles (336) 349-3511

Ridgeway Chapel of the Good Shepherd **M** (4) 1202 Ridgeway-Warrenton Road 27570-0070 (Mail to: PO Box 70 27570-0070) (252) 456-2412

Roanoke Rapids All Saints Episcopal Church **P** (224) 635 Hamilton Street 27870-2703 (Mail to: 635 Hamilton St 27870-2703) (252) 537-3610

Roanoke Rapids St Mark Episcopal Church **P** (19) C/O Senior Warden PO Box 234 27870-0234 (Mail to: C/O Senior Warden PO Box 234 27870) Ben Duffey (252) 537-8835

Rockingham Church of the Messiah **P** (19) 202 Lawrence St 28379-3668 (Mail to: PO Box 1313 28380-1313) (910) 895-4739

Rocky Mount Church of the Epiphany **M** (11) 500 Fairview Rd 27801 (Mail to: Earnestine Lloyd-Battle. P.O. Box 1471 27802) (252) 442-7516

Rocky Mount Church of the Good Shepherd **P** (496) 231 Church St 27804-5404 (Mail to: 231 Church St 27804-5404) Louise Anderson Matthew Johnson (252) 442-1134

Rocky Mount St Andrews Episcopal Church **P** (493) 301 S Circle Dr 27804-3613 (Mail to: 301 S Circle Dr 27804-3613) George Greer (252) 443-2070

Roxboro St Marks Episcopal Church **M** (66) 422 Main St 27573-5037 (Mail to: PO Box 1071 27573-1071) (336) 597-2171

Salisbury St Lukes Episcopal Church **P** (589) 131 W Council St 28144-4320 (Mail to: 131 W Council St 28144-4320) Robert Black Bonnie Duckworth (704) 633-3221

Salisbury Saint Matthew Church **M** (54) 4401 Statesville Blvd 28147-7463 (Mail to: 4401 Statesville Blvd 28147-7463) Edwin Cox (704) 636-0821

Salisbury St Pauls Church **M** (44) 930 S Main St 28144-6453 (Mail to: PO Box 1852 28145-1852) (704) 637-9404

Sanford St Thomas Episcopal Church **P** (402) 312 Steele St 27330-3922 (Mail to: 312 Steele St 27330-3922) Bruce Heyvaert (919) 774-8644

Scotland Neck Trinity Episcopal Church **P** (37) 1305 Main St 27874-1346 (Mail to: PO Box 372 27874-0372) Elmer Malone John Fulton (252) 826-4616

Smithfield St Paul's Episcopal Church **P** (245) 218 S 2nd St 27577-4532 (Mail to: 218 S 2nd St 27577-4532) James Melnyk (919) 934-2675

Smithfield San Jose Mission **M** (120) 218 South Second St 27577 (Mail to: 218 S 2nd St 27577-4532) (910) 989-9742

Southern Pines Emmanuel Parish Episcopal Church **P** (745) 340 S Ridge St 28387-6036 (Mail to: 340 S Ridge St 28387-6036) Mary Dunlap Randal Foster Randal Foster John Talk (910) 692-3171

Speed St Marys Episcopal Church **M** (41) 169 Kilquick Rd 27886 (Mail to: 1264 Rogister Rd 27886-4366) (252) 903-3555

Statesville Trinity Episcopal Church **P** (271) 801 Henkel Rd 28677-3215 (Mail to: PO Box 1103 801 Henkel Rd 28687-1103) Robert Mullis (704) 872-6314

Tarboro Calvary Episcopal Church **P** (332) § 411 E Church St 27886-4403 (Mail to: PO Box 1245 27886-1245) (252) 823-8192

Tarboro St Luke Episcopal Church **M** (24) PO Box 64 27886-0064 (Mail to: PO Box 64 27886-0064) Louise Anderson (252) 641-5853

Tarboro St Michael Episcopal Church **M** (114) 3204 Western Blvd 27886-1828 (Mail to: PO Box 331 27886-0331) (252) 823-4926

Troy St Mary Magdalene Episcopal Church **M** (58) PO Box 613 27371-0613 (Mail to: PO Box 456 27376-0456) (910) 673-3838

Wadesboro Calvary Episcopal Church **P** (149) 223 E Morgan St 28170-2222 (Mail to: PO Box 942 28170-0942) Timothy Hushion (704) 694-3223

Wake Forest St Johns Episcopal Church **P** (767) 830 Durham Rd 27587-8792 (Mail to: 834 Durham Rd 27587-8792) Sarah Phelps Margaret Silton (919) 556-3656

Walnut Cove Christ Church **P** (52) 412 Summit Ave. 27052-0476 (Mail to: PO Box 476 27052-0476) (336) 591 7727

Warrenton Emmanuel Episcopal Church **M** (57) 133 Main St 27589-1921 (Mail to: PO Box 704 27589-0704) (252) 257-2557

Waxhaw St Margarets Episcopal Church **P** (349) 8515 Rea Rd 28173-6801 (Mail to: 8515 Rea Rd 28173-6801) Todd Dill Elenito Santos Paul Winton (704) 243-3523

Weldon Grace Episcopal Church **P** (26) Washington Ave & 5th St 27890 (Mail to: PO Box 308 27890-0308) (252) 536-4312

Wilson La Iglesia de la Guadalupana **M** (974) 106 Reid St SE 27893-6230 (Mail to: PO Box 4032 27893-0032) (252) 206-9996

Wilson St Marks Episcopal Church **M** (91) C/O Louie Tabron 2404 Nash St 27896-1309 (Mail to: C/O Louie Tabron 2404 E Nash Street 27893) (252) 291-6076

Wilson St Timothys Church **P** (641) 202 Goldsboro Street 27893 (Mail to: PO Box 1527 27894-1527) Martha Stebbins Robert Thomas (252) 291-8220

Winston Salem St Annes Episcopal Church **P** (377) 2690 Fairlawn Dr 27106-3802 (Mail to: Attn Treasurer PO Box 11437 27116-1437) Virginia Wilder (336) 768-0174

Winston Salem St Pauls Episcopal Church **P** (2707) 520 Summit St 27101-1115 (Mail to: 520 Summit St 27101-1195) Sara Ardrey-Graves Darby Everhard David Kinser Nancy Vaders Lauren Villemuer-Drenth (336) 723-4391

Winston Salem St Stephen Episcopal Church **P** (119) 810 Highland Ave 27101-4209 (Mail to: 810 Highland Ave 27101-4209) Hector Sintim (336) 724-2614

Winston Salem St Timothys Episcopal Church **P** (1058) 2575 Parkway Dr 27103-3522 (Mail to: 2575 Parkway Dr 27103-3522) Steven Rice Mary Kroohs (336) 765-0294

DIOCESE OF NORTH DAKOTA
(PROVINCE VI)
Comprises the State of North Dakota and Clay County, Minnesota
DIOCESAN OFFICE 3600 South 25th St Fargo ND 58104-6861
TEL (701) 235-6688　WEB http://www.ndepiscopal.org/

Previous Bishops—
Wm D Walker 1883-96, Samuel C Edsall 1899-1901, Cameron Mann 1901-13, John P Tyler 1914-31, Fredk B Bartlett 1931-35, Douglass H Atwill 1937-51, Richard R Emery 1951-64, George T Masuda 1965-79, Harold A Hopkins Jr 1980-88
Andrew H Fairfield 1989-2003

Bishop—The Rt Rev Michael G Smith (998)
(Dio 18 May 04)

Conv Sec J Helgaas; *Treas* D Williams; *Chanc* K Venhuizen; *Dio Admin* L Woltjer; *Indian Work* E McLaughlin; *Fin* vacant; *ER&D* vacant; *Evang Off* vacant; *UTO* M Zaharia

Stand Comm—Cler: Pres J Floberg M Strobel T Overbo; *Lay:* R Fox D Henderson C Iverson

PARISHES, MISSIONS, AND CLERGY

Bismarck Saint George's Episcopal Church **P** (325) 601 4th St 58501-3685 (Mail to: PO Box 1241 58502-1241) (701) 223-1942

Cannon Ball St James Episcopal Church **P** (122) General Delivery 58528 (Mail to: PO Box 612 58528) Neil Two Bears (701) 854-7325

Cartwright St Michael & All Angels Church **P** (47) 14 Route 1 Box Box 58838 (Mail to: General Delivery 58838-9999) (701) 572-9278

Devils Lake Episcopal Church of the Advent **P** (24) 501 6th St NE 58301-2523 (Mail to: PO Box 703 58301-0703) (701) 662-3726

Dickinson St Johns Episcopal Church **P** (27) 822 5th Ave W 58601-3832 (Mail to: PO Box 48 58602-0048) (701) 225-5026

Dunseith St Sylvans Church **P** (77) 1025 61st Ave Nw 58329 (Mail to: PO Box 10337 58106-0337) (701) 891-2911

✛ **Fargo** Gethsemane Cathedral **O** (371) 3600 25th St S 58104-6861 (Mail to: 3600 25th St S 58104-6861) Mark Strobel Terry Overbo Charlotte Robbins Crystal Towers Glenn Williams (701) 232-3394

Fargo St Stephens Episcopal Church **P** (153) 120 21st Ave 58102-2015 (Mail to: 120 21st Ave 58102-2015) Jamie Parsley (701) 232-2076

Fort Totten St Thomas Church **P** (119) PO Box 43 58335-9999 (Mail to: C/O Mr William Mckay General Delivery 58335-9999) (701) 766-4630

Fort Yates St Lukes Church **P** (297) 501 S River Rd 58538 (Mail to: P.O. Box 612 58538-0612) Lindsey Dwarf Sloane Floberg Virginia Luger Neil Two Bears (701) 854-2323

Garrison St Pauls Church **P** (86) 1025 61st Ave NW 58540-9384 (Mail to: PO Box 10337 58106-0337)

Grand Forks St Pauls Episcopal Church **P** (202) 319 S 5th St 58201-4607 (Mail to: 319 S 5th St 58201-4607) James Shannon (701) 775-7955

Jamestown Grace Episcopal Church **P** (135) 405 2nd Ave Ne 58401-3308 (Mail to: 405 2nd Ave NE 58401-3308) (701) 252-4499

Minot All Saints' Episcopal Church **P** (58) 301 Main St S 58701-3917 (Mail to: 301 Main St S 58701-3917) (701) 839-1037

Moorhead St John the Divine Episcopal Church **P** (265) 120 8th St S 56560-2809 (Mail to: PO Box 641 56561-0641) (218) 233-0423

Oakes St Mary and St Mark Epis Church **M** (26) 211 6th St 58474-1218 (Mail to: 9034 111th Avenue SE 58474-9105) (701) 742-2213

Selfridge Church of the Cross **P** (29) 25 Main St 58568-6801 (Mail to: PO Box 73 58568-0073) John Floberg (701) 891-2911

Valley City All Saints Episcopal Church **P** (19) 516 Central Ave 58072-2544 (Mail to: PO Box 366 58072-0366) (701) 845-0819

Walhalla St Peters Church **P** 508 Delano Ave 58282 (Mail to: 12707-109th St Ne 58282-9460) Elsie Magnus

Williston St Peters Episcopal Church **P** (96) 111 East 14th Street 58802-1181 (Mail to: PO Box 1181 58802-1181) Michael Paul (701) 572-9278

DIOCESE OF NORTHERN CALIFORNIA
(PROVINCE VIII)
Comprises the northern third of the State of California
DIOCESAN OFFICE 350 University Avenue, Suite 280, Sacramento CA 95825
TEL (916) 442-6918　FAX (916) 442-6927
E-MAIL info@norcalepiscopal.org　WEB www.norcalepiscopal.org

Previous Bishops—
John HD Wingfield 1874-98; William H Moreland m 1899 Bp 1910-33; Archie WN Porter coadj 1933 Bp 1933-57; Edward McNair suffr 1967-73; Clarence R Haden coadj 1957 Bp 1958-78; John L Thompson III 1978-91; Jerry A Lamb coadj 1991 Bp 1992-2006; Barry L Beisner coad 2006 Bp 2006

Bishop—Rt. Rev Barry Leigh Beisner (1008) (Dio Sep 2006)

Sec Conv Rev M Warren; *Canon to Ord* Rev Cn A McMillin; *Board of Trustees Pres* Rt Rev B Beisner; *Board of Trustees VP* Rev M Monnot; *Treas* J Nykamp; *Chanc* Cn C Mack; *Dir of Ops* K Braak; *Comm on Min* R Simas; *Cong Dev* Rev B Monnot; *Epis Comm Serv* Rev L Jevne; *Health Min* S Wahlstrom; *Companion Diocese* Rev D Green; *Sust Dev Goals* Rev L Jevne; *ERD* J Snibbe; *Chap to Ret Clergy* Rev C Leigh-Taylor

Stand Comm—Cler: Pres B Clark *Sec* S Kellerman *Comm* J Richardson; *Lay:* C Allen C Hill N Mack J Sargent

PARISHES, MISSIONS, AND CLERGY
Alturas St Michaels Episcopal Church **M** (27) 310 W North St 96101-3957 (Mail to: 310 W North

St 96101-3957) David Cohen James Young (530) 233-2251

Anderson St. Michael's Episcopal Church **P** (82) 3001 Rupert Rd 96007-3746 (Mail to: PO Box 144 96007-0144) (530) 365-4344

Antelope St. Andrew's Episcopal Church **M** (56) 7850 Watt Ave 95843-2001 (Mail to: 7850 Watt Ave 95843-2001) Peter Rodgers (916) 332-1476

Arcata St Albans Episcopal Church **P** (257) 1675 Chester Ave 95521-6827 (Mail to: 1675 Chester Ave 95521-6827) Sara Potter Nancy Streufert (707) 822-4102

Auburn St Lukes Church **P** (193) 124 Orange St 95603-5233 (Mail to: 124 Orange St 95603-5233) Jana Branson Brian Rebholtz (530) 885-2316

Benicia St Pauls Episcopal Church **P** (281) 120 East J Street 94510-3235 (Mail to: 120 E J St 94510-3298) Anne Mertz Mary Goshert Arthur Holder (707) 745-0307

Calistoga St Lukes Episcopal Church **M** (94) 1504 Myrtle St 94515-1633 (Mail to: PO Box 381 94515-0381) Susan Napoliello (707) 942-6007

Cameron Park Faith Episcopal Church **P** (523) 2200 Country Club Dr 95682-7703 (Mail to: PO Box 966 95682-0966) Sean Cox Sonya Reichel (530) 676-5348

Carmichael St Georges Church **P** (82) 5600 Winding Way 95608-1213 (Mail to: 5600 Winding Way 95608-1213) Robert Olsen (916) 487-5600

Carmichael St Michaels Episcopal Church **P** (678) §
2140 Mission Ave 95608-5635 (Mail to: 2140 Mission Ave 95608-5699) Rodney Davis George Foxworth Mary Hudak Cynthia Long (916) 488-3550

Chico St John the Evangelist Church **P** (325) 2341
Floral Ave 95926-7311 (Mail to: 2341 Floral Ave 95926-7311) Richard Yale Lewis Powell (530) 894-1971

Cloverdale Church of the Good Shepherd **M** (38)
122 Main St 95425-3346 (Mail to: PO Box 337 95425-0337) (707) 891-6015

Colusa St Stephens Episcopal Church **P** (49)
642 5th St 95932-2611 (Mail to: PO Box 1044 95932-1044) John Vafis (530) 458-2470

Corning St Andrew Episcopal Church **M** (14)
820 Marin St 96021-3230 (Mail to: PO Box 276 96021-0276) (530) 680-0353

Crescent City St Pauls Episcopal Church **M** (69)
220 E Macken Ave 95531-2745 (Mail to: 220 E Macken Ave 95531-2745) (707) 464-2708

Davis Church of St Martin **P** (559) 640 Hawthorne
Ln 95616-3463 (Mail to: 640 Hawthorne Ln 95616-3463) Anne Beatty Pamela Dolan Margaret Grayden Leah Hallisey Ernest Lewis (530) 756-0444

Eureka Christ Episcopal Church **P** (194) 625 15th
St 95501-2328 (Mail to: PO Box 861 95502-0861) Daniel London Nancy Streufert (707) 442-1797

Fair Oaks St Francis Episcopal Church **P** (143)
11430 Fair Oaks Blvd 95628-5157 (Mail to: 11430 Fair Oaks Blvd 95628-5157) Aileen Aidnik Diana Lueckert (916) 966-2261

Fairfield Grace Episcopal Church **P** (352) 1405
Kentucky St 94533-4715 (Mail to: 1405 Kentucky St 94533-4715) David Cavanagh Karen Freeman (707) 425-4481

Ferndale St Mary Episcopal Church **M** (6) 400
Shaw Ave 95536 (Mail to: PO Box 366 95536-0366) (707) 786-9843

Folsom Trinity Episcopal Church **P** (374) 803
Figueroa St 95630-2404 (Mail to: 801 Figueroa St 95630-2404) Jason Bruce Patricia Kempster Charles Knuth (916) 985-2495

Fort Bragg St Michael & All Angels Parish **P** (72)
201 Fir St 95437-3110 (Mail to: PO Box 124 95437-0124) Tansy Chapman Randy Knutson (707) 964-1900

Fortuna St Francis Episcopal Church **M** (130)
568 16th St 95540-2415 (Mail to: 568 16th St 95540-2415) Mara Arack Kathleen Mccloghrie (707) 725-4686

Galt St Lukes Episcopal Church **M** (78) 200 Third
St 95632 (Mail to: PO Box 897 95632-0897) Barbara Nixon (209) 745-2784

Grass Valley Emmanuel Episcopal Church **P**
(415) 235 S Church St 95945-6703 (Mail to: 235 S Church St 95945-6793) Alan Kellermann Anne Powell (530) 273-7876

Gridley St Timothys Episcopal Church **M** (87)
410 Jackson St 95948-2513 (Mail to: PO Box 176 95948-0176) (530) 846-4147

Gualala Shepherd by the Sea MIssion **M** (62)
39141 Church St 95445-8306 (Mail to: PO Box 691 95445-0691) (707) 785-3682

Healdsburg St Pauls Episcopal Church **P** (294)
209 Matheson St 95448-4109 (Mail to: 209 Matheson St 95448-4109) Sally Hubbell (707) 433-2107

Kenwood St Patricks Episcopal Church **P** (378)
9000 Sonoma Hwy 95452-9028 (Mail to: PO Box 247 95452-0247) Doyle Dietz Allen George Hunt Karen King Leslie King (707) 833-4228

Lake Almanor Holy Spirit Mission **M** (11) 3767
Hwy A 13 96137 (Mail to: 3767 Hwy A-13 96137) John Palmer Matthew Warren (530) 375-0994

Lakeport St Johns Episcopal Church **P** (82) 1190
Forbes St 95453-3824 (Mail to: 1190 Forbes St 95453-3824) (707) 263-4785

Lincoln St James Episcopal Church **P** (122) 479 L
St 95648-1633 (Mail to: 490 K St 95648-1627) Richard Henry Sarah Quinney (916) 645-1739

Marysville St Johns Episcopal Church **P** (86) 800
D St 95901-5321 (Mail to: 800 D St 95901-5321) (530) 742-8829

Monte Rio St Andrews in the Redwoods **M** 20329
Highway 116 95462-9747 (Mail to: PO Box 721 95462-0721) (707) 865-0834

Mount Shasta St Barnabas **M** (95) 701 Lassen Ln
96067-9711 (Mail to: 701 Lassen Ln 96067-9711) Lawrence Holben (530) 926-5326

Napa St Marys Episcopal Church **P** (391) 1917
Third St 94558 (Mail to: 1917 3rd St 94559-2312) Vanessa Glass John Morris (707) 255-0991

Nevada City Holy Trinity Episcopal Church **P**
(401) 201 Nevada St 95959-2605 (Mail to: 201 Nevada St 95959-2605) Bradley Helmuth (530) 265-8836

Oroville St Pauls Episcopal Church **P** (58) 1430
Pine St 95965-4836 (Mail to: 1430 Pine St 95965-4836) David Englund Susan Fay (530) 533-5035

Paradise Church of St Nicholas **P** (159) 5872
Oliver Rd 95969-3835 (Mail to: 5872 Oliver Rd 95969-3835) Ann Sullivan David Alves (530) 877-7006

Petaluma St Johns Episcopal Church **P** (100) 40
5th St 94952-3042 (Mail to: 40 5th St 94952-3042) Daniel Green (707) 762-8872

Placerville Episcopal Church of Our Saviour **P**
(155) 2979 Coloma St 95667-4440 (Mail to: PO Box 447 95667-0447) Debra Warwick-Sabino Susan Plucker (530) 622-2441

Quincy Christ the King Episcopal Church **M** (35)
545 Lawrence St 95971-9432 (Mail to: 545 Lawrence St 95971-9432) Matthew Warren (530) 283-0254

Rancho Cordova St Clements Episcopal Church
P (130) 2376 Zinfandel Dr 95670-4953 (Mail to: 2376 Zinfandel Dr 95670-4953) Kenneth Katona Charles Rines (916) 635-5282

Red Bluff Saint Peter's Episcopal Church **P** (91) 510 Jefferson St 96080-3408 (Mail to: 510 Jefferson St 96080-3408) Aidan Rontani (530) 527-5205

Redding All Saints Episcopal Church **P** (291) 2150 Benton Dr 96003-2151 (Mail to: 2150 Benton Dr 96003-2151) Carren Sheldon (530) 243-1000

Rio Vista St Brigid of Kildare **P** 218 California Street 94571-1923 (Mail to: PO Box 580 94571-0580) Susan Reeve (707) 374-2667

Rocklin St Augustine of Canterbury **P** (146) 1800 Wildcat Blvd. 95765 (Mail to: 1800 Wildcat Blvd 95765-5471) Elizabeth Armstrong Maryellen Garnier Thomas Gartin (916) 435-9552

Roseville St Johns Episcopal Church **P** (439) 2351 Pleasant Grove Blvd 95747-8918 (Mail to: c/o The Rev Cliff Haggenjos 2351 Pleasant Grove Blvd 95747-8918) Clifford Haggenjos Babette Haggenjos (916) 786-6911

Sacramento All Saints Episcopal Church **P** (207) 2076 Sutterville Rd 95822-1320 (Mail to: 2076 Sutterville Rd 95822-1384) Virginia Mcneely Michael Monnot (916) 455-0643

Sacramento St Matthews Episcopal Church **P** (112) 2300 Edison Ave 95821-1714 (Mail to: 2300 Edison Ave 95821-1796) Cynthia Long Rik Rasmussen Chana Tetzlaff (916) 927-0115

Sacramento St Pauls Episcopal Church **P** (59) 1430 J St 95814-2918 (Mail to: PO BOX 160914 95816) Michael Backlund Rik Rasmussen Anne Slakey Lynell Walker (916) 446-2620

Sacramento St Marys Church **P** (128) 9085 Calvine Rd 95829-9451 (Mail to: 9085 Calvine Rd 95829-9451) Anne Slakey Anne Smith (916) 689-1099

✠ **Sacramento** Trinity Episcopal Cathedral **O** (1749) 2620 Capitol Ave 95816-5905 (Mail to: 2620 Capitol Ave 95816-5991) James Richardson Steven Skiffington Jesse Vaughan Lynell Walker (916) 446-2513

Saint Helena Grace Episcopal Church **P** (460) 1314 Spring St 94574-2050 (Mail to: 1314 Spring St 94574-2050) Anne Clarke Amy Denney-Zuniga Michael Erhard (707) 963-4157

Santa Rosa The Church of the Incarnation **P** (612) 550 Mendocino Ave 95401-5213 (Mail to: 550 Mendocino Ave 95401-5213) Stephen Shaver James Knutsen Margaret Moore (707) 579-2604

Sebastopol St Stephens Episcopal Church **P** (140) 500 Robinson Rd 95472-4110 (Mail to: 500 Robinson Rd 95472-4110) Christy Laborda Harris (707) 823-3281

Sonoma Trinity Episcopal Church **P** (159) 275 East Spain Street 95476-5732 (Mail to: 275 E Spain St 95476-5732) James Thomas (707) 938-4846

Susanville Good Shepherd Episcopal Church **M** (26) 1155 North St 96130-4051 (Mail to: 1155 North St 96130-4051) David Cohen (530) 257-6002

Sutter Creek Trinity Episcopal Church **P** (124) 430 Highway 49 95685 (Mail to: 430 State Highway 49 95685-4144) Paul Colbert (209) 267-0255

Tahoe City St Nicholas Episcopal Church **M** (93) 855 W. Lake Blvd Hwy 89 96145 (Mail to: PO Box 855 96145-0855) (530) 583-4713

Ukiah Holy Trinity Episcopal Church **P** (77) 640 South Orchard Avenue 95482-5012 (Mail to: Barbara Webster 640 S Orchard Ave 95482-5012) (707) 462-8042

Vacaville Epiphany Episcopal Church **P** (292) 300 West St 95688-4516 (Mail to: 300 West St 95688-4516) Thomas Olson Beatryce Clark (707) 448-2275

Vallejo Ascension Episcopal Church **P** (167) 2420 Tuolumne St 94589-2345 (Mail to: 2420 Tuolumne St 94589-2345) Bayani Rico Richard Von Grabow (707) 644-5505

Wheatland Grace Episcopal Church **M** (27) 610 3rd St 95692-9459 (Mail to: 610 3rd St 95692-9459) Paul Hancock (530) 483-7050

Willits St Francis in the Redwoods Mission **M** (91) 1 Main Street 95490 (Mail to: 66 E Commercial St 95490-3102) Betsy Bruneau Mary Fisher Donnalee Hart (707) 459-3066

Willows Holy Trinity Episcopal Church **P** (33) 556 East Sycamore Street 95988-3250 (Mail to: Mrs R W Danley PO Box 339 95988) (530) 934-3778

Woodland St Lukes Episcopal Church **P** (126) 515 Second Street 95695-4029 (Mail to: 515 2nd St 95695-4029) Terri Hobart Frank Chacon George Foxworth (530) 662-7152

Yuba City St James of Jerusalem Mission **M** (37) 556 George Washington Blvd 95993 (Mail to: 556 George Washington Blvd 95993-8995) (530) 673-1790

DIOCESE OF NORTHERN INDIANA
(PROVINCE V)
Comprises Northern Indiana
DIOCESAN OFFICE 117 N Lafayette Blvd South Bend IN 46601
TEL (574) 233-6489   FAX (574) 287-7914
E-MAIL info@ednin.org   WEB www.ednin.org

Previous Bishops—
John H White 1895-1925, Campbell Gray 1925-44, Reginald Mallett 1944-63, Walter Conrad Klein 1963-72, William CR Sheridan 1972-87, Francis C Gray 1987-98, Edward S Little II 2000-2016

Bishop—Rt Rev Dr Douglas E Sparks (Dio 25 Jun 16)

Miss for Admin and Comm Rev Cn M Walker; *Miss for Gov and Trans* Rev Cn TL Bays; *Miss for Fin* Cn C Bianchini & Cn S Katona; *Miss for Form* Rev Cn H Randolph; *Miss for Dcns* Rev Cn A Wietstock; *Miss for Comm Eng* Cn A Niyongabo

Officers: Sec Rev JH Warnock; *Treas* J Walker; *Chanc* Daniel H Pfeifer 53600 N Ironwood Dr South Bend IN 46635 (574) 272-2870

Stand Comm: Cler: J Czolgosz R Lightsey P Nesta; *Lay:* M Goodwin T McLaughlin R Powers

Depts: COM Rev JH Warnock

PARISHES, MISSIONS, AND CLERGY

Angola Church of the Holy Family **P** (81) 909 A S Darling St 46703-1857 (Mail to: 909 S Darling St 46703-1857) Thomas Adamson (260) 665-5067

Berne St George Episcopal Church **M** (31) 1195 Hendricks St 46711-2391 (Mail to: 1195 Hendricks St 46711-2391) (260) 589-3315

Bristol Saint John Of The Cross **P** (127) 601 E Vistula St 46507-8904 (Mail to: PO Box 433 46507-0433) Jennifer Fulton (574) 848-7114

Chesterton St Francis Episcopal Church **P** (90) 237 E 1200 N 46304-9360 (Mail to: PO Box 621 46304-0621) David Pearson (219) 926-3497

Crown Point St Christophers Episcopal Church **P** (72) 12718 Marshall St 46307-8386 (Mail to: 12718 Marshall St 46307-8386) (219) 663-0559

Culver St Elizabeths Episcopal Church **M** (18) 820 Academy Rd 46511-1106 (Mail to: 515 State St 46511-1131) Clark Miller (574) 339-0235

East Chicago Church of the Good Shepherd **P** (149) 4525 Baring Ave 46312-3208 (Mail to: 4525 Baring Ave 46312-3208) (219) 397-4597

Elkhart St David Episcopal Church **P** (135) 26824 County Road 4 46514-5851 (Mail to: 26824 County Road 4 46514-5851) Joshua Nelson (574) 264-4039

Elkhart Church of St John the Evangelist **P** (238) 226 W Lexington Ave 46516-3128 (Mail to: 226 W Lexington Ave 46516-3128) (574) 295-1725

Fort Wayne Grace Episcopal Church **P** (132) 10010 Aurora Pl 46804-8500 (Mail to: 10010 Aurora Pl 46804-8500) (260) 432-9221

Fort Wayne St Alban Episcopal Church **P** (165) 7308 Saint Joe Rd 46835-1581 (Mail to: 7308 Saint Joe Rd 46835-1596) Daniel Layden (260) 485-8022

Fort Wayne Trinity Episcopal Church **P** (391) 611 W Berry St 46802-2105 (Mail to: 611 W Berry St 46802-2192) TJ Freeman Chandler Randall Gordon Samra (260) 423-1693

Gary St Augustine Episcopal Church **P** (128) 2425 W 19th Ave 46404-2749 (Mail to: PO Box 4156 46404-4156) (219) 944-8383

Gary St Barnabas in the Dunes **P** (38) PO Box 2608 46403-0608 (Mail to: 1125 Pike St 46403-1380) Michael Dwyer (219) 938-2834

Gas City St Paul Episcopal Church **P** (15) 121 E South A St 46933-1706 (Mail to: PO Box 46 46933-0046) (765) 674-2670

Goshen St James Episcopal Church **P** (70) 105 S 6th St 46528-3303 (Mail to: 105 S 6th St 46528-3398) (574) 533-4984

Griffith St Timothy Episcopal Church **P** (87) 1115 Cline Ave 46319-1563 (Mail to: 1115 Cline Ave 46319-1563) (219) 838-8379

Hobart St Stephen Episcopal Church **P** (94) 1360 State St 46342-6056 (Mail to: PO Box 647 46342-0647) John Blakslee (219) 696-4819

✣ **Howe** St Mark's Episcopal Church **O** (35) 5755 State Road 9 46746-9228 (Mail to: PO Box 336 46746-0336) (260) 497-9718

Huntington Church of Christ the King **P** (64) § 1224 Jefferson St 46750-1848 (Mail to: 1224 Jefferson St 46750-1848) Theodore Neidlinger (260) 356-3570

Kokomo St Andrew Episcopal Church **HC** (242) 602 W Superior Street 46901-5299 (Mail to: 602 W Superior St 46901-5299) Richard Lightsey (765) 457-2075

Laporte St Pauls Episcopal Church **P** (238) 708 Harrison St 46350-3418 (Mail to: 708 Harrison St 46350-3418) Joel Steiner (219) 362-2784

Logansport Trinity Episcopal Church **P** (114) 319 7th St 46947-3128 (Mail to: 319 7th St 46947-3128) Clark Miller (574) 753-2733

Marion Gethsemane Episcopal Church **P** (100) 111 E 9th St 46953-1968 (Mail to: 803 S Washington St 46953-1968) James Warnock (765) 664-4638

Michigan City St Andrew by the Lake Episcopal Ch **P** (29) 1007 Moore Rd 46360-1762 (Mail to: PO Box 8766 46361-8766) Robert Dorow (219) 872-6984

Michigan City Trinity Episcopal Church **P** (112) 600 Franklin St 46360-3412 (Mail to: 600 Franklin St 46360-3412) Joseph Czolgosz (219) 874-4355

Mishawaka St Paul Episcopal Church **P** (163) 616 Lincolnway E 46544-2210 (Mail to: 616 Lincolnway E 46544-2210) Susan Haynes Stewart Clem Michael Cover (574) 255-9090

Munster St Paul Episcopal Church **P** (71) 1101 Park Dr 46321-2544 (Mail to: 1101 Park Dr 46321-2544) (219) 838-3803

Plymouth St Thomas Church Episcopal **HC** (144) N. Center Street at Adams 46563-1728 (Mail to: PO Box 421 46563-0421) Thomas Haynes (574) 936-2735

Rensselaer St Peter Episcopal Church **M** (6) 402 S Melville St 47978-3202 (Mail to: PO Box 244 47978-0244) (219) 866-8225

South Bend Church of the Holy Trinity **P** (51) 915 Olive St 46628-2521 (Mail to: PO Box 3679 46619-0679) Terri Bays (574) 234-9582

South Bend St Michael & All Angels Episcopal Ch **P** (231) 53720 Ironwood Rd 46635-1532 (Mail to: 53720 Ironwood Rd 46635-1532) Matthew Cowden Cynthia Van Parys (574) 243-0632

✤ **South Bend** Cathedral of St James **O** (223) 117 Lafayette Blvd 46601-1507 (Mail to: 117 Lafayette Blvd 46601-1587) Brian Grantz Janice Miller (574) 232-4837

Syracuse All Saints Episcopal Church **M** (77) 7812 E Vawter Park Rd 46567-9515 (Mail to: 7830 E Vawter Park Rd 46567-9515) (574) 457-2178

Valparaiso St Andrew's Episcopal Church **P** (259) 505 Bullseye Lake Rd. 46383-4813 (Mail to: 505 Bullseye Lake Rd 46383-1951) Roger Bower (219) 462-4946

Warsaw St Anne Episcopal Church **P** (246) 424 W Market St 46580-2831 (Mail to: 424 W Market St 46580-2831) (574) 267-6266

DIOCESE OF NORTHERN MICHIGAN
(PROVINCE V)
Comprises the northernmost part of the State in the Upper Peninsula of Michigan
DIOCESAN OFFICE 131 E Ridge St Marquette MI 49855
TEL (906) 228-7160   FAX (906) 228-7171
E-MAIL diocese@upepiscopal.org   WEB www.upepiscopal.org

Previous Bishops—
Gershom M Williams 1896-1919, Robt L Harris coadj 1918 Bp 1919-29, Hayward S Ablewhite 1930-39, Herman Page prov 1940-42, Herman R Page 1942-64, George R Selway 1964-71, Sam J Wylie 1972-74, Wm A Dimmick 1975-82, Thomas K Ray 1982-99, James A Kelsey 1999-2007

Bishop—Rayford J Ray (April 1, 2011)

Treas R Graybill; *Chanc* P Micklow; *Stewardship* T Lippart; *District Ministry Developers* Rev M Padilla Rev K Thew Forrester Rev Cathy Clark *COM* J Martindale; *Trans* M Padilla & LK Bucklin; *Cn to Ord* J Cisluycis; *Cn for Disc & Vit* LK Bucklin

PARISHES, MISSIONS, AND CLERGY

Crystal Falls St Marks Church **P** (29) 809 Crystal Ave 49920-1104 (Mail to: C/O T R Harrison Treasurer 127 Iron St 49920-1124) Christine Mello-Maki Carolyn Orchard Margaret Padilla (906) 875-3921

De Tour Village St Stephens Episcopal Church **P** (17) 124 S Ontario St 49725 (Mail to: PO Box 413 49725-0413) (906) 297-3207

Eagle Harbor St Peters by the Sea **SC** (7) 435 Front Street 49950 (Mail to: PO Box 265 49950-0265) (906) 289-4567

Escanaba St Stephens Episcopal Church **P** (301) 500 Ogden Ave 49829-3930 (Mail to: 510 Ogden Ave 49829-3930) (906) 786-7970

Gladstone Trinity Episcopal Church **P** (135) 901 Dakota Ave 49837-1616 (Mail to: PO Box 428 49837-0428) Dale Jamison Maria Maniaci Suzanne Ray (906) 428-4116

Houghton Trinity Episcopal Church **P** (49) 205 E Montezuma Ave 49931-2110 (Mail to: 205 E Montezuma Ave 49931-2110) (906) 482-2010

Iron Mountain Church of the Holy Trinity **P** (78) 221 W B St 49801-3336 (Mail to: PO Box 805 49801-0805) Candice Lauk Norris Satterly (906) 774-3722

Iron River St Johns Church **P** (17) 527 2nd Ave 49935-1446 (Mail to: 527 2nd Ave 49935-1446) (906) 265-9013

Ironwood Church of the Transfiguration **P** (52) 336 E Aurora St 49938-2114 (Mail to: 334 E Aurora St 49938-2114) Geri Sola John Kangas (906) 932-4395

Ishpeming Grace Episcopal Church **P** (83) & 1st Canda Sts 49849 (Mail to: PO Box 601 49849-0601) (906) 485-1623

Larium Christ Episcopal Church **P** (74) 57031 Fifth St 49913 (Mail to: 3906 5th St 49913-1809) Laura Eaton (906) 337-5242

Mackinac Island Trinity Episcopal Church **P** (32) 1623 Fort St 49757 (Mail to: PO Box 472 49757-0472) (906) 847-3798

Manistique St Albans Church **P** (35) 301 Range St 49854-1562 (Mail to: PO Box 302 49854-0302) (906) 286-2881

Marquette Holy Innocents Episcopal Church **P** (19) 131 E Ridge St 49855-4208 (Mail to: PO Box 333 49833-0333) (906) 942-7178

Marquette St Pauls Episcopal Church **P** (340) 201 E Ridge St 49855-4210 (Mail to: 201 E Ridge St 49855-4210) Marcia Franz Coralie Hambleton Kevin Thew Forrester (906) 226-2912

Menominee Grace Episcopal Church **P** (54) 922 10th Ave 49858-3033 (Mail to: 922 10th Ave 49858-3033) Mary Miron Bonnie Turner (906) 863-2385

Munising St Johns Church **P** (18) 121 W Onota Street 49862-1119 (Mail to: 121 W Onota St 49862-1119) Virginia Mannisto Marion Luckey Thomas Luckey Kimberly Moote (906) 387-2468

Negaunee St Johns Episcopal Church **P** (56) 101 W Main St 49866-1607 (Mail to: PO Box 29 49866-0029) John Lenten James Martindale Kevin Thew Forrester (906) 475-4012

Newberry All Saints Church **P** (23) 314 W Truman St 49868-1227 (Mail to: 314 W Truman St 49868-1227) (906) 293-3180

Pointe Aux Pins Church of the Tranfiguration **SC** (3) Island Rd 49775 (Mail to: PO Box 850 49775-0850) (231) 634-7323

Sault Sainte Marie St James Episcopal Church **P** (86) 533 Bingham Ave 49783-2141 (Mail to: 533 Bingham Ave 49783-2199) Dawn Aldrich Robert Aldrich Susan Harries Diane Horst Lawrence Rice (906) 632-2451

DIOCESE OF NORTHWEST TEXAS
(PROVINCE VII)
Comprises 80 counties of Texas
DIOCESAN OFFICE The Hulsey Episcopal Center 1802 Broadway Lubbock TX 79401-3016
TEL (806) 763-1370   FAX (806) 472-0641
E-MAIL ethames@nwtdiocese.org   WEB www.nwtdiocese.org

Previous Bishops—
Edward A Temple 1910-24, Eugene C Seaman 1925-45, George H Quarterman 1946-72, Willis R Henton 1972-80, Sam B Hulsey 1980-1997, Charles Wallis Ohl Jr 1997-2008

Bishop—J Scott Mayer (1035)
(Dio 21 Mar 09)

Cn to Ord JM Ehmer; *Dio Adm* E Thames; *Fin Mgr* A Mora; *Treas* F Deaderick; *Asst* C Holley; *Reg* E Thames; *Chanc* T Choate; *COM* JM Ehmer

Stand Comm—Cler: C Ellery D Perdue J Walters; *Lay*: Y Batts M Emeny C Holeva

PARISHES, MISSIONS, AND CLERGY

Abilene Church of the Heavenly Rest Abilene **P** (605) 602 Meander St 79602-1027 (Mail to: 602 Meander St 79602-1099) Robert Hennagin Claire Makins Douglas Thomas Douglas Thomas Amanda Watson Amanda Watson (325) 677-2091

Abilene Saint Mark's Episcopal Church **P** (53) 3150 Vogel St 79603-2128 (Mail to: 3150 Vogel St 79603-2199) Mary Glover Mary Glover James Smart Peggy Valentine (325) 677-1471

Albany Trinity Episcopal Church **M** (15) 140 Ave B 76430 (Mail to: PO Box 818 76430-0818) (325) 513-7983

Amarillo St Andrews Episcopal Church **P** (1102) 1601 S Georgia St 79102-2315 (Mail to: 1601 S Georgia St 79102-2315) Nina Jo Craig Robert Pace Diedre Ballou Dave Blakley Erin Jones Mildred Rugger Jill Walters-Pace Christopher Wrampelmeier (806) 376-6316

Amarillo St Peters Episcopal Church **P** (152) 4714 Nw 4th Ave 79106-5220 (Mail to: 4714 NW 4th Ave 79106-5220) (806) 353-9594

Big Spring St Mary the Virgin Episcopal Church **P** (66) 1001 Goliad St 79720-2848 (Mail to: PO Box 2949 79721-2949) Christian Rabone Connetta Fowler John Marshall (432) 267-8201

Borger St Peters Church **P** (22) 620 Hemlock St 79007-4554 (Mail to: PO Box 138 79008-0138) (806) 274-2944

Brownfield Good Shepherd Mission **M** (41) 304 E. Lanny 79316-0334 (Mail to: PO Box 334 79316-0334) James Haney (806) 637-6827

Canyon St Georges Episcopal Church **M** (27) 2516 4th Ave 79015-4146 (Mail to: 2516 4th Ave 79015-4146) Beverly Couzzourt (806) 655-3121

Clarendon St John the Baptist Mission **M** (29) 301 South Park 79226 (Mail to: Attn Kade L Matthews PO Box 1078 79226) (806) 874-2511

Coleman St Marks Episcopal Church **M** (61) 601 S Neches St 76834-4026 (Mail to: PO Box 838 76834-0838) Russell Fisher (325) 625-4995

Colorado City All Saints Episcopal Church **M** (25) 304 Locust St 79512-6428 (Mail to: PO Box 336 79512-0336) (325) 728-2243

Dalhart St James Church **P** (158) 801 Denver Ave 79022-3625 (Mail to: 801 Denver Ave 79022-3625) (806) 244-2396

Dumas St Pauls Episcopal Church **M** (22) 815 E 3rd St 79029-4155 (Mail to: PO Box 71 79029-0071) (806) 935-3139

Levelland St Lukes Episcopal Church **M** (19) 1103 Sundown Hwy 79336 (Mail to: 1103 W. Street Rd 300 79336) (804) 894-8097

Lubbock Canterbury Episcopal Campus Ministry at Texas Tech **CC** (50) 2407 16th St 79401-4434 (Mail to: 2407 16th St 79401-4434) (806) 765-0037

Lubbock St Christophers Episcopal Church **P** (325) 2807 42nd St 79413-3223 (Mail to: 2807 42nd St 79413-3223) Jennifer Holder Alvin Stofel (806) 799-8208

Lubbock St Pauls Church on the Plains **P** (782) 1510 Ave X 79401 (Mail to: 1510 Avenue X 79401-4423) James Haney (806) 762-2893

Lubbock St Stephens Episcopal Church **HC** (310) 1101 Slide Rd 79416-5419 (Mail to: 1101 Slide Rd 79416-5419) James Perdue Paige McKay (806) 799-3439

Midland Church Of The Holy Trinity **P** (502) 1412 W Illinois Ave 79701-6537 (Mail to: 1412 W Illinois Ave 79701-6593) David Galletly Barbara Kirk-Norris (432) 683-4207

Midland St Nicholas Episcopal Church **P** (96) 4000 W Loop 250 79707-3419 (Mail to: 4000 W Loop 250 79707-3419) Nancy Springer Thomas Burns (432) 694-8856

Odessa St Barnabas Episcopal Church **P** (122) 4141 Tanglewood Ln 79762-7224 (Mail to: 4141 Tanglewood Ln 79762-7224) David Mossbarger (432) 362-3881

Odessa St Johns Episcopal Church **P** (179) 401 County Road West 79763 (Mail to: 401 County Rd W PO Box 3346 79763-3741) (432) 333-6022

Odessa San Miguel Arcangel Episcopal Church **M** (375) 907 Adams Ave 79761-4111 (Mail to: 907 Adams Ave 79761-4111) (432) 332-2074

Pampa St Matthews Episcopal Church **P** (215) 727 W Browning Ave 79065-6204 (Mail to: 727 W Browning Ave 79065-6204) Mark Lang (806) 665-0701

Plainview St Marks Episcopal Church **M** (15) 710 Joliet St 79072-7716 (Mail to: 710 Joliet St 79072-7716) (806) 296-7185

San Angelo Emmanuel Episcopal Church **P** (417) 3 S Randolph St 76903-5828 (Mail to: 3 S Randolph St 76903-5828) Matthew Rowe (325) 653-2446

San Angelo Church of the Good Shepherd **P** (54) 720 S. Abe Street 76903 (Mail to: 720 S Abe St 76903-6734) Celia Ellery Celia Ellery (325) 659-3800

Shamrock St Michaels & All Angels Church **PS** (7) 304 S Madden St 79079-2518 (Mail to: 304 S Madden St 79079-2518) (806) 256-5181

Sweetwater St Stephens Episcopal Church **M** (31) 505 Locust St 79556-3249 (Mail to: 502 Locust St 79556-3250) Jared Houze (325) 235-8408

Vernon Grace Episcopal Church **M** (20) 3207 Indian St 76384-5923 (Mail to: PO Box 1404 76385-1404) (940) 552-7008

DIOCESE OF NORTHWESTERN PENNSYLVANIA
(PROVINCE III)
Comprises 13 counties in Northwest PA
DIOCESAN OFFICE 145 W 6th St Erie PA 16501
TEL (814) 456-4203　FAX (814) 454-8703
WEB www.dionwpa.org

Previous Bishops— Rogers Israel 1911-21, John C Ward 1921-43, Edward P Wroth 1943-46, Harold E Sawyer 1946-51, Wm Crittenden 1952-1973, Donald J Davis coadj 1973 Bp 1974-91 Robt D Rowley Jr coadj 1989-1991 Bp 1991-2007

Bishop—Rt Rev Sean Rowe (1019) (Dio 8 Sep 07)

Archdcn GG Winslow; *Cn for Miss Dev & Trans* Rev M Ishman; *Cn for Admin* V Butler; *Treas* R

Armstrong 381 Armstrong Dr New Castle PA 16101; *Chanc* J Steadman 24 Main St Girard PA 16417; *Deans: SW* Rev M Ishman *NE* Rev S Fussell *NW* Rev M Norton *SE* Rev B Ellis; *Cn for Fin* C Dougan; *Asst for Form* Rev J Piatko; *Cn for Cong Vit & Innovation* Rev A Johnson; *Comm* M Sewak

Stand Comm—Cler: J Downey S Fussell J Shank M Norton *Lay: Pres* J Malovich D Billioni C Dressler *Sec* A Bardol

PARISHES, MISSIONS, AND CLERGY

Bradford Church of the Ascension **P** (139) 26 Chautauqua Pl 16701-1915 (Mail to: PO Box

337 16701-0337) Stacey Fussell Gail Winslow (814) 368-8915

Brookville Church of the Holy Trinity **M** (52) 62 Pickering St 15825-1246 (Mail to: 62 Pickering St 15825-1246) (814) 849-7235

Clearfield St Andrews Church **M** (25) 102 E Cherry St 16830-2350 (Mail to: 102 E Cherry St 16830-2350) (814) 849-7235

Corry Emmanuel Episcopal Church **P** (48) 327 Center St 16407-1628 (Mail to: 327 Center St 16407-1676) Mary Norton (814) 665-7535

Dubois Church of Our Saviour **P** (130) 400 Liberty Blvd 15801-2408 (Mail to: PO Box 503 15801-0503) Melinda Hall (814) 371-8810

Edinboro St Augustine of Canterbury Church **M** (74) 427 W Plum St 16412-2145 (Mail to: PO Box 479 16412-0479) David Fulford (814) 734-4116

Emporium Emmanuel Episcopal Church **P** (75) 144 E 4th St 15834-1445 (Mail to: PO Box 88 15834-0088) Matthew Ryan (814) 486-0711

✤ **Erie** Cathedral of St Paul **O** (484) 134 W 7th St 16501-1004 (Mail to: 134 W 7th St 16501-1004) John Downey (814) 452-3779

Erie St Marks Episcopal Church **P** (207) 4701 Old French Rd 16509-3631 (Mail to: 4701 Old French Rd 16509-3699) (814) 868-9704

Erie St Marys Episcopal Church **M** (62) 662 Silliman Ave 16511-2057 (Mail to: 662 Silliman Ave 16511-2057) (814) 899-0118

Fairview St Stephens Church **P** (221) 1070 Dutch Rd 16415-1627 (Mail to: 1070 Dutch Rd 16415-1627) Shawn Clerkin (814) 474-5490

Foxburg Memorial Church of Our Father **M** (39) 110-136 Church Rd R 16036 (Mail to: PO Box 332 16036-0332) Patricia Lavery (724) 659-4541

Franklin St Johns Episcopal Church **P** (232) 1145 Buffalo St 16323-1254 (Mail to: PO Box 550 16323-0550) Elizabeth Yale (814) 432-5161

Greenville St Clements Episcopal Church **P** 103 Clinton St 16125-2051 (Mail to: 103 Clinton St 16125-2051) (724) 588-6440

Grove City Church of the Epiphany **M** (47) 870 Liberty St Ext 16127-6438 (Mail to: Rd 3 PO Box 287 16127) Patricia Lavery (724) 458-6720

Hermitage Church of the Redeemer **P** 5130 E State St 16148-9447 (Mail to: 5130 E State St 16148-9489) (724) 347-4602

Houtzdale Church of the Holy Trinity **M** (40) 222 Brisbin St 16651-1301 (Mail to: 222 Brisbin St 16651) William Ellis (814) 378-8543

Kane St Johns Episcopal Church **P** (9) 427 Chase St 16735-1320 (Mail to: 427 Chase St 16735-1320) (814) 837-6351

Lake City Grace Episcopal Church **M** (39) 10121 Hall Avenue 16423 (Mail to: 10121 Hall Ave 16423-1220) Donald Baxter (814) 774-8288

Meadville Christ Episcopal Church **P** (103) 870 Diamond Park 16335-2606 (Mail to: 870 Diamond Park 16335-2606) Rebecca Lash (814) 724-7389

New Castle Trinity Episcopal Church **P** 212 Mill St 16101-3612 (Mail to: 212 Mill St 16101-3612) Robert Reed (724) 654-8761

New Castle Trinity Episcopal Church **Cluster** 212 Mill St 16101-3612 (Mail to: 212 Mill St 16101-3612) Erin Betz Shank (724) 654-8761

North East Holy Cross Episcopal Church **M** (44) 51 W Main St 16428-1103 (Mail to: 51 W Main St 16428-1103) (814) 725-2910

Oil City Christ Church **P** (56) 16 Central Ave 16301-2734 (Mail to: 16 Central Ave 16301-2734) Mark Elliston (814) 677-3023

Osceola Mills St Laurence Episcopal Church **M** (43) 501 Lingle St 16666-1121 (Mail to: R.R. Box 569 16666) (814) 342-2379

Port Allegan St Joseph Church **M** (38) 116 E Arnold Ave 16743-1247 (Mail to: PO Box 117 16743) Joann Piatko (814) 558-5876

Ridgway Grace Episcopal Church **P** (63) 216 Center St 15853-1203 (Mail to: PO Box 404 15853-0404) Alan Coudriet Bonnie Skellen (814) 776-6132

Saint Marys St Agnes Episcopal Church **P** (57) 209 Saint Marys St 15857-1237 (Mail to: 209 Saint Marys St 15857-1271) (814) 781-1909

Sharon St Johns Episcopal Church **P** (545) 226 W State St 16146-1341 (Mail to: 226 W State St 16146-1395) Adam Trambley Randall Beck (724) 347-4501

Smethport Saint Luke's Episcopal Church **P** (78) 600 W Main & Church 16749 (Mail to: PO Box 1475 16749-1146) (814) 887-5841

Titusville St James Memorial Church **P** (98) 112 E Main St 16354-1849 (Mail to: 112 E Main St 16354-1849) (814) 827-3590

Warren Trinity Memorial Church **P** (122) 444 Pennsylvania Ave W 16365-2238 (Mail to: 444 Pennsylvania Ave W 16365-2238) Matthew Scott Timothy Dyer (814) 723-9360

Waterford St Peters Church **M** (42) 100 E 3rd St 16441-9766 (Mail to: PO Box 804 16441-0804) (814) 796-9011

Youngsville St Francis of Assisi Epis Church **P** (62) 343 E Main St 16371-1125 (Mail to: 343 E Main St 16371-1177) (814) 563-7586

STATE OF OHIO

Dioceses of Ohio and Southern Ohio

DIOCESE OF OHIO

(PROVINCE V)
Comprises the northern portion of Ohio
DIOCESAN OFFICE Trinity Commons 2230 Euclid Ave Cleveland OH 44115-2499
TEL (216) 771-4815   FAX (216) 623-0735
WEB www.dohio.org

Previous Bishops—
Philander Chase 1819-31, Chas P McIlvaine 1832-73, Gregory T Bedell coadj 1859 Bp 1873-89, Wm A Leonard 1889-30, Frank De Moulin coadj 1914-24, Warren L Rogers coadj 1925 Bp 1930-38, Beverley D Tucker coadj 1938 Bp 1938 -52, Nelson M Burroughs coadj 1949 Bp 1952-68, John H Burt coadj 1967 Bp 1968-1984, William Davidson asst 1980-86, James R Moodey coadj 1983 Bp 1984-93, Arthur Benjamin Williams Jr Bp Suffr 1986-2002, J Clark Grew II Bp 1994-2004

Bishop—Rt Rev Mark Hollingsworth Jr (997)
(Dio 17 Apr 04)

Assisting Bishop—Rt Rev William D Persell (999)

Assisting Bishop—Rt Rev Arthur B Williams Jr (812)

Cn to Ord WA Powel III; *Sec* D Arrington; *Treas* PT Austin; *Chanc* WA Powel III; *Archiv* B Wilbert; *Cn for Cong* B Purdom; *Cn for Min* P Grant; *Cn for Chr Frm* V Black; *Cn for Mission* M D'Anieri; *CFO* S Leishman; *Comm* J Rocha; *Development* L Hnat; *Camp & Retreat Proj Dir* K Ong-Landini; *Bps Admin Asst* E Cole

Stand Comm—Cler: G Catinella V Clark C McCann C Reed; *Lay:* J Bing D Coughlin G Daniels R Preston

PARISHES, MISSIONS, AND CLERGY

Akron Church Of Our Saviour **P** (213) 471 Crosby St 44302-1518 (Mail to: 471 Crosby St 44302-1500) Debra Bennett (330) 535-9174

Akron St Andrews Church **P** (52) 765 Thayer St 44315-0001 (Mail to: 765 Thayer St 44310-3099) (330) 253-6447

Akron St Pauls Church **P** (2109) 1361 W Market St 44313-7123 (Mail to: C/O Tom Valtman 1361 W Market St 44313-7123) Mark Pruitt Polly Glanville Susan Tiffany (330) 836-9327

Akron St Philips Church **P** (94) 1130 Mercer Ave 44320-3646 (Mail to: 1130 Mercer Ave 44320-3646) (330) 535-7295

Alliance Trinity Church **P** (84) 1200 S Union Ave 44601-4021 (Mail to: 1200 S Union Ave 44601-4021) Jerome Colegrove (330) 821-8498

Ashland St Matthews Church **P** (89) 1515 Mifflin Ave 44805-3648 (Mail to: 1515 Mifflin Ave 44805-3648) Alice Kay Ashby (419) 281-1420

Ashtabula St Peters Church **P** (231) 4901 Main Ave 44004-7018 (Mail to: PO Box 357 44005-0357) C David Evans Peter Nielsen (440) 992-8100

Barberton St Andrews Episcopal Church **P** (156) 267 5th St Nw 44203-2103 (Mail to: 583 W Hopocan Ave 44203-2256) Michael Petrochuk (330) 753-9026

Bellevue St Pauls Church **P** (77) 285 W Main St 44811-1333 (Mail to: PO Box 372 44811-0372) John Reinheimer (419) 483-4628

Berea Church of St Thomas **P** (285) 50 E Bagley Rd 44017-2009 (Mail to: 50 E Bagley Rd 44017-2009) David Radzik (440) 234-5241

Boardman St James Church **P** (110) 7640 Glenwood Ave 44512-5897 (Mail to: 7640 Glenwood Ave 44512-5897) Jessica Phillips Mary Vidmar John Wigle (330) 758-2727

Bowling Green St Johns Church **P** (29) 1505 E Wooster St 43402-3392 (Mail to: 1505 E Wooster St 43402-3392) (419) 353-0881

Brecksville St Matthews Church **P** (190) 9549 Highland Dr 44141-2729 (Mail to: 9549 Highland Dr 44141-2799) Stephanie Pace (440) 526-9865

Brunswick St Patricks Church **P** (100) 3611 Center Rd 44212-0397 (Mail to: PO Box 397 44212-0397) (330) 220-2777

Canton St Marks Church **P** (340) 515 48th St Nw 44709-1369 (Mail to: 515 48th St NW 44709-1369) Elizabeth Frank (330) 449-2662

Canton St Pauls Church **P** (217) 425 Cleveland Ave Sw 44702-1625 (Mail to: PO Box 21333 425 Cleveland Ave SW 44701-1333) (330) 455-0286

Chagrin Fall St Martin's Episcopal Church **P** (482) 6295 Chagrin River Rd 44022-3544 (Mail to: 6295 Chagrin River Rd 44022-3599) John Cerrato (440) 247-7406

Chardon St Lukes Church **P** (223) 11519 Wilson Mills Rd 44024-9406 (Mail to: 11519 Wilson

Mills Rd PO Box 244 44024-9406) Christopher McCann (440) 285-4641

Cleveland All Saints Church **P** (272) 8911 W Ridgewood Dr 44130-4122 (Mail to: 8911 W Ridgewood Dr 44130-4100) (440) 888-4055

Cleveland St Albans Church **P** (30) 2555 Euclid Heights Blvd 44106-2709 (Mail to: 2555 Euclid Heights Blvd 44106-2799) (216) 932-8080

Cleveland St Andrews Church **P** (132) 2171 E 49th St 44103-4401 (Mail to: 2171 E 49th St 44103-4401) Sharon Williams (216) 391-2632

Cleveland St Bartholomew's Episcopal Church **P** (107) 435 Som Center Rd 44143-1519 (Mail to: 435 Som Center Rd 44143-1519) Stephen Secaur (440) 449-2290

Cleveland St Johns Church **P** 2600 Church Ave 44113-2908 (Mail to: PO Box 309 44107-0309) (216) 781-5546

Cleveland St Pauls Episcopal Church **P** (1643) 2747 Fairmount Blvd 44106-3606 (Mail to: 2747 Fairmount Blvd 44106-3696) Philip Anderson Dale Grandfield Jessie Gutgsell Jeanne Leinbach (216) 932-5815

✣ **Cleveland** Trinity Cathedral **O** (1031) 2021 E 22nd St 44115-2401 (Mail to: 2230 Euclid Ave 44115-2405) Bernard Owens Nancy Rich Sarah Shofstall (216) 771-3630

Coshocton Trinity Episcopal Church **P** (85) 705 Main St 43812-1616 (Mail to: 705 Main St 43812-1616) (740) 622-0860

Cuyahoga Fls St Johns Episcopal Church **P** (128) 2220 2nd St 44221-2502 (Mail to: 2220 2nd St 44221-2502) William Tompkin (330) 928-2139

Defiance Grace Church **P** (62) 308 W 2nd St 43512-2131 (Mail to: 308 Second Street 43512) (419) 782-0766

E Liverpool St Stephens Church **P** (109) 220 W 4th St 43920-4510 (Mail to: 220 W 4th St 43920-4510) Mary Vidmar (330) 385-3828

Elyria St Andrews Church **P** (271) 300 3rd St 44035-5618 (Mail to: 300 3rd St 44035-5693) Martha June Dorsey (440) 322-2126

Euclid Church of the Epiphany **P** (313) 21000 Lakeshore Blvd 44123-1800 (Mail to: 21000 Lake Shore Blvd 44123-1800) Rosalind Hughes (216) 731-1316

Findlay Trinity Episcopal Church **P** (253) 128 W Hardin St 45840-3104 (Mail to: C/O Todd Russell 128 W Hardin St 45840-3104) John Drymon (419) 422-3214

Fremont St Pauls Church **P** (170) 206 Park Ave 43420-2430 (Mail to: 206 Park Ave 43420-2430) Matthew Wahlgren (419) 332-3032

Gambier Harcourt Parish **P** (123) Church of the Holy Spirit 102 College-Park St 43022 (Mail to: PO Box 377 43022-0377) Rachel Kessler (740) 427-2187

Gates Mills St Christophers by the River Church **P** (249) 7601 Old Mill Rd 44040 (Mail to: PO Box 519 44040) Ann Kidder (440) 423-4451

Geneva Christ Church **P** (96) 66 South Eagle St 44041-1547 (Mail to: 66 S Eagle St 44041-1547) (440) 466-3706

Hudson Christ Church Episcopal **P** (308) 21 Aurora St 44236-2902 (Mail to: Attn: Kathy Garber 21 Aurora St 44236-2902) Charlotte Collins Reed (330) 650-4359

Huron Christ Episcopal Church **P** (260) 120 Ohio St 44839-1537 (Mail to: 120 Ohio St 44839-1537) Michael Floyd (419) 433-4701

Kent Christ Episcopal Church **P** (194) 118 S Mantua St 44240-3437 (Mail to: 118 S Mantua St 44240-3437) Julie Fisher William Lyle (330) 673-4604

Lakewood Church of the Ascension **P** (239) 13216 Detroit Ave 44107-2842 (Mail to: 13216 Detroit Ave 44107-2894) Vincent Black (216) 521-8727

Lakewood St Peters Episcopal Church **P** (609) 18001 Detroit Ave 44107-3417 (Mail to: 18001 Detroit Ave 44107-3491) Gordon Owen Kelly Aughenbaugh Nancy Wittig (216) 226-1772

Lisbon Holy Trinity Church **P** (43) 310 E Lincoln Way 44432-1420 (Mail to: PO Box 323 44432-0323) (330) 424-5442

Lorain Church of the Redeemer **P** (164) 647 Reid Ave 44052-1737 (Mail to: PO Box 521 44052-0521) Mary Carson Alexander Barton (440) 244-3134

Lyndhurst Church of the Good Shepherd **P** (285) 23599 Cedar Rd 44122-1065 (Mail to: 23599 Cedar Rd 44122-1065) Aaron Collins Anne Pillot (216) 382-7770

Macedonia St Timothys Church **P** (300) 8667 Shepard Rd 44056-2010 (Mail to: PO Box 560204 44056-0204) Albert Jennings Anne Pillot (330) 467-1103

Mansfield Grace Church **P** (319) 41 Bowman St 44903-1650 (Mail to: 41 Bowman St 44903-1650) Joe Ashby Daniel Orr (419) 524-2661

Marion St Pauls Episcopal Church **P** (25) 197 E Center St 43302-3813 (Mail to: 197 E Center St 43302-3876) (740) 387-6220

Massillon St Timothys Church **P** (442) 226 3rd St Se 44646-6702 (Mail to: 226 3rd St SE 44646-6702) George Baum (330) 833-3183

Maumee St Pauls Church **P** (624) 310 Elizabeth St 43537-3322 (Mail to: 310 Elizabeth St 43537-3322) John Board (419) 893-3381

Medina St Pauls Church **P** (539) 317 E Liberty St 44256-2108 (Mail to: 317 E Liberty St 44256-2108) (330) 725-4131

Mentor St Andrews Church **P** (256) 7989 Little Mountain Rd 44060-7802 (Mail to: 7989 Little Mountain Rd 44060-7802) Lisa O'Rear (440) 255-8842

Mentor St Huberts Church **P** (293) 8870 Baldwin Rd 44060-7835 (Mail to: 8870 Baldwin Rd 44060-7835) Daniel Schoonmaker John Hayden (440) 256-1280

Mount Vernon St Paul's Episcopal Church **HC** (99) 100 E High St 43050-3402 (Mail to: 100 E High St 43050-3402) Karl Stevens (740) 392-8601

Napoleon St Johns Church **P** (26) 1400 Glenwood Ave 43545-9032 (Mail to: PO Box 227 43545-0227) (419) 592-8466

New Phila Trinity Church **P** (66) 122 3rd St Nw 44663-3719 (Mail to: 122 3rd St Nw 44663-3719) (330) 339-6439

Niles St Lukes Church **P** (118) 348 Robbins Ave 44446-2408 (Mail to: 348 Robbins Ave 44446-2489) (330) 652-2952

Norwalk St Pauls Church **P** (65) 87 W Main St 44857-1439 (Mail to: 87 W Main St 44857-1439) Margaret D'Anieri (419) 668-1937

Oberlin Christ Church **P** (90) 162 S Main St 44074-1629 (Mail to: 162 S Main St 44074-1629) Brian Wilbert Nancy Roth Gregory Stark (440) 775-2501

Oregon St Pauls Church **P** (146) 798 S Coy Rd 43616-3008 (Mail to: 798 S Coy Rd 43616-3008) (419) 691-9400

Painesville St James Church **P** (216) 131 State St 44077-3939 (Mail to: 131 State St 44077-3991) Vanessa Clark (440) 354-3526

Perrysburg St Timothys Church **P** (212) 871 E Boundary St 43551-2451 (Mail to: 871 E Boundary St 43551-2451) Jeffry Bunke (419) 874-5704

Port Clinton Church of St Thomas **P** (57) 214 E 2nd St 43452-1117 (Mail to: 214 E 2nd St 43452-1117)

Put In Bay St Pauls Church **P** (46) 623 Catawba Ave 43456-6539 (Mail to: PO Box 248 43456-0248) Mary Staley (419) 285-5981

Ravenna Grace Church **P** (139) 250 Cedar Ave 44266-2740 (Mail to: 250 Cedar Ave 44266-2740) Carol Evans William Snyder James Wichman (330) 296-3443

Salem Church of Our Saviour **P** (51) 870 E State St 44460-2224 (Mail to: PO Box 120 44460-0120) Jerome Colegrove (330) 332-5701

Sandusky Grace Church **P** (244) 315 Wayne St 44870-2619 (Mail to: 315 Wayne St 44870-2658) Jan Wood (419) 625-6919

Shaker Heights Christ Church **P** (305) 3445 Warrensville Center Rd 44122-5206 (Mail to: 3445 Warrensville Center Rd 44122-5206) Peter Faass James Greer (216) 991-3432

Shelby St Marks Episcopal Church **P** (87) 31 Gamble St 44875-1201 (Mail to: 31 Gamble St 44875-1201) (419) 347-7701

Sidney St Mark's Episcopal Church **P** (54) 231 Miami Ave 45365-2707 (Mail to: 231 Miami Ave 45365-2707) Stephanie Brugger Arthur Good (937) 492-8584

Steubenville St Pauls Church **P** (98) 415 Adams St 43952-2809 (Mail to: 415 Adams St 43952-2809) (740) 282-5366

Steubenville St Stephens Episcopal Church **P** (104) 284 Lovers Ln 43953-3401 (Mail to: 284 Lovers Ln 43953-3401) (740) 264-5005

Tiffin Old Trinity Church **P** (65) 125 E Market St 44883-3903 (Mail to: 125 E Market St 44883-3903) Aaron Gerlach (419) 447-0728

Toledo All Saints Episcopal Church **P** (135) 563 Pinewood Ave 43602-1009 (Mail to: 563 Pinewood Ave 43604-8009) (419) 246-2461

Toledo St Andrew's Episcopal Church **P** (202) 2770 W. Central Ave 43606-3462 (Mail to: 2770 W Central Ave 43606-3462) Bridget Coffey (419) 473-1367

Toledo St Matthews Church **P** (307) 5240 Talmadge Rd 43623-2138 (Mail to: 5240 Talmadge Rd 43623-2138) Nancy Kin (419) 473-1187

Toledo St Michaels in the Hills Church **P** (483) 4718 Brittany Rd 43615-2314 (Mail to: 4718 Brittany Rd 43615-2314) (419) 531-1616

Toledo Trinity Church **P** (112) 1 Trinity Plz 43604-1503 (Mail to: 316 Adams St Fl 1 43604-1585) Lisa Tucker-Gray (419) 243-1231

Uniontown New Life Episcopal Church **P** (132) 13118 Church Ave Nw 44685-8452 (Mail to: 13118 Church Ave NW 44685-8452) (330) 699-3554

Wadsworth St Marks Episcopal Church **P** (52) 146 College St 44281-1852 (Mail to: 146 College St 44281-1852) Allan Belton (330) 336-0212

Warren Christ Episcopal Church **P** (344) 2627 Atlantic St Ne 44483-4423 (Mail to: 2627 Atlantic St NE 44483-4498) J Jeffrey Baker (330) 372-4998

Westlake Church of the Advent **P** (139) 3760 Dover Center Rd 44145-5433 (Mail to: 3760 Dover Center Rd 44145-5433) (440) 871-6685

Willoughby Grace Church **P** (94) 36200 Ridge Rd 44094-4161 (Mail to: 36200 Ridge Rd 44094-4194) Rose Anne Lonsway (440) 942-1015

Wooster Saint James Episcopal Church **P** (280) 122 E. North St. 44691 (Mail to: 122 E North St. 44691) Evan Fischer (330) 262-4476

Youngstown St Augustines Church **P** (40) C/O Leonard Mc Cormick Treas 614 Parmalee Ave 44510-1603 (Mail to: C/O Leonard Mc Cormick,Treas 614 Parmalee Ave 44510) Jane McDermott (330) 747-7225

Youngstown St Johns Church Episcopal **P** (304) 323 Wick Ave 44503-1003 (Mail to: 323 Wick Ave 44503-1095) Gayle Catinella (330) 743-3175

DIOCESE OF OKLAHOMA
(PROVINCE VII)
Comprises the State of Oklahoma
DIOCESAN OFFICE 924 N Robinson Oklahoma City 73102
TEL (405) 232-4820   FAX (405) 232-4912
WEB www.epiok.org

Previous Bishops—
Theology P Thurston 1919-27, Thomas Casady m 1927 dio 1937-53, WR Chilton Powell 1953-77, Frederick W Putnam suffr 1963-79, Gerald N McAllister 1977-89, William J Cox asst 1980-88, Robert Manning Moody 1988-2007

Bishop—Rt Rev Dr Edward Joseph Konieczny DMin (1020) (Dio 15 Sep 07)

Staff: Cn for Cler Trans & Cong Life W Carroll; *Cn for Church Growth & Dev* SB Snook; *Bp Exec Asst* L Graft *Admin Asst to Cns* D Ellsworth; *Prison Miss* N Brock; *Dir of Christian Form* S Evans; *CFOlCn for Fin & Admin* W Buchanan; *Payroll & Benefits* M Smith; *Dir of Comm* N Baxley; *Arch* P Bell.

Officers: Conv Sec M Wignall 9177 E 117th Pl Bixby OK; *Chanc* W Cathcart 2807 Classen Blvd OK; *Vice Chanc* G Derrick, T Williams; *Treas* H Baer

Stand Comm—Cler: Pres MA Hill S Scott E Lees; *Lay:* M Whaley R Yadon M Moon

PARISHES, MISSIONS, AND CLERGY

Ada St Lukes Episcopal Church **P** (148) 110 E 17th St 74820-7802 (Mail to: PO Box 890 74821-0890) Erin Warde (580) 332-6429

Altus St Pauls Episcopal Church **P** (58) 721 Thomas St 73521-2871 (Mail to: 721 Thomas St 73521-2800) Carol Mollison Michael Trachman (580) 482-2102

Antlers St James Episcopal **M** (51) 700 High St 74523-2245 (Mail to: 700 High St 74523-2245) (580) 298-5123

Ardmore St Philips Episcopal Church **P** (464) 516 Mclish St 73401-4710 (Mail to: 516 Mclish St 73401-4742) Michael Stephenson Joyce Spurgin (580) 226-2191

Bartlesville St Lukes Episcopal Church **P** (390) 210 E 9th St 74003-4905 (Mail to: 210 E 9th St 74003-4961) Stephen Hood (918) 336-1212

Broken Arrow St Patricks Episcopal Church **P** (550) 4250 W Houston St 74012-4538 (Mail to: 4250 W Houston St 74012-4538) Shelby Scott Spencer Brown (918) 294-9444

Chickasha St Lukes Episcopal Church **M** (83) 124 S 6th St 73018-3420 (Mail to: 124 S 6th St 73018-3420) (405) 224-1296

Claremore St Pauls Episcopal Church **P** (130) 1310 Sioux Ave 74017-4416 (Mail to: 1310 Sioux Ave 74017-4416) (918) 341-0168

Clinton St Pauls Episcopal Church **M** (54) 321 S 7th St 73601-3903 (Mail to: 321 S 7th St 73601-3903) Lynn Borrego (580) 323-2160

Coalgate St Peters Episcopal Church **M** (16) 107 W Hanover Ave 74538-1839 (Mail to: PO Box 165 74538-0165) (580) 927-3310

Cushing St Albans Episcopal Church **M** (8) 112 S Thompson Ave 74023-4040 (Mail to: PO Box 1248 74023-1248) Paul Ostrander (918) 225-2170

Duncan All Saints' Episcopal Church **P** (131) 809 W Cedar Ave 73533-4135 (Mail to: 809 W Cedar Ave 73533-4135) Gary Templeton (580) 255-6165

Durant St Johns Episcopal Church **P** (96) 515 W Beech St 74701-4335 (Mail to: PO Box 1168 74702-1168) James Blagg (580) 924-1332

Edmond St Marys Episcopal Church **P** (745) 325 E 1st St 73034-4544 (Mail to: 325 E 1st St 73034-4500) Mark Story William Hesse (405) 341-3855

El Reno Christ Memorial Episcopal Church **M** (59) 500 S Bickford Ave 73036-3844 (Mail to: 500 S Barker Ave 73036-3801) (405) 262-1710

Enid St Matthews Church **P** (200) 518 W Randolph Ave 73701-3828 (Mail to: 518 W Randolph Ave 73701-3897) John Toles Janie Koch (580) 237-4737

Eufaula Trinity Episcopal Church **M** (74) S 3rd & High Sts 74432 (Mail to: PO Box 759 74432-0759) Therese Starr (918) 689-2369

Grove St Andrews Episcopal Church **P** (141) 555 E 3rd St 74344-7139 (Mail to: 555 E 3rd St 74344-7139) David Bridges Philip Lawrence Melissa Harris Philip Lawrence (918) 786-4113

Guthrie Trinity Church **P** (117) 310 E Noble Ave 73044-3311 (Mail to: 310 E Noble Ave 73044-3311) (405) 282-0982

Guymon St Stephens Episcopal Church **M** (19) 1803 Lelia St 73942-2832 (Mail to: PO Box 1952 73942-1952) (580) 338-8747

Holdenville St Pauls Episcopal Church **M** (11) 8th And Oak Sts 74848 (Mail to: PO Box 69 74848-0069) Elizabeth Davis Cyntha Gilks (405) 379-5879

Hugo St Mark's Episcopal Church **P** (43) 803 S 3rd St 74743-6809 (Mail to: 803 South 3rd 74743) Arlen Fowler (580) 326-9197

Idabel St Luke the Beloved Physician **M** (22) 211 Se Ave 74745-5728 (Mail to: 211 Se Ave 74745) (580) 286-3672

Langston Holy Family Episcopal Church **M** (6) 308 West Hale 73050 (Mail to: PO Box 727 73050-0727) (405) 521-8839

Lawton St Andrews Episcopal Church **P** (252) 1313 Sw D Ave 73501-4252 (Mail to: PO Box 1256 73502-1256) Shelley Forrester Katherine Dutcher Patricia Kardaleff (580) 355-9543

Lindsay St Michael & All Angels **M** (10) 1505 Nw 4th St 73052-1803 (Mail to: PO Box 134 73052-0134) (405) 756-3433

Mcalester All Saints Episcopal Church **P** (98) 325 E Washington Ave 74501-4757 (Mail to: PO Box 534 74502-0534) (918) 423-1915

Miami All Saints Episcopal Church **P** (103) 225 B St Nw 74354-5806 (Mail to: 225 B St NW 74354-5806) (918) 542-3662

Midwest City St Christophers Church **P** (226) 800 S Midwest Blvd 73110-4730 (Mail to: PO Box 10722 73140-1722) Emily Schnabl (405) 732-4802

Muskogee Grace Episcopal Church **HC** (235) Attn Mary Emily Basolo 218 6th St 74401-6209 (Mail to: 218 6th St 74401-6209) Charles Wickizer Thomas Harrington (918) 687-5416

Norman St Anselm Canterbury Assn **CM** 800 Elm Ave 73069-8837 (Mail to: 800 Elm Ave 73069-8837) Kay Greenshields (405) 360-6453

Norman St Johns Episcopal Church **P** (1018) 235 W Duffy St 73069-5827 (Mail to: PO Box 2088 73070-2088) Dwight Helt (405) 321-3020

Norman St Michaels Episcopal Church **P** (261) 1601 W. Imhoff Rd 73072-7408 (Mail to: 1601 W Imhoff Rd 73072-7408) Jason Haddox (405) 321-8951

Oklahoma City All Souls Episcopal Church **P** (1667) 6400 Pennsylvania Ave 73116-5626 (Mail to: 6400 Pennsylvania Ave 73116-5694) Patrick Bright James Easter Christopher Yoder (405) 842-1461

Oklahoma City Church of the Redeemer **P** (152) 2100 Martin Luther King Ave 73111 (Mail to: PO Box 11272 73136-0272) Morgan Ibe (405) 427-2106

Oklahoma City Episcopal Church Of The Resurrection **P** (317) 13112 Rockwell Ave Attn: Administrator 73142-2717 (Mail to: Attn Administrator 13112 Rockwell Ave 73142-2700) Sean Ekberg Beth Bell Melva Bridges Dion Crider (405) 721-2929

Oklahoma City St Augustine of Canterbury **M** (247) 14700 May Ave 73134-5009 (Mail to: 14700 May Ave 73134-5008) Joseph Alsay Anthony Moon Robert Trammell (405) 751-7874

Oklahoma City St Davids Episcopal Church **M** (52) 3333 No Meridian Ave 73112 (Mail to: 3333 Meridian Ave 73112-3198) Tracey Carroll (405) 942-1740

Oklahoma City St James Episcopal Church **M** (111) 8400 S Pennsylvania Ave 73159-5205 (Mail to: 924 Robinson Ave 73102-5814) Nathan Carr Jeffrey Huston (405) 682-3405

Oklahoma City St Johns Episcopal Church **P** (296) § 5401 Brookline Av 73112-3514 (Mail to: 5401 Brookline Ave 73112-3598) David Stock George Back Lisa Chronister Dana Orwig (405) 943-8548

✠ **Oklahoma City** St Pauls Cathedral **O** (1070) 127 Nw 7th St 73102-6004 (Mail to: 127 NW 7th St 73102-6004) Susan Joplin (405) 235-3436

Oklahoma City Santa Maria Virgen **M** (863) 5500 S Western Ave. 73109 (Mail to: 5500 S Western Ave 73109-4511) (405) 631-6747

Okmulgee Church of the Redeemer **M** (44) 213 Seminole Ave 74447-7334 (Mail to: PO Box 1012 74447-1012) (918) 756-2384

Owasso Church of the Holy Cross **M** (58) 9309 129th East Ave 74055-5314 (Mail to: 9309 129th East Ave 74055-5314) (918) 271-1075

Pauls Valley St Timothys Church **M** (23) 1820 S Walnut St 73075-6902 (Mail to: PO Box 485 73075-0485) Stanley Upchurch (405) 238-2133

Pawhuska St Thomas Episcopal Church **M** (44) 817 Leahy Ave 74056-3219 (Mail to: PO Box 1476 74056-1476) (918) 287-3513

Pawnee Church of the Ascension **M** (11) Seventh And Ash Sts 74058 (Mail to: PO Box 26 74058-0026) (918) 762-2771

Perry St Mark Episcopal Church **M** (22) 701 7th St 73077-4227 (Mail to: PO Box 507 73077-0507) William Powell (580) 336-9720

Ponca City Grace Episcopal Church **P** (208) 109 13th St 74601-7314 (Mail to: 109 13th St 74601-7314) Steven Mallory (580) 765-7609

Poteau St Barnabas Episcopal Church **M** 506 College Ave 74953-3114 (Mail to: Rr 3 Box 100 74953-9803) (918) 647-9092

Pryor St Martin of Tours Episcopal Church **M** (65) 612 SE 1st St 74361-4614 (Mail to: PO Box 1153 74362-1153) (918) 825-1115

Sand Springs St Matthews Episcopal Church **M** (27) 601 Lake Dr 74063-8716 (Mail to: 601 Lake Dr 74063-8716) (918) 245-7552

Sapulpa Church of the Good Shepherd **P** (191) 1420 E Dewey Ave 74066 (Mail to: PO Box 335 74067-0335) Nancy Brown Robert Fallis (918) 224-5144

Seminole St Marks Episcopal Church **M** (21) 800 Highland St 74868 (Mail to: PO Box 1304 74818-1304) Lynn Borrego William Bales Elizabeth Davis (405) 382-2192

Shawnee Emmanuel Episcopal Church **P** (345) 501 Broadway Ave 74801-6926 (Mail to: PO Box 1905 74802-1905) Thomas Dahlman John Belzer (405) 273-1374

Stillwater St Andrews Church **P** (397) 516 W 3rd Ave 74074-3001 (Mail to: 516 W 3rd Ave 74074-3001) James Cook Jeffrey Huston (405) 372-3357

Stillwater St Augustine Canterbury Ctr **CM** 519 W University Ave 74074-3033 (Mail to: 519 W University Ave 740743033) (405) 624-0141

Tahlequah St Basils Episcopal Church **M** (81) 814 Vinita Ave 74464-2235 (Mail to: 814 Vinita Ave 74464-2235) Debora Jennings (918) 456-3649

✤ **Tulsa** Chapel of All Saints **O** 5666 E 81st St 74136 (Mail to: 5666 E. 81st St. 74137-2001) Robert Bibens (918) 481-1111

Tulsa Christ Episcopal Church **M** (148) 10901 S Yale Ave 74137-7211 (Mail to: 10901 S Yale Ave 74137-7211) Everett Lees Judith Gann (918) 299-7510

Tulsa St Adrian of Canterbury **CM** 1115 S Florence Ave 74104-4104 (Mail to: 1115 S Florence Ave 74104-4104) (918) 631-2993

Tulsa Saint Aidan's Episcopal Church **M** (76) 4045 Martin L King Jr Blvd 74106-6452 (Mail to: PO Box 480874 74148-0874) William Holly William Holly (918) 425-7882

Tulsa St Dunstans Episcopal Church **P** (523) 5635 E 71st St 74136-6538 (Mail to: 5635 E 71st St 74136-6538) Alan Barrow Mary Hill Alberto Moreno Casas (918) 492-7140

Tulsa St Johns Episcopal Church **P** (1186) 4200 S Atlanta Pl 74105-4331 (Mail to: 4200 S Atlanta Pl 74105-4300) John Rule (918) 742-7381

Tulsa St Lukes Episcopal Church **P** (124) 4818 E 9th St 74112-4240 (Mail to: 4818 E 9th St 74112-4240) Robert Scott (918) 834-4800

Tulsa St Peters Episcopal Church **P** (89) 9100 E 21st St 74129-1421 (Mail to: 9100 E 21st St 74129-1421) Mary Lord (918) 627-2713

Tulsa Trinity Church **P** (1859) § 501 S Cincinnati Ave 74103-4801 (Mail to: 501 S Cincinnati Ave 74103-4800) Kristina Maulden (918) 582-4128

Vinita Saint John's Episcopal Church **M** (51) 522 W Canadian Ave 74301-3612 (Mail to: PO Box 165 74301-0165) (918) 256-3766

Wagoner St James Church **M** (41) 303 E Church St 74467-5209 (Mail to: 303 E Church St 74467-5209) Edmund James (918) 485-5681

Watonga Whirlwind Mission of the Holy Family **M** (64) 1000 E Russworm Dr 73772 (Mail to: PO Box 26 73772-0026) James Kee-Rees (580) 623-5585

Westport St Bedes Episcopal Church **M** (55) 1 2 Miles North Hwy 64 74020 (Mail to: RR 3 Box 4A 74020-9502) John Powers (918) 743-2686

Woodward St Johns Episcopal Church **M** (73) 917 Texas St 73801-3125 (Mail to: 917 Texas St 73801-3125) Mary Davis (580) 256-7713

Yukon Grace Church - Episcopal **P** (54) 720 S Yukon Parkway 73099-3300 (Mail to: 720 S Yukon Pkwy 73099-4585) Timothy Baer (405) 354-7277

DIOCESE OF OLYMPIA
(PROVINCE VIII)
Comprises western Washington
DIOCESAN OFFICE 1551 10th Ave E Seattle WA 98102
TEL (206) 325-4200   FAX (206) 325-4631
E-MAIL info@ecww.org   WEB ecww.org

Previous Bishops— John A Paddock 1880-94, Wm M Barker 1894-1901, Frederic W Keator 1902-24, S Arthur Huston 1925-47, Stephen F Bayne Jr 1947-60, Wm F Lewis 1960-64, Ivol I Curtis 1964-76, Robt H Cochrane 1976-89, Sanford ZK Hampton asst 1996-2004, Vincent W Warner 1990-2007, Bavi Edna Rivera Suff 2004-10

Bishop—Rt Rev Gregory H Rickel (1021) (Dio 15 Sep 2007)

Cn to Ord Rev M Steedman Sanborn; *Cn for Operations* D Moore; *Cn for Stew & Dev* Rev L Ousley; *Cn for Faith Formation* Rev R Kirkpatrick; *Cn for Cong Dev* Rev A Newton; *Cn for Multicultural Min* Rev A Davison; *Dir of Fin* vacant; *Commun Dir* J Hornbeck; *Dir Resource Ctr* S Tait; *Ex Asst to Bis & Cn to Ord* M MacKinnon; *Dio Property Mgr* Rev D Tierney; *Iona School Dean* M McLaughlin-Crawford; *Int Strategist* K Allman; *Veterans Min Missioner* Rev B Wright; *Refugee Resettl* G Hope; *Mission to Seafarers Exec Dir* K Hawkins; *Huston Ctr Dir* B Tubbs; *SA Hse Mgr* D Oberg

Officers—Treas B Fox; *Sec* K Gusse; *Chanc* J Andrews; *V Chanc* M Reynvaan; *Hist Br* C Griffin; *Archive* D Wells

Stand Comm—Cler: C Espeseth B Fulton; A Feregrino H McPeak *Lay:* K Rickert D Woods *Pres* K Casey J Beckwith

Bd of Dir—Cler: Pres G Rickel C Jillard J Weldon *Lay:* W Brent M Dickinson *Treas* B Fox G Garcia *Sec* K Gusse C Liska P McGuire *VP* G Robertson

Dio Coun—Cler: R Barrett L Breckinridge E Clendenin D Conn J Fox B Malone M Miller D Tierney M Wright M Yabroff *Lay:* J Akin J Balducci N Baxter L Brice J Collins L Donato S Farrell J Harris-Gane D Patrick J Whitworth

PARISHES, MISSIONS, AND CLERGY

Aberdeen St Andrews Episcopal Church **P** (343) 400 E 1st St 98520-4116 (Mail to: 400 E 1st St 98520-4116) Evan Clendenin Sarah Monroe (360) 533-2511

Allyn St Hugh of Lincoln Episcopal Church **M** (95) 280 E Wheelwright St S 98524 (Mail to: PO Box 156 98524-0156) Sylvia Haase Christie Logan Jennifer Pratt (360) 275-8450

Anacortes Christ Episcopal Church **M** (113) 1216 7th St 98221-1809 (Mail to: 1216 7th St 98221-1809) Eric Johnson Brian Lennstrom (360) 293-5790

Auburn St Matthews Episcopal Church **P** (206) 123 L St Ne 98002-4434 (Mail to: 123 L St NE 98002-4434) Patricia Trytten (253) 833-0890

Bainbridge Island Grace Episcopal Church **M** (510) 8595 Ne Day Rd 98110-1395 (Mail to: C/O Trustee For Human Resource 8595 NE Day Rd 98110-1395) Mary Anderson Wren Blessing William Maxwell (206) 842-9997

Bainbridge Island St Barnabas Episcopal Church **P** (460) 1187 Wyatt Way Nw 98110-2722 (Mail to: 1187 Wyatt Way NW 98110-2722) Daniel Fowler Martha Haig Patricia Robertson Nancy Tiederman (206) 842-5601

Battle Ground Church of the Holy Spirit **M** (118) 2400 NW 9th Ave 98604-1117 (Mail to: PO Box 1117 98604-1117) (360) 687-3301

Bellevue All Saints Church **M** (29) 1307 120th Ave Ne 98005-2124 (Mail to: 1307 120th Ave NE 98005-2124) Christina Robertson (425) 646-1136

Bellevue Church of the Holy Apostles **M** (76) 15220 Main St 98007-5228 (Mail to: Attn Mr Torres Hui 15220 Main St 98007-5228) (425) 351-1423

Bellevue Church of the Resurrection **P** (138) 15220 Main St 98007-5228 (Mail to: 15220 Main St 98007-5228) (425) 746-0322

Bellevue St Margarets Episcopal Church **P** (625) 4228 Factoria Blvd Se 98006-1929 (Mail to: 4228 Factoria Blvd SE 98006-1929) Christina Jillard Christine Demura (425) 746-6650

Bellingham St Paul's Episcopal Church **P** (1041) 2117 Walnut St 98225-2836 (Mail to: 2117 Walnut St 98225-2836) Jonathan Weldon Lindsay Ross-Hunt Marsha Vollkommer Jonathan Weldon Charles Whitmore (360) 733-2890

Blaine Christ Episcopal Church **M** (78) 382 Boblett St 98230-4003 (Mail to: 382 Boblett St 98230-4003) Dawn Foisie (360) 332-4113

Bremerton St Pauls Episcopal Church **P** (200) 700 Callahan Dr 98310-3304 (Mail to: 700 Callahan Dr 98310-3304) Kathleen Kingslight Susan Stroup (360) 377-0106

Castle Rock St Matthew Church **M** (55) 412 Pioneer Ave Ne 98611-9234 (Mail to: PO Box 1467 98611-1467) Elizabeth Cochran Linda Santman Suzanne Streiff (360) 274-9393

Cathlamet Saint James Episcopal Church **M** (40) 1134 Columbia St 98612-9535 (Mail to: 1134 Columbia St 98612-9535) Irene Martin Joann Prestegard Rachael Wolford (360) 795-8612

Chehalis St Timothy Episcopal Church **P** (127) 1826 Sw Snively Ave 98532-4022 (Mail to: PO Box 277 98532-0277) Katherine Flores (360) 748-8232

Darrington Church of the Transfiguration **M** (23) 836 Commercial St 98241 (Mail to: PO Box 55 98241-0055) Janet Loyd (360) 436-1552

Eastsound Emmanuel Episcopal Church **P** (199) 242 Main St 98245 (Mail to: PO Box 8 98245-0008) Jose Gandara-Perea Hugh Grant Kathleen Kinney (360) 376-2352

Edmonds St Albans Episcopal Church **P** (300) 21405 82nd Pl W 98026-7434 (Mail to: 21405 82nd Pl W 98026-7434) Gregory Peters (425) 778-0371

Edmonds St Hilda-St Patrick Church **M** (147) 15224 52nd Ave W 98026-4304 (Mail to: 15224 52nd Ave W 98026-4304) Elisabeth Fitzgibbons (425) 743-4655

Elma St Lukes Episcopal Church **M** (46) 626 E Young St 98541-9357 (Mail to: C/O Mr Steve Brown 103 Heritage Dr 98541-9339) Steven Brill John Nemes (360) 482-3231

Everett Trinity Episcopal Church **P** (332) 2301 Hoyt Ave 98201-2898 (Mail to: 2301 Hoyt Ave 98201-2898) Rachel Taber-Hamilton (425) 252-4129

Federal Way Church of the Good Shepherd **P** (180) 345 S 312th St 98003-4031 (Mail to: PO Box 3108 98063-3108) Joshua Hosler (253) 839-6100

Forks St Swithin **M** Prince of Peace Lutheran Ch 98362-6938 (Mail to: 660 G St 98331) (360) 457-4862

Freeland St Augustines in-the-Woods Episcopal **P** (200) 5217 Honeymoon Bay Rd 98249-9712 (Mail to: PO Box 11 98249-0011) Nigel Taber-Hamilton Malcolm Davis (360) 331-4887

Friday Harbor St Davids Episcopal Church **P** (90) 780 Park St 98250-9609 (Mail to: PO Box 2714 98250-2714) Margaret Lewis-Headden Douglas Simonsen (360) 378-5360

Gig Harbor St Johns Episcopal Church **P** (547) 7701 Skansie Ave 98335-8330 (Mail to: 7701 Skansie Ave 98335-8330) Marilyn Behrens Eric Stelle (253) 858-3777

Hoodsport St Germain Episcopal Church **M** 600 Lake Cushman Rd 98548-9781 (Mail to: PO Box 222 98548) Peter Van Zanten (360) 866-9870

Issaquah St Michael and All Angels Church **P** (354) 325 Se Darst St 98027-4326 (Mail to: 325 SE Darst St 98027-4326) Katherine Sedwick (425) 392-3215

Kenmore Church of the Redeemer **P** (687) 6211 Ne 182nd St 98028-9419 (Mail to: PO Box 82677 98028-0677) Jedediah Fox Jill Zimmerschied (425) 486-3777

Kent St Columba's Episcopal Church **M** (88) 26715 Military Rd S 98032-7011 (Mail to: 31811 Pacific Hwy S Ste B342 98003) Alissabeth Newton (253) 854-9912

Kent St James Episcopal Church **P** (848) 24447 94th Ave S 98030-4746 (Mail to: 24447 94th Ave S 98030-4746) Joyce Parry-Moore (253) 852-4450

Kingston Faith Episcopal Church **M** (25) 9900 Ne Shorty Campbell Rd 98346-9614 (Mail to: PO Box 1362 98370-0136) Raymond Sheldon Laura Murray (360) 471-7522

Kirkland St Johns Episcopal Church **P** (280) 105 State St S 98033-6610 (Mail to: 127 State St S 98033-6687) Patrick Ousley (425) 827-3077

Lacey St Benedicts Episcopal Church **M** (238) 910 Bowker St Se 98503-1212 (Mail to: PO Box 3811 98509-3811) Eldwin Lovelady (360) 456-2240

Lakewood St Joseph & St John Church **P** (58) 11111 Old Military Rd Sw 98498 (Mail to: PO Box 88550 98388-0550) Zula Johnston Joseph Peters-Mathews (253) 584-6143

Lakewood St Marys Episcopal Church **P** (305) 10630 Gravelly Lake Dr Sw 98499-1328 (Mail to: Attn Rosemary Doupe 10630 Gravelly Lake Dr SW 98499-1328) Genevieve Grewell Eldwin Lovelady Marian Stinson (253) 588-6621

Longview St Stephens Episcopal Church **P** (125) 1428 22nd Ave 98632-2828 (Mail to: 1428 22nd Ave 98632-2828) Kathleen Patton Nicholas Mather (360) 423-5600

Lopez Island Grace Church **P** (156) 70 Sunset Ln 98261 (Mail to: PO Box 324 98261-0324) (360) 468-3477

Maple Valley St Georges Episcopal Church **M** (129) § 24219 Witte Rd Se 98038-6827 (Mail to: PO Box 510 98038-0510) Bonnie Malone (425) 432-5481

Marysville St Philip Episcopal Church **P** (72) 4312 84th St Ne 98270-3447 (Mail to: 4312 84th St NE 98270-3447) Rebecca Kirkpatrick (360) 659-1727

Medina St Thomas Episcopal Church **P** (1164) § 8398 Ne 12th St 98039-3100 (Mail to: PO Box 124 98039-0124) Alexander Breckinridge Kathryn Ballinger Stephen Best Sarah Ginolfi (425) 454-9541

Mercer Island Emmanuel Episcopal Church **P** (357) 4400 86th Ave SE 98040-4146 (Mail to: 4400 86th Ave SE 98040-4146) Elizabeth Riley Beverly Hosea Jonathan Myers (206) 232-1572

Monroe Church of Our Saviour Episcopal **M** (33) 331 S Lewis St 98272-2320 (Mail to: PO Box 99 98272-0099) Curtis Zimmerman (360) 794-4816

Montesano St Marks Episcopal Church **M** (25) 124 Sylvia St 98563-3717 (Mail to: C/O Joyce Avery 124 Sylvia St 98563-3717) Joyce Avery F Lorraine Dierick (360) 249-3281

Mount Vernon St Pauls Episcopal Church **P** (97) 415 S 18th St 98273 (Mail to: 415 S 18th Street 98274-4658) (360) 424-1822

Oak Harbor St Stephens Episcopal Church **P** (17) 555 SE Regatta Dr 98277-3981 (Mail to: PO Box 2754 98277-6754) Rilla Barrett Richard Scott (360) 279-0715

Olympia St John's Episcopal Church **P** (878) 114 20th Ave SE 98501-2923 (Mail to: 114 20th Ave SE 98501-2999) Albin Fogelquist Robert Laird (360) 352-8527

Olympia St Christophers Community Church **M** (169) 7902 Steamboat Island Rd NW 98502-9101 (Mail to: 7902 Steamboat Island Rd NW 98502-9101) Patricia Sells James Thibodeaux (360) 866-2111

Port Angeles Saint Andrews Episcopal Church **P** (217) 510 E Park Ave 98362-8687 (Mail to: 510 E Park Ave 98362-6938) Gail Wheatley (360) 457-4862

Port Orchard St Bede Episcopal Church **M** (175) 1578 SE Lider Rd 98367-7516 (Mail to: PO Box 845 98366-0845) Arienne Davison (360) 876-1182

Port Townsend St Pauls Episcopal Church **P** (350) 1020 Jefferson St 98368-6618 (Mail to: PO Box 753 98368-0753) Dianne Andrews Francis Holly William Maxwell (360) 385-0770

Puyallup Christ Episcopal Church **P** (305) 210 5th St Sw 98371-5383 (Mail to: 210 5th St SW 98371-5383) Rachel Endicott (253) 848-2323

Redmond Church of the Holy Cross **P** (826) 11526 162nd Ave NE 98052-2645 (Mail to: 11526 162nd Ave NE 98052-2645) James Eichner Carlos Caguiat Jane Rohrer (425) 885-5822

Renton St Luke Episcopal Church **P** (125) 99 Wells Ave S 98055-2153 (Mail to: C/O Kate Martin 99 Wells Ave S 98057-2153) Kevin Pearson Sara Carlson Susan Dean (425) 255-3323

Rockport St Martin-St Francis **M** 55223 Conrad Rd 98283-9740 (Mail to: 55223 Conrad Rd 98283-9740) (425) 876-4628

Sammamish Good Samaritan Episcopal Church **P** (458) 1757 244th Ave NE 98074-3323 (Mail to: 1757 244th Ave NE 98074-3323) Charles Danzey Brian Gregory (425) 868-4379

Seattle Christ Church **P** (191) 4548 Brooklyn Ave NE 98105-4537 (Mail to: 4548 Brooklyn Ave NE 98105-4537) Shelly Fayette Carla Robinson (206) 633-1611

Seattle Church of the Apostles **M** 4272 Fremont Avenue 98103 (Mail to: 4272 Fremont Ave 98103-7279) (206) 851-8962

Seattle Church of the Ascension **P** (308) 2330 Viewmont Way W 98199 (Mail to: 2330 Viewmont Way W 98199-3939) Mary MacKenzie Mary Shehane (206) 283-3967

Seattle Epiphany Parish of Seattle **P** (710) 1805 38th Ave 98122-3447 (Mail to: 1805 38th Ave

98122-3447) Doyt Conn Ruth Anne Garcia (206) 324-2573

Seattle St Andrews Episcopal Church **P** (599) 111 Ne 80th St 98115-4033 (Mail to: 111 Ne 80th St 98115-4033) Danae Ashley Kay Kessel-Hanna Richard Weyls (206) 523-7476

Seattle St Clement of Rome Episcopal Church **P** (271) 1501 32nd Ave S 98144-3917 (Mail to: 1501 32nd Ave S 98144-3917) Thomas Bigelow Robert Gallagher Kevin Smith (206) 324-3072

Seattle St Elizabeths Episcopal Church **P** (100) 1005 Sw 152nd St 98166-1845 (Mail to: PO Box 66579 98166-0579) John Forman (206) 243-6844

Seattle Church of St John the Baptist **P** (225) 3050 California Ave Sw 98116-3302 (Mail to: 3050 California Ave SW 98116-3302) Kate Wesch (206) 937-4545

Seattle St Lukes Episcopal Church **P** (131) 5710 22nd Ave Nw 98107-3144 (Mail to: 5710 22nd Ave NW 98107-3144) Britt Olson (206) 784-3119

✣ **Seattle** St Marks Episcopal Cathedral **O** (1390) 1245 10th Ave E 98102-4323 (Mail to: 1245 10th Ave E 98102-4398) Steven Thomason Cristi Chapman Jennifer Daugherty Earl Grout Nancy Ross Richard Weyls (206) 323-0300

Seattle St Pauls Episcopal Church **P** (261) 15 Roy St 98109-4019 (Mail to: PO Box 9070 98109-0070) Sara Fischer Kerry Kirking Robert Rhodes Charles Ridge Jay Rozendaal (206) 282-0786

Seattle St Stephens Episcopal Church **P** (717) 4805 Ne 45th St 98105-3803 (Mail to: 4805 Ne 45th St 98105-3897) (206) 522-7144

Seattle St Peter's Episcopal Parish **P** (107) 1610 S King St 98144-2115 (Mail to: 1610 S King St 98144-2115) Richard Buhrer Edmund Harris (206) 323-5250

Seattle Trinity Church Episcopal **P** (362) 609 8th Ave 98104-1921 (Mail to: 609 8th Ave 98104-1997) Robert Davidson Malcolm Davis Jeffrey Gill (206) 624-5337

Seaview St Peters Episcopal Church **M** (38) 5000 Place 98644 (Mail to: PO Box 268 98644-0268) (360) 642-3115

Sedro Woolley St James Church **P** (20) 1013 Polte Rd 98284-1142 (Mail to: 1013 Polte Rd 98284-9478) (360) 424-1822

Sequim St Lukes Episcopal Church **P** (257) 525 5th Ave 98382-3079 (Mail to: PO Box 896 98382-4314) ClayOla Gitane (360) 683-4862

Shelton Church of St David of Wales **P** (217) 324 W Cedar St 98584-0339 (Mail to: PO Box 339 98584-0339) Joseph Mikel (360) 426-8472

Shoreline St David Emmanuel Episcopal Church **M** (48) 18842 Meridian Ave 98133-4232 (Mail to: PO Box 77322 98177-0322) Gerald Hanna (206) 362-2565

Shoreline St Dunstans Church **P** (209) 722 145th St 98133-6502 (Mail to: PO Box 33029 98133-0029) David Marshall (206) 363-4319

Silverdale St Antony of Egypt Episcopal Church **P** (159) § 10239 Old Frontier Rd Nw 98383-8895 (Mail to: PO Box 2822 98383-2822) William Fulton Craig Vocelka (360) 698-0555

Snohomish St John's Episcopal Church **P** (252) 913 2nd St 98290-2918 (Mail to: 913 2nd St 98290-2918) Eliacin Rosario-Cruz (360) 568-4622

Snoqualmie St Clare of Assisi Episcopal Church **M** (105) 8650 Railroad Ave SE 98065 (Mail to: PO Box 369 98065-0369) Patricia Baker (425) 831-6175

Stanwood St Aidans Episcopal Church **M** (191) 1318 E State Route 532 98292 (Mail to: PO Box 145 98292-0145) Stephen Foisie (360) 629-3969

Tacoma All Saints' Episcopal Church **M** (70) 205 E 96th St 98445-2003 (Mail to: 205 E 96th St 98445-2003) Jeffrey Sharp (253) 537-2970

Tacoma Christ Church **P** (253) 310 K St 98403-1617 (Mail to: 310 K St 98403-1696) Robert Carver Samuel Torvend William Tudor (253) 383-1569

Tacoma Holy Family of Jesus Epis Church **M** (13) 1427 E 40th St 98411-2376 (Mail to: Attn Sue Bernsteiin PO Box 112376 98411) (253) 471-9838

Tacoma St Andrews Episcopal Church **P** (230) 7410 S 12th St 98465-1500 (Mail to: 7410 S 12th St 98465-1500) Martin Yabroff Meghan Mullarkey Edward Sterling (253) 564-4402

Tacoma St Lukes Episcopal Church **P** (372) 3615 Gove St 98407-4815 (Mail to: 3615 Gove St 98407-4899) Marlene Jacobs (253) 759-3534

Tacoma Saint Matthew Church **P** (120) 6800 East Side Dr Ne 98422-1116 (Mail to: 6800 E Side Dr NE 98422-1116) Kendall Haynes (253) 927-9808

Tahuya St Nicholas Episcopal Church **M** (19) 15000 Ne North Shore Rd 98588 (Mail to: PO Box 101 98588-0101) Robert Williams (360) 275-7141

Vancouver All Saints Episcopal Church **M** (44) 2206 NW 99th St 98665-6253 (Mail to: PO Box 65825 98665-0028) Joseph Scheeler (360) 573-8106

Vancouver Church of the Good Shepherd **P** (606) § 805 SE Ellsworth Rd 98664-5120 (Mail to: 805 SE Ellsworth Rd 98664-5120) William Warne (360) 892-7770

Vancouver St Lukes Church **P** (310) 426 E Fourth Plain Blvd 98663-3040 (Mail to: 426 E Fourth Plain Blvd Ste 11 98663-3085) Jaime Case Dennis Cole (360) 696-0181

Vashon Church of the Holy Spirit **P** (295) 15420 Vashon Hwy Sw 98070-3841 (Mail to: PO Box 508 98070-0508) Sarah Colvin (206) 567-4488

Washougal St Anne Episcopal Church **M** (84) 2350 Main St 98671 (Mail to: PO Box 62 98671-0062) Kathleen Patton (360) 835-5301

STATE OF OREGON

Dioceses of Oregon and Eastern Oregon

DIOCESE OF OREGON

(PROVINCE VIII)
Comprises Oregon west of the Cascade Mountains
DIOCESAN OFFICE 11800 SW Military Ln Portland OR 97219-8436
TEL (503) 636-5613   FAX (503) 636-5616
E-MAIL marieb@diocese-oregon.org   WEB www.diocese-oregon.org

Previous Bishops—
Thomas F Scott 1854-67, Benj W Morris m 1868 (OR and WA) 1880 (OR) dio 1889-1906, Chas Scadding 1906-14, Walter T Sumner 1915-35, Benj D Dagwell 1936-58, James WF Carman 1958-74, Hal R Gross suffr 1965-79, Matthew P Bigliardi 1974-85, Robert L Ladehoff coadj 1985 Bp 1986-2003, Johncy Itty 2003-08

Bishop—Rt Rev Michael Joseph Hanley (1041)
(Dio 10 Apr 2010)

Cn Ord N Ellgren; *Treas* M Stone; *Ex Asst* M Bagwell; *Chanc* M Dotten 568 9th St Lake Oswego OR 97034 *Fin* T Lee; *Archdcn* C Hawley; *C Ed* C Sedlacek; *Comm* H Pitts; *Prog/Budg* T Phipps; *COM* H Crandall; *Archivist* M Bagwell

Deans: Metro-East Rev J Joiner; *Columbia* Rev D Sweeney; *Sunset* Rev J Littlefield; *Willamette* Rev F Heard; *Central* Rev B Powell; *South* Rev T Hutchinson; *S Coast* Rev C Close-Erskine

Stand Comm—Cler: Pres D Sweeney S Justice L Peeler N Gallager; *Lay:* J Johnson J Simpson L Arnoldt S Rogers

PARISHES, MISSIONS, AND CLERGY

Albany St Albans Episcopal Church **M** (137) 1730 Hill St Se 97322-4246 (Mail to: PO Box 1556 97321-0465) Robert Morrison (541) 967-7051

Ashland Trinity Episcopal Church **P** (317) 44 2nd St 97520-1927 (Mail to: 44 2nd St 97520-1927) Bert Anderson Anne Bartlett Anthony Hutchinson Meredith Pech (541) 201-3418

Astoria Grace Episcopal Church **P** (92) 1545 Franklin Ave 97103-3717 (Mail to: 1545 Franklin Ave 97103-3717) Lance Peeler Patricia Morris-Rader Lance Peeler (503) 325-4691

Bandon Church of St John by the Sea **M** (70) 795 Franklin Avenue 97411-0246 (Mail to: PO Box 246 97411-0246) Beth Hoffmann (541) 347-2152

Beaverton Saint Bartholomew's Church **P** (456) 11265 SW Cabot St 97005-2295 (Mail to: 11265 SW Cabot St 97005-2219) Jeffrey Littlefield Janis Hansen Philippa Lindwright Mikel Mcclain (503) 644-3468

Boring Holy Cross Episcopal Church **M** (82) 10351 SE Orient Dr 97009 (Mail to: PO Box 669 97009-0669) Roberto Maldonado-Mercado (503) 663-4223

Brookings St Timothy Episcopal Church **M** (123) 401 Fir St 97415-9222 (Mail to: PO Box 1237 97415-0115) James Lindley (541) 469-3314

Cave Junction Church of St Matthias **M** (7) 25904 97523-0805 (Mail to: PO Box 805 97523-0805) (541) 592-2006

Coos Bay Emmanuel Episcopal Church **P** (214) 370 Market Ave 97420-2229 (Mail to: PO Box 1028 97420-0226) Christine Close Erskine (541) 269-5829

Coquille St James Episcopal Church **M** (38) 210 E 3rd St 97423-1871 (Mail to: Attn Treasurer 210 E 3rd St 97423) Timothy Hannon (541) 396-2322

Corvallis St Anselm of Canterbury Episcopal Ch **CC** 2615 NW Arnold Way 97330-5308 (Mail to: 2615 Nw Arnold Way 97330-5308) Douglas Hale (541) 752-3734

Corvallis Church of the Good Samaritan **P** (649) § 333 Nw 35th St 97330-4908 (Mail to: 333 Nw 35th St 97330-4956) Abigail Buckley Simon Justice (541) 757-6647

Cottage Grove St Andrews Episcopal Church **M** (23) 1301 W Main St 97424-1802 (Mail to: 1301 W Main St 97424-1802) (541) 767-9050

Dallas Church of St Thomas **M** (72) 1486 SW Levens St 97338-0144 (Mail to: PO Box 144 97338-0144) Frederick Heard Addyse Palagyi (503) 623-8522

Drain St Davids Episcopal Church **M** (5) 239 East B Ave 97436 (Mail to: C/O Jane B Stewart PO Box 97 97435-0097) (541) 972-7085

Eugene Church of the Resurrection **P** (236) 3925 Hilyard St 97405-3957 (Mail to: 3925 Hilyard St 97405-3957) Brent Was Nancy Gallagher Maron Van (541) 686-8462

Eugene St Marys Episcopal Church **P** (631) 1300 Pearl St 97401-3539 (Mail to: 1300 Pearl St 97401-3539) Robert Powell Nancy Crawford Thomas English Douglas Hale Christine Marie Nancy Muhlheim Ann Rose (541) 343-9253

Eugene St Matthews Episcopal Church **P** (174) 4110 River Rd 97404-1235 (Mail to: 4110 River Rd 97404-1235) Patricia Hale (541) 689-4010

Eugene St Thomas Episcopal Church **P** (163) 1465 Coburg Rd 97401-5006 (Mail to: 1465 Coburg Rd Ste 2 97401-5006) (541) 343-5241

Florence St Andrews Episcopal Church **M** (108) 2135 19th St 97439-9730 (Mail to: PO Box 15 97439-0001) John Crocker (541) 997-6600

Forest Grove St Bede Episcopal Church **M** (130) 1609 Elm St 97116-2503 (Mail to: 1609 Elm St 97116-2503) (503) 357-5300

Gardiner St Mary Episcopal Church **M** (29) North 2nd & High Sts 97441 (Mail to: PO Box 208 97441-0208) (541) 271-0413

Gold Beach St Matthews Episcopal Church **M** (43) 94261 Moore St 97444 (Mail to: PO Box 651 97444-0651) George Walter (541) 247-7878

Grants Pass St Lukes Episcopal Church **P** (192) 244 NW 'D' St 97526-2042 (Mail to: 224 NW D St 97526-2042) Ernestein Flemister Joan Bristol Mary Piper Mary Piper (541) 476-2493

Gresham St Lukes Episcopal Church **P** (119) 120 Sw Towle Ave 97080-6750 (Mail to: 120 SW Towle Ave 97080-6750) (503) 665-9442

Hillsboro All Saints Parish of Hillsboro **P** (111) 372 Ne Lincoln St 97124-3146 (Mail to: 372 NE Lincoln St 97124-3196) David Brownmiller (503) 648-2514

✣ **Hillsboro** Todos Los Santos **O** (137) 372 Ne Lincoln St 97124-3146 (Mail to: 372 Ne Lincoln St 97124-3146) (503) 640-9425

Lake Oswego Christ Episcopal Church **P** (1189) § 1060 Chandler Rd 97034-2874 (Mail to: C/O Charles Mansfield PO Box 447 97034-0048) Carolynne Fairweather Shannon Leach Jeremy Lucas Alison Schultz Iain Stanford (503) 636-5618

Lebanon St Martins Episcopal Church **P** (162) 257 E Milton St 97355-3493 (Mail to: 1461 Grove St 97355-3428) Melodie Kimball Helen Richard (541) 451-1159

Lincoln City St James Episcopal Parish **P** (82) 2490 Ne Highway 101 97367-4148 (Mail to: PO Box 789 97367-0789) Kristina Burbank Christine Hertlein (541) 994-2426

McMinnville St Barnabas Episcopal Church **P** (261) 822 W Second St 97128 (Mail to: PO Box 539 97128-0539) Helen Durany (503) 472-5831

Medford St Marks Episcopal Parish **P** (369) 140 Oakdale Ave 97501-2629 (Mail to: 426 W 6th St 97501-2713) Jedediah Holdorph Betty Pinnock Linda Potter Thomas Sramek (541) 773-3111

Milwaukie Church of St John the Evangelist **P** (404) 2036 Se Jefferson St 97222-7660 (Mail to: 2036 SE Jefferson St 97222-7660) Stephen Denny Richard Simpson (503) 653-5880

Monmouth St Hildas Episcopal Church **M** (67) 245 Main St W 97361-2024 (Mail to: 245 Main St W 97361-2024) William Mosier Ronald Wynn (503) 838-6087

Nehalem St Catherine Episcopal Church **M** (182) 36335 Highway 101 97131-9732 (Mail to: PO Box 251 97130) (503) 368-7890

Newberg St Michael/San Miguel **M** (195) 110 S Everest Rd 97132-2113 (Mail to: PO Box 358 97132-0358) Juan Guerra-Diaz (503) 538-3080

Newport St Stephens Episcopal Church **P** (88) 331 SW 9th St 97365-0076 (Mail to: PO Box 1014 97365-0076) Susan Church George Goold Janis Goold (541) 265-5251

Oregon City St Pauls Episcopal Church **P** (191) 822 Washington St 97045-1945 (Mail to: 822 Washington St 97045-1945) Shawn Dickerson Davis Fisher

Port Orford St Christophers Church **M** (48) 9th & Washington Sts 97465 (Mail to: PO Box 214 97465-0214) Norman Goldman (541) 347-1504

Portland All Saints Episcopal Church **P** (303) 4033 Se Woodstock Blvd 97202-7661 (Mail to: 4033 SE Woodstock Blvd 97202-7661) Andria Skornik (503) 777-3829

Portland Ascension Parish **P** (235) 1823 Sw Spring St 97201-2345 (Mail to: 1823 SW Spring St 97201-2345) Claude Craig Robert Ladehoff (503) 227-7806

Portland Parish of St John the Baptist **P** (469) 6300 Sw Nicol Rd 97223-7566 (Mail to: 6300 SW Nicol Rd 97223-7566) Robert Bryant Julia Jensen Heather Wenrick Colin Williams (503) 245-3777

Portland Grace Memorial Church **P** (474) 1535 Ne 17th Ave 97232-1417 (Mail to: 1535 NE 17th Ave 97232-1417) Darrah Clark Martin Elfert Lucy Houser (503) 287-0418

Portland St Aidan's Episcopal Church **P** (225) 17405 NE Glisan St 97230-6414 (Mail to: 17405 NE Glisan St 97230-6414) Esme Jo Culver (503) 252-6128

Portland St Andrew Episcopal Church **M** (75) 7600 Hereford Ave 97203-3432 (Mail to: 7600 Hereford Ave 97203-3498) (503) 285-0631

Portland St Barnabas Episcopal Church **P** (151) 2201 Sw Vermont St 97219-1935 (Mail to: 2201 SW Vermont St 97219-1935) Sean Wall (503) 246-1949

Portland St Davids Episcopal Church **P** (183) 2800 Se Harrison St 97214-5650 (Mail to: 2800 SE Harrison St 97214-5699) John Nesbitt P Joshua Griffin James Joiner Kerlin Richter (503) 232-8461

Portland St Gabriel the Archangel Episcopal **M** (411) 17435 Nw West Union Rd 97229-2190

(Mail to: AttnRevCraig Mac Coll 17435 Nw West Union Road 97229) Louann Pickering Thomas Lang Louann Pickering Roger Reynolds (503) 645-0744

Portland St James Episcopal Church **P** (185) 11511 Sw Bull Mountain Rd 97224-2716 (Mail to: 11511 SW Bull Mountain Rd 97224-2716) Beth Mallon Robert Williams (503) 639-3002

Portland St Matthews Episcopal Church **P** (59) 11229 Ne Prescott St 97220-2457 (Mail to: 11229 NE Prescott St 97220-2457) (503) 252-5720

Portland St Michael & All Angels Church **P** (796) 1704 Ne 43rd Ave 97213-1402 (Mail to: 1704 NE 43rd Ave 97213-1402) Christopher Craun Samuel Borbon Sallie Bowman James Joiner David Perry (503) 284-7141

Portland Saints Peter and Paul **P** (426) 247 SE 82nd Ave 97216-1005 (Mail to: 247 SE 82nd Ave 97216-1005) Tracy LeBlanc (503) 254-8168

Portland St Philip the Deacon Epis Church **P** (81) 120 Ne Knott St 97212-3010 (Mail to: 120 NE Knott St 97212-3010) MARIA MCDOWELL (503) 281-5802

Portland St Stephens Episcopal Parish **P** (193) 1432 Sw 13th Ave 97201-3356 (Mail to: 1432 SW 13th Ave 97201-3390) Dale Carr (503) 223-6424

✠ **Portland** Trinity Episcopal Cathedral **O** (937) 147 NW 19th Ave 97209-1901 (Mail to: 147 NW 19th Ave 97209-1901) Phillip Ayers Joseph Dubay Valerie Ivey Matthew Lawrence Nathanael LeRud Julia McCray-Goldsmith John Scannell Maureen Tighe Patrick Tomter (503) 222-9811

Riddle Church of the Ascension **M** (14) 135 D St 97469 (Mail to: PO Box 460 97469-0460) (541) 874-2936

Roseburg St Georges Episcopal Church **P** (221) 1024 Se Cass Ave 97470-4912 (Mail to: 1024 SE Cass Ave 97470-4984) (541) 673-4048

Saint Helens Christ Episcopal Church **M** (102) 35350 E Division Rd 97051-3202 (Mail to: PO Box 478 97051-0478) (503) 397-1033

Salem St Pauls Episcopal Church **P** (1059) 1444 Liberty St Se 97302-4344 (Mail to: 1444 Liberty St SE 97302-4384) Anne Emry (503) 362-3661

Salem St Timothys Episcopal Church **P** (160) 3295 Ladd Ave Ne 97301-1750 (Mail to: PO Box 7416 97303-0089) Brandon Filbert Donald Wilson (503) 363-0601

Salem The Episcopal Church Of The Prince Of Peace **M** (148) 1525 Glen Creek Rd NW PO Box 5757 97304-2726 (Mail to: PO Box 5757 97304-2726) Margaret McMurren Anne Moore (503) 585-1479

Seaside Calvary Parish **P** (146) 503 Holladay Dr 97138-6923 (Mail to: 503 Holladay Dr 97138-6923) David Sweeney (503) 738-5773

Shady Cove St Martins Church **M** (55) 95 Cleveland St 97539-9730 (Mail to: PO Box 786 97539-0786) (541) 878-2166

Silverton St Edwards Episcopal Church **M** (108) 211 W Center St 97381-1905 (Mail to: PO Box 344 97381-0344) Shana Mccauley (503) 873-6188

Springfield Church of St John the Divine **P** (50) 2537 Game Farm Rd 97477-7577 (Mail to: PO Box 1537 97477-0166) (541) 746-3322

Stayton Christ the King on the Santiam **M** (12) 550 W Regis St 97383-1164 (Mail to: PO Box 403 97383-0403) Thomas Moehl (503) 394-4113

Sutherlin Church of the Holy Spirit **M** (22) 120 S Umatilla St 97479-9548 (Mail to: PO Box 1398 97479-1398) Nancy Gallagher (541) 459-4697

Tillamook St Albans Episcopal Parish **P** (169) 2102 6th St 97141-3900 (Mail to: PO Box 285 97141-0285) (503) 842-6192

Toledo St Johns Episcopal Church **M** (38) 110 Ne Alder St 97391-1520 (Mail to: PO Box 332 97391-0332) Pauline Morrison Jonathan Shumate (541) 336-3161

Waldport Saint Luke's Church **M** (79) 1353 Highway 101 S 97394 (Mail to: PO Box 422 97394-0422) (541) 563-4812

Wilsonville St Francis of Assisi Episcopal **P** (607) 8818 Sw Miley Rd 97070 (Mail to: PO Box 445 97070-0445) Kenneth Russell (503) 678-5422

Woodburn St Marys Episcopal Church **M** (78) 1560 W Hayes St 97071-4314 (Mail to: PO Box 362 97071-0362) Samuel Borbon (503) 982-6262

STATE OF PENNSYLVANIA

Dioceses of Bethlehem (Be), Central Pennsylvania (CPA), Northwestern Pennsylvania (NWPA), Pennsylvania (PA), and Pittsburgh (Pgh)

Abington—PA	Archbald—Be	Bala Cynwyd—PA	Berwick—CPA
Allentown—Be	Ardmore—PA	Bedford—CPA	Bethlehem—Be
Altoona—CPA	Ashland—Be	Bellefonte—CPA	Blairsville—Pgh
Ambler—PA	Athens—Be	Benton—CPA	Bloomsburg—CPA

Blue Bell—PA
Blue Ridge Summit—CPA
Boothwyn—PA
Brackenridge—Pgh
Bradford—NWPA
Bridgeport—PA
Brighton Heights—Pgh
Bristol—PA
Brookland—CPA
Brookville—NWPA
Bryn Mawr—PA
Buckingham—PA
Camp Hill—CPA
Canonsburg—Pgh
Carbondale—Be
Carlisle—CPA
Carnegie—Pgh
Chambersburg—CPA
Chester—PA
Clarks Summit—Be
Clearfield—NWPA
Clifton Hts—PA
Coatesville—PA
Collegeville—PA
Columbia—CPA
Conshohocken—PA
Corry—NWPA
Coudersport—CPA
Dallas—Be
Danville—CPA
Donora—Pgh
Downingtown—PA
Douglassville—Be
Doylestown—PA
Drexel Hill—PA
Drifton—Be
Dubois—NWPA
Eagles Mere—CPA
East Liberty—Pgh
Easton—Be
Edinboro—NWPA
Elkins Pk—PA
Emmaus—Be
Emporium—NWPA
Erie—NWPA
Essington—PA
Exchange—CPA
Exton—PA
Fairview—NWPA
Forest City—Be
Ft Washington—PA
Foxburg—NWPA
Frackville—Be
Franklin—NWPA
Franklin Park—Pgh
Gap—PA
Gettysburg—CPA
Gladwyne—PA

Glen Mills—PA
Glenmoore—PA
Glenside—PA
Greensburg—Pgh
Greenville—NWPA
Grove City—NWPA
Hamlin—Be
Hanover—CPA
Harleysville—PA
Harrisburg—CPA
Hatboro—PA
Havertown—PA
Hawk Run—CPA
Hazelwood—Pgh
Hazleton—Be
Hellertown—Be
Hermitage—NWPA
Hershey—CPA
Highland Park—Pgh
Hilltown—PA
Hollidaysburg—CPA
Homestead—Pgh
Honesdale—Be
Honey Brook—PA
Houtzdale—NWPA
Hulmeville—PA
Huntingdon—CPA
Huntingdon Valley—PA
Indiana—Pgh
Jeannette—Pgh
Jenkintown—PA
Jersey Shore—CPA
Jim Thorpe—Be
Johnstown—Pgh
Kane—NWPA
Kennett Sq—PA
King of Prussia—PA
Kingston—Be
Kittanning—Pgh
Kutztown—Be
Lafayette Hill—PA
Lake City—NWPA
Lancaster—CPA
Langhorne—PA
Lansdale—PA
Lansdowne—PA
Lansford—Be
Lebanon—CPA
Lehighton—Be
Levittown—PA
Lewisburg—CPA
Lewistown—CPA
Ligonier—Pgh
Lock Haven—CPA
Lower Gwynedd—PA
Malvern—PA
Manheim—CPA
Mansfield—CPA
Maple Glen—PA

Marietta—CPA
McKeesport—Pgh
Meadville—NWPA
Mechanicsburg—CPA
Media—PA
Milford—Be
Milton—CPA
Monogehela—Pgh
Montoursville—CPA
Montrose—Be
Morgantown—Be
Morrisville—PA
Moscow—Be
Mountaintop—Be
Mt Carmel—CPA
Mt Joy—CPA
Mt Lebanon—Pgh
Mt Pocono—Be
Muncy—CPA
Nanticoke—Be
Narvon—CPA
Nazareth—Be
New Castle—NWPA
New Hope—PA
New Milford—Be
Newport—CPA
Newtown—PA
Newtown Sq—PA
Norristown—PA
North East—NWPA
North Hills—Pgh
North Side—Pgh
North Versailles—Pgh
Northern Cambria—Pgh
Northumberland—CPA
Norwood—PA
Oakmont—Pgh
Oaks—PA
Oil City—NWPA
Oreland—PA
Osceola Mills—NWPA
Oxford—PA
Palmerton—Be
Paoli—PA
Parkesburg—PA
Pen Argyl—Be
Penn Hills—Pgh
Peters Township—Pgh
Philadelphia—PA
Philipsburg—CPA
Phoenixville—PA
Pittston—Be
Pittsburgh—Pgh
Pt Alleghany—NWPA
Pottstown—PA
Pottsville—Be
Prospect Pk—PA
Quakertown—PA
Reading—Be

Renovo—CPA
Ridgway—NWPA
Ridley Pk—PA
Rockledge—PA
Rosemont—PA
Royersford—PA
St Clair—Be
St Marys—NWPA
Sayre—Be
Schuylkill Haven—Be
Scottdale—Pgh
Scranton—Be
Selinsgrove—CPA
Shamokin—CPA
Sharon—NWPA
Shippensburg—CPA
Smethport—NWPA
Solebury—PA
Somerset—Pgh
Southampton—PA
Springfield—PA
Squirrel Hill—Pgh
State College—CPA
Stroudsburg—Be
Sunbury—CPA
Susquehanna—Be
Swarthmore—PA
Tamaqua—Be
Thompsontown—CPA
Tioga—CPA
Titusville—NWPA
Towanda—Be
Trexlertown—Be
Troy—Be
Tunkhannock—Be
Tyrone—CPA
University Pk—CPA
Valley Forge—PA
Villanova—PA
Warren—NWPA
Waterford—NWPA
Wayne—PA
Waynesboro—CPA
Wayne Township—CPA & Pgh
Wellsboro—CPA
W Chester—PA
Westfield—CPA
Whitehall—Be
Wilkes-Barre—Be
Williamsport—CPA
Wind Gap—Be
Wrightstown—PA
Wyncote—PA
Wynnewood—PA
Yardley—PA
York—CPA
Youngsville—NWPA

DIOCESE OF PENNSYLVANIA
(PROVINCE III)
Comprises Bucks, Chester, Delaware, Montgomery, and Philadelphia Counties
DIOCESAN OFFICE Church House 3717 Chestnut Street, Suite 300, Philadelphia 19104
Tel (215) 627-6434   FAX (267) 900-2928
E-MAIL mail@diopa.org   WEB www.diopa.org

Previous Bishops—
Wm White 1787-1836, Henry
U Onderdonk coadj 1827 Bp
1836-44, Alonzo Potter 1845-
65, Samuel Bowman suffr 1858-
61, Wm B Stevens coadj 1862 Bp
1865-87, Ozi W Whitaker coadj
1886 Bp 1887-1911, Alexander
Mackay-Smith coadj 1902 Bp
1911, Philip McRhinelander coadj 1911 Bp 1911-23,
Thomas J Garland suffr 1911 Bp 1924-31, Francis
M Taitt coadj 1929 Bp 1931-43, Wm P Remington
suffr 1945-51, Oliver J Hart coadj 1942 Bp 1943-63, J
Gillespie Armstrong suffr 1949 coadj 1960 Bp1963-
64, Robert L DeWitt coadj 1964 Bp 1964-73, Lyman
C Ogilby coadj 1973 Bp 1974-87, Allen L Bartlett
Jr coadj 1986 Bp 1987-98, Franklin D Turner suffr
1988-2000, Charles E. Bennison Jr coadj 1997-98 Bp
1998-2012, Clifton Daniel Bp prov 2013-2016

Bishop—Daniel G.P. Gutiérrez

Chanc M Kohart; *Treas* J Pope; *Bp's Staff: Exec Asst*
C Fisher; *Cn for Fin* D Horner; *Cn for Trans Min* A
Benoit Joseph; *Property Manager* S McCauley; *Cn
Growth and Support* B Ivey; *Cn Growth and Support*
K Berlenbach; *Cn for Miss* T Smyth; *Cn for Comm* J
Tucker; *Cn to Ord* S Wamsley; *Conv Sec* J Buescher

Deans: Brandywine RT Morgan; *Bucks* M Ruk;
Delaware D Whitfield; *Merion* D Romanik;
Montgomery L Hade; *Pennypack* S Murangi;
Schuylkill M Shaw; *Southwark* G Reid; *Valley Forge*
K Andonian; *Wissahickon* J Kerbel

Stand Comm—Cler: H Raining L Colton J Jones M
Rau M Ruk *Lay: Pres* N McCausland G Vosburgh E
Rabe P Smith C Johnstone

PARISHES, MISSIONS, AND CLERGY

Abington St Annes Episcopal Church **P** (433)
2119 Welsh Rd 19001-1013 (Mail to: 2119 Old
Welsh Rd 19001-1013) Winston Smith (215)
659-1674

Ambler Trinity Episcopal Church **P** (506) 708
S Bethlehem Pike 19002-5809 (Mail to:
708 S Bethlehem Pike 19002-5899) Mary
Mccullough (215) 646-0416

Ardmore Nevil Memorial Church of St George **P**
(350) 1 W Ardmore Ave 19003-1017 (Mail to: 1
W Ardmore Ave # C 19003-1017) Joel Daniels
(610) 642-3500

Ardmore Saint Mary's Episcopal Church **P** (390)
36 Ardmore Ave 19003-1334 (Mail to: 36
Ardmore Ave 19003-1334) Karen Kaminskas
Joseph Schaller (610) 649-1486

Bala Cynwyd Church of St Asaphs **P** (296) § 27
Conshohocken State Rd 19004-2400 (Mail to:
27 Conshohocken State Rd 19004-2496) Barry
Harte (610) 664-0966

Bala Cynwyd St Johns Episcopal Church **P** (119)
404 Levering Mill Rd 19004-2703 (Mail to: 404
Levering Mill Rd 19004-2700) Frank Wallner
(610) 664-4517

Blue Bell St Dunstans Episcopal Church **P** (161)
750 Skippack Pike 19422-1712 (Mail to: 750
Skippack Pike 19422-1712) (215) 643-0522

Boothwyn Trinity Church **P** (103) 700
Meetinghouse Rd 19061-3503 (Mail to: 700
Meetinghouse Rd 19061-3503) Paul Gitimu
(610) 213-9587

Bridgeport Christ Episcopal Church **P** (44) 740
Schuylkill River Rd 19405-1761 (Mail to: 740
River Rd 19405-1761) Theodore Henderson
(610) 272-6036

Bristol St James Church Episcopal **P** (120) 225
Walnut St 19007-4940 (Mail to: 225 Walnut St
19007-4940) Marlee Norton (215) 788-2228

Bryn Mawr Church of the Redeemer **P** (2349) 230
Pennswood Rd 19010 (Mail to: 230 Pennswood
Rd 19010-3616) Peter Vanderveen JoAnn
Jones David Romanik (610) 525-2486

Buckingham Trinity Episcopal Church **P** (305)
2631 Durham Rd 18912 (Mail to: PO Box 387
18912-0387) Nancy Dilliplane (215) 794-7921

Chester St Mary Episcopal Church **M** (85) 703
Edwards St 19013 (Mail to: PO Box 595 19016-
0595) Deirdre Whitfield (610) 874-8565

Chester St Pauls Episcopal Church **P** (90) 301 E
9th St 19013-6020 (Mail to: 301 E 9th St 19013-
6088) Zachary Smith (610) 872-5711

Clifton Hgts Saint Stephen's Episcopal Church **P**
(114) 119 W Baltimore Ave 19018-1405 (Mail
to: 199 W Baltimore Ave 19018-1494) (610)
622-3636

Coatesville The Church of the Trinity **P** (111)
323 E Lincoln Hwy 19320-3409 (Mail to: 323 E
Lincoln Hwy 19320-3409) Sherry Deets (610)
384-4771

Collegeville St James Church Collegeville **P** (428)
3768 Germantown Pike 19426-3151 (Mail to:
3768 Germantown Pike 19426-3151) William
Sowards (610) 489-7564

Conshohocken Calvary Episcopal Church **P** (119)
325 Fayette St 19428-0546 (Mail to: PO Box 546
19428-0546) Thomas McClellan (610) 825-5959

Downingtown St James Episcopal Church **P** (354)
409 E Lancaster Ave 19335-2722 (Mail to: 409
E Lancaster Ave 19335-2722) John Symonds
(610) 269-1774

Doylestown St Pauls Episcopal Church **P** (616) 84 E Oakland Ave 18901-4647 (Mail to: 84 E Oakland Ave 18901-4647) Daniel Moore (215) 348-5511

Drexel Hill Incarnation Holy Sacrament Episcopal **P** (244) 3000 Garrett Rd 19026-2217 (Mail to: 3000 Garrett Rd 19026-2217) Diane Faison Benjamin Wallis (610) 259-5148

Drexel Hill The Church of the Holy Comforter **P** (253) 1000 Burmont Rd 19026-4533 (Mail to: 1000 Burmont Rd 19026-4533) Thomas Eoyang (610) 789-6754

Elkins Park St Paul's Episcopal Church **P** (181) 7809 Old York Rd 19027-2508 (Mail to: 7809 Old York Rd 19027-2593) Paul Reid (215) 635-4185

Essington Church of St John the Evangelist **P** (172) 16 W 3rd St 19029-1200 (Mail to: 16 W 3rd St 19029-1200) Denise Leo Zachary Smith Harry White (610) 521-3612

Exton St Pauls Episcopal Church **P** (420) 901 E Lincoln Hwy 19341-2806 (Mail to: 1105 E Lincoln Hwy 19341-2824) (610) 363-2363

Fort Washington St Thomas Church Whitemarsh **P** (1379) 7020 Camp Hill Rd 19034-2202 (Mail to: 610 Bethlehem Pike 19034) Marek Zabriskie Elizabeth Costello Tommy Thompson (215) 233-3970

Gap St Johns Episcopal Church **P** (122) 1520 W Kings Hwy 17527-9009 (Mail to: 1520 W Kings Hwy 17527-9009) Nina George-Hacker John Obenchain (717) 442-4302

Gladwyne Saint Christopher's Church **P** (602) § 226 Righters Mill Rd 19035-1533 (Mail to: 226 Righters Mill Rd 19035-1597) Hillary Raining Callie Swanlund (610) 642-8920

Glen Mills St Johns Episcopal Church **P** (753) 576 Concord Rd 19342-1402 (Mail to: 576 Concord Rd 19342-1402) John Sorensen Jill Laroche Wilson (610) 459-2994

Glenmoore St Andrews Episcopal Church **P** (509) 7 Saint Andrews Ln 19343-9559 (Mail to: 7 Saint Andrews Ln 19343-9559) Tommy Thompson (610) 458-5277

Glenside St Peters Episcopal Church **P** (332) 654 Easton Rd 19038-4310 (Mail to: 654 Easton Rd 19038-4391) Emily Richards (215) 887-1765

Harleysville The Church of the Holy Spirit **P** (632) 2871 Barndt Rd 19438-1150 (Mail to: PO Box 575 19438-0575) Kathryn Andonian (215) 234-8020

Hatboro Church of the Advent **P** (243) 12 Byberry Rd 19040-3405 (Mail to: 12 Byberry Rd 19040-3405) Lynn Hade (215) 675-5737

Hilltown Good Shepherd Epis Church **P** (131) 1634 Hilltown Pike 18927-9701 (Mail to: PO Box 132 18927-0132) Catherine Kerr (215) 822-3930

Honey Brook St Marks Church **P** (108) 1040 Chestnut Tree Rd 19344-9645 (Mail to: 1040 Chestnut Tree Rd 19344-9645) (610) 942-2365

Hulmeville Grace Episcopal Church **P** (134) 313 Main St 19047-5801 (Mail to: 313 Main St 19047-5801) E Morgan Marlee Norton (215) 757-6025

Huntingdon Valley Saint John's Church **P** (90) 1309 Old Welsh Rd 19006-5899 (Mail to: 1309 Old Welsh Rd 19006-5899) Eric Bond (215) 947-3212

Jenkintown Church of Our Saviour **P** (81) Old York & Homestead Rds 19046 (Mail to: Homestead & Old York Roads 19046) Eric Bond (215) 887-0500

Jenkintown Memorial Church Of The Holy Nativity **P** (223) 205 Huntingdon Pike 19046-4444 (Mail to: C/O Heather Sherman 205 Huntingdon Pike 19046-4444) Michael Rau (215) 663-9903

Kennet Sq Church of the Advent **P** (1234) 401 Union St 19348-2427 (Mail to: 401 Union St 19348-2427) Nancy Hauser Gregory Wilson (610) 444-4624

King of Prussia Grace Church and the Incarnation **P** (89) C/O John Loftus 966 Trinity Lane 19406 (Mail to: Treasurer 2645 E Venango St 19134-5529) (610) 828-1500

Kng Of Prussia Trinity Church Gulph Mills **P** (199) 966 Trinity Ln 19406-3636 (Mail to: Attn J. Smith 966 Trinity Ln 19406-3636) Deborah Payson (610) 828-1500

Lafayette Hill Church of St Jude and the Nativity **P** (90) 203 Germantown Pike 19444-1323 (Mail to: 203 Germantown Pike 19444-1323) (610) 941-6666

Langhorne St James Episcopal Church **P** (240) 330 S Bellevue Ave 19047-2808 (Mail to: 330 S Bellevue Ave 19047-2808) Barbara Kelley (215) 757-3766

Lansdale Holy Trinity Church **P** (171) 407 Broad St 19446-2413 (Mail to: 407 Broad St 19446-2450) (215) 855-4431

Lansdowne St Michaels Episcopal Church **P** (71) 813 Longacre Blvd 19050-3319 (Mail to: 813 Longacre Blvd 19050-3319) Jordan Casson (610) 259-7871

Levittown All Saints Episcopal Church **P** (58) 9 Old Locust Ave 19054-1107 (Mail to: 9 Old Locust Ave 19054-1107) Sean Slack (215) 295-5196

Levittown St Paul Church **P** (128) 89 Pinewood Dr 19054-3609 (Mail to: 89 Pinewood Dr 19054-3609) Sean Slack (215) 946-8559

Lower Gwynedd Church of the Messiah **P** (929) 1001 Dekalb Pike 19002-1941 (Mail to: 1001 Dekalb Pike 19002-1941) Keith Marsh MaryJo Melberger (215) 699-9204

Malvern St Peters Church in the Great Valley **P** (622) 2475 Saint Peters Rd 19355-8791 (Mail to: PO Box 334 19301-0334) Kyle Babin Abigail Nestlehutt (610) 644-7967

Malvern St Francis-in-the Field **P** (524) 689 Sugartown Rd 19355-3305 (Mail to: 689

Sugartown Rd 19355-3305) Kevin Dellaria Diane Faison (610) 647-0130

Maple Glen Saint Matthew's Church **P** (596) § 919 Tennis Ave 19002-2312 (Mail to: 919 Tennis Ave 19002-2312) David Robinson James Walton (215) 646-4092

Media Christ Episcopal Church **P** (402) 311 S Orange St 19063-3111 (Mail to: 311 S Orange St 19063-3190) Ernest Galaz (610) 566-7525

Morrisville Church of the Incarnation **P** (145) 1505 Makefield Rd 19067-3149 (Mail to: 1505 Makefield Rd 19067-3149) Harriet Kollin (215) 295-2259

New Hope St Philips Episcopal Church **P** (149) 10 Chapel Rd 18938-1006 (Mail to: 10 Chapel Rd 18938-1006) Michael Ruk (215) 862-5782

Newtown Saint Luke's Church In The County Of Buck **P** (400) 100 E Washington Ave 18940-1980 (Mail to: 100 E Washington Ave 18940-1980) Ernest Curtin (215) 968-2781

Newtown Square Saint Alban's Church **P** (207) 3625 Chapel Rd 19073-3602 (Mail to: 3625 Chapel Rd 19073-3698) Matthew Dayton-Welch (610) 356-0459

Norristown All Saints Episcopal Church **P** (183) 535 Haws Ave 19401-4542 (Mail to: 535 Haws Ave 19401-4542) Sandra Etemad Geoffrey West (610) 279-3990

Norristown St Augustine of Hippo Church **P** (126) 1208 Green St 19401-3402 (Mail to: 1208 Green St 19401-3402) (610) 279-8890

Norristown St Johns Episcopal Church **P** (88) 23 E Airy St 19401-4815 (Mail to: 23 E Airy St 19401-4815) Scott Albergate (610) 272-4092

Norwood St Stephen Episcopal Church **P** (126) 128 Chester Pike 19074-1702 (Mail to: 128 Chester Pike 19074-1702) (610) 461-0490

Oaks St Pauls Episcopal Church **P** (134) 126 Black Rock Rd 19456 (Mail to: PO Box 404 19456) Daniel Olsen (610) 650-9336

Oreland St Philip in the Fields **P** (136) Lorraine Ave & Oreland Mill Rd 19075 (Mail to: 317 Oreland Mill Rd 19075-2256) (215) 233-0409

Oxford St Christophers Episcopal Church **P** (242) 116 Lancaster Pike 19363-1171 (Mail to: 116 Lancaster Pike 19363-1171) Mary Mertz (610) 932-8134

Paoli Church of the Good Samaritan **P** (1104) § 212 W Lancaster Ave 19301-1723 (Mail to: 212 W Lancaster Ave 19301-1758) Benjamin Capps Richard Morgan John Whitnah (610) 644-4040

Parkesburg Church of the Ascension **P** (94) 406 W 2nd Ave 19365-1402 (Mail to: PO Box 193 19365-0193) (610) 857-9176

Philadelphia All Saints Church Torresdale **P** (372) 9601 Frankford Ave 19114-2813 (Mail to: 9601 Frankford Ave 19114-2895) Elizabeth Colton Robert Smith (215) 637-8787

Philadelphia All Saints Church (Rhawnhurst) **P** (71) 7939 Frontenac St 19111 (Mail to: 1811 Loney St 19111-2911) James Morris (215) 342-6310

Philadelphia Calvary-St Augustine Church **P** (189) 814 41st St 19104-4813 (Mail to: 814 41st St 19104-4813) Isaac Miller (215) 222-2070

✣ **Philadelphia** Cathedral Church of Our Saviour **O** (150) 13-19 S 38th St 19104 (Mail to: 23 S 38th St 19104-3189) Judith Sullivan Phillip Bennett Sarah Hedgis Pamela Nesbit Robert Tate (215) 386-0234

Philadelphia La Iglesia de Christo § San Ambrosio **M** (2172) 3552 6th St 19140-4506 (Mail to: 6th And Venango Sts 19140) (215) 226-1444

Philadelphia Christ Church & St Michaels Church **P** (227) 29 W Tulpehocken St 19144-2607 (Mail to: 29 W Tulpehocken St 19144-2607) (215) 844-7274

Philadelphia Christ Church **P** (544) 20 American St 19106-4509 (Mail to: 20 American St 19106-4592) Timothy Safford Susan Richardson (215) 922-1695

Philadelphia St Andrew & St Monica Church **M** (181) 3600 Baring St 19104-2333 (Mail to: 3600 Baring St 19104-2333) Samuel Adu-Andoh (215) 222-7606

Philadelphia Church of St Luke & the Epiphany **P** (253) 330 S 13th St 19107-5916 (Mail to: 330 S 13th St 19107-5916) Rodger Broadley (215) 732-1918

Philadelphia Church of St Martin in the Fields **P** (800) 8000 Saint Martins Ln 19118-4101 (Mail to: 8000 Saint Martins Ln 19118-4101) Walter Kerbel Carol Duncan James Taylor Anne Thatcher (215) 247-7466

Philadelphia Church of the Annunciation **P** (94) 324 Carpenter Ln 19119-3003 (Mail to: 324 Carpenter Ln 19119-3003) (215) 844-3059

Philadelphia Memorial Church of the Good Shepherd **P** (121) 3820 The Oak Road 19129-1030 (Mail to: 3820 the Oak Rd 19129-1030) (215) 844-0580

Philadelphia Emmanuel Church **P** (92) 8201 Frankford Ave 19136-2735 (Mail to: 8201 Frankford Ave 19136-2735) Samuel Murangi (215) 624-8520

Philadelphia George W South Ch of Advocate **P** (75) 1801 W Diamond St 19121-1519 (Mail to: PO Box 50480 19132-6480) (215) 978-8000

Philadelphia Gloria Dei Episcopal Church **P** (220) 916 S Swanson St 19147-4332 (Mail to: 916 S Swanson St 19147-4396) Patricia Cashman (215) 389-1513

Philadelphia Grace Epiphany Church **P** (174) 224 E Gowen Ave 19119-1020 (Mail to: 224 E Gowen Ave 19119-1020) (215) 248-2950

Philadelphia Holy Apostles And Mediator **P** (133) Spruce & 51st Sts 19139 (Mail to: 260 S 51st St 19139) Joseph Garrigan (215) 472-3000

Philadelphia Holy Innocents St Pauls Church **P** (150) 7001 Torresdale Ave 19135-1914 (Mail to: 7001 Torresdale Ave 19135-1914) (215) 624-1144

Philadelphia House of Prayer **P** (99) 1747 Church Ln 19141-1309 (Mail to: 1747 Church Ln 19141-1309) (215) 549-7650

Philadelphia Memorial Church of St Luke **P** (112) 1946 Welsh Rd 19115-4654 (Mail to: 1946 Welsh Rd 19115-4712) Timothy Griffin (215) 969-3645

Philadelphia St Albans Church Roxborough **P** (160) 6769 Ridge Ave 19128-2444 (Mail to: 6769 Ridge Ave 19128-2444) Paul Adler (215) 482-2627

Philadelphia St Andrews in the Field Church **P** (117) 500 Somerton Ave 19116-2027 (Mail to: 500 Somerton Ave 19116-2027) (215) 673-5938

Philadelphia St Clements Church **P** (105) 2013 Appletree St 19103-1409 (Mail to: 2013 Appletree St 19103-1409) Richard Alton (215) 563-1876

Philadelphia St Davids Episcopal Church **P** (44) 156 Dupont St 19127 (Mail to: PO Box 29102 19127-0102) Frank Wallner (215) 482-2345

Philadelphia St Dismas Episcopal Mission **M** (20) 3717 Chestnut St 19104 (Mail to: PO Box 244 19426-0244) George Master (215) 985-5751

Philadelphia St Gabriels Episcopal Church **M** (125) 101 E Roosevelt Blvd 19120-4243 (Mail to: 101 E Roosevelt Blvd 19120-4243) Nancy Deming Joseph Schaller (215) 329-3807

Philadelphia St George & St Barnabas **P** (191) 520 S 61st St 19143-2234 (Mail to: 520 S 61st St 19143-2234) James Wynn (215) 747-2605

Philadelphia St James of Kingsessing Episcopal Ch **P** (207) 6838 Woodland Ave 19142-1822 (Mail to: 6838 Woodland Ave 19142-1822) (215) 727-5265

Philadelphia St Lukes Church Germantown **P** (615) 5421 Germantown Ave 19144-2223 (Mail to: 5421 Germantown Ave 19144-2223) David Morris (215) 844-8544

Philadelphia St Mark's Episcopal Church **P** (392) 1625 Locust St 19103-6304 (Mail to: 1625 Locust St 19103-6388) Kyle Babin Sean Mullen Nicholas Phelps (215) 735-1416

Philadelphia St Marks Church Frankford **P** (190) 4442 Frankford Ave 19124-3659 (Mail to: 4442 Frankford Ave 19124-3659) Jonathan Clodfelter (215) 535-0635

Philadelphia St Marys Church Cathedral Road **P** (189) 630 E Cathedral Rd 19128-1935 (Mail to: 630 E Cathedral Rd 19128-1935) Peter Carey (215) 482-6300

Philadelphia St Marys Church Hamilton Village **P** (205) 3916 Locust Walk 19104-6152 (Mail to: 3916 Locust Walk 19104-6152) Mariclair Partee Carlsen (215) 386-3916

Philadelphia St Marys Episcopal Church **P** (35) 1831 Bainbridge St 19146-1429 (Mail to: 1831 Bainbridge St 19146-1429) (215) 985-0360

Philadelphia St Pauls Church Chestnut Hill **P** (486) 22 E Chestnut Hill Ave 19118-2715

(Mail to: 22 E Chestnut Hill Ave 19118-2764) E Clifford Cutler Robert Davidson Joseph Wolyniak (215) 242-2055

Philadelphia St Peter's Church **P** (413) 313 Pine St 19106-4212 (Mail to: 313 Pine St 19106-4299) Sean Lanigan Claire Nevin-Field (215) 925-5968

Philadelphia St Simon the Cyrenian Church **P** (106) 22nd And Reed Sts 19146 (Mail to: 1401 S 22nd St 19146-4530) (215) 468-1926

Philadelphia St Stephens Church **HC** (29) 19 S 10th St 19107-4224 (Mail to: 19 S 10th St PO Box 1103 19107-4280) (215) 922-3807

Philadelphia St Timothy Episcopal Church **HC** (320) 5720 Ridge Ave 19128-1734 (Mail to: 5720 Ridge Ave 19128-1734) Bonnie McCrickard (215) 483-1529

Philadelphia The African Epis Ch of St Thomas **P** (983) 6361 Lancaster Ave 19151-2622 (Mail to: 6361 Lancaster Ave 19151-2622) Martini Shaw Samuel Ndungu (215) 473-3065

Philadelphia The Church of the Holy Trinity **HC** (531) 1904 Walnut St 19103-5733 (Mail to: 1904 Walnut St 19103-5796) John Gardner Rachel Wenner Gardner (215) 567-1267

Philadelphia Church of St John the Free **M** (77) 3089 Emerald St 19134-0498 (Mail to: PO Box 14798 19134-0498) David Faccio (215) 425-2933

Philadelphia Trinity Church, Oxford **P** (147) 601 Longshore Ave 19111 (Mail to: 601 Longshore Ave 19111-4330) (215) 745-1258

Philadelphia Trinity Memorial Church **P** (99) 2212 Spruce St 19103-6503 (Mail to: 2212 Spruce St 19103-6503) Donna Maree (215) 732-2515

Phoenixville St Peters Episcopal Church **P** (381) 121 Church St 19460-3438 (Mail to: 121 Church St 19460-3438) Koshy Mathews Joseph Dietz (610) 933-2195

Pottstown Christ Episcopal Church **P** (326) 316 E High St 19464-5538 (Mail to: 316 E High St 19464-5538) Joshua Caler John Houghton (610) 323-2895

Prospect Park St James Church Episcopal **P** (153) 11th & Lincoln Aves 19076 (Mail to: 732 11th Ave 19076-1313) (610) 461-6698

Quakertown Emmanuel Episcopal Church **P** (100) 560 S Main St 18951-1570 (Mail to: 560 S Main St 18951-1570) (215) 536-3040

Ridley Park Christ Church Episcopal **P** (1130) 104 Nevin St 19078-2108 (Mail to: 104 Nevin St 19078-2195) Judith Buck-Glenn (610) 521-1626

Rosemont The Church of the Good Shepherd **P** (40) 1116 E Lancaster Ave 19010-2615 (Mail to: 1116 E Lancaster Ave 19010-2693) Nazareno Javier (610) 525-7070

Royersford Church of the Epiphany **P** (103) 209 S 3rd Ave 19468-2551 (Mail to: 209 S 3rd Ave 19468-2551) Beth Hixon (610) 948-9655

Solebury Trinity Episcopal Church **P** (490) § 6587 Upper York Rd 18963 (Mail to: PO Box 377 18963-0377) Emory Byrum Virginia Sheay Richard Vinson (215) 297-5135

Southampton Church of the Redemption **P** (161) 1101 2nd Street Pike 18966-3956 (Mail to: 1101 2nd Street Pike 18966-3956) Emmanuel Williamson (215) 357-0303

Springfield Church of the Redeemer **P** (326) 145 W Springfield Rd 19064-1414 (Mail to: 145 W Springfield Rd 19064-1414) David Beresford (610) 544-8113

Swarthmore Trinity Church **P** (252) N Chester Rd & College Ave 19081 (Mail to: 301 Chester Rd 19081-1496) Edward Thompson Joyce Tompkins (610) 544-2297

Valley Forge Washington Memorial Chapel **P** (206) RR 23 19481-0098 (Mail to: PO Box 98 19481-0098) (610) 783-0120

Villanova Christ Church **P** (275) 536 Conestoga Rd 19085-1131 (Mail to: 536 Conestoga Rd 19085-1131) John Sosnowski (610) 688-1110

Wayne St David Episcopal Church **P** (3330) 763 Valley Forge Rd 19087-4724 (Mail to: 763 Valley Forge Rd 19087-4794) William Allen Elizabeth Colton Amanda Eiman Harvey McCaslin (610) 688-7947

Wayne St Martins Church **P** (238) 400 King Of Prussia Rd 19087-2342 (Mail to: 400 King of Prussia Rd 19087-2342) Christopher Bishop (610) 688-4830

Wayne St Marys Episcopal Church **P** (449) 104 Louella Ave 19087-4121 (Mail to: 104 Louella Ave 19087-4195) Joseph Smith (610) 688-1313

West Chester The Church of the Holy Trinity **P** (399) 212 S High St 19382-3404 (Mail to: 212 S High St 19382-3499) Paul Hunt (610) 696-4640

Wrightstown Church of the Holy Nativity **M** (46) 749 Durham Rd 18940-9679 (Mail to: 749 Durham Rd 18940-9679) Lisa Keppeler (215) 598-3405

Wyncote All Hallows Church **P** (192) 262 Bent Road 19095 (Mail to: 262 Bent Rd 19095-1503) Mark Ainsworth (215) 885-1641

Wynnewood All Saints Episcopal Church **P** (148) Montgomery Ave & Gypsy Ln 19096 (Mail to: 1325 Montgomery Ave 19096-1037) (610) 642-4098

Wynnewood Church of the Holy Apostles **P** (243) 1020 Remington Rd 19096-2326 (Mail to: 1020 Remington Rd 19096-2394) James Stambaugh (610) 642-6617

Yardley St Andrews Church Episcopal **P** (458) 47 W Afton Ave 19067-1444 (Mail to: 47 W Afton Ave 19067-1444) Hilary Greer Lloyd Winter (215) 493-2636

DIOCESE OF PITTSBURGH

(PROVINCE III)
Comprises the southwestern portion of Pennsylvania
DIOCESAN OFFICE 325 Oliver Avenue, Suite 300, Pittsburgh, PA 15222
TEL (412) 721-0853
E-MAIL office@episcopalpgh.org   WEB www.episcopalpgh.org

Previous Bishops—
John B Kerfoot 1866-81, Cortlandt Whitehead 1881-1922, Alexander Mann 1923-43, Austin Pardue 1944-68, William S Thomas suffr 1954-70, Robert B Appleyard 1968-82, Alden M Hathaway 1983-97, Robert Duncan 1997-2008, Kenneth L Price 2009-2012

Bishop—Rt Rev Dorsey McConnell (1070) (Dio 21 Oct 2012)

Treas & Dir of Admin K Workman; *Cn Pastor* S Quinn; *Cn for Ordained Vocations* J Geisler; *Cn for Miss* K Karashin; *Cn for Evangelism & Faith Formation* N Hall; *Exec Asst* J Rogers; *Fin and Prop Admin* M Rihn; *Dir of Ext Relations* R Creehan; *Web Admin* A Muhl; *Chanc* A Roman, Cohen & Grigsby PC 625 Liberty Ave Pittsburgh PA 15222 (412) 297-

4867; *Pres Brd of Trustees* J Stephenson; *Child Min Team Coord* J Yoon ; *Univ Chaplain* Rev D Isadore; *Comm on Min Chr* Rev K Opat; *Comm on Race and Reconciliation Chr* Rev M Foley; *Disaster Prep Coords* J Gundersen & Rev H Gillette; *Ed for Min Coord* V Sterling; *Epis Ch Women Pres* B Hetzler; *Epis Relief & Dev Rep* D Duntley; *Social Justice Comm* M Novy

Stand Comm—Cler: E McIntosh L Reimer N Evans A Rogers; *Lay:* R Ayres R Johnston D Powell-Williams L Brown

PARISHES, MISSIONS, AND CLERGY

Blairsville St Peters Episcopal Church **P** (24) 36 W Campbell St 15717-1312 (Mail to: 36 W Campbell St 15717-1312) Joseph Baird (724) 459-9804

Brackenridge St Barnabas Episcopal Church **P** (80) 989 Morgan St 15014-1164 (Mail to: 989 Morgan St 15014-1197) Kamila Blessing Francis Yesko (724) 224-9280

Brighton Heights All Saints Episcopal Church **P** (91) 3577 McClure Ave 15212-2147 (Mail to: 3577 McClure Ave 15212-2147) (412) 766-8112

Canonsburg St Thomas Episcopal Church **P** (116) 139 Jefferson Ave 15317-1307 (Mail to: 139 Jefferson Ave 15317-1307) Catherine Brall (724) 745-2013

Carnegie Church of the Atonement **P** (27) 618 Washington Ave 15106-2837 (Mail to: 618 Washington Ave 15106-2837) (412) 279-1944

Carnegie Old St Luke's Church **P** 330 Old Washington Pike 15106-3730 (Mail to: PO Box 9089 15224-0089)

Donora St Johns Episcopal Church **P** (29) 998 Thompson Ave 15033-2146 (Mail to: 998 Thompson Ave 15033-2146) (724) 379-8871

Franklin Park Saint Brendan's Episcopal Church **P** (251) 2365 McAleer Rd 15143-8762 (Mail to: 2365 McAleer Rd 15143-8762) Regis Smolko (412) 364-5974

Greensburg Christ Episcopal Church **P** (34) 132 Sherwood Drive 15601 (Mail to: 122 Maple Ave 15601-2580) (724) 216-4717

Homestead St Matthews Episcopal Church **P** (63) 336 E 10th Ave 15120-1613 (Mail to: 336 E 10th Ave 15120-1613) (412) 461-5291

Indiana Christ Episcopal Church **P** (114) 902 Philadelphia St 15701-3912 (Mail to: 902 Philadelphia St 15701-3912) William Geiger (724) 465-6129

Jeannette Church of the Advent **P** (36) 51 S 1st St 15644-2102 (Mail to: 51 S 1st St 15644-2102) Martin Wright (724) 836-5116

Johnstown St Marks Episcopal Church **P** (145) 335 Locust St 15901-1606 (Mail to: 335 Locust St 15901-1606) Nancy Threadgill (814) 535-6797

Kittanning St Pauls Episcopal Church **P** (109) 112 Water St 16201-1516 (Mail to: 112 Water St 16201-1516) (724) 543-5402

Ligonier St Michaels of the Valley **P** (245) 2535 Route 381 15658 (Mail to: PO Box 336 15658-0336) James Simons (724) 238-9411

Mckeesport St Stephens Episcopal Church **P** (78) 220 8th St 15132-2744 (Mail to: 220 8th St 15132-2744) (412) 664-9379

Monongahela St Pauls Episcopal Church **P** (42) § 130 W. Main Street 15063-2332 (Mail to: 130 W Main St 15063-2332) Teresa Hunt (724) 258-7792

N Versailles All Souls Church **P** (26) 215 Canterbury Ln 15137-2111 (Mail to: 215 Canterbury Ln 15137-2198) Linda Wilson (412) 823-1440

Northern Cambria St Thomas Episcopal Church **P** (20) § 1201 Chestnut Ave 15714-1469 (Mail to: PO Box 91 15714-0091) Ann Staples (814) 948-5230

Oakmont St Thomas Memorial Church **P** (686) 378 Delaware Ave 15139-1618 (Mail to: 378 Delaware Ave 15139-1618) Jeffrey Murph (412) 828-9680

Peters Township St Davids Episcopal Church **P** (134) 905 E McMurray Rd 15367-1094 (Mail to: 905 E Mcmurray Rd 15367-1094) Kristian Opat Kristian Opat (724) 941-4060

Pittsburgh Calvary Episcopal Church **P** (1139) 315 Shady Ave 15206-4388 (Mail to: 315 Shady Ave 15206-4388) Charles Esposito Carol Henley Jonathon Jensen Neil Raman Leslie Reimer Walter Szymanski (412) 661-0120

Pittsburgh Christ Episcopal Church **P** (1425) 5910 Babcock Blvd 15237-2548 (Mail to: 5910 Babcock Blvd 15237-2588) James Shoucair Wade Lawrence Jean McIlvain Lorena Ringle (412) 364-2442

Pittsburgh Church of the Good Shepherd **P** (25) 124 Johnston Ave 15207-1739 (Mail to: PO Box 55054 15207-0054) Huett Fleming (412) 421-8497

Pittsburgh Church of the Holy Cross **P** (119) 7507 Kelly St 15208-1914 (Mail to: C/O Rev Willa Dean Lowery MD 7507 Kelly St 15208-1914) Moni McIntyre (412) 242-3209

Pittsburgh Church of the Nativity **P** (263) 33 Alice St 15205-2801 (Mail to: 33 Alice St 15205-2801) Douglas Kinsey Shawn Malarkey (412) 921-4103

Pittsburgh Emmanuel Episcopal Church **P** (204) 957 W North Ave 15233-1693 (Mail to: 957 W North Ave 15233-1693) Don Youse (412) 231-0454

Pittsburgh St James Episcopal Church **P** (18) 11524 Frankstown Rd 15235-3199 (Mail to: 11524 Frankstown Rd 15235-3199) Eric Mcintosh (412) 242-2300

Pittsburgh St Pauls Episcopal Church **P** (1443) 1066 Washington Rd 15228-2061 (Mail to: 1066 Washington Rd 15228-2024) Noah Evans Christopher Yates (412) 531-7153

Pittsburgh St Peters Episcopal Church **P** (380) 4048 Brownsville Rd 15227-3499 (Mail to: 4048 Brownsville Rd 15227-3499) William Geisler (412) 884-5225

Pittsburgh St Stephens Episcopal Church **P** (128) 600 Pitt St 15221-3136 (Mail to: 600 Pitt St 15221-3136) (412) 243-6100

Pittsburgh St Andrews Episcopal Church **P** (465) 5801 Hampton St 15206-1615 (Mail to: 5801 Hampton St 15206-1615) Bruce Robison Jean Chess (412) 661-1245

Pittsburgh Church of the Redeemer **P** (231) 5700 Forbes Ave 15217-1526 (Mail to: 5700 Forbes Ave 15217-1526) Michael Foley (412) 422-7100

✠ **Pittsburgh** Trinity Cathedral **O** (154) 325 Oliver Avenue 15222-2403 (Mail to: 325 Oliver Ave 15222-2467) Scott Quinn (412) 232-6404

Scottdale St Bartholomew Trinity Church **P** (28) 149 Walnut Ave 15683-1936 (Mail to: C/O The Rev Charles Martin 220 Columbia St 15905-3420) (724) 832-5110

Somerset St Francis in the Fields Epis Church **P** (59) 2081 Husband Rd 15501-7253 (Mail to: 2081 Husband Rd 15501-7253) Lennel Anderson (814) 445-7149

Wayne Township St Michaels Episcopal Church **P** (11) 274 Saint Michaels Rd 16249-0218 (Mail to: PO Box 544 16249-0544) Arthur Dilg (724) 783-7194

DIOCESE OF PUERTO RICO
(PROVINCE IX)
Comprises the Island of Puerto Rico
DIOCESAN CENTER Carr 848 Km 1.1, Saint Just, Trujillo Alto, PR 00976
(MAIL: PO Box 902 • Saint Just, PR 00978-0902)
TEL (787) 761-9800   FAX (787) 761-0320
E-MAIL iep@episcopalpr.org   WEB www.episcopalpr.org

Previous Bishops—
WW Jackson (Antigua) in charge 1860-1895, James H Van Buren 1902-1912, Charles B Colmore 1913-1947, Charles F Boynton 1948-1950, Albert E Swift 1951-1964, Francisco Reus Froylan 1964-1986, David Andres Alvarez Velazquez 1986-2013, Wilfrido Ramos Orench 2013-2017
(Prov Bp)

Bishop—Rt Rev Rafael L. Morales Maldonado (July 22, 2017)

Archdcns: Northeastern Cn D Muñoz; *North I* Rev F Guzmán; *North II* Rev F Rivera; *Southern* F Morales; *Southwest* Rev J Franco; *Southeastern* Rev I Linares; *Mountains* Rev C Vélez

Staff Off: Bp Exec Asst Y Torres; *Ord* Cn R Zorrilla; *Supp & Cong Dev* Cn A Dávila; *Miss, Pastoral & Evang* Cn G. Garcés; *Comm* Rev E Giraldo; *Admin* Y Salinas

Sec of Conv Rev E Desueza; *Treas* Rev N Lopez; *Chanc* Lic F Nives; *Chaplains of Cler* Rev M Santos Rev J Velázquez; *Extradiocesan Min* Rev A Rivera; *Stew & Dev Min* Cn A Dávila; *Evan & Christian Ed* Cn A Álvarez ; *Community Serv* Rev AR Mendez; *Hist* Rev I Buxeda; *Yth Min* C Olán

Dean: Very Rev J Rabell

Stand Comm—Cler: R Líz A Araque J Muñoz L Alvarado; *Lay:* A Cruz C Olán L Candelario T Vega

PARISHES, MISSIONS, AND CLERGY
Aibonito Espiritu Santo la Tea **M** Bo. Caonillas Sector La Tea Carr. 726, Km 4.2 00705 (Mail to: PO Box 127 00705-0127) (787) 313-7015
Aibonito Mision San Judas Tadeo **M** (114) Barrio Pasto Carr. 717 Km. 0.9 Sector La Playita 00705 (Mail to: PO Box 612 00705-0612) (787) 735-2299
Añasco San Jose de Arimatea **P** Carr. 109 Km. 2.4 00610 (Mail to: PO Box 239 00610-0239) (787) 645-3971

Arecibo Mision San Pablo **M** (158) Carr. 653 Avenida Universidad Barrio Villa Los Santos 00613 (Mail to: Apartado 1051 00613) (787) 878-2084
Bayamon Parroquia San Pedro § San Pablo **P** (61) IC33 Ave Lomas Verdes 00956 (Mail to: IC33 Ave. Lomas Verdes 00956) (787) 785-6472
Bayamon Mision San Bernabe **M** (18) Carr 167 Km 14.7 Bo Buena Vista 00956 (Mail to: RR 5, Box 8100 Bo. Buena Vista 00956) (787) 730-8265
Bayamon San Timoteo **P** 49-13 Calle 36 Esq North Main Urb Sierra Bayamon 00961 (Mail to: 49-13 Calle 36 Esq North Main Urb Sierra Bayamon 00961)
Cabo Rojo Nuestra Senora de Walsingham **M** Carr. 103 Residencia #3 Bario Bajura Sector Coqui 00623 (Mail to: PO Box 1271 00623) (787) 685-6766
Caguas Mision Cristo Rey **M** (64) Calle Mayagüez, Esquina Ponce Urb Villa del Carmen 00725 (Mail to: PO Box 6271 00726) Juan Garcia De Jesus (787) 746-2543
Carolina Mision El Adviento **M** (42) Urb Villa Fontana Calle Via 19 QR 16 00985 (Mail to: Condominio La Rada Ashford 1020 Apt. 23 Condado 00907) (787) 724-9217
Carolina Mision Santo Tomas Apostol **M** (50) Bo Martin Gonzalez Carr 860 KM 1.1 00987 (Mail to: PO Box 757 00986-0757) (787) 276-1283
Coamo Nueva Mision San Simon de Cirineo **M** (9) Bo. Las Flores #47 A Paseo Los Tulipanes 00769 (Mail to: Urb. Valle de Andalucia 3143 Calle Almeria 00728) (787) 387-0889
Dorado Mision Emmanuel **M** (46) Bo Maguayo, Sector Maysonet II Carr 694 00646 (Mail to: HC 46 Box 5667 00646) (787) 466-8970
Ensenada Mision Santa Cecilia **M** (62) Calle Brandon #1 00647 (Mail to: PO Box 445 00647-0445) Jacqueline Ponce Martinez (787) 821-1201
Fajardo Mision El Buen Pastor **M** (50) 399 Ave General Valero 00738-3990 (Mail to: 399 Ave. General Valero 00738) (939) 400-1278

Guayama Mision San Pedro **M** (41) Hospital Epis S Lucas Guayama Ave Pedro Albizu Campos 00785 (Mail to: Hospital Epis San Luca Guayama Ave Pedro Albizu Campos 00784) (787) 989-2369

Guaynabo Mision San Esteban El Martir **M** (43) Urb. San Ramón Calle Nogal Final 00970 (Mail to: Urb Santiago Iglesias 1308 Ave Paz Granela Pmb 160 00921-4183) (787) 367-1128

Hato Rey Parroquia la Encarnacion **P** (45) Calle Juan Davila Esq Juan BR Urb Roosevelt 00918 (Mail to: GPO Box 361067 00936-1067) (787) 459-8374

Humacao Mision San Gabriel Arcangel **M** (49) Ave. Los Sauces Lote B 00792 (Mail to: Villa Humacao A-2 00791) (787) 645-3971

Lares Mision la Santa Cruz **M** (73) Carr 135 KM 64.4 Poblado de Castañer 00631 (Mail to: PO Box 1012 00631-1012) Tomas Pixcar-Pol (787) 439-7111

Lares Mision San Bartolome **M** (40) Carr. 128 KM. 37.9 Bo. Bartolo 00631 (Mail to: PO Box 1005 00631-1005) (787) 553-0401

Lares Mision San Matias **M** (62) Carr 111 KM 2.4 Ave. Los Patriotas 00669 (Mail to: PO Box 499 00669) (787) 800-3960

Levittown Mision Santa Maria Magdalena **M** (26) Ave Boulevard Esq Paseo Conde 00949 (Mail to: PO Box 580497 00950) (787) 604-3135

Loiza Mision San Felipe § Santiago Apostol **M** (53) Carr 187 KM 5.8 Mediania Alta 00772 (Mail to: HC - 01 Buzon 5460 00772-9726) (787) 536-1700

Manati Parroquia la Resurreccion **P** (160) Bo. Cantera Carr. 2 KM 47 00674 (Mail to: 88 Bo Cantera 00674-4805) (787) 368-1625

Maricao Mision la Epifania **M** (44) Barrio Indiera Alta Sector 30 Km 128 Carr 428 00606 (Mail to: HC-01 Box 4766 00606) (787) 553-0401

Maricao Mision La Transfiguracion **M** (78) Carr. 365, Int 105 Sector Indiera Baja 00606 (Mail to: PO Box 551 00606-0551) (787) 838-2629

Mayaguez Parroquia San Andres **P** (205) 156 Calle Santiago R Palmer 00680 (Mail to: PO Box 4297 00681-4297) (787) 832-1116

Morovis Parroquia Ayudada La Ascencion **P** (112) Carr 633 Km 3.9 Bo. Barahona 00674 (Mail to: HC-02 Box 5830 00687) (787) 862-4206

Penuelas San Mateo Apostol § Evangelista **M** (65) KM 2.3 Sector La Gelpa Bo Quebrada Ceiba 00624 (Mail to: HC - 01 Buzon 8219 00624) (787) 969-0164

Ponce Mision San Lucas Evangelista **M** 909 Ave Tito Castro Torre Medica Hosp Epis S Lucas 00716 (Mail to: 2703 Paseo De La Reina 00717) (787) 996-4504

Ponce Parroquia Ayudada La Reconciliacion **P** (235) Bo. Quebrada Limon Carr. 502, Km. 4.5 00728 (Mail to: Parcelas Pastillo Canas 818 Calle Jesus T Pineiro 00728-3601) (787) 612-0381

Ponce Mision Principe de Paz **M** (31) 469 Calle 13 Urb Brisas del Caribe El Tuque 00728 (Mail to: PO Box 271 Brisas del Caribe 00728-5312) (787) 514-5994

Ponce Mision San Marcos Evangelista **M** (72) Carr 123 Km. 10 Hm. 5 Bo. Magueyes 00731 (Mail to: PO Box 8453 00732-8453) (787) 844-4681

Ponce Mision San Miguel Arcangel **M** (76) Calle Lolita Tizol #49 00731 (Mail to: HC - 01 Box 10100 00624) (787) 470-5894

Ponce Parroquia Ayudada Santa Maria Virgen **M** (196) Bo. Clausells Calle Central #15 00780 (Mail to: PO Box 10010 00732-0010) (787) 454-9161

Ponce Parroquia Santisima Trinidad **P** (389) Calle Marina Esq Abolicion 732 (Mail to: Apartado 335693 00732) (787) 841-6719

Ponce Parroquia Santo Nombre de Jesus **P** (120) Parcelas Pastillos Canas 806 Calle Jesus T Pineiro 00728-3601 (Mail to: Parcelas Pastillo Canas 806 Calle Jesus T Pineiro 00728-3601) (787) 844-3955

Rio Piedras Mision San Francisco de Asis **M** (17) Urb El Comandante 876 Calle Manuel Guerra 00924-2534 (Mail to: Urb El Comandante 876 Calle Manuel Guerra 00924) (787) 762-0835

Rio Piedras Parroquia San Jose **P** (80) Carr 842 KM 2.4 Caimito 00926 (Mail to: RR 6 Box 9615 00926) (787) 720-5834

Sabana Grande Mision Santa Ana **M** (41) Urb El Arrendado 97 Calle A 00637 (Mail to: PO Box 445 00647) (787) 821-1201

✠ **Santurce** Catedral San Juan Bautista **O** (171) Ave Ponce de León Esq. Calle Canals Pda. 20 00908 (Mail to: PO Box 9262 00908-9262) (787) 721-2395

✠ **Santurce** Cathedral St John the Baptist **O** (175) 1401 Ponce de Leon Ave Esquina Calle Canals Parada 20 00907 (Mail to: Box 9262 Santurce 00708) (787) 722-3254

Trujillo Alto Parroquia la Sagrada Familia **P** (65) Carr 848 KM 1.1 Bo Saint Just 00978 (Mail to: PO Box 360145 00936-0145) (787) 616-9174

Trujillo Alto Parroquia Ayudada Santa Hilda **P** (106) Carr 848 Bo Saint Just 00978 (Mail to: Apartado 902 00978) (787) 755-7675

Utuado Los Santos Apostoles **M** Calle Dr Cueto 81 00641 (Mail to: PO Box 2729 00613) (787) 516-9438

Vieques Mision Todos los Santos **M** (62) Calle Plinion Peterson 557 765 (Mail to: PO Box 308 00765-0308) (787) 741-2668

Yauco Mision la Anunciacion a la Virgen **M** (99) Bo Rancheras Carr 371 Km 12.2 00698 (Mail to: 1925 Calle Afrodita Urb Alta Vista 00716-2945) (787) 856-6256

Yauco Mision San Juan Apostol § Evangelist **M** (39) Calle Marcial Santana, #73 Parcelas Viejas,Barinas 00698 (Mail to: HC 03 Box 15683 00698) (787) 460-1001

Yauco Mision San Rafael Arcangel **M** (114) Calle Barbosa #21 00698 (Mail to: PO Box 1967 00698-1967) (787) 460-1001

DIOCESE OF RHODE ISLAND
(PROVINCE I)
Comprises the State of Rhode Island
DIOCESAN OFFICE 275 N Main St Providence 02903-1298
TEL (401) 274-4500   FAX (401) 331-9430
E-MAIL Diocese@episcopalri.org   WEB www.episcopalri.org

Previous Bishops—
Samuel Seabury 1790-96, Edward Bass 1798-1803, Alexander V Griswold 1811-43, John PK Henshaw 1843-52, Thomas M Clark 1854-1903, Wm M McVickar coadj 1898 Bp 1903-10, James D Perry 1911-46, Granville G Bennett suffr 1939 Bp 1946-54, John S Higgins coadj 1953 Bp 1955-72, Frederick H Belden coadj 1971 Bp 1972-79, George N Hunt 1980-94, Geralyn Wolf 1996-2012

Bishop—The Very Rev W Nicholas Knisely SOSc (1071) (Dio 17 Nov 2012)

Bps Exec Asst/Sec E Crawley; *Epis Char* B Fornal; *Sec Conv Rev* A Schell; *Treas* R Batchelor 275 N Main Providence 02903; *Cn to Ord* L Grenz; *CFO* Dennis Burton

Stand Comm—Cler: Pres G Getlein D Ames J Testin J Higginbotham; *Lay:* N McNamara D Whitman M Ballard J Gilmartin

PARISHES, MISSIONS, AND CLERGY

Barrington St Johns Episcopal Church **P** (996) 191 County Rd 02806-4501 (Mail to: 191 County Rd 02806-4501) Patrick Greene (401) 245-4065

Barrington Sts Matthew & Mark Episcopal Church **P** (182) 3 Chapel Rd 02806-1807 (Mail to: 5 Chapel Rd 02806-1861) (401) 245-3690

Block Island St Anns by the Sea **M** (69) 25 Spring St 02807-0622 (Mail to: PO Box 622 02807-0622) Eletha Buote-Greig (401) 466-2911

Bristol St Michaels Church **P** (260) 399 Hope St 02809-1803 (Mail to: 399 Hope St # 414 02809-1803) Paul Twelves (401) 253-7717

Central Falls St George & San Jorge **P** (710) 12 Clinton St 02863-2906 (Mail to: 12 Clinton St 02863-2906) (401) 722-9449

Charlestown Church Of The Holy Spirit **M** (75) 4150 Old Post Rd 02813-2551 (Mail to: PO Box 241 02813-0241) (401) 364-6368

Coventry St Francis Episcopal Church **M** (252) 132 Peckham Ln 02816-5125 (Mail to: PO Box 142 02816-0003) Sean Manchester (401) 397-7757

Cranston Church of the Ascension **P** (400) 390 Pontiac Ave 02910-3322 (Mail to: 390 Pontiac Ave 02910-3322) Michael Coburn (401) 461-5811

Cranston St Davids on the Hill Epis Ch **P** (546) 200 Meshanticut Valley Pkwy 02920-3917 (Mail to: 200 Meshanticut Valley Pkwy 02920-3997) Andrea Wyatt (401) 942-4368

Cranston Trinity Episcopal Church **P** (453) 139 Ocean Ave 02905-3628 (Mail to: 139 Ocean Ave 02905-3628) Mitchell Lindeman (401) 941-4324

Cumberland Emmanuel Episcopal Church **P** (439) § 120 Nate Whipple Hwy 02864-1410 (Mail to: 120 Nate Whipple Hwy 02864-1410) Joan Testin (401) 658-1506

E Greenwich Saint Luke's Episcopal Church **P** (1199) 99 Peirce St 02818-3814 (Mail to: 99 Peirce St 02818-3814) Noel Bailey John Higginbotham Timothy Rich Dante Tavolaro (401) 884-4116

East Providence St Marys Episcopal Church **M** (40) 81 Warren Ave 02914-5165 (Mail to: 81 Warren Ave 02914-5165) Peter Michaelson Mary Canavan Michele Matott (401) 434-7456

Greenville St Thomas Episcopal Church **P** (350) 1 Smith Avenue 02828 (Mail to: PO Box 505 02828-0505) Susan Carpenter Susan Carpenter Donald Parker (401) 949-0261

Hope Valley St Elizabeths Church **M** (115) 63 Canonchet Rd 02832-2401 (Mail to: Attn Robert Olsen PO Box 48 02832-0048) Edward Beaudreau (401) 539-7346

Jamestown St Matthews Parish **P** (418) § 87 Narragansett Ave 02835-1149 (Mail to: PO Box 317 02835-0317) Kevin Lloyd William Locke (401) 423-1762

Kingston St Augustines Church **P** (139) 35 Lower College Rd 02881-1307 (Mail to: 15 Lower College Rd 02881-1307) Elizabeth Sherman William Dobbins Janice Grinnell (401) 783-2153

Lincoln Christ Church in Lonsdale **P** (199) 1643 Lonsdale Ave 02865-1707 (Mail to: 1643 Lonsdale Ave 02865-1707) Veronica Tierney (401) 725-1920

Little Compton St Andrew's by-the-Sea **P** (248) § 182 Willow Ave 02837-1535 (Mail to: PO Box 491 02837-0491) Lynn Orville (401) 635-2452

Middletown St Columbas Chapel **P** (486) § 55 Vaucluse Ave 02842-5742 (Mail to: 55 Vaucluse Ave 02842-5742) Everett Greene Erik Larsen (401) 847-5571

Middletown Church of the Holy Cross **M** (62) 1439 West Main Rd 02842-7315 (Mail to: PO Box 4121 02842-0121) (401) 846-7076

N **Kingstown** St Pauls Wickford **P** (1960) 55 Main St 02852-5017 (Mail to: 55 Main St 02852-5017) Virginia Heistand (401) 294-4357

N **Providence** St James Episcopal Church **M** (55) § 474 Fruit Hill Ave 02911-2636 (Mail to: 474 Fruit Hill Ave 02911-2636) (401) 353-2079

N **Scituate** Trinity Church **P** (291) 251 Danielson Pike 02857-1906 (Mail to: 249 Danielson Pike 02857-1906) Johanna Marcure (401) 647-2322

Narragansett St Peters-by-the-Sea Church **P** (453) § 72 Central St 02882-3647 (Mail to: 72 Central St 02882-3647) Craig Swan (401) 783-4623

Newport Emmanuel Church **P** (297) § 42 Dearborn St 02840-3408 (Mail to: 42 Dearborn St 02840-3408) Anita Schell Anita Schell (401) 847-0675

Newport St Johns Church **P** (63) 61 Poplar St 02840-2434 (Mail to: 61 Poplar St 02840-2434) Nathan Humphrey (401) 848-2561

Newport Trinity Church **P** (402) 1 Queen Anne Sq 02840-6855 (Mail to: 1 Queen Anne Sq 02840-6855) Anne Richards (401) 846-0660

Pawtucket Church of the Good Shepherd **P** (167) 490 Broadway 02860-1340 (Mail to: 490 Broadway 02860-1340) (401) 723-0408

Pawtucket St Lukes Episcopal Church **P** (234) 670 Weeden St 02860-1649 (Mail to: 670 Weeden St 02860-1649) Dennis Bucco Joyce Thorne (401) 723-9216

Pawtucket St Pauls Church **P** (333) 50 Park Pl 02860-4010 (Mail to: 50 Park Pl 02860-4010) Greta Getlein (401) 728-4300

Portsmouth St Marys Episcopal Church **P** (995) 324 East Main Rd. 02871-2113 (Mail to: 324 E Main Rd 02871-2113) Jennifer Pedrick (401) 846-9700

Portsmouth St Pauls Episcopal Church **P** (32) 2679 E Main Rd 02871-2613 (Mail to: 2679 E Main Rd 02871-2613) (401) 683-1164

Providence All Saints Memorial Church **P** (84) 674 Westminster St 02903-4066 (Mail to: 674 Westminster St 02903-4066) Julianne Hanavan Maryalice Sullivan (401) 751-1747

Providence Cathedral of St John **P** (384) 271 Main St 02903-1237 (Mail to: 271 Main St 02903-1237) (401) 274-4500

Providence Church of the Redeemer **P** (81) 655 Hope St 02906-2652 (Mail to: 655 Hope St 02906-2652) Patrick Campbell (401) 331-0678

Providence Church of the Transfiguration **P** (929) § 1665 Broad St 02905-2727 (Mail to: 1665 Broad St 02905-2727) Michele Matott (401) 461-3142

Providence Grace Episcopal Church **P** (680) 175 Mathewson St 02903-3410 (Mail to: 300 Westminister St 02903) Jonathan Huyck (401) 331-3225

Providence St Martins Episcopal Church **P** (630) § 50 Orchard Ave 02906-5418 (Mail to: 50 Orchard Ave 02906-5418) Mark Sutherland Lawrence Bradner Linda Griggs (401) 751-2141

Providence St Peters & St Andrews Episcopal **P** (122) 25 Pomona Ave 02908-5255 (Mail to: 25 Pomona Ave 02908-5244) (401) 272-9649

Providence St Stephens Church **P** (130) § 114 George St 02906-1189 (Mail to: 114 George St Attention: George Ryan 02906-1189) John Alexander Leroy Close (401) 421-6702

Rumford Church of the Epiphany **P** (325) 1336 Pawtucket Ave 02916-1412 (Mail to: 1336 Pawtucket Ave 02916-1412) Jennifer Zogg Dorothy Brightman (401) 434-5012

Saunderstown Chapel of St John the Divine **P** (184) 10 Church Way 02874-3807 (Mail to: PO Box 541 02874-0541) (401) 295-0193

Tiverton Church of the Holy Trinity **P** (242) 1956 Main Rd 02878-4637 (Mail to: 1956 Main Rd 02878-4698) John Higginbotham (401) 624-4759

Wakefield Church of the Ascension **P** (218) 370 Main St 02879-7407 (Mail to: 370 Main St 02879-7407) Robert Travis (401) 783-2911

Warwick All Saints Church in Pontiac **P** (63) 111 Greenwich Ave 02886-1279 (Mail to: 111 Greenwich Ave 02886-1279) (401) 739-1238

Warwick St Barnabas Episcopal Church **P** (414) 3257 Post Rd 02886-7145 (Mail to: 3257 Post Rd 02886-7196) Scott Lee (401) 737-4141

Warwick St Marks Church **P** (460) 111 W Shore Rd 02889-1102 (Mail to: 111 W Shore Rd 02889-1145) Susan Wrathall (401) 737-3127

Westerly Christ Church **P** (338) 7 Elm St 2891 (Mail to: Attn: Treasurer 7 Elm St 02891-2198) Kuruvilla Chandy John Barrett Sandra Haines-Murdocco David Joslin Richard Morgan (401) 596-0197

Wood River Jct St Thomas Episcopal Church **M** (73) 322 Church St 02894-1119 (Mail to: PO Box 33 02894-0033) Bettine Besier (401) 364-3113

Woonsocket St James Church **P** (201) § 24 Hamlet Ave 02895-4408 (Mail to: 24 Hamlet Ave 02895-4427) Peter Tierney (401) 762-2222

DIOCESE OF THE RIO GRANDE
(PROVINCE VII)
Comprises New Mexico and Far West Texas
DIOCESAN OFFICE 6400 Coors Blvd NW Albuquerque NM 87120
TEL (505) 881-0636   FAX (505) 883-9048
E-MAIL office@dioceserg.org   WEB www.dioceserg.org

Previous Bishops—
John M Kendrick 1889 (NM and AZ) 1892-1911, Frederick B Howden 1914-40, James M Stoney M 1942 dio 1952-56, Charles James Kinsolving III 1956-72, Richard M Trelease Jr 1972-87 Terence Kelshaw 1989-2005, Jeffrey N Steenson 2005-07, Michael L. Vono 2010-18

Bishop—Rt Rev Michael B. Hunn (1110) (Dio 3 November 2018)

Treas J Perner; *Chanc for NM* K Aubrey; *Chanc for TX* C Pine; *Archivist* CE Davies; *Reg* M Jewell; *ECW* C Davis; *Recov Min* R Murphy; *Jubliee* Min D Martin; *Inv Bd* J Perner; *Cn to Ord* Rev Cn R Raney; *Archdcn* P Soukup; *Cn Theol* Very Rev Cn C McGowan; *Trans Off* Rev Cn R Raney; *Bosque Ctr* Rev Cn R Raney; *Bishop's Ridge: Stoney Camp and Rec Ctr* C Jewell; *Yth Min* P Mote; *Border Min* TBA; *Comm* Rev Cn R Rancy; *Hispano Min* Rev Cn J Bernal; *School for Min* Rev Cn C McGowan; *Disciplinary Board* S Pine; *COMB* J Alarid

Stand Comm—Cler: R Hurst D Tuton J Hosea; *Lay:* P Mote J Gaige *Pres* K Pittman

Regional Deans: NE Very Rev C Adams; *NW* Very Rev K Kopren; *SE* Very Rev A Brockmeier; *SW* Very Rev Dcn L Benavides

PARISHES, MISSIONS, AND CLERGY

Alamogordo St Johns Episcopal Church **P** (187) § 1114 Indiana Ave 88310-6720 (Mail to: PO Box 449 88311-0449) (575) 437-3891

Albuquerque Hope in the Desert Episcopal Church **P** (136) 8700 Alameda Blvd NE 87122-3789 (Mail to: 8700 Alameda Blvd NE 87122-3789) Daniel Tuton Ruth Morgan (505) 830-0572

Albuquerque Our Lady in the Valley Epis Ch **M** (68) 2805 Don Felipe Rd 87105-6748 (Mail to: PO Box 4126 87196-4126) (505) 873-2011

Albuquerque St Chads Episcopal Church **P** (382) 7171 Tennyson St Ne 87122-1081 (Mail to: 7171 Tennyson St NE 87122-1081) Jeremiah Griffin Janice Hosea (505) 856-9200

✠ **Albuquerque** Cathedral Church of St John **O** (1150) 318 Silver Ave Sw 87102-3328 (Mail to: PO Box 1246 87103-1246) Charles Jones Arthur Lovekin Daniel Webster (505) 247-1581

Albuquerque St Marks Episcopal Church **P** (198) 431 Richmond Pl Ne 87106-2150 (Mail to: 431 Richmond Pl NE 87106-2150) Christopher

Mclaren David Martin Patricia Soukup (505) 262-2484

Albuquerque St Marys Episcopal Church **P** (308) 1500 Chelwood Park Blvd Ne 87112-4620 (Mail to: 1500 Chelwood Park Blvd NE 87112-4620) James Hunter Ernest St Johns Samuel Stearns (505) 293-1911

Albuquerque St Michael and All Angels Church **P** (665) 601 Montano Rd Nw 87107-5226 (Mail to: 601 Montano Rd Nw 87107-5226) Mary Allison-Hatch Jean Arrossa Joseph Britton Paul Strid (505) 345-8147

Albuquerque St Thomas of Canterbury Church **P** (75) 425 University Blvd Ne 87106-4556 (Mail to: 425 University Blvd NE 87106-4556) Edward Curtis Sylvia Miller-Mutia (505) 247-2515

Alpine St James Church **M** 510 6th St # 877 79830-3510 (Mail to: 510 6th St # 877 79830-3510) (432) 837-7313

Anthony St Luke's Episcopal Church **P** (218) 7050 Mcnutt Rd 88021-9221 (Mail to: 7050 McNutt Rd 88021-9221) Daniel Cave (575) 874-3972

Artesia St Pauls Church **P** (24) 807 S 10th St 88210-2388 (Mail to: PO Box 1308 88211-1308) Maurice Geldert (575) 746-3380

Carlsbad Grace Episcopal Church **P** (169) 508 W Fox St 88220-5721 (Mail to: PO Box Pp 88221-7529) Rodney Hurst (575) 885-6200

Chama St Jeromes Church **M** (25) 331 North Pine 87520 (Mail to: PO Box 399 87575-0399) (575) 753-1503

Cloudcroft Church of the Ascension **SC** (7) 60 Chipmunk Ave 88317 (Mail to: PO Box 263 88317-0263) (575) 404-1590

Clovis Curry St James Episcopal Church **P** (112) 1117 N. Main St 88102-0249 (Mail to: PO Box 249 88102-0249) Alan Brockmeier (575) 763-4638

Corrales San Gabriel the Archangel **P** (54) 4908 Corrales Rd. Suite B 87048-9312 (Mail to: 4908 Corrales Rd. Ste B 87048-8613) Bonnie Edwards (505) 933-5931

Deming St Lukes Episcopal Church **M** (39) 419 W. Spruce Street 88030-3640 (Mail to: PO Box 1258 88031-1258) Susan Hutchins (575) 546-8088

Edgewood Church of the Holy Cross **P** (222) 367 State Road 344 87015-1090 (Mail to: PO Box 1090 87015-1090) Kristin Kopren (505) 281-7722

El Paso All Saints Episcopal Church **P** (131) 3500 Mcrae Blvd 79925-2807 (Mail to: 3500 Mcrae Blvd 79925-2897) Chester King (915) 598-0721

El Paso Holy Spirit Episcopal Church **P** (90) 10500 Kenworthy St 79924-1738 (Mail to: 10500 Kenworthy St 79924-1738) (915) 821-1362

El Paso St Albans Episcopal Church **P** (120) 1810 Elm St 79930-3110 (Mail to: 1810 Elm St 79930-3110) Linda Lilley Francis Perko (915) 565-2727

El Paso Saint Christopher's Episcopal Church **P** (91) 300 Riverside Dr 79915-4527 (Mail to: 300 Riverside Dr 79915-4527) Jose Bernal (915) 859-9329

El Paso St Francis on the Hill Episcopal Church **M** (116) § 6280 Los Robles Dr 79912-1958 (Mail to: 6280 Los Robles Dr 79912-1958) Justin Gibson (915) 581-9500

Espanola St Stephens Episcopal Church **M** (35) 703 Bond St 87532-2729 (Mail to: PO Box 1303 87532-1303) Douglas Bleyle Constance Delzell (505) 753-3010

Farmington St Johns Episcopal Church **P** (312) 312 Orchard Ave 87401-6227 (Mail to: 312 Orchard Ave 87401-6227) Guy Mackey (505) 325-5832

Fort Stockton St Stephens Episcopal Church **M** (19) 401 East Second St 76054-2941 (Mail to: PO Box 330 79735-0330) (432) 336-3180

Fort Sumner St Johns Episcopal Church **M** (21) 113 S 7th St 88119-9218 (Mail to: PO Box 392 88119-0392) (575) 355-2800

Gallup Church of the Holy Spirit **M** (73) 1334 S Country Club Dr 87301-5665 (Mail to: 1334 S Country Club Dr 87301-5665) Charleen Hill Lynn Perkins Roger Perkins (505) 863-4695

Glencoe St Anne Chapel **HC** Highway 70 88355-7367 (Mail to: 121 Mescalero Trl 88345-6090) (575) 257-2356

Hillsboro Christ Episcopal Church **M** (5) Eleanora St 88042 (Mail to: PO Box 91 88042) (575) 895-5644

Hobbs St Christophers Church **M** (30) 207 E Permian Dr 88240-4434 (Mail to: 207 E Permian Dr 88240-4434) Beverly Tasy (575) 393-3237

Las Cruces St Andrews Episcopal Church **P** (487) Canon Scott A Ruthven 518 Alameda Blvd 88005 (Mail to: PO Box 266 88004-0266) Scott Ruthven Walter LaLonde (575) 526-6333

Las Cruces St James Episcopal Church **P** (445) 102 Saint James 88005-3713 (Mail to: PO Box 2427 88047-2427) Francis Williams (575) 526-2389

Las Vegas St Pauls Peace Church **M** (53) 810 8th St 87701-4242 (Mail to: PO Box 2576 87701-2576) William Mckay Thomas Woodward (505) 425-8479

Los Alamos Trinity on the Hill Episcopal Church **P** (474) 3900 Trinity Dr 87544-1871 (Mail to: 3900 Trinity Dr 87544-1871) Christopher Adams Alicia Pope (505) 662-5107

Los Lunas St Matthews Episcopal Church **M** (166) 400 Huning Ranch Loop W 87031-4325 (Mail to: 400 Huning Ranch Loop W 87031-4325) Robert Mundy (505) 865-6548

Lovington St Marys Episcopal Church **M** (4) 417 W Avenue C 88260-4337 (Mail to: Attn Charlie Painter PO Box 883 88260-0883) (575) 396-5222

Marfa St Paul's Church **M** (35) 101 E Washington 79843-0175 (Mail to: PO Box 175 79843-0175) (830) 660-2971

Milan All Saints Episcopal Church **M** (33) 600 Hwy 605 87021 (Mail to: PO Box 157 87020-0157) Patricia Eustis (505) 285-5074

Pecos St Marks Episcopal Church **M** (8) 416 S Plum St 79772-3832 (Mail to: 416 S Plum St 79772-3832) (915) 445-3812

Portales Trinity Episcopal Church **M** (7) § 1116 W 3rd St 88130-6618 (Mail to: 1116 W 3rd St 88130-6618) Larry Mote (575) 356-6860

Raton Holy Trinity Episcopal Church **HC** (74) 240 Rio Grande Ave 87740-3945 (Mail to: PO Box 1016 87740-1016) Timothy Sexton (575) 445-9884

Rio Communities St Philips Episcopal Church **M** (98) 113 La Luna Pl 87002 (Mail to: 113 La Luna Place 87002-1096) (505) 864-7954

Rio Rancho St Francis Episcopal Church **P** (162) 2903 Cabezon Blvd Se 87124-1741 (Mail to: 2903 Cabezon Blvd SE 87124-1741) Alexander Lenzo (505) 896-1999

Roswell St Andrews Church **P** (250) § 505 Pennsylvania Ave 88201-4736 (Mail to: PO Box 1495 88202-1495) Dale Plummer (575) 622-1353

Ruidoso Epis Church in Lincoln County **P** (210) 121 Mescalero Trl 88345-6090 (Mail to: 121 Mescalero Trl 88345-6090) Judith Burgess Laurie Benavides (575) 257-2356

Santa Fe Church of the Holy Faith **P** (866) § 311 E Palace Ave 87501-2221 (Mail to: C/O Amy Jones 311 E Palace Ave 87501-2221) Robin Dodge James Gordon (505) 982-4447

Santa Fe Episcopal Church Of The Holy Family **M** (26) 10A Bisbee Ct 87508-4865 (Mail to: 10A Bisbee Ct 87508-4865) Corinne Hodges Elisabeth Noland (505) 424-0095

Santa Fe St Bedes Episcopal Church **P** (245) 1601 S Saint Francis Dr 87505-4051 (Mail to: Attn Jenny Langston 1601 S Saint Francis Dr 87505-4099) Randall Lutz Edward Fellhauer Sheila Fellhauer Mary Volland (505) 982-1133

Silver City Church of the Good Shepherd **P** (145) 615 Texas St 88061-5422 (Mail to: PO Box 2795 88062-2795) Thomas Bates Francoise Gelineau (575) 538-2015

Socorro Church of the Epiphany **M** (102) 908 Leroy Pl 87801-4744 (Mail to: PO Box 692 87801-0692) Morrill Peabody (575) 835-1818

Taos St James Episcopal Church **P** (223) 214 Camino De Santiago 87571-4306 (Mail to: 208 Camino De Santiago 87571-4306) Walter Allen Loren Olsen Pamela Tyler (575) 758-2790

Terlingua Santa Inez Episcopal Church **M** Terlingua Ghost Town & Ivey Rd 79852 (Mail to: PO Box 88 79830) (432) 371-4399

Truth Consq St Pauls Episcopal Church **M** (47) 407 Cedar St 87901-2335 (Mail to: PO Box 949 87901-0949) (575) 894-9596

Tucumcari St Michaels Episcopal Church **M** (41) 2602 S 2nd St 88401-4221 (Mail to: 2602 S 2nd St 88401-4221) Mark Lake (575) 461-4222

DIOCESE OF ROCHESTER
(PROVINCE II)
Comprises 8 western New York counties
DIOCESAN OFFICE 3825 E Henrietta Rd, Ste 100, Henrietta, NY 14467
TEL (585) 473-2977
E-MAIL communications@episcopaldioceseofrochester.org
WEB www.episcopalrochester.org

Previous Bishops—
David L Ferris 1931-38, Bartel H Reinheimer coadj 1936 Bp 1938-49, Dudley S Stark 1950-62, Geo W Barrett 1963-69, Robert R Spears Jr 1970-84, William G Burrill 1984-99, Jack M McKelvey 1999-2008

Bishop—Rt Rev Prince Grenville Singh (1029) (Dio 31 May 2008)

Cn to Ord J Ross; *Cn for Stew & Fin CFO* T Rubiano; *Operations & Benefits* K Estey; *Exec to the Bishop* C McConnell; *Audit* C Shoemaker; *Comm* S Richards; *Accounting* K Woodward; *Sec to Conv* Rev A Stridiron; *Treas* T Butwid; *Asst Treas* B Owen; *Chanc* PR Fileri; *Asst Chanc* CT Wright, FP Greene; *Reg* C McConnell

Stand Comm— *Cler:* R Hamlin L Burkardt C Miller R Picken; *Lay:* Pres S Peters J DaBall-Lavoie C Mok S Woodhouse

PARISHES, MISSIONS, AND CLERGY

Addison Church of the Redeemer **P** (60) 1 Wombaugh Sq 14801-1032 (Mail to: 1 Wombaugh Sq 14801-1032) (607) 359-2300

Angelica St Pauls Church **P** (21) 1 Park Cir 14709 (Mail to: PO Box 472 14709) (585) 466-3546

Avon Zion Church **P** (110) 10 Park Pl 14414-1055 (Mail to: 10 Park Pl 14414-1055) Virginia Mazzarella (585) 226-3722

Bath St Thomas Church **P** (199) 122 Liberty St 14810-1509 (Mail to: 122 Liberty St 14810-1509) (607) 776-4503

Bloomfield St Peters Episcopal Church **P** (45) 44 Main St 14469-9231 (Mail to: PO Box 67 14469-0067) Richard Krapf C Denise Yarbrough (585) 657-6715

Branchport St Lukes Church **P** (63) § 121 West Lake Rd 14418-9754 (Mail to: 187 W Lake Rd 14418-9768) Philip Kasey Philip Kasey (315) 595-6162

Brockport Saint Luke's Church **P** (191) 14 State St 14420-1922 (Mail to: 14 State St 14420-1922) (585) 637-6650

Caledonia St Andrews Episcopal Church **M** (53) 175 North St 14423-1036 (Mail to: C/O Laurie Mcmeremy 175 North St 14423-1036) (585) 538-2112

Canandaigua St Johns Church **P** (305) 183 Main St 14424-1226 (Mail to: 183 Main St 14424-1226) David Hefling (585) 394-4818

Canaseraga Trinity Church **P** (5) 20 N. Church St 14822 (Mail to: PO Box 202 14822-0202) Bruce Torrey (607) 545-6211

Clifton Springs Saint John's Church **P** (68) 32 E Main St 14432-1233 (Mail to: PO Box 622 14432-0622) Andrew VanBuren (315) 462-6611

Corning Christ Episcopal Church **P** (219) 33 East First St. 14830-2620 (Mail to: 33 E 1st St 14830-2699) Troy Preston (607) 937-5449

Cuba Christ Church **P** (13) 19 South St 14727-1411 (Mail to: PO Box 112 14727-0112) (585) 268-7622

Dansville St Peters Memorial **P** (22) 25 Clara Barton Street 14437 (Mail to: PO Box 127 14437-0127) John Thompson (585) 335-5434

Fairport Saint Luke's Church **P** (206) 77 Country Corner Ln 14450-3034 (Mail to: PO BOX 146 14450-0146) Kenneth Pepin (585) 223-2796

Gates Ephphatha Mission of the Deaf **M** 3285 Buffalo Rd 14624-2413 (Mail to: Mr Edwin Bevinsma 81 Linden Ave Apt 613 14610) Nancy Stevens (585) 247-4190

Gates The Church of the Epiphany **P** (225) 3285 Buffalo Rd 14624-2413 (Mail to: 3285 Buffalo Rd 14624-2483) Jimmie Sue Deppe (585) 247-4190

Geneseo Saint Michael's Episcopal Church **P** (228) 23 Main St 14454-1213 (Mail to: 23 Main St 14454-1213) William Daniel Terrell Price (585) 243-1220

Geneva St Johns Chapel **M** South Main St 14456 (Mail to: 300 Pulteney St 14456-3304) Lesley Adams (315) 781-3671

Geneva St Peters Memorial **P** (370) 149 Genesee St 14456 (Mail to: PO Box 147 14456-0147) James Adams (315) 789-4910

Geneva Trinity Church **P** (54) 78 Castle Street 14456-3107 (Mail to: PO BOX 287 14456-3196) (315) 325-4216

Hammondsport St James Church **P** (119) 38 Lake St 14840 (Mail to: PO Box 249 14840-0249) Lynne Sharp (607) 569-2647

Henrietta St Peter's **P** (154) 3825 E Henrietta Rd 14467-9147 (Mail to: 3825 E Henrietta Rd 14467-9147) Catherine Tatem (585) 334-1110

Hilton St Georges Church **P** (92) 635 Wilder Rd 14468-9701 (Mail to: 635 Wilder Rd 14468-9701) (585) 392-4099

Honeoye Falls St Johns Episcopal Church **P** (80) 11 Episcopal Ave 14472-1001 (Mail to: 11 Episcopal Ave 14472-1001) Virginia Tyler Smith (585) 624-4074

Hornell Christ Episcopal Church **P** (92) Main And Center St 14843 (Mail to: PO Box 336 14843-0336) John Andrews (607) 324-3620

Keuka Park Garrett Chapel **SC** C/O John Barden 213 West Main St 14478 (Mail to: Skyline Dr 14478) (315) 536-3955

Lyons Grace Episcopal Church **P** (44) 7 Phelps St 14489-1420 (Mail to: 9 Phelps St 14489-1509) Richard Witt (315) 946-9687

Newark St Marks Church **P** (88) 400 S Main St 14513-1723 (Mail to: 400 S Main St Ste 3 14513-1795) Gretchen Ratterree (315) 331-3610

Odessa Saint John's Church **HC** (33) 4938 County Route 14 14869-9729 (Mail to: Interchurch Office 112 Sixth Street 14891) (607) 535-2321

Palmyra Zion Episcopal Church **P** (134) 120 E Main St 14522-1018 (Mail to: 120 E Main St 14522-1018) Susan Kohlmeier (315) 597-9236

Penfield Church of the Incarnation **P** (233) 1957 Five Mile Line Rd 14526-1000 (Mail to: 1957 Five Mile Line Rd 14526-1000) Christopher Streeter Miriam Owens (585) 586-7860

Penn Yan St Marks Episcopal Church **P** (105) 179 Main St 14527-1202 (Mail to: PO Box 424 14527-0424) Dan Burner (315) 536-3955

Pittsford Christ Church **P** (1051) 36 S Main St 14534-1939 (Mail to: 36 S Main St 14534-1999) Joshua Walters Ronald Young (585) 586-1226

Rochester Christ Church **P** (253) 141 East Ave 14604-2521 (Mail to: 141 East Ave 14604-2597) Ruth Ferguson (585) 454-3878

Rochester Church of the Ascension **P** (137) 2 Riverside St 14613-1222 (Mail to: 2 Riverside St 14613-1222) Dahn Gandell (585) 458-5423

Rochester St Luke & St Simon Cyrene Episcopal **P** (164) 17 Fitzhugh St S 14614-1401 (Mail to: 17 Fitzhugh St S Attn: Keith Patterson 146141401) Keith Patterson (585) 546-7730

Rochester St Marks & St Johns Church **P** (88) 1245 Culver Rd 14609-5340 (Mail to: 1245 Culver Rd 14609-5340) Cynthia Rasmussen Julie Cicora Michael Finn (585) 654-9229

Rochester St Pauls Church **P** (745) § 41 Westminster Rd 14607-2223 (Mail to: 25 Westminster Rd 14607-2223) Robert Picken Jay Burkardt (585) 271-2240

Rochester St Stephens Episcopal Church **P** (55) 350 Chili Ave 14611-2555 (Mail to: 350 Chili Ave 14611-2555) Gloria Fish (585) 328-0856

Rochester St Thomas Episcopal Church **P** (705) 2000 Highland Ave 14618-1125 (Mail to: 2000 Highland Ave 14618-1125) Leslie Burkardt Christa Moore-Levesque (585) 442-3544

Rochester South Wedge Mission **M** 125 Caroline St 14620-2127 (Mail to: 125 Caroline St 14620-2127) (585) 746-0348

Rochester The Chapel of the Good Shepherd **Chapel** 505 Mount Hope Ave 14620-2251 (Mail to: 505 Mount Hope Ave 14620-2251) (585) 546-8400

Rochester Trinity Episcopal Church **P** (239) § 3450 Ridge Rd W 14626 (Mail to: Attn: Aministrative Asst 3450 W Ridge Rd 14626-3432) Deborah Duguid-May (585) 225-7848

Savona Church of the Good Shepherd **HC** (55) § 31 Church St 14879-9658 (Mail to: PO Box 466 14879-9658) (607) 569-2647

Scottsville Grace Episcopal Church **P** (105) 9 Browns Ave 14546-1345 (Mail to: PO Box 158 14546-0158) Kenneth Pepin (585) 889-2028

Sodus St Johns Episcopal Church **P** (56) 54 West Main St 14551-1134 (Mail to: 54 W Main St 14551-1134) Michael Laver (315) 483-4235

Sodus Point Christ Church **SC** 8350 Bay St 14555-9533 (Mail to: 935 East Ave 14607-2216) (315) 331-8251

Watkins Glen Saint James' Church **HC** (78) 597 S Decatur St 14891-1610 (Mail to: 112 6th St 14891-1359) Abidhananthar John (607) 535-2321

Webster Church of the Good Shepherd **P** (458) 1130 Webster Rd 14580-9320 (Mail to: 1130 Webster Rd 14580-9321) Lance Robbins (585) 872-2281

Webster St Andrews by the Lake **SC** 1206 Lake Rd 14580-9708 (Mail to: 935 East Ave 14607-2216) (716) 872-2281

Wellsville St John Episcopal Church **P** (34) 12 E Genesee St 14895-1032 (Mail to: 12 E Genesee St 14895-1032) Carol Stewart (585) 593-5592

DIOCESE OF SAN DIEGO
(PROVINCE VIII)
Comprises San Diego, Imperial and part of Riverside Counties, CA and Yuma County, AZ
DIOCESAN OFFICE 2083 Sunset Cliffs Blvd, San Diego CA 92107
TEL (619) 291-5947 FAX (619) 481-3091
E-MAIL info@edsd.org WEB www.edsd.org

Previous Bishops—
Robert M Wolterstorff 1974-82, C Brinkley Morton 1982-92, Gethin B Hughes 1992-2005, James R. Mathes 2005-17

Ecclesiastical Authority—The Rev Gwynn Lynch, President, Standing Committee (Nov 2018)

Assisting Bishop—Rt Rev Katharine Jefferts Schori

Assisting Bishop—Rt Rev John B Chane

Cn to Ord N Holland; *Ecum Off* E Ellsworth; *Sec* D Peralta; *Treas* K Smith; *Reg* A Terry; *Hist* J Will; *Chanc* D Bagley

Standing Comm—Cler: Pres M McKone-Sweet G Lynch K Branstetter B Sol; *Lay:* J Stiven J Gamboa C Levien S Turnbull

PARISHES, MISSIONS, AND CLERGY

Alpine Church of Christ the King **P** (66) 1460 Midway Dr 91901-3714 (Mail to: 1460 Midway Dr 91901-3714) Jason Samuel (619) 445-3419

Bonita Epis Church of the Good Shepherd **P** (109) 3990 Bonita Rd 91902-1260 (Mail to: 3990 Bonita Rd 91902-1260) George Calvert (619) 479-8391

Borrego Spgs St Barnabas Episcopal Church **P** (121) 2680 Country Club Rd 92004 (Mail to: PO Box 691 92004-0691) Laura Brecht (760) 767-4038

Brawley All Saints Episcopal Church **M** (20) 305 H St 92227-2517 (Mail to: PO Box 1811 92227-1308) (760) 344-8806

Carlsbad Holy Cross Episcopal Church **M** (66) 2510 Gateway Road 92009-1727 (Mail to: 2510 Gateway Rd Ste 101 92009-1727) Roger Haenke (760) 930-1270

Carlsbad Church of St Michaels-by-the-Sea **P** (877) 2775 Carlsbad Blvd 92008-2210 (Mail to: 2775 Carlsbad Blvd 92008-2210) Doran Stambaugh Doran Stambaugh (760) 729-8901

Chula Vista St Johns Epis Ch **P** (477) § 760 1st Ave 91910-6012 (Mail to: 760 1st Ave 91910-6012) (619) 422-4141

Coronado Christ Episcopal Church **P** (581) § 1114 Ninth St 92118 (Mail to: 1114 9th St 92118-2602) Anne Bridgers (619) 435-4561

Del Mar St Peters Episcopal Church **P** (891) 334 14th St 92014-2519 (Mail to: PO Box 336 92014-0336) Paige Blair-Hubert Martha Anderson (858) 755-1616

El Cajon St Albans Episcopal Church **P** (203) 490 Farragut Cir 92020-5203 (Mail to: 490 Farragut Cir 92020-5203) David Madsen (619) 444-8212

El Centro Sts Peter & Paul Episcopal Church **P** (60) 500 S 5th St 92243-3333 (Mail to: PO Box 3446 92244-3446) Paul Gambling (760) 352-6531

Encinitas St Andrew-the-Apostle Church **P** (781) 890 Balour Dr 92024-3943 (Mail to: 890 Balour Dr 92024-3943) Brenda Sol Richard Hogue (760) 753-3017

Escondido Trinity Episcopal Church **P** (300) 845 Chestnut St 92025-5257 (Mail to: 845 Chestnut St 92025-5257) Margaret Decker Robert Lucent Carolyn Richardson (760) 743-1629

Fallbrook St Johns Episcopal Church **P** (133) § 434 Iowa St 92028-2109 (Mail to: 434 Iowa St 92028-2109) Leland Jones (760) 728-2908

Hemet The Church of the Good Shepherd **P** (214) § 308 E Acacia Ave 92543-4228 (Mail to: 308 E Acacia Ave 92543-4228) (951) 929-1152

Idyllwild St Hugh of Lincoln Episcopal Church **M** (37) § 25525 Tahquitz Rd 92549 (Mail to: PO Box 596 92549-0506) (951) 659-4471

Indio St Johns Episcopal Church **P** (133) 45319 Deglet Noor St 92201-4315 (Mail to: 45319 Deglet Noor St 92201-4315) Brian Johnson (760) 347-3265

La Jolla St James by-the-Sea Episcopal Church **P** (1174) 743 Prospect St 92037-4229 (Mail to: 743 Prospect St 92037-4290) Darlyn Dinovo Mark Hargreaves Steven Strane (858) 459-3421

La Mesa Saint Andrew's Church **P** (236) 4816 Glen St 91941-5498 (Mail to: 4816 Glen St 91941-5498) Robert Blessing Harold Reed (619) 460-7272

Lake Elsinore St Andrews by the Lake Epis Church **M** (51) 111 S. Kellogg St 92530-3538 (Mail to: 111 S. Kellogg Street 92530) W Clarke Prescott Kenneth Simon (951) 674-4087

Lemon Grove Church of St Philip the Apostle **P** (416) § 2660 Hardy Dr 91945-2936 (Mail to: 2660 Hardy Dr 91945-2936) Carlos Garcia-Tuiran (619) 466-8055

Menifee St Stephen's Episcopal Church **M** (22) § 26704 Murrieta Rd 92585-9545 (Mail to: 26704 Murrieta Road 92585) Kenneth Simon (951) 679-3010

National City St Matthews Episcopal Church **P** (242) § 521 E 8th St 91950-2343 (Mail to: 521 E 8th St 91950-2398) Maria Borges (619) 474-8916

Palm Desert St Margarets Episcopal Church **P** (807) § 47-535 Highway 74 92260 (Mail to: 47-

535 Highway 74 92260-5946) Lane Hensley Kathleen Dale Joseph Lund Deborah Seles Clark Trafton Richard Wilmington (760) 346-2697

Palm Springs St Paul in the Desert **P** (533) § 125 W El Alameda 92262-5662 (Mail to: 125 W El Alameda 92262-5662) Marvin Green (760) 320-7488

Pauma Valley St Francis Episcopal Church **P** (128) § 16608 State Highway 76 92061 (Mail to: PO Box 1220 92061-1220) (760) 742-1738

Poway St Bartholomews Episcopal Church **P** (1739) § 16275 Pomerado Rd 92064-1826 (Mail to: 16275 Pomerado Rd 92064-1826) Mark McKone-Sweet Mary Coulson Allisyn Thomas (858) 487-2159

Ramona St Marys in the Valley Church **M** (159) § 1010 12th St 92065-2848 (Mail to: PO Box 491 92065-0491) Janet Wheelock (760) 789-7948

San Diego All Saints Church **P** (182) § 625 Pennsylvania Ave 92103-4321 (Mail to: 625 Pennsylvania Ave 92103-4393) Robert Eaton Victor Krulak Anthony Noble (619) 298-7729

San Diego All Souls' Episcopal Church **P** (386) 1475 Catalina Blvd 92107-3763 (Mail to: Attn: Finance Office 1475 Catalina Blvd 92107-3798) Joseph Dirbas James Carroll Terry Dirbas (619) 223-6394

✢ **San Diego** Cathedral Church of St Paul **O** (1156) 2728 6th Ave 92103-6301 (Mail to: 2728 6th Ave 92103-6301) Penelope Bridges Susan Astarita Carlos Exposito Irrarragorri Jeffrey Martinhauk Brooks Mason Jacqueline Pippin (619) 298-7261

San Diego Good Samaritan Episcopal Church **P** (282) § 4321 Eastgate Mall 92121-2102 (Mail to: 4321 Eastgate Mall 92121-2102) Janine Schenone (858) 458-1501

San Diego St Andrews by the Sea Church **P** (147) § 1050 Thomas Ave 92109-4161 (Mail to: 1050 Thomas Ave 92109-4194) Janet Wheelock (858) 273-3022

San Diego St Anthony of-the-Desert Mission **M** (96) § 2083 Sunset Cliffs Blvd 92107 (Mail to: PO Box 40 92240-0040) (760) 329-2755

San Diego St Davids Episcopal Church **P** (307) § 5050 Milton St 92110-1250 (Mail to: 5050 Milton St 92110-1299) Michael Tinnon (619) 276-4567

San Diego St Dunstans Episcopal Church **P** (568) 6556 Park Ridge Blvd 92120-3236 (Mail to: 6556 Park Ridge Blvd 92120-3297) Kent Branstetter Henry Mann (619) 460-6442

San Diego St Lukes Episcopal Church **P** (215) 3725 30th St 92104-3607 (Mail to: 3725 30th St 92104-3697) Susan Astarita Colin Mathewson Laurel Mathewson (619) 298-2130

San Diego St Marks Episcopal Church **P** (167) § 4227 Fairmount Ave 92105-1243 (Mail to: PO Box 5788 92165-5788) Richard Lee (619) 283-6242

San Diego St Timothy's Episcopal Church **P** (120) § 10125 Azuaga St 92129-4000 (Mail to: 10125 Azuaga St 92129-4000) Wilfredo Crespo Judith Allison Edward Busch (858) 538-1267

San Marcos Grace Episcopal Church **M** (182) § 1020 Rose Ranch Rd 92069-1161 (Mail to: 1020 Rose Ranch Rd 92069-1161) William Lieber Gwynn Lynch (760) 744-7667

Santee St Columbas Episcopal Church **M** (35) § 9720 Cuyamaca St 92071-2626 (Mail to: 9720 Cuyamaca St 92071-2626) (619) 857-6749

Temecula Saint Thomas of Canterbury Epis Church **M** (488) § 44651 Avenida De Missiones 92592-3098 (Mail to: 44651 Avenida De Missiones 92592-3098) Timothy True (951) 302-4566

Vista All Saints Episcopal Church **P** (131) § 651 Eucalyptus Ave 92084-6241 (Mail to: 651 Eucalyptus Ave 92084-6298) Virginia Benson (760) 726-4280

Yuma St Pauls Episcopal Church **P** (350) 1550 S 14th Ave 85364-4414 (Mail to: 1550 S 14th Ave 85364-4498) Paul Gambling (928) 782-5155

DIOCESE OF SAN JOAQUIN
(PROVINCE VIII)
Comprises the central third of California
DIOCESAN OFFICE 1528 Oakdale Rd Modesto CA 95355
TEL (209) 576-0104   FAX (209) 576-0114
E-MAIL emeyer@diosanjoaquin.org   WEB www.diosanjoaquin.org

Previous Bishops—
Louis C Sanford 1911-42, Sumner FD Walters 1944-68, Victor M Rivera 1968-88, John-David Schofield 1989-2008, Jerry A Lamb 2008-11, Chester L Talton (2011-14)

Bishop—Rt Rev. David C. Rice (2014)

Cn to Ord Rev Dr AR Carmichael; *Chanc* MO Glass 1101 Fifth Avenue Suite 100 San Rafael CA 94901; *Treas* M Austin, C Peck; *Dio Admin* E Meyer; *Comm* E Ray

Stand Comm—Cler: Pres S Ward N Key R Woods C Woodall *Lay: Sec* N Voorhees N Fitzgerald J Peck

Dio Coun—Cler: VPres N Lorenzetti G Bernthal *Lay: Sec* B Inderbitzen-G Glenn J March B Greer G Sitts S Gilmer

Comm on Min: Chair Rev K Galicia N Silva Rev G Bernthal N Fitzgerald W Bentley Rev N Lorenzetti Rev V Walter W Patterson M Ashburn T Poindexter

Deaneries—Southern: Pres Jan Dunlap *VPres* TBD; *Central: Pres* Rev G Bernthal *V Pres* T Poindexter *Northern: Pres* Rev K Galicia *VPres* Carolyn List

PARISHES, MISSIONS, AND CLERGY

Avery St Clare of Assisi **M** (41) 4351 Highway 4 95224 (Mail to: PO Box 278 95224-0278) Michael Backlund (209) 795-5970

Bakersfield St Paul's Episcopal Church **P** (209) 2216 17th St 93301-3605 (Mail to: 2216 17th St 93301-3605) Vernon Hill Luis Rodriguez (661) 869-1630

Hanford Church of the Saviour Parish **P** (106) 519 Douty St 93230-3910 (Mail to: 519 Douty St 93230-3910) (559) 584-7706

Kernville St Sherrian Episcopal Church **M** (18) Meets at 251 Big Blue Road 93238 (Mail to: 50 Tobias St 93238) Robert Woods (760) 376-2455

Lodi Church of St John The Baptist **P** (299) 1055 S Lower Sacramento Rd 95242 (Mail to: 1055 S Lower Sacramento Rd 95242-9339) Elaine Breckenridge (209) 369-3381

Madera Holy Trinity Episcopal Church **M** (21) 500 Sunset Ave 93637-3012 (Mail to: PO Box 517 93639-0517) (559) 975-9037

Modesto St Pauls Episcopal Church **P** (170) § 1528 Oakdale Rd 95355-3306 (Mail to: Attn Allison 1528 Oakdale Rd 95355-3306)

Dominick Lorenzetti (209) 522-3267

Oakhurst St Raphael Episcopal Church **M** (17) PO Box 13 93644 (Mail to: PO Box 13 93644-0013) (559) 683-4023

Ridgecrest St Michaels Episcopal Church **P** (57) 200 Drummond Ave 93555-3119 (Mail to: 200 Drummond Ave 93555-3119) (760) 446-5816

San Andreas St Matthew's Church **P** (62) 414 Oak Street 95249-9612 (Mail to: PO Box 520 95249-0520) (209) 754-3878

Sonora St James Episcopal Church **P** (33) 42 Snell St 95370-5600 (Mail to: 42 Snell St 95370-5600) (209) 532-1580

Stockton Church of St Anne **P** (226) 1020 W Lincoln Rd 95207-2516 (Mail to: 1020 W Lincoln Rd 95207-2516) Lynette Morlan Justo Andres Lynette Morlan Carolyn Woodall (209) 473-2313

Taft St Andrews Mission **M** (32) 703 5th St 93268-2407 (Mail to: 703 5th St 93268-2407) Heather Mueller (661) 765-2378

Tulare St Johns Episcopal Church **P** (70) § 1701 E Prosperity Ave 93274-2345 (Mail to: 1701 E Prosperity Ave 93274-2345) (559) 631-3663

Turlock St Francis Episcopal Church **M** (54) 915 East Main Street 95380 (Mail to: 915 E Main St 95380-3404) Kathryn Galicia Kathryn Galicia Donald Rees (209) 324-1677

Visalia St Pauls Epis Fellowship **P** (45) 1039 S Chinowth St 93277-1609 (Mail to: PO Box 7446 93290-7446) Suzanne Ward (559) 627-8265

STATE OF SOUTH CAROLINA

Diocese of Upper South Carolina and The Episcopal Church in South Carolina

---

THE EPISCOPAL CHURCH IN SOUTH CAROLINA

(PROVINCE IV)

Comprising churches in Southern and Eastern South Carolina
DIOCESAN OFFICE: 98 Wentworth St Charleston SC 29401
(MAIL: Box 20485 Charleston SC 29413)
TEL: (843) 259-2016   E-MAIL: info@episcopalchurchsc.org
WEB: www.episcopalchurchsc.org

Previous Bishops—
Charles vonRosenberg (provisional) 2013-16

Provisional Bishop: The Right Reverend Gladstone B Adams (972) (Prov Bp 10 Sep 2016)

Archdcn C Walpole; *Chancellor* T S Tisdale; *Treas* J Taylor; *Exec Asst to Bp* L Kinard; *Comm* H Behre; *Min Dev* A McKellar, *Miss for Returning Congregations* W Coyne

Stand Comm: Cler—W Keith J Richardson G Moyser F Thompson P Fahrner C Lee; *Lay*— C Grish R

Lovelace E Guess R Stall D Wilson T Richardson

Diocesan Council—Cler: C Huff M McCormick R Donehue W Merchant A Shoemaker R Tripp; *Lay:* P Neumann W Rutter R Sabalis C Wingard S Mayse A Bush

Trustees—Lay: B Beak B Mann D Billings *Cler:* D McPhail M Brinkmann P Linder

Comm on Ministry—Cler: J McGraw W Keith R Lindsey C Walpole D Sanderson; *Lay:* C Hayes A Webb JH Lewis MA Foy

PARISHES, MISSIONS, AND CLERGY

Allendale Church of Holy Communion **M** (24) 401 Main St 29810-3717 (Mail to: PO Box 202 29810-0202) William Rose (803) 812-9912

Charleston Calvary Episcopal Church **P** (268) 106 Line St 29403-5305 (Mail to: 106 Line St 29403-5305) Matthew McCormick (843) 723-3878

Charleston Church of the Holy Communion **P** (499) 218 Ashley Ave 29403-5245 (Mail to: 218 Ashley Ave 29403-5245) Jeffrey Richardson Michael Smith (843) 722-2024

Charleston Grace Church Cathedral **P** (1979) § 98 Wentworth St 29401-1424 (Mail to: 98 Wentworth St 29401-1473) Jonathan Wright Lisa Walpole Alberry Cannon Caleb Lee Charles Minifie Bryce Wandrey (843) 723-4575

Charleston St Marks Episcopal Church **P** (100) 18 Thomas St 29403-6024 (Mail to: 16 Thomas St 29403-6024) (843) 722-0267

Charleston St. Stephen's Episcopal Church **P** (499) 67 Anson St 29401-1529 (Mail to: 67 Anson St 29401-1529) Adam Shoemaker Gregory Smith Gregory Smith (843) 723-8818

Charleston St Francis Episcopal Church **M** (8) Stuhr's Chapel 3360 Glenn McConnell Pkwy 29414-5759 (Mail to: 2245 C Ashley Crossing Dr PMB 174 29414-7034) James Shaffer Gregory Smith (843) 442-2692

Cheraw St Davids Church **P** (115) 420 Market St 29520-2637 (Mail to: PO Box 926 29520-0926) (843) 537-3832

Conway St Anne's Episcopal Church **P** (110) Lackey Chapel 105 University Dr 29526-8832 (Mail to: PO Box 752 29528-0752) Robertson Donehue (843) 246-1247

Denmark Christ Episcopal Church **M** (43) 5266 Carolina Hwy 29042-1684 (Mail to: PO Box 237 29042-0237) (803) 793-4837

Denmark St Philip Episcopal Church **CC** (18) 386 Porter Dr 29042 (Mail to: PO Box 678 290420678) James Yarsiah (803) 780-1264

Edisto Island Episcopal Church on Edisto **P** (208) 1650 Hwy 174 29438 (Mail to: PO Box 239 29438-0239) Fred Thompson (843) 869-3568

Estill Church of the Heavenly Rest **M** (7) 152 Corley Rd 29918-0152 (Mail to: PO Box 1190 29918-1190) William Rose (843) 524-1644

Florence St Catherine's Episcopal Church **M** (49) 3123 W Palmetto St 29501-5937 (Mail to: c/o Earl Phillips 4205 Byrnes Blvd 29506-8335) Philip Emanuel (843) 259-2016

Hampton All Saints Episcopal Church **M** (42) § 511 Jackson Ave E 29924-3605 (Mail to: Attn Mr Wes Shore 511 Jackson Ave E 29924-3605) (803) 943-2300

Hilton Head Island All Saints Episcopal Church **P** (411) § 3001 Meeting St 29926-1673 (Mail to: 3001 Meeting St 29926-1673) Mark Brinkmann (843) 681-8333

Kingstree St Albans Church **M** (37) 305 Hampton Ave 29556-3417 (Mail to: PO Box 866 29556-0866) (843) 355-7575

Mc Clellanville St James Santee **M** (110) 144 Oak St 29458-9746 (Mail to: PO Box 123 29458-0123) Jill Williams (843) 887-4386

Mount Pleasant The East Cooper Episcopal Church **M** (50) 1494 Mathis Ferry Road 29464-9727 (Mail to: P.O Box 511 29464) William Coyne (843) 614-0679

Myrtle Beach Episcopal Church of the Messiah **M** 6200 North Kings Highway St. Philip Lutheran Church 29572-3576 (Mail to: PO Box 70367 29572-0025) Randolph Ferebee (843) 582-2866

N Charleston St Thomas Episcopal Church **P** (249) 1150 E Montague Ave 29405-4719 (Mail to: 1150 E Montague Ave 29405-4719) James Taylor Charles Jett (843) 747-0479

N Myrtle Bch St Stephens Episcopal Church **P** (203) 801 11th Ave 29582-2644 (Mail to: 801 11th Ave 29582-2644) Wilmot Merchant (843) 249-1169

Orangeburg Church of the Redeemer **P** (292) 1606 Russell St 29115-6065 (Mail to: PO Box 9 29116-0009) (803) 534-3794

Pawleys Island Holy Cross Faith Mem Epis Ch **P** (547) 88 Baskervill Dr 29585-6191 (Mail to: PO Box 990 29585-0990) William Keith Donald Fishburne Jason Roberson (843) 237-3459

Pinewood St Augustines Episcopal Church **M** (46) 5450 Milford Plantation Rd 29125 (Mail to: Attn Mr John Spann PO Box 247 29168-0247) (803) 259-2016

Port Royal St Mark's Episcopal Church **M** 1110 Paris Ave Ste A 29935-2322 (Mail to: PO Box 761 29935-0761) Roy Tripp (843) 379-1020

Ridgeland The Episcopal Church in Okatie **M** Ste 1 & 2 231 Hazzard Creek Vlg 29936-8285 (Mail to: 4467 Spring Is 29909-4756) (843) 259-2016

Saint Stephen St Stephens Episcopal Church **M** (45) 245 Mendel St 29479 (Mail to: PO Box 517 29479-0517) (843) 567-3419

Summerville Episcopal Church of the Good Shepherd **M** (85) 119b W Luke Ave 29483-6423 (Mail to: 119b W Luke Ave 29483-6423) Marshall Sanderson (843) 225-7590

Summerville St Georges Episcopal Church **P** (390) 9110 Dorchester Rd 29485-8647 (Mail to: 9110 Dorchester Rd 29485-8647) Christopher Huff Hugh Wallace (843) 873-0772

Summerville Church of the Epiphany **M** (95) 212 Central Ave 29483-6004 (Mail to: 807 W 2nd North St 29483-3829) Robert Switz (843) 851-3467

Sumter Church of the Good Shepherd **M** (39) 401 Dingle St 29150-5155 (Mail to: PO Box 1701 29151-1701) (803) 773-8341

DIOCESE OF SOUTH DAKOTA
(PROVINCE VI)
Comprises South Dakota, 2 churches in Nebraska, and 1 church in Minnesota
DIOCESAN OFFICE 408 N Jefferson Ave Pierre SD 57501-2626
TEL (605) 494-2020   FAX (605) 494-2025
E-MAIL office@episcopalchurchsd.org   WEB www.episcopalchurchsd.org

Previous Bishops—
Wm H Hare 1873-1909, Fred F
Johnson asst 1905 Bp 1910-11, Geo
Biller Jr 1912-15, Hugh L Burleson
1916-31, Wm P Remington suffr
1918-22, W Blair Roberts suffr
1922 Bp 1931-53, Conrad H Gesner
coadj 1945-54 Bp 1954-69, Lyman C
Ogilby coadj 1967-70, Harold S Jones suffr 1970-75,
Walter H Jones 1970-83, Craig B Anderson 1984-92,
Creighton L Robertson Bp 1994-2009

Bishop—Rt Rev John T Tarrant (1038) (Dio 31
Oct 09)

Fin Off K Parker; *Admin Asst* M Fratzke; *Archdcn* P
Sneve; *Treas* E Walker; *Chan* S Sanford PO Box 2498
Sioux Falls SD 57105; *Miss for Camping & Retreats* P
Corbin; *Miss for Ldrshp Dev & Trad Min* C Corbin;
Miss for Property P LeBeau; *Miss of Supp* T Fountain

Stand Comm—Cler Pres D Hussey *Sec* L Stanley A
Henninger Hal Weidman; *Lay:* P LeBeau J Sutton T
Fonder T Salisbury

Counc: K Fonder C Roussell R Thompson Jr M
Keppen H Eagle Bull R Zephier D Metcalf T
Woundedhead E Geboe

Departments: COM: J Flagstad; *Theol Edu:* C Corbin;
Chm Niobrara Council: R. Zephier

PARISHES, MISSIONS, AND CLERGY

Aberdeen St Marks Episcopal Church **P** (137)
1410 Kline St 57401-2103 (Mail to: 1410 Kline
St 57401-2103) (605) 225-0474

Batesland St Michaels Episcopal Church **M** (129)
Hwy 18 57716 (Mail to: PO Box 74 57752-
0074) (605) 455-2140

Bear Creek St James Church **M** 5 Miles North of
Hwy 212 57636 (Mail to: PO Box 534 57625-
0534) (605) 964-6180

Belle Fourche St James Episcopal Church **P** (47)
806 6th Ave 57717-1707 (Mail to: PO Box 414
57717-0414) (605) 892-2446

Blackfoot Church of the Ascension **M** Blackfoot
57601 (Mail to: PO Box 80 57625-0080) (605)
964-6180

Brookings St Pauls Episcopal Church **P** (130) 725
5th St 57006-2102 (Mail to: 726 6th St 57006-
2108) Larry Ort (605) 692-2617

Browns Valley St Johns Church **M** (278) Browns
Valley 56219 (Mail to: Sisseton Mission 56219)
(605) 698-6528

Bullhead St John the Baptist **PS** (15) Bullhead Rd
57642 (Mail to: PO Box 264 57642-0264) (605)
338-9751

Chamberlain Christ Episcopal Church **M** (21)
207 S Main St 57325-1420 (Mail to: PO Box
221 57325-0221) (605) 234-6327

Cherry Creek St Andrews Station **M** Cherry
Creek 57623 (Mail to: PO Box 80 57625-0080)
(605) 964-6180

Deadwood St Johns Episcopal Church **P** (57) 401
Williams St 57732-1113 (Mail to: PO Box 130
57732-0130) Michael Johnson (605) 920-8818

DeSmet St Stephens Church **M** (20) 411 Calumet
Ave NW 57231 (Mail to: 408 Jefferson Ave
57501-2626) (605) 338-9751

Dupree St Philips Church **M** Main St & Hwy 212
57623 (Mail to: Main St & Hwy 212 57623)
(605) 964-6180

✠ **Eagle Butte** Cheyenne River Episcopal Mission **O**
Eagle Butte 57625 (Mail to: PO Box 812 57625-
0812) (605) 964-7283

Eagle Butte St John the Evangelist **M** (417) N
Main Street 57625-0080 (Mail to: North Main
St. & Hwy 212 57625) (605) 964-6180

Firesteel Church of the Holy Spirit **M** (101) State
Rte 20 57633 (Mail to: c/o John Red Bear PO
Box 336 57642-0336) (605) 338-9751

Flandreau St Mary & Our Blessed Redeemer **M**
(47) 217 E 2nd St 57028 (Mail to: C/O Rev
Allen Lewis 4705 S Wildwood Cir 57105-7122)
(605) 270-3560

Fort George Holy Name Church **M** Iron Nation St
57548 (Mail to: c/o The Rev. Craig West 209 S
Main 57325) (605) 730-0626

Fort Pierre St Peters Episcopal Church **M** (36)
713 S 1st St 57532-2074 (Mail to: PO Box 391
57532-0391) (605) 670-7195

Fort Thompson Christ Episcopal Church **M** (147)
Ft Thompson 57339 (Mail to: PO Box 457
57339-0457) (605) 730-0626

Gregory Church of the Incarnation **M** (17) 1117
Main St 57533-1147 (Mail to: PO Box 225
57533) (605) 835-8144

Herrick All Saints Episcopal Church **M** (26) 352
Avenue 57538 (Mail to: 105 E 12the St 57533-
1140) (605) 835-8144

Hot Springs St Lukes Episcopal Church **M** (69)
Hammond Ave & Minnekah 57747 (Mail to:
PO Box 716 57747-0716) (605) 745-3323

Huron Grace Episcopal Church **P** (83) 1617
McClellan Dr 57350-1361 (Mail to: PO Box
1361 57350-1361) Jean Mornard (605) 352-3096

Ideal Church of the Holy Spirit **M** (88) Rural Tripp Co Gravel Rd 57541 (Mail to: 590 W 9th St 57580-2406) (605) 842-2211

Iron Lightning St Lukes Church **SC** Iron Lightning 57623 (Mail to: PO Box 1593 57625-1593) (605) 964-6180

Kyle Church of the Mediator **M** (414) Kyle Village Rd 57752 (Mail to: PO Box 354 57772-0354) (605) 455-2140

Lake Andes Saint Philip the Deacon Church **M** (24) 29273 383rd Ave 57356 (Mail to: East & South of Lake Andes 57356) (605) 384-5294

Lead Christ Episcopal Church **P** (59) 631 W. Main Avenue 57754 (Mail to: PO Box 675 57754-0675) (605) 584-3607

Little Eagle St Pauls Episcopal Church **M** (43) Little Eagle 57639 (Mail to: PO Box 722 57601-0722) (605) 338-9751

Little Oak Creek Church of the Good Shepherd **M** (87) Little Oak Creek 57639 (Mail to: PO Box 722 57601-0722) (605) 338-9751

Lower Brule Holy Comforter Episcopal Church **M** (450) 412 Spotted Tail Lane 57548 (Mail to: PO Box 242 57325-0242) (605) 441-6812

Lower Brule Messiah Episcopal Church **P** Iron Nation 57548 (Mail to: PO Box 227 57548-0227)

Madison Grace Episcopal Church **M** (17) 306 Nw 3rd St 57042-2115 (Mail to: 804 Best Point Dr 57042-9001) (605) 256-2325

Martin St Katharines Episcopal Church **M** (214) 4th Avenue & School Street 57551-0207 (Mail to: PO Box 207 57551-0207) (605) 685-6173

McLaughlin St Peters Episcopal Church **M** (100) 307 3rd Ave W 57642 (Mail to: PO Box 534 57642-0534) (605) 823-2269

Milbank Christ Episcopal Church **M** (36) 203 4th St 57252 (Mail to: 1114 Washington Dr 57252-3420) (605) 438-2101

Mission St Philip and St James Station **M** (36) PO Box 256 57579 (Mail to: PO Box 256 575550256) (605) 828-3892

✠ **Mission** Rosebud Episcopal Mission **O** Bishop Hare Rd 57555 (Mail to: PO Box 257 57570-0257) (605) 828-3892

Mission Trinity Episcopal Church **M** (207) 180 Main Street 57601 (Mail to: PO Box 188 57555-0188) (605) 828-3892

Mitchell St Marys Episcopal Church **P** (132) 214 W 3rd Ave 57301-2547 (Mail to: PO Box 866 57301-0866) (605) 996-3025

Mobridge St James Episcopal Church **P** (59) 802 Main St 57601 (Mail to: PO Box 722 57601-0722) (605) 845-3281

Niobrara Church of the Blessed Redeemer **M** (39) 535 Ave Howe Creek 68760 (Mail to: PO Box 686 57380-0686) (605) 384-5294

Norris Tiwahe ed wacekiyapi **M** S Main St 57560 (Mail to: S Main St 57560)

Oglala St Johns Episcopal Church **M** Pine Ridge Mission 57764 (Mail to: PO Box 207 57551-0207) (650) 867-1502

Okreek Calvary Episcopal Church **M** (29) Highway 18 57563 (Mail to: c/o The Rev Annie Henninger 105 East 12th Street 57533) (605) 835-8144

On The Tree St Thomas Station **PS** Green Grass-Whitehorse Rd Rural Dewey County 57265 (Mail to: PO Box 80 57625-0080) (605) 964-6180

Parmelee Holy Innocents Episcopal Church **M** (237) 7 1st St 57566 (Mail to: PO Box 257 57555-0188) (605) 828-3892

Peever St Marys Episcopal Church **M** (106) 12889 Whipple Rd 57257-7628 (Mail to: 716 7th Ave W 57262-1248) (605) 698-6528

Pierre Trinity Episcopal Church **P** (158) 408 Jefferson Ave 57501-2626 (Mail to: 408 Jefferson Ave 57501-2626) Mercy Hobbs Judith Flagstad (605) 224-5237

Pine Ridge Church of the Advent **PS** (102) Calico 57770 (Mail to: Attn Craig West PO Box 532 57551-0532) (605) 685-6631

Pine Ridge Holy Cross Episcopal Church **M** (95) Highway 407 57770 (Mail to: PO Box 14 57770-0014) (605) 685-6631

✠ **Pine Ridge** Pine Ridge Episcopal Mission **O** Pine Ridge Reservation 57551 (Mail to: Box J 57770) (605) 685-6173

Porcupine St Julias Episcopal Church **PS** (50) 92 Main St 57772 (Mail to: The Reverend C Apple P O Box 56 57772) (605) 685-6631

Promise St Marys Episcopal Church **M** Whitehorse-Promise Rd 57625 (Mail to: PO Box 80 57625-0080) (605) 964-6180

Pukwana St John the Baptist Episcopal Church **M** (62) Crow Creek Reservation 57370 (Mail to: 209 S Main St 57325-1420) (605) 730-0626

Rapid City Emmanuel Episcopal Parish **P** (484) Attention: Rev. Chris Roussell 717 Quincy St 57701-3631 (Mail to: Attention Rev. Chris Roussell 717 Quincy St 57701-3631) Christopher Roussell (605) 342-0909

Rapid City St Andrew's Episcopal Church **P** (321) 910 Soo San Dr 57702-8115 (Mail to: 910 Soo San Dr 57702-8115) Martha Garwood Hal Weidman (605) 343-4210

Rapid City St Matthews Episcopal Church **M** (430) 620 Haines Ave 57701 (Mail to: PO Box 1606 57709-1606) (605) 342-6199

Red Scaffold St Stephens Station **SC** Red Scaffold 57626 (Mail to: PO Box 80 57625-0080) (605) 964-6180

Red Shirt Table Christ Episcopal Church **SC** (214) RR 57701 (Mail to: PO Box 168 57744-0168) (605) 255-4914

Reliance St Albans Episcopal Church **P** 23792 340th Ave 57569-5622 (Mail to: 23792 340th Ave 57569-5622) (605) 730-0626

Rosebud Church of Jesus **M** (187) Rosebud Mission 57570 (Mail to: C/O Frank Gangone PO Box 897 57555) (605) 828-3892

Santee Church of Our Most Merciful Savior **M** (209) 65 Santee Rt. 22 68760 (Mail to: PO Box 686 57380-0686) (605) 384-5294

✠ **Sioux Falls** Calvary Cathedral **O** (774) 500 S Main Ave 57104-6814 (Mail to: 500 S Main Ave 57104-6814) Ward Simpson (605) 336-3486

Sioux Falls Church of the Good Shepherd **P** (417) 2707 W 33rd St 57105-4302 (Mail to: 2707 W 33rd St 57105-4302) Christina O'Hara (605) 332-1474

Sioux Falls Church of the Holy Apostles **M** (188) 1415 S Bahnson Ave 57103-3443 (Mail to: 3316 E 28th St 57103-4402) (605) 332-4828

Sioux Falls Dow Rummel Village **NH** 1321 W DOW RUMMEL ST 57104-7808 (Mail to: 1321 W DOW RUMMEL ST 57104-7808) (605) 336-1491

Sioux Falls Waterford At All Saints **NH** 111 W 17th St 57104-4972 (Mail to: 111 W 17th St 57104-4972)

Sisseton Gethsemane Episcopal Church **M** (52) Sisseton 57262 (Mail to: 7 5th Ave E 57262-2014) (605) 698-6528

Soldier Creek Grace Station **PS** (32) Soldier Creek Rd 57570 (Mail to: Bishop Hare Rd 57566) (605) 382-3892

Spearfish Church of All Angels **P** (192) 1044 5th St 57783-2009 (Mail to: 1044 5th St 57783-2009) John Riley (605) 642-4349

Sturgis St Thomas Episcopal Church **P** (105) 1222 Junction Ave 57785-1937 (Mail to: 1222 Junction Ave 57785-1937) (605) 347-5683

Thunder Butte St Peters Church **M** Thunder Butte Rd 57623 (Mail to: PO Box 80 57625-0456) (605) 964-6180

Vermillion St Pauls Episcopal Church **M** (53) 10 Linden Ave 57069-3203 (Mail to: 10 Linden Ave 57069-3203) (605) 624-3379

Wagner Church of the Holy Spirit **M** (105) 613 S Main St 57380 (Mail to: 500 S. Main 57102) (605) 384-5294

Wakpala St Elizabeths Episcopal Church **M** (131) Standing Rock Mission 57658 (Mail to: PO Box 105 57658-0105) (605) 845-7131

Wanblee Gethsemane Episcopal Church **M** (90) 210 1st St 57577 (Mail to: 6th & Main St 57577) (605) 685-6631

Watertown Trinity Episcopal Church **P** (34) 202 E Kemp 57201-3642 (Mail to: 612 3rd St NE 57201) Isaiah Brokenleg (605) 280-4927

Waubay St James Episcopal Church **M** (259) Enemy Swim Lake 57273 (Mail to: 716 7th Ave W 57262-1248) (605) 698-6528

Webster St Marys Episcopal Church **M** (19) 8th & Main St 57275 (Mail to: PO Box 71 57261-0071) (605) 486-4587

White Horse Emmanuel Episcopal Church **M** White Horse 57661 (Mail to: PO Box 5 57625-0053) (605) 964-6180

Yankton Christ Episcopal Church **P** (227) 513 Douglas Ave 57078-4030 (Mail to: Attn: Richard Unruh 513 Douglas Ave 57078-4030) Timothy Fountain (605) 665-2456

DIOCESE OF SOUTHEAST FLORIDA
(PROVINCE IV)
Comprises 7 counties in SE Florida
DIOCESAN OFFICE 525 NE 15th St Miami FL 33132
TEL (305) 373-0881   FAX (305) 375-8054
E-MAIL info@diosef.org   WEB www.diosef.org

Previous Bishops— Wm C Gray 1892-1913, Cameran Mann m 1913 dio 1922-32, John D Wing coadj 1925 Bp 1932-50, Martin J Bramm suffr 1951-56, Wm F Moses suffr 1956-61, Henry I Louttit suffr 1945 coadj 1948 Bp 1951-69, Wm L Hargrave suffr 1961-69, James L Duncan suffr 1961-69 Bp 1970-80, Calvin O Schofield Jr Bp 1980-2000, John Said suffr 1995-2002, James Ottley Asst Bp 2002-2006, Leopold Frade 2000-2016, Peter Eaton coadj 2015-16

Bishop Rt Rev Peter Eaton 1087 (2016)

Cn to Ord Rev Cn J Tidy; *Archdcn for Imm and Soc Just Ven* JF Bazin; *Sec* K Neely; *Treas Cn* T Huston;

Chanc C Johnson ESQ; *Vice Chanc* B Reid; K Grantham; WT Muir ESQ; D Anderson ESQ; *Chanc Em*; RD Tylander; JR Gillespie; *COO* C Valdes; *Interim Pres Episc Charities* Rev R Taylor; *ComM* Rev P Rasmus

Deans: N Palm Beach Very Rev J Cook; *South Palm Beach* Very Rev P Kane; *Broward* Very Rev A Cutie; *North Dade* Very Rev G Mansfield; *South Dade* Very Rev M E Cassini; *Keys* Very Rev L Hooper; *Trinity Cathedral* Vicar M Busto

Stand Comm—Cler: Pres A Holder N Blasco C Olson R Knowles; *Lay:* J Miller M Mathis J Villiers L Avery

PARISHES, MISSIONS, AND CLERGY

Big Pine Key St Francis in the Keys Church **M** (29) 1600 Key Deer Blvd 33043 (Mail to: PO

Box 430645 33043-0645) Christopher Todd Christopher Todd (305) 872-2547

Biscayne Park Santa Cruz-Resurrection Episcopal Church **M** (613) 11173 Griffing Blvd 33161 (Mail to: 11173 Griffing Blvd 33161-7249) Jose Ortez (305) 893-8523

Boca Raton Chapel Of Saint Andrew **M** (100) 2707 Nw 37th St 33434-4497 (Mail to: "3900 Jog Rd, Building 13" 33434) Winnie Bolle Charles Browning Anne Harris Faye Somers Charles Wissink (561) 210-2700

Boca Raton St Gregorys Episcopal Church **P** (1071) § 100 Ne Mizner Blvd 33432-4008 (Mail to: PO Box 1503 33429-1503) Andrew Sherman Benjamin Thomas (561) 395-8285

Boynton Beach St Cuthberts Episcopal Church **M** (46) Attn Mrs Barbara Smith 417 Nw 7th Ave 33435-3754 (Mail to: Attn Mrs Barbara Smith 417 Nw 7th Ave 33435-3754) (561) 732-7422

Boynton Beach St Josephs Episcopal Church **P** (871) § 3300a S Seacrest Blvd 33435-8661 (Mail to: 3300A S Seacrest Blvd 33435-8661) Martin Zlatic Gwendolyn Tobias (561) 732-3060

Clewiston St Martins Episcopal Church **M** (97) 207 Nw Cowen Ave 33440 (Mail to: 207 W C Owens Ave 33440-3030) (863) 983-7960

Coral Gables Chapel of the Venerable Bede **CC** (88) 1150 Stanford Dr 33146-2002 (Mail to: 1150 Stanford Dr 33146-2002) Frank Corbishley (305) 284-2333

Coral Gables St Philips Episcopal Church **P** (440) 1121 Andalusia Avenue 33134-4799 (Mail to: 1121 Andalusia Ave 33134-5509) Mary Conroy Michael Sahdev (305) 444-6176

Deerfield Beach St Marys Episcopal Church **M** (122) 417 S Dixie Hwy 33441-4627 (Mail to: 417 S Dixie Hwy 33441-4627) (954) 428-3040

Delray Beach St Matthews Episcopal Church **M** (140) 404 SW 3rd St 33444-2402 (Mail to: 404 SW 3rd St 33444-2402) Marcia Beam (561) 272-4143

Delray Beach St Pauls Church **P** (973) § 188 S Swinton Ave 33444-3656 (Mail to: 188 S Swinton Ave 33444-3698) Paul Kane Kathleen Gannon (561) 276-4541

Fort Lauderdale St Ambrose Episcopal Church **M** (110) 2250 Sw 31st Ave 333124398 (Mail to: 2250 SW 31st Ave 33312-4398) Andrew Hudson Ralph Klingenberg Rosa Lindahl (954) 583-0603

Fort Lauderdale St Mark the Evangelist Church **P** (551) 1750 E Oakland Park Blvd 33334 (Mail to: 1750 E Oakland Park Blvd 33334-5299) Ronald Hayde Eliza Ragsdale Robert Trache (954) 563-5155

Ft Lauderdale All Saints Episcopal Church **P** (1087) § 333 Tarpon Dr 33301-2337 (Mail to: 333 Tarpon Dr 33301-2337) Carl Beasley Leslie Hague (954) 467-6496

Ft Lauderdale St Christophers Episcopal Church **M** (117) 318 Nw 6th Ave 33311-9154 (Mail to: PO Box 228 33302-0228) (954) 306-6148

Ft Lauderdale Episcopal Church of the Atonement **P** (718) § 4401 W Oakland Park Blvd 33313-1826 (Mail to: 4401 W Oakland Park Blvd 33313-1826) (954) 731-6100

Ft Lauderdale St Benedicts Episcopal Church **P** (1066) 7801 Nw 5th St 33324-1911 (Mail to: 7801 NW 5th St 33324-1999) Albert Cutie (954) 473-6578

Hallandale Beach St. Anne's Episcopal Church **M** (60) 705 NW 1st Avenue 33020 (Mail to: PO Box 695 33004-0695) (301) 253-2130

Hallandale Beach St Anne's Episcopal Church **M** (181) 705 Nw 1st Ave 33009-2301 (Mail to: 705 NW 1st Ave 33009-2301) (954) 454-2811

Hobe Sound Christ Memorial Chapel **SC** (46) 52 S Beach Rd 33455-2225 (Mail to: PO Box 582 33475-0582) Heidi Kinner (772) 546-8329

Hollywood Holy Sacrament Episcopal Church **P** (665) § 2801 University Dr 33024-2547 (Mail to: 2801 University Dr 33024-2547) Anthony Holder William Eaton (954) 432-8686

Hollywood St James in the Hills Church **P** (151) 3329 Wilson St 33021-4836 (Mail to: 3329 Wilson St 33021-4836) (954) 987-2203

Hollywood St Johns Episcopal Church **P** (136) § 1704 Buchanan St 33020-4030 (Mail to: 1704 Buchanan St 33020-4030) (954) 921-3721

Homestead St Johns Episcopal Church **M** (506) § 145 Ne 10th St 33030-4633 (Mail to: 145 NE 10th St 33030-4698) (305) 247-5343

Islamorada St James the Fisherman **P** (232) § 87500 Overseas High 33036 (Mail to: PO Box 509 33036-0509) (305) 852-2161

Jensen Beach All Saints Episcopal Church **P** (554) 2303 Ne Seaview Dr 34957-5533 (Mail to: 2303 Ne Seaview Dr 34957) Alan Gellert (772) 334-0610

Key Biscayne St Christophers By The Sea Church **P** (148) § 95 Harbor Dr 33149-1411 (Mail to: 95 Harbor Dr 33149-1499) Susan Bruttell Miguel Baguer Susan Bruttell (305) 361-5080

Key West St Pauls Episcopal Church **P** (490) 401 Duval St 33040-6550 (Mail to: 401 Duval St 33040-6550) Larry Hooper (305) 296-5142

Key West St Peters Episcopal Church **M** (100) 807 Center St 33040-7435 (Mail to: 800 Center St 33040-7435) (305) 296-2346

Lake Worth St Johns Episcopal Church **M** (34) 810 Washington Ave 33460-5555 (Mail to: 1524 Douglas St 33460-5510) (561) 547-4480

Lake Worth Holy Redeemer Episcopal Church **M** (257) 3730 Kirk Rd 33461-3431 (Mail to: 3730 Kirk Rd 33461-3431) (561) 965-8632

Lake Worth St Andrews Episcopal Church **P** (390) 100 Palmway 33460-3515 (Mail to: 100 Palmway 33460-3515) Brenda Masterman Paul Rasmus (561) 582-6609

Marathon St Columba Episcopal Church **P** (110) § 451 52nd Street Gulf 33050-2614 (Mail to: PO Box 500426 451 52nd Street Gulf 33050-0426) Debra Andrew-maconaughey (305) 743-6412

Miami All Angels Episcopal Church **M** (215) § 1801 Ludlam Dr 33166-3165 (Mail to: 1801 Ludlam Dr 33166-3165) Ann Kathleen Goraczko (305) 885-1780

Miami Christ Church **P** (400) § 3481 Hibiscus St 33133-5717 (Mail to: 3481 Hibiscus St 33133-5717) Jonathan Archer Vivian Hopkins (305) 442-8542

Miami Episcopal Church of the Ascension **P** (498) § 11201 Sw 160th St 33157-2701 (Mail to: 11201 SW 160th St 33157-2701) Milton Cooper (305) 238-5151

Miami Holy Comforter Episcopal Church **M** (483) § 150 Sw 13th Ave 33135-2412 (Mail to: 150 SW 13th Ave 33135-2491) Sixto Garcia (305) 643-2711

Miami Episcopal Church of the Incarnation **P** (863) 1835 Nw 54th St 33142-3065 (Mail to: PO Box 420050 33242-0050) Roberta Knowles (305) 633-2446

Miami Church of the Holy Family **P** (595) 18501 Nw 7th Ave 33169-4441 (Mail to: 18501 NW 7th Ave 33169-4441) Horace Ward Ledly Moss (305) 652-6797

Miami Iglesia Epis de Todos Los Santos **P** (378) 1023 Sw 27th Ave 33135-4614 (Mail to: 1023 SW 27th Ave 33135-4614) Alejandro Hernandez (305) 642-2951

Miami Iglesia Episcopal Santisima Trinidad **P** (612) 6744 Miami Ave 33150-4030 (Mail to: 6744 Miami Ave Suite 201 33150-4030) Marivel Milien (305) 758-8546

Miami Historic St Agnes Episcopal Church **P** (483) 1750 Nw 3rd Ave 33136-1610 (Mail to: PO Box 12943 33101-2943) Doris Ingraham Denrick Rolle (305) 573-5330

Miami St Andrews Episcopal Church **P** (545) 14260 Old Cutler Rd 33158-1347 (Mail to: 14260 Old Cutler Rd 33158-1347) Spencer Potter George Ronkowitz (305) 238-2161

Miami St Faith Episcopal Church **P** (251) 10600 Caribbean Blvd 33189-1361 (Mail to: 10600 Caribbean Blvd 33189-1361) (305) 235-3621

Miami St Luke the Physician **M** (346) 12355 Sw 104th St 33186-3602 (Mail to: 12355 SW 104th St 33186-3602) Corinna Olson (305) 279-4265

Miami Church of St Matthew the Apostle **P** (172) § 7410 Sunset Dr 33143-4130 (Mail to: 7410 Sunset Dr 33143-4130) James Jones (305) 665-7333

Miami St Simons Episcopal Church **M** (112) 10950 Sw 34th St 33165-3542 (Mail to: 10950 SW 34th St 33165-3542) Carlos Sandoval Cros Rohani Weger (305) 221-4753

Miami St Stephens Episcopal Church **P** (535) § 2750 Mcfarlane Rd 33133-6026 (Mail to: 2750 McFarlane Rd 33133-6026) Wilifred Allen-Faiella Jo-Ann Murphy Jo-Ann Murphy (305) 448-2601

Miami St Thomas Episcopal Church **P** (957) § 5690 Sw 88th St 33156-2199 (Mail to: 5690 SW 88th St 33156-2199) Richard Maxwell Harold

Walker (305) 661-3436

Miami St Paul et Les Martyrs D'Haiti **M** (179) 6744 Miami Ave 33150-4030 (Mail to: 6744 Miami Ave 33150-4000) Marivel Milien Smith Milien (305) 758-8546

✠ **Miami** Trinity Cathedral **O** (985) 464 Ne 16th St 33132-1222 (Mail to: 464 Ne 16th St 33132-1222) Richard Benedict Mercedes Busto Elaine Jessup John Stanton (305) 374-3372

Miami Beach All Souls' Episcopal Church **P** (106) § 4025 Pine Tree Dr 33140-3601 (Mail to: 4025 Pine Tree Dr 33140-3677) Charles Humphries (305) 520-5410

Miami Lakes Church of the Epiphany **M** (160) § 15650 Miami Lakeway 33014-5517 (Mail to: 15650 Miami Lakeway 33014-5517) (305) 558-3961

N Miami Beach St Bernard de Clairvaux Episcopal Church **P** (729) § 16711 W Dixie Hwy 33160-3714 (Mail to: 16711 W Dixie Hwy 33160-3714) Gregory Mansfield Ann Kathleen Goraczko (305) 945-1461

Opa Locka Church of the Transfiguration **M** (146) 15260 Nw 19th Ave 33054-2960 (Mail to: PO Box 272 33054) Terrence Taylor (305) 681-1660

Opa Locka St Kevins Episcopal Church **M** (120) 3280 Nw 135th St 33054-4812 (Mail to: PO Box 540668 33054-0668) Simeon Newbold Simeon Newbold (305) 688-8517

Palm Beach The Episcopal Church Of Bethesda-By-The-Sea **P** (1198) 141 S County Rd 33480 (Mail to: 141 S County Rd 33480-1057) James Harlan Margaret McGhee Walter Salmon Cecily Titcomb (561) 655-4554

Palm Beach Garden Saint Mark's Church **P** (1303) § 3395 Burns Rd 33410-4322 (Mail to: Attn Treasurer Accounting Dept 3395 Burns Rd 33410-4322) James Cook Sanford Groff Jean Wright (561) 622-0956

Palm City Church of the Advent **M** (184) 4484 SW Citrus Blvd 34990 (Mail to: 4484 SW Citrus Blvd 34990-8760) (772) 283-6221

Pompano Beach St Nicholas Episcopal Church **P** (433) 1111 E Sample Rd 33064-5113 (Mail to: 1111 E Sample Rd 33064-5113) Mark Jones (954) 942-5887

Pompano Beach St Martins Episcopal Church **P** (349) 140 Se 28th Ave 33062-5441 (Mail to: 140 SE 28th Ave 33062-5441) Bernard Pecaro Ralph Klingenberg (954) 941-4843

Pompano Beach St Mary Magdalene Episcopal **P** (840) § 1400 Riverside Dr 33071-6070 (Mail to: 1400 Riverside Dr 33071-6070) Natalie Blasco Lorna Goodison Ruth Hahne Todd Hoover (954) 753-1400

Pompano Beach St Philips Episcopal Church **M** (50) 465 Nw 15th St 33060-5416 (Mail to: 465 NW 15th St 33060-5416) (954) 785-2437

Riviera Beach St Georges Episcopal Church **P** (70) 21 W 22nd St 33404-5509 (Mail to: PO Box 10584 33419-0584) (561) 844-7713

Stuart St Lukes Episcopal Church **P** (400) 5150 Se Railway Ave 34997-3305 (Mail to: PO Box 117 34992-0117) Carol Barron (772) 286-5455

Stuart St Marys Episcopal Church **P** (1377) 623 South East Ocean Blvd 34994-2329 (Mail to: 623 SE Ocean Blvd 34994-2376) Todd Cederberg Christian Anderson (772) 287-3244

Stuart St Monicas Episcopal Church **M** (59) PO Box 1798 34995-1798 (Mail to: PO Box 1798 33494) (772) 221-0552

Tequesta Church of the Good Shepherd **P** (1516) § 400 Seabrook Road 33469-2685 (Mail to: 400 Seabrook Rd 33469-2685) Douglas Scharf (561) 746-4674

West Palm Bch Grace Episcopal Church **P** (561) 3600 Australian Ave 33407-4513 (Mail to: 3600 Australian Ave 33407-4599) Winston Wright (561) 845-6060

West Palm Bch Holy Spirit Episcopal Church **P** (304) § 1003 Allendale Rd 33405-1347 (Mail to: 1003 Allendale Rd 33405-1347) Donna Hall (561) 833-7605

West Palm Bch Holy Trinity Episcopal Church **P** (532) § 211 Trinity Pl 33401-6119 (Mail to: 211 Trinity Pl 33401-6119) (561) 655-8650

West Palm Bch St Christophers Episcopal Church **M** (220) § 1063 Haverhill Rd 33417-5844 (Mail to: PO Box 222068 33422-2068) (561) 683-8167

West Palm Bch St David in the Pines Epis Church **P** (431) § 465 W Forest Hill Blvd 33414-4705 (Mail to: 465 W Forest Hill Blvd 33414-4705) William Thomas (561) 793-1976

West Palm Beach Saint Patricks Church **P** (321) § 418 North Sapodilla Avenue 33401-4138 (Mail to: 418 Sapodilla Ave 33401-4138) Winston Joseph (561) 833-1903

DIOCESE OF SOUTHERN OHIO
(PROVINCE V)
Comprises 40 counties of Southern Ohio
DIOCESAN OFFICE 412 Sycamore St Cincinnati OH 45202-4179
TEL (513) 421-0311; (800)   582-1712 FAX (513) 421-0315
WEB www.diosohio.org

Previous Bishops—
Thomas A Jaggar 1875-1904, Boyd Vincent coadj 1889 Bp 1904-29, Theodore I Reese coadj 1913 Bp 1929-31, Henry W Hobson coadj 1930 Bp 1931-59, Roger W Blanchard coadj 1958 Bp 1959-70, John M Krumm 1971-80, WG Black coadj 1979 Bp 1980-91, Herbert Thompson Jr coadj 1988 Bp 1992-05, Kenneth Price Jr suffr 1994-2012

Bishop—Rt Rev Thomas E Breidenthal (1016)
(Dio 28 April 2007)

Cn to Ord Rev Cn L Carter-Edmands; *Cn for Transitions & Cong Vit* Rev Cn J Leo; *Cn for Form & Soc Just* L A Reat; *Op Exec* C deLange *CFO* D Robinson; *Yth Min & Sum Camp* A Foote; *Dir of Comm* D Dreisbach; *Pres of Trustees* J Boss; *Sec to Conv* A Sabo; *Chanc* JJ Dehner 3300 Great American Tower 301 E Fourth St Cincinnati 45202; *Hist* Rev AW Wilson; *Ecum & Interfaith* M Zacharia 318 E Fourth St Cincinnati OH 45202; *Treas* R Krantz

Stand Comm—Cler: E Cook P DeVaul C Graves; *Lay: Pres* M Lentz C Bagot L Hayes

PARISHES, MISSIONS, AND CLERGY
Amelia Church of the Good Samaritan **M** (31) 25 Amelia-Olive Branch Rd 45102-0889 (Mail to:

PO Box 889 45102-0889) (513) 753-4115

Athens Church Of The Good Shepherd **P** (153) § 64 University Ter 45701-2913 (Mail to: 64 University Ter 45701-2982) Deborah Woolsey (740) 593-6877

Bellaire Trinity Episcopal Church **M** (39) § 4310 Noble St 43906-1448 (Mail to: 4310 Noble St 43906-1448) (740) 676-4472

Cambridge St Johns Episcopal Church **M** (33) 1025 Steubenville Ave 43725-2401 (Mail to: PO Box 1044 43725-6044) Robert Howell (740) 432-7508

Chillicothe St Pauls Episcopal Church **P** (94) 33 E Main St 45601-2504 (Mail to: 33 E Main St 45601-2595) Paul Daggett (740) 772-4105

Cincinnati All Saints Episcopal Church **P** (171) 6301 Parkman Pl 45213-1123 (Mail to: 6301 Parkman Pl 45213-1123) Eileen O'Reilly (513) 531-6333

Cincinnati Calvary Episcopal Church **P** (411) 3766 Clifton Ave 45220-1238 (Mail to: 3766 Clifton Ave Ste B 45220-1255) Allison English Gary Givler (513) 861-4437

Cincinnati Holy Child Chapel-Childrens Hospital **PS** 3333 Burnet Ave # 5022 45229-3026 (Mail to: 3333 Burnet Ave MLC 5022 45229) (513) 636-4200

Cincinnati Christ Church - Glendale **P** (512) 965 Forest Ave 45246-4405 (Mail to: 965 Forest Ave 45246-4499) David Pfaff Nicholas Evancho Anne Reed (513) 771-1544

✤ **Cincinnati** Christ Church Cathedral **O** (562) 318 E 4th St 45202-4202 (Mail to: C/O Judy Hering 318 E 4th St 45202-4202) Gail Greenwell Noel Julnes-Dehner Karen Montagno Sherilyn Pearce Manoj Zacharia (513) 621-1817

Cincinnati Church of Our Saviour **P** (103) 65 E Hollister St 45219-1703 (Mail to: 65 E Hollister St 45219-1796) Paula Jackson (513) 241-1870

Cincinnati Church of the Advent **HC** (85) 2366 Kemper Lane 45206-2686 (Mail to: 2366 Kemper Ln 45206-2686) Stacy Salles (513) 961-2100

Cincinnati Grace Episcopal Church **M** (49) 5501 Hamilton Ave 45224-3111 (Mail to: 5501 Hamilton Ave 45224-3301) (513) 541-2415

Cincinnati Holy Trinity Episcopal Church **M** (36) 7190 Euclid Ave 45243-2544 (Mail to: 7190 Euclid Ave 45243-2544) Karen Sherrill (513) 984-8400

Cincinnati Indian Hill Church **P** (165) 6000 Drake Rd 45243-3308 (Mail to: 6000 Drake Rd 45243-3395) George Sherrill (513) 561-6805

Cincinnati St Andrews Episcopal Church **P** (238) 1809 Rutland Ave 45207-1219 (Mail to: 1809 Rutland Ave 45207-1219) John Agbaje Anne Reed (513) 531-4337

Cincinnati St Barnabas Church **P** (705) 10345 Montgomery Rd 45242-5113 (Mail to: PO Box 42642 45242-0642) Nancy Turner-Jones (513) 984-8401

Cincinnati St James Episcopal Church **P** (218) 3207 Montana Ave 45211-6609 (Mail to: 3207 Montana Ave 45211-6697) Mary Carson (513) 661-1154

Cincinnati St Simon of Cyrene Episcopal **P** (206) 810 Matthews Dr 45215-1837 (Mail to: 810 Matthews Dr 45215-1837) Theorphlis Borden Colenthia Hunter James Mobley (513) 771-4828

Cincinnati St Timothys Episcopal Church **P** (903) § 8101 Beechmont Ave 45255-3190 (Mail to: 8101 Beechmont Ave 45255-3196) Roger Greene (513) 474-4445

Cincinnati Ascension and Holy Trinity **P** (458) § 334 Burns Ave 45215-4320 (Mail to: 334 Burns Ave 45215) Eric Miller (513) 821-5341

Cincinnati The Church of the Redeemer **P** (871) 2944 Erie Ave 45208-2404 (Mail to: 2944 Erie Ave 45208-2404) Philip Devaul Mitchell Bojarski Joyce Keeshin Melanie Slane (513) 321-6700

Circleville St Philips Episcopal Church **HC** (142) § 129 W Mound St 43113-1623 (Mail to: PO Box 484 43113-0484) David Getreu (740) 474-4525

Columbus St Edwards Church Whitehall **M** (108) 214 Fairway Blvd 43213-2012 (Mail to: 214 Fairway Blvd 43213-2012) Fredric Shirley (614) 861-1777

Columbus St Albans Epis Church of Bexley **P** (506) 333 S Drexel Ave 43209-2139 (Mail to: 333 S Drexel Ave 43209-2139) James Rodgers Harry Harper John Jupin Meribah Mansfield (614) 253-8549

Columbus St James Episcopal Church **P** (334) § 3400 Calumet St 43214-4106 (Mail to: 3400 Calumet St 43214-4106) Elise Feyerherm Phillip Harris (614) 262-2360

Columbus St Johns Episcopal Church **M** (293) 1003 W Town St 43222-1438 (Mail to: 1003 W Town St 43222-1438) Meribah Mansfield (614) 221-9328

Columbus Saint Mark's Episcopal Church **P** (783) § 2151 Dorset Rd 43221-3103 (Mail to: 2151 Dorset Rd 43221-3194) Kenneth St Germain Christopher Richardson (614) 486-9452

Columbus St Philip Episcopal Church **P** (289) 166 Woodland Ave 43203-1774 (Mail to: 166 Woodland Ave 43203-1774) Karl Ruttan Brenda Taylor Charles Wilson (614) 253-2771

Columbus Saint Stephen's Episcopal Church And University **P** (250) 30 W Woodruff Ave 43210-1118 (Mail to: 30 W Woodruff Ave 43210-1118) Susan Michelfelder Pamela Elwell (614) 294-3749

Columbus Trinity Episcopal Church **P** (355) 125 E Broad St 43215-3605 (Mail to: 125 E Broad St 43215-3605) Richard Burnett Brian Shaffer (614) 221-5351

Dayton Christ Episcopal Church **P** (434) § 20 W 1st St 45402-1213 (Mail to: 20 W 1st St 45402-1269) Joanna Leiserson (937) 223-2239

Dayton St Andrews Episcopal Church **P** (121) 1060 Salem Ave 45406-5130 (Mail to: 1060 Salem Ave 45406-5198) Connie Mccarroll (937) 278-7345

Dayton St Georges Episcopal Church **P** (585) 5520 Far Hills Ave 45429-2204 (Mail to: 5520 Far Hills Ave 45429-2232) Benjamin Phillips C David Cottrill Lewis Lane (937) 434-1781

Dayton St Margarets Episcopal Church **P** (286) 3010 Mccall St 45417-2034 (Mail to: 5301 Free Pike 45426-2441) Benjamin Speare-Hardy Jeanette Manning (937) 837-7741

Dayton St Marks Episcopal Church **P** (102) 456 Woodman Dr 45431-2099 (Mail to: 456 Woodman Dr 45431-2099) Michael Kreutzer George Snyder (937) 256-1082

Dayton St Pauls Church Episcopal **P** (625) 33 W Dixon Ave 45419-3431 (Mail to: 33 W Dixon Ave 45419-3431) John Atkins (937) 293-1154

Delaware St Peters Episcopal Church **P** (221) 45 W Winter St 43015-1947 (Mail to: 45 West Winter St 43015) David Kendall-Sperry (740) 369-3175

Dublin St Patricks Episcopal Church **P** (901) 7121 Muirfield Dr 43017-2863 (Mail to: 7121 Muirfield Dr 43017-2863) Stephen Smith Lori O'Riley Robert Rideout (614) 766-2664

Fairborn St Christophers Church **P** (1501) 1501 Broad St 45324-5575 (Mail to: PO Box 1026 45324-1026) John Paddock (937) 878-5614

Gallipolis St Peters Episcopal Church **P** (58) 541 2nd Ave 45631-1250 (Mail to: 541 2nd Ave 45631-1250) Gene Stack (740) 446-2483

Granville St Luke Episcopal Church **P** (394) 107 Broadway E 43023-1303 (Mail to: PO Box 82 43023-0082) Doris Westfall (740) 587-0167

Greenville St Pauls Episcopal Church **P** (67) 201 S Broadway St 45331-1978 (Mail to: 201 South Broadway & Water 45331) David Brower Richard Larsen (937) 548-5575

Hamilton Trinity Church **P** (165) § 115 6th St 45011-3541 (Mail to: 115 6th St 45011-3541) Suzanne Levesconte (513) 896-6755

Hillsboro St Marys Episcopal Church **P** (91) § 234 High St 45133-1129 (Mail to: 234 High St 45133-1129) Judi Wiley (937) 393-2043

Ironton Christ Church **M** (72) 501 Park Ave 45638-1546 (Mail to: PO Box 555 45638-0555) (740) 532-3528

Lancaster St Johns Episcopal Church **P** (271) 134 Broad St 43130-3701 (Mail to: 134 Broad St 43130-3701) Robert Clarke (740) 653-3052

Lebanon St Patricks Church **P** (170) 232 E Main St 45036-2230 (Mail to: 232 E Main St 45036-2230) Jacqueline Matisse (513) 932-7691

Logan St Pauls Episcopal Church **M** (36) 375 E Main St 43138-1307 (Mail to: PO Box 736 43138-0736) (740) 385-1005

London Christ Chapel **SC** 11235 State Route 38 SE 43140-9716 (Mail to: 11235 State Route 38 Se 43140-9716)

London Trinity Episcopal Church **P** (74) Corner of 4th and Main St 43140-0468 (Mail to: PO Box 468 43140-0468) Frank Edmands George Glazier (740) 852-9298

Maineville St Mary Magdalene Church **M** (29) § 2757 W US Route 22 45039 (Mail to: PO Box 352 45039-0352) (513) 677-1777

Marietta St Lukes Episcopal Church **P** (241) § 320 2nd St 45750-2919 (Mail to: 320 2nd St 45750-2919) William Field Dale Sheppard (740) 373-5132

Mc Arthur Trinity Church **M** (8) 202 W High St 45651-1009 (Mail to: 202 W High St 45651-1009) (740) 596-5562

Mechanicsburg Church of Our Saviour **M** (65) § 56 S Main St 43044-1111 (Mail to: 230 Scioto St 43078-2128) (937) 653-3497

Middletown Church of the Ascension **P** (186) § 2709 Mcgee Ave 45044-4836 (Mail to: 2709 Mcgee Ave 45044-4899) Thomas Fehr (513) 424-1254

Nelsonville Church of the Epiphany **M** (32) 193 Jefferson St 45764-1207 (Mail to: 193 Jefferson St 45764-1207) (740) 753-3434

New Albany All Saints Episcopal Church **P** (366) PO Box 421 5101 Johnstown Road 43054-0421 (Mail to: PO Box 421 43054-0421) Kevin Beesley Jason Prati (614) 855-8267

Newark Trinity Episcopal Church **P** (191) 76 E Main St 43055-5604 (Mail to: 76 E Main St 43055-5672) (740) 345-5643

Oxford Holy Trinity Episcopal Church **P** (236) 25 E. Walnut St. 45056-1892 (Mail to: 25 E Walnut St 45056-1892) Sara Palmer (513) 523-7559

Pickerington Saint Andrew's Church **P** (120) 8630 Refugee Rd 43147-9509 (Mail to: 8630 Refugee Rd 43147-9509) Paul Williams Seth Wymer (614) 626-2720

Piqua St James Episcopal Church **P** (138) 200 W High St 45356-2218 (Mail to: 200 W High St 45356-2218) Robert Hill (937) 773-1241

Pomeroy Grace Episcopal Church **M** (31) 326 E Main St 45769-1023 (Mail to: 326 E Main St 45769-1023) (740) 992-3968

Portsmouth All Saints' Episcopal Church **P** (207) 610 4th St 45662-3921 (Mail to: 610 4th St 45662-3921) Stephen Cuff Richard Schisler (740) 353-7919

Springboro St Francis Episcopal Church **P** (143) 225 Main St 45066-9255 (Mail to: 225 Main St 45066-9255) (937) 748-2592

Springfield Christ Episcopal Church Of Springfield **P** (374) 409 E High St 45505-1007 (Mail to: 409 E High St 45505-1007) Otto Anderson Rick Incorvati Margaret Leidheiser-Stoddard (937) 323-8651

Terrace Park St Thomas Episcopal Church **P** (1467) § 100 Miami Ave 45174-1175 (Mail to: 100 Miami Ave 45174-1175) Darren Elin Daniel Grossoehme Noel Julnes-Dehner Robert Reynolds (513) 831-2052

Troy Trinity Episcopal Church **P** (123) § 60 S Dorset Rd 45373-5616 (Mail to: 60 S Dorset Rd 45373-5616) Nancy Hardin Joan Smoke (937) 335-7747

Urbana Church of the Epiphany **M** (84) § 230 Scioto St 43078-2128 (Mail to: 230 Scioto St 43078-2128) (937) 653-3497

Waynesville St Marys Episcopal Church **M** (28) 107 S 3rd St 45068-9011 (Mail to: PO Box 653 45068-0653) Pamela Gaylor (513) 897-2435

West Chester St Anne Episcopal Church **P** (441) § 6461 Tylersville Rd 45069-1435 (Mail to: 6461 Tylersville Rd 45069-1435) Phyllis Spiegel (513) 779-1139

Westerville St Matthews Episcopal Church **M** (98) § 30 E College Ave 43081-1601 (Mail to: 30 E College Ave 43081-1601) Joseph Kovitch (614) 882-2706

Worthington St Johns Episcopal Church **P** (494) 700 High St 43085-4137 (Mail to: 700 High St 43085-4152) Alice Herman Denise Mueller Denise Mueller Karl Stevens (614) 846-5180

Wshngtn Ct Hs St Andrews Episcopal Church **M** (216) 733 State Route 41 Sw 43160-8797 (Mail to: 733 State Route 41 SW 43160-8797) (740) 335-2129

Xenia Christ Episcopal Church **P** (74) 63 E Church St 45385-3001 (Mail to: 68 E Church St 45385-3002) Jennifer Oldstone-Moore (937) 372-1594

Zanesville St James Episcopal Church **P** (142) 155 6th St 43701-3603 (Mail to: 155 6th St 43701-3688) Robert Willmann (740) 453-9459

DIOCESE OF SOUTHERN VIRGINIA
(PROVINCE III)
Comprises 26 southern VA counties
DIOCESAN OFFICE 11827 Canon Blvd Ste 101 Newport News VA 23606
TEL (757) 423-8287 In VA only (800) 582-8292   FAX (757) 595-0783
E-MAIL 600@diosova.org   WEB www.diosova.org

Previous Bishops—
Alfred M Randolph 1892-1918,
Beverley D Tucker coadj 1906 Bp
1918-30, Arthur C Thomson suffr
1917 coadj 1919 Bp 1930-37, Wm
A Brown 1938-50, Geo P Gunn
coadj 1948 Bp 1950-71, David
S Rose suffr 1958 coadj 1964
Bp 1971-1978, C Charles Vaché
coadj 1976 Bp 1978-91, O'Kelley
Whitaker asst 1992-97 Frank H Vest Jr coadj 1989
Bp 1991-98 Donald P Hart asst 1998-2001, Carol
Joy WT Gallagher suffr 2002-2005, David C Bane
coadj 1997 Bp 1998-2006, John C Buchaman Bp Int
2006-09

Bishop—Herman Hollerith IV (1034) (Dio 13
Feb 2009)

Sec Rev RE Haines; *Chanc* T Coyle; *Vice Chancs*
S Webster; *Cn for Deploy* C Robinson; *Treas* A
Kirchmier

Stand Comm—Cler: Pres C Alexander S Grimm
S Sawyer; *Lay:* S Norris J Rector M Easton *Deans:*
1st or Eastern Shore V Rev B Ford; *2nd or Virginia
Beach* V Rev S Sawyer; *3rd or Norfolk* V Rev J Rohrs;
4th V Rev K Emerson; *5th or Jamestown* V Rev Dr R
Ramsey *6th or Petersburg* V C Moore; *7th or South
Richmond* V Rev D Custer; *8th or Farmville* V Rev N
Meck; *9th or Danville* V Rev Dr S Grimm

PARISHES, MISSIONS, AND CLERGY

Accomac St James Episcopal Church **P** (52) 23309
Back St 23301-1742 (Mail to: PO Box 540
23301-0540) (757) 787-4892

Amelia Ct Hs Christ Church **P** (82) 16401 Court
St 23002-4870 (Mail to: PO Box 468 23002-
0468) Michael Stone (804) 561-2441

Appomattox St Anne Episcopal Church **P** (72)
311 Oakleigh Ave 24522 (Mail to: PO Box 387
24522-0387) (434) 352-8296

Baskerville St Andrew Episcopal Church **M** (8)
4118 Baskerville Rd 23915-2045 (Mail to: PO
Box 124 23915-0124) (434) 447-4914

Blackstone St Lukes Episcopal Church **P** (68)
Corner Of S Main & Church 23824 (Mail to:
PO Box 36 23824-0036) (434) 292-4265

Bon Air St Michael Episcopal Church **P** (261) §
2040 McRae Rd 23235 (Mail to: 2040 McRae
Rd 23235) Jeunee Godsey (804) 272-0992

Bracey St Mark Episcopal Church **M** (30) 3906
Highway Nine O Three 23919-9997 (Mail to:
James A Mckeathern PO Box 227 23919-0227)
(434) 689-2219

Buckingham Emmanuel Episcopal Church **M**
(18) 7825 Howardsville Rd 23921-2459 (Mail
to: 637 Williams Rd 24562-4115) Halley
Willcox (434) 969-4814

Cape Charles Emmanuel Episcopal Church **M**
(31) 601 Tazewell Ave 23310-0601 (Mail to: PO
Box 601 23310-0601) Robert Coniglio (757)
678-7802

Cartersville St James Episcopal Church **P** (52)
C/O Mr John R Martin 35 Boone Trl 23027-
9630 (Mail to: C/O Mr John R Martin 35
Boone Trl 23027-9630) (804) 375-3019

Chase City St John Episcopal Church **P** (33) 338 E
4th St 23924-1226 (Mail to: 338 E 4th St 23924-
1226) (434) 372-3318

✠ **Chatham** St Marys Chapel **O** 800 Chatham Hall
Cir 24531-3084 (Mail to: 800 Chatham Hall
Cir 24531-3084) (757) 489-9096

Chatham Emmanuel Episcopal Church **P** (65)
66 North Main Street 24531-0026 (Mail to:
PO Box 26 24531-0026) Rebecca Crites (434)
432-0316

Chesapeake St Bride Episcopal Church **P** (118)
621 Sparrow Rd 23325-2504 (Mail to: 621
Sparrow Rd 23325-2504) (757) 420-7033

Chesapeake St Thomas Episcopal Church **P** (594)
§ 233 Mann Dr 23322-5215 (Mail to: 233 Mann
Dr 23322-5215) James Young (757) 547-4662

Chesapeake Church of the Messiah **M** 816
Kempsville Rd 23320-5002 (Mail to: 816
Kempsville Rd 23320-5002) (757) 436-2545

Chester Saint John's Church **P** (336) 12201
Richmond St 23831-4440 (Mail to: PO Box
3886 23831-8471) Raymond Custer (804) 748-
2182

Chesterfield St Matthew Episcopal Church **P**
(175) 9300 Shawonodasee Rd 23832-6330
(Mail to: PO Box 2187 23832-9111) (804) 790-
1211

✠ **Claremont** Ritchie Memorial Episcopal Church
O 115 Virginian 23899 (Mail to: PO Box 27
23899-0027) (804) 866-8629

Clarksville St Timothy Episcopal Church **P** (100)
111 6th St 23927-9285 (Mail to: 111 6th St
23927-9285) Susan Grimm (434) 374-8611

Colonial Heights St Michael Episcopal Church **P**
(303) § 501 Old Town Dr 23834-1734 (Mail to:
501 Old Town Dr 23834-1734) (804) 526-1790

Courtland St Luke Episcopal Church **M** (38)
22430 Main St 23837-1027 (Mail to: PO Box
156 23837-0156) (757) 653-2442

Danville Christ Episcopal Church **P** (174) 9
Ridgecrest Dr 24540-0115 (Mail to: PO Box
10355 24543-5006) Cleon Ross (434) 836-2060

Danville Church of the Epiphany **P** (291) 781 Main St 24541-1803 (Mail to: 115 Jefferson Ave 24541-1921) Jon Anderson (434) 792-4321

Disputanta Brandon Episcopal Church **P** (34) 18706 James River Dr 23842-9045 (Mail to: 18706 James River Dr 23842-9045) Macon Walton (757) 866-8977

Drakes Branch Grace Episcopal Church **M** (5) 250 Proctor St 23937-2936 (Mail to: Attn Susan M Miale Treasurer PO Box 467 23937-0467) (434) 568-5861

Eastville Christ Church **P** (80) 16304 Courthouse Rd 23347 (Mail to: PO Box 367 23347-0367) Robert Johnson

Emporia St James Episcopal Church **M** (41) 609 Halifax St 23847-1305 (Mail to: PO Box 821 23847-0821) (434) 634-5351

Farmville Johns Memorial Episcopal Church **P** (191) 400 High St 23901-1812 (Mail to: 400 High St 23901-1812) Nancy Meck (434) 392-5695

Franklin Emmanuel Episcopal Church **P** (280) 400 High St 23851-1420 (Mail to: PO Box 146 23851-0146) (757) 562-4542

Freeman St Thomas Episcopal Church **M** (58) § 6271 Belfield Rd 23856-2413 (Mail to: PO Box 71 23856-0071) (434) 336-1132

Gretna St Johns Episcopal Church **M** (16) 1357 Hickeys Rd 24557-4689 (Mail to: 1357 Hickeys Rd 24557-4689) (434) 656-1735

Halifax Christ Church **M** (10) 545 Main St 24558 (Mail to: 545 Main St 24558) (434) 476-4421

Halifax Emmanuel Episcopal Church **M** 3120 Mountain Rd 24558-2228 (Mail to: PO Box 905 24558-0905) (434) 476-6696

Halifax St John Episcopal Church **P** (141) § 197 Mountain Rd 24558-2010 (Mail to: PO Box 905 24558-0905) Cleon Ross (434) 476-6696

Hampton Emmanuel Episcopal Church **P** (367) 179 E Mercury Blvd 23669-2461 (Mail to: 179 E Mercury Blvd 23669-2461) Rhonda Wheeler (757) 723-8144

Hampton St Cyprian Episcopal Church **P** (215) 1242 W Queen St 23669-3843 (Mail to: PO Box 65 23669-0065) Ronald Ramsey (757) 723-8253

Hampton St John Church **P** (436) 100 W Queens Way 23669-4014 (Mail to: 100 W Queens Way 23669-4014) Mark Riley Samantha Vincent-Alexander (757) 722-2567

Hampton St Mark Episcopal Church **P** (129) 2605 Cunningham Dr 23666-2370 (Mail to: PO Box 7430 23666-0430) Warren Hicks (757) 826-3515

Hopewell St John Episcopal Church **P** (184) 505 Cedar Ln 23860-1517 (Mail to: 505 Cedar Ln 23860-1517) William Taylor (804) 458-8142

Java St Paul Episcopal Church **M** (9) 13953 Halifax Rd 24565 (Mail to: C/O P Banksdale PO Box 43 24565-0043) (804) 432-3776

Kenbridge Church of St Paul and St Andrew **P** (115) 512 S Broad St 23944-2012 (Mail to: PO Box 248 23944-0248) (434) 676-3448

Lawrenceville St Andrew Episcopal Church **P** (37) 400 Windsor Ave 23868-1202 (Mail to: PO Box 26 23868-0026) (434) 848-3939

Lawrenceville Saint Paul's Memorial Chapel **CC** (76) § 115 James Solomon Russell Dr 23868-1299 (Mail to: PO Box 268 23868-1200) (434) 848-2544

Machipongo Hungars Parish **P** (181) 10107 Bayside Rd 23405-1816 (Mail to: PO Box 367 23347-0367) Harry Crandall Daniel Crockett (757) 678-7837

Mc Kenney Church of the Good Shepherd **P** (61) 7800 Lew Jones 23872 (Mail to: PO Box 357 23872-0357) (804) 478-4280

Midlothian Episcopal Church of the Redeemer **P** (961) 2341 Winterfield Rd 23113-4157 (Mail to: 2341 Winterfield Rd 23113-4157) Robert Marshall (804) 379-8899

Midlothian Manakin Episcopal Church **P** (494) 985 Huguenot Trl 23113-9224 (Mail to: 985 Huguenot Trl 23113-9224) Rebecca Dean Virginia Distanislao Judith Lee (804) 794-6401

Midlothian St Matthias Episcopal Church **P** (667) 11300 W Huguenot Rd 23113-1121 (Mail to: 11300 W Huguenot Rd 23113-1121) Brenda Overfield (804) 272-8588

Newport News St Andrew Episcopal Church **P** (716) § 45 Main St 23601-4011 (Mail to: 45 Main St 23601-4088) Anne Kirchmier Lorna Williams (757) 595-0371

Newport News St Augustine Episcopal Church **P** (160) 2515 Marshall Ave 23607-4605 (Mail to: 2515 Marshall Ave 23607-4605) Terry Edwards (757) 245-4613

Newport News St George Episcopal Church **P** (75) § 15446 Warwick Blvd 23608-1506 (Mail to: 15446 Warwick Blvd 23608-1506) (757) 877-0088

Newport News St Paul Episcopal Church **P** (90) 221 34th St 23607-2903 (Mail to: 221 34th St 23607-2903) Bruce Cheney (757) 247-5086

Newport News St Stephen Episcopal Church **P** (273) 372 Hiden Blvd 23606-2934 (Mail to: 372 Hiden Blvd 23606-2934) (757) 595-5521

Norfolk Christ & St Lukes Epis Church **P** (1340) § 560 W Olney Rd 23507-2135 (Mail to: 560 W Olney Rd 23507-2135) Irwin Lewis Jess Stribling (757) 627-5665

Norfolk Episcopal Church of the Ascension **P** (290) § 405 Talbot Hall Rd 23505-4309 (Mail to: 405 Talbot Hall Rd 23505-4309) Alan Mead Stewart Tabb (757) 423-6715

Norfolk Church of the Epiphany **P** (106) 1530 Lafayette Blvd 23509-1112 (Mail to: 1530 Lafayette Blvd 23509-1112) Julia Ashby (757) 622-7672

Norfolk Church of the Good Shepherd **P** (527) 7400 Hampton Blvd 23505-1775 (Mail to: Attn

Accounting Dept 7400 Hampton Boulevard 23505) James Medley (757) 423-3230

Norfolk Grace Episcopal Church **P** (857) 1400 E Brambleton Ave 23504-4394 (Mail to: PO Box 1003 23501-1003) Harold Cobb (757) 625-2868

Norfolk St Andrew Episcopal Church **P** (458) 1009 W Princess Anne Rd 23507-1219 (Mail to: 1009 W Princess Anne Rd 23507-1219) John Rohrs Joshua Stephens Andrea Wigodsky (757) 622-5530

Norfolk St Paul Episcopal Church **P** (459) § 201 St Pauls Blvd 23510 (Mail to: C/O Judy Best 201 Saint Pauls Blvd 23510-2701) Frank Hennessy (757) 627-4353

Norfolk St Peter's Episcopal Church **P** (542) § 224 S Military Hwy 23502-5231 (Mail to: 224 S Military Hwy 23502-5231) John Eidam (757) 466-9392

Norfolk St Stephen's Episcopal Church **P** (79) 1445 Norview Ave 23513-1552 (Mail to: 1445 Norview Ave 23513-1552) Gwynneth Mudd Carlotta Cochran (757) 855-2788

Norfolk Episcopal Church of the Advent **P** (102) 9620 Sherwood Pl 23503-1723 (Mail to: 9629 Norfolk Ave 23503-1701) Anne Dale (757) 587-0125

North Chesterfield St Barnabas Episcopal Church **P** (113) 5155 Iron Bridge Rd 23234-4703 (Mail to: 5155 Iron Bridge Rd 23234-4703) (804) 275-1648

North Chesterfield St David Episcopal Church **P** (285) § 1801 Camborne Rd 23236-2126 (Mail to: 1801 Camborne Rd 23236-2126) Elizabeth Felicetti (804) 276-4348

North Prince George Merchants Hope Episcopal Church **M** (96) 11500 Merchants Hope Rd 23860-8933 (Mail to: 11500 Merchant Hope Rd 23860-8933) Charles Moore (804) 458-1356

Onancock Holy Trinity Episcopal Church **P** (140) 66 Market St 23417-4224 (Mail to: PO Box 338 23417-0338) Calvin Ford (757) 787-4430

Petersburg Christ & Grace Epis Church **P** (389) 1545 S Sycamore St 23805-1314 (Mail to: 1545 S Sycamore St 23805-1314) Robin Teasley (804) 733-7202

Petersburg St John Episcopal Church **P** (64) 842 W Washington St 23804-1187 (Mail to: 842 W Washington St 23803-3060) (804) 732-8107

Petersburg St Paul's Episcopal Church **P** (323) 110 Union St 23803 (Mail to: PO Box 564 23804-0564) Daniel Greenwood (804) 733-3415

Petersburg St Stephen Episcopal Church **P** (121) 228 Halifax St 23803-6312 (Mail to: 228 Halifax St 23803-6312) Willis Foster (804) 733-6228

Portsmouth Saint Christopher's Episcopal Church **P** (114) 3300 Cedar Ln 23703-4104 (Mail to: 3300 Cedar Ln 23703-4104) Eileen Walsh (757) 484-5155

Portsmouth St James Episcopal Church **M** (118) 928 Effingham St 23704-3438 (Mail to: 928

Effingham St 23704-3438) Frederick Walker (757) 399-7707

Portsmouth St John Episcopal Church **P** (250) 424 Washington St 23704-2435 (Mail to: 424 Washington St 23704-2435) J Derek Harbin (757) 399-4967

Portsmouth Trinity Episcopal Church **P** (434) 500 Court St 23704-3606 (Mail to: 500 Court St 23704-3606) Robert Davenport James Sell Grant Stokes (757) 393-0431

Powhatan St Luke Episcopal Church **P** (252) 2245 Huguenot Trl 23139-4403 (Mail to: 2245 Huguenot Trl 23139-4403) Sandra Kerner (804) 794-6953

Pungoteague St George Episcopal Church **P** (70) 30241 Bobtown Rd 23422 (Mail to: PO Box 540 23301-0540) (757) 787-4892

Richmond Church of the Good Shepherd **P** (347) 4206 Springhill Ave 23225-3345 (Mail to: 4206 Springhill Ave 23225-3345) Ross Wright (804) 233-2278

Smithfield Christ Episcopal Church **P** (141) 111 S Church St 23430-1332 (Mail to: 111 S Church St 23430-1332) Connie Gilman (757) 357-2826

South Boston Trinity Episcopal Church **P** (95) § 520 Yancey St 24592-3322 (Mail to: 520 Yancey St 24592-3323) Timothy Fulop (434) 572-4513

South Hill All Saints Episcopal Church **P** (71) 203 Franklin St 23970-2009 (Mail to: PO Box 58 23970-0058) Terrence Walker (434) 955-2271

South Hill Trinity Episcopal Church **P** (49) 926 Thomason Ln 23970 (Mail to: P O Box 903 Attn: Treasurer 23970-0903) Terrence Walker (434) 447-6533

Suffolk Glebe Episcopal Church **P** (143) § 4400 Nansemond Pkwy 23435-2136 (Mail to: 440 Manesmond Parkway 23435) Ross Keener (757) 538-8842

Suffolk St John Episcopal Church **P** (126) 828 Kings Hwy 23432-1112 (Mail to: C/O Susan Kirkpatrick 828 Kings Hwy 23432-1112) Leslie Ferguson (757) 255-4168

Suffolk St Mark Episcopal Church **P** (74) 142 Tynes St 23434-4625 (Mail to: 142 Tynes St 23434-4625) (757) 934-0830

Suffolk St Paul Episcopal Church **P** (221) 213 North Main Street 23434-4420 (Mail to: 213 Main St 23434-4420) Keith Emerson (757) 539-2478

Surry St Paul Episcopal Church **M** (63) 11891 Rolfe Hwy 23883-2738 (Mail to: PO Box 298 23883-0298) (757) 569-6280

Temperanceville Emmanuel Episcopal Church **M** (70) 26405 Horsey Rd 23442 (Mail to: PO Box 186 23416-0186) (757) 824-5043

Toano Hickory Neck Episcopal Church **P** (509) 8300 Richmond Rd 23168-9206 (Mail to: 8300 Richmond Rd 23168-9206) Jennifer Andrews-Weckerly Charles Bauer (757) 566-0276

Victoria St Luke Episcopal Church **M** (9) C/O Charlie W Allen 601 Mecklenburg Avenue

23974-0437 (Mail to: C/O Cathy Johnson PO Box 437 23974) (434) 676-3432

Virginia Bch Church of the Holy Apostles **P** (114) 1598 Lynnhaven Pkwy 23453-2008 (Mail to: 1593 Lynnhaven Pkwy 23453-2008) Alan Mead (757) 427-0963

Virginia Bch Galilee Episcopal Church **P** (865) § 3928 Pacific Ave 23451-2636 (Mail to: 3928 Pacific Ave 23451-2636) Andrew Buchanan Kathleen Bobbitt Patrick Bush (757) 428-3573

Virginia Bch Good Samaritan Episcopal Church **P** (35) 848 Baker Rd 23462-1035 (Mail to: 848 Baker Rd 23462-1035) Wendy Wilkinson (757) 497-0729

Virginia Bch Old Donation Episcopal Church **P** (973) § 4449 Witchduck Rd 23455-6151 (Mail to: 4449 Witchduck Rd 23455-6151) Robert Randall Ashley Urquidi (757) 497-0563

Virginia Bch St Aidan Episcopal Church **P** (458) 3201 Edinburgh Dr 23452-5803 (Mail to: 3201 Edinburgh Dr 23452-5803) Mark Wilkinson Josephine Taylor (757) 340-6459

Virginia Bch St Francis Episcopal Church **P** (274) 509 S Rosemont Rd 23452-4131 (Mail to: 509 S Rosemont Rd 23452-4131) Conor Alexander (757) 340-6884

Virginia Bch St Simons by the Sea **M** (43) 308 Sandbridge Rd 23456-4522 (Mail to: 312 Pintail Cres 23456-4448) Marni Schneider Dale Hirst (757) 426-5427

Virginia Beach All Saints' Episcopal Church **P** (480) 1969 Woodside Ln 23454-1031 (Mail to: 1969 Woodside Ln 23454-1031) Stanley Sawyer (757) 481-0577

Virginia Beach Eastern Shore Chapel **P** (1109) 2020 Laskin Rd 23454-4208 (Mail to: 2020 Laskin Rd 23454-4208) Julia Messer Cameron Randle (757) 428-6763

Virginia Beach Emmanuel Episcopal Church **P** (824) § 5181 Singleton Way 23462-4241 (Mail to: 5181 Singleton Way 23462-4241) Mary Lacy (757) 499-1271

Warfield St James Episcopal Church **M** (39) 275 Waqua Creek Rd 23889-2048 (Mail to: C/O Mrs Lena G Pierson PO Box 248 23868-0248) (434) 949-7720

Waverly Christ Episcopal Church **M** (27) 203 E Main St 23890-3240 (Mail to: PO Box 928 23890-0928) (804) 834-2393

Williamsburg Bruton Parish Church **HC** (1994) 331 E Duke Of Gloucester St 23185-4251 (Mail to: PO Box 3520 23187-3520) Christopher Epperson Daniel McClain Lauren McDonald Joshua Stephens (757) 229-2891

Williamsburg St Martins Episcopal Church **P** (566) 1333 Jamestown Rd 23185-3335 (Mail to: 1333 Jamestown Rd 23185-3335) Catherine Boyd Elizabeth Green (757) 229-1111

Yorktown Christ the King Church **P** (220) 4109 Big Bethel Rd 23693-3821 (Mail to: 4109 Big Bethel Rd 23693-3821) (757) 865-7227

Yorktown Grace Episcopal Church **P** (687) § 111 Church St 23690-4002 (Mail to: PO Box 123 23690-0123) Carleton Bakkum Jacqueline Soltys (757) 898-3261

DIOCESE OF SOUTHWEST FLORIDA

(PROVINCE IV)

Comprises 12 counties of SW Florida

DIOCESAN OFFICE 8005 25th St E Parrish FL 34219

TEL (941) 556-0315　FAX (941) 556-0321

E-MAIL jnothum@episcopalswfl.org　WEB www.episcopalswfl.org

Previous Bishops–
Francis H Rutledge 1851–1866, John F Young 1867-1885, Edwin G Weed 1886-1924, Wm C Gray 1892-1914, Cameron Mann 1914-1932, John D Wing coadj 1925 Bp 1932-1950, Martin J Bramm suffr 1951-1956, Wm F Moses suffr 1956-1961, Henry I Louttit suffr 1945 coadj 1948 Bp 1951-1969, James L Duncan suffr 1961-1969, Wm L Hargrave suffr 1961-1969 Bp 1970-1975, E Paul Haynes 1975-1988, Rogers S Harris 1989-1997, Telesforo A Issac assist 1991-1996, John B Lipscomb 1997-2007

Bishop—Rt Rev Dabney T Smith (1014) (Dio 15 Sep 07)

Assisting Bishops—Rt Rev J Michael Garrison and Rt Rev Barry R Howe

Chanc TL Tripp Jr; *Cn for Fin & Admin/CFO* AM Vickers; *Archdeacon* Ven Dr KM Moore; *COM Chair* V Rev C Olivero; *Cn for Stew & Pastoral Care* Rev CN Gray; *Cn for Mis & Min* Rev RH Norman; *Dir Yth Min & Prog* GM Randall; *Mis for Church Extension* Rev AM Hymes; *Dir Comm* JG Pollard; *Dir Cong Supp* Rev ME Goodwill; *Ex Dir DaySpring* CJ Odell

Deans: Clearwater V Rev S Robbins-Penniman; *Ft Myers* V Rev AC Cannon III; *St Petersburg* V Rev SB Morris; *Manasota* V Rev CB McCook; *Tampa* V Rev

CE Connelly; *Naples* V Rev ES Cooter; *Venice* V Rev C Olivero

Stand Comm–Cler: Pres C Connelly F Robinson CB McCook EM Sloan ES Cooter; *Lay: VP* RU Stoll MG Duffy M Alford JH Corn

PARISHES, MISSIONS, AND CLERGY

Arcadia Church of St Edmund the Martyr **M** (123) 327 W Hickory St 34266-3905 (Mail to: 327 W Hickory St 34266-3905) James McConnell (863) 494-0485

Boca Grande St Andrews Church **P** (316) 390 Gilchrist Avenue 33921 (Mail to: PO Box 272 33921-0272) Michelle Robertshaw (941) 964-2257

Bonita Springs Saint Mary's Episcopal Church **P** (373) § 9801 Bonita Beach Rd 34135-4628 (Mail to: PO Box 1923 34135-1923) Michael Rowe Barbara Parini Alfred Salt Gail Tomei (239) 992-4343

Bradenton Christ Church **P** (964) 4030 Manatee Ave West 34205-1789 (Mail to: 4030 Manatee Ave W 34205-1789) Gretchen Platt Micheal Sircy (941) 747-3709

Bradenton St George's Episcopal Church **P** (130) 912 63rd Ave W 34207-4849 (Mail to: 912 63rd Ave W 34207-4800) (941) 755-3606

Bradenton St Mary Magdalene **P** (330) 11315 Palmbrush Trail 34202-2938 (Mail to: 11315 Palmbrush Trl 34202-2938) James Hedman (941) 751-5048

Brooksville St John Episcopal Church **P** (173) § 200 S Brooksville Ave 34601-3311 (Mail to: 200 S Brooksville Ave 34601-3311) Kenneth Taber (352) 796-9112

Cape Coral Church of the Epiphany **P** (205) 2507 Del Prado Blvd South 33904-5768 (Mail to: 2507 Del Prado Blvd S 33904-5768) Aubrey Cort Susan Henderson Ryan Wright (239) 574-3200

Clearwater Episcopal Church of the Ascension **P** (985) 701 Orange Ave 33756-5232 (Mail to: 701 Orange Ave 33756-5232) John Hiers Linda Barley Hugh Bell Leo Crawford Norman Howard Daniel Lemley Carol Schwenke William Shiflet (727) 447-3469

Clearwater Epis Ch of Good Samaritan **M** (150) 2165 Ne Coachman Rd 33765-2616 (Mail to: 2165 NE Coachman Road 33765-2616) Brian Beno (727) 461-1717

Clearwater Holy Trinity Episcopal Church **P** (440) § 3200 Mcmullen Booth Rd 33761-2009 (Mail to: 3200 McMullen Booth Road 33761-2009) Randall Hehr (727) 796-5514

Clearwater St Johns Episcopal Church **P** (512) § 1676 South Belcher Rd 33764-6517 (Mail to: 1676 S Belcher Rd 33764-6517) Kathleen Walter (727) 531-6020

Dade City St Marys Episcopal Church **P** (311) Attn Sandra Sartain 37637 Magnolia Ave

33523-3744 (Mail to: C/O Kim Bulmanski 37637 Magnolia Ave 33523-3744) James De Fontaine-Stratton (352) 567-3888

Dunedin Church of the Good Shepherd **P** (227) 639 Edgewater Dr 34698-6916 (Mail to: 639 Edgewater Dr 34698-6916) Sylvia Robbins-Penniman Cynthia Roehl (727) 733-4125

Englewood St Davids Episcopal Church **P** (264) 401 South Broadway 34223-3802 (Mail to: 401 S Broadway 34223-3802) Vickie McDonald Vincent Scotto Micki-Ann Thomas (941) 474-3140

Fort Myers Iona-Hope Episcopal Church **P** (161) 9650 Gladiolus Dr 33908-7616 (Mail to: 9650 Gladiolus Dr 33908-7616) Herman Buchanan John Gamble Margaret Harker Suzanne Post (239) 454-4778

Fort Myers Lamb Of God Episcopal Church **P** (480) § 19691 Cypress View Dr 33967-6217 (Mail to: 19691 Cypress View Dr 33967-6217) (239) 267-3525

Fort Myers St Hilarys Episcopal Church **P** (509) § 5011 Mcgregor Blvd 33901-8840 (Mail to: 5011 McGregor Blvd 33901-8840) Alberry Cannon Cynthia Montooth (239) 936-1000

Fort Myers St Lukes Episcopal Church **P** (846) § 2635 Cleveland Ave 33901-5803 (Mail to: 2635 Cleveland Ave 33901-5803) Philip Read Robert Browning Richard Grady Alan Kelmereit (239) 334-2479

Fort Myers Bch St Raphaels Church **M** (51) 5601 Williams Dr 33931-4031 (Mail to: 5601 Williams Dr 33931-4097) John Adler (239) 463-6057

Holmes Beach Episcopal Church of Annunciation **P** (150) 4408 Gulf Dr 34217-1829 (Mail to: 4408 Gulf Dr 34217-1829) Matthew Grunfeld John Franklin Bruce Gillies Kathlyn Gilpin (941) 778-1638

Hudson Saint Martin's Episcopal Church **P** (283) § 15801 U.S. 19 34667-3602 (Mail to: PO Box 7199 34674-7199) Ronald Kowalski (727) 863-8560

Indian Rk Bc Calvary Episcopal Church **P** (324) 1615 1st St 33785-2809 (Mail to: 1615 1st St 33785-2809) Hugh Bell Michael Day Charles Roberts (727) 595-2374

Labelle The Church of the Good Shepherd **M** (73) 1098 Collingswood Pkwy 33935-2306 (Mail to: 1098 Collingswood Pkwy 33935-2306) Panel Guerrier (863) 675-0385

Largo Resurrection Episcopal Church **M** (41) 10888 126th Ave 33778-2710 (Mail to: 10888 126th Ave 33778-2710) Nathan Speck-Ewer Marcia Tremmel (727) 586-6968

Lehigh Acres St Anselms Church **M** (124) 2201 E 6th Street 33936-4376 (Mail to: 2201 E 6th St 33936-4399) Marcel Algernon (239) 369-1916

Longboat Key All Angels by the Sea **P** (214) 563 Bay Isles Rd 34228-3142 (Mail to: 563 Bay Isles Rd Attn Sandy L Wood 34228-3142) Michael

Durning Frederick Emrich Margaret Gat (941) 383-8161

Marco Island St Mark's Episcopal Church **P** (626) 1101 Collier Blvd 34145-2507 (Mail to: 1101 Collier Blvd 34145-2507) Jessica Babcock Alden Burhoe John Ineson Kathryn Schillreff (239) 394-7242

Naples St Johns Episcopal Church **P** (485) 500 Park Shore Dr 34103-3537 (Mail to: 500 Park Shore Dr 34103-3537) Joseph Maiocco (239) 261-2355

Naples St Monica Episcopal Church **P** (482) 7070 Immokalee Rd 34119-8845 (Mail to: 7070 Immokalee Rd 34119-8845) Eric Cooter (239) 591-4550

Naples St Pauls Episcopal Church **P** (190) 3901 Davis Blvd 34104-5010 (Mail to: 3901 Davis Blvd 34104-5010) Thomas Thoeni Panel Guerrier Wendel Meyer (239) 643-0197

Naples Trinity by the Cove **P** (1416) 553 Galleon Dr 34102-7639 (Mail to: 553 Galleon Dr 34102-7639) Edward Gleason Nicholas Caccese Edward Gleason Jean Hite Stephen Zimmerman (239) 262-6581

New Prt Rchy St Stephens Episcopal Church **P** (219) 5326 Charles St 34652-3906 (Mail to: 5326 Charles St 34652-3906) Walcott Hunter (727) 849-4330

North Fort Myers All Souls Episcopal Church **M** (47) 14640 Cleveland Ave 33903-3806 (Mail to: 14640 Cleveland Ave 33903-3806) Sandra Johnson Christian Maxfield Walter Mycoff Nancy Smith (239) 997-7685

North Port St Nathaniel Episcopal Church **P** (180) 4200 S Biscayne Dr 34287-1626 (Mail to: 4200 S Biscayne Dr 34287-1626) Andrea Hayden Margaret Koor Margaret Koor (941) 426-2520

Osprey Church of the Holy Spirit **P** (109) § 129 S Tamiami Trl 34229-9211 (Mail to: 129 S Tamiami Trl 34229-9211) Michael Todd (941) 966-1924

Palm Harbor St Alfreds Episcopal Church **P** (443) 1601 Curlew Rd 34683-6515 (Mail to: 1601 Curlew Rd 34683-6515) Peter Lane (727) 785-1601

Palmetto St Marys Episcopal Church **P** (212) 1010 24th Ave W 34221-3540 (Mail to: 1010 24th Ave W 34221-3540) William De la Torre Glen Graczyk (941) 722-5292

Pinellas Park St Giles Episcopal Church **P** (342) 8271 52nd St 33781-1518 (Mail to: 8271 52nd St 33781-1558) Hipolito Fernandez-Reina (727) 544-6856

Plant City St Peters Episcopal Church **P** (562) 302 N. Carey St. 33563-4316 (Mail to: 302 Carey Street 33563) (813) 752-5061

Pt Charlotte Saint James Episcopal Church **P** (448) 1365 Viscaya Dr 33952-2519 (Mail to: 1365 Viscaya Dr 33952-2519) Arthur Lee Cesar Olivero Cesar Olivero (941) 627-4000

Punta Gorda Church of the Good Shepherd **P** (525) § 401 W Henry St 33950-5905 (Mail to: 401 W Henry St 33950-5905) Roy Tuff Jane Kelly Patricia Powers (941) 639-2757

Safety Harbor Church of the Holy Spirit **P** (131) 601 Phillippe Pkwy 34695-3148 (Mail to: 601 Phillippe Pkwy 34695-3148) Raynald Bonoan (727) 725-4726

Sanibel Church of Saint Michael & All Angels Episcopal Church **P** (327) 2304 Periwinkle Way 33957-3209 (Mail to: 2304 Periwinkle Way 33957-3209) Ellen Sloan Paul Goddard Alan Kelmereit Anne Kimball Douglass Lind (239) 472-2173

Sarasota Church of the Nativity **P** (380) 5900 Lockwood Ridge Rd 34243-2523 (Mail to: 5900 Lockwood Ridge Rd 34243-2523) Charles Mann Rosalind Hall (941) 355-3262

Sarasota Church of the Redeemer **P** (1976) 222 S Palm Ave 34236-6727 (Mail to: 222 S Palm Ave 34236-6799) Fredrick Robinson Mario Castro Arthur Cheney Charleston Wilson Christian Wood (941) 955-4263

Sarasota Saint Boniface Church **P** (883) § 5615 Midnight Pass Rd 34242-1721 (Mail to: 5615 Midnight Pass Rd 34242-1721) John Chrisman Jonathan Evans Wayne Farrell Elisa Hansen Ralph Mcgimpsey (941) 349-5616

Sarasota St Margaret of Scotland Church **P** (103) 8700 State Road 72 34241-9578 (Mail to: 8700 State Road 72 34241-9578) Carla McCook (941) 925-2525

Sarasota St Wilfred Episcopal Church **P** (199) 3773 Wilkinson Rd 34233-3607 (Mail to: 3773 Wilkinson Rd 34233-3608) Virginia Herring (941) 924-7436

Seminole St Anne of Grace Church **M** (335) 6650 113th St North 33772-6214 (Mail to: 6650 113th St 33772-6214) Robert Crow Pamela Milhan (727) 392-4483

Spring Hill St Andrews Episcopal Church **P** (383) § 2301 Deltona Blvd 34606 (Mail to: PO Box 5026 34611-5026) Lance Wallace Elaine Cole Donald Lillpopp Frederick Scharf Ludwig Wallner (352) 683-2010

St James City St Johns Episcopal Church **M** (60) 7771 Stringfellow Rd 33956-2805 (Mail to: 7771 Stringfellow Rd 33956-2805) Aubrey Cort Susan Henderson (239) 283-1820

St Petersburg St Albans Episcopal Church **P** (157) 330 85th Ave 33706-1525 (Mail to: 330 85th Ave 33706-1546) Georgene Conner Muriel deBussy (727) 360-8406

St Petersburg St Augustine's Episcopal Church **P** (83) § 2920 26th Ave South 33712-3328 (Mail to: 2920 26th Ave S 33712-3328) Mack Bauknight Josefa Rose (727) 867-6774

St Petersburg St Bartholomews Episcopal Church **P** (298) § 3747 34th St South 33711-3836 (Mail to: 3747 34th St S 33711-3836) William Burkett Alfred Montalto Lucien Watkins (727) 867-7015

St Petersburg St Matthews Church **M** (78) 738 Pinellas Point Dr S 33705-6255 (Mail to: 738 Pinellas Point Dr S 33705-6255) Harry Parsell Kevin Mort (727) 866-2187

St Petersburg St Thomas Episcopal Church **P** (1116) 1200 Snell Isle Blvd NE 33704-3036 (Mail to: 1200 Snell Isle Blvd NE 33704-3036) Ryan Whitley Martha Goodwill John Suhar (727) 896-9641

St Petersburg St Vincents Episcopal Church **P** (303) § 5441 Ninth Ave 33710-6546 (Mail to: 5441 9th Ave 33710-6599) Alexander Andujar Richard Earle Chester Trow (727) 321-5086

St. Petersburg St Peters Episcopal Cathedral **O** (915) 140 4th St 33701-3807 (Mail to: PO Box 1581 33731-1581) Earl Beshears Ronald Brokaw Katherine Churchwell Peter Fleming Stephen Morris Henry Robinson Samuel Tallman Thomas Williams (727) 822-4173

St. Petersburg St Bede Episcopal Church **P** (162) 2500 16th St 33704-3132 (Mail to: 2500 16th St 33704-3132) Marcus Crim Jonathan Percival (727) 823-7649

Sun City Center St John the Divine Episcopal Church **P** (329) 1015 Del Webb East 33573 (Mail to: 1015 E Del Webb Blvd 33573-6673) Leewin Miller Kevin Warner (813) 633-3970

Tampa Grace Episcopal Church **P** (478) 15102 Amberly Dr 33647-1618 (Mail to: 15102 Amberly Dr 33647-1618) Benjamin Twinamaani Lynn Grinnell (813) 971-8484

Tampa St Andrews Episcopal Church **P** (889) 509 E Twiggs St 33602-3916 (Mail to: 509 E Twiggs St 33602-3934) John Reese (813) 221-2035

Tampa St Chads Episcopal Church **M** (122) 5609 Albany Ave 33603-1005 (Mail to: 5609 Albany Ave 33603-1005) (813) 872-7545

Tampa St Clement's Church **P** (228) 706 W 113th Ave 33612-5605 (Mail to: 706 W 113th Ave 33612-5605) Andrew Heyes (813) 932-6204

Tampa St Francis Episcopal Church **M** (234) 912 E Sligh Ave 33604-5636 (Mail to: PO Box 9332 33674-9332) Livan Echazabal (813) 238-1098

Tampa St James House of Prayer **P** (161) § 2708 Central Ave 33602-1602 (Mail to: 2708 Central Ave 33602-1699) (813) 223-6090

Tampa Saint Mark's Episcopal Church Of Tampa **P** (225) 13312 Cain Rd 33625-4004 (Mail to: 13312 Cain Rd 33625-4004) Robert Douglas (813) 962-3089

Tampa St Marys Episcopal Church **P** (300) § 4311 W San Miguel St 33629-5623 (Mail to: 4311 W San Miguel St 33629-5691) Eric Kahl (813) 251-1660

Tampa St Johns Episcopal Church **P** (1667) 906 S Orleans Ave 33606-2941 (Mail to: 906 S Orleans Ave 33606-2941) Chase Ackerman Robert Baker Charles Connelly Kathleen Moore (813) 259-1570

Tarpon Spgs All Saints Episcopal Church **P** (286) 1700 Keystone Rd 34688-4928 (Mail to: 1700 Keystone Rd 34688-4928) Robert Kinney Robert Kinney Janet Tunnell (727) 937-3881

Temple Terrace St Catherine of Alexandria Ch **P** (479) 502 Druid Hills Rd 33617-3853 (Mail to: 502 Druid Hills Rd 33617-3853) Susan Latimer Ralph Campbell Allen Farabee Allen Farabee (813) 988-6483

Valrico Church Of the Holy Innocents **P** (596) 604 Valrico Rd 33594 (Mail to: 604 Valrico Rd 33594-6874) Bryan O'Carroll Denise Healy Stephen Rudacille (813) 689-3130

Venice St Marks Episcopal Church **P** (711) § 513 Nassau St South 34285-2816 (Mail to: 513 Nassau St S 34285-2816) James Puryear Oliver Backhaus Leonard Brusso John Lawrence Judith Roberts Margaret Sullivan Joyce Treppa John Warfel (941) 488-7714

Venice The Episcopal Church Of The Good Shepherd **P** (346) 1115 Center Rd 34292-3812 (Mail to: 1115 Center Rd 34292-3812) Gary Wilde Michael Kitt Robert Miller (941) 497-7286

Zephyrhills St Elizabeths Episcopal Church **P** (111) § 5855 16th St 33542-3761 (Mail to: 5855 16th St 33542-3761) Edward Rich Hugh Wilkes (813) 782-1202

DIOCESE OF SOUTHWESTERN VIRGINIA

(PROVINCE III)

Comprises 32 Southwestern VA counties

DIOCESAN OFFICE 1002 1st St. SW Roanoke VA 24016 (MAIL: Box 2279 Roanoke VA 24009-2279)

TEL (540) 342-6797, (800) 346-7982   FAX (540) 343-9114

E-MAIL mfurlow@dioswva.org   WEB www.dioswva.org

Previous Bishops—
Robt C Jett 1920-38, Henry D Phillips 1938-54, Wm H Marmion 1954-79, A Heath Light 1979-96, F Neff Powell 1996-2013

Bishop—Rt Rev Mark Allen Bourlakas (1077) (Dio 20 Jul 2013)

COO Cn Mark Furlow; *Treas* J Hall 614 Academy Salem 24153; *Chanc* M Loftis PO Box 14125 Roanoke VA 24038; *Reg* K Kroeger PO Box 2279 Roanoke VA 24009; *Hist* Rev S West PO Box 164 Blacksburg VA 24063; *Ecum* Rev SR Stanley 1826 Mount Vernon Road SW Roanoke VA 24015

Stand Comm—Cler: Pres S West E Long E Edmondson; *Lay:* J Ackley J Kappes D Williams

PARISHES, MISSIONS, AND CLERGY

Abingdon Church of St Thomas **P** (151) Attn Elizabeth K Hurley 124 E Main St 24210-2808 (Mail to: Attn: Treasurer 124 E Main St 24210-2808) Boyd Evans (276) 628-3606

Altavista St Peters Episcopal Church **P** (37) 1010 Broad St 24517-1806 (Mail to: PO Box 207 24517-0207) (434) 369-5291

Amherst Ascension Episcopal Church **P** (38) 253 S. Main St 24521-0810 (Mail to: PO Box 810 24521-0810) (434) 946-5498

Amherst Saint Mark's Church **P** (42) 670 Patrick Henry Hwy 24521-3982 (Mail to: PO Box 36 24533-0036) Francis Crittenden David Perkins (434) 946-1121

Amherst St Pauls Episcopal Mission **M** (155) 2009 Kenmore Road 24521-3239 (Mail to: PO Box 2279 24009-2279) (434) 946-2531

Arrington Trinity Episcopal Church **P** (37) 475 Oak Ridge Rd 22922-2610 (Mail to: 475 Oak Ridge Rd 22922-2610) (434) 263-5721

Bedford St Johns Episcopal Church **P** (207) 314 Bridge St 24523-1928 (Mail to: 314 Bridge St 24523-1928) Francis Brown (540) 586-9582

Bedford St Thomas Episcopal Church **M** (21) 9575 Big ISland Highway 24523 (Mail to: C/O Edward Marshall PO Box 695 24523-0695) (540) 586-4768

Big Stone Gap Christ Episcopal Church **P** (44) 106 Clinton Avenue PO Box 778 24219 (Mail to: PO Box 778 24219-0778) Robert Moore (276) 523-0401

Blacksburg Christ Episcopal Church **P** (550) 120 Church St Ne 24060-3923 (Mail to: PO Box 164 24063-0164) Scott West (540) 552-2411

Blue Grass Epis Church of the Good Shepherd **P** (34) 3678 Blue Grass Valley Rd 24413-0007 (Mail to: PO Box 7 24413-0007) Robert Gilman (540) 474-2175

Bluefield St Marys Episcopal Church **P** (69) 30 Logan St 24605-1404 (Mail to: PO Box 990 24605-0990) (276) 322-0487

Bristol Emmanuel Episcopal Church **P** (237) 700 Cumberland Street 24201 (Mail to: PO Box 1376 24203-1376) Joe Dunagan (276) 669-9488

Buchanan Trinity Episcopal Church **P** (27) 19460 Main St 24066-2701 (Mail to: PO Box 459 24066-0459) (540) 254-1574

Buena Vista Christ Episcopal Church **P** (27) 2246 Walnut Ave 24416-2702 (Mail to: 2246 Walnut Ave 24416-2702) (540) 261-3929

Callaway St Peters Episcopal Church **P** (109) 65 Rock Ridge Rd 24067-5701 (Mail to: 65 Rock Ridge Rd 24067-5701) John Heck (540) 483-5370

Christiansbrg St Thomas Episcopal Church **P** (238) 103 E Main St 24073-3032 (Mail to: 103 E Main St 24073-3032) Phyllis Spiegel Mark Frazier (540) 382-4365

Clifton Forge St Andrews Episcopal Church **P** (11) 516 Mccormick Blvd 24422-1137 (Mail to: 516 McCormick Blvd 24422-1137) (540) 863-3041

✠ **Covington** All Saints Chapel **O** 414 Boys' Home Rd 24426-5539 (Mail to: 414 Boys' Home Rd 24426-5539) Connie Gilman (540) 965-7700

Covington Emmanuel Episcopal Church **P** (41) 138 Maple Ave 24426-1545 (Mail to: PO Box 709 24426-0709) Lebaron Taylor (540) 965-5626

Fincastle St Marks Episcopal Church **P** (123) 111 S Roanoke St 24090 (Mail to: PO Box 277 24090-0277) George Logan (540) 473-2370

Forest St Stephens Episcopal Church **P** (106) 1695 Perrowville Rd 24551-2258 (Mail to: 1695 Perrowville Rd 24551-2258) Kathryn Bast (434) 525-5511

Galax Church of the Good Shepherd **P** (71) 9441 Grayson Parkway 24333 (Mail to: PO Box 1266 24333-1266) (276) 236-4957

Glasgow Saint John's Episcopal Church **M** (24) 1002 Blue Ridge Rd 24555-2160 (Mail to: C/O Elaine S Massie PO Box 507 24555-0607) (540) 258-2959

Hot Springs St Lukes Episcopal Church **P** (93) Rte 220 24445 (Mail to: Attn Treasurer PO Box 779 24445-0779) Russell Cox Jerry Heidel (540) 839-2279

Lexington Grace Episcopal Church **P** (426) 123 W Washington St 24450-2122 (Mail to: 123 W Washington St 24450-2122) Robert Crewdson James Hubbard (540) 463-4981

Lynchburg Grace Memorial Episcopal Church **P** (226) 1021 New Hampshire Ave 24502-1216 (Mail to: 1021 New Hampshire Ave 24502-1216) Alan Cowart (434) 846-3156

Lynchburg St Johns Episcopal Church **P** (1256) § 200 Boston Ave 24503-0123 (Mail to: PO Box 3123 24503-0123) Kim Glenn (434) 528-1138

Lynchburg St Pauls Episcopal Church **P** (510) 7th & Clay St 24504 (Mail to: 605 Clay St 24504-2460) William Bumgarner Diane Vie Todd Vie (434) 845-7301

Lynchburg Trinity Episcopal Church **P** (128) 104 Walnut Hollow Rd. 24503-4213 (Mail to: PO Box 3278 24503-0278) Nina Salmon (434) 384-2257

Marion Christ Episcopal Church **P** (103) 401 W Main St 24354-2417 (Mail to: 401 W Main St 24354-2417) Emily Edmondson (276) 783-8050

Martinsville Christ Episcopal Church **P** (287) 321 E. Church Street 24112-2981 (Mail to: 311 E Church St 24112-2981) Nicholas Hull (276) 632-2896

Martinsville St Pauls Episcopal Church **M** (27) 904 Fayette St 24112-3432 (Mail to: 904 West Fayette 24112) Gene Anderson (276) 790-2612

Massies Mill Grace Episcopal Church **P** (50) 1934 Crabtree Falls Hwy 22967-2008 (Mail to: PO Box 762 22958-0762) Marion Kanour (434) 277-8926

Moneta Trinity Ecumenical Parish **P** (118) 40 Lakemount Dr 24121-1915 (Mail to: 40 Lakemount Dr 24121-1915) (540) 721-4330

Monroe St Lukes Episcopal Church **M** (5) 3788 Buffalo Springs Tpke 24574-3104 (Mail to: C/O Mr Thomas C Wallace Iv PO Box 688 24572-0688) (434) 845-3446

Norton All Saints Episcopal Church **P** (64) Virginia Ave & 11th St 24273 (Mail to: PO Box 227 24273-0227) (276) 679-3185

Pearisburg Christ Episcopal Church **P** (39) 529 Wenonah Ave. 24134 (Mail to: PO Box 360 24134-0360) Sarah Morris (540) 921-3033

Pocahontas Christ Episcopal Church **M** (23) Water St 24635-0322 (Mail to: PO Box 322 24635-0322) (276) 322-0487

Pulaski Christ Episcopal Church **P** (76) 144 Washington Ave 24301-0975 (Mail to: PO Box 975 24301-0975) (540) 980-2413

Radford Grace Episcopal Church **P** (150) 210 4th St 24141-1523 (Mail to: 210 4th St 24141-1523) Katherine Dunagan Sarah Morris (540) 639-3494

Richlands Trinity Episcopal Church **P** (46) 107 Hill Creek Rd 24641-2032 (Mail to: 107 Hill Creek Rd 24641-2032) (276) 963-9600

Roanoke Christ Episcopal Church **P** (408) 1101 Franklin Rd Sw 24016-4309 (Mail to: 1101 Franklin Rd SW 24016-4397) Alexander MacPhail Melissa Hays-Smith (540) 343-0159

Roanoke St Elizabeths Episcopal Church **P** (73) 2339 Grandin Rd Sw 24015-3916 (Mail to: PO Box 4706 24015-0706) Karin MacPhail (540) 774-5183

Roanoke St James Episcopal Church **P** (228) 4515 Delray St Nw 24012-2209 (Mail to: 4515 Delray St NW 24012-2209) Susan Bentley William Eanes (540) 366-4157

Roanoke St John Episcopal Church **P** (1672) 1 Mountain Ave Sw 24016-5109 (Mail to: PO Box 257 24002-0257) Whitney Burton Eric Long Mary Mackin (540) 343-9341

Rocky Mount Trinity Episcopal Church **P** (160) 15 East Church Street 24151 (Mail to: PO Box 527 24151) David Taylor (540) 483-5038

Saint Paul St Marks Episcopal Church **P** (23) Broad And Fifth Ave 24283 (Mail to: PO Box 1138 24283-1138) (276) 679-3185

Salem St Pauls Episcopal Church **P** (477) § 42 E Main St 24153-3807 (Mail to: 42 E Main St 24153-3807) David Dixon (540) 389-9307

Saltville St Pauls Episcopal Church **M** (15) 370 E Main St 24370-2808 (Mail to: Attn Helen W Barbrow PO Box 235 24370-0235) (276) 791-3175

Staunton Good Shepherd Folly Mills **M** (44) 809 Lee Jackson Hwy 24401-5510 (Mail to: 809 Lee Jackson Hwy 24401-5510) (540) 377-9449

Staunton Emmanuel Episcopal Church **P** (192) 300 W Frederick St 24401-3328 (Mail to: 300 W Frederick St 24401-3328) Shelby Owen (540) 886-8172

Staunton Trinity Episcopal Church **P** (482) 214 W Beverley St 24401-4205 (Mail to: PO Box 208 24402-0208) Paul Nancarrow (540) 886-9132

Tazewell Stras Memorial Epis Church **P** (67) 211 Central Ave 24651-1005 (Mail to: PO Box 563 24651-0563) (540) 988-2889

Waynesboro St Johns Episcopal Church **P** (398) 473 S Wayne Ave 22980-4739 (Mail to: PO Box 945 22980-0693) Benjamin Badgett (540) 942-4136

Wytheville St John's Episcopal Church **P** (209) § 275 E Main St 24382-2323 (Mail to: 275 E Main St 24382-2323) Thomas Rambo (276) 228-2562

DIOCESE OF SPOKANE
(PROVINCE VIII)
Comprises Eastern Washington and North Idaho
DIOCESAN OFFICE 245 E 13th Ave Spokane WA 99202-1114
TEL (509) 624-3191 FAX (509) 747-0049
E-MAIL malloryw@spokanediocese.org WEB www.spokanediocese.org

Previous Bishops—
Lemuel H Wells 1892-1913, Herman Page 1915-23, Edward M Cross 1924-54, Russell S Hubbard m 1954 dio 1964-67, John R Wyatt 1967-78, Leigh A Wallace Jr 1979-90, Frank J Terry coadj 1990-91 Bp 91-99, James E Waggoner Jr 2000-17

Bishop — Gretchen M Rehberg (1099) (Dio 18 Mar 2017)

Cn to Ord Rev Cn K Schomburg; *Trans Min* Rev Cn S Cleveley; *Sec Conv* Rev J Neuberger; *Treas* G Durrie; *Chanc* S Miller of J Scott Miller, PS 201 W No River Dr Ste 500 Spokane WA 99201; *Arch and Reg* G Lund; *Arch dcn* Rev T Nitz; *Trustee Bd Chair Foundation* M Henneberry; *Fin Off* L Boss; *B Exec Asst* M Ware; *COM Chair* Rev Cn Robin Biffle

Stand Comm The Rev MaryBeth Rivetti

PARISHES, MISSIONS, AND CLERGY

Bonners Ferr St Marys Church **Chapel** (23) 6633 Buchanan St 83805-8616 (Mail to: 6633 Buchanan St 83805-8616) (208) 267-3202

Cashmere St James Episcopal Church **M** (68) 222 Cottage Ave 98815-1004 (Mail to: PO Box 351 98815-0351) Carol Forhan Robert Hasseries (509) 782-1590

Chelan St Andrews Episcopal Church **P** (69) 120 East Wooden Ave 98816 (Mail to: PO Box 1226 98816-1226) Linda Mayer (509) 682-2851

Cheney St Pauls Episcopal Church **M** (38) 625 C St 99004-1747 (Mail to: 625 C St 99004-1747) Achilles Balabanis Judith Soule (509) 235-6150

Coeur D Alene St Lukes Episcopal Church **P** (293) 501 E Wallace Ave 83814-2955 (Mail to: 501 E Wallace Ave 83814-2955) David Gortner Robert Runkle (208) 664-5533

Dayton Grace Episcopal Church **M** (17) 301 S 3rd St 99328-1332 (Mail to: 301 S 3rd St 99328-1332) (509) 382-4795

Dover Holy Spirit Episcopal Church **M** (57) 55 Rocky Point Road 83825 (Mail to: 217 Cedar St PMB 336 83864-1410) Marjorie Stanley (208) 263-7078

Ellensburg Grace Episcopal Church **P** (158) 1201 B Street 98926-2578 (Mail to: PO Box 644 98926-1918) Anthony Green Christianne McKee (509) 962-2951

Ephrata St John the Baptist Epis Church **M** (68) 701 1st Ave Nw 98823-1504 (Mail to: PO Box 295 98823-0295) Anthony Green (509) 754-4949

Grand Coulee St Dunstans Episcopal Church **M** (48) 328 Grand Coulee E 99133 (Mail to: 326 E Grand Coulee Ave 99133-9755) (509) 989-9672

Grangeville Holy Trinity Episcopal Church **M** (32) 311 S Hall St 83530-2011 (Mail to: 311 S Hall St 83530-2011) Chris Hagenbuch (208) 451-0645

Kennewick St Paul's Episcopal Mission **P** (357) 1609 W 10th Ave 99336-5200 (Mail to: PO Box 6857 99336-0529) Marilynn Yule (509) 582-8365

Lewiston Church of the Nativity **P** (112) 731 8th St 83501-2626 (Mail to: 731 8th St 83501-2626) Mary Ayers (208) 743-9121

Moscow St Marks Episcopal Church **P** (134) 111 S Jefferson St 83843-2859 (Mail to: 111 S Jefferson St 83843-2859) Robin Biffle (208) 882-2022

Moses Lake St Martins Episcopal Church **P** (88) 416 E Nelson Rd 98837-2383 (Mail to: 416 E Nelson Rd 98837-2383) Gayle Gaither (509) 765-3369

Omak St Annes Episcopal Church **M** (72) 639 W Ridge Dr 98841-3251 (Mail to: PO Box 3251 98841-3251) Stanalee Wright (509) 826-5815

Oroville Trinity Episcopal Church **M** (103) 604 Central Ave. 98844-0186 (Mail to: PO Box 1270 98844-1270) (509) 476-2230

Pomeroy St Peters Church **P** (39) 710 High St 99347 (Mail to: PO Box 490 99347-0490) William Totten (509) 843-1871

Prosser St Matthews Episcopal Church **M** (61) 317 7th St 99350-1180 (Mail to: PO Box 828 99350-0828) (509) 830-6318

Pullman Saint James **P** (172) § 1410 Ne Stadium Way 99163-3841 (Mail to: 1410 NE Stadium Way 99163-4619) Dianne Lowe Theodore Nitz Wilhelmina Sarai-Clark Linda Young (509) 332-1742

Republic Episcopal Church of the Redeemer **M** (6) 3 Klondike Rd 99166-9701 (Mail to: PO Box 342 99166-0342) (509) 775-3096

Richland All Saints Episcopal Church **P** (500) 1322 Kimball Ave 99354-3206 (Mail to: 1322 Kimball Ave 99354-3206) Jane Schmoetzer (509) 943-1169

South Cle Elum Church of the Resurrection **M** (82) Kelly Clift PO Box 23 98943-0023 (Mail to: PO Box 701 98941-0701) (509) 649-2283

✠ **Spokane** Cathedral of St John the Evangelist **O** (650) 127 E 12th Ave 99202-1105 (Mail to: C/O Rosie Banta 127 E 12th Ave 99202-1105) Heather VanDeventer (509) 838-4277

Spokane St Andrews Episcopal Church **P** (145) 2404 Howard St 99205-3215 (Mail to: 2404 Howard St 99205-3215) (509) 325-5252

Spokane Saint David's Church **P** (373) 7315 Wall St 99208-6102 (Mail to: PO Box 18917 99228-0917) (509) 466-3100

Spokane St Stephens Episcopal Church **P** (268) 5720 S Perry St 99223-6349 (Mail to: 5720 S Perry St 99223-6349) William Osborne Elaine Pitzer (509) 448-2255

Spokane West Central Episcopal Mission **M** (60) § 245E 13th AVE 99202 (Mail to: PO Box 8508 99203-0508) (509) 326-6471

Sunnyside Holy Trinity Episcopal Church **P** (117) 327 E Edison Ave 98944-1435 (Mail to: 327 E Edison Ave 98944-1435) Peter Kalunian (509) 837-4727

Veradale Church of the Resurrection **P** (196) 15319 E 8th Ave 99037-8828 (Mail to: PO Box

14771 99214-0771) Linda Bartholomew (509) 926-6450

Walla Walla Saint Paul's Church **P** (502) 323 Catherine St 99362-3021 (Mail to: 323 Catherine St 99362-3082) David Sibley Ernest Campbell Robert Kaye (509) 529-1083

Wenatchee St Luke's Episcopal Church **P** (150) § 428 King St 98801-2846 (Mail to: PO Box 1642 98807-1642) Frances Twiggs (509) 662-5635

Yakima St Michaels Episcopal Church **P** (67) 5 S Naches Ave 98901-2726 (Mail to: 5 S Naches Ave 98901-2726) Frank Cowell David Hacker (509) 453-4881

Yakima St Timothys Episcopal Church **P** (473) 4105 Richey Rd 98908-2662 (Mail to: 4105 Richey Rd 98908-2662) (509) 966-7370

Zillah Christ Episcopal Church **M** (28) Second & 4th 98953 (Mail to: PO Box 356 98953-0356) Joan Dahl Elisabeth Kuhr (509) 829-3020

DIOCESE OF SPRINGFIELD
(PROVINCE V)
Comprises 60 counties of central and southern Illinois
DIOCESAN CENTER 821 S Second St Springfield IL 62704
TEL (217) 525-1876   FAX (217) 525-1877
E-MAIL diocese@episcopalspringfield.org   WEB www.episcopalspringfield.org

Previous Bishops—
Geo F Seymour 1878-1906, Chas R Hale coadj 1892-1900, Edward W Osborne coadj 1904 Bp 1906-16, Granville H Sherwood 1917-23, John C White 1924-47, Richard T Loring 1947-48, Chas A Clough 1948-61, Albert A Chambers 1962-72, Albert W Hillestad 1972-81, Donald M Hultstrand 1982-91, Peter H Beckwith 1992-2010

Bishop—The Rt Rev Daniel H Martins (Dio 19 March 2011)

Archdcn The Ven SW Denney; *V Pres* The Very Rev RA Swan; *Sec* The Rev GW Howard III; *Asst Sec* Rev SL Howard; *Treas* R Matthews; *Chanc* KJ Babb; *Trustee* D Monty; *COM* The Rev JR Henry; *ECW* C King; *Dio Admin* S Spring; *Depts—Fin* C Rice; *Audit* The Rev Dr TW Langford; *Miss* R Winn & G Smith

Stand Comm—Cler: Pres RA Swan BH Maynard ME Evans BD Hankinson *Lay:* C McCrary J Patterson K Babb H Williams

Deans—Darrow IC Wetmore; *Eastern* BD Hankinson; *Hale* SL Black; *Northern* ME Evans; *Northeastern* SD Ferrell; *Northwestern* RA Swan

PARISHES, MISSIONS, AND CLERGY

Albion St Johns Episcopal Church **M** (15) 20 E Cherry St 62806-1302 (Mail to: 146 7th St 62806-1043) George Howard (618) 242-6594

Alton St Pauls and Trinity Chapel **P** (352) § 10 E 3rd St 62002-6201 (Mail to: 10 E 3rd St 62002-6201) Cynthia Sever (618) 465-9149

Alton Trinity Chapel **SC** 1901 State St 62002-6201 (Mail to: 10 E 3rd St 62002-6201) (618) 465-9149

Belleville St Georges Episcopal Church **P** (539) § 105 E D St 62220-1205 (Mail to: 105 E D St 62220-1295) Dale Coleman (618) 233-6320

Bloomington St Matthews Episcopal Church **P** (513) § 1920 E Oakland Ave 61701-5755 (Mail to: 1920 E Oakland Ave 61701-5798) Bruce DeGooyer David Halt Gregory Leighton (309) 662-4646

Cairo Church Of The Redeemer **M** (8) 600 Washington Ave 62914-2229 (Mail to: C/O Diocese of Springfield 821 S 2nd St 62704-2601) James Muriuki (618) 734-1443

Carbondale St Andrews Episcopal Church **P** (72) § 402 W Mill St 62901-2728 (Mail to: 402 W Mill St 62901-2728) Kathryn Jeffrey (618) 529-4316

Carlinville St Pauls Episcopal Church **P** (48) § 415 S Broad St 62626-2111 (Mail to: 415 S Broad St 62626-2111) John Henry (217) 854-6431

Centralia St Johns Episcopal Church **M** (21) 700 E Broadway 62801-3261 (Mail to: Attn Craig Mattson PO Box 96 62801) Sylvia Howard Gene Tucker (618) 532-3767

Champaign Chapel Of Saint John The Divine **P** (217) § 1011 S Wright St 61820-6249 (Mail to: 1011 S Wright St 61820-6249) Sean Ferrell (217) 344-1924

Champaign Emmanuel Memorial Episcopal Church **P** (407) 102 State St 61820-3908 (Mail to: 208 W University Ave 61820-3997) Beth Maynard Caleb Roberts (217) 352-9827

Chesterfield St Peters Episcopal Church **M** 110 East Lincoln Ave 62630 (Mail to: C/O St Paul's Church 415 S Broad St 62626-2111) (217) 854-6431

Danville Church of the Holy Trinity **P** (154) § 308 Vermilion St 61832-4770 (Mail to: 308 Vermilion St 61832-4770) (217) 442-3498

Decatur St Johns Episcopal Church **P** (232) § 130 W Eldorado St 62522-2111 (Mail to: 130 W Eldorado St 62522-2111) Richard Swan (217) 428-4461

Edwardsville St Andrews Episcopal Church **P** (227) 406 Hillsboro Ave 62025-1730 (Mail to: 406 Hillsboro Ave 62025-1730) Joel Morsch (618) 656-1929

Elkhart Church of St John the Baptist **SC** c/o Trinity Episcopal Church 402 Pekin St 62656-2033 (Mail to: PO Box 386 62656-0386) James Cravens Janet Lombardo (217) 732-7609

Glen Carbon St Thomas Episcopal Church **M** (54) § 182 Summit Ave 62034-1446 (Mail to: 182 Summit Ave 62034-1446) (618) 288-5620

Granite City St Bartholomews Episcopal Church **M** (25) § 2167 Grand Ave 62040-4724 (Mail to: 2165 Grand Ave 62040-4724) (618) 876-9097

Harrisburg St Stephen's Church **P** (32) § 101 E Church St 62946-1704 (Mail to: 101 E Church St 62946-1704) Timothy Goodman (618) 252-8239

Havana St Barnabas Episcopal Church **M** (38) § 420 Plum St 62644-1129 (Mail to: PO Box 343 62644-0343) (309) 543-2430

Jacksonville Trinity Episcopal Church **P** (87) § 359 W State St 62650-2007 (Mail to: 359 W State St 62650-2007) Zachary Brooks Thomas Langford (217) 245-5901

Lincoln Trinity Episcopal Church **P** (61) 402 Pekin St 62656-2033 (Mail to: PO Box 386 62656-0386) Mark Evans (217) 732-7609

Marion St James Episcopal Church **Chapel** (8) § 301 E Thorn St 62959-3159 (Mail to: 301 E Thorn St 62959-3159) (618) 993-2074

Mattoon Trinity Episcopal Church **M** (27) PO Box 302 61938-0302 (Mail to: PO Box 302 61938-0302) Anne Flynn Jeffrey Kozuszek (217) 234-4514

Morton All Saints Episcopal Church **M** (63) § 201 W Chicago St 61550-1909 (Mail to: 329 S Plum Ave 61550-1856) Matthew Dallman Laurie Kellington (309) 266-9894

Mount Carmel St John the Baptist Episcopal Church **P** (39) § 600 Mulberry St 62863-2045 (Mail to: PO Box 674 62863-0674) Brant Hazlett (618) 262-7382

Mount Vernon Trinity Episcopal Church **P** (114) 1100 Harrison St 62864-3814 (Mail to: 1100 Harrison St 62864-3814) Benjamin Hankinson (618) 242-3434

Normal Christ The King Episcopal Church **P** (77) § 1210 S Fell Ave 61761-3641 (Mail to: 1210 S Fell Ave 61761-3641) (309) 310-9574

O Fallon St Michaels Episcopal Church **M** (169) 111 Ofallon Troy Rd 62269-6703 (Mail to: 111 Ofallon Troy Rd 62269-6703) Ian Wetmore (618) 632-6168

Pekin St Pauls Church Episcopal **P** (48) § 349 Buena Vista Ave 61554-4288 (Mail to: 343 Buena Vista Ave 61554-4227) Matthew Dallman Laurie Kellington (309) 346-2615

Rantoul St Christopher Episcopal Church **M** (24) § 1501 E Grove Ave 61866-2735 (Mail to: 1501 E Grove Ave 61866-2735) Steven Thorp (217) 892-2476

Robinson St Marys Episcopal Church **M** (17) § 8996 E 1050th Ave 62454-4822 (Mail to: PO Box 442 62454-0442) Ann Tofani Ann Tofani Kenneth Truelove (618) 544-8974

Salem St Thomas Episcopal Church **M** (41) § 512 W Main St 62881-0622 (Mail to: PO Box 622 62881-0622) (618) 548-3560

Springfield Christ Episcopal Church **P** (141) § 611 E Jackson St 62701-1815 (Mail to: 611 E Jackson St 62701-1898) Gregory Tournoux (217) 523-1871

Springfield St Lukes Episcopal Church **M** (165) § 1218 S Grand Ave E 62703-2621 (Mail to: 1218 S Grand Ave E 62703-2621) Shawn Denney (217) 528-5915

✠ **Springfield** Cathedral Church of St Paul **O** (414) § 815 So 2nd St 62704 (Mail to: 815 S 2nd St 62704-2696) Martha Bradley Gus Franklin Andrew Hook Gerald Raschke (217) 544-5135

W Frankfort St Marks Episcopal Church **M** (48) § 212 Ida St 62896-2311 (Mail to: PO Box 97 62896-0097) Sheryl Black (618) 937-4976

SWITZERLAND
See Europe

DIOCESE OF TAIWAN
(PROVINCE VIII)
Comprises Taiwan and neighboring islands
DIOCESAN OFFICE 7 Ln 105 Hangchow S Rd Sec 1 Taipei Taiwan 10060 ROC
TEL 886-2-2341-1265   FAX 886-2-2396-2014
E-MAIL skh.tpe@msa.hinet.net   WEB www.episcopalchurch.org.tw

Previous Bishops—
Harry S Kennedy 1954-60, Chas
P Gilson suffr 1961-64, James CL
Wong 1965-70, James TM Pong
1971-79, PY Cheung 1980-87
John Chien 1988-2001

Bishop—Rt Rev David Jung-Hsin Lai (962) (Dio 25 Nov 2000)

Sec Conv CN Yang *Treas* Amy BH Lin *Chanc* HHP Ma

Stand Comm—Cler: LF Lin YR Chang LL Chang TS Tsou WB Tzeng ML Wu *Lay:* BS Hu CN Young G Chern YC Chiu HW Chuang YH Ti *Honorable Chairperson* HHP Ma

PARISHES, MISSIONS, AND CLERGY

✠ **Taipei** St John Cathedral **O** 280 Fu-Hsing S Rd Sec 2 TAIWAN 10663 (Mail to: 280 Fu-Hsing S Rd Sec 2 Taipei TAIWAN 10663) Philip Lin, Anthony Liang

Keelung Holy Trinity **P** 163 Tung-Ming Road TAIWAN 20141 (Mail to: 163 Tung-Ming Road Keelung TAIWAN 20105) Justin Lin

Keelung St Stephen **M** 1F No29 Aly 6 Ln 168 Zhonghe Rd Zhongshan Dist TAIWAN 20347 (Mail to: 1F No29 Aly 6 Ln 168 Zhonghe Rd Zhongshan Dist Keelung TAIWAN 20347) Julia Lin

Taipei Good Shepherd **P** 509 Chung-Cheng Rd Shihlin Dist TAIWAN 11168 (Mail to: 509 Chung-Cheng Rd Shihlin Dist Taipei TAIWAN 11168) Keith Lee

New Taipei City Advent **P** 499 Sec 4 Tam King Rd Tamsui TAIWAN 25135 (Mail to: 499 Sec 4 Tam King Rd Tamsui New Taipei City TAIWAN 25135) Lennon Chang, Irving Wu

Taoyuan City Christ **M** No.33, Chongyi 3rd St., Pingzhen Dist., Taoyuan City, TAIWAN 32453, (Mail to: No.33, Chongyi 3rd St., Pingzhen Dist., Taoyuan City, TAIWAN 32453) Deledda Tsai

Taichung St James **P** No 23 Wu-Chuan West Road Sec 1 TAIWAN 40348 (Mail to: No 23 Wu-Chuan West Road Sec 1 Taichung TAIWAN 40348) Lily Chang

Taichung Leading Star **M** No8 Ln 530 Guangxing Rd Taiping Dist TAIWAN 41148 (Mail to: No8 Ln 530 Guangxing Rd Taiping Dist Taichung AIWAN 41148) Lily Chang

Chiayi St Peters **M** 8 Hsing Chung St TAIWAN 60047 (Mail to: 8 Hsing Chung St Chiayi TAIWAN 60047) Simon Tsou

Chiayi County Goubei Mission **PS** No 70-1 Goubei Village Dalin Township TAIWAN 62245 (Mail to: No 70-1 Goubei Village Dalin Township Chiayi County TAIWAN 62245) Simon Tsou

Tainan Grace **M** No24 Ln 550 Chongde Rd East Dist TAIWAN 70171 (Mail to: No24 Ln 550 Chongde Rd East Dist Tainan TAIWAN 70171) Philip Ho

Kaohsiung St Andrew **PS** No311 Sec 2 Jiading Rd Qieding Dist TAIWAN 85241 (Mail to: No311 Sec 2 Jiading Rd Qieding Dist Kaohsiung TAIWAN 85241) Philip Ho

Kangshan All Saints **P** No5 Jieshou Rd Gangshan Dist TAIWAN 82044 (Mail to: No5 Jieshou Rd Gangshan Dist Kaohsiung TAIWAN 82044) Leo Tzeng

Kaohsiung St Paul **M** 200 Tzu Chiang 1 Rd San Min Dist TAIWAN 80749 (Mail to: 200 Tzu Chiang 1 Rd San Min Dist Kaohsiung TAIWAN 80749) Chen-Chang Cheng

Kaohsiung St Timothy **P** 3F # 262 Chung-Hsiao 1 Rd Hsin-Hsing Dist TAIWAN 80055 (Mail to: 3F # 262 Chung-Hsiao 1 Rd Hsin-Hsing Dist Kaohsiung TAIWAN 80055) Richard Lee

Pingtung St Mark **M** 120-11 Chung Hsiao Rd TAIWAN 90063 (Mail to: 120-11 Chung Hsiao Rd Pingtung Taiwan 90063) Joseph Wu

Hualien St Luke **M** No 1-6 Ming Hsin St TAIWAN 97050 (Mail to: 1-6 Ming Hsin St Hualien TAIWAN 97050) Joseph Ho

STATE OF TENNESSEE
Dioceses of East Tennessee (ETN), Tennessee (TN), and West Tennessee (WTN)

Antioch—TN
Athens—ETN
Atoka—WTN
Battle Creek—ETN
Bolivar—WTN
Brentwood—TN
Bristol—ETN
Brownsville—WTN
Chattanooga—ETN
Clarksville—TN
Cleveland—ETN
Collierville—WTN
Columbia—TN
Cookeville—TN
Copperhill—ETN
Cordova—WTN
Covington—WTN
Cowan—TN
Crossville—ETN
Cumberland Furnace—
  TN
Dechard—TN

Dickson—TN
Dyersburg—WTN
Elizabethton—ETN
Fayetteville—TN
Franklin—TN
Ft Ogelthorpe—ETN
Gallatin—TN
Gatlinburg—ETN
Germantown—WTN
Greeneville—ETN
Harriman—ETN
Hendersonville—TN
Hixson—ETN
Humboldt—WTN
Jackson—WTN
Jefferson City—ETN
Johnson City—ETN
Jonesborough—ETN
Kingsport—ETN
Knoxville—ETN
LaFollette—ETN
La Grange—WTN

Lebanon—TN
Lookout Mtn—ETN
Loudon—ETN
Madison—TN
Manchester—TN
Maryville—ETN
Mason—WTN
McMinnville—TN
Memphis—WTN
Millington—WTN
Monteagle—TN
Morristown—ETN
Murfreesboro—TN
Nashville—TN
Newport—ETN
New Johnsonville—TN
Norris—ETN
Oak Ridge—ETN
Ooltewah—ETN
Paris—WTN
Pulaski—TN
Ripley—WTN

Rogersville—ETN
Rossview—TN
Rugby—ETN
Saint Andrews—TN
Sevierville—ETN
Sewanee—TN
Seymour—ETN
Shelbyville—TN
Sherwood—TN
Signal Mtn—ETN
Smyrna—TN
Somerville—WTN
So Pittsburg—ETN
Spring Hill—TN
Springfield—TN
Tracy City—TN
Tullahoma—TN
Union City—WTN
Winchester—TN

DIOCESE OF TENNESSEE
(PROVINCE IV)
Comprises the middle section of the State of Tennessee
DIOCESAN OFFICE 3700 Woodmont Blvd Nashville TN 37215
TEL (615) 251-3322   FAX (615) 251-8010
E-MAIL info@edtn.org   WEB http://edtn.org/

Previous Bishops—
James H Otey 1834-63, Chas T Quintard 1865-98, Thomas F Gailor coadj 1893 Bp 1898-1935, Troy Beatty coadj 1919-22, James hM Maxon coadj 1922 Bp 1935-47, Edmund P Dandridge coadj 1938 Bp 1947-53,

Theodore N Barth coadj 1948 Bp 1953-61, John Vander Horst suffr 1955-1961 coadj 1961 Bp 1961-1977, William E Sanders coadj 1962 Bp 1977-1984, W Fred Gates Jr suffr 1966-1982, Geo L Reynolds 1985-91, Bertram N Herlong 1993-2006

Bishop—Rt Rev John C Bauerschmidt (1013)
(Dio 27 Jan 2007)

Cn to Ord Rev Cn A Petiprin; *Cn to Ord* Rev Cn PP Snare; *Cn for Spec Proj* Rev Cn F Dettwiller; *Treas* WA Stringer; *Chanc* GS Aden; *V Chanc* W Longmire; *Asst Treas* J Ramsey; *COM Chair* E Arning; *AF* S Abington; *Exec Asst and Comm* K Dougherty

Stand Comm—Cler: C Bowhay V Burgess K Blaess J Terhune; *Lay:* D Clayton R Riggar K Vickers

PARISHES, MISSIONS, AND CLERGY

Antioch St Marks Episcopal Church **P** (100) 3100 Murfreesboro Pike 37013-2202 (Mail to: PO Box 741 37011-0741) Battle Beasley (615) 361-4100

Brentwood Church of the Good Shepherd **P** (953) § 1420 Wilson Pike 37027-7701 (Mail to: 1420 Wilson Pike 37027-7701) (615) 661-0890

Clarksville Grace Chapel **M** (25) 1950 Rossview Rd 37043-1516 (Mail to: C/O Julia Meadows Treasurer 3270 Port Royal Rd 37010-9018) (931) 3582111

Clarksville Trinity Episcopal Church **P** (401) § 317 Franklin St 37040-3421 (Mail to: 317 Franklin St 37040-3421) Meghan Holland (931) 645-2458

Columbia St Peters Episcopal Church **P** (432) 311 W 7th St 38401-3132 (Mail to: 311 W 7th St 38401-3132) Christopher Bowhay (931) 388-3331

Cookeville St Michael Episcopal Church **P** (300) 640 Washington Ave 38501-2659 (Mail to: 640 Washington Ave 38501-2659) (931) 526-4654

Cowan St Agnes Mission **M** (27) England At Cherry 37318 (Mail to: P.O.Box 356 37318) (931) 636-6313

Cumberland Furnace Calvary Episcopal Church **M** (22) 1086 Old Highway 48 37051-5000 (Mail to: 1086 Old Highway 48 37051-5000) (615) 566-5247

Decherd Christ Episcopal Church **M** (20) 9616 Old Alto Hwy 37324 (Mail to: Leona Hawk 311 Kelly Dr 37324-3803) (931) 967-0898

Dickson St James Episcopal Church **M** (30) § 205 Church Street 37055 (Mail to: PO Box 1196 37056-1196) David Yancey David Yancey (615) 446-8916

Fayetteville St Mary Magdalene Episcopal Church **P** (155) § 106 Washington St E 37334-2544 (Mail to: PO Box 150 37334-0150) Jason Terhune (931) 433-2911

Franklin St Pauls Episcopal Church **P** (1442) § 510 W Main St 37064-2722 (Mail to: 510 W Main St 37064-2722) William McCown Monna Mayhall (615) 790-0527

Franklin Church of the Resurrection **P** (110) § 1216 Sneed Rd W 37069-6927 (Mail to: 1216 Sneed Rd W 37069-6927) Stephen Jones (615) 377-9144

Gallatin Church Of Our Saviour **P** (120) 704 Hartsville Pike 37066-2525 (Mail to: PO Box 307 37066-0307) Jacob Bottom (615) 452-7146

Hendersonvlle St Joseph of Arimathea Episcopal Church **P** (129) 103 Country Club Dr 37075-4024 (Mail to: 103 Country Club Dr 37075-4024) Joseph Howard (615) 824-2910

Lebanon Episcopal Church of the Epiphany **P** (112) § 1500 Hickory Ridge Rd 37087-5702 (Mail to: 1500 Hickory Ridge Rd 37087-5702) Cynthia Seifert (615) 444-7336

Madison St James The Less **P** (83) 411 W Due West Ave 37115-4403 (Mail to: 411 W Due West Ave 37115-4403) Robert Arning (615) 865-4496

Manchester St Bedes Episcopal Church **P** (67) § 93 Saint Bedes Dr 37355-5900 (Mail to: PO Box 305 37349-0305) (931) 728-4463

Mcminnville St Matthews Episcopal Church **M** (65) 105 Edgewood Ave 37110-1565 (Mail to: 105 Edgewood Ave 37110-1565) (931) 473-8233

Monteagle Church of the Holy Comforter **M** (14) 1st Ave & Fairmont 37356 (Mail to: PO Box 541 37356-0541) (931) 967-0898

Murfreesboro Church of the Holy Cross **M** (92) 1140 Cason Ln 37128-7660 (Mail to: 1140 Cason Ln 37128-7660) James Teets (615) 867-7116

Murfreesboro Saint Paul's Episcopal Church **P** (986) 116 Academy St 37130-3717 (Mail to: 116 Academy St 37130-3717) Colin Ambrose Colin Ambrose (615) 893-3780

✣ **Nashville** Christ Church Cathedral **O** (2025) 900 Broadway 37203-3807 (Mail to: 900 Broadway 37203-3854) Timothy Kimbrough Hassell Hurst Timothy Kimbrough Matthew Lewis Aleathia Nicholson Melissa Smith (615) 255-7729

Nashville Church of the Advent **P** (654) 5501 Franklin Pike 37220-2115 (Mail to: 5501 Franklin Pike 37220-2115) James McVey (615) 373-5630

Nashville Church of the Holy Trinity **P** (102) 615 6th Ave S 37203 (Mail to: 615 6th Ave S 37203-4613) William Dennler (615) 256-6359

Nashville Church of the Holy Spirit **P** (140) 222 Franklin Limestone Rd 37217-3004 (Mail to: 5325 Nolensville Pike 37211-6415) (615) 333-9979

Nashville St Anns Episcopal Church **P** (208) 419 Woodland St 37206-4207 (Mail to: 419 Woodland St 37206-4207) Kira Schlesinger Richard Wineland (615) 254-3534

Nashville St Anselms Episcopal Chapel **M** (78) 2008 Meharry Blvd 37208-2916 (Mail to: 2008 Meharry Blvd 37208-2916) Cynthia Seifert (615) 329-9640

Nashville Saint Augustine's Chapel **CC** (300) 200 24th Ave S 37235 (Mail to: PO Box 6330B 37235-0001) Ian Cron Alison Lutz Rebecca Stevens-Hummon Rebecca Stevens-Hummon (615) 322-4783

Nashville St Bartholomews Episcopal Church **P** (1058) § 4800 Belmont Park Terrace 37215-4422 (Mail to: 4800 Belmont Park Ter 37215-4422) Travis Hines Sammy Wood (615) 377-4750

Nashville Saint David's Episcopal Church **P** (126) § 6501 Pennywell Dr 37205-3005 (Mail to: 6501 Pennywell Dr 37205-3005) Carolyn Coleman (615) 352-0293

Nashville Saint George's Church **P** (3685) § 4715 Harding Pike 37205-2809 (Mail to: 4715 Harding Pike 37205-2896) Robert Spruill Samuel Adams Kristine Blaess Michael Blaess Clinton Wilson (615) 385-2150

Nashville Saint Philip's Church **P** (365) 85 Fairway Dr 37214-2148 (Mail to: 85 Fairway Dr 37214-2148) Vicki Burgess (615) 883-4595

New Johnsonville St Andrews Episcopal Church **M** (30) 539 Hillcrest Dr 37134-9668 (Mail to: PO Box 522 37134-0522) (931) 535-2314

Pulaski Church of the Messiah **P** (104) § 114 3rd St 38478-3203 (Mail to: 114 3rd St 38478-3203) Jess Reeves (931) 363-1454

Saint Andrews St Andrews-Sewanee **SC** 290 Quintard Rd 37375-3000 (Mail to: 290 Quintard Rd 37375-3000) (931) 598-5651

Sewanee Otey Memorial Episcopal Church **P** (420) 216 University Ave 37375-2202 (Mail to: PO Box 267 37375-0267) Robert Lamborn Elizabeth Carpenter Elizabeth Carpenter (931) 598-5926

Sewanee St James Episcopal Church **P** (65) 898 Midway Rd 37375-2701 (Mail to: PO Box 336 37375-0336) John Runkle (931) 598-0153

Shelbyville Church of the Redeemer **P** (55) 203 E Lane St 37160-3429 (Mail to: PO Box 274 37162-0274) Regan Schutz (931) 619-5493

Sherwood Church of the Epiphany **M** (102) 62 Mountain Ave E 37376 (Mail to: 62 Mountain Ave W 37376-2000) (931) 967-0898

Smyrna All Saints Episcopal Church **M** (273) 1401 Lee Victory Pkwy 37167-6299 (Mail to: 1401 Lee Victory Pkwy 37167-6299) (615) 223-7157

Spring Hill Grace Episcopal Church **M** (71) 5291 Main St 37174-2449 (Mail to: 5291 Main St

37174-2449) Joseph Davis (931) 486-3223

Springfield St Lukes Church **M** (36) 103 7th Ave W 37172-2826 (Mail to: 103 7th Ave W 37172-2826) (615) 382-7505

Tracy City Christ Episcopal Church **M** (147) PO Box 457 37387-0457 (Mail to: PO Box 457 37387-0457) (931) 967-0898

Tullahoma St Barnabas Episcopal Church **P** (234) 110 E Lincoln St 37388-3631 (Mail to: 110 E Lincoln St 37388-3632) Michael Murphy (931) 455-3170

Winchester Trinity Episcopal Church **P** (27) § 213 1st Ave NW 37398-1645 (Mail to: 213 1st Ave NW 37398-1645) William Barton (931) 967-0898

STATE OF TEXAS
Dioceses of Dallas (Dal), Fort Worth (FtW), Northwest Texas (NT), Rio Grande (RG), Texas (TX), and West Texas (WT)

Abilene—NT	Burnet—TX	Denton—Dal	Hearne—TX
Albany—NT	Calvert—TX	De Soto—Dal	Hebbronville—WT
Alamogordo—RG	Cameron—TX	Devine—WT	Hempstead—TX
Albuquerque—RG	Canton—Dal	Dickinson—TX	Henderson—TX
Aledo—FtW	Canyon—NT	Dripping Spgs—WT	Hereford—NT
Alice—WT	Canyon Lake—WT	Dumas—NT	Hillsboro—FtW & RG
Allen—Dal	Carlsbad—RG	Eagle Lake—TX	Hitchcock—TX
Alpine—RG	Carrizo Spgs—WT	Eagle Pass—WT	Hobbs—RG
Alvin—TX	Carthage—TX	Edgewood—RG	Houston—TX
Amarillo—NT	Cedar Hill—Dal	Edinburg—WT	Humble—TX
Angleton—TX	Cedar Pk—TX	Edna—WT	Huntsville—TX
Anthony—RG	Center—TX	El Paso—RG	Hurst—FtW & RG
Aransas Pass—WT	Chama—RG	Ennis—Dal	Irving—Dal
Arlington—FtW	Clarendon—NT	Espanola—RG	Jacksonville—TX
Artesia—RG	Cloudcroft—RG	Farmington—RG	Jasper—TX
Athens—Dal	Clovis—RG	Fort Sumner—RG	Jefferson—TX
Atlanta—Dal	Coleman—NT	Flower Mound—Dal	Junction—WT
Austin—TX	College Sta—TX	Ft McKavett—WT	Katy—TX
Bandera—WT	Colorado City—NT	Ft Worth—FtW	Kaufman—Dal
Bastrop—TX	Columbus—TX	Fredericksburg—WT	Keller—FTW
Bay City—TX	Comfort—WT	Freeport—TX	Kemp—Dal
Baytown—TX	Conroe—TX	Friendswood—TX	Kenedy—WT
Beaumont—TX	Coppell—Dal	Frisco—Dal	Kerrville—WT
Beeville—WT	Copperas Cove—TX	Gallup—RG	Kilgore—TX
Bellville—TX	Corpus Christi—WT	Galveston—TX	Killeen—TX
Big Spg—NT	Corrales—RG	Garland—Dal	Kingsville—WT
Blanco—WT	Corsicana—Dal	Georgetown—TX	LaGrange—TX
Boerne—WT	Cotulla—WT	George West—WT	LaMarque—TX
Bonham—Dal	Crockett—TX	Gilmer—Dal	LaPorte—TX
Borger—NT	Cuero—WT	Glencoe—RG	Lake Corpus Christi—
Bracketville—WT	Cypress—TX	Goliad—WT	WT
Brady—WT	Cypress Mill—WT	Gonzales—WT	Lake Jackson—TX
Brenham—TX	Dalhart—NT	Granbury—FtW	Lampasas—TX
Brownfield—NT	Dallas—Dal	Greenville—Dal	Lancaster—Dal
Brownsville—WT	Del Rio—WT	Hallettsville—WT	Laredo—WT
Bryan—TX	Deming—RG	Hamilton—FtW	Las Cruces—RG
Buda—WT	Denison—Dal	Harlingen—WT	Las Vegas—RG

League City—TX
Leander—TX
Levelland—NT
Lewisville—Dal
Liberty—TX
Lindale—TX
Livingston—TX
Llano—WT
Lockhart—WT
Longview—TX
Los Alamos—RG
Los Lunas—RG
Lovington—RG
Lubbock—NT
Lufkin—TX
Luling—WT
Madisonville—TX
Manor—TX
Marble Falls—TX
Marfa—RG
Marlin—TX
Marshall—TX
Matagorda—TX
McAllen—WT
McKinney—Dal
Menard—WT
Mexia—TX
Midland—NT
Milan—RG
Mineola—Dal
Mission—WT
Missouri City—TX

Montell—WT
Mt Pleasant—Dal
Murphy—Dal
Nacogdoches—TX
Navasota—TX
New Braunfels—WT
Odessa—NT
Orange—TX
Palacios—TX
Palestine—TX
Pampa—NT
Paris—Dal
Pasadena—TX
Pearland—TX
Pecos—RG
Perryton—NT
Pflugerville—TX
Pharr—WT
Pittsburg—Dal
Plainview—NT
Plano—Dal
Pleasanton—WT
Portales—RG
Pt Aransas—WT
Pt Isabel—WT
Pt Lavaca—WT
Portland—WT
Pt Neches—TX
Pottsboro—Dal
Prairie View—TX
Prosper—Dal
Raton—RG

Raymondville—WT
Refugio—WT
Richardson—Dal
Richmond—TX
Rio Communities—RG
Rio Rancho—RG
Rockdale—TX
Rockport—WT
Rockwall—Dal
Roswell—RG
Round Rock—TX
Ruidoso—RG
Salago—TX
San Antonio—WT
San Angelo—NT
San Augustine—TX
San Benito—WT
San Marcos—WT
San Saba—WT
Santa Fe—RG
Sealy—TX
Seguin—WT
Shamrock—NT
Sherman—Dal
Silsbee—TX
Silver City—RG
Socorro—RG
Sonora—WT
Spring—TX
Stafford—TX
Stephenville—FtW
Sugar Land—TX

Sulphur Spgs—Dal
Sweetwater—NT
Taos—RG
Taylor—TX
Temple—TX
Terlingua—RG
Terrell—Dal
Texas City—TX
The Colony—Dal
The Woodlands—TX
Tomball—TX
Truth Consq—RG
Tucumcari—RG
Tyler—TX
Universal City—WT
Uvalde—WT
Vernon—NT
Victoria—WT
Waco—TX
Waxahachie—Dal
Weatherford—FtW
Weslaco—WT
W Columbia—TX
Wharton—TX
Wichita Falls—FtW
Wimberley—WT
Windcrest—WT
Winnie—TX
Winnsboro—Dal
Woodville—TX

DIOCESE OF TEXAS
(PROVINCE VII)
Comprises 57 counties of southeast and central Texas
DIOCESAN OFFICE 1225 Texas Ave Houston TX 77002-3504
TEL (713) 520-6444, (800) 318-4452   FAX (713) 520-5723
E-MAIL Individual e-mail addresses may be found on the diocesan website   WEB www.epicenter.org

Previous Bishops—
Alexander Gregg 1859-93, Geo H Kinsolving coadj 1892 Bp 1893-1928, Clinton S Quin coadj 1918 Bp 1928-55, F Percy Goddard suffr 1955-72, James P Clements suffr 1956-60, Scott Field Bailey suffr 1964-75, John E Hines coadj 1945 Bp 1955-64, James M Richardson 1965-80, Roger H Cilley suffr 1976-85, Gordon T Charlton suffr 1982-89, Maurice M Benitez 1980-95, William E Sterling suffr 1989-99 James B Brown asst Bp 2000-2003, Claude E Payne Bp 1995-2003, Leopoldo J Alard suffr 1995-2003, Rayford B High Jr suffr 2003-2011, Don A Wimberly Bp 2003-09, Dena A Harrison suffr 2006-2019

Bishop—Rt Rev C Andrew Doyle (1033) (Dio 7 June 09)

Bishop Suffragan—Rt Rev Jeff W Fisher (1068) (6 Oct 2012)

Bishop Assistant-Rt Rev Hector F Monterroso (7 June 2003)

Cn to Ord Rev Cn KM Ryan; *Sec* Rev Cn JA Logan Jr; *Treas and CFO* L Mitchell; *Chanc* DT Harvin; *Chief of Staff* Rev Cn C Faulstich; *Cn for Wellness & Care* Rev Cn L Hines; *Trans Off* Rev B Rider; *Dir Fdns* D Fisher; *Chr Form* J Martin-Currie; *Yth* S Townes; *Missional Communities* J Evans; *Comm* LK Eaglin; *Camps* G Dehan; *Mission Amp* Rev Cn J Saylors; *Archdcn* R Oechsel; *Intercultural Dev* D Trevino

Deans: Austin B Pearson; *Central* D Hay; *Northeast* M Tollett; *Northwest* J Jones; *San Jacinto* GSevick; *Southeast* K Giblin; *Southwest* T Smith; *West Harris* J Condon; *East Harris* V Thomas; *Galveston* J Liberatore

Stand Comm—Cler: Sec M Tollett J Pevehouse G Razim; *Lay: Pres* D Bollinger M Quintanilla E Ziegler

PARISHES, MISSIONS, AND CLERGY

Alvin Grace Episcopal Church **P** (234) 200 W Lang St 77511-2396 (Mail to: 112 W Lang St 77511-2300) Carol Mills Joseph Mills Suzanne Smith (281) 331-5657

Angleton Church of the Holy Comforter **P** (178) § 234 South Arcola 77515 (Mail to: PO Box 786 77516-0786) Travis Smith (979) 849-1269

Austin All Saints Episcopal Church **P** (1377) § 209 W 27th St 78705-1043 (Mail to: 209 W 27th St 78705-1043) Michael Adams Cynthia Caruso (512) 476-3589

Austin Church of the Resurrection **P** (321) 2200 Justin Ln 78757-2417 (Mail to: 2200 Justin Ln 78757-2417) William Tweedie (512) 459-0027

Austin Episcopal Church of the Cross **P** PO Box 340821 78734-0014 (Mail to: PO Box 340821 78734-0014) Paul Johnson

Austin Iglesia San Francisco de Asis **M** (997) 7000 Woodhue Dr 78745-5454 (Mail to: 7000 Woodhue Dr 78745-5454) Albert Pearson (512) 439-0721

Austin St Albans Episcopal Church **P** (597) 11819 S I H 35 78747-1804 (Mail to: PO Box 368 78652-0368) Erin Hensley (512) 282-5631

Austin St Christophers Episcopal Church **P** (244) 8724 Travis Hills Dr 78735-8171 (Mail to: 8724 Travis Hills Dr 78735-8171) Madeline Hawley Sharon Williams (512) 288-0128

Austin St Davids Episcopal Church **P** (2000) § 301 E 8th St 78701-3203 (Mail to: 301 E 8th St 78701-3280) William Treadwell Robert Gribble Robert Gribble Michael Horvath Chad McCall Catherine Wright (512) 610-3500

Austin St Georges Episcopal Church **P** (128) 4301 I H 35 78722-1103 (Mail to: 4301 Interstate 35 78722-1103) Kevin Schubert (512) 454-2523

Austin St James' Episcopal Church **P** (700) 1941 Webberville Rd 78721-1679 (Mail to: 1941 Webberville Rd 78721-1679) Albert Rodriguez (512) 926-6339

Austin St Johns Episcopal Church **P** (237) 11201 Parkfield Dr 78758-4264 (Mail: 11201 Parkfield Dr 78758-4264) Victoria Mason (512) 836-3974

Austin St Lukes on the Lake Epis Church **P** (953) § 5600 Ranch Road 620 78732-1823 (Mail to: 5600 Ranch Road 620 78732-1823) Janice Krause (512) 266-2455

Austin St Marks Episcopal Church **P** (758) 2128 Barton Hills Dr 78704-4651 (Mail to: 2128 Barton Hills Dr 78704-4651) Zachary Koons (512) 444-1449

Austin St Matthews Episcopal Church **P** (1404) 8134 Mesa Dr 78759-8615 (Mail to: 8134 Mesa Dr 78759-8678) John Wade Jerry Chapman Christian Hawley William Helms George Wilson (512) 345-8314

Austin St Michaels Episcopal Church **P** (678) 6317 Bee Caves Rd 78746-5148 (Mail to: 1500 Capital of Texas Hwy 78746-3320) Hope Benko John Newton Nancy Ricketts Sharon Williams (512) 327-1474

Austin The Church of the Good Shepherd **P** (3307) 3201 Windsor Dr 78703-2239 (Mail to: PO Box 5176 78763-5176) Morgan Allen Holmes Adams Cynthia Kittredge James Lawrence Marcea Paul Kathleen Pfister Shannon Preston (512) 476-3523

Bastrop Calvary Episcopal Church **P** (400) § 603 Spring St 78602-3226 (Mail to: PO Box 721 78602-0721) Kenneth Kesselus (512) 303-7515

Bay City St Marks Episcopal Church **P** (372) 2200 Avenue E 77414-5009 (Mail to: 2200 Avenue E 77414-5009) John Myers (979) 245-2557

Baytown Trinity Episcopal Church **P** (442) 2701 W Main St 77520-6220 (Mail to: 5010 Main St 77521-9606) Meredith Crigler Lajunta Rios (281) 421-0090

Beaumont St Mark's Episcopal Church **P** (763) § 680 Calder St 77701-2303 (Mail to: 680 Calder St 77701-2398) Anthony Clark (409) 832-3405

Beaumont St Stephens Episcopal Church **P** (531) 4090 Delaware St 77706-7801 (Mail to: 4090 Delaware St 77706-7801) Steven Balke Patricia Ritchie (409) 892-4227

Bellville St Marys Episcopal Church **P** (103) 24 Masonic St 77418-1444 (Mail to: 24 Masonic St 77418-1444) Rohani Weger (979) 865-2330

Brenham St Peters Episcopal Church **P** (232) 2310 Airline Dr 77833 (Mail to: PO Box 937 77834-0937) Stephen Whaley (979) 836-7248

Bryan St Andrews Episcopal Church **P** (343) 217 W 26th St 77803-3215 (Mail to: PO Box 405 77806-0405) Daryl Hay David Hoster Matthew Stone (979) 822-5176

Burnet Epis Church of the Epiphany **P** (247) 601 Wood St 78611-0002 (Mail to: PO Box 2 78611-0002) (512) 756-2334

Calvert Church Of The Epiphany **M** (21) 700 E Gregg St 77837-7801 (Mail to: PO Box 129 77837) (512) 217-6314

Cameron All Saints Episcopal Church **M** (30) 200 Travis St 76520 (Mail to: PO Box 510 76520) Durwood Bagby (254) 697-2167

Carthage St Johns Episcopal Church **M** (52) Attn Maudie Leach 904 Daniels St 75633-1126 (Mail to: Attn Maudie Leach 904 Daniels St 75633-1126) Jennene Laurinec Richard Mcleon (903) 693-5566

Cedar Park Christ Episcopal Church **P** (293) 3520 W Whitestone Blvd 78613 (Mail to: PO Box 638 78630-0638) Trawin Malone (512) 267-2428

Center St Johns Episcopal Church **M** (26) 1063 Southview Circle 75935 (Mail to: PO Box 1026 75935-1026) Jane Barker (936) 598-4101

College Station St Francis Episcopal Church **P** (95) 1101 Rock Prairie Rd 77845-8344 (Mail to: 1101 Rock Prairie Rd 77845-8344) Lacy Largent (979) 696-1491

College Station St Thomas Episcopal Church **P** (562) § 906 George Bush Dr 77840-3056 (Mail to: 906 George Bush Dr 77840-3056) Angela Cortinas (979) 696-1726

Columbus Saint John's Episcopal Church **P** (30) 913 Travis St 78934-2436 (Mail to: PO Box 746 78934-0746) (979) 732-2590

Conroe Saint James The Apostle Episcopal Church **P** (524) 1803 Highland Hollow Dr 77304-4092 (Mail to: C/O Financial Secretary 1803 Highland Hollow Dr 77304-4092) Jerald Hyche Phyllis Hartman (936) 756-8831

Copperas Cove St Martins Episcopal Church **M** (67) 1602 S Fm 116 76522-4204 (Mail to: 1602 S Fm 116 76522-4204) (254) 547-0331

Crockett All Saints Episcopal Church **M** (26) 1301 E Houston Ave 75835-1749 (Mail to: PO Box 103 75835-0103) John Chase (936) 544-8914

Cypress St Aidans Episcopal Church **M** (406) 13131 Fry Rd 77433-3339 (Mail to: 13131 Fry Rd 77433-3339) Leslie Carpenter Warren Miedke (281) 373-3203

Cypress St Marys Episcopal Church **P** (520) 15415 Eldridge Pkwy 77429-2005 (Mail to: 15415 Eldridge Pkwy 77429-2005) Russell Oechsel (281) 370-8000

Dickinson Holy Trinity Episcopal Church **P** (273) 4613 Highway 3 77539-6852 (Mail to: 4613 Highway 3 77539-6852) Michael Gemignani Vivian Orndorff (281) 337-1833

Eagle Lake Christ Church **P** (98) PO Box 577 77434-0577 (Mail to: PO Box 577 77434-0577) Stephen Spicer (979) 234-3437

Freeport St Pauls Episcopal Church **P** (95) 1307 W 5th St 77541-5311 (Mail to: 1307 W 5th St 77541-5311) Robert Dohle (979) 233-3673

Friendswood Church of the Good Shepherd **P** (720) § 1207 Winding Way Dr 77546-4808 (Mail to: 1207 W Winding Way Dr 77546-4808) Geoffrey Gwynne (281) 482-7630

Galveston Grace Episcopal Church **P** (289) 1115 36th St 77550-4113 (Mail to: 1115 36th St 77550-4113) Nicholas Earl (409) 762-9676

Galveston St Augustine of Hippo Church **M** (89) § 1410 Jack Johnson Blvd 77550-3953 (Mail to: 1410 Jack Johnson Blvd 77550-3953) Chester Makowski (409) 763-4254

Galveston Trinity Episcopal Church **P** (455) 2216 Ball St 77550-2224 (Mail to: Finance Office 2216 Ball St 77550-2224) Susan Kennard Edward Thompson (409) 765-6317

✠ **Galveston** William Temple Episcopal Center **O** 427 Market St 77550-2703 (Mail to: Attn. Mr. Tim R. Mack, Treas. 427 Market St 77550-2703) (409) 539-2077

Georgetown Grace Episcopal Church **P** (509) 1314 E University Ave 78626-6115 (Mail to: 1314 E University Ave 78626-6115) Mary Ann Huston Albert Pearson (512) 863-2068

Hearne St Philips Episcopal Church **M** (3) 408 Cedar St 77859-2545 (Mail to: Ina F Boyle PO Box 952 77859) (979) 279-3234

Hempstead St Bartholomews Church **P** (87) 811 14th St 77445-5146 (Mail to: PO Box 961 77445-0961) (979) 826-2525

Henderson St Matthews Episcopal Church **P** (70) 214 College Ave 75654-4131 (Mail to: 214 College Ave 75654-4131) Patsy Barham (903) 657-3154

Hitchcock All Saints Episcopal Church **M** (41) 10416 Highway 6 77563-4580 (Mail to: 10416 Highway 6 77563-4580) Mark Marmon (409) 925-2544

✠ **Houston** Christ Church Cathedral **O** (3608) § 1117 Texas St 77002-3113 (Mail to: C/O J David Simpson 1117 Texas St 77002-3113) Barkley Thompson Arthur Callaham Simon Bautista Glenice Robinson-Como Glenice Robinson-Como Gregory Seme Rebecca Zartman (713) 590-3308

Houston Christ the King Episcopal Church **M** (251) 15325 Bellaire Blvd 77083-3110 (Mail to: 15325 Bellaire Blvd 77083-3110) (281) 933-6800

Houston Church of the Ascension **P** (725) 2525 Seagler Rd 77042-3119 (Mail to: 2525 Seagler Rd 77042-3119) (713) 781-1330

Houston Church of the Epiphany **P** (704) § 9600 S Gessner Dr 77071-1002 (Mail to: 9600 S Gessner Rd 77071-1099) (713) 774-9619

Houston Church of the Redeemer **M** (75) § 5700 Lawndale 77023-1898 (Mail to: PO Box 9564 77261-9564) James Kearney Lacy Largent (713) 928-3221

Houston Emmanuel Church **P** (472) § 16000 Barkers Point Ln 77079-4023 (Mail to: 16000 Barkers Point Ln Ste 175 77079-4000) Bradley Sullivan (281) 493-3161

Houston Grace Episcopal Church **M** (157) 4040 W Bellfort Ave 77025-5307 (Mail to: 4040 W Bellfort St 77025-5307) Randall Painter (713) 666-1408

Houston Church of the Holy Spirit **P** (1207) 12535 Perthshire Rd 77024-4106 (Mail to: 12535 Perthshire Rd 77024-4186) Joshua Condon Korey Wright (713) 468-7796

Houston Hope Episcopal Church **P** (170) 1613 W 43rd St 77018-1849 (Mail to: 1613 W 43rd St 77018-1849) (713) 681-6422

Houston Santa Maria Virgen Episcopal Church **M** (1028) § 9600 Huntington Place Dr 77099-2316 (Mail to: 9600 Huntington Place Dr 77099-2316) Uriel Osnaya-Jimenez (281) 879-6000

Houston Iglesia San Mateo **M** (1282) 6635 Alder Dr 77081-5201 (Mail to: 6635 Alder Dr 77081-5201) Janssen Gutierrez (713) 664-7792

Houston Lord of the Streets Episcopal Church **M** (23) 3401 Fannin St. 77004-3806 (Mail to: 3401 Fannin St 77004-3806) (713) 526-0311

Houston Palmer Memorial Episcopal Church **P** (2648) 6221 Main St 77030-1506 (Mail to: 6221 Main St 77030-1506) Elizabeth Parker John Price Linda Shelton Henry Strobel Katharine Wallingford Neil Willard (713) 529-6196

Houston St Albans Episcopal Church **M** (129) 420 Woodard St 77009-1824 (Mail to: 420 Woodard St 77009-1824) William Laucher (713) 692-3080

Houston St Barnabas Episcopal Church **P** (107) 107 E Edgebrook Dr 77034-1401 (Mail to: 107 E Edgebrook Dr 77034-1496) (713) 946-8058

Houston St Christophers Episcopal Church **P** (185) 1656 Blalock Rd 77080-7396 (Mail to: 1656 Blalock Rd 77080-7396) Portia Sweet (713) 465-6015

Houston St Cuthbert Episcopal Church **P** (1108) § 17020 West Rd 77095-7758 (Mail to: 17020 West Rd 77095-5578) Bruce Bonner Margaret Williams (281) 463-7330

Houston St Dunstans Episcopal Church **P** (1240) § 14301 Stuebner Airline Rd 77069-3529 (Mail to: 14301 Stuebner Airline Rd 77069-3529) Randall Trego (281) 440-1600

Houston St Francis Episcopal Church **P** (1187) 345 Piney Point Rd 77024-6505 (Mail to: 345 Piney Point Rd 77024-6505) Stuart Bates David Price Robert Wismer (713) 782-1270

Houston St James Episcopal Church **P** (519) § 3129 Southmore Boulevard 77004-6298 (Mail to: 3129 Southmore Blvd 77004-6298) Elizabeth Divine Victor Thomas (713) 526-9571

Houston St John the Divine Episcopal Church **P** (4486) § 2450 River Oaks Blvd 77019-5826 (Mail to: 2450 River Oaks Blvd 77019-5826) Clay Lein Reagan Cocke Charles Holt Matthew Marino Louise Samuelson (713) 622-3600

Houston St Luke the Evangelist Church **P** (164) 3530 Wheeler St 77004-5527 (Mail to: 3530 Wheeler St 77004-5527) Francene Young (713) 748-5974

Houston St Marks Episcopal Church **P** (838) § 3816 Bellaire Blvd 77025-1209 (Mail to: 3816 Bellaire Blvd 77025-1296) Patrick Miller Samantha Smith (713) 664-3466

Houston St Martin's Episcopal Church **P** (9400) § 717 Sage Rd 77056-2111 (Mail to: 717 Sage Rd 77056-2111) Jonathan Adams Russell Levenson Martin Bastian Sarah Condon James Cunningham Alexander Graham Rutger-Jan Heijmen Alexander Large Chad Martin Susannah Mcbay (713) 985-3802

Houston St Pauls Episcopal Church **P** (514) § 7843 Park Place Blvd 77087-4639 (Mail to: 7843 Park Place Blvd 77087-4698) (713) 645-5031

Houston Saint Stephen's Episcopal Church **P** (365) § 1805 W Alabama St 77098-2601 (Mail to: Attn Deborah Waugh 1805 W Alabama St 77098-2601) Lisa Hunt Isaias Ginson Sarah Knoll Sweeney (713) 528-6665

Houston Saint Thomas Church **P** (411) § 4900 Jackwood St 77096-1505 (Mail to: 4900 Jackwood St 77096-1599) David Browder Geoffrey Simpson (713) 666-3111

Houston St Thomas the Apostle Episcopal Church **P** (1091) § 18300 Upper Bay Rd 77058-4110 (Mail to: 18300 Upper Bay Rd 77058-4110) Michael Stone Jennifer Scott (281) 333-2384

Houston St Timothys Episcopal Church **P** (202) 13125 Indianapolis St 77015-3600 (Mail to: 13125 Indianapolis St 77015-3600) (713) 451-2909

Houston St Andrews Episcopal Church **P** (282) § 1819 Heights Blvd 77008-4025 (Mail to: 1819 Heights Blvd 77008-4025) James Grace Carissa Baldwin-Mcginnis (713) 861-5596

Houston Trinity Episcopal Church **P** (677) 1015 Holman St 77004-3810 (Mail to: 1015 Holman St 77004-3899) Hannah Atkins Richard Houser (713) 528-4100

Humble Christ the King (Atascocita) **P** (207) 19330 Pinehurst Trail Dr 77346-2224 (Mail to: 19330 Pinehurst Trail Dr 77346-2224) David Nelson (281) 852-1990

Huntsville St Stephens Episcopal Church **P** (295) 5019 Sam Houston Ave 77340-6653 (Mail to: PO Box 388 77342-0388) Kellaura Johnson (936) 295-7226

Jacksonville Trinity Episcopal Church **M** (63) 1000 S Jackson St 75766-3016 (Mail to: PO Box 472 75766-0472) (903) 586-4336

Jasper Trinity Episcopal Church **P** (22) § 800 Main St 75951-3018 (Mail to: PO Box 1598 75951-0016) (409) 384-3719

Jefferson Christ Episcopal Church **M** (18) 703 S Main St 75657-2227 (Mail to: 703 S Main St 75657-2227) (903) 665-2693

Katy Holy Apostles Episcopal Church-Katy **P** (597) 1225 S Grand Pkwy 77494-8283 (Mail to: 1225 W Grand Pkwy S 77494-8283) (281) 392-3310

Katy Saint Paul's Church **P** (259) § 5373 Franz Rd 77493-1732 (Mail to: 5373 Franz Rd 77493-1732) Gillian Keyworth (281) 391-2785

Kilgore St Pauls Episcopal Church **P** (58) § 314 Henderson Blvd 75662-2712 (Mail to: 314 Henderson Blvd 75662-2712) (903) 984-3929

Killeen St Christophers Episcopal Church **P** (435) 2800 Trimmier Rd 76542-6003 (Mail to: 2800 Trimmier Rd 76542-6003) (254) 634-7474

Kingwood Church of the Good Shepherd **P** (931) 2929 Woodland Hills Dr 77339-1406 (Mail to: 2929 Woodland Hills Dr Attn: JenstikesW# 77339-1406) William Richter (281) 358-3154

La Grange St James Episcopal Church **P** (129) 156 Monroe St 78945-2651 (Mail to: PO Box 507 78945-0507) Eric Hungerford (979) 968-3910

La Marque St Michaels Episcopal Church **HC** (102) § 1601 Lake Rd 77568-5242 (Mail to: 1601 Lake Rd 77568-5242) Robert Moore (409) 935-3559

La Porte St Johns Episcopal Church **P** (244) 815 S Broadway St 77571-5323 (Mail to: 815 S Broadway St 77571-5323) Viktoria Gotting Nan Doerr (281) 471-0383

Lake Jackson St Timothys Episcopal Church **P** (593) § 200 Oyster Creek Dr 77566-4402 (Mail to: 200 Oyster Creek Dr 77566-4402) Brendan Kimbrough (979) 297-6003

Lampasas St Marys Episcopal Church **P** (147) 501 S Chestnut St 76550-3225 (Mail to: PO Box 29 76550-0001) Susanne Comer Mildred Williams (512) 556-5433

League City St Christopher Episcopal Church **P** (358) 2508 St Christopher Ave 77573-4258 (Mail to: 2508 St Christopher Ave 77573-4258) Brian Cannaday (281) 332-5553

Leander St Peters Episcopal Church **P** (49) 3305 Pinnacle Cv 78645-6567 (Mail to: 3305 Pinnacle Cv 78645-6567) (512) 267-2744

Liberty St Stephens Episcopal Church **P** (139) 2041 Trinity St 77575-4831 (Mail to: PO Box 10357 77575-7857) Ted Smith Glennda Hardin (936) 336-3762

Lindale St Lukes Episcopal Church **M** (51) 16292 FM 849 75771 (Mail to: PO Box 1766 75771-1766) John Carr Kenneth Martin (903) 882-8118

Livingston St Lukes Episcopal Church **P** (70) 832 W Jones St 77351-2721 (Mail to: 836 W Jones St 77351-2721) Leonard Hullar (936) 327-8467

Longview St Michael & All Angels Episcopal Ch **P** (168) 909 Reel Rd 75604-2528 (Mail to: 909 Reel Rd 75604-2528) Ryan Mails (903) 759-2051

Longview Trinity Episcopal Church **P** (402) § 906 Padon St 75601-6734 (Mail to: 906 Padon St 75601-6797) Frank Hughes (903) 753-3366

Lufkin St Cyprians Episcopal Church **P** (588) § 919 S John Redditt Dr 75904-4326 (Mail to: 919 S John Redditt Dr 75904-4326) Ralph Morgan (936) 639-1253

Madisonville Holy Innocents Episcopal Church **M** (25) 600 McIver St 77864-3270 (Mail to: Attn Treasurer PO Box 1344 77864-1344) (936) 348-2034

Manor St Mary Magdalene Episcopal Church **M** (65) 12800 Lexington St 78653-3333 (Mail to: P.O. Box 33 78653) Alex Montes (512) 423-8897

Marble Falls Trinity Episcopal Church **P** (170) § 909 Avenue D 78654-5217 (Mail to: 909 Avenue D 78654-5217) Nan Kennedy David Sugeno (830) 693-2822

Marlin St Johns Episcopal Church **P** (59) 514 Carter St 76661-2326 (Mail to: 514 Carter St 76661-2326) Judy Filer (254) 803-3800

Marshall St Pauls Church **P** (11) Fm Rd 134 75670 (Mail to: 4512 Fern Ave 71105-3116) (903) 407-0117

Marshall Trinity Episcopal Church **P** (427) 106 Grove St 75670-3237 (Mail to: 106 Grove St 75670-3237) John Himes Andrew Ellison (903) 938-4246

Matagorda Christ Episcopal Church **M** (68) § 206 Cypress St 77457 (Mail to: PO Box 673 77457-0673) Lawrence Gwin (979) 863-7239

Mexia Christ Episcopal Church **M** (50) 505 E Commerce St 76667-2862 (Mail to: 505 E Commerce St 76667-2862) (254) 562-5918

Missouri City St Catherine of Sienna Epis Church **M** (437) 4747 Sienna Pkwy 77459-6052 (Mail to: 4747 Sienna Pkwy 77459-6052) Michael Besson (281) 778-2046

Nacogdoches Christ Church **P** (394) 1430 N. Mound St. 75961-4052 (Mail to: 1320 Mound St 75961-4029) Howard Castleberry Michael Caldwell Wanda Cuniff (936) 564-0421

Navasota St Pauls Episcopal Church **P** (76) 414 E Mcalpine St 77868-3645 (Mail to: 414 E McAlpine St 77868-3645) Cynthia Engle (936) 825-7726

Orange St Pauls Episcopal Church **P** (105) 1401 W Park Ave 77630 (Mail to: 1401 W Park Ave 77630-4950) Petroula Ruehlen (409) 883-2969

Palacios St Johns Episcopal Church **M** (55) 3rd & Main Sts 77465 (Mail to: PO Box 895 77465-0895) (361) 972-2744

Palestine St Philips Episcopal Church **P** (227) 106 E Crawford St 75801-2805 (Mail to: 106 E Crawford St 75801-2805) Justin Briggle (903) 729-4214

Pasadena St Peters Episcopal Church **M** (290) 705 Williams St 77506-3639 (Mail to: 705 Williams St 77506-3694) David Goldberg Pedro Lopez (713) 473-8090

Pearland St Andrews Episcopal Church **P** (762) 2535 Broadway St 77581-4901 (Mail to: 2535 Broadway St 77581-4901) James Liberatore (281) 485-3843

Pflugerville St Paul's Episcopal Church **M** (91) § 507 E Pflugerville Loop 78660-1904 (Mail to: PO Box 28 78691-0028) Kelly Koonce (512) 990-1350

Port Neches Holy Trinity Episcopal Church **P** (242) § 2425 Nall St 77651-4703 (Mail to: 2425 Nall St 77651-4703) Mark Chambers (409) 722-6238

Prairie View St Francis of Assisi Epis Church **P** (29) § PO Box 246 77446-0246 (Mail to: PO Box 246 77446-0246) Cynthia Engle (936) 857-3272

Richmond Calvary Episcopal Church **P** (337) § 806 Thompson Rd 77469-3334 (Mail to: 806 Thompson Rd 77469-3334) Paul Wehner Lecia Brannon Neil Innes (281) 342-2147

Richmond Saint Mark's Episcopal Church **P** (135) § 7615 FM 762 77469 (Mail to: 7615 Fm 762 Rd 77469-9505) Susanne Comer Susanne Comer (281) 545-1661

Rockdale St Thomas Episcopal Church **M** (27) 302 E Davilla Ave 76567-2986 (Mail to: PO Box 997 76567-0997) (512) 446-5932

Round Rock St Richards Episcopal Church **P** (898) 1420 E Palm Valley Blvd 78664-4549 (Mail to: 1420 E Palm Valley Blvd 78664-4549) Franck Shelby (512) 255-5436

Round Rock St Julian of Norwich Episcopal Church **M** 7700 Cat Hollow Dr Ste 204 78681-5799 (Mail to: 7700 Cat Hollow Dr Ste 204 78681-5799) Miles Brandon (512) 284-7983

Salado St Joseph's Episcopal Church **M** (94) 881 North Main Street 76571-0797 (Mail to: PO Box 797 76571-0797) Robert Bliss (254) 947-3160

San Augustine Christ Episcopal Church **M** (29) 201 Ayish St 75972-2105 (Mail to: PO Box 85 75972-0085) (936) 275-6993

Sealy St Johns Episcopal Church **M** (83) 311 6th St 77474-2719 (Mail to: PO Box 1477 77474-1477) Eric LeBrocq (979) 885-2359

Silsbee St Johns Episcopal Church **P** (225) 1305 Roosevelt Dr 77656-3309 (Mail to: 1305 Roosevelt Dr 77656-3309) (409) 385-4371

Spring Holy Comforter Episcopal Church **P** (250) 2322 Spring Cypress Rd 77388-4717 (Mail to: 2322 Spring Cypress Rd 77388-4717) James Abbott (281) 288-8169

Stafford All Saints Episcopal Church **P** (239) § 605 Dulles Ave 77477-5222 (Mail to: 607 Dulles Ave 77477-5222) (281) 499-9602

Sugar Land Holy Cross Episcopal Church **P** (223) 5653 W River Park Dr 77479-7900 (Mail to: 5653 W River Park Dr 77479-7900) Scott Thompson (281) 633-2000

Taylor St James Episcopal Church **M** (35) 612 Davis St 76574-2729 (Mail to: C/o Treasurer PO Box 268 76574-0268) Terry Pierce (512) 352-2330

Temple Christ Episcopal Church **P** (497) § 300 Main St 76501-3210 (Mail to: 300 Main St 76501-3210) James Wilburn James Wilburn Justin Yawn (254) 773-1657

Temple St Francis Episcopal Church **P** (181) 5001 Hickory Rd 76502-3012 (Mail to: 5001 Hickory Rd 76502-3099) Tamara Clothier David Krause (254) 773-4255

Texas City St. George's Episcopal Church **P** (218) § 510 13th Ave 77590-6250 (Mail to: 510 13th Ave 77590-6250) Robin Reeves (409) 945-2583

The Woodlands Trinity Episcopal Church **P** (1353) § 3901 S. Panther Creek Dr. 77381-2736 (Mail to: 3901 S Panther Creek Dr 77381-2736) Gerald Sevick Frank Samuelson Sean Steele (281) 367-8113

Tomball Church of the Good Shepherd **P** (211) 715 Carrell St 77375-4899 (Mail to: 715 Carrell St 77375-4899) Cecil McGavern (281) 351-1609

Tyler Christ Episcopal Church **P** (1084) § 118 S Bois D Arc Ave 75702-7101 (Mail to: 118 S Bois D Arc Ave 75702-7199) David Luckenbach Matthew Boulter (903) 597-9854

Tyler St Francis Episcopal Church **P** (257) 3232 Jan Ave 75701-9115 (Mail to: 3232 Jan Ave 75701-9115) Fenton Kovic Mitchell Tollett (903) 593-8459

Tyler St John's Episcopal Church **M** (34) 514 W Vance St 75702-3251 (Mail to: 514 W Vance St 75702-3251) ML Agnew (903) 597-5923

Waco Episcopal Church of the Holy Spirit **P** (338) § 1624 Wooded Acres Dr 76710-2852 (Mail to: 1624 Wooded Acres Dr 76710-2852) Jason Ingalls Roberta Kraft Thomas Rardin (254) 772-1982

Waco St. Alban's Episcopal Church **P** (519) 305 30th St 76710-7225 (Mail to: 2900 W. Waco Drive 76610) Aaron Zimmerman Neal McGowan (254) 752-1773

Waco St Pauls Episcopal Church **P** (1118) 515 Columbus Ave 76701-1347 (Mail to: 601 Columbus Ave 76701-1347) James Pevehouse Raymond Waldon (254) 753-4501

West Columbia St Marys Episcopal Church **P** (32) 16th & Clay Sts 77486 (Mail to: PO Box 786 77486-0786) Sharron Cox (979) 345-3456

Wharton St Thomas Church **P** (129) § 207 Bob O Link Lane 77488-3205 (Mail to: PO Box 586 77488-0586) (979) 532-1723

Winnie Trinity Episcopal Church **M** (82) 1324 Highway 124, 77665-0630 (Mail to: C/O Travis Pair PO Box 630 77665-0630) (409) 267-6582

Woodville St Pauls Episcopal Church **M** (110) Hwy 190 W 75979 (Mail to: PO Box 546 75979-0546) (409) 283-3710

DIOCESE OF UPPER SOUTH CAROLINA
(PROVINCE IV)
Comprises Northwestern South Carolina
DIOCESAN OFFICE 1115 Marion St Columbia SC 29201
TEL (803) 771-7800   FAX (803) 799-5119
E-MAIL diocese@edusc.org   WEB www.edusc.org

Previous Bishops—
Kirkman G Finlay 1922-38; John J Gravatt 1939-53; C Alfred Cole 1953-63; John A Pinckney 1963-72; George M Alexander 1973-79; Rogers S Harris suffr 1985-89; Wm A Beckham 1979-94; Wm F Carr asst 1991-94; Dorsey F Henderson Jr 1995-2009

Bishop—Rt Rev W Andrew Waldo (1046) (Dio 22 May 2010)

Chanc K Shealy; *Asst Chanc* JP Lee; *Sec* N Grimball; *Asst to BP* M Sweet; *Cn for Vis & Min Dev* Rev DM Hazel; *Cn for Lead/Chr Form* Rev J Hartley; *Cn for Evan & Miss* Rev A Bentrup; *Aging Min* Rev W Kinyon; *Pres ECW* P Webb; *Cursillo* W Lee; *DOK* P Batten; *ER&D* M Jennings-Todd; *Com* G Kennedy; *Treas* B Sandberg; *Sec to Conv* R Ratterree

Stand Comm—Cler: D Apoldo N Beasley D del Priore J Hardaway P Sexton J Biedenharn S Rhoades M Smith; *Lay:* N Grimball M Martin L Moore S Palmer C Williams M Darnell M Haile R Kenner M Langford

PARISHES, MISSIONS, AND CLERGY

Abbeville Trinity Episcopal Church **M** (39) 200 Church Street 29620-0911 (Mail to: PO Box 911 29620-0911) (864) 366-5186

Aiken St Augustine of Canterbury **M** (132) 1630 Silver Bluff Rd 29803-9200 (Mail to: 1630 Silver Bluff Rd 29803-9200) Dale Klitzke Daniel Wagner (803) 641-1913

Aiken St Thaddeus Episcopal Church **P** (569) § 125 Pendleton St Sw 29801-3861 (Mail to: 125 Pendleton St SW 29801-3861) Grant Wiseman Joseph Whitehurst (803) 648-5497

Anderson Grace Episcopal Church **P** (410) § 711 S Mcduffie St 29624-2334 (Mail to: 711 S McDuffie St 29624-2334) John Hardaway (864) 225-8011

Anderson St George Episcopal Church **P** (80) 2206 Highway 81 29621-2548 (Mail to: 2206 E Greenville St 29621) Susan Hardaway (864) 224-1104

Batesburg St Pauls Episcopal Church **PS** 116 S Perry St 29006-2244 (Mail to: 116 S Perry St 29006-2244) Teddy Higgins (803) 532-0950

Beech Island All Saints Episcopal Church **M** (31) 305 Williston Rd 29842-8407 (Mail to: 137 Summerwood Way 29803-7702) (803) 302-9900

Boiling Springs St Margarets Episcopal Church **P** (225) 4180 Highway 9 29316-8580 (Mail to: PO Box 160024 29316-0002) Henry Leonard (864) 578-3238

Camden Grace Episcopal Church **P** (507) 1315 Lyttleton St 29020-3617 (Mail to: 1315 Lyttleton St 29020-3600) Michael Bullock Henry Wall (803) 432-7621

Cayce All Saints' Episcopal Church **P** (150) 1001 12th St 29033-3302 (Mail to: 1001 12th St 29033-3302) Patricia Sexton (803) 796-5735

Chapin St Francis of Assisi **P** (542) 735 Old Lexington Hwy 29036-7980 (Mail to: PO Box 265 29036-0265) Slaven Manning (803) 345-1550

Chester Saint Mark's Church **M** (12) 132 Center St 29706-1703 (Mail to: PO Box 41 29706-0041) (803) 581-3273

Clemson Holy Trinity Episcopal Parish **P** (474) § 193 Old Greenville Hwy 29631-1335 (Mail to: 193 Old Greenville Hwy 29631-1335) Suzanne Cate Christopher Wilkerson (864) 654-5071

Clinton All Saints Episcopal Church **P** (122) § 505 Calvert Ave 29325-2620 (Mail to: 505 Calvert Ave 29325-2620) (864) 833-1388

Columbia Church of the Cross **M** (69) 7244 Patterson Rd PO Box 9561 29209-2626 (Mail to: PO Box 9561 29290-0561) Simon Bautista Herbert Johnson (803) 776-1864

Columbia Church of the Good Shepherd **P** (353) 1512 Blanding St 29201-2907 (Mail to: 1512 Blanding St 29201-2907) James Lyon (803) 779-2960

✛ **Columbia** Finlay House **O** 2100 Blossom St 29205-2248 (Mail to: 2100 Blossom St 29205-2248) (803) 799-6524

Columbia St Davids Episcopal Church **P** (373) 605 Polo Rd 29223-2905 (Mail to: 605 Polo Rd 29223-2905) William Brock (803) 736-0866

Columbia St Johns Episcopal Church **P** (1385) § 2827 Wheat St 29205-2515 (Mail to: 2827 Wheat St 29205-2515) Nicholas Beasley Scott Fleischer Louis Wheeler William Wight (803) 799-4767

Columbia St Lukes Episcopal Church **P** (266) § 1300 Pine St 29204-1846 (Mail to: 1300 Pine St 29204-1846) Jill Zook-Jones (803) 254-2327

Columbia St Martins-in-the-Fields **P** (757) 5220 Clemson Ave 29206-3011 (Mail to: 5220 Clemson Ave 29206-3011) Charles Petit Susan Prinz Mitchell Smith (803) 787-0392

Columbia St Marys Episcopal Church **P** (680) § 170 Saint Andrews Rd 29210-4107 (Mail to: 170 Saint Andrews Rd 29210-4107) Jill Beimdiek Alfredo Gonzalez Alice Mills (803) 798-2776

Columbia St Michael and All Angels **P** (190) §
6408 Bridgewood Rd 29206-2126 (Mail to:
6408 Bridgewood Rd 29206-2198) Charles
Smith (803) 782-8080

Columbia St Timothys Episcopal Church **P** (117)
900 Calhoun St 29201-2308 (Mail to: 900
Calhoun St 29201-2308) Dimitrula Henson
(803) 765-1519

✙ **Columbia** Trinity Episcopal Cathedral **O** (3834)
§ 1100 Sumter St 29201-3717 (Mail to: 1100
Sumter St 29201-3717) Charles Davis Micah
Del Priore Andrew Grosso Timothy Jones Tina
Lockett Patricia Malanuk (803) 771-7300

Easley St Michaels Episcopal Church **P** (163) 1200
Powdersville Rd 29642-2422 (Mail to: 1200
Powdersville Rd 29642-2422) Thomas Dudley
(864) 859-6296

Eastover St Thomas Church **M** (59) 115 Yelton Rd
29044-9770 (Mail to: PO Box 614 29044-0614)
(803) 479-4101

Fort Mill Saint Paul's Episcopal Church **P** (329)
501 Pine St 29715-1750 (Mail to: PO Box 753
29716-0753) Sarah Franklin (803) 547-5968

Gaffney Episcopal Church of the Incarnation **P**
(110) 308 College Dr 29340-3007 (Mail to: 308
College Dr 29340-3007) Jeannette Gettys (864)
489-6183

Graniteville St Pauls Episcopal Church **P** (50) 111
Hard St 29829 (Mail to: PO Box 276 29829-
0276) Douglas Puckett (803) 663-9457

Great Falls St Peters Episcopal Church **M** (32) 30
Hampton St 29055-1636 (Mail to: PO Box 521
29055-0521) Charles Davis (803) 482-6755

Greenville Christ Episcopal Church **P** (3498) §
10 Church St 29601-2809 (Mail to: 10 Church
St 29601-2864) Harrison McLeod James
Biedenharn Kellie Wilson (864) 271-8773

Greenville Church of the Redeemer **P** (335) 120
Mauldin Rd 29605-1257 (Mail to: 120 Mauldin
Rd 29605-1257) (864) 277-4562

Greenville St Andrews Episcopal Church **P** (187)
1002 S Main St 29601-3335 (Mail to: 1002 S
Main St 29601-3335) John Eichelberger (864)
235-5884

Greenville St Francis Episcopal Church **P** (378)
301 Piney Mountain Rd. 29609 (Mail to: 506
Edwards Rd 29615-1247) (864) 268-2845

Greenville St James Episcopal Church **P** (651) §
301 Piney Mountain Rd 29609-3035 (Mail to:
Attn Accounts Payable 301 Piney Mountain
Rd 29609-3035) Stephen Rhoades (864) 244-
6358

Greenville St Peters Episcopal Church **P** (555) §
910 Hudson Rd 29615-3430 (Mail to: PO Box
25817 29616-0817) Furman Buchanan Marie
Cope (864) 268-7280

Greenville Saint Philip's Episcopal Church **M** (44)
31 Allendale Ln 29607-2208 (Mail to: PO Box
17521 29606-8521) (864) 271-1382

Greenwood Church of the Resurrection **P** (484)
700 Main St W 29646-3211 (Mail to: PO Box

3283 29648-3283) Timothy Ervolina (864)
223-5426

Greer Church of the Good Shepherd **P** (189) 200
Cannon St 29651-3705 (Mail to: PO Box 1408
29652-1408) Michael Schnatterly (864) 877-
2330

Hopkins St Johns Episcopal Church **P** (168) 1151
Elm Savannah Rd 29061-8938 (Mail to: 1151
Elm Savannah Rd 29061-8938) Daniel Hank
(803) 776-9292

Irmo Church of St Simon and St Jude **P** (278) 1110
Kinley Rd 29063-9633 (Mail to: 1110 Kinley Rd
29063-9633) Mark Abdelnour (803) 732-0153

Jenkinsville St Barnabas Episcopal Church **M**
(71) 1056 St Barnabas Rd 29065-9400 (Mail to:
PO Box 18 29065-0018) (803) 635-4995

Lancaster Christ Episcopal Church **P** (111) 534
Plantation Rd 29720 (Mail to: PO Box 488
29721-0488) (803) 286-5224

Laurens Church of the Epiphany **P** (81) 225 W
Main St 29360-2940 (Mail to: 225 W Main St
29360-2940) (864) 984-7000

Lexington St Albans Episcopal Church **P** (343)
403 Park Rd 29072-9060 (Mail to: PO Box 882
29071-0882) Thomas Dimarco (803) 359-2444

Newberry St Lukes Episcopal Church **P** (108)
1605 Main St 29108-3456 (Mail to: 1605 Main
St 29108-3456) (803) 276-8513

North Augusta St Bartholomews Episcopal
Church **P** (539) 471 W Martintown Rd 29841-
3105 (Mail to: 471 W Martintown Road 29841-
3105) Nancee Cekuta (803) 279-4622

Pauline Calvary Episcopal Church **M** (55) C/O
Claude Finney 305 Quinn Rd 29374-2834
(Mail to: C/O Claude Finney 305 Quinn Rd
29374-2834) (864) 582-3952

Ridgeway St Stephens Episcopal Church **M** (67)
335 Longtown Rd 29130-6814 (Mail to: PO Box
26 29130-0026) Mark Werner (803) 337-2905

Rock Hill Church Of Our Saviour **P** (565) § 144
Caldwell St 29730-4534 (Mail to: 144 Caldwell
St 29730-4534) Jane Wilson (803) 327-1131

Seneca Church of the Ascension **P** (159) 214
Northampton Road 29672-2221 (Mail to: 214
Northampton Rd 29672-2221) Carol Marshall
(864) 882-2006

Simpsonville Holy Cross Episcopal Church **P**
(677) § 205 E College St 29681-2616 (Mail to:
PO Box 187 29681-0187) Michael Flanagan
Erin Rath (864) 967-7470

Spartanburg Episcopal Church of the Advent **P**
(1499) § 141 Advent St 29302-1904 (Mail to:
141 Advent St 29302-1904) Jonathan Morris
Pauline Griffin (864) 585-2268

Spartanburg Episcopal Church of the Epiphany
M (53) 121 W Park Dr 29306-5010 (Mail to:
PO Box 726 29304-0726) (864) 583-0405

Spartanburg St Christophers Church Episcopal
M (169) 400 Dupre Dr 29307-2976 (Mail to:
400 Dupre Dr 29307-2976) Leslie Horvath
(864) 585-2858

Spartanburg St Matthews Episcopal Church **P** (501) 101 Saint Matthews Ln 29301-1378 (Mail to: 101 Saint Matthews Ln 29301-1378) Robert Brown Mia Chelynn McDowell (864) 576-0424

Trenton Episcopal Church of the Ridge **M** (105) 117 Watson St 29847-0206 (Mail to: PO Box 206 29847-0206) (803) 275-3934

Union Church of the Nativity **M** (61) 320 S Church St 29379-2307 (Mail to: PO Box 456 293790456) (864) 427-8610

Winnsboro St Johns Episcopal Church **P** (105) 301 W Liberty St 29180-1423 (Mail to: 301 W Liberty St 29180-1423) (803) 635-4398

York Church of the Good Shepherd **P** (202) 108 E Liberty St 29745-1549 (Mail to: PO Box 437 29745-0437) Paul Greeley (803) 684-4021

DIOCESE OF UTAH
(PROVINCE VIII)
Comprises the State of Utah, excluding Navajoland and including Page, AZ
DIOCESAN OFFICE 75 South 200 East Salt Lake City UT 84111-2147
TEL (801) 322-4131,   FAX (801) 322-5096
E-MAIL mdaly@episcopal-ut.org   WEB www.episcopal-ut.org

Previous Bishops—
Daniel S Tuttle 1867-86, Abiel Leonard 1888-1903, Franklin S Spalding 1904-14, Paul Jones 1914-18, Arthur W Moulton 1920-46, Stephen C Clark 1946-50, Richard S Watson 1951-71, E Otis Charles 1971-86, George E Bates 1986-97, Carolyn T Irish coadj 1996-97 Bp 1997-2010

Bishop—Rt Rev Scott B Hayashi (1038) (Dio 6 Nov 2010)

Bp Exec Asst M Daly; *Comm* C Wirth; *Chanc* S Hutchinson; *Treas* D Lingo; *Conv Sec* D Sakrison; *Fin Off* S Andersen; *Cn to the Ordinary & Exec Off* vacant; *Latino Missioner* P Ramos

Stand Comm—Cler: Pres P Ramos; *Lay: VP* N Tanner

Diocesan Council—Cler: Pres SB Hayashi *VP* T Browning

Comm on Min: Lay: Chair M LeTourneau

PARISHES, MISSIONS, AND CLERGY

Brigham City St Michaels Episcopal Church **M** (96) 589 S 200 E 84302-2903 (Mail to: 80 S 300 E 84111-1607) (801) 391-2185

Cedar City St Judes Episcopal Church **M** (35) 70 200 W 84720-2570 (Mail to: 70 200 W 84720-2570) (435) 586-3623

Centerville Church of the Resurrection **P** (182) 1131 S Main St 84014-2217 (Mail to: 92 E Pages Lane 84014-2216) (801) 295-1360

Clearfield St Peters Episcopal Church **P** (116) 1204 E 1450 S 84015-1643 (Mail to: 80 S 300 E 84111-1607) (801) 825-0177

Ivins Spirit of the Desert **M** (20) 873 Coyote Gulch Ct Ste D 84738-6708 (Mail to: 873 Coyote Gulch Ct Ste D 84738-6708) (435) 592-0034

Logan St Johns Episcopal Church **P** (287) 85 E 100 84321-4624 (Mail to: 85 E 100 84321-4624) (435) 752-0331

Midvale St James Episcopal Church **P** (510) 7486 Union Park Ave 84047-4164 (Mail to: 7486 S Union Park Ave 84047-4164) Christopher Szarke John Dillon (801) 566-1311

Moab Mision de San Francisco **P** 250 Kane Creek Blvd 84532-2538 (Mail to: PO Box 596 84532-0596) (435) 259-3113

Moab St Francis Episcopal Church **P** (156) 250 Kane Creek Blvd 84532-2950 (Mail to: PO Box 96 84532-0096) (435) 259-5831

Ogden Church of the Good Shepherd **P** (214) 2374 Grant Ave 84401-1408 (Mail to: 2374 Grant Ave 84401-1408) Vanessa Cato Nancy Groshart Lewis Poggemeyer (801) 392-8168

Page St Davids Episcopal Church **M** (162) 421 S Lake Powell Blvd 86046 (Mail to: PO Box 125 86040-0125) (928) 645-4965

Park City St Lukes Church **P** (283) 4595 N. Silver Springs Dr. 84098 (Mail to: PO Box 981208 84098-1208) (435) 649-4900

Price Ascension St Matthew's Episcopal Church **M** (143) 522 Homestead Blvd 84501-2261 (Mail to: PO Box 881 84501-0881) (435) 637-0106

Provo Saint Mary's Church **P** (96) 50 W 200 84601-2806 (Mail to: 50 W 200 84601-2806) Craig Klein Timothy Yanni (801) 373-3090

Randlett Church of the Holy Spirit **M** (221) 4250 South 10000 E 84063 (Mail to: PO Box 630016 84063) (435) 545-2400

Salt Lake City All Saints Episcopal Church **P** (394) 1710 Foothill Dr 84108-3052 (Mail to: 1710 S Foothill Dr 84108-3052) Tracy Browning Garang Atem Ernest Bebb Antoinette Catron Miner Deborah Hughes-Habel (801) 581-0380

✠ **Salt Lake City** Cathedral Church Of Saint Mark **O** (832) 231 E 100 S 84111-1604 (Mail to: 231 E 100 S 84111-1604) Tyler Doherty Tyler

Doherty Elizabeth Hunter Michael Milligan (801) 322-3400

Salt Lake City St Pauls Episcopal Church **P** (680) 261 S 900 E 84102-2308 (Mail to: C/O Selma Afridi 261 S 900 E 84102-2308) Kurt Wiesner Tracy Browning Christine Contestable (801) 322-5869

St George Grace Episcopal Church **P** (360) 1072 East 900 South 84790-4042 (Mail to: 1072 E 900 S 84790-4042) (435) 628-1181

Vernal St Pauls Episcopal Church **P** (63) 226 W Main St 84078-2506 (Mail to: 226 W Main St 84078-2506) (435) 781-1806

West Valley City Iglesia Episcopal San Esteban **P** 4615 S 3200 W 84119-5943 (Mail to: 4615 S 3200 W 84119-5943) (801) 968-2731

West Valley City St Stephens Episcopal Church **P** (153) 4615 S 3200 W 84119-5943 (Mail to: 4615 S 3200 W 84119-5943) (801) 968-2731

Whiterocks St Elizabeths Episcopal Church **P** (122) 11700 3900 E 84085 (Mail to: 80 S 300 E 84111-1607) (435) 353-4279

DIOCESE OF VENEZUELA
IGLESIA ANGLICANA/EPISCOPAL EN VENEZUELA
(PROVINCE IX)
DIOCESAN OFFICE Centro Diocesano, Ave Caroni No 100, Colinas de Bello Monte Caracas
(Mail: 49-143 Colinas de Bello Monte Caracas 1042-a Venezuela)
TEL: (58) 212-7513046 or (58) 212-7530723   FAX (58) 212-7513180
E-MAIL: obispoguerrero@iglesianglicanavzla.org   WEB www.iglesianglicanavzla.org

Previous Bishops—
Guy Marshall 1967-76, Hyden Jones 1976-1986, Onell Soto 1987-1995

Bishop—Rt Rev Orlando JT Guerrero (1004)

Dio Admin: Sr Marco A Ramos C; *Treas:* Sr José Francisco; *Chris Ed:* Lic Adrían E Cárdenas T

PARISHES, MISSIONS, AND CLERGY

Barquisimeto Misión San Judas Tadeo **M** Av. Florencio Jimenez - KM14 Via Quibor (Mail to: Ave Florencio Jimenez Manzana Caja No. L-95)

Caraballeda Misión Anglicana San Mateo **M** Vista al Mar (Mail to: Centro Diocesano) (212) 615-4440

Caracas Capilla de la Reconciliacion **P** Ave Caroni #100, Colinas Bello Monte (Mail to: Ave Caroni #100, Colinas Bello Monte) (212) 753-0723

Caripe Misión de la Sagrada Familia **M** El Potrero de Teresen (Mail to: Calle El Cementerio Arriba No. 27- Teresen) 2925551022

Caripe Misión de San Miguel Arcangel **M** Sector Alto de las Brisas (Mail to: Sector Alto de las Brisas) (281) 808-0882

Caripe 6224 Misión Bendita Virgen Maria **M** Sector La Sabana (Mail to: Sector La Sabana) 2925551022

El Callao, 8017 Misión de San Agustin de Cantorbery **M** Via Santa Elena de Uairen Km 72 (Mail to: Calle Orinoco #3) 2887621206

El Callao, 8056 Iglesia de la Resurreccion **M** Calle Heres Con Bolivar #14 (Mail to: Calle Heres # 14) 2887621206

Puerto La Cruz, 6023 Iglesia de la Santisima Trinidad **M** Valdez No. 46- Tierra Adentro (Mail to: Valdez No. 102- Tierra Adentro)

San Felix, 8050 Iglesia de la Santisima Cruz **M** Tumutu, Urb Bella Vista (Mail to: Calle Bakairies, Detras Semaforo El Roble) (414) 894-9254

San Flaviano Misión de San Flaviano **M** Carretera Nacional via la Gran Sabana (Mail to: Calle Orinoco #3) 2887621206

Steenrijk, Curacao Iglesia de Todos los Santos **P** Heelsumstraat #18 (Mail to: Heelsumstraat #18)

INSTITUTIONS

ISTESAC Insituto Superior de Teología San Agustine de Cantórbery *E-mail* istesac@ iglesianglicanavzla.org; *Web* www. iglesianglicanavzla.org/ISTESAC.htm

DIOCESE OF VERMONT
(PROVINCE I)
Comprises the State of Vermont
DIOCESAN OFFICE 5 Rock Pt Rd Burlington VT 05408-2735
TEL (802) 863-3431   FAX (802) 860-1562
E-MAIL adminasst@diovermont.org   WEB http://diovermont.org/

Previous Bishops—
John H Hopkins 1832-68, Wm
HA Bissell 1868-93, Arthur AC
Hall 1894-1929, Wm F Weeks
coadj 1913-14, Geo Y Bliss
coadj 1915-24, Samuel B Booth
coadj 1925 Bp 1929-35, Vedder
Van Dyck 1936-60, Harvey
D Butterfield 1961-74 Robert
S Kerr 1974-86, Daniel L Swenson coadj 1986 Bp
1987-93, Mary Adelia R McLeod Bp 1993-2001

Bishop—Rt Rev Thomas Clark Ely (965) (Dio
28 April 2001)

Cn to Ord L Bates; *Archdcn* C Cooke; *Fin-Property
Adm* R Sagui; *Bishop Booth Conf Ctr Mgr* A
Drapelick; *Reg/Hist* E Allison;; *Off Asst* A Carroll;
Bishop's Asst P Van de Graaf; *Off Admin* M Sandul;
Comm Min M Harris; *Conv Sec* J Cheney; *Treas* G
Davis; *Chanc* T Little; *V Chanc* W Meub; *Deploy
Off /Trans Min* L Bates; *COM COD Chair* LA
Crawford; *Dio Altar Guild Chair* E Maynard; *Earth
Stew Convener* W Grace; *Dismantling Racism Chairs*
The Rev R Spainhour M Harris; *Outreach & Social
Just Chair* LA Crawford; *Oversight & Audit Comm* L
Buel; *UTO Coord* W. Grace

Stand Comm—Cler: Pres R Swanson J Anderson
T Bennett K Hardy; *Lay:* S Ginn P Harrington L
Hunter B Murphy

PARISHES, MISSIONS, AND CLERGY

Alburg St Lukes Episcopal Mission **M** (11) 33
Main St 05440-9726 (Mail to: Attn Senior
Warden PO Box 113 05440-0113) (802) 863-
8036

Arlington St James Episcopal Church **P** (166) 46
Church St 05250-4457 (Mail to: PO Box 25
05250-0025) Christopher David (802) 375-
9952

Barre Church of the Good Shepherd **P** (84) 39
Washington St 05641-4236 (Mail to: PO Box
726 05641-0726) William Kooperkamp (802)
476-3929

Bellows Falls Immanuel Episcopal Church **HC**
(50) 20 Church St 05101-1515 (Mail to: PO
Box 64 05101-0064) Steven Fuller Charles
Mansfield (802) 463-3100

Bennington St Peters Episcopal Church **P** (443)
200 Pleasant St 05201-2526 (Mail to: 200
Pleasant St 05201-2526) Justin Lanier Penelope
Hawkins (802) 442-2911

Bethel Christ Episcopal Church **P** (30) 5 Main St
05032-9002 (Mail to: PO Box 383 05032-0383)
(802) 234-5680

Brandon St Thomas and Grace Church **P** (62) 19
Conant Sq 05733-1011 (Mail to: 19 Conant Sq
05733-1011) (802) 247-6759

Brattleboro St Michaels Episcopal Church **P** (314)
16 Bradley Ave 05301-3429 (Mail to: 16 Bradley
Ave 05301-3429) Mary Lindquist Duncan
Hilton Jean Jersey Jean Smith (802) 254-6048

✠ **Burlington** Cathedral Church of St Paul **O** (345)
2 Cherry St 05401-7304 (Mail to: 2 Cherry St
05401-7304) Joseph Baker Laura Bryant (802)
864-0471

Canaan St Paul-Border Parish **P** (3) 55 Power
House Rd 05903 (Mail to: 55 Power House Rd
05903) Robert Lee (802) 266-8269

Chester St Lukes Episcopal Church **P** (142) 313
Main St 05143-9864 (Mail to: PO Box 8 05143-
0008) Heidi Edson (802) 875-6000

Colchester Saint Andrew's Episcopal Church **P**
(188) 1063 Prim Rd 05446 (Mail to: PO Box 78
05446-0078) Robert Leopold (802) 658-0533

Enosburg Fls St Matthews Episcopal Church **P**
(24) C/O Michael Burfoot Md 1650 Water
Tower Rd 05450-5422 (Mail to: PO Box 276
05450-0276) Jane Presler (802) 933-6127

Essex Jct St James Episcopal Church **P** (328) 4 St
James Pl 05452-3223 (Mail to: 4 St James Pl
05452-3223) G David Ganter Kim Hardy (802)
878-4014

Fair Haven St Marks-St Lukes Episcopal Mission
M (24) 13 East Main St 05743 (Mail to: PO Box
535 05735-0535) (203) 788-6965

Fairlee St Martins Episcopal Church **P** (90) 1 Lake
Morey Rd 05045-9595 (Mail to: PO Box 158
05045-0158) Mark Preece (802) 333-9725

Hardwick Church of St John the Baptist **P** (43)
PO Box 424 05843-0424 (Mail to: PO Box 424
05843-0424) (802) 472-5979

Island Pond Christ Church Episcopal Mission **M**
(26) 5 Walnut Ave 05846 (Mail to: PO Box 341
05846-0341) (802) 723-6381

Killington Church of Our Saviour **M** (22) 316
Mission Farm Rd 05751-9451 (Mail to: PO Box
272 05751-0272) Lee Crawford (802) 422-9064

Lyndonville St Peter Episcopal Mission **M** (46) 51
Elm St 05851-9255 (Mail to: PO Box 41 05851-
0041) (802) 626-5705

Manchestr Ctr Zion Church **P** (631) 5167 Main St
05255-9772 (Mail to: PO Box 717 05255-0717)
John Mitchell (802) 362-1987

Middlebury St Stephens Episcopal Church **P** (464) 3 Main St 05753-1450 (Mail to: 3 Main St 05753-1450) Donald Morris Lucy Pellegrini (802) 388-7200

Montpelier Christ Episcopal Church **P** (229) 64 State St 05602-2933 (Mail to: 64 State St 05602-2933) Paul Habersang (802) 223-3631

Newport St Marks Episcopal Church **HC** (183) 44 2nd St 05855-2178 (Mail to: PO Box 125 05855-0125) Robert Wilson (802) 334-7365

Northfield St Marys Episcopal Church **P** (42) 203 S. Main St. 05663-5670 (Mail to: 203 S Main St 05663-5670) M P Schneider (802) 485-8221

Norwich St Barnabas Episcopal Church **P** (58) 262 Main St 05055 (Mail to: PO Box 306 05055-0306) Jennie Anderson Todd Mckee (802) 649-1923

Proctorsville Gethsemane Church **P** (41) Depot St 05153 (Mail to: PO Box 217 05153-0217) (802) 226-7967

Randolph St Johns Episcopal Church **P** (80) 15 Summer St 05060-1162 (Mail to: PO Box 278 05060-0278) (802) 728-9910

Rutland Trinity Episcopal Church **P** (471) 85 West St 05701-3452 (Mail to: 85 West St 05701-3452) William Muller (802) 775-1004

S Burlington All Saints Episcopal Church **P** (207) 1250 Spear St 05403-7407 (Mail to: 1250 Spear St 05403-7407) David Hamilton Daniel MacDonald Margaret Mathauer (802) 862-9750

Saint Albans St Lukes Church **P** (165) 8 Bishop St 05478-1639 (Mail to: 8 Bishop St 05478-1639) James Ballard (802) 524-6212

Shelburne Trinity Episcopal Church **P** (475) 5171 Shelburne Rd 05482-6509 (Mail to: 5171 Shelburne Rd 05482-6509) Frederick Moser (802) 985-2269

Sheldon Grace Church **M** (12) Beth Crane Senior Warden 215 Pleasant St 05483-9801 (Mail to: 215 Pleasant St 05483-9696) (802) 899-1188

Springfield St Marks Church **P** (37) 33 Fairground Rd 05156-2112 (Mail to: 33 Fairground Rd 05156-2112) (802) 885-2723

St Johnsbury St Andrews Episcopal Church **P** (40) 1265 Main St 05819-2697 (Mail to: 1265 Main St 05819-2697) (802) 748-2121

Stowe St Johns in the Mountains **P** (125) 1994 Mountain Road 05672-1175 (Mail to: PO Box 1175 05672-1175) Richard Swanson (802) 253-7578

Swanton Holy Trinity Episcopal Church **P** (141) 38 Grand Ave 05488-0273 (Mail to: 38 Grand Ave 05488-1427) John Spainhour (802) 868-7185

Underhill Calvary Episcopal Church **P** (80) 372 Vermont Route 15 05489-0057 (Mail to: PO Box 57 05489-0057) (802) 899-2326

Vergennes St Paul's Episcopal Church **P** (117) 6 Park St 05491-1129 (Mail to: PO Box 196 05491-0196) Alan Kittelson (802) 877-3322

Waitsfield St Dunstans Episcopal Mission **M** (14) § 6307 Main Street 05673 (Mail to: PO Box 1133 05673-1133) Laurian Seeber (802) 479-7920

Wells St Pauls Episcopal Church **M** (45) 587 E Wells Rd 05774-3847 (Mail to: PO Box 726 05774-0726) William Davidson (518) 499-1850

White Riv Jct St Pauls Episcopal Church **P** (204) 749 Hartford Ave 05001-8037 (Mail to: 749 Hartford Ave 05001-1693) Scott Neal (802) 295-5415

Wilmington St Mary in the Mountain Epis **P** (53) 13 E Main St 05363-9645 (Mail to: PO Box 1366 05363-1366) Nicholas Porter (802) 464-9341

Windsor St Pauls Episcopal Church **P** (29) 27 State St 05089-1201 (Mail to: PO Box 725 05089-0725) (802) 674-6576

Woodstock St James Episcopal Church **P** (125) 2 St. James Place 05091-1214 (Mail to: 2 St. James Place 050911214) Lisa Ransom (802) 457-1727

DIOCESE OF THE VIRGIN ISLANDS
(PROVINCE II)
Comprises the American and British Virgin Islands
DIOCESAN OFFICE #13 Commandant Gade Charlotte Amalie St Thomas
US Virgin Islands 00801
(MAIL: PO Box 7488 St Thomas VI 00801)
TEL (340) 776-1797   FAX (340) 777-8485

Previous Bishops— Cedric E Mills 1963-72, Edward M Turner 1972-86, Richard B Martin int 1985-87, E Don Taylor 1987-94, Telesforo A Isaac int (1996-May 1997) Theodore A Daniels

1997-2003 Telesforo Issac 2004-05

Bishop—E Ambrose Gumbs (1003) (Dio 11 June 05)

Treas J Williams; *Hist* B Hodge-Smith; *Chanc* Atty R Simmonds-Ballentine; *Conv Sec* L Turnbull; *Fin Comm Chr* R Javois; *COM Chr* Rev E Georges

Stand Comm—Cler: E George S Malone G Gibson
Lay: Pres M Hennessey L Claxton M Jacobs

PARISHES, MISSIONS, AND CLERGY

Christiansted St Croix St John's Episcopal Church **P** (151) 27 King St 00820 (Mail to: PO Box 486 00821-0486) (340) 778-8221 Rev Gregory Gibson

Christiansted St Croix St Peter's Episcopal Church **P** (185) Castle Coakley 38-40 00820 (Mail to: PO Box 7974 00823-7974) Rev Alric Francis (340) 778-6471

Cruz Bay St John St Ursula Church **M** (33) 295 Contant 00831 (Mail to: PO Box 199 00831-0199) (340) 777-6306 Cn Lionel Rymer Dcn Reginald Hodge

Frederiksted St Croix Iglesia San Francisco Episcopal **M** (19) 20 Estate Diamond 00840 (Mail to: PO Box 1796 00851-1796) (340) 776-1797 Dcn Aida Nieves

Frederiksted St Croix St Paul's Episcopal Church **P** (103) 25-26-27 Prince St 00841-0745 (Mail to: PO Box 745 00841-0745) (340) 772-0818 Cn Samuel Knight

Kingshill St Croix Episcopal Church of the Holy Cross **P** (35) Estate Upper Love 00850 (Mail to: RR 1 Box 8005 00850-9860) (340) 778-3272 Rev Amonteen Doward

SCB St Paul's Episcopal Church **M** (85) (Mail to: PO Box 3066 Tortola VG1110) (284) 494-4732 Rev Sandra Walters Malone

St Thomas Cathedral Church of All Saints **P** (227) § PO Box 1148 Charlotte Amalie Street 00804 (340) 774-0217 Dcn Clarence Scipio

St Thomas Church of the Holy Spirit **M** (36) (Mail to: PO Box 301827 00803-1827) (340) 776-1797 Bishop Ambrose Gumbs

St Thomas Nazareth by the Sea **M** 6501 Red Hook Ste 201 St Thomas VI 00802 (44) (340) 776-1797

St Thomas St Andrew's Episcopal Church **P** (450) 31-33 Frist Ave Sugar Estate 00802 (Mail to: PO Box 7386 008010386) (340) 774-1223 Rev Lenroy Cabey Dcn B Bartlett Dcn Marigold Browne

St Thomas St Luke's Episcopal Church **P** (49) Smith Bay #10A & 115A 00801 (Mail to: PO Box 7335 00801-0335) (340) 775-3100 Rev Stedwart Lee

Tortola St George the Martyr Church **P** (229) 170 Main St Road Town VG1110 (Mail to: PO Box 28 Road Town VG1110) (284) 3894 Rev Dr Ian Rock

Virgin Gorda VG 1150 St Mary the Virgin Church (40) **P** Church Hill Road The Valley VG 1150 (Mail to: PO Box 65 The Valley VG 1150) (284) 495-5769 Rev Esther Georges

STATE OF VIRGINIA

Dioceses of Southern Virginia (SV), Southwestern Virginia (SwV), and Virginia (VA)

Abingdon—SwV
Accomac—SV
Afton—VA
Aldie—VA
Alexandria—VA
Altavista—SwV
Amelia Court House—SV
Amherst—SwV
Annandale—VA
Appomattox—SV
Arlington—VA
Arrington—SwV
Ashburn—VA
Ashland—VA
Aylett—VA
Baskerville—SV
Bedford—SwV
Berryville—VA
Big Stone Gap—SwV
Blacksburg—SwV
Blackstone—SV
Blue Grass—SwV

Bluefield—SwV
Bluemont—VA
Boonesville—VA
Bowling Green—VA
Bracey—SV
Brandy Sta—VA
Bremo Bluff—VA
Bristol—SwV
Buchanan—SwV
Buckingham—SV
Buena Vista—SwV
Burke—VA
Callaway—SwV
Cape Charles—SV
Cartersville—SV
Casanova—VA
Catlett—VA
Centreville—VA
Charles City—VA
Charlottesville—VA
Chase City—SV
Chatham—SV
Chesapeake—SV

Chester—SV
Chesterfield—SV
Christchurch—VA
Christiansburg—SwV
Claremont—SV
Clarksville—SV
Clifton Forge—SwV
Colonial Bch—VA
Colonial Hts—SV
Columbia—VA
Courtland—SV
Covington—SwV
Culpeper—VA
Danville—SV
Delaplane—VA
Disputanta—SV
Doswell—VA
Drakes Branch—SV
Dunn Loring—VA
Earlysville—VA
Eastville—SV
Elkton—VA
Emporia—SV

Fairfax—VA
Fairfax Sta—VA
Falls Church—VA
Farmville—SV
Farnham—VA
Fincastle—SwV
Forest—SwV
Franconia—VA
Franklin—SV
Fredericksburg—VA
Freeman—SV
Front Royal—VA
Galax—SwV
Glasgow—SwV
Glen Allen—VA
Gloucester—VA
Goochland—VA
Gordonsville—VA
Great Falls—VA
Greenwood—VA
Gretna—SV
Grottos—VA
Hague—VA

Halifax—SV	Marion—SwV	Petersburg—SV	Staunton—SwV
Hampton—SV	Markham—VA	Pocahontas—SwV	Sterling—VA
Hanover—VA	Martinsville—SwV	Pt Royal—VA	Suffolk—SV
Harrisonburg—VA	Massies Mill—SwV	Portsmouth—SV	Surry—SV
Haymarket—VA	Mathews—VA	Powhatan—SV	Tappahannock—VA
Heathsville—VA	McKenney—SV	Pulaski—SwV	Tazewell—SwV
Henrico—VA	McLean—VA	Pungoteague—SV	Temperanceville—SV
Herndon—VA	Mechanicsville—VA	Purcellville—VA	The Plains—VA
Hopewell—SV	Middleburg—VA	Radford—SwV	Toano—SV
Hot Spgs—SwV	Midlothian—SV	Rapidan—VA	Upperville—VA
Ivy—VA	Millers Tavern—VA	Reedville—VA	Victoria—SV
Java—SV	Millwood—VA	Remington—VA	Vienna—VA
Kenbridge—SV	Mineral—VA	Reston—VA	Virginia Bch—SV
Keswick—VA	Moneta—SwV	Richlands—SwV	Warfield—SV
Kilmarnock—VA	Monroe—SwV	Richmond—VA & SV	Warrenton—VA
King and Queen	Montpelier—VA	Rixeyville—VA	Warsaw—VA
Cthse—VA	Montross—VA	Roanoke—SwV	Washington—VA
King George—VA	Mt Jackson—VA	Rocky Mt—SwV	Waverly—SV
Lancaster—VA	Mt Vernon—VA	St Paul—SwV	Waynesboro—SwV
Lawrenceville—SV	New Kent—VA	Salem—SwV	West Pt—VA
Leesburg—VA	Newport News—SV	Saltville—SwV	White Marsh—VA
Lexington—SwV	Norfolk—SV	Scottsville—VA	White Post—VA
Loretto—VA	Norton—SwV	Shenandoah—VA	Wicomico Church—VA
Lorton—VA	N Chesterfield—SV	Smithfield—SV	Williamsburg—SV
Louisa—VA	N Prince George—SV	S Boston—SV	Winchester—VA
Luray—VA	Oak Grove—VA	S Hill—SV	Woodbridge—VA
Lynchburg—SwV	Oak Hill—VA	Spotsylvania—VA	Woodstock—VA
Machipongo—SV	Onancock—SV	Springfield—VA	Wytheville—SwV
Madison—VA	Orange—VA	Stafford—VA	Yorktown—SV
Manakin Sabot-VA	Orkney Spgs—VA	Stanardsville—VA	
Manassas—VA	Pearisburg—SwV	Stanley—VA	

DIOCESE OF VIRGINIA
(PROVINCE III)
Comprises 38 northern and northwestern VA counties
DIOCESAN OFFICE 110 W Franklin St Richmond VA 23220
TEL (804) 643-8451, 1-800-DIOCESE   FAX (804) 644-6928
E-MAIL bishopsoffice@thediocese.net

NORTHERN VA OFFICE 115 E Fairfax St Falls Church VA 22046
TEL (703) 241-0441   FAX (703) 531-0082
WEB www.thediocese.net

Previous Bishops—
James Madison 1790-1812, Richard C Moore 1814-41, Wm Meade coadj 1829 Bp 1842-62, John Johns coadj 1842 Bp 1862-76, Francis M Whittle coadj 1868 Bp 1876-1902, Alfred M Randolph coadj 1883-1892, John B Newton coadj 1894-97, Robt A Gibson coadj 1897 Bp 1902-19, Arthur S Lloyd coadj 1909-10, Wm C Brown coadj 1914 Bp 1919-27, Henry StG Tucker coadj 1926 Bp 1927-44, Wiley R Mason suffr 1942-50, Fredk D Goodwin coadj 1930 Bp 1944-60, Robt F Gibson Jr suffr 1949-54 coadj 1954 Bp 1960-74, Samuel B Chilton suffr 1960-69, Phil A Smith suffr 1970-73, John A Baden suffr 1973-79, Robt B Hall coadj 1966 Bp 1974-85, David H Lewis Jr suffr 1980-87, Robt P Atkinson asst 1989-93, FC Matthews suff 1993-99, Francis C Gray ret asst 1999-2006, Peter James Lee coadj 1984 Bp 1985-2009, David C Jones suff 1995-2012, Edwin F Gulick Jr ret asst 2011-17

Bishop—Rt Rev Shannon S Johnston (1017)
(Coadjutor 2007, Bp 1 Oct 2009-3 Nov 2018)

Bishop Suffragan—Rt Rev Susan E Goff (1066)

Chanc JP Causey Jr Esq; *Pres Exec Bd* Rt Rev S Goff; *Dio Sec* T Smith; *Treas* T Smith; *Cn to Ord* Rev M

Thorpe; *Dir Chr Form* P Ball; *Dep Off* Rev M Thorpe; *Stew* J Simonton; *Comm Off* N Chafin

Stand Comm—Cler: Pres G Ambrose C Hancock D Niemeyer P Roaf A Merrow B Willis; *Lay:* B Anderson B Davenport S Walker D Wright A Cameron C Thomas

Deans of Regions: K Coleman R Alexander H Smith C Bailey B Shelton C Hicks C Tibbetts M Feather C McKinney D Trogdon C Newlun L Lloyd K Guin T Heflin S Smith Graham M Rhodes

PARISHES, MISSIONS, AND CLERGY

Afton Holy Cross Church **M** (85) 190 Rockfish School Ln 22920 (Mail to: PO Box 12 22924-0012) Anthony Andres Ryan Lesh (540) 456-6305

Aldie Church of Our Redeemer **M** (548) § PO Box 217 20105-0217 (Mail to: PO Box 217 20105-0217) John Sheehan (703) 327-4060

Alexandria All Saints Sharon Chapel **P** (222) 3421 Franconia Rd 22310-2320 (Mail to: 3421 Franconia Rd 22310-2320) Valerie Hayes Bernard Ramey (703) 960-4808

Alexandria Christ Church **P** (2496) § 118 Washington St 22314-3023 (Mail to: 118 Washington St 22314-3078) Diane Murphy Lyndon Shakespeare Seldon Walker Noelle York-Simmons (703) 549-1450

Alexandria Church Of The Resurrection **P** (189) PO Box 11210 22312-0210 (Mail to: 2280 Beauregard St 22311-2299) Jo Belser (703) 998-0888

Alexandria Church of the Spirit **P** (172) § C/O Olivet Episcopal Church 6107 Franconia Rd 223102542 (Mail to: C/O Olivet Episcopal Church 6107 Franconia Rd 223102542) Cornelia Weierbach (703) 971-5242

Alexandria Emmanuel Church **P** (648) § 1608 Russell Rd 22301-1926 (Mail to: 1608 Russell Rd 22301-1998) Charles Mccoart Joan Peacock (703) 683-0798

Alexandria Grace Episcopal Church **P** (885) § 3601 Russell Rd 22305-1731 (Mail to: 3601 Russell Rd 22305-1799) Robert Malm Pedro Cuevas Feliz (703) 549-1980

Alexandria La Iglesia de San Marcos **M** (100) 6744 S Kings Hwy 22306-1318 (Mail to: 6744 S Kings Hwy 22306-1318) (703) 765-3949

Alexandria Immanuel Church on the Hill **P** (837) 3606 Seminary Rd 22304-5200 (Mail to: 3606 Seminary Rd 22304-5200) Joseph Alexander Patricia Alexander John Hogg Rachel Rickenbaker (703) 370-6555

Alexandria Meade Memorial Church **P** (120) § 322 Alfred St 22314-2423 (Mail to: 322 Alfred St 22314-2423) Collins Asonye (703) 549-1334

Alexandria Olivet Church **P** (82) § 6107 Franconia Rd 22310-2508 (Mail to: 6107 Franconia Rd 22310-2508) John Cadaret Robert Tedesco (703) 971-4733

Alexandria St Aidans Church **P** (277) 8531 Riverside Rd 22308-2206 (Mail to: 8531 Riverside Rd 22308-2200) John Baker (703) 360-4220

Alexandria St Luke's Church **P** (439) § 8009 Fort Hunt Road 22308-1207 (Mail to: 8009 Fort Hunt Rd 22308-1293) Ellis Bowerfind Michael Moore Veronika Travis (703) 765-4342

Alexandria Saint Mark's Church **P** (257) § 6744 S Kings Hwy 22306-1318 (Mail to: 6744 S Kings Hwy 22306-1318) Donna Foughty John Hall Juan Valderrama Sanabria (703) 765-3949

Alexandria Saint Paul's Episcopal Church **P** (2000) § 228 S. Pitt Steet 22314 (Mail to: 228 S Pitt St 22314-3797) Oran Warder Rosemary Beales Anne Monahan Elizabeth Rees Alyse Viggiano (703) 549-3312

Alexandria Church of St Clement **P** (276) § 1701 Quaker Ln 22302-2339 (Mail to: 1701 Quaker Ln 22302-2339) Cynthia Park Robin Razzino (703) 998-6166

Annandale St Albans Church **P** (526) 6800 Columbia Pike 22003-3431 (Mail to: 6800 Columbia Pike 22003-3431) Paul Moberly Jeffrey Shankles (703) 256-2966

Annandale St Barnabas' Church **P** (420) 4801 Ravensworth Rd 22003-5551 (Mail to: 4801 Ravensworth Rd 22003-5551) Carol Flanagan (703) 941-2922

Arlington La Iglesia de Cristo Rey **M** (147) 415 S Lexington St 22204-1226 (Mail to: 415 S Lexington St 22204-1226) (703) 524-4716

Arlington St Andrews Church **P** (200) 4000 Lorcom Ln 22207-3937 (Mail to: 4000 Lorcom Ln 22207-3937) Dorota Pruski Alfred Moss (703) 522-1600

Arlington St Georges Church **P** (481) § 915 Oakland St 22203-1916 (Mail to: 915 Oakland St 22203-1916) Shearon Williams John Shellito (703) 525-8286

Arlington St Johns Episcopal Church **P** (67) 415 S Lexington St 22204-1226 (Mail to: 415 S Lexington St 22204-1226) Ann Barker (703) 671-6834

Arlington Saint Mary's Episcopal Church **P** (1900) 2609 Glebe Rd 22207-3501 (Mail to: 2609 Glebe Rd 22207-3501) Andrew Merrow Christopher Cole Amy Slater (703) 527-6800

Arlington Saint Michael's Episcopal Church **P** (306) 1132 Ivanhoe St 22205-2445 (Mail to: 1132 Ivanhoe St 22205-2499) Elizabeth Franklin (703) 241-2474

Arlington St Peters Episcopal Church **P** (1079) § 4250 Glebe Rd 22207-4508 (Mail to: 4250 Glebe Rd 22207-4500) Craig Phillips Howard Kempsell Daniel Spors (703) 536-6606

Arlington San Jose Church **M** (192) 911 Oakland St 22203-1916 (Mail to: 911 Oakland St 22203-1916) (703) 524-4716

Arlington Trinity Church **P** (183) 2217 Columbia Pike 22204-4405 (Mail to: 2217 Columbia Pike

22204-4497) Kim Coleman Timothy Malone Elliott Waters (703) 920-7077

Ashburn Saint David's Church **P** (820) § 43600 Russell Branch Pkwy 20147-2903 (Mail to: C/O Lisa Gager 43600 Russell Branch Pkwy 20147-2903) Mary Brown William Packard (703) 729-0570

Ashland Church of St James the Less **P** (441) 125 Beverly Rd 23005-1821 (Mail to: 125 Beverly Rd 23005-1821) Jeffrey Higgins (804) 798-6336

Aylett St Davids Church **M** (45) 11291 W River Rd 23009-3000 (Mail to: PO Box 125 23009-0125) (804) 737-6685

Berryville Grace Episcopal Church **P** (360) 110 Church St 22611-1109 (Mail to: PO Box 678 22611-0678) Justin Ivatts (540) 955-1610

Berryville St Marys Church **M** (31) N Buckmarsh St 22611 (Mail to: PO Box 252 22611-0252) (540) 955-1610

Bluemont Church of the Good Shepherd **M** (37) 27 Good Shepherd Rd 20135-4725 (Mail to: PO Box 324 20135-0324) Ralph Bayfield (540) 554-8351

Boonesville Good Shepherd-of-the-Hills **M** (23) Intersection of SR601 & SR810 22940 (Mail to: PO Box 31 22940-0031) (434) 973-7688

Bowling Green St Asaphs Church **P** (109) 130 S Main St 22427-9424 (Mail to: PO Box 1178 22427-1178) (804) 633-5660

Brandy Station Christ Church **P** (73) 14586 Alanthus Rd 22714-0025 (Mail to: PO Box 25 22714-0025) (434) 286-3914

Bremo Bluff Grace Episcopal Church **M** (55) 754 Bremo Bluff Rd 23022-2104 (Mail to: PO Box 95 23022-0095) Thomas Hendrickson (804) 266-1410

Burke Church of the Good Shepherd **P** (1200) 9350 Braddock Rd 22015-1521 (Mail to: 9350 Braddock Rd 22015-1521) Charles Cowherd Philip Johnston Christine Mendoza (703) 323-5400

Burke St Andrews Church **P** (1237) § 6509 Sydenstricker Rd 22015-4210 (Mail to: 6509 Sydenstricker Rd 22015-4210) Timothy Heflin Margaret Peel (703) 455-2500

Casanova Grace Church Emmanuel Parish **P** (47) 5108 Weston Rd 20139 (Mail to: PO Box 18 20139-0018) James Cirillo (540) 788-4419

Catlett St Stephens Church **P** (206) 8695 Old Dumfries Road 20119-1922 (Mail to: 8695 Old Dumfries Rd 20119-1943) Peter Gustin (540) 788-4252

Centreville Saint John's Church **P** (175) § 5649 Mount Gilead Rd 20120-1906 (Mail to: 5649 Mount Gilead Rd 20120-1906) Carol Hancock (703) 803-7500

Charles City Westover Parish Church **P** (296) 6401 John Tyler Mem High 23030 (Mail to: 6401 John Tyler Memorial Hwy 23030-3310) April Greenwood (804) 829-2488

Charlottesville Mcilhany Parish **M** (66) 960 Monacan Trail Rd 22903-7704 (Mail to: 960 Monacan Trail Rd 22903-7704) (434) 293-3455

Charlottesville Saint Luke's, Simeon **M** (73) 1333 Thomas Jefferson Pkwy 22902-7518 (Mail to: PO Box 694 22902-0694) Brian Hutcherson (434) 970-5020

Charlottesville St Paul's Ivy Church **P** (796) 773 Neves Ln 22901-9594 (Mail to: PO Box 37 22945-0037) Justin Mcintosh Richard Lord (434) 979-6354

Charlottesville Christ Episcopal Church **P** (1453) 120 W High St 22902 (Mail to: 100 W Jefferson St 22902-5023) Paul Walker Joshua Bascom Marilu Thomas (434) 977-1227

Charlottesville Church of Our Saviour **P** (566) § 1165 Rio Rd E 22901-1810 (Mail to: 1165 E Rio Rd 22901-1810) David Stoddart Kathleen Sturges (434) 973-6512

Charlottesville St Pauls Memorial Church **P** (1662) 1700 University Ave 22903-2619 (Mail to: 1700 University Ave 22903-2619) William Peyton Heather Warren Mark Wastler (434) 295-2156

Charlottesville Trinity Episcopal Church **M** (120) 1118 Preston Ave 22903-2002 (Mail to: 1118 Preston Ave 22903-2002) Bertram Bailey (434) 293-3157

Christchurch Christ Church Parish **P** (155) 56 Christchurch Labe Rt 33 & 638 23031 (Mail to: PO Box 476 23149-0476) Stuart Wood (804) 758-2006

Colonial Beach St Mary's Church **P** (313) 203 Dennison St 22443-2311 (Mail to: 203 Dennison St 22443-2311) Nicholas Szobota Thomas Hughes (804) 224-7186

Columbia St Johns Church **M** (28) 43 Washington St 23038 (Mail to: C/O B A Jones PO Box 853 23038-0853) Richard Singleton (434) 842-3715

Culpeper St Stephens Episcopal Church **P** (287) 115 East St 22701-3021 (Mail to: 115 East St 22701-3021) Benson Shelton (540) 825-8786

Delaplane Emmanuel Episcopal Church, Delaplane **P** (180) 9668 Maidstone Rd 20144-2211 (Mail to: 9668 Maidstone Rd 20144-2211) Amanda Knouse (540) 364-2772

Doswell St Martins Church **M** (11) 10523 Doswell Rd 23047-1800 (Mail to: Attn Cecelia Wade PO Box 214 23047-0214) (804) 233-8120

Doswell The Fork Church **P** (154) 12566 Old Ridge Rd 23047-1710 (Mail to: 12566 Old Ridge Rd 23047-1710) Kenneth Forti (804) 227-3413

Dunn Loring Church of the Holy Cross **P** (481) 2455 Gallows Road 22027-1225 (Mail to: 2455 Gallows Rd 22027-1225) Robert Becker Jamie Samilio Denise Trogdon (703) 698-6991

Earlysville Buck Mountain Church **P** (189) 4133 Earlysville Rd 22936-2504 (Mail to: PO Box 183 22936-0183) Constance Clark (434) 973-2054

Elkton St Stephen & the Good Shepherd **P** (37) 7078 Rocky Bar Rd 22827-3503 (Mail to: 7078 Rocky Bar Road 22827) Laura Minnich-Lockey Stuart Wood (540) 249-4121

Fairfax Holy Cross Korean Epis Church **M** (37) 10520 Main St 22030-3380 (Mail to: 10520 Main St 22030-3380) (703) 563-6333

Fairfax Station St Peters in the Woods **M** (374) § 5911 Fairview Woods Dr 22039-1427 (Mail to: 5911 Fairview Woods Dr 22039-1427) Marlene Forrest Susan Hartzell (703) 503-9210

Falls Church La Iglesia de Santa Maria **M** (314) 7000 Arlington Blvd 22042-1827 (Mail to: 7000 Arlington Blvd 22042-1827) Roberto Orihuela (703) 533-9220

Falls Church St Patricks Episcopal Church **M** (126) § 3241 Brush Dr 22042-2569 (Mail to: 3241 Brush Dr 22042-2569) Tinh Huynh (703) 532-5656

Falls Church St Pauls Episcopal Church **P** (73) § 3439 Payne St 22041-2019 (Mail to: 3439 Payne St 22041-2019) Elizabeth Tomlinson (703) 820-2625

Falls Church The Falls Church Episcopal **P** (266) 115 E Fairfax St 22046-2903 (Mail to: 115 E Fairfax St 22046-2903) Michael Hinson Kelly Moughty John Ohmer (703) 241-0003

Farnham North Farnham Parish Church **P** (37) 231 Farnham Church Rd 22460 (Mail to: PO Box 343 22460-0343) (804) 333-4333

Fredericksbrg Church of the Messiah **M** (135) 5875 Plank Rd 22407-6229 (Mail to: 12201 Spotswood Furnace Ln 22407-2265) Kyle Tomlin (540) 786-3100

Fredericksbrg Trinity Church **P** (794) 825 College Ave 22401-5469 (Mail to: PO Box 3400 22402-3400) Kent Rahm David Casey (540) 373-2996

Fredericksburg St Georges Episcopal Church **P** (1195) § 905 Princess Anne St 22401-5821 (Mail to: 905 Princess Anne St 22401-5821) Joseph Hensley Areeta Bridgemohan Robert Miller (540) 373-4133

Front Royal Calvary Church **P** (362) 132 Royal Avenue 22630-2603 (Mail to: 132 Royal Ave 22630-2614) Valerie Hayes Jane Piver (540) 635-2763

Glen Allen Christ Episcopal Church **P** (1990) 5000 Pouncey Tract Rd 23059-5301 (Mail to: 5000 Pouncey Tract Rd 23059-5301) Shirley Smith Graham Richard Pelkey Darren Steadman (804) 364-0394

Gloucester Ware Episcopal Church **P** (318) 7825 John Clayton Memorial Hwy 23061-5108 (Mail to: PO Box 616 23061-0616) Theodore Ambrose (804) 693-3821

Goochland Grace Church **P** (228) 2955 River Road West 23063-0698 (Mail to: PO Box 698 23063-0698) Emily Dunevant (804) 556-3051

Gordonsville Christ Church **P** (78) 310 High Street 22942 (Mail to: PO Box 588 22942-0588) Jane Barr Mary Wells (540) 832-3209

Great Falls St Francis Church **P** (625) 9220 Georgetown Pike 22066-2726 (Mail to: 9220 Georgetown Pike 22066-2726) Tracey Kelly David Lucey (703) 759-2082

Greenwood Emmanuel Episcopal Church **P** (576) 7500 Rockfish Gap Tpke 22943-1802 (Mail to: 7599 Rockfish Gap Tpke 22943-1802) (540) 456-6334

Grottoes Grace Memorial Church **P** (76) C/O Sally Jensen 1203 Randall Rd Apt A6 24441-2433 (Mail to: 7120 Ore Bank Rd 24471-2206) Stuart Wood (540) 249-4121

Hague Cople Parish **P** (162) 72 Coles Point Rd 22469 (Mail to: PO Box 110 22469-0110) Rita White (804) 472-2593

Hanover Calvary Episcopal Church **P** (104) 13312 Courthouse Road 23069-0307 (Mail to: PO Box 307 23069-0307) (804) 537-5061

Hanover St Paul's Episcopal Church **P** (391) 8050 St Paul's Church Rd 23069 (Mail to: PO Box 441 23069-0441) Connor Newlun (804) 537-5516

Harrisonburg Emmanuel Church **P** (510) 660 S Main St 22801-5819 (Mail to: 660 S Main St 22801-5819) Edward Bachschmid (540) 434-2357

Haymarket St Pauls Church **P** (167) St. Paul's Episcopal Church 6750 Fayette Street 20169-2916 (Mail to: 6750 Fayette St 20169-2913) Sean Rousseau (703) 753-2443

Heathsville St Stephens Episcopal Church **P** (71) 6807 Northumberland Hwy 22473-3334 (Mail to: PO Box 40 22473-0040) Lucia Lloyd (804) 724-4238

Henrico Varina Church **P** (232) 2385 Mill Rd 23231-7019 (Mail to: 2385 Mill Rd 23231-7019) Catherine McKinney (804) 795-5340

Herndon St Timothys Church **P** (1353) § 432 Van Buren St 20170-5104 (Mail to: 432 Van Buren St 20170-5199) Richard Bardusch (703) 437-3790

Ivy St John the Baptist Church **M** (56) § State Route 637 22945 (Mail to: Attn: Treasurer PO Box 351 22945-0351) Kathleen Sturges (434) 295-0744

Keswick Grace Church **P** (222) 5607 Gordonsville Rd 22947-1906 (Mail to: PO Box 43 22947-0043) Gary Smith (434) 293-3549

Kilmarnock Grace Church **P** (533) § 303 S Main St 22482-9595 (Mail to: PO Box 1059 22482-1059) Pilar Parnell John Thomas (804) 435-1285

King and Queen Courthouse Immanuel Church **M** (5) 190 Allens Cir 23085 (Mail to: General Delivery 23085) (804) 785-6461

King George Emmanuel Church **P** (8) 17062 James Madison Pkwy 22485-2613 (Mail to: PO Box 134 22485-0134) (540) 775-3635

King George Hanover With Brunswick Parish - Saint John **P** (69) 9403 Kings Hwy 22485-3425 (Mail to: PO Box 134 22485-0134) Richard Fichter (540) 775-3635

King George Saint Paul's, Owens **P** (173) 5486 Saint Pauls Rd 22485-5436 (Mail to: 5486 Saint Pauls Rd 22485-5436) Leonard Gandiya (540) 663-3085

Lancaster St Marys Whitechapel **P** (75) 5940 White Chapel Rd 22503-3029 (Mail to: 5940 White Chapel Rd 22503-3029) Megan Limburg (804) 462-5908

Lancaster Trinity Episcopal Church **P** (66) § 8484 Mary Ball Rd, Lancaster 22503 (Mail to: C/O Craig H Giese PO Box 1546 22503) (804) 462-0610

Leesburg Christ Church Lucketts **M** (35) 14861 Newvalley Church Rd 20176-6031 (Mail to: 14861 Newvalley Church Rd 20176-6031) (703) 771-2196

Leesburg St Gabriels Episcopal Church **M** (129) 14 Cornwall St Nw 20176-2801 (Mail to: 14 Cornwall St NW 20176-2801) Daniel Velez-Rivera (703) 779-3616

Leesburg St James Church **P** (1240) § 14 Cornwall St NW 20176-2801 (Mail to: 14 Cornwall St NW 20176-2801) Mark Feather Katherine Bryant Katherine Bryant (703) 777-1124

Loretto Vauters Church **P** (81) § 3661 Tidewater Trl 22438 (Mail to: PO Box 154 22438-0154) Scott Parnell (804) 443-4788

Lorton Pohick Church **P** (637) § 9301 Richmond Hwy 22079-1519 (Mail to: 9301 Richmond Hwy 22079-1519) Donald Binder Lynn Ronaldi (703) 339-6572

Louisa St James Church **P** (183) 102 Ellisville Dr 23093-6550 (Mail to: PO Box 1216 23093-1216) Rodney Caulkins Charles Riffee (540) 967-1665

Luray Christ Church **P** (79) § PO Box 231 22835-0231 (Mail to: 16 Amiss Ave 22835-1310) Catherine Tibbetts (540) 743-5734

Madison Piedmont Bromfield Parish **P** (174) 214 Church St 22727-3013 (Mail to: PO Box 305 22727-0305) William Miller (540) 948-6787

Manakin Sabot St Francis Episcopal Church **P** (58) 1484 Hockett Rd 23103-2603 (Mail to: PO Box 303 23103-0303) John Maher (804) 784-6116

Manassas Trinity Church **P** (1156) 9325 West St 20110-5128 (Mail to: 9325 West St 20110-5197) Stuart Schadt Vinnie Lainson (703) 368-4231

Markham Episcopal Church of Leeds Parish **P** (299) 4332 Leeds Manor Rd 22643-1906 (Mail to: 4332 Leeds Manor Rd 22643-1906) (540) 364-2849

Mathews Kingston Parish **P** (286) 370 Main Street 23109-0471 (Mail to: PO Box 471 23109-0471) Gary Barker (804) 725-2175

Mc Lean St Dunstans Church **P** (659) § 1830 Kirby Rd 22101-5323 (Mail to: 1830 Kirby Rd 22101-5399) Stephen Shepherd Anna Scherer (703) 356-7533

Mc Lean St Johns Episcopal Church **P** (1302) § 6715 Georgetown Pike 22101-2243 (Mail to: PO Box 457 22101-0457) Martha Johns Stuart Kenworthy Dina Widlake (703) 356-4902

Mclean St Thomas Church **P** (367) § 8991 Brook Rd 22102-1510 (Mail to: 8991 Brook Rd 22102-

1599) Fran Gardner-Smith Anne Turner (703) 442-0330

McLean St Francis Korean Church **M** (30) 1830 Kirby Rd 22101-5323 (Mail to: 1830 Kirby Rd 22101-5323) Young Kwon Choi (804) 2210153

Mechanicsville All Souls Episcopal Church **M** (189) 9077 Atlee Rd 23116-2501 (Mail to: PO Box 2798 23116-0021) Katherine Dougherty (804) 229-4998

Mechanicsvlle Church of the Creator **P** (172) 7159 Mechanicsville Tpke 23111-3663 (Mail to: 7159 Mechanicsville Tpke 23111-3663) William Burk (804) 746-8765

Mechanicsvlle Immanuel Church **P** (281) 3263 Old Church Rd. 23111 (Mail to: 3263 Old Church Rd 23111-6224) Christopher Miller (804) 779-3454

Middleburg Emmanuel Church **P** (141) 105 E Washington St 20117 (Mail to: C/O Norris Beavers PO Box 306 20118-0306) Eugene LeCouteur (540) 687-6297

Millers Tavern Grace Church **P** (33) 604 Howerton Road 23115 (Mail to: PO Box 126 23115-0126) (804) 843-3587

Millers Tavern St Paul's Episcopal Church **P** (175) 360 Highway 23115 (Mail to: PO Box 278 23115-0278) Theodore McConnell Sarah Miller (804) 443-2341

Millwood Cunningham Chapel Parish **P** (135) 809 Bishop Meade Road 22646-0153 (Mail to: PO Box 153 22646-0153) Matthew Rhodes (540) 837-1112

Mineral Church of the Incarnation **M** (59) Rt 552 & Lee St 23117 (Mail to: PO Box 307 23117-0307) Lura Kaval (540) 894-0136

Montpelier Church of Our Saviour **M** (148) 17102 Mountain Rd 23192-2550 (Mail to: PO Box 11 23192-0011) Emily Krudys (804) 883-5943

Montross St James Church **P** (146) 15870 Kings Hwy 22520 (Mail to: PO Box 177 22520-0177) Alan Hooker (804) 493-8285

Montross St Pauls Church Nomini Grove **P** (34) 21983 Kings Hwy 22520-2912 (Mail to: Attn Treasurer 1819 Neenah Rd 22520-3115) (804) 493-8994

Mount Jackson St Andrews Church **P** (52) 5890 Main St 22842-9406 (Mail to: PO Box 117 22842-0117) Kathleen Murray (540) 477-3335

Mount Vernon St James' Episcopal Church **P** (114) 5614 Old Mills Rd 22309 (Mail to: 5614 Old Mill Rd 22309-3300) Charles Brock (703) 780-3081

New Kent St Peters Parish Church **P** (332) 8400 Saint Peters Ln 23124-2718 (Mail to: 8400 St Peters Ln 23124-2718) John Wigner (804) 932-4846

Oak Grove St Peters **P** (138) 2961 Kings Hwy 22443-5310 (Mail to: Attn: Alice Payne PO Box 757 22520) Rodney Gordon Linda Murphy (804) 224-0163

Oak Hill Church of the Epiphany **P** (126) 3301 Hidden Meadow Drive 20171 (Mail to: 3301

Hidden Meadow Dr 20171-4068) Hillary West (703) 466-5200

Orange St Thomas Episcopal Church **P** (179) 119 Caroline St 22960-1532 (Mail to: 119 Caroline St 22960-1532) Linda Hutton (540) 672-3761

✛ **Orkney Springs** Cathd Shrine of the Transfiguration **O** (9) 221 Shrine Mont Cir 22845 (Mail to: 221 Shrine Mont Cir 22845) (540) 856-2141

Port Royal St Peters Church **P** (66) § 823 Water St 22535 (Mail to: PO Box 399 22535-0399) Catherine Hicks (804) 742-5908

Purcellville St Peters Church **P** (416) 37018 Glendale St 20132-3422 (Mail to: PO Box 546 20134-0546) Thomas Simmons (540) 338-7307

Rapidan Emmanuel Church **P** (60) 28279 Rapidan Rd 22733-2431 (Mail to: PO Box 81 22733-0081) Philip Morgan Philip Morgan (540) 672-1395

Reedville St Marys Church **P** (65) 3020 Fleeton Rd 22539-4221 (Mail to: PO Box 278 22539-0278) Sandra Mizirl (804) 453-6712

Remington St Lukes Church **P** (45) 400 Church St 22734-9708 (Mail to: PO Box 267 22734-0267) Nancy Betz (540) 439-3733

Reston St Anne's Church **P** (1100) 1700 Wainwright Dr 20190-5500 (Mail to: 1700 Wainwright Dr 20190-5500) Laura Cochran Harold Johnson (703) 437-6530

Richmond All Saints Church **P** (1608) 8787 River Rd 23229-8303 (Mail to: 8787 River Rd 23229-8303) Brent Melton Judith Davis (804) 288-7811

Richmond Christ Ascension Church **P** (123) § 1704 W Laburnum Ave 23227-4312 (Mail to: 1704 W Laburnum Ave 23227-4312) David Keill (804) 264-9474

Richmond Church of the Holy Comforter **P** (293) 4819 Monument Ave 23230-3615 (Mail to: 4819 Monument Ave 23230-3615) Joseph Klenzmann Hilary Smith (804) 355-3251

Richmond Emmanuel Church at Brook Hill **P** (349) § 1214 Wilmer Ave 23227-2405 (Mail to: 1214 Wilmer Ave 23227-2405) (804) 266-2431

Richmond Epiphany Church **P** (310) 8000 Hermitage Rd 23228-3704 (Mail to: 8000 Hermitage Road 23228) Andrew Reinholz (804) 266-2503

Richmond Grace and Holy Trinity Church **P** (900) 8 Laurel St 23220-4700 (Mail to: 8 Laurel St 23220-4797) Bollin Millner Kimberly Reinholz (804) 359-5628

Richmond St Andrews Church **P** (195) 240 S Laurel St 23220 (Mail to: 236 S Laurel St 23220-6229) Barbara Ambrose Bruce Gray Andrew Moore (804) 648-7980

Richmond St Bartholomews Episcopal Church **P** (229) § 10627 Patterson Ave 23238-4701 (Mail to: PO Box 29626 23242-0626) Andrew Dunks (804) 740-2101

Richmond St Johns Church **P** (220) 2401 E Broad St 23223-7128 (Mail to: 2319 E Broad St 23223-7126) Sandra Levy Amelie Wilmer Anne Lane Witt (804) 649-7938

Richmond St Johns Episcopal Church **P** (267) 2401 E Broad St 23223 (Mail to: PO Box 336 22560-0336) Robert Friend Candine Johnson (804) 649-7938

Richmond St Marks Church **P** (300) 520 Boulevard 23220-3309 (Mail to: 520 Boulevard 23220-3309) John Niemeyer (804) 358-4771

Richmond St Martins Episcopal Church **M** (297) 9000 Saint Martin Ln 23294-4448 (Mail to: 9000 St Martins Ln 23294-4448) Lee Hutchson (804) 270-6786

Richmond St Mary's Episcopal Church **P** (1902) § Attn Gina M Alexander 12291 River Rd 23238-6112 (Mail to: 12291 River Rd 23238-6112) David May (804) 784-5678

Richmond St Matthews Episcopal Church **P** (702) § 1101 Forest Ave 23229-5845 (Mail to: 1101 Forest Ave 23229-5800) Stephen Schlossberg (804) 288-1911

Richmond St Pauls Church **P** (684) 815 E Grace St 23219-3409 (Mail to: 815 E Grace St 23219-3409) Molly Bosscher Molly Bosscher Susan Eaves William Queen (804) 643-3589

Richmond St Peters Episcopal Church **M** (50) 1719 22nd St 23223-4431 (Mail to: 1719 22nd St 23223-4431) Andrew Terry (804) 643-2686

Richmond St Philips Church **P** (293) 2900 Hanes Avenue 23222-3607 (Mail to: 2900 Hanes Ave 23222-3607) Phoebe Roaf (804) 321-1266

Richmond St Stephens Church **P** (4200) 6000 Grove Ave 23226-2601 (Mail to: 6000 Grove Ave 23226-2601) Gary Jones Eleanor McDaniel Stephen McGehee Claudia Merritt Penny Nash William Sachs (804) 288-2867

Richmond St Thomas Church **P** (654) 3602 Hawthorne Ave 23222-1824 (Mail to: 3602 Hawthorne Ave 23222-1824) Herbert Jones (804) 321-9548

Richmond St James Church **P** (2891) 1205 W Franklin St 23220-3711 (Mail to: 1205 W Franklin St 23220-3793) John McCard Carmen Germino Hilary Streever (804) 355-1779

Rixeyville Little Fork Episcopal Church **P** (144) 16471 Oak Shade Rd 22737-2927 (Mail to: PO Box 367 22737-0367) Emmetri Beane (540) 937-4306

Scottsville St Annes Parish **P** (179) § 410 Harrison St 24590 (Mail to: PO Box 337 24590-0337) (434) 286-3437

Shenandoah St Pauls Church **P** (12) 3075 Comertown Rd 22849-4047 (Mail to: 1012 Wahmona Ave 22849-1023) (540) 962-7112

Spotsylvania Christ Church **P** (577) 8951 Courthouse Rd 22553-2517 (Mail to: 8951 Courthouse Rd 22553-2517) William Queen (540) 582-5033

Springfield St Christophers Church **P** (561) 6320 Hanover Ave 22150-4009 (Mail to: 6320 Hanover Ave 22150-4099) Peter Ackerman (703) 451-1088

Stafford Aquia Church **P** (1157) 2938 Jefferson Davis Hwy 22554-1730 (Mail to: PO Box 275 22555-0275) John Morris James Rickenbaker (540) 659-4007

Stanardsville Grace Church **M** (117) 97 Main St 22973 (Mail to: PO Box 112 112 Main St 22973-0112) Anne West Grace Cangialosi (434) 985-7716

Stanley St Georges Church **M** (34) The Diocese Of Virginia 3380 Pine Grove Rd 22851-5411 (Mail to: The Diocese Of Virginia 110 W Franklin St 23220-5010) Stuart Smith (540) 778-3462

Sterling St Matthews Church **P** (738) § 201 E Frederick Dr 20164-2387 (Mail to: 201 E Frederick Dr 20164-2387) Carl Merola Robert Mansfield (703) 430-2121

The Plains Grace Church **P** (291) 6507 Main St 20198 (Mail to: PO Box 32 20198-0032) Edward Mathews (540) 253-5177

Upperville Trinity Church **P** (458) 9108 John S Mosby Hwy 20184-1776 (Mail to: PO Box 127 20185-0127) Edward Miller (540) 592-3343

Vienna Church of the Holy Comforter **P** (2045) § 543 Beulah Rd Ne 22180-3510 (Mail to: 543 Beulah Rd NE 22180-3599) Jon Strand (703) 938-6521

Warrenton St Andrews Church **M** (65) Attn Mr Ordie L Frazier 75 Frazier Rd 20186-2704 (Mail to: 75 Frazier Rd 20186-2704) (540) 675-3616

Warrenton St James Church **P** (641) § 73 Culpeper St 20186-3321 (Mail to: 73 Culpeper St 20186-3321) Benjamin Maas (540) 347-4342

Warsaw St Johns Church **P** (138) 5987 Richmond Rd 22572-1093 (Mail to: C/O Anne Douglas PO Box 1093 22572-1093) (804) 333-4333

Washington Trinity Church **P** (208) 379 Gay St 22747-1978 (Mail to: PO Box 299 22747-0299) Herschel Hunter (540) 675-3716

West Point St Johns Episcopal Church **P** (90) § C/O H V Perry 916 Main St 23181-0249 (Mail to: PO Box 629 23181-0629) Barbara Marques (804) 843-4594

West Point St Pauls Church **P** (57) 532 15th St 23181-0767 (Mail to: PO Box 767 23181-0767) (804) 843-3587

White Marsh Abingdon Church **P** (271) 4645 Geo Washington Mem Hwy 23183 (Mail to: PO Box 82 23183-0082) Sven Vanbaars (804) 693-3035

White Post Meade Memorial Church **M** (36) 192 White Post Road 22663-0007 (Mail to: PO Box 7 22663-0007) (540) 837-2354

Wicomico Church Wicomico Parish Church **P** (219) § 5195 Jessie B Dupont Mem Hwy 22579 (Mail to: PO Box 70 22579-0070) James Silcox (804) 580-6445

Winchester Christ Episcopal Church **P** (642) § 114 W Boscawen St 22601-4116 (Mail to: 114 W Boscawen St 22601-4116) Webster Gibson Jane Piver (540) 662-5843

Winchester St Pauls on the Hill Church **P** (184) 1527 Senseny Rd 22602-6423 (Mail to: 1527 Senseny Rd 22602-6423) Susan Macdonald (540) 667-8110

Woodbridge St Margaret's Episcopal Church **P** (120) 5290 Saratoga Ln 22193-3455 (Mail to: 5290 Saratoga Ln 22193-3455) Kathy Rowe-Guin (703) 590-3990

Woodstock Emmanuel Church **P** (93) 122 E Court St 22664-1727 (Mail to: 122 E Court St 22664-1727) Kathleen Murray (540) 459-2720

STATE OF WASHINGTON

Dioceses of Olympia and Spokane

DIOCESE OF WASHINGTON
(PROVINCE III)
Comprises DC and 4 counties of Maryland
DIOCESAN OFFICE Episcopal Church House Mt S Alban Washington DC 20016-5094
TEL (202) 537-6555 (800) 642-4427   FAX (202) 364-6605
E-MAIL newspaper@edow.org   WEB www.edow.org

Previous Bishops—
Henry Y Satterlee 1896-1908, Alfred Harding 1909-23, James E Freeman 1923-43, Angus Dun 1944-62, William F Creighton coadj 1959 Bp 1962-77, Paul Moore Jr suffr 1964-70, John T Walker suffr 1971-76 coadj 1976 Bp 1977-89, Ronald H Haines suffr 1986-90 Bp 1990-2000, Jane H Dixon suffr 1992-2002; John Bryson Chane 2002-2011

Bishop —Rt Rev Mariann Edgar Budde (1061)
(Dio 12 Nov 2011)

Cn to Ord & COO P Cooney ; *Cler Dev, Multicultural & Justice* Rev Cn P Clark; *Chanc* M Kostel; *V Chanc* A Coe; *Treas* P Barkett; *Hist* S Stonesifer; *Sec* K Roachford; *Strategic Fin Res Comm Prog Mgr* J Anderson; *Latino Miss* Rev S Goodwin; *Cn for Min Initiatives* Rev Cn M Hagans; *Miss for Evan & Community Engagement* Rev P Lyons; *Assoc for Lead Dev & Cong Care* Rev Dr R Phillips; *Archddcn* Ven S von Rautenkranz; *Strategic Comm Adv* Rev R Weinberg; *Miss for Collaborative Form* M Reyes; *Miss for Comm* D Lobban

Stand Comm—Cler: Pres S McJilton J Harmon K Lucas E O'Callaghan *Lay:* E Gilmore L Puricelli A Vanterpool vacancy

PARISHES, MISSIONS, AND CLERGY

Accokeek Christ Church, Saint John's Parish **P** 600 Farmington Rd W 20607-9732 (Mail to: 600 Farmington Rd W 20607-9732) Brian Vander Wel (301) 292-5633

✠ **Aquasco** St Mary **O** 13500 Baden Westwood Rd 20608 (Mail to: C/O St Pauls Church 20613) Mary McCarty (301) 579-2643

Avenue All Saints Church **P** (218) 22598 Oakley Rd 20609 (Mail to: PO Box 307 20609-0307) (301) 769-4288

Beltsville St Johns Church **P** (293) 11040 Baltimore Ave 20705-2118 (Mail to: PO Box 14 20704-0014) Joseph Constant John Price (301) 937-9242

Bethesda St Dunstans Episcopal Church **P** (369) 5450 Massachusetts Ave 20816-1653 (Mail to: 5450 Massachusetts Ave 20816-1653) Jeffrey Macknight (301) 229-2960

Bethesda St Lukes Church Trinity Parish **P** (369) 6030 Grosvenor Ln 20814-1852 (Mail to: 6030 Grosvenor Ln 20814-1852) Jessica Hitchcock Owen Thompson (301) 530-1800

Bethesda Church of the Redeemer **P** (173) 6201 Dunrobbin Dr 20816-1044 (Mail to: 6201 Dunrobbin Dr 20816-1044) Ciritta Park David Schlafer (301) 229-3770

Bowie Holy Trinity Episcopal Church **P** (390) § 13106 Annapolis Rd 20720-3829 (Mail to: 13106 Annapolis Rd 20720-3829) Leslie St Louis (301) 262-5353

Brandywine St Pauls Parish **P** (111) 13500 Baden Westwood Rd 20613-8419 (Mail to: 13500 Baden Westwood Rd 20613-8419) Christian Lehrer (301) 579-2643

Brandywine St Philips Church **P** (120) 13801 Baden Westwood Rd 20613-8426 (Mail to: 13801 Baden Westwood Rd 20613-8426) Christopher Wilkins Christopher Wilkins (301) 888-1536

Brookeville St Lukes Church **P** (125) PO Box 131 20833-0131 (Mail to: PO Box 131 20833-0131) Victoria Clayton (301) 570-3834

California St Andrews Church **P** (310) 44078 St Andrews Church Rd 20619 (Mail to: 44078 Saint Andrews Church Rd 20619-2100) Beverly Weatherly (301) 862-2247

Chaptico Christ Church **P** (369) 25390 Maddox Rd 20621 (Mail to: 37497 Zach Fowler Road P.O. Box 8 20621) Christopher Jubinski (301) 884-3451

Charlotte Hall All Faith Episcopal Church **P** (105) 38885 New Market Turner Rd 20659 (Mail to: PO Box 24 20622-0024) (301) 884-3773

Chevy Chase All Saints Episcopal Church **P** (1580) § 3 Chevy Chase Cir 20815-3408 (Mail to: 3 Chevy Chase Cir 20815-3400) Edward Kelaher Matthew Kozlowski Nathaniel Lee (301) 654-2488

Chevy Chase St Johns Church **P** (1175) 6701 Wisconsin Ave 20815-5351 (Mail to: 6701 Wisconsin Ave 20815-5399) Sari Ateek Hershey Mallette Stephens (301) 654-7767

Clinton Christ Church **P** (106) 8710 Old Branch Ave 20735-2522 (Mail to: 8710 Old Branch Ave 20735-2522) (301) 868-1330

College Park St Andrews Episcopal Church **P** (477) 4510 College Ave 20740-3302 (Mail to: 4512 College Ave 20740-3302) Timothy Johnson Kristen Pitts (301) 864-8881

College Park University of Maryland Mission **CC** University Of Maryland 2116 Memorial Chapel 20742 (Mail to: 2116 Memorial Chapel 20740) (301) 405-8453

Damascus St Anne's Church **P** (280) 25100 Ridge Rd 20872-1832 (Mail to: 25100 Ridge Rd 20872-1832) Ronald Davis (301) 253-2130

Ft Washington St Johns Broad Creek **P** (169) § 9801 Livingston Rd 20744-4925 (Mail to: 9801 Livingston Rd 20744-4925) (301) 248-4290

Gaithersburg Church of the Ascension **P** (1084) 205 S Summit Ave 20877-2315 (Mail to: Attn: Linett Keene 205 S Summit Ave 20877-2399) Kimberly Becker (301) 948-0122

Gaithersburg St Barnabas Church of the Deaf **M** (15) c/o Church of the Ascension 205 S Summit Ave 20877-2315 (Mail to: c/o Church of the Ascension 205 S Summit Ave 20877-2315) Elizabeth Anne Bagioni (301) 907-2955

Gaithersburg St Bartholomews Church **P** (160) 21615 Laytonsville Rd 20882-1627 (Mail to: PO Box 5005 20882-0005) Linda Calkins Margaret Pollock (301) 355-7189

Germantown St Nicholas Episcopal Church **P** (591) 15575 Germantown Road 20874-3012 (Mail to: 15575 Germantown Rd 20874-3012) Elizabeth O'Callaghan (240) 631-2800

Glenn Dale St Georges Church Glenn Dale Parish **P** (266) 7010 Glenn Dale Rd 20769 (Mail to: PO Box 188 20769-0188) Constance Reinhardt (301) 262-3285

✠ **Hughesville** Old Fields Chapel **O** 15837 Prince Frederick Road 20637-9801 (Mail to: PO Box 178 20637-0178) (301) 934-1424

Hughesville Trinity Parish **P** (215) PO Box 178 20637-0178 (Mail to: PO Box 178 20637-0178) (301) 934-1424

Hyattsville St Matthews Episcopal Church **P** (650) § 5901 36th Ave 20782-2925 (Mail to: 5901 36th Ave 20782-2925) Vidal Rivas Elena Thompson (301) 559-8686

Hyattsville St Michael and All Angels Church **P** (250) 8501 New Hampshire Ave 20783-2411 (Mail to: 8501 New Hampshire Ave 20783-2411) (301) 434-4646

Indian Head St James' Church **P** (153) 7 Potomac Ave 20640-1714 (Mail to: 7 Potomac Ave 20640-1798) Denise Cabana Roberta Taylor (301) 743-2366

Kensington Christ Church Parish **P** (663) 4001 Franklin St 20895-3827 (Mail to: 4001 Franklin St 20895-3827) Emily Guthrie (301) 942-4673

La Plata Christ Church **P** (164) 112 E Charles Street 20646-0760 (Mail to: PO Box 760 20646-0760) Katherine Heichler Steven Seely Eric Shoemaker (301) 392-1051

Laurel St Philips Church **P** (479) 522 Main St 20707-4118 (Mail to: 522 Main St 20707-4118) Sheila Mcjilton Robert Bunker (301) 7765151

Leonardtown St Georges Church **P** (264) 44965 Blake Creek Rd 20650 (Mail to: PO Box 30 20692-0030) Gregory Syler (301) 994-0585

Lexingtn Park The Church of the Ascension **P** (267) 21641 Great Mills Rd 20653-1239 (Mail to: 21641 Great Mills Rd 20653-1239) Harry Harper (301) 863-8551

Mount Rainier St Johns Episcopal Church **P** (285) 4104 34th St 20712-1948 (Mail to: 4112 34th St 20712-1948) (301) 927-1156

Nanjemoy Christ Church (Durham Parish) **P** (182) 8700 Ironsides Rd 20662-3430 (Mail to: 8685 Ironsides Rd 20662-3430) Catharine Gibson Arnold Taylor (301) 743-7099

New Carrollton Saint Christopher's Church **P** (212) 8001 Annapolis Rd 20784-3009 (Mail to: 8001 Annapolis Rd 20784-3009) Melana Nelson-Amaker (301) 577-1281

Newburg Christ Church Wayside William and Mary Parish **P** (99) 13050 Rock Point Rd 20664 (Mail to: PO Box 177 20664-0177) Steven Seely (301) 259-4327

Olney St Johns Church **P** (1153) § 3427 Olney Laytonsville Rd 20832-1743 (Mail to: PO Box 187 20830-0187) Henry McQueen John Price (301) 774-6999

Poolesville St Peters Parish **P** (333) 20100 Fisher Ave 20837-2080 (Mail to: PO Box 387 20837-0387) Emily Lloyd (301) 349-2073

Potomac St Francis Church **P** (1200) § 10033 River Rd 20854-4902 (Mail to: 10033 River Rd 20854-4975) Mark Michael James Stewart (301) 365-2055

Potomac St James Church **P** (268) § 11815 Seven Locks Rd 20854-3340 (Mail to: 11815 Seven Locks Rd 20854-3340) Meredith Heffner James Isaacs (301) 762-8040

✠ **Ridge** St Marys Chapel **O** 12960 Point Lookout Road 20687 (Mail to: PO Box 207 20686-0207) John Ball (301) 862-4597

Rockville Christ Church, Rockville **P** (592) § 107 S Washington St 20850-2319 (Mail to: 107 S Washington St 20850-2319) Debra Kissinger Cynthia Simpson (301) 762-2191

Silver Spring Our Saviour Hillandale **P** (560) 1700 Powder Mill Rd 20903-1514 (Mail to: 1700 Powder Mill Rd 20903-1500) Jose Valle (301) 439-5900

Silver Spring Church of the Ascension **P** (735) 633 Sligo Ave 20910-4764 (Mail to: 634 Silver Spring Ave 20910-4657) Joan Beilstein Terri Murphy (301) 587-3272

Silver Spring Church of the Transfiguration **P** (641) 13925 New Hampshire Ave 20904-6218 (Mail to: 13925 New Hampshire Ave 20904-6218) (301) 384-6264

Silver Spring Good Shepherd Episcopal Church **P** (281) § 818 University Blvd W 20901-1039 (Mail to: 818 University Blvd W 20901-1095) David Wacaster (301) 593-3282

Silver Spring Grace Episcopal Church **P** (780) § 1607 Grace Church Rd 20910-1509 (Mail to: Attn Gib Baily 1607 Grace Church Rd 20910-1563) Andrew Walter Amanda Akes Richard Meadows (301) 585-3515

Silver Spring St Marks Church Fairland **P** (231) 12621 Old Columbia Pike 20904-1614 (Mail to: 12621 Old Columbia Pike 20904-1614) Isaac Bonney (301) 622-5860

Silver Spring St Mary Magdalene Church **P** (185) 3820 Aspen Hill Rd 20906-2904 (Mail to: 3820 Aspen Hill Rd 20906-2904) Sarah Lamming (301) 871-7660

St Marys City St Marys Parish **HC** (237) PO Box 145 20686-0145 (Mail to: PO Box 207 20686-0207) John Ball (301) 862-4597

Temple Hills St Barnabas Episcopal Church **P** (117) 5203 St Barnabas Rd 20748-5837 (Mail to: 5203 Saint Barnabas Rd 20748-5837) Shell Kimble (301) 894-9100

✠ **Uppr Marlboro** Chapel of the Incarnation **O** 14300 Thomas Church 20772 (Mail to: 14300 St Thomas Church Rd 20772-8222) (301) 627-8469

Uppr Marlboro St Barnabas Church **P** (252) § 14111 Oak Grove Rd 20774-8424 (Mail to: 14111 Oak Grove Rd 20774-8424) Phillip Cato Robyn Franklin-Vaughn (301) 249-5001

Uppr Marlboro St Thomas Parish **P** (96) 14300 Saint Thomas Church Rd 20772 (Mail to: 14300 Saint Thomas Church Rd 20772-8222) Peter Antoci (301) 627-8469

Uppr Marlboro Trinity Episcopal Church **P** (351) 14515 Church St 20772-3039 (Mail to: PO Box 187 20773-0187) (301) 627-2636

Waldorf St Pauls Episcopal Church **P** (368) Piney Church Rd @ St Pauls Dr 20604 (Mail to: 4535 Piney Church Rd 20604-0272) Maria Kane Steven Seely (301) 645-5000

Washington All Souls Memorial Church **P** (406) 2300 Cathedral Ave Nw 20008-1505 (Mail to: 2300 Cathedral Ave NW 20008-1505) Diana Gustafson Jadon Hartsuff Elizabeth Orens (202) 232-4244

Washington Calvary Church **P** (334) 509 I St Ne 20002-4345 (Mail to: 820 6th St Ne 20002-4326) Gayle Fisher-Stewart Peter Jarrett-Schell (202) 546-8011

✠ **Washington** Washington National Cathedral **O** (1126) Attn Human Resources Dept 3101 Wisconsin Ave NW 20016 (Mail to: 3101 Wisconsin Ave NW Mt Saint Alban 20016-5015) Andrew Barnett Eva Maria Cavaleri Jeannette Cope Dana Corsello Rosemarie Duncan Randolph Hollerith Brooks Hundley Richard Kukowski Cameron Soulis Charles Walthall (202) 537-6200

Washington Christ Church Washington Parish **P** (357) 620 G St Se 20003-2722 (Mail to: C/O Washington Parish 620 G St Se 20003-2722) Cara Spaccarelli Mary Flowers Serena Sides (202) 547-9300

Washington Christ Church Georgetown **P** (1469) 3116 O St NW 20007-3116 (Mail to: 3116 O St NW 20007-3198) Timothy Cole Elizabeth Gardner Elizabeth Keeler Peter Lee (202) 333-6677

Washington Church of Our Saviour **P** (102) 1616 Irving St Ne 20018-3826 (Mail to: 1616 Irving St NE 20018-3826) (202) 635-7804

Washington Church Of Saint Stephen And The Incarnation **P** (210) 1525 Newton St Nw 20010-3103 (Mail to: 1525 Newton St Nw 20010-3199) Frank Dunn Linda Kaufman Dessordi Leite (202) 232-0900

Washington Church of the Ascension & St Agnes **P** (211) 1217 Massachusetts Ave Nw 20005-5301 (Mail to: 1217 Massachusetts Ave NW 20005-5396) Mary McCue Dominique Peridans (202) 347-8161

Washington Church of the Atonement **P** (281) 5073 E Capitol St Se 20019-5327 (Mail to: 5073 E Capitol St SE 20019-5327) (202) 582-4200

Washington Church of the Epiphany **P** (163) Rock Crk Ch Rd & Webster St NW 20747-4434 (Mail to: 3111 Ritchie Rd 20747-4434) Prince Decker (202) 726-2080

Washington Church of the Holy Comforter **P** (287) 701 Oglethorpe St Nw 20011-2021 (Mail to: 701 Oglethorpe St NW 20011-2021) Charles Wynder (202) 726-1862

Washington Church of the Holy Communion **P** (46) 3640 Martin L King Jr Ave SE 20032-1546 (Mail to: 3640 Martin L King Jr Ave SE 20032-1546) Rondesia Jarrett-Schell (202) 562-8153

Washington Howard University Episcopal Mission **CC** 2225 Georgia Ave 20059-1014 (Mail to: Howard University MS 59017 20059-0001) (202) 806-5747

Washington Grace Church **P** (365) 1041 Wisconsin Ave Nw 20007-3635 (Mail to: 1041 Wisconsin Ave NW 20007-3635) John Graham Sarah Fischer Shearon Williams (202) 333-7100

Washington Parish of St Monica and St James **P** (80) 222 8th St NE 20002-6106 (Mail to: 222 8th St NE 20002-6188) John Coleman Marilyn Jenkins William Stafford-Whittaker (202) 546-1746

Washington St Albans Episcopal Parish **P** (1857) 3001 Wisconsin Ave Nw 20016-5095 (Mail to: Attn: Doug Dykstra 3001 Wisconsin Ave NW Bldg 1 20016-5069) Emily Griffin Geoffrey Hoare Deborah Kirk James Quigley (202) 363-8286

Washington Saint Augustine's Episcopal Church **P** (119) 555 Water St SW 20024 (Mail to: 555 Water St SW 20024) Martha Clark (202) 554-3222

Washington St Columba's Episcopal Church **P** (3996) § 4201 Albemarle St Nw 20016-2009 (Mail to: 4201 Albemarle St NW 20016-2098) Ledlie Laughlin Jason Cox Susan Flanders Amanda Molina-Moore (202) 363-4119

Washington St Davids Episcopal Church **P** (407) 5150 Macomb St Nw 20016-2612 (Mail to: 5150 Macomb St NW 20016-2699) Kristen Hawley (202) 966-2093

Washington St Georges Church **P** (241) 160 U St Nw 20001-1606 (Mail to: C/O James O Williams 160 U St NW 20001-1606) John Hayden Stephen Marcoux Stephen Marcoux (202) 387-6421

Washington St Johns Church **P** (457) § Georgetown Parish 3240 O St Nw 20007-2842 (Mail to: 3240 O St NW 20007-2880) Sarah Duggin Virginia Gerbasi (202) 338-1796

Washington St Johns Church **P** (500) 1525 H St NW 20005-1005 (Mail to: 1525 H St NW 20005-1098) David Olivo (202) 347-8766

Washington St Lukes Church **P** (312) 1514 15th St NW 20036 (Mail to: 1514 15th St NW 20005-1922) Raymond Massenburg (202) 667-4394

Washington St Margarets Church **P** (449) 1820 Connecticut Ave Nw 20009-5732 (Mail to: 1830 Connecticut Ave NW 20009-5706) Kimberly Lucas Peter Antoci Richard Weinberg (202) 232-2995

Washington St Marks Church **P** (920) 301 A St SE 20003-3812 (Mail to: Attn P Schans or M Morgan 301 A St SE 20003-3812) Marcella Gillis Leonard Lipscomb Michele Morgan (202) 543-0053

Washington St Marys Church **P** (108) 728 23rd St Nw 20037-2501 (Mail to: 728 23rd St NW 20037-2598) (202) 333-3985

Washington St Patricks Church **P** (472) § 4700 Whitehaven Pkwy NW 20007-1554 (Mail to: 4700 Whitehaven Pkwy NW 20007-1586) Kurt Gerhard Jenifer Gamber (202) 342-2800

Washington St Pauls Parish **P** (750) 2430 K St Nw 20037-1703 (Mail to: 2430 K St NW 20037-1703) Douglas Greenaway James Jelinek Lloyd Lewis John Pham Shawn Strout Richard Wall (202) 337-2020

Washington St Pauls Rock Creek Parish **P** (159) 201 Allison St Nw 20011-7305 (Mail to: 201 Allison St NW 20011-7305) Allan Johnson-Taylor Gerald Cope Douglas Greenaway (202) 726-2080

Washington St Philip the Evangelist Episcopal **P** (109) § 2001 14th St Se 20020-4817 (Mail to: 2001 14th St SE 20020-4817) (202) 678-4300

Washington St Thomas Parish **P** (252) 1777 Church St NW 20036-1302 (Mail to: 1777 Church St Nw 20036-1302) Charles Dyer (202) 332-0607

Washington St Timothys Church **P** (310) § 3601 Alabama Ave Se 20020-2425 (Mail to: 3601 Alabama Ave SE 20020-2425) Jeanie Martinez-Jantz (202) 582-7740

Washington The Church of the Epiphany **P** (320) 1317 G St Nw 20005-3102 (Mail to: 1317 G St Nw 20005-3165) Glenna Huber Timothy Johnson (202) 347-2635

Washington Trinity Church **P** (604) 7005 Piney Branch Rd Nw 20012-2417 (Mail to: 7005 Piney Branch Rd NW 20012-2417) John Harmon (202) 726-7036

DIOCESE OF WEST MISSOURI

(PROVINCE VII)

Comprises counties of the western half of Missouri

DIOCESAN OFFICE 420 W 14th St Kansas City MO 64105

TEL (816) 471-6161

E-MAIL info@diowestmo.org   WEB www.diowestmo.org

Previous Bishops—
Edward R Atwill 1890-1911, Sidney C Partridge 1911-30, Robert N Spencer 1930-49, Robt R Spears Jr suffr 1967-70, Edward R Welles 1950-72, Arthur A Vogel 1973-89, John C Buchanan coadj 1989 Bp 1989-99 Barry R Howe 1998-2011

Bishop—Martin Scott Field (Dio 5 March 11)

Cn Ord & Cong Dev S Rottgers; *Sec* C Hamilton *Comm Dir* G Allman; *Treas* T Kokjer; *Chanc* D Powell; *Reg Min Dev* W Fasel T Coppinger S Breese

Stand Comm—Cler: Pres J Frazier L Ehren A Kyle J Spicer; *Lay:* G Leabo S Bolden M Christiano C Pryor

Deans: D Lynch C Marks J Tharakan

Chairs: COM R Maynard; *Yth* J Trader; *Lit; Hist* C Neuman; *ECW* J Turner; *Comp Dio* D Robinson; *Christian Form* K Snodgrass

PARISHES, MISSIONS, AND CLERGY

Blue Springs Church of the Resurrection **P** (225) § 1433 Nw R D Mize Rd 64015-3666 (Mail to: 1433 NW R D Mize Rd 64015-3666) David Lynch (816) 228-4220

Bolivar St Albans Episcopal Church **M** (61) 201 South Killingsworth 65613 (Mail to: PO Box 844 65613-0844) Catherine Cox Brenda Sickler (417) 777-2233

Boonville Christ Episcopal Church **M** (37) 524 4th St 65233-1552 (Mail to: 524 4th St 65233-1552) Martha Byer (660) 882-6444

Branson Shepherd of the Hills Church **P** (55) 107 Walnut Ln 65616-2220 (Mail to: 107 Walnut Ln 65616-2220) (417) 334-3968

Camdenton St George Episcopal Church **Chapel** (89) § 423 North Business Route 5 65020-9591 (Mail to: PO Box 1043 65020-1043) Lauretta Hughes (573) 346-4686

Carthage Grace Church **P** (808) 820 Howard St 64836-2318 (Mail to: PO Box 596 64836-0596) Steven Wilson (417) 358-4631

Cassville St Thomas a Becket Epis Ch **M** (30) 13628 State Highway AA 65625-8529 (Mail to: PO Box 613 65625-0613) (417) 846-2155

Chillicothe Grace Episcopal Church **P** (62) 421 Elm St 64601-2610 (Mail to: 421 Elm St 64601-2610) (660) 646-4288

Clinton St Pauls Episcopal Church **M** (78) 181 E Highway 7 64735-9504 (Mail to: PO Box 453 64735-0453) (660) 885-8008

Excelsior Springs St Luke Episcopal Church **M** (97) § 404 Regents Street 64024-2649 (Mail to: PO Box 551 64024-0551) John Coil (816) 630-2309

Fayette St Marys Episcopal Church **M** (18) 104 W Davis St 65248-1453 (Mail to: PO Box 57 65248-0057) (660) 248-3219

Harrisonville St Peters Episcopal Church **P** (106) 400 W Wall St 64701-2251 (Mail to: PO Box 425 64701-0425) John Richardson (816) 884-4025

Independence Saint Michael's Episcopal Church **P** (174) § 4000 S Lees Summit Rd 64055-4005 (Mail to: 4000 S Lees Summit Rd 64055-4005) (816) 373-5333

Independence Trinity Episcopal Church **P** (130) 409 Liberty St 64050-2701 (Mail to: PO Box 58 64051-0058) Karen Mann (816) 254-3644

Joplin St Philips Episcopal Church **P** (250) § 706 Byers Ave 64801-4304 (Mail to: 706 Byers Ave 64801-4304) Francisco Sierra (417) 623-6893

Kansas City Bishop Spencer Place Inc **Retirement Home** 4301 Madison Ave 64111-3488 (Mail to: Rev Kathleen Hall 4301 Madison Ave 64111-3471) Kathleen Hall (816) 931-4277

Kansas City Church of the Good Shepherd **P** (355) § 4947 Ne Chouteau Dr 64119-4815 (Mail to: 4947 NE Chouteau Dr 64119-4815) Galen Snodgrass (816) 452-0745

Kansas City Church of the Redeemer **P** (263) § 7110 State Route 9 64152-2930 (Mail to: 7110 State Route 9 64152-2930) Ralph Behen Ralph Behen Elisabeth Sinclair (816) 741-1136

✣ **Kansas City** Grace And Holy Trinity Cathedral **O** (977) § 415 W 13th St 64105-1350 (Mail to: 415 W 13th St 64105-1350) Christy Dorn Evelyn Hornaday Marco Serrano (888) 902-4482

Kansas City St Andrews Episcopal Church **P** (1478) 6401 Wornall Ter 64113-1755 (Mail to: 6401 Wornall Ter 64113-1789) John Spicer Jeffrey Stevenson (816) 523-1602

Kansas City St Augustines Church **P** (84) 2732 Benton Blvd 64128-1130 (Mail to: 2732 Benton Blvd 64128-1130) Charles Marks (816) 921-8534

Kansas City Saint Mary's Episcopal Church **P** (218) 1307 Holmes St 64106-2845 (Mail to: 1307 Holmes St 64106-2845) Charles Everson (816) 842-0975

Kansas City St Matthews Episcopal Church **P** (105) 9349 E 65th St 64133-4907 (Mail to: 9349 E 65th St 64133-4907) (816) 353-4592

Kansas City St Pauls Church **P** (659) § 11 E 40th St 64111-4909 (Mail to: 11 E 40th St 64111-4909) Rufus Runnels (816) 931-2850

Kansas City St Luke's Chapel **Hospital** 4401 Wornall Rd 64111-3220 (Mail to: 4401 Wornall Rd 64111-3241) Mark Jeske Marshall Scott Ronald Verhaeghe (816) 932-2180

Kansas City St. Peter & All Saints Episcopal Church **P** (187) § 100 E Red Bridge Rd 64114-5412 (Mail to: 100 E Red Bridge Rd 64114-5499) Jonathan Frazier Kathleen Hall (816) 942-1066

Kimberling City St Marks Episcopal Church **M** (64) 3 Northwoods Blvd 65686 (Mail to: PO Box 153 65686-0153) (417) 739-2460

Lebanon Trinity Episcopal Church **M** (41) PO Box 1615 65536-1615 (Mail to: PO Box 1615 65536-1615) Jerry Miller (417) 532-3433

Lees Summit St Annes Church **P** (249) § 1815 Ne Independence Ave 64086-5415 (Mail to: 1815 NE Independence Ave 64064-6586) Margaret Rhodes (816) 524-5552

Lees Summit St Pauls Episcopal Church **P** (166) 416 Grand St 64063 (Mail to: PO Box 372 64063-0372) Robert Estes Nancy Nevins (816) 524-3651

Lexington Christ Episcopal Church **P** (96) 13th And Franklin St 64067 (Mail to: PO Box 307 64067-0307) (660) 259-3605

Liberty Grace Episcopal Church **P** (217) 520 S State Route 2 64068-1915 (Mail to: 520 S State Route 291 64068-1915) Ruth Baker John McCann (816) 781-6262

Maryville St Pauls Episcopal Church **M** (23) 901 Main St 64468 (Mail to: 901 Main St 64468-0675) (660) 582-5832

Monett St Stephens Episcopal Church **M** (58) 601 E Benton St 65708-1770 (Mail to: PO Box 126 65708-0126) (417) 235-3330

Mountain Grove Church of the Transfiguration **M** (57) 215 Wall St 65711-1766 (Mail to: PO Box 160 65689-0160) Bradford Ellsworth Linda Milholen (417) 926-5217

Neosho St Johns Church **M** (36) 305 W Spring St 64850-1762 (Mail to: c/o The Rev Daniel Erdman 929 E Hawthorne Loop 64870-7228) (417) 451-3644

Nevada All Saints Episcopal Church **P** (135) 425 E Cherry St 64772-3418 (Mail to: PO Box 456 64772-0456) James Lile (417) 667-2607

Belton St Mary Magdalene **P** (302) 16808 S Holmes Road 64012 (Mail to: 16808 S State Route D 64012-9661) Lawrence **Noel** St Nicholas Episcopal Church **M** (95) § 101 Sulphur St 64854 (Mail to: PO Box 248 64854-0248) (417) 475-3852

Overland Park St Luke's South Chapel **Chapel** 12300 Metcalf Ave 66213-1324 (Mail to: Spiritual Wellness Dept 12300 Metcalf Ave 66213-1324) (816) 932-2190

Ozark St Matthews Episcopal Church **P** 203A E Brick St 65721-8906 (Mail to: 203A E Brick St 65721-8906) (417) 581-1350

Saint Joseph Christ Episcopal Church **P** (128) 207 7th St 64501-1905 (Mail to: 207 7th St 64501-1975) (816) 279-6351

Savannah St Marys Episcopal Church **M** (18) 401 W Chestnut St 64485-1439 (Mail to: 401 W Chestnut St 64485-1439) (816) 324-5532

Sedalia Calvary Episcopal Church **P** (140) 713 S Ohio Ave 65301-4415 (Mail to: 713 S Ohio Ave 65301-4415) Anne Kyle (660) 826-4873

Skidmore St Oswalds in the Field Church **M** (7) 30996 X Ave 64487-8191 (Mail to: Route 1 Box 123 64487) (660) 442-5897

Springfield Christ Episcopal Church **P** (1144) 601 E Walnut St 65806-2419 (Mail to: 601 E Walnut St 65806-2491) Kenneth Chumbley Mark Ohlemeier (417) 866-5133

Springfield St James Episcopal Church **P** (117) 2645 E Southern Hill Blvd 65804-3433 (Mail to: 2645 E Southern Hills Blvd 65804-3433) Suzanne Lynch Jos Tharakan (417) 881-3073

Springfield St Johns Episcopal Church **P** (229) § 515 E Division St 65803-2815 (Mail to: 515 E Division St 65803-2815) David Kendrick (417) 869-6351

Trenton St Philips Church **M** (10) 205 E 9th St 64683-2202 (Mail to: PO Box 46 64683-0046) (660) 359-5309

Warrensburg Christ Episcopal Church **P** (161) 136 E Gay St 64093-1810 (Mail to: PO Box 3 64093-0003) Ronald Verhaeghe (660) 429-1133

West Plains All Saints Church **P** (74) 107 S Curry St 65775-3943 (Mail to: PO Box 1012 65775-1012) Teresa Deokaran (417) 256-2215

DIOCESE OF WEST TENNESSEE
(PROVINCE IV)

Comprises twenty counties lying west of the Tennessee River including all of Hardin County

DIOCESAN OFFICE 692 Poplar Ave Memphis TN 38105

TEL (901) 526-0023　FAX (901) 526-1555

E-MAIL diocese@episwtn.org　WEB www.episwtn.org

Previous Bishops—
Alex D Dickson 1983-94, James M Coleman 1994-2001

Bishop — Rt Rev Don E Johnson (967) (Dio 30 June 01)

Cn to Ord ZA Davis III; *Sec* Rev D Wells; *Asst* M Jones; *Treas* J Shipley; *Asst Treas* PA Calame Jr; *Asst Treas* B Rolfes Jr; *Chanc* MA Cobb Jr; *V Chanc* M Marshall *Hist* R Thompson; *Reg* Z Davis

Stand Comm—Cler: G Meade O Rencher D Wells DN Campbell; *Lay:* S Cheney C Walsh M Webb L Wilhite

Bishop & Council—Cler: B Gordon G McCarty K Stillings S Webb D Brooks S Walters G Endicott; *Lay:* J Danley K Gordon H Peyton CB Miller M Miller K Trammell

PARISHES, MISSIONS, AND CLERGY

Atoka Ravenscroft Chapel **M** (41) C/O Shelly Nichols 33 Sarah Cove 38004-4904 (Mail to: PO Box 251 C/O Brenda F Scott 38011-0251) (901) 837-1312

Bolivar St James Episcopal Church **M** (50) PO Box 85 38008-0085 (Mail to: PO Box 85 38008-0085) Walter Gordon (731) 658-4439

Brownsville Christ Episcopal Church **HC** (28) 140 Washington Ave 38012-2519 (Mail to: 140 Washington Ave 38012-2519) (901) 772-9156

Collierville Church of the Holy Apostles **P** (434) 1380 Wolf River Blvd 38017-8687 (Mail to:

1380 Wolf River Blvd 38017-8687) John Leach Robert Calhoun (901) 937-3830

Collierville Saint Andrew's Episcopal Church **P** (357) 106 Walnut St 38017-2672 (Mail to: PO Box 38 38027-0626) Jeffery Marx Joseph Butler (901) 853-0425

Cordova Church of the Annunciation **P** (150) 8282 Macon Rd 38018-8532 (Mail to: 8282 Macon Rd 38018-8532) (901) 753-0142

Covington St Matthew Episcopal Church **HC** (41) 303 S Munford St 38019-2555 (Mail to: 303 S Munford St 38019-2555) (901) 476-6577

Dyersburg St Mary's Episcopal Church **P** (161) 108 King Ave 38024-4610 (Mail to: 108 King Ave 38024-4610) Gary Meade (731) 285-3522

Germantown St George Episcopal Church **P** (540) § 2425 S Germantown Rd 38138-5946 (Mail to: 2425 S Germantown Rd 38138-5946) Dorothy Wells David Campbell (901) 754-7282

Humboldt St Thomas the Apostle **M** (38) 6 Esquire Lewis Rd 38343-6426 (Mail to: PO Box 442 38343-0442) Bill Burks (901) 784-2872

Jackson St Lukes Episcopal Church **HC** (371) 309 E Baltimore St 38301-6304 (Mail to: 309 E Baltimore St 38301-6304) Patricia Mccarty Tommy Rhoads (731) 424-0556

La Grange Immanuel Episcopal Church **HC** (37) PO Box 21 38046-0021 (Mail to: PO Box 21 38046-0021) (901) 754-7282

Mason St Paul Episcopal Church **M** (28) 2406 Highway 59 38049-7522 (Mail to: C/O John Cochran PO Box 158 38049-0158) (901) 294-2641

Mason Trinity Episcopal Church **M** (9) 260 Main St 38049 (Mail to: 206 North Main Street 38049) (901) 594-5012

Memphis All Saints Episcopal Church **P** (49) 1508 S White Station Rd 38117-6826 (Mail to: 1508 S White Station Rd 38117-6899) Nancy O'Shea (901) 685-7333

Memphis Calvary Episcopal Church **HC** (1005) 102 2nd St 38103-2203 (Mail to: 102 2nd St 38103-2287) Robert Bartusch Amber Carswell Lewis McKee Paul Mclain James Walters (901) 525-6602

Memphis Church of the Holy Communion **P** (1153) 4645 Walnut Grove Rd 38117-2537 (Mail to: 4645 Walnut Grove Rd 38117-2597) Jonathan Chesney Eyleen Farmer Hester Mathes Alexander Webb (901) 767-6987

Memphis Emmanuel Episcopal Church **P** (109) 4150 Boeingshire Dr 38116-6007 (Mail to: 4150 Boeingshire Dr 38116-6007) Colenzo Hubbard (901) 346-7434

Memphis Grace - St Lukes Church **P** (1086) § 1720 Peabody Ave 38104-6124 (Mail to: 1720 Peabody Ave 38104-6100) Ollie Rencher Meredith Day Amy George (901) 272-7425

Memphis Holy Trinity Episcopal Church **P** (42) 3749 Kimball Ave 38111-6420 (Mail to: 3749 Kimball Ave 38111-6420) (901) 743-6421

Memphis St Elisabeths Episcopal Church **P** (250) 6033 Old Brownsville Rd 38135-0722 (Mail to: 6033 Old Brownsville Rd 38135-0722) (901) 372-2753

Memphis St Johns Episcopal Church **P** (864) 3245 Central Ave 38111-4409 (Mail to: 3245 Central Ave 38111-4409) Miranda Griffin Charles Taylor (901) 323-8597

✠ **Memphis** St Joseph Episcopal Church **O** (6) 604 Saint Paul Ave 38126-2865 (Mail to: 604 Saint Paul Ave 38126-2865) Colenzo Hubbard (901) 523-2617

✠ **Memphis** St Mary's Episcopal Cathedral **O** (702) 692 Poplar Ave 38105-4512 (Mail to: 692 Poplar Ave 38105-4512) William Andrews Laura Gettys Patrick Williams (901) 527-3361

Memphis St Philip Episcopal Church **P** (256) 9380 Davies Plantation Rd 38133-4250 (Mail to: 9380 Davies Plantation Rd 38133-4250) Terry Street (901) 388-9830

Memphis Church of the Good Shepherd **P** (51) 1971 Jackson Ave 38107-4614 (Mail to: 1971 Jackson Ave 38107-4614) (901) 725-9768

Millington St Annes Church **P** (111) 4063 Sykes Rd 38053-7930 (Mail to: 4063 Sykes Rd 38053-7930) Jack Rogers (901) 872-0303

Paris Grace Episcopal Church **P** (107) 103 S Poplar St 38242-4103 (Mail to: PO Box 447 38242-0447) (731) 642-1721

Ripley Immanuel Episcopal Church **M** (51) 153 Highland St Ro Winslow 38063-1815 (Mail to: PO Box 513 38063-0513) Richard Fletcher (731) 635-5593

Somerville St Thomas Episcopal Church **M** (49) Attn Rev William Fry 203 W Market St 38068-1593 (Mail to: Attn Rev William Fry 10 North Highland 38068) (901) 465-7112

Union City St James Episcopal Church **P** (80) 422 E Church St 38261-3906 (Mail to: PO Box 838 38281-0838) William Mcmillen (731) 885-9575

DIOCESE OF WEST TEXAS

(PROVINCE VII)

Comprises 60 West Texas counties

DIOCESAN OFFICE 111 Torcido Dr San Antonio TX 78209 (MAIL: Box 6885)

TEL (210) 824-5387 (888) 824-5387 FAX (210) 824-2164

E-MAIL general.mail@dwtx.org WEB www.dwtx.org

Previous Bishops—
Robt WB Elliott miss 1874-87, James S Johnston miss 1888-1904 dio 1905-16, Wm T Capers 1916-43, Everett H Jones 1943-69, R Earl Dicus suffr 1955-75, Harold C Gosnell coadj 1968 dio 1969-77, Scott Field Bailey 1976-87, Stanley F Hauser suffr 1979-87, John H MacNaughton coadj 1986, dio 1987-95 Earl N McArthur suffr 1988-93, James Folts coadj 1994-96, dio 1996-2006, Robert B Hibbs 1996-2003; Gary R Lillibridge (coadj 2004; Dio 2006-17)

Bishop—Rt Rev David M Reed (1005) (suff 2006-14; coadj 2014-17; Dio June 2017)

Bishop Suffragan—Rt Rev Jennifer Brooke-Davidson (1104) (Cons 29 July 2017)

Lay Cn C Mowen; *Sec* Rev D Read; *Treas* T Burkhart; *Reg* L Woodall; *Chanc* K Kimble 11 Tanglewood St Uvalde TX 78801-6502; *Asst Chanc* J Norman; *Comm* E Kittrell and L McGrew; *Stew* N Stinson; *Camp& Conf* R Watson; *Cong Dev* J Brooke-Davidson; *Hisp Off* vacant; *Hist* M George; *Deploy Off* vacant

Stand Comm—Cler: *Pres* M Marsh P Frey R Hardaway *Lay:* L Nisbet C Mowen S Alwais

Deans: Central D Read; *Eastern* V Frnka; *North Eastern* C Caddell; *Northern* B Dobbins; *Southern* S Maloney; *Valley* C Sharrow; *Western* P Frey

PARISHES, MISSIONS, AND CLERGY

Alice The Epis Church of the Advent **P** (30) 200 Wright 78332 (Mail to: PO Box 1937 78333-1937) Thomas Turner (361) 664-7881

Aransas Pass The Episcopal Church of Our Saviour **M** (59) 822 S McCampbell St 78336-2316 (Mail to: 822 S McCampbell St 78336-2316) (361) 727-9101

Bandera St Christophers Church **P** (156) 395 State Highway 173 78003 (Mail to: PO Box 314 78003-0314) Robert Harris (830) 796-4387

Beeville St Philip's Episcopal Church **P** (142) § 311 E Corpus Christi St 78102-4813 (Mail to: 311 E Corpus Christi St 78102-4813) Brian Tarver (361) 358-2730

Blanco St Michaels and All Angels Episcopal **M** (77) 218 Pittsburg St 78606-5768 (Mail to: PO Box 684 78606-0684) (830) 833-4816

Boerne St Helena's Episcopal Church and School **P** (570) § 410 Main St 78006 (Mail to: PO Box 1765 78006-6765) David Read (830) 249-3228

Brackettville St Andrews Episcopal Church **M** (27) 300 E Henderson St 78832 (Mail to: PO Box 927 78832) (830) 563-3666

Brady St Pauls Episcopal Church **P** (67) 1111 S Blackburn 76825 (Mail to: PO Box 1148 76825-1148) (325) 597-1330

Brownsville Church of the Advent **P** (472) § 104 W Elizabeth St 78520-5547 (Mail to: 104 W Elizabeth St 78520-5594) Laurie McKim (956) 542-4123

Brownsville St Pauls Episcopal Church **M** (50) 16th and Taft St 78521-3132 (Mail to: PO Box 4191 78523-4191) Charles Sharrow (956) 542-3869

Buda St Elizabeths Episcopal Church **M** (116) 723 Ranch Road 967 78610-9297 (Mail to: PO Box 292 78610-0292) Daniel Strandlund (512) 295-3674

Canyon Lake St Francis-by-the-Lake Epis Church **P** (304) 13250 Farm to Market 306 78133 (Mail to: PO Box 2031 78133-0023) David Chalk (830) 964-3820

Carrizo Springs Holy Trinity Episcopal Church **M** (49) 1807 Pena 78834 (Mail to: Attn Treasurer PO Box 919 78834-6919) Nicholas Mayer (830) 876-9729

Comfort St Boniface Episcopal Church **Chapel** (81) § 116 US 87 78013 (Mail to: PO Box 676 78013-0676) (830) 995-3897

Corpus Christi All Saints Episcopal Church **P** (300) 3026 S Staples 78404 (Mail to: 3026 S Staples St 78404-3691) Jonathan Wickham Cynthia McKenna (361) 855-6294

Corpus Christi Church of the Good Shepherd **P** (1171) § 700 S Upper Broadway 78401-3521 (Mail to: 700 S Upper Broadway St 78401-3521) Milton Black William Campbell Philip May (361) 882-1735

Corpus Christi St Andrews Episcopal Church **M** (193) 13026 Leopard St 78410-4515 (Mail to: 13026 Leopard St 78410-4515) (361) 241-9240

Corpus Christi St Bartholomews Episcopal Church **P** (345) § 622 Airline Rd 78412 (Mail to: 622 Airline Rd 78412-3156) Sean Maloney (361) 991-2954

Corpus Christi The Church of the Reconciliation **P** (90) 4518 Saratoga Blvd 78413-2151 (Mail to: 4518 Saratoga Blvd 78413-2151) (361) 852-9677

Cotulla St Timothys Church **M** (18) 305 North Choctaw Ave 78014 (Mail to: PO Box 738 78014-0738) (830) 879-2239

Crp Christi St Marks Episcopal Church **P** (225) 2727 Airline Rd 78414-3306 (Mail to: 2727 Airline Rd 78414-3306) John Hardie (361) 994-0285

Cuero Grace Episcopal Church **P** (57) 102 E Live Oak St 77954 (Mail to: 102 E Live Oak St 77954-2957) Charles Sumners (361) 275-3423

Cypress Mill St Lukes Episcopal Church **M** (121) 263 Spur 962 78663-8486 (Mail to: 263 Spur 962 78663-8486) Tommy Bye (830) 825-8001

Del Rio St James Episcopal Church **P** (294) § 206 W Greenwood St 78841-1129 (Mail to: PO Box 1129 78841-1129) John Fritts (830) 775-7292

Devine St Matthias **M** (31) 901 N. Teel Dr. 78016-1701 (Mail to: PO Box B 78016-0684) (210) 385-7668

Dripping Spgs The Church Of The Holy Spirit **P** (203) § 301 Hays Country Acres Rd 78620-4282 (Mail to: 301 Hays Country Acres Rd 78620-4282) Christopher Caddell (512) 858-4924

Eagle Pass Church of the Redeemer **P** (150) § 648 Madison St 78852 (Mail to: 648 Madison St 78852-4246) Matthew Frey (830) 773-5122

Edinburg St Matthews Episcopal Church **P** (123) § 2620 Crestview Dr 78539-6296 (Mail to: C/O Rev Charles Mahan 2620 Crestview Dr 78539-6219) (956) 383-4202

Edna Trinity Episcopal Church **P** (29) 102 W Church St 77957 (Mail to: PO Box 305 77957-0305) (361) 782-2204

Fort McKavett St James Episcopal Church **M** (18) 3232 Runge Ranch Rd 76841-2020 (Mail to: 2685 County RD 76935) (325) 387-2955

Fredricksburg St Barnabas Episcopal Church **P** (613) 601 W Creek St 78624 (Mail to: 601 W Creek St 78624-3117) Richard Elwood Burford Dobbins Jeffrey Hammond (830) 997-5762

George West Church of the Good Shepherd **Chapel** (75) 809 San Antonio St 78022 (Mail to: PO Box 1582 78022-1582) John Rayls Joyce Wilkinson George Keeble (361) 449-2737

Goliad St Stephens Episcopal Church **M** (13) 152 Chilton Ave 77963-3906 (Mail to: PO Box 739 77963-0739) (361) 645-2234

Gonzales Episcopal Church of the Messiah **P** (100) 721 St Louis St 78629-4154 (Mail to: PO Box 139 78629-0139) Shanna Neff (830) 672-3407

Hallettsville St James Episcopal Church **M** (24) 1103 E 4th St 77964-3219 (Mail to: 1103 E 4th St 77964-3219) (361) 798-4119

Harlingen St Albans Episcopal Church **P** (890)
§ 1417 E Austin Ave 78550 (Mail to: 1417 E
Austin Ave 78550-8855) John Inserra (956)
428-2305

Hebbronville St James Episcopal Church **M**
(44) 112 W North 78361 (Mail to: PO Box 68
78361-0068) Ernest Buchanan (361) 527-3433

Junction Trinity Episcopal Church **M** (74) 1119
Main 76849 (Mail to: Attn: Pat Thomson,
Treasurer PO Box 3 76849-0003) (325) 446-4416

Kenedy St Matthews Episcopal Church **M** (25)
309 S 5th 78119 (Mail to: 315 S 5th St 78119-
2607) (830) 583-2589

Kerrville St Peters Episcopal Church **P** (968) §
956 Main St 78028-3549 (Mail to: 320 Saint
Peter St 78028-4650) Bertrand Baetz (830)
257-8162

Kingsville Episcopal Church of the Epiphany
P (171) 206 3rd St 78363 (Mail to: 206 3rd St
78363-4409) Janet Dantone (361) 595-5535

Lake Corpus Christi St Michaels Episcopal
Church **M** (3) 99109 FM 534 78383 (Mail to:
PO Box 180 78383-0180) (361) 547-6658

Laredo Christ Episcopal Church **P** (187) 2320
Lane St 78043-2711 (Mail to: 2320 Lane St
78043-2711) Paul Frey (956) 723-5714

Llano Grace Episcopal Church **P** (98) 1200
Oatman St 78643-2730 (Mail to: 1200 Oatman
St 78643-2730) (325) 247-5276

Lockhart Emmanuel Episcopal Church **P** (132)
118 Church St 78644 (Mail to: 118 Church St
78644-2102) (512) 398-3342

Luling Church of the Annunciation **P** (87) 301 S
Walnut Ave 78648-2925 (Mail to: PO Box 106
78648-0106) Mark Bigley (830) 875-5155

McAllen St Johns Episcopal Church **P** (651) §
2500 N. 10th St. 78501-4008 (Mail to: 2500
10th St 78501-4090) (956) 687-6191

Menard Calvary Episcopal Church **M** (12) 201
Callan St 76859 (Mail to: PO Box 863 76859-
0863) (325) 396-2696

Mission St Peter & St Paul Church **M** (166) 2310
Stewart Rd 78574 (Mail to: 2310 Stewart Rd
78574-8842) William Clark (956) 585-5005

Montell Church of the Ascension **M** (33) 27851
Hwy 55 78802-0808 (Mail to: C/O June Smith
206 5th St 78801-5425) (830) 597-4284

New Braunfels St Johns Episcopal Church **P** (242)
312 S Guenther Ave 78130-5639 (Mail to: 312
S Guenther Ave 78130-5639) Ripp Hardaway
(830) 625-2532

Pharr Trinity Episcopal Church **P** (171) 210 W
Caffery Ave 78577-4713 (Mail to: PO Box 692
78577-1613) Richard Speer (956) 787-1243

Pleasanton All Saints Episcopal Church **M** (40)
1435 W Oaklawn Rd 78064 (Mail to: PO Box
732 78064-0732) (830) 277-2222

Port Aransas Trinity by the Sea **P** (127) § 431
Trojan St. 78373 (Mail to: PO Box 346 78373-
0346) John Derkits Douglas Schwert (361)
749-6449

Port Isabel St Andrews by the Sea **HC** (87) 1022
Yturria 78578 (Mail to: PO Box 1168 78578-
1168) Claudia Nalven (956) 943-1962

Port Lavaca Grace Episcopal Church **P** (36) 213
E Austin St 77979 (Mail to: PO Box 172 77979-
0172) Robert DeWolfe (361) 552-2805

Portland St Christophers by the Sea **P** (154) 720
7th St 78374 (Mail to: PO Box 386 78374-0386)
(361) 643-3514

Raymondville Church of the Epiphany **M** (92)
688 W Kimball Ave 78580-2309 (Mail to: 688
W Kimball Ave 78580-2309) Robert McAllen
(956) 689-9582

Refugio Church of the Ascension **M** (20) 602 E
Plasuela St 78377-3241 (Mail to: PO Box 903
78377-0903) (361) 526-4262

Rockport Saint Peter's Episcopal Church **P** (235)
555 Enterprise Blvd 78382 (Mail to: PO Box
1807 78381-1807) James Friedel (361) 729-2649

San Antonio Christ Episcopal Church **P** (1108)
510 Belknap Pl 78212-3400 (Mail to: 510
Belknap Pl 78212-3493) William Gahan Scott
Kitayama Justin Lindstrom (210) 736-3132

San Antonio Church of Reconciliation **P** (460)
8900 Starcrest Dr 78217-4741 (Mail to: 8900
Starcrest Dr 78217-4700) Robert Woody (210)
655-2731

San Antonio Church of the Holy Spirit **P** (244)
§ 11093 Bandera Road 78250-6814 (Mail to:
11093 Bandera Rd 78250-6806) Jason Roberts
Andrew Green (210) 314-6729

San Antonio Grace Episcopal Church **M** All
Saints Chapel at TMI 20955 W Tejas Trail
78257 (Mail to: 6275 Camp Bullis Road 78257)
Jacob George (210) 462-6901

San Antonio St Andrews Episcopal Church **P**
(278) 6110 NW Loop 410 78238-3305 (Mail
to: 6110 NW Loop 410 78238-3399) David
Archibald David Archibald (210) 684-0845

San Antonio St Davids Episcopal Church **P** (583)
§ 1300 Wiltshire Ave 78209-6049 (Mail to:
1300 Wiltshire Ave 78209-6049) Lisa Mason
Joshua Woods (210) 824-2481

San Antonio St George Episcopal Church **P** (743)
§ 6904 West Ave 78213-1820 (Mail to: 6904
West Ave 78213-1893) Ramiro Lopez (210)
342-4261

San Antonio St Lukes Episcopal Church **P** (1648)
§ Jane Crowley 11 Saint Lukes Ln 78209-4445
(Mail to: David Thomas 11 Saint Lukes Ln
78209-4445) Irving Cutter Michael Koehler
(210) 828-6425

San Antonio St Margarets Episcopal Church **M**
(141) § 5310 Stahl Rd 78247-1522 (Mail to:
5310 Stahl Rd 78247-1500) (210) 657-3328

San Antonio St Marks Episcopal Church **P** (1475)
315 E Pecan St 78205-1819 (Mail to: 315 E
Pecan St 78205-1819) Elizabeth Knowlton
Christopher Wise (210) 226-2426

San Antonio Saint Paul's Episcopal Church **P**
(164) § 1018 E Grayson St 78208-1224 (Mail

to: 1018 E Grayson St 78208-1299) Robert Carabin Bradley Landry Martha Vasquez Joseph Webb (210) 226-0345

San Antonio St Philips Episcopal Church **P** (94) 1310 Pecan Valley Dr 78210-3416 (Mail to: 1310 Pecan Valley Dr 78210-3416) (210) 333-6256

San Antonio St Stephens Episcopal Church **P** (53) 3726 S. New Braunfels Ave. 78223 (Mail to: 3726 S New Braunfels Ave 78223-1706) (210) 534-5400

San Antonio St Thomas Epis Church & School **P** (1228) § 1416 Loop 1604 E 78232-1427 (Mail to: 1416 Loop 1604 E 78232-1400) Beth Wyndham (210) 494-3507

San Antonio Sante Fe Episcopal Church **M** (175) 1108 Brunswick Blvd 78211-1502 (Mail to: 1108 Brunswick Blvd 78211-1502) John Wauters Donald Wilkinson (210) 923-0822

San Antonio St Francis Episcopal Church **Chapel** (272) 4242 Bluemel Rd 78240-1063 (Mail to: PO Box 690670 78269) Patricia Riggins (210) 696-0834

San Benito All Saints Episcopal Church **P** (47) 499 Reagan 78586 (Mail to: PO Box 1948 78586-0041) (956) 399-1795

San Marcos St Marks Episcopal Church **P** (519) § 3039 Ranch Road 12 78666-2488 (Mail to: 3039 Ranch Road 12 78666-2488) Benjamin Nelson Michael Woods (512) 353-1979

San Saba St Lukes Episcopal Church **P** (34) 601 W Dry St 76877-5611 (Mail to: 601 W Dry St 76877-5611) William Grusendorf (325) 372-4731

Seguin Saint Andrew's Episcopal Church **P** (569) 201 E Nolte 78155 (Mail to: 201 E Nolte St 78155-6123) Alexandra Easley (830) 372-4330

Sonora St Johns Episcopal Church **P** (158) 404 E Poplar St 76950 (Mail to: PO Box 1100 76950-1100) Casey Berkhouse (325) 387-2955

Universal City St Matthews Episcopal Church **P** (162) 810 Kitty Hawk Rd 78148-3822 (Mail to: PO Box 2337 78148-1337) Timothy Vellom (210) 658-5956

Uvalde St Philips Episcopal Church **P** (244) § 343 Getty St 78801-4690 (Mail to: 343 Getty St 78801-4690) Michael Marsh (830) 278-5223

Victoria St Francis Episcopal Church **P** (168) 3002 Miori Ln 77901-3618 (Mail to: 3002 Miori Ln 77901-3618) Stephen Carson (361) 575-0441

Victoria Trinity Episcopal Church **P** (602) § 1501 Glass St 77901 (Mail to: 1501 Glass St 77901-5130) Carrie Guerra James Kee-Rees (361) 573-3228

Weslaco Grace Episcopal Church **P** (186) 701 S Missouri 78596 (Mail to: 701 S Missouri Ave 78596-6941) Thomas Murray (956) 968-7014

Wimberley Saint Stephen's Episcopal Church **P** (722) § 6000 Fm 3237 78676-5832 (Mail to: 6000 FM 3237 Unit A 78676-6386) Sandra Casey-Martus (512) 847-9956

Windcrest Church of the Resurrection **P** (390) § 5909 Walzem Rd 78218-2197 (Mail to: 5909 Walzem Rd 78218-2197) Christopher Cole (210) 655-5484

DIOCESE OF WEST VIRGINIA
(PROVINCE III)
Comprises State of West Virginia
DIOCESAN OFFICE 1608 Virginia St E Charleston WV 25311-2114
(MAIL: PO Box 5400 Charleston WV 25361-0400)
TEL (304) 344-3597; Toll-free (866) 549-8346   FAX (304) 343-3295
E-MAIL [use first initial and last name]@wvdiocese.org   WEB www.wvdiocese.org

Previous Bishops—
Geo W Peterkin 1878-1916, Wm L Gravatt coadj 1899 Bp 1916-39, Robt EL Strider coadj 1923 Bp 1939-55, WC Campbell coadj 1950 Bp 1955-76, Robt P Atkinson coadj 1973 Bp 1976-88, W Franklin Carr suffr 1985-90, John H Smith 1989-99

Bishop—Rt Rev W Michie Klusmeyer (970)
(Dio 13 Oct 2001)

Treas TC Farnsworth 111 McCulloch Dr Wheeling WV 26003; *Chanc* K Klein; Co-*VChanc* T Dinsmore & J Canfield; *Fin Asst* A Combs; *CFO* D Ramkey; *COM* J Harris; *Publications* L Comins; *Dio Admin* M Bailey

Stand Comm—Cler: J Saxe M Remington C Slater J Valentine; *Lay:* B Hardesty D Redfield R Lowther B Hinkle

PARISHES, MISSIONS, AND CLERGY

Ansted Church of the Redeemer **M** (25) 102 Taylor St 25812 (Mail to: PO Box 625 25812-0625) (304) 658-5857

Beckley St Stephens Episcopal Church **P** (149) § 200 Virginia St 25801-5243 (Mail to: 200 Virginia St 25801-5299) (304) 253-9672

Berkeley Spg St Marks Episcopal Church **P** (76) 180 S Washington St 25411-1646 (Mail to: 180 S Washington St 25411-1646) David Shoda (304) 258-2440

Bluefield Christ Episcopal Church **P** (195) 200 Duhring St 24701-2910 (Mail to: 200 Duhring St 24701-2910) Chadwick Slater (304) 327-6861

Buckhannon Church of the Transfiguration **M** (42) 65 S Kanawha St 26201-2636 (Mail to: 65 S Kanawha St 26201-2636) (304) 472-4418

Bunker Hill Christ Episcopal Church **HC** Runnymeade Rd 25413 (Mail to: Runnymeade Road 25413) (304) 344-3597

Charles Town St Philips Episcopal Church **M** (25) 411 S Lawrence St 25414-1645 (Mail to: PO Box 368 25414-0368) Elwyn Mackov (304) 725-4236

Charles Town Zion Episcopal Church **P** (424) 301 East Congress Street 25414 (Mail to: 221 E Washington St 25414-1073) John Willard (304) 725-5312

✣ **Charleston** Chapel of the Resurrection **O** 1608 Virginia St E 25311-2114 (Mail to: 1608 Virginia St E 25311-2114) (304) 344-3597

Charleston St Johns Episcopal Church **P** (430) 1105 Quarrier St 25301-2410 (Mail to: 1105 Quarrier St 25301-2493) Marquita Hutchens (304) 346-0359

Charleston St Matthews Episcopal Church **P** (504) 36 Norwood Rd 25314-1327 (Mail to: 36 Norwood Rd 25314-1399) Alan Webster (304) 343-3837

Charleston St Christopher Episcopal Church **P** (170) 821 Edgewood Dr 25302-2811 (Mail to: 821 Edgewood Dr 25302-2811) Melissa Remington (304) 342-3272

Clarksburg Christ Episcopal Church **P** (92) 123 S 6th St 26302 (Mail to: PO Box 1492 26302-1492) Nora Becker (304) 622-3694

Colliers Olde St John Episcopal Church **M** (77) 2308 Eldersville Rd 26035 (Mail to: P O Box 347 26035) (304) 527-4746

Elkins Grace Episcopal Church **P** (78) 212 John St 26241-3823 (Mail to: Attn E W Carter Treasurer 212 John St 26241-3823) Frederick Bird (304) 636-4251

Fairmont Christ Church **P** (182) 824 Fairmont Avenue 26554-5138 (Mail to: 824 Fairmont Ave 26554-5190) Jordan Trumble (304) 366-3471

Glenville St Mark Episcopal Church **M** (9) 607 Main St 26351 (Mail to: 607 W Main St 26351-1057) Teresa Wayman (304) 462-7455

Grafton St Matthias Episcopal Church **M** (13) 330 W Francis St 26354-1720 (Mail to: PO Box 27 26354-0027) Frederick Bird (304) 265-3112

Hansford Church of the Good Shepherd **P** (78) 1203 Center St 25103 (Mail to: C/O Donald L Smith Treasurer PO Box 41 25103-0041) (304) 595-6224

Harpers Ferry St Johns Episcopal Church **M** (33) 898 W Washington St 25425-6910 (Mail to: PO Box 999 25425-0999) (304) 579-5586

Hedgesville Mt Zion Episcopal Church **M** (28) PO Box 2246 1 Zion Street 25427 (Mail to: PO Box 2246 25427-2246) (304) 702-7111

Hinton Ascension Episcopal Church **M** (29) 222 5th Ave 25951-2210 (Mail to: 222 5th Ave 25951-2210) (304) 627-1232

Huntington St John Episcopal Church **P** (266) 3000 Washington Blvd 25705-1633 (Mail to: 3000 Washington Blvd 25705-1633) Lisa Graves (304) 525-9105

Huntington St Peters Episcopal Church **P** (136) 2248 Adams Ave 25704-1424 (Mail to: 435 23rd St W 25704-1349) (304) 429-2241

Huntington Trinity Episcopal Church **P** (297) 520 11th St 25701-2211 (Mail to: 520 11th St 25701-2292) James Morgan (304) 529-6084

Hurricane Church St Timothys in the Valley **P** (243) 3434 Teays Valley Rd 25526-0424 (Mail to: PO Box 424 25526-0424) Cheryl Winter (304) 562-9325

Kearneysville Grace Episcopal Church **M** (60) East & Church St 25430 (Mail to: Attn William W Grantham 159 East St 25430-5691) (304) 725-7073

Kearneysville St Bartholomews Church **M** (18) PO Box 896 25430 (Mail to: C/O Judith Schroder PO Box 684 25414-0684) (304) 725-1707

Keyser Emmanuel Episcopal Church **P** (57) 303 S Mineral St 26726-2641 (Mail to: 303 S Mineral St 26726-2641) Martin Townsend (304) 788-4475

Kingwood St Michaels Episcopal Church **M** (38) 107 Mcdonald St 26537-1017 (Mail to: Attn Richard V Wolfe PO Box 543 26537-0543) (304) 329-3207

Lewisburg St James Episcopal Church **P** (239) 218 Church St 24901-1330 (Mail to: 468 Church Street 24901-1330) Joshua Saxe (304) 645-2588

Logan Holy Trinity Church **P** (32) 604 Stratton St 25601-4029 (Mail to: 604 Stratton St 25601) (304) 752-6900

Marlinton St Johns Church **M** 415 9th St 24954-1236 (Mail to: 717 8th Ave 24954-1214) James Lanter (304) 704-2014

Martinsburg Trinity Episcopal Church **P** (264) 200 West King Street 25401-3212 (Mail to: 200 W King St 25401-3212) Julie Harris (304) 263-0994

Moorefield Emmanuel Episcopal Church **M** (31) 309 Winchester Ave 26836 (Mail to: PO Box 692 26836-0692) Stephen Haptonstahl (304) 530-5226

Morgantown St Thomas a Becket Episcopal **P** (366) Old Cheat Rd And Rt 26505 (Mail to: 75 Old Cheat Rd 26508-4103) (304) 296-0270

Morgantown Trinity Episcopal Church **P** (198) 247 Willey St 26505-5522 (Mail to: 247 Willey St 26505-5522) E Morgan (304) 292-7364

Moundsville Trinity Church **P** (114) 1 Oak Ave 26041-1107 (Mail to: PO Box P 26041-0966) Bruce Bevans (304) 845-5982

N Martinsvlle St Anns Episcopal Church **P** (74) 453 Maple Ave 26155-7000 (Mail to: PO Box 161 26155-0161) Richard Heller (304) 455-5143

Oak Hill St Andrews Episcopal Church **P** (131) 345 Kelley Ave 25901-2916 (Mail to: 345 Kelly Ave 25901-2916) (304) 469-3223

Parkersburg Memorial Church of the Good Shepherd **P** (575) 903 Charles St 26101-4825 (Mail to: 903 Charles St 26101-4825) Marjorie Bevans (304) 428-1525

Parkersburg Trinity Episcopal Church **P** (203) 430 Juliana St 26101-5335 (Mail to: 430 Juliana St 26101-5335) Paul Hicks (304) 422-3362

Point Pleasat Christ Church **P** (104) C/O Jack Sturgeon 804 Main St 25550-1229 (Mail to: C/O Jack Sturgeon PO Box 819 25550) Katharine Foster Raymond Hage (304) 675-3120

Princeton Church of the Heavenly Rest **M** (62) 1207 Mercer St 24740-3031 (Mail to: 1207 Mercer St 24740-3031) (304) 425-9345

Ravenswood Grace Episcopal Church **M** (32) 405 Walnut St 26164-1649 (Mail to: 405 Walnut St 26164-1649) Marie Mulford (304) 273-0980

Ripley St Johns Episcopal Church **M** (30) 702 Main St W 25271-1110 (Mail to: PO Box 558 25271-0558) Katharine Foster (304) 372-9183

Romney St Stephens Church **M** (42) 316 E Main St 26757-1822 (Mail to: 332 E Main St Apt A 26757-1845) (304) 822-5054

Ronceverte Church of the Incarnation **M** (34) 707 W Main St 24970-1754 (Mail to: PO Box 276 24970-0276) (304) 536-3320

Salem Prince of Peace Episcopal Church **M** (25) 53 Sacred Heart Ln 26426-8647 (Mail to: PO Box 215 26426-0215) Pamela Shier (304) 906-7540

Shepherdstown Trinity Church **P** (470) 200 W German St 25443 (Mail to: PO Box 308 25443-0308) George Schramm Frank Coe (304) 876-6990

Sistersville St Pauls Episcopal Church **P** (24) 313 Wells St 26175-1437 (Mail to: PO Box 79 26175-0079) (304) 652-1801

✣ **Snowshoe** Chapel on the Mount **O** (16) 10 Snowshoe Dr. 26209 (Mail to: 354 Locust Glen Drive 26291) James Lanter (304) 572-3333

St Albans St Marks Episcopal Church **P** (141) 405 B St 25177-2716 (Mail to: 405 B St 25177-2716) (304) 722-4284

St Marys Grace Episcopal Church **P** (25) 317 Riverside Dr 26170-1030 (Mail to: 317 Riverside Drive 26170-1030) Richard Heller (304) 684-7976

Summersville St Martins in the Fields **M** (29) § 221 Mckees Creek Rd 26651-1601 (Mail to: 221 Mckees Creek Rd 26651-1601) (304) 872-5594

Union All Saints Church **M** (50) 1 Greenhill Rd 24983 (Mail to: PO Box 401 24983-0401) (304) 772-3120

Weirton St Thomas Episcopal Church **P** (38) 300 Three Springs Dr 26062-4922 (Mail to: PO Box 2232 Three Springs Dr 26062) (304) 723-4120

Welch St Lukes Episcopal Church **M** PO Box 204 24801-2414 (Mail to: 71 Riverside Dr 24801-2544) (304) 436-2641

Wellsburg Christ Episcopal Church **P** (61) 1014 Main St 26070-1632 (Mail to: 1014 Main St 26070-1632) (304) 737-1866

Weston St Pauls Church **P** (195) 206 E 2nd St 26452-1927 (Mail to: 206 E 2nd St 26452-1927) John Valentine (304) 269-5266

Wheeling St Lukes Episcopal Church **M** (79) 200 S Penn St 26003-2028 (Mail to: 200 S Penn St 26003-2028) Theresa Kelley (304) 232-2395

Wheeling St Matthews Church **P** (397) PO Box 508 26003-0064 (Mail to: PO Box 508 26003-0064) Mark Seitz (304) 233-0133

Wheeling Lawrencefield Parish Church **P** (133) Table Rock Ln 44 Kirkside Dr 26003 (Mail to: PO Box 4063 26003-0414) (304) 277-2353

Wht Sphr Spgs St Thomas Episcopal Church **P** (128) 205 W Main St 24986-2411 (Mail to: PO Box 148 24986-0148) (304) 536-3320

Williamson St Pauls Episcopal Church **M** (36) 411 Prichard St 25661-3140 (Mail to: 415 Prichard St 25661-3140) Nick England (304) 235-4056

Williamstown Christ Memorial Episcopal Church **M** (57) 409 Columbia Ave 26187-1122 (Mail to: 409 Columbia Ave 26187-1122) Richard Heller (304) 375-6506

DIOCESE OF WESTERN KANSAS
(PROVINCE VII)
Comprises Western Kansas
DIOCESAN OFFICE 1 North Main Ste 418 Hutchinson KS 67504
TEL (620) 669-0006   FAX (620) 259-6151
WEB http://www.diowks.org

Previous Bishops—
Sheldon M Griswold 1903-17, John C Sage 1918-19, Robt H Mize 1921-38, Shirley H Nichols 1943-55, Arnold M Lewis 1956-64, Wm Davidson mb 1966-71, Bp 1971-80, John F Ashby 1981-95, Vernon E Strickland 1995-2002, James M Adams Jr 2002-10, Michael Milliken 2011-18

Current Bishop- The Rt. Rev. Mark A. Cowell (Dio 1 Dec 2018)

Dio Admin T Cottrell; *Chanc* M Kliewer1717 Old Manor Rd,Garden City KS 67846; *Treas* M Wamsley; *Bus & Fin* M Wamsley; *COM* Rev M Milliken; *Sec Dio Conv* T Cottrell *Dispatch of Busines sfor Dio Conv* C Peterson; *ECW* vacant; *UTO Chair* K Milliken; *Yth* A & B Long; *Cn to Ord* Rev Cn J Jones 1113 Pinehurst Hays KS 67601 (785) 623-1736

Stand Comm—Cler: Pres K Lemon D Gilhousen C Ballinger; *Lay:* L Boone H Smith S Russell

PARISHES, MISSIONS, AND CLERGY

Anthony Grace Episcopal Church **M** (19) § 401 Anthony Ave 67003-2012 (Mail to: 401 Anthony Ave 67003-2012) Mary Hixson (620) 842-3254

✠ **Bavaria** St Onesimus Chapel **O** St Francis Academy 5097 W Cloud St 67401-9743 (Mail to: 5097 W Cloud St 67401-9743) (913) 825-0563

Colby Ascension-on-the-Prairie Episcopal **P** (31) 1170 Wheat Ridge Rd 67701-3530 (Mail to: PO Box 842 67701-0842) Donald Martin (785) 462-7198

Concordia Church of the Epiphany **M** (17) 117 W 8th St 66901-3401 (Mail to: PO Box 466 66901-0466) Dale Lumley (785) 243-2947

Dodge City Saint Cornelius Episcopal Church **P** (159) 200 W Spruce St 67801-4425 (Mail to: PO Box 1414 67801-1414) John Seatvet (620) 227-6975

Ellsworth Holy Apostles Church **M** (21) 104 W 4th St 67439-3212 (Mail to: 103 W 4th St 67439-3212) Phyllis Flory (785) 472-5477

Garden City St Thomas Episcopal Church **M** (57) 710-712 Main St 67846-5433 (Mail to: PO Box 2410 67846-8410) (620) 276-3173

Goodland St Pauls Episcopal Church **M** (31) 121 W 13th St 67735-2926 (Mail to: PO Box 452 67735-0452) Donald Martin (785) 890-2115

Great Bend St Johns Episcopal Church **M** (21) 2701 17th St 67530-2303 (Mail to: 2701 17th St 67530-2303) Basil Price (620) 792-4288

Hays St Andrews Episcopal Church **M** (24) 2422 Hyacinth Ave 67601 (Mail to: Attn Mrs Gwen Johnson PO Box 247 67601-0247) Harvey Hillin (785) 625-6476

Hays St Michaels Episcopal Church **P** (39) 2900 Canal Blvd 67601-1704 (Mail to: PO Box 1352 2900 Canal Blvd 67601-1352) Harvey Hillin (758) 628-8442

Hutchinson Grace Episcopal Church **P** (418) § 2 Hyde Park Dr 67502-2824 (Mail to: 2 Hyde Park Dr 67502-2824) James Blakley Larry Carver Larry Steadman William Waln (620) 662-8024

Kingman Christ Episcopal Church **M** (10) 332 Spruce St 67068-1651 (Mail to: PO Box 323 67068-0323) Charles Kerschen (620) 532-2488

Kinsley Holy Nativity Episcopal Church **M** (10) 714 E 8th St 67547-1326 (Mail to: PO Box 233 67547-0233) (620) 659-2539

Lakin Epis Church of the Upper Room **M** (29) 406 W Kingman Ave 67860-9463 (Mail to: PO Box 634 67860-0634) (620) 355-6077

Larned Sts Mary and Martha of Bethany **M** (45) PO Box 333 67550-0333 (Mail to: PO Box 333 67550-0333) Kevin Schmidt (620) 285-6503

Liberal St Andrews Church **M** (44) 521 Sherman Ave 67901-3205 (Mail to: PO Box 250 67905-0250) Charles Schneider (620) 624-3944

Logan Church of the Transfiguration **HC** (14) 20 Washington St 67646 (Mail to: PO Box 284 67646-0284) (785) 689-4627

Lyons Saint Mark's Church **M** (64) 524 East Ave S 67554-3804 (Mail to: 524 East Ave S 675543804) Brian Viel Kevin Schmidt (620) 257-5955

Mcpherson St Annes Episcopal Church **M** (75) 105 W Sutherland St 67460-4719 (Mail to: 105 W Sutherland St # 577 67460-4719) (866) 363-8850

Meade St Augustine Episcopal Church **M** (6) 2127 18 Road 67864 (Mail to: 2127 18 Rd 67864-9403) (620) 646-5420

Medicine Ldg St Marks Episcopal Church **M** (7) 204 Walnut St 67104-1325 (Mail to: 1109 Goodview St 67104-1040) Karen Lemon (620) 866-5131

Norton Trinity Episcopal Church **M** (61) § 319 N. State St. 67654 (Mail to: 319 State St 67654-1811) Charles Schneider (785) 877-2589

Pratt All Saints Episcopal Church **M** (44) 218 Main St 67124-1739 (Mail to: C/O Warden Gary Skaggs 542 Terrace Dr 67124-1354) Karen Lemon (620) 672-2308

Russell St Elizabeth's Episcopal Church **M** (8) 66 S Culp St 67665-3134 (Mail to: 629 Margaret 67665) Harvey Hillin (785) 483-4889

Russell Springs St Francis Episcopal Church **M** (18) 525 Hilts Ave 67764 (Mail to: Hilts Street 67764) Donald Martin (785) 751-4278

Salina Armstrong Memorial Chapel **CC** 110 E Otis Ave 67402 (Mail to: PO Box 827 67402-0827) (785) 823-7231

✠ **Salina** Christ Cathedral Church **O** (188) § 138 S 8th St 67401-2808 (Mail to: 138 S 8th St 67401-2808) Shay Craig David Hodges Bruce Le Barron Basil Price Charles Schneider Robert Seaton (785) 825-0974

Salina Church of the Incarnation **M** (58) 639 Max Ave 67401-6662 (Mail to: 639 Max Ave 67401-6662) Randy McIntosh Basil Price (785) 823-2850

Salina St Francis of Assisi Chapel **Special Needs Ministry** 509 E Elm St 67401-2348 (Mail to: PO Box 1340 67402-1340) (800) 423-1342

Scott City St Lukes Episcopal Church **M** (35) 303 Epperson Dr 67871-1841 (Mail to: Attn Harriet Jones 303 Epperson Dr 67871-1841) Donald Martin (620) 872-3666

Ulysses St Johns Episcopal Church **M** (26) 104 S Maxwell St 67880-2327 (Mail to: 104 S Maxwell St 67880-2327) Floyd Daharsh (620) 356-3690

DIOCESE OF WESTERN LOUISIANA
(PROVINCE VII)

Comprises Thirty-Four Civil Parishes and Ten Missions in Western Louisiana

DIOCESAN OFFICE 335 Main St Pineville LA 71360 (MAIL: Box 4330 Pineville LA 71361)

TEL (318) 442-1304   FAX (318) 442-8712

E-MAIL bishopjake@diocesewla.org   WEB www.epiwla.org

Previous Bishops—
Willis R Henton 1980-90, Robert J Hargrove 1990-2002, D Bruce MacPherson 2002-12

Bishop—Rt Rev Jacob W Owensby (21 July 2012)

Sec N Shaw; *Chanc* K McInnis 1080 Avery St Shreveport 71106; *Treas* G Easterling 128 Versailles Blvd Alexandria 71303; *Reg* H Davis; *Ecum* Rev WE Carter

Standing Comm—Cler: Pres A Etheredge M Richard R Heying; *Lay:* J Thompson R Myers J Robert

Deans: Acadiana M McLain; *Alexandria* R Snow; *Lake Charles* S Donald; *Monroe* D Stodghill; *Shreveport* J Flowers

PARISHES, MISSIONS, AND CLERGY

Abbeville St Pauls Episcopal Church **P** (80) 101 E Vermilion St 70510 (Mail to: PO Box 1101 70511-1101) Madge McLain (337) 893-3195

Alexandria St Timothy's Episcopal Church **P** (309) 2627 Horseshoe Dr 71301-2664 (Mail to: 2627 Horseshoe Dr 71301-2664) Walter Friese George Snow (318) 487-0875

Alexandria St James Episcopal Church and School **P** (372) § 1620 Murray Street 71301-6882 (Mail to: 1620 Murray St 71301-6882) (318) 445-9845

Bastrop Christ Episcopal Church **P** (133) 204 S Locust St 71220-4554 (Mail to: 206 S Locust St 71220-4554) Christie Fleming (318) 281-5276

Bossier City St Georges Episcopal Church **P** (226) 1959 Airline Dr 71112-2407 (Mail to: 1959 Airline Dr 71112-2407) James Flowers (318) 746-2571

Bunkie Calvary Church **P** (53) 401 S Lexington Ave 71322-1842 (Mail to: PO Box 679 71322-0679) (318) 445-7651

Cheneyville Trinity Episcopal Church **M** (15) PO Box 223 71325-0223 (Mail to: PO Box 223 71325-0223) Joseph Bordelon (318) 473-9811

Crowley Trinity Episcopal Church **P** (46) 1303 Hoffpauir Ave 70526-2625 (Mail to: PO Box 342 70527-0342) Herman Ogea (337) 783-3615

Deridder Trinity Episcopal Church **P** (46) C/O Marjorie H Adams PO Box 661 70634-0661 (Mail to: C/O Marjorie H Adams PO Box 661 70634) (337) 463-6322

Grambling St Lukes Chapel **M** (26) 1991 S Main & Adams St 71245 (Mail to: PO Box 365 71245-0365) Dawnell Stodghill (318) 247-6669

Jennings St Lukes Mission Episcopal Church **M** (21) PO Box 461 70546-0461 (Mail to: PO Box 461 70546-0461) Johnny Clark (337) 824-4397

Lafayette Episcopal Church of the Ascension **P** (722) § 1030 Johnston St 70501-7810 (Mail to: C/O Frank Limouze 1030 Johnston St 70501-7810) Joseph Daly (337) 232-2732

Lafayette St Barnabas Episcopal Church **HC** (300) § 400 Camellia Blvd 70503-4316 (Mail to: 400 Camellia Blvd 70503-4316) Michael Bordelon (337) 984-3848

Lake Charles Church of the Good Shepherd **P** (438) § 715 Kirkman St 70601-4350 (Mail to: C/O Ann Lindsay 715 Kirkman St 70601-4350) John Myers Frances Kay Frances Kay James Lueckenhoff (337) 433-5244

Lake Charles St Andrews Episcopal Church **M** (108) 1532 Sam Houston Jones Pkwy 70611 (Mail to: 1532 Sam Houston Jones Pkwy 70611-5457) (337) 855-1344

Lake Charles St Michael & All Angels Episcopal Ch **P** (296) 123 W Sale Rd 70605-2821 (Mail to: 123 W Sale Rd 70605-2821) David Donald (337) 477-1881

Lecompte Holy Comforter Episcopal Church **M** (67) 1708 Hardy St 71346 (Mail to: 3215 Madonna Dr 71301-4816) Joseph Bordelon (318) 776-5287

Leesville Leonidas Polk Memorial Episcopal Mission **M** (23) PO Box 1546 71496-1546 (Mail to: PO Box 1546 71496-1546) (337) 239-3083

Lk Providence Grace Episcopal Church **M** (26) PO Box 566 71254-0566 (Mail to: PO Box 566 71254-0566) William Echols (318) 559-1620

Mansfield Christ Memorial Episcopal Church **P** (114) 401 Washington Ave 71052-3103 (Mail to: 401 Washington Ave 71052-3103) (318) 872-1144

Mer Rouge St Andrews Episcopal Church **P** (112) 201 Davenport Ave 71261 (Mail to: PO Box 65 71261-0065) (318) 647-3683

Minden St Johns Episcopal Church **P** (181) § 1107 Broadway St 71055-3314 (Mail to: 1107 Broadway St 71055-3314) (318) 377-1259

Monroe Grace Episcopal Church **P** (697) § 405 Glenmar Ave 71201-5307 (Mail to: 405 Glenmar Ave 71201-5307) James Popham Jo Popham (318) 387-6646

Monroe St Albans Episcopal Church **P** (167) 2816 Deborah Dr 71201-1942 (Mail to: 2816 Deborah Dr 71201-1942) Thomas Stodghill (318) 323-3139

Monroe St Thomas Episcopal Church **P** (68) 3706 Bon Aire Dr 71203-3009 (Mail to: 3706 Bon Aire Dr 71203-3009) Dawnell Stodghill (318) 343-4089

Natchitoches Trinity Episcopal Church **P** (147) § 533 Second Street 71457-4619 (Mail to: 148 Touline St 71457-4639) Mary Wolfenbarger (318) 352-3113

New Iberia Episcopal Church of the Epiphany **P** (224) 303 W Main St 70560-3642 (Mail to: 303 W Main St 70560-3698) Donald Woollett (337) 369-9966

Oak Ridge Church of the Redeemer **M** (21) 206 Oak St 71264-9385 (Mail to: PO Box 238 71264-0238) (318) 647-3683

Opelousas Church of the Epiphany **P** (153) 1103 S. Union St 70570-5972 (Mail to: 1103 S Union St 70570-5952) John Bedingfield (337) 942-3336

Pineville Mount Olivet Chapel **HC** 335 Main St 71360-6929 (Mail to: PO Box 2031 71309) Jacob Owensby (318) 442-1304

Pineville St Michael's Episcopal Church **P** (323) 500 Edgewood Dr 71360-4525 (Mail to: 500 Edgewood Dr 71360-4525) (318) 640-0030

Rayville St Davids Episcopal Church **P** (77) 834 Louisa St 71269-2633 (Mail to: PO Box 276 71269-0276) (318) 728-2367

Ruston Church of the Redeemer **P** (122) 504 Tech Dr 71270-4938 (Mail to: 504 Tech Dr 71270-4938) William Easterling (318) 255-3925

Shreveport Church Of The Holy Cross **P** (100) 875 Cotton St. 71101 (Mail to: PO Box 1627 71165-1627) Mary Richard Donald Heacock (318) 222-3325

Shreveport St James Episcopal Church **P** (137) 2050 Bert Kouns Loop 71118-3315 (Mail to: 2050 Bert Kouns Loop 71118-3315) Morgan Macintire (318) 686-1261

✠ **Shreveport** St Marks Episcopal Cathedral **O** (1774) § 908 Rutherford St 71104-4246 (Mail to: 908 Rutherford St 71104-4297) Russell Boylan William Bryant Wayne Carter Andrew Christiansen Alston Johnson Thomas Nsubuga Rowena White (318) 221-3360

Shreveport St Matthias Episcopal Church **P** (252) 3301 St Matthias Dr 71119-5600 (Mail to: 3301 Saint Matthias Dr 71119-5600) (318) 635-5354

Shreveport St Pauls Episcopal Church **P** (648) § 275 Southfield Rd 71105-3608 (Mail to: 275 Southfield Rd 71105-3608) Sean Duncan Paul Martin (318) 865-8469

St Joseph Christ Episcopal Church **P** (25) 120 Hancock St 71366 (Mail to: PO Box 256 71366-0256) Gregg Riley (318) 766-3518

Sulphur Church of the Holy Trinity **P** (173) C/O Mrs Heather Reddoch 1700 Maplewood Dr 70663-6002 (Mail to: C/O Mrs Heather Reddoch 1700 Maplewood Dr 70663-6002) Ally Perry (337) 625-4288

Tallulah Trinity Episcopal Church **P** (57) PO Box 208 71284-0208 (Mail to: PO Box 208 71284-0208) William Echols (318) 362-9728

West Monroe St Patricks Episcopal Church **P** (97) 1712 Wellerman Rd 71291 (Mail to: 1712 Wellerman Rd 71291-7429) Dawnell Stodghill Thomas Stodghill (318) 396-1341

Winnfield St Pauls Episcopal Church **M** (5) 206 Pecan St 71483-3363 (Mail to: PO Box 206 71483-0206) Richard Taylor (318) 628-6971

Winnsboro St Columbas Episcopal Church **M** (11) 201 Franklin St 71295-2245 (Mail to: PO Box 83 71378-0083) (318) 435-6269

DIOCESE OF WESTERN MASSACHUSETTS
(PROVINCE I)
Comprises the central and western half of the state of Massachusetts
DIOCESAN OFFICE 37 Chestnut St Springfield MA 01103
TEL (413) 737-4786, 737-4787, (800) 332-8513   FAX (413) 746-9873
E-MAIL diocese@diocesewma.org   WEB www.diocesewma.org

Previous Bishops—
Alexander H Vinton 1902-11, Thomas F Davies 1911-36, William A Lawrence 1937-57, Robert M Hatch 1957-70, Alexander D Stewart 1970-84, Andrew F Wissemann 1984-92, Robert S Denig 1993-95, Gordon P Scruton 1996-2012

Bishop—Rt Rev Douglas John Fisher (1073) (Dio 1 Dec 2012)

Sec of Conv Rev Wm Murray; *Cns to Ord* Rev Dr R Simpson Rev P Mott; *Cn for Mission Resources* S Abdow; *Exec Asst to Bp Dio* J Senecal; *Treas* W Gass; *Asst Treas* S Abdow; *Chanc* D Allison 69 S Pleasant St Suite 201 Amherst MA 01002; *Exec Dir Trustees* N Kalber

Stand Comm—Cler: Chair N Webb Stroud C Jones C Munz S Smith; *Lay:* L Cheek P Kite N Lowry C Loy

PARISHES, MISSIONS, AND CLERGY

Amherst Grace Episcopal Church **P** (635) 14 Boltwood Ave 01002-2301 (Mail to: 14 Boltwood Ave 01002-2301) (413) 256-6754

Ashfield St Johns Episcopal Church **M** (133) Main & South St 01330-9602 (Mail to: PO Box 253 01330-0253) (413) 628-4402

Athol St Johns Episcopal Church **P** (93) 15 Park Ave 01331-2515 (Mail to: 15 Park Ave 01331-2500) (978) 249-9553

Auburn Church of St Thomas **P** (96) 35 School St 01501-2917 (Mail to: 35 School St 01501-2917) (508) 832-2598

Chicopee Trinity Church **P** (130) 27 Streiber Dr 01020-3055 (Mail to: 27 Streiber Dr 01020-3055) (413) 533-7872

Clinton Church Of The Good Shepherd **P** (263) 209 Union St 01510-2903 (Mail to: 209 Union St 01510-2903) (978) 365-5169

E Longmeadow Saint Mark's Episcopal Church **P** (353) 1 Porter Rd 01028-1348 (Mail to: 1 Porter Rd 01028-1348) James Swarr (413) 525-6341

Easthampton Saint Philip's Church **P** (169) 128 Main St 01027-2023 (Mail to: 128 Main St 01027-2023) Jill Rierdan (413) 527-0862

Feeding Hills St Davids Episcopal Church **P** (128) 699 Springfield St 01030-2134 (Mail to: 699 Springfield St 01030-2134) Benjamin Hill (413) 786-6133

Fitchburg Christ Church **P** (697) 569 Main St 01420-8012 (Mail to: 569 Main St 01420-8057) Bennett Jones Carolyn Jones (978) 342-0007

Gardner St Pauls Episcopal Church **P** (140) 79 Cross St 01440-2214 (Mail to: 79 Cross St 01440-2214) (978) 632-0925

Great Barrington Grace Church in the Southern Berkshires **P** (111) 67 State Road 01230 (Mail to: 352 Main St 01230-1814) Ray Wilson (413) 644-0022

Greenfield Epis Ch of St James & Andrew **P** (228) 8 Church St 01301-2901 (Mail to: 8 Church St 01301-2901) Heather Blais Laura Goodwin (413) 773-3925

Holden St Francis Episcopal Church **P** (695) 70 Highland St 01520-2594 (Mail to: 70 Highland St 01520-2594) (508) 829-3344

Holyoke St Pauls Episcopal Church **P** (309) 485 Appleton St 01040-3255 (Mail to: 485 Appleton St 01040-3295) Marisa Egerstrom (413) 532-5060

Lanesboro St Lukes Episcopal Church **M** (39) 20 S Main St 01237-9656 (Mail to: 20 S Main St box 593 01237-9656) Noreen Suriner (413) 443-0165

Lenox St Helenas Chapel **M** (137) 245 New Lenox Rd 01240-2242 (Mail to: 221 New Lenox Rd 01240-2223) (413) 637-1483

Lenox Trinity Parish **P** (203) 88 Walker St 01240-2725 (Mail to: Attn Eugenie Fawcett 88 Walker St 01240-2797) (413) 637-0073

Leominster St Marks Episcopal Church **P** (572) 60 West St 01453-5653 (Mail to: 60 West St 01453-5653) James Craig (978) 537-3560

Longmeadow St Andrews Episcopal Church **P** (542) 335 Longmeadow St 01106-1367 (Mail to: 335 Longmeadow St 01106-1367) Robert Fetz Benjamin Hill Francis Howard (413) 567-5901

Milford Trinity Episcopal Church **HC** (515) 17 Congress St 01757-4152 (Mail to: Dio of Western Massachusetts 37 Chestnut St 01103-1705) William Murray (508) 473-8464

Millville Saint John's Church **M** (149) 49 Central St 01529-1714 (Mail to: PO Box 395 01529-0395) (508) 883-4480

North Adams All Saints Ch of the Berkshires **P** (218) 59 Summer St 01247-4009 (Mail to: PO Box 374 01247-0374) James Duncan Stephen White (413) 663-5389

North Adams St Andrews Episcopal Church **M** (23) PO Box 327 01247-0327 (Mail to: 1438 Massachusetts Ave 01247-2261) (413) 662-2775

North Brookfield Christ Memorial Church **P** (92) 133 Main St 01535-1413 (Mail to: 65 E Huron St 60611-2728) (508) 867 2789

Northampton St Johns Episcopal Church **P** (587) 48 Elm St 01060-2903 (Mail to: 48 Elm St 01060-2932) Catherine Munz Michael Ramsey-Musolf (413) 584-1757

Northborough Church of the Nativity **P** (363) 45 Howard St 01532-1441 (Mail to: 45 Howard St 01532-1441) (508) 393-3146

Oxford Grace Episcopal Church **P** (165) 270 Main St 01540-2359 (Mail to: 268 Main Street 01540) Alfred Zadig (508) 987-1004

Pittsfield St Stephens Episcopal Church **P** (550) 67 East St 01201-5313 (Mail to: 67 East St 01201-5383) Charlotte Cooper Gwen Sears (413) 448-8276

Rochdale Christ Episcopal Church **P** (154) 1089 Stafford St 01542-1003 (Mail to: PO Box 142 01542-0142) Mary Scherm (508) 892-8460

Sheffield Christ Episcopal Trinity Lutheran Church **P** (105) 180 S Main St 01257 (Mail to: PO Box 127 01257-0127) (413) 229-8811

Shrewsbury Trinity Episcopal Church **P** (197) 440 Main St 01545-2208 (Mail to: 440 Main St 01545-2208) (508) 842-6040

South Hadley All Saints Church **P** (335) 7 Woodbridge St 01075-1117 (Mail to: 7 Woodbridge St 01075-1117) (413) 532-8917

Southbridge Holy Trinity Episcopal Church **P** (81) 446 Hamilton St 01550-1859 (Mail to: 446 Hamilton St 01550-1859) (508) 765-9559

Southwick Southwick Community Episcopal Ch **M** (196) PO Box 1069 01077-1069 (Mail to: PO Box 1069 01077-1069) J Taylor Albright (413) 569-9650

✠ **Springfield** Christ Church Cathedral **O** (558) 35 Chestnut St 01103-1705 (Mail to: 37 Chestnut St 01103-1786) (413) 736-2742

Springfield St Peters Church **P** (198) 45 Buckingham St 01109-3926 (Mail to: 45 Buckingham St 01109-3926) Michael Devine (413) 736-8567

Stockbridge St Pauls Episcopal Church **P** (163) 29 Main St 01262 (Mail to: PO Box 784 01262-0784) Jane Tillman (413) 298-4913

Sutton Holy Spirit Episcopal Church **P** (392) 3 Pleasant St 01590-3890 (Mail to: 3 Pleasant St 01590-3890) Laura Goodwin (508) 865-6448

W Springfield Church of the Good Shepherd **P** (150) 214 Elm St 01089-2709 (Mail to: PO Box 483 01090-0483) (413) 734-1976

Ware Trinity Episcopal Church **P** (106) PO Box 447 01082-0447 (Mail to: PO Box 447 01082-0447) (413) 967-6100

Webster The Church of the Reconciliation **P** (310) 5 Main St 01570-2229 (Mail to: 5 Main St 01570-2229) Janice Ford Janice Ford (508) 943-8714

Westborough Saint Stephen's Church **P** (278) 3 John St 01581-2510 (Mail to: 3 John St 01581-2510) Jesse Abell (508) 366-4134

Westfield Church of the Atonement **P** (374) 36 Court St 01085-3503 (Mail to: 36 Court St 01085-3594) (413) 562-5461

Whitinsville Trinity Episcopal Church **P** (127) 33 Linwood Ave 01588-2309 (Mail to: 29 Linwood Ave 01588-2309) (508) 234-5303

Wilbraham Church of the Epiphany **P** (272) 10 Highland Ave 01095-1932 (Mail to: 20 Highland Ave 01095-1932) (413) 596-6080

Williamstown St Johns Church **P** (466) 35 Park St 01267-2114 (Mail to: 35 Park St 01267-2114) (413) 458-8144

Worcester All Saints Episcopal Church **P** (1020) 10 Irving St 01609-3210 (Mail to: 10 Irving St 01609-3229) Bernard Poppe (508) 752-3766

Worcester St Lukes Episcopal Church **P** (275) 921 Pleasant St 01602-1908 (Mail to: c/o Dio of W Massachusetts 37 Chestnut St 01103) (508) 756-1990

Worcester St Marks Episcopal Church **P** (74) 0 Freeland St 01603-2603 (Mail to: 0 Freeland St 01603-2603) William Hobbs (508) 791-6027

Worcester St Matthews Church **P** (261) 695 Southbridge St 01610-2914 (Mail to: 695 Southbridge St 01610-2914) (508) 755-4433

Worcester St Michaels on the Heights **P** (167) 340 Burncoat St 01606-3101 (Mail to: 340 Burncoat St 01606-3101) David Woessner (508) 853-9400

DIOCESE OF WESTERN MICHIGAN
(PROVINCE V)
Comprises the western half of the Lower Peninsula
DIOCESAN OFFICE Diocese of Western Michigan
535 S Burdick Ste 1 Kalamazoo MI 49007
TEL (269) 381-2710 Bishop's Office (269) 381-2710 x14   FAX (269) 381-7067
E-MAIL info@edwm.org   WEB www.edwm.org

Previous Bishops—
Geo deN Gillespie 1875-1909,
John McCormick coadj 1906 Bp
1909-37, Lewis B Whittemore
coadj 1936 Bp 1937-53, Dudley
B McNeil 1953-59, Chas E
Bennison 1960-84, Howard S
Meeks coadj 1984 Bp 1984-88,
Edward L Lee Jr 1989-2002,
Robert R Gepert 2002-2013

Bishop—Rt Rev Whayne M Hougland Jr (1078)
(Dio 28 Sept 2013)

Sec Conv WJ Spaid; *Chanc* WJ Fleener Jr *Admin
Staff: Bp Admin Asst* M Ettwein; *Cn Missioner ~~to Ord~~*
WJ Spaid; *Cn Missioner* V Ambrose; *Cn Missioner* A
Hallmark; *Bus & Fin* T Mazure; *Child Yth & Young
Adult Min* G Callard; *Cn for Evang and Networking* K
Forsyth; *Fin Asst* C Rhodes

Stand Comm—Cler: J Baron Z Char B Heyboer
R Warren *Lay:* D Croal A Davidson J Fleener M
Bartlett

Council: Pres The Bishop; B Kelly C Nawrocki G
Stackhouse D Pike L Stifler L Marx R Schorle L
Marx C Baron P Foster L Atwater J Buchanan T
McPherson S Pattok

Extended Staff: Past Couns K Reid; *Dcn for MDGs*
B Drew; *Dcn forDom Miss* C Nawrocki; *Jubilee Ofcr*
M Bartlett

Comm on Ministry—Cler: Chair M Ryan; F Schark
D Kuhn M Fedewa J Gockerman D Stier; *Lay:*
M Simpson L Cox J Lemieux S Lund-Coyle K
Varanauskas

PARISHES, MISSIONS, AND CLERGY

Albion St James Church **P** (86) 119 W Erie St
49224-1756 (Mail to: 119 W Erie St 49224-
1756) Darlene Kuhn (517) 629-8710

Allegan Church of the Good Shepherd **P** (79) 101
Walnut St 49010-1249 (Mail to: 101 Walnut
St 49010-1249) Thomas Toeller-Novak (269)
673-2254

Battle Creek Church of the Resurrection **P** (30)
2589 Capital Ave Sw 49015-4160 (Mail to: 2589
Capital Ave SW 49015-4160) (269) 965-2840

Battle Creek Church of St Thomas **P** (334) 16
E Van Buren St 49017-3916 (Mail to: 16 Van
Buren St E 49017-3916) Brian Coleman (269)
965-2244

Beaver Island St James Episcopal Mission **M**
26055 Pine St 49782 (Mail to: PO Box 281
49782-0281) (231) 448-2241

Belmont Church of the Holy Spirit **P** (103) 1200
Post Dr Ne 49306-9723 (Mail to: 1200 Post Dr
Ne 49306-9723) David Meyers Nurya Parish
(616) 784-1111

Benton Harbor St Augustine's Church **P** (150)
1753 Union St 49022-6261 (Mail to: 1753
Union Ave 49022-6298) Barbara Wilson (269)
925-2670

Beulah St Philips Church **P** (96) 785 Beulah
Hwy 49617-9297 (Mail to: PO Box 26 49617-
0026) Christian Baron Jodi Baron Marilou
Schlotterbeck (231) 882-4506

Big Rapids St Andrews Episcopal Church **P** (47) §
323 S State St 49307-1760 (Mail to: 323 S State
St 49307-1760) Gary Hamp (231) 796-5473

Boyne City Church of the Nativity **P** (16) 209
E Main St 49712-1306 (Mail to: PO Box 228
49712-0228) (231) 582-5045

Cadillac St Marys Church **P** (60) 815 Lincoln St
49601-2033 (Mail to: 815 Lincoln St 49601-
2033) (231) 775-9641

Charlevoix Christ Church **P** (76) PO Box 385
49720-0385 (Mail to: PO Box 385 49720-0385)
(231) 547-6322

Charlotte St Johns Episcopal Church **P** (47) 201
W Shepherd St 48813-1868 (Mail to: 201 W
Shepherd St 48813-1868) (517) 543-4440

Coldwater St Marks Church **P** (256) § 27 E Chicago
St 49036-1605 (Mail to: 27 E Chicago St 49036-
1605) Frederick Schark (517) 278-5752

Dowagiac St Pauls Episcopal Church **P** (82)
306 Courtland St 49047-1198 (Mail to: 306
Courtland St 49047-1198) (269) 782-7033

Elk Rapids St Pauls Episcopal Church **P** (102)
§ 403 Traverse St 49629-9721 (Mail to: 403
Traverse St 49629-9721) (231) 264-8871

Fremont St Johns Episcopal Church **P** (56) 124 S
Sullivan Ave 49412-1546 (Mail to: PO Box 277
49412-0277) (231) 924-3280

Grand Haven St Johns Episcopal Church **P** (314)
524 Washington Ave 49417-1455 (Mail to: 524
Washington Ave 49417-1455) Jared Cramer
(616) 842-6260

Grand Ledge Trinity Church **P** (104) 201 E
Jefferson St 48837-0116 (Mail to: PO Box 116
48837-0116) (517) 627-6287

Grand Rapids Grace Church **P** (434) 1815 Hall St
Se 49506-4005 (Mail to: 1815 Hall St SE 49506-
4099) Stephen Holmgren (616) 241-4631

Grand Rapids Grace Sudanese Episcopal Church **M** 2345 Robinson Rd SE 49506-1851 (Mail to: PO Box 9502 49509-0502) (616) 328-3752

Grand Rapids St Andrews Church **P** (498) 1025 3 Mile Rd Ne 49505-3419 (Mail to: 1025 3 Mile Rd NE 49505-3419) (616) 361-7887

Grand Rapids St Marks Episcopal Church **P** (876) 134 Division Ave 49503-3103 (Mail to: 134 Division Ave 49503-3173) Christian Brocato Albert Dickinson Susan York (616) 456-1684

Grand Rapids St Philips Church **P** (84) 550 Henry Ave Se 49503-5547 (Mail to: 550-558 Henry Ave Se 49503-5547) John English (616) 451-9865

Greenville St Paul the Apostle Epis Ch **P** (120) 305 S Clay St 48838-1917 (Mail to: 305 S Clay St 48838-1917) (616) 754-3163

Harbert Church of the Mediator **P** (102) 14280 Red Arrow Hwy 49115 (Mail to: PO Box 223 49115-0223) Paula Durren (269) 469-1441

Harbor Spgs St Johns Chapel **SC** Third & Traverse 49740 (Mail to: PO Box 52 49740-0052) Phillip Ellsworth (231) 526-3914

Hastings Emmanuel Church **P** (125) 315 W Center St 49058-1615 (Mail to: 315 W Center St 49058-1615) William Ericson Linnea Stifler (269) 945-3014

Holland Grace Church **P** (665) 555 Michigan Ave 49423-4748 (Mail to: 555 Michigan Ave 49423-4794) Jennifer Adams Henry Idema (616) 396-7459

Ionia St John the Apostle Episcopal Church **P** (71) 107 W Washington St 48846-1623 (Mail to: PO Box 307 48846-0307) (616) 527-2290

Kalamazoo St Lukes Church **P** (416) § 247 W Lovell St 49007-5207 (Mail to: 247 W Lovell St 49007-5276) Randall Warren (269) 345-8553

Kalamazoo St Martin of Tours Episcopal Church **P** (118) 2010 Nichols Rd 49004-3200 (Mail to: 2010 Nichols Rd 49004-3200) Mary Perrin (269) 381-3188

Kentwood Church of the Holy Cross **P** (125) 4252 Breton Rd Se 49512-3858 (Mail to: 4252 Breton Rd Se 49512-3858) Michael Wernick (616) 949-7034

Lansing St Davids Church **P** (303) 1519 Elmwood Rd 48917-1543 (Mail to: 1519 Elmwood Rd 48917-1543) David Pike Andrew Downs Carol Spangenberg (517) 323-2272

Leland St Peters Chapel **SC** PO Box 3 49654-0003 (Mail to: 3309 Lake Leelanau Dr 49653-9622) (231) 271-3081

Ludington Grace Episcopal Church Of Ludington **P** (77) 301 James St 49431-1723 (Mail to: 301 James St 49431-1723) Domingo Shriver (231) 843-9366

Manistee Holy Trinity Episcopal Church **P** (105) 410 2nd St 49660-1534 (Mail to: PO Box 577 49660-0577) Everett Klein (231) 723-2078

Marshall Trinity Episcopal Church **P** (194) 101 E Mansion St 49068-1117 (Mail to: 101 E Mansion St 49068-1186) Anne Schnaare (269) 781-7881

Montague St Peters by the Lake Episcopal **P** (102) 8435 Old Channel Trl 49437-1360 (Mail to: 8435 Old Channel Trl 49437-1360) David Meyers (231) 893-2425

Mt Pleasant St Johns Church Episcopal **P** (193) 206 W Maple St 48858-3103 (Mail to: 206 W Maple St 48858-3103) Nancy Fulton (989) 773-7448

Muskegon St Pauls Episcopal Church **P** (170) 1006 3rd St 49440-1206 (Mail to: 1006 3rd St 49440-1206) (231) 722-2112

Newaygo St Marks Church **P** (100) 30 Justice St 49337-8519 (Mail to: PO Box 211 49337-0211) Bobbi Heyboer (231) 652-7284

Niles Trinity Episcopal Church **P** (99) § 9 S 4th St 49120-2708 (Mail to: 9 S 4th St 49120-2708) Diane Pike (269) 683-6060

Northport St Christophers Church **P** (38) § 701 Warren St 49670 (Mail to: PO Box 98 49670-0098) (231) 386-5037

Norton Shores St Gregorys Episcopal Church **P** (167) 1200 Seminole Rd 49441-4375 (Mail to: 1200 Seminole Rd 49441-4375) Lily Marx (231) 780-2955

Onekama St Johns by the Lake Chapel **SC** 4663 Highway 22 49675-9748 (Mail to: Chuck Andrews 1131 Conlon Ave. S.E. 49506-3566) (231) 935-1898

Paw Paw St Marks Episcopal Church **P** (73) § 412 Cedar St 49079 (Mail to: PO Box 307 49079-0307) Rebecca Crise (269) 657-3762

Pentwater St James Church **P** (35) 82 S Wythe St 49449-7526 (Mail to: PO Box 412 49449-0412) (231) 869-7351

Petoskey Emmanuel Episcopal Church **P** (298) 1020 E Mitchell St 49770-2636 (Mail to: Attn Office Manager 1020 E Mitchell St 49770-2636) Alan James (231) 347-2350

Plainwell St Stephens Episcopal Church **P** (155) 309 Union St 49080-1248 (Mail to: 309 Union St 49080-1248) Terry Haughn (269) 685-8230

Portage St Barnabas Episcopal Church **P** (200) 929 E Centre Ave 49002-5571 (Mail to: 929 E Centre Ave 49002-5571) Michael Wood (269) 327-7878

Richland St Timothys Church **P** (68) 9800 E Bc Ave 49083-9577 (Mail to: 9800 E BC Ave 49083-9577) Joel Turmo (269) 629-9436

Saugatuck All Saints Church **P** (276) 252 Grand St 49453-9627 (Mail to: PO Box 189 49453-0189) Gerald Stoppel (269) 857-5201

Shelbyville St Francis Episcopal Church **P** (34) 11850 9 Mile Rd 49344-9441 (Mail to: 11850 9 Mile Rd 49344-9441) (269) 664-4345

South Haven Church of the Epiphany **P** (62) 410 Erie St 49090-1324 (Mail to: 410 Erie St 49090-1324) Michael Ryan (269) 637-2521

St Joseph St Pauls Episcopal Church **P** (114) § 914 Lane Dr 49085-2053 (Mail to: 914 Lane Dr 49085-2053) (269) 983-4761

Sturgis St John Episcopal Church **P** (135) 110 S Clay St 49091-1711 (Mail to: 110 S Clay St 49091-1711) (269) 651-5811

Three Rivers Trinity Episcopal Church **P** (85) 321 Main St 49093-1422 (Mail to: 321 Main St 49093-1422) (269) 273-3795

Traverse City Grace Episcopal Church **P** (576) 341 Washington St 49684-2547 (Mail to: 341 Washington St 49684-2547) Janis Costas Louise Kountze (231) 947-2330

Wyoming Holy Trinity Episcopal Church **P** (155) 5333 Clyde Park Ave Sw 49509-9527 (Mail to: 5333 Clyde Park Ave SW 49509-9527) Bradley Allard David Brower Peter Homeyer (616) 538-0900

DIOCESE OF WESTERN NEW YORK
(PROVINCE II)
Comprises 7 Western New York counties
DIOCESAN OFFICE 1064 Brighton Rd Tonawanda NY 14150
TEL (716) 881-0660   FAX (716) 881-1724
E-MAIL diocesanoffice@episcopalwny.org   WEB www.episcopalwny.org

Previous Bishops—
Wm H Delancey 1839-65, Arthur C Coxe coadj 1865 Bp 1865-96, Wm D Walker 1897-1917, Chas H Brent 1918-29, David L Ferris suffr 1920-24 coadj 1924 Bp 1929-31, Cameron J Davis coadj 1930 Bp 1931-47, Lauriston L Scaife 1948-70, Harold B Robinson coadj 1968 Bp 1970-1987, David C Bowman coadj 1986 Bp 1987-98, J Michael Garrison 1999-2011

Bishop—Rt Rev R William Franklin (1057) (Dio 30 Apr 2011)

Ex Sec Trustees H Gondree; *Sec* H Gondree; *Treas* R Matson; *Chanc* C Fisher; *Archdcn* T Tripp

Standing Comm—Cler: Pres T Broad E Brauza L Fodor D Leiker; *Lay:* B Fortune E Hill E Boron J Robbins

Deans: Cattaraugus T Broad; *Central Erie* E Brauza; *Cattaraugus & Chautauqua* T Broad; *Eastern Erie* B Price; *Genesee Region* C O'Connor; *Northern Region* R Rowe; *Southern Erie* A Tillman; *St. Paul's Catherdral* D Fetz

PARISHES, MISSIONS, AND CLERGY

Albion Christ Episcopal Church **P** (29) § 26 S Main St 14411-1401 (Mail to: 26 S Main St 14411-1401) Judith Hefner (585) 589-5314

Alden St Aidans Church **M** (45) 13021 Main St 14004-1225 (Mail to: 13021 Main St 14004-1225) (716) 937-6922

Angola St Pauls Episcopal Church **P** (117) 930 Lake St 14006-9200 (Mail to: PO Box 344 14006-0344) (716) 549-0063

Attica St Luke's Episcopal Church **P** (340) 30 Favor St 14011-1257 (Mail to: P.O. Box 178 14011) (585) 591-0301

Batavia St James Church **P** (262) 405 E Main St 14020-2496 (Mail to: 405 E Main St 14020-2496) Steven Metcalfe Bonnie Morris (585) 343-6802

Buffalo Church of the Advent **P** (332) § 54 Delaware Rd 14217-2402 (Mail to: 54 Delaware Rd 14217-2402) Terry Bull Penelope Foster (716) 876-6504

Buffalo Church of the Ascension **P** (39) 96 Jewett Parkway 14214 (Mail to: Treasurer 16 Linwood Ave 14209-2204) Catherine Dempesy-Sims (716) 884-6362

Buffalo St Andrews Church **P** (34) 3107 Main St 14214-1305 (Mail to: 3107 Main St 14214-1305) Ellen Brauza (716) 834-9337

Buffalo St Davids Episcopal Church **P** (246) 3951 Seneca St 14224-3412 (Mail to: 3951 Seneca St 14224-3412) Claudia Scheda (716) 674-4670

Buffalo St Johns Grace Church **P** (108) 51 Colonial Cir 14222-1399 (Mail to: 51 Colonial Cir 14222-1399) Jon Lavelle (716) 885-1112

Buffalo St Judes Episcopal Church **P** (192) 124 Macamley St 14220-1242 (Mail to: 124 Macamley St 14220-1242) (716) 824-4322

Buffalo St Marks and All Saints Episcopal Church **P** (63) 311 Ontario St 14207-1548 (Mail to: 311 Ontario St 14207-1548) (716) 875-8374

Buffalo St Matthews Church **P** (48) 1182 Seneca St 14210-1545 (Mail to: 1182 Seneca St 14210-1545) Patricia Guinn (716) 822-4830

Buffalo St Michael and All Angels Church **P** (75) 81 Burke Dr 14215-1305 (Mail to: 81 Burke Dr 14215-1305) (716) 836-0220

Buffalo St Patricks Episcopal Church **P** (102) 1395 George Urban Blvd 14225-3807 (Mail to: 1395 George Urban Blvd 14225-3807) (716) 684-4206

✠ **Buffalo** Saint Paul's Cathedral **O** (270) 4 Cathedral Park 14202-4094 (Mail to: 4 Cathedral Park 14202-4094) Robert Fetz (716) 855-0900

Buffalo St Pauls Episcopal Church **P** (448) 4275 Harris Hill Rd 14221-7437 (Mail to: 4275 Harris Hill Rd 14221-7437) Vicki Zust Leann McConchie (716) 632-8221

Buffalo St Peters Episcopal Church **P** (217) 205 Longmeadow Rd 14226-2905 (Mail to: Rev. Wayne J. Knockel 205 Longmeadow Rd 14226-2905) Wayne Knockel (716) 832-9764

Buffalo St Philips Episcopal Church **P** (184) 18 Sussex Street 14215 (Mail to: PO Box 1254 14215-6254) Lillian Davis-Wilson Stephen Lane Katherine Lwebuga-Mukasa (716) 833-0444

Buffalo St Simons Episcopal Church **P** (140) 200 Cazenovia St 14210-2451 (Mail to: 200 Cazenovia St 14210-2499) Thomas Hawkins Ralph Strohm Linda Malia (716) 822-1901

Buffalo The Church of the Good Shepherd **P** (152) § 96 Jewett Pkwy 14214-2322 (Mail to: 96 Jewett Pkwy 14214-2322) Michael Hadaway Leann McConchie (716) 833-1151

Buffalo Trinity Episcopal Church **P** (628) 371 Delaware Ave 14202-1601 (Mail to: 371 Delaware Ave Ste 1 14202-1699) Stephen Lane Matthew Lincoln (716) 852-8314

Burt St Andrews Episcopal Church **P** (159) 2239 W Creek Rd 14028-9724 (Mail to: PO Box 133 14028-0133) Randi Rowe (716) 778-7633

Chautauqua Chapel of the Good Shepherd **SC** Clark Ave 14722 (Mail to: PO Box 81 14722-0081) (716) 753-2172

Dunkirk Church of St John the Baptist **P** (96) 16 W 4th St 14048-2056 (Mail to: PO Box 14 14048-0014) (716) 366-1979

East Aurora St Matthias Episcopal Church **P** (376) § 374 Main St 14052-1715 (Mail to: 374 Main St 14052-1715) Ann Tillman (716) 652-0377

Ellicottville St Johns Episcopal Church **P** (16) Washington & Jefferson Sts 14731 (Mail to: PO Box 137 14731-0137) Michael Lonto (716) 945-1820

Franklinville St Barnabas Episcopal Church **M** (14) PO Box 105 14737-0105 (Mail to: PO Box 105 14737-0105) (716) 676-3468

Fredonia Trinity Episcopal Church **P** (214) 11 Day St 14063-1813 (Mail to: 11 Day St PO Box 467 14063-1813) James Clement (716) 679-7901

Gowanda St Marys Episcopal Church **P** (41) 75 Center St 14070-1106 (Mail to: PO Box 166 14070-0166) W David Noves (716) 532-4352

Grand Island Church of St Martin in the Fields **P** (272) § 2587 Baseline Rd 14072-1656 (Mail to: 2587 Baseline Rd 14072-1656) Christopher O'Connor (716) 773-3335

Hamburg Trinity Episcopal Church **P** (340) § 261 E Main St 14075-5345 (Mail to: 261 E Main St 14075-5345) Shannon Collis (716) 649-4320

Holley St Pauls Episcopal Church **P** (39) 2 Jackson St 14470-1106 (Mail to: 2 Jackson St 14470-1106) John Boyer (585) 638-5142

Irving Church of the Good Shepherd **M** (105) 12114 Route 438 Ext 14081-9661 (Mail to: PO Box 179 14081-0179) (716) 934-3328

Jamestown St Lukes Episcopal Church **P** (375) § 410 Main St 14701-5008 (Mail to: 410 Main St 14701-5008) Barbara Baxter Lucas Fodor Cathleen Smith (716) 483-6405

Lake View Church of the Holy Communion **M** (122) 5381 Old Lake Shore Rd 14085-9746 (Mail to: PO Box 158 14085-0158) (716) 627-5951

Lancaster Trinity Church **P** (198) 5448 Broadway 14086-2124 (Mail to: 5448 Broadway St 14086-2124) Ann Markle (716) 683-1111

Le Roy St Marks Episcopal Church **P** (203) § 1 E Main St 14482-1209 (Mail to: 1 E Main Street 14482-1209) Mary McHale O'Connor (585) 768-7200

Lewiston St Pauls Episcopal Church **P** (128) § 400 Ridge St 14092-1206 (Mail to: PO Box 354 14092-0354) Neil Johnson Daniel Pinti Barbara Price Barbara Price (716) 754-4591

Lockport Christ Church **P** (245) 7145 Fieldcrest Dr 14094-1613 (Mail to: 7145 Fieldcrest Dr 14094-1613) Jeffery Edmister Thomas Mitchell (716) 433-9229

Lockport Grace Episcopal Church **P** (109) 100 Genesee St 14094-4318 (Mail to: 100 Genesee St 14094-4395) Samuel Colley-Toothaker Leann McConchie (716) 433-2878

Mayville St Pauls Episcopal Church **P** (141) 99 S Erie St 14757-1120 (Mail to: 99 S Erie St 14757-1120) Claudia Scheda (716) 753-2172

Medina St Johns Church **P** (51) 200 E Center St 14103-1623 (Mail to: 200 E Center St 14103-1623) Nancy Guenther (585) 798-0920

Niagara Falls Niagara Falls Episcopal Urb Ministry **Ministry** (109) 140 Rainbow Blvd 14303-1214 (Mail to: 140 Rainbow Blvd 14303-1214) Helen Harper (716) 282-1717

Niagara Falls St Stephen's Episcopal Church **P** (244) 616 Cayuga Drive 14304-3499 (Mail to: 616 Cayuga Dr 14304-3499) (716) 283-2774

North Tonawanda St Mark Episcopal Church **P** (340) 61 Payne Ave 14120-6012 (Mail to: 61 Payne Ave 14120-6012) (716) 692-3735

Olean St Stephens Church **P** (108) 109 S Barry St 14760-3626 (Mail to: Attn Treasurer PO Box 446 14760-0446) Kim Rossi (716) 372-5628

Orchard Park St Marks Episcopal Church **P** (616) 6595 E Quaker St 14127-2501 (Mail to: 6595 E Quaker St 14127-2585) John Marshall Leland Rose (716) 662-4418

Perry Holy Apostle Episcopal Church **P** (50) 88 Main St S 14530-1524 (Mail to: 88 Main St S 14530-1524) (585) 237-5883

Randolph Grace Episcopal Church **P** (101) 21 Washington St 14772 (Mail to: Attn Elizabeth A Jackson 21 Washington Street 14772) Thomas Broad (716) 358-6124

Salamanca St Marys Episcopal Church **P** (112) 99 Wildwood Ave 14779-1523 (Mail to: 99 Wildwood Ave 14779-1523) Michael Lonto (716) 945-1820

Silver Creek St Albans Episcopal Church **P** (57) 4 Lake Ave 14136-1012 (Mail to: PO Box 214 14136-0214) (716) 934-2174

Springville St Pauls Episcopal Church **M** (138) § 591 E Main St 14141-1437 (Mail to: 591 E Main St 14141-1437) Gerald Hilfiker (716) 592-2153

Stafford St Pauls Episcopal Church **P** (39) § 6188 Main Rd 14143-9546 (Mail to: 6188 Main Rd 14143-9546) (585) 356-0769

✠ Tonawanda St Anthony of Padua Chapel **O** 1064 Brighton Road 14150 (Mail to: 1064 Brighton Rd 14150) (716) 881-0660

Warsaw Trinity Church **P** (26) 62 W Buffalo St 14569-1209 (Mail to: PO Box 396 14569-0396)

Sarah Anuszkiewicz (585) 786-5285

Westfield St Peters Episcopal Church **P** (110) § 12 Elm St 14787-1402 (Mail to: 12 Elm St 14787-1402) Virginia Carr (716) 326-2064

Williamsville Calvary Episcopal Church **P** (1226) 20 Milton St 14221-6704 (Mail to: 20 Milton St 14221-6704) Robert Harvey (716) 633-7800

Wilson St Johns Episcopal Church **P** (61) 431 Lake St 14172-9798 (Mail to: C/O A Malangelo PO Box 28 14172-0028) Randi Rowe (716) 751-6109

Youngstown St Johns Episcopal Church **P** (86) 110 Chestnut St 14174-1002 (Mail to: PO Box 366 14174-0366) (716) 745-3369

DIOCESE OF WESTERN NORTH CAROLINA
(PROVINCE IV)
Comprises the 28 westernmost counties of North Carolina
DIOCESAN OFFICE 900-B Centre Park Dr Asheville NC 28805
TEL (828) 225-6656   FAX (828) 225-6657
E-MAIL bishopjose@diocesewnc.org   WEB www.diocesewnc.org

Previous Bishops—
Junius M Horner 1898-1933, Robt E Gribbin 1934-47, Matt G Henry 1948-75, Wm G Weinhauer coadj 1973 Bp 1975-89, Robert H Johnson 1990-2004, Granville Porter Taylor 2004-2016

Bishop — Rt Rev José McLoughlin (1096) (Dio 1 Oct 2016)

Cn to Ord and Deploy Rev Cn A Anderson; *Treas* H Cole; *Chanc* GS Hilderbran 72 Patton Ave Asheville NC 28801; *Ecum* Rev B Norris; *Outreach Min* A Ware; *Prog Min* E Clarke; *Cn Yth Min* Rev J Myers; *Cong Dev* Rev C Beebe & Rev G Butterworth; *Archdcn* K Neal

Stand Comm—Cler: Chair L Walton M Morrow S White; *Lay:* A Fullwood N Wilson C Stover G Sweet Jr

Deans: Asheville Rev T Donatelli; *Foothills* Rev A Dieterle; *Hendersonville* Rev R Adams; *Mountain* Rev R Biega; *Piedmont* Rev R Taylor; *Western* Rev B Breedlove

PARISHES, MISSIONS, AND CLERGY

Asheville St Matthias Episcopal Church **P** (82) 1 Dundee Street 28802-7375 (Mail to: PO Box 7375 28802-7375) Gerald Prickett David Sailer (828) 285-0033

✠ Asheville Church of the Advocate **O** (225) 60 Church St 28801-3622 (Mail to: PO Box 5978 28813-5978) (828) 243-3932

Asheville Church of the Redeemer **P** (144) 1201 Riverside Dr 28804-3019 (Mail to: 1201 Riverside Dr 28804-3019) (828) 253-3588

Asheville Grace Church **P** (704) 871 Merrimon Ave 28804-2404 (Mail to: 871 Merrimon Ave 28804-2492) Gary Butterworth Wendy Cade Robert Reese (828) 254-1086

Asheville St Johns Episcopal Church **P** (76) 290 Old Haw Creek Rd 28805-1436 (Mail to: 290 Old Haw Creek Rd 28805-1436) Joan Grant (828) 298-3553

Asheville Saint Luke's Episcopal Church **P** (133) 219 Chunn's Cove Rd 28805-1210 (Mail to: 219 Chunns Cove Rd 28805-1210) Patricia Mouer (828) 254-2133

Asheville St Marys Church **P** (167) 337 Charlotte Street 28801-1437 (Mail to: 337 Charlotte St 28801-1437) Michael Norris William Austin Otis Edwards Gary Kovach Stephen Weissman Harry Woggon (828) 254-5836

Asheville St Georges Episcopal Church **P** (33) 1 School Rd 28806-1633 (Mail to: 1 School Rd 28806-1633) Carol Jablonski Harry Woggon (828) 258-0211

✠ Asheville Cathedral of All Souls **O** (909) § 9 Swan St 28803-2674 (Mail to: 9 Swan St 28803-2674) Todd Donatelli Brian Cole Rosa Harden Nancy Mccarthy Mildred Morrow Nontombi Tutu (828) 274-2681

Asheville Trinity Episcopal Church **P** (1049) 60 Church St 28801-3622 (Mail to: 60 Church St 28801-3690) Robert White David Henson (828) 253-9361

Bat Cave Church of the Transfiguration **P** (97) 106 Saylor Lane 28710 (Mail to: PO Box 130 28710-0130) John Shields (828) 625-9244

Bessemer City St Andrews Episcopal Church **P** (50) 1303 12th St 28016-6739 (Mail to: PO Box 611 28016-0611) (704) 629-3021

Black Mtn Saint James Church **P** (372) 424 W State St 28711-3345 (Mail to: PO Box 1087 28711-1087) Judith Whelchel (828) 669-2754

Blowing Rock St Mary of the Hills Church **P** (276) § 140 Chestnut Cir 28605-9214 (Mail to: PO Box 14 28605-0014) James Gloster Linda Hawkins Samuel Tallman Samuel Tallman (828) 295-7323

Boone St Lukes Episcopal Church **P** (342) 170 Councill St 28607-3727 (Mail to: 170 Councill St 28607-3727) Cynthia Banks (828) 264-8943

Brevard St Philip's Episcopal Church **P** (554) 317 E Main St 28712-3834 (Mail to: 256 E Main St 28712-3724) Thomas Murphy (828) 884-3666

Burnsville St Thomas Episcopal Church **P** (96) PO Box 591 28714-0591 (Mail to: PO Box 591 28714-0591) Alicia Turner (828) 682-0037

Canton St Andrews Church **P** (271) 99 Academy St 28716-4445 (Mail to: PO Box 947 28716-0947) Timothy Mcree (828) 648-7550

Cashiers Church Of The Good Shepherd **P** (581) 1448 Highway 107 S 28717 (Mail to: PO Box 32 28717-0032) Erin Johnson Robert Wood (828) 743-2359

Cherokee St Francis of Assisi Church **P** (40) Hwy 441 At Oconaluftee Bridge 28719 (Mail to: PO Box 585 28719-0585) Elizabeth O'Callaghan (828) 507-5992

Cullowhee St Davids Episcopal Church **P** (122) P.O. Box 152 28723 (Mail to: PO Box 152 28723-0152) Valori Sherer (828) 293-9496

Denver Epis Ch of St Peters by the Lake **P** (492) 8433 Fairfield Rd 28037-9130 (Mail to: 8433 Fairfield Forest Rd 28037-9166) Ronald Taylor Judith Cole (704) 483-3460

Edneyville St Pauls Episcopal Church **P** (76) 1659 St Pauls Rd 28727 (Mail to: PO Box 70 28727-0070) Richard Rowe Harriet Shands (828) 685-3644

Flat Rock Church Of Saint John In The Wilderness **P** (482) 1895 Greenville Hwy 28731-9646 (Mail to: PO Box 185 28731-0185) Joyce Beschta William Mccleery John Roberts Harry Viola (828) 693-9783

Fletcher Calvary Episcopal Church **P** (388) PO Box 187 Hwy 25 28732-0187 (Mail to: PO Box 187 28732-0187) James Clarkson (828) 684-6266

Franklin All Saints Episcopal Church **P** 216 Roller Mill Rd 28734-9089 (Mail to: 84 Church Street 28734-2946) Jonathan Stepp

Franklin St John's Episcopal Church **P** (75) 542 St John's Church Rd 28734-8201 (Mail to: 542 Saint Johns Church Rd 28734-8201) (828) 524-6370

Gastonia All Saints Episcopal Church **P** (162) 1201 S New Hope Rd 28054-5833 (Mail to: 1201 S New Hope Rd 28054-5833) (704) 864-7201

Gastonia St Marks Episcopal Church **P** (540) 258 W Franklin Blvd 28052-4108 (Mail to: 258 W Franklin Blvd 28052-4108) Shawn Griffith (704) 864-4531

Glendale Springs Parish of Holy Communion **P** (98) 120 Glendale School Rd 28629 (Mail to: PO Box 177 28629-0177) Kimberly Becker Shirley Long (336) 982-3076

Hayesville Church of the Good Shepherd **P** (282) 495 Herbert Hills Dr 28904-4716 (Mail to: PO Box 677 28904-0677) William Breedlove (828) 389-3397

Hendersonvlle La Capilla de Santa Maria **P** (165) P.O. Box 296 28793 (Mail to: C/O Mrs Margaret Dowsett Rt 9 Box 313 28792) (828) 697-5292

Hendersonvlle St James Episcopal Church **P** (809) 766 Main St 28792-5078 (Mail to: 766 Main St 28792-3612) Joel Hafer Timothy Jones Christiana Olsen (828) 693-7458

Hickory Church Of The Ascension **P** (398) § 726 1st Ave Nw 28601-6062 (Mail to: 726 1st Ave NW 28601-6062) Karla Woggon (828) 328-5393

Hickory St Albans Episcopal Church **P** (739) 130 39th Ave Pl NW 28601-8029 (Mail to: 130 39th Avenue Pl NW 28601-8029) Tryggvi Arnason (828) 324-1351

Highlands Church of the Incarnation **P** (307) 520 Main St 28741 (Mail to: PO Box 729 28741-0729) William Manning (828) 526-2968

Lenoir St James Episcopal Church **P** (249) 806 College Ave Sw 28645-5426 (Mail to: 806 College Ave SW 28645-5426) Susan Buchanan (828) 754-3712

Lincolnton Our Saviour Episcopal Church **P** (21) P O Box 203 28092 (Mail to: PO Box 203 28093-0203) (704) 732-3585

Lincolnton St Lukes Church **P** (161) § 325 Cedar St 28092-2802 (Mail to: 315 Cedar St 28092-2802) (704) 732-9179

Linville All Saints Episcopal Chapel **SC** Carolina Ave 28646 (Mail to: C/O Edgar A Terrell Jr 2820 Rothwood Drive 28646) (828) 733-4311

Little Switzerland Church of the Resurrection **SC** PO Box 217 160 High Ridge Rd 28749-0217 (Mail to: PO Box 217 160 High Ridge Rd 28749-0217) Robert Hansel (828) 765-1808

Marion St Johns Episcopal Church **P** (117) 311 S Main St 28752-4526 (Mail to: PO Box 968 28752-0968) Michael Cogsdale Richard Rowe (828) 652-4144

Mars Hill Episcopal Church Of The Holy Spirit **P** (176) 433 Bone Camp Rd 28753 (Mail to: C/O Treasurer PO Box 956 28754-0956) David McNair Otis Edwards Robert Magnus (828) 689-2517

Mills River Church of the Holy Family **P** (128) 419 Turnpike Rd 28729 (Mail to: 419 Turnpike Rd 28759-9548) (828) 891-9375

Morganton Grace Episcopal Church **P** (216) 303 S King St 28655-3536 (Mail to: 303 S King St 28655-3536) Michael Jenkins Marshall Jolly (828) 437-1133

Morganton St Pauls Episcopal Church **P** (92) 4656 E Shores Dr 28655-8278 (Mail to: 4656 E Shores Dr 28655-8278) Harry Rains (704) 584-0955

Morganton St Marys & St Stephen's Episcopal Ch **P** (140) 140 Saint Marys Church Rd 28655-9096 (Mail to: 140 Saint Marys Church Rd 28655-9096) James Dahlin James Dahlin (828) 448-8490

Murphy Church of the Messiah **P** (119) 76 Peachtree St 28906-2940 (Mail to: Attn Ann Taaffe PO Box 67 28906-0067) (828) 837-2021

Newland Church of the Savior **P** (17) 2118 Elk Park Hwy 28657-8827 (Mail to: 2118 Elk Park Hwy 28657-8827) David Booher (828) 733-2513

Newton Episcopal Church of the Epiphany **P** (104) 750 W 13th St 28658-3826 (Mail to: PO Box 270 28658-0270) (828) 464-1876

Robbinsville Grace Mountainside Lutheran Episcopal Church **P** (20) 129 S. Main St. 28771-9802 (Mail to: Route 2 Box 7 28771) (828) 479-1184

Rutherdforton St Gabriels Episcopal Church **P** (42) P.O. Box 2121 28139 (Mail to: C/O Debbie Johnson 311 Mt View Street 28043) Bobby Lynch (828) 980-1466

Rutherfordton St Francis Episcopal Church **P** (130) § 395 Main Street 28139-2415 (Mail to: 395 Main St 28139-2505) (828) 287-3888

Saluda Church of the Transfiguration **P** (133) 72 Church St 28773-9716 (Mail to: PO Box 275 28773-0275) (828) 749-9740

Shelby Church of the Redeemer **P** (183) 502 W Sumter St 28150-4329 (Mail to: 502 W Sumter St 28150-4329) (704) 487-5404

Sparta Christ Episcopal Church **P** (108) 2543 US Hwy 21 S 28675 (Mail to: PO Box 1866 28675-1866) Stephanie Parker (336) 372-7983

Spruce Pine Trinity Episcopal Church **P** (211) 15 Hemlock Ave 28777-2981 (Mail to: 15 Hemlock Ave 28777-2981) Richard Biega (828) 520-1151

Sylva St Johns Episcopal Church **P** (93) 18 Jackson St 28779-3034 (Mail to: PO Box 175 28779-0175) Patricia Curtis (828) 586-8358

Tryon Church of the Good Shepherd **P** (75) § 814 Markham Rd 28782-2819 (Mail to: PO Box 186 27925-0186) (828) 859-9961

Tryon Church of the Holy Cross **P** (164) 150 Melrose Ave 28782-3327 (Mail to: PO Box 279 28782-0279) Robert Ard Mary Turner (828) 859-9741

Valle Crucis Church of the Holy Cross **P** (320) § 122 Skiles Way 28604 (Mail to: PO Box 645 28691-0645) Robert Mccaslin Anna Shine (828) 963-4609

Waynesville Grace Church in the Mountains **P** (256) § 394 Haywood St 28786-5718 (Mail to: 394 Haywood St 28786-5718) Joslyn Schaefer (828) 456-6029

Wilkesboro St Pauls Episcopal Church **P** (339) 200 W Cowles St 28697-2410 (Mail to: PO Box 95 28697-0095) Kedron Nicholson (336) 667-4231

STATE OF WISCONSIN

Dioceses of Eau Claire (EauC), Fond du Lac (FdL), and Milwaukee (Mil)

Algoma—FdL
Amherst—FdL
Antigo—FdL
Appleton—FdL
Ashland—EauC
Baraboo—Mil
Bayfield—EauC
Beaver Dam—Mil
Beloit—Mil
Brookfield—Mil
Brown Deer—Mil
Burlington—Mil
Chippewa Falls—EauC
Clear Lake—EauC
Conrath—EauC
Delafield—Mil
Delavan—Mil
De Pere—FdL
Eagle River—FdL
Eau Claire—EauC
Elkhorn—Mil
Fish Creek—FdL
Fond du Lac—FdL
Ft Atkinson—Mil

Gardner—FdL
Green Bay—FdL
Greendale—Mil
Hartford—Mil
Hartland—Mil
Hayward—EauC
Hudson—EauC
Janesville—Mil
Kenosha—Mil
La Crosse—EauC
Lake Geneva—Mil
Madison—Mil
Manitowoc—FdL
Marinette—FdL
Menasha—FdL
Menomonee Falls—Mil
Menomonie—EauC
Merrill—FdL
Milwaukee—Mil
Mineral Pt—Mil
Minocqua—FdL
Monroe—Mil
Mosinee—FdL
New London—FdL

New Richmond—EauC
Oconomowoc—Mil
Oneida—FdL
Oshkosh—FdL
Owen—EauC
Pewaukee—Mil
Phillips—EauC
Platteville—Mil
Plymouth—FdL
Pt Washington—Mil
Portage—Mil
Prairie du Chien—Mil
Racine—Mil
Rhinelander—FdL
Rice Lake—EauC
Richland Ctr—Mil
Ripon—FdL
Shawano—FdL
Sheboygan—FdL
Sheboygan Falls—FdL
Sister Bay—FdL
So Milwaukee—Mil
Sparta—EauC
Spooner—EauC

Springbrook—EauC
Stevens Pt—FdL
Sturgeon Bay—FdL
Suamico—FdL
Summit—Mil
Sun Prairie—Mil
Superior—EauC
Sussex—Mil
Thiensville—Mil
Tomah—EauC
Tomahawk—FdL
Watertown—Mil
Waukesha—Mil
Waupaca—FdL
Waupun—FdL
Wausau—FdL
Wautoma—FdL
W Bend—Mil
Whitefish Bay—Mil
Whitewater—Mil
Wis Dells—Mil
Wis Rapids—FdL

DIOCESE OF WYOMING
(PROVINCE VI)
Comprises the State of Wyoming
DIOCESAN OFFICE 123 S Durbin Casper WY 82601
TEL (307) 265-5200   FAX (307) 577-9939
E-MAIL Jessica@wyomingdiocese.org   WEB www.wyomingdiocese.org

Previous Bishops—
Ethelbert Talbot 1887-98, Na-
thaniel S Thomas 1909-27, Elmer
N Schmuck 1929-36, Winifred H
Ziegler 1936-49, James W Hunter
1949-69, David R Thornberry
1969-77, Bob G Jones 1977-96,
Bruce Caldwell 1997-2010

Bishop — Rt Rev John S Smylie (1048) (Dio
31 July 2010)

Deploy Cn J Dingman; *Sec/Treas* J Hotle; *Chanc* P
Nicolaysen; *Comm* B Fitzhugh; *Admin* J Reynolds;
Cn to Ordinary J Dingman; *Ed* L Modesitt; *Rec* G
Easton;

Stand Comm—Cler: Pres B Gross S Dyer S Boyd;
Lay: P Clark N St Clair L McElwain

COM—Cler: L Modesitt L Fleming C Clarke D
Wasinger J Zimmerschied *Lay: Sec* J Reynolds J
Dominick M Tepper C Lev

Diocesan Council: *Cler:* A Davenport E Farmer J
Shumard *Lay:* J Wildman L Seaton K McAtee K Lowe
M Appel T Johnson P Hotchkiss P Larson J Angst

PARISHES, MISSIONS, AND CLERGY

Atlantic City St Andrews Episcopal Church **M**
(20) 50 E Forbes St 82520-8812 (Mail to: 123 S
Durbin St 82601-2511) (307) 332-4327

Basin St Andrews Episcopal Church **P** (75) 401 S
8th St 82410-9550 (Mail to: PO Box 407 82410-
0407) Jean McLean (307) 568-2072

Big Piney St John the Baptist Episcopal Church **M**
(46) 340 Smith Ave 83113 (Mail to: PO Box 205
83113-0205) Jami Anderson (307) 276-3805

Bondurant St Hubert the Hunter **SC** US 191 189
82922 (Mail to: 104 S 4th St 82070-3162) (307)
733-4166

Buffalo St Lukes Episcopal Church **P** (335) 178
S Main St 82834-0909 (Mail to: PO Box 909
82834-0909) Douglas Wasinger (307) 684-
7529

Casper St Marks Church **P** (576) § 701 S Wolcott
St 82601-3159 (Mail to: 701 S Wolcott St
82601-3159) James Shumard (307) 234-0831

Casper St Stephens Church **P** (50) 4700 S Poplar
St 82601-6257 (Mail to: 4700 S Poplar St 82601-
6257) Katherine Flores Judy Likwartz Wendy
Owens (307) 265-4105

Cheyenne St Christophers Church **P** (178) 2602
Deming Blvd 82001-5708 (Mail to: 2602
Deming Blvd 82001-5708) (307) 632-4488

Cheyenne St Marks Episcopal Church **P** (247) §
1908 Central Ave 82001-3743 (Mail to: 1908
Central Ave 82001-3743) Richard Veit David
Mcelwain David Mcelwain James Stewart
(307) 634-7709

Cody Christ Church **P** (597) 825 Simpson Avenue
82414-1718 (Mail to: PO Box 1718 82414-
1718) Mary Caucutt David Fox Douglas
Sunderland (307) 587-3849

Cokeville St Bartholomews Church **M** (7) 220
Pine St 83114 (Mail to: PO Box 365 83114-
0365) (307) 279-3519

Dixon St Pauls Episcopal Church **M** (123) PO
Box 68 82323-0068 (Mail to: PO Box 68 82323-
0068) (307) 383-7645

Douglas Christ Episcopal Church **P** (92) 411 E
Center St 82633-2438 (Mail to: PO Box 1419
82633-1419) (307) 358-5609

Dubois St Thomas Episcopal Church **P** (80) 5 S
1st St 82513 (Mail to: PO Box 735 82513-0735)
Lyndie Duff (307) 455-2313

Encampment St James Church **M** (6) 812
Mccaffrey 82325 (Mail to: 1318 Montana St
82301-4341) (307) 710-5464

Evanston St Pauls Episcopal Church **P** (160) §
10th And Sage Sts 82930 (Mail to: PO Box 316
82931-0316) Constance Clark Suzanne Mac
Ewen George Snow (307) 444-2601

Fort Bridger St Davids Episcopal Church **M**
(3) 95 Carter St 82933 (Mail to: PO Box 144
82933-0144) (307) 782-3454

Fort Washakie Shoshone Mission **M** (179) 189 Trout
Creek Rd 82514 (Mail to: PO Box 175 82514-
0175) Velma Chavez Carl Means (307) 332-7925

Gillette Holy Trinity Episcopal Church **P** (120)
5101 Tanner Drive 82718 (Mail to: 5101
Tanner Dr 82718-4332) Anetta Davenport
(307) 682-4296

Glendo St John the Baptist Church **M** (29) § Attn
Mrs John H Hughes PO Box 412 82213-0008
(Mail to: PO Box 412 82213-0412) (307) 331-8405

Glenrock Christ Episcopal Church **M** (128) § 415
W Cedar St 82637-0849 (Mail to: PO Box 298
82637-0298) Leigh Earle (307) 436-8804

Green River St Johns Episcopal Church **P** (45)
350 Mansface St 82935-4904 (Mail to: PO Box
400 82935-0321) (307) 875-3419

Hartville Our Saviour Church **M** (40) 9 Lincoln
St 82215 (Mail to: PO Box 64 82215-0064) Rex
Martin William Walker (307) 836-2321

Jackson Chapel of the Transfiguration **SC** 170
Glenwood 83001 (Mail to: PO Box 1690 83001-
1690) (307) 733-2603

Jackson St Johns Episcopal Church **P** (1035) § 170 Glenwood St 83001-8761 (Mail to: PO Box 1690 83001-1690) James Bartz Brian Nystrom (307) 733-2603

Kaycee All Souls Episcopal Church **M** (37) 414 Sullivan St 82639 (Mail to: PO Box 12 82639-0012) (307) 738-2416

Kemmerer St James Episcopal Church **M** (76) 506 Cedar Ave 83101-3015 (Mail to: 506 Cedar Ave 83101-3015) Walt Seeley (307) 877-3652

Kinnear Holy Nativity Church **M** (30) 10925 US Hwy 26 82516-0160 (Mail to: PO Box 160 82516-0160) Sally Bub

Lander Our Father's House **M** (144) 3 Saint Michael Cir 82520-9373 (Mail to: PO Box 8610 82520-8060) Patricia Bergie (307) 332-2660

Lander Trinity Episcopal Church **P** (125) 806 S 3rd St 82520-3712 (Mail to: 860 S 3rd St 82520-3712) Raymond Price Terry Robeson Walt Seeley (307) 332-5977

✠ **Laramie** St Matthews Episcopal Cathedral **O** (296) 104 S 4th St 82070 (Mail to: 104 S 4th St 82070-3102) Patricia Askew Candice Corrigan Richard Naumann (307) 742-6608

Lusk St Georges Episcopal Church **P** (61) 120 West 5th St 82225 (Mail to: PO Box 38 82225-0038) (307) 334-2870

Medicine Bow St Lukes Church **M** (12) 220 Pine Street 82329 (Mail to: PO Box 23 82329-0085) (307) 745-8472

Meeteetse St Andrews Episcopal Church **M** (50) 1116 Park Ave 82433 (Mail to: PO Box 88 82433-0088) (307) 868-2534

Newcastle Christ Episcopal Church **M** (23) 310 S Summit Ave 82701-0519 (Mail to: PO Box 519 82701-0519) (307) 746-9684

Pinedale St Andrews in the Pines **P** (289) 524 West Pine St 82941 (Mail to: PO Box 847 82941-0847) Melinda Bobo Raleigh Denison (307) 367-2674

Powell St Johns Episcopal Church **M** (77) 308 Mountain View St 82435-2231 (Mail to: PO Box 846 82435-0846) Megan Nickles (307) 754-4000

Rawlins St Thomas Episcopal Church **P** (84) 6th And Pine Sts 82301 (Mail to: PO Box 608 82301-0608) Karen Buckingham (307) 324-5447

Riverton St James Episcopal Church **P** (169) § 519 E Park Ave 82501-3652 (Mail to: 519 E Park Ave 82501-3652) (307) 856-2369

Rock Springs Church of the Holy Communion **P** (147) 205 2nd St 82901 (Mail to: PO Box 567 82902-0567) (307) 362-3002

Saratoga St Barnabas Episcopal Church **M** (27) 204 West Main 82331 (Mail to: PO Box 250 82331-0250) (307) 326-8514

Sheridan St Peters Episcopal Church **P** (692) One S Tschirgi St 82801 (Mail to: 1 S Tschirgi St 82801-4229) Ronald Johnson Andrew Cruz Lillegard John Meyer (307) 674-7655

Sundance Good Shepherd Episcopal Church **M** (31) 120 North 6th St 82729 (Mail to: Attn Norma Lambert Treas PO Box 246 82729-0246) Katherine Moore (307) 283-1863

Thermopolis Holy Trinity Episcopal Church **P** (122) § 642 Arapahoe St 82443-2712 (Mail to: PO Box 950 82443-0950) Joseph Galligan Anetta Davenport (307) 864-3629

Torrington All Saints Episcopal Church **P** (195) 2601 Main St 82240-1925 (Mail to: 2601 Main St 82240-1925) Brian Gross (307) 532-5495

Wheatland All Saints Episcopal Church **P** (150) § 605 11th Street 82201-2805 (Mail to: PO Box 997 82201-0997) Lori Modesitt Jill Zimmerschied (307) 322-9067

Worland St Albans Episcopal Church **P** (102) § 1126 Us Highway 16 82401-3011 (Mail to: PO Box 84 82401-0084) (307) 347-4704

Wright Saint Francis On The Prairie Church **M** (51) 357 Willow Creek Dr 82732 (Mail to: PO Box 161 82732-0161) Sally Boyd (307) 464-0028

The Succession of American Bishops

See end of list for lettered entries.

		Consecrators			Born	Date Consecrated	Died
1	SEABURY SAMUEL	AAA	AAB	AAC	1729	1784	1796
2	WHITE WILLIAM	AAD	AAE	AAF	1748	1787	1836
3	PROVOOST SAMUEL	AAD	AAE	AAF	1742	1787	1815
4	MADISON JAMES	AAG	AAD	AAH	1749	1790	1812
5	CLAGGETT THOMAS JOHN	3	1	2	1743	1792	1816
6	SMITH ROBERT	2	3	4	1732	1795	1801
7	BASS EDWARD	2	3	5	1726	1797	1803
8	JARVIS ABRAHAM	2	3	7	1739	1797	1813
9	MOORE BENJAMIN	2	5	8	1748	1801	1816
10	PARKER SAMUEL	2	5	8	1744	1804	1804
11	HOBART JOHN HENRY	2	3	8	1775	1811	1830
12	GRISWOLD ALEXANDER V	2	3	8	1766	1811	1843
13	DEHON THEODORE	2	8	11	1776	1812	1817
14	MOORE RICHARD C	2	11	12	1762	1814	1841
15	KEMP JAMES	2	11	14	1764	1814	1827
16	CROES JOHN	2	11	15	1762	1815	1832
17	BOWEN NATHANIEL	2	11	15	1779	1818	1839
18	CHASE PHILANDER	2	11	15	1775	1819	1852
19	BROWNELL THOMAS C	2	11	12	1779	1819	1865
20	RAVENSCROFT JOHN S	2	12	15	1772	1823	1830
21	ONDERDONK HENRY U	2	11	15	1789	1827	1858
22	MEADE WILLIAM	2	11	12	1789	1829	1862
23	STONE WILLIAM MURRAY	2	14	21	1779	1830	1838
24	ONDERDONK BENJAMIN T	2	19	21	1791	1830	1861
25	IVES LEVI SILLIMAN	2	21	24	1797	1831	1867
26	HOPKINS JOHN HENRY	2	12	17	1792	1832	1868
27	SMITH BENJAMIN B	2	19	21	1794	1832	1884
28	MCILVAINE CHARLES P	2	12	22	1799	1832	1873
29	DOANE GEORGE W	2	24	25	1799	1832	1859
30	OTEY JAMES HERVEY	2	21	24	1800	1834	1863
31	KEMPER JACKSON	2	14	18	1789	1835	1870
32	MCCOSKRY SAMUEL ALLEN	21	29	31	1804	1836	1886
33	POLK LEONIDAS	22	27	28	1806	1838	1864
34	DELANCEY WILLIAM H	12	21	24	1797	1839	1865
35	GADSDEN CHRISTOPHER E	12	29	32	1785	1840	1852
36	WHITTINGHAM WILLIAM R	12	14	24	1805	1840	1879
37	ELLIOT STEPHEN	22	25	35	1806	1841	1866
38	LEE ALFRED	12	14	18	1807	1841	1887
39	JOHNS JOHN	12	22	25	1796	1842	1876
40	EASTBURN MANTON	12	19	24	1801	1842	1872
41	HENSHAW JOHN P K	19	24	26	1792	1843	1852
42	CHASE CARLTON	18	19	24	1794	1844	1870
43	COBBS NICHOLAS HAMNER	18	22	28	1795	1844	1861
44	HAWKS CICERO STEPHENS	18	31	32	1812	1844	1868
45	BOONE WILLIAM JONES	18	29	30	1811	1844	1864
46	FREEMAN GEORGE W	18	31	33	1789	1844	1858
47	SOUTHGATE HORATIO	18	36	37	1812	1844	1894
48	POTTER ALONZO	18	19	29	1800	1845	1865
49	BURGESS GEORGE	18	19	40	1809	1847	1866
50	UPFOLD GEORGE	27	28	31	1796	1849	1872
51	GREEN WILLIAM MERCER	30	33	43	1798	1850	1887
52	PAYNE JOHN	22	38	39	1815	1851	1874
53	RUTLEDGE FRANCIS H	35	37	43	1799	1851	1866
54	WILLIAMS JOHN	19	26	34	1817	1851	1899
55	WHITEHOUSE HENRY JOHN	19	38	40	1803	1851	1874
56	WAINWRIGHT JONATHAN M	19	29	31	1792	1852	1854
57	DAVIS THOMAS F	19	26	27	1804	1853	1871
58	ATKINSON THOMAS	19	28	29	1807	1853	1881
59	KIP WILLIAM INGRAHAM	31	38	45	1811	1853	1893
60	SCOTT THOMAS FIELDING	37	43	57	1807	1854	1867
61	LEE HENRY WASHINGTON	26	32	34	1815	1854	1874
62	POTTER HORATIO	19	26	29	1802	1854	1887
63	CLARK THOMAS MARCH	19	26	29	1812	1854	1903
64	BOWMAN SAMUEL	31	34	38	1800	1858	1861
65	GREGG ALEXANDER	26	27	30	1819	1859	1893
66	ODENHEIMER WILLIAM H	22	32	39	1817	1859	1879

		Consecrators			Born	Cons.	Died
67	BEDELL GREGORY T	22	28	39	1817	1859	1892
68	WHIPPLE HENRY B	31	34	43	1822	1859	1901
69	LAY HENRY C	22	28	33	1823	1859	1885
70	TALBOT JOSEPH C	31	27	44	1816	1860	1883
71	STEVENS WILLIAM B	26	38	48	1815	1862	1887
72	WILMER RICHARD H	22	37	39	1816	1862	1900
73	VAIL THOMAS H	31	55	61	1812	1864	1889
74	COXE ARTHUR CLEVELAND	26	49	58	1818	1865	1896
75	QUINTARD CHARLES T	26	49	58	1824	1865	1898
76	CLARKSON ROBERT H	26	31	32	1826	1865	1884
77	RANDALL GEORGE M	26	27	40	1810	1865	1873
78	KERFOOT JOHN B	26	28	36	1816	1866	1881
79	WILLIAMS CHANNING M	26	38	39	1829	1866	1910
80	WILMER JOSEPH P B	26	51	72	1812	1866	1878
81	CUMMINS GEORGE D	26	27	61	1822	1866	1876
82	ARMITAGE WILLIAM E	31	32	61	1830	1866	1873
83	NEELY HENRY A	26	54	62	1830	1867	1899
84	TUTTLE DANIEL S	26	62	66	1837	1867	1923
85	YOUNG JOHN F	26	52	65	1820	1867	1885
86	BECKWITH JOHN W	51	58	72	1831	1868	1890
87	WHITTLE FRANCIS M	39	38	67	1823	1868	1902
88	BISSELL WILLIAM H A	32	54	62	1814	1868	1893
89	ROBERTSON CHARLES F	27	32	39	1835	1868	1886
90	MORRIS BENJAMIN W	38	66	73	1819	1868	1906
91	LITTLEJOHN ABRAM N	62	39	66	1824	1869	1901
92	DOANE WILLIAM C	62	66	83	1832	1869	1913
93	HUNTINGTON FREDERIC D	27	40	62	1819	1869	1904
94	WHITAKER OZI W	28	38	40	1830	1869	1911
95	PIERCE HENRY N	51	55	72	1820	1870	1899
96	NILES WILLIAM W	27	54	83	1832	1870	1914
97	PINKNEY WILLIAM	27	39	58	1810	1870	1883
98	HOWE WILLIAM B W	27	36	57	1823	1871	1894
99	HOWE MARK A DE W	27	28	38	1809	1871	1895
100	HARE WILLIAM H	27	38	54	1838	1873	1909
101	AUER JOHN GOTTLIEB	27	38	52	1832	1873	1874
102	PADDOCK BENJAMIN H	27	38	54	1828	1873	1891
103	LYMAN THEODORE B	36	58	69	1815	1873	1893
104	SPALDING JOHN F	32	67	70	1828	1873	1902
105	WELLES EDWARD R	27	54	58	1830	1874	1888
106	ELLIOTT ROBERT W B	65	72	75	1840	1874	1887
A	HOLLY JAMES THEODORE	27	38	62	1829	1874	1911
107	WINGFIELD JOHN H D	39	58	69	1833	1874	1898
108	GARRETT ALEXANDER C	76	84	100	1832	1874	1924
109	ADAMS WILLIAM F	51	80	86	1833	1875	1920
110	DUDLEY THOMAS U	27	39	71	1837	1875	1904
111	SCARBOROUGH JOHN	62	71	78	1831	1875	1914
112	GILLESPIE GEORGE D	32	70	88	1819	1875	1909
113	JAGGAR THOMAS A	27	38	62	1839	1875	1912
114	MC LAREN WILLIAM E	32	67	68	1831	1875	1905
115	BROWN JOHN H H	62	88	92	1831	1875	1888
116	PERRY WILLIAM S	71	74	78	1832	1876	1898
117	PENICK CHARLES C	58	87	97	1843	1877	1914
118	SCHERESCHEWSKY SAMUEL	27	62	67	1831	1877	1906
119	BURGESS ALEXANDER	27	54	63	1819	1878	1901
120	PETERKIN GEORGE W	67	78	87	1841	1878	1916
121	SEYMOUR GEORGE F	62	66	69	1829	1878	1906
B	RILEY HENRY CHAUNCEY	38	67	71		1879	1904
122	HARRIS SAMUEL S	72	70	76	1841	1879	1888
123	STARKEY THOMAS A	63	73	91	1818	1880	1903
124	GALLEHER JOHN N	51	71	89	1839	1880	1891
125	DUNLOP GEORGE K	68	89	102	1830	1880	1888
126	BREWER LEGH R	93	84	88	1839	1880	1916
127	PADDOCK JOHN A	27	38	62	1825	1880	1894
128	WHITEHEAD CORTLANDT	71	67	99	1842	1882	1922
129	THOMPSON HUGH M	51	72	122	1830	1883	1902
130	KNICKERBACKER DAVID B	74	89	103	1833	1883	1894
131	POTTER HENRY C	27	54	63	1835	1883	1908
132	RANDOLPH ALFRED M	38	98	110	1836	1883	1918
133	WALKER WILLIAM D	63	74	76	1839	1883	1917
134	WATSON ALFRED A	51	83	98	1818	1884	1905
135	BOONE WILLIAM J	79	AAK	AAL	1846	1884	1891

		Consecrators		Born	Cons.	Died
136	RULISON NELSON S	38	99	114	1842	1884	1897
137	PARET WILLIAM	38	71	99	1826	1885	1911
138	WORTHINGTON GEORGE	74	100	114	1840	1885	1908
139	FERGUSON SAMUEL DAVID	38	71	91	1842	1885	1916
140	WEED EDWIN GARDNER	75	98	106	1847	1886	1924
141	GILBERT MAHLON NORRIS	38	67	68	1848	1886	1900
142	THOMAS ELISHA SMITH	68	73	84	1834	1887	1895
143	TALBOT ETHELBERT	68	73	84	1848	1887	1928
144	JOHNSTON JAMES S	72	110	122	1843	1888	1924
145	LEONARD ABIEL	73	75	84	1848	1888	1903
146	COLEMAN LEIGHTON	99	94	109	1837	1888	1907
147	KENDRICK JOHN MILLS	84	110	130	1836	1889	1911
148	VINCENT BOYD	104	110	117	1845	1889	1935
149	KNIGHT CYRUS F	114	116	119	1831	1889	1891
150	GRAFTON CHARLES C	114	119	121	1832	1889	1912
151	LEONARD WILLIAM A	54	68	92	1848	1889	1930
152	DAVIES THOMAS F	54	68	84	1831	1889	1905
153	GRAVES ANSON ROGERS	84	100	119	1842	1890	1931
154	NICHOLS WILLIAM FORD	54	75	83	1849	1890	1924
155	ATWILL EDWARD ROBERT	84	114	111	1840	1890	1911
156	JACKSON HENRY M	72	98	120	1848	1891	1900
157	SESSUMS DAVIS	75	84	108	1858	1891	1929
158	BROOKS PHILLIPS	54	63	68	1835	1891	1893
159	NICHOLSON ISAAC LEA	114	94	109	1844	1891	1906
160	NELSON CLELAND K	75	98	103	1852	1892	1917
161	HALE CHARLES REUBEN	116	121	133	1837	1892	1900
162	KINSOLVING GEORGE H	72	75	94	1849	1892	1928
163	WELLS LEMUEL HENRY	54	83	90	1841	1892	1936
164	GRAY WILLIAM CRANE	75	110	140	1835	1892	1919
165	BROOKE FRANCIS KEY	84	95	104	1852	1893	1918
166	BARKER WILLIAM MORRIS	90	104	114	1854	1893	1901
167	MCKIM JOHN	91	103	110	1852	1893	1936
168	GRAVES FREDERICK R	91	103	110	1858	1893	1940
169	CAPERS ELLISON	103	134	140	1837	1893	1908
170	GAILOR THOMAS FRANK	75	110	116	1856	1893	1935
171	LAWRENCE WILLIAM	54	63	83	1850	1893	1941
172	CHESHIRE JOSEPH B	103	134	169	1850	1893	1932
173	HALL ARTHUR CRAWSHAY	83	96	146	1847	1894	1930
174	NEWTON JOHN B	87	110	120	1839	1894	1897
175	WHITE JOHN HAZEN	84	114	128	1849	1895	1925
176	MILLSPAUGH FRANK R	68	84	104	1848	1895	1916
177	ROWE PETER TRIMBLE	92	94	123	1856	1895	1942
178	BURTON LEWIS WILLIAM	110	120	132	1852	1896	1940
179	JOHNSON JOSEPH H	152	138	143	1847	1896	1928
180	SATTERLEE HENRY YATES	74	93	110	1843	1896	1908
181	WILLIAMS GERSHOM MOTT	84	75	114	1857	1896	1923
182	MORRISON JAMES DOW	92	93	111	1844	1897	1934
183	BREWSTER CHAUNCEY B	91	92	94	1848	1897	1941
184	GIBSON ROBERT A	87	117	120	1846	1897	1919
185	MC VICKAR WILLIAM N	92	94	113	1843	1898	1910
186	BROWN WILLIAM M	114	121	128	1855	1898	1937
187	HORNER JUNIUS MOORE	172	134	169	1859	1898	1933
C	KINSOLVING LUCIEN LEE	110	92	111	1862	1899	1929
188	MORELAND WILLIAM HALL	154	145	147	1861	1899	1946
189	EDSALL SAMUEL COOK	114	121	133	1860	1899	1917
190	MORRISON THEODORE N	114	121	133	1850	1899	1929
191	FUNSTEN JAMES BOWEN	84	94	117	1856	1899	1918
192	FRANCIS JOSEPH M	114	121	152	1862	1899	1939
193	WILLIAMS ARTHUR L	138	104	153	1853	1899	1919
194	GRAVATT WILLIAM L	87	117	120	1858	1899	1942
195	PARTRIDGE SIDNEY C	167	118	168	1857	1900	1930
196	CODMAN ROBERT	96	92	93	1859	1900	1915
197	ANDERSON CHARLES P	114	112	121	1863	1900	1930
198	BARNWELL ROBERT W	129	140	144	1849	1900	1902
199	WELLER REGINALD H	150	114	159	1857	1900	1935
200	TAYLOR FREDERICK W	121	150	159	1853	1901	1903
201	MANN CAMERON	84	143	155	1851	1901	1932
202	BRENT CHARLES H	92	131	171	1862	1901	1929
203	KEATOR FREDERIC W	114	100	159	1855	1902	1924
204	BURGESS FREDERICK	131	92	111	1853	1902	1925
205	INGLE JAMES A	168	167	195	1867	1902	1903

		Consecrators			Born	Cons.	Died
206	VINTON ALEXANDER H	152	93	173	1852	1902	1911
207	OLMSTED CHARLES S	84	144	145	1853	1902	1918
208	MACKAY SMITH A	92	111	128	1850	1902	1911
209	VAN BUREN JAMES H	120	171	173	1850	1902	1917
210	RESTARICK HENRY B	154	113	147	1854	1902	1933
211	OLMSTED CHARLES T	93	96	131	1842	1902	1924
212	BECKWITH CHARLES M	110	108	157	1851	1902	1928
213	GRISWOLD SHELDON M	92	121	133	1861	1903	1930
214	BRATTON THEODORE D	110	140	144	1862	1903	1944
215	LINES EDWIN S	84	92	111	1845	1903	1927
216	FAWCETT EDWARD	84	121	150	1865	1904	1935
217	GREER DAVID H	131	92	94	1844	1904	1919
218	NELSON RICHARD H	92	94	133	1859	1904	1931
219	OSBORNE EDWARD W	121	131	150	1845	1904	1926
220	STRANGE ROBERT	169	132	172	1857	1904	1914
221	ROOTS LOGAN H	168	167	171	1870	1904	1945
222	SPALDING FRANKLIN S	84	94	111	1865	1904	1914
223	AVES HENRY D	108	144	157	1853	1904	1936
224	KNIGHT ALBION W	84	140	157	1859	1904	1936
225	WOODCOCK CHARLES E	84	121	138	1854	1905	1940
226	DARLINGTON JAMES H	94	121	128	1856	1905	1930
227	JOHNSON FREDERIC F	84	94	113	1866	1905	1943
228	WILLIAMS CHARLES D	84	113	148	1860	1906	1923
229	PARKER EDWARD M	96	171	173	1855	1906	1925
230	MC CORMICK JOHN N	84	112	160	1863	1906	1939
231	WEBB WILLIAM W	159	150	175	1857	1906	1933
232	SCADDING CHARLES	84	121	128	1861	1906	1914
233	TUCKER BEVERLEY D	132	120	172	1846	1906	1930
234	GUERRY WILLIAM A	84	140	170	1861	1907	1928
235	PADDOCK ROBERT L	84	131	180	1869	1907	1939
236	KNIGHT EDWARD J	111	143	208	1864	1907	1908
237	ROBINSON HENRY D	84	150	189	1859	1908	1913
238	REESE FREDERICK F	160	140	170	1854	1908	1936
239	KINSMAN FREDERICK J	84	94	96	1868	1908	1944
240	HARDING ALFRED	84	109	111	1852	1909	1923
241	THOMAS NATHANIEL S	84	94	111	1867	1909	1937
242	BREWSTER BENJAMIN	84	154	183	1860	1909	1941
243	MURRAY JOHN G	137	109	132	1857	1909	1929
244	LLOYD ARTHUR S	84	120	132	1857	1909	1936
245	BEECHER GEORGE A	84	108	153	1868	1910	1951
246	TEMPLE EDWARD A	84	108	144	1867	1910	1924
247	PERRY JAMES D	84	126	171	1871	1911	1947
248	ATWOOD JULIUS W	171	173	183	1857	1911	1945
249	THURSTON THEODORE P	84	126	165	1867	1911	1941
250	SANFORD LOUIS C	154	179	188	1867	1911	1948
251	BURCH CHARLES S	217	92	111	1855	1911	1920
252	ISRAEL ROGERS	128	143	148	1854	1911	1921
253	WINCHESTER JAMES R	84	140	162	1852	1911	1941
254	DAVIES THOMAS F	84	171	183	1872	1911	1936
255	RHINELANDER PHILIP M	84	128	171	1869	1911	1939
256	GARLAND THOMAS J	84	111	128	1866	1911	1931
257	TOLL WILLIAM E	84	151	175	1843	1911	1915
258	TUCKER HENRY ST G	167	AAM	AAN	1874	1912	1959
259	HUNTINGTON DANIEL T	168	221	AAO	1868	1912	1950
260	BILLER GEORGE JR	84	126	165	1874	1912	1915
261	LONGLEY HARRY S	84	190	193	1868	1912	1944
262	MC ELWAIN FRANK A	84	189	193	1875	1912	1957
263	WEEKS WILLIAM F	173	218	229	1859	1913	1914
264	REESE THEODORE I	148	151	171	1873	1913	1931
265	BABCOCK SAMUEL G	171	196	202	1851	1913	1942
266	COLMORE CHARLES B	84	140	170	1879	1913	1950
267	TYLER JOHN P	84	120	132	1862	1914	1931
268	DU MOULIN FRANK	151	128	148	1870	1914	1947
269	HOWDEN FREDERICK S	84	143	148	1869	1914	1940
270	CAPERS WILLIAM T	84	140	144	1867	1914	1943
271	BROWN WILLIAM C	84	132	184	1861	1914	1927
272	FABER WILLIAM F	84	126	151	1860	1914	1934
273	HUNTING GEORGE C	84	154	179	1871	1914	1924
274	JONES PAUL	84	154	179	1880	1914	1941
275	DARST THOMAS C	84	172	187	1875	1915	1948
276	SUMNER WALTER T	197	151	175	1873	1915	1935

		Consecrators			Born	Cons.	Died
277	HULSE HIRAM RICHARD	217	151	163	1868	1915	1938
278	MATTHEWS PAUL	148	151	192	1866	1915	1954
279	PAGE HERMAN	84	163	171	1866	1915	1942
280	BLISS GEORGE YEMENS	173	196	229	1864	1915	1924
281	FISKE CHARLES	84	199	211	1868	1915	1942
282	STEARLY WILSON REIFF	215	128	143	1869	1915	1941
283	ACHESON EDWARD C	183	171	215	1858	1915	1934
284	WISE JAMES	84	162	177	1875	1916	1939
285	BURLESON HUGH LATIMER	84	171	189	1865	1916	1933
286	JOHNSON IRVING PEAKE	84	189	193	1866	1917	1947
287	TOURET FRANK HALE	84	270	272	1875	1917	1945
288	SHERWOOD GRANVILLE H	84	190	193	1878	1917	1923
289	SAPHORE EDWIN W	84	162	195	1854	1917	1944
290	THOMSON ARTHUR C	84	132	172	1871	1917	1946
291	MOORE HARRY TUNIS	84	108	162	1874	1917	1955
292	MIKELL HENRY JUDAH	170	140	164	1873	1917	1942
293	REMINGTON WILLIAM P	84	228	249	1879	1918	1963
294	SAGE JOHN CHARLES	84	190	193	1866	1918	1919
295	HARRIS ROBERT LE ROY	84	151	175	1874	1918	1948
296	DEMBY EDWARD THOMAS	84	170	195	1869	1918	1957
297	QUIN CLINTON SIMON	84	223	225	1883	1918	1956
298	DELANY HENRY B	172	233	275	1858	1918	1928
299	GREEN WILLIAM M	84	157	170	1876	1919	1942
300	SHAYLER ERNEST V	203	163	272	1868	1919	1947
301	BEATTY TROY	84	170	253	1866	1919	1922
302	PARSONS EDWARD L	154	179	188	1868	1919	1960
303	OVERS WALTER H	84	226	252	1870	1919	1934
304	MORRIS JAMES C	84	170	224	1870	1920	1944
305	MOSHER GOUVERNEUR F	168	259	258	1871	1920	1941
306	JETT ROBERT C	84	233	194	1865	1920	1950
307	MOULTON ARTHUR W	84	171	173	1873	1920	1962
308	DAVENPORT GEORGE W	84	233	151	1870	1920	1956
309	STEVENS WILLIAM B	179	154	167	1884	1920	1947
310	FERRIS DAVID L	202	128	173	1864	1920	1947
311	COOK PHILIP	84	143	201	1875	1920	1938
312	FOX HERBERT H H	84	184	262	1871	1920	1943
313	BENNETT GRANVILLE G	84	151	192	1882	1920	1975
314	MIZE ROBERT HERBERT	84	213	245	1870	1921	1956
315	FINLAY KIRKMAN GEORGE	234	172	238	1877	1921	1938
316	MANNING WILLIAM T	84	148	171	1866	1921	1949
317	INGLEY FRED	84	286	128	1878	1921	1951
318	GARDINER THEOPHILUS M	84	170	244	1870	1921	1941
319	LA MOTHE JOHN D	84	243	233	1868	1921	1928
320	WARD JOHN C	84	128	148	1873	1921	1949
321	SHIPMAN HERBERT	84	316	215	1869	1921	1930
322	PENICK EDWIN A	172	234	275	1887	1922	1959
323	MAXON JAMES M	170	216	225	1875	1922	1948
324	MC DOWELL WILLIAM G	170	210	233	1882	1922	1938
325	OLDHAM GEORGE A	218	151	316	1877	1922	1963
326	SLATTERY CHARLES L	171	233	265	1867	1922	1930
327	ROBERTS WILLIAM BLAIR	84	285	286	1881	1922	1964
328	CARSON HARRY R	84	170	316	1869	1923	1948
329	MANN ALEXANDER	201	171	215	1860	1923	1948
330	FREEMAN JAMES E	170	171	243	1866	1923	1943
331	STRIDER ROBERT E L	194	271	329	1887	1923	1969
332	STERRETT FRANK W	143	226	194	1885	1923	1976
D	FERRANDO MANUEL	170	316	244	1866	1923	1934
333	REIFSNIDER CHARLES S	167	179	151	1875	1924	1958
334	CROSS EDWARD MAKIN	262	261	330	1880	1924	1965
335	WHITE JOHN CHANLER	143	216	197	1867	1924	1956
336	COLEY EDWARD H	143	244	310	1861	1924	1949
337	JUHAN FRANK A	143	253	315	1887	1924	1967
338	SEAMAN EUGENE CECIL	170	162	270	1881	1925	1950
339	BOOTH SAMUEL B	173	229	247	1883	1925	1935
340	GILMAN ALFRED A	168	259	221	1878	1925	1966
341	ROGERS WARREN L	151	279	148	1877	1925	1938
342	GRAY CAMPBELL	199	216	231	1879	1925	1944
343	IVINS BENJAMIN F P	231	199	213	1884	1925	1962
344	HUSTON SIMEON A	162	270	309	1876	1925	1963
345	WING JOHN D	201	238	170	1882	1925	1960
346	STIRES ERNEST M	143	243	316	1866	1925	1951

		Consecrators			Born	Cons.	Died
347	CAMPBELL ROBERT E	143	170	303	1884	1925	1977
348	THOMAS WILLIAM M M	143	172	C	1878	1925	1951
349	BARNWELL MIDDLETON S	143	170	212	1882	1925	1957
350	MITCHELL WALTER	243	278	248	1876	1926	1971
351	CREIGHTON FRANK W	243	218	256	1879	1926	1948
352	NICHOLS SHIRLEY HALL	167	333	AAN	1884	1926	1964
353	DALLAS JOHN T	243	173	171	1880	1926	1961
354	HELFENSTEIN EDWARD T	243	194	233	1865	1926	1947
355	CASADY THOMAS	243	190	245	1881	1927	1958
356	THOMAS ALBERT S	243	172	214	1873	1928	1967
357	BINSTED NORMAN S	243	167	258	1890	1928	1961
358	JENKINS THOMAS	243	177	250	1871	1929	1955
359	LARNED JOHN I B	243	177	250	1883	1929	1955
360	WILSON FRANK E	243	170	197	1885	1929	1944
361	ABBOTT HENRY P A	243	178	225	1881	1929	1945
362	TAITT FRANCIS M	256	226	241	1862	1929	1943
363	STURTEVANT HARWOOD	199	213	231	1888	1929	1977
364	SCHMUCK ELMER N	197	238	241	1882	1929	1936
365	DAVIS CAMERON J	310	281	285	1873	1930	1952
366	LITTELL SAMUEL H	285	167	210	1873	1930	1967
367	ABLEWHITE HAYWARD S	285	230	279	1887	1930	1964
368	HOBSON HENRY W	148	151	194	1891	1930	1983
369	SCARLETT WILLIAM	148	227	248	1883	1930	1973
370	GOODEN ROBERT B	309	188	250	1874	1930	1976
371	STEWART GEORGE C	247	213	225	1879	1930	1940
372	SHERRILL HENRY KNOX	247	171	221	1890	1930	1980
373	GOODWIN FREDERICK D	258	194	244	1888	1930	1968
374	GILBERT CHARLES K	247	224	244	1878	1930	1958
375	SPENCER ROBERT N	270	216	227	1877	1930	1961
376	KEMERER BENJAMIN T	269	230	262	1874	1930	1960
377	WYATT BROWN HUNTER	247	310	320	1884	1931	1952
378	KEELER STEPHEN E	269	230	262	1887	1931	1956
379	BENTLEY JOHN B	247	170	177	1896	1931	1989
380	SALINAS Y VELASCO E	247	170	244	1886	1931	1968
381	BUDLONG FREDERICK G	247	183	242	1881	1931	1953
382	BARTLETT FREDERICK B	285	250	317	1882	1931	1941
383	WASHBURN BENJAMIN M	247	224	244	1887	1932	1966
384	URBAN RALPH E	247	224	278	1875	1932	1935
385	PORTER ARCHIE W N	188	250	302	1885	1933	1963
386	GRIBBIN ROBERT E	247	322	275	1887	1934	1976
387	NICHOLS JOHN WILLIAMS	AAI	168	340	1878	1934	1940
388	LUDLOW THEODORE R	247	282	311	1883	1936	1961
389	DAGWELL BENJAMIN D	278	177	250	1890	1936	1963
390	KROLL LEOPOLD	247	244	316	1874	1936	1946
391	VAN DYCK VEDDER	247	353	372	1889	1936	1960
392	REINHEIMER BARTEL H	247	281	310	1889	1936	1949
393	CLINGMAN CHARLES	247	178	225	1883	1936	1971
394	WHITTEMORE LEWIS B	247	230	342	1885	1936	1965
395	GARDNER WALLACE J	278	188	311	1883	1936	1954
396	ESSEX WILLIAM L	247	192	261	1886	1936	1959
397	ZIEGLER WINFRED H	371	177	245	1885	1936	1972
398	LAWRENCE WILLIAM A	171	247	242	1889	1937	1968
399	BEAL HARRY	309	250	370	1885	1937	1944
400	ATWILL DOUGLASS H	378	261	262	1881	1937	1960
401	FENNER GOODRICH R	284	270	286	1891	1937	1966
402	ROBERTS WILLIAM P	AAI	168	AAJ	1888	1937	1971
403	WILNER ROBERT F	305	333	AAK	1889	1938	1960
404	HERON RAYMOND A	258	171	242	1886	1938	1960
405	BROWN WILLIAM A	258	275	306	1878	1938	1965
406	CARPENTER CHARLES C J	258	214	270	1899	1938	1969
407	DANDRIDGE EDMUND P	258	214	266	1881	1938	1961
408	PHILLIPS HENRY D	258	275	292	1882	1938	1955
409	TUCKER BEVERLEY D	258	194	275	1882	1938	1969
410	PEABODY MALCOLM E	258	248	307	1888	1938	1974
411	BLOCK KARL M	302	309	358	1886	1938	1958
412	MITCHELL RICHARD B	350	214	289	1887	1938	1961
413	KIRCHHOFFER RICHARD A	258	342	349	1890	1939	1977
414	MC KINSTRY ARTHUR R	258	309	320	1894	1939	1991
415	BLANKINGSHIP A H	258	266	328	1894	1939	1975
416	BURTON SPENCE	258	247	286	1881	1939	1966
417	GRAVATT JOHN J	258	194	275	1881	1939	1965

			Consecrators			Born	Cons.	Died
418	MC CLELLAND WILLIAM		258	268	308	1883	1939	1949
419	DANIELS HENRY HEAN		312	307	344	1885	1939	1958
420	RANDALL EDWIN J		258	177	262	1869	1939	1962
421	BRINKER HOWARD R		258	245	300	1893	1940	1965
422	PITHAN ATHALICIO T		348	380	415	1898	1940	1966
423	JACKSON JOHN L		258	275	292	1884	1940	1948
424	GRAY WALTER H		258	247	381	1898	1940	1973
425	CRAIGHILL LLOYD R		402	AAI	AAL	1886	1940	1971
426	CONKLING WALLACE E		258	347	395	1896	1941	1979
427	LORING OLIVER L		258	247	391	1904	1941	1979
428	POWELL NOBLE C		258	354	330	1891	1941	1968
429	STONEY JAMES M		258	406	412	1888	1942	1965
430	RHEA FRANK A		307	334	358	1887	1942	1963
431	DE WOLFE JAMES P		258	316	346	1895	1942	1966
432	LEWIS WILLIAM F		258	307	358	1902	1942	1964
433	MASON WILEY R		258	306	373	1879	1942	1967
434	WALKER JOHN M		258	337	412	1888	1942	1951
435	HART OLIVER J		258	330	362	1892	1942	1977
436	PAGE HERMAN R		258	351	394	1892	1942	1977
437	GRAY DUNCAN M		258	214	412	1898	1943	1966
438	HEISTAND JOHN T		258	332	435	1895	1943	1979
439	WROTH EDWARD P		258	329	331	1889	1943	1946
440	JONES EVERETT H		258	401	414	1902	1943	1995
441	VOEGELI CHARLES A		258	325	383	1904	1943	1984
442	BOYNTON CHARLES F		266	343	395	1906	1944	1999
443	WALTERS SUMNER F D		258	250	309	1898	1944	1979
444	KENNEDY HARRY S		258	317	350	1901	1944	1986
445	PARDUE AUSTIN		258	365	421	1899	1944	1981
446	DUN ANGUS		258	372	368	1892	1944	1971
447	CARRUTHERS THOMAS N		258	323	356	1900	1944	1960
448	HAINES ELWOOD L		258	406	423	1893	1944	1949
449	HORSTICK WILLIAM W		258	363	420	1902	1944	1973
450	MALLETT JAMES R		343	363	395	1893	1944	1965
451	HARRIS BRAVID W		258	405	322	1896	1945	1965
452	GESNER CONRAD H		258	327	378	1901	1945	1993
453	ALDRICH DONALD B		258	251	374	1892	1945	1961
454	GOODEN REGINALD H		258	370	415	1910	1945	2003
455	LOUTTIT HENRY I		345	350	416	1903	1945	1984
456	KINSOLVING II ARTHUR		258	350	409	1894	1945	1964
457	BARRY FREDERICK L		258	325	346	1897	1945	1960
458	MASON CHARLES A		258	291	426	1904	1945	1970
459	BANYARD ALFRED L		258	383	395	1908	1945	1992
460	WRIGHT THOMAS H		258	275	428	1904	1945	1997
461	HINES JOHN E		258	297	411	1910	1945	1997
462	MOODY WILLIAM R		258	393	368	1900	1945	1986
463	EMRICH RICHARD S M		258	262	351	1910	1946	1997
464	SAWYER HAROLD E		258	320	410	1890	1946	1969
465	BARTON Ln W		258	368	378	1899	1946	1997
466	QUARTERMAN GEORGE H		258	355	401	1906	1946	2002
467	CLARK STEPHEN C		258	307	309	1892	1946	1950
468	NASH NORMAN B		372	353	398	1888	1947	1963
469	BAYNE JR STEPHEN F		372	344	424	1908	1947	1974
470	BOWEN HAROLD L		372	317	426	1886	1947	1967
471	LORING JR RICHARD T		372	335	426	1900	1947	1948
472	DONEGAN HORACE W B		372	374	468	1900	1947	1991
473	GUNN GEORGE P		372	306	405	1903	1948	1973
474	HALL CHARLES F		372	353	468	1908	1948	1992
475	MELCHER LOUIS C		372	407	417	1898	1948	1965
476	HUNTER JAMES W		372	397	440	1904	1948	1987
477	BLOY FRANCIS E I		258	302	370	1904	1948	1993
478	SCAIFE LAURISTON L		372	365	420	1907	1948	1970
479	GORDON JR WILLIAM J		372	322	379	1918	1948	1994
480	HUBBARD RUSSELL S		343	335	445	1902	1948	1972
481	CLOUGH CHARLES A		343	335	427	1903	1948	1961
482	BARTH THEODORE N		372	323	407	1898	1948	1961
483	HENRY MATTHEW G		258	408	447	1910	1948	1975
484	WEST EDWARD H		372	337	349	1906	1948	1977
485	HIGLEY WALTER M		372	336	410	1899	1948	1969
486	SHERMAN JONATHAN G		372	394	431	1907	1949	1989
487	CAMPBELL DONALD J		372	302	477	1903	1949	1973
488	JONES GIRAULT M		372	337	417	1904	1949	1998

		Consecrators			Born	Cons.	Died
489	CLAIBORNE RANDOLPH R	258	406	428	1906	1949	1986
490	GIBSON JR ROBERT F	258	373	433	1906	1949	1990
491	ARMSTRONG JOSEPH G	372	293	435	1901	1949	1964
492	St CHARLES L	372	343	426	1891	1949	1968
493	MILLER ALLEN J	428	446	464	1901	1949	1991
494	BURROUGHS NELSON M	258	368	408	1899	1949	1998
495	KRISCHKE EGMONT M	475	379	422	1909	1950	1972
496	STARK DUDLEY S	372	368	378	1894	1950	1971
497	WELLES EDWARD R	372	375	428	1907	1950	1991
498	SMITH GORDON V	372	327	394	1906	1950	1997
499	CAMPBELL WILBURN C	258	331	373	1910	1950	1997
500	BURRILL G FRANCIS	258	291	432	1906	1950	2001
501	SHIRES HENRY H	372	370	411	1886	1950	1961
502	BAKER RICHARD H	372	322	428	1897	1951	1981
503	LICHTENBERGER A C	372	340	369	1900	1951	1968
504	HATCH ROBERT M	372	381	424	1910	1951	2009
505	WATSON RICHARD S	372	307	430	1902	1951	1987
506	SWIFT A ERVINE	372	379	442	1913	1951	2003
507	EMERY RICHARD R	372	378	400	1910	1951	1964
508	RICHARDS DAVID E	372	347	451	1921	1951	2018
509	BRAM MARTIN J	455	458	416	1897	1951	1956
510	POWELL CHILTON	372	355	421	1911	1951	1994
511	WALTHOUR JOHN B	372	322	435	1904	1952	1952
512	HALLOCK DONALD H V	343	426	363	1908	1952	1996
513	KELLOGG HAMILTON H	372	297	378	1899	1952	1977
514	CRITTENDEN WILLIAM	372	368	409	1908	1952	2003
515	NOLAND IVESON B	488	412	437	1916	1952	1975
516	OGILBY LYMAN C	357	403	424	1922	1953	1990
517	HIGGINS JOHN S	372	313	378	1904	1953	1992
518	WARNECKE FREDERICK J	372	332	383	1906	1953	1977
519	BRADY WILLIAM H	363	481	343	1912	1953	1996
520	STARK LELAND	372	378	383	1907	1953	1986
521	MURRAY GEORGE M	406	393	498	1919	1953	2006
522	MC NEIL DUDLEY B	372	394	470	1908	1953	1977
523	THOMAS WILLIAM S	445	435	478	1901	1953	1986
524	COLE CLARENCE ALFRED	322	417	447	1909	1953	1963
525	KINSOLVING III C J	429	401	456	1904	1953	1984
526	MOSLEY J BROOKE	372	368	414	1915	1953	1988
527	MARMION CHARLES G	372	393	458	1905	1954	2000
528	MARMION WILLIAM H	372	408	414	1907	1954	2002
529	HARTE JOSEPH M	500	297	510	1914	1954	1999
530	MINNIS JOSEPH S	470	421	449	1904	1954	1977
531	CROWLEY ARCHIE H	372	436	468	1907	1954	1996
532	STUART ALBERT R	372	347	488	1906	1954	1973
533	STOKES JR ANSON P	372	368	468	1905	1954	1986
534	VANDERHORST JOHN	372	407	482	1912	1955	1980
535	DOLL HARRY L	372	373	428	1903	1955	1984
536	DICUS RICHARD E	440	350	412	1910	1955	1996
537	GODDARD FREDERICK P	297	440	461	1903	1955	1983
538	BROWN ROBERT R	412	414	373	1910	1955	1994
539	LEWIS ARNOLD M	372	337	484	1904	1956	1994
540	CARMAN JAMES W F	372	389	293	1903	1956	1979
541	HONAMAN EARL M	372	438	435	1904	1956	1982
542	SIMOES PLINIO L	475	379	495	1915	1956	1994
543	TURNER EDWARD C	401	470	421	1915	1956	1997
544	CLEMENTS JAMES P	372	297	461	1911	1956	1977
545	MOSES WILLIAM F	372	455	345	1898	1956	1961
546	STERLING CHANDLER W	419	421	530	1911	1956	1984
547	LAWRENCE FREDERIC C	372	398	533	1899	1956	1989
548	FOOTE NORMAN L	372	430	449	1915	1957	1974
549	CRAINE JOHN P	413	411	368	1911	1957	1977
550	HADEN CLARENCE R	372	385	497	1910	1957	2000
551	SAUCEDO JOSE G	372	380	440	1924	1958	
552	MC NAIRY PHILIP F	372	368	513	1911	1958	1989
553	ESQUIROL JOHN HENRY	372	424	504	1900	1958	1970
554	CORRIGAN DANIEL	372	530	449	1900	1958	1994
555	PIKE JAMES ALBERT	372	302	472	1913	1958	1969
556	ROSE DAVID S	372	473	405	1913	1958	1997
557	LICKFIELD FRANCIS W	500	396	519	1908	1958	1997
558	MACADIE DONALD	383	520	503	1899	1958	1963
559	BLANCHARD ROGER W	372	368	484	1909	1958	1998

		Consecrators			Born	Cons.	Died
560	SHERRILL EDMUND K	372	495	542	1925	1959	2015
561	BROWN ALLEN W	503	457	410	1908	1959	1990
562	CABANBAN BENITO C	516	444	587	1911	1959	1990
563	CADIGAN GEORGE L	503	496	538	1910	1959	2005
564	CREIGHTON WILLIAM F	503	446	480	1909	1959	1987
565	MILLARD G RICHARD	503	432	443	1914	1960	2018
566	WRIGHT WILLIAM G	503	432	443	1904	1960	1973
567	BENNISON SR CHARLES E	503	394	470	1917	1960	2004
568	KELLOGG PAUL A	503	441	506	1910	1960	1999
569	WETMORE JAMES STUART	503	472	478	1915	1960	1999
570	CURTIS IVOL I	503	370	477	1908	1960	1994
571	CHILTON SAMUEL B	503	373	490	1900	1960	1984
572	FRASER JR THOMAS A	503	373	502	1915	1960	1989
573	DE WITT ROBERT L	503	446	468	1916	1960	2003
574	THAYER EDWIN B	530	470	498	1905	1960	1989
575	TEMPLE GRAY	503	424	427	1914	1961	1999
576	BUTTERFIELD HARVEY D	503	424	427	1908	1961	1998
577	RAUSCHER RUSSELL T	503	421	510	1908	1961	1989
578	GILSON CHARLES P	503	444	402	1899	1961	1980
579	GONZALEZ AGUEROS R	503	415	379	1906	1961	1966
580	BROWN JR DILLARD H	503	446	564	1912	1961	1969
581	ALLIN JOHN M	503	488	437	1921	1961	1998
582	HUTCHENS JOSEPH W	424	427	553	1913	1961	1979
583	DUNCAN JAMES L	503	455	534	1913	1961	2000
584	HARGRAVE WILLIAM L	503	455	424	1903	1961	1975
585	MAC LEAN CHARLES W	431	472	486	1903	1962	1985
586	SANDERS WILLIAM E	503	534	532	1919	1962	
587	MONTGOMERY JAMES WINCHESTER	503	500	492	1921	1962	
588	CHAMBERS ALBERT A	503	472	450	1906	1962	1993
589	MCCREA THEODORE H	503	458	500	1908	1962	1986
590	BURGESS JOHN MELVILLE	503	526	446	1909	1962	2003
591	LONGID EDWARD G	503	516	533	1908	1963	1993
592	PERSELL JR CHARLES B	503	561	478	1909	1963	1988
593	MILLS CEDRIC EARL	428	379	506	1903	1963	1992
594	BARRETT GEORGE W	472	496	554	1908	1963	2000
595	PUTNAM JR FREDERICK W	538	510	543	1917	1963	2007
596	KLEIN WALTER C	450	500	549	1904	1963	1980
597	PINCKNEY JOHN A	483	356	417	1905	1963	1972
598	MOORE JR PAUL	503	549	564	1919	1964	2003
599	ROMERO LEONARDO	503	551	506	1930	1964	1986
600	SAUCEDO MELCHOR	503	551	506	1920	1964	
601	RATH GEORGE E	503	472	520	1913	1964	1995
602	COLE JR NED	503	410	485	1917	1964	2000
603	REED DAVID B	503	454	529	1927	1964	
604	BAILEY SCOTT FIELD	461	466	537	1916	1964	2005
605	MYERS C KILMER	549	463	531	1914	1964	1981
606	RUSACK ROBERT C	477	370	570	1926	1964	1986
607	SELWAY GEORGE R	549	529	436	1905	1964	1989
608	REUS FROYLAN F	503	506	442	1919	1964	2008
609	WONG JAMES CHANG L	AAK	AAO	AAP		1960	1970
610	MASUDA GEORGE T	452	476	546	1913	1965	1995
611	RICHARDSON J MILTON	461	604	537	1913	1965	1980
612	GROSS HAL R	461	540	550	1914	1965	2002
613	DAVIDSON WILLIAM	461	466	610	1919	1966	2006
614	VAN DUZER ALBERT W	461	459	486	1917	1966	1999
615	GATES JR WILLIAM F	461	534	586	1912	1966	1987
616	BARNDS WILLIAM PAUL	461	458	589	1904	1966	1973
617	STEVENSON DEAN T	461	438	518	1915	1966	1994
618	HALL ROBERT BRUCE	461	490	500	1921	1966	1985
619	TAYLOR GEORGE A	461	493	414	1903	1966	1978
620	MARTIN RICHARD B	461	486	478	1913	1967	2012
621	BURT JOHN HARRIS	461	494	409	1918	1967	2009
622	MOORE JR WILLIAM M	532	572	502	1916	1967	1998
623	WYATT JOHN R	461	529	605	1913	1967	2004
624	SPEARS JR ROBERT R	461	472	497	1918	1967	2008
625	WOOD JR MILTON L	461	406	489	1922	1967	2015
626	KELLER CHRISTOPH JR	461	581	538	1916	1967	1995
627	FREY WILLIAM C	461	508	507	1930	1967	
628	MCNAIR EDWARD	461	477	550	1913	1967	1986
629	HANCHETT EDWIN LANI	461	444	540	1919	1967	1975
630	BROWNING EDMOND LEE	461	AAQ	444	1929	1968	2016

		Consecrators			Born	Cons.	Died
631	APPLEYARD ROBERT B	461	445	523	1917	1968	1999
632	ROBINSON HAROLD B	461	478	AAR	1922	1968	1994
633	GOSNELL HAROLD C	461	440	494	1908	1968	1999
634	GILLIAM JACKSON EARL	461	521	546	1920	1968	2000
635	RIVERA VICTOR MANUEL	461	443	570	1916	1968	2005
636	ELEBASH HUNLEY AGEE	461	460	484	1923	1968	1993
637	WOLF FREDERICK BARTO	461	424	517	1922	1968	1998
638	MEAD WILLIAM HENRY	461	414	526	1921	1968	1974
639	LEIGHTON DAVID K SR	461	535	523	1922	1968	2013
640	HAYNSWORTH GEORGE E	608	508	510	1925	1969	2012
641	RAMOS JOSE ANTONIO	461	608	508	1937	1969	
642	MANGURAMAS C B	562	591	630	1933	1969	
643	SPOFFORD WILLIAM B J	461	548	465	1921	1969	2013
644	THORNBERRY DAVID R	461	368	476	1911	1969	1995
645	ATKINS STANLEY H	449	512	519	1912	1969	1996
646	REEVES GEORGE PAUL	532	455	Nassau	1918	1969	2010
647	SMITH PHILIP A	461	490	618	1920	1970	2010
648	FOLWELL WILLIAM H	455	583	646	1924	1970	
649	HOSEA ADDISON	462	527	488	1914	1970	1986
650	DAVIES A DONALD	461	577	581	1920	1970	
651	JONES WALTER H	498	452	610	1925	1970	2003
652	BROWNE GEORGE D	461	520	441	1933	1970	1993
653	STEWART ALEXANDER D	461	590	504	1926	1970	1999
654	GRESSLE LLOYD EDGAR	461	526	518	1918	1970	1999
655	PONG JAMES T M	461	AAK	AAJ	1911	1971	1988
656	HOBGOOD CLARENCE E	461	539	572	1914	1971	2008
657	CACERES V ADRIAN D	461	627	600	1922	1971	2006
658	STOUGH FURMAN C	461	521	581	1928	1971	2004
659	KRUMM JOHN MC GILL	461	474	559	1913	1971	1995
660	GARNIER LUC A J	461	527	620	1928	1971	1999
661	VARLEY ROBERT P	461	577	619	1921	1971	2000
662	VOGEL ARTHUR ANTON	461	497	512	1924	1971	2012
663	HENTON WILLIS RYAN	461	466	599	1925	1971	2006
664	WALKER JOHN THOMAS	461	564	590	1925	1971	1989
665	CHARLES EDGAR OTIS	461	505	582	1926	1971	2013
666	BELDEN FREDERICK H	461	517	561	1909	1971	1979
667	MCGEHEE HARRY C JR	461	490	463	1923	1971	2013
668	PORTEUS MORGAN	461	582	424	1917	1971	
669	TRELEASE JR RICHARD M	461	526	621	1921	1971	2005
670	JONES HAROLD STEPHEN	461	452	651	1909	1972	2002
671	RIGHTER WALTER C	461	474	498	1923	1972	2011
672	ARNOLD MORRIS F	461	590	659	1915	1972	1992
673	FRANKLIN WILLIAM A	603	514	454	1916	1972	1998
674	HILLESTAD ALBERT W	461	588	637	1924	1972	2007
675	SHIRLEY LEMUEL B	454	603	584	1916	1972	1999
676	SIMS BENNETT J	461	489	613	1920	1972	2006
677	FRENSDORFF WESLEY	461	505	566	1926	1972	1988
678	ISAAC TELESFORO A	461	568	441	1929	1972	
679	WYLIE SAMUEL J	461	472	659	1918	1972	1974
680	TURNER EDWARD MASON	461	593	506	1918	1972	1996
681	KING HANFORD L JR	461	548	651	1921	1972	1986
682	SHERIDAN WILLIAM CR	461	587	AAQ	1917	1972	2005
683	PRIMO QUINTIN E JR	461	587	463	1913	1972	1998
684	COX WILLIAM JACKSON	461	639	535	1921	1972	
685	ALEXANDER GEORGE M	461	521	583	1914	1973	1983
686	CARRAL-SOLAR ANSELMO	600	675	514	1925	1973	2002
687	ATKINSON ROBERT P	461	499	586	1927	1973	2012
688	BADEN JOHN ALFRED	490	618	556	1913	1973	1983
689	GASKELL CHARLES T	461	512	645	1919	1973	2000
690	WEINHAUER WILLIAM G	461	636	572	1924	1973	2007
691	PARSONS DONALD JAMES	461	587	512	1922	1973	2016
692	DAVIS DONALD JAMES	461	514	549	1929	1973	2007
693	BIGLIARDI MATTHEW P	540	612	570	1920	1974	1996
694	WRIGHT HAROLD LOUIS	598	590	472	1929	1974	1978
695	HOGG WILBUR EMORY JR	461	561	637	1918	1974	1986
696	KERR ROBERT SHAW	461	576	624	1917	1974	1988
697	WOLTERSTORFF ROBERT M	461	477	552	1914	1974	2007
698	GRAY DUNCAN M JR	461	581	515	1926	1974	2016
699	CERVENY FRANK S	461	543	484	1933	1974	
700	COCHRAN DAVID REA	581	479	610	1915	1974	2001
701	HAYNES EMERSON PAUL	581	584	455	1918	1974	1988

		Consecrators			Born	Cons.	Died
702	BELSHAW GEORGE PHELPS MELLICK	581	614	444	1928	1975	
703	WITCHER ROBERT CAMPBELL	581	486	515	1926	1975	
704	JONES WILLIAM AUGUSTUS JR	581	563	614	1927	1975	
705	CLARK WILLIAM HAWLEY	581	590	613	1919	1975	1997
706	DIMMICK WILLIAM ARTHUR	581	534	582	1919	1975	1984
707	ABELLON RICHARD ABELARDO	562	591	614	1924	1975	
708	TERWILLIGER ROBERT ELWIN	581	560	699	1917	1975	1991
709	COCHRANE ROBERT HUME	581	570	677	1924	1976	2010
710	CILLEY ROGER HOWARD	581	611	537	1918	1976	1986
711	BROWN JAMES BARROW	581	488	454	1932	1976	
712	VACHE CLAUDE CHARLES	581	556	564	1926	1976	2009
713	SPONG JOHN SHELBY	581	601	618	1931	1976	
714	HEISTAND JOSEPH THOMAS	581	438	618	1924	1976	2008
715	COBURN JOHN BOWEN	581	590	472	1914	1976	2009
716	MAYSON HENRY IRVING	581	667	683	1925	1976	1995
717	WARNER JAMES DANIEL	581	519	543	1924	1976	2009
718	McALLISTER GERALD NICHOLAS	581	613	633	1923	1977	2014
719	JONES EDWARD WITKER	581	549	617	1929	1977	2007
720	LUMPIAS MANUEL CAPUYAN	562	707	655	1930	1977	
721	JONES BOBBY GORDON	581	644	479	1932	1977	
722	ANDERSON ROBERT MARSHALL	581	552	665	1933	1978	2011
723	CHILD CHARLES JUDSON	581	676	489	1923	1978	2004
724	BURGREEN CHARLES LEE	581	539	633	1924	1978	2006
725	PINA HUGO LUIS	581	675	648	1938	1978	2018
726	THOMPSON JOHN LESTER	581	550	635	1926	1978	2004
727	WALLACE LEIGH ALLEN	581	623	634	1927	1979	2010
728	SCHOFIELD CALVIN ONDERDONK	581	583	455	1933	1979	
729	LIGHT ARTHUR HEATH	581	528	516	1929	1979	
730	MERINO BERNARDO	581	675	657	1930	1979	
731	HAUSER STANLEY FILLMORE	581	604	670	1922	1979	1989
732	SWING WILLIAM EDWIN	581	605	664	1936	1979	
733	BECKHAM WILLIAM ARTHUR	581	685	586	1927	1979	2005
734	DENNIS WALTER DECOSTER	598	472	569	1932	1979	2003
735	SANDERS BRICE SIDNEY	581	460	636	1930	1979	1997
736	WALMSLEY ARTHUR EDWARD	581	668	637	1928	1979	2017
737	BLACK WILLIAM GRANT	581	368	659	1920	1979	2013
738	CHEUNG PUI-YEUNG	581	655	642	1919	1980	1987
739	LEWIS DAVID H JR	581	618	490	1918	1980	2002
740	HOPKINS HAROLD A JR	581	610	637	1930	1980	2019
741	ESTILL ROBERT W	581	572	650	1927	1980	
742	MARTINEZ-RESENDEZ ROBERTO	581	551	600	1938	1980	
743	HUERTA-RAMOS CLARO	581	551	600	1929	1980	
744	HUNT GEORGE N III	581	732	517	1931	1980	
745	KIMSEY RUSTIN R	581	465	643	1935	1980	2015
746	STEVENS WILLIAM L	581	519	689	1932	1980	1997
747	BENITEZ MAURICE M	581	461	604	1928	1980	2014
748	DONOVAN HERBERT A JR	581	626	538	1931	1980	
749	ALLISON C FITZSIMONS	581	575	685	1927	1980	
750	WANTLAND WILLIAM C	581	645	718	1934	1980	
751	MALLORY C SHANNON				1936	1972	2018
752	McNUTT CHARLIE FULLER JR	581	617	687	1931	1980	
753	HULSEY SAM BYRON	581	466	663	1932	1980	
754	WOLFRUM WILLIAM H	581	627	574	1926	1981	2007
755	DUVALL CHARLES F	581	521	733	1935	1981	
756	WHITAKER O'KELLEY	581	602	648	1926	1981	2015
757	ASHBY JOHN F	581	718	750	1929	1981	2001
758	GREIN RICHARD F	581	543	552	1932	1981	
759	HARRIS GEORGE C	581	700	651	1925	1981	2000
760	HUCLES HENRY B III	581	703	486	1923	1981	1989
761	HATHAWAY ALDEN M	581	631	618	1933	1981	
762	ESPINOZA-VENEGAS SAMUEL	581	600	551	1942	1981	2013
763	COLERIDGE CLARENCE L	581	736	AAA	1930	1981	
764	HASTINGS W BRADFORD	581	736	AAA	1919	1981	1992
765	GUERRA-SORIA ARMANDO R	675	686	678	1949	1982	
766	HULTSTRAND DONALD M	581	689	719	1927	1982	2018
767	EASTMAN ALBERT THEODORE	581	639	535	1928	1982	2018
768	BIRNEY DAVID B IV	581	654	681	1929	1982	2004
769	RAY THOMAS K	581	567	706	1934	1982	2018
770	CHARLTON GORDON T JR	581	747	650	1923	1982	
771	MORTON CHARLES B	581	697	658	1926	1982	1994
772	DYER JM MARK	581	654	590	1930	1982	2014

		Consecrators			Born	Cons.	Died
773	DICKSON ALEX D JR	581	698	586	1926	1983	
774	MOODEY JAMES R	581	621	494	1932	1983	2005
775	SORGE ELLIOTT L				1929	1971	2011
776	PATTERSON DONIS D	581	604	724	1930	1983	2006
777	LONGID ROBERT LEE OMENGAN	707	591	720	1935	1983	1996
778	SHIPPS HARRY WOOLSTON	581	646	773	1926	1984	2016
779	OTTLEY JAMES HAMILTON	581	730	599	1936	1984	
780	FRADE LEOPOLD	581	711	765	1943	1984	
781	PETTIT VINCENT KING	581	702	734	1924	1984	2006
782	BALL DAVID STANDISH	581	508	695	1926	1984	2017
783	WISSEMANN ANDREW FREDERICK	581	782	504	1928	1984	2014
784	BURRILL WILLIAM GEORGE	581	500	550	1934	1984	
785	LEE PETER JAMES	581	741	618	1938	1984	
786	ANDERSON CRAIG BARRY	581	452	634	1942	1984	
787	WHITE ROGER JOHN	581	766	587	1941	1984	2012
788	CHALFANT EDWARD COLE	581	559	659	1937	1984	
789	WIMBERLY DON ADGER	581	749	699	1937	1984	
790	MEEKS HOWARD SAMUEL	581	567	776	1932	1984	2016
791	POPE CLARENCE CULLAM JR	581	645	711	1929	1985	
792	GARCIA-MONTEIL MARTINIANO	581	650	762	1933	1985	
793	DOWNS-HIGGS STURDIE WYMAN	599	787	678	1947	1985	
794	GRISWOLD FRANK TRACY III	581	500	587	1937	1985	
795	HARRIS ROGERS SANDERS	581	733	773	1930	1985	2017
796	VEST FRANK HARRIS JR	581	741	572	1936	1985	2008
797	GARVER OLIVER BAILEY JR	581	745	746	1925	1985	1996
798	CARR WILLIAM FRANKLIN	581	687	499	1938	1985	
799	REYNOLDS GEORGE LAZENBY JR	581	722	773	1927	1985	1991
800	JOHNSON DAVID ELLIOT	581	538	500	1933	1985	1995
801	LADEHOFF ROBERT LOUIS	581	693	755	1932	1985	
802	MacNAUGHTON JOHN HERBERT	630	604	731	1929	1986	
803	JONES CHARLES IRVING	630	634	603	1943	1986	
804	BARTLETT ALLEN LYMAN JR	630	516	603	1929	1986	
805	THEUNER DOUGLAS EDWIN	630	647	736	1938	1986	2013
806	SWENSON DANIEL LEE	630	722	696	1928	1986	2014
807	TICOBAY NARCISCO VALENTIN	692	707	777	1932	1986	2014
808	MILLER ROBERT ORAN	630	698	608	1935	1986	2009
809	ZABRISKIE STEWART CLARK	677	740	771	1936	1986	1999
A810	VALENTINE BARRY						
811	BOWMAN DAVID CHARLES	630	494	621	1932	1986	2015
812	WILLIAMS ARTHUR BENJAMIN JR	630	774	621	1935	1986	
813	BATES GEORGE EDMOND	677	745	643	1933	1986	1999
814	HAINES RONALD HAYWARD	630	664	690	1934	1986	2008
815	GRAY FRANCIS CAMPBELL	630	648	719	1940	1986	
816	TENNIS CALVIN CABELL	729	804	712	1932	1986	
817	HART DONALD PURPLE	630	479	647	1937	1986	
818	ALLAN FRANK KELLOGG	723	586	676	1935	1987	
819	TAYLOR EGBERT DON	630	632	680	1937	1987	2014
820	MARTINEZ-MARQUEZ GERMAN	802	779	551	1933	1987	
821	ROWTHORN JEFFERY WILLIAM	630	657	736	1934	1987	
822	McARTHUR EARL NICHOLAS	630	802	718	1925	1988	2016
823	MacBURNEY EDWARD HARDING	630	746	813	1927	1988	
824	MOODY ROBERT MANNING	630	718	785	1939	1988	
825	CHIEN JOHN CHIH-TSUNG	630	817		1923	1988	2013
826	WALKER ORRIS GEORGE	630	812	703	1942	1988	2015
827	CAISAPANTA LUIS	779	692	657	1932	1988	1991
828	BORSCH FREDERICK HOUK	630	702	664	1935	1988	2017
829	THOMPSON HERBERT	630	737	620	1933	1988	2006
830	EPTING C CHRISTOPHER	630	648	671	1946	1988	
831	TURNER FRANKLIN D	630	804	664	1933	1988	2013
832	SCHOFIELD DAVID MERCER	630	635	732	1938	1988	2013
833	WOOD RAYMOND STEWART	664	667	659	1934	1988	
834	HARRIS BARBARA CLEMENTINE	630	800	804	1930	1989	
835	BUCHANAN JOHN CLARK	630	755	622	1933	1989	
836	KELSHAW TERENCE	630	761	747	1936	1989	
837	JOHNSON ROBERT HODGES	630	690	723	1934	1989	
838	HAMPTON SANFORD ZANGWILL KAYE	630	722	834	1935	1989	
839	HOWE JOHN W	630	761	627	1942	1989	
840	ROWLEY ROBERT D	630	692	772	1941	1989	2010
841	SMITH JOHN H	630	690	774	1939	1989	2012
842	HARGROVE ROBERT JEFFERSON	630	663	711	1937	1989	2005
843	WARNER VINCENT WAYDELL JR	709	637	800	1940	1989	

		Consecrators			Born	Cons.	Died
844	CARRANZA-GOMEZ SERGIO	678	826	675	1941	1989	
845	STERLING WILLIAM E	630	747	686	1927	1989	2005
846	KROTZ JAMES E	630	717	830	1948	1989	
847	LEE EDWARD L JR	719	769	516	1934	1989	
848	LONGEST CHARLES L	630	639	767	1933	1989	
849	ZABALA ARTEMIO MASLENG	707	777	807		1989	
850	FAIRFIELD ANDREW H	630	610	740	1943	1989	
851	SMALLEY WILLIAM E	630	758	767	1940	1989	
852	SALMON EDWARD L JR	630	749	640	1934	1990	2016
853	PLUMMER STEVEN T	630	670	595	1944	1990	2005
854	KEYSER CHARLES L	630	699	785	1930	1990	
855	WILLIAMS HUNTINGTON JR	630	741	676	1925	1990	2013
856	LARREA-MORENO JOSE N	630	779	780	1949	1990	
857	THORNTON JOHN STUART	658	745	801	1932	1990	
858	SHIMPFKY RICHARD LESTER	630	834	713	1940	1990	2011
859	TERRY FRANK JEFFREY	630	516	623	1939	1990	1999
860	WINTERROWD WILLIAM JERRY	630	627	754	1938	1991	
861	TALTON CHESTER LOVELLE	630	722	826	1941	1991	
862	WIEDRICH WILLIAM W	719	587	794	1931	1991	2014
863	ROCKWELL HAYS HAMILTON	630	758	704	1936	1991	
864	SCANTLEBURY VICTOR A	630	779	675	1945	1991	
865	CHARLESTON STEVEN	630	853	750	1949	1991	
866	MCKELVEY JACK MARSTON	756	713	831	1941	1991	
867	THARP ROBERT G	630	648	586	1928	1991	2003
868	LAMB JERRY A	630	726	801	1940	1991	
869	MARBLE ALFRED CLARK JR	581	698	735	1936	1991	2017
870	HOLGUIN-KHOURY JULIO CESAR	856	779	678	1948	1991	
871	JOSLIN DAVID BRUCE	630	631	838	1936	1991	
872	BECKWITH PETER HESS	630	829	794	1939	1991	
873	BARAHONA-PASCASIO MARTIN DE JESUS	630	779	856	1943	1992	
874	HUGHES GETHIN BENWIL	630	828	842	1942	1992	
875	SHAHAN ROBERT R	630	529	714	1939	1992	
876	DIXON JANE HOLMES	630	814	834	1937	1992	2012
877	TOWNSEND MARTIN GOUGH	630	775	772	1943	1992	
878	DENIG ROBERT S	630	847	783	1946	1993	1995
879	STANTON JAMES M	630	828	832	1946	1993	
880	IKER JACK L	630	791	659	1949	1993	
881	DURACIN JEAN Z	630	660	867	1947	1993	
882	HERLONG BERTRAM N	630	785	752	1934	1993	2011
883	MATTHEWS FRANK CLAY	630	785	687	1947	1993	
884	PAYNE CLAUDE E	630	461	581	1932	1993	
885	JELINEK JAMES L	630	722	838	1942	1993	
886	DOSS JOE MORRIS	630	732	780	1943	1993	
887	MCLEOD MARY ADELIA R	630	808	834	1938	1993	
888	COLEMAN JAMES MALONE	630	711	773	1929	1993	
889	FOLTS JAMES EDWARD	630	802	604	1940	1994	
890	GREW JOSEPH CLARK	630	812	794	1939	1994	
891	GULICK EDWIN FUNSTEN JR	630	796	883	1948	1994	
892	JECKO STEPHEN HAYS	630	699	661	1940	1994	2007
893	JOHNSON ROBERT CARROLL JR	630	741	855	1938	1994	2014
894	JACOBUS RUSSELL EDWARD	630	746	787	1944	1994	
895	MAZE LARRY EARL	630	698	748	1943	1994	
896	ROBERTSON CREIGHTON LELAND	630	786	670	1944	1994	2014
897	ACKERMAN KEITH LYNN	630	691	823	1946	1994	
898	SHAW MARVIL THOMAS III SSJE	630	800	834	1945	1994	2014
899	ESPAÑA ALFREDO TERENCIO MORANTE	D	A906	856	1947	1994	
900	PRICE KENNETH LESTER	630	829	841	1943	1994	
901	LOUTITT HENRY IRVING JR	630	778	675	1938	1995	
902	HENDERSON DORSEY FELIX JR	630	583	746	1939	1995	
903	SAID JOHN LEWIS	630	728	583	1932	1995	2019
904	STRICKLAND VERNON EDWARD	630	721	830	1938	1995	
905	HAYES CLARENCE WALLACE	630	454	730	1928	1995	
A906	SOTO ONELL ASISELO	779	648	730	1932	1987	2015
907	JONES DAVID COLIN	630	785	687	1943	1995	
908	ALARD LEOPOLDO J	630	884	845	1941	1995	2003
909	IHLOFF ROBERT W	630	763	834	1941	1995	
910	CREIGHTON MICHAEL W	630	752	843	1940	1995	
911	HIBBS ROBERT B	630	889	802	1932	1996	2017
912	ROSKAM CATHERINE A	630	834	758	1943	1996	
913	WOLF GERALYN	630	794	744	1947	1996	
914	LIPSCOMB JOHN B	630	888	795	1950	1996	

		Consecrators			Born	Cons.	Died
915	SKILTON WILLIAM J	630	852	575	1940	1996	
916	DUNCAN ROBERT WILLIAM	630	761	785	1948	1996	
917	SMITH ANDREW DONNAN	630	763	736	1944	1996	
918	IRISH CAROLYN TANNER	630	813	665	1940	1996	
919	MARSHALL PAUL VICTOR	840	772	654	1947	1996	
920	GLOSTER JAMES GARY	630	893	741	1936	1996	
921	LEIDEL JR EDWIN MAX	630	833	719	1938	1996	
922	DANIEL III CLIFTON	630	735	712	1947	1996	
923	PARSLEY JR HENRY NUTT	630	808	785	1948	1996	
924	SCRUTON GORDON PAUL	630	653	783	1947	1996	
925	POWELL FRANK NEFF	630	729	796	1947	1996	
926	CHANG RICHARD SUI ON	630	744	745	1941	1997	2017
927	BENNISON JR CHARLES ELLSWORTH	630	804	831	1943	1997	
928	MICHEL RODNEY RAE	630	826	703	1943	1997	
929	WAYNICK CATHERINE MAPLES	812	719	667	1948	1997	
930	OHL JR CHARLES WALLIS	752	753	860	1943	1997	
931	DANIELS THEODORE ATHELBERT	734	819	675	1944	1997	
932	BANE JR DAVID CONNER	829	796	687	1942	1997	
933	MACDONALD MARK LAWRENCE	630	853	750	1954	1997	
934	CALDWELL BRUCE EDWARD	846	721	850	1947	1997	
935	HERZOG DANIEL	630	782	924	1941	1997	
936	JENKINS CHARLES EDWARD III	794	711	852	1951	1998	
937	HOWE BARRY ROBERT	794	835	795	1942	1998	
938	KNUDSEN CHILTON ABBIE RICHARDSON	794	637	913	1946	1998	
939	SISK MARK SEAN	794	758	734	1942	1998	
940	BAINBRIDGE HARRY BROWN	812	867	857	1939	1998	2010
941	WRIGHT WAYNE PARKER	840	936	887	1951	1998	
942	RABB JOHN LESLIE	840	909	767	1944	1998	
943	CRONEBERGER JOHN PALMER	812	713	866	1938	1998	
944	VONROSENBERG CHARLES GLENN	867	586	733	1947	1999	
945	PERSELL WILLIAM D	794	812	890	1943	1999	
946	WHITMORE KEITH BERNARD	794	750	904	1945	1999	
947	GARRISON J MICHAEL	794	811	809	1945	1999	
948	KELSEY JAMES ARTHUR	794	769	847	1952	1999	2007
949	MACPHERSON DAVID BRUCE	851	879	828	1940	1999	2017
950	GIBBS WENDELL NATHANIEL	812	587	834	1954	2000	
951	PACKARD GEORGE ELDEN	794	854	758	1944	2000	
952	LITTLE EDWARD STUART	812	815	832	1947	2000	
953	BRUNO JOSEPH JON	858	828	861	1946	2000	
954	BENA DAVID JOHN	794	935	782	1943	2000	
955	CURRY MICHAEL BRUCE	837	920	834	1953	2000	
956	GRAY III DUNCAN MONTGOMERY	794	869	698	1949	2000	
957	GREGG WILLIAM OTIS	630	745	801	1951	2000	
958	SAULS STACY FRED	837	789	891	1955	2000	
959	CURRY JAMES E.	805	917	763	1948	2000	
960	RAMOS-ORENCH WILFRIDO	805	917	763	1940	2000	
961	WAGGONER JAMES EDWARD	868	687	900	1947	2000	
962	LAI DAVID JUNG-HSIN	926	825		1948	2000	
963	SCHORI KATHARINE JEFFERTS	868	801	918	1954	2001	
964	CEDARHOLM ROY FREDERICK JR	805	898	834	1944	2001	
965	ELY THOMAS CLARK	805	887	806	1951	2001	
966	DUNCAN PHILIP MENZIE II	794	755	937	1944	2001	
967	JOHNSON DON EDWARD	794	888	586	1949	2001	
968	ALEXANDER JOHN NEIL	794	818	723	1954	2001	
969	DUQUE FRANCISCO JOSÉ	794	730	856	1950	2001	
970	KLUSMEYER WILLIAM MICHIE	794	945	687	1955	2001	
971	ALLEN LLOYD EMMANUEL	779	780		1956	2001	
972	ADAMS GLADSTONE BAILEY III	866	671	891	1952	2001	
973	WHALON PIERRE WELTÉ	794	821	839	1952	2001	
974	ANDRUS MARK HANDLEY	794	923	785	1956	2002	
975	SMITH GEORGE WAYNE	890	863	830	1955	2002	
976	ADAMS JAMES MARSHALL JR	851	904	894	1948	2002	
977	GALLAGHER CAROL JOY WT	840	932	834	1955	2002	
978	GEPERT ROBERT R	812	847	772	1948	2002	
979	CHANE JOHN BRYSON	794	876	814	1944	2002	
980A	SCRIVEN HENRY WM	AAD			1951	1995	
981	HARRIS GAYLE ELIZABETH	812	898	834	1951	2003	
982	SHAND JAMES JOSEPH	909	877	775	1946	2003	
983	SCARFE ALAN	885	830	981	1950	2003	
984A	ALVAREZ DAVID ANDRES	779	772	608	1941	1987	
985	BURNETT JOE GOODWIN	885	717	846	1948	2003	

		Consecrators			Born	Cons.	Died
986	ITTY JOHNCY	794	630	801	1963	2003	
987	BROOKHART C FRANKLIN	794	970	854	1948	2003	
988	HIGH RAYFORD BAINES JR	949	789	884	1941	2003	
989	O'NEILL ROBERT JOHN	885	860	898	1955	2003	
990	COUNCELL GEORGE EDWARD	794	783	945	1949	2003	2018
991	MILLER STEVEN ANDREW	950	787	662	1957	2003	
992	HOWARD SAMUEL JOHNSON	936	892	699	1951	2003	
993	ROBINSON V GENE	794	630	767	1947	2003	
994	WOLFE DEAN ELLIOTT	949	851	758	1956	2003	
995	LILLIBRIDGE GARY	794	889	911	1956	2004	
996	HOLLINGSWORTH MARK JR	950	890	898	1954	2004	
997	SMITH KIRK STEVAN	794	875	953	1951	2004	
998	SMITH MICHAEL GENE	794	850	740	1955	2004	
999	TAYLOR GRANVILLE PORTER	893	968	818	1950	2004	
1000	STEENSON JEFFREY NEIL	794	836	791	1952	2005	
1001	RIVERA BAVI EDNA	940	843	732	1946	2005	
1002	MATHES JAMES ROBERT	926	874	995	1959	2005	
1003	GUMBS EDWARD AMBROSE	812	678	826	1949	2005	
1004A	GUERRERO ORLANDO JESUS	AAS	870	AAT		2005	
1005	REED DAVID MITCHELL	949	995	889	1957	2006	
1006	OUSLEY STEVEN TODD	950	921	948	1961	2006	
1007	LOVE WILLIAM H	794	935	954	1957	2006	
1008	BEISNER BARRY L	940	963	868	1951	2006	
1009	HARRISON DENA A	949	789	988	1947	2006	
1010	BAXTER NATHAN D	794	910	979	1948	2006	
1011	BENFIELD LARRY R	963	748	895	1955	2007	
1012	BECKWITH MARK M	963	722	943	1951	2007	
1013	BAUERSCHMIDT JOHN C	922	882	711	1959	2007	
1014	SMITH DABNEY T	922	914	648	1953	2007	
1015	FITZPATRICK ROBERT L	963	926	962	1958	2007	
1016	BREIDENTHAL THOMAS E	963	900	737	1951	2007	
1017	JOHNSTON SHANNON S	963	785	907	1958	2007	
1018	AHRENS LAURA J	963	959	912	1962	2007	
1019	ROWE SEAN W	963	840	772	1975	2007	
1020	KONIECZNY EDWARD J	963	952	824	1954	2007	
1021	RICKEL GREGORY	926	843	1001	1963	2007	
1022	GRAY-REEVES MARY	963	1027	728	1962	2007	
1023	EDWARDS DAN	963	968	868	1950	2008	
1024	SLOAN JOHN MCKEE	963	923	808	1955	2008	
1025	LAWRENCE MARK	922	870	897	1950	2008	
1026	LEE JEFFREY	963	950	938	1957	2008	
1027A	ROMERO SYLVESTRE	AAU			1943	1994	
1028	LN STEPHEN	963	866	938	1949	2008	
1029	SINGH PRINCE	963	866	1012	1962	2008	
1030	SUTTON EUGENE	963	979	1010	1954	2008	
1031	LAMBERT PAUL	949	879	998	1950	2008	
1032	THOM BRIAN	963	940	868	1955	2008	
1033	DOYLE CHARLES A	963	789	1009	1966	2008	
1034	HOLLERITH HERMAN	963	785	925	1955	2009	
1035	MAYER J SCOTT	963	753	930	1955	2009	
1036	RUIZ LUIS F	963	969	960	1956	2009	
1037	PROVENZANO LAWRENCE	963	924	990	1955	2009	
1038	TARRANT JOHN J	963	896	786	1952	2009	
1039	BENHASE SCOTT A	963	901	1030	1957	2010	
1040	PRIOR BRIAN N	963	885	961	1959	2010	
1041	HANLEY MICHAEL J	963	1021	1001	1954	2010	
1042	DOUGLAS IAN T	963	955	952	1958	2010	
1043	THOMPSON MORRIS K	963	958	956	1955	2010	
1044	BRUCE DIANE	963	953	1037	1956	2010	
1045	GLASSPOOL MARY D	963	953	997	1954	2010	
1046	WALDO ANDRE W	963	881	923	1953	2010	
1047	MAGNESS JAMES B	963	891	951	1947	2010	
1048	SMYLIE JOHN S	963	1040	955	1952	2010	
1049	BAILEY DAVID E	963	918	745	1940	2010	
1050	LATTIME MARK A	963	1029	866	1966	2010	
1051	WHITE TERRY ALLEN	963	891	937	1959	2010	
1052	VONO MICHAEL LOUIS	963	906	973	1949	2010	
1053	HAYASHI SCOTT B	963	918	1008	1953	2010	
1054	MILLIKEN MICHAEL P	963	994	1011	1947	2011	
1055	FIELD MARTIN S	963	937	994	1956	2011	
1056	MARTINS DANIEL H	963	952	894	1951	2011	

		Consecrators			Born	Cons.	Died
1057	FRANKLIN RALPH WILLIAM	963	939	973	1947	2011	
1058	RAY RAYFORD JEFFREY	963	1006	950	1956	2011	
1059	YOUNG GEORGE DIBRELL III	963	1013	967	1955	2011	
1060	BARKER JOSEPH SCOTT	963	985	939	1964	2011	
1061	BUDDE MARIANN EDGAR	963	1040	1012	1959	2011	
1062	DIETSCHE ANDREW ML	963	939	990	1953	2012	
1063	BREWER GREGORY O	922	839	1007	1951	2012	
1064	BEAUVOIR OGÉ	963	881	939	1956	2012	
1065	OWENSBY JACOB W	963	949	975	1957	2012	
1066	GOFF SUSAN E	963	1017	891	1953	2012	
1067	HIRSCHFELD ALFRED ROBERT	963	993	924	1961	2012	
1068	FISHER JEFF W	963	1033	1009	1964	2012	
1069	WRIGHT ROBERT C	963	968	955	1964	2012	
1070	MCCONNELL DORSEY WM	963	900	898	1953	2012	
1071	KNISELY W NICHOLAS JR	963	996	1028	1960	2012	
1072	MARRAY SANTOSH KUMAR					2005	
1073	FISHER DOUGLAS J	963	924	939	1954	2012	
1074	HAHN WILLIAM DOUGLAS	963	968	1051	1952	2012	
1075	LAMBERT WILLIAM JAY III	963	894	1063	1948	2013	
1076	HODGES-COPPLE ANNIE ELLIOTT	963	955	1039	1957	2013	
1077	BOURLAKAS MARK ALLEN	963	955	968	1963	2013	
1078	HOUGLAND WHAYNE MILLER JR	963	955	958	1962	2013	
1079	STOKES WILLIAM HALLOCK	963	990	780	1957	2013	
1080	RICE DAVID	963			1961	2014	
1081	GUNTER MATTHEW ALAN	963	1026	991	1957	2014	
1082	SHIN ALLEN KUNHO	963	1062	1037	1956	2014	
1083	COOK HEATHER ELIZABETH	963	1030	982		2014	
1084	GATES ALAN MCINTOSH	1028	898	990	1958	2014	
1085	SEAGE BRIAN RICHARD	963	956	953	1963	2014	
1086	SKIRVING ROBERT	963	1006	870	1960	2014	
1087	EATON PETER DAVID	963	780	989	1958	2015	
1088	KENDRICK JAMES RUSSELL	963	966	1033	1960	2015	
1089	SCANLAN AUDREY CADY	963	1042	1018	1958	2015	
1090	SUMNER GEORGE ROBINSON	955	1031	1013	1955	2015	
1091	MOTA MOISES QUEZADA	955	870	678	1956	2016	
1092a	VAN KOEVERING MARK				1957	2016	
1093	BELL PATRICK WILLIAM	955	1001	961	1952	2016	
1094	SPARKS DOUGLAS EVERETT	955	952	1040	1956	2016	
1095	GUTIERREZ DANIEL GEORGE POLYCARP	955	922	1052	1964	2016	
1096	MCLOUGHLIN JOSÉ ANTONIO	955	999	1020	1969	2016	
1097	DUNCAN-PROBE DEDE	955	1017	834	1962	2016	
1098	WRIGHT CARL WALTER	955	1047	1030	1959	2017	
1099	REHBERG GRETCHEN MARY	955	961	1016	1964	2017	
1100	BASKERVILLE-BURROWS JENNIFER	955	929	1094	1966	2017	
1101	TAYLOR JOHN HARVEY	955	953	1044	1954	2017	
1102	RODMAN SAMUEL SEWELL	955	1084	1076	1959	2017	
1103	MORALES MALDONADO RAFAEL LUIS	955	960	984	1963	2017	
1104	DAVIDSON JENNIFER BROOKE	955	1005	1018	1960	2017	
1105a	MONTERROSO GONZALEZ HECTOR FIDEL					2017	
1106	COLE BRIAN LEE	955	950	1077	1967	2017	
1107	BROWN KEVIN SCOTT	955	967	941	1968	2017	
1108	NICHOLS KEVIN DONNELLY	955	1019	1067	1962	2018	
1109	HUGHES CARLYE JEAN	955	1097	1035	1958	2018	
1110	HUNN MICHAEL BUERKEL	955	1052	1022	1970	2018	
1111	COWELL MARK ANDREW	955	1054	1055	1965	2018	

Codes for other Anglican and Old Catholic Consecrators

AAA Aberdeen	AAE York	AAI North China	AAM Rangoon	AAQ Rowinski (PNC)
AAB Ross	AAF Bath and Wells	AAJ Singapore	AAN Kyushu	AAR Zielinski (PNC)
AAC Skinner	AAG London	AAK Hong Kong	AAO Borneo	AAS Costa Rica
AAD Canterbury	AAH Rochester	AAL Honan	AAP Korea	AAT Colombia
				AAU Belize

Key to Single-Letter Entries

These entries refer to Bishops consecrated for foreign lands which subsequently became missionary jurisdictions of this church: A Haiti; B Mexico; C Brazil; D Puerto Rico.

Key to "A" + Number

These entries refer to Bishops consecrated outside the American episcopate, later transferred in as Assistant Bishops under Canon III.12.(b)(2) or a Bishop whose diocese has joined The Episcopal Church under Article V of the Constitution.

A Table of Presiding Bishops*

1. WILLIAM WHITE (2) (Bishop of Pennsylvania), from July 28, 1789, to October 3, 1789.

2. SAMUEL SEABURY (1) (Bishop of Connecticut), from October 5, 1789 to September 8, 1792.

3. SAMUEL PROVOOST (3) (Bishop of New York), from September 13, 1792, to September 8, 1795.

4. WILLIAM WHITE (2) (Bishop of Pennsylvania), from September 8, 1795, to July 17, 1836.

5. ALEXANDER VIETS GRISWOLD (12) (Bishop of the Eastern Diocese), from July 17, 1836, to February 15, 1843.

6. PHILANDER CHASE (18) (Bishop of Illinois), from February 15, 1843, to September 20, 1852.

7. THOMAS CHURCH BROWNELL (19) (Bishop of Connecticut), from September 20, 1852, to January 13, 1865.

8. JOHN HENRY HOPKINS (26) (Bishop of Vermont), from January 13, 1865, to January 9, 1868.

9. BENJAMIN BOSWORTH SMITH (27) (Bishop of Kentucky), from January 9, 1868, to May 31, 1884.

10. ALFRED LEE (38) (Bishop of Delaware), from May 31, 1884, to April 12, 1887.

11. JOHN WILLIAMS (54) (Bishop of Connecticut), from April 12, 1887, to February 7, 1899.

12. THOMAS MARCH CLARK (63) (Bishop of Rhode Island), from February 7, 1899, to September 7, 1903.

13. DANIEL SYLVESTER TUTTLE (84) (Bishop of Missouri), from September 7, 1903, to April 17, 1923.

14. ALEXANDER CHARLES GARRETT (108) (Bishop of Dallas), from April 17, 1923, to February 18, 1924.

15. ETHELBERT TALBOT (143) (Bishop of Bethlehem), from February 18, 1924, to January 1, 1926.

ELECTIVE

16. JOHN GARDNER MURRAY (243) (Bishop of Maryland), from January 1, 1926, to October 3, 1929 (died in office).

17. CHARLES PALMERSTON ANDERSON (197) (Bishop of Chicago), from November 13, 1929, to January 30, 1930 (died in office).

18. JAMES DEWOLF PERRY (247) (Bishop of Rhode Island), from March 26, 1930, to serve until General Convention of 1931. Reelected September 23, 1931, at General Convention held in Denver, Colo., for a term of six years to end December 31, 1937.

19. HENRY ST. GEORGE TUCKER (258) (Bishop of Virginia, resigned** in 1944), from January 1, 1938, to December 31, 1946.

20. HENRY KNOX SHERRILL (372) (Bishop of Massachusetts, resigned June 1, 1947), from January 1, 1947, to November 14, 1958.

21. ARTHUR LICHTENBERGER (503) (Bishop of Missouri, resigned in 1959), from November 15, 1958. Resigned for ill health, October, 1964.

22. JOHN ELBRIDGE HINES (461) (Bishop of Texas, resigned December 31, 1964), from January 1, 1965 to May 31, 1974.

23. JOHN MAURY ALLIN (581) (Bishop of Mississippi, resigned 1974), from June 1, 1974 to December 31, 1985.

24. EDMOND LEE BROWNING (630) (Bishop of Hawaii, resigned 1986) from January 1, 1986 to December 31, 1997.

25. FRANK TRACY GRISWOLD III (794) (Bishop of Chicago, resigned 1998) from January 1, 1998 to October 31, 2006.

26. KATHARINE JEFFERTS SCHORI (963) (Bishop of Nevada, resigned October 31, 2006) from November 1, 2006, to October 31, 2015.

27. MICHAEL BRUCE CURRY (955) (Bishop of North Carolina, resigned October 31, 2015), from November 1, 2015.

*NOTE—The title *Presiding Bishop* was not used in the Journals of General Convention until 1795. This table is based on the premise that the Bishop who was President of General Convention or of the House of Bishops before 1795 was *de facto* Presiding Bishop.

The General Convention of 1789 during its first session (July 28-August 8), and for the first five days (September 29-October 3) of its second session (September 29-October 16), consisted of one House only. Bishop White was *President of the General Convention* throughout its first session and for the first five days of its second session, and as such signed the minutes of the first session.

When, on October 5, 1789, a separate House of Bishops was first organized, Bishop Seabury became President of the House of Bishops in accordance with the rule of seniority, based on the date of consecration to the episcopate.

On September 13, 1792, Bishop Provoost became President of the House of Bishops by the adoption of the rule that the office should "be held in rotation, beginning from the North."

In 1795, under the above rule, Bishop White automatically became President of the House of Bishops, and for the first time the title *Presiding Bishop* appears in the signing of the minutes of that

House. In 1799, "the Bishop whose turn it would have been to preside" not being present, "Bishop White was requested to preside." In 1801 the rule of rotation was suspended. On September 12, 1804, the rule of seniority was again adopted and continued in effect for 115 years.

The General Convention of 1919 provided for the election of the Presiding Bishop by the Convention. The first such election took place at the General Convention of 1925.

**NOTE—The Presiding Bishop is currently elected by and from the House of Bishops and confirmed by the House of Deputies. The Presiding Bishop resigns from being a Diocesan within six months of taking office and retires after nine years (or at age seventy). The term begins on the first day of November following the election. (See Canon I.2 for further detail.)

RECENTLY CONSECRATED BISHOPS

KEVIN D. NICHOLS

The Rt. Rev. Kevin D. Nichols was ordained and consecrated as the IX Bishop of Bethlehem on September 15, 2018. He was elected on the first ballot of a Special Electing Convention held on April 28 at the Cathedral Church of the Nativity. Prior to his election, Nichols was chief operating officer and canon for mission resources in the Diocese of New Hampshire. Nichols was formerly president of the Diocese of New Hampshire's Standing Committee and a member of the churchwide Task Force to Reimagine the Episcopal Church.

Nichols began his ministry as a bivocational priest, serving a small rural parish while working full time as an account manager and management trainer for Sealed Air Corporation, a packaging company. A former Roman Catholic priest who received his master of divinity degree from St. Mary's Seminary and University in Baltimore, he was received into the Episcopal priesthood in 1999 and has served as rector of St. Stephen's in Pittsfield, New Hampshire, and St. Andrew's in Hopkinton, New Hampshire.

The bishop's wife, Patti, is a licensed clinical social worker. They have four adult children—Graham, Lindsay, Bryan, and Keaton—and three grandchildren.

CARLYE J. HUGHES

On May 19, 2018, the Rev. Carlye J. Hughes was elected as the 11th Bishop of the Diocese of Newark on the first ballot. Upon her consecration on September 22, 2018 at NJPAC, she became the first woman and African American to serve as bishop of this diocese.

A life-long Episcopalian, Hughes was born Tulsa, Oklahoma, and raised in Ft. Worth, Texas. She earned a BA in Drama from the University of Texas in Austin, and for 20 years she made her home in New York City while pursuing a career in Human Resources as a corporate trainer, mostly in the hotel industry.

While in NYC she discerned a call to the priesthood and attended Virginia Theological seminary, earning an MDiv in 2005. After a Lilly Fellowship at St. James' Church in New York City, she was called to serve as rector first at St. Peter's Church, Peekskill, New York, and most recently at Trinity Church, Ft. Worth, Texas. Hughes describes her ministry there as one in which she helped others "discover the ways they are called to serve God and God's people . . . supporting, encouraging, and empowering them to go and do what God created them to do." Because, Hughes stated, "today's church is not one that can rest on the past while waiting for people to come and ask about the faith. Instead God is guiding us to be active participants in the world. An important element of my ministry . . . is to nurture and guide our capacity to build relationships with neighbors locally or on the other side of the globe."

Hughes has been active on the Board of Trustees of the Virginia Theological Seminary; as a member of the Standing Committee, Commission on Ministry, Diocesan Convention Chaplain in the Diocese of New York, and in the Episcopal Diocese of Fort Worth as a member of the Standing Committee and as a General Convention Delegate. At the national level, she has served the General Convention on the Task for the Study of Marriage and the Racial Justice & Reconciliation.

Hughes is married to David Smedley and they have a dog, Abbey.

MICHAEL BUERKEL HUNN

The Rt. Rev. Michael Buerkel Hunn grew up in New Mexico and Texas. He was elected Bishop of the Episcopal Diocese of the Rio Grande on May 5, 2018. He was ordained and consecrated bishop on November 3, 2018, in Albuquerque, New Mexico, by Presiding Bishop the Most Rev.

Michael Bruce Curry, whom he had served as canon for more than a decade.

In twenty years of ordained ministry he has served as a parish priest, a school chaplain, college chaplain, canon to Bishop Michael Curry in the Diocese of North Carolina, and as canon to the presiding bishop.

In North Carolina, he designed and led diocesan systems in the areas of congregational support and development, youth ministry, pastoral response, transition ministry, clergy discipline, misconduct prevention training, priestly ordination process, and conflict transformation. As a lecturer, keynote speaker, and preacher, he has spoken on subjects such as public speaking, nonviolent communication, canon law, stewardship, and nonviolent approaches to conversations about race.

Ordained in 1996, Bishop Hunn first served The Kent School in Connecticut as chaplain, head baseball coach, and chair of the Theology Department. He went on to serve as senior associate rector of the Church of the Holy Comforter in Kenilworth, Illinois, and as Episcopal chaplain to Davidson College, and associate rector of St. Alban's, Davidson, North Carolina.

Bishop Hunn holds degrees from Middlebury College (Bachelor of Arts, History, and Religion) and Cambridge University (Master of Arts, Theology) and a Certificate of Advanced Theological Study from Seabury Western Theological Seminary.

He loves his work for the church and also loves spending time with his family, baseball, digging in his vegetable garden, writing fiction, and riding bicycles. His short story "Al's Garage and Soul Repair Shop" won the 2009 Middlebury Magazine Fiction Contest.

He is married to the Rev. Meg Buerkel Hunn. They have three children, Dexter, Murphy, and Dosie.

MARK A. COWELL

The Rev. Mark A. Cowell is familiar to the people of the Episcopal Diocese of Western Kansas. He is the vicar of Sts. Mary and Martha of Bethany, Larned, and Holy Nativity, Kinsley.

Mark began his education at Drew University in Madison, New Jersey, complet-ing a Bachelor's Degree in Political Science in 1990. While at Drew, Mark played rugby, which resulted in the most spectacularly broken leg. While an upper classman studying at Drew, Mark enrolled in semi-nary classes but chose the study of law over seminary.

Mark earned his *juris doctorate* degree in 1994 from Washburn University School of Law in Topeka, Kansas, and graduated with honors. He was admitted to the Kansas bar in 1994. He was soon recruited to prosecute gangs in Dodge City, and he moved there in 1995. After gang members shot out his car windows, he moved his family to Larned in 1996. He has lived there ever since, and has commuted back and forth to Dodge City. Mark now works part time as the City of Dodge City municipal prosecutor. He is also the Hodgeman County attorney, and was just reelected to his second term.

After law school, Mark still knew that God was calling him, but Mark was faced with a problem. He had incurred his fair share of student loan debt, and there was no means to go to seminary. In 1997, Mark sought out Bishop Strickland and finally acknowledged that he wanted to be a priest. Bishop Strickland offered Mark a solution. Father Tom Keith, who was both a priest and a college professor, was putting together a class called Education for Vocation. The class was designed to incubate budding students who were discerning their calls to ordination. Mark agreed to study with Father Keith.

After two years of classes with Father Keith, Mark was approved as a postulant. Mark began serving the Central Region in the diocese, preaching weekly in rotation at Sts. Mary and Martha in Larned, and at St. John's Episcopal Church in Great Bend. After several additional years of study, Mark was ordained as a transitional deacon in October 2003. He was ordained as a priest in June 2004. He continued to serve the Central Region until its dissolution. He continues to serve Sts. Mary and Martha, Larned, today.

Mark began his service to the Diocese of Western Kansas before his ordination. He was senior warden at Sts. Mary and Martha, elected to Diocesan Council, served as the diocesan youth coordinator, and served as the adult representative to the Provincial Youth Network for Province VII while a member of the laity. Since ordination, Mark has served on Diocesan Council, the Commission on Ministry, and numerous times on Standing Committee, including eighteen months as president of the latter in the absence of a bishop after Bishop Adams resigned.

During that time, Mark oversaw the election of the next bishop, Bishop Milliken. Before that election,

Mark met with Presiding Bishop Jefferts Schori in New York to discuss and consult on the idea of a dual role Episcopacy. This is the model our diocese has pursued, and this was the role to which Bishop Milliken was elected. This new vision of the Episcopacy as both a bishop and a priest serving both the diocese and a church has been a successful solution, and a model which other dioceses, faced with similar problems, may employ.

Mark began to serve Holy Nativity, Kinsley, as well as Sts. Mary and Martha in Larned when Father Dennis Zimmerman fell ill. Mark continues to serve Holy Nativity. When Father Zimmerman passed away, Mark and Father Larry Carver served St. Cornelius, Dodge City, for over two years while St. Cornelius searched for a new rector.

Mark served both Bishop Adams and Bishop Milliken as the co-chancellor of the diocese with his wife Julie. Mark continues to be the diocesan youth coordinator.

Mark is married to Julie, who is the district magistrate judge in Larned, and they have three children, Gabriel, Cathleen and Gryffin.

The Anglican Communion

Introduction

The Anglican Communion comprises 40 self-governing *Member Churches* or *Provinces* that share several things in common including doctrine, ways of worshipping, mission, and a focus of unity in the Archbishop of Canterbury. Formal mechanisms for meeting include the Lambeth Conference, the Anglican Consultative Council, and the Primates' Meeting, together with the Archbishop, known as the *Instruments of Communion*.

Most Communion life, however, is found in the relationships between Anglicans at all levels of church life and work around the globe; dioceses linked with dioceses, parishes with parishes, people with people, all working to further God's mission. There are tens of millions of people on six continents who call themselves Anglican (or Episcopalian), in more than 165 countries. These Christian brothers and sisters share prayer, resources, support and knowledge across geographical and cultural boundaries.

As with any family, the Anglican Communion's members have a range of differing opinions. The Anglican Christian tradition has long valued its diversity, and has never been afraid to tackle publicly the hard questions of life and faith.

History

In continuity with the ancient Celtic and Saxon churches of the British Isles, and Britain's place within Catholic Europe, Anglicanism found its distinctive identity in the 16th and 17th centuries. At the Reformation national Churches emerged in England, Ireland and Scotland. With the American Revolution an autonomous Episcopal Church was founded in the United States and later Anglican or Episcopal Churches were founded across the globe as a result of the missionary movements of the 18th and 19th centuries. Many of these Churches became autonomous Provinces in the course of the 19th and 20th centuries. In South Asia, the United Churches formed between Anglican and Protestant denominations, joined the Anglican Communion, as did Churches elsewhere such as the Spanish Episcopal Reformed Church and the Lusitanian Church of Portugal.

Official structures

It was in 1867 that Lambeth Palace hosted the first conference for Anglican bishops from around the world. From 1948 each Archbishop of Canterbury has called a *Lambeth Conference* every ten years. The last, in 2008, saw more than 800 bishops from around the world invited to Canterbury. The Conference has no authority of itself: rather it is a chance for bishops to meet and explore aspects of Anglican Communion life and ministry. The next Lambeth Conference takes place in July and August 2020.

Bishops attending the 1968 Lambeth Conference called for a body representative of all sections of the churches—laity, clergy and bishops—to co-ordinate aspects of international Anglican ecumenical and mission work. The resulting body was the *Anglican Consultative Council*. This council comprising elected and appointed members from around the globe meets approximately every three years.

Since 1979 the Archbishop of Canterbury has also regularly invited the chief bishops of the Provinces (known as *Primates*) to join him in a meeting for consultation, prayer and reflection on theological, social and international matters. These *Primates' Meetings* take place approximately every two years.

These Instruments of Communion are served by a secretariat with staff based at the Anglican Communion Office in London, England, and New York.

(See below for more information on the Anglican Communion Office)

Beliefs

There can be many differences between individual Anglican churches, but all uphold and proclaim the Catholic and Apostolic faith, proclaimed in the Scriptures, interpreted in the light of tradition and reason. Anglicans hold these things in common:

- The Holy Bible, comprising the Old and New Testament, as a basis of our faith;

- The Nicene and Apostles' Creeds as the basic statements of Christian belief;

- Recognition of the Sacraments of Baptism and Holy Communion; and

- The Historic Episcopate—ours is a Christian tradition with bishops.

This *quadrilateral*, drawn up in the 19th Century, is one of the definitions of Anglican faith and ministry. Another is a style of worship which has its roots in the Book of Common Prayer and the Services of Ordination (the Ordinal). Anglicans also celebrate the Eucharist (also known as the Holy Communion, the Lord's Supper or the Mass), the Sacrament of Baptism and other rites including Confirmation, Reconciliation, Marriage, Anointing of the Sick, and Ordination.

Anglicanism rests on the three pillars of Scripture, Tradition and Reason as it seeks to chart 'a middle way' among the other Christian traditions.

Mission

Following the teachings of Jesus Christ, Anglicans are committed to proclaiming the good news of the Gospel to all creation as expressed in the Marks of Mission:

- To proclaim the Good News of the Kingdom;

- To teach, baptise and nurture new believers;

- To respond to human need by loving service;

- To seek to transform unjust structures of society, to challenge violence of every kind and to pursue peace and reconciliation

- To strive to safeguard the integrity of creation and sustain and renew the life of the earth.

These Marks are to be expressed in all areas of a Christian's life: their words and their actions. Therefore, members of the Anglican Communion around the world are involved with a range of life-changing activities that include evangelism and church growth; providing food, shelter and clothing to those in need; speaking out with and for the oppressed; and setting up schools, hospitals, clinics and universities.

PROVINCES

The Anglican Church in Aotearoa,
New Zealand & Polynesia
The Anglican Church of Australia
The Church of Bangladesh
Igreja Episcopal Anglicana do Brasil
The Anglican Church of Burundi
The Anglican Church of Canada
The Church of the Province of Central Africa
Iglesia Anglicana de la Region Central de America
Iglesia Anglicana de Chile
Province de L'Eglise Anglicane Du Congo
The Church of England
Hong Kong Sheng Kung Hui
The Church of the Province of the Indian Ocean
The Church of Ireland
The Nippon Sei Ko Kai
(The Anglican Communion in Japan)
The Episcopal Church in Jerusalem
& the Middle East
The Anglican Church of Kenya
The Anglican Church of Korea
The Church of the Province of Melansia
La Iglesia Anglicana de Mexico
The Church of the Province of Myanmar (Burma)
The Church of Nigeria (Anglican Communion)
The Church of North India (United)
The Church of Pakistan (United)
The Anglican Church of Papua New Guinea
The Episcopal Church in the Philippines
Province de l'Eglise Episcopal au Rwanda
The Scottish Episcopal Church
Church of the Province of South East Asia

The Church of South India (United)
The Anglican Church of Southern Africa
The Anglican Church of South America
Province of the Episcopal Church of South Sudan
Province of the Episcopal Church of Sudan
The Anglican Church of Tanzania
The Church of the Province of Uganda
The Episcopal Church *(Includes 100 dioceses in the United States, and 12 additional dioceses or jurisdictions in 1 nations)*
The Church in Wales
The Church of the Province of West Africa
The Church in the Province of the West Indies

Extra-Provincial Churches and other dioceses
The Church of Ceylon
(Extra-Provincial to Canterbury)
Bermuda (Extra-Provincial to Canterbury)
The Lusitanian Church
(Extra-Provincial to Canterbury)
The Reformed Episcopal Church of Spain (Extra-Provincial to Canterbury)
Falkland Islands (Extra-Provincial to Canterbury)

Churches in Communion
The Mar Thoma Syrian Church of Malabar
The Old Catholic Churches of the Union of Utrecht
The Philippine Independent Church
(Iglesia Filipina Independiente—IFI)
NB: Anglicans/Episcopalians in certain parts of the Communion are in full communion with some Lutheran Churches.

THE ANGLICAN COMMUNION OFFICE

Sec Gen for Ang Com Archbishop Dr Josiah Idowu-Fearon; *Dir for Unity Faith and Order* Revd Cn Dr John Gibaut; *Co-Executive Dir for Anglican Alliance* Revd Andy Bowerman *and* Revd Rachel Carnegie; *Dir for Com* Adrian Butcher; *Dir for Finance and Resources* Michaela Southworth; *Dir for Mission* Rev John Kafwanka; *Dir for Women in Church and Society* Revd Terrie Robinson; *Rep to UN institutions in Geneva* Revd Cn Jack Palmer-White - Anglican Communion; *Wdn of the Gst Hse* Stefan Tkaczek; *Chief Operating Officer:* David White

Anglican Communion Office: St Andrew's House, 16 Tavistock Crescent, London, W11 1AP
Tel: +44 (0)207 313 3900   *Fax:* +44 (0)207 313 3999
E-mail: aco@anglicancommunion.org
Web: www.anglicancommunion.org   ACNS: www.anglicannews.org/

The permanent secretariat (the Anglican Communion Office) serves the Anglican Communion and is responsible for facilitating all meetings of the conciliar Instruments of Communion as well as the commissions, working groups and networks of the Communion. Anglican Communion Office staff from countries including Canada, Colombia, Nigeria, the United States, and Zambia also maintain the Anglican Communion website where visitors can find the official prayer cycle (daily prayer intentions for the dioceses of the Communion) and vast amounts of official information and documentation about the Anglican Communion's Instruments and its ministries. The very latest news from around the Anglican world is available via the Anglican Communion News Service (ACNS) website. Most of the funding for the work of the office comes from the Inter- Anglican budget supported by all Member Churches according to their means.

The Anglican Episcopate

THE ANGLICAN CHURCH IN AOTEAROA, NEW ZEALAND AND POLYNESIA
General Secretary The Revd Michael M Hughes PO BOX 87188 Meadowbank Auckland 1742 NEW ZEALAND *Tel:* + 64 (0)9 521 4439 *Email:* gensecm@anglicanchurch.org.nz *Web:* www.anglican.org.nz

Aotearoa Vacant Aotearoa is the overall See for all the Maori diocese in NZ PO Box 568 Gisborne 4040 NEW ZEALAND *Tel:* + 64 (0)6 867 8856

Auckland The Rt Revd Ross Bay Bishop of Auckland PO Box 37 242 Parnell Auckland 1151 NEW ZEALAND *Tel:* + 64 (0)9 302 7201 *Email:* bishop.office@auckanglican.org.nz

Auckland The Rt Revd James White Assistant bishop of Auckland PO Box 37 242 Parnell Auckland 1151 NEW ZEALAND *Tel:* + 64 (09) 302 7288 *Web:* www.auckanglican.org.nz

Christchurch The Rt Revd Victoria Matthews Bishop of Christchurch PO Box 4438 Christchurch 8140 NEW ZEALAND *Tel:* + 64 (0)3 379 5950 *Fax:* + 64 (0)3 372 3357 *Email:* bishopsa@anglicanlife.org.nz *Web:* www.anglicanlife.org.nz

Dunedin The Rt Revd Steven Benford Bishop of Dunedin 1A Howden Street Green Island Dunedin 9052 NEW ZEALAND *Tel:* + 64 (0)3 488 0820 *Fax:* + 64 (0)3 488 2038 *Email:* bishop.steven@calledsouth.org.nz *Web:* www.calledsouth.org.nz

Nelson The Rt Revd Victor Richard Ellena Bishop of Nelson PO Box 100 Nelson 7040 NEW ZEALAND *Tel:* + 64 (0)3 548 3124 *Fax:* + 64 (0)3 548 2125 *Email:* bprichard@nelsonanglican.org.nz *Web:* www.nelsonanglican.org.nz

Polynesia The Most Revd Winston Halapua Bishop of Polynesia and Primate and Archbishop of the Anglican Church in Aotearoa, New Zealand and Polynesia Box 35 Suva Fiji *Tel:* + 679 3 304 716 *Fax:* + 679 3 302 553 *Email:* archbishop@dioceseofpolynesia.org *Web:* www.dioceseofpolynesia.org

Polynesia The Rt Revd Apimeleki Nadoki Qiliho Bishop of Vanua Levu and Taveuni, Fiji PO Box 117 Lautoka FIJI *Tel:* + 679 666 0124 *Email:* qiliho@gmail.com *Web:* www.dioceseofpolynesia.org

Polynesia The Rt Revd Gabriel Sharma Bishop of Viti Levu West, Fiji PO Box 117 Lautoka FIJI *Email:* gabsharma@yahoo.com *Web:* www.dioceseofpolynesia.org

Polynesia The Rt Revd Afa Vaka Bishop in Tonga Box 35 Suva FIJI *Email:* afavaka@yahoo.co.nz

Te Pihopatanga o Manawa o Te Wheke The Rt Revd Ngarahu Katene Pihopa ki Te Manawa o Te Wheke (Bp Central North Island Region) Po Box 146 Rotorua 3040 NEW ZEALAND *Tel:* + 64 (0)7 348 4043 *Email:* ngarahukatane@ihug.co.nz

Te Pihopatanga o Tai Tokerau The Rt Revd Te Kitohi Wiremu Pikaahu Pihopa ki Te Tai Tokerau (Bp, Northern Region) PO Box 25 Paihia Bay of Islands 247 NEW ZEALAND *Tel:* + 64 (0)9 402 6788 *Fax:* + 64 (0)9 402 6663 *Email:* tkwp@tokerau.ang.org.nz

Te Pihopatanga o Tairawhiti The Rt Revd Don Tamihere Bishop of Te Hui Amorangi ki Te Tairawhiti PO Box 568 Gisborne 4040 NEW ZEALAND *Tel:* + 64 (0)6 867 8856 *Fax:* + 64 (0)6 867 8859 *Email:* bishop@tairawhiti.org.nz

Te Pihopatanga o Upoko o Te Ika The Rt Revd Muru Walters Pihopa ki Te Upoko o Te Ika (Bp, Wellington / Taranaki Region) 14 Amesbury Drive Churton Park Wellington 6037 NEW ZEALAND *Tel:* + 64 (0)4 478 3549 *Email:* muru.walters@xtra.co.nz

Te Pihopatanga o Upoko o Te Waipounamu The Rt Revd Richard R Wallace Pihopa ki Te Waipounamu (Bp, South Island) PO Box 10 086 Christchurch 8145 NEW ZEALAND *Tel:* + 64 (0)3 389 1683 *Fax:* + 64 (0)3 389 0912

Waiapu The Rt Revd Andrew Hedge Bishop of Waiapu PO Box 227 Napier 4140 NEW ZEALAND *Tel:* + 64 (0)6 835 8230 *Fax:* + 64 (0)6 835 0680 *Web:* www.waiapu.anglican.org.nz

Waikato & Taranaki The Most Revd Philip Richardson Bishop of Taranaki and Senior Bishop of New Zealand Dioceses and Primate and Archbishop of the Anglican Church in Aotearoa, New Zealand and Polynesia PO Box 547 566 Mangorei Road New Plymouth 4340 NEW ZEALAND *Tel:* + 64 (0)6 759 1178 *Fax:* + 64 (0)6 759 1180 *Email:* bishop@taranakianglican.org.nz

Waikato & Taranaki The Rt Revd Helen-Ann Hartley Bishop of Waikato PO Box 21 Hamilton 3240 NEW ZEALAND *Tel:* + 64 (0)7 857 0020 *Email:* bishopspa@waikatoanglican.org.nz *Web:* www.waikatotaranakianglican.org.nz/

Wellington The Rt Revd Justin Duckworth Bishop of Wellington PO Box 12-046 Wellington 6144 NEW ZEALAND *Tel:* + 64 04 472 1057 *Fax:* + 64 04 499 1360 *Email:* reception@wn.ang.org.nz *Web:* wn.anglican.org.nz

Wellington The Rt Revd Eleanor Sanderson Assistant Bishop of Wellington PO Box 12-046 Wellington 6144 NEW ZEALAND *Tel:* + 64 04 472 1057 *Email:* reception@wn.ang.org.nz *Web:* wn.anglican.org.nz

THE ANGLICAN CHURCH OF AUSTRALIA

General Secretary Ms Anne Hywood General Synod Office Suite 4 Level 5 189 Kent Street Sydney 2000 AUSTRALIA *Tel:* + 61 (0)2 8267 2701 *Fax:* + 61 (0)2

8267 2727 *Email:* generalsecretary@anglican.org.au

Finance and Administration Manager Ms Marianne Yacoel General Synod Office Suite 4 Level 5 189 Kent Street Sydney 2000 AUSTRALIA *Tel:* + 61 2 8267 2700 *Fax:* + 61 2 8267 2727 *Web:* www.anglican.org.au

Adelaide-South Australia The Rt Revd Geoffrey Martyn Smith Archbishop elect of Adelaide 18 King William Road North Adelaide 5006 AUSTRALIA *Tel:* + 61 (0)8 8305 9350 *Email:* office@adelaideanglicans.com

Adelaide-South Australia The Rt Revd Christopher McLeod Assistant Bishop of Adelaide & National Aboriginal Bishop 18 King William Road North Adelaide 5006 AUSTRALIA *Tel:* + 61 (0)8 305 9350 *Web:* www.adelaide.anglican.com.au

Adelaide-South Australia The Rt Revd Tim J Harris Bishop for Mission and Evangelism 18 King William Road North Adelaide 5006 AUSTRALIA *Tel:* + 61 8 8305 9352 *Email:* tharris@adelaide.anglican.com.au

Armidale-New South Wales The Rt Revd Richard Lewers Bishop of Armidale Anglican Diocesan Registry PO Box 198 Armidale 2350 AUSTRALIA *Tel:* + 61 (02) 6772 4491 *Fax:* + 61 (02) 6772 9261 *Email:* bishop@armidaleanglicandiocese.com *Web:* www.armidaleanglicandiocese.com

Ballarat-Victoria The Rt Revd Garry Weatherill Bishop of Ballarat PO Box 89 Ballarat 3352 AUSTRALIA *Tel:* + 61 (0)35 331 1183 *Fax:* + 61 (0)35 333 2982 *Email:* bishop@ballaratanglican.org.au *Web:* www.ballaratanglican.org.au

Bathurst-New South Wales The Rt Revd Ian Palmer Bishop of Bathurst PO Box 23 Bathurst 2795 AUSTRALIA *Tel:* + 61 (0)26 331 1722 *Fax:* + 61 (0)26 332 2772 *Web:* www.bathurst.anglican.org

Bendigo-Victoria The Rt Revd Andrew William Curnow Bishop of Bendigo PO Box 2 Post office Bendigo 3552 AUSTRALIA *Tel:* + 61 (0)35 443 4711 *Fax:* + 61 (0)35 441 2173 *Email:* bishop@bendigoanglican.org.au *Web:* www.bendigoanglican.org.au/

Brisbane-Queesland The Most Revd Phillip John Aspinall Archbishop of Brisbane PO Box 421 Brisbane 4001 AUSTRALIA *Tel:* + 61 (0)7 3835 2218 *Fax:* + 61 (0)7 3832 5030 *Email:* ajoseph@anglicanbrisbane.org.au *Web:* www.brisbane.anglican.org

Brisbane-Queensland The Rt Revd Ian Keese Lambert Aglican Bishop to the Australian Defence Force PO Box 421 Brisbane 4001 AUSTRALIA

Brisbane-Queensland The Rt Revd Cameron Venables Bishop of Brisbane - Western Region PO Box 2600 Toowoomba 4350 AUSTRALIA *Tel:* + 61 (0)7 4639 1875 *Fax:* + 61 (0)7 4632 6882

Brisbane The Rt Revd Alison Taylor Bishop of Brisbane - Southern Region PO Box 5384 Gold Coast Mail Centre 9726 Queensland AUSTRALIA

Brisbane-Queensland The Rt Revd Jonathan Holland Bishop of Brisbane - Northern Region GPO Box 421 Brisbane 4001 AUSTRALIA *Tel:* + 61 (0)7 3835 2213 *Fax:* + 61 (0)7 3832 5030 *Email:* jholland@anglicanbrisbane.org.au

Bunbury-Western Australia The Rt Revd Alan Ewing Bishop of Bunbury Bishopscourt PO Box 15 Bunbury 6231 AUSTRALIA *Tel:* + 61 9721 2100 *Email:* office@bunbury.org.au *Web:* www.bunbury.org.au

Canberra & Goulburn-ACT The Rt Revd Stuart Robinson Bishop of Canberra & Goulburn Jamieson House 43 Constitution Avenue Reid 2612 AUSTRALIA

Canberra & Goulburn-ACT The Rt Revd Trevor W Edwards Assistant Bishop of Canberra & Goulburn 28 McBryde Crescent Wanniassa 2903 AUSTRALIA *Tel:* + 61 (0)2 6231 7347 *Fax:* + 61 (0)2 6231 7500 *Email:* trevor@stmattswanniassa.org.au

Canberra & Goulburn-ACT Vacant Regional Bishop in Wagga Wagga Jamieson House 43 Constitution Avenue Reid 2612 AUSTRALIA

Gippsland-Victoria The Rt Revd Kay Goldsworthy Bishop of Gippsland PO Box 928 Sale 3850 AUSTRALIA *Tel:* + 61 (0)35 144 2044 *Fax:* + 61 (0)35 144 7183 *Email:* bishopkay@gippsanglican.org.au *Web:* www.gippsanglican.org.au

Grafton-New South Wales The Rt Revd Sarah Macneil Bishop of Grafton Bishopsholme PO Box 4 Grafton 2460 AUSTRALIA *Tel:* + 61 (0)2 6642 4122 *Fax:* + 61 (0)2 6643 1814 *Email:* bishop@graftondiocese.org.au *Web:* www.graftondiocese.org.au

Melbourne-Victoria The Most Revd Philip Leslie Freier Archbishop of Melbourne & Primate of Australia The Anglican Centre 209 Flinders Lane Melbourne 3000 AUSTRALIA *Tel:* + 61 (0)3 9653 4204 *Email:* archbishopsoffice@melbourneanglican.org.au *Web:* www.melbourne.anglican.com.au/

Melbourne-Victoria The Rt Revd Genieve Blackwell Bishop of Melbourne - Marmingatha Episcopate The Anglican Centre 209 Flinders Lane Melbourne 3000 AUSTRALIA *Tel:* + 61 (0)3 9653 4220

Melbourne-Victoria The Rt Revd Philip J Huggins Bishop of Melbourne - Oodthenong Episcopate The Anglican Centre 209 Flinders Lane Melbourne 3000 AUSTRALIA *Tel:* + 61 (0)3 9653 4220 *Fax:* + 61 (0)3 9653 4266 *Email:* phuggins@melbourne.anglican.com.au

Melbourne-Victoria The Rt Revd Paul White Bishop of Melbourne - Jumbunna Episcopate The Anglican Centre 209 Flinders Lane Melbourne 3000 AUSTRALIA *Tel:* + 61 3 9653 4220 *Fax:* + 61 3 9650 2184 *Email:* paulwhite49@iinet.net.au

Newcastle (AUS)-New South Wales The Rt Revd Greg E Thompson Bishop of Newcastle The Bishop's Registry PO Box 817 Newcastle 2300 AUSTRALIA *Tel:* + 61 (0)2 4926 3733 *Fax:* + 61 (0)2 4926 1968 *Web:* www.newcastleanglican.org.au

Newcastle (AUS)-NEW SOUTH WALES The Rt Revd Peter Stuart Assistant Bishop of Newcastle The Diocesan Office PO Box 817 Newcastle 2300 AUSTRALIA *Tel:* + 61 (02) 4926 3733 *Email:* bishoppeter@newcastleanglican.org.au *Web:* www.newcastleanglican.org.au

North Queensland-Queensland The Rt Revd William J Ray Bishop of North Queensland PO Box 1244 Townsville 4810 AUSTRALIA *Tel:* + 61 (0)7 4771 4175 *Fax:* + 61 (0)7 4721 1756 *Email:* bishop@anglicannq.org *Web:* www.anglicannq.com

North West Australia-Western Australia The Rt Revd Gary Nelson Bishop of North West AUSTRALIA PO Box 2783 Geraldton 6531 AUSTRALIA *Tel:* + 61 (0)8 9921 7277 *Fax:* + 61 (0)8 9964 2220 *Email:* bishop@anglicandnwa.org *Web:* www.anglicandnwa.org

Northern Territory, The- NT The Rt Revd Greg Anderson Bishop of the Northern Territory GPO Box 2950 Darwin 801 AUSTRALIA *Tel:* + 61 (0)8 8941 7440 *Fax:* + 61 (0)8 8941 7446 *Email:* ntdiocese@internode.on.net *Web:* www.anglicanchurchnt.org.au

Perth-Western Australia The Most Revd Roger A Herft Archbishop of Perth GPO Box W2067 Perth 6846 AUSTRALIA *Tel:* + 61 (0)8 9425 7201 *Fax:* + 61 (0)8 9325 6741 *Email:* archbishop@perth.anglican.org *Web:* www.perth.anglican.org/

Perth-Western Australia The Rt Revd Tom Wilmot Assistant Bishop of Perth, Eastern and Rural Region GPO Box W2067 Perth 6846 AUSTRALIA *Tel:* + 61 08 9325 7455 *Fax:* + 61 08 9325 6741 *Email:* twilmot@perth.anglican.org

Perth-Western Australia The Rt Revd Jeremy James Assistant Bishop of Perth Goldfields-Country Region GPO Box W2067 Perth 6846 AUSTRALIA *Tel:* + 61 (0)8 9430 7224 *Fax:* + 61 (0)8 9336 3374

Perth-Western Australia The Rt Revd Kate Wilmot Assistant Bishop of Perth GPO Box W2067 Perth 6846 AUSTRALIA *Tel:* + 1 (0)8 9425 7201 *Web:* www.perth.anglican.org

Riverina-New South Wales The Rt Revd Rob Gillion Bishop of Riverina PO Box 10 58 Arthur Street Narrandera 2700 AUSTRALIA *Tel:* + 61 (0)2 6959 1648 *Fax:* + 61 (0)2 6959 2903 *Email:* bishoprob@anglicanriverina.com *Web:* www.riverina.anglican.org

Rockhampton-Queensland The Rt Revd David Robinson Bishop of Rockhampton PO Box 6158 Central Queensland Mail Centre Rockhampton 4702 AUSTRALIA *Tel:* + 61 (0)7 4927 3188 *Fax:* + 61 (0)7 4922 4562 *Email:* bishop@anglicanrock.org.au *Web:* www.anglicanrock.org.au

Sydney-New South Wales The Most Revd Glenn N Davies Archbishop of Sydney PO Box 190 Q.V.B Post Office Sydney 1230 AUSTRALIA *Tel:* + 61 2 9265 1527 *Fax:* + 61 2 9265 1543 *Email:* gdavies@sydney.anglican.asn.au *Web:* www.sydneyanglicans.net

Sydney-New South Wales The Rt Revd Robert C Forsyth Assistant Bishop of Sydney - South PO Box Q190 QVB Post Office Sydney 1230 AUSTRALIA *Tel:* + 61 (0)292 651 523 *Fax:* + 61 (0)292 651 543 *Email:* robforsyth@sydney.anglican.asn.au *Web:* www.anglicanmediasydney.asn.au/

Sydney-New South Wales The Rt Revd Ivan Y Lee Assistant Bishop of Sydney - West PO Box Q190 QVB Post Office 1230 AUSTRALIA *Tel:* + 61 (0)296 353 186 *Fax:* + 61 (0)296 333 636 *Email:* office@westernsydney.anglican.asn.au

Sydney-New South Wales The Rt Revd Al Stewart Assistant Bishop of Sydney - Wollongong 74 Church Street PO Box A287 Wollongong 2500 AUSTRALIA *Tel:* + 61 (0)2 4225 2800 *Fax:* + 61 (0)2 4228 4296 *Email:* office@wollongong.anglican.asn.au *Web:* www.anglicanmediasydney.asn.au

Sydney-New South Wales The Rt Revd Peter J Tasker Assistant Bishop of Sydney - Liverpool PO Box Q190 QVB Post Office Sydney 1230 AUSTRALIA *Tel:* + 61 2 9265 1572 *Fax:* + 61 2 9265 1543 *Email:* ptasker@sydney.anglican.asn.au

Sydney-New South Wales The Rt Revd Chris Edwards Assistant Bishop of Sydney - North PO Box Q190 QVB Post Office Sydney 1230 AUSTRALIA *Tel:* + 61 2 9265 1527 *Fax:* + 61 2 9265 1543 *Web:* www.sydneyanglicans.net

Tasmania-Tasmania The Rt Revd Richard Condie Bishop of Tasmania GPO 748H Hobart 7001 AUSTRALIA *Tel:* + 61 (0)3 6220 2020 *Email:* bishop@anglicantas.org.au *Web:* www.anglicantas.org.au

Tasmania-Tasmania The Rt Revd Christopher R J Jones Assistant Bishop of Tasmania GPO Box 1620 Hobart 7001 AUSTRALIA *Tel:* + 61 (0)3 6231 9602 *Fax:* + 61 (0)3 6231 9589 *Email:* c.jones@anglicare-tas.org.au *Web:* www.anglicare-tas.org.au

Tasmania-Tasmania The Rt Revd Ross J Nicholson Assistant Bishop of Tasmania 157 St John Street Launceston 7250 AUSTRALIA *Tel:* + 61 (0)3 6331 4896 *Fax:* + 61 (0)3 6334 1719 *Email:* rnicholson@stjohns.net.au

The Murray-South Australia The Rt Revd John Frank Ford Bishop of The Murray Po Box 269 Murray Bridge 5253 AUSTRALIA *Tel:* + 61 (0)8 8532 2270 *Fax:* + 61 (0)8 8532 5760 *Email:* registry@murray.anglican.org *Web:* www.murray.anglican.org

Wangaratta-Victoria The Rt Revd John Parkes Bishop of Wangaratta Bishop's Lodge PO Box 457 Wangaratta 3677 AUSTRALIA *Tel:* + 61 (0)3 5721

3643 *Email:* bishop@wangaratta.anglican.org *Web:* www.wangaratta-anglican.org.au

Willochra-South Australia The Rt Revd John Stead Bishop of Willochra PO Box 96 Gladstone 5497 AUSTRALIA *Tel:* + 61 (0)8 8662 2249 *Fax:* + 61 (0)8 8662 2027 *Email:* bishop@diowillochra.org.au *Web:* www.willochra.anglican.org

THE CHURCH OF BANGLADESH
Provincial Secretary Dr James Tejosh Das 54/1 Barobagh Mirpur-2 Dhaka 1216 Bangladesh *Email:* tejoshd@gmail.com

Hon Treasurer Mr Lawrence Mondol 54/1 Barobagh Mirpur-2 Dhaka 1216 Bangladesh *Email:* lorance_mondol@yahoo.com

Barisal The Rt Revd Shourabh Pholia Bishop of Barisal Awaiting Details

Dhaka The Most Revd Paul Shishir Sarker Moderator, Church of Bangladesh & Bishop of Dhaka 54/1 Barobagh Mirpur-2 Dhaka 1216 Bangladesh *Tel:* + 880 2 805 3729 *Email:* pssarker19@gmail.com

Kushtia The Rt Revd Samuel Sunil Mankhin Bishop of Kushtia St Thomas Church 391 New Eskaton Road Moghbazar Dhaka 1000 Bangladesh *Tel:* + 880 2 711 6546 *Fax:* + 880 2 712 1632

IGREJA EPISCOPAL ANGLICANA DO BRASIL
Provincial Secretary The Revd Arthur P Cavalcante Praça Olavo Bilac nº 63-Campos Elseos São Paulo SP 01201-050 BRAZIL *Email:* arthurieab@gmail.com

Provincial Treasurer Mrs Silvia Fernandes Campos Elíseos São Paulo SP 01201-050 BRAZIL *Tel:* + 55 (0)11 3667 8161 *Fax:* + 55 (0)11 3667 8161 *Email:* sec.geral@ieab.org.br

Amazon The Rt Revd Saulo Mauricio de Barros Bishop of the Amazon Avenida Serzedelo Corrêa 514 Batista Campos Belem PA 66033-265 BRAZIL *Tel:* + 55 (0)91 3241 9720 *Email:* saulomauricio@gmail.com *Web:* www.daa.ieab.org.br/

Brasilia The Rt Revd Maurício Jose Araujo De Andrade Bishop of Brasilia Gabinete Episcopal - Catedral Anglicana EQS 309/310 sala 1 - Asa Sul Brazilia DF 70362-400 BRAZIL *Tel:* + 55 (0)61 3443 4305 *Fax:* + 55 (0)61 3443 4337 *Email:* mandrade@ieab.org.br *Web:* www.dab.ieab.org.br

Curitiba The Rt Revd Naudal Alves Gomes Bishop of Curitiba Av. Sete de Setembro 3927 sl. 8 Centro Curitiba PR 80250-210 BRAZIL *Tel:* + 55 (0)41 3079 9992 *Fax:* + 55 (0)41 3079 9992 *Email:* naudal@yahoo.com.br *Web:* www.dac.ieab.org.br

Missionary District of Oeste-Brasil Vacant The Most Revd Francisco de Assis da Silva is currently Bishop in Charge Av. Rio Branco 880 Santa Maria RS 97010-422 BRAZIL *Tel:* + 55 (0)55 3221 4328 *Fax:*

+ 55 (0)55 8131 0709 *Email:* xicosilva@gmail.com *Web:* www.dmo.ieab.org.br/

Pelotas The Rt Revd Renato Da Cruz Raatz Bishop of Pelotas Rua Goncalves Chaves, 665 Pelotas RS 96015-560 BRAZIL *Tel:* + 55 (0)53 3202 8618 *Email:* rcaatz@ieab.org.br *Web:* www.dapsul.com.br/

Recife The Rt Revd João Cancio Peixoto Bishop of Recife Av. Boa Viagem 5130 apto 701 Recife PE 51.030-000 BRAZIL *Tel:* + 55 (0)81 33410791 *Fax:* + 55 (0)81 88330791 *Email:* joao.peixoto01@uol.com.br *Web:* www.dar.ieab.org.br

Rio de Janeiro The Rt Revd Filadelfo Oliviera Neto Bishop of Rio de Janeiro Rua Haddock Lobo 258 Rio de Janeiro RJ 20260-142 BRAZIL *Tel:* + 55 (0)21 2220 2148 *Fax:* + 55 (0)21 2252 9686 *Email:* oliveira.ieab@gmail.com *Web:* www.anglicanarj.org

Sao Paulo The Rt Revd Flavio Augusto Borges Irala Bishop of São Paulo Rua Borges Lagoa 172 Vila Clementino Sao Paulo SP 04038-030 BRAZIL *Tel:* + 55 (0)11 5549 9086 *Email:* flavioirala@ieab.org.br

South Western Brazil The Most Revd Francisco De Assis Da Silva Primate of Brazil & Bishop of South-Western Brazil Av. Rio Branco 880 Santa Maria RS 97010-422 BRAZIL *Tel:* + 55 55 3221 4328 *Fax:* + 55 55 3221 4328 *Email:* xicoasilva@gmail.com *Web:* www.ieab.org.br

Southern Brazil The Rt Revd Humberto Maiztegue Bishop of Southern Brazil Av Eng Ludolfo Boehl 278 Teresópolis Porto Alegre RS 91720-150 BRAZIL *Tel:* + 55 (0)51 3318 6199 *Fax:* + 55 (0)51 3318 6199 *Email:* humbertox@uol.com.br *Web:* www.dm.ieab.org.br

THE ANGLICAN CHURCH OF BURUNDI
Provincial Secretary The Revd Félibien Ndintore BP 2098 Bujumbura Burundi *Tel:* + 257 22 22 9129

Provincial Treasurer Mrs Christine Niyonkuru BP 2098 Bujumbura Burundi

Buhiga The Rt Revd Evariste Nijimbere Bishop of Buhiga Awaiting Details

Bujumbura The Rt Revd Eraste Bigirimana Bishop of Bujumbura BP 1300 Bujumbura Burundi *Tel:* + 257 22 249 104 *Fax:* + 257 22 227 496 *Email:* eraste@bethesdaburundi.org

Buye The Rt Revd Sixbert Macumi Bishop of Buye Eglise Episcopale du Burundi BP 94 Ngozi Burundi *Tel:* + 257 22 302 210 *Fax:* + 257 22 302 317 *Email:* buyedioc@yahoo.fr

Gitega The Rt Revd John W Nduwayo Bishop of Gitega BP 23 Gitega Burundi *Tel:* + 257 22 402 247 *Fax:* + 257 22 402 247 *Email:* eab.diogitega@gmail.com

Gitega The Rt Revd Aimé Joseph Kimararungu Coadjutor Bishop of Gitega BP 23 Gitega Burundi *Tel:* + 257 22 402 247

Makamba The Most Revd Martin B Nyaboho Archbishop of Burundi & Bishop of Makamba BP 96 Makamba Burundi *Tel:* + 257 22 508 080 *Fax:* + 257 22 229 129 *Email:* mgrmartinyaboho@gmail.com

Matana The Rt Revd Seth Ndayirukiye Bishop of Matana DS 30 Bujumbura Burundi *Tel:* + 257 79923832 *Email:* canonseth@gmail.com *Web:* www. anglicanburundi.org

Muyinga The Rt Revd Paisible Ndacayisaba Bishop of Muyinga BP 55 Muyinga Burundi *Tel:* + 257 22 306 019 *Fax:* + 257 22 306 157 *Email:* ndacp@yahoo. com *Web:* www.anglicanchurchmuyinga.moonfruit. com

Rumonge The Rt Revd Pedaculi Birakengana Bishop of Rumonge Awaiting Details *Tel:* + 257 79 970 926 *Email:* birakepeda@yahoo.fr

Rutana The Rt Revd Pontien Ribakare Bishop of Rutana Awaiting Details

THE ANGLICAN CHURCH OF CANADA

The Most Revd Frederick J Hiltz Primate of the Anglican Church of Canada 80 Hayden Street Toronto ON M4Y 3G2 CANADA *Tel:* + 1 416 924 9199 *Fax:* + 1 416 924 0211 *Email:* primate@ national.anglican.ca *Web:* www.anglican.ca/

General Secretary of the General Synod The Ven Michael Thompson 80 Hayden Street Toronto ON M4Y 3G2 CANADA *Tel:* + 1 416 924 9199 *Fax:* + 1 416 924 0211 *Email:* mthompson@national. anglican.ca

General Treasurer of the General Synod Ms Hanna Goschy 80 Hayden Street Toronto ON M4Y 3G2 CANADA *Tel:* + 1 416 924 9199 *Email:* hgoschy@ national.anglican.ca

Algoma-Ontario The Rt Revd Anne Germond Bishop of Algoma PO Box 1168 619 Wellington Street East Sault Ste. Marie ON P6A 5N7 CANADA *Tel:* + 1 705 256 5061 *Fax:* + 1 705 673 4979 *Email:* bishop@dioceseofalgoma.com *Web:* www. dioceseofalgoma.com

Anglican Parishes of the Central Interior (formerly Cariboo)-British Columbia The Rt Revd Barbara Jean Andrews Bishop of Anglican Parishes of the Central Interior 360 Nicola Street Kamloops BC V2C 2P5 CANADA *Tel:* + 1 778 471 5573 *Fax:* + 1 778 471 5586 *Email:* apcibishop@shaw.ca *Web:* www.territoryofthepeople.ca

Athabasca-Alberta The Rt Revd Fraser W Lawton Bishop of Athabasca Box 6868 Peace River AB T8S 1S6 CANADA *Tel:* + 1 780 624 2767 *Fax:* + 1 780 624 2365 *Email:* bpath@telusplanet.net *Web:* www. dioath.ca

Brandon-MB The Rt Revd William Cliff Bishop of Brandon 403 13th Street Brandon MB R7A 4P9 CANADA *Tel:* + 1 204 727 2380 *Fax:* + 1 204 724 4135 *Email:* bishop@brandon.anglican.ca *Web:* www.dioceseofbrandon.org

British Columbia-British Columbia The Rt Revd Logan McMenamie Bishop of British Columbia 900 Vancouver Street Victoria BC V8V 3V7 CANADA *Tel:* + 1 250 386 7781 *Fax:* + 1 250 386 4013 *Email:* bishop@bc.anglican.ca *Web:* www.bc.anglican.ca

Caledonia-British Columbia The Revd David TJ Lehmann Bishop elect of Caledonia #201 - 4716 Lazelle Avenue Terrace BC V8G 1T2 CANADA *Tel:* + 1 250 635 6016 *Fax:* + 1 250 635 6026 *Email:* caledonia@telus.net *Web:* www.caledoniaanglican.ca

Calgary-Alberta The Most Revd Gregory Kerr-Wilson Metropolitan of Rupert's Land & Archbishop of Calgary 180 1209 - 59th Avenue SE Calgary AB T2H 2P6 CANADA *Tel:* + 1 403 243 3673 *Fax:* + 1 403 243 2182 *Email:* info@calgary.anglican.ca *Web:* www.calgary.anglican.ca

Central Newfoundland-Canada The Rt Revd John Watton Bishop of Central Newfoundland 34 Fraser Road Gander NL A1V 2E8 CANADA *Tel:* + 1 709 256 2372 *Fax:* + 1 709 256 2396 *Email:* centraldiocese@ bellaliant.com *Web:* www.centraldiocese.ca

Eastern Newfoundland & Labrador-Canada The Rt Revd Geoffrey Peddle Bishop of Eastern Newfoundland & Labrador 16 King's Bridge Road St John's NL A1C 3K4 CANADA *Tel:* + 1 709 576 6697 *Fax:* + 1 709 576 7122 *Email:* geoffpeddle48@gmail. com *Web:* www.anglicanenl.net

Edmonton-Alberta The Rt Revd Jane Alexander Bishop of Edmonton 10035-103 Street Edmonton AB T5J 0X5 CANADA *Tel:* + 1 780 439 7344 *Fax:* + 1 780 439 6549 *Email:* bishop@edmonton.anglican.ca *Web:* www.edmonton.anglican.org

Fredericton-Canada The Rt Revd David Edwards Bishop of Fredericton 115 Church Street Fredericton NB E3B 4C8 CANADA *Tel:* + 1 506 459 1801 *Fax:* + 1 506 460 0520 *Email:* bishop@anglican.nb.ca *Web:* www.fredericton.anglican.org

Huron-Ontario The Rt Revd Linda Nicholls Bishop of Huron 190 Queen's Avenue London ON N6A 6H7 CANADA *Tel:* + 1 519 434 6893 *Fax:* + 1 519 673 4151 *Email:* lnicholls@huron.anglican.ca

Huron-Ontario The Rt Revd Terrance Arthur Dance Suffragan Bishop of Huron 190 Queens Avenue London ON N6A 6H7 CANADA *Tel:* + 1 519 434 6893 *Fax:* + 1 519 673 1451 *Email:* bishops@ huron.anglican.ca *Web:* www.diohuron.org

Keewatin-Ontario The Rt Revd David Norman Ashdown Bishop of Keewatin 915 Ottawa Street PO Box 567 Keewatin ON P0X 1C0 CANADA *Tel:* + 1 807 547 3353 *Fax:* + 1 807 547 3356 *Email:* keewatinbishop@shaw.ca *Web:* www. dioceseofkeewatin.ca/

Kootenay-British Columbia The Most Revd John Elswood Privett Metropolitan of BC and Yukon and Archbishop of Kootenay #201 - 380 Leathead Road Kelowna BC V1X 2H8 CANADA *Tel:* + 1 250 762 3306 *Fax:* + 1 250 762 4150 *Email:* diocese_of_kootenay@telus.net *Web:* www.kootenay.anglican.ca/

Mishamikoweesh-Ontario The Rt Revd Lydia Mamakwa Bishop of Indigenous Spiritual Ministry of Mishamikoweesh P.O. Box 65 Kingfisher Lake ON P0V 1Z0 CANADA *Tel:* + 1 807 532 2085 *Fax:* + 1 807 532 2344 *Email:* lydiam@kingfisherlake.ca

Montreal-Canada The Rt Revd Mary Irwin-Gibson Bishop of Montreal 1444 Union Avenue Montreal QCH3A 2B8 CANADA *Tel:* + 1 514 843 6577 *Fax:* + 1 514 843 3221 *Email:* bishops.office@montreal.anglican.ca *Web:* www.montreal.anglican.ca

Moosonee-Ontario The Rt Revd Thomas A Corston Bishop of Moosonee 113 Third St PO Box 735 Cochrane ON P0L 1C0 CANADA *Tel:* + 1 705 360 1129 *Fax:* + 1 705 360 1120 *Email:* bishop@moosoneeanglican.ca *Web:* www.moosonee.anglican.org

National Indigenous Bishop-Ontario The Rt Revd Mark Lawrence MacDonald National Indigenous Anglican Bishop 80 Hayden Street Toronto ON M4Y 3G2 CANADA *Tel:* + 1 416 924 9199 *Fax:* + 1 416 968 7983 *Email:* mmacdonald@national.anglican.ca *Web:* www.anglican.ca

New Westminster-British Columbia The Rt Revd Melissa M Skelton Bishop of New Westminster 1410 Nanton Avenue Vancouver BC V6H 2E2 CANADA *Tel:* + 1 604 684 6306 *Fax:* + 1 604 684 7017 *Email:* bishop@vancouver.anglican.ca *Web:* www.vancouver.anglican.ca

Niagara-Ontario The Rt Revd Michael Allan Bird Bishop of Niagara Cathedral Place 252 James Street North Hamilton ON L8R 2L3 CANADA *Tel:* + 1 905 527 1316 *Fax:* + 1 905 527 1281 *Email:* bishop@niagara.anglican.ca *Web:* www.niagara.anglican.ca

Nova Scotia & Prince Edward Island-Canada The Most Revd Ronald Wayne Cutler Metropolitan of the Ecclesiastical Province of Canada & Bishop of Nova Scotia & Prince Edward Island 1340 Cathedral Lane Halifax NS B3H 2Z1 CANADA *Tel:* + 1 902 420 0717 *Fax:* + 1 902 425 0717 *Email:* rcutler@nspeidiocese.ca *Web:* www.nspeidiocese.ca

Ontario-Ontario The Rt Revd Michael D Oulton Bishop of Ontario 90 Johnson Street Kingston ON K7L 1X7 CANADA *Tel:* + 1 613 544 4774 *Fax:* + 1 613 547 3745 *Email:* moulton@ontario.ca *Web:* www.ontario.anglican.ca

Ottawa-Ontario The Rt Revd John Holland Chapman Bishop of Ottawa 71 Bronson Avenue Ottawa ON K1R 6G6 CANADA *Tel:* + 1 613 232 7124 *Fax:* + 1 613 232 7088 *Email:* bishopsoffice@ottawa.anglican.ca *Web:* www.ottawa.anglican.ca

Ottawa-Ontario The Rt Revd Nigel Shaw Anglican Bishop Ordinary to the Canadian Armed Forces N.D.H.Q. (CFSU Ottawa – Uplands) 101 Colonel By Drive Ottawa ON K1A 0K2 CANADA *Email:* Nigel.Shaw@gc.forces.ca

Qu'Appelle-Rupert's Land The Rt Revd Robert Hardwick Bishop of Qu'Appelle 1501 College Avenue Regina SK S4P 1B8 CANADA *Tel:* + 1 306 522 1608 *Fax:* + 1 306 352 6808 *Email:* bishop.rob@sasktel.net *Web:* www.quappelle.anglican.ca/

Quebec-Canada The Rt Revd Bruce Myers Bishop of Quebec 31 rue des Jardins Quebec QC G1R 4L6 CANADA *Tel:* + 1 418 692 3858 *Email:* bishopqc@quebec.anglican.ca *Web:* www.quebec.anglican.org

Rupert's Land-Rupert's Land The Rt Revd Donald David Phillips Bishop of Rupert's Land 935 Nesbitt Bay Winnipeg MB R3T 1W6 CANADA *Tel:* + 1 204 992 4200 *Fax:* + 1 204 992 4219 *Email:* dphillips@rupertsland.anglican.ca *Web:* www.rupertsland.ca/

Saskatchewan-Rupert's Land The Rt Revd Michael William Hawkins Bishop of Saskatchewan 1308 Fifth Avenue East Prince Albert SK S6V 2H7 CANADA *Tel:* + 1 306 763 2455 *Fax:* + 1 306 764 5172 *Email:* synod@sasktel.net *Web:* www.saskatchewan.anglican.org

Saskatchewan-Rupert's Land The Rt Revd Adam Halkett Suffragan Bishop of Saskatchewan - Indigenous Ministry 1308 Fifth Avenue East Prince Albert SK S6V 2H7 CANADA *Tel:* + 1 306 763 2455 *Fax:* + 1 306 764 5172 *Web:* www.saskatchewan.anglican.org

Saskatoon-Rupert's Land The Rt Revd David M Irving Bishop of Saskatoon PO Box 1965 1403 9th Avenue North Saskatoon SK S7K 3S5 CANADA *Tel:* + 1 306 244 5651 *Fax:* + 1 306 933 4606 *Email:* bishopdavid@sasktel.net *Web:* www.saskatoon.anglican.org

The Arctic-Rupert's Land The Rt Revd David Parsons Bishop of the Diocese of the Arctic Box 190 Yellowknife NT X1A 2N2 CANADA *Tel:* + 1 867-873-5432 *Email:* arctic@arcticnet.org *Web:* www.arcticnet.org

The Arctic-Rupert's Land The Rt Revd Darren McCartney Suffragan Bishop of the Diocese of the Arctic PO Box 57 Iqaluit NU X0A 0H0 CANADA *Tel:* + 1 867-979-5595 *Email:* darren@arcticnet.org

Toronto-Ontario The Most Revd Colin Robert Johnson Metropolitan of Ontario and Archbishop of Toronto 135 Adelaide St East Toronto ON M5C 1L8 CANADA *Tel:* + 1 416 363 6021 *Fax:* + 1 416 363 7678 *Email:* cjohnson@toronto.anglican.ca *Web:* www.toronto.anglican.ca

Toronto-Ontario The Rt Revd Riscylla Shaw Suffragan Bishop of Toronto - Trent-Durham Area Suite 207 965 Dundas St. West Whitby ON L1P 1G8 CANADA *Tel:* + 1 905 668 1558 *Fax:* + 1 905 668 8216 *Email:* rshaw@toronto.anglican.ca *Web:* www. trentdurhamanglicans.ca

Toronto-Ontario The Rt Revd Peter Fenty Suffragan Bishop of Toronto - York - Simcoe 2174 King Road Unit 2 King City ON L7B 1L5 CANADA *Tel:* + 1 905 833 8327 *Fax:* + 1 905 833 8329 *Email:* ysimcoe@ toronto.anglican.ca

Toronto-Ontario The Rt Revd Jenny Andison Suffragan Bishop of Toronto - York-Credit Valley 135 Adelaide St East Toronto ON M5C 1L8 CANADA *Tel:* + 1 416 363 6021 *Fax:* + 1 416 363 7678 *Email:* jandison@toronto.anglican.ca

Toronto-Ontario The Rt Revd Kevin Robertson Suffragan Bishop of Toronto - York - Scarborough 135 Adelaide St East Toronto ON M5C 1L8 CANADA *Tel:* + 1 416 363 6021 *Email:* krobertson@ toronto.anglican.ca

Western Newfoundland-Canada The Rt Revd Percy David Coffin Bishop of Western Newfoundland 25 Main Street Corner Brookl NF A2H 1C2 CANADA *Tel:* + 1 709 639 8712 *Email:* dsown@nf.aibn.com *Web:* www.westernnewfoundland.anglican.org/

Yukon-Yukon The Rt Revd Larry David Robertson Bishop of Yukon Box 31136 Whitehorse YK Y1A 5P7 CANADA *Tel:* + 1 867 667 7746 *Fax:* + 1 867 667 6125 *Email:* synodoffice@klondiker.com *Web:* www.yukon.anglican.org

THE CHURCH OF THE PROVINCE OF CENTRAL AFRICA

Acting Provincial Secretary **Eastern Zambia** The Rt Revd William Mchombo Bishop of Eastern Zambia & PO Box 510154 Chipata ZAMBIA *Tel:* + 260 216 221 294 *Email:* dioeastzm@zamnet.zm

Provincial Treasurer Mr Evans Mwewa CPCA P.O. Box 22317 Kitwe ZAMBIA *Tel:* + 260 267 351 081 *Fax:* + 260 267 351 668

Botswana The Rt Revd Metlhayotlhe Rawlings Belemi Bishop of Botswana PO Box 769 Gaaborone BOTSWANA *Tel:* + 267 (0)3 953 779 *Fax:* + 267 (0)3 913 015 *Email:* angli_diocese@info.bw *Web:* www. diobot.bw

Central Zambia The Rt Revd Derek Gary Kamukwamba Bishop of Central Zambia PO Box 70172 Ndola ZAMBIA *Tel:* + 260 (0)2 612 431 *Fax:* + 260 (0)2 615 954 *Email:* adcznla@zamnet.zm

Central Zimbabwe The Rt Revd Ishmael Mukuwanda Bishop of Central Zimbabwe PO Box 25 Gweru ZIMBABWE *Tel:* + 263 (0)5 421 030 *Fax:* + 263 (0)5 421 097 *Email:* diocent@telconet.co.zw

Harare The Rt Revd Chad Nicholas Gandiya Bishop of Harare Diocese of Harare CPCA 2nd Floor Paget House 87 Kwame Nkurumah Avenue Harare ZIMBABWE *Tel:* + 263 4 702 253 *Fax:* + 263 4 300 419 *Web:* www.hreanglicancpca.org.zw

Lake Malawi The Rt Revd Francis Kaulanda Bishop of Lake Malawi PO Box 30349 Lilongwe 3 MALAWI *Tel:* + 265 1 797 858 *Fax:* + 265 1 797 548

Luapula The Rt Revd Robert Mumbi Bishop of Luapula PO Box 710 210 Mansa ZAMBIA *Tel:* + 260 (0)2 821 680 *Email:* diopula@zamtel.zm

Lusaka The Rt Revd David Njovu Bishop of Lusaka Bishop's Lodge PO Box 30183 Lusaka ZAMBIA *Tel:* + 260 (0)1 264 515 *Fax:* + 260 (0)1 262 379

Manicaland The Rt Revd Erick Ruwona Bishop of Manicaland 113 Herbert Chitepo Street Mutare ZIMBABWE *Tel:* + 263 20 68418 *Email:* ruwonaerick@gmail.com

Masvingo The Rt Revd Godfrey Tawonezwi Bishop of Masvingo PO Box 1421 Masvingo ZIMBABWE *Tel:* + 263 39 362 536 *Email:* bishopgodfreytawonezvi@ gmail.com *Web:* www.masvingo.anglican.org/

Matabeleland The Rt Revd Cleophas Lunga Bishop of Matabeleland PO Box 2422 Bulawayo ZIMBABWE *Tel:* + 263 09 613 70 *Fax:* + 263 09 683 53 *Email:* clunga@aol.com

Northern Malawi The Rt Revd Fanuel Emmanuel Magangani Bishop of Northern Malawi PO Box 120 Mzuzu MALAWI *Tel:* + 265 (0) 1312 858 *Email:* anglicandnm@gmail.com *Web:* www. nmalawianglican.org

Northern Zambia The Most Revd Albert Chama Archbishop of Central Africa & Bishop of Northern Zambia PO Box 20798 Kitwe ZAMBIA *Tel:* + 260 2 223 264 *Fax:* + 260 2 224 778 *Email:* chama_albert@ yahoo.ca

Southern Malawi The Rt Revd Alinafe Kalemba Bishop of Southern Malawi PO Box 30220 Chichiri Blantyre 3 MALAWI *Tel:* + 265 1 841 218 *Fax:* + 265 1 841 235 *Email:* dean@sdnp.org.mw

Upper Shire The Rt Revd Brighton Vitta Malasa Bishop of Upper Shire Bishop's House Private Bag 1 Chilema Zomba MALAWI *Email:* malasab@ yahoo.co.uk *Web:* www.malawipartnership.co.uk/ uppershire/

IGLESIA ANGLICANA DE LA REGION CENTRAL DE AMERICA

Provincial Treasurer Mr Harold Charles Apartado R Balboa REPUBLIC OF PANAMA *Tel:* + 507 262 2052 *Email:* iarcahch@sinfo.net

Costa Rica The Rt Revd Hector Monterroso Gonzalez Bishop of Costa Rica & Provincial Secretary Apartado 2773-1000 San José COSTA

RICA *Tel:* + 506 22250209 *Fax:* + 506 22538331 *Email:* iarca@me.com

El Salvador The Rt Revd Juan David Alvarado Melgar Bishop of El Salvador 47 Avenida Sur 723 Col Flor Blanca Apt Postal (01) San Salvador 274 EL SALVADOR *Tel:* + 503 2 223 2252 *Email:* anglican. es@gmail.com

Guatemala The Most Revd Armando R Guerra Soria Bishop of Guatemala Apartado 58a Avenida La Castellana 40-06 Guatemala City Zona 8 GUATEMALA *Tel:* + 502 (0)2 472 0852 *Fax:* + 502 (0)2 472 0764 *Email:* agepiscopal@yahoo.com

Guatemala The Revd Silvestre Romero Bishop Coadjutor elect of Guatemala Apartado 58a Avenida La Castellana 40-06 Guatemala City Zona 8 Guatemala *Tel:* + 502 (0)2 472 0852 *Email:* agepiscopal@yahoo.com

Nicaragua The Most Revd Sturdie Downs Primate of IARCA & Bishop of Nicaragua Apartado 1207 Managua NICARAGUA *Tel:* + 505 22225174 *Fax:* + 505 22545248 *Email:* secretaria_diocesana@hotmail. com

Panama The Rt Revd Julio Murray Bishop of Panama Box R Balboa REPUBLIC OF PANAMA *Tel:* + 507 212 0062 *Email:* bpmurray@hotmail.com

PROVINCE DE L'EGLISE ANGLICANE DU CONGO

Provincial Secretary The Ven Anthonio Kibwela The Province of the Anglican Church of Congo 11 AV Basalakala Commune de Kalamu Kinshasa DR CONGO *Tel:* + 243 995412138 *Email:* anthoniokibwela@gmail.com

Provincial Treasurer Mr Alain Batondela PO Box 16482 Kinshasa 1 DR CONGO

Aru The Rt Revd Georges Titre Ande Bishop of Aru PO Box 226 Arua UGANDA *Tel:* + 243 8 1039 3071 *Email:* revdande@yahoo.co.uk

Boga The Rt Revd Mugenyi William Bahemuka Bishop of Boga Awaiting Details *Email:* mugenywiliam@yahoo.com

Bukavu The Rt Revd Sylvestre Bahati Bishop of Bukavu Evache Anglican Av. Pagni No2 Q/ Nyalukemba, C/ Ibanda Bukavu DR CONGO *Email:* bahati_bali@yahoo.fr

Kamango The Rt Revd Sabiti Tibafa Daniel Bishop of Kamango c/o The Congo Church Liaison Office PO Box 25586 Kampala UGANDA *Tel:* + 243 99 779 1013 *Email:* revsabiti@yahoo.fr

Kasai The Rt Revd Marcel Kapinga Bishop of Kasai No. 05, Avenue Makenga District Bonzola Common Dibindi Mbuji-Mayi Kasai Oriental DR CONGO *Tel:* + 243 8160 61423 *Email:* anglicanekasai2@ gmail.com

Katanga The Rt Revd Bertin Subi Bishop of Katanga C/O U.M.M PO Box 22037 Kitwe ZAMBIA *Tel:* + 342 97 047 173 *Email:* peacbertinsubi@yahoo.fr *Web:* www.katanga.anglican.org

Kindu The Most Revd Zacharie Masimango Katanda Archbishop of the Congo & Bishop of Kindu Av. Penemisenga No 4, C/ Kasuku Kindu Maniema RWANDA *Email:* angkindu@yahoo.fr

Kinshasa The Rt Revd Achille Mutshindu Bishop of Kinshasa PO Box 16482 Kinshasa 1 DR CONGO

Kisangani The Rt Revd Lambert F Botolome Bishop of Kisangani Bowane Street, No 10 Quartier des Musiciens C/ Makiso BP 861 Kisangani DR CONGO

Nord Kivu The Rt Revd Muhindo Isesomo Bishop of Nord Kivu CAZ Butembo PO Box 506 Bwera-Kasese UGANDA *Fax:* + 871 166 1121

Nord Kivu The Rt Revd Enoch WM Kayeeye Assistant Bishop of Nord Kivu C/O Po Box 506 Bwera/Kasese UGANDA *Tel:* + 243 09 9414 8579 *Email:* bpkayeeye@hotmail.com

THE CHURCH OF ENGLAND

Provincial Secretary Mr William Nye Church House Great Smith Street London SW1P 3NZ UK *Tel:* + 44 (0)207 898 1360 *Fax:* + 44 (0)207 898 1369 *Email:* william.nye@churchofengland.org

Bath & Wells-Canterbury The Rt Revd Peter Hancock Bishop of Bath & Wells The Palace Wells Somerset BA5 2PD ENGLAND *Tel:* + 44 (0)1749 672 341 *Fax:* + 44 (0)1749 679 355 *Email:* bishop@ bathwells.anglican.org *Web:* www.bathwells. anglican.org

Bath & Wells- Canterbury The Rt Revd Ruth Worsley Suffragan Bishop of Taunton The Palace Wells Somerset BA5 2PD ENGLAND *Tel:* + 44 (0)1749 672 341 *Fax:* + 44 (0)1749 679 355 *Email:* bishop.taunton@bathwells.anglican.org *Web:* www. bathandwells.org.uk

Birmingham-Canterbury The Rt Revd David Andrew Urquhart Bishop of Birmingham Birmingham Diocese Office 1 Colmore Row Birmingham B3 2BJ ENGLAND *Tel:* + 44 (0)121 427 1163 *Fax:* + 44 (0)121 426 1322 *Email:* bishop@ birmingham.anglican.org *Web:* www.birmingham. anglican.org

Birmingham-Canterbury The Rt Revd Anne Elizabeth Hollinghurst Suffragan Bishop of Birmingham - Aston Birmingham Diocese Office 1 Colmore Row Birmingham B3 2BJ ENGLAND *Tel:* + 44 (0)121 426 0400 *Fax:* + 44 (0)121 428 1114 *Email:* bishopofaston@birmingham.anglican.org *Web:* www.birmingham.anglican.org

Blackburn-York The Rt Revd Julian Tudor Henderson Bishop of Blackburn Bishop's House Ribchester Road Clayton-le-Dale Blackburn BB1

9EF ENGLAND *Tel:* + 44 (0)1254 248 234 *Fax:* + 44 (0)1254 246 668 *Email:* bishop@bishopofblackburn. org.uk *Web:* www.blackburn.anglican.org

Blackburn-York The Rt Revd Philip North Suffragan Bishop of Blackburn - Burnley Church House Cathedral close Blackburn BB1 5AA ENGLAND *Tel:* + 44 01254 503087 *Email:* bishop.burnley@ blackburn.anglican.org

Blackburn-York The Rt Revd Geoffrey Seagrave Pearson Suffragan Bishop Lancaster The Vicarage Whinney Brow Lane Shireshead, Forton Preston PR3 0AE ENGLAND *Tel:* + 44 (0)1524 799 900 *Fax:* + 44 (0)1524 799 901 *Email:* bishop.lancaster@ ukonline.co.uk

Bristol-Canterbury The Rt Revd Michael Arthur Hill Bishop of Bristol 58a High Street Winterbourne Bristol BS36 1JQ ENGLAND *Tel:* + 44 (0)1454 777 728 *Fax:* + 44 (0)1454 777 814 *Email:* bishop@ bristoldiocese.org *Web:* www.bristol.anglican.org

Bristol-Canterbury The Rt Revd Lee Stephen Rayfield Bishop of Swindon Mark House Field Rise Swindon SN1 4HP England *Tel:* + 44 (0)1793 538 654 *Fax:* + 44 (0)1793 525 181 *Email:* bishop. swindon@bristoldiocese.org

Canterbury-Canterbury The Most Revd and Rt Hon Justin Welby Archbishop of Canterbury Lambeth Palace London SE1 7JU United Kingdom *Tel:* + 44 (0)20 7898 1238 *Fax:* + 44 (0)20 7261 9836 *Email:* pa.archbishop@lambethpalace.org.uk *Web:* www.archbishopofcanterbury.org/

Canterbury-Canterbury The Rt Revd Roderick Charles Howell H Thomas Suffragan Bishop of Maidstone Bishop's House Pett Lane Charing Ashford TN27 0DL ENGLAND *Tel:* + 44 (0)1233 712 950 *Fax:* + 44 (0)1233 713 543 *Email:* bishop@ bishmaid.org *Web:* www.bishopofmaidstone.org

Canterbury-Canterbury The Rt Revd Trevor Willmott Bishop in Canterbury and Bishop of Dover The Old Palace The Precincts Canterbury CT1 2EE ENGLAND *Tel:* + 44 (0)1227 459 382 *Fax:* + 44 (0)1227 784 985 *Email:* bishop@bishcant.org

Canterbury-Canterbury The Rt Revd Norman N Banks Suffragan Bishop of Richborough Parkside House Abbey Mill Lane St Albans AL3 4HE ENGLAND *Tel:* + 44 (0)1727 836 358 *Email:* bishop@richborough.org.uk

Canterbury-Canterbury The Rt Revd Jonathan Goodall Suffragan Bishop of Ebbsfleet Hill House The Mount Caversham Reading RG4 7RE UK *Tel:* + 44 (0)1865 288 030 *Email:* bishop@ebbsfleet.org.uk

Carlisle-York The Rt Revd James Scobie WS Newcome Bishop of Carlisle Bishop's House Ambleside Road Keswick CA12 4DD ENGLAND *Tel:* + 44 (0)1768 773 430 *Email:* bishop.carlisle@ carlislediocese.org.uk *Web:* www.carlislediocese.org. uk

Carlisle-York The Rt Revd Robert Freeman Suffragan Bishop of Penrith Holm Croft 13 Castle Road Kendal LA9 7AU ENGLAND *Tel:* + 44 (0)1539 727 836 *Email:* bishop.penrith@carlislediocese.org.uk

Chelmsford-Canterbury The Rt Revd Stephen Geoffrey Cottrell Bishop of Chelmsford Bishopscourt Main Road Margretting Ingatestone Essex CM4 0HD ENGLAND *Tel:* + 44 (0)1277 352 001 *Fax:* + 44 (0)1277 355 374 *Email:* bishopscourt@chelmsford. anglican.org *Web:* www.chelmsford.anglican.org

Chelmsford-Canterbury The Rt Revd Peter Hill Bishop of Barking Barking Lodge 35A Verulam Avenue Walthamstow London E17 8ES ENGLAND *Tel:* + 44 (0)20 8509 7377 *Fax:* + 44 (0)20 8514 6049 *Email:* b.barking@chelmsford.anglican.org

Chelmsford-Canterbury The Rt Revd Anthony Brett Morris Bishop of Colchester 1 Fitzwalter Road Colchester CO3 3SS ENGLAND *Tel:* + 44 (0)1206 576 648 *Fax:* + 44 (0)1206 763 868 *Email:* b.colchester@chelmsford.anglican.org *Web:* www. chelmsford.anglican.org

Chelmsford-Canterbury Vacant Bishop elect of Bradwell Bishop's House Orsett Road Hordon-on-the-Hill Stanford-le-Hope SS17 8NS ENGLAND *Tel:* + 44 (0)1375 673 806 *Fax:* + 44 (0)1375 674 222 *Email:* b.bradwell@chelmsford.anglican.org

Chester-York The Rt Revd Peter Robert Forster Bishop of Chester Bishop's House Abbey Square Chester CH1 2JD ENGLAND *Tel:* + 44 (0)1244 350 864 *Fax:* + 44 (0)1244 314 187 *Email:* bpchester@ chester.anglican.org *Web:* www.chester.anglican.org/

Chester-York The Rt Revd Keith Sinclair Bishop of Birkenhead Bishops Lodge 67 Bidston Road Prenton Wirral CH43 6TR ENGLAND *Tel:* + 44 (0)151 652 2741 *Fax:* + 44 (0)151 651 2330 *Email:* bpbirkenhead@chester.anglican.org

Chester-York The Rt Revd Libby Lane Suffragan Bishop of Chester - Stockport Bishop's Lodge Back Lane Dunham Town Altrincham WA14 4SG ENGLAND *Tel:* + 44 (0)161 928 5611 *Fax:* + 44 (0)161 929 0692 *Email:* bpstockport@chester. anglican.org

Chichester-Canterbury The Rt Revd Martin C Warner Bishop of Chichester The Palace Canon Lane Chichester West Sussex PO19 1PY ENGLAND *Tel:* + 44 (0)1243 782 161 *Fax:* + 44 (0)1243 531 332 *Email:* bishop@chichester.anglian.org *Web:* www. chichester.anglican.org

Chichester-Canterbury The Rt Revd Mark Sowerby Suffragan Bishop of Horsham Bishop's House 21 Guildford Road Horsham Sussex RH12 1LU ENGLAND *Tel:* + 44 (0)1403 211 139 *Fax:* + 44 (0)1403 217 349 *Email:* bishop.horsham@chichester. anglican.org

Chichester-Canterbury The Revd Richard Charles Jackson Suffragan Bishop of Lewes The Palace

Canon Lane Chichester West Sussex PO19 1PY ENGLAND

Coventry-Canterbury The Rt Revd Christopher J Cocksworth Bishop of Coventry Bishop's House 23 Davenport Road Coventry CV5 6PW ENGLAND *Tel:* + 44 (0)2476 672 244 *Fax:* + 44 (0)24 76 713 271 *Email:* bishop@bishop-coventry.org *Web:* www.dioceseofcoventry.org

Coventry-Canterbury The Rt Revd John RA Stroyan Suffragan Bishop of Warwick Warwick House School Hill Offchurch Leamington Spa CV33 9AL UK *Tel:* + 44 (0)1926 427465 *Email:* Bishop.Warwick@covcofe.org

Derby-Canterbury The Rt Revd Alastair Redfern Bishop of Derby The Bishop's House 6 King Street Duffield Belper DE56 4EU ENGLAND *Tel:* + 44 (0)1332 840 132 *Fax:* + 44 (0)1332 842 743 *Email:* pa@bishopofderby.org *Web:* www.derby.anglican.org/

Derby-Canterbury The Rt Revd Janet Elizabeth McFarlane Suffragan Bishop of Derby - Repton Repton House Lea Matlock Derby DE4 5JP ENGLAND *Tel:* + 44 (0)1629 534 644 *Fax:* + 44 (0)1629 534 003 *Email:* bishop@repton.free-online.co.uk

Diocese in Europe The Rt Revd Robert Innes Bishop of Gibraltar in Europe 47 rue Capitaine Crespel - boite 49 Brussels 1050 Belgium *Tel:* + 32 2 213 7480 *Email:* robert.innes@churchofengland.org *Web:* www.europe.anglican.org

Diocese in Europe The Rt Revd David Hamid Suffragan Bishop of the Diocese in Europe 14 Tufton Street Westminster London SW1P 3QZ ENGLAND *Tel:* + 44 (0)20 7898 1160 *Fax:* + 44 (0)20 7898 1166 *Email:* david.hamid@churchofengland.org

Durham-York The Rt Revd Paul R Butler Bishop elect of Durham Auckland Castle Bishop Auckland Durham DL14 7NR ENGLAND *Tel:* + 44 (0)1388 602 576 *Fax:* + 44 (0)1388 605 264 *Email:* bishop.of.durham@durham.anglican.org *Web:* www.durham.anglican.org

Durham-York The Rt Revd Mark Watts Bryant Suffragan Bishop of Jarrow Bishop's House Ivy Lane Low Fell Gateshead NE9 6QD ENGLAND *Tel:* + 44 (0)191 491 0917 *Fax:* + 44 (0)191 491 5116 *Email:* bishop.of.jarrow@durham.anglican.org *Web:* www.durham.anglican.org

Ely-Canterbury The Rt Revd Stephen David Conway Bishop of Ely The Bishop's House Ely Cambs CB7 4DW ENGLAND *Tel:* + 44 (0)1353 662 749 *Fax:* + 44 (0)1353 669 477 *Email:* bishop@ely.anglican.org *Web:* www.ely.anglican.org

Ely-Canterbury The Rt Revd David Thomson Suffragan Bishop of Huntingdon 14 Lynn Road Ely CB6 1DA ENGLAND *Tel:* + 44 (0)1353 662 137 *Fax:* + 44 (0)1353 662 137 *Email:* bishop.huntingdon@ely.anglican.org

Exeter-Canterbury The Rt Revd Robert Atwell Bishop of Exeter The Palace Exeter EX1 1HY ENGLAND *Tel:* + 44 (0)1392 272 362 *Fax:* + 44 (0)1392 430 923 *Email:* sarah.johnson@exeter.anglican.org *Web:* www.exeter.anglican.org

Exeter-Canterbury The Rt Revd Sarah Mullally Suffragan Bishop of Crediton 32 The Avenue Tiverton Devon EX16 4HW ENGLAND *Tel:* + 44 (0)1884 250 002 *Fax:* + 44 (0)1884 257 454 *Email:* Sarah.mullally@exeter.anglican.org

Exeter-Canterbury The Rt Revd Nick McKinnel Suffragan Bishop of Plymouth 31 Riverside Walk Tamerton Foliot Plymouth PL5 4AQ ENGLAND *Tel:* + 44 (0)1752 769 836 *Fax:* + 44 (0)1752 769 818 *Email:* bishop.of.plymouth@exeter.anglican.org

Gloucester-Canterbury The Rt Revd Rachel Treweek Bishop of Gloucester Church House 2 College Green Gloucester GL1 2LR ENGLAND *Tel:* + 44 (0)1452 835 512 *Email:* bgloucester@glosdioc.org.uk *Web:* www.gloucester.anglican.org

Gloucester-Canterbury The Rt Revd Robert Wilfrid WS Springett Suffragan Bishop of Gloucester-Tewkesbury Bishop's House Church Road Staverton Gloucester GL51 0TW ENGLAND *Tel:* + 44 (0)1242 680 188 *Email:* btewkesbury@glosdioc.org.uk *Web:* www.gloucester.anglican.org

Guildford-Canterbury The Rt Revd Andrew John Watson Bishop of Guildford Willow Grange Woking Road Guildford Surrey GU4 7QS ENGLAND *Tel:* + 44 01483 590 500 *Fax:* + 44 01483 590 501 *Email:* bishop.guildford@cofeguildford.org.uk *Web:* www.cofeguildford.org.uk

Guildford-Canterbury The Rt Revd Jo Bailey Wells Suffragan Bishop of Guildford-Dorking Dayspring 13 Pilgrim's Way Guildford GU4 8AD ENGLAND *Tel:* + 44 01483 570829 *Email:* muriel.mulvany@cofeguildford.org.uk

Hereford-Canterbury The Rt Revd Richard MC Frith Bishop of Hereford Bishop's House The Palace Hereford HR4 9BN ENGLAND *Tel:* + 44 (0)1432 373 300 *Email:* diooffice@hereford.anglican.org

Hereford-Canterbury The Rt Revd Alistair James Magowan Suffragan Bishop of Ludlow Bishops' House Corvedale Road Cavern Arms Shropshire SY7 9BT ENGLAND *Tel:* + 44 (0)1588 673 571 *Fax:* + 44 (0)1588 673 571 *Email:* bishopalistair@btinternet.com

Leeds-York The Rt Revd Nicholas Baines Bishop of Leeds St Mary's Street Leeds West Yorkshire LS9 7DP ENGLAND *Tel:* + 44 01274 545414 *Fax:* + 44 01274 544831 *Email:* bishop.nick@leeds.anglican.org *Web:* www.leeds.anglican.org

Leeds-York The Rt Revd Anthony W Robinson Area Bishop of Wakefield 181A Manygates Lane Sandal Wakefield WF2 7DR ENGLAND *Tel:* + 44 (0)1924 250 781 *Fax:* + 44 (0)1924 240 490 *Email:* bishop.tony@leeds.anglican.org

Leeds-York The Rt Revd James H Bell Area Bishop of Ripon Thistledown Exelby Bedale DL8 2HD ENGLAND *Tel:* + 44 (0)1677 423 525 *Fax:* + 44 (0)1677 427 515 *Email:* bishop.james@leeds. anglican.org

Leeds-York The Rt Revd Paul Slater Area Bishop of Richmond St Mary's Street Leeds West Yorkshire LS9 7DP ENGLAND *Tel:* + 44 (0)113 284 4304 *Email:* bishop.paul@leeds.anglican.org

Leeds-York The Rt Revd Jonathan Gibbs Area Bishop of Huddersfield Stone Royd 9 Valley Head Huddersfield HD2 2DH ENGLAND *Tel:* + 44 (0)1484 471801 *Email:* bishop.jonathan@leeds. anglican.org

Leeds-York The Rt Revd Toby Howarth Area Bishop of Bradford 47 Kirkgate Shipley BD18 3EH ENGLAND *Email:* bishop.toby@leeds.anglican.org

Leicester-Canterbury The Rt Revd Martyn James Snow Bishop of Leicester Bishop's Lodge 10 Springfield Road Leicester LE2 3BD ENGLAND *Tel:* + 44 (0)116 270 8985 *Email:* leicester@leccofe.org *Web:* www.leicester.anglican.org

Leicester-Canterbury The Revd Canon Guli Francis-Dehqani Bishop elect of Loughborough Bishop's Lodge 10 Springfield Road Leicester LE2 3BD ENGLAND *Web:* www.leicester.anglican.org

Leicester-Canterbury The Rt Revd Christopher John Boyle Assistant Bishop in the Diocese of Leicester Church House St Martin's East Leicester LE1 5FX ENGLAND *Tel:* + 44 (0) 116 248 7411 *Email:* bishop.boyle@leccofe.org

Lichfield-Canterbury The Rt Revd Michael Ipgrave Bishop of Lichfield The Bishop's House 22 The Close Lichfield WS13 7LG ENGLAND *Tel:* + 44 (0)1543 306 000 *Fax:* + 44 (0)1543 306 009 *Email:* bishop. lichfield@lichfield.anglican.org *Web:* www.lichfield. anglican.org

Lichfield-Canterbury The Rt Revd Mark James Rylands Bishop of Shrewsbury Athlone House 68 London Road Shrewsbury SYZ 6PG ENGLAND *Tel:* + 44 (0)1743 235 867 *Fax:* + 44 (0)1743 243 296 *Email:* bishop.shrewsbury@lichfield.anglican.org *Web:* www.lichfield.anglican.org

Lichfield-Canterbury The Rt Revd Geoffrey Peter Annas Suffragan Bishop of Stafford Ash Garth 6 Broughton Crescent Barlaston Stoke on Trent ST12 9DD ENGLAND *Tel:* + 44 (0)1782 373 308 *Fax:* + 44 01782 373 705 *Email:* bishop.stafford@lichfield. anglican.org

Lichfield-Canterbury The Rt Revd Clive Gregory Bishop of Wolverhampton 61 Richmond Road Merridale Wolverhampton WV3 9JH ENGLAND *Tel:* + 44 (0)1902 824 503 *Fax:* + 44 (0)1902 824 504 *Email:* bishop.wolverhampton@lichfield.anglican. org

Lincoln-Canterbury The Rt Revd Christopher Lowson Bishop of Lincoln The Old Palace Minster Yard Lincoln LN2 1PU ENGLAND *Tel:* + 44 (0)1522 504 090 *Fax:* + 44 (0)1522 511 095 *Email:* bishop. lincoln@lincoln.anglican.org *Web:* www.lincoln. anglican,org

Lincoln-Canterbury The Rt Revd David Eric Court Suffragan Bishop of Grimsby Bishop's House Church Lane Irby Upon Humber Grimsby DN37 7JR ENGLAND *Tel:* + 44 (0)1472 371 715 *Fax:* + 44 (0)1472 371 716 *Email:* bishop.grimsby@lincoln. anglican.org

Lincoln-Canterbury The Rt Revd Nicholas Alan Chamberlain Suffragan Bishop of Grantham Saxonwell Vicarage Church Street Long Bennington Newark NG23 5ES ENGLAND *Tel:* + 44 (0)1400 283 344 *Fax:* + 44 (0)1400 283 321 *Email:* bishop. grantham@lincoln.anglican.org

Liverpool-York The Rt Revd Paul Bayes Bishop of Liverpool Bishop's Lodge Woolton Park Liverpool L25 6DT ENGLAND *Tel:* + 44 (0)151 421 0831 *Fax:* + 44 (0)151 428 3055 *Email:* Bishopslodge@ liverpool.anglican.org *Web:* www.liverpool.anglican. org

Liverpool-York The Rt Revd Richard Finn Blackburn Suffragan Bishop of Warrington St James House 20 St James Road Liverpool L1 7BY ENGLAND *Tel:* + 44 (0)151 705 2140 *Fax:* + 44 (0)151 709 2885 *Email:* bishopofwarrington@liverpool.anglican.org

London-Canterbury The Rt Revd & Rt Hon Richard John Carew Chartres Bishop of London The Old Deanery Dean's Court London EC4V 5AA ENGLAND *Tel:* + 44 (0)20 7248 6233 *Fax:* + 44 (0)20 7248 9721 *Email:* bishop@londin.clara.co.uk *Web:* www.london.anglican.org

London-Canterbury The Rt Revd Adrian Newman Suffragan Bishop of London - Stepney 63 Coborn Road Bow London Kent E3 2DB ENGLAND *Tel:* + 44 (0)1634 843 366 *Fax:* + 44 (0)1634 401 410 *Email:* bishop.stepney@london.anglican.org

London-Canterbury The Rt Revd Peter Allan Broadbent Bishop of Willesden 173 Willesden Lane London NW6 7YN ENGLAND *Tel:* + 44 (0)20 8451 0189 *Fax:* + 44 (0)20 8451 4606 *Email:* bishopwillesden.pa@btinternet.com

London-Canterbury The Rt Revd Graham Tomlin Suffragan Bishop of London - Kensington Dial House Riverside Twickenham Middlesex TW1 3DT ENGLAND *Tel:* + 44 (0)208 8892 7781 *Fax:* + 44 (0)208 8891 3969 *Email:* bishop.kensington@ london.anglican.org

London-Canterbury The Rt Revd Robert Wickham Suffragan Bishop of London - Edmonton 27 Thurlow Road Hampstead London NW3 5PP ENGLAND *Tel:* + 44 (0)20 7435 5890 *Fax:* + 44 (0)20 7435 6049 *Email:* bishop.edmonton@london.anglican.org

London-Canterbury The Rt Revd Ric Thorpe Suffragan Bishop of London - Islington Bishop of Islington's Office St Edmund the King Lombard Street London EC3V 9EA ENGLAND *Tel:* + 44 020 3837 5275 *Email:* bishop.islington@london.anglican. org

London-Canterbury The Rt Revd Jonathan Mark Richard Baker Suffragan Bishop of Fulham The Old Deanery Dean's Court London EC4V 5AA ENGLAND *Tel:* + 44 (0)20 7932 1130 *Email:* bishop. fulham@london.anglican.org

Manchester-York The Rt Revd David S Walker Bishop of Manchester Bishopscourt Bury New Road Salford Manchester M7 4LE ENGLAND *Tel:* + 44 (0)161 792 2096 *Fax:* + 44 (0)161 792 6826 *Email:* bishop@bishopscourt.manchester.anglican.org *Web:* www.manchester.anglican.org

Manchester-York The Rt Revd Mark Davies Suffragan Bishop of Middleton The Hollies Manchester Road Rochdale OL11 3QY ENGLAND *Tel:* + 44 (0)1706 358 550 *Fax:* + 44 (0)1706 354 851 *Email:* bishopmark@manchester.anglican.org

Manchester-York The Rt Revd Mark David Ashcroft Suffragan Bishop of Bolton Bishop's Lodge Walkden Road Worsley Manchester M28 2WH ENGLAND *Tel:* + 44 (0)161 790 8289 *Fax:* + 44 (0)161 703 9157 *Email:* bishopofbolton@manchester.anglican.org *Web:* www.manchester.anglican.org

Newcastle-York The Rt Revd Christine Hardman Bishop of Newcastle Bishop's House 29 Moor Road South Gosforth Newcastle upon Tyne NE3 1PA ENGLAND *Tel:* + 44 (0)191 285 2220 *Fax:* + 44 (0)191 284 6933 *Email:* bishop@newcastle.anglican. org *Web:* www.newcastle.anglican.org

Newcastle-York The Rt Revd Mark Tanner Suffragan Bishop of Berwick Bishop's House 29 Moor Road South Gosforth Newcastle upon Tyne NE3 1PA ENGLAND*Email:* bishopofberwick@newcastle. anglican.org

Norwich-Canterbury The Rt Revd Graham James Bishop of Norwich Bishop's House Norwich Norfolk NR3 1SB ENGLAND *Tel:* + 44 (0)1603 629 001 *Fax:* + 44 (0)1603 761 613 *Email:* bishop@norwich. anglican.org *Web:* www.norwich.anglican.org

Norwich-Canterbury The Rt Revd Jonathan Meyrick Suffragan Bishop of Lynn The Old Vicarage Castle Acre King's Lynn Norfolk PE32 2AA ENGLAND *Tel:* + 44 (0)1760 755 553 *Fax:* + 44 (0)1760 755 085 *Email:* bishop.lynn@norwich. anglican.org

Norwich-Canterbury The Rt Revd Alan Peter Winton Suffragan Bishop of Thetford The Red House 53 Norwich Street Stoke Holy Cross Norwich Norfolk NR14 8AB ENGLAND *Tel:* + 44 (0)1508 491 014 *Fax:* + 44 (0)1508 492 105 *Email:* bishop. thetford@norwich.anglican.org

Oxford-Canterbury The Rt Revd Steven Croft Bishop of Oxford Diocesan Church House North Hinksey Oxford OX2 0NB ENGLAND *Tel:* + 44 (0)1865 208 222 *Fax:* + 44 (0)1865 790 470 *Email:* bishopoxon@dch.oxford.anglican.org *Web:* www. oxford.anglican.org

Oxford-Canterbury The Rt Revd Alan Thomas Lawrence Wilson Suffragan Bishop of Buckingham Sheridan Grimms Hill Great Missenden Bucks HP16 9BD ENGLAND *Tel:* + 44 (0)1494 862 173 *Fax:* + 44 (0)1494 890 508 *Email:* bishopbucks@ oxford.anglican.org

Oxford-Canterbury The Rt Revd Colin William Fletcher Suffragan Bishop of Dorchester Arran House Sandy Lane Yarnton Kidlington OX5 1PB ENGLAND *Tel:* + 44 (0)1865 208 218 *Fax:* + 44 (0)1865 379 890 *Email:* bishopdorchester@oxford. anglican.org

Oxford-Canterbury The Rt Revd Andrew Proud Suffragan Bishop of Reading Bishop's House Tidmarsh Lane Reading Berks RG8 8HA ENGLAND *Tel:* + 44 (0)118 984 1216 *Fax:* + 44 (0)118 984 1218 *Email:* bishopreading@oxford.anglican.org

Peterborough-Canterbury The Rt Revd Donald Spargo Allister Bishop of Peterborough Bishop's Lodging The Palace Peterborough Cambs PE1 1YA ENGLAND *Tel:* + 44 (0)1733 562 492 *Fax:* + 44 (0)1733 890 077 *Email:* bishop@peterborough-diocese.org.uk *Web:* www.peterborough-diocese. org.uk

Peterborough-Canterbury The Rt Revd John E Holbrook Suffragan Bishop of Brixworth Orchard Acre 11 North Street Mears Ashby Northampton NN6 0DW ENGLAND *Tel:* + 44 (0)1733 562 492 *Email:* bishop.brixworth@peterborough-diocese. org.uk

Portsmouth-Canterbury The Rt Revd Christopher RJ Foster Bishop of Portsmouth Bishopsgrove 26 Osborn Road Fareham Hants PO16 7DQ ENGLAND *Tel:* + 44 (0)1329 280 247 *Fax:* + 44 (0)1329 231 538 *Email:* bishports@portsmouth. anglican.org *Web:* www.portsmouth.anglican.org/

Rochester-Canterbury The Rt Revd James H Langstaff Bishop of Rochester Bishopscourt 24 St Margaret's Street Rochester K entME1 1TS ENGLAND *Tel:* + 44 (0)1634 842 721 *Fax:* + 44 (0)1634 831 136 *Email:* bishop.rochester@rochester. anglican.org *Web:* www.rochester.anglican.org/

Rochester-Canterbury Vacant Suffragan bishop elect of Rochester - Tonbridge Bishop's Lodge 48 St Botolph's Road Sevenoaks TN13 3AG ENGLAND *Tel:* + 44 (0)1732 456 070 *Fax:* + 44 (0)1732 741 449 *Email:* bishop.tonbridge@rochester.anglican.org

Salisbury-Canterbury The Rt Revd Nicholas R Holtam Bishop of Salisbury South Canonry 71 The Close Salisbury Wiltshire SP1 2ER ENGLAND *Tel:* +

44 (0)1722 334 031 *Fax:* + 44 (0)1722 413 112 *Email:* bishop.salisbury@salisbury.anglican.org *Web:* www.salisbury.anglican.org

Salisbury-Canterbury The Rt Revd Karen Gorham Suffragan Bishop of Sherborne The Sherborne Area Office St Nicholas' Church Centre 30 Wareham Road Corfe Mullen Dorset BH21 3LE ENGLAND *Tel:* + 44 (0)1202 691 418 *Email:* gsherborne@salisbury. anglican.org *Web:* www.salisbury.anglican.org

Salisbury-Canterbury The Rt Revd Edward Condry Suffragan Bishop of Ramsbury Diocesan Office Church House Crane Street Salisbury Wilts SP1 2QB ENGLAND *Tel:* + 44 (0)1722 438 662 *Fax:* + 44 (0)1380 848 247 *Email:* ramsbury.office@salisbury. anglican.org

Sheffield-York The Rt Revd Pete Wilcox Bishop of Sheffield Bishopscroft Snaithing Lane Sheffield S10 3LG ENGLAND *Tel:* + 44 (0)114 230 2170 *Email:* bishop@sheffield.anglican.org *Web:* www.sheffield. anglican.org

Sheffield-York The Rt Revd Peter Burrows Suffragan Bishop of Doncaster Doncaster House Church Lane Fishlake Doncaster DN7 5JW ENGLAND *Tel:* + 44 (0)1302 846 610 *Fax:* + 44 (0)1709 730 230 *Email:* bishoppeter@bishopofdoncaster.org.uk

Sodor & Man-York The Rt Revd Peter Eagles Bishop elect of Sodor & Man Thie yn Aspick 4 The Falls Tromode Road Douglas IM4 4PZ Isle of Man *Tel:* + 44 (0)1624 622 108 *Fax:* + 44 (0)1624 672 890 *Email:* bishop@sodorandman.im *Web:* www.sodorandman. im

Southwark-Canterbury The Rt Revd Christopher T Chessun Bishop of Southwark Trinity House 4 Chapel Court Borough High Street London SE1 1HW ENGLAND *Tel:* + 44 (0)207 939 9241 *Email:* bishop.christopher@southwark.anglican.org *Web:* www.southwark.anglican.org

Southwark-Canterbury The Rt Revd Richard I Cheetham Suffragan Bishop of Kingston 620 Kingston Road Raynes Park London SW20 8DN ENGLAND *Tel:* + 44 (0)20 8545 2440 *Fax:* + 44 (0)20 8545 2441 *Email:* bishop.richard@southwark. anglican.org

Southwark-Canterbury The Rt Revd Johnathan Clark Suffragan Bishop of Croydon St Matthew's House 100 George Street Croydon Surrey CR0 1PE ENGLAND *Tel:* + 44 (0)208 256 9630 *Fax:* + 44 (0)208 256 9631 *Email:* bishop.jonathan@ southwark.anglican.org

Southwark-Canterbury The Rt Revd Karowei Dorgu Suffragan Bishop of Woolwich Trinity House 4 Chapel Court Borough High Street London SE1 1HW ENGLAND *Tel:* + 44 (0)207 939 9405 *Fax:* + 44 (0)207 939 9467 *Email:* bishop@southwark. anglican.org *Web:* www.southwark.anglican.org

Southwell & Nottingham-York The Rt Revd Paul Gavin Williams Bishop elect of Southwell & Nottingham Bishop's Manor Southwell Notts NG25 0JR ENGLAND *Tel:* + 44 (0)1636 812 112 *Fax:* + 44 (0)1636 815 401 *Email:* bishop@southwell.anglican. org *Web:* www.southwell.anglican.org

Southwell & Nottingham-York The Rt Revd Anthony Porter Suffragan Bishop of Southwell - Sherwood Dunham House 8 Westgate Southwell Notts NG25 0JL ENGLAND *Tel:* + 44 (0)1636 819 133 *Fax:* + 44 (0)1636 819 085 *Email:* bishopsherwood@ southwell.anglican.org

St Albans-Canterbury The Rt Revd Alan GC Smith Bishop of St Albans Abbey Gate House 4 Abbey Mill Lane St Albans Herts AL3 4HD ENGLAND *Tel:* + 44 (01727 853 305 *Fax:* + 44 (01727 846 715 *Email:* bishop@stalbans.anglican.org *Web:* www.stalbans. anglican.org/

St Albans-Canterbury The Rt Revd Richard Atkinson Bishop of Bedford Bishop's Lodge Bedford Road Cardington MK44 3SS ENGLAND *Tel:* + 44 (0)1234 831 432 *Fax:* + 44 (0)1234 831 484 *Email:* bishopbedford@stalbans.anglican.org

St Albans-Canterbury The Rt Revd Michael Beasley Suffragan Bishop of Hertford Bishopswood 3 Stobarts Close Knebworth Herts SG3 6ND ENGLAND *Tel:* + 44 (0)1438 817 260 *Email:* bishophertford@stalbans. anglican.org

St Edmundsbury & Ipswich-Canterbury The Rt Revd Martin Seeley Bishop of St Edmundsbury & Ipswich The Bishop's House 4 Park Road Ipswich Suffolk IP1 3ST ENGLAND *Tel:* + 44 01473 252829 *Fax:* + 44 01473 232552 *Email:* bishops.office@ cofesuffolk.org *Web:* www.stedmundsbury.anglican. org

St Edmundsbury & Ipswich-Canterbury The Rt Revd Michael Harrison Suffragan Bishop of Dunwich The Bishop's House 4 Park Road Ipswich Suffolk IP1 3ST ENGLAND *Tel:* + 44 (0)1473 222 276 *Email:* bishop.mike@cofesuffolk.org

Truro-Canterbury The Revd Christopher David Goldsmith Suffragan Bishop of St Germans 32 Falmouth Road Truro Cornwall TR1 2HX ENGLAND *Tel:* + 44 (0)1872 273 190 *Fax:* + 44 (0)1872 277 883 *Email:* bishop@stgermans.truro. anglican.org

Winchester-Canterbury The Rt Revd Tim Dakin Bishop of Winchester Wolvesey Winchester Hampshire SO23 9ND ENGLAND *Tel:* + 44 (0)1962 854 050 *Fax:* + 44 (0)1962 897 088 *Email:* joyce.cockell@winchester.anglican.org *Web:* www. winchester.anglican.org

Winchester-Canterbury The Rt Revd David Grant Williams Suffragan Bishop of Basingstoke Bishop's Lodge Colden Lane Old Alresford Hampshire SO24

9DY ENGLAND *Tel:* + 44 (0)1962 737 330 *Email:* lindsey.demaudave@winchester.anglican.org

Winchester-Canterbury The Rt Revd Jonathan H Frost Suffragan Bishop of Southampton Bishop's House St Mary's Church Close Wessex Lane Southampton Hants SO18 2ST ENGLAND *Tel:* + 44 (0)23 8067 2684 *Email:* bishop.jonathan@winchester.anglican.org

Worcester-Canterbury The Rt Revd John G Inge Bishop of Worcester The Bishop's Office The Old Palace Deans Way Worcester Worcs WR1 2JE ENGLAND *Tel:* + 44 (0)1905 731 599 *Fax:* + 44 (0)1299 250 027 *Email:* generalinfo@cofe-worcester.org.uk

Worcester-Canterbury The Rt Revd Graham B Usher Suffragan Bishop of Dudley Bishop's House 60 Bishop's Walk Cradley Heath Warley West Midlands B64 7RH ENGLAND *Tel:* + 44 (0)121 550 3407 *Fax:* + 44 (0)121 550 7340 *Email:* bishop.dudley@cofe-worcester.org.uk

York-York The Most Revd & Rt Hon Dr John TM Sentamu Archbishop of York Bishopthorpe Palace Bishopthorpe York North Yorks YO23 2GE ENGLAND *Tel:* + 44 (0)1904 707 021 *Fax:* + 44 (0)1904 709 204 *Email:* alison.cundiff@archbishopofyork.org *Web:* www.dioceseofyork.org.uk/

York-York The Rt Revd Glyn Webster Suffragan Bishop of Beverley Holy Trinity Rectory Micklegate York YO1 6LE ENGLAND *Tel:* + 44 (0)113 265 4280 *Fax:* + 44 (0)113 265 4281 *Email:* bishopofbeverley@yorkdiocese.org

York-York The Rt Revd Paul John Ferguson Bishop of Whitby 21 Thornton Rd Middlesbrough TS8 9DS ENGLAND *Tel:* + 44 (0)1642 593273 *Fax:* + 44 (0)1642 710 685 *Email:* bishopofwhitby@yorkdiocese.org

York-York The Rt Revd John Bromilow Thomson Bishop of Selby Bishop's House Barton-le-Street Malton YO17 6PL ENGLAND *Tel:* + 44 (0)1653 627 191 *Fax:* + 44 (0)1653 627 193 *Email:* bishselby@clara.net

York-York The Rt Revd Alison White Suffragan Bishop of Hull Hullen House Woodfield Lane Hessle HU13 0ES ENGLAND *Tel:* + 44 (0)1482 649 019 *Fax:* + 44 (0)1482 647 449 *Email:* bishopofhull@yorkdiocese.org

HONG KONG SHENG KUNG HUI

Provincial Secretary The Revd Peter D Koon 16/F Tung Wai Commercial Building 109-111 Gloucester Road Wan Chai Hong Kong PEOPLE'S REPUBLIC OF CHINA *Tel:* + 852 25 265 355 *Fax:* + 852 25 212 199 *Email:* peter.koon@hkskh.org

Hong Kong Island The Most Revd Paul Kwong Archbishop of Hong Kong Sheng Kung Hui & Bishop of Hong Kong Island 71 Bonham Road Shek Tong Tsui Hong Kong PEOPLE'S REPUBLIC OF CHINA *Tel:* + 852 2526 5366 *Fax:* + 852 2523 3344 *Email:* paul.kwong@hkskh.org *Web:* dhk.hkskh.org

Western Kowloon The Rt Revd Andrew Chan Bishop of Western Kowloon 11 Pak Po Street Mongkok Kowloon Hong Kong PEOPLE'S REPUBLIC OF CHINA *Tel:* + 852 27 830 811 *Fax:* + 852 27 830 799 *Email:* dwk@hkskh.org *Web:* dwk.hkskh.org

THE CHURCH OF THE PROVINCE OF THE INDIAN OCEAN

Provincial Secretary The Revd Canon Samitiana J Razafindralambo Jhonson Diocesan Church House 37th St Paul Road Vacoas MAURITIUS *Tel:* + 230 686 5158 *Fax:* + *Email:* psec.acio@gmail.com

Provincial Treasurer Mr Philip Tse Rai Wai 21 Dr, J. Riviere St Port Louis REPUBLIC OF MAURITIUS *Tel:* + 230 465 1235 *Fax:* + *Email:* pptrw@intnet.mu

Antananarivo The Rt Revd Samoela Jaona Ranarivelo Bishop of Antananarivo Evêché Anglican Lot VK57 ter Ambohimanoro 101 Antananarivo MADAGASCAR *Tel:* + 261 (0)20 222 0827 *Fax:* + 261 (0)2 226 1331 *Email:* eemdanta@yahoo.com

Antananarivo The Rt Revd Todd Andrew McGregor Bishop of Tulear and Assistant Bishop of Antananarivo Evêché Anglican Lot VK57 ter Ambohimanoro 101 Antananarivo MADAGASCAR*Email:* revmctodd@yahoo.com

Antsiranana The Rt Revd Theophile Botomazava Bishop of Antsiranana Evêché Anglican BP 278 4 Rue Grandidier Antsiranana 201 MADAGASCAR *Tel:* + 261 (0)20 822 2776

Fianarantsoa The Rt Revd Gilbert Rateloson Rakotondravelo Bishop of Fianarantsoa Eveque du Diocese Fianarantsoa BP 1418 Fianarantsoa 301 MADAGASCAR *Tel:* + 261 20 755 1583 *Email:* eemdiofianara@yahoo.fr

Mahajanga The Rt Revd Jean Claude Andrianjafimanana Bishop of Mahajanga Eveche Anglican 401 Mahajanga B.P 570 Mahajanga 501 MADAGASCAR *Email:* andrianjajc@yahoo.fr

Mauritius The Rt Revd Ian Gerald James Ernest Bishop of Mauritius Bishops House Nallatamby Road Phoenix MAURITIUS *Tel:* + 230 686 5158 *Fax:* + 230 697 1096 *Email:* dioang@intnet.mu

Seychelles The Most Revd James Richard Wong Yin Song Archbishop, Province of Indian Ocean & Bishop of the Seychelles PO Box 44 Victoria Mahe SEYCHELLES *Tel:* + 248 321 977 *Fax:* + 248 323 879 *Email:* angdio@seychelles.net

Toamasina The Rt Revd Jean Paul Solo Bishop of Toamasina Evêché Anglican Lot VK57 ter Ambohimanoro Antananarivo 101 MADAGASCAR *Tel:* + 261 20 533 1663 *Fax:* + 261 20 533 1689 *Email:* eemdtoam@wanadoo.mg

Toliara The Rt Revd Todd McGregor Bishop of Toliara Awaiting Details *Email:* Bishopmctodd@ yahoo.com

THE CHURCH OF IRELAND

Provincial Secretary Mr David Ritchie Church of Ireland House Church Avenue Rathmines Dublin 6 REPUBLIC OF IRELAND *Tel:* + 353 (0)1 497 8422 *Fax:* + 353 (0)1 497 8792 *Email:* chiefofficer@rcbdub. org

Armagh-Dublin The Most Revd Richard Lionel Clarke Archbishop of Armagh and Primate of All Ireland and Metropolitan Church House 46 Abbey Street Armagh BT61 7DZ NORTHERN IRELAND *Tel:* + 44 (0)28 375 27144 *Fax:* + 44 (0)28 375 1059 *Email:* archbishop@armagh.anglican.org *Web:* www. armagh.anglican.org/

Cashel & Ossory-Dublin The Rt Revd Michael Andrew James J Burrows Bishop of Cashel, Ferns & Ossory Bishop's House Troysgate Kilkenny REPUBLIC OF IRELAND *Tel:* + 353 (0)56 778 6633 *Fax:* + 353 (0)56 775 1813 *Email:* cashelossorybishop@eircom.net *Web:* www.cashel. anglican.org/

Clogher-Armagh The Rt Revd John McDowell Bishop of Clogher The See House 152A Ballagh Road Fivemiletown Co Tyrone BT75 0QP NORTHERN IRELAND *Tel:* + 44 (0)28 6634 7879 *Fax:* + 44 (0)28 8952 2475 *Email:* bishop@clogher.anglican.org *Web:* www.clogher.anglican.org

Connor-Armagh The Rt Revd Alan Francis Abernethy Bishop of Connor Bishop's House 1 Marlborough Gate Marlborough Park Malone, Belfast BT9 6GB NORTHERN IRELAND *Tel:* + 44 (0)28 902 33188 *Fax:* + 44 (0)28 902 37802 *Email:* bishop@connor.anglican.org *Web:* www.connor. anglican.org/

Cork, Cloyne & Ross-Dublin The Rt Revd William Paul Colton Bishop of Cork, Cloyne & Ross The Palace Bishop Street Cork REPUBLIC OF IRELAND *Tel:* + 353 (0)21 5005 080 *Fax:* + 353 (0)21 4320 960 *Email:* bishop@ccrd.ie *Web:* www.cork.anglican.org

Derry & Raphoe-Armagh The Rt Revd Kenneth Raymond Good Bishop of Derry & Raphoe The See House 112 Culmore Road Londonderry BT48 8JF NORTHERN IRELAND *Tel:* + 44 (0)28 7135 1206 *Fax:* + 44 (0)28 7135 2554 *Email:* bishop@derry. anglican.org *Web:* www.derry.anglican.org

Down & Dromore-Armagh The Rt Revd Harold Creeth Miller Bishop of Down & Dromore The See House 32 Knockdene Park South Belfast BT5 7AB

NORTHERN IRELAND *Tel:* + 44 (0)28 9082 885 *Fax:* + 44 (0)28 902 31902 *Email:* bishop@dowr anglican.org *Web:* www.down.anglican.org

Dublin & Glendalough-Dublin The Most Rev Michael Geoffrey St Aubyn Jackson Archbishop o Dublin & Glendalough The See House 17 Templ Road Dartry Dublin 6 REPUBLIC OF IRELANI *Tel:* + 353 (0)1 497 6981 *Fax:* + 353 (0)1 497 635 *Email:* archbishop@dublin.anglican.org *Web:* www dublin.anglican.org

Kilmore, Elphin & Ardagh-Armagh The Rt Rev Ferran Glenfield Bishop of Kilmore, Elphin & Ardagh The Rectory Cootehill Co Cavan IRELANI *Tel:* + 353 49 555 9954 *Email:* bishop@kilmore anglican.org *Web:* www.kilmore.anglican.org

Limerick & Killaloe-Dublin The Rt Revd Kennetl Kearon Bishop of Limerick & Killaloe Rien Ro Adare Co Limerick REPUBLIC OF IRELAND *Te* + 353 (0)61 396 244 *Fax:* + 353 (0)66 451 100 *Emai* bishop@limerick.anglican.org *Web:* www.limerick anglican.org

Meath & Kildare-Dublin The Rt Revd Patrici Louise Storey Bishop of Meath & Kildare Bishop' House Mayglare Maynooth Co Kildare REPUBLIC OF IRELAND *Tel:* + 353 (0)1 629 2163 *Fax:* + 35 (0)1 628 9354 *Email:* bishop@meath.anglican.org *Web:* www.meath.anglican.org/

Tuam, Killala & Achonry-Armagh The Rt Rev Patrick William Rooke Bishop of Tuam, Killala & Achonry Bishop's House 2 Summerfield Cahergowar Claregalway Co Galway IRELAND *Tel:* + 353 (0)9 799 359 *Email:* bishop@tuam.anglican.org *Web* www.tuam.anglican.org

THE NIPPON SEI KO KAI (THE ANGLICAN COMMUNION IN JAPAN)

General Secretary The Revd Jesse Shin-Ichi Yahag 65-3 Yarai Cho Shinjuku-Ku Tokyo 162-0805 JAPAN *Tel:* + 81 (0)3 5228 3171 *Fax:* + 81 (0)3 5228 3175 *Email:* general-sec.po@nskk.org

Provincial Treasurer Mr Shigeo Ozaki Provincial Office 65-3 Yarai-cho Shinjuku-ku Tokyo 162-0805 JAPAN *Tel:* + 81 (0)3 5228 3171 *Fax:* + 81 (0)3 5228 3175

Chubu The Rt Revd Peter Ichiro Shibusawa Bishop of Chubu 2-28-1 Meigetsu-cho Showa-ku Nagoyashi Aichi-ken 466-0034 JAPAN *Tel:* + 81 (0)52 858 1007 *Fax:* + 81 (0)52 858 1008 *Email:* bishop.chubu@ nskk.org

Hokkaido The Most Revd Nathaniel Makoto Uematsu Primate of The Nippon Sei Ko Kai & Bishop of Hokkaido Kita 15 Jo Nishi 5-1-12 Kita-Ku Sapporo 001-0015 JAPAN *Tel:* + 81 (0)11 717 8181 *Fax:* + 81 (0)11 736 8377 *Email:* fwjh6169@ mb.infoweb.ne.jp *Web:* www.nskk.org/hokkaido

Kita Kanto The Rt Revd Zerubbabel Katsuich Hirota Bishop of Kita Kanto 2-172 Sakuragi-cho

Omiya-ku Saitama-shi Saitama-ken 330-0854 JAPAN *Tel:* + 81 (0)48 642 2680 *Fax:* + 81 (0)48 648 0358 *Email:* horotaz@nifty.com

Kobe The Rt Revd Andrew Yatuka Nakamura Bishop of Kobe 5-11-1 Shimo Yamate Dori Chuo-ku Kobe City Hyogo 650 0011 JAPAN *Tel:* + 81 (0)78 351 5469 *Fax:* + 81 (0)78 382 1095 *Email:* nakamurayutaka6@msn.com *Web:* www.kobe.anglican.org

Kyoto The Rt Revd Stephen Takashi Kochi Bishop of Kyoto 380 Okakuen-cho, Shimotachiuri-agaru Karasumadori Kamikyo-ku Kyoto-shi Kyoto-hu 602-8011 JAPAN *Tel:* + 81 (0)75 431 7204 *Fax:* + 81 (0)75 441 4238 *Email:* aset@kje.biglobe.ne.jp *Web:* www.nskk.org/kyoto

Kyushu The Rt Revd Luke Ken-ichi Muto Bishop of Kyushu 2-9-22 Kusagae Chuo-ku Fukuoka-shi Fukuoka-ken 810 -0045 JAPAN *Tel:* + 81 (0)92 771 2050 *Fax:* + 81 (0)92 771 9857 *Web:* www.kyushu.anglican.org

Okinawa The Rt Revd David Eisho Uehara Bishop of Okinawa 3-3-5 Aza Meada Urasoe-shi Okinawa-ken 901-2102 JAPAN *Tel:* + 81 (0)98 942 1101 *Fax:* + 81 (0)98 942 1102 *Email:* rtrev.david-uehara@anglican-okinawa.jp

Osaka The Rt Revd Andrew Haruhisa Iso Bishop of Osaka 2-1-8 Matsuzaki-cho Abeno-ku Osaka-shi Osaka-fu 545-0053 JAPAN *Tel:* + 81 (0)6 6621 6530 *Fax:* + 81 (0)6 6621 9148 *Email:* iso.osaka@nskk.org *Web:* www.nskk.org/osaka/

Tohoku The Rt Revd John Hiromichi Kato Bishop of Tohoku 2-13-15 Kokubun-cho Aoba-ku Sendai-shi Miyagi-ken 980-0803 JAPAN *Tel:* + 81 (0)22 223 2349 *Fax:* + 81 (0)22 223 2387 *Email:* bishop.tohoku@nskk.org *Web:* www.tohoku.anglican.org

Tokyo The Rt Revd Andrew Yoshimichi Ohata Bishop of Tokyo 3-6-18 Shiba Koen Minato-ku Tokyo Tokyo-to 105-0011 JAPAN *Tel:* + 81 (0)3 3433 0987 *Fax:* + 81 (0)3 3433 8678 *Email:* bishop.tko@nskk.org *Web:* www.tokyo.anglican.org

Yokohama The Rt Revd Laurence Yutaka Minabe Bishop of Yokohama 14-57 Mitsuzawa Shimo-cho Kanagawa-ku Yokohama-shi Kanagawa-ken 221-0852 JAPAN *Tel:* + 81 (0)45 321 4988 *Fax:* + 81 (0)45 321 4978 *Email:* laurence.yokohama@anglican.jp *Web:* www.anglican.jp/yokohama/

THE EPISCOPAL CHURCH IN JERUSALEM AND THE MIDDLE EAST

Provincial Secretary Ms Georgia K Katsantonis 2 Grigori Afxentiou Nicosia P O Box 22075 1515 CYPRUS *Email:* georgia@spidernet.com.cy

Provincial Treasurer The Ven Canon William Schwartz PO Box 3210 Doha QATAR *Tel:* + 974 4416 5726 *Email:* archdeacon.bill@cypgulf.org

Cyprus and the Gulf The Rt Revd Michael Augustine Owen A O Lewis Bishop of Cyprus and the Gulf Bishop's Office PO Box 22075 CY 1517 Nicosia CYPRUS *Tel:* + 357 (0)22 332 206 *Fax:* + 357 (0)22 672 241 *Email:* bishop@spidernet.com.cy *Web:* www.cypgulf.org/

Egypt The Rt Revd Mouneer Hanna Anis Bishop in Egypt with North Africa and the Horn of Africa Diocesan Office PO Box 87 Zamalek Distribution 11211 Cairo EGYPT *Tel:* + 20 (0)2 738 0821/3/9 *Fax:* + 20 (0)2 735 894 *Email:* bishopmouneer@gmail.com *Web:* www.dioceseofegypt.org/

Egypt The Rt Revd Grant Lemarquand Area Bishop for the Horn of Africa Gambella Anglican Centre Gambella Town Gambella ETHIOPIA *Tel:* + 20 (0)2 738 0821/3/9 *Fax:* + 20 (0)2 735 894 *Email:* bishopgrant777@gmail.com

Egypt The Rt Revd Samy Fawzy Area Bishop for North Africa Diocesan Office PO Box 87 Zamalek Distribution 11211 Cairo EGYPT *Tel:* + 20 (0)2 738 0821/3/9

Iran Vacant Bishop elect of Iran St Thomas Center Raiwind Road PO Box 688 Lahore Punjab 54000 PAKISTAN *Tel:* + 92 (0)42 542 0452

Jerusalem The Most Revd Suheil S Dawani Archbishop, Jerusalem & the Middle East & Archbishop in Jerusalem St George's Cathedral Close Nablus Road Box 19122 Jerusalem 91191 ISRAEL *Tel:* + 972 (0)2 627 1670 *Fax:* + 972 (0)2 627 3847 *Email:* bishop@j-diocese.org *Web:* www.j-diocese.org

THE ANGLICAN CHURCH OF KENYA

Provincial Secretary The Revd Canon Rosemary Mbogo Bishops Road Off Ngong Road P. O. Box 40502 - 00100 Nairobi KENYA *Tel:* + 254 20 271 4752/3/4 *Fax:* + 254 20 2718442 *Email:* ackpsoffice@ackenya.org

Provincial Treasurer Mr William Ogara PO Box 40502 Bishop's Gardens Bishop's Road Nairobi KENYA *Tel:* + 254 (0)20 2333 324/5 *Fax:* + 254 (0)20 2728 139

Provincial Accountant Mr John Muhoho PO Box 40502 Bishop's Gardens Bishop's Road Nairobi KENYA *Tel:* + 254 (0)20 2714 755 *Fax:* + 254 (0)20 2718 442

All Saints Cathedral Diocese The Most Revd Jackson Ole Sapit Primate and Archbishop of All Kenya PO Box 678 Kericho 20200 KENYA *Tel:* + 254 (0)20 2714 752/3/5 *Fax:* + 254 (0)20 2718 442 *Email:* archoffice@ackenya.org

All Saints Cathedral Diocese The Rt Revd Cleti Ogeto Suffragan Bishop - All Saints Cathedral Diocese PO Box 40502 Nairobi 100 KENYA

All Saints Cathedral Diocese The Rt Revd David Mutisya Suffragan Bishop of All Saints Cathedral Diocese - Garissa Missionary Area All Saints Cathedral PO Box 60 Garissa 70100 KENYA

Bondo The Rt Revd Johannes O Angela Bishop of the Diocese of Bondo PO Box 240 Bondo 40601 KENYA *Tel:* + 254 (0)335 20415 *Email:* ackbondo@swiftkenya.com

Bungoma The Revd George Mechumo Bishop elect of Bungoma PO Box 2392 Bungoma 50200 KENYA *Tel:* + 254 (0)337 30 481 *Fax:* + 254 (0)337 30 481 *Email:* ackbungoma@swiftkenya.com

Butere The Rt Revd Timothy Wambunya Bishop of Butere PO Box 54 Butere 50101 KENYA *Tel:* + 254 056 620 412 *Fax:* + 254 056 620 038 *Email:* ackbutere@swiftkenya.com

Eldoret The Rt Revd Christopher Ruto Bishop of Eldoret PO Box 3404 Eldoret 30100 KENYA*Email:* ackeldoret@africaonline.co.ke

Embu The Rt Revd David Muriithi Ireri Bishop of Embu PO Box 189 Embu 60100 KENYA *Tel:* + 254 068 30614 *Email:* ack-embu@swiftkenya.com

Kajiado The Rt Revd Gadiel Katanga Lenini Bishop of Kajiado P.O. Box 203-01100 Kajiado 1100 KENYA *Tel:* + 254 (0)45 21105 *Email:* ackajiado@swiftkenya.com

Kapsabet The Rt Revd Paul Korir Bishop of Kapsabet Awaiting Details

Katakwa The Rt Revd John OKude Omuse Bishop of Katakwa PO Box 68 Amagoro 50244 KENYA *Tel:* + 254 (0)337 54 079 *Fax:* + 254 (0)337 54 017 *Email:* ackatakwa@swiftkenya.com

Kericho The Rt Revd Ernest Kiprotich Bishop of Kericho PO Box 678 Kericho 20200 KENYA *Tel:* + 254 (0)52 20112

Kirinyaga The Rt Revd Joseph Kibuchua Bishop of Kirinyaga PO Box 95 Kutus 10304 KENYA *Tel:* + 254 (0)163 44 221 *Fax:* + 254 (0)163 44 020 *Email:* ackirinyaga@swiftkenya.com

Kitale The Rt Revd Stephen Kewasis Bishop of Kitale PO Box 4176 Kitale KENYA *Tel:* + 254 054 31631 *Email:* ack.ktl@gmail.com

Kitui The Rt Revd Josephat V Mule Bishop of Kitui PO Box 1054 Kitui 90200 KENYA *Tel:* + 254 (0)141 226 82 *Fax:* + 254 (0)141 221 19 *Email:* ackitui@swiftkenya.com

Machakos The Rt Revd Joseph Mutungi Bishop of Machakos PO Box 282 Machakos 90100 KENYA *Tel:* + 254 044 21379 *Fax:* + 254 044 20178 *Email:* ackmachakos@gmail.com

Makueni The Rt Revd Joseph M Kanuku Bishop of Makueni PO Box 282 Machakos KENYA *Tel:* + 254 044 21379 *Fax:* + 254 044 20178 *Email:* ackmachakos@swiftkenya.com

Malindi The Rt Revd Lawrence K Dena Bishop of Malindi Ukumbusho House Nkrumah Road PO Box 80072 Mombasa KENYA *Web:* www.ackenya.org

Marsabit The Rt Revd Robert Martin Bishop of Marsabit PO Box 51 Marsabit 6500 KENYA *Email:* ackbishopmarsabit@gmail.com

Maseno North The Rt Revd Simon M Oketch Bishop of Maseno North PO Box 416 Kakemega 50100 KENYA *Tel:* + 254 56 2/3 *Email:* ackmnorth@jambo.co.ke

Maseno South The Rt Revd Francis Abiero Bishop of Maseno South PO Box 114 Kisumu 40100 KENYA *Tel:* + 254 (0)35 45 147 *Fax:* + 254 (0)35 21 009 *Email:* ackmsouth@swiftkenya.com

Maseno West The Rt Revd Joseph J Wasonga Bishop of Maseno West PO Box 793 Siaya 40600 KENYA *Email:* wbishopjoseph@yahoo.com

Mbeere The Rt Revd Moses Masamba Nthukah Bishop of Mbeere PO Box 122 Siakago 60104 KENYA *Tel:* + 254 721423840 *Email:* bishopmbeere@gmail.com *Web:* http://www.ackenya.org/dioceses/mbeere.html

Meru The Rt Revd Charles N Mwendwa Bishop of Meru PO Box 427 Meru 60200 KENYA *Tel:* + 254 16 430 719 *Email:* ackmeru@swiftkenya.com

Mombasa The Rt Revd Julius R M Katio Kalu Bishop of Mombasa Ukumbusho House Mkrumah Road PO Box 80072 Mombasa 80100 KENYA *Tel:* + 254 (0)11 311 105 *Fax:* + 254 (0)11 227 837 *Email:* ackmombasa@swiftmombasa

Mount Kenya Central The Rt Revd Isaac M Ng'ang'a Bishop of Mount Kenya Central PO Box 1040 Muranga 10200 KENYA *Tel:* + 254 (0)60 30559 *Fax:* + 254 (0)60 30148 *Email:* ackmkcentral@wananchi.com

Mount Kenya Central The Rt Revd Allen M Waithaka Suffragan Bishop of Mount Kenya Central PO Box 1040 Muranga 10200 KENYA *Tel:* + 254 156 305 59

Mount Kenya South The Rt Revd Timothy Ranji Bishop of Mount Kenya South PO Box 886 Kiambu 900 KENYA *Tel:* + 254 (0)154 22 997 *Fax:* + 254 (0)154 22 408 *Email:* ackmtksouth@swiftkenya.com

Mount Kenya South The Rt Revd Charles Muturi Suffragan Bishop Mt Kenya South Mount Kenya South Diocese PO Box 886 Kiambu 900 KENYA *Email:* ackmtkenyasouth@swiftkenya.com

Mount Kenya West The Rt Revd Joseph M Kagunda Bishop of Mount Kenya West PO Box 229 Nyeri 10100 KENYA *Tel:* + 254 (0)171 302 14 *Fax:* + 254 (0)171 2954 *Email:* ackmtkwest@wananchi.com

Mumias The Rt Revd Beneah Okumu Salala Bishop of Mumias PO Box 213 Mumias 50102 KENYA *Fax:* + 254 333 41232 *Email:* ackmumias@swiftkenya.com *Web:* www.ackmumiasdiocese.org

Muranga South The Rt Revd Julius Karanu Wa Gicheru Bishop of Muranga South Awaiting Details

Nairobi The Rt Revd Joel Waweru Mwangi Bishop of Nairobi PO Box 72846 Nairobi 200 KENYA *Tel:* + 254 020 4440524 *Fax:* + 254 2 226259

Nakuru The Rt Revd Joseph Muchai Bishop of Nakuru PO Box 56 Moi Road Nakuru 20100 KENYA *Tel:* + 254 (0)37 212 155 *Fax:* + 254 (0)37 44 379

Nakuru The Rt Revd Musa Kamuren Suffragan Bishop of Nakuru - Baringo Area PO Box 56 Moi Road Nakuru 20100 KENYA *Tel:* + 254 (0)37 212 155

Nambale The Rt Revd Robert Magina Barasa Bishop of Nambale PO Box 4 Nambale 50409 KENYA *Tel:* + 254 (0)336 24040 *Fax:* + 254 (0)336 24071 *Email:* acknambale@swiftkenya.com

Nyahururu The Rt Revd Stephen Kabora Bishop of Nyahururu PO Box 926 Nyahururu 20300 KENYA *Tel:* + 254 365 32179 *Email:* nyahu_dc@africaonline.co.ke

Nyahururu The Rt Revd Jacob Lesuuda Suffragan Bishop of Maralal Area PO Box 42 Maralal KENYA*Email:* jlesuuda@yahoo.com

Southern Nyanza The Rt Revd James Ochiel Bishop of Southern Nyanza PO Box 65 Homa Bay 40300 KENYA *Tel:* + 254 0385 221 27 *Fax:* + 254 0385 220 56 *Email:* acksnyanza@swiftkenya.com

Taita-Taveta The Rt Revd Samson Mwaluda Bishop of Taita Taveta ACK Taita-taveta Diocese PO Box 75 Voi 80300 KENYA *Tel:* + 254 (0)147 30 096 *Fax:* + 254 (0)147 30 364 *Email:* acktaita@swiftmombasa.com

Taita-Taveta The Rt Revd Liverson Mng'onda Coadjutor Bishop of Taita-Taveta ACK Taita-taveta Diocese PO Box 75 Voi 80300 KENYA

Thika The Rt Revd Julius Njuguna Wanyoike Bishop of Thika PO Box 214 Thika 1000 KENYA *Tel:* + 254 (0)151 217 35 *Fax:* + 254 (0)151 315 44

THE ANGLICAN CHURCH OF KOREA

General Secretary The Revd Stephen Si-Kyung Yoo 16, Sejong-daero 19-gil Jung-gu Seoul 100-120 KOREA *Tel:* + 82 (0)2 738 8952 *Fax:* + 82 (0)2 737 4210 *Email:* 08skyoo@naver.com *Web:* www.skh.or.kr

Busan The Most Revd Onesimus Dongsin Park Primate of the Anglican Church of Korea & Bishop of Busan Bishop's Office 18 Daecheong-dong 2Ga Jung-Ku Busan 600-092 KOREA *Tel:* + 82 (0)51 463 5742 *Fax:* + 82 (0)51 463 5957 *Email:* primate.ack@gmail.com *Web:* skhpusan.onmam.com/

Daejeon The Revd Moses Nak Jun Yoo Bishop elect of Daejeon Bishop's Office 87-6 Sunhwa 2-dong Jung-gu Daejeon 301-823 KOREA *Tel:* + 82 (0)42 256 9988 *Fax:* + 82 (0)42 255 8918 *Email:* tdio@unitel.co.kr *Web:* www.djdio.or.kr

Seoul The Rt Revd Peter Lee Bishop of Seoul Bishop's Office 16 Sejong-daero 19-gil Jung-gu Seoul 100-120 KOREA *Tel:* + 82 (0)2 735 6157 *Fax:* + 82 (0)2 723 2640 *Web:* www.skhseoul.or.kr

THE CHURCH OF THE PROVINCE OF MELANESIA

Tel: +

Provincial Secretary Dr Abraham Hauriasi Anglican Church of Melanesia P.O.Box 19 Honiara SOLOMON ISLANDS *Tel:* + 677 20407

Provincial Accountant Mr Jimmy Maeigoa Po Box 19 Dogura MBP PAPUA NEW GUNIEA *Tel:* + 677 21 892 *Fax:* + 677 23 301

Banks & Torres The Rt Revd Alfred Patterson Worek Bishop of Banks & Torres C/O PO Box 19 Sola Vanualava Torba Province VANUTU *Tel:* + 678 38520 *Fax:* + 678 38520 *Email:* worek_p@comphq.org.sb

Central Melanesia The Most Revd George Takeli Archbishop of the Anglican Church of Melanesia and Bishop of Central Melanesia Church of Melanesia PO Box 19 Honiara SOLOMON iSLANDS *Tel:* + 677 242 10 *Email:* g.takeli@comphq.org.sb

Central Solomons The Rt Revd Ben Seka Bishop of Central Solomons PO Box 52 Tulagia CIP SOLOMON ISLANDS *Tel:* + 677 32 042 *Email:* d.bindon@xtra.co.nz

Guadalcanal The Rt Revd Nathan Tome Bishop of Guadalcanal Awaiting Details *Tel:* + 677 23337 *Email:* ntome4080@gmail.com

Hanuato'o The Rt Revd Alfred Karibongi Bishop of Hanuato'o C/O Post Office Kirakira Makira/Ulawa Province SOLOMON ISLANDS

Malaita The Rt Revd Samuel Sahu Bishop of Malaita Bishops House PO Box 7 Auki Malaita Province SOLOMON ISLANDS *Tel:* + 611 45 121 071 *Fax:* + 677 21 098

Malaita The Revd Rickson George Maomaoru Assistant Bishop elect of Malaita Bishops House PO Box 7 Auki Malaita Province SOLOMON ISLANDS

Temotu The Rt Revd Leonard Dawea Bishop of Temotu PO Box 50 Lata Santa Cruz Temotu Province SOLOMON ISLANDS *Tel:* + 677 530 80 *Fax:* + 677 530 92 *Email:* bjdawea@gmail.com

Vanuatu The Rt Revd James M Ligo Bishop of Vanuatu Bishop's House PO Box 238 Luganville Santo VANUATU *Tel:* + 678 370 65 *Fax:* + 678 363 31 *Email:* comdov@vanuatu.com.vu

Ysabel The Revd Ellison Quity Bishop elect of Ysabel Bishop's House PO Box 6 Buala Jejevo Ysabel Province SOLOMON ISLANDS *Tel:* + 677 350 34 *Fax:* + 677 350 71 *Email:* ellison.jejevo@gmail.com

LA IGLESIA ANGLICANA DE MEXICO

Provincial Secretary The Revd Canon Alfonso Walls Acatlán 102 Oriente Col. Mitras Centro Monterrey Nuevo Leon 64460 MEXICO *Tel:* + 52 81 8333 0992 *Fax:* + 52 81 8348 7362 *Email:* awalls@anglicanmx. org

Ms Laura Gracia Provincial Treasurer Acatlán 102 Ote Mitras Centro Monterrey NL 64460 MEXICO *Tel:* + 52 (0)81 8333 0992 *Email:* lgracia@anglicanmx.org

Cuernavaca The Rt Revd Enrique Treviño Cruz Bishop of Cuernavaca Minerva #1 Fracc. Delicias Cuernavaca Morelos 62330 MEXICO *Tel:* + 52 777 315 2870 *Email:* diocesisdecuernavaca@hotmail. com

Mexico The Rt Revd Carlos Touche-Porter Bishop of Mexico San Jeronimo #117 Col. San Angel Delegacion Alvaro Obregón MEXICO City DF 1000 MEXICO *Tel:* + 52 (0)33 5616 2205 *Email:* diocesisdemexico@gmail.com

Northern Mexico The Most Revd Francisco Moreno Presiding Bishop of La Iglesia Anglicana de Mexico & Bishop of Northern Mexico Acatlán 102 Oriente Col. Mitras Centro Monterrey Nuevo Leon 64460 MEXICO *Tel:* + 52 81 8333 0992 *Fax:* + 52 81 8348 7362 *Email:* primado@anglicanmx.org

Southeastern Mexico The Rt Revd Benito Juarez-Martinez Bishop of Southeastern Mexico Av Las Americas #73 Col. Aguacatal Xalapa Veracruz 91130 MEXICO *Tel:* + 52 (0)228 814 6951 *Email:* obispobenito.49@gmail.com

Western Mexico The Rt Revd Lino Rodriguez-Amaro Bishop of Western Mexico Torres Quintero # 15 Col. Seattle Zapopan Jalisco 45150 MEXICO *Tel:* + 52 333 560 4727 *Fax:* + 52 333 560 4726 *Email:* obispolino@hotmail.com *Web:* www.iamoccidente. org.mx

THE CHURCH OF THE PROVINCE OF MYANMAR (BURMA)

General Secretary The Revd Paul Myint Htet Htin Ya No 140 Pyidaungsu Yeiktha Street PO Box 11191 Yangon MYANMAR *Tel:* + 95 1 395 279 *Email:* myinthtet@gmail.com

Provincial Treasurer Ms Helen Myint Htwe Yee 140 Pyidaungsu-Yeiktha Road Dagon PO Yangon MYANMAR *Tel:* + 95 (0)1 395 279 *Email:* cpm.140@mptmail.com.mm

Hpa-an The Rt Revd Saw Stylo Bishop of Hpa-an Bishop Kone: Ward 4 Hpa-an Kayin State MYANMAR *Tel:* + 95 58 216 96

Mandalay The Rt Revd David Nyi Nyi Naing Bishop of Mandalay Diocesan Office 22 Pinya Road Mandalay MYANMAR *Tel:* + 95 (0)2 341 10 *Email:* davidnaing@gmail.com

Mytikyina The Rt Revd John Zau Li Bishop of Mytikyina 147 Thankin Net Pe Road Thinda Quarters Mytikyina Kachin State MYANMAR *Tel:* + 95 (0)74 231 04 *Email:* john.zauli@gmail.com

Mytikyina The Rt Revd Vacant Assistant Bishop elect of Mytikyina Diocesan Office 147 Thakin Net Pe Road Thida Quarter Mytikyina Kachin State MYANMAR *Tel:* + 95 074 25428

Sittwe The Rt Revd James Min Dein Bishop of Sittwe May Yu Stree Sittwe Rakhine StateMYANMAR *Tel:* + 95 43 536 22 *Email:* mindein3@gmail.com

Toungoo The Rt Revd Saw Wilme Bishop of Toungoo Diocesan Office Nat-shin-Naung Street Ward 20 Toungoo Myanamar *Tel:* + 95 54 231 59 *Email:* bishop.wilme@gmail.com

Yangon The Most Revd Stephen Than Myint Oo Archbishop of Myanmar and Bishop of Yangon No 140 Pyidaungsu Yeiktha Street PO Box 11191 Yangon MYANMAR *Tel:* + 95 (0)1 395 279 *Fax:* + 95 (0)1 395 314 *Email:* stephenthan777@gmail.com

Yangon The Rt Revd Samuel Htang Oak Assistant Bishop of Yangon No 44 Bishop Home Pyay Road Yangon MYANMAR *Tel:* + 95 1 372 300 *Email:* sthangoak40@gmail.com

THE CHURCH OF NIGERIA (ANGLICAN COMMUNION)

Provincial Secretary Vacant Episcopal House 24 Doula Street P.O. Box 212 ADCP Abuja NIGERIA *Tel:* + 234 9 5236950 *Email:* communicator1@anglican-nig.org

Provincial Treasurer Chief O Adekunle PO Box 78 Lagos NIGERIA *Tel:* + 234 (0)1 263 3581

The Rt Revd Michael Olurohunbi Episcopal House 24 Douala Street Wuse District, Zone 5 P.O.Box 212 ADCP, Garki, Abuja NIGERIA *Tel:* + 234 (0)9 523 6950 *Email:* mikefarohunbi08@gmail.com

Aba-Province of the Niger Delta The Most Revd Ugochukwu U Ezuoke Archbishop of the Province of Niger Delta & Bishop of Aba Bishopscourt 70-72 St Michael's Road PO Box 212 Aba NIGERIA *Tel:* + 234 (0)82 227 666 *Email:* aba@anglican-nig.org

Aba Ngwa North-Province of Niger Delta The Rt Revd Nathan C Kanu Bishop of Aba Ngwa North Bishopscourt - All Saints Cathedral Abayi-Umuocham No. 161-165 Owerri Road PO Box 43 Aba Abia State NIGERIA *Email:* odinathnfe@sbcglobal.net

Abakaliki-Province of Enugu The Rt Revd Monday C Nkwoagu Bishop of Abakaliki All Saints Cathedral PO Box 112 Abakaliki Ebonyi State NIGERIA *Tel:* + 234 (0)43 20 762 *Email:* abakaliki@anglican-nig.org

Abuja-Province of Abuja The Most Revd Nicholas Okoh Metropolitan & Primate of all Nigeria &

Bishop of Abuja Episcopal House 24 Douala Street Wuse District, Zone 5, PO Box 212 Abuja ADCP Garki NIGERIA *Tel:* + 234 (0)56 280 682 *Email:* nickorogodo@yahoo.com

Afikpo-Province of Enugu The Rt Revd Paul Uduogu Bishop of Afikpo Bishop's House PO Box 699 Afikpo Ebonyi State NIGERIA *Email:* udogupaul@yahoo.com

Aguata-Province of Niger The Most Revd Christian O Efobi Archbishop of the Province of the Niger & Bishop of Aguata Bishopscourt PO Box 1128 Ekwulobia Anambra State Rivers State NIGERIA *Tel:* + 234 (0)803 750 1077 *Email:* christianefobi@yahoo.com

Ahoada-Province of Niger Delta The Rt Revd Clement Ekpeye Bishop of Ahoada Bishopscourt PO Box 4 Ahoada Rivers State NIGERIA *Tel:* + 234 (0)806 357 6242 *Email:* ahoada@anglican-nig.org

Ajayi Crowther-Province of Ibadan The Rt Revd Olugbenga Oduntan Bishop of Ajayi Crowther Bishopscourt PO Box 430 Iseyin Oyo State NIGERIA *Tel:* + 234 (0)803 719 8182 *Email:* ajayicrowtherdiocese@yahoo.com

Akoko-Province of Ondo The Rt Revd Gabriel Akinbiyi Bishop of Akoko Bishopscourt PO Box 572 Ikare-Akoko Ondo State NIGERIA *Tel:* + 234 (0)31 801 011 *Email:* bishopgabrielakinbiyi@yahoo.com

Akoko Edo-Province of Bendel The Rt Revd Jolly Oyekpen Bishop of Akoko Edo Bishopscourt PO Box 10 Igarra Edo State NIGERIA *Tel:* + 234 (0)803 470 5941 *Email:* venjollye@yahoo.com

Akure-Province of Ondo The Rt Revd Simeon O Borokini Bishop of Akure Bishopscourt PO Box 1622 Akure Ondo state NIGERIA *Tel:* + 234 (0)34 241 572 *Fax:* + 234 (0)34 241 572

Amichi-Province of Niger The Rt Revd Ephraim Ikeakor Bishop of Amichi Bishopscourt PO Box 13 Amichi Anambra State NIGERIA *Tel:* + 234 (0)803 317 0916 *Email:* eoikeakor@yahoo.com

Arochukwu/Ohafia-Province of Aba The Rt Revd Johnson Onuoha Bishop of Arochukwu/ Ohafia Bishopscourt PO Box 193 Arochukwu Abia State NIGERIA *Tel:* + 234 (0)802 538 6407 *Email:* aroohafia@anglican-nig.org

Asaba-Province of Bendel The Rt Revd Justus N Mogekwu Bishop of Asaba Bishopscourt PO Box 216 Asaba Delta State NIGERIA *Tel:* + 234 (0)802 819 2980 *Email:* justusmogekwu@yahoo.com

Awgu/Aninri-Province of Niger The Rt Revd Emmaunuel Ugwu Bishop of Awgu/Aniniri Bishopscourt PO Box 305 Agwu Enungu State NIGERIA *Tel:* + 234 (0)803 334 9360 *Email:* afamnonye@yahoo.com

Awka-Province of Niger The Rt Revd Alexander C Ibezim Bishop of Awka Bishopscourt PO Box 130 Awka Anambra State NIGERIA *Tel:* + 234 (0)48 550 058 *Email:* chioma1560@aol.com

Awori-Province of Lagos The Rt Revd J Akin Atere Bishop of Awori Bishopscourt PO Box 10 Ota Ogun State NIGERIA *Tel:* + 234 (0)803 553 7284 *Email:* dioceseofawori@yahoo.com

Badagry-Province of Lagos The Rt Revd Joseph B Adeyemi Bishop of Badagry Bishopscourt PO Box 7 Badagry Lagos State NIGERIA *Email:* badagary@anglican-nig.org

Bari-Province of Kaduna The Rt Revd Idris A Zubairu Bishop of Bari Bishopscourt Gidan Mato Bari Kano State NIGERIA *Tel:* + 234 (0)808 559 7183

Bauchi-Province of Jos The Rt Revd Musa Tula Bishop of Bauchi Bishop's House 2 Hospital Road PO Box 2450 Bauchi NIGERIA *Tel:* + 234 (0)77 543 460 *Email:* bauchi@anglican-nig.org

Benin-Province of Bendel The Rt Revd Peter J Imasuen Bishop of Benin Bishopscourt PO Box 82 Benin City Edo State NIGERIA *Tel:* + 234 30799560 *Email:* Beninanglican@yahoo.com

Bida-Province of Abuja The Rt Revd Jonah G E Kolo Bishop of the Missionary Diocese of Bida Bishop's House St John's Mission Compound PO Box 14 Bida NIGERIA *Tel:* + 234 (0)66 461 694

Bukuru-Province of Jos The Rt Revd Jwan Zhumbes Bishop of Bukuru Bishopscourt Citrus Estate PO Box 605 Sabon Bariki Plateau State NIGERIA

Calabar-Province of Niger Delta The Rt Revd Tunde Adeleye Bishop of Calabar Bishopscourt PO Box 74 Calabar Cross Rivers State NIGERIA *Tel:* + 234 (0)87 232 812 *Fax:* + 234 (0)88 220 835 *Email:* calabar@anglican-nig.org

Damaturu-Province of Jos The Rt Revd Abiodun Ogunyemi Bishop of Damaturu PO Box 312 Damaturu Yobe State NIGERIA *Tel:* + 234 (0)74 522 142 *Email:* damaturu@anglican-nig.org

Diocese on the Coast formerly (Ikale-Ilaje)-Province of Ondo The Rt Revd Joshua E Ogunele Bishop of the Diocese on the Coast Bishopscourt Ikoya Road PMB 3 Ilutitun-Osooro Ondo State NIGERIA *Tel:* + 234 (0)803 467 1879 *Email:* joshuaonthecoast@yahoo.ca

Doko-Province of Lokoja The Rt Revd Uriah Kolo Bishop of Doko PO Box 1513 Bida Niger State NIGERIA *Tel:* + 234 (0)803 590 6327 *Email:* uriahkolo@gmail.com

Dutse-Province of Kaduna The Rt Revd Yesufu I Lumu Bishop of Dutse PO Box 67 Yadi Dutse Jigawa State NIGERIA *Tel:* + 234 (0)64 721 379 *Email:* dutse@anglican-nig.org

Egba-Province of Lagos The Rt Revd Emmanuel O Adekunle Bishop of Egba Bishopscourt Cathedral of St Peter PO Box 46 Ile-oluji Ondo State NIGERIA

Egba West-Province of Lagos The Rt Revd Samuel O Ajani Bishop of Egba-West Bishopscourt Oke-Ata Housing Estate PO Box 6204 Sapon Abeokuta NIGERIA *Tel:* + 234 (0)80 5518 4822 *Email:* samuelajani@yahoo.com

Egbu-Province of Owerri The Rt Revd Geoffrey E Okoroafor Bishop of Egbu PO Box 1967 Owerri Imo State NIGERIA *Tel:* + 234 (0)83 231 797 *Email:* egbu@anglican-nig.org

Eha-Amufu-Province of Enugu The Rt Revd Daniel Olinya Bishop of Eha - Amufu St Andrews Cathedral Bishopscourt PO Box 85 Eha-Amufu Enugu State NIGERIA *Tel:* + 234 (0)803 089 2131 *Email:* dankol@yahoo.com

Ekiti-Province of Ondo The Most Revd Samuel Abe Archbishop of the Province of Ondo & Bishop of Ekiti Bishopscourt PO Box 12 Okesa Street Ado-Ekiti Ekiti State NIGERIA *Tel:* + 234 (0)30 250 305 *Email:* adedayoekiti@yahoo.com

Ekiti Kwara-Province of Ibadan The Rt Revd Andrew O Ajayi Bishop of Ekiti Kwara Awaiting Details *Tel:* + 234 (0)803 470 3522 *Email:* andajayi@yahoo.com

Ekiti Oke-Province of Ondo The Rt Revd Isaac Olubowale Bishop of Ekiti - Oke PMB 207 Usi-Ekiti Ekiti State NIGERIA *Email:* ekitioke@anglican-nig.org

Ekiti West-Province of Ondo The Rt Revd Samuel Oke Bishop of the Diocese of Ekiti West Bishop's Residence 6 Ifaki Street PO Box 477 Ijero-Ekiti NIGERIA *Tel:* + 234 (0)30 850 314

Enugu-Province of Niger The Rt Revd Emmanuel C Chukwuma Bishop of Enugu Bishop's House PO Box 418 Enugu NIGERIA *Tel:* + 234 (0)42 435 804 *Fax:* + 234 (0)42 259 808 *Email:* enugu@anglican-nig.org

Enugu North-Province of Niger Delta The Rt Revd Sosthenes Eze Bishop of Enugu North Bishopscourt St Marys Cathedral Ngwo-Enugu NIGERIA *Tel:* + 234 (0)803 870 9362 *Email:* bishopsieze@yahoo.com

Esan-Province of Bendel The Most Revd Friday J Imaekhai Archbishop of Bendel Province & Bishop of Esan Bishopscourt Ojoelen PO Box 921 Ekpoma Edo State NIGERIA *Tel:* + 234 (0)55 981 079 *Email:* bishopimaekhai@yahoo.com

Etche-Province of Niger Delta The Rt Revd Precious Nwala Bishop of Etche Bishopscourt PO Box 89 Okehi Etche Rivers State NIGERIA

Etsako-Province of Bendel The Rt Revd Jacob Bada Bishop of Etsako Bishopscourt PO Box 11 Jattu Auchi Edo State NIGERIA

Evo-Province of Niger Delta The Rt Revd Innocent Ordu Bishop of Evo Bishopscourt PO Box 3576 Port Harcourt Rivers State NIGERIA *Tel:* + 234 (0)803 715 2706 *Email:* innocent-ordu@yahoo.com

Gboko-Province of Abuja The Rt Revd Emmanuel Nyitsse Bishop of Gboko Awaiting Details

Gombe-Province of Jos The Rt Revd Henry Ndukuba Bishop of Gombe Cathedral Church of St Peter PO Box 39 Gombe NIGERIA *Tel:* + 234 (0)72 221 212 *Fax:* + 234 (0)72 221 141 *Email:* gombe@anglican-nig.org

Gusau-Province of Kaduna The Rt Revd John Garba Bishop of Gusau PO Box 64 Gusau Zamfara State NIGERIA *Tel:* + 234 (0)63 204 747 *Email:* gusau@anglican.skannet.com

Gwagwalada-Province of Abuja The Rt Revd Moses Tabwaye Bishop of Gwagwalada Diocesan Headquarters Secretariat Road PO Box 287 Gwagwalada Abuja NIGERIA *Tel:* + 234 (0)9 882 2083 *Email:* anggwag@skannet.com.ng

Ibadan-Province of Ibadan The Most Revd Joseph Akinfenwa Archbishop of Ibadan Province & Bishop of Ibadan PO Box 3075 Mapo Ibadan NIGERIA *Tel:* + 234 (0)2 810 1400 *Fax:* + 234 (0)2 810 1413 *Email:* ibadan@anglican.skannet.com.ng

Ibadan North-Province of Ibadan The Rt Revd Segun Okubadejo Bishop of Ibadan North Bishopscourt Moyede PO Box 182 Dugbe Ibadan NIGERIA *Tel:* + 234 (0)2 810 7482 *Email:* angibn@skannet.com

Ibadan South-Province of Ibadan The Rt Revd Jacob Ajetunmobi Bishop of Ibadan South Bishopscourt PO Box 166 St David's Compound Kudeti Ibadan NIGERIA *Tel:* + 234 (0)2 231 9141 *Fax:* + 234 (0)2 231 9141 *Email:* jacajet@skannet.com.ng

Idah-Province of Abuja The Rt Revd Joseph Musa Bishop of Idah Bishopscourt PO Box 25 Idah Kogi State NIGERIA *Email:* idah@anglican-nig.org

Ideato-Province of Owerri The Rt Revd Caleb A Maduoma Bishop of Ideato Bishopscourt PO Box 2 Ndizuogu Imo State NIGERIA *Email:* bpomacal@hotmail.com

Idoani-Province of Ondo The Rt Revd Ezekiel B Dahunsi Bishop of Idoani Bishopscourt PO Box 100 Idoani Ondo State NIGERIA *Tel:* + 234 (0)803 384 4029 *Email:* bolaezek@yahoo.com *Web:* www.dioceseofidoani.org

Ife-Province of Ibadan The Rt Revd Oluwole Odubogun Bishop of Ife Bishopscourt PO Box 312 Ife Osun State NIGERIA *Tel:* + 234 (0)36 230 046 *Email:* rantiodubogun@yahoo.com

Ife East-Province of Ibadan The Rt Revd Oluseyi Oyelade Bishop of Ife East Bishop's House PMB

505 Modakeke-Ife Osun State NIGERIA *Tel:* + 234 (0)802 332 4962 *Email:* seyioyelade@yahoo.com

Ifo-Province of Lagos The Rt Revd Nathaniel Oladejo Ogundipe Bishop of Ifo Bishopscourt Trinity House KM1 Ibogun Road Ifo Ogun State NIGERIA *Tel:* + 234 (0)802 778 4377 *Email:* dioceseofifo@gmail.com

Igbomina-Province of Kwara The Ven Emmanuel Adekola Bishop elect of Igbomina Bishopscourt PO Box 102 Oro Kwara State NIGERIA *Tel:* + 234 (0)803 669 1940

Igbomina-West-Province of Kwara The Rt Revd James O Akinola Bishop of Igbomina West Bishop's House PO Box 32 Oke Osin Kwara State NIGERIA *Tel:* + 234 (0)803 392 3720 *Email:* olaotimuyiwa@yahoo.com *Web:* www.dioceseofigbominawest.org/igbomina/

Ijebu-Province of Lagoa The Rt Revd Ezekiel Awosoga Bishop of Ijebu Bishopscourt Ejirin Road PO Box 112 Ijebu-Ode NIGERIA

Ijeb-North-Province of Lagos The Rt Revd Solomon Kuponu Bishop of Ijebu - North Bishopscourt Oke-Sopen Ijebu-Igbo NIGERIA *Tel:* + 234 (0)803 741 9372 *Web:* www.ijebunorthdiocese.org

Ijesa North East-Province of Ibadan The Rt Revd Joseph A Olusola Bishop of Ijesa North East PO Box 40 Ipetu Ijesa Osun State NIGERIA *Tel:* + 234 (0)803 942 8275 *Email:* bpjafsola@gmail.com *Web:* www.ijesanortheastdiocese.org

Ijesha North-Province of Ibadan The Rt Revd Isaac Oluyamo Bishop of Ijesha North Bishopscourt PO Box 4 Ijebu-Jesa Osun State NIGERIA *Tel:* + 234 (0)802 344 0333

Ijumu-Province of Lokoja The Rt Revd Ezekiel Ikupolati Bishop of Ijumu Bishopscourt PO Box 90 Iyara-Ijumi Kogi State NIGERIA *Tel:* + 234 (0)807 500 8780 *Email:* efikupolati@yahoo.com

Ikara-Province of Kaduna The Rt Revd Yusuf I Janfalan Bishop of Ikara Bishopscourt PO Box 23 Ikara Kaduna State NIGERIA *Tel:* + 234 (0)803 679 3865 *Email:* ikara@anglican-nig.org

Ikeduru-Province of Owerri The Rt Revd Emmanuel C Maduwike Bishop of Ikeduru Bishop's House PO Box 56 Atta Imo State NIGERIA *Tel:* + 234 (0)803 704 4686 *Email:* emmamaduwike@yahoo.com

Ikka-Province of Bendel The Rt Revd Peter Onekpe Bishop of Ikka St John's Cathedral PO Box 5 Agbor Delta State NIGERIA *Tel:* + 234 (0)55 250 14

Ikwerre-Province of Niger Delta The Rt Revd Blessing Enyindah Bishop of Ikwerre Bishopscourt St Peter's Cathedral PO Box 14229 Port Harcourt Rivers State NIGERIA *Tel:* + 234 (0)802 321 2824 *Email:* blessingenyindah@yahoo.com

Ikwo-Province of Enugu The Rt Revd Kenneth C Ifemene Bishop of Ikwo Bishops Residence PO Box 998 Agubia Ikwo Abakaliki Ebonyi State NIGERIA *Tel:* + 234 (0)805 853 4849 *Email:* bishopikwoanglican@yahoo.com

Ikwuano-Province of Aba The Rt Revd Chigozirim Onyegbule Bishop of Ikwuano Bishopscourt St Phillip's Cathedral PO Box 5 Ahaba-Oloko Abia State NIGERIA *Tel:* + 234 (0)803 085 9319 *Email:* ikwuano@anglican-nig.org

Ilaje-Province of Ondo The Rt Revd Fredrick I Olugbemi Bishop of Iiaje Bishopscourt PO Box 147 Igbokoda Ondo State NIGERIA *Tel:* + 234 (0)806 624 8662 *Email:* forogbemi@yahoo.com

Ile-Oluji-Province of Ondo The Rt Revd Samson O Adekunle Bishop of Ile - Oluji Bishopscourt Cathedral of St PEter PO Box 46 Ile-Oluji Ondo State NIGERIA *Tel:* + 234 (0)803 454 1236 *Email:* adekunlesamson86@yahoo.co.uk

Ilesa-Province of Ibadan The Rt Revd Olubayu Sowale Bishop of Ilesa Diocesan Headquarters Muroko Road PO Box 237 Ilesa Osun State NIGERIA *Tel:* + 234 (0)36 460 138 *Email:* ilesha@anglican-nig.org

Ilesa South West-Province of Ibadan The Rt Revd Samuel Egbebunmi Bishop of Ilesa South West Bishopscourt Cathedral of the Holy Trinity Imo Ilesa Osun State NIGERIA *Tel:* + 234 (0)803 307 1876 *Email:* segbebunmi@yahoo.com

Irele-Eseodo-Province of Ondo The Rt Revd Felix O Akinbuluma Bishop of Irele - Eseodo Bishopscourt Sabomi Road Ode Irele Ondo State NIGERIA *Tel:* + 234 (0)805 671 2653 *Email:* felixgoke@yahoo.com

Isiala-Ngwa-Province of Aba The Rt Revd Owen N N Azubuike Bishop of Isiala-Ngwa Bishopscourt St Georges Cathedral Compound PNB 2033 Mbawsi Abia State NIGERIA *Tel:* + 234 (0)805 467 0528 *Email:* bpowenazubuike@yahoo.com

Isial-Ngwa South-Province of Aba The Rt Revd Isaac Nwaobia Bishop of Isiala-Ngwa South St Peter's Cathedral Compound PO Box 15 Owerrinta Abia State NIGERIA *Tel:* + 234 (0)803 711 9317 *Email:* isialangwasouth@anglican-nig.org

Isikwuato-Province of Aba The Rt Revd Manasses Chijiokem Okere Bishop of Isikwuato Bishopscourt PO Box 350 Ovim Abia State NIGERIA *Tel:* + 234 (0)803 386 221 *Email:* isiukwuato@anglican-nig.org

Jalingo-Province of Jos The Rt Revd Timothy Yahaya Bishop of Jalingo PO Box 4 Magami Jalingo Tabara State NIGERIA *Tel:* + 234 806 594 4694 *Email:* timothyyahaya@yahoo.com

Jebba-Province of Kwara The Rt Revd Timothy S Adewole Bishop of Jebba Bishopscourt PO Box 2 Jebba Kwara State NIGERIA *Tel:* + 234 (0)803 572 5298 *Email:* bishopadewole@yahoo.com

Jos-Province of Jos The Most Revd Benjamin A Kwashi Archbishop of the Province of Jos & Bishop of Jos Bishopscourt PO Box 6283 Jos Plateau State NIGERIA*Email*: benkwashi@gmail.com

Kabba-Province of Lokoja The Rt Revd Steven K Akobe Bishop of Kabba Bishopscourt Obara Way PO Box 62 Kabba Kogi State NIGERIA *Tel*: + 234 (0)58 300 633 *Fax*: + 234 (0)803 471 4759

Kaduna-Province of Kaduna Vacant Bishop elect of Kaduna PO Box 72 Kaduna NIGERIA *Tel*: + 234 (0)62 240 085 *Fax*: + 234 (0)62 244 408

Kafanchan-Province of Abuja The Rt Revd Marcus Dogo Bishop of Kafanchan Bishopscourt PO Box 29 Kafanchan Kaduna State NIGERIA *Tel*: + 234 (0)61 20 634*Web*: www.anglicankafanchan.blogspot.co.uk

Kano-Province of Kaduna The Rt Revd Zakka L Nyam Bishop of Kano Bishopscourt PO Box 362 Kano Kano State NIGERIA *Tel*: + 234 (0)64 647 816 *Fax*: + 234 (0)64 647 816 *Email*: kano@anglican. skannet.com.ng

Katsina-Province of Kaduna The Rt Revd Jonathan S Bamaiyi Bishop of Katsina Bishop's Lodge PO Box 904 Katsina Katsina State NIGERIA

Kebbi-Province of Kaduna The Most Revd Edmund E Akanya Archbishop of the Province of Kaduna & Bishop of Kebbi Bishops Residence PO Box 701 Birnin Kebbi Kebbi State NIGERIA *Tel*: + 234 (0)68 321 179 *Fax*: + 234 (0)803 586 1060 *Email*: eekanya@ yahoo.com

Kontagora-Province of Lokoja The Rt Revd Jonah Ibrahim Bishop of Kontagora Bishop's House GPA PO Box 1 Kontagora Niger State NIGERIA *Tel*: + 234 (0)803 625 2032 *Email*: jonahibrahim@yahoo.co.uk

Kubwa-Province of Abuja The Rt Revd Duke Akamisoko Bishop of Kubwa Bishop's House PO Box 67 Kubwa Abuja FCT NIGERIA *Tel*: + 234 (0)803 651 9437 *Email*: dukesoko@yahoo.com

Kutigi-Province of Lokoja The Rt Revd Jeremiah N N Kolo Bishop of Kutigi Bishop's House St John's Mission Compound PO Box 14 Bida NIGERIA *Tel*: + 234 (0)803 625 2032 *Email*: bishopkolo@yahoo.com

Kwara-Province of Kwara The Most Revd Olusegun S Adeyemi Archbishop of Province of Kwara & Bishop of Kwara Bishopscourt Fate Road PO Box 1884 Ilorin Kwara State NIGERIA *Tel*: + 234 (0)31 220 879 *Fax*: + 234 (0)803 325 8068 *Email*: bishopolusegun@yahoo.com

Kwoi-Province of Abuja The Rt Revd Paul S Zamani Bishop of Kwoi Bishop's Residence Cathedral Compound Samban Gida P.O. Box 173 Kwoi Kaduna State NIGERIA *Tel*: + 234 (0)80 651 8160 *Email*: paulzamani@yahoo.com

Lafia-Province of Abuja The Rt Revd Miller K Maza Bishop of the Missionary Diocese of Lafia PO Box

560 Lafia Nasarawa State NIGERIA *Tel*: + 234 (0)803 973 5973 *Email*: anglicandioceseoflafia@yahoo.com

Lagos-Province of Lagos The Most Revd Ephraim Ademowo Archbishop of the Province of Lagos & Bishop of Lagos 29 Marina PO Box 13 Lagos NIGERIA *Tel*: + 234 (0)1 263 6026 *Fax*: + 234 (0)803 403 1358 *Email*: adebolaademowo@dioceseoflagos.org

Lagos Mainland-Province of Lagos The Rt Revd Adebayo Akinde Bishop of Lagos Mainland Bishops House PO Box 849 Ebute Lagos State NIGERIA *Tel*: + 234 (0)703 390 5522 *Email*: adakinde@gmail.com *Web*: www.lagosmainlanddiocese.org

Lagos West-Province of Lagos The Rt Revd James Odedeji Bishop of Lagos West Vining House 3rd Floor Archbishop Vining Memorial Cathedral Oba Akinjobi Road GRA Ikeja NIGERIA *Tel*: + 234 (0)1 493 7333 *Fax*: + 234 (0)1 493 7337 *Email*: dioceseoflagoswest@yahoo.com

Langtang-Province of Jos The Rt Revd Stanley D Fube Bishop of Langtang No 87 Solomon Lar Road PO Box 38 Langtang Plateau State NIGERIA *Tel*: + 234 (0)803 605 8767 *Email*: stanleyfube@gmail.com

Lokoja-Province of Lokoja The Most Revd Emmanuel Sokowamju Egbunu Archbishop of the Province of Lokoja & Bishop of Lokoja Bishopscourt PO Box 11 bethany Lokoja Koji State NIGERIA *Tel*: + 234 (0)58 220 588 *Fax*: + 234 (0)803 592 5698 *Email*: emmanuelegbunu@yahoo.co.uk *Web*: www. anglican-lokojadiocese.org

Maiduguri-Province of Jos The Ven Emmanuel Morris Bishop elect of Maiduguri Bishopscourt PO Box 1693 Maiduguri Borno State NIGERIA *Tel*: + 234 (0)76 234 010 *Email*: bishope-45@yahoo.com

Makurdi-Province of Abuja The Rt Revd Nathan Nyitar Inyom Bishop of Makurdi Bishopscourt PO Box 1 Makurdi Benue State NIGERIA *Tel*: + 234 (0)44 533 349 *Fax*: + 234 (0)803 614 5319 *Email*: makurdi@anglican.skannet.com.ng

Mbaise-Province of Owerri The Rt Revd Chamberlain Chinedu Ogunedo Bishop of Mbaise Bishopscourt PO Box 10 Ife Imo State NIGERIA *Tel*: + 234 (0)803 336 9836 *Email*: ogunedochi@yahoo. com

Mbamili-Province of Niger The Rt Revd Henry S Okeke Bishop of Mbamili Bishopscourt PO Box 2653 Onitsha Anambra State NIGERIA *Tel*: + 234 (0)803 644 9780 *Email*: bishopokeke@yahoo.com

Minna-Province of Lokoja The Rt Revd Daniel Abu Yisa Bishop of Minna Bishopscourt Dutsen Kura PO Box 2469 Minna NIGERIA *Tel*: + 234 (0)803 588 6552 *Email*: danyisa2007@yahoo.com

Ndokwa-Province of Bendel The Rt Revd David Obiosa Bishop of Ndokwa Bishopscourt 151 Old Sapele Road Obiaruka Delta State NIGERIA *Tel*: + 234 (0)803 776 9464 *Email*: dfao1963@yahoo.com

New Busa-Province of Kwara The Rt Revd Israel Amoo Bishop of New Busa Bishoscourt PO Box 208 New Busa Niger State NIGERIA *Tel:* + 234 (0)803 677 3839 *Email:* bishopamoo@yahoo.com

Ngbo-Province of Enugu The Rt Revd Christian Ebisike Bishop of Ngbo Bishop's House PO Box 93 Abakaliki Ebonyi State NIGERIA *Tel:* + 234 (0)806 979 4899 *Email:* vendchris@yahoo.com

Niger Delta North-Province of Niger Delta The Most Revd Ignatius C O Kattey Archbishop of Niger Delta Province & Bishop of Niger Delta North PO Box 53 Diobu Port Harcourt Rivers State NIGERIA *Tel:* + 234 (0)803 309 4331 *Email:* bishopicokattey@yahoo.com

Niger Delta West-Province of Niger Delta The Rt Revd Emmanuel Oko-Jaja Bishop of Niger Delta West PO Box 10 Yenagoa Bayelsa NIGERIA *Tel:* + 234 (0)803 870 2099 *Email:* nigerdelta-west@anglican-nig.org

Niger Delta, The-Province of the Niger Delta The Rt Revd Ralph Ebirien Bishop of the Niger Delta Bishopscourt PO Box 115 Port Harcourt Rivers State NIGERIA *Tel:* + 234 (0)708 427 9095 *Email:* revpalph_ebirien@yahoo.com

Niger West-Province of Niger The Rt Revd Johnson Ekwe Bishop of Niger West Bishop's House Anambra Anambra State NIGERIA *Tel:* + 234 (0)803 384 3339

Nike-Province of Enugu The Rt Revd Evans Jonathan Ibeagha Bishop of Nike Bishopscourt Trans-Ekulu PO Box 2416 Enugu Enugu State NIGERIA *Tel:* + 234 (0)803 324 1387 *Email:* pnibeagha@yahoo.com

Nnewi-Province of Niger The Rt Revd Godwin Izundu Nmezinwa Okpala Bishop of Nnewi Bishopscourt (opp Total filling station) PO Box 2630 Uruagu-Nnewi Anambra State NIGERIA *Tel:* + 234 (0)803 348 5714 *Fax:* + 234 (0)46 462 676 *Email:* okpalagodwin@yahoo.co.uk

Northern Izon-Province of Niger Delta The Rt Revd Fred Nyanabo Bishop of Northern Izon Bishopscourt PO Box 705 Yenagoa Bayelsa State NIGERIA *Tel:* + 234 (0)803 316 0938 *Email:* fred_nyanabo@yahoo.co.uk

Nsukka-Province of Enugu The Rt Revd Aloysius Agbo Bishop of Nsukka Bishopscourt St Cypran's Compound PO Box 516 Nsukka Enugu State NIGERIA *Tel:* + 234 (0)803 932 7840 *Email:* nsukka@anglican-nig.org

Offa-Province of Kwara The Rt Revd Akintunde Popoola Bishop of Offa Bishop's House 78-80 Ibrahim Road PO Box 21 Offa Kwara State NIGERIA *Tel:* + 234 (0)805 925 0011 *Email:* tpopoola@anglican-nig.org

Ogbaru-Province of Niger The Rt Revd Samuel Ezeofor Bishop of Ogbaru Bishopscourt PO Box 46 Atani Anambra State NIGERIA *Web:* www.ogbaruanglicandiocese.org

Ogbia-Province of Niger Delta The Rt Revd James Oruwori Bishop of Ogbia Bishop's House No 10 Queens Street Ogbia Town Bayelsa State NIGERIA *Tel:* + 234 (0)803 73 4746 *Email:* jaoruwori@yahoo.com

Ogbomoso-Province of Ibadan The Rt Revd Matthew Osunade Bishop of Ogbomoso Bishopscourt St David's Anglican Cathedral PO Box 1909 Ogbomoso NIGERIA *Tel:* + 234 (0)805 593 6164 *Email:* maaosunade@yahoo.com

Ogoni-Province of Niger Delta The Rt Revd Solomon Gberegbara Bishop of Ogoni Bishopscourt PO Box 73 Bori Rivers State NIGERIA *Tel:* + 234 (0)803 339 2545 *Email:* ogoni@anglican-nig.org

Ogori-Magongo-Province of Lokoja The Rt Revd Festus Davies Bishop of Ogori-Magongo Bishop's House St Peter's Cathedral Ogori Kogi State NIGERIA *Tel:* + 234 (0)803 451 0378 *Email:* fessyoladiran@yahoo.com

Ohaji/Egbema-Province of Owerri The Rt Revd Chidi Collins Oparaojiaku Bishop of Ohaji/Egbema Bishop's House PO Box 8026 New Owerri Imo State NIGERIA *Tel:* + 234 (0)803 312 1063 *Email:* chidioparachiaku@yahoo.com

Oji River-Province of Enugu The Most Revd Amos Amankechinelo Madu Archbishop of the Province of Enugu & Bishop of Oji River St Paul's Cathedral Church PO Box 123 Oji River Enuga NIGERIA *Tel:* + 234 (0)803 670 4888 *Email:* amosmadu@yahoo.com

Okene-Province of Lokoja The Ven Emmanuel Onsachi Bishop elect of Okene Bishopscourt PO Box 43 Okene Kogi State NIGERIA *Tel:* + 234 (0)803 700 0016 *Email:* okenediocese@yahoo.com

Oke-Ogun-Province of Ibadan The Rt Revd Solomon Amusan Bishop of Oke-Ogun Bishopscourt PO Box 30 Saki Oyo State NIGERIA *Tel:* + 234 (0)802 323 3365 *Email:* solomonamusan@yahoo.com

Oke-Osun-Province of Ibadan The Rt Revd Abraham Akinlalu Bishop of Oke-Osun Bishopscourt PO Box 251 Gbongan Osun State NIGERIA *Tel:* + 234 (0)803 771 7194 *Email:* abrahamakinlalu@yahoo.com *Web:* www.okeosunanglicandiocese.org

Okigwe-Province of Owerri The Rt Revd Edward Osuegbu Bishop of Okigwe Bishopscourt PO Box 156 Okigwe Imo State NIGERIA *Tel:* + 234 (0)803 724 6374 *Email:* edchuc@justice.com

Okigwe North-Province of Owerri The Rt Revd Godson Udochukwu Ukanwa Bishop of Okigwe North Bishopscourt PO Box 127 Anara Imo State NIGERIA *Tel:* + 234 (0)803 672 4314 *Email:* venukanwa@yahoo.com

Okigwe South-Province of Owerri The Rt Revd David Onuoha Bishop of Okigwe South Bishopscourt PO Box 235 Nsu Imo State NIGERIA *Email:* okisouth@yahoo.com

Okrika-Province of Niger Delta The Rt Revd Tubokosemie Atere Bishop of Okrika Bishopscourt PO Box 11 Okrika Rivers State NIGERIA *Tel:* + 234 (0)803 312 5226 *Email:* dioceseofokrika@yahoo.com

Oleh-Province of Bendel The Rt Revd John Usiwoma Aruakpor Bishop of Oleh Bishopscourt PO Box 8 Oleh Delta State NIGERIA *Tel:* + 234 (0)53 701 062 *Fax:* + 234 (0)802 307 4008 *Email:* angoleh2000@yahoo.com

Omu-Aran-Province of Kwara The Rt Revd Philip Adeyemo Bishop of Omu-Aran Bishop's House PO Box 224 Omu-Aran Kwara State NIGERIA *Tel:* + 234 (0)806 592 4891 *Email:* rtrevadeyemo@yahoo.com

On the Lake-Province of Owerri The Rt Revd Chijioke Oti Bishop of on the Lake Bishopscourt PO Box 36 Oguta Imo State NIGERIA *Tel:* + 234 (0)802 788 8738 *Email:* chijiokeoti72@yahoo.com

On the Niger-Province of Niger The Rt Revd Owen Chidozie Nwokolo Bishop of On the Niger Bishopscourt Ozala Road Onitsha Anambra State NIGERIA *Tel:* + 234 (0)803 726 0548 *Email:* owenelsie@yahoo.com

Ondo-Province of Ondo The Rt Revd George Lasebikan Bishop of Ondo Bishopscourt PO Box 265 Ife Road Ondo Ondo State NIGERIA *Tel:* + 234 (0)34 610 718 *Fax:* + 234 (0)803 472 1813 *Email:* ondoanglican@yahoo.co.uk

Ondo-Province of Ondo The Rt Revd Christopher Tayo Omotunde Suffragan Bishop of Ondo Bishopscourt PO Box 265 Ife Road Ondo Ondo State NIGERIA *Tel:* + 234 (0)802 919 1866 *Email:* chrisomotunde@yahoo.com

Orlu-Province of Owerri The Most Revd Bennett C I Okoro Archbishop of Province of Owerri & Bishop of Orlu Bishopscourt PO Box 260 Nkwerre Imo State NIGERIA *Tel:* + 234 (0)82 440 538 *Fax:* + 234 (0)803 671 1271 *Email:* anglicannaorlu@yahoo.com

Oru-Province of Owerri The Rt Revd Geoffrey Chukwunenye Bishop of Oru PO Box 191 Mgbidi Imo State NIGERIA *Tel:* + 234 (0)803 308 1270 *Email:* geoinlagos@yahoo.com

Osun-Province of Ibadan The Rt Revd James Afolabi Popoola Bishop of Osun Bishopscourt PO Box 285 Osogbo Osun State NIGERIA *Tel:* + 234 (0)35 240 325 *Fax:* + 234 (0)803 356 1628 *Email:* folapool@yahoo.com

Osun North East-Province of Ibadan The Rt Revd Humphery Olumakaiye Bishop of Osun North East Bishopscourt PO Box 32 Otan Ayegbaju Osun State NIGERIA *Tel:* + 234 (0)803 388 2678

Email: bamisebi2002@yahoo.co.uk *Web:* www. osunnortheastdiocese.org

Otukpo-Province of Abuja The Rt Revd David Bello Bishop of Otukpo Bishopscourt Po Box 360 Otukpo Benue State NIGERIA *Tel:* + 234 (0)803 309 1778 *Email:* bishopdkbello@yahoo.com

Owerri-Imo State The Rt Revd Cyril Chuk-wunonyerem Okorocha Bishop of Owerri Bishop's Bourne PMB 1063 Owerri NIGERIA *Tel:* + 234 (0)83 230 784 *Fax:* + 234 (0)803 338 9344 *Email:* owerri_anglican@yahoo.com

Owo-Province of Ondo The Rt Revd Stephen Ayo-deji Fagbemi Bishop of Owo Bishopscourt PO Box 472 Owo Ondo State NIGERIA *Tel:* + 234 (0)51 241 463 *Fax:* + 234 (0)803 475 4291

Oyo-Province of Ibadan The Rt Revd Williams Oluwarotimi Aladekugbe Bishop of Oyo PO Box 23 Oyo Oyo State NIGERIA *Tel:* + 234 (0)38 240 225 *Fax:* + 234 (0)803 857 2120 *Email:* oyo@anglican-nig.org

Pankshin-Province of Jos The Rt Revd Olumuyiwa Ajayi Bishop of Pankshin Diocesan Secretariat PO Box 196 Pankshin Plateau State NIGERIA *Tel:* + 234 (0)803 344 7318 *Email:* olumijayi@yahoo.com

Remo-Province of Lagos The Rt Revd Michael Fape Bishop of Remo Bishopscourt PO Box 522 Sagama Ogun State NIGERIA *Tel:* + 234 (0)37 640 598 *Fax:* + 234 (0)803 726 7949 *Email:* remo@anglican-nig.org

Sabongidda-Ora-Province of Bendel Vacant Bishop elect of Sabongidda-Ora Bishopscourt PO Box 13 Sabongidda-Ora - Edo State NIGERIA *Tel:* + 234 (0)57 54 132

Sapele-Province of Bendel The Rt Revd Blessing A Erifeta Bishop of Sapele Bishopscourt PO Box 52 Sapele Delta State NIGERIA *Tel:* + 234 (0)803 662 4282 *Email:* dioceseofsapele@yahoo.com

Sokoto-Province of Kaduna The Rt Revd Augustin Omole Bishop of Sokoto Bishop's Lodge 68 Shuni Road PO Box 3489 Sokoto Sokoto State NIGERIA *Tel:* + 234 (0)60 234 639 *Fax:* + 234 (0)803 542 3765 *Email:* akin_sok@yahoo.com *Web:* www.dosac.org

Udi-Province of Enugu The Rt Revd Chjioke Augustine Aneke Bishop of Udi Bishopscourt PO Box 30 Udi Enugu State NIGERIA *Tel:* + 234 (0)806 908 9690 *Email:* bpchijiokeudi@yahoo.com

Ughelli-Province of Bendel The Rt Revd Cyril Odutemu Bishop of Ughelli Bishopscourt PO Box 760 Ughelli Delta State NIGERIA *Tel:* + 234 (0)53 600 403 *Fax:* + 234 (0)803 530 7114 *Email:* ughellianglican@yahoo.com

Ukwa-Province of Aba The Rt Revd Samuel Kelechi Eze Bishop of Ukwa PO Box 20468 Aba Abia State NIGERIA *Tel:* + 234 (0)803 789 2431 *Email:* kelerem53878@yahoo.com

Umuahia-Province of Aba The Most Revd Ikechi Nwachukwu Nwosu Archbishop of Province of Aba & Bishop of Umuahia St Stephen's Cathedral Church Compound PO Box 96 Umuahia Abia State NIGERIA *Tel:* + 234 (0)88 221 037 *Fax:* + 234 (0)803 549 9066

Uyo-Province of Niger Delta The Rt Revd Prince Asukwo Antai Bishop of Uyo Bishopscourt PO Box 70 Uyo Akwa Ibom State NIGERIA *Tel:* + 234 (0)802 916 2305 *Email:* uyo@anglican-nig.com

Warri-Province of Bendel The Rt Revd Christian Esezi Ideh Bishop of Warri Bishopscourt 17 Mabiaku Road PO Box 4571 Warri Delta State NIGERIA *Tel:* + 234 (0)53 255 857 *Fax:* + 234 (0)805 102 2680 *Email:* angdioceseofwarri@yahoo.com

Western Izon-Province of Bendel The Rt Revd Edafe B Emamezi Bishop of Western Izon Bishopscourt PO Box 5 Patani Delta State NIGERIA *Tel:* + 234 (0)822 05 6228 *Email:* anglizon@yahoo.co.uk

Wusasa-Province of Kaduna The Rt Revd Ali Buba Lamido Bishop of Wusasa PO Box 28 Wusasa Zaria Kaduna State NIGERIA *Tel:* + 234 (0)69 334 594 *Fax:* + 234 (0)803 727 2504 *Email:* lamido2sl@aol.co.uk

Yewa (form. Egbado)-Province of Lagos The Rt Revd Michael Adebayo Oluwarohunbi Bishop of Yewa Bishopscourt PO Box 484 Ilaro Ogun State NIGERIA *Tel:* + 234 (0)39 440 695

Yola-Province of Jos The Rt Revd Markus A Ibrahm Bishop of Yola PO Box 601 Yola Adamawa State Adamawa State NIGERIA *Tel:* + 234 (0)75 624 303 *Fax:* + 234 (0)803 045 7576 *Email:* marcusibrahim2002@yahoo.com

Zaki-Biam-Province of Abuja The Rt Revd Benjamin A Vager Bishop of Zaki-Biam Bishopscourt PO Box 600 Yam Market Road Zaki-biam Benue State NIGERIA *Tel:* + 234 (0)803 676 0018 *Email:* rubavia@yahoo.com

Zaria-Province of Kaduna The Rt Revd Cornelius Salifu Bello Bishop of Zaria Bishopscourt PO Box 507 Zaria Kaduna State NIGERIA *Tel:* + 234 (0)802 708 9555 *Email:* cssbello@hotmail.com

Zonkwa-Province of Abuja The Rt Revd Jacob W Kwashi Bishop of Zonkwa Bishop's Residence PO Box 26 Zonkwa 802002 Kaduna State NIGERIA *Tel:* + 234 (0)803 331 0252 *Email:* zonkwa@anglican-nig.org

THE CHURCH OF NORTH INDIA

Provincial Secretary Mr Alwan Masih CNI Synod Post Box 311 16 Pandit Pant Marg New Delhi 110 001 INDIA *Tel:* + 91 11 2373 1079 *Fax:* + 91 11 2371 6901 *Email:* alwanmasih@cnisynod.org *Web:* www. cnisynod.org

Provincial Treasurer Mr Prem Masih CNI Synod Post Box 311 16 Pandit Pant Marg New Delhi 110 001 INDIA *Tel:* + 91 11 4321 4000 *Fax:* + 91 11 4321 4006 *Email:* ucnita1@gmail.com

Agra The Rt Revd Prem Prakash Habil Bishop of Agra Bishop's House 4/116-B Church Road Civil Lines Agra Uttarr Pradesh 282 002 INDIA *Tel:* + 91 (0)562 285 4845 *Fax:* + 91 (0)562 252 0074 *Email:* doacni@gmail.com

Amritsar The Rt Revd Pradeep K Samantaroy Bishop of Amritsar 26 R B Prakash Chand Road Opp Police Ground Amritsar Punjab 143 001 INDIA *Tel:* + 91 (0)183 256 2010 *Fax:* + 91 (0)183 222 2910 *Email:* bishoppradeep@gmail.com *Web:* www. amritsardiocese.org/

Andaman & Car Nicobar Islands The Rt Revd Christopher Paul Bishop of Andaman & Car Nicobar Islands Cathedral Church Compound Car Nicobar MUS 744 301 ANDAMAN & NICOBAR ISLANDS *Tel:* + 91 (0)319 223 1362 *Fax:* + 91 (0)319 223 1362 *Email:* cniportblair@yahoo.co.in

Barrackpore The Rt Revd Brojen Malakar Bishop of Barrackpore Bishop's Lodge 86 Middle Road Barrackpore Kolkata West Bengal 700 120 INDIA *Tel:* + 91 (0)332 593 1852 *Fax:* + 91 (0)332 593 1852 *Email:* malakar.brojen@rediffmail.com *Web:* www. barrackporediocesecni.org

Bhopal The Rt Revd Robert Ali Bishop of Bhopal Bishop's House 57 Residency Area Behind Narmada Water Tank Indore Madhya Pradesh 452 001 INDIA *Tel:* + 91 (0)731 271 0551 *Fax:* + 91 (0)731 405 5452 *Email:* bhopal_diocese@yahoo.com

Calcutta The Rt Revd Ashok Biswas Bishop of Kolkata Bishop's House 51 Chowringhee Road Kolkata West Bengal 700 071 INDIA *Tel:* + 91 (0)336 534 7770 *Fax:* + 91 (0)332 282 6340 *Email:* ashoke.biswas@vsnl.net

Chandigarh The Rt Revd Younas Massey Bishop of Chandigarh Bishop's House CNI Mission Compound Brown Road Ludhiana Punjab 141 008 INDIA *Tel:* + 91 (0)161 222 5706 *Fax:* + 91 (0)161 222 5706 *Email:* massey.younas@yahoo.in

Chhattisgarh The Rt Revd Purna Sagar Nag Bishop of Chhattisgarh Opp. Rajbhavan Gate No 1 Civil Lines Raipur Chhattisgarh 492 001 INDIA *Tel:* + 91 (0)771 221 0015 *Email:* doccni@reiffmail.com

Chotanagpur The Rt Revd B Baskey Bishop of Chotanagpur Bishop's Lodge PO Box 1 Old Hazari Bagh Road Ranchi Jharkhand 834 001 INDIA *Tel:* + 91 651 235 1181 *Fax:* + 91 651 235 1184 *Email:* rch_cndta@sancharnet.in

Cuttack The Rt Revd Surendra Kumar Nanda Bishop of Cuttack Bishop's House Mission Road Cuttack Orissa 753 001 INDIA *Tel:* + 91 6712300102 *Email:* doccni@gmail.com

Delhi Vacant Bishop elect of Delhi 1 Church Lane Off North Avenue New Delhi Delhi 110 001 INDIA *Tel:* + 91 (0)112 371 7471 *Fax:* + 91 (0)112 335 8006

Durgapur The Rt Revd Probal K Dutta Deputy Moderator of CNI & Bishop of Durgapur St Michael's Church Compound Alderin Path Bidhan Nagar Durgapur West Bengal 713 212 INDIA *Tel:* + 91 (0)343 253 4552 *Email:* probaldutta@ymail.com

Eastern Himalayas Vacant Bishop elect of Eastern Himalayas Bishop's House 1B K Gongba Road Darjeeling West Bengal 734 001 INDIA *Tel:* + 91 (0)354 225 8183 *Email:* easternhimalaya2004@ yahoo.co.in

Gujarat The Rt Revd Silvans S Christian Bishop of Gujarat Bishop's House I.P Mission Compound Ellis Bridge Ahmedabad Gujarat State380 006 INDIA *Tel:* + 91 (0)792 656 1950 *Fax:* + 91 (0)792 656 1950 *Email:* gujdio@yahoo.co.in

Jabalpur The Most Revd Dr Prem Chand P C Singh Moderator of CNI & Bishop of Jabalpur Bishop's House 2131 Napier Town Jabalpur Madhya Pradesh 482 001 INDIA *Tel:* + 91 (0)761 262 2109 *Fax:* + 91 (0)761 262 2109 *Email:* bishoppcsingh@yahoo.co.in

Kolhapur The Rt Revd Bathuel R Tiwade Bishop of Kolhapur Bishop's House EP School Compound Nagala Park Kolhapur Maharashatra 416 003 INDIA *Tel:* + 91 (0)231 265 4832 *Fax:* + 91 (0)231 265 4832 *Email:* kdcdbss@yahoo.com

Lucknow The Rt Revd Peter Baldev Bishop of Lucknow Bishop's House 25/11 Mahatma Gandhi Marg Allahabad Uttar Pradesh 211 001 INDIA *Tel:* + 91 (0)532 242 7053

Marathwada The Rt Revd Madhukar Kasab Bishop of Marathwada Bungalow 28/A Mission Compound Cantt Aurangabad Maharashtra 431 002 INDIA *Tel:* + 91 (0)240 237 3136 *Email:* revmukasab@yahoo. co.in

Mumbai (Form. Bombay) The Rt Revd Prakash D Patole Bishop of Mumbai Bishop's House 19 Hazarimal Somani Marg Mumbai Maharashtra 400 001 INDIA *Tel:* + 91 (0)222 206 0248 *Fax:* + 91 222 206 0248 *Email:* cnibombaydiocese@yahoo.com

Nagpur The Rt Revd Paul B K Dupare Bishop of Nagpur Bishop's House Cathedral House, Opp Indian Coffee House Sadar Nagpur Maharashtra 440 001 INDIA *Tel:* + 91 (0)712 255 3351 *Fax:* + 91 (0)712 255 3351 *Email:* nagpurdiocese@rediffmail.com

Nasik The Rt Revd Pradip Kamble Bishop of Nasik Bishop's House 1 Outram Road Tarakpur Ahmednagar Maharashtra 414 003 INDIA *Tel:* + 91 (0)241 241 1806 *Fax:* + 91 (0)241 242 2314 *Email:* bishopofnasik@rediffmail.com

North East India The Rt Revd Michael Herenz Bishop of North East India Bishop's Kuti Shillong Meghalaya 1 793 001 INDIA *Tel:* + 91 (0)364 222 3155 *Fax:* + 91 (0)364 250 1178

Patna The Rt Revd Philip P Marandih Bishop of Patna Bishop's House Christ Church Compound Bhagalpur Bihar 812 001 INDIA *Tel:* + 91 (0)641 240 0033 *Email:* cnipatna@rediffmail.com

Phulbani The Rt Revd Bijay K Nayak Bishop of Phulbani Bishop's House, Mission Compound Gudripori G. Udayagiri Phulbani Kandhmal 762 100 INDIA *Tel:* + 91 (0)684 726 0569 *Email:* bpnayakbijaykumar@gmail.com *Web:* www. cniphulbanidiocese.org

Pune The Rt Revd Andrew B K Rathod Bishop of Pune 1A Stavley Road General Bhagat Marg Pune Maharashtra 411 001 INDIA *Tel:* + 91 (0)202 633 4374 *Email:* punediocese@yahoo.co.in

Rajasthan The Rt Revd Darbara Singh Bishop of Rajasthan 2/10 Civil Lines Opp. Bus Stand Jaipur Road Ajmer Rajasthan 305 001 INDIA *Tel:* + 91 (0)145 242 0633 *Fax:* + 91 (0)145 262 1627

Sambalpur The Rt Revd Pinuel Dip Bishop of Sambalpur Bishop's House Mission Compound Bolangir Orissa 767 001 INDIA *Tel:* + 91 (0)665 223 0625 *Email:* pinuel_dip@rediffmail.com

THE CHURCH OF PAKISTAN (UNITED)

General Secretary Mr Anthony Lamuel Bishopsbourne Cathedral Close The Mall Lahore 54000 PAKISTAN

Provincial Treasurer Mr Irshad Nawab 113 Quasim Road PO Box 204 Multan Cantt PAKISTAN *Email:* treasurersynod.cop@gmail.com

Faisalabad The Rt Revd John Samuel Bishop of Faisalabad and Deputy Moderator of the Church of Pakistan Bishop's House PO Box 27 Mission road Gojra Dist Toba Tek Sing PAKISTAN *Tel:* + 92 (0)46 351 4689 *Email:* jsamuel51@hotmail.com

Hyderabad The Rt Revd Kaleem John Bishop of Hyderabad 27 - Liaqat Road Civil Lines Hyderabad 71000 PAKISTAN *Email:* kaleemjohn@aol.com

Karachi The Rt Revd Sadiq Daniel Bishop of Karachi Trinity Close Abdullah Haroon Road Karachi 4 PAKISTAN *Tel:* + 92 021 356556913 *Email:* sadiqdaniel@hotmail.com

Lahore The Rt Revd Irfan Jamil Bishop of Lahore Bishopsbourne Cathedral Close The Mall Lahore 54000 PAKISTAN *Tel:* + 92 (0)42 3723 3560 *Fax:* + 92 (0)42 3712 0766 *Email:* 9thbishopoflahore@ gmail.com *Web:* www.dol.com.pk

Multan The Rt Revd Leo Roderick Paul Bishop of Multan 113 Quasim Road PO Box 204 Multan Cantt PAKISTAN *Tel:* + 92 (0)61 458 3694 *Email:* bishop_ mdcop@live.com

Peshawar The Most Revd Humphrey S Peters Bishop of Peshawar & Moderator of the Church of Pakistan St Johns Cathedral 1 Sir Syed Road Peshawar 25000 PAKISTAN *Tel:* + 92 (0)91 527 6519 *Email:* bishopdop@hotmail.com

Raiwind The Rt Revd Azad Marshall Bishop of Raiwind 17 Warris Road Lahore 54000 PAKISTAN *Tel:* + 92 (0)42 3758 8950 *Email:* bishop@saintthomascenter.org

Sialkot The Rt Revd Alwin John Samuel Bishop of Sialkot Lal Kothi Bara Pathar Christian Town Sialkot 2 PAKISTAN *Tel:* + 92 052 4264828 *Email:* alwinsialkot@gmail.com

THE ANGLICAN CHURCH OF PAPUA NEW GUINEA

The Most Revd Allan Migi Archbishop of Papua New Guinea P.O.Box 673 Lae 411 Morobe Province PAPUA NEW GUINEA *Tel:* +*Email:* archbishopmigi95@gmail.com

Provincial Secretary Mr Dennis Kabekabe P.O.Box 673 Lae 411 Morobe Province PAPUA NEW GUINEA *Tel:* + 675 4724262 *Email:* dpk07jan@gmail.com

Aipo Rongo The Rt Revd Nathan Ingen Bishop of Aipo Rongo PO Box 893 Mount Hagen Western Highlands Province PAPUA NEW GUINEA *Tel:* + 675 54 211 31 *Fax:* + 675 54 211 81 *Email:* bishopnathan2@gmail.com

Dogura The Rt Revd Tennyson Bogar Bishop of Dogura Po Box 19 Dogura MBP PAPUA NEW GUINEA *Tel:* + 675 641 1530

New Guinea Islands, The Vacant Bishop elect of The New Guinea Islands Bishop's House PO Box 806 Kimbe NGIP PAPUA NEW GUINEA *Tel:* + 675 9 835 120 *Fax:* + 675 9 835 120

Popondota The Rt Revd Lindsley Ihove Bishop of Popondota Diocese of Popondota PO Box 26 Popondetta Oro Province PAPUA NEW GUINEA *Tel:* + 675 329 7194 *Fax:* + 675 329 7476 *Email:* bplndsleyihove@gmail.com

Port Moresby The Rt Revd Denny Bray Guka Bishop of Port Morsby PO Box 6491 Boroko NCD PAPUA NEW GUINEA*Email:* dennyguka@gmail.com

THE EPISCOPAL CHURCH IN THE PHILIPPINES

Provincial Secretary Mr Floyd Lalwet P.O Box 10321 Broadway Centrum Quezon City 1112 PHILIPPINES *Fax:* + 63 (0)2 721 1923 *Email:* flaw997@gmail.com

Provincial Treasurer Mrs Bridget Lacdao Provincial Office PO Box 10321 Broadway Centrum 1112 Quezon City PHILIPPINES *Tel:* + 63 (0)2 722 8510 *Fax:* + 63 (0)2 721 1923

Central Philippines The Rt Revd Dixie Copanut Taclobao Central Philippines 281 E Rodriguez Sr Avenue 1102 Quezon City PHILIPPINES *Tel:* + 63 (0)2 412 8561 *Fax:* + 63 (0)2 721 1923 *Email:* central@i-next.net

Davao The Rt Revd Jonathan Labasan Casimina Bishop of Davao Km. 3 McArthur Highway Matina Davao City PHILIPPINES *Tel:* + 63 82 299 1511 *Fax:* + 63 82 296 9629 *Email:* episcopaldioceseofdavao@yahoo.com *Web:* www.eddphilippines.com

North Central Philippines The Most Revd Joel Atiwag Pachao Prime Bishop of the Philippines & Bishop of North Central Philippines 358 Magsaysay Avenue Baguio City 2600 PHILIPPINES *Tel:* + 63 27228481 *Fax:* + 63 (0)74 442 2432 *Email:* bpjoelpachao@yahoo.com

Northern Luzon Vacant Bishop elect of Northern Luzon Bulanao Tabuk Kalinga-Apayao 3800 PHILIPPINES

Northern Philippines- Mt Province The Rt Revd Brent W Alawas Bishop of Northern Philippines Diocesan Office Bontoc 2616 PHILIPPINES *Tel:* + 63 (0)74 602 1026 *Fax:* + 63 (0)74 462 4099 *Email:* ednpvic@hotmail.com

Northern Philippines The Rt Revd Miguel P Yamoyam Suffragan Bishop of the Northern Philippines PO Box 10321 Broadway Centrum Quezon City 1112 PHILIPPINES *Tel:* + 63 (0)2 722 8481/8460 *Fax:* + 63 (0)2 721 1923 *Email:* ecpnational@yahoo.co.ph

Santiago-Isabela The Rt Revd Alexander A Wandag Bishop of Santiago Episcopal Diocese of Santiago Maharlika Highway 3311 Divisoria Santiago City 3311 PHILIPPINES *Tel:* + 63 (0)78 682 3756 *Fax:* + 63 (0)78 682 1256 *Email:* alexwandageds@yahoo.com

Southern Philippines The Rt Revd Danilo Labacanacruz Bustamante Bishop of Southern Philippines 186 Sinsuat Avenue Cotabato City 9600 PHILIPPINES *Tel:* + 63 (0)64 421 2960 *Fax:* + 63 (0)64 421 1703 *Email:* edsp_ecp@yahoo.com *Web:* www.edspphilippines.com

L'EGLISE EPISCOPAL AU RWANDA

Provincial Secretary The Revd Francis Karemera PO Box 2487 Kigali RWANDA *Email:* frkaremera@yahoo.co.uk

Butare The Rt Revd Nathan K Gasatura Bishop of Butare BP 255 Butare RWANDA *Tel:* + 250 30 710 *Fax:* + 250 30 504 *Email:* nathan.gasatura@gmail.com

Byumba The Rt Revd Emmanuel Ngendahayo Bishop of Byumba BP 17 Byumba RWANDA *Tel:* + 250 64 242 *Fax:* + 250 64 242 *Email:* engendahayo@ymail.com

Cyangugu The Rt Revd Nathan Amooti Rusengo Bishop of Cyangugu PO Box 52 Cyangugu RWANDA *Tel:* + 250 788 409 061 *Email:* nathanamooti@gmail.com

Gahini The Rt Revd Alexis Bilindabagabo Bishop of Gahini BP 22 Gahini RWANDA *Tel:* + 250 67 422

Fax: + 250 77 831 *Email:* abilindabagabo@gmail.com

Gasabo The Most Revd Onesphore Rwaje Archbishop of L'Eglise Episcopal au Rwanda and Bishop of Gasabo PO Box 2487 Kigali RWANDA *Fax:* + 250 64 242 *Email:* onesphorerwaje@yahoo.fr

Kibungo The Rt Revd Emmanuel Ntazinda Bishop of Kibungo BP 719 Kibungo RWANDA *Tel:* + 250 566 194

Kigali The Rt Revd Louis Muvunyi Bishop of Kigali PO Box 61 Kigali RWANDA *Tel:* + 250 576 340 *Fax:* + 250 573 213 *Email:* louismuvunyi@hotmail.com

Kigeme The Rt Revd Augustin Mvunabandi Bishop of Kigeme BP 67 Gikongoro RWANDA *Tel:* + 250 535 086 *Email:* dkigemeear@yahoo.fr

Kivu The Rt Revd Augustin Ahimana Bishop of Kivu PO Box 166 Gisenyi RWANDA *Tel:* + 250 78 830 5119 *Email:* aamurekezi@gmail.com

Shyira The Rt Revd Laurent Mbanda Bishop of Shyira EER - Shyira PO Box 52 Ruhengeri RWANDA *Tel:* + 250 466 02 *Fax:* + 250 546 449 *Email:* mbandalaurent@yahoo.com

Shyira The Rt Revd Samuel Mugisha Mugiraneza Coadjutor Bishop of Shyira EER - Shyira PO Box 52 Ruhengeri RWANDA *Tel:* + 250 466 02

Shyogwe The Rt Revd Jered Kalimba Bishop of Shyogwe BP 27 Gitarama RWANDA *Tel:* + 250 62 372 *Fax:* + 250 62 460 *Email:* kalimbaj60@yahoo.fr

THE SCOTTISH EPISCOPAL CHURCH

Secretary General Mr John Stuart 21 Grosvenor Crescent Edinburgh EH12 5EE SCOTLAND *Tel:* + 44 (0)131 225 6357 *Fax:* + 44 (0)131 346 7247 *Email:* secgen@scotland.anglican.org

Provincial Treasurer Mr Malcolm G Bett 21 Grosvenor Crescent Edinburgh EH12 5EE SCOTLAND *Tel:* + 44 (0)131 225 6357 *Fax:* + 44 (0)131 346 7247

Aberdeen & Orkney The Rt Revd Robert Gillies Bishop of Aberdeen & Orkney Diocesan Office St Clement's Church House Mastrick Drive Aberdeen AB16 6UF SCOTLAND *Tel:* + 44 (0) 1224 662 247 *Fax:* + 44 (0)1224 662 168 *Email:* bishop@aberdeen. anglican.org *Web:* www.aberdeen.anglican.org

Argyll & The Isles-Argyll The Rt Revd Kevin Pearson Bishop of Argyll & The Isles St Moluag's Diocesan Centre Croft Avenue Oban PA34 5JJ SCOTLAND *Tel:* + 44 (0)1631 570 870 *Fax:* + 44 (0)1631 570 411 *Email:* bishop@argyll.anglican.org *Web:* www.argyllandtheisles.org.uk

Brechin The Rt Revd Nigel Peyton Bishop of Brechin The Brechin Diocesan Office 38 Langlands Street Dundee DD4 6SZ SCOTLAND *Tel:* + 44 (0)1382 562 24 *Email:* office@brechin.anglican.org *Web:* www.thedioceseofbrechin.org

Edinburgh The Rt Revd John Armes Bishop of Edinburgh Diocesan Centre 21A Grosvenor Crescent Edinburgh EH12 5EL SCOTLAND *Tel:* + 44 (0)131 538 7044 *Fax:* + 44 (0)131 538 7088 *Email:* bishop@edinburgh.anglican.org *Web:* www.edinburgh.anglican.org

Glasgow & Galloway The Rt Revd Gregor Duncan Bishop of Glasgow & Galloway Bishop's Office Diocesan Centre 5 St Vincent Place Glasgow G1 2DH SCOTLAND *Tel:* + 44 (0)141 221 6911 *Fax:* + 44 (0)141 221 7014 *Email:* bishop@glasgow.anglican. org *Web:* www.glasgow.anglican.org

Moray, Ross & Caithness The Most Revd Mark Strange Primus of the Scottish Episcopal Church & Bishop of Moray, Ross & Caithness Diocesan Office 9-11 Kenneth Street Inverness IV3 5NR SCOTLAND *Tel:* + 44 (0)1463 237503 *Fax:* + *Email:* bishop@moray.anglican.org *Web:* www.moray. anglican.org

St Andrews Dunkeld & Dunblane Vacant Bishop of St Andrews, Dunkeld & Dunblane Diocesan Office 28A Balhousie Street Perth PH1 5HJ SCOTLAND *Tel:* + 44 01738 580426 *Email:* bishopsec@standrews. anglican.org

CHURCH OF THE PROVINCE OF SOUTHEAST ASIA

Provincial Secretary The Revd Kenneth Thien Su Yin PO Box 10811 88809 Kota Kinabalu Sabah 88809 MALAYSIA *Email:* kenneththien@gmail.com

Provincial Treasurer Mr Keith Chua 35 Ford Avenue Singapore 268714 SINGAPORE *Tel:* + 65 (0)2 6235 3344 *Fax:* + 65 (0)2 6736 1201 *Email:* keithchu@ singnet.com.sg

Kuching The Rt Revd Danald Jute Bishop of Kuching Bishop's House PO Box 347 Kuching Sarawak 93704 MALAYSIA *Tel:* + 60 (0)82 240 187 *Fax:* + 60 (0)82 426 488 *Email:* bpofkuching@gmail.com *Web:* www. diocesekuching.org

Kuching The Rt Revd Solomon Cheong Sung Voon Assistant Bishop of Kuching Bishop's House PO Box 347 Kuching Sarawak 93704 MALAYSIA *Tel:* + 60 (0)82 429 755

Sabah The Rt Revd Melter Jiki Tais Bishop of Sabah PO Box 10811 88809 Kota Kinabalu Sabah 88809 MALAYSIA *Tel:* + 60 (0)89 521 448 *Fax:* + 60 (0)89 521 448 *Email:* uskupmjtais@gmail.com

Sabah The Rt Revd John Yeo Assistant Bishop of Sabah 201 Jalan Dunlop Tawau sabah 91000 MALAYSIA *Tel:* + 60 (0)89 772 212 *Fax:* + 60 (0)89 761 451 *Email:* ad.johnyeo@gmail.com

Singapore The Rt Revd Rennis Ponniah Bishop of Singapore St Andrew's Village 1 Francis Thomas Drive #01-01 Singapore 359340 SINGAPORE *Tel:* + 65 6288 7585 *Fax:* + 65 6288 5574 *Email:* bpoffice@ anglican.org.sg

West Malaysia The Most Revd Ng Moon Hing Archbishop of South East Asia & Bishop of West Malaysia 16 Jalan Pudu Kuala Lumpur 50200 MALAYSIA *Tel:* + 60 (0)32 031 3213 *Fax:* + 60 (0)32 031 2728 *Email:* canonmoon@gmail.com

West Malaysia The Rt Revd Charles K Samuel Assistant Bishop of West Malaysia St George's Church 1 Lebuh Farquhar Georgetown Pulau Pinang 10200 MALAYSIA *Tel:* + 60 (0)16 922 1618 *Email:* vencan.cs@gmail.com

West Malaysia The Rt Revd Jayson Selvaraj Assistant Bishop of West Malaysia Christ Church Melaka 48 Jalan Gereja Melaka 75000 West MALAYSIA *Tel:* + 60 06 2848 804 *Email:* jasondaphne101@gmail.com

CHURCH OF SOUTH INDIA

General Secretary CSI The Revd D R Sadananda CSI Centre, No 5 Whites Road Royapettah Chennai 6000 014 INDIA *Tel:* + 91 044 2852 1566 *Email:* synodcsi@gmail.com

Provincial Treasurer Advocate C. Robert Bruce 5 Whites Road Royapettah Chennai 600014 INDIA *Tel:* + 91 044 2852 1566 *Email:* treasurercsi@eth.net

Cochin The Rt Revd Baker Ninan Fenn Bishop of Cochin CSI Diocesan Office P.B. No. 104 Shoranur Palakkad Kerala 679 121 INDIA *Tel:* + 91 (0)466 222 4454 *Fax:* + 91 (0)466 222 2545 *Email:* revbnfenn@gmail.com

Coimbatore The Rt Revd Timothy Ravinder Bishop of Coimbatore Bishop's House 256 Race Course Road Coimbatore TN 1 641018 INDIA *Tel:* + 91 (0)422 221 3605 *Fax:* + 91 (0)422 221 3369 *Email:* csi.bpcbe@gmail.com

Dornakal The Rt Revd Vadapalli Prasada Rao Deputy Moderator of CSI & Bishop of Dornakal Bishop's House Epiphany Cathedral Compound SC Railway Dornakal Andhra Pradesh 506 381 INDIA *Tel:* + 91 (0) 8719 227 535 *Fax:* + 91 (0) 8719 227 376 *Email:* dkbpoff@hotmail.com

East Kerala The Rt Revd Kayalakkakathu George Daniel Bishop of East Kerala CSI Bishop's House Melukavumattom - Kerala 686 652 INDIA *Tel:* + 91 (0)4822 219 044 *Email:* bishopkgdaniel@rediffmail.com

Jaffna The Rt Revd Daniel Selvaratnam Thiagarajah Bishop of Jaffna Bishop's House Vaddukoddai SRI LANKA *Tel:* + 94 (0)60 221 2424 *Email:* dsthiagarajah@yahoo.com

Kanyakumari The Rt Revd Gnanasigamony Devakadasham Bishop of Kanyakumari 71-A Dennis Street Nagercoil Tamil Nadu629 001 INDIA *Tel:* + 91 (0)4652 231 539 *Fax:* + 91 (0)4652 226 560 *Email:* csikkd@bsnl.com

Karimnagar The Rt Revd Reuben Mark Bishop of Karimnagar 2-8-95 CV Raman Road PO Box 40 Makarampura Karimnagar Andhra Pradesh 505 001 INDIA *Tel:* + 91 878 226 2971 *Fax:* + 91 878 226 2972

Karnataka Central The Rt Revd Prasana Kumar Samuel Bishop of Karnataka Central Diocesan Office 20 Third Cross CSI Compound Bangalore Karnataka 560 027 INDIA *Tel:* + 91 (0)80 2222 3766 *Email:* admin@csikcd.org

Karnataka North The Rt Revd Ravikumar J. Niranjan Bishop of Karnataka North Bishop's House All Saints Church Compound Dharwad - Karnataka 580 008 INDIA *Tel:* + 91 (0)836 244 7733 *Email:* haradoni.rn@gmail.com

Karnataka South The Rt Revd Mohan Manoraj Bishop of Karnataka South Bishop's House Balmatta Mangalore 575 002 INDIA *Tel:* + 91 (0)824 2432 657 *Fax:* + 91 (0)824 2432 363 *Email:* csikcd2014@gmail.com

Kollam-Kottarakkara Vacant Bishop elect of Kollam - Kottarakkara CSI Kollam - Kottarakkara Diocesan Office N. H. 208 Chinnakkada Kollam-Kerala 691001 INDIA *Email:* revbhanusamuel@gmail.com

Krishna-Godavari The Rt Revd Govada Dyvasirvadam Bishop of Krishna-Godavari St Andrew's Cathedral Compound Main Road Machilipatnam - Andhra Pradesh 521 002 Krishna-Godaviri District INDIA *Tel:* + 91 (0)8672 220 623 *Fax:* + 91 (0)8672 220 771 *Email:* bishopkrishna@yahoo.com

Madhya Kerala The Most Revd Thomas Kanjirappally Oommen Moderator of CSI & Bishop of Madhya Kerala CSI Bishop's House Cathedral Road Kottayam Kerala State 686 001 INDIA *Tel:* + 91 (0)481 2566 536 *Fax:* + 91 (0)481 2566 531 *Email:* csimkdbishopsoffice@gmail.com

Madras The Rt Revd George Stephen Jeyaraj Bishop of Madras Diocesan Office PB No 4914 226 Cathedral Road Chennai Tamil Nadu 600 086 INDIA *Tel:* + 91 (0)44 2811 3933 *Fax:* + 91 (0)44 2811 0608 *Web:* www.csimadrasdiocese.org

Madurai-Ramnad The Rt Revd Marialouis Joseph Bishop of Madurai-Ramnad #5 Bhulabai Road Chockikulam Madurai District Tamil Nadu 625 002 INDIA *Tel:* + 91 (0)452 256 3196 *Fax:* + 91 (0)452 256 0864 *Email:* bishop@csidmr.net

Malabar The Rt Revd Royce Manoj Victor Bishop of Malabar CSI Diocesan Office Bank Road Calicut Kerala 673001 INDIA *Tel:* + 91 495 2721748 *Email:* csimalabardiocese@gmail.com

Medak Vacant Bishop elect of Medak 10-3-65, Church House Golden Jubilee Bhavan Old Lancer Lane Secunderabad Andhra Pradesh 500 025 INDIA *Tel:* + 91 (0)40 2783 3151 *Fax:* + 91 (0)40 2782 0843 *Email:* medakdiocese@yahoo.com

Nandyal The Rt Revd Eggoni Pushpalalitha Bishop of Nandyal Bishop's House Nandyal RS Kurnool District Andhra Pradesh 518 502 INDIA *Tel:* + 91 (0)8514 222 477 *Fax:* + 91 (0)8514 242 255

Rayalaseema The Rt Revd B D Prasada Rao Bishop of Rayalaseema CSI Compound Kadapa Andhra Pradesh 516 001 INDIA *Tel:* + 91 (0) 8562 325320 *Fax:* + 91 (0) 8562 275200 *Email:* lbd_prasad@ yahoo.com

South Kerala The Rt Revd Dharmaraj Rasalam Bishop of South Kerala Bishop's House LMS Compound Trivandrum Kerala State 695 033 INDIA *Tel:* + 91 (0)471 231 5490 *Fax:* + 91 (0)471 231 6439

Thoothukudi-Nazareth The Rt Revd Samuel Devasahayam Ebenezer E Clement Bishop of Thoothukudi - Nazareth Diocesan Road Caldwell Hr. Sec. School Campus Beach Road Thoothukudi Tamil Nadu 628 001 INDIA *Tel:* + 91 (0) 461 2329 408 *Fax:* + 91 (0)461 2328 408 *Email:* csitnd@bsnl.in

Tirunelveli The Rt Revd Jayaraj J Christdoss Bishop of Tirunelveli Bishopstowe PO Box 118 Palayamkottai Tirunelveli Tamil Nadu 627 002 INDIA *Tel:* + 91 (0)462 2578 744 *Fax:* + 91 (0)462 2574 525

Trichy-Tanjore The Rt Revd Gnanamuthu Paul Vasanthakumar Bishop of Trichy-Tanjore CSI Diocesan Office Allithurai Road Pathur Tiruchirappalli Tamil Nadu 620 017 INDIA *Tel:* + 91 (0)431 771 254 *Email:* csittd@tr.net.in

Vellore The Rt Revd A Rajavelu Bishop of Vellore 3/1 Anna Salai Vellore Tamil Nadu 632 001 INDIA *Tel:* + 91 (0)416 2232 160 *Fax:* + 91 (0)416 2223 835 *Email:* csi.vlrdiocese@gmail.com

THE CHURCH OF THE PROVINCE OF SOUTHERN AFRICA

Provincial Executive Officer The Ven Horace Arenz 20 Bishopscourt Drive Claremont Western Cape 7708 SOUTH AFRICA *Tel:* + 27 (0)21 763 1325 *Fax:* + 27 (0)21 797 1329 *Email:* peo@ anglicanchurchsa.org.za

Provincial Treasurer and Diocesan Secretary of Cape Town Mr Rob S Rogerson P O Box 53014 Kenilworth 7745 SOUTH AFRICA *Tel:* + 27 (0)21 797 8324 *Fax:* + 27 (0)21 683 4603 *Email:* rogerson@cpsa-province. org.za

Angola (Missionary Diocese) The Rt Revd Andre Soares Bishop of Angola Off Caixa Postal No. 10341 Luanda ANGOLA *Tel:* + 244 946463780 *Email:* anglicangola@yahoo.com

Cape Town The Most Revd Thabo C Makgoba Archbishop of Capetown and Primate of Southern Africa 20 Bishopscourt Drive Bishopscourt Claremont Cape Town Western Cape 7708 SOUTH AFRICA *Tel:* + 27 021 763 1320 *Fax:* + 27 021 761

4193 *Email:* archpa@anglicanchurchsa.org.za *Web:* www.anglicanchurchsa.org/

Cape Town The Rt Revd Garth Q Counsell Bishop of Table Bay PO Box 1932 Cape Town 8000 SOUTH AFRICA *Tel:* + 27 (0)21 469 3774 *Fax:* + 27 (0)21 469 3774 *Email:* bishop.suffragan@ctdiocese.org.za

Christ the King The Rt Revd Peter J Lee Bishop of Christ the King Diocese of Christ the King PO Box 1653 Rosettenville Gauteng 2130 SOUTH AFRICA *Tel:* + 27 (0)11 435 0097 *Fax:* + 27 (0)11 435 2868 *Email:* bishop@ctkdiocese.co.za *Web:* www. christthekingdiocese-anglican.org

Diocese of the Free State (formerly Bloemfontein) The Rt Revd Dintoe Letloenyane Bishop of Diocese of the Free State PO Box 411 Bloemfontein 9300 SOUTH AFRICA *Tel:* + 27 (0)51 447 6053 *Fax:* + 27 (0)51 447 5874 *Email:* bishopdintoe@dsc.co.za *Web:* www.dsc.co.za

False Bay The Rt Revd Margaret Brenda Vertue Bishop of False Bay PO Box 2804 Somerset West 7129 SOUTH AFRICA *Tel:* + 27 (0)21 852 5243 *Fax:* + 27 (0)21 852 9430 *Email:* bishopm@falsebaydiocese. org.za *Web:* www.falsebaydiocese.org.za

George The Rt Revd Brian Marajh Bishop of George PO Box 227 George Cape Province 6530 SOUTH AFRICA *Tel:* + 27 (0)44 873 5680 *Fax:* + 27 (0)44 873 5680 *Email:* bishopbrian@georgediocese.org.za

Grahamstown The Rt Revd Ebenezer StM Ntlali Bishop of Grahamstown Bishopsbourne PO Box 181 Grahamstown Eastern Cape 6140 SOUTH AFRICA *Tel:* + 27 (0)46 636 1996 *Fax:* + 27 (0)46 622 5231 *Email:* bpgtn@intekom.co.za

Highveld The Rt Revd David H Bannerman Bishop of the Highveld PO Box 17642 Benoni West Gauteng 1503 SOUTH AFRICA *Tel:* + 27 (0)11 422 2231/2 *Fax:* + 27 (0)11 420 1336 *Email:* diohveld@iafrica. com *Web:* www.diocesehighveld.org.za

Johannesburg The Rt Revd Stephen Mosimanegape Moreo Bishop of Johannesburg Diocesan Office P O Box 157 Westhoven Gauteng 2142 SOUTH AFRICA *Tel:* + 27 (0)11 375 2700 *Fax:* + 27 (0)11 477 1337 *Email:* steve.moreo@anglicanjoburg.org.za

Kimberley & Kuruman The Rt Revd Oswald P P Swartz Bishop of Kimberley and Kuruman PO Box 45 Kimberley 8300 SOUTH AFRICA *Tel:* + 27 (0)53 833 2433 *Fax:* + 27 (0)53 831 2730 *Email:* oppswartz@onetel.com

Lebombo The Rt Revd Carlos Simao Matsinhe Bishop of Lebombo Caixa Postale 120 Maputo MOZAMBIQUE *Tel:* + 258 860 278 712 *Email:* carlosmatsinhe@rocketmail.com

Lesotho The Rt Revd Adam Mallane A Taaso Bishop of Lesotho PO Box 87 Maseru 100 LOSOTO *Tel:* + 266 (0)22 3311 974 *Fax:* + 266 (0)22 310 161 *Email:* dioceselesotho@ecoweb.co.ls

Matlosane (formerly Klerksdorp) The Rt Revd Stephen M Diseko Bishop of Matlosane PO Box 11417 Klerksdorp 2570 SOUTH AFRICA *Tel:* + 27 (0)18 464 2260 *Fax:* + 27 (0)18 462 4939 *Email:* diocesematlosane@telkomsa.net

Mbhashe The Rt Revd Elliot S Williams Bishop of Mbhashe PO Box 1184 Butterworth 4960 SOUTH AFRICA *Tel:* + 27 (0)47 491 8127 *Fax:* + 27 (0)47 491 9218 *Email:* dioceseofmbhashe@telkomsa.net

Mpumalanga The Rt Revd Daniel M Kgomosotho Bishop of Mpumalanga PO Box 4327 White River 1240 SOUTH AFRICA *Tel:* + 27 (0)13 751 1960 *Fax:* + 27 (0)13 751 3638 *Email:* bishopdan@telkomsa.net

Mthatha (formerly St John's) The Rt Revd Sitembele T Mzamane Bishop of Mthatha PO Box 25 Umtata Transkei 5100 SOUTH AFRICA *Tel:* + 27 (0)47 532 4450 *Fax:* + 27 (0)47 532 4191 *Email:* anglicbspmthatha@intekom.co.za   *Web:*   www. mthatha.anglican.org

Namibia The Rt Revd Natanael Nakwatumba Bishop of Namibia PO Box 57 Windhoek 9000 NAMIBIA *Tel:* + 264 (0)61 238 920 *Fax:* + 264 (0)61 225 903 *Email:* bishop@anglicanchurchnamibia.com

Namibia The Rt Revd Petrus Hilukiluah Suffragan Bishop of Namibia PO Box 65 Windhoek NAMIBIA *Tel:* + 264 (0)61 236 009 *Fax:* + 264 (0)61 225 903 *Email:* bpertus@iafrica.com.na

Natal The Rt Revd Dino Gabriel Bishop of Natal PO Box 47439 Greyville Durban 4023 SOUTH AFRICA *Tel:* + 27 (0)31 308 9302 *Fax:* + 27 (0)31 308 9316 *Email:* bishop@dionatal.org.za *Web:* www.anglican-kzn.org.za

Natal The Rt Revd Hummingfield C Ndwandwe Suffragan Bishop of the South Episcopal Area PO Box 889 Pietermaritzburg 3200 SOUTH AFRICA *Tel:* + 27 (0)33 394 1560 *Fax:* + 27 (0)33 394 8785 *Email:* bishopndwandwe@dionatal.org.za

Natal The Rt Revd Tsietse Edward Seleoane Suffragan Bishop of the North West Episcopal Area P O Box 463 Ladysmith 3370 SOUTH AFRICA *Tel:* + 27 (0)36 631 4650 *Fax:* + 27 (0)36 637 4949 *Email:* seleoanet@vodamail.co.za

Niassa The Revd Vicente Msossa Bishop elect of Niassa Diocese of Niassa CP 264 Lichinga Niassa MOZAMBIQUE *Tel:* + 258 2712 0735 *Email:* bishop. niassa@gmail.com

Niassa The Rt Revd Manuel Ernesto Suffragan Bishop of Niassa Diocese of Niassa CP 264 Lichinga Niassa MOZAMBIQUE *Tel:* + 258 27 121 377 *Email:* mernesto.diocese.niassa@gmail.com

Port Elizabeth The Rt Revd Nceba B Nopece Bishop of Port Elizabeth PO Box 7109 Newton Park 6055 SOUTH AFRICA *Tel:* + 27 (0)41 365 1387 *Fax:* + 27 (0)41 365 2049 *Email:* pebishop@iafrica.com *Web:* www.anglicandiocepe.org.za

Pretoria The Rt Revd Allan John Kannemeyer Bishop of Pretoria PO Box 1032 Pretoria 1 SOUTH AFRICA *Tel:* + 27 (0)12 430 2345 *Fax:* + 12 (0)12 430 2224 *Email:* ptabish@dioceseofpretoria.org *Web:* www.pretoriadiocese.org.za

Saldanha Bay The Rt Revd Raphael B V Hess Bishop of Saldanha Bay PO Box 420 Malmesbury Cape Province 7299 SOUTH AFRICA *Tel:* + 27 (0)22 487 3885 *Fax:* + 27 (0)22 487 3187 *Email:* bishop@dioceseofsaldanhabay.org.za

St Helena The Rt Revd Richard D Fenwick Bishop of St Helena Bishopsholme PO Box 62 St Helena Island South Atlantic *Tel:* + 290 4471 *Fax:* + 290 4728 *Email:* bishop@helanta.sh *Web:* www.sthelena.anglican.org

St Mark the Evangelist The Rt Revd Martin A Breytenbach Bishop of St Mark the Evangelist PO Box 643 Polokwane 700 SOUTH AFRICA *Tel:* + 27 (0)15 297 3297 *Fax:* + 27 (0)15 297 0408 *Email:* martin@stmark.org.za *Web:*

Swaziland The Rt Revd Ellinah Ntfombi Wamukoya Bishop of Swaziland PO Box 118 Mbabane SWAZILAND *Tel:* + 268 4 04 3624 *Fax:* + 268 404 6759 *Email:* bishopen@swazilanddiocese.org.sz *Web:*

Ukhahlamba The Rt Revd Mazwi E Tisani Bishop of Ukhahlamba PO Box 1673 Queenstown Eastern Cape 116 SOUTH AFRICA *Tel:* + 27 (0)45 838 3261 *Fax:* + 27 (0)45 838 2874 *Email:* bishopmazwi@mweb.co.za

Umzimvubu The Rt Revd Mlibo M Ngewu Bishop of Umzimvubu PO Box 644 Kokstad 4700 SOUTH AFRICA *Tel:* + 27 (0)39 727 4117 *Fax:* + 27 (0)39 727 4117 *Email:* mzimvubu@futurenet.co.za *Web:*

Zululand The Rt Revd Monument Makhanya Bishop of Zululand PO Box 147 Eshowe Zululand 3815 SOUTH AFRICA *Tel:* + 27 (0)35 474 2047 *Fax:* + 27 (0)35 474 2047 *Email:* bishopzld@nctactive.co.za

IGLESIA ANGLICANA DEL CONO SUR DE AMERICA

Provincial Secretary Mrs Cristina Daly Awaiting Details *Email:* cristindaly@gmail.com

Provincial Treasurer The Revd Walter Toro Awaiting Details *Email:* wabricii@gmail.com

Argentina The Most Revd Gregory James Venables Presiding Bishop of the Anglican Church of South America & Bishop of Argentina 25 de Mayo 282 Capital Federal Buenos Aires 1001 ARGENTINA *Tel:* + 54 11 4342 4618 *Fax:* + 54 11 4784 1277 *Email:* bpgreg@fibertel.com.ar *Web:* www.anglicana.org.ar

Bolivia The Rt Revd Raphael Samuel Bishop of Bolivia Inglesia Anglicana Episcopal de Bolivia Casilla 848 Cochabamba BOLIVIA *Tel:* + 591 4440 1168 *Email:* raphaelsamuel@gmail.com

Chile The Rt Revd Hector Zavala Muñoz Bishop of

Chile Casilla 50675 Correo Central Santiago CHILE *Tel:* + 56 (0)2 638 3009 *Fax:* + 56 (0)2 639 4581 *Email:* tzavala@iach.cl *Web:* www.iach.cl

Chile The Rt Revd Abelino Manuel Apeleo Suffragan Bishop of Chile Pasaje Viña Poniente 4593 Puente Alto Santiago CHILE *Tel:* + 56 (0)2 638 3009 *Email:* aapeleo@gmail.com *Web:* www.iach.cl

Northern Argentina The Rt Revd Nicholas James Quested Drayson Bishop of Northern Argentina Iglesia Anglicana Casilla 187 Salta 4400 ARGENTINA *Tel:* + 54 387 431 1718 *Fax:* + 54 371 142 0100 *Email:* nicobispo@gmail.com

Northern Argentina The Rt Revd Cristiano Rojas Suffragan Bishop of Northern Argentina Iglesia Anglicana Casilla 187 Salta 4400 ARGENTINA

Northern Argentina The Rt Revd Mateo Alto Suffragan Bishop of Northern Argentina Iglesia Anglicana Casilla 187 Salta 4400 ARGENTINA

Northern Argentina The Rt Revd Urbano Duarte Suffragan Bishop of Northern Argentina Iglesia Anglicana Casilla 187 Salta 4400 ARGENTINA

Paraguay The Rt Revd Peter John Henry Bartlett Bishop of Paraguay Iglesia Anglicana Paraguya Casilla de Correo 1124 Asuncion Paraguya PARAGUAY *Tel:* + 595 (0)21 200 933 *Fax:* + 595 (0)21 214 328 *Email:* peterparaguay@gmail.com

Paraguay The Rt Revd Andrés Rodríguez Erben Assistant Bishop of Paraguay España # 1357 (casi Gral. Santos) Asuncion 1124 PARAGUAY *Tel:* + 59 5331 242 533

Peru The Rt Revd Jorge Luis Aguilar Bishop of Peru Calle Doña María 141 Los Rosales Surco Lima 33 PERU *Tel:* + 51 (0)1 449 0600 *Email:* cocosac59@ hotmail.com

Peru The Rt Revd Eulogio Alejandro Mesco Suffragan bishop of Peru Residencial Monte Bello D4 Cerro Colorado Arequipa PERU *Tel:* + 51 054 9943 51781 *Email:* alejandromesco@hotmail.com

Peru The Rt Revd Juan Carlos Revilla Suffragan Bishop of Peru Calle Doña María 141 Los Rosales Surco Lima 33 PERU *Tel:* + 51 (0)1 449 0600 *Email:* jucareli1208@hotmail.es

Uruguay The Rt Revd Michael Pollesel Bishop of Uruguay Reconquista # 522 Montevideo 11000 URUGUAY *Tel:* + 598 (0)2 915 9627 *Fax:* + 598 (0)2 916 2519 *Email:* iglesiaau@gmail.com *Web:* www. anglicanchurch.uy

Uruguay The Rt Revd Gilberto Obdulio Porcal Martínez Suffragan Bishop of Uruguay Reconquista # 522 Montevideo 11000 URUGUAY *Tel:* + 598 (0)2 915 9627 *Fax:* + 598 (0)4 732 8237 *Email:* gilbertoporcal@hotmail.com

THE EPISCOPAL CHURCH OF SOUTH SUDAN

Acting Provincial Secretary Mr John Augustino Lumori PO Box 110 Juba SOUTH SUDAN *Email:* provincialsecretary@sudan.anglican.org

Provincial Treasurer Mr Evans Sokiri PO Box 110 Juba SOUTH SUDAN *Email:* ecsprovince@hotmail. com

Akot-Bahr El Ghazal The Rt Revd Isaac Dhieu Ater Bishop of Akot PO Box 110 Juba SOUTH SUDAN *Email:* bishop@akot.anglican.org *Web:* www.akot. anglican.org

Attooch-Upper NIle The Rt Revd Moses Anur Bishop of Attooch Awaiting Details *Tel:* + 211 91489017 *Email:* athoochdiocese@gmail.com

Aweil-Bahr El Ghazal The Rt Revd Abraham Yel Nhial Bishop of Aweil e/o ECS PO Box 110 Northern Bah el Ghazal SOUTH SUDAN *Tel:* + 211 (0)955 621 584 *Email:* bishop@aweil.anglican.org *Web:* www. aweil.anglican.org

Aweil-Bahr El Ghazal The Rt Revd Michael Deng Assistant Bishop of Aweil - Abyei Area Awaiting Details *Tel:* + 211 (0)9257 73333 *Email:* mbol55@ hotmail.com

Awerial -Bahr El Ghazal The Rt Revd David Akau Kuol Bishop of Awerial Awaiting Details *Tel:* + 211 (0)955 526 396 *Email:* bpkuol2@gmail.com

Bor-Upper NIle The Rt Revd Ruben Akurdid Ngong Bishop of Bor C/O ECS PO Box 110 Juba SOUTH SUDAN *Tel:* + 211 (0)926 572 471 *Web:* www.bor. anglican.org

Cueibet-Bahr El Ghazal The Rt Revd Elijah Matueny Awet Bishop of Cueibet C/O ECS PO Box 110 Juba SOUTH SUDAN *Tel:* + 211 (0)926 572 471 *Email:* bishop@cueibet.anglican.org *Web:* www. cueibet.anglican.org

Duk-Upper Nile The Rt Revd Daniel Deng Abot Bishop of Duk Awaiting Details *Email:* danieldengabot@gmail.com

Duk-Upper Nile The Rt Revd Thomas Tut Assistant Bishop of Duk - Ayod Area Awaiting Details*Email:* tutgany@gmail.com

Ezo-Minye The Rt Revd John Kereboro Zawo Bishop of Ezo C/O ECS PO Box 110 Juba SOUTH SUDAN *Tel:* + 211 (0)818 593 217 *Web:* www.ezo. anglican.org

Ibba-Minye The Rt Revd Wilson Elisa Kamani Bishop of Ibba C/O ECS PO Box 110 Juba SOUTH SUDAN *Email:* bishopkamani@gmail.com *Web:* www.ibba.anglican.org

Juba-Loryco The Most Revd Daniel Deng Bul Yak Archbishop of the Province of the Episcopal Church of South Sudan & Bishop of Juba Province of the Episcopal Church of South Sudan PO Box 110 Juba

SOUTH SUDAN *Email:* archbishopdeng@gmail.com *Web:* www.juba.anglican.org

Juba-Loryco The Rt Revd Fraser Yugu Elias Assistant Bishop of Juba Episcopal Church of Sudan PO Box 110 Juba SOUTH SUDAN *Email:* bishopyugu@gmail.com

Kajo Keji-Loryco The Rt Revd Emmanuel Murye Bishop of Kajo Keji C/O ECS PO Box 110 Juba SOUTH SUDAN *Email:* bishop@kajokeji.anglican.org *Web:* www.kajokeji.anglican.org

Kongor-Upper Nile The Rt Revd Gabriel Thuch Agoth Deng Bishop of Kongor St Peter's Cathedral Panyagor SOUTH SUDAN *Tel:* + 211 955225139 *Email:* ecsdkongor@gmail.com

Lainya-Loryco The Rt Revd Eliaba Lako Obed Bishop of Lainya C/O ECS PO Box 110 Juba SOUTH SUDAN *Email:* eliabalakoobed@gmail.com

Lomega-Loryco The Rt Revd Paul Yugusuk Bishop of Lomega Awaiting Details *Email:* lomegarea@yahoo.com

Lui-Central The Rt Revd Stephen Dokolo Ismail Bishop of Lui C/O ECS PO Box 110 Juba SOUTH SUDAN *Email:* stephen.dokolo@gmail.com *Web:* www.lui.anglican.org

Malakal-Upper Nile The Rt Revd Hilary Garang Deng Bishop of Malakal PO Box 114 Malakal SOUTH SUDAN *Email:* bishop@malakal.anglican.org *Web:* www.malakal.anglican.org

Malakal-Upper Nile The Rt Revd Peter Gatbel Kunen Assistant Bishop of Malakal - Nasir Area PO Box 114 Malakal SOUTH SUDAN *Email:* pgkunen2014@gmail.com

Malakal-Upper Nile The Rt Revd John Gettek Assistant Bishop of Malakal - Bentiu Area PO Box 114 Malakal SOUTH SUDAN *Tel:* + 211 (0)955 039476 *Email:* jgattek@yahoo.com

Malakal-Upper Nile The Rt Revd David Kiir Mayath Assistant Bishop of Malakal - Pariang Area PO Box 114 Malakal SOUTH SUDAN

Malek-Upper Nile The Rt Revd Peter Joh Mayom Bishop of Malek C/O P.O. Box 110 Diocese of Malek SOUTH SUDAN *Email:* malekdiocese@gmail.com

Maridi-Minye The Rt Revd Justin Badi Arama Bishop of Maridi C/O ECS Office PO Box 7576 Kampala UGANDA *Tel:* + 256 77 3304 965 *Email:* bishop@maridi.anglican.org *Web:* www.maridi.anglican.org

Mundri-Central The Rt Revd Bismark Monday Avokaya Bishop of Mundri P.O. Box 127 Juba SUDAN *Tel:* + 88 216 2197 4812 *Email:* bishop@mundri.anglican.org *Web:* www.mundri.anglican.org

Nzara-Minye The Rt Revd Samuel Enosa Peni Bishop of Nzara c/o ECS P.O. Box 110, WES/Yambio SOUTH SUDAN *Email:* samuelpeni@yahoo.com *Web:* www.nzara.anglican.org

Olo-Minye The Rt Revd Tandema O Andrew Bishop of Olo Awaiting Details *Email:* bishopolo65@gmail.com

Pacong-Bahr El Ghazal The Rt Revd Joseph Maker Atot Bishop of Pacong C/O CMS PO Box 40360 Nairobi KENYA *Email:* ecs.pacongdiocese@yahoo.com *Web:* www.pacong.anglican.org

Rejaf-Loryco The Rt Revd Enock Tombe Bishop of Rejaf PO Box 110 Juba SOUTH SUDAN *Tel:* + 249 811 20040 *Fax:* + 249 183 20065 *Web:* www.rejaf.anglican.org

Renk-Upper Nile The Rt Revd Joseph Garang Atem Bishop of Renk c/o ECS P.O. Box 110 S Upper Nile State SOUTH SUDAN *Email:* josephatem@gmail.com *Web:* www.renk.anglican.org

Rokon-Loryco The Rt Revd Francis Loyo Mori Bishop of Rokon c/o ECS P.O.Box 110CES-Juba SOUTH SUDAN *Tel:* + 211 928 122 065 *Email:* bployo@yahoo.co.uk *Web:* www.rokon.anglican.org

Rumbek-Bahr El Ghazal The Rt Revd Alapayo Manyang Kuctiel Bishop of Rumbek c/o ECS P.O.Box 110Lake State SOUTH SUDAN*Email:* kuctiel@yahoo.com *Web:* www.rumbek.anglican.org

Terekeka-Loryco The Rt Revd Paul Modi Bishop of Terekeka PO Box 110 Juba SOUTH SUDAN*Email:* modipaul5@gmail.com *Web:* www.terekeka.anglican.org

Torit-Loryco The Rt Revd Bernard Oringa Balmoi Diocesan Bishop of Torit Awaiting Details *Email:* bishop@torit.anglican.org *Web:* www.torit.anglican.org

Torit-Loryco The Rt Revd Isaac Deu Chon Assistant Bishop of Torit - Kapoeta Area Awaiting Details

Torit-Loryco The Rt Revd Martin Abuni Assistant Bishop of Torit - Magwi Area Awaiting Details

Twik East-Upper Nile The Rt Revd Ezekiel Diing Bishop of Twik East Awaiting Details *Tel:* + 211 (0)955 682118 *Email:* malangajang@gmail.com

Wau-Bahr El Ghazal The Rt Revd Moses Deng Bol Bishop of Wau c/o ECS P.O. Box 110 Western Bahr El Ghazal SOUTH SUDAN*Email:* mosesdengbol@gmail.com *Web:* www.wau.anglican.org

Wondurba-Loryco The Rt Revd Matthew Taban Peter Bishop of Wondurba Awaiting Details *Email:* bp.matthewpeter@gmail.com

Yambio-Minye The Rt Revd Peter Munde Yacoub Bishop of Yambio c/o ECS P.O. Box 110 WES/Yambio SOUTH SUDAN *Email:* mundepeter@gmail.com *Web:* www.yambio.anglican.org

Yei-Loryco The Rt Revd Hilary Luate Adeba Bishop of Yei c/o ECS P.O. Box 110 CES-Juba SOUTH SUDAN *Email:* hill_shepherd@yahoo.com *Web:* www.yei.anglican.org

Yirol-Bahr El Ghazal The Rt Revd David Akau Bishop of Yirol C/O ECS P.O. Box 110 Lakes State SOUTH SUDAN *Email:* ecsyiroldiocese@yahoo.com *Web:* www.yirol.anglican.org

Yirol-Bahr El Ghazal The Rt Revd Isaac Nyaryiel Aleth Assistant Bishop of Yirol - Aluakluak Area C/O ECS P.O. Box 110 Lakes State SOUTH SUDAN *Tel:* + 211 (0)923 045451 *Email:* aluakluakarea@gmail.com

Yirol-Bahr El Ghazal The Rt Revd Paul Tokmach Lual Assistant Bishop of Yirol - Nyang Area C/O ECS P.O. Box 110 Lakes State SOUTH SUDAN *Tel:* + 211 (0)955 990351 *Email:* nyangarea@gmail.com

THE EPISCOPAL CHURCH OF SUDAN

Provincial Secretary The Revd Musa Abujam Awaiting Details *Email:* msabujam@gmail.com

El-Obeid The Rt Revd Ismail Gabriel Abudigin Bishop of El-Obeid PO Box 211 El Obeid SUDAN *Web:* www.elobeid.anglican.org

Kadugli & Nuba Mountains The Rt Revd Andudu Adam Elnail Bishop of Kadugli and Nuba Mountains PO Box 35 Kadugli SUDAN *Tel:* + 249 63 182 2898 *Fax:* + 249 63 182 2898 *Email:* bpkadugli@gmail.com *Web:* www.kadugli.anglican.org

Kadugli & Nuba Mountains The Rt Revd Hassan J Osman Assistant Bishop of Kadugli & Nuba Mountains PO Box 35 Kadugli SUDAN *Email:* Hassan.ojamis@gmail.com *Web:* kadugli.anglican.org

Khartoum The Most Revd Ezekiel Kumir Kondo Archbishop of the Province of Sudan & Bishop of Khartoum PO Box 65 Omdurman SUDAN *Email:* bishop@khartoum.anglican.org *Web:* www.khartoum.anglican.org

Port Sudan The Rt Revd Abdu Elnur Kodi Bishop of Port Sudan PO Box 278 Red Sea State SUDAN *Tel:* + 249 31 212 24 *Email:* bunukaa@live.com *Web:* www.portsudan.anglican.org

Wad Medani The Rt Revd Saman Farajalla Mahdi Bishop of Wad Medani Awaiting Details *Email:* bishop@wadmedani.anglican.org *Web:* www.wadmedani.anglican.org

THE ANGLICAN CHURCH OF TANZANIA

Provincial Secretary The Revd Canon Capt. Johnson Chinyong'ole PO Box 899 Dodoma TANZANIA *Tel:* + 255 (0) 26 232 4574 *Fax:* + 255 (0) 26 232 4565 *Email:* chinyongole@gmail.com *Web:* www.anglican.or.tz

Central Tanganyika The Rt Revd Dickson Chilongani Bishop elect of Central Tanganyika

Makay House PO Box 15 Dodoma TANZANIA *Tel:* + 255 (0)26 232 4518 *Email:* chilongani@anglican.or.tz *Web:* www.d-c-t.org

Dar-es-Salaam The Rt Revd Valentino Mokiwa Bishop of Dar-es-Salaam St Mark's Theological College pO Box 25016 Dar es Salaam TANZANIA *Fax:* + 255 (0)22 286 5840 *Email:* mokiwa_valentine@hotmail.com *Web:* www.diodar.org

Kagera The Rt Revd Aaron Kijanjali Bishop of Kagera PO Box 18 Ngara TANZANIA *Tel:* + 255 (0)28 222 3624 *Fax:* + 255 (0)28 222 2518 *Email:* dkagera@gmail.com *Web:* www.kageradiocese.info

Kibondo The Rt Revd Awaiting Details Bishop of Kibondo P.O. Box 15 Kibondo Kigoma TANZANIA

Kiteto The Rt Revd Isaiah Chambala Bishop of Kiteto PO Box 74 Kibaya Kiteto TANZANIA *Email:* bishopiofkiteto@yahoo.com

Kondoa The Rt Revd Given Gaula Bishop of Kondoa PO Box 7 Kondoa TANZANIA *Tel:* + 255 687424428 *Fax:* + 255 762080083 *Email:* gmguala@gmail.com

Lake Rukwa The Rt Revd Mathayo Kasagara Bishop of Lake Rukwa PO Box 19 Mpanda TANZANIA *Email:* kasagarajr@gmail.com

Lweru The Rt Revd Jackton Yeremiah Lugumira Bishop of Lweru PO Box 12 Muleba TANZANIA *Tel:* + 255 (0)28 222 2796 *Email:* act@bukobaonline.com

Mara The Rt Revd George Okoth Bishop of Mara PO Box 131 Musoma TANZANIA *Tel:* + 255 (0)28 262 2376 *Email:* frokoth@yahoo.com

Masasi The Rt Revd James Almasi Bishop of Masasi Private Bag PO Masasi Mtwara Region TANZANIA *Tel:* + 255 (0)23 251 0016 *Fax:* + 255 (0)23 251 0351 *Email:* Bishopjamesalmasi@yahoo.com

Morogoro The Rt Revd Godfrey Sehaba Bishop of Morogoro PO Box 320 Morogoro TANZANIA *Tel:* + 255 (0)23 260 3356 *Fax:* + 255 (0)23 260 4602 *Email:* bishopgsehaba@yahoo.com

Mount Kilimanjaro The Rt Revd Stanley Elilekia Hotay Bishop of Mount Kilimanjaro PO Box 1057 Arush TANZANIA *Tel:* + 255 (0)27 254 8396 *Fax:* + 255 (0)27 254 4187 *Email:* hotaystanley@gmail.com *Web:* www.mountkilimanjaro.anglican.org

Mpwapwa The Most Revd Jacob Erasto Chimeledya Archbishop of Tanzania & Bishop of Mpwapwa PO Box 2 Mpwapwa TANZANIA *Tel:* + 255 (0)26 232 0117 *Fax:* + 255 (0)26 232 0063 *Email:* jacobchimeledya@hotmail.com *Web:*

Newala The Rt Revd Oscar Mnung'a Bishop of Newala PO Box 92 Newala TANZANIA *Email:* oscarnewala.diocese@yahoo.com

Rift Valley The Rt Revd John Daudi Lupaa Bishop of the Rift Valley PO Box 16 Manyoni TANZANIA *Tel:* + 255 (0)26 254 0013 *Fax:* + 255 (0)26 250 3014 *Email:* jlupaa@yahoo.com *Web:* www.dioceseofriftvalley.

weebly.com

Rorya The Rt Revd John Adiema Bishop of Rorya PO Box 38 Musoma TANZANIA *Tel:* + 255 (0)752 893957

Ruaha The Rt Revd Joseph D Mgomi Bishop of Ruaha PO Box 1028 Iringa TANZANIA *Email:* sanbalatchisewo@yahoo.com

Ruvuma The Rt Revd Maternus Kapinga Bishop of Ruvuma Bishop's Office PO Box 1357 Songea TANZANIA *Tel:* + 255 (0)25 260 0090 *Fax:* + 255 (0)25 260 2987 *Email:* matemask@gmail.com

Shinyanga The Rt Revd Charles Kija Ngusa Bishop of Shinyanga C/O PO Box 421 Shinyanga TANZANIA *Tel:* + 255 (0)28 276 3584 *Email:* ckngusa@yahoo.com

South West Tanganyika The Rt Revd Matthew Mhagama Bishop of South West Tanganyika Bishop's House PO Box 32 Njombe TANZANIA *Tel:* + 255 (0)26 278 2010 *Fax:* + 255 (0)26 278 2403

Southern Highlands The Rt Revd John Mwela Bishop of Southern Highlands PO Box 198 Mbeya TANZANIA *Tel:* + 255 (0)25 250 0216 *Email:* mwelajohn@yahoo.co.uk

Tabora The Rt Revd Elias S Chakupewa Bishop of Tabora Diocese of Tabora PO Box 1408 Tabora TANZANIA *Tel:* + 255 (0)26 260 4124 *Fax:* + 255 (0)26 260 4899 *Email:* chakupewalucy@yahoo.com *Web:* www.anglicantabora.wordpress.com

Tanga The Rt Revd Maimbo Mndolwa Bishop of Tanga PO Box 35 Korogwe Tanga TANZANIA *Tel:* + 255 (0)27 264 0631 *Fax:* + 255 (0)27 264 0631

Tarime The Rt Revd R Mwita Akiri Bishop of Tarime PO Box 410 Tarime TANZANIA *Tel:* + 255 (0)28 269 0153 *Fax:* + 255 (0)28 269 0153 *Email:* bishop.tarime@gmail.com *Web:* www.anglicantarime.org/

Victoria Nyanza The Rt Revd Boniface Kwangu Bishop of Victoria Nyanza PO Box 278 Mwanza TANZANIA *Tel:* + 255 (0)75 439 6020 *Fax:* + 255 (0)28 250 0676 *Email:* bandmkwangu@yahoo.co.uk

Western Tanganyika The Rt Revd Sadock Makaya Bishop of Western Tanganyika PO Box 13 Kasulu TANZANIA *Tel:* + 255 (0)26 260 4124 *Fax:* + 255 (0)26 260 4899

Zanzibar The Rt Revd Michael Hafidh Bishop of Zanzibar PO Box 5 Mkunazini Zanzibar TANZANIA *Tel:* + 255 (0)24 223 5348 *Fax:* + 255 (0)24 223 6772 *Email:* secactznz@zalink.com

THE CHURCH OF THE PROVINCE OF UGANDA

Provincial Secretary The Revd Canon Amos Magezi Wills Road Namirembe P.O. Box 14123 Kampala UGANDA *Tel:* + 256 414 272 757 *Email:* pschurchofuganda@gmail.com

Provincial Treasurer Mr Richard M Obura Box 14123 Kampala UGANDA *Tel:* + 256 (0)41 270 218 *Fax:* + 256 (0)41 251 925 *Email:* richardobura@gmail.com

Ankole The Rt Revd Sheldon F Mwesigwa Bishop of Ankole PO Box 14 Mbarara UGANDA *Tel:* + 256 787 084 301 *Email:* ruharo@utlonline.co.ug *Web:* www.ankolediocese.org

Bukedi The Rt Revd Samuel Egesa Bishop of Bukedi PO Box 170 Tororo UGANDA *Tel:* + 256 772 542 164 *Email:* bukedidiocese@yahoo.com

Bunyoro-Kitara The Rt Revd Samuel Kahuma Bishop of Bunyoro-Kitara PO Box 20 Hoima UGANDA *Tel:* + 256 772 55 83 83 *Email:* can.kahuma@gmail.com

Busoga The Rt Revd Paul Moses Samson Naimanhye Bishop of Busoga PO Box 1658 Jinja UGANDA *Tel:* + 256 0752 598 955 *Fax:* + 256 (0)43 20 547 *Email:* busogadiocese@gmail.com

Central Buganda The Rt Revd Michael Lubowa Bishop of Central Buganda PO Box 1200 Kanoni-Gomba Mpigi UGANDA *Tel:* + 256 772 475 640 *Fax:* + 256 772 242 742 *Email:* michaelluwalira@yahoo.com *Web:* www.centralbuganda.com

Central Busoga The Rt Revd Patrick Wakula Bishop of Central Busoga Awaiting Details *Tel:* + 256 782 510 482

East Ruwenzori The Rt Revd Edward Bamucwanira Bishop of East Ruwenzori PO Box 1439 Kamwenge UGANDA *Tel:* + 256 772 906 236 *Email:* edward_bamu@yahoo.com

Kampala The Most Revd Stanley Ntagali Archbishop of Uganda & and Bishop of Kampala Box 335 Kampala UGANDA *Tel:* + 256 (0)41 270 218 / 9 *Fax:* + 256 (0)41 251 925 *Email:* abpcou@gmail.com

Kampala The Rt Revd Hannington Mutebi Assistant Bishop of Kampala Box 335 Kampala UGANDA *Tel:* + 256 (0)414 342 601 *Email:* mutebihanning@gmail.com

Karamoja The Rt Revd Joseph Abura Bishop of Karamoja PO Box 44 Moroto UGANDA *Tel:* + 256 782 658 502 *Email:* loukomoru@gmail.com

Kigezi The Rt Revd George Bagamuhunda Bishop of Kigezi PO Box 3 Kabale UGANDA *Tel:* + 256 772 450 019 *Email:* bishopkigezi@infocom.co.ug

Kinkiizi The Rt Revd Dan J Zoreka Bishop of Kinkizi PO Box 77 Kanungu UGANDA *Tel:* + 256 782 316 238 *Email:* zoekadan@gmail.com *Web:* www.kinkiizidiocese.com

Kitgum Vacant Bishop elect of Kitgum PO Box 187 Kitgum UGANDA *Tel:* + 256 772 959 924

Kumi The Rt Revd Thomas E Irigei Bishop of Kumi PO Box 18 Kumi UGANDA *Tel:* + 256 772 659 460 *Fax:* + 256 (0)45 613 25 *Email:* kumimothersunion@yahoo.com

Lango The Revd Canon Alfred Olwa Bishop elect of Lango PO Box 6 Lira UGANDA *Tel:* + 256 772 614 000 *Email:* bishoplango@yahoo.com

Luwero The Rt Revd Eridard Kironde Nsubuga Bishop of Luwero PO Box 125 Luwero UGANDA *Tel:* + 256 772 349 669 *Email:* eridard.nsubuga@gmail.com

Madi & West Nile The Rt Revd Charles Collins Andaku Bishop of Madi & West Nile PO Box 370 Arua UGANDA *Tel:* + 256 772 382 324 *Email:* andakucollins@gmail.com

Masindi-Kitara The Rt Revd George Kasangaki Bishop of Masindi-Kitara PO Box 515 Masindi UGANDA *Tel:* + 256 772 624 461 *Email:* georgewakasa@gmail.com

Mbale The Rt Revd Patrick M Gidudu Bishop of Mbale Bishop's House PO Box 473 Mbale UGANDA *Tel:* + 256 782 625 619 *Email:* mbalediocese7@rocketmail.com

Mityana The Rt Revd Stephen Kaziimba Bishop of Mityana PO Box 102 Mityana UGANDA *Tel:* + 256 772 512 175 *Email:* skaziimba@yahoo.com

Muhabura The Rt Revd Cranmer Mugisha Bishop of Muhabura PO Box 22 Kisoro UGANDA *Tel:* + 256 712 195 891 *Email:* cranhopmu@yahoo.co.uk

Mukono The Rt Revd William K Ssebaggala Bishop of Mukono PO Box 39 Mukono UGANDA *Tel:* + 256 772 603 348 *Email:* jamesebagala@yahoo.co.uk *Web:* www.mukonodiocese.or.ug

Namirembe The Rt Revd Wilberforce Kityo Luwalira Bishop of Namirembe PO Box 14297 Kampala UGANDA *Tel:* + 256 712 942 161 *Email:* omulabirizi@gmail.com *Web:* www.namirembediocese.org

Nebbi The Rt Revd Alphonse Watho-kudi Bishop of Nebbi PO Box 27 Nebbi UGANDA *Tel:* + 256 772 650 032 *Email:* bpalphonse@ekk.org

North Ankole The Rt Revd Stephen Namanya Bishop of North Ankole PO Box 1 Rushere-Kiruhura UGANDA *Tel:* + 256 772 622 116 *Email:* Nadsrushere@yahoo.com

North Karamoja The Rt Revd James Nasak Bishop of North Karamoja PO Box 26 Kotido UGANDA *Tel:* + 256 772 660 228 *Email:* jn.nasak@yahoo.com

North Kigezi The Rt Revd Benon Magezi Bishop of North Kigezi PO Box 23 Kinyasano-Rukungiri UGANDA *Tel:* + 256 782 561 217 *Email:* northkigezi@infocom.co.ug

North Mbale The Rt Revd Samuel Gidudu Bishop of North Mbale PO Box 2357 Mbale UGANDA *Tel:* + 256 782 853 094 *Email:* northmbalediocese@yahoo.com

Northern Uganda The Rt Revd Johnson Gakumba Bishop of Northern Uganda PO Box 232 Gulu UGANDA *Tel:* + 256 772 601 421 *Email:* dnu@utlonline.co.ug *Web:* dioceseofnorthernuganda.blogspot.co.uk

Ruwenzori The Rt Revd Reuben Kisembo Bishop of Ruwenzori PO Box 37 Fort Portal UGANDA *Tel:* + 256 (0)45 51 072 *Email:* dioruwenzori@yahoo.com *Web:* www.ruwenzoridiocese.com

Sebei The Rt Revd Paul Kiptoo Masaba Bishop of Sebei PO Box 23 Kapchorwa UGANDA *Tel:* + 256 772 312 502 *Email:* revpkmasaba@yahoo.com

Soroti The Rt Revd George Erwau Bishop of Soroti Soroti Diocese PO Box 107 Soroti UGANDA *Tel:* + 256 772 653 607 *Email:* georgeerwau@yahoo.com *Web:* www.soroti.anglican.org

South Ankole The Rt Revd Nathan Ahimbisibwe Bishop of South Ankole PO Box 39 Ntungamo UGANDA *Tel:* + 256 772 660 636 *Email:* revnathan2000@yahoo.com

South Rwenzori The Rt Revd Jackson Nzerebende Bishop of South Rwenzori PO Box 142 Kasese UGANDA *Tel:* + 256 772 713 736 *Email:* srdiocese@gmail.com *Web:* www.southrd.org

West Ankole The Rt Revd Johnson Twinomujuni Bishop of West Ankole PO Box 140 Bushenyi UGANDA *Tel:* + 256 752 377 192 *Email:* wad@westankolediocese.org

West Buganda The Rt Revd Henry Katumba-Tamale Bishop of West Buganda PO Box 242 Masaka UGANDA *Tel:* + 256 772 770 828 *Email:* hkatumbatamale@gmail.com

West Lango The Rt Revd Alfred Acur Okodi Bishop of West Lango Awaiting Details *Tel:* + 256 772 523 153 *Email:* revalfredac@yahoo.co.uk

THE CHURCH IN WALES

Provincial Secretary Canon Simon Lloyd 2 Callaghan Square Cardiff CF10 5BT WALES *Tel:* + 44 (0)2920 348 200 *Email:* simonlloyd@churchinwales.org.uk *Web:* www.churchinwales.org.uk

Bangor The Rt Revd Andrew T G John Bishop of Bangor Ty'r Esgob Upper Garth Road Bangor Gwynedd LL57 2SS WALES *Tel:* + 44 (0)1248 362 895 *Fax:* + 44 (0)1248 372 454 *Email:* bishop.bangor@churchinwales.org.uk *Web:* bangor.churchinwales.org.uk

Llandaff The Rt Revd June Osborne Bishop of Llandaff Llys Esgob The Cathedral Green Llandaff Cardiff CF5 2YE WALES *Tel:* + 44 (0)292 056 2400 *Fax:* + 44 (0)292 057 7129 *Email:* bishop.llandaff@churchinwales.org.uk *Web:* llandaff.churchinwales.org.uk

Monmouth The Rt Revd Richard R Pain Bishop of Monmouth Bishopstow 91 Stow Hill Newport Gwent NP20 4EA WALES *Tel:* + 44 (0)1633 263 510 *Fax:* + 44 (0)1633 259 946 *Email:* bishop. monmouth@churchinwales.org.uk *Web:* monmouth. churchinwales.org.uk

St Asaph The Rt Revd Gregory K Cameron Bishop of St Asaph Esgobty St Asaph Denbighshire LL17 0TW WALES *Tel:* + 44 (0)1745 583 503 *Fax:* + 44 (0)1745 584 301 *Email:* Bishop.stasaph@churchinwales.org. uk *Web:* stasaph.churchinwales.org.uk

St Davids The Rt Revd Joanna Penberthy Bishop of St Davids Llys Esgob Abergwili Carmarthen SA31 2JG WALES *Tel:* + 44 (0)1267 236 597 *Fax:* + 44 (0)1267 243 403 *Email:* bishop.stdavids@churchinwales.org. uk *Web:* stdavids.churchinwales.org.uk

Swansea & Brecon The Most Revd John E Davies Archbishop of Wales & Bishop of Swansea & Brecon Bishop's House Ely Tower Castle Square Brecon Powys LD3 9DJ WALES *Tel:* + 44 (0)1874 622 008 *Fax:* + 44 (0)1874 610 927 *Email:* archbishop@ churchinwales.org.uk *Web:* swanseaandbrecon. churchinwales.org.uk

THE CHURCH IN THE PROVINCE OF WEST AFRICA

Provincial Secretary The Revd Canon Anthony M K Eiwuley PO Box KN 2023 Kaneshie Accra GHANA *Email:* morkeiwuley@gmail.com

Provincial Treasurer The Revd Canon Andrew Torgbor P. O. Box GP8 Accra GHANA *Tel:* + 233 208 237 424 *Email:* ayorkor33@yahoo.com

Accra-Ghana The Rt Revd Daniel Sylvanus Mensah Torto Bishop of Accra Bishopscourt PO Box 8 Accra 233 GHANA *Tel:* + 233 302 662 292 *Fax:* + 233 277 496 479 *Email:* dantorto@yahoo.com *Web:* http:// www.accraanglican.org/

Asante-Mampong-Ghana The Rt Revd Cyril K Ben-Smith Bishop of Asante-Mampong PO Box 220 Mampong Ashanti GHANA*Email:* bishop. mampong@yahoo.co.uk *Web:* www.mampong. anglican.org

Bo (Sierra Leone)-West Africa The Rt Revd Emmanuel J S Tucker Bishop of Bo PO Box 21 Bo Southern Province SIERRA LEONE *Tel:* + 232 766 778 62 *Fax:* + 232 (0)32 605 *Email:* ejstucker@gmail. com

Cameroon-West Africa The Rt Revd Dibo T B Elango Bishop of Cameroon BP 15705 Akwa Douala CAMEROON *Tel:* + 237 7 555 8276 *Email:* revdibo2@yahoo.com

Cape Coast-Ghana The Rt Revd Victor R Atta-Baffoe Bishop of Cape Coast Bishopscourt PO Box A233 Adiadel Estates Cape Coast GHANA *Tel:* + 233 20 650 2319 *Email:* victorattabaffoe@yahoo.com

Dunkwa-on-Offin-Ghana The Rt Revd Edmund K Dawson Ahmoah Bishop of Dunkwa-on-Offin PO Box DW42 Dukwa-on-Offin GHANA *Tel:* + 233 244 464 764 *Email:* papacy11@yahoo.co.uk

Freetown (Sierra Leone)-West Africa The Rt Revd Thomas Arnold Ikunika Wilson Bishop of Freetown (Sierra Leone) Bishopscourt PO Box 537 105 Fourah Bay Road Freetown SIERRA LEONE *Tel:* + 232 (0)22 251 307 *Email:* vicnold2003@gmail.com

Gambia-West Africa The Rt Revd James Allen Yaw Odico Bishop of the Gambia Bishopscourt PO Box 51 Banjul THE GAMBIA *Tel:* + 220 4227084 *Email:* jayawodico@gmail.com

Guinea-West Africa The Rt Revd Jacques Boston Bishop of Guinea BP 1187 Conakry GUINEA *Tel:* + 224 632 204 660 *Email:* dioceseanglicanguinee@ yahoo.fr

Ho-Ghana The Rt Revd Matthias K Mededues-Badohu Bishop of Ho Bishopslodge PO Box MA300 Ho Volta Region GHANA *Tel:* + 233 20 816 2246 *Email:* matthiaskwab@gmail.com

Koforidua-Ghana The Rt Revd Francis F B Quashie Bishop of Koforidua PO Box 980 Koforidua GHANA *Tel:* + 233 26 681 9414 *Email:* fbquashie@yahoo.com

Kumasi-Ghana The Most Revd Daniel Y Sarfo Primate & Metropolitan, CPWA; Archbishop of the Internal province of Ghana and Bishop of Kumasi Bishop's House PO Box 144 Kumasi GHANA *Tel:* + 233 32 204 7717 *Email:* anglicandioceseofkumasi@ yahoo.com *Web:* www.anglicandioceseofkumasi.com

Liberia-West Africa The Most Revd Jonathan Bau-Bau Bonaparte Hart Archbishop for the internal province of West Africa and Bishop of Liberia PO Box 10-0277 1000 Monrovia 10 LIBERIA West Africa *Tel:* + 231 88 651 6343 *Email:* bishopecl12@ yahoo.com

Sekondi-Ghana The Rt Revd Alexander K Asmah Bishop of Sekondi PO Box 85 Sekondi GHANA *Tel:* + 233 208 378 295 *Email:* alexasmah@yahoo.com

Sunyani=Ghana The Rt Revd Festus Yeboah-Asuamah Bishop of Sunyani PO Box 23 Sunyani GHANA *Tel:* + 233 208 124 378 *Email:* fyasuamah@ yahoo.com

Tamale-Ghana The Rt Revd Jacob K Ayeebo Bishop of Tamale PO Box 110 Tamale NR GHANA *Tel:* + 233 24 341 9864 *Email:* ayeebojacob@gmail.com

Wiawso-Ghana The Rt Revd Abraham K Ackah Bishop of Wiawso PO Box 4 Sefwi Wiawso GHANA *Tel:* + 233 20 816 1826 *Email:* bishopackah@yahoo. com

THE CHURCH IN THE PROVINCE OF THE WEST INDIES

Provincial Secretary Mrs Elenor I Lawrence Bamford House Society Hill St John BB2008 BARBADOS *Tel:* + 1 246 423 0842 *Fax:* + 1 246 423 0855 *Email:* cpwi@caribsurf.com

Barbados The Most Revd & The Hon John W D Holder Archbishop of West Indies & Bishop of Barbados Mandeville House Henry's Lane Collymore Rock St Michael BARBADOS *Tel:* + 1 246 426 2761 *Fax:* + 1 246 426 0871 *Email:* jwdh@outlook.com *Web:* www.barbados.anglican.org

Belize The Rt Revd Philip S Wright Bishop of Belize Diocesan Office 2 Rectory Lane PO Box 535 Belize City BELIZE *Tel:* + 11 501 227 3029 *Fax:* + 11 501 227 6898 *Email:* bzediocese@btl.net *Web:* anglicandioceseofbelize.com

Diocese of The Bahamas and The Turks and Caicos Islands The Rt Revd Laish Z Boyd Bishop of The Bahamas and The Turks and Caicos Islands Addington House Sands Road PO Box N-7107 New Providence Nassau BAHAMAS *Tel:* + 1 (0)242 322 3015/6/ *Fax:* + 1 (0)242 322 7943 *Email:* bishop@bahamasanglican.org *Web:* www.bahamasanglicans.org

Guyana The Rt Revd Charles Davidson Bishop of Guyana Diocesan Office 49 Barrack Street PO Box 10949 Georgetown GUYANA *Tel:* + 592 226 4183 *Fax:* + 592 226 6091 *Email:* dioceseofguyana@gmail.com

Jamaica & The Cayman Islands The Rt Revd Howard K A Gregory Bishop of Jamaica & The Cayman Islands Church House 2 Caledonia Avenue Kingston JAMAICA *Tel:* + 1 876 920 2712 *Email:* hkagregory@hotmail.com *Web:* www.anglicandioceseja.org

Jamaica & The Cayman Islands The Rt Revd Robert M Thompson Suffragan Bishop of Kingston 3 Duke Street Kingston JAMAICA *Tel:* + 1 876 924 9044 *Fax:* + 1 876 948 5362 *Email:* bishop.kingston@anglicandiocese.com

Jamaica & The Cayman Islands Vacant Suffragan Bishop elect of Mandeville 8 Morningside Drive PO Box 346 Montego Bay JAMAICA *Tel:* + 1 876 625 6817 *Fax:* + 1 876 625 6819

Jamaica & The Cayman Islands The Rt Revd Leon Paul Golding Suffragan Bishop of Montego Bay 8 Clieveden Avenue Kingston 6 JAMAICA *Tel:* + 876 920 2712

North Eastern Caribbean & Aruba The Rt Revd Leroy E Brooks Bishop of North Eastern Caribbean & Aruba Bishop's Lodge Redcliffe Street PO Box 23 St John's ANTIGUA *Tel:* + 1 268 462 0151 *Fax:* + 1 268 462 2090 *Email:* brookx@anguillanet.com

Trinidad & Tobago The Rt Revd Claude Berkley Bishop of Trinidad & Tobago Diocesian Office 21 Maraval Road Port of Spain TRINIDAD *Email:* claberk@yahoo.com

Windward Islands The Rt Revd Calvert L Friday Bishop of the Windward Islands Diocesan Pastoral Centre Montrose PO Box 502 Kingstown ST VINCENT *Tel:* + 1 784 456 1895 *Fax:* + 1 784 456 2591 *Email:* diocesewi@vincysurf.com

THE CHURCH OF CEYLON

Mrs Ramola Sivasunderam Secretary to General Assembly c/o The Polytechnic Galle Road Colombo 600 Sri Lanka *Tel:* + 94 1 1258 6603 *Fax:* + 94 (0) 777 35 23 73

Colombo The Rt Revd Dhiloraj Ranjit Canagasabey Bishop of Colombo Bishop's Office 368/3A Bauddhaloka Mawatha Colombo - 07 Sri Lanka *Fax:* + 94 (0)11 268 4811 *Email:* anglican@sltnet.lk

KurunagalaVacant Bishop elect of Kurunagala Bishop's House 31 Kandy Road Kurunagala 60000 Sri Lanka *Tel:* + 94 (0)37 222 2191 *Email:* bishopkg@sltnet.lk

IGLESIA EPISCOPAL DE CUBA

Provincial Secretary Mr Francisco De Arazoza Calle 6 No 273 Vedado Plaza de la revolucion Ciudad de la Habana CUBA *Tel:* + 53 7 832 1120 *Fax:* + 53 7 834 3293 *Email:* episcopal@enet.cu

Cuba The Rt Revd Griselda Delgado Del Carpio Bishop of Cuba Calle 6 No 273 Vedado Plaza Cuidad de La Habana 10400 CUBA *Tel:* + 53 (0)7 833 5760 *Email:* griselda@enet.cu

Cuba The Rt Revd Ulises A Prendes Suffragan Bishop of Cuba Calle Escario No. 459 entre 3 Y 4 Santiago de Cuba 90100 CUBA *Tel:* + 53 (0)22 627 815 *Email:* bpulises@enet.cu

BERMUDA (EXTRA-PROVINCIAL TO CANTERBURY)

Provincial Treasurer HM CX Mr Campbell McBeath PO Box HM769 Hamilton BERMUDA *Tel:* + 1 441 292 6987 *Fax:* + 1 441 292 5421 *Email:* diocese@anglican.bm *Web:* www.anglican.bm

Bermuda The Rt Revd Nicholas Dill Bishop of Bermuda Diocesan Office PO Box HM769 Hamilton HM CX BERMUDA *Tel:* + 1 441 292 6987 *Fax:* + 1 441 292 5421 *Email:* bishop@anglican.bm *Web:* www.anglican.bm

THE LUSITANIAN CHURCH (EXTRA-PROVINCIAL TO CANTERBURY)

Provincial Treasurer The Revd Sérgio Filipe Pinho Alves Diocesan Centre of Lusitanian Church Rua Afonso de Albuquerque, No 86 4430-003 Vila Nova de Gaia PORTUGAL *Tel:* + 351 22 375 4018 *Fax:* + 351 22 375 2016 *Email:* sergioalves@igreja-lusitana.org *Web:* www.igreja-lusitana.org

Lusitanian Church The Rt Revd José Jorge De Pina Cabral Bishop of the Lusitanian Church Diocesan

Centre of Lusitanian Church Rua Afonso de Albuquerque, No 86 4430-003 Vila Nova de Gaia PORTUGAL *Tel:* + 351 (0)22 375 4018 *Fax:* + 351 (0)22 375 2016 *Email:* bispopinacabral@igreja-lusitana.org *Web:* www.igreja-lusitana.org

THE REFORMED CHURCH OF SPAIN

Senor Jose Antonio Rodriguez Provincial Treasurer Calle Beneficencia 18 Madrid 28004 SPAIN *Tel:* + 34 91 445 25 60 *Email:* secretario@anglicanos.org *Web:* www.anglicanos.org

The Reformed Episcopal Church of Spain The Rt Revd Carlos López-Lozano Bishop of Spanish Reformed Episcopal Church Calle Beneficencia 18 Madrid 28004 SPAIN *Tel:* + 34 (0)91 445 2560 *Fax:* + 34 (0)91 594 4572 *Email:* eclesiae@arrakis.es

PARISH OF THE FALKLAND ISLANDS

Falkland Islands (Parish of) The Rt Revd Timothy M Thornton Bishop to the Forces and Bishop to the Falkland Islands Lambeth Palace London SE1 7JU United Kingdom *Email:* tim.thornton@lambethpalace.org.uk

CHURCHES IN FULL COMMUNION WITH THE EPISCOPAL CHURCH

The Episcopal Church seeks the full, visible unity of Christ's Church in one Eucharistic fellowship. The Episcopal Church notes that in full communion, "churches become interdependent while remaining autonomous. Diversity is preserved, but this diversity is not static. Neither church seeks to remake the other in its own image, but each is open to the gifts of the other as it seeks to be faithful to Christ and his mission."

The Office of Ecumenical and Interreligious Relations promotes relationships between the Episcopal Church and other Christian communities and supports interreligious relationships globally and locally.

The Presiding Bishop is the Ecumenical Officer of the Episcopal Church. The Rev. Margaret Rose is the Deputy to the Presiding Bishop for Ecumenical and Interreligious Relations. Email: mrose@episcopalchurch. org. Mr. Richard Mammana is Associate for Ecumenical and Interreligious Relations. Email: rmammana@ episcopalchurch.org.

EVANGELICAL LUTHERAN CHURCH IN AMERICA

In 2001, the Episcopal Church and the Evangelical Lutheran Church in America (ELCA) entered into a relationship of full communion on the basis of the document *Called to Common Mission*, culminating thirty years of dialogue with one another. The two churches have committed themselves to joint mission and witness, including mutual participation in consecrations and installations of bishops and the free movement of clergy between the two churches. The Lutheran Episcopal Coordinating Committee meets regularly to support this relationship, and maintains a directory of documentation and other resources at lutheran-episcopal.org.

THE MORAVIAN CHURCH (Northern and Southern Provinces)

Following centuries of friendly relations between the two traditions, the Episcopal Church and the Moravian Church in America's Northern and Southern Provinces established an official dialogue in 1997. In 2003, the two churches entered into an agreement on interim Eucharistic sharing. In 2009, the General Convention approved *Finding Our Delight in the Lord*, a proposal for full communion between the two churches. While presbyters and bishops may be shared interchangeably, Moravian and Episcopal deacons may not be interchanged because of differences over the nature and role of the diaconate. The ELCA is also in full communion with these Moravian provinces. The Moravian Episcopal Coordinating Committee supports this relationship, and provides background material at moravian-episcopal.org.

TTHE OLD CATHOLIC CHURCHES OF THE UNION OF UTRECHT

The Old Catholic Churches of the Union of Utrecht are our oldest and longest termed Full Communion partners. (They are not to be confused with the various groups in the United States and elsewhere who call themselves Old Catholic but are not related to Utrecht.) In 1934, the Episcopal Church entered full communion with the Old Catholic Churches in communion with the See of Utrecht during the ratification of the Bonn Agreement of 1931, which stipulated that:

- Each Communion recognizes the catholicity of the other and maintains its own.

- Each Communion agrees to admit members of the other communion to participate in the sacraments.

- Intercommunion does not require from either communion the acceptance of all doctrinal opinion, sacramental devotion, or liturgical practice characteristic of the other, but implies that each believes the other to hold all the essentials of the Christian faith.

Mutual ministry, primarily in Europe, is being accomplished by our cooperation and shared ministries.

The Presiding Bishop has designated a permanent representative to the annual Old Catholic Bishops' Conference in order to assure continued communication, mutual ministry and understanding as well as a shared understanding of the Gospel of Jesus Christ.

PHILIPPINE INDEPENDENT CHURCH

In 1961, the Philippine Independent Church, also known as the Iglesia Filipina Independiente (IFI), and the Episcopal Church agreed to "establish a concordat of full communion." As part of that agreement, the Episcopal Church assists the IFI in its efforts to minister to members in the United States, and IFI members assist and participate in the broader life and work of the Episcopal Church. A Concordat Panel supports this relationship, and members of the IFI often attend the General Convention of the Episcopal Church as observers.

MAR THOMA SYRIAN CHURCH OF MALABAR

Following an agreement acknowledged by the General Convention in 1976, the Episcopal Church is in full communion with the Mar Thoma Syrian Church of Malabar, based in southern India. When requested by the Metropolitan of the Mar Thoma Church, bishops of dioceses of the Episcopal

Church shall exercise episcopal oversight of clergy and laity of the Mar Thoma Church within their jurisdictions. Members of the Mar Thoma Church in the jurisdiction of an Episcopal diocese shall be treated as members of the Episcopal Church, with the understanding that they also remain members of the Mar Thoma Church.

THE CHURCH OF SWEDEN

The Episcopal Church maintains close relations with the Church of Sweden. Most recently, both churches agreed to work together to mitigate climate change; in 2013, Presiding Bishop Katharine Jefferts Schori and Church of Sweden Archbishop Anders Wejryd, along with then-ELCA Presiding Bishop Mark Hanson, signed a joint statement affirming their commitment to advocate for governmental policies

that encourage renewable energy and support just economic systems. Through the Lutheran World Federation, the Church of Sweden is in fellowship with all other Lutheran member churches. The General Convention adopted a resolution in 2015 accepting a report identifying the grounds for ongoing shared mission in the following areas: in practical work in parishes; in areas of tripartite interest with common partners; in issues of common concern in the strategy and programmatic work of the World Council of Churches; and in specific questions which the two churches prioritize, such as climate change, peace, gender justice, etc. General Convention 2018's Resolution D085 requested that the Presiding Bishop prepare "a memorandum of understanding setting forth the terms and procedures of the full communion between The Episcopal Church and the Church of Sweden."

ECUMENICAL RELATIONS

The Episcopal Church maintains ecumenical relations through dialogues with other Christian traditions; coordinating committees or concordat panels supporting existing full communion relationships; membership in the World Council of Churches and the National Council of Churches as well as other national and international conciliar or ecumenical bodies; and diocesan and local ecumenical efforts conducted through the network of Episcopal Diocesan Ecumenical and Interreligious Officers (EDEIO).

ECUMENICAL DIALOGUES

The Episcopal Church is engaged in formal bilateral talks with the following churches. These dialogues have been established by act of General Convention and are provided with oversight by the Office of Ecumenical and Interreligious Relations (EIR) in conjunction with clergy and laity appointed by the EIR and the Office of General Convention.

United Methodist-Episcopal Dialogue

The United Methodist-Episcopal dialogue was The United Methodist-Episcopal dialogue was established by act of the 2000 General Convention and began meeting in 2002. The 2006 General Convention approved interim Eucharistic sharing with the United Methodist Church. Episcopal parishes are now authorized to hold joint celebrations of the Eucharist with United Methodist churches under the guidelines established by General Convention. The Episcopal Church participated with the United Methodist Church as part of the Consultation on Church Union. The ecumenical work of the United Methodist Church is carried out by the Council of Bishops Office of Christian Unity and Interreligious Relationships. The committee's proposal for full communion is under discussion in the 2018-2012 triennium.

Presbyterian-Episcopal Dialogue

The Presbyterian Church (U.S.A.) was formed in 1983 through the merger of the United Presbyterian Church and the Presbyterian Church in the United

States. The Episcopal Church participated in dialogue with the Presbyterian Church (U.S.A.) within the context of the earlier Consultation on Church Union. A bilateral dialogue was established in 2000 and began meeting in 2002. General Convention in 2009 approved an agreement with the Presbyterian Church (U.S.A.). While this relationship is not full communion or Eucharistic sharing, the agreement encourages cooperation and joint ministry. General Convention 2018 also authorized a further round of ongoing dialogue.

Anglican-Roman Catholic Dialogue

The Episcopal Church has been in dialogue with the Roman Catholic Church for more than 40 years through the Anglican-Roman Catholic Dialogue in the USA (ARC-USA), and on the international level through the Anglican Communion Office in the Anglican-Roman Catholic International Consultations (ARCIC). In a common declaration signed in 2006 by Rowan Williams, then Archbishop of Canterbury, and Pope Benedict XVI, the two leaders renewed the historic commitment to the goal of "full visible communion in the truth of Christ." ARC-USA continues its discussions through its current round of dialogue on the topic of reconciliation.

OTHER ECUMENICAL RELATIONS
Evangelical Lutheran Church in Bavaria

Beginning in 2015, members of the Episcopal Church and the Evangelical Lutheran Church in

Bavaria (Evangelisch-Lutherische Kirche in Bayern/ELKB) have conducted conversations about areas of shared mission and ministry, particularly in Europe. Observers from the Anglican Communion Office; the Inter-Anglican Standing Commission for Unity, Faith and Order; the Lutheran World Federation; the Convocation of Episcopal Churches in Europe; and the United Evangelical Lutheran Church of Germany have joined in these ongoing conversations. General Convention 2018's Resolution C059 commended "the process of exploring deeper relations and the dialogue toward full communion between The Episcopal Church and the ELKB."

The Polish National Catholic Church

The Episcopal Church was in a relationship of full communion with the Polish National Catholic Church (PNCC) on the basis of the Bonn Agreement and a supplemental concordat of intercommunion by the 1946 General Convention. In 1978, the PNCC terminated this full communion agreement after the ordination of women in the Episcopal Church. The Episcopal Church did not take a similar action. In 2003, the PNCC ceased to be in communion with the Archbishop of Utrecht and is no longer a member of the Old Catholic Churches of the Union of Utrecht. The PNCC is a member of the World Council of Churches.

Episcopal Diocesan Ecumenical and Interreligious Officers

EDEIO is the national network of individuals designated by their diocesan bishops with special responsibility for encouraging the visible unity of Christ's Church and collegial relationships with members of other religions. It maintains a website (edeio.org) with a wide variety of resources, including the Ecumenical Handbook. EDEIO is also a sponsor of the annual National Workshop on Christian Unity (nwcu.org), a gathering of ecumenical officers from several denominations for education, formation, mutual encouragement, and worship. Each province of the Episcopal Church has an EDEIO-elected provincial coordinator supporting regional ecumenical and interreligious work.

WORLD COUNCIL OF CHURCHES

The World Council of Churches (WCC) is a fellowship of churches which confess the Lord Jesus Christ as God and Savior according to the Scriptures and therefore seeks to fulfill together their common calling to the glory of the one God: Father, Son, and Holy Spirit. The WCC is constituted by member churches to serve the ecumenical movement. It incorporates the work of the world movements for Faith and Order and Life and Work, the International Missionary Council, and the World Council of Christian Education. The primary purpose of the fellowship of churches in the WCC is to call one another to visible unity in one faith

and in one Eucharistic fellowship, expressed in worship and common life in Christ, through witness and service to the world. The WCC has more than 350 member churches. Almost every province of the Anglican Communion is included, together with most independent Orthodox churches and Protestant traditions. The Roman Catholic Church has sent official observers to all main WCC meetings since 1960. In the United States, most churches that belong to the National Council of Churches belong to the WCC.

NATIONAL COUNCIL OF CHURCHES OF CHRIST IN THE USA

The National Council of Churches (NCC) is a major expression in the U.S. of the movement toward Christian unity. The NCC's 38 member communions, including Protestant, Orthodox, and Anglican church bodies, work together on a wide range of activities that further Christian unity, that promote peace and justice, and that serve people throughout the world. The council was formed in 1950 by the action of representatives of the member churches and by the merger of 12 previously existing ecumenical agencies, each of which had a different program focus. Episcopalians participate annually in the NCC's Christian Unity Gathering and convening tables on Christian education, Faith and Order, and interreligious relations.

CHRISTIAN CHURCHES TOGETHER IN THE USA

In 2006, 34 churches and national Christian organizations officially formed the broadest fellowship of Christian churches and organizations in the U.S. Those participating as founding members represent the Episcopal Church, Orthodox, Roman Catholic, Evangelical, Pentecostal, and Charismatic churches, among others. Christian Churches Together (CCT) provides a context in which churches can develop relationships, share common work, make public witness, and pray together. Its website is christianchurchestogether.org.

CHURCHES UNITING IN CHRIST

After 40 years of study and prayer through the Consultation on Church Union (COCU), nine churches—the African Methodist Episcopal Church, the African Methodist Episcopal Zion Church, the Christian Church (Disciples of Christ), the Christian Methodist Episcopal Church, the Episcopal Church, International Council of Community Churches, the Presbyterian Church (U.S.A.), the United Church of Christ, and the United Methodist Church—in 2002 agreed to start living their unity in Christ more fully through a relationship called Churches Uniting in Christ (CUIC). In 2006, the Moravian Church (Northern Province) became a full member. The ELCA is a CUIC partner in mission and dialogue. Each church maintains its own identity and decision-making structures, but each also pledges to draw closer in sacred things and common mission, especially the mission to combat racism. Recent work has focused on issues of racial justice among our churches. On Pentecost of 2017, a joint celebration in Dallas acknowledged and deepened this work while proclaiming the recognition of ministries among our member denominations.

CONSULTATION ON COMMON TEXTS

The Episcopal Church is a member of the Consultation on Common Texts, an ecumenical group of liturgical scholars and denominational representatives from the United States and Canada who produce liturgical materials and a three-year lectionary for common use by Christian churches worldwide. Through the CCT, the Episcopal Church is also represented in the international corollary body, the English Language Liturgical Consultation. Its website is www.commontexts.org.

INTERRELIGIOUS RELATIONS

The Episcopal Church's primary participation in interreligious dialogue focuses principally on:

- Ecumenical efforts with other Christians through the Interfaith Relations Commission of the National Council of Churches of Christ (NCC). The 1999 Assembly of the NCC unanimously approved a policy statement giving a theological rationale for participating in interreligious dialogue;

- International efforts through the Anglican Communion Office, including the Network for Interfaith Concerns;

- Particular initiatives taken by the Presiding Bishop as primate of the church;

- Task force initiatives and programs created by Episcopal Church institutions, such as Episcopal Relief and Development;

- Diocesan, congregational, and individual efforts in peacemaking and interreligious dialogue.

In 2003, the General Convention officially located oversight of the church's interreligious work with the Standing Commission on Ecumenical Relations, which was renamed the Standing Commission on Ecumenical and Interreligious Relations (SCEIR). During the 2006-2009 triennium, the Interreligious Relations Subcommittee of the SCEIR worked to develop a more substantive statement to clarify the theological and historical rationale for the Episcopal Church's interreligious engagement, and in 2009 a resolution was adopted by General Convention—and reaffirmed in 2012—establishing a canonical teaching on interreligious relations known as "Toward Our Mutual Flourishing."

RELIGIONS FOR PEACE USA

The Episcopal Church actively participates in Religions for Peace USA (RfPUSA). Religions for Peace USA works to contribute to the well-being of civil society and to advance peace-building efforts and reconciliation in the U.S. and internationally. Religions for Peace USA is part of a network of Religions for Peace with nearly 100 affiliates globally. The Presiding Bishop is a member of the organization's Council of Presidents, and representatives from the Episcopal Church are members of its Executive Council. This organization's website is at www.rfpusa.org.

THE ANTI-DEFAMATION LEAGUE

The Anti-Defamation League (ADL) was founded in 1913 "to stop the defamation of the Jewish people and to secure justice and fair treatment to all." It is a major civil rights and human relations agency fighting anti-Semitism and all forms of bigotry. It defends democratic ideals and protects civil rights for all. The Episcopal Church partners with the ADL in advocacy. ADL members attend the General Convention as invited observers.

THE AMERICAN JEWISH COMMITTEE

The American Jewish Committee (AJC) is an international advocacy organization, founded in 1906 to protect the human rights of Jewish persons throughout the world. The AJC sends an observer to the General Convention of the Episcopal Church, and consults with the Episcopal Church's Office of Government Relations on matters of common interest and concern. The AJC's website is at www.ajc.org.

THE ISLAMIC CIRCLE OF NORTH AMERICA

Established in 1968, the Islamic Circle of North America (ICNA) is an umbrella organization focusing on development, education, outreach and social services. The Episcopal Church participates in conversation with ICNA through the National Council of Churches Muslim-Christian Dialogue. ICNA is online at www.icna.org.

THE ISLAMIC SOCIETY OF NORTH AMERICA

The goal of the Islamic Society of North America (ISNA), founded in 1982, is "to be an exemplary and unifying Islamic organization in North America that contributes to the betterment of the Muslim community and society at large." The Episcopal Church participates in conversation with ISNA through the National Council of Churches Muslim-Christian Dialogue, and has sent an observer to the General Convention of the Episcopal Church. The Episcopal Church also partners with ISNA in special events and educational initiatives. ISNA is online at www.isna.net.

SHOULDER TO SHOULDER

Shoulder to Shoulder (shouldertoshouldercampaign.org) is an interfaith organization dedicated to ending anti-Muslim sentiment by strengthening the voice of freedom and peace. Founded in November 2010 by over 20 national religious groups, Shoulder to

Shoulder works not only on a national level, but offers strategies and support to local and regional efforts to address anti-Muslim sentiment and seeks to spread the word abroad. Episcopalians serve on the steering committee of Shoulder to Shoulder and engage in advocacy work as well as the development of congregational resources.

BREAD FOR THE WORLD

Bread for the World (www.bread.org) provides nonpartisan policy analysis on hunger and strategies to end it. The Episcopal Church works with Bread for the World in its poverty and hunger initiatives. The Circle of Protection, of which the Episcopal Church is a member, is an alliance of Christian leaders working to monitor policy, legislation, and programs addressing the needs of the most vulnerable in society.

CHURCHES FOR MIDDLE EAST PEACE

Churches for Middle East Peace (CMEP) is a coalition of 27 national Church denominations and organizations in Catholic, Orthodox and Protestant traditions. Each of these denominations and organizations is represented on the CMEP Board of Directors, which sets CMEP's mission, positions and policy. Decisions are made by consensus of this group. The Episcopal Church is on the Executive Committee and the board of this organization. CMEP works to encourage U.S. policies that actively promote a just, lasting, and comprehensive resolution of the Israeli-Palestinian conflict, ensuring security, human rights and religious freedom for all the people of the region. The Episcopal Church primarily works through CMEP on Middle East-related policy advocacy. CMEP is online at cmep.org.

Clergy List of
The Episcopal Church

Any changes to this list should be addressed to the
Recorder of Ordinations, Church Pension Group,
19 East 34th Street, New York, NY 10016.

The symbol ✠ indicates bishop.

CLERGY LIST

The names, addresses, and canonical residences in the Clergy List section are supplied by The Recorder of Ordinations and reflect changes reported by **31 December 2018**. Any request for a change in the Clergy List should be addressed to The Recorder of Ordinations, CHURCH PENSION GROUP, 19 East 34th Street, New York, NY 10016.

NECROLOGY
1/18-12/18

Bishops

COUNCELL, George	5/21/18
EASTMAN, Albert Theodore	4/26/18
HULTSTRAND, Donald Maynard	12/21/18
MALLORY, Charles Shannon	4/4/18
MILLARD, George Richard	6/15/18
PINA-LOPEZ, Hugo Luis	9/20/18
RAY, Thomas Kreider	2/7/18
RICHARDS, David Emrys	8/21/18

Priests and Deacons

AITON JR, Alexander A	7/30/18
ALBURY, Ronald Graham	10/24/18
ALEXANDER, Bruce Ames	3/27/18
ALFRIEND, John Daingerfield	5/22/18
ALLING, Frederic Augustus	10/22/18
AMAYA, Adrian A	4/15/18
ANDERHEGGEN, George Curtis	9/27/18
ANDERSON JR, Otto Harold	12/29/18
ANGUS, Caroline Helen	12/2/18
ARQUES, Rafael	5/2/18
ASKREN, Robert Darling	11/24/18
AYCOCK JR, Marvin	12/15/18
BAIRD, Stephen Earl	3/10/18
BAKER, Bruce D'Aubert	12/26/18
BALL JR, John Coming	4/26/18
BALLENTINE JR, George Young	6/3/18
BARNES JR, Bennett Herbert	7/10/18
BARNUM, Malcolm McGregor	1/17/18
BAUM, Denis	4/2/18
BECKER, Arthur Paul	6/22/18
BEEM, Charles Lee	10/5/18
BELLIS, Elaine	11/15/18
BIGFORD, Jack Norman	10/12/18
BISHOP, Barbara Elaine	1/30/18
BLAKEMORE, Barbara	7/16/18
BOOKER, Vaughan P L	6/23/18
BOSS WOLLNER, Ernesto Sieghard	6/25/18
BOWDEN, Teresa Thomas	5/3/18
BRANDENBURG, John Paul	3/10/18
BRANSCOMB JR, William Maurice	1/13/18
BRANSCOME III, Dexter Arno	10/24/18
BRATHWAITE, Percy Alphonso	8/23/18
BRECHNER, Eric Lonell	4/29/18
BREZNAU, Jack Charles	9/7/18

BROCK, Velma Elaine	12/9/18
BROOKFIELD, Christopher Morgan	6/15/18
BROWNELL, Leona Weiss	12/16/18
BUCKLEY, Herbert Wilkinson	8/22/18
BUNN III, George Strother	4/21/18
BURNS JR, Jervis Oliver	1/6/18
BURTENSHAW, Noel C	7/17/18
BUSLER, George Warren	11/18/18
BUXTON JR, Eugene Harvey	8/11/18
CADY III, Mark Stone	11/25/18
CARLSON, William Douglas	9/30/18
CARRENO-GAMBOA, Bladimir	5/13/18
CARTWRIGHT JR, Howard Mott	4/12/18
CAVE JR, George Harold	10/29/18
CAYLESS, F(Rank) Anthony	9/9/18
CHANDLER-WARD, Constance	4/2/18
CLABUESCH, Ward Henry	12/26/18
CLARK, Adelaide	3/5/18
CLIFT JR, Wallace B	2/5/18
COAN, Barbara Frances Smith	8/20/18
COLLINS, Judith Tindall	2/16/18
COONEY, James Francis	10/11/18
CORBETT, John Philip	1/2/18
COWARDIN, Stephen Paul	7/31/18
COX JR, James Stanley	11/2/18
CROFT, Charles Carter	12/2/18
CROSBY, Derrill Plummer	8/8/18
CRYSLER, Kenneth W	11/3/18
CUNNINGHAM, Marcus	8/25/18
CURRAN, Michael Joseph	8/28/18
D'AMICO, Samuel Robert	4/7/18
DANNELLEY, James Preston	11/28/18
DAVIS, Ronald C.	4/23/18
DAVIS JR, Thomas Clark	1/13/18
DAVIS, Thomas Preston	7/9/18
DAY III, Charles V.	10/23/18
DAY, Robert Charles	1/23/18
DECHAMPLAIN, Mitties	5/8/18
DECKER, Clarence Ferdinand	11/29/18
DEMOTT, Richard Arthur	3/31/18
DE WOLF, Mark Anthony	4/9/18
DIEFENBACHER, Fred H	5/29/18
DIEHL, Robert Edward	12/19/18
DIELY, Elizabeth Barrett Hanning	2/3/18
DONAHUE, Ray Lawrence	11/22/18
DORMAN, Jane	3/8/18
DORR JR, Erwin John	12/13/18
DOUGLASS, James Herford	7/15/18
DROBIN, Frederick A	7/14/18
DUNKERLEY, James Hobson	8/16/18
DUPLESSIE, Thomas Frederick	3/20/18

DURHAM, Eugenia M	7/30/18
DWYER, Martin James	10/22/18
ELLINGTON, William Ferrell	9/21/18
EVANS JR, Creighton	5/18/18
FENTON, Arnold Aidan	10/20/18
FERGUSON, Vergie Rae	10/15/18
FERRELL, Davis Marion	8/15/18
FINSTER, Mary Ruth	1/31/18
FITZGERALD III, John H	3/8/18
FLEMING, John C	11/2/18
FOLSOM, Henry Titus	5/8/18
FONTAINE, Ann Kristin	4/18/18
FORD, Austin Mcneill	8/18/18
FORTUNE, Dwight Chapman	10/21/18
FOX, Deborah	9/6/18
FREEMAN, Robert Arthur	10/15/18
FRELUND, Warren	2/13/18
FRENCH, William A	7/13/18
FURGERSON, John Arthur	3/22/18
FUSELIER, Donald Paul	5/27/18
GALLAGHER, Elvin Ross	1/18/18
GARCIA, Louis Fernando	5/26/18
GARLICHS, Richard Walbridge	7/21/18
GARTIG, William George	3/6/18
GARY, Hobart Jude	5/14/18
GATCHELL, Lois Harvey	12/5/18
GIFFORD, Lance Allen Ball	11/20/18
GILLMAN, Paula Ruth	10/22/18
GINGHER, Richard Hammond	2/28/18
GLEASON, David Thomas	6/18/18
GOMPERTZ, Charles Bates	10/3/18
GOODRICH III, Daniel Hillman	8/13/18
GOSNELL, Linda	7/25/18
GOWEN, Eleanore Louise	10/18/18
GRANFELDT SR, Robert C	1/27/18
GRAUMLICH, Nancy Rice	4/16/18
GRIMES, Daphne B	3/11/18
GROFF, Addison Keiper	1/21/18
GROSS, Don	7/25/18
GUTHRIE, Donald Angus	2/22/18
HALL, George	11/14/18
HALL, John	10/7/18
HALL, Karen	12/1/18
HAMILTON, Michael Pollock	1/10/18
HANCKEL, Ellen	10/6/18
HARDMAN, Louise O'Kelley	6/22/18
HART, Fred	8/10/18
HAYDEN, Robert Stoddard	5/29/18
HEATH, Glendon Edward	3/9/18
HENRY, David Winston	11/1/18
HETHCOCK, William Hoover	1/9/18
HIGHAM, Jack	6/27/18
HOBBS, Edward Craig	4/4/18
HODGKINS, Lewis	2/19/18
HOHLT, Allan Hunter	6/14/18
HORTON, Edward Robert	5/17/18
HOSTETLER, Hugh Steiner	12/15/18
HUGHES, Alan	4/11/18
HULSE JR, Granvyl G	8/18/18
IJAMS, Carl Phillip	1/3/18
IRELAND, Clyde Lambert	1/16/18
JACKSON, Eric Michael Colin	11/28/18
JANKOWSKI, John A	9/24/18
JARVIS III, Frank Washington	10/7/18
JENKINS, David P	4/18/18
JENKINS, George Washburn	9/27/18
JEROME, Douglas Darrel	2/25/18
JOHNSON, Emmanuel W	3/2/18

JOHNSON III, Roberts Poinsett	5/25/18
JOHNSON, William Francis	9/19/18
JOHNSTON, Roy Wayne	7/11/18
JONES, Nikki Lou	1/23/18
JONES, Patsy Ann	10/29/18
JORDAN, Katherine	3/11/18
JOSEPH, Augustine	6/16/18
KAPP, Charl Ann	5/16/18
KEELER, Charles Bobo	1/9/18
KEENEY-MULLIGAN, Gail	1/24/18
KEITH, Thomas Frederick	7/4/18
KERR JR, Tom	12/19/18
KIMBALL, John Charles	1/13/18
KING JR, Frank H	5/21/18
KING, Joseph Willet	11/28/18
KINGSLEY MURRAY, Miguel	5/19/18
KLAAS III, Anthony Rudolph	3/10/18
KNUDSON, James Clarence	2/11/18
KOHLBECKER, Eugene Edmund	12/5/18
KORATHU, Anna Maria	4/10/18
KOSTAS, George Agapios	2/25/18
KOTRC, Ronald Fred	4/7/18
KOUMRIAN, Paul Sprower	1/25/18
KRAFT, Harry Bishop	2/19/18
KUHLMANN, Frederick Jennings	11/27/18
LACEY, John Howard	12/1/18
LACRONE, Frederick Palmer	3/30/18
LAKE JR, Orloff Levin	7/20/18
LAREMORE, Richard Thomas	1/17/18
LAWRENCE, Charles Kane Cobb	1/4/18
LEEHAN, Jim	11/16/18
LEFEBVRE, Eugene Francis	8/30/18
LESEURE, Laurence James	3/2/18
LEWIS JR, Giles Floyd	11/19/18
LEWIS JR, Howarth Lister	11/11/18
LIEBENOW, Robert Ervin	6/18/18
LIPSEY, Howard Martin	11/25/18
LITZENBURG JR, Thomas Vernon	5/19/18
LLOYD, John Janney	12/18/18
LOFMAN, Donald Stig	11/11/18
LOGAN, William Stevenson	3/11/18
LONERGAN, Robert Thomas	6/17/18
LONERGAN JR, Willis Gerald	3/11/18
MAESEN, William August	1/2/18
MAGNUSON, George Peter	10/18/18
MANDERBACH, Aaron	4/29/18
MARSHALL JR, Bill	8/8/18
MARTIN, Charles Percy	2/16/18
MARTIN, William Henderson	5/11/18
MARTINEZ-RAPALO, Ramon	6/21/18
MASQUELETTE, Eizabeth Daggett	11/20/18
MAYBIN, Maxine Roberta	11/11/18
MCCONNEY, J Anne	12/15/18
MCMURREN, Jay Junior	1/31/18
MCNULTY, Lynne Herrick	6/5/18
MEAD, Loren	5/5/18
MICHNO, Dennis Glen	9/26/18
MILLAR, Chuck	12/21/18
MILLER, James Lower	1/16/18
MINIFIE, Thomas Richardson	8/17/18
MINTURN, Benjamin Bradshaw	2/21/18
MIONSKE, Wayne Allan Robert	4/30/18
MITCHELL, Judy	12/2/18
MOORE, James Wesley	8/25/18
MORRIS, Richard Melvin	12/14/18
MOSHER, David Rike	1/5/18
MOULDEN, Michael Mackreth	9/24/18
MOWERY, Donald	6/12/18

MUELLER, Susan Richards	8/12/18
MULAC, Pam	9/23/18
MURCHISON, Joel Williams	6/10/18
MURRAY, Lewellyn St Elmo	4/1/18
MURRAY, Robin George Ellis	10/11/18
MUTH, David Philip	9/15/18
MYERS III, Bruns M	11/2/18
NAKATSUJI, Dorothy Masako Kamigaki	1/9/18
NEVILLE, Barry Paige	10/8/18
NOISY HAWK SR, Lyle Maynard	11/20/18
ONKKA SR, Paul William	4/17/18
PAGLIARO, Lois Anne	12/8/18
PARAN, William John	3/22/18
PARK III, Howard Franklin	3/13/18
PARKER, Andy	12/18/18
PATTERSON, John	7/28/18
PAYNE, Samuel Houston	12/31/18
PETERSEN, Judith	1/25/18
PHILLIPS-MATSON, Wesley A	10/14/18
PITTMAN, Albert Calhoun	7/10/18
PREBLE, Joan Nelson	4/13/18
PRESSEY, Stephen Palmer	2/19/18
PRITCHARD, David Gatlin	5/26/18
PURKS III, James Harris	2/19/18
QUINBY, Congreve Hamilton	6/14/18
RANSOM, Charles Wilfred	2/8/18
RATHMAN, William E	6/3/18
RED BIRD, Hazel	11/24/18
REDMON, William Jessie	8/19/18
REED SR, James A	1/12/18
REID JR, Raymond W	8/2/18
REUSCHLING, Walter Edward	1/24/18
RHODES, Erroll Franklin	11/24/18
RICE, Charles L	10/8/18
RICH JR, Ernest Albert	3/20/18
RICHARDS, Anne Frances	1/12/18
RIDDLE, Hill Carter	7/29/18
RIDGWAY, George Edward	8/17/18
ROACH, Robert Eugene	3/9/18
ROBERTS, William Allan	9/22/18
ROBINSON, Grant Harris	9/5/18
ROBY JR, Jesse	6/10/18
ROCKABRAND, Walter Ralph	7/26/18
ROGERS, Allan Douglas	2/2/18
ROSE, Roger Franklin	9/11/18
ROSE, Shirley Jean	7/17/18
RUPP, Lloyd Gary	8/26/18
SAUSSY JR, Hugh	4/8/18
SCHAUBLE, Jack	11/12/18
SCHLEGEL, Stuart Allen	11/8/18
SCHROEDER, Donald John	3/29/18
SELLE, Kevin Dwight	8/6/18
SHAEFER III, Harry Frederick	8/28/18
SHAFFER, Paul	6/22/18
SHEARS, Sidney Herbert	9/3/18
SHELTON, Joan Adams	11/15/18
SHEPHERD, Richard Golder	4/7/18
SHIRES, Robert A	1/8/18
SHUCKER II, Courtney A	8/1/18
SIEFFERMAN, Norman Clyde	2/23/18
SIMPSON, Geoffrey Sedgwick	2/9/18
SIMPSON JR, John Patrick	5/3/18
SIMS, Elizabeth Erringer	4/16/18
SISK JR, Edwin Kerr	12/5/18
SMITH, Charles Howard	3/4/18
SMITH, Dennis Lee	11/23/18
SMITH JR, Elton Osman	11/17/18
SMITH, James Albert	2/23/18
SMITH, John Harmon	2/6/18
SMITH, Robert Angus	3/12/18
SMITH, Samuel Earl	10/21/18
SPANGENBERG, Ronald Wesley	10/5/18
SPELLMAN, Robert Garland Windsor	7/20/18
SPRUILL JR, William Arthur	6/12/18
STEED, John Griffith	5/8/18
STEINFELD, John Wilfred	6/30/18
STEVENS III, Halsey	1/15/18
STINGLEY, Elizabeth Anne	6/18/18
STOY, Carol Berry	1/29/18
STROMWELL, Gloria Regina	12/10/18
STUART JR, Calvin Truesdale Biddison	4/6/18
SUMMERS, Charlie	2/8/18
SWANN, Stephen Barham	9/17/18
SWEENY, Thomas Edward	6/13/18
TARWATER, Thomas William	9/18/18
THEODORE, Pamela Hillis	5/2/18
THIERING, Barry Bernard	4/1/18
THOMAS, Samuel Sutter	10/15/18
THOMPSON, Doug	1/27/18
TINKLEPAUGH, John	7/11/18
TOLAND JR, William Leslie	7/1/18
TREMAINE, Gordon Hyde	3/21/18
TREMBATH, Jack Graham	3/28/18
TRIPP, Arthur Davis	9/29/18
UNDERWOOD, Robert Franklin	3/5/18
VAN CULIN, Thomas Meyers	11/4/18
VANDEVELDER, Frank Radcliff	11/18/18
VAN DUSEN, David Buick	10/16/18
VAN HOOK, Peter	12/16/18
VAN VALKENBURGH, William Burton	5/14/18
VOORHEES, Jonathan Andrew	7/28/18
WAGNER, Dick	6/10/18
WALKER, Charles Henry	8/2/18
WALKER, David Charles	12/3/18
WANCURA, Paul Forsyth	4/16/18
WARD, Katherine	10/12/18
WAY, Peter Trosdal	10/6/18
WAYNE, David Boyd	1/11/18
WEAVER, Joseph Clyde	4/29/18
WEST, Craig	11/2/18
WHITAKER, James Stewart	4/22/18
WHITESELL, Hugh A	7/7/18
WHITFIELD, Mary Dean	5/24/18
WHITFIELD, Raymond Palmer	3/22/18
WILDSMITH, Joseph Ned	2/5/18
WILEY, Ronald Lee	10/8/18
WILKINS JR, Aaron Ellis	1/19/18
WILKINSON, John Preston	7/23/18
WILLIAMS, James Armstrong	5/1/18
WILLIAMS, Richard Alan	4/20/18
WILLIAMS, Robert Bruce	11/26/18
WILLIAMS, Tracey Mark	5/27/18
WILSON JR, Charles Alexander	11/24/18
WILSON, Henry H	1/21/18
WILSON, John Morris	4/23/18
WIPFLER, William Louis	10/3/18
WOLFF, Pierre Maurice	1/31/18
WOODRUM, Lawrence Paul	5/22/18
YOUNGER, Leighton Keith	5/20/18

CLERGY RECEIVED FROM ROMAN CATHOLIC CHURCH OR OTHER CHURCHES IN FULL COMMUNION
1/18-12/18

CONNOR, The Rev. Stephen J. (RC) — 6/30/18
FERNANDEZ, Jureck Zamudio (RC) — 7/21/18
LOPEZ, Ricardo Ramirez (RC) — 5/25/18
SCHRANZ, Donald Jerome (RC) — 3/22/18
WYMER, Seth Thomas (RC) — 5/8/18

CLERGY RECEIVED FROM EVANGELICAL LUTHERAN CHURCH IN AMERICA
1/18-12/18

ALBERTI, Brian Christopher — 5/30/18
FISCHER, Ryan David — 3/25/18
MOORE, Scott Alan — 10/16/18
STROBEL, Mark Alan — 3/25/18

CLERGY TRANSFERRED FROM OTHER PROVINCES OF THE ANGLICAN COMMUNION
1/18-12/18

ACKERMANN, Frauke — 6/7/18
(Ch of the Prov of Sthrn Afr)
ACKERMANN, Lutz — 6/7/18
(Ch of the Prov of Sthrn Afr)
BUCHANAN, Ernest Ray (Dio Nthrn Mex) — 8/29/18
FREEMAN, Karen Lynn (Ch Of Engl) — 11/19/18
KRUGER, Andrew David — 3/23/18
(Ch of the Prov of Sthrn Afr)
LAVELLE, Jon Frederick — 7/27/18
(The Epis Ch in Jerusalem and the Middle E)
LEE, Hyangnam (Angl Comm In Japan) — 11/13/18
NAPIER, Graeme Stewart Patrick Columbanus — 6/4/18
(Ch Of Engl)
PAGER, Deng Alaak — 10/11/18
(The Epis Ch of the Sudan)
RAMOS HUERTA, Habacuc — 2/22/18
(Dio Wstrn Mex)

SHUKAIR, Halim Adel — 10/11/18
(The Epis Ch in Jerusalem and the Middle E)
STANSFIELD, Patricia Janette — 8/9/18
(Angl Ch of Can)
STEELE, David Regan — 1/10/18
(Ch in the Prov Of The W Indies)
THORNLEY, Edward Charles (Ch Of Engl) — 8/29/18
WANDREY, Bryce Philip (Ch Of Engl) — 5/6/18

RESTORATIONS
1/18-12/18

BARNES, Simon (Pgh) — 8/13/18
BUSSEY, Lawrence Day (Minn) — 6/26/18

SUSPENSIONS
1/18-12/18

BAUGH, Jonathan Earle (NC) — 12/21/18
LASITER JR, Douglas Norman (La) — 3/21/18
LISBY, Gregory C (WMass) — 3/27/18
MOERMOND, Curt (Ia) — 11/4/18
RACINE, Jean-Joel (Hai) — 12/7/18
SPENCER, Peter Levalley (RI) — 5/14/18
WALLER, Ryan Casey (Dal) — 10/30/18

DEPOSITIONS
1/18-12/18

ARCHER, Michael (Los) — 11/9/18
BENDER, Richard E (ECR) — 11/15/18

REMOVALS
1/18-12/18

BISSOONDIAL, Dinesh (CFla) — 9/11/18
CORDOVA RUIZ, Santiago David (EcuC) — 5/31/18
DEMMON, Michael David Scott (Colo) — 8/29/18
EGAN, Adam DJ (Alb) — 5/21/18
GILLILAND, Jonathon Shea (Dal) — 5/8/18
HYER, Darin Stant (CGC) — 1/30/18
LANNON, Nicholas Jewett (Ky) — 8/31/18
LOWNEY, James Edward (Ind) — 11/21/18
MASON, Bruce Edmund (Alb) — 7/2/18
MCLEOD, Timothy Reeves (NC) — 5/22/18
SILVA-GONZALEZ, Alvaro (PR) — 7/31/18
VILLAMARIN-GUTIERREZ, Washington — 8/6/18
Rigoberto (EcuC)
WAIT III, Benjamin Wofford (CFla) — 11/15/18
WILSON, Frank K (RG) — 2/13/18
WOOLARD, Lynn Phillip (CFla) — 10/16/18

CLERGY REPORTED AS ORDAINED
Not included in the Clergy List

The following is a list of names of Clergy who have been reported as ordained. At deadline date no data had been received from them. Because they could not be properly entered in the files of THE CHURCH PENSION FUND, they are not a part of the Clergy List.

CORDOVA RUIZ, Santiago (EcuC)   **MASON**, John (RG)

CLERGY:
BISHOPS, PRIESTS, AND DEACONS

The names, addresses, and canonical residences in the Clergy List, as well as the preceding list (Necrology, Receptions, Transfers, Restorations, Suspensions, Depositions, Removals, and Clergy Reported as Ordained), are supplied by The Recorder of Ordinations and reflect changes reported by 31 December 2018. Any request for a change in the Clergy List should be addressed to The Recorder of Ordinations, CHURCH PENSION GROUP, 19 East 34th Street, New York, NY 10016.

A

AALAN, Joshua Canon (Pa) 2013 Appletree St, Philadelphia, PA 19103

AARON, Stephen Craig (Wyo) 618 Saunders Cir, Evanston, WY 82930

AARON LUDWIG, Stephanie (Wyo)

ABBOTT, Barbara Leigh (Pa) 110 Llanfair Rd, Ardmore, PA 19003

ABBOTT, Dick (VI) Po Box 686, Frederiksted, VI 00841

ABBOTT, Gail Eoline (Mil)

ABBOTT SR, Gary Louis (Ga) 92 Camden Way, Hawkinsville, GA 31036

ABBOTT, Grant H (Minn) 2163 Carter Ave, Saint Paul, MN 55108

ABBOTT, James Michael (Tex) 6507 Allentown Dr, Spring, TX 77389

ABBOTT, Samuel Bassett (Alb) 1 Church St, Cooperstown, NY 13326

ABBOTT, Sefton Frank James (WNC) 27 Hildebrand St, Asheville, NC 28801

ABDELNOUR, Mark Anthony (USC) St. Simon & St. Jude Epis Church, 1110 Kinley Rd., Irmo, SC 29063

ABDY, Anne (Ore) PO Box 1398, Sutherlin, OR 97479

ABELL, Jesse W (WMass) 3 John Street, Westborough, MA 01581

ABER, Jack Albert (Q) 522 Portsmouth Ct, Doylestown, PA 18901

ABERNATHEY, James Milton (Tex) 1903 E. Bayshore Dr., Palacios, TX 77465

ABERNATHY, Paul (WA) 1050 Willis Rd, Spartanburg, SC 29301

ABERNATHY JR, W Harry (NY) 50 Bedford Rd, Armonk, NY 10504

ABERNETHY-DEPPE, David Edward (Cal) 19938 Josh Pl, Castro Valley, CA 94546

ABERNETHY-DEPPE, Jonathan (Cal) 2322 Oakcrest Dr, Palm Springs, CA 92264

ABEYARATNE, Keshini Anoma (Mass) 4 Greenough Cir, Brookline, MA 02445

ABIDARI, Mehrdad (Cal) Cathedral School for Boys, 1257 Sacramento St, San Francisco, CA 94108

ABRAHAM, Billie (Miss) P.O. Box 921, Vicksburg, MS 39181

ABRAHAM, John Laurence (Az) 9138 North Palm Brook Dr., Tucson, AZ 85743

ABRAHAMSON, Wendy (Ia) St. John's Episcopal Church, 120 First St. NE, Mason City, IA 50401

ABRAMS, Mary Elizabeth (Ky) 4100 Southern Pkwy, Louisville, KY 40214

ABRAMS, Ronald (EC) 3309 Upton Ct, Wilmington, NC 28409

ABREU ABREU, JoseMartinAltagracia (DR (DomRep))

ABSHIER, Patsy Ann (Kan) Po Box 1175, Wichita, KS 67201

ABSHIRE, Lupton P (Colo) Saint Luke's Episcopal Church, 2000 Stover St, Fort Collins, CO 80525

ABSTEIN II, W(Illiam) Robert (Tenn) 9210 Sawyer Brown Rd, Nashville, TN 37221

ABT, Audra (NC) 2105 W Market St, Greensboro, NC 27403

ABUCHAR CURY, Rafael (Colom)

ACCIME, Max (Hai) C/O Lynx Air, PO Box 407139, Fort Lauderdale, FL 33340

ACEVEDO, Miriam (NH) 92 Nashua Rd, Pelham, NH 03076

ACEVEDO, Sheila Devine (SeFla) St. Andrew's Episcopal Church, 100 N Palmway, Lake Worth, FL 33460

ACKAAH, Vincent Abisi (NY) PO Box 950A, Bronx, NY 10451

ACKER, Patricia Small (CFla) PO Box 290245, Pt Orange, FL 32129

ACKERMAN, Chase Dumont (SwFla)

ACKERMAN, Patricia Elizabeth (NY) 86 Piermont Ave, Nyack, NY 10960

ACKERMAN, Peter (Va) 101 N. Quaker Ln, Alexandria, VA 22304

ACKERMAN, Thomas Dieden (Mil) 4875 Easy St, Unit # 12, Hartland, WI 53029

ACKERMANN, Frauke (Eur)

ACKERMANN, John Frederick (Oly)

ACKERMANN, Lutz (Eur) Garmischer Str. 2A, Augsburg, 86163, Germany

ACKERSON, Charles Garrett (LI) Po Box 113, Mastic Beach, NY 11951

ACKLAND III, Lauren Dreeland (Nwk) 321 N Wyoming Ave Apt 1b, South Orange, NJ 07079

ACKLEY, Susan M (NH) 28 River St, Ashland, NH 03217

ACOSTA RODRIGUEZ, Richard (Colom)

ACOSTA-ZAPATA, Pedro Jose (Mil)

ACREE, Nancy Pickering (Ga) 207 High Pt, Saint Simons Island, GA 31522

ADAIR, Maryly S (The Episcopal NCal)

ADAM, Barbara Ann (Kan) 10500 W 140th Ter, Overland Park, KS 66221

ADAM, Betty (Tex) 3501 Chevy Chase Dr, Houston, TX 77019

ADAM, John Todd (Neb) 2621 CR 59, Alliance, NE 69301

ADAMIK, George F (NC) 221 Union St, Cary, NC 27511

ADAMS, Chris (RG) 231 Amberleigh Dr Apt 102, Wilmington, NC 28411

ADAMS JR, David Morrison (Spr)

ADAMS, David Robert (NJ)

ADAMS, Deanna Sue (U) 603 W 2350 S, Perry, UT 84302

ADAMS, Debra Jeanne (Ida)

ADAMS, Eloise Ellen (Ct) 495 Laurel Hill Rd Apt 4B, Norwich, CT 06360

ADAMS JR, Enoch (Ak)

ADAMS, Frank George (NJ) 107 Devon Dr, Chestertown, MD 21620

ADAMS, Gary Jay (ECR) 3002 Hauser Ct, Carson City, NV 89701

✠ **ADAMS III**, Gladstone Bailey (CNY) The Episcopal Church in South Carolina, PO Box 20485, Charleston, SC 29413

ADAMS, Helen Kandl (CFla) 103 Shady Branch Trl, Ormond Beach, FL 32174

ADAMS JR, Holmes S (Miss) All Saints' Church, 608 W Jefferson St, Tupelo, MS 38804

ADAMS, James Harold (Roch) 517 Castle St, Geneva, NY 14456

✠ **ADAMS JR**, James Marshall (CFla) 428 W Cobblestone Loop, Hernando, FL 34442

ADAMS, James Patrick (NC) 120 East Edenton Street, Raleigh, NC 27601

ADAMS, Jennifer Lin (WMich) 536 College Ave, Holland, MI 49423

ADAMS JR, Jesse Roland (La) 6306 Prytania St, New Orleans, LA 70118

ADAMS, John (Neb) 450 Bordeaux St., Chadron, NE 69337

ADAMS JR, John Davry (Va) 1731 Cloister Dr, Richmond, VA 23238

ADAMS, John Stockton (ECR) 24745 Summit Field Road, Carmel, CA 93923

ADAMS, John Torbet (Alb) 262 Center Rd, Lyndeborough, NH 03082

ADAMS, Jonathan Vaughn (Tex)

ADAMS, Lesley (Roch) 6200 Mount Rd, Trumansburg, NY 14886

ADAMS, Margaret Louise (Tenn) 411 Annex Ave Apt F-1, Nashville, TN 37209

ADAMS, Mary Lynn (FdL)

ADAMS, Michael K (Tex) 209 W 27th St, Austin, TX 78705

ADAMS, Patricia Wessels (Ak) 3506 Cherokee Dr S, Salem, OR 97302

ADAMS, Richard Carl (Oly) Po Box 336, Hinesburg, VT 05461

ADAMS, Samuel Bowman (Tenn) 4715 Harding Pike, Nashville, TN 37205

ADAMS JR, Thomas Edwin (Mass) PO Box 522, Falmouth, MA 02541

ADAMS, William J (The Episcopal NCal) 95 Malaga Ct, Ukiah, CA 95482

ADAMS, William Rian (WNC) 6329 Frederica Rd, St Simons Island, GA 31522

ADAMS, William Seth (Oly) 2707 Silver Crest Court, Langley, WA 98260

ADAMS-HARRIS, Anne Jane (Wyo) Po Box 4086, Santa Barbara, CA 93140

ADAMS-MASSMANN, Jennifer Helen (Eur) Sebastian-Rinz-Str 22, Frankfurt, Germany, Germany

ADAMSON, Thomas I (NI) 909 S Darling St, Angola, IN 46703

ADAMS-RILEY, Gena D (Fla) 815 E Grace St, Richmond, VA 23219

ADAMS-RILEY, Wallace (USC) 815 E Grace St, Richmond, VA 23219

ADAMS-SHEPHERD, Kathleen E (Mo) Christ Church Cathedral, 1210 Locust St, Saint Louis, MO 63103

ADDIEGO, Jeffrey Clark (Nev) 1429 Bronco Rd, Boulder City, NV 89005

ADDISON, Orlando J (CFla) 6990 S US Highway 1, Port St Lucie, FL 34952

ADE, Daniel Gerard George (Los) 242 E Alvarado St, Pomona, CA 91767

ADEBONOJO, Mary Bunton (Pa) 50 Bagdad Rd, Durham, NH 03824

ADELIA, Laura A (Az) 100 W Roosevelt St, Phoenix, AZ 85003

ADER, Thomas Edmund (At) 3596 Liberty Ln, Marietta, GA 30062

ADERS, Magdalena Mary (NJ) 18 Ryers Ln, Matawan, NJ 07747

ADESSA, Denise Mcgovern (Ct) 311 Broad St, Windsor, CT 06095

ADINOLFI, Debora (At) 901 W. Eire St, Chandler, AZ 85225

ADINOLFI JR, Jerry (Kan) 131 Country Estates Rd, Greenville, NY 12083

ADKINS, Edna Fishburne (Ga) Po Box 1601, Tybee Island, GA 31328

ADKINS JR, Robert Frederick (CNY) 956 Graylea Cir, Elmira, NY 14905

ADLER, John Stuart (SwFla) 1406 S. Larkwood Square, Fort Myers, FL 33919

ADLER, Paul (Pa) 6769 Ridge Ave, Philadelphia, PA 19128

ADOLPHSON, Donald Richard (Cal) 552 Old Orchard Dr, Danville, CA 94526

ADORNO ANDINO, Hector Luis (PR) Iglesia Episcopal Puertorriquena, PO Box 902, Saint Just, PR 00978

ADU-ANDOH, Samuel (Pa) 1121 Serrill Ave, Yeadon, PA 19050

ADWELL, Lynn (Minn) 334 E Fremont Dr, Tempe, AZ 85282

ADZIMA, Melissa Lian (Colo) 2015 Glenarm Pl, Denver, CO 80205

AFANADOR-KAFURI, Hernan (Ala) 176 Ridgewood Dr., Remlap, AL 35133

AFFER, Licia (At) 3098 Saint Annes Ln NW, Atlanta, GA 30327

AGAR JR, Ralph Wesley (Neb) 2315 Georgetown Pl, Bellevue, NE 68123

AGBAJE, John (SO) 1 Paddle Ct, Portsmouth, VA 23703

AGBO, Godwin (Ct) 61 Grove St, Putnam, CT 06260

AGGELER, Harold Griffith (Ida)

AGIM, Emeka Ngozi (Tex) 16203 Dryberry Ct, Houston, TX 77083

AGNER, Georgia Ellen (Eau) 17823 57th Ave, Chippewa Falls, WI 54729

AGNEW, Christopher Mack (Va)

AGNEW JR, ML (WLa) 113 Whispering Pines Dr, Bullard, TX 75757

AGUILAR, Norman (Hond)

AGUILAR DE RAMIREZ, Ana Roselia (Hond)

AHLENIUS, Robert Orson (Dal) 2541 Pinebluff Drive, Dallas, TX 75228

AHLVIN, Judith L (ECR) 18325 Crystal Dr, Morgan Hill, CA 95037

AHN, Matthew Y (Los) 10555 Bel Air Dr, Cherry Valley, CA 92223

AHN, Paul C (Chi) 5801 N Pulaski Rd #348, Chicago, IL 60646

✠ **AHRENS**, Laura J (Ct) 2 Cannondale Dr, Danbury, CT 06810

AHRON, Linda W (Los) 31641 La Novia Ave, San Juan Capistrano, CA 92675

AIDNIK, Aileen Marie (The Episcopal NCal) 988 Collier Dr, San Leandro, CA 94577

AIKEN JR, Charles Duval (Va) 4210 Hanover Ave, Richmond, VA 23221

AIKEN, Richard Lloyd (Ct) P.O. Box 1130, Truro, MA 02666

AIN, Judith Pattison (ECR) 286 Thompson Rd Rear, Watsonville, CA 95076

AINSLEY, Matthew Brian (CFla)

AINSWORTH, Mark J (Pa) 262 Bent Road, Wyncote, PA 19095

AIS, Jean Nesly (Hai) Eglesi Episcopal D'Haiti, Boite Postale 1309, Port-au-Prince, Haiti

AJAX, Kesner (Hai) C/O Agape Flights Acc. #2519, 100 Airport Avenue, Venice, FL 34285

AKAMATSU, Mary Catherine (Ala) St Matthew's Episcopal Church, 786 Hughes Rd, Madison, AL 35758

AKER, Edwina Sievers (Mont) 32413 Skidoo Ln, Polson, MT 59860

AKES, Amanda Ann (WA) Grace Church, 1607 Grace Church Rd, Silver Spring, MD 20910

AKIN, Mary Anne (Ala) 3525 Great Oak Lk Ln, Birmingham, AL 35223

AKINKUGBE, Felix Olagboye (FtW) 2995 Celian Dr, Grand Prairie, TX 75052

AKIYAMA, Diana D (The Episcopal Church in Haw) PO Box 44915, Kamuela, HI 96743

AKRIDGE, Alan M (Ga) 108 Worthing Rd, St Simons Island, GA 31522

ALAGNA, Frank J (NY) Po Box 1, Rhinecliff, NY 12574

ALAN, Stacy (Chi) 5540 S Woodlawn Ave, Chicago, IL 60637

ALAVA VILLAREAL, Geronimo (Litoral Ecu) Casilla 0901-5250, Guayaquil, Ecuador

ALBANO, Randolph Nolasco (The Episcopal Church in Haw) St. Paul's Episcopal Church, 229 Queen Emma Square, Honolulu, HI 96813

ALBERCA MERINO, Francisco Venito (Eur) Via Napoli, 58, Roma, Italy, 00184, Italy

ALBERGATE, Scott P (Pa) 249 N. Belfield Ave, Havertown, PA 19083

ALBERS, Barbara Ann (RG) 8540 S Southpoint Rd, Empire, MI 49630

ALBERT II, Edwin Edward (SO) 1924 Timberidge Dr., Loveland, OH 45140

ALBERT, Hilario (NY) 535 King St, Port Chester, NY 10573

ALBERT III, Jules Gilmore (La) 6249 Canal Blvd, New Orleans, LA 70124

ALBERTI, Brian Christopher (Fla)

ALBINGER JR, Bill (The Episcopal Church in Haw)

ALBOM, Sandra Janet (NH) 51 Concord St, Peterborough, NH 03458

ALBRECHT, John Herman (Mich) 293 Scottsdale Dr, Troy, MI 48084

ALBRETHSEN, Karen Anne (Nev) 777 Sage St, Elko, NV 89801

ALBRIGHT, J Taylor Taylor (Ct) 525 Suffield St, Agawam, MA 01001

ALBRIGHT, Meredyth L (FdL)

ALBRIGHT, Timothy Scott (Be) 383 N Hunter Hwy, Drums, PA 18222

ALDANA ROJAS, Javier (Colom)

ALDAY, Kristen Nowell (CFla) 1017 E. Robinson Street, Orlando, FL 32801

ALDER, Steve (U) 2215 Molino Ave Apt A, Signal Hill, CA 90755

ALDRICH, Dawn Marie (NMich) 1310 Ashmun St, Sault Sainte Marie, MI 49783

ALDRICH JR, Kenneth Davis (NJ) 400 4th St., Huntingdon, PA 16652

ALDRICH, Robert Paul (NMich)

ALEXANDER, Brantley (Ind)

ALEXANDER, Conor Matthew (SVa)

ALEXANDER II, George Wilson (At) 3468 Summerford Ct, Marietta, GA 30062

ALEXANDER, Gerald G (Fla) 4311 Ortega Forest Dr, Jacksonville, FL 32210

✠ **ALEXANDER**, J Neil (At) 335 Tennessee Avenue, Sewanee, TN 37383

ALEXANDER, Jane Biggs (WLa) 2015 East Northside Dr., Jackson, MS 39211

ALEXANDER, Jason L (Ark) The Episcopal Diocese of Arkansas, P.O. Box 164668, Little Rock, AR 72216

ALEXANDER, John David (RI) 974 Pine St, Seekonk, MA 02771

ALEXANDER, Jonna Ruth (Ore) 247 SE 82nd Ave, Portland, OR 97216

ALEXANDER, Kathryn Bellm (Ark) CHRIST CHURCH, 509 SCOTT ST, LITTLE ROCK, AR 72201

ALEXANDER, Patricia Phaneuf (WA) 8804 Postoak Rd, Potomac, MD 20854

ALEXANDER JR, Randy (Va) 3606 Seminary Rd, Alexandria, VA 22304

ALEXANDER, Sharon Ann (La) 3552 Morning Glory Ave, Baton Rouge, LA 70808

ALEXANDER, Stephen Gray (Lex) 5300 Hamilton Ave Apt 906, Cincinnati, OH 45224

ALEXANDER, William David (Okla)

ALEXANDRE, Hickman (LI) 260 Beaver Dam Road, Brookhaven, NY 11719

ALEXANDRE, Soner (Hai)

ALEXIS, Alicia (NC) PO Box 20427, Greensboro, NC 27420

ALEXIS, Judith (Ct) 628 Main St, Stamford, CT 06901

ALFORD, Billy J (Ga) 3041 Hummingbird Ln, Augusta, GA 30906

ALFORD JR, Harold Bennett (Ala) 680 Calder St, Beaumont, TX 77701

ALFORD, Joseph Stanley Trowbridge (Kan) 2618 W 24th Terrace, Lawrence, KS 66047

ALFORD, William T (CPa) 302 S Liberty St, Centreville, MD 21617

ALFORD-HARKEY, April L (Ct)

ALGERNON, Marcel Glenford (SwFla) 2055 Woodsong Way, Fountain, CO 80817

ALIMOLE, Chisara Rose (NY) 1415 Pelhamdale Ave, Pelham, NY 10803

ALLAGREE, The Rev. Harry R. (The Episcopal NCal) 361 Lincoln Avenue, Cotati, CA 94931

ALLAIN, Thomas A (Miss) 615 18th St S, Birmingham, AL 35233

✠ **ALLAN**, Frank Kellogg (At) 1231 Briarcliff Rd Ne, Atlanta, GA 30306

ALLARD, Bradley Richard (WMich) 1145 N Hampton Dr NE, Grand Rapids, MI 49505

ALLEE, Roger G (SeFla) 2212 S Cypress Bend Dr Apt 107, Pompano Beach, FL 33069

ALLEMAN, Timothy Lee (Be) 20B Buckingham Street, Luzerne, PA 18709

ALLEMEIER, James Elmer (Chi) 4306 34th Avenue Pl, Moline, IL 61265

ALLEN, Abraham Claude (Mass) 17 Winthrop St, Marlborough, MA 01752

ALLEN, Barbara (WA) 6919 Strathmore St Apt C, Bethesda, MD 20815

ALLEN, Charles William (Ind) 4118 Byram Ave, Indianapolis, IN 46208

ALLEN, Curtis Tilley (WTenn) 133 Jefferson Sq, Nashville, TN 37215

ALLEN, David Eastman (Mass) 980 Memorial Dr, Cambridge, MA 02138

ALLEN, David Edward (Mass) PO Box 1052, Barnstable, MA 02630

ALLEN, Donald Frederick (Ct) 34 Ashlar Vlg, Wallingford, CT 06492

ALLEN, E(arl) Michael (Nwk) 55 George St, Allendale, NJ 07401

ALLEN II, George Curwood (SO) 988 Duxbury Ct, Cincinnati, OH 45255

ALLEN JR, John (Ky) 1512 Valley Brook Rd, Louisville, KY 40222

ALLEN, John M (Oly) 4415 Colebrooke Lane SE, Lacey, WA 98513

ALLEN, John Shepley (NH) 229 Shore Dr, Laconia, NH 03246

ALLEN, John Tait (Mil) 515 Oak St., South Milwaukee, WI 53172

ALLEN, Larry J (WMo) 3212 S. Jeffrey Cir., Independence, MO 64055

✠ **ALLEN**, Lloyd Emmanuel (Hond) Diocese of Honduras, PO Box 523900, Miami, FL 33152

ALLEN, Mark (The Episcopal NCal) 5872 Oliver Rd, Paradise, CA 95969

ALLEN, Mary (Del) 3 Thornberry Dr, Ocean View, DE 19770

ALLEN, Morgan S (Tex) 3201 Windsor Rd, Austin, TX 78703

ALLEN, Patrick Scott (SC) 886 Seafarer Way, Charleston, SC 29412

ALLEN JR, Radford Bonnie (FtW) 1804 Dakar Rd W, Fort Worth, TX 76116

ALLEN, Robert Edward (Ark) 1101 Glenwood Dr, El Dorado, AR 71730

ALLEN, Roger D (At) St. James Episcopal Church, 161 Church St NE, Marietta, GA 30060

ALLEN, Russell Harvey (Ct) 28 Seaward Ln, Harwich, MA 02645

ALLEN, Stephanie Perry (NC) Church of the Nativity, 8849 Ray Road, Raleigh, NC 27613

ALLEN, Susan Van Leunen (ECR) PO Box 173, King City, CA 93930

ALLEN, Thomas Scott (Be) 713 Cherokee St, Bethlehem, PA 18015

ALLEN, Thomas Wynn (Md) 1 St. Mary's Church Rd., Abingdon, MD 21009

ALLEN, W Frank (Pa) 763 Valley Forge Rd, Wayne, PA 19087

ALLEN, Walter Drew (Colo) Po Box 5958, Vail, CO 81658

ALLEN-FAIELLA, Willie (SeFla) 16745 Southwest 74th Avenue, Miami, FL 33157

ALLEN-HERRON, Dawn (Ak) 3886 S Tongass Hwy, Ketchikan, AK 99901

ALLEY, Ann Leonard (Spr) 913 W Washington St, Champaign, IL 61821

ALLEY, Charles Dickson (Va) 1101 Forest Ave, Richmond, VA 23229

ALLEY, Marguerite Cole (SVa) 1917 Indian Run Rd, Virginia Beach, VA 23454

ALLEYNE, Edmund Torrence (LI) 972 E 93rd St, Brooklyn, NY 11236

ALLICK, Paul Delain (Cal) 162 Hickory St, San Francisco, CA 94102

ALLIN, Hailey Wile (Miss) PO Box 1366, Jackson, MS 39215

ALLING JR, Roger (Ct) 125 N 28th St, Camp Hill, PA 17011

ALLISON II, C Roy (CFla) 38 S Halifax Dr, Ormond Beach, FL 32176

✠ **ALLISON**, Christopher FitzSimons (SC) 1081 Indigo Ave, Georgetown, SC 29440

ALLISON, John Leroy (Me) PO Box 186, Hulls Cove, ME 04644

ALLISON, Judith Anne (SanD)

ALLISON, Marianne Stirling (Ore) 17435 NW West Union Rd, Portland, OR 97229

ALLISON, Nancy Jean (NC) 3110 Belvin Dr, Raleigh, NC 27609

ALLISON-HATCH, Mary Susan (RG) 1625 Escalante Ave SW, Albuquerque, NM 87104

ALLMAN, Denny Paul (Miss) 8008 Bluebonnet Blvd Apt 13-2, Baton Rouge, LA 70810

ALLMAN, Mary Katherine (SanD) 7946 Calle De La Plata, La Jolla, CA 92037

ALLMAN, Susan (U) 1016 E. High Cedar Highlands Dr., Cedar City, UT 84720

ALLPORT II, Bill (Nwk) 113 Engle St, Englewood, NJ 07631

ALLRED, Jennifer Allison (Minn) 901 Portland Ave, Saint Paul, MN 55104

ALLTOP, Bob (Mich) Cathedral Church of St Paul, 4800 Woodward Ave, Detroit, MI 48201

ALMENDAREZ BAUTISTA, Javier E (NC)

ALMODIEL JR, Arsolin Diones (Nev) Dioces of Nevada, 9480 S Eastern Ave, Las Vegas, NV 89123

ALMON JR, Austin Albert (RI) 116 Daggett Ave, Pawtucket, RI 02861

ALMONO ROQUE, Joel (Mass) 1524 Summit Ave, Saint Paul, MN 55105

ALMONTE, Salvador (DR (DomRep)) Calle Santiago #114 Gazcue, Santo Domingo, Dominican Republic

ALMOS, Richard Wayne (La) 996 Marina Dr, Slidell, LA 70458

ALMQUIST, Curtis Gustav (Mass) St. John the Evangelist, 980 Memorial Drive, Cambridge, MA 02138

ALONGE-COONS, Katherine Grace (Alb) Grace Church, 34 3rd St, Waterford, NY 12188

ALONSO MARINA, Jesus Daniel (EcuC) Ava Y Maldonado, Guayaquil, Ecuador

ALONZO, Mary Parsons (Roch) 541 Linden St, Rochester, NY 14620

ALONZO MARTINEZ, Gerardo Antonio (Hond)

ALSAY, Joseph Caldwell (Okla) 14700 N MAY AVE, OKLAHOMA CITY, OK 73134

ALTENBACH, Julie Kay (CFla)

ALTIZER, Aimee Marie (U) PO Box 651572, Salt Lake Cty, UT 84165

ALTIZER, Caryl Jean (WTenn) 1830 S 336th St Apt C-202, Federal Way, WA 98003

ALTON, Frank (Los) 840 Echo Park Ave, Los Angeles, CA 90026

ALTON, Richard (Pa) St. Clement's Church, 2013 Appletree Street, Philadelphia, PA 19103

ALTOPP, Whitney F (Ct) Saint Stephen's Church, 351 Main St, Ridgefield, CT 06877

ALVARADO FIGUEROA, Luis A (PR)

ALVARADO-PALADA, Carlos (Hond)

ALVAREZ, Miguel (WNC) 5383 E Owens Ave, Las Vegas, NV 89110

ALVAREZ-ADORNO, Aida-Luz (PR)

✠ **ALVAREZ-VELAZQUEZ**, David Andres (PR) 4735 Ave. Isla Verde, Villas del Mar Oeste- Apt 3-E, Carolina, PR 00979

ALVAREZ VELEZ, Sergio Leon (Colom) Cra 6 #49-85, Bogota, Colombia

ALVES, David Alan (The Episcopal NCal) 13840 Tulsa Ct, Magalia, CA 95954

ALVES, Robert (EC) St John's Episcopal Church, 302 Green St, Fayetteville, NC 28301

ALVEY JR, John Thomas (Ala) 110 W Hawthorne Rd, Birmingham, AL 35209

ALWINE, David W (Tex) 527 Shem Butler Ct., Charleston, SC 29414

AMADIO, Carol M (FdL) Po Box 51, Washington Island, WI 54246

AMBELANG, John (Eau) 506 Fairway Dr, Sheboygan, WI 53081

AMBLER V, John Jaquelin (SwVa) 507 Sunset Dr, Amherst, VA 24521

AMBLER JR, Michael (Me) 912 Middle St, Bath, ME 04530

AMBROISE, Rospignac (Mass) Box 1309, Port-Au-Prince, Haiti

AMBROSE, Barbara (Va) 236 S Laurel St, Richmond, VA 23220

AMBROSE, Colin Moore (Tenn) 116 N. Academy St., Murfreesboro, TN 37130

AMBROSE, Theodore (Va) 2609 N Glebe Rd # P, Arlington, VA 22207

AMBROSE, Val Twomey (WMich) 6308 Greenway Drive SE, Grand Rapids, MI 49546

AMBURGEY, Cristina Goubaud (Oly) 3213 17th Street Pl Se, Puyallup, WA 98374

AMEND, Russell Jay (WNY) 25 Caspian Ct, Amherst, NY 14228

AMERMAN, Lucy S.L. (Pa) PO Box 57, Buckingham, PA 18912

AMES, David A (RI) 130 Slater Ave, Providence, RI 02906

AMES, Richard Kenneth (SeFla) 4917 Ravenswood Dr Apt 1709, San Antonio, TX 78227

AMMONS JR, B Wiley (Fla) 7500 Southside Blvd, Jacksonville, FL 32256

AMPAH, Rosina A (NY) 3042 Eagle Dr, Augusta, GA 30906

AMPARO TAPIA, Milton Mauricio (DR (DomRep)) Juan Luis Franco Bido #21, Santo Domingo, Dominican Republic

AMSDEN, Helen Prince (Neb) 9459 Jones Cir, Omaha, NE 68114

AMUZIE, Charles (WA) 3601 Alabama Ave SE, Washington, DC 20020

ANCHAN, Israel D (Chi) 298 S. Harrison Ave., Kankakee, IL 60901

ANDERS, Florence Kay Houghton (RG) Holy Family Episcopal Church, 10 A Bisbee Court, Santa fe, NM 87508

ANDERSEN, Francis Ian (Cal) 5 Epsom Court, Donvale Victoria, VI 3111, Australia

ANDERSEN, John Day (CNY) 2702 W Old State Road 34, Lizton, IN 46149

ANDERSEN, Judith Ann (NMich) 500 Ogden Ave, Escanaba, MI 49829

ANDERSEN, Paul (Va)

ANDERSEN, Raynor Wade (Ct) 199 Eastgate Dr, Cheshire, CT 06410

ANDERSEN, Richard Belden (Nwk) 275 E Franklin Tpke, Ho Ho Kus, NJ 07423

ANDERSEN, Steven C (U) 75 South 200 East, P.O. Box 3090, Salt Lake City, UT 84110

ANDERSON, Alissa Goudswaard (Ind) 802 Broadway, New York, NY 10003

ANDERSON, Angela Mary (Nev)

ANDERSON, Ann Johnston (ND) 2405 W Country Club Dr S, Fargo, ND 58103

ANDERSON, Anthony Dennis (Neb)

ANDERSON, Augusta (WNC) 2 Cedarcliff Road, Asheville, NC 28803

ANDERSON, Becky (RI) 719 Hope St Apt 1, Bristol, RI 02809

ANDERSON JR, Bert A (Los) 612 Chestnut St, Ashland, OR 97520

ANDERSON, Betsy (Los) 315 Lorraine Blvd, Los Angeles, CA 90020

ANDERSON, Bettina Galer (Colo) 822 Fox Hollow Ln, Golden, CO 80401

ANDERSON, Bill (At) 2510 Two Oaks Dr, Charleston, SC 29414

ANDERSON, Carmen Marie (Kan) 375 Lake Shore Drive, Alma, KS 66401

ANDERSON, Carol (NY) 115 E 87th St Apt 6B, New York, NY 10128

ANDERSON, Christian S (SeFla) St Marys Episcopal Church, 623 Se Ocean Blvd, Stuart, FL 34994

ANDERSON JR, C Newell (At) 1884 Rugby Ave, College Park, GA 30337

✠ **ANDERSON**, Craig Barry (SD) PO Box 1316, Ranchos de Taos, NM 87557

ANDERSON, David (Ct) Saint Luke's Parish, 1864 Post Rd, Darien, CT 06820

ANDERSON, Devon (Minn) 4644 Upton Ave S, Minneapolis, MN 55410

ANDERSON, Douglas Evan (Dal) 413 Olive St, Texarkana, TX 75501

ANDERSON, Douglas Reid (Mont) 408 Westview Dr, Missoula, MT 59803

ANDERSON JR, E Bernard (Md) 3800 Rodman St NW Apt 304, Washington, DC 20016

ANDERSON, Eldon Wayne (Episcopal SJ) P O Box 146, 18232 Smoke St, Jamestown, CA 95327

ANDERSON III, Elenor Lucius 'Andy' (Ala) 447 McClung Ave SE, Huntsville, AL 35801

ANDERSON, Elizabeth May (Chi) 141 Main St Unit 323, Racine, WI 60046

ANDERSON, Eric A (WMo) 2001 Windsor Dr, Newton, KS 67114

ANDERSON, Forrest E (USC) 3333 Oakwell Ct Apt 529, San Antonio, TX 78218

ANDERSON, Gene (SwVa) 5631 Warwood Dr, Roanoke, VA 24018

ANDERSON, Gordon James (Ind) 2522 E Elm St, New Albany, IN 47150

ANDERSON, Hannah (NH) 54 Dunklee St, Concord, NH 03301

ANDERSON, Howard (Los) PO Box 37, Pacific Palisades, CA 90272

ANDERSON, James Arthur (Mil) 10041 Beckford St, Pickerington, OH 43147

ANDERSON, James Desmond (WA) 9556 Chantilly Farm Ln, Chestertown, MD 21620

ANDERSON, James Russell (WA) 3111 Ritchie Rd, Forestville, MD 20747

ANDERSON, Jami (Wyo) PO Box 847, Pinedale, WY 82941

ANDERSON, Jennie (Vt) PO Box 265, Norwich, VT 05055

ANDERSON, Jerry (Los) 339 West Avenue 45, Los Angeles, CA 90065

ANDERSON, Joan Wilkinson (ECR) 425 Carmel Ave, Marina, CA 93933

ANDERSON, Jon (ETenn) 663 Douglas Street, Chattanooga, TN 37403

ANDERSON, Judith Kay Finney (Mont) 408 Westview Dr, Missoula, MT 59803

ANDERSON, Juliana Collins (Mass) 1770 Massachusetts Ave, Cambridge, MA 02140

ANDERSON, Karen Sue (Neb) 1517 Broadway Ste 104, Scottsbluff, NE 69361

ANDERSON, Kenneth Edwin (RG) 258 Riverside Dr, El Paso, TX 79915

ANDERSON, Kent Howard (Ia)

Clergy List

ANDERSON III, Lennel Vincent (Pgh) 2081 Husband Rd, Somerset, PA 15501
ANDERSON, Linda Lee (Wyo)
ANDERSON, Louise Thomas (NC) 901 N Main St, Tarboro, NC 27886
ANDERSON, Marilyn Lea (Ct) 180 Cross Highway, Redding, CT 06896
ANDERSON, Mark S (Dal)
ANDERSON, Martha O (SanD) P. O. Box 334, Del Mar, CA 92014
ANDERSON, Mary Petty (Oly) 10450 NE Yaquina Ave, Bainbridge Island, WA 98110
ANDERSON, Mary Sterrett (O) 2581 Norfolk Rd, Cleveland Heights, OH 44106
ANDERSON, Megan Elizabeth (The Episcopal NCal) Trinity Cathedral, 2620 Capitol Ave, Sacramento, CA 95816
ANDERSON, Michael Eddie (Chi) 1225 Asbury Ave, Evanston, IL 60202
ANDERSON, Otto Suen (SO) 409 E High St, Springfield, OH 45505
ANDERSON III, Paul Kemper (At) 302 West Avenue, P.O. Box 85, Cedartown, GA 30125
ANDERSON, Philip Alden (O) 2581 Norfolk Rd, Cleveland Heights, OH 44106
ANDERSON, Polly Chambers (WLa) 4037 Highway 15, Calhoun, LA 71225
ANDERSON JR, Ralph W (WMass) 114 Lake St, Shrewsbury, MA 01545
ANDERSON, Richard John (NY) 2635 2nd Ave Apt 203, San Diego, CA 92103
ANDERSON, Robert Jay (WVa) 1006 Frostwood St, Huntsville, TX 77340
ANDERSON, Robert Melville (CFla) 350 Lake Talmadge Rd., Deland, FL 32724
ANDERSON, Rosemarie (ECR) 355 Redwood Dr, Boulder Creek, CA 95006
ANDERSON, Scott C (USC) Episcopal Church Of The Redeemer, 120 Mauldin Rd, Greenville, SC 29605
ANDERSON JR, Theodore Lester (NJ) 47 S Ensign Dr, Little Egg Harbor, NJ 08087
ANDERSON, Tim (Neb) P.O. Box 64, Ashland, NE 68003
ANDERSON, William C (Md) 415 Helmsman Way, Severna Park, MD 21146
ANDERSON III, William Marcellus (NY)
ANDERSON-KRENGEL, William Erich (Ct) 191 Margarite Rd, Middletown, CT 06457
ANDERSON-SMITH, Susan (Az) Third Floor, 232 E 11th St, New York, NY 10003
ANDONIAN, Kathryn Ann (Pa) 942 Masters Way, Harleysville, PA 19438
ANDRE, Wildaine (Hai)
ANDRES, Justo Rambac (Episcopal SJ) 115 E Miner Ave, Stockton, CA 95202

ANDRES, Michael James (NH) 106 Lowell St, Manchester, NH 03101
ANDRES, Tony (Ind) 795 Elk Mountain Rd, Afton, VA 22920
ANDREW, Carol (Ga) 3042 Eagle Dr, Augusta, GA 30906
ANDREW SR, Robert Nelson (O) 3800 W 33rd St, Cleveland, OH 44109
ANDREW-MACONAUGHEY, Debra Elaine (SeFla) 111 W Indies Dr, Ramrod Key, FL 33042
ANDREWS, Alfred John (Neb) PO Box 141, Sidney, NE 69162
ANDREWS III, Andy (WTenn) St Mary's Cathedral, 692 Poplar Ave, Memphis, TN 38105
ANDREWS, Arthur Edward (Ore) 1704 Se 22nd Ave, Portland, OR 97214
ANDREWS, Carl Machin (Colo) The Diocese of Colorado, 1300 Washington Street, Denver, CO 80203
ANDREWS JR, David Tallmadge (Del) 732 Nottingham Rd, Wilmington, DE 19805
ANDREWS, David Thomas (WA) 500 Merton Woods Way, Millersville, MD 21108
ANDREWS, Dianne (Oly) 1613 California Ave SW #301, Seattle, WA 98116
ANDREWS II, George Edward (SeFla) 20 Vine St, Marion, MA 02738
ANDREWS II, George Strafford (Chi) 102 Starling Ln, Longwood, FL 32779
ANDREWS III, James Allen (Ia)
ANDREWS, John (Colo) 5968 S Zenobia Ct, Littleton, CO 80123
ANDREWS, John Anthony (NY) PO Box 547, Lima, NY 14485
ANDREWS, Lyde Coley (Ga) St Philips Episcopal Church, 302 E General Stewart Way, Hinesville, GA 31313
ANDREWS, Pati Mary (Va) 8217 Roxborough Loop, Gainesville, VA 20155
ANDREWS, Robert Forrest (Colo) 30 Hutton Ln, Colorado Springs, CO 80906
ANDREWS, Shirley May (Mass) 2 Palmer St, Barrington, RI 02806
ANDREWS-WECKERLY, Jennifer N. (SVa) 8300 Richmond Rd, Toano, VA 23168
ANDRUS, Archie Leslie (HB) 2701 Bellefontaine St, Houston, TX 77025
✠ **ANDRUS**, Marc (Cal) Episcopal Diocese Of California, 1055 Taylor St, San Francisco, CA 94108
ANDUJAR, Alexander (SwFla)
ANEI, Abraham Muong (WMich)
ANGELICA, David M (Mass) 15 Colonial Club Dr Apt 300, Boynton Beach, FL 33435
ANGELL, Debra Lanning (Colo) 13866 W 2nd Ave, Golden, CO 80401
ANGELL, Michael R (Mo) 7401 Delmar Blvd, Saint Louis, MO 63130
ANGELO, Patrice Lonnette (Los) 1818 Monterey Blvd, Hermosa Beach, CA 90254

ANGERER JR, John David (La) 112 Hazel Drive, River Ridge, LA 70123
ANGLE, Nancy Scott (Colo) 150 Sipprelle Dr, Battlement Mesa, CO 81635
ANGULO ZAMORA, Gina Mayra (Litoral Ecu) Iglesia Episcopal del Ecuador Diocese Litoral, Amarilis Fuente 603, Avenida 09015250, Guayaquil, Ecuador, Ecuador
ANGUS, David E (WMo) Grace Cathedral, 415 W 13th St, Kansas City, MO 64105
ANGUS, Joslyn Lloyd (Ga) 88 Oakwood Dr., Hardeeville, SC 29927
ANSCHUTZ, Mark Semmes (Mass) 162 Pleasant Street, South Yarmouth, MA 02664
ANSCHUTZ, Maryetta Madeleine (Los) P.O. Box 691404, Los Angeles, CA 90069
ANSLOW-WILLIAMS, Susan (Mich) Saint Stephen's Church, 5500 N Adams Rd, Troy, MI 48098
ANTHONY, Benjamin J (At)
ANTHONY, Carol (Pa) 627 Kenilworth St, Philadelphia, PA 19147
ANTHONY II, Henry F (RI) 727 Hampton Woods Ln SW, Vero Beach, FL 32962
ANTHONY, Joan (Oly) 1549 MW 57th St., Seattle, WA 98107
ANTHONY JR, Joseph Daniel (At) 389 Dorsey Cir Sw, Lilburn, GA 30047
ANTHONY, Lloyd Lincoln (LI) 9910 217th Ln, Queens Village, NY 11429
ANTHONY, Robert Williams (RI) 104 Old Stage Rd, Centerville, MA 02632
ANTHONY-CHARLES, Ana Graciela (Ve)
ANTOCI, Peter M (WA) 3117 Perry St, Mount Rainier, MD 20712
ANTOLINI, Holly Lyman (Mass) 11 Quincy St, Arlington, MA 02476
ANTTONEN, Jennifer Parker (Ida) 288 E Kite Dr, Eagle, ID 83616
ANUSZKIEWICZ, Sarah Elisabeth (WNY) St Paul's Episcopal Church, 4275 Harris Hill Rd, Williamsville, NY 14221
ANZILOTTI, Laura Niemann (Mo)
APARICIO, Paul Douglas (FdL)
APOLDO, Deborah D (USC)
APPELBERG, Helen Marie Waller (Tex) 301 University Blvd, Galveston, TX 77555
APPLEGATE, Stephen Holmes (SO) 117 S Plum St, Granville, OH 43023
APPLEQUIST, Alice Mae (Minn) 17221 Highway 30 SE, Chatfield, MN 55923
APPLETON, Mary Ellen (CFla) 200 Saint Andrews Blvd Apt 1406, Winter Park, FL 32792
APPLEYARD, Dan (Mo) 9 S Bompart Ave, Webster Groves, MO 63119
APPLEYARD, Jonathan Briggs (Me) 26 Montsweag Road, Woolwich, ME 04579

APPLEYARD JR, Robert Bracewell (Mass) 2036 Acton Ridge Rd, Acton, ME 04001

APPLING, Elizabeth Faragher (Oly) St. Paul's Episcopal Church, P.O. Box 753, Port Townsend, WA 98368

APPOLLONI, Sharyn L (Nev) 1965 Golden Gate Dr, Reno, NV 89511

ARACK, Mara (The Episcopal NCal) St Francis Episcopal Church, 568 16th St, Fortuna, CA 95540

ARAICA, Alvaro (Chi) 4609 Main St, Skokie, IL 60076

ARAMBULO, Arnulfo (NY) 231 City View Ter, Kingston, NY 12401

ARAQUE GALVIS, Alirio (PR) Iglesia Episcopal Puertorriquena, PO Box 902, Saint Just, PR 00978

ARBOGAST, Stephen Kirkpatrick (WA) St. Mark's School of Texas, 10600 Preston Rd, Dallas, TX 75230

ARBOLEDA, Guillermo Alejandro (Ga)

ARBUCKLE, Jacquelyn Fenelon (Vt) 54 Morse Pl, Burlington, VT 05401

ARCHER, Arthur William (Del) 650 Willow Valley Sq # K-401, Lancaster, PA 17602

ARCHER, Carolyn (Ct)

ARCHER, John Richard (Cal) 80 Harmon St, Hamden, CT 06517

ARCHER, Jonathan Gurth Adam (SeFla) 3481 Hibiscus St, Miami, FL 33133

ARCHER, Melinda (Az) 5265 NE 3rd Court, Lincoln City, OR 97367

ARCHER, Nell B (LI) 199 Carroll St, Brooklyn, NY 11231

ARCHIBALD, David Jost (Del) 32216 Bixler Rd, Selbyville, DE 19975

ARCHIBALD, David Roberts (WTex) 6110 NW Loop 410, San Antonio, TX 78238

ARCHIE, Andrew John (Mo) 6345 Wydown Blvd, Saint Louis, MO 63105

ARCINIEGA, Roberto (Ore) 2065 Se 44th Ave Apt 248, Hillsboro, OR 97123

ARD, Eddie Jackson (At) 3880 Glenhurst Dr Se, Smyrna, GA 30080

ARD JR, Robert (WNC) 6518 Michigan Ave, St. Louis, MO 63111

ARD, Roger Hoyt (At) 104 Sequoia Dr SE, Rome, GA 30161

ARDREY-GRAVES, Sara (NC) St Paul Episc Church, 520 Summit St, Winston Salem, NC 27101

ARELLANO, Donna (The Episcopal NCal)

ARENAS TORO, William Henry (Colom)

ARENTS, Gina (Md) 1511 Long Quarter Ct, Lutherville, MD 21093

ARGUE, Douglas (SO) 22 Glencoe Rd, Columbus, OH 43214

ARLEDGE JR, Thomas Lafayette (At) 909 Massee Ln, Perry, GA 31069

ARLIN, Charles Noss (Nwk) 1078B Long Beach Blvd, Long Beach Twp., NJ 08008

ARMENTROUT, Katharine Jacobs (At) 202 Griffith Rd, Jasper, GA 30143

ARMER, Mary Carolyn (Mo) 8170 Halsey St, Lenexa, KS 66215

ARMER, Susan Charlee (Oly) 10064 E Durham Rd, Dewey, AZ 86327

ARMINGTON, Shawn Aaron (NJ) 118 Jefferson Rd, Princeton, NJ 08540

ARMSTRONG, Barbara Keegan (NC) 509 Sleepy Valley Rd, Apex, NC 27523

ARMSTRONG, Elizabeth (The Episcopal NCal) 1008 Linier Ct., Roseville, CA 95678

ARMSTRONG, Geoffrey Macgregor (NY) 10 Lanes End, Mervin Village, NH 03850

ARMSTRONG, Michael N (Fla) 2349 SW Bascom Norris Dr, Lake City, FL 32025

ARMSTRONG, Phyllis (SO) 2841 Urwiler Ave, Cincinnati, OH 45211

ARMSTRONG, Richard Sweet (Mass) 35 Old Fields Way, Castine, ME 04421

ARMSTRONG, Robert Hancock (SVa) 4600 Bruce Rd, Chester, VA 23831

ARMSTRONG, Susan J (The Episcopal NCal) 1765 Virginia Way, Arcata, CA 95521

ARMSTRONG, William H (WVa) 320 Old Bluefield Rd, Princeton, WV 24740

ARMSTRONG, Zenetta (Mass) 58 Crawford St Apt 2, Dorchester, MA 02121

ARMY, Virginia (Ct) The Rectory School, Pomfret, CT 06258

ARNASON, Tryggvi Gudmundur (WNC) 130 39th Avenue Pl NW, Hickory, NC 28601

ARNEY, Carol Mary (The Episcopal Church in Haw) 1840 University Ave W, Apt. 104, Saint Paul, MN 55104

ARNHART, James Rhyne (Tenn) 1710 Riverview Dr, Murfreesboro, TN 37129

ARNING, Robert W (Tenn) 411 W Due West Ave, Madison, TN 37115

ARNOLD, Beth Kelly (Los) 1231 E. Chapman Ave., Fullerton, CA 92831

ARNOLD, Christopher John (FdL) St Andrew's, 828 Commercial Street, Emporia, KS 66801

ARNOLD, Donna J (Alb) 4 Pine Ledge Ter, Gansevoort, NY 12831

ARNOLD, Duane Wade-Hampton (NY) 5815 Lawrence Dr., Indianapolis, IN 46226

ARNOLD, Kimball Clark (Az) 3150 Spence Springs Rd, Prescott, AZ 86305

ARNOLD, Margaret L (Mass) 149 High St Apt 1, Wareham, MA 02571

ARNOLD, Robert D (WNY) 29 University Park, Fredonia, NY 14063

ARNOLD, Robyn Elizabeth (Ala) 2146 Santa Clara Ave Apt 1, Alamed, CA 94501

ARNOLD, Scott A (Ala) 1204 Valridge N, Prattville, AL 36066

ARNOLD, Susan Louise (ECR) Church Divinity School Of The Pacific, Morro Bay, CA 93442

ARNOLD, William Bruce (SwFla) 114 Fairway Ct, Greenwood, SC 29649

ARNOLD JR, William Stevenson Maclaren (Nev) 1855 Baring Blvd Apt 301, Sparks, NV 89434

ARNOLD-BOYD, Annette Ruth (Oly) 12420 SW Tremont St, Portland, OR 97225

ARPEE, Stephen T Rowbridge (WA) 3810 39th St NW Apt A-121, Washington, DC 20016

ARRINGTON, Sandra Clark (Roch) 20 Trumbull Lane, Pittsford, NY 14534

ARROSSA, Jean Pierre (RG)

ARROYO, Jose Del Carmen (Chi) 25291 W Lehmann Blvd, Lake Villa, IL 60046

ARROYO, Margarita Eguia (WTex) 721 S Missouri Ave, Weslaco, TX 78596

ARROYO-SANCHEZ, Jose (PR)

ARRUNATEGUI, Herbert (CFla) 3468 Capland Ave, Clermont, FL 34711

ARSENIE, Linda Sue (Ct)

ARTHUR, Amelia Ruth (Minn) 4439 W 50th St, Edina, MN 55424

ARTHUR, Anne Tilley (The Episcopal NCal) 2620 Capitol Ave, Sacramento, CA 95816

ARTHUR, Richard Winston (At) 6780 James B Rivers Dr, Stone Mountain, GA 30083

ARTMAN, Melinda M (Be) 201 S Wilbur Ave, Sayre, PA 18840

ARTRESS, Lauren (Cal) 309 Coleridge St, San Francisco, CA 94110

ASEL, John Kenneth (Wyo) 407 F Street Suite 104, North Wilkesboro, NC 28659

ASGILL, Edmondson Omotayo (CFla) 381 N Lincoln St, Daytona Beach, FL 32114

ASH JR, Evan Arnold (Kan) 1114 E Northview St, Olathe, KS 66061

ASH, Gerald Arnold (Md) 10450 Lottsford Rd Apt 1101, Mitchellville, MD 20721

ASH, Linda D (EMich) 111 S Shiawassee St, Corunna, MI 48817

ASH, Patricia Bryan (Los)

ASHBY, Alice Kay Neel (O) 344 Shepard Rd, Mansfield, OH 44907

ASHBY, Joe Lyn (O) 402 Channel Rd, N Muskegon, MI 49445

ASHBY, Julia Sizemore (SVa) 4205 Cheswick Ln, Virginia Beach, VA 23455

ASHBY, Lucinda Beth (Ida) 1858 Judith Ln, Boise, ID 83705

ASHCRAFT, Brandon Cole (NY)

ASHCROFT, Ernie (Minn) 4015 Sunnyside Road, Edina, MN 55424

ASHCROFT, Mary Ellen (Minn) PO Box 1093, Grand Marais, MN 55604

ASHER, Charles William (Los)

ASHFORD, Raphiell (Miss) 643 Beasley Rd, Jackson, MS 39206

ASHLEY, Danae (Oly) 4805 NE 45th Street, Seattle, WA 98105

ASHMORE, Christopher Lee (Spr) 17 Forest Park W, Jacksonville, IL 62650

ASHMORE JR, Robert Michael (WNC) PO Box 956, Mars Hill, NC 28754

ASIS, Debra (Az) 12111 N La Cholla Blve, Oro Valley, AZ 85755

ASKEW, Angela Victoria (NY) 659 E 17th St, Brooklyn, NY 11230

ASKEW, Jerry Wayne (ETenn) 600 S Chestnut St, Knoxville, TN 37914

ASKEW, Patricia Tanzer (Wyo)

ASKEW, Stephen (Wyo) 104 S 4th St, Laramie, WY 82070

ASMAN, Mark Elliott (Los) 1500 State St, Santa Barbara, CA 93101

ASONYE, Collins Enyindah (Va)

ASSON, Marla Lynn (Nev) Holy Cross/ St Christopher, 3740 Meridian St N, Huntsville, AL 35811

ASTARITA, Susan Gallagher (WA) PO Box 816, Del Mar, CA 92014

ASTLEFORD, Elise Linder (Oly) 2515 NE 80th St, Vancouver, WA 98665

ASTON, Geraldine Patricia (Ala) 544 S Forest Dr, Homewood, AL 35209

ATAMIAN, Thomas Michael (Chi) 272 Presidential Ln, Elgin, IL 60123

ATCHESON, Charles (Oly) 8529 Caroline Ave N, Seattle, WA 98103

ATCHLEY, Joyce Eileen (EO)

ATCITTY, Janice Nacke (Ida) Po Box 388, Fort Hall, ID 83203

ATEEK, Sari N (WA) 6701 Wisconsin Ave, Chevy Chase, MD 20815

ATEM, Garang Gabriel (U) 1710 S Foothill Dr, Salt Lake City, UT 84108

ATHEY JR, Kenneth F (Del) PO Box 88, 10719 Grove St, Delmar, DE 19940

ATKINS, Hannah (Tex) Trinity Episcopal Church, 1015 Holman St, Houston, TX 77004

ATKINS JR, Henry (NJ) 3210 Louisiana St, Apt 1413, Houston, TX 77006

ATKINS, John Merritt (SO) 33 W Dixon Ave, Dayton, OH 45419

ATKINSON, Andrew James (EC) 321 Pettigrew Dr, Wilmington, NC 28412

ATKINSON, Herschel Robert (At) 509 Rhodes Dr, Elberton, GA 30635

ATKINSON JR, Joel Walter (Be) 321 Wyandotte St, Bethlehem, PA 18015

ATKINSON, Kate Bigwood (NH)

ATKINSON, Mark W (Fla) 7801 Lone Star Rd, Jacksonville, FL 32211

ATKINSON, William Harold (Vt) 40 Water St, Meredith, NH 03253

ATTEBURY, Rich Earl (EO) Po Box 123, Lostine, OR 97857

ATWOOD, Mary Hill (Los) 546 Bradford Ct, Claremont, CA 91711

ATWOOD JR, Theodore Oertel (Ga) 6785 El Banquero Pl, San Diego, CA 92119

AUBERT, Keri T (Ct) 830 Whitney Ave, New Haven, CT 06511

AUBREY, Norman Edward (WMass) 5 College View Hts, South Hadley, MA 01075

AUCHINCLOSS, R Anne (NY) 250 W 94th St # 4F, New York, NY 10025

AUCHINCLOSS, Susan Carpenter (NY) 2342 Glasco Tpk., Woodstock, NY 12498

AUELUA, Royston Toto'A Stene (The Episcopal NCal) 6963 Riata Dr, Redding, CA 96002

AUER, Dorothy Kogler (NJ) 320 Glenburney Dr Apt 106, Fayetteville, NC 28303

AUER, Nancy Ann (NMich)

AUGHENBAUGH, Kelly Anne (O) 18001 Detroit Ave, Lakewood, OH 44107

AUGUSTE, Pierre (Hai)

AUGUSTE, Roldano (Hai)

AUGUSTIN, Dale Lee (Nev) 422 Red Canvas Pl, Las Vegas, NV 89144

AUGUSTINE, Patrick Parvez (Eau) 427 14th St S, La Crosse, WI 54601

AUGUSTINE, Peter John (Eau) 111 9th St N, La Crosse, WI 54601

AULENBACH JR, William Hamilton (The Episcopal Church in Haw) The Groves 59, 5200 Irvine Blvd, Irvine, CA 92620

AULETTA, Kimberlee (NY)

AURAND, Benjamin Kyte (Tex) 2421 Gate 11 Rd, Two Harbors, MN 55616

AUSAS-COMBES, Jose (PR)

AUSTIN, Dorothy Ann (Nwk) Harvard Yard, Cambridge, MA 02138

AUSTIN, Evette Eliene (Alb) 9 E Main St, Canton, NY 13617

AUSTIN, Henry Whipple (Neb) 4509 Anderson Cir, Papillion, NE 68133

AUSTIN, Jean E (Vt) 545 Shore Road, Digby, B0V 1A0, Canada

AUSTIN, Margaret (Colo) 2526 Gates Cir, Apt. 2611, Baton Rouge, LA 70809

AUSTIN JR, Vernon Arthur (Pa) 4397 Buttercup Cir, Collegeville, PA 19426

AUSTIN, Victor (Dal) 3966 Mckinney Ave, Dallas, TX 75204

AUSTIN, Wilborne Adolphus (Ct) 18 Richard Rd, East Hartford, CT 06108

AUSTIN, William Bouldin (CFla) 3508 Lakeshore Dr SW, Smyrna, GA 30082

AUSTIN, William Paul (WNC) 112 Trotter Pl, Asheville, NC 28806

AVCIN, Janet Elaine (CPa) 228 Charles St, Harrisburg, PA 17102

AVENI JR, James Vincent (NwT) Po Box 1064, Clarendon, TX 79226

AVERY, Daniel Thomas (SVa) 118 Nina Lane, Williamsburg, VA 23188

AVERY, Gail (NH) Seafarer's Friend, 77 Broadway, Chelsea, MA 02150

AVERY, Harold Dennison (CNY) 112 Arbordale Pl, Syracuse, NY 13219

AVERY, Joyce Marie (Oly) 1022 Monte Elma Rd, Elma, WA 98541

AVERY, Richard Norman (Los) 1026 Goldenrod St, Placentia, CA 92870

AVERY, Steven Walter (Ore) PO Box 2617, Florence, OR 97439

AVILA, Ricardo (ECR) 20 University Ave, Los Gatos, CA 95030

AVILA-NATIVI, Rigoberto (NY) PO Box 3786, Poughkeepsie, NY 12603

AVRIL, Wilky (Hai)

AWAN, Abraham Kuol (Chi) 7100 N Ashland Blvd, Chicago, IL 60626

AXBERG, Keith (Mont) Trinity Church Jeffers, PO Box 336, Ennis, MT 59729

AYALA TORRES, Carlos Anibal (EcuC) Bogota S/N Jose Vicente Trujillo, Guayaquil, Ecuador

AYBAR-MARTE, Pantaleon (PR)

AYER, Kelly Lane (Roch) 10 Park Pl, Avon, NY 14414

AYERBE, Reynaldo (SwFla) 4012 Penhurst Park, Sarasota, FL 34235

AYERS, Barbara (Alb)

AYERS, John Cameron (Cal) 13601 Saratoga Ave, Saratoga, CA 95070

AYERS, Margaret (WLa) St James Episcopal Church, PO Box 494, Port Gibson, MS 39150

AYERS, Mary L (Spok) 7315 N Wall St, Spokane, WA 99208

AYERS, Phillip (Ore) 3232 NE 12th Ave, Portland, OR 97212

AYERS, Robert Curtis (CNY) 6010 E. Lake Rd., Cazenovia, NY 13035

AYERS, Russell C (Mass) 3737 Seminary Rd, Alexandria, VA 22304

AYMERICH, Ramon (Mass)

AYRES, Steve (Mass) 193 Salem St, Boston, MA 02113

AZAR, Antoinette Joann (Lex) 201 Providence Hill, Ashland, KY 41101

AZARIAH, Khushnud M (Los) 6563 East Ave, Etiwanda, CA 91739

B

BAAR, David Josef (The Episcopal Church in Haw)

BABB, Trevor (NY) 76 Franklin Ave, Staten Island, NY 10301

BABCOCK, Harold Ross Manly (NH) Old Rossier Farm, 238 Rossier Rd., Montgomery Center, VT 05471

BABCOCK, Jessica H (CGC) St Marks Episcopal Church, 4129 Oxford Ave, Jacksonville, FL 32210

BABCOCK, Linda Mae (WMo) Saint Anne'S Church, Lebanon, MO 65536

BABCOCK, Lori Hale (Md) 1700 South Rd, Baltimore, MD 21209

BABCOCK, Margaret (Wyo) 4230 S Oak St, Casper, WY 82601

BABCOCK, Mary Kathleen (Kan) 400 E. Maple St, Independence, KS 67301

BABCOCK, Ted (Pgh) The Episcopal Diocese of Pittsburgh, 325 Oliver Ave, Pittsburgh, PA 15222

BABENKO-LONGHI, Julie P (Chi) 1850 Landre Ct, Burlington, WI 53105

BABIN, Alexander Raymond (Mich) 69440 Brookhill Dr, Romeo, MI 48065

BABIN, Alice Elizabeth Duffy (Md) 65 Verde Valley School Rd, Apt C-13, Sedona, AZ 86351

BABIN, Kyle James (Pa)

BABLER, Emmett John (Minn) 9411 E Parkside Dr, Sun Lakes, AZ 85248

BABNEW JR, Rodger Allan (Az) 969 W Country Club Dr, Nogales, AZ 85621

BABNIS, Mariann (WA) 33203 W Batten St, Lewes, DE 19958

BABSON, Katharine E (Me) 149 Pennellville Rd, Brunswick, ME 04011

BACAGAN, Magdaleno K (Los) 225 W Linfield St, Glendora, CA 91740

BACHMANN, Douglas P (Cal) 419 Orchard View Ave, Martinez, CA 94553

BACHSCHMID, Edward Karl (RG) 9024 N Congress St, New Market, VA 22844

BACIGALUPO, Joseph Andrew (ECR) 1343 Wylie Way, San Jose, CA 95130

BACK, George (Okla) 2520 NW 59 St, Oklahoma City, OK 73112

BACK, Heather Back (Ky) 744 Sherwood Dr, Bowling Green, KY 42103

BACK, Luke (Chi) 400 E Westminster, Lake Forest, IL 60045

BACKER, Karri Anne (Los) 1231 E. Chapman Ave., Fullerton, CA 92832

BACKHAUS, Oliver Keith (SwFla) St Mark's Episcopal Church, 513 Nassau St S, Venice, FL 34285

BACKLUND, Michael Anders (Episcopal SJ) 10449 Oak Valley Rd, Angels Camp, CA 95222

BACKSTRAND, Brian E (Mil) 804 E Juneau Ave, Milwaukee, WI 53202

BACKUS, Brett Paul (ETenn) The Episcopal Church of the Ascension, 800 S. Northshore Drive, Knoxville, TN 37919

BACKUS, Howard G (NC) 600 South Central Avenue, Laurel, DE 19956

BACKUS, Timothy Warren (CGC) PO Box 12683, Pensacola, FL 32591

BACON JR, James Edwin (Ala) 3239 Heathrow Downs, Hoover, AL 35226

BACON, Lynne Lazier (Neb) 719 Crestridge Rd, Omaha, NE 68154

BACON JR, Robert (Mass) 51 Ledgelawn Ave, Lexington, MA 02420

BADDERS JR, John David (WTex) 11 Saint Lukes Ln, San Antonio, TX 78209

BADE, James Robert (Az) 6300 N Central Ave, Phoenix, AZ 85012

BADER-SAYE, Demery Letisha (Be) 334 Knapp Rd, Clarks Summit, PA 18411

BADGETT, Benjamin R (WTenn)

BAER, Kirsten Herndon (Okla) 13316 SW 3rd St, Yukon, OK 73099

BAER, Timothy Christopher (Okla) 13316 SW 3rd St, Yukon, OK 73099

BAER, Walter Jacob (Eur) Convocation of Episcopal Churches in Europe, 23 avenue George V, Paris, AS 75008, France

BAETZ III, Bertrand O (WTex) 320 Saint Peter St, Kerrville, TX 78028

BAGAY, Martin (At) all saints episcopal church, 1708 Watson boulevard, warner robins, GA 31093

BAGBY, Durwood Ray (Tex) PO Box 510, Cameron, TX 76520

BAGBY, John Blythe (Ala) 3516 Country Club Road, Birmingham,, AL 35213

BAGGETT, Heather Kathleen (ND) 601 N 4th St, Bismarck, ND 58501

BAGIONI, Elizabeth A B (WA) 6701 Wisconsin Ave, Chevy Chase, MD 20815

BAGLEY, Robert Chambers (Mil) 4701 Erie St, Racine, WI 53402

BAGUER II, Miguel A (SeFla) 300 Sunrise Dr Apt 1b, Key Biscayne, FL 33149

BAGUYOS, Avelino (Kan) PO Box 40222, Overland Park, KS 66204

BAGWELL, Rob (Mass) 401 E 60th St, Savannah, GA 31405

BAHLOW, Harry (ETenn) 4026 Starview Lane, Evans, GA 30809

BAILEY, Anne Cox (Cal) 750 Adella Ave, Coronado, CA 92118

BAILEY, Audrey Veronica (NY) 777 E 222nd St, Bronx, NY 10467

BAILEY, B(Ertram) Cass (Va) 1118 Preston Ave, Charlottesville, VA 22903

BAILEY, Charles James (Lex)

BAILEY, Charles Leroy (Alb) 15 Richards Ave, Oneonta, NY 13820

BAILEY, David Bruce (SO) 9097 Cascara Dr, West Chester, OH 45069

✠ **BAILEY**, David Earle (NAM) PO Box 720, Farmington, NM 87499

BAILEY III, Douglass Moxley (NC)

BAILEY, Frank Hudson (Md) 7474 Washington Blvd, Elkridge, MD 21075

BAILEY, Gregory Bruce (Alb) Trinity Episcopal Church, 30 Park St, Gouverneur, NY 13642

BAILEY, Jefferson Moore (Az) PO Box 492, Tucson, AZ 85702

BAILEY, Lydia Collins (O) 21000 Lake Shore Blvd, Euclid, OH 44123

BAILEY, Max (Colo) 1303 S Bross Ln, Longmont, CO 80501

BAILEY, Noel (RI) St Luke's Episcopal Church, 99 Pierce St, East Greenwich, RI 02818

BAILEY, Paul Milton (La) Po Box 1086, Hammond, LA 70404

BAILEY, Pauline Rose (Alb) 15 Richards Ave, Oneonta, NY 13820

BAILEY, Ricardo Z (At) 2744 Peachtree Rd NW, Atlanta, GA 30305

BAILEY, Sarah E (WVa) 401 S Washington St, Berkeley Springs, WV 25411

BAILEY, Stephanie Abbott (Cal) C/O Diocese of California, 1055 Taylor St, San Francisco, CA 94108

BAILEY III, Theodore Harbour (SVa) 133 Leon Dr, Williamsburg, VA 23188

BAILEY FISCHER, Valerie Dianne (Nwk) 283 Herrick Avenue, Teaneck, NJ 07666

BAILLARGEON JR, Henri Albert (SVa) 4604 Sewaha St, Tampa, FL 33617

BAIN, Robert Walker (WMass) 1673 Huasna Dr, San Luis Obispo, CA 93405

BAIRD, Carolyn Mroczkowski (Cal) 1026 Springhouse Dr, Ambler, PA 19002

BAIRD, Gary Clifton (Ark) 617 Tahleguah, Siloan Springs, AR 72761

BAIRD, Joseph Paul (Pgh) St. Peter's Episcopal Church, 36 W Campbell St, Blairsville, PA 15717

BAIRD, Kathryn Jo Anne (Az) 4442 E Bermuda St, Tucson, AZ 85712

BAKAL, Pamela (Nwk) 200 Highfield Ln, Nutley, NJ 07110

BAKELY, Catherine Mae (SVa) P.O. Box 186, Oak Hall, VA 23416

BAKER, Andrea (The Episcopal NCal) 2620 Capitol Ave, Sacramento, CA 95816

BAKER, Brian (The Episcopal NCal) 1160 Los Molinos Way, Sacramento, CA 95864

BAKER, Brock (Alb) PO Box 1374, Lake Placid, NY 12946

BAKER, Carenda D (CPa) 206 E Burd St, Shippensburg, PA 17257

BAKER JR, Charles Mulford (Ct) PO Box 296, Gales Ferry, CT 06335

BAKER, Clarence Dawson (Ark) 692 Poplar Ave, Memphis, TN 38105

BAKER, Douglas Macintyre (NJ)

BAKER, J Jeffrey (O) 160 Keagler Dr, Steubenville, OH 43953

BAKER, Johanna M (Az) 62 Pickering St., Brookville, PA 15825

BAKER, John (Va) 8531 Riverside Rd, Alexandria, VA 22308

BAKER JR, John Thurlow (Cal) 2055 Northshore Rd, Bellingham, WA 98226

BAKER, Joseph Scott (SVa) St. Stephen's Episcopal Church, 372 Hiden Blvd., Newport News, VA 23606

BAKER, Joseph Stannard (Vt) 2 Cherry St., Burlington, VT 05401

BAKER, Josephine Louise Redenius (Pa) Po Box 429, Wayne, PA 19087

BAKER, K. Drew (SwVa) 2411 Shiraz Lane, Charleston, SC 29414

BAKER, Kim Turner (Ia) 2338 Lincoln Way, Ames, IA 50014

BAKER, Mark James (At) 126 wild horse cove circle, cleveland, GA 30528

BAKER, Mathew Scott (Alb) PO Box 183, Greenwich, NY 12834

BAKER, M Clark (Tenn) 780 Laurel Branch Trl, Sewanee, TN 37375

BAKER, Milledge Leonard (CGC) 699 S Hwy 95A, Cantonment, FL 32533

BAKER, Patricia Thomas (Oly) PO Box 369, Snoqualmie, WA 98065

BAKER, Paul Edgar (Alb) 4 St Lukes Pl, Cambridge, NY 12816

Clergy List

BAKER, Powell E (Dal) 14500 Marsh Lane, Apt. 176, Addison, TX 75001
BAKER, Rhonda (Va) Po Box 59, Goochland, VA 23063
BAKER, Richard Henry (Mo) 3139 Barrett Station Rd, Saint Louis, MO 63122
BAKER, Robert (SwFla) 906 S Orleans Ave, Tampa, FL 33606
BAKER, Ruth Louise (Mont) 52120 Lake Mary Ronan Rd, Proctor, MT 59929
BAKER, Shireen R (Chi) 116 E Church St, Elmhurst, IL 60126
BAKER, Thomas Joseph (Kan)
BAKER, Ursula Paula (Az)
BAKER, William M (NY) 1 Kingsley Ave, Staten Island, NY 10314
BAKER-BORJESON, Susan C (Alb) 3425 South Atlantic Avenue, #1006, Daytona Beach Shores, FL 32118
BAKER-WRIGHT, Michelle (Los) 1325 Monterey Rd, South Pasadena, CA 91030
BAKEWELL JR, Grant McNeill (The Episcopal NCal)
BAKKER, Cheryl Anne (CFla) 7416 W Seven Rivers Dr, Crystal River, FL 34429
BAKKER, Gregory Kendall (Episcopal SJ) 41 Station Road, Sholing, Southampton, SO19 8FN, Great Britain (UK)
BAKKER, Joseph Harold (Fla) 211 N Monroe St, Tallahassee, FL 32301
BAKKUM, Carleton (SVa) PO Box 123, Yorktown, VA 23690
BALABANIS, Achilles (Spok)
BALDERSON, Scott (NC) 304 E Franklin St, Chapel Hill, NC 27514
BALDRIDGE SR, Kempton Dunn (Eur) 605 Woodland Drive, Paducah, KY 42001
BALDWIN, Frederick (NJ) 1710 Restoration Court, Charleston, SC 29414
BALDWIN, Gary (CGC) 188 Grindstone Creek Dr, Clarkesville, GA 30523
BALDWIN, Gayle R (Wyo) ????, Greybull, WY 82426
BALDWIN, Jerome M (SO) 9477 N Maura Ln., Brown Deer, WI 53223
BALDWIN, John Anson (SVa) 5181 Singleton Way, Virginia Beach, VA 23462
BALDWIN, Judith Anne (Nwk) 119 Main St, Millburn, NJ 07041
BALDWIN, Marilyn E (Minn) 12336 Eagle Cir NW, Coon Rapids, MN 55448
BALDWIN, Rob (Kan) 1011 Vermont St, Lawrence, KS 66044
BALDWIN, Victoria Evelyn (Ct) 27 Babcock Ave, Plainfield, CT 06374
BALDWIN-MCGINNIS, Carissa E. (Los) 1220 Omar St, Houston, TX 77008
BALDYGA, Andrea (Be) 22c Castle Hill Rd, Agawam, MA 01001
BALE, Harvey Edgar (WA)

BALES, Janice Stebing (RG) 3112 La Mancha Pl Nw, Albuquerque, NM 87104
BALES, Joshua Morris (CFla) 130 N Magnolia Ave, Orlando, FL 32801
BALES, William Oliver (SO) 29405 Blosser Rd, Logan, OH 43138
BALFE, Martin Kevin (Minn) 315 State St W, Cannon Falls, MN 55009
BALICKI, John (Me) 104 Echo Rd, Brunswick, ME 04011
BALIIRA, Nelson Kuule (CPa)
BALKE JR, Steven M (Tex) 4090 Delaware St, Beaumont, TX 77706
BALL, Edwin (CFla) 3740 Pinebrook Cir, Bradenton, FL 34209
BALL, John Arthur (WA) 46455 Hyatt Ct, Drayden, MD 20630
BALL, Raymond Carl (Dal) 5421 Victor St, Dallas, TX 75214
BALLANTINE, Lucia (NY) 402 Route 22, North Salem, NY 10560
BALLARD, Chris Christopher (LI) St Lukes and St Matthew's Episcopal Church, 520 Clinton Ave, Brooklyn, NY 11238
BALLARD, James David (Vt) 139 Sanderson Rd, Milton, VT 05468
BALLARD JR, Joseph Howard (Tenn) 17525 Shady Elm Ave, Baton Rouge, LA 70816
BALLARD, Kathleen Miller (Nwk)
BALL-DAMBERG, Sarah (NC) 1014 Monmouth Ave, Durham, NC 27701
BALLENTINE, Jabriel Simmonds (CFla) 1000 Bethune Dr, Orlando, FL 32805
BALLERT JR, Irving Frank (Alb) 25 Sharon St, Sidney, NY 13838
BALLEW, Thelma Johnanna (NH) 1 Park Ct, Durham, NH 03824
BALLING, Valerie L (NJ) 142 Sand Hill Road, Monmouth Junction, NJ 08852
BALLINGER, Carolyn Tucker (WK)
BALLINGER, Kathryn Elisabeth (Oly) 9210 Ne 123rd St, Kirkland, WA 98034
BALLOU, Diedre Schuler (NwT) 6304 Roadrunner Ct, Amarillo, TX 79119
BALMER, Randall (Ct) 720 Pattrell Road, Norwich, VT 05055
BALMER, William John (NJ) 380 Sycamore Ave, Shrewsbury, NJ 07702
BALTUS, Donald Barrington (NY) 123 E 15th St # 1504, New York, NY 10003
BALTZ, Ann Marie Halpin (Ida) 8947 Springhurst Dr, Boise, ID 83704
BALTZ, Francis Burkhardt (At) 369 Merrydale Dr SW, Marietta, GA 30064
BAMBERGER, Michael Andrew (Los) 241 Ramona Ave, Sierra Madre, CA 91024
BAMBRICK, Barbara Nichols (SeFla) 1802 Pine St, Perry, IA 50220
BAMBROOK II, Walter Earl (RG)
BAMFORD, Marilyn Halverson (Minn) PO Box 3247, Duluth, MN 55803

BANAKIS, Kathryn Loretta (Chi) 939 Hinman Ave, Evanston, IL 60202
BANCROFT, John Galloway (At) 1865 Highway 20 W, Mcdonough, GA 30253
BANCROFT, Stephen Haltom (Mich) 27310 Wellington Rd, Franklin, MI 48025
BANDY, Talmage Gwaltney (NC) 22 Bogie Dr, Whispering Pines, NC 28327
✠ **BANE JR**, David Conner (SVa) 163 Pelican Pointe Dr, Elizabeth City, NC 27909
BANKOWSKI, Thomas (CFla)
BANKS, Cynthia Kay Rauh (WNC) 272 Maple Ridge Dr, Boone, NC 28607
BANKS JR, Frederick David (Ky) 2541 Southview Dr, Lexington, KY 40503
BANKS JR, Ralph Alton (SeFla) 940 Eucalyptus Rd, North Palm Beach, FL 33408
BANKS, Richard Allan (La) 1444 Cabrini Ct, New Orleans, LA 70122
BANKSTON, Van (Be) 509 W Pine St, Hattiesburg, MS 39401
BANNER, Daniel Lee (Chi) 2431 Bradmoor Dr, Quincy, IL 62301
BANNER, Shelly Ann (CNY) 41 Highmore Dr, Oswego, NY 13126
BANSE JR, Robert (Va) 221 Orr Rd, Pittsburgh, PA 15241
BAPTISTE-WILLIAMS, Barbara Jeanne (SeFla) 6041 Sw 63rd Ct, Miami, FL 33143
BARBARE, Mikel J (Fla) 7801 Lone Star Rd, Jacksonville, FL 32211
BARBARITO, Melanie Repko (FtW) 5005 Dexter Ave, Fort Worth, TX 76107
BARBER, Barbara Jean (Kan) 5518 Sw 17th Ter, Topeka, KS 66604
BARBER, Elaine Elizabeth Rybak (Minn) 4830 Acorn Ridge Rd, Minnetonka, MN 55345
BARBER, Grant (Mass) 102 Branch St., Scituate, MA 02066
BARBER, Grethe Ann (Oly) 690 N Shepherd Rd, Washougal, WA 98671
BARBER, James Frederick (FtW) 3217 Chaparral Ln, Fort Worth, TX 76109
BARBERIA, Kristin Neily (Los) c/o St. Matthew's Parish School, 1031 Bienveneda Avenue, Pacific Palisades, CA 90272
BARBOUR, Grady Frederic Waddell (Ala) 565 12th Ct, Pleasant Grove, AL 35127
BARBUTO, Judith Steele (U) 11146 S Heather Grove Ln, South Jordan, UT 84095
BARDEN III, Albert A (Ct) 254 Father Rasle Rd, Norridgewock, ME 04957
BARDOS, Gordon (Vt) 9449 N 110th Ave, Sun City, AZ 85351
BARDSLEY, Nancy Louise (Ida) 1154 Camps Canyon Rd, Troy, ID 83871
BARDUSCH JR, Rich (Va) PO Box 149, Taunton, MA 02780

BAREBO, Charles Vincent (Be) 333 Wyandotte St, Bethlehem, PA 18015

BARFIELD, Bill (Ind) PO Box 141, Danville, IN 46122

BARFIELD, David S (Ala) 4908 Masters Rd, Pell City, AL 35128

BARFIELD, DeOla Edwina (Ct) 744 Lakeside Dr, Bridgeport, CT 06606

BARFIELD, Karen (NC) 501 E Poplar Ave, Carrboro, NC 27510

BARFORD, Lee Alton (ECR) 561 Keystone Ave #434, Reno, NV 89503

BARGER, Rebecca Sue (Mo)

BARGETZI, David Michael (O) 1417 Larchmont Ave, Lakewood, OH 44107

BARGIEL, Mary Victoria (Ind) 3243 N Meridian St, Indianapolis, IN 46208

BARHAM, Michael (Cal) PO Box 555, Half Moon Bay, CA 94019

BARHAM, Patsy Griffin (Tex) St Matthew's Episcopal Church, 214 College Ave, Henderson, TX 75654

BARKER, Ann Biddle (Va) 6231 Kilmer Ct, Falls Church, VA 22044

BARKER, Christie Dalton (NC) 981 Valiant Dr., Statesville, NC 28677

BARKER, Christopher Haskins (Pgh) 1062 Old Orchard Dr, Gibsonia, PA 15044

BARKER, Daniel W (CNY) 324 Harding Ave, Vestal, NY 13850

BARKER, Gary Joseph (Va) 111 S Church St, Smithfield, VA 23430

BARKER, Herbert James (SanD) 11727 Mesa Verde Dr, Valley Center, CA 92082

BARKER, Jane Daugherty (Tex)

BARKER, Jo Ann D (Del) 241 Louisiana Circl, Sewanee, TN 37375

BARKER, Kenneth Lee (CGC) 9409 E 65th St, Tulsa, OK 74133

BARKER, Lynn Kay (Miss) 29 Melody Ln, Purvis, MS 39475

BARKER, Patrick Morgan (Ark) 1521 Mcarthur Dr, Jacksonville, AR 72076

✠ **BARKER**, Scott Scott (Neb) 109 N 18th St, Omaha, NE 68102

BARLEY, Linda Elizabeth (SwFla) 10922 106th Ave, Largo, FL 33778

BARLOWE, Michael (Cal) 815 Second Avenue, New York City, NY 10017

BARNARD, Nancy Alexandra Sandra (ECR) 1267 Black Sage Cir, Nipomo, CA 93444

BARNES, Chuck (EO) Po Box 317, Hermiston, OR 97838

BARNES, Jeffry Parker (SD) 21285 E Highway 20 Apt 127, Bend, OR 97701

BARNES, John David (Ala) 401 N Main Ave, Demopolis, AL 36732

BARNES, Rebecca A (Be) 20 Cumming St, New York, NY 10034

BARNES, Simon (Pgh)

BARNES, Susan Johnston (Minn) St John The Baptist Episc Ch, 4201 Sheridan Ave S, Minneapolis, MN 55410

BARNETT, Andrew K (WA) Washington National Cathedral, 3101 Wisconsin Ave NW, Washington, DC 20016

BARNETT, Becca Fleming (Cal) 435 Euclid Ave Apt 1, San Francisco, CA 94118

BARNETT, Edwin Wilson (FtW) 808 Voltamp Dr., Fort Worth, TX 76108

BARNETT, Maxine Maria Veronica (LI) Church of Saint Jude, 3606 Lufberry Ave, Wantagh, NY 11793

BARNETT, Thomas (EC) 1219 Forest Hills Dr., Wilmington, NC 28403

BARNEY, David Marshall (Mass) 310 Hayward Mill Rd, Concord, MA 01742

BARNEY, Roger Alexander (ECR) 19040 Portos Dr, Saratoga, CA 95070

BARNHILL JR, James W (Fla) 5043 Timuquana Rd, Jacksonville, FL 32210

BARNHOUSE, David H (Los) 6844 Penham Pl, Pittsburgh, PA 15208

BARNICLE, Brendan John (Ore) 1432 SW 13th Ave, Portland, OR 97201

BARNS, George Stewart (Mass) PO Box 381164, Cambridge, MA 02238

BARNUM, Barbara Coxe (Los) 11359 Perris Blvd, Moreno Valley, CA 92557

BARNUM, Elena (Ct) 112 Bentwood Dr, Stamford, CT 06903

BARNWELL, William (La) 1917 Audubon St, New Orleans, LA 70118

BARON, Christian John (WMich) 555 Michigan Ave, Holland, MI 49423

BARON, Jodi Lynn (WMich) 555 Michigan Ave, Holland, MI 49423

BAROODY, Roger Anis (NY) 218 Luke Mountain Rd, Covington, VA 24426

BARR, David Lee (Fla) 8227 Bateau Rd S, Jacksonville, FL 32216

BARR, Donna Faulconer (Lex) 2140 Woodmont Dr, Lexington, KY 40502

BARR, Gillian Rachel (RI) 275 N Main St, Providence, RI 02903

BARR, Jane Wallace (Va) 209 Macarthur Rd, Alexandria, VA 22305

BARR, Norma Margaret (Chi)

BARRAGAN, Juan (Los) 9046 Gallatin Rd., Pico Rivera, CA 90660

BARRAZA, Rene (Los) St Athanasius and St Paul's, 840 Echo Park Ave, Los Angeles, CA 90026

BARRE, James Lyman (Vt) 1009 Robert E. Lee Drive, Wilmington, NC 28412

BARRERA FLORES, Olga I (Hond) IMS SAP Dept 215, PO BOX 523900, Miami, FL 33152-3900, Honduras

BARRETT, Constance Yvonne (Mil) 3560 N Summit Ave, Shorewood, WI 53211

BARRETT, Jo (Mass) Trinity Church, 124 River Road, Topsfield, MA 01983

BARRETT, John Hammond (WTex) 3527 Vancouver Dr, Dallas, TX 75229

BARRETT JR, John Henry (CNY) 41 S Woody Hill Rd, Westerly, RI 02891

BARRETT, John Richard (Tex) St Martin's Episcopal Church, 1602 S Fm 116, Copperas Cove, TX 76522

BARRETT, Patricia Callan (Mass)

BARRETT, Rilla (Oly) 670 Rainbow Dr, Sedro-Woolley, WA 98284

BARRETT, Robin Carter (EO) 9310 Parakeet Dr, Bonanza, OR 97623

BARRETT, Sr Helena (Nwk)

BARRETT, Timothy Lewis (Nwk) 10 Crestmont Rd, Montclair, NJ 07042

BARRIE, David Paul (NY) 2109 Broadway # 1241, New York, NY 10023

BARRINGTON, Dominic M J (Chi) 65 E Huron St, Chicago, IL 60611

BARRINGTON JR, Tom (Mass) 27 6th Ave, North Chelmsford, MA 01863

BARRIOS, Luis (NY) 295 Saint Anns Ave, Bronx, NY 10454

BARRIOS, Maria Trevino (Dal) 534 W 10th St, Dallas, TX 75208

BARRON JR, Caldwell Alexander (SC) 168 Club Cir, Pawleys Island, SC 29585

BARRON, Carol Dunn (SeFla) 3954 SE Fairway E, Stuart, FL 34997

BARRON, Scott William (Chi) 1148 N Douglas Ave, Arlington Heights, IL 60004

BARRON, Thomas Lemuel (Ga) PO Box 211106, Augusta, GA 30917

BARROW, Alan Lester (Okla) 5635 E. 71st St., Tulsa, OK 74136

BARROW, Colin Vere (SO) 8592 Roswell Rd Apt.218, Sandy Springs, GA 30350

BARROW, John Condict Hurst (Ind) 8920 Washington Blvd West Dr, Indianapolis, IN 46240

BARROW, John Thomas (Episcopal SJ) Po Box 3231, Mammoth Lakes, CA 93546

BARROW, Suzanne (Ky)

BARROWCLOUGH, Lisa Shirley (SeFla) St. Mark's Episcopal Church and School, 3395 Burns Road, Palm Beach Gardens, FL 33410

BARROWS, Jennifer Eve (NY) 1585 Route 9 West, West Park, NY 12493

BARRY, Brian Clark (LI) St Ann's Episcopal Church, 262 Middle Rd, Sayville, NY 11782

BARRY, Eugenia Clare Mackenzie (WNC) 11 Lone Pine Rd, Asheville, NC 28803

BARRY, Peggy Sue (Ark) 400 Hill St, Forrest City, AR 72335

BARRY-MARQUESS, Richard Livingston (SeFla) 19540 Nw 8th Ave, Miami, FL 33169

BARTA, Heather Marie (EMich) 156 Guanonocque St, Auburn Hills, MI 48326

BARTELS, Judith Tallman (Oly) none----moved from there, lacey, WA 98117

BARTH, Barbara L (Me) 42 Tailwind Ct Apt 78 D, Auburn, ME 04210

BARTHELEMY, Paul Berge (Ore) 4524 Trillium Woods, Lake Oswego, OR 97035

BARTHOLOMEW, Adam Gilbert Leinbach (NY) 802 Broadway, New York, NY 10003

BARTHOLOMEW, Linda Milavec (Spok) Church Of The Resurrection, 15319 E 8th Ave, Spokane Valley, WA 99037

BARTHOLOMEW, Tara Anne (Az)

BARTLE, Edward Bartholomew (CFla) 330 Hickory Ave, Orange City, FL 32763

BARTLE, John Dixon (Alb) Po Box E, Richfield Springs, NY 13439

BARTLE, Kevin B (CFla) 700 Rinehart Rd, Lake Mary, FL 32746

BARTLE, Leonard William (CFla) 3520 Curtis Dr, Apopka, FL 32703

BARTLE, Phyllis (CFla) 330 Hickory Ave, Orange City, FL 32763

✠ **BARTLETT JR**, Allen Lyman (Pa) 600 E. Cathedral Rd, Apt L-209, Philadelphia, PA 19128

BARTLETT, Anne Kristin (Ore) 281 Talent Ave, Talent, OR 97540

BARTLETT, Basil A (VI) PO Box 7386, St Thomas, VI 00801

BARTLETT, Harwood (At) 4345 Erskine Rd, Clarkston, GA 30021

BARTLETT, Laurie Lee (Alb) Calvary Church, PO Box 41, Burnt Hills, NY 12027

BARTLETT, Lois Sherburne (Be) 2716 Tennyson Ave, Sinking Spring, PA 19608

BARTLETT, Stephen I Ves (WMich) 8975 Shawbacoung Trail, Shelby, MI 49455

BARTLETT, Susan Mansfield (Mo) 906 Mallard Sq, Rolla, MO 65401

BARTLETT, Thomas Albert (Mass) 25 Monmouth St, Brookline, MA 02446

BARTOLOMEO, Michael Edward (LI) 124 Balaton Ave, Lake Ronkonkoma, NY 11779

BARTON, Alexander Doyle (O) PO Box 521, Lorain, OH 44052

BARTON, Anne (Spok) 5205 Sycamore Dr, Yakima, WA 98901

BARTON III, Bill (Tenn) Trinity Episcopal Church, 213 1st Ave NW, Winchester, TN 37398

BARTON, Charles Denis Hampden (Mass) 3602 Stembridge Ct, Wilmington, NC 28409

BARTON JR, John Clib (Ark) 1024 Stanford Dr Ne, Albuquerque, NM 87106

BARTON JR, Lane Wickham (Cal) 12616 Se 11th St, Vancouver, WA 98683

BARTUSCH, Robert Frederic (WTenn) 2851 Neeley St # 113, Batesville, AR 72501

BARTZ, James Perkins (Wyo) St John's Church, 170 N Glenwood St, Jackson, WY 83001

BARWICK III, Frederick Ernest (NC) 5941 Leasburg Rd., Roxboro, NC 27574

BARWICK, Mark (Eur) avenue du Préau 16, Brussels, 01040, Belgium

BASCOM, Cathleen (Ia) Cathedral Church of St. Paul, 815 High Street, Des Moines, IA 50309

BASCOM, Joshua L (Va)

BASDEN, Michael (SwFla) 495 Galleon Dr, Naples, FL 34102

BASINGER JR, Elvin David (Ala) 21526 Silver Oaks Circle, Athens, AL 35613

✠ **BASKERVILLE-BURROWS**, Jennifer (Ind)

BASKIN, Cynthia Oppen (WA) 10924 Citreon Ct, N Potomac, MD 20878

BASS, Francis Arthur (ETenn)

BASS-CHOATE, Yamily (NY) 4 Gateway Rd, Unit 1-D, Yonkers, NY 10703

BASSETT-JELLEMA, Alice (Md) 1401 Carrollton Ave, Ruxton, MD 21204

BASSUENER, Barbara A. (Colo) 20 3rd St, Pocomoke City, MD 21851

BAST, Kathryn Ana Terra (SwVa) PO Box 164, Blacksburg, VA 24063

BAST, Robert Lee (Eas) 201 Crosstown Dr Apt 3013, Peachtree City, GA 30269

BASTIAN, Martin James (Tex) 5714 Jackwood St, Houston, TX 77096

BATARSEH, Peter Bahjat (Tenn) 312 Battle Avenue, Franklin, TN 37064

BATCHELDER JR, Kelsey Chase (NY)

BATEMAN, David (CPa) 3312 Brisban St, Harrisburg, PA 17111

BATES, Allen Layfield (Ark) 1902 W Magnolia St, Rogers, AR 72758

BATES, Charlotte McKnight (Mich) 15136 S. Dillman, Plainfield, IL 60544

BATES, J Barrington (Nwk) 15 Warren St Unit 117, Jersey City, NJ 07302

BATES, James Brent (Nwk) 31 Woodland Ave, Summit, NJ 07901

BATES, Percy Quin (La)

BATES, Robert Seaton (Chi) 121 W Macomb St, Belvidere, IL 61008

BATES, Steven Byron (CGC) 508 S Market St, Scottsboro, AL 35768

BATES, Stuart Alan (Tex) 345 Piney Point Rd, Houston, TX 77024

BATES, Thomas Justin (RG)

BATES, Toppie (CNY) 5623 Mack Rd, Skaneateles, NY 13152

BATIZ MEJIA, José David (Hond) IMS SAP Dept 215, PO BOX 523900, Miami, FL 33152-3900, Honduras

BATSON, Lloyd Samuel (Nwk) 160 W South Orange Ave, South Orange, NJ 07079

BATSON, Sara Chapman (Pa) 6102 Treyburn Point Dr, Durham, NC 27712

BATSON III, Stephen Radford (NY) 3721 Wares Ferry Rd Apt 500, Montgomery, AL 36109

BATTEN, Stephen John (EC) PO Box 332, Chocowinity, NC 27817

BATTERMAN, Stephanie Jane (Me) 3 FAIRVIEW LN, Bath, ME 04530

BATTLE, Michael Jesse (NC) 1611 East Millbrook Rd, Raleigh, NC 27609

BATTON JR, Robert Nolton (RG) 4304 Carlisle Blvd NE, Albuquerque, NM 87107

BAUER, Audrey T (NMich) 6837 Lahti Ln, Pellston, MI 49769

BAUER, Charles (SVa)

BAUER, Charles David (Eau)

BAUER, Kathryn Ann (WMo) Po Box 996, Kremmling, CO 80459

BAUER, Richard C (SeFla) 1608 Russell Rd, Alexandria, VA 22301

BAUER, Ronald Coleman (Los) 27292 Via Callejon Unit B, San Juan Capistrano, CA 92675

BAUER, Thomas William (Md) 3148 Gracefield Rd Apt CL412, Silver Spring, MD 20904

✠ **BAUERSCHMIDT**, John (Tenn) 50 Vantage Way Ste 107, Nashville, TN 37228

BAUGHMAN, David Lee (Chi) 804 James Court, Wheaton, IL 60189

BAUKNIGHT JR, Mack Miller (SwFla) 2440 26th Ave S, Saint Petersburg, FL 33712

BAUM, George R (O) 13415 Ardoon Ave, Cleveland, OH 44120

BAUM, Nancy Louise (Mich) 411 Walnut St # 3371, Green Cove Springs, FL 32043

BAUMAN, Dwayne Ray (Ark) 176 State Road YY, Tunas, MO 65764

BAUMAN, Ward J (Minn) 1111 Upton Ave N, Minneapolis, MN 55411

BAUMANN, David Michael (Spr) PO Box 303, Salem, IL 62881

BAUMGARTEN, Betsy (Ark) 14294 John Lee Road, Biloxi, MS 39532

BAUMGARTEN, Jonathan David (Chi) 41 E. 8th St. Apt. 2001, Chicago, IL 60605

BAUMGARTEN, William Paul (Mont) 845 2nd Ave E, Kalispell, MT 59901

BAUSCHARD, Michael Robert Thomas (NwPa) 5 Cottage Pl, Warren, PA 16365

BAUSTIAN, Donald Edward (Ark) 1801 20th St Unit K-15, Ames, IA 50010

BAUTISTA, Gina (CPa)

BAUTISTA, Simon (Tex) Christ Church Cathedral, 1117 Texas St, Houston, TX 77002

BAVARO, Carolyn Margaret (Chi) P.O. Box 30247, Chicago, IL 60630

BAXLEY, Todd Lee (NwT) 1601 S Georgia St, Amarillo, TX 79102

BAXTER, Barbara (WNY) 16 N Phetteplace St, Falconer, NY 14733

BAXTER JR, Donald Leslie (NwPa) 300 Hilltop Rd, Erie, PA 16509

BAXTER, Jane Ann (CNY) 151 Hawkins Rd, Ferrisburgh, VT 05456

BAXTER, Lisette Dyer (Vt) 112 Lakewood Pkwy, Burlington, VT 05408

BAXTER, Nancy Julia (At) 1223 Clifton Rd NE, Atlanta, GA 30307

✠ **BAXTER**, Nathan Dwight (CPa) 115 N Duke St, Lancaster, PA 17602

BAXTER, Rae Lee (Mich) 430 Nicolet St, Walled Lake, MI 48390

BAYACA, Greg G(uerrero) (Los)

BAYANG, Martin Eugenio (RG) 1406 S Cliff Dr, Gallup, NM 87301

BAYFIELD, Ralph Wesley (Va) 300 Westminster Canterbury Dr Apt 405, Apt 405, Winchester, VA 22603

BAYLES, Joseph Austin (Kan) 1341 N River Blvd, Wichita, KS 67203

BAYLES, Richard Allen (Oly) Po Box 1115, South Bend, WA 98586

BAYNE, Bruce George Cuthbert (Cal) 2875 Idledwild Dr, #108, Reno, NV 89505

BAYNES, Leopold Cornelius (LI) 2306 98th St, East Elmhurst, NY 11369

BAYS, Terri (NI) 117 N Lafayette Blvd, South Bend, IN 46601

BAZIN, Jean Jacques Emmanuel Fritz (SeFla) 525 NE 15 Street, Miami, FL 33132

BEACH, Deborah Elizabeth (Alb) 132 Duanesburg - Churches Road, Duanesburg, NY 12056

BEACH, Diana (Nwk) 88 Main Street, Thomaston, ME 04861

BEACH, John Tappan (Mass) 39, Route De Malagnou, Geneva, 01208, Switzerland

BEACH, Joseph Lawrence (ETenn) 4768 Edens View Rd, Kingsport, TN 37664

BEACH, Kay Joan (Ia) 201 E Church St, Marshalltown, IA 50158

BEACHAM III, Albert Burton (U) 1420 N 3000 W, Vernal, UT 84078

BEACHY, William Nicholas (WMo) 431 W 60th Ter, Kansas City, MO 64113

BEAL, Jennifer D (Mass) 1745 Wedgewood Cmn, Concord, MA 01742

BEAL, Stephen Thomas (The Episcopal NCal) 2301 Polk St, Apt 3, San Francisco, CA 94109

BEALE, Mary I (NH) 45 Derryfield Ct, Manchester, NH 03104

BEALES, Rosemary Elizabeth (Va) St Stephen's & St Agnes School, 400 Fontaine St, Alexandria, VA 22302

BEALL, Nathan A (WA) PO Box 207, St Marys City, VA 20686

BEAM, Barbara (WMo) 6336 SE Hamilton Rd, Lathrop, MO 64465

BEAM, Marcia Mckay (SeFla) 805 SW 6th Ave, Delray Beach, FL 33444

BEAMER, Charles Wesley (O) 3920 Spokane Ave, Cleveland, OH 44109

BEAN, Kathleen Tedrow (Cal)

BEAN, Kevin D (WMass) All Saints Church, 10 Irving St., Worcester, MA 01609

BEAN, Rebecca Anne (EC) PO Box 1333, Goldsboro, NC 27533

BEANE, Emmetri Monica (Va) PO Box 367, Rixeyville, VA 22737

BEAR, Susan (Miss) 3600 Arlington Loop, Hattiesburg, MS 39402

BEARD, Bryan Benjamin (Okla) 9309 N 129th East Ave, Owasso, OK 74055

BEARDEN, Jane Bostick (Miss) 77 Westchester Dr, Haverhill, MA 01830

BEASLEY, Battle Alexander (Tenn) 1613 Fatherland St, Nashville, TN 37206

BEASLEY, Carl H (Eas) 720 NE 4th Ave Apt 506, Fort Lauderdale, FL 33304

BEASLEY, Christopher Ryan (Ind)

BEASLEY, Helen Roberts (SwVa) Po Box 1266, Galax, VA 24333

BEASLEY, Nicholas (USC) 126 Blyth Avenue, Greenwood, SC 29649

BEASLEY, Robert (ETenn) 121 E. Harper Avenue, Maryville, TN 37804

BEASLEY JR, Thomas Edward (Fla) 6003 Brookridge Rd, Jacksonville, FL 32210

BEATTIE, Richard Edward (Ct) 438 Old Tavern Rd, Orange, CT 06477

BEATTY, Anne M (The Episcopal NCal) 1515 Shasta Dr Apt 1335, Davis, CA 95616

BEATTY, Steve (Va) 10267 Lakeridge Square CT, Apt B, Ashland, VA 23005

BEATY, Maureen Kay (Colo) St Mary Magdalene, 4775 Cambridge St, Boulder, CO 80301

BEAUCHAMP, Robert William (SwVa) PO Box 227, Norton, VA 24273

BEAUDREAU JR, Edward Gil (RI) 63 Canonchet Rd, Hope Valley, RI 02832

BEAUHARNOIS, Patricia Ann (Alb) 18 Butternut St, Champlain, NY 12919

BEAULAC, David Armand (Alb) St Mary's Church, PO Box 211, Lake Luzerne, NY 12846

BEAULIEU, Cynthia Rae (Me) 650 Main St, Caribou, ME 04736

BEAULIEU, Delores Joyce (Minn) Rr 2 Box 246, Bagley, MN 56621

BEAULIEU, Joyce (Chi) 223 W Royal Dr, Dekalb, IL 60115

BEAUMONT, Jerrold Foster (CFla) 8494 Ridgewood Ave Apt 4201, Cape Canaveral, FL 32920

BEAUMONT, Katharine Jenetta (Az)

BEAUVOIR, Jonas (Hai) Eglesi Episcopal D'Haiti, Boite Postale 1309, Port-au-Prince, Haiti

✠ **BEAUVOIR**, Oge (Hai) 76 Avenue Christophe, Port-Au-Prince, Haiti

BEAVEN, John Clinton (Me) 22 Willow Grove Rd, Brunswick, ME 04011

BEAZLEY, Robert William (La) PO Box 409, Sewanee, TN 37375

BEBB JR, Ernest Leo (U) 6452 South 1650 East, Murray, UT 84121

BEBBER, Gerald King (Q) 1821 Mcgougan Rd, Fayetteville, NC 28303

BECHERER, Carl John (Minn)

BECHTOLD, Bryant Coffin (FtW) 3290 Lackland Rd, Fort Worth, TX 76116

BECK, Brien Patrick (FdL) 347 Libal St, De Pere, WI 54115

BECK, Judith Taw (Pa) 3300 W Penn St, Philadelphia, PA 19129

BECK, Laura E (Colo)

BECK, Randall Alan (NwPa) St John's Episcopal Church, 226 W State St, Sharon, PA 16146

BECK, Sue Ann (Los) St. John The Divine, 183 E. Bay St., Costa Mesa, CA 92627

BECK, Tanya (Ind) 5810 Kingsley Dr., Indianapolis, IN 46220

BECK, Thomas Francis (Ct) 4 Willow Ct, Cromwell, CT 06416

BECKER, CS Honey (The Episcopal Church in Haw) PO Box 819, Kailua, HI 96734

BECKER, Kim (WNC) PO Box 177, Glendale Springs, NC 28629

BECKER, Mary Clovis (Kan)

BECKER, Mary Elizabeth (Ind) 2076 E County Rd 375 S, Winslow, IN 47598

BECKER, Nora A (WVa)

BECKER, Robert Andrew (Va) 1124 Handlebar Rd, Reston, VA 20191

BECKER, Stephen David (Va) 13 Braxton Dr, Sterling, VA 20165

BECKETT, Kimberly Youngblood (Ala) 113 Brown Ave, Rainbow City, AL 35906

BECKETT JR, Norman James (Los) 3157 E Avenue, #B-4, Lancaster, CA 93535, Costa Rica

BECKHAM JR, M Edwin (At) 3172 Legion Dr SE, Covington, GA 30014

BECKLES, William Anthony (NY) Po Box 1067, Mount Vernon, NY 10551

✠ **BECKWITH**, Mark M (Nwk) Episcopal Diocese of Newark, 312 Mulberry St, Newark, NJ 07102

✠ **BECKWITH**, Peter Hess (Spr) 7451 E Bacon Rd, Hillsdale, MI 49242

BEDARD, Caren Marie (Minn) 408 N 7th St, Brainerd, MN 56401

BEDDINGFIELD, John (NY) 316 E 88th St, New York, NY 10128

BEDELL, Bryan Douglas (Roch) 28 Village Trl, Honeoye Falls, NY 14472

BEDFORD, Michael John (Mich) 25831 Lexington Dr Unit 1, South Lyon, MI 48178

BEDINGFIELD, John Davis (WLa) 400 Camellia Blvd, Lafayette, LA 70503

BEE, Robert D (Neb) 5109 N Jefferson St, Gladstone, MO 64118

BEEBE, Christine Fair (Minn) 395 N Main St, Rutherfordton, NC 28139

BEEBE SR, Fred H (Fla) 124 Peninsular Dr, Crescent City, FL 32112

BEEBE, James Russell (Nev) 205 Mackinaw Ave, Akron, OH 44333

BEEBE, Jane Alice (WMass)

BEEBE SR, Jeffrey (SeFla) 151 S County Rd, Palm Beach, FL 33480

BEEBE, Susan Rafter (SeFla) 151 S County Rd, Palm Beach, FL 33480

BEEBE-BOVE, Polly (Vt) 3 Cathedral Sq Apt 2G, Burlington, VT 05401

BEECHAM, Troy (Ia) 815 High St, Des Moines, IA 50309

BEECHER, Jo (Oly) 7134 Steelhead Ln, Burlington, WA 98233

BEELEY, Christopher Alfred (Tex) 1527 Sunnymede Ave, South Bend, IN 46615

BEER, David Frank (Tex) 6810 Thistle Hill Way, Austin, TX 78754

BEERS, William Rogers (Chi) 120 1st St, Lodi, WI 53555

BEERY, Bill (NY) 905 Osprey Ct, New Bern, NC 28560

BEERY, Susan Beem (U) 228 S Pitt St, Alexandria, VA 22314

BEESLEY, Kevin D (SO)

BEHEN, Ralph Joseph (WMo)

BEHM, Nancy Anne (FdL) 1703 Doemel St, Oshkosh, WI 54901

BEHNKE, Cathleen Ann (Mich) 4800 Woodward Ave, Detroit, MI 48201

BEHNSTEDT, Patrice Faith (CFla) 500 W Floral Ave, Bartow, FL 33830

BEHRENS, Marilyn Jean (Oly) 7417 Hill Ave Apt 2, Gig Harbor, WA 98335

BEIKIRCH, Paula Marie (CFla) 4915 Deter Rd, Lakeland, FL 33813

BEILSTEIN, Joan Elizabeth (WA) 400 Hinsdale Ct, Silver Spring, MD 20901

BEIMDIEK, Jill (USC) St. Stephen's Episcopal Church, 200 North James St, Goldsboro, NC 27530

BEIMES, Phyllis Mahilani (The Episcopal Church in Haw) St Matthew's Episcopal Church, Po Box 70, Waimanalo, HI 96795

✠ **BEISNER**, Barry (The Episcopal NCal) Episcopal Diocese Of Northern California, 350 University Ave Ste 280, Sacramento, CA 95825

BEITZEL, Wallace Dickens (U) 9475 Brookside Ave, Ben Lomond, CA 95005

BEIZER, Lance Kurt (ECR) P.O. Box 1047, 9 Blackberry Way, Canaan, CT 06018

BEK, Susan (Los) 3290 Loma Vista Rd, Ventura, CA 93003

BELA, Robert (Mass) 475 Breeding Loop, Breeding, KY 42715

BELANGER, Fanny Sohet (Va)

BELCHER, Nancy Spencer (Mo) PO Box 6065, Fulton, MO 65251

BELCHER, Sandra Alves (Ct) 165 Grassy Hill Rd, Woodbury, CT 06798

BELKNAP, Charles (Los) 1386 Beddis Road, Salt Spring Island, V8K 2C9, Canada

BELKNAP, Sarah (Los) 2066 Empress Ave, South Pasadena, CA 91030

BELL, Beth Ann (Okla) 13112 N Rockwell Ave, Oklahoma City, OK 73142

BELL, Daniel Peter (Mass) Tufts University Protestant Chaplaincy, 3 The Green, Medford, MA 02155

BELL, Emily Susan Richardson (Los) 190 Avenida Aragon, San Clemente, CA 92672

BELL, Gerald Michael (Miss) 602 Riverview Dr, Florence, AL 35630

BELL JR, Hugh Oliver (Tex) 919 S John Redditt Dr, Lufkin, TX 75904

BELL, Jocelyn (ETenn) 643 Westview Rd, Chattanooga, TN 37415

BELL JR, John Robinson (Oly) 2454 E Palm Canyon Dr # 4d, Palm Springs, CA 92264

BELL, Mary Cynthia (Mass) 22 Hathaway Pond Circle, Rochester, MA 02770

BELL, Michael S (Los) 5801 Crestridge Rd, Rancho Palos Verdes, CA 90275

BELL, Mike (WMich) 406 2nd St, Manistee, MI 49660

✠ **BELL**, Pat (EO) 501 E Wallace Ave, Coeur D Alene, ID 83814

BELL, Roger C (Pgh) 56500 Abbey Rd, Three Rivers, MI 49093

BELL JR, William R (Md) 2901 Boston St Apt 601, Baltimore, MD 21224

BELL, Winston Alonzo (LI) 2263 Sedgemont Dr, Winston Salem, NC 27103

BELLAIMEY, John Edward (Minn) 4233 Linden Hills Blvd, Minneapolis, MN 55410

BELLAIS, William (WMo) 440 Dickinson St, Chillicothe, MO 64601

BELLISS, Richard (Los) 25454 Via Heraldo, Santa Clarita, CA 91355

BELLNER, Elisabeth Ann (Md)

BELLOWS, Carol Hartley (WMass) 33 Fernald Street, Wilton, ME 04294

BELLOWS, Richard (WMass) 21 Briarcliff Dr, Westfield, MA 01085

BELLOWS, Scott P (Md) Saint Davids Church, 4700 Roland Ave, Baltimore, MD 21210

BELL-WOLSKI, Dedra Ann (Ga) 32464 Willow Parke Circle, Fernandina Beach, FL 32034

BELMONT JR, Jack (NJ) 300 S Main St, Pennington, NJ 08534

BELMONTES, Mervyn Lancelot (LI) 812 Nebraska Ave, Bay Shore, NY 11706

BELMORE JR, Buck (Nev) 4626 Grand Dr Unit 2, Las Vegas, NV 89169

BELMORE, Constance (Nev) 4626 Grand Drive #2, Las Vegas, NV 89169

BELNAP, Ronald Victor (U) 8952 Golden Field Way, Sandy, UT 84094

BELSER, Jo J (Va) 2280 N Beauregard St, Alexandria, VA 22311

✠ **BELSHAW**, George Phelps Mellick (NJ) 15 Boudinot St, Princeton, NJ 08540

BELSHAW, Richard W (NH) 18 Highland Street, Ashland, NH 03217

BELSKY, Emil Eugene (U) 2714 Sierra Vista Road, Grand Junction, CO 81503

BELT, Michel (Ct) 119 Huntington St, New London, CT 06320

BELTON, Allan Edgar (O) 3490 E Prescott Cir, Cuyahoga Falls, OH 44223

BELTON, Colin Charles (Alb) 18 Trinity Pl., Plattsburgh, NY 12901

BELTON, Randy Samuel (Wyo) Church Of Saint Andrew's In The Pines, Po Box 847, Pinedale, WY 82941

BELZER, John Alfred (Okla) 13 Lake Ln, Shawnee, OK 74804

BENAVIDES, Laurie Pauline (RG) 112 Goldenrod Ln, Alto, NM 88312

BENBROOK, James Gordon (WLa) 125 Woodstone Dr., Ruston, LA 71270

BENCKEN, Cathi Head (Ia) 211 Walnut St., Muscatine, IA 52761

BENCKEN, Charles F (WNY) 2461 Longhurst Ct., Muscatine, IA 52761

BENDALL, Douglas (Nwk) 26 Howard Court, Newark, NJ 07103

BENDER, David Randa (NY) 104 Fairview Avenue, Poughkeepsie, NY 12601

BENDER, Jane (Be) 557 W 3rd St Apt K, Bethlehem, PA 18015

BENDER, John Charles (Tenn) Our Saviour Episcopal Church, 704 Hartsville Pike, Gallatin, TN 37066

BENDER, William (Ala) 402 S Scott St, Scottsboro, AL 35768

BENDER-BRECK, Barbara (Cal) 3226 Adeline St, Oakland, CA 94608

BENEDICT, Richard Alan Davis (NJ) 1625 SE 10th Ave Apt 602, Fort Lauderdale, FL 33316

BENES, Sandra S (Mich) 122 White Lake Dr, Brooklyn, MI 49230

BENESH, Jimi Brown (The Episcopal NCal) 334 D St, Redwood City, CA 94063

✠ **BENFIELD**, Larry (Ark) Episcopal Diocese Of Arkansas, 310 W 17th St, Little Rock, AR 72206

BENHAM, David D (Ark) 2701 Old Greenwood Rd, Fort Smith, AR 72903

✠ **BENHASE**, Scott Anson (Ga) 611 E Bay St, Savannah, GA 31401

BENISTE, Jean C (Ind) 2430 K St NW, Washington, DC 20037

BENITEZ, Wilfredo (LI) St George's Church, 13532 38th Ave, Flushing, NY 11354

BENITZ, Stephen M (Ia) 120 1st St NE, Mason City, IA 50401

BENJAMIN, Judy (Cal) 1400 Loma Drive, Ojai, CA 93023

BENKO, Andrew G (FtW) 908 Rutherford St, Shreveport, LA 71104

BENKO, Hope (FtW) 9700 Saints Cir, Fort Worth, TX 76108

BENNER, Stephen Thomas (Ind) 636 W Grace St Apt 2w, Chicago, IL 60613

BENNET, Richard Wilson (FdL) 7220 Newell Road, Hazelhurst, WI 54531

BENNETT III, Arthur Lasure (WVa) 16 Ashwood Dr, Vienna, WV 26105

BENNETT JR, Bertram George (NY) 384 E 160th St, Bronx, NY 10451

BENNETT, Betsy Blake (Neb) 325 W. 11th St., Hastings, NE 68901

BENNETT, Christine Aikens (Me) 30 Turtle Cove Rd, Raymond, ME 04071

BENNETT, Dale Koch (WMich) 110 Quail St, Battle Creek, MI 49037

BENNETT, Debra Q (O) 1933 Kingsley Ave, Akron, OH 44313

BENNETT, Denise Harper (Roch) 2882 Country Road 13, Clifton Springs, NY 14432

BENNETT, Ernest L (CFla) Diocese of Central Florida, 1017 E Robinson St, Orlando, FL 32801

BENNETT JR, Franklin Pierce (EMich) 1051 Virginia Ave, Marysville, MI 48040

BENNETT, Gail Louise (NJ) 803 Prospect Ave, Spring Lake, NJ 07762

BENNETT, Gerald L (SwFla) 5134 Wedge Ct E, Bradenton, FL 34203

BENNETT, JoAnne (Ore) PO Box 1791, Roseburg, OR 97470

BENNETT, Kyle Vernon (Miss) St. Mark's Episcopal Church, 1101 N. Collier Blvd, Marco Island, FL 34145

BENNETT, Lisa Carol (ECR)

BENNETT, Marionette Elvena (Colo) 15625 E Atlantic Cir, Aurora, CO 80013

BENNETT, Pattiann (Mont) 324 Terning Dr W, Eureka, MT 59917

BENNETT, Phillip (Pa) 2001 Hamilton St Apt 303, Philadelphia, PA 19130

BENNETT, Rachel Marybelle (ECR) 201 Glenwood Cir Apt 19e, Monterey, CA 93940

BENNETT, R Dudley (Nwk) 16 Warwick Way, Jackson, NJ 08527

BENNETT, Robert Avon (Mass) Po Box 380367, Cambridge, MA 02238

BENNETT, Sarah (Tex) 7002 Rusty Fig Dr, Austin, TX 78750

BENNETT, Susan P (Ind) 610 Perry St, Vincennes, IN 47591

BENNETT, Thad (Vt) 17 Lane Dr, Newfane, VT 05345

BENNETT, Virginia Lee (Spr) 1404 Gettysburg Lndg, Saint Charles, MO 63303

BENNETT, Vivian Rose Kerr (Pa) 934 Overfield RD, Meshoppen, PA 18630

BENNETT, William (Tex) 3711 Hidden Holw, Austin, TX 78731

BENNETT JR, William Doub (NC) Po Box 28024, Raleigh, NC 27611

✠ **BENNISON JR**, Charles Ellsworth (Pa) 279 S 4th St, Philadelphia, PA 19106

BENO, Brian Martin (FdL) 17 Yorkshire Dr, Fond du Lac, WI 54935

BENOIT JOSEPH, Arlette Dierdre (At) 294 Peyton Rd SW, Atlanta, GA 30311

BENSHOFF, Bruce L (Mass) 11 Meadowlark Dr, Middleboro, MA 02346

BENSON, E Heather (CNY) 60 Elm St, Ilion, NY 13357

BENSON, George Andrew (Neb) 8800 Holdrege St, Lincoln, NE 68505

BENSON, J(Ohn) Bradley (CNY) 110 Robie St, Bath, NY 14810

BENSON, Kathleen (Del) 4830 Kennett Pike Apt 2537, Wilmington, DE 19807

BENSON, Patricia B (Minn) PO Box 5888, Collegeville, MN 56321

BENSON, Ricky Lynn (Tex) 1616 Driftwood Ln, Galveston, TX 77551

BENSON, Virginia (Los) 1432 Engracia Ave, Torrance, CA 90501

BENTER JR, Harry William (SwFla) 1010 American Eagle Blvd, Apt 348, Sun City Center, FL 33573

BENTLEY JR, John R (Tex) 15410 Misty Forest Ct., Houston, TX 77068

BENTLEY, Stephen Richard (Episcopal SJ) 316 N El Dorado St, Stockton, CA 95202

BENTLEY, Susan Bliss Emmons (SwVa) 4515 Delray St Nw, Roanoke, VA 24012

BENTLEY-SHELTON, Elizabeth Michael (Wyo) 2511 Coffeen Ave, Sheridan, WY 82801

BENTRUP, Alan Dale (USC) 1115 Marion St, Columbia, SC 29201

BENVENUTI, Anne Cecilia (Chi) 4945 S Dorchester Ave, Chicago, IL 60615

BENZ, Charles Frederick (NC) 4118 Pin Oak Dr, Durham, NC 27707

BERARD, Jeffrey Jerome (Mil) 1622 Quincy Ave, Racine, WI 53405

BERBERICH, Gloria Carroll Kennedy (Va) 673 Evergreen Ave, Charlottesville, VA 22902

BERCOVICI, Hillary Rea (NY) 8 Sound Shore Dr Ste 130, Greenwich, CT 06830

BERDAHL, Peder (Ind) 5 Oak Brook Club Dr. Apr P2S, Oak Brook, IL 60523

BERENDS, April (ETenn) St. Mark's Episcopal Church, 2618 N. Hackett Ave., Milwaukee, WI 53211

BERESFORD, David Charles (Pa) 145 W Springfield Rd, Springfield, PA 19064

BERESFORD, Ruth (Del) P. O. Box 3510, Greenville, 507 East Buck Road, Wilmington, DE 19807

BERG, Dustin (The Episcopal Church in Haw) Saint Mark's Church, 515 48th St NW, Canton, OH 44709

BERG, James Christopher (Mich) 642 Woodcreek Dr, Waterford, MI 48327

BERGE JR, William Clark (Oly) P.O. Box 399, Mount Sinai, NY 11766

BERGEN, Franklyn Joseph (Az) 4076 N Hidden Cove Pl, Tucson, AZ 85749

BERGER, Fred (Ia) 25111 Valley Drive, Pleasant Valley, IA 52767

BERGER, Jere Schindel (Alb) Montvert Road #1125, Middletown Springs, VT 05757

BERGER, Martha (Mil) 1616 Martha Washington Dr, Wauwatosa, WI 53213

BERGERON, Mary Lee (ETenn) 6823 Sheffield Dr, Knoxville, TN 37909

BERGH JR, Palmer A (Ida) 180 kings court, mountain home, ID 83647

BERGHUIS, Michael Robert (WMich)

BERGIE, Patricia Ann (Wyo) Po Box 903, Fort Washakie, WY 82514

BERGIN, Joseph Alphonsus (CNY) 6312 N Manlius Rd, Kirkville, NY 13082

BERGMANN, William (WMass) 85 E Main St, Ayer, MA 01432

BERGMANS, Susan Estelle (Cal) 1320 Addison St Apt C130, Berkeley, CA 94702

BERGNER, Mario J (Spr) 149 Asbury St, South Hamilton, MA 01982

BERGNER, Robert A (Ct) 200 Seabury Dr, Bloomfield, CT 06002

BERGSTROM, Fiona Mabel (NC) 11 Fleet St, Umina Beach NSW, NC 02257, Australia

BERGSTROM, Jeremy W (Dal) St John's Church, 1 W Macon St, Savannah, GA 31401

BERITELA, Gerry (CNY) 360 S Collingwood Ave, Syracuse, NY 13206

BERK, Dennis Bryan Alban (Be) 27 Grace Avenue, Schuylkill Haven, PA 17972

BERKHOUSE, Casey Stephen (WTex) 343 N Getty St, Uvalde, TX 78801

BERKLEY, John Clayton Ashton (NI) 26824 County Road 4, Elkhart, IN 46514

BERKOWE, Kathleen (NY) 16 Truesdale Dr, Croton On Hudson, NY 10520

BERKTOLD, Brenda Clare (Ore) 170 Brookside Dr, Eugene, OR 97405

BERKTOLD, Ted (Ore) 170 Brookside Dr, Eugene, OR 97405

BERLENBACH, Betty Lorraine (Vt) 1961 Plains Rd., Perkinsville, VT 05151

BERLENBACH, Kirk Thomas (Pa) 6429 Sherwood Rd, Philadelphia, PA 19151

BERLIN II, George Albert (Colo) 3155 Kendall St, Wheat Ridge, CO 80214

BERLIN, Sarah Aline (Colo) 3155 Kendall St, Wheat Ridge, CO 80214

BERMAN, Elizabeth Sievert (Mass) 6 Heritage Dr, Lexington, MA 02420

BERNACCHI, Jacqueline A (Minn) 1730 Clifton Pl Ste 201, Minneapolis, MN 55403

BERNACKI, Jim (NC) P.O. Box 657, Albemarle, NC 28002

BERNAL, Jose Juan (RG) 635 N Story Rd, Irving, TX 75061

BERNARD, Michael Allen (Kan) 305 Old Colony Ct, North Newton, KS 67117

BERNARDEZ JR, Teogenes Kalaw (Nev) 832 N Eastern Ave, Las Vegas, NV 89101

BERNARDI, Frank Alan (Episcopal SJ) 1815 S Teddy St, Visalia, CA 93277

BERNHARD, Margaret (Ore) 1180 NW Country Ct, Corvallis, OR 97330

BERNIER, Daniel L (Mass) PO Box 719, Wareham, MA 02571

BERNIER, Noe (Hai)

BERNTHAL, Gail Elizabeth (Episcopal SJ) 519 N Douty St, Hanford, CA 93230

BERRA, Robert M (Az) St Augustine's Episcopal Church, 1735 S College Ave, Tempe, AZ 85281

BERRY, Beverly (Pa) 212 W Lancaster Ave, Paoli, PA 19301

BERRY JR, Charles (WTex) 1100 Grand Blvd Apt 223, Boerne, TX 78006

BERRY JR, Graham Gardner (Chi) 1021 S Orange Grove Blvd, Unit 107, Pasadena, CA 91105

BERRY, John Emerson (NMich)

BERRY, Mary Helen (Miss)

BERRYMAN II, Jerome Woods (Colo) 5455 Landmark PL Unit 807, Greenwood Village, CO 80111

BERSIN, Ruth Ann Hargrave (Ct) 4 Holmes Rd, Boxford, MA 01921

BERTOLOZZI, Michael Alan (Nev) 3625 Marlborough Ave, Las Vegas, NV 89110

BERTRAND, Michael Elmore (WTex) 2310 N Stewart Rd, Mission, TX 78574

BESCHTA, Gerald Thomas (WNC) 175 Mimosa Way, Hendersonville, NC 28739

BESCHTA, Joyce Marie (WNC) 65 Mimosa Way, Hendersonville, NC 28739

BESENBRUCH, Peter Ray (The Episcopal Church in Haw) 1679 California Ave, Wahiawa, HI 96786

BESHEARS, Earl D (SwFla) 331 56th Ave S, St Petersburg, FL 33705

BESHEER, Kimbrough Allan (Oly) 600 1st Ave Ste 632, Seattle, WA 98104

BESIER, Bettine Elisabeth (RI) 30 Scotch Cap Rd, Quaker Hill, CT 06375

BESS JR, Walter (Cal) 118 Tamalpais Rd, Fairfax, CA 94930

BESSLER, Jeffrey L (Ind)

BESSON JR, Michael Wallace (Tex) 9610 Roarks Psge, Missouri City, TX 77459

BEST, Steve (Oly) 17421 Ne 139th Pl, Redmond, WA 98052

BETANCES, Gregoria Cedano de (At) 6216 Love St, Austell, GA 30168

BETANCES, Ramon Antonio (At) 925 Whitlock Ave Apt 1308, Marietta, GA 30064

BETANCUR ORTIZ, Ricardo Antonio (Colom) c/o Diocese of Colombia, Cra 6 No. 49-85 Piso 2, Bogota, BDC, Colombia

BETE, Vincent Songaben (Ia) 204 E. 5th St., Ottumwa, IA 52501

BETENBAUGH, Helen R (CGC)

BETHANCOURT JR, A Robert (Los) 1145 W Valencia Mesa Dr, Fullerton, CA 92833

BETHEA, Mary (Los) 31641 La Novia Ave, San Juan Capistrano, CA 92675

BETHELL, John Christian (USC) Holy Trinity, 193 Old Greenville Hwy, Clemson, SC 29631

BETHELL, Talbot James (Tex) 290 Fall Creek Dr., Oceanside, OR 97134

BETIT, John D (LI) 5 Pleasant St, Sutton, MA 01590

BETSINGER, Vicki Lynn (Oly) 280 E Wheelright St, Allyn, WA 98524

BETTINGER, Robert Louis (Cal) 3940 Park Blvd Apt 911, San Diego, CA 92103

BETTS, Ian Randolph (NY) 6515 Palisade Ave Apt 201, West New York, NJ 07093

BETTS, Robert Hamilton (Pa) 1126 Foulkeways, Gwynedd, PA 19436

BETZ, David Emanuel (NwPa)

BETZ, Nancy Elizabeth (CNY) 412 Hugunin St, Clayton, NY 13624

BETZ SHANK, Erin L (NwPa)

BEUKMAN, Christian Arnold (Mass) 12 Quincy Ave, Quincy, MA 02169

BEVANS, Bruce Sinclair (WVa) PO Box P, Moundsville, WV 26041

BEVANS, Marjorie (WVa) 903 Charles St, Parkersburg, WV 26101

BEVENS, Myrna Eloise (Colo) 46 N Albion St, Colorado Springs, CO 80911

BEVERIDGE, Robin Lorraine (NY)

BEYER, Jeanie Tillotson (Fla) 2872 N. Hannon Hill Dr., Tallahassee, FL 32309

BEZILLA, Gregory (NJ) 134 Mercer Street, Princeton, NJ 08540

BEZY, Bernard Anthony (Lex) 1407 Gemstone Blvd, Hanahan, SC 29410

BIANCHI, Mary Elizabeth (Nev) 1674 Harper Drive, Carson City, NV 89701

BIBENS, Robert Lee (Okla) 4642 E 57th Pl, Tulsa, OK 74135

BICE, Michael Kenneth (Chi) 1244 N Astor St, Chicago, IL 60610

BICKERTON, Frances Catherine Baur (NJ) 164 Buttonwood Dr, Fair Haven, NJ 07704

BICKFORD, Wayne Elva (HB) 8212 Kelsey Whiteface Rd, Cotton, MN 55724

BICKING, David (WVa) 813 Bowling Green Rd, Front Royal, VA 22630

BIDDLE, Blair Charles (Alb) Po Box 1029, Plattsburgh, NY 12901

BIDDLE III, Craig (Va) 364 Friar Trl, Annapolis, MD 21401

BIDDY, Eric (Chi) 545 S East Ave, Oak Park, IL 60304

BIDWELL, Mary Almy (NH) 1145 Jerusalem Rd, Bristol, VT 05443

BIDWELL-WAITE, Davidson (Cal) 3641 20th St., San Francisco, CA 94110

BIEDENHARN III, Jay (USC) 10 N Church St, Greenville, SC 29601

BIEGA, Richard (WNC) 426 English Rd, Spruce Pine, NC 28777

BIEGLER, James Cameron (FdL) 1632 Jensen Dr, Ellison Bay, WI 54210

BIELSKI, Diane Irene (Colo) P O Box 1558, Fraser, CO 80442

BIEVER, Robert Ray (Oly) 3310 N Bennett St, Tacoma, WA 98407

BIFFLE, Robin Lee (Spok) 111 S. Jefferson St., Moscow, ID 83843

BIGELOW, Thomas Seymour (Oly) Box 20489, Seattle, WA 98102

BIGGADIKE, Maylin Teresa (Nwk) 398 Shelbourne Ter, Ridgewood, NJ 07450

BIGGERS, Helen Hammond (Spok) 4803 W Shawnee Ave, Spokane, WA 99208

BIGGERS, Jackson Cunningham (Miss) 10100 Hillview Dr Apt 537, Pensacola, FL 32514

BIGGS, Carolyn (CFla) 6071 Sabal Hammock Cir, Port Orange, FL 32128

BIGGS, John (WMo) 2632 S Wallis Smith Blvd, Springfield, MO 65804

BIGLEY, Mark Charles (WTex) Church of the Annunciation, PO Box 106, Luling, TX 78648

BILBY, Gary Eugene (NwT) 1501 S Grinnell St, Perryton, TX 79070

BILLER, Larry Ray (NI) 9064 E Koher Rd S, Syracuse, IN 46567

BILLINGSLEA, Wendy Ward (Fla) 400 San Juan Dr, Ponte Vedra Beach, FL 32082

BILLINGSLEY, Michael (Mass) Saint Paul's Episcopal Church, 61 Wood St., Hopkinton, MA 01748

BILLINGTON, James Hadley (Cal) 1 S El Camino Real, San Mateo, CA 94401

BILLMAN, Daniel Robert (Ind) 8165 Gwinnett Pl., Indianapolis, IN 46250

BILLMAN, Sharon Lynn (Kan) 1738 24000 Rd, Parsons, KS 67357

BILLOW JR, William Pierce (WA) PO Box 242, Barboursville, VA 22923

BILLUPS, Beatrice Moore (Md) 1514 Gordon Cove Dr, Annapolis, MD 21403

BIMBI, Jim (Del) 4828 Hogan Dr, Wilmington, DE 19808

BINDER, Donald Drew (Va) 9301 Richmond Hwy, Lorton, VA 22079

BINDER, Thomas Francis (Mil)

BINGHAM, Elizabeth Jane (Mich)

BINGHAM, John Pratt (The Episcopal NCal) 17538 Caminito Balata, San Diego, CA 92128

BINGHAM, Sally Grover (Cal) 7 Laurel St, San Francisco, CA 94118

BIORNSTAD, Nathan A (Los) 122 S California Ave, Monrovia, CA 91016

BIPPUS JR, William Lloyd (Ky) 917 Church St, Marinette, WI 54143

BIRCHER, Victor Malcolm (Miss) 102 Edie St, Columbia, MS 39429

BIRD, David John (ECR) 81 North 2 Street, San Jose, CA 95113

BIRD, Edith (Mo) 1325 Margaret St, Cape Girardeau, MO 63701

BIRD IV, Edward T (Chi) 306 S Prospect Ave, Park Ridge, IL 60068

BIRD, Frederick L (WVa) 1009 S Henry Ave, Elkins, WV 26241

BIRD JR, John Edwin (NJ) 304 S Girard St, Woodbury, NJ 08096

BIRD, Julie Childs (SC)

BIRD, Michael (NY) 7 Library Ln, Bronxville, NY 10708

BIRD, Patricia A (Del) 30851 Crepe Myrtle Dr Unit 60, Millsboro, DE 19966

BIRD, Robert Dale (Mich) 824 W Maple Ave, Adrian, MI 49221

BIRD, Robert Vincent (Los) 2701 Blue Fox Dr, Ontario, CA 91761

BIRD, Virginia Lee (SD) PO Box 9412, Rapid City, SD 57709

BIRDSALL, James (Ct) PO Box 2252, Orleans, MA 02653

BIRDSALL, John Burton (Eas) 419a Evans St Apt 2, Williamsville, NY 14221

BIRDSEY, Robert B (EC) 2206 Rosewood Ave, Richmond, VA 23220

BIRDSONG, Jerre Eugene (Mo) 4714 Clifton Ave, Saint Louis, MO 63109

BIRKBY, Charles H (CNY) 1505 Pershing Pl Apt A, Rolla, MO 65401

BIRKENHEAD, Harold George (Mass) 8 Nevin Rd, South Weymouth, MA 02190

BIRNBAUM, Rachelle (Va) 942A Heritage Vlg, Southbury, CT 06488

BIRNEY, Edith Hazard (Me) 11 Perkins St, Topsham, ME 04086

BIRNEY III, James Gillespie (Me) 1110 North Rd, North Yarmouth, ME 04097

BIRTCH, John Edward McKay (SwFla) 1001 Carpenters Way Apt H108, Lakeland, FL 33809

BISHOP, Christopher (Pa)

BISHOP, Edwin (Ore) 1900 Lauderdale Dr Apt D115, Henrico, VA 23238

BISHOP, Genevieve R (NJ)

BISHOP JR, Harold Ellsworth (Md) Box 128, Cottage 505-B, Quincy, PA 17247

BISHOP, Kathleen Gayle (NJ) St Mary's by-the-sea, 804 Bay Ave, Point Pleasant Beach, NJ 08742

BISSELL-THOMPSON, Geraldine Vina (Alb) 225 Back West Creek Rd, Newark Valley, NY 13811

BITTNER, Merrill (Me) 118 Lone Pine Rd, Newry, ME 04261

BJORNBERG JR, Philip John (Ct) Trinity Episcopal Church, 345 Main St, Portland, CT 06480

BLACK, Cynthia (Nwk) 36 South St, Morristown, NJ 07960

BLACK, George Donald (At) 215 N Edenfield Ridge Dr, Rome, GA 30161

BLACK, Katharine C (Mass) 13 Louisburg Sq, Boston, MA 02108

BLACK JR, Milton England (WTex) 149 Cordula St, Corpus Christi, TX 78411

BLACK, Rebecca Lynn (Mass) 128 Village St, Millis, MA 02054

BLACK, Robert E. (HB) 21Jerimoth Dr., Bradford, CT 06405

BLACK JR, Robert William (NC) 131 West Council Street, Salisbury, NC 28144

BLACK, Ruth Buck Wallace (Miss) 1704 Poplar Blvd, Jackson, MS 39202

BLACK, Sherry Leonard (Spr) 12806 Mallard Dr., Whittington, IL 62897

BLACK, Timothy H (At) 4393 Garmon Rd NW, Atlanta, GA 30327

BLACK, Vicki Kay (Me) 73 Bristol Rd, Damariscotta, ME 04543

BLACK, Vincent (O) 2230 Euclid Ave, Cleveland, OH 44115

BLACKBURN, Elliot Hillman (Spr) 603 South Grant, Mason City, IA 50401

BLACKBURN, Gerald Jackson (EC) 4212 Stratton Village Ln, Wilmington, NC 28409

BLACKBURN, Gregory Benjamin (SeFla) 1121 Andalusia Ave, Coral Gables, FL 33134

BLACKBURN, Terry Gene (NJ) 35-50 85th Street 5J, Jackson Heights, NY 11372

BLACKERBY JR, William (Ala) 4307 Clairmont Ave S, Birmingham, AL 35222

BLACKHAM, Todd Patten (Los) 1325 Monterey Rd, South Pasadena, CA 91030

BLACKLOCK, Martha Grace (NJ) POBox 2973, Silver City, NM 88062

BLACKMER, Stephen D (NH) Kairos Earth, 107 Hackleboro Road, Canterbury, NH 03224

BLACKMON, Andrew Thomas (La) 120 S New Hampshire St, Covington, LA 70433

BLACKWELL, Norma Lee (WA) 10754 Main St Apt 202, Fairfax, VA 22030

BLACKWELL, Robert Hunter (Ala) 1016 Broadway Ave SW, Cullman, AL 35055

BLACKWOOD, Deb (NC) 14103 Wilford Ct, Charlotte, NC 28277

BLADON, Doyle Gene (Az) 310 W Union Ave, Monticello, AR 71655

BLAESS, Kristine Amend (Tenn) 4715 Harding Pike, Nashville, TN 37205

BLAESS, Michael (Tenn)

BLAGG, James Raymond (Okla) 117 Sandpiper Cir, Durant, OK 74701

BLAIES-DIAMOND, Sarah (NC) 3430 Old US 70 PO BOX 37, Cleveland, NC 27013

BLAINE, Carol McGown (Tex) 307 Palm Dr, Marlin, TX 76661

BLAINE, Patti (Roch) 3825 E Henrietta Rd Ste 100, Henrietta, NY 14467

BLAINE-WALLACE, Bill (Me) 161 Wood Street, Lewiston, ME 04240

BLAIR, Alexander (Cal) 1801 Marin Ave, Berkeley, CA 94707

BLAIR, Rebecca H (RI) 40 Hoppin Hill Avenue, North Attleboro, MA 02760

BLAIR JR, Thom Williamson (Va) Po Box 1059, Kilmarnock, VA 22482

BLAIR-HUBERT, Paige (SanD) PO Box 336, Del Mar, CA 92014

BLAIR-LOY, Mary Frances (SanD) 747 W University Ave, San Diego, CA 92103

BLAIS, Heather Jeanette (WMass) 73 Federal St, Wiscasset, ME 04578

BLAKE, Sandra Jean (Colo)

BLAKE, Susan Lynn (CFla) 460 N Grandview St, Mount Dora, FL 32757

BLAKE JR, Thomas (Ind)

BLAKELY, Wayne Allen (Kan) 2805 Woodmont Dr, Louisville, KY 40220

BLAKLEY, Dave Edward (NwT)

BLAKLEY, J. Ted (WK) 402 N Topeka St, Wichita, KS 67202

BLAKLEY, Raymond Leonard (WTenn) 761 Spaulding Dr, Roseville, CA 95678

BLAKSLEE, John Charles (NI) 15606 W 103rd Lane, Dyer, IN 46311

BLANCH, Paul F (The Episcopal NCal) 2150 Benton Dr, Redding, CA 96003

BLANCHARD, Louise Browner (Colo) 600 Gilpin St, Denver, CO 80218

BLANCHARD, Louise Sharon (Colo) 6774 Tabor St, Arvada, CO 80004

BLANCHARD, Margaret (WVa)

BLANCHARD, Sudie Mixter (Me) St. George's Episcopal Church, PO Box 364, York Harbor, ME 03911

BLANCHETT, David Harvey (The Episcopal Church in Haw) 1100 Pullman Dr, Wasilla, AK 99654

BLANCK, Charles Kenneth (WNC) 977 Collins Rd, Sparta, NC 28675

BLANCO, Patricia Dugan (Los) 3455 Mountain Ave, San Bernardino, CA 92404

BLANCO-MONTERROSO, Leonel (Okla) 5500 S Western Ave., Oklahoma City, OK 73109

BLAND, John Dilkes (Minn) 1431 Cherry Hill Rd, Mendota Heights, MN 55118

BLAND, Leslie Rasmussen (NC)

BLAND SR, Thomas James (NC) 4608 Pine Cove Rd, Greensboro, NC 27410

BLASCO, Natalie (SeFla) 1801 Ludlam Dr, Miami Springs, FL 33166

BLASDELL, Machrina Loris (Cal) 804 Cottonwood Dr., Lansing, KS 66043

BLATZ, Edward Nils (LI) 79 Zophar Mills Road, Wading River, NY 11792

BLAUSER, Dennis Alan (NwPa) 215 Dermond Rd, Hermitage, PA 16148

BLAUVELT II, Charles (NH) 162 Sagamore St., Manchester, NH 03104

BLAUVELT, Jeremy David (USC) 125 Church Ave, Pass Christian, MS 39571

BLAVIER JR, Donald Charles (WTex) 404 Salisbury Ln, Victoria, TX 77904

BLAYER, Brian David (Ct) 15117 14 Rd, Whitestone, NY 11357

BLAYLOCK, Joy Harrell (CGC) 7125 Hitt Rd, Mobile, AL 36695

Clergy List

BLAZEK, Laura Sue (Okla) 1601 W Imhoff Rd, Norman, OK 73072

BLEDSOE, Alwen Grace (Colo)

BLEDSOE, Faith E (WTex) St. Francis Episcopal Church, 3002 Miori Lane, Victoria, TX 77901

BLEDSOE, Sharon Calloway (SVa) 116 Victorian Lane, Jupiter, FL 33458

BLEND, Jennifer Davis (Colo) 4775 Cambridge St, Boulder, CO 80301

BLESSING, Kamila Abrahamova (Pgh) 6211 Wrightsville Ave. Unit 147, Wilington, NC 28403

BLESSING, Pastor Mary (ECR) 5271 Scotts Valley Dr, Scotts Valley, CA 95066

BLESSING, Robert Alan (SanD) 12539 Sundance Ave, San Diego, CA 92129

BLESSING, Wren Tyler (Oly) Grace Episcopal Church, 8595 NE Day Rd E, Bainbridge Island, WA 98110

BLEVINS, Isaac (ETenn)

BLEYLE, Douglas Karl (RG) 318 Silver Ave SW, Albuquerque, NM 87102

BLINDHEIM, Mark (Oly)

BLINMAN, Clifford Louis (Ore) 2092 E. Bighorn Mountain Dr, Oro Valley, AZ 85755

BLISS, John Derek Clegg (Cal) 4 Edgewater Hillside, Westport, CT 06880

BLISS, Robert Francis (Tex) 881 North Main Street, PO Box 797, Salado, TX 76571

BLISS, Vernon Powell (CNY) 86 E Taylor Hill Rd, Montague, MA 01351

BLIZZARD, Charles Fortunate-Eagle (Okla) 1301 Andover Ct, Oklahoma City, OK 73120

BLOOM, Barry Moffett (Mass) 3030 Union St, Oakland, CA 94608

BLOOMER, Nancy Hester (NY) 4 Grant St, Essex Junction, VT 05452

BLOSSOM JR, John Dickson (Chi) 125 Sw Jefferson Ave, Peoria, IL 61602

BLOTTNER, William Eugene (Chi) 510 First Ave, Farmville, VA 23901

BLUBAUGH, Susan Jo (NI) 1305 S 2nd St, Lafayette, IN 47905

BLUE, Eddie Michael (Md) 7 Park Ave Apt 1, Westminster, MD 21157

BLUE, Gordon K (Ak) 2902 Sawmill Creek Rd, Sitka, AK 99835

BLUE, Susan (WA) 270 El Diente Dr., Durango, CO 81301

BLUE COAT TRAVERSIE, Iva (SD)

BLUME, Andrew C (NY) 160 West 95th Street, Apt. 8B, New York, NY 10025

BLUMENSTOCK, Robert (The Episcopal NCal) 732 Shoreside Dr, Sacramento, CA 95831

BLUMER, Gary R (Be) Po Box 623, Portland, PA 18351

BLUNDELL, Gayle Ann (ECR) 2100 Emmons Rd, Cambria, CA 93428

BLUNT, Elizabeth E (Az) Christ Church of the Ascension, 4015 E Lincoln Dr, Paradise Valley, AZ 85253

BLUNT JR, Howard Elton (LI) 125 Eastern Parkway #5D, Brooklyn, NY 11238

BOARD, John Curtis (Mont) 2704 Gold Rush Ave, Helena, MT 59601

BOARD III, Paul (O) 313 E Wayne St, Maumee, OH 43537

BOASE, David John (Spr) 4902 Blu Fountain Dr, Godfrey, IL 62035

BOATRIGHT-SPENCER, Angela (NY) 801 Willow St, Wadesboro, NC 28170

BOATWRIGHT, William (NJ) 1901 N. DuPont Highway, New Castle, DE 19720

BOBBITT, Kathleen Morrisette (SVa) 1005 Windsor Rd, Virginia Beach, VA 23451

BOBO, Melinda (Wyo) P.O. Box 1177, Dubois, WY 82513

BOCCHINO, Jim (RI) 589 Smithfield Rd, North Providence, RI 02904

BOCCINO, Kenneth Robert (Nwk) 550 Ridgewood Rd, Maplewood, NJ 07040

BOCK, Susan Kay (Mich) 529 E Kirby St, Detroit, MI 48202

BOCKUS, Ian Lawrence (Me) 496 N Searsport Rd, Prospect, ME 04981

BODIE, Park McDermit (NY) 235 W 56th St Apt 11m, New York, NY 10019

BOEGER, Daniel Edward (The Episcopal NCal)

BOEGER, Mary Rose Steen (The Episcopal NCal)

BOELTER, Phillip R (Minn) Gethsemane Episcopal Church, 905 4th Avenue South, Minneapolis, MN 55402

BOELTER, Sally (Cal) 41485 S. I-94 Service Drive, Belleville, MI 48111

BOESCHENSTEIN, Kathryn C (Colo)

BOESSER, Mark Alan (Ak) 17585 Point Lena Loop Rd, Juneau, AK 99801

BOEVE, Phillip Dale (Spr) 303 Merchants Avenue, Fort Atkinson, WI 53538

BOGAL-ALLBRITTEN, Rose (Ky) 1504 Kirkwood Dr, Murray, KY 42071

BOGAN III, Leslie Eugene (CGC) 1336 Greenvista Ln, Gulf Breeze, FL 32563

BOGEL, Marianne (Oly) 11844 Bandera Rd #148, HELOTES, TX 78023

BOGERT-WINKLER, Hilary Megan (WMass) 14 Boltwood Ave., Amherst, MA 01002

BOGGS, Timothy A (Me) 12 Oakhurst Road, Cape Elizabeth, ME 04107

BOGHETICH, Barbara Ann (Hond) IMC-SAP 564, PO Box 52-3900, Miami, FL 33152

BOHLER JR, Lewis Penrose (Los) PO Box 16216, Augusta, GA 30919

BOHNER, Charles Russell (Del) 1309 Grinnell Rd # N33, Wilmington, DE 19803

BOIVIN, Barbara Ann (Nev)

BOJARSKI, Mitchell T (SanD) 116 S. Columbia St., Campbellsville, KY 42718

BOLAND, Geoffrey Allan (CFla) 1861 Peninsular Dr, Haines City, FL 33844

BOLDINE, Charles Stanley (RG) 6009 Costa Brava Ave NW, Albuquerque, NM 87114

BOLI, Judith Davis (EMich) 4444 State St Apt F-318, Saginaw, MI 48603

BOLIN, William Eugene (Md) 244 Braeburn Cir, Walkersville, MD 21793

BOLLE, Stephen (NY) 1 Chipping Ct, Greenville, SC 29607

BOLLE, Winnie Mckenzie Hoilette (SeFla) 6055 Verde Trl S Apt H316, Boca Raton, FL 33433

BOLLES-BEAVEN, Anne (Nwk) 32 Yale St, Maplewood, NJ 07040

BOLLING, Angelique (Mont)

BOLLINGER II, David Glenn (CNY) 206 John St, Binghamton, NY 13905

BOLLINGER, Matthew D (NJ) 514 W Adams Blvd, Los Angeles, CA 90007

BOLMAN DWIGHT, Robert Bolman (SO) 115 W Monument Ave, #1201, Dayton, OH 45402

BOLT, Michelle Warriner (ETenn) 413 Cumberland Ave, Knoxville, TN 37902

BOLTON, Carolyn Marie (Cal) 1125 Brush St, Oakland, CA 94607

BOLTON, John Donald (At) 16245 Birmingham Hwy, Milton, GA 30004

BOLTON, Virginia Cassady (CFla)

BOMAN, Ruth Kay (Okla) 424 E St Nw, Miami, OK 74354

BOMAN, Samuel Ratliff (Neb) 262 Parkside Ln, Lincoln, NE 68521

BON, Brin Carol (Tex) 1500 N Capital Of Texas Hwy, Austin, TX 78746

BONADIE, LeRoy Rowland (Md) 609 Wellington Ln, Cumberland, ND 21502

BOND, Barbara Lynn (O) 455 Santa Clara St Nw, Canton, OH 44709

BOND, Eric (Pa) 2122 Washington Ln, Huntingdon Valley, PA 19006

BOND, Jeremy William (CPa) 676 N 12th Street Unit 25, Grover Beach, CA 93433

BOND, Leonard Wayne (Oly) 5810 Fleming St Unit 66, Everett, WA 98203

BOND, Michael David (Chi) PO Box 438, Cedar Lake, IN 46303

BOND, Michele (Eas) 19524 Meadowbrook Rd, Hagerstown, MD 21742

BONDURANT, Stephen Bryce (SO) 785 Ludlow Ave, Cincinnati, OH 45220

BONE, Patrick Joseph (ETenn) Po Box 129, Church Hill, TN 37642

BONEBRAKE, Aletha Green (EO) 2347 Campbell St, Baker City, OR 97814

BONELL, John Winston (NH) 332 US Route 202, Rindge, NH 03461

BONEY, Samuel Ashford (Miss) 10100 Hillview Dr. Apt 433, Pensacola, FL 32514

BONIN, Raymond Thomas (NH) 1 Hood Rd, Derry, NH 03038

BONNER, Bruce (Tex) 3520 W. Whitestone Blvd., Cedar Park, TX 78613

BONNER, George Llewellyn (LI) 783 E 35th St, Brooklyn, NY 11210

BONNER III, John Hare (ETenn) Holy Trinity Episcopal Church, 207 S Church St, Hertford, NC 27944

BONNER-STEWART, Ann (NC) St Mary's Chapel, 900 Hillsborough St, Raleigh, NC 27603

BONNEVILLE, Jerome (Spok)

BONNEY, Isaac Kojo Nyame (WA) Saint Mark's Church, 12621 Old Columbia Pike, Silver Spring, MD 20904

BONNYMAN, Anne Berry (Mass) 50 Sonnet Lane, Asheville, NC 28804

BONOAN, Raynald Sales (SwFla) 18612 Chemille Dr, Lutz, FL 33558

BONSEY, Steven Charles (Mass) 138 Tremont St, Boston, MA 02111

BONSEY, W(Illiam) Edwin (The Episcopal Church in Haw) 401 SAnta Clara Av e Apt 309, Oakland, CA 94610

BONSTEEL, Susan Layh (NY) 94 Clifton Ave, Kingston, NY 12401

BONWITT, Martha (WA) 14303 Old Marlboro Pike, Upper Marlboro, MD 20772

BOODT, Mary Ione (Ind) 100 Oakview Dr, Mooresville, IN 46158

BOOHER, David Lewis (SVa) 724 West H St., Elizabethton, TN 37643

BOOK, Robert TM (At) 170 Trinity Ave SW, Atlanta, GA 30303

BOOKER JR, James Howard (Az) 700 E Georgia Ave, Deland, FL 32724

BOOKSTEIN, Nancey Johnson (Colo) 110 Johnson St, Frederick, CO 80530

BOONE, Arthur Robinson (Vt) 1616 Harmon St, Berkeley, CA 94703

BOONE, Connie Louise (EO) 42893 Pocahontas Rd, Baker City, OR 97814

BOONE JR, Robert Augustus (WNC) 41 Cobblers Way Apt 333, Asheville, NC 28804

BOOTH, Errol Kent (WA) 2811 Deep Landing Rd, Huntingtown, MD 20639

BOOTH, James Alexander (ECR) 48 Miramoute Rd., Carmel Valley, CA 93924

BOOTH, Karen (Lex) 7423 San Jose Blvd, Jacksonville, FL 32217

BOOTH, Stephen P (WMass)

BOOZER, Alcena Elaine Caldwell (Ore) 5256 NE 48th Ave, Portland, OR 97218

BORBON, Samuel (Ore) 1704 NE 43rd Ave, Portland, OR 97213

BORDADOR, Noel Estrella (NY)

BORDELON, Andre Alan (WLa)

BORDELON, Joseph Ardell (WLa) 5704 Monroe Hwy, Ball, LA 71405

BORDELON, Michael Joseph (WLa)

BORDEN, Robert Bruce (Vt) P0 Box 554, East Middlebury, VT 05740

BORDEN, Theorphlis Marzetta (SO) St Simon Of Cyrene, 810 Matthews Dr, Cincinnati, OH 45215

BORDENKIRCHER, Amanda (CFla) 942 Cobbler Ct, Longwood, FL 32750

BORDNER, Ken (Roch) 3471 Cerrillos Rd Trlr 78, Santa Fe, NM 87507

BORG, Manuel (Chi) 1072 Ridge Ave, Elk Grove Village, IL 60007

BORG, Marianne (Ore) 1133 Nw 11th Ave Apt 403, Portland, OR 97209

BORGEN, Linda Suzanne (CGC)

BORGES, Maria Cristina (SanD) 521 E 8th St, National City, CA 91950

BORGESON, Josephine (The Episcopal NCal) 458 Occidental Cir, Santa Rosa, CA 95401

BORGMAN, Dean Wylie (Mass) 5 Heritage Dr, Rockport, MA 01966

BORNT, Lisa Ashley (Md)

BORREGO, John Edward (Okla) 422 E Noble Ave, Guthrie, OK 73044

BORREGO, Lynn Griffith (Okla) 422 E Noble Ave, Guthrie, OK 73044

BORSCH, Kathleen Ann (Ore)

BORZUMATO, Judith Alice (NY) 500 State Rte 299 Apt 24C, Highland, NY 12528

BOSBYSHELL, William (SwFla) 106 21st Ave Ne, Saint Petersburg, FL 33704

BOSLER, Sarah Mather (Be) 1188 Ben Franklin Hwy E, Douglassville, PA 19518

BOSS, Bruce William (Ind) 133 Belvedere Dr, Georgetown, KY 40324

BOSSCHER, Molly Boscher (Va) 251 E Lake Brantley Dr, Longwood, FL 32779

BOST, Emily Catherine (Ark) 217 N East Ave, Fayetteville, AR 72701

BOSTIAN, Nathan Louis (WTex) 20955 W Tejas Trl, San Antonio, TX 78257

BOSTOCK, Jasmine Hanakaulani (The Episcopal Church in Haw) 1020 Green St Apt 204, Honolulu, HI 96822

BOSTON, Dane E (Alb) 69 Fair St, Cooperstown, NY 13326

BOSTON, James Terrell (Ore) 518 NE Dean Dr, Grants Pass, OR 97526

BOSWELL JR, Frederick Philip (Colo) 9200 W 10th Ave, Lakewood, CO 80215

BOSWELL, Kathryn Mary (Alb) 21 Cherry St., Potsdam, NY 13676

BOTH, M Blair (Ec) 305 S 5th Ave, Wilmington, NC 28401

BOTTOM, Jacob A (Tenn) Saint David's Episcopal Church, 623 Ector St, Denton, TX 76201

BOTTONE, Doreen Ann (Ct) 68 Main St, Berlin, CT 06037

BOUCHER, Edward Charles (RI) 341 Seaview Ave, Swansea, MA 02777

BOUCHER, John (SVa) 600 Farnham Ct, North Chesterfield, VA 23236

BOULTER, Matthew Rutherford (Tex) 118 S. Bois d'Arc, Tyler, TX 77702

BOULTER, Richard Ottmuller (Mich) 11575 Belleville Rd, Belleville, MI 48111

BOULTER, Robert J (Md) Cathedral of the Incarnation, 4 E University Pkwy, Baltimore, MD 21218

BOURDEAU, Mary Ellen (Md) 2 Saint Peters Pl, Lonaconing, MD 21539

BOURGEAULT, Cynthia Warren (Colo) HC 2 Box 16, Sunset, ME 04683

BOURHILL, John William (NY) 26 Huron Rd, Yonkers, NY 10710

✠ **BOURLAKAS**, Mark (SwVa) 421 S 2nd St, Louisville, KY 40202

BOURNE, Nathaniel Francis (NH)

BOURNE-RAISWELL, Margaret Lafayette (ECR) 20025 Glen Brae Dr, Saratoga, CA 95070

BOURQUE, Mary Elizabeth (Me) 20 Union St., Hallowell, ME 04347

BOURQUIN, Eugene Alphonse (NY) 296 9th Ave, New York, NY 10001

BOUSFIELD, Nigel J (FdL) 1432 Foxfire Ct, Waupaca, WI 54981

BOUSQUET, Michael (Mass) PO Box 395, Barnstable, MA 02630

BOWDEN, George Edward (Mo) 624 Saffron Ct, Myrtle Beach, SC 29579

BOWDEN JR, Talmadge Arton (Ga) 3409 Wheeler Rd, Augusta, GA 30909

BOWDISH, Lynn Eastman (Cal) 172 Northgate Ave, Daly City, CA 94015

BOWEN, Anthony DeLisle (LI) 180 Kane St, Brooklyn, NY 11231

BOWEN, Carol Staley (Cal) 2019 Monroe Ave, Belmont, CA 94002

BOWEN, Elizabeth Anne (Mo) Trinity Episcopal Church, 318 S Duchesne Dr, Saint Charles, MO 63301

BOWEN, George Harry (Nwk) 308 River Oaks Dr, Rutherford, NJ 07070

BOWEN, Kristin Elaine (Mich)

BOWEN, Paul Roger (Tex) 324 Sherwood Ave, Staunton, VA 24401

BOWEN, Pauline Mason (WNY) 138 Castle Hill Rd, East Aurora, NY 14052

BOWEN, Peter Scott (Me) 20 Sky Harbor Dr, Biddeford, ME 04005

BOWEN, Shirley Williams (Me) 20 Sky Harbor Drive, Biddeford, ME 04005

BOWER, Alice W (Oly) 2400 NW 9th Ave, Battle Ground, WA 98604

BOWER, Bruce E (WMo) 6401 Wornall Ter, Kansas City, MO 64113

BOWER, Jeffrey L (Ind) 4160 Broadway St, Indianapolis, IN 46205

BOWER, John Allen (SO) 418 Sugar Maple Ln, Springdale, OH 45246

BOWER, Richard Allen (CNY) 681 N Hill Cross Rd, Ludlow, VT 05149

BOWER, Roger Andrew (NI) 505 Bullseye Lake Rd, Valparaiso, IN 46383

BOWERFIND, Ellis Tucker (Va) 8727 Bluedale St, Alexandria, VA 22308

BOWERS, Albert Wayne (NJ) 17 Woodbridge Ave, Sewaren, NJ 07077

BOWERS, David Douglas (SwFla) 513 Nassau St S, Venice, FL 34285

BOWERS, John Edward (SO) 1276 Coonpath Rd Nw, Lancaster, OH 43130

BOWERS, Marvin Nelson (The Episcopal NCal) 202 Tucker St, Healdsburg, CA 95448

BOWERS, Terry L. (Chi) 1900 Etton Dr, Fort Collins, CO 80526

BOWERS, Thomas Dix (NY) 304 Lord Granville Dr, Morehead City, NC 28557

BOWERSOX, Ned Ford (WTex) 8607 Tomah Dr, Austin, TX 78717

BOWERSOX, Sally (Colo) 620 S Alton Way Apt 4d, Denver, CO 80247

BOWES, Bruce (NY) 254 Bloomer Rd, Lagrangeville, NY 12540

BOWHAY, Chris (Tenn) St. Peter's Episcopal Church, 311 W 7th St, Columbia, TN 38401

BOWLIN, Howard B (ETenn) PO Box 6259, Maryville, TN 37802

BOWMAN, Andrea C (Spok) 104 E 17th Ave, Ellensburg, WA 98926

BOWMAN, Lani Louise (The Episcopal Church in Haw)

BOWMAN, Sallie W (Ore) Department Of Spiritual Care, 1015 NW 22nd Ave, Portland, OR 97210

BOWMAN, susan (Alb) 16 Mansion Blvd, Apt B, Delmar, NY 12054

BOWRON, Josh (At) 1623 Carmel Rd, Charlotte, NC 28226

BOWYER, Charles Lester (NwT) 5806 Emory St, Lubbock, TX 79416

BOYCE, Ryan Antonio (NJ) 1709 Arctic Ave, Atlantic City, NJ 08401

BOYD, Catherine Tyndall (SVa) 1333 Jamestown Rd, Williamsburg, VA 23185

BOYD, David (Tex) 104 Cove Point Ln, Williamsburg, VA 23185

BOYD, James Richard (WTenn) 6367 Shadowood Ln, Memphis, TN 38119

BOYD, Jeffrey Howard (Mass) 57 Bethany Woods Rd, Bethany, CT 06524

BOYD JR, John Alexander (La)

BOYD, Julia Woolfolk (NC) Po Box 6124, Charlotte, NC 28207

BOYD, Justin Andrew (Okla) 5666 E 81st St, Tulsa, OK 74137

BOYD, Karen Pisarz (NwT) 602 Meander St, Abilene, TX 79602

BOYD, Larry (Neb) 2325 S 24th St, Lincoln, NE 68502

BOYD, Linda Koerber (Md)

BOYD, Sally Ann (Wyo) 436 Sundance Circle, Wright, WY 82732

BOYD, Samuel L (Tex) Po Box 1884, Chandler, TX 75758

BOYD, Sandra Hughes (Colo) 8251 E Phillips Pl, Englewood, CO 80112

BOYD, Virginia Ann (Md) 10901 Farrier Rd, Frederick, MD 21701

BOYD, William Marvin (Fla) 338 River Rd, Carrabelle, FL 32322

BOYD-ELLIS, Sue (WNY) 1439 Schoellkopf Rd, Lake View, NY 14085

BOYDEN-EDMONDS, Marjorie Jennifer (LI) 10017 32nd Ave, East Elmhurst, NY 11369

BOYER JR, Ernest l (ECR) PO Box 360832, Milpitas, CA 95036

BOYER, Geoffrey Thomas (Mich) 2600 Milscott Dr Apt 1335, Decatur, GA 30033

BOYER, John Paul (WNY) 3885 Teachers Ln Apt 8, Orchard Park, NY 14127

BOYER, Marcia M (Vt) Po Box 494, Woodstock, VT 05091

BOYER, William James (CFla) 126 E Palmetto Ave, Howey in the Hills, FL 34737

BOYLAN, Russell Brooks (WLa)

BOYLE, Patton Lindsay (Spok) 1342 Bartlett Ave, Wenatchee, WA 98801

BOYLE, Peter (Nwk) 185 Newman St, Metuchen, NJ 08840

BOYLES, David Joseph (Fla) St Mary's Episcopal Church, PO Box 611, Madison, FL 32341

BOYNTON, Caroline Cochran (NY)

BOYTE, James Garrett Asa (WLa) 335 Tennessee Ave, Sewanee, TN 37383

BOZARTH, Alla Renée (Minn) 43222 SE Tapp Rd, Sandy, OR 97055

BOZZUTI-JONES, Mark Francisco (NY) 74 Trinity Place, New York, NY 10006

BRACKETT, Thomas L (WNC) 13 Kent Pl, Asheville, NC 28804

BRADA, Netha Nadine (Ia) 345 Lincoln Ave, Iowa Falls, IA 50126

BRADBURY, Bill (Mass) 133 School Street, New Bedford, MA 02740

BRADBURY, John Saferian (Ind)

BRADBURY, Stephanie (Mass) 390 Main St, North Andover, MA 01845

BRADEN, Anita (Mil) PO Box 2938, Tappahannock, VA 22560

BRADEN, Lawrence Frank (Ark)

BRADFORD, Kathleen Diane Ross (Cal) 1713 Daisy Way, Antioch, CA 94509

BRADFORD, Larry (Colo) 4131 E 26th Ave, Denver, CO 80207

BRADFORD, Lewis Gabriel (Md) 2900 E Fayette St, Baltimore, MD 21224

BRADLEY, Amy Smith (Ga)

BRADLEY, Carolyn Ann (NJ) 503 Asbury Ave, Asbury Park, NJ 07712

BRADLEY, Charles Eldwyn (Okla)

BRADLEY, Gary J (Los) Immanuel Mission, 4366 Santa Anita Ave., El Monte, CA 91731

BRADLEY, James (Ct) 95 Cornwall Ave, Cheshire, CT 06410

BRADLEY, Martha Jean (Spr) 3621 Troon DR, Springfield, IL 62712

BRADLEY, Matthew Bryant (Ky) St. John's Episcopal Church, 1620 Main St, Murray, KY 42071

BRADLEY, Michael Lee (NH) 15 Park Court, Durham, NH 03824

BRADLEY, Patrick John (WNY) 505 Riverdale Ave, Lewiston, NY 14092

BRADLEY, Peg (Los) 619 W Roses Rd, San Gabriel, CA 91775

BRADLEY, Raymond Earle (Ind) 15914 Blush Drive, Fishers, IN 46037

BRADNER, Lawrence Hitchcock (RI) 500 Angell St Apt 504, Providence, RI 02906

BRADSEN, Kate (Colo)

BRADSHAW, Charles Robbins (Me) 54 Thorsen Rd, Hancock, ME 04640

BRADSHAW, Katie Ann (Miss)

BRADSHAW, Mark D (Los) PO Box 93096, Pasadena, CA 91109

BRADSHAW, Michael Ray (NC) St Paul's Episcopal Church, 520 Summit St, Winston Salem, NC 27101

BRADSHAW, Paul Frederick (NI) University of Notre Dame, 1 Suffolk Street, London, SW1Y 4HG, Great Britain (UK)

BRADTMILLER, Katharine (Minn)

BRADY, Amanda B Mandy (At) 1501 Ridge Ave., Evanston, IL 60201

BRADY, Christian Mark (Tenn) 18 Hampton Ct, State College, PA 16803

BRADY, Susan Jane (Colo) 3250 Lee Hill Dr., Boulder, CO 80302

BRADY II, William Donald (CFla) 10780 W Yulee Dr Unit 198, Homosassa, FL 34487

BRADY-CLOSE, Jane (NJ)

BRAINARD, Cheryl Elaine (EC) 25 S 3rd St, Wilmington, NC 28401

BRAINARD, Mary-Lloyd (Ct) 3A Gold St, Stonington, CT 06378

BRAINE, Beverly Barfield (Md) 1314 Second Avenue, Tybee Island, GA 31328

BRAKE, Mary Wood (Va)

BRAKEMAN, Lyn G (Mass) 203 Pemberton St Unit #, Cambridge, MA 02140

BRALL, Cathy (Pgh) 321 Parkside Ave, Pittsburgh, PA 15228

BRAMBILA, Gerardo Brambila (Az) 483 W. 80Th. Avenue, Denver, CO 80221

BRAMBLE, Peter Wilkin Duke (LI) 1417 Union St, Brooklyn, NY 11213

BRAMBLE, Sandra Russline (WA)

BRAMLETT, Bob (Mil) 419 E Court St, Janesville, WI 53545

BRAMLETT, Bruce (ECR) 6028 El Dorado Street, El Cerrito, CA 94530

BRANCH, Caroline E (At) 2089 Ponce De Leon Ave NE, Atlanta, GA 30307

BRANCHE, Ronald Clifford (VI) PO Box 28, Main Street, Tortola, British Virgin Islands

BRANDENBURG, Nancy Lee Hamman (SO) Saint John'S Church, Worthington, OH 43085

BRANDON, Bonnie P (Los) 1874 W Nutwood Pl, Anaheim, CA 92804

BRANDON, Karen Dale (RG) 226 Jupiter Dr, White Sands Missile Range, NM 88002

BRANDON II, Miles (Tex) 1501 W 30th St, Austin, TX 78703

BRANDT JR, George Walter (NY) 16 Park Ave, Apt 9C, New York, NY 10016

BRANDT, Robert G (LI) 414 SW Horseshoe Bay, Port Saint Lucie, FL 34986

BRANNOCK, Chris (Lex) PO Box 27, Paris, KY 40362

BRANNOCK-WANTER JR, Henry Paul (Vt) 257 Us Route 5, Hartland, VT 05048

BRANNON, Kenneth Hoffman (Ida) St. Thomas Episcopal Church, PO Box 1070, Sun Valley, ID 83353

BRANNON, Lecia Elaine (ECR)

BRANNON, Stephen Nave (The Episcopal NCal) 19275 Robinson Rd, Sonoma, CA 95476

BRANSCOMBE, Mike (SwFla) 1010 Charles St, Clearwater, FL 33755

BRANSON, Jana Mauck (The Episcopal NCal) 124 Orange St, Auburn, CA 95603

BRANSON, John (Ct) 827 Fearrington Post, Pittsboro, NC 27312

BRANSTETTER, Kent A (SanD) St Dunstans Episcopal Church, 6556 Park Ridge Blvd, San Diego, CA 92120

BRANT, George Henry (Nwk) 601 Park St Apt 11-D, Bordentown, NJ 08505

BRANTINGHAM, Nancy Marie (Minn) 3185 County Road 6, Long Lake, MN 55356

BRASWELL, James H (Fla)

BRATHWAITE, Christopher Ethelbert (CFla) 102 North 9Th Street, Haines City, FL 33844

BRAUN, James Richard (Mil) 5900 7th Avenue, Kenosha, WI 53140

BRAUNSCHNEIDER, Karl Nicholas (CFla) 202 Pontotoc St, Auburndale, FL 33823

BRAUZA, Ellen Lederer (WNY) 4210 Gunnville Road, Clarence, NY 14031

BRAWLEY, Anna (Ala) 1900 Darby Drive, Florence, AL 35630

BRAWLEY, Joan Biddles Kirby (CFla) 631 W Lake Elbert Dr, Winter Haven, FL 33881

BRAXTON JR, Louis (Nwk) 480 Warwick Ave, Teaneck, NJ 07666

BRAY, Doris S (Be) 443 Franklin Ave, Palmerton, PA 18071

BRDLIK, Chris (Nwk) 914 Ridge Rd, Newton, NJ 07860

BREAKEY, Pamela Jean (WMich) 54581 California Rd, Dowagiac, MI 49047

BRECHT, Laura Berger (SanD) 3425 Santa Saba Rd, Borrego Springs, CA 92004

BRECKENRIDGE, Allen (Az) 2721 N Dos Hombres Rd, Tucson, AZ 85715

BRECKENRIDGE, Elaine (Episcopal SJ) 2927 Sweetwood Dr, Lodi, CA 95242

BRECKENRIDGE, Ella Huff (WLa) 1825 Albert Street, Alexandria, LA 71301

BRECKINRIDGE IV, Alexander Negus (Oly) 8398 NE 12th St, Medina, WA 98039

BREDLAU, Mary Theresa (Nev) 8520 W Hammer Ln, Las Vegas, NV 89149

BREEDEN, James Pleasant (Mass) 29 Rope Ferry Rd # 3755, Hanover, NH 03755

BREEDLOVE, William L (WNC) Church Of The Good Shepherd, PO Box 677, Hayesville, NC 28904

BREEDLOVE II, William Otis (NJ) 10 Winthrop Road, Somerset, NJ 08873

BREESE, Mary Schrom (WMo) 606 Woodcrest Dr, Saint Joseph, MO 64506

BREESE, Sidney Samuel (WMo) 2533 Francis St, Saint Joseph, MO 64501

BREHE, Steve (Mont) 912 Stuart St., Helena, MT 59601

✠ **BREIDENTHAL**, Thomas Edward (SO) Diocese Of Southern Ohio, 412 Sycamore St, Cincinnati, OH 45202

BREINER, Bert Fredrick (NY) 401 W 24th St, New York, NY 10011

BRELSFORD, Diane Bowyer (Oly) 507 5th Ave W, Seattle, WA 98119

BRENEMEN, Betty Jo (CGC) 18 West Wright Street Street, Pensacola, FL 32501

BRENES VARGAS, Luis Gustavo (Hond) Iglesia Episcopal Custo Redentor, Apartado Postal 15029 Col. Kennedy, Tegucigalpa, 11101, Honduras

BRENMARK-FRENCH, Regina Kay (Chi) 2105 Cumberland St, Rockford, IL 61103

BRENNEIS, Michael Joseph (Va) 2309 N Kentucky St, Arlington, VA 22205

BRENNOM, Kesha Mai (Los) 4366 Santa Anita Ave., El Monte, CA 91731

BRENTLEY, David J (SO) 804 Clearfield Ln, Cincinnati, OH 45240

BRENTNALL, Burden (Oly) 9086 Chickadee Way, Blaine, WA 98230

BRENY, Judith Mary (WNY) 745 Ashland Ave, Buffalo, NY 14222

BRERETON, Thomas Frederick (Colo) 2741 Freedom Heights, Colorado Springs, CO 80904

BRESCIANI, Eduardo Roberto (Los) 9037 Park St, Bellflower, CA 90706

BRESNAHAN, Paul B (Mass) 17 King Street, Unit 1, Lynn, MA 01902

BRETSCHER, Robert George (SwFla) 240 Hancock Ln, Athens, GA 30605

BRETTMANN, William Sims (EC) 557 Fearnington Post, Pittsboro, NC 27312

BREUER, David R (ECR) 20 University Ave, Los Gatos, CA 95030

BREWER, Aaron Keith (Ga) PO Box 273, Hawkinsville, GA 31036

BREWER, Anne (NY) 1275 Summer St, Stamford, CT 06905

✠ **BREWER**, Gregory Orrin (CFla) 1017 East Robinson St, Orlando, FL 32801

BREWER, Johnny Lyvon (CGC) 7810 Navarre Pkwy, Navarre, FL 32566

BREWER JR, Luther Gordon (ETenn) 1417 Warpath Dr Ste B, Kingsport, TN 37664

BREWER, Richard Elliott (Okla) 6606 E 99th Pl, Tulsa, OK 74133

BREWER III, Richard Frederick (LI) Prestwick Farm, 2260 County Route 12, Whitehall, NY 12887

BREWER, Todd H (Pgh) 4048 Brownsville Rd, Pittsburgh, PA 15227

BREWIN-WILSON, Debbie (Nwk) St Mary's Church, 85 Conestoga Trl, Sparta, NJ 07871

BREWSTER, John Pierce (At) 1064 Can Tex Dr, Sewanee, TN 37375

BREWSTER JR, William (O) 7 Bond Rd, Kittery Point, ME 03905

BREWSTER-JENKINS, Regina (La) 6249 Canal Blvd, New Orleans, LA 70124

BREYER, Chloe Anne (NY) 1800 Adam Clayton Powell Blvd., Apartment 7B, New York, NY 10026

BREYFOGLE, Elizabeth Elain (Dal) 511 Foote St., McKinney, TX 75069

BREZNAU, Nancy Ann (EMich) PO Box 1882, Caseville, MI 48725

BRICE, Jonathan Andrew William (Colo) Christ Episcopal Church, 536 W North St, Aspen, CO 81611

BRICE, Theresa (At) 302 West Avenue, Cedartown, GA 30125

BRICKSON, Cynthia Jean (Minn) 905 4th Ave S, Minneapolis, MN 55404

BRIDGE, Melvin Alden (FtW) 729 Carette Dr, Fort Worth, TX 76108

BRIDGE, Michael James (WK)

BRIDGE, Peter (NJ) 1509 Esther Ln, Yardley, PA 19067

BRIDGEMOHAN, Areeta D (Mich)

BRIDGERS, Anne (SanD) 1114 9th St, Coronado, CA 92118

BRIDGES, Christopher Mark (The Episcopal Church in Haw) 5286 Kalanianaole Hwy, Honolulu, HI 96821

BRIDGES, David Leslie (Okla)

BRIDGES, Melva Gayle (Okla) 12719 S Couts Dr, Mustang, OK 73064

BRIDGES, Nancy Kilbourn (Okla) 408 Ridge Rd, Edmond, OK 73034

BRIDGES, Penelope Maud (SanD) 6935 Camino Pacheco, San Diego, CA 92111

Clergy List

BRIDGFORD, Peter W (WNY) 18 Harbour Pointe Cmn, Buffalo, NY 14202

BRIDGFORD, Richard Oliver (SVa) 707 Steiner Way, Norfolk, VA 23502

BRIGGLE, Justin David (Tex) 311 Glenwood Dr, Palestine, TX 75801

BRIGGS, Barbara (NJ) 306 S Main St, Pennington, NJ 08534

BRIGGS, Lyn (U) 661 Redondo Ave, Salt Lake City, UT 84105

BRIGGS, Michael (Ark) PO Box 954, Granby, CO 80446

BRIGGS II, Paul R (Ct) 306 S Main St, Pennington, NJ 08534

BRIGHAM, Richard Daniel (At) 208 Edgewater Way, Peachtree City, GA 30269

BRIGHT, Barbara Pamela (WNC) Episcopal Church of the Redeemer, 502 W Sumter St, Shelby, NC 28150

BRIGHT, Carl Connell (CGC) 198 Beardsley Court, Muscle Shoals, AL 35661

BRIGHT SR, Dee (CFla) 511 South Cabin Lake Drive, San Antonio, TX 78244

BRIGHT, John Adams (Cal) 812 Southwest Saint Clair Ave. Apt 1, Portland, OR 97209

BRIGHT, Pamela (Wyo)

BRIGHT, Patrick Edmund (Okla) 11901 Maple Hollow Ct, Oklahoma City, OK 73120

BRIGHT, Wheigar J (NC) PO Box 858, Yanceyville, NC 27379

BRIGHTMAN, Dorothy Louise (RI) 17 N Country Club Dr, Warwick, RI 02888

BRILL, Steven G (Oly) St Luke's Episcopal Church, PO Box 1294, Elma, WA 98541

BRIMM, Martha Carol (NC) 7 Surrey Ln, Durham, NC 27707

BRINDLEY, Thomas (Cal) 704 Sutro Ave, Novato, CA 94947

BRINKMAN, Charles Reed (Pa) 219 Hanover Rd, Phoenixville, PA 19460

BRINKMANN, Mark (SC) All Saints Episcopal Church, 3001 Meeting St, Hilton Head Island, SC 29926

BRINKMOELLER, Leonard Joseph (WMich) 312 Maple Street, Paw Paw, MI 49079

BRINSON, Katherine Herrington (Ga) 4227 Columbia Rd, Martinez Branch, GA 30907

BRION, Theresa Markley (Va) 5726 Colfax Ave, Alexandria, VA 22311

BRIONES, Miguel Angel (Chi) 5101 W Devon Ave, Chicago, IL 60646

BRISBANE, Paul Owen (Colo) 513 N. Union City Rd., Coldwater, MI 49036

BRISBIN, James A (Alb) 2647 Brookview Rd., Castleton, NY 12033

BRISON, William Stanly (Ct) 2 Scott Ave, Bury, BL9 9RS, Great Britain (UK)

BRISSON JR, James L (Az) 868 Satinwood Ct, Fayetteville, NC 28312

BRISTOL II, Henry Platt (NJ) St David's Church, 90 S Main St, Cranbury, NJ 08512

BRISTOL, Joan Esther (Ore) 2529 Bel Abbes Ave, Medford, OR 97504

BRITCHER, Sharon Ann (CFla) 1010 Pennsylvania Ave, Fort Pierce, FL 34950

BRITNELL, Offie Wayne (Ak) 18609 S. Lowrie Loop, Eagle River, AK 99577

BRITO, Antonio P (At) 1015 Old Roswell Rd, Roswell, GA 30076

BRITO, Napoleon Ramon (DomRep)) Box 764, Santo Domingo, Dominican Republic

BRITT, Diane (LI) St Ann's Church, 257 Middle Rd, Sayville, NY 11782

BRITT, Larry (WNC) 236 Camelot Dr, Morganton, NC 28655

BRITT, Marc Lawrence (WA) 2 Amy Ct, Pittsfield, MA 01201

BRITT, Sarah Eugenia Swiss (At) 253 Lake Somerset Dr Nw, Marietta, GA 30064

BRITT, Stephen (Fla) San Jose Episcopal, 7423 San Jose Blvd., Jacksonville, FL 32217

BRITTON, John Clay (Chi) 680 Madrona Ave S, Salem, OR 97302

BRITTON, Joseph Harp (RG) St. Michael and All Angels Church, 601 Montano Road, NW, Albuquerque, NM 87107

BRITTON SR, Judith Ann (NMich) 365 Kirkpatrick Ln, Gwinn, MI 49841

BRITTON JR, Richard (Tenn) 509 Laurel Park Dr, Nashville, TN 37205

BRO, Andrew Harmon (Chi) Po Box 111, Mount Carroll, IL 61053

BROAD, Thomas Michael (WNY) 19 N Washington St, Randolph, NY 14772

BROADBENT, Anna Lynn (Va) 65 E Huron St, Chicago, IL 60611

BROADFOOT III, Walter Marion (EC) 200 S. McMorrine Street, Elizabeth City, NC 27909

BROADHEAD, Alan John (ND) 107 Heartwood Drive, Lansdale, PA 19446

BROADLEY, Rodger Charles (Pa) 336 S Camac St, Philadelphia, PA 19107

BROCATO, Christian (WMich) St. Peter's Episcopal Church, 838 Mass Ave., Cambridge, MA 02139

BROCHARD, Philip Thomas (Cal) 2729 Kinney Dr, Walnut Creek, CA 94595

BROCK, Charles F. (Va) St. James' Episcopal Church, Alexandria, VA 22309

BROCK, Laurie M (Lex) 2025 Bellefont Dr, Lexington, KY 40503

BROCK, Scott (USC) 230 Pinecrest Dr Apt 25, Fayetteville, NC 28305

BROCKENBROUGH, Sarah (Va) PO Box 3520, Williamsburg, VA 23187

BROCKMAN, Bennett Albert (Ct) 362 Lake St, Vernon, CT 06066

BROCKMAN, John Martin (Ind) 82 E. Colony Acres Dr., Brazil, IN 47834

BROCKMANN, Robert (Mass) 78 Mann Hill Rd, Scituate, MA 02066

BROCKMANN, Sarah (Mass) 78 Mann Hill Road, Scituate, MA 02066

BROCKMEIER, Alan Lee (RG) 8516 N Prince St, Clovis, NM 88101

BROCKMEIER, Suzanne Carroll (RG) St James Episcopal Church, PO Box 249, Clovis, NM 88102

BRODERICK, Janet (Nwk) 268 2nd St, Jersey City, NJ 07302

BRODERICK, Rosemarie (NJ) P.O. Box 326, Navesink, NJ 07752

BRODERICK Y GUERRA, Cecily (LI) 3495 Hawthorne Dr N, Wantagh, NY 11793

BRODIE, Robert (SwVa) 1612 Valhalla Ct, Salem, VA 24153

BRODY, Mary Ann (Roch) 190 Penarrow Rd., Rochester, NY 14618

BROEREN, Erik Stephanus Simon (ETenn)

BROGAN, Betty Jean (Mich) 17665 E Kirkwood Dr, Clinton Township, MI 48038

BROGAN, Margaret C (Cal) 1432 Eastshore Dr, Alameda, CA 94501

BROKAW, Ronald Gene (CFla) 1106 Dorchester St, Orlando, FL 32803

BROKENLEG, Isaiah Elias (SD) PO Box 936, Minocqua, WI 54548

BROME, Henderson LeVere (Mass) 1201 Davenport Ave, Canton, MA 02021

BROMILEY, Hugh Philip (CFla) 1250 Paige Pl, The Villages, FL 32159

BRONDSTED, Linda J (Eur) 1880 Taylor Ave, Winter Park, FL 32789

BRONOS, Sarah L (CFla) 7718 White Ash Street, Orlando, FL 32819

BRONSON, David Louis (NY) 414 Cottekill Rd, Stone Ridge, NY 12484

BROOK, Robert Charles (Mich) 6112 W Longview Dr, East Lansing, MI 48823

✠ **BROOKE-DAVIDSON**, Jennifer (WTex) 6000 Fm 3237 Unit A, Wimberley, TX 78676

✠ **BROOKHART JR**, Frank (Mont) PO Box 2020, Helena, MT 59624

BROOKMAN, Cathleen Anne (Chi) 29 West 410 Emerald Green Drive, Warrenville, IL 60555

BROOKS, Albert (Hond) Aptd 28, La Ceiba Atlantida, 31101, Honduras

BROOKS, Ashton Jacinto (VI) C/O Cathedral Church of the Epiphany, P O BOX 764, Santo Domingo, Dominican Republic

BROOKS, Donald Edgar (WTenn) 1436 Forest Drive, Union City, TN 38261

BROOKS, Dub (Tex) 1718 Wentworth St, Houston, TX 77004

BROOKS, James Buckingham (Ida) Po Box 36, Letha, ID 83636

BROOKS, Rebecca Rae (Ky)

BROOKS, Reverend Kimberly Brooks (CPa) 248 Seneca St, Harrisburg, PA 17110

BROOKS, Richard Smith (WK) 1333 Crescent Ln, Concordia, KS 66901

BROOKS JR, Robert Brudon (NY) 4 Quail Ridge Rd, Hyde Park, NY 12538

BROOKS, Robert Johnson (Ct) 140 Christopher Cv, Kyle, TX 78640

BROOKS, Robert Thomas (RI) 285 W Main Rd, Little Compton, RI 02837

BROOKS, Teddy (NY) 750 Kelly St, Bronx, NY 10455

BROOKS, Thomas Gerald (NY) 35 Cambridge Ct, Highland, NY 12528

BROOKS, Weldon Timothy (NH) 113 Main St, Lancaster, NH 03584

BROOKS, Zachary D (Spr) 359 W State St, Jacksonville, IL 62650

BROOME JR, William Bridges (Chi) 504 E Earle Street, Landrum, SC 29356

BROOMELL, Ann Johnson (Ct) 28 Long Hill Farm, Guilford, CT 06437

BROSEND II, William Frank (Ky) 335 Tennessee Ave., Sewanee, TN 37383

BROTHERTON, E Ann (Tex) 12101 Bluebonnet Ln, Manchaca, TX 78652

BROUCHT, Mary Louise (CPa) 126 N. Water St., Lancaster, PA 17603

BROUGHTON, Jacalyn Irene (Eau) E4357 451st Ave, Menomonie, WI 54751

BROUGHTON, William (SanD) 1830 Avenida Del Mundo, Unit 712, Coronado, CA 92118

BROWDER, David O'Neal (Tex) St Dunstan's Episcopal Church, 14301 Stuebner Airline Rd, Houston, TX 77069

BROWDER III, James Wilbur (SVa) Po Box 133, Courtland, VA 23837

BROWER, David (WMich) 7895 Adams St, Zeeland, MI 49464

BROWER, Gary (Colo) 2050 E Evans Ave Ste 29, Denver, CO 80208

BROWER, George C (Ct) 503A Heritage Village, Southbury, CT 06488

BROWER, Katherine Moore (WMich) 335 Bridge St NW Apt 2301, Grand Rapids, MI 49504

BROWER, Meaghan M (RI) Episcopal Diocese of Rhode Island, 275 N Main St, Providence, RI 02903

BROWER, Sally (NC) 164 Fairview Rd, Mooresville, NC 28117

BROWN, Aston George (Tex)

BROWN, Barton (NJ)

BROWN, Becky (Colo) 6820 W 84th Cir Unit 26, Arvada, CO 80003

BROWN, Bernard Owen (Chi) 5417 S Blackstone Ave, Chicago, IL 60615

BROWN JR, Bill (Ida) 5605 Lynwood Pl., Boise, ID 83706

BROWN, Charles Homer (Okla) 1416 Stoneridge Pl, Ardmore, OK 73401

BROWN, Christopher Aubrey (Alb) 437 Old Potsdam Parishville Road, Potsdam, NY 13676

BROWN, Claire (ETenn) 305 W 7th St, Chattanooga, TN 37402

BROWN, Cliff (Mass) 351 Pearl St # 1, Cambridge, MA 02139

BROWN, Colin (Los) 1024 Beverly Way, Altadena, CA 91001

BROWN, Craig Howard (WK) 3710 Summer Ln, Hays, KS 67601

BROWN, Daniel Aaron (NC) 936 Cannock St, Grovetown, GA 30813

BROWN, Daniel Barnes (At) Po Box 490, Clarkesville, GA 30523

BROWN, David Crane (NY) 125 Prospect Ave Apt 9G, Hackensack, NJ 07601

BROWN, David Wooster (Ct) 729 W Beach Rd, Charlestown, RI 02813

BROWN, Debbie (Minn) 1297 Wilderness Curv, Eagan, MN 55123

BROWN, Deborah (Ore) Diocese of Oregon, 11800 SW Military Ln, Portland, OR 97219

BROWN, Deborah Bennett (SwFla)

BROWN, Dennis Roy Alfred (CGC) 306 Grant St, Chickasaw, AL 36611

BROWN JR, Dewey (SwFla) 37637 Magnolia Ave, Dade City, FL 33523

BROWN, Don (La) 224 Pecan Ave, New Roads, LA 70760

BROWN, Donald Gary (Cal) 2821 Claremont Blvd, Berkeley, CA 94705

BROWN, Donn H (At) 217 Booth St Apt 119, Gaithersburg, MD 20878

BROWN, Donna Hvistendahl (WA) 1318 Charlottesville Blvd, Knoxville, TN 37922

BROWN, Dorothy (At) 1197 Skyline Drive, Toccoa, GA 30577

BROWN, Dwight (Va) 489 Ridge Rd, Moscow, ID 83843

BROWN, Elly Sparks (WA) 5006-B Barbour Dr, Alexandria, VA 22304

BROWN, Enrique (WA) 5248 Colorado Ave Nw, Washington, DC 20011

BROWN JR, F Wilson (SwVa) 715 Sunset Drive, Bedford, VA 24523

BROWN, Freda Marie (Tex) St. Vincent's Episcopal House, 2817 Alfreda Houston Place, Galveston, TX 77550

BROWN, Frederick Ransom (Vt) 346 Gladys Avenue, Long Beach, CA 90814

BROWN, Gary N (The Episcopal NCal)

BROWN, Gaye (NC) 308 W Main St, Elkin, NC 28621

BROWN III, George W (Dal) 409 Prospect St, New Haven, CT 06511

BROWN, Greg (NC) 1020 E Mitchell St, Petoskey, MI 49770

BROWN, Greg (Los) St Cross Episcopal Church, 1818 Monterey Blvd, Hermosa Beach, CA 90254

BROWN III, Henry William (CFla) Po Box 1420, Homosassa Springs, FL 34447

BROWN JR, H (Horace) Frederick (WTex) 309 S Someday Dr, Boerne, TX 78006

BROWN III, Hugh Eldridge (NJ) 16 All Saints Rd, Princeton, NJ 08540

BROWN, Ian Frederick (Mich) 26 Tower Dr., Saline, MI 48176

✠ **BROWN**, James Barrow (La) 2136 Octavia St, New Orleans, LA 70115

BROWN, James Louis (O) 1533 N 85th Ct, Kansas City, KS 66112

BROWN, James Thompson (Cal) 6225 Vine Hill School Rd, Sebastopol, CA 95472

BROWN, Jan Michelle (SVa)

BROWN, Janet Easson (CPa) 140 N Beaver St, York, PA 17401

BROWN, Janet Kelly (Vt) Po Box 351, Jericho, VT 05465

BROWN, Jennifer (NY) 1558 Unionport Rd Apt 7E, Bronx, NY 10462

BROWN, Jennifer Clarke (NC) 2212 Tyson Street, Raleigh, NC 27612

BROWN JR, John Ashmore (USC) 9 Sweet Branch Ct, Columbia, SC 29212

BROWN, John Clive (Ore) 431-A Red Blanket Rd, Prospect, OR 97536

BROWN, John Daniel (Dal) 7610 Rockingham Rd, Prospect, KY 40059

BROWN, John Thompson (Ala) 4157 Winston Way, Birmingham, AL 35213

BROWN, Keith B (Episcopal SJ) 1776 S Homsy Ave, Fresno, CA 93727

BROWN, Ken (WA) 1318 Charlottesville Blvd, Knoxville, TN 37922

✠ **BROWN**, Kevin S (Del) 2106 N Grant Ave, Wilmington, DE 19806

BROWN, Kirk (WNC) 500 Christ School Rd, Arden, NC 28704

BROWN, Lawrence Mitchell (Los) 44550 Denmore Ave, Lancaster, CA 93535

BROWN, Lila Byrd (Fla) 2358 Riverside Ave. #704, Jacksonville, FL 32204

BROWN, Linda (Ark)

BROWN, Linda Josephine (Colo) 1700 W 10th Ave, Broomfield, CO 80020

BROWN, Lydia Huttar (Minn) 10 Buffalo Rd, North Oaks, MN 55127

BROWN, Lyle L (Ia) 605 Avenue E, Fort Madison, IA 52627

BROWN, Mac Macdonald (ETenn) Good Shepherd Episcopal Church, 211 Franklin Rd, Lookout Mountain, TN 37350

BROWN, Marilynn (Ore) 332338 109Th Pl SE Apt 102, Auburn, WA 98092

BROWN, Marion Mackey (SwFla) 208 Ne Monroe Cir N Apt 103-C, Saint Petersburg, FL 33702

BROWN, Mark (Mass) 980 Memorial Dr, Cambridge, MA 02138

BROWN, Mary K (Va) 228 Pitt St, Alexandria, VA 22314

BROWN, Nancy (Okla) 3914 E. 37th Street, Tulsa, OK 74135

BROWN, Nancy (Los) 2095 Stoneman St, Simi Valley, CA 93065

BROWN, Neva Wilkins (Md)

BROWN, Peter (Minn)

BROWN, Ralph Douglas (Ind) Po Box 1596, Old Fort, NC 28762

Clergy List

BROWN, Ray (EC) 205 Bedell Pl, Fayetteville, NC 28314

BROWN, Raymond Dutson (Mont) 6162 Lazy Man Gulch, Helena, MT 59601

BROWN, Reed Haller (Vt) 49 Brewer Pkwy, South Burlington, VT 05403

BROWN, Rob (USC) 531 Old Iron Works Rd, Spartanburg, SC 29302

BROWN, Robert Charles (Ark) 501 S Phoenix Ave, Russellville, AR 72801

BROWN, Robert Henry (Pa) 117 Pine Lake Dr, Whispering Pines, NC 28327

BROWN, Robert Labannah (Neb) 9302 Blondo St, Omaha, NE 68134

BROWN, Rodney K (Eas) 32659 Seaview Loop, Millsboro, DE 19966

BROWN, Rosa Maria (Az) 50 N Illinois St, Indianapolis, IN 46204

BROWN, Royce Walter (Wyo) Central Wyoming Hospice, 319 S Wilson, Casper, WY 82601

BROWN, Ruth Ellen (Az) 9071 E Old Spanish Trl, Tucson, AZ 85710

BROWN, Sally Sims (Colo) 85 Rampart Way Uniit 510, Denver, CO 80230

BROWN, Scott Jeffrey (WTex) 1417 E Austin Ave, Harlingen, TX 78550

BROWN, Sharman Jones (Mont)

BROWN, Spencer Wade (Okla)

BROWN, Thomas James (Mass) 70 Church St., Winchester, MA 01890

BROWN, Virginia Dabney (WMo) 874 Yorkchester, # 108, Houston, TX 77079

BROWN, Virginia Wood (Colo) 706 E. 3rd Avenue, Durango, CO 81301

BROWN JR, Walter R (Ark) 12415 Cantrell Rd, Little Rock, AR 72223

BROWN, Wendy Jo (EMich) 409 W Randolph St, Lansing, MI 48906

BROWN, William Garland (Lex) 311 Washington St, Frankfort, KY 40601

BROWN, Willis Donald (Ky) 2402 Glenview Ave, Louisville, KY 40222

BROWN III, Wm Hill (Va) 5103 Harlan Cir, Richmond, VA 23226

BROWN DOUGLAS, Kelly Delaine (WA) 12519 Hawks Nest Ln, Germantown, MD 20876

BROWNE, Bliss Williams (Chi) 7743 SE Loblolly Bay Dr, Hobe Sound, FL 33455

BROWNE, Frances Louise (NC) 303 Eastchester Dr, High Point, NC 27262

BROWNE, Gayle (SO) 212 Tulane Ave, Oak Ridge, TN 37830

BROWNE III, Joseph M (EC) 200 NC Highway 33 W, Chocowinity, NC 27817

BROWNE, Joy Elizabeth (Ky) 922 Milford Ln, Louisville, KY 40207

BROWNE, Marigold Sandreen (VI)

BROWNING JR, Bob (Nwk) Grace Church, 128 W Passaic Ave, Rutherford, NJ 07070

BROWNING II, Charles Alex (SeFla) 2707 NW 37th Street, Boca Raton, FL 33434

BROWNING, Peter (Los) 2 HIdalgo, Irvine, CA 92620

BROWNING JR, Robert Guy Shipton (SwFla) 7038 West Brandywine Circle, Fort Myers, FL 33919

BROWNING, Trace (U) All Saints Episcopal Church, 1710 S Foothill Dr, Salt Lake City, UT 84108

BROWNLEE, Annette Geoffrian (Colo) 410 W 18th St, Pueblo, CO 81003

BROWNMILLER, David Clark (Ore) 16379 Nw Charlais St, Beaverton, OR 97006

BROWN-NOLAN, Virginia (WA) 12613 Meadowood Dr, Silver Spring, MD 20904

BROWNRIDGE, Walter Bruce Augustine (Md) The Episcopal Diocese of Maryland, 4 East Parkway Ave., Baltimore, MD 21202

BROYLES, Elizabeth Ruth (NY) 37 Chipmunk Hollow Rd, Kerhonkson, NY 12446

BRUBAKER GARRISON, Tasha Vache (Ore) 418 Stonewood Dr, Eugene, OR 97405

BRUCE, David Allison (Me) Brigham'S Cove Road, Box 243 HCR 63, West Bath, ME 04530

✠ **BRUCE**, Diane Jardine (Los) 5 W Trenton, Irvine, CA 92620

BRUCE, Jane (NC) 750 Weaver Dairy Rd Apt 1225, Chapel Hill, NC 27514

BRUCE, Todd (The Episcopal NCal)

BRUCE, Tracy Ann (Md) 5814 19th St N, Arlington, VA 22205

BRUCKART, Robert Monroe (CFla) 2327 Saint Andrews Cir, Melbourne, FL 32901

BRUGGER, Stephanie Black (SO) 335 Lincoln Ave, Troy, OH 45373

BRUMBAUGH, Charlie (Colo) PO Box 2166, Breckenridge, CO 80424

BRUNDIGE, Allyson Paige (Nwk) 333 Christian St, Wallingford, CT 06492

BRUNEAU, Betsy (The Episcopal NCal) 66 E. Commercial St., Willits, CA 95490

BRUNELLE, Denis Charles (LI) PO Box 2733, East Hampton, NY 11937

BRUNETT, Harry (Md) 9855 S Iris Ct, Littleton, CO 80127

BRUNNER, Arthur Fischer (Pa) Po Box 1190, N Cape May, NJ 08204

BRUNO, James Ernest (Ark)

BRUNO, Jean M (DR (DomRep)) Box 1309, Port-Au-Prince, Haiti

✠ **BRUNO**, Joseph Jon (Los) 3505 Grayburn Rd., Pasadena, CA 91107

BRUNO, Suzanne Lee (NC) 9528 Spurwig Ct, Charlotte, NC 28278

BRUNS, Thomas Charles (Mo) 222 Montwood, Seguin, TX 78155

BRUNSON, Catherine E (NJ) 124 Harrow Dr, Somerset, NJ 08873

BRUSCO, Kathleen Kyle (Minn) 112 Crestridge Dr, Burnsville, MN 55337

BRUSSO, Leonard George (SeFla) 1225 Knollcrest Ct, Venice, FL 34285

BRUTTELL, Susan Margaret (SeFla) 706 Glenwood Ln, Plantation, FL 33317

BRUTTELL, Thomas Allen (SeFla) 706 Glenwood Ln, Plantation, FL 33317

BRUTUS, Joseph Mathieu (Hai) Box 1309, Port-Au-Prince, Haiti

BRYAN, Elizabeth (SD) 1521 Forest Dr, Rapid City, SD 57701

BRYAN, Joan C (Fla) PO Box 1584, Ponte Vedra Beach, FL 32004

BRYAN, Jonathan (Va) 7815 Midday Ln, Alexandria, VA 22306

BRYAN, Michael John Christopher (Tenn) The School of Theology, The University of the South, 335 Tennessee Ave, Sewanee, TN 37398

BRYAN, Nancy Henry (Cal) 2111 Hyde St # 404, San Francisco, CA 94109

BRYAN, Peggy L (ECR) 5038 Hyland Ave, San Jose, CA 95127

BRYAN, Walter Lee (WNC) PO Box 1356, Columbus, NC 28722

BRYANT, Bronson Howell (Miss) 5408 Vinings Lake View, SW, Mableton, GA 30126

BRYANT, Julie Diane (Los) Church of the Transfiguration, 1881 South First Avenue, Arcadia, CA 91006

BRYANT, Katherine Seavey (Va) 14 Cornwall St NW, Leesburg, VA 20176

BRYANT, Laura Annette (At) 2456 Tanglewood Rd, Decatur, GA 30033

BRYANT, Peter F (Roch) 4160 Back River Rd, Scio, NY 14880

BRYANT, Richard Gordon (Md) 678 Dave Ct, Covington, KY 41015

BRYANT, Robert (Ore) 6300 Sw Nicol Rd, Portland, OR 97223

BRYANT, Todd (Cal) 5826 Doliver Dr, Houston, TX 77057

BRYANT, William Reid (WLa) 715 Lewisville Rd, Minden, LA 71055

BRYCE, Christopher David Francis (USC) 819 Angela Ln, Cross, SC 29436

BRYSON, Nancy Gretchen (CFla)

BRZEZINSKI, James (Chi) 401 N Cherry St, Morrison, IL 61270

BUB, Sally Letchworth (Wyo) 30 Diversion Dam Rd, Kinnear, WY 82516

BUCCHERI, Matthew Paul (NY) 14 E 109th St, New York, NY 10029

BUCCO, Dennis M (RI) 58 Arrowhead Ln, West Greenwich, RI 02817

BUCHAN III, Thomas Nicholson (CFla) 1716 River Lakes Rd N, Oconomowoc, WI 53066

BUCHANAN, Andrew (SVa) 3928 Pacific Ave, Virginia Beach, VA 23451

BUCHANAN, Ernest Ray (WTex) PO Box 68, Hebbronville, TX 78361

BUCHANAN, Furman Lee (USC) 910 Hudson Road, Greenville, SC 29615

BUCHANAN, H Ray (SwFla) 9650 Gladiolus Dr, Fort Myers, FL 33908

✠ **BUCHANAN**, John Clark (WMo) 1Bishop Gadsden Way Apt 332, Charleston, SC 29412

BUCHANAN, Margaret Grace (WNC) 827 Montreat Rd, Black Mountain, NC 28711

BUCHANAN, Susan Jill (WNC) 806 College Ave Sw, Lenoir, NC 28645

BUCHHOLZ, Paige (ETenn) 1211 Oakdale Trl, Knoxville, TN 37914

BUCHIN, Daniel Arthur (Mich) 2260 Baltic Ave, Idaho Falls, ID 83404

BUCK, David E (NC) 616 Watson St., Davidson, NC 28036

BUCK, Elizabeth Salmon (EC) 744 Lakeside Dr Se, Bolivia, NC 28422

BUCK, Leonard Frank (HB)

BUCK, Martha (ECR) 651 Sinex Ave Apt L115, Pacific Grove, CA 93950

BUCK, Robert Allen (Colo) 3070 Indiana St, Golden, CO 80401

BUCK-GLENN, Judith (Pa) 1031 N Lawrence St, Philadelphia, PA 19123

BUCKINGHAM, Carole Sylmay (Wyo) PO Box 12, Kaycee, WY 82639

BUCKINGHAM, Karen Burnquist (Wyo) 608 6th St, Rawlins, WY 82301

BUCKLEY, Abigail J (Ore) St Barnabas Episcopal Church, 822 SW 2nd St, Mcminnville, OR 97128

BUCKLEY, Terrence Patrick (LI) 64 S Country Rd, Bellport, NY 11713

BUCKLIN, Lydia K (Ia) 225 37th St, Des Moines, IA 50312

BUCKWALTER, Georgine (Ky) 2511 Cottonwood Dr, Louisville, KY 40242

BUDD, Dorothy Reid (Dal) 3707 Crescent Ave, Dallas, TX 75205

BUDD, Richard Wade (SVa) 120 Cypress Crk, Williamsburg, VA 23188

✠ **BUDDE**, Mariann (WA) Diocese of Washington, Episcopal Church House-Mount St Alban, Washington, DC 20016

BUDEZ, Jorge Horacio (WNY)

BUDHU, Esar (Nwk) 206 Renshaw Ave, East Orange, NJ 07017

BUDNEY, Karen Vickers (CNY) 18 Cross St., Dover, MA 02030

BUECHELE, Thomas John (The Episcopal Church in Haw) 15-2686 Hinalea St, Pahoa, HI 96778

BUECHNER, Deborah Ann (CFla) 1078 Coastal Cir, Ocoee, FL 34761

BUECHNER, Frederick Alvin (Ga) Po Box 2626, Thomasville, GA 31799

BUEHLER, Lynnsay Anne (At) 147 Shadowmoor Dr, Decatur, GA 30030

BUEHRENS, Gwen Langdoc (Mass) 1333 Gough St. Apt 1-D, San Francisco, CA 94109

BUELL, Susan Davies (NwPa) 75 Perry St. 2A, New York City, NY 10014

BUELOW, Peggy Butterbaugh (SVa) 23397 Owen Farm Road, Carrollton, VA 23314

BUENO BUENO, Francisco Javier (Colom) Kra 80 #53a-78, Medellin, Colombia

BUENTING, Julianne (Chi) 3857 N Kostner Ave, Chicago, IL 60641

BUENZ JR, John Frederick (ECR) 22115 Dean Ct, Cupertino, CA 95014

BUFFONE, Gregory James (Tex)

BUHRER, Richard Albert (Oly) 2021 15th Ave S Apt 1, Seattle, WA 98144

BUICE, Bonnie Carl (At) 115 Maplewood Ave Sw, Milledgeville, GA 31061

BUICE, Samuel Walton (At) 3 Westridge Rd, Savannah, GA 31411

BUICE, William Ramsey (Hond) 10100 Hillview Dr #4A, Pensacola, FL 32514

BUIE, Delinda Stephens (Ky) 2341 Strathmoor Blvd, Louisville, KY 40205

BUISSON, Pierre-Henry Paul (Az) 375 Benfield Rd, Severna Park, MD 21146

BUKER, Karen Elaine (Mil) 3380 S Jeffers Dr, New Berlin, WI 53146

BULL, Julian (Los) 5049 Gloria Ave, Encino, CA 91436

BULL, Terry Wayne (WNY) 633 Harrison Ave, Buffalo, NY 14223

BULLARD, Carol Ann (Neb) 1603 17th St, Mitchell, NE 69357

BULLARD, Jill Staton (NC) 403 E Main St, Durham, NC 27701

BULLARD, Lynn Huston (Ala) 8020 Whitesburg Dr S, Huntsville, AL 35802

BULLER, Reverend Deacon Alberta Brown (Cal) P.O. Box 494, Fairfax, CA 94978

BULLION, James Regis (Ga) 512 Flamingo Ln., Albany, GA 31707

BULLITT-JONAS, Margaret (WMass) 83 Bancroft Rd, Northampton, MA 01060

BULLOCK, Ashley Michelle Workman (Pa)

BULLOCK, Debra K (Chi) St. Mark's Episcopal Church, 1509 Ridge Avenue, Evanston, IL 60201

BULLOCK, Jeff (Los) 3474 NW Bryce Canyon Ln, Bend, OR 97703

BULLOCK, Kenneth R (Pa) 213 Stable Rd, Carrboro, NC 27510

BULLOCK, Michael Anderson (WMass) 1040 Brentwood Dr, Columbia, SC 29206

BULSON, William Lawrence (Minn) 13000 Saint Davids Rd, Minnetonka, MN 55305

BUMGARNER, William Ray (SwVa) 605 Clay St, Lynchburg, VA 24504

BUMILLER, William Norton (SO) 320 Lonsdale Ave, Dayton, OH 45419

BUMP, Anne Glass (Mich) 1708 Jamestown Place, Pittsburgh, PA 15235

BUMSTED, David S (CFla) Church Of The Redeemer, 222 S Palm Ave, Sarasota, FL 34236

BUNCH, Linda Lauren (Cal) 600 Colorado Ave, Palo Alto, CA 94306

BUNCH, Wilton Herbert (Ala) Samford University, Birmingham, AL 35229

BUNDER, Peter J (Ind) 610 Meridian St, West Lafayette, IN 47906

BUNKE, Jeff L (O) 871 E Boundary St, Perrysburg, OH 43551

BUNKER, Oliver Franklin (Kan) Grace Episcopal Church, 209 S Lincoln Ave, Chanute, KS 66720

BUNKER, Robert Monroe (Md) 522 Main St, Laurel, MD 20707

BUNSY, Martin (Episcopal SJ) 1327 N Del Mar Ave, Fresno, CA 93728

BUNTING, Drew Andrew (Mil) 290 Quintard Rd # 19, Sewanee, TN 37375

BUNTING SR, Norman Richard (Eas) St Paul's Episcopal Church, 3 Church St, Berlin, MD 21811

BUNYAN, Frederick Satyanandam (Colo) 1749 Stove Prairie Cir, Loveland, CO 80538

BUOTE-GREIG, Eletha (Mass) Po Box 192, North Scituate, RI 02857

BUQUOR, Anthony Francis (SD) 1357 Old Marlboro Rd, Concord, MA 01742

BURACKER II, William Joseph (CFla)

BURBANK, Kristina Dawn (Ore)

BURCH, Charles Francis (Mil) 3254 Silver Arrow Cir, Lake Havasu City, AZ 86406

BURCH, Ian C (Mil) 1424 N Dearborn St, Chicago, IL 60610

BURCH, Suzanne (ETenn) 4111 Albemarle Ave, Chattanooga, TN 37411

BURCHARD, Russell Church (SwVa) 51 Mayapple Gln, Dawsonville, GA 30534

BURCHILL, George Stuart (SwFla) 2611 Bayshore Blvd, Tampa, FL 33629

BURDEKIN, Edwina Amelia (Colo) 4566 Winewood Village Dr, Colorado Springs, CO 80917

BURDEN, Richard James (Mass) 1789 Beacon St Unit 1, Brookline, MA 02445

BURDESHAW, Charles Abbott (Tenn) 139 Brighton Close, Nashville, TN 37205

BURDETT, Audrey Brown (At) 3223 Rilman Rd Nw, Atlanta, GA 30327

BURDETTE, Matthew E (Dal) 11122 Midway Rd, Dallas, TX 75229

BURDICK III, Henry C (Ct) 152 Wharf Landing Dr Unit A, Edenton, NC 27932

BURG, Michael John (FdL) 2515 Lakeshore Dr, Sheboygan, WI 53081

BURGDORF, David (Los) 36270 Avenida De Las Montanas, Cathedral City, CA 92234

BURGER, Charles Sherman (Ida) 9640 W. Sleepy Hollow Ln, Garden Valley, ID 83714

BURGER, Douglas Clyde (RI) 214 Oakley Rd, Woonsocket, RI 02895

BURGER, Robert Franz (Wyo) Po Box 579, Estes Park, CO 80517

BURGER, Tim (WMass) 11 Berkeley Pl, Glen Rock, NJ 07452

BURGESS, Brian (NJ) The Rectory of Christ Church, 62 Delaware Street, Woodbury, NJ 08096

BURGESS, Candis (NC) Po Box 1547, Clemmons, NC 27012

BURGESS, Carol Jean (NC) 721 7 Lks N, Seven Lakes, NC 27376

BURGESS, Judith Fleming (RG) 134 Hillcrest Loop, Capitan, NM 88316

BURGESS, Vicki Tucker (Tenn) 4016 Brush Hill Rd, Nashville, TN 37216

BURGESS, Walter F (Eas) 105 Gay St, Denton, MD 21629

BURGOS, Joe A (Tex) 305 Sunset Drive, North Manchester, IN 46962

BURHANS III, Rick (CFla)

BURHOE, Alden Read (Mass) 54 Grant Ave, Somerset, MA 02726

BURK, John H (Episcopal SJ) 599 Colton St, Monterey, CA 93940

BURK, William H (Va) 7159 Mechanicsville Tpke, Mechanicsville, VA 23111

BURKARDT, Jay P (Roch) St Paul Episcopal Church, 25 Westminster Rd, Rochester, NY 14607

BURKARDT, Leslie S (Roch) 2000 Highland Ave, Rochester, NY 14618

BURKE, Anne B (RI) 66 Elm St Apt 1, Westerly, RI 02891

BURKE, Celine (WMich) 1033 NW Stannium Rd, Bend, OR 97701

BURKE, Cyril Casper (Ct) 26 Hoskins Rd, Bloomfield, CT 06002

BURKE, Geneva Frances (Mich) 21514 Deguindre, #202, Warren, MI 48091

BURKE, Michael (Ak) 3221 Amber Bay Loop, Anchorage, AK 99515

BURKE, Norman Charles (Az) 9552 West Wild Turkey Lane, Strawberry, AZ 85544

BURKE, Patrick (Ind)

BURKE, Richard Early (Mass) 3279 Flamingo Blvd, Hernando Beach, FL 34607

BURKE, Robert Thomas (NwPa) Grace Episcopal Church, 10121 Hall Ave, Lake City, PA 16423

BURKE, Sean Dennis (Ia) 201 Hollihan St, Decorah, IA 52101

BURKERT-BRIST, Monica Anne (FdL) 315 E Jefferson St, Waupun, WI 53963

BURKETT, William Vernard (SwFla) 2902 Weset San Rafael Street, Tampa, FL 33629

BURKHART, John Delmas (Lex) 701 E Engineer St, Corbin, KY 40701

BURKS, Bill (WTenn) 98 Jim Dedmon Rd., Dyer, TN 38330

BURKS, Tami Louise (NY)

BURLEIGH, Judith Cushing (Me) PO Box 8, Presque Isle, ME 04769

BURLESON, Saul Lars (RG) Unit 100341 Box 41, FPO AE, 09564

BURLEY, Aloysius Englebert John Timothy (Minn) 615 W Tanglewood Dr, Arlington Heights, IL 60004

BURLEY III, Clarence Augustus (ECR) 651 Broadway, Gilroy, CA 95020

BURLINGTON, Robert Craig (RI) 2070 Homewood Blvd Apt 306, Delray Beach, FL 33445

BURMAN, Susan Crandall (FdL) 315 E Jefferson St, Waupun, WI 53963

BURMEISTER, Melissa Lynne (Mil) 5556 E. Colonial Oaks Dr., Monticello, IN 47960

BURNARD, Karen (SO) PO Box 284, Little Switzerland, NC 28749

BURNER, Dan E (Roch)

✠ **BURNETT**, Joe Goodwin (Neb) PO Box 540617, Omaha, NE 68154

BURNETT, Joseph or Jody Goodwin (Miss) St. Peter's Episcopal Church, 113 S 9th St, Oxford, MS 38655

BURNETT, Richard Alvin (SO) 125 E Broad St, Columbus, OH 43215

BURNETTE, Marc (Ala) 1930 Fairfax Dr, Florence, AL 35630

BURNHAM, Fred (NY) 556 Lakeshore Drive Ext, Asheville, NC 28804

BURNHAM, Karen Lee (Colo) 2029 Pine St, Pueblo, CO 81004

BURNS, A(Nn) Lyn (Colo) PO Box 635, La Veta, CO 81055

BURNS, Deborah Stansbrough (Kan) 3021 Steven Dr, Lawrence, KS 66049

BURNS, Duncan Adam (LI) 209 Albany Ave, Kingston, NY 12401

BURNS, Jacquelyn Mae (SO) St John's Episcopal Church, 700 High St, Worthington, OH 43085

BURNS, James Lee (NY) 1029 Arrowhead Rd, Camano Island, WA 98282

BURNS, Jerome (SO) 1316 Villa Paloma Blvd, Little Elm, TX 75068

BURNS, Leonetta Faye (Me) 52 Dondero Rd, Chelsea, ME 04330

BURNS, Steven Thomas (Eau)

BURNS, Thomas Dale (NwT) 3402 W Ohio Ave, Midland, TX 79703

BURNS LAGRECA, Allison Marie (NJ)

BURR, John Terry (Roch) 594 Stearns Rd, Churchville, NY 14428

BURR, Whitney Haight (Mass) 175 Shane Dr, Chatham, MA 02633

✠ **BURRILL**, William George (Az) 7550 N. 16th Street #5204, Phoenix, AZ 85020

BURRIS, Holly Jean (Miss) PO Box 224, Tunica, MS 38676

BURRIS, Richard R (Okla) 900 Schulze Dr., Norman, OK 73071

BURROUGHS, Joseph Parker (Md) 7236 Gaither Rd, Sykesville, MD 21784

BURROWS, Judith Anne (WNY) 106 Hickory Hill Rd Apt A, Buffalo, NY 14221

BURROWS, Paul Anthony (Cal) 474 48th Avenue, Apt 23A, Long Island City, NY 11109

BURRUSS, John (Ala) 8282 Macon Rd, Cordova, TN 38018

BURT, William R (Ct) 813 Marla Dr, Point Pleasant Boro, NJ 08742

BURTON, Anthony John (Dal) 3966 McKinney Ave, Dallas, TX 75204

BURTON, Bob (Az) 9502 W. Hutton Drive, Sun City, AZ 85351

BURTON, Cassandra Yvonne (WA)

BURTON, Christine Hazel (RI) PO Box 48, Hope Valley, RI 02832

BURTON, Jack C (SO) Norton Orchard Rd, PO Box 5195, Edgartown, MA 02539

BURTON, James M (SC) 126 Taylor Cir, Goose Creek, SC 29445

BURTON, John (Ct)

BURTON, John (Ark) 807 COUNTY ROAD 102, EUREKA SPRINGS, AR 72632

BURTON, John Peter (Chi) 4839 W Howard, Skokie, IL 60076

BURTON, Kenneth William Fowler (Colo) 472 Crystal Hills Blvd, Manitou Springs, CO 80829

BURTON, Laurel Arthur (Ark)

BURTON, Whitney A (SwVa)

BURTON-EDWARDS, Grace (At) St Thomas Episcopal Church, 2100 Hilton Ave, Columbus, GA 31906

BURTS, Ann Horton (NC) 8804 Broadmore Ct, Raleigh, NC 27613

BUSBY, Lisa Jo (CNY) PO Box 561, Cape Vincent, NY 13618

BUSCH, Edward Leonard (SanD) 11650 Calle Paracho, San Diego, CA 92128

BUSCH, Glenn (NC) 3024 Cardinal Pl, Lynchburg, VA 24503

BUSCH, Richard Alan (Los) 4125 36th St S, Arlington, VA 22206

BUSH JR, Arnold (CGC) 1109 Bristol Way, Birmingham, AL 35242

BUSH, Emilie Chaudron (Los) St. Paul's, PO Box 726, Barstow, CA 92312

BUSH, Katherine McQuiston (WTenn) 718 Charles Place, Memphis, TN 38112

BUSH, Patricia (SanD) 4642 Utah Street #1, San Diego, CA 92116

BUSH, Patrick M (Ct) 11 Church St, Tariffville, CT 06081

BUSHEE, Grant Sartori (Cal) 1225 Rosefield Way, Menlo Park, CA 94025

BUSHEY JR, Howard (La) 8833 Goodwood Blvd, Baton Rouge, LA 70806

BUSHNELL, Peter Emerson (Ct) Holy Trinity Church, 383 Hazard Ave., Enfield, CT 06082

BUSHONG JR, Edward Stuart (SVa) 2806 E. Marshall St., Richmond, VA 23223

BUSSE, Mary Ruth (Fla) 3580 Pine St, Jacksonville, FL 32205

BUSSEY, Lawrence Day (Minn)

BUSTARD-BURNSIDE, Carol (Md) 1106 Woodheights Ave, Baltimore, MD 21211

BUSTO, Mercedes (SeFla)

BUSTRIN, Robert C (Az) 118 Lafayette Ave, Brooklyn, NY 11217
BUTCHER, Geoffrey (Ky) 607 5th Ave W, Springfield, TN 37172
BUTCHER, Gerald Alfred (Okla) 1720 W Carolina Ave, Chickasha, OK 73018
BUTCHER, Julie Ann (WMass)
BUTCHER, Kenneth Pf (Colo) 3306 Morris Ave, Pueblo, CO 81008
BUTCHER, William (Minn)
BUTERBAUGH, Matthew L (Mil) St Matthew's Church, 5900 7th Ave, Kenosha, WI 53140
BUTIN, John Murray (Ga) 303 Cannon Ct, St Simons Island, GA 31522
BUTLER III, Andrew Garland (NY) 59 Montclair Ave, Montclair, NJ 07042
BUTLER, Barbara Thayer (Minn) 2324 Branch St, Duluth, MN 55812
BUTLER, Charles Roger (CNY) 28205 Nc 73 Hwy, Albemarle, NC 28001
BUTLER, Clarence Elliot (Roch) 19 Russell Ave., Watertown, MA 02472
BUTLER, David Floyd (Kan) PO Box 65, Independence, KS 67301
BUTLER, Joseph Gilbert (WTenn)
BUTLER, Joseph Green (O) 471 Crosby St, Akron, OH 44302
BUTLER, Marilyn M (Ida) 4251 N 1800 E, Buhl, ID 83316
BUTLER, Mark Hilliard (LI) 225 Arbutus Ln, Hendersonville, NC 28739
BUTLER, Oliver Martin (Dal) 8011 Douglas Ave, Dallas, TX 75225
BUTLER, Pauline Felton (CFla) 815 E Graves Ave, Orange City, FL 32763
BUTLER, Robert Mitchell (Me) 35821 Pradera Dr, Zephyrhills, FL 33541
BUTLER, Susan J (ETenn) 20 Belvoir Ave, Chattanooga, TN 37411
BUTLER, Tony Eugene (Cal) Po Box 4380, Sparks, NV 89432
BUTLER-GEE, Eve (SVa) Martin's Brandon Episcopal Church, 18706 James River Dr, Disputanta, VA 23842
BUTTERWORTH, Gary (WNC) 3587 Fieldstone Dr, Gastonia, NC 28056
BUTTON, Roger Dee (Dal) 9845 McCree Rd, Dallas, TX 75238
BUTTS, Stephen Jack (Tex) 314 N Henderson Blvd, Kilgore, TX 75662
BUTWILL, Norman M (Cal)
BUXEDA-DIAZ, Ivan R (PR)
BUXO, David Carlysle (Mich) 3601 W 13 Mile Rd, Royal Oak, MI 48073
BUXTON-SMITH, Sarah Wallace (WNY) 100 Beard Ave, Buffalo, NY 14214
BUZZARD, Henry Lewis (NY) 71 Wayne Ave, White Plains, NY 10606
BWECHWA, Oswald (Mil) 3400 E Debbie Drive, Oak Creek, WI 53154
BYE, Mike (NC) P.O. Box 942, wadesboro, NC 28170
BYE, Tommy Frank (FtW) 1201 Overhill St, Bedford, TX 76022
BYER, Martha Russell (WMo) 3907 Ivanhoe Blvd, Columbia, MO 65203

BYERS, Mark (Ct) 38 Grove St, Thomaston, CT 06787
BYERS, Sara Shovar (Ga) PO Box 925, Moultrie, GA 31776
BYERS, William (WMass) 35 Nedwied Rd, Tolland, CT 06084
BYRD, Bear (CGC) 403 W College St, Troy, AL 36081
BYRD, Frederick Colclough (USC) 1115 Marion St, Columbia, SC 29201
BYRD, Katherine H (Mil) 166 Market St, Lexington, KY 40507
BYRD, Nita Charlene Johnson (NC) St Paul Episcopal Church, 221 Union St, Cary, NC 27511
BYRD SR, Ronald Charles (Mich) 634 Canoga, Haslett, MI 48840
BYRER, Johnine Vaughn (Pa) 6 Juniper Dr, Whitehouse Station, NJ 08889
BYRNE, Anne SC (Md) 126 E. Liberty St., Oakland, MD 21550
BYRNE, Larry (LI) 21433 40th Ave., Bayside, NY 11361
BYRUM, Emory Etheridge (Nwk) Trinity Episcopal Church, 6587 Upper York Rd. PO Box 377, Solebury, PA 18963
BYRUM, Philip Robert (NC) 1207 Cambridge Rd Nw, Wilson, NC 27896
BYRUM, Rick Edward Yervant (Los) 28648 Greenwood Pl, Castaic, CA 91384

C

CABALLERO, Daniel (Mil) 4305 Rolla Ln, Madison, WI 53711
CABANA, Denise (Ct) 2584 Main St, Glastonbury, CT 06033
CABEY, Lenroy Kirtley (VI)
CABRERA AMADOR, Fredy (Hond) IMS SAP Dept 215, PO Box 523900, Miami, FL 22152-3900, Honduras
CABRERO-OLIVER, Juan (LI) 443 Maren St, West Hempstead, NY 11552
CABUSH, David Walter (Nwk) 2 Pond Hill Rd # 7960, Morristown, NJ 07960
CACCESE, Nicholas Michael (SwFla) 553 Galleon Dr, Naples, FL 34102
CACOPERDO, Peter Anthony (RG) PO Box 1747, Elephant Butte, NM 87935
CADARET, John Michael (Va) 8411 Freestone Ave, Richmond, VA 23229
CADDELL, Christopher Len (WTex) The Episcopal Church of the Holy Spirit, 301 Hays Country Acres Rd, Dripping Springs, TX 78620
CADE, Wendy P (At) 1323 N Dupont St, Wilmington, DE 19806
CADENA, Enrique (Az) 2801 N 31st Street, Phoenix, AZ 85008
CADIGAN, Charles Richard (Mo) 1625 Masters Drive, DeSoto, TX 75115
CADIGAN, Katherine (Los) 1227 4th St, Santa Monica, CA 90401

CADWALLADER, Doug (Tex) PO Box 35303, Houston, TX 77235
CADWELL, Matthew P (Mass) 94 Newbury Ave Apt 309, Quincy, MA 02171
CADY, Donald Holmes (Va) Grace Episcopal Church, PO Box 43, Keswick, VA 22947
CAFFERATA, Gail Lee (The Episcopal NCal) 4794 Hillsboro Cir, Santa Rosa, CA 95405
CAFFREY, David (Los) PO Box 514, Joshua Tree, CA 92252
CAGE JR, Stewart B (La) 8932 Fox Run Ave, Baton Rouge, LA 70808
CAGGIANO, Diane Ruth (Ct) 11 Overvale Rd, Wolcott, CT 06716
CAGGIANO, Joyce (Mass) 27 Curtis Rd., Milton, MA 02186
CAGUIAT, Carlos J (Mich) 10901 176 Circle NE apt 2421, Redmond, WA 98052
CAGUIAT, Julianna (Oly) 20 Oakwood Road, Saranac Lake, NY 12983
CAHILL, Patricia Ann Bytnar (ETenn) 317 Windy Hollow Dr, Chattanooga, TN 37421
CAHOON, Vernon John (NC) 428 Pee Dee Ave, Albemarle, NC 28001
CAIMANO, Catherine Anne (NC) 13804 Hill St, Huntersville, NC 28078
CAIN, Donavan G (Fla) St Mark's Episcopal Church, 4129 Oxford Ave, Jacksonville, FL 32210
CAIN JR, Everett Harrison (Tex) 7705 Merrybrook Circle, Austin, TX 78731
CAIN, George Robert (SwFla) 1813 Echo Pond Pl, Wesley Chapel, FL 33543
CAIRES, Joy MarieLouise (Minn) 12671 Woodside Drive, Chesterland, OH 44026
CAIRNS, Fr John (Alb) 316 Valentine Pond Rd, Pottersville, NY 12860
CALAFAT, Karen A (FtW) 2647 Mayflower Ave, Arcadia, CA 91006
CALCOTE, A(Lan) Dean (Tex) 5615 Duff St, Beaumont, TX 77706
CALDBECK, Elaine S (Ia) 2400 Middle Rd, Bettendorf, IA 52722
CALDWELL, Brenda Ann (Wyo) 1167 Hidalgo Dr, Laramie, WY 82072
✠ **CALDWELL**, Bruce (Wyo) 104 S 4th St, Laramie, WY 82070
CALDWELL, Edward Frederick (Alb) 100 Farmington Dr, Camillus, NY 13031
CALDWELL, George M (Va) 501 Slaters Ln Apt 521, Alexandria, VA 22314
CALDWELL, James Hardy (Chi) 1307nW Logan St, Freeport, IL 61032
CALDWELL, Kevin Lee (CFla) 905 E Mcmurray Rd, Venetia, PA 15367
CALDWELL, Margaret Caldwell (ETenn) 1264 Duane Rd, Chattanooga, TN 37405
CALDWELL, Michael L (Tex) 1430 N Mound St, Nacogdoches, TX 75961

Clergy List

CALDWELL, Steve (RG) 9632 Allande Rd. NE, Albuquerque, NM 87109

CALDWELL, Wallace Franklin (Mo) 1115 Woodleigh Ct, Harrisonburg, VA 22802

CALER, Joshua M (Tenn) 900 Broadway, Nashville, TN 37203

CALEY BOWERS, Elizabeth Ann Ann (Fla) 9252 San Jose Blvd. Apt. 3703, Jacksonville, FL 32257

CALHOUN, Annie (Los) 2400 N Canal St, Orange, CA 92865

CALHOUN, Dolores Moore (CPa) Po Box 32, Jersey Mills, PA 17739

CALHOUN, Joseph William (ETenn) 9420 States View Dr, Knoxville, TN 37922

CALHOUN, Nancy Ellen (Del) 31 Dresner Cir, Boothwyn, PA 19061

CALHOUN, Ora (WK) 26627 Midland Rd, Bay Village, OH 44140

CALHOUN, Robert Clay (WTenn)

CALHOUN, Royce (WTex) 103 Bluff Vista, Boerne, TX 78006

CALHOUN-BRYANT, Julie Elizabeth (CNY) Po Box 91, Camillus, NY 13031

CALKINS, Linda R (WA) 10617 Eastwood Ave, Silver Spring, MD 20901

CALKINS, Matthew H(amilton)) (NY) PO Box 366, Millbrook, NY 12545

CALLAGHAN, Alice Dale (Los) 307 E 7th St, Los Angeles, CA 90014

CALLAGHAN, Carol L (Eas) 308 Elm Ave, Easton, MD 21601

CALLAHAM, Arthur A (Tex) 6167 Olympia Drive, Houston, TX 77057

CALLAHAN, Gary Edward (ETenn) Po Box 21275, Chattanooga, TN 37424

CALLARD, Tom Adams (WMass) 35 Chestnut St, Springfield, MA 01103

CALLAWAY, James Gaines (NY) 549 W 123rd St Apt 13A, New York, NY 10027

CALLAWAY, Richard H (At) 6513 Blue Creek Ct, Douglasville, GA 30135

CALLENDER, Francis Charles (Episcopal SJ) 1060 Cottage Ave, Manteca, CA 95336

CALLENDER, Randy (Md) Saint Philip's Church, 730 Bestgate Rd, Annapolis, MD 21401

CALLISON, Donald Walter (The Episcopal NCal)

CALLISON, Jonathan David (WMo) 11 E 40th St, Kansas City, MO 64111

CALVERT, George (SanD) 3990 Bonita Rd, Bonita, CA 91902

CALVO PEREZ, Antonis De Jesus (Colom) C165 No. 36 A-30, Bogota, Colombia

CAMERON, David Albert (SD) 2417 Holiday Ln, Rapid City, SD 57702

CAMERON, Euan Kerr (NY)

CAMERON, Jackie (Chi) 513 W Aldine Ave Apt 2h, Chicago, IL 60657

CAMERON, Krista (Roch) 3345 Edgemere Dr, Rochester, NY 14612

CAMERON, Meigan Cameron (Chi) 4140 N Lavergne Ave, Chicago, IL 60641

CAMMACK, David Walker (Md) 7200 3rd Ave, Sykesville, MD 21784

CAMPBELL, Anne (Oly) 3438 161st Pl Se Apt 51, Bellevue, WA 98008

CAMPBELL, Benjamin Pfohl (Va) 1310 Whitby Rd, Richmond, VA 23227

CAMPBELL, Bruce Alan (Mich) 160 Walnut St, Wyandotte, MI 48192

CAMPBELL, Catherine (Va) 3420 Flint Hill Place, Woodbridge, VA 22192

CAMPBELL, Dana L(Ou) (Ct) 58 Greenwood St, East Hartford, CT 06118

CAMPBELL, David N (WTenn)

CAMPBELL, Dennis Gail (Ark) 1501 32nd Ave S, Seattle, WA 98144

CAMPBELL, Ernest Francis (Spok) 825 Wauna Vista Dr, Walla Walla, WA 99362

CAMPBELL, Ernestina Rodriguez (The Episcopal NCal) 1617 32nd Ave, Sacramento, CA 95822

CAMPBELL III, George Latimer (NJ) 257 4th St, South Amboy, NJ 08879

CAMPBELL, James Donald (La) 525 N Laurel St, Amite, LA 70422

CAMPBELL, Janet Bragg (Oly) 6509 80th St SW, Lakewood, WA 98499

CAMPBELL, Jean (RG) 42 Timberline Dr, Poughkeepsie, NY 12603

CAMPBELL, Karen (LI) PO Box 570, Hampton & East Union Street, Sag Harbor, NY 11963

CAMPBELL, Kathryn Sue (Ia) 106 3rd Ave, Charles City, IA 50616

CAMPBELL, Kenneth Stuart B (WMass) 5 Peace Lane, Box 306, South Orleans, MA 02653

CAMPBELL, Linda (ECR) 2065 Yosemite St., Seaside, CA 93955

CAMPBELL, Lynn Marie (Mass) 1132 Highland Ave, Needham, MA 02494

CAMPBELL, Maurice Bernard (Episcopal SJ) 1151 Park View Ct, Sheridan, WY 82801

CAMPBELL, Patrick Alan (RI) St Paul's Church, 50 Park Pl, Pawtucket, RI 02860

CAMPBELL, Peter Nelson (Chi) 519 Franklin Ave, River Forest, IL 60305.

CAMPBELL II, Ralph (LI) 9825 Georgetown St. N.E., Louisville, OH 44641

CAMPBELL, Scott (Colo) PO Box 1961, Monument, CO 80132

CAMPBELL, Solomon Sebastian (SeFla) P.O. Box 50222, Nassau, Bahamas

CAMPBELL, Thomas Wellman (SD) 234 W Kansas St, Spearfish, SD 57783

CAMPBELL, William Thomas (WTex) Church of the Good Shepherd, 700 S Upper Broadway St, Corpus Christi, TX 78401

CAMPBELL-DIXON, Robert A (NY) PO Box 99, West Park, NY 12493

CAMPBELL-LANGDELL, Alene L (Los) 144 S C St, Oxnard, CA 93030

CAMPBELL-LANGDELL, Melissa (Los) 144 S. C St, Oxnard, CA 93030

CAMPBELL-PEARSON, Constance (Mont)

CAMPO, JoAnne Crocitto (NY) 48 Spring St S, South Salem, NY 10590

CAMPO, Joseph John (NY)

CAMPO CAMAYO, Omar Julio (Colom)

CANADY III, Hoyt Paul (EC) Christ Church, P.O. Box 1246, New Bern, NC 28563

CANAN, Dave (Pa) 708 S Bethlehem Pike, Ambler, PA 19002

CANAVAN, Mary Ann (RI)

CANDLER, Samuel Glenn (At) 2744 Peachtree Rd Nw, Atlanta, GA 30305

CANELA CANELA, Ramon (DR (DomRep)) Ms Digna Valdez, Box 764, Dominican Republic, Dominican Republic

CANGIALOSI, Grace Louise (Va) 2209 E Grace St, Richmond, VA 23223

CANHAM, Liz (WNC) 51 Laurel Ln, Black Mountain, NC 28711

CANION, Gary Yates (Tex) 5435 Whispering Creek Way, Houston, TX 77017

CANNADAY, Brian W (Tex) 410 N Main St, Boerne, TX 78006

CANNADY, Jessie Edmonia (Colo)

CANNAN, Andrew (EC) St Lukes Episc Church, 435 Peachtree St NE, Atlanta, GA 30308

CANNELL, John Edward (WTex) 11107 Wurzbach Rd Ste 401, San Antonio, TX 78230

CANNING, Michael Jacob Brinton (Ida) 2333 W Duck Alley Rd, Eagle, ID 83616

CANNON JR, Alberry Charles (USC) 51 Roper Rd, Flat Rock, NC 28731

CANNON III, Alberry Charles (SwFla) 87500 Overseas Highway, Islamorada, FL 33036

CANNON, Carl Thomas (La) 10622 Masters Dr, Clermont, FL 34711

CANNON, Charles Wilcken (The Episcopal Church in Haw) 291 Shady Glen Ave., Point Roberts, WA 98281

CANNON, David Lawrence (Ct) #93 Route 2-A Pouquetanuck, Preston, CT 06365

CANNON, Justin R (Cal) 911 Dowling Blvd, San Leandro, CA 94577

CANNON, Michael David Winslow (USC) 210 S Indian River Dr, Fort Pierce, FL 34950

CANNON, Thomas Kimball (Chi) 141 S Taylor Ave, Oak Park, IL 60302

CANO, George Luciano (Episcopal SJ) 3605 Shady Valley Ct, Modesto, CA 95355

CANTELLA, Frances French (Los) 30015 Buchanan Way, Castaic, CA 91384

CANTER, Matthew A (SanD) PO Box 127, Carlsbad, CA 92018

CANTERBURY, Marion Lucille (RG) 5304 Rincon Rd Nw, Albuquerque, NM 87105

CANTOS DELGADO, Jose (NJ)

CANTRELL, Darla (Nev) PO Box 181, Austin, NV 89310

CANTRELL, Laura (Ga) Christ Church, 1521 N Patterson St, Valdosta, GA 31602

CANTRELL, Patricia Martin (Miss) PO Box 316, West Point, MS 39773

CANTRELL, Spencer (ETenn)

CAPALDO, Christopher James (La) 801 Atlantic Ave, Fernandina Beach, FL 32034

CAPELLARO, John (Los) 13029 Central Ave Unit 304, Hawthorne, CA 90250

CAPITELLI, Stephen Richard (Mil) St John in the Wilderness, 13 S Church St, Elkhorn, WI 53121

CAPPEL, Jerry (Ky) 344 Reed Ln, Simpsonville, KY 40067

CAPPER, Steve (Tex) 4405 McKinney St, Houston, TX 77023

CAPPERS, Linda Frances (Me) 30 Hemlock Dr, Saco, ME 04072

CAPPS, Benjamin (Pa)

CAPWELL, Kim (Del) 2400 W 17th St, Wilmington, DE 19806

CARABIN, Robert Jerome (WTex) 203 Panama Ave, San Antonio, TX 78210

CARADINE, Billie Charles (Ala) Po Box 787, Asotin, WA 99402

CARBERRY, Timothy Oliver (SO) 49 Dipper Cove Rd, Orrs Island, ME 04066

CARCEL-MARTINEZ, Antonio (Hond) Apdo 52, Camino Rio Mar, Puerto Cortes, Honduras

CARDEN, Larry Edward (Tenn) University Of The South, Spo, Sewanee, TN 37375

CARDONE, Susan Holliday (Los) 6125 Carlos Ave, Los Angeles, CA 90028

CARDOZA, Edward Miguel (Mass) 116 South St, Foxboro, MA 02035

CARDWELL, Emily Marie (Lex) 210 N Main St, Versailles, KY 40383

CARDWELL, Sarah L (ETenn)

CAREY, Brent (SanD) 2561 Wexford Rd, Upper Arlington, OH 43221

CAREY, Pamela Hann (Cal) 525 29th St, Oakland, CA 94609

CAREY, Peter (Pa) 5602 Cary Street Rd, Richmond, VA 23226

CAREY, Peter R (NY) 150 9th Ave Apt 1, New York, NY 10011

CAREY, Tom (Los) 888 N Alameda St, Los Angeles, CA 90012

CARHARTT, Forrest Andrew (Colo) 4737 Mckinley Dr, Boulder, CO 80303

CARL, Elizabeth (WA) 1414 Montague St NW, Washington, DC 20011

CARLETON, Ellen Diane (Wyo) 519 E Park Ave, Riverton, WY 82501

CARLETTA, David M (WTenn) St Andrew's Church, 17 South Ave, Beacon, NY 12508

CARLIN, Christine (EC) 810 Fisher St Apt 4, Morehead City, NC 28557

CARLIN II, William B (Okla) 3508 Robert Drive, Duncan, OK 73533

CARLING, Paul Joseph (Ct) Saint Paul's Episcopal Church, 661 Old Post Road, Fairfield, CT 06824

CARLISLE, Christopher Arthur Elliott (WMass) 758 N Pleasant St, Amherst, MA 01002

CARLISLE, Corky (Lex) 85 Mikell Ln, Sewanee, TN 37375

CARLISLE, David Paul Christian (Az)

CARLISTO, John Bradley (Ala) 121 Radley Ln, Beaufort, NC 28516

CARLSEN, Gail (Az) 3756 E Marble Peak Pl, Tucson, AZ 85718

CARLSEN, Stephen Earl (Ind) 55 Monument Cir Ste 600, Indianapolis, IN 46204

CARLSON, Carol Emma (NwPa) Po Box 328, Mount Jewett, PA 16740

CARLSON, Constance (Oly) St Andrew's Episc Church, 111 NE 80th St, Seattle, WA 98115

CARLSON, David John (Mich) 28217 Edward Ave, Madison Heights, MI 48071

CARLSON, David Lee (NY) 84 Seward Ave, Port Jervis, NY 12771

CARLSON, Geraldine Beatrice (WMich) 1287 La Chaumiere Drive # 5, Petoskey, MI 46770

CARLSON, Jeremy Lloyd (Ala)

CARLSON, Kelly B (Mo) Saint Peter's Episcopal Church, 110 N Warson Rd, Saint Louis, MO 63124

CARLSON, Kit (Mich) 907 Southlawn Ave, East Lansing, MI 48823

CARLSON, Monica (Ala) 2310 Skyland Blvd E, Tuscaloosa, AL 35405

CARLSON, Philip Lawrence (Az) 7147 N 78th St, Scottsdale, AZ 85258

CARLSON, Reed Anthony (Minn)

CARLSON, Robert Bryant (Ore) 15242 Sw Millikan Way Apt 517, Beaverton, OR 97006

CARLSON, Robert Warren (Pa) 1001 Cresthaven Dr, Silver Spring, MD 20903

CARLSON, Sally (Oly) 17320 97th Pl Sw Apt 603, Vashon, WA 98070

CARLTON, Cathleen Ann (Az)

CARLTON-JONES, Anne Helen (SwFla) 15608 Fiddlesticks Blvd, Fort Myers, FL 33912

CARLYON, Robert David (Be) P.O.Box 262, Orwigsburg, PA 17961

CARMAN, Charles Churchill (RG) 94 Winterhaven Drive, Nellysford, VA 22958

CARMICHAEL, Alisa Roberts (SwFla) 502 Druid Hills Rd, Temple Terrace, FL 33617

CARMICHAEL, Anna R (Episcopal SJ) 1528 Oakdale Rd, Modesto, CA 95355

CARMICHAEL, Mary Jean (Oly) 1600 Marshall Cir Unit 328, Dupont, WA 98327

CARMIENCKE JR, Bayard Collier (LI) 1145 Walnut Ave, Bohemia, NY 11716

CARMODY, Alison Cutter (Ala) 1708 Wickingham Cv, Vestavia, AL 35243

CARMONA, Paul B (SanD) -, San Diego, CA 92115

CARNAHAN, Patricia King (Pgh) 4201 Saltsburg Rd, Murrysville, PA 15668

CARNES, Valerie Folts (Mil) 4507 Dayton Blvd, Chattanooga, TN 37415

CARNEY, Georgia Martyn (Roch) 350 Chili Ave, Rochester, NY 14611

CARNEY, Michael (U) PO Box 55, Whiterocks, UT 84085

CARNEY, Paul Martin (Alb) 146 1st St, Troy, NY 12180

CARNEY, Paulette Louise (WNY) 131 Lincoln Blvd, Kenmore, NY 14217

CARNEY, Susan Roberta (RI) 9924 Pointe Aux Chenes Road, Ocean Springs, MS 39564

CARON, Donald Raymond (NJ) 116 Forte Dr Nw, Milledgeville, GA 31061

CARON II, Joseph A (Alb) 271 Stevenson Rd, Greenwich, NY 12834

CARPENTER, Allen Douglas (Alb) 62 S. Swan St., Albany, NY 12210

CARPENTER, Catherine E (CNY) PO Box 6, Baldwinsville, NY 13027

CARPENTER, Charles Monroe (Ind) 91 Smiths Rd, Mitchell, IN 47446

CARPENTER, Doug (Ala) 3037 Overton Rd, Birmingham, AL 35223

CARPENTER, Elizabeth Kincaid (Tenn) 216 University Ave, Sewanee, TN 37375

CARPENTER, Francis Newton (Chi) 337 Ridge Rd, Barrington Hills, IL 60010

CARPENTER, Gene (EC) 1603 E Walnut St, Goldsboro, NC 27530

CARPENTER, George Harrison (Oly) Po Box 343, Medina, WA 98039

CARPENTER, John Paul (Pa) 3937 Netherfield Rd, Philadelphia, PA 19129

CARPENTER, Judith Perry (Mass) 192 N. Main Street, Rockland, ME 04841

CARPENTER, Leslie Scott (Tex) 6050 N. Meridian St., Indianapolis, IN 46208

CARPENTER II, Marion George (NI) Saint Annes, 424 W Market St, Warsaw, IN 46580

CARPENTER, Nicholas (Los) 15757 Saint Timothy Rd, Apple Valley, CA 92307

CARPENTER, Stephen (The Episcopal NCal) 1020 Westview Dr, Napa, CA 94558

CARPENTER, Susan (RI) PO Box 505, Greenville, RI 02828

CARR, Clifford Bradley (Be) 526 11th Avenue, Bethlehem, PA 18018

CARR, Dale Robert (Ore) 5223 NE Everett St, Portland, OR 97213

CARR, John Joseph (WNY) 56 Mckinley Ave, Kenmore, NY 14217

CARR, John Philip (Tex)

CARR, Michael (SanD) 651 Eucalyptus Ave, Vista, CA 92084

CARR, Michael Leo (Mich) 9132 Pine Valley Dr, Grand Blanc, MI 48439

CARR, Nathan Daniel (Okla) 6400 N Pennsylvania Ave, Nichols Hills, OK 73116

CARR, Spencer (Colo) 4661 Wilson Dr, Broomfield, CO 80023

CARR, Timothy Patrick (Nwk) St John's Episcopal Church, 226 Cornelia St, Boonton, NJ 07005

CARR, Virginia Rose (WNY) 12 Elm St, Westfield, NY 14787

✠ **CARR**, William Franklin (USC) 4249 Cedar Grove Rd, Murfreesboro, TN 37127

✠ **CARRANZA-GOMEZ**, Sergio (Los) PO Box 512164, Los Angeles, CA 90051

CARREKER, Michael Lyons (Ga) 1 West Macon Street, Savannah, GA 31401

CARRICK, Judith Trautman (LI) 4 Kenny St, Hauppauge, NY 11788

CARRIERE, Anne Stone (WTenn) 31 Stonecrest Ct, Mountain Home, AR 72653

CARRINGTON, James Henry (ECR)

CARR-JONES, Philip (NJ) 3 Haytown Rd, Lebanon, NJ 08833

CARROCCINO, Michael Jonathan (Oly) 541 W Morondo Ave, Ajo, AZ 85321

CARROLL III, Bill William (Okla) 924 N Robinson Ave, Oklahoma City, OK 73102

CARROLL, Charles Moisan (Me) PO Box 195, Brunswick, ME 04011

CARROLL, Christian (Nwk) 173 Oakland Rd, Maplewood, NJ 07040

CARROLL, Diana (Md) St. Luke's Church, 1101 Bay Ridge Avenue, Annapolis, MD 21403

CARROLL, Diane Phyllis (Va) 10360 Rectory Ln, King George, VA 22485

CARROLL, James Earle (SanD) 3750 Amaryllis Dr, San Diego, CA 92106

CARROLL, Kevin Charles (Mil) 3309 N Knoll Terrace, Wauwatosa, WI 53222

CARROLL, Michael Edward (Ct) 16 Church St, Waterbury, CT 06702

CARROLL, Steve (NJ) 618 S Hazel Ct, Gilbert, AZ 85296

CARROLL, Tracey Fiore (Okla) 335 Tennessee Ave, Sewanee, TN 37383

CARROLL, Vincent John (SwVa) 2518 2nd St, Richlands, VA 24641

CARROLL, William Wesley (Fla) 465 11th Ave N, Jacksonville, FL 32250

CARROON, Robert Girard (Ct) 24 Park Pl, Apt 8F, Hartford, CT 06106

CARRUBBA, Amity (Chi) 1434 W Thome Ave Apt 1A, Chicago, IL 60660

CARSKADON, Garrett Harvey (Md) 32 Main St, Westernport, MD 21562

CARSON, Boyd Rodney (SwFla) 1875 Massachusetts Ave Ne, Saint Petersburg, FL 33703

CARSON, Julie Ann (Mass) 500 Brook St, Framingham, MA 01701

CARSON, Mary Claypoole (SO) 3207 Montana Ave, Cincinnati, OH 45211

CARSON, Rebecca Jayne (CGC) 1707 Government St, Mobile, AL 36604

CARSON, Stephen Wilson (WTex) 3002 Miori Ln, Victoria, TX 77901

CARSWELL, Amber B (WTenn) 102 N 2nd St, Memphis, TN 38103

CARTAGENA MEJIA DE AREVALO, Maria Consuelo (Hond) San Angel B-26, C4202, Tegucigalpa, C, Honduras

CARTER, Bente (Cal) 60 Pinehurst Way, San Francisco, CA 94127

CARTER, Charles Robert (Eau) 1001 McLean Ave, Tomah, WI 54660

CARTER, David (Ct) 521 Pomfret Street (Box 21), Pomfret, CT 06258

CARTER, Davis Blake (WTex) Po Box 707, Aberdeen, MS 39730

CARTER JR, Frederick Leroy (U) 472 Gordon Cir, Tooele, UT 84074

CARTER, Grayson Leigh (RG) 1602 Palmcroft Dr Sw, Phoenix, AZ 85007

CARTER, Halcott Richardson (USC) 4708 Seahurst Ave, Everett, WA 98203

CARTER, James Currie Mackechnie (Va) 3510 Hastings Dr, Richmond, VA 23235

CARTER, James Lee (SwFla) 9925 Ulmerton Rd Lot 40, Largo, FL 33771

CARTER JR, James Robert (Ga) 601 Washington Ave, Savannah, GA 31405

CARTER, John Franklin (Ct) John Carter, 19 Willow Dr, Lakeville, CT 06039

CARTER, L Susan (Mich) 1102 Portage Path, East Lansing, MI 48823

CARTER, Lynda Anne (Mich) 2803 1st St, Wyandotte, MI 48192

CARTER III, Philander Lothrop (WMich) 1296 Siena Way, Boulder, CO 80301

CARTER JR, Richard Blair (ETenn) PO Box 5104, Knoxville, TN 37928

CARTER, Robert Douglas (SwFla) Berkeley Preparatory School, 4811 Kelly Road, Tampa, FL 33615

CARTER, Stanley Edward (ETenn) 1930 Chelsea Jo Ln., Sevierville, TN 37876

CARTER, Thomas Brooke (Md) 2860 Hill Top Dr, Salisbury, MD 21801

CARTER, Wayne (WLa) 396 Country Club Circle, Minden, LA 71055

CARTER-EDMANDS, Lynn (SO) 55 S Vernon Ln, Fort Thomas, KY 41075

CARTIER, Fred Claire (NY) 222 Starbarrack Rd, Red Hook, NY 12571

CARTWRIGHT, Gary Earle (SwFla) 2202 Wildwood Hollow Dr, Valrico, FL 33594

CARTWRIGHT, Thomas Lisson (Ore) 1720 Ten Oaks Ln, Woodburn, OR 97071

CARTY, Shawn (Nwk) PO Box 117, Bellevue, ID 83313

CARUSO, Cynthia Woodham (Tex) 209 W 27th St, Austin, TX 78705

CARUSO, Frank (Mass) 112 Spring St, Hopkinton, MA 01748

CARUSO, Kevin (Chi) 647 Dundee Ave, Barrington, IL 60010

CARUTHERS, Mary C (Ark) 509 Scott St, Little Rock, AR 72201

CARVER, Barbara Schenkel (Spok) 1904 Browning Way, Sandpoint, ID 83864

CARVER, J.P. (Spok) 1904 Browning Way, Sandpoint, ID 83864

CARVER, Larry A (WK) 18 E 28th Ave, Hutchinson, KS 67502

CARVER, Lynne (Ia) St. Peter's Episcopal Church, 2400 Middle Rd., Bettendorf, IA 52722

CARVER, Robert Cody (Oly) 1701 N Juniper St, Tacoma, WA 98406

CARVER, Sarah Frances (NC) 4795 Silver Creek Dr., Greensboro, NC 27410

CASE, Jaime J (Oly) 426 E Fourth Plain Blvd, Vancouver, WA 98663

CASE, James J (At) Holy Innocents Episcopal Church, 805 Mount Vernon Hwy, Atlanta, GA 30327

CASE, Margaret Timothy (RG)

CASE, Michael Allen (Ida) 704 S Latah St, Boise, ID 83705

CASEY, David P (SeFla)

CASEY, Dayle Alan (Colo) 2059 Glenhill Rd, Colorado Springs, CO 80906

CASEY, Stephen Charles (CPa) 429 Camp Meeting Rd, Landisville, PA 17538

CASEY-MARTUS, Sandra (WTex) St. Stephen's Episcopal Church, Wimberley, TX 78676

CASHELL, Douglas Hanson (NwT)

CASHMAN, Patricia (Pa) 2 Riverside St, Rochester, NY 14613

CASIANO, Ruth Arelys (PR)

CASILLAS, Laina Wood (Cal) 4942 Thunderhead Ct, El Sobrante, CA 94803

CASKEY, Charles C (Chi) 24410 Reserve Ct Apt 103, Bonita Springs, FL 34134

CASON JR, Charles Edward (FdL) 1805 Arlington Dr, Oshkosh, WI 54904

CASPARIAN, Peter (LI) 705 Snyder Hill Dr, San Marcos, TX 78666

CASSELL JR, John Summerfield (Md) 708 Milford Mill Rd, Baltimore, MD 21208

CASSELL, Jonnie Lee (Mo) 12025 Willow Ln Apt 916, Overland Park, KS 66213

CASSELL JR, Mike (SeFla) 2718 Sw 6th St, Boynton Beach, FL 33435

CASSELS, Christine Helen (RI) 99 Peirce St, East Greenwich, RI 02818

CASSEUS, Frantz (Hai) 7835 Jean Vincent, Montreal, H1E 3C4, Canada

CASSINI, Mary Ellen (SeFla) 2805 Duncan Dr Apt C, Boca Raton, FL 33434

CASSON, Jordan Francis Martin (Pa) 813 Longacre Blvd, Yeadon, PA 19050

CASSON, Lloyd S (Del) 902 N Market St Apt 1327, Wilmington, DE 19801

CASTELLAN, Megan (CNY) 11 E 40th St, Kansas City, MO 64111

CASTELLI, Paul Henry (Mich)

CASTELLO, Kenneth August (Mil)

CASTELLON, Paul Frank (NJ) 7403 Dress Blue Cir, Mechanicsville, VA 23116

CASTILLO, Guillermo Antonio (Ark) 406 W Central Ave, Bentonville, AR 72712

CASTILLO, Sandra Ann (Okla) 322 N Water St, Sparta, WI 54656

CASTLEBERRY, Howard Glen (Tex) 300 N Main St, Temple, TX 76501

CASTLES, Charles William (Ga) 1552 Pangborn Station Dr, Decatur, GA 30033

CASTO, David Cameron (Pgh) 9 Cliff Rd. Apt. B2, Woodland Park, NJ 07424

CASTO, R Richard (CFla) Po Box 2068, Dunnellon, FL 34430

CASTRO, Jose Roberto (DR (DomRep))

CASTRO, Mario (SwFla) Church of the Redeemer, 222 S Palm Ave, Sarasota, FL 34236

CASTRO, Reinel (CFla) 29655 Circle R Greens Drv, Escondido, CA 92026

CATALANO, Patricia (ECR)

CATCHINGS, Robert Mitchell (WA)

CATE, Rex Vasa (Ga) 615 Mallery St, St Simons Is, GA 31522

CATE, Suzanne (USC) Holy Trinity Parish, 193 Old Greenville Hwy, Clemson, SC 29631

CATES, Susanna (NJ) 602 Meander St, Abilene, TX 79602

CATHERS, Robert Earl (SwFla) 2291 Hebron Rd, Hendersonville, NC 28739

CATINELLA, Gayle (O) 16507 S Red Rock Dr, Strongsville, OH 44136

CATIR JR, Norman Joseph (FtW) 31 John St, Providence, RI 02906

CATO, Brooks (CNY) St. Thomas', 12 1/2 Madison St, Hamilton, NY 13346

CATO, Phillip Carlyle (WA) 8617 Hidden Hill Ln, Potomac, MD 20854

CATO, Vanessa Gisela (U) 2374 Grant Ave, Ogden, UT 84401

CATON, Lisa Elfers (NJ) 23 E Welling Ave, Pennington, NJ 08534

CATRON MINER, Antoinette (U) 1710 Foothill Dr, Salt Lake City, UT 84108

CAUCUTT, Mary (Wyo) 820 River View Dr, Cody, WY 82414

CAUDLE, Stephen (WLa) 7714 Albany Ave Apt B, Lubbock, TX 79424

CAULFIELD, Dorothee Renee (NY)

CAULKINS, Rodney LeRoy (SVa) 267 Jefferson Dr, Palmyra, VA 22963

CAUSTON, Michele Lynn (Be) 205 N 7th St, Stroudsburg, PA 18360

CAVAGNARO, Deborah Daggett (NwPa) St Luke's Church, 600 W Main St, Smethport, PA 16749

CAVALCANTE, Jose Ivanildo (Los) 48 Old Post Rd, Mount Sinai, NY 11766

CAVALERI, Eva Maria K (WA) 3612 Woodley Rd NW, Washington, DC 20016

CAVALIERE, Denise B (NJ) 15 Paper Mill Rd., Cherry Hill, NJ 08003

CAVANAGH, David Nathan (The Episcopal NCal) 2901 Owens Ct, Fairfield, CA 94534

CAVANAUGH, Bill (Dal) 421 Custer Road, Richardson, TX 75080

CAVANAUGH, Sean Harris (Va) 1795 Johnson Ferry Rd, Marietta, GA 30062

CAVANNA, Robert Charles (Minn) 6910 43rd Ave Se, Saint Cloud, MN 56304

CAVE, Daniel Eugene (RG) 7052 McNutt Rd, La Union, NM 88021

CAVE, Jeffrey Paull (At)

CAVENDISH, John Claude (Lex) 240 Cedar Cliff Rd, Waco, KY 40385

CAVIN, Barbara (EMich) Saint Paul's Episcopal Church, 711 S Saginaw St, Flint, MI 48502

CAWTHORNE, John Harry (Md) 1597 Amberlea Dr. S, Dunedin, FL 34698

CAZDEN, Jan (Cal) 2901 Verona Ct, Arlington, TX 76012

CEDERBERG, Todd (SeFla) 623 SE Ocean Blvd, Stuart, FL 34994

✠ **CEDERHOLM JR**, Roy Frederick (Mass) 499 Webster St, Needham, MA 02494

CEKUTA, Nancee A (USC) 471 W Martintown Rd, North Augusta, SC 29841

CELESTIN, Jois Goursse (Hai)

CELL, John Albert (FdL) 825 N Webster Ave, Green Bay, WI 54302

CELLA, Richard L (Colo) 4935 Hahns Peak Dr Apt 104, Loveland, CO 80538

CEMBALISTY INNES, Susan Eve (Be) 108 Fern Way, Clarks Summit, PA 18411

CENCI, Daniel M (EC) 110 W Main St, Clinton, NC 28328

CENDESE, William Ivan (U) 521 9th Ave, Salt Lake City, UT 84103

CERRATO III, John A (O) 2813 Market Bridge Ln Unit 101, Raleigh, NC 27608

CERTAIN, Robert (At) 3776 Loch Highland Pkwy NE, Roswell, GA 30075

✠ **CERVENY**, Frank Stanley (Fla) 3711 Ortega Blvd, Jacksonville, FL 32210

CESAR, Gerard David (Hai) Box 1309, Port-Au-Prince, Haiti

CESARETTI, Charles Antony (NJ) Po Box 408, New Milford, PA 18834

CEYNAR, Marlene Hruby (Minn) 1811 Southbrook Ln, Wadena, MN 56482

CHABOT, Bruce Guy (Tex) 5919 Wild Horse Run, College Station, TX 77845

CHACE, Alston Rigby (WMass) 144 Pine Bluff Rd, Brewster, MA 02631

CHACE, Brian David (EMich) Trinity Episcopal Church, PO Box 83, West Branch, MI 48661

CHACE, Elizabeth Marian Maxwell (EMich) PO Box 109, Frederic, MI 49733

CHACON, Frank Joe (The Episcopal NCal)

CHACON-RODRIGUEZ, Dagoberto (Hond)

CHADWICK, Leslie (WA) 11290 Spyglass Cove Lane, Reston, VA 20191

CHADWICK, Loring William (CFla) 11440 SW 84th Avenue Rd, Ocala, FL 34481

CHADWICK, Thora Louise Libbey (Vt) 267 Hildred Dr, Burlington, VT 05401

CHAFFEE, Adna Romanza (Ga) 302 E General Stewart Way, Hinesville, GA 31313

CHAFFEE, Barbara B (EC) 10618 Peppermill Dr, Raleigh, NC 27614

CHALAKANI, Paul Scott (NJ) 7 Lincoln Ave, Rumson, NJ 07760

CHALARON, Janice Belle Melbourne (USC) 144 Caldwell St, Rock Hill, SC 29730

✠ **CHALFANT**, Edward Cole (Me) PO Box 2056, Ponte Vedra Beach, FL 32004

CHALFANT-WALKER, Nancy Oliver (Pgh) 33 Thorn St, Sewickley, PA 15143

CHALK, David Paul (WTex) 651 Pecan St, Canyon Lake, TX 78133

CHALK, Michael Dulaney (WTex) 155 El Rancho Way, San Antonio, TX 78209

CHALKER, Gae M (The Episcopal Church in Haw) 400 S. Old Litchfield Rd., Litchfield Park, AZ 85340

CHALMERS, Glenn (NY) 296 9th Ave, New York, NY 10001

CHAMBERLAIN, Carol Moore (Pa) 22 Pin Oak Rd, Newport News, VA 23601

CHAMBERLAIN, David Morrow (EC) 136 Fairway Oaks Dr, Perry, GA 31069

CHAMBERLAIN, Eve Yorke (NJ) 325 Little Silver Point Rd, Little Silver, NJ 07739

CHAMBERLAIN-HARRIS, Naomi Redman (Cal) 4467 Crestwood Cir, Concord, CA 94521

CHAMBERS, Joseph Michael Cortright (Mo) 3906 Tropical Ln, Columbia, MO 65202

CHAMBERS, Mark Ellis (Tex) 2329 12th St, Port Neches, TX 77651

CHAMBERS, Rex (Colo) PO BOX 237, WINDSOR, CO 80550

CHAMBERS, Richard Graeff Mark (CFla) 91 Church St, Seymour, CT 06483

CHAMBERS, Robert Karl (NY)

CHAMBERS, Stanford Hardin (Dal) PO Box 540562, Dallas, TX 75354

CHAMBLISS, Arrington (Mass) 7 Eldridge Rd, Jamaica Plain, MA 02130

CHAMPION, Peter (Cal) 703 Mariposa Avenue, Rodeo, CA 94572

CHAMPION, Susan Manley (Cal) 703 Mariposa Ave., Rodeo, CA 94572

CHAMPION-GARTHE, Mo Vinck (Mont) 2101 W Broadway, #103-190, Columbia, MO 65203

CHAMPLIN, Jeffrey Fletcher (Ark) 2701 Old Greenwood Rd, Fort Smith, AR 72903

CHAN, Charles Yang-Ling Ping-Fai (Colo) Po Box 662, Mukwonago, WI 53149

CHAN, Henry Albert (LI) 1212 Foulk Rd Apt 4c, Wilmington, DE 19803

CHANCE, Robin (Wyo) 6516 Weaver Rd, Cheyenne, WY 82009

CHANCELLOR JR, Donald Wood (Miss) PO Box 391, Como, MS 38619

CHANDLER, Belinda (Chi) 3025 Walters Ave, Northbrook, IL 60062

CHANDLER, Gail Stearns (Me) St. David's Episcopal Church, 138 York St, Kennebunk, ME 04043

CHANDLER, John Herrick (Los) 2286 Vasanta Way, Los Angeles, CA 90068

CHANDLER, Nan Elizabeth (EC) 301 Bretonshire Rd, Wilmington, NC 28405

CHANDLER, Paul-Gordon (Spok)

CHANDLER JR, Richard Anthony (CFla) Saint Anne's Church, 9870 W Fort Island Trl, Crystal River, FL 34429

CHANDLER, Susan (Mass) 195 Patmos Rd., Sawyer's Island, Rowley, MA 01969

CHANDY, Sunil Kulangana (RI) 1115 New Pear St, Vineland, NJ 08360

CHANE, John Bryson (WA) 5309 Pendleton St, San Diego, CA 92109

CHANEY JR, Michael Jackson (Ga) 1802 Abercorn St, Savannah, GA 31401

CHANEY, Myrna Faye (Mont) 14 September Dr, Missoula, MT 59802

CHANG, Hsin Fen (Los) 15694 Tetley St, Hacienda Heights, CA 91745

CHANG, Lennon Yuan-Rung (Tai) Wen-Hua 3rd Road, 4th Place #75, Pei-Tan, Taiwan

CHANG, Ling-Ling (Tai) 280 Fu-Hsing South Road, Sec 2, Taipei, Taiwan

CHANG, Mark Chung-Moon (Nwk) 11 Foakes Drive, Ajax, LIT 3K5, Canada

CHANGO, Georgianna (NwPa) Rr 6 Box 324, Punxsutawney, PA 15767

CHANNON, Ethel M (Del) 2304 County Ave, Texarkana, AR 71854

CHAPMAN, Alton James (SwFla) 12905 Forest Hills Dr, Tampa, FL 33612

CHAPMAN JR, Chuck (Ark) 1721 Monzingo, Magnolia, AR 71753

CHAPMAN, Colin (NH) Christ Church, 2 Rectory St, Rye, NY 10580

CHAPMAN, Cristi Elizabeth (Oly) 3434 39th Ave W, Seattle, WA 98199

CHAPMAN, George (Mass) 41 Garth Road, West Roxbury, MA 02132

CHAPMAN, Hugh William (Fla) 13 Bb Misgunsi, St. Thomas, VI 802

CHAPMAN, James Dreger (Mass) 201 Washington Ave, Chelsea, MA 02150

CHAPMAN, Jennifer Marie (NMich)

CHAPMAN, Jerry Wayne (Dal) 11201 Pickfair Dr, Austin, TX 78750

CHAPMAN, Justin P (Minn) 1430 15th Ave NW, Rochester, MN 55901

CHAPMAN, Michael (Alb) 22 Bergen St, Brentwood, NY 11717

CHAPMAN, Phillip (Neb) 322 S 15th St, Plattsmouth, NE 68048

CHAPMAN, Rebecca Ann (CFla)

CHAPMAN, Tansy (Mass) PO Box 832, Mendocino, CA 95460

CHAPPELL, Annette Mary (Md)

CHAPPELL, Veronica Donohue (CPa) 1118 State Route 973 E, Cogan Station, PA 17728

CHAPPELLE, Laurinda (Nev) 1230 Riverberry Dr, Reno, NV 89509

CHAR, Zachariah Jok (WMich) 4232 Alpinehorn Dr Nw, Comstock Pk, MI 49321

CHARD JR, Arthur Cameron (WVa) 1206 Maple Lane, Anchorage, KY 40223

CHARLES, D Maurice (Roch) 412 Euclid Avenue, Oakland, CA 94610

CHARLES, Kathy (Eau) 1001 McLean Ave, Tomah, WI 54660

CHARLES, Leonel (SeFla) Box 1309, Port-Au-Prince, Haiti

CHARLES, Randolph (WA) 11178 Kilkenny Rd, Marshall, VA 20115

CHARLES, Winston Breeden (NC) 114 East Drewry Lane, Raleigh, NC 27609

✠ **CHARLESTON**, Steven (Okla) 2702 Silvertree Dr, Oklahoma City, OK 73120

✠ **CHARLTON**, Gordon Taliaferro (Tex) 132 Lancaster Dr Apt 310, Irvington, VA 22480

CHASE, Alexis M (At) PO Box 286, Decatur, GA 30031

CHASE JR, Benjamin Otis (Vt) 95 Worcester Village Rd, Worcester, VT 05682

CHASE, Christopher (Cal) 10885 Caminito Cuesta, San Diego, CA 92131

CHASE IV, Edwin Theodore Ted (LI) 432 Lakeville Road, The Church of St. Philip and St. James, Lake Success, NY 11042

CHASE JR, John Garvey (Tex) P.O. Box 103, Crockett, TX 75835

CHASE, Katharine Barnhardt (SwVa) PO Box 810, Amherst, VA 24521

CHASE, Peter Gray Otis (Mass) 258 Concord St, Newton, MA 02462

CHASE JR, Ran (Mass) PO Box 924, Barnstable, MA 02630

CHASSE, Richard P (Nwk) 176 Palisade Ave, Jersey City, NJ 07306

CHASSEY JR, George Irwin (USC) 9b Exum Dr, West Columbia, SC 29169

CHASTAIN, Gordon Lee (Ind) 1769 Dunaway Ct, Indianapolis, IN 46228

CHATFIELD, Jane Sheldon (Me) 11 White St, Rockland, ME 04841

CHATFIELD, Jenifer (Los)

CHATHAM, Charles Erwin (Az) 500 S Jackson St, Wickenburg, AZ 85390

CHATTIN, Mark Haney (NJ) 839 Haddon Ave., Collingswood, NJ 08108

CHAVEZ, Chloe Ann Tischler (RG)

CHAVEZ, David Ulloa (Az)

CHAVEZ, Karen Sue (Los) 3160 Graceland Way, Corona, CA 92882

CHAVEZ, Rafael (Hond)

CHAVEZ, Velma (Wyo) 29 Shipton Lane, Fort Washakie, WY 82514

CHAVEZ FRANCO, Juan Eloy (Litoral Ecu) Amarilis Fuente 603/, Ave. Vicente Trujillo y la D, Apartado Postal 09015250, Guayaquil, Ecuador

CHECO, Antonio (LI) 2510 30th Rd Apt 2L, Astoria, NY 11102

CHEE, David T (Los) 700 Devils Drop Ct, El Sobrante, CA 94803

CHEEK, Alison Mary (Mass) Po Box 356, Tenants Harbor, ME 04860

CHEESMAN JR, Benbow Palmer (Mil) 2501 S 60th St, Milwaukee, WI 53219

CHEFFEY, Anne Davis (WMo) 3 Northwoods Dr, Kimberling City, MO 65686

CHEN, Charles Chin-Ti (Tai) 23 Wu-Chuan West Road, 403, Taichung, Taiwan

CHEN, Luke Hh (Tai) No 67 Lane 314 Ming Shen Rd, Shin Hua County, Tainan Hsien, 71246, Taiwan

CHENEY III, Arthur Milton (WMass) 38 Barnes Ln, West Greenwich, RI 02817

CHENEY, Barbara T (Ct) 90 Rogers Rd, Hamden, CT 06517

CHENEY SR, Bruce David (SVa) St Paul Episcopal Church, 221 34th St, Newport News, VA 23607

CHENEY, Dexter (Ct) 90 Rogers Rd, Hamden, CT 06517

CHENEY, Michael Robert (Mass) 117 Forest St, Malden, MA 02148

CHENEY, Peter Gunn (Az) 5090 N Via Gelsomino, Tucson, AZ 85750
CHENG, Chen Chang (Tai) 499, Sec 4 Tam King Rd, Tamsui Dist, New Taipei City Taiwan, 25135, Taiwan
CHENG, Ching-Shan (Tai) 40 Ta Tung Rd, Wu Feng, Taichung County, 852, Taiwan
CHENG, Patrick S (NY) 19 E 34th St, New York, NY 10016
CHERBONNEAU, Allen Robert (Ala) 4367 East River Road, Box 282, Mentone, AL 35984
CHERISME, Charles M. (Hai) 472 Beech St, Roslindale, MA 02131
CHERRY, Charles Shuler (Minn) 734 7th St S, Breckenridge, MN 56520
CHERRY, Jacqueline Ann (Cal) 1076 De Haro St, San Francisco, CA 94107
CHERRY, Mary Jane (Ky) Episcopal Church Home, 7504 Westport Rd, Louisville, KY 40222
CHERRY, Timothy B (Dal) 56 Cedar Ln, Osterville, MA 02655
CHERY, Jean Fils (Hai)
CHERY, Marie Carmel (Hai)
CHESHIRE, Grady Patterson (WNC) 1131 S Edgemont Ave, Gastonia, NC 28054
CHESNEY, Jonathan C (WTenn) 4577Billy Maher Rd., Bartlett, TN 38135
CHESNUT, Mark Douglas (Alb)
CHESS, Jean D (Pgh) 1500 Cochran Rd Apt 901, Pittsburgh, PA 15243
CHESTERMAN JR, Thomas Charles (DR (DomRep)) 2418 Hidden Valley Dr, Santa Rosa, CA 95404
CHEVES, Henry Middleton (SC) 635 Foredeck Lane, Edisto Island, SC 29438
CHILDERS, Robert T J (ETenn) Church of the Good Shepherd, P.O. Box 145, Lookout Mountain, TN 37350
CHILDRESS JR, John (Ark) 10702 Crestdale Ln, Little Rock, AR 72212
CHILES, Bob (USC) The Reverend Robert L Chiles, 103 Underwood Dr, Hendersonville, NC 28739
CHILESE, Sandra Lee (Az)
CHILLINGTON, Joseph Henry (Ind) 215 N 7th Street, Terre Haute, IN 47807
CHILTON, Bruce (NY) Bard College, Annandale-on-Hudson, NY 12504
CHILTON, Mary Habel (Alb) 3 Woods Edge Ln, West Sand Lake, NY 12196
CHILTON, William Parish (Eas) 214 Wye Ave, Easton, MD 21601
CHIN, Mary Louise (LI) Po Box 650397, Fresh Meadows, NY 11365
CHINERY, Edwin Thomas (NJ) 165 Essex Ave Apt 102, Metuchen, NJ 08840
CHINLUND, Stephen James (NY) 445 W 19th St Apt Ph-D, New York, NY 10011
CHIPPS, Kathleen Dawn (Va) 3604 Secret Grove Ct, Dumfries, VA 22025

CHIRAN QUINONEZ, Jairo Ernesto (Litoral Ecu) Santiago Apostol, Parroquia La Pila Calle Mexico, La Pila, 593, Ecuador
CHIRINOS-HERNANDEZ, Jose A (Hond)
CHISHAM, Anne Beardsley (SanD) 47568 Hawley Boulevard, San Diego, CA 92116
CHISHOLM, Alan Laird (NY) 209 S Broadway, Nyack, NY 10960
CHITTENDEN, Nils Philip (NY) St Stephens Church, 50 Bedford Rd, Armonk, NY 10504
CHO, Francis Soonhwan (NJ) 16 Rodak Cir, Edison, NJ 08817
CHOATE JR, Horace (NY) 4 Gateway Rd., Unit 1-D, Yonkers, NY 10703
CHOI, Beryl Turner (WNY) 51 Virginia Pl, Buffalo, NY 14202
CHOI, Stephen Young Sai (NY) 5 77th St # 7047, North Bergen, NJ 07047
✠ **CHOI**, William Chul-Hi (Los) 8105 232nd St Se, Woodinville, WA 98072
CHOI, Young Kwon Kwon (Va) 1830 Kirby Rd, Mclean, VA 22101
CHOLLET, Mariclea Joaquim (Mo) 232 South Woods Mill Rd., Chesterfield, MO 63017
CHORNYAK, Christopher John (Me) 3 Spring House Ln, Ellsworth, ME 04605
CHOU, Yun-Kuang (Tai) St. Mark, 120-11 Chung Hsiao Road, Ping Tung, 900, Taiwan
CHOYCE, George (ETenn) 27 Cool Springs Rd, Signal Mountain, TN 37377
CHRISMAN JR, John Aubrey (RI) 7118 Treymore Ct, Sarasota, FL 34243
CHRISMAN, Robert (Oly) 1214 184th Pl, Long Beach, WA 98631
CHRISNER, Marlen Ronald (At) 6517 SW 85th St, Ocala, FL 34476
CHRISTENSEN, Bonniejean Mcguire (ND) 4001 Beneva Rd Apt 334, Sarasota, FL 34233
CHRISTIAN, Carol Jean (SO) 5701 Makati Cir Apt E, San Jose, CA 95123
CHRISTIAN, Charles Ellis (Ind) 3627 E Crystal Valley Dr, Vincennes, IN 47591
CHRISTIAN, David Victor (WTenn) 8282 Macon Rd, Cordova, TN 38018
CHRISTIAN, Earl Rix (SVa) 25 Tripp Ter, Hampton, VA 23666
CHRISTIAN JR, Frank Stanaland (Ga) 212 W Pine St, Fitzgerald, GA 31750
CHRISTIANSEN, Andrew Lee (EMich) 908 Rutherford St, Shreveport, LA 71104
CHRISTIANSEN, Anthony (Colo)
CHRISTIANSON, Regina (Vt) PO Box 57, Underhill, VT 05489
CHRISTIANSSEN, Paul Jerome (The Episcopal NCal) 1016 W. Arrow Hwy, Apt. C, Upland, CA 91786

CHRISTIE, Robert Lusk (Oly) 6350 Portal Way Unit 72, Ferndale, WA 98248
CHRISTOFFERSEN, Timothy Robert (Cal) 611 Foxwood Way, Walnut Creek, CA 94595
CHRISTOPHER JR, Chuck (EO) 19529 Sugar Mill Loop, Bend, OR 97702
CHRISTOPHER, Cynthia Ann (Md) Holy Trinity Episcopal Church, 1131 Mace Ave, Essex, MD 21221
CHRISTOPHER, John S (Az) 5143 E Karen Dr, Scottsdale, AZ 85254
CHRISTOPHER, Mary (Ia) 2110 Summit St, Sioux City, IA 51104
CHRISTOPHER, Melanie (Colo) 371 Upham St, Lakewood, CO 80226
CHRISTOPHERSON, Paul Conrad (Minn) Wildlife Run, New Vernon, NJ 07976
CHRISTY, Christine Lavon (Az)
CHRISTY, Stephen James (Wyo)
CHRONISTER, Lisa Marie (Okla)
CHRYSTAL, Susan (Nwk) 33 Woodstone Cir, Short Hills, NJ 07078
CHUBB JR, Donald Allen (Kan) 1011 SW Cambridge Ave, Topeka, KS 66604
CHUBOFF, Esther Lois (Ct) 83 E Main St, Clinton, CT 06413
CHUMBLEY, Ken (WMo) 601 E Walnut St, Springfield, MO 65806
CHUN, Franklin (The Episcopal Church in Haw) 1163 Lunaanela St, Kailua, HI 96734
CHURCH, Susan (Ore) Po Box 605, John Day, OR 97845
CHURCH, Susan Jean (NMich) Christ Church, 3906 5th St, Calumet, MI 49913
CHURCHILL, Gregg Hardison (Los) Po Box 1082, Lompoc, CA 93438
CHURCHMAN, Michael Arthur (Neb) 300 W Broadway Ste 108, Council Bluffs, IA 51503
CHURCHMAN, Nina Wood (Colo) 3224 S Eudora St, Denver, CO 80222
CHURCHWELL, Katherine C (SwFla) PO Box 1581, St Petersburg, FL 33731
CIANNELLA, J oseph Domenic Kennith (Mass) 13 Park Dr, West Springfield, MA 01089
CICCARELLI, Sharon Lynn (Mass) 13 Turner Ter, Newton, MA 02460
CICORA, Julie Anne (Roch) 556 Forest Lawn Dr, Webster, NY 14580
CIESEL, Barbara Bitney (SD) 126 N Park St Ne, Wagner, SD 57380
CIESEL, Conrad Henry (SD) Po Box 216, Lake City, SD 57247
CIHAK, Susan Elizabeth (Az) 12990 E Shea Blvd, Scottsdale, AZ 85259
CILLEY, Norman H (CFla) 23 E Hampton Dr, Auburndale, FL 33823
CIMIJOTTI, Jerry Anthony (SD) 2822 S Division St, Spokane, WA 99203
CINTRON, Julio A (PR)
CIOSEK, Scott Andrew (Mass) 351 Elm St, South Dartmouth, MA 02748

CIPOLLA, Angela Marie (NJ) 650 Rahway Dr., Woodbridge, NJ 07095

CIRIELLO, Mary Anne (Ct) 3768 Anslow Drive, Leland, NC 28451

CIRILLO, James Hawthorne (Va) Po Box 847, Buckingham, PA 18912

CIRVES, Judith Melanie (Mil) 510 Ludington Ave, Madison, WI 53704

CISNEROS, Hilario (WNC) 2657 Chimney Rock Rd, Hendersonville, NC 28792

CITARELLA, Kenneth Christopher (NY) PO Box 459, North Salem, NY 10560

CIVALIER, Rick (NJ) 161 Lakebridge Dr., Deptford, NJ 08096

CLAASSEN, Scott Allen (Los) 714 Mission Park Dr, Santa Barbara, CA 93105

CLADER, Linda Lee (The Episcopal NCal) 5555 Montgomery Dr Apt N201, Santa Rosa, CA 95409

CLAGGETT III, Thomas West (Md) 1123C Jefferson Pike, Knoxville, MD 21758

CLANCE, Bennett Bolton (Fla)

CLAPP JR, Schuyler Lamb (EMich) 2830 Arborview Dr Apt 2, Traverse City, MI 49685

CLARAGE, Thelma Lou (NMich)

CLARK, Anthony P (Tex) 5525 N Circuit Dr, Beaumont, TX 77706

CLARK, Beatryce Arlene (The Episcopal NCal) 581 Ridgewood Dr, Vacaville, CA 95688

CLARK, Brad (Mass) Po Box 25, Arlington, VT 05250

CLARK, Carol Ruth (NMich) 10401 V.05 Rd, Rapid River, MI 49878

CLARK, Carole Sue (Okla) Hc 67 Box 82, Indianola, OK 74442

CLARK, Cathy A (NMich) P.O. Box 601, Ishpeming, MI 49849

CLARK, Charles Halsey (NH) 5 Timber Ln Apt 228, Exeter, NH 03833

CLARK, Cheryl (Ark) 1106 Deer Run N, Pine Bluff, AR 71603

CLARK, Cindy Lou (Tex) 501 E Gregg St, Calvert, TX 77837

CLARK, Constance Lee (Va) PO Box 183, Earlysville, VA 22936

CLARK, Corbet (Oly) 11520 Sw Timberline Dr, Beaverton, OR 97008

CLARK, David Norman (Md) 12265 Boyd Rd, Clear Spring, MD 21722

CLARK, Diana (Nwk) 59 Montclair Ave, Montclair, NJ 07042

CLARK, Diane Catherine FitzGerald (WA) 13 Eleanor Avenue, Saint Albans, Hertfordshire, AL35TA, Great Britain (UK)

CLARK, Douglas Burns (SeFla) 116 Prospect Park W # 2r, Brooklyn, NY 11215

CLARK, Frances M (NJ) 201 Penbryn Rd, Berlin, NJ 08009

CLARK, Frank H (Az) 7810 W Columbine Dr, Peoria, AZ 85381

CLARK, Holly Christine (Me)

CLARK, Jacqueline (Mass) St Elizabeth's Episcopal Church, 1 Morse Rd, Sudbury, MA 01776

CLARK II, James Boyd (Az) 6715 N Mockingbird Lane, Paradise Valley, AZ 85253

CLARK, Jane (Chi) 1608 W Plymouth Dr, Arlington Heights, IL 60004

CLARK, Jason (ETenn)

CLARK, Joan Bonnell (CFla) 231 Waters Edge Dr, Kissimmee, FL 34743

CLARK, John E (CFla) 414 Pine St, Titusville, FL 32796

CLARK, John Leland (SO) #1712 - 8888 Riverside Dr E, Windsor, N8S 1H2, Canada

CLARK SR, John Warren (WLa) 321 Horseshoe Drive, Crowley, LA 70526

CLARK, Joseph Madison (WA) 402 Grove Ave, po box 1098, Washington Grove, MD 20880

CLARK, Judith Freeman (Mass) 10 Ida Rd., Worcester, MA 01604

CLARK, Katherine Hampton (Los) 3969 Bucklin Pl, Thousand Oaks, CA 91360

CLARK, Marlene M (Mich) 1180 S Durand Rd, Lennon, MI 48449

CLARK, Martha (WA) 600 M St SW, Washington, DC 20024

CLARK, Paula E (WA) 3001 Orion Ln, Upper Marlboro, MD 20774

CLARK, Philip C (Minn) 128 Canterbury Cir, Le Sueur, MN 56058

CLARK, Ralph (EC) 801 Bobby Jones Drive, Fayetteville, NC 28312

CLARK JR, Richard Johnston (SwFla) 315 41st St W, Bradenton, FL 34209

CLARK, Richard Neece (WMich) 900 Pivot Rock Rd, Eureka Springs, AR 72632

CLARK, Richard Tilton (Mass) 16 Timothy St, Fairhaven, MA 02719

CLARK, Robbin (Cal) 36 Larkhay Road, Hucclecote Gloucester, AE GL3 3NS, Great Britain (UK)

CLARK, Susan Mccarter (EMich) W180N7890 Town Hall Rd Apt D315, Menomonee Falls, WI 53051

CLARK, Taylor Brooks (EO) 991 Normandy Ave S, Salem, OR 97302

CLARK, Vance Norman (CPa) 925 S. Lincoln Ave., Apt. G, Tyrone, PA 16686

CLARK, Vanessa E B (O) St. James Episcopal Church, 131 N State St, Painesville, OH 44077

CLARK, William Roderick (WTex) 1417 E Austin Ave, Harlingen, TX 78550

CLARK, William Whittier (Alb) Po Box 56, Medusa, NY 12120

CLARKE, Anne Elizabeth (The Episcopal NCal) 350 University Ave Ste 280, Sacramento, CA 95825

CLARKE, Barbara Jean (Me) 11 Daisey Ln, Brewer, ME 04412

CLARKE, Charles Ray (Wyo) 796 Garner Dr, Lander, WY 82520

CLARKE JR, Daniel L (SC) 94 Willow Oak Cir, Charleston, SC 29418

CLARKE, Debra M (NJ) 187 Aster Ct, Whitehouse Station, NJ 08889

CLARKE, Gervaise Angelo Morales (Nwk) 34 Orane Ave, Meadowbrook Mews, Kingston 19, Jamaica

CLARKE, James Munro (Alb) Po Box 405, Downsville, NY 13755

CLARKE, Janet Vollert (SeFla) 33406 Fairway Rd, Leesburg, FL 34788

CLARKE, John David Blackmore (NY) 790 11th Ave Apt 29a, New York, NY 10019

CLARKE, John Robert (Mass) 2 Ridgewood Rd, Malden, MA 02148

CLARKE, Julian Maurice (VI) 123 Circle Dr, Saint Simons Island, GA 31522

CLARKE, Kenneth Gregory (SO) 3090 Montego Ln. Apt. 1, Maineville, OH 45039

CLARKE, Richard Kent (WMass) 162 Laurelwood Dr, Hopedale, MA 01747

CLARKE, Robert (Chi) 524 Sheridan Sq Apt 3, Evanston, IL 60202

CLARKE, Sheelagh (Nwk) 119 Main St, Millburn, NJ 07041

CLARKE, Thomas George (Los) 1549 E Lobo Way, Palm Springs, CA 92264

CLARK-KING, Ellen Jane (Cal) 1100 California St, San Francisco, CA 94108

CLARK-KING, Jeremy ()

CLARKSON, Frederick C (EC) 4401 Statesville Blvd., Salisbury, NC 28147

CLARKSON, J (WNC)

CLARKSON, Julie Cuthbertson (NC) 1420 Sterling Rd, Charlotte, NC 28209

CLARKSON, Ted Hamby (Ga) Po Drawer 929, Darien, GA 31305

CLARKSON IV, William (WA) 1424 W Paces Ferry Rd Nw, Atlanta, GA 30327

CLASSEN, Ashley Molesworth (Dal) 635 N Story Rd, Irving, TX 75061

CLAUSEN, Kathryn (SO) 3623 Sellers Drive, Millersport, OH 43046

CLAUSEN, Ruth Lucille (Mich) 100 N. College Row Apt. 165, Brevard, NC 28712

CLAVIER, Anthony Forbes Moreton (Spr) 193 Summit Avenue, Glen Carbon, IL 62034

CLAVIJO, Joseph Maria (La) 4600 Saint Charles Ave, New Orleans, LA 70115

CLAWSON, Donald Richard (SeFla) 1605 Pasos Del Lago Ln, Vero Beach, FL 32967

CLAWSON, Jeffrey David (Los) 3 Bayview Ave., Belvedere, CA 94920

CLAXTON, Constance Colvin (Minn) 312 Church St, Audubon, IA 50025

CLAXTON, Leonard Cuthbert (Minn) RR #2, Box 207, Truman, MN 56088

CLAY, Thomas Davies (WA) 15003 Reserve Rd, Accokeek, MD 20607

CLAYTON JR, Paul Bauchman (NY) 4 Townsend Farm Rd, Lagrangeville, NY 12540

CLAYTON, Sharon Hoffman Chant (NY) 4 Townsend Farm Rd, Lagrangeville, NY 12540

CLAYTON, Vikki (WA) 20100 Fisher Ave, Poolesville, MD 20837

CLAYTOR, Susan Quarles (CPa) 310 Elm Avenue, Hershey, PA 17033

CLEAVER-BARTHOLOMEW, Dena (CNY) 4566 Stoneledge Ln, Manlius, NY 13104

CLEAVES JR, George Lucius (WMo) 9020 South Saginaw Road, Grand Blanc, MI 48439

CLECKLER, Michael Howard (Ala) 1513 Edinburgh Way, Birmingham, AL 35243

CLEGHORN, Charlotte Dudley (WNC) 37 Cherry St., Arden, NC 28704

CLEGHORN, Maxine Janetta (NY) 4401 Matilda Ave, Bronx, NY 10470

CLELAND, Carol Elaine (Cal) 1550 Portola Avenue, Palo Alto, CA 94306

CLEM, Stewart Douglas (Okla) 616 Lincolnway E, Mishawaka, IN 46544

CLEMENT, Betty Cannon (Dal) 4120 Jasmine St, Paris, TX 75462

CLEMENT, James Marshall (WNY) Trinity Episcopal Church, 11 Day St, Fredonia, NY 14063

CLEMENTS, C(Harles) Christopher (USC) 1523 Delmar St, West Columbia, SC 29169

CLEMENTS, Elaine Gant (La) St Andrew's Episcopal Church, 1101 S Carrollton Ave, New Orleans, LA 70118

CLEMENTS, Michael Stuart (Okla) 515 W Beech St, Durant, OK 74701

CLEMENTS, Robert (Ct) PO Box 809, Litchfield, CT 06759

CLEMMONS, Geraldine Dobbs (Alb) 105 23rd St., Troy, NY 12180

CLEMONS, D. David (The Episcopal NCal) 8148 Emerson Ave, Yucca Valley, CA 92284

CLEMONS, Roland (NJ) 132 S Adelaide Ave Apt 1b, Highland Park, NJ 08904

CLENDENIN, Evan Graham (Oly) 719 West 2nd St, Erie, PA 16507

CLENDINEN JR, James H (Ga) 2621 Cotuit Ln, Tallahassee, FL 32309

CLERKIN, Shawn J (NwPa) 662 Silliman Ave, Erie, PA 16510

CLEVELAND, Jennifer B (Oly) 125 SW Eckman St, McMinnville, OR 97128

CLEVELAND, Thomas Grover (Mass) 28 Grover Ln, Tamworth, NH 03886

CLEVELEY, Susan Lynn (Spok) 1005 E B St, Moscow, ID 83843

CLEVENGER, Mark R (U) PO Box 606, Shoreham, NY 11786

CLICK, Barbara Gail (Mo) 600 N Euclid Ave, Saint Louis, MO 63108

CLIFF, Frank Graham (Be) 15 Bede Circle, Honesdale, PA 18431

CLIFF, Wendy Dawson (Cal) 77 Kensington Rd, San Anselmo, CA 94960

CLIFFORD III, George Minott (The Episcopal Church in Haw)

CLIFT, Jean Dalby (Colo) 2130 E Columbia Pl, Denver, CO 80210

CLIFT, Joe Walter (Ga) 343 Gander Rd, Dawson, GA 39842

CLIFTON JR, Ellis Edward (Mich) St. Clement'S Episcopal Church, 4300 Harrison Road, Inkster, MI 48141

CLIFTON, Steve (CFla) 3137 Denham Ct, Orlando, FL 32825

CLINEHENS JR, Hal (The Episcopal NCal) 714 Lassen Lane, Mount Shasta, CA 96067

CLINGENPEEL, Ronald H (La) 1911 Cypress Creek Road #222, New Orleans, LA 70123

CLIVER, Stanley Cameron (Wyo) Po Box 176, Sundance, WY 82729

CLODFELTER, Jon (Pa) 4442 Frankford Ave, Philadelphia, PA 19124

CLOSE, David Wyman (Ore) 7990 Headlands Way, Clinton, WA 98236

CLOSE, Leroy Springs (RI) 316 W Main Rd, Little Compton, RI 02837

CLOSE, Pat (NJ) Grace Episcopal Church, 19 Kings Hwy E, Haddonfield, NJ 08033

CLOSE ERSKINE, Christine Elaine (Ore) 60960 Creekstone Loop, Bend, OR 97702

CLOTHIER, Tamara A (Tex) 5001 Hickory Rd, Temple, TX 76502

CLOUGHEN JR, Charles (Md) PO Box 313-, Hunt Valley, MD 21030

CLOWERS, Grantland Hugh (Kan) 2007 Miller Dr, Lawrence, KS 66046

CLUETT JR, Rick (Be) 119 W. Johnston St., Allentown, PA 18103

COATS, Bleakley Irving (Ida)

COATS, Christopher Vincent (CGC) Wharf Marina Slip #38, Orange Beach, AL 36561

COATS, John Rhodes (Cal) 15814 Champion Forest Dr, Spring, TX 77379

COATS, William Russell (Nwk) 19 Elmwood Ave., Ho Ho Kus, NJ 07423

COBB, Christina Rich (Mo) 1212 Ringo St, Mexico, MO 65265

COBB, David (Chi) 34 Running Knob Hollow Rd, Sewanee, TN 37375

COBB JR, Harold James (SVa) 1931 Paddock Rd, Norfolk, VA 23518

COBB, Julia Kramer (NwT) St Barnabas Episcopal Church, 4141 Tanglewood Ln, Odessa, TX 79762

COBB, Matthew M (Kan) 1915 Montgomery Dr, Manhattan, KS 66502

COBB-ANDERSON, Vienna (Va) 1138 West Ave, Richmond, VA 23220

COBDEN JR, Edward Alexander Morrison (Mich) Po Box 295, South Egremont, MA 01258

COBDEN III, Edward Alexander Morrison (NY) 374 Sarles St, Bedford Corners, NY 10549

COBLE JR, John Reifsnyder (Be) 1929 Pelham Rd, Bethlehem, PA 18018

COBLE, Robert Henry (Pa) 36 Crescent Cir, Harleysville, PA 19438

COBURN, Ann Struthers (Mass) PO Box 1988, Berkeley, CA 94709

COBURN, Michael (RI) 55 Linden Road, Barrington, RI 02806

COCHRAN, Elizabeth Jane (Oly) St Matthew's Episcopal Church, 412 Pioneer Ave, Castle Rock, WA 98611

COCHRAN, Joseph M (Md)

COCHRAN, Laura (Va) 1700 Wainwright Dr, Reston, VA 20190

COCHRAN, Lottie (SVa) 713 Seagrass Reach, Chesapeake, VA 23320

COCKBILL, Douglas J (Chi) 3310 Coventry Ct, Joliet, IL 60431

COCKE, Reagan Winter (Tex) 2450 River Oaks Blvd, Houston, TX 77019

COCKERILL, Ernest William (ECR) 1538 Koch Ln, San Jose, CA 95125

COCKRELL, John Grafton (SC) 275 Warden Ave, Bluefield, WV 24701

COCKRELL, Richard (USC) 8700 N La Cholla Blvd Apt 2137, Anderson, SC 29625

CODE, David (NJ) 729 Partridge Ln, State College, PA 16803

CODY, Daphne C (Chi) 380 Hawthorn Ave, Glencoe, IL 60022

COE III, Frank S (WVa) 74 Rhodes Court, Harpers Ferry, WV 25425

COE, Wayland Newton (Tex) 5934 Rutherglenn Dr, Houston, TX 77096

COENEN, Susan Ann (FdL)

COERPER, Becky (CNY) 98 East Genesee St, Skaneateles, NY 13152

COERPER, Milo George (Md) 7315 Brookville Rd, Chevy Chase, MD 20815

COFFEY, Bridget (O) 2112 Harvest Dr, Winchester, VA 22601

COFFEY, E Allen (Va) 10231 Fenholloway Dr, Mechanicsville, VA 23116

COFFEY, Gary (WNC) 23 Forest Knoll Dr, Weaverville, NC 28787

COFFEY JR, Jon (Fla) 4903 Robert D Gordon Rd, Jacksonville, FL 32210

COFFEY, Kevin (Nwk) 2-06 31st St, Fair Lawn, NJ 07410

COFFEY, Paris (Chi) 240 S. Marion St., 1N, Oak Park, IL 60302

COFFIN, Peter R (NH) 35 Woodbury St, Keene, NH 03431

COFFMAN, Daniel Brian (Neb) Holy Trinity Episcopal Church, 6001 A St, Lincoln, NE 68510

COFFMAN, Mary Ann (Okla) 3333 N Meridian Ave, Oklahoma City, OK 73112

COGAN, Timothy Bernard (NJ) 38 The Blvd/RFD659, Edgartown, MA 02539

COGAR, Carolyn Christine (SO) 541 2nd Ave, Gallipolis, OH 45631

COGGI, Lynne Marie Madeleine (NY) 3206 Cripple Creek St Apt 39b, San Antonio, TX 78209

COGGIN, Bruce W (FtW) 3700 Ellsmere Ct, Fort Worth, TX 76103

COGILL, Richard Leonard (Minn) Cathedral of St George the Martyr, 5 Wales St, Cape Town, 8001, South Africa

COGSDALE, Mike (WNC) 845 Cherokee Place, Lenoir, NC 28645

COHEE, William Patrick (Az) 114 W Roosevelt St, Phoenix, AZ 85003

COHEN, David Michael (The Episcopal NCal) 310 W North St, Alturas, CA 96101

COHEN, Georgia S (NJ) Po Box 5, Blawenburg, NJ 08504

COHOON, Richard Allison (CPa) 500 E Guardlock Dr, Lock Haven, PA 17745

COIL, Doug (At) 4141 Wash Lee Ct Sw, Lilburn, GA 30047

COIL, John Albert (WMo) 7917 Lamar Ave, Prairie Village, KS 66208

COKE, Paul Tyler (Tex) 9426 Peabody Ct, Boca Raton, FL 33496

COLANGELO, Preston Hart (Ala) 1663 Bradford Ln, Bessemer, AL 35022

COLAVINCENZO, Sue (EMich) St Dunstan's Episcopal Church, 1523 N Oak Rd, Davison, MI 48423

COLBERT, Paul (The Episcopal NCal) 230 S Church St, Grass Valley, CA 95945

COLBURN, Suzanne (Mass) Po Box 185, Boothbay Harbor, ME 04538

COLBURN, Therese Jean (Colo)

COLBY, Richard Everett (Me) 3702 Haven Pines Dr, Kingwood, TX 77345

COLE, Allan Hunter (Colo) 9200 W 10th Ave, Lakewood, CO 80215

COLE, Anson Dean (O) 565 S Cleveland Massillon Rd, Akron, OH 44333

COLE, Anthony Richard (Eur) 3 Rue de Monthoux, Geneva, 1201, Switzerland

✠ **COLE**, Brian (ETenn) Church of the Good Shepherd, 533 E Main St, Lexington, KY 40508

COLE JR, C Alfred (CFla) 125 Larkwood Dr, Sanford, FL 32771

COLE JR, Cecil T (Mass) 2210 E Tudor Rd, Anchorage, AK 99507

COLE, Christopher A (At) Holy Innocents Episcopal Church, 805 Mt Vernon Hwy NW, Atlanta, GA 30327

COLE, Christopher Owen (WTex) 5909 Walzem Rd, San Antonio, TX 78218

COLE, Dennis Curtis (Oly) 3917 Ne 44th St, Vancouver, WA 98661

COLE, Elaine Agnes (SwFla) 330 Forest Wood Ct, Spring Hill, FL 34609

COLE, Enid Omodele (WA)

COLE, Ethan J (WNY) 5083 Thompson Rd, Clarence, NY 14031

COLE, Frantz (Hai) Box 1309, Port-Au-Prince, Haiti

COLE JR, Howard Milton (Pa) 2001 S. 40th Court, West Des Moines, IA 50265

COLE, Judith Hampton Poteet (WNC) 8015 Island View Ct, Denver, NC 28037

COLE, Lisa Jeanne (The Episcopal NCal) 275 E Spain St, Sonoma, CA 95476

COLE, Marguerite June (Nev) 5268 Jodilyn Ct Apt 150, Las Vegas, NV 89103

COLE, Patrice Clark (Az)

COLE JR, Ray (WTex) 3614 Hunters Dove, San Antonio, TX 78230

COLE, Roy Allen (NY) 1333 Bay St, Staten Island, NY 10305

COLE III, Roy W (USC) 184 Clifton Ave, Spartanburg, SC 29302

COLE, Sue (Me) 42 Gardiner Pl, Walton, NY 13856

COLE, Timothy Alexander Robertson (WA) Christ Church, 3116 O St NW, Washington, DC 20007

COLE-DUVALL, Mary Duvall (Ia) 2001 S 40th Ct, West Des Moines, IA 50265

COLEGROVE, Jerome Higgins (O) 475 Laurel Drive, Kent, OH 44240

COLEMAN, Bernice (LI) 10206 Farmers Blvd, Hollis, NY 11423

COLEMAN, Betty Ellen Gibson (SO) 4325 Skylark Dr, Englewood, OH 45322

COLEMAN, Brian Ray (WMich) 252 Chestnut St, Battle Creek, MI 49017

COLEMAN, Carolyn (Tenn) Holy Cross Episcopal Church, 1140 Cason Land, Murfreesboro, TN 37128

COLEMAN JR, Dale D (Spr) 105 E. D St., Belleville, IL 62220

COLEMAN, Dennis E (Pa) 121 Church St, Phoenixville, PA 19460

COLEMAN, Edwin Cabaniss (Tenn) 4715 Harding Pike, Nashville, TN 37205

COLEMAN JR, Fred George (NY) 2048 Lorena Ave., Akron, OH 44313

✠ **COLEMAN**, James Malone (WTenn) 3052 Tyrone Dr, Baton Rouge, LA 70808

COLEMAN, James Patrick (CFla) 4820 Lake Gibson Park Rd, Lakeland, FL 33809

COLEMAN, John Charles (CGC) 2 Chateau Place, Dothan, AL 36303

COLEMAN, Karen (Mass) 59 Fayerweather St # 2138, Cambridge, MA 02138

COLEMAN, Kim (Va) 912 S Veitch St, Arlington, VA 22204

COLEMAN, M Joan (Spr) 9 Teakwood Dr, Belleville, IL 62221

✠ **COLERIDGE**, Clarence Nicholas (Ct) 29 Indian Rd, Trumbull, CT 06611

COLES, Clifford Carleton (NC) 3927 Napa Valley Dr, Raleigh, NC 27612

COLES, Constance C (NY) 73 Waterside Lane, Clinton, CT 06413

COLETON, John M (Kan) 7224 Village Dr, Prairie Village, KS 66208

COLLAMORE JR, Harry Bacon (Ct) 899 Turtle Ct, Naples, FL 34108

COLLEGE, Philip (SO) 5691 Great Hall Ct, Columbus, OH 43231

COLLER, Patricia Marie (Ct) Church Pension Group, 19 E 34th St, New York, NY 10016

COLLEY-TOOTHAKER, Sam Scott (WNY) 437 Hawthorne Drive, Danville, VA 24541

COLLIER, Catherine (Ala) 605 Lurleen B Wallace Blvd N, Tuscaloosa, AL 35401

COLLIER, Daniel R (NH) 155 Salem Rd, Billerica, MA 01821

COLLIER, Mary Anne (NwT) 1605 W Pecan Ave, Midland, TX 79705

COLLIN, Winifred Nohmer (Roch) 2696 Clover St, Pittsford, NY 14534

COLLINS, Charles Blake (WTex) 431 Richmond Pl Ne, Albuquerque, NM 87106

COLLINS, David William (SeFla) 365 La Villa Dr., Miami Springs, FL 33166

COLLINS, Diana Garvin (Vt) 535 Woodbury Rd, Springfield, VT 05156

COLLINS, Emily Selden (NMich) 1628 W Town Line Rd, Pickford, MI 49774

COLLINS, Gerald (Pa) 4700 City Avenue, Apt. 11310, Philadelphia, PA 19131

COLLINS, Guy J(Ames) D(Ouglas) (NH) 9 W Wheelock St, Hanover, NH 03755

COLLINS, James Edward (ECR) 615 Santa Paula Dr, Salinas, CA 93901

COLLINS, Jean Griffin (Mont) 1000 Fountain Terrace, 402, Lewistown, MT 59457

COLLINS III, John Milton (SanD) 701 Kettner Blvd Unit 94, San Diego, CA 92101

COLLINS, John Robert (EO) PO Box 130, Sisters, OR 97759

COLLINS, Loretta L (Eas) 21 S Main St, Lewistown, PA 17044

COLLINS, Lynn (LI) 21 Eldridge Ave, Hempstead, NY 11550

COLLINS, Mac (SanD) 3847 Balsamina Dr, Bonita, CA 91902

COLLINS, Mark R (Nwk) 40 Central Ave, Glen Rock, NJ 07452

COLLINS, Patrick (Eas) 640 N 67th St, Harrisburg, PA 17111

COLLINS, Paul (O) 2387 Edgerton Rd, University Heights, OH 44118

COLLINS, Paul Michael (Oly) PO Box 1204, Summerland, CA 93067

COLLINS, Stanley Penrose (Episcopal SJ) 1401 Locke Rd, Modesto, CA 95355

COLLINS, Victoria Lundberg (CFla) 688 Ebony St, Melbourne, FL 32935

COLLINS, William Gerard (Ga) 209 Maple St, Saint Simons Island, GA 31522

COLLINS-BOHRER, Padraic Michael (Roch) 111 East Ave Apt 330, Rochester, NY 14604

COLLINS REED, Charlotte Collins (O) 409 E High St, Springfield, OH 45505

COLLINSWORTH, Beverly (NI)

COLLIS, Geoffrey (NJ) 32 Lafayette St, Rumson, NJ 07760

COLLIS, Shannon J (WNY) 11305 Hesperia Rd., Hesperia, CA 92345

COLMENAREZ, Gustavo Adolfo (Ve) Iglesia Episcopal de Venezuela, Colinas de Bello Monte, Centro Diocesano Av. CaronÃ No. 100, Caracas, 1042A, Venezuela

COLMORE III, Charles Blayney (SanD) Po Box 516, Jacksonville, VT 05342

COLON TORRES, Lydia (PR) PO Box 902, Saint Just, PR 00978

COLTON, Elizabeth Wentworth (Pa) 966 Trinity Lane, King of Prussia, PA 19406

COLVILL, Lea Nadine (Mont)

COLVIN, Jeremi Ann (Mass) 160 Rock St, Fall River, MA 02720

COLVIN, Sarah M (Oly) 131 Waterbury Court, Charlottesville, VA 22902

COLWELL, Charles Richard (NY) 172 Ivy St, Oyster Bay, NY 11771

COLWELL II, Kirby O (O) 4449 Lander Rd, Chagrin Falls, OH 44022

COMBS, Carrie A (Ct) 36 Main St, Newtown, CT 06470

COMBS, Jaqueline Suzanne (WNC)

COMBS, Leslie David (NY) 123 Franklin St., Concord, NH 03301

COMBS, Nikolaus M (Ida)

COMBS, William (At) 2920 Landrum Education Dr, Oakwood, GA 30566

COMEAU, Molly Stata (Vt) 70 Poor Farm Rd, Alburg, VT 05440

COMEAUX, Andrew Anthony (WLa) 3728 Sabine Pass Dr, Bossier, LA 71111

COMER, Fletcher (Ala) 898 Running Brook Dr, Prattville, AL 36066

COMER, Judith Walton (Ala) 2813 Godfrey Ave NE, Fort Payne, AL 35967

COMER, Kathleen Susan (La) 4105 Division St, Metairie, LA 70002

COMER, Skip (WMich) 1231 Fran Dr, Frankfort, MI 49635

COMER, Susie (Tex) 1941 Webberville Rd, Austin, TX 78721

COMFORT, Alexander Freeman (WNC) 105 Sunny Ln, Mars Hill, NC 28754

COMINOS, Peter Mitchell (EMich) 508 Hart St, Essexville, MI 48732

COMMINS, Gary (Los) 954 Avenue C, Bayonne, NJ 07002

COMPIER, Don Hendrik (Kan) 835 SW Polk St, Topeka, KS 66612

COMPTON, William Hewlett (Miss) 674 Mannsdale Rd, Madison, MS 39110

CONANT, Louise Ritchey (Mass) 24 Bowdoin St, Cambridge, MA 02138

CONAWAY, Arthur Clarence (Lex) 1403 Providence Rd, Richmond, KY 40475

CONDON, Joshua T (Tex) Holy Spirit Episcopal Church, 12535 Perthshire Rd, Houston, TX 77024

CONDON, Sarah Taylor (Tex)

CONES, Bryan Matthew (Chi) 1140 Wilmette Ave, Wilmette, IL 60091

CONGDON, William Hopper (Ct)

CONGER, George AM (CFla) 3086 N Barton Creek Cir, Lecanto, FL 34461

CONGER, George Mallett (NY) 9 Angel Rd, New Paltz, NY 12561

CONGER, John Peyton (Cal)

CONIGLIO, Robert Freeman (SVa) 21313 Metompkin View Lane, Parksley, VA 23421

CONKLIN, Andrea Caruso (Tex) 1819 Heights Blvd, Houston, TX 77008

CONKLIN, Caroline Elizabeth (Mont) 13231 15th Ave N.E., Seattle, WA 98125

CONKLIN, Daniel (Oly) Neue Jakob Str 1, Berlin, 10179, Germany

CONKLING JR, Allan (WTex) PO Box 314, Bandera, TX 78003

CONKLING, Kelly S (WTex) 10642 Newcroft Pl, Helotes, TX 78023

CONLEY, Alan Bryan (WTex) P.O. Box 350, 231 Cave Springs Dr. W., Hunt, TX 78024

CONLEY, Joan Frances (Nwk) 169 Fairmount Rd, Ridgewood, NJ 07450

CONLEY, Kristina Mellor (Me) 17 Littlefield Dr, Kennebunk, ME 04043

CONLEY, Patricia Ann (Chi) 1993 Yasgur Dr, Woodstock, IL 60098

CONLIFFE, Mario Romain Marvin (Md) 2434 Capehorn Rd, Hampstead, MD 21074

CONN JR, Doyt Ladean (Oly) 1805 38th Ave, Seattle, WA 98122

CONN, John Hardeman (Mass) 4 Alton Court, Brookline, MA 02446

CONN, Rodney Carl (Be) 108 N. 5th St., Allentown, PA 18102

CONNELL, George Patterson (Ky) 11 Saint Lukes Ln, San Antonio, TX 78209

CONNELL, John Baade (The Episcopal Church in Haw) 95-1050 Makaikai St. Apt. 17M, Mililani, HI 96789

CONNELL, Susan (Okla) 57200 E Hwy 125, Unit 3431, Monkey Island, OK 74331

CONNELLY III, Albert Pinckney (CFla) 16 Hawks Lndg, Weaverville, NC 28787

CONNELLY, Charles Evans (SwFla) 2401 Bayshore Blvd., Unit 505, Tampa, FL 33629

CONNELLY, Constance R (NC) 1950 S Wendover Rd, Charlotte, NC 28211

CONNELLY, John Vaillancourt (Chi) 3500 Lacey Rd, Suite 700, Downers Grove, IL 60515

CONNELLY JR, Walter (Mass) 231 Bowdoin St, Winthrop, MA 02151

CONNER, Georgene Davis (SwFla) 2926 57th Street S, Gulfport, FL 33707

CONNER, Lu-Anne (Mo) Church Of The Transfiguration, 1860 Lake Saint Louis Blvd, Lake St Louis, MO 63367

CONNER, Martha (Az) 11102 W. Kolina Lane, Sun City, AZ 85351

CONNER JR, Sarah A (Mass) 4 Ernest Rd # 3, Arlington, MA 02474

CONNERS, John H (EC) 14703 Dorset Dr, Noblesville, IN 46062

CONNOLLY, Emma French (WTenn) 480 S. Greer St., Memphis, TN 38111

CONNOR, Alice Elizabeth (SO) 5751 Marmion Ln, Cincinnati, OH 45212

CONNOR, The Rev. Stephen J. (NJ)

CONNORS, Carey D (Va) 905 Princess Anne St, Fredericksburg, VA 22401

CONRAD JR, James Wallace (Az) 2540 Ontario Dr, Las Vegas, NV 89128

CONRAD, John (Los) All Saints Episcopal Church, 3847 Terracina Dr, Riverside, CA 92506

CONRAD JR, Larry Brown (NC)

CONRAD, Matthew MacMillan (ECR) 7620 Cristobal Ave, Atascadero, CA 93422

CONRAD, Pamela Gales (Md) 105 1st Ave SW, Glen Burnie, MD 21061

CONRADO VARELA, Victor H (Chi)

CONRADS, Alexandra (Los)

CONRADS, Nancy Alice (Chi) 4801 Spring Creek Rd, Rockford, IL 61114

CONRADT, James Robert (FdL) W1693 Echo Valley Rd, Kaukauna, WI 54130

CONROE, Jon Wallace (RG)

CONROY, Mary E (SeFla) 1121 Andalusia Ave, Coral Gables, FL 33134

CONSIDINE, H James (NwPa) 11733 SW 17th CT, Miramar, FL 33025

CONSTANT, Donna Rittenhouse (Pa) 167 Hermit Hollow Lane, Middleburg, PA 17842

CONSTANT, Joseph (WA) 701 Oglethorpe St NW, Washington, DC 20011

CONTESTABLE, Christine Marie (U) 673 Wall St, Salt Lake City, UT 84103

CONTI, Ann (NY) 22 Coulter Ave, Pawling, NY 12564

CONWAY, Cooper (NY) 1514 Palisade Ave, Union City, NJ 07087

CONWAY, Marta Therese-Peña (RG)

CONWAY, Natalie Hall (Md)

CONWAY, Thomas Bradley (NJ) 22 Wickapecko Dr, Interlaken, NJ 07712

CONYERS, Kacei (The Episcopal NCal)

COOK, Ashley Michele (Tex) 919 S John Redditt Dr, Lufkin, TX 75904

COOK, Bill E (Tex) 11245 Shoreline Dr., Apt 308, Tyler, TX 75703

COOK, Carol Lee (Cal) 2235 3rd St, Livermore, CA 94550

COOK, Charles James (Tex) Po Box 2247, Austin, TX 78768

COOK, Charles Robert (Neb) 2666 El Rancho Rd, Sidney, NE 69162

COOK, Debbie (NJ) 202 Navesink Avenue, Atlantic Highlands, NJ 07716

COOK, Ellen Piel (SO) 2768 Turpin Oaks Ct, Cincinnati, OH 45244

COOK, Harvey Gerald (Lex) 20129 N Painted Sky Dr, Surprise, AZ 85374

COOK, James (Okla) Saint Andrew's Church, 516 W 3rd Ave, Stillwater, OK 74074

COOK, Jim (SeFla) 3395 Burns Road, Palm Beach Gardens, FL 33410

COOK JR, Joe (Mass) 28 Highland Ave, Roxbury, MA 02119

COOK, Johnny Walter (CGC) 206 Fig Ave, Fairhope, AL 36532

COOK, Kay Kellam (U) 2425 Colorado Ave, Boulder, CO 80302

COOK, Nancy Bell (Ark) 1112 Alcoa Rd, Benton, AR 72015

COOK, Patricia Ann (NAM) PO Box 85, Bluff, UT 84512

COOK, Paul Raymond (WMo) 4 Burton Rd, Kingston, KT25TE, Great Britain (UK)

COOK, Peter John Arthur (WLa) 4100 Bayou Rd, Lake Charles, LA 70605

COOK JR, Robert (NC) 8400 Goose Landing Ct, Browns Summit, NC 27214

COOK, Thomas R (Minn) 4439 W 50th St, Edina, MN 55424

COOK, Winifred Rose (Mich) PO Box 287, Onsted, MI 49265

COOKE, Barbara (NC) 5205 Ainsworth Dr, Greensboro, NC 27410

COOKE, Catherine Cornelia Hutton (Vt) 500 South Union, Burlington, VT 05401

COOKE, Douglas Tasker (Ct) 19 Ridgebrook Dr, West Hartford, CT 06107

COOKE, Hilary (Ind)

COOKE, Hugh Mabee (Episcopal SJ) 67 W Noble St, Stockton, CA 95204

COOKE JR, James Coffield (EC) 309 Mary Lee Ct, Winterville, NC 28590

COOKE, James Daniel (Ct) 23 Parsonage Road, HIgganum, CT 06441

COOKE, Philip Ralph (ECR) 17740 Peak Ave, Morgan Hill, CA 95037

COOK-QUARRY, Cassandra (Minn)

COOL, Opal Mary (Neb) 3525 N. 167Th Cir. Apt. 206, Omaha, NE 68116

COOLEY, Andrew A (Colo) 1315 Figueroa St, Walla Walla, WA 99362

COOLIDGE, Robert T (Cal) PO Box 282, Westmount, H3Z 2T2, Canada

COOLIDGE, Ted (Ct) 43 Spruce Ln, Cromwell, CT 06416

COOLIDGE, William Mccabe (NC) 118 Cumberland Ave, Asheville, NC 28801

COOLING, David Albert (USC) 280 Holcombe Way, Lambertville, NJ 08530

COOMBER, Matthew J.M. (ND)

COON, David Paul (The Episcopal Church in Haw) Po Box 690, Kamuela, HI 96743

COON, Nancy (WTex) 200 Crossroads Drive, Dripping Springs, TX 78620

COOPER JR, A(Llen) William (Alb) 1365 County Route 60, Onchiota, NY 12989

COOPER, Cricket S (WMass) 67 East Street, Pittsfield, MA 01201

COOPER, Deborah Silas (Ark)

COOPER IV, Francis Marion (CGC) Po Box 1677, Santa Rosa Beach, FL 32459

COOPER, Gale Hodkinson (NC) 1636 Headquarters Plantation Drive, Charleston, SC 29455

COOPER, James Herbert (Fla) 1314 Ponte Vedra Blvd, Ponte Vedra Beach, FL 32082

COOPER, Joseph Wiley (EC) 4925 Oriole Dr, Wilmington, NC 28403

COOPER, Michael Francis (Los) 4018 Vista Ct, La Crescenta, CA 91214

COOPER, Michael Scott (CPa) 181 S 2nd St, Hughesville, PA 17737

COOPER, Miles Oliver (CFla) 423 Forest Ridge Dr, Aiken, SC 29803

COOPER, Milton Norbert (SeFla) 11201 Sw 160th St, Miami, FL 33157

COOPER, Richard Randolph (Tex) 4805 E Columbary Dr, Rosenberg, TX 77471

COOPER, Robert Norman (WLa) 108 Blue Ridge, Site 41, Comfort, TX 78013

COOPER, Stephenie Rose (ECR) 1205 Pine Ave, San Jose, CA 95125

COOPER-WHITE, Pamela (NY) Union Theological Seminary, 3041 Broadway, New York, NY 10027

COOTE, Laurel Eileen (Los) 2200 Via Rosa, Palos Verdes Estates, CA 90274

COOTER, Eric Shane (SwFla) 4309 Trout River Xing, Ellenton, FL 34222

COPE, Gerald D (Ga)

COPE, Jan Naylor (WA) Washington National Cathedral, 3101 Wisconsin Avenue, NW, Washington, DC 20016

COPE, Marie (USC) 101 St. Matthew's Ln, Spartanburg, SC 29301

COPELAND, Richard (Dal) 1141 N Loop 1604 E, Suite 105-614, San Antonio, TX 78232

COPELAND, Wanda Ruth (CNY) St Matthews Episcopal Church, 408 S Main St, Horseheads, NY 14845

COPENHAVER, Robert Thomas (SwVa) 50 Draper Place, Daleville, VA 24083

COPLAND, Edward Mark (SwFla) 5462 Shadow Lawn Dr, Sarasota, FL 34242

COPLEY, David (NY) 10 West Elizabeth Street, Tarrytown, NY 10591

COPLEY, Susan Kay (NY) 10 W Elizabeth St, Tarrytown, NY 10591

COPP, Ann (Md) 444 Garrison Forest Rd, Owings Mills, MD 21117

COPPEL JR, Stanley Graham (Episcopal SJ) Po Box 1431, Twain Harte, CA 95383

COPPEN, Christopher J (Spok) 5108 W Rosewood Ave, Spokane, WA 99208

COPPINGER, Tim (WMo) 107 W Perimeter Dr, San Antonio, TX 78227

CORAM, James M (NC) 12109 Park Shore Ct, Woodbridge, VA 22192

CORBETT, Father James (Los) 10819 SE Rex St, Portland, OR 97266

CORBETT, Ian (NAM) Po Box 28, Bluff, UT 84512

CORBETT-WELCH, Kathy (WA) 2218 Hillhouse Rd, Baltimore, MD 21207

CORBIN, Christopher Wesley (SD) 631 W Main St, Lead, SD 57754

CORBIN, Portia Renae (SD) 500 S Main Ave, Sioux Falls, SD 57104

CORBISHLEY, Frank J. (SeFla) 921 Sorolla, Coral Gables, FL 33134

CORDERO JIMENEZ, Angel Daniel (MexSE)

CORDINGLEY, Saundra Lee (Roch) 23 Seneca Road, Rochester, NY 14622

CORDOBA, Guillermo (Fla) 2961 University Blvd N, Jacksonville, FL 32211

CORIOLAN, Simpson (Hai) Box 1309, Port-Au-Prince, Haiti

CORKERN, Matthew Thomas Locy (Nwk) 41 Woodland Avenue, Summit, NJ 07901

CORKLIN, Stanley Earl (Vt) 744 Parker Road, West Glover, VT 05875

CORL, James Alexander (CNY) 2435 Fleming Scipio Town Line Road, Auburn, NY 13021

CORLETT, Diane Bishop (NC) 6901 Three Bridges Cir, Raleigh, NC 27613

CORLEY, Kathryn S (CNY) 97 Underhill Rd, Ossining, NY 10562

CORLEY, Robert M (Dal) 10837 Colbert Way, Dallas, TX 75218

CORNEJO, Quirino H. (Colo) 193 Bristlecone St, Brighton, CO 80601

CORNELL, Allison Lee (Az) 2252 Cherry Hills Dr, Sierra Vista, AZ 85635

CORNELL, Amy S (NJ)

CORNELL, Charles Walton (The Episcopal NCal) 813 Mormon St, Folsom, CA 95630

CORNELL, Peter Stuart (NJ) 5 Paterson St, New Brunswick, NJ 08901

CORNER, Cynthia Ruth (Mich) PO Box 287, Onsted, MI 49265

CORNEY, Richard Warren (NY) 12 Hartford Ave Apt B, Glens Falls, NY 12801

CORNILS, Calvin Stanley (The Episcopal NCal)

CORNMAN, Jane Elizabeth (Me) Po Box 105, Northeast Harbor, ME 04662

CORNNER, Robert Wyman (Los) 8170 Manitoba St., Unit #1, Playa Del Rey, CA 90293

CORNTHWAITE, Hannah Elyse (Ia)

CORNWELL, Marilyn (Oly) Church of the Ascension, 2330 Viewmont Way Weat, Seattle, WA 98199

CORREA, Trino Cortes (Episcopal SJ) 3345 Sierra Madre, Clovis, CA 93619

CORREA AMARILES, Maria Ofelia (Colom) Parroquia San Lucas, Cr 80 No 53A-78, Medellin, Antioguia, Colombia

CORREA GALVEZ, Jose William (Colom) Carrera 6 No 49-85, Piso 2, Bogota, Colombia

CORRELL, Ruth E (Va) 15639 John Diskin Cir, Woodbridge, VA 22191

CORRIGAN, Candice Lyn (Oly) 506 21st St SW, Austin, MN 55912

CORRIGAN, Michael (Mass) Northfield Mount Hermon School, 1 Lamplighter Way #4702, Mt. Hermon, MA 01354

CORRIGAN, Michael Edward (Los) 1500 State St, Santa Barbara, CA 93101

CORRY, Lisa Marie (Ark)

CORRY, Richard Stillwell (Va) 214 E King St, Quincy, FL 32351

CORSELLO, Dana Colley (WA) 1755 Clay St, San Francisco, CA 94109

CORT, Aubrey Ebenezer (SwFla) 2507 Del Prado Blvd S, Cape Coral, FL 33904

CORTINAS, Angela Maria (Tex) 333 Tarpon Dr, Fort Lauderdale, FL 33301

CORTRIGHT, Amy Ethel Marie Chambers (Mo) Christ Church Cathedral, 1210 Locust Street, St. Louis, MO 63103

COSBY, Arlinda (Cal) 36458 Shelley Ct, Newark, CA 94560

COSMAN, Sandra Lee (Ct) 220 Prospect St, Torrington, CT 06790

COSSLETT, Ashley Cosslett (WNC) 449 Crowfields Dr, Asheville, NC 28803

COSTA, Steven James (The Episcopal Church in Haw) St Timothy's Episcopal Church, 98-939 Moanalua Rd, Aiea, HI 96701

COSTAS, Catherine Stephenson (Cal) 905 W Middlefield Rd Apt 946, Mountain View, CA 94043

COSTAS, J Kathryn (Ind) 838 Ridgewood Dr NE, Lenoir, NC 28645

COSTELLO, Elizabeth R (Colo) St John's Cathedral, 1350 Washington St, Denver, CO 80203

COSTIN, Richard Banks (CFla) 1601 Alafaya Trl, Oviedo, FL 32765

COTTER, Barry Lynn (SO) 1864 Sherman Ave Apt 5SE, Evanston, IL 60201

COTTRELL, Jan M. (Lex) 1445 Copperfield Court, Lexington, KY 40514-175

COTTRILL, Dave (SO) 3724 Mengel Dr, Kettering, OH 45429

COUCH, Michelle Allen (Oly) 105 State St, Kirkland, WA 98033

COUDRIET, Alan P (NwPa) 10 Woodside Ave, Oil City, PA 16301

COUFAL, M(ary) Lorraine (Ind) 3819 Green Arbor Way #812, Indianapolis, IN 46220

COUGHLIN, Christopher Anthony (O) 7640 Glenwood Ave, Boardman, OH 44512

COULOUTE, Schneyder (Hai)

COULSON, Mary Lynn (SanD) 16275 Pomerado Rd, Poway, CA 92064

COULTAS, Amy (Ky) 612 Myrte St, Louisville, KY 40208

COULTER, Clayton Roy (Ore) 7430 Sw Pineridge Ct, Portland, OR 97225

COULTER, Elizabeth (Ia) 3148 Dubuque St. NE, Iowa City, IA 52240

COULTER, Linda M (CFla)

COULTER, Sherry Lynn (At) 681 Holt Rd Ne, Marietta, GA 30068

COUNSELMAN, Robert Lee (NJ) 119 S Hondo St, P O Box 1478, Sabinal, TX 78881

COUNTRYMAN, L(Ouis) William (Cal) 5805 Keith Avenue, Oakland, CA 94618

COUPER, David Courtland (Mil) 5282 County Road K, Blue Mounds, WI 53517

COUPLAND, Geoffrey D (Va) 5110 Park Ave., Richmond, VA 23226

COURTNEY, Joseph Bradley (Los) 4533 Laurel Canyon Blvd, Studio City, CA 91607

COURTNEY, Larry Edward (Ky)

COURTNEY, Michael David (Ark) 235 Caroline Acres Road, Hot Springs, AR 71913

COURTNEY, Peter (At) 339 Reeds Landing, 807 Wilbraham Rd, Springfield, MA 01109

COURTNEY II, Robert Wickliff (La) 1025 Beverly Garden Drive, New Orleans, LA 70002

COURTRIGHT, Alice Hodgkins (NH)

COURTRIGHT, Andrew Michael (NH) 21 Centre St, Concord, NH 03301

COUVILLION, Brian Neff (Chi) 4370 Woodland Ave, Western Springs, IL 60558

COUZZOURT, Beverly Schmidt (NwT) 2516 4th Ave, Canyon, TX 79015

COVENTRY, Donald Edgar (Spr) 246 Southmoreland Pl, Decatur, IL 62521

COVER, Michael Benjamin (Dal) 616 Lincolnway E., Mishawaka, IN 46544

COVERSTON, Harry Scott (ECR) 630 Roberta Ave, Orlando, FL 32803

COVERT, Edward Martin (SwVa) Po Box 126, Fort Defiance, VA 24437

COVINGTON, John E (NY) 410 West 24th Street, Apartment 8K, New York, NY 10011

COWARDIN, Eustis Barber (ND) 510 E Lake County Rd, Jamestown, ND 58401

COWART, Alan B (SwVa) 1021 New Hampshire Ave, Lynchburg, VA 24502

COWDEN, Matthew D (NI) 16341 Parkwood Ct, Granger, IN 46530

COWELL, Curtis Lyle (Kan) 2601 Sw College Ave, Topeka, KS 66611

COWELL, Frank Bourne (Nev) 7300 W Van Giesen St, West Richland, WA 99353

✠ **COWELL**, Mark Andrew (WK) 501 W 5th St, Larned, KS 67550

COWEN, Charles Lane (RI) 1108 N Adams St, Wilmington, DE 19801

COWHERD, Charles Robison (Va)

COWPER, Judith Ann (Ct) 54 Dora Dr, Middletown, CT 06457

COWPERTHWAITE, Robert W (Fla) 7001 Charles St., St. Augustine, FL 32080

COX, Amy Eleanor (WMo) St. Francis of Assisi in the Pines, 17890 Metcalf Ave, Overland Park, KS 66085

COX, Amy Gabrielle (Los)

COX, Anne Elizabeth (Mich) 8 Ridge Rd, Tenants Harbor, ME 04860

COX IV, Brian (Los) 871 Serenidad Pl, Goleta, CA 93117

COX, Catherine Susanna (WMo) 365 E 372nd Rd, Dunnegan, MO 65640

COX, Celeste O'Hern (Del) 568 Willowwood Dr, Smyrna, DE 19977

COX, Christopher Edward (NJ) 801 W State St, Trenton, NJ 08618

COX, David (Kan) 1455 E 37th St, Sedalia, MO 65301

COX, Edwin Manuel (NC) 4510 Highberry Rd, Greensboro, NC 27410

COX, Frances (Md) 4510 Highberry Rd, Greensboro, NC 27410

COX, Gary (Chi)

COX, James Richard (WK) Po Box 827, Salina, KS 67402

COX, Jason (Los) 8201 16th St Apt 1024, Silver Spring, MD 20910

COX, Mildred Louise (Minn) 1210 Washburn Ave N, Minneapolis, MN 55411

COX, Nancy L J (NC) 525 Lake Concord Road NE, Concord, NC 28025

COX, R. David (SwVa) 107 Lee Ave., Lexington, VA 24450

COX, Raymond L (Ct) 461 Mill Hill Ter, Southport, CT 06890

COX, Sean Armer (The Episcopal NCal) 3601 Sudbury Rd, Cameron Park, CA 95682

COX, Sharron Leslie (Tex) 601 Columbus Ave, Waco, TX 76701

COYNE, William (SC) 1615 Ellsworth St, Mount Pleasant, SC 29466

COZZOLI, John David (Md) 17524 Lincolnshire Rd, Hagerstown, MD 21740

CRAFT, Bernadine Louise (Wyo) Po Box 567, Rock Springs, WY 82902

CRAFT, Carolyn Martin (SVa) 1702 Briery Rd, Farmville, VA 23901

CRAFT, John Harvey (La) 4505 S Claiborne Ave, New Orleans, LA 70125

CRAFT, Stephen Frank (La) 3101 Plymouth Pl, New Orleans, LA 70131

CRAFTON, Barbara Cawthorne (NY) 53 McCoy Ave, Metuchen, NJ 08840

CRAFTS JR, Robert (SanD) 13030 Birch Ln, Poway, CA 92064

CRAIG, Carrie (EC) 820 Lake Park Dr Apt 101, Davidson, NC 28036

CRAIG SR, Claude Phillip (EC) 214 Twain Ave, Davidson, NC 28036

CRAIG JR, Claude Phillip (Ore) 6300 SW Nicol Road, Portland, OR 97223

CRAIG JR, Harry Walter (Kan) 5041 Sw Fairlawn Rd, Topeka, KS 66610

Clergy List

CRAIG, Idalia S (NJ) 85 Stone Rd, Mcdonough, GA 30253

CRAIG III, James (WMass) 11 Cotton St, Leominster, MA 01453

CRAIG, Jo Roberts (NwT) 2401 Parker St, Amarillo, TX 79109

CRAIG III, Richard (Mil) 4417 Westway Ave, Racine, WI 53405

CRAIG, Shay (WK)

CRAIGHEAD, Thomas Gray (Chi) St Andrew's Church, 1125 Franklin St, Downers Grove, IL 60515

CRAIGHEAD JR, Tom Thomas (Oly) 23404 107th Ave SW, Vashon, WA 98070

CRAIGHILL, Peyton Gardner (Pa) 25 Sycamore Lane, Lexington, VA 24450

CRAIN II, Lee Bryan (LI) 518 Brooklyn Blvd, Brightwaters, NY 11718

CRAIN, William Henry (WMo) 9208 Wenonga Rd, Leawood, KS 66206

CRAM, Donald Owen (RG) Po Box 45000, Rio Rancho, NM 87174

CRAM JR, Norman Lee (The Episcopal NCal) Po Box 224, Vineburg, CA 95487

CRAMER, Alan Barry (Ind)

CRAMER, Alfred Anthony (Vt) 47 Morningside Commons, Brattleboro, VT 05301

CRAMER, Jared C (WMich) 524 Washington Ave, Grand Haven, MI 49417

CRAMER, Roger Weldon (Mass) 16 Aubin Street, Amesbury, MA 01913

CRAMMER, Margaret Corinne (Chi) 927 Scott Blvd Apt 205, Decatur, GA 30030

CRAMPTON, Susan H (WMass) 16595 Warren Ct Apt 305, Chagrin Falls, OH 44023

CRANDALL, Harry Wilson (SVa) PO Box 275, 9115 Franktown Road, Franktown, VA 23354

CRANDALL, John Davin (Mass) 404 Juniper Way, Tavares, FL 32778

CRANE, Linda Sue (EMich) 1213 6th St, Port Huron, MI 48060

CRANE, Rebecca Mai (Mass) 13 Trinity St., Danvers, MA 01923

CRANSTON, Dale L (NY) 21 Stone Fence Road, Mahwah, NJ 07430

CRANSTON, Pamela Lee (Cal) 207 Taurus Ave, Oakland, CA 94611

CRAPSEY II, Marc (Mass) 77 L Drew Rd, Derry, NH 03038

CRARY, Kathleen (Cal) 733 Baywood Rd, Alameda, CA 94502

CRAUN, Chris (Ore) 3236 NE Alberta St., Portland, OR 97211

CRAVEN III, James Braxton (NC) 17 Marchmont Ct, Durham, NC 27705

CRAVEN, Sam (Tex) 6221 Main St, Houston, TX 77030

CRAVENS, James Owen (Spr) 4 Canterbury Ln, Lincoln, IL 62656

CRAVER III, Marshall P (CGC) 613 Highland Woods Dr E, Mobile, AL 36608

CRAWFORD, Alicia Leu Lydon (Chi) 550 N Green Bay Rd, Lake Forest, IL 60045

CRAWFORD II, Gerald Gene (Ark)

CRAWFORD JR, Grady J (At) 2602 Oglethorpe Cir NE, Atlanta, GA 30319

CRAWFORD, Hayden G (SeFla) 701 45th Ave S, Saint Petersburg, FL 33705

CRAWFORD, Karen Graham (Ia) 223 E 4th St N, Newton, IA 50208

CRAWFORD JR, Kelly (Los) 450 NW Ivy Ave, Dallas, OR 97338

CRAWFORD, Lee (Vt) POB 67, Plymouth, VT 05056

CRAWFORD, Leo Lester (SwFla) 2694 Grove Park Rd, Palm Harbor, FL 34583

CRAWFORD, Malia (Mass) 21 Marathon St., Arlington, MA 02474

CRAWFORD, Mark (Tex) PO Box 20269, Houston, TX 77225

CRAWFORD, Nancy Rogers (Ore) 1595 E 31st Ave, Eugene, OR 97405

CRAWFORD, Sidnie White (Be)

CRAWFORD, Stephen Howard (La) 3552 Morning Glory Ave, Baton Rouge, LA 70808

CRAWFORD, Susan Kaye (Miss) 1026 S Washington Ave, Greenville, MS 38701

CRAWLEY, Clayton D (ECR) 20 Pine St Apt 2106, New York, NY 10005

CREAN, Charleen (Los) 931 E. Walnut St. #114, Pasadena, CA 91106

CREAN JR, John Edward (Los) 1735 La Paz Rd, Altadena, CA 91001

CREASY, James Arthur (Ala) 3228 Lee Road 56, Auburn, AL 36832

CREASY, William Charles (O) 65 E Maple Ave, New Concord, OH 43762

CRECCA, Kimberly Diane (Az)

CREED, Christopher Duflon (ECR) 501 Portola Rd Apt 8185, Portola Valley, CA 94028

✠ **CREIGHTON**, Michael Whittington (CPa) 2716 Gingerview Lane, Annapolis, MD 21401

CREIGHTON, Susan (Oly) 15 Huckleberry Court, Bellingham, WA 98229

CRELLIN, Timothy Edward (Mass) 25 Boylston St, Jamaica Plain, MA 02130

CRERAR, Patrick (Los) 202 Avenida Aragon, San Clemente, CA 92672

CRESPO, Willy (SanD) 10125 Azuaga St, San Diego, CA 92129

CRESS, Katherine E (Los) 3903 Wilshire Blvd, Los Angeles, CA 99010

CRESSMAN, Lisa Suzanne Kraske (Minn) 3 Blue Iron Dr, Missouri City, TX 77459

CRESSMAN, Louise A (NJ) 25 Lakeshore Dr, Hammonton, NJ 08037

CRESSMAN, Naomi May (NJ) 305 Main St, Riverton, NJ 08077

CRESWELL, Carl Edward (NwT) 2113 S Lipscomb St, Amarillo, TX 79109

CRESWELL, Jennifer M (Ore) 4411 NE Beech St., Portland, OR 97213

CRETEN, Claude Daniel (NMich) E4929 State Highway M35, Escanaba, MI 49829

CREWDSON, Robert (SwVa) 6 Miley Ct, Lexington, VA 24450

CREWS, Norman Andrew (SwVa) 1125 Spindle Xing, Virginia Beach, VA 23455

CREWS, Norman Dale (CPa) 201 Porter Dr, Annapolis, MD 21401

CREWS, Warren Earl (Mo) 2 Algonquin Wood, Saint Louis, MO 63122

CREWS, William Eugene (Colo) 4042 Xerxes Ave. S., Minneapolis, MN 55410

CRICHLOW, Neville Joseph (CFla) 381 N Lincoln St, Daytona Beach, FL 32114

CRIDER, Dion Gregory (Okla)

CRIGLER, Meredith (Tex) 1115 36th St, Galveston, TX 77550

CRIM, Marcus Jacob (Cal) 385 Eddy St Apt 613, San Francisco, CA 94102

CRIMI, Lynne B (Alb) 7 Sweet Rd, Stillwater, NY 12170

CRIPPEN, David Wells (ETenn) 4617 County Road 103, Florence, CO 81226

CRIPPEN, Stephen Daniel (Oly) 2631 Jamestown Ln Apt 104, Alexandria, VA 22314

CRIPPS, David Richard (Roch) 139 Lake Bluff Rd, Rochester, NY 14622

CRISE, Rebecca Ann (WMich) Saint Mark's Episcopal Church, PO Box 307, Paw Paw, MI 49079

CRISP, Justin E (Ct) 111 Oenoke Rdg, New Canaan, CT 06840

CRISS, Carthur Paul (Kan) 4138 E 24th St N, Wichita, KS 67220

CRIST, John (Chi) P.O. Box, 131 Fifth St., McNabb, IL 61335

CRIST, Mary Frances (Los) St Michael's Episcopal Church, 4070 Jackson St, Riverside, CA 92503

CRIST JR, William Harold (Los) 2091 Business Center Dr Ste 130, Irvine, CA 92612

CRISTE-TROUTMAN, Bob (Be) 137 Trinity Hill Rd., Mt. Pocono, PA 18344

CRISTOBAL, Robert S (Chi) 1000 West Rt 64, Oregon, IL 61061

CRITCHFIELD, Margot Dunlap (Mass) PO Box 524, Cohasset, MA 02025

CRITCHLOW II, Fitzgerald St Clair Jerry (Tex) 3700 Kingwood Dr Apt 1806, Kingwood, TX 77339

CRITELLI, Robert J (NJ) 13 King Arthurs Ct, Sicklerville, NJ 08081

CRITES, Becky (SVa) Emmanuel Episcopal Church, PO Box 26, Chatham, VA 24531

CRITES, Karry D (Nev) 1035 Munley Dr, Reno, NV 89503

CRITTENDEN, Joan Marie (WA)

CRITTENDEN, Tom Thomas Glasgow (SwVa) 22 Whitmore ST, Lexington, VA 24450

CRITTENDEN, William S (WNY) Po Box 93, Chautauqua, NY 14722

CROCKER, Byron Grey (Tex) 2025 Hanover Cir, Beaumont, TX 77706

CROCKER, Edna Irene (Fla) 10560 Fort George Rd, Jacksonville, FL 32226

CROCKER, George Neville (Ct) 29 Powder Horn Hl, Brookfield, CT 06804

CROCKER JR, John Alexander Frazer (U) 3541 Ocean View Dr, Florence, OR 97439

CROCKER, Ronald Conrad (Va) 3 Hamilton Court, Uxbridge, MA 01569

CROCKETT, Daniel L (SVa) PO Box 102, Conyers, GA 30012

CROCKETT, Jennie L (SO) 2700 Kenview Rd S, Columbus, OH 43209

CROCKETT, Larry Joe (Minn) 4525 Alicia Dr, Inver Grove Heights, MN 55077

CROES, John Rodney (NJ) 20 Claremont Ave, South River, NJ 08882

CROFT, Jay Leslie (WA) 5595 Teakwood Ct, Frederick, MD 21703

CROMEY, Edwin Harry (NY) St. Luke's Church, 850 Wolcott Ave. Box 507, Beacon, NY 12508

CROMEY, Robert Warren (Cal) 3839 - 20th, San Francisco, CA 94114

CROMMELIN-DELL, Sally Huntress (SVa) 500 Court St., Portsmouth, VA 23704

CROMWELL, Peggy Lynn (Ark)

CROMWELL, Richard (The Episcopal Church in Haw) 322 Aoloa St Apt 1103, Kailua, HI 96734

CRON, Ian Morgan (Ct) 226 5th Ave S, Franklin, TN 37064

✠ **CRONEBERGER**, John Palmer (Be) 1079 Old Bernville Rd, Reading, PA 19605

CRONIN, Audrey Ann (WMass)

CROOK II, Jerry V (Ga) 4027 Dumaine Way, Memphis, TN 38117

CROOK, Senter Cawthon (WTenn) 2796 Lombardy Ave, Memphis, TN 38111

CROOM, James (NC) 2795 Riley Ridge Road, Holland, MI 49424

CROSBY, David (Va) Immanuel Church-on-the-Hill, 3606 Seminary Rd, Alexandria, VA 22304

CROSBY, Karen Ann (Md) 52 S Broadway, Frostburg, MD 21532

CROSIER, Allen Duane (Spok)

CROSKEY, Christine Lucille (CFla) Holy Apostles Episcopal Church, 505 Grant Ave, Satellite Beach, FL 32937

CROSS, Carol (SwVa)

CROSS II, Eugenia Sealy (NC) 1032 Wessyngton Rd, Winston Salem, NC 27104

CROSS JR, Freeman Grant (Ga) 5424 Hill Rd, Albany, GA 31705

CROSS, Kevin (Eas) P.O. Box 387, Oxford, MD 21654

CROSS, Myrick Tyler (SO) 52 Pleasant St., Freedom, ME 04941

CROSS, Samuel Otis (NY) 330 Fletcher Hollow Rd, Collierville, TN 38017

CROSSETT, Judith Hale Wallace (Ia) 320 E College St, Iowa City, IA 52240

CROSSNOE, Marshall E (Mo) 217 ADAMS ST, JEFFERSON CITY, MO 65101

CROSSWAITE, John (CNY) 700 Quinlan Dr., Pewaukee, WI 53072

CROTHERS, John-Michael (NY) 214 Burntwood Trl, Toms River, NJ 08753

CROTHERS, Kenneth Delbert (Ida) Po Box 374, Shoshone, ID 83352

CROUCH, Billy Gene (NY) 3604 Balcones Dr, Austin, TX 78731

CROW, Lyn (Los) 1145 W Valencia Mesa Dr, Fullerton, CA 92833

CROW, Robert B (SwFla) St. Andrews By-the-Sea Episcopal Church, PO Box 1658, Destin, FL 32540

CROWDER, James Robert (Md) 13801 York Rd Apt E9, Cockeysville, MD 21030

CROWE, Amy Beth (The Episcopal Church in Haw)

CROWE, Kathleen A (ECR) The Rev Kathleen Crowe, 4271 N 1st St Spc 74, San Jose, CA 95134

CROWELL, Larry A (SO)

CROWELL, Paul L (Az) 2800 Huntsman Ct, Jamestown, NC 27282

CROWLEY, Daniel Fenwick (Mass) 76 Olde Towne Lane, West Chatham, MA 02669

CROWNOVER, Richard Matthew (Dal)

CROWSON, Steve (LI) 1778 Hallowell Rd, Litchfield, ME 04350

✠ **CROWTHER**, CE (Los) 289 Moreton Bay Ln Apt 2, Goleta, CA 93117

CROZIER, Richard Lee (USC) 125 Pendleton St Sw, Aiken, SC 29801

CRUIKSHANK, Charles Clark (CPa) 208 W Foster Ave, State College, PA 16801

CRUM, Robert James Howard (EO) 700 SW Eastman Pkwy Ste B110, Gresham, OR 97080

CRUMB, Lawrence Nelson (Ore) 1674 Washington St, Eugene, OR 97401

CRUMBAUGH III, Frank (NJ) 410 S Atlantic Ave, Beach Haven, NJ 08008

CRUMLEY, Carole Anne (WA) 3039 Beech St Nw, Washington, DC 20015

CRUMMEY, Rebecca (Colo) 967 Marion St Apt 7, Denver, CO 80218

CRUMP, Carl Calvin (ETenn) St Martin's/ St Stephen's, 15801 US Highway 19, Hudson, FL 34667

CRUMPTON IV, Alvin Briggs (Ga) 6230 Laurel Island Pkwy, Kingsland, GA 31548

CRUPI, Hilary (FdL) Our Lady of the Northwoods, W 704 Alft Rd, White Lake, WI 54491

CRUSE, William Clayton (NH) PO Box 382, North Conway, NH 03860

CRUSOE, Lewis D (EMich)

CRUZ, Hector (PR)

CRUZ-DIAZ, Nora (At) 5148 Victor Trail, Norcross, GA 30071

CRUZ LILLEGARD, Andrew R (Eau)

CRUZ MENDEZ, Manuel Ramon (DR (DomRep))

CRYSLER JR, Fred (Ct) PO Box 9324, Louisville, KY 40209

CUBILLAS, Angelito Conde (Az) PO Box 8667, Phoenix, AZ 85066

CUBINE, James W (WTenn) 7910 Gayle Ln, Memphis, TN 38138

CUDD, Anne Grover (Ida) 3024 SW 98th Way, Gainesville, FL 32608

CUEVAS FELIZ, Pedro G (RG) Blvd Benitez #99, El Pedregal Tijuana, BCN 22104, Mexico

CUFF, Steve (SO) 2140 Grandview Ave, Portsmouth, OH 45662

CUFF, Victoria Slater Smith (NJ) 45 2nd St, Keyport, NJ 07735

CUFFIE, Karen Ann (ECR) 2094 Grant Rd, Mountain View, CA 94040

CULBERTSON, David Paul (CPa) 210 S Washington St, Muncy, PA 17756

CULBERTSON, Thomas Leon (Md) 6 Yearling Way, Lutherville, MD 21093

CULBREATH, Leeann Drabenstott (Ga) PO Box 889, Tifton, GA 31793

CULBREATH, Lola Annette (Nev)

CULHANE, Suzanne M (LI)

CULLEN, Kathleen Mary (NH) St. Andrew's Episcopal Church, 102 N Main St., Manchester, NH 03102

CULLEN, Peter (LI) 199 Carroll St, Brooklyn, NY 11231

CULLINANE, Kathleen Jean (The Episcopal Church in Haw) 6221 Keokea Pl. Apt 132, Honolulu, HI 96825

CULLIPHER III, James Robert (USC) 800 Stillpoint Way, Balsam Grove, NC 28708

CULMER, Ronald D (Cal) 3350 Hopyard Rd, Pleasanton, CA 94588

CULP JR, Robert S (Roch) 19 Arbor Ct, Fairport, NY 14450

CULPEPPER, Charles Leland (Miss) 1832 Saint Ann St, Jackson, MS 39202

CULPEPPER, Judith (Ind) 6736 Prince Regent Ct, Indianapolis, IN 46250

CULPEPPER, Polk (Ind) 1301 Summit Ave, Washington, NC 27889

CULTON, Douglas (Del) 1212 E Holly St, Goldsboro, NC 27530

CULVER, Carson Kies (Mil) 590 N Church St, Richland Center, WI 53581

CULVER, Esme Jo R (Ore) Grace Memorial Church, 1535 Ne 17th Ave, Portland, OR 97232

CUMBIE II, Walter Kenneth (CGC) 172 Hannon Ave, Moile, AL 36604

CUMMER, Edwin West (SwFla)

CUMMINGS, Carolsue J (NJ) 322 So Second St, Surf City, NJ 08008

CUMMINGS, Patricia L (Cal) 110 Wood Rd Apt C-104, Los Gatos, CA 95030

CUMMINGS, Sally Ann (Minn) 520 N Pokegama Ave, Grand Rapids, MN 55744

CUMMINGS, Sudduth (NC) 3990 Meandering Ln., Tallahassee, FL 32308

CUMMINS, James Michael (Kan)

CUMMINS, Thomas W (Ore) 11100 Sw Riverwood Rd, Portland, OR 97219

CUNIFF, Wanda Wood (Tex) Christ Episcopal Church, 1320 Mound St., Nacogdoches, TX 75961

CUNNINGHAM, Arthur Leland (Mil) 1320 Mill Rd, Delafield, WI 53018

CUNNINGHAM, Chris (Mich) 400 High St, Farmville, VA 23901

CUNNINGHAM, James Earl (Tex) 2227 Woodland Springs Dr, Houston, TX 77077

CUNNINGHAM, Joyce Corbin (NC)

CUNNINGHAM, Lynn Edward (Wyo) 3403 Ordway St Nw, Washington, DC 20016

CUNNINGHAM, Margaret Taylor (Los) 1122 Wabash St, Pasadena, CA 91103

CUNNINGHAM, Michael Ray (Los) St Marys Episcopal Church, 2800 Harris Grade Rd, Lompoc, CA 93436

CUNNINGHAM, Philip John (Mil) 2500 N. 10th St., McAllen, TX 78501

CUNNINGHAM, Trish (Cal) 1668 Bush St, San Francisco, CA 94109

CUNNINGHAM, William Wallace (Ala)

CUPP, Jean Carol (EO) 1239 Nw Ingram Ave, Pendleton, OR 97801

CURL, James Fair (WNC) 461 Crowfields Dr., Asheville, NC 28803

CURNS, Mary S (WMass) All Saints Episcopal Church, PO Box 374, North Adams, MA 01247

CURREA, Luis Alejandro (SwFla) Po Box 9332, Tampa, FL 33674

CURRIE, Ryan Daniel (CGC)

CURRY, Dorothy Reed (Cal) 4351 Ridgeway Dr, San Diego, CA 92116

CURRY, Gene E (Mich) 2735 Manchester Rd, Ann Arbor, MI 48104

CURRY, Glenda (Ala) 2670 Southgate Dr, Birmingham, AL 35243

☩ **CURRY**, James Elliot (Ct) 14 Linwold Dr, West Hartford, CT 06107

☩ **CURRY**, Michael B (NC) 200 W Morgan Ste 300, Raleigh, NC 27601

CURT, George (SwFla) 1204 Westlake Blvd, Naples, FL 34103

CURTIN, Anne (Alb) Healing a Woman's Soul, Inc., 68 S.Swan St., Albany, NY 12210

CURTIN JR, Ernest Albert (Pa) St Luke's Episcopal Church, 100 E Washington Ave, Newtown, PA 18940

CURTIS, Chuck (EMich) 3260 E Midland Rd, Bay City, MI 48706

CURTIS, David (Va)

CURTIS, Edward W (Chi) 637 S Dearborn Ste 1, Chicago, IL 60605

CURTIS, Frederick L (Alb) 262 Main St N, Southbury, CT 06488

CURTIS, Jim (At) 1100 Hampton Way NE, Atlanta, GA 30324

CURTIS, Kenton (NY) 200 Bennett Ave #3G, New York, NY 10040

CURTIS, Lynne Marsh Piret (Alb) 912 Route 146, Clifton Park, NY 12065

CURTIS, Mary Page (NC) 212 Edinboro Dr, Southern Pines, NC 28387

CURTIS, Patricia H (WNC) St John's Episcopal Church, PO Box 175, Sylva, NC 28779

CURTIS, Sandra King (Roch) 10 Shether St # 272, Hammondsport, NY 14840

CURTIS, Sandra O (Ark) Episcopal Collegiate School, 1701 Cantrell Rd, Little Rock, AR 72201

CURTIS III, William L (Ind) 2407 Cascade Rd SW, Atlanta, GA 30311

CURTIS JR, William Shepley (Nev) 1654 County Rd, Minden, NV 89423

CURTIS, Yvonne Marie (WNY) PO Box 14, Dunkirk, NY 14048

CURTISS, Geoff (Nwk) 202 3RD AVE, Bradley Beach, NJ 07720

CUSANO, William Alan (NY) 2500 Jerome Ave, Bronx, NY 10468

CUSHING, Nan Chenault Marshall (NC) 69 Crystal Oaks Ct, Durham, NC 27707

CUSHINOTTO, Susan Elizabeth (NJ) 9425 3rd Ave, Stone Harbor, NJ 08247

CUSHMAN, Mary Toohey (NY) PO Box 211, Chebeague Island, ME 04017

CUSHMAN, Thomas Spaulding (NY) PO Box 211, Chebeague Island, ME 04017

CUSIC, Georgeanne Hill (FdL) 1510 N Broadway Ave, Marshfield, WI 54449

CUSTER, Dale (SVa) 14404 Roberts Mill Court, Midlothian, VA 23113

CUTAIAR, Michael Louis (NMich)

CUTIE, Albert R (SeFla) 11173 Griffing Blvd, Miami, FL 33161

CUTLER, Donald Robert (NY) 38 Chestnut St, Salem, MA 01970

CUTLER, E Clifford (Pa) 18 E Chestnut Hill Ave, Philadelphia, PA 19118

CUTLER, Howard Taylor (HB) 1124 Westhampton Glen Dr, Richmond, VA 23238

CUTOLO, Mark Anthony (WNY) 351 E 74th St, New York, NY 10021

CUTSHALL, Jason Edward (Minn) 2801 Westwood Rd, Minnetonka Beach, MN 55391

CUTTER IV, Irv (Okla) 4200 S Atlanta Pl, Tulsa, OK 74105

CYR, Gary A (CNY) 3 J St, Bangor, ME 04401

CYR, Mark Bernard (Eas) 25 Addy Road, P.O. Box 191, Bethany Beach, DE 19930

CZARNETZKY, Sylvia Yale (Miss) 148 French Br, Madison, MS 39110

CZARNIECKI, Lynn (Pa) 30 Gildersleeve Pl, Watchung, NJ 07069

CZOLGOSZ, Joseph Tamborini (NI) 707 S Chester Ave, Park Ridge, IL 60068

D

DABNEY, Elizabeth Ruth (Tex) PO Box 746, Columbus, TX 78934

DAGG, Kay (Kan) 1427 SW Macvicar Ave, Topeka, KS 66604

DAGGETT, Paul (So) 115 North 6th Street, Hamilton, OH 45011

DAHARSH, Floyd Arthur (Okla) 112 West 9th Street, Hugoton, KS 67951

DAHL, Joan Elizabeth (Spok) 8991 State Route 24, Moxee, WA 98936

DAHLIN, James G (WNC) 140 Saint Marys Church Rd, Morganton, NC 28655

DAHLMAN, Thomas A (Okla) 4250 W Houston St, Broken Arrow, OK 74012

DAIGLE, Deborah Heft (Tex) PO Box 1344, Madisonville, TX 77864

DAILEY, Beulah Huffman (Dal) 2929 Hickory St, Dallas, TX 75226

DAILEY, Douglas G (At) 3603 Tradition Drive, Gainesville, GA 30506

DAILY JR, Charles W (FdL) N 6945 Ash Road, Shawano, WI 54166

DAILY, Teresa Wooten (Ark) 925 Mitchell St, Conway, AR 72034

DAISA IV, George Donald John (Los) PO Box 37, Pacific Palisades, CA 90272

DAKAN, Karen Nugent (SwFla) 14 Sandy Hook Rd N, Sarasota, FL 34242

DALBY, Marti (Ark)

D'ALCARAVELA, Joao Antonio Alpalhao (Mass) Palmoinho, Serra do Louro, Palmela, 2950-305, Portugal

DALE, Anne (SVa)

DALE, Cortney H (EC)

DALE, Kathleen Askew (Los) St. Margaret's Episcopal Church, 47-535 HWY 74 at Haystack Rd., Palm Desert, CA 92260

DALES, Randolph Kent (NH) PO Box 1363, Wolfeboro, NH 03894

DALEY, Joy (Dal) 13355 Pandora Cir, Dallas, TX 75238

DALFERES, Craig (La) 624 Winfield Blvd, Houma, LA 70360

DALGLISH, William Anthony (Tenn) 1911 Hampton Dr, Lebanon, TN 37087

DALLMAN, Matthew Christian (Spr)

DALLY, John A (Chi) 2650 N Lakeview Ave Apt 2501, Chicago, IL 60614

DALMASSO, Gary Lee (Chi) 215 29th Ave, East Moline, IL 61244

DALMASSO, Judith Connie (Ia) Renewal in Christ Ministries, PO Box 94, East Moline, IL 61244

DALRYMPLE, Sharon Gladwin (ECR) 5147 Show Low Lake Rd, Lakeside, AZ 85929

DALTON, Harlon L (Ct) 329 Greene St Unit 9, New Haven, CT 06511

DALTON JR, James Albert (Ark) 94 Cherrywood Dr., Cabot, AR 72023

DALTON, Joyce Foley (Ark) St Stephen's Episcopal Church, 2413

Northeastern Ave, Jacksonville, AR 72076

DALY JR, Herbert T (Fla) 209 E. Adkins St., Starke, FL 32091

DALY, Joseph Erin (WLa) 1030 Johnston St, Lafayette, LA 70501

DALY III, Raymond Ernest (Fla) 160 Sea Island Dr, Ponte Vedra Beach, FL 32082

DALY, Richard R (Dal) 5323 N Mulligan Ave, Chicago, IL 60630

DALY JR, Robert (Md) 13801 York Rd Apt D5, Cockeysville, MD 21030

DALZON, Wilfrid (Hai)

D'AMARIO, Matthew Justin (Eas) 302 North Baltimore Avenue, Ocean City, MD 21842

DAMON, Robert Edward (SeFla) 3329 Wilson St, Hollywood, FL 33021

DAMROSCH, Thomas Hammond (WMass) PO Box 612, Stockbridge, MA 01262

DAMUS, Pierre Gasner (LI) 1227 Pacific St, Brooklyn, NY 11216

DANAHER JR, William Joseph (Mich) 470 Church Rd, Bloomfield Hills, MI 48304

DANCER, Kathleen Ruth (WMich) 501 Se 50th Ave, Ocala, FL 34471

DANDRIDGE, Robert Floyd (WLa) 702 Elm St, Minden, La 71055

DANFORD, Nicholas Chase (NY) 4 Fountain Sq, Larchmont, NY 10538

DANFORTH, John Claggett (Mo) 911 Tirrill Farms Rd, Saint Louis, MO 63124

DANGELO, Michael B (Mass) 10600 Preston Rd, Dallas, TX 75230

D'ANGIO, Peter David (Lex) 16 E 4th St, Covington, KY 41011

✠ **DANIEL III**, Clifton (NY) 1047 Amsterdam Ave, New York, NY 10025

DANIEL, Joshua Timothy Kenyon (Ark) 531 W College Ave, Jonesboro, AR 72401

DANIEL, Wilfred (VI) 112 Estate La Reine, Christiansted, Saint Croix, VI 00823

DANIEL JR, William Otis (Roch) 23 Main St, Geneseo, NY 14454

DANIELEY, Teresa Kathryn Mithen (Mo) 3664 Arsenal St, Saint Louis, MO 63116

DANIELS, Janet (NJ) St Mary's by the Sea, 804 Bay Ave, Point Pleasant, NJ 08742

DANIELS, Joel C. (NY) 1 W. 53rd St., New York, NY 10019

DANIELS, John D (WA) 1001 E Lincoln Hwy, Exton, PA 19341

✠ **DANIELS**, Theodore Athelbert (VI) 3208 Prairie Clover Path, Austin, TX 78732

DANIEL-TURK, Patricia (Fla) 15 East Manor, Beaufort, SC 29906

D'ANIERI, Margaret C (O) 18369 State Route 58, Wellington, OH 44090

DANITSCHEK, Thomas K (Colo) 6930 E 4th Ave, Denver, CO 80220

DANKEL, Rainey (Mass) 233 Clarendon St., Boston, MA 02115

DANNALS, James Clark (SC) 1979 Long Branch Rd, Marshall, NC 28753

DANNALS, Robert S (Dal) 8011 Douglas @ Colgate, Dallas, TX 75225

DANNER, David Lawrence (SwFla) All Angels by the Sea Episcopal Church, 563 Bay Isles Rd, Longboat Key, FL 34228

DANNHAUSER, Adrian (NY) St James' Church, 865 Madison Ave, New York, NY 10021

DANSDILL, Dorothy Newton (NMich) 501 N Ravine St, Sault Sainte Marie, MI 49783

DANSON, Michelle Anne (Colo) 7776 Country Creek Dr, Longmont, CO 80503

DANTONE, Jan (WTex)

DANZEY, Charles (Oly) St Peter's Episcopal Church, 621 W Belmont Ave, Chicago, IL 60657

D'AOUST, Jean J (Colo) 1515 W 28th St Apt 114, Loveland, CO 80538

DARBY, Steven Lanier (Ga) 114 W Mockingbird Ln, Statesboro, GA 30461

DARDEN, John Webster (Dal) 3852 E Mulberry, PPrescott Valley, AZ 89314

DARISME, Joseph Wilkie (Hai) Boite Postale 1309, Port-Au-Prince, Haiti

DARKO, Daniel Dodoo (WA) 1510 Erskine St, Takoma Park, MD 20912

DARLING, Beth (WNC) 118 Clubwood Ct, Asheville, NC 28803

DARLING, Laura (Cal) 724 Valle Vista Avenue, Vallejo, CA 94590

DARLING, Mary (Roch) 2704 Darnby Dr, Oakland, CA 94611

DARLINGTON, Diane Lillie (NMich) 301 N 1st St, Ishpeming, MI 49849

DARROW, Robert Michael (Colo) 3275 S Pontiac St, Denver, CO 80224

DARVES-BORNOZ, James (NY) Church Pension Group, 19 E 34th St, New York, NY 10016

DARVILLE, Nathaniel Kirk Michael (Ala) 906 Pike Rd, Pike Road, AL 36064

DASS, Stephen (CFla) 1108 SE 9th Ave, Ocala, FL 34471

DATOS-ROBYN, Richard James (NY) St Mary's-in-Tuxedo, PO Box 637, Tuxedo Park, NY 10987

DATSKO, Paula Suzanne (Md) St Alban's Church, 105 1st Ave SW, Glen Burnie, MD 21061

DAUER-CARDASIS, Joade (NY) 227 E 87th St Apt 1B, New York, NY 10128

DAUGHERTY, Jennifer King (Oly) 1245 Tenth Ave E, Seattle, WA 98102

DAUGHTRY, James Robert (RG) 205 Augusta Way, Melbourne, FL 32940

DAUGHTRY, Susan (Minn) 1325 Nottoway Ave, Apt. A, Richmond, VA 23227

DAUNT, Francis Thomas (La) 815 E Guenther St, San Antonio, TX 78210

DAUPHIN, Joanne Coyle (Eur) 51 rue d'Amsterdam, Paris, 75008, France

DAUTEL, Terrence Pickands (O) Po Box 62, Gates Mills, OH 44040

DAVENPORT, Anetta Lynn (Wyo) Holy Trinity Episcopal Church, PO Box 950, Thermopolis, WY 82443

DAVENPORT, Carrol Kimsey (Mo) 17 Broadview, Kirksville, MO 63501

DAVENPORT JR, Charles Richard (NH) PO Box 85, Colebrook, NH 03576

DAVENPORT, Dave (SVa) 6051 River Road Pt, Norfolk, VA 23505

DAVENPORT, Elizabeth Jayne Louise (Chi)

DAVENPORT, Karen Geddes (CFla) 3840 Lakeview Dr, Sebring, FL 33870

DAVENPORT, Marcia EM (SwFla) 1606 Chickasaw Rd, Arnold, MD 21012

DAVENPORT, Robert (SVa) 1509 N Shore Rd, Norfolk, VA 23505

DAVENPORT III, Stephen Rintoul (WA) 4700 Whitehaven Pkwy Nw, Washington, DC 20007

DAVID, Charles Wayne Laskin (Mass) 6390 Sagewood Way, Delray Beach, FL 33484

DAVID, Christopher (LI) PO Box 110, 482 County Route 30, Salem, NY 12865

DAVID, Jacob Thandasseril (Nwk) 1 Paddock Court, Dayton, NJ 08810

DAVID, John Spencer (WMich) 157 Lost Creek Lane, Kalispell, MT 59901

DAVID, Ronald (Los) 1225 Wilshire Blvd, Los Angeles, CA 90017

DAVIDSON, Charles Alexander (Pa) 814 N 41st St, Philadelphia, PA 19104

DAVIDSON, Donald F (EMich) 9020 S Saginaw Rd, Grand Blanc, MI 48439

DAVIDSON, Jon Paul (Nev) PO Box 8822, Incline Village, NV 89452

DAVIDSON, Mark Alan (NC) 3205 S Main St, Winston Salem, NC 27127

DAVIDSON, Patricia Foote (Ct) 118 Bill Hill Rd, Lyme, CT 06371

DAVIDSON, Robert Michael (Pa) 22 E Chestnut Hill Ave, Philadelphia, PA 19118

DAVIDSON, Robert Paul (Colo) 1005 Cimmaron Dr, Loveland, CO 80537

DAVIDSON, Susan (Ct) 61 Hunter Ct, Torrington, CT 06790

DAVIDSON, Thomas Walter (Az) 4041 N 164th Dr, Goodyear, AZ 85395

DAVIDSON, William Albert (Vt) Prestwick Farm, 2260 County Route 12, Whitehall, NY 12887

DAVIDSON-METHOT, David G (Los) 2945 Bell Rd Pmb 325, Auburn, CA 95603

DAVIES, Ian E (Los) 7501 Hollywood Blvd, Los Angeles, CA 90046

DAVIES JR, Richard Wood (Pgh) 300 Madison Ave, Apt 309, Pittsburgh, PA 15243

DAVIES-ARYEEQUAYE, Eliza Ayorkor (NY) 23 Water Grant St. Apt. 9E, Yonkers, NY 10701

DAVILA, Mary Fisher (Va) 117 Rivana Terr SW, Leesburg, VA 20175

DAVILA, Willie Rodriguez (SeFla) 1063 Haverhill Rd N, Haverhill, FL 33417

DAVILA COLON, Angel Michael (PR)

DAVILA FIGUEROA, Wilson Jaime (Colom) c/o Diocese of Colombia, Cra 6 No. 49-85 Piso 2, Bogota, BDC, Colombia

DAVINICH, George Lawrence (Mich) 945 Palmer St, Plymouth, MI 48170

DAVIOU, Albert G (At) 432 Noelle Lane, Dahlonega, GA 30533

DAVIS JR, Albin P (Los) 209 S. Detroit St., Los Angeles, CA 90036

DAVIS, Alice Downing (Va) P.O. Box 622, Luray, VA 22835

DAVIS, Angus Kenneth (Pa) PO Box 329, Kimberton, PA 19442

DAVIS, Bancroft Gherardi (Pa) 419 Chandlee Dr, Berwyn, PA 19312

DAVIS, Calvin Lee (SwFla) 725 Nokomis Ave S, Venice, FL 34285

DAVIS, Catherine Ward (EC) St James Parish, 25 S 3rd St, Wilmington, NC 28401

DAVIS, Charles Lee (Ak) ST MATTHEW'S EPISCOPAL CHURCH, 1030 2ND AVE, FAIRBANKS, AK 99701

DAVIS SR, Charles Meyer (USC) 232 Elstow Rd, Irmo, SC 29206

DAVIS JR, Charles Meyer (USC) 3709 Greenbriar Dr, Columbia, SC 29206

DAVIS, Charlotte Murray (NC) 3120 Sunnybrook Dr, Charlotte, NC 28210

DAVIS III, Chip Alfred (WTenn) 2225 Jefferson Ave, Memphis, TN 38104

DAVIS, Clifford Bruce (Kan) 1070 W Antelope Creek Way, Tucson, AZ 85737

DAVIS, David Joseph (EC) 208 Country Club Dr., Shallotte, NC 28470

DAVIS, Donald Henry Kortright (WA) 11414 Woodson Ave, Kensington, MD 20895

DAVIS, Doyal (Okla) P.O. Box 1905, Shawnee, OK 74802

DAVIS, Elizabeth Hill (Okla)

DAVIS, Emily (Mo) 9441 Engel Ln, St. Louis, MO 63132

DAVIS, Fletcher (WMass) 4490 Smugglers Cove Rd, Freeland, WA 98249

DAVIS, Gae K (EC)

DAVIS, Gail E (Kan) 1228 Auburn Village Dr, Durham, NC 27713

DAVIS, Gale Davis (Mass) 25 Central St, Andover, MA 01810

DAVIS, Gena Lynn (Tex) 5010 N Main St, Baytown, TX 77521

DAVIS, Gordon Bell (Va) 1201 Rothesay Cir, Richmond, VA 23221

DAVIS, James Lloyd (Ia) 6617 Romford Ct, Johnston, IA 50131

DAVIS, Jane Lowe (EC) PO Box 7386, St Thomas, VI 00801

DAVIS, John Bartley (ND) 7940 45r Street Southeast, Jamestown, ND 58401

DAVIS, John William (Be) Church of the Good Shepherd, 1780 N Washington Ave, Scranton, PA 18509

DAVIS JR, Johnnie (USC) PO Box 2959, West Columbia, SC 29171

DAVIS, Jon (CFla) 1412 Palomino Way, Oviedo, FL 32765

DAVIS, Joseph N (Tenn) 8215 Planters Grove Dr, Cordova, TN 38018

DAVIS, Joy Ruth (Ga) St Patrick's Episcopal Church, 4800 Old Dawson Rd, Albany, GA 31721

DAVIS, Judith Anne (Mass) 671 Route 28, Harwich Port, MA 02646

DAVIS, Judy (Va) 236 S Laurel St, Richmond, VA 23220

DAVIS, Margaret Callender (CFla) 19924 W Blue Cove Dr, Dunnellon, FL 34432

DAVIS, Mary Alice (Okla) 3200 Shady Brook Rd, Woodward, OK 73801

DAVIS, Mary Elizabeth (Nwk) 200 Main St, Chatham, NJ 07928

DAVIS, Maryan Elizabeth (NH)

DAVIS, Matthew Steven (Episcopal SJ) 1710 Verde St, Bakersfield, CA 93304

DAVIS, Michael (WTex) 8401 Kearsarge Dr, Austin, TX 78745

DAVIS, Milbrew (WTex) 338 Hub Ave, San Antonio, TX 78220

DAVIS, Orion Woods (Nwk) 2 Pasadena St, Canton, NC 28716

DAVIS, Patricia Rhoads (Ga) 215 Grimball Point Rd, Savannah, GA 31466

DAVIS, Philip Arthur (SwFla) 1603 52nd St W, Bradenton, FL 34209

DAVIS, Rodney (The Episcopal NCal) 2140 Mission Ave., Carmichael, CA 95608

DAVIS, Ronald Lee (WA) Saint Anne's Church, 25100 Ridge Rd, Damascus, MD 20872

DAVIS, Roy Jefferson (Tex)

DAVIS, Steven (Wyo)

DAVIS, Vicki (Ct) 4551 Pennsylvania Ave Unit 1523, Kansas City, MO 64111

DAVIS, West Richard (Oly) 790 Smugglers Cove Rd, Friday Harbor, WA 98250

DAVIS-HELLER, Lisa Ann (WVa)

DAVIS-LAWSON, Karen Dm (LI) 1420 27th Ave, Astoria, NY 11102

DAVISON, Arienne Siu Ling (Oly) 2151 4th St, Bremerton, WA 98312

DAVIS-SHOEMAKER, Courtney D (NC) 1019 E Willowbrook Drive, Burlington, NC 27215

DAVISSON, Mary Thomsen (Md) 2363 Hamiltowne Cir., Baltimore, MD 21237

DAVIS-WILSON, Lillian Juanita (WNY) St Philip's Episc Church, 15 Fernhill Ave, Buffalo, NY 14215

DAVY, Brian Kendall (At) 589 Martins Grove Rd, Dahlonega, GA 30533

DAW JR, Carl Pickens (Ct) 171 Highland Ave, Watertown, MA 02472

DAWSON, Adrien P (Md) 4412 Eastway, Baltimore, MD 21218

DAWSON, Barbara Louise (Cal) 399 Gregory Ln, Pleasant Hill, CA 94523

DAWSON, Cynthia Louise (Me)

DAWSON, Eric Emmanuel (VI) 19-5 Hope, Saint Thomas, VI 00801

DAWSON JR, Frank Prescott (Md) 9422 Penfield Rd N, Columbia, MD 21045

DAWSON, George (WTex) 4426 Dolphin Pl, Corpus Christi, TX 78411

DAWSON, Margaret G (La) 320 Sena Dr, Metairie, LA 70005

DAWSON, Mark Douglas (Los) 514 W Adams Blvd, Los Angeles, CA 90007

DAWSON JR, Marshall Allen (Lex) 1375 Weisenberger Mill Rd, Midway, KY 40347

DAWSON, Paul Sweeting (Md) 145 Main St., Apt. A1, Vineyard Haven, MA 02568

DAWSON JR, Tucker Edward (La) 321 State St, Bay Saint Louis, MS 39520

DAWSON, Walter (Mich) 18017 Grand Lake Blvd, Presque Isle, MI 49777

DAY, Christine Jane (CNY) 35 Second St, Johnson City, NY 13790

DAY, Dennis Lee (CGC) PO Box 2066, Fairhope, AL 36533

DAY, James Meredith (Eur)

DAY, Jeremiah (EC) 109 Skipper Circle, Oriental, NC 28571

DAY, John Edward (The Episcopal NCal) 9843 Derby Way, Elk Grove, CA 95757

DAY JR, John Warren (Wyo) 441 Highland Dr, Bellingham, WA 98225

DAY, Kate Lufkin (CNY) 106 Ardsley Dr, Syracuse, NY 13214

DAY, Margaret Ann (Me) 777 Stillwater Ave Lot 63, Old Town, ME 04468

DAY, Marshall Benjamin (At) 2089 Ponce de Leon Ave NE, Atlanta, GA 30307

DAY, Meredith Jane (WTenn) 1747 Peabody Ave - R, Memphis, TN 38104

DAY, Michael Henry (SwFla) 1070 54th St N, Saint Petersburg, FL 33710

DAY, Randall Carl Kidder (Los) 2901 Nojoqui Avenue, P.O. Box 39, Los Olivos, CA 93441

DAY, Stephen Crayton (Mont) PO Box 1526, Miles City, MT 59301

DAY, Thomas Leighton (Tex) 320 N Kansas Ave, League City, TX 77573

DAY, Virginia Rex (Be) 1006 Eisenhower Way, Tobyhanna, PA 18466

DAYNES, Taylor Darlington (CNY) 25 Westminster Rd, Rochester, NY 14607

DAYTON, Douglas Kennedy (NwPa) 3600 Mcconnell Rd, Hermitage, PA 16148

DAYTON-WELCH, Matthew H (Pa) 3625 Chapel Rd, Newtown Square, PA 19073

DEACON JR, Charles Alexander (WNY) 84 Rosedale Blvd., Amherst, NY 14226

DEACON, Jonathan (NJ) 12 Bryan Dr, Voorhees, NJ 08043

DEADERICK, Dianna LaMance (USC) 1300 Pine St, Columbia, SC 29204

DEAKLE, David Wayne (La) 4350 SE Brooklyn St, Portland, OR 97206

DEAN, Aelred B (Lex) PO, 131 Edgewood Rd, Middlesboro, KY 40965

DEAN, Bobby Wayne (CGC) PO Box 1677, Santa Rosa Beach, FL 32459

DEAN JR, Edward Carroll (RI) St Davids Episcopal Church, 200 Meshanticut Valley Pkwy, Cranston, RI 02920

DEAN, Gordon Joy (WMass) 10 Fox Rd, Shelburne Falls, MA 01370

DEAN, Jay Judson (Me) 33 Baker St, Dover, NH 03820

DEAN, Rebecca Anderson (SVa) 985 Huguenot Trl, Midlothian, VA 23113

DEAN, Steve (Los) 25211 Via Tanara, Santa Clarita, CA 91355

DEAN, Susan Chanda (Oly) 3714 90th Avenue SE, Mercer Island, WA 98040

DE ANAYA, Nilda Lucca (PR) 2100 Washington Ave Apt 2c, Silver Spring, MD 20910

DEANE JR, William Boyd (Pa) 812 Lombard St, Philadelphia, PA 19147

DEAR, Tyrrel (CFla) Po Box 668, New Smyrna, FL 32170

DEARING, Trevor (Oly) 4 Rock House Gardens, Radcliffe Road, Stamford, PE9 1AS, Great Britain (UK)

DEARMAN, David (Tex) 90 Island Psge, Galveston, TX 77554

DEARMAN JR, William Benjamin (NY) 7 Oakridge Pkwy, Peekskill, NY 10566

DEASY, James Scott (Az) Epiphany Episcopal Church, 423 N Beaver St, Flagstaff, AZ 86001

DEATON JR, Charles Milton (Miss) 1616 52nd Ct, Meridian, MS 39305

DEATON, Jennifer Deaton (Miss) PO Box 23107, Jackson, MS 39225

DEATRICK, George Edward (NJ) 215 Philadelphia Blvd, Sea Girt, NJ 08750

DEATS, Cathy (NC) 6625 Battleford Dr, Raleigh, NC 27613

DEAVOURS, Cipher A (NJ) 112 Union St, Montclair, NJ 07042

DE AZEVEDO, Guilherme Barbosa (U)

DE BARY, Edward Oscar (Miss) 11 Wakefield Dr Apt 2105, Asheville, NC 28803

DEBBOLI, Walter Anthony (Ct) 80 Rockwell Ave, Plainville, CT 06062

DE BEER, John Michael (Mass) 2905 Wynnewood Drive, Greensboro, NC 27408

DE BEER, Patricia Jean (Mass) 2905 Wynnewood Dr., Greensboro, NC 27408

DEBENHAM JR, Warren Warren (Cal) 143 Arlington Ave, Berkeley, CA 94707

DEBLASIO, Diane L (LI) 100 46th St, Lindenhurst, NY 11757

DEBOW, Rebecca (Ala) 3519 W Lakeside Dr, Birmingham, AL 35243

DEBUSSY, Muriel S (NJ) 825 Summerset Dr, Hockessin, DE 19707

DEBUYS III, John Forrester (Ala) 2501 Country Club Cir, Birmingham, AL 35223

DECAMPS, Walin (Hai)

DECARLEN, Marya Louise (Mass) same, Boxford, MA 01921

DECARVALHO, Maria Elena (RI) 18 Vassar Ave, Providence, RI 02906

DE CHAMBEAU, Franck Alsid (Ct) 163 Belgo Rd, P.O. Box 391, Lakeville, CT 06039

DECKER, Dallas (The Episcopal Church in Haw) 18218 Paradise Mountain Rd Spc 88, Valley Center, CA 92082

DECKER, Georgia Ann (WK) 509 16th Ter, Hutchinson, KS 67501

DECKER, Linda McCullough (The Episcopal Church in Haw) 307 S Alu Rd, Wailuku, HI 96793

DECKER, Margaret Sharp (SanD) 1651 S Juniper St Unit 26, Escondido, CA 92025

DECKER, Prince A (WA) 3918 Wendy Ln, Silver Spring, MD 20906

DECOSS, Donald Albion (Cal) 26 Overlake Ct, Oakland, CA 94611

DEDDE, Joseph Colin (WNY) 233 Brantwood Rd, Amherst, NY 14226

DEDEAUX JR, James Terrell (Miss) 5303 Diamondhead Cir, Diamondhead, MS 39525

DEDMON JR, Robert Aaron (Chi) 1804 Sycamore Circle, Manchester, TN 37355

DEERY, Laurel Pierson (Mass) 44 School St, Manchester, MA 01944

DEETHS, Margaret Edith (Cal) 576 Cedarberry Ln, San Rafael, CA 94903

DEETS, Sherry (Pa) 2717 Shelburne Road, Downingtown, PA 19335

DEETZ, Susan Maureen (Minn) 4210 Robinson St, Duluth, MN 55804

DE FONTAINE-STRATTON, James Bruce (NY) 161 Mansion St, Poughkeepsie, NY 12601

DEFOOR II, Allison (Fla) 325 N Market St, Jacksonville, FL 32202

DEFOREST, John William (Tex) 3535 Whittaker Ln, Beaumont, TX 77706

DEFOREST, Nancy (Tex) 3535 Whittaker Ln, Beaumont, TX 77706

DEFRANCO JR, Peter (NJ) 396 Clifton Ave, Clifton, NJ 07011

DEFRIEST, Jeannette (Chi) 400 Main St Apt 5A, Evanston, IL 60202

DEGAVRE, Susan Williams (Va) 7120 S. Wenatchee Way Unit C, Aurora, CO 80016

DEGENHARDT, Terri Walker (Ga) St Michael's Episcopal Church, 515 S Liberty St, Waynesboro, GA 30830

DEGOOYER, Bruce Underwood (The Episcopal Church in Haw) 2816 Greenfield Rd, Bloomington, IL 61704

DE GRAVELLES, Charlie (La) 3651 Broussard St, Baton Rouge, LA 70808

DEGWECK, Stephen William (Ala) 1336 Round Hill Rd, Birmingham, AL 35216

DEHART, Benjamin Robert (NY) Calvary and St George, 61 Gramercy Park N Fl 2, New York, NY 10010

DEHART, Elsa Arp (Ak) St James the Fisherman, PO Box 1668, Kodiak, AK 99615

DEHART, Steven Darrell (Mont)

DEHETRE, Donna (Chi) 31 Edgehill Rd, New Haven, CT 06511

DEHLER, Debra Rae (Ind) St Albans Episcopal Church, 4601 N Emerson Ave, Indianapolis, IN 46226

DEJARDIN, Wisnel (Hai)

DE JESUS, Gerardo James (CFla) 6316 Matchett Rd, Orlando, FL 32809

DE JESUS-JIMENEZ, Justo (PR) Parroquia Santo Nombre de Jesus, 806 Calle Jesus T Pineiro, Ponce, PR 00728

DE JESUS LAGARES, Jose Joaquin (DR DomRep))

DEJOHN, Kathleen Ann Gillespie (NJ) 138 Rector St, Perth Amboy, NJ 08861

DE KAY, Charles Augustus (Chi) 901 Forest Avenue 1E, Evanston, IL 60202

DEKKER, Bob Peter (Chi) 15145 Smarty Jones Drive, Noblesville, IN 46060

DE LA CRUZ, Luis Manuel (CFla) 1709 N John Young Pkwy, Kissimmee, FL 34741

DELAFIELD, Audrey Sawtelle (Me) 32 Ship Channel Rd, South Portland, ME 04106

DELAMATER, Joanie (Minn) 6287 Crackleberry Trl, Woodbury, MN 55129

DELANCEY, Mary Louise (CFla) 510 SE Broadway St, Ocala, FL 34471

DE LANEROLLE, Nihal Chandra (Ct) 500 Prospect St Apt 2-F, New Haven, CT 06511

DELANEY, Conrad Todd (SanD)

DELANEY, Mary Joan (Az) 5611E Alta Vista St, Tucson, AZ 85712

DELANEY, Mary Timothea Kathleen (EMich) 1038 W Center St, Alma, MI 40001

DELANEY, Michael F (LI) 191 Kensington Road, Garden City, NY 11530

DELANEY, Ryan Ray (Alb) 340 S Elm St, Oconomowoc, WI 53066

DE LA TORRE, Carlos Enrique (Ct)

DE LA TORRE, William Jhon (SwFla) 8271 52nd St N, Pinellas Park, FL 33781

Clergy List

DELAURA, Gilbert Frank (Alb) Church of the Messiah, 296 Glen St, Glens Falls, NY 12801

DELAUTER, Joseph Halvor (CPa) 598 Longbarn Rd, State College, PA 16803

DE LA VARS, Gordon (Md) 115 S Erie St, Mayville, NY 14757

DEL BENE, Ronald Norman (Ala) 2841 Floyd Bradford Rd, Trussville, AL 35173

DEL CASTILLO, Gloria R (Cal) 622 Lois Lane, El Sobrante, CA 94803

DELCUZE, Mark Stewart (Eas) 623 Cloverfields Dr, Stevensville, MD 21666

DELEERY, Seth Mabry (Tex) 9002 Clithea Cv, Austin, TX 78759

DE LEEUW, Gawain (NY) 95 Ralph Ave, White Plains, NY 10606

DELEUSE, Betsey W (Me) 27 Arlington St. Unit 1, Portland, ME 04101

DELFS, Carin Bridgit (SO) 11 Rosemary Run, Delaware, OH 43015

DELGADO, Joseph Anthony (Cal) 2220 Cedar St, Berkeley, CA 94709

DELGADO-MARKSMAN, Adams Felipe (Ve)

DELGADO-MILLER, Diego (NY) 260 W 231st St, Bronx, NY 10460

DELGADO-VERA, Ramiro Mario (WTex) 697 W White Ave, Raymondville, TX 78580

DELICAT, Joseph Kerwin (Hai)

DELINGER, Ian Michael (ECR)

DE LION, Lawrence Raymond (LI) 15 Greenwich Rd, Smithtown, NY 11787

DELK, Michael (SVa) 205 Castle Ln, Williamsburg, VA 23185

DELL, Jacob William (NY) 504 E 79th St Apt 4H, New York, NY 10075

DELL, Mary Lynn (O) 2741 Sherbrooke Road, Shaker Heights, OH 44122

DELLARIA, Kevin (Pa) Saint Francis-In-The-Fields, 689 Sugartown Rd, Malvern, PA 19355

DELLENBARGER, Leslie Ann (Ga)

DELMAS, Hailey Lynne (Cal) 28 Cobblestone Ln, Belmont, CA 94002

DEL PRIORE, Dorian (USC) 910 Hudson Rd, Greenville, SC 29615

DEL VALLE-ORTIZ, Efrain Edgardo (PR) 557 Calle Plinio Peterson, Vieques, PR 00765

DEL VALLE-TIRADO, Jose A (PR)

DELZELL, Constance Kay Clawson (Colo) 3 Calle de Montanas, Santa Fe, NM 87507

DEMAREST, Richard Alan (Ida) 518 N. Eighth Street, Boise, ID 83702

DEMBI, Megan E (Be) 6030 Grosvenor Ln, Bethesda, MD 20814

DE MEL, Chitral S (Mass)

DEMENT, Thomas Erik (Oly) 1118 E Baldwin Ave, Spokane, WA 99207

DEMING, Nancy James (Pa) 518 Hilaire Rd, Saint Davids, PA 19087

DEMING, Robert (Ct) 20 Shepherd Ln, Orange, CT 06477

DE MIRANDA, Mario Eugenio (SeFla) 15650 Miami Lakeway N, Miami Lakes, FL 33014

DEMLER, Maureen Ann (Alb) 912 Route 146, Clifton Park, NY 12065

DEMMLER, Mary Reynolds Hemmer (At) 995 E Tugalo St, Toccoa, GA 30577

DEMO, Gar R (Kan) 8144 Rosehill Rd, Lenexa, KS 66215

DEMO, Kelly Marie (Kan) 8144 Rosehill Rd, Lenexa, KS 66215

DE MONTMOLLIN, Dee Ann Ann (SwFla) 394 N. Main Street, Rutherfordton, NC 28139

DEMPESY-SIMS, Catherine Biggs (WNY) St Pauls Cathedral, 128 Pearl St, Buffalo, NY 14202

DEMPZ, Julia A (Mich) 61 Grosse Pointe Blvd, Grosse Pointe Farms, MI 48236

DEMURA, Christie (Oly) 10042 Main St Apt 410, Bellevue, WA 98004

DE MUTH, Steven H (Los) Holy Trinity Parish, PO Box 4195, Covina, CA 91723

DENARO, John (LI) 157 Montague St, Brooklyn, NY 11201

DENDTLER, Robert Blanchard (At) 1011 Cedar Ridge, Greensboro, GA 30642

DENEAU, Elizabeth Ann (NMich) 500 Ogden Ave, Escanaba, MI 49829

DENEKE, Kelly (At) 515 E Ponce De Leon Ave, Decatur, GA 30030

DENG DENG, William (Oly) 4759 Shattuck Pl S Unit B101, Renton, WA 98055

DENHAM, John (WA) 767 N Cambridge Way, Claremont, CA 91711

DENISON, Charles Wayne (Wyo) 2502 Overland Road, Laramie, WY 82070

DENISON JR, Raleigh Edmond (Dal) 1504 S Ash St, Georgetown, TX 78626

DENMAN, Scott (Cal) 7917 Outlook Ave, Oakland, CA 94605

DENNEY, Robin (ECR)

DENNEY, Shawn W (Spr) 3813 Bergamot Dr, Springfield, IL 62712

DENNEY, Shelley Booth (ECR) PO Box 1317, Lake Arrowhead, CA 92352

DENNEY-ZUNIGA, Amy E (ECR)

DENNIS, Alan Godfrey (NY) 45 orchard lane, Torrington, CT 06790

DENNIS, Fredrick Hogarth (Alb) 455 Park Ave, Saranac Lake, NY 12983

DENNIS, Loretta Anne (Roch) 240 S 4th St, Philadelphia, PA 19106

DENNIS, William J (WLa) 501 Springfield Ave, Eutaw, AL 35462

DENNISON JR, Bryant Whitman (Mich) PO Box 3974, Ann Arbor, MI 48106

DENNLER, William David (Tenn) 615 6th Ave. S., Nashville, TN 37203

DENNY, Stephen Michael (Ore) 10143 Se 49th Ave, Milwaukie, OR 97222

DENSON JR, John (Ind) 5 Granite St, Exeter, NH 03833

DENTON, Edna Marguerite (SO) 1021 Crede Way, Waynesville, OH 45068

DENTON, Jean (Ind) 607 Alden Rd, Claremont, CA 91711

DENTON, Maria Anna (Colo) 7068 Kiowa Rd, Larkspur, CO 80118

DEOKARAN, Teresa J (WK) 209 S Walnut St, Medicine Lodge, KS 67104

DEPHOUSE, John R (Los) 1325 Monterey Rd, South Pasadena, CA 91030

DEPPE, Jimmie Sue Marie (Roch) 3285 Buffalo Rd, Rochester, NY 14624

DEPPE, Thomas W (SVa) 2020 Laskin Rd, Virginia Beach, VA 23454

DEPPEN, G(ehret) David (NJ) 35 Queens Way, Wellfleet, MA 02667

DEPRIEST, Sandra Moss (Miss) 510 7th St N, Columbus, MS 39701

DEPUE, Karen Lynn Joanna (NY) 7 Heather Ln, Orangeburg, NY 10962

DE PUY KERSHAW, Susan Lynn (NH) P.O. Box 485, Walpole, NH 03608

DERAVIL, Jean-Jacques (Hai) Diquini 63b #8, Carrefour, Haiti

DERBY, William (NY) 14 E 109th St, New York, NY 10029

DERBYSHIRE, John Edward (CNY) 229 Twin Hills Dr, Syracuse, NY 13207

DERKITS III, J James (WTex) Trinity by the Sea Episcopal Church, PO Box 346, Port Aransas, TX 78373

DEROSE, Kathryn Pitkin (Los) 2621 6th St Apt 5, Santa Monica, CA 90405

DERRICK, John Burton (Ga) 1512 Meadows Ln, Vidalia, GA 30474

DERSE, Anne Elizabeth (WA)

DERSNAH, Donald L (Mich) 4354 Weber Rd, Saline, MI 48176

DE RUFF, Elizabeth Anslow (Cal) PO Box 1137, Ross, CA 94957

DESALVO, David (Del) 350 Noxontown Rd, Middletown, DE 19709

DESAULNIERS, John Joseph (Va) 406 Haven Lake Ave, Milford, DE 19963

DESCHAINE, Thomas Charles (Me) Po Box 467, Augusta, ME 04332

DESHAIES, Robert Joseph (SeFla)

DE SHEPLO, Louis John (NJ) 551 Saint Kitts Dr, Williamstown, NJ 08094

DE SILVA, Sumi (Az) 9533 E. Kokopelli Circle, Tucson, AZ 85748

DESIR, Jean Nephtaly (DR (DomRep)) Iglesia Episcopal Dominicana, Apartado 764, Santo Domingo, Dominican Republic

DESIRE, Fritz (Hai)

DESMARAIS, Susanna (Neb) 4545 S 58th St, Lincoln, NE 68516

DESMITH, David John (Nwk) 90 Kiel Ave, Kinnelon, NJ 07405

DESROSIERS JR, Norman (CFla) St Sebastian By The Sea, 2010 Oak St, Melbourne Beach, FL 32951

DESUEZA, Edmond (NY) 271 Broadway, Newburgh, NY 12550

DESUEZA-SAVINON, Edmond (PR) Urb. Fairview, D11 Calle 10, San Juan, PR 00926

DETRICH, James Paul (Dal) 1524 Smirl Dr, Heath, TX 75032

DETTWILLER II, George Frederick (Tenn) 108 Savoy Cir., Nashville, TN 37205

DEVALL IV, Frederick D (La) St. Martin's Episcopal Church, 2216 Metairie Road, Metairie, LA 70001

DEVATY, Jean M (Alb) 508 4th Ave, Beaver Falls, PA 15010

DEVAUL, Philip H (SO) 31641 La Novia Ave, San Juan Capistrano, CA 92675

DEVEAU, Peter (WMo) 5916 Oak St, Kansas City, MO 64113

DEVENS, Philip (RI) 111 Greenwich Ave # 2886, Warwick, RI 02886

DEVINE, Michael Francis (WMass) 47 Ruskin St, Springfield, MA 01108

DEVINE, Taylor Poindexter (Va)

DEVINE, Whitney Alford Jones (Oly) 4420 - 137th Avenue Northeast, Bellevue, WA 98005

DE VOLDER, Luk Jozef (Ct) 950 Chapel St Fl 2, New Haven, CT 06510

DEVORE, Kirk Eugene (Md) 2 E High St, Hancock, MD 21750

DEWEES, Herbert Reed (Dal) 9511 Meadowknoll Dr, Dallas, TX 75243

DE WETTER, Robert Emerson (Colo) PO Box 5310, Snowmass Village, CO 81615

DEWEY, Camie Marie (Colo)

DEWEY, Edward Robinson (SC) 598 E Hobcaw Dr, Mount Pleasant, SC 29464

DEWEY JR, Sanford Dayton (NY) B908 New Providence Wharf, 1 Fairmont Ave, London, E14 9PB U.K., Great Britain (UK)

DEWITT, Edward Leonard (NMich) 90 Croix St Apt 2, Negaunee, MI 49866

DEWITT, Phyllis M (NMich) 301 N 1st St, Ishpeming, MI 49849

DEWITT, William Henry (NMich) 301 N 1st St, Ishpeming, MI 49849

DEWLEN, Janet Marie (Colo) 2500 22nd Drive, Longmont, CO 80503

DEWOLFE, Robert F (WTex) 3412 Pebblebrook Dr, Tyler, TX 75707

DEXTER, Beverly Liebherr (SanD) 325 Kempton St Apt 400, Spring Valley, CA 91977

DEYO, Bonnie (Wyo)

DEYOUNG, Lily April (Mass) 12408 Main Campus Drive, Lexington, MA 02421

DEZHBOD, Esmail Shahrokh (Ct) 294 Main St S, Woodbury, CT 06798

DIAS, Krista K (Colo) Church Of Our Saviour, 8 4th St, Colorado Springs, CO 80906

DIAZ, George (NY) 257 Clinton St Apt 19n, New York, NY 10002

DIAZ, Gladys (NY) Po Box 617, Bronx, NY 10473

DIAZ, Jose (Pa) 3554 N 6th St, Philadelphia, PA 19140

DIAZ, Joseph Herbert (SwFla) 3396 Deerfield Ln, Clearwater, FL 33761

DIAZ, Juan Jose (Hond)

DIAZ, Narciso Antonio (Chi) 400 E Westminster Rd, Lake Forest, IL 60045

DIAZ ESTEVEZ, Manuel (DR (DomRep))

DIBENEDETTO, Aileen Elizabeth (WMass) 8 Cedar Rd, Shrewsbury, MA 01545

DICARLO, Michael Joseph (Los) 1400 W. 13th St. Spc 139, Upland, CA 91786

DICE, Daniel (Mass) St John the Evangelist, PO Box 2893, Duxbury, MA 02331

DICK, Brandt (Miss) 1026 S. Washing Ave, Greenville, MS 38701

DICKERSON, Shawn E (Ore) 822 Washington St, Oregon City, OR 97045

DICKEY, Michael Patrick (CGC)

DICKEY, Robert William (Va) 108 Forest Garden Rd, Stevensville, MD 21666

DICKHAUT, Walter R (Me)

DICKINSON, Albert Hugh (Pa) 2510 Lake Michigan Dr, NW Apt. A-205, Grand Rapids, MI 49504

DICKINSON, Garrin William (Dal) 3804 Carrizo Dr, Plano, TX 75074

DICKS, Paul Richard (Spr) 422 E 1st South St, Carlinville, IL 62626

✠ **DICKSON**, Alex Dockery (WTenn) 1 Bishop Gadsden Way Apt 356, Charleston, SC 29412

DICKSON JR, Elton Robert (Mass) 6102 Buckhorn Rd, Greensboro, NC 27410

DICKSON, Patricia Joan (Va) 3883 Connecticut Ave Nw Apt 715, Washington, DC 20008

DIEBEL, Mark H (Alb) 68 Troy Rd., East Greenbush, NY 12061

DIEGUE, Joseph Tancrel (Hai) Box 1309, Port-Au-Prince, Haiti

DIEGUE, Joseph Tancrel (Hai)

DIEHL, Jane Cornell (EMich) 3201 Gratiot Ave, Port Huron, MI 48060

DIELE, Joseph (LI) 4301 Avenue D, Brooklyn, NY 11203

DIERICK, F Lorraine (Oly) 102 Glenn Ln, Montesano, WA 98563

DIETER, David D (Mich) 847 Grand Marais St, Grosse Pointe Park, MI 48230

DIETERLE, Ann (WNC) 200 W Cowles St, Wilkesboro, NC 28697

DIETRICH, Seth (Mil) 4234 N Larkin St, Milwaukee, WI 53211

✠ **DIETSCHE**, Andy (NY) 1047 Amsterdam Ave, New York, NY 10025

DIETZ, Joseph Bland (Pa) 2619 N Charlotte St, Pottstown, PA 19464

DIETZ ALLEN, Doyle (The Episcopal NCal) Saint Patricks Episcopal Church, PO Box 247, Kenwood, CA 95452

DIGGS, Thomas Tucker (USC) 2313 Kestrel Dr, Rock Hill, SC 29732

DILEO, John (Fla) 1505 NW 91st Ter, Gainesville, FL 32606

DILG, Arthur Charles (Pgh) 1371 Washington St, Indiana, PA 15701

DILL, David S (Colo) Church of the Good Shepherd, 3809 Spring Avenue SW, Decatur, AL 35603

DILL, Todd R (NC) 8515 Rea Rd, Waxhaw, NC 28173

DILLARD, Walter Scott (Va) 9 Deerfield Dr, Luray, VA 22835

DILLER, Sallie Winch (NMich) 733n E Gulliver Lake Rd, Gulliver, MI 49840

DILLEY, John S (HB)

DILLIPLANE, Nancy Burton (Pa) PO Box 245, Buckingham, PA 18912

DILLON, Gwendolyn J (Chi) 446 E 95th St, Chicago, IL 60619

DILLON, John Lawrence (U) 8738 Oakwood Park Cir, Sandy, UT 84094

DILLON, Karla Lewis (Okla)

DILLON II, Tommy J (La) 1715 Saint Rose Ave Apt 3, Baton Rouge, LA 70808

DILLS, Robert Scott (Oly) 919 - 21st Avenue East, Seattle, WA 98112

DILLS-MOORE, Amy Sarah (At) 3110 Ashford Dunwoody Rd NE, Brookhaven, GA 30319

DI LORENZO, Anthony (LI) 40 Warren Avenue, Lake Ronkonkoma, NY 11779

DIMARCO, Thomas Edgar (USC) PO Box 206, Trenton, SC 29847

DIMMICK, Kenneth Ray (Tex) Lorenzstaffel 8, Stuttgart, 70182, Germany

DINGES, John Albert (Mil) Box 27671, West Allis, WI 53227

DINGLE, John Hausmann (NY) 143 Kent I, Century Village, West Palm Beach, FL 33417

DINGLEY, Alison M. (The Episcopal Church in Haw) 1255 Nuuanu Ave., #E1513, Honolulu, HI 96817

DINGMAN, Joel (Wyo) 419 Circle Dr, Gillette, WY 82716

DINKINS, David Duane (RG) Unit 100175 Box 2314, FPO AP, 96615

DINNERVILLE, Robert Raymond (CFla) 6400 N Socrum Loop Rd, Lakeland, FL 33809

DINOTO, Anthony Charles (Ct) PO Box 810, Niantic, CT 06357

DINOVO, Darlyn Rebecca (SanD) St John The Evangelist Episcopal Church, 2036 SE Jefferson St, Milwaukie, OR 97222

DINSMORE, Taylor Whitehead (ETenn) 9125 Candlewood Dr, Knoxville, TN 37923

DINSMORE, Virginia Carol (Nwk) 681 Prospect Ave, West Orange, NJ 07052

Clergy List

DINWIDDIE, Donald H (Fla) 1113 Fleet Landing Blvd, Atlantic Beach, FL 32233

DINWIDDIE, Philip Matthew (Mich) 25150 East River, Grosse Ile, MI 48138

DIRBAS, Joseph James (SanD) 1475 Catalina Blvd, San Diego, CA 92106

DIRBAS, Terry Shields (SanD) 1114 9th St, Coronado, CA 92118

DISBROW, Jimmie Lynn (Okla) 1737 Churchill Way, Oklahoma City, OK 73120

DISHAROON, Susan Clay (Miss) 3030 Highway 547, Port Gibson, MS 39150

DISTANISLAO, Virginia Gates (SVa) 512 S. Broad St., Kenbridge, VA 23944

DITTERLINE, Richard Charles (Pa) 1350 Spring Valley Rd, Bethlehem, PA 18015

DITZENBERGER, Christopher Steven (Colo) 6190 E. Quincy Avenue, Englewood, CO 80111

DIVINE, Elizabeth Baird (Tex) 1616 Fountainview Dr #203, Houston, TX 77057

DIVIS, Mary Lou (Be) 408 E Main St, Nanticoke, PA 18634

DIXON, David Lloyd (SwVa) 42 E Main St, Salem, VA 24153

DIXON, Elizabeth Lovette (WA)

DIXON JR, John Henry (RG) Av. C. Leon de Nicaragua 1, Esc. 3, 1-B, Alicante, 03015, Spain

DIXON, Mary Lenn (Tex) 1101 Rock Prairie Rd, College Station, TX 77845

DIXON, Robert Keith (Nwk) 73 Fernbank Ave, Delmar, NY 12054

DIXON, Robert P (CGC) Saint Stephen's Church, 1510 Escambia Ave, Brewton, AL 36426

DIXON, Valerie Wilde (Ct) 23 Bayview Ave, Niantic, CT 06357

DMYTRIW, Carey-Lea (Wyo)

DOAR, Katherine Baginski (ECR) 1225 Pine Ave, San Jose, CA 95125

DOBBIN, Robert A (Cal) 24 Van Gordon Pl, Danville, CA 94526

DOBBINS, Burford C (WTex) 1501 N. Glass St., Victoria, TX 77901

DOBBINS JR, David David (RI) 205 Lindley Ave, North Kingstown, RI 02852

DOBBINS, Timothy (Pa) 292 Militia Dr, Radnor, PA 19087

DOBSON, Marc (Dal) 6021 Shady Valley Court, Garland, TX 75043

DOBYNS, Nancy (Ind) 1021 Sw 15th St, Richmond, IN 47374

DOBYNS, Richard (Ind) 1021 Sw 15th St, Richmond, IN 47374

DOCKERY, Nancy Lynn (Nev) 501 Bianca Bay St, Las Vegas, NV 89144

DOCTOR, Virginia Carol (Ak) PO Box 93, Tanana, AK 99777

DOD, David Stockton (ECR) 8294 Carmelita Ave, Atascadero, CA 93422

DODD, Debra (Dee) Anne (Ct) 37 Bailey Dr, North Branford, CT 06471

DODD, Jean Carrison (Fla) 1860 Edgewood Ave S, Jacksonville, FL 32205

DODDEMA, Peter (Lex) 118 West Poplar Street, Harrodsburg, KY 40330

DODGE, Jeffrey A (Cal) 1944 Trinity Ave, Walnut Creek, CA 94596

DODGE, Robin Dennis (RG) Church Of The Holy Faith, 311 E Palace Ave, Santa Fe, NM 87501

DODSON, Wayne J (NY) 9 W 130th St, New York, NY 10037

DOERR, Nan (Tex) 901 S. Johnson, Alvin, TX 77511

DOGARU, Vickie A (Oly) 22405 Ne 182nd Ave, Battle Ground, WA 98604

DOGGETT, William Jordan (WA) 1209 East Capitol Street SE, Washington, DC 20003

DOHERTY, Anna Clay (Minn) 670 E Monroe Ave, Hartford, WI 53027

DOHERTY, Jerry Clay (Minn) 201 Bayberry Avenue Ct, Stillwater, MN 55082

DOHERTY, John S (Ia) CATHEDRAL CHURCH OF ST PAUL, 815 HIGH ST, DES MOINES, IA 50309

DOHERTY, Maureen Catherine (Ia) 417 Olive St, Cedar Falls, IA 50613

DOHERTY, Noel James (Okla) 6910 E 62nd St, S, Tulsa, OK 74133

DOHERTY, Tyler Britton (U) 231 E 100 S, Salt Lake City, UT 84111

DOHERTY-OGEA, Kathleen Lambert (WLa) 206 South Street, Bastrop, LA 71220

DOHLE, Robert Joseph (Tex) St Paul's Episcopal Church, 1307 W 5th St, Freeport, TX 77541

DOHONEY, Ed (WTex) 14906 Grayoak Frst, San Antonio, TX 78248

DOING JR, Robert Burns (SwFla) 36 Barkley Circle Apt 205, Fort Myers, FL 33907

DOLACK, Craig A (Ga) Saint Michael And All Angels, 3101 Waters Ave, Savannah, GA 31404

DOLAN, Mary Ellen (Eur) Frankfurter Strasse 3, Wiesbaden, 65189, Germany

DOLAN, Pamela (The Episcopal NCal) 9 S Bompart Ave, Saint Louis, MO 63119

DOLAN-HENDERSON, Susan Mary (Tex) 3104 Harris Park Ave, Austin, TX 78705

DOLEN, William Kennedy (Ga) 605 Reynolds St, Augusta, GA 30901

DOLL, Gregory Allen (Kan)

DOLLAHITE, Damian DeWitt Gene (Dal) 226 Oakhaven Dr, Grand Prairie, TX 75050

DOLLHAUSEN, Matthew Mark (CGC) 6849 Oak St, Milton, FL 32570

DOLNIKOWSKI, Edie (Mass) The Episcopal Diocese Of Massachusetts, 138 Tremont St, Boston, MA 02111

DOLPH, Scott (Ore) 4233 S. E. Ash Street, Portland, OR 97215

DOLS, Timothy Walters (Va) 5705 Oak Bluff Ln, Wilmington, NC 28409

DOLS JR, William Ludwig (Va) 300 Aspen St, Alexandria, VA 22305

DOMBEK, Timothy (Az) 11242 N 50th Ave, Glendale, AZ 85304

DOMENICK JR, W(arren) L(ee) (Minn) St Luke's Church, 4557 Colfax Ave S, Minneapolis, MN 55419

DOMIENIK, Steven B (Mich) St. John's Episcopal Church, 555 S Wayne Rd, Westland, MI 48186

DONAHOE, Melanie (Cal) Church of the Epiphany, 1839 Arroyo Avenue, San Carlos, CA 94070

DONALD, David Seth (WLa) 715 Kirkman St, Lake Charles, LA 70601

DONALD, James (WA) 1 Peachtree Battle Ave. , NW #5, Unit #5, Atlanta, GA 30305

DONALDSON, Audley (LI) 1345 President St, Brooklyn, NY 11213

DONALDSON, Walter Alexander (Los) 7631 Klusman Ave, Rancho Cucamonga, CA 91730

DONATELLI, Todd M (WNC) Cathedral of All Souls, 9 Swan St, Asheville, NC 28803

DONATHAN, William Larry (WA) 105 15th Street SE, Washington, DC 20003

DONCASTER, Diana (The Episcopal NCal) 495 Albion Ave, Cincinnati, OH 45246

DONDERO, Christina Downs (At) 879 Clifton Rd Ne, Atlanta, GA 30307

DONECKER, Paul (CPa) 351 Bull Run Crossing, Lewisburg, PA 17837

DONEHUE, Robertson Carr (SC)

DONELSON JR, Frank Taylor (WTenn) 475 N Highland St Apt 7e, Memphis, TN 38122

DONNELLY, Frances (Nwk) 852 Bullet Hill Rd, Southbury, CT 06488

DONNELLY, Jeffrey Joseph (Cal)

DONNELLY, John Allen (Ct) 470 Quaker Farms Road, Oxford, CT 06478

DONNELLY, Richard Colonel (Ct) 430 Quaker Drive, York, PA 17402

DONOHUE, Alison (The Episcopal Church in Haw)

DONOHUE, Mary Jane (Mass) 51 Ryder Ave, Melrose, MA 02176

DONOHUE-ADAMS, Amy (Oly) 11703 Oakwood Dr, Austin, TX 78753

✠ **DONOVAN JR**, Herbert Alcorn (NY) 3085 Mill Vista Rd Unit 2322, Highlands Ranch, CO 80129

DONOVAN, John Carl (Tex) 2908 Avenue O Apt 1, Galveston, TX 77550

DONOVAN, Nancy Lu (SD) 9412 Saint Joseph St, Silver City, SD 57702

DONOVAN, William Patrick (Minn) 684 Mississippi River Blvd S, Saint Paul, MN 55116

DOOLEY, Martha M (NJ) 4735 Cedar Ave, Philadelphia, PA 19143

DOOLITTLE, Geoffrey Douglas (CNY) 117 Main St, Owego, NY 13827

DOPP, Cynthia Hill (WA) 301 A St SE, Washington, DC 20003

DOPP, William Floyd (SwFla) 818 Chamise Ct, San Marcos, CA 92069

DORAN, Judith Ann (Chi) 1350 N Western Ave Apt 111, Lake Forest, IL 60045

DORAN, Michelle Stuart (Md) All Saints, PO Box 40, Sunderland, MD 20689

DORCEUS, Jean Moiise (Hai)

DORN, Christy (WMo) 13134 Lamar Ave, Overland Park, KS 66209

DORN III, James M (CFla) 574 West Montrose St, Clermont, FL 34711

DORNEMANN, Deanna Maxine (EC) 60 Bethlehem Pike Rm 1401, Philadelphia, PA 19118

DORNER, Mary Anne (SwFla) 27127 Fordham Dr, Wesley Chapel, FL 33543

DORNHECKER, Douglas Boyd (Oly) 114 20th Ave SE, Olympia, WA 98501

DOROW, Robert M (NI) 1007 Moore Rd, Michigan City, IN 46360

DORR JR, Erwin John (Ind) 256 51st St Cir E, Palmetto, FL 34221

DORR, Kathleen (Ct) 39 Whalers Pt, East Haven, CT 06512

DORRIEN, Gary John (NY) Union Theological Seminary, 3041 Broadway, New York, NY 10027

DORSCH, Ken (Ore) 15625 Nw Norwich St, Beaverton, OR 97006

DORSEY, Laura Miller (Eas) 28333 Mount Vernon Rd, Princess Anne, MD 21853

DORSEY, Martha June Hardy (O) 3602 Hawthorne Ave, Richmond, VA 23222

DOSHER, Joy (EC)

✠ **DOSS**, Joe (NJ) 15 Front St, Mandeville, LA 70448

DOSTAL FELL, Margaret Ann (Minn) 1765 Upper 55th St E, Inver Grove Heights, MN 55077

DOSTER, Daniel Harris (Ga) 724 Victoria Cir, Dublin, GA 31021

DOTY, D(Avid) Michael (ETenn) 143 Caledonia Rd, Landrum, SC 29356

DOTY, Phyllis Marie (Fla) P.O. Box 4366, Dowling Park, FL 32064

DOUBLEDAY, William Alan (NY) 31 Croton Avenue, MOUNT KISCO, NY 10549

DOUGHARTY, Phil (WNY) 427 Loma Hermosa Dr NW, Albuquerque, NM 87105

DOUGHERTY JR, Edward Archer (SeFla) 10 Eighth St., Biddeford Pool, ME 04006

DOUGHERTY, Janet Hayes (Minn) 5844 Deer Trail Cir, Woodbury, MN 55129

DOUGHERTY, Katherine G (Va)

DOUGLAS, Alan David (Colo) 5409 Fossil Creek Dr, Fort Collins, CO 80526

DOUGLAS, Ann Leslie (NY) 201 Scarborough Rd, Briarcliff Manor, NY 10510

DOUGLAS, Carole Robinson (Md) 7521 Rockridge Rd, Pikesville, MD 21208

DOUGLAS, Dorothy Ruth (CGC) 5904 Woodvale Dr, Mobile, AL 36608

✠ **DOUGLAS**, Ian (Ct) Episcopal Diocese Of Connecticut, 290 Pratt Street, Box 52, Meriden, CT 06450

DOUGLAS, Jeff (EC) 907 Colony Ave N, Ahoskie, NC 27910

DOUGLAS, Michael John (Az) 400 S Old Litchfield Rd, Litchfield Park, AZ 85340

DOUGLAS, Robert Charles (SwFla)

DOUGLAS, Roger Owen (Az) 47280 Amir Dr, Palm Desert, CA 92260

DOUGLASS, David George (NI) 6085 N 190 W, Howe, IN 46746

DOULOS, William Lane (Los) 535 W Roses Rd, San Gabriel, CA 91775

DOVER III, John Randolph (SC) 231 Cedar Berry Ln, Chapel Hill, NC 27517

DOW, Neal (Colo) 3296 S Heather Gardens Way, Aurora, CO 80014

DOWARD, Amonteen Ravenden (VI) PO Box 486, Christiansted, VI 00821

DOWDESWELL, Eugenia Hedden (WNC) Po Box 132, Flat Rock, NC 28731

DOWDLE, Catherine Ellen (SanD) 726 2nd Ave, Chula Vista, CA 91910

DOWER, Ronny W (NJ) 3500 Penny Ln, Zanesville, OH 43701

DOWER, Sandra Nichols (WNY)

DOWLING, Shelley (Ia)

DOWLING-SENDOR, Elizabeth (NC) 6 Davie Cir, Chapel Hill, NC 27514

DOWNER, Gretchen Marie (Ida) 1419 Butte View Cir, Emmett, ID 83617

DOWNEY, John (NwPa) 220 W 41st St, Erie, PA 16508

DOWNIE, Elizabeth Morris (EMich) 668 Elder Ln, Winnetka, IL 60093

DOWNING, John W (Mil)

DOWNING, LaRue (WNC) 21 Indigo Way, Hendersonville, NC 28739

DOWNING, Patricia S (Del) 1108 N Adams St, Wilmington, DE 19801

DOWNING, Richard E (WA) 2602 N Harrison St, Wilmington, DE 19802

DOWNS, Alice Lacey (NJ) 14 Winding Lane, Southwest Harbor, ME 04679

DOWNS, Andrew D (Ind) Saint Stephen's Church, 215 N 7th St, Terre Haute, IN 47807

DOWNS, Dalton Dalzell (WA) 703 Carmel Lane, Poinciana, FL 34759

DOWNS, Donna (Ct) 64 Philip Dr, Shelton, CT 06484

DOWNS JR, Joseph Thomas (EMich) 3225 N Branch Dr, Beaverton, MI 48612

DOWNS, Lee Daniel (Mil) N77W17700 Lake Park Dr Apt 311, Menomonee Falls, WI 53051

DOWNS, Thomas Alexander (CFla) 390 Lake Lenelle Drive, Chuluota, FL 32766

DOYLE, Ann K (Ky) Calvary Episcopal Church, 821 S 4th St, Louisville, KY 40203

✠ **DOYLE**, C Andrew (Tex) 1225 Texas Ave, Houston, TX 77002

DOYLE, Henry Lovelle (Minn) 1000 Shumway Ave, Faribault, MN 55021

DOYLE, Margaret E (Ala) 429 Cloudland Dr, Hoover, AL 35226

DOYLE, Ralph Thomas (Mo) 1432 Kearney St, El Cerrito, CA 94530

DOYLE, Seamus (Ark) 1802 W Cambridge Dr, Harrison, AR 72601

DRACHLIS, David Bernard (Ala) 1103 Shades Cir Se, Huntsville, AL 35803

DRAEGER JR, Walter Raymond (WMich) 3957 Sherwood Forest Dr, Traverse City, MI 49686

DRAESEL JR, Herbert Gustav (NY) 215 W 84th St #515, New York, NY 10024

DRAKE, Deborah Rucki (Nwk) 380 Clifton Ave, Clifton, NJ 07011

DRAKE, Jo-Ann Jane (RI) 104 Lafayette St, Pawtucket, RI 02860

DRAKE, Lesley-Ann (At) 2160 Cooper Lake Rd SE, Smyrna, GA 30080

DRAKE, Leslie Sargent (USC) 1630 Silver Bluff Rd., Aiken, SC 29803

DRAPER, Rick (Ind) 11974 State Highway M26, Eagle Harbor, MI 49950

DRAZDOWSKI, Tar (Ga) 408 S 1st St, Cordele, GA 31015

DREBERT, Kay Marie (CNY) 227 W Walnut Dr, Sturgeon Bay, WI 54235

DREBERT, Rebecca Ellen (CNY) St. Peter's Episcopal Church, 1 Church St, Bainbridge, NY 13733

DREISBACH, Christopher (Md) Old St. Paul's Episcopal Church, Charles & Saratoga, Baltimore, MD 21201

DRENNEN, Zachary Polk (WVa) c/o Katakwa Diocese, PO Box 68, Amagoro, 50244, Kenya

DRESBACH, Michael (ECR) 490 Vivienne Dr, Watsonville, CA 95076

DRESSEL, Marilyn Kaye (EMich) 3725 Woodside Dr, Traverse City, MI 49684

DRESSER, Deborah Metcalf (NY) 105 Grand St, Newburgh, NY 12550

DREWRY, John Colin (EC) 2513 Confederate Dr, Wilmington, NC 28403

DRINKWATER, Michael (RG) PO Box 1246, Albuquerque, NM 87103

DRINO, Jerry William (ECR) 14801 Whipple Ct, San Jose, CA 95127

DRISCOLL, Janine (NC) PO Box 1071, Roxboro, NC 27573

DRISKILL, Lorinda Elizabeth (Tex) Trinity Episcopal Church, PO Box 777, Anahuac, TX 77514

DRIVER, Bess D (Az) 2137 W. University Ave., Flagstaff, AZ 86001

DROST, Pat (Eas)

DROSTE, Rob (NJ) 911 Dowling Blvd, San Leandro, CA 94577

DRUBE, Bruce James (Ala) 1219 Quail Run Dr Sw, Jacksonville, AL 36265

DRUCE, Glenn Edward (NJ) 1450 Iris Ave Unit 14, Imperial Beach, CA 91932

DRUMM, Elizabeth Prentice (Kan)

DRURY, Susan R (Kan) 7311 Legler Road, Shawnee, KS 66217

DRYMON, John A (O) Trinity Church, 128 W Hardin St, Findlay, OH 45840

DRYNAN, Thomas Steele (Ore) 6431 Ganon St Se, Salem, OR 97317

DRYSDALE, Jessie Cookson (Me) 136 Butterfield Landing Rd., Weston, ME 04424

DRYSDALE-SCHRUTH, Sherry (Minn) Grace Memorial Episcopal Church, PO Box 27, Wabasha, MN 55981

DUBAY, Joe (Ore) 1805 NW 34th Ave, Portland, OR 97210

DUBOIS, Charles Holgate (NJ) 33509 Anns Choice Way, Warminster, PA 18974

DUBOSE, Georgia (WVa) Po Box 999, Harpers Ferry, WV 25425

DUBOSE, Jerry Davis (USC) 50 Keoway Dr Apt F7, Seneca, SC 29672

DUBOVENKO, Sandra Raye (NMich)

DUCKWORTH, Bonnie Wagner (NC)

DUCKWORTH, Penelope (Cal) Trinity Cathedral, 81 North Second Street, San Jose, CA 94115

DUDDING II, Burton Arthur (Nev) 7000 Mae Anne Ave Apt 1521, Reno, NV 89523

DUDLEY, Michael Devere (O) 28 Perry Place, Canandaigua, NY 14424

DUDLEY JR, Thomas Lee (USC) 134 Boscawen, Winchester, VA 22601

DUER, Don Rey (CFla) 2005 Harrison Ave, Orlando, FL 32804

DUERR, Robert Edward (Mass) 15 Millbrook Rd, Beverly, MA 01915

DUFF, Eric Towle Moore (The Episcopal NCal) 524 Old Wagon Road, Trinidad, CA 95570

DUFF, Lyndie (Wyo) 1117 West Ramshorn Boulevard, Box 844, Dubois, WY 82513

DUFFEY, Ben Rosebro (SVa) 1401 N High St., Apt. 102, Franklin, VA 23851

DUFFEY, Bill (Pa) 3300 Darby Rd, Cottage 304, Haverford, PA 19041

DUFFIELD, Sue (U) St Eliizabeth Episcopal Church, PO Box 100, Whiterocks, UT 84085

DUFFTY, Bryan (ECR) 3020 Daurine Ct, Gilroy, CA 95020

DUFFUS, Cynthia Slaughter (EC) 48 W High St, Mt Sterling, KY 40353

DUFFY, Christopher Gregory (NJ) 338 Ewingville Rd., Trenton, NJ 08628

DUFFY, Glenn Alan (Eas) 63 Battersea Rd., Berlin, MD 21811

DUFORD, Donald John (Mich) 16889 Club Drive, Southgate, MI 48195

DUFOUR, Matthew John (Ak) PO Box 773223, Eagle River, AK 99577

DUGAN II, Haynes Webster (Okla) 305 Camino Norte, Altus, OK 73521

DUGAN, Jeffrey Scott (Ct) 102 Seabury Drive, Bloomfield, CT 06002

DUGAN, Raymond Paul (Az) 534 W Wilshire Dr, Phoenix, AZ 85003

DUGARD, Debra Harris (WTenn) Emmanuel Episcopal Church, 4150 Boeingshire Dr, Memphis, TN 38116

DUGGAN, Joe F (The Episcopal NCal) 1644 Shadow Wood Road, Reno, NV 93103

DUGGAR, Marilyn (Ak) St Mark's Episcopal Church, PO Box 469, Nenana, AK 99760

DUGGER, Clinton George (Alb) Po Box 148, New Lebanon, NY 12125

DUGGER, Rita Jacqueline Carney (WNY) 24 Linwood Ave, Buffalo, NY 14209

DUGGER, Tracy Michelle (CFla) 241 N Main St, Winter Garden, FL 34787

DUGGIN, Sarah Helene (WA) 3240 O St NW, Washington, DC 20007

DUGGINS, Amy E (NC)

DUGGINS, Gordon Hayes (NY) P.O. Box 670, Colfax, NC 27235

DUGHI, Lorraine Mazuy (Nwk)

DUGUID-MAY, Deborah Lee (Roch) 3450 WT Ridge Rd, Rochester, NY 14626

DUH, Michael Yung-Che (Tai) 952 Sec 2 Chading Road Chading, Kaohsiung Hsien 85202, Taiwan, China

DUKE, Brandon (At) Saint Julian's Episcopal Church, 5400 Stewart Mill Rd, Douglasville, GA 30135

DUKE, Ceci (At) 597 Haralson Dr Sw, Lilburn, GA 30047

DUKES, John (At) 626 Mississippi Ave, Signal Mountain, TN 37377

DUKES, Lynne Adair Slane (WMich) 115 3rd St S Apt 913, Jacksonville Beach, FL 32250

DULFER, John Guidi (NY) 110 W 15th St Apt 1, New York, NY 10011

DULGAR, Sandra Lee (Nev) P.O. Box 3522, Tonopah, NV 89049

DULL, Stanley Lynn (Pa) 2215 Palm Tree Dr, Punta Gorda, FL 33950

DUMKE, Barbara A (Colo) 11684 Eldorado St Nw, Coon Rapids, MN 55433

DUMKE, Edward John (Cal) 805 Barneson Ave, San Mateo, CA 94402

DUMOLT, Elizabeth Ann (Los) 122 S. California Ave., Monrovia, CA 91016

DUNAGAN, Joe (SwVa) 116 Alabama Ave, Macon, GA 31204

DUNAGAN, Katherine K (SwVa) 1 Mountain Ave SW, Roanoke, VA 24016

DUNBAR, Donald Machell (Mass) 160 Longmeadow Rd, Fairfield, CT 06824

DUNBAR, Gavin Gunning (Ga) 1 W Macon St, Savannah, GA 31401

DUNBAR, Julia Brown (WMass) 20 Whitney Ave, Cambridge, MA 02139

DUNBAR, Pamela (Dal) 9221 Flickering Shadow Dr, Dallas, TX 75243

DUNBAR, Philip Craig (CFla) 2505 Gramercy Dr, Deltona, FL 32738

DUNBAR, Robert Barron (USC) PO Box 36155, Rock Hill, SC 29732

DUNBAR, Timothy Andrew (Colo)

DUNBAR, Veronica (Mich) 4800 Woodward Ave, Detroit, MI 48201

DUNCAN, Barbara Tompkins (WA) 8103 Langley Dr, Glen Allen, VA 23060

DUNCAN, Carol (Pa) 503 W Springer St, Philadelphia, PA 19119

DUNCAN, Carrie Barnes (Miss) PO Box 267, Leland, MS 38756

DUNCAN, Christopher R (Tex) PO Box 5176, Austin, TX 78763

DUNCAN, David (Los) 6700 Woodland Hills Rd, Rushville, IL 62681

DUNCAN, Hugh C (Ida) 5120 W Overland Rd PMB-276, Boise, ID 83705

DUNCAN, James Bruce (Los) 45 Chestnut St Unit A, North Adams, MA 01247

DUNCAN, John L (The Episcopal NCal) 110 San Benito Avenue, Aptos, CA 95003

✠ **DUNCAN II**, Philip Menzie (CGC) 7208 Mitra Dr, Austin, TX 78739

DUNCAN, Rosemarie Logan (WA) 1329 Hamilton St Nw, Washington, DC 20011

DUNCAN, Sean David (CFla) 275 Southfield Rd, Shreveport, LA 71105

DUNCAN, Shawn P (LI) 722 E 22nd St, Brooklyn, NY 11210

DUNCAN, Victoria D (LI) 722 E 22nd St, Brooklyn, NY 11210

DUNCAN-O'NEAL III, William McKinley (Ark) 9669 Wedd St, Overland Park, KS 66212

✠ **DUNCAN-PROBE**, DeDe (CNY) 2 Audubon Drive, Cazenovia, NY 13035

DUNEVANT, Emily Hope (Va) 2955 River Rd W, Goochland, VA 23063

DUNFEE, Mikayla S (Nev)

DUNHAM, Richard Eldon (WTex) 4137 Harry St, Corpus Christi, TX 78411

DUNKLE, Kurt (Fla)

DUNKS, Andrew Andrew (Va) Saint Bartholomew's Church, 10627 Patterson Ave, Richmond, VA 23238

DUNLAP, Daniel K (Eas) 715 Carrell St., Tomball, TX 77375

DUNLAP, Dennis Joe (Chi) 326 W. Northland Ave, Peoria, IL 61614

DUNLAP, Eunice R (Del) 403 Northview Dr, Fayetteville, NC 28303

DUNLAP, Garland Edward (Va) 537 Chattooga Place Dr, Wilmington, NC 28412

DUNLAP, Mary Balfour (NC) Emmanuel Episcopal Church, 340 S Ridge St, Southern Pines, NC 28387

DUNLOP, William Henry (Mil) 413 S 2nd St, Watertown, WI 53094

DUNN JR, Carlton Willard (NJ) St Andrew's Church, 121 High St, Mount Holly, NJ 08060

DUNN III, D(ouglas) (SVa) 2000 Huguenot Trl, Powhatan, VA 23139

DUNN, Douglas Robert (Colo) 1270 Poplar St, Denver, CO 80220

DUNN, Frank (WA) St Stephen and the Incarnation Parish, 1525 Newton St NW, Washington, DC 20010

DUNN, George Mervyn (Ga) 8 Woodbridge Crescent, Kanata, K2M 2N6, Canada

DUNN, Matilda Eeleen Greene (ETenn) 7013 Rocky Trl, Chattanooga, TN 37421

DUNN, Patrick Hall (Miss) 4030 Perch Point Dr, Mobile, AL 36605

DUNN, Prentiss Carroll (La) 422 W Hickory Ave, Bastrop, LA 71220

DUNN, Robert Ellis (Oly) Po Box 1377, Granite Falls, WA 98252

DUNN, Sharon Kay Estey (Nev) 3500 San Mateo Ave, Reno, NV 89509

DUNN, William (Los) 1803 Highland Hollow Dr # 559, Conroe, TX 77304

DUNNAM, Thomas Mark (Eur) Via Bernardo Rucellai 9, Firenze, 50123, Italy

DUNNAN, Donald Stuart (Md) Saint James School, Saint James, MD 21781

DUNNAVANT, Charles Randall (Tenn) 817 Stonebrook Blvd, Nolensville, TN 37135

DUNNETT, Walter McGregor (Chi) 2127 Hallmark Ct, Wheaton, IL 60187

DUNNING, Jane Romeyn (WMass) 44 Main St, Shelburne Falls, MA 01370

DUNNING, William (Md) 1612 Trebor Ct, Lutherville, MD 21093

DUNNINGTON, Michael Gerard (Mo) 1620 Forestview Ridge Ln, Ballwin, MO 63021

DUNPHY, Martha-Jane (NY) 190 Pinewood Rd Apt 78, Hartsdale, NY 10530

DUNST, Earl Walter (Mil) 8121 N Seneca Rd, Milwaukee, WI 53217

DUPLANTIER, David Allard (La) 2037 South Carrollton Avenue, New Orleans, LA 70118

DUPREE, Charlie (Ind) 111 S. Grant St., Bloomington, IN 47408

DUPREE, Hugh Douglas (Ga) 325 N Market St, Jacksonville, FL 32202

DUPREY, David Luke (Wyo) 1 S Tschirgi St, Sheridan, WY 82801

DU PRIEST, Travis Talmadge (Mil) 508 DeKoven, Racine, WI 53403

✠ **DUQUE-GOMEZ**, Francisco (Colom) Calle 122-A #1211, Bogota, Colombia

✠ **DURACIN**, Zache (Hai) Box 1309, Port-Au-Prince, Haiti

DURAIKANNU, Yesu (Colo) St.James' Church, 1 St. James' Place, Goshen, NY 10924

DURAND, Sally Elaine (Az) 7813 N. Via De La Luna, Scottsdale, AZ 85258

DURANT, Jack Davis (NC) 3001 Old Orchard Rd, Raleigh, NC 27607

DURANY, Helen Marie (Colo)

D'URBANO, Faith Jeanne (Be) 340 W. Orange Street, Lancaster, PA 17603

DURBIDGE, Andrew John (LI) 50 Cathedral Ave, Garden City, NY 11530

DURE, Lucy Ann (Nwk) 46 Montrose Ave, Verona, NJ 07044

DURHAM, Martha Hemenway (Az) St Mary's Episcopal Church, 306 S Prospect Ave, Park Ridge, IL 60068

DURNING, Michael (SwFla) 12002 Summer Meadow Dr, Bradenton, FL 34202

DURREN, Paula Ellen (WMich) 19 S Jameson St, New Buffalo, MI 49117

DURST, Ted (Chi) 4900 N Marine Dr Apt 411, Chicago, IL 60640

DUTCHER, Katherine Grant (Okla) St Andrew's Episcopal Church, PO Box 1256, Lawton, OK 73502

DUTTON-GILLETT, Matthew Richard (Cal) 330 Ravenswood, Menlo Park, CA 94025

DUVAL, Linda Marie (NY) 16 Boulder Ave, Kingston, NY 12401

DUVAL JR, Richard Henri (Episcopal SJ) 813 Lassen View Dr, Lake Almanor, CA 96137

✠ **DUVALL**, Charles Farmer (CGC) 104 Wildeoak Trl, Columbia, SC 29223

DUVEAUX, Irnel (Hai) Box 1309, Port-Au-Prince, Haiti

DUVERT, Pierre-Andre (NY) 331 Hawthorne St, Brooklyn, NY 11225

DVARISHKIS, Dorcie Della Kafka (Mont) Church Of The Holy Spirit, 130 S 6th St E, Missoula, MT 59801

DWARF, Lindsey Craig (ND) PO Box 45, Cannon Ball, ND 58528

DWYER, Beatrice Mary (Eau) Christ Church Cathedral, 510 S Farwell St, Eau Claire, WI 54701

DWYER, John F (Minn) 2300 Hamline Ave N, Roseville, MN 55113

DWYER, Michael W (Chi) 1101 Park Drive, Munster, IN 46321

DWYER, Patricia Marie (Be)

DWYER, Tommy (CGC) 800 22nd St, Port St Joe, FL 32456

DYAKIW, Alexander Raymond (CPa) St John's Episc Ch, 120 W Lamb St, Bellefonte, PA 16823

DYCHE, Bradley (FtW) 6 Old Post Road North, Croton on Hudson, NY 10520

DYER, Alex (WA) 51 Crown St, New Haven, CT 06510

DYER, Susan Jeinine (Wyo) PO Box 399, Saratoga, WY 82331

DYER, Timothy D (NwPa) 444 Pennsylvania Ave W, Warren, PA 16365

DYER-CHAMBERLAIN, Margaret Elizabeth (Cal)

DYKE, Nicolas Roger David (Tex) 3815 Echo Mountain Dr, Humble, TX 77345

DYKES, Deborah White (Miss) 3524 Old Canton Rd, Jackson, MS 39216

DYKSTRA, Danny Jon (Ky) 9616 Westport Rd, Louisville, KY 40241

DYNER, Marthe (NH) Po Box 347, Charlestown, NH 03603

DYSON, Elizabeth Wheatley (Mass) 451 Birchbark Dr, Hanson, MA 02341

DYSON, Martha Lynn (Vt) 123 Caroline St, Burlington, VT 05401

DYSON, Thack Harris (CGC) 28788 N Main St, Daphne, AL 36526

E

EADE, Christopher K (Los) 1031 Bienveneda Ave, Pacific Palisades, CA 90272

EADES, Susan Tindall (Mont) 218 E Chapman St, Dillon, MT 59725

EAGER, Donald Bates (SO) 2102 Scenic Dr Ne, Lancaster, OH 43130

EAGLEBULL, Harold L (SD) Po Box 1149, Cass Lake, MN 56633

EAKINS, Bill (Ct) 25 Scarborough St, Hartford, CT 06105

EAKINS, Hope Howlett (Ct) 25 Scarborough St, Hartford, CT 06105

EAMES, Marc Gilbert (Mass) 28 Pleasant St., The Church of the Advent, Medfield, MA 02052

EANES II, William Raymond (SwVa) St James Episcopal Church, 4515 Delray St NW, Roanoke, VA 24012

EARL, John Keith (WNC) 1650 5th St Nw, Hickory, NC 28601

EARL, Nicholas Edward (Tex)

EARLE, Charles Douglas (WTex) 7302 Robin Rest Dr, San Antonio, TX 78209

EARLE, Leigh Christensen (Wyo) 1745 Westridge Cir, Casper, WY 82604

EARLE, Mary Colbert (WTex) 7302 Robin Rest Dr, San Antonio, TX 78209

EARLE, Patty Ann Trapp (NC) Po Box 1103, Statesville, NC 28687

EARLE III, Richard Tilghman (SwFla) 555 13th Avenue NE, Saint Petersburg, FL 33701

EARLS, John G (USC)

EARLY, Nancy Davis (WA) 402 Montrose Ave, Catonsville, MD 21228

EARLY, Thomas M (Ia)

EASLEY, Alexandra (WTex)

EASLEY, Barbara Ann (Ia) 605 Avenue E, Fort Madison, IA 52627

EASLEY, Julia Kathleen (Ia) 26 E Market St, Iowa City, IA 52245

EASTER, James Dennis (WMo)

EASTER, James Hamilton (Okla) 11308 N Miller Ave, Oklahoma City, OK 73120

EASTER, Mary Kathleen (WMo) 973 Evergreen Ave, Hollister, MO 65672

EASTER, William Burton (Chi) 594 Eastlake Dr Se, Rio Rancho, NM 87124

EASTERDAY, Pamela Kay (CFla) 1830 S. Babcock St, Melbourne, FL 32901

EASTERDAY, Stephen Wayne (CFla) 1830 S. Babcock St., Melbourne, FL 32901

EASTERLING JR, Richard Brooks (La) 4600 Saint Charles Ave, New Orleans, LA 70115

EASTERLING SR, William Ramsay (WLa) 504 Tech Dr, Ruston, LA 71270

EASTES, Suzanne Hardey (Mo) 312 Clayton Crossing Dr., #108, Ellisville, MO 63011

EASTHILL, Christopher Mark (Eur) Schuetzenstrasse 2, Wiesbaden, 65195 DE, Germany

EASTMAN, Susan Grove (NC) 4604 Brodog Ter, Hurdle Mills, NC 27541

EASTON, Elizabeth Lavender (Neb) 9302 Blondo St., Omaha, NE 68134

EASTON, Stanley Evan (Ala) 1104 Church Avenue Northeast, Jacksonville, AL 36265

EASTWOOD, Jack (Cal) 30 Ogden Ave, San Francisco, CA 94110

EATON, Bert (EC) PO Box 337, Swansboro, NC 28584

EATON, Carol Ann (EC) St Francis By the Sea Church, 920 Salter Path Rd, Salter Path, NC 28512

EATON, Cornelia Kay (NAM) PO Box 720, Farmington, NM 87499

EATON, Karen A (Oly) PO Box 753, Port Townsend, WA 98368

EATON, Laura Mary (NMich)

✠ **EATON**, Peter David (SeFla) 525 NE 15th Street, Miami, FL 33132

EATON, Robert G (Episcopal SJ) 1571 E Glenwood Ave, Tulare, CA 93274

EATON, William Albert (SeFla) 10914 Nw 8th Ct, Plantation, FL 33324

EAVES, Lindon John (Va) 10835 Old Prescott Rd, Richmond, VA 23238

EAVES, Sue (Va) 3207 Hawthorne Ave, Richmond, VA 23222

EBEL, Ann Teresa (PR)

EBENS, Richard Frank (Mass) 4-C Autumn Dr, Hudson, MA 01749

EBERHARDT, Karen Anne (Nwk) 18 Ute Ave., Lake Hiawatha, NJ 07034

EBERHARDT, Timothy Charles (Vt) 2460 Braintree Hill Rd, Braintree, VT 05060

EBERLE, William Edward (Va) P.O. Box 367, Rixeyville, VA 22737

EBERLY, George Douglas (NJ) 500 19th St, Ocean City, NJ 08226

EBERT, Bernhard (Colo) 802 Raton Ave, La Junta, CO 81050

ECCLES, M E (Chi) 311 N. Westgate Rd., Mount Prospect, IL 60056

ECCLES, Mark Eldon (Ia) 1619 21st St Nw, Cedar Rapids, IA 52405

ECHAZABAL, Livan (SwFla) 6709 N Nebraska Ave, Tampa, FL 33604

ECHOLS, Mary W (SwFla) 917 11th St N, Naples, FL 34102

ECHOLS, William Joseph (WLa) 104 Ingram St, Lake Providence, LA 71254

ECKART JR, Richard James (Roch) 38 Dale Rd, Rochester, NY 14625

ECKEL, Malcolm David (Mass) 11 Griggs Ter., Brookline, MA 02446

ECKIAN, Deirdre (WA) 4000 Tunlaw Road NW Apt 1005, Washington, DC 20007

EDDY, Charles H. (Ak) P.O. Box 747, Willow, AK 99688

EDDY, Diane Lynn (Ia) 1458 Locust St, Dubuque, IA 52001

EDDY, Elizabeth (NJ) 913 Fassler Ave, Pacifica, CA 94044

EDDY, William Welles (Mass) PO Box 3615, Waquoit, MA 02536

EDELMAN, Walter Lucian (SanD) 17427 Gibraltar Ct, San Diego, CA 92128

EDEN, Holly (CNY) 120 W 5th St, Oswego, NY 13126

EDEN, Jonathan T (Mass) 865 Madison Ave, New York, NY 10021

EDENS III, Henry Harman (NC) 8011 Douglas Ave, Dallas, TX 75225

EDINGTON, Mark David Wheeler (Mass) PO Box 455, Hardwick, MA 01037, Dominican Republic

EDELMAN JR, Samuel Warren (Md) 1257 Weller Way, Westminster, MD 21158

EDMAN, David Arthur (FtW) 47 Acorn Hollow Ln, Ardmore, OK 73401

EDMAN, Elizabeth Marie (Nwk) 690 Fort Washington Ave, Apt 1L, New York, NY 10040

EDMANDS II, Frank A (SO) 55 S Vernon Lane, Fort Thomas, KY 41075

EDMINSTER, Beverley Beadle (Az) 1810 E Camino Cresta, Tucson, AZ 85718

EDMISTER, Jeffery Ray (WNY) Christ Episcopal Church, 7145 Fieldcrest Dr, Lockport, NY 14094

EDMISTON, Alan James (LI) 3939 Ocean Dr, Vero Beach, FL 32963

EDMONDS, Curtis M (Nev) Po Box 70342, Las Vegas, NV 89170

EDMONDS, John B (NY) Po Box 1535, Blue Hill, ME 04614

EDMONDSON, Emily F (SwVa)

EDMUNDS, Robert Douglas (Mass) PO Box 9000, Edgartown, MA 02539

EDSON, Heidi L (Vt) 6795 W 19th Pl Apt 304, Lakewood, CO 80214

EDSON, Lawrence Neil (Eau) 608 Madison St, Stanley, WI 54768

EDSON, Robert Bruce (Mass) 4 Home Meadows Ln, Hingham, MA 02043

EDWARD, Gadi M (ND) 120 8th St S, Moorhead, MN 56560

EDWARDS, Bonnie (RG) 4908 Corrales Rd Ste B, Corrales, NM 87048

EDWARDS, Carl Norris (Md) 201 Box Turtle Trl, Chapel Hill, NC 27516

✠ **EDWARDS**, Dan Thomas (Nev) 9480 S Eastern Ave Ste 236, Las Vegas, NV 89123

EDWARDS, Doug (Los) 4255 Harbour Island Ln, Oxnard, CA 93035

EDWARDS, Fitzroy Foster (NY) 72 Carnegie Ave, Elmont, NY 11003

EDWARDS, Halbert D (Okla) 1728 NW 42nd St, Oklahoma City, OK 73118

EDWARDS, James Dennison (LI) 4 S Aspen Pl, Lewisburg, PA 17837

EDWARDS, James Paul (Nev) 1400 Ebbetts Dr, Reno, NV 89503

EDWARDS, Jamie L (NC) 1902 N Holden Rd, Greensboro, NC 27408

EDWARDS, John Garry (CFla) 102 N 9th St, Haines City, FL 33844

EDWARDS II, Justin Sargent (Episcopal SJ) 765 Mesa View Dr Spc 98, Arroyo Grande, CA 93420

EDWARDS, Kathleen Louise (Minn)

EDWARDS, Laura MacFarland (WA) 13118 Collingwood Ter, Silver Spring, MD 20904

EDWARDS, Lloyd (USC) 4628 Datura Rd, Columbia, SC 29205

EDWARDS, Lydia Alice (NJ) 81 Hillside Ave, Metuchen, NJ 08840

EDWARDS, Nancy Beltz (The Episcopal NCal) Po Box 10202, Bainbridge Is, WA 98110

EDWARDS JR, Otis Carl (WNC) 115 Murphy Hill Rd, Weaverville, NC 28787

EDWARDS, Paul David (Los) 734 W Maplewood Ave, Fullerton, CA 92832

EDWARDS, Rebecca (Cal) 4321 Eastgate Mall, San Diego, CA 92121

EDWARDS, Robert Daniel (Los) 31641 La Novia, San Juan, CA 92675

EDWARDS, Terry Ann (SVa) 2515 Marshall Ave, Newport News, VA 23607

EDWARDS JR, Theodore Whitfield (SwFla) 114 John Pott Dr, Williamsburg, VA 23188

EDWARDS III, Tilden Hampton (WA) 9615 Page Ave, Bethesda, MD 20814

EDWARDS, Whitney (Va) St Jame's Episcopal, 1205 W Franklin St, Richmond, VA 23220

EDWARDS, William Glover (WNC) 38 Wildwood Ave, Asheville, NC 28804

EDWARDS, William Patrick (LI) St John's Episc Ch, Po Box 5069, Southampton, NY 11969

EDWARDS-ACTON, Jaime Kendall (Los) 727 Olympic Ave, Costa Mesa, CA 92626

EFFINGER, Richard W (SeFla) 141 S County Rd, Palm Beach, FL 33480

EGBERT, David (Okla) 2817 Natchez Trl, Edmond, OK 73012

EGBERT, Paula Sue (Ida) 5780 Millwright Ave, Boise, ID 83714

EGERSTROM, Marisa (WMass)

EGERTON, Karen (CFla) 1404 Chapman Cir, Winter Park, FL 32789

EHMER, Joseph Michael (NwT) Diocese of Northwest Texas, 1802 Broadway, Lubbock, TX 79401

EHREN, Lawrence Glenn (WMo)

EHRICH, Thomas Lindley (NC) 505 W 54th St Apt 812, New York, NY 10019

EIBIN, Julian Raymond (Nwk) 284 Island Ave., Ramsey, NJ 07446

EIBNER, Susan (NH) 97 Halls Mill Rd, Newfields, NH 03856

EICH III, Wilbur Foster (Ala) 1600 Darby Dr, Florence, AL 35630

EICHELBERGER JR, J Gary (USC) 10 N Church St, Greenville, SC 29601

EICHENLAUB, Patricia (Mich) 2745 Lake Pine Apt 219, Saint Joseph, MI 49085

EICHLER, Stephen (ETenn) 1151 Gudger Rd, Sewanee, TN 37375

EICHNER, James F (Oly)

EICK, John David (WMo) 8030 Ward Pkwy, Kansas City, MO 64114

EICK, Mary Herron (Ore) 11511 SW Bull Mountain Rd, Tigard, OR 97224

EIDAM JR, John Mahlon (SVa) 224 S Military Hwy, Norfolk, VA 23502

EIMAN, Amanda (Pa) St Davids Church, 763 Valley Forge Rd, Wayne, PA 19087

EINERSON, Dean Alfred (FdL) 29 S Pelham St, Rhinelander, WI 54501

EISENSTADT-EVANS, Elizabeth Anne (Pa) 50 Fleming Drive, Glenmoore, PA 19343

EKBERG, Sean A (Okla) 210 E 9th St, Bartlesville, OK 74003

EKEVAG, Ellen Poole (Chi) 209 N Pine St, New Lenox, IL 60451

EKIZIAN, Hagop J (NY) 137 N Division St, Peekskill, NY 10566

EKLO, Thomas (Minn) 8064 Golden Valley Rd, Golden Valley, MN 55427

EKLUND, Carolyn Hassig (Me) Episcopal Church St Paul, PO Box 195, Brunswick, ME 04011

EKLUND, Virginia Jane Rouleau (Lex) 130 Winterhawk Rd, Danville, KY 40422

EKREM, Katherine Boyle (Mass) 12 White Pine Ln, Lexington, MA 02421

EKSTROM, Ellen Louise (Cal) 1017 Virginia Street, Berkeley, CA 94710

EKUNWE, Sylvester Osa (Nwk)

ELAM III, Walter L (CGC) 153 Orange Ave, Fairhope, AL 36532

ELBERFELD, Katherine Ann Fockele (At) 123 Church St NE # 150, Marietta, GA 30060

ELBERFELD, Richard (NwPa) 3105 Springland Terrace, Erie, PA 16506

ELCOCK, Frank Ulric (LI) 257 Leaf Ave, Central Islip, NY 11722

ELDER, Clayton L (Dal) 311 E Corpus Christi St, Beeville, TX 78102

ELDER, Paul Robert (Los) 580 Hilgard Ave, Los Angeles, CA 90024

ELDER, Robert Macrum (Va) 218 2nd St, Huntingdon, PA 16652

ELDER, Ruth Annette (Md) 4238 Pimlico Rd, Baltimore, MD 21215

ELDER-HOLIFIELD, Donna Ellen Carter (ECR) 64 San Pedro St, Salinas, CA 93901

ELDREDGE, Martha Josephine (WA) 19167 Poplar Hill Ln, Valley Lee, MD 20692

ELDRIDGE, Barbara Adelle (CFla) 2143 Kings Cross St, Titusville, FL 32796

ELDRIDGE, Buel (EMich)

ELDRIDGE JR, Robert William (USC) Hq Forscom, 1777 Hardee Ave Sw, Fort Mcpherson, GA 30330

ELEK, Hentzi (Pa) 3625 Chapel Rd, Newtown Square, PA 19073

ELEY, Gary W (Vt) 33 Adams Ct, Burlington, VT 05401

ELFERT, Martin (Ore) 127 E 12th Ave, Spokane, WA 99202

ELFRING-ROBERTS, Jess (Chi) Church of our Saviour, 530 W Fullerton Pkwy, Chicago, IL 60614

ELFVIN, Robert Roger (Ia) 8 Poinciana Lane, Palm Coast, FL 32164

ELIN, Darren (SO) 100 Miami Ave, Terrace Park, OH 45174

ELIOT, Mary (Md) 1930 Brookdale Rd, Baltimore, MD 21244

ELKINS-WILLIAMS, Stephen John (NC) 100 Black Oak Pl, Chapel Hill, NC 27517

ELL, Marianne (Del) 4751 Highway 1804, Williston, ND 58801

ELLEDGE II, Clyde (Mass) 54 Robert Road, Marblehead, MA 01945

ELLEDGE, Kathryn (Mass) 54 Robert Road, Marblehead, MA 01945

ELLER, Ruth (U) 700 S Silver Ridge St Spc 85, Ridgecrest, CA 93555

ELLERY, Celia (NwT) 2661 Yale Ave, San Angelo, TX 76904

ELLESTAD, Charles Dwight (Lex) 837 Isaac Shelby Cir E, Frankfort, KY 40601

ELLEY, Eric M (WMass) PO Box 528, Somersville, CT 06072

ELLGREN SHEPLEY, Neysa (Ore) 11800 SW Military Ln, Portland, OR 97219

ELLINGBOE, Shirley Kay (RG) 5794 Ndcbu, Taos, NM 87571

ELLINGTON, Meta Louise Turkelson (NC) 521 Marlowe Rd, Raleigh, NC 27609

ELLIOTT, Annie (Miss) 370 Old Agency Rd, Ridgeland, MS 39157

ELLIOTT, Barb (Minn) St Paul's Episcopal Church, 1710 E Superior St, Duluth, MN 55812

ELLIOTT, Beverley Florence (At) 5458 E Mountain St, Stone Mountain, GA 30083

ELLIOTT, Bianca Lynn (Kan)

ELLIOTT III, David Augustus (Miss) 205 Autumn Ridge Dr, Jackson, MS 39211

ELLIOTT, Diane Lynn (Minn)

ELLIOTT, Gates Safford (Miss) 4130 Crestview Dr, 118 N Congress St, Jackson, MS 39201

ELLIOTT III, Harry Arnold (Ct) Grace Episcopal Church, 311 Broad St, Windsor, CT 06095

ELLIOTT, James Lawrence (Ga) PO Box 864, Quitman, GA 31643

ELLIOTT JR, Jim (Ala) 2714 Hilltop Cir, Gadsden, AL 35904

ELLIOTT, Jim (The Episcopal NCal) 1407 N Anderson St, Tacoma, WA 98406

ELLIOTT, Lawrence (Va)

ELLIOTT, Luz Adriana (Dal) St Anne Episcopal Church, 1700 N Westmoreland Rd, Desoto, TX 75115

ELLIOTT, Paul Alexander (At) 5458 E Mountain St, Stone Mountain, GA 30083

ELLIOTT, Paul C (At) 3131 Dale Dr Ne, Atlanta, GA 30305

ELLIOTT III, Richard G (EC) 2322 Metts Ave, Wilmington, NC 28403

ELLIOTT, Robert James (O) 4141 Bayshore Blvd Apt 101, Tampa, FL 33611

ELLIOTT, Rodger Neil (Minn) 1262 Birch Pond Trail, White Bear Lake, MN 55110

ELLIOTT, Scott Fuller (Chi) 2222 W Belmont Ave, # 205, Chicago, IL 60618

ELLIOTT, William Tate (EMich) 6757 Middle Rd, Hope, MI 48628

ELLIS JR, Bill (Spok) 128 E 12th Ave, Spokane, WA 99202

ELLIS, Jane Fielding (Ala) 556 Mohave Cir, Huntington, CT 06484

ELLIS, Kassinda Rosalind Tabia (LI)

ELLIS, Malcolm (Md) 232 Saint Thomas Ln, Owings Mills, MD 21117

ELLIS, Michael Elwin (Fla) 6126 Cherry Lake Dr N, Jacksonville, FL 32258

ELLIS, Michael Warren (Md) 4803 Leybourne Dr, Hilliard, OH 43026

ELLIS, Nana Kwasi (Md) All Saints Episcopal Church, Po Box 279, Reisterstown, MD 21136

ELLIS, Richard Alvin (Ct) 15 Piper Rd Apt J313, Scarborough, ME 04074

ELLIS, Russell Ray (Vt) 328 Shore Rd, Burlington, VT 05408

ELLIS, Steven MacDonald (ECR) 1408 Beaumont St NW, Salem, OR 97304

ELLIS, Walter L (Tex) 2419 Lansing Cir, Pearland, TX 77584

ELLIS, William Joseph (NwPa) 222 Brisbin St, Houtzdale, PA 16651

ELLISON, Andrew Duncan (FtW) 4321 Us Highway 80 W, Marshall, TX 75670

ELLISON, Monique (Md) 6060 Charles Edward Terrace, Columbia, MD 21045

ELLISTON, Mark Sanford (NwPa) 16 Central Ave, Oil City, PA 16301

ELLSWORTH, Anne (Az) 6300 N Central Ave, Phoenix, AZ 85012

ELLSWORTH, Bradford Edwin (WMo) Po Box 160, Cabool, MO 65689

ELLSWORTH, Eleanor (SanD) 2205 Caminito Del Barco, Del Mar, CA 92014

ELLSWORTH JR, Phillip C (Cal) 10033 River Rd, Potomac, MD 20854

ELLSWORTH, Scott Anthony (Ida) 2887 Snowflake Dr, Boise, ID 83706

ELMER-ANTHONY, Betty Lou (Ak) 11641 Hebron Dr, Eagle River, AK 99577

Clergy List

ELMIGER-JONES, Mary Kathleen (Cal) St Timothy's Church, 1550 Diablo Rd, Danville, CA 94526

ELPHEE, David T (SwVa)

ELSBERRY, Terry (NY) PO Box 293, Bedford, NY 10506

ELSE, John David (Pgh) 272 Caryl Dr, Pittsburgh, PA 15236

ELSENSOHN, David Dirk (Ak) 1714 Edgecumbe Dr, Sitka, AK 99835

ELVIN, Peter Thurston (WMass) 35 Park St, Williamstown, MA 01267

ELWELL, Pamela (SO) 321 East Kanawha Ave, Columbus, OH 43214

ELWOOD, Frederick Campbell (Mich) 1334 Riverside Dr, Buhl, ID 83316

ELWOOD, Richard Hugh (Tex) 308 E San Antonio St, Fredericksburg, TX 78624

ELY, Elizabeth Wickenberg (NC) Dunwyck, 64 Peniel Road, Columbus, NC 28722

ELY, James Everett (Tex) 1700 Golden Ave, Bay City, TX 77414

✠ **ELY**, Thomas C (Vt) 11 Rock Point Rd, Burlington, VT 05408

EMANUEL, Philip Grantham (Nev) PO Box 990, Pawleys Island, SC 29585

EMBLER-BEAZLEY, Liz (La) 6249 Canal Blvd, New Orleans, LA 70124

EMENHEISER, Ed (WMich) 174 Wakulat Ln, Traverse City, MI 49686

EMERSON, Angela Angela (Vt) Gates Briggs Blgd. Ste. 315, White River Junction, VT 05001

EMERSON, James Carson (Q) 1625 Hershey Ct, Columbia, MO 65202

EMERSON, Jason (ETenn) 9932 Bedford Ave., Omaha, NE 68134

EMERSON, Keith Roger (SVa) St. Paul's Church, 213 N. Main Street, Suffolk, VA 23434

EMERSON, Mary Beth (Mass) 8991 Brook Rd, McLean, VA 22102

EMERSON, Richard Clark (ECR) 1412 Maysun Ct, Campbell, CA 95008

EMERY, Dana Karen (Minn) 1400 Corbett Rd, Detroit Lakes, MN 56501

EMERY-GINN, Margaret Elizabeth (Alb) 10215 Carriage Dr, Plymouth, IN 46563

EMGE, Kevin Ray (Ia)

EMMERT, John Howard (CPa) 648 Laurel View Dr., Manheim, PA 17545

EMPSALL, Glenda Mascarella (Spok) 501 E Wallace Ave, Coeur D Alene, ID 83814

EMPSALL, Nathan Santway (Spok)

EMRICH III, Frederick Ernest (WMass) 7 Smith St, P.O. Box 318, North Haven, ME 04853

EMRICH III, Richard S M (Chi) 755 Hinchman Rd, Baroda, MI 49101

EMRY, Anne D (Ore) 1444 Liberty St SE, Salem, OR 97302

ENCARNACION-CARABALLO, Felix Antonio (DR (DomRep)) C/ Santiago 114, Santo Iomingo, Dominican Republic

ENCINOSA, Christina (SeFla) 68 Paxford Ln, Boynton Beach, FL 33426

ENDER, Sinclair C (Ia) 829 21st Ave, Moline, IL 61265

ENDICOTT, Gerri LaVerne (WTenn) PO Box 318, Somerville, TN 38068

ENDICOTT, Rachel (Oly) 15114 SE 48th Dr., Bellevue, WA 98006

ENGDAHL JR, Frederick Robert (Mich) 6490 Clarkston Rd., Clarkston, MI 48346

ENGELHARDT, Hanns Christian Joachim (Eur) Stephanienstrasse, 72, Karlsruhe, 76133, Germany

ENGELHORN, Paula Elaine (Chi)

ENGELS, Allen Robert (Colo) 3081 Evanston Ave, Grand Junction, CO 81504

ENGELS, Jimichael (Mass) 1190 Adams St Apt 213, Dorchester Center, MA 02124

ENGFER, Michael John (Nev) 4201 W Washington Ave, Las Vegas, NV 89107

ENGLAND, Edward Gary (ETenn) 408 Oak Ave, South Pittsburg, TN 37380

ENGLAND, Gary William (Ky) 7404 Arrowwood Rd, Louisville, KY 40222

ENGLAND, Loy David (WTex) Po Box 1025, Pflugerville, TX 78691

ENGLAND, Margaret Jefferson (Az) 11058 Portobelo Dr, San Diego, CA 92124

ENGLAND, Nicholas B (SO) 134 N Broad St, Lancaster, OH 43130

ENGLAND JR, Nick Arnold (WVa) 411 Prichard St, Williamson, WV 25661

ENGLAND, Otis Bryan (WMo) 315 E Partridge Ave, Independence, MO 64055

ENGLE, Cynthia L (Tex) 414 E. McAlpine, Navasota, TX 77868

ENGLE SR, Mark Christoph (NMich) 22975 Pine Lake Rd, Battle Creek, MI 49014

ENGLEBY, Matt (NJ) 379 Mount Harmony Rd, Bernardsville, NJ 07924

ENGLISH, Allison Rainey (Los) 504 N Camden Dr, Beverly Hills, CA 90210

ENGLISH, Ann Cantwell (Spok) Rr 1 Box 241-B, Touchet, WA 99360

ENGLISH, John Lyle (WMich) 1045 Woodrow Ave Nw, Grand Rapids, MI 49504

ENGLISH, Linda (WK) 114 W Roosevelt, Phoenix, AZ 85003

ENGLISH, Rev Carrie (Fla) 11601 Longwood Key Dr W, Jacksonville, FL 32218

ENGLISH, Thomas Ronald (Ore) 2530 Fairmount Blvd, Eugene, OR 97403

ENGLISH, Tristan Clifford (Minn) Christ Church, 321 West Ave, Red Wing, MN 55066

ENGLISH, William H (Roch) 248 Commons Lane, Foster City, CA 94404

ENGLUND, David (The Episcopal NCal) 1624 10th St, Oroville, CA 95965

ENGLUND, Henry C (NJ) 90 Dillon Way, Washington Crossing, PA 18977

ENGSTROM, Marilyn Jean (Wyo) 1714 Mitchell St, Laramie, WY 82072

ENGWALL, Douglas Brian (Ct) Trinity Episcopal Church, 55 River Rd, Collinsville, CT 06019

ENNIS, Kathleen Knox (SwFla) 6180 Golden Oaks Ln, Naples, FL 34119

ENSOR, Amelia Jeanne (Oly) 8235 36th Ave Ne, Seattle, WA 98115

ENSOR, Peter Crane (Los) 111 Westview Drive, Dubois, WY 82513

EOYANG JR, Thomas (Pa) 6622 Germantown Ave Unit 3A, Philadelphia, PA 19119

EPES, Gail E (Va) 1200 N Quaker Ln, Alexandria, VA 22302

EPPERSON, Christopher Larry (SVa) PO Box 3520, Williamsburg, VA 23187

EPPLE, Jogues Fred (Okla) 1830 University Ave W, Apt 201, Saint Paul, MN 55104

EPPLY-SCHMIDT, Joanne (NJ) 26 Nelson Ridge Rd, Princeton, NJ 08540

✠ **EPTING**, Chris Christopher (Ia) 86 Broadmoor Ln, Iowa City, IA 52245

ERB, Edward Kenneth (Be) 827 Church St., Honesdale, PA 18431

ERDELJON, Lisa Michele (Chi) 647 Dundee Ave, Barrington, IL 60010

ERDMAN, Dan (Mich) 929 E Hawthorne Loop, Webb City, MO 64870

ERDMAN, Nathan (Md) St Thomas Episcopal Church, 232 Saint Thomas Ln, Owings Mills, MD 21117

ERHARD, Michael Edward Charles (Cal) 2421 Day Dr, The Villages, FL 32163

ERICKSON, David L (Cal) 1818 Monterey Blvd, Hermosa Beach, CA 90254

ERICKSON, Frederick David (Los) 10700 Keswick St, Garrett Park, MD 20896

ERICKSON, Gregory Charles (WNC) 1359 Lamb Mountain Rd, Hendersonville, NC 28792

ERICKSON, Heather B (Los) St Margaret's Episcopal Church, 31641 La Novia Ave, San Juan Capistrano, CA 92675

ERICKSON JR, Joseph Austin (Los) 764 Valparaiso Dr, Claremont, CA 91711

ERICKSON, Ken (Mich) 711 Wooddale Rd, Bloomfield Hills, MI 48301

ERICKSON, Lori Jean (Ia)

ERICKSON, Mary (At) 4 Jones St, Cartersville, GA 30120

ERICKSON, Mary Cobb (Wyo) PO Box 1690, Jackson, WY 83001

ERICKSON, Richard Paul (Alb) 901 Ridge View Circle, Castleton-On-Hudson, NY 12033

ERICKSON, Scott (Cal) 420 Eureka St, San Francisco, CA 94114

ERICKSON, Winifred Jean (NMich) 1506 Us #2 Highway West, Crystal Falls, MI 49920

ERICSON, Bill (Mich) Po Box 267, Dewitt, MI 48820

ERIXSON, Lorna Lloyd (At) 316 Spyglass Hill Dr, Perry, GA 31069

ERQUIAGA, Trudel Nada (Nev) 1128 Green Valley Drive, Fallon, NV 89406

ERSKINE, Jack Arthur (EO) 69787 Pine Ridge Road, Sisters, OR 97759

ERVOLINA, Timothy Mark (USC) 120 Ridgewood Cir, Greenwood, SC 29649

ERWIN, Ginny (Los) 2157 Birdie Dr, Banning, CA 92220

ERWIN JR, James Walter (NY) 5 Second St, Warwick, NY 10990

ESBENSHADE, Burnell True (Mo) 1116 E Linden Ave, Saint Louis, MO 63117

ESCALERA, Jose Refugio (Okla) 8400 S Pennsylvania Ave, Oklahoma City, OK 73159

ESCOTT, Raymond Philip (WNC) 12 Misti Leigh Ln, Waynesville, NC 28786

ESKAMIRE-JACKSON, Joyce (La) 1313 Esplanade Ave, New Orleans, LA 70116

ESONU, Clinton Chukwuemeka (WA) 2031 Powhatan Rd, Hyattsville, MD 20782

ESPERANCE, Jabnel (Hai)

ESPESETH, Cynthia A (Colo) 13613 178TH Ave NE, Redmond, WA 98052

ESPINOSA-AREVALO, Carlos (EcuC) Apartado Postal 10-04-21, Atuntaqui-Imbabura, Ecuador

ESPOSITO, Catherine Patricia (NJ) 14 Edgemere Dr, Matawan, NJ 07747

ESPOSITO, Charles Paul (Pgh) 315 Shady Ave, Pittsburgh, PA 15206

ESTES, Anthony Carlos (Mich)

ESTES, Diane (La)

ESTES, James Gray (SanD) 1427 Rimrock Dr, Escondido, CA 92027

ESTES, Robert Theodore (WMo) 425 East Cherry St, Nevada, MO 64772

ESTES, William Thomas (FtW) Grace Church, 405 Glenmar Ave, Monroe, LA 71201

ESTEY, Lawrence Mitchell (Me) 3 Greenhead Lane, PO Box 646, Stonington, ME 04681

ESTIL, Colbert (Hai) Eglesi Episcopal D'Haiti, Boite Postale 1309, Port-au-Prince, Haiti

✠ **ESTILL**, Robert Whitridge (NC) 8601 Cypress Lakes Dr # A302, Raleigh, NC 27615

ESTRADA, Carolyn Sullivan (Los) 2516 E Willow St Unit 108, Signal Hill, CA 90755

ESTRADA, Richard Roger (Los) 2808 Altura St, Los Angeles, CA 90031

ESWEIN, Nancy G (Cal) 5040 E Timrod St, Tucson, AZ 85711

ETEMAD, Sandra L (Pa) 535 Haws Ave, Norristown, PA 19401

ETHEREDGE, Annie (WLa) 905 Dafney Drive, Lafayette, LA 70503

ETHRIDGE, Forrest Eugene (Ga) 2408 Forest Ave NW, Fort Payne, AL 35967

ETTENHOFER, Karen Ruth (NMich) 500 Ogden Ave, Escanaba, MI 49829

EUSTACE, Warren Paul (ECR) 1604 E. Nectarine Ave., Lompoc, CA 93436

EUSTIS, Patricia Anne (ND) 2200 Koch Dr Apt 313, Bismarck, ND 58503

EVANCHO, Nicholas James (NwPa) 3116 O St NW, Washington, DC 20007

EVANGREENE, Gaelyn Lei (WNC)

EVANS, Aaron (WMich) 1115 W Summit Ave, Muskegon, MI 49441

EVANS, Amber (Cal) 1357 Natoma St, San Francisco, CA 94103

EVANS, Bill (Ga) 675 Holly Drive, Marietta, GA 30064

EVANS III, Boyd McCutchen (SwVa) Church of St Thomas, 124 E Main St, Abingdon, VA 24210

EVANS, Carol (O) 246 Cedar Ave, Ravenna, OH 44266

EVANS, Caryllou Deedee (Kan) St. James Episcopal Church, 3750 E. Douglas, Wichita, KS 67208

EVANS II, C David (NwPa) 506 Young Rd, Erie, PA 16509

EVANS, David Hugh (Mich) 1926 Morris St, Sarasota, FL 34239

EVANS, Dolores Elaine (Be) 184 Meadow Lane, Conestoga, PA 17516

EVANS, Gareth C (Mass) 148 Newtown Rd, Acton, MA 01720

EVANS, Gary T (NMich) 1000 Bluff View Dr Apt 112, Houghton, MI 49931

EVANS, Geoffrey Parker (Ala) 1727 Post Oak Ct., Auburn, AL 36830

EVANS, Haydn Barry (Pa) 214 New Street, 4N, Philadelphia, PA 19106

EVANS, Holly Sue (CNY) PO Box 319, Copenhagen, NY 13626

EVANS, Jacob Joseph (Alb) 5 Simpson Ave, Round Lake, NY 12151

EVANS, James Eston (Pa) 1013 Balfour Cir, Phoenixville, PA 19460

EVANS, James W (Dal) 401 S. Crockett, Sherman, TX 75092

EVANS, Jeffrey Keith (Ala) St Timothy's Episcopal Church, 207 E Washington St, Athens, AL 35611

EVANS, John Frederick (WA) 10450 Lottsford Rd Apt 3115, Mitchellville, MD 20721

EVANS, John Miles (Md) PO Box 1272, PO Box 1272, Portsmouth, NH 03802

EVANS, Jonathan W (SwFla)

EVANS, Karen (Ar) 675 Holly Drive, Marietta, GA 30064

EVANS, Katharine Cope (Mass) 18 Lafayette Rd, Ipswich, MA 01938

EVANS, Len (U) 515 S 1000 E Apt 506, Salt Lake City, UT 84102

EVANS, Maria Louise (Mo) 12776 Suncrest Way, Greentop, MO 63546

EVANS, Mark E (Spr) 402 Pekin St., P.O. Box 386, Lincoln, IL 62656

EVANS, Noah H (Pgh) 240 Woodhaven Dr., Pittsburgh, PA 15228

EVANS, Norman Dean (Pa) 304 Lexington, Media, PA 19063

EVANS, Paul Fredric (Cal) 23 Seward St Apt C2, Saratoga Springs, NY 12866

EVANS JR, Ralph Easen (CFla) 2804 Coral Shores Dr, Fort Lauderdale, FL 33306

EVANS, Scott Charles (Alb) 15 W High St, Ballston Spa, NY 12020

EVANS, Steven A (Ga) 4625 Sussex Pl, Savannah, GA 31405

EVANS, Theodore H. (WMass) 235 Walker St. Apt. 236, Lenox, MA 01240

EVENSON, Bruce (SC) 34 Krier Ln, Mt Pleasant, SC 29464

EVERETT, Isaac J (Mass) 138 Tremont St, Boston, MA 02111

EVERETT, Sherman Bradley (SO) 3206 Brandon Rd, Columbus, OH 43221

EVERHARD, Darby Oliver (NC) 520 Summit Street, Winston Salem, NC 27101

EVERSLEY, Walter VL (Md) 214 Lambeth Rd, Baltimore, MD 21218

EVERSMAN, Karen Lynn (O) 2041 W. Reserve Cir., Avon, OH 44011

EVERSON, Charles Webster (Kan) 4224 Charlotte St, Kansas City, MO 64110

EVERSON, Jacquelyn (NMich) 711 11th Ave, Menominee, MI 49858

EWART, Craig Kimball (NY)

EWING, Elizabeth (CNY) St Andrew's Episcopal Church, 4512 College Ave, College Park, MD 20740

EWING, Judith (SC) 203 Magnolia Bluff Dr, Columbia, SC 29229

EWING, Ward Burleson (ETenn) P O Box 6, 213 Baker Cemetery Road, Ten Mile, TN 37880

EXLEY, Lori Tucker (Pa)

EXNER, William Edward (NH) 19 W Union St, Goffstown, NH 03045

EXPOSITO IRRARRAGORRI, Carlos Eduardo (SanD)

EYER-DELEVETT, Aimee (Los) All Saints By The Sea, 83 Eucalyptus Lane, Santa Barbara, CA 93108

EYLERS, David Edward (NY) PO Box 352, Harwinton, CT 06791

EYTCHESON, Gerald Leonard (Kan) 2400 Gary Ave, Independence, KS 67301

EZELL II, Jim (ECR) 105 Dogwood Trl, Elizabeth City, NC 27909

F

FAASS, Peter (O) 3566 Avalon Rd, Shaker Heights, OH 44120

FABIAN, Rick (Cal) 2525 Lyon St, San Francisco, CA 94123

FABRE, John P (Az) 18083 W Douglas Way, Surprise, AZ 85374

FABRE, Julie Kilbride (U) 38105 Redwood Road #2191, West Valley City, UT 84119

FACCIO, David Franceschi (Pa)

FACKLER, Phillip Joseph Augustine (Pa) 1104 Mayberry Place, Raleigh, NC 27609

FACTOR, Beverly A (Los) 2620 Catherine Rd, Altadena, CA 91001

FADELY, Diane Camille (Md) Trinity Episcopal Church, 120 Allegheny Ave, Towson, MD 21204

FAETH, Margaret Ann (Va) 4529 Peacock Ave, Alexandria, VA 22304

FAGEOL, Suzanne Antoinette (Oly) Po Box 303, Langley, WA 98260

FAGG, Randy Jay (Ida) PO Box 324, Rupert, ID 83350

FAHRNER, Pamela Henry (SC) Saint John's Episcopal Church, 5234 Maryland Hwy, Deer Park, MD 21550

FAIN, Beth Ann Jernigan (Tex) 10515 Laneview Dr, Houston, TX 77070

FAIN, Robert Duncan (Ga) 2230 Walton Way, Augusta, GA 30904

FAIR, Verna M (Chi) 1134 Highpointe Dr, Dekalb, IL 60115

FAIRBANKS, Barbara Jean (Minn) 3044 Longfellow Ave, Minneapolis, MN 55407

FAIRFIELD, Roger Louis (EO) 69793 Pine Glen Rd, Sisters, OR 97759

FAIRLESS, Caroline (NH) 8 Whispering Pines Rd, Wilmont, NH 03287

FAIRLEY, Pamela Sue (Dal) 6400 McKinney Ranch Pkwy, McKinney, TX 75070

FAIRMAN, Henry Francis (RI) 73 Touisset Ave, Swansea, MA 02777

FAIRWEATHER, Carolynne Marie (Ore) 4061 Hayes St. #28, Newberg, OR 97132

FAISON, Dee Doheny (Pa) 405 Warren Rd, West Chester, PA 19382

FAISON, Diane Elizabeth (Pa) 657 11th Ave, Prospect Park, PA 19076

FAIT JR, Harold Charles (Minn)

FALCIANI, Justin Anthony (NJ) 16 W. Wilmont Ave, Somers Point, NJ 08244

FALCONE, John Francis (O) 7513 W 33rd St, Tulsa, OK 74107

FALCONER, Allan (Miss) 11593 Avondale Dr, Fairfax, VA 22030

FALES, Stephen Abbott (Ind) 1402 W Main St, Carmel, IN 46032

FALLIS, Robert Keith (Okla) 10901 S Yale Ave, Tulsa, OK 74137

FALLON, Amy L (Mo) Grace Place Campus Ministry, 401 Normal Rd, Dekalb, IL 60115

FALLOWFIELD, William Harris (Md) 2622 N Calvert St, Baltimore, MD 21218

FALLS, Michael Lee (Tex) 5831 Secrest Dr, Austin, TX 78759

FAMULARE JR, Joseph Anthony (Alb) 119 Southern Ave, Little Falls, NY 13365

FAN, Peter Sheung-Mau (The Episcopal Church in Haw) St Elizabeth Episcopal Church, 720 N King St, Honolulu, HI 96817

FANFAN, Luckner (Hai)

FANGUY, Mabel Matheny (Pgh) 1114 1st St, Canonsburg, PA 15317

FANNING, Thomas H (Miss) 24 Greystone Dr, Madison, MS 39110

FARABEE, Allen (WNY) 310 Norwood Ave, Buffalo, NY 14222

FARAMELLI, Norman Joseph (Mass) 29 Harris St, Waltham, MA 02452

FARBER, Joseph W (EO) 1420 E Dewey Ave, Sapulpa, OK 74066

FARGO, David Rolland (La) 17 Hastings Ct, Asheville, NC 28803

FARGO, Valerie Mae (EMich)

FARIA III, Manuel P (Mass) 4 Ocean St, Beverly, MA 01915

FARINA, Gaspar Miran (Mil) 154 Club Wildwood, Hudson, FL 33568

FARKAS, Hazel Daphne Martin (SVa) 111 Montrose, Williamsburg, VA 23188

FARLEY, Nancy Stone (Lex) 151 Vine St, Sadieville, KY 40370

FARMER, Edward Dean (Wyo)

FARMER, Eyleen Hamner (WTenn) 102 N 2nd St, Memphis, TN 38103

FARMER, Gary Clayton (WNC) Po Box 633, Arden, NC 28704

FARMER, Jennie Marietta (EMich) 453 S 26th St, Saginaw, MI 48601

FARNES, Joseph E (Ida) 67 East St, Pittsfield, MA 01201

FARONE, Martha Jeanette (WNY) 7145 Fieldcrest Dr, Lockport, NY 14094

FARQUHAR-MAYES, Alice Fay (Ida) 1560 Lenz Ln, Boise, ID 83712

FARQUHAR-MAYES, Thomas (Ida) 1115 W Clarinda Dr, Meridian, ID 83642

FARR, Beau Anthony (At)

FARR, Curtis Andrew (Ct) St James' Church, 19 Walden St, West Hartford, CT 06107

FARR, Elizabeth (ETenn)

FARR, Matthew R (ETenn)

FARR, Meghan J (CFla) St Luke's Episcopal Church, PO Box 605, Gladstone, NJ 07934

FARRAND, Gregory C (NC)

FARRAR, Charles Thomas (Me) 2390 Rfd 201, Gardiner, ME 04345

FARRAR III, Dean (Los) 4091 E La Cara St, Long Beach, CA 90815

FARRELL JR, Reid Dwyer (Vt) PO Box 273, Swanton, VT 05488

FARRELL, Wayne (SwFla) 1700 Keystone Rd, Tarpon Springs, FL 34688

FARSTAD, Joan Elizabeth (Ia) 2410 Melrose Dr, Cedar Falls, IA 50613

FARWELL JR, James William (At) Virginia Theological Seminary, Alexandria, VA 22304

FASEL, William Jay (WMo) 824 W 62nd St, Kansas City, MO 64113

FAST SR, Todd Howard (Oly) 8756 Sylvan Pl Nw, Seattle, WA 98117

FAUCETTE, Louis H (At) 2998 Kodiak Ct, Marietta, GA 30062

FAULKNER, David M (Dal) The Episcopal Church of the Good Shepherd, 200 West College Street, Terrell, TX 75160

FAULKNER, Tom (NY) 131 E 66th St Apt 10b, New York, NY 10065

FAULSTICH, Christine Marie (Tex) 9600 South Gessner Rd., Houston, TX 77071

FAULSTICH, Matthew (SeFla) 1704 Buchanan St, Hollywood, FL 33020

FAUPEL, David William (SeFla) 7447 Emilia Ln, Naples, FL 34114

FAUSAK, Frederick Emil (NY) 41 Alter Ave, Staten Island, NY 10304

FAVAZZA, Gregory Emanuel (CFla)

FAY, Michael (Colo) 8010 W Us Highway 50, Salida, CO 81201

FAY, Susan D (The Episcopal NCal) 3878 River Rd, Colusa, CA 95932

FAYETTE, Shelly Lynn (Oly) 805 SE Ellsworth Rd, Vancouver, WA 98664

FEAGIN JR, Jerre Willis (WNY) 3751 N Franklin Ave, Loveland, CO 80538

FEAMSTER JR, Thomas Otey (NC) 1805 Virginia Ct, Tavares, FL 32778

FEATHER, Mark (Va) 14 Cornwall St NW, Leesburg, VA 20176

FECHT, Dustin Michael (Mil) St John's Episcopal Church, 405 N Saginaw Rd, Midland, MI 48640

FEDEWA, Mike (WMich) 1025 3 Mile Rd Ne, Grand Rapids, MI 49505

FEDOCK, Maria Michele (Md) 2115 Southland Rd, Baltimore, MD 21207

FEDORCHAK, Karen Christina Russell (Ct) 48 S Hawthorne St, Manchester, CT 06040

FEELY, Mary Josephine (Minn) 8055 Morgan Ave N, Stillwater, MN 55082

FEHR, Thomas James (SO) Community of the Transfiguration, 495 Albion Ave., Cincinnati, OH 45246

FEHR, Wayne L (Mil) 8220 Harwood Ave Apt 334, Wauwatosa, WI 53213

FEIDER, Paul A (FdL) 1511 Cedarhurst Dr, New London, WI 54961

FELICETTI, Elizabeth Marshall (SVa) 1217 Yarbrough Way, Virginia Beach, VA 23455

FELLHAUER, Edward William (Miss) 9B Deans Court, Santa Fe, NM 87508

FELLHAUER, Sheila Rose (Miss) 9B Deans Court, Santa Fe, NM 87508

FELLOWS, Richard Greer (SwFla) 15801 Country Lake Drive, Tampa, FL 33624

FELLOWS, Robert Hayden (Okla) 5820 W Garden Pointe Dr, Stillwater, OK 74074

FELS, Charles Wentworth Baker (ETenn)

FELSOVANYI, Andrea (The Episcopal NCal) 4 Bishop Ln, Menlo Park, CA 94025

FELTNER, Allan L (EMich) 1287 Adams Dr, West Branch, MI 48661

FELTY, Rose Ann (Alb) PO Box 114, Columbiaville, NY 12050

FENLON, Mathew Charles (Tex) 2450 River Oaks Blvd, Houston, TX 77019

FENN, Richard Kimball (Pa) 43 Hibben Rd, Princeton, NJ 08540

FENN, Richard Lewis (WNY) 19 Pradas Way, Edgartown, MA 02539

FENNER, Renee Lynette (Mo)

FENTON, David Henry (SanD) 3962 Josh St, Eugene, OR 97402

FENTON, Douglas (NY) 1410 Nanton St, Vancouver, V6H 2E2, Canada

FENTON, Eric (WTex) 606 W Cleveland St, Cuero, TX 77954

FENTON, Fred (Los) 1670 Interlachen Rd Apt 43g, Seal Beach, CA 90740

FENTON, Graham (Minn) 4720 Zenith Ave S, Minneapolis, MN 55410

FENWICK, Robert Donald (SO) 6439 Bethany Village Dr., Box 307, Centerville, OH 45459

FEREBEE, Randy (WNC) 127 42nd Avenue Dr NW, Hickory, NC 28601

FEREGRINO, Alfredo (Oly)

FERGUESON, John Frederick (Oly) 14449 90th Ct Ne, Bothell, WA 98011

FERGUSON, Anthony David Norman (Fla) 5128 Falling Water Rd, Nolensville, TN 37135

FERGUSON, Dina McMullin (Los) St. Michael the Archangel, El Segundo, CA 90245

FERGUSON, Dru (NwT) 510 Newell Ave, Dallas, TX 75223

FERGUSON, Fred-Munro (Alb) 6 Spences Trce, Harwich, MA 02645

FERGUSON, Judith Ann (NY) 391 Main St, Highland Falls, NY 10928

FERGUSON, Katherine (Va)

FERGUSON JR, Lawrence C (EO) Po Box 1344, Prineville, OR 97754

FERGUSON, Les (SVa) 5537 Greenefield Dr S, Portsmouth, VA 23703

FERGUSON, Linda Jean (Mich) 1434 E 13 Mile Rd, Madison Heights, MI 48071

FERGUSON, Ronald L (Chi)

FERGUSON, Ruth (Roch) 377 Rector Pl Apt 95, New York, NY 10280

FERGUSON, Sheila Saward (Chi) 1709 Indian Knoll Rd, Naperville, IL 60565

FERGUSON, Stephen Keith (Tex) 20171 Chasewood Park Drive, Houston, TX 77070

FERGUSON, Thomas C (Mass) 583 Sheridan Ave, Columbus, OH 43209

FERGUSON, Virginia Alice (Nev) 6773 W Charleston Blvd, Las Vegas, NV 89146

FERLO, Roger Albert (NY) 1700 E 56th Street, Apartment 2601, Chicago, IL 60637

FERNANDEZ, Jose Pascual (NY) 107 Se Superior Way, Stuart, FL 34997

FERNANDEZ, Jureck Zamudio (Cal)

FERNANDEZ, Linda Jean Pell (Md) 1930 Brookdale Rd, Baltimore, MD 21244

FERNANDEZ-LIRANZO, Hipolito Secundino (DR (DomRep)) Calle 10 No. 30, Villa Olga, Santiago, Dominican Republic

FERNANDEZ-POLA, Rosali (PR)

FERNANDEZ-REINA, Hipolito (SwFla)

FERNER, Dave (Ind) 180 Red Coat Ln, Stoddard, NH 03464

FERREIRA-SANDOVAL, Wilson (Ore) 372 NE Lincoln St, Hillsboro, OR 97124

FERREL, Artis Louise (Ia) 15102 Pinehurst Dr, Council Bluffs, IA 51503

FERRELL, Nathan Wilson (Me) 41 Foreside Road, Falmouth, ME 04105

FERRELL, Sean Daniel (Spr) 2018 Boudreau Dr, Urbana, IL 61801

FERRER, Gabriel V (Los) All Saints Parish, 504 N Camden Dr, Beverly Hills, CA 90210

FERRIANI, Nancy Ann (Ind) 5010 Washington Blvd, Indianapolis, IN 46205

FERRITO, Michael Louis (ECR) 1391 Market St, Santa Clara, CA 95050

FERRO, Mauricio (Colom) Carrera 16 #94-A-30, Bogota, Colombia

FERRY, Daniel Whitney (NH) 1465 Hooksett Rd Unit 280, Hooksett, NH 03106

FESQ, John Alfred (Mass) 2708 Salem Church Rd Apt 217, Apt 222, Fredericksburg, VA 22407

FESSLER, Robert H (Mil) 2275 De Carlin Dr, Brookfield, WI 53045

FETTERMAN, James Harry (WLa) 1755 Ne 46th St, Oakland Park, FL 33334

FETZ, Robert D (WMass) 30 Warren Ter, Longmeadow, MA 01106

FEUERSTEIN, John Mark (Pgh) 1066 Washington Rd, Mt Lebanon, PA 15228

FEUERSTEIN, Paul (NY) 431 E 118th St, New York, NY 10035

FEUS, William Frederick (USC) St. Mark's Church, 132 Center Street, Chester, SC 29706

FEYERHERM, Elise Anne (Mass) 3400 Calumet St, Columbus, OH 43214

FEYRER, David Allport (Ct) 70 S. Dogwood Trail, Southern Shores, NC 27949

FHUERE, Brenda Lee (Colo) 520 Jaylee St Unit A, Clifton, CO 81520

FICHTER JR, Richard E (Va) 10360 Rectory Ln, King George, VA 22485

FICKS III, Robert Leslie (Ct) 8166 Mount Air Place, Columbus, OH 43235

FIDDLER, Andrew (Ct) 215 Highland St, New Haven, CT 06511

FIDLER, Brian Ernest (SanD) The Bishop's School, 7607 La Jolla Blvd, La Jolla, CA 92037

FIEBKE, Edward John (Alb) 6014 7th Ave W, Bradenton, FL 34209

FIEFIE, Guilene ()

FIELD, Claire Cowden (NwT) 1601 S Georgia St, Amarillo, TX 79102

☫ **FIELD**, Martin Scott (WMo) 420 W. 14th St, Kansas City, MO 64105

FIELD, Norman Grover (NwPa) 747 E 41st St, Erie, PA 16504

FIELD, Rachel E (Ct)

FIELD, Robert Durning (WNC) 256 E. Main St., Brevard, NC 28712

FIELD, William Overstreet (Del) 1611 Spring Dr Apt 5B, Louisville, KY 40205

FIELDS, Kenneth L (Tex) 1227 Wellshire Dr, Katy, TX 77494

FIELDS, Laddie B (Tex) 431 Pace Rd, Hendersonville, NC 28792

FIELDSTON, Heidi A (Mass) 24 Court St, Dedham, MA 02026

FIFE, Richard (SwVa) 2250 Maiden Ln Sw, Roanoke, VA 24015

FIGGE, Diane (RG) 3900 Trinity Dr, Los Alamos, NM 87544

FIGLEWSKI, Brett Michael (Ct) 770 E Main St, Waterbury, CT 06702

FIKE, Christopher John (Mass) 24 Oakland St, Medford, MA 02155

FIKES, Gerald David (Tex) PO Box 100014, Arlington, VA 22210

FILBERT, Brandon Lee (Ore) 2090 High St. SE, Salem, OR 97302

FILER, Judy Kathleen (Tex) St John's Episcopal Church, 514 Carter St, Marlin, TX 76661

FILL, Michael (Be) 151 Prospect Ave Apt 16d, Hackensack, NJ 07601

FILLER, John Arthur (U) 514 Americas Way #4603, Box Elder, SD 57719

FINAN, Alice Jeanne (Vt) Cathedral Church of St. Paul, 2 Cherry St, Burlington, VT 05401

FINCH, Barbara Jo (Ore) 11865 SW Tualatin Rd Apt 45, Tualatin, OR 97062

FINCH JR, Floyd William (SC) 1 Bishop Gadsden Way Apt 119, Charleston, SC 29412

FINCH, Robin Lee (Ida) All Saints' Episcopal Church, 704 S Latah St, Boise, ID 83705

FINCHER, Michael (Los) 1242 E 4th St Unit 8, Long Beach, CA 90802

FINEANGANOFO, Sosaia Ala (Cal) 2565 Redbridge Rd, Tracy, CA 95377

FINKENSTAEDT JR, Harry Seymour (WMass) 13761 Charismatic Way, Gainesville, VA 20155

FINLEY IV, John Huston (Mass) 717 Atlantic Ave Apt 3B, Boston, MA 02111

FINLEY, Rosamond Stelle (Los) 212 W Franklin St, Tucson, AZ 85701

FINN, Anne Marie (NwT) 2630 S 11th St, Abilene, TX 79605

FINN, Emilie Aurora (Az) 13150 W Spanish Garden Dr, Sun City West, AZ 85375

FINN, Michael John (Roch) 1245 Culver Rd, Rochester, NY 14609

FINN, Patrick Shawn (WMich) 1006 3rd Street, Muskegon, MI 49440

FINN, Robert Patrick (EMich) PO Box 83, West Branch, MI 48661

FINNERUD, Margaret A (Ct) St Philip's Episcopal Church, 205 E Moore St, Southport, NC 28461

FINNIN, Nathan Mcbride (NC) Canterbury School, 5400 Old Lake Jeanette Rd, Greensboro, NC 27455

FIRESTINE, Susan Lee (WNY)

FIRTH, Harry Warren (WMo) 4024 W 100th Ter, Overland Park, KS 66207

FISCHBECK, Lisa Galen (NC) 8410 Merin Rd, Chapel Hill, NC 27516

FISCHER III, Charles L (At) St. Paul's Episcopal Chur, 294 Peyton Rd., SW, Atlanta, GA 30311

FISCHER, Evelyn (O) 127 W. North Street, Wooster, OH 44691

FISCHER, John Denny (Mil) 920 E Courtland Pl, Milwaukee, WI 53211

FISCHER, Ryan David (ND) PO Box 83, Crystal, ND 58222

FISCHER, Sara (Oly) 2800 SE Harrison Street, Portland, OR 97214

FISCHER, Sarah Motley (WA) Grace Episcopal Church, 1041 Wisconsin Ave NW, Chevy Chase, MD 20815

FISCHER-DAVIES, Clare (RI) 50 Orchard Ave, Providence, RI 02906

FISH, Cameron Hoover (CNY) 6 Canberra Ct, Mystic, CT 06355

FISH, Charles (Tad) Cramer (Ct) PO Box 67724, Albuquerque, NM 87193

FISH, Gloria Hoyer (Roch) 46 Azalea Rd, Rochester, NY 14620

FISH, Sonnie (Ct) PO Box 67724, Albuquerque, NM 87193

FISHBAUGH-LOONEY, Kristen Fishbaugh (Md) 11232 Falls Rd, Timonium, MD 21093

FISHBECK, Nadine B (Tenn)

FISHBURNE, Donald Allston (SC) 57 Sweet Water Ct, Pawleys Island, SC 29585

FISHER, Barbara Anne (Eas)

FISHER, David Hickman (Chi) 1012 Churchill Dr, Naperville, IL 60563

FISHER, Davis Lee (Chi) 430 SW 13th Ave, #1015, Portland, OR 97205

FISHER, Doug (WMass) 37 Chestnut St, Springfield, MA 01103

FISHER, Elizabeth B (NY) Po Box 974, Millbrook, NY 12545

FISHER, Ernest Wilkin (SwFla) 550 1st Ave S Apt 514, #514, Saint Petersburg, FL 33701

FISHER, James Alfred (NJ) 15 Maple Street, South Seaville, NJ 08246

FISHER, Jeff (Tex) 2695 S Southwest Loop 323, Tyler, TX 75701

FISHER, Jerry William (NC) 635 Galashiels Place, Wake Forest, NC 27587

FISHER, Jill Carmen (ETenn) 1175 Pineville Rd Apt 85, Chattanooga, TN 37405

FISHER, John Coale (SC) 8244 Crooked Creek Ln, Edisto Island, SC 29438

FISHER, Joy (Ga) 147 SouthSecond Street, Cochran, GA 31014

FISHER, Julie Blake (O) 475 Laurel Drive, Kent, OH 44240

FISHER, Margaret (Spok) 522 West Park Place, Spokane, WA 99205

FISHER, Mary Carlton (The Episcopal NCal) 72 Mill Creek Dr, Willits, CA 95490

FISHER, Paige Ford (Mass) 206 Clarendon St, Boston, MA 02116

FISHER, Richard Lingham (WNC) 175 Vinal St, Rockport, ME 04856

FISHER, Robert William (ECR) PO Box 101, Carmel Valley, CA 93924

FISHER, Ronald Spencer (Md) 24 Evergreen Trail, Severna Park, MD 21146

FISHER JR, Russell Ellsworth (FtW) Po Box 192, Santa Anna, TX 76878

FISHER, Sarah (At) 4755 N Peachtree Rd, Atlanta, GA 30338

FISHER, Scott Owen (Ak) 1030 2nd Ave, Fairbanks, AK 99701

FISHER, William A (Colo) 200 Elk Run Dr, Basalt, CO 81621

FISHER-STEWART, Gayle Antoinette (WA) 820 6th St Ne, Washington, DC 20002

FISHWICK, Jeffrey Palmer (Va) 1260 River Chase Ln, Charlottesville, VA 22901

FISKE, Thomas W (U) 123 Linden Avenue, Fairmont, MN 56031

FITCH, William Babcock (USC) 6342 Yorkshire Dr, Columbia, SC 29209

FITZGERALD, John P (HB) 1551 10th Ave E, Seattle, WA 98102

FITZGERALD, Joseph Michael (Az) 2288 W Silverbell Tree Dr, Tucson, AZ 85745

FITZGERALD, Todd (Tex) St Stephens School, 6528 Saint Stephens Dr, Austin, TX 78746

FITZGIBBONS, Michael John (Spok) 8505 W Hood Ave, Kennewick, WA 99336

FITZGIBBONS, Sabeth S (NwPa) 1706 NW 60th St, Seattle, WA 98107

FITZHUGH, Bobbe Kay (Wyo) PO Box 1419, Douglas, WY 82633

FITZHUGH, Mark L (LI) 325 Lattingtown Road, Locust Valley, NY 11560

✠ **FITZPATRICK**, Bob (The Episcopal Church in Haw) Office of the Bishop, 229 Queen Emma Sq, Honolulu, HI 96813

FITZPATRICK, Michael Carl (Mich) 24699 Grand River Ave, Detroit, MI 48219

FITZPATRICK, Robert (NY) 179 East Main st, Washingtonville, NY 10992

FITZSIMMONS, Daniel (Be) 16 Allenberry Dr, Wilkes Barre, PA 18706

FITZSIMMONS, James (Az) 1741 North Camino Rebecca, Nogales, AZ 85621

FITZSIMMONS, James Patrick (Az) 969 W Country Club Dr, Nogales, AZ 85621

FLAGSTAD, Judith Marie (SD) 101 W Prospect Ave Apt 3, Pierre, SD 57501

FLAHERTY, Jane (SVa) 614 E 7th St, Alton, IL 62002

FLAHERTY, Jessica Barbara (Mass)

FLAHERTY, Philip John (Mass) 44 Park Ave, Whitman, MA 02382

FLAMINIO, Robert Joseph (NMich)

FLANAGAN, Carol Cole (WA) St. Barnabas' Episcopal Church, 4801 Ravensworth Rd, Annandale, VA 22003

FLANAGAN, Jakki Renee (Ct)

FLANAGAN, Michael P (USC) 104 Brockman Dr, Mauldin, SC 29662

FLANAGAN JR, R Daniel ()

FLANAGAN, Robert D (NY) PO Box 267, Bridgewater, CT 06752

FLANDERS, Alden Beaman (Mass) 145 Weyland Cir, North Andover, MA 01845

FLANDERS JR, James W (WA) 3714 Harrison St Nw, Washington, DC 20015

FLANDERS, Susan Mann (WA) Susan Flanders, 3714 Harrison St., NW, Washington, DC 20015

FLANIGEN, John Monteith (Ida) Po Box 71027, Tuscaloosa, AL 35407

FLECK, Timothy R (Me) Saint Saviour's Parish, 41 Mount Desert St, Bar Harbor, ME 04609

FLEENER SR, William Joseph (WMich) 297 W Clay Ave Apt 214, Muskegon, MI 49440

FLEENOR, David (NY) 4310 48th Ave Apt 2f, Woodside, NY 11377

FLEENOR, Ryan C (NY) 865 Madison Ave, New York, NY 10021

FLEETWOOD, Zachary William Maddrey (Eur) 28 Castle Terrace, Edinburgh, EH1 2EL, Great Britain (UK)

FLEISCHER, Marie Moorefield (NC) 8241 Allyns Landing Way Apt 304, Raleigh, NC 27615

FLEISCHER, Scott (USC) 2827 Wheat St, Columbia, SC 29205

FLEISCHMAN, Donald M (Mil) 297 N Main St, Richland Center, WI 53581

FLEMING, Carol (NI) 70865 Wayne St, Union, MI 49130

FLEMING, Christie Shelburne (WLa) PO Box 52, Bastrop, LA 71221

FLEMING JR, Huett Maxwell (Pgh) 3000 William Penn Hwy, Pittsburgh, PA 15235

FLEMING, Joan (NJ) 183 Hartley Ave., Princeton, NJ 08540

FLEMING, Linda Lee (Wyo) St Paul's Episcopal Church, PO Box 68, Dixon, WY 82323

FLEMING JR, Peter Wallace (SwFla) 1 Beach Dr SE Apt 2214, Saint Petersburg, FL 33701

FLEMING JR, Raymond Edgar (Los) 484 Cliff Dr Apt 10, Laguna Beach, CA 92651

FLEMISTER, Ernestein (SwFla) 212 W Idlewild Avenue, Tampa, FL 33604

FLEMMING, Leslie (SO) 1 Kent Dr, Athens, OH 45701

FLENTJE, Gregory Laurence (WMich) 4210 Honey Creek Ave Ne, Ada, MI 49301

FLES, Jacob C (Me) 2 Dresden Ave, Gardiner, ME 04345

FLETCHER, Margaret Ann Laurie (Vt) St. Peter's Episcopal Church, 300 Pleasant St., Bennington, VT 05201

FLETCHER JR, Richard James (WTenn) 108 N King Ave, Dyersburg, TN 38024

FLETCHER, Wayne Alexander (WLa) 500 Edgewood Dr, Pineville, LA 71360

FLETT, Carol (WA) retired, Washington, DC 20016

FLEXER, Katharine Grace (NY) 225 W 99th St, New York, NY 10025

FLICK, Robert Terry (Tex) 1410 Cambridge Dr, Friendswood, TX 77546

FLINTOM, Jack Glenn (Md) 2030 Marshall Ln, Hayes, VA 23072

FLOBERG, John (ND) Po Box 612, Fort Yates, ND 58538

FLOBERG, Sloane R (ND) 820 West Central Ave, Bismarck, ND 58501

FLOCKEN, Robin (CNY) 1721 Stanley Rd, Cazenovia, NY 13035

FLOOD, Charles Ta (Pa) 19 S 10th St, Philadelphia, PA 19107

FLOOD, James Andrew (CFla)

FLORES, Katherine Doris (Wyo) 4700 S Poplar St, Casper, WY 82601

FLORY, Carol Inez (Fla) 9645 Old Baymeadows Rd Apt 750, Jacksonville, FL 32256

FLORY, Phyllis Brannon (WK) 1551 Briargate Dr, Salina, KS 67401

FLOWERS JR, James Byrd (CGC)

FLOWERS JR, James Edgar (WLa) 946 Ockley Dr, Shreveport, LA 71106

FLOWERS, Lauren F (Ga) 3 Ridge Rd, Savannah, GA 31405

FLOWERS, Mary Miller (WA)

FLOYD JR, Charles K(amper) (Miss) 4400 King Road, Meridian, MS 39305

FLOYD, Charles Rhein (CGC) 117 Rusty Gans Dr, Panama City Beach, FL 32408

FLOYD, Donna (Tenn)

FLOYD, Michael Hinnant (DR (DomRep)) 5505 B Stuart Cir Unit B, Austin, TX 78721

FLOYD, Michael Stephen (O) 120 Ohio St, Huron, OH 44839

FLOYD, Peter M (Colo) 7408 Tudor Rd, Colorado Springs, CO 80919

FLOYD, Peter Winslow (Ct) 18 Hidden Lake Rd, Higganum, CT 06441

FLOYD, Theresa Ann (Ore) 4177 Nw Thatcher Rd, Forest Grove, OR 97116

FLY, David Kerrigan (Mo) 4400 Lindell Blvd Apt 11n, Saint Louis, MO 63108

FLYNN, Anne Regina (Kan) 21 Copperfield Ln, Charleston, IL 61920

FLYNN, Michael T (Los) 4406 El Corazon Ct, Camarillo, CA 93012

FLYNN, Peggy Rishel (Kan)

FODOR, Luke (WNY) 410 N Main St, Jamestown, NY 14701

FOERSTER III, Frederick Henry (CNY) 183 Capn Crosby Rd, Centerville, MA 02632

FOGELQUIST, Albin Hilding (Spok) 1307 Regents Blvd Apt D, Fircrest, WA 98466

FOISIE, Dawn Ann Campbell (Oly) 5757 Solomons Island Rd, Lothian, MD 20711

FOISIE, Stephen D (Oly) 228 Wall St, Camano Island, WA 98282

FOLEY, Kristen C (NJ) 2136 Woodbridge Ave, Edison, NJ 08817

FOLEY, Michael (Pgh) 5700 Forbes Ave, Pittsburgh, PA 15217

FOLEY, Theodore Archer (NJ) Christ Church, 415 Washington St, Toms River, NJ 08753

✠ **FOLTS**, James Edward (WTex) PO Box 6885, San Antonio, TX 78209

FOLTS, Jonathan (Ct) 3 Windswept Ridge Road, Ivoryton, CT 06442

FOLTS, Kimberly S (Ct) 40 Main St, Essex, CT 06426

FOLTZ, Marvin Lee (Mo) 12424 Cape Cod Dr, Saint Louis, MO 63146

✠ **FOLWELL**, William Hopkins (CFla) 600 Carolina Village Rd Unit 25, Hendersonville, NC 28792

FONCREE, Rose Mary Ivas (Miss) 4526 Meadow Hill Road, Jackson, MS 39206

FONDER SR, Kim Michael (SD) Holy Comforter/Messiah, PO Box 242, Lower Brule, SD 57548

FONES, Peter Alden (Ore) 723 S. 48th St, Springfield, OR 97478

FOOSE, Elizabeth Boutwell (Miss) 6697 Bee Lake Rd, Tchula, MS 39169

FOOTE, Beth (Cal) 705 Grand St, Alameda, CA 94501

FOOTE, Margaret Lloyd Foster (SO) 334 Burns Ave, Wyoming, OH 45215

FOOTE, Roger (SO) 7 E Interwood Pl, Cincinnati, OH 45220

FOOTE, Stephen Williams (Me) 574 Turner Rd, Bremen, ME 04551

FORAKER, Greg (Colo) St Luke's Episc Ch, 2000 Stover St, Fort Collins, CO 80525

FORAKER-THOMPSON, Jane (Nev) P.O. Box 2665, Gardnerville, NV 89410

FORBES, David Reineman (Cal) 22 Delmar St, San Francisco, CA 94117

FORBES, Elizabeth Faye (Ga) 3321 Wheeler Rd, Augusta, GA 30909

FORBES, Mark S (Ala) 156 Lavender Bloom Loop, Mooresville, NC 28115

FORBES, Michael Philip (Minn) 402 31st St Ne Apt 224, Rochester, MN 55906

FORD, Berkley (SVa) 68 Market Street, Onancock, VA 23417

FORD, Charles Allan (NY) 205 Stone Rd, West Hurley, NY 12491

FORD, Cheri Lynn (NMich) Rr 2 Box 939-A, Newberry, MI 49868

FORD, Denis B (Colo) 3231 Olive St., Jacksonville, FL 32207

FORD, Janet Carol (Nev)

FORD, Janice Celeste (WMass)

FORD, Joan B (SanD) 838 4th St, Encinitas, CA 92024

FORD, Joann (Colo) 3231 Olive St, Jacksonville, FL 32207

FORD, John Mark (Ala) PO Box 614, Chelsea, AL 35043

FORD, Richard Barlow (Cal) 2165 West Dry Creek Road, Healdsburg, CA 95448

FORD, Robert Lawrence (Oly) PO Box 3276, Bellevue, WA 98009

FORD, Stanley Eugene (Spok)

FORD, Steven E (NMich) Rr 2 Box 939-A, Newberry, MI 49868

FORD, Steven R (Az) 3436 N 43rd Pl, Phoenix, AZ 85018

FORDHAM, James Frederick (EC) 1579 Bayview Rd, Bath, NC 27808

FOREMAN JR, Harold Vandon (Ala) 3013 Boundary Oaks Dr SE, Owens Cross Roads, AL 35763

FORESMAN, R Scott (Ia) Po Box 306, Bishop, CA 93515

FORHAN, Carol Lynn (Spok) 9327 E Leavenworth Rd, Leavenworth, WA 98826

FORINASH JR, Joseph Lynn (Colo) PO Box 1026, Eagle, CO 81631

FORMAN, John P (Oly) 1005 S.W. 152nd Street, Burien, WA 98166

FORNALIK, Barbara Horn (Roch) 1130 Webster Rd, Webster, NY 14580

FORNARO, Frank (Mass) 11 Alaska Ave, Bedford, MA 01730

FORNEA, Stanley Wayne (EC) 2111 Jefferson Davis Hwy, Apt 603S, Arlington, VA 22202

FORNEY, John C (Los) 316 W Green St., Claremont, CA 91711

FORREST, Louise Louise (Mass) 41 Hall Ave, Watertown, MA 02472

FORREST, Marlene E (Va)

FORREST, William (FdL) 56500 Abbey Rd, Three Rivers, MI 49093

FORREST, William Clifford (Az) 24922 S Lakewood Dr, Sun Lakes, AZ 85248

FORRESTER, Shelley (Okla) St. Andrew's Church, PO Box 1256, 1313 SW D Ave, Lawton, OK 73502

FORSHAW, Lee (Ct) 2000 Main St, Stratford, CT 06615

FORSYTHE, Margaret Ann Kroy (NJ) 687 Donald Dr S, Bridgewater, NJ 08807

FORSYTHE, Mary Louise (Neb) 420 Shorewood Ln, Waterloo, NE 68069

FORTE, Jeanne (The Episcopal NCal) 700 Wellfleet Dr, Vallejo, CA 94591

FORTI, Nicholas (Va) 1700 University Ave, Charlottesville, VA 22903

FORTNER, Marian Dulaney (Miss) 509 W Pine St, Hattiesburg, MS 39401

FORTUNA, Lisa (Mass) Christ Church Iglesia San Juan, 1220 River St, Hyde Park, MA 02136

FORTUNA, Virgilio (Mass) 2112 County St, Somerset, MA 02726

FORTUNATO, Susan (NY) 82 Ehrhardt Rd, Pearl River, NY 10965

FOSS, Charlie (USC) 1646 SW Spence Ave, Troutdale, OR 97060

FOSTER III, Andrew William (NY) 790 Plymouth Rd, Claremont, CA 91711

FOSTER, Craig Arthur (SO) 508 Thistle Dr, Delaware, OH 43015

FOSTER, Guy Roland (NY) 12408 Cambridge Village Loop, Apex, NC 27502

FOSTER, Katharine K (SO) 7919 N Coolville Ridge Rd, Athens, OH 45701

FOSTER JR, Kenneth Earl (Mil) 1418 Valley Dr, Wisconsin Dells, WI 53965

FOSTER, Margaret Reidpath (WNY) 1088 Delaware Ave Apt 5a, Buffalo, NY 14209

FOSTER, Pamela LaMotte (Mass) 19 Warren Point Rd, Wareham, MA 02571

FOSTER, Penelope Hope (WNY) 54 Delaware Rd, Kenmore, NY 14217

FOSTER, Randal Arthur (NC) 105 Pettingill Pl, Southern Pines, NC 28387

FOSTER, Simon (LI) 808 Driggs Ave Apt 5B, Brooklyn, NY 11211

FOSTER, Steve Leslie (LI) 13728 244th St, Rosedale, NY 11422

FOSTER, Todd E (NJ)

FOSTER, Willis Renard (SVa) 228 Halifax St, Petersburg, VA 23803

FOTCH JR, Charlton Harvey (Cal) 681 S Eliseo Dr, Greenbrae, CA 94904

FOTINOS, Dennis George (Tex) 248 Birchbark Dr., Mills River, NC 28759

FOUGHTY, Donna (Va) 7414 Heatherfield Ln, Alexandria, VA 22315

FOUKE, Scherry Vickery (ETenn) 1601 Forest Dr, Morristown, TN 37814

FOULKE, Mary Lova (NY) 521 West 126th Street, New York, NY 10027

FOUNTAIN, Timothy L (SD) 2707 W. 33rd St, Sioux Falls, SD 57105

FOUT, Jason A (WMich) 591 Sheridan Ave, Bexley, OH 43209

FOUTS, Guy (WA) 603 Ramapo Ave, Pompton Lakes, NJ 07442

FOWLE, Elizabeth Heller (WMass) 15 Old Hancock Rd., Hancock, NH 03449

FOWLER, Anne Carroll (Mass) 39 Prospect Street, Portland, ME 04103

FOWLER, Arlen Lowery (Okla) 817 Virginia Ln, Ardmore, OK 73401

FOWLER, Connetta Bertrand (NwT) 430 Dallas St, Big Spring, TX 79720

FOWLER, Daniel Lewis (Oly) 4335 NE Rhodes End Rd, Bainbridge Island, WA 98110

FOWLER III, Robert (Ala) St Margaret's Episcopal Church, 606 Newnan St, Carrollton, GA 30117

FOWLER, Stanley Gordon (Oly) 111 Ne 80th St, Seattle, WA 98115

FOWLER IV, William Young (Tex) Po Box 292, Buda, TX 78610

FOWLKES, Tyrone (NC) 530 W Fullerton Pkwy, Chicago, IL 60614

FOX, Carol Rogers (NY) 312 West 22nd Street, New York, NY 10011

FOX, Cheryl Lynn (NY) 175 9th Ave # 262, New York, NY 10011

FOX, David Coblentz (Okla) 2455 Sulphur Creek St, Cody, WY 82414

FOX, Don (Cal) 185 Baltimore Way, San Francisco, CA 94112

FOX III, Frederick Carl (Nwk) 441 Lockhart Mountain Rd Unit 4, Lake George, NY 12845

FOX, Jed (Oly) 6345 Wydown Blvd, Saint Louis, MO 63105

FOX, Loren Charles (CFla) Tang-Lin, Minden Road, 248816, Singapore

FOX, Matthew Timothy (Cal) 287 17th St Ste 400, Oakland, CA 94612

FOX, R. Steven (U) 6230 Hyderabad Pl., Dulles, VA 20189

FOX, Richard George (Mil) South 24 West 26835 Apache Pass, South 24 W 26835 Apache Pass, Waukesha, WI 53188

FOX, Ronald Napoleon (SeFla) 3464 Oak Ave, Miami, FL 33133

FOX, Sarah (Mich) 8500 Jackson Square Blvd Apt 5D, Shreveport, LA 71115

FOX, Stephanie Donaldson (Ark) 20900 Chenal Pkwy, Little Rock, AR 72223

FOX, Susann (Pa) 76 S Forge Manor Dr, Phoenixville, PA 19460

FOX SR, Wesley D (ND) HC 2, Box 176, Garrison, ND 58540

FOXWORTH, George Marion (The Episcopal NCal) 4338 Walali Way, Fair Oaks, CA 95628

FOXX, Louis N (Mass) 397 Putnam Ave., Cambridge, MA 02139

✠ **FRADE**, Leo (SeFla) 525 NE 15th St, Miami, FL 33132

FRAIOLI, Karen Ann (Mass) 20 Rhodes Ave, Sharon, MA 02067

FRALEY, Anne (Ct) 1500 Hickory Ridge Rd, Lebanon, TN 37087

FRANCE JR, Andrew Menaris (CPa) 651 Harding Ave, Williamsport, PA 17701

FRANCES, Martha (Tex) 6405 Westward #65, Houston, TX 77081

FRANCIS SR, Alric H (VI) PO Box 7974, Christiansted, VI 00823

FRANCIS, Desmond (Alb) 2011 Trotter Ln, Bloomington, IL 61704

FRANCIS, James Woodcock (Mich) 1404 Joliet Pl, Detroit, MI 48207

FRANCIS, John Robert (Be) 435 Court St, P.O. Box 1094, Reading, PA 19603

FRANCIS, Mary Jane Jane (Oly) 725 9th Ave., Apt. 2109, Seattle, WA 98104

FRANCISCO VILAR, Jose (PR)

FRANCKS, Robert Christopher (NY) 360 W 21st St, New York, NY 10011

FRANCO ESTEVEZ, Juan Bautista (PR) Iglesia Episcopal Puertorriquena, PO Box 902, Saint Just, PR 00978

FRANCOIS, Yvan (Hai) Box 1309, Port-Au-Prince, Haiti

FRANDSEN, Charles Frederick (WMich) 509 Ship St, Saint Joseph, MI 49085

FRANK, Anna (Ak) 1578 Bridgewater Dr, Fairbanks, AK 99709

FRANK, Beth (O) New Life Episcopal Church, 13188 Church Ave NW, Uniontown, OH 44685

FRANK, Richard Lloyd (U) 13640 N 21st Ave, Phoenix, AZ 85029

FRANK, Travis Ray (Ark) 14 Haslingden Ln, Bella Vista, AR 72715

FRANK JR, William George (Va) 11 Wakefield Dr Apt 2004, Asheville, NC 28803

FRANKEN, Robert Anton (Colo) PO Box 2073, 101 E Main Street, Unit 204, Frisco, CO 80443

FRANKFURT, Dawn M (Kan) 3750 E Douglas Ave, Wichita, KS 67208

FRANKLIN, Ann Hope (Mass) 143 Gillespie Circle, Brevard, NC 28712

FRANKLIN, Beth (Va) 301 E 8th St, Austin, TX 78701

FRANKLIN III, Gus Lee (Spr) 6508 Willow Springs Rd, Springfield, IL 62712

FRANKLIN III, James (NC) Winston Salem Young Adult Ministry, PO Box 7204, Winston Salem, NC 27109

FRANKLIN, John Thomas (Mich)

✠ **FRANKLIN**, Ralph William (WNY) 1064 Brighton Road, Tonawanda, NY 14150

FRANKLIN, Sally (USC) 7128 Caggy Ln, Fort Mill, SC 29707

FRANKLIN-VAUGHN, Robyn (WA) 319 Bryant St Ne, Washington, DC 20002

FRANKS, Laurence Edward Alexander (FdL) 299 Corey St, Boston, MA 02132

FRANSON, Marna (Ark)

FRANTZ-DALE, Heidi Hallett (NH) 247 Pound Road, Madison, NH 03849

FRANZ, Marcia Wheatley (NMich)

FRASER, Anders (Miss) St. Paul's Episcopal Church, P.O. Box 1225, Corinth, MS 38835

FRASER, Richard Trent (Colo) 1400 S University Blvd, Denver, CO 80210

FRASER, Thomas A (Chi) 60 Akenside Rd, Riverside, IL 60546

FRASER SR, William Carson (ETenn) 4487 Post Place, #129, Nashville, TN 37205

FRAUSTO, Nancy Aide (Los) 861 S Mariposa Ave, Los Angeles, CA 90005

FRAZELLE, David C (NC) 304 E Franklin St, Chapel Hill, NC 27514

FRAZER, Candice Burk (Ala) St John's Episcopal Church, 113 Madison Ave, Montgomery, AL 36104

FRAZIER JR, Allie Washington (SVa) 1124 Dryden Lane, Charlottesville, VA 22903

FRAZIER, John T (EC) 5324 Bluewater Pl, Fayetteville, NC 28311

FRAZIER, Jonathan E (WMo) 422 W 111th Ter, Kansas City, MO 64114

FRAZIER, Mark (SwVa) 905 Highland Ave, Bristol, VA 24201

FRAZIER, Raymond Malcom (SwFla) 8017 Fountain Ave, Tampa, FL 33615

FREARSON, Andrew Richard (At) 3136 Lynnray Dr, Doraville, GA 30340

FREDERIC, Eliot Garrison (Eas) 51 Columbine Ave N, Hampton Bays, NY 11946

FREDERICK, John Bassett Moore (Ct) 32 Chestnut St, Princeton, NJ 08542

FREDERICK, Robert John (Md) 1930 Brookdale Rd, Baltimore, MD 21244

FREDERICK, Sherman Richardson (Nev) 2724 Brienza Way, Las Vegas, NV 89117

FREDERICK, Warren Charles (WMass) 19 Rydal St, Worcester, MA 01602

FREDERIKSEN III, Victor (EC) Po Box 7672, Wilmington, NC 28406

FREDHOLM, Everett Leonard (Tex) 201 Nicholas Dr, Asheville, NC 28806

FREDIE JR, Julian Von Kessel (Mass)

FREDRICK, Lawrence Edward (EO) 1220 Tasman Dr Spc 1k, Sunnyvale, CA 94089

FREDRICKSON, David A (Mass) 149 Court Street, Plymouth, MA 02360

FREE JR, Horace D (NY) PO Box 125, Johns Island, SC 29457

FREEBERN, Douglas Wayne (Okla) 210 E 9th St, Bartlesville, OK 74003

FREEMAN, Ashley B (La)

FREEMAN, Bruce A (Los) 2944 Erie Ave, Cincinnati, OH 45208

FREEMAN JR, De (CGC) St James Church, 860 N Section St, Fairhope, AL 36532

FREEMAN, Diana G (Dal) 6400 Stonebrook Pkwy, Frisco, TX 75034

FREEMAN, John (WMass)

FREEMAN, Karen Lynn (The Episcopal NCal) 1405 Kentucky St, Fairfield, CA 94533

FREEMAN, Len (Minn) 190 Cygnet Pl, Long Lake, MN 55356

FREEMAN, Lindsay Hardin (Minn) 190 Cygnet Pl, Long Lake, MN 55356

FREEMAN, Monroe (NC) 1706 Highlands Vw SE, Smyrna, GA 30082

FREEMAN JR, Norman (Los) St George's Church And Academy, 23802 Avenida de la Carlota, Laguna Hills, CA 92653

FREEMAN, Reed H (Fla) 12614 Muirfield Blvd S, Jacksonville, FL 32225

FREEMAN, Sarah (Colo) 726 W Elati Cir, Littleton, CO 80120

FREEMAN, Sollace Mitchell (At) 5194 Glenstone Ct, Gainesville, GA 30504

FREEMAN, T.J. (NI) 611 W Berry St, Fort Wayne, IN 46802

FREES, Mooydeen Claire (SO) 3826 Portrush Way, Amelia, OH 45102

FREGEAU, Stephen Alfred (Mass) 7719 SE Sugar Sand Cir, Hobe Sound, FL 33455

FREGOSO, Krista (Cal) 1707 Gouldin Rd, Oakland, CA 94611

FREIRE-SOLORZANO, Luis Hernan (EcuC) Barrio El Tambo, Sector Bomba De Aqua, Pelileo, 24, Ecuador

FRENCH, Alan C (NJ) 237 Summer Winds Cir, Aiken, SC 29803

FRENCH, Clarke (NC) 814 Churchill Dr, Chapel Hill, NC 27517

FRENCH, Dick (Oly) 23500 Cristo Rey Dr Unit 520G, Cupertino, CA 95014

FRENCH, Jonathan D (CFla) 2304 SE 12th ST, Ocala, FL 34471

FRENCH, Peter (NJ) 53 University Pl., Princeton, NJ 08540

FRENCH, Sally (NC) 407 E. Seneca St., Manlius, NY 13104

FRENS, Mary Jean (WMich) 934 Clubview Dr, Fremont, MI 49412

FRENSLEY, James Monroe (Colo) 3506 Armstrong Ave, Dallas, TX 75205

FREW, Randolph Lloyd (NY) 332 Bleecker St #K80, New York, NY 10014

FREY, Louane Florence Virgilio (NC) 801 Footbridge Pl, Cary, NC 27519

FREY, Matthew Vincent (WTex) 2620 Crestview Dr, Edinburg, TX 78539

FREY, Paul Anthony (WTex) 139 Kentucky St, Laredo, TX 78041

✠ **FREY**, William Carl (Colo) 23315 Eagle Gap, San Antonio, TX 78255

FRIAS, Miguel (Chi) 941 W Lawrence Ave, Chicago, IL 60640

FRIBOURGH, Cindy (Ark) 11123 Bainbridge Dr, Little Rock, AR 72212

FRICK, Matthew M (Dal) 2627 Horseshoe Dr, Alexandria, LA 71301

FRIDAY, Rawlin (Wyo)

FRIDAY, Roxanne L (Wyo)

FRIEDEL, James (WTex) 11905 E Maple Dr, Claremore, OK 74019

FRIEDMAN, Anna Russell (Ala) PO Box 27, Minter, AL 36761

FRIEDMAN, Maurice Lane (WTex) 4934 Lakeway Dr, Brownsville, TX 78520

FRIEDRICH, James Louis (Los) 4685 Taylor Ave Ne, Bainbridge Island, WA 98110

FRIEDRICH JR, Robert E (Ct) 23 Friend Ct, Wenham, MA 01984

FRIEND, Robert Douglas (Va) 4011 College Valley Ct, Richmond, VA 23233

FRIESE JR, Walter Edward (WLa) 107 Shady Ave., Pineville, LA 71360

FRINK, James Phillip (RI) 3a Grouse Trl, Smithfield, RI 02917

FRISCH, Floyd Charles (ECR) 2 N Santa Cruz Ave, Los Gatos, CA 95030

FRITCH, Charles Oscar (CFla) 324 S Lost Lake Ln, Casselberry, FL 32707

FRITSCH, Andrew John (WMo) 3702 Poplar Dr, Joplin, MO 64804

FRITSCH, Peter Louis (Ore) 6310 W Ford Ave, Las Vegas, NV 89139

FRITSCHE, Janet Yvonne (NMich) 122 Hunter Rd, Iron River, MI 49935

FRITSCHNER, Annie (WNC) Po Box 2818, Hendersonville, NC 28793

FRITSCHNER, John (Ky) Church of the Advent, 901 Baxter Ave, Louisville, KY 40204

FRITTS, John Clinton (WTex) St Paul's Episcopal Church, PO Box 1148, Brady, TX 76825

FRITTS, Julia Anne (Ct) 702 Brookwood Rd, Baltimore, MD 21229

FRITZ, Janice Vary (CPa) 109 Hope Dr, Boiling Springs, PA 17007

FRITZ, Susan Cheryl (WA) 7 Potomac Ave, Indian Head, MD 20640

FRIZZELL, Judith Ann (Dal) 5200 Fairway Circle, Granbury, TX 76049

FRNKA, Virginia H (WTex) 314 W Gayle St, Edna, TX 77957

FROEHLICH, Burt H (SeFla) 406-B Coopers Cove Rd, St Augustine, FL 32095

FROEHLICH, Meghan F (O) Presiding Bishop's Staff, 815 2nd Ave, New York, NY 10017

FROILAND, Paul Vincent (Minn) 12525 Porcupine Ct, Eden Prairie, MN 55344

FROLICK, Betty Roberson (NI) 6334 Bennington Dr, Fort Wayne, IN 46815

FROLICK, Paul (CNY) St Matthew's Episcopal Chruch, 300 Vine St, Liverpool, NY 13088

FROMBERG, Paul D (Cal) 500 De Haro Street, San Francisco, CA 94107

FRONTJES, Rich (Chi) 910 Normal Rd, DeKalb, IL 60115

FROST, Gregory Hayden (Los) 18354 Superior St, Northridge, CA 91325

FROST, Jeffrey Louis (Cal) Saint Timothy's Church, 1550 Diablo Rd, Danville, CA 94526

FROST-PHILLIPS, Lisa (NC) 128 Creekview Cir, Carrboro, NC 27510

FROTHINGHAM, Christen Struthers (Mass) 6 Sunset Ave, North Reading, MA 01864

FROWE, Jeanne Shelton (Nev) 384 Sunset Dr, Reno, NV 89703

FROYEN, Jeremy C (Chi) St John the Evangelist, 2640 Park Dr, Flossmoor, IL 60422

FRUEHWIRTH, Robert Alan (FdL) 66 Ella Road, Norwich, NR1 4BS, Great Britain (UK)

FRY, Gwenneth Jeri (Ark) 7604 Apache Road, Little Rock, AR 72205

FRY, Lisa D (Me) 1000 N Mississippi St, Little Rock, AR 72207

FRY III, William Nall (WTenn) 10 N Highland St, Memphis, TN 38111

FRYE, Don Jay (Chi) 2843 Gypsum Cir, Naperville, IL 60564

FRYE, Linda Lou (Eau) 21836 Gladestone Ave, Tomah, WI 54660

FULFORD, David Edward (NwPa)

FULGHUM, Charles Benjamin (At) 759 Loridans Dr Ne, Atlanta, GA 30342

FULGHUM, Peter Clopper (Md) 13007 Still Meadow Rd, Smithsburg, MD 21783

FULGONI, Dina Loreen (Los) PO Box 1681, Big Bear Lake, CA 92315

FULK, Michael Thomas (WTex) 909 S. Darling St., Angola, IN 46703

FULKS, William B (Pa) 112 Elite Hts, Hurricane, WV 25526

FULLER, Betty WL Works (WTex) 823 S Water St Apt 3G, Corpus Christi, TX 78401

FULLER, Edward Beaty (At) 3826 Courtyard Drive, Atlanta, GA 30339

FULLER JR, Frank (WLa)

FULLER III, Frank E (Tex) 823 S Water St #3G, Corpus Christi, TX 78401

FULLER, Glen C (WNY)

FULLER, Jan (SwVa) 2247 Saddle Club Rd, Burlington, NC 27215

FULLER, John Paul (Los) 940 Ivywood Dr, Oxnard, CA 93030

FULLER, Lynnette Burley (NJ) 8 Sargent Street, #4, Nutley, NJ 07110

FULLER SR, Steven George (Vt) 10 South St # 5101, Bellows Falls, VT 05101

FULLER, Walter Harry (LI) 1692 Bellmore Ave, North Bellmore, NY 11710

FULLMER, Janet (Colo) 1700 Esther Way, The Dalles, OR 97058

FULOP, Timothy Earl (SVa)

FULTON, Bill (Oly) 32 NE Tracy Hill Way, Bremerton, WA 98311

FULTON JR, Charles Britton (Fla) 1580 Murdock Rd, Marietta, GA 30062

FULTON III, Charles Newell (NY) 815 2nd Ave, New York, NY 10017

FULTON, Jennifer (NI)

FULTON, John Gary (EC) 307 N Main St, Farmville, NC 27828

FULTON, Nancy Casey (WMich) 807 South University, Mt Pleasant, MI 48858

FULTON, Norman Hamilton (NY) Macaulay Road, Rd #2, Katonah, NY 10536

FULTON, Sharline Alahverde (Pa) 1207 Foulkeways, Gwynedd, PA 19436

FUNK, Delmar Gerald (Neb) 3668 - 18th, Columbus, NE 68601

FUNK, Jeffrey Lawrence (Be) 46 S Laurel St, Hazleton, PA 18201

FUNK, Kathyleen Allen (Nev) PO Box 1385, Pahrump, NV 89041

FUNK, Nicholas (Dal) 8320 Jack Finney Blvd, Greenville, TX 75402

FUNKHOUSER, David Franklin (Pa) 456 66th St, Oakland, CA 94609

FUNSTON, A Patrick K (Kan) 601 Poyntz Avenue, Manhattan, KS 66502

FUNSTON, Charles Eric (O) St. Paul's Episcopal Church, 317 E. Liberty Street, Medina, OH 44256

FURLOW, Mark D (SwVa)

FURMAN, James Edmund (Los) 13131 Moorpark St Apt 412, Sherman Oaks, CA 91423

FURNISS III, Robert Hosmer (Minn) 2132 Cameron Dr, Woodbury, MN 55125

FURRER, Thomas (Ct) 5 Trout Drive, Granby, CT 06035

FUSSELL, Stacey Marie (NwPa) 462 Congress St, Bradford, PA 16701

G

GABAUD, Pierre Simpson (SeFla) St Paul et Les Martyrs d'Haiti, 6744 N Miami Ave, Miami, FL 33150

GABB, James Neil (Neb) 21724 Oldgate Rd, Elkhorn, NE 68022

GABBARD, Justin E (Lex)

GABEL, Mark Francis (Fla) 5139 Marbella Isle Dr, Orlando, FL 32837

GABLE, David Lee (Nwk) 24 Harmony Dr, Pt Jefferson Station, NY 11776

GABLE, Stephen Louis (Ind) 1045 E Sassafras Cir, 1129 Linden Dr, Bloomington, IN 47408

GADDIS, Mona Elaine (WNY) 4275 Harris Hill Rd, Williamsville, NY 14221

GADDY, Anna Lee (RG) Po Box 648, Ruidoso Downs, NM 88346

GADSDEN, Carol D (NY) 168 W Boston Post Rd, Mamaroneck, NY 10543

GAEDE, Lee A (Chi) 342 Custer Ave. Apt. 2, Evanston, IL 60202

GAEDE, Sarah (Ala) 830 Willingham Rd, Florence, AL 35630

GAESTEL, Bob (Los) 1100 Avenue 64, Pasadena, CA 91105

GAFFORD, Donna Elizabeth Goodman (Ala) 38 Longview Ct, Seale, AL 36875

GAFFORD, Happy Lawton (CFla) 1330 Arthur St, Orlando, FL 32804

GAFNEY, Wilda Clydette (Pa) 7301 Germantown Ave, Philadelphia, PA 19119

GAFOUR, Ayyoubawaga Bushara (Colo) Sudanese Community Church, 1350 Washington St, Denver, CO 80203

GAGE, Bartlett Wright (Ct) 26 Edmond St, Darien, CT 06820

GAGE, Nancy Elizabeth (Ct) Grace Church, 5958 Main St, Trumbull, CT 06611

GAHAGAN, Susan Elisabeth (Ga) 1802 Abercorn St, Savannah, GA 31401

GAHAN III, W(Illiam) Patrick (WTex) Christ Episcopal Church, 510 Belknap Pl, San Antonio, TX 78212

GAHLER, Robert Edward (NY) 67 Woodmere Rd, Stamford, CT 06905

GAILLARD, Ann (Ore)

GAINES, Elizabeth Juliet (The Episcopal NCal)

GAINES, Mary Moore Thompson (Cal) 128 Beaumont Ave, San Francisco, CA 94118

GAISER, Ted J (Me) 641 Allen Ave, Portland, ME 04103

GAITHER, Gayle Lee (Spok) 416 E Nelson Rd, Moses Lake, WA 98837

GALAGAN, Christine Kay (Wyo) PO Box 1718, Cody, WY 82414

GALANTOWICZ, Deena McHenry (Fla) 49 Ocean Ct, Saint Augustine, FL 32080

GALAZ, Ernest M (Az) 969 W Country Club Dr, Nogales, AZ 85621

GALBREATH, Janet Louise (CFla) 01236 Miller Blvd, Fruitland Park, FL 34731

GALEANO FRANCO, Gustavo Adolfo (SeFla)

GALEY, Hilary (NMich)

GALEY, Patrick (NMich)

GALGANO, Hollis H (NY) 311 Huguenot St, New Rochelle, NY 10801

GALGANOWICZ, Henry (Pa) 432 Bluestone Ct, PO Box 714, Lake Harmony, PA 18624

GALICIA, Kathie (Episcopal SJ) 3308 Swallow Dr, Modesto, CA 95356

GALINDO-PAZ, Elvia Maria (Hond)

GALIPEAU, Steven Arthur (Los) 8805 Azul Drive, West Hills, CA 91304

✠ **GALLAGHER**, Carol (NY) 40 Charlotte St, Haverhill, MA 01830

GALLAGHER, Daniel P (NY) 29 Halcyon Rd, Millbrook, NY 12545

GALLAGHER, Gerald J (NY) 1001 Leesburg Dr, Leland, NC 28451

GALLAGHER, John Merrill (Cal) 212 Riviera Cir, Larkspur, CA 94939

GALLAGHER, Mary Ellen Turner (Ida) 13118 W Picadilly St, Boise, ID 83713

GALLAGHER, Nancy Elizabeth (Ore) 1800 Lakewood Ct, Spc 58, Eugene, OR 97402

GALLAGHER, Patricia Marie-Portley (Ct) 9134 Town Walk Dr, Hamden, CT 06518

GALLAGHER, Robert A (Me) 1640 18th Ave, Apt 2, Seattle, WA 98122

GALLAGHER, Robert Joseph (Mich) 78 Nason St, Maynard, MA 01754

GALLARDO-LUCENA, Antonio Jose (Los) 132 N Euclid Ave, Pasadena, CA 91101

GALLEHER, Stephen C (Nwk) 7855 Kennedy Blvd E, Apt. 21D, North Bergen, NJ 07047

GALLETLY, David P (NwT) 1412 W Illinois Ave, Midland, TX 79701
GALLIGAN, Joseph Edward (Wyo) PO Box 950, Thermopolis, WY 82443
GALLOWAY, David Alan (At) 845 Edgewater Dr Nw, Atlanta, GA 30328
GALLOWAY, Denise Althea (LI) 35 Cathedral Ave, Garden City, NY 11530
GALLOWAY, Richard Kent (NC) 120 Mauldin Rd, Greenville, SC 29605
GALVIN, Kathleen M (Ore) 2293 NW Mcgarey Dr, McMinnville, OR 97128
GALVIN, Mike Joseph (Ind) 9621 Claymount Ln, Fishers, IN 46037
GAMBER, Jenifer Chestora (WA) 4700 Whitehaven Pkwy NW, Washington, DC 20007
GAMBLE, Deborah Elizabeth (SO) 4234 Hamilton Ave, Cincinnati, OH 45223
GAMBLE, John Robert (SwFla) 1005 Sleepy Hollow Rd, Venice, FL 34285
GAMBLE, Robert David (Ia) ul. Pasieka 24, Poznan, 61657, Poland
GAMBLING, Paul (SanD) 5079 E 30th Pl, Yuma, AZ 85365
GAMBRILL, James Howard (Nwk) PO Box 1929, York Beach, ME 03910
GAME, Dick (At) Trinity Episcopal Church, 1130 First Ave, Columbus, GA 31901
GAMEZ-CARDONA, Rosa Angelica (Hond)
GAMMONS JR, Edward Babson (NJ) 7 Oak St, Warren, RI 02885
GANDARA-PEREA, José Roberto (Oly) PO Box 8, Eastsound, WA 98245
GANDELL, Dahn Dorann Dean (Roch) 21 Warwick Dr, Fairport, NY 14450
GANDIYA, Leonard F (Va) 5486 Saint Pauls Rd, King George, VA 22485
GANN, Judith Fara Walsman (Okla) 6335 S 72nd East Ave, Tulsa, OK 74133
GANNON, Kathleen (SeFla) 2014 Alta Meadows Ln Apt 302, Delray Beach, FL 33444
GANNON, William Sawyer (Nwk) 11 French Dr, Bedford, NH 03110
GANTER, G David (Vt) 12 Beechwood Lane, Jericho, VT 05465
GANTER-TOBACK, Gail Sage (NY) 32 Center St, New Paltz, NY 12561
GANTZ, Jay John (EMich) 10095 E Coldwater Rd, Davison, MI 48423
GARAFALO, Robert Christopher (Los) 19988 Promenade Cir, Riverside, CA 92508
GARBARINO, Harold William (Mass) 2038 Laurel Park Hwy, Laurel Park, NC 29739
GARCEAU, John Earle (Alb) 2050 N San Clemente Rd, Palm Springs, CA 92262
GARCES TORRES, Gilberto Goen (PR) Iglesia Episcopal Puertorriquena, PO Box 902, Saint Just, PR 00978
GARCIA, Carlos Alberto ()

GARCIA, Christine Joyce (Va) 1704 W Laburnum Ave, Richmond, VA 23227
GARCIA, Christopher (Md) Emmanuel Church, Greenwood Parish, PO Box 38, Greenwood, VA 22943
GARCIA, David Allen (PR) 165 Hoyt St, Brooklyn, NY 11217
GARCIA, Emily J (Mass) 379 Hammond St, Chestnut Hill, MA 02467
GARCIA JR, Francisco J (Los) Holy Faith Episcopal Church, 260 N Locust St, Inglewood, CA 90301
GARCIA, Hope Jufiar (ECR) Po Box 3994, Salinas, CA 93912
GARCIA, Michael George (Az)
GARCIA, Ruth Anne (NY) Grace Episcopal Church, 116 City Island Avenue, Bronx, NY 10464
GARCIA, Sixto Rafael (SeFla) 150 SW 13th Ave, Miami, FL 33135
GARCIA, Teodosio R (HB)
GARCIA-APONTE, Jorge (PR)
GARCIA CARDENAS, Pastor Elias (Colom)
GARCIA CORREA, Luis Alberto (DR (DomRep))
GARCIA DE JESUS, Juan (PR)
GARCIA DE LOS SANTOS, Ramon Antonio (DR (DomRep)) Guarionex #19, Ensanche Quisqueya, La Romana, Dominican Republic
GARCIA-PEREZ, Jose Rafael (PR)
GARCIA-TUIRAN, Carlos Alfredo (SanD) 2660 Hardy Drive, Lemon Grove, CA 91945
GARD, Mary Anne (Ore) 147 NW 19th Ave, Portland, OR 97209
GARDE, Mary Ann (LI) 573 Roanoke Ave, Riverhead, NY 11901
GARDNER, Albutt Lorian (Pa) 600 E. Cathedral Rd., # H-304, Philadelphia, PA 19128
GARDNER, Anne (Mass) Phillips Academy, 180 Main Street, Andover, MA 01810
GARDNER, Bruce Norman (Eau) 221 Twin Oak Dr, Altoona, WI 54720
GARDNER, Calvin George (SVa) 1405 Bruton Ln, Virginia Beach, VA 23451
GARDNER, Carol Hartsfield (WTenn) 215 Windsor Terrace Dr, Nashville, TN 37221
GARDNER, Daniel Wayne (EO) 571 Yakima St S, Vale, OR 97918
GARDNER, Edward Morgan (WNC) 118 Clubwood Ct, Asheville, NC 28803
GARDNER, Elizabeth (WA) St John's Church, 6715 Georgetown Pike, McLean, VA 22101
GARDNER, Este (Cal) 1105 High Ct, Berkeley, CA 94708
GARDNER, E Ugene Clifton (Dal) 6505 Brook Lake Dr., Dallas, TX 75248
GARDNER, Harry Huey (Ala) 1910 12th Ave. South, Birmingham, AL 35205

GARDNER, James Edward (CPa) 839 Fraternity Rd, Lewisburg, PA 17837
GARDNER III, James Wynn (Ala) 61 Gramercy Park N Apt 201, New York, NY 10010
GARDNER, Joan Margiotta (ECR) 1970 Cerra Vista Dr, Hollister, CA 95023
GARDNER, John (Cal) 1340 Dolores St, San Francisco, CA 94110
GARDNER, John (Pa) Ch Of The Ascension & Holy Trinity, 420 W 18th St, Pueblo, CO 81003
GARDNER, Mark William (Los) 1031 Lanza Ct, San Marcos, CA 92078
GARDNER, Randal B (Cal) 769 Joaquin Ave, San Leandro, CA 94577
GARDNER, Van (Md) 89 Murdock Rd, Baltimore, MD 21212
GARDNER-SMITH, Fran (Va) 2217 Koa Ct, Antioch, CA 94509
GARFIELD, Elizabeth Ann (Colo) St Luke's Episcopal Church, 1270 Poplar St, Denver, CO 80220
GARFIELD, Liston Alphonso (Ala) 2060 Mohican Dr, Auburn, AL 36879
GARGIULO, Mariano (Nwk) 384 Hilltop Ave # 7605, Leonia, NJ 07605
GARLAND III, John G (Tex) 251 E Lake Brantley Dr, Longwood, FL 32779
GARMA, Joann Marie (La) 1014 Marigny Ave, Mandeville, LA 70448
GARMAN, Cynthia (Mich) 426 Cottonwood Ln., Saline, MI 48176
GARNER, Evan D (Ark) 2411 13th St SE, Decatur, AL 35601
GARNER, Jeffery Ray (CGC)
GARNER, Mary P (Eas) 302 S Liberty St, Centreville, MD 21617
GARNER, Terry (Mil) 10328 N Stanford Dr, Mequon, WI 53097
GARNIER, Maryellen (The Episcopal NCal) 1800 Wildcat Blvd, Rocklin, CA 95765
GARNO, Arthur Scott (Alb) 5828 State Highway 68, Ogdensburg, NY 13669
GARNO, Scott (Alb) Po Box 537, Unadilla, NY 13849
GARNSEY, Elizabeth H (NY) Church of the Heavenly Rest, 2 E 90th St, New York, NY 10128
GARRAMONE, Laurie Marie (Alb) 28 S. Market Street, Johnstown, NY 12095
GARRATT, Steve (Oly) 19247 40th Pl NE, Lake Forest Park, WA 98155
GARREN, Ben (Az)
GARRENTON, Linwood Wilson (Roch) 599 E 7th St Apt 6E, Brooklyn, NY 11218
GARRETT, David (ETenn) 515 5th St, Newport, TN 37821
GARRETT, George Kenneth (Mass) 12 Academy Ave, Fairhaven, MA 02719
GARRETT, Jane Nuckols (Vt) 206 Fairway Vlg, Leeds, MA 01053
GARRETT, Mary Ann (La) PO Box 126, Baton Rouge, LA 70821

GARRETT, Paul (Colo) 2530 Leyden St., Denver, CO 80207

GARRIGAN, Edward (Pa) PO Box 1681, Doylestown, PA 18901

✠ **GARRISON**, Michael (WNY) 207 Pineneedle Dr, Bradenton, FL 34210

GARRISON, Thomas Martin (Minn)

GARRISON, William (Los) 7056 Washington Ave, Whittier, CA 90602

GARRISON, William Brian (CFla) 212 Brevity Ln, DeLand, FL 32724

GARRITY, Clelia Pinza (CGC) 3081 Margarita Ave, Pahrump, NV 89048

GARTIN, Thomas R (The Episcopal NCal) 1800 Wildcat Blvd, Rocklin, CA 95765

GARTON, Mary Pamela (CFla) 190 Interlachen Rd, Melbourne, FL 32940

GARVIN, Grayson Barry (CFla) 3000 Nw 42nd Ave Apt B401, Coconut Creek, FL 33066

GARWOOD, Martha Jayne (SD) 4640 Sturgis Rd Lot 49, Rapid City, SD 57702

GARZA JR, Frederico Eloy (Va) 2900 Hanes Ave, Richmond, VA 23222

GARZA LOPEZ, Carlos (Hond) Santa Maria Virgen, Bamo San Pedrito, Copan Ruinas, Copan, Honduras

GARZA SALVADOR, Sergio Danilo (Hond) San Juan Bautista, Carrizalito Copan Ruinas, Copan Ruinas, Copan, Honduras

GASKILL JR, John Joseph (EC) 174 Windy Point Rd, Beaufort, NC 28516

GASQUET, Mark Cordes (La) 308 Central Ave, Jefferson, LA 70121

GASTON, Katherine Elizabeth (Neb) 7625 Lafayette Ave, Omaha, NE 68114

GASTON III, Paul Lee (O) 2389 Brunswick Lane, Hudson, OH 44236

GAT, Maggie (Nwk) 4230 Cascade Falls Dr, Sarasota, FL 34243

GATCH JR, Milton Mccormick (NY) 575 W End Ave Apt 7C, New York, NY 10024

GATELEY, Gail Nicholson (Dal) 15264 SW Peachtree Drive, Tigard, OR 97224

◄ **GATES**, Alan (Mass) Episcopal Diocese of Massachusetts, 138 Tremont St, Boston, MA 02111

GATES, Alan K (Cal)

GATES, Mary May (Ct) 16 Church St, Waterbury, CT 06702

GATES JR, Robert J (Okla)

GATTA, Julia Milan (Ct) 243 Tennessee Ave, Sewanee, TN 37375

GATTIS, Larry R (Chi) 20326 Harding Ave, Olympia Fields, IL 60461

GATZA, Mark Francis (Md) Po Box 628, Bel Air, MD 21014

GAUMER, Susan Salot (La) 7820 Jeannette St., New Orleans, LA 70118

GAUVIN, Joseph Henri Armand (NJ) 25 Southwood Drive, St Catharine'S, L2M 4M5, Canada

GAVENTA, Sarah Kinney (Va)

GAVIN, Craig Edmonds (Ark) 196 Dawn Dr, Centerton, AR 72719

GAVIN, Timothy (Pa) The Episcopal Academy, 1785 Bishop White Dr, Newtown Square, PA 19073

GAVIT, Sara B (Me) 2222 E Tudor Rd, Anchorage, AK 99507

GAY, Jean Ricot (SeFla) 465 Ne 100th St, Miami Shores, FL 33138

GAY, Judith S (Mass) 59 Fenno St, Cambridge, MA 02138

GAY, Karen (La) Episcopal Church of the Holy Communion, P. O. Box 474, Plaquemine, LA 70764

GAY, Margaret Worcester (CNY)

GAY, Robert George (SVa)

GAYLE JR, William Gedge (La) 227 Helios Avenue, Metairie, LA 70005

GAYLOR, Pamela Elaine (SO) 3149 Indian Ripple Rd, Dayton, OH 45440

GDULA, Peter Barry (CPa) St Luke's Episcopal Church, 8 E Keller St, Mechanicsburg, PA 17055

GEARHART, Robert James (Neb) 665 4th St., PO Box 56, Syracuse, NE 68446

GEARING, Charles Edward (At) 6525 Gardenia Way, Stone Mountain, GA 30087

GEARS, Wallace E (Minn) 3240 Jersey Ave S, Minneapolis, MN 55426

GEDDES, Robert Douglas (Va) 269 Johnson Point Road, Hallieford, VA 23068

GEDRICK III, John Paul (At) 700 Route 22, Pawling, NY 12564

GEEN, Russell Glenn (HB) 4 Shad Bush Dr, Columbia, MO 65203

GEER, Francis Hartley (NY) Po Box 158, Garrison, NY 10524

GEERDES, Patricia Seney (WVa) 900 Hillsborough St, Raleigh, NC 27603

GEFFRARD, Ricot (Hai)

GEHLSEN, Tom (Minn) 1232 Lakemoor Dr., Woodbury, MN 55129

GEHRIG, Stephen James (Oly) 1828 Field Place NE, Renton, WA 98059

GEIB, Lanny Roland (Tex) 5087 Galileo Dr, Colorado Springs, CO 80917

GEIGER, Clifford T (Me) 2800 Se Fairway W, Stuart, FL 34997

GEIGER, Martin (Mo)

GEIGER, William Linwood (Pgh) 3079 Warren Rd, Indiana, PA 15701

GEISLER, Jay (Pgh) 1283 Earlford Drive, Pittsburgh, PA 15227

GEISLER, Mark (Chi) 113 E. Lafayette St., Ottawa, IL 61350

GEISLER, William Fredric (Cal) PO Box 2624, San Anselmo, CA 94979

GEISSLER-O'NEIL, Susan (Mass) 3350 Hopyard Rd, Pleasanton, CA 94588

GEITZ, Elizabeth Rankin (NJ) 431 Twin Lakes Rd, Shohola, PA 18458

GELDERT, Maurice William (RG) 121 Mescalero Tr, Ruidoso, NM 88345

GELFER, Miriam Carmel (Mass) 8 Saint Johns Rd, Cambridge, MA 02138

GELIEBTER, Phillip Lincoln (Pa) 4442 Frankford Ave, Phila, PA 19124

GELINEAU, Francoise (Mich) P.O. Box 351, Roscommon, MI 48653

GELLER, Maggie (Mass) 160 Farm St, Millis, MA 02054

GELLERT, Alan Cranston (SeFla) 2303 NE Seaview Dr, Jensen Beach, FL 34957

GEMIGNANI, Michael (Tex) 1816 Dublin Dr., League City, TX 77573

GEMINDER, Randolph Jon (LI) 175 Broadway, Amityville, NY 11701

GENEREUX, Patrick Edward (Ia) 3700 S Westport Ave #530, Sioux Falls, SD 57106

GENNETT JR, Paul (Del) 413 Terra Dr, Newark, DE 19702

GENNUSO JR, George (WLa) 500 Edgewood Dr, Pineville, LA 71360

GENSZLER, Mark (LI)

GENTLE, Judith Marie (Pgh) 315 Turnpike St, North Andover, MA 01845

GENTRY, Bryan Massey (Tex) 209 Orange Avenue, Fairhope, AL 36532

GENTRY, Keith Alan (Nwk) 11 Hinchman Avenue, Wayne, NJ 07470

GENTY, Marc Daniel (Colo) St Luke's Episcopal Church, 2000 Stover St, Fort Collins, CO 80525

GEORGE, Allen Winnie Sie (NY) 781 Castle Hill Ave, Bronx, NY 10473

GEORGE, Amy Martin (WTenn) Grace - Saint Luke's Church, 1720 Peabody Ave, Memphis, TN 38104

GEORGE, Clarence Davis Dominic (NY) 797 Corbett Ave Apt 3, San Francisco, CA 94131

GEORGE, Eldred (Chi)

GEORGE, Erminie A (VI) PO Box 1148, Charlotte Amalie, VI 00804

GEORGE JR, Jay Charles (WTex) 7714 Moss Brook Dr, San Antonio, TX 78255

GEORGE, Joanna Elizabeth (Dal) St Philip's Episcopal Church, 6400 Stonebrook Pkwy, Frisco, TX 75034

GEORGE, Johannes (Tex) 15325 Bellaire Boulevard, Houston, TX 77083

GEORGE, John C (CGC)

GEORGE, Juan (Del) Trinity Episcopal Church, 1108 N Adams St, Wilmington, DE 19801

GEORGE, Mitzi (WLa) 1020 Sutherland Rd, Lake Charles, LA 70611

GEORGE, Reverend Cathy Hagstrom George (Mass) 409 Prospect St., New Haven, CT 06511

GEORGE, Susanne T (Cal) 60 Brunswick Park, Melrose, MA 02176

GEORGE-HACKER, Nina (Alb) PO Box 125, Cornwall, PA 17016

GEORGES, Esther Mathilda (VI)

GEORGI, Geoffrey Mack (NC) Po Box 13, Rougemont, NC 27572

✠ **GEPERT**, Robert R (WMich) Episcopal Diocese of Central Pennsylvania, 101 Pine St, Harrisburg, PA 17101

GERBASI, Virginia Kaye (WA) 1525 H St., N.W, St. John's Church, Lafayette Square, Washington, DC 20005

GERBER, Ronald D (Alb) 36 General Torbert Dr, Milford, DE 19963

GERBRACHT-STAGNARO, Madge (NH) 106 Lowell St, Manchester, NH 03101

GERDING, Susan Ann (Tex) 836 W. Jones St., Livingston, TX 77351

GERDSEN, Elizabeth Jane (SO) 1219 Amherst Pl, Dayton, OH 45406

GERHARD, Ernest J (Neb) 14214 Briggs Cir, Omaha, NE 68144

GERHARD, Kurt (WA) Saint Patrick's Episcopal Church, 4700 Whitehaven Pkwy NW, Washington, DC 20007

GERHARDT, Michael Joseph (NJ) 171 Larch Ave., Bogota, NJ 07603

GERHART JR, John James (CFla) 4315 Longshore Dr, Land O Lakes, FL 34639

GERHART, Stacey P (Ia) 1308 S Cleveland St, Sioux City, IA 51106

GERHART, William James (NJ) 2131 Woodbridge Ave, PO Box 1286, Edison, NJ 08817

GERLACH, Aaron R (O) 125 East Market St, Tiffin, OH 44883

GERMAN, Kenneth L (Episcopal SJ) 329 Mannel Ave, Shafter, CA 93263

GERMINO, Carmen (NC) 1205 W Franklin St, Richmond, VA 23220

GERNS, Andrew (Be) 14 Midland Dr, Easton, PA 18045

GEROLD, Donna (Ala) St Stephen's Episcopal Church, 3775 Crosshaven Dr, Vestavia, AL 35223

GERTH JR, Stephen (NY) Church of Saint Mary the Virgin, 145 West 46th Street, New York, NY 10036

GERVAIS JR, Sidney Joseph (Tex) 1210 E Mesa Park Dr, Round Rock, TX 78664

GESTON, Alejandro Sumadin (The Episcopal Church in Haw) 91-1746 Bond St, Ewa Beach, HI 96706

GETCHELL, Philip Armour (ECR) 6524 Hercus Ct, San Jose, CA 95119

GETLEIN, Greta (RI) Saint Paul's Church, 50 Park Pl, Pawtucket, RI 02860

GETREU, David Edward (SO) 127 W Mound Street, Circleville, OH 43113

GETTEL, Becky (Mass) Trinity Church, 81 Elm St, Concord, MA 01742

GETTS, Sarah Jane (Az)

GETTYS, Jeannette Cooper (USC) 308 College Dr., Gaffney, SC 29340

GETTYS, Laura (WTenn) 692 Poplar Ave, Memphis, TN 38105

GETZ, Peter Richard Remsen (Dal) 808 Oak Hollow Lane, Rockwall, TX 75087

GHEEN, Stephen Harris (Minn)

GHINAGLIA SOCORRO, Florencio Armando (Ct) PO Box 2321, Bristol, CT 06011

GIACOBBE, Georgia Bates (EO) 3564 E. Second St. #26, The Dalles, OR 97058

GIACOMA, Claudia Louder (U) 7362 Tall Oaks Dr, Park City, UT 84098

GIANNINI, Robert Edward (Ind) 55 Monument Cir Ste 600, Indianapolis, IN 46204

GIANSIRACUSA JR, Michael (Pa) 225 S 3rd St, Philadelphia, PA 19106

GIARDINA, Denise Diana (WVa)

GIBBES, Joseph A (Fla) 12236 Mandarin Rd, Jacksonville, FL 32223

GIBBONS, David Austen (Chi) 339 Ridge Rd, Barrington, IL 60010

GIBBONS, Ro (CPa) 64 Mayflower Ln, Mansfield, PA 16933

GIBBS, Charles Philip (Cal) 9900 Kensington Pkwy, Kensington, MD 20895

GIBBS, Dennis (Los) 840 Echo Park Ave, Los Angeles, CA 90026

GIBBS, Lee Wayland (O) 2413 Weymouth Dr, Springfield, VA 22151

✠ **GIBBS JR**, Wendell (Mich) 19594 Renfrew Rd, Detroit, MI 48221

GIBLIN, Keith Fredrick (Tex) 1401 W Park Ave, Orange, TX 77630

GIBSON, Alan (Mich) St Andrew Episcopal Church, 306 N Division St, Ann Arbor, MI 48104

GIBSON, Barbara Jean (Kan) 400 Sutton Dr, Newton, KS 67114

GIBSON, Beverly Findley (CGC) 24 Blacklawn St, Mobile, AL 36604

GIBSON, Catharine (WA)

GIBSON, Catherine S (ETenn) Carlene Cottage, Tarland, Aboyne, Aberdeenshire, Scotland, AB34 4YX, Great Britain (UK)

GIBSON, Earl Dodridge (Az) 31641 La Novia Ave., San Juan Capistrano, CA 92675

GIBSON, Emily Stearns (Me) 732 Nottingham Rd, Wilmington, DE 19805

GIBSON, Gregory H (VI) St John's Episcopal Church, PO Box 486, Christiansted, VI 00821

GIBSON, John Kenneth (NC) 1520 Canterbury Rd, Raleigh, NC 27608

GIBSON, John Noel Keith (VI) Box 65, Valley, Virgin Gorda, VI, British Virgin Islands

GIBSON, Justin Thomas (RG)

GIBSON, Libby (Mass) Saint Mary's Episcopal Church, 3055 Main St, Barnstable, MA 02630

GIBSON III, Owen S (HB) 2926 Maple Springs Blvd, Dallas, TX 75235

GIBSON, Robert Burrows (At) 20 Lucky Ln, Blairsville, GA 30512

GIBSON, Tom (CFla) Po Box 320026, 139 S. Atlantic Avenue, Cocoa Beach, FL 32932

GIBSON, Webster S (Va) 111 Stonebrook Rd, Winchester, VA 22602

GIDDINGS, Monte Carl (Kan) 26755 W 103rd St, Olathe, KS 66061

GIERLACH, David Joseph (The Episcopal Church in Haw) 231 Miloiki Pl, Honolulu, HI 96825

GIESELER, Mary Morgret (Miss)

GIESELMANN, Rob (ETenn) Church of the Ascension, 800 S. Northshore Drive, Knoxville, TN 37919

GIFFORD II, Gerald Gerard (The Episcopal Church in Haw) 446 Kawaihae St Apt 119, Honolulu, HI 96825

GIFFORD-COLE, Irene Margarete (Minn) 225 Hoylake Rd W, Qualicum Beach, V9K 1K5, Canada

GILBERT, Brenda Marie (WNC) 8433 Fairfield Forest Rd, Denver, NC 28037

GILBERT, Carol Beverly (NJ) 34 Mystic Way, Burlington, NJ 08016

GILBERT JR, George Asbury (CGC) 10100 Hillview Dr Apt 432, Pensacola, FL 32514

GILBERT, Lara (Wyo)

GILBERT, Marilynn D (Ct) 28 Windemere Pl, Grosse Pointe Farms, MI 48236

GILBERT, Paul (LI) 1760 Parc Vue Ave, Mount Pleasant, SC 29464

GILBERT, Thomas F (Me) 118 Morrill St, Pittsfield, ME 04967

GILBERT, Trimble (Ak) General Delivery, Arctic Village, AK 99722

GILBERTSEN, George Eugene (Lex) Courthouse Sq, Tiffin, OH 44883

GILBERTSON, Gary Raymond (WMo) 12301 West 125th Terr, Overland Park, KS 66213

GILCHRIST, James Edwin (Neb) 124 1st Ave Se, Ronan, MT 59864

GILCHRIST, James F (Colo) 5478 S Idalia Ct, Centennial, CO 80015

GILCHRIST, John Richard (Ct) Po Box 361, Winter Harbor, ME 04693

GILDERSLEEVE, Robert K (Be) 435 Center Street, Jim Thorpe, PA 18229

GILES, James D (CFla)

GILES, Richard Stephen (Pa) 105 Lansdowne Ct, Lansdowne, PA 19050

GILES, Walter Crews (FtW) 1649 Park Ln, Alvarado, TX 76009

GILES, Walter Edward (CNY) 12914 US Route 11, Adams Center, NY 13606

GILFEATHER, Gordon Grant (Az) 12990 E Shea Blvd, Scottsdale, AZ 85259

GILHOUSEN, Dennis Ray (Kan) 6501 Mapel Dr, Mission, KS 66202

GIL JIMENEZ, Ramon Antonio (DR (DomRep))

GILKES, Overton Weldon (Ct) 262 Shelton Ave, New Haven, CT 06511

GILKEY JR, Sam (CFla) 3670 Northgate Dr Apt 1, Kissimmee, FL 34746

GILKS, Cyntha Ann (Okla) 903 E Main St, Holdenville, OK 74848

GILL JR, Charles (Eur) 3451 South Washington Ave., Titusville, FL 32780

GILL, Cynthia Elizabeth (SeFla) 2750 Mcfarlane Rd, Miami, FL 33133

GILL, Jeffrey Shilling (Oly) Trinity Parish, 609 8th Ave, Seattle, WA 98104

GILL, Jim (Be) PO Box 214, East Winthrop, ME 04343

GILL JR, John Nicholas (SO) 3429 Live Oak Place, Columbus, OH 43221

GILL, Jule Carlyle (WA) 4 Milford Ave, Lewes, DE 19958

GILL, Robert Clarence (CPa) 139 N Findlay St, York, PA 17402

GILLESPIE, Ann (Va) Christ Church, 118 N Washington St, Alexandria, VA 22314

GILLESPIE, David Marston (RI) 2206 N Hollow Rd, Rochester, VT 05767

GILLESPIE JR, Robert Schaeffer (WA) 14702 W Auburn Rd, Accokeek, MD 20607

GILLETT, Elizabeth (CNY) 1213 River Rd, Hamilton, NY 13346

GILLETT, Kathryn Sarah (CFla) 18 W Wright St, Pensacola, FL 32501

GILLETT, Richard Walker (Oly) 719 N 67th St, Seattle, WA 98103

GILLETTE, Howard Dennis (Pgh) 3414 Ventana Dr, Coraopolis, PA 15108

GILLETTE, Martha Carol (Chi) 154 Timber Ridge Ln, Lake Barrington, IL 60010

GILLIAM, John Malone (EC) 101 W Gale St, Edenton, NC 27932

GILLIES, Bruce Nelson (WNY) 1082 Brookwood Dr, Derby, NY 14047

GILLIES, Clara (WNY) 18 N Pearl St, Buffalo, NY 14202

GILLIS, Marcella R (WA) 55 Myrtle Ave, Westport, CT 06880

GILLISS, Columba (Md) 3200 Baker Cir Unit I209, Adamstown, MD 21710

GILL-LOPEZ, John Herbert (LI) 80 La Salle St Apt 21-H, New York, NY 10027

GILLOOLY, Bryan Charles (O) 19636 Scottsdale Blvd, Cleveland, OH 44122

GILMAN, Bob (SwVa) 16918 Paynes Creek Dr, Cypress, TX 77433

GILMAN, Connie (SVa) 306 Boys Home Rd, Covington, VA 24426

GILMAN, James Earl (SwVa) 719 Opie St, Staunton, VA 24401

GILMER, Lyonel Wayman (NC) 2924 Wellesley Tree, Nashville, TN 37215

GILMORE, Elizabeth Lameyer (Me) 24 Fairmount St, Portland, ME 04103

GILMORE, William Kennedy (SwFla)

GILPIN, John Mitchell (Ct) St John's Episcopal Church, 7 Whittlesey Ave, New Milford, CT 06776

GILPIN, Kathlyn Castiglion (SwFla)

GIL RESTREPO, Silvio (Colom) Carrera 6 No 49-85, Piso 2, Bogota, Colombia

GILSDORF, John Walter (EO) 1971 Sw Quinney Ave, Pendleton, OR 97801

GILSON, Anne Elizabeth (WA) 5 Fernwood Cir, Harwich, MA 02645

GILSON, Christine (Kan) Po Box 883, El Dorado, KS 67042

GILTON, Michael R (Dal)

GINN JR, Robert Jay (WMass) Oratory Of Saint Francis, Box 300, Templeton, MA 01468

GINNEVER, Richard Arthur (Md) 9259 Brush Run, Columbia, MD 21045

GINOLFI, Priscilla Grant (CPa) 321 W Chestnut St, Lancaster, PA 17603

GINOLFI, Sarah C (Oly) 6050 N Meridian St, Indianapolis, IN 46208

GINSON, Isaias Gonzales (LI) 1805 W.Alabama st., Houston, TX 77098

GIOVANGELO, Steven Michael (Ind) 337 North Kenyon Street, Indianapolis, IN 46219

GIRALDO OROZCO, Edgar (PR)

GIRARD, Jacques Andre (Nwk) 8 Shore Rd, Staten Island, NY 10307

GIRARDEAU, Charles Michael (At) 1446 Edinburgh Dr, Tucker, GA 30084

GIRARDEAU, Doug (Eas) 211 E Isabella St, Salisbury, MD 21801

GIRARDIN, Barbara Jeanine (Colo) 2604 S Troy Ct, Aurora, CO 80014

GIRATA, Christopher D (Dal) St Michael & All Angels Church, 8011 Douglas Ave, Dallas, TX 75225

GIROUX, Mark Alan (CNY) 355 Hyde St, Whitney Point, NY 13862

GIRVIN, Calvin Shields (NwT) 4541 County Road 127, Colorado City, TX 79512

GITANE, ClayOla (SanD) 5412 Wales Avenue, Fort Worth, TX 76133

GITAU, Samson Njuguna (Ark) 243 N Mcneil St, Memphis, TN 38112

GITHITU, James Kimari (Mass) 740 Princeton Blvd Apt 3, Lowell, MA 01851

GITIMU, Paul Wainaina (Pa) 1747 Church Ln, Philadelphia, PA 19141

GIVEN, Mark E (Ct) 1113 Abrams Road, #4-121, Richardson, TX 75081

GIVLER, Gary Bruce (SO) 6215 Kenwood Rd, Madeira, OH 45243

GLANCEY, Bryan Eaton (Eas) 1205 Frederick Ave, Salisbury, MD 21801

GLANDON, Clyde Calvin (Okla) 4223 E 84th St, Tulsa, OK 74137

GLANVILLE, Polly Ann (O) 1945 26th Street, Cuyahoga Falls, OH 44223

GLASER, David Charles (Mich) 20500 W OLD US HIGHWAY 12, Chelsea, MI 48118

GLASER, Geoffrey Scott (ECR) 3631 W Avenida Obregon, Tucson, AZ 85746

GLASS, Rosalee Tyree (Me)

GLASS, Vanessa (Cal) St. Francis of Assisi Episcopal Church, 967 5th Street, Novato, CA 94945

GLASSER, Joanne Kathleen (Eau) 111 9th St N, La Crosse, WI 54601

☩ **GLASSPOOL**, Mary Douglas (NY) Episcopal Diocese of New York, 1047 Amsterdam Ave, New York, NY 10025

GLAUDE, Ron (Ct) 125 Grand View Ter, Brooklyn, CT 06234

GLAZIER JR, George H (SO) 10 E. Weber Rd #305, Columbus, OH 43202

GLAZIER II, William Stuart (Ct) 30 Ice House Ln, Mystic, CT 06355

GLEASON, Dorothy Jean (Episcopal SJ) Po Box 399, Ambridge, PA 15003

GLEASON, Edward Campbell (SwFla) 553 Galleon Dr, Naples, FL 34102

GLEAVES, Donna Jeanne (Mont) 5 West Olive St, Bozeman, MT 59715

GLEAVES, Glen Lee (Mont) 1226 Wildflower Trl, Livingston, MT 59047

GLEESON, Terry Patrick (ECR) All Saints Church, 555 Waverley Street, Palo Alto, CA 94301

GLENDENNING, Audrey Geraldine (SeFla) 3322 Meridian Way N Apt A, Palm Beach Gardens, FL 33410

GLENDINNING, David Cross (Me) 221 Shelburne Rd, Burlington, VT 05401

GLENN JR, Charles Leslie (Mass) 1 Robeson St, Boston, MA 02130

GLENN, Kim B (SwVa) 200 Boston Ave, Lynchburg, VA 24503

GLENN, Lawrance Gail (FdL) 1230 Sandpebble Dr., Rockton, IL 61072

GLENN, Michael Eugene (Okla) 106 E Crawford St, Palestine, TX 75801

GLENN, Patricia Foster (Mo) 19424 Highway 54, Louisiana, MO 63353

GLENNIE, Jannel (Mich) 294 Willoughby Rd, Mason, MI 48854

GLICK, Phillip Randall (EC) 184 Watersedge Drive, Kill Devil Hills, NC 27948

GLIDDEN, Charles Aelred (FdL) 56500 Abbey Rd, Three Rivers, MI 49093

GLIDDEN, Richard Mark (Chi) 49 Larbert Rd # 6490, Southport, CT 06890

GLOFF, Holly (NC) 1520 Canterbury Rd, Raleigh, NC 27608

GLOSSON HAMMONS, Jamesetta (Los) 1508 W 145th St, Compton, CA 90220

☩ **GLOSTER**, James Gary (NC) 2236 Fernbank Dr, Charlotte, NC 28226

GLOVER, Beth Faulk (Nwk) 29 Village Gate Way, Nyack, NY 10960

GLOVER, Betty Marie (Ak) Saint David's Episcopal Church, 3916 SW 17th St, Topeka, KS 66604

GLOVER, Hazel (At) 606 Newnan St, Carrollton, GA 30117

GLOVER, Marsha Bacon (NY) 122 Grandview Ave, White Plains, NY 10605

GLOVER, Mary Elizabeth (NwT) 891 Davis Dr, Abilene, TX 79605

GOBER, Jane A (Spok) 323 Catherine St, Walla Walla, WA 99362

GOBER, Patricia Derr (Mass) 17 Leroy St, Attleboro, MA 02703

GOBER, Wallace Gene (Mass) 17 Leroy St, Attleboro, MA 02703

GOCHA, Teresa Payne (NH) 477 Main St, Plymouth, NH 03264

GOCKERMAN, Janet Pierce (WMich) 134 Division Ave N, Grand Rapids, MI 49503

GOCKLEY, Mary Jane (Neb) PO Box 353, Broken Bow, NE 68822

GODBOLD, Richard Rives (Ind) 829 Wiltshire Dr, Evansville, IN 47715

GODDARD, John R (Nev) 10465 SE Waverly Ct Apt 2018, Milwaukie, OR 97222

GODDARD, Paul Dillon (Chi) 742 Sand Dollar Dr, Sanibel, FL 33957

GODDEN, Edward Eastman (Del) 610 Lindsey Rd, Wilmington, DE 19809

GODDERZ, Michael John (Mass) 209 Ashmont Street, Boston, MA 02124

GODFREY, Samuel Bisland (Miss) 1115 Main St., Vicksburg, MS 39183

GODFREY, Steven R (Ia) 339 Hickory Dr, Ames, IA 50014

GODFREY, William Calvin (LI) 102 Thompson Blvd, Greenport, NY 11944

GODLEY, Robert James (NY) 4440 E Lady Banks Ln, Murrells Inlet, SC 29565

GODSEY, Jeunee (SVa) 8706 Quaker Ln, North Chesterfield, VA 23235

GODWIN, JD D (Oly) 2630 46th Ave SW, Seattle, WA 98116

GOEKE, Randall Fred (Neb) 87993 482nd Ave, Atkinson, NE 68713

GOERTZ, Linda Ruth (Ore)

GOETSCH, Richard William (Ida) 213 E Avenue D, Jerome, ID 83338

GOFF, Nancy L (Alb) The Adirondack Mission Episcopal Churches, PO Box 119, Brant Lake, NY 12815

✠ **GOFF**, Susan (Va) 110 W Franklin St, Richmond, VA 23220

GOFF, Terry Lynn (CGC) 7125 Hitt Rd, Mobile, AL 36695

GOFORTH, Lisa (Az) 1310 N. Sioux Ave., Claremore, OK 74017

GOFORTH, Thomas Robert (Chi) 1126 W Wolfram St, Chicago, IL 60657

GOGLIA, Bette Mack (CFla) 9203 Glascow Dr, Fredericksburg, VA 22408

GOING, Virginia Lee (NC) 400 S Boylan Ave, Raleigh, NC 27603

GOKEY, Mary Jordheim (ND) 1742 9th St S, Fargo, ND 58103

GOLDBERG, David Michael (Tex) 705 Williams St, Pasadena, TX 77506

GOLDBERG, Mike William (CFla) 460 38th Sq Sw, Vero Beach, FL 32968

GOLDBERG, Rebecca Lee (Cal) 777 Southgate Ave, Daly City, CA 94015

GOLDBLOOM, Ruth Alice (Md) 52 S Broadway, PO Box 229, Frostburg, MD 21532

GOLDEN JR, John Anthony (Pgh) 5 Devon Ave, Lawrenceville, NJ 08648

GOLDEN, Peter (LI) 2115 Albemarle Terrace, Brooklyn, NY 11226

GOLDFARB, Ronald Allen (WTenn) 8853 Mission Hills Dr Apt 104, Memphis, TN 38125

GOLDFEDER, Deborah Baker (Mo) 4520 Lucas and Hunt Rd, Saint Louis, MO 63121

GOLDHOR, Andrew (Mass) 6 Meriam St, Lexington, MA 02420

GOLDING, Christopher PJ (La) The Parish of St Clement, 1515 Wilder Ave, Honolulu, HI 96822

GOLDMAN, Norman Clifford (Ore) 94416 Langlois Mountain Rd, Langlois, OR 97450

GOLDSBOROUGH, Neal Neal (Va) PO Box 12683, Pensacola, FL 32591

GOLDSMITH, Gail Austin (Va)

GOLDSMITH, Maurice Rusty (Tex) Saint Luke's Episcopal Church, 3736 Montrose Rd., Birmingham, AL 35213

GOLDSMITH, Michael (Ala) 113 Brown Ave, Rainbow City, AL 35906

GOLDSMITH III, Robert (Eas) 314 North St, Easton, MD 21601

GOLENSKI, John Donald (Cal) 1360 Montgomery St Apt 1, San Francisco, CA 94133

GOLLIHER, Jeff (NY) 150 W End Ave Apt 30-M, New York, NY 10023

GOLUB, Elizabeth Kress (Nwk) 18 Wittig Ter # 7470, Wayne, NJ 07470

GOMAN, Jon Gifford (Ore) 2615 Nw Arnold Way, Corvallis, OR 97330

GOMER JR, Richard Henry (CFla) 6400 N Socrum Loop Rd, Lakeland, FL 33809

GOMES, Elizabeth (Kan) 912 N Amidon Ave, Wichita, KS 67203

GOMEZ, Ed (Tex) 2404 Marcus Abrams Blvd, Austin, TX 78748

GOMEZ, Luis Enrique (NY) 26 W 84th St, New York, NY 10024

GOMEZ ALMONTE, Lorenzo (DR (DomRep)) Calle Las Mercedes #66, Bigalindo, Hato Mayor Del Rey, DR

GONZALES, Pat Marie (Okla) PO Box 26, Watonga, OK 73772

GONZALES JR, Ricardo (Los) 859 Jessica Pl, Nipomo, CA 93444

GONZALEZ, Alfredo Pedro (USC) 1115 Marion St, Columbia, SC 29201

GONZALEZ, Betsy Carmody (WA) 1200 N Quaker Ln, Alexandria, VA 22302

GONZALEZ, Isabel Tapia (U) 4024 Red Hawk Rd, West Valley City, UT 84119

GONZALEZ, Reagan Len (Mont) 2325 S 24th St, Lincoln, NE 68502

GONZALEZ, Richard (CFla)

GONZALEZ AQUDELO, Luis Mariano (Colom) Carrera 84 North 50 A-112, Ap 301, Medellin, Antioquia, Colombia

GONZALEZ DEL SOLAR, Mario Sebastian (Va) 800 Brantley Rd, Richmond, VA 23235

GONZALEZ-FIGUEROA, Efrain (PR)

GONZALEZ GARAVITO, Jose Pio (PR) PO Box 902, Saint Just, PR 00978

GONZALEZ HERNANDEZ, Yoimel (WA) 1525 Newton St NW, Washington, DC 20010

GONZALEZ-MESA, Gustavo (Ore) 700 Se 7th St, Gresham, OR 97080

GONZALEZ SANTOS, Rosa Ari (PR)

GOOCH, Gary Duane (Kan) 117 E Sierra Cir, San Marcos, TX 78666

GOOD, Arthur Allen (FdL) 1068 Misty Meadow Circle, De Pere, WI 54115

GOOD, Elizabeth (Mass) 17 Church St, Hanover, MA 02339

GOODALE-MIKOSZ, Desiree Ann (Chi) 20913 W Snowberry Ln, Plainfield, IL 60544-416

GOODFELLOW, Willa Marie (EO) 1745 5th St., #8, Coralville, IA 52241

GOODHEART, Donald P (NC) 1303 Hwy A1A #201, Satellite Beach, FL 32937

GOODHOUSE-MAUAI, Angela (ND)

GOODING, Ludwick E (Pa) 5910 Cobbs Creek Pkwy, Philadelphia, PA 19143

GOODISON, Lorna Fay (SeFla) 1400 Riverside Dr, Coral Springs, FL 33071

GOODKIND, Caroline Cox (USC) 45 Crooked Island Circle, Murrells Inlet, SC 29576

GOODLETT, Cal Calvin (Fla)

GOODMAN, James Mark (RG) P.O. Box 1246, Albuquerque, NM 87103

GOODMAN, Kevin M (Chi) 6033 N Sheridan Rd Apt 29g, Chicago, IL 60660

GOODMAN, Timothy Allen (Spr) 9267 HERRIN RD, JOHNSTON CITY, IL 62951

GOODNESS, DONALD (NY) 4800 Fillmore Ave Apt 651, Alexandria, VA 22311

GOODPANKRATZ, Gretchen (WK) Po Box 851, Liberal, KS 67905

GOODPASTURE, Terrance Martin (Episcopal SJ) 2315 Merriment Ct., Turlock, CA 95380

GOODRICH, Kevin P (Ia) St John Episc Ch, 1458 Locust St, Dubuque, IA 52001

GOODRIDGE, Rob (CFla) 4791 Longbow Drive, Titusville, FL 32796

GOODWILL, Martha Elizabeth (SwFla) 8005 25th St E, Parrish, FL 34219

GOODWIN, Joan Carolyn (Az) 413 N San Francisco St, Flagstaff, AZ 86001

GOODWIN, Laura Bishop (WMass) St Andrew's Church, 53 N Main St, North Grafton, MA 01536

GOODWIN, Marilyn Marie (Minn) 27309 County Road 4, Naytahwaush, MN 56566

GOODWIN, Sarabeth (WA) 1721 Lamont St NW, Washington, DC 20010

GOOLD, George Charles (Ore) St Stephen's Church, SW Ninth & Hurbert Sts, Newport, OR 97365

GOOLD, Janis Leigh (Ore) 16530 Nottingham Dr, Gladstone, OR 97027

GOOLSBEE, Arthur Leon (NwT) 602 Meander St., Abilene, TX 79602

GOOLSBY, Bob (Fla) 1656 Blalock Rd., Houston, TX 77080
GOOLTZ, Janet R (Az) 12607 W Westgate Dr, Sun City West, AZ 85375
GOONESEKERA, Desmond Joel Peter (Tex) 2806 Belham Creek Dr, Katy, TX 77494
GOORAHOO, Ephraim Basant (LI) 111-16 116th St, South Ozone Park, NY 11420
GORACZKO, Ann Kathleen R (SeFla) 1801 Ludlam Drive, Miami Springs, FL 33166
GORANSON, Paul Werner (WMass) 130 Sachem Ave., Worcester, MA 01606
GORCHOV, Michael Ivan (Alb) 58 3rd St, Troy, NY 12180
GORDAY, Peter J (WNC) 34 Lullwater Pl Ne, Atlanta, GA 30307
GORDON, Billie Mae (Mass) 290 Kingstown Way Unit 395, Duxbury, MA 02332
GORDON, Constance Leigh (U) 789 White Pine Dr, Tooele, UT 84074
GORDON, David Walter (Cal) 130 Avenida Barbera, Sonoma, CA 95476
GORDON JR, Harrington Manly (RI) 108 Columbia Ave, Warwick, RI 02888
GORDON, Jay Holland (NY) 382 Central Park W Apt 17p, New York, NY 10025
GORDON, Jim (RG) St Paul's Episcopal Church, PO Box 175, Marfa, TX 79843
GORDON, Rodney E (SVa) 701 S Providence Rd, North Chesterfield, VA 23236
GORDON, Walt (Minn) 834 Marshall Ave, Saint Paul, MN 55104
GORDON, Walter Bernard (WTenn) PO Box 622, Grand Junction, TN 38039
GORDON-BARNES, Janice E (Md) 3117 Raven Croft Terrace, The Villages, FL 32163
GORE, Gina Lee (Los) 18631 Chapel Ln, Huntington Beach, CA 92646
GORE, Kevin W (Ore) 511 Coley Dr, Mountain Home, AR 72653
GORES, Ariail Fischer (Dal) 4229 Tomberra Way, Dallas, TX 75220
GORMAN, James Michael (Chi) 5388 W Harvey Rd, Oregon, IL 61061
GORMAN, W Kenneth (NJ) 684 Sunrise Dr, Avalon, NJ 08202
GORMLEY, Shane P (Alb)
GORTNER, David Timothy (WA) 3737 Seminary Road, Alexandria, VA 22304
GOSHERT, Mary Linda (The Episcopal NCal) 882 Oxford Way, Benicia, CA 94510
GOSHGARIAN, Martin John (Mass) 85 Glenwood Rd, Somerville, MA 02145
GOSHORN, Alice Elizabeth Gill (Ind) 4921 E State Road 252, Franklin, IN 46131

GOSS, Frank (NJ) Po Box 1, Bradley Beach, NJ 01/01/7720
GOSS III, James Paul (Cal) 792 Penny Royal Ln, San Rafael, CA 94903
GOSSARD, Pamela Ann (The Episcopal NCal)
GOSSETT JR, Earl Fowler (Ala) 1811 Cedar Crest Rd, Birmingham, AL 35214
GOSSLING, Nancy (Mass) 25 Chapman Dr, Glastonbury, CT 06033
GOTAUTAS, Patricia Marie (USC)
GOTCHER, Vernon Alfred (FtW) 1904 Westcliff Dr, Euless, TX 76040
GOTKO, Raymond (At) 501 Sweet Berry Drive, Mont Eagle, TN 37356
GOTT, Amanda Katherine (Neb)
GOTTARDI-LITTELL, Laura (Chi) Church of Our Saviour, Chicago, IL 60614
GOTTING, Viktoria Johanna Petra (Tex) Saint John's Church, 815 S Broadway St, La Porte, TX 77571
GOTTLICH, Samuel Grier (WTex) 5857 Timbergate Dr Apt 1149, Apt 1149, Corpus Christi, TX 78414
GOUGH, Karen (WNY) 315 Oakbrook Dr, Williamsville, NY 14221
GOULD, Glenn Hamilton (USC) 30 Moise Dr, Sumter, SC 29150
GOULD, Jane (Los) 19 Nahant Pl, Lynn, MA 01902
GOULD, Jennie Ruth (NH) 19 Maplewood St, Watertown, MA 02472
GOULD, Mary Dolores (Oly) Po Box 1193, Maple Valley, WA 98038
GOWDY-JAEHNIG, Christine Annette (Ia) 506 W Broadway St, Decorah, IA 52101
GOWETT, Randall James (Episcopal SJ) 1224 E Sample Ave, Fresno, CA 93710
GOWING, Michael LeVern (Mich) 2696 Indian Trl, Pinckney, MI 48169
GOWLAND, James David (NJ) 11 N Monroe Ave, Wenonah, NJ 08090
GOWTY, Richard Newton (Tex) 21 Mclean Street, Brighton, 4017, Australia
GRAB, Virginia (NY) 74 Montgomery St, Tivoli, NY 12583
GRABHER, Jerald (WMo) 4635 Campbell St, Kansas City, MO 64110
GRABINSKI, Kenneth Lee (Oly) 5240 46th Ave Sw, Seattle, WA 98136
GRABNER, John David (Spok) 165 SW Spruce St, Apt 1, Pullman, WA 99163
GRABNER-HEGG, Linnae Marie (Minn) 1619 31st Ave S, Fargo, ND 58103
GRACE JR, Harry Tyler (WNY) 36 Parkside Ct, Buffalo, NY 14214
GRACE, Holt Buff (Minn) 215 4th St N, Stillwater, MN 55082
GRACE SR, James McKay Lykes (Tex) 2428 Swift Blvd, Houston, TX 77030
GRACE, Patricia M. (ETenn) 4753 Scepter Way, Knoxville, TN 37912

GRACEN, Sharon Kay (Ct) 1109 Main St, Branford, CT 06405
GRACIA, Kesner (Hai)
GRACZYK, Glen Gerard (SwFla) St Marys Episcopal Church, 1010 24th Ave W, Palmetto, FL 34221
GRADY, Ann (EMich) 815 N. Grant St, Bay City, MI 48708
GRADY, Richard C. (SwFla) 6985 Edgewater Cir, Fort Myers, FL 33919
GRAEBNER, Brooks (NC) Po Box 628, Hillsborough, NC 27278
GRAF, Thomas W (SeFla) St Faith's Episcopal Church, 10600 Caribbean Blvd, Cutler Bay, FL 33189
GRAFF, Donald T (Pa) 1434 Alcott St, Philadelphia, PA 19149
GRAFF, Stephen John (SeFla) 2871 N Ocean Blvd Apt C513, Boca Raton, FL 33431
GRAHAM III, Alexander D (Dal) 2783 Valwood Pkwy, Farmers Branch, TX 75234
GRAHAM, Carolyn Jane (Kan) 1107 W 27th Ter, Lawrence, KS 66046
GRAHAM, Deborah Marie Therese (Ida) 1867 W Belmont St, Boise, ID 83706
GRAHAM III, Earnest N (NC) 828 Kings Hwy, Suffolk, VA 23432
GRAHAM, John (WA) 1041 Wisconsin Ave. NW, Washington, DC 20007
GRAHAM, John Kirkland (Tex) 6231 Ella Lee Ln, Houston, TX 77057
GRAHAM, Julie Ann (Cal) 1104 Mills Ave, Burlingame, CA 94010
GRAHAM III, Robert Lincoln (Alb) 153 Billings Ave, Ottawa, K1H 5K8, Canada
GRAHAM IV, Sandy (The Episcopal Church in Haw) 563 Kamoku St, Honolulu, HI 96826
GRAHAM, Suzanne H (NY) 279 Piermont Ave, Nyack, NY 10960
GRAHAM, Tim (At) 1130 First Ave, Columbus, GA 31901
GRAHAM, Wells Newell (CGC) 771 Simon Park Cir, Lawrenceville, GA 30045
GRAHAM JR, William James (Neb) 607 Toluca Ave, Alliance, NE 69301
GRAMBSCH, Mary Frances (NY) 20 Seaman Ave Apt 1k, New York, NY 10034
GRAMLEY, Thomas S (Roch) 13 Prospect Ave, Canisteo, NY 14823
GRANDFIELD, Dale Terence (O) 2747 Fairmount Blvd, Cleveland Heights, OH 44106
GRANGER JR, Charles Irving (Okla) 305 E Douglas Dr, Midwest City, OK 73110
GRANT JR, Blount (SeFla) 8500 Bluebonnet Blvd Apt 31, Baton Rouge, LA 70810
GRANT, Hugh M (At) PO Box 632, Eastsound, WA 98245
GRANT, Joan (WNC) 290 Old Haw Creek Rd, Asheville, NC 28805

GRANT, Priscilla (Percy) R (O) 2230 Euclid Ave., Cleveland, OH 44115

GRANT, Rebecca Ann (Me) 16 Alton Road, Apt 219, Augusta, ME 04330

GRANT, Sandra Marceau (SC)

GRANTZ, Brian Glenn (NI) 117 N Lafayette Blvd, South Bend, IN 46601

GRATZ, Louis Paul (Vt) 208 Silver St, Bennington, VT 05201

GRAUER, David Ernst (Chi) 808 S Seminary Ave, Park Ridge, IL 60068

GRAUNKE, Kristine (WTex) PO Box 68, Hebbronville, TX 78361

GRAVATT, Jacqueline Segar (SVa) 301 49th St, Virginia Beach, VA 23451

GRAVES, Carol Carson (NMich) 4341 Se Satinleaf Pl, Stuart, FL 34997

GRAVES IV, Charles Cornelius (SO) 2366 Kemper Ln, Cincinnati, OH 45206

GRAVES, Chip C (WVa) 210 S McHenry Ave, Crystal Lake, IL 60014

GRAVES JR, Farrell (Los) 5 Mill Pond Rd, Stony Brook, NY 11790

GRAVES JR, Leonard Roberts (CGC) 1302 E Avery St, Pensacola, FL 32503

GRAVES, Lisa Beyer (WVa) 290 Grove St., Crystal Lake, IL 60014

GRAVES, Rena B (Pa) 5421 Germantown Ave, Philadelphia, PA 19144

GRAVES, Richard W (Ia) 1247 7th Ave N, Fort Dodge, IA 50501

GRAY, Bruce Alan (Va) 8525 Burgundy Rd, Richmond, VA 23235

GRAY, Bruce William (Ind) Episcopal Diocese of Indianapolis, 1100 W 42nd St, Indianapolis, IN 46208

GRAY, Calvin (Colo) 1625 Larimer Street #2501, Denver, CO 80202

GRAY, Cathy J (Ind) 11120 El Arco Dr, Whittier, CA 90604

GRAY, Chris (SwFla) 8005 25th Street East, Parrish, FL 34219

GRAY, Cindra Dee (Ore) PO Box 358, Newberg, OR 97132

GRAY, Donna Claire (Ct)

GRAY, Douglas Alan (SVa) 3100 Shore Dr, Virginia Beach, VA 23451

✠ **GRAY III**, Duncan (Miss) 110 Philip Rd, Oxford, MS 38655

✠ **GRAY**, Frank (NI) 3820 Nall Ct, South Bend, IN 46614

GRAY, Giulianna C (Miss) 4600 Saint Charles Ave, New Orleans, PA 70115

GRAY, Katherine Tupper (SVa) 84 Post St, Newport News, VA 23601

GRAY, Marie Theresa (FdL) N63W29046 Tail Band Ct, Hartland, WI 53029

GRAY, Melvin Kelly (Fla) 715 Sleepyvale Ln, Houston, TX 77018

GRAY, Michael Fred (Va) 712 Amanda Ct, Culpeper, VA 22701

GRAY, Patrick Terrell (Mass) 151 Asbury St, South Hamilton, MA 01982

GRAY, Peter Hanson (Va) 1800 Old Meadow Rd Apt 321, McLean, VA 22102

GRAY, Peter Whittlesey (Miss) Trinity Church, 1329 Jackson Ave, New Orleans, LA 70130

GRAY, Priscilla Grace-Gloria (Minn) 611 19th St N, Sartell, MN 56377

GRAY, Svea Blomquist (Mich) 306 N Division St, Ann Arbor, MI 48104

GRAY, Thomas Weddle (RG) 108 E Orchard Ln, Carlsbad, NM 88220

GRAY, Victoria Stephanie (Cal)

GRAYBILL, Richard Martin (NMich) First And Canda St, Ishpeming, MI 49849

GRAYBILL, Virginia K (NMich) 301 N 1st St, Ishpeming, MI 49849

GRAYDEN, Margaret Miller (The Episcopal NCal)

GRAY-FOW, Michael John Gregory (Mil) 120 S Ridge St, Whitewater, WI 53190

✠ **GRAY-REEVES**, Mary (ECR) 154 Central Ave, Salinas, CA 93901

GRAYSON, Timothy Holiday (Md) 536 Kinsale Rd, Timonium, MD 21093

GREATHOUSE, William Matthew (WTenn) 103 S Poplar St, Paris, TN 38242

GREATWOOD, Richard Neil (CFla) 1167 Adair Park Place, Orlando, FL 32804

GRECO, John Anthony (LI) 333 E 53rd St Apt 5m, New York, NY 10022

GREELEY, Horace (Cal)

GREELEY III, Paul William (USC) 206 Kings Mountain St, York, SC 29745

GREEN, Andrew (SanD) 2004 East Calle Lileta, Palm Springs, CA 92262

GREEN, Andrew T (WTex) Church of the Holy Spirit, 11093 Bandera Rd, San Antonio, TX 78250

GREEN III, Anthony Roy (Spok) 1705 5th St, Wenatchee, WA 98801

GREEN, Daniel Currie (The Episcopal NCal) 40 5th St, Petaluma, CA 94952

GREEN, David Edward (Cal) 6103 Harwood Ave, Oakland, CA 94618

GREEN, David Keith (CGC)

GREEN, David Robert (Be) 623 Cloverfields Dr., Stevensville, MD 21666

GREEN, Dru (Chi) 971 First St, Batavia, IL 60510

GREEN, Elizabeth A (SVa) 1333 Jamestown Rd, Williamsburg, VA 23185

GREEN, Frazier L (Ga) 1041 Fountain Lake Dr, Brunswick, GA 31525

GREEN, Gary (Mil) 6502 51st Ave, Kenosha, WI 53142

GREEN, Gretchen Hall (O) 35 Cohasset Dr, Hudson, OH 44236

GREEN JR, Joseph Nathaniel (SVa) 3826 Wedgefield Ave, Norfolk, VA 23502

GREEN, Kenneth William (Spok) 539 3rd Ave, Havre, MT 59501

GREEN, Kuulei Mobley (ETenn) 3975 E Clocktower Ln Apt 236, Meridian, ID 83642

GREEN, Larry A (Chi) 1424 N Dearborn St, Chicago, IL 60610

GREEN, Lawrence Joseph (Minn) Saint Pauls Episcopal Church, 265 Lafayette St, Winona, MN 55987

GREEN, Linda (Chi) 971 First St, Batavia, IL 60510

GREEN, Mary Emily (Tex) 4633 Tanner View Dr, Clinton, WA 98236

GREEN, Patricia Anne (WMich) 160 Main St, Somerset, MA 02726

GREEN, Patricia Lynn (RG) 1678 Tierra Del Rio NW, Albuquerque, NM 87107

GREEN, Randy (WNC) 343 Dogwood Knl, Boone, NC 28607

GREEN, Richard (Oly) 1645 24th Avenue, Longview, WA 98632

GREEN JR, Roy Donald (EO) 275 N Main St, Providence, RI 02903

GREEN, Susan Louise (SanD) 125 W El Alameda, Palm Springs, CA 92262

GREEN, Tamara Melanie (Cal) 7211 Garden Glen Ct Apt 318, Huntington Beach, CA 92648

GREENAWAY, Douglas Andrew Gordon (WA) 1116 Lamont St Nw, Washington, DC 20010

GREENE, Adam S (Fla) 4620 Algonquin Ave, Jacksonville, FL 32210

GREENE, Catie (Colo) 1300 Washington St, Denver, CO 80203

GREENE, Dorothy Anne (NY) 27 Willow Ave, Larchmont, NY 10538

GREENE, Edward Rideout (WVa) 19 Valley Rd, Bath, ME 04530

GREENE, Everett Henry (RI) 1117 Capella S, Newport, RI 02840

GREENE, George Burkeholder (Alb) 53 West St, Whitesboro, NY 13492

GREENE III, Joe (NY) 1451 Carriage Ridge Dr., Greensboro, GA 30642

GREENE, Jon Alan (SwVa)

GREENE, Judith (Ct) 60 Bywatyr Ln, Bridgeport, CT 06605

GREENE, Kim Harlene (WNY) St Paul's Cathedral, 128 Pearl St, Buffalo, NY 14202

GREENE, Lynne Tuthill (SwFla) 1369 Vermeer Drive, Nokomis, FL 34275

GREENE, Mary Carter (Cal) 330 Ravenswood Ave, Menlo Park, CA 94025

GREENE, Michael Paul Thomas (Eau) St Luke's Episcopal Church, 221 W 3rd St, Dixon, IL 61021

GREENE, Patrick (RI) 55 Main St, N Kingstown, RI 02852

GREENE, Roger Stewart (SO) 8101 Beechmont Ave, Cincinnati, OH 45255

GREENE-MCCREIGHT, Kathryn (Ct) 198 Mckinley Ave, New Haven, CT 06515

GREENEY, Dawnlynn (Minn)

GREENFIELD, Peter Alan (CPa) 122 Greenview Dr, Lancaster, PA 17601

GREENLAW, William A (NY) 529 West 42nd St. Apt. 4J, New York, NY 10036

GREENLEAF, Debra Lynn (Ida)

GREENLEAF, Richard Edward (NH) 325 Pleasant St, Concord, NH 03301

GREENLEE, Malcolm Blake (Ct) 32 Old Wagon Rd, Wilton, CT 06897

GREENMAN, Elizabeth Travis Rees (Fla) 2959 Apalachee Parkway, Unit J6, Tallahassee, FL 32301

GREENSHIELDS, Kay Conner (Okla) 405 Roserock Dr, Norman, OK 73026

GREENWELL, Gail (SO) 318 E 4th St, Cincinnati, OH 45202

GREEN-WITT, Margaret Evelyn Ashmead (SwFla) 2499 Mapleleaf Ct, Spring Hill, FL 34606

GREENWOOD, April Valeria Trew (Va) 2910 Stratford Rd, Richmond, VA 23225

GREENWOOD III, Daniel R (SVa) 2910 Stratford Rd, Richmond, VA 23225

GREENWOOD, Don Robert (SO) 10414 Nw 13th Pl, Vancouver, WA 98685

GREENWOOD JR, Eric Sutcliffe (Tenn) 404 Northridge Ct, Nashville, TN 37221

GREENWOOD, Jody (EC) 4925 Oriole Dr, Wilmington, NC 28403

GREENWOOD, Susan A (Colo) 53 Paradise Rd, Golden, CO 80401

GREENWOOD, Walter Merritt (O) 1473 Brighton Ave, Arroyo Grande, CA 93420

GREER, Broderick L (Colo) 1720 Peabody Ave, Memphis, TN 38104

GREER, David (WLa) 208 Bruce Ave, Shreveport, LA 71105

GREER JR, George Holeman (NC) 301 S Circle Dr, Rocky Mount, NC 27804

GREER, Hilary (Ct) 42 N Eagleville Rd, Storrs, CT 06268

GREER JR, James Gossett (O) 13710 Shaker Blvd Apt 404, Cleveland, OH 44120

GREGG, Catherine (Nev) 2235 S. 1400 E Unit 19, Saint George, UT 84790

GREGG, Jennifer E (WMass) St Stephen's Episcopal Church, 67 East St, Pittsfield, MA 01201

GREGG, Robert Clark (Cal) 659 Salvatierra St, Stanford, CA 94305

✠ **GREGG**, William O (NC) St. Paul's Church, 220 N. Zapatta Hwy11, PMB141A, Laredo, TX 78043

GREGORIUS, Mary B (NY) 378 Bedford Rd, Pleasantville, NY 10570

GREGORY, Brian Joseph (Oly) 1757 244th Ave NE, Sammamish, WA 98074

GREGORY, Emma Jean (Nev) 4201 W Washington Ave, Las Vegas, NV 89107

GREGORY, Marie Christine (Spr) 130 W Eldorado St, Decatur, IL 62522

GREGORY, Pam (RI) 251 Danielson Pike, North Scituate, RI 02857

GREGORY, Phillip Richard (Chi) 2612 Gateshead Dr, Naperville, IL 60564

GREGORY, Rachael (Chi) 410 Grand Ave, Waukegan, IL 60085

✠ **GREIN**, Richard Frank (NY) 150 West End Avenue, Apt. 9H, New York, NY 10013

GREINER, Robert Charles (Mass) 138 Tremont St, Boston, MA 02111

GREISER, Ronald Edmond (WNC) 5601 Oak Ridge Ave, New Port Richey, FL 34652

GREMILLION, Dorothy (Tex) 2708 Butler National Dr, Pflugerville, TX 78660

GRENNEN, Thomas Kyle (Alb) Grace Church, 32 Montgomery St, Cherry Valley, NY 13320

GRENZ, Linda (RI) 275 N Main St, Providence, RI 02903

GRESSLE, Richard (NY) 130 1st Ave, Nyack, NY 10960

GREVE, John Haven (Ia) New Song Episcopal Church, 912 20th Ave, Coralville, IA 52241

GREVE JR, Paul Andrew (NI) 611 W Berry St, Fort Wayne, IN 46802

✠ **GREW II**, J Clark (O) One Huntington Avenue, # 304, Boston, MA 02116

GREWELL, Genevieve Michael (Oly) 1551 Tenth Ave. E, Seattle, WA 98102

GRIBBLE, Robert Leslie (Tex) 301 E 8th St, Austin, TX 78701

GRIBBON, Robert T (Eas) PO Box 1493, Salisbury, MD 21802

GRIEB, Anne Katherine (WA) 3737 Seminary Rd, Alexandria, VA 22304

GRIEB, Ray Kline (Wyo) 487 Goodrich Rd, Wheatland, WY 82201

GRIESBACH, Sigrid Jane (WMass) 921 Pleasant St, Worcester, MA 01602

GRIESER, Jonathan (Mil) 116 W Washington Ave, Madison, WI 53703

GRIESHEIMER, James Cade (Ia) 506 W Broadway St, Decorah, IA 52101

GRIEVES, Brian (The Episcopal Church in Haw) 7007 Hawaii Kai Drive Apt A21, Honolulu, HI 96825

GRIFFIN, Barry (At) Po Box 169, Morrow, GA 30260

GRIFFIN, Calvin Russell (USC) 200 Tyborne Cir, Columbia, SC 29210

GRIFFIN, Christopher E (Chi) 1356 W Jarvis Ave # 1, Chicago, IL 60626

GRIFFIN, Donald J (Del)

GRIFFIN, Emily (WA) St. Alban's Episcopal Church, 3001 Wisconsin Ave Nw, Washington, DC 20016

GRIFFIN, Horace Leeolphus (Cal)

GRIFFIN, Jan (Spok) 803 Symons St, Richland, WA 99354

GRIFFIN, Jeremiah (RG) PO Box 175, Marfa, TX 79843

GRIFFIN, Jon Edward (Spr) 449 State Highway 37, West Frankfort, IL 62896

GRIFFIN, Mary-Carol Ann (Me) 862 Eagle Lake Rd, Bar Harbor, ME 04609

GRIFFIN, Miranda Cully (WTenn) 3245 Central Ave, Memphis, TN 38111

GRIFFIN, Patrick Corrigan (Colo) 127 W Archer Pl, Denver, CO 80223

GRIFFIN, Pauline Ruth (USC) 605 Woodland St, Spartanburg, SC 29302

GRIFFIN, P Joshua (Cal) St David Of Wales, 2800 SE Harrison St, Portland, OR 97214

GRIFFIN, Ronald Wayne (ECR) 1007 Persimmon Ave, Sunnyvale, CA 94087

GRIFFIN, Russell Agnew (NJ) 219 Philadelphia Blvd, Sea Girt, NJ 08750

GRIFFIN, Tim (Pa) 2730 Cranston Rd, Philadelphia, PA 19131

GRIFFIN JR, William Leonard (Ark) 40 Cliffdale Dr, Little Rock, AR 72223

GRIFFIS SR, Terrell Hathorn (La) 316 Driftwood Dr, Meridian, MS 39305

GRIFFITH, Bernard Macfarren (SeFla) 15100 Sw 141st Ter, Miami, FL 33196

GRIFFITH, Bruce Derby (LI) Po Box 145, Pultneyville, NY 14538

GRIFFITH, Charles (WK) 8631 Beulah Land Dr, Ozark, AR 72949

GRIFFITH, David M (Los) 821 Valley Crest St, La Canada, CA 91011

GRIFFITH, Gregory Erwin (O) 705 Main St, Coshocton, OH 43812

GRIFFITH, Nickolas Clay (Los)

GRIFFITH JR, Norman Early (WTex) 1601 E 19th St, Georgetown, TX 78626

GRIFFITH JR, Robert L (LI) 199 Carroll St, Brooklyn, NY 11213

GRIFFITH, Robert Talmadge (CFla) 601 S Highland Ave, Apopka, FL 32703

GRIFFITH, Shawn Lynn (WNC) 3658 Gaston Day School Rd, Gastonia, NC 28056

GRIFFITHS, Robert Stephen (Fla) 2613 Vista Cove Rd, Saint Augustine, FL 32084

GRIFO, Lynne (Ct)

GRIGG, Joel Thomas (Alb) 145 Main Street, Massena, NY 13662

GRIGGS, Linda Mackie (RI) 50 Orchard Avenue, Providence, RI 02906

GRIM, Leland Howard (Minn) 2636 County Road 94, International Falls, MN 56649

GRIMES, Charles Gus (Tenn) 510 W Main St, Franklin, TN 37064

GRIMES, Eve Lyn (Colo) 624 W 19th St, Pueblo, CO 81003

GRIMM, Susan (SVa) 1104 Lakepoint Dr, Clarksville, VA 23927

GRIMSHAW, Gretchen Sanders (Mass) 28 Robbins Rd, Watertown, MA 02472

GRINDON, Carri Patterson (Los) 1014 E. Altadena Dr., Altadena, CA 91001

GRINDON, Sharon Lee (Vt) 386South St, Middlebury, VT 05753

GRINER, Robert (Nwk) 115 Cedar Dr, Newton, NJ 07860

GRINNELL, Janice Louise (RI) 263 Orchard Woods Drive, Saunderstown, RI 02874

GRINNELL, Lynn Dean (SwFla) 15102 Amberly Dr, Tampa, FL 33647

GRISCOM, Donald Wayne (SwFla) 3324 Chicago Ave, Bradenton, FL 34207

GRISHAM JR, Lowell (Ark) Po Box 1190, Fayetteville, AR 72702

GRISWOLD, David Alton (WA) 4201 Albemarle St NW, Washington, DC 20016

✠ **GRISWOLD III**, Frank Tracy (Chi)

GRISWOLD-KUHN, Karl E (Alb) 6 Silvester St, Kinderhook, NY 12106

GRITTER, Joshua Michael (CFla) 1875 19th Ave SW, Vero Beach, FL 32962

GRIZZLE, Anne Fletcher (SwVa) 123 W Washington St, Lexington, VA 24450

GROB, Bruce Russell (Fla) 151 Nc Highway 9 Pmb 227, Black Mountain, NC 28711

GRODT, Eileen Patricia (Oly) 722 N 145th St, Shoreline, WA 98133

GROENINGER, Mary (Minn)

GROFF JR, John Weldon (Ala) 12656 N Shoreland Pkwy, Mequon, WI 53092

GROFF, Mary Elizabeth (Ala) 6141 Sherry Dr, Guntersville, AL 35976

GROFF JR, Sanford (SeFla) 3395 Burns Rd, Palm Beach Gardens, FL 33410

GROH, Clifford Herbert (Mich)

GRONEK, Marianna L (Az) Church of the Epiphany, 423 N Beaver St, Flagstaff, AZ 86001

GRONEMAN, Leslie Joyce (Alb)

GROSCHNER, Peter Kingston (Mich) 19759 Holiday Rd, Grosse Pointe Woods, MI 48236

GROSE, Fayette Powers (O) 310 E Lincoln Way, Lisbon, OH 44432

GROSH, Christine Marie (Neb) 7921 N Hazelwood Dr, Lincoln, NE 68510

GROSHART, Nancy Louise (U) 1051 Allen Peak Cir, Ogden, UT 84404

GROSJEAN, Lyle Wood (ECR) 3255 Amber Dr, Paso Robles, CA 93446

GROSKOPH, Elizabeth May (Roch) PO Box 541, Hancock, NY 13783

GROSKOPH, Ralph Gordon (Roch) PO Box 541, 211 Somerset Lake Rd, Hancock, NY 13783

GROSS, Bob (Neb) 1009 Bedford Ct W, Hurst, TX 76053

GROSS, Brian K (Wyo) 2625 Main St, Torrington, WY 82240

GROSS, Daniel La Rue (NY) 76 Saint Albans St, Staten Island, NY 10312

GROSSMAN, Stacey (Cal) St. Timothy's Episcopal Church, 1550 Diablo Rd, Danville, CA 94526

GROSSO, Andrew (USC) 1100 Sumter St, Columbia, SC 29201

GROSSOEHME, Daniel Huck (SO) Pulmonary Medicine Mlc2021, Cchmc, Cincinnati, OH 45229

GROSSOEHME, Henrietta H (Ind) 111 S Grant St, Bloomington, IN 47408

GROTH, Justin C (Dal)

GROTZINGER, Terri (Mont) 130 S 6th St E, Missoula, MT 59801

GROUBERT, Gerri Helen (Nev) 3665 Largo Verde Way, Las Vegas, NV 89121

GROUT III, Earl Leroy (Oly) 6801 30th Ave Ne, Seattle, WA 98115

GROVER III, Charles Lowell (Roch) 4006 Brick Kiln Dr, Chittenango, NY 13037

GROVES, Barbara T (CNY) 141 Main St, Whitesboro, NY 13492

GRUBAUGH, Lauren DH (Los) 125 Monument Cir, Indianapolis, IN 46204

GRUBB, Sarah Ann (Neb) 8800 Holdrege St, Lincoln, NE 68505

GRUBBS, Lucas (Colo) 630 Gilpin St, Denver, CO 80218

GRUBE, David Quinn (Nev) 777 Sage St., Elko, NV 89801

GRUBERTH, Cole (CNY)

GRUMAN, Stephen Cowles (Ala) 131 Silver Lake Cir, Madison, AL 35758

GRUMHAUS, Jennifer Wood (Mass) 23 Loew Cir, Milton, MA 02186

GRUNDY, Elizabeth A (Mass) 421 Wianno Ave, Osterville, MA 02655

GRUNDY, Sandra A (Colo) 9345 Carr St, Westminster, CO 80021

GRUNFELD, Matthew (SwFla) Church of Annunciation, 4408 Gulf Dr, Holmes Beach, FL 34217

GRUSELL, Katrina L (Md) 5057 Stone Hill Dr, Ellicott City, MD 21043

GRUSENDORF, William Connor (WTex) 401 W Dry St, San Saba, TX 76877

GRYGIEL, Janet Carol (Chi) 1415 Temple Cir, Rockford, IL 61108

GUAILLAS CARANGUI, Raul (DR (DomRep)) Cafetos Oe-3-76 Y Nazareth, Quito, 00593, Ecuador

GUAMAN AYALA, Francisco (EcuC) Brasilia Y Buenos Aires, Ambato, Ecuador

GUANSON, Lou Ann (The Episcopal Church in Haw)

GUBACK, Thomas Henry (WMich) 6300 North ManitouTrail, Northport, MI 49670

GUCK, Sarah St John (RG) PO Box 2795, Silver City, NM 88062

GUENTHER, Nancy Louise (WNY) 200 East Center St., Medina, NY 14103

GUERNSEY, Jacqueline Louise (CFla) 25510 Belle Alliance, Leesburg, FL 34748

GUERNSEY, Justine Marie (Alb) 563 Kenwood Ave, Delmar, NY 12054

GUERRA, Carrie Lee (WTex) Trinity Episcopal Church, 1501 N Glass St, Victoria, TX 77901

GUERRA, Irma N (At) 400 Holcomb Bridge Rd, Norcross, GA 30071

GUERRA, Norma Yanira (Los)

GUERRA-DIAZ, Juan Antonio (Ore) Po Box 1731, Hillsboro, OR 97123

✠ **GUERRERO**, Orlando Jesus (Ve) Centro Diocesano, Avenue Caroni No. 100, Colinas de Bello Monte, Caracas, Venezuela

GUERRERO-STAMP, Carmen Bruni (Az) 114 W Roosevelt, Phoenix, AZ 85003

GUERRIER, Michel Marguy (Hai)

GUERRIER, Panel Marc (SwFla) 3901 Davis Blvd, Naples, FL 34104

GUEVARA RODRIGUEZ, Carlos Eduardo (Colom) Calle 30 No 17-08, Barrio Armenia, Teusaquillo, Bogota, Colombia

GUFFEY, Andrew Ryan (Va)

GUFFEY, Emily Williams (Va) 4550 N Hermitage Ave, Chicago, IL 60640

GUGLIERMETTO, Gian Luigi Luigi (Los)

GUIBORD, Gwynne Marlyn (Los) 146 S Beachwood Dr, Los Angeles, CA 90004

GUIDA, Angela G (Az) 2480 Virginia St Apt 4, Berkeley, CA 94709

GUIDRY, Robert Turner (WNC) 869 Daylily Dr, Hayesville, NC 28904

GUILFOYLE, David Martin (Ind)

GUILLAUME-SAM, Sully (LI) 1405 Bushwick Ave, Brooklyn, NY 11207

GUILLEN, Anthony Anthony (Los) 198 Via Baja, Ventura, CA 93003

GUINN, Patricia J (WNY) 2753 Eastwood Rd, East Aurora, NY 14052

GUINTA, Denise (SwVa) 5011 McGregor Blvd, Fort Myers, FL 33901

GUISTOLISE, Kathryn Jean Mazzenga (Chi) 5555 N Sheridan Rd #608, Chicago, IL 60640

✠ **GULICK JR**, Ted (Va) 425 S 2nd St, Louisville, KY 40202

GULLETT, John Manford (CFla)

GUMBS, Delores Elvida (VI) PO Box 6454, Christiansted, St Croix, VI 00823

✠ **GUMBS**, Edward (VI) P.O. Box 7488, St Thomas, VI 00801

GUNDERSON, David John (Mont) 313 S Yellowstone St, Livingston, MT 59047

GUNDERSON, Gretchen Anne (Oly) 629 Taft Ave, Raymond, WA 98577

GUNN, Daniel Cube (NJ) 201 Crestview Rd, Bridgewater, NJ 08807

GUNN, Kevin Paul (Los) All Saints Parish, 5619 Monte Vista St, Los Angeles, CA 90042

GUNN, Sally Watkins Pope (Va)

GUNN, Scott Alan (SO) Forward Movement, 412 Sycamore St, Cincinnati, OH 45202

✠ **GUNTER**, Matthew A (FdL) 22w400 Hackberry Dr, Glen Ellyn, IL 60137

GUNTHORPES, Alexander (LI) 2666 E 22nd St, Brooklyn, NY 11235

GURRY, Jane Todd (NC) 817 Rosemont Ave, Raleigh, NC 27607

GUSTAFSON, Diana Vivian (Wa) 2300 Cathedral Ave NW, Washington, DC 20008

GUSTAFSON, Elyse Marie (Chi) 4901 N Mesa St Apt 4206, El Paso, TX 79912

GUSTAFSON III, Karl Edmund (Nev) 4201 W Washington Ave, Las Vegas, NV 89107

GUSTAFSON, Mary (WMass) 1840 University Ave W Apt 201, Saint Paul, MN 55104

GUSTIN, Pete (Va) 301 W Broad St Apt 762, Falls Church, VA 22046

GUTGSELL, Jessie D (O) 2747 Fairmount Blvd, Cleveland Heights, OH 44106

GUTHRIE, Bill (Nwk) 2812 Sequoyah Drive, Haines City, FL 33844

GUTHRIE, Emily (WA) 7215 Arthur Dr, Falls Church, VA 22046

GUTHRIE, Suzanne Elizabeth (The Episcopal NCal) 31 Oriole Drive, 105 Federal Hill Road, Woodstock, NY 12498

✠ **GUTIERREZ**, Daniel (Pa) 601 Montano Rd. N.W., Albuquerque, NM 87107

GUTIERREZ, Hayr (PR) Villas De Castro, Calle 25 Ee-19, Caguas, PR 00726

GUTIERREZ, Janssen J (Tex) 895 Palm Valley Rd, Ponte Vedra, FL 32081

GUTIERREZ, Jorge Martin (Roch) 48 Whitcomb Road, Boxborough, MA 01719

GUTIERREZ, Jorge Pablo (SeFla) 1003 Allendale Rd, West Palm Beach, FL 33405

GUTIERREZ-DUARTE, Edgar (Mass) 32 Franklin Ave, Chelsea, MA 02150

GUTWEIN, Martin (NJ) 527 N 2nd St, Camden, NJ 08102

GUY, Kenneth Gordon (FdL) N11052 Norway Ln, Tomahawk, WI 54487

GUZMAN, Pedro S (NJ) 7709 Piersanti Ct, Pennsauken, NJ 08109

GUZMAN VELEZ, Francisco Inocencio (PR) PO Box 902, Saint Just, PR 00978

GWIN, Connor Brindley (SwVa) 1002 1st St SW, Roanoke, VA 24016

GWIN JR, Lawrence Prestidge (Tex) Po Box 404, Bay City, TX 77404

GWINN, Thomas Wallace (Alb) PO Box 286, North Stratford, NH 03590

GWYN III, Lewis R. (CFla) 5855 39th Ln, Vero Beach, FL 32966

GWYN, Roxane S (NC) 115 Sherman Pines Drive, Fuquay-Varina, NC 27526

GWYNN, Caron A (WA) St. Timothy's Episcopal Church, 3601 Alabama Avenue, S.E., Washington, DC 20020

GWYNNE, Geoff Carrington (Tex) 1104 Peregrine Dr, Friendswood, TX 77546

H

HAACK, Christopher Allyn (Minn) 877 Jessie St, Saint Paul, MN 55130

HAACK, Marcus John (Ia)

HAAS, Kirk (WVa) 112 South Walnut St., Morgantown, WV 26501

HAAS, Margaret Ann (Mich) 2923 Roundtree Blvd Apt A2, Ypsilanti, MI 48197

HAAS, Michael James (NI) 2006 E Broadway, Logansport, IN 46947

HAASE, Sylvia Anne (Oly) Po Box 208, Vaughn, WA 98394

HABECKER, Elizabeth A (RI) PO Box 743, Bristol, RI 02809

HABECKER, John Christian (Nwk) 47 Av Sur #723 Colonia Flor Blanca, Apartado (01) 274, San Salvador, CA 000

HABERKORN, Violet Marie (Ind) 5045 W 15th Street, Speedway, IN 46224

HABERSANG, Paul Matthew (Vt) 605 Getz Rd, Williamstown, VT 05679

HABIBY, Samir Jamil (Ga) 24 Sawyers Crossing Rd, Swanzey, NH 03446

HACKBARTH, Michael George (FdL)

HACKER, Craig A (Alb) Po Box 775, Waddington, NY 13694

HACKER, David (Spok) PO Box 356, Zillah, WA 98953

HACKETT, Ann Riley (At) Po Box 169, Morrow, GA 30260

HACKETT JR, Charles Dudleigh (At) 10298 Big Cnoe, Big Canoe, GA 30143

HACKETT, Christopher James (ETenn) 413 Cumberland Ave, Knoxville, TN 37902

HACKETT, David Robert (ETenn) 7994 Prince Dr., Ooltewah, TN 37363

HACKETT, Michael George (La)

HACKLER, Wendy Kaye Douglas (Az) 10486 N. Autumn Hill Lane, Tucson, AZ 85737

HACKNEY, Lisa E (Chi) 2954 Essex Rd, Cleveland Heights, OH 44118

HADAWAY, Elizabeth Leigh (WNY) 913 Briarwood Ct, Morgantown, WV 26505

HADAWAY JR, Michael (WNY) PO Box 205, Kingsville, MD 21087

HADDAD, Mary E (Eur) 4 Rue Henri Duchene, Paris, 75015, France

HADDIX JR, Theodore R (Va) 3825 Indianview Ave, Cincinnati, OH 45227

HADDOX, Jason M (Okla) 1512 Vine St, Norman, OK 73072

HADE, Lynn Augustine (Pa) Church of the Advent, 12 Byberry Rd, Hatboro, PA 19040

HADEN JR, Robert Lee (NC) 798 Evans Rd., Hendersonville, NC 28739

HADLER JR, Jacques Bauer (WA) 1736 Columbia Rd NW Apt 201, Washington, DC 20009

HADLEY, Arthur Clayton (SO) 1500 Shasta, McAllen, TX 78504

HAENKE, Roger Alan (SanD)

HAFER, Joel (WNC) 776 N. Main St., Hendersonville, NC 28792

HAGAN JR, John (WVa) 1001 Loudon Heights Rd, Charleston, WV 25314

HAGANS, Michele Victoria (WA) 1645 Myrtle St Nw, Washington, DC 20012

HAGBERG, Joe (CGC) 9101 Panama City Beach Parkway, Panama City Beach, FL 32407

HAGE, Raymond Joseph (WVa) 2105 Wiltshire Blvd, Huntington, WV 25701

HAGEN, Amelia (Me) 39 Highland Ave, Millinocket, ME 04462

HAGEN, Jim (NY) 21-15 34th Ave apt 14C, Astoria, NY 11106

HAGEN, Maureen (Ore) 3030 Se Bybee Blvd, Portland, OR 97202

HAGENBUCH, Chris (Spok) 311 South Hall St, Grangeville, ID 83530

HAGER, Marty Monroe (Va) St Thomas Episcopal Church, 8991 Brook Rd, McLean, VA 22102

HAGERMAN, Steven William (Colo) 1110 Saint Stephens Church Rd, Crownsville, MD 21032

HAGERTY, Stephen P (NY) 84 Ehrhardt Rd, Pearl River, NY 10965

HAGGENJOS, Babette Florence (The Episcopal NCal)

HAGGENJOS JR, Cliff (The Episcopal NCal) 1905 Third Street, Napa, CA 94559

HAGLER, James Robert (ETenn) 933 S. 17th St., Newark, NJ 07108

HAGNER, Nancy (Mass)

HAGOOD II, Monroe Johnson (CFla) 7745 Indian Oaks Dr Apt H114, Vero Beach, FL 32966

HAGUE, Betsy (WA) 4507 Leland St, Chevy Chase, MD 20815

HAGUE, Bill (WA) 4001 Franklin St, Kensington, MD 20895

HAGUE, Jane (WA)

HAGUE, Leslie (SeFla) 1132 N Ivanhoe St, Arlington, VA 22205

HAGUE, Sarah Anne (NH) 23 Alice Peck Day Dr Unit 247, Lebanon, NH 03766

HAHN, Dorothee Elisabeth (Eur) 815 2nd Ave, New York, NY 10017

✠ **HAHN**, Doug (Lex) 2134 Wells Dr, Columbus, GA 31906

HAHNE, Ruth Olive (CFla) 9260-C Sw 61st Way, Boca Raton, FL 33428

HAHNEMAN, Geoffrey (Ct) 180 Battery Park Dr, Bridgeport, CT 06605

HAHNEMAN, Lisa (Ct) 154 Jackman Ave, Fairfield, CT 06825

HAIG, David William (Alb) PO Box 1834, Orleans, MA 02653

HAIG, Karen (Oly) 4685 Taylor Ave NE, Bainbridge Island, WA 98110

HAILEY, Victor (Md) 1110 Saint Stephens Church Rd, Crownsville, MD 21032

HAIN, John Walter (NJ) 13 Madison Ave, Flemington, NJ 08822

HAINES, Harry Jeffrey (WNY) 24 Cobb Ter, Rochester, NY 14620

HAINES, Mike (Pa) 31 Kleyona Ave, Phoenixville, PA 19460

HAINES III, Ralph Edward (SVa) 42 Park Ave, Newport News, VA 23607

HAINES-MURDOCCO, Sandra (RI) 109 Old Post Rd, Wakefield, RI 02879

HAIRSTON, Raleigh Daniel (EC) 3183 Kings Bay Cir, Decatur, GA 30034

HAKIEL, Nicholas Edward (Ida) 1014 Wildwood St, Sultan, WA 98294

HALE, Douglas J (Ore) 2785 Elysium Ave, Eugene, OR 97401

HALE, Jane Currie Linnard (Ct) Trinity Episcopal Church, Po Box 276, Brooklyn, CT 06234

HALE, Linda Mosier (Spok) PO Box 456, Sunnyside, WA 98944

HALE, Patricia Ann (Ore) 2785 Elysium Avenue, Eugene, OR 97401

HALE, William Charles (Mich) 1067 Hubbard St, Detroit, MI 48209

HALEY-RAY, Judith (Pa) 163 Colket Ln, Devon, PA 19333

HALFORD, Cathrine Nance (Miss) 147 Daniel Lake Blvd, Jackson, MS 39212

HALKETT, Thomas (Me) PO Box 564, Machias, ME 04654

HALL, Addison Curtis (Mass) 79 Denton Rd, Wellesley, MA 02482

HALL, Albert Benjamin (WMass) 775 Columbia Northwest, Port Charlotte, FL 33952

HALL, Allen Keith (Colo) 3950 W 12th St Nr 10, Greeley, CO 80634

HALL, Caroline J A (ECR) Po Box 6359, Los Osos, CA 93412

HALL, Charlotte Melissa (Nwk) 11 S Kingman Rd, South Orange, NJ 07079

HALL, Daniel Charles (NJ) 114 Willow Dr, North Cape May, NJ 08204

HALL, Daniel Emerson (Pgh) 412 Locust St, Pittsburgh, PA 15218

HALL, David A (Ala) 2753 11th Ave S, Birmingham, AL 35205

HALL, David Moreland (WMass) 20 Winchester Ave, Auburn, MA 01501

HALL, Dianne Costner (Ga) 212 N Jefferson St, Albany, GA 31701

HALL, Donna (SeFla) 941 Allendale Rd, West Palm Beach, FL 33405

HALL, Ernest Eugene (Spr) 1808 Lakeside Dr Unit A, Champaign, IL 61821

HALL, Gary (Los) Cathedral of St Peter & St Paul, 3101 Wisconsin Ave NW, Washington, DC 20016

HALL, John C N (Va) 124 Quietwalk Ln, Herndon, VA 20170

HALL, John Liston (Ia) 20 Mcclellan Blvd, Davenport, IA 52803

HALL, Jon (Mo) 15764 Clayton Rd, Ellisville, MO 63011

HALL, Karen (SD) 302 S.Maple, Watertown, SD 57201

HALL, Kathleen (WMo) 100 E Red Bridge Rd, Kansas City, MO 64114

HALL, Laurens Allen (Tex) 3725 Chevy Chase Dr, Houston, TX 77019

HALL, Leigh (NY) P.O. Box 74, Swainsboro, GA 30401

HALL, Lisbeth Jordan (Mass) 1239 Peterkin Hl, South Woodstock, VT 05071

HALL, Mark (Episcopal SJ) 2212 River Dr, Stockton, CA 95204

HALL, Mark R (Dal) 5100 Ross Ave, Dallas, TX 75206

HALL, Mavis Ann (Neb) 3214 Davy Jones Dr, Plattsmouth, NE 68048

HALL, Melinda (NwPa) Holy Trinity Church, 62 Pickering St, Brookville, PA 15825

HALL, Michael Gregory (CFla) Shepherd of the Hills, 2540 W Norvell Bryant Hwy, Lecanto, FL 34461

HALL, Patrick Mckenzie (Tex) 915 Saulnier St # B, Houston, TX 77019

HALL, Paula Claire (WLa) 361 Cypress Loop, Farmerville, LA 71241

HALL, Richard Hastings (Me) 29 Tarratine Dr, Brunswick, ME 04011

HALL, Rosalind Katherine (SwFla) Episcopal Church of Nativity, 5900 N Lockwood Ridge Rd, Sarasota, FL 34243

HALL, Ryan Ashley (SD) St. Paul's Episcopal Church, 726 6th St, Brookings, SD 57006

HALL, Samuel Leslie (RG) 1023 Acequia Trl Nw, Albuquerque, NM 87107

HALL, Stephen Monteith (Ga) PO Box 69, Clayton, GA 30525

HALL, Tod Latham (NH) 140 Muzzy Hill Rd, Milan, NH 03588

HALL, Vernon Donald (O) 3510 Lee Run Rd, Hermitage, PA 16148

HALL, Virginia (Ind) 3436 E. Longview, Bloomington, IN 47408

HALLADAY, Richard Allen (Ind) 448 Freeman Ridge Rd, Nashville, IN 47448

HALLAHAN, T Mark (Los)

HALLANAN, Sunny (Eur) Chaussee de Charleroi 2, 1420 Braine-l'Alleud, Belgium

HALLAS, Cynthia Johnston (Chi) 3025 Walters Ave, Northbrook, IL 60062

HALLE, Michael Addenbrooke (Az) 241 S.Beverly Street, Chandler, AZ 85225

HALLENBECK, Edwin F (RI) 101 Larchmont Rd, Warwick, RI 02886

HALLER, Robert Bennett (NJ) Trinity Episcopal Church, Vincentown, NJ 08088

HALLER, Tobias Stanislas (NY) 305 West Lafayette Avenue, Baltimore, MD 21217

HALLETT, Timothy Jerome (Spr) 3007 N Ramble Rd W, Bloomington, IN 47408

HALLEY, Marcus George (Minn) 6401 Wornall Ter, Kansas City, MO 64113

HALLISEY, L Ann (The Episcopal NCal) 1711 Westshore St, Davis, CA 95616

HALLMARK, Charlotte A (WMich) PO Box 306, Middleburg, VA 20118

HALLOCK JR, Harold H (Va) 920 Flordon Dr, Charlottesville, VA 22901

HALLY, Jane Eloise (At) 18 Lenox Pointe NE Ste A, Atlanta, GA 30324

HALSTEAD, Jan (Tex) Christ Episcopal Church, 3520 Whitestone Blvd, Cedar Park, TX 78613

HALT, David Jason Andrew (Spr) 2153 Crest Rd, Cincinnati, OH 45240

HALTER, Karl Stuttgart (WA) 2059 Huntington Ave Apt 1203, Alexandria, VA 22303

HALVERSON-RIGATUSO, Kathryn (Ia) 111 N Vine St, Glenwood, IA 51534

HALVERSTADT JR, Albert Nast (Colo) 1244 Detroit St, Denver, CO 80206

HALVORSEN, Douglas C (NJ) 28 Oakhurst Ln, Mount Laurel, NJ 08054

HAMBLETON, Coralie Voce (NMich) St Paul's Episcopal Church, 201 E Ridge St, Marquette, MI 49855

HAMBLIN, Fr Jeffrey L (LI) 423 West 46th Street, New York, NY 10036

HAMBLIN, Sheldon Neilson (LI) 4301 Avenue D, Brooklyn, NY 11203

HAMBY, Daniell C (Pa) 10 Lorile Cir, Eufaula, AL 36027

HAMBY, Timothy Christopher (Lex) 25 S 3rd St, Wilmington, NC 28401

HAMER, Donald (Ct) 240 Kenyon St, Hartford, CT 06105

HAMERSLEY, Andrew C (NJ) 414 East Broad Street, Westfield, NJ 07090

HAMES, Patty Margaret (Ct) 21 N Main St, Niantic, CT 06357

HAMILL, Allardyce Armstrong (CFla) Church of our Saviour, 200 NW 3rd St, Okeechobee, FL 34972

HAMILL, Charles BW (Ct) Christ Episcopal Church North Hills, 5910 Babcock Blvd, Pittsburgh, PA 15237

HAMILL, Jan Elizabeth (Md) 703 Peppard Dr, Bel Air, MD 21014

HAMILTON, Abigail W (Nwk) 681 Prospect Ave # 7052, West Orange, NJ 07052

HAMILTON, David George (Vt) 129 Cumberland Rd, Burlington, VT 05408

HAMILTON, David Hendry (Nwk) 75 Summerhill Dr, Manahawkin, NJ 08050

HAMILTON, Gordon (USC) 101 Woodside Dr, Gaffney, SC 29340

HAMILTON SR, James (Tex) 13618 Brighton Park Drive, Houston, TX 77044

HAMILTON, James G (Md) Canton/ Fells Point Church Plant, 1025 S Potomac St, Baltimore, MD 21224

HAMILTON, Jamie L (NH) 20 Main St, Exeter, NH 03833

HAMILTON, John M (At) 248 Arcadia St Apt B, Dahlonega, GA 30533

HAMILTON, Lucy B (SwFla) 626 Hibiscus Dr, Venice, FL 34285

HAMILTON, Paul Edward Connell (LI) 176 Davis Ln, Hamden, NY 13782

HAMILTON, Reid (Mich) 4657 Dexter Ann Arbor Road, Ann Arbor, MI 48103

HAMILTON, Robert Earl (NC) 1200 N Elm St, Greensboro, NC 27401

HAMILTON, Roger John (CFla) 4018 Shorecrest Drive, Orlando, FL 32804

HAMILTON, Terrell Eugene (Episcopal SJ) 401 N Marilyn Ave, Wenatchee, WA 98801

HAMILTON, William Edward (SeFla) 1728 13th Ave N, Lake Worth, FL 33460

HAMILTON, W Michael (Mass) 19 Bradford Rd, Natick, MA 01760

HAMLIN, Richard Lee (Roch) 6258 County Road 31a, Friendship, NY 14739

HAMLIN, W Richard (Mich) 1016 Poxson Ave, Lansing, MI 48910

HAMLYN, Robert Cornelius (NY) 127 Fulton Ave Apt J1, Poughkeepsie, NY 12603

HAMMATT JR, Edward Augustus (SeFla) 16330 Sw 80th Ave, Miami, FL 33157

HAMMETT, Robert Lee (Mass) P.O. Box 224, Oak Bluff, MA 02557

HAMMON, LeRoy R (Ore) 820 Berwick Ct, Lake Oswego, OR 97034

HAMMOND, Blaine Randol (ECR) PO Box 293, Ben Lomond, CA 95005

HAMMOND, Constance Ann (Ore) 4045 S.E. Pine St., Portland, OR 97214

HAMMOND, David Murray (Cal) 11 Mesa Ave, Mill Valley, CA 94941

HAMMOND, Henry L (Md) 6705 Maxalea Rd, Baltimore, MD 21239

HAMMOND, James Allen (Va) 102 Cottage Drive, Winchester, VA 22603

HAMMOND, Jeff (WTex) 14526 Spaulding Dr, Corpus Christi, TX 78410

HAMMOND, Marion Junior (Colo) 9 Chusco Rd, Santa Fe, NM 87508

HAMMONDS, Joanie (Ala) 755 Plantation Dr, Selma, AL 36701

HAMNER IV, James Edward (At) 6785 Hunters Trace Cir, Atlanta, GA 30328

HAMP, Gary (WMich) 245 Rose Bud Ct, Traverse City, MI 49696

HAMPTON, Carol McDonald (Okla) 1414 N Hudson Ave, Oklahoma City, OK 73103

HAMPTON, Cynthia Marie (SO) 410 Torrence Ct, Cincinnati, OH 45202

HAMPTON, Roger Keith (Los) Po Box 260304, Corpus Christi, TX 78426

✠ **HAMPTON**, Sanford Zangwill Kaye (Oly) La Vida Real, 11588 Via Rancho San Diego Apt D 3049, El Cajon, CA 92019

HAN, Heewoo Daniel (Va) 4060 Championship Dr, Annandale, VA 22003

HAN, Valentine S (Va) 4060 Championship Dr, Annandale, VA 22003

HANAHAN, Gwin Hunter (At) 2744 Peachtree Rd NW, Atlanta, GA 30305

HANAVAN, Julianne (RI) 674 Westminster St, Providence, RI 02903

HANBACK, Holly (Va) 14 Cornwall St NW, Leesburg, VA 20176

HANCHEY, Howard (SVa) 3003 Larkspur Run, Williamsburg, VA 23185

HANCOCK, Art (Eau) 13705 Perry Lake Road, Cable, WI 54821

HANCOCK, Carol Jean (Va) 10730 Scott Dr, Fairfax, VA 22030

HANCOCK, Melinda Bowne ()

HANCOCK, Paul B (Ga) 1317 Gordon Ave, Thomasville, GA 31792

HAND, Gary Dean (Los) 69/659 Moo Ban Far Rangsit, Bungyeetho, Thanyaburi, Pathum Thani Thailand, 12130, Thailand

HANDLOSS, Pattie (Mass) 115 Bayridge Lane, Duxbury, MA 02332

HANDS, Don (Mil) 6 Becks Retreat, Savannah, GA 31411

HANDSCHY, Daniel John (Mo) 9373 Garber Rd, Saint Louis, MO 63126

HANDWERK, Larry Wayne (Chi) 9517 Springfield Ave, Evanston, IL 60203

HANEN, Pat (O) 3785 W 33rd St, Cleveland, OH 44109

HANEY, Jack Howard (NH) 2 Leeward Way, Fairhaven, MA 02719

HANEY, James Paul (NwT) 4904 14th Street, Lubbock, TX 79416

HANEY V, James Paul (NwT) St. Paul's-on-the-Plains, 1510 Avenue X, Lubbock, TX 79401

HANISIAN, Jim (SO) 1409 W Gantry Ct, Leland, NC 28451

HANISIAN, Matthew R (Md) St Martins-in-the-Field, 375 Benfield Rd, Severna Park, MD 21146

HANK, Daniel Hayman (USC) 1151 Elm Savannah Rd, Hopkins, SC 29061

HANKINS, Samuel Scott (Az) 2501 W. Zia Road, #8205, Santa Fe, NM 87505

HANKINSON JR, Benjamin D (Spr)

HANKS JR, Alexander Hamilton (WNC) Po Box 8893, Asheville, NC 28814

HANKS, Paige Alvarez (NC)

HANLEY, Elise Ashley (NY) 860 Orange St, New Haven, CT 06511

HANLEY, Ian David (Los) 59131 Wilcox Ln, Yucca Valley, CA 92284

✠ **HANLEY**, Michael (Ore) Episcopal Diocese of Oregon, 11800 SW Military Ln, Portland, OR 97219

HANNA, Daniel Bassett (Chi) 760 Magazine Street #205, New Orleans, LA 70130

HANNA, Gerald Benson (Oly) 11527 9th Ave Ne, Seattle, WA 98125

HANNA, Nancy Wadsworth (NY) 100 Edward Bentley Rd., Lawrence, NY 11559

HANNA, Raymond J (EC) Po Box 1043, Mount Airy, NC 27030

HANNA, William James (Miss) 783 Rosewood Pointe, Madison, MS 39110

HANNIBAL, Preston Belfield (WA) Washington National cathedral, Mount St. Alban, Washington, DC 20016

HANNON, Timothy Robert (Ore)

HANNUM, Christopher Cary Lee (At) 2148 Winding Creek Ln Sw, Marietta, GA 30064

HANSEL, Bob (SO) PO Box 217, Little Switzerland, NC 28749

HANSELL, Susan Kay (CFla) 2048 Ryan Way, Winter Haven, FL 33884

HANSELMAN, David (CNY) PO Box 88, Greene, NY 13778

HANSEN, Carl R (ECR) 959 Vista Cerro Dr., Paso Robles, CA 93446

HANSEN, Elisa Marie (SwFla) 5615 Midnight Pass Rd, Sarasota, FL 34242

HANSEN, Janis Lee Harney (Mont) 2430 Sw Crestdale Dr, Portland, OR 97225

HANSEN, Jessica V (Cal) 1532 Burlingame Ave, Burlingame, CA 94010

HANSEN, Karen Sue (Okla) 310 E. Noble Ave., Guthrie, OK 73044

HANSEN, Knute Coates (Ct)

HANSEN, Michelle H (Ct) 125 Parklawn Dr, Waterbury, CT 06708

HANSEN JR, Robert F (ECR) 16 Salisbury Dr Apt 7217, Asheville, NC 28803

HANSEN, Thomas Parker (NI) 3717 N Washington Rd, Fort Wayne, IN 46802

HANSKNECHT, Jeanne Marie (CNY) 10 Mill St, Cazenovia, NY 13035

HANSLEY, Mary (SVa) 6219 Chelsea Crescent, Williamsburg, VA 23188

HANSON III, Aquilla (Fla) 406 Glenridge Rd, Perry, FL 32348

HANSON, Deborah Ann (Miss) 5400 Old Canton Rd, Jackson, MS 39211

HANSON, Norma (Del) 405 Sadly Huntingdon Ln, Asheville, NC 28803

HANSON-FOSS, Patricia Jean (Alb) PO Box 237, Au Sable Forks, NY 12912

HANSTINE, Barbara Ann (Alb) 287 Leonard St, Hancock, NY 13783

HANTEN, Helen Bailey (Minn) 66 E. St. Marie St. #205, Duluth, MN 55803

HANWAY JR, Donald Grant (Neb) 128 N 13th St Apt #1009, Lincoln, NE 68508

HANYZEWSKI, Andrew J (Mil) 303 Merchants Ave, Fort Atkinson, WI 53538

HAPTONSTAHL, Stephen R (Minn) 807 Louisiana Ave, Cumberland, MD 21502

HARBIN, J Derek (SVa) 424 Washington St, Portsmouth, VA 23704

HARBOLD, Sally (NC) 221 Union St, Cary, NC 27511

HARBORT, Raymond Louis (Be) 1841 Millard St, Bethlehem, PA 18017

HARDAWAY IV, John Benjamin (USC) 795 Wilson St, Anderson, SC 29621

HARDAWAY, Ripp Barton (WTex) 312 S Guenther Ave, New Braunfels, TX 78130

HARDAWAY, Susan (USC) 404 North St, Anderson, SC 29621

HARDEN, Rosa Lee (Cal) 15 Riparian Way, Ashevile, NC 28778

HARDENSTINE, Autumn Hecker (Pa) 126 Grist Mill Rd, Schuylkill Haven, PA 17963

HARDER, Cheryl Anne (Minn) 10 E Penton Blvd, Duluth, MN 55808

HARDIE JR, John Ford (WTex) 6709 Pharaoh Dr, Corpus Christi, TX 78412

HARDIN, Glennda Cecile (Tex) PO Box 10357, Liberty, TX 77575

HARDIN, Nancy H (SO)

HARDING, Kerith (The Episcopal Church in Haw)

HARDING, Leander Samuel (Alb) Trinity School For Ministry, 311 Eleventh Street, Ambridge, PA 15003

HARDING, Rona (WA) 22968 Esperanza Drive, Lexington Park, MD 20653

HARDING, Sahra Megananda (O) 3004 Belvedere Blvd, Omaha, NE 68111

HARDING, Scott (At) 25 Bonner Dr, Queensbury, NY 12804

HARDING, Stephen Riker (Mass) 1047 Amsterdam Ave, New York, NY 10025

HARDMAN, Bob (Minn) 2338 Como Ave, Saint Paul, MN 55108

HARDMAN, J(Ohn) (Chi) 222 Kenilworth Ave., Kenilworth, IL 60043

HARDWICK, Bill (Oly) 19 1/2 Murray St, Norwalk, CT 06851

HARDWICK, Dana (Lex) 7620 Summerglen Dr, Raleigh, NC 27615

HARDWICK, Lada Eldredge (Colo) 4490 Hanover Ave, Boulder, CO 80305

HARDWICK, Linda C (Mo) 1001 Pheasant Hill Drive, Rolla, MO 65401

HARDY, Cameron (NY) 696 Deep Hollow Rd., Millbrook, NY 12545

HARDY JR, Jerry Edward (Mass) 51 John Ward Ave, Haverhill, MA 01830

HARDY, Karen (WNY) 200 Cazenovia St, Buffalo, NY 14210

HARDY, Kim (Vt) 4 St James Pl, Essex Junction, VT 05452

HARDY, Mary Elizabeth Holsberry (La) Po Box 3654, Durango, CO 81302

HARDY, (Patricia) Joyce (Ark) 2114 Center St, Little Rock, AR 72206

HARDY, Stanley P (Mass) Po Box 657, Humarock, MA 02047

HARDY, Velinda Elaine (NC) P.O. Box 86, 4880 Highway 561 East, Tillery, NC 27887

HARE, Ann DuBuisson (NY) 255 Huguenot St Apt 1712, New Rochelle, NY 10801

HARE, Delmas (At) 104 Sequoyah Hills Drive, Fletcher, NC 28732

HARER, Mark P (CPa) 251 S Derr Dr, Lewisburg, PA 17837

HARGIS, James Frederick (The Episcopal NCal) 742 El Granada Blvd, Half Moon Bay, CA 94019

HARGIS, Kathleen A (Neb) PO Box 1414, Dodge City, KS 67801

HARGREAVES, Helen (Ark) 10 Camp Mitchell Rd, Morrilton, AR 72110

HARGREAVES, Mark Kingston (SanD) St James Episcopal Church, 743 Prospect St, La Jolla, CA 92037

HARGREAVES, Robert Alan (Me) Po Box 96, Nobleboro, ME 04555

HARGROVE, Thomas J (Pa) 1628 Prospect St, Ewing, NJ 08638

HARING, Charlotte (Az) 3942 E Monte Vista Dr, Tucson, AZ 85712

HARKER, Margaret Ann Griggs (NI) 1364 N Pinebluff Dr, Marion, IN 46952

HARKINS, James Robert (NY) 235 Walker Street, Apt. 43, Lenox, MA 01240

HARKINS III, J William (At) 1703 Grace Ct SE, Smyrna, GA 30082

HARLACHER, Richard Charles (CPa) 486 Fencepost Ln, Palmyra, PA 17078

HARLAN, Barry Stephen (WVa) 3887 Carriage Ln SW, Conyers, GA 30094

HARLAN, James (SeFla) 141 S County Rd, Palm Beach, FL 33480

HARLAND, Mary Frances (Spok) Po Box 1510, Medical Lake, WA 99022

HARMAN, Torrence (Va) 1927 Stuart Ave, Richmond, VA 23220

HARMON, Andrew Miles (Mil) 3506 Lawndale Dr, Greensboro, NC 27408

HARMON, Elsa Wittmack (Ia) 3131 Fleur Dr Apt 901, Des Moines, IA 50321

HARMON, John (WA) 7005 Piney Branch Rd NW, Washington, DC 20012

HARMON, Joseph Albion (Nwk) 8 Rosemont Ct, West Orange, NJ 07052

HARMON, Jude Aaron (Cal) Grace Cathedral, 1100 California St, San Francisco, CA 94108

HARMON, Judith Lynn (Mich) 8874 Northern Ave, Plymouth, MI 48170

HARMON, Robert Dale (Spr) 1119 Oakland Ave, 1119 Oakland Ave, Mount Vernon, IL 62864

HARMON, Zachary C (NH) 1444 Liberty St SE, Salem, OR 97302

HARMS, Richard Benjamin (Los) 2731 Jody Pl, Escondido, CA 92027

HARMUTH, Karl Michael (Dal) 9021 Church Rd, Dallas, TX 75231

HARNEY, Margaret Ferris (At) 4393 Garmon Rd Nw, Atlanta, GA 30327

HARPER, Anna Katherine (CFla) St Mary's Church, 5750 SE 115th St, Belleview, FL 34420

HARPER, Barbara Anne (ETenn) 1155 Woodlawn Rd, Lenoir City, TN 37771

HARPER, Catherine Ann (Mass) 124 Front St, Marion, MA 02738

HARPER, David Scott (CPa) 5598 Arminda St, Harrisburg, PA 17109

HARPER, Fletcher (Nwk) 241A Johnson Ave Apt M1, Hackensack, NJ 07601

HARPER, Harry Taylor (WA) 36303 Notley Manor Ln, Chaptico, MD 20621

HARPER, Helen Othelia (WNY) 210 Drummond Ave, Ridgecrest, CA 93555

HARPER, John Brammer (Ia) 1310 Bristol Dr, Iowa City, IA 52245

HARPER, John Harris (Ala) 2600 Arlington Ave S Apt 62, Birmingham, AL 35205

HARPER, Katherine Stuart (Ala) 12200 Bailey Cove Rd SE, Huntsville, AL 35803

HARPER, William Roland (Oly) 5836 Packard Lane, Bainbridge Island, WA 98110

HARPFER, Nancy Jean Fuller (EMich) St Andrews Episcopal Church, PO Box 52, Harrisville, MI 48740

HARPSTER, Chris (ETenn) St Paul's Episcopal Church, 161 E Ravine Rd, Kingsport, TN 37660

HARRELL, Linda J (Ore) 99 Brattle St, Cambridge, MA 02138

HARRELSON JR, Ernie (Spok) 915 S 22nd Ave, Yakima, WA 98902

HARRELSON, Larry Eugene (Ida) 3095 W. Ravenhurst St., Meridian, ID 83646

HARRES, Elisa P (At) 13479 Spring View Dr, Alpharetta, GA 30004

HARRIES, Susan Gratia (NMich) 1111 Bingham Ave, Sault Sainte Marie, MI 49783

HARRIES, Thomas (Minn) 10520 Beard Ave S, Bloomington, MN 55431

HARRIGAN, Kate (CPa) 1105 Old Quaker Rd, Etters, PA 17319

HARRIMAN, Barbara June (Nwk)

HARRINGTON, Debra Lynn (Chi) 1250 Averill Dr, Batavia, IL 60510

HARRINGTON, Lynn Beth (NY) 203 Salem Rd, Pound Ridge, NY 10576

HARRINGTON, Thomas Anthony (Okla) 2961 N 23rd St W, Muskogee, OK 74401

HARRIS, Anne (Miss) 705 Rayburn Ave, Ocean Springs, MS 39564

✠ **HARRIS**, Barbara Clementine (Mass) 11 Atherton Rd., Foxboro, MA 02035

HARRIS, Carl Berlinger (Md) 1506 Eton Way, Crofton, MD 21114

HARRIS, Carl Burton (Va) 2727 Fairview Ave E Apt 3b, Seattle, WA 98102

HARRIS, Cheryl Jeanne (Neb) 820 Weat 9th Street, Alliance, NE 69301

HARRIS, Christopher Ross (SanD)

HARRIS, Donald Bell (SVa) 121 Jordans Journey, Williamsburg, VA 23185

HARRIS, Edmund Immanuel (Oly) 1336 Pawtucket Ave, Rumford, RI 02916

HARRIS, Edward Ridgway (Minn) 2225 Crest Ln Sw, Rochester, MN 55902

HARRIS, Gareth Scott (At) Po Box 191708, Atlanta, GA 31119

✠ **HARRIS**, Gayle (Mass) 138 Tremont St, Boston, MA 02111

HARRIS, Gerald Joaquin (NwPa) 2604 Toucan Ave., McAllen, TX 78504

HARRIS, Henry G (O) 735 Woodrich St SW, Massillon, OH 44646

HARRIS, Herman (USC) 633 Swallow Rd, Elgin, SC 29045

HARRIS JR, James Wesley (Dal) 1700 N Westmoreland Rd, Desoto, TX 75115

HARRIS, John Carlyle (WA) 3050 Military Rd NW #2104, Washington, DC 20015

HARRIS, John E (Ga) 30 Anderson Ave., Holden, MA 01520

HARRIS, John T. (The Episcopal NCal) P.O. Box 1291, Gridley, CA 95948

HARRIS, Jonathan (SwVa) 3286 Avenham Ave Sw, Roanoke, VA 24014

HARRIS, Julie (WVa) 200 W King St, Martinsburg, WV 25401

HARRIS, Ladd Keith (WMich) 5527 N Sierra Ter, Beverly Hills, FL 34465

HARRIS JR, Lawrence (WA) 10450 Lottsford Road, #1218, Mitchellville, MD 20721

HARRIS, Lorraine Denise (NJ) PO Box 1551, Camden, NJ 08101

HARRIS, Margaret Stilwell (Ia) 1120 45th St, Des Moines, IA 50311

HARRIS, Mark (Del) 207 E Market St, Lewes, DE 19958

HARRIS, Mark Hugh (Ore) 385 Doral Place, Pinehurst, NC 28374

HARRIS, Mark P (Ark) 200 N Elm St, Searcy, AR 72143

HARRIS, Marsue (RI) 99 Main St, North Kingstown, RI 02852

HARRIS, Martha Caldwell (CGC) 79 6th St., Apalachicola, FL 32320

HARRIS, Melissa Anderson (Okla)

HARRIS, Michael William Henry (SwFla) 24311 Narwhal Lane, Port Charlotte, FL 33983

HARRIS JR, Paul Sherwood (Pa) 810 Pine St, Philadelphia, PA 19107

HARRIS, Paula (Mil) St. Luke's Episcopal Church, 4011 Major Ave, Madison, WI 53716

HARRIS, Phillip Jay (SO) Po Box 484, Circleville, OH 43113

HARRIS, Robert Carradine (WTex) 510 Belknap Pl, San Antonio, TX 78212

HARRIS, Robert Charles (Kan) 6649 Nall Dr, Mission, KS 66202

HARRIS, Rory Hb (CFla) 827 Tomlinson Ter, Lake Mary, FL 32746

HARRIS, Stephen Dirk (CPa) 1138 Boyds School Rd, Gettysburg, PA 17325

HARRIS, Suzanne Love (NJ) Box 864, Wilson, WY 83014

HARRIS, Thomas G (Chi) 5749 N Kenmore Ave, Chicago, IL 60660

HARRIS, Vincent Powell (WA) 3917 Peppertree Ln, Silver Spring, MD 20906

HARRIS, William Henry (NwPa) 940 Route 46, Emporium, PA 15834

HARRIS-BAYFIELD, Maeva Hair (Tex) 300 Westmnstr Cantrbry Dr, Apt 405, Winchester, VA 22603

✠ **HARRISON**, Dena Arnall (Tex) 3402 Windsor Rd, Austin, TX 78703

HARRISON JR, Edward (SanD) 1114 9th St., Coronado, CA 92118

HARRISON, Elizabeth Arendt (CFla) 215 S Lake Florence Dr, Winter Haven, FL 33884

HARRISON JR, G Hendree (Lex) 533 E Main St, Lexington, KY 40508

HARRISON, Harold Donald (At) 3823 Cherokee Frd, Gainesville, GA 30506

HARRISON, Jim (FdL) All Saints Episcopal Church, 100 N Drew St, Appleton, WI 54911

HARRISON, Merle Marie (Colo) 816 Harrison Ave, Canon City, CO 81212

HARRISON, Merritt Raymond (Mass) 12 Remington St Apt 105, Cambridge, MA 02138

HARRISON JR, Robert (WA) Churchillplein 6, The Hague, 2517 JW, Netherlands

HARRISON, Ronald Edward (Alb) 24 Summit Ave, Latham, NY 12110

HARRISON, Sherridan (WTex) 2431 Michele Jean Way, Santa Clara, CA 95050

HARRISS, Mary L (Chi) 2338 Country Knolls Ln, Elgin, IL 60123

HARRISS, Susan Carol (NY) 2 Rectory St, Rye, NY 10580

HARRITY, Alison (CFla) 5151 Lake Howell Rd, Winter Park, FL 32792

HARRON II, Frank Martin (WA) 10708 Brewer House Rd, North Bethesda, MD 20852

HARROP, Stephen (Tai) 16 W 3rd St, Essington, PA 19029

HART, Alan Reed (Alb) 120 Waters Rd, Scotia, NY 12302

HART, Benjamin James (Ky) Grace Episcopal Church, 216 E 6th St, Hopkinsville, KY 42240

HART, Curtis Webb (NY) 132 N Broadway 1NW, Tarrytown, NY 10591

✠ **HART**, Donald Purple (The Episcopal Church in Haw) P.O. Box 461, Peterborough, NH 03458

HART, Donnalee (The Episcopal NCal) St Francis in the Redwoods, 66 E Commercial St, Willits, CA 95490

HART JR, George Barrow (Ark) 3802 Hwy 82 W, Crossett, AR 71635

HART, J. Joseph (Md) 6701 N Charles St, Towson, MD 21204

HART, Lois Ann (Me) 1100 Washington St, Bath, ME 04530

HART, Lorraine M (Alb) 1154 Hedgewood Ln, Niskayuna, NY 12309

HART, Mary Carol (Alb) 120 Waters Rd, Scotia, NY 12302

HART, Robert (Colo) 1471 Bennavile Ave, Birmingham, MI 48009

HART, Stephen Anthony (Alb) 2849 Laurel Park Hwy, Hendersonville, NC 28739

HART, Valerie (ECR) 8 Daytona Dr, Laguna Niguel, CA 92677

HART, William Gardner (NY) 414 Haines Rd # 4, Mount Kisco, NY 10549

HARTE, Barry Jay (Pa) 27 Conshohocken State Rd, Bala Cynwyd, PA 19004

HARTE JR, John Joseph Meakin (Az) 1000 E. Ponderosa Parkway, Flagstaff, AZ 86001

HARTE, Kathleen Audrey (LI)

HARTE, Susan Brainard (Az) 1000 E. Ponderosa Parkway, Flagstaff, AZ 86001

HART GARNER, Eleanor E (Be) 125 Mount Joy St, Mount Joy, PA 17552

HARTJEN JR, Raymond Clifton (Kan) 7115 S. 5th St., Leavenworth, KS 66048

HARTL, Palmer (Pa) 240 S 3rd St, Philadelphia, PA 19106

HARTLEY, Chris (Ala) 1000 W 18th St, Anniston, AL 36201

HARTLEY, Harold Aitken (Mich) 1106 Riverview St, Rogers City, MI 49779

HARTLEY, James Peyton (USC)

HARTLEY, Loyde Hobart (CPa) St James Church, 119 N Duke St, Lancaster, PA 17602

HARTLEY, Melissa M (At) 735 University Ave, Sewanee, TN 37383

HARTLEY, Robert Henry (The Episcopal NCal) 14530 N Line Post Ln, Tucson, AZ 85755

HARTLING, David Charles (CFla) 1606 Fort Smith Blvd, Deltona, FL 32725

HARTLING, Gardner J (Lex) 1013 Marshall Park Dr, Georgetown, KY 40324

HARTMAN, Anthony Eden (EMich) 3458 E Mckinley Rd, Midland, MI 48640

HARTMAN, Holly H (Mass) PO Box 920372, Needham, MA 02492

HARTMAN, John Franklin (Be) 30 Butler St, Kingston, PA 18704

HARTMAN, Kathleen Thomas (Vt) PO Box 383, Bethel, VT 05032

HARTMAN, Phyllis Colleen (Tex) 1803 Highland Hollow Dr, Conroe, TX 77304

HARTMAN, Samuel Henry (Eas) 5 School House Lane, North East, MD 21901

HARTMANS, Robert Gerrit (ETenn) 5008 14th Ave, Chattanooga, TN 37407

HARTNETT, John Godfrey (Nwk) 169 Fairmount Rd, Ridgewood, NJ 07450

HARTNEY, Michael Elton (Roch) 210 Reading Rd, Watkins Glen, NY 14891

HARTSFIELD, Paula Kindrick (Mo)

HARTSUFF, Jadon (WA) All Souls Memorial Episcopal Church, 2300 Cathedral Ave NW, Washington, DC 20008

HARTT, Paul Jonathan (Alb) 8 Loudon Hts S, Loudonville, NY 12211

HARTT, Walter Fred (NJ) 408 Kingfisher Rd, Tuckerton, NJ 08087

HARTWELL, Edward Mussey (Tex) 5502-B Buffalo Pass, Austin, TX 78745

HARTWELL, Michael (Mass) 620 Flick Cir., Thomasville, NC 27360

HARTZELL, Susan (Va) 5911 Fairview Woods Dr, Fairfax Station, VA 22039

HARTZOG, Dorothy Chatham (Tenn) 211 Chip N Dale Dr., Clarksville, TN 37043

HARTZOG, Howard Gallemore (WTex) 2229 Aiken Way, El Dorado Hills, CA 95762

HARVALA, Eileen Gay (Minn) Trinity Episcopal Church, 345 Main St, Portland, CT 06480

HARVEY, Edwin Edward (WTex) 868 Porter Rd, Cochran, GA 31014

HARVEY, Errol Allen (NY) 800 North Miami Ave., Apt. 302, Miami, FL 33136

HARVEY, Rick E (Ida) 2080 Bodine Ct, Boise, ID 83705

HARVEY, Robert William (WNY) Episcopal Church of Our Saviour, 1700 Powder Mill Road, Silver Spring, MD 20903

HARVEY, Robert William (Az) 9901 Penn Ave S Apt 336, Bloomington, MN 55431

HARWOOD, John Thomas (CPa) 137 3rd St, Renovo, PA 17764

HARY, Barbara A (CPa) 20 Heatherland Rd, Middletown, PA 17057

HASEN, Elizabeth Sorchan (Spok) 409 W 22nd Ave, Spokane, WA 99203

HASKELL, Robert Finch (Alb) 9 Long Creek Dr, Burnt Hills, NY 12027

HASLETT III, William Warner (Pgh) 418 Jerad Ln., Windber, PA 15963

HASS, Caroline Vada (WNY) Po Box 161, Alexander, NY 14005

HASSAN, Rose Cohen (Nwk) 954 Ave C, Bayonne, NJ 07002

HASSE III, Ed (Nwk) 4 Woodland Rd, Montvale, NJ 07645

HASSELBROOK, Audrey Caroline (Nwk) 18 Shepard Pl, Nutley, NJ 07110

HASSELL, Mariann Barbara (Tenn) 1204 Jackson Dr, Pulaski, TN 38478

HASSEMER, Donald William (RG) Po Box 747, Medanales, NM 87548

HASSERIES, Robert Alan (Spok) East 360 Springview Drive, Coeur D'Alene, ID 83814

HASSETT, Miranda Katherine (Mil) 6325 Shoreham Dr, Madison, WI 53711

HASSETT, Steve (Cal)

HASTINGS, Brian J (Chi) 857 W. Margate Terrace, #1-W, Chicago, IL 60640

HASTINGS, Mark Wayne (Mich) PO Box 287, Onsted, MI 49265

HATCH, Jessica Ann (U) 2586 Elizabeth St Apt 6, Salt Lake City, UT 84106

HATCH, Mark (WMass) 267 Locust Street, Apt 2K, Florence, MA 01062

HATCH, Rebekah (Ct) 2852 Kimmeridge Dr, Atlanta, GA 30344

HATCH, Victoria Theresa (Los) 1095 Dysar, Banning, CA 92220

HATCHER, Spencer Elizabeth (Md)

HATFIELD, Adele Dees (Eas) 221 Boulevard, Mountain Lakes, NJ 07046

HATFIELD JR, Chuck (Eas) 221 Boulevard, Mountain Lakes, NJ 07046

HATFIELD, Joel (Dal)

HATFIELD, Russ (SwVa) 101 Logan St, Bluefield, VA 24605

☩ **HATHAWAY**, Alden Moinet (SC) 107 Laurens St., Beaufort, SC 29902

HATHAWAY, Dale Caldwell (The Episcopal Church in Haw) 1863 Rock Glen DR Apt 103, Rock Hill, SC 29732

HATZENBUEHLER, Robin Ritter (WTenn) 1544 Carr Ave, Memphis, TN 38104

HAUCK, Barbara Horsley (Minn) 32 W College St, Duluth, MN 55812

HAUCK, Mary Rockett (The Episcopal NCal) 11489 Phoebe Ct, Penn Valley, CA 95946

HAUERT, Robert Harold (Los) 1419 Jorn Ct, Ann Arbor, MI 48104

HAUFF, Bradley S (Minn) 9601 Frankford Ave, Philadelphia, PA 19114

HAUG, Phillip (Lex) 100 Daisey Dr, Richmond, KY 40475

HAUGAARD, Jeffrey James (CNY) 101 E Williams St, Waterloo, NY 13165

HAUGEN, Alice Bordwell Fulton (Ia) 1483 Grand Ave, Iowa City, IA 52246

HAUGHN, Terry Lee (WMich) 111 W Brighton St, Plainwell, MI 49080

HAUSER, NancyTayler (Pa) Episcopal Church of the Advent, 201 Crestline Dr, Kennett Square, PA 19348

HAUSMAN, Sharon (Nwk)

HAUTTECOEUR, Mario Alberto (ECR) 95 Stillbreeze Ln, Watsonville, CA 95076

HAVENS, Helen Markley Morris (Tex) 2401 Dryden Rd, Houston, TX 77030

HAVERKAMP, Heidi (Chi) 365 Rolfe Rd, Dekalb, IL 60115

HAVERLY, Tom P (NJ) Saint Andrew's Episcopal Church, 419 South St, New Providence, NJ 07974

HAWES III, Charles M (NC) 6 Fountain View Cir Apt C, Greensboro, NC 27405

HAWES, Peter Wortham (USC) 32 Locust Ln, Tryon, NC 28782

HAWKES, Daphne (NJ) 50 Patton Ave, Princeton, NJ 08540

HAWKINS IV, Barney Barney (WNC) 3737 Seminary Rd, Alexandria, VA 22304

HAWKINS, Charles Thomas (Miss) 3003 Curran Rd, Louisville, KY 40205

HAWKINS, Deborah (Cal) 280 Country Club Dr., South San Francisco, CA 94080

HAWKINS JR, Frank Jay (Tex) 1827 Green Gate Dr, Rosenberg, TX 77471

HAWKINS, Gary Altus (WVa) 1803 New Windsor Road, New Windsor, MD 21776

HAWKINS, Jodene (The Episcopal Church in Haw) 203 Kulipuu St, Kihei, HI 96753

HAWKINS, Linda (Va) 4801 Ravensworth Rd, Annandale, VA 22003

HAWKINS, Penelope Elizabeth (Vt) Po Box 492, North Bennington, VT 05257

HAWKINS, Richard Thurber (Pa) W396 n5918 Meadow Ln, Oconomowoc, WI 53066

HAWKINS, Tom (WNY) 14900 Mark Twain St, Detroit, MI 48227

HAWKINS, William Mills (Ark)

HAWKS, Shanna Elizabeth (Spok)

HAWLEY, Carter R (Ore) St Thomas Episcopal Church, 1465 Coburg Rd, Eugene, OR 97401

HAWLEY, Christian N (Tex) 800 S Northshore Dr, Knoxville, TN 37919

HAWLEY, Frank Martin (WTex) 4518 Winlock Dr, San Antonio, TX 78228

HAWLEY, Kristen (WA) Christ Church, 3116 O St NW, Washington, DC 20007

HAWLEY, Madeline Shelton (Tex)

HAWLEY, Oral Robers (Ak)

HAWORTH, Mark (The Episcopal Church in Haw)

HAWS, Howard Eugene (ETenn) 1418 Lonas Dr, Maryville, TN 37803

HAWS, Molly Elizabeth (Cal) Episcopal Church of the Redeemer, 123 Knight Dr, San Rafael, CA 94901

HAWTHORNE, Nanese Arnold (Eas) All Hallows Episcopal Church, 109 W Market St, Snow Hill, MD 21863

HAY, Audrey Leona (NMich) 4955 12th Rd, Escanaba, MI 49829

HAY, Charles (Ga) 1014 Shore Acres Dr, Leesburg, FL 34748

HAY, Daryl (Tex) 2917 Fairfax Dr, Tyler, TX 75701

HAY, Lesley J H (Cal) 1100 California St, San Francisco, CA 94108

HAYASHI, Koji (Ida) 2282 S Southshore Way, Boise, ID 83706

☩ **HAYASHI**, Scott (U) 2649 E. Chalet Circle, Cottonwood Heights, UT 84093

HAYCOCK, Randall Hilton (Chi) 935 Dorchester Pl Apt 301, Charlottesville, VA 22911

HAYDE, Ronald Edward (SeFla) St Mark the Evangelist, 1750 E Oakland Park Blvd, Oakland Park, FL 33334

HAYDEN, Andrea Rose-Marie (NJ) 1002 4th Ave, Asbury Park, NJ 07712

HAYDEN JR, Daniel Frank (Mass)

HAYDEN, John (O) 206 S Oval Dr, Chardon, OH 44024

HAYDEN, John Carleton (WA) 3710 26th St Ne, Washington, DC 20018

HAYDEN JR, Louis Harold (FtW) 7193 Neshoba Cir, Germantown, TN 38138

HAYEK, Hal T (Ia) 220 40th St NE, Cedar Rapids, IA 52402

HAYES III, Christopher Thomas (Va) 1131 Oaklawn Dr, Culpeper, VA 22701

HAYES, E Perren (NY) 33165 W Chesapeake St, Lewes, DE 19958

HAYES, John Michael (Md) 217 N Carey St, Baltimore, MD 21223

HAYES, Margaret Leigh (CFla)

HAYES, Pamela T. (EC) 1004 Bonner Bussells Dr, Southport, NC 28461

HAYES, Valerie Jean (Va) 543 Beulah Rd NE, Vienna, VA 22180

HAYES-MARTIN, Gianetta Marie (Cal) 2650 Sand Hill Rd, Menlo Park, CA 94025

HAYMAN, Robert Fleming (Oly) 1102 E Boston St, Seattle, WA 98102

HAYNES, Alice (USC) 3136 Cimarron Trl, West Columbia, SC 29170

HAYNES, Argola Electa (Los) 1979 Newport Ave, Pasadena, CA 91103

HAYNES, Elizabeth Stephenson (Be) 621 Prices Dr, Cresco, PA 18326

HAYNES, Frank James (EMich) 2518 Woodstock Dr, Port Huron, MI 48060

HAYNES, John Connor (NJ) 45 W Broad St, Burlington, NJ 08016

HAYNES, Kendall Thomas (Oly) PO Box 6906, Tacoma, WA 98417

HAYNES SR, Larry Lee (NY) 34 Point St, New Hamburg, NY 12590

HAYNES, Peter (Los) 4300 Park Newport, Newport Beach, CA 92660

HAYNES, Rachel Fowler (NC) Po Box 504, Davidson, NC 28036

HAYNES, Susan (NI) 616 Lincolnway East, Mishawaka, IN 46544

HAYNES, Thomas E (NI) St. Thomas Episcopal Church, PO Box 421, Plymouth, IN 46563

HAYNES, Warren Edward (LI) 429 E 52nd St Apt 27h, New York, NY 10022

HAYNIE, Amy Peden (FtW) 771 Lakewood Ct, Highland Village, TX 75077

HAYS, Bret (Mass) 48 Middle St, Gloucester, MA 01930

HAYS, Joseph Spurgeon (At) 666 E College St, Griffin, GA 30224

HAYS, Lloyd Philip Whistler (Pgh) Po Box 43, Ambridge, PA 15003

HAYS, Louis B (Pgh) 505 Kingsberry Cir, Pittsburgh, PA 15234

HAYS-SMITH, Melissa B (SwVa) Christ Episcopal Church, 1101 Franklin Rd SW, Roanoke, VA 24016

HAYWARD, Dennis Earl (Vt) 511 Rankinville Rd, Mabou, B0E1X0, Canada

HAYWARD, Stephen H (WA) Stephen H Hayward, 154 Mills Point Rd, Brooksville, ME 04617

HAYWORTH, Joseph Allison (NC) 910 Croyden St, High Point, NC 27262

HAZEL, d'Rue (USC) 546 Woodland Hills West, Columbia, SC 29210

HAZEL, Jim (FtW) 6828 Woodstock Road, Fort Worth, TX 76116

HAZELETT, William Howard (CFla) 1666 Parkgate Dr., Kissimmee, FL 34746

HAZEN, Albie (Ore) 5944 SE Glen Eagle Way, Stuart, FL 34997

HAZEN, Susan Marcotte (Be) St John's Episcopal Church, PO Box 246, Bandon, OR 97411

HAZLETT, Brant Vincent (Spr) 600 N Mulberry St # 674, Mount Carmel, IL 62863

HEACOCK, Donald Dee (WLa) 3218 Line Ave # 101, Shreveport, LA 77104

HEAD, Janice (Colo)

HEAD, Paul Anthony (CFla) 656 Avenue L, NW, Winter Haven, FL 33881

HEALD, David Stanley (Me) 8 Pine Ln, Cumberland Foreside, ME 04110

HEALEY, Joseph Patrick (NY) 1045 Cook Rd, Grosse Pointe, MI 48236

HEALY, Catherine Elizabeth (Mass) 79 Denton Rd, Wellesley, MA 02482

HEALY, Denise Catherine (SwFla) 1502 Paddock Dr, Plant City, FL 33566

HEALY, Linda (Miss)

HEALY, Ruth (At) 1403 Oakridge Cir, Decatur, GA 30033

HEANEY, David Lloyd (SanD) 690 Oxford St, Chula Vista, CA 91911

HEARD, Fred (Ore) 1239 Wigh St SE, Salem, OR 97302

HEARD, Thomas (CGC)

HEARD, Victoria R.T. (Dal) 1630 N Garrett Ave, Diocese of Dallas, Dallas, TX 75206

HEARN, Arnold Withrow (Ark) 232 Pearl St., Marianna, AR 72360

HEARN, Roger Daniel (Va) 2201 Foresthill Rd, Alexandria, VA 22307

HEARNSBERGER, Keith (Ark) 1304 S Schiller St, Little Rock, AR 72202

HEATH, Claudia H (U) 326 Fairfax Dr, Little Rock, AR 72205

HEATH, Susan Blackburn (USC) 1115 Marion Street, Columbia, SC 29201

HEATHCOCK, Deborah Beth (WLa) 404 Ansley Blvd Apt B, Alexandria, LA 71303

HEATHCOCK, J Edwin (Mo) 14485 Brittania Dr, Chesterfield, MO 63017

HEATHERLY, Rose Temple (Wyo) 4700 S Poplar St, Casper, WY 82601

HEATHMAN, Sharron Gae (WMo) Box 307, Lexington, MO 64067

HEBERT, Frank (NJ) 33 Throckmorton St., Freehold, NJ 07728

HECK, John Hathaway (SwVa) 65 Rock Ridge Rd, Callaway, VA 24067

HECKEL, Deborah Lee (FdL) Church of the Holy Apostles, 2937 Freedom Rd, Oneida, WI 54155

HECOCK, Georgia Ingalis (Minn) St. Luke's Episcopal Church, P.O. Box 868, Detroit Lakes, MN 56502

HECTOR JR, Bob (WMich) 348 Waltonia Road, Drake, CO 80515

HEDEN, Eileen (WK) 311 N 4th St, Sterling, KS 67579

HEDGER, John Spencer (Me) 524 Lake Louise Cir Apt 501, Naples, FL 34110

HEDGES, David Benedict (Az) 602 N Wilmot Rd, Tucson, AZ 85711

HEDGES, Merry Helen (Ark) 8201 Hood Rd, Roland, AR 72135

HEDGIS, Sarah Emily (Pa) 5421 Germantown Ave, Philadelphia, PA 19144

HEDGPETH, Marty (NC) 1412 Providence Rd, Charlotte, NC 28207

HEDIN, Joanne Christine (SD) 802 E Iowa St, Rapid City, SD 57701

HEDLUND, Arnold Melvin (ECR) PO Box 2131, Salinas, CA 93902

HEDMAN, James Edward (SwFla) 9719 33rd Ave E, Palmetto, FL 34221

HEDQUIST, Ann Whitney (Kan) 3205 Sw 33rd Ct, Topeka, KS 66614

HEE, Malcolm Keleawe (The Episcopal Church in Haw) 229 Queen Emma Sq, Honolulu, HI 96813

HEFFNER, John H (Be) 129 Fairfax Rd, Bryn Mawr, PA 19010

HEFFNER, Meredith (WA) 11815 Seven Locks Rd, Potomac, MD 20854

HEFFRON, Judy (Los) 4959 Ridgeview St, La Verne, CA 91750

HEFLIN, Tim (Va) St Andrew's Episcopal Church, 6509 Sydenstricker Rd, Burke, VA 22015

HEFLING JR, Charles (Mass) 1619 Massachusetts Ave, Cambridge, MA 02138

HEFLING, David (Roch) St. John's Episcopal Church, 183 North Main Street, Canandaigua, NY 14424

HEFNER, Judith Ann (WNY) 1307 Ransom Rd, Grand Island, NY 14072

HEFTI, William Joseph (The Episcopal NCal) 24300 Green Valley Rd, Auburn, CA 95602

HEGE, Andrew Joseph (Lex)

HEGEDUS, Frank (Los) 12340 Seal Beach Blvd Ste B, Seal Beach, CA 90740

HEGG, Camille (At) 753 College St, Macon, GA 31201

HEGLUND, Janice N (Cal) 84 San Gabriel Dr, Fairfax, CA 94930

HEGNEY, Georgina (CNY) 210 Twin Hills Dr, Syracuse, NY 13207

HEHR, Randy (SwFla) 3200 McMullen Booth Road, Clearwater, FL 33761

HEICHLER, Katherine (WA) Saint Columba's Church, 4201 Albemarle St NW, Washington, DC 20016

HEIDECKER, Eric Vaughn (Nev) 14645 Rim Rock Dr, Reno, NV 89521

HEIDEL, Jerry (SwVa) PO Box 779, Hot Springs, VA 24445

HEIDMANN, Tina Jeanine (ECR) 98 Kip Dr, Salinas, CA 93906

HEIDT, James Kevin (CNY) St John's Church, 341 Main St, Oneida, NY 13421

HEIGHTON JR, Robert Herbert (Alb) St Stevens, 16 Elsmere Ave, Delmar, NY 12054

HEIJMEN, Rutger-Jan Spencer (Tex) St Martin's Episcopal Church, 717 Sage Rd, Houston, TX 77056

HEILIGMAN, Sara (Sally) (CNY) 187 Brookside Ave., Amsterdam, NY 12010

HEIN, Charles Gregory (CGC) 533 Woodleaf Ct, Saint Louis, MO 63122

HEINE, Mary Anne (La) 15249 Brandon Dr, Ponchatoula, LA 70454

HEINE JR, William AJ (La) 436 Jefferson Ave., Metaire, LA 70005

HEINEMANN, Ann E (Ga) 539 N Westover Blvd Apt 103, Albany, GA 31707

HEINRICH, Judith Capstaff (Chi) 853 Oak Hill Rd, Barrington, IL 60010

HEISCHMAN, Daniel R (Ct) 20 Park Ave, #9A, New York, NY 10016

HEISTAND, Virginia (RI) Saint Paul's Church, 55 Main St, North Kingstown, RI 02852

HEITMANN, Katherine A (Dal) 511 Foote St, McKinney, TX 75069

HEKEL, Dean (Mil) 7017 Colony Dr, Madison, WI 53717

HELFERTY, Scott Hanson (Mass) 57 Hillside Ave, Salt Lake City, UT 84103

HELGESON, Gail Michele (Oly) 2909 7th St, Port Townsend, WA 98368

HELLER, Amy Groves (Dal) 6119 Black Berry Ln, Dallas, TX 75248

HELLER, Jan C (Oly) 1663 Bungalow Way NE, Poulsbo, WA 98370

HELLER, Richard C (WVa) 266 Paw Paw Ln, Saint Marys, WV 26170

HELLMAN, Gary L (NY) 224 W 11th St Apt 2, New York, NY 10014

HELMAN, Peter Alan (Az) 131 Edgewood Rd, Middlesboro, KY 40965

HELMER, Ben Edward (Ark) 28 Prospect Ave, Eureka Springs, AR 72632

HELMER, Richard Edward (Cal) Church of Our Saviour, 10 Old Mill St, Mill Valley, CA 94941

HELMS III, David Clarke (SO) 1 Marlborough Avenue, Bromsgrove, B60 2PG, Great Britain (UK)

HELMS, William Travis (Tex) 602 Park Blvd, Austin, TX 78751

HELMUTH, Bradley M (The Episcopal NCal) Holy Trinity Church, 202 High St, Nevada City, CA 95959

HELT, Dwight Neil (Okla) 130 Rue de Montserrat, Norman, OK 73071

HEMINGSON, Celeste (NH) 340 Main St # 3229, Hopkinton, NH 03229

HEMMERS, Louis Emanuel (Los) 1634 Crestview Rd, Redlands, CA 92374

HEMPHILL, Margaret Ayars (Chi) 53 Loveland Rd, Norwich, VT 05055

HEMPSTEAD, James Breese (Ind) 512 Woodland Ave, Petoskey, MI 49770

HENAULT JR, Armand Joseph (Vt) 374 Spring Street, St Johnsbury, VT 05819

HENAULT, Rita (At)

HENDERSON, Catherine Ann Graves (Ga) St Francis of the Islands, 590 Walthour Rd, Savannah, GA 31410

HENDERSON III, Charles (CNY) 39 E Church St, Adams, NY 13605

HENDERSON, Don Keith (Colo) 40 Cougar Trl, Ridgway, CO 81432

✠ **HENDERSON**, Dorsey (USC) 1115 Marion St, Columbia, SC 29201

HENDERSON, Dumont Biglar (Me) 65 Eustis Pkwy., Waterville, ME 04901

HENDERSON JR, George Raymond (Fla) 1516 Marsh Inlet Ct, Jacksonville Beach, FL 32250

HENDERSON, Harvey George (ND) 801 2nd St N, Wahpeton, ND 58075

HENDERSON, Jane Pataky (Chi) 624 Colfax St, Evanston, IL 60201

HENDERSON, Luther Owen (WMo) 288 Cedar Glen Dr Unit 4B, Camdenton, MO 65020

HENDERSON, Mark William (Cal) 795 Buena Vista Ave W Apt 6, San Francisco, CA 94117

HENDERSON, Michael Brant (Lex) 381 Bon Haven Rd, Maysville, KY 41056

HENDERSON, Michael Jack (Fla) 1746 Hillgate Ct, Tallahassee, FL 32308

HENDERSON, Patricia Ann (Tex) St. Francis Episcopal Church, 432 Forest Hill Rd, Macon, GA 31210

HENDERSON, Robert Bobo (Ala) 5375 US Highway 231, Wetumpka, AL 36092

HENDERSON III, Samuel G (Me) 134 Park St, Portland, ME 04101

HENDERSON, Sterling Archibald (Fla) 1746 Hillgate Ct, Tallahassee, FL 32308

HENDERSON, Susan (SwFla) 12630 Panasoffkee Dr, North Fort Myers, FL 33903

HENDERSON JR, Theodore Herbert (Pa) 236 Glen Pl, Elkins Park, PA 19027

HENDRICK, Elizabeth (At) 1520 Oak Rd, Snellville, GA 30078

HENDRICKS III, Frisby (SeFla) 2303 N.E. Seaview Drive, Jensen Beach, FL 34957

HENDRICKS, Mary D (Neb)

HENDRICKS, Rebecca Lanham (EO) Po Box 293, Milton Freewater, OR 97862

HENDRICKSON, Patricia Dee (Los) 265 W Sidlee St, Thousand Oaks, CA 91360

HENDRICKSON III, Robert J (Az) Saint John's Cathedral, 1350 Washington St Fl 3, Denver, CO 80203

HENDRICKSON, Thomas Samuel (Va) 3845 Village Views Pl, Glen Allen, VA 23059

HENERY, Charles Robert (Mil) 20 Oakwood Dr, Delafield, WI 53018

HENKING, Patricia Ellen (NH) 2 Lavender Ct, Merrimack, NH 03054

HENLEY, Carol Eileen (Pgh) 1212 Trevanion Ave, Pittsburgh, PA 15218

HENLEY, Charles Wilbert (ND) PO Box 524, Valley City, ND 58072

HENLEY JR, Edward Joseph (SwFla) 404 Park Ridge Ave, Temple Terrace, FL 33617

HENLEY, Robert P (ETenn) 351 Hardin Ln, Sevierville, TN 37862

HENNAGIN, Bob (Ala) Church Of The Holy Comforter, 2911 Woodley Rd, Montgomery, AL 36111

HENNE, Bruce Charles (Minn) 1270 118th Ave NW, Coon Rapids, MN 55448

HENNESSEY, Nancy H (Md) 66 Highland Ave, Short Hills, NJ 07078

HENNESSY, F(rank) Scott (SVa) 132 Blue Ridge Dr, Orange, VA 22960

HENNESSY, Jeanne Katherine (Minn) 4875 Boatman Ln, Inver Grove Heights, MN 55076

HENNIES, Ronald Gene (SD) 3004 S West Ave, Sioux Falls, SD 57105

HENNING, Joel Peter (HB) 2607 Grant St, Berkeley, CA 94703

HENNING, Kristina Louise (FdL) 6426 S. 35th Street, Franklin, WI 53132

HENNINGER, Annie (SD) 105 E 12th St, Gregory, SD 57533

HENRICHSEN, Robert Anton (Neb)

HENRICK, Mother Joan (Ala) 5789 Tydan Ln, Gadsden, AL 35907

HENRICKSON, Mark (Los) 32A Wingate Street, Avondale, Auckland, 0600, New Zealand (Aotearoa)

HENRY, Barbara Dearborn (WA) 5333 N Sheridan Rd Apt.8H, Chicago, Chicago, IL 60640

HENRY, Dean (NJ) 14 Winding Lane, Southwest Harbor, ME 04679

HENRY, Earl (SeFla) 4401 W Oakland Park Blvd, Fort Lauderdale, FL 33313

HENRY, Eric Lynn (CPa) 1 N Hanover St, Carlisle, PA 17013

HENRY, George Kenneth Grant (NC) 34 Red Fox Lane, Brevard, NC 28712

HENRY, James Russell (SwVa) 4647 Prince Trevor Dr, Williamsburg, VA 23185

HENRY, John R (Spr) 415 S Broad St, Carlinville, IL 62626

HENRY II, John W (Alb) P.O. Box 175, Clifton Park, NY 12065

HENRY, Karen E J (NY) St John's Church, 365 Strawtown Rd, New City, NY 10956

HENRY, Lloyd I (LI) 4607 Avenue H, Brooklyn, NY 11234

HENRY, Richard Arlen (Episcopal SJ) 1155 Leavell Park Cir, Lincoln, CA 95648

Clergy List

HENRY, Richard Lynn (Nev) 228 Hillcrest Dr, Henderson, NV 89015

HENRY JR, Wayman Wright (USC) 116 Sedgewood Ct, Easley, SC 29642

HENSARLING JR, Reid (CFla) 146 Oak Sq S, Lakeland, FL 33813

HENSEL, Charles Howard (Chi) 2625 TEchny Rd Apt 620, Northbrook, IL 60062

HENSHAW, Richard Aurel (Roch) 199 Crosman Terr., Rochester, NY 14620

HENSLEY, Erin S (Tex) PO Box 368, Austin, TX 78767

HENSLEY JR, Joseph H (Va) 905 Princess Anne St, Fredericksbrg, VA 22401

HENSLEY, Lane Goodwin (SanD) 47535 State Highway 74, Palm Desert, CA 92260

HENSLEY, Paul Michael (Episcopal SJ)

HENSLEY, Rob (Chi) 701 N Randall Rd, Aurora, IL 60506

HENSLEY-ECHOLS, Beth Marie (WA) Brooke Army Medical Center, 3851 Roger Brooke Dr, San Antonio, TX 78234

HENSON, David R (WNC) 471 W Martintown Rd, North Augusta, SC 29841

HENSON, Paula (The Episcopal Church In NAM) Good Shepherd Mission, PO Box 618, Fort Defiance, AZ 86504

HENSON, Tula (USC) 253 Bridleridge Rd, Lexington, SC 29073

HENWOOD, Karen Lee (Colo) 5604 E Nichols Pl, Centennial, CO 80112

HENWOOD, William Arthur (Colo) 5604 E Nichols Pl, Centennial, CO 80112

HERALD, Erin Carol (NwPa) St Jude's Episc Church, PO Box 1714, Hermitage, PA 16148

HERBST, Gary (Dal) 8320 Jack Finney Blvd., Greenville, TX 75402

HERGENRATHER, Lynda May Stevenson (Va) 5904 Mount Eagle Dr Apt 318, Alexandria, VA 22303

HERKNER JR, Robert Thomas (O) 328 Windsor Ct, Huron, OH 44839

HERLOCKER SR, John Robert (Ida) 3700 NW Orchard Dr, Terrebonne, OR 97760

HERLOCKER, Thomas Dean (Kan) 1704 E 10th Ave, Winfield, KS 67156

HERMAN, Alice McWreath (SO) 345 Ridgedale Dr N, Worthington, OH 43085

HERMAN, Elizabeth Frances (Minn) 615 Vermillion St, Hastings, MN 55033

HERMANSON, David Harold (NJ) 56 Grace Drive, Old Bridge, NJ 08857

HERMERDING, Joseph R (Dal) Church Of The Incarnation, 3966 Mckinney Ave, Dallas, TX 75204

HERMES, Jonathan Robert (ETenn) PO Box 3248, Kingsport, TN 37664

HERNANDEZ, Alejandro Felix (SeFla) 9460 Fontainebleau Blvd, Apt 334, Miami, FL 33172

HERNANDEZ, Gustavo (Los) Po Box 893, Downey, CA 90241

HERNANDEZ, Jorge A (Nev) 2000 S Maryland Pkwy, Las Vegas, NV 89104

HERNANDEZ, Luis Alfonso (Hond)

HERNANDEZ, Miguel Angel (Nwk)

HERNANDEZ JR, Nicolas (Alb) Trinity Episcopal Church, 1336 1st Ave, Watervliet, NY 12189

HERNANDEZ ROJAS, Martin Antonio (Colom) Carrera 6 No 49-85, Piso 2, Bogota, Colombia

HERNDON, James C (Ida) 1055 Riverton Rd, Blackfoot, ID 83221

HERON, James (NY) 54 Angela Ct, Beacon, NY 12508

HERON, Marsha S (U) 4447 E Lake Cir S, Centennial, CO 80121

HERRERA, Lourdes del Carmen (Hond) IMS SAP Dept 215. PO Box 523900, Miami, FL 33152-3900, Honduras

HERRERA, Maria I (Pa) Po Box 40382, Philadelphia, PA 19106

HERRERA CHAGNA, Raul (EcuC) Avenue Amazonas #4430, Igl Epis Del Ecuador, Quito, Ecuador

HERRICK, Robert Frank (NY) 159-00 Riverside Drive West, Apt 6K-70, New York, NY 10032

HERRING, Dianne Lerae (Wyo) PO Box 12, Kaycee, WY 82639

HERRING, Holly (Az) All Saints' Episcopal Church and Day School, 6300 N Central Ave, Phoenix, AZ 85012

HERRING, John Foster (At) 634 W Peachtree St NW, Atlanta, GA 30308

HERRING, Joseph Dahlet (At) 5575 N Hillbrooke Trce, Johns Creek, GA 30005

HERRING, Virginia (NC) 428 S Shore Dr, Osprey, FL 34229

HERRINGTON III, Willet Jeremiah (Mich) 30420 Rush St, Garden City, MI 48135

HERRMANN, H W (Dal) 623 Ector St, Denton, TX 76201

HERRON, Daniel Peter (Az) St Mark's Church, 322 N Horne, Mesa, AZ 85203

HERRON-PIAZZA, Katharine Ann (Ct) 22 Coulter Ave, Pawling, NY 12564

HERSHBELL, Jackson Paul (SwVa) 274 Still House Dr, Lexington, VA 24450

HERTH, Daniel Edwin (Cal) 32 Mallorie Park Drive, The Garden House, Ripon North Yorkshire, HG42QF, Great Britain (UK)

HERTLEIN, Chris (Ore) 2490 NE Highway 101, Lincoln City, OR 97367

HERVEY JR, Ted (Tex) 933 N Fm 1174, Bertram, TX 78605

HERZOG, Carole Regina (Los) 1471 Cloister Dr, La Habra Heights, CA 90631

✠ **HERZOG**, Daniel William (Alb) 612 S Shore Rd, Delanson, NY 12053

HERZOG, Kenneth Bernard (Fla) 3545 Olympic Dr, Green Cove Springs, FL 32043

HESCHLE, John Henry (Chi) 7100 North Ashland Blvd, Chicago, IL 60626

HESS, Elizabeth Parker (NH) PO Box 545, Berlin, NH 03570

HESS, George Robert (HB)

HESS, Howard (ETenn) 8500 Cambridge Woods Ln, Knoxville, TN 37923

HESS III, Raymond Leonard (The Episcopal NCal) 9001 Crowley Way, Elk Grove, CA 95624

HESSE, Alan Roger (Mass) 409 Common St, Walpole, MA 02081

HESSE JR, Rayner Wilson (NY) 415 Collins St, Bethany Beach, DE 19930

HESSE, Vicki K (Mich) Episcopal Diocese of Michigan, 4800 Woodward Ave, Detroit, MI 48201

HESSE, William Arthur (Okla) 1805 N Canary Dr, Edmond, OK 73034

HETHERINGTON, Robert Gunn (Va) 1500 Westbrook Ct Apt 2133, Richmond, VA 23227

HETLER, Gwendolyn Kay (NMich) 3135 County Road 456, Skandia, MI 49885

HETRICK JR, Budd Albert (Ida) 7470 Sundance Dr, Boise, ID 83709

HETZEL, Alan Dorn (WNC) Po Box 442, Highlands, NC 28741

HEUETT, Bradley Allen (WMo)

HEUSS, William Beresford (Mass) 15 Thimbleberry Rd, South Yarmouth, MA 02664

HEVERLY, Craig Brian (Ore) 925 Se Center St, Portland, OR 97202

HEWETSON, Richard Walton (Cal)

HEWIS, Clara Mae (CGC) 7979 N 9th Ave, Pensacola, FL 32514

HEWITT, Emily Clark (NY) 1848 Commonwealth Ave Apt 56, Boston, MA 02135

HEYBOER, Bobbi Jo (WMich) 30 Justice St, Newaygo, MI 49337

HEYD, Matthew F (NY) 74 Trinity Pl, New York, NY 10006

HEYDT, Charles Read (SwFla) 523 S Palm Ave Apt 7, Sarasota, FL 34236

HEYDUK, Terri (U) St James Episcopal Church, 7486 S Union Park Ave, Midvale, UT 84047

HEYES, Andrew Robin (SwFla) 706 W 113th Ave, Tampa, FL 33612

HEYING, R Christopher (WLa) 3301 Saint Matthias Dr, Shreveport, LA 71119

HEYVAERT, Bruce T (NC) Saint James Church, PO Box 846, Magnolia, AR 71754

HEYWARD, Isabel Carter (Mass) PO Box 449, Cedar Mountain, NC 28718

HIATT, Anthony Ray (FtW) PO Box 22, Decatur, TX 76234

HIATT, Kathleen Mary (Nev) Po Box 146, Pioche, NV 89043

HICKENLOOPER, Morgan (CGC) Po Box 27120, Panama City, FL 32411

HICKEY, John D (Mil) 7845 N River Rd, River Hills, WI 53217

HICKEY-TIERNAN, Joseph (Oly) 3415 S 45th St Apt G, Tacoma, WA 98409

HICKMAN, Clare L (Mich) 851 Reagan St, Canton, MI 48188

HICKS, Catherine D (Va) PO Box 399, Port Royal, VA 22535

HICKS, Janice Marie (WA)

HICKS, John Wellborn (CGC) 502 La Rose Dr, Mobile, AL 36609

HICKS, Mary Kohn (WMass) 88 Masonic Home Rd, #R404, Charlton, MA 01507

HICKS, Paul L (WVa) 430 Juliana St., Parkersburg, WV 26101

HICKS, Richard William (La) 2507 Portola Ave Apt 20, Livermore, CA 94551

HICKS, Warren Earl (SVa) PO Box 7430, Hampton, VA 23666

HIEBERT, Cornelius A (Dal) 8105 Fair Oaks Xing, Dallas, TX 75231

HIERS JR, John (SwFla) 1004 Woodcrest Ave, Clearwater, FL 33756

HIERS, Sharon (At) 2089 Ponce de Leon Ave NE, Atlanta, GA 30307

HIGGINBOTHAM, John E (RI) 99 Pierce St, East Greenwich, RI 02818

HIGGINBOTHAM, Richard Cann (Chi) 3800 N Lake Shore Dr # 1j, Chicago, IL 60613

HIGGINBOTHAM, Stuart Craig (At) 2900 Paces Ferry Rd SE Bldg D, Atlanta, GA 30339

HIGGINS, Kent (WVa) St Matthews Episcopal Church, 36 Norwood Rd, Charleston, WV 25314

HIGGINS, Pam (Cal) 272 W I St, Benicia, CA 94510

HIGGINS, Rock (Va)

HIGGINS, Teddy John (USC)

HIGGINS, Timothy John (Me) 25 Twilight Ln, Gorham, ME 04038

HIGGINS, William Harrison (Va) 8000 Hermitage Rd, Richmond, VA 23228

HIGGINSON, Paul Howard (NH) 472 Swazey La, Bethlehem, NH 03574

HIGGINS-SHAFFER, Diane Hazel (Ore) 503 N Holladay Dr, Seaside, OR 97138

HIGGITT, Noel (ECR) 1325 San Mateo Dr, Menlo Park, CA 94025

✠ **HIGH JR**, Rayford (Tex) 4709 Marbella Cir, Fort Worth, TX 76126

HIGHLAND, Terrence Irving (Pa)

HIGHSMITH, Jennifer Lynn (Ga) 102 Borrell Blvd, Saint Marys, GA 31558

HILDEBRAND, Nancy Steakley (WA) St Nicholas Episcopal Church, 14100 Darnestown Rd Ste B, Germantown, MD 20874

HILDEBRANDT, Lise (NH) 1400 1st Avenue, Longmont, CO 80501

HILDESLEY, Christopher Hugh (NY) 570 Park Ave Apt 6-D, New York, NY 10021

HILE, Jeanette Theresa (Nwk) 16 Day Rd, Landing, NJ 07850

HILEMAN, Mary E sther (Okla) 2809 W 28th Ave, Stillwater, OK 74074

HILFIKER, Gerald Milton (WNY) 10085 Pfarner Road, Boston, NY 14025

HILGARTNER, Elizabeth (Vt) Po Box 6, Orford, NH 03777

HILL, C(harleen) Diane (RG) 1806 Meadows Dr, Birmingham, AL 35235

HILL, David Ernest (Minn) 103 West Oxford Street, Duluth, MN 55803

HILL, Deborah (Ala) Cathedral Church of the Advent, 2017 6th Ave N, Birmingham, AL 35203

HILL, Derrick C (ETenn) 626 Mississippi Ave, Signal Mountain, TN 37377

HILL, Donald B (Roch) 321 E Market St, Jeffersonville, IN 47130

HILL, Ellen R. (Los) 5066 Berean Ln, Irvine, CA 92603

HILL, Gary Hill (Tex) 9541 Highland View Dr., Dallas, TX 75238

HILL III, George Aldrich (SO) 22 Vintage Walk, Cincinnati, OH 45249

HILL, Gordon Carman (Az) 2257 E Becker Ln, Phoenix, AZ 85028

HILL III, Harry Hargrove (Dal) Church Of The Incarnation, 3966 McKinney Ave, Dallas, TX 75204

HILL IV, Harvey (WMass) 19 Ward Avenue, Northampton, MA 01060

HILL, Heather L (The Episcopal Church in Haw) 8911 W Ridgewood Dr, Parma, OH 44130

HILL, H Michael (CGC) 2255 Valle Escondido Dr, Pensacola, FL 32526

HILL, Jerry Echols (Dal) 281 Becky Ln, Waxahachie, TX 75165

HILL, John Spencer (WTex) St Margaret's Episcopal Church, 5310 Stahl Rd, San Antonio, TX 78247

HILL, Joshua Ashton (NH) 950 Episcopal School Way, Knoxville, TN 37932

HILL, Jude (Cal) 573 Dolores St, San Francisco, CA 94110

HILL, Mary Ann (Okla) 5635 E. 71st. St., Tulsa, OK 74136

HILL, Nicholas Thomas (Minn) 4 Saint Paul Ave, Duluth, MN 55803

HILL, Ralph Julian (SD) 1224 Junction Ave, Sturgis, SD 57785

HILL, Renee Leslie (NY) 575 Grand St Apt 1801, New York, NY 10002

HILL, Robert Samuel (Lex)

HILL, Susan Diane (Ga) 3101 Waters Ave, Savannah, GA 31404

HILL, Susan Elizabeth (NY) 225 W 99th St., New York, NY 10025

HILL, Vernon Willard (Episcopal SJ) PO Box 153, Bakersfield, CA 93302

HILLEBRAND, Walter V (LI) 23 Cedar Shore Dr, Massapequa, NY 11758

HILLEGAS, Eric (Mass) Parish of St. Chrysostom, 1 Linden Street, Quincy, MA 02170

HILLENBRAND, Pam (Chi) 412 North Church St, Rockford, IL 61103

HILLER, Michael T. (Cal) 278 Hester Ave, San Francisco, CA 94134

HILLGER, Cindy Lou (Minn) 2801 Westwood Rd, Minnetonka Beach, MN 55361

HILLIARD-YNTEMA, Katharine Arnold (At) 737 Woodland Ave SE, Atlanta, GA 30316

HILLIN JR, Harvey Henderson (WK)

HILLMAN, George Evans (FdL) P O Box 215, Sturgeon Bay, WI 54235

HILLMAN, Harry Randall (Ak) PO Box 870995, Wasilla, AK 99687

HILLQUIST, Kitty (Mo) same, same, MO 63124

HILLS, Frances Ann (WMass) 2 Amy Ct, Pittsfield, MA 01201

HILLS, John Bigelow (WMich) 1450 S Ferry St Apt 104, Grand Haven, MI 49417

HILLS, Julian Victor (Mil) 3046 N Cambridge Ave, Milwaukee, WI 53211

HILLS, Nancy Hays (Mil)

HILLS, Wes (Chi) 221 W 3rd St, Dixon, IL 61021

HILLS JR, William Leroy (SC) 727 Atlantic St, Mt Pleasant, SC 29454

HILSABECK, Polly H (NC) 184 Grey Elm Trl, Durham, NC 27713

HILTON, Duncan Lindsley (Mass) 16 Bradley Ave, Brattleboro, VT 05301

HILTON, Elizabeth Grant (At) PO Box 169, Morrow, GA 30260

HILTON, Olivia Parsons Lillich (WA)

HILYARD, Jack (Ore) 311 NW 20th Ave, Portland, OR 97209

HIMES, John Martin (Tex) 106 N Grove St, Marshall, TX 75670

HIMMERICH, Maurice Fred (Mil) 107 Fairview St, Watertown, WI 53094

HINCAPIE LOAIZA, David Hernan (Colom) Manzana 26 Barrio Simon Bolivar, Armenia-Quindio, Columbia, Colombia

HINCHLIFFE, George Lewis (Fla) PO Box 1238, Live Oak, FL 32064

HINDLE, Darren E (RG)

HINDS, Eric (Cal) 1 S El Camino Real, San Mateo, CA 94401

HINDS, Gilberto Antonio (LI) 9707 Horace Harding Expy Apt 8L, Corona, NY 11368

HINES, Caroline V (NH) 2 Wentworth St, Exeter, NH 03833

HINES JR, Chester (Mo) 1210 Locust St, St. Louis, MO 63103

HINES, John C (Tex) 4603 Pro Ct, College Station, TX 77845

HINES, John Moore (Ky) 5722 Coach Gate Wynde, Louisville, KY 40207

HINES, John S (WNC) 219 Chunns Cove Rd, Asheville, NC 28805

HINES, Lisa Stolley (Tex) Calvary Episcopal Church, PO Box 721, Bastrop, TX 78602

Clergy List

HINES, Travis S (Tenn) 4800 Belmont Park Ter, Nashville, TN 37215

HINKLE, Daniel Wayne (Be) 234 High St, Atglen, PA 19310

HINKLE, Robin Hansen (Ala)

HINMAN, Allen (Nwk) 149 Pennington Ave, Passaic, NJ 07055

HINO, Moki (The Episcopal Church in Haw) Cathedral of St. Andrew, 229 Queen Emma Sq, Honolulu, HI 96813

HINRICHS, William Roger (Alb) 1201 Vineyard St., Cohoes, NY 12047

HINSE, Mary N (Cal) 2230 Huron Dr., Concord, CA 94519

HINSON, Bryan T (At) 582 Walnut St, Macon, GA 31201

HINSON, Jerome Andrew (WMo) 5 Averil Ct, Fredericksburg, VA 22406

HINSON, Michael Bruce (Va) 6033 Queenston St, Springfield, VA 22152

HINTON, Brad (Del) 2320 Grubb Road, Wilmington, DE 19810

HINTON, Gregory (CPa) PO Box 701, Wellsboro, PA 16901

HINTON, Michael (VI) Box 199, Cruz Bay, Saint John, VI 00831

HINTON, Wesley Walker (SO) 5907 Castlewood Xing, Milford, OH 45150

HINTZ, Mary Louise (Cal) 623 28th Street, Richmond, CA 94804

HINXMAN, Frederic William (Lex) 5639 Highway #1, Granville Ferry, B0S 1K0, Canada

HIPP JR, Thomas Allison (USC) 910 Hudson Rd, Greenville, SC 29615

HIPPLE, Judy Kay (Chi) 4511 Newcastle Rd, Rockford, IL 61108

HIPPLE, Maureen (Be) 298 Country View Drive, Towanda, PA 18848

☩ HIRSCHFELD, A Robert (NH) 103 Hedgerose Ln, Hopkinton, NH 03229

HIRSCHMAN, Portia Royall Conn (Md) 11860 Weller Hill Dr, Monrovia, MD 21770

HIRST, Dale Eugene (SVa) 4127 Columbus Ave, Norfolk, VA 23504

HIRST, Robert Lynn (Kan) Po Box 1859, Wichita, KS 67201

HITCH, Catherine Elizabeth (Colo) 1320 Arapahoe Street, Golden, CO 80401

HITCH, Kenneth R (EMich) 405 N Saginaw Rd, Midland, MI 48640

HITCHCOCK JR, H(Orace) Gaylord (The Episcopal Church in Haw) 1030 Aoloa Place, Apt 206A, Kailua, HI 96734

HITCHCOCK, Jessica (WA) 5225 Pooks Hill Rd Apt 1208 South, Bethesda, MD 20814

HITE, Jean (SwFla) St Nathaniel's Episcopal Church, 4200 S Biscayne Dr, North Port, FL 34287

HITE SPECK, Nancy J (NJ) 201 Meadow Ave, Point Pleasant, NJ 08742

HIXON, Beth (Pa) 1201 Lower State Rd, North Wales, PA 19454

HIXSON, Mary Louise (WK) 19 Deer Creek Tr, Anthony, KS 67003

HIYAMA, Paul Shoichi (Mich) 734 Peninsula Ct, Ann Arbor, MI 48105

HIZA, Douglas William (Minn) 10 Meynal Crescent, South Hackney, London, E97AS, Great Britain (UK)

HIZER, Cynthia A (NAM) 550 Jenkins Rd, Covington, GA 30014

HLASS, Lisa (Ark) 2606 Beach Head Ct, Richmond, CA 94804

HLAVACEK, Frances (Be) 110 W Catherine St, Milford, PA 18337

HO, Edward HC (Mass) 24 Greenleaf St, Malden, MA 02148

HO, Jeng-Long Philip (Tai) #200 Ziqiang 1st Rd, Samin Dist, Kaohsiung, Taiwan

HO, Jui-En (Tai)

HOAG, David Stewart (NY) 503 North Causeway #102, New Smyrna Beach, FL 32169

HOARE, Geoffrey Michael St John (WA)

HOBART, James (Nev)

HOBART, Terri (The Episcopal NCal) 967 5th St, Novato, CA 94945

HOBBS, Bryan Arthur (SeFla) 751 Sw 98th Ter, Pembroke Pines, FL 33025

HOBBS, Mercy (SD) 405 N Madison Ave, Pierre, SD 57501

HOBBS, William (WMass) 45 Park Ave., Athol, MA 01331

HOBBS, William Ebert (O) 18 Donlea Dr, Toronto, M4G 2M2, Canada

HOBBY, Kim A (ETenn) Christ Church Episcopal, P.O. Box 347, South Pittsburg, TN 37380

HOBDEN, Brian Charles (RG) 3160 Executive Hills Rd, Las Cruces, NM 88011

HOBGOOD, Bob (EC) 1870 Holly St SW, Ocean Isle Beach, NC 28469

HOBGOOD JR, Walter P (Ga) 1036 Cherry Creek Dr, Valdosta, GA 31605

HOBSON, Carol Gordon (Dal)

HOBSON JR, George Hull (Eur) 119 Blvd. Du Montparnasse, Paris, 75006, France

HOBSON III, Jennings Wise (Va) Po Box 247, Washington, VA 22747

HOBSON, Patricia Shackelford (SO) 2955 Thrushfield Terrace, Cincinnati, OH 45238

HOBSON, Thomas Prunty (Colo) 1236 S High St, Denver, CO 80210

HOCH, Helen Elizabeth (Kan) 314 N 3rd St, Burlington, KS 66839

HOCHE-MONG, Raymond (Cal) Box 937, Montara, CA 94037

HOCKENSMITH, David Albert (Pa) PO Box 90, Morgan, VT 05853

HOCKER, Will (Cal) 6135 Laird Ave, Oakland, CA 94605

HOCKING, Charles Edward (NC) 632 Hughes Rd, Hampstead, NC 28443

HOCKRIDGE, Ann Elizabeth (Pa) Po Box 716, Lyndonville, VT 05851

HODAPP, Tim Leo (Ct) 1335 Asylum Ave, Hartford, CT 06105

HODGE, Reginald Roy (VI)

HODGE, Sonia H (Mass) 111 High St, Taunton, MA 02780

HODGE SR, Vincent (Va) Po Box 767, West Point, VA 23181

HODGE SR, Wayne Carlton (SVa) 114 Cross Ter, Suffolk, VA 23434

HODGES, Corinne (RG) St. Anne's Episcopal Church, 424 W. Market St., Warsaw, IN 46580

HODGES, david.hodges@st-francis.org (WK) 520 Summit St., Winston Salem, NC 27101

HODGES, Michael John (Mass) 29 Central St, Andover, MA 01810

☩ HODGES-COPPLE, Anne (NC) 1104 Watts St, Durham, NC 27701

HODGKINS, Margaret S R (Ct) Trinity Episcopal Church, PO Box 400, Southport, CT 06890

HODGKINS, Nelson (NC) 874 Simmons Grove Church Rd, Pilot Mountain, NC 27041

HODGSON, Carla (Minn)

HODGSON, Gregory Scott (SVa) 11940 Fairlington Lane, Midlothian, VA 23113

HODSDON, Douglas Graham (Fla) 1439 N Market St, Jacksonville, FL 32206

HOEBERMANN, Christine Marie (Oly) 123 L St NE, Auburn, WA 98002

HOECKER, Maria Janine (Me) 32 Emery Ln, Boothbay Harbor, ME 04538

HOECKER, Marsha (Mass) 188 Center Road, Shirley, MA 01464

HOEDEL, Barbara Anne (Ak) PO Box 1661, Kodiak, AK 99615

HOEKSTRA, Robert Bruce (Eau) 909 Summit Ave, Chippewa Falls, WI 54729

HOELTZEL, George Anthony (NY) 721 Warburton Ave, Yonkers, NY 10701

HOELZEL III, William Nold (Chi) 3257 Anika Dr, Fort Collins, CO 80525

HOEY, Anne Knight (Tex) 5608-A Jim Hogg Ave., Austin, TX 78756

HOEY, Lori Jean (CFla) 901 Clearmont St, Sebastian, FL 32958

HOFER, Christopher David (LI) 1400 Poulson St, Wantagh, NY 11793

HOFER, Larry John (CPa) 32801 Ocean Reach Dr, Lewes, DE 19958

HOFF, Timothy Joseph (Ala) 2601 Lakewood Cir, Tuscaloosa, AL 35405

HOFFACKER, Charles (WA) 9A Parkway #202, Greenbelt, MD 20770

HOFFACKER, Michael Paul Niblett (Pa) PO Box 765, Devon, PA 19333

HOFFER, Jack Lee (CPa) 830 Washington Avenue, Tyrone, PA 16686

HOFFER, Wilma Marie (EO) 64849 Casa Ct, Bend, OR 97701

HOFFMAN, Arnold R (Spr) 1226 Olive St Unit 505, Saint Louis, MO 63103

HOFFMAN, Charles Lance (Ct) 8 Sharon Ln, Old Saybrook, CT 06475

HOFFMAN JR, Edgar Henry Hap (Ark) 7 Rubra Ct, Little Rock, AR 72223

HOFFMAN, Ellendale Mccollam (Ct) 8 Sharon Ln, Old Saybrook, CT 06475

HOFFMAN, Jeffrey Paul (CNY)

HOFFMAN, Lisa A (NJ) St. Barnabas by the Bay Church, 13 W. Bates Avenue, Villas, NJ 08251

HOFFMAN, Mary E (Ia) 2704 E garfield, Davenport, IA 52803

HOFFMAN, Michael Patrick (CGC) Christ Episcopal Church, 18 W Wright St, Pensacola, FL 32501

HOFFMAN, Roy Everett (SVa) 2 BL Jackson Road, Newport, RI 02840

HOFFMANN, Beth Borah (Ore) 2409 Crescent Rd, Navarre, FL 32566

HOFMANN, Therese Marie (Mass) 108 Stratford St, West Roxbury, MA 02132

HOGAN, Claudia S M (Eau)

HOGAN, Faye (Los) 1237 Laguna Ln, San Luis Obispo, CA 93035

HOGAN, Lucy Lind (WA) 4500 Massachusetts Ave Nw, Washington, DC 20016

HOGG, Douglas (EC) 347 South Creek Drive, Osprey, FL 34229

HOGG, John Edwin (Va)

HOGG JR, Peter (SVa) 7858 Sunset Dr, Hayes, VA 23072

HOGIN, Christopher W (ETenn) Church Of The Ascension, 800 S Northshore Dr, Knoxville, TN 37919

HOGUE, Kelsey (Colo) 9 W 35th St, Scottsbluff, NE 69361

HOGUE, Marlene Christine Harshfield (Eau) PO Box 637, Hayward, WI 54843

HOGUE JR, Richard R (SanD) 575 Kearny Ave, Kearny, NJ 07032

HOHENFELDT, Robert John (Mil) 1310 Rawson Ave, South Milwaukee, WI 53172

HOIDRA, Carol (Ct) 245 East 72nd Street, Apt. 2D, New York, NY 10021

HOKE, Stuart Hubbard (NY) 536 Fearrington Post, Pittsboro, NC 27312

HOLBEN, Lawrence Robert (The Episcopal NCal) 701 Lassen Ln, Mount Shasta, CA 96067

HOLBERT, John Russell (La) 1645 Carol Sue Ave, Terrytown, LA 70056

HOLBROOK JR, Paul Evans (Lex) 308 Madison Pl, Lexington, KY 40508

HOLCOMB, Justin S (CFla) 100 W Jefferson St, Charlottesville, VA 22902

HOLCOMB, Steve A-Retired (WNC) 1500 Maltby Rd, Marble, NC 28905

HOLCOMBE, Matthew P (Pa) 1412 Providence Road, Charlotte, NC 28207

HOLCOMBE, Scott (CFla) 4146 Millstone Dr, Melbourne, FL 32940

HOLDBROOKE, Charles Henry (LI) Calvary & St. Cyprian's Church, Brooklyn, NY 11221

HOLDEN, Elizabeth G (Tex) 4709 Laurel St, Bellaire, TX 77401

HOLDER, Anthony Brian (SeFla) 2801 N University Dr, Pembroke Pines, FL 33024

HOLDER, Arthur Glenn (Cal) 2400 Ridge Rd, Berkeley, CA 94709

HOLDER, Charles Richard (Md) PO Box A, Rohrersville, MD 21779

HOLDER, Jennifer Sutton (NwT) 1318 Amarilla St, Abilene, TX 79602

HOLDER, Lauren R (At) 435 Peachtree St Ne, Atlanta, GA 30308

HOLDER, Michael Rawle (SVa) 926 Thomasson Lane, South Hill, VA 23970

HOLDER, Timothy (ETenn) 142 Lovers Ln, Elizabethton, TN 37643

HOLDER-JOFFRION, Kerry Elizabeth (Ala) 3009 Barcody Rd Se, Huntsville, AL 35802

HOLDING, Megan (Mass) 15 Saint Paul St, Brookline, MA 02446

HOLDING, Suzann (Chi) 2728 6th Ave, San Diego, CA 92103

HOLDORPH, Jedediah D (EO) 2203 Dollarhide Way, Ashland, OR 97520

HOLE, Jeremy (Fla) 4141 Nw 18th Dr, Gainesville, FL 32605

✠ **HOLGUIN-KHOURY**, Julio (DR (DomRep)) Agape Flights Dms 13602, 100 Airport Ave E, Venice, FL 34285

HOLLAND, Albert L (Del) 4858 Smick St, Philadelphia, PA 19127

HOLLAND JR, Bud (Pa) 121 Penns Grant Dr, Morrisville, PA 19067

HOLLAND, Carol L (Va) P.O. Box 1626, Kilmarnock, VA 22482

HOLLAND, Clayton Theodore (Dal) 517 W Hull St, Denison, TX 75020

HOLLAND, David Wesley (Dal) Po Box 292365, Lewisville, TX 75029

HOLLAND, Donald Keith (Ga)

HOLLAND, Eleanor Lois (Md) 3204 Bayonne Ave, Baltimore, MD 21214

HOLLAND, J Mark (ETenn) 601 W Main St, Morristown, TN 37814

HOLLAND, Janet M (Cal) 1042 Dead Indian Memorial Road, Ashland, OR 97520

HOLLAND, John Stewart (HB)

HOLLAND III, Jule Carr (Nwk) 7404 Halifax Rd, Youngsville, NC 27596

HOLLAND, Katharine Grace (Ore) 13265 Nw Northrup St, Portland, OR 97229

HOLLAND, Meg (Tenn) Trinity Episcopal Church, 317 Franklin St, Clarksville, TN 37040

HOLLAND, Nancy R (SanD)

HOLLAND-SHUEY, Marilyn Basye (Ala) 3740 Meridian St N, Huntsville, AL 35811

HOLLAR, Sarah (NC) 19107 Southport Drive, Cornelius, NC 28031

HOLLEMAN, Virginia Falconer (Dal) 5518 Merrimac Ave, Dallas, TX 75206

HOLLENBECK, Jon Nelson (Dal) 2215 Tracey Ann Ln, Killeen, TX 76543

HOLLENBECK, Scott Warren (Colo) 820 2nd Street, Meeker, CO 81641

✠ **HOLLERITH IV**, Herman (SVa) 600 Talbot Road, Norfolk, VA 23505

HOLLERITH, Melissa Kaye Zuber (Va) 5503 Toddsbury Rd, Richmond, VA 23226

HOLLERITH, Randolph M (WA) 1205 W Franklin St, Richmond, VA 23220

HOLLEY, Richard Hedge (SVa) 202 Devils Den Road, Hampton, VA 23669

HOLLIDAY, Charles Thomas (Va) 3001 Stonewall Avenue, Richmond, VA 23225

HOLLIDAY, Fran (Chi) 5057 W. Devon Ave, Chicago, IL 60646

HOLLIGER, John Charles (O) 70 Welshire Court, Delaware, OH 43015

✠ **HOLLINGSWORTH JR**, Mark (O) 2230 Euclid Ave, Cleveland, OH 44115

HOLLINGSWORTH-GRAVES, Judy Lynn (SD) 1508 S Rock Creek Dr # 168, Sioux Falls, SD 57103

HOLLIS, Joanna (NJ) 5 Paterson St, New Brunswick, NJ 08901

HOLLIS, Robin Buckholtz (Az) St James the Apostle Episcopal Church, 975 E Warner Rd, Tempe, AZ 85284

HOLLIS, Tony (Md) 712 Murdock Rd, Baltimore, MD 21212

HOLLOWAY, Eric Andre Cole (Tex)

HOLLOWELL II, James Rhoads (Colo) 11675 Flatiron Dr, Lafayette, CO 80026

HOLLY, Francis Eugene (Nev) 2481 Anderson Lake Rd # 417, Chimacum, WA 98325

HOLLY, William David (Okla)

HOLLYWOOD, Trula Louise (CNY) 701 S Main St, Athens, PA 18810

HOLM, Marjorie H (SVa) 400 N High St, Franklin, VA 23851

HOLMAN, Emily Clark (NJ) 96 Fairacres Dr, Toms River, NJ 08753

HOLMAN, John Earl (Tex) 2400 Spring Raindrive, #1018, Spring, TX 77379

HOLMAN, J(oseph) Lawrence (Be) RR 1 Box 125A, Towanda, PA 18848

HOLMAN, Kathryn Daneke (At) 1883 Clinton Dr, Marietta, GA 30062

HOLMBERG, Sandi (Minn) 14266 E Fox Lake Rd, Detroit Lakes, MN 56501

HOLMES, Anna Rilla (USC) 205 Meadowlark Ln, Fountain Inn, SC 29644

HOLMES, Forrest Milton (Ida) 1100 Burnett Dr Unit 416, Nampa, ID 83651

HOLMES, Francine Reynolds (NY) 944 Thistlegate Rd, Oak Park, CA 91377

HOLMES, James Colomb (WA) 10450 Lottsford Rd Apt 5005, Mitchellville, MD 20721

HOLMES, Jane Victoria Frances (NC) 2540 Bricker Drive, Charlotte, NC 28273

HOLMES, Joyce Ann Woolever (Kan) Grace Episcopal Church, 209 South Lincoln, Chanute, KS 66720

HOLMES, Kristine Marie (Mass) 91 Main St, Bridgewater, MA 02324

HOLMES, Marsha Evans (Fla) 400 San Juan Dr, Ponte Vedra Beach, FL 32082

HOLMES, Martha Hixson (Ala) 5712 1st Ave N, Birmingham, AL 35212

HOLMES, Phillip Wilson (WNY) 418 Virginia St, Buffalo, NY 14201

HOLMES, Rebecca Elizabeth (NC) 237 N Canterbury Rd, Charlotte, NC 28211

HOLMES, Stanley W (WVa) Po Box 79, Hansford, WV 25103

HOLMGREN, Stephen Carl (WMich) 2200 Thornapple River Dr Se, Grand Rapids, MI 49546

HOLMQUIST, David Wendell (Neb) St Augustine of Canterbury, 285 S 208th St, Elkhorn, NE 68022

HOLMS, Christopher Michael (Ct)

HOLROYD, David D (Me) 3 Elizabeth Rd, South Berwick, ME 03908

HOLSAPPLE, Kevin G (Me) 7208 W Milwe Lane, Crystal Rivet, FL 34429

HOLSTON III, George Wilson (Fla) 804 Doubles Ct, Harker Heights, TX 76548

HOLSTROM, Sue (Chi) 1218 Avery Ranch Rd, Silver City, NM 88061

HOLT, Ann Case (NJ) 60 Main St, Clinton, NJ 08809

HOLT, Charles L (CFla) 700 Rinehart Road, Lake Mary, FL 32746

HOLT, Jane L (Bonnie) (Minn) 224 2nd St N, Cannon Falls, MN 55009

HOLT, Joseph (Cal) 2237 Fulton #103, San Francisco, CA 94117

HOLT, William Mayes (Tenn) 202 Kimberly Dr, Dickson, TN 37055

HOLT III, William Therrel (Az) 854 E Florida Saddle Dr, Green Valley, AZ 85614

HOLTHUS, Jess (Md) 106 W Church St, Frederick, MD 21701

HOLTKAMP, Patrick John (LI) 7712 35th Ave Apt A64, Jackson Heights, NY 11372

HOLTMAN, Kimberly Erica (Nwk) 655 W Briar Pl, Apt 1, Chicago, IL 60657

HOLTON, Edie H (Md) 120 E J St, Benicia, CA 94510

HOLTON, Stephen C (Ct) Christ Episcopal Church, 84 Broadway, New Haven, CT 06511

HOLTON, Steve (NY) 91 Greenwood Lane, White Plains, NY 10607

HOLTZEN, Thomas Lee (Mil) 2777 Mission Rd, Nashotah, WI 53058

HOLZ JR, John Clifford (Ak)

HOLZHALB, Leon (La) 100 Christwood Blvd, Covington, LA 70433

HOMEYER, Charles Frederick (WMich) 3539 Quiggle Ave Se, Ada, MI 49301

HOMEYER, Peter Carey (WMich) Holy Trinity Episcopal Church, 5333 Clyde Park Ave SW, Wyoming, MI 49509

HONAKER, Martha (Ind) 111 Ivy Lane, Sparta, NC 28675

HONDERICH, Thomas E (Ind) 3941 N Delaware St, Indianapolis, IN 46205

HONEA, Janice Bailey (CFla) 6246 Tremayne Dr, Mount Dora, FL 32757

HONEYCHURCH, John Robert (Los) 1000 Concha St, Altadena, CA 91001

HONNOLD, Sandra Elizabeth (The Episcopal NCal) PO Box 7063, PMB 295, Ocean View, HI 96737

HONODEL, Jill (Cal) 285 Kaanapali Dr, Napa, CA 94558

HONSE, Robert Wayne (Kan)

HOOD, Nancy E (Dal) 6883 Lagoon Dr, Grand Prairie, TX 75054

HOOD, Stephen D (Ala) 3648 Dabney Drive, Vesatvia Hills, AL 35243

HOOD, William Rienks (La) 1808 Prospect St, Houston, TX 77004

HOOGERHYDE, Scott Matthew (Nwk) 7 E Main St, Mendham, NJ 07945

HOOK, Andrew S (Spr) Cathedral Church of Saint Paul the Apostle, 815 South Second Street, Springfield, IL 62704

HOOK, Edward Lindsten (Colo) PO Box 1388, Green Valley, AZ 85622

HOOKE, Ruthanna Brinton (WMass) 3737 Seminary Rd, Alexandria, VA 22304

HOOKER, Alan Bruce (Va) 6645 Northumberland Hwy, Heathsville, VA 22473

HOOKER, Hannah G (Ark) St Marks Episcopal Church, 531 W College Ave, Jonesboro, AR 72401

HOOKER, John L (WMass) 22c Castle Hill Rd, Agawam, MA 01001

HOOP, Kimberly Ann (WMich) 4155 S Norway St Se, Grand Rapids, MI 49546

HOOPER, Elizabeth E (Los) 1014 E. Altadena Drive, Altadena, CA 91001

HOOPER, John Kontz (Mich) 42 Cottage Circle, West Lebanon, NH 03784

HOOPER, Larry Donald (SeFla) 401 Duval St, Key West, FL 33040

HOOPER, Phillip Russell (Nev)

HOOPER III, Robert Channing (Ct) 10 Cumberland Rd, West Hartford, CT 06119

HOOPER, Ruth Isabelle (Az) 1710 W. Dalehaven Cir, Tucson, AZ 85704

HOOPES, David Bryan (LI) Church of St Edward the Martyr, 14 E 109th St, New York, NY 10029

HOOVER, Greg T (Ark) 107 Walnut Ln, Branson, MO 65616

HOOVER, John (CPa) 99 Willowbrook Blvd, Lewisburg, PA 17837

HOOVER, Joshua Aaron (Mich) 355 W Maple Rd, Birmingham, MI 48009

HOOVER, Judy Verne Hanlon (Minn) 2020 Orkla Dr, Golden Valley, MN 55427

HOOVER, Melvin Aubrey (SO) 1870 Commonwealth Ave., Auburndale, MA 02466

HOOVER, Richard A (CFla) 209 S Iowa Ave, Lakeland, FL 33801

HOOVER, Todd (SeFla) 952 SW 7th St, Ft Lauderdale, FL 33315

HOOVER-DEMPSEY, Randy (Tenn) 1829 Hudson Rd, Madison, TN 37115

HOPEWELL, Gloria (Chi) 939 Hinman Ave, Evanston, IL 60202

HOPKINS, Christine Carroll (Spr) 102 E Mchenry St, Urbana, IL 61801

HOPKINS, Daniel W (Colo) 7127 S. Quemoy St., Aurora, CO 80016

✠ **HOPKINS JR**, Harold Anthony (ND) 15 Piper Rd Apt K211, Scarborough, ME 04074

HOPKINS, John Leonard (Alb) 34 Velina Dr, Burnt Hills, NY 12027

HOPKINS, Lydia Elliott (La)

HOPKINS, Michael Warren (Roch) 67 E Main St, Hornell, NY 14843

HOPKINS, Terry Robert (Minn) P.O. Box 402, Monticello, MN 55362

HOPKINS, Vivian Louise (Oly) 32820 20th Ave S #61, Federal Way, WA 98003

HOPKINS-GREENE, Nancy (SO) 6255 Stirrup Rd, Cincinnati, OH 45244

HOPLAMAZIAN, Julie M (LI) The Church of St. Luke and St. Matthew, 520 Clinton Ave, Brooklyn, NY 11238

HOPNER, Kathryn Ann (The Episcopal NCal) St Paul's Episcopal Church, PO Box 737, Sparks, NV 89432

HOPPE, Robert Donald (FdL) 806 4th St, Algoma, WI 54201

HOPPER, Edgar Wilson (NY) St Augustines, 333 Madison St, New York, NY 10002

HOPWOOD, Alfred Joseph (Minn) 1417 Blue Flag Ct, Northfield, MN 55057

HORD, Christine D (CGC)

HOREN, Anna Lynn (Cal) 4529 Lakewood St, Pleasanton, CA 94588

HORGAN, Daniel E (Mass) 204 Monument Rd, Orleans, MA 02653

HORKEY, Patricia Lynn (SanD) PO Box 506, Idyllwild, CA 92549

HORLE, Garrison Locke (Colo) 720 Downing St, Denver, CO 80218

HORN, John C (Ia) Trinity Episcopal Cathedral, 121 W. 12th St., Davenport, IA 52803

HORN, Mike (ND) 15757 N 90th Pl Apt 2053, Scottsdale, AZ 85260

HORN, Raisin (Ia) Trinity Church, 320 E College St, Iowa City, IA 52240

HORN, S Huston (Los) 334 S Parkwood Ave, Pasadena, CA 91107

HORNADAY, Evelyn (WMo) St. Peter & All Saints Episcopal Church, 100 E. Red Bridge Rd., Kansas City, MO 64114

HORNBECK, Jen (Cal) PO Box 274, Kenwood, CA 95452

HORNE, Lance Cameron (Fla) 3275 Tallavana Trl, Havana, FL 32333

HORNE, Martha (Va) 3809 Fort Worth Ave, Alexandria, VA 22304

HORNER, John (O) 813 West Main St, Elizabeth City, NC 27909

HORNER, Robert William (Tex) 8 Coralvine Ct, The Woodlands, TX 77380

HORNER, William McKinley (Miss) 14981 W Verde Ln, Goodyear, AZ 85338

HORNING, David J (Mich) 104 Mount Homestake Dr., Leadville, CO 80461

HORNSBY, James Harmon (Mass) 260 Lake Ave, Fall River, MA 02721

HORST, Diane Elizabeth (NMich) 12769 W Lakeshore Dr, Brimley, MI 49715

HORTON, Carol J (NJ) 3 Plumstead Ct, Annandale, NJ 08801

HORTON, Fred Lane (NC) 2622 Weymoth Rd, Winston Salem, NC 27103

HORTON JR, James Taylor (FtW) 7413 Hillstone Dr, Benbrook, TX 76126

HORTON, Jim (EC) 1060 Dixie Trl, Williamston, NC 27892

HORTON, Sarah (Vt) 17 Mack Ave, West Lebanon, NH 03784

HORTON-HOWE, Carole Lee (Los) 7056 Washington Ave, Whittier, CA 90602

HORTON-SMITH, Sandra (Kan) St Paul's Episcopal Church, 601 Poyntz Ave, Manhattan, KS 66502

HORTUM, John (Va) 1407 N Gaillard St, Alexandria, VA 22304

HORVATH, Leslie Ferguson (USC) 400 Dupre Dr., Spartanburg, SC 29307

HORVATH, Michael J (NY)

HORVATH, Victor John (Vt) 6 South St, Bellows Falls, VT 05101

HOSEA, Beverly Ann (Oly) 215 14th Ave E Apt 401, Seattle, WA 98112

HOSEA, Janice Forney (RG) 7171 Tennyson St NE, Albuquerque, NM 87122

HOSKINS, Charles L (Ga) 4629 Sylvan Dr, Savannah, GA 31405

HOSKINS, Jo Ann Smith (Fla) 4241 Duval Dr, Jacksonville Beach, FL 32250

HOSLER, Carol Smith (Az) PO Box 171, 408 Jamestown Road, Kearny, AZ 85137

HOSLER, Joshua Luke (Oly) 2117 Walnut St, Bellingham, WA 98225

HOSLER, Samuel Odyth (Az) 408 Jamestown Road, Kearny, AZ 85137

HOSPADOR, Dorothea Cecelia (NJ) 247 Carr Ave, Keansburg, NJ 07734

HOSTER JR, David (Tex) 30003 Edgewood Drive, Georgetown, TX 78628

HOSTER, Elizabeth M (O) Trinity Episcopal Church, 316 Adams Street, Toledo, OH 43604

HOSTETLER, Hugh Steiner (WMich) 313B 15th Ave S, Surfside Bch, SC 29575

HOSTETTER, Jane (USC) 2303 NE Seaview Dr, Jensen Beach, FL 34957

HOTCHKISS, Margaret (Wyo)

HOTCHKISS, Thomas S (Dal) 11122 Midway Rd, Dallas, TX 75229

HOTRA, Nancy Louise (WMich) 9733 Sterling, Richland, MI 49083

HOTZE, Janice A (Ak) Po Box 91, Haines, AK 99827

HOUCK III, Ira Chauncey (USC) 120 Norse Dr, Columbia, SC 29229

HOUCK, John Bunn (Chi) 5236 S Cornell Ave, Chicago, IL 60615

HOUCK, Kay M (EMich)

HOUGH III, Charles (Dal) 2900 Alemeda St, Fort Worth, TX 76108

HOUGH, George Willard (NwPa) 904 Holiday Hills Dr, Hollidaysburg, PA 16648

HOUGHTON, Frederick Lord (EMich) 4138 N Francis Shores Ave, Sanford, MI 48657

HOUGHTON, John William (NI) 609 Houghton St., Culver, IN 46511

HOUGHTON, William Clokey (NwT) 27 Painted Canyon Place, The Woodlands, TX 77381

HOUGLAND, Erin Elizabeth (Ind)

✠ **HOUGLAND JR**, Whayne (WMich) Episcopal Diocese of Western Michigan, 535 S Burdick St, Kalamazoo, MI 49007

HOUI-LEE, Samuel Sroun (Oly) 34608 8th Ave Sw, Federal Way, WA 98023

HOUK, David Stangebye (Dal) 848 Harter Road, Dallas, TX 75218

HOULE, Michael Anthony (EMich) 4525 Birch Run Rd, Birch Run, MI 48415

HOULIK, Michael Andrew (Colo) 2712 Geneva Place, Longmont, CO 80503

HOUPT, Cameron Wheeler (Colo) 10222 W Ida Ave Unit 238, Littleton, CO 80127

HOUSE, Karen Ellen (CFla) 1120 Sunshine Ave, Leesburg, FL 34748

HOUSER, Lucy Anne Latham (Ore) 11476 SW Riverwoods Rd., Portland, OR 97219

HOUSER III, Richard Truett (Tex) 13131 Fry Rd, Cypress, TX 77433

HOUSER, Teresa (Neb)

HOUSNER-RITTER, Jenny Lee (Mich)

HOUSTON, Barbara Pearce (EC) 206 North Fairlane Drive, Box 939, Grifton, NC 28530

HOUZE, Jared Foster (NwT)

HOVENCAMP, Otis (WNY) 85 Wide Beach Rd, Irving, NY 14081

HOVEY JR, Frederick Franklin (WNC) 724 Cobblestone Dr, Ormond Beach, FL 32174

HOWANSTINE JR, John Edwin (Md) 3090 Broomes Island Road, Port Republic, MD 20676

HOWARD, Anne (Los) 950 Dena Way, Santa Barbara, CA 93111

HOWARD, Charles Lattimore (Pa)

HOWARD, Coleen Gayle (Ore) PO Box 1319, Gresham, OR 97030

HOWARD, Cynthia A (CGC) 2005 Boxwood Ave, Andalusia, AL 36421

HOWARD, Dave (SO)

HOWARD, Francis Curzon (Ct) 116 Terry's Plain Road, Box 423, Simsbury, CT 06070

HOWARD III, George Williams (Spr) 1811 Highland Vw, Mount Vernon, IL 62864

HOWARD, Harry Lee (ETenn) 2668 Karenwood Dr, Maryville, TN 37804

HOWARD II, Joseph B (Tenn) 2458 Center Point Rd, Hendersonville, TN 37075

HOWARD, Karin D (SwVa) 4461 S Main St Apt 111, Acworth, GA 30101

HOWARD, Ken Wayne (WA) 9 Liberty Heights Court, Germantown, MD 20874

HOWARD, Leonard Rice (The Episcopal Church in Haw) 98-1128 Malualua St, Aiea, HI 96701

HOWARD, Lois Waser (Lex) 713 Dicksonia Ct, Lexington, KY 40517

HOWARD, Mary Merle (SeFla)

HOWARD, Noah B (NC) 206 Maryland Ave, Tarboro, NC 27886

HOWARD, Norman (SwFla) 766 Lake Forest Rd, Clearwater, FL 33765

HOWARD, Sally Anne (Los) 132 N Euclid Ave, Pasadena, CA 91101

✠ **HOWARD**, Samuel Johnson (Fla) 325 N Market St, Jacksonville, FL 32202

HOWARD, Sylvia Lord (Spr) 1811 Highland Vw, Mount Vernon, IL 62864

HOWARD, Theodore B (Colo) 1419 Pine St., Boulder, CO 80302

HOWARD, William Alexander (Colo) 7168 Burnt Mill Rd, Beulah, CO 81023

HOWCOTT, Jeffernell Ophelia Green (Mich) 19320 Santa Rosa Dr, Detroit, MI 48221

✠ **HOWE**, Barry (WMo) PO Box 413227, Kansas City, MO 64141

HOWE, Garth (Chi) 637 S Dearborn St, Chicago, IL 60605

HOWE, Gregory Michael (Del) 7 Conway St, Provincetown, MA 02657

HOWE, Heath (Chi) 1229 Hinman Ave, Evanston, IL 60202

HOWE, Jeffrey Newman (Lex) 201 Price Rd Apt 216, Lexington, KY 40511

✠ **HOWE**, John Wadsworth (CFla) 5583 Jessamine Lane, Orlando, FL 32830

HOWE, Karen Elvgren (CFla) 5583 Jessamine Ln, Orlando, FL 32839

HOWE JR, Ralph (La) 8965 Bayside Ave, Baton Rouge, LA 70806

HOWE, Raymond Jordan (Be) 833 Gillinder Place, Cary, NC 27519

HOWE, Wendy Salisbury (ECR) 203 Lighthouse Ave, Pacific Grove, CA 93950

HOWELL, Edward Allen (The Episcopal NCal) 1953 Terry Rd, Santa Rosa, CA 95403

HOWELL, Laura (Be) 44 E Market St, Bethlehem, PA 18018

HOWELL, Margery E (SVa) 3316 Hyde Cir, Norfolk, VA 23513

HOWELL, Miguelina (Ct) Christ Church Cathedral, 45 Church St, Hartford, CT 06103

HOWELL, Peggy Ann (Mass) Po Box 134, North Billerica, MA 01862

HOWELL, Robert M (SO) 69081 Mount Herman Rd, Cambridge, OH 43725

HOWELL, Sydney C (Va) 495 Melrose Dr, Monticello, FL 32344

HOWELL, Terry Robert (At) 2135 Zelda Dr Ne, Atlanta, GA 30345

HOWELL-BURKE, Undine Jean (Neb) 7425 Stevens Ridge Rd, Lincoln, NE 68516

HOWELLS, Donald Arthur (Be) 1936 Chestnut Hill Road, Mohnton, PA 19540

HOWLETT, Louise (NH) 131 E Harrisville Rd, Dublin, NH 03444

HOWSER, Carol Louise Jordan (Ore) 192 Harrison St, Ashland, OR 97520

HOWZE, Lynn Corpening (CFla) 215 West Park, Lakeland, FL 33803

HOXIE, George (Dal)

HOY, Lois (Cal) 36 Dos Posos, Orinda, CA 94563

HOY, Mary Ann (Me) 6 Old Mast Landing Rd, Freeport, ME 04032

HOYT, Calvin Van Kirk (CPa) 1418 Walnut St, Camp Hill, PA 17011

HOYT, Tim (WNC) 479 Whispering Woods Dr, Saluda, NC 28773

HROSTOWSKI, Susan (Miss) 1861 Tryon Dr Unit 3, Fayetteville, NC 28303

HSIEH, Nathaniel (Eur) 44 Rue Docteur Robert, Chatillon Sur Seine, 21400, France

HU, Kuo-Hua (Tai) Chieh Shou Road 5, Kangshan, 82018, Taiwan

HUACANI, Amy J (NC) PO Box 2263, Durham, NC 27702

HUAL, Jeffrey C (Md) 3600 Solomons Island Rd, Edgewater, MD 21037

HUANG, Peter P (Los) 2200 Via Rosa, Palos Verdes Estates, CA 90274

HUBBARD, Carol Murphy (WNC) 211 Montford Ave, Asheville, NC 28801

HUBBARD JR, Charles Clark (Ga) 227 McDuffie Drive, Richmond Hill, GA 31324

HUBBARD, Colenzo (WTenn) 604 Saint Paul Ave, Memphis, TN 38126

HUBBARD, Cynthia (Mass) 45 White Trellis, Plymouth, MA 02360

HUBBARD, Francis Appleton (NJ) 5 North Rd, Berkeley Heights, NJ 07922

HUBBARD, James (SwVa) 384 Waughs Ferry Rd, Amherst, VA 24521

HUBBARD, Lani Marie (Oly) 225 Mar Vista Way, Port Angeles, WA 98362

HUBBARD, Martha (Mass) St. Paul's Church, 166 High St., Newburyport, MA 01950

HUBBARD, Mavourneen Ann (NY) 17 South Ave, 855 Wolcott Ave, Beacon, NY 12508

HUBBARD, Philip R (LI) 20309 W 219th Ter, Spring Hill, KS 66083

HUBBARD, Tom (Los) 621 Mayflower Rd 104, Claremont, CA 91711

HUBBELL, Gilbert Leonard (O) 1094 Clifton Ave # 2, Akron, OH 44310

HUBBELL, Sally Hanes (The Episcopal NCal) 209 Matheson St, Healdsburg, CA 95448

HUBBY III, Turner Erath (Tex) 329 Meadowbrook Dr, San Antonio, TX 78232

HUBER, Amy Whitcombe (Eau) 234 Avon St, La Crosse, WI 54603

HUBER, Donald Marvin (Neb) 10807 Scott Peddler Rd, Cattaraugus, NY 14719

HUBER, E Wendy (Colo) 76 Spring Ridge Ct, Glenwood Springs, CO 81601

HUBER, Ellen (Ct) 171 Old Tannery Rd # 6468, Monroe, CT 06468

HUBER, Frank A (Colo) 12295 West Applewood Drive, Lakewood, CO 80215

HUBER, Glenna (WA) 1820 Greenberry Rd, Baltimore, MD 21209

HUBER, Kurt J (Ct) 171 Old Tannery Rd, Monroe, CT 06468

HUBER, Steve (Los) 506 N. Camden Drive, Beverly Hills, CA 90210

HUBERT, Deven Ann (Roch) 66 Little Briggins Circle, Fairport, NY 14450

HUBERT, Lawrence William (Alb) 970 State St, Schenectady, NY 12307

HUCK, Beverly (Nwk) 155 Rainbow Dr # 5549, Livingston, TX 77399

HUCKABAY JR, Harry Hunter (ETenn) 1706 Glenroy Ave., Chattanooga, TN 37405

HUDAK, Bob (EC) St Paul's Church, 401 E. 4th St, Greenville, NC 27858

HUDAK, Mary L (The Episcopal NCal) 1240 Mission Ave., Sacramento, CA 95608

HUDDLESTON, Kevin (Mil) 216 E Chandler Blvd, Burlington, WI 53105

HUDDLESTON, Nathan (Nwk)

HUDLOW, A Kelley (Ala) 521 20th St N, Birmingham, AL 35203

HUDSON, Aaron (NY) St. Paul's Episcopal Church, 22 Dillman Drive, Council Bluffs, IA 51503

HUDSON, Andrew (SeFla) 7538 Granville Dr, Tamarac, FL 33321

HUDSON, Andrew George (SeFla) 2250 SW 31st Ave, Fort Lauderdale, FL 33312

HUDSON, Betty (SVa) 120 John Bratton, Williamsburg, VA 23185

HUDSON, Daniel Mark (La) 1329 Jackson Ave, New Orleans, LA 70130

HUDSON, Henry Lee (Ala) 1424 4th St, New Orleans, LA 70130

HUDSON, Joel Pinkney (At) 1225 N Shore Dr, Roswell, GA 30076

HUDSON, Joseph Dale (SwFla)

HUDSON, Kimberly Karen (WA) 11403 Trillum St, Bowie, MD 20721

HUDSON, Linda Ann (Wyo) 860 S 3rd St, Lander, WY 82520

HUDSON, Mary Bowen (CFla) 4345 Indian River Dr, Cocoa, FL 32927

HUDSON, Mary Jo (EMich)

HUDSON, Michael (WNC) Po Box 152, Cullowhee, NC 28723

HUDSON, Thomas James (Md)

HUDSON-LOUIS, Holly (ECR) 65 Highway 1, Carmel, CA 93923

HUDSPETH, Denise (CFla) 208 Nw Avenue H, Belle Glade, FL 33430

HUERTA, Efrain (FtW) 12607 Banchester Ct, Houston, TX 77070

HUERTA GARCIA, Huerta (Tex) Chamela 33 A, Tlaquepaque, JAL 45589, Mexico

HUFF, Carolyn Tuttle (Pa) 1121 N Trooper Rd, Eagleville, PA 19403

HUFF, Christopher Mercer (SC) 1612 Dryden Ln, Charleston, SC 29407

HUFF, Clark Kern (Tex) 2252 Garden Court, San Marcos, TX 78666

HUFF, Susan Ellen (At) 1031 Eagles Ridge Ct, Lawrenceville, GA 30043

HUFFMAN, Charles Howard (Tex) 8124 Greenslope Dr, Austin, TX 78759

HUFFMAN, Robert Nelson (SVa) 2212 Lynnwood drive, Wilmington, NC 28403

HUFFORD, Robert Arthur (SO) 52 Bishopsgate Dr Apt 703, Cincinnati, OH 45246

HUFFSTETLER, Joel W (ETenn) 3920 Clairmont Dr Ne, Cleveland, TN 37312

HUFT, Jerry Ray (CGC) Po Box 595, Wewahitchka, FL 32465

HUGGARD, Linda (Episcopal SJ) 4300 Keith Way, Bakersfield, CA 93309

✠ **HUGHES**, Carlye J (Nwk) Trinity Episcopal Church, 3401 Bellaire Drive South, Fort Worth, TX 76109

HUGHES, Frank W (WLa) 1107 Broadway St, Minden, LA 71055

✠ **HUGHES**, Gethin Benwil (SanD) 461 Quail Run Rd, Buellton, CA 93427

HUGHES, James Anthony (Va) 9320 West St, Manassas, VA 20110

HUGHES, J Daniel (Chi)

HUGHES, Jennifer Scheper (Mass) 1147 Walnut St, Berkeley, CA 94707

HUGHES, John Richard (Lex) 2449 Larkin Rd, Lexington, KY 40503

HUGHES, Laura K (WMo) St. George Episcopal Church, 423 N Highway 5, Camdenton, MO 65020

HUGHES, Linda M (Ia) 103 Melissa St, Elizabethtown, KY 42701

HUGHES, Malcolm Albert (FdL) Saint John's Episcopal Church, 139 South Smalley, Shawano, WI 54166

HUGHES, Mary London Carswell (ECR) 902 California Ave, San Jose, CA 95125

HUGHES III, Robert Davis (SO) 335 Tennessee Ave, Sewanee, TN 37383

HUGHES, Rosalind Claire (O)

HUGHES, Thomas Downs (WNC) 16 Salisbury Dr Apt 7206, Asheville, NC 28803

HUGHES JR, Thomas Roddy (Eas) 852 Spring Valley Dr, Fredericksburg, VA 22405

HUGHES-EMPKE, Sheryl Ann (Ia) PO Box 486, Perry, IA 50220

HUGHES-HABEL, Deborah Jean (U) 4615 S 3200 W, West Valley City, UT 84119

HUGHS, Leslie Curtis (LI) 16 Birch Road, Danbury, CT 06811

HUGUENIN, Robert (Fla) 4224 Coastal Hwy, Crawfordville, FL 32327

HUINER, Peter Bruce (Del) 500 Woodlawn Rd, Wilmington, DE 19803

HULBERT, Edward R (Los) St Richard of Chichester Church, PO Box 1317, Lake Arrowhead, CA 92352

HULEN, Jennifer L (Mo) 9 S Bompart Ave, Saint Louis, MO 63119

HULET, Jefferson R (NJ) 14 Saint Remy Ct, Newport Coast, CA 92657

HULIN, Kathy Elizabeth (CFla) 209 S Iowa Ave, Lakeland, FL 33801

HULL, Carol Wharton (SO) 14590 Wilmot Way, Lake Oswego, OR 97035

HULL, George (Chi) 509 Brier St, Kenilworth, IL 60043

HULL, Nicholas Andrew (SwVa) PO Box 1146, Columbus, GA 31902

HULL, S (Los) 13025 Bloomfield St., Studio City, CA 91604

HULL IV, William Franklin (Fla) 630 S Sapodilla Ave Apt 214, West Palm Beach, FL 33401

HULLAR, Leonard Earl (Ct) 115 W Main St, Plainville, CT 06062

HULLINGER, Jon M (Kan) 3750 E Douglas Ave, Wichita, KS 67208

HULL-RYDE, Norman Arthur (WNC) 2535 Sheffield Dr, Gastonia, NC 28054

HULME, Steven Edward (Ct) 26 Colony Road, East Lyme, CT 06333

HULME, Thomas Stanford (Ia) 1617 W Benton St, Iowa City, IA 52246

HULS II, Frederick Eugene (Az) 2812 N 69th Pl, Scottsdale, AZ 85257

HULS, Patricia Taylor (Az) 2310 N 56th St, Phoenix, AZ 85008

✠ **HULSEY**, Sam Byron (NwT) 801 Hillcrest St, Fort Worth, TX 76107

HULTMAN, Eugene Bradlee (Mass) 255 N Central Ave, Quincy, MA 02170

HUMBER, Michael R (Colo) 2201 Dexter St, Denver, CO 80207

HUMKE, Richard Herbert (Ky) 200 S Galt Ave, Louisville, KY 40206

HUMM, Richard (Md) St Paul's Church, 25 Church St, Prince Frederick, MD 20678

HUMMEL, Gini (Ct) 30 Woodland Street, #6D, Hartford, CT 06105

HUMMEL, Thomas Charles (Va) 1200 N Quaker Ln, Alexandria, VA 22302

HUMMELL, Mark William (NY) 160 Cabrini Blvd Apt 36, New York, NY 10033

HUMPHREY, Christine Ann (Mich) 544 W Iroquois Rd, Pontiac, MI 48341

HUMPHREY, Georgia Lehman (Ia) 15064 Sheridan Ave, Clive, IA 50325

HUMPHREY JR, Howard MacKenzie (O) 6295 Chagrin River Rd, Chagrin Falls, OH 44022

HUMPHREY, Marian Teresa (WA) 9801 Livingston Rd, Fort Washington, MD 20744

HUMPHREY, M(ary) Beth (WA) St Albans School, Mount St Albans, Washington, DC 20016

HUMPHREY, Nathan J A (RI) The Zabriskie Memorial Church of Saint John the Evangelist, 61 Poplar St, Newport, RI 02840

HUMPHREYS, Eugene L (NC) 425 E 17th St, Charlotte, NC 28206

HUMPHREYS, Walter Lee (ETenn) 7113 Hampshire Dr, Knoxville, TN 37909

HUMPHRIES, Charles Emerson (SeFla)

HUMPHRIES JR, John Curtis (CNY) 405 Euclid Avenue, Elmira, NY 14905

HUNDLEY, Brooks (WA)

HUNGATE, Carla Valinda (At) 4318 Windmill Tree, Douglasville, GA 30135

HUNGERFORD, Eric Paul (Tex) 3901 S Panther Creek Dr, The Woodlands, TX 77381

HUNGERFORD, Roger (Chi) 2805 32nd Avenue Dr, Moline, IL 61265

HUNKINS, Claire (SVa) PO Box 186, Oak Hall, VA 23416

HUNKINS, Orin James (Okla) 3724 Bonaire Pl, Edmond, OK 73013

HUNLEY, Deborah (SwVa) 2042 Lee HI Rd SW, Roanoke, VA 24018

HUNN, Meg Buerkel (NC) 412 N East Street, Raleigh, NC 27604

✠ **HUNN**, Michael (RG) 412 N East St, Raleigh, NC 27604

HUNSINGER, Jimmie Ruth Coffey (Fla) 350 Sw Stallion Gln, Lake City, FL 32024

HUNT, Ashley Stephen (EC) 1 Palmerston Road, Melton Mowbray, Great Britain (UK)

HUNT, Barnabas John William (SanD) PO Box 34548, San Diego, CA 92163

HUNT, Donald Aldrich (Mass) 221 Atlantic Ave, Marblehead, MA 01945

HUNT, Edward (SD) 20475 Sunningdale Park, Grosse Pointe Woods, MI 48236

HUNT III, Ernest Edward (Eur) 3310 Fairmount St Apt 9b, Dallas, TX 75201

✠ **HUNT III**, George Nelson (RI) 1401 Fountain Grove Pkwy #107, Santa Rosa, CA 95403

HUNT, Hazel Bailey (Be) Po Box 86, Towanda, PA 18848

HUNT, J Patrick (NJ) 57 Putters Pl, Savannah, GA 31419

HUNT, John C (O) 44267 Route 511 East, Oberlin, OH 44074

HUNT, Karla ()

HUNT, Katherine Ann (Ak) 2006 W 31st Ave, Anchorage, AK 99517

HUNT, Lisa (Tex) 419 Woodland St, Nashville, TN 37206

HUNT, Marshall William (Mass) Po Box 1205, East Harwich, MA 02645

HUNT, Mary (ETenn) 100 Steven Ln., Harriman, TN 37748

HUNT, Meredith (WMich) 4708 State Park Hwy, Interlochen, MI 49643

HUNT, Paul Stuart (Pa) 212 S High St, West Chester, PA 19382

HUNT, Teresa Gioia (Pgh) 1335 Berryman Avenue, Bethel Park, PA 15102

HUNT, Terry Lynn (Nev) 79 Northwood Commons Pl, Chico, CA 95973

HUNT, Victoria Wells (Mass) Po Box 1205, East Harwich, MA 02645

HUNT, William Gilbert (Miss) 510 Godsey Rd., Apt. 183, Bristol, TN 37620

HUNTER, Christina M (Alb) 2331 15th St, Troy, NY 12180

HUNTER, Colenthia (SO) 8387 Vicksburg Dr, Cincinnati, OH 45249

HUNTER, Elizabeth Lane (Miss) 327 N First St, Rolling Fork, MS 39159

HUNTER, Elizabeth Sue (U) 231 E 100 S, Salt Lake City, UT 84111

HUNTER JR, Herschel Miller (Va) Box 37, Ivy, VA 22945

HUNTER II, James Nathaniel (Ak) 3223 Cross Way, North Pole, AK 99705

HUNTER, James Wallace (RG) St Mary's Church, 1500 Chelwood Park Blvd NE, Albuquerque, NM 87112

HUNTER, Karen (Ida) 204 Courthouse Dr, Salmon, ID 83467

HUNTER, Kay Smith (WLa) 401 Washington Ave, Mansfield, LA 71052

HUNTER, Kenneth (Alb) 29 Walnut St., Oneonta, NY 13820

HUNTER, Lawrence Scott (Cal) 1042 Dead Indian Memorial Road, Ashland, OR 97520

HUNTER, Marcia G (Lex) 104 Dellwood Dr, Berea, KY 40403

HUNTER, Mary Veronica (Alb) 305 Main St, Oneonta, NY 13820

HUNTER, Paul A (Alb) Christ Episcopal Church, 69 Fair St, Cooperstown, NY 13326

HUNTER SR, Robert Fulton Boyd (WA) 12213 Rolling Hill Ln, Bowie, MD 20715

HUNTER, S Scott (Mich) The Cathedral Church of St. Paul, 4800 Woodward Ave, Detroit, MI 48201

HUNTER JR, Victor Edward (Dal) 1115 S. Bryan St., Mesquite, TX 75149

HUNTER, Walcott Wallace (SwFla) Po Box 646, Kinderhook, NY 12106

HUNTER-SPENCER, Dorothy Elaine (CFla)

HUNTINGTON, Carol L (Me) 121 Bowery St, Bath, ME 04530

HUNTINGTON, Francis Cleaveland (NY) 11 Rassapeague, Saint James, NY 11780

HUNTINGTON, Frederic DuBois (Va) 219 Wolfe St, Alexandria, VA 22314

HUNTLEY, Stuart Michael (LI) 9 Carlton Ave, Port Washington, NY 11050

HUPF, Jeffrey Lee (Minn) 2801 Westwood Rd S, Minnetonka Beach, MN 55361

HUR, Won-Jae (Cal) 206 Arborway Apt 3, Boston, MA 02130

HURD JR, Austin Avery (Pgh) 102 Fountain Cv, 160 Marwood Rd Apt 3314, Cabot, PA 16023

HURLBERT, Sarah (Mich) 765 Grove Street, East Lansing, MI 48823

HURLBURT, Martha Cornue (EO) 801 Jefferson St, Klamath Falls, OR 97601

HURLBUT, Terence James (WMass) 7 Woodbridge St, South Hadley, MA 01075

HURLEY, Hal Owen (SeFla) 418 N Sapodilla Ave, West Palm Beach, FL 33401

HURLEY, Janet (Los) St John the Evangelist Episcoapl Church, PO Box 183, Needles, CA 92363

HURLEY, Thomas James (Neb) 113 N 18th St, Omaha, NE 68102

HURST, Hassell J (Ga) PO Box 50555, Nashville, TN 37205

HURST, Michael W (Dal) 400 S Church St, Paris, TX 75460

HURST, Rodney Shane (RG) 508 W Fox St, Carlsbad, NM 88220

HURST, William George (NH) 108 Wecuwa Dr, Fort Myers, FL 33912

HURST, William Jeffrey (WMo)

HURTADO, Homero (EcuC) Guallabamba 214, Cuenca, Ecuador

HURTT, Annie Lawrie (Pa) 659 W Johnson St, Philadelphia, PA 19144

HURWITZ, Ellen Sara (Md) 12147 Pleasant Walk Rd, Myersville, MD 21773

HUSBAND, John Frederick (Minn) 16533 Long Beach Dr, Detroit Lakes, MN 56501

HUSBY, Mary Eloise Brown (SD) 1504 S Park Ave, Sioux Falls, SD 57105

HUSHION, Timothy V (NC) 328 6th St, Pittsburgh, PA 15215

HUSSEY, David Payne (SD) 405 N Madison Ave, Pierre, SD 57501

HUSSEY-SMITH, Teddra R (EC) 5071 Voorhees Rd, Denmark, SC 29042

HUSSON, Brenda G (NY) 865 Madison Ave, New York, NY 10021

HUSTAD, Siri Hauge (Minn) 519 Oak Grove St, Minneapolis, MN 55403

HUSTON, Jeffrey Clayton (Okla)

HUSTON, Julie Winn (At) 2950 Mt. Wilkinson Pkwy, Unit 817, Atlanta, GA 30339

HUSTON, Mary Ann (Tex) 3816 Bellaire Blvd, Houston, TX 77025

HUSTON, Nancy Williams (Neb) 923 S 33rd St, Omaha, NE 68105

HUTCHENS, Holly Blair (WMo) St Ninians Cottage, Melton, Drumnadrochit, SCOTLAND IV63 6UA, Great Britain (UK)

HUTCHENS, Marquita L (WVa) St. John's Episcopal Churh, 1105 Quarrier Street, Charleston, WV 25301

HUTCHERSON, Anne V (WMo) 624 W 61st Ter, Kansas City, MO 64113

HUTCHERSON, Brian (Va) 74 Peterson Pl, Fishersville, VA 22939

HUTCHERSON, Robert M (WMo) 624 West 64th Terrace, Kansas City, MO 64113

HUTCHINS, Margaret Smith (EC) 7909 Blue Heron Dr W Apt 2, Wilmington, NC 28411

HUTCHINS, Susan Ellen (RG) St Luke's Episcopal Church, Po Box 1258, Deming, NM 88031

HUTCHINSON, Anthony Alonzo (Ore) Trinity Episcopal Church, 44 N 2nd St, Ashland, OR 97520

HUTCHINSON, Barbara (CPa) 9 Carlton Ave, Port Washington, NY 11050

HUTCHINSON JR, John Fuller (Del) 350 Noxontown Rd, Middletown, DE 19709

HUTCHINSON, Ninon N (CNY) 7029 Texas Road, Croghan, NY 13327

HUTCHISON, Hal (ETenn) 309 Quail Dr., Johnson City, TN 37601

HUTCHISON, Jonathan (Ind) Hc 81 Box 6009, Questa, NM 87556

HUTCHISON, Sheldon Butt (ECR) 921 Eton Way, Sunnyvale, CA 94087

HUTCHSON, Lee Allen (Va) 18256 Oxshire Ct, Montpelier, VA 23192

HUTH, Harvey Checketts (Alb) St Stephen's Church, 16 Elsmere Ave, Delmar, NY 12054

HUTJENS, Dale Henry (FdL) 123 Nob Hill Ln, De Pere, WI 54115

HUTSON, Blake Robert (Ala) Church Of The Holy Apostles, 424 Emery Dr, Hoover, AL 35244

HUTSON, Linda Darlene (Az) 12111 N La Cholla Blvd, Oro Valley, AZ 85755

HUTSON, Thomas Milton (ETenn) 3502 Wood Bridge Dr, Nashville, TN 37217

HUTTAR BAILEY, Julia Ruth (Mich)

HUTTO, Kelsey (Ind) 422 N 13th Ave, Beech Grove, IN 46107

HUTTON, Linda Arzelia (Tenn) Box 3167, Sewanee, TN 37375

HUTTON, Linda Vaught (Va)

HUTTON III, Skip (SVa) 3429 Boyce Court, Norfolk, VA 23509

HUXLEY, Dave (NwT) Saint Luke's Church, 146 S Church St, Whitewater, WI 53190

HUYCK, Jonathan Taylor (RI) 175 Mathewson St, Providence, RI 02903

HUYNH, Tinh Trang (Va) 64 Horseshoe Ln N, Columbus, NJ 08022

HYATT, David (Pa) 404 Donna Ln, Phoenixville, PA 19460

HYBL, Andrew David (Ark) 925 Mitchell St, Conway, AR 72034

HYCHE, Jerald (Tex) 1803 Highland Hollow Drive, Conroe, TX 77304

HYDE, John Ernest Authur (SwFla) 4650 Cove Cir Apt 407, Madeira Beach, FL 33708

HYDE, Lillian (Tex) Po Box 580117, Houston, TX 77258

HYDE, Pamela Willson (Az) 75 Church Ln, Westport, CT 06880

HYDE III, Robert Willis (Tex) 208 Seawall Blvd, Galveston, TX 77550

HYLDEN, Emily R (Dal) 1302 W Kiest Blvd, Dallas, TX 75224

HYLDEN, Jordan (Dal) 6345 Wydown Blvd, Saint Louis, MO 63105

HYMES, Adrienne Renita (SwFla) 8005 25th St E, Parrish, FL 34219

HYNDMAN, David Lee (NI) 8981 E 5th Ave Apt 101, Gary, IN 46403

I

IALONGO, Donna Marie (Chi) 2s697 Parkview Dr, Glen Ellyn, IL 60137

IBE, Morgan Kelechi (Okla) 2424 Pinon Pl, Edmond, OK 73013

IDEMA III, Henry (WMich) 13562 Redbird Ln, Grand Haven, MI 49417

IDICULA, Mathew (Chi) The Church of St Columba of Iona, 1800 Irving Park Rd, Hanover Park, IL 60133

IFILL, Angela Sylvia S (O) 64 Bayley Ave, Yonkers, NY 10705

IGO, Nancy Elle (NwT) Episcopal Diocese of Northwest Texas, 1802 Broadway, Lubbock, TX 79401

IHIASOTA, Isaac (WNY) 8283 Effie Drive, Niagara Falls, NY 14304

✠ **IHLOFF**, Robert Wilkes (Md) 1200 Steuart St Unit 1020, Baltimore, MD 21230

IKENYE, Ndungu John Brown (Chi) 1930 Darrow Ave, Evanston, IL 60201

ILLAS, Antonio (WTex) PO Box 1948, San Benito, TX 78586

ILLES, Joseph Paul (NI) 56869 Sundown Rd, South Bend, IN 46619

ILLINGWORTH, David Paul (Me) 28 Wayne St, Portland, ME 04102

ILLUECA, Marta Del Carmen (Del)

IMBODEN, Stanley Franklin (CPa) 315 Dead End Rd, Lititz, PA 17543

IMMEL, Otto Wigaart (NJ) Po Box 2379, Tybee Island, GA 31328

IMPICCICHE, Frank S (Ind)

INAPANTA PAEZ, Lourdes Esther (EcuC)

INCORVATI, Rick (SO)

INESON JR, John Henry (Me) 53 High St., Damariscotta, ME 04543

INFANTE PINZON, John Edwin (WMich) 524 Washington Ave, Grand Haven, MI 49417

INGALLS JR, Arthur B (Md) PO Box 25, Churchville, MD 21028

INGALLS, Clayton Dean (Tenn) 5501 Franklin Pike, Nashville, TN 37220

INGALLS, Jason T (Tex) 1100 N. 15th St., Waco, TX 76707

INGALLS, Meg (WA) Transfiguration Church, 13925 New Hampshire Ave, Silver Spring, MD 20904

INGEMAN, Peter Lyle (Ga) 3128 Huntington Ridge Circle, Valdosta, GA 31602

INGERSOLL, Russ (WNC) 52 Sturbridge Lane, Greensboro, NC 27408

INGRAHAM, Doris Williams (SeFla) 15955 Nw 27th Ave, Opa Locka, FL 33054

INIESTA-AVILA, Bernardo (Nev) 4201 W Washington Ave, Las Vegas, NV 89107

INMAN, John Wesley (WMich) 135 Old York Road, New Hope, PA 18938

INMAN, Virginia Bain (NC) 607 N Greene St, Greensboro, NC 27401

INNES, Neil Fraser (WTex) 1702 S Medio River Cir, Sugar Land, TX 77478

INSCOE, Laura D (Va) 2319 E. Broad Street, Richmond, VA 23223

INSERRA, John Michael (WTex) 1417 E Austin Ave, Harlingen, TX 78550

IRELAND, Joel T (LI) 532 E 1st St, Tucson, AZ 85705

✠ **IRISH**, Carolyn Tanner (U) 1930 South State, Salt Lake City, UT 84115

IRIZARRY, J E (PR)

IRONSIDE, Susan R (Nwk) 414 E Broad St, Westfield, NJ 07090

IRSCH, Leona M (WNY) 108 S Thomas Ave, Edwardsville, PA 18704

IRVIN, Cynthia Diane (Colo) 546 N Elm St #1496, Cortez, CO 81321

IRVINE, Peter Bennington (NI) 1140 Blaine Ave, Janesville, WI 53545

IRVING, Anthony Tuttle (Oly) 5445 Donnelly Dr Se, Olympia, WA 98501

IRVING, Jocelyn (WA) 9713 Summit Cir Apt 1B, Upper Marlboro, MD 20774

IRVING, Stanley Herbert (Vt) 5205 Georgia Shore Rd, Saint Albans, VT 05478

IRWIN, Margaret Bertha (Mil) 6989 Apprentice Pl, Middleton, WI 53562

IRWIN, Sara (Pgh)

IRWIN, Zachary Tracy (NwPa) 4216 E South Shore Dr, Erie, PA 16511

ISAAC III, Frank Reid (O) 2181 Ambleside Drive, Apartment 412, Cleveland, OH 44106

✠ **ISAAC**, Telesforo A (SwFla) JP 8600, PO Box 02-5284, Miami, FL 33102

ISAACS, James Steele (WA) St James Church, 11815 Seven Locks Rd, Potomac, MD 20854

ISADORE, Daniel Joseph (Pgh) 5801 Hampton St, Pittsburgh, PA 15206

ISHIZAKI, Norman Yukio (Los) 580 Hilgard Ave, Los Angeles, CA 90024

ISHMAN, Martha S. (NwPa) 245 Valley Trails Ln, Franklin, PA 16323

ISLEY, Carolyn W (ETenn) 118 Oak Grove Rd, Greeneville, TN 37745

ISRAEL, Carver Washington (LI) 322 Clearbrook Ave, Lansdowne, PA 19050

ISRAEL JR, Fielder (Md) 4720 Winterberry Ct, Williamsburg, VA 23188

ISWARIAH, James Chandran (Va) 465 Walnut Ln, King William, VA 23086

✠ **ITTY**, Johncy (Ore) 10 Avalon Road, Garden City, NY 11530

IVATTS, Justin Anthony (Va)

IVES (Mass) 23 Monmouth St., Brookline, MA 02446

IVES, Nathan W (Ct)

IVEY, Betsy (Pa) 1401 S 22nd St, Philadelphia, PA 19146

IVEY, Valerie Ann (Ore) 15240 Nw Courting Hill Dr, Banks, OR 97106

IWICK, Richard Edward (Mich) 25755 Kilreigh Ct, Farmington Hills, MI 48336

IX, Victoria Shippee (WMass) 37 Chestnut St, Springfield, MA 01103

IZADI, Samira (Dal) 6941 kingdom estates drive, Dallas, TX 75236

IZQUIERDO-VELAZQUEZ, Jesus B (EcuC)

IZUTSU, Margaret W (Mich) 18 Fairview Ave, Arlington, MA 02474

IZZI SR, Robert Peter (RI)

IZZO, Joanne (NY) 8411 13th Ave # 2nd Floor, Brooklyn, NY 11228

J

JABLONSKI, Carol J (WA) 4512 College Ave, College Park, MD 20740

JACKSON, Brad (Va) Po Box 305, Madison, VA 22727

JACKSON, Bruce A (Az) 7719 W Bluefield Ave, Glendale, AZ 85308

JACKSON, Carl Thomas (Va) 2940 Corries Way, Conneaut, OH 44030

JACKSON III, Chandler Cheshire (WMo) 515 E Division St, Springfield, MO 65803

JACKSON, David (SwFla) All Souls Episcopal Church, 14640 N Cleveland Ave, North Fort Myers, FL 33903

JACKSON, David G (Chi) 203 S Kensington Ave, La Grange, IL 60525

JACKSON, David Hilton (NC) 245 Cavalier Drive, Greenville, SC 29650

JACKSON, Deborah Mitchell (Fla) 4849 Hampshire Pl, Hixson, TN 37343

JACKSON JR, Gary (CFla) 500 W Stuart St, Bartow, FL 33830

JACKSON, Gary Jon (Ga) St Mark's Episcopal Church, 900 Gloucester St, Brunswick, GA 31520

JACKSON, Hugo T (At) 4246 Glenforest Way Ne, Roswell, GA 30075

JACKSON, Ira Leverne (Ga) Grace Episcopal Church, PO Box 617, Sandersville, GA 31082

JACKSON, Jared Judd (Pgh) 903 Orchard Park Dr., Gibsonia, PA 15044

JACKSON, Jeffery R (At) 69 Mobley Road, PO Box 752, Hamilton, GA 31811

JACKSON, Jimmy (Kan) Saint Matthew's Episcopal Church, 2001 Windsor Dr, Newton, KS 67114

JACKSON, Judy Ann (Chi)

JACKSON, Kimberly (At) 3737 Seminary Rd, Alexandria, VA 22304

JACKSON, Margaret Ruth Brosz (Ia)

JACKSON, Micah (Tex) 501 E 32nd St, Austin, TX 78705

JACKSON, Patricia Gladys (Ct) 120 Sigourney St, Hartford, CT 06105

JACKSON, Paul Phillip (CFla) 1620 Mayflower Ct. A-211, Winter Park, FL 32789

JACKSON, Paula Marie (SO) 65 E Hollister St, Cincinnati, OH 45219

JACKSON, Peter (Nwk) 130 Bessida St, Bloomfield, NJ 07003

JACKSON, Peter Jonathan Edward (WA) 1 The Green, London, N14 7EG, Great Britain (UK)

JACKSON, Phillip A (NY) 50 Pine St, New York, NY 10005

JACKSON, Reginald Fitzroy (LI) 1695 E 55th St, Brooklyn, NY 11234

JACKSON, Rhea E (Ark) PO Box 36, Roland, AR 72135

JACKSON, Robert Sumner (Mass) 339 S Madison St, Woodstock, IL 60098

JACKSON, Rosemary Herrick (WNC) 145 Old Mt Olivet Rd, Zirconia, NC 28790

JACKSON, Terry Allan (NY) 600 W 246th St Apt 1515, Bronx, NY 10471

JACKSON, Thomas C (Cal) Christ Episcopal Church, 1700 Santa Clara Avenue, Alameda, CA 94501

JACKSON, Thomas Lee (Ala) Po Box 4155, Tyler, TX 75712

JACKSON-MCKINNEY, Statha Frances (SwFla) 484 E Shade Dr, Venice, FL 34293

JACOB, James Neithelloor (RI)

JACOB, Jerry Elias (Ala) 305 Arnold St NE, Cullman, AL 35055

JACOBS, Allston Alexander (Md) 2019 Division St, Baltimore, MD 21217

JACOBS, Connie Hartquist (Episcopal SJ) 2635 2nd Ave Apt 730, San Diego, CA 92103

JACOBS, Gregory Alexander (Nwk) 31 Mulberry St., Newark, NJ 07102

JACOBS, John Ray (NC) 21 Riviera Dr, Pinehurst, NC 28374

JACOBS, Marlene (Oly) 1917 Logan Ave S, Minneapolis, MN 55403

JACOBS III, Philip (Mass) 203 Chapman St, Canton, MA 02021

JACOBS, Robert Alexander (NY) 20 Trestle Way, Dayton, NJ 08810

JACOBSON, Harold Knute (Mo) 123 S. Ninth Street, Columbia, MO 65201

JACOBSON, Jeanne (CPa) 616 Spruce St., Hollidaysburg, PA 16648

JACOBSON, Marc R (Pgh) 4604 Crew Hall Ln, Quezon City, Waxhaw, NC 28173

JACOBSON, Matthew Daniel (NY) 145 W 46th St, New York, NY 10036

JACOBSON, Mr. Jacobson (Pa) 9 Esty Way, Groveland, MA 01834

JACOBSON, Paul Alan (Ct) 859 East Broadway, Stratford, CT 06515

JACOBSON, Steve (Pa) 155 Bayside Drive, Eastham, MA 02642

✠ **JACOBUS**, Russell Edward (FdL) 17786 Valley View Rd, Townsend, WI 54175

JACOBY, Lisa Anne (Los) St George Episcopal Church, 23802 Avenida De La Carlota, Laguna Hills, CA 92653

JACQUES, Mary Martha (Mont) 13100 Highway 41 North, Dillon, MT 59725

JAEGER, Nick (Ky) 2502 Jefferson St., Paducah, KY 42001

JAEKLE, Charles Roth (WA) 7446 Spring Village Dr Apt 307, Springfield, VA 22150

JAENKE, Karen Ann (NJ) 24 Woodland Road, Fairfax, CA 94930

JAIKES, Donald William (Mass) 1095 Pinellas Pt Dr So Unit 327, Saint Petersburg, FL 33705

JAKOBSEN, Wilma (ECR) St Jude the Apostle Church, 20920 McClellan Rd, Cupertino, CA 95014

JALLOUF, Georges (Okla) 5850 E 78th Pl, Tulsa, OK 74136

JAMBOR, Christopher Noel (FtW) 1805 Malibar Rd, Fort Worth, TX 76116

JAMES, Alan (Chi) 400 E Westminster, Lake Forest, IL 60045

JAMES, Charles (CGC) Po Box 29, Bon Secour, AL 36511

JAMES, Claudia Jan (Az) 423 N. Beaver St., Flagstaff, AZ 86001

JAMES, Darryl Farrar (LI) 3312 S Indiana Ave, Chicago, IL 60616

JAMES, Edmund Ludwig (Okla) 104 W Hanover St, Hoyt, OK 74472

JAMES, Jay C (NC) 4523 Six Forks Road, Raleigh, NC 27609

JAMES, John Hugh Hugh (Ct) Christ Episc Church, 78 Washington St, Norwich, CT 06360

JAMES, Marcus Gilbert (Roch)

JAMES, Molly F (Ct) 37 Griswold Dr, West Hartford, CT 06119

JAMES, Nancy (WA) 713 E St Ne, Washington, DC 20002

JAMES JR, Ralph Matthew (WVa) PO Box 145, Union, WV 24983

JAMES, Reynelda Cordelia (Nev)

JAMES, Robert Arthur (LI) 5 Fig Ct E, Homosassa, FL 34446

JAMES, Robin L (NY) 660 S 500 E, Salt Lake City, UT 84102

JAMES, Sally Patricia (NMich) 402 W Fleshiem St, Iron Mountain, MI 49801

JAMES, William Evans (CGC) 1530 University Dr NE Apt 15, Atlanta, GA 30306

JAMESON, Elizabeth Butler (Chi) 232 S. Dwyer, Arlington Heights, IL 60005

JAMESON, J Parker (Tex) 8 Troon Dr, Lakeway, TX 78738

JAMIESON, Sandra Swift Cornett (SwFla) 301 Jasmine Way, Clearwater, FL 33756

JAMIESON JR, William Stukey (WNC) 15 Macon Ave, Asheville, NC 28801

JAMIESON-DRAKE, Vicky (NC) 304 E Franklin St, Chapel Hill, NC 27514

JAMISON, Dale Martin (NMich) 901 Dakota Ave, Gladstone, MI 49837

JAMISON, Dorothy Lockwood (Cal) 501 Portola Rd Apt 12J, Portola Valley, CA 94028

JAMISON, Walter Kay (Fla)

JANDA, Mary Sheridan (U)

JANELLE, Nicole (Los) St. Michael's University Church, 6586 Picasso Rd., Isla Vista, CA 93117

JANE REDDICK, Mary (Tex) 2525 Seagler Rd, Houston, TX 77042

JANESS, Nancy Kingswood (Nev)

JANG, Teduan Vincent (Cal) 5072 Diamond Heights Blvd, San Francisco, CA 94131

JANIEC, Thomas Daniel (Chi) 342 E Wood St, Palatine, IL 60067

JARA, Francisco Gonzalo (EcuC)

JARRELL, Robin Campbell (CPa) 229 Alana Ln, Lewisburg, PA 17837

JARRETT III, John J (SeFla) 1052 Nw 65th St, Miami, FL 33150

JARRETT-SCHELL, Peter (WA) 1700 Powder Mill Rd, Silver Spring, MD 20903

JARRETT-SCHELL, Rondesia (WA) 13925 New Hampshire Ave, Silver Spring, MD 20904

JARVIS, Leon Gerald (NMich) 1300 West Ave, Marquette, MI 49855

JASMER, Gerald Bruce (Mont) 36 30th St W, Billings, MT 59102

JASPER SR, John Weaver (CFla) 1151 Sw Del Rio Blvd, Port Saint Lucie, FL 34953

JASPER, Michael Angelo (Okla) 13112 N Rockwell Ave, Oklahoma City, OK 73142

JAVIER, Nazareno C (Pa)

JAY, Lynn (Los) 26084 Viento Ct, Valencia, CA 91355

JAYAWARDENE, Thomas Devashri (Los) 1141 Westmont Rd, Santa Barbara, CA 93108

JAYNES, Ronald P (Pa) 431 Atkins Ave, Lancaster, PA 17603

JAYNES, Ruth (Neb) 1322 S 52nd St, Omaha, NE 68106

JEAN, Jean Junior (Hai)

JEAN, Macdonald (Hai) Box 1309, Port-Au-Prince, Haiti

JEANES III, Paul (NJ) 33 Mercer St, Princeton, NJ 08540

JEAN-JACQUES, Harry Musset (Hai) Boite Postale 1309, Port-Au-Prince, Haiti

JEAN-PHILIPPE, Jean-Alphonse (Hai) PO Box 407139, C/O Lynx Air, Fort Lauderdale, FL 33340

JEFFERS, Mary Elisabeth (USC) 711 S McDuffie St, Anderson, SC 29624

JEFFERSON, Paul (La) 1329 Jackson Ave, New Orleans, LA 70130

JEFFERSON, Lee Goodrich (WLa)

✠ **JEFFERTS SCHORI**, Katharine (Nev) Episcopal Diocese of San Diego, 2083 Sunset Cliffs Blvd, San Diego, CA 92107

JEFFERY, Anne-Marie (NJ) St Peters Episcopal Church, 183 Rector St, Perth Amboy, NJ 08861

JEFFERY, David Luce (Fla) 1843 Seminole Rd, Atlantic Beach, FL 32233

JEFFERY, Vincent James (Nev) 1500 Mount Rose St, Reno, NV 89509

JEFFREY, Kathryn G (Spr) 29 Nord Circle Rd, North Oaks, MN 55127

JEFFREY, Peter Leigh (Mass) 8 Kirk St, Lowell, MA 01852

JEKABSONS, Wendie Susan Scudds (ETenn) 334 Sourwood Hill Rd, Bristol, TN 37620

✠ **JELINEK**, James Louis (Minn) 957 25th St NW, Washington, DC 20037

JELLISON, Mary Lavon (Wyo) 3129 Pinewood Ave, Bellingham, WA 98225

JEMMOTT, Brian Anthony Lester (NJ) 2005 South Columbia Place, Decatur, GA 30032

JENCKS, Jeff (CGC) 7979 N 9th Ave, Pensacola, FL 32514

JENKINS, Al W (CFla) 103 W Christina Blvd, Lakeland, FL 33813

✠ **JENKINS III**, Charles Edward (La) P.O. Box 3000, St. Francisville, LA 70775

JENKINS JR, Harry (La) 1534 7th St, Slidell, LA 70458

JENKINS, James Leonard (Minn) 5250 Vernon Ave S Apt 232, Edina, MN 55436

JENKINS, James Morgan (CPa) St. Paul's Episcopal Church, 101 E Main St, Bloomsburg, PA 17815

JENKINS, John Stone (La) 708 Forest Point Dr, Brandon, MS 39047

JENKINS, John William Andrew (Ga)

JENKINS, Judith Ann (RG) 601 Montano Rd. N.W., Albuquerque, NM 87107

JENKINS, Kathryn E (Va) 3507 Pond Chase Dr, Midlothian, VA 23113

JENKINS, Kit Reid (WVa) 3000 Washington Blvd, Huntington, WV 25705

JENKINS, Marilyn Hamilton (WA)

JENKINS, Mark A (NH) 20260 Williamsville Rd, Gregory, MI 48137

JENKINS, Martha L (SVa) 120 Reykin Dr, Richmond, VA 23236

JENKINS, Michael Lemon (WNC) 5165 Hayes Waters Rd, Morganton, NC 28655

JENKINS, Stephanie (Kan) 835 SW Polk St, Topeka, KS 66612

JENKINS, William David (Kan) 314 N Adams St, Junction City, KS 66441

JENKS, Alan W (WVa) 450 Elm St, Morgantown, WV 26501

JENKS, Glenn B (Az) 5417 E Milton Dr, Cave Creek, AZ 85331

JENKS, Peter Q (Me) 200 Main St, Thomaston, ME 04861

JENNEKER, Bruce (WA) St George's Cathedral, 5 Wale St, Cape Town, 8001, South Africa

JENNER, Helen McLeroy (NC) 1079 Ridge Dr, Clayton, NC 27520

JENNEY, Joe Allen (EMich)

JENNINGS, Albert Arthur (O) 8667 Shepard Rd # 204, Macedonia, OH 44056

JENNINGS, Debora (Okla) 814 N Vinita Ave, Tahlequah, OK 74464

JENNINGS, Gay Clark (O) 168 Hiram College Dr, Sagamore Hills, OH 44067

JENNINGS, James Courtney (HB) 5701 Snead Rd, Richmond, VA 23224

JENNINGS, Kelly Kathleen (Tex)

JENNINGS, Margaret Herring (USC) 301 W Liberty St, Winnsboro, SC 29180

JENNINGS, Mary Kay (RG) Yankton Mission Cluster, 126 N Park NE, Wagner, SD 57380

JENNINGS, Nathan Grady (Tex) PO Box 2247, Austin, TX 78768

JENNINGS, Robert Tallmadge (Ky) 2002 High Ridge Rd, Louisville, KY 40207

JENNINGS III, William Worth (NC) 702 Hillandale Ln, Garner, NC 27529

JENSEN, Anne (Cal) 865 Walavista Ave., Oakland, CA 94610

JENSEN, Barbara Ann (NJ) 238 Main St, South River, NJ 08882

JENSEN, Jan D (Tex) 11 Sherwood St, Dayton, TX 77535

JENSEN, Jonathon W (Pgh) 315 Shady Avenue, Pittsburgh, PA 15206

JENSEN, Julia Kooser (Ore) 2020 SW Knollcrest Dr., Portland, OR 97225

JENSEN, Patricia Ann (CFla) 9301 Hunters Park Way, Tampa, FL 33647

JENSON, Constance (WA) 17413 Audrey Road, Cobb Island, MD 20625

JERAULD, Philip Eldredge (Mass) 1 Concord Coach Ln, Litchfield, NH 03052

JERGENS, Andrew MacAoidh (SO) 2374 Madison Rd, Cincinnati, OH 45208

JERNAGAN III, Luke (Mo) 110 N Warson Rd, Saint Louis, MO 63124

JEROME, Joseph (LI) 3956 44th St, Sunnyside, NY 11104

JERSEY, Jean Staffeld (Vt) 32 Liberty St, Montpelier, VT 05602

JESION, Lawrence Michael (Ga) Christ Episcopal Church, 1904 Greene St, Augusta, GA 30904

JESKE, Mark William (WMo) 4401 Wornall Rd, Kansas City, MO 64111

JESSE JR, Henry (Colo) 7787 E Gunnison Pl, Denver, CO 80231

JESSETT, Frederick Edwin (Oly) 5309 S. Myrtle Lane, Spokane, WA 99223

JESSUP, Dorothy Margaret Paul (Pa) 278 Friendship Dr, Paoli, PA 19301

JESSUP, Elaine Anderson (SeFla) 464 NE 16th St, Miami, FL 33132

JESTER, Pamela Jean (Cal) 911 Dowling Blvd, San Leandro, CA 94577

JETT, Charles D (SC) 107 Sea Lavender Ln, Summerville, SC 29486

JETT, Mary J (NY) Church of St Mary the Virgin, 145 W 46th St, New York, NY 10036

JEULAND, Eric Vincent (Ct) 25 Church St, Shelton, CT 06484

JEULAND, Jane Catherine Eppley (Ct) 300 Main St, Wethersfield, CT 06109

JEVNE, Lucretia (The Episcopal NCal) 120 Loraine Ct, Vacaville, CA 95688

JEW, Cynthia Lynne (Los) Trinity Episcopal Church, 600 Saratoga, Fillmore, CA 93016

JEWELL, Kenneth Arthur (Nev) 732 Aesop Dr, Spring Creek, NV 89815

JEWETT, Ethan A (Chi) 2013 Appletree St, Philadelphia, PA 19103

JEWISS, Tony (Los) 1290 Kent Street, Brooklyn, NY 11222

JEWSON, Alfred Joseph (WMo) 7511 Rannells Ave, Saint Louis, MO 63143

JEWSON, Dayna (Mo) 7511 Rannells Ave, Saint Louis, MO 63143

JILLARD, Christina Liggitt (Oly) Saint Margaret's Episcopal Church, 4228 Factoria Blvd SE, Bellevue, WA 98006

JIM, Rosella A (NAM) Po Box 5854, Farmington, NM 87499

JIMENEZ, Darla Sue (NwT)

JIMENEZ, Juan (Los) 311 W South St, Anaheim, CA 92805

JIMENEZ-IRIZARRY, Edwin (Ct) Urb. El Vedado, Calle 12 de Octubre #428-A, San Juan, PR 00918

JIMENEZ-MESENBRING, Maria Jesus (Oly) 2020 E. Terrace St., Seattle, WA 98122

JINETE, Alvaro E (Chi) 3241 Calwagner St, Franklin Park, IL 60131

JIZMAGIAN, Mary Gibson (Cal) 2570 Chestnut St, San Francisco, CA 94123

JODKO, Juliusz Siegmond (Ct) St. Michael's Parish, 210 Church St, Naugatuck, CT 06770

JOE-KINALE, Rose Mary (Nev)

JOFFRION JR, Felix Hughes (Ala) 1180 11th Ave S, Birmingham, AL 35205

JOHANNSEN, Carole (NY) 8 Pine Road, Bedford Hills, NY 10507

JOHANNSON, Johanna-Karen (NY) PO Box 1412, Bucksport, ME 04416

JOHANSEN, Paul Charles (SwFla) 504 3rd St Nw, New Philadelphia, OH 44663

JOHANSON, Norman Lee (Neb) 116 S Sunset Pl, Monrovia, CA 91016

JOHANSSEN, John (SO) 9429 Lighthouse Cut, Thornville, OH 43076

JOHN, Abidhananthar (Roch) PO Box 466, Savona, NY 14879

JOHN, James Howard (Kan) 7603 E Morris St, Wichita, KS 67207

JOHN, Rene (NJ) 16 Fanning Way, Pennington, NJ 08534

JOHNS, Ernest William (SwFla) 20024 Behan Ct, Port Charlotte, FL 33952

JOHNS, Martha (Los) 30382 Via Con Dios, Rancho Santa Margarita, CA 92688

JOHNS III, Norman S (Oly) 5787 Lenea Dr Nw, Bremerton, WA 98312

JOHNS, Richard Gray (Los) 1199 Marinaside Crescent, Apt. 1701, Vancouver, V6Z 2Y2, Canada

JOHNSON JR, Al (Chi) 212 Biltmore Dr, N Barrington, IL 60010

JOHNSON, Alston Boyd (WLa) 140 Devereaux Dr, Madison, MS 39110

JOHNSON, Andrew (Roch) 1957 Five Mile Line Rd., Penfield, NY 14526

JOHNSON, Andy (Dal) Saint John's Episcopal Church, 848 Harter Rd, Dallas, TX 75218

JOHNSON, Ann L (Ct) 1105 Quarrier St, Charleston, WV 25301

JOHNSON, Ann Ruth (Az) 701 North Apollo Way, Flagstaff, AZ 86001

JOHNSON, Ann Elizabeth Simmons (Az) PO Box 40, 13803 North Watts Lane, Fort Thomas, AZ 85536

JOHNSON, Arthur Everitt (Miss) 1052 Deer Dr, Bay Saint Louis, MS 39520

✠ **JOHNSON**, Bob (WNC) 21 Lincolnshire Loop, Asheville, NC 28803

JOHNSON, Brian David (SanD) 1836 N Mira Loma Way, Palm Springs, CA 92262

JOHNSON, Candine E (Va)

JOHNSON, Carolynn Elayne (Mich)

JOHNSON, Charlie (Va) 132 Lancaster Dr Apt 626, Irvington, VA 22480

JOHNSON, Christopher Allen (Mich) 45 Woodland Ave, Glen Ridge, NJ 07028

JOHNSON, David (Miss) 116 Cedar Pointe, Fairhope, AL 36532

JOHNSON, David Allen (Ga) 1700 Ashwood Blvd, Charlottesville, VA 22911

JOHNSON, David George (NMich) 1021 E E St, Iron Mountain, MI 49801

JOHNSON, Dennis Lee (Wyo) Po Box 3485, Jackson, WY 83001

JOHNSON, Deon K (Mich) 200 W Saint Paul St, Brighton, MI 48116

JOHNSON, Diana P (U) 1854 Kensington Avenue, Salt Lake City, UT 84108

✠ **JOHNSON**, Don (WTenn) 692 Poplar Ave, Memphis, TN 38105

JOHNSON, Donald Keith (Dal) 2026 Cherrywood Ln, Denton, TX 76209

JOHNSON, Doris (Ga) 3 Westridge Rd, Savannah, GA 31411

JOHNSON, Douglas Peter (WMo) 9905 N Hawthorne Ave, Kansas City, MO 64157

JOHNSON, Edwin (Mass) 14 Cushing Ave, Dorchester, MA 02125

JOHNSON, Eric N (Oly) Christ Episcopal Anacortes, 1216 7th St, Anacortes, WA 98221

JOHNSON, Erin Minta (Va) PO Box 32, Cashiers, NC 28717

JOHNSON, Frances Kay Carter (The Episcopal Church in Haw) 959 W 41st Street, Houston, TX 77018

JOHNSON, Frank T (SanD) 651 Eucalyptus Ave, Vista, CA 92084

JOHNSON, Franklin Orr (Mont) 355 Francis Way, Jackson, WY 83001

JOHNSON JR, Fred Hoyer (NY) 118 Lake Emerald Drive - #409, Oakland Park, FL 33309

JOHNSON, Greg (The Episcopal Church in Haw) PO Box 893788, Mililani, HI 96789

JOHNSON JR, Harold Vance (WA) 12194 Cathedral Dr, Lake Ridge, VA 22192

JOHNSON JR, Harrel Brown (NC) 210 South Chestnut Street, Henderson, NC 27536

JOHNSON, Herbert Alan (WNC) 245 Laurel Falls Rd, Franklin, NC 28734

JOHNSON, Horace S (Ct) 3404 Castlebar Cir, Ormond Beach, FL 32174

JOHNSON, Ida (Cal) 535 Joaquin Ave #D, San Leandro, CA 94577

JOHNSON, Ira Joseph (WTenn) 4150 Boeingshire Dr, Memphis, TN 38116

JOHNSON, James Baxter (Colo) 1715 Holly Way, Fort Collins, CO 80526

JOHNSON, Jane Margaret (FdL) 1316 Ellis St., Stevens Point, WI 54481

JOHNSON, Janis Lynn (Oly) 1541 Vista Loop SW #33-101, Tumwater, WA 98512

JOHNSON, Jay Brooks (NC) 2690 Fairlawn Dr, Winston Salem, NC 27106

JOHNSON, Jay Emerson (Cal) 632 38th St, Richmond, CA 94805

JOHNSON, Joan Cottrell (Mass) 4833 Europa Dr, Naples, FL 34105

JOHNSON, Johan (NY) 521 W 126th St, New York, NY 10027

JOHNSON, John Brent (Tex) St. John's Episcopal Church, 1305 Roosevelt, Silsbee, TX 77656

JOHNSON JR, John Romig (NY) 1020 Tyron Cir, Charleston, SC 29414

JOHNSON, Juanita Hanger (Neb) 10761 Izard St, Omaha, NE 68114

JOHNSON, Julie Anna (Tenn) St Mary Magdalene Church, PO Box 150, Fayetteville, TN 37334

JOHNSON, June (Ga) 519 Parker Ave, Decatur, GA 30032

JOHNSON, June B (Oly) 114 20th Ave SE, Olympia, WA 98501

JOHNSON, Karen Brown (WA) 18404 Tea Rose Pl, Gaithersburg, MD 20879

JOHNSON, Katherine Bradley (NC) 2504 Englewood Ave, Durham, NC 27705

JOHNSON, Kellaura Beth Jones (Tex) 235, Royal Oaks, Huntsville, TX 77320

JOHNSON, Kenneth William (Mass) 11699 Bennington Woods Rd, Reston, VA 20194

JOHNSON, Kent William (LI) 6626 52nd Rd, #1, Maspeth, NY 11378

JOHNSON, Kevin Allen (FtW) St. Alban's Episcopal Church, 316 W Main St, Arlington, TX 76010

JOHNSON, Kristine Ann (Va) 6715 Georgetown Pike, Mclean, VA 22101

JOHNSON, Lee (Episcopal SJ) 310 Audubon Dr, Lodi, CA 95240

JOHNSON, Linda Catherine (Ind) IU Episcopal Campus Ministry, PO Box 127, Bloomington, IN 47402

JOHNSON, Linda Marie (Oly) Po Box 354, Westport, WA 98595

JOHNSON, Lori Elaine (EMich) 315 1/2 N Maple St, Flushing, MI 48433

JOHNSON JR, Lucius Curtis (Ga) 552 Hunterdale Rd, Evans, GA 30809

JOHNSON, Lynn H (NJ) 3 Azalea Dr, Lumberton, NJ 08048

JOHNSON, Maeve Maud Vincent (Az) 114 W Roosevelt St., Phoenix, AZ 85003

JOHNSON, Malinda Margaret Eichner (Ct) 9 Arrow Head Rd, Westport, CT 06880

JOHNSON, Marcus Peter (CFla)

JOHNSON, Marietta (Mont) Po Box 78, Red Lodge, MT 59068

JOHNSON, Marta D. V. (Md) 4603 Rocks Road, PO Box 103, Street, MD 21154

JOHNSON, Mary Peterson (ND) All Saints' Church, 301 Main St S, Minot, ND 58701

JOHNSON, Mary Richardson (NMich) 1021 E E St, Iron Mountain, MI 49801

JOHNSON, Matt (NC) 231 N Church St, Rocky Mount, NC 27804

JOHNSON, Michael R (SD) PO Box 434, Deadwood, SD 57732

JOHNSON, Michaela (Kay) (RI) 1214 Noyes Dr, Silver Spring, MD 20910

JOHNSON, Neil Edward (WNY) 18 Harrogate Square, Williamsville, NY 14221

JOHNSON, Nora (Pa)

JOHNSON, Patricia A (Ia) 2222 McDonald St, Sioux City, IA 51104

JOHNSON, Paul (Tex) 17706 Linkview Dr, Dripping Springs, TX 78620

JOHNSON, Randy Wayne (Minn) 2175 1st St, White Bear Lake, MN 55110

JOHNSON, R Dean (At) 1480 Pineview Ln Nw, Conyers, GA 30012

JOHNSON, Richard E (Mont) 902 Logan St, Helena, MT 59601

JOHNSON, Robert Gaines (SVa) 1411 25th St, Galveston, TX 77550

JOHNSON, Robert Wallace (CFla)

JOHNSON, Ronald A (SwFla) 4030 Manatee Ave W, Bradenton, FL 34205

JOHNSON, Ronald Norman (SeFla) 320 Dudley Creek Rd, Hardy, VA 24101

JOHNSON, Russell L (SwFla) 13555 Heron Cir, Clearwater, FL 33762

JOHNSON, Russell Michael (The Episcopal Church in Haw) 296 Nikolau Pl, Hilo, HI 96720

JOHNSON JR, Russell Woodrow (WMo) 409 E Liberty, Independence, MO 64050

JOHNSON, Sandra Parnell (SwFla) 14640 N Cleveland Ave, N Ft Myers, FL 33903

JOHNSON, Sanford (WMass) 50 Shaker Farm Rd N, Marlborough, NH 03455

JOHNSON, Simeon O (NY) 165 Saint Marks Pl Apt 10H, Staten Island, NY 10301

JOHNSON, Stephanie McDyre (Ct) 37 Avon Street, New Haven, CT 06511

JOHNSON, Susan (At) 571 Holt Road, Marietta, GA 30068

JOHNSON, Susan Elaine (Eur) Schiesstaettberg 44, Eichstatt, AL 498421-4125, Germany

JOHNSON, Sydney (Wyo)

JOHNSON, Thalia Felice (Mich) 8261 Cypress Way, Dexter, MI 48130

JOHNSON, Theodore Arthur (Nev) P.O. Box 4551, South Lake Tahoe, CA 95729

JOHNSON, Theodore William (WA) PO Box 386, Basye, VA 22810

JOHNSON, Tim (WA) Washington Episcopal School, 5600 Little Falls Parkway, Bethesda, MD 20816

JOHNSON, Vicki Lynn (Spok) 1322 Kimball Ave, Richland, WA 99354

JOHNSON, Walter S (Los) 1264 N Kings Rd Apt 17, West Hollywood, CA 90069

JOHNSON, Ward Kendall (ND) 1003 Crescent Ln, Bismarck, ND 58501

JOHNSON, William Alexander (NY) 27 Fox Meadow Rd, Scarsdale, NY 10583

JOHNSON, William Gerald (Az) 11,000 east Calle Vaqueros, Tucson, AZ 85749

JOHNSON III, William Pegram (WA) 2004 Floyd Ave, Richmond, VA 23220

JOHNSON RUSSELL, Tracy Johnson (Ct) 89 Lenox St Unit N, New Haven, CT 06513

JOHNSON-TAYLOR, Allan (WA) 4211 Enterprise Rd, Bowie, MD 20720

JOHNSON-TOTH, Louise M (Roch) 243 Genesee Park Blvd, Rochester, NY 14619

JOHNSTON, Cathy Lynn (ETenn) 2152 Hawthorne St, Kingsport, TN 37664

JOHNSTON, Clifford A (CPa) 3147 Grahamton Rd, Morrisdale, PA 16858

JOHNSTON, Copeland David (U)

JOHNSTON, David Knight (Mass) 78 Bishop Dr, Framingham, MA 01702

JOHNSTON, Duncan (NJ) 414 E Broad St, Westfield, NJ 07090

JOHNSTON, Edward (NY) 1215 5th Ave Apt 12d, New York, NY 10029

JOHNSTON, Frank Norman (LI) PO Box 566, Onset, MA 02558

JOHNSTON, Gregory B (Mass) 147 Concord Rd, Lincoln, MA 01773

JOHNSTON, Hewitt (NJ) 41087 Calla Lily St, Indian Land, SC 29707

JOHNSTON, Laurel (ECR) 2767 Delpha Court, Thousand Oaks, CA 91362

JOHNSTON, Lewis Tyra (WMo) 2105 Quail Creek Dr, Lawrence, KS 66047

JOHNSTON, Madelynn (RG) Po Box 8716, Santa Fe, NM 87504

JOHNSTON, Mark Wylie (Ala) 105 Delong Rd, Nauvoo, AL 35578

JOHNSTON, Martha Suzanne (Tenn) 1216 Sneed Rd W, Franklin, TN 37069

JOHNSTON, Nature (Colo)

JOHNSTON, Philip Gilchrist (Va) 4773 Thornbury Dr, Fairfax, VA 22030

JOHNSTON III, Robert Hugh (Dal) 5311 Ridgedale Dr, Dallas, TX 75206

JOHNSTON JR, Robert Hugh (WTex) 102 E. Live Oak St., Cuero, TX 77954

JOHNSTON, Robert Owen (SVa) 207 Marshall St, Petersburg, VA 23803

JOHNSTON, Sally (USC) 392 Stonemarker Rd, Mooresville, NC 28117

✠ **JOHNSTON**, Shannon Sherwood (Va) 110 W Franklin St, Richmond, VA 23220

JOHNSTON, Suzanne Elaine (Roch) 1245 Culver Rd., Rochester, NY 14609

JOHNSTON, William Merrill (FdL) 1010 Congress St, Neenah, WI 54956

JOHNSTON, Zula J (Oly) 8527 46th Ct Ne, Olympia, WA 98516

JOHNSTONE, Elise (Lex)

JOHNSTONE, Mary (RI) 39 Washington St, Newport, RI 02840

JOINER, James (Ore) St David Of Wales Epis Ch, 2800 SE Harrison St, Portland, OR 97214

JOLLY, Anne B (Chi) 3201 Windsor Rd, Austin, TX 78703

JOLLY, Marshall A (WNC) Grace Episcopal Church, 303 S King St, Morganton, NC 28655

JONES, Abram Paschal (Miss)

JONES, Adrea (Okla) 1901 Skyline Place, Bartlesville, OK 74006

JONES, Alan (Cal) 1100 California St, San Francisco, CA 94108

JONES, Andrew Lovell (Ct) Po Box 1083, Norwalk, CT 06856

JONES, Andy (Mil) 2920 Pelham Rd, Madison, WI 53713

JONES, Angela Louise (Neb) 1555 14Th St, Mitchell, NE 69357

JONES, Anthony Edward (LI) St Jone's Episcopal Church, 12 Prospect St, Huntington, NY 11743

JONES III, Arthur L (Ga)

JONES II, Ben (WMass) 569 Main Street, Fitchburg, MA 01420

JONES, Bernie (Mass) PO Box 260321, Brooklyn, NY 11226

JONES, Beverly Jean (CNY) 7460 Se Concord Pl, Hobe Sound, FL 33455

✠ **JONES**, Bob Gordon (Wyo) 900 Cottonwood Dr, Fort Collins, CO 80524

JONES, Bonnie Quantrell (Lex) 1801 Glenhill Dr, Lexington, KY 40502

JONES, Bryan (Los) 5306 Arbor Road, Long Beach, CA 90808

JONES, Carolyn G (WMass) 4 Carousel Ln, Lunenburg, MA 01462

JONES JR, Cecil Baron (Miss) 117 Demontluzin Ave Apt 25, Bay St Louis, MS 39520

✠ **JONES III**, Charles I (Mont) PO Box 86, Gulf Shores, AL 36547

JONES, Charles James (CNY) 9 Jutland Road, Binghamton, NY 13903

JONES, Christine Ann (NY)

JONES, Christopher David (Mass) 464 NE 16th St, Miami, FL 33132

JONES, Chuck (RG) 318 Silver Ave SW, Albuquerque, NM 87102

JONES, Claiborne (At) 5668 Stillwater Court, Stone Mountain, GA 30087-1645, Virgin Islands (U.S.)

JONES, Connie (SVa) 6214 Monroe Pl, Norfolk, VA 23508

JONES, Corey Matthew (Ala)

JONES, Curtis Carl (Ark) 20900 Chenal Pkwy, Little Rock, AR 72223

JONES, Daniel Gwilym (Be) 315 Calvin St, Dunmore, PA 18512

JONES SR, Daniel L (Alb) 15 Center St, Deposit, NY 13754

✠ **JONES**, David Colin (Va) 6043 Burnside Landing Drive, Burke, VA 22015

JONES, David G (ECR) 1061 Garcia Rd, Santa Barbara, CA 93103

JONES, David James (ECR) Le Bourg, 47120 Loubes-Bernac, Duras, 47120 FR, France

JONES, David Lyall (Nwk) 200 Main St, Chatham, NJ 07928

JONES, David P (Chi) 1229 Hinman Avenue, Evanston, IL 60202

JONES, Derek Leslie (Cal) 786 Tunbridge Rd, Danville, CA 94526

JONES, Donald Avery (Ind) 2652 E Windermere Woods Dr, Bloomington, IN 47401

JONES, Dorothy Kovacs (Cal) Po Box 768, Tiburon, CA 94920

JONES, Duncan Haywood (NC) 102 E Calhoun St, Jackson, NC 27845

JONES JR, Eddie Ellsworth (Fla) 160 Bear Pen Rd, Ponte Vedra Beach, FL 32082

JONES, Edward Wilson (Va) Diocese Of Virginia, 110 W Franklin St, Richmond, VA 23220

JONES, Erin Courtney (NwT) 1601 S Georgia St, Amarillo, TX 79102

JONES, Eustan Ulric (LI) 721 E 96th St Apt 2, Brooklyn, NY 11236

JONES, Frederick Lamar (At) 901 Stewart Lake Rd, Kent, OH 44240

JONES, Gary (Va) 412 Maple Ave, Richmond, VA 23226

JONES, Gary H (Tex) 3806 Kiamesha Dr, Missouri City, TX 77459

JONES, Greg (NC) 1520 Canterbury Rd, Raleigh, NC 27608

JONES, Helen Hammon (Ky) 30 River Hill Rd, Louisville, KY 40207

JONES, Herbert H (Va)

JONES JR, Hugh Burnett (ETenn) PO Box 1408, Ridgeland, MS 39158

JONES, Jack Monte (WTex) 1615 S Monroe St, San Angelo, TX 76901

JONES, Jacqueline Sydney (Alb) 8 Byard St, Johnstown, NY 12095

JONES, James (NJ) Oceanview Towers 30, 510 Ocean Ave, Long Branch, NJ 07740

JONES, James Place (SeFla) 9013 SW 62nd Ter, Miami, FL 33173

JONES, James Walter (Mont)

JONES, Jane Denton (Los) 457 W 39th St, San Pedro, CA 90731

JONES, Janice (Tex) 1314 E University Ave, Georgetown, TX 78626

JONES, Jared Lane (CFla)

JONES, Jerry Steven (WK) 1113 Pinehurst St, Hays, KS 67601

JONES, JoAnn Bradley (Pa) 230 Pennswood Rd, Bryn Mawr, PA 19010

JONES, John Tyler (WA) 11040 Baltimore Ave, Beltsville, MD 20705

JONES, Judith A (Ore) 4929 SW Seneca Pl., Waldport, OR 97394

JONES, Judith Gay (Tex) PO Box 28, Pflugerville, TX 78691

JONES, Kenneth Leon (Mass) 62 Hopetown Road, Mt.Pleasant, SC 29464

JONES, Kent Trevor (Chi) 3706 W Saint Paul Ave, McHenry, IL 60050

JONES, Leland Bryant (SanD) 1118 W Country Club Ln, Escondido, CA 92026

JONES, Liz (Miss) 621 Briarwood Dr, Long Beach, MS 39560

JONES, Lynne Elizabeth (SeFla) 206 Pendleton Ave, Palm Beach, FL 33480

JONES, Margaret W (WTenn) 4757 Walnut Grove Rd, Memphis, TN 38117

JONES, Mark Andrew (SeFla) 2707 NW 37th St, Boca Raton, FL 33434

JONES, Mark Stephen (Ga) 212 N Jefferson St, Albany, GA 31701

JONES, Mary Alice (Mont)

JONES, Mary-Frances (Minn) 911 - 8th Avenue Northwest, Austin, MN 55912

JONES, Michael Stephen (CNY) 785 Forest Ridge Dr, Youngstown, OH 44512

JONES, Nelson Bradley (Alb) 970 State St, Schenectady, NY 12307

JONES, Patricia Loraine (Alb) 1295 Myron St, Schenectady, NY 12309

JONES, Patricia Wayne (WNC) 260 21st Ave Nw, Hickory, NC 28601

JONES, Peter Hoyt (HB) 7571 Greenlake Way #B, Lantana, FL 33462

JONES, Rebecca (Colo) 8235 W. 44th Ave, Wheat Ridge, CO 80033

JONES, Rich (SwVa) 2455 N Stevens St, Alexandria, VA 22311

JONES, Richmond A (At) 432 Forest Hill Rd, Macon, GA 31210

JONES, Robert Michael (WNC) PO Box 729, Highlands, NC 28741

JONES, Ross (Okla) 385 Racquet Club Rd., Asheville, NC 28803

JONES, Ruth Elise (NwT) 3010 - 60th, Lubbock, TX 79413

JONES, Sandra Lee Spoar (U) PO Box 981208, Park City, UT 84098

JONES, Scott Daniel (Az) 10716 E Medina Ave, Mesa, AZ 85209

JONES, Stephen Bradley (ETenn)

JONES, Stephen Chad (Tenn) 1216 Sneed Rd W, Franklin, TN 37069

JONES JR, Stewart H (Colo) 2421 S Krameria St, Denver, CO 80222

JONES, Tammy Lynn (Ida) PO Box 324, Rupert, ID 83350

JONES, Teresa Crawford (NY) 5 Christopher Ave, Highland, NY 12528

JONES, Theodore Grant (Md) 2604 Halcyon Avenue, Baltimore, MD 21214

JONES, Thomas A (Neb)

JONES, Thomas Glyndwr (At) 4425 Colchester Ct, Columbus, GA 31907

JONES, Timothy Dale (WNC) 290 Old Haw Creek Rd, Asheville, NC 28805

JONES, Timothy Kent (USC) St Georges Church, 4715 Harding Pike, Nashville, TN 37205

JONES, Tyler (NY) 161 Mansion St., Poughkeepsie, NY 12601

JONES, Vern Edward (Cal) 3814 Jefferson Ave, Emerald Hills, CA 94062

JONES, Walton (Miss) 308 South Commerce St., Natchez, MS 39120

JONES JR, William Augustus (Mo) 58 Kendal Dr, Kennett Square, PA 19348

JONES, William Henry (O) 2651 Cheltenham Rd, Toledo, OH 43606

JONES, William Ogden (SVa) 8137 Brown Rd, Bon Air, VA 23235

JOO, Indon Paul (Chi) 1300 Hallberg Ln, Park Ridge, IL 60068

JOOS, Heidi L (Minn) 3105 W 40th St, Minneapolis, MN 55410

JOPLIN, Susan Colley (Okla) 2513 Sw 123rd St, Oklahoma City, OK 73170

JOPLING, Mal (Fla)

JORDAN, Elizabeth Joy (Mass)

JORDAN SR, John E (Nev) 7560 Splashing Rock Dr., Las Vegas, NV 89131

JORIS, Stan (Okla) 2141 Sw 25th St, Oklahoma City, OK 73108

JOSE, Nancy (WA) 8213 Bald Eagle Ln, Wilmington, NC 28411

JOSEPH, Annette Beth (Mo) 420 N Main St, Poplar Bluff, MO 63901

JOSEPH, Arthur E (NY) 450 Convent Ave, New York, NY 10031

JOSEPH, Hyvenson (NJ)

JOSEPH, Jean Jeannot (Hai) P.O. Box 1390, Port-Au-Prince, Haiti

JOSEPH, Pierre Jean (Ve) Calle Tiuna y Callejon, Sta Elena, Venezuela, Venezuela

JOSEPH, Rogenor ()

JOSEPH, Winston (SeFla)

✠ **JOSLIN**, David Bruce (CNY) 10 Meadow Ridge Rd, Westerly, RI 02891

JOSLIN, Roger (LI) 13225 Sound Ave, Mattituck, NY 11952

JOSLYN-SIEMIATKOSKI, Daniel Edmond (Cal) 501 E 32nd St, Austin, TX 78705

JOY, Charles Austin (SVa) 1009 W Princess Anne Rd, Norfolk, VA 23507

JOYCE, Thomas Joseph (Chi) 214 Hillside Dr., East Berlin, PA 17316

JOYNER, Thomas Roland (Ala) 1170 11th Ave S, Birmingham, AL 35205

JOYNER JR, William Henry (NC) 309 N Boundary St, Chapel Hill, NC 27514

JOYNER-GIFFIN, Sally (Md) 13736 Catoctin Furnace Rd, Thurmont, MD 21788

JUAREZ, Jose Martin (ECR) 113 Morcroft Ln, Durham, NC 27705

JUAREZ VILLAMAR, Betty Marlene (Litoral Ecu) Coop Esperanza Mz.1 Sl.7, Canton Catarama, Ecuador

JUBINSKI, Chris (WA) Christ Episcopal Church, PO Box 8, Chaptico, MD 20621

JUCHTER, Mark Russell (NwPa) 5007 Lions Gate Lane, Killeen, TX 76549

JUDD, Steven William (Minn) 460 Willow Creek Dr, Owatonna, MN 55060

JUDSON, Donald Irving (Chi) 425 E May St, Elmhurst, IL 60126

JUDSON, Horace Douglas (Los) 1065 Lomita Blvd Spc 197, Harbor City, CA 90710

JUDSON, Marguerite Anne (Cal)

JULIAN, Mercedes I (RI) Ascension Church, 390 Pontiac Ave, Cranston, RI 02910-3322, Panama

JULNES-DEHNER, Noel (SO) 3491 Forestoak Court, Cincinnati, OH 45208

JUMP, Douglas Brian (CFla)

JOPLIN / *column 3*

JUNK, Dixie (Kan) 2701 W 51st Ter, Westwood, KS 66205

JUNKIN, Hays Maclean (NH) Church of Our Saviour, P.O. Box 237, Milford, NH 03055

JUPIN, J Michael (SO) 70 S Remington Rd, Columbus, OH 43209

JURADO, Ruben Dario (Nwk) 326 Westervelt Pl, Lodi, NJ 07644

JURKOVICH-HUGHES, Jocelynn Lena (The Episcopal NCal) 216 A Street, Davis, CA 95616

JUSTICE, Simon (Ore) 445 NW Elizabeth Drive, Corvallis, OR 97330

JUSTIN, Daniel (Los) 14311 Dickens St Apt 111, Sherman Oaks, CA 91423

K

KADEL, Andrew (NY) 1 Alexander Street, Yonkers, NY 10701

KAEHR, Michael G (SanD) 9503 La Jolla Farms Rd, La Jolla, CA 92037

KAESTNER, James Andrew (Mil) N52w37111 Washington St, Oconomowoc, WI 53066

KAETON, Elizabeth (Nwk) 35647 Joann Dr, Millsboro, DE 19966

KAHL, Eric (SwFla) 1142 Coral Way, Coral Gables, FL 33134

KAHL JR, Robert Mathew (NJ) 107 E Tampa Ave, Villas, NJ 08251

KAHLE, George Frank (SVa) 16711 Holly Trail Dr, Houston, TX 77058

KAHLER, Jerome Evans (Los) 9061 Santa Margarita Rd, Ventura, CA 93004

KAHN, Paul Stewart (NY) 552 West End Avenue, New York, NY 10024

KAIGHN, Reuel Stewart (Be) 145 The Hideout, Lake Ariel, PA 18436

KAISCH, Kenneth Burton (Los) 2112 Camino Del Sol, Fullerton, CA 92833

KALAS, Steven Curtis (Nev) 3607 Blue Dawn Dr, North Las Vegas, NV 89032

KALEMKERIAN, Louise Knar (Ct) 5030 Main St, Trumbull, CT 06611

KALLENBERG, Richard Arthur (NI) 55805 Oak Manor Pl, Elkhart, IN 46514

KALLIO, Craig (ETenn) 119 Newell Lane, Oak Ridge, TN 37830

KALOM, Judith Christine Lilly (At)

KALUNIAN, Peter John (Spok) 5506 W. 19th Ave., Kennewick, WA 99338

KAMANO, Charles Lansana (Ct) 28 Church St, West Haven, CT 06516

KAMINSKAS, Karen A (Pa)

KAMINSKI, Neil (Ark) 188 Elcano Dr, Hot Springs Village, AR 71909

KAMM, Wayne Kenneth (Ia) 1451 Salem Rd., Salem, IA 52649

KANE, E Ross (Va) 3737 Seminary Rd, Alexandria, VA 22304

KANE, Maria A (WA) 4535 Piney Church Rd, Waldorf, MD 20602

KANE, Paul (SeFla) St James In The Hills Episcopal, 3329 Wilson St, Hollywood, FL 33021

KANELLAKIS, Theodore (NY) 10 Rawson Ave, Camden, ME 04843

KANESTROM, Glenn Walter (FdL) 6443 Estelle Ave, Riverbank, CA 95367

KANG, Peter (La) PO Box 28, St Francisvle, LA 70775

KANGAS, John Gilbert (NMich) 302 E Arch St, Ironwood, MI 49938

KANNENBERG, James Gordon (Ia) 605 Avenue E, Fort Madison, IA 52627

KANOUR, Marion Elizabeth (SwVa) 732 S Chestnut Ave, Arlington Heights, IL 60005

KANYI, Peter (ETenn) 630 Mississippi Ave, Signal Mtn, TN 37377

KANZLER JR, Jay Lee (Mo) 20 Southmoor Dr, Clayton, MO 63105

KAOMA, Kapya John (Mass) Christ Church, Po Box 366202, Hyde Park, MA 02136

KAPP, John Deane (Az) 2800 W Ina Rd, Tucson, AZ 85741

KAPPEL, Roger D (EC) 1313 Deer Creek Dr, Denison, TX 75020

KAPURCH, Linda Marie (Pa) 343 Elizabeth Dr, Kennett Square, PA 19348

KARANJA, Daniel Njoroge (Spr) PO BOX 534, BLYTHEWOOD, SC 29016

KARCHER, David Pirritte (SeFla) 5374 Sw 80th St, Miami, FL 33143

KARCHER, Steven Michael (Neb)

KARDA, Margaret (Nwk) 6095 Summerlake Dr, Port Orange, FL 32127

KARDALEFF, Patricia Payne (Okla) 777 Chosin, Lawton, OK 73507

KAREFA-SMART, Rena Joyce Weller (WA) 4601 N Park Ave Apt 1202, Chevy Chase, MD 20815

KARELIUS, Bradford Lyle (Los) 29602 Via Cebolla, Laguna Niguel, CA 92677

KARKER, Arthur Lee (Me) Po Box 277, West Rockport, ME 04865

KARL JR, John Charles (Roch) 995 Park Ave, Rochester, NY 14610

KARL, Sharon Leith (Roch) 995 Park Ave, Rochester, NY 14610

KARNEY JR, George James (Del) 2812 Faulkland Rd, Wilmington, DE 19808

KARPF, Jessie Olive (Ct) 345 Main St, Portland, CT 06480

KARPF, Ted (WA) PO Box 6654, Santa Fe, NM 87502

KASEY, Philip Howerton (NJ) 4326 Teall Beach Rd, Geneva, NY 14456

KASEY, Polly Mcwilliams (NJ) 4326 Teall Beach Rd, Geneva, NY 14456

KASIO, Joseph Lelit (Nev)

KASSABIAN, Robin Lynn (Los) 25 E Laurel Ave, Sierra Madre, CA 91024

KASSEBAUM, John Albert (NY) 53 S Clinton Ave, Hastings On Hudson, NY 10706

KASWARRA, George (NY) 23 N Willow St, Montclair, NJ 07042

KATER JR, John (Cal) 2116 Tice Creek Drive #2, Walnut Creek, CA 94595

KATHMANN, Charmaine M (La) St. John's Episcopal Church, 2109 17th Street, Kenner, LA 70062

KATON, Joanne Catherine (SeFla) 1800 Southwest 92nd Place, Miami, FL 33165

KATONA, Kenneth J (The Episcopal NCal)

KATZ, Nathaniel Peter (Los) 514 W Adams Blvd, Los Angeles, CA 90007

KAUFFMAN, Bette Jo (WLa) 79 Quail Ridge Dr, Monroe, LA 71203

KAUFMAN, Linda Margaret (WA) 701 S Wayne St, Arlington, VA 22204

KAUTZ, Richard Arden (Ind) 913 Brentwood Ct, New Albany, IN 47150

KAVAL, Lura M (Va) 8522 Light Moon Way, Laurel, MD 20723

KAVROS, Peregrine Murphy (NC) 1311 Lawrence Rd, Hillsborough, NC 27278

KAY, Frances Creveling (WLa) 2914 W Prien Lake Rd, Lake Charles, LA 70605

KAYE, Robert Pleaman Skarpmoen (EO) 365 SE Highland Park Dr, College Place, WA 99324

KAYIGWA, Beatrice Mbatudoe (WMass) 209 Union St, Clinton, MA 01510

KAYNOR, Bob (NC) 82 Kimberly Dr, Durham, NC 27707

KAZANJIAN, Rosanna (Mass) Po Box 1215, Sonoita, AZ 85637

KAZANJIAN JR, Victor Hanford (Mass) Wellesley College, 106 Central St, Wellesley, MA 02481

KE, Jason Chau-sheng (Tai) 37 Jen-Chih St., Nanton City, Taiwan

KEAN, Melissa Lee (Colo)

KEARLEY, David Arthur (Ala) 154 Morgans Steep Rd, Sewanee, TN 37375

KEARNEY, James A (NY) 4410 1/2 Leeland St, Houston, TX 77023

KEARNS, Jada Dart (CFla) 1601 Alafaya Trl, Oviedo, FL 32765

KEATOR, Marnie Knowles (The Episcopal Church in Haw) PO Box 2037, 1 Carley Lane, South Londonderry, VT 05155

KEBBA, Elaine Marguerite Bailey (NC) 6003 Quail Ridge Dr, Greensboro, NC 27455

KEBLESH JR, Joe (O) 4617 Crestview Dr, Sylvania, OH 43560

KECK, Carolyn (Tenn) Church of the Messiah, 114 N 3rd St, Pulaski, TN 38478

KEEBLE, Mac (WTex) 4201 Adina Way, Corpus Christi, TX 78413

KEECH, April Irene (NY)

KEEDY, Susan Shipman (SeFla) 1200 Heron Ave, Miami Springs, FL 33166

KEEFER, John S (Pa) 124 High St, Sharon Hill, PA 19079

KEEHN, Randy P (ND)

KEEL, Ron (WMo)

KEELER, Donald Franklin (Ia) 121 W Marina Rd, Storm Lake, IA 50588

KEELER, Elizabeth Franklin (Va) 3116 O St NW, Washington, DC 20007

KEELER, John Dowling (At) 225 Brookhaven Cir, Elberton, GA 30635

KEEN JR, Charles Ford (Dal) 206 Mansfield Blvd., Sunnyvale, TX 75182

KEEN, George Comforted (CFla) 1225 W Granada Blvd, Ormond Beach, FL 32174

KEEN, Lois (Ct) 20 Hudson St, Norwalk, CT 06851

KEENAN, John P (Vt) 73 Oak St, Newport, VT 05855

KEENE, Benita (Md)

KEENE, Christopher Paul (Del) Immanuel Church, 100 Harmony St, New Castle, DE 19720

KEENE, Claire Claire (ETenn) 4000 Shaw Ferry Rd, Lenoir City, TN 37772

KEENE, Katheryn C (Ct) 92 Bryn Mawr Ave, Auburn, MA 01501

KEENER, E Michaella (Pa) P.O. Box 594, 36 Bayview Avenue, Stonington, ME 04681

KEENER JR, Ross Fulton (SVa) 117 Cove Road, Newport News, VA 23608

KEENEY, Albert J (Roch) 2901 Capen Dr, Bloomington, IL 61704

KEENEY, Randall James (NC) Po Box 1547, Clemmons, NC 27012

KEE-REES, James Louis (WTex) 1501 N Glass St, Victoria, TX 77901

KEESE, Peter Gaines (ETenn) 905 Chateaugay Rd., Knoxville, TN 37923

KEESHIN, Joyce Jenkins (SO) St James Episcopal Church, 3207 Montana Ave, Cincinnati, OH 45211

KEESTER, John Carl (Los) 627 Leyden Ln, Claremont, CA 91711

KEGGI, J John (Me) 62 Crest Rd, Wellesley, MA 02482

KEILL, David (Va) 8212 Pilgrim Ter, Richmond, VA 23227

KEIM, Robert (ECR) 301 Trinity Ave, Arroyo Grande, CA 93420

KEITH, Briggett (Nwk) 3004 Overton Rd, Henrico, VA 23228

KEITH, George Arthur (SanD) 4424 44th St Apt 305, San Diego, CA 92115

KEITH JR, John Matthew (Ala) 15001 Searstone Dr Apt 111, Cary, NC 27513

KEITH, Judith Ann (Ga) PO Box 33, 216 Remington Avenue, Thomasville, GA 31799

KEITH III, Stuart Brooks (Colo) Po Box 1591, Edwards, CO 81632

KEITH, Thomas Aaron (NwT)

KEITH, William (SC) PO Box 145, Lookout Mountain, TN 37350

KEITH-LUCAS, Diane Dorothea (Mass)

KEITHLY JR, Thomas Graves (Dal) 1612 Kiltartan Dr, Dallas, TX 75228

KEIZER, Garret John (Vt) 770 King George Farm Rd, Sutton, VT 05867

KELAHER, Edward Thomas (WA) 3 Chevy Chase Cir, Chevy Chase, MD 20815

KELDERMAN, Kate E (Ct) Kent School, 1 Macedonia Rd, Kent, CT 06757

KELLAM, Patricia Marie (SVa) Po Box 468, Amelia Court House, VA 23002

KELLAWAY, James L (Ct) 123 Babbitt Hill Road, Pomfret Center, CT 06259

KELLER, Anthony (Los) 808 Foothill Blvd, La Canada, CA 91011

KELLER JR, Charles Edward (Nwk) 711 S Custer Ave, Miles City, MT 59301

KELLER III, Christoph (Ark) 5224 Country Club Blvd, Little Rock, AR 72207

KELLER JR, David Gardiner Ross (WNC) 31 Alexander Farms Lane, Alexander, NC 28701

KELLER, John Speake (O) 20508 Hilliard Blvd, Rocky River, OH 44116

KELLER SR, Patterson (Oly) Po Box 1808, Cody, WY 82414

KELLER, Susan (Md) Trinity And Saint Philip's Cathedral, 24 Rector St, Newark, NJ 07102

KELLERMANN, Alan Seth (The Episcopal NCal) 245 S Church St, Grass Valley, CA 95945

KELLETT, James William (SVa) 11233 Tierrasanta Blvd, #40, San Diego, CA 92124

KELLEY, Barbara A (Pa) 159 Windsor Ave, Southampton, PA 18966

KELLEY, Brian Scott (Mass) 47 Concord Sq, Boston, MA 02118

KELLEY, Carlton F (WMich) 57607 M-51 South, Dowagiac, MI 49047

KELLEY, James Vincent (Nev)

KELLEY, Theresa M (Mont) 3350 Keokuk St, Butte, MT 59701

KELLIHER, James William (RI)

KELLINGTON, Brian T (Spr) 17085 SE 93rd Yondel Cir, The Villages, FL 32162

KELLINGTON, Laurie R (Spr) 17085 SE 93rd Yondel Cir, The Villages, FL 32162

KELLNER, Andrew L (Pa)

KELLO, Rebecca Ruth (Ky) 1215 State St, Bowling Green, KY 42101

KELLOGG, Alicia Sue (Me) 27 Forest Ave, Winthrop, ME 04364

KELLOGG III, Edward Samuel (SanD) 3407 Larga Cir, San Diego, CA 92110

KELLOGG, John A (La) 7215 Zimpel St, New Orleans, LA 70118

KELLUM, Rose Edna (Miss)

KELLY, Arthur James (Pa) 1171 Sandy Ridge Rd, Doylestown, PA 18901

KELLY, Christopher Douglas (SeFla) 110 Selfridge Rd, Gansevoort, NY 12831

KELLY III, Colin Purdie (RG) 4 Inca Ln, Los Alamos, NM 87544

KELLY, Francis J (CFla) 1250 Paige Pl, The Villages, FL 32159

KELLY, James Lester (Nev) 1075 Oxen Rd, Incline Village, NV 89451

KELLY, Jane Young (SwFla) The Church of the Good Shepherd, 401 W. Henry St., Punta Gorda, FL 33950

KELLY, Joan Hickey (Md) 303 N Main St, Bel Air, MD 21014

KELLY, Karen Joy (WMich)

KELLY, Kathleen M (SanD) 308 E Acacia Ave, Hemet, CA 92543

KELLY, Linda (NwT) 218 Oak Hill Dr, Kerrville, TX 78028

KELLY, Margaret I (Ida) 1800 N Cole Rd Apt E204, Boise, ID 83704

KELLY, Roger K (Ga) 3101 Waters Ave, Savannah, GA 31404

KELLY, Sarah Elizabeth (O) 9160 Putnam Rd, Pandora, OH 45877

KELLY, Shannon (Mass) 37 Grandwood Dr, Forestdale, MA 02644

KELLY, Steven Joseph Patrick (Mich) 791 Westchester Rd, Grosse Pointe Park, MI 48230

KELLY, Tracey (Va) 9220 Georgetown Pike, Great Falls, VA 22066

KELLY, Verneda Joan (Neb) 1014 N 6th St, Seward, NE 68434

KELM, Mark William (Minn) 109 Lawn Terrace, Golden Valley, MN 55416

KELMEREIT, Alan (SwFla) 4554 Springview Cir, Labelle, FL 33935

KELSEY, Anne (Mo) Po Box 4740, Saint Louis, MO 63108

KELSEY, Julie Vietor (Ct) 38 Brocketts Point Rd, Branford, CT 06405

KELSEY II, Preston Telford (Ct) 80 Lyme Rd, Apt 213, Hanover, NH 03755

KELSEY, Stephen (Az) 138 N White Willow Pl, Tucson, AZ 85710

KELSON, Laura Jayne (CGC) 1 Saint Francis Dr, Gulf Breeze, FL 32561

KELTON, Barbara Smoot (Dal) 719 Pampa Street, Sulphur Springs, TX 75482

KEM, Bob (Ia) 538 NW Scott St, Ankeny, IA 50023

KEMEZA, Maureen (Mass) 17 Munroe Pl., Concord, MA 01742

KEMMERER, Stanley Courtright (Ct) Po Box 2025, Burlington, CT 06013

KEMMLER, Richard Sigmund (NY) 1420 Pine Bay Dr, Sarasota, FL 34231

KEMP, Drusilla Rawlings (Ky) Church Of The Advent, 901 Baxter Ave, Louisville, KY 40204

KEMP, Matthew Benjamin (Spr) 138 S 8th St, Salina, KS 67401

KEMP, Rowena Jessica (Ct) 55 New Park Ave, Hartford, CT 06106

KEMPF, Barb (Ind) Saint Christopher's Episcopal Church, 1402 W Main St, Carmel, IN 46032

KEMPF, Victoria Nystrom (Colo) 2220 Katahdin Dr, Fort Collins, CO 80525

KEMPSELL JR, Howard Frederic (Va) Post Office Box 2360, Centreville, VA 20122

KEMPSON-THOMPSON, Deborah (Nev) 1776 US Highway 50, Glenbrook, NV 89413

KEMPSTER, Jane (WNC) 10450 Lottsford Rd Apt 355, Mitchellville, MD 20721

KEMPSTER, Patricia Sue (The Episcopal NCal) 2098 Tracy Court, Folsom, CA 95630

KENDALL, Michael Jonah (NC) 403 E Main St, Durham, NC 27701

KENDALL, Michael Samuel (NY) 9 1/2 Church St, Bristol, RI 02809

KENDALL-SPERRY, David (SO) St Paul Episcopal Church, 100 E High St, Mount Vernon, OH 43050

KENDRICK, David (WMo) St Johnh's Church, 515 E Division St, Springfield, MO 65803

✠ **KENDRICK**, Russell (CGC) 3557 Hampshire Drive, Birmingham, AL 35223

KENDRICK, William Barton (The Episcopal NCal) 19 Five Iron Ct, Chico, CA 95928

KENNA, Jennifer Anne (CNY) 235 John St, Clayton, NY 13624

KENNARD, Susan (Tex) 3000 Ave L, Bay City, TX 77414

KENNEDY, Arthur Thomas (Ida) 261 Los Lagos, Twin Falls, ID 83301

KENNEDY, David Crichton (SeFla) 7231 Hearth Stone Ave, Boynton Beach, FL 33437

KENNEDY, David Kittle (The Episcopal Church in Haw) 1 Keahole Pl Apt 3409, Honolulu, HI 96825

KENNEDY, Dennis (Colo)

KENNEDY, Ellen Kathleen (Ct) 243 Harbor St, Branford, CT 06405

KENNEDY, Gary Grant (Kan) 1900 E Front St, Galena, KS 66739

KENNEDY, Hilda L (WVa) Po Box 665, Northfork, WV 24868

KENNEDY, John Ira (Ala)

KENNEDY, Karen (Oly)

KENNEDY, Nan N (At) 304 Krupp Ave, Liberty Hill, TX 78642

KENNEDY, Palmer Bourne (CFla)

KENNEDY, Thomas B (Mass) 46 Glen Road, Brookline, MA 02445

KENNELLY, Margery (Mass) 379 Hammond St, Chestnut Hill, MA 02467

KENNEY, Christine Swarts (Okla) 505 Fieldstone Dr, Georgetown, TX 78633

KENNINGTON, Curtis A (CGC)

KENNINGTON, Spergeon Albert (CGC) 212 Margaret Dr, Fairhope, AL 36532

KENNY JR, John Roy (Md) 9106 River Crescent Dr, Annapolis, MD 21401

KENNY, Susie Fowler (Los) 1020 N. Brand Blvd., Glendale, CA 91202

KENT, David Williamson (Kan) 1900 Spyglass Court, Lawrence, KS 66047

KENT, Stuart Matthews (Dal) PO Box 429, North Stonington, CT 06359

KENWORTHY, Stuart (WA) 2801 Mexico Avenue NW, Apt 711, Washington DC, DC 20007

KENYI, Alex Lodu (ND) 3725 30th St, San Diego, CA 92104

KENYON, James Howard Benjamin (Alb) 1606 5th St, Rensselaer, NY 12144

KEPLINGER, Steve (Az) 2331 E Adams St, Tucson, AZ 85719

KEPPELER, Lisa Leialoha (Pa) 124 S Main Street, Coopersburg, PA 18036

KEPPY, Susan (WNY) 419 Cherry Ln, Lewiston, NY 14092

KERBEL, Carol Ann (NJ) 232 Camino De La Sierra, Santa Fe, NM 87501

KERBEL, Walter Jarrett (Pa) 1418 E 57th St, Chicago, IL 60637

KERN, David Paul (Nwk) Po Box 1703, North Eastham, MA 02651

KERN, Karl Lee (Be) 182 Gable Dr/, Myerstown, PA 17067

KERN, Roy Allen (CPa) 613 Eschol Ridge Rd, Elliottsburg, PA 17024

KERNER, Sandra Barbary (SVa) 2755 Buckstone Dr, Powhatan, VA 23139

KERR, Catherine D (Pa) Good Shepherd Church, P.O. Box 132, Hilltown, PA 18927

KERR, Denniston Rupert (SwFla) 5609 N Albany Ave, Tampa, FL 33603

KERR, Kyra Anne (RG) P.O. Box 188, Tesuque, NM 87574

KERR, Lauri Ann (CPa) 1435 Scott St, Williamsport, PA 17701

KERR, Linda (Pa) 1603 Yardley Commons, Yardley, PA 19067

KERR, Richard S (Cal) 442 34th Ave, San Francisco, CA 94121

KERR, Robert Anthony (Mich) 21731 Southfield Rd, Southfield, MI 48075

KERR, Verdery (NC) Po Box 6124, Charlotte, NC 28207

KERRICK, Mike (The Episcopal NCal) 2612 Colin Rd, Placerville, CA 95667

KERSCHEN, Charles Thomas (WK) 520 East Ave S, Lyons, KS 67554

KERTLAND, Gail Ellen (LI) 36 Cathedral Ave, Garden City, NY 11530

KESHGEGIAN, Flora A (Pa) 601 Montgomery Ave Apt 308, Bryn Mawr, PA 19010

KESLER, Walter Wilson (FtW) 3937 Anewby Way, Fort Worth, TX 76133

KESSEL-HANNA, Kay Lynn (Oly) 11527 9th Ave NE, Seattle, WA 98125

KESSELUS, Kenneth William (Tex) 1301 Church St., Bastrop, TX 78602

KESSLER, Edward Scharps (Pa) 44 Hinde Street, Sheffield, S4 8HJ, Great Britain (UK)

KESSLER, Judith Maier (CNY) 17 Elizabeth St, Binghamton, NY 13901

KESSLER, Rachel Cheryl (O) Harcourt Parish, Po Box 377, Gambier, OH 43022

KESTER, Martha (Ia) 1916 Merklin Way, Des Moines, IA 50310

KETNER, Thomas Howard (Wyo) 411 E Center St, Douglas, WY 82633

KETTLEWELL, John Michael (Alb) 110 Monument Dr, Schuylerville, NY 12871

KETTLEWELL, Paula Swaebe (Va) 705 Wilder Dr, Charlottesville, VA 22901

KEUCHER, Gerald Werner (LI) 1 Pendleton Pl, Staten Island, NY 10301

KEVERN, John (WVa) C/O Trinity Epis Church, PO Box P, Moundsville, WV 26041

KEW, William Richard (Tenn) 2272 Lewisburg Pike, Franklin, TN 37064

KEY, Nancy Anne (Episcopal SJ) PO Box 7446, Visalia, CA 93279

KEY, Sandy (Ct) St. Luke's Church, POB 94, Somers, NY 10589

KEYDEL JR, John F (Mich) 6981 Lindsay Ln, Easton, MD 21601

KEYES, Charles Don (NY) 5801 Hampton St, Pittsburgh, PA 15206

KEYES, John Irvin (SD) 513 Douglas Ave, Yankton, SD 57078

KEYES, Samuel N (Md) Saint Paul's Church, 905 Church St, Greensboro, AL 36744

KEYS, Joel Thompson (Tenn) PO Box 24183, Saint Simons Island, GA 31522

KEYSE, Andrew Carl (Ala) 262 Creekside Dr, Florence, AL 35630

✠ **KEYSER**, Charles Lovett (Fla) 4719 Ivanhoe Rd, Jacksonville, FL 32210

KEYWORTH, Gill (Tex) 1215 Ripple Creek Dr, Houston, TX 77057

KEZAR, Dennis Dean (SwFla) 4030 Manatee Ave W, Bradenton, FL 34205

KHALIL, Adeeb Mikhail (WVa) 127 Brookwood Ln, Beckley, WV 25801

KHAMIN, Alexei (Nwk) All Saints Episcopal Church, 230 E. 60th St., New York, NY 10022

KHOO, Oon-Chor (Tex) 3203 W Alabama St, Houston, TX 77098

KIBLER SR, Bryant C (Lex) 607 HWY 1746, 607 Highway 1746, Irvine, KY 40336

KIBLINGER, Charles Edward (Va) 651 Rivendell Blvd, Osprey, FL 34229

KIDD, Paul David (At) 10952 NW 32nd Ave, Gainesville, FL 32606

KIDD, Reggie M (CFla)

KIDD, Sandra (SO)

KIDD, Saundra Kay (Fla) 4129 Oxford Ave, Jacksonville, FL 32210

KIDD, Scott (At) 557 Yonah Mountain Rd., Cleveland, GA 30528

KIDD, Stephen Willis (Miss) 11322 E Taylor Rd, Gulfport, MS 39503

KIDDER, Ann (O) PO Box 519, Gates Mills, OH 44040

KIDDER, Frederick Elwyn (PR)

KIEFER, Lee (EO) 428 King St, Wenatchee, WA 98801

KIENZLE, Edward Charles (Mass) 165 Pleasant St Apt 303, Cambridge, MA 02139

KIESCHNICK, Frannie (Cal) 134 La Goma St, Mill Valley, CA 94941

KIESSLING, Donna Jean (Del) 22 N. Union Street, Smyrna, DE 19977

KIKER, Norman Wesley (Okla) 5705 Earl Dr, Shawnee, OK 74804

KILBOURN, Lauren Michelle (NC) 221Union St, Cary, NC 27511

KILBOURN, Thomas Lewis (Ct) 51 Paddy Hollow Rd, Bethlehem, CT 06751

KILBOURN-HUEY, Mary Esther (Lex) 310 Edgemont Rd, Maysville, KY 41056

KILBY, John Irvine (Ia) 4903 California St Apt 5, Omaha, NE 68132

KILGORE, John W (Mo) 320 Union Blvd, Saint Louis, MO 63108

KILIAN, Joan M (Ga) 9003 Oakfield Dr, Statesboro, GA 30461

KILLEEN, David Charles (Fla) St. John's Episcopal Church, 211 North Monroe St., Tallahassee, FL 32301

KILLIAN, David Allen (Mass) 882 Watertown St, West Newton, MA 02465

KILLIAN, Kathleen Erin (Me)

KILLINGSTAD, Mary Louise (Spok) 502 Hillside Dr, Yakima, WA 98903

KIM, Andrew (Los) 13091 Galway St, Garden Grove, CA 92844

KIM, John D (Los) St James Episcopal Church, 3903 Wilshire Blvd, Los Angeles, CA 90010

KIM, John Jong-Kun (Pa) 3204 Ashy Way, Drexel Hill, PA 19026

KIM, Jonathan Jang-Ho (WNY) Kumi Box 1039, Kumi Kyungbuk, 730-600, Korea (South)

KIM, Richard (Mich) 19983 E Doyle Pl, Grosse Pointe, MI 48236

KIM, Sean (WMo)

KIM, Stephen Yongchul (Los) 45267 Sancroft Ave, Lancaster, CA 93535

KIM, Yein Esther (Los) 840 Echo Park Ave, Los Angeles, CA 90026

KIM, Yong Gul Ninian (LI) 2235 36th St, Astoria, NY 11105

KIMBALL, Anne (Ct) 14890 David Drive, Fort Myers, FL 33908

KIMBALL JR, George Allen (Mil) 320 E Pleasant St Unit 301, Oconomowoc, WI 53066

KIMBALL, Jennifer Warfel (Va) 125 Beverly Rd, Ashland, VA 23005

KIMBALL, Melodie Irene (Ore) 257 E Milton St, Lebanon, OR 97355

KIMBLE, Shell Teyssier (WA) 5316 Taylor Rd, Riverdale, MD 20737

KIMBROUGH, Brendan Lee (Tex) 200 Oyster Creek Dr, Lake Jackson, TX 77566

KIMBROUGH, Timothy Edward (Tenn) 435 Patina Circle, Nashville, TN 37209

KIMES, Nicki Sagendorf (Ct) 134 East Ave, New Canaan, CT 06840

KIMMELMAN, Sandra Sue (Miss)

KIMMEY, Jimmye Elizabeth (NY) 928 W Hickory St, Denton, TX 76201

KIMMICK, Donald William (Nwk) 9625 Miranda Dr, Raleigh, NC 27617

KIMURA, Gregory W (Los) 9900 Toakee Cir, Eagle River, AK 99577

KIN, Nancy E (O) 1249 3rd St, Rensselaer, NY 12144

KINARD III, George Oscar (SeFla)

KINCAID III, S Thomas (Dal) 708 Harrison St, La Porte, IN 46350

KINDEL JR, William H (Colo) 802 Navajo Avenue, Fort Morgan, CO 80701

KINDERGAN, Walter Bradford (CGC)

KING, Allan Brewster (Mass) 222 Sayre Drive, Princeton, NJ 08540

KING, Benjamin John (Mass) School of Theology University of the South, 335 Tennessee Ave., Sewanee, TN 37383

KING JR, Charles Baldwin (Alb) 5 Jodiro Ln Apt 100, Colonie, NY 12205

KING, Chester W (RG) 10033 Cork Dr, El Paso, TX 79925

KING, Christopher (ECR) 220 W Penn St, Long Beach, NY 11561

KING, Darlene Dawn (EMich) 3201 Gratiot Ave, Port Huron, MI 48060

KING JR, Earle (WNY) 2595 Baseline Rd, Grand Island, NY 14072

KING, Ed (WMass) 4571 Lakeshore Rd, Lexington, MI 48450

KING, Francis Marion Covington (WNC) 140 Saint Marys Church Rd, Morganton, NC 28655

KING, Frank Walter (WNC) 4425 Huntington Dr, Gastonia, NC 28056

KING, Giovan Venable (The Episcopal Church in Haw) 93 N Kainalu Dr, Kailua, HI 96734

KING, Janet Gay Felland (Ida) 678 E 400 N, Rupert, ID 83350

KING, Jonathan LeRoy (NY) 340 Godwin Ave, Ridgewood, NJ 07450

KING, Kale Francis (Wyo) 3107 Summit Hills Trl, Mount Airy, NC 27030

KING, Karen (Chi) 125 E 26th St, Chicago, IL 60616

KING, Karen Gail (Mont) P.O. Box 158, Troy, MT 59935

KING, Karen L (Ind) 3401 Lindel Ln, Indianapolis, IN 46268

KING, Kathryn Louise (Nwk) 28 Ralph St, Bergenfield, NJ 07621

KING JR, Kenneth Vernon (EO) 702 Grant Street, Summit, MS 39666

KING, Leslie Anne (The Episcopal NCal) 55 Maria Dr Ste 837, Petaluma, CA 94954

KING, Leyla (ETenn) 1607 W 43rd St, Chattanooga, TN 37409

KING, Margaret Creed (Fla) 704 Vauxhall Dr, Nashville, TN 37221

KING, Mary Howard (Miss) PO Box 1225, Corinth, MS 38835

KING, Robert Andrew (Ky) 3935 Sunnyside Dr, Harrisonburg, VA 22801

KING, Steven (Neb) 113 N 18th St, Omaha, NE 68102

KING, Tom Earl (NC) 2725 SE 39th ST, MOORE, OK 73160

KING, William Michael (Ala) 905 Castlemaine Drive, Birmingham, AL 35226

KINGDON, Arthur M (Vt) 334 Oak Grove Rd, Vassalboro, ME 04989

KINGMAN, Donna Watkins (WMass) 3 Newington Ln, Worcester, MA 01609

KINGSLEY, Josh (Ore) 11229 NE Prescott St, Portland, OR 97220

KINGSLEY, Myra Jessica (Az) 100 W Roosevelt St, Phoenix, AZ 85003

KINGSLEY, Timothy Miles (Minn) 519 Oak Grove St, Minneapolis, MN 55403

KINGSLIGHT, Kathleen Anne (Oly) 700 Callahan Dr, Bremerton, WA 98310

KINGSTON, Louise (NJ) 85 Westcott Rd, Princeton, NJ 08540

KINMAN, Mike (Los) 6209 Pershing Ave, Saint Louis, MO 63130

KINMAN, Thomas David (Az) PO Box 40126, Tucson, AZ 85717

KINNER, Heidi Ellen (Mont) St. Peters Episcopal Cathedral, 511 N. Park Avenue, Helena, MT 59601

KINNEY, Elise (Mass) 193 Clifton St, Malden, MA 02148

KINNEY, Genie (Cal) 1746 29th Ave, San Francisco, CA 94122

KINNEY, Kathleen (Oly) 610-906-9690, Eastsound, WA 98245

KINNEY, Patricia (CNY)

KINNEY, Robert Paul (SwFla)

KINNEY, Robert Sturgis (Okla) 5231 Wedgefield Rd, Granbury, TX 76049

KINNEY, Stephen W (Tex) 2306 Cypress Pt W, Austin, TX 78746

KINNUNEN, Victor J (NwPa)

KINSER, Dixon (NC) St Paul's Episcopal Church, 520 Summit St, Winston Salem, NC 27101

KINSEY, Douglas Andrew (Pgh)

KINSEY, Kevin Lee (Me) 650 Main St Ste A, Caribou, ME 04736

KINSEY, Theron Harvey (Cal) 917 Avis Dr, El Cerrito, CA 94530

KINSEY, Thomas Burton (SO) 5004 Upton Ave S, Minneapolis, MN 55410

KINSOLVING, John Armistead (RG) 107 Washington Ave, Santa Fe, NM 87501

KINYON, Brice Wayne (USC) 1900 Woodvalley Drive, Columbia, SC 29212

KIRBY, Elisa Mabley (EC) 320 Pollock St, New Bern, NC 28560

KIRBY, Erin C (FdL) PO Box 936, Minocqua, WI 54548

KIRBY, Harry Scott (Eau) 1712 Lehman St., Eau Claire, WI 54701

KIRBY, Jacquelyn Walsh (RI) PO Box 317, Jamestown, RI 02835

KIRBY, Kelly Ellen (Ky) 330 N Hubbards Ln, Louisville, KY 40207

KIRBY, Richard Allen (Neb)

KIRBY, Whitney B (Az) 100 W. Roosevelt, Phoenix, AZ 85003

KIRCHER, Kathleen L (SwFla) 1741 Winding Oaks Way, Naples, FL 34109

KIRCHHOFFER, James Hawley (Cal) 922 Valle Vista Ave, Vallejo, CA 94590

KIRCHMIER, Anne Ruth (SVa) 45 Main Street, Newport News, VA 23601

KIRK, Deborah (WA) 14300 Saint Thomas Church Rd, Upper Marlboro, MD 20772

KIRK, Jeffrey Malcolm (NJ) 102 Pearlcroft Rd, Cherry Hill, NJ 08034

KIRK, Patricia Lanier (USC) 501 S La Posada Cir Apt 118, Green Valley, AZ 85614

KIRK, Richard Joseph (Pa) 189 Kendal Dr, Kennett Square, PA 19348

KIRKALDY, David (Tex) 612 Duroux Rd, La Marque, TX 77568

KIRKHAM II, Hall (Mass) 112 Randolph Avenue, Milton, MA 02186

KIRKING, Kerry Clifton (Spok) 2900 3rd Ave W Apt 317, Seattle, WA 98119

KIRKLAND, Patricia Ann (Ia)

KIRKLEY, John Lawrence (Cal) 4616 California St, San Francisco, CA 94118

KIRKMAN, John Raymond (WMich) 4713 Rockvalley Dr NE, Grand Rapids, MI 49525

KIRK-NORRIS, Barbara (NwT) PO Box 2949, Big Spring, TX 79721

KIRKPATRICK, Daisy (CNY) 741 West Second St, Elmira, NY 14905

KIRKPATRICK, Frank Gloyd (Ct) 154 Clearfield, Wethersfield, CT 06109

KIRKPATRICK, Martha G (Del) St Barnabas Church, 2800 Duncan Rd, Wilmington, DE 19808

KIRKPATRICK, Nathan Elliott (NC) 8410 Merin Rd, Chapel Hill, NC 27516

KIRKPATRICK, Rebecca Blair (Oly) 111 NE 80th St, Seattle, WA 98115

KIRKPATRICK JR, Robert Jr Frederick (Lex) 9801 Germantown Pike, Apt 115, Lafayette Hill, PA 19444

KISNER, Mary (CPa) 712 E 16th St, Berwick, PA 18603

KISS, Margaret Mary (Mil) 3775 S 27th St Apt 210, Milwaukee, WI 53221

KISSAM, Todd William (Eas) 105 Church Lane, Church Hill, MD 21623

KISSINGER, Debra Jean (Ind) 1100 W. 42nd St., Indianapolis, IN 46208

KITAGAWA, Chisato (WMass) 5 Hickory Ln, Amherst, MA 01002

KITAGAWA, John Elliott (Az) 1700 E Chula Vista Rd, Tucson, AZ 85718

KITAYAMA, Scott D (WTex)

KITCH, Anne E (Be) 333 Wyandotte St, Bethlehem, PA 18015

KITCH, Sarah Underhill (Los) 280 Royal Ave, Simi Valley, CA 93065

KITT, Michael (Chi) 523 Courtland Ave, Park Ridge, IL 60068

KITTELSON, Alan Leslie (Vt) 6 Park St, Vergennes, VT 05491

KITTREDGE, Cynthia Briggs (Tex) Seminary of the Southwest, 501 East 32nd Street, Austin, TX 78705

KIVEL, Virginia McDermott (Dal)

KLAM, Warren Peter (Va) 4200 Harbor Blvd., Oxnard, CA 93035

KLEE, George Martin (Ark) 1516 Willow St., Blytheville, AR 72315

KLEFFMAN, Todd Aaron (Ind) 5757 Rosslyn Ave, Indianapolis, IN 46220

KLEIN, Craig Alan (Kan) 67 SW Pepper Tree Ln, Topeka, KS 66611

KLEIN, Everett H (WMich) 7521 Anthony St, Whitehall, MI 49461

KLEIN, John Conrad (Mich) 231 E Grand Blvd, Detroit, MI 48207

KLEIN, John Harvey (SeFla) 3586 Woods Walk Blvd, Lake Worth, FL 33467

KLEIN, Susan Webster (Los) 9606 Oakmore Rd, Los Angeles, CA 90035

KLEIN-LARSEN, Martha Susan (Ct) 117 Oenoke Ridge, New Canaa, CT 06840

KLEMMT, Pierce (Va) 1208 N Pitt St, Alexandria, VA 22314

KLENZMANN, Joseph G. (Va)

KLEVEN, Terence J (Ia) 1334 N. Prairie St., Pella, IA 50219

KLICKMAN, John Michael (Dal) 4017 Hedgerow Dr, Plano, TX 75024

KLIMAS, Marcella Louise (CPa) 4355 Georgetown Square Apt 141, Atlanta, GA 30338

KLINE, Andy (Colo) 5 Brookside Dr, Greenwood Village, CO 80121

KLINE, John William (NwPa) 825 Matilda Dr, Plano, TX 75025

KLINE, Nancy Wade (CFla) St. Barnabas Episcopal Church, 319 W. Wisconsin Ave., Deland, FL 32720

KLINE, Timothy Eads (WK) 50 Oyster Bay Dr, Graford, TX 76449

KLINE-MORTIMER, Sandra L (Md) Po Box 3298, Shepherdstown, WV 25443

KLINGELHOFER, Stephan Ernest (Eas) 545 Fey Rd # 21620-, Chestertown, MD 21620

KLINGENBERG, Ralph Gerard (SeFla) 1400 Riverside Dr, Coral Springs, FL 33071

KLINGENSMITH, Roxanne Elizabeth Pearson (Mont) 1715 South Black, Bozeman, MT 59715

KLITZKE, Dale (USC) 1816 Crestwood Ln, Menomonie, WI 54751

KLITZKE, Paul Kenneth (Dal) 8787 Greenville Avenue, Dallas, TX 75243

KLOPFENSTEIN, Timothy David (CGC) 106 Galaxy Ave, Bonaire, GA 31005

KLOTS, Stephen Barrett (Ct) 40 Bulls Bridge Rd, South Kent, CT 06785

KLOZA, Wanda Margaret (CPa) 101 Pine St, Harrisburg, PA 17101

✠ **KLUSMEYER**, William (WVa) 1 Roller Rd, Charleston, WV 25314

KLUTTERMAN, David Lee (FdL) 330 McClellan, Wausau, WI 54401

KNAPICK, Veronica Helene (Ak) 6816 E. Riverwood Cir, Palmer, AK 99645

KNAPP, Carl Jude (Pa) 584 Fairway Ter, Philadelphia, PA 19128

KNAPP, Clayton L (WMass) 3003 Dick Wilson Dr., Sarasota, FL 34240

KNAPP, Cynthia Clark (At) 43 Twin Oak Ln, Wilton, CT 06897

KNAPP, Donald Hubert (Be) 162 Springhouse Rd, Allentown, PA 18104

KNAPP, Gretchen Bower (Mont) Po Box 794, Hilger, MT 59451

KNAPP, Ron (Eas) 11240 Gail Dr, Princess Anne, MD 21853

KNAUFF, Elizabeth Ann (Ct) 155 Wyllys St, Hartford, CT 06106

KNAUP JR, Daniel Joseph (O) 2341 Ardleigh Drive, Cleveland Heights, OH 44106

KNEE, Jacob S (Mont) St Stephen's Episcopal Ch, 1241 Crawford Dr, Billings, MT 59102

KNEIPP, Lee Benson (WTenn) Po Box 3874, Pineville, LA 71361

KNIGHT, Arthur James (NJ) 3 Blueberry Rd, Shamong, NJ 08088

KNIGHT, David Hathaway (Va) 6005 S Crestwood Ave, Richmond, VA 23226

KNIGHT, Frank Lauchlan (NY) 3859 Dogwood Trl, Allentown, PA 18103

KNIGHT IV, Frank Michael (Pa) 803 Montbard Dr, West Chester, PA 19382

KNIGHT, Harold Stanley (Az) 145 N Fraser Dr, Mesa, AZ 85203

KNIGHT, Hollinshead T (Cal) 485 Bridgeway Apt 1, Sausalito, CA 94965

KNIGHT, J David (CGC) Saint Simon's On The Sound, 28 Miracle Strip Pkwy SW, Fort Walton Beach, FL 32548

KNIGHT, Joseph Sturdevant (CGC) 436 Lapsley Street, Selma, AL 36701

KNIGHT, Kimberly Adonna (La) 200 Chapel Crk Apt 116, Mandeville, LA 70471

KNIGHT, Samuel Theodore (Mich) 28725 Sunset Boulevard West, Lathrup Village, MI 48076

KNIGHT, Skully (La) 3200 Woodland Ridge Blvd, Baton Rouge, LA 70816

KNIGHT II, Steve (SanD) 403 Shalimar Drive, Prescott, AZ 86303

KNIGHT, Theolinda Lenore Johnson (Cal) 806 Jones St, Berkeley, CA 94710

KNIGHT, W Allan (Md) 58 Hanson Rd, Chester, NH 03036

KNISELY, Harry Lee (Ct) 365 Hickory Rd, Carlisle, PA 17015

✠ **KNISELY JR**, W Nicholas (RI) Episcopal Diocese of Rhode Island, 275 N Main St, Providence, RI 02903

KNOCKEL, Wayne J (WNY) Saint Peter's Episcopal Church, 205 Longmeadow Rd, Eggertsville, NY 14226

KNOLL LENON, Katherine G (Kan)

KNOLL SWEENEY, Sarah Jacqueline (Tex) 4120 Clinton Pkwy, Lawrence, KS 66047

KNOTT, Joseph Lee (Ala) 5528 - 11th Court South, Birmingham, AL 35222

KNOTTS, Harold Wayne (Mich) 26431 W Chicago, Redford, MI 48239

KNOUSE, Amanda (Va) 9668 Maidstone Rd, Delaplane, VA 20144

KNOWLES, Bobbie (SeFla) 2704 Rossedale Street, Houston, TX 77004

KNOWLES II, Harold Frank (Los) 623 El Centro St, South Pasadena, CA 91030

KNOWLES, Melody D (Chi) 3737 Seminary Rd, Alexandria, VA 22304

KNOWLES, Walter Roy (Oly) 11020 Ne 64th St, Kirkland, WA 98033

KNOWLTON, Beth (WTex) 315 E Pecan St, San Antonio, TX 78205

KNOX, David Paul (CFla) 216 Sheridan Ave, Longwood, FL 32750

KNOX, Floyd L (La) 10587 Birchwood Dr, Baton Rouge, LA 70807

KNOX, Jannet Marie (Mont) 59 Mill Creek Rd # 463, Sheridan, MT 59749

KNOX, Jeffrey Donald (CNY) 1755 State Route 48, Fulton, NY 13069

KNOX, John Michael (WK) 16019 W 80th St, Lenexa, KS 66219

KNOX, Regina G (Me) 143 State St, Portland, ME 04101

✠ **KNUDSEN**, Chilton Richardson (Me) Diocese of Maryland, 4 E University Pkwy, Baltimore, MD 21218

KNUDSON, Kay Francis (Neb) 1304 Wade St, Lexington, NE 68850

KNUTH, Charles H (The Episcopal NCal)

KNUTSEN, Jamie (The Episcopal NCal) P.O. Box 3601, Santa Rosa, CA 95402

KNUTSON, Randy A (The Episcopal NCal) 201 E. Fir St. (P.O. Box 124), Fort Bragg, CA 95437

KOCH, Adrienne Marie (NC) 3216 Idlewood Village Drive, Raleigh, NC 27610

KOCH, Eunice Jane (Minn) PO Box 513, Ely, MN 55731

KOCH, Janie Layne (Okla) 518 W Randolph Ave, Enid, OK 73701

KOCH JR, John Dunbar (Ky) 5301 Francis In The Fields, PO Box 225, Harrods Creek, KY 40027

KOCH, William Christian (RG) P.O. Box 1614, Blue Hill, ME 04614

KOCHENBURGER, Philip A (Tex) 24011 Sunset Sky, Katy, TX 77494

KOCHTITZKY, Rodney Morse (Tenn) The Pastoral Center for Healing, 1024 Noelton Ave, Nashville, TN 37204

KODERA, T James (Mass) 212 Old Lancaster Rd, Sudbury, MA 01776

KOEHLER, Anne E (Nwk) PO Box 611, East Orleans, MA 02643

KOEHLER, Michael Alban Collins (WTex) 6000 FM 3237 Unit A, Wimberley, TX 78676

KOEHLER III, Norman Elias (Pgh) 408 Forest Highlands Dr, Pittsburgh, PA 15238

KOEHLER, Robert Brien (Spr) 19206 Boca del Mar, San Antonio, TX 78258

KOELLIKER, Karulynn Travis (Ga)

KOELLN, Theodore Frank (CFla) 505 Ne 1st Ave, Mulberry, FL 33860

KOENIG, Diane L (Chi) 86 Pomeroy Ave # 2, Crystal Lake, IL 60014

KOENIG, John (NJ) 17546 Drayton Hall Way, San Diego, CA 92128

KOENIGER, Margaret Smithers (Nwk) 574 Ridgewood Rd, Maplewood, NJ 07040

KOEPKE, Jack (SO) 412 Sycamore Street, Cincinnati, OH 45202

KOERNER, Travers (NY) 314 Lincoln Ave, Rockville, MD 20850

KOFFRON-EISEN, Elizabeth Mary (Ia) 945 Applewood Ct #1, Coralville, IA 52241

KOH, Aidan Y (Los) 4344 Lemp Ave, Studio City, CA 91604

KOHL, Stacey (Ct)

KOHLMEIER, Susan (Roch) 1017 Silvercrest Dr, Webster, NY 14580

KOHN, George Frederick (ECR) 980 W Franklin St, Monterey, CA 93940

KOHN-PERRY, Ellen Marie (Nwk)

KOLANOWSKI, Ron (Ct) St. James Episcopal Church, 95 Route 2A, Preston, CT 06365

KOLB, Jerry Warren (WMo) 8256 Outlook Lane, Prairie Village, KS 66208

KOLB, William Albert (WTenn) 531 S. Prescott St, Memphis, TN 38111

KOLBET, Paul Robert (Oly) 8 Ivy Cir., Wellesley, MA 02482

KOLLIN, Harriet (Pa) 3738 W Country Club Rd, Philadelphia, PA 19131

KOLLIN JR, James T (NJ) 120 Sussex St Apt 1b, Hackensack, NJ 07601

KONDRATH, William Michael (Mass) 25 Richards Ave, Sharon, MA 02067

✠ **KONIECZNY**, Ed (Okla) Episcopal Diocese Of Oklahoma, 924 N Robinson Ave, Oklahoma City, OK 73102

KONYHA, Dorothy Margaret (NwPa) 134 W 7th St, Erie, PA 16501

KOONCE, Kelly Montgomery (Tex) 6625 Whitemarsh Valley Walk, Austin, TX 78746

KOONS, Zachary Gunnar (Tex) 1420 E Palm Valley Blvd, Round Rock, TX 78664

KOOPERKAMP, Sarah Jennifer (LI) 612 Greenwood Ave, Brooklyn, NY 11218

KOOPERKAMP, William Earl (Vt) Church Of The Good Shepherd, 39 Washington St, Barre, VT 05641

KOOR, Margaret Platt (SwFla) 4017 Heaton Ter, North Port, FL 34286

KOPERA, Dorothy Jean (NMich) 214 E Avenue A, Newberry, MI 49868

KOPP, Vincent Joseph (NC) 4523 Six Forks Rd, Raleigh, NC 27609

KOPPEL, Mary E (Okla) PO Box 5176, Austin, TX 78763

KOPREN, Kristin C (RG) 1055 Route 6, Mahopac, NY 10541

KORIENEK, Martha (Cal) 802 Broadway, New York, NY 10003

KORN, Elizabeth Louise (NMich) N2809 River Dr, Wallace, MI 49893

KORTE, Mary (Kan) Saint Stephen's Church, 7404 E Killarney Pl, Wichita, KS 67206

KOSHNICK, Loxley Jean (Minn) PO Box 868, Detroit Lakes, MN 56502

KOSKELA, David Michael (Colo) 5433 South Buckskin Pass, Colorado Springs, CO 80917

KOSKELA, Robert N (Mil) 1260 Deming Way Apt 310, Madison, WI 53717

KOSKELA, Ruth Alma (Mil) 1260 Deming Way Apt 310, Madison, WI 53717

KOSKI, John Arthur (FdL)

KOSSLER, Robert Joseph (Cal)

KOSTIC, Elizabeth M (Pa) 2523 E Madison St, Philadelphia, PA 19134

KOTUBY, Janice (NY) 860 Wolcott Ave, Beacon, NY 12508

KOULOURIS, Beulah (Mass) 12 Sunrise Ave, Plymouth, MA 02360

KOUNTZ, Peter James (Pa)

KOUNTZE, Louise Priscilla (WMich) 255 Ivanhoe Street, Denver, CO 80220

KOVACH, Gary David (WNC) 19 Old Youngs Cove Rd, Candler, NC 28715

KOVALOVICH, Kurt Kriztofer (Be) 200 S 2nd St, Pottsville, PA 17901

KOVIC, Fenton Hubert (Tex) 821 Pam Dr, Tyler, TX 75703

KOVITCH, Joseph Gerard (SO) PO Box 176, Westerville, OH 43086

KOVOOR, George Iype (Ct) 400 Humphrey St, New Haven, CT 06511

KOWALEWSKI, Mark Robert (Los) 841 Kodak Dr., Los Angeles, CA 90026

KOWALEWSKI, Paul James (Los) 54280 Avenida Montezuma, La Quinta, CA 92253

KOWALSKI, Jim (NY) The Cathedral Church of Saint John the Divine, 1047 Amsterdam Ave, New York, NY 10025

KOWALSKI, Mark Joseph (Neb) Diocese of Nebraska, 109 N 18th St, Omaha, NE 68102

KOWALSKI, Ronald Chester (SwFla) 7349 Ulmerton Rd, Lot# 1398 Balboa St., Largo, FL 33771

KOWALSKI, Vesta (Me) Po Box 598, Mount Desert, ME 04660

KOZAK, Jan (EO) PO Box 214, Madras, OR 97741

KOZIELEC, Mark A (Mo) Saint Mark's Church, 4714 Clifton Ave, Saint Louis, MO 63109

KOZIKOWSKI, Mary Carol (NMich) 922 10th Ave, Menominee, MI 49858

KOZLOWSKI, Joseph Felix (WNY)

KOZLOWSKI, Matthew William (SeFla) 623 SE Ocean Blvd, Stuart, FL 34994

KOZUSZEK, Jeffrey Frank (Spr) 512 W Main St, Salem, IL 62881

KRADEL, Adam (Pa) 311 S Orange St, Media, PA 19063

KRAEMER, C Jeff (Dal) 760 Burchart Dr, ., Prosper, TX 75078

KRAFT, Carol Joyce (Chi) 124 West Prairie Street, Wheaton, IL 60187

KRAFT, Roberta A (FdL)

KRAKOWSKY, Posey (NY) 12 W 11th St, New York, NY 10011

KRAMER, Caroline Anne (SwVa)

KRAMER, Charles Edward (NY) 4536 Albany Post Rd, Hyde Park, NY 12538

KRAMER, Esther Ann (Mil) 1111 Genesee St, Delafield, WI 53018

KRAMER, Frederick Ferdinand (Ia) 1304 S 4th Ave W, Newton, IA 50208

KRAMER, Linda Jean (SD) 23120 S Rochford Rd, Hill City, SD 57745

KRANTZ, Jeffrey Hoyt (LI) 43 Cedar Shore Dr, Massapequa, NY 11758

KRANTZ, Kristin (Md) 1307 N Main St, Mount Airy, MD 21771

KRANTZ, Saralouise Camlin (LI) 555Advent Street, Westbury, NY 11590

KRAPF, Richard David (Roch) 15 Granger Street, Canandaigua, NY 14424

KRASINSKI, Joseph Alexander (Ct) 2 Cannondale Dr, Danbury, CT 06810

KRATOVIL, Mildred Elsie Ida Johanna (Md) 204 West St Apt A4, Williamsburg, IA 52361

KRAULAND, Lesley Werner (WA)

KRAUS, Susan (Me) 65 Eddy Rd, Edgecomb, ME 04556

KRAUSE, David (Dal) 12109 Mossygate Trl, Manor, TX 78653

KRAUSE, Janice (Tex) 10043 Boyton Canyon Rd, Frisco, TX 75035

KRAUSS, Harry Edward (NY) 2 West 90th St Apt 5B, New York, NY 10024

KREAMER, Martha (CGC) Po Box 57, Lillian, AL 36549

KREFT, Armand John (Mass) 1717 E. Vista Chino, #A7-266, Palm Springs, CA 92262

KREITLER, Peter Gwillim (Los) 16492 El Hito Ct, Pacific Palisades, CA 90272

KREJCI, Richard Scott (Va) 346 Laurel Farms Ln, Urbanna, VA 23175

KRELL, Thomas William (Mich) 16200 W 12 Mile Rd, Southfield, MI 48076

KRELLER, Daniel Ward (Nwk) 161 W Prospect St, Waldwick, NJ 07463

KREUTZER, Michael Alan (SO) 7 Lonsdale Avenue, Dayton, OH 45419

KRIEGER, Frederick Gordon (SO) 5538 Sebastian Place, Halifax, B3K 2K6, Canada

KRIEGER, Walter Lowell (Be) Fifth & Court, Reading, PA 19603

KRISS, Gary W (Alb) PO Box 26, Cambridge, NY 12816

KROH, Timothy Edward (Md)

KROLL, Brenda M (Ark) 1402 Pagosa Trl, Carrollton, TX 75007

KROM, Judith Sue (NJ) 410 S Atlantic Ave, Beach Haven, NJ 08008

KROMHOUT, Linda Adams (CFla) 2104 Golden Arm Rd, Deltona, FL 32738

KROOHS, Kenneth (NC) 700 Sunset Drive, High Point, NC 27262

KROOHS, Mary (NC) 1700 Queen St, Winston Salem, NC 27103

KROPP, Catherine Amy (Me)

✠ **KROTZ**, James Edward (Neb) 3484 520th Road, Rushville, NE 69360

KRUDYS, Emily Judin (Va) PO Box 11, Montpelier, VA 23192

KRUEGER, Albert Peter (Ore) 1926 W Burnside St Unit 909, Portland, OR 97209

KRUEGER, James Gordon (Alb) 55 Lake Delaware Dr, Delhi, NY 13753

KRUGER, Andrew David (NJ) 205 North Ave E, Cranford, NJ 07016

KRUGER, Ann (CFla) 167 Clear Lake Cir, Sanford, FL 32773

KRUGER, Diane Renee (Kan) 7404 E Killarney Pl, Wichita, KS 67206

KRUGER, Matthew Carl (Mass) 81 Elm St, Concord, MA 01742

KRUGER, Susan Marie (Minn) 1711 Stanford Ave, Saint Paul, MN 55105

KRULAK JR, Victor Harold (SanD) 3118 Canon St Apt 4, San Diego, CA 92106

KRULAK, William Morris (Md) 113 W Hughes St, Baltimore, MD 21230

KRUMBHAAR, Andrew Ramsay (CFla) 144 Carretera Chapala-Ajijic, Pmb 108, San Antonio Tlaycapan, JAL 45900, Mexico

KRUMLAUF, Dennis Skyler (Eur)

KRUMME, Judith Sterner (Mass) 349 Simon Willard Rd, Concord, MA 01742

KRUSE, William G (Chi) 1413 Potomac Ct, Geneva, IL 60134

KRUTZ, Charles (La) 527 North Boulevard, Fourth Floor, Baton Rouge, LA 70802

KRYDER-REID, Thomas Marshall (Ind) 5354 Olympia Dr, Indianapolis, IN 46228

KRYZAK, Andrew Astwood (RI) 254 E Putnam Ave, Greenwich, CT 06830

KUBBE, AnnaLeigh (EMich) Diocese of Eastern Michigan, 924 N Niagara St, Saginaw, MI 48602

KUBICEK, Chief (Md) 8400 Greenspring Ave, Stevenson, MD 21153

KUBLER, Barry P(Aul) (SwFla) 340 Shade Tree Circle, Woodstock, GA 30188

KUEHL JR, H August (RI) 40 Bagy Wrinkle Cv, Warren, RI 02885

KUEHN, Craig (The Episcopal NCal) 2821 Bronzecrest St, Placerville, CA 95667

KUEHN, Jerome Frederick (FdL) 806 4th St, Algoma, WI 54201

KUENKLER, Richard Frederick (CNY) 1 W Church St, Elmira, NY 14901

KUENNETH, John (Tenn) 538 Hickory Trail Drive, Nashville, TN 37209

KUHLMANN, Martha Chandler (Cal) 107 Franciscan Dr, Danville, CA 94526

KUHN, Darlene (WMich)

KUHN, Michael (La) Trinity Episcopal School, 1315 Jackson Ave, New Orleans, LA 70130

KUHN, Philip James (Mass) 25 Wood lane, Maynard, MA 01754

KUHN, Thomas Randall (EC) 328 Kelly Ave, Oak Hill, WV 25901

KUHR, Carolyn S. (Mont) 2409 West Irene Street, Boise, ID 83702

KUHR, Elisabeth Schader (Spok) 2490 Thompson Rd, Cowiche, WA 98923

KUJAWA-HOLBROOK, Sheryl Anne (Los) 1644 Carmel Cir E, Upland, CA 91784

KUKOWSKI, Rich (WA) 412 Colesville Manor Dr, Silver Spring, MD 20904

KULP, John Eugene (SwFla) 17 W Vernon Ave Unit 301, Phoenix, AZ 85003

KUNDINGER, Hazel Doris (CFla) 2404 Fairway Dr, Melbourne, FL 32901

KUNHARDT III, Philip B (NY) Po Box 33, Waccabuc, NY 10597

KUNKLE, George Owen (RG) 1914 Tijeras Rd, Santa Fe, NM 87505

KUNZ JR, Andy (Va) 1006 Greenway Ln, Richmond, VA 23226

KUNZ JR, Carl (Del) Po Box 5856, Wilmington, DE 19808

KUNZ, Phyllis Ann (Minn) 67982 260th Ave, Kasson, MN 55944

KUNZ, Rich (NY) Grace Church, 33 Church St, White Plains, NY 10601

KUOL, Agook Kon () 1225 Texas St, Houston, TX 77002

KUOL, Daniel Kuch (Ky) 8701 Shepherdsville Rd, Louisville, KY 40219

KURATKO, Lauren (NY) 3110 Ashford Dunwoody Rd NE, Atlanta, GA 30319

KURATKO, Ryan (NY) P.O. Box 788, Mechanicsville, VA 23111

KURIA, Janet Kabui (Md) 6515 Loch Raven Blvd, Loch Hill, MD 21239

KURTH, Michael Benjamin Evington (NY) 2 Rectory St, Rye, NY 10580

KURTZ, James Edward (CFla) 1352 Seburn Rd, Apopka, FL 32703

KURTZ, Kelli Grace (Los) 408 Greenfield Ct, Glendora, CA 91740

KURTZ, Margaret Eileen (Ida) 3185 E Rivernest Dr, Boise, ID 83706

KUSCHEL, Catherine Mary (Eau) 3774 Goodwin Ave N, Oakdale, MN 55128

KUSKY, Donna Lee Stewart (EMich) 13685 Block Rd, Birch Run, MI 48415

KWAN, Franco (Cal) 425 Swallowtail Ct, Brisbane, CA 94005

KWIATKOWSKI, Jan (Mil) 9333 W Goodrich Ave, Milwaukee, WI 53224

KYGER JR, Paul Scholl (Chi) 2304 Finwick Ct, Kissimmee, FL 34743

KYLE, Anne Meredith (WMo) Calvary Episcopal Church, 713 S Ohio Ave, Sedalia, MO 65301

KYLE, Michael Raymond (Mo) 3932 Oxford Rd, Jefferson City, MO 65109

L

LABARRE, Barbara L Root (Okla) 10901 S Yale Ave, Tulsa, OK 74137

LABATT, Walter Bruce (Mo) 520 Coventry Cir, Dexter, MI 48130

LABELLE, Philip N (Mass) 27 Main St, Southborough, MA 01772

LABORDA HARRIS, Christy (The Episcopal NCal) St. Stephen's Episcopal Church, PO Box 98, Sebastopol, CA 95472

LABORDE, Jean Jonas (Hai)

LABUD, Richard John (CFla) 28097 Se Highway 42, Umatilla, FL 32784

LACEY, John Howard (SwFla) 851 Moonlight Ln, Brooksville, FL 34601

LACEY, Maryanne (SanD) 3208 Old Heather Rd, San Diego, CA 92111

LACOMBE, Edgar A (Alb) 5708 State Highway 812, Ogdensburg, NY 13669

LACROSSE, Diana Parsons (Dal) 2700 Warren Cir, Irving, TX 75062

LACY, Mimi (SVa) 107 Louis St, Greenville, NC 27858

LACY II, Thomas Alonzo (Ga) St. Anne's Episcopal Church, P.O. Box 889, Tifton, GA 31793

✠ **LADEHOFF**, Robert Louis (Ore) 1330 SW 3rd Ave., Apt. P8, Portland, OR 97201

LAFFLER, Brian H (Nwk) 72 Lodi St, Hackensack, NJ 07601

LAFLER, Mark Alan (CFla) 414 Pine St, Titusville, FL 32796

LAFON, Kirk David (Miss) 950 Episcopal School Way, Knoxville, TN 37932

LAFOND II, Charles (Colo) 1023 Pleasant Street, Webster, NH 03303

LAFONTANT, Fritz Raoul (Hai) Eglise Street Pierre, Mirebalais, Haiti

LAFOREST, Charlotte Henning (Ct) 19 Walden St, West Hartford, CT 06107

LAFORTUNE, Patrick (Mass) 74 S Common St, Lynn, MA 01902

LAFRANCE, Shawn Vincent (NH)

LAGANA, Gaye Lynn (Nev) PO Box 18917, Spokane, WA 99228

LAGER, Michael Alan (Ark) 16816 Summit Vista Way, Louisville, KY 40245

LAGO, Ana Mercedes (PR)

LAHAR, Teresa Roseanne (WK)

LAHEY, Stephen Edmund (Neb) 1935 Sewell St, Lincoln, NE 68502

Clergy List

✠ **LAI**, Jung-Hsin (Tai) 7- Lane 105, Hangchow S - Road Sec 1, Taipei, 10060, Taiwan

LAI, Paul C (LI) 1321 College Point Blvd, College Point, NY 11356

LAINE, Jeanty (SeFla) 404 SW 3rd St, Delray Beach, FL 33444

LAING, Chris (Ore) 8275 Sw Canyon Ln, Portland, OR 97225

LAINSON, Vinnie (Va) 9325 West Street, Manassas, VA 20110

LAIRD, Daniel Dale (NC) 1737 Hillandale Rd, Durham, NC 27705

LAIRD, I Bruce (Colo) 606 Newnan St, Carrollton, GA 30117

LAIRD, Lucinda Rawlings (Eur) 330 N Hubbards Ln, Louisville, KY 40207

LAIRD, Robert C (Oly) 316 E 88th St, New York, NY 10128

LAITE JR, Robert Emerson (Me) 200 Main St, Thomaston, ME 04861

LAKE, Mark William (RG) 2602 S 2nd St, Tucumcari, NM 88401

LAKEMAN, Thomas Edmund (CGC) 127 Oak Bend Ct, Fairhope, AL 36532

LALONDE, Kathryn Nan (Pgh) 100 Great Pl Ne, Albuquerque, NM 87113

LALONDE, Walter Joseph (Pgh) 139 N Jefferson Ave, Canonsburg, PA 15317

LALOR, Donald Jene (Minn)

LAM, Peter (LI) 33 Howard Pl, Waldwick, NJ 07463

LAM, Vivian P (LI) 500 S Country Rd, Bay Shore, NY 11706

LA MACCHIA, James R (Mass) 32 Mountain Ash Dr, Kingston, MA 02364

LAMAZARES, Gabriel (NY) 4312 46th St, Sunnyside, NY 11104

LAMB, Jan M (NC) 3064 Colony Rd Apt D, Durham, NC 27705

✠ **LAMB**, Jerry Alban (The Episcopal NCal) 1065 Villita Loop, Las Cruces, NM 88007

LAMB, Ridenour Newcomb (Ga) 2425 Cherry Laurel Ln., Albany, GA 31705

LAMB, Thomas Jennings (Chi) 503 Macon Dr, Rockford, IL 61109

LAMB, Trevor Vanderveer (CFla) 316 Ocean Dunes Rd, Daytona Beach, FL 32118

LAMB, Watson (La) 10701 Saint Francis Dr, Philadelphia, MS 39350

LAMBERT, Bob (Mil) 6303 Partridge Hills Dr, Mount Pleasant, WI 53406

LAMBERT, Dave (Ala) Episcopal Church of the Epiphany, 1338 Montevallo Rd, Leeds, AL 35094

LAMBERT, Gary (Mil) 205 Nichols Rd, Monona, WI 53716

LAMBERT, George A (Me) 259 Essex St. Apt. 3, Bangor, ME 04401

LAMBERT, John Peck (Oly) 26621 128th Ave South East, Kent, WA 98030

LAMBERT, Leandra Thelma Lisa (LI) 18 James Ln, East Hampton, NY 11937

✠ **LAMBERT**, Paul Emil (Dal) 1439 Tranquilla Dr., Dallas, TX 75218

✠ **LAMBERT III**, William Jay (Eau) 510 S Farwell St, Eau Claire, WI 54701

LAMBORN, Amy (Tenn) The General Theological Seminary, 440 West 21st Street, New York, NY 10011

LAMBORN, Rob (Tenn) Otey Memorial Parish, Po Box 267, Sewanee, TN 37375

LAMKIN, Melissa Warren (Ct) 139 W 91st St, NY, NY 10024

LAMMING, Sarah Rebecca (WA) 3820 Aspen Hill Rd, Silver Spring, MD 20906

LAMONTAGNE, Allen Allen (Eas) 2019 Featherwood Dr W, Jacksonville, FL 32233

LAMPE, Christine Kay (WK) 710 N Main St, Garden City, KS 67846

LAMPERT, Richard B (SwFla) 826 Hampton Wood Ct, Sarasota, FL 34232

LAMPHERE, Mary Kathryn (Spok) 15319 E 8th Ave, Spokane Valley, WA 99037

LANCASTER, James Mansell (Miss) 2721 Brumbaugh Rd, Ocean Springs, MS 39564

LANCE, Philip J (Los) 6464 Sunset Blvd., Suite 845, Los Angeles, CA 90028

LANDER, Barbara Temple (ND) 319 S 5th St, Grand Forks, ND 58201

LANDER III, James Rollin (Los) 1101 E Terrace St. #202, Seattle, WA 98122

LANDER, Stephen King (Minn) 5029 Girard Ave S, Minneapolis, MN 55419

LANDERS, Davidson Texada (Ala) 5220 Midway Cir, Tuscaloosa, AL 35406

LANDERS JR, Edward Leslie (Tenn) 6536 Jocelyn Hollow Rd, Nashville, TN 37205

LANDERS, Gail Joan (Md) 12400 Manor Road, PO Box 4001, Glen Arm, MD 21057

LANDERS, Greg Leroy (NY) 2150 Baileys Corner Rd, Wall Township, NJ 07719

LANDERS, Kay Marie (Los) 1136 Scenic View St, Upland, CA 91784

LANDERS, Sylvia C (Neb) 206 Westridge Drive, Norfolk, NE 68701

LANDRETH, Robert Dean (Mass) 7 Mechanic Sq, Marblehead, MA 01945

LANDRITH, Richard Stanley (EO) 123 S G St, Lakeview, OR 97630

LANDRY, Brad (WTex) St Paul's Episcopal Church, 1018 E Grayson St, San Antonio, TX 78208

LANDRY, Robert W (Me)

LANE III, Calvin (SO) St George's Episcopal Church, 5520 Far Hills Ave, Dayton, OH 45429

LANE, Charles Lewis (Ia)

LANE III, Edward Jacob (Ky)

LANE, John Charles (Oly) 311 Ridge Dr, Port Townsend, WA 98368

LANE, John David (SwVa) 307 Rainbow Dr, Staunton, VA 24401

LANE, Johnny (Ga) Route #4, Leslie Road, Box 1455, Americus, GA 31709

LANE, Joseph Andrew (Cal) 527 E Woodbury Rd, Altadena, CA 91001

LANE, Keith Cecil (NY) 487 Hudson St, New York, NY 10014

LANE, Nancy Upson (CNY)

LANE, Peter Austin (SwFla) 200 Meshanticut Valley Pkwy, Cranston, RI 02920

LANE, Peter Carlson (Chi) 4945 S Dorchester Ave, Chicago, IL 60615

LANE, Stephen Edward (WNY) 371 Delaware Ave, Buffalo, NY 14202

✠ **LANE**, Stephen Taylor (Me) 84 Parsons Rd., Portland, ME 04103

LANE, Wendy (Chi) 1775 W Newport Ct, Lake Forest, IL 60045

LANE, William Benjamin (Del) 614 Loveville Rd., B-1-I, Hockessin, DE 19707

LANG, Anne Adele (FdL)

LANG, Ellen Davis (SD) 3504 E. Woodsedge St., Sioux Falls, SD 57108

LANG, Mark William (NwT) 727 W Browning Ave, Pampa, TX 79065

LANG, Martha Ellen (Ia) 2101 Nettle Ave, Muscatine, IA 52761

LANG, Nicholas Gerard (Ct) 14 France St, Norwalk, CT 06851

LANG, Thomas Andrew (Ore) 2812 Ne Kaster Dr, Hillsboro, OR 97124

LANGDON, Clarence (Chi) 1249 Hedgerow Dr, Grayslake, IL 60030

LANGDON, David Stetson (Miss) PO Box 40, Parchman, MS 38738

LANGENFELD, Robert Joseph (Minn) 615 Vermillion St, Hastings, MN 55033

LANGE-SOTO, Anna Beatriz (Cal) 1503 E Campbell Ave, Campbell, CA 95008

LANGEVIN, Ann Elizabeth (Nev) St Thomas Episcopal Church, 5383 E Owens Ave, Las Vegas, NV 89110

LANGFELDT, John Addington (EO) 1000 Vey Way Apt 361, The Dalles, OR 97058

LANGFORD, Thomas William (Spr) 873 S Park Ave, Springfield, IL 62704

LANGI, Viliami (The Episcopal Church in Haw) 720 N King St, Honolulu, HI 96817

LANGILLE, David (Minn) Messiah Episcopal Church, 1631 Ford Pkwy, Saint Paul, MN 55116

LANGLE, Susan (NH) Unit 6, 26 Myrtle St, Claremont, NH 03743

LANGLEY III, Raleigh (CFla)

LANGLOIS, Donald Harold (Spr) 916 W Loughlin Dr, Chandler, AZ 85225

LANGSTON, Michael Griffith (NC) 203 Denim Dr, Erwin, NC 28339

LANIER, Justin (Vt) 200 Pleasant St, Bennington, VT 05201

LANIER, Stanley Lin (At) PO Box 637, Waycross, GA 31502

LANIGAN, Sean Robert (Pa) 525 E 7th St, Long Beach, CA 90813

LANNING JR, James Clair (Chi) 1315 W. Roosevelt Rd., Wheaton, IL 60187

LANPHERE, Lynette (Ala) 8132 Becker Ln, Leeds, AL 35094

LANTER, James Joseph (WVa) HC 69 Box 88, Slatyfork, WV 26291

LAPENTA-H, Sarah (ECR) 4775 Cambridge St, Boulder, CO 80301

LAPRE, Alfred Charles (Ct) 616 Shamrock Dr, Fredericksburg, VA 22407

LAQUINTANO, David (NJ) 2998 Bay Ave, Ocean City, NJ 08226

LARA, Juana (Dal) St Barnabas Episcopal Church, 1200 N Shiloh Rd, Garland, TX 75042

LARA, Lino (Dal) 5923 Royal Lane, Dallas, TX 75230

LARA, Pedro DJ (Dal) 635 N Story Rd, Irving, TX 75061

LARCOMBE, David John (Vt) 37 Premo Rd, Roxbury, VT 05669

LAREMORE, Darrell Lee (SeFla) 6003 Back Bay Ln, Austin, TX 78739

LARGE, Alexander R (Tex) 717 Sage Rd, Houston, TX 77056

LARGENT, Lacy (Tex) Po Box 10603, Houston, TX 77206

LARIBEE JR, Richard (CNY) 20 Masonic Ave Apt A4, Camden, NY 13316

LARIVE, Armand Edward (Spok) 4812 Fremont Ave, Bellingham, WA 98229

LARKIN, Gregory Bruce (Los) 1251 Las Posas Rd, Camarillo, CA 93010

LARKIN, Lauren Renee Ellis (CFla)

LARKIN, Patrick (ETenn)

LAROCCA, Lucy D(riscoll) (Ct) 1109 Main St, Branford, CT 06405

LAROCHE WILSON, Jill Monica (Pa) 246 Fox Rd, Media, PA 19063

LAROM JR, Richard U (NY) Po Box 577, Ivoryton, CT 06442

LARRIMORE, Chip Barker (Cal) 61 Santa Rosa Ave., Sausalito, CA 94965

LARSEN, Amy Louise (Episcopal SJ)

LARSEN, Erik W (RI) Saint Columba's Chapel, 55 Vaucluse Ave, Middletown, RI 02842

LARSEN, Gilbert Steward (Ct) 9160 Sw 193rd Cir, Dunnellon, FL 34432

LARSEN JR, Jim (Pa) PO Box 341490, Dayton, OH 45434

LARSEN, Matthew David (Dal) 3966 McKinney Ave, Dallas, TX 75204

LARSEN, Peter Michael (LI) 515 Eastlake Dr, Muscle Shoals, AL 35661

LARSON, Donna (WMass) 19 Pleasant St, Chicopee, MA 01013

LARSON, Frances Jean (Minn) 1010 1st Ave N, Wheaton, MN 56296

LARSON, John Milton (Los) 2665 Tallant Rd Apt W307, Santa Barbara, CA 93105

LARSON, Laurence (Chi) 2424 41st St Apt 48, Moline, IL 61265

LARSON JR, L(awrence) John (Cal) 1835 NW Lantana Dr., Corvallis, OR 97330

LARSON, Robert Anton (Colo) P.O. Box 563, Ouray, CO 81427

LARSON, Steven Shaw (Ga) PO Box 74, Swainsboro, GA 30401

LARSON, Wayne (Md) 15 East Bishop's Road, Baltimore, MD 21218

LARSON-MILLER, Lizette (Cal) 926 Santa Fe Ave, Albany, CA 94706

LA RUE, Howard Arlen (Va) PO Box 72, Searsport, ME 04974

LA RUE, Michael Dreyer (FtW)

LASCH, Ian (Mo) 8605 Spoon Dr, Saint Louis, MO 63132

LASCH, Loren V (Mo) Diocese Of Missouri, 1210 Locust St # 3, Saint Louis, MO 63103

LASH, Rebecca Henry (NwPa) 870 Diamond Park, Meadville, PA 16335

LASKE, Holger (Los) Riehler Strasse 7, Koeln, 50668, Germany

LASLEY, Jerry Drew (NC)

LASSALLE, David Fredric (SVa) 1336 Bolling Ave, Norfolk, VA 23508

LASSEN, Corrie (Cal) 409 Topa Topa Dr, Ojai, CA 93023

LASSITER, Richard Bruce (Nev) 1311 Ramona Ln, Boulder City, NV 89005

LATHAM, Betty Craft (ETenn) 628 Magnolia Vale Dr, Chattanooga, TN 37419

LATHROP, Brian Albert (NY) 63 Downing St Apt 4-A, New York, NY 10014

LATHROP, John (Me) 101 Paseo Encantado Ne, Santa Fe, NM 87506

LATIMER, Susan (SwFla) 502 Druid Hills Road, Temple Terrace, FL 33617

LATTA, Dennis James (Ind) 2742 S Hickory Corner Rd, Vincennes, IN 47591

✠ **LATTIME**, Mark A (Ak) 1205 Denali Way, Fairbanks, AK 99701

LAU, Ronald Taylor Christensen (LI) 326 Clinton St, Brooklyn, NY 11231

LAUCHER, Bill (Tex) 417 Avenue Of Oaks St, Houston, TX 77009

LAUDISIO, Patricia Devin (Colo) 3328 Sentinel Dr, Boulder, CO 80301

LAUER, Daniel Donald (WTex) 2006 Pinetree Ln, San Antonio, TX 78232

LAUGHLIN III, Ledlie (WA) 4201 Albemarle St NW, Washington, DC 20016

LAUGHLIN JR, Ledlie Irwin (Eur) 63 Ford Hill Rd, West Cornwall, CT 06796

LAUGHLIN, Ophelia (NJ) Waterman Avenue, Rumson, NJ 07760

LAUGHMAN JR, Richard (The Episcopal NCal) St. James of Jerusalem Episcopal Church, 556 N George Washington Blvd, Yuba City, CA 95993

LAUK, Candice Ruth (NMich) 1003 Wickman Dr, Iron Mountain, MI 49801

LAURA, Ronald Samuel (Vt) 158 Concord Rd Apt K9, Billerica, MA 01821

LAURINEC, Jennene Ellen (Tex) 308 Cottage Rd., Carthage, TX 75633

LAURITZEN, Ruth (Wyo)

LAUTENSCHLAGER, Paul John (Colo) 11 W. Madison Street, Colorado Springs, CO 80907

LAUZON, Marcia (Mont)

LAVALLEE, Armand Aime (Ct) 5523 Birchhill Rd, Charlotte, NC 28227

LAVALLEE, Donald Alphonse (RI) 1665 Broad St, Cranston, RI 02905

LAVANN, Jason Gary (Mil) 216 E Chandler Blvd, Burlington, WI 53105

LAVELLE, Jon Frederick (WNY) 51 Colonial Cir, Buffalo, NY 14222

LAVENGOOD, Henrietta Louise (NJ) 211 Falls Ct, Medford, NJ 08055

LAVENGOOD, Martin (NJ) 211 Falls Ct, Medford, NJ 08055

LAVER, Michael Scott (Roch) 54 W Main St, Sodus, NY 14551

LAVERONI, Alfred Frank (Md) 312 Cigar Loop, Hvre De Grace, MD 21078

LAVERY, Patricia Anne (NwPa) PO Box 287, Grove City, PA 16127

LAVETTY, Denise Jean (NY) 224 Waverly Pl, New York, NY 10014

LAVINE, Patricia Iva (Alb) 323 Lakeshore Dr, Norwood, NY 13668

LAVOE, John F (CNY) 210 Yoxall Ln, Oriskany, NY 13424

LAW, Eric Hung-Fat (Los) 351 Sandpiper St, Palm Desert, CA 92260

LAWBAUGH, William (CPa) 813 Franklin Avenue, Aliquippa, PA 15001

LAWLER, Gary Elwyn Andrew (Chi) 6033 North Sheridan Road - 27J, Chicago, IL 60660

LAWLER, Rick (WNC) Po Box 2680, Blowing Rock, NC 28605

LAWLER, Steven William (Mo) 33 N Clay Ave, Saint louis, MO 63135

LAWLOR, Jay R (WMich) Diocese of Western Michigan, 535 S. Burdick Street, Suite 1, Kalamazoo, MI 49007

LAWRENCE JR, Albert Sumner (Tex) 14 Sedgewick Pl, The Woodlands, TX 77382

LAWRENCE, Amy (Cal) 2711 Harkness St, Sacramento, CA 95818

LAWRENCE, Bruce Bennett (NC) C/ O Department Of Religion, Duke University, Durham, NC 27706

LAWRENCE, Catherine Abbott (NY) 1415 Pelhamdale Ave, Christ Church, Pelham, NY 10803

LAWRENCE, Dean (Tex) 1101 Rock Prairie Road, College Station, TX 77845

LAWRENCE, Eric John (Nev) 2306 Paradise Dr Apt 222, Reno, NV 89512

LAWRENCE, Gerard Martin (Mass) 22874 NE 127th Way, Redmond, WA 98053

LAWRENCE JR, Harry Martin (ETenn) 1800 Lula Lake Rd, Lookout Mountain, GA 30750

LAWRENCE, John Arthur (Chi) 712 Mockingbird Lane, Kerrville, TX 78028

LAWRENCE, John Elson (WA) 4336 Wordsworth Way, Venice, FL 34293

Clergy List

LAWRENCE, Matt (The Episcopal NCal) 18 Foremast Cv, Corte Madera, CA 94925

LAWRENCE, Novella E (NY) 20 Laguardia Ave Apt 4f, Staten Island, NY 10314

LAWRENCE, Phil (Okla) 32251 S 616 Rd, Grove, OK 74344

LAWRENCE JR, Raymond Johnson (SwVa) 913 Ash Tree Ln., Niskayuna, NY 12309

LAWRENCE, Wade William (Pgh) 6911 Prospect Ave, Pittsburgh, PA 15202

LAWS III, Robert J (Eas) 30513 Washington St, Princess Anne, MD 21853

LAWS, Tom (Nwk) 11 Harvard St, Montclair, NJ 07042

LAWSON, Daniel Matthew Custance (Mich)

LAWSON, Frederick Quinney (U) 4294 Adonis Dr, Salt Lake City, UT 84124

LAWSON, Neil-St Barnabas J (Episcopal SJ) P.O. Box 7606, Stockton, CA 95267

LAWSON, Paul David (Los) 567 Mayflower Rd, Claremont, CA 91711

LAWSON, Peter Raymond (Cal) 805 North Webster Street, Petaluma, CA 94952

LAWSON, Richard (Colo) 1350 N Washington St, Denver, CO 80203

LAWSON, Rolfe Adrian (Vt)

LAWSON, Shirley May (NY)

LAWSON, Victor Freeman (WVa) 64 Barley Lane, Charles Town, WV 25414

LAWSON-BECK, David Roswell (NJ) 143 W Milton Ave, Apt 4, Rahway, NJ 07065

LAWTON, John Keith (Ak) Po Box 530, Palmer, AK 99645

LAWYER, Evelyn Virden (Minn) 4539 Keithson Dr, Arden Hills, MN 55112

LAYCOCK JR, Brad (SwVa) 2725 Wilshire Ave SW, Roanoke, VA 24015

LAYCOCK, John (Mich) 7112 Kauffman Blvd., Presque Isle, MI 49777

LAYDEN, Daniel Keith (NI) 11009 Brandy Oak Run, Fort Wayne, IN 46845

LAYNE, Najah Suzanne (Kan) 631 E. Marlin St., McPherson, KS 67460

LAYNE, Robert Patterson (Kan) The Cedars, 807 N Maxwell St, Mc Pherson, KS 67460

LAZARD, Amirold (Hai)

LEA, Gail Ann (U) PO Box 96, Moab, UT 84532

LEA, William Howard (Ga) 1 Fair Hope Ln, Savannah, GA 31411

LEACH, Duane Lamar (The Episcopal Church in Haw) 57-077 Eleku Kuilima Pl Apt 97, Kahuku, HI 96731

LEACH, JoAnn Zwart (Ore) 8400 Paseo Vista Dr, Las Vegas, NV 89128

LEACH, John Philip (WTenn) 1380 Wolf River Blvd, Collierville, TN 38017

LEACH, Marilyn May (Minn)

LEACH, Shannon Paul (Nev) 8400 Paseo Vista Dr, Las Vegas, NV 89128

LEACOCK, Rob (Ark) 8605 Verona Trl, Austin, TX 78749

LEAMAN, Kris (Ia) 120 1st St Ne, Mason City, IA 50401

LEANILLO, Ricardo Ivan (SwFla) 5033 9th St, Zephyrhills, FL 33542

LEANNAH, Scott Robert (Mil) 3734 S. 86th St., Milwaukee, WI 53228

LEARY, Charles Randolph (SO) 133 Croskey Boulevard, Medway, OH 45341

LEARY, Kevin David (Ct) 15 Rimmon Rd, Woodbridge, CT 06525

LEAS, Bercry Eleanor (Mich) 7051 Wakan Ln., Corryton, TN 37721

LEATHERMAN, Daniel Lee (The Episcopal Church in Haw) 7 Pursuit, Aliso Viejo, CA 92656

LEAVITT, Christie Plehn (Nev) 1739 Carita Ave, Henderson, NV 89014

LE BARRON, Bruce Erie (WK) 3218 White Tail Way, Salina, KS 67401

LEBEAU, Philip Henry (ECR) 23 Millar Ave, San Jose, CA 95127

LEBENS ENGLUND, Paul (Minn) 7315 N Wall St, Spokane, WA 99208

LE BLANC, Fran Andre Telles (Md) 204 Monument Rd, Orleans, MA 02653

LEBLANC, Tracy Jean (Ore) 15416 Ne 90th St, Vancouver, WA 98682

LEBRIJA, Lorenzo (Los) 840 Echo Park Ave, Los Angeles, CA 90026

LEBROCQ JR, Eric Francis (Tex) St. John's Episcopal Church, PO Box 1477, Sealy, TX 77474

LEBRON, Robert Emmanuel (Mil) 409 E. Court St., Janesville, WI 53545

LEBUS, Jesse Williams (LI) 1670 Route 25a, Cold Spring Harbor, NY 11724

LECHE III, Edward Douglas (Oly) 205 Olympic View Dr, Friday Harbor, WA 98250

LECLAIR, Arthur Anthony (Colo) 8221 E Fremont Cir, Englewood, CO 80112

LECLAIR, Paul Joseph (Mich) 1434 E 13 Mile Rd, Madison Heights, MI 48071

LECLAIRE, Patrick Harry (Nev) 620 W B St, Fallon, NV 89406

LECLERC, Charles Edward (NH) 1873 Dover Rd, Epsom, NH 03234

LECOUTEUR II, Eugene Hamilton (Va) 6000 Grove Ave, Richmond, VA 23226

LEDERHOUSE, Susan (Mass) PO Box 1586, Orleans, MA 02653

LEDERMAN, Maureen Elizabeth (Ct) 124 Midland Dr, Meriden, CT 06450

LEDFORD, Marcia (Mich) 959 Sherman St, Ypsilanti, MI 48197

LEDGERWOOD, Mary Jayne (CGC) 860 N Section St, Fairhope, AL 36532

LEDIARD SR, Daniel E (EO) PO Box 681, Virginia City, NV 89440

LEDIARD, Jo Anne (Spok) 1609 W 10th Ave, Kennewick, WA 99336

LEDYARD, Christopher Martin (Az) 2331 E Adams St, Tucson, AZ 85719

LEDYARD, Flo (Md) 1021 Bosley Rd, Cockeysville, MD 21030

LEE, Alison Ruth (Az) 602 N Wilmot Rd, Tucson, AZ 85711

LEE III, Arthur Randall (SwFla) 7304 Van Lake Dr, Englewood, FL 34224

LEE, Betsy A. (Minn) 4901 Triton Dr, Golden Valley, MN 55422

LEE, Caleb J (SC) 215 Ann St, Beaufort, NC 28516

LEE, Chen-Cheng (Tai) No. 311 Sec.2, Chieding Rd, Chieding District, Kaohsiung City, 85241, Taiwan

LEE, Christine Kim (NY) St Mary's Episcopal Church, 521 W 126th St, New York, NY 10027

LEE, Darry Kyong Ho (Los) 5950 Imperial Hwy Apt 47, South Gate, CA 90280

LEE, David Edward (Va) 2343 Highland Ave, Charlottesville, VA 22903

LEE, Deborah Annette (NY) 50 Guion Pl Apt 5h, New Rochelle, NY 10801

LEE, Donald DeArman (WTex) Po Box 545, Bandera, TX 78003

✠ LEE JR, Edward Lewis (WMich) 123 Glenwood Rd, Merion Station, PA 19066

LEE, Enoch (Tai) North 1-6, Ming-Shin Street, Hualien, Taiwan

LEE, George (The Episcopal Church in Haw) 2468 Lamaku Pl, Honolulu, HI 96816

LEE, Grace (Va)

LEE, Hosea Mun-Yong (Nwk) 1600 Parker Ave Apt 3-D, Fort Lee, NJ 07024

LEE, Hyacinth Evadne (NY) 50 Guion Pl, 5H, New Rochelle, NY 10801

LEE, Hyangnam (Los) 408 S Broadway, Redondo Beach, CA 90277

LEE, James Kyung-Jin (Los) Episcopal Church of the Messiah, 614 N Bush St, Santa Ana, CA 92701

LEE JR, James Oliver (Dal) 1729 S Beckley Ave, Dallas, TX 75224

✠ LEE, Jeff (Chi) 65 E Huron St, Chicago, IL 60611

LEE JR, John E (NMich) Rr 1 Box 586, Newberry, MI 49868

LEE, Judith (WNY) 36 Marion Rd E # 8540, Princeton, NJ 08540

LEE, Jui-Chiang (U) 163 Tung-Ming Rd., Keelung, Taiwan

LEE, Julia Hamilton (Ala)

LEE, Kirk A (At) 1195 Village Run NE, Atlanta, GA 30319

LEE, Marc DuPlan (Kan) 4515 W Moncrieff Pl, Denver, CO 80212

LEE, Margaret Will (Chi) 3412 54th St, Moline, IL 61265

LEE, Mark Chong (RG)

LEE, Maurice Charles (Spr) 3231 Alton Rd, Atlanta, GA 30341

LEE, Nathaniel Jung-Chul (WA) Church of the Holy Spirit, 1624 Wooded Acres Dr, Waco, TX 76710

✠ **LEE**, Peter J (Va) 511 E Rosemary St, Chapel Hill, NC 27514

LEE, Rhonda Mawhood (NC) 914 Green St, Durham, NC 27701

LEE, Richard Stanley (SanD) 4036 Ampudia St, San Diego, CA 92110

LEE, Robert Bruce (Vt) 51 Park St., Canaan, VT 05903

LEE III, Robert Vernon (Fla) 1131 N Laura St, Jacksonville, FL 32206

LEE, Sang (Dal) 2783 Valwood Pkwy, Farmers Branch, TX 75234

LEE, Scott Charles (Ct) 2000 Main Street, Stratford, CT 06615

LEE, Scott R (RI) St James the Apostle Epis Ch, 1803 Highland Hollow Dr, Conroe, TX 77305

LEE, Shiane Marlena (NY) 191 S Greeley Ave, Chappaqua, NY 10514

LEE, Shirley Lynne (Ak) 1205 Denali Way, Fairbanks, AK 99701

LEE, Solomon Sang-Woo (Chi) 9227 Cameron Ln, Morton Grove, IL 60053

LEE, Stedwart Warren Rubinstein (VI) 261 Mount Pleasant, Frederiksted, VI 00840

LEE, Steven Yong (NY) 1047 Amsterdam Ave, New York, NY 10025

LEE, Susan Hagood (Mass) 336 Maple St, New Bedford, MA 02740

LEE, Tammy (NC) 304 E Franklin St, Chapel Hill, NC 27514

LEE, Terence A (NY) 204 W 134th St, New York, NY 10030

LEE III, Thomas Carleton (LI) 3000 Galloway Ridge Apt D104, Pittsboro, NC 27312

LEE, Thomas Moon (Tenn) 510 Mable Mason Cv, La Vergne, TN 37086

LEE, Wanhong Barnabas (Md) St John's Episcopal Church, 9120 Frederick Rd, Ellicott City, MD 21042

LEE, Wen-Hui (Tai) 5F No. 7 Kee-King 2nd Road, Kee Lung City, 20446, Taiwan

LEE III, William Forrest (Md) Po Box 2188, Mountain Lake Park, MD 21550

LEECH, John (Oly) PO Box 65807, Tucson, AZ 85728

LEED, Rolf (WMo) 226 N Main St, Clinton, MO 64735

LEEMHUIS, Guy Anthony (Los) 260 N Locust St, Inglewood, CA 90301

LEES, Everett (Okla) 2613 W Broadway St, Broken Arrow, OK 74012

LEESON, Gary William (Los) 4457 Mont Eagle Pl, Los Angeles, CA 90041

LEFEVRE, Ann Raynor (Be) 1190 Bianca Dr Ne, Palm Bay, FL 32905

LEGER, Don Curtis (WLa) 919 Anthony Ave, Opelousas, LA 70570

LEGNANI, Bob (NJ) 22 Ashley Dr, Delran, NJ 08075

LEHMAN, Kitty (Cal) 705 W Main St, Kerrville, TX 78028

LEHMAN, Susan (SwVa) 550 E 4th St #U, Cincinnati, OH 45202

LEHMANN, Richard B (Alb) 24 Summit Ave, Latham, NY 12110

LEHRER, Christian Anton (Cal) 800 Pomona St, Crockett, CA 94525

LEIBHART, Linda Dianne (Roch) 9406 Chipping Dr, Richmond, VA 23237

✠ **LEIDEL JR**, Ed (EMich) 430 W Brentwood Ln, Milwaukee, WI 53217

LEIDER, Jennifer (O) St. Paul's Episcopal Church, 798 S. Coy Rd., Oregon, OH 43616

LEIDHEISER-STODDARD, Margaret Clare (SO) St. John's Episcopal Church, 700 High St, Worthington, OH 43085

LEIFUR, Teresa (CGC) 1110 E Gadsden St, Pensacola, FL 32501

LEIGH, W Joseph (NJ) 238 Twilight Ave, Keansburg, NJ 07734

LEIGH-KOSER, Charlene M (CPa) 6219 Lincoln Hwy, Wrightsville, PA 17368

LEIGH-TAYLOR, Christine (The Episcopal NCal) 4231 Oak Meadow Rd, Placerville, CA 95667

LEIGHTON, Christopher (Ct) 33 Dora Cir, Bridgeport, CT 06604

LEIGHTON, Jack Lee (Tex) 135 E Circuit Dr, Beaumont, TX 77706

LEIGHTON, Tim (Spr) 1920 E Oakland Avenue, Bloomington, IL 61705

LEIKER, Diana Louise (WNY)

LEIN, Clay A (Tex) 1102 Highland St., Houston, TX 77009

LEINBACH, Jeanne A (O) 2747 Fairmount Blvd, Cleveland Heights, OH 44106

LEININGER, Austin L (ECR) 532 Center St, Santa Cruz, CA 95060

LEIP, Harry Louis (Mo) 600 N Euclid Ave, Saint Louis, MO 63108

LEISERSON, Joanna (SO) 2218 Oakland Ave, Covington, KY 41014

LEITE, Dessordi Peres (WA)

LEMA, Julio M (At) 1379 Craighill Ct, Norcross, GA 30093

LEMAIRE JR, Michael E (Cal) 2220 Cedar St, Berkeley, CA 94709

LEMAY, Anne Rae (NJ) 576 West Ave, Sewaren, NJ 07077

LEMBURG, David (Ga) 1350 Courthouse Rd, Gulfport, MS 39507

LEMBURG, Melanie Dickson (Ga) 1909 15th Street, Gulfport, MS 39501

LEMERY, Gary Conrad (RI) 45 Bay View Drive North, Jamestown, RI 02835

LEMLER, James (Ct) Christ Church, 254 E Putnam Ave, Greenwich, CT 06830

LEMLEY, Daniel James (SwFla) 701 Orange Ave, Clearwater, FL 33756

LEMLEY, Kent Christopher (At) 764 Springlake Ln NW, Atlanta, GA 30318

LEMMING, Craig P (Minn) St John The Evangelist Episcopal Church, 60 Kent St, Saint Paul, CO 55102

LEMON, Karen Dillenbeck (WK) 20081 Sw 20th Ave, Pratt, KS 67124

LEMONS, Catherine (Minn) 12621 Old Columbia Pike, Silver Spring, MD 20904

LENNE, Laurent Pierre (Eur)

LENNON, Evelyn Cromartie (Minn) 65a Lovell Rd, Fryeburg, ME 04037

LENNOX, Daniel Duncan (Nwk) 707 Washington St, Hoboken, NJ 07030

LENNSTROM, Brian (Oly) 1216 7th St, Anacortes, WA 98221

LENOIR, Robert Scott (Miss) 2005 Lauban Ln, Gautier, MS 39553

LENOW, Joseph Earl (Va)

LENT, Morris J (SC) 1855 Houghton Dr, Charleston, SC 29412

LENTEN, John William (NMich) 11 Longyear Dr, Negaunee, MI 49866

LENTZ, Benjamin Lee (Be) 9758 N. Rome Rd., Athens, PA 18810

LENTZ III, Julian Carr (ECR) 1001 Sleepy Hollow Ln, Plainfield, NJ 07060

LENTZ, Preston (The Episcopal Church in Haw) 999 Wilder Ave Apt 1204, Honolulu, HI 96822

LENZO, Alex (RG) 1525 33rd Cir SE, Rio Rancho, NM 87124

LEO, Agnes Patricia (The Episcopal Church in Haw) 665 Paopua Loop, Kailua, HI 96734

LEO, Denise Florence (Pa) 400 S Jackson St, Media, PA 19063

LEO, Jason (SO) 3780 Clifton Ave, Cincinnati, OH 45220

LEO, John (Be) 295 Brown St, Wilkes Barre, PA 18702

LEON, Luis (WA) 1525 H St NW, Washington, DC 20005

LEON, Sadoni (Hai) Eglesi Episcopal D'Haiti, Boite Postale 1309, Port-au-Prince, Haiti

LEONARD, Alan (USC) 254 Crooked Tree Dr, Inman, SC 29349

LEONARD, Jaime (Va) 8991 Brook Rd, McLean, VA 22102

LEONARD, Sean T (Mass) Saint Dunstans Episcopal Church, 18 Springdale Ave, Dover, MA 02030

LEONARD, Thomas Edgar (Az) 11 Avineda de la Herran, Tubac, AZ 85646

LEONARD-PASLEY, Tricia (Ct) 680 Racebrook Rd, Orange, CT 06477

LEONCZYK JR, Kenneth George (Dal) 425 D St SE Apt 304, Washington, DC 20003

LEONETTI, Stephen James (The Episcopal NCal) PO Box 6194, Vacaville, CA 95696

LEON-LOZANO, Cristobal (EcuC) Casilla 13-05-179, Manta, Ecuador

LEOPOLD, Bobby (ETenn) 1616 Read Ave, Chattanooga, TN 37408

LEPLEY, Rebecca Ruth Baird (EMich) 539 N William St, Marine City, MI 48039

LEROUX, Donald Francis (ND) 319 S 5th St, Grand Forks, ND 58201

Clergy List

LEROUX JR, Grant Meade (Ga) 5 Mooregate Square, Atlanta, GA 30327

LE ROY, Melinda Louise Perkins (WNC) 4 Flycatcher Way Unit 302, Arden, NC 28704

LERUD, Nathanael D (Ore) Trinity Episcopal Cathedral, 147 NW 19th Ave, Portland, OR 97209

LESCH, Robert Andrew (Minn) 828 5th St Ne, Minneapolis, MN 55413

LESESNE JR, Gray (Ind) 1100 W 42nd Street, Suite 235, Indianapolis, IN 46208

LESH, Ryan Edwin (NY) 7423 S Broadway, Red Hook, NY 12571

LESIEUR, Betsy Ann (RI) 200 Heroux Blvd # 2001, Cumberland, RI 02864

LESLIE, Jo Marie (Md) 130 W Seminary Ave, Lutherville, MD 21093

LESLIE, Joanne (Los) 1351 Grant St, Santa Monica, CA 90405

LESLIE III, Richard B (ECR) 520 Lobos Ave, Pacific Grove, CA 93950

LESSMANN, Mary (Dal) 8011 Douglas Avenue, Dallas, TX 75225

LESTER, Elmore William (LI) 1440 Tanglewood Pkwy, Fort Myers, FL 33919

LE SUEUR, Susan Dianne Lassey (NH) 18 Gaita Dr, Derry, NH 03038

LESWING, James Bartholomew (Chi) 1125 Franklin St, Downers Grove, IL 60515

LETHIN, Judith Lynn Wegman (Ak) 3509 Wentworth St, Anchorage, AK 99508

LETHIN, Kris Walter (Ak) 175 Main St, Seldovia, AK 99663

LEVENSALER, Kurt H (The Episcopal NCal) St Timothy's Church, 1550 Diablo Rd, Danville, CA 94526

LEVENSON JR, Russell J (Tex) St Martin's Episcopal Church, 717 Sage Rd, Houston, TX 77056

LEVESCONTE, Suzanne (SO) Trinity Episcopal Church, 115 N 6th St, Hamilton, OH 45011

LEVINE, Paul H (ECR) 720 S 3rd St Apt 5, San Jose, CA 95112

LEVY, Sandra Maria (Va) 9107 Donora Dr, Richmond, VA 23229

LEVY, William Turner (NY) 22121 Lanark St, Canoga Park, CA 91304

LEWALLEN, Jerrie (Ala) 174 Carpenter Cir, Sewanee, TN 37375

LEWALLEN, Theresa Cammarano (Va) St Albans Episcopal Church, 6800 Columbia Pike, Annandale, VA 22003

LEWELLEN, Donald S (Chi) 523 W Glen Ave, Peoria, IL 61614

LEWELLIS, Bill (Be) 3235 Clear Stream Dr, Whitehall, PA 18052

LEWIS III, Adam (Del) 115 E 90th St Apt 5C, New York, NY 10128

LEWIS III, Albert Davidson (ETenn) 340 Chamberlain Cove Rd, Kingston, TN 37763

LEWIS, Alice LaReign (EMich) 437n County Road 441, Manistique, MI 49854

LEWIS, Allen Lee (SD) 4705 S Wildwood Cir, Sioux Falls, SD 57105

LEWIS, Barbara (Tex) 1401 Calumet St. unit 12, Houston, TX 77004

LEWIS, Barbara Ann (Nev) 1511 Cardinal Peak Ln Unit 101, Las Vegas, NV 89144

LEWIS, Barbara J (Pa) 19115 Avalon Way, Lawrenceville, NJ 08648

LEWIS, Catherine Blanc (Roch) 7086 Salmon Creek Rd, Williamson, NY 14589

LEWIS, Charles Robert (Alb) 3711 Glen Oaks Manor Dr, Sarasota, FL 34232

LEWIS, Cynthia Jean (RG)

LEWIS, Earl James (Del) 1313 Lee St E Apt 112, Charleston, WV 25301

LEWIS, Edwin L (Ct) 1864 Post Rd, Darien, CT 06820

LEWIS, Ernest Loran (The Episcopal NCal) 640 Hawthorne Ln, Davis, CA 95616

LEWIS, Harold Thomas (Pgh) 315 Shady Ave, Pittsburgh, PA 15206

LEWIS JR, Irwin Morgan (SVa) 4449 N Witchduck Rd, Virginia Beach, VA 23455

LEWIS, Jason (Ky) 204 Monroe Ave, Belton, MO 64012

LEWIS, Jeffrey Clement (ECR) St George's School, PO Box 1910, Newport, RI 02840

LEWIS, John (WTex) St. Benedict's Workshop, 315 E Pecan St, San Antonio, TX 78205

LEWIS, John Walter (Me) 33 Knowlton St, Camden, ME 04843

LEWIS, Karen Burke (NJ) PO Box 605, Gladstone, NJ 07934

LEWIS, Karen Cichowski (Mich) 218 W Ottawa St, Lansing, MI 48933

LEWIS, Kate (Los) 265 W Sidlee St, Thousand Oaks, CA 91360

LEWIS, Katherine (Minn) 13000 St. Davids Rd, Minnetonka, MN 55305

LEWIS, Ken (Mass) 309 New York Ave, Jersey City, NJ 07307

LEWIS, Kenneth Rutherford (Ala) 708 Fairfax Dr, Fairfield, AL 35064

LEWIS, Laurie Ann (Kan) 3705 Edgemont St, Wichita, KS 67208

LEWIS, Lawrence Bernard (WMo) 415 Market Street, Osceola, MO 64776

LEWIS JR, Lloyd Alexander (LI) 5501 Seminary Rd Apt 812, Falls Church, VA 22041

LEWIS, Mabel (NY) 40 Barton St, Newburgh, NY 12550

LEWIS, Mark (Nwk) PO Box 93, Rensselaerville, NY 12147

LEWIS, Matthew W (Tenn) 900 Broadway, Nashville, TN 37203

LEWIS, Maurine Ann (Mil) 1717 Carl St, Fort Worth, TX 76103

LEWIS III, Philip Gregory (Oly)

LEWIS, Philip M (Spr) 420 N. Plum St., Havana, IN 62644

LEWIS, Richard H (CNY) none, none, NY 13442

LEWIS, Richard Irvin (Spr)

LEWIS, Robert Michael (Neb) 11251 SW Highway 484, Dunnellon, FL 34432

LEWIS, Sarah Elizabeth (Md) 576 Johnsville Rd, Eldersburg, MD 21784

LEWIS, Sarah V (CNY) PO Box 4353, Rome, NY 13442

LEWIS, Sharon (SwFla) 3773 Wilkinson Rd, Sarasota, FL 34233

LEWIS, Stephen Charles (Okla)

LEWIS, Theodore Longstreet (WA) 20235 Laurel Hill Way, Germantown, MD 20874

LEWIS, Thom (SVa) 2702 W Market St, Greensboro, NC 27403

LEWIS, Timothy J (LI) Po Box 264, Wainscott, NY 11975

LEWIS, Walter England (Nwk) 60 Dryden Rd, Montclair, NJ 07043

LEWIS, William Benjamin (WA) 14110 Royal Forest Ln, Silver Spring, MD 20904

LEWIS, William George (CFla) 442 Sanderling Dr, Indialantic, FL 32903

LEWIS-HEADDEN, Margaret (Oly) P.O. Box 1997, 1036 Golf Course Rd., Friday Harbor, WA 98250

LEWIS-THEERMAN, Kristina D (NY) 91 Church St, Seymour, CT 02630

LEY, James Lawrence (Pa) 101 Lydia Ln, West Chester, PA 19382

LEYS, Donovan I (LI) 20931 111 Avenue, Queens Village, NY 11429

L'HOMME, Robert Arthur (Chi) 8501 Timber Ln, Lafayette, IN 47905

L'HOMMEDIEU, J Gary (CFla) 1433 Fairview St, Orlando, FL 32804

LIANG, Fan-Wei (Tai)

LIAO KING-LING, Samuel (Tai) 1-105-7 Hangchow South Road, Taipei, Taiwan

LIBBEY, Elizabeth Weaver (USC) 1140 Fork Creek Rd, Saluda, NC 28773

LIBBEY, Robert Edward (USC) 16 Salisbury Drive #7410, Asheville, NC 28803

LIBBY, Glenn (Los) 835 W 34th Street 203, Los Angeles, CA 90089

LIBBY, Richardson Armstrong (Ct) 235 King George Street, Annapolis, MD 21401

LIBBY, Robert Meredith Gabler (SeFla) 200 Ocean Lane Dr Apt 408, Key Biscayne, FL 33149

LIBERATORE, James Vincent (Tex) 2535 Broadway St, Pearland, TX 77581

LICARI, Luigi (Cal) 904-9 Deer Park Crescent, Toronto, M4V 2C4, Canada

LIDDY, Jeffery T (Pa) 922 Main Street, Ste. 406, Lynchburg, VA 24504

LIEB, James Marcus (ECR) PO Box 293, Ben Lomond, CA 95005

LIEBER, William Louis (SanD) 8975 Lawrence Welk Dr Spc 77, Escondido, CA 92026

LIEBERT-HALL, Linda Ann (CFla) Shepherd of the Hills, 2540 W Norvell Bryant Hwy, Lecanto, FL 34461

LIEBLER, John (CFla) 2254 6th Avenue SE, Vero Beach, FL 32962

LIEF, Richard C (SanD) 3212 Eichenlaub St, San Diego, CA 92117

LIEM, Jennifer E (The Episcopal NCal) PO Box 855, Tahoe City, CA 96145

LIERLE, Deane Kae (Okla) 5037 E Via Montoya Dr, Phoenix, AZ 85054

LIESKE, Mark Stephen (Los) 3833 Artadi Dr, Spanish Springs, NV 89436

LIETZ, Dennis Eugene (Chi) 935 Knollwood Rd, Deerfield, IL 60015

LIGGETT JR, Jim (NwT) 3518 Hyde Park Ave, Midland, TX 79707

✠ **LIGHT**, Arthur Heath (SwVa) 2524 Wycliffe Ave Sw, Roanoke, VA 24014

LIGHTCAP, Torey Lynn (Kan) 835 SW Polk St, Topeka, KS 66612

LIGHTSEY, Pamela Sue Willis (Ga) 2700 Pebblewood Dr, Valdosta, GA 31602

LIGHTSEY, Richard Brian (NI) 602 W Superior St, Kokomo, IN 46901

LIGON, Michael Moran (EC) 517 Brandywine Cir, Greenville, NC 27858

LIKOWSKI, James Boyd (Ore) 2818 Lilac St, Longview, WA 98632

LIKWARTZ, Judy Saima (Ore) Po Box 51447, Casper, WY 82605

LILE JR, James Elbert (WMo)

LILES, Allison Sandlin (Ala) 6615 Saddleback Ct, Crozet, VA 22932

LILES, Eric (Va) 6605 Bevington Rd, Dallas, TX 75248

LILES, Linda Kathleen (NY) 120 W 69th St, New York, NY 10023

LILLARD SR, Eddie Lee (NJ) 1819 Columbus Ave, Neptune, NJ 07753

LILLEY, Lin S (RG) St. Alban's Episcopal Church, 1810 Elm St, El Paso, TX 79930

✠ **LILLIBRIDGE**, Gary Richard (WTex) PO Box 6885, San Antonio, TX 78209

LILLICRAPP, Arthur Reginald (The Episcopal NCal) 9401 Century Oaks Ln, Elk Grove, CA 95758

LILLIE, Paul Andrew (The Episcopal Church in Haw) 3311 Campbell Avenue, Honolulu, HI 96815

LILLIS, Rosemary (Roch) 1222 Sunset Ave, Asbury Park, NJ 07712

LILLPOPP, Donald R (Ct) 7314 Aloe Dr, Spring Hill, FL 34607

LILLVIS, David (Mich) 4708 State Park Hwy, Interlochen, MI 49643

LILLY, Beth Cobb (WNC) 2953 Ninth Tee Dr, Newton, NC 28658

LIM, You-Leng Leroy (Los) 12172 9th St, Garden Grove, CA 92840

LIMA, Roy Allen (Fla) 259 Duncan Dr, Crawfordville, FL 32327

LIMATO, Richard Paul (NY) 225 W 99th St, New York, NY 10025

LIMATU, Hector Roberto (Los) Chapantongo, Col Chapantongo Centro, Chapantongo, HID 42900, Mexico

LIMBACH, Mary Evelyn (Eau) 2034 Upper Ridge Road, Port Washington, WI 53074

LIMBURG, Megan (Va) St Christopher's School, 711 Saint Christophers Rd, Richmond, VA 23226

LIMEHOUSE III, Frank F (Ala) 3538 Lenox Rd, Birmingham, AL 35213

LIMO, John Edward (Los) 15757 Saint Timothy Rd, Apple Valley, CA 92307

LIMOZAINE, Bruce John (Ark) 30 Gettysburg N, Cabot, AR 72023

LIMPERT JR, Robert Hicks (Alb) 731 Old Piseco Road, Piseco, NY 12139

LIMPITLAW, John Donald (Ct) 140 Whidah Way, Wellfleet, MA 02667

LIN, Justin Chun-Min (Tai) 3/F, 262 Chung-Hsiao I Road, Hsin Hsing Dis, Kaohsiung, 800, Taiwan

LIN, Philip Li-Feng (Tai) 23 Wu-Chuan West Road Sec. 1, Taichung, TAIWAN, Taiwan

LIN, Samuel Ying-Chiu (Tai) #280 Fuhsing S Rd, Sec 2, C/O Diocese Of Taiwan, Taipei, Taiwan

LIN, Shu-Hwa (Tai) 1 F #29 Alley 6, Lane 168 Chung-her Rd, Keelung, 20347, Taiwan

LINARES-RIVERA, Ivette (PR)

LINBOOM, Bradley A. (Chi)

LINCOLN, Matt (WNY) Trinity Church, 371 Delaware Ave, Buffalo, NY 14202

LINCOLN, Richard (Los) 15114 Archwood St, Van Nuys, CA 91405

LINCOLN, Thomas Clarke (Nwk) 1156 Carolina Cir Sw, Vero Beach, FL 32962

LIND, Douglass Theodore (Ct) 17080 Harbour Point Dr, Apt 1017, Fort Myers, FL 33908

LIND, Tracey (O) 80 E. 252nd St., Euclid, OH 44132

LINDAHL, Rosa Vera (Ala)

LINDBERG, Robert Morris (CPa) 16 Winch Hill Rd, Swanzey, NH 03446

LINDELL, John Allen (Mont) 6629 Merryport Ln, Naples, FL 34104

LINDELL, Thomas Jay (Az) 4460 N Camino Del Rey, Tucson, AZ 85718

LINDEMAN, Eileen Cornish (RI) 830 Mohican Way, Redwood City, CA 94062

LINDEMAN, Matthew James (Ct) PO Box 400, Southport, CT 06890

LINDEMAN, Mitchell James (Cal) 139 Ocean Avenue, Cranston, RI 02905

LINDENBERG, Juliana T (NC) 231 N Church St, Rocky Mount, NC 27804

LINDER, Callie Maebelle (Mich) 2034 S 69th East Pl, Tulsa, OK 74112

LINDER, Mark (Ky) 2500 Crossings Blvd # 518, Bowling Green, KY 42104

LINDER, Philip Conrad (SC) 25 Otranto Lane, Columbia, SC 29209

LINDH-PAYNE, Kristofer Hans (Md) 2216 Pot Spring Rd., Timonium, MD 21093

LINDLEY, James B (Ore) 97955 Hallway Rd, PO Box 3190, Harbor, OR 97415

LINDLEY, Susie (Okla) 1202 W Elder Ave, Duncan, OK 73533

LINDQUIST, Mary Dail (Vt) 16 Bradley Ave, Brattleboro, VT 05301

LINDSAY JR, Spencer Hedden (La) 273 Monarch Dr Apt L-26, Houma, LA 70364

LINDSEY, Kenneth Lewis (Me) 649 W River Rd, Augusta, ME 04330

LINDSEY, Richard Carroll (SC) 3001 Meeting St, Hilton Head Island, SC 29926

LINDSLEY, James Elliott (NY) Maplegarth, Box 881, Millbrook, NY 12545

LINDSTROM JR, Donald Fredrick (CGC) 269 Rainbow Falls Road, Franklin, NC 28734

LINDSTROM, Justin (WTex) 510 Belknap Pl, San Antonio, TX 78212

LINDSTROM, Marjorie Dawson (Nwk) 91 Francisco Ave, Rutherford, NJ 07070

LINDWRIGHT, Philippa Elin (Ore) 3600 SW 117th Ave Apt 149, Beaverton, OR 97005

LINEBAUGH, Jonathan Andrew (CFla) 5910 NE 22nd Ter, Fort Lauderdale, FL 33308

LING, James K (Tai) 4149 N Kenmore Ave # 28, Chicago, IL 60613

LING, Steven (Ct) Trinity Episcopal Church, 345 Main St, Portland, CT 06480

LINGLE, Mark Duane (Ct) 503 Old Long Ridge Rd, Stamford, CT 06903

LINK, Mike (Nev) 11844 Orense Dr, Las Vegas, NV 89138

LINLEY, Eliza (ECR) 210 Lake Court, Aptos, CA 95003

LINNENBERG, Daniel (Roch) 267 Brooklawn Dr, Rochester, NY 14618

LINSCOTT, John Burton (NC) 830 Durham Rd, Wake Forest, NC 27587

LINSCOTT, Stephanie (Tex) 3838 N Braeswood Blvd, Apt 257, Houston, TX 77025

LINTON, Adam Stuart (Mass) 204 Monument Rd, Orleans, MA 02653

LINVILLE, Harriet Burton (ECR) 10372 S W Windwood Way, Portland, OR 97225

LINZEL, Claire Benedict (SwFla) 411 Nottinghill Gale St. #805, #1207, Arlington, TX 76014

LIOTTA, Thomas Mark (NY) 629 County Route 12, New Hampton, NY 10958

LIPP, Beth Ann (ND) P.O. Box 1241, Bismarck, ND 58502

LIPPART, Thomas Edward (NMich) 5207 Eleuthra Circle, Vero Beach, FL 32967

LIPPE, Amanda J (ETenn) PO Box 29, Norris, TN 37828

LIPPITT, Dudley Hand (Ga) 1704 11th Ave, Albany, GA 31707

LIPSCOMB III, C(Harles) Lloyd (SwVa) 501 V E S Rd Apt B513, Lynchburg, VA 24503

LIPSCOMB III, John W (CFla) 317 S Mary St, Eustis, FL 32726

LIPSCOMB, Leonard Scott (Md) 301 A St SE, Washington, DC 20003

LIPSCOMB, Steve (Kan) 3324 NW Bent Tree Ln, Topeka, KS 66618

LIRIANO MARTINEZ, Jorge Antonely (NJ) 3050 River Rd, Camden, NJ 08105

LIRO, Judith Reagan (Tex) 4301 N I H 35, Austin, TX 78722

LITMAN, Eric Robert (Mass) 1 Linden St, Quincy, MA 02170

LITSEY, Kim Jeanne (Ct) 915 Main St, South Glastonbury, CT 06073

✠ **LITTLE II**, Edward Stuart (NI) 52231 Brendon Hills Dr, Granger, IN 46530

LITTLE, Geoffery Alan (Ct) 358 Lenox Street, New Haven, CT 06513

LITTLE, Harry Robert (CNY) 22366 County Route 42, Carthage, NY 13619

LITTLE, Tracie L (EMich) 543 Michigan Ave, Marysville, MI 48040

LITTLEFIELD, Jeff (Ore) 11265 SW Cabot St, Beaverton, OR 97005

LITTLEJOHN, Luchy (Tex) 6307 Hickory Holw, Windcrest, TX 78239

LITTLEJOHN, Norman Richard (Alb)

LITTLEPAGE, Dorothella Michel (Mass) 74 S Common St, Lynn, MA 01902

LITTLETON, William Harvey (Ga) PO Box 20633, Saint Simons Island, GA 31522

LITTMAN, Val J (Eur) Altos Del Maria,, 314 Toscana II, Sora, Panama

LITTRELL, James H (Pa) 339 Dover Rd, South Newfane, VT 05351

LITWINSKI, Anthony (Eur) Mauritiusplatz 1, Wiesbaden, MI D65183, Germany

LITZENBERGER, Caroline Jae (Ore) 1605 NE Clackamas St Apt 300C, Portland, OR 97232

LIU, Ting-Hua (Tai) I-105-7 Hang Chou South Road, Silo, Taiwan

LIVELY, James W (SwVa) 11610 Chantilly Ct, Clermont, FL 34711

LIVELY, Paula Kay (WMo) 601 E Benton St, Monett, MO 65708

LIVERMORE, Charles Whittier (ETenn) 7604 Windwood Dr, Powell, TN 37849

LIVINGSTON, Bill (Miss) 37 Sheffield Place, Brevard, NC 28712

LIVINGSTON, Diane Howard (WNC) 37 Sheffield Place, Brevard, NC 28712

LIVINGSTON, James John (Los) 31641 La Novia Ave, San Juan Capistrano, CA 92675

LIVINGSTON, James Leo (NMich) 3135 County Road 456, Skandia, MI 49885

LIZ LOPEZ, Ramon A (PR) PO Box 6814, Elizabeth, NJ 07202

LJUNGGREN, M Lorraine (NC) 5400 Crestview Rd, Raleigh, NC 27609

LJUNGGREN, Timothy Merle (Mont) 62 Greenway Dr, Goshen, IN 46526

LLERENA FIALLOS, Angel Polivio (EcuC) Apartado 89, Guaranda, Provincia De Bolivar, Ecuador

LLOYD, Bonnie Jean (Tenn) 1420 Wilson Pike, Brentwood, TN 37027

LLOYD, Dennis (Pa) 811 Dover Rd, Wynnewood, PA 19096

LLOYD, Elizabeth Anne (Chi) 322 Farragut St, Park Forest, IL 60466

LLOYD, Emily (WA) 487 Hudson St, New York, NY 10014

LLOYD, James Edward (NJ) Apdo Postal 803, La Cristina 50-5, Chapala, JAL 45920, Mexico

LLOYD, John Janney (NY) 115 Iroquois Rd, Yonkers, NY 10710

LLOYD, Kevin (RI) 67 Mount Hope Ave, Jamestown, RI 02835

LLOYD, Lucia Kendall (Va) PO Box 158, Tappahannock, VA 22560

LLOYD, Margaret Ewing (Mass) 115 Standish Ave, Plymouth, MA 02360

LLOYD, Robert Baldwin (SwVa) 3204 Mathews Ln., Blacksburg, VA 24060

LLOYD III, Samuel Thames (Mass) 206 Clarendon St, Boston, MA 02116

LLUMIGUANO AREVALO, Nancy (EcuC) Sarmiento, Quito, Ecuador

LO, Kwan (Los) 133 E Graves Ave, Monterey Park, CA 91755

LOBBAN, Andy (Cal) Grace Cathedral, 1100 California St, San Francisco, CA 94108

LOBDELL, Gary Thomas (Oly) 2610 E Section St Unit 92, Mount Vernon, WA 98274

LOBS, Donna Burkard (CFla) 128 Legacy Dr, Advance, NC 27006

LOBS III, George Richard (CFla) 128 Legacy Dr, Advance, NC 27006

LOCH, C Louanne (Fla) Holy Trinity Episcopal Church, 100 NE 1st St, Gainesville, FL 32601

LOCH, Jerry Lynn (Chi) 446 Somonauk St, Sycamore, IL 60178

LOCHER, Elizabeth A (Va) Msalato Theological College, PO Box 264, Dodoma, Tanzania

LOCHNER, Charlie (NJ) 2106 5th Ave, Spring Lake, NJ 07762

LOCK, John Mason (NJ) Trinity Episcopal Church, 65 W Front St, Red Bank, NJ 07701

LOCKE, Carol Ann (Los) 61 Painter St Apt 1, Pasadena, CA 91103

LOCKE, Kathleen Newell (Nwk) 15 Norwood Ave, Summit, NJ 07901

LOCKE, William Russell (RI) 63 Pidge Avenue, Pawtucket, RI 02860

LOCKETT, Donna A (CGC) 102 Shadow Ln, Troy, AL 36079

LOCKETT, Harold J (At)

LOCKETT, Tina (USC) Trinity Episcopal Cathedral, 1100 Sumter St, Columbia, SC 29201

LOCKLEY, Linda Sue (SwFla) 6006 Braden Run, Bradenton, FL 34202

LOCKWOOD II, Frank Robert (Alb) 14 Spencer Blvd, Coxsackie, NY 12051

LOCKWOOD, Marcia (ECR) PO Box 345, Carmel Valley, CA 93924

LODDER, Herbert Kingsley (Md) 130 W Seminary Ave, Lutherville, MD 21093

LODER, Debra Jayne (Az)

LODWICK, James Nicholas (NY) 925 W Washington St, South Bend, IN 46601

LOESCHER, Candyce Jean (Ky) St. Mark's Episcopal Church, 2822 Frankfort Ave, Louisville, KY 40206

LOEWE, Richard (Los) 1907 W West Wind, Santa Ana, CA 92704

LOFGREN, Claire (NY) St. Joseph of Arimathea, 2172 Saw Mill River Road, White Plains, NY 10607

LOGAN, Christie Larson (Oly) 720 E Road Of Tralee, Shelton, WA 98584

LOGAN, Jeffery Allen (FtW) Psc 817 Box 43, Fpo, AE 09622

LOGAN JR, John Alexander (Tex) 2808 Sunset Blvd, Houston, TX 77005

LOGAN, Linda Marie (CNY) 405 N Madison Ave, Pierre, SD 57501

LOGAN JR, Willis (SwVa) 100 W Jefferson St, Charlottesville, VA 22902

LOGAN, Yvonne Luree (NY) 1185 Park Ave Apt 12j, New York, NY 10128

LOGSDON, Tami Davis (NwT) 4207 Emil Ave, Amarillo, TX 79106

LOGUE, Frank (Ga) 111 Clinton Ct, Saint Marys, GA 31558

LOGUE, Mary Ann Willson (Ct) 173 Livingston St, New Haven, CT 06511

LOHMANN, John J (Mich) 296 Ackerson Lake Dr., Jackson, MI 49201

LOHSE, Dana May (Wyo) Po Box 291, Kaycee, WY 82639

LOKEN, Gail Mitchell (Ak) 5101 Omalley Rd, Anchorage, AK 99507

LOKEY, Michael Paul (Eas) 29618 Polks Rds, Princess Anne, MD 21853

LOLCAMA, Thirza A (Oly) 10630 Gravelly Lake Dr SW, Lakewood, WA 98499

LOLK, Otto Lothar Manfred (Pa) 3135 Clark Ave, Trevose, PA 19053

LOMAS, Bruce (Mass) 3 Gould St, Melrose, MA 02176

LOMBARDO, Janet Marie Vogt (NH) 67 Ridge Rd, Concord, NH 03301

LONDON, Daniel Deforest (The Episcopal NCal) 2451 Ridge Rd, Berkeley, CA 94709

LONDON, Gary Loo (Los) 122 S California Ave, Monrovia, CA 91016

LONE, Jose Francisco (Hond)

LONERGAN, Kathleen Guthrie (Mass) 119 Washington Street, c/o St James Episcopal Church, Groveland, MA 01834

LONERGAN, Wallace Gunn (Ida) 812 E Linden St, Caldwell, ID 83605

LONG, Amy Lauren (WK)

LONG, Benjamin Isaac (Tex) 1941 Webberville Rd, Austin, TX 78721

LONG, Beth (At) 165 Meredith Ridge Rd, Athens, GA 30605

LONG, Betty Ann (Ct) 2 Viking Ln, Sandwich, MA 02563

LONG, Cynthia A (The Episcopal NCal) 7041 Verdure Way, Elk Grove, CA 95758

LONG, Eric (SwVa) PO Box 257, Roanoke, VA 24002

LONG, Gail (SVa) 2441 Tuxedo Pl, Albany, GA 31707

LONG II, John Michael (Neb) 1615 Brent Blvd, Lincoln, NE 68506

LONG, Michael Richardson (Chi) Amargura 2, San Miguel De Allende, San Miguel de Allende, GUA 37700, Mexico

LONG, Shirley Dube (WNC) Po Box 72, Deep Gap, NC 28618

LONG, Thomas Mcmillen (Colo) 4155 E Jewell Ave Ste 1117, Denver, CO 80222

LONGACRE, Seth T (SanD) 3508 Alander Court, Carlsbad, CA 92010

LONGBOTTOM, Rob (CFla) 3891 Cedar Hammock Trl, Saint Cloud, FL 34772

LONGE, Neal Patrick (Alb) 58 Reber St, Colonie, NY 12205

✠ **LONGEST**, Charles Lindsay (Md) 7200 3rd Ave., C-035, Sykesville, MD 21784

LONGHI, Anthony Peter (Chi) 1850 Landre Ct, Burlington, WI 53105

LONGHITANO, Maria Vittoria (Eur) via Benevenuto Cellini 24, Corsico MI, 20094, Italy

LONGSTAFF, Thomas Richmond Willis (Me) 39 Pleasant St, Waterville, ME 04901

LONGSTRETH, William Morris (Pa) 1146 Handview Circle, Pottstown, PA 19464

LONSWAY, Rose Anne (O) St Peter's Episcopal Church, 45 W Winter St, Delaware, OH 43015

LONTO, Michael J (WNY) 99 Wildwood Av, Salamanca, NY 14779

LOOMIS, Julia Dorsey (SVa) 416 Court St, Portsmouth, VA 23704

LOOP, Dick (Ore) 36489 Florence Ct., Astoria, OR 97103

LOOR CEDENO, Mariana De Jesus (Litoral Ecu) 22 Ava & 3er Callejon P, Bahia De Caraquez, Ecuador

LOPER, Jerald Dale (Minn) 1524 Country Club Rd, Albert Lea, MN 56007

LOPEZ, Abel E (Los) 2396 Mohawk St Unit 7, Pasadena, CA 91107

LOPEZ, Antonio (Nev) 832 N Eastern Ave, Las Vegas, NV 89101

LOPEZ, Bienvenido Taveras (DR (DomRep)) Iglesia Episcopal Divina Providencia, Calle Marcos Del Rosario #39, Republica Dominicana, Dominican Republic

LOPEZ JR, Eddie (Ct) 35 S Franklin St, Wilkes Barre, PA 18701

LOPEZ, Mary Alice (SwFla) 504 Columbia Dr, Tampa, FL 33606

LOPEZ, Oscar Obdulio (Hond) 12 Calle B, 10-11 Ave SE, Casa No 1023, San Pedro Sula, Honduras

LOPEZ, Pedro (Tex) Saint Peter's Church, 705 Williams St, Pasadena, TX 77506

LOPEZ JR, Ramiro Eduardo (WTex) 1247 Vista Del Juez, San Antonio, TX 78216

LOPEZ, Ricardo Ramirez (NwT) 907 Adams Ave, Odessa, TX 79761

LOPEZ, Sarah (Ia)

LOPEZ, Sunny (Chi) 3115 W Jerome St, Chicago, IL 60645

LOPEZ, Uriel (Tex) 40 Center St, Elgin, IL 60120

LOPEZ-CHAVERRA, Hector (SwFla) Episc Ch St. Francis, P.O. Box 9332, Tampa, FL 33674

LOPEZ ZAMUDIO, Rocio Patricia (Okla) PO Box 10722, Midwest City, OK 73140

LOPOSER, Ellen Fogg (Spok) St Andrew's Episcopal Church, 2404 N Howard St, Spokane, WA 99205

LOR, Cher John (Minn) Holy Apostles Episcopal Church, 2200 Minnehaha Ave E, Saint Paul, MN 55119

LOR, Nor Annie (Minn)

LORA, Juan B (Ct) 16 Paul St, Danbury, CT 06810

LORD, James Raymond (Ky) 3001 Myrshine Dr, Pensacola, FL 32506

LORD, Mary George (NwPa) 2425 Glendale Ave, Erie, PA 16510

LORD, Philip Warren (WNY) 5013 Van Buren Rd, Dunkirk, NY 14048

LORD, Richard (Va) 543 Beulah Road Northeast, Vienna, VA 22180

LORD, Robert (CFla) 1312 Bridgeport Drive, Winter Park, FL 32789

LORENSON, Ruth Lorraine (LI) 9 Warton Pl, Garden City, NY 11530

LORENZ, Constance (LI) 49 Hudson Watch Dr, Ossining, NY 10562

LORENZE, James Dennis (Eau) 2304 Country Club Ln, Eau Claire, WI 54701

LORENZETTI, Dominick J (Episcopal SJ)

LORING III, Richard Tuttle (Mass) 114 Badger Ter, Bedford, MA 01730

LORING, William Delano (Ct) 15 Pleasant Drive, Danbury, CT 06811

LOSCH, Richard Rorex (Ala) Po Box 1560, Livingston, AL 35470

LOUA, Cece Alfred-S (Mich) 1021 Norwich Drive, Troy, MI 48084

LOUD JR, Johnson D (Minn) 740 Shane Park Cir Apt 2, Prescott, WI 54021

LOUDEN, Molly O'Neill (Ct) 37 Gin Still Ln, West Hartford, CT 06107

LOUDENSLAGER, Samuel Charles (Ark) 20000 Hwy 300-Spur, Bigelow, AR 72016

LOUGHRAN JR, Eugene James (SwFla) 633 Coquina Court, Fort Myers, FL 33908

LOUGHREN, James Patrick (Dal) 4879 Lake Shore Dr, Bolton Landing, NY 12814

LOUIS, Richard Mortimer (Nwk) 2395 Quill Ct, Mahwah, NJ 07430

LOUIS DEAN SKIPPER, James Louis Dean (Ala) 1426 Gilmer Ave, Montgomery, AL 36104

LOUISE, Sister Catherine (Mass) 17 Louisburg Sq, Boston, MA 02108

LOUTREL, William Frederic (Ct) 1090 Ridge Rd, Hamden, CT 06517

✠ **LOUTTIT**, Henry (Ga) 611 E Bay St, Savannah, GA 31401

LOUTTIT SR, James William (CFla) 331 Lake Ave, Maitland, FL 32751

LOVE, Leon Lewis (CNY) 5 Gail Dr, Waverly, NY 14892

✠ **LOVE**, William Howard (Alb) PO Box 211, Lake Luzerne, NY 12846

LOVEJOY, Margaret Helen (WLa)

LOVEKIN, Arthur Adams (RG) 10501 Lagrima De Oro Rd NE, Apt 4208, Albuquerque, NM 87111

LOVELACE, David (CPa) 140 N Beaver St, York, PA 17401

LOVELADY, Eldwin M (Oly) 3700 14th Ave SE, Unit 3, Olympia, WA 98501

LOVELESS, Phillip Lyman (SanD) Episcopal Community Center, 2083 Sunset Cliffs Blvd, San Diego, CA 92107

LOVETT, G David (ETenn) 7900 High Heath, Knoxville, TN 37919

LOVING, John Harnish (NwT) 8009 Ladera Verde, Austin, TX 78739

LOW, James Robert (Ct) 60 Shadagee Rd Unit 22, Saco, ME 04072

LOW, Melvin Leslie (Ia) 1310 Sierra Dr NE Apt 14, Cedar Rapids, IA 52402

LOW, Raymond Albert (Mass) 5 Buttonwood Rd, Marshfield, MA 02050

LOW, Salin Miller (Ct) 12 Meadowview Ct, Canton, CT 06019

LOWE, Dianne Louise (Spok) St James Episcopal Church, 1410 NE Stadium Way, Pullman, WA 99163

LOWE, Edward Charles (Ga) PO Box 168, Saint Marys, GA 31558

LOWE JR, Eugene Yerby (NY) 624 Colfax St, Evanston, IL 60201

LOWE, Harold Chapin (Dal) 2212 Saint Andrews, McKinney, TX 75070

LOWE JR, J Fletcher (Del) 1600 Westbrook Ave Apt G-27, Richmond, VA 23227

LOWE, John Leon (Ind) 200 Glennes Ln Apt 205, Dunedin, FL 34698

LOWE, Lori (Chi) 5116 W Malibu Ct, McHenry, IL 60050

LOWE, Robert Steven (Chi) 2009 Regency Ct, Geneva, IL 60134

LOWE JR, Thomas (RG) Episcopal Church of St. John, P.O. Box 449, Alamogordo, NM 88310

LOWE, Walter James (At) 1647 N Rock Springs Rd NE, Atlanta, GA 30324

LOWERY, Don (NC) 210 S Chestnut St, Henderson, NC 27536

LOWERY, Hermon Lee (Ga) 2705 Michael Rd, Albany, GA 31721

LOWREY, Edward Sager (NwPa) Box 54, 107 Harvey Road, Foxburg, PA 16036

LOWREY III, Pierce Lang (At) 3830 Randall Farm Rd, Atlanta, GA 30339

LOWRY, David B (LI) Po Box 51777, New Orleans, LA 70151

LOWRY, Robert Lynn (Tex) Trinity in the Woodland Texas, 3901 S Panther Creek Dr, The Woodlands, TX 77381

LOWRY III, William M (Ark) PO Box 224, Tunica, MS 38676

LOW-SKINNER, Debbie (Cal) 137 Redding Rd Apt C, Campbell, CA 95008

LOY, Reed J (NH) 885 Shore Rd, Cape Elizabeth, ME 04107

LOYA, Craig William (Neb) 113 N 18th St, Omaha, NE 68102

LOYD, Janet Ellen (Oly) 56738 Sturgeon Rd, Darrington, WA 98241

LOYD, Michael Corman (Kan) 8021 W 21st St N, Wichita, KS 67205

LOYOLA, Leo (The Episcopal Church in Haw) Diocese o f Hawaii, 229 Queen Emma Sq, Honolulu, HI 96813

LOZAMA, Abiade (Hai)

LOZANO, Kathleen Barbara (Los) St Matthias Episcopal Church, 7056 Washington Ave, Whittier, CA 90602

LUAL, Anderia Arok (Az) Diocese of Arizona, 114 W Roosevelt St, Phoenix, AZ 85003

LUBELFELD, Nicholas (Va) 4460 Edan Mae Ct, Annandale, VA 22003

LUBIN, Gary Robert (SO)

LUCAS, Alison C (ECR) 19315 Vineyard Ln, Saratoga, CA 95070

LUCAS, Jason Bryan (Minn) St. Edward Episcopal Church, 865 Ferndale Rd. N, Wayzata, MN 55391

LUCAS, Jeremy P (Ore) 1060 Chandler Rd, Lake Oswego, OR 97034

LUCAS, Kimberly Danielle (WA) 1830 Connecticut Ave NW, Washington, DC 20009

LUCAS, Mary Louise (Mass) 136 Bay Street #501, Hamilton, L8P 3H8, Canada

LUCAS, Paul Nahoa (The Episcopal Church in Haw) 47-074 Lihikai Dr, Kaneohe, HI 96744

LUCAS, Rigal (Hai) Box 1309, Port-Au-Prince, Haiti

LUCAS, T Stewart (Md) Church of the Nativity, 419 Cedarcroft Rd, Baltimore, MD 21212

LUCAS, Wanda Beth (Ga) 524 Suncrest Blvd, Savannah, GA 31410

LUCENT, Robert Brian (SanD) 629 Judson St, Escondido, CA 92027

LUCEY, David (Va) 399 Hope St., Bristol, RI 02809

LUCHS, Lewis Richard (Chi) 6417 81st St, Cabin John, MD 20818

LUCK, Diana Nelson (Dal) 6912 Merrilee Ln, Dallas, TX 75214

LUCK, G Thomas (CNY) 310 Montgomery St., Syracuse, NY 13202

LUCK JR, George Edmund (Dal) 6912 Merrilee Ln, Dallas, TX 75214

LUCKENBACH, David Andrew (Tex) 1709 S College Ave, Tyler, TX 75701

LUCKETT JR, David Stafford (Miss) 4241 Otterlake Cove, Niceville, FL 32578

LUCKEY, Marion Isabelle Aiken (NMich) 1531 Vardon Rd, Munising, MI 49862

LUCKEY III, Thomas Hannan (NMich) E9430 E. Munising Ave. #2, Munising, MI 49862

LUCKRITZ, Denzil John (Chi) 558 Kingsway Dr, Aurora, IL 60506

LUDBROOK, Helen Christine (Mo) 1422 Lawnwood Dr, Des Peres, MO 63131

LUECKENHOFF, James Joseph (WLa) 1518 Griffith St, Lake Charles, LA 70601

LUECKERT, Diana Rowe (The Episcopal NCal) 4800 Olive Oak Way, Carmichael, CA 95608

LUEDDE, Christopher S (Roch) 31 Kitty Hawk Dr, Pittsford, NY 14534

LUETHE, Robin Lewis (Oly) 789 Highway 603, Chehalir, WA 98532

LUFKIN, Alison C (Colo) PO Box 1305, Leadville, CO 80461

LUFKIN, George S (Colo) PO Box 243, Leadville, CO 80461

LUGER, Virginia M (ND) 821 N 4th St Apt 3, Bismarck, ND 58501

LUGO, Beverley Lee (Ida) 411 10th Ave S, Nampa, ID 83651

LUHRING, Peggy Williams (SVa) 4449 N Witchduck Rd, Virginia Beach, VA 23455

LUI, David Suikwei (Cal) 1011 Harrison St # 202, Oakland, CA 94607

LUJAN, Mary (EO) Po Box 25, Hood River, OR 97031

LUKANICH, Emily A (Colo) Christ Episcopal Church, PO Box 1000, Vail, CO 81658

LUKAS, Arlene (WNC) 416 N Haywood St, Waynesville, NC 28786

LUKAS, Randolph Edgar (Alb) PO Box 827, New Lebanon, NY 12125

LUKENS JR, Alexander M (Colo) 536 Seneca Cir, Walsenburg, CO 81089

LUKENS, Ann Pierson (Oly) 2015 Killarney Way, Bellevue, WA 98004

LUKENS, Matthew M (Mich) 183 Alala Rd, Kailua, HI 96734

LULEY, William Tracy (Mo) 1101 Sulphur Spring Rd, Manchester, MO 63021

LULLO, Milania (WNY) 200 Cazenovia St, Buffalo, NY 14210

LUMBARD, Carolyn Mary Dunsmore (Roch) 326 Frederick Douglas St, Rochester, NY 14608

LUMLEY, Dale Allen (WK) 906 W Wheat Ave, Ulysses, KS 67880

LUNA JR, Eulalio Gallardo (WTex) 234 W Mariposa Dr, San Antonio, TX 78212

LUNA, Julie (Minn) 60 Kent St, Saint Paul, MN 55102

LUND, Joseph (WA) 70381 Placerville Rd, Rancho Mirage, CA 92270

LUND, Judith Ann (Ark) 8280 Spanker Ridge Dr, Bentonville, AR 72712

LUND, Virginia U Sapienza (Mil) 1101 Greenough Dr W, Apt. E-6, Missoula, MT 59802

LUNDELIUS, Carolyn Sparks (WA) 5801 Nicholson Lane Apt 1923, Rockville, MD 20852

LUNDEN, Michael Carl (NY) 118 S Church St, Goshen, NY 10924

LUNDGREN, Linda Lou (The Episcopal Church in Haw) 8 3rd St, Proctor, MN 55810

LUNDGREN, Richard John (Chi) 13129 Lake Mary Dr., Plainfield, IL 60585

LUNDIN, George Edward (Miss) 705 Southern Ave, Hattiesburg, MS 39401

LUNDQUIST, Rob (WNC) 419 Turnpike Rd, Mills River, NC 28759

LUNNUM, Lindsay (LI) Zion Episcopal Church, 243-01 Northern Blvd, Douglaston, NY 11363

LUNTSFORD, Sharon Lorene (ND) Po Box 18, Alexander, ND 58831

LUONI, Rick (CFla) 2499 N Westmoreland Dr, Orlando, FL 32804

LUPFER JR, William B (NY) 120 Broadway Fl 38, New York, NY 10271

LUPTON JR, James Harold (Ark) 241 Riverview St., Belhaven, NC 27810

LUSIGNAN, Louise Jennet (WA) 10450 Lottsford Road, Mitchellville, MD 20721

LUSK JR, Karl (Ky) 236 Ridgeview Dr, New Haven, KY 40051

LUTAS, Donald Mckenzie (Mich) 6114 28th St, Detroit, MI 48210

LUTES, Kathy (Mil) 2224 Cedar Dr, Rapid City, SD 57702

LUTHER, Carol Luther (Cal) St Paul's Episcopal School, 46 Montecito Ave., Oakland, CA 94610

LUTTER, Linda F (Chi) 5725 Stearns School Rd, Gurnee, IL 60031

LUTTRELL, John Sidney (LI) 295 Old Kings Hwy, Downingtown, PA 19335

LUTZ, Alison W (NY) National Route 3, Cange Haiti, Haiti

LUTZ, Bill (CNY) 82 Scott Ave, Elmira, NY 14905

LUTZ, Randall Robert (RG) 2365 Brother Abdon Way, Santa Fe, NM 87505

LUTZ, Richard Herbert (LI) Cashelmara 40, 23200 Lake Road, Bay Village, OH 44140

LUTZ, Ruth Jeanne (RG) 1330 Renoir Ct., Las Cruces, NM 88007

LWEBUGA-MUKASA, Katherine N (WNY) 168 Schimwood Ct, Getzville, NY 14068

LYCETT, Horace Abbott (Colo) 1223 Center St, Goodland, KS 67735

LYGA, Robert Michael (Minn) N36457 State Road 93/121, Independence, WI 54747

LYLE, Jerry (Tex) St. Joseph's Episcopal Church, PO Box 797, Salado, TX 76571

LYLE, Patsy Rushworth (La) 19344 Links Ct, Baton Rouge, LA 70810

LYLE, Randall Robert (Ia) 2350 Glass Rd NE, Cedar Rapids, IA 52402

LYLE, William Edward (SO) 1547 Stratford Dr, Kent, OH 44240

LYMAN, Janyce Rebecca (Cal) 115 Sheridan Way, Woodside, CA 94062

LYNCH JR, Bobby (WNC) Po Box 561, Rutherfordton, NC 28139

LYNCH, Daniel Luke (WVa) 123 Hidden Valley Ests, Scott Depot, WV 25560

LYNCH, David (WMo) 16808 S State Route D, Belton, MO 64012

LYNCH, Gwynn (SanD) 13319 Fallen Leaf Rd, Poway, CA 92064

LYNCH, John J (RI) 4109 Big Bethel Rd, Tabb, VA 23693

LYNCH, Pam (EMich) 525 Weiss Rd, Gaylord, MI 49735

LYNCH, Suzanne Mchugh Stryker (WMo) 1342 S Ventura Ave, Springfield, MO 65804

LYNCH, William David (NC) 8849 Ray Rd, Raleigh, NC 27613

LYNN, Connor Kay (Los) 1902 Park Ave Apt 316, Los Angeles, CA 90026

LYNN, Jackie (Chi)

LYON, Don (CFla) 1628 Bent Oaks Blvd, DeLand, FL 32724

LYON IV, James Fraser (USC) 1512 Blanding St, Columbia, SC 29201

LYON, Lauren (Ia) Trinity Church, 320 E College St, Iowa City, IA 52240

LYON, Susan Loy (Ark) 1000 N Mississippi St, Little Rock, AR 72207

LYONS JR, James Hershel (Nev) All Saint's Episcopal Church, 4201 W Washington Ave, Las Vegas, NV 89107

LYONS, Leroy A (NJ) 1208 Prospect Ave, Plainfield, NJ 07060

LYONS, Patricia M (WA)

LYTHGOE, Amy U (Colo)

LYTLE, Ashley Alexandra Gabriella (At) 515 E Ponce De Leon Ave, Decatur, GA 30030

M

MAAS, Benjamin Wells (Va) 1374 S Brook St, Louisville, KY 40208

MAAS, Jan Alfred (NY) 2121 Jamieson Ave Unit 1909, Alexandria, VA 22314

MABERRY, Lois Rayner (WLa)

MACARTHUR II, Robert Stuart (Mo) 334 Maple Ridge Road, Center Sandwich, NH 03227

MACATEE, Louise Mae (Los) Church of the Epiphany, 5450 Churchwood Dr, Oak Park, CA 91377

MACAULEY JR, Robert Conover (Vt) 175 Hills Point Road, Charlotte, VT 05445

MACBETH, Andy (WTenn) 1640 Harbert Ave, Memphis, TN 38104

MACCOLL, Craig (Colo) 5876 E Kettle Pl, Centennial, CO 80112

MACCONNELL, James Stuart (Wyo) 403 15th St #1, Dallas Center, IA 50063

MACDONALD, Daniel (Mass) 147 Concord Rd, Lincoln, MA 01773

MACDONALD, David Roberts (LI) 253 Glen Ave, Sea Cliff, NY 11579

MACDONALD, Gilbert John (EMich) 331 West Mill Street, Oscoda, MI 48750

MACDONALD, Heyward Hunter (Md) 2551 Summit Ridge Trail, Charlottesville, VA 22911

MACDONALD, Jean A (Vt) 7 N College St, Montpelier, VT 05602

MACDONALD, John Alexander (Spok)

MACDONALD, Linda Jean (Mich) 1780 Nemoke Trl, Haslett, MI 48840

✠ **MACDONALD**, Mark Lawrence (Ak) 2228 Penrose Ln., Fairbanks, AK 99709

MACDONALD, Susan Savage (Va) 1527 Senseny Rd, Winchester, VA 22602

MACDONALD, Terrence Cameron (O) 207 Weed St, New Canaan, CT 06840

MACDONALD, Walter Young (Mich) 2796 Page Ave, Ann Arbor, MI 48104

MACDONELL, Alexander Harrison (Nwk) 216 Heath Vlg, Hackettstown, NJ 07840

MACDOUGALL, Matthew Bradstock (NwPa) 343 E Main St, Youngsville, PA 16371

MACDOWELL, Barry Scott (Ind) 138 S 18th St, Richmond, IN 47374

MACDUFFIE, Bruce Lincoln (CNY) 836 5th Ave. West, Dickinson, ND 58601

MACEK, Kathy (EO) PO Box 1001, La Grande, OR 97850

MAC EWEN, Suzanne Marie (Wyo) Po Box 137, Evanston, WY 82931

MACFARLANE, Robert John (Chi) 3724 Farr Ave, Fairfax, VA 22030

MACFIE JR, Tom (Tenn) 117 Carruthers Rd, Sewanee, TN 37375

MACGILL, Martha (Md)

MACGILL III, William D (WVa) 5909 cedar landing rd, Wilmington, NC 28409

MACGOWAN JR, Kenneth Arbuthnot (Colo) 3440 S Jefferson St Apt 1136, Falls Church, VA 22041

MACGREGOR, Laird S (WK) 322 S Ash St, Mcpherson, KS 67460

MACIAS PEREZ, Franklin Oswaldo (Litoral Ecu) CALLE AMARILIS FUENTES N, 603 Y CALLE D, GUAYAQUIL, 09-01-5250, Ecuador

MACINNIS, Elyn G (NY) 64 Memorial Rd, Providence, RI 02906

MACINTIRE, Morgan Montelepre (La) 2050 Bert Kouns, Shreveport, LA 71118

MACINTOSH, Neil Keith (Kan) Charismead, 11A Browns Road, The Oaks, NSW, 2570, Australia

MACK, Arthur Robert (Mich) 13 Dover Ln., Hendersonville, NC 28739

MACK, Ross Julian (NI) Po Box 462, Valparaiso, IN 46384

MACKAY III, Donald (Oly) 9727 NE Juanita Dr, Unit #311, Kirkland, WA 98034

MACKE, Beth (Ind) 4713 Housebridge Rd, Corydon, KY 42406

MACKENDRICK, Gary Winfred (Ore) 3014 Main Street, Forest Grove, OR 97116

MACKENZIE JR, Albert Harold (SO) 37 Abbey Ln, Washington, NC 27889

MACKENZIE, A(Lexander) James (The Episcopal NCal) 3988 NW Walnut Ct., Corvallis, OR 97330

MACKENZIE, Andrea Shortal (ECR) 13601 Saratoga Ave, Saratoga, CA 95070

MACKENZIE, John Anderson Ross (WNY) 11819 Eastkent Sq, Richmond, VA 23238

MACKENZIE, Jon (NH) 52 Brick Kiln Rd, Chelmsford, MA 01824

MACKENZIE, Katharine Helen (Los) 948 W Sierra Nevada Way, Orange, CA 92865

MACKENZIE, Lester V (Los) 428 Park Ave, Laguna Beach, CA 92651

MACKENZIE, Mary (Oly) 16060 Ne 28th St, Bellevue, WA 98008

MACKENZIE, Vanessa Mildred (Los) 1739 Buckingham Rd, Los Angeles, CA 90019

MACKEY, George Rudolph (Los) 801 Haslam Dr, Santa Maria, CA 93454

MACKEY, Guy (RG) 312 N. Orchard Ave., Farmington, NM 87401

MACKEY, Jeffrey A (Fla) 500 Grove Street, Melrose, FL 32666

MACKEY, Judith P (Los) 801 Haslam Dr, Santa Maria, CA 93454

MACKEY, Kyle Christopher (At) 576 Roscoe Rd, Newnan, GA 30263

MACKEY, Peter David (Mich) 614 Company St, Adrian, MI 49221

MACKILLOP, Alan (SanD) 73 Windward Ln, Manchester, NH 03104

MACKIN, Mary Ruetten (SwVa) St John's Episcopal Church, PO Box 257, Roanoke, VA 24002

MACKINTOSH, Leigh (NY) St Michael's Church, 225 W 99th St, New York, NY 10025

MACKNIGHT, Jeff (WA) 5450 Massachusetts Ave, Bethesda, MD 20816

MACKOV, Elwyn Joseph (WVa) 118 Five Point Ave, Martinsburg, WV 25404

MACLEAN, Peter Duncan (LI) P.O. Box 848, Colchester, VT 05446

Clergy List

MACLEOD, Jay (NH) Episcopal Church Of St Andrew, PO Box 294, New London, NH 03257

MACLEOD III, Norman (Vt) 2 Church St, Woodstock, VT 05091

MACLIN, Charles Waite (Me) Po Box 1259, Portland, ME 04104

MACMILLAN, Cameron P (CFla)

MACNABB, Anne St Clair Coghill (Md) 20370 Marguritte Sq, Sterling, VA 20165

MACNALLY, Janet Lee (Minn)

✠ **MACNAUGHTON**, John Herbert (WTex) 230 W Sunset Rd Apt 1113, San Antonio, TX 78209

MACNEICE, Alan Donor (The Episcopal Church in Haw) 29Eo Street 178, Commond Choy Chom, Phnom Penh, Cambodia

MACORT, John Gilbert (Ct) 5227 Rancho Ave, Sarasota, FL 34234

MACPHAIL, Alexander Douglas (SwVa) 1101 Franklin Rd SW, Roanoke, VA 24016

MACPHAIL, Karin L (SwVa) 335 Eagle Street, Woodstock, VA 22664

MACQUEEN, Karen (Los) 23730 Gold Nugget Ave, Diamond Bar, CA 91765

MACSWAIN, Robert Carroll (EC) University Of The South School Of Theology, 335 Tennessee Ave., Sewanee, TN 37383

MACVEAN-BROWN, Shannon (Ind) 8850 Woodward Ave, Detroit, MI 48202

MACWHINNIE II, Anthony Eugene (CGC) 7810 Navarre Pkwy, Navarre, FL 32566

MADDISON, Benjamin B (NJ)

MADDON, Ernest Clinton (Okla) 1411 the Lakes Ct, Keller, TX 76248

MADDOX III, William Edward (NC) 5718 Catskill Court, Durham, NC 27713

MADDUX, Carole Frauman (At) 9695 Hillside Dr, Roswell, GA 30076

MADDUX, Donald Jess (Oly) 706 West Birch Street, Shelton, WA 98584

MADDY, Marta Tuff (Minn)

MADER, Carol Ann (Mich) 6092 Beechwood Drive, Haslett, MI 48840

MADISON, David (FtW) 1420 4th Ave Ste 29, Canyon, TX 79015

MADISSON LOPEZ, Vaike Marika (Hond) Km. 119 Crr al Norte, Jugo de Cane, Siguatepeque, 21105, Honduras

MADRID, Hector (Hond) Apartado Postal 30, Siguatepeque, Comayagua, Honduras

MADSEN, David Lloyd (SanD) Saint Alban's Episcopal Church, 490 Farragut Cir, El Cajon, CA 92020

MADSON, Peter G (CFla) 509 Derby Dr, Altamonte Springs, FL 32714

MAFLA SILVA, Daniel Antonio (Colom) Carrera 6 No 49-85, Piso 2, Bogota, Colombia

MAGALA, Joy (Los) 8341 De Soto Ave, Canoga Park, CA 91304

MAGDALENE, Deborah (NY) 12 Saterlee Pl, Wappingers Falls, NY 12590

MAGEE, Frederick Hugh (Spok) 17 North Street, ST. ANDREWS, - KY16 9PW, Great Britain (UK)

MAGEE JR, Lynwood Cresse (SC) 98 Wentworth St, Charleston, SC 29401

MAGERS, James Hugh (WTex) 4934 Lakeway Dr, Brownsville, TX 78520

MAGGIANO, Grey (Md) Memorial Episcopal Church, 1407 Bolton St, Baltimore, MD 21217

MAGIE, William Walter (Ia) 301 S 2nd St, Polk City, IA 50226

MAGILL, Peter George (CFla) 8310 Crosswicks Dr, Orlando, FL 32819

MAGLIULA, Robert James (NY) Holy Cross Monastery, PO Box 99, West Park, NY 12493

✠ **MAGNESS**, James Beattie (SVa) Diocese of Southern Virginia, 11827 Canon Blvd Ste 101, Newport News, VA 23606

MAGNUS, Elsie Linda (ND) PO Box 704, Walhalla, ND 58282

MAGNUS, Robert Frederick (Be) 105 Baird Rd, Mars Hill, NC 28754

MAGNUSON, Paulette Williams (Tex)

MAGUIRE III, Bernard Leonard (Pa) 224 Flourtown Rd, Plymouth Meeting, PA 19462

MAHAFFEY, Glenn G (CNY) 201 S Wilbur Ave, Sayre, PA 18840

MAHAFFY II, Richard James (WMass)

MAHAN, Charles Earl (Mo) 444 Brightfield Trl, Manchester, MO 63021

MAHER JR, John (Va) 14331 Forest Row Trl, Midlothian, VA 23112

MAHER III, John Francis (NJ) 414 E Broad St, Westfield, NJ 07090

MAHER, Joseph Anthony (CFla) 5997 Heron Pond Dr, Port Orange, FL 32128

MAHON, Paul Kelly (SanD)

MAHONEY, James Michael (Ida) 1912 Delmar St, Boise, ID 83713

MAHONEY, William D (LI)

MAHOOD, Sharon M (Ia) 3705 Washington Ave, Des Moines, IA 50310

MAHURIN, Shanda M (SwFla) 1021 Greenturf Rd., Spring Hill, FL 34608

MAIER, Andrea R (Oly) 10841 Whipple Street, No. 105, North Hollywood, OR 91602

MAIER, Beth Ann (Vt) 1924 Blake St A, Berkeley, CA 94704

MAIL, Mary Jean (Mil) 509 East University, Bloomington, IN 47401

MAILS, Ryan Fredrick (NC) 407 Hillmont Ave, Longview, TX 75601

MAINWARING, Monica B (At) 1114 9th St, Coronado, CA 92118

MAINWARING, Simon J (At) Christchurch School, 49 Seahorse Ln, Christchurch, VA 23031

MAIOCCO III, Joseph F (SwFla) 500 Park Shore Dr, Naples, FL 34103

MAITREJEAN, J Patrick (Cal) 1549 Circulo Jacona, Rio Rico, AZ 85648

MAJKRZAK, Albert Walter (Chi) 1222 Carpenter Street, Madison, WI 53704

MAJOR, John Charles (Be) 220 Montgomery Ave, West Pittston, PA 18643

MAJOR, Joseph Kenneth (SeFla) 1835 Nw 54th St, Miami, FL 33142

MAJOR, Philip S (CNY) St Paul's Syracuse, 310 Montgomery St Ste 1, Syracuse, NY 13202

MAKINS, Claire T (NwT)

MAKOWSKI, Chester Joseph (Tex) 1410 Jack Johnson Blvd., Galveston, TX 77550

MALANUK, Patsy (USC) 6045 Lakeshore Dr, Columbia, SC 29206

MALARKEY, Shawn O (Pgh) 33 Alice St, Pittsburgh, PA 15205

MALAVE TORRES, Hector (PR)

MALCOLM, Frieda (Eas) 1006 Beaglin Park Dr Apt 201, Salisbury, MD 21804

MALCOLM, Karen Gottwald (Alb)

MALCOLM, Kenneth A (Colo) 910 E 3rd Ave, Durango, CO 81301

MALCOLM, Patricia Ann (Del) PO Box 1374, Dover, DE 19903

MALDONADO-MERCADO, Roberto (Ore) 2700 W Powell Blvd Apt 3144, Gresham, OR 97030

MALE JR, Henry Alfred (Be) 80 Kal Shore Rd, Norway, ME 04268

MALERI, Karen D (Me) 112 Randolph Avenue, Milton, MA 02186

MALIA, Linda Merle (WNY) 209 Columbus Ave, Buffalo, NY 14220

MALIA, Phyllis Terri (CFla)

MALIAMAN, Irene Egmalis (The Episcopal Church in Haw) ECIM, 911 N Marine Corps Dr, Tamuning, GU 96913

MALIN, Katherine Murphy (NY) 2 Rectory St, Rye, NY 10580

MALIONEK, Judith (Alb) 21 Hackett Blvd, Albany, NY 12208

MALIONEK, Thomas V (Alb) St Paul Church, Po Box 637, Kinderhook, NY 12106

MALLARY JR, Raymond DeWitt (NY) 80 Lyme Rd #161, Hanover, NH 03755

MALLETTE STEPHENS, Hershey A (NC)

MALLIN, Caroll Sue Driftmeyer (SeFla) 1150 Stanford Dr, Coral Gables, FL 33146

MALLON, Beth Kohlmeyer (Ore) 11511 SW Bull Mountain Rd, Tigard, OR 97224

MALLONEE, Anne Floyd (NY) 19 E 34th St, New York, NY 10016

MALLORY, Richard Deaver (Az) 455 Hope St Apt 3-D, Stamford, CT 06906

MALLORY, Steven Michael (Okla) 1808 Cedar Ln, Ponca City, OK 74604

MALLOW, Sherod Earl (SeFla) 2131 Sw 23rd Ave, Fort Lauderdale, FL 33312

MALLOY, Nancy (Colo) Saint Laurence's Episcopal Mission, 26812 Barkley Rd, Conifer, CO 80433

MALLOY, Patrick L (NY) The General Theological Seminary, 440 W 21st St., New York, NY 18102

MALM, Robert Hiller (Va) 3601 Russell Rd, Alexandria, VA 22305

MALONE, Bonnie (Oly) 24219 Witte Rd SE, Maple Valley, WA 98038

MALONE JR, Elmer Taylor (NC) 308 Wilcox St., Warrenton, NC 27589

MALONE, Michael James (Dal) 430 Greenwood Drive, Petersburg, VA 23805

MALONE, Tim (WA) 2609 N Glebe Rd, Arlington, VA 22207

MALONE, Trawin E (Tex) 4115 Paint Rock Dr., Austin, TX 78731

MALONEY, Linda M (Vt) Po Box 294, Enosburg Falls, VT 05450

MALONEY, Sean Patrick Henry (WTex) 622 Airline Rd, Corpus Christi, TX 78412

MALSEED, Caroline Frey (Ak) 4032 Deborah Dr., Juneau, AK 99801

MALTBIE, Colin Snow (Minn) 1000 Shumway Ave, Faribault, MN 55021

MANASEK, Robert Wesley (Neb) St Francis Episcopal Church, PO Box 1201, Scottsbluff, NE 69361

MANASTERSKI, Myron Julian (CFla) 2901 Sw 91st St # 2907, Ocala, FL 34476

MANCHESTER, Sean (RI) 19 Trinity Pkwy, Providence, RI 02908

MANCIL, Eric Nathan (Ala)

MANDELL, Cuthbert Heneage (Eas) 2010 Schooner Dr, Stafford, VA 22554

MANDEVILLE, Kathleen C (NY) Po Box 450, Tivoli, NY 12583

MANDRELL, H Dean (Ak)

MANGELS III, John (The Episcopal NCal) 6725 Hillglen Way, Fair Oaks, CA 95628

MANGUM, Frank Burnett (Tex) 14041 Horseshoe Cir, Woodway, TX 76712

MANIACI, Maria Kathleen (NMich) 824 Dakota Ave, PO Box 411, Gladstone, MI 49837

MANION, James Edward (Del) 20 Olive Ave, Rehoboth Beach, DE 19971

MANIYATT, John Kuriakose (Md) 4 E University Pkwy, Baltimore, MD 21218

MANLEY JR, Derrill Byrne (NwT) 1615 S Carpenter Ln, Cottonwood, AZ 86326

MANLEY, Wendy T (Cal) 1090 Brookfield Rd., Berlin, VT 05602

MANN, Alice (Mass) 51 Leroy Ave, Haverhill, MA 01835

MANN, Carl Douglas (Ia) 19372 140th St, Danville, IA 52623

MANN, Charles Henry (SwFla) 5900 N Lockwood Ridge Road, Sarasota, FL 34243

MANN, Fred (SwFla) 7835 Moonstone Dr, Sarasota, FL 34233

MANN III, Harold Vance (WNC) 15 Creekside View Dr, Asheville, NC 28804

MANN, Henry Rezin (SanD) 7981 Hemingway Ave, San Diego, CA 92120

MANN, Karen L (WMo) 16608 S Holmes, Belton, MO 64012

MANN, Louise (Mass) 8399 Breeding Rd, Edmonton, KY 42129

MANN, Lucretia Winslow (ECR) 5271 Scotts Valley Dr, Scotts Valley, CA 95066

MANN, Mary Anne (Ct) 36 Convent Drive 1a31, Bethesda, MD 20892

MANNEN, Daniel Joseph (CFla) 414 Pine St, Titusville, FL 32796

MANNING, Gary Briton (Mil) 1717 Church St., Wauwatosa, WI 53213

MANNING, Gene Bentley (Tenn) 900 Broadway, Nashville, TN 37203

MANNING, Jean Louise (NMich) 1344 M-64, Ontonagon, MI 49953

MANNING, Jeanette Belle (SO) 164 Community Dr, Dayton, OH 45404

MANNING, Ronald Francis (CFla) 70 Town Ct Apt 307, Palm Coast, FL 32164

MANNING, Shannon (La) 5335 Suffolk Dr, Jackson, MS 39211

MANNING, Slaven L (USC) PO BOX 220, Prosperity, SC 29127

MANNING, William B (WNC)

MANNING-LEW, Sharon Janine (NY) 522 Washington St, Peekskill, NY 10566

MANNISTO, Virginia Lee (NMich) N4354 Black Creek Rd, Chatham, MI 49816

MANNSCHRECK, Mary Lou Cowherd (SwVa) St Luke's Episcopal Church, 801 S Osage Ave, Bartlesville, OK 74003

MANOLA, John Edwin (NJ)

MANOOGIAN, Phyllis (Cal) 2300 Bancroft Way, Berkeley, CA 94704

MANSELLA, Thomas G (Va) 3705 S George Mason Dr, Apt 2105-S, Falls Church, VA 22041

MANSFIELD, Charles Kirk (Vt) 157 Parker Hill Rd, Bellows Falls, VT 05101

MANSFIELD, Gregory James Edward (SeFla) St. Bernard de Clairvaux Episcopal Church, 16711 West Dixie Highway, North Miami Beach, FL 33160

MANSFIELD, Meribah Ann (SO) 2282 Fernleaf Lane, Columbus, OH 43235

MANSFIELD JR, Richard Huntington (Ct) 41 Gatewood, Avon, CT 06001

MANSFIELD, Robert Grant (Va) 201 E Frederick Dr, Sterling, VA 20164

MANSFIELD, Vic (WNC) PO Box 531, Skyland, NC 28776

MANSIR, Kerry Rhoads (Me) 2 Dresden Ave, Gardiner, ME 04345

MANSON, Anne Leslie Yount (Va) The Prestwould, 612 West Franklin St. #12C, Richmond, VA 23220

MANSON, Malcolm (Cal) 35 Keyes Avenue, San Francisco, CA 94129

MANTILLA-BENITEZ, Haydee (EcuC) Avenue Libertad Parada 8, Esmeralda, Ecuador

MANUEL, Anandsekar Joseph (LI) 3907 61st St, Woodside, NY 11377

MANZANARES, Zoila Manzanares-Rodriguez (Ind) 6613 El Paso Dr, Indianapolis, IN 46214

MANZO, Barbara A (Eau) 510 S Farwell St, Eau Claire, WI 54701

MANZO, Peter (NJ) 69 Penn Rd, Voorhees, NJ 08043

MAPPLEBECKPALMER, Richard Warwick (Cal) 472 Dale Rd, Martinez, CA 94553

MARANVILLE, Irvin Walter (Vt) 6809 23rd Ave W, Bradenton, FL 34209

MARANVILLE, Joyce Margaret (Vt) 6809 23rd Ave W, Bradenton, FL 34209

MARCANTONIO, John (Nwk) 39 Johnson Rd, West Orange, NJ 07052

MARCETTI, Alvin Julian (RI) 81 Warren Ave, East Providence, RI 02914

MARCH, Amanda (Mass) 1135 Walnut St, Newton, MA 02461

MARCH, Bette Ann (Wyo) 34 Thomas The Apostle Rd, Cody, WY 82414

MARCHAND, R Richard (NY) 1 Kingsley Ave, Staten Island, NY 10314

MARCHL III, William Henry (NC) 719 S 1st St, Smithfield, NC 27577

MARCIALES ARENAS, Alberto Camilo (Colom) Carrera 6 No 49-85, Piso 2, Bogota, Colombia

MARCOUX, Kent (WA) St George's Parish, 160 U St NW, Washington, DC 20001

MARCURE, Johanna M (RI) 209 E Main St, Waterville, NY 13480

MARCUSSEN, Bjorn Birkholm (SanD) 731 G St C3, Chula Vista, CA 91910

MAREE, Donna L (Pa) 2112 Delancey St, Philadelphia, PA 19103

MAREK, Joseph J (Tenn) 204-A Courthouse Dr., Salmon, ID 83467

MARGERUM, Michael C (Nev) 11205 Carlsbad Rd, Reno, NV 89506

MARGRAVE, Thomas Edmund Clare (NY) 29 William St, Cortland, NY 13045

MARICONDA, Thomas Nicholas (Ct) 36 Main St, Newtown, CT 06470

MARIE, Christine Anna (Ak)

MARIN, Carlos Heli (CFla) 438 Magpie Ct, Kissimmee, FL 34759

MARIN, Mario R (Cal)

MARIN, Nora (Cal)

MARINCO, Judith Ann (EMich) 1434 E 13 Mile Rd, Madison Heights, MI 48071

MARINCO, Vincent Michael (Mich) 1434 E 13 Mile Rd, Madison Heights, MI 48071

MARINO, Matthew A (Tex) 114 W Roosevelt Street, Phoenix, AZ 85003

MARIS, Margo (Ore) 13201 Se Blackberry Cir, Portland, OR 97236

MARKEVITCH, Diane (Mil) 17 Dumont Rd, Madison, WI 53711

MARKHAM, Eva Melba Roberts (Ky) 1604 Whippoorwill Rd., Louisville, KY 40213

MARKHAM, Ian (Va) 3737 Seminary Rd, Alexandria, VA 22304

MARKIE, Patrick Gregory (Minn) 770 Parkview Ave, Saint Paul, MN 55117

MARKLE, Ann (ETenn) 1076 Sparta Hwy, Crossville, TN 38572

MARKS, Chas (WMo) 2732 Benton Blvd, Kansas City, MO 64128

MARKS, Patrica (Ga) 814 W Alden Ave, Valdosta, GA 31602

MARKS, Sharla J (FtW) 2431 St Gregory St, Arlington, TX 76013

MARKS SR, William Parker (USC) 51 Otterside Ct, Middlebury, VT 05753

MARLER, Malcolm Lewis (Ala)

MARLIN, John Henry (Okla) 1818 Coventry Lane, Oklahoma City, OK 73120

MARMON, Mark Mccarter (Tex) 10416 Highway 6, Hitchcock, TX 77563

MARONDE, James A (Los)

MARONEY III, Gordon Earle (Ark) PO Box 202, Smackover, AR 71762

MARQUAND, Betty Harlina (Colo) 1521 Windsor Way Unit 8, Racine, WI 53406

MARQUES, Barbara (Va) 7411 Moss Side Ave, Richmond, VA 23227

MARQUEZ, Juan I (DR (DomRep)) Calle Santiago 114, Gazcue, Santo Domingo, Dominican Republic

MARQUIS JR, James F (ETenn) 2017 Kirby Rd, Memphis, TN 38119

MARR JR, Andrew (Chi) 56500 Abbey Rd, Three Rivers, MI 49093

MARR, Jon Aidan (RG) 906-B Old Las Vegas Hwy, Santa Fe, NM 87505

✠ **MARRAY**, Santosh K (Eas) The Diocese of Easton, 314 North St, Easton, MD 21601

MARRERO CAMACHO, Luis Fernando (PR)

MARRONE, Michael J (Mass) 410 Washington St, Duxbury, MA 02332

MARRS JR, James David (SD)

MARSDEN, Richard Conlon (SwFla) 222 S Palm Ave, Sarasota, FL 34236

MARSH, Abigail (Colo) 6931 E Girard Ave, Denver, CO 80224

MARSH, Caryl A (U) 829 E 400 S Apt 110, Salt Lake City, UT 84102

MARSH, Elizabeth (Mass) 368 Kings Hwy W, 358 Farwood Rd, Haddonfield, NJ 08033

MARSH, Gayle (Minn) 1644 Cohansey St, Saint Paul, MN 55117

MARSH, Graham Alan (NJ)

MARSH, Karl Edwin (Neb) 1873 S Cherry Blossom Ln, Suttons Bay, MI 49682

MARSH, Keith A (Pa) Church of the Messiah, PO Box 127, Gwynedd, PA 19436

MARSH, Mike (WTex) 343 N. Getty, Uvalde, TX 78801

MARSH JR, Robert Francis (Fla) 2462 C H Arnold Rd, Saint Augustine, FL 32092

MARSH IV, Wallace (At) St. James' Episc Church, 161 Church St. N.E., Marietta, GA 30060

MARSHALL, Carol Phillips (USC) Christ Episcopal Church, PO Box 488, Lancaster, SC 29721

MARSHALL, David Allen (Oly) P.O. Box 33029, Seattle, WA 98133

MARSHALL, David J (SanD) Grace Episcopal Church, 1020 Rose Ranch Road, San Marcos, CA 92069

MARSHALL III, Elliott Wallace (Chi) 710 Crab Tree Lane, Bartlett, IL 60103

MARSHALL, John Anthony (WNY) 7145 Fieldcrest Dr, Lockport, NY 14094

MARSHALL, John Harris (NwT)

MARSHALL, Lewis Edwin (NY) 176 Dean St, Brooklyn, NY 11217

MARSHALL, McAlister Crutchfield (Va) 2316 E Grace St # 8011, Richmond, VA 23223

MARSHALL, Mercedes Concepcion (SwFla)

✠ **MARSHALL**, Paul Victor (Be) 2234 Overlook Ln, Fogelsville, PA 18051

MARSHALL, Richard G (Ala) 6944 Cypress Spring Ct, Saint Augustine, FL 32086

MARSHALL, Robert K (SVa) 191 County Rd, Barrington, RI 02806

MARSTON, Robert Dandridge (SVa) 128 Prince St Unit 47, Tappahannock, VA 22560

MARTA, Dale Charles (Mo) 112 N Ray Ave, Maryville, MO 64468

MARTENS, Ann F (Va) 3050 N Military Rd, Arlington, VA 22207

MARTIN, Alexander D (O) St Timothy's Episcopal Church, 8101 Beechmont Ave, Cincinnati, OH 45255

MARTIN, Alison Jane (WNY) PO Box 234, Youngstown, NY 14174

MARTIN, Andrea Brooke (WA) 163 Oak Street, Hillsdale, MI 49242

MARTIN, Chad (Tex) 4900 Jackwood St, Houston, TX 77096

MARTIN, Christopher (Cal) 1123 Court St, San Rafael, CA 94901

MARTIN, Christopher S (Fla) PO Box 330500, Atlantic Beach, FL 32233

MARTIN, David Aaron (RG) 431 Richmond Pl NE, Albuquerque, NM 87106

MARTIN, Derrick Antonio (SeFla) 17 Fernhill Ave, Buffalo, NY 14215

MARTIN, Donald Graham (WK) 1715 W 5th St, Colby, KS 67701

MARTIN JR, Ed (NJ) 1281 Venezia Ave, Vineland, NJ 08361

MARTIN, George H (Minn) 12305 Chinchilla Ct W, Rosemount, MN 55068

MARTIN JR, George Oliver (WK)

MARTIN, Gregory Alexander (Cal) 162 Hickory St, San Francisco, CA 94102

MARTIN, Hallock (SeFla) 5042 El Claro N, West Palm Beach, FL 33415

MARTIN, Irene Elizabeth (Oly) PO Box 83, Skamokawa, WA 98647

MARTIN, James Mitchell (WVa) 177 Edison Dr, Huntington, WV 25705

MARTIN JR, John Charles (Md) 610 Brookfield Ave, Cumberland, MD 21502

MARTIN, John Gayle (Pa) 8114 Heacock Ln, Wyncote, PA 19095

MARTIN, Kathleen A (NY) 900 W End Ave, New York, NY 10025

MARTIN, Kenneth Earl (Fla) 125 Holly View, Holly Lake Ranch, TX 75765

MARTIN, Kevin E (Dal) 202 Kickapoo Creek Ln, Georgetown, TX 78633

MARTIN, Lydia Adriana Peter (Md) 10800 Greenpoint Rd, Lavale, MD 21502

MARTIN, Mary J (NY) 900 W End Ave Apt 10-C, New York, NY 10025

MARTIN, Mary Nadine (Az) 7750 E Oakwood Cir, Tucson, AZ 85750

MARTIN, Nancee (Fla) 10560 Fort George Road, Fort George Island, FL 32226

MARTIN, Nancy D (WVa) 222 5th Ave, Hinton, WV 25951

MARTIN, Patricia L (NMich)

MARTIN, Paul Dexter (WLa) 275 Southfield Road, Shreveport, LA 71105

MARTIN, Rene Elizabeth (Md) Buckingham's Choice, 3200 Baker Cir, Adamstown, MD 21710

MARTIN, Rex L (Wyo) PO Box 64, Hartville, WY 82215

MARTIN JR, Robert James (SwFla) 9727 Bay Colony Dr, Riverview, FL 33578

MARTIN, Robin Pierce (Pa) 8114 Heacock Ln, Wyncote, PA 19095

MARTIN, Terry L (NJ) 220 Fairview Ave, Hammonton, NJ 08037

MARTIN, Tom (At) 3207 Pristine View, Williamsburg, VA 23188

MARTIN, William (Okla) PO Box 1153, Pryor, OK 74362

MARTIN, William Jeffrey (Az) 7750 E Oakwood Cir, Tucson, AZ 85750

MARTIN, William L (Be) 5114 Hilltop Cir, East Stroudsburg, PA 18301

MARTINDALE, James Lawrence (NMich) 14 Stonegate Hts, Marquette, MI 49855

MARTINDALE, Kyle Thomas (Neb) 9302 Blondo St, Omaha, NE 68134

MARTINDALE, Richard James (Ky) 5 S Green St, Henderson, KY 42420

MARTINER, John William (Del) 65 Continental Dr, Harwich, MA 02645

MARTINEZ, Gregorio Bernardo (NwT) 907 Adams Ave, Odessa, TX 79761

MARTINEZ, Jose (Ct) 155 Wyllys St, Hartford, CT 06106

MARTINEZ, Kim Renee (RG) Po Box 1434, Santa Cruz, NM 87567

MARTINEZ, Lucy (At) 539 Wagner Way Ne, Kennesaw, GA 30144

MARTINEZ, Mario Ancizar (NY) 802 Broadway, New York, NY 10003

MARTINEZ AMENGUAL, Margarita (Hond)

MARTINEZ AMENGUAL, Roberto Aaron (Hond)

MARTINEZ-JANTZ, Jeanie (Va) 5821 Bush Hill Dr, Alexandria, VA 22310

MARTINEZ-MORALES, Roberto (Los) 1011 S Verdugo Rd, Glendale, CA 91205

MARTINEZ RAPALO, Arturo (Hond) IMS SAP Dept 215, PO BOX 523900, Miami, FL 33152-3900, Honduras

MARTINEZ TOLEDO, Eduardo (PR)

MARTINEZ TORO, Jorge De Jesus (Colom) Carrera 80 #53a-78, Medellin, Antioquia, Colombia

MARTIN FUMERO, Emilio Samuel (DR (DomRep))

MARTINHAUK, Jeff (SanD) 2728 6th Ave, San Diego, CA 92103

MARTINICHIO, John Robert (CNY) 89 Fairview Ave, Binghamton, NY 13904

MARTINO, Rose Marie (LI) 612 Forest Ave, Massapequa, NY 11758

MARTIN-RHODES, Lilla Rebecca (LI) 27002 Arrowbrook Way, Wesley Chapel, FL 33544

✠ **MARTINS**, Daniel Hayden (Spr) 821 S 2nd St, Springfield, IL 62704

MARTZ, Jeannie (Los) 3107 Pepperwood Ct, Fullerton, CA 92835

MARTZ, Steve (Chi) 947 Oxford Rd, Glen Ellyn, IL 60137

MARVIC, Paula A (NMich) 501 Ogden Ave, Escanaba, MI 49829

MARX, Jeffery Wayne (WTenn) 484 Riding Brook Way, Collierville, TN 38017

MARX, Lily Esther (WMich) 1200 Seminole Rd, Norton Shores, MI 49441

MASADA, Jennifer Ann (Ia) 912 20th Ave, Coralville, IA 52241

MASILLEM, Benedict Baguyos (Ak) 6510 E 10th Ave Apt B, Anchorage, AK 99504

MASON, Alan Newell (Ct) 211 Senexet Rd, Woodstock, CT 06281

MASON, Brooks Kevin (SanD) Cathedral Church of Saint Paul, 2728 6th Ave, San Diego, CA 92103

MASON, Bruce (Ct) PO Box 443, Litchfield, CT 06759

MASON JR, Charles Thurston (Ind) 224 N Alden Rd, Muncie, IN 47304

MASON, Christopher P (SwVa) 128 Laurel Mountain Estates Drive, Todd, NC 28684

MASON, David Raymond (O) 2277 N Saint James Pkwy, Cleveland Heights, OH 44106

MASON, Eric (Oly) Church of the Redeemer, 6211 NE 182nd St, Kenmore, WA 98028

MASON, Jack Malleroyal (Eas) 114 S Harrison St, Easton, MD 21601

MASON, Joan M (NJ) 417 Washington St, Toms River, NJ 08753

MASON, Joel Clark (NY) 39 Morton Pl, Chappaqua, NY 10514

MASON, John Skain (HB) Rr 2 Box 542b, Inwood, WV 25428

MASON, Lawrence Walker (SVa) 2355 Brookwood Rd, Richmond, VA 23235

MASON, Lisa P (WTex) 1300 Wiltshire Ave, San Antonio, TX 78209

MASON, Marilyn (Los) PO Box 743, Bristol, RI 02809

MASON, Philip Caldwell (Colo) 280 Peregrine Dr, San Marcos, TX 78666

MASON, Samuel Alison (NC) 2181 Jameson Ave Unit 1207, Alexandria, VA 22314

MASON, Victoria Anne (Tex) 6500 Halsey Court, Austin, TX 78739

MASSENBURG, Barbara Jean (Ak) 7962 N Tongass Hwy, Ketchikan, AK 99901

MASSENBURG, Raymond Douglas (WA) 1514 15th St NW, Washington, DC 20005

MASSEY, Hoyt B (SwFla) Po Box 2161, Franklin, NC 28744

MASSEY, Nigel John (NY) 111 E 60th St Penthouse, New York, NY 10022

MASSIE IV, Robert Kinloch (Mass) 140 Sycamore St, Somerville, MA 02145

MASTER II, George (Pa) 6838 Woodland Avenue, Philadelphia, PA 19142

MASTERMAN, Brenda Patricia (RG) 119 N Golfview Road, Box 9, Lake Worth, FL 33460

MASTERMAN, Frederick James (SeFla) 15170 N Rugged Lark Dr, Tucson, AZ 85739

MASTERS, Ralph Leeper (Tex) 459 Medina Dr, Highland Village, TX 75077

MASTERSON, Liz Rust (Del) 1 Southerly Ct., Apt. 606, Towson, MD 21286

MASZTAL, Gregory Thomas (Episcopal SJ)

MATAMOROS, Delia Patricia (Hond) Iglesia Episcopal San Isidro, Colonia Florencia Norte, Primeraentrada Boulevard Suyapa, Tegucigalpa M.DC, 11101, Honduras

MATARAZZO, Laura Rice (Nwk) 10 Doe Hollow Lane, Belvidere, NJ 07823

MATHAUER, Margaret Ann (Vt) 7 Holy Cross Rd, Colchester, VT 05446

MATHENY, Clint Michael (CFla) 130 N Magnolia Ave, Orlando, FL 32801

MATHER, Nicholas S (Oly) 1428 22nd Ave, Longview, WA 98632

MATHER-HEMPLER, Portia (ECR) 950 - 30th Street, Port Townsend, WA 98368

MATHES, Hester (WTenn) 4645 Walnut Grove Rd, Memphis, TN 38117

✠ **MATHES**, Jim (SanD) 2083 Sunset Cliffs Blvd, San Diego, CA 92107

MATHESON, M Jennings Jennings (Ct) 74 South St # 809, Litchfield, CT 06759

MATHEUS, Rob (SO) 6300 Kinver Edge Way, Columbus, OH 43213

MATHEW, Cherian (ND)

MATHEWS, Keith (SO) 662 N 600 E, Firth, ID 83236

MATHEWS, Koshy (Pa) 103 Potters Pond Dr, Phoenixville, PA 19460

MATHEWS, Miriam Atwell (Md) 3433 Manor Ln, Ellicott City, MD 21042

MATHEWS, Ranjit (Ct) 76 Federal St, New London, CT 06320

MATHEWS JR, Tom (Nwk) 5 Surrey Ln, Madison, NJ 07940

MATHEWS, Weston (Va) 6000 Grove Ave, Richmond, VA 23226

MATHEWSON, Colin J (SanD) St Paul's Episcopal Cathedral, 2728 6th Ave, San Diego, CA 92103

MATHEWSON, Kathryn Carroll (ETenn) 412 silverberry, Pittsboro, NC 27312

MATHEWSON, Laurel (SanD) St Paul's Cathedral, 2728 6th Ave, San Diego, CA 92103

MATHIAS, Barbara Helen (Minn) 110 S Oak St, Lake City, MN 55041

MATHIESON, James West (SVa) 183 Grove Park Cir, Danville, VA 24541

MATHIS, Judy (CFla) 86 Dianne Dr., Ormond Beach, FL 32176

MATHIS, Thelma Monique (At) 306 Peyton Rd SW, Atlanta, GA 30311

MATHISON, Mary Alice (CGC) 28788 N Main St, Daphne, AL 36526

MATIJASIC, Ernie (SwFla) 401 W Shoreline Dr #253, Sandusky, OH 44870

MATIS, Glenn Marshall (Pa) 45 Latham Ct, Doylestown, PA 18901

MATISSE, Jackie (SO) 232 E Main St, Lebanon, OH 45036

MATLACK, David Russell (NY) Po Box 703, Southwest Harbor, ME 04679

MATLAK, David John (Md) 1101 Forest Ave, Richmond, VA 23229

MATNEY, Rex H (Kan) The Church of the Covenant, PO Box 366, Junction City, KS 66441

MATO, Sarah (Mass) Church of the Holy Spirit, 204 Monument Rd, Orleans, MA 02653

MATOTT, Michele Louise (RI) 80 Fisher Road Unit 90, Cumberland, RI 02864

MATSON, David John (Me) 26 Heron Lane, Harpswell, ME 04079

MATTER, Janice Louise (Me) 5 Boynton Ln, Billerica, MA 01821

MATTERS, Rick (ECR) 181 S Corinth Ave, Lodi, CA 95242

MATTHEW, John Clifford (Ida) 5301 E Warm Springs Ave E102, Boise, ID 83716

MATTHEWS JR, Allen Russel (WTex) Po Box 348, Luling, TX 78648

MATTHEWS, Anne (Miss) P. O. Box 804, Brookhaven, MS 39602

MATTHEWS, Bonnie Anne (Ct) Trinity Episc Church, 120 Sigourney St, Hartford, CT 06105

✠ **MATTHEWS**, Clay (Va) PO Box 12686, New Bern, NC 28561

MATTHEWS, Daniel Paul (NY) 1047 Amsterdam Ave, New York, NY 10025

MATTHEWS JR, Daniel Paul (At) 435 Peachtree St, Atlanta, GA 30308

MATTHEWS, Donald William (CNY) 375 W Clinton St, Elmira, NY 14901

MATTHEWS III, James Houston (WNC) 2232 Water Oak Ln, Gastonia, NC 28056

MATTHEWS, Joyce (Mich) 37906 Glengrove Dr, Farmington Hills, MI 48331

MATTHEWS, Kevin (NC) 625 Candlewood Drive, Greensboro, NC 27403

MATTHEWS, Mary Theresa (RI) Woodson Dr 2721, 2721 Woodson Dr, Mckinney, TX 75070

MATTHEWS, Patricia Gail (Ark)

MATTHEWS, Richard L (Minn) 8895 Bradford Pl, Eden Prairie, MN 55347

MATTHEWS, William Thompson (CFla)

MATTIA, Joan Plubell (Va) 1 Egyetem Ter, Debrecen, 4032, Hungary

MATTIA JR, Louis Joseph (Va) 622 Worchester St, Herndon, VA 20170

MATTILA, Daniel E (Ct) 104 Walnut Tree Hill Rd, Sandy Hook, CT 06482

MATTLIN, Margaret Baker (Minn) 2085 Buford Ave, Saint Paul, MN 55108

MATTSON, Jennifer Elizabeth (CPa) 33 Wilson Dr, Lancaster, PA 17603

MATTSON, Sherry (Ind) 11974 State Highway M26, Eagle Harbor, MI 49950

MATYLEWICZ, Stephen Jerome (Be) 116 Riverview Ln, Jermyn, PA 18433

MAUAI, Brandon Lee (ND) 500 S Main Ave, Sioux Falls, SD 57104

MAUGHAN III, Webster (O) 1226 Waverly Rd, Sandusky, OH 44870

MAULDEN, Kristina Ann (Okla) 501 S Cincinnati Ave, Tulsa, OK 74103

MAUMUS, Priscilla Guderian (La) Episcopal Diocese of Louisiana, 1623 Seventh St., New Orleans, LA 70115

MAUNEY, James Patrick (RI) P.O Box 1236, Sagamore Beach, MA 02562

MAURAIS, Robert Irwin (CFla) 175 Groveland Rd, Mount Dora, FL 32757

MAURER, Karen (Los) 777 N. Acacia Ave., Rialto, CA 92376

MAURER, Sally Beth (NJ) St Johns Episcopal Church, 76 Market St, Salem, NJ 08079

MAURY, James L (Ga) PO Box 61297, Savannah, GA 31420

MAXFIELD, Christian D (SwFla) 14640 N Cleveland Ave, North Fort Myers, FL 33903

MAXSON, John Hollis (The Episcopal Church in Haw) 447 Kawaihae St, Honolulu, HI 96825

MAXWELL, Anne M (La) 259 W Hickory St, Ponchatoula, LA 70454

MAXWELL, Barbara Jean (O) 120 Charles Ct, Elyria, OH 44035

MAXWELL, Elizabeth Gail (NY) 225 W. 99th St., New York, NY 10025

MAXWELL JR, George (At) 2744 Peachtree Road NW, Atlanta, GA 30305

MAXWELL, James (Mich) 281 W Drayton St, Ferndale, MI 48220

MAXWELL, Kevin Burns (Cal) 2 Meadow Park Circle, Belmont, CA 94002

MAXWELL, Max (Ct) Grace Episcopal Church, 4 Madison Ave, Madison, CT 06443

MAXWELL, Sally Dawn (Minn) St David's Episcopal Church, 304 E 7th St, Austin, TX 78701

MAXWELL, William F (U) 515 Van Buren St, Port Townsend, WA 98368

MAY, Amanda Rutherford (Cal) 613 Parkhaven Ct, Pleasant Hill, CA 94523

MAY, Charles Scott (At) 3750 Peachtree Rd NE Apt 811, Atlanta, GA 30319

MAY, David Hickman (Va) 93 Eubank Dr, Kilmarnock, VA 22482

MAY JR, Frederick Barnett (NJ) 916 Lagoon Ln., Mantoloking, NJ 08738

MAY JR, Jim (Fla) 16178 Williams Pl, King George, VA 22485

MAY IV, Lynde Eliot (Mil) 982 Hunters Trl, Sun Prairie, WI 53590

MAY, Philip Walter (WTex) 700 S Upper Broadway St, Corpus Christi, TX 78401

MAY, Richard Ernest (Va) Po Box 155, Campton, NH 03223

MAY, Richard Leslie (SVa) 349 Archers Mead, Williamsburg, VA 23185

MAY, Thomas Richard (NJ) 65 W Front St, Red Bank, NJ 07701

MAYBERRY, Richard (Ct) 16 Southport Woods Drive, Southport, CT 06890

MAYCOCK, Roma (Va) 5210 Patriots Colony Dr, Williamsburg, VA 23188

MAYEN, John Mabior (SD) 1415 S Bahnson Ave, Sioux Falls, SD 57105

MAYER, Annette Cleary (Chi)

MAYER, Charles D (NY)

MAYER, Linda Margaret (Spok) PO Box 1226, Chelan, WA 98816

MAYER JR, Nicholas Max (WTex) Po Box 1265, Castroville, TX 78009

MAYER, Peter Woodrich (Md) 1601 Pleasant Plains Rd, Annapolis, MD 21409

MAYER, Sandra (CGC) 5158 Border Dr N, Mobile, AL 36608

✠ **MAYER**, Scott (NwT) 1802 Broadway, Lubbock, TX 79401

MAYERS, Tom (Mich) 3837 W. 7 Mile Rd., Detroit, MI 48221

MAYES, Amy Kathryn (Wyo) 519 E Park Ave, Riverton, WY 82501

MAYFIELD, Donna Jeanne (O) 515 N Chillicothe Rd, Aurora, OH 44202

MAYFIELD JR, Ellis (ETenn) 1449 Stagecoach Rd, Sewanee, TN 37375

MAYHALL, Monna (Tenn) 1509 Jaybee Ct, Franklin, TN 37064

MAYHEW, Nancy (EMich)

MAYHOOD, Gary William (LI) 509 W Plane St, Hackettstown, NJ 07840

MAYNARD, Beth H (Spr) 702 W Green St, Champaign, IL 61820

MAYNARD, Dennis Roy (SanD) 49 Via Del Rossi, Rancho Mirage, CA 92270

MAYNARD, Jane (Oly) 6732 N Parkside Ln, Tacoma, WA 98407

MAYNARD, Joan Pearson (So) 2661 Haverford Rd, Columbus, OH 43220

MAYO, H(Arold) Jonathan (Be) 3900 Mechancsville Rd, Whitehall, PA 18052

MAYOM, Abraham Mabior (SD)

MAYOR, Mike (Oly) 10630 Gravelly Lake Dr SW, Lakewood, WA 98499

MAYORGA-GONZALEZ, Mary (Ct) 3 Oakwood Ave., Lawrence, MA 01841

MAYPOLE, Sara (Va) 6988 Woodchuck Hill Rd, Fayetteville, NY 13066

MAYRER, Jane Goodhue (Md) 2010 Sulgrave Ave, Baltimore, MD 21209

MAYS, Foster (Kan) Epiphany Episcopal Church, P.O. Box 367, Sedan, KS 67361

MAYS-STOCK, Barbara L (RI) 50 Charles St, Cranston, RI 02920

✠ **MAZE**, Larry (Ark) 102 Midland St, Little Rock, AR 72205

MAZINGO, Stephen L (Fla) Saint Peter's Church, 801 Atlantic Ave, Fernandina Beach, FL 32034

MAZUJIAN, Harry (NJ) 44 Broad St, Flemington, NJ 08822

MAZZA, Joseph (Colo) 1737 Mayview Rd, Jacksonville, FL 32210

MAZZA, Joseph Edward (FdL) 4569 Glidden Dr, Sturgeon Bay, WI 54235

MAZZACANO, Leslie G (NJ) 379 Huntington Drive, Delran, NJ 08075

MAZZARELLA, Virginia Teresa (Roch) 327 Mendon Center Rd, Pittsford, NY 14534

MCADAMS, James Lee (Ala) 3775 Crosshaven Dr, Birmingham, AL 35223

MCADAMS, Kathy (Mass) PO Box 287, Franklin, MA 02038

MCAFEE JR, Ernest (Dal) 1106 Richland Oaks Drive, Richardson, TX 75081

MCALHANY, Julie Ann (Me) St John's Episcopal Church, 234 French St, Bangor, ME 04401

MCALISTER, Donald Beaton (Chi)

MCALLEN, Robert (WTex) 1112 S Westgate Dr, Weslaco, TX 78596

MCALLISTER, Loring William (Minn)

MCALPINE, James Paul (Mass) 2 Victoria Ct Apt 208, York, ME 03909

MCALPINE, Thomas Hale (FdL) PO Box 46017, Madison, WI 53744

MCAULAY, Roderick Neil (The Episcopal NCal) 7803 Stefenoni Ct, Sebastopol, CA 95472

MCBAY, Susannah E (Tex) 717 Sage Rd, Houston, TX 77056

MCBEATH, Susan Audrey (Ind) 13088 Tarkington Commons, Carmel, IN 46033

MCBRIDE, Bill (WLa) 9105 Colonial Gdns, Shreveport, LA 71106

MCBRIDE, Ronald Winton (Cal) 34043 Calle Mora, Cathedral City, CA 92234

MCBRYDE, Greer (CFla) 1155 C.R. 753 South, Webster, FL 33597

MCCABE, Chad P (WMass)

MCCABE III, Charles Peyton (WMich) 325 West Center, Hastings, MI 49058

MCCABE, Paul Charles (At) 1785 Benningfield Dr Sw, Marietta, GA 30064

MCCAFFREY, Susan Maureen (CFla) 4110 S Ridgewood Ave, Port Orange, FL 32127

MCCAIN, Michael T. (Ark)

MCCALEB, Doug (SeFla) 464 NE 16th Street, Miami, FL 33132

MCCALL, Chad (Tex)

MCCALL JR, Jack Keith William (Me) 300 Page St, San Francisco, CA 94102

MCCALL, Ramelle Lorenzo (Md) 730 Bestgate Rd, Annapolis, MD 21401

MCCALL, Richard David (LI) 5117 N Chatham Dr, Bloomington, IN 47404

MCCALL, Terry A (Mass) 5117 N Chatham Dr, Bloomington, IN 47404

MCCALLISTER, Katlin E (The Episcopal Church in Haw) 3738 N Old Sabino Canyon Rd, Tucson, AZ 85750

MCCALLUM, Bruce Allan (FdL) PO Box 561, Waupaca, WI 54981

MCCANDLESS, Clelie Fleming (Miss) 8245 Getwell Rd, Southaven, MS 38672

MCCANDLESS, Richard Lawrence (O) 1106 Bell Ridge Rd., Akron, OH 44303

MCCANDLESS, Richard William (Kan) 3028 Washington Ave, Parsons, KS 67357

MCCANN, Christopher Richard (O) 16267 Oakhill Rd, Cleveland Heights, OH 44112

MCCANN, John Harrison (WMo) 1492 Hemlock Ct, Liberty, MO 64068

MCCANN, Michael Louis (HB)

MCCANN, Michael Wayne (At) 975 Longstreet Cir, Gainesville, GA 30501

MCCANN, Robert Emmett (Cal) 4023 Canyon Rd, Lafayette, CA 94549

MCCANN, Sandy (At)

MCCANN, Susan Griffen (WMo) 1492 Hemlock Ct, Liberty, MO 64068

MCCARD, John (Va) 3110 Ashford Dunwoody Rd Ne, Atlanta, GA 30319

MCCARLEY, Melanie (Mass) Zion Church, 221 E. Washington St., Charles Town, WV 25414

MCCARROLL, Connie Jo (SO) 4381 S.Rangeline Rd., West Milton, OH 45383

MCCARROLL, Sandra Kim (Nev) 1806 Hilton Head Dr, Boulder City, NV 89005

MCCARRON, Charles F (LI) 11 Violet Ave, Mineola, NY 11501

MCCARTHY, Bartlett A (Dal) 7335 Inwood Rd, Dallas, TX 75209

MCCARTHY, Bill (Ore) 5060 SW Philomath Blvd, PMB 165, Corvallis, OR 97333

MCCARTHY, Ian (Fla) St. Mary's Episcopal Church, 623 SE Ocean Blvd, Stuart, FL 34994

MCCARTHY, Jean Elizabeth Rinner (Ia) 2906 39th St, Des Moines, IA 50310

MCCARTHY, Martin (NC) 4205 Quail Hunt Lane, Charlotte, NC 28226

MCCARTHY, Melissa (Los) 6860 Poppyview Dr, Oak Park, CA 91377

MCCARTHY, Nancy Horton (SeFla) 24 Highbridge Xing, Apt 1002, Asheville, NC 28803

MCCARTHY JR, Stephen Joseph (Mass) 2017 6th Ave N, Birmingham, AL 35203

MCCARTY, Marjorie McDonall (EC) 100 E Sherwood Dr, Havelock, NC 28532

MCCARTY, Mary Sharon (WA) 1831 Parkers Creek Road, Port Republic, MD 20676

MCCARTY, Patricia (WTenn) 1720 Peabody Ave., Memphis, TN 38104

MCCARTY, Steven Lynn (Md) Saint Andrew's Episcopal Church, 22 Cumberland St, PO Box 189, Clear Spring, MD 21722

MCCARTY, Willis Barnum Coker (Fla) 5303 Ortega Blvd Apt 208, Jacksonville, FL 32210

MCCASLIN, H Kenneth (Pa) 694 Kennedy Ln, Wayne, PA 19087

MCCASLIN, Robert Allan (WNC) 5198 NC Highway 194 S, Banner Elk, NC 28604

MCCAUGHAN, Patricia Susanne (Los) 1554 N. Shelley Avenue, Upland, CA 91786

MCCAULEY, Margaret Hudley (Los) 4215 W 61st St, Los Angeles, CA 90043

MCCAULEY, Shana (Ore) 1550 Diablo Rd, Danville, CA 94526

MCCAULLEY, Barbara Marie (Ia) 620 Briarstone Dr Apt 28, Mason City, IA 50401

MCCAUSLAND, John Lesher (NH) 457 Reservoir Dr, Weare, NH 03281

MCCAW, Mary Ann (Oly) 6 Lincoln Rd, Wellesley, MA 02481

MCCLAIN, Daniel W (SVa) 4 E University Pkwy, Baltimore, MD 21218

MCCLAIN, Marion Roy Sam (FtW) 3650 Chicora Ct Apt 330, Fort Worth, TX 76116

MCCLAIN, Mikel (Ore) 7875 SW Alden St, Portland, OR 97223

MCCLAIN, Rebecca Lee (Oly) Saint Paul's Cathedral, 2728 6th Ave, San Diego, CA 92103

MCCLAIN, William Allen (The Episcopal NCal) 6825 Sterchi Ln, Montague, CA 96064

MCCLASKEY, Steven Lloyd (Q) 2020 21st St, Rock Island, IL 61201

MCCLATCHY, Johnny Edward (Nev)

MCCLEERY III, Bill (SO) 7265 Edgewood Ln, Athens, OH 45701

MCCLELLAN, Robert Farrell (NMich) Po Box 841, Saint Helena, CA 94574

MCCLELLAN, Thomas Lee (Pa) Po Box 642, Lafayette Hill, PA 19444

MCCLELLAND, Carol Jean (EO) 12019 SE 15th St, Vancouver, WA 98683

MCCLENAGHAN, Malcolm Eugene (The Episcopal NCal) 2020 Brady Ln, Roseville, CA 95747

MCCLOGHRIE, K(athleen) Lesley (NY) 4259 Forest Hills Dr, Fortuna, CA 95540

MCCLOSKEY JR, Robert Johnson (SeFla) Po Box 1691, West Jefferson, NC 28694

MCCLOUD, Christine L (Nwk) 816 Prospect St, Union, NJ 07083

MCCLOUD, Linda (Lex) 4057 Mooncoin Way Apt 7102, Lexington, KY 40515

MCCLOUGH, Jeffrey David (Chi) 3801 Central Ave, Western Springs, IL 60558

MCCLOY, Randolph McKellar (WTenn) 42 S Goodlett St, Memphis, TN 38117

MCCLURE, Robert Coke (Neb) Saint Matthew's Church, 312 W 16th St, Alliance, NE 69301

MCCLURE JR, William James (EMich) 232 North 'E' Street, Cheboygan, MI 49721

MCCOART JR, Charles Carroll (Va) Emmanuel Episcopal Church, 1608 Russell Rd, Alexandria, VA 22301

MCCOLL, Scott Joseph (Eur)

MCCOMAS, Scot A (FtW) 223 S Pearson Ln, Keller, TX 76248

MCCOMBS, Lauren (Cal) 1040 Border Rd, Los Altos, CA 94024

MCCONCHIE, Leann P (WNY) 119 Royal Pkwy E, Williamsville, NY 14221

MCCONE, Susan (Ct) 80 Green Hill Rd, Washington, CT 06793

MCCONKEY, David Benton (Alb) 6 Albion Place, Northampton, NN1 1UD, Great Britain (UK)

Clergy List

✠ **MCCONNELL**, Dorsey (Pgh) Episcopal Diocese of Pittsburgh, 4099 William Penn Hwy, Suite 502, Monroeville, PA 15146

MCCONNELL JR, James Bert (SwFla) 2916 Palm Dr, Punta Gorda, FL 33950

MCCONNELL, Theodore A (Alb) 106 East Farm Woods Ln, Fort Ann, NY 12827

MCCONNELL, Theodore Howard (Va) 7319 Habeas Ct., Mechanicsville, VA 23111

MCCONNEY, J Anne (Neb) 413 S 78th St Apt 8, Omaha, NE 68114

MCCOOK, Carla Benae (SwFla) 1929 Par Pl, Sarasota, FL 34240

MCCORMICK, Brendan (Ct) 5 Sea Ln, Old Saybrook, CT 06475

MCCORMICK, Matthew W (SC) Calvary Episcopal Church, 106 Line St, Charleston, SC 29403

MCCORMICK, Phyllis Ann (SwFla) 2850 Countrybrook Dr Apt 13, Apt. 13, Palm Harbor, FL 34684

MCCORMICK, Reid T (CFla) 210 Church St, Greenville, AL 36037

MCCORMICK, Thomas Ray (Del) PO Box 1478, Bethany Beach, DE 19930

MCCOWN, William R (Tenn) 510 W Main St, Franklin, TN 37064

MCCOY, Adam (NY) Mount Calvary Monastery, 505 E Los Olivos St, Santa Barbara, CA 93105

MCCOY, David Ormsby (SO) 24 Old Coach Road, Athens, OH 45701

MCCOY, Elaine K (O) 3785 W 33rd St, Cleveland, OH 44109

MCCOY, Frances Jean (SwVa) 1001 Virginia Ave NW, Norton, VA 24273

MCCOY, Robert Martin (Md) 521 Sixth St., Annapolis, MD 21403

MCCOY, William Keith (NJ) 14 Second Street, Edison, NJ 08837

MCCRACKEN, Jennifer Anne (Mass) 112 Randolph Ave, Milton, MA 02186

MCCRACKEN-BENNETT, Richard J (SO) 9019 Johnstown Alexandria Rd, Johnstown, OH 43031

MCCRAY-GOLDSMITH, Julia (Ore) 147 NW 19th Ave, Portland, OR 97209

MCCREARY, Ernest Cannon (USC) 8530 Geer Hwy, Cleveland, SC 29635

MCCREATH, Amy (Mass) 23 Gilbert St, Waltham, MA 02453

MCCRICKARD, Bonnie Mixon (Pa) Church of the Nativity, 208 Eustis Ave SE, Huntsville, AL 35801

MCCRUM, Lewis Lamb (NJ) 415 Washington St, Toms River, NJ 08753

MCCUE, Allan Homer (Mass) 12 Regwill Ave, Wenham, MA 01984

MCCUE, Mary Madeline (WA)

MCCUE, Michael Edlow (WMass) 123 Eileen Dr, Rochester, NY 14616

MCCULLOCH, Kent Thomas (Oly) 10630 Gravelly Lake Dr Sw, Lakewood, WA 98499

MCCULLOUGH, Brian Duncan (SanD) 332 N Massachusetts St, Winfield, KS 67156

MCCULLOUGH, Mary (Pa) 708 S. Bethlehem Pike, Ambler, PA 19002

MCCUNE, Henry Ralph (Dal) 11560 Drummond Dr, Dallas, TX 75228

MCCURDY III, Alexander (Pa) 613 Maplewood Avenue, Wayne, PA 19087

MCCURRY MILLIKEN, Cathleen Ann (Mil) 1734 Fairhaven Dr., Cedarburg, WI 53012

MCCURTAIN, Glad (SwFla) 261 1st Ave SW, Largo, FL 33770

MCCUSKER III, Thomas Bernard (Va) Orchid Garden Homes, 229/103 Thepprasit Rd Moo 12, Chonburi, 20260, Thailand

MCDADE, Shelley D (LI) 12 W 11th St, New York, NY 10011

MCDANIEL, Eleanor B (SwVa)

MCDANIEL, Elna Irene (Eau) 408 W Nott St, Tomah, WI 54660

MCDANIEL, Judith Maxwell (Oly) 3971 Point White Dr NE, Bainbridge Island, WA 98110

MC DARBY, Mark Daniel (Alb) 8 Summit St, Philmont, NY 12565

MCDERMOT, Joanna (NwPa) 19556 E Cole Rd, Meadville, PA 16335

MCDERMOTT, James Patrick (LI) 1709 Rue Saint Patrick Apt 504, Montreal, H3K 3G9, Canada

MCDERMOTT, Jane Leslie (O) 2918 Kirkhaven Dr, Youngstown, OH 44511

MCDERMOTT, John Roy (Md) 4493 Barberry Ct, Concord, CA 94521

MCDERMOTT, Matthew (Cal) 580 Colorado Ave, Palo Alto, CA 94306

MCDERMOTT, Nelda Grace (Ark) 1204 Hunter St, Conway, AR 72032

MCDONALD, Catherine Jane Walter (Minn) 9671 Clark Cir, Eden Prairie, MN 55347

MCDONALD, David Forrest (NY) PO Box 783, Cornwall, NY 12518

MCDONALD, Dawn (CFla) 1457 Barn Owl Loop, Sanford, FL 32773

MCDONALD, Durstan R (Tex) 811 E 46th St, Austin, TX 78751

MCDONALD, James Ross (Alb) 1937 The Plz, Schenectady, NY 12309

MCDONALD, James Roy (NY) PO Box 161897, Austin, TX 78716

MCDONALD, James Wallace (Episcopal SJ) 627 Goshen Ave, Clovis, CA 93611

MCDONALD, Janet Strain (Va) Po Box 233, Free Union, VA 22940

MCDONALD, Jim (Ark) 511 Coley Dr, Mountain Home, AR 72653

MCDONALD, Karen Loretta (WMich) 89513 Shorelane Dr, Lawton, MI 49065

MCDONALD, Lauren (SVa) Spiritworks Foundation, 5800 Mooretown Rd, Williamsburg, VA 23188

MCDONALD, Marc Edwin (Kan) 828 Commercial St, Emporia, KS 66801

MCDONALD, Mark William (CGC) Church Of The Advent, 12099 County Road 99, Lillian, AL 36549

MCDONALD III, Norval Harrison (Md) 309 Royal Oak Dr, Bel Air, MD 21015

MCDONALD, Vickie Lynn (SwFla)

MCDONALD, William Kenneth (Mich) 421 East Ellen Street, Fenton, MI 48430

MCDONNELL, Brian K (Md) 8 Loveton Farms Ct, Sparks, MD 21152

MCDONNELL, George Anne (ECR) PO Box 3811, Lacey, WA 98509

MCDONNELL III, Richard P (Ga) 3 Wexford on the Green, Hilton Head Island, SC 29928

MCDOUGLE, Jane (Cal) 537 Chenery Street, San Francisco, CA 94131

MCDOWELL, Glenda Irene (WNC) Cathedral of All Souls, 9 Swan St, Asheville, NC 28803

MCDOWELL, Harold Clayton (LI) 27 Private Rd, Medford, NY 11763

MCDOWELL JR, John Sidebotham (CPa) 125 Beverly Rd, Ashland, VA 23005

MCDOWELL, Joseph Lee (CFla) 116 Jamaica Dr, Cocoa Beach, FL 32931

MCDOWELL, Lynn (SwFla) 2808 Valley Park Dr., Little Rock, AR 72212

MCDOWELL, Maria Gwyn (Ore) 5301 NE 73rd Ave, Portland, OR 97218

MCDOWELL, Mia Chelynn Drummond (USC) 101 Saint Matthews Ln, Spartanburg, SC 29301

MCDOWELL, Todd S (Mo) Grace Episcopal Church, 514 E Argonne Dr, Kirkwood, MO 63122

MCDOWELL-FLEMING, Dave (CGC) 3560 Briar Cliff Dr, Pensacola, FL 32505

MCDUFFIE, John Stouffer (WA) 5320 Westpath Way, Bethesda, MD 20816

MCELRATH, James Devoe (WNC) 22 Edgewater Ln, Canton, NC 28716

MCELROY, Catherine DeLellis (NY) 191 Larch Ave, Teaneck, NJ 07666

MCELROY, Gary Austin (O) 8437 Eaton Dr, Chagrin Falls, OH 44023

MCELROY, Jamie (Miss) 3921 Oakridge Dr, Jackson, MS 39216

MCELWAIN, David Marc (Wyo) 3594 Stampede Ranch, Cheyenne, WY 82007

MCEWEN JR, Billy Wayne (ND)

MCEWEN, Michael Thomas (Okla) 514 Big Rock Rd, PO Box 338, Medicine Park, OK 73557

MCFADDEN, Cheryl Culley (EC) 203 Vandemere St, Oriental, NC 28571

MCFARLAND, Earl Everett (RG) 8960 Stetson Pl, Las Cruces, NM 88011

MCFARLANE, Robert Bruce (Mass) 21 Euclid Ave, Lynn, MA 01904

MCGARRY, Susan Ellen (Vt) Saint Stephen's Church, 3 Main St, Middlebury, VT 05753

MCGARRY-LAWRENCE, Marla (Ore) 2136 NE Cesar E Chavez Blvd., Portland, OR 97212

MCGARVEY, Philip Peter (Md) 3671 Lily St, Oakland, CA 94619

MCGAVERN III, Cecil George (Tex) 15015 Memorial Dr, Houston, TX 77079

MCGAVRAN, Frederick Jaeger (SO) 3528 Traskwood Cir, Cincinnati, OH 45208

MCGEE JR, Hubert (Ind) 1609 Rivershore Rd, Elizabeth City, NC 27909

MCGEE, Kyle Marland (Ct) 11133 Town Walk Dr, Hamden, CT 06518

MCGEE, Robert Maurice (CFla)

MCGEE, William Earl (ETenn) 3404-A Taft Hwy, Signal Mountain, TN 37377

MCGEE-STREET, Eleanor Lee (Ct) 35 Killdeer Rd, Hamden, CT 06517

MCGEHEE, Andrew Austin (At) 1790 Lavista Rd NE, Atlanta, GA 30329

MCGEHEE, J Pittman (Tex) 1307 Westover Rd, Austin, TX 78703

MCGEHEE, Lionel Eby (NY) 225 W 99th St, New York, NY 10025

MCGEHEE, Stephen (Va) 6000 Grove Ave, Richmond, VA 23226

MCGHEE, Margaret Evalyn (NY)

MCGILL JR, Dennis Madison (Ga)

MCGILL, Jim (Tex) 6339 E Mystic Mdw, Houston, TX 77021

MCGILL JR, William James (CPa) Po Box 682, Cornwall, PA 17016

MCGIMPSEY, Ralph Gregory (Mich) 8207 Nice Way, Sarasota, FL 34238

MCGINLEY, Charles Richard (Md) 18024 Sand Wedge Dr, Hagerstown, MD 21740

MCGINN, John Edward (Mass) 29 Oak Ridge Rd, East Sandwich, MA 02537

MCGINNIS, Richard H(Arry) (Fla) 1312 Wisconsin St., Apt. 137, Hudson, WI 54016

MCGINTY, John P (LI) 33 Jefferson Street, Garden City, NY 11530

MCGINTY, William Joseph (Be) 110 Ave M., Matamoras, PA 18336

MCGIRR, Joyce Bearden (Nwk)

MCGLANNAN, Dorian (Mich) 6217 137th Pl SW, Edmonds, WA 98026

MCGLASHON JR, Hugh (CFla) PO Box 3303, Haines City, FL 33845

MCGOWAN, Carole (RG) 425 University Blvd NE, Albuquerque, NM 87106

MCGOWAN, Diane Darby (Minn) 5029 2nd Ave S, Minneapolis, MN 55419

MCGOWAN, Neal Scott (Tex) 305 N 30th St, Waco, TX 76710

MCGOWAN, Sandra Maria (Alb)

MCGOWEN, Willetta Hulett (Ga) 900 Gloucester St, Brunswick, GA 31520

MCGRADY, Jacqueline Ann (Mass) PO Box 2847, Nantucket, MA 02584

MCGRANE, Kevin John (Mo) 3664 Arsenal St, Saint Louis, MO 63116

MCGRATH, Victoria (Nwk) 113 Center Ave, Chatham, NJ 07928

MCGRAW, Jean (SC) 2341 Wofford Rd, Charleston, SC 29414

MCGRAW, Stanley Earle (At) 1878 Oleander Ct., Charleston, SC 29414

MCGRAW, Tara L (SwFla)

MCGREGOR, Patricia Cox (SeFla) PO Box 399, Ambridge, PA 15003

MCGUGAN, Terry (Colo) 2950 S University Blvd, Denver, CO 80210

MCGUINNESS, David (NC) 4330 Pin Oak Dr, Durham, NC 27707

MCGUIRE, Malcolm (Pa) 1300 Lombard St Apt 711, Philadelphia, PA 19147

MCGUIRE, Mark Alan (WMo) 908 SW Hackney Ct, Lees Summit, MO 64081

MCGURK, Brian (Mass) 625 Main St, Chatham, MA 02633

MCHALE, Stephen (Cal) 1700 Santa Clara Ave, Alameda, CA 94501

MCHALE O'CONNOR, Mary Colleen (WNY) 1 East Main Street, Le Roy, NY 14482

MCHENRY, Richard Earl (FtW) 1010 Willowcreek Rd, Cleburne, TX 76033

MCHUGH III, John Michael (NJ) 324 Rio Grande Blvd Nw, Albuquerque, NM 87104

MCILHINEY, David B (NH) 701 E High St Apt 211, Charlottesville, VA 22902

MCILMOYL, Mac (The Episcopal NCal) 1314 Spring St, Saint Helena, CA 94574

MCILVAIN, Jean Christine (Pgh) 5622 Alan St, Aliquippa, PA 15001

MCILVEEN, Richard William (Me) 26 Concord St, Portland, ME 04103

MCINDOO, Lisa (ECR) Diocese Of West Tennessee, 692 Poplar Ave, Memphis, TN 38105

MCINERNEY, Joseph Lee (Cal) 1421 Oxford St, Berkeley, CA 94709

MCINNIS, Victor Erwin (Miss) Po Box 63, Lexington, MS 39095

MCINTIRE, Rhonda (RG) 17 Camino Redondo, Placitas, NM 87043

MCINTOSH, David Kevin (Ct) 1 North Main Street, PO Box 309, Kent, CT 06757

MCINTOSH, Eric (Pgh) St James Episcopal Church, 11524 Frankstown Rd, Pittsburgh, PA 15235

MCINTOSH, Justin M (Va) 4332 Leeds Manor Road, Markham, VA 22643

MCINTOSH, Kendra Lea (Nwk) 26 W 84th St, New York, NY 10024

MCINTOSH, Mark Allen (Chi) 65 E Huron St, Chicago, IL 60611

MCINTOSH, Randy (WK) 138 S 8th St, Salina, KS 67401

MCINTOSH, Wayne S (SD) Trinity Episcopal Church, 500 14th Ave NW, Watertown, SD 57201

MCINTYRE, Calvin Carney (NY) 4401 Matilda Ave, Bronx, NY 10470

MCINTYRE, Gregory Edward (NC) 258 W Franklin Blvd, Gastonia, NC 28052

MCINTYRE, John George (Md) 326 Pintail Dr, Havre De Grace, MD 21078

MCINTYRE, Moni (Pgh) 4601 5th Ave #825, Pittsburgh, PA 15213

MCJILTON, Sheila N (WA) St Philip's Church, 522 Main St, Laurel, MD 20707

MCKAY IV, Bob (NwPa) 1267 Treasure Lk, Du Bois, PA 15801

MCKAY, Judy Aileen (Ida) 6251 S Paperbirch Ave, Boise, ID 83716

MCKAY, Paige Higley (NwT) 1101 Slide Rd, Lubbock, TX 79416

MCKAY, William Martin (RG)

MCKEAN, Deborah Adams (Me) PO Box 137, Cushing, ME 04563

MCKEAN, Samantha K (Ga)

MCKEE, Christianne (Spok) 1909 W. Clearview Dr., Ellensburg, WA 98926

MCKEE, Elizabeth Shepherd (NC) 408 Woodlawn Ave, Greensboro, NC 27401

MCKEE, Helen Louise (SVa) 405 Avondale Dr., Danville, VA 24541

MCKEE, Lewis Kavanaugh (WTenn) 57 Wychewood Dr, Memphis, TN 38117

MCKEE, Martha Marcella (NJ) 11 Exeter Ct, East Windsor, NJ 08520

MCKEE, Michael Dale (Los) 815 Emerald Bay, Laguna Beach, CA 92651

MCKEE, Stephen (Okla) 501 S Cincinnati Ave, Tulsa, OK 74103

MCKEE, Susan Rose (CGC) PO Box 29, Bon Secour, AL 36511

MCKEE, Todd Anderson (Vt) 105 Hickory Rdg, White River Junction, VT 05001

MCKEEVER, Anne Dryden (The Episcopal NCal) 2620 Capitol Ave., Sacramento, CA 95816

MCKELLER, Dwayne Allen (SeFla) 705 NW 1st Ave, Hallandale Beach, FL 33009

✠ **MCKELVEY**, Jack Marston (Roch) 8 Grove St, Rochester, NY 14605

MCKENNA, Cynthia Ann (Okla) P.O. Box 187, Boerne, TX 78006

MCKENNA, Keith (NY) 429 Lakeshore Drive, Putnam Valley, NY 10579

MCKENNEY, Mary Lou R (ECR)

MCKENNEY, Walter (Ct) 38 Clover Dr, West Hartford, CT 06110

MCKENZIE, Bryan Keith (FtW) 2117 Ruea St, Grand Prairie, TX 75050

MCKENZIE, Jennifer Gaines (Va) Christ Church, 118 N Washington St, Alexandria, VA 22314

MCKENZIE JR, William Bruce (Ore) 1873 Sw High St, Portland, OR 97201

MCKENZIE-HAYWARD, Renee (Pa) 34 East Hodges Ave, Philadelphia, PA 19121

MCKEON, Julia McKay (Cal) 1590 Cabrillo Hwy S, Half Moon Bay, CA 94019

MCKEON JR, Richard (NY) Church of the Messiah, PO Box 248, Rhinebeck, NY 12572

MCKIM, Laurie J. (WTex) Church of the Advent, 104 W Elizabeth St, Brownsville, TX 78520

MCKINLEY, Ellen Bacon (Ct) 47 Valley Rd # B1, Cos Cob, CT 06807

MCKINLEY, Mele Senitila Tuineau (Ore) 1817 E Alsea Hwy, Waldport, OR 97394

MCKINNEY, Catherine R (Va) Varina Episcopal Church, 2385 Mill Rd, Henrico, VA 23231

MCKINNEY, Chantal (NC) 242 Flintshire Rd., Winston-Salem, NC 27104

MCKINNEY, Douglas Walton (Los) 401 S Detroit St Apt 311, Los Angeles, CA 90036

MCKINNEY, Helen Katherine (Mass)

MCKINNON, Michael John (Mass) 9 Svenson Ave, Worcester, MA 01607

MCKINNON, Stanley A (Ark) PO Box 767, Siloam Springs, AR 72761

MCKNIGHT, Jim (Cal) 801 S Plymouth Ct Unit 817, Chicago, IL 60605

MCKNIGHT, Leta Jeannette Zimmer (Vt) 75 South, Box 434, Lyndonville, VT 05851

MCKONE-SWEET, Mark C. (SanD) 16275 Pomerado Rd, Poway, CA 92064

MCLACHLAN, Devin Shepard (Mass) 38 Beaufort Place, Thompsons Lane, Cambridge, CB5 8AG, Great Britain (UK)

MCLAIN, Madge (WLa) PO Box 1101, Abbeville, LA 70511

MCLAIN III, Paul King (WTenn) 102 N 2nd St, Memphis, TN 38103

MCLAREN, Christopher Todd (RG) 6730 Green Valley Place NW, Los Ranchos, NM 87107

MCLAUGHLIN, Debra Kay (SeFla) 1704 Buchanan St, Hollywood, FL 33020

MCLAUGHLIN, Eleanor (NH) 38 Nekal Ln, Randolph, NH 03593

MCLAUGHLIN, John Norris (Mass) 406 Paradise Rd Apt 1b, Swampscott, MA 01907

MCLAUGHLIN, Marlys Jean (Az) 10926 W Topaz Dr, Sun City, AZ 85351

MCLEAN JR, James Rayford (Ark) PO Box 524, Leland, MI 49654

MCLEAN, Jean Medding (Mont)

MCLEAN, Katherine Sharp (La)

MCLEAN, Richard (WTex) 3821 Sandia Dr, Plano, TX 75023

MCLEAVEY, Lauren (Mass) St Anne's Episcopal Church, PO Box 134, North Billerica, MA 01862

MCLELLAN, Brenda Jean (Mont) 350 Janet St Apt 2b Apt 2b, Helena, MT 59601

MCLEMORE, Ann Rossington (Miss) 3921 Oakridge Dr, Jackson, MS 39216

MCLEMORE, William Pearman (Chi) 5116 W Malibu Ct, McHenry, IL 60050

MCLEOD, Harrison Marvin (USC) Christ Church, 10 N Church St, Greenville, SC 29601

MCLEOD III, Henry Marvin (Vt) 301 Georgetown Cir, Charleston, WV 25314

MCLEOD, James Wallace (ECR) 34400A Mission Blvd Apt 1109, Union City, CA 94587

✠ **MCLEOD**, Mary Adelia Rosamond (Vt) 301 Georgetown Cir, Charleston, WV 25314

MCLEOD, Robert Boutell (CFla) 6661 N Placita Alta Reposa, Tucson, AZ 85750

MCLEOD, Sandra Kirby (CGC) St Agath's Church, 150 Circle Dr, DeFuniak Springs, FL 32435

MCLEON IV, Richard (WTex) PO Box 698, Henderson, TX 75653

✠ **MCLOUGHLIN**, Jose Antonio (WNC) 924 N Robinson Ave, Oklahoma City, OK 73102

MCLUEN, Roy Emery (CGC) 25450 144th Place SE, Kent, WA 98042

MCMAHAN, Larry Wayne (CGC) 3902 E Jamie Ln, Bloomington, IN 47401

MCMAHON, Kathryn Evans (WA)

MCMANIS, Dennis Ray (SwFla) 12606 Rockrose Glen, Lakewood Ranch, FL 34202

MCMANUS, Bridget (CNY) 531 Cumberland Ave, Syracuse, NY 13210

MCMANUS, Mary Christie (Cal) 215 10th Ave, San Francisco, CA 94118

MCMANUS, Michael (Colo) P. O. Box 33022, Palm Beach Gardens, FL 33420

MCMICHAEL JR, Ralph Nelson (Spr) 1210 Locust St, Saint Louis, MO 63103

MCMILLAN, Bruce Dodson (Miss) Po Box 596, Holly Springs, MS 38635

MCMILLAN, John N (Alb) 4531 Ethel St, Okemos, MI 48864

MCMILLAN, Marilyn Ayres (Mass) 205 Old Main St, South Yarmouth, MA 02664

MCMILLEN II, Chuck (WTenn) St James Episcopal Church, PO Box 838, Union City, TN 38281

MCMILLIN, Andrea McMillin (The Episcopal NCal) 1600 Knox Ave, Bellingham, WA 98225

MCMULLEN, Andrew L (The Episcopal Church in Haw) Saint Matthias Episcopal Church, 18320 Furrow Rd, Monument, CO 80132

MCMURREN, Margaret (Ore) 1525 Glen Creek Rd Nw, Salem, OR 97304

MCMURTRY, Herbert Charles (Ak) 1915 Lindsay Loop, Mount Vernon, WA 98274

MCNAB, Charles Bruce (Colo) 2 Park Plaza Rd, Bozeman, MT 59715

MCNAB, Joan T (Colo) 536 W North St, Aspen, CO 81611

MCNABB, Christopher Ward (NJ) 33 Mercer St, Princeton, NJ 08540

MCNAIR, David (WNC) The Episcopal Church of the Holy Spirit, PO Box 956, Mars Hill, NC 28754

MCNAIR, Kent Stevens (The Episcopal NCal) 2200 Country Club Dr., Cameron Park, CA 95682

MCNAIRY, Philip Edward (Minn) 2287 Bevans Cir, Red Wing, MN 55066

MCNALLY, Jennifer Steckel (Minn) 2035 Charlton Rd, Sunfish Lake, MN 55118

MCNAMARA, Beth Cooper (Md) 8015 Rider Ave, Towson, MD 21204

MCNAMARA, Joseph Francis (CPa) Po Box 474, Mansfield, PA 16933

MCNAMARA, Kim (Oly) PO Box 156, Allyn, WA 98524

MCNAMARA, Patrick (NH) Holy Trinity, 768 Main St, Greenport, NY 11944

MCNAUGHTON, Bonnie Eleanor (Los) 2571 Via Campesina Unit G, Palos Verdes Estates, CA 90274

MCNAUGHTON, Margaret (WA) 720 Upland Pl, Alexandria, VA 22314

MCNAUL, Bob (Nev) 1909 Camino Mirada, North Las Vegas, NV 89031

MCNEELEY, David Fielden (Hai) 566 Standish Rd, Teaneck, NJ 07666

MCNEELY, Virginia Diane (The Episcopal NCal) Trinity Cathedral, 2620 Capitol Ave, Sacramento, CA 95816

MCNEER, Charles Conrad (SwVa) 490 Court St Apt 6, Abingdon, VA 24210

MCNEILL, Nayan (ECR) 20 University Ave, Los Gatos, CA 95030

MCNELLIS, Kathleene Kernan (RG) 6200 Coors NW, Albuquerque, NM 87120

MCNIEL, Donna (Episcopal SJ) 4401 4th St N Apt 242, Arlington, VA 22203

MCNISH, Jill L (Pa) 199 W Baltimore Ave, Clifton Heights, PA 19018

✠ **MCNUTT JR**, Charlie Fuller (CPa) 5225 Wilson Ln Apt 2137, Mechanicsburg, PA 17055

MCNUTT, Robin Lee (Neb) 3020 Belvedere Blvd, Omaha, NE 68111

MCPARTLIN, Julie (Alb) Harbour Island Club #203, 5101 Highway A1a, Vero Beach, FL 32963

MCPEAK, Helen C (Oly) 415 S 18th St, Mount Vernon, WA 98274

MCPHAIL, Donald Stewart (SC) 22 Saint Augustine Dr., Charleston, SC 29407

MCPHEE, Gizelle Valencia (SeFla) PO Box 12943, Miami, FL 33101

MCPHERSON, Bruce (Md) 214 Wardour Drive, Annapolis, MD 21401

MCPHERSON, Clair W (NY) 1234 Midland Ave #5E, Bronxville, NY 10708

MCPHERSON, Phebe Lewald (Md) 214 Wardour Dr, Annapolis, MD 21401

MCPHERSON, Thomas Dale (WMich) 224 Chauncey Ct, Marshall, MI 49068

MCQUADE, Lynne (NY) 900 Palmer Rd Apt 7-L, Bronxville, NY 10708

MCQUEEN, Dale (Oly) 3230 Chanute Dr., Lake Havasu city, AZ 86406

MCQUEEN, Henry (WA) St John's Church, 3427 Olney Laytonsville Rd, Olney, MD 20832

MCQUEEN, Paul (CFla) 1332 Bramley Ln, Deland, FL 32720

MCQUERY, Andy (Ore)

MCQUIN, Randall Lee (Kan) 3141 Fairview Park Dr Ste 250, Falls Church, VA 22042

MCQUITTY, Elizabeth Grace (Los)

MCRAE, Marcia O (EC) 511 E Broughton St, Bainbridge, GA 39817

MCREE, Tim (WNC) 274 Sunset Hts, Canton, NC 28716

MCSWAIN, William D (SC) 7313 Highway 162, Hollywood, SC 29449

MCTERNAN, Vaughan Durkee (Colo) 2609 Rigel Drive, Colorado Springs, CO 80906

MCVEY, Arthur William (Kan) 9218 Cherokee Pl, Leawood, KS 66206

MCVEY, Brian (Tenn) 4403 High Ct, Davenport, IA 52804

MCWHORTER, Betty (NY) 1304 NW Meadows Drive, McMinnville, OR 97128

MCWHORTER, Shirley R (Mich) St Thomas Episcopal Church, 2441 Nichols Drive, Trenton, MI 48183

MCWHORTER, Stephen (Va) 570 Lovely Ln, Sylacauga, AL 35151

MEACHAM, Carlyle Haynes (Vt) Po Box 115, Washburn, IL 61570

MEACHEN, Jerome Webster (Ct) 20 W Canal St Apt 423, Winooski, VT 05404

MEAD, Alan Champ (CPa) 3159 Silver Sands Circle #103, Virginia Beach, VA 23451

MEAD, Andrew Craig (NY) 321 Wandsworth Street, Narragansett, RI 02882

MEAD, Carol Lynn (Miss) 105 Montgomery Hl, Starkville, MS 39759

MEAD, Matthew Hoxsie (NY) 1415 Pelhamdale Avenue, Pelham, NY 10803

MEADE, Elizabeth G (Chi) 406 Peck Rd, Geneva, IL 60134

MEADE, Gary J (WTenn) St. Mary's Episcopal Church, 108 N. King Ave., Dyersburg, TN 38024

MEADE, Jean (La) 1314 Jackson Ave, New Orleans, LA 70130

MEADERS JR, Calvin Judson (Miss) 200 E Academy St., Canton, MS 39046

MEADERS III, Calvin Judson (Miss) 305 S Commerce St, Natchez, MS 39120

MEADOWCROFT, Jeffrey Whittaker (USC)

MEADOWS JR, Richard (WA) Grace Episcopal Church, 1607 Grace Church Rd, Silver Spring, MD 20910

MEAIRS, Babs Marie (SanD) 11650 Calle Paracho, San Diego, CA 92128

MEANS, Carl T (Wyo) 300 Mt. Arter Loop, Lander, WY 82520

MEANS, Jackie (Ind) 834 Mount Dora Ln, Indianapolis, IN 46229

MEARS JR, Preston Kennard (NH) 15101 Candy Hill Rd, Upper Marlboro, MD 20772

MEASE, Carole Ann (CPa) 359 Schoolhouse Rd, Middletown, PA 17057

MEAUX, Amy Dafler (Lex) 320 W Main St, Danville, KY 40422

MEBANE JR, Will (Mass) St. Paul's Cathedral, 4 Cathedral Park, Buffalo, NY 14202

MECK III, Daniel Stoddart (Md) 5620 Greenspring Avenue, Baltimore, MD 21209

MECK, Nancy E (SVa) 13530 Heathbrook Rd, Midlothian, VA 23112

MECKLING, Jude (Pa) 730 S Highland Ave, Merion Station, PA 19066

MEDELA, Jean Milor (Hai) Eglesi Episcopal D'Haiti, Boite Postale 1309, Port-au-prince, Haiti

MEDINA, Ernesto (Neb) 16611 Castelar St, Omaha, NE 68130

MEDINA, Felix R (PR) Po Box 2156, Bridgeport, CT 06608

MEDINA MEJIA, Jorge Reynaldo (Hond)

MEDLEY, James W (SVa) 808 Gates Ave Apt B5, Norfolk, VA 23517

MEECH, Michelle (NY) 4800 Woodward Ave, Detroit, MI 48201

MEEKS, Edward Gettys (USC) 405 S. Chapel Street, Baltimore, MD 21231

MEENGS, John Richard (WMich) 622 Lawndale Ct, Holland, MI 49423

MEGEATH, Sally Holme (Colo) 343 Canyon St, Lander, WY 82520

MEGGINSON JR, Marshall Elliot (HB) 5689 Utrecht Rd, Baltimore, MD 21206

MEGINNISS, David Hamilton (Ala) 801 Pin Brook Lane, Tuscaloosa, AL 35406

MEHEUX, Sybil Adlyn (CFla) 543 Corporation St, Holly Hill, FL 32117

MEIER, Kermit Irwin (Ore) 1209 Fleet Landing Blvd, Atlantic Beach, FL 32233

MEIROW, Lisa Marie (Fla)

MEISS, Marion (Be) 46 S. Laurel St., Hazleton, PA 18201

MEISTER, Deborah (Ct) 3001 Wisconsin Ave. NW, Washington, DC 20016

MEISTER, Stephen George (Roch) 400 S Main St, Newark, NY 14513

MEISTER BOOK, Nancy D (Az)

MEJIA, Jairo (ECR) 12149 Saddle Road, Carmel Valley, CA 93924

MEJIA, Jose Arnaldo (Hond) Calle Principal, La Estrada, HN, Honduras

MEJIA, Nelson Yovany (Hond) Roatan Islas De La Bahia, Apartado 193, Roatan, Coxen Hole, Honduras

MEJIA BALLESTEROS, Francisco Javier (Colom) Calle 1 N 48-95 Barrio Leon XIII, Villavicencio Meta, Colombia

MEJIA ESPINOSA, Jose Vicente (EcuC) Avenue La Castellana 40-06, Zona 8, Guatemala City, 01008, Guatemala

MEJIA-MONTESDEOCA, Marco (EcuC) P.O. Box 588, Ibarra, Ecuador

MELBERGER, MaryJo (Pa) 734 Twining Way, Collegeville, PA 19426

MELCHER, John Robert (Mich) 2441 Nichols St, Trenton, MI 48183

MELCHIONNA, Elizabeth Marie Marie (NC) 104 Nuttal Pl, Chapel Hill, NC 27514

MELENDEZ, Michael Paul (Mass) 138 Tremont St, Boston, MA 02111

MELIN, Marilyn Joyce (Chi) 206 South Maple Street, Libertyville, IL 60048

MELIS, Alberto Manuel (Tex) 305 N 30th St, Waco, TX 76710

MELLISH, Roy Whyle (La) PO Box 1825, Morgan City, LA 70381

MELLO, Iris Elaine (RI) 88 Albert Ave, Cranston, RI 02905

MELLO, Jeffrey William (Mass) 130 Aspinwall Ave, Brookline, MA 02446

MELLO, Mary Ann (RI)

MELLO-MAKI, Christine Helene (NMich) 470 North Us 141, Crystal Falls, MI 49920

MELLON, Bob (Pa) 10551 Machrihanish Cir, San Antonio, FL 33576

MELLOTT, Emily Alice (NJ) 207 W Main St, Moorestown, NJ 08057

MELNYK, James (NC) 5400 Crestview Rd, Raleigh, NC 27609

MELTON, Betty Anne (Miss)

MELTON, Brent (Va) 210 Ellington St, Fayetteville, NC 28305

MELTON, Heather L (NAM) 288 Harrison Ave, Harrison, NY 10528

MELTON, Jk (Colo) Fordham University, 441 E Fordham Rd, Bronx, NY 10458

MELTON, Jonathan Randall (Mil) 1360 Regent St # 157, Madison, WI 53715

MELTON, Mark Randall (Dal) Saint James' Episcopal Church, 10707 County Road 4022, Kemp, TX 75143

MEMBA, Joseluis (NJ) PO Box 502, Red Bank, NJ 07701

MENAUL, Marjorie Ann (CPa) 6288 Peach Tree Rd, Columbus, OH 43213

MENDENHALL, Elborn E (Kan) 2477 SW Brookhaven Ln, Topeka, KS 66614

MENDEZ, Noe (Dal) The Holy Nativity Episcopal Church, 2200 18th St, Plano, TX 75074

MENDEZ, Richard (U) RR2 Box 64, Pocatello, ID 83202

MENDEZ, Troy Douglas (Az) Trinity Cathedral, 100 W Roosevelt St, Phoenix, AZ 85003

Clergy List

MENDEZ COLON, Ana Rosa (PR) Urbanizacion Venus Gardens, 1770 Calle Peliux, San Juan, PR 00926

MENDOZA, Christine L (Va) 3201 Windsor Rd, Austin, TX 78703

MENDOZA, Lidia ()

MENDOZA, Loretta (Mil) 2708 Red Fawn Ct, Racine, WI 53406

MENDOZA CEDENO, Eduardo (Litoral Ecu)

MENDOZA MARMOLEJOS, Milquella Rosanna (DR (DomRep))

MENDOZA PEREZ, Julio Cesar (Ve) Iglesia Episcopal de Venezuela, Centro Diocesano Av. Caroní No. 100, Colinas de Bello Monte Caracas 1042-A, Venezuela

MENDOZA QUIROZ, Hugo Eligio (Litoral Ecu) Calle #19, #208, Calderon, Ecuador

MENEELEY, Beverly Ann (Be)

MENELAS, Frederic (Hai)

MENGER, James Andrew (Ga) 3521 Nassau Dr, Augusta, GA 30909

MENJIVAR, Natividad (Okla) St Mark's Episcopal Church, 6744 S Kings Hwy, Alexandria, VA 22306

MENJIVAR, Nicholas (NC) Po Box 218, Durham, NC 27702

MENNELL, John A (Nwk) 75 S Fullerton Ave, Montclair, NJ 07042

MENZI, Donald Wilder (Mich) 5 E 10th St, New York, NY 10003

MERCADO GALARZA, Wilfredo (PR)

MERCER JR, Charles Spencer (Md) The Episcopal Church Of St Mary The Virgin, 3121 Walbrook Ave, Baltimore, MD 21216

MERCER, Emmanuel A (Md) Saint Paul's Church, 22 E Chestnut Hill Ave, Philadelphia, PA 19118

MERCER JR, Roy Calvin (CFla) 4932 Willowbrook Cir, Winter Haven, FL 33884

MERCER, Thomas Robert (NY) Po Box A, Granite Springs, NY 10527

MERCER LADD, Morgan (LI)

MERCHANT, John Edward (At) 474 Sunset Dr., Asheville, NC 28804

MERCHANT, Patricia (At) 120 Warren St NE, Atlanta, GA 30317

MERCHANT II, Wilmot (SC) 801 11th Avenue North, North Myrtle Beach, SC 29582

MERCURE, Joan Carol (Minn) 4557 Colfax Ave S, Minneapolis, MN 55419

MEREDITH, Carol Ann (Colo) 316 Oakland St, Aurora, CO 80010

MERFY, Florence Martha (Nev) 1515 Shasta Dr Apt 1510, Davis, CA 95616

MERINO-BOTERO, Bernardo (Colom) Calle 97 - No 16-51, Apt 303 Edificio Royal Plaza, Bogota, Colombia

MEROLA SR, Carl Robert (CFla) 705 Victory Lane, Hendersonville, NC 28739

MEROLA JR, Carl Robert (Va) 402 Valencia Cir, Oviedo, FL 32765

MERONEY, Anne Elrod (At) 4919-B Rivoli Dr, Macon, GA 31210

MERRELL, Robin Nicholas (Cal) 3886 Balcom Rd, San Jose, CA 95148

MERRICK, Barbara Robinson (Ky) 8110 Saint Andrews Church Rd, Louisville, KY 40258

MERRILL, George Richard (Md) 9046 Quail Run Rd, Saint Michaels, MD 21663

MERRILL JR, Robert Clifford (Tex) 1321 Upland Dr #5192, Houston, TX 77043

MERRILL, Russell Walter (EMich) 262 Raleigh Pl, Lennon, MI 48449

MERRIMAN, Michael Walter (Minn) 2012 Stain Glass Dr, Plano, TX 75075

MERRIN, Susie (Colo)

MERRITT, Claudia W (Va) 3401 Hawthorne Avenue, Richmond, VA 23222

MERRITT, Frederick Deen (Neb)

MERRITT, Robert E (CFla) 864 Summerfield Dr, Lakeland, FL 33803

MERROW, Andrew T P (Va) 2609 North Glebe Road, Arlington, VA 22207

MERTZ, Annie Pierpoint (The Episcopal NCal) St. Paul's Episcopal School, 116 Montecito Ave, Oakland, CA 94610

MERTZ, Mary Ann (Pa) 116 Lancaster Pike, Oxford, PA 19363

MERZ, John (LI) 129 Kent Street, Brooklyn, NY 11222

MESENBRING, David Gary (Oly) 1245 10th Ave E, Seattle, WA 98102

MESERVEY, Norman Rix (WNC) 84 Church St, Franklin, NC 28734

MESLER JR, Raymond Clyde (NY) 7470 W Glenbrook Rd Apt 313, Milwaukee, WI 53223

MESLEY, Gordon Warwick (WMo) 2021 S Hummel Dr, Independence, MO 64055

MESSENGER, Ray Stillson (CNY) 3877 Milton Ave Apt 235, Camillus, NY 13031

MESSENGER, William Glen (Mass) 84 Lexington St, Belmont, MA 02478

MESSENGER-HARRIS, Beverly Ann (CNY) 124 W Hamilton Ave, Sherrill, NY 13461

MESSER, Chuck (NJ) PO Box 452, Glen Riddle, PA 19037

MESSER, Julia (SVa) 5181 Princess Anne Rd, Virginia Beach, VA 23462

MESSER, Kenneth Blaine (Ia)

MESSERSMITH, Daphne S (CPa) PO Box 125, Cornwall, PA 17016

MESSERSMITH, Merton (CPa) 909 Alison Ave, Mechanicsburg, PA 17055

MESSICK, Joshua E (Miss) 20 3rd St, Pocomoke City, MD 21851

MESSIER, Daniel Joseph (Az) 600 S La Canada Dr, Green Valley, AZ 85614

MESSINA JR, Michael Frank (CFla) 94 Pecan Run, Ocala, FL 34472

MESTETH, Rhoda Yvonne (SD) Po Box 9, Pine Ridge, SD 57770

MESTRE JR, José Wilfredo (Ct) 2340 North Ave Apt. 7D, Bridgeport, CT 06614

METCALF, Michael Patrick (Dal) 3205 Landershire Ln, Plano, TX 75023

METCALFE, Steven (WNY) 20 Milton St, Williamsville, NY 14221

METELLUS, Donald (Hai)

METHENY JR, Lloyd Erwin (The Episcopal NCal) 11070 Hirschfeld Way #66, Rancho Cordova, CA 95670

METHVEN, Susanne (Okla) PO Box 1783, Salina, KS 67402

METHVIN, Thomas G (Dal) 3966 McKinney Ave, Dallas, TX 75204

METIVIER, Catherine A (Okla)

METOYER, Eric (Cal) Episcopal Diocese Of California, 1055 Taylor St, San Francisco, CA 94108

METRO, Michael (Be)

METTLER, Garrett (NY) PO Box 484, Fishkill, NY 12524

METZ, susanna (ETenn) 335 Tennessee Ave, Sewanee, TN 37383

METZGER, Carl (Pa) 100 E Lehigh Ave, Philadelphia, PA 19125

METZGER, Curtis (NH) PO Box 1541, Concord, NH 03302

METZGER, Jim (Mo) 3402 Sawgrass Ln, Cincinnati, OH 45209

METZLER, Carolyn (Me) 1611 Sunset Gardens Rd SW, Albuquerque, NM 87105

METZLER, Martie (Mo) 5305 Kenrick View Drive, Saint Louis, MO 63119

METZLER, Paul Arthur (CNY) 5305 Kenrick View Dr, Saint Louis, MO 63119

MEUSCHKE, Marty O (Ga) 145 River Ridge Loop, Hortense, GA 31543

MEYER, Alan King (Az) 5909 SW Karla Ct, Portland, OR 97239

MEYER, Erika K (NY) 240 E. 31st St., New York, NY 10016

MEYER, John (Mich) 1353 Labrosse St, Detroit, MI 48226

MEYER, John Anthony (LI) 423 Falcon Ridge Drive, Sheridan, WY 82801

MEYER, Kerri Ann (Cal)

MEYER, Mark David (Colo) 1365 Fairview Ave, Canon City, CO 81212

MEYER, Nancy Ruth (Chi) St Peter's Episcopal Church, 621 W Belmont Ave, Chicago, IL 60657

MEYER, Robert (FdL) PO Box 184, Tremont, IL 61568

MEYER, Wendel William (Mass) 347 Emerald Bay Cir Unit S7, Naples, FL 34110

MEYERS, David Craig (WMich) Church Of The Holy Spirit, 1200 Post Dr NE, Belmont, MI 49306

MEYERS, Frederick W (Rick) (Colo) 420 Cantril St, Castle Rock, CO 80104

MEYERS, Michael William (Az) 300 N Constitution Dr, Tucson, AZ 85748

MEYERS, Ruth (Cal) Church Divinity School Of The Pacific, 2451 Ridge Rd, Berkeley, CA 94709

MEYERS, Timothy M (NC)

MEZACAPA, Nicklas A (Minn) 111 3rd Ave SW, Rochester, MN 55902

MICHAEL, Mark A (WA) 10033 River Rd, Potomac, MD 20854

MICHAELS, Glen Francis (Alb) Po Box 2123, Plattsburgh, NY 12901

MICHAELS, Laurie Jane (Chi) 647 Dundee Ave, Barrington, IL 60010

MICHAELSON, Peter Ruhl (RI) 2 Gaspee Point Dr, Warwick, RI 02888

MICHAUD, Bruce Alan (EMich) 2090 Wyndham Ln, Alpena, MI 49707

MICHAUD, David Norman (Eas) St Peter's Church, 115 Saint Peters St, Salisbury, MD 21801

MICHAUD, Eleanor Jean (Eau)

MICHAUD, Jean Fruitho (Hai) Eglesi Episcopal D'Haiti, Boite Postale 1309, Port-au-Prince, Haiti

✠ **MICHEL**, Rodney Rae (LI) 600 E Cathedral Rd Apt G304, Philadelphia, PA 19128

MICHELFELDER, Susan Rebecca (SO) 30 W Woodruff Ave, Columbus, OH 43210

MICHELL, Neal O (Dal) 5100 Ross Ave, Dallas, TX 75206

MICHELS, Sandie B (Ind) 5910 Black Oak Lane, Ft. Worth, TX 76114

MICHIE, Mike (Dal) 8701 Tiercels Dr, Mckinney, TX 75070

MICKELSON, Margaret Belle (Ak) PO Box 849, Cordova, AK 99574

MICKLOW, Patricia L (NMich)

MIDDLETON, Mark Leslie (Chi) 509 Hessel Blvd, Champaign, IL 61820

MIDDLETON III, Richard Temple (Miss) 944 Royal Oak Dr, Jackson, MS 39209

MIDDLETON, Tracie Gail (FtW) PO Box 24761, Fort Worth, TX 76124

MIDENCE VALDES, Jose Francisco (Hond) Comercio, Tela, Honduras

MIDWOOD JR, John Earle (Pa) 300 North Lawrence, Philadelphia, PA 19106

MIDYETTE III, Charles Thomas (EC) 122 Queen St, Beaufort, NC 28516

MIEDKE, Warren Giles (Tex) 13131 Fry Rd, Cypress, TX 77433

MIESCHER III, Walter Henry (Kan) 2630 N Ridgewood Ct, Wichita, KS 67220

MIHALYI, David (CNY) 472 Washington St, Geneva, NY 14456

MIKAYA, Henry C (WMich) Box 1315, Gabrone, Botswana

MIKEL, Joseph F (Oly) 15945 Cascade Ln Se, Monroe, WA 98272

MILAM, David Ross (Mass) 108 Lakeside Ave, Lakeville, MA 02347

MILAM, Thomas Richerson (SwVa) 715 Forest Hills Dr, Wilmington, NC 28403

MILAN JR, Jesse (Kan) 7103 Waverly Ave, Kansas City, KS 66109

MILANO, Mary Lucille (Chi) 8765 W Higgins Rd, Chicago, IL 60631

MILES, Allan Wayne (Ore)

MILES, Frank William (Colo) 1175 Vine St Apt 207, Denver, CO 80206

MILES, Glenworth Dalmane (LI) 2714 Lurting Ave, Bronx, NY 10469

MILES, James B (HB)

MILES JR, John Pickett (SVa) 268 Mill Stream Way, Williamsburg, VA 23185

MILES, Kristin K (NY) 120 Broadway Fl 38, New York, NY 10271

MILES, Richard Alan Knox (NC) 634 Parkway Blvd, Reidsville, NC 27320

MILES, Thomas Dee (Kan) 1308 Overlook Dr, Manhattan, KS 66503

MILFORD, Sara M (Ark) 228 Spring St, Hot Springs, AR 71901

MILHAN, Pamela Hope Arnold (SwFla)

MILHOAN, Charles Everett (Az) 4102 W Union Hills Dr, Glendale, AZ 85308

MILHOLEN, Linda Scott (WMo) PO Box 109, Houston, MO 65483

MILHOLLAND, Nancy Elizabeth (Mass) 58 Stanford Heights Ave, San Francisco, CA 94127

MILHON-MARTIN, Jana (Los) 569 Carleton Pl, Claremont, CA 91711

MILIAN, Mario Emilio (SeFla) 5690 N Kendall Dr, Coral Gables, FL 33156

MILIEN, Marivel (SeFla) 6744 N Miami Ave, Miami, FL 33150

MILIEN, Smith Baptiste Smith (SeFla) 6744 North Miami Ave, Miami, FL 33150

MILKOVICH, Edward Frank (Los) 28211 Pacific Coast Hwy, Malibu, CA 90265

MILLAR, John Dunne (Az) 7245 E Manzanita Dr, Scottsdale, AZ 85258

MILLER, Alan Clayborne (Fla) 1637 Nw 19th Cir, Gainesville, FL 32605

MILLER, Alden Scott (Oly) 211 Calle del Verano, Palm Desert, CA 92260

MILLER, Alfred Franklin (Colo) 2701 S York St, Denver, CO 80210

MILLER, Anthony Glenn (Los) 350 S Madison Ave Apt 207, Pasadena, CA 91101

MILLER, Arthur Burton (ECR) 2050 California St Apt 20, Mountain View, CA 94040

MILLER, Barbara Ruth (ECR) 5318 Palma Ave, Atascadero, CA 93422

MILLER, Barry William (Ct) 99 Timberwood Rd, West Hartford, CT 06117

MILLER, Bill (La) PO Box 1745, Lihue, HI 96766

MILLER, Caroline Joy (CFla)

MILLER, Charlene Ida (Tex) 14300 66th St N Lot 900, Clearwater, FL 33764

MILLER, Christopher H (Va) 1000 Saint Stephens Rd, Alexandria, VA 22304

MILLER, Christopher James-Alan (At) 3098 Saint Annes Ln Nw, Atlanta, GA 30327

MILLER, Clark Stewart (NI) 319 7th St, Logansport, IN 46947

MILLER, David Dallas (Dal) 1700 N Westmoreland Rd, Desoto, TX 75115

MILLER, David Walton (Los) 1037 16th St Apt 1, Santa Monica, CA 90403

MILLER, Donald Stewart (Cal) 45602 State Highway 14, Stevenson, WA 98648

MILLER, Duane Alexander (WTex)

MILLER JR, Ed (Va) 6715 Georgetown Pike, Mclean, VA 22101

MILLER JR, Edwin Lee (Okla) 3300 N Vermont Ave, Oklahoma City, OK 73112

MILLER, Elizabeth (Me) 286 Lincoln St, South Portland, ME 04106

MILLER, Elizabeth M (Be) 44 E Market St, Bethlehem, PA 18018

MILLER, Eric Lee (SO) 321 Worthington Ave., Cincinnati, OH 45215

MILLER JR, Ernest Charles (NY) 611 Broadway Rm 520, New York, NY 10012

MILLER, Fred (CPa) 547 Brighton Place, Mechanicsburg, PA 17055

MILLER, Frederic (LI) 41 Reid Ave., Port Washington, NY 11050

MILLER, Isaac J (Pa) 18th & Diamond, Philadelphia, PA 19121

MILLER, James Barrett (The Episcopal NCal) 550 Seagaze Dr Apt 19, Oceanside, CA 92054

MILLER, Janice Mary Howard (NI) 2117 E Jefferson Blvd, South Bend, IN 46617

MILLER, Jason Michael (WNY) 64 Green Forest Ct, East Amherst, NY 14051

MILLER, Jean Louise (EC) 9191 Daly Rd., Cincinnati, OH 45231

MILLER, Jerry (WMo) 4258 E Whitehall Dr, Springfield, MO 65809

MILLER, Jo Anne (Ore) P.O. Box 413, Bandon, OR 97411

MILLER, Joe Ted (Okla) 2732 Walnut Rd, Norman, OK 73072

MILLER, Joel (ECR) 160 Robideaux Rd, Aptos, CA 95003

MILLER, John Edward (Alb) PO Box 12, Ancram, NY 12502

MILLER, John Edward (Va) 4209 Monument Ave, Richmond, VA 23230

MILLER, John Leonard (NY) 23 Cedar Ln, Princeton, NJ 08540

MILLER JR, John Meredith (Vt) 34 County Route 59, Buskirk, NY 12028

MILLER, John Sloan (La) 12679 N Highmeadow Ct, Baton Rouge, LA 70816

MILLER, Joseph Potter (Los)

MILLER, Judith Joelynn Walker (Oly) PO Box 1782, Westport, WA 98595

MILLER JR, Kenny (Mil) 3906 W Mequon Rd, Mequon, WI 53092

MILLER, Kurt David (Ga) 3665 Bermuda Cir, Augusta, GA 30909

MILLER, Laura Jean (Alb) 41 Gardiner Pl, Walton, NY 13856

MILLER, Laurence Henry (Be) 31 Tecumseh Pass, Millsboro, DE 19966

MILLER, Leewin Glen (SwFla) 4279 70th St Cir E, Palmetto, FL 34221

MILLER JR, Louis (USC) 129 Heathwood Rd, Union, SC 29379

MILLER, Marion R (Tenn) Po Box 1903, Monterey, CA 93942

MILLER, Mark Joseph (Oly) 913 2nd St, Snohomish, WA 98290

MILLER, Mary Scott (Mass) 54 Robert Rd, Marblehead, MA 01945

MILLER, Michaelene M (Ark) 501 S Phoenix Ave, Russellville, AR 72801

MILLER, Nancy (Ct) 99 Timberwood Rd, West Hartford, CT 06117

MILLER, Nancy Fay (RI) 82 Rockmeadow Rd, Westwood, MA 02090

MILLER, pastor (Be) 2227 NW 79th Ave, Doral, FL 33122

MILLER, Patricia L (WMo) 1840 Hickory Station Cir, Snellville, GA 30078

MILLER, Patrick Jameson (Tex) 3514 Corondo Ct., Houston, TX 77005

MILLER, Paula (Mich) 1325 Champaign Rd, Lincoln Park, MI 48146

MILLER, R Cameron (Roch) 164 Washington St, Geneva, NY 14456

MILLER, Rich (NI) 17716 Downing Dr, Lowell, IN 46356

MILLER, Richard (Pa) 1521 Ashby Rd, Paoli, PA 19301

MILLER, Robert Mcgregor (Pa) 2039 Serendipity Way, Schwenksville, PA 19473

MILLER, Robert William (Minn) 11030 Batello Dr, Venice, FL 34292

MILLER, Roger Edward (CFla) 11620 Claymont Circle, Windermere, FL 34786

MILLER, Ronald Homer (Md) 830 W 40th St. Apt 860, Baltimore, MD 21211

MILLER, Sarah HT (Tex) 5286 Santa Maria Dr, Mechanicsville, VA 23116

MILLER, Sarah L (Neb) PO Box 2421, Fremont, NE 68026

MILLER, Stephen Arthur (WNC) 290 Hillside Oaks Dr, Jefferson, NC 28640

MILLER, Stephen Howard (Okla) 701 N 7th St, Perry, OK 73077

✠ **MILLER**, Steve (Mil) 804 E Juneau Ave, Milwaukee, WI 53202

MILLER, Susan Heilmann (ECR) 25020 Pine Hills Dr, Carmel, CA 93923

MILLER, Thomas Paul (NY) 165 Christopher St Apt 5W, New York, NY 10014

MILLER, Todd (Mass) 12 Ridge Ave., Newton, MA 02459

MILLER, Victoria C (Ct) 350 Sound Beach Ave, Old Greenwich, CT 06870

MILLER, William Charles (Pgh) 18297 W 155th Ter, Olathe, KS 66062

MILLER, William Robert (CPa) 182 Dew Drop Rd Apt G, York, PA 17402

MILLER, William T (Fla) 25928 Kilreigh Dr, Farmington Hills, MI 48336

MILLER IV, Woodford Decatur (CFla) 2508 Creekside Dr., Fort Piece, FL 34981

MILLER-MUTIA, Sylvia J (RG) 425 University Blvd NE, Albuquerque, NM 87106

MILLETTE, Carol Leslie (RI) 19 Midway Dr, Warwick, RI 02886

MILLICAN JR, Ford Jefferson (La) 3919 Morris Pl, Jefferson, LA 70121

MILLIEN, Jean (Hai) Ecole Le Bon Samaritan, 26 Rue Jonathas, Carrefour, 06134, Haiti

MILLIEN, Wilner (PR)

MILLIGAN, Donald Arthur (Mass) 222 Bowdoin St, Winthrop, MA 02152

MILLIGAN, Kathleen Sue (Ia) 3714 Pennsylvania Ave Apt. I-86, Dubuque, IA 52002

MILLIGAN, Michael (U) 28 Ridgeview Drive, Bountiful, UT 84010

MILLIKEN, Jean Louise (Va) 3732 N Oakland St, Arlington, VA 22207

✠ **MILLIKEN**, Mike (WK) 1 N. Main Sreet - Suite 418, Hutchinson, KS 67501

MILLIKIN, Gregory L (Chi) 228 S Pitt St, Alexandria, VA 22314

MILLNER JR, Bo (Va) 8 N Laurel St, Richmond, VA 23220

MILLOTT, Diane Lynn (SwFla) 4510 Pilgrim Mill Road, Cumming, GA 30041

MILLOTT, Donna Evans (SwFla) 1236 Santa Barbara Blvd, Cape Coral, FL 33991

MILLOTT, Robert Thomas (SwFla) 4510 Pilgrim Mill Road, Cumming, GA 30041

MILLS, Alice Marie (USC) St Mary's Episcopal Church, 170 Saint Andrews Rd, Columbia, SC 29210

MILLS JR, Arthur Donald (SO) 2696 Cedarbrook Way, Beavercreek, OH 45431

MILLS, Byron Keith (Az) 596 W. Ord Mountain Rd, Globe, AZ 85501

MILLS, Carol Ann (Tex) 205 Hillcrest Dr, Alvin, TX 77511

MILLS, Christen H (Mass)

MILLS, David Knight (SO) 172 Clark Point Rd # 696, Southwest Harbor, ME 04679

MILLS III, Edward James (ETenn) 2104 Lamont St, Kingsport, TN 37664

MILLS, Eric Christopher (FdL) 347 Libal St, De Pere, WI 54115

MILLS, Fred Thomas (Ky) 685 West Dr, Madisonville, KY 42431

MILLS III, Joseph Edmund (LI) 1118 9th St Apt 9, Santa Monica, CA 90403

MILLS JR, Joseph Milton (Tex) 205 Hillcrest Dr, Alvin, TX 77511

MILLS, Joy Anna Marie (Pa) 2103 Quail Ridge Dr, Paoli, PA 19301

MILLS III, Ladson Frazier (SC) 3114 Mayfair Ln, Johns Island, SC 29455

MILLS, Michael S (Dal) 11122 Midway Rd, Dallas, TX 75229

MILLS, Nancy Thompson (Ga) PO Box 3136, Thomasville, GA 31799

MILLS, Stephen (ECR) 713 Helen Drive, Hollister, CA 95023

MILLS, Susan Patricia (SO) 9222 Garrison Dr Apt 203c, Indianapolis, IN 46240

MILLS, Wallace Wilson (Ida)

MILLSAP, William Richard (Nev) PO Box 2246, Reno, NV 89505

MILLS-CURRAN, Lori (Mass) 7 Kimball Rd, Westborough, MA 01581

MILLS-POWELL, Mark Oliver Mclay (Eur)

MILNER JR, Raymond Joseph (SanD) 200 E 22nd St Apt 32, Roswell, NM 88201

MILTENBERGER, Gordon (Dal) 10 Oak Village Rd, Greenville, TX 75402

MINARIK JR, Harry J (ETenn) 69 Hickory Trail, Norris, TN 37828

MINDRUM, Alice Anderson (Ct) 60 Range Rd, Southport, CT 06890

MINEAU, Charles Douglas (NMich)

MINER, Bob (Ct) 15 Morningside Ter, Wallingford, CT 06492

MINER, Darren R (Cal) 1750 29th Ave, San Francisco, CA 94122

MINER, David R. (Fla) 3212 Wind Lake Ln, Tallahassee, FL 32312

MINER II, James Stevens (SO) 276 North Ardmore Road, Columbus, OH 43209

MINER-PEARSON, Anne Arlene (Minn) 15601 Island Road, Burnsville, MN 55306

MINERVA SR, Royal Edward (Fla)

MINGLEDORFF, Paschal Schirm (Ga) 9541 Whitfield Ave, Savannah, GA 31406

MINICH, Henry Nichols Faulconer (SeFla) 250 Pantops Mountain Rd Apt 5406, Charlottesville, VA 22911

MINIFIE, Charles Jackson (NY) 23 Sherman Dr, Hilton Head Island, SC 29928

MINNICH-LOCKEY, Laura (Va) 79 Laurel St, Harrisonburg, VA 22801

MINNICK, Margaret (Ct) 381 Main St Box 187, Middletown, CT 06457

MINOR, Al (ETenn) 7006 Brickton Way, Knoxville, TN 37919

MINOR, Cheryl Vasil (Mass) 65 Common Street, Belmont, MA 02478

MINOR, Paul Lawrence (Mass) 65 Common St., Belmont, MA 02478

MINSHEW, Jim (SeFla) Po Box 1596, Port Salerno, FL 34992

MINSHEW, Nancy Elizabeth (CFla) 3735 Us Highway 17 92 N, Davenport, FL 33837

MINTER, Larry Clifton (Ky) 5409 Hickory Hill Rd, 5409 Hickory Hill Rd, Louisville, KY 40214

MINTER, Michael William (FdL) 314 Bellevue Rd, Highland, NY 12528

MINTER, Russell Deane (Tex) 364 Beckett Point Rd, Port Townsend, WA 98368

MINTON, Anne Mansfield (Mass) 35 Riverwalk Way Unit 303, Lowell, MA 01854

MINTURN, Sterling Majors (NY) 5555 N Sheridan Rd Apt 607, Chicago, IL 60640

MINTZ, Elsa H (Pa) 3716 Abercrombie Court, Mount Pleasant, SC 29466

MINX, Patricia Ann (Kan) 105 S Indian Wells Dr, Olathe, KS 66061

MIRATE, Galen Alderman (Ga) 3338 Plantation Dr, Valdosta, GA 31605

MIRON, Jane Elizabeth (CPa)

MIRON, Mary Louise (NMich)

MISKELLEY, Audrey (Cal)

MISNER, Mary Jane Brain (Mil) N1639 Six Corners Rd, Walworth, WI 53184

MISSNER, Heath McDonell (Chi) 470 Maple St, Winnetka, IL 60093

MITCHEL III, Glen Henry Hank (Los) 1072 Casitas Pass Road #317, Carpinteria, CA 93014

MITCHELL, Barbara Louise (Alb) 172 Ottawa St, Lake George, NY 12845

MITCHELL JR, Charles Albert (Los) 111 S 6th St, Burbank, CA 91501

MITCHELL, Dawn-Victoria (Mo) 3206 Pleasant St, Hannibal, MO 63401

MITCHELL, Jeffrey Jay (WK) PO Box 250, Liberal, KS 67905

MITCHELL, Joe T (NC) 505 Mountain Rd, Asheboro, NC 27205

MITCHELL, John Patrick (NJ) PO Box 261, Cape May, NJ 08204

MITCHELL, John Stephen (Vt) 372 Canterbury Rd, Manchester Center, VT 05255

MITCHELL, Karin Rasmussen (NJ) 125 Orchard Ave, Hightstown, NJ 08520

MITCHELL, Katherine N (EC) 515 Pamlico River Dr, Washington, NC 27889

MITCHELL, Lisa Sauber (NJ) 380 Sycamore Ave, Shrewsbury, NJ 07702

MITCHELL, Marilyn Dean (NC) 90 Worcester Rd Unit 12, Washington Depot, CT 06794

MITCHELL, Pat Rhonda (LI) 732 Scarsdale Rd, Tuckahoe, NY 10707

MITCHELL, Preston Wade (SwVa)

MITCHELL JR, Richard Cope (Colo) 3107 Nevermind Ln, Colorado Springs, CO 80917

MITCHELL, R(Obert) James (Kan) Via Roma, Wichita, KS 67230

MITCHELL, Sadie S (Pa) 600 E Cathedral Rd, Apt H320, Philadelphia, PA 19128

MITCHELL, Thomas James (WNY) 7145 Fieldcrest Drive, Lockport, NY 14094

MITCHELL, Tim (Ky) 901 Baxter Ave, Louisville, KY 40204

MITCHELL, Winnie (Colo) 3821 Elk Ln, Pueblo, CO 81005

MITCHENER, Gary Asher (O) 13800 Shaker Blvd Apt 206, Cleveland, OH 44120

MITCHICAN, Jonathan A (Pa) 1000 Burmont RD, Drexel Hill, PA 19026

MITHEN III, Thomas Scott (Ga) 516 E Broughton St, Bainbridge, GA 39817

MITMAN, John Louis (Ct) 31 Steep Hollow Ln, West Hartford, CT 06107

MIX, Lucas John (Az) Lucas Mix, 26 Oxford St, Cambridge, MA 02138

MIZIRL, Sandra M (Tex) 3015 Fleeton Rd, Reedville, VA 22539

MKHIZE, Danana Elliot (La) 1222 N Dorgenois St, New Orleans, LA 70119

MOBERLY, Paul Benjamin (Va)

MOBLEY, James E (SO) 955 Matthews Dr, Cincinnati, OH 45215

MOCZYDLOWSKI, Ann Louise Hare (WA) 10120 Brock Dr, Silver Spring, MD 20903

MODESITT, Lori Jane (Wyo) 1357 Loomis St, Wheatland, WY 82201

MOEHL, Thomas Joseph (Ore) 12360 Summit Loop SE, Turner, OR 97392

MOELLER, Linda Lee Breitung (NJ) 13 Blossom Dr, Ewing, NJ 08638

MOHN, Michael Collver (Va) 1527 Senseny Rd, Winchester, VA 22602

MOIR, Tory Kuepper (Colo)

MOISE, Burnet (SeFla)

MOISE, Joe (LI) 1227 Pacific St, Brooklyn, NY 11216

MOJALLALI, Darius (Alb) 13 High St, Delhi, NY 13753

MOLEGODA, Niranjani S (Ct) 232 Durham Rd, Madison, CT 06443

MOLINA-MOORE, Amanda E (WA) PO Box 3510, Wilmington, DE 19807

MOLINE, Mark Edwin (Az) 2000 Shepherds Lane, Prescott, AZ 86301

MOLITORS, Elizabeth A (Chi) 393 N Main St, Glen Ellyn, IL 60137

MOLLARD, Elizabeth McCarter (CPa) 235 N Spruce St, Elizabethtown, PA 17022

MOLLER, Nels D (Ida) 902 E Lakeview Ln, Spokane, WA 99208

MOLLISON, Carol Suzanne (Okla) 721 N Thomas St, Altus, OK 73521

MOLNAR, Annette June (RG) St Elizabeth's Episcopal Church, 1 Morse Rd, Sudbury, MA 01776

MOLNAR, Joshua ()

MOLONY, Roberta Diane (Chi) 2009 Boehme St, Lockport, IL 60441

MOMBERG, Tom (WTenn) 3235 Overland Place, Memphis, TN 38111

MONAHAN, Anne (WA) 404 S Lee St, Alexandria, VA 22314

MONASTIERE, Sally Melczer (Los) 1335 North Hills Drive, Upland, CA 91784

MONCRIEFF, Stephanie Christen Patterson (Ia) 4535 Kimball Ave, Waterloo, IA 50701

MONETTE, Ruth Alta (Los) 104-5990 E Blvd, Vancouver, V6T 1Z3, Canada

MONGE-MANCIA, Israel (Hond)

MONGE-SANTIAGO, Juan (NJ) 213 Madison Ave, Lakewood, NJ 08701

MONICA, Ted (Fla) 6661 Man O War Trail, Tallahassee, FL 32309

MONICA, Teri (Alb) Trinity Episc Church, 18 Trinity Pl, Plattsburgh, NY 12901

MONK, Edward R (Dal) Saint John's Church, 101 N 14th Street, Corsicana, TX 75110

MONNAT, Thomas Leonard (Pa) 213 Earlington Road, Havertown, PA 19083

MONNOT, Elizabeth Lockwood (The Episcopal NCal) 1225 41st Avenue, Sacramento, CA 95922

MONNOT, Michael John (The Episcopal NCal) 1225 41st Ave, Sacramento, CA 95822

MONREAL, Anthony A (Episcopal SJ) 9323 South Westlawn, Fresno, CA 93706

MONREAL, Linda Carey (Episcopal SJ)

MONROE, George Wesley (Chi) 2866 Vacherie Ln, Dallas, TX 75227

MONROE, Sarah Beth (Oly) PO Box 1248, Westport, WA 98595

MONROE, Virginia Hill (Ala) 430 Newman Ave. Se, Huntsville, AL 35801

MONROE LOES, Brenda Frances (At) 304 E 6th St, West Point, GA 31833

MONSON, Scott B (Minn) 1015 Sibley Memorial Hwy Apt 303, Saint Paul, MN 55118

MONSOUR, John (SwFla) 2114 W Destiny Point Cir, St George, UT 84790

MONTAGNO, Karen (Mass) 536 Main St # 2, Medford, MA 02155

MONTAGUE, Cynthia Russell (ECR) 17574 Winding Creek Rd, Salinas, CA 93908

MONTALTO, Alfred Patrick (NY) 841 4th Ave, North, Apt 65, St. Petersburg, FL 33701

MONTANARI, Albert Ubaldo (WNY) 135 Old Lyme Dr Apt 4, Williamsville, NY 14221

MONTELLA, Christopher (Los)

✠ **MONTERROSO GONZALEZ**, Hector (Tex) 12 Avenue 6-86, Zona 1, Zacapa, Guatemala

MONTES, Alejandro Sixto (Tex) 10426 Towne Oak Ln, Sugar Land, TX 77478

MONTES, Alex G (Tex) 11608 Glen Knoll Dr, Manor, TX 78653

MONTES, Eli (Kan) St Francis Community Services, 4155 E Harry St, Wichita, KS 67218

MONTGOMERY, Brandt Leonard (WLa) Episcopal Church of the Ascension, 1030 Johnston Street, Lafayette, LA 70501

MONTGOMERY, Bruce (NJ) 1310 Tullo Rd, Martinsville, NJ 08836

MONTGOMERY, Cathy (SwVa) 2231 Timberlake Dr, Lynchburg, VA 24502

Clergy List

MONTGOMERY, Ellen Maddigan (WNY) 41 Saint Georges Sq, Buffalo, NY 14222

MONTGOMERY JR, Errol (Miss) 3706 Bon Aire Dr, Monroe, LA 71203

MONTGOMERY, Fletcher (Fla) 100 NE 1st St, Gainesville, FL 32601

MONTGOMERY, Ian (FdL) 26 Gaskill Rd, Chester, VT 05143

MONTGOMERY, Ian (ECR) 19 Montrose Avenue, Bryn Mawr, PA 19010

✠ **MONTGOMERY**, James Winchester (Chi) 5555 N Sheridan Rd Apt 809, Chicago, IL 60640

MONTGOMERY, Jennifer Born (Va) 4000 Lorcom Ln, Arlington, VA 22207

MONTGOMERY, John Alford (Lex)

MONTGOMERY, Lee Allen (U) 70 N 200 W, Cedar City, UT 84720

MONTGOMERY, Tyler Lindell (SVa) PO Box 3520, Williamsburg, VA 23187

MONTIEL, Robert Michael (WTenn) 103 S Poplar St, Paris, TN 38242

MONTILEAUX, Charles Thomas (SD) Po Box 246, Kyle, SD 57752

MONTJOY IV, Gid (Md) 609 Collins Creek Dr., Murrells Inlet, SC 29576

MONTOOTH, Cynthia Hooton (SwFla) 15 Knob Hill Circle, Decatur, GA 30030

MONTOYA CARPIO, S Leonardo (EcuC) Apartado #17-01-3108, Quito, Ecuador

MONZON-MOLINA, Eduardo (Hond) Apartado 2598, San Pedro, Honduras

MOODY, John Wallace (NY) 42 W 9th St Apt 18, New York, NY 10011

✠ **MOODY**, Robert Manning (Okla) 4001 Oxford Way, Norman, OK 73072

MOON, Abigail White (Fla) 211 N Monroe St, Tallahassee, FL 32301

MOON, Anthony Bernard (Okla) 2401 N. Westminster Road, Arcadia, OK 73007

MOON, Catherine Joy (Cal) The Curate's House, 7 Walton Village, Liverpool, AL L4 6TJ, Great Britain (UK)

MOON JR, Don Pardee (Chi) 438 N Sheridan Rd # A500, Waukegan, IL 60085

MOON, James Fred (WMo) 43 Old Mill Ln, South Greenfield, MO 65752

MOON, Mary Louise (Oly) 927 S Sheridan Ave, Tacoma, WA 98405

MOON, Richard Warren (Neb) Po Box 1012, West Plains, MO 65775

MOON, Robert Michael (Los) 1294 Westlyn Pl, Pasadena, CA 91104

MOONEY, Michelle Puzin (Mil) 2633 N Hackett Ave Apt A, Milwaukee, WI 53211

MOONEY, Noreen O'Connor (LI) 1 Berard Blvd, Oakdale, NY 11769

MOORE, Albert Lee (NC) 8705 Gleneagles Dr, Raleigh, NC 27613

MOORE, Allison (Nwk) 11 N Broadway, Irvington, NY 10533

MOORE, Andrew Y (Va) 240 S Laurel St, Richmond, VA 23220

MOORE, Andy J (NJ) 229 Goldsmith Ave, Newark, NJ 07112

MOORE, Anne Elizabeth Olive (Ore) 630 B St, Silverton, OR 97381

MOORE, Bob (Tex) 3285 Park Falls Ct., League City, TX 77573

MOORE JR, Charles Nottingham (SVa) 12800 Nightingale Drive, Chester, VA 23836

MOORE, Charles Owen (Pa) 4631 Ossabaw Way, Naples, FL 34119

MOORE, Charlotte Elizabeth (Eas)

MOORE, Cheryl P (U) 2378 East 1700 South Street, Salt Lake City, UT 84108

MOORE, Christopher Chamberlin (Pa) 51 Springhouse Ln, Media, PA 19063

MOORE, Clifford Allan (Wyo) P.O. Box 1086, #3 Valley Dr., Sundance, WY 82729

MOORE III, Clint (Chi) 750 Pearson Street Apt 902, Des Plaines, IL 60016

MOORE, Courtland Manning (FtW) 2341 Monticello Cir, Plano, TX 75075

MOORE, Daniel T (Pa) 553 Galleon Dr, Naples, FL 34102

MOORE, David (Oly) 116 Rossel Lane, PO Box 702, Eastsound, WA 98245

MOORE, Delrece Lorraine (Colo) 3665 Overton St, Colorado Springs, CO 80910

MOORE, Denise Maureen (Alb)

MOORE, Diane Marquart (WLa) 211 Celeste Dr, New Iberia, LA 70560

MOORE, Dominic C (Az) 533 E Main St, Lexington, KY 40508

MOORE, Donald Ernest (Eas) 3946 Rock Branch Rd, North Garden, VA 22959

MOORE, Frederick Ashbrook (Ore) 1675 Chester Ave, Arcata, CA 95521

MOORE, Helen (Ct) 24 Goodwin Circle, Hartford, CT 06105

MOORE, James Raymond (The Episcopal Church in Haw) 911 N Marine Corps Dr, Tamuning, GU 96913

MOORE, Jan Marie (Miss) PO Box 1483, Hattiesburg, MS 39403

MOORE, Judith (O) 7125 North Hills Blvd NE, Albuquerque, NM 87109

MOORE, Julia Gibert (Miss) 208 S Leflore Ave, Cleveland, MS 38732

MOORE, Katherine JoAnne (Wyo) PO Box 246, Sundance, WY 82729

MOORE, Kathleen Mary (SwFla)

MOORE, Linda Turman (The Episcopal NCal) 155-A Derek Dr, Susanville, CA 96130

MOORE, Lynda Foster (WNC) 138 Murdock Ave, Asheville, NC 28801

MOORE, Margaret Jo (The Episcopal NCal) 516 Clayton Ave, El Cerrito, CA 94530

MOORE, Mark (Mil) ST PAUL'S EPISCOPAL CHURCH, 413 S 2ND ST, WATERTOWN, WI 53094

MOORE, Mark Ross (Ct) 85 Viscount Dr Unit 12c, Milford, CT 06460

MOORE, Mary Diane (Oly) 7796 S Harrison Cir, Centennial, CO 80122

MOORE, Mary Navarre (ETenn) 715 E Brow Rd, Lookout Mountain, TN 37350

MOORE, Matthew Edward (LI) 139 Saint Johns Pl, Brooklyn, NY 11217

MOORE, Melvin Leon (Va) 219 Cornwallis Ave, Locust Grove, VA 22508

MOORE, Michael D (Fla)

MOORE, Michael Osborn (NH) 7321 Brad St, Falls Church, VA 22042

MOORE, Nancy Lee (Me) 403 Harrison Rd, Norway, ME 04268

MOORE, Orral Margarite (Neb) 714 N 129th Plz, Omaha, NE 68154

MOORE, Pamela Andrea (The Episcopal NCal) Po Box 4791, Santa Rosa, CA 95402

MOORE, Patricia Elaine (The Episcopal NCal) 342 Wilson St, Petaluma, CA 94952

MOORE, Paul R (RG) Church Of The Good Shepherd, PO Box 2795, Silver City, NM 88062

MOORE JR, Ralph M (Me) 191 West Meadow Rd., Rockland, ME 04841

MOORE, Richard Wayne (La) 4500 Lake Borgne Ave, Metairie, LA 70006

MOORE, Robert Allen (Minn) 19 Lea Road, Whittle-le-Woods, Chorley, Lancs, PR6-7PF, Great Britain (UK)

MOORE, Robert B (Cal) 4230 Langland St, Cincinnati, OH 45223

MOORE JR, Robert Raymond (SwVa) 110 Clinton Avenue, Big Stone Gap, VA 24219

MOORE, Robin Adair (Oly) Po Box 584, Grapeview, WA 98546

MOORE, Rodney Allen (Colo) 221 S Salem Ct, Aurora, CO 80012

MOORE, Scott Alan (Eur)

MOORE, Stephen Edward (Oly) 350 sunset ave n, Edmonds, WA 98020

MOORE, Steven Paul (CNY) St Mary's Episcopal Church, 1917 3rd St, Napa, CA 94559

MOORE, Theodore Edward (NJ) 17 Cray Ter., Fanwood, NJ 07023

MOORE, Trenton Scott (Fla)

MOORE, Vassilia Shelton (SwFla) 16500 Gulf Blvd Apt 755, North Redington Beach, FL 33708

MOORE JR, W Taylor (Miss) 22002 Halliburton Cv, Oxford, MS 38655

MOORE JR, William Henry (Spr) 141 Candlewood Dr, Wallace, NC 28466

MOOREHEAD, Kate Bingham (Fla) 240 N Belmont St, Wichita, KS 67208

MOORE-LEVESQUE, Christa Marie (Roch) 2000 Highland Ave, Rochester, NY 14618

MOORER, Dawson Delayne (O) 281 E 244th St Apt D5, Euclid, OH 44123

MOORHEAD, Bill (Ia) 107 Washington Park Rd, Iowa City, IA 52245

MOOTE, Kimberly Ann (NMich) E9494 Maple St, Munising, MI 49862

MOQUETE, Clemencia Rafaela (NY) 821 Central Trinity Avenue, Bronx, NY 10456

MORALES, Carlton Owen (NC) Po Box 21011, Greensboro, NC 27420

MORALES, Evelyn Ruth (NC) 2009 Hickswood Rd, High Point, NC 27265

MORALES JR, Frank R (NY) 3115 S High St, Arlington, VA 22202

MORALES, Loyda (NY) 347 Chiquita Court, Kissimmee, FL 34758

MORALES, Roberto (Va)

MORALES COLON, Francisco Javier (PR)

MORALES GAVIRIA, Jose Ricardo (Colom) Barrio Las Delicias, El Bagne, Antioquia, Colombia

✠ **MORALES MALDONADO**, Rafael L (PR) Iglesia Episcopal Puetorriquene, PO Box 902, Saint Just, PR 00978

MORALES-VEGA, Emilia (PR) D10 Calle Pomarrosa, Guaynabo, PR 00969

MORAN, John Jay (Mont) 2415 Hauser Blvd, Helena, MT 59601

✠ **MORANTE-ESPANA**, Terencio Alfredo (Litoral Ecu) Ulloa 213 Y Carrion, Box 17-0-353-A, Quito, Ecuador

MORA VILLEGA, Carlos Donato (Litoral Ecu) Amarilis Fuentes 603 Calle D Ave Trujillo, Guayaquil, Ecuador

MORCK, Christopher Robert (Mass) Grace Episcopal Church, 133 School St, New Bedford, MA 02740

MOREAU, Joseph Raoul (LI) 15524 90th Ave, Jamaica, NY 11432

MOREAU, Walter Jerome (NJ) 211 Willow Valley Sq # D-319, Lancaster, PA 17602

MOREHEAD, Carol (Mass) Grace Church, 160 High St, Medford, MA 02155

MOREHOUS, Amy Hodges (ETenn) 800 S. Northshore Dr., Knoxville, TN 37919

MOREHOUSE JR, Merritt Dutton (FdL) 1920 Green Tree Road, Washington Island, WI 54246

MOREHOUSE, Rebecca (Cal) 21 Sonora Way, Corte Madera, CA 94925

MOREHOUSE, Timothy Lawrence (NY) 200 Riverside Dr Apt 7B, New York, NY 10025

MORELL, Ellen Jones (Az) 8110 Saint Andrews Church Rd, Louisville, KY 40258

MORELLI, John (NY) 210 E 181 St Apt 1A, Bronx, NY 10457

MORELLI, Thomas Carlo Anthony (SanD) 1114 9th St, Coronado, CA 92118

MORELL MONTALVO, Louise Esthella (PR)

MORENO CASAS, Alberto Moreno (Okla) San Miguel Arcangel, 907 N Adams Ave, Odessa, TX 79761

MORESCHI, Alexander Thomas (Ga)

MORETZ, Matthew John (NY) 325 Park Ave, New York, NY 10022

MORETZSOHN, Jeffrey Paul (Pa)

MOREY, Gordon Howell (Mil) N4111 Pine St, Brodhead, WI 53520

MORFORD, Norman L (Ind) PO Box 55085, Indianapolis, IN 46205

MORFORD, Samuel Allen (Neb) 9302 Blondo St, Omaha, NE 68134

MORGAN, Barbara Jean (Alb) 24 Silver St Apt G8, Great Barrington, MA 01230

MORGAN, Daniel (Ct) 489 Mansfield Ave, Darien, CT 06820

MORGAN, David Forbes (Colo) 740 Clarkson St, Denver, CO 80218

MORGAN, Dennis Lee (Eas) 6242 Oxbridge Dr, Salisbury, MD 21801

MORGAN, Diane Elizabeth (Mich) 25710 Beech Ct, Redford, MI 48239

MORGAN, Dwight Dexter (SeFla) 2201 S.W. 25th Street, Coconut Grove, FL 33133

MORGAN, Ed (Colo) 5952 E Irish Pl, Centennial, CO 80112

MORGAN, E F Michael (Pa) 33 Baltusrol Way, Springfield, NJ 07081

MORGAN, Elaine Ludlum (Nev) 402 W Robinson St, Carson City, NV 89703

MORGAN III, Harold Edgar (USC) 204 Derby Ln, Clinton, SC 29325

MORGAN, Heather (Mo) 1400 Forum Boulevard, Suite 38, Columbia, MO 65203

MORGAN, J. Gregory (NY) St. Simon the Cyrenian Church, 135 Remington Place, New Rochelle, NY 10801

MORGAN, James Charles (Tex) 235 Royal Oaks St, Huntsville, TX 77320

MORGAN JR, James Hanly (WVa) 520 11th Ave., Huntington, WV 25701

MORGAN, Keely (Minn) 60 Kent St, Saint Paul, MN 55102

MORGAN, Kimberly Ann (Nev) 305 N Minnesota St, Carson City, NV 89703

MORGAN, Mamie Elizabeth (USC) 204 Derby Lane, Clinton, SC 29325

MORGAN, Marilyn Kay (Ark) 1475 Stone Crest Dr, Conway, AR 72034

MORGAN, Michael T (Mont) West 3817 Fort Wright Drive 1-204, Spokane, WA 99204

MORGAN, Michele H. (WA) 301 A St NE, Washington, DC 20002

MORGAN, Pam (Ark) 1410 E Walnut St., Rogers, AR 72756

MORGAN, Philip (Va) 17476 Hawthorne Ave, Culpeper, VA 22701

MORGAN, Ralph Baier (Tex)

MORGAN, Randall Carl (SC) St Jude's Episcopal Church, 907 Wichman St, Walterboro, SC 29488

MORGAN V, Richard (RI) 19 Castle Way, Westerly, RI 02891

MORGAN, Richard (Pa) Church of the Good Samaritan, 212 W Lancaster Ave, Paoli, PA 19301

MORGAN, Ruth Margaret (RG) 8017 Krim Dr. NE, Albuquerque, NM 87109

MORGAN, Walter (ETenn) 3475 Edgewood Cir Nw, Cleveland, TN 37312

MORGAN-HIGGINS, Stanley Ethelbert (Nwk) 3828 Leprechaun Ct, Decatur, GA 30034

MORICAL, Robin E (CFla) 1631 Ford Pkwy, Saint Paul, MN 55116

MORIN, Geoffrey S (Pa) 841 Shenton Road, West Chester, PA 19380

MORISSEAU, Robert Edward Lee (NY) 502 Forest Gln, Pompton Plains, NJ 07444

MORITZ III, Bernard Eugene (SwVa) 4022 Fauquier Ave, Richmond, VA 23227

MORIYAMA, Jerome Tomokazu (WA) Rossbrin Cove, Schull, Co. Cork, Ireland

MORLAN, Lynette K (Episcopal SJ) 2803 Stratford Dr, San Ramon, CA 94583

MORLEY, Anthony J (Minn) 825 Summit Ave #806, Minneapolis, MN 55403

MORLEY, Richard Matthew (NJ) 140 S Finley Ave, Basking Ridge, NJ 07920

MORLEY, William Harris (NC) 3454 Rugby Rd, Durham, NC 27707

MORNARD, Jean Elisabeth (SD) 1400 21st St SW Lot 110, 208, Huron, SD 57350

MORONEY, Kevin John (Pa) 440 W 21st St, New York, NY 10011

MORONTA, Buddelov Adolfo (NY)

MORPETH, Robert Park (Ala) 521 20th St N, Birmingham, AL 35203

MORRIGAN, Cedar Abrielynne (Minn) 309 13th St Sw, Little Falls, MN 56345

MORRILL, Bonnie G (Dal) 5314 Somerset Dr., Rowlett, TX 75089

MORRIS, Bob (Fla) 601 Alhambra Ln N, Ponte Vedra Beach, FL 32082

MORRIS, Bonnie (WNY) 20 Milton Street, Williamsville, NY 14221

MORRIS, Charles Henry (Be) 24 Forsythia Dr, Harwich, MA 02645

MORRIS, Clayton L (Cal) 30 Devoe St Apt 2B, Brooklyn, NY 11211

MORRIS, Danielle DuBois (CFla) 444 Covey Cv, Winter Park, FL 32789

MORRIS, David John (Pa) 449 Newgate Ct Apt B2, Andalusia, PA 19020

MORRIS, David Wayne (NY) 15 Pine St, Lake Peekskill, NY 10537

MORRIS, Donald Richard (Vt) 280 Round Rd, Bristol, VT 05443

MORRIS, Gregg A (Chi) 1125 Franklin St, Downers Grove, IL 60515

MORRIS, Janie Kirt (Tex) 439 NW 44th Street, Oklahoma City, OK 73118

MORRIS, Jim (Pa) 203 Devon Dr, Exton, PA 19341

MORRIS, John (Vt) 37 Thompson Rd, East Corinth, VT 05040

MORRIS, John (CPa) St. John's Episcopal Church, 321 W. Chestnut St., Lancaster, PA 17603

MORRIS III, John Glen (Va) 1021 Aquia Dr, Stafford, VA 22554

MORRIS, John Karl (The Episcopal NCal) 3663 Solano Ave Apt 204, Napa, CA 94558

MORRIS, Jonathan Edward (USC) 717 Dupre Dr, Spartanburg, SC 29307

MORRIS, Julie H. (Los) P.O. Box 2305, Camarillo, CA 93011

MORRIS, Kevin L (LI) 176 Palisade Ave, Jersey City, NJ 07306

MORRIS, Richard Melvin (O) 55 Countryside Dr, Cumberland, RI 02864

MORRIS, Robert Corin Vesal (Nwk) 422 Clark, South Orange, NJ 07079

MORRIS III, Robert Lee (Va)

MORRIS, Roberta Louise (Los) 1733 N New Hampshire Ave, Los Angeles, CA 90027

MORRIS, Sarah (SwVa) 1962 Tyler Rd, Christiansburg, VA 24073

MORRIS, Stephen B (SwFla) 140 4th St N, St Petersburg, FL 33701

MORRIS, Thomas (Tex) PO Box 173, Sewanee, TN 37375

MORRIS-KLIMENT, Nicholas M (Mass) 44 Seminole Rd, Acton, MA 01720

MORRISON, Alistair James (Alb) 132 Duanesburg Churches Rd, Duanesburg, NY 12056

MORRISON, Enid Ann (Ind) 8320 E. 10th St., Indianapolis, IN 46219

MORRISON, Glenn David (Mich) 171 W Pike St, Pontiac, MI 48341

MORRISON JR, Henry T Nick (Az) Po Box 610, Ketchum, ID 83340

MORRISON, James R (La) 1329 Jackson Ave, New Orleans, LA 70130

MORRISON, John Ainslie (SO) Calvary Episcopal Church, 3766 Clifton Ave, Cincinnati, OH 45220

MORRISON III, John E (LI) 510 Manatuck Blvd, Brightwaters, NY 11718

MORRISON, Karl Frederick (NJ) 75 Linwood Circle, Princeton, NJ 08540

MORRISON, Larry Clair (NJ) PO Box 100, Front Royal, VA 22630

MORRISON, Leroy Oran (NwT) 6535 Amber Dr, Odessa, TX 79762

MORRISON, Mary K (ECR) 443 Alberto Way Unit B221, Los Gatos, CA 95032

MORRISON, Mikel Anne (Oly) 760 Kristen Ct, Santa Barbara, CA 93111

MORRISON, Paul Charles (NC) 77 W Coolidge St #227, Phoenix, AZ 85013

MORRISON, Pauline (Ore) St John's Episcopal Church, 110 NE Alder St, Toledo, OR 97391

MORRISON, Richard (Az) 720 West Elliot Road, Gilbert, AZ 85233

MORRISON, Robert (Ore) Po Box 789, Lincoln City, OR 97367

MORRISON JR, Robert Dabney (EC) 119 Briarwood St., Lynchburg, VA 24503

MORRISON, Sam (FdL) 101 S Wythe St, Pentwater, MI 49449

MORRISON-CLEARY, Douglas Vaughn (Minn)

MORRIS-RADER, Patricia (Ore) 8045 Sw 56th Ave, Portland, OR 97219

MORRISS, Jerry Davis (Dal) 132 Baywood Blvd, Mabank, TX 75156

MORRISSETTE, Paul E (WMass) 14 Enaya Circle, Worcester, MA 01606

MORROW, Andrea (Mich) 2803 1st St, Wyandotte, MI 48192

MORROW, Dan (CPa) 101 Pine St, Harrisburg, PA 17101

MORROW, Gabriel Charles Daniel (Alb) PO Box 41, Burnt Hills, NY 12027

MORROW JR, Harold Frederick (CPa) 2453 Harrisburg Pike, Lancaster, PA 17601

MORROW, Jerry Dean (Mass) 89 Msgr Patrick J Lydon Way, Dorchester, MA 02124

MORROW, John Thomas (NJ) Po Box 424, Pine Beach, NJ 08741

MORROW, Mildred K (WNC) 9 Swan St, Asheville, NC 28803

MORROW, Penelope (Eas) St Paul's by-the-Sea Episcopal Church, PO Box 1207, Ocean City, MD 21843

MORROW, Quintin Gregory (FtW) 917 Lamar St, Fort Worth, TX 76102

MORSCH, Joel James (Spr) 1903 - 85th Court NW, Bradenton, FL 34209

MORSE, Alice Janette (Mich) 3899 Ryan's Ridge, Monroe, MI 48161

MORSE, Davidson Rogan (FtW) 2916 Caprock Ct, Grapevine, TX 76051

MORSE, Elizabeth Bovelle (Ore) 661 NW Kersey Dr, Dallas, OR 97338

MORT, Kevin Duane (SwFla)

MORTON, James Parks (NY) 285 Riverside Dr Apt 13-B, New York, NY 10025

MORTON, John (WNC) Po Box 185, Flat Rock, NC 28731

MORTON SR, Kell (Pa) 316 High St, Pottstown, PA 19464

MORTON, Paula (WNC) 901 Big Raven Ln, Saluda, NC 28773

MORTON, Ronald Dean (ETenn) 5401 Tiffany Ln, Knoxville, TN 37912

MORTON, William Paul (EO) 1025 NE Paula Dr, Bend, OR 97701

MORTON III, Woolridge Brown (Va) 212 Wirt St NW, Leesburg, VA 20176

MOSCOSO, Servio Rhadames (NJ) 38 W End Pl, Elizabeth, NJ 07202

MOSELEY, Christine Carr (Vt) PO Box 125, Newport, VT 05855

MOSER, Albert E (Alb) 133 Saratoga Rd Apt. 109-8, Glenville, NY 12302

MOSER, Frederick Perkins (Vt) 5167 Shelburne Rd, Shelburne, VT 05482

MOSER, Gerard Stoughton (Eur) 15 Hoopoe Ave., Camps Bay, Cape Town, 8005, South Africa

MOSER, Patricia Mariann (Chi) 621 W Belmont Ave, Chicago, IL 60657

MOSER, Paul Henry (Md) 15 Brooks Rd, Bel Air, MD 21014

MOSES, Donald Harwood (Kan) 2201 Sw 30th St, Topeka, KS 66611

MOSES, George David (WVa) 20 Alexander Drive, Morgantown, WV 26508

MOSES, Michael David (Minn) 11078 Nichols Spring Dr, Chatfield, MN 55923

MOSES, Robert Emilio (CFla) 145 E Edgewood Dr, Lakeland, FL 33803

MOSES, Sarah Marie (Miss)

MOSHER, Steve (Eas) 301 S Talbot St, Saint Michael, MD 21663

MOSIER, James David (EO) 1237 Sw 12th St, Ontario, OR 97914

MOSIER, William (Ore) 39361 Mozart Ter Unit 101, Fremont, CA 94538

MOSKAL, Jason Edward (LI) 3350 82nd St, Jackson Heights, NY 11372

MOSLEY, Carl Ernest (Eas) 111 76th St Unit 205, Ocean City, MD 21842

MOSQUEA, Jose Luis (DR DomRep))

MOSS JR, Alfred Alfonso (Chi) 1500 N Lancaster St, Arlington, VA 22205

MOSS III, David M (At) 3880 N Stratford Rd Ne, Atlanta, GA 30342

MOSS, Denise S (At)

MOSS, Eliot (WMass) 7 Kestrel Ln, Amherst, MA 01002

MOSS III, Frank (WMass) 17910 NW Chestnut Lane, Portland, OR 97231

MOSS SR, Ledly Ogden (SeFla) 4020 Nw 187th St, Carol City, FL 33055

MOSS, Susan Maetzold (Minn) 175 Woodlawn Ave, Saint Paul, MN 55105

MOSSBARGER, David (NwT) 1402 Wilshire Dr, Odessa, TX 79761

MOSSO, Karen Ann (Ind) 721 Roma Ave., Jeffersonville, IN 47130

MOTE, Donna Susan (At) 1296 Fork Creek Trl, Decatur, GA 30033

MOTE, Doris (Ind) 2018 Locust St, New Albany, IN 47150

MOTE, Larry H. (RG) 1016 E 1st St, Portales, NM 88130

MOTES, Brantley Eugene (Ala) Po Box 5556, Decatur, AL 35601

MOTHERSELL, Lawrence Lavere (Roch) Po Box 1, Geneseo, NY 14454

MOTIS, John Ray (CFla) Church of the Good Shepherd, 221 S 4th St, Lake Wales, FL 33853

MOTT, Pam (WMass) 148 Dorwin Dr, West Springfield, MA 01089

MOTTL, Christine Elizabeth (Pa) 27074 St. Peter's Church Rd., Crisfield, MD 21817

MOTTL, Paul Edward (Neb) 27074 St. Peters Church Road, Crisfield, MD 21817

MOUA, Bao (Minn) Holy Apostles Episcopal Church, 2200 Minnehaha Ave E, Saint Paul, MN 55119

MOUER, Patty (WNC) 500 Christ School Road, Asheville, NC 28704

MOUGHTY, Kelly Patricia (Va) 115 E Fairfax Street, Falls Church, VA 22046

MOUILLE, David Ronald (Kan) 4786 Black Swan Dr, Shawnee, KS 66216

MOULINIER, Deirdre Ward (Az)

MOULTON, Elizabeth Jean (Be) 109 Cruser St, Montrose, PA 18801

MOULTON, Eric Morgan (EC) 1219 Forest Hills Dr, Wilmington, NC 28403

MOULTON II, John (Fla) 1631 Blue Heron Ln, Jacksonville Beach, FL 32250

MOULTON, Roger Conant (Mass) 291 Washington St, Arlington, MA 02474

MOUNCEY, Perry (CNY) 127 Brookview Ln, Liverpool, NY 13088

MOUNTFORD, Helen Harvene (Los) 1566 Edison St, Santa Ynez, CA 93460

MOUNTFORD SR, Robert Tatton (CFla) 160 Heron Bay Cir, Lake Mary, FL 32746

MOURADIAN, Victoria Kirk (Los) 1411 Dalmatia Dr., San Pedro, CA 90732

MOUSIN, Thomas Nordboe (Mass) 29 Lakeview Rd, Winchester, MA 01890

MOWERS, Culver Lunn (CNY) Po Box 130, Brooktondale, NY 14817

MOWERS, David M (Mil) 111 Sixth St., Baraboo, WI 53913

MOYER, Dale Luther (SeFla) 4851a Nursery Rd, Dover, PA 17315

MOYER, J Douglas (Be) 205 North Seventh Street, Stroudsburg, PA 18360

MOYER, Laureen H (Cal) 412 Centre Ct, Alameda, CA 94502

MOYER, Michael David (Eas) 1 Church St, Berlin, MD 21811

MOYER, Michelle M (Be) 321 Wyandotte St, Bethlehem, PA 18015

MOYERS, William Riley (SwFla) 2008 Isla De Palma Cir, Naples, FL 34119

MOYLE, Sandra K (Fla) Holy Cross Faith Memorial Episcopal Church, 88 Baskervill Dr, Pawleys Island, SC 29585

MOYSER, George H (SC) 58 Raven Glass Ln, Bluffton, SC 29909

MOZELIAK JR, Leon (CNY) St. Paul's Church and All Saints Church, 204 Genesee Street and 153 South First Street, Chittenango, NY 13037

MOZINGO, Brandon Thomas (Pgh) 325 Oliver Ave, Pittsburgh, PA 15222

MRAZ, Barbara E (Minn) 4201 Sheridan Ave S, Minneapolis, MN 55410

MROCZKA, Mary Ann (Roch) 77 Plum Drive Apt F, Dansville, NY 14437

MUDD, Gwynneth Jones (SVa) 797 Casual Ct, Virginia Beach, VA 23454

MUDGE, Hannah (Alb) Oaks of Righteousness Episcopal Ministry, 2331 15th St, Troy, NY 12180

MUDGE, Hiram Thomas (Kan) PO Box 99, West Park, NY 12493

MUDGE, Julia Hamilton (Alb) 204 Worthington Ter, Wynantskill, NY 12198

MUDGE, Melanie (NC) 2820 Rue Sans Famille, Raleigh, NC 27607

MUDGE JR, Shaw (Alb) 25 Rushforde Dr, Manchester, CT 06040

MUELLER, Denise Ray (SO) 412 Sycamore St., Cincinnati, OH 45202

MUELLER, Heather (The Episcopal Church in Haw) PO Box 628, Kapa'au, HI 96755

MUELLER, Kay (CFla)

MUELLER, Mary Margaret (WTex) 1045 Shook Ave Apt 105, San Antonio, TX 78212

MUES, Steve (Kan) 144 Lake Mountain Dr, Boulder City, NV 89005

MUGAN JR, Robert Charles (WNC) 894 Indian Hill Rd, Hendersonville, NC 28791

MUHLHEIM, Nancy Colleen Collins (Ore) 98 Fairway Loop, Eugene, OR 97401

MUINDE, Sandra Laverne (FdL) 311 Division St, Oshkosh, WI 54901

MUIR, George Daniels (Ga) St. Paul's Church, 605 Reynolds St., Augusta, GA 30901

MUIR, Richard Dale (Chi) 181 Wildwood Rd, Lake Forest, IL 60045

MUKHWANA-NAFUMA, Joel Eric (NY)

MULDER, Timothy John (Nwk) 2 Hunt Lane, Gladstone, NJ 07934

MULDOON, Maggie R (Minn) 18350 67 Avenue, Cloverdale, V3S 1E5, Canada

MULFORD, Marie Lynne (WVa) 2585 State Route 7 N, Gallipolis, OH 45631

MULKIN, Suzanne Devine (CFla) 875 Brock Rd, Bartow, FL 33830

MULL, Judson Gary (At) 499 Trabert Ave Nw, Atlanta, GA 30309

MULLALY JR, Charles (Va) 888 Summit View Ln, Charlottesville, VA 22903

MULLARKEY, Meghan Kathleen (Oly) 44000 86th Ave SE # AE, Mercer Island, WA 98040

MULLEN, Melanie B (WA) St Paul's Episcopal Church, 815 E Grace St, Richmond, VA 23219

MULLEN, Sean E (Pa) St Mark's Church, 1625 Locust St, Philadelphia, PA 19103

MULLER, Denise (Az)

MULLER, Donald (NJ) 4 Christopher Mill Rd, Medford, NJ 08055

MULLER JR, John (Colo) 513 E 19th St, Delta, CO 81416

MULLER, Michael A (Nwk) St Peter's Episc Church, 215 Boulevard, Mountain Lakes, NJ 07046

MULLER, Thomas G (Eur) Via Bernardo Rucellai, 9, Florence, Italy

MULLER JR, William C (Vt) 522 W 4th Ave, Mitchell, SD 57301

MULLIGAN IV, Edward B (At) Holy Innocents' Episc Ch, 805 Mount Vernon Hwy NW, Atlanta, GA 30327

MULLIN, Mark Hill (Okla) 2091 Brownstone Ln, Charlottesville, VA 22901

MULLINS, Andrew Jackson W (NY) 230 E 50th St Apt 4C, New York, NY 10022

MULLINS, Earl (Md) 6922 Hollenberry Rd, Sykesville, MD 21784

MULLINS, Edward L (Mich) 730 E Knot Ct, Corolla, NC 27927

MULLINS, Judith Pierpont (Oly) 80 E Roanoke St Apt 16, Seattle, WA 98102

MULLINS, Perry Emerson (Dal)

MULLIS, Robert Bradley (NC) 405 Baymount Dr., Statesville, NC 28625

MULVEY, Dorian L (Az) 8951 E. Sutton Drive, Scottsdale, AZ 85260

MULVEY JR, Thomas Patrick (Mass)

MUMFORD, Nigel William David (SVa)

MUMITA, Joseph Thairu (Mass) Grace Episcopal Church, 67 Norwood St, Everett, MA 02149

MUMMA-WAKABAYASHI, Diane Carole (Spr)

MUN, Paul Shinkyu (Tenn) Church Of The Holy Spirit, 5325 Nolensville Pike, Nashville, TN 37211

MUNCEY, Marilee Elliott (Episcopal SJ) 915 E Main St, Turlock, CA 95380

MUNCIE, Margaret Ann (NY) 1 Chipping Court, Greenville, SC 29607

MUNCIE, Steve D. (LI) 65 Joralemon Street, Brooklyn, NY 11201

MUNDIA, Wilberforce Omusala (NC) 204 W Salisbury St, Pittsboro, NC 27312

MUNDY, Robert (RG)

MUNGOMA, Stephen Masette (Los) 1401 W 123rd St, Los Angeles, CA 90047

MUNOZ, Antonio (Dal) 5100 Ross Ave, Dallas, TX 75206

MUNOZ, Frank Peter (SanD) Navy Region Southwest, San Diego, CA 92136

MUNOZ, Maria E (Los) Nuestra Senora de Las Americas, 2610 N. Francisco, Chicago, IL 60647

MUNOZ-LABRA, Manuel J (PR)

MUNOZ PENA, Munoz (PR) Paseo De La Reina 2703, Ponce, PR 00716

MUNOZ QUINTANA, Dimas D (PR) Po Box 8106, Humacao, PR 00792

MUNRO, Edward Henry (Md) 12310 Firtree Ln, Bowie, MD 20715

MUNRO, Michael (Kan) 804 Cottonwood Dr, Lansing, KS 66043

MUNROE, Jim (WMass) 235 State St Apt 413, Springfield, MA 01103

MUNROE, Sally G (Colo) 1127 Westmoreland Rd, Colorado Springs, CO 80907

MUNSELL, Richard Francis (Colo)

MUNSON, Peter (Colo) 9972 W 86th Ave, Arvada, CO 80005

MUNZ, Cat (WMass) 5 Willow Circle, Easthampton, MA 01027

MURANGI, Samuel Bacwa (Pa) 8201 Frankford Ave, Philadelphia, PA 19136

MURASAKI-WEKALL, Ellen S (Los) 330 East Cordova St Unit 366, Pasadena, CA 91101

MURAY, Leslie Anthony (Mich) 241 Douglas Ave, Lansing, MI 48906

MURBARGER, Jason Andrew (CFla) Trinity Episcopal Church, 2365 Pine Ave, Vero Beach, FL 32960

MURCHIE, Alan Cameron (Ct) 78 Green Hill Rd, Washington, CT 06793

MURDOCH, Judith Carolyn (Fla) 4227 Columbia Rd, Martinez, GA 30907

MURDOCH, Julie (WVa) 75 Old Cheat Rd., Morgantown, WV 26508

MURDOCH, Richard Dorsey (SVa) 214 Archers Mead, Williamsburg, VA 23185

MURDOCH JR, William Henry (Me) Po Box 639, Damariscotta, ME 04543

MURDOCK, Audrey (Ct) 831 Stafford Ave, Bristol, CT 06010

MURDOCK, Linda Lee (EC) PO Box 626, Havelock, NC 28532

MURGUIA, James Raphael (WTex) 6904 West Ave, San Antonio, TX 78213

MURIUKI, James (Spr) 493 S Jackson St, Montgomery, AL 36104

MURPH, Jeffrey David (Pgh) 530 10th St, Oakmont, PA 15139

MURPHEY, William Frederick (CPa) 2306 Edgewood Rd, Harrisburg, PA 17104

MURPHREE, James Willis (Dal) 5426 Meadowcreek Dr Apt 2037, Dallas, TX 75248

MURPHY, Diane Gensheimer (Va) 9374 Mount Vernon Cir, Alexandria, VA 22309

MURPHY, Edward John (NJ) 10 Rupells Rd, Clinton, NJ 08809

MURPHY JR, Edward John (CNY) 7639 Reed Ter, Lowville, NY 13367

MURPHY, Gwyneth MacKenzie (NY) St Mary the Virgin Episcopal Church, 191 South Greeley Ave, Chappaqua, NY 10514

MURPHY JR, Hartshorn (Los) 1630 Greenfield Ave. Apt 105, Los Angeles, Los Angeles, CA 90025

MURPHY, James T (SwFla) 1605 Banchory Cir, Walhalla, SC 29691

MURPHY, Jo-Ann (Va) 3605 S Douglas Rd, Miami, FL 33133

MURPHY, Linda Estelle (Va) 15 Hamilton St, Colonial Beach, VA 22443

MURPHY, Michael John (Tenn) 219 Jennings Cir, Tullahoma, TN 37388

MURPHY, Michael Robert (SVa) 2315 Mary Goodwyn Rd., Powhatan, VA 23139

MURPHY JR, P L (Dal)

MURPHY, Patricia Ann (Kan) 7515 W 102nd St, Overland Park, KS 66212

MURPHY, Richard William (RG) 4717 Sundial Way, Santa Fe, NM 87507

MURPHY, Robert A (WMo) 4225 Sw Clipper Ln, Lees Summit, MO 64082

MURPHY JR, Russell Edward (Wyo) 11506 Wornall Rd, Kansas City, MO 64114

MURPHY, Sue (Me) 37 Chancery Lane, Sanford, ME 04073

MURPHY, Susan (Ind)

MURPHY, T Abigail (LI) 15 Stewart Ave, Stewart Manor, NY 11530

MURPHY, Terri Marie (WA) 15575 Germantown Rd, Germantown, MD 20874

MURPHY, Thomas Christopher (WA) 3700 Massachusetts Avenue, NW, Apartment 531, Washington, DC 20016

MURPHY, Thomas Edward (Spok) 215 Tolman Creek Rd Unit 34, Ashland, OR 97520

MURPHY, Thomas Lynch (WNC) 9 Swan St, Asheville, NC 28803

MURPHY, Thomas M (Nwk) 38 Duncan Avenue, Jersey City, NJ 07304

MURPHY, Timothy Hunter (Ala) 801 The Trce W, Jasper, AL 35504

MURPHY, Warren Charles (Wyo) 50 Diamond View Rd, Cody, WY 82414

MURPHY, William McKee (WMich) N 2794 Summerville Park Road, Lodi, WI 53555

MURRAY, Ann Elena Williams (Okla) 325 E 1st St, Edmond, OK 73034

MURRAY, Austin B (The Episcopal Church in Haw) 2853 Panepoo St, Kihei, HI 96753

MURRAY IV, Bill S (At) 8011 Douglas Avenue, Dallas, TX 75225

MURRAY, Cicely Anne (Pa) 600 E Cathedral Rd Apt D104, Philadelphia, PA 19128

MURRAY, Diane Marie (FdL) W5766 Winooski Rd, Plymouth, WI 53073

MURRAY, Elizabeth Ann (CFla) 144 Sea Park Blvd, Satellite Beach, FL 32937

MURRAY JR, George Ralph (Eas) 4453 Eastwicke Dr, Salisbury, MD 21804

MURRAY III, John William (CGC) 1326 Live Oak Ln, Jacksonville, FL 32207

MURRAY, Kat (SO) 1255 Canterbury Blvd, Altus, OK 73521

MURRAY, Kathleen (Va)

MURRAY, Laura Jane (Oly) 7701 Skansie Ave, Gig Harbor, WA 98335

MURRAY, Lois Thompson (SeFla) 1521 Alton Rd # 219, Miami Beach, FL 33139

MURRAY, Mac (WMass) 23 Dana Park, Hopedale, MA 01747

MURRAY, Michael Hunt (Va) 700 Port St Apt 226, Easton, MD 21601

MURRAY, Milton Hood (Fla) 3750 Peachtree Rd NE # 422, Atlanta, GA 30319

MURRAY, Noland Patrick (Ark) 14300 Chenal Pkwy Apt 1316, Little Rock, AR 72211

MURRAY, Robert Scott (Episcopal SJ) 1104 Kitanosho-Cho, Ohmihachiman, Shiga, 523-0806, Japan

MURRAY III, Roderic Lafayette (Ala) 634 Timber Ln, Nashville, TN 37215

MURRAY III, Thomas Holt (WTex) 1120 Lake Dr, Kerrville, TX 78028

MURRAY, Thomas P (Fla) 4129 Oxford Ave, Jacksonville, FL 32210

MURRAY, Trilby Ometa (Chi) 3801 S Wabash Ave, Chicago, IL 60653

MURRAY, Vincent Devitt (Oly) 306 Lopez Ave, Port Angeles, WA 98362

MURRAY-SMITH, Jihan Brittany (Chi) 1424 N Dearborn St, Chicago, IL 60610

MURRELL, William Lewis (NY) 2400 Johnson Ave Apt 10c, Bronx, NY 10463

MURSULI, Modesto (SeFla) 399A Himrod St, Brooklyn, NY 11237

MUSCO, John Robert (LI) 1099 Ocean Ave, Brooklyn, NY 11230

MUSGRAVE, David Charles (Chi) 11112 Bayberry Hills Dr, Raleigh, NC 27617

MUSHORN, Richard C (LI) 2206 Cloverleaf Cir SE, Cleveland, TN 37311

MUSOKE-LUBEGA, Benjamin Kiwomutemero (NY) 27 Compton Dr, East Windsor, NJ 08520

MUSSATTI, David James (Nev) Po Box 5572, Incline Village, NV 89450

MUSSER, Jonathan David (Ark) 3737 Seminary Rd # 107, Alexandria, VA 22304

MUSSER, Lisa (WTenn) 8011 Douglas Avenue, Dallas, TX 75225

MUSTARD, George Thomas (SwVa) 6437 Monarch Ct, Hoschton, GA 30548

MUSTERMAN, Amanda E (Lex) 206 W Columbia St, Somerset, KY 42501

MUTCHLER, Marlene Kay-Scholten (Ore) 147 Nw 19th Ave, Portland, OR 97209

MUTH, Donald Charles (La) 4920 Cleveland Pl, Metairie, LA 70003

MUTOLO, Frances (Colo) 85 Long Bow Cir, Monument, CO 80132

MYCOFF JR, Walt (SO) 892 W Webster Rd, Summersville, WV 26651

MYERS, Amy Slaughter (Md) Epiphany Episcopal Church, 2216 Pot Spring Rd, Timonium, MD 21093

MYERS, Annwn (Miss) 335 Tennessee Avenue, Sewanee, TN 37383

MYERS, Bethany Leigh (Colo) 800 N Saint Asaph St # 202, Alexandria, VA 22314

MYERS, Brooke (Mo) 4141 Flora Pl, Saint Louis, MO 63110

MYERS, David John (Ark) 12599 Timberline Dr, Garfield, AR 72732

MYERS, Elizabeth Williams (Be) 798 Willow Grove St # 3a, Hackettstown, NJ 07840

MYERS, Fredrick Eugene (SanD) 1111 E Ramon Rd Unit 80, Palm Springs, CA 92264

MYERS, Jeannette (The Episcopal NCal) 38 Payran Street, Petaluma, CA 94952

MYERS, John Geenwood (WLa) 833 Clarence St, Lake Charles, LA 70601

MYERS, Jonathan (Spok) St Stephen Episcopal Church, 4805 NE 45th St, Seattle, WA 98105

MYERS, Max Arthur (Ct) 247 New Milford Tpke, Marble Dale, CT 06777

MYERS, Nicholas A (Colo) 6050 N Meridian St, Indianapolis, IN 46208

MYERS, Rebecca (CPa) St John's Church, 701 Engineer St, Corbin, KY 40701

MYERS II, Robert (Ind) 8014 River Bay Drive West, Indianapolis, IN 46240

MYERS JR, Robert Keith (Chi) 7050 N Oakley Ave, Chicago, IL 60645

MYERS, Roy (WLa) 1906 Evangeline Dr, Bastrop, LA 71220

MYERS, Thomas (NJ) 2502 Central Ave, North Wildwood, NJ 08260

MYERS, William Francis (Va) 11142 Beaver Trail Ct, Reston, VA 20191

MYHR, Laura Parmer (WNC) 100 Summit Street, Marion, NC 28752

MYNATT, Belva Charlene (WMo) 3523 S Kings Hwy, Independence, MO 64055

MYRICK, Bill (Mil) 503 E Walworth Ave, P.O. Box 528, Delavan, WI 53115

MYSEN, Andrea Leigh (Chi) 411 Laurel Ave, Highland Park, IL 60035

MYSINGER, Kellie (Ky)

N

NABE, Clyde Milton (Mo) 4742 Burlington Ave N, Saint Petersburg, FL 33713

NACHTRIEB, John David (Chi) 131 N Brainard Ave, La Grange, IL 60525

NAECKEL, Lynn Miles (Minn) Po Box 43, Ranier, MN 56668

NAEF, Linda (Miss) 655 Eagle Ave, Jackson, MS 39206

NAEGELE III, John Aloysius (CPa) 982 Spa Rd. Apt. 201, Annapolis, MD 21403

NAGARAJAH, Bertram (ECR)

NAGATA, Ada (Los) Church of Our Saviour, 535 West Roses Road, San Gabriel, CA 91775

NAGEL, Virginia Otis Wight (CNY) 100 Wilson Pl, Syracuse, NY 13214

NAGLE, George Overholser (CNY) 65 Glenwood Dr, Saranac Lake, NY 12983

NAGLEY, Stephanie Jane (WA) 6030 Grosvenor Lane, Bethesda, MD 20814

NAGY, Robert A (NJ) 33396 Alagon Street, Temecula, CA 92592

NAILOR, Willis Michael (CPa) 221 N Front St, Harrisburg, PA 17101

NAIRN, Frederick William (Minn) 5895 Stoneybrook Dr, Minnetonka, MN 55345

NAKAMURA RENGERS, Katherine Toshiko (Ala) 521 20th St N, Birmingham, AL 35203

NAKAYAMA, Timothy Makoto (Oly) 700 6th Ave S Apt 321, Seattle, WA 98104

NAKO, Jim (Chi) 9300 S Pleasant Ave, Chicago, IL 60643

NALVEN, Claudia (WTex) 327 S 4th St, Geneva, IL 60134

NANCARROW, Arthur Paul (Mich) 148 W Eagle Lake Dr, Maple Grove, MN 55369

NANCARROW, Paul Steven (SwVa) 25 Church St, Staunton, VA 24401

NANCEKIVELL, Diane (NJ) 1008 Hemenway Rd, Bridport, VT 05734

NANNY, Susan Kathryn (Mo) 2831 Eads Ave, Saint Louis, MO 63104

NANTHICATTU, Jacob Philip (NY) 182 Ridge Rd, Valley Cottage, NY 10989

NANTON-MARIE, Allan Anselm (Fla) PO Box 1-5442, Fort Lauderdale, FL 33318

NAPIER, Graeme Stewart Patrick Columbanus (NY)

NAPOLIELLO, Susan Foster (The Episcopal NCal) 2412 Foothill Blvd No. 31, Calistoga, CA 94515

NARAIN, Errol (Chi) 125 E 26th St, Chicago, IL 60616

NARVAEZ, Alfonso Anthony (WTex) PO Box 8004, Reston, VA 20195

NARVAEZ ADORNO, Jose A (PR)

NASH, Cynthia Gordon (WNC) 15 Hemlock Ave, Spruce Pine, NC 28777

NASH, Penny Annette (Va) 6000 Grove Ave, Richmond, VA 23226

NATHANIEL, Mary (Ak) PO Box 56, Chalkyitsik, AK 99788

NATIONS, Christopher Cameron (Ala) 338 E Lyman Ave, Winter Park, FL 32789

NATOLI, Anne Marie (EC) 305 Myrtle St, Ashland, VA 23005

NATTERMANN, Margaret Ann (WMich) 06685 M-66n, Charlevoix Estates Lot 124, Charlevoix, MI 49720

NATZKE, Vicki (FdL) 7221 Country Village Dr, Wisconsin Rapids, WI 54494

NAUGHTON, Ezra A (VI) 398 N St Sw, Washington, DC 20024

NAUGHTON, Mary Anne (SeFla) 3300A S Seacrest Blvd, Boynton Beach, FL 33435

NAUGHTON, Sharon Yvonne (EMich) St Paul's Episcopal Church, 711 S Saginaw St, Flint, MI 48502

NAUGLE, Gretchen Rohn (Neb) I535 North 69th Stret, Lincoln, NE 68505

NAUMANN, John Robert (Mont) 1241 Crawford Dr., Billings, MT 59102

NAUMANN, Richard Donald (Wyo) 1251 Inca Dr, Laramie, WY 82072

NAUSKA, Gayle (Ak) 1703 Richardson Dr, Anchorage, AK 99504

NAWROCKI, Cynthia Lynn (WMich) 3006 Bird Ave Ne, Grand Rapids, MI 49525

NAYLOR, Susan B (Mo) 2905 Wingate Ct, Saint Louis, MO 63119

NDAI, Domenic M (Pa) 801 Macdade Blvd, Collingdale, PA 19023

NDISHABANDI, William K (NJ) 147 Daniel Lake Blvd, Jackson, MS 39212

NDUNGU, Samuel Kirabi (Pa) 6361 Lancaster Ave, Philadelphia, PA 19151

NEAD III, Prescott Eckerman (USC) 714 Michaels Creek, Evans, GA 30809

NEAKOK, Willard Payne (Ak)

NEAL, Deonna Denice (WA) eSchool of Graduate PME, 600 Chennault Cir, Maxwell Afb, AL 36112

NEAL, James Frederick (Oly) 1831 E South Island Dr, Shelton, WA 98584

NEAL, Kristi Hasskamp (WNC) 100 Spring Ln, Black Mountain, NC 28711

NEAL, Linda (ECR) 41-884 Laumilo St, Waimanalo, HI 96795

NEAL JR, Millard Fillmore (SwFla) 14820 Rue De Bayonne, Clearwater, FL 33762

NEAL, Scott (Vt) PO Box 410, Arlington, VT 05250

NEAL, William Everett (FdL)

NEALE, Alan James Robert (Pa) 316 S 16th St, Philadelphia, PA 19102

NEARY, Marlyn Mason (NH) 1935 Us Route 3, Colebrook, NH 03576

NEAT, William Jessee (Lex) 311 Washington St, Frankfort, KY 40601

NEBEL, Sue (Chi) 2023 Lake Ave, Wilmette, IL 60091

NECKERMANN, Ernest Charles (Los) 1107 Foothills Dr, Newberg, OR 97132

NEDELKA, Jerome Joseph (LI) PO Box 2016, Miller Place, NY 11764

NEED, Merrie Anne Dunham (Colo) 7726 S Trenton Ct, Englewood, CO 80112

NEEL, Doug (Colo) 225 S Pagosa Blvd, Pagosa Springs, CO 81147

NEELEY II, Harry Edwin (Mont) 100 W Glendale St #8, Dillon, MT 59725

NEEL-RICHARD, Joanne Louise (Ct) 39 Mckinley Ave, New Haven, CT 06515

NEELY, Christopher Fones (SO) 3580 Shaw Ave 409, Cincinnati, OH 45208

NEFF, Shanna (WTex) St Pauls Episcopal Church, PO Box 1148, San Antonio, TX 78294

NEFSTEAD, Eric (Cal) 275 Burnett Ave Apt 8, San Francisco, CA 94131

NEGLIA, Dwight (Nwk) 116 Oakmont Dr, Mays Landing, NJ 08330

NEGRON CARABALLO SR, Luis (PR)

NEIDLINGER, Theodore (NI) 125 S Mccann St, Kokomo, IN 46901

NEIGHBORS, Dolores (Chi) 5555 S Everett Ave Apt C-4, Chicago, IL 60637

NEIL, Earl Albert (WA) 4545 Connecticut Ave Nw, Apt 929, Washington, DC 20008

NEIL, Judy Kay (Ala) Grace Episcopal Church, 5712 1st Ave N, Birmingham, AL 35212

NEILSEN, Eloise (RI) 20 Exeter Blvd, Narragansett, RI 02882

NEILSON, Albert Pancoast (Del) 10 Chickadee Dr, Topsham, ME 04086

NEILSON, John Robert (NJ) 39 Yarmouth Ct, Scotch Plains, NJ 07076

NEILSON, Kurt (Ore) 2736 SE 63rd Ave, Portland, OR 97206

NEILSON, Lisa (FtW) 902 George Bush Dr, College Station, TX 77840

NEILY, Robert Edward (Mich) 704 15th St Apt 360, Durham, NC 27705

NEIMAN, Judi Ann (WMich) 34462 1st St, Paw Paw, MI 49079

NEITZEL, Anna C (Dal) 6525 Inwood Road, Dallas, TX 75209

NELSON, Ann Jean (Colo) 2002 Warwick Ln, Colorado Springs, CO 80909

NELSON III, Benjamin Howard (WTex) 3039 Ranch Rd 12, San Marcos, TX 78666

NELSON SR, Bob (SanD) 330 11th St, Del Mar, CA 92014

NELSON, Charles Herbert (LI) 194-51 Murdock Ave, Saint Albans, NY 11412

NELSON, Charles Nickolaus (Minn) Rt 2 Box 283, Park Rapids, MN 56470

NELSON, David Scott (Tex) 19330 Pinehurst Trail Dr, Humble, TX 77346

NELSON, Elizabeth Anne (Ida)

NELSON, Elizabeth Lane (CFla) 705 Jefferson Ave, Lehigh Acres, FL 33936

NELSON, Genevieve Elizabeth (SVa) 7400 Hampton Blvd, Norfolk, VA 23505

NELSON, Geri Lee (Ga) 129 Viewcrest Dr, Hendersonville, NC 28739

NELSON, J Douglas (SD) 21 rue du Sourdonnet, Les Mathes, SD 17570, France

NELSON, James Craig (WTex) 2500 N 10th St, McAllen, TX 78501

NELSON, Jeffrey Scott (Neb) 1714 Short Street, North Platte, NE 69101

NELSON, Jennifer Claire (Cal)

NELSON, Joseph Reed Peter (NJ) 715 Magie Ave, Elizabeth, NJ 07208

NELSON, Joshua D (NI)

NELSON, Julie (ECR) 532 Tyrella Ave Apt 30, Mountain View, CA 94043

NELSON, Leilani Lucas (Cal) 3973 17th St, San Francisco, CA 94114

NELSON JR, Levine S (Pa) Po Box 1105, Norristown, PA 19404

NELSON, Raymond A (SVa) 3850 Pittaway Dr, Richmond, VA 23235

NELSON JR, Rich (NwT) Po Box 82, Burton, TX 77835

NELSON, Richard A (Ga) 7607 Lynes Ct, Savannah, GA 31406

NELSON, Rita (Del) 30895 Crepe Myrtle Dr Unit 66, Millsboro, DE 19966

NELSON JR, Robert Mitchell (Nev) 3609 Casa Grande Ave, Las Vegas, NV 89102

NELSON, Robert William (Ak) 93 Laukahi St, Kihei, HI 96753

NELSON, Roger (Mass) 557 Salem St, Malden, MA 02148

NELSON, Sarah Lee (Del) Saint James Episcopal Church, 2 S Augustine St, Newport, DE 19804

NELSON-AMAKER, Melana (WA) 8001 Annapolis Rd, New Carrollton, MD 20784

NELSON-LOW, Jane (Spok) 719 W. Montgomery Ave, Spokane, WA 99205

NEMBHARD, Ralston Bruce (CFla) 8413 Clematis Ln, Orlando, FL 32819

NEMES, John Dale (Oly) 16920 Se 40th Pl, Bellevue, WA 98008

NERN JR, William B (Cal)

NERUD, Barbara Jeanne (Neb)

NESBIT, Pamela (Pa) 16 Belmont Sq, Doylestown, PA 18901

NESBIT JR, William (Chi) 917 Wildwood Ct, St. Charles, IL 60174

NESBITT, John Russell (EO) 3846 NE Glisan St, Portland, OR 97232

NESBITT, Margot Lord (Okla) 1703 N Hudson Ave, Oklahoma City, OK 73103

NESBITT, Paula Diane (Cal) 577 Forest St., Oakland, CA 94618

NESHEIM, Donald Oakley (Minn) 10785 Valley View Rd #114, Eden Prairie, MN 55344

NESIN, Leslie Frances (Me) Po Box 358, Howland, ME 04448

NESMITH, Elizabeth Clare (LI) 305 Carlls Path, Deer Park, NY 11729

NESS, Jerry (Neb) 803 Avenue E Pl, Kearney, NE 68847

NESS, Louisett Marie (Chi) 466 W Jackson St, Woodstock, IL 60098

NESS, Zanne Bartlett (ND) 1971 Mesquite Loop, Bismarck, ND 58503

NESTA, Paul Anthony (NI)

NESTLEHUTT, Abigail Crozier (Pa) Po Box 517, Saint Michaels, MD 21663

NESTLEHUTT, Mark S (Eas) 115 West Chestnut, PO Box 517, Saint Michaels, MD 21663

NESTLER, Mary June (U) St. George's College, 31 Salahedeen Street, Jerusalem, Jerusalem District 91000, Israel

NESTOR, Elizabeth M (RI) 57 South Rd, Wakefield, RI 02879

NESTROCK, Frederick Richard (Chi) 4633 Fairway Ct, Waterford, MI 48328

NETTLETON, Edwin Bewick (Colo) Po Box 22, Lake City, CO 81235

NETTLETON, Jerome Paul (Eas) 525 E 6th St, Cookeville, TN 38501

NETZLER, Sherryl Kaye (Nev) 1631 Esmeralda Pl, Minden, NV 89423

NEUBAUER, Nicholas Lawrence (Nev)

NEUBAUER, Zachary D (CFla)

NEUBERGER, Jeffrey Lynn (Spok) 9106 N Bradbury St, Spokane, WA 99208

NEUBURGER, James Edward (USC) 301 W Liberty St, Winnsboro, SC 29180

NEUFELD, Ellen Christine (Alb) 6349 Milgen Rd Apt 12, Columbus, GA 31907

NEUFELD, Michael John (Alb) 52 Sacandaga Rd, Scotia, NY 12302

NEUHARDT, Kerry (Az) 975 E Warner Rd, Tempe, AZ 85284

NEUHAUS, Theodore James (Minn) 290 Dayton Ave Apt 1w, Saint Paul, MN 55102

NEVELS JR, Harry V (O) 2532 Potomac Hunt Ln Apt 1B, Richmond, VA 23233

NEVILLE, Robert E (ECR) 5170 Madison Ave, Trumbull, CT 06611

NEVILLE, Robyn M (Va) 1299 Quaker Hill Dr, Alexandria, VA 22314

NEVIN-FIELD, Claire Margaret (Pa) 816 Derby Dr, West Chester, PA 19380

NEVINS, Nancy Ruth (WMo) 416 SE Grand, Lee's Summit, MO 64063

NEWAGO, Michael Jeffrey (Spr) PO Box 816, Bayfield, WI 54814

NEWBERRY, Hancella Warren (SO) 840 Middlebury Dr N, Worthington, OH 43085

NEWBERRY III, Jay Lamar (Mass) 205 Oxbow Rd, Wayland, MA 01778

NEWBERT, Russell Anderson (WNY) 185 Norwood Ave, Buffalo, NY 14222

NEWBERY, Charles Gomph (LI) 1322 Shattuck Ave., #306, Berkeley, CA 94709

NEWBOLD SR, Simeon Eugene (Va) PO Box 540668, Opa Locka, FL 33054

NEWBY, Robert LaVelle (Colo) 18 Folsom Pl, Durango, CO 81301

NEWCOMB, Blair Deborah (Md) PO Box 301, Center Sandwich, NH 03227

NEWCOMB, Deborah Johnson (Va) 25260 County Route 54, Dexter, NY 13634

NEWCOMB, Tom (NY) 35 Parkview Ave 4L, Bronxville, NY 10708

NEWCOMBE, David Gordon (NY) 113 Gilbert Road, Cambridge, CB4 3NZ, Great Britain (UK)

NEWELL, Tige John E. (SVa) 1562 Heathrow Ln, KESWICK, VA 22947

NEWHART, David George (CFla) 120 Larchmont Ter, Sebastian, FL 32958

NEWLAND, Ben (Colo) Saint John's Episcopal Church, 1419 Pine St, Boulder, CO 80302

NEWLIN, Melissa Dollie (ECR) 1965 Luzern St, Seaside, CA 93955

NEWLUN, Connor J (Va) Aquia Episcopal Church, PO Box 275, Stafford, VA 22555

NEWMAN, Georgia Ann (At)

NEWMAN II, James Arthur (Los) 1445 Westerly Ter, Los Angeles, CA 90026

NEWMAN, Michael Werth (Pa) 1806 Half Mile Post South, Garnet Valley, PA 19060

NEWMAN, Richard Barend (Pa) 14 Princess Ln, Newtown, PA 18940

NEWMAN, Ryan D (Episcopal SJ) PO Box 429, Kapaa, HI 96746

NEWMAN, Thomas Frank (SD) 10 Red Oak Rd, Shawnee, OK 74804

NEWNAM, Elizabeth (Cal) 555 4th St Unit 530, San Francisco, CA 94107

NEWSOM, James Cook (WTenn) St George's Independent School, 3749 Kimball Ave, Memphis, TN 38111

NEWTON, Alissabeth Anne (Oly) Diocese Of Olympia, 1551 10th Ave E, Seattle, WA 98102

NEWTON IV, John (Tex) 209 W 27th St, Austin, TX 78705

NEWTON, John David (Minn) 1631 Ford Pkwy, Saint Paul, MN 55116

NEYLAND, Thomas Allen (Colo) PO Box 228, Hygiene, CO 80533

NEYLON, Jean Carla (Md)

NG, Joshua (Los) 15930 Annellen St, Hacienda Heights, CA 91745

NG-LAM, Connie M Ng (Los) 133 E Graves Ave, Monterey Park, CA 91755

NGUYEN, Herman Hong Xuan (Los) 10795 Garza Ave, Anaheim, CA 92804

NI, Huiliang (Los) St Edmunds Episcopal Church, 1175 S San Gabriel Blvd, San Marino, CA 91108

NICHOLS, Alice (Ky) 216 E 6th St, Hopkinsville, KY 42240

NICHOLS, Catherine Palmer (Vt) PO Box 554, East Middlebury, VT 05740

NICHOLS JR, Charlie (NH) 43 Pine St, Exeter, NH 03833

✠ **NICHOLS**, Kevin Donnelly (Be) 21 Hampshire Hills Dr, Bow, NH 03304

NICHOLS, Liane Christoffersen (Ia) 2013 Minnetonka Dr, Cedar Falls, IA 50613

NICHOLS III, Robert George (Tex) 15 Hannon Ave, Mobile, AL 36604

NICHOLS, Sarah (Los) 837 S Orange Grove Blvd, Pasadena, CA 91105

NICHOLSON, Aleathia Dolores (Tenn) 3729 Creekland Ct, Nashville, TN 37218

NICHOLSON, Anne L (Md) 1830 Connecticut Ave NW, Washington, DC 20009

NICHOLSON, Kedron (WNC) 245 Kingsley Ave, Orange Park, FL 32073

NICHOLSON, Wayne Philip (WMich) 405 E High St, Mount Pleasant, MI 48858

NICKEL, Rebecca (Ind) St. Timothy's Episcopal Church 2601 E. Thompson Road, Indianapolis, IN 46227

NICKELSON, Marian L (Ak) 1133 Walnut Ave, Kenai, AK 99611

NICKERSON, Audra M (WMich) 141 Broad St N, Battle Creek, MI 49017

NICKERSON, Bruce Edward (Mass) 77 South Rd, Bedford, MA 01730

NICKERSON JR, Donald Albert (Me) Po Box 855, Intervale, NH 03845

NICKLES, Amanda L (Fla) PO Box 10472, Tallahassee, FL 32302

NICKLES, Brenda Joyce (Alb) 12 Woodbridge Ave., Chatham, NY 12037

NICKLES, Megan Woods (Wyo) 349 N Douglas St, Powell, WY 82435

NICOLL, Tom (NY) 16 Claret Dr, Greenville, SC 29609

NICOLOSI, Gary (Az) St. James Westminster Church, 115 Askin Street, London, N6C 1E7, Canada

NIEHAUS, Tom (WNC) 12503 N Woodberry Dr, Mequon, WI 53092

NIELSEN III, Peter W (O) 5811 Vrooman Rd, Painesville, OH 44077

NIEMAN, John S (Me) PO Box 234, Newcastle, ME 04553

NIEMEYER, David (Va) 501 W Nine Mile Rd, Highland Springs, VA 23075

NIESE JR, Alfred Moring (NJ) 6 Apple Tree Dr, Brunswick, ME 04011

NIETERT, Jack Frederick (SC) 2830 W Royal Oaks Dr, Beaufort, SC 29902

NIPPS, Leslie (Cal) 592 Jean St #202, Oakland, CA 94610

NISBETT, Joshua (LI) 11738 Cross Island Pkwy, Cambria Heights, NY 11411

NISSEN, Peter Boy (WK) 312 S Kansas Ave, Norton, KS 67654

NITZ, Theodore Allen (Spok) 2300 NW Ridgeline Drive, Pullman, WA 99163

NIX JR, William Dale (NwT) 11355 Nix Ranch Road, Canadian, TX 79014

NIXON, Barbara Elizabeth (Ct) 399 Windward Way, Sacramento, CA 95831

NIXON, James Thomas (At) 2700 Bennington Dr Ne, Marietta, GA 30062

NIXON, Thomas E (CGC) 1580Deese Road, Ozark, AL 36360

NNAJI, Udochukwu Benjamin (NY) 1905 Morris Ave, Bronx, NY 10453

NOALL, Nancy Jo (WA) 312 Hillmoor Dr, Silver Spring, MD 20901

NOBLE, Anthony Norman (SanD) 625 Pennsylvania Ave, San Diego, CA 92103

NOBLE, Mitzi McAlexander (WA) 508 Tranquility Rd., Moneta, VA 24121

NOBLE, William Conner (NJ) 1941 Wayside Rd, Tinton Falls, NJ 07724

NOCHER, Janet Gregoire (FtW) 4408 Foxfire Way, Fort Worth, TX 76133

NOE, William Stanton (Va) Po Box 2078, Ashland, VA 23005

NOEL, Virginia Lee (Mo) 15826 Clayton Rd Apt 131, Ellisville, MO 63011

NOLAN, Daryce (Chi) 7600 Wolf Rd, Burr Ridge, IL 60527

NOLAN, Richard Thomas (Ct) 451 Heritage Drive, Apt 1014, Pompano Beach, FL 33060

NOLAND, Elisabeth Hooper (RG) 2 Pino Pl, Santa Fe, NM 87508

NOLEN, Kenneth (CFla) 414 Pine St, Titusville, FL 32796

NONKEN, Scott Eugene (SwFla)

NOON, Anna C (NJ) 5203 Falls Road Ter Apt 1, Baltimore, MD 21210

NOONAN, Deborah Anne (Az) 2331 E. Adams St., Tucson, AZ 85719

NORBY, Laura L (Mil) 508 Rupert Rd, Waunakee, WI 53597

NORCROSS, Steve (Ore) 8949 SW Fairview Pl, Portland, OR 97223

NORD, Christina Virginia (Pa) 108 N. 5th St., Allentown, PA 18102

NORDQUIST, Conrad (Los) 4063 Ruis Ct, Jurupa Valley, CA 92509

NORDSTROM JR, Eugene Alexander (HB)

NORDWICK, Brian P (ECR) 670 Clearview Dr, Hollister, CA 95023

NORGARD, David Lee (Los) PO Box 691458, West Hollywood, CA 90069

NORGREN, William Andrew (NY) 120 East 79th Street Apt. 2D, New York, NY 10075

NORMAN, Curt (EMich) St. John's Episcopal Church, 123 N Michigan Ave, Saginaw, MI 48602

NORMAN, Harold Gene (Dal) 406 Dula Cir., Duncanville, TX 75116

NORMAN, Joseph Gary (Alb) PO Box 800, Morris, NY 13808

NORMAN, Lynn (CGC) Trinity Episcopal Church, 1900 Dauphin St, Mobile, AL 36606

NORMAN JR, Richard (SwFla) 405 Glenmar Ave, Monroe, LA 71201

NORMAN, Tex (CFla)

NORMAND, Ann (Tex) 1225 Texas Ave., Houston, TX 77002

NORMANN, Margaret Ella Monroe (Ct) 888 B Heritage Vlg, Southbury, CT 06488

NORRIS, David (Ct) 5 Briar Brae Rd, Stamford, CT 06903

NORRIS JR, Edwin Arter (Chi) 2866 Vacherie Ln, Dallas, TX 75227

NORRIS, M Brent (WNC) 337 Charlotte St, Asheville, NC 28801

NORRIS, Mark Joseph Patrick (Neb) 155 Strozier Rd # B, West Monroe, LA 71291

NORRIS III, Paul Haile (At) 951 Williams St, Madison, GA 30650

NORRIS, Rollin Bradford (Mich) 1626 Strathcona Dr, Detroit, MI 48203

NORRIS, Stephen Allen (Ga) 2493 Chandler Dr, Valdosta, GA 31602

NORRIS, Susy (NJ) 6355 Pine Dr., Chincoteague, VA 23336

NORRO, Hugo Pablo (Los) 4200 Summers Ln Unit 15, Klamath Falls, OR 97603

NORTH JR, Bill (Tex) 570 Marietta Ave, Swarthmore, PA 19081

NORTH, Bob (Chi) 7 Huron Trce, Galena, IL 61036

NORTH, Joseph James (Alb) 144 Prospect Ave, Gloversville, NY 12078

NORTHCRAFT, Linda Louise (Mich) 19120 Eldridge Ct, Southfield, MI 48076

NORTHRUP, Michael C (Nev) 507 Churchill St, Fallon, NV 89406

NORTHUP, Frederick Bowen (At) 1118 Chicory Lane, Asheville, NC 28803

NORTHUP, Lesley Armstrong (NY) 1298 NE 95th St, Miami, FL 33138

NORTHWAY, Daniel Page (Kan) 3531 SW Ashworth Ct, Topeka, KS 66614

NORTON, Ann Elizabeth (EMich) PO Box 217, Otter Lake, MI 48464

NORTON JR, James Frederick (Ia) 1621 E River Ter, Minneapolis, MN 55414

Clergy List

NORTON, Jerry R (Ak)
NORTON, Marlee R (Va) 2416 N Florida St, Arlington, VA 22207
NORTON, Mary (NwPa) 218 Center St, Ridgway, PA 15853
NORTON, Mary Julyan (Ak) St Georges In the Arctic Church, Po Box 269, Kotzebue, AK 99752
NORVELL, John David (Okla) 530 Northcrest Dr, Ada, OK 74820
NOVAK, Barbara Ellen Hosea (Spok) 1107 E 41st Ave, Spokane, WA 99203
NOVAK, Margaret Anne (Oly) 15502 30th Ave Ne, Shoreline, WA 98155
NOVAK, Nick (Tex) 5215 Honey Creek, Baytown, TX 77523
NOVAK-SCOFIELD, Eleanor Patricia (SwVa) 124 E Main St, Abingdon, VA 24210
NOVES, W David Peter (WNY) 840 Bataan Ave, Dunkirk, NY 14048
NOWLIN, Ben Gary (Mo) 61 Dames Ct, Ferguson, MO 63135
NOYES, Daphne B (Mass) Church of the Advent, 30 Brimmer St, Boston, MA 02108
NSENGIYUMVA, Samuel (Md) 1223 Huron Trail, Sheboygan Falls, WI 53085
NSUBUGA, Thomas (WLa) 538 Main St, Grambling, LA 71245
NTAGENGWA, Jean Baptiste (Mass) 138 Tremont St, Boston, MA 02111
NUAMAH, Reggie (LI) 3607 Glenwood Rd, Brooklyn, NY 11210
NULL, John A (WK) 636 East Iron, Salina, KS 67401
NUNEZ, Carlos E (Ore) 3052 Se 158th Ave, Portland, OR 97236
NUNEZ, Tim (CFla) 10481 Se 68th Ct, Belleview, FL 34420
NUNLEY, Jan (NY) 137 N Division St, Peekskill, NY 10566
NUNN, Frances Louise (Va) Po Box 206, Monterey, VA 24465
NURDING, Brian Frank (The Episcopal Church in Haw) 1144 Kumukumu St. Apt. E, Honolulu, HI 96825
NUSSER-TELFER, Hiltrude Maria (O) 9868 Ford Rd, Perrysburg, OH 43551
NUTTER, James Wallace (Tex) 6221 Main St, Houston, TX 77030
NWACHUKU, Chukwuemeka Polycarp (Chi) St Andrew's - Pentecost Evanston, 1928 Darrow Ave, Evanston, IL 60201
NWANKWO, Chizoba Uzoamaka (NJ)
NYATSAMBO, Tobias Dzawanda (NH) PO Box 737, Ashland, NH 03217
NYBACK, Rachel (Los) 1818 Monterey Blvd, Hermosa Beach, CA 90254
NYBERG, Kristina Yvette (Los) 700 S. Myrtle Avenue, Apt 514, Monrovia, CA 91016
NYE, Linda Wade (NC) Grace Memorial Episcopal Church, 871 Merrimon Ave, Asheville, NC 28804

NYE, Max Ormsbee (Nev) 150 Cortona Way Apt 331, Brentwood, CA 94513
NYEIN, Zachary C (ETenn) 20 Belvoir Ave, Chattanooga, TN 37411
NYGAARD, Richard Lowell (NwPa)
NYGAARD, Steven Bickham (NMich) 6144 Westridge 21.25 Dr, Gladstone, MI 49837
NYRE-THOMAS, Beryl Jean (Los) 1117 Bennett Ave, Long Beach, CA 90804
NYSTROM, Brian Eric (Wyo) PO Box 1690, Jackson, WY 83001

O

OAK, Carol Pinkham (Md) St. John's Episcopal Church, 9120 Frederick Road, Ellicott City, MD 21042
OAKES, Leonard (Cal) 777 Southgate Ave, Daly City, CA 94015
OAKES, Louise K (NC) 201 N Walbridge Ave Apt 335, Madison, WI 53714
OAKES, Sara Elizabeth Herr (Cal) 622 Terra California Dr Apt 7, Walnut Creek, CA 94595
OAKLAND, Mary Jane (Ia) 1612 Truman Dr, Ames, IA 50010
OASIN, Elizabeth Jayne (NJ) 344 B Delancey Pl, Mount Laurel, NJ 08054
OATS, Louis (NC) 1325 Hickory Lane, Dandridge, TN 37725
OBARSKI, Sandra Ruth (Minn) 1111 Lowell Cir, Apple Valley, MN 55124
OBENCHAIN, John Colin (Pa) 98 Ayers Dr, Rising Sun, MD 21911
OBERHEIDE, Richard Dean (Ala) 155 N Twining St, Montgomery, AL 36112
OBIER, Cynthia Andrews (La) 4255 Hyacinth Ave, Baton Rouge, LA 70808
OBREGON, Ernesto M (Ala) 5424 Wisteria Trce, Trussville, AL 35173
O'BRIEN, Charles Harold (WMass) 738 Simonds Rd, Williamstown, MA 01267
O'BRIEN, Craig Edward (Ga) 201 E 49th St, Savannah, GA 31405
O'BRIEN, Donald Richard (SwFla)
O'BRIEN, Eileen Elizabeth (Tex)
O'BRIEN, Julie Lynn (Az) 1735 S College Ave, Tempe, AZ 85281
O' BRIEN, Richard L (Nev) Christ Church, 200 S Maryland Pkwy, Las Vegas, NV 89101
O'BROCHTA, Joseph William (Lex)
O'CALLAGHAN, Beth (WA) 15575 Germantown Rd, Germantown, MD 20874
O'CARROLL, Bryan (SwFla) 912 63rd Ave W, Bradenton, FL 34207
OCCHIUTO, Joseph John (LI)
O'CONNELL, Kelly (Mass) 138 Tremont St, Boston, MA 02111
O'CONNELL, Patricia Marie (WMass) 36 Court St, Westfield, MA 01085

O'CONNOR, Andrew T (Kan) 9605 W Greenspoint St, Wichita, KS 67205
O'CONNOR, Christopher Duane (WNY) 30 Favor St, Attica, NY 14011
O'CONNOR, Maureen Nicole (Chi)
O'CONNOR JR, Terrence (NJ) 2998 Bay Ave, Ocean City, NJ 08226
ODA-BURNS, John MacDonald (Cal) 611 La Mesa Dr, Portola Valley, CA 94028
ODDERSTOL, Sarah Dodds (WA) St. Mary's Episcopal Church, 306 S Prospect Avenue, Park Ridge, IL 60068
ODEKIRK, Dennis Russell (Los) 830 Columbine Ct, San Luis Obispo, CA 93401
O'DELL, Thomas Peyton (WMich) 123 W Washington St, Lexington, VA 24450
ODEN, Jason D (SO)
ODGERS, Marie Christine Hanson (Neb) 8800 Holdrege St, Lincoln, NE 68505
ODIERNA, Robert William (NH) Po Box 412, Nashua, NH 03061
ODOM, Robert (Dal) 5923 Royal Ln, Dallas, TX 75230
O'DONNELL, Elizabeth Gibbs (Me) 16726 Lauder Ln, Dallas, TX 75248
O'DONNELL, John J (NH) 315 Mason Rd, Milford, NH 03055
O'DONNELL, Michael Alan (Alb) 4940 Shirley Pl, Colorado Springs, CO 80920
OECHSEL JR, Russell Harold (Tex) 13011 Broken Brook Ct, Cypress, TX 77429
OESTERLIN, Peter William (RG) 3232 Renaissance Dr SE, Rio Rancho, NM 87124
OETJEN, Sandra Lee (Nev) 4613 Steeplechase Ave, North Las Vegas, NV 89031
OFFINGER, Julia Macy (NY)
O'FLINN, Nancy C (Ala)
O'FLYNN, Donnel (Mont) Christ Church, 215 3rd Ave E, Kalispell, MT 59901
OFOEGBU, Daniel Okwuchukwu (Dal) Church Of The Ascension, 8787 Greenville Ave., Dallas, TX 75243
OGBURN JR, John Nelson (NC) 330 W Presnell St Apt 44, Asheboro, NC 27203
OGBURN, William L (NY) 55 Main St, North Kingstown, RI 02852
OGDEN, Virginia Louise (Alb) 51 Brockley Dr, Delmar, NY 12054
OGEA, Herman Joseph (WLa) 110 W 13th St, PO Box 912, Jennings, LA 70546
OGIER JR, Dwight (At) 125 Betty Street, Clarkesville, GA 30523
OGLE, Albert Joy (NY) 3634 Seventh Ave Unit 6B, San Diego, CA 92103
OGLE SR, Louis Knox (La) 43 Hyacinth Dr, Covington, LA 70433
OGLESBY, Charles Lucky (NC) 325 Glen Echo Ln Apt J, Cary, NC 27518
OGLESBY, Keith W (At)

OGLESBY, Patricia A (Pa) 1734 Huntington Tpke, Trumbull, CT 06611

OGUIKE, Martin (NJ) 17 Woodbridge Ave, Sewaren, NJ 07077

OGUS, Mary Hutchison (EC) 175 9th Ave, New York, NY 10011

OGWAL-ABWANG, Benoni Y (NY) 135 Remington Pl, New Rochelle, NY 10801

OH, David Yongsam (Nwk) 1224 McClaren Drive, Carmichael, CA 95608

OH, KyungJa (SO) Bexley Seabury Seminary Federation, 1407 E 60th St, Chicago, IL 60637

O'HAGIN, Zarina Eileen Suarez (Vt) 215 Corner Rd, Hardwick, VT 05843

O'HARA, Christina Swenson (SD) 2707 W 33rd St, Sioux Falls, SD 57105

O'HARA, Ellen (NY) 141 Fulton Ave Apt 609, Poughkeepsie, NY 12603

O'HARA-TUMILTY, Anne (Los) 26029 Laguna Court, Valencia, CA 91355

✠ **OHL**, C Wallis (NwT) 3205 Skye Ridge Dr, Norman, OK 73069

OHLEMEIER, Mark William (Kan) 601 E Walnut St, Springfield, MO 65806

OHLIDAL, Susan Marie (Vt)

OHLSON, Elizabeth Anderson (NJ) 5752 West Ave, Ocean City, NJ 08226

OHLSTEIN, Allen Michael (Kan) 310 W 17th St, Leavenworth, KS 66048

OHMER, John (Va) The Falls Church Episcopal, 115 E Fairfax St, Falls Church, VA 22046

O'KEEFE, Lloyd Frost (O) 970 Cottage Gate Dr, Kent, OH 44240

OKEREKE, Ndukaku Shadrack (Dal) 9624 Valley Mills Ln, Dallas, TX 75227

OKRASINSKI, Ronald Stanley (Va) Po Box 420, Colonial Beach, VA 22443

OKTOLLIK, Carrie Ann (Ak) PO Box 446, Point Hope, AK 99766

OKUNSANYA, Adegboyega Gordon (At) 711 Saint Saginaw Street, Flint, MI 48502

OKUSI, George Otiende (Los) 312 S Oleander Ave, Compton, CA 90220

OLANDESE, Jan Susan (Nev) 2830 Phoenix St, Las Vegas, NV 89121

OLBRYCH, Jennie Clarkson (SC) 26 Saint Augustine Dr, Charleston, SC 29407

OLDFATHER, Susan Kay (Md) PO Box 187, Kingsville, MD 21087

OLDHAM ROBINETT, Lynn Margaret (Cal) 211 Forbes Ave, San Rafael, CA 94901

OLDS, Kevin (Ct) 4670 Congress St, Fairfield, CT 06824

OLDSTONE-MOORE, Jennifer (SO) St Anne Episcopal Church, 6461 Tylersville Rd, West Chester, OH 45069

O'LEARY, Jane (Md) 6011 Chesworth Rd., Baltimore, MD 21228

OLIVER, Kyle M (NY) St. Michael's Church, 225 W 99th St, New York, NY 10025

OLIVER, Nancy Diesel (CFla) 2951 Mulberry Dr, Titusville, FL 32780

OLIVERO, Cesar Olivero (SwFla) 17241 Edgewater Dr, Port Charlotte, FL 33948

OLIVO, David A (WA) 1525 H St NW, Washington, DC 20005

OLLER, Janet Petrey (Ind) St John's Episcopal Church, PO Box 445, Crawfordsville, IN 47933

OLMEDO-JAQUENOD, Nina (Cal) 1321 Webster St, Alameda, CA 94501

OLMSTED, Nancy Kay Young (RI) Po Box 245, Lincoln, RI 02865

OLOIMOOJA, Edith Ipiso (Los) 3303 W Vernon Ave, Los Angeles, CA 90008

OLOIMOOJA, Joseph Mtende (Los) 1501 N Palos Vevoler Dr. #128, Harbor City, CA 90710

OLSEN, Christie (WNC) 1812 Lower Ridgewood Blvd., Hendersonville, NC 28791

OLSEN, Daniel Kevin (Pa) Box 681, Oaks, PA 19456

OLSEN, David Logie (Ore) 10445 Sw Greenleaf Ter, Tigard, OR 97224

OLSEN, Donna Jeanne Hoover (Ind) 2601 East Thompson Road, Indianapolis, IN 46227

OLSEN, Jean Barry (RI) 35-C W Castle Way, Charlestown, RI 02813

OLSEN, L Michael (RG) St James Episcopal Church, 208 Camino de Santiago, Taos, NM 87571

OLSEN JR, Lloyd Lein (CFla) 992-B E Michigan St, Orlando, FL 32806

OLSEN, Meredith DK (Md) 4127 Chadds Crossing, Marietta, GA 30062

OLSEN, Robert M (The Episcopal NCal) 8070 Glen Creek Way, Citrus Heights, CA 95610

OLSON, Alice Ingrid (Minn) 7218 Hill Rd, Two Harbors, MN 55616

OLSON, Anna Burns (Los) 4274 Melrose Ave, Los Angeles, CA 90029

OLSON, Barbara Jane (ND)

OLSON, Britt Elaine (Oly) 262 Swenson Ct., Auburn, CA 95603

OLSON, Cori (SeFla) 8888 SW 131st Ct Apt 205, Miami, FL 33186

OLSON, Ellen Elizabeth (Neb) 609 Avenue C, Plattsmouth, NE 68048

OLSON, John Seth (Ala) 202 Gordon Dr SE, Decatur, AL 35601

OLSON, Thomas Mack (The Episcopal NCal) 300 West St, Vacaville, CA 95688

OLSSON, Paul V (Nwk) 32 Hillview Ave, Morris Plains, NJ 07950

OLULORO, Emmanuel Bola (Az) 848 E Dobbins Rd, Phoenix, AZ 85042

OLVER, Matthew S C (Dal) 6431 Vista Ave, Wauwatosa, WI 53213

O'MALLEY, Donald Richard (WNC) 101 Piney Rd, Hayesville, NC 28904

OMERNICK, Marilyn (Los) 1418 Montecito Dr, Los Angeles, CA 90031

OMONIYI, Ayodeji Oloyede (FtW)

ONATE-ALVARADO, Gonzalo Antonio (EcuC) Apartado Postal #5250, Guayaquil, Ecuador

O'NEIL, Janet Anne (Mo) 808 N Mason Rd, Saint Louis, MO 63141

O'NEILL, Bruce Douglas (Cal) 2833 Claremont Blvd, Berkeley, CA 94705

O'NEILL, Joanne Carbone (Nwk) 97 Highwood Ave., Tenafly, NJ 07670

✠ **O'NEILL**, Robert John (Colo) 7937 E 24th Ave, Denver, CO 80238

O'NEILL, Vince (The Episcopal Church in Haw) 98-939 Moanalua Rd, Aiea, HI 96701

ONG, Dian Marie (Ia) 803 W Tyler Ave, Fairfield, IA 52556

ONG, Merry (Cal) 1011 Harrison St, Oakland, CA 94607

ONKKA, Marcia Rauls (Minn) 1200 Autumn Dr Apt 211, Faribault, MN 55021

ONYENDI, Matthias E (Tex)

OPARE-ADDO, Frederick Akwetey (LI) 13304 109th Ave, South Ozone Park, NY 11420

OPAT, Kris (Pgh) 1066 Washington Rd, Pittsburgh, PA 15228

OPEL, William A (NH) 395 Locust Road, Eastham, MA 02642

O'PRAY, Denis Michael (Minn) 2412 Seabury Ave, Minneapolis, MN 55406

OPRENDEK, Matt (NY) 33 Jefferson ave, Garden City, NY 11530

ORBAUGH, Phyllis Rae (RG) 6626 Shpaati Ln, Cochiti Lake, NM 87083

ORCHARD, Carolyn Gertrude (NMich) 311 S 4th St, Crystal Falls, MI 49920

O'REAR, Lisa (O)

O'REILLY, Eileen (SO) 6873 Fieldstone Pl, Mason, OH 45040

O'REILLY, John Thomas Jack (SwFla) 5321 Laurelwood Pl, Sarasota, FL 34232

O'REILLY, Patricia (Los) 402 S. Oakland Ave Apt 6, Pasadena, CA 91101

OREM, Becky Jane Tilton (NwT) St Paul's on-the-Plains Episcopal Church, 1510 Avenue X, Lubbock, TX 79401

ORENS, Elizabeth Mills Pickering (Md) St James Church, 19200 York Rd, Parkton, MD 21120

ORESKOVICH JR, Steve John (Mont) 1405 Sunflower Dr, Missoula, MT 59802

ORIHUELA, Roberto Opolinar (Va) 7000 Arlington Blvd, Falls Church, VA 22042

O'RILEY, Lori Cameron (At)

ORLANDO, Helen Marie (NJ) 10 Iris Ct, Marlton, NJ 08053

ORME-ROGERS, Charles Arthur (Mil) 7634 Mid Town Rd - #212, Madison, WI 53719

ORMOS, Patrick Patrick (WTex) 12933 Latchwood Ln, Austin, TX 78753

ORNDORFF, Vivian (Tex) 3901 S Panther Creek Dr, The Woodlands, TX 77381

O'ROURKE, Brian (Los) 1325 Monterey Road, South Pasadena, CA 91030

O'ROURKE, David Carter (Colo) 2840 Signal Creek Pl, Thornton, CO 80241

OROZCO, Benjamin Manuel (SanD) 3568 Elmwood Ct, Riverside, CA 92506

ORPEN JR, J Robert (Chi) 5550 S Shore Dr Apt 512, Chicago, IL 60637

ORR, Daniel Longsworth (O) 433 E Maple St, Bryan, OH 43506

ORR, Kristin Elizabeth (Mont) P. O. Box 25, Flossmoor, IL 60422

ORRALA MONCADA, Francisco (Litoral Ecu)

ORRIN, Dyana Vail (Ak) 1501 N Adams St, Fredericksburg, TX 78624

ORSBURN, Kenneth Ray (Okla)

ORSO, Thomas Ray (NY) 100 DeHaven Drive #405, Yonkers, NY 10703

ORT, Larry Victor (SD) St. Paul's Episcopal Church, 726 6th St, Brookings, SD 57006

ORTEGA, Guido Andres (EcuC) Avenue Amazonas 4430 Y Villalengua, Casilla, 17116165, Ecuador

ORTEGA CABALLERO, Hector Amilcar (Hond) Catedral Episcopal El Buen Pastor, 21 Calle 23 Ave C. Col. Trejo, San Pedro Sula, Honduras

ORTEZ, Leonel (SeFla)

ORTIZ, Michelle (At) Holy Innocents' Episcopal Church, 604 N Valrico Rd, Valrico, FL 33594

ORTT, William (Eas) 111 S Harrison St, Easton, MD 21601

ORTUNG, Thomas Edward (Oly) 105 State St, Kirkland, WA 98033

ORVILLE, Lynn D (RI) PO Box 491, Little Compton, RI 02837

ORWIG, Dana Lynn Maynard (Okla) 2710 Nw 17th St, Oklahoma City, OK 73107

OSBERGER, Charles Edward (Eas) 14084 Old Wye Mills Rd, Wye Mills, MD 21679

OSBORN, Mary Anne (Ct) 560 Lake Dr., Guilford, CT 06437

OSBORN, Sherrell E (Vt) 1142 Prindle Rd Apt B, Charlotte, VT 05445

OSBORN DE ANAYA, Chan (NAM) 1115 Main St, Vicksburg, MS 39183

OSBORNE, Bill (Spok) 5720 S Perry St, Spokane, WA 99223

OSBORNE, Charles Edward (ETenn) 1540 Belmeade Dr, Kingsport, TN 37664

OSBORNE, Jamie (Ala) 113 Madison Ave, Montgomery, AL 36104

OSBORNE, Janne Alr (Tex) PO Box 150535, Austin, TX 78715

OSBORNE, Ralph Everett (FdL) 2420 Marathon Ave, Neenah, WI 54956

OSBORNE, Richard L (RG) 102 Southfork Cir, Pottsboro, TX 75076

OSBORNE, Robert Allen (CFla)

OSBORNE, Ronald Douglas (Ia) 2325 E Highview Dr., Des Moines, IA 50320

OSBORNE-MOTT, Susan Elizabeth (NJ) 503 Asbury Ave, Asbury Park, NJ 07712

OSGOOD, John A (NY) 201 Old Mountain Rd N, Nyack, NY 10960

OSGOOD, Thomas Marston (Cal) 6471 Coopers Hawk Rd, Klamath Falls, OR 97601

O'SHEA, Nancy Corinne Tucker (WTenn) 6294 Venus Ave, Bartlett, TN 38134

O'SHEA, Susan J (Oly) 234 Wood Ave SW #410, Bainbridge Island, WA 98110

OSHRY, Michael A (Spok) 5225 S Cree Dr, Spokane, WA 99206

OSMUN, Andrew (Ct) 41 Park Circle, Milford, CT 06460

OSNAYA-JIMENEZ, Uriel (Tex) 9600 Huntington Place Dr, Houston, TX 77099

OSORIO-CAMACHO, Nabor (Ve)

OST, Gary (Cal) 499 Ellsworth St Apt A, San Francisco, CA 94110

O'STEEN, Joe (LI) 1665 Waterford Dr, Lewisville, TX 75077

OSTENSO MOORE, Anna Victoria (Minn) 519 Oak Grove St, Minneapolis, MN 55403

OSTLUND, Holly Lisa (SeFla) 15730 88th Pl N, Loxahatchee, FL 33470

OSTRANDER, Paul Copeland (Okla) 2321 Northwest 48th Street, Oklahoma City, OK 73112

OSTUNI, Elizabeth Ellen (Nwk) 10 Hampton Downes, Newton, NJ 07860

O'SULLIVAN, Ann Kathlyn (Me)

OSWALD, Todd D (USC) 2200 Wilson Rd, Newberry, SC 29108

OTA, David Yasuhide (Cal) 900 Edgewater Blvd, Foster City, CA 94404

OTIS, Violetta Lansdale (Me) 17 Foreside Rd, Falmouth, ME 04105

OTT, Janet Sanderson (Miss) 1200 Meadowbrook Rd Apt 44, Jackson, MS 39206

OTT, Luther (Miss) 1200 Meadowbrook Road, #44, Jackson, MS 39206

OTT, Paula Lee (Lex) 2410 Lexington Rd, Winchester, KY 40391

OTT, Robert Michael (ECR) 1490 Mark Thomas Dr., Monterey, CA 93940

OTTAWAY, Richard Napoleon (NJ) 16 Bell Ter, Bernardsville, NJ 07924

OTTERBURN, Margaret (Nwk) 50 Route 24, Chester, NJ 07930

✠ OTTLEY, Jim (LI) 3 E Fairway Ct, Bay Shore, NY 11706

OTTO, Ronald Lee (EMich) St Andrews Church, PO Box 52, Harrisville, MI 48740

OTTO, Susan Wanty (EMich) St Andrews Church, PO Box 52, Harrisville, MI 48740

OTTSEN, David (Tex) 3007 Live Oak Dr., Brenham, TX 77833

OU, Chun-Shih Shih (Tai) 200 Chu Chang 1st Road, Kaohsiung, Taiwan

OUGHTON, Marjorie Knapp (Pa) Church St Paul's, 301 E 9th St, Chester, PA 19013

OUSLEY, David Kenneth (Alb) Saint Eustace Episcopal Church, 2450 Main St, Lake Placid, NY 12946

OUSLEY, John Douglas (NY) 209 Madison Ave, New York, NY 10016

OUSLEY, Patrick Lance (Oly) 1551 10th Ave E, Seattle, WA 98102

✠ OUSLEY, Steven Todd (EMich) 1821 Avalon Ave, Saginaw, MI 48638

OUTMAN-CONANT, Robert Earl (Mass) 482 Beech St, Rockland, MA 02370

OUTWIN, Edson Maxwell (WNY) 316 Park Ave, Medina, NY 14103

OVENSTONE, Jenni (SanD) 810 Mockingbird Ln Apt 301, Towson, MD 21286

OVERALL, Martha Rollins (NY) 345 E 86th St Apt 16-D, New York, NY 10028

OVERBO, Terry (ND)

OVERFIELD, Brenda (SVa) 2817 Mohawk Drive, North Chesterfield, VA 23235

OVERGAARD, Emily Lodine (Minn)

OWEN, Charles Bryan (La) St Luke's Episcopal Church, 8833 Goodwood Blvd, Baton Rouge, LA 70806

OWEN, David Allen (Ct) 92 E Hill Rd, Canton, CT 06019

OWEN, Donald Edward (Ala) 1921 Chandaway Ct, Pelham, AL 35124

OWEN II, G Keith (O) 18001 Detroit Ave, Lakewood, OH 44107

OWEN, Harrison Hollingsworth (WA)

OWEN, Jennifer Marie (NY)

OWEN, Ron (Fla) 1100 Stockton Street, Jacksonville, FL 32204

OWEN, Sam (NY) 661 E 219th St, Bronx, NY 10467

OWEN, Shelby Ochs (SwVa) 222 Fayette St, Staunton, VA 24401

OWEN, Stephen Lee (Miss) PO Box 3400, Meridian, MS 39303

OWEN, William Bonner (NY) PO Box 99, West Park, NY 12493

OWENS IV, Bernard J (NC) 4407 Westbourne Rd, Greensboro, NC 27410

OWENS, Brent (Lex) Christ Church Cathedral, 166 Market St, Lexington, KY 40507

OWENS JR, Donald P (La) 712 Saddleridge Drive, Wimberley, TX 78676

OWENS, John Alfred (Fla) 4180 Julington Creek Rd, Jacksonville, FL 32223

OWENS, Jonathan Michael (SeFla) 777 Southgate Ave, Daly City, CA 94015

OWENS, Michael (At) P.O. Box 86, 637 University Ave, Sewanee, TN 37375

OWENS, Miriam Elizabeth (Roch) 515 Oakridge Dr, Rochester, NY 14617

OWENS, U'Ne\`io Yvette (Ga) 4033 Foxborough Blvd, Valdosta, GA 31602

OWENS, Wendy S (Wyo)

✠ **OWENSBY**, Jacob W (WLa) 335 Main St, Pineville, LA 71360

OWREN, David (The Episcopal NCal) 99 Pampas Ln, Fortuna, CA 95540

OWSLEY, Rebecca D (EMich) Christ Episcopal Church, 202 W Westover St, East Tawas, MI 48730

OWUSU-AFRIYIE, Kwabena (Pa) 811 Longacre Blvd, Yeadon, PA 19050

OXFORD, Scott (WNC) 520 New Haw Creek Rd, Asheville, NC 28805

OXLEY, Sara McCracken (CFla)

P

PACE, Bradley Warren (Ind) St Johns Episcopal Church, 600 Ferry St, Lafayette, IN 47901

PACE, David Frederick (ECR) 514 Central Ave, Menlo Park, CA 94025

PACE, David Taylor (Ore) 1729 Northeast Tillamook St, Portland, OR 97212

PACE, James Conlin (NY) 145 W 46th St Apt 5, New York, NY 10036

PACE, Joseph Leslie (Ct) 1 Gold St, Apt 16E, Hartford, CT 06103

PACE, Robert F (NwT) 6200 Adirondack Trl, Amarillo, TX 79106

PACE, Stephanie Anne Heflin (O) 3677 Hughstowne Dr, Akron, OH 44333

PACHECO, Jose (SanD) 209 Clay St, Weed, CA 96094

✠ **PACKARD**, George Elden (NY) 26 Oakwood Ave, Rye, NY 10580

PACKARD, Jeff (CPa) 208 W Foster Ave, State College, PA 16801

PACKARD, Laurence Kent (Va) 9350 Braddock Rd, Burke, VA 22015

PACKARD, Linda (Chi) 2 Currant Ct, Galena, IL 61036

PACKARD, Nancy Meader (Be) 359 Whitehall Rd, Hooksett, NH 03106

PACKARD, William Laurence (Va) 43600 Russell Branch Pkwy, Ashburn, VA 20147

PACKER, Barbara J (Nwk) Po Box 240, Mendham, NJ 07945

PADASDAO, Imelda Sumaoang (The Episcopal Church in Haw) 1326 Konia St, Honolulu, HI 96817

PADDOCK, Andrea Lee (Los) 31551 Catalina St,, Laguna Beach, CA 92651

PADDOCK, John Sheldon (SO) 1837 Ruskin Rd, Dayton, OH 45406

PADGETT, John Elliott (WTex) 12431 Modena Bay, San Antonio, TX 78253

PADGETT, Judy Malinda Pitts (At) 980 W Mill Bnd Nw, Kennesaw, GA 30152

PADILLA, Manuel Jack (NMich) 711 Michigan Ave, Crystal Falls, MI 49920

PADILLA, Margaret E (NMich) 711 Michigan Ave, Crystal Falls, MI 49920

PADILLA-MORALES, Luis (PR)

PADZIESKI, Virginia Sue (Minn) 7 Terrace Point, P. O. Box 788, Grand Marais, MN 55604

PAE, Joseph S (LI) 191 Kensington Rd, Garden City, NY 11530

PAE, Keun-Joo (Nwk) 76 E Main St, Newark, OH 43055

PAGANO, Joseph Samuel (Md)

PAGE, Donald Richard (Ct) 11 Nassau Rd., Somers Point, NJ 08244

PAGE JR, Hugh Rowland (NI) 1526 Cedar Springs Ct, Mishawaka, IN 46545

PAGE, Marilyle Sweet (Roch) 6 Cadence Ct, Penfield, NY 14526

PAGE, Michelle Rene (EC) 18115 State Road 23 Ste 112, South Bend, IN 46637

PAGE, Rufus Lee (The Episcopal NCal) 2525 11th Ave, Sacramento, CA 95818

PAGE JR, William Russell (Mass) 217 Holland St Pt 2A, Somerville, MA 02144

PAGER, Deng Alaak (Dal) 8787 Greenville Ave, Dallas, TX 75243

PAGLIARO, Lois Anne (NY) 18818 89th Ave, Hollis, NY 11423

PAGLINAUAN, Cristina (Md) 5603 N Charles St, Baltimore, MD 21210

PAGUIO, Ruth Alegre (ECR) 212 Swain Way, Palo Alto, CA 94304

PAHL JR, James Larkin (NC) 302 College St, Oxrford, NC 27565

PAIN, Mary Reed (Mil) 10400 W Dean Rd Apt 102, Milwaukee, WI 53224

PAINE, Michael Jackson (WVa) 13 Byron St, Boston, MA 02108

PAINTER JR, Borden Winslow (Ct) 110 Ledgewood Rd, West Hartford, CT 06107

PAINTER, R Scott (Tex) 1805 W Alabama St, Houston, TX 77098

PALACIN, Manuel Enrique (PR)

PALACIO BEDOYA, Luis Hernan (Colom) Carrera 6 No 49-85, Piso 2, Bogota, Colombia

PALAGYI, Addyse Lane (Ore) 3697 Croisan Creek Rd S, Salem, OR 97302

PALARINE, John R (Fla) 12236 Mandarin Rd, Jacksonville, FL 32223

PALASI, Dario (LI) 13424 96th St, Ozone Park, NY 11417

PALLARD SR, John J (CFla) PO Box 142, Peckham Lane RR#2, Coventry, RI 03/01/2816

PALLARES ARELLANO, Jorge Enrique (Los) 10154 Mountair Ave, Tujunga, CA 91042

PALMA, Jose (WMo) 420 West 14th St, Kansas City, MO 64105

PALMER, Alison (WA) 70 Lookout Rd, Wellfleet, MA 02667

PALMER JR, Archie (Nwk) 459 Passaic Ave Apt 315, West Caldwell, NJ 07006

PALMER, Beth (Miss) 1415 Baum St, Vicksburg, MS 39180

PALMER, Brian (ECR) 2700 Eton Rd, Cambria, CA 93428

PALMER, John Avery (ECR) 981 South Clover Ave, San Jose, CA 95128

PALMER, John M (NY) 33 E 10th St Apt 2-G, New York, NY 10003

PALMER, Richard Rainer (Colo) 400 Summit Blvd Unity 1503, Broomfield, CO 80021

PALMER, Richard William (Wyo) 4753 Estero Blvd Apt 1601, Fort Myers Beach, FL 33931

PALMER, Sara (SO) 108 W Farriss Ave, High Point, NC 27262

PALMGREN, Charles Leroy (At) 4482 Hunters Ter, Stone Mountain, GA 30083

PALUMBO, Candace Ann (Alb)

PANASEVICH, Eleanor Jones (Mass) 104 Oak St, Weston, MA 02493

PANG, Lisa A (The Episcopal Church in Haw) 911 N Marine Corps Dr, Tamuning, GU 96913

PANG, Pui-Kong Thomas (Mass) 138 Tremont St, Boston, MA 02111

PANKEY, Steven J (Ky) 1780 Abbey Loop, Foley, AL 36535

PANNELL, Terry (Mass) 519 Commercial St, Provincetown, MA 02657

PANTLE, Thomas Alvin (Dal) 617 Star St # 81, Bonham, TX 75418

PANTON, Rosalyn Way (Ga) 2200 Birnam Pl, Augusta, GA 30904

PAOLOZZI, Joann (Oly) 211 Summit Ave E Apt 212, Seattle, WA 98102

PAPANEK, Nicolette (Kan) 545 Greenup St #3, Covington, KY 41011

PAPAZOGLAKIS, Elizabeth Brumfield (Alb) 912A Route 146, Clifton Park, NY 12065

PAPAZOGLAKIS, Thomas W (Alb) 912a Route 146, Clifton Park, NY 12065

PAPE, Cynthia Dale (Mass) 1 Linden St, Quincy, MA 02170

PAPILE, Jim (Va) 3241 Brush Dr, Falls Church, VA 22042

PAPINI, Heber Mauricio (Okla) 9100 E 21st St, Tulsa, OK 74129

PAPPAS, Christopher A (RI) 211 Galland Close NW, Edmonton, T5T 6P6, Canada

PAPPAS III, Jim (At) 735 University Ave, Sewanee, TN 37383

PARACHINI, David Charles (Ct) 42 Blue Jay Dr, Northford, CT 06472

PARADINE, Philip James (Va) 118 Monte Vista Ave., Charlottesville, VA 22903

PARADISE, Gene Hooper (Ga) 10 Iron Bound Pl NW, Atlanta, GA 30318

PARAISON, Edwin Mardochee (DR (DomRep)) Calle Tony Mota Ricart #16, Box 132, Barahona, Dominican Republic

PARAISON, Maud (Hai) PO Box 5826, Fort Lauderdale, FL 33310

Clergy List

PARDO ARCINIEGAS, Angel Maria (Colom) c/o Diocese of Colombia, Cra 6 No. 49-85 Piso 2, Bogota, BDC, Colombia

PARDOE III, Edward Devon (Ct) St Barnabas Episcopal Church, 954 Lake Ave, Greenwich, CT 06831

PAREDES MUNGUIA, Delma Ibel (Hond) La Visitacion De La Bendita Virgen Maria, 23 Ave C, 21 Calle S.O. Colonia Trejo, San Pedro Sula, Honduras

PARHAM, Alfred Philip (RG) 6148 Los Robles Dr, El Paso, TX 79912

PARINI, Barbara Dennison (Mass) 2957 Barbara St., Ashland, OR 97520

PARISH, Nurya (WMich) 1025 3 Mile Rd NE, Grand Rapids, MI 49505

PARK, Ciritta Boyer (WA) 6201 Dunrobbin Dr, Bethesda, MD 20816

PARK, Cynthia B (At) 13560 Cogburn Road, Milton, GA 30004

PARK, John Hayes (Hond) 520 Park Rd, Ambridge, PA 15003

PARK, Patricia Ann (The Episcopal NCal) 124 Orange St, Auburn, CA 95603

PARK, Stephen Radcliffe (NH) 4060 Barrows Point Rd, Nisswa, MN 56468

PARK, Theodore A(llen) (Minn) 19 S 1st St Apt B2208, Minneapolis, MN 55401

PARKER, Betsee (Va) 110 W Franklin St, Richmond, VA 23220

PARKER, Carol Ann (EO) 9333 Nw Winters Ln, Prineville, OR 97754

PARKER, David Clinton (Ind) 224 Davis Ave, Elkins, WV 26241

PARKER, Dennis J (Ore) 4320 SW Corbett Ave, Unit # 317, Portland, OR 97239

PARKER, Donald Harry (Mass) 28 Cambridge Cir., Smithfield, RI 02917

PARKER, Elizabeth (Tex) 200 Oyster Creek Dr, Lake Jackson, TX 77566

PARKER, Gary Joseph (LI) 9 Barrow St. #3B, New York, NY 10014

PARKER III, George Leonard (Los) 5700 Rudnick Ave, Woodland Hills, CA 91367

PARKER, James Frank (HB) 2409 Cheshire Woods Rd, Toledo, OH 43617

PARKER, Jesse Leon Anthony (Md) 105 W 6th St, New Castle, DE 19720

PARKER JR, Jim (Ga) 402 E 46th St, Savannah, GA 31405

PARKER, Mark (The Episcopal NCal)

PARKER, Matthew Ross (Dal)

PARKER, Phillip Don (Miss)

PARKER, Robert Coleman (Tex) 832 W Jones St, Livingston, TX 77351

PARKER, Ronald Mark (FtW) 200 N Bailey Ave, Fort Worth, TX 76107

PARKER, Ronald Wilmar (Pa) 254 Williams Rd, Bryn Mawr, PA 19010

PARKER JR, Roy Earl (Mass) Holy Cross Monastery, West Park, NY 12493

PARKER, Stephanie Eve (Oly) 2543 US Hwy 21 S, Sparta, NC 28675

PARKER JR, Stephen Dwight (Ct) 4607 Chandlers Forde, Sarasota, FL 34235

PARKER, Susan Dozier (Az)

PARKER, William Curtis (Ky) 200 Armitage Court, Lincoln University, PA 19352

PARKIN, Jason Lloyd (Chi) 222 Kenilworth Ave, Kenilworth, IL 60043

PARKINSON, Caroline (Va) 4614 Riverside Drive, Richmond, VA 23225

PARKS, James Joseph (Fla)

PARKS, Ken Thomas (Ark) 1001 Kingsland Rd, Bella Vista, AR 72714

PARKS, Larry Joseph (EMich) St John the Baptist, PO Box 217, Otter Lake, MI 48464

PARKS, Sarah J (EMich) St John the Baptist, PO Box 217, Otter Lake, MI 48464

PARKS, Theodore Edward Michael (Mil) PO Box 590, Milwaukee, WI 53201

PARLIER, Susan Taylor (USC) 1238 Evergreen Ave, West Columbia, SC 29169

PARMAN IV, Fritz Quinn (ETenn) St. Paul's Episcopal Church, 305 W 7th St, Chattanooga, TN 37402

PARMETER JR, George (SD) Po Box 1361, Huron, SD 57350

PARNELL, Pilar Felicia Padron (WNY) 303 S Main St, Kilmarnock, VA 22482

PARNELL, Scott Daniel (Va) Christchurch School, 49 Seahorse Ln, Christchurch, VA 23031

PARNELL, William Clay (Mass) 138 Tremont St, Boston, MA 02111

PARR, Heather Katheryn (Ore) 835 E 43rd Ave, Eugene, OR 97405

PARRIS, Cheryl (Ga) 1401 Martin Luther King Jr Blvd, Savannah, GA 31415

PARRIS, Kenneth W (Cal)

PARRISH, David LeRoy (Neb) 647 Sussex Dr, Janesville, WI 53546

PARRISH JR, Joe (NJ) 300 E 56th St Apt 2B, New York, NY 10022

PARRISH, Judy (SwVa) 989 Pigeon Hill Rd, Roseland, VA 22967

PARRISH, Larry (Neb) PO Box 117, Falls City, NE 68355

PARRISH, William Potter (SwVa) 3708 Manton Dr, Lynchburg, VA 24503

PARROTT, Sally F (USC) 100 Deerfield Dr, Greer, SC 29650

PARRY, James William (ETenn) 2740 Joneva Rd, Knoxville, TN 37932

PARRY-MOORE, Joyce (Oly) St James Episcopal Church, 24447 94th Ave S, Kent, WA 98030

PARSELL, Harry Irvan (SwFla) 738 Pinellas Point Dr S, St Petersburg, FL 33705

✠ **PARSLEY JR**, Henry (Ala) Episcopal Diocese of Easton, 314 North St, Easton, MD 21601

PARSLEY, Jamie A (ND) 117 20 Ave. N., Fargo, ND 58102

PARSONS, Ann Roberts (Ak) Po Box 1445, Sitka, AK 99835

PARSONS, Berry Ed (LI) 20 Apache Ln, Sedona, AZ 86351

PARSONS, Susan Diane (Cal)

PARSONS, Timothy Hamilton (CNY) 12 Oak Ave, Norway, ME 04268

PARSONS-CANCELLIERE, Rebecca Anne (Be) Episcopal Parish Of Saint Mark And, 21 Race St, Jim Thorpe, PA 18229

PARTANEN, Robert Carl (Cal) 62 Valais Ct, Fremont, CA 94539

PARTEE CARLSEN, Mariclair Elizabeth (Pa) Saint Mary's Church Hamilton Village, 3916 Locust Walk, Philadelphia, PA 19104

PARTENHEIMER, Gary Hoffman (Pa) East Hall - Northfield Mt Hermon, Northfield, MA 01360

PARTHUM III, Charles Frederick (Mass) 1415 N Victoria Cir, Elm Grove, WI 53122

PARTINGTON, Richard Ogden (Pa) 4116 Twin Silo Dr, Blue Bell, PA 19422

PARTLOW, John Michael Owen (WVa) 809 Chestnut Ct, Winnetka, IL 60093

PARTLOW, Ruth Goodrich (SVa) 3409 W Point Ct, North Chesterfield, VA 23235

PARTRIDGE, Cameron Elliot (Cal) 34 Hatch Rd, Medford, MA 02155

PARTRIDGE, Edmund Bruce (Nwk) 9849 Martingham Cir, St Michaels, MD 21663

PARTRIDGE JR, Henry Roy (Me) 3 Old Colony Ln, Scarborough, ME 04074

PASALO, Annalise C (The Episcopal Church in Haw)

PASALO JR, Ernesto Castro (The Episcopal Church in Haw)

PASAY, Marcella Claire (CFla) 11251 SW Highway 484, Dunnellon, FL 34432

PASCHALL JR, Fred William (NC) 4341 Bridgewood Ln, Charlotte, NC 28226

PASHTURRO, James Joseph (Mich)

PATIENCE, Rodger L (FdL) 130 Cherry Ct, Appleton, WI 54915

PATNAUDE, Robert J (O) 7146 Hesperides Dr, Warrenton, VA 20186

PATRONIK JR, Joseph Andrew (SanD) PO Box 1283, Marina, CA 93933

PATSTON, John Ralph Ansell (NI) 502 N James St, Ludington, MI 49431

PATTEN, Kenneth Lloyd (Hond)

PATTERSON JR, Baldo Alfred Kaleo (The Episcopal Church in Haw) 229 Queen Emma Sq, Honolulu, HI 96813

PATTERSON, Barbara Anne Bowling (At) 437 S Candler St, Decatur, GA 30030

PATTERSON, Beverly A (WTex) 3701 Cimarron Blvd Apt 2604, Corpus Christi, TX 78414

PATTERSON JR, Dennis Delamater (At) St Luke's Episc Ch, 435 Peachtree St NE, Atlanta, GA 30308

PATTERSON, Jane (WTex) Seminary of the Southwest, P.O. Box 2247, Austin, TX 78768

PATTERSON, John Willard (NJ) 2885 Citrus Lake Dr, Naples, FL 34109

PATTERSON, Keith F (Roch)

PATTERSON, Michael Steven (Nev) PO Box 1041, Fernley, NV 89408

PATTERSON, Peggy Pittman (Del) 10 Concord Ave, Wilmington, DE 19802

PATTERSON, Robert Place (Md) 3 Cobb Ln, Topsham, ME 04086

PATTERSON, Sharon (NJ)

PATTERSON, Tim (NC) 607 N Greene St, Greensboro, NC 27401

PATTERSON JR, William Brown (NC) 195 N Carolina Ave, Sewanee, TN 37375

PATTERSON-URBANIAK, Penelope Ellen (CFla) 676 Nettles Ridge Rd, Banner Elk, NC 28604

PATTISON, Benno David (At) 634 W Peachtree St Nw, Atlanta, GA 30308

PATTISON, Ruth Lindberg (At) 1501 Dinglewood Dr, Columbus, GA 31906

PATTON, David C (Mich)

PATTON, Kathleen (Oly) 1645 24th Ave, Longview, WA 98632

PATTON, Thomas Dunstan (Spr)

PATTON-GRAHAM, Heather Lynn (The Episcopal Church in Haw) 2611 Ala Wai Blvd Apt 1206, Honolulu, HI 96815

PAUL, Jeffrey (Nev) 305 N Minnesota St, Carson City, NV 89703

PAUL, Kenneth Wayne (WLa) 720 Wilder Pl, Shreveport, LA 71104

PAUL, Linda Joy (Okla) 501 S Cincinnati Ave, Tulsa, OK 74103

PAUL, Marcea E (SeFla) 10600 Caribbean Blvd, Cutler Bay, FL 33189

PAUL, Michael (ND) 6419 15th St S, Fargo, ND 58104

PAUL, Richard (Colo)

PAUL, Rocks-Anne (SwFla) 1200 4th St W, Palmetto, FL 34221

PAUL, Wectnick (Ct) Box 1309, Port-Au-Prince, Haiti

PAULIKAS, Steven D (LI) 286-88 7th Ave, Brooklyn, NY 11215

PAULIS, Marion Helen (SD) 201 S 4th St, Milbank, SD 57252

PAULSON, Diane Theresa (Ida) 1785 Arlington Dr, Pocatello, ID 83204

PAULSON, Donald Leonard (Ida) 1785 Arlington Dr, Pocatello, ID 83204

PAULUS, Ruth B (SO)

PAVIA, Jennifer Lynne (Los)

PAVLAC, Brian Alexander (Be) 365 Rutter Ave, Kingston, PA 18704

PAXTON, Richard Edwin (Ky) 820 Broadway St, Paducah, KY 42001

PAYDEN-TRAVERS, Christine (SwVa) 1711 Link Rd, Lynchburg, VA 24503

PAYER, Donald R (Ia) 2205 Green Hills Dr, Ames, IA 50014

✠ **PAYNE**, Claude Edward (Tex) 2702 Charter House Dr, Abilene, TX 79606

PAYNE, Edward Thomas (SO) 8363 Cannon Knoll Ct, West Chester, OH 45069

PAYNE, Harold Womack (Ark) 3412 W 7th St, Little Rock, AR 72205

PAYNE, John Douglas (FtW) 4902 George St, Wichita Falls, TX 76302

PAYNE, No Saluation-- Pam (Be)

PAYNE, Richard Leeds (Mass) Po Box 289, Brewster, MA 02631

PAYNE, Susan Strauss (Ark) 1723 Center St, Little Rock, AR 72206

PAYNE-CARTER, Gloria (WNY) 15 Fernhill Ave, Buffalo, NY 14215

PAYNE-HARDIN, Mary Elizabeth (CGC) 1608 Baker Ct, Panama City, FL 32401

PAYNE-WIENS, Reginald A (NC) 1941 Webberville Rd, Austin, TX 78721

PAYSON, Charles Beck (Chi) N1133 Vinne Haha Rd, Fort Atkinson, WI 53538

PAYSON, Deborah (Pa) 531 Maison Place, Bryn Mawr, PA 19010

PAYSON, Evelyn (Mil) N1133 Vinne Ha Ha Rd, Fort Atkinson, WI 53538

PEABODY, Morrill (RG) Po Box 247, Lemitar, NM 87823

PEABODY, S Walton (Pa) 234 Yahoola Shoals Dr, Dahlonega, GA 30533

PEABODY, William Nelson (Mo) 852 Water Andric Rd, Saint Johnsbury, VT 05819

PEACOCK, Andrea Coffee (Ala)

PEACOCK, Caroline (NY) St Luke In The Fields Episcopal Church, 487 Hudson St, New York, NY 10014

PEACOCK, Joan Louise (Va) 7515 Snowpea Ct Unit M, Alexandria, VA 22306

PEACOCK, Margaret Ann (NMich) Po Box 66, Saint Ignace, MI 49781

PEACOCK, Virginia A (NMich) PO Box 305, Deer Isle, ME 04627

PEAK, Ronald Robert (Kan) 609 Gould St, Eustis, FL 32726

PEALER, Judson Paul (Me) 2614 Main St, Rangeley, ME 04970

PEARCE, Clyde Willard (Ala) 1301 Paradise Cove Ln, Wilsonville, AL 35186

PEARCE JR, Robert Charles (Kan) 1720 Westbank Way, Manhattan, KS 66503

PEARCE, Sherilyn (SO) Christ Church Cathedral, 318 E 4th St, Cincinnati, OH 45202

PEARCE, William Philip Daniel (ECR) 1037 Olympic Ln, Seaside, CA 93955

PEARSALL, Arlene Epp (SD) 115 N Dakota Ave Apt 117, Sioux Falls, SD 57104

PEARSALL, Martin A (Colo) 4939 Harvest Rd, Colorado Springs, CO 80917

PEARSON, Albert Claybourn (Tex) 261 Fell St, San Francisco, CA 94102

PEARSON II, Alonzo Lawrence (FdL) 421 Lowell Pl, Neenah, WI 54956

PEARSON JR, Andrew C (Ala) Cathedral Church of the Advent, 2017 Sixth Avenue North, Birmingham, AL 35203

PEARSON, Anna (NY) 78 Main St, Hastings On Hudson, NY 10706

PEARSON, Bryan Austin (Mass)

PEARSON, Cedric Eugene (O) 14778 Dexter Falls Rd, Perrysburg, OH 43551

PEARSON, Daniel (Minn) 1970 Nature View Lane, W. St. Paul, MN 55118

PEARSON, David Ernest (HI)

PEARSON, Francis J (Be) 10 Chapel Rd, New Hope, PA 18938

PEARSON, Jan (Colo)

PEARSON, Jim (SD) Christ Episcopal Church, 513 Douglas Ave, Yankton, SD 57078

PEARSON, John Norris (Oly) 2831 Marietta St, Steilacoom, WA 98388

PEARSON, Joseph Herbert (At) 1280 Berkeley Rd, Avondale Estates, GA 30002

PEARSON, Katie Curran (Colo) 1350 N Washington St, Denver, CO 80203

PEARSON, Kevin David (Oly) 16617 Marine View Dr SW, Burien, WA 98166

PEARSON, Michael A (Pa) 2 Blount Circle, Barrington, RI 02806

PEARSON, Patricia Waychus (Cal) 1219 Dutch Mill Drive, Danville, CA 94526

PEARSON, William Arthur (Alb) 27 Trottingham Road, Saratoga Springs, NY 12866

PEASE JR, Edwin C (Mass) 2 Kennedy Ln, Walpole, MA 02081

PEAY, Steven Allen (Mil) 8513 Jackson Park Blvd, WAUWATOSA, WI 53226

PECARO, Bernie (SeFla) 140 Se 28th Ave, Pompano Beach, FL 33062

PECH, Meredith Ayer (Ore) 371 Idaho St, Ashland, OR 97520

PECK, David W (CPa) 119 N Duke St, Lancaster, PA 17602

PECK SR, Donald Morrow (Ore) 304 Spyglass Dr, Eugene, OR 97401

PECK JR, Edward Jefferson (CPa) 7041 Fairway Oaks, Fayetteville, PA 17222

PECK, Felicity Lenton Clark (ETenn) 3333 Love Cir, Nashville, TN 37212

PECK, Frederick (Ore) 18205 SE 42nd St, Vancouver, WA 98683

PECK, Maryjane (Mich) Christ Episcopal Church, 120 N Military St, Dearborn, MI 48124

PECKHAM, Ashley Hall (RI) 31 W Main St, Portsmouth, RI 02871

PECKHAM, Laura (Me) St Martin's Episcopal Church, 900 Main St, Palmyra, ME 04965

Clergy List

PECKHAM CLARK, Margaret A (LI) 1579 Northern Boulevard, Roslyn, NY 11576

PEDERSEN, John Charles (Kan) 9408 San Rafael Ave Ne, Albuquerque, NM 87109

PEDRAZA ARIAS, Bladimir Ivan (Colom) Kra 15 # 71-15, Barrio 7 de Agosto, Cartagena Bolivar, 472, Colombia

PEDRICK, Jennifer (RI) 1336 Pawtucket Ave, Rumford, RI 02916

PEEK, Charles Arthur (Neb) 2010 Fifth Avenue, Kearney, NE 68845

PEEL, Margaret (Va) 543 Beulah Rd NE, Vienna, VA 22180

PEEL, Richard Charles (Mont) 1726 Cannon St Apt 4, Helena, MT 59601

PEELER, Amy Lauren (Chi) 320 Franklin St, Geneva, IL 60134

PEELER, Lance Vernon (Ore) 333 NW 35th St, Corvallis, OR 97330

PEEPLES, David H (Ala) 2354 Wildwood Dr, Montgomery, AL 36111

PEERMAN III, C(Harles) Gordon (Tenn) 4416 Harding Pl, Nashville, TN 37205

PEET, Donald Howard (Ct) PO Box 681, Sandisfield, MA 01255

PEETE, Brandon Ben (SwFla) 5503 Effingham Dr, Houston, TX 77035

PEETE, Nan (WA) 3001 Veazey Ter Nw Apt 1208, Washington, DC 20008

PEETS, Patricia Ann Dunne (Mo) 429 Martindale Dr, Albany, GA 31721

PELKEY, Richard Elwood (Fla) 7860 SW 86th Way, Gainesville, FL 32608

PELKEY, Wayne Lloyd (Ia) 13218 State Road #17, West Plains, MO 65775

PELLA, Diane Maria (Az) Po Box 753, Hartsdale, NY 10530

PELLATON, Thomas JP (NY) 2186 5th Ave Apt 7D, New York, NY 10037

PELLEGRINI, Lucy Carr Bergen (Vt) 48 East St, Bristol, VT 05443

PELLETIER, Ann Dietrich (RI) 57 Grandeville Ct, Apt#3323, Wakefield, RI 02879

PELNAR, William Donald (Mil) 2544 Tilden Ave, Delavan, WI 53115

PEMBERTON, Barbara Louise (CFla) 668 Whispering Pines Ct, Inverness, FL 34453

PENA-REGALADO JR, Jose (Hond) Col Victoria, Bloque J-3, Choloma Cortes, Honduras

PENA TAVAREZ, Vicente A (DR (DomRep)) Iglesia Episcopal Todos Los Santos, Calle Dr. Ferry Esq Eugenio Miranda, La Romna, Dominical Republic, Dominican Republic

PENCE, George E (Spr) 8103 Donna Lane, Edwardsville, IL 62025

PENDERGAST, Margaret McShane (Be) PO Box 1094, Reading, PA 19603

PENDERGRAFT, Randall Scott (Mont) Po Box 367, Red Lodge, MT 59068

PENDLETON, Mark (NH) Christ Church, 43 Pine St, Exeter, NH 03833

PENDLETON, William Beasley (NC) 1205-B Brookstown Ave. NW, Winston Salem, NC 27101

PENFIELD, Joyce A. (RI) 25 Pomona Ave, Providence, RI 02908

PENICK, Fern Marjorie (Eau) 538 N 4th St, River Falls, WI 54022

PENLAND, Michael R (SeFla) 236 Fennel Dun Cir, Biltmore Lake, NC 28715

PENN, John William (RG) 116 Kansas City Rd, Ruidoso, NM 88345

PENNEKAMP, Nancy (Cal)

PENNER, Henry Andrews (FtW) 222 S Pearson Ln, Keller, TX 76248

PENNER, Loree (Md) 623 Monkton Rd, Monkton, MD 21111

PENNINGTON, Jasper Green (Mich) 204 Elm St, Ypsilanti, MI 48197

PENNINGTON, John Joseph (Lex) 24 Thompson Ave, Ft Mitchell, KY 41017

PENNOYER II, Robert Morgan (NY)

PENNYBACKER, Kathleen Joanne (CFla) 320 S Canaday Dr, Inverness, FL 34450

PENROD, Scott (WTex) 114 S. Cypress Cir, Pharr, TX 78577

PEOPLES, David Brandon (CFla) 2627 Brookside Bluff Loop, Lakeland, FL 33813

PEPE, Carol Ann (NJ)

PEPIN, Ken (Roch) 53 Lee Road 974, Phenix City, AL 36870

PEPPLER, Connie Jo (Ind) 4131 W Woodyard Rd, Bloomington, IN 47404

PERALTA, Ercilia (DR (DomRep))

PERCIVAL, Joanna Vera (ECR) Flat 5 Waterside, Mill Lane, Uplyme, Lyme Regis, Dorset, DT7 3TZ, Great Britain (UK)

PERCIVAL, Jonathan (NJ) 4051 Westbourne Cir, Sarasota, FL 34238

PERCIVAL, Michael John (Colo) 381 Baltusrol Dr, Aptos, CA 95003

PERDUE, David (NwT) 1101 Slide Rd, Lubbock, TX 79416

PERDUE, Lane (Az) Trinity Cathderal, 100 W Roosevelt St, Phoenix, AZ 85003

PERDUE, Thomas Hayes (EC) 3981 Fairfax Sq, Fairfax, VA 22031

PEREIRA ALVAREZ, Rafael Alexis (Nev) 4201 W Washington Ave, Las Vegas, NV 89107

PEREZ, Greg (Nwk) 141 Broadway, Bayonne, NJ 07002

PEREZ, Jon Arnold (ECR)

PEREZ JR, Juan Francisco (NY)

PEREZ-BULLARD, Altagracia (NY) 1047 Amsterdam Ave, New York, NY 10025

PEREZ MACIAS, Jesus Eduardo (Colom) Ap Aer 2704, Barranquilla, Atlantico, Colombia

PEREZ MOREIRA, Hector Amado (EcuC) Cd Sauces 5 Mz 225 V2, Guayaquil, Ecuador

PEREZ-QUINONES, Juan Pablo (PR)

PEREZ-VEGA, Rodrigo (Nwk) 214 Washington St, Hackettstown, NJ 07840

PERICA, Raymond William (CFla) 145 E Edgewood Dr, Lakeland, FL 33803

PERIDANS, Dominique F (WA) 1217 Massachusetts Ave NW, Washington, DC 20005

PERINE, Everett Craig (Ct) 60 Church St, Hebron, CT 06248

PERKINS, Aaron C (Me) 26 Moulton Ln, York, ME 03909

PERKINS III, Albert Dashiell (Ala) 425 N Moye Dr, Montgomery, AL 36109

PERKINS, Cecil Patrick (FdL) 1307 Holmes St, Kansas City, MO 64106

PERKINS, David W (Ga) None, 5157 Five Points Jewell Rd, Mitchell, GA 30820

PERKINS, Ezgi S (FdL) 420 W 14th St, Kansas City, MO 64105

PERKINS, Jesse S (Chi) St Michael's Episcopal Church, 647 Dundee Ave, Barrington, IL 60010

PERKINS, Lynn Jones (Az) PO Box 4330, Gallup, NM 87305

PERKINS, Patrick R (WMass) 679 Farmington Ave, West Hartford, CT 06119

PERKINS, Roger S (Az) 1409 Linda Drive, Gallup, NM 87301

PERKINSON, Edward M (O) 3 Fox Hollow, Plymouth, MA 02360

PERKO, F Michael (RG) 2 Paa Ko Ct, Sandia Park, NM 87047

PERO, David Edward (Ore) 1609 Elm St, Forest Grove, OR 97116

PERRA, James Francis (Md) 1401 Towson St, Baltimore, MD 21230

PERRIN, Charlie (LI) 27521 Pine Straw Rd, Leesburg, FL 34748

PERRIN, Henry Keats (SO) 10129 Springbeauty Ln, Cincinnati, OH 45231

PERRIN, Mary Elizabeth (WMich) 2512 Highpointe Dr, Kalamazoo, MI 49008

PERRIN, Ronald Van Orden (NY) 3409 Hollywood Ave, Austin, TX 78722

PERRIN, Susan Elizabeth (USC)

PERRINO, Robert Anthony (SeFla) 1103 Duncan Cir Apt 103, Palm Beach Gardens, FL 33418

PERRIS, John David (NY) 581 Valley Rd, Upper Montclair, NJ 07043

PERRIZO, Faith Crook (WVa) 541 Deer Ridge Ln S, Maplewood, MN 55119

PERROTT, Ann Marie (Ct)

PERRY, Ally (WLa) 3125 Debra Ln, Westlake, LA 70669

PERRY, Bonnie Anne (Chi) 4550 N Hermitage Ave # 103, Chicago, IL 60640

PERRY, Cecilia Carolyn (RI) PO Box 872, Bristol, RI 02809

PERRY, David Warner (Ore) 715 Se 34th Ave, Portland, OR 97214

PERRY, John Wallis (Vt) 431 Union St, Hudson, NY 12534

PERRY, Kenneth M (Roch) PO Box 147, Geneva, NY 14456

PERRY, Margaret Rose (Az) St Francis in-the-Valley, 600 S La Canada Dr, Green Valley, AZ 85614

PERRY, Nandra Loraine (Tex)

PERRY, Raymond Glenn (NMich) 251 Monongahela Rd, Crystal Falls, MI 49920

PERRY, Robert Kendon (Ida) 411 Capitol Ave, Salmon, ID 83467

PERSCHALL JR, Donald Richard (Dal) 909 W Gandy St, Denison, TX 75020

✠ **PERSELL**, Bill (Chi) 28 Haskell Dr., Bratenahl, OH 44108

PERSON, Dorothy Jean (NMich) 208 Lane Ave, Kingsford, MI 49802

PERSON, Kathryn Jeanne (NY) 1803 Glenwood Rd, Brooklyn, NY 11230

PESSAH, Elizabeth Jayne (Fla) 1225 W Granada Blvd, Ormond Beach, FL 32174

PESSAH, Stephen Michael (CFla) 1225 W Granada Blvd, Ormond Beach, FL 32174

PETERMAN, Lynn C (EC) 115 John L Hurst Dr, Swansboro, NC 28584

PETERS, Albert Fitz-Randolph (Del) c/o Manor House, 1001 Middleford Rd Apt 106, Seaford, DE 19973

PETERS, Arthur Edward (Alb) 35 North St, Granville, NY 12832

PETERS JR, August William (WA) 1000 Hilton Ave, Catonsville, MD 21228

PETERS, David W (Tex) PO Box 178, Mount Vernon, IL 62864

PETERS, Diana Wray (Colo) 13495 Monroe St, Thornton, CO 80241

PETERS, Greg (Oly) 4424 SW 102nd Street, Seattle, WA 98146

PETERS, Helen Sarah (Ak) 1340 23rd Ave, Fairbanks, AK 99701

PETERS, John (Minn) 14434 Fairway Dr, Eden Prairie, MN 55344

PETERS, Patrick (CPa) 465 Zachary Dr, Manheim, PA 17545

PETERS, Peter William (Roch) 239 Yarmouth Rd, Rochester, NY 14610

PETERS, Thomas Word (Ct)

PETERS, Yejide (NY) 1414 Greycourt Ave, Richmond, VA 23227

PETERSEN, Barbara Jean (WNC) 2047 Paint Fork Rd, Mars Hill, NC 28754

PETERSEN, Carolyn Sherman (CFla) 4708 Waterwitch Point Dr, Orlando, FL 32806

PETERSEN, Duane Eric (WLa) 1030 Johnston Street, Lafayette, LA 70501

PETERSEN, Scott (At) All Saints Church, 1708 Watson Blvd, Warner Robins, GA 31093

PETERSEN, William Herbert (Roch) 49 Winding Brook Dr., Fairport, NY 14450

PETERSEN-SNYDER, Christine (LI) 290 Conklin St, Farmingdale, NY 11735

PETERS-MATHEWS, Joseph (Oly) 11111 Old Military Rd SW, Lakewood, WA 98498

PETERSMEYER, Julie Andrews (WA)

PETERSON, Barbara (Mass) 17 Sandy Neck Rd, East Sandwich, MA 02537

PETERSON, Bryan Anthony (Neb) 9302 Blondo St, Omaha, NE 68134

PETERSON, Carol Elizabeth (Wyo) 1908 Central Ave, Cheyenne, WY 82001

PETERSON, Diane Mildred (Ct) 5160 Madison Avenue, 4670 Congress Street, Trumbull, CT 06611

PETERSON JR, Frank Lon (NY) 969 Park Ave Apt 8C, New York, NY 10028

PETERSON, Iris E (Be) 56 Franklin St Unit 16, Danbury, CT 06810

PETERSON JR, John Henry (FdL) 129 5th St, Neenah, WI 54956

PETERSON, John Louis (WA) 1001 Red Oak Dr, Hendersonville, NC 28791

PETERSON JR, John Raymond (SwFla) 5020 Bayshore Blvd Apt 301, Tampa, FL 33611

PETERSON, Ralph (NY) 235 Walker Sreet Apt 134, Lenox, MA 01240

PETERSON, Richard Trenholm (Cal) 883 Roble Dr, Sunnyvale, CA 94086

PETERSON, Suzanne (Ia) Diocese of Cape Town, PO Box 1932, Cape Town, 8000, South Africa

PETERSON-WLOSINSKI, Cindy (Minn) 1121 W Morgan St, Duluth, MN 55811

PETERSON ZUBIZARRETA, Dorenda C (SeFla)

PETIPRIN, Andrew Kirk (Tenn) 3700 Woodmont Blvd, Nashville, TN 37215

PETIT, Charles David (USC) 5220 Clemson Ave, Columbia, SC 29206

PETITE, Robert (Chi) 4717 S. Greenwood Ave. Unit 1, Chicago, IL 60615

PETIT.FRERE, Mondesir (Hai)

PETIT-HOMME, Jean Pierre (Hai)

PETLEY, Dale Alfred (Okla) 1813 Westminster Pl, Oklahoma City, OK 73120

PETRASH, David (Dal) 1300 Overlook Dr, Kaufman, TX 75142

PETROCCIONE, Jim (Nwk) 28 Ross Rd, Stanhope, NJ 07874

PETROCHUK, Michael Aaron (O) St Andrew's Episcopal Church, 583 W Hopocan Ave, Barberton, OH 44203

PETROTTA, Anthony Joseph (Ore) PO Box 445, Wilsonville, OR 97070

PETTEE, Abigail Bower (Me) 33 Chestnut St, Camden, ME 04843

PETTENGILL, David Eugene (Az) 1558 E Gary St, Mesa, AZ 85203

PETTENGILL-RASURE, Rachael Marie (Mass) 453 Adams St, Milton, MA 02186

PETTERSON, Ted Ross (La) 25 Signature Dr, Brunswick, ME 04011

PETTIGREW, Thomas John (Alb) 3764 Main St, Warrensburg, NY 12885

PETTITT, Robert Riley (ND) 1201 49th Avenue, Rt 6, Fargo, ND 58103

PETTY, Carol Ross (Tex) Episcopal Diocese of Texas, PO Box 2247, Austin, TX 78768

PETTY JR, Jess Joseph (O) 35 B Pond St, Marblehead, MA 01945

PETTY JR, Tyrus Cecil (Kan) 5841 Sw 26th St, Topeka, KS 66614

PETZAK, Rodney Ross (Nev) 1965 Golden Gate Dr, Reno, NV 89511

PEVEHOUSE, James Melvin (Tex) 24 N Masonic St, Bellville, TX 77418

PEVERLEY, Stephen Richard (LI) 1 Araca Ct, Babylon, NY 11702

PEYTON III, Allen Taylor (Alb) 2401 Ben Hill Rd, Atlanta, GA 30344

PEYTON IV, Francis Bradley (WA) 1919 York Road, 2nd Floor, Timonium, MD 21093

PEYTON, Linda (Me) 42 Flying Point Rd, Freeport, ME 04032

PEYTON JR, Robert Lee (At) PO Box 207, Hartwell, GA 30643

PEYTON, Susan Carroll (SwVa) 300 W Frederick St, Staunton, VA 24401

PEYTON, William Parish (Va) 865 Madison Ave., New York, NY 10021

PFAB, Martin William (Fla) 724 Lake Stone Cir, Ponte Vedra Beach, FL 32082

PFAB, Penny (Fla) 724 Lake Stone Cir, Ponte Vedra Beach, FL 32082

PFAFF, Brad Hampton (NY) 126 W 83rd St Apt 3-P, New York, NY 10024

PFAFF, David Anthony (SO) 985 Forest Ave, Glendale, OH 45246

PFEIFFER, Dorothea Koop (WNC) 2 Sweet Gum Ct, Hilton Head, SC 29928

PFISTER, Kathleen Rock (Tex) PO Box 5176, Austin, TX 78763

PFOTENHAUER, Leon Henry (Ia) 1613 S Nicollet St, Sioux City, IA 51106

PHALEN, John Richard (Los) 5772 Garden Grove Blvd Spc 487, Westminster, CA 92683

PHAM, J Peter (Chi) St. Paul's Episcopal Church, 2430 K St, N.W., Washington, DC 20037

PHANORD, Jean Berthold (Hai)

PHARES, Nicholas Isaac (WMich) 3200 N 12th Ave, Pensacola, FL 32503

PHELAN, Shane (Nwk) 43 Massachusetts Ave., Haworth, NJ 07641

PHELPS, Cecil Richard (NI) 4525 Baring Ave, Box 2293, East Chicago, IN 46312

PHELPS, Joan (Ct) 15 Freedom Way Unit 101, Niantic, CT 06367

PHELPS, John Edward (Me) 4 Glendale Rd, Kennebunk, ME 04043

PHELPS JR, Kenneth Oliver (Md) PO Box 40, Sunderland, MD 20689

PHELPS, Mary M (Minn) 1415 6th Ave. South, Anoka, MN 55303

PHELPS, Nicholas Barclay (Pa) 1906 Trenton Ave, Bristol, PA 19007

PHELPS, Sarah E (NC) 306 Bayoak Dr, Cary, NC 27513

PHELPS, Shannon David (SanD) Po Box 234, Del Mar, CA 92014

PHENNA, Timothy Peter (Colo) 1320 Arapahoe St, Golden, CO 80401

PHILIP, Kristi (Spok) 22 W 37th Ave, Spokane, WA 99203

PHILIPS, J Kevin (ECR) 1190 Alta Mesa Road, Monterey, CA 93940

PHILIPS, Ronald K (Wyo) PO Box 950, Thermopolis, WY 82443

PHILLIPS III, Arthur William (WLa) Diocese Of Western Louisiana, PO Box 20131, Alexandria, VA 22320

PHILLIPS, Benjamin T. S. (SO)

PHILLIPS, Beth (Cal) 815 Portola Rd, Portola Valley, CA 94028

PHILLIPS, Catharine Seybold (Chi) 458 Dee Ln, Roselle, IL 60172

PHILLIPS, Craig Arnold (Va) 4818 Old Dominion Dr, Arlington, VA 22207

PHILLIPS, Deborah Anne (Mass) 35 Settlers Way, Salem, MA 01970

PHILLIPS, Douglas Cecil (Ind) 40 Trapelo St, Brighton, MA 02135

PHILLIPS, Jennifer Mary (Mass) 2903 Cabezon Blvd SE, Rio Rancho, NM 87124

PHILLIPS, Jerry Ray (La) PO Box 199, Rosedale, LA 70772

PHILLIPS, John Bradford (Cal) 891 Skeel Drive, Camarillo, CA 93010

PHILLIPS II, John Walter (CGC) 590 Parker Dr, Pensacola, FL 32504

PHILLIPS, Julia Coleman (CGC) 127 Hamilton Ave, Panama City, FL 32401

PHILLIPS, Kevin Alan (Va) 2094 Grant Rd, Mountain View, CA 94040

PHILLIPS, Linda (Nwk) 50 State Route 24, Chester, NJ 07930

PHILLIPS, Marie (O) 50 Sunnycliff Dr, Euclid, OH 44123

PHILLIPS, Michael Albin (NY) 316 E 88th St, New York, NY 10128

PHILLIPS, Paul (SVa) 1416 S Grand Blvd Apt 3, Spokane, WA 99203

PHILLIPS JR, Raymond Leland (USC) 701 Unity St, Fort Mill, SC 29715

PHILLIPS, Richard Oliver (NY) 10 Badger St, Littleton, NH 03561

PHILLIPS, Robert Taylor (WA) 1525 Newton St NW, Washington, DC 20010

PHILLIPS, Robert W (CFla) 1620 Mayflower Ct Apt A-610, Winter Park, FL 32792

PHILLIPS, Roger V (Minn) 1801 Santa Maria Pl, Orlando, FL 32806

PHILLIPS, Sara Dulaney (CGC) 4875 Highway 188, Coden, AL 36523

PHILLIPS, Stuart John Tristram (Tenn) 654 Long Hollow Pike, Goodlettsville, TN 37072

PHILLIPS, Susan Elizabeth (Del) 18 Olive Ave, Rehoboth Beach, DE 19971

PHILLIPS, Thomas Larison (Spr) 1015 Frank Dr, Champaign, IL 61821

PHILLIPS, Thomas M (CFla)

PHILLIPS, Wendell Roncevalle (NC) 4211 Sharon View Rd, Charlotte, NC 28226

PHILLIPS-GAINES, Lynn (Miss) 105 N Montgomery St, Starkville, MS 39759

PHILPUTT JR, Frederick Chapman (Dal) 5811 Penrose Ave, Dallas, TX 75206

PHINNEY, James Mark (Oly) 4246 South Discovery Road, Port Townsend, WA 98368

PHIPPS, Joy Ogburn (Ala) 3919 Westminster Ln, Birmingham, AL 35243

PHIPPS, Marion Elizabeth (Chi) 5403 W Greenbrier Dr, McHenry, IL 60050

PHIPPS JR, Robert Stirling (Va) Po Box 33430, San Antonio, TX 78265

PIATKO, Joann M (NwPa) 26 Chautauqua Pl, Bradford, PA 16701

PICKARD, Joe (Nwk) 91 Ann Rustin Dr, Ormond Beach, FL 32176

PICKEN, Robert Andrew (Roch) 191 Kensington Road, Garden City, NY 11530

PICKENS, Gregory Doran (Dal) 8011 Douglas, Dallas, TX 75225

PICKERAL, Gretchen (Minn) 404 Trout Lake Rd, Grand Rapids, MN 55744

PICKERING, LouAnn (Ore) 7610 Sw 49th Ave, Portland, OR 97219

PICKERING, William Todd (Va) 208 N 28th St, Richmond, VA 23223

PICKERRELL, Nina (Cal) 1100 California St, San Francisco, CA 94108

PICKUP JR, Ed (SVa) Po Box 146, Franklin, VA 23851

PICKUP JR, Ezra Alden (Vt) 37 S Main St, Alburgh, VT 05440

PICOT, Katherine Frances (Tex) The Harnhill Centre, Harnhill, Cirencester, TX GL75PX, Great Britain (UK)

PICOU, Michael David (SeFla) St Stephen's Episc Ch, 2750 McFarlane Rd, Coconut Grove, FL 33133

PIERCE, Adam Miller (EC) 16 N 16th St, Wilmington, NC 28401

PIERCE, Charles Christian (Chi) Grace Episcopal Church, 120 E 1st St, Hinsdale, IL 60521

PIERCE, Dorothy Kohinke (CNY) PO Box 458, Chenango Bridge, NY 13745

PIERCE, Graham Towle (Me) 35 Pine Ledge Dr, Scarborough, ME 04074

PIERCE, Jacob E (NC)

PIERCE, Kenneth Allen (Lex)

PIERCE, Nathaniel (Eas) 3864 Rumsey Dr, Trappe, MD 21673

PIERCE, Patricia Daniels (NJ) 203 Wildwood Ave, Pitman, NJ 08071

PIERCE, Patrick Arthur (CPa) 306 N Main Street, Mercersburg, PA 17236

PIERCE, Roderick John (Tex) 4435 S FARM ROAD 125, SPRINGFIELD, MO 65810

PIERCE, Terry Lee (Tex) PO Box 268, Taylor, TX 76574

PIERRE, Yonel (Hai)

PIERSON, Anne Susan (The Episcopal NCal)

PIERSON, Peter (Alb) PO Box 183, 156 Josh Hall Pond Road, Grafton, NY 12082

PIERSON, Robert Michael (Los) PO Box 27, Marlboro, NY 12542

PIERSON, Stewart (Vt) 232 High Rock Rd, Hinesburg, VT 05461

PIETSCH, Louise Parsons (NY) 80 Lyme Rd Apt 347, Hanover, NH 03755

PIETTE, Joseph Leroy (Minn) 204 8th St, Cloquet, MN 55720

PIFKE, Lauran Kretchmar (Ak) 3400 Stevenson Blvd. #Q37, Fremont, CA 94538

PIGGINS, Deborah Hanwell (NJ)

PIKE, Clifford Arthur Hunt (Pa) 105 Elm St, Lawrenceburg, KY 40342

PIKE, David (WMich) 1519 Elmwood Rd, Lansing, MI 48917

PIKE, Diane M (WMich) 925 S 84th St, Omaha, NE 68114

PIKE, Richard S (NY) St Matthew's Episcopal Church, PO Box 293, Bedford, NY 10506

PIKE, Stephen Phillip (Ky) RCT 1 HQ Co, UIC 40145, FPO AP, 96426

PIKE, Thomas Frederick (NY) 26 Gramercy Park S Apt 9h, New York, NY 10003

PILARSKI, Terri C (Mich) 120 N Military St, Dearborn, MI 48124

PILAT, Ann Ferres (USC) St Mary's Episcopal Church, 170 St Andrews Rd, Columbia, SC 29210

PILLOT, Anne (O) 4292 Elmwood Rd, South Euclid, OH 44121

PILLSBURY, Jeannette Noyes (Ia) PO Box 4, Decorah, IA 52101

PILLSBURY, Samuel Hale (Los) 919 Albany St, Los Angeles, CA 90015

PILTZ, Guy H (The Episcopal Church in Haw) 62-2145 Ouli St, Kamuela, HI 96743

PINDER, Churchill (CPa) St. Stephens Episcopal Cathedral, 221 N. Front St., Harrisburg, PA 17101

PINDER, Nelson Wardell (CFla) 2632 Marquise Ct, Orlando, FL 32805

PINEO, Linda Baker (At) 3404 Doral Ln, Woodstock, GA 30189

PINHO, Joseph T (Mass) 1 Summit Dr Apt 48, Reading, MA 01867

PINKERTON, Patricia Edith Long (ECR) The Vicarad,St Annes Way, St.Briavels., Gloucestershire, GL15 6UE, Great Britain (UK)

PINKERTON, Susan B (Ct) 400 East Westminster Road, Lake Forest, IL 60045

PINKSTON JR, Frederick William (NC) 7225 Saint Clair Dr, Charlotte, NC 28270

PINNER JR, Joseph (ETenn) 818 Hill St, Kingston, TN 37763

PINNOCK, Betty Lou (Ore) 459 Herbert St, Ashland, OR 97520

PINTI, Daniel John (WNY) 13021 W. Main St., Alden, NY 14004

PINTO DE ARIZA, Myriam (Colom) CRA 6 #49-85, Bogota, D.C., Colombia

PINZON, Samuel E(duardo) (WA) 15570 Sw 143rd Ter, Miami, FL 33196

PINZON CASTRO, Luis Alberto (Colom) Carrera 6 No 49-85, Piso 2, Bogota, Colombia

PIOTROWSKI, Mary Triplett (Az) 2035 N Southern Hills Dr, Flagstaff, AZ 86004

PIOVANE, Michael (Be) Po Box 368, Trexlertown, PA 18087

PIPER, Charles Edmund (NMich) 1676 Lander Ln, Lafayette, CO 80026

PIPER, Geoffrey Tindall (Mass) 124 Front St, Marion, MA 02738

PIPER, Katherine Mae (Colo) 390 Garnet Ave, Granby, CO 80446

PIPER, Linda Lee (NMich) 1676 Lander Lane, Lafayette, CO 80026

PIPER, Mary Elizabeth Meacham (Ore) 4757 Highway 66, Ashland, OR 97520

PIPKIN, Michael (Minn) 1730 Clifton Pl Ste 201, Minneapolis, MN 55403

PIPPIN, Jacqueline Lynne (SanD)

PIPPIN, Tina (At) 25 Second Avenue, Atlanta, GA 30317

PIRET, Michael John (LI) Christ Church, 61 E Main St, Oyster Bay, NY 11771

PISANI JR, Gerard Alexander (Nwk) 8602 Forester Lane, Apex, NC 27539

PITA-PARRALES, Ubaldo Abilito (EcuC) Manabi Y Tayapi, Puyo, Ecuador

PITCHER, Trenton Langland (Chi) 145 E Columbia Ave, Elmhurst, IL 60126

PITMAN JR, Ralph William (O) 3044 Edgehill Rd, Cleveland Heights, OH 44118

PITT JR, Louis Wetherbee (Mass) 59 Dartmouth Ct, Bedford, MA 01730

PITT-HART, Barry Thomas (SD) 1409 S 5th Ave, Sioux Falls, SD 57105

PITTMAN, David West (NC) 218 Pine Cove Drive, Inman, SC 29349

PITTMAN, Warren (NC) 2903 County Clare Rd, Greensboro, NC 27407

PITTS, John Robert (Tex) 3652 Chevy Chase, Houston, TX 77019

PITTS, Kristen Tossell (WA) St Andrew's Episcopal Church, 4512 College Ave, College Park, MD 20740

PITZER, Elaine Virginia (Spok) St Stephen's Episcopal Church, 5720 S Perry St, Spokane, WA 99223

PITZER, John M (La)

PIVER, Jane Duncan (Va) 53 Ridgemont Road, Ruckersville, VA 22968

PIXCAR-POL, Tomas (PR) PO Box 3184, Guayama, PR 00785

PIZZONIA, Wanda (Mass) Post Road & Ring'S End Road, Darien, CT 06820

PIZZUTO, Vincent Anthony (Cal) 171 Forrest Ave, Fairfax, CA 94930

PLACE, Donald Gordon (WMass) 52 County Road, Pownal, VT 05261

PLANK, David Bellinger (LI) 26 Hampton Towne Estates, Hampton, NH 03842

PLANTIN, Jean Wilfrid ()

PLANTZ, Chris (Neb) 605 S Chestnut St, Kimball, NE 69145

PLASKE, Susan Ann (Alb) 68 S Swan St, Albany, NY 12210

PLATSON, Julie L (Ak) PO Box 1130, Sitka, AK 99835

PLATT, Gretchen Mary (SwFla) 1562 Dormie Dr, Gladwin, MI 48624

PLATT, Nancy Grace Van Dyke (Me) 192 Cross Hill Rd, Augusta, ME 04330

PLATT, Thomas Walter (Pa) 824 S New St, West Chester, PA 19382

PLATT, Warren Christopher (NY) 255 W 23rd St Apt 3-DE, New York, NY 10011

PLATT-HENDREN, Barbara (NC) 554 Shuford Circle Dr, Newton, NC 28658

PLAZAS, Carlos Alberto (Chi) 1333 W Argyle St, Chicago, IL 60640

PLESTED, Robert William Harvey (LI) 5402 Timber Trace St, San Antonio, TX 78250

PLIMPTON, Barbara Wilson (WNC) PO Box 968, Marion, NC 28752

PLOVANICH, Ede Marie (CGC)

PLUCKER, Susan (The Episcopal NCal) 1200 Fulton Ave Apt 227, Sacramento, CA 95825

PLUMMER, Alton (NC) Grace Episcopal Church, 419 S Main St, Lexington, NC 27292

PLUMMER, Catherine B (NAM) Episcopal Church in Navajoland, PO Box 720, Farmington, NM 87499

PLUMMER, Cathlena Arnette (NAM) PO Box 720, Farmington, NM 87499

PLUMMER, Dale Wilkinson (RG) 505 N. Pennsylvania, Roswell, NM 88201

PLUMMER, Lynn Whitman (NC) 8600 Mount Holly Hntrsvlle Rd, Huntersville, NC 28078

PLUNKET-BREWTON, Callie Dawn (Ala) 410 N Pine St, Florence, AL 35630

PLUNKETT, Phillip Riley (Ark) 7 Sonata Trail, Little Rock, AR 72205

POBJECKY, Richard Richard (CFla) 414 Pine St, Titusville, FL 32796

POCALYKO, Richard Peter (Pgh) 415 Stone Mill Trl Ne, Atlanta, GA 30328

POGGEMEYER JR, Lewis Eugene (U) 2849 Polk Ave, Ogden, UT 84403

POGOLOFF, Stephen Mark (NC) 218 Forestwood Dr, Durham, NC 27707

POGUE, Blair Alison (Minn) 2136 Carter Avenue, Saint Paul, MN 55108

POGUE, Ronald D (Tex) 5616 Shady Hill, Arlington, TX 76017

POIRIER, Esther (Oly) 4426 133rd Ave SE, Bellevue, WA 98006

POISSON, Ellen Francis (USC) Convent of St. Helena, 414 Savannah Barony Drive, North Augusta, SC 29841

POIST, David Hahn (Va) 341 Woodlands Rd, Charlottesville, VA 22901

POKORNY, Wayne (Ct) 30 Woodland St Apt 11NP, Hartford, CT 06105

POLANCO DE LA CRUZ, Leonel (Ga)

POLGLASE, Kenneth Alexis (Nwk) 2796 Rudder Dr, Annapolis, MD 21401

POLING, Jason Alder (Md)

POLK, Perry Willis (The Episcopal NCal) Grace Episcopal Church, 1405 Kentucky St, Fairfield, CA 94533

POLK, Thomas Robb (RG) 90 S Longspur Dr, The Woodlands, TX 77380

POLLACH, Gideon Liam (LI) 125 Court Street, 11SH, Brooklyn, NY 11201

POLLARD, Richard Allen (Pgh) 1750 Hastings Mill Rd, Pittsburgh, PA 15241

POLLARD III, Robert (NY) 400 S Ocean Blvd PHB, Palm Beach, FL 33480

POLLEY, Bonnie Bonnabel (Nev) 1631 Ottawa Drive, Las Vegas, NV 89169

POLLEY, Seth (Az) 5 Gardner St, Bisbee, AZ 85603

POLLINA, Roy (SwVa) 311 E Church St, Martinsville, VA 24112

POLLITT, Michael James (Chi) 1376 Telegraph Rd., West Caln, MI 19320

POLLOCK, Douglas Stephen (Oly) 7701 Skansie Ave, Gig Harbor, WA 98335

POLLOCK, John (EC) 1912 Shepard St, Morehead City, NC 28557

POLLOCK, Margaret (Va) 21517 Laytonsville Rd, Laytonsville, MD 20882

POLLOCK, Ronald Neal (NJ) 154 W High St, Somerville, NJ 08876

POLLOCK, Ryan Edward (Dal) 5100 Ross Ave, Dallas, TX 75206

POLVINO, Andrea Regina (WNY) 515 Columbus Ave., Waco, TX 76701

POLYARD, Karen Marie (Minn) PO Box 27, Wabasha, MN 55981

POMPA, Tony (Be) 19 E Cochran St, Middletown, DE 19709

PONADER, Martha Downs (Ind) 1337 Eagle Run Dr, Sanibel, FL 33957

PONCE MARTINEZ, Jacqueline (PR) 1 Calle Brandon, Ensenada, PR 00647

POND, Finn Richard (Spok) 7315 N Wall St, Spokane, WA 99208

POND JR, Walter Edward (WNY) 171 N Maple St, Warsaw, NY 14569

PONDER, James Brian (Miss) 118 N Congress St, Jackson, MS 39201

PONG, Tak Yue (Tai) 11 Pak Po Street, Homantin, Hong Kong

PONSOLDT, Megan Hollaway (Va) Grace Episcopal Church, 301 S Main St, Kilmarnock, VA 22482

POOL, Jayne (Ala) 106 Stratford Road, Birmingham, AL 35209

POOLE, Charles Lane (The Episcopal NCal) 6342 Paso Dr, Redding, CA 96001

POOLE, John Huston (CFla) 603 Spring Island Way, Orlando, FL 32828

POOLEY, Nina Ranadive (Me) 152 Princes Point Rd, Yarmouth, ME 04096

POOSER, William Craig (Chi) 2423 Blue Quail, San Antonio, TX 78232

POPE, Alicia Hale (RG) Trinity on the Hill, 3900 Trinity Dr, Los Alamos, NM 87544

POPE, Charles Maurice (Ia) 505 Edgehill Dr, Saint Albans, WV 25177

POPE III, Daniel Stuart (Roch) 406 Canandaigua St, Palmyra, NY 14522

POPE, Nadine Karen (At) PO Box 1010, Cumming, GA 30028

POPE, Robert Gardner (Colo) 108 Sawmill Cir, Bayfield, CO 81122

POPE, Steven Myron (Tex) 905 Whispering Wind, Georgetown, TX 78633

POPE, Stina (Cal) 934 W 14th St, Port Angeles, WA 98363

POPHAM, James J (CGC) Saint David's Episcopal Church, 401 S Broadway, Englewood, FL 34223

POPHAM, Jo P (CGC)

POPLE, David (Ct) 95 Greenwood Ave, 22 Golden Hill St, Bethel, CT 06801

POPPE, Bernie (WMass) 18 De Hart Rd, Maplewood, NJ 07040

POPPE, Kenneth Welch (Vt) 2 Cherry St, Burlington, VT 05401

POPPLEWELL, Elizabeth (Ia) 1808 Nw 121st Cir, Clive, IA 50325

POPPOFF, Robin Marie (ECR) 7269 Santa Teresa Blvd, San Jose, CA 95139

PORCHER, Philip (SC) 1494 Stratton Pl, Mount Pleasant, SC 29466

PORRAS, Samuel Edison (At) 498 Prince Ave, Athens, GA 30601

PORTARO JR, Sam Anthony (Chi) 1250 N Dearborn St Apt 19C, Chicago, IL 60610

PORTER, Elizabeth Streeter (Ark) 10 Thunderbird Dr, Holiday Island, AR 72631

PORTER III, Fulton Louis (Chi) 2720 2nd Private Rd, Flossmoor, IL 60422

PORTER, George Vernon (Ga) 1201 Fairfield St, Cochran, GA 31014

PORTER, Gerry (Oly) 5555 Montgomery Dr Apt N103, Santa Rosa, CA 95409

PORTER, James Robert (Az) 2200 Lester Dr NE Apt 460, Albuquerque, NM 87112

PORTER, Joe Thomas (WTenn) 43 Carriage Ln, Sewanee, TN 37375

PORTER, John Harvey (Cal) 551 Ivy St, San Francisco, CA 94102

PORTER, John Joseph (At) 215 Abington Dr NE, Atlanta, GA 30328

PORTER, Lloyd Brian (Tex) 1701 W TC Jester Blvd, Houston, TX 77008

PORTER, Nicholas (Ct) Trinity Church, 651 Pequot Ave, P.O. Box 400, Southport, CT 06890

PORTER, Pam (WMass) Po Box 19, Heath, MA 01346

PORTER, Roger Cliff (CGC) 6500 Middleburg Ct, Mobile, AL 36608

PORTER, Shirley (At)

PORTER-ACEE III, John (EC) 107 Louis St, Greenville, NC 27858

PORTEUS, Bev (Eas) 27 Woods Way, Elkton, MD 21921

PORTEUS, Christopher (Eas) 27 Woods Way, Elkton, MD 21921

PORTEUS, James Michael (Az) Triskele, Rinsey, Ashton, Helston, TR13 9TS, Great Britain (UK)

✠ **PORTEUS**, Morgan (Ct) PO Box 782, Wellfleet, MA 02667

PORTILLA GOMEZ, Israel Alexander (Colom)

POST, Suzanne Marie (SwFla) 14511 Daffodil Dr Apt 1402, Fort Myers, FL 33919

POSTON, Ronald Glen (Az) 2174 E Loma Vista Dr, Tempe, AZ 85282

POST VAN DER BURG, Melissa (Me)

POTEAT, Sally Tarler (EC) 4181 Cambridge Cove Cir SE # 2, Southport, NC 28461

POTEET, David Bertrand (Tex) Po Box 6828, Katy, TX 77491

POTEET, Fred (SVa) 2508 Shepherds Ln, Virginia Beach, VA 23454

POTTER, Frances Dickinson (NH) 1010 Waltham St Apt 352, Lexington, MA 02421

POTTER, Jack C (U) 231 E 100 S, Salt Lake City, UT 84111

POTTER, Linda (Chi) 1240 NE 64th Ln, Hillsboro, OR 97124

POTTER, Lorene Heath (WNY) 537 S Park Ave, Buffalo, NY 14204

POTTER, Meredith (Chi) 317 Satinwood Ct S, Buffalo Grove, IL 60089

POTTER, Paul Christopher (Los) 37 Sepulveda, RANCHO SANTA MARGARITA, CA 92688

POTTER, Raymond J (The Episcopal NCal) 2224 Gateway Oaks Dr. #355, Sacramento, CA 95833

POTTER, Sara (The Episcopal NCal) 1776 Old Arcata Road, Bayside, CA 95524

POTTER JR, Spencer B (SeFla) 19000 SW 89th Ave, Cutler Bay, FL 33157

POTTER-NORMAN, Ricardo T (DR (DomRep)) Camila Alvarez #7 Urb. Mallen, San Pedro De Macoris, Dominican Republic

POTTERTON, Carol Thayer (SO) 5825 Woodmont Ave, Cincinnati, OH 45213

POTTS, David G (SD) 1728 Mountain View Rd, Rapid City, SD 57702

POTTS, Kathleen (Miss) 1421 Goodyear Blvd., Picayune, MS 39466

POTTS, Matthew L (WMich) P.O. Box 298, Falmouth, MA 02541

POULIN, Sue (NH) Saint John the Baptist, 118 High St, Sanbornville, NH 03872

POULOS, George William (NC) 3308 Northampton Dr, Greensboro, NC 27408

POUNDERS, Marci J (Dal) St James Episcopal Church, 9845 McCree Rd, Dallas, TX 75238

POVEY, John Michael (Mass) 3901 Glen Oaks Drive E, Sarasota, FL 34232

POWELL, Anne Margrete (The Episcopal NCal) 20248 Chaparral Cir, Penn Valley, CA 95946

POWELL, Anthony F (Fla) 657 SE 2nd Ave, Melrose, FL 32666

POWELL, Armistead Christian (Tex) 58 St. Andrews Dr., Jackson, MS 39211

POWELL, Arthur Pierce (NJ) 16 Copperfield Dr, Hamilton, NJ 08610

POWELL, Betty (WA) 2361 Elliott Island Rd, Vienna, MD 21869

POWELL, Blanche Lee (Del) 304 Taylor Ave, Hurlock, MD 21643

POWELL, Brent Cameron (WTenn) 346 Hawthorne St, Memphis, TN 38112

POWELL, Catherine Ravenel (EC) 25 Vivian Ave, Asheville, NC 28801

POWELL, Christopher (Chi) Christ Church, 470 Maple St, Winnetka, IL 60093

POWELL, David Brickman (Ala) PO Box 467, Selma, AL 36702

POWELL, David Richardson (The Episcopal NCal) 122 Main, Cloverdale, CA 95425

POWELL, Elizabeth Jennings (Ala) P.O. Box 467, Selma, AL 36742

POWELL, Everett (Cal) 417 44th Ave, San Francisco, CA 94121

POWELL JR, Festus Hilliard (Ark) Po Box 21162, Hot Springs, AR 71903

POWELL, Greg (Eas) 29497 Hemlock Ln, Easton, MD 21601

POWELL, John Charles (NJ) 307 Red Lion Road, Southampton, NJ 08088

POWELL, John Lynn (Cal) 180 Westbury Cir Apt 327, Folsom, CA 95630

POWELL, Kenneth James (Cal) All Saints Parish, 1355 Waller St, San Francisco, CA 94117

POWELL, Lewis (The Episcopal NCal) 20248 Chaparral Cir, Penn Valley, CA 95946

POWELL, Marilyn (SC) 577 Water Turkey Retreat, Charleston, SC 29412

POWELL, Mark M (EC) St Andew's On-The-Sound Episcopal Church, 101 Airlie Rd, Wilmington, NC 28403

POWELL, Murray Richard (Tex) 951 Curtin St, Houston, TX 77018

✠ **POWELL**, Neff (SwVa) 295 W 22nd Ave, Eugene, OR 97405

POWELL JR, Peter Ross (Ct) 6 Gorham Ave, Westport, CT 06880

POWELL, R Bingham (Ore) St Mary's Episcopal Church, 1300 Pearl St., Eugene, OR 97401

POWELL, Rita Teschner (Mass) Trinity Church Episcopal, 206 Clarendon St, Boston, MA 02116

POWELL IV, Robert Jefferson (ETenn) 1101 N Broadway St, Knoxville, TN 37917

POWELL, Sydney Roswell (NY) 3405 Grace Ave, Bronx, NY 10469

POWELL, William Vincent (Okla) 124 Randolph Ct, Stillwater, OK 74075

POWELL IV, Woodson Lea (NC) 560 Water Tower Road, Moncure, NC 27559

POWER, William Joseph Ambrose (Dal) 8011 Douglas Ave, Dallas, TX 75225

POWERS JR, Clarence (LI) 139 Saint Johns Pl, Brooklyn, NY 11217

POWERS, David Allan (CGC) 959 Charleston St, Mobile, AL 36604

POWERS, Elizabeth Ann (SD) 209 S Main S, Chamberlain, SD 57325

POWERS, Fairbairn (Nwk) 531 Harrison Ave, Claremont, CA 91711

POWERS, Jack (Okla) 2431 Terwilleger Blvd, Tulsa, OK 74114

POWERS, Lee (NJ) 119 St. Georges Drive, Galloway, NJ 08205

POWERS, Nancy Chambers (Dal) 1023 Addison Ave, Pottsboro, TX 75076

POWERS, Patricia Ann (SwFla) Caixa Postal 11510, Porto Alegre, 91720-15, Brazil

POWERS, Sharon Kay (Mass) 49 Puritan Rd, Buzzards Bay, MA 02532

POWERS, Steve (FdL) 311 Division St, Oshkosh, WI 54901

POZO, Francisco (NJ) 61 Kristopher Dr, Yardville, NJ 08620

POZZUTO, Keith Allen (Tex) 220 8th St., Mckeesport, PA 15132

PRADAT, Paul Gillespie (Ala) 12200 Bailey Cove Rd SE, Huntsville, AL 35803

PRAKTISH, Carl Robert (Va) 2572 Lemon Rd Apt 903, Honolulu, HI 96815

PRALL, Brian R (Chi)

PRATER, Willard Gibbs (O) 50 Green St, Thomaston, ME 04861

PRATHER, Joel A (Mil) 503 E Walworth Ave, Delavan, WI 53115

PRATHER, Lynn (Ga) 3504 Professional Cir Ste A, Martinez, GA 30907

PRATI, Jason M (SO) PO Box 421, New Albany, OH 43054

PRATOR, Lloyd (Eugene) (NY) 15620 Riverside Dr W Apt 13i, New York, NY 10032

PRATT, Dorothy (ETenn) 5409 Jacksboro Pike, Knoxville, TN 37918

PRATT JR, Earle (LI) 3240 N Caves Valley Path, Lecanto, FL 34461

PRATT, Grace Atherton (Va) 8009 Fort Hunt Rd, Alexandria, VA 22308

PRATT, Jennifer Julian (Oly) 2109 N Lafayette Ave, Bremerton, WA 98312

PRATT, Mary Florentine Corley (Vt) 865 Otter Creek Hwy, New Haven, VT 05472

PRAY, Frederick Russell (NJ) 221 Ivy Rd, Edgewater Park, NJ 08010

PREAS, Barbara Jean (Nev) 10328 SUMMER RIVER AV., Las Vegas, NV 89144

PREBLE, Charles William (Minn) PO Box 844, Saint Joseph, MN 56374

PRECHTEL, Daniel L (Chi) 2337 Greenwich Rd, San Pablo, CA 94806

PREECE, Mark (Vt) 220 E 6th Ave, Conshohocken, PA 19428

PREGNALL, William Stuart (WA) 132 Lancaster Dr #410, Irvington, VA 22480

PREHM, Katherine T. (Spok) 3401 W Lincoln Ave, Yakima, WA 98902

PREHN III, Walter Lawrence (NwT) 5308 Carrington Ct, Midland, TX 79707

PRENDERGAST, James David (Los) 1325 Monterey Rd, South Pasadena, CA 91030

PRENTICE, David Ralph (Mass) All Saints Episcopal Church, 46 Cherry St, Danvers, MA 01923

PRESCOTT, Vicki (Roch) 2500 East Avenue, Apartment 5H, Rochester, NY 14610

PRESCOTT, W Clarke (Los) 8830 Mesa Oak Dr, Riverside, CA 92508

PRESLER, Henry Airheart (NC) Po Box 293, Monroe, NC 28111

PRESLER, Jane Crosby (Vt) 2534 Hill West Rd., Montgomery, VT 05471

PRESLER, Titus Leonard (Vt) PO Box 501, Montgomery, VT 05471

PRESSENTIN, Elsa Ann (EMich) 7562 Alex Ct, Freeland, MI 48623

PREST JR, Alan Patrick Llewellyn (Va) 3920 Custis Rd, Richmond, VA 23225

PRESTEGARD, Joann Maxine (Oly) 55 Irving St, Cathlamet, WA 98612

PRESTON, Elizabeth Cone (Ia) PO Box 85, Spirit Lake, IA 51360

PRESTON II, James Montgomery (Tex) 1310 Malmaison Ridge Dr, Spring, TX 77379

PRESTON, Leigh (ETenn) 305 W 7th St, Chattanooga, TN 37402

PRESTON, Robert George (SeFla) 401 SW 6th Ave, Hallandale Beach, FL 33009

PRESTON, Shannon E (Tex)

PRESTON, Troy Lynn (Roch) Christ Episcopal Church, 33 E 1st St, Corning, NY 14830

PRETTI, Victoria (NJ) 893 Main St, West Newbury, MA 01985

PREVATT JR, James Thomas (NC) 5104 Ainsworth Dr, Greensboro, NC 27410

PREVIL, Myldred (LI) 1227 Pacific St, Brooklyn, NY 11216

PREVIL, Philome (LI) 1227 Pacific St, Brooklyn, NY 11216

PREVOST, Edward Simpson (Chi) 6 Brookshire Rd, Worcester, MA 01609

PRICE, Barbara Deane (Ak) Po Box 56419, North Pole, AK 99705

PRICE, Barbara Jean (WNY) 77 Huntington Ave, Buffalo, NY 14214

PRICE, Basil Hayes (WK)

PRICE, Darwin Ladavis (LI) PO Box 280, Brewster, MA 02631

PRICE, David William (Tex) 302 S Hardie St, Alvin, TX 77511

PRICE, George (SeFla) 2300 Spanish River Rd, Boca Raton, FL 33432

PRICE, George N (Me) 290 Baxter Blvd Apt B3, Portland, ME 04101

PRICE, Gloria Maccormack (EC) 130 Quail Dr, Dudley, NC 28333

PRICE, Harold Thomas (Ky) 409 Wendover Ave, Louisville, KY 40207

PRICE, John Randolph (Md) 772 Ticonderoga Ave, Severna Park, MD 21146

PRICE, John W (Tex) 2312 Steel Street, Houston, TX 77098

PRICE, Joyce Elizabeth (WNC) 75 Echo Lake Dr, Fairview, NC 28730

PRICE, Kathie (WA) 199 Rolfe Rd, Williamsburg, VA 23185

✠ **PRICE**, Kenneth Lester (SO) 4754 Shire Ridge Rd. W, Hilliard, OH 43026

PRICE, Marston (Ct) 33 Old Field hill Rd. Unit48, Southbury, CT 06488

PRICE, Paul Alexander (Los) 113 Tierra Plano, Rancho Santa Margarita, CA 92688

PRICE, Phyllis Anne (Mass) 12191 Clipper Dr, Lake Ridge, VA 22192

PRICE, Raymond Estal (Wyo) 417 S 2nd St, Lander, WY 82520

PRICE JR, Richard Elwyn (WNC) 185 Macon Ave Apt A-3, Asheville, NC 28804

PRICE, Robert Paul (Tex) 1023 Compass Cove Cir, Spring, TX 77379

PRICE, Sarah (Va)

PRICE, Stephen Marsh (NY) 133 Grove Street, Peterborough, NH 03458

PRICE, Susan Medlicott (Spok) 2029 Sheridan Pl, Richland, WA 99352

PRICE, Terrell Wells (Roch) 23 Main St, Geneseo, NY 14454

PRICE-HADZOR, Robert Baylor (La)

PRICHARD, Albert Hughes (WVa) 75 Old Cheat Rd, Morgantown, WV 26508

PRICHARD, Robert W (Va) Virginia Theological Seminary, 3737 Seminary Rd., Alexandria, VA 22304

PRICHARD, Thomas Morgan (Pgh) 809 18th St, Ambridge, PA 15003

PRICKETT, Gerald Stanley (WNC) 360 Asheville School Rd., Asheville, NC 28806

PRIDEMORE JR, Charles Preston (NY) PO Box 149, Ossining, NY 10562

PRIEST JR, W(Illiam) Hunt (Ga) 4400 86th Ave SE, Mercer Island, WA 98040

PRINCE, Elaine (Md) 10913 Knotty Pine Dr, Hagerstown, MD 21740

PRINGLE, Amy (Los) 5332 Mount Helena Ave, Los Angeles, CA 90041

PRINGLE, Charles Derek (SVa) 419 Elizabeth Lake Dr, Hampton, VA 23669

PRINZ, Susan Moore (USC) 6408 Bridgewood Rd, Columbia, SC 29206

✠ **PRIOR**, Brian N (Minn) 1730 Clifton Place Suite 201, Minneapolis, MN 55403

PRIOR, Eleanor N (Me) PO Box 68, Tivoli, NY 12583

PRIOR, Greg (RI) 7 Trillium Ln, Hilton Head Island, SC 29926

PRIOR, Randall Leavitt (Va) 9515 Holly Prospect Ct, Burke, VA 22015

PRITCHER, Joan Jean (At) 1098 Saint Augustine Pl Ne, Atlanta, GA 30306

PRITCHETT JR, Harry Houghton (NY) 1290 Peachtree Battle Ave Nw, Atlanta, GA 30327

PRITCHETT JR, James Hill (WNC) 209 Nut Hatch Loop, Arden, NC 28704

PRITTS, Clarence Edward (NJ) 7 E Maple Ave, Merchantville, NJ 08109

PRIVETTE, William Herbert (EC) 1119 Hendricks Ave., Jacksonville, NC 28540

PRIVITERA, Linda Fisher (Mass) 21 Marathon St, Arlington, MA 02474

PROBERT, Walter Leslie (Mil) 125 Cedar Ridge Dr, West Bend, WI 53095

PROBST, David (At) 169 Lakeport Rd., Macon, GA 31210

PROCTOR, F Rederick Gregory (Miss) 5527 Ridgewood Rd, Jackson, MS 39211

PROCTOR, Judith Harris (Va) St Paul's Episcopal Church, 228 S Pitt St, Alexandria, VA 22314

PROCTOR, Richard Gillespie (CGC) 4129 Oxford Ave., Jacksonville, FL 32210

PROFFITT, Darrel D (Tex) 1225 W Grand Pkwy S, Katy, TX 77494

PROFFITT III, John (Ark) 1608 McEntire Circle, Chatsworth, GA 30705

PROUD, James (Pa) 111 W Walnut Ln, Philadelphia, PA 19144

✠ **PROVENZANO**, Larry C (LI) Episcopal Diocese of Long Island, 36 Cathedral Avenue, Garden City, NY 11530

PROVINE, Marion Kay (Minn) 3424 Willow Ave, White Bear Lake, MN 55110

PRUITT, Albert (CGC) 729 Brown Pl, Decatur, GA 30030

PRUITT, Alonzo Clemons (Chi) 6552 W Shakespeare Avenue, Apt 2W, Chicago, IL 60707

PRUITT JR, George Russell (Md) 1246 Summit Ave SW, Roanoke, VA 24015

PRUITT, Mark J (O) Po Box 1910, Newport, RI 02840

PRUITT, R Allen (At) 301 N Greenwood St, Lagrange, GA 30240

PRUSKI, Dorota (Va) St Andrew Church, 4000 Lorcom Ln, Arlington, VA 22207

PRYNE, Carla Valentine (Oly) 1745 Ne 103rd St, Seattle, WA 98125

PUCA JR, Anthony J (Nwk) 9 Harrington Ave, Westwood, NJ 07675

PUCHALLA, Daniel Andrew (Chi) 4180 N Marine Dr Apt 410, Chicago, IL 60613

PUCKETT, David Forrest King (Tex) 12535 Perthshire Rd, Houston, TX 77024

PUCKETT, Douglas Arnold (USC) 111 Aiken Rd # 323, Graniteville, SC 29829

PUCKLE, Donne Erving (Az) 125 E Kayetan Dr, Sierra Vista, AZ 85635

PUGH, Charles Dean (Md) 128 S Hilltop Rd, Catonsville, MD 21228

PUGH II, Joel Wilson (Ark) 9, The Close, Salisbury, SP12E B, Great Britain (UK)

PUGH III, Willard Jerome (HB) 1700 E 56th St Apt 3806, Chicago, IL 60637

PUGLIESE, Richard A (Spr) 744 Parker Road, West Glover, VT 05875

PUGLIESE, William Joseph (Ia) 108 Eden Way Ct, Cranberry Twp, PA 16066

PULIMOOTIL, Cherian Pilo (Va) 7124 Dijohn Court Dr, Alexandria, VA 22315

PULLIAM, James Millard (WMo) 80 Council Trl, Warrensburg, MO 64093

PUMMILL, Joseph Howard (Cal) 2550 Dana St Apt 2D, Berkeley, CA 94704

PUMPHREY, Charles Michael (Ia) Naval Medical Center, Portsmouth, 620 John Paul Jones Cir, Portsmouth, VA 23701

PUMPHREY, David William (O) 2385 Covington Rd, Apt 201, Akron, OH 44313

PUMPHREY, John Blair (Del) PO Box 1374, Dover, DE 19903

PUMPHREY, Margaret K (Del) 146 Fairhill Dr, Wilmington, DE 19808

PUMPHREY, Patricia Tilton (Nev) Trinity Episcopal Church, PO Box 2246, Reno, NV 89505

PUMPHREY, Thomas Claude (At) 64 Powderhorn Dr, Phoenixville, PA 19460

PUNNETT, Ian Case (Minn) 901 Portland Ave, Saint Paul, MN 55104

PUNZO, Thomas Edward (WMo) 7055 N Highland Ct, Gladstone, MO 64118

PUOPOLO JR, Angelo (SO) 2366 Kemper Ln, 1801 Rutland Ave., Cincinnati, OH 45207

PURCELL, Christine (Los) 1031 BIENVENEDA AVENUE, 1031, Pacific Palisades, CA 90272

PURCELL, Mary Frances Fleming (Lex) 835 Pinkney Dr, Lexington, KY 40504

PURCELL-CHAPMAN, Diana Barnes (Roch) Po Box 492, Wellsville, NY 14895

PURCHAL, John Jeffrey (LI) 45 Willow St. Apt. 420, Springfield, MA 01103

PURDOM III, Allen Bradford (O) 6809 Mayfield Rd Apt 1071, Cleveland, OH 44124

PURDUM, Ellen Echols (At) 3098 Saint Annes Ln Nw, Atlanta, GA 30327

PURDY, Jim (Mo) 448 Conway Meadows Dr, Chesterfield, MO 63017

PURDY, Tom Clayton (Ga) Christ Church, 6329 Frederica Rd, Saint Simons Island, GA 31522

PURNELL, Erl Gould (Ct) 46 Overlook Ter, Simsbury, CT 06070

PURNELL, Susan Ann (Los) 19682 Verona Ln, Yorba Linda, CA 92886

PURRINGTON, Sandra Jean (NMich) 201 E Ridge St, Marquette, MI 49855

PURSER, Phil Philip (USC) 635 Timberlake Dr, Chapin, SC 29036

PURSLEY, George William (SO) 332 Mount Zion Rd NW, Lancaster, OH 43130

PURVIS, Robert David (Ind) 31 Hampshire Ct, Noblesville, IN 46062

PURYEAR, Jim (SwFla) 339 Meadow Beauty Ct, Venice, FL 34293

PURYEAR, Sarah Elizabeth (Tenn) St. George's Episcopal Church, 4715 Harding Rd, Nashville, TN 32705

PUTMAN, Richard Byron (Ala) 408 Thornberry Cir, Birmingham, AL 35242

PUTNAM, Kevin Todd (Cal) 849 Spruance Ln, Foster City, CA 94404

PUTNAM, Sarah Thompson (SC) Po Box 888, Marion, SC 29571

PUTNAM, Thomas Clyde (Ia) 397 Huron Ave, Cambridge, MA 02138

PUTZ, Shirley Joyce Baynham (Nev) 1453 Rawhide Rd, Boulder City, NV 89005

PYATT, Petrina Margarette (NJ) 100 East Maple Ave, Penns Grove, NJ 08069

PYLES, Chris (CPa) 707 Park Ave, Baltimore, MD 21201

PYRON JR, Wilson Nathaniel (Mo) 1422 Shady Creek Ct, Saint Louis, MO 63146

Q

QUACKENBUSH, Margaret Haight (Alb) 7610 Heths Salient St Apt 200, Spotsylvania, VA 22553

QUAINTON, Rodney F (Chi) 1725 Northfield Square, Northfield, IL 60093

QUATORZE, Jean Lenord (Hai)

QUEEN, Jeffrey Denver (Lex) 3 Chalfonte Place, Fort Thomas, KY 41075

QUEEN, Laura Virginia (Los) Church Pension Group, 19 E 34th St, New York, NY 10016

QUEEN JR, William L (Va) 514 N 25th St, Richmond, VA 23223

QUEHL-ENGEL, Catherine Mary (Ia) 103 Oak Ridge Dr Se, Mount Vernon, IA 52314

QUESENBERRY-NELSON, Jane E (Minn) 4903 Maple Grove Rd, Hermantown, MN 55811

QUEVEDO-BOSCH, Juan A (LI) 3014 Crescent St S, Astoria, NY 11102

✠ **QUEZADA MOTA**, Moises (DR (DomRep)) Calle Costa Rica No 21, Ens. Ozama, Santo Domingo, Dominican Republic

QUICK, Judy Goins (Ala) 224 Bentley Cir, Shelby, AL 35143

QUIGGLE, George Willard (Ala) 384 Windflower Dr, Dadeville, AL 36853

QUIGLEY, James E (WA) St Alban's Church, 3001 Wisconsin Ave NW, Washington, DC 20016

QUIJADA-DISCAVAGE, Thomas Damian (Los) 2563 Sale Pl, Walnut Park, CA 90255

QUILA GARCIA, Pedro Perfecto (EcuC) Box 235, Tena, Ecuador

QUILL, Margaret (Chi) Guardian Angels of Elk River, Inc., 400 Evans Avenue, Elk River, MN 55330

QUIN, Alison (NY) 3021 State Route 213 E, Stone Ridge, NY 12484

QUINES JR, Brent B (Los) Holy Trinity and St Benedict, 416 N Garfield Ave, Alhambra, CA 91801

QUINN, Carolee Elizabeth Sproull (USC) 1402 Wenwood Ct, Greenville, SC 29607

QUINN, Catherine Alyce Rafferty (Nwk) 66 Pomander Walk, Ridgewood, NJ 07450

QUINN, Eugene Frederick (WA) 5702 Kirkside Dr, Chevy Chase, MD 20815

QUINN, Michele (Colo) 3153 S Forest St, Denver, CO 80222

QUINN, Peter Darrell (Ct) 120 Ford Ln, Torrington, CT 06790

QUINN, Scott (Pgh) 537 Hamilton Rd, Pittsburgh, PA 15205

QUINNELL, Carolyn T (CFla) PO Box 2373, Belleview, FL 34421

QUINNELL, Robert Douglass (CFla) PO Box 2373, Belleview, FL 34421

QUINNEY, Sarah Howell (The Episcopal NCal) 2351 Pleasant Grove Blvd, Roseville, CA 95747

QUINONEZ-MERA, Juan Carlos (EcuC)

QUINTON, Dean Lepidio (Nev) 8500 Doniphan Dr, Unit 17, Anthony, TX 79821

QUIROGA, Luis Alberto (LI) 14755 Sw 154th Ct, Miami, FL 33196

R

RAASCH, Timothy (Minn) 8323 N Shannon Rd Unit 19206, Tucson, AZ 85742

RABAGO-NUNEZ, Luis Antonio (U) 1211 N Redwood Rd Apt 165, Salt Lake City, UT 84116

✠ **RABB**, John L (Md) 4 E University Pkwy, Baltimore, MD 21218

RABONE, Christian Robert (NwT)

RABY, Edith Gilliam (CFla) 111 S Church St, Smithfield, VA 23430

RACHAL, Paula C (NC) 2803 Watauga Dr, Greensboro, NC 27408

RACHAL, Robert T (NC) 2803 Watauga Dr, Greensboro, NC 27408

RACIOPPI, Gerard Andrew (Nwk) 73 S Fullerton Ave, Montclair, NJ 07042

RACKLEY, M Kathryn (O) 1730 Wright Ave, Rocky River, OH 44116

RACUSIN, Michele (Los) 5267 San Jacinto Ave, Clovis, CA 93619

RADANT, William Fred (Mil) PO Box 442, Manitowish Waters, WI 54545

RADCLIFF III, Cecil Darrell (CFla) 3010 Big Sky Blvd, Kissimmee, FL 34744

RADCLIFF, Irene Evelyn (SO)

RADCLIFFE, Ernest Stanley (Oly) 3732 Colonial Ln Se, Port Orchard, WA 98366

RADCLIFFE JR, William Eugene (Md) 2846 Angus Circle, Molino, FL 32577

RADKE, Pamela Kay (Nev) St Matthew's Episcopal Church, 4709 S Nellis Blvd, Las Vegas, NV 89121

RADLEY, Charles Perrin (Me) 3701 R St NW, Washington, DC 20007

RADNER, Ephraim Louis (Colo) 410 W 18th St, Pueblo, CO 81003

RADTKE, Warren Robert (Mass) 111 Perkins St Apt 213, Jamaica Plain, MA 02130

RADZIK, David Robert (O)

RAEHN, J Sid (CFla) 106 Jim Dedmon Rd, Dyer, TN 38330

RAFFALOVICH, Francis Dawson (Dal) 306 Cobalt Cv, Georgetown, TX 78633

RAFFERTY, Joseph Patrick (Be) 220 Montgomery Ave, West Pittston, PA 18643

RAFFERTY, Robert Douglas (NMich) 421 Cherry St, Iron River, MI 49935

RAFTER, John Wesley (Me) PO Box 527, Camden, ME 04843

RAGAN, Raggs (Ore) 640 Southshore Blvd., Lake Oswego, OR 97034

RAGLAND, Rebecca B (Mo) 1210 Locust St, Saint Louis, MO 63103

RAGSDALE, Eliza Robinson (SeFla) 1750 E Oakland Park Blvd, Fort Lauderdale, FL 33334

RAGSDALE, James Lewis (Colo) 3143 S Nucla St, Aurora, CO 80013

RAGSDALE, Katherine H (Nwk) 99 Brattle St, Cambridge, MA 02138

RAGSDALE III, Lee Morris (ETenn)

RAHHAL, Michele Duff (Okla) 721 Franklin Dr, Ardmore, OK 73401

RAHM, Kent David (Va) 6604 Willow Pond Dr, Fredericksburg, VA 22407

RAHN, Gaynell M (Va) 905 Princess Anne St, Fredericksburg, VA 22401

RAICHE, Brian Michael (Mass) 26 White St, Haverhill, MA 01830

RAILEY, Robert Macfarlane (NMich) 3029 N Lakeshore Blvd, Marquette, MI 49855

RAINING, Hillary (Pa) 226 Righters Mill Rd, Gladwyne, PA 19035

RAINS JR, Harry James (WNC) 8 Nicole Lane, Weaverville, NC 28787

RAISH, John Woodham (WLa) 211 Linden St, Shreveport, LA 71104

RAJ, Seelam Sujanna (Mo)

RAJ, Vincent (ECR) P.O. Box 551, Carmel Valley, CA 93950

RAJAGOPAL, Doris Elizabeth (Pa) 763 Valley Forge Rd, Wayne, PA 19087

RALPH, Michael Jay (LI) 28 Highland Rd, Glen Cove, NY 11542

RALPH, Samuel Lester (Mass) 88 King St, Reading, MA 01867

RALSTON, Betty Marie (Colo) Po Box 773627, Steamboat Springs, CO 80477

RALSTON, D Darwin (O) 711 College Ave, Lima, OH 45805

RAMAN, Neil K (Pgh)

RAMBO JR, Charles B (CFla) Po Box 46, Rutherfordton, NC 28139

RAMBO, Thomas (SwVa) 323 Catherine St, Walla Walla, WA 99362

RAMBOW, George (NJ) 16 All Saints Rd, Princeton, NJ 08540

RAMERMAN, Diane Gruner (Oly) 1216 7th St, Anacortes, WA 98221

RAMEY, Bernard (Va) St Alban's Episcopal Church, 6800 Columbia Pike, Annandale, VA 22003

RAMIREZ, Lucia (PR)

RAMIREZ, Mark Lloyd (Chi) St Barnabas Epis Church, 22W415 Butterfield Rd, Glen Ellyn, IL 60137

RAMIREZ-MILLER, Gerardo Carlos (NY) 351 W 24th St Apt 6-C, New York, NY 10011

RAMIREZ-NIEVES, Aida Iris (VI) PO Box 1796, Kingshill, VI 00851

RAMIREZ-SEGARRA, Cesar E (Pa) PO Box 1967, Yauco, PR 00698

RAMNARAINE, Barbara Allen (Minn) St. Luke's Episcopal Church, 4557 Colfax Ave. 5, Minneapolis, MN 55403

RAMOS, Leon (PR)

RAMOS, Mary Serena (Minn) 700 S 2nd Street, Unit 41, Minneapolis, MN 55401

RAMOS, Pablo (U) 1904 Dale Ridge Ave, Salt Lake City, UT 84116

RAMOS, Waldemar F (PR) 560 Calle Napoles Apt 2c, San Juan, PR 00924

RAMOS-GARCIA, Ramon (PR)

RAMOS HUERTA, Habacuc (NC) Avenue Ruiz 2090-6, Priv Los

Clergy List

Girasoles, Ensenada, BCN 22800, Mexico

✠ **RAMOS-ORENCH**, Wilfrido (PR) 77 Linnmoore St, Hartford, CT 06114

RAMSDEN, Charlie (Cal)

RAMSEY, Ron (SVa) 8 Meacham Rd, Cambridge, MA 02140

RAMSEY, Walter Albert (Cal) 162 Hickory St, San Francisco, CA 94102

RAMSEY-MUSOLF, Michael Jeffrey (Los) Department Of Physics, U. Mass Amherst, 710 N Pleasant St 416, Amherst, MA 01003

RAMSHAW, Lance Arthur (Del) 106 Alden Rd, Concord, MA 01742

RAMSHAW, Lynn Cecelia Homeyer (Chi) 12 Jolynn Drive, Ormond Beach, FL 32174

RAMSTAD, Philip Robert (Minn) 901 Como Boulevard East, #304, Osceda, WI 54020

RANDALL, Anne E (Dal) 421 Custer Rd, Richardson, TX 75080

RANDALL, Catharine Louise (Ct) 91 Minortown Rd, Woodbury, CT 06798

RANDALL II, Chandler Corydon (SanD) PO Box 15605, Fort Wayne, IN 46885

RANDALL, Elizabeth Penney (Colo) 735 S Vine St, Denver, CO 80209

RANDALL, Jeanne Rice (Ala)

RANDALL, Richard Alan (CPa) 222 N 6th St, Chambersburg, PA 17201

RANDALL JR, Robert James (SVa) 716 Abbey Dr, Virginia Beach, VA 23455

RANDALL, Sarah Archais (Mass) P.O. Box C, Duxbury, MA 02331

RANDLE, Cameron D (SVa) 6125 Carlos Ave, Los Angeles, CA 90028

RANDOLPH, Barry Trent (Mich) 231 E Grand Blvd, Detroit, MI 48207

RANDOLPH JR, Henry G (NI) 117 N Lafayette Blvd, South Bend, IN 46601

RANEY III, Raymond Raymond (RG) 04 Tano Road, Santa Fe, NM 87506

RANK, Andrew Peter Robert (SanD) Po Box 34548, San Diego, CA 92163

RANKIN, Annette Reiser (Ore) 10 Old Mill St, Mill Valley, CA 949410

RANKIN, Deborah (O) 2220 Second St., Cuyahoga Falls, OH 44221

RANKIN, Edward Harris (Oly) 11510 NE 35th Ave, Vancouver, WA 98686

RANKIN, Glenn Edger (Ia) 2206 Frontier Rd, Denison, IA 51442

RANKIN, Jerry Dean (Kan) 406 Hillside St, Abilene, KS 67410

RANKIN II, William Wright (Cal) 13 Mara Vista Ct, Tiburon, CA 94920

RANKIN-WILLIAMS, Chris (Cal) Po Box 217, Ross, CA 94957

RANNA, Claire Dietrich (Cal)

RANNENBERG, Pamela Lamb (RI) 442 Wickford Point Rd, North Kingstown, RI 02852

RANSOM, Jim (Md) 89 Hilltop Pl, New London, NH 03257

RANSOM, Lisa (Vt) 2016 Us Rr 2, Waterbury, VT 05676

RAO, Chitra Dasu Sudarshan (Los) 10833 Le Conte Ave, Los Angeles, CA 90095

RAPALO DE RUIZ, Jaqueline Siomara (Hond) 23 Ave 21 Calle SO. Col. Trejo, San Pedro Sula Cortes, Honduras

RAPP, Phillip James (WK) 6529 Clifton Rd, Clifton, VA 20124

RARDIN, Thomas Michael (Tex) 332 Oklahoma Ave, Hewitt, TX 76643

RASCHKE, Gerald Wesley (Spr) 2921 Haverford Rd, Springfield, IL 62704

RASCHKE, Vernon Joseph (SD) 625 W Main, Lead, SD 57754

RASICCI, Michael Dominic (Chi) 222 S Batavia Ave, Batavia, IL 60510

RASKOPF, Roger William (LI) 1250 Newport Dr., Oconomowoc, WI 53066

RASMUS, John Edward (Eau) 5318 Regent St, Madison, WI 53705

RASMUS, Paul (SeFla) 3740 Holly Dr, Palm Beach Gardens, FL 33410

RASMUSSEN, Cynthia M (Roch) 215 Parkview Dr, Rochester, NY 14625

RASMUSSEN, Jeanne Louise (Az) 520 N Pokegama Ave, Grand Rapids, MN 55744

RASMUSSEN, Rik Lorin (The Episcopal NCal) St Paul's Episcopal Church, PO Box 160914, Sacramento, CA 95816

RASNER, Richard Lewis (SO) 143 State St, Portland, ME 04101

RASNICK, Kenneth Wayne (Mich)

RASNICK, Thomas (ETenn) 6804 Glenbrook Cir, Knoxville, TN 37919

RATCLIFF, Elizabeth Rogers (WLa)

RATH, Erin (USC) PO Box 187, Simpsonville, SC 29681

RATHBONE, Cristine F (Mass) 138 Tremont St., Boston, MA 02111

RATHBUN JR, Arthur John (Kan) 138 S 8th St, Salina, KS 67401

RATLIFF, Ruth Evelyn (Ia) St Luke's Episcopal Church, 2410 Melrose Dr, Cedar Falls, IA 50613

RATTERREE, Gretchen S (Roch)

RAU, Michael S (Pa) St Mark's Episcopal Church, 111 Oenoke Rdg, New Canaan, CT 06840

RAULERSON, Aaron D (Ala) 5529 Cedar Mill Dr, Guntersville, AL 35976

RAUSCHER JR, William V. (NJ) 663 N Evergreen Ave, Woodbury, NJ 08096

RAVEN, Margaret Hilary (NJ) 324 Edgewood Dr, Toms River, NJ 08755

RAVNDAL III, Eric (CFla) 1302 Country Club Oaks Cir, Orlando, FL 32804

RAWLINS, Allister (LI) 744 Havemeyer Ave, Bronx, NY 10473

RAWLINSON, John Edward (Cal) 891 Dowling Blvd, San Leandro, CA 94577

RAWSON, William Leighton (Nwk) 10960 Big Canoe, Jasper, GA 30143

RAY, Andrew M (Pgh) PO Box 38342, Pittsburgh, PA 15238

RAY, Douglass E (Colo) 5601 Collins Ave Apt 706, Miami Beach, FL 33140

RAY, Harvey H (Cal) 1354 Primavera Dr E, Palm Springs, CA 92264

RAY, John Sewak (At) 4808 Glenwhite Dr, Duluth, GA 30096

RAY, Michael Fleming (Ct) 830 Whitney Avenue, New Haven, CT 06511

RAY, Philip Carroll (NwT) 1608 Monte Vista Dr, Dalhart, TX 79022

RAY, Pratik Kumar (RG)

✠ **RAY**, Rayford J (NMich) 9922 U 65 Lane, Rapid River, MI 49878

RAY, Suzanne Patricia (NMich) 9922 U 65 Lane, Rapid River, MI 49878

RAY, Wanda (O) 312 Park St, Huron, OH 44839

RAY, Wayne Allen (Miss) 116 Siowan Ave, Ocean Springs, MS 39564

RAYBOURN JR, Fred Loren (Neb) 1204 Sunshine Blvd, Bellevue, NE 68123

RAYBURG-ELLIOTT, Jason Alan (WNY) 128 Pearl St, Buffalo, NY 14202

RAYLS, John William (WTex) PO Box 6885, San Antonio, TX 78209

RAYMOND, Bob (Me) Po Box 215, Hulls Cove, ME 04644

RAYMOND, Patrick (Chi) 647 Dundee Ave, Barrington, IL 60010

RAYMOND, Seth (Mil) Christ Episcopal Church, 5655 N Lake Dr, Whitefish Bay, WI 53217

RAYMOND, Sue Ann (Ia) Lot 17A, 1771 Golf Course Blvd., Independence, IA 50644

RAYSA, Mary G (SO)

RAZEE, George Wells (Ct) 234 Essex Mdws, Essex, CT 06426

RAZIM, Genevieve (Tex)

RAZZINO, Robin (Va) 1701 N Quaker Ln, Alexandria, VA 22302

REA, Robert Allen (NC) 1226 21st Ave, San Francisco, CA 94122

READ, Allison (Ct) 300 Summit St, Hartford, CT 06106

READ, David Glenn (WTex) PO Box 1765, Boerne, TX 78006

READ, Nancy Ann (Nwk) 12 Northfield Ter, Clifton, NJ 07013

READ II, Philip Daugherty (SwFla) 11698 Pointe Cir, Fort Myers, FL 33908

REANS, Douglas J (NJ) 512 Sycamore Ter, Cinnaminson, NJ 08077

REARDIN, Lois Arline (NC) 221 Union St, Cary, NC 27511

REARDON, John Paul (RI) 474 Fruit Hill Ave, North Providence, RI 02911

REASONER, Rand (Los) 5700 Rudnick Ave, Woodland Hills, CA 91367

REAT, Lee Anne (SO) 2318 Collins Dr, Worthington, OH 43085

REBHOLTZ, Brian (The Episcopal NCal) 79 Denton Rd, Wellesley, MA 02482

RECHTER, Elizabeth (Los) 2744 Peachtree Rd Nw, Atlanta, GA 30305

RECTENWALD, Marion Bridget (SD) 371 New College Dr, Sewanee, TN 37375

REDDALL, Jennifer Reddall (NY) 500 E 77th St Apt 1622, New York, NY 10162

REDDELL, Ronald Kirk (Oly) 910 Harris Ave Unit 408, Bellingham, WA 98225

REDDIE, Grover Tyrone (Alb) 11192 State Route 9W, Coxsackie, NY 12051

REDDIG, Mike (Cal) 1400 Geary Blvd., #3A, San Francisco, CA 94109

REDDIMALLA, Samuel (NY) 4673 Flatlick Branch Drive, Chantilly, VA 20151

REDDING, Pamela J (Cal) 2925 Bonifacio Street, Concord, CA 94519

REDFIELD, William (CNY) 225 Pelham Rd, Syracuse, NY 13214

REDMAN, Nolan Bruce (Spok) 3020 E Flintlock Ct, Mead, WA 99021

REDMON, Caroline (Los) 1050 E Ramon Rd Unit 125, Palm Springs, CA 92264

RED OWL, Cordelia (SD) Po Box 354, Porcupine, SD 57772

REDPATH, Valerie Jean (NJ) 329 Estate Point Rd, Toms River, NJ 08753

REECE, Herbert Anderson (O) 9522 Lincolnwood Dr, Evanston, IL 60203

REECE, Jennifer M (Me) 41 Mount Desert St, Bar Harbor, ME 04609

REECE, Mark Spencer (SeFla) Iglesia Catedral del Redentor, Calle Beneficancia #18, Madrid, 28004, Spain

REECE, Nathaniel Treat (Mass) 60 Edward Rd, Raynham, MA 02767

REED, Anne L (SO) Diocese of Southern Ohio, 412 Sycamore St., Cincinnati, OH 45202

REED, Bobette P (O) Deer Hill Rr#1, East Hampton, CT 06424

REED, Craig Andrew (Dal) 9714 Lanward Dr, Dallas, TX 75238

✠ **REED**, David (Ky) 5226 Moccasin Trl, Louisville, KY 40207

✠ **REED**, David (WTex) P. O. Box 6885, San Antonio, TX 78209

REED, Davies (Ind) St. Christopher's Church, 1402 W. Main Street, Carmel, IN 46032

REED, Elizabeth H (Be) 108 N 5th St, Allentown, PA 18102

REED, Harold Vincent (Alb) 1802 Sonoma Ln, Lemon Grove, CA 91945

REED, Jeffrey Bruce (Az) Po Box 42618, Tucson, AZ 85733

REED, Jim (EC) PO Box 985, Washington, DC 27889

REED, Juan Y (Chi) 1617 E 50th Place, Apt 4D, Chicago, IL 60615

REED, Loreen Hayward Rogers (At) 355 Porter St, Madison, GA 30650

REED JR, Poulson (Az) 6300 N Central Ave, Phoenix, AZ 85012

REED, Richard Wayne (RG) Hc 31 Box 17-B, Las Vegas, NM 87701

REED, Robert Cooper (NwPa) 105 Waugh Ave Unit 1106, New Wilmington, PA 16142

REED, Ronald Lind (Kan) 4810 W 67th St, Prairie Village, KS 66208

REED, Stephen K (Ak) 1722 Linden St, Longmont, CO 80501

REED, Thomas Louis (Pa) 16 Nestlenook Dr, Middleboro, MA 02346

REEDER, Tom (Fla) 400 San Juan Dr, Ponte Vedra, FL 32082

REEMAN, Karen Baehr (NJ) 69 Broad St, Eatontown, NJ 07724

REES, Donald Joseph (Episcopal SJ) 12358 Newport Rd, Ballico, CA 95303

REES, Elizabeth (Va) 1501 River Farm Dr, Alexandria, VA 22308

REES, Emily Frances (At) Po Box 223, Braselton, GA 30517

REESE, Carol Sue (Chi) 1525 W Birchwood Ave, Chicago, IL 60626

REESE, Donnis Jean (EMich) 200 E Page St, Rose City, MI 48654

REESE, Frederic William (Miss) 373 Edenbrook, Brookhaven, MO 39601

REESE, Jeannette Ellis (WNC) 45 Spooks Branch Extension, Asheville, NC 28804

REESE, John (SwFla) 509 E Twiggs St, Tampa, FL 33602

REESE, John Victor (Ark) 406 W Central Ave, Bentonville, AR 72712

REESE, Judith Foster (WTenn) 800 Rountree Avenue, Kinston, NC 28501

REESE, Mary (EC) 404 E. New Hope Rd., Goldsboro, NC 27534

REESE, Robert Emory (WNC) 45 Spooks Branch Ext, Asheville, NC 28804

REESE, Thomas Francis (LI) 141 Ascan Ave, Forest Hills, NY 11375

REESON, Geoffrey Douglas (EcuC) Casilla 17-16-95, Quito, Ecuador

REESON, Marta Lidia (EcuC) Casilla 17-16-95, Quito, Ecuador

REEVE, Keith John (NC) 3613 Clifton Ct, Raleigh, NC 27604

REEVE, Susan Margaret (The Episcopal NCal) 146 Saint Gertrude Ave, Rio Vista, CA 94571

REEVES, Bernice Brysch (WTex)

REEVES, Daniel J (NC) 1737 Hillandale Rd, Durham, NC 27705

REEVES, Diane Delafield (Fla) 13588 NE 247th Lane, Box 18, Orange Springs, FL 32182

REEVES, Frank B (FtW) 2204 Collington Dr, Roanoke, TX 76262

REEVES, Jack William (LI) 23 Old Mamaroneck Rd Apt 5R, White Plains, NY 10605

REEVES, Jess (SeFla) 8619 North Liston Avenue, Kansas City, MO 64154

REEVES, Robin K (Tex) 523 E 4th St, Tyler, TX 75701

REEVES JR, William (Va) The Collegiate Schools, Richmond, VA 23229

REGAN, Thomas Francis (SD) 708 Sawyer St, Lead, SD 57754

REGAS, George Frank (Los) 807 Las Palmas Rd., Pasadena, CA 91105

REGEN, Catharine Louise Emmert (Tenn) 306 Broadview Dr, Dickson, TN 37055

REGISFORD, Sylvanus Hermus Alonzo (SeFla) 7580 Derby Ln, Shakopee, MN 55379

REGIST, Antonio Alberto (WTex) 1310 Pecan Valley Dr, Antonio, TX 78210

REHAGEN, Gerry (EMich) 2093 Michaywe Dr, Gaylord, MI 49735

REHBERG, Gloria Irene (RG) 7104 Montano Rd Nw, Albuquerque, NM 87120

✠ **REHBERG**, Gretchen (Spok) 245 E 13th Ave, 731 E 8th Ave, Spokane, WA 99202

REHO, James Hughes (SwFla) Lamb Of God Episcopal Church, 19691 Cypress View Dr, Fort Myers, FL 33967

REICH, Jeffrey Walker (Miss) 834 N. 5th Ave, laurel, MS 39440

REICHARD, Bernice Dorothy (Be) P.O. Box 368, Trexlertown, PA 18087

REICHEL, Sonya Joan (The Episcopal NCal)

REICHERT, Elaine Starr Gilmer (Cal) 1605 Vendola Dr, San Rafael, CA 94903

REICHMAN, Amy L (Ct) PO Box 698, Sharon, CT 06069

REICHMANN, Jeffrey H (At) 26 Oakwood Ct, Jacksonville Beach, FL 32250

REID, Brian S (NwPa) 415 4th Ave, Warren, PA 16365

REID, Catharine Brannan (Oly) 1123 19th Ave East, Seattle, WA 98112

REID, Dennis Joseph (Be)

REID, Franklin Lionel (NY) 1064 E 219th St, Bronx, NY 10469

REID, Gordon (Pa) 1027 Arch St, Apt 406, Philadelphia, PA 19107

REID, Jennie Lou (SeFla) 3840 Alhambra Ct, Coral Gables, FL 33134

REID, M Sue (Oly) 315 Burns Lane, Williamsburg, VA 23185

REID, Michael Edgar (ECR) 146 12th St, Pacific Grove, CA 93950

REID, Paul (Pa) 7809 Old York Rd, Elkins Park, PA 19027

REID, Richard P (NI) 44591 San Rafael Ave, Palm Desert, CA 92260

REID, Richard William (Vt) Po Box 70070, North Dartmouth, MA 02747

REID-LEVY, Schelly (Md) 3002 Holly St, Edgewater, MD 21037

REIDT, Donna (Vt) 124 Willis Rd, West Charleston, VT 05872

REILEY, Jennifer B S (Mass) 48 Prospect St, North Andover, MA 01845

REIMER, Leslie (Pgh) 5426 Wilkins Ave, Pittsburgh, PA 15217

REIMER, Susan (RG) 184 Boutwell Ct, Loveland, CO 80537

REIN, Lily A (At) 1105-L Clairemont Ave, Decatur, GA 30030

REINECKE, Rod (NC) 3810 Heritage Dr Rm 104, Burlington, NC 27215

REINERS JR, Alwin (Va) 1600 Westbrook Ave, Richmond, VA 23227

REINERS, Diane (NY)

REINHARD, Kathryn Louise (NY) Christ Church, 84 Broadway, New Haven, CT 06511

REINHARDT, Connie (WA) 27 Broad St, Newburyport, MA 01950

REINHEIMER, John Jay (NH) 227 W 6th St, Port Clinton, OH 43452

REINHEIMER, Philip (The Episcopal NCal) 13948 Gold Country Drive, Penn Valley, CA 95945

REINHOLZ, Andrew C (Va) Epiphany Episcopal Church, 8000 Hermitage Rd, Henrico, VA 23228

REINHOLZ, Kimberly (Va) Christ Church, 205 N 7th St, Stroudsburg, PA 18360

REINKEN, Dirk Christian (NJ) 5208 Biltmore Dr, Freehold, NJ 07728

REISCHMAN, Charles J (Spr) 4767 Redbud Ct, Decatur, IL 62526

REISHUS, John William (WMich) 5161 E 50 N, Kokomo, IN 46901

REISNER, Terry Ralph (Dal)

REJOUIS, Mary Kate (Colo) 2700 University Heights Ave, Boulder, CO 80302

RELLER, Wilfred Herman (Colo) 71 Aspen Ln, Golden, CO 80403

RELYEA, Michael Johl (NY) 127b east terminal blvd, Atlantic Beach, NC 28512

REMBOLDT, Cherry Ann (SanD) 47535 State Highway 74, Palm Deset, CA 92260

REMENTER, Nancy Sandra (CPa) 239 E Market St, Marietta, PA 17547

REMER, Douglas E (SwFla) 5231 S Jules Verne Ct, Tampa, FL 33611

REMINGTON, Melissa (WVa) 821 Edgewood Dr, Charleston, WV 25302

REMPPEL, Paulette Evelyn (NY) 52 Brookside Pl, New Rochelle, NY 10801

REMY, Joseph Michel Jean (Hai) 5935 Del Lago Circle, Sunrise, FL 33313

RENCHER, Ollie (WTenn) 1720 Peabody Ave, Memphis, TN 38104

RENDON OSPINA, Gonzalo Antonio (Colom) Cra 80 No. 53a-78, Medelin Antioquia, 99999, Colombia

RENDOR OSPINA, Gonzalo () Cra 80 No. 53a-78, Medellin, ANTIOQUIA, Colombia

RENEGAR, Douglas Mcbane (Ga) 224 Lakefield Rd., Waterloo, SC 29384

RENFREW, William Finch (Mich) 2101 Wellesley Dr, Lansing, MI 48911

RENG, Zecharia (ND)

RENGERS, Josiah Daniel (Ala) 109 Woodcrest Circle, Eutaw, AL 35462

RENICK, Van Taliaferro (SwVa) 170 Mountain Ave, Rocky Mount, VA 24151

RENN, Wade (Nwk) 558 Highland Ave, Montclair, NJ 07043

RENNA, Pamela Stacey (EMich) 123 N Michigan Ave, Saginaw, MI 48602

REPLOGLE, Jennifer (Chi) 33 Mercer St, Princeton, NJ 08540

REPP, Jeanette (Los) 1648 W 9th St, San Pedro, CA 90732

RESSLER, Richard Alan (SD) St. Paul's Episcopal Church, 309 S. Jackson St., Jackson, MI 49201

RESTREPO CARDONA, Juan Carlos (Colom) Calle 51 # 6-49, Bogota, 111166, Colombia

RETAMAL, M Regina (Mass) 59 Lawrence St, Framingham, MA 01702

RETTGER, John Hubbard (Minn) 65 - 104th Avenue Northwest, Coon Rapids, MN 55448

RETZLAFF, Georg (USC) 1612 Goldfinch Ln, West Columbia, SC 29169

REUMAN, Eugene Frederic (CFla) 2915 W Henley Ln, Dunnellon, FL 34433

REUSS, Patricia Ann Osborne (WNC) 133 Liberty Ct, Oak Ridge, TN 37830

REUSS, Robert Julius (WNC) 133 Liberty Ct, Oak Ridge, TN 37830

REVEL, Anna Carter (Ky) 5146 Sunnybrook Dr, Paducah, KY 42001

REX III, Charles Walton (Chi) 2739 Prairie Ave, Evanston, IL 60201

REX JR, William Moyer (Pa) 407 N Broad St, Lansdale, PA 19446

REXFORD, William Nelson (Mich) 7213 Meadow Wood Way, Clarksville, MD 21029

REYES, Jesus (ECR) P.O. Box 1903, Monterey, CA 93942

REYES, Juan P (WA) 3001 Wisconsin Ave NW, Washington, DC 20016

REYES, Julia Sierra (Colo) Christ Church Episcopal, 18 Abercorn St, Savannah, GA 31401

REYES GUILLEN, Karla Patricia (Hond) Catedral Episcopal Santa Maria De Los Angeles, Colonia Florencia Norte Primera, Entrada Boulevard Suyapa, Tegucigalpa M.DC, 11101, Honduras

REYES PEREZ, Jose R (WMass) 6744 S Kings Hwy, Alexandria, VA 22306

REYNES, Stephen Alan (Vt) 64 State St, Montpelier, VT 05602

REYNOLDS, Bettye (The Episcopal NCal) 4706 Oakbough Way, Carmichael, CA 95608

REYNOLDS, Bo Daniel (NY) 487 Hudson St, New York, NY 10014

REYNOLDS, Bob (Cal) 6832 Treeridge Dr, Cincinnati, OH 45244

REYNOLDS JR, Edward Charles (Mich) 2112 Melrose Road, Ann Arbor, MI 48104

REYNOLDS, Eleanor Francis (Nwk) PO Box 240, Mendham, NJ 07945

REYNOLDS, Fred (Roch) 579 Sagamore Ave Unit 84, Portsmouth, NH 03801

REYNOLDS, Gail Ann (Kan) 9119 Dearborn St, Overland Park, KS 66207

REYNOLDS, James Ronald (FtW) 3717 Cook Ct, Fort Worth, TX 76244

REYNOLDS, Joe D (Tex) 145 15th St NE Apt 1006, Atlanta, GA 30309

REYNOLDS, Katharine Sylvia (Minn) Loring Green East, 1201 Yale Place #610, Minneapolis, MN 55403

REYNOLDS, Kay (ETenn) 4017 Sherry Dr, Knoxville, TN 37918

REYNOLDS, Max Midgley (WTex) 4485 Medina Hwy, Kerrville, TX 78028

REYNOLDS, Richard Seaver (Mont) 4530 Asa Trl, Stevensville, MT 59870

REYNOLDS, James (Ore) 18271 SW Ewen Dr, Aloha, OR 97003

REYNOLDS, Sarah Anne (Los) 9415 Culver Blvd Ste 9, Culver City, CA 90232

REYNOLDS JR, Wallace Averal (CFla) 500 W Stuart St, Bartow, FL 33830

REZACH, Karen Beverly (Nwk) 74 Edgewood Pl, Maywood, NJ 07607

REZIN, Mary Ellen (Eau) 27042 State Highway 21, Tomah, WI 54660

RHEA, Pamela Towery (Miss) 318 College St, Columbus, MS 39701

RHEA, Robert E (Tenn) 1401 Lee Victory Pkwy, Smyrna, TN 37167

RHOADES, Mary Ann (Chi) PO Box 494, Dixon, IL 61021

RHOADES, Stephen James (USC) Saint James Episcopal Church, 301 Piney Mountain Rd, Greenville, SC 29609

RHOADS, Bob (Oly) 181 W Maple St, Sequim, WA 98382

RHOADS, Tommy L (WTenn) 309 E Baltimore St, Jackson, TN 38301

RHODENHISER, Imogen Leigh (Mich) 410 Church Rd, Bloomfield Hills, MI 48304

RHODENHISER, James Cousins (Mich) St. Clare of Assisi Episcopal Church, 2309 Packard Road, Ann Arbor, MI 48104

RHODES, Charlotte Dimmick (CFla) 414 Pine St, Titusville, FL 32796

RHODES, David Hughes (Ct) 47535 Highway 74, Palm Desert, CA 92260

RHODES, Diane Lynn (Nwk) 38 Lynn St, Harrington Park, NJ 07940

RHODES, Judith Louise (Ct) 661 Old Post Rd, Fairfield, CT 06824

RHODES, Margaret Diana Clark (WMo) 1815 NE Independence Ave, Lees Summit, MO 64086

RHODES, Matthew W (Va) PO Box 153, Millwood, VA 22646

RHODES, Robert Richard (Oly) 9 Harrington Ave., Westwood, NJ 07675

RHODES, Robert Wayne (Oly) 300 W 8th Street Unit 314, Vancouver, WA 98660

RHYNE, Patty (NC) Christ Church, 1412 Providence Rd, Charlotte, NC 28207

RICE, Arianne V (Md) 1405 Boyce Ave, Towson, MD 21204

✠ **RICE**, David C (Episcopal SJ) Diocese Of San Joaquin, 1528 Oakdale Rd, Modesto, CA 95355

RICE, Debra Harsh (WNC) PO Box 2319, Franklin, NC 28744

RICE, Doreen Ann (Kan)

RICE, Edward G (NH) 37 Harbor Way Unit 13, Wolfeboro, NH 03894

RICE, Glenda Ann (Ak) PO Box 1130, Sitka, AK 99835

RICE, John David Sayre (WNC) 51 North View Circle, Hayesville, NC 28904

RICE JR, John Fay (Va) 240 Old Main St, South Yarmouth, MA 02664

RICE, Lawrence Allen (NMich) 5526 S Baker Side Rd, Sault Sainte Marie, MI 49783

RICE, Randolf James (ECR) 2534 Dumbarton Ave, San Jose, CA 95124-717

RICE, Rodney Vincent (NY) 914 Adana Road, Pikesville, MD 21208

RICE, Sandra Kay (Md) Retired, Frederick, MD 21701

RICE, Steven C (NC) 2575 Parkway Dr, Winston Salem, NC 27103

RICE, Whitney (Ind) St. David's Episcopal Church, P.O. Box 1798, Nashville, IN 47448

RICE, Winston Edward (La) 512 E Boston St, Covington, LA 70433

RICH, Bill (Mass) 333 Ricciuti Drive Unit 1526, Quincy, MA 02169

RICH III, Edward Robins (SwFla) 11315 Linbanks Pl, Tampa, FL 33617

RICH, Michael Glenn (Ala) 408 Church Ave SE, Jacksonville, AL 36265

RICH, Nancy Willis (O) 5650 Grace Woods Dr Unit 203, Willoughby, OH 44094

RICH, Noel David (Minn) 808 Eldo Ln SW, Alexandria, MN 56308

RICH, Sue (EMich) Grace Episcopal Church, 735 W. Nepessing, Lapeer, MI 48446

RICH, Tim (RI) St Luke's Episc Ch, 99 Pierce St, East Greenwich, RI 02818

RICHARD, Helen Taylor (Ore) 123 Grove St, Lebanon, OR 97355

RICHARD, Mary B (WLa) PO Box 1627, Shreveport, LA 71165

RICHARDS, Anne Marie (RI) 7 Cowsill Ln, Newport, RI 02840

RICHARDS, Daniel P (Az) 1031 E Sahuaro Dr, Phoenix, AZ 85020

RICHARDS, Dennison Sherman (LI) 107-66 Merrick Blvd, Jamaica, NY 11433

RICHARDS, Edward Thomas (CGC) PO Box 7359, Panama City Beach, FL 32413

RICHARDS, Emily Barr (Pa) 654 N Easton Rd, Glenside, PA 19038

RICHARDS, Erin Kathleen (ND) 301 Main St S, Minot, ND 58701

RICHARDS, Fitzroy Ivan (Oly) 12499 Eagle Dr, Burlington, WA 98233

RICHARDS, Gerald Wayne (Be) 265 Old Mine Rd, Lebanon, PA 17042

RICHARDS, Jeffery Martin (O) 2510 Olentangy Dr, Akron, OH 44333

RICHARDS, Michael Gregory (Los) PO Box 220383, Newhall, CA 91322

RICHARDS, Rosalie (Ct) 536 Old Glen Avenue, Berlin, NH 03570

RICHARDS, Susan M (Pa) 1074 BROADMOOR RD, BRYN MAWR, PA 19010

RICHARDS, Tyler Clayton (EMich) 324 Hickory Knl, Birmingham, AL 35226

RICHARDSON, Carolyn Garrett (SanD) 3515 Lomas Serenas Dr., Escondido, CA 92029

RICHARDSON, Christopher C (SO) 2151 Dorset Rd., Columbus, OH 43221

RICHARDSON, David Anthony (Az) 3111 Silver Saddle Dr, Lake Havasu City, AZ 86406

RICHARDSON, Ellen H (EC) 311 10th St W, Tifton, GA 31794

RICHARDSON JR, Grady Wade (Ala) 605 Country Club Dr, Gadsden, AL 35901

RICHARDSON, Janet Beverly (Ind) 310 Del Mar Dr, Lady Lake, FL 32159

RICHARDSON, Jeffrey Roy (SC)

RICHARDSON, Jim (The Episcopal NCal) 1700 University Ave, Charlottesville, VA 22903

RICHARDSON JR, John Dowland (CGC) 19 Gaywood Circle, Birmingham, AL 35213

RICHARDSON, John Marshall (WMo) 23405 S Waverly Rd, Spring Hill, KS 66083

RICHARDSON, Jon (Nwk) 3820 the Oak Rd, Philadelphia, PA 19129

RICHARDSON, Marcia Ann Kelley (Me) 6 Jewett Cove Rd, Westport Is, ME 04578

RICHARDSON, Mark Stanton (Fla)

RICHARDSON, Mary M (Cal) 5833 College Ave, San Diego, CA 92120

RICHARDSON, Michael Wm (Colo) 16181 Parkside Dr, Parker, CO 80134

RICHARDSON, Susan (Pa) 20 N American St, Philadelphia, PA 19106

RICHARDSON, W Mark (Cal) Church Divinity School of the Pacific, 2451 Ridge Rd, Berkeley, CA 94709

RICHAUD III, Reynold Hobson (Tenn) P.O. Box 808, Townsend, TN 37882

RICHEY, Donald Delose (Ct) 99 Willowbrook Rd, Cromwell, CT 06416

RICHEY, Leon Eugene (O) 2727 Barrington Dr, Toledo, OH 43606

RICHMOND III, Allen Pierce (Ak) 2602 Glacier St, Anchorage, AK 99508

RICHMOND, John David (Spr) 4105 S Lafayette Ave, Bartonville, IL 61607

RICHMOND, Seth Gunther (Colo) 460 Prospector Ln, Estes Park, CO 80517

RICHMOND, Susan (Mass) 197 8th St Apt 801, Charlestown, MA 02129

RICHNOW, Douglas Wayne (Tex) 4014 Meadow Lake Ln, Houston, TX 77027

RICHTER, Amy Elizabeth (Md) St. Anne's Episcopal Church, 199 Duke of Gloucester St, Annapolis, MD 21401

RICHTER, Kerlin J (Ore) 399A Himrod St, Brooklyn, NY 11237

RICHTER JR, William Thompson (Tex) 2929 Woodland Hills Dr, Kingwood, TX 77339

RICK II, John William (Ct) 625 S St Andrews Pl, Los Angeles, CA 90005

RICKARDS JR, Joseph Asher (Ind) Spring Mills, 109 Jamestown Dr, Falling Waters, WV 25419

RICKARDS, Reese Stanley (Eas) 115 Nentego Dr, Fruitland, MD 21826

✠ **RICKEL**, Gregory Harold (Oly) 3209 42nd Ave SW, Seattle, WA 98116

RICKENBAKER, James Robert (Va) PO Box 275, Stafford, VA 22555

RICKENBAKER, Rachel Amelia (Va) PO Box 127, Upperville, VA 20185

RICKENBAKER, Thomas (EC) Box 548, Edenton, NC 27932

RICKER, Linda Seay (SVa)

RICKER, Mark (Colo) St Andrews Episcopal Church, PO Box 427, Ashland, WI 54806

RICKERT, David (The Episcopal NCal)

RICKETTS, Linda (Mass) 12607 Cascade Hls, San Antonio, TX 78253

RICKETTS, Marcia Carole Couey (NwT) 133 Olivias Ct, Tuscola, TX 79562

RICKETTS, Nancy Lee (Tex) 1500 N Capital of Texas Hwy, Austin, TX 78746

RICKEY, David (Cal) 430 29th Ave, San Francisco, CA 94131

RICO, Bayani Depra (The Episcopal NCal) 2420 Tuolumne St, Vallejo, CA 94589

RIDDICK, Daniel Howison (SwVa) 240 Blackwater Ridge Ln, Glade Hill, VA 24092

RIDDLE III, Charles Morton (SVa) 1102 Botetourt Gdns Apt B-5, Norfolk, VA 23507

RIDDLE, Jennifer Lynne (Ala) 530 Hurst Rd, Odenville, AL 35120

RIDEOUT, Robert Blanchard (SO) 7121 Muirfield Dr., Dublin, OH 43017

RIDER, David M (NY) 424 W End Ave Apt 9c, New York, NY 10024

RIDER, Joe (CFla) 400 18th St, E 4, Vero Beach, FL 32960

RIDER, Paul G (Minn) 401 S 1st St Unit 610, Minneapolis, MN 55401

RIDER, Wm Blake (Tex) Diocese of Texas, 1225 Texas St, Houston, TX 77002

RIDGE, Charles Searls (Oly) 2658 48th Ave SW, Seattle, WA 98116

RIDGWAY, Michael Wyndham (ECR) 365 Stowell Ave, Sunnyvale, CA 94085

RIEBE, Norman W (SanD) 5633 Chalyce Ln, Charlotte, NC 28270

RIEGEL, Robert Gambrell (USC) 1100 Sumter St, Columbia, SC 29201

RIEGER, Pamela Ann (SanD)

RIERDAN, Pastor Jill (WMass) 128 Main St, Easthampton, MA 01027

RIETH, Sarah Melissa (NC) 500 East Rhode Island Avenue, Southern Pines, NC 28387

RIETMANN, Paul David (Oly) 3615 N Gove St, Tacoma, WA 98407

RIFFEE, Charles Alexander (Va) 1205 W Franklin St, Richmond, VA 23220

RIGGALL, Daniel John (Me) Po Box 165, Kennebunk, ME 04043

RIGGALL, George Gordon (CGC) 3811 Old Shell Rd., Mobile, AL 36608

RIGGIN, Jean Monroe Porter (NC)

RIGGIN, John Harris (CGC) 4051 Old Shell Rd, Mobile, AL 36608

RIGGINS, Patricia Readon (WTex) 1310 Pecan Valley Dr, San Antonio, TX 78210

RIGGLE JR, John Field (SwFla) 9267 Sun Isle Dr Ne, Saint Petersburg, FL 33702

RIGHTMYER, Tom (WNC) 16 Salisbury Dr 7304, Asheville, NC 28803

RIIS, Susan (SO) 144884 Harbor Dr E, Thornville, OH 43076

RIKER JR, William Chandler (Nwk) 249 Hartshorne Rd, Locust, NJ 07760

RILEY, Clay (SD) 1333 Jamestown Rd, Williamsburg, VA 23185

RILEY, Diane Napolitano (Nwk)

RILEY, Elizabeth R (Oly)

RILEY, George Daniel (NY) 39 Minnesota Ave, Long Beach, NY 11561

RILEY, Gregg Les (WLa) 3203 Claiborne Cir, Monroe, LA 71201

RILEY JR, James Foster (Minn) 132 Maj Hornbrook Road, Christchurch, Canterbury, New Zealand (Aotearoa)

RILEY, Linda (Ak)

RILEY, Mark D (SVa) 3928 Pacific Ave, Virginia Beach, VA 23451

RILEY, Reese Milton (Los) 1414 East Grovemont, Santa Ana, CA 92705

RIMASSA, Paul Stephen (NJ) 215 Briner Ln, Hamilton Square, NJ 08690

RIMER, Kathleen Pakos (Mass) 330 Brookline Ave., Boston, MA 02115

RIMKUS, William Allen (Chi) 14755 Eagle Ridge Dr, Homer Glen, IL 60491

RINCON, Virginia M (Me) 121 Margaret St Apt C, South Portland, ME 04106

RINEHART, Jim (Be) 108 Arbor Dr, Myerstown, PA 17067

RINES, Charles Tedford (The Episcopal NCal) 3641 Mari Dr, Lake Elsinore, CA 92530

RING, Anthony Richard (Eau) W10601 Pine Rd, Thorp, WI 54771

RING, Bonnie (Cal) 2011 Carlos Street, Moss Beach, CA 94038

RINGLAND, Robin Lynn (Oly) 415 S 18th St, Mount Vernon, WA 98274

RINGLE, Lorena May (Pgh) Christ Episcopal Church, 5910 Babcock Blvd, Pittsburg, PA 15237

RIOS, Austin Keith (Eur) Diocese of Western North Carolina, 900-B Centre Park Dr., Asheville, NC 28805

RIOS, Lajunta Michelle (Tex) Trinity Episcopal Church, 5010 N Main St, Baytown, TX 77521

RISARD, Frederick William (Episcopal SJ) 1541 Bristol Ln, Hanford, CA 93230

RISK III, Jay (Chi) 901 N Delphia Ave, Park Ridge, IL 60068

RITCHIE, Anne Gavin (Va) 1002 Janney's Lane, Alexandria, VA 22302

RITCHIE, Harold (Fla) 12013 SW 1st St, Micanopy, FL 32667

RITCHIE, Patricia Ritter (Tex) 4090 Delaware St, Beaumont, TX 77706

RITCHIE, Robert Joseph (Pa) 7712 Brous Ave, Philadelphia, PA 19152

RITCHIE, Sandra Lawrence (Pgh) 1808 Kent Rd, Pittsburgh, PA 15241

RITCHINGS, Frances Anne (Pa) 36 E Abington Ave, Philadelphia, PA 19118

RITONIA, Ann (Md) 9120 Frederick Rd, Ellicott City, MD 21042

RITSON, Veronica Merita (Az) 6556 N Villa Manana Dr, Phoenix, AZ 85014

RITTER, Christine (Pa) 1771 Sharpless Rd, Meadowbrook, PA 19046

RITTER, Cynthia Anne (Okla) 1604 S Fir Ave, Broken Arrow, OK 74012

RITTER, Kenneth Phillip (Miss) 20 Belvoir Ave, Chattanooga, TN 37411

RITTER, Nathan (LI) 414 E Broad St, Westfield, NJ 07090

RIVAS, Vidal (WA) Episcopal Church House, Mount Saint Alban, Washington, DC 20016

RIVERA, Aristotle C (Cal) PO Box 101, Brentwood, CA 94513

✠ **RIVERA**, Bavi Edna (Oly) PO Box 1548, The Dalles, OR 97058

RIVERA, Jorge Juan (PR)

RIVERA, Victor M ()

RIVERA-GEORGESCU, Ana Maria (Alb) St. James Episcopal Church, 14216 NYS RT 9N, Au Sable Forks, NY 12912

RIVERA PEREZ, Francisco Javier (PR) PO Box 902, Saint Just, PR 00978

RIVERA-RIVERA, Luis Antonio (NY) 550 W 155th St, New York, NY 10032

RIVERA RIVERA, Luis Guillermo (PR)

RIVERA-RODRIGUEZ, Angel (PR)

RIVEROS MAYORGA, Jose Aristodemus (Colom) c/o Diocese of Colombia, Cra 6 No. 49-85 Piso 2, Bogota, BDC, Colombia

RIVERS, Barbara White Batzer (Pa) 378 Paoli Woods, Paoli, PA 19301

RIVERS, David Buchanan (Pa) 148 Heacock Ln, Wyncote, PA 19095

RIVERS, John (WNC) 55 Wingspread Dr, Black Mountain, NC 28711

RIVERS III, Joseph Tracy (Pa) 2902 Monterey Ct, Springfield, PA 19064

RIVET, E (Colo) 7102 E Briarwood Dr, Centennial, CO 80112

RIVETTI, Mary Beth (Spok) 1436 Pine Cone Rd Apt 3, Moscow, ID 83843

RIVOLTA, Agostino Cetrangolo (NJ) 69 Broad St, Eatontown, NJ 07724

ROACH, Kenneth Merle (Fla) 92 Atari Rd, Waynesville, NC 28786

ROACH, Michelle Mona (CFla)

ROADMAN, Betsy Johns (NY) 91 Mystic Dr, Ossining, NY 10562

ROAF, Phoebe Alison (Va) 2900 Hanes Ave, Richmond, VA 23222

ROANE, Wilson Kessner (FdL) E2382 Pebble Run Rd, Waupaca, WI 54981

ROARK III, Hal (NY) PO Box 350, Granite Springs, NY 10527

ROBAYO HIDALGO, Daniel Dario (NC) 200 W Morgan St Ste 300, Raleigh, NC 27601

ROBB, George Kerry (SeFla) 521 Rhine Rd, Palm Beach Gardens, FL 33410

ROBB, Stephen (Roch)

ROBBINS, Anne Wilson (SO) 10831 Crooked River Rd., #101, Bonita Springs, FL 34135

ROBBINS, Buckley (ETenn) 781 Shearer Cove Rd, Chattanooga, TN 37405

ROBBINS, Charlotte Ann (ND) 3600 25th St. S., Fargo, ND 58104

ROBBINS, Herbert John (RG) 104 East Circle Drive, Ruidoso Downs, NM 88346

ROBBINS, Janice M (ETenn) 3425 Alta Vista Dr, Chattanooga, TN 37411

ROBBINS, Lance (Roch) 1130 Webster Rd, Webster, NY 14580

ROBBINS, Mary Elizabeth (Tex) 562 Elkins lk, Huntsville, TX 77340

ROBBINS-COLE, Adrian (Mass) Saint Andrew's Church, 79 Denton Rd, Wellesley, MA 02482

ROBBINS-COLE, Sarah Jane (Mass) 49 Concord St, Peterborough, NH 03458

ROBBINS-PENNIMAN, Sylvia Beckman (SwFla) Church of the Good Shepherd, 639 Edgewater Dr, Dunedin, FL 34698

ROBERSON, Jason D (SC)

ROBERSON, Mary Moore Mills (USC) 3123 Oakview Rd, Columbia, SC 29204

ROBERT, Mary Christopher (CGC) 551 W Barksdale Dr, Mobile, AL 36606

ROBERTS, Alice (NH) 2 Moore Rd, Newport, NH 03773

ROBERTS, Caleb S (Spr) 208 W University Ave, Champaign, IL 61820

ROBERTS, Charles Jonathan (SwFla) Calvary Episcopal Church, 1615 First St., Indian Rocks Beach, FL 33785

ROBERTS, George C (Ct) Saint James Episcopal Church, 3 Mountain Rd, Farmington, CT 06032

ROBERTS, Harold (Miss) 7417 Falcon Cir., Ocean Springs, MS 39564

ROBERTS, Harvey William (Ky)

ROBERTS III, Henry Pauling (EC) 260 Houser Road, Blacksburg, SC 29702

ROBERTS, James Beauregard (Miss) 2441 S Shore Dr, Biloxi, MS 39532

ROBERTS, J Ames Christopher (Mont) PO BOX 2020, Helena, MT 59624

ROBERTS, Jason Thomas (WTex) 8642 Cheviot Hts, San Antonio, TX 78254

ROBERTS JR, John Bannister Gibson (CFla) 860 Ohlinger Rd, Babson Park, FL 33827

ROBERTS, John Charles (WNC) PO Box 185, Flat Rock, NC 28731

ROBERTS, Jose (RI) 236 Central Ave, Pawtucket, RI 02860

ROBERTS, Judith S (Ind) 342 Red Ash Cir, Englewood, FL 34223

ROBERTS, Katherine Alexander (At) 18 Clarendon Ave, Avondale Estates, GA 30002

ROBERTS, Kim Elaine (Neb) 2312 J St, Omaha, NE 68107

ROBERTS, Leonard (Nwk)

ROBERTS, Linda L (Mont) 16404 72nd St, Plattsmouth, NE 68048

ROBERTS III, Malcolm (EC) 520 Taberna Way, New Bern, NC 28562

ROBERTS, Mollie (Ala) 3702 Mays Bend Rd., Pell City, AL 35128

ROBERTS, Patricia Joyce (Ia) 3226 S Clinton St, Sioux City, IA 51106

ROBERTS, Patricia Kant (CFla) 35 Willow Dr, Orlando, FL 32807

ROBERTS, Paul Benjamin (At) 33 Cross Crk E, Dahlonega, GA 30533

ROBERTS, Peter (CFla) 5500 N Tropical Trl, Merritt Island, FL 32953

ROBERTS, Steven Michael (La) 1613 7th St, New Orleans, LA 70115

ROBERTS, Susan Jean (U) 261 S 900 E, Salt Lake City, UT 84102

ROBERTS, Suzanne Grondin (Me) 143 State St, Portland, ME 04101

ROBERTS, William Bradley (Va) 3737 Seminary Rd, Alexandria, VA 22304

ROBERTS, William D (Chi) 720 Ambria Drive, Mundelein, IL 60060

ROBERTS, William Tudor (Mich) 584 E Walled Lake Dr, Walled Lake, MI 48390

ROBERTSHAW III, Arthur Bentham (Ct) 88 Notch Hill Rd Apt 240, North Branford, CT 06471

ROBERTSHAW, Michelle (SwFla) St Andrew's Episcopal Church, PO Box 272, Boca Grande, FL 33921

ROBERTSON, Amanda Kucik (NC) 2701 Park Rd, Charlotte, NC 28209

ROBERTSON IV, Ben G. (Miss) The Chapel Of The Cross, 674 Mannsdale Rd, Madison, MS 39110

ROBERTSON, Bruce Edward (NMich) 452 Silver Creek Rd, Marquette, MI 49855

ROBERTSON, Charles Kevin (Az) 815 2nd Avenue, New York, NY 10017

ROBERTSON, Claude Richard (Ark) 1605 E Republican Rd, Jacksonville, AR 72076

ROBERTSON JR, Edward Ray (La) 212 Spencer Ave, New Orleans, LA 70124

ROBERTSON, Frederick W (Kan) 626 E Montclaor St Apt 1D, Springfield, MO 65807

ROBERTSON, James Bruce (CPa) 4824 Bell Street, Kansas City, MO 64112

ROBERTSON, John (Minn) 38378 Reservation Highway 101, PO Box 369, Morton, MN 56270

ROBERTSON, John Brown (EC) St Timothy's Epis Church, 107 Louis St, Greenville, NC 27858

ROBERTSON, Josephine (Oly) St John's Kirkland, 105 State St S, Kirkland, WA 98033

ROBERTSON, Karen (Suzi) Sue (FtW) 1757 244th Ave NE, Sammamish, WA 98074

ROBERTSON, Marilyn Sue (Okla) 127 NW 7th St, Oklahoma City, OK 73102

ROBERTSON, Patricia Rome (Oly) 313 Bromley Place NW, Bainbridge Island, WA 98110

ROBESON, Terry Ann (Wyo) 665 Cedar St, Lander, WY 82520

ROBILLARD, Roger Manuel (Va) 400 S Cedar Ave, Highland Springs, VA 23075

ROBINSON, Allen (Md) 2729 Moores Valley Dr, Baltimore, MD 21209

✠ **ROBINSON**, Bishop Gene Gene (NH) Diocese Of New Hampshire, 63 Green St., Washington, DC 20005

ROBINSON, Carla Lynn (Oly) 15220 Main St, Bellevue, WA 98007

ROBINSON, Charles (SVa) 2124 Benomi Dr., Williamsburg, VA 23185

ROBINSON, Charles Edward (U) PO Box 981208, Park City, UT 84098

ROBINSON, Chris (Miss) 113 S 9th St, Oxford, MS 38655

ROBINSON, Constance Diane (Eas) 5820 Haven Ct, Rock Hall, MD 21661

ROBINSON, Cristopher (WTex) 1621 Santa Monica St, Kingsville, TX 78363

ROBINSON, David (Me) Po Box 7554, Ocean Park, ME 04063

ROBINSON JR, David Gordon (NH) 1035 Lafayette Rd, Portsmouth, NH 03801

ROBINSON, David Gordon (Eas) 5820 Haven Ct, Rock Hall, MD 21661

ROBINSON, David Scott (Pa) 603 Misty Hollow Dr, Maple Glen, PA 19002

ROBINSON, Dorothy Linkous (Tex) 7700 Pleasant Meadow Cir, Austin, TX 78731

ROBINSON, Franklin Kenneth (Ct) 305 Golden Ginkgo Lane, Salisbury, MD 21801

ROBINSON, Fredrick Arthur (SwFla) 222 South Palm Avenue, Sarasota, FL 34236

ROBINSON JR, Henry Jefferson (Fla) 314 Glen Ridge Ave, 939 Beach Dr. NE Unit 1502, Temple Terrace, FL 33617

ROBINSON, Janet Rohrbach (Ga) 3565 Bemiss Rd., Valdosta, GA 31605

ROBINSON, Joe (Mass) Po Box 1366, Jackson, MS 39215

ROBINSON, Katherine Sternberg (Wyo) 2350 S Poplar St, Casper, WY 82601

ROBINSON, Linda Gail H Hornbuckle (Ala) 6324 Woodlake Dr., Buford, GA 30518

ROBINSON, Mark (Ct) 82 Shore Rd, Old Lyme, CT 06371

ROBINSON, Michael Eric (Mass) 171 Goddard Ave, Brookline, MA 02445

ROBINSON, Michael Kevin (Ark) 305 Pointer Trl W, Van Buren, AR 72956

ROBINSON, Paula (Mo) 123 S 9th St, Columbia, MO 65201

ROBINSON, Sonja Douglas (EC) 1009 Midland Dr, Wilmington, NC 28412

ROBINSON JR, Virgil Austin Anderson (Chi) 1527 Chapel Ct, Northbrook, IL 60062

ROBINSON-COMO, Glenice (Tex) 1117 Texas St, Houston, TX 77002

ROBISON, Bruce Monroe (Pgh) 5801 Hampton Street, Pittsburgh, PA 15206

ROBISON, Jeannie (Ala) Church of the Nativity, 208 Eustis Ave SE, Huntsville, AL 35801

ROBISON, Ronald Livingston (CFla) 331 Lake Avenue, Maitland, FL 32751

ROBISON, Sandra L(ee) (Spok) 1407 Thayer Dr, Richland, WA 99354

ROBLES, Daniel (DR (DomRep)) 651 Broadway, Gilroy, CA 95020

ROBSON, David (CPa) 2985 Raintree Rd, York, PA 17404

ROCCOBERTON, Marjorie Ruth Smith (Ct) 82 Shoddy Mill Rd, Bolton, CT 06043

ROCK, Ian Eleazar (VI) St. George's Episcopal (Anglican) Church, 170 Main Street, Road Town, Miami, VI 00801, British Virgin Islands

ROCK, Jean-Baptiste Kenol (NY) 3061 Bainbridge Ave, Bronx, NY 10467

ROCK, J Konrad (WK) 706 E 74th Ave, Hutchinson, KS 67502

ROCK, John Sloane (Minn) PO BOX 1178, Bemidji, MN 56619

ROCKHILL, Cara M (RI)

ROCKMAN, Jane Linda (NJ) 559 Park Ave, Scotch Plains, NJ 07076

ROCKWELL, Cristine Van Kirk (WMass) 51 Perkins St, Springfield, MA 01118

✠ **ROCKWELL**, Hays H. (Mo) Po Box 728, West Kingston, RI 02892

ROCKWELL, Melody Neustrom (Ia) 220 40th St NE, Cedar Rapids, IA 52402

ROCKWELL, Raymond Eugene (Alb)

ROCKWELL III, Reuben L (CGC) 4051 Old Shell Road, Mobile, AL 36608

ROCKWELL, Sarah (NH) 10 Pond Rd, Derry, NH 03038

ROCKWOOD, David Alan (Ak) Po Box 23003, Ketchikan, AK 99901

RODDY, Bonnie Joia (Ore) 266 4th Ave, #601, Salt Lake City, UT 84103

RODDY, Jack Edward (Ore) 266 4th Ave. Apt 601, Salt Lake City, UT 84103

RODENBECK, Benjamin Daniel (Az) Trinity Episcopal Church, PO Box 590, Kingman, AZ 86402

RODGERS, Billy Wilson (CFla) 13465 SE 93rd Court Rd, Summerfield, FL 34491

RODGERS, James Devin (SO) St. Gregory of Nyssa, 500 De Haro St, San Francisco, CA 94107

RODGERS, Paul Benjamin (Mass) 359 Elm St, Dartmouth, MA 02748

RODGERS, Peter R (Ct) 400 Humphrey St, New Haven, CT 06511

RODGERS, Robert Christopher (Dal) 5023 Lindale Dr, Wichita Falls, TX 76310

RODGERS, Stephen M (NY) 14160 SW Teal Blvd. 32 B, Beaverton, OR 97008

RODIN, Carol Jane Strandoo (Oly) Christ Episcopal Church, 1216 7th St, Anacortes, WA 98221

RODMAN, Edward Willis (Mass) 8 Yorks Rd, Framingham, MA 01701

RODMAN, Janet Laura (EC) 218 Fairway Drive, Washington, DC 27889

RODMAN, Reginald Cary (Ore) 10434 Brackenwood Ln NE, Bainbridge Island, WA 98110

RODMAN III, Samuel (NC) 112 Randolph Ave, Milton, MA 02186

RODRIGUEZ, Al (Tex) 2503 Ware Rd, Austin, TX 78741

RODRIGUEZ, Christopher Michael (CFla) 2365 Pine Ave, Vero Beach, FL 32960

RODRIGUEZ, Gladys (CFla) 1601 Alafaya Trl, Oviedo, FL 32765

RODRIGUEZ, Hector Raul (Md) 6960 Sunfleck Row, Columbia, MD 21045

RODRIGUEZ, Isa?as (At) 3004 Mccull Dr NE, Atlanta, GA 30345

RODRIGUEZ, Luis Mario (Episcopal SJ) 5286 Kalanianaole Hwy, Honolulu, HI 96821

RODRIGUEZ JR, Pedro Luis (NY)

RODRIGUEZ, Ramiro (Los) 7540 Passons Blvd, Pico Rivera, CA 90660

RODRIGUEZ ESPINEL, Neptali (Minn) 1524 Summit Ave, Saint Paul, MN 55105

RODRIGUEZ-HOBBS, Joshua (Md) Episcopal Church of the Good Shepherd, 1401 Carrollton Ave, Ruxton, MD 21204

RODRIGUEZ-PADRON, Francisco (LI) 418 50th St, Brooklyn, NY 11220

RODRIGUEZ SANCHEZ, Mario Hiram (PR) 1308 Ave Paz Granela, San Juan, PR 00921

RODRIGUEZ-SANJURJO, Jose (CFla) Church of the Incarnation, 1601 Alafaya Trl, Oviedo, FL 32765

RODRIGUEZ-SANTOS, Carlos (Hond)

RODRIGUEZ-SANTOS, Toribio (NJ) 38 W End Pl, Elizabeth, NJ 07202

RODRIGUEZ TOUCET, Maritza (PR)

RODRIGUEZ VALLECILLO, Digna Suyapa (Hond) Barrio Zaragoza, Calle De La Shell, Siguatepeque, Honduras

RODRIGUEZ-YEJO, Ruben (Del) 1005 Pleasant St, Wilmington, DE 19805

ROECK, Gretchen Elizabeth (Minn) 5330 Oliver Ave South, Minneapolis, MN 55419

ROEGER JR, William Donald (Mo) 419 N 6th St, Hannibal, MO 63401

ROEHL, Cynthia Ann (SwFla) 639 Edgewater Dr, Dunedin, FL 34698

ROEHNER, Rodney (CFla) 6249 Canal Blvd, New Orleans, LA 70124

ROESCHLAUB, Robert Friedrich (Ind) 20 Pannatt Hill, Millom, Cumbria, LA18 5DB, Great Britain (UK)

ROESKE, Michael Jerome (Mass) 35 Bowdoin St, Boston, MA 02114

ROFF, Lucinda Lee (Ala) 812 5th Ave, Tuscaloosa, AL 35401

ROFINOT, Laurie Ann (Mass) 88 Lexington Ave # 2, Somerville, MA 02144

ROGERS, Annis Humphries (Pgh) 335 Locust St, Johnstown, PA 15901

ROGERS, Diana (Ct) 20 Shepherd Ln, Orange, CT 06477

ROGERS, Douglas K (Chi) 412 N Church St, Rockford, IL 61103

ROGERS III, George M (Alb) 325 East 80th Street, 1D, New York, NY 10021

ROGERS, Henry Stanley Fraser (Oly) 4770 116th Ave Se, Bellevue, WA 98006

ROGERS JR, Jack A (WTenn) 2185 Aztec Dr, Dyersburg, TN 38024

ROGERS, James Arthur (FtW) 4302 Wynnwood Dr, Wichita Falls, TX 76308

ROGERS, James Luther (Tenn) 935 Mount Olivet Rd, Columbia, TN 38401

ROGERS JR, John (Ct) 69 Butternut Ln, Rocky Hill, CT 06067

ROGERS, John Sanborn (RI) 106 Osprey Dr, Saint Marys, GA 31558

ROGERS, Joy Edith Stevenson (Chi) 65 E. Huron, Chicago, IL 60611

ROGERS, Larry Samuel (Okla) 1310 N Sioux Ave, Claremore, OK 74017

ROGERS, Linda Franks (SVa) 66 Market St, Onancock, VA 23417

ROGERS, Marcus Brayton (Ct) 5601 County Route 30, Granville, NY 12832

ROGERS, Martha C (Ia) 235 Partridge Ave, Marion, IA 52302

ROGERS, Matthew Arnold (Md) 3100 Monkton Rd, Monkton, MD 21111

ROGERS, Norma Jean (Az) PO Box 4567, Tubac, AZ 85646

ROGERS, Page (Ct) 99 Lee Farm Dr, Niantic, CT 06357

ROGERS, Robert Gerald (La) Po Box 233, Clinton, LA 70722

ROGERS III, Sampson (FtW) 828-28 Avenue North #4, Menomonie, WI 54751

ROGERS III, Thomas Sherman (Chi) 1653 West Congress Parkway, Chicago, IL 60612

ROGERS, Tim (Mass) 2920 NE 8th Ter, Apt 101, Wilton Manors, FL 33334

ROGERS, Victor (Ct) 111 Whalley Ave, New Haven, CT 06511

ROGERS, William Burns (Tenn) 510 W Main St, Franklin, TN 37064

ROGERSON, George William (Ia) 11536 Wild Rose Dr, West Burlington, IA 52655

ROGGE, Joel Jay (WA) PO Box 1396, 27 Smith St, Marblehead, MA 01945

ROGINA, Julius M (Nev) 1080 Del Webb Pkwy West, Reno, NV 89523

ROGNAS, Alice Anita (Mont) 713 8th St, Lewiston, ID 83501

ROHDE, John W (CNY)

ROHDE, Kay M. (NAM) 1326 East A St., Casper, WY 82601

ROHLEDER, Catherine Christine (Kan)

ROHMAN, Suzannah (Ct) St. Paul's Episcopal Church, 145 Main St., Southington, CT 06489

ROHRBACH, Marissa S (Ct) St. Andrew's Episcopal Church, 20 Catlin St, Meriden, CT 06450

ROHRER, Glenn E (CGC) 5636 Firestone Dr, Pace, FL 32571

ROHRER, Jane Carolyn (Oly) Episcopal Church Of The Holy Cross, 11526 162nd Ave NE, Redmond, WA 98052

ROHRS, John D (SVa)

ROJAS-ARROYO, Padre Sergio (PR)

ROJAS POVEDA, Jesus A (EC) 737 Delma Grimes Rd, Coats, NC 27521

ROLAND, Carla (NY) Church of St Matthew & St Timothy, 26 W 84th St, New York, NY 10024

ROLDAN, Roman D (La) 11621 Ferdinand St, Saint Francisville, LA 70775

ROLES, ELIZABETH J (Az) 175 9th Ave # 123, New York, NY 10011

ROLFE-BOUTWELL, Suzan Jane (Mass) 7588 N Meredith Blvd, Tucson, AZ 85741

ROLLE, Denrick Ephriam (SeFla)

ROLLE, Yolanda Antoinette (WA)

ROLLINS, Andrew Sloan (La) 640 Carriage Way, Baton Rouge, LA 70808

ROLLINS, Belle Frances (WLa) 1001 Berry St, Pineville, LA 71360

ROLLINS, Everette Wayne (SO) 10 Alton St., Portland, ME 04103

ROLLINS, John August (Nwk) 11 Fine Road, High Bridge, NJ 08829

ROLLINSON, John Thomas (RG) 1120 Gidding St, Clovis, NM 88101

ROMACK, Gay Harpster (Az) 609 N Old Litchfield Rd, Litchfield Park, AZ 85340

ROMANIK, David F (Pa) 230 Pennswood Rd, Bryn Mawr, PA 19010

ROMANS, Nicholas J (Chi) 514 S Mountain Road, Mesa, AZ 85208

ROMER, William Miller (NH) 128 Audubon Dr, Acton, MA 01720

ROMERIL, Gwendolyn Jane (Be) 26 W Market St, Bethlehem, PA 18018

✠ **ROMERO**, Sylvestre Donato (NJ) 808 W State St, Trenton, NJ 08618-5326, Guatemala

ROMERO-GUEVARA, Antonio N (EcuC) Dias De La Madrid 943, Quito, Ecuador

ROMERO MARTE, Francisco Alfredo (DR (DomRep))

ROMO-GARCIA, Gerardo (Los) 4 Indian Wells Hwy, P, O, Box 139, Amagansett, NY 11930

RONALDI, Lynn P (Miss) Episcopal Church Of The Advent, PO Box 366, Sumner, MS 38957

RONDEAU, Daniel James (SanD) 44910 Calle Placido, La Quinta, CA 92253

RONKOWITZ, George (SeFla) 8310 SW 60th Ave, South Miami, FL 33143

RONN, Denise Marie (Ga) 2600 Rolling Hill Dr, Valdosta, GA 31602

RONTANI, Aidan M (The Episcopal NCal)

RONTANI JR, William (The Episcopal NCal) 104 Main St., Wheatland, CA 95692

ROOD JR, Peter (Los) 702 W Alegria Ave, Sierra Madre, CA 91024

ROOS, Carl A (Ind) 6920 Mohawk Ln, Indianapolis, IN 46260

ROOS, Michelle Kate (Ind) 720 Dr. Martin Luther King Jr St., Indianapolis, IN 46202

ROOS, Richard John (Ind) 2033 Paradise Oaks Ct, Atlantic Beach, FL 32233

ROOSEVELT, Nancy (O) 17100 Van Aken Blvd, Shaker Heights, OH 44120

ROOSEVELT, Nick (Ga)

ROOT, Diane Eleanor (Vt) 2 Jones Avenue, West Lebanon, NH 03784

ROPER, Charles Murray (At) 128 River Ridge Ln, Roswell, GA 30075

ROPER, Jeffrey Howard (Kan) 3750 E Douglas Ave, Wichita, KS 67208

ROPER, John Dee (Kan) 14802 E Willowbend Cir, Wichita, KS 67230

ROPER, Terence Chaus (Pa) 1815 John F Kennedy Blvd, Philadelphia, PA 19103

ROQUE, Christopher Collin (WTex) 3500 N 10th St, Mcallen, TX 78501

RORKE, Stephen Ernest (Roch) 6727 Royal Thomas Way, Alexandria, VA 22315

ROS, Salvador Patrick (NJ)

ROSA, Thomas Phillip (Chi) 121 W Macomb St, Belvidere, IL 61008

ROSADA, Miguel Andres (Fla)

ROSANAS, Louis Toussaint (Hai) Box 1309, Port-Au-Prince, Haiti

ROSARIO-CRUZ, Eliacin (Oly) 111 NE 80th St, Seattle, WA 98115

ROSARIO DE LA CRUZ, Juan Antonio (Nwk) 3901 Park Ave, Union City, NJ 07087

ROSE, Ann W (Ore) 7 Saint Johns Rd Apt 30, Cambridge, MA 02138

ROSE, Carol Benson (EO) 2133 N Cajeme Ave, Casa Grande, AZ 85222

ROSE, Christopher Lee (Ct) 30 Woodland Street Unit 10NP, Hartford, CT 06106

ROSE, David D (SwVa) 210 4th St., Radford, VA 24141

ROSE, David Jonathan (Ga) St. Anne's Episcopal Church, PO Box 889, Tifton, GA 31793

ROSE, Josie Rodriguez (NwT) 5539 7th Ave N, Saint Petersburg, FL 33710

ROSE, Joy Ann (Nwk) Saint Mary's Episcopal Church, 216 Orange Ave, Daytona Beach, FL 32114

ROSE, Leland Gerald (WNY) 602 Crescent Ave, East Aurora, NY 14052

ROSE, L(oran) A(nson) Paul (WA) 6101 Edsall Rd Apt 508, Alexandria, VA 22304

ROSE, Margaret Rollins (NY) 531 E 72nd St Apt 3c, New York, NY 10021

ROSE, Philip John (Minn) 7708 Upton Ave S, Minneapolis, MN 55423

ROSE, William Harrison (SC) 20 Riverview Dr, Beaufort, SC 29907

ROSE-CROSSLEY, Ramona (Vt) 327 University Ave, Sewanee, TN 37375

ROSE-CROSSLEY, Remington (Vt)

ROSEN, Carolyn (Mont) 119 N 33rd St, Billings, MT 59101

ROSEN, Elisabeth Payne (Cal) P O Box 1306, Ross, CA 94957

ROSENBAUM, Richard Lemoine (Okla) 9804 Cisler Lane, Manassas, VA 20111

ROSENBERG, Elma Joy Van Fossen (SwFla) 125 56th Ave S Apt 314, Saint Petersburg, FL 33705

ROSENBLUM, Nancy Jo (Alb) 22 Buckingham Dr, Albany, NY 12208

ROSENDAHL, Mary (CFla) 1043 Genesee Avenue, Sebastian, FL 32958

ROSENDALE, Mary (WMass)

ROSENGREN, Linda W (Fla) 5054 Ripple Rush Dr N, Jacksonville, FL 32257

ROSENZWEIG, Edward Charles (Md) 83 Harriman Point Road, Brooklin, ME 04616

ROSERO-NORDALM, Ema (Mass) St Stephen's Episcopal Church, 419 Shawmut Ave, Boston, MA 02118

ROSHEUVEL, Terrence Winst (NJ) 25 Sunset Ave E, Red Bank, NJ 07701

✠ **ROSKAM**, Catherine Scimeca (NY) 15502 Friar St, Van Nuys, CA 91411

ROSOLEN, Emil J (SeFla) 100 Ne Mizner Blvd # 1503, Boca Raton, FL 33432

ROSOLOWSKI, Robert (Eau)

ROSS, Anne M (NY) 88 Ridge Rd, Valley Cottage, NY 10989

ROSS, Cleon (SVa) 196 Homeport Ln, Danville, VA 24540

ROSS, David Jeffrey (Cal) Po Box 774, Pinole, CA 94564

ROSS, Donna Baldwin (ECR) 3291 Pickwick Ln, Cambria, CA 93428

ROSS, Ellen Marie (Neb) 106 Robin Rd, Council Bluffs, IA 51503

ROSS, George Crawford Lauren (Cal) 19815 Windwood Dr, Woodbridge, CA 95258

ROSS, George Mark (Minn) Po Box 1231, Cass Lake, MN 56633

ROSS, Jeffrey Austin (Del) 213 W Third St, Lewes, DE 19958

ROSS, John C (ETenn) 413 Cumberland Ave, Knoxville, TN 37902

ROSS, Johnnie (Roch) 250 Danbury Cir S, Rochester, NY 14618

ROSS, Nancy J (Oly) 1245 10th Ave E, Seattle, WA 98102

ROSS, Patricia Lynn (Cal) 215 10th Ave, San Francisco, CA 94118

ROSS, Robert (Ct) 91 Miry Brook Rd, Danbury, CT 06810

ROSS, Robert Layne (Ala) 2636 River Grand Cir, Vestavia, AL 35243

ROSS, Rowena Jane (RG)

ROSS, Sue (Dal) 2679 Orchid Dr, Richardson, TX 75082

ROSSER SR, James Bernard (At) 2703 Sanibel Ln Se, Smyrna, GA 30082

ROSS-HUNT, Lindsay S (Ore)

ROSSI, Anna Elaine (Cal)

ROSSI, Kim Elizabeth (WNY) St Stephen's Episcopal Church, PO Box 446, Olean, NY 14760

ROTCHFORD, Lisa Marie (Los) 24352 Via Santa Clara, Mission Viejo, CA 92692

ROTH, Frank Alwin (Ala) 2310 Skyland Blvd E, Tuscaloosa, AL 35405

ROTH, Marilyn Lee (EO) 1805 Minnesota St, The Dalles, OR 97058

ROTH, Nancy Leone (O) 330 Morgan St, Oberlin, OH 44074

ROTH JR, Ralph Carl (Be) Phoebe Berks Village, 9 Reading Dr Apt 242, Wernersville, PA 19565

ROTHAUGE, Arlin John (Ore) 197 Lighthouse Ln, Friday Harbor, WA 98250

ROTTGERS, Steven Robert (WMo) 3521 NW Winding Woods Drive, Lees Summit, MO 64064

ROUFFY, Edward Albert (Colo) 950 SW 21st Ave Apt 402, Portland, OR 97205

ROUMAS, Peisha Geneva (WMo) 913 E 100th Ter, Kansas City, MO 64131

ROUNDS, James Arlen (Wyo) PO Box 1194, Laramie, WY 82073

ROUNDTREE, Ella Louise (NY) 311 Huguenot St, New Rochelle, NY 10801

ROUNDTREE, Philip (Cal) 60 Martinez Ct, Novato, CA 94945

ROUSE, Charles Ernest (The Episcopal NCal)

ROUSER, John Richard (ETenn) 7555 Ooltewah Georgetown Rd, Ooltewah, TN 37363

ROUSSEAU, Sean Kenneth (Va) St Paul's Episcopal Church, 6750 Fayette St, Haymarket, VA 20169

ROUSSELL, Chris (SD) Emmanuel Episcopal Church, 717 Quincy St, Rapid City, SD 57701

ROWAN, Mary Elizabeth (Minn)

ROWE, Deryl Tobias (Ark)

ROWE, Gary (Del) 913 Wilson Road, Wilmington, DE 19803

ROWE, Grayce O'Neill (Az) 1423 E Blue Wash Rd, New River, AZ 85087

ROWE, Jacquelyn (NJ) PO Box 326, Pine Beach, NJ 08741

ROWE, Mary Stone (Mont)

ROWE, Matthew (NwT) Emmanuel Episcopal Church, 3 S Randolph St, San Angelo, TX 76903

ROWE, Michael (SwFla) 9213 Estero River Cir, Estero, FL 33928

ROWE, Randi Hicks (WNY) 9 Cedar St, Lockport, NY 14094

ROWE, Richard (WNC) 64 Oak Gate Dr, Hendersonville, NC 28739

ROWE, Richard Charles (NwPa) 706 Wilhelm Rd, Hermitage, PA 16148

ROWE, Sandra Jeanne (CFla) PO Box 2206, Breckenridge, CO 80424

✠ **ROWE**, Sean (NwPa) 4024 State St, Erie, PA 16508

ROWE-GUIN, Kathy (Va) 5911 Fairview Woods Dr, Fairfax Station, VA 22039

ROWELL, Emily Elizabeth (Va) 526 Fontana Dr, Charlottesville, VA 22911

ROWELL, Melanie Gibson (At)

ROWELL, Rebecca E (Ga) 6329 Frederica Rd, St Simons Island, GA 31522

ROWINS, Charles Howard (Los) 1 Warrenton Rd, Baltimore, MD 21210

ROWLAND, Kenneth George (Ga) 6463 Cobbham Rd, Appling, GA 30802

ROWLAND, Thomas Dayle (RG) St Paul's Episcopal Church, PO Box 949, Truth Or Consequences, NM 87901

ROWLES, Stephen Paul (Va) 9116 Shewsbury Dr, New Kent, VA 23124

ROWLEY, Angela (Ct) Yale New Haven Hospital, 20 York Street, New Haven, CT 06510

✠ **ROWTHORN**, Jeffery William (Ct) 17 Woodland Dr, Salem, CT 06420

ROY, Byron Willard (Roch) 19 Abbotswood Crescent, Penfield, NY 14526

ROY JR, Derik Justin Hurd (Alb) 10 W High St, Ballston Spa, NY 12020

✠ **RUIZ RESTREPO**, Luis Fernando (DR (DomRep)) Carrera 80 #53 A 78, Medellin, Colombia

ROY, Jeffrey A (NJ) 7 Lincoln Ave, Rumson, NJ 07760

ROY, Robert Royden (Minn) 1289 Galtier St, Saint Paul, MN 55117

ROYAL, Dorothy Kaye (Neb) St Mary's Episcopal Church, 116 S 9th St, Nebraska City, NE 68410

ROYALS, Debbie (Az) 7945 N Village Ave, Tucson, AZ 85704

ROYALTY, Beth (Minn) 901 W Emery St, Dalton, GA 30720

ROZENDAAL, Jay Calvin (Oly) 1134 Finnegan Way # 302, Bellingham, WA 98225

ROZENE, Wendy Anne (Me) 17 Fox Run Rd, Cumberland, ME 04021

ROZO, Oscar A (Mil) 409 S 2nd St, Watertown, WI 53094

ROZZELLE, Stephen (Nwk) 400 Ramapo Avenue, Pompton Lakes, NJ 07442

RUBEL, Christopher Scott (Los) 250 N Live Oak Ave, Glendora, CA 91741

RUBIANO-ALVARADO, Raul (CFla) 2851 Afton Cir, Orlando, FL 32825

RUBIN, Richard Louis (Los) 163 W. 11th St., Claremont, CA 91711

RUBINSON, Rhonda Joy (NY) 400 W 119th St Apt 11-L, New York, NY 10027

RUBRIGHT, Elizabeth Alice Shemet (SwFla)

RUBY, Lorne Dale (Pa) 20 N 2nd St, Columbia, PA 17512

RUCKER, James Cliff (Tex) 203 Ivy Terrace St, Lufkin, TX 75901

RUDACILLE, Stephen L (SwFla) 2702 Saint Cloud Oaks Dr, Valrico, FL 33594

RUDE, David B (Nwk) 5 Estate Drive, Wantage, NJ 07461

RUDER, John Williams (Oly) 602 6th St., Castlegar, V1N2G1, Canada

RUDER, Rhonda (Minn)

RUDINOFF, Jan Charles (The Episcopal Church in Haw) 2775 Kanani St, Lihue, HI 96766

RUDOLPH, Patrick Charles (FdL) 1036 Pine Beach Rd, Marinette, WI 54143

RUEDY, Shirley Eloise (SwVa)

RUEHLEN, Petroula Kephala (Tex) 3541 Adrienne Ln, Lake Charles, LA 70605

RUFFIN, Hunter (Az) 8011 Douglas Ave, Dallas, TX 75225

RUFFINO, Russell Gabriel (Eur) Corso Cavour, 110, C.P. #81, Orvieto, 05018, Italy

RUGGABER, Michael Paul (Nev)

RUGGER, Mildred Susan (NwT) St Andrew's Episcopal Church, 1601 S Georgia St, Amarillo, TX 79102

RUGGLES, Roxanne (Lex) Church of the Nativity, 31 E. Third St, PO Box 3, Maysville, KY 41056

RUGH, Nathan (Los) 1227 4th St, Santa Monica, CA 90401

RUHLE, Kay West (CFla)

✠ **RUIZ RESTREPO**, Luis Fernando (DR (DomRep)) Carrera 80 #53 A 78, Medellin, Colombia

RUIZ-RIQUER, Cynthia S (FtW) 5910 Black Oak Ln, River Oaks, TX 76114

RUK, Michael (Pa) 10 Chapel Rd, New Hope, PA 18938

RULE, Alan R (CFla) 216 Orange Ave, Daytona Beach, FL 32114

RULE II, John Henry (Okla) 1122 E 20th St, Tulsa, OK 74120

RUMPLE, John G (Ind) 550 University Blvd # 1410, Indianapolis, IN 46202

RUNDLETT, Brad (Va) St Timothy's Episcopal Church, 432 Van Buren St, Herndon, VA 20170

RUNGE, Phillip Diedrich (Ga) 338 Lakeview Dr, Baxley, GA 31513

RUNGE, Thomas Leonard (Lex) 7 Court Pl, Newport, KY 41071

RUNKLE, John Ander (Tenn) St Mary's Sewanee, 770 St. Mary's Lane, Sewanee, TN 37375

RUNKLE, Robert Scott (Spok) 501 E Wallace Ave, Coeur D Alene, ID 83814

RUNNELS, Stan (WMo) 11 E 40th St, Kansas City, MO 64111

RUNNER, Paul W (NJ) 370 Main St, Wakefield, RI 02879

RUNNING JR, Joseph Martin (EC) 3207 Notting Hill Rd, Fayetteville, NC 28311

RUPP, Lawrence Dean (SO) 13 Balsam Acres, New London, NH 03257

RUPP, Tuesday Jane (Ct) 249 Main St S, Woodbury, CT 06798

RUPPE, David (SO) 25005 SR 26, New Matamoras, OH 45767

RUPPE-MELNYK, Glyn Lorraine (Pa) 689 Sugartown Road, Malvern, PA 19355

RUSCHMEYER, Henry Cassell (NY) 2929 SE Ocean Blvd Apt M9, Stuart, FL 34496

RUSH, Joyce Anne (Minn) 407 NW 7th St, Brainerd, MN 56401

RUSHTON, Joseph (Eas) P O BOX 602, Georgetown, DE 19947

RUSK, Michael Frederick (Eur) 3 rue de Monthoux, Geneva, 01201, Switzerland

RUSLING, Julia G (At) 432 Lockwood Ter., Decatur, GA 30030

RUSS JR, Frank D (SC) 1159 Wyndham Rd, Charleston, SC 29412

RUSSELL, Ann Veronica (VI) Box 3066, Sea Cow's Bay, Tortola, British Virgin Island VG 1110, British Virgin Islands

RUSSELL JR, Carl Asa (Me) 9 Perkins Rd, Boothbay Harbor, ME 04538

RUSSELL, Carlton Thrasher (Mass) 27 Abnaki Way, Stockton Springs, ME 04981

RUSSELL, Jack Dempsey (Tex) 800 E Hudson St, Tyler, TX 75701

RUSSELL, John Alan (WNY) 768 Potomac Ave, Buffalo, NY 14209

RUSSELL, Kathleen Sams (Tex) 1823 Montana Sky Drive, Austin, TX 78727

RUSSELL, Kenneth Paul (Ore) 5311 Sw Wichita St, Tualatin, OR 97062

RUSSELL, Margaret Ellen Street (Me) 9 Perkins Rd, Boothbay Harbor, ME 04538

RUSSELL, Michael Bennett (Tex) 3112 James St, San Diego, CA 92106

RUSSELL, Patricia Griffith (NwT) 1802 Broadway, Lubbock, TX 79401

RUSSELL, Scott (NJ) 2365 McAleer Rd, Sewickley, PA 15143

RUSSELL, Sherrill Ann (WMo) 7110 N State Route 9, Kansas City, MO 64152

RUSSELL, Steven Scott (Eau)

RUSSELL, Susan (Los) 680 Mountain View St, Altadena, CA 91001

RUSSELL, Susan Hayden (Mass) 72 Cavendish Circle, Salem, MA 01970

RUTENBAR, C Harles Mark (WTenn) 7774 Grand Point Rd., Presque Isle, MI 49777

RUTENBAR, LaRae (WMich) 8238 Greengate Cove, Cordova, TN 38018

RUTHERFORD, Allen (Ind) 420 Locust Street, Mt. Vernon, IN 47620

RUTHERFORD, Ellen C (NJ) 1115 New Pear St, Vineland, NJ 08360

RUTHERFORD, Thomas Houston (CFla) 1260 Log Landing Drive, Ocoee, FL 34761

RUTHVEN, Carol (Lex) 926 Mason Headley Rd, Lexington, KY 40504

RUTHVEN, Scott (RG) 805 Lenox Ave., Las Cruces, NM 88005

RUTHY, Rosemary (Eau)

RUTLEDGE, Andrew Brooks (WA)

RUTLEDGE, Fleming (NY) 38 Hillandale Rd, Rye Brook, NY 10573

RUTLEDGE, Lynn V (Me) 13 Garnet Head Rd, Pembroke, ME 04666

RUTTAN, Karl D (Ky) 125 E Broad St, Columbus, OH 43215

RUTTER, Deborah Wood (Va) PO Box 1306, Front Royal, VA 22630

RUYAK, Mark A (Cal) 5 Weatherly Drive Apt 109, Mill Valley, CA 94941

RUYLE, Everett Eugene (At) 1195 Terramont Dr, Roswell, GA 30076

RWAMASIRABO, Nfikije Mugisha (NJ)

RYAN, Adele Marie (Mass) 50 Harden Hill Rd, Box C, Duxbury, MA 02331

RYAN, Bartholomew Grey (Chi) 2713 6 3/16 Ave, New Auburn, WI 54757

RYAN, Dennis L (Miss) 3507 Pine St, Pascagoula, MS 39567

RYAN III, Frances Isabel Sells (Az) 3150 N Winding Brook Rd, Flagstaff, AZ 86001

RYAN, Katherine (WNC) 1223 Sea Pines Dr, Aubrey, TX 76227

RYAN, Kathryn McCrossen (Tex) 8787 Greenville Ave, Dallas, TX 75243

RYAN, Matthew Ryan (NwPa) 67 Thomas-Ryan Road, Emporium, PA 15834

RYAN, Michael James (WMich) The Church of the Epiphany, 410 Erie Street, South Haven, MI 49090

RYAN, Michelle A (Ky)

RYAN, William Wilson (WTenn) 9233 Speerberry Ln, #14101, Cordova, TN 38016

RYDER, Anne Elizabeth (WMass) PO Box 1294, Sheffield, MA 01257

RYDER, Barbara (SVa) 12 Spring St, Decatur, GA 30030

RYMER, Lionel Simon (VI) Po Box 7335, St Thomas, VI 00801

S

SAAGER, Rebecca Ann (Lex) 311 Washington St, Frankfort, KY 40601

SAARE, Keith Robert (RG)

SABETTI III, Henry Martin (Eas) 12822 Shrewsbury Church Rd, Kennedyville, MD 21645

SABOGAL GUTIERREZ, Diego Fernando (Colom)

SABOM, William Stephen (At) 1143 Sanden Ferry Dr, Decatur, GA 30033

SABUNE, Petero Aggrey Nkurunziza (NY) 293 Highland Ave, Newark, NJ 07104

SACCAROLA FAVARO, Flavio (EcuC) Apdo 08-01-404, Esmeraldas, Ecuador

SACHS, Patti Luann (Md) 5757 Solomons Island Rd, Lothian, MD 20711

SACHS, William Lewis (Va) 509 Saint Christophers Road, Richmond, VA 23226

SACQUETY JR, Charles William (Los) 8402 Castilian Dr, Huntington Beach, CA 92646

SAFFORD, Timothy Browning (Pa) 20 N American St, Philadelphia, PA 19106

SAHDEV, Michael Clifford (SeFla) 1121 Andalusia Ave, Coral Gables, FL 33134

SAID, James T (Ga) 3321 Wheeler Rd, Augusta, GA 30909

✠ **SAID**, John Lewis (SeFla) 6508 Nw Chugwater Cir, Port Saint Lucie, FL 34983

SAIK, Robert (Az) 514 S Mountain Rd, Mesa, AZ 85208

SAILER, David Walter (WNC) 3 Oak Leaf Ln, Arden, NC 28704

SAINTILVER, Margarette (Hai)

SAINT JUSTE, Vanel (DR (DomRep))

SAINT-PIERRE, Nathanael L B (NY) Haitian Congregation of the Good Samaritan, 661 E 219th St, Bronx, NY 10467

SAINT ROMAIN, Brad (Tex) 3333 Castle Ave, Waco, TX 76710

SAINT-VIL, Renaud (Hai)

SAJNA, Barbara Jean Reiser (FdL) 2100 Ridges Rd., Baileys Harbor, WI 54202

SAKIN, Charles Robert (NJ) 1812 Rue De La Port Drive, Wall, NJ 07719

SAKRISON, David L (U) 280 E 300 S, Moab, UT 84532

SALAMONE, Robert Emmitt (At) 2490 Orchard Walk, Bogart, GA 30622

SALAZAR-SOTILLO, Orlando Rafael (Ve)

SALAZAR-VASQUEZ, Jose (Ve)

SALBADOR, Gus William (Wyo) 2510 Stonebridge Way, Mount Vernon, WA 98273

SALCEDO, Federico B (PR)

SALIK, Lamuel Gill (Dal) 138 Liveoak St, Hereford, TX 79045

SALINARO, Katherine Ella Mae (Cal) 121 Sheffield, Hercules, CA 94547

SALISBURY, Katherine Ann (LI) 157 Montague St, Brooklyn, NY 11201

SALLES, Stacy D (Mich) 67640 Van Dyke Rd # 10, Washington, MI 48095

SALLEY JR, George Bull (Ga) 310 McLaws Street, Savannah, GA 31405

SALMON JR, Abraham Dickerson (Md) 7351 Willow Rd Apt 2, Frederick, MD 21702

SALMON, Alan Kent (NJ) 4 Tara Ln, Delran, NJ 08075

SALMON JR, John Frederick (Nwk) 195 Woodside Dr, Lumberton, NJ 08048

SALMON, Nina (SwVa)

SALMON, Walter Burley Stattmann (At)

SALT, Alfred Lewis (Nwk) 4822 Martinique Way, Naples, FL 34119

SALTZGABER, Jan Mcminn (Ga) 225 W Point Dr, Saint Simons Island, GA 31522

SALVATIERRA SERIAN, Juan E (EcuC) Apdo 17-11-6165, Quito, Ecuador

SAM, Albert Abuid Samuel (WNY) 7469 Dysinger Rd, Lockport, NY 14094

SAM, Helen (WNY) PO Box 14, Dunkirk, NY 14048

SAM, Rachelle Divonne (WA)

SAMILIO, Jamie Suzanne (Va) 2455 Gallows Rd, Dunn Loring, VA 22027

SAMMIS, Robert Lyle (Los)

SAMMONS, Gregory P (O) 4684 Brittany Rd, Toledo, OH 43615

SAMMONS, Margaret Holt (O) 208 Lewiston Rd., Kettering, OH 45429

SAMPEY, Amanda L (FdL) St James Episcopal Church, 402 2nd St, Mosinee, WI 54455

SAMPSON, Leon (NAM) PO Box 28, Bluff, UT 84512

SAMPSON, Paula Kathryn (Ak) 4317 Birch Avenue, Terrace, V8G 1X2, Canada

SAMRA, Gordon L (NI) 14823 Waterbrook Rd, Fort Wayne, IN 46814

SAMS, David Lee (Minn) 203 Aspenwood Drive, Redwood Falls, MN 56283

SAMS, Jonathan Carter (Mich) 6402 Fredmoor Dr, Troy, MI 48098

SAMSON, Clive E P (Mo)

SAMUEL, Amjad John (Ct) 1361 W Market St, Akron, OH 44313

SAMUEL, Daniel (DR (DomRep)) Aptd 764, Santo Domingo, Dominican Republic

SAMUEL, Jason (SanD) Saint David's Epis Church, 5050 Milton St, San Diego, CA 92110

SAMUEL, Pauline Ann (LI)

SAMUELS, Robert Marshall (WNY) 201 Saint Francis Dr, Green Bay, WI 54301

SAMUELSON, Frank W (CFla) 3901 S Panther Creek Dr, The Woodlands, TX 77381

SAMUELSON, Louise B (CFla) 2450 River Oaks Blvd, Houston, TX 77019

SANBORN, Calvin (Me) Po Box 823, York Harbor, ME 03911

SANBORN, Victoria B M (NY) 3919 Pocahontas Ave, Cincinnati, OH 45227

SANCHEZ, Jose D (Tex) 525 NE 15th St, Miami, FL 33132

SANCHEZ, Patricia Anne (U) 1579 S State St, Clearfield, UT 84015

SANCHEZ NAVARRO, Connie (Hond)

SANCHEZ NAVARRO, Jose Israel (Hond)

SANCHEZ NUNEZ, Carlos A (PR) PO Box 327, Manati, PR 00674

SANCHEZ PUJOL, Augusto Sandino (DR (DomRep)) Santiago #114, Santo Domingo, Dominican Republic

SANCHEZ-SHABAZZ, Jacqueline Marie (NY) 236 E 31st St, New York, NY 10016

SAND, David Allan (NMich) PO Box 805, Iron Mountain, MI 49801

SAND, Lynn Ann (NMich) PO Box 805, Iron Mountain, MI 49801

SANDERS, Edwin Benjamin (Ky) 3812 Burning Bush Rd, Louisville, KY 40241

SANDERS, Harvel Ray (Mo) 110 Walnut Park Dr, Sedalia, MO 65301

SANDERS, Jaime Mw (Ore) 2190 Crest Dr, Lake Oswego, OR 97034

SANDERS, Joanne Marie (Cal) Stanford Memorial Church, Stanford University, Stanford, CA 94305

SANDERS, John Clarke (At) 2744 Peachtree Rd Nw, Atlanta, GA 30305

SANDERS, Lynn Coggins (NY) St. Bartholomew's Church, 325 Park Avenue, New York, New York 10022

SANDERS, Marilyn Mae (CNY) 33092 Bay Ter, Lewes, DE 19958

SANDERS, Megan (NY) 40 Old Mill Rd, Staten Island, NY 10306

SANDERS, Patrick W (Miss)

SANDERS, Richard Devon (At)

SANDERS, Richard Evan (Ga) 605 Reynolds St, Augusta, GA 30901

SANDERS, Wayne Francis Michael (SanD) 3563 Merrimac Ave, San Diego, CA 92117

✠ **SANDERS**, William Evan (ETenn) 404 Charlesgate Ct, Nashville, TN 37215

SANDERSON, Dow (SC) 218 Ashley Avenue, Charleston, SC 29403

SANDERSON, Holladay Worth (Ida) All Saints Episcopal Church, 704 S Latah St, Boise, ID 83705

SANDERSON, Peter O (Ia) 410 Brentwood Dr, Alamogordo, NM 88310

SANDFORT, Candace C (Nwk)

SANDLIN, Allan (At) 1881 Edinburgh Terrace NE, Atlanta, GA 30307

SANDOE, Deirdre Etheridge (WA) 400 Rouen Dr Apt H, Deland, FL 32720

SANDOVAL, Juan (At) 161 Church St NE, Marietta, GA 30060

SANDOVAL CROS, Carlos (SeFla) 1000 NW North River Drive #110, Miami, FL 33136

SANDS, Robin Osborne (NC)

SANDWELL-WEISS, Rosa Leah (Az) 8502 N Deer Valley Dr, Tucson, AZ 85742

SANFORD, Carol Webb (WMo)

SANFORD, Gary Lee (NwT) 1801 Edmund Blvd, San Angelo, TX 76901

SANG, Clive Oscar (NJ) 205 North Ave, Cranford, NJ 07016

SANGREY, William Frederick (SO)

SANON, Jean-Louis Felix (NY) 2757 Jacob Lane, Douglasville, GA 30135

SANTANA, Carlos Enrique (DR (DomRep))

SANTANA, Margarita (Md) Apartado 128, San Pedro De Macoris, Dominican Republic

SANTANA-RUIZ, Benjamin (PR) 222 S Palm Ave, Sarasota, FL 34236

SANTIAGO, Vicente C (Pgh) 132 Sherwood Drive, Greensburg, PA 15601

SANTIAGO-PADILLA, Gilberto (PR) Carr 187 KM 5.8, Mediana Alta, Loiza, PR 00772

SANTIBANEZ, Susana (Az)

SANTIVIAGO-ESPINAL, Maria Isabel (NY) 2453 78th St # 2, East Elmhurst, NY 11370

SANTMAN, Linda (Oly)

SANTOS, Elenito Bravo (NC) 221 Union St, Cary, NC 27511

SANTOS ABREGO, Concepcion (Hond) Espiritu Santo, Barrio Las Brisas, Santa Rita, Honduras

SANTOS-MONTES, Margarita (PR)

SANTOS-RIVERA, Carlos (Pa) 3554 N 6th St, Philadelphia, PA 19140

SANTOSUOSSO, John Edward (SwFla) 4860 Highlands Place Drive, Lakeland, FL 33813

SANTUCCI, Mark Albert (Ct) 166 Lambtown Rd, Ledyard, CT 06339

SANZO, Maria B (NJ) 318 Huxley Dr, Brick, NJ 08723

SAPP, Rose Marie (CFla)

SARAI-CLARK, Wilhelmina Olivia (Spok) 503 E D St, Moscow, ID 83843

SARGENT, Arthur Lloyd (Dal) 213 Sierra Ridge Dr, San Marcos, TX 78666

SARGENT GREEN, Nancy Hunnewell (EO) 18160 Cottonwood Rd Pmb 719, Sunriver, OR 97707

SARKISSYIAN, Sabi Kamel (Mo) 524 Fox Run Estates Ct, Ballwin, MO 63021

SARRAZIN, Victor (NY) 12 Depot St, Middletown, NY 10940

SARTIN, Nancy Avera (Ga) 1521 N Patterson St, Valdosta, GA 31602

SARTIN, Randall Randall (Fla) 3480 Lakeshore Drive, Tallahassee, FL 32312

SASSER JR, Howell Crawford (CPa) Saint Paul's Church, PO Box 764, Bloomsburg, PA 17815

SASTRE, Iane M (Ga) 21268 US Highway 17, White Oak, GA 31568

SATERSTROM, Roger Thomas (Tenn) Christ Church Cathedral, 900 Broadway, Nashville, TN 37203

SATHER, Jerry Earl (SwFla) Psc 47 Box 366, Apo, AE 09470

SATO, Judith Ann (Colo) 13741 Windrush dr, Colorado Springs, CO 80921

SATORIUS, Joanna (Los) Po Box 512164, Los Angeles, CA 90051

SATTERLY, Norris Jay (NMich) 132 Henford Ave, Kingsford, MI 49802

SATULA, John A (Mass) 6Schoolhouse Hill Road, Newtown, CT 06470

SAUCEDO SICA, Susan Teresa (Nwk) 407 N Broad St, Lansdale, PA 19446

SAUERZOPF, Richard Creighton (Mich) 110 Rocking Chair Rd, Horseheads, NY 14845

✠ **SAULS**, Stacy F (Lex) 815 Second Ave., New York, NY 10017

SAUNDERS, Cora Germaine (At) 607 River Run Dr, Sandy Springs, GA 30350

SAUNDERS, Elizabeth Goodwin (NC) 3029 Mountainbrook Rd, Charlotte, NC 28210

SAUNDERS, James (NJ) 8113 Rugby St, Philadelphia, PA 19150

SAUNDERS, John (Ga) General Theological Seminary, 175 9th Ave, New York, NY 10011

SAUNDERS III, Kenneth H. (ETenn) 305 Park St, GREENEVILLE, TN 37743

SAUNDERS, Lisa Ann (Tex) 833 W Wisconsin Ave, Milwaukee, WI 53233

SAUNDERSON, Ann Marie (Oly) 3918 N 24th St, Tacoma, WA 98406

SAUNKEAH, Bobby Reed (Okla) 110 E 17th St, Ada, OK 74820

SAVAGE, Harley Stewart (Tex) 180 CR 222, Bay City, TX 77414

SAVAGE, Jack Laverne (Mich) 1157 E Buckhorn Cir, Sanford, MI 48657

SAVAGE-KING, Ruthann (Mass) 487 Boston Rd, Groton, MA 01450

SAVIDGE, Karen F (WMo) 207 N. 7th, St. Joseph, MO 64501

SAVILLE III, John (Los) Po Box 152, Corona, CA 92878

SAVILLE, Milton (SO) 3580 Shaw Avenue #323, Cincinnati, OH 45208

SAVINO, Bella Jean (Ak) Po Box 70786, Fairbanks, AK 99707

SAWICKY, Blake A (Cal) The Church of St. Michael & St. George, 6345 Wydown Blvd, St. Louis, MO 63105

SAWTELLE, Gary Donald (Roch) 2171 Scottsville Rd, Scottsville, NY 14546

SAWYER, Alice Sherman (CGC) 205 Holly Ln, Dothan, AL 36301

SAWYER, Anne M (NY) St Mark's Church in the Bowery, 131 E 10th St, New York, NY 10003

SAWYER, Frank D (CFla) 210 S Indian River Dr, Fort Pierce, FL 34950

SAWYER, Gary Alan (Az)

SAWYER, Robert Claremont (NC) Po Box 28024, Raleigh, NC 27611

SAWYER, Stanley Whitfield (SVa) 2200 Cape Arbor Dr, Virginia Beach, VA 23451

SAWYER, Susan (Kan) 1640 Sunflower Rd, Clay Center, KS 67432

SAWYER HARMON, Cecily Judith (Del) 262 S College Ave, Newark, DE 19711

SAXE, Joshua Andrew (WVa) 218 Church St, Lewisburg, WV 24901

SAXE, Sarah E (EC) 7302 Us Highway 264 E, Washington, NC 27889

SAXON, Mary-Margaret (Colo) 5527 Harrison Street, Kansas City, MO 64110

SAXON, Miriam (NC) 2214 Buck Quarter Farm Rd, Hillsborough, NC 27278

SAXTON II, Carl Millard (Ala) 256 E Church St, Jacksonville, FL 32202

SAYLOR, Kristin Lee (NY)

SAYLORS, Joann L (Tex) 1225 Texas St, Houston, TX 77002

SCALES, Linda (Ga) 4344 Miller Dr, Evans, GA 30809

SCALES JR, Louie Grady (Ga) 4344 Miller Drive, Evans, GA 30809

SCALIA, Deborah White (La) 10136 Walden Dr, River Ridge, LA 70123

SCALISE, Margaret Mary (Ala) 8816 Old Greensboro Rd Apt 19103, Tuscaloosa, AL 35405

✠ **SCANLAN**, Audrey (CPa) 124 Brindle Rd, Mechanicsburg, PA 17055

SCANLAN, Paul Joseph (SO)

SCANLON, Geoffrey Edward Leyshon (Spr) 2910 E Stone Creek Blvd, Urbana, IL 61802

SCANNELL, Alice Updike (Ore) 1500 NE 15th Ave Apt 336, Portland, OR 97232

SCANNELL, John Scott (Ore) 1500 NE 15th Ave Apt 336, Portland, OR 97232

✠ **SCANTLEBURY**, Victor Alfonso (Chi) 6167 Westwind Rd, Jackson, MS 39206

SCARBOROUGH, Anjel Lorraine (Md) 2711 Flintridge Ct, Myersville, MD 21773

SCARCIA, Steven Angelo (Alb) PO Box 592, Little Falls, NY 13365

✠ **SCARFE**, Alan (Ia) 225 37th St, Des Moines, IA 50312

SCARFF, Stephen D (Alb) 129 Ledge Hill Rd, Guilford, CT 06437

SCARLETT, William George (Md)

SCARPACE, Ramona (Minn) 2035 Charlton Rd, Sunfish Lake, MN 55118

SCHAAL, Richard (CNY) 1504 76th Rd, Berkshire, NY 13736

SCHACHT, Lawrence Arthur (NY) 525 W End Ave Apt 4-H, New York, NY 10024

SCHADT, Stuart Everett (Va) 6070 Greenway Ct, Manassas, VA 20111

SCHAEFER III, John (Neb) 7236 County Road 34, Fort Calhoun, NE 68023

SCHAEFER, Joslyn (WNC) 349 N Haywood St, Waynesville, NC 28786

SCHAEFER, Lee (Ind) 444 South Harbour Drive, Noblesville, IN 46062

SCHAEFER, Lynette Golderman (The Episcopal Church in Haw) PO Box 1233, Kaunakakai, HI 96748

SCHAEFER, Norma Jane (Chi) 417 N. Beck Road, Lindenhurst, IL 60046

SCHAEFER, Philip David (Roch) 47 Brougham Dr, Penfield, NY 14526

SCHAEFFER, John R (Eas) All Saints Episcopal Church, 3577 McClure Ave, Pittsburgh, PA 15212

SCHAEFFER, Phillip Negley (NMich) 1803 N Schaeffer Rd, N4244 Gladhaven Road, Moran, MI 49760

SCHAEFFER, Susan Edwards (NY) 17 Perkins Ave, Northampton, MA 01060

SCHAFFENBURG, Karl Christian (FdL) 1011 N. 7th St., 103 W. Broad Street, Sheboygan, WI 53081

SCHAFFNER, Philip Perry (Minn) 2401 33rd Ave. S, Minneapolis, MN 55406

SCHAFROTH, Stephen Louis (EO) 1107 Lewis St, The Dalles, OR 97058

SCHAIBLE II, Donald J (Be) Christ and Trinity Parishes, 58 River St, Carbondale, PA 18407

SCHAITBERGER, Stephen Harold (Minn) 1402 S 8th St, Brainerd, MN 56401

SCHALLER, Joseph G (Pa) 303 W. Lancaster Avenue, Suite 2C, Wayne, PA 19087

SCHALLER JR, Warren August (Va) 7 Lost Ridge Lane, Galena, IL 61036

SCHAPER, Richard (Cal) 646 Ridgewood Avenue, Mill Valley, CA 94941

SCHARF, Douglas Frederick (SeFla) 3714 Cystal Dew St, Plant City, FL 33567

SCHARF JR, Frederick E (SwFla) 11644 Spindrift Loop, Hudson, FL 34667

SCHARK, Frederick J (WMich) St Mark Episcopal Church, 27 E Chicago St, Coldwater, MI 49036

SCHEDA, Claudia (WNY) 54 Linwood Ave, Williamsville, NY 14221

SCHEEL, William Preston (Ark) 26 Cypress Point, Wimberley, TX 78676

SCHEELER, Joseph L (Oly) All Saints Episc Church, 2206 Nw 99th St, Vancouver, WA 98665

SCHEELER, Richard Edward Gerhart (Mil) 1540 S 166th St, New Berlin, WI 53151

SCHEEPERS, Noble F (Mass) 62 Cedar St, Dedham, MA 02026

SCHEFF, Tanya Lynn (Eau) 620 3rd St W, Ashland, WI 54806

SCHEIBLE, Anne Clare Elsworth (Minn) 225 5th St Se, Chatfield, MN 55923

SCHEIBLE, Gordon Kenneth (SanD) 2151 Bella Vista, Canyon Lake, TX 78133

SCHEID, Daniel S (EMich) 922 Blanchard Ave, Flint, MI 48503

SCHEIDE, Diana Southwick (NY) PO Box 296, Callicoon, NY 12723

SCHEIDER, Dave (Tex) 130 Sobrante Rd Unit 116, Belton, TX 76513

SCHELB, Holly Greenmam (NC) 1323 Irving St, Winston Salem, NC 27103

SCHELL, Anita Louise (RI) 42 Dearborn St, Newport, RI 02840

SCHELL, Donald J (Cal) 555 De Haro St Ste 330, San Francisco, CA 94107

SCHELL, Richardson Whitfield (Ct) Kent School, Kent, CT 06757

SCHELLENBERG, Roger Thomas (Va) 5775 Barclay Drive Suite G, Kingstowne, VA 22315

SCHELLHAMMER, Judith Lynn (Mich) PO Box 287, Onsted, MI 49265

SCHELLING, Robert Louis (Colo) 393 Private Road 5730, Jefferson, TX 75657

SCHELLINGERHOUDT, Liz (At) 450 Clairmont Ave, Atlanta, GA 30030

SCHEMBS, Lois Jean (Nwk) 321 Lamberts Mill Rd, Westfield, NJ 07090

SCHENCK, Timothy E (Mass) 172 Main St, Hingham, MA 02043

SCHENEMAN, Mark (CPa) 226 Acre Dr, Carlisle, PA 17013

SCHENKEL JR, Robert Downes (Be) 6539 Betsy Ross Cir, Bethlehem, PA 18017

SCHENONE, Janine L (SanD) 4321 Eastgate Mall, San Diego, CA 92121

SCHERCK, Steven H (Alb) P.O. Box 397, Guilderland, NY 12084

SCHERER, Anna (SVa) 1830 Kirby Rd, McLean, VA 22101

SCHERER-HOOCK, Joyce Lynn (Mass) Po Box 308, Topsfield, MA 01983

SCHERFF, Holly D (Ia)

SCHERM, Mary Cecelia (WMass) 48 Amity Pl, Amherst, MA 01002

SCHEYER, Joyce (NJ) Grace Church Rectory, 423 W 8th St, Plainfield, NJ 07060

SCHIEFFELIN JR, John Jay (WMass)

SCHIEFFLER, Daniel Kent (Ark) 19 Woodberry Rd., Little Rock, AR 72212

SCHIERING, Janet Christine (EO) PO Box 1323, Hood River, OR 97031

SCHIESLER, Robert Alan (WMich) 30 Kerry Ct, Mechanicsburg, PA 17050

SCHIESS, Betty Bone (CNY) 6987 Van Antwerp Dr, Cicero, NY 13039

SCHIESZ, Catherine Murdock (Ala) PO Box M, Florence, AL 35631

SCHIFFMAYER, Jeffrey Paul (Tex) 8739 Serenade Ln, Houston, TX 77040

SCHILLING III, Walter Bailey (CFla) 1803 Crane Creek Blvd, Melbourne, FL 32940

SCHILLREFF, Kathy (SwFla) 278 Sawgrass Ct, Naples, FL 34110

SCHINDLER, Gary (WNY) 591 E Main St, Springville, NY 14141

SCHINK, Susan Alma (Nwk) 481 Airmount Avenue, Ramsey, NJ 07446

SCHIRMACHER, Michael (Md) 3202 Lake St Apt 2, Houston, TX 77098

SCHISLER, Richard Thomas (SO) 2210 Cleveland Ave, Portsmouth, OH 45662

SCHISLER, Sallie Chellis (SO) 2210 Cleveland Ave, Portsmouth, OH 45662

SCHISSER, Janet (Mo) 1203 Castle Bay Pl, Columbia, MO 65203

SCHIVELY, John Alrik (The Episcopal NCal) 1441 Marseille Ln, Roseville, CA 95747

SCHJONBERG, Mary Frances Frances (Nwk) 407 Seaview Circle, Neptune, NJ 07753

SCHLACHTER, Melvin Harlan (Ia) 7 Glenview Knl NE, Iowa City, IA 52244

SCHLAFER, David John (Mil) 5213 Roosevelt Street, Bethesda, MD 20814

SCHLESINGER, Kira (Tenn) 4220 Harding Pike, Nashville, TN 37205

SCHLEY JR, Joseph Hastings (FtW) 1300 S Harrison St Apt 1008, Amarillo, TX 79101

SCHLISMANN, Robert (Neb) 1309 R St, Lincoln, NE 68508

SCHLOSSBERG, Stephen KK (Alb) 1574 Spring Ave., Wynantskill, NY 12198

SCHLOTTERBECK, Marilou Jean (WMich) 12530 Cinder Rd, Beulah, MI 49617

SCHMALING, Pamela Jane (Oly) 7913 W Golf Course Dr, Blaine, WA 98230

SCHMIDT, Ann W (Ark) 726 Davemar Dr, Saint Louis, MO 63123

SCHMIDT, Carolyn Jean Decker (Minn) PO Box 278, 1633 Croftville Rd, Grand Marais, MN 55604

SCHMIDT JR, Frederick William (WA) Garrett-Evangelical Theological Seminary, 2121 Sheridan Rd, Evanston, IL 60201

SCHMIDT, John David (Dal)

SCHMIDT, Kenneth John (Mass)

SCHMIDT, Kenneth L (Cal) 1350 Waller St, San Francisco, CA 94117

SCHMIDT, Kevin Lynn (Kan) 15309 W 153rd St, Olathe, KS 66062

SCHMIDT, Linda Marie (FdL) N2592 State Highway 17, Merrill, WI 54452

SCHMIDT, Norma (Ct) 661 Old Post Rd, Fairfield, CT 06824

SCHMIDT, Richard (CGC) 101 Fairwood Blvd., Fairhope, AL 36532

SCHMIDT, Wayne Roy (NY) 3 Ashley Dr, Newburgh, NY 12550

SCHMIDTETTER, Todd T (CFla)

SCHMITT, Barbara Joyce (SO) 115 N 6th St, Hamilton, OH 45011

SCHMITT, Geoffrey (WLa) 3910 Parkway Dr, 1605 Gray Lake Dr, Princeton, LA 71067

SCHMITT, Jackie (Mass) 31 Ely Dr., Fayetteville, NY 13066

SCHMITZ, Barbara G (CNY)

SCHMOETZER, Jane Ellen (Spok) 1940 Thayer Dr., Richland, WA 99354

SCHNAARE, Anne Elizabeth (WMich) 115 Hart St., Marshall, MI 49068

SCHNABEL, Charles Edward (LI) 143 Lakeside Trail, Ridge, NY 11961

SCHNABL, Emily (Okla) 4036 Neptune Dr, Oklahoma City, OK 73116

SCHNACK, Peggy Ellan (Oly)

SCHNATTERLY, Michael Dean (USC) 5 Mountain Vista Rd, Taylors, SC 29687

SCHNAUFER, Dennis Eric (USC) 6 Del Norte Blvd, Greenville, SC 29615

SCHNEIDER, Charles W (WK) 317 Stoney Hill Rd, San Antonio, TX 67401

SCHNEIDER, Edward Nichols (EMich) 7039 W. Saint John Rd., Glendale, AZ 85308

SCHNEIDER, Gregg Alan (NC) 703 Milwaukee Road, Beloit, WI 53511

SCHNEIDER, Judith Irene (Colo) 2187 Canyon Ct W, Grand Junction, CO 81503

SCHNEIDER, Marian Helen (Roch) 13 E Water St, Friendship, NY 14739

SCHNEIDER, Marilyn Butler (Colo) 7900 E Dartmouth Ave Apt 58, Denver, CO 80231

SCHNEIDER, Marni Jacqueline (Los) 2972 Cadence Way, Virginia Beach, VA 23456

SCHNEIDER, Matthew C (Ala) 2017 6th Ave N, Birmingham, AL 35203

SCHNEIDER, M P (Vt) 164 Milton Road, Warwick, RI 02888

SCHNEIDER, Stephen (Ore) 2427 Ne 17th Ave, Portland, OR 97212

SCHNEIDER, Thomas Carl (ETenn) 1038 Sparta Hwy, Crossville, TN 38572

SCHNEIDER, William J (Mass) 276 Riverside Dr Apt 4e, New York, NY 10025

SCHNITZER, William Lawton (NY) 26 N Manheim Blvd, New Paltz, NY 12561

SCHOECK, Lauren L (CPa) 6300 N Central Ave, Phoenix, AZ 85012

SCHOECK, Robert H (CPa) 119 N Duke St, Lancaster, PA 17602

SCHOENBRUN, Zoila Collier (Cal) 327 San Rafael Ave, Belvedere, CA 94920

✠ **SCHOFIELD JR**, Calvin Onderdonk (SeFla) 7900 East Dartmouth Ave. # 77, Denver, CO 80231

SCHOFIELD, Kathlyn Elizabeth (CNY) St Paul's Episcopal Church, 204 Genesee St, Chittenango, NY 13037

SCHOFIELD, Peter (Alb) 39 Imperial Dr., Niskayuna, NY 12309

SCHOFIELD-BROADBENT, Carrie (CNY) 941 Euclid Ave., Syracuse, NY 13210

SCHOLER, Linda Carlson (NJ) P O Box 1206, Chincoteague Island, VA 23336

SCHOMAKER, Kenneth Elmer (Ind) 2030 Chester Blvd IH 7B, Richmond, IN 47374

SCHOMBURG, Karen (Spok) Episcopal Diocese Of Spokane, 245 E 13th Ave, Spokane, WA 99202

SCHOOLER, William Thomas (Cal) 352 Bay Rd, Atherton, CA 94027

SCHOONMAKER, Dan (O) 18426 Winslow Rd, Shaker Heights, OH 44122

SCHOONMAKER, Lisa Katherine (CPa) 21 S Main St, Lewistown, PA 17044

SCHRAMM, George T (WVa) Po Box 308, Shepherdstown, WV 25443

SCHRAMM, John Eldon (NI) P. O. Box 695, Plymouth, IN 46563

SCHRANZ, Donald Jerome (Spr)

SCHRAPLAU, Frederick William (NY) 182 Nixon Avenue, Staten Island, NY 10304

SCHREIBER, Mary (WMass) 6 Wall St, Shelburne Falls, MA 01370

SCHREIBER, Michael Nelson (Cal) 162 Hickory St, San Francisco, CA 94102

SCHREINER, Shawn M (Chi) 5 North 047 Route 83, Bensenville, IL 60106

SCHRIDER, James Edward (Los) 620 D Street, SE, Washington, DC 20003

SCHRIMSHER, Alyce Marie (Dal) 6132 Yellow Rock Trl, Dallas, TX 75248

SCHRODER, Edward Amos (Fla) 15 Hickory Lane, Amelia Island, FL 32034

SCHROEDER, CC (Va) 314 Ayrlee Avenue Nw, Leesburg, VA 20176

SCHROEDER, H.B.W. (Va)

SCHROETER, George Hieronymus (CGC) 500 Spanish Fort Blvd Apt 29, Spanish Fort, AL 36527

SCHUBERT, Jill Marie (Minn) 520 N Pokegama Ave, Grand Rapids, MN 55744

SCHUBERT, Kevin Lane Johnson (Tex) 3307 Garden Villa Ln, Austin, TX 78704

SCHUBERT, Rebecca Malcolm (WMo) 3700 West 83 Terrace, Prairie Village, KS 66206

SCHUEDDIG JR, Louis Charles (At) 345 9th St Ne, Atlanta, GA 30309

SCHUETZ, Mary (EMich) 3536 West River Road, Sanford, MI 48657

SCHUILING, Alice Catherine (NMich) 1100 Sunview Dr Apt 201, Saint Johns, MI 48879

SCHULENBERG, George W (ND) 135 Skogmo Blvd, Fergus Falls, MN 56537

SCHULENBERG, Michael A (Minn) 715 N High St, Lake City, MN 55041

SCHULER, Rock Hal (Md) St Andrew The Fisherman Episcopal, PO Box 175, Mayo, MD 21106

SCHULTZ, Alison M (Ore) 5560 Chemin de Vie, Atlanta, GA 30342

SCHULTZ, Gregory Allen (FdL) West 7145 County Road U, Plymouth, WI 53073

SCHULTZ, Mark Daniel (NY) PO Box 65840, Tucson, AZ 85728

SCHULTZ, Thomas Haines (Cal) St. Mary's Retreat House, 505 E. Los Olivos St., Santa Barbara, CA 93105

SCHULZ, David Allen (Del) 224 N Bayshore Dr, Frederica, DE 19946

SCHUNEMAN, Steven Lawrence (Chi) 200 N El Camino Real Spc 179, Oceanside, CA 92058

SCHUNIOR, Rebecca J (Colo) St Mark's Church, 301 A St SE, Washington, DC 20003

SCHUNK, Steven Wendell (NY) 3021 State Route 213 E, Stone Ridge, NY 12484

SCHUSTER III, Franklin Phillip (RG) 28231 Pine Lake St, Edwardsburg, MI 49112

SCHUSTER WELTNER, Alicia Dawn (At) 2744 Peachtree Rd NW, Atlanta, GA 30305

SCHUTZ, Christine Elizabeth (O) 843 Tarra Oaks Dr, Findlay, OH 45840

SCHUTZ, Regan M. (Ore) PO Box 3331, Sewanee, TN 37375

SCHUYLER, William Kearns (Me) 19 Ridgeway Ave, Sanford, ME 04073

SCHWAB, Susan Mary Brophy (Mass) 280 Village St Apt G1, Medway, MA 02053

SCHWAB, Wayne Stephen (Nwk) PO Box 294, Hinesburg, VT 05461

SCHWAHN, Vincent (Los) 117 Avenida San Jeronimo, San Angel, Mexico City, CMX 01000, Mexico

SCHWARTZ, William Edward (Mil) PO Box 3210, Doha, QATAR, Qatar

SCHWARTZ CROUCH, Emily (Ky) 7304 Westport Rd, Louisville, KY 40222

SCHWARZ, Robert Carl (SD) 500 S Main Ave, Sioux Falls, SD 57104

SCHWARZ, Robert Louis (LI) 324 Fairington Dr, Summerville, SC 29485

SCHWARZER, Margaret (Mass) 321 Tappan St Apt 5, Brookline, MA 02445

SCHWEINSBURG JR, Richard Lyle (RI) 46 Fairway Dr, Washington Village, Coventry, RI 02816

SCHWENKE, Carol (SwFla) 3000 S Schiller St, Tampa, FL 33629

SCHWENZFEIER, Paul Macleod (Mass) 32 Arlington Rd., Wareham, MA 02571

SCHWERT, Douglas Peters (WTex) 433 Trojan St, Port Aransas, TX 78373

SCHWOYER, Robin Lynn Vanhorn (Pa) 232 American Dr, Richboro, PA 18954

SCIAINO, Elizabeth Rauen (NJ) 88 Claremont Rd, Bernardsville, NJ 07924

SCIME, Michael S (Ind)

SCIPIO, Clarence Tyrone (VI) PO Box 1148, St Thomas, VI 00804

SCISSONS, Anne (EO) 17 Fairview Heights Loop, Burns, OR 97720

SCOFIELD, Lawrence Frederick (NwPa) 24 W Frederick St, Corry, PA 16407

SCOFIELD, Susan M (NwPa) Nonparochial, 24 W. Frederick St., Corry, PA 16407

SCOLARE, Michael Charles (FdL)

SCOOPMIRE, Leslie Barnes (Mo) 11538 Patty Ann Drive, Saint Louis, MO 63146

SCOTT, Andrew T (Okla)

SCOTT JR, Benjamin Ives (Minn) 8429 55th St Sw, Byron, MN 55920

SCOTT, Catherine F (Neb) 1903 Pleasantview Ln, Bellevue, NE 68005

SCOTT, Cathy Ann (Ind) Holy Family Episcopal Church, 11445 Fishers Point Blvd, Fishers, IN 46038

SCOTT, David Thomas (NwT) Po Box 88, Perryton, TX 79070

SCOTT, Dick (Oly) 4885 NW Chad Ct, Silverdale, WA 98383

SCOTT, Donna Jeanne (Tenn) 404 Siena Drive, Nashville, TN 37205

SCOTT, Douglas Gordon (Pa) PO Box 1914, Ranchos De Taos, NM 87557

SCOTT, Edward C (NC) 525 Lake Concord Rd Ne, Concord, NC 28025

SCOTT, George Michael (Ga) PO Box 294, Cochran, GA 31014

SCOTT, Horton James (NY) 489 Saint Pauls Pl, Bronx, NY 10456

SCOTT JR, James Edward (Tex) 8407 Glenscott St., Houston, TX 77061

SCOTT, Jean Pearson (NwT) 1101 Slide Rd., Lubbock, TX 79416

SCOTT, Jennifer M (Be) 18300 Upper Bay Rd, Houston, TX 77058

SCOTT, John Charles (Ala) St Stephens Episcopal Church, PO Box 839, Eutaw, AL 35462

SCOTT III, John Llewellyn (Alb) 86 Lake Hill Rd, Burnt Hills, NY 12027

SCOTT, Keith Elden (RI) 103 Union Ave S, Delmar, NY 12054

SCOTT, Marshall (WMo) 1256 W 72nd Ter, Kansas City, MO 64114

SCOTT, Matthew Rhoades (NwPa) 209 West St, Warren, PA 16365

SCOTT, Michael B (NMich)

SCOTT, Nolie Edward (ETenn) 12026 Pine Cove Dr, Soddy Daisy, TN 37379

SCOTT, Norma J (Nev) Po Box 750, Hawthorne, NV 89415

SCOTT, Peggy King (La) 607 E Main St, New Roads, LA 70760

SCOTT, Rebecca Jean (Oly)

SCOTT II, Robert Alfred (Okla)

SCOTT, Robert W (Neb) 13054 Thomas Drive, Bellevue, NE 68005

SCOTT, Roger Timothy (Az)

SCOTT, Sheila Maria (Mil) 4700 W. Deer Run Dr # 103, Brown Deer, WI 53223

SCOTT, Shelby Hudson (Okla) 9119 S 89th E Ave, Broken Arrow, OK 74133

SCOTT, Thomas Crawford Hunt (WMich) 2327 park place #2, evanston, IL 60201

SCOTT JR, William Tayloe (Cal) 95 Winfield St, San Francisco, CA 94110

SCOTT-HAMBLEN, Shane (NY) 1 Chestnut St, Cold Spring, NY 10516

SCOTTO, Vincent Francis (SwFla) 23465 Harborview Rd Apt634, Port Charlotte, FL 33980

SCRANTON, Susan Lee (Los) 1420 E Foothill Blvd, Glendora, CA 91741

SCRIBNER, Jean Mary (Neb) 1725 Old Haywood Rd., Asheville, NC 28806

SCRIVEN, Elizabeth A (Mo) 2309 Packard St, Ann Arbor, MI 48104

SCRIVENER, William Eugene (SO) 7193 Foxview Dr, Cincinnati, OH 45230

SCRUGGS JR, Charles Perry (ETenn) 540 Bryant Rd, Chattanooga, TN 37405

SCRUTCHINS, Arthur Paul (Okla) Holland Hall School, 5666 E 81st St, Tulsa, OK 74137

✠ **SCRUTON**, Gordon (WMass) 40 Carriage Hill Dr, Wethersfield, CT 06109

SCULLY, Fred (SwFla) 311 Irwin Ave, Albion, MI 49224

SCUPHOLME, Anne (SeFla) 1990 English Oaks Cir N, Charlottesville, VA 22911

SEABURY, Scott Hamor (WMass) 10 Rawlings Brook Rd, Suffield, CT 06078

SEADALE, Vincent Gerald (Mass)

✠ **SEAGE**, Brian (Miss) 106 Vinson Cv, Madison, MS 39110

SEAGE, Kyle Dice (Miss) 106 Vinson Cv, Madison, MS 39110

SEAGLE, Teresa Ryan (Fla) 301 Brooks Cir E, Jacksonville, FL 32211

SEAL, Chris Houston (The Episcopal NCal) 201 Nevada St, Nevada City, CA 95959

SEALES, Hea Suk (Ala)
SEALS, William Frederick (CFla) 23 Surrey Run, Hendersonville, NC 28791
SEAMAN, Kelly S (NH) 52 Gould Rd, New London, NH 03257
SEAMAN, Martha Lee (Az) 7419 E Palm Ln, Scottsdale, AZ 85257
SEAMANS, Timothy Joseph Sommer (At) 1200 N Quaker Ln, Alexandria, VA 22302
SEARLE, S Elizabeth (Nwk) 200 W 79th St Apt 14-P, New York, NY 10024
SEARS III, Albert Nelson (Mass) 98 Ridgewood Dr, Rocky Hill, CT 06067
SEARS, Barbara (Md) 7030 Upland Ridge Dr, Adamstown, MD 21710
SEARS, Barbara Anne (Md) 1000 Weller Cir Apt 221, Westminster, MD 21158
SEARS, Gwen W (WMass) 235 Walker St. Apt. 162, Lenox, MA 01240
SEATON, Anne Christine (Minn) 168 W Arizona St, Holbrook, AZ 86025
SEATON, Robert Deane (WK) 137 Aspen Rd, Salina, KS 67401
SEATVET, John (WK) St Cornelius Episcopal Church, 200 W Spruce St, Dodge City, KS 67801
SEAVER, Maurice Blanchard (WNC) 3500 Carmel Rd, Charlotte, NC 28226
SEAVEY, Suzanne E (ETenn) 135 Fountainhead Ct, Lenoir City, TN 37772
SEAY, Donald Robert (CFla) 247 N Main St #14, Dousman, WI 53118
SEBRO, Jacqueline Marie (ECR) 815 Sycamore Canyon Rd, Paso Robles, CA 93446
SECAUR, Stephen (Mil) 435 SOM Center Rd., Mayfield Village, OH 44143
SEDDON, Anne Christine (Ct) 4 Maybury Rd, Suffield, CT 06078
SEDDON, Matt (Tex) St. John's Episcopal Church, 11201 Parkfield Drive, Austin, TX 78758
SEDGWICK, Roger Stephen (O) 647 Reid Ave, Lorain, OH 44052
SEDLACEK, Carol Westerberg (Ore) 2103 Desiree Pl, Lebanon, OR 97355
SEDLACEK, Wes (Ore) 2103 Desiree Pl, Lebanon, OR 97355
SEDWICK, Katherine L (Oly) 5128 40th Avenue South, Minneapolis, MN 55417
SEEBER, Laurian (Vt) 47 Shadow Lang Berlin, Barre, VT 05641
SEEFELDT, Scott Allen (Mil)
SEEGER, Elisabeth Ann (Oly) 4467 S. 172nd St., SeaTac, WA 98188
SEEGER, Sue Fisher (Mass) 28 Seagrave Rd, Cambridge, MA 02140
SEEKINS, Sheila (Me)
SEELEY, Janet Lynne (Wyo)
SEELEY JR, Walt (Wyo) 2024 Rolling Hills Road, Kemmerer, WY 83101
SEELY, Shirley Ann (EMich) 3201 Gratiot Ave, Port Huron, MI 48060

SEELY, Steven (WA)
SEELYE FOREST, Elizabeth Jane (Mich) 14191 Ivanhoe Dr Apt 3, Sterling Heights, MI 48312
SEFCHICK, Frank Stephen (Be) 1498 Quakake Rd, Weatherly, PA 18255
SEFTON, Kate (The Episcopal NCal)
SEGAL, Joy Joy (Pa) 916 South Swanson Street, Philadelphia, PA 19147
SEGER, David L (NI) 13259 Hisega Dr, Rapid City, SD 57702
SEGER, Nikki Elizabeth Louise (Mich)
SEGERBRECHT, Stephen Louis (Kan) 1715 Prestwick Dr, Lawrence, KS 66047
SEIBERT, Joanna Johnson (Ark) 27 River Ridge Rd, Little Rock, AR 72227
SEIBERT, Thomas E (Colo) 145 W 5th St, Delta, CO 81416
SEIDMAN, Kim (NwT) Holy Comforter Episcopal Church, PO Box 412, Broomfield, CO 80038
SEIFERT, Cynthia (Tenn) 5041 English Village Dr, Nashville, TN 37211
SEIFERT, Robert Joseph (ECR) 161 Palo Verde Ter, Santa Cruz, CA 95060
SEIFERT, Sarah Lavonne (Kan) 14301 S Blackbob Rd, Olathe, KS 66062
SEILER, Jeffrey Hamilton (Va) 4003 St Erics Turn, Williamsburg, VA 23185
SEILER, Michael S (Los) 300 W Ocean Blvd Apt 6203, Long Beach, CA 90802
SEILER-DUBAY, Noreen (WA) 1510 Oakview Dr, Silver Spring, MD 20903
SEILS, Donald Davis (Colo) 5749 N Stetson Ct, Parker, CO 80134
SEIPEL, James Russell (Los) 25769 Player Dr, Valencia, CA 91355
SEIPP, Vivian (NY) 39 Cumberland Rd, Fishkill, NY 12524
SEITER, Claudia (U) 540 W 2350 S, Brigham City, UT 84302
SEITZ, Christopher R (Dal) Wycliffe College, University Of Toronto, Toronto, M5S 1H7, Canada
SEITZ, Mark Ellis (WVa) PO Box 508, Wheeling, WV 26003
SEITZ, Phil (EMich) 3003 Mill Station Road, Hale, MI 48739
SEITZ JR, Tom (CFla) 221 S 4th St, Lake Wales, FL 33853
SELDEN, Elizabeth Ann (Minn) 6212 Crest Ln, Edina, MN 55436
SELES, Deb (SanD) 1172 Woodriver Dr, Twin Falls, ID 83301
SELF, Debbie (SwFla)
SELFE-VERRONE, Ann Christine (NY) Chapel of St. Francis, 3621 Brunswick Ave., Los Angeles, CA 90039
SELL, James William Henry (SVa) 239 Duke St Unit 207, Norfolk, VA 23510

SELLERS, Robert (Tex) 1401 S PALMETTO AVE, APT 207, DAYTONA BEACH, FL 32114
SELLERY, David F (NC) PO Box 393, Salisbury, CT 06068
SELL-LEE, William Merle (WA) 965 Winslow Way E Unit 103, Bainbridge Island, WA 98110
SELLS, Jeffery Edward (Oly) Po Box 3090, Salt Lake City, UT 84110
SELLS, Michael Gregory (NAM)
SELLS, Patti (Oly)
SELNICK, Thomas Conrad (O) 5040 Wright Terrace, Skokie, IL 60077
SELVAGE, Dan (CPa) 102 Faust Cir, Bellefonte, PA 16823
SELVEY, Mark F (Neb) 3310 16th Ave, Omaha, NE 68022
SELZER, David Owen (WNY) 4 Phylis St, NEPEAN, K2J 1V2, Canada
SEME, Gregory (SeFla)
SEME, Yves (Hai)
SEMES, Robert Louis (Ore) 1354 Primavera Drive E, Palm Springs, CA 92264
SEMON-SCOTT, Deborah Anne (Mich) 3 N Broad St, Hillsdale, MI 49242
SEMPARI, Izabella Lilli (Cal) 1540 12th Ave, Oakland, CA 94606
SENECHAL, Roger (WMass) 7601 Harper Road, Joelton, TN 37080
SENEY, Robert William (Miss) 14165 Denver West Cricle #3407, Lakewood, CO 80401
SENUTA, Lisa Ann (Chi) 550 Sunset Ridge Rd, Northfield, IL 60093
SENYONI, Christian (ND) Grace Episcopal Church, 405 2nd Ave NE, Jamestown, ND 58401
SERACUSE, Linda Kay (Tex) Po Box 559, Conroe, TX 77305
SERAS, Barbara (Md) 67 River Bend Park, Lancaster, PA 17602
SERFES, Patricia May (Me) 2524 Casa Dr, New Port Richey, FL 34655
SERIO, Robert Andrew (Ala) Church of the Nativity, 208 Eustis Ave Se, Huntsville, AL 35801
SERMON, William Todd (Colo) 1612 E Custer St, Laramie, WY 82070
SERPA-ORDONEZ, Pedro Abel (EcuC) Casilla Postal 533, Riobamba, Ecuador
SERRA-LIMA, Federico (Alb) 28 Harrington Lane, Old Chatham, NY 12136
SERRANO, Marco Gabriel (WMo)
SERRANO POREDA, Nelson Evelio (Colom) c/o Diocese of Colombia, Cra 6 No. 49-85 Piso 2, Bogota, BDC, Colombia
SERVAIS, Jean Neal (Okla) PO Box 165, Coalgate, OK 74538
SERVELLON, Maria Filomena (NY) 30 Pine Grove Avenue, 20 Carroll Street, Poughkeepsie, Kingston, NY 12401
SERVETAS, Linda Anne (Alb) 16 Dean St, Deposit, NY 13754

SERVETAS, Nickolas (Alb) 16 Dean St, Deposit, NY 13754

SESSIONS, Judy Karen (WTex) 2910 Treasure Hills Blvd Apt B, Harlingen, TX 78550

SESSIONS, Marcia Andrews (RI) 15 Hattie Ave, Greenville, RI 02828

SESSUM, Bob (Lex) 12000 Diamond Creek Rd Apt 102, Raleigh, NC 27614

SETMEYER, Robert Charles (Chi) 711 S River Rd Apt 508, Des Plaines, IL 60016

SETTLES, Russell Lee (NC) 9118 Kings Canyon Dr, Charlotte, NC 28210

SETZER, Stephen F (Del) 5100 Ross Ave, Dallas, TX 75206

SEUFERT, Carmen Rae (Roch) 103 Williams St, Newark, NY 14513

SEVAYEGA, Reginald Delano (HB) 4701 Belfiore Rd, Warrensville Heights, OH 44128

SEVER, Cynthia A (Spr) 3390 Lyell Rd, Rochester, NY 14606

SEVICK, Gerald (Tex) 3901 S. Panther Creek, The Woodlands, TX 77381

SEVILLE, John C (Chi) 802 Foxdale Ave, Winnetka, IL 60093

SEVILLE, Joseph Yates (CPa) 1405 Wedgewood Way, Mechanicsburg, PA 17050

SEWARD, Barbara J (Chi) Church of St Benedict, 909 Lily Cache Ln, Bolingbrook, IL 60440

SEWELL, Edith (The Episcopal Church in Haw) 1212 Punahou #2504, Honolulu, HI 96826

SEWELL, John Wayne (WTenn) 53 Shepherd Ln, Memphis, TN 38117

SEXTON, Jessica Elaine (Md) 1401 Carrollton Ave, Baltimore, MD 21204

SEXTON, Patricia (USC) 1001 12th St, Cayce, SC 29033

SEXTON, Tim (The Episcopal Church in Haw) PO Box 181, Des Moines, NM 88418

SEYMOUR, John Jack David (Chi) 1631 N Tripp Ave, Chicago, IL 60639

SEYMOUR, Marlyne Joyce (Mil) 862 No. Sandy Lane, Elkhorn, WI 53121

SGRO, Anthony Huston (At)

SHACKELFORD, Lynn Clark (Okla) 404 Washington Avenue, Sand Springs, OK 74063

SHACKLEFORD, Richard Neal (LI) Timber Ridge, 711 John Green Rd, Jonesborough, TN 37659

SHACKLETT JR, Richard L (Kan) 6535 Maple Dr, Mission, KS 66202

SHADLE, Jennifer L (Colo)

SHADOW, Burton Alexander (FtW) 3540 Manderly Place, Fort Worth, TX 76109

SHAEFER, Susan A (Mich) 1605 E. Stadium Blvd., Ann Arbor, MI 48104

SHAFER, Gail Ann (Mich)

SHAFER, Lee Franklin (Ky) 821 S 4th St, Louisville, KY 40203

SHAFER, Linda Jean (Mich) 151 N Main St, Brooklyn, MI 49230

SHAFER, Michael Gales (NY) 21 Decker Road, Stanfordville, NY 12581

SHAFER, Samuel H (RG) 630 66th St, Oakland, CA 94609

SHAFFER, Brian Keith (Mich) Cathedral Church of St. Paul, Detroit, MI 48201

SHAFFER, Charles Omer (Md) 7200 3rd Ave, Cot. C119, Eldersburg, MD 21784

SHAFFER, Dallas Bertrand (WVa) 1415 Cornell St, Keyser, WV 26726

SHAFFER, Dee (Ga) 299 Ga Episcopal Conference Ctr Rd, Waverly, GA 31565

SHAFFER, James M (WMo) PO Box 2714, Friday Harbor, WA 98250

SHAFFER, John Alfred (CNY) PO Box 1219, Shepherdstown, WV 25443

SHAH, Anil Virendra (Los)

☩ **SHAHAN**, Robert Reed (Az) 10175 S North Lake Ave, Olathe, KS 66061

SHAHINIAN, Katharine Anne (Md) St Martin's In The Field, 375 Benfield Rd, Severna Park, MD 21146

SHAIN-HENDRICKS, Christy (Colo) Po Box 10000, Silverthorne, CO 80498

SHAKESPEARE, Lyndon (WA) 543 Beulah Rd NE, Vienna, VA 22180

SHALLCROSS, Lexa Herries (Be) 150 Elm St, Emmaus, PA 18049

SHAMBAUGH, Benjamin Albert (Me) 143 State St, Portland, ME 04101

SHAMEL, Andrew (Cal) 55 Monument Cir Ste 600, Indianapolis, IN 46204

SHAMO, Vincent (Los) 3225 Hollypark Dr Apt 4, Inglewood, CA 90305

SHAN, Becky (ECR) 450 Old San francisco Rd Apt A110, Sunnyvale, CA 94086

SHANAHAN, Thomazine Weinstein (CPa) 4426 Reservoir Rd Nw, Washington, DC 20007

☩ **SHAND**, Bud (Eas) 208 Somerset Ct, Queenstown, MD 21658

SHAND III, William Munro (WA) PO Box 326, Saluda, NC 28773

SHANDS III, Alfred Rives (Ky) 8915 Highway 329, Crestwood, KY 40014

SHANDS, Harriet Goodrich (WNC) 21 Chestnut Ridge Road, Pisgah Forest, NC 28768

SHANE, Janette (Chi) 102 Marquette St, Park Forest, IL 60466

SHANK, Jason Nathaniel (NwPa)

SHANK, Michael Joseph (Alb) 87 E Main St, Sidney, NY 13838

SHANK, Nancy (CPa) 111 Pine St, Danville, PA 17821

SHANKLES, Jeffrey Scott (Va) 6800A Columbia Pike, Annandale, VA 22003

SHANKS, Estelle (Nev) PO Box 98, Austin, NV 89310

SHANKS, Margaret R (Lex) 367 Stratford Dr, Lexington, KY 40503

SHANKS, Stephen Ray (Ala) 112-C King Valley Rd, Pelham, AL 35124

SHANLEY-ROBERTS, Eileen (Chi) 326 N Martin Luther King Jr Ave, Waukegan, IL 60085

SHANNON JR, Carl (Tex) 102 Pecan Grv Apt 121, Houston, TX 77077

SHANNON, Carolyn Louise (Nev) 2366 Aqua Vista Ave, Henderson, NV 89014

SHANNON, James (Pa) 112 Lansdowne Ct, Lansdowne, PA 19050

SHANNON, James Michael (ND) 319 S 5th St, Grand Forks, ND 58201

SHANNON, Johnson (FtW) Po Box 5555, Laguna Park, TX 76644

SHANNON II, Robert Lloyd (Roch) 17 Uncle Bens Way, Orleans, MA 02653

SHAON, Gerald E (Cal) 911 Main St Unit 2908, Kansas City, MO 64105

SHAPTON, Eleanor (Spok) 240 Maringo Rd, Ephrata, WA 98823

SHARP, Carolyn Jackson (Ct) Yale Divinity School, 409 Prospect St., New Haven, CT 06511

SHARP, James L (ETenn) 135 Scenic Shores Dr, Dandridge, TN 37725

SHARP, Jeffrey Robert (Oly) 205 East 96th St, Tacoma, WA 98445

SHARP, Lynne (Roch) PO Box 249, Hammondsport, NY 14840

SHARP, Virginia Gale (ETenn) PO Box 1780, Dandridge, TN 37725

SHARP, Wesley Eric (Ala) 700 Rinehart Rd, Lake Mary, FL 32746

SHARPE, Sheila Gast (Del) 65 East Stephen Drive, Newark, DE 19713

SHARPE, Virginia Edna (CFla) 210 Fallen Timber Trl, Deland, FL 32724

SHARPTON, Larry (Ala) 8501 Olde Gate, Montgomery, AL 36116

SHARROW, Charles (WTex) 960 Toledo Dr, Brownsville, TX 78526

SHATAGIN, Theodore Ivan (Vt) Po Box 1807, Ardmore, OK 73402

SHATTUCK JR, Gardiner Humphrey (RI) 190 North St, Warwick, RI 02886

SHAUBACH, Sheila Kathryn (Episcopal SJ) Po Box 164, Raymond, CA 93653

SHAVER, Ellen M (Me) 139 High Head Rd, Harpswell, ME 04079

SHAVER, John (Minn) 3448 Rum River Dr, Anoka, MN 55303

SHAVER, Stephen (The Episcopal NCal) 550 Mendocino Ave, Santa Rosa, CA 95401

SHAVER, Thomas Ronald (SO) 25 State Rd 13 Apt H8, Saint Johns, FL 32259

SHAW, Adrianna S (Kan) St Philip's Episcopal Church, 302 E. General Stewart Way, Hinesville, GA 31314

SHAW, Jane Alison (Cal) 110 California St, San Francisco, CA 94111

SHAW, Martini (Pa) 6361 Lancaster Ave, Philadelphia, PA 19151

SHAW, Philip Algie (Az) Trinity Episcopal Church, P.O. Box 590, Kingman, AZ 86402

Clergy List

SHAW, Robert Clyde (Mil) 46 New Cross N, Asheville, NC 28805

SHAW, Samuel Gates (Ala) 4112 Abingdon Ln, Birmingham, AL 35243

SHAW, Timothy Joel (CFla) 901 Thompson Cir Nw, Winter Haven, FL 33881

SHAW, Warren Ervin (Pa) 1029 Bristlecone Ln, Charlottesville, VA 22911

SHEARER, Donald Robert (Nwk) 156 Mountain Dr, Greentown, PA 18426

SHEARER, Robert L (Nwk) 2077 Center Ave Apt 20A, Fort Lee, NJ 07024

SHEAY, Virginia M (NJ) 12 Glenwood Ln, Stockton, NJ 08559

SHECTER, Teri Ann (Colo) 2461 F 1/4 Road #231, Grand Junction, CO 81505

SHEEHAN JR, David (Del) 3401 Greenbriar Ln, West Grove, PA 19390

SHEEHAN, John (Va) 512 Duff Rd Ne, Leesburg, VA 20176

SHEEN RODRIGUEZ, Juan Enrique (DR (DomRep))

SHEETZ, David Allan (Cal) 250 Baldwin Ave Apt 303, San Mateo, CA 94401

SHEFFIELD III, Earl J (Tex) 325 Apache Run Road, Wallisville, TX 77597

SHEFFIELD, John Joseph (Tex) PO Box 12615, San Antonio, TX 78212

SHEFFIELD, Sharon (Los) 10354 Downey Ave, Downey, CA 90241

SHEHANE, Mary (Oly) 9416 1st Ave Ne Apt 408, Seattle, WA 98115

SHELBY, Franck Stuart (Tex) Saint Richard's Episcopal Church, 1420 E Palm Valley Blvd, Round Rock, TX 78664

SHELBY, Jason (Miss) 106 Sharkey Ave, Clarksdale, MS 38614

SHELDON, Carren (The Episcopal NCal) 1500 State Street, Santa Barbara, CA 93101

SHELDON, Jaclyn Struff (Ct) 85 Holmes Rd, East Lyme, CT 06333

SHELDON III, Joseph Victor (Spr) 1220 Uss Daniel Boone Ave, Kings Bay, GA 31547

SHELDON, Karen Sears (Vt) 86 S Main St, Hanover, NH 03755

SHELDON, Patricia Lu (Neb) 3818 N 211th St, Elkhorn, NE 68022

SHELDON, Peggy Ann (SeFla) 2000 Sw Racquet Club Dr, Palm City, FL 34990

SHELDON, Raymond S (Oly) 1075 Alexander Pl Ne, Bainbridge Island, WA 98110

SHELDON, Terry Lynn (CNY) 21 White St, Clark Mills, NY 13321

SHELL, Lawrence S (NMich) 201 E. Ridge St., Marquette, MI 49855

SHELLITO, John (Va) St George's Church, 915 N Oakland St, Arlington, VA 22203

SHELLY, Marshall Keith (NJ) 505 Main St, Spotswood, NJ 08884

SHELTON, Benson Eldridge (Va) 9220 Georgetown Pike, Great Falls, VA 22066

SHELTON, Edna S (Mich) 18270 Northlawn St, Detroit, MI 48221

SHELTON, Linda Ross (Tex) 3507 Plumb St, Houston, TX 77005

SHEMATEK, Jon Paul (Md) 9120 Frederick Rd, Ellicott City, MD 21042

SHEMAYEV, Roman Aeired (Mil) 3528 Valley Ridge Rd, Middleton, WI 53562

SHEPARD, Alfred Hugh (Colo) 3013 Taos Meadows Dr NE, Rio Rancho, NM 87144

SHEPARD, Diane Elise Rucker (Pgh) 1155 Brintell St, Pittsburgh, PA 15201

SHEPARD, Kenneth (Neb)

SHEPARD, Margaret Smith (CGC) 1608 Baker Ct, Panama City, FL 32401

SHEPHERD, Angela Fontessa (At) Episcopal Diocese of Maryland, 4 E University Pkwy, Baltimore, MD 21218

SHEPHERD, Burton Hale (WTex) 185 Towerview Dr Apt 1101, Saint Augustine, FL 32092

SHEPHERD, Karlyn Ann (RG) 22 Bowersville Rd, Algodones, NM 87001

SHEPHERD, Nancy Delane (At) 1100 Pine Valley Road, Griffin, GA 30224

SHEPHERD, Nancy Hamilton (Mass) 172 Harvard Rd, Stow, MA 01775

SHEPHERD, Stephen (Va) 6019 Hibbling Ave, Springfield, VA 22150

SHEPHERD, Thomas Charles (Mass) 6600 Ne 22nd Way Apt 2323, Fort Lauderdale, FL 33308

SHEPHERD, Thomas E (WMo) 1107 Saratoga Drive, Euless, TX 76040

SHEPHERD JR, William Henry (At) 1100 Pine Valley Rd, Griffin, GA 30224

SHEPHERD, William John (Pa) 110 W Johnson St, Philadelphia, PA 19144

SHEPIC, Charlotte Louise (Colo) 14031 W Exposition Dr, Lakewood, CO 80228

SHEPLER, Dawn (Colo)

SHEPLEY, Joseph (Ct) 65 Grey Rock Road, Southbury, CT 06488

SHEPPARD, Dale Eugene (WVa) 1051 Walker Road, Follansbee, WV 26037

SHEPPARD, Patricia (Fla) 919 San Fernando St., Fernandina Beach, FL 32034

SHEPPARD, Ricardo Wayne (NJ)

SHERARD, Susan (NC) 402 West Smith Street, 4J, Greensboro, NC 27401

SHERER, Valori (WNC) 506 W Sumter St, Shelby, NC 28150

SHERFICK, Kenneth L (WMich) 1517 Emoriland Blvd, Knoxville, TN 37917

SHERIDAN, Dennis Arnol (Los) 242 E Alvarado St, Pomona, CA 91767

SHERIDAN-CAMPBELL, Laura M (SanD) 6540 Ambrosia Ln Apt 1128, Carlsbad, CA 92011

SHERMAN, Andrew James (SeFla) 245 NE 2nd St., Boca Raton, FL 33432

SHERMAN, Beth (RI) St. Francis Episcopal Church, San Francisco, CA 94127

SHERMAN, Clark Michael (Mont) 5 W Olive St, Bozeman, MT 59715

SHERMAN, Guy Charles (Oly) 12527 Roosevelt Way NE Apt 405, Seattle, WA 98125

SHERMAN JR, Levering Bartine (Me) 130 Cedar St, Bangor, ME 04401

SHERMAN, Russell E (WTex) 202 Primera Dr, San Antonio, TX 78212

SHERMAN, Walter (Ind) 5023 N. Pennsylvania St, Indianapolis, IN 46205

SHERRER, Wayne (Be) 150 Elm Street, Emmaus, PA 18049

SHERRILL, Christopher Ralph (NJ) P.O. Box 45, Southport, ME 04576

SHERRILL II, Edmund Knox (NH) Church Farm School, 1001 E Lincoln Hwy, Exton, PA 19341

SHERRILL JR, George (SO) 906 Main St Apt 412, Cincinnati, OH 45202

SHERRILL, Joan Lee (NC)

SHERRILL, Karen F Lynt (SO) St. John's Episcopal Church, 3000 Washington Blvd, Huntington, WV 25705

SHERROUSE, Wanda Gail (CFla) 121 W 18th St, Sanford, FL 32771

SHERWIN, Lawrence Alan (Vt) 54 E State St, Montpelier, VT 05602

SHERWOOD, Robert Leon (Mass) 165 Main St, Buzzards Bay, MA 02532

SHERWOOD, Zalmon Omar (Mich) PO Box 1342, Arcadia, FL 34265

SHEVLIN, James Charles (CFla) Saint Paul's Church, 25 River St, Sidney, NY 13838

SHEW, Debbie (Colo) 910 E 3rd Ave, Durango, CO 81301

SHEWMAKER, David Paul (The Episcopal NCal) St Paul's Episcopal Ch, 220 E. Macken, Crescent City, CA 95531

SHIELD, Catherine Ann (Kan) 13420 E Harry St, Wichita, KS 67230

SHIELDS, James Mark (Md) 6153 Waiting Spg, Columbia, MD 21045

SHIELDS, John (NC) 520 Summit St, Winston Salem, NC 27101

SHIELDS, Kelly Ann (Ia)

SHIELDS, Richard Edward (The Episcopal Church in Haw) 1441 Victoria St Apt 403, Honolulu, HI 96822

SHIELDS, Wes (WNC) 2508 Amity Ave, Gastonia, NC 28054

SHIER, Marshall (Los) 1348 E Wilshire Ave, Fullerton, CA 92831

SHIER, Nancy Katherine (Los) 224 Bradbury Dr, San Gabriel, CA 91775

SHIER, Pamela C (WVa) 164 Mason Ridge Rd, Mount Morris, PA 15349

SHIFLET JR, Bill (Md) 4520 Cornflower Ct, Ellicott City, MD 21043

SHIGAKI, Jerry Moritsune (Oly) 6963 California Ave Sw Unit 102, Seattle, WA 98136

SHIGAKI, Pauline Yuri (Oly)

SHIKE, Charles Wesley (Nwk) 601 Kappock St Apt 1F, Bronx, NY 10463

SHILEY, Ed (Pa) 145 West Springfield Road, Springfield, PA 19064

✠ **SHIN**, Allen (NY) Episcopal Diocese of New York, 1047 Amsterdam Ave, New York, NY 10025

SHINE, Anna Colleen (WNC) PO Box 645, Valle Crucis, NC 28691

SHIODE, Jimmy H (Los)

SHIPMAN, Bruce MacDonald (Ct) 241 Monument St Apt 6, Groton, CT 06340

SHIPMAN, Josh (Colo)

SHIPP, Mary Jane Mccoy (Mont) 120 Antelope Dr, Dillon, MT 59725

SHIPPEE, Richard C (RI) 3330 E Main St Lot 109, Mesa, AZ 85213

SHIPPEN II, Joseph J (At) PO Box 1213, Griffin, GA 30224

SHIPPEN, Sallie Elliot (Cal) 756 14th Way Sw, Edmonds, WA 98020

SHIPPEY, Edgar Elijah (Ore) 940 N Dean St, Coquille, OR 97423

SHIRLEY, Diana Frangoulis (SO) 664 Glacier Pass, Westerville, OH 43081

SHIRLEY, Fredric C (SO) 664 Glacier Pass, Westerville, OH 43081

SHIRLEY, John Robert (LI) 520 Clinton Ave, Brooklyn, NY 11238

SHIRLEY, Mike (Mass) 28 Amherst St, Lawrence, MA 01843

SHIRLEY, Sarah A (WA) 4851 W Gandy Blvd Lot B1025, Tampa, FL 33611

SHIRLEY, Sylvia (Okla) St John's Episcopal Church, 5201 N Brookline Ave, Oklahoma City, OK 73112

SHIROTA, Andrew Kunihito (Ky) 4700 Lowe Rd, Louisville, KY 40220

SHISLER, Sara (The Episcopal Church in Haw) 480 Olinda Rd, Makawao, HI 96768

SHIVES, Beverly Mason (SeFla) 159 Biscayne Ave, Tampa, FL 33606

SHIVES, Robert Edward (WVa) 154 East St, Kearneysville, WV 25430

SHOBE, Melody W (RI) 2407 Cranston St., Cranston, RI 02920

SHOBE, Robert Casey (Dal) 14115 Hillcrest Road, Dallas, TX 75254

SHOBERG, Warren E (SD) 3316 E 28th St, Sioux Falls, SD 57103

SHOCKLEY, Stephanie Elizabeth (NJ) 316 E 88th St, New York, NY 10128

SHODA, David Brian (WVa) 108 S Washington St, Berkeley Springs, WV 25411

SHOEMAKE, Daniel O (Ga) 4346 Ridge Rd, Buford, GA 30519

SHOEMAKER, Adam (SC) The Episcopal Church of the Holy Comforter, 320 East Davis Street, Burlington, NC 27215

SHOEMAKER, Eric Wayne (WA) 8795 Lowell Road, Pomfret, MD 20675

SHOEMAKER, Patricia Ross Pittman (NC) 22 Mayflower Ln, Lexington, NC 27295

SHOEMAKER, Stephanie (RI) 96 Washington St, Newport, RI 02840

SHOFSTALL, Sarah J (O) Saint Barnabas Church, 468 Bradley Rd, Bay Village, OH 44140

SHOLANDER, Mark Earl (CFla) 907 Oakway Dr, Auburndale, FL 33823

SHOLTY JR, Henry Edward (Dal) 5942 Abrams Rd # 209, Dallas, TX 75231

SHORT, James Healy (Colo) 797 Tower Hill Rd., Appomattox, VA 24522

SHORT, James Ritchie (Episcopal SJ) Casanova & ocean, Carmel, CA 93921

SHORT, Molly (NC) 290 Quintard Rd, Sewanee, TN 37375

SHORTELL, Bruce Mallard (At) PO Box 1293, Flowery Branch, GA 30542

SHORTES, Stephen Edward (The Episcopal NCal) 2883 Coloma St, Placerville, CA 95667

SHORTESS, Stephen A (La)

SHORTRIDGE, Delores J (Nev) 973 S. Fulton St., Denver, CO 80247

SHORTT, Mary J (EMich) P.O. Box 151, West Branch, MI 48661

SHOUCAIR, James Douglas (Pgh) 130 Westchester Dr, Pittsburgh, PA 15215

SHOULAK, Jim (Minn) 20475 County Road 10, Corcoran, MN 55340

SHOULDERS, David Ira (Ind) 3415 Windham Lake Place, Indianapolis, IN 46214

SHOWERS, David (Md) Middleham & St. Peter Ep. Parish, PO Box 277, Lusby, MD 20657

SHOWS, William Derek (NC) 1077 Fearrington Post, Pittsboro, NC 27312

SHOWS CAFFEY, Elizabeth Kristen (At) 634 W Peachtree St NW, Atlanta, GA 30308

SHRIVER, Domingo Frances (WMich) 301 N James St, Ludington, MI 49431

SHRIVER JR, Frederick Hardman (NY) 37 W. 12th Street, Apt. 4K, New York, NY 10011

SHUART, Steve (NwPa) Po Box 368, South Harwich, MA 02661

SHUFORD, Carlton Lamont (Ga) 131 Avondale Dr, Augusta, GA 30907

SHUFORD, Sheila Cathcart (Nwk) 12 Sorman Ter, Randolph, NJ 07869

SHUKAIR, Halim Adel (Mich) 120 N Military St, Dearborn, MI 48124

SHULDA, David Leroy (Ore) 2139 Berwin Ln, Eugene, OR 97404

SHUMAKER, Jack (Episcopal SJ) 1317 Gold Hunter Rd, San Andreas, CA 95249

SHUMARD, James B (Wyo) 701 S Wolcott St, Casper, WY 82601

SHUMATE, Jonathan Kale Gavin (Ore)

SIBERINE, Katherine H (NH) 1704 Ne 43rd Ave, Portland, OR 97213

SIBLEY, David C (LI) 910 E. Sumach St, Walla Walla, WA 99362

SICHANGI, Nicholas Nyongesa (Eas)

SICILIANO, Elizabeth Diana (Md)

SICKELS, Peter L (Ia) 4814 Amesbury Ct, Davenport, IA 52807

SICKLER, Brenda Pamela (WMo) 5 E 337th Rd, Humansville, MO 65674

SICKLES, Clarence William (Nwk) 68 Heath Village, Hackettstown, NJ 07840

SIDEBOTHAM, John Nelson (EC) 16 W Fayetteville St, Wrightsville Beach, NC 28480

SIDERIUS, Donna-Mae Amy (SVa) 3 Mizzen Cir, Hampton, VA 23664

SIDES, Serena Wille (WA) 620 G St SE, Washington, DC 20003

SIEGEL II, Carl De Haven (WMo) 1405 Boyce Ave, Baltimore, MD 21204

SIEGENTHALER, David John (Mass) 54 Concord Ave Apt 102, Cambridge, MA 02138

SIEGFRIEDT, Karen (The Episcopal NCal) 170 Verdon St, Morro Bay, CA 93442

SIEGMUND, Mary Kay (Kan) 3 Ne 83rd Ter, Kansas City, MO 64118

SIENER, George Richard (NH) 6 Whippoorwill Ln, Exeter, NH 03833

SIERACKI, Emily (Ida) 518 N 8th Street, Boise, ID 83702

SIERRA, Federico (Los) 425 N Stoneman Ave Apt A, Alhambra, CA 91801

SIERRA, Frank (WMo) 2718 Alabama Ct, Joplin, MO 64804

SIERRA, Jesus (NC) Iglesia Episcopal Puertorriquena, PO Box 902, Saint Just, PR 00978

SIERRA ECHEVERRY, Gabriel Alcides (Colom) Parroquia La Anunciacion, El Bagre, Apartado Aereo 52964, Bogota, Colombia

SIFFORD, Thomas Andrew (Ark) 74 Sierra Dr, Hot Springs Village, AR 71909

SIGAFOOS, Richard Vaughn (Colo) 131 31 Rd, Grand Junction, CO 81503

SIGAMONEY, Christopher (LI)

SIGLER, James (The Episcopal NCal) P.O. Box 467, Wimberley, TX 78676

SIGLER JR, Richard Eugene (NC) 930 Walker Ave, Greensboro, NC 27403

SIGLOH, Jane Engleby (SwVa) 4068 Garth Rd, Crozet, VA 22932

SIGNORE, Richard S (WMass) 19 Briggs Ave., Bourne, MA 02532

SIGNORELLI, Barry M (NY) 278 Monmouth St Apt 4-L, Jersey City, NJ 07302

SILBAUGH, Morgan Collins (Cal) 914 Mountain Meadows Cir, Ashland, OR 97520

SILBEREIS, Richard M (Ct) 155 Wyllys St, Hartford, CT 06106

SILCOX JR, James Heyward (Va) Wicomico Parish Church, PO Box 70, Wicomico Church, VA 22579

SILIDES JR, George Constantine (Los) 830 W Bonita Ave, Claremont, CA 91711

SILIDES, Hunter (Los) 411 Gold St, Juneau, AK 99801

SILK-WRIGHT, Margaret E (CFla) 1813 Palo Alto Ave, Lady Lake, FL 32159

SILLA, SuzeAnne Marie (NI) Diocese of Northern Indiana, 117 N Lafayette Blvd, South Bend, IN 46601

SILTON, Margaret Kanze (NC) PO Box 608, Wake Forest, NC 27588

SILVER, Deborah Lee (At) 3005 St James Pl, Grovetown, GA 30813

SILVER, Gay (Fla) 14557 Basilham Ln, Jacksonville, FL 32258

SILVERSTRIM, Elaine Margaret (CPa) 110 Dry Run Rd., Coudersport, PA 16915

SIMEONE, Richard John (Mass) 203 Pemberton St Unit 3, Cambridge, MA 02140

SIMMONS, Charles Winston (NY) St Andrew's Church, 781 Castle Hill Ave, Bronx, NY 10473

SIMMONS, David (Mil) 808 S East Ave, Waukesha, WI 63186

SIMMONS, David Clark (NMich) 5976 Whitney 19.8 Blvd, Gladstone, MI 49837

SIMMONS, Elizabeth (Ak) PO Box 1668, Kodiak, AK 99615

SIMMONS, Harriet (Miss) 4911 Country Club Dr, Meridian, MS 39305

SIMMONS, Harriette (At) Saint Paul'S Church, 605 Reynolds Street On The Riverwalk, Augusta, GA 30901

SIMMONS, Kenneth William (Minn) 11 Kellogg Blvd E Apt 715, Saint Paul, MN 55101

SIMMONS, Mary Rose (NMich) 5976 Whitney 19.8 Blvd, Gladstone, MI 49837

SIMMONS, Ned Allen (Ga) 109 Flint River Circle, Quitman, GA 31643

SIMMONS IV, Tom (Va) 1807 Hungary Rd, Richmond, VA 23228

SIMMONS, Walter Clippinger (Md) 514 Limerick Cir. Unit 201, Lutherville Timonium, MD 21093

SIMMONS, Warren Reginald (At) 13560 Cogburn Rd, Milton, GA 30004

SIMON JR, Ken (SanD) 6556 Park Ridge Boulevard, San Diego, CA 92120

SIMONIAN, Marlene Jenny (RI) 1346 Creek Nine Dr, North Port, FL 34290

SIMONS, Daniel J (NY) 74 Trinity Pl, New York, NY 10006

SIMONS, James Burdette (Pgh) 731 Laurel Dr, Ligonier, PA 15658

SIMONSEN, Douglas C (Oly) P.O. Box 1974, Anacortes, WA 98221

SIMOPOULOS, Nicole M (SanD) 563 Kamoku St, Honolulu, HI 96826

SIMPLE, Margaret (Ak)

SIMPSON, Cindy (WA) Christ Episcopal School, 107 S Washington St, Rockville, MD 20850

SIMPSON, Dawn Marie (Colo) Po Box 291, Monte Vista, CO 81144

SIMPSON, Elizabeth Bass (Mo) St Matthew's Episcopal Church, 1100 Grove St, Mexico, MO 65265

SIMPSON, Geoffrey Stewart (Pa) Church Of The Good Samaritan, 212 W Lancaster Ave, Paoli, PA 19301

SIMPSON, Matthew David (Pa) PO Box 387, Buckingham, PA 18912

SIMPSON, Richard Edmund (LI) 754 Main St, Islip, NY 11751

SIMPSON, Richard Michael (WMass) 88 Highland St, Holden, MA 01520

SIMPSON, Richard Roy (RI) 7009 SE 117th Pl., Portland, OR 97266

SIMPSON, Sallie O'Keef (NC) 1725 N New Hope Rd, Raleigh, NC 27604

SIMPSON, Ward Howard (SD) 500 South Main Ave, Sioux Falls, SD 57104

SIMRILL, Spenser (At) 4945 Dupont Ave S, Minneapolis, MN 55419

SIMS, Carol Carruthers (SVa) 3929 Ocean Cut Lane, Virginia Beach, VA 23451

SIMS, Gregory Brian (Chi) 4233 Ahlstrand Dr, Rockford, IL 61101

SIMS, Gregory Knox (Cal) Po Box 1, Boonville, CA 95415

SIMS, Kenneth Harry (SeFla) 3970 Nw 188th St, Opa Locka, FL 33055

SIMS, Mark (SeFla) 1165 Ne 105th St, Miami Shores, FL 33138

SIMS, Richard Osborn (Nev) 24 Elysium Dr, Ely, NV 89301

SIMS, Ronald Frank (Wyo) 200 Country Brook Dr Apt 2427, Keller, TX 76248

SIMS, William David (Ark) 28 Prospect Avenue, Eureka Springs, AR 72632

SIMSON, John Everett (Mass) 4773 Abargo St, Woodland Hills, CA 91364

SINCLAIR, Barbara Louise (Chi) St James Episcopal Church, 425 E MacArthur Ave, Lewistown, IL 61542

SINCLAIR, Elisabeth Anne (Mil) 7110 N State Route 9, Kansas City, MO 64152

SINCLAIR, Gregory Lynn (NwT) 801 Ross Ave, Abilene, TX 79605

SINCLAIR, Nancy (Los) 502 Hawk Ln, Fountain Valley, CA 92708

SINCLAIR, Scott Gambrill (Cal) 663 Coventry Rd, Kensington, CA 94707

SINCLAIR, William Carter (SVa)

SINGER, Allen Michael (EC) 800 Rountree St, Kinston, NC 28501

SINGER, Susanna Jane (Cal) 1233 Howard Street #714, San Francisco, CA 94103

☩ **SINGH**, Prince Grenville (Roch) 4 Cathedral Oaks, Fairport, NY 14450

SINGH, Simon Peter (Chi) 261 W Army Trail Rd, Bloomingdale, IL 60108

SINGLETON, Jill (Nwk) 38 Duncan Ave, Jersey City, NJ 07304

SINGLETON, Lester Brian (Fla) 18120 Southeast 59 Street, Micanopy, FL 32667

SINGLETON, Richard Oliver (Mich) 1520 W River Rd, Scottsville, VA 24590

SINISI, Gabriel Arcangelo (Az) 17025 W Aberdeen Dr, Surprise, AZ 85374

SINK, Thomas Leslie (NJ) Po Box 3010, Pt Pleasant, NJ 08742

SINNING, Thomas John (Minn) 1517 Rosewood Cir, Alexandria, MN 56308

SINNOTT, Lynn (Roch) 2842 Hawks Rd, Wellsville, NY 14895

SINTIM, Tim (NC) 1925 waters DR, Raleigh, NC 27610

SIPE, Robert Billie (Ore) 59048 Whitetail Ave., Saint Helens, OR 97051

SIPES, David Sheldon (O) 446 Shepard Rd, Mansfield, OH 44907

SIPOS, Elizabeth Anne Margaret (Md) 11901 Belair Rd, Kingsville, MD 21087

SIPPLE, Peter Warren (Pa) 45 Bay View Avenue, Cornwall on Hudson, NY 12520

SIRCY, Micheal John (SwFla)

SIRENO, Robert (Ct)

SIRIANI, Laura Eustis (Los) 1221 Wass St, Tustin, CA 92780

SIRMON JR, Thomas Forbes (CGC) 28 Miracle Strip Pkwy SW, Fort Walton Beach, FL 32548

SIROTA, Victoria R (NY) Cathedral Church of St John the Divine, 1047 Amsterdam Ave, New York, NY 10025

☩ **SISK**, Mark (NY) PO Box 53, Jefferson, NY 12093

SISK, Robert Buchanan (Mont) Rr 1 Box 241, Wilsall, MT 59086

SISSON, Duane (Cal) 2973 California St, Oakland, CA 94602

SISSON, Penny Ray (Miss) 414 Turnberry Cir, Oxford, MS 38655

SITTON, Gary William (Colo) 7695 Quitman St, Westminster, CO 80030

SITTS, C Joseph (CFla) 271 New Waterford Pl, Longwood, FL 32779

SIVE, Marian Mae (Alb) PO Box 41, Burnt Hills, NY 12027

SIVLEY, John Stephen (CPa) 869E Rhue Haus Ln, Hummelstown, PA 17036

SIVRET, David Otis (Me) 46 Oak Lane, Alexander, ME 04694

SIWEK, Peter (Chi) 733 Hayes Ave, Oak Park, IL 60302

SIX, George (Los) PO Box 235, Horse Shoe, NC 28742

SIZE, Patricia Barrett (Mil) 2215 Commonwealth Ave, Madison, WI 53726

SKAGGS, Richard Lee (WVa) 1410 Chapline St, Wheeling, WV 26003

SKALA, Kira (Va) 241 Signal Ridge Ln, Winchester, VA 22603

SKALESKI, Elizabeth Harris (Ct)

SKAU, Laurie Jean (Minn) 6727 France Ave N, Brooklyn Center, MN 55429

SKAUG, Jon (Az)

SKEATES, Winifred June (NH) 270 Stark Hwy N, Dunbarton, NH 03046

SKEITH, Paul (Tex) SoCo Episcopal Community, 1502 Eva St, Austin, TX 78704

SKELLEN, Bonnie Jean (NwPa) 425 E Main St, Ridgway, PA 15853

SKELLY, Herbert Cope (Mass) 40 Woodland Way, Eastham, MA 02642

SKEWES-COX, Peter Dunne (Nev)

SKIDMORE, Joanne Louise (FdL) 2389 Penny Lane, Sister Bay, WI 54234

SKIFFINGTON, Steven Wayne (Episcopal SJ) Trinity Cathedral, 2620 Capitol Ave, Sacramento, CA 95816

SKILLICORN, Gerald Amos (WMo) 2207 Conrad Way, Somerset, NJ 08873

SKILLINGS, Thomas (Cal) 1104 Mills Ave, Burlingame, CA 94010

✠ **SKILTON**, William Jones (DR (DomRep)) 4969 Parkside Dr, North Charleston, SC 29405

SKINNER, Beatrice (SD)

SKINNER, Jean Mary (CNY) 40 Faxton St, Utica, NY 13501

SKINNER, Susan (Mo) 400 Mark Dr, Saint Louis, MO 63122

✠ **SKIRVING**, Robert Stuart (EC) Episcopal Diocese of East Carolina, PO Box 1336, Kinston, NC 28503

SKOGLUND, Lars David Jackson (Mil) 670 E Monroe Ave, Hartford, WI 53027

SKORNIK, Andria (Chi) St Andrew's Episcopal Church, 1125 Franklin St, Downers Grove, IL 60515

SKRAMSTAD, Dawn Marie (Alb) St. Mary's Church, P.O. Box 211, Lake Luzerne, NY 12846

SKUTCH, Patrick J (Chi) 306 S Prospect Ave, Park Ridge, IL 60068

SKYLES, Benjamin Henry (Tex) 2110 Canyon Lake Dr, Deer Park, TX 77536

SLABACH, Brock Allen (WMo) 16808 S State Route D, Belton, MO 64012

SLACK, James Cooper Simmons (Dal) 1019 Sassafras Lane, Niles, MO 49120

SLACK, Sean C (Pa) St Paul's Church, 89 Pinewood Dr, Levittown, PA 19054

SLADE, Debra Katherine Ann (Ct) 503 Old Long Ridge Rd, Stamford, CT 06903

SLADE, Kara N (NJ) Saint David's Episcopal Church, PO Box 334, Laurinburg, NC 28353

SLAKEY, Anne Elisa Margaret (Ida) 110 N. 10th St., Payette, ID 83661

SLANE, Christopher D (Neb)

SLANE, Melanie W (Mo) 3737 Seminary Rd, Alexandria, VA 22304

SLANGER, George Comfort (ND) 8435 207th St. W., Lakeville, MN 55044

SLATER, Amy A (Fla)

SLATER, Chadwick M (WVa) 200 Duhring St, Bluefield, WV 24701

SLATER, Joan (NMich) PO Box100, Mackinac Island, MI 49757

SLATER, Jo Ann Kennedy (Mich) 5416 Parkgrove Rd, Ann Arbor, MI 48103

SLATER, Michael (Nev) 7900 Pueblo Drive, Stagecoach, NV 89429

SLATER, Sarah Elizabeth (WA)

SLATER, Scott Gerald (Md) 4 East University Parkway, Baltimore, MD 21218

SLAUGHTER, Susan (FtW) 1612 Boardwalk Ct, Arlington, TX 76011

SLAUSON, Holley B (NY) 75 de Maio Dr Apt B12, Milford, CT 06460

SLAVIN, Nancy (Cal)

SLAWNWHITE, Virginia Ann (NH) Po Box 433, Portsmouth, NH 03802

SLAWSON III, H Thomas (Md) 3695 Rogers Avenue, Ellicott City, MD 21043

SLAY, Pearlean Boykin (Ala) PO Box 560, Demopolis, AL 36732

SLAYMAKER, Lorraine P (Ark) 1112 Alcoa Rd, Benton, AR 72015

SLAYTER, Malcolm Franklin (NwT) 2809 Moss Ave, Midland, TX 79705

SLEMMER, Amy Whitcomb (Mass)

SLEMP, Dennett Clinton (SVa) 11001 Ashburn Rd, North Chesterfield, VA 23235

SLENSKI, Mary (Ind) 5256 Central Ave., Indianapolis, IN 46220

SLIGH, John Lewis (SeFla) 2422 W Stroud Ave, Tampa, FL 33629

SLOAN III, Carey Erastus (O) 2390 N Orchard Rd NE, Bolivar, OH 44612

SLOAN, Ellen Margaret (SwFla) St. Michael & All Angels, 2304 Periwinkle Way, Sanibel, FL 33957

✠ **SLOAN SR**, John Mckee (Ala) 521 North 20th Street, Birmingham, AL 35203

SLOAN, Richard D (NY) 90 Gilbert Road, Ho-Ho-Kus, NJ 07423

SLOAN, Stan Jude (Chi) 2313 N Kedzie Blvd # 2, Chicago, IL 60647

SLOAN, Susan (Ala) 821 Baylor Drive, Huntsville, AL 35802

SLOCOMBE, Iris Ruth (Mich) Apdo Postal 673, Col Ajijic Centro, Chapala, JAL 45920, Mexico

SLOCUM, Robert Boak (Lex) PO Box 2505, Danville, KY 40423

SLONE, Remington (Fla) 400 San Juan Dr., Ponte Vedra Beach, FL 32082

SLOVAK, Anita M (Az) Christ The King Episcopal Church, 2800 W Ina Rd, Tucson, AZ 85741

SLUSHER, Montie Bearl (Ak) 1133 Park Dr., Fairbanks, AK 99709

SLUSS, Mark (Mo) 2918 Victor St, Saint Louis, MO 63104

SMALL, Timothy K (CPa) 370 Spring Hill Ln, Columbia, PA 17512

SMALLEY, H Bud (Ida) 5170 Leonard Rd, Pocatello, ID 83204

SMALLEY, Nancy T (Dal) 416 Victorian Dr, Waxahachie, TX 75165

SMALLEY, Richard Craig (Ala) 2017 6th Avenue North, Birmingham, AL 35203

SMALLEY, Stephen Mark (Pgh) 210 Strawberry Circle, Cranberry Township, PA 16066

✠ **SMALLEY**, William Edward (Ind) 13809 E 186th St, Noblesville, IN 46060

SMALLWOOD, Richard Lewis (Nev) 4709 S Nellis Blvd, Las Vegas, NV 89121

SMART, Dennis (At) 442 Euclid Terrace N.E., Atlanta, GA 30307

SMART JR, James Hudson (NwT) 1826 Elmwood Dr, Abilene, TX 79605

SMART, John A (Pa) 5100 N Northridge Cir, Tucson, AZ 85718

SMART, LuLa Grace Grace (Pa) 147 7th Ave, Folsom, PA 19033

SMEDLEY IV, Walter (Chi) Saint Chrysostom's Church, 1424 N Dearborn St, Chicago, IL 60610

SMELSER, Todd Dudley (At) 1358 E Rock Springs Rd Ne, Atlanta, GA 30306

SMERCINA, Eugene Edward (O) 4307 Cleveland Rd E, Huron, OH 44839

SMIRAGLIA, Richard Paul (Pa) 340 Fitzwater Street, Philadelphia, PA 19147

SMITH, Aaron William (Fla) 4775 Godwin Ave, Jacksonville, FL 32210

SMITH, Adeline (NY)

SMITH, Aidan (Alb)

SMITH, A Lan Bruce (SO) 627 Yaronia Dr N, Columbus, OH 43214

SMITH, Aloha Lee (Los) 5848 Tower Rd, Riverside, CA 92506

SMITH, Andrea (Ct) 16 Clam Shell Alley, P.O. Box 412, Vinalhaven, ME 04863

SMITH, Ann Robb (Pa) 816 Castlefinn Ln, Bryn Mawr, PA 19010

SMITH, Anne Largent (The Episcopal NCal) 9085 Calvine Rd., Sacramento, CA 95829

SMITH, Ann-Lining (Cal) 750 47th Ave Spc 34, Capitola, CA 95010

SMITH, Arthur Wells (CNY) 341 Main St, Oneida, NY 13421

SMITH, Barbara Joan (U) c/o Episcopal Carmel of Saint Teresa, 123 Little New York Rd, Rising Sun, MD 21911

SMITH, Bardwell Leith (Minn) 104 Maple St, Northfield, MN 55057

SMITH JR, Ben Huddleston (Md) 1401 Carrollton Ave, Baltimore, MD 21204

SMITH, Bert Orville (At) 841 Kings Grant Dr NW, Atlanta, GA 30318

SMITH, Betty Lorraine (NMich) 8114 Trout Lake Rd, Naubinway, MI 49762

SMITH, Bill (Ore) 17320 Quaker Ln Apt B21, Sandy Spring, MD 20860

SMITH, Bob (Pa) 2033 Bainbridge St, Philadelphia, PA 19146

SMITH, Bob (Eas) 35 Spruance Ct, Elkton, MD 21921

SMITH, Bobby (Chi) 217 Houston St, Ripon, WI 54971

SMITH, Bonnie (EC) 501 S Harding Dr Apt 1002, Goldsboro, NC 27534

SMITH, Bradford Ray (NC) 116 S Church St, PO Box 293, Monroe, NC 28111

SMITH, Brian Eliot (Fla) 655 W Jefferson St, Tallahassee, FL 32304

SMITH, Bruce (Cal) 14 Ardmore Ct, Pleasant Hill, CA 94523

SMITH, Carol Diane (Minn) 1211 Jackson Ave, Detroit Lakes, MN 56501

SMITH, Carol Kay Huston (Mil) 4522 Aztec Trail, Fitchburg, WI 53711

SMITH, Carter Austin (CFla) 2499 N Westmoreland Dr, Orlando, FL 32804

SMITH, Cathleen Anne (WNY) 410 N Main St, Jamestown, NY 14701

SMITH, Cecilia Mary Babcock (Tex) PO Box 2247, Austin, TX 78768

SMITH, Channing (ECR) 13601 Saratoga Avenue, Saratoga, CA 95070

SMITH, Charles J (SVa) St Michael and All Angels, 6408 Bridgewood Rd, Columbia, SC 29206

SMITH, Charles L (Ak) PO Box 3346, Odessa, TX 79760

SMITH, Charles Rodney (Tex) 156 Fairacres Ln, Sewanee, TN 37375

SMITH, Charles Stuart (Alb) 45 Pierrepont Ave., Potsdam, NY 13676

SMITH, Christopher Atkins (Alb) 12 Main St., Hagaman, NY 12086

SMITH, Claude (Mass) 160 River Street, Norwell, MA 02061

SMITH, Claudia L (Me) 810 Morgan Bay Rd, Blue Hill, ME 04614

SMITH, Coleen Haas (SO)

SMITH III, Colton Mumford (SC) 1 Bishop Gadsden Way Apt 346, Charleston, SC 29412

SMITH, Craig (Vt) 5167 Shelburne Road, Shelburne, VT 05482

✠ **SMITH**, Dabney (SwFla) The Diocese of Southwest Florida, 8005 25th Street East, Parrish, FL 34219

SMITH, Dale Leroy (Los) 10451 Jordan Parkway, Hopewell, VA 23860

SMITH, David Grant (Roch) St. Mark's Episcopal Church, P.O. Box 424, Penn Yan, NY 14527

SMITH, David Gregory (Mont) 5 W Olive St, Bozeman, MT 59715

SMITH, David Hayes (Va) 800 Chatham Hall Cir., Chatham, VA 24531

SMITH, David Lester (WNY) 5448 Broadway St, Lancaster, NY 14086

SMITH, Don Leland (Oly) 8989 S Pine Dr, Beulah, CO 81023

SMITH, Donald Hedges (Roch) 2492 Keystone Lake Drive, Cape Coral, FL 33909

SMITH III, Donald M (Ala) 860 N Section St, Fairhope, AL 36532

SMITH, Doris Graf (At) 11210 Wooten Lake Rd, Kennesaw, GA 30144

SMITH, Douglas Cameron (CPa) 21 Cornell Dr, Hanover, PA 17331

✠ **SMITH**, Drew (Ct) 106 Vista Way, Bloomfield, CT 06002

SMITH, Duane Andre (Lex) 110 Chestnut Ct, Berea, KY 40403

SMITH, Edward D (CFla) 1210 Locust St, Saint Louis, MO 63103

SMITH, Edwin Ball (FdL) 1060 S Westhaven Dr, Oshkosh, WI 54904

SMITH, Edwin Earl St Clair (Pa) 154 Locksley Rd, Glen Mills, PA 19342

SMITH JR, Frank Warner (Neb) 2303 Elk, Beatrice, NE 68310

SMITH, Gail S (Mass) 35 Skyline Drive, Chatham, MA 02633

SMITH, Geoffrey T (NH) 400 E 58th St Apt 3c, New York, NY 10022

SMITH III, George Dresser (Chi) 792 Forest Ave, Glen Ellyn, IL 60137

SMITH, Georgianna (Minn)

SMITH, Glenn Colyer (Chi) 754 Main St, Islip, NY 11751

SMITH, Graham (Chi) St George's College Jerusalem, PO Box 1248, Jerusalem ISRAEL, OR 91000

SMITH, Gregory Louis (SC) 314 Grove Street, Charleston, SC 29403

SMITH, H Alan (CNY) 2891 Oran Delphi Rd, Manlius, NY 13104

SMITH JR, Harmon Lee (NC) 3510 Randolph Rd, Durham, NC 27705

SMITH, Harold Vaughn (Ind) 8328 Hawes Ct, Indianapolis, IN 46256

SMITH, H Gregory (Pa) 5421 Germantown Ave, Philadelphia, PA 19144

SMITH, Hilary Borbon (Va) 4924 Bethlehem Rd., Richmond, VA 23230

SMITH, H Mark (Mass) 10 Linda Lane, #2-8, Dorchester, MA 02125

SMITH, Howard Louis (Alb) 970 State St., Schenectady, NY 12307

SMITH, Jacob Andrew (NY) 61 Gramercy Park N APT 7, 209 E 16th St, New York, NY 10003

SMITH, Jacqueline Kay (Oly) 6208 83rd St Sw, Lakewood, WA 98499

SMITH, James Clare (Be) 302 Pine St, Ashland, PA 17921

SMITH, James Drinard (SVa) 3235 Sherwood Ridge Dr, Powhatan, VA 23139

SMITH JR, James Owen (EC) 113 S Woodlawn Ave, Greenville, NC 27858

SMITH, Jane Gravlee (WNC) 40 Wildwood Ave., Asheville, NC 28804

SMITH, Jay (NY) 145 W 46th St #4, New York, NY 10036

SMITH, Jean (Ia) Saint Timothy's Epscopal Church, 1020 24th St, West des Moines, IA 50266

SMITH, Jean Ann (Ind) 6033 Gladden Dr, Indianapolis, IN 46220

SMITH, Jean Reinhart (NJ) 58 Jenny Ln, Brattleboro, VT 05301

SMITH, Jeffry Bradford (Episcopal SJ) 10 St Theresa'S Avenue, W Roxbury, MA 02132, Great Britain (UK)

SMITH, Jennifer Dorothy (Dal) 3609 Steven Dr, Plano, TX 75023

SMITH, Jerry W (Fla) 4800 Belmont Park Ter, Nashville, TN 37215

SMITH IV, Jess Wayne (Wyo) 33 Windy Ridge Rd, Laramie, WY 82070

SMITH, Jesse George (FtW) 2825 Winterhaven Dr, Hurst, TX 76054

SMITH, Jessica (Oly) St Anne's Episcopal Church, 2350 Main St, Washougal, WA 98671

SMITH, Jethroe Larrie (At) 46 S Main St, Wadley, GA 30477

SMITH, Joan (Ky) 1077 Merrick Dr, Lexington, KY 40502

SMITH, John (Md) 1204 Maple Ave, Annapolis, MD 21401

SMITH, John Cutrer (NY) 45 E 85th St, New York, NY 10028

SMITH, John Ferris (Mass) Box 3064, Wellfleet, MA 02667

SMITH, John Moffett (Va) 3000 S Randolph St Apt 284, Arlington, VA 22206

SMITH, John Perry (Fla) 256 E Church St, Jacksonville, FL 32202

SMITH, John Peterson (WLa) 1904 Jasmine Dr, Opelousas, LA 70570

SMITH JR, John Robert (Az) 602 N Wilmot Rd, Tucson, AZ 85711

SMITH, Joseph Kershaw (Pa) 101 Shelton Dr, Spartanburg, SC 29307

SMITH, Juanita Dawn (Wyo) 15 S Tschirgi St, Sheridan, WY 82801

SMITH, Julie (Ore) 335 SE 8th Ave, Hillsboro, OR 97123

SMITH, Julie Lynn (Pgh)

SMITH, Karen (Ore) St John the Baptist, 100 S French St, Breckenridge, CO 80424

SMITH, Kathryn Barr (Ala) St Stephen's Episcopal Church, 3775 Crosshaven Dr, Vestavia, AL 35223

SMITH, Kent Clarke (Ct) 112 Sconset Ln, Guilford, CT 06437

SMITH, Kermit Wade (WMo) PO Box 634, Kimberling City, KS 65086

SMITH, Kerry Jon (Md) 6097 Franklin Gibson Rd, Tracys Landing, MD 20779

SMITH, Kevin Corbin (Oly) 507 Mcgraw St, Seattle, WA 98109

SMITH, Kirby (Los) 27802 El Lazo Rd., Laguna Niguel, CA 92677

✠ **SMITH**, Kirk Stevan (Az) 114 W Roosevelt St, Phoenix, AZ 85003

SMITH, Kristy K (Ia) 4339 W Sawmill Ct, Castle Rock, CO 80109

SMITH, Larry Phillip (Dal) 17236 Lechlade Lane, Dallas, TX 75252

SMITH, Leslie Carl (NJ) 153 Seamans Rd, New London, NH 03257

SMITH, Letitia Lee (NC) 2725 Wilshire Ave. S.W., Roanoke, VA 24015

SMITH, Linda Becker (Nev) St Paul's Episcopal Church, PO Box 737, Sparks, NV 89432

SMITH, Lisa White (Minn) 4900 Nathan Lane, Plymouth, MN 55442

SMITH, Lizabeth Patterson (Nwk) 653 Courtney Hollow Lane, Madison, VA 22727

SMITH, Lora Alison (Alb) 531 County Route 59, Potsdam, NY 13676

SMITH, Manning Lee (Md) PO Box 2157, Mountain Lake Park, MD 21550

SMITH, Marc D (Mo) 4520 Lucas and Hunt Rd, Saint Louis, MO 63121

SMITH, Mark (Pa) 1904 Walnut St, Philadelphia, PA 19103

SMITH, Martin L (WA) 429 N St SW Apt S306, Washington, DC 20024

SMITH, Mary Jo (Vt) 973 Route 106, Reading, VT 05062

SMITH, Melissa M (Tenn) 84 Broadway, New Haven, CT 06511

SMITH JR, Merle Edwin (Ia) 715 W 7th St S, Newton, IA 50208

✠ SMITH, Michael (ND) Po Box 8, Naytahwaush, MN 56566

SMITH, Michael Allen (Az) 2800 W Ina Rd, Tucson, AZ 85741

SMITH, Michael John (SO)

SMITH, Michael W (SC) 218 Ashley Ave., Charleston, SC 29403

SMITH, Miles Miles (Va) Grace Church, 5607 Gordonsville Rd, PO Box 43, Keswick, VA 22947

SMITH, Mitchell T (USC) 1329 Jackson Ave, New Orleans, LA 70130

SMITH, Molly Dale (NJ) 805 Timber Ln., Nashville, TN 37215

SMITH III, Murdock Murdock (NC) St. Martin's Church, 1510 E. Seventh Street, Charlotte, NC 28204

SMITH, Myrl Elden (O) 4541 Gilhouse Rd, Toledo, OH 43623

SMITH, Nancy Metze (SwFla) 13011 Sandy Key Bend, Apt 1, North Fort Myers, FL 33903

SMITH, Nancy Spencer (Mass) 29 W Cedar St, Boston, MA 02108

SMITH, Nora (NY) 11 N. Broadway, Irvington, NY 10533

SMITH, Paul Bruce (Ak) 9631 Noaya, Eagle River, AK 99577

SMITH, Paul Weeghman (Ky) 3724 Hillsdale Rd, Louisville, KY 40222

SMITH, Perry Michael (WA) 15 Charles Plz Apt 2307, Baltimore, MD 21201

SMITH, P(Hilip) Kingsley (Md) 8339 Carrbridge Cir, Towson, MD 21204

SMITH, Ralph (NY) 219 Old Franklin Grove Dr Apt 6-A, Chapel Hill, NC 27514

SMITH JR, Ralph Wood (ETenn) Po Box 476, Mountain Home, TN 37684

SMITH, Raymond Robert (Colo) 23321 E Dry Creek Cir, Aurora, CO 80016

SMITH, Richard Byron (NC) 6 Natchez Court, Greensboro, NC 27455

SMITH, Richard Leslie (Cal) 226 Clinton Park, San Francisco, CA 94103

SMITH JR, Richard Winton (Pa) 305 E 83rd St Apt 4g, New York, NY 10028

SMITH JR, Robert Adrian (Me) 35 Prospect St, Caribou, ME 04736

SMITH, Robert E (Mich) 22326 Cherry Hill St, Dearborn, MI 48124

SMITH, Robert Kennedy (CFla) 3224 Carleton Circle East, Lakeland, FL 33803

SMITH, Roberts (Los)

SMITH, Robin (Pa) 107 Allison Rd, Oreland, PA 19075

SMITH, Robin Penman (Dal) 2712 E Aspen CT, Plano, TX 75075

SMITH, Roger Stilman (Me) 70 Country Club Rd, Manchester, ME 04351

SMITH, Roger W (SC) 15 Newpoint Rd, Beaufort, SC 29907

SMITH, Ron (Tex) 1403 Preston Ave, Austin, TX 78703

SMITH, Rose Ann (NwT) 3500 Barclay Dr, Amarillo, TX 79109

SMITH, Samantha Ruth Elizabeth (Tex)

SMITH, Samuel J (WMass) 1047 Amsterdam Ave, New York, NY 10025

SMITH, Sarah K (EC) 917 Gordon Woods Rd, Wilmington, NC 28411

SMITH, Stanley James (O) 249 E 7th St, New York, NY 10009

SMITH, Stephen (SO) 7121 Muirfield Dr., Dublin, OH 43017

SMITH, Stephen (Tex) 3310 Nathanael Rd., Greensboro, NC 27408

SMITH, Stephen H (FtW)

SMITH, Stephen John Stanyon (WNY) 100 Beard Ave, Buffalo, NY 14214

SMITH, Stephen Vaughn (Mass) 32 Popponesset Ave, Mashpee, MA 02649

SMITH, Stephen R Richard (Cal)

SMITH, Steven Ronald (Eur) Church of the Ascension, Seybothstrasse 4, 81545 Munich, Germany

SMITH, Stuart (Nwk) 653 Courtney Hollow Ln, Madison, VA 22727

SMITH, Susan M (SO) 333 S. Drexel Avenue, Bexley, OH 43209

SMITH, Susan Sims (Ark) 1809 Canal Pointe, Little Rock, AR 72202

SMITH, Susannah (NY) 219 Old Franklin Grove Dr, Chapel Hill, NC 27514

SMITH, Suzanne Gail (Tex) 200 W Lang St, Alvin, TX 77511

SMITH, Taylor Magavern (Md) 3608 Horned Owl Ct, Ellicott City, MD 21042

SMITH, Ted William (Tex) PO Box 10357, Liberty, TX 77575

SMITH, Thee (At) 3530 Fairlane Dr NW, Atlanta, GA 30331

SMITH, Thomas A (Dal)

SMITH, Thomas Eugene (EMich) P.O. Box 86, Dryden, MI 48428

SMITH, Thomas Gibson (Chi) 118 Tanglewood Dr, Elk Grove Village, IL 60007

SMITH JR, Thomas Parshall (NY) 225 W 99th St, New York, NY 10025

SMITH JR, Thomas Richard (Va) 1500 Westbrook Ct Apt 3142, Richmond, VA 23227

SMITH, Timothy Clarke (Cal) 2325 Union St, San Francisco, CA 94123

SMITH, Travis H (Tex) Holy Comforter Episcopal Church, 227 S Chenango PO BOX 786, Angleton, TX 77515

SMITH, Travis K (Md) St. Michael's Episcopal Church, 1520 Canterbury Rd., Raleigh, NC 27608

SMITH, Twila J (Be) 2451 Ridge Rd, Berkeley, CA 94709

SMITH, Vicki (Kan) 10104 Sorrills Creek Lane, Raleigh, NC 27614

SMITH, Vickie Mitchel (Ark) 601 Brookside Dr Apt 12, Little Rock, AR 72205

SMITH, Walter E (At) 3750 Peachtree Rd.NE, Atlanta, GA 30319

SMITH III, Walter Frederick (RG) 10328, Albuquerque, NM 87114

✠ SMITH, Wayne (Mo) 823 Carillon Ct, Saint Louis, MO 63141

SMITH, Wendy M (ECR) 4061 Sutherland Dr, Palo Alto, CA 94303

SMITH, Wesley Wesley (At) 210 Willie Six Road, Sewanee, TN 37375

SMITH, Whitney B (Ind) 2020 Bundy Ave, New Castle, IN 47362

SMITH, WillaMarie Eileen (CFla) 381 N Lincoln St, Daytona Beach, FL 32114

SMITH, William Charles (NwT) St Matthew's Episcopal Church, 727 W Browning Ave, Pampa, TX 79065

SMITH, William Herbert (WMich) 2073 SE North Blackwell Dr, Port St Lucie, FL 34952

SMITH, William Louis (Md) 24 Lake Drive, Bel Air, MD 21014

SMITH III, William Paul (Fla) PO Box 1005, Hilliard, FL 32046

SMITH, Willie (Nwk)

SMITH, Winston Teal (Pa)

SMITH-ALLEN, Serita Verner (EO) Po Box 186, Union, OR 97883

SMITH BOOTH, Rebecca Lee (Tex) Trinity Episcopal Church, 5010 N Main St, Baytown, TX 77521

SMITH-CRIDDLE, Linda C (O) 19 Pent Road, Madison, CT 06443

SMITHDEAL JR, Foss Tyra (NC) 8050 Ravenwood Ln, Stanley, NC 28164

SMITHERMAN, Gene R (ETenn) 211 Brookwood Dr, Chattanooga, TN 37411

SMITHERMAN, Suzanne Nichols (ETenn) 1108 Meadow Ln, Kingsport, TN 37663

SMITH GRAHAM, Shirley Elizabeth (Va) 5000 Pouncey Tract Rd, Glen Allen, VA 23059

SMITHGRAYBEAL, Felicia Marie (Colo) 8738 Triple Crown Dr., Frederick, CO 80504

SMITH-KURTZ, Mary Bonnagean (WMich) 7280 Deepwater Point Rd, Williamsburg, MI 49690

SMITH-MORAN, Barbara Putney (Mass) 93 Anson Road, Concord, MA 01742

SMODELL, George (CFla) 2394 Lakes of Melbourne Dr, Melbourne, FL 32904

SMOKE, Joan Claire (Ind) Trinity Episcopal Church, 60 S Dorset Rd, Troy, OH 45373

SMOLKO, Regis Joseph (Pgh) 2365 Mcaleer Rd, Sewickley, PA 15143

SMUCKER III, John Reed (Mich) 108 N Quaker Ln, Alexandria, VA 22304

SMULLEN, Thelma Alice (Md) 15708 Bradford Drive, Laurel, MD 20707

✠ **SMYLIE**, John (Wyo) 123 S Durbin St, Casper, WY 82601

SMYTH, Margaret Emma Ferrell (NJ) 53 Mulberry St, Medford, NJ 08055

SMYTH, Toneh Alana (Pa)

SMYTH, William E (NC) PO Box 615, Columbia, NC 27925

SMYTHE JR, Colville (Az) 2103 Hill Ave, Altadena, CA 91001

SMYTHE, Sally Lee (ND) 301 Main St S, Minot, ND 58701

SNAPP, J(Ames) Russell (Ark)

SNARE, Pamela Porter (Tenn) 1024 Chicamauga Ave, Nashville, TN 37206

SNEARY, Jerry (WTex) 164 Fox Rdg, Canyon Lake, TX 78133

SNELLING, Kathryn Sue (Ak) PO Box 1130, Sitka, AK 99835

SNEVE, Paul (SD) 12 Linden Ave, Vermillion, SD 57069

SNICKENBERGER, Patricia Wolcott (Chi) 179 School Street, Libertyville, IL 60048

SNIDER II, Mike (Fla) St Patrick's Episcopal Church, 1532 Stratford Ct, Saint Johns, FL 32259

SNIDER, Stephen B (Pa) 10527 W Albany St, Boise, ID 83704

SNIECIENSKI, Ed (Los) 908 N AVENUE 65, LOS ANGELES, CA 90042

SNIFFEN, Ernest Timothy (Me) P0 Box 368, Readfield, ME 04355

SNIFFEN, Michael Thomas (LI) 520 Clinton Ave, Brooklyn, NY 11238

SNIVELY, Candace Foley (NC)

SNODGRASS, A Bowie (NY) 60 Knollwood Road, Short Hills, NJ 07078

SNODGRASS, Cynthia Jean (SO) 5146 SW 9th Lane, Gainesville, FL 32607

SNODGRASS, Galen D (WMo) 3317 N 103rd Ct, Kansas City, KS 66109

SNODGRASS, Thomas James (PR) 705 Gladstone Ave, Baltimore, MD 21210

SNOOK, Susan Brown (Okla) 3116 NW 21st St, Oklahoma City, OK 73107

SNOW, George Richard (WLa) 151 Washakie Dr, Evanston, WY 82930

SNOW, Peter David (Oly) 927 36th Ave, Seattle, WA 98122

SNOW, Robert Gerald (Neb) Po Box 407052, Fort Lauderdale, FL 33340

SNYDER, Belinda Ann Wright (WTenn) 539 Cherry Rd, Memphis, TN 38117

SNYDER, David L (NJ) St. Andrew's Episcopal Church, 121 High Street, Mt. Holly, NJ 08060

SNYDER, Erick (Be) 290 Conklin St, Farmingdale, NY 11735

SNYDER, George Lewis (SO)

SNYDER, Judith (Be) 4621 Ashley Ln, Bethlehem, PA 18017

SNYDER, Larry Alan (Chi) 240 S 4th St, Warsaw, IN 62379

SNYDER, Paul Leech (Okla) PO Box 10722, Midwest City, OK 73140

SNYDER, Philip L (Dal) 2220 Susan Cir, Plano, TX 75074

SNYDER, Philip Wiseman (CNY) 248 Buckfield Dr, Lititz, PA 17543

SNYDER, Richard (NAM) PO Box 22771, Carson City, NV 89721

SNYDER, Robert Paul (Ind) 3221 - 29th, Bedford, IN 47421

SNYDER, Sharon Boublitz (Eas) 12842 Fox Ridge Ct, Bishopville, MD 21813

SNYDER, Susanna Jane (Mass) 99 Brattle St, Cambridge, MA 02138

SNYDER, William Delpharo (O) 4920 Woodview Rd, Ravenna, OH 44266

SOARD II, John Robert (Tex) 207 Bob O Link Ln, Wharton, TX 77488

SOJWAL, Imlijungla (NY) 27 Church St, Stonington, CT 06378

SOJWAL, Milind (NY) 16 All Saints Rd, Princeton, NJ 08540

SOL, Brenda (SanD) 8011 Douglas Ave, Dallas, TX 75225

SOLA, Geri Ely (Eau) 6579 W Center Dr, Hurley, WI 54534

SOLAK, Ketlen A (Del) 913 Wilson Rd, Wilmington, DE 19803

SOLBAK, Mary Martha (CPa) 1001 E. Oregon Rd, Lititz, PA 17543

SOLDWEDEL, Erik Gustav (Nwk) 31 Mulberry St, Newark, NJ 07102

SOLLER, Robin (NH) 23 Old Bristol Rd, New Hampton, NH 03256

SOLOMON, Dana Lee (Colo) St Stephen's Episcopal Church, 1303 S Bross Ln, Longmont, CO 80501

SOLON JR, Robert Francis (Md) 1301 S Charles St, Baltimore, MD 21230

SOLON, Terry Tim (Wyo) 3251 Acacia Dr, Cheyenne, WY 82001

SOLTER, Katrina Howard (NH) St Patrick's Episcopal Church, 4700 Whitehaven Pkwy NW, Washington, DC 20007

SOLTYS, Jacqueline Rebecca (Chi) 65 E Huron St, Chicago, IL 60611

SOMERS, Daniel E (NJ)

SOMERS, David Wayne (CFla) 5873 N Dean Rd, Orlando, FL 32817

SOMERS, Faye Veronica (SeFla) 2707 NW 37th St, Boca Raton, FL 33434

SOMERVILLE II, Ben (Az) 542 Raymond Dr, Sierra Vista, AZ 85635

SOMERVILLE, David James (Ga) 128 King Cotton Rd, Brunswick, GA 31525

SOMES, Norman (ECR) 85 Anna Laura Rd., 85 Anna Laura Drive, Jacksonville, OR 97530

SOMMER, Robert Lane (ECR) All Saints Church/Cristo Rey, 437 Rogers Ave, Watsonville, CA 95076

SOMMER, Sue (Chi) 2410 Glenview Rd, Glenview, IL 60025

SOMODEVILLA, Rene Francisco (Dal) 4018 S Lakewood Dr, Memphis, TN 38128

SONDEREGGER, Kathrine Ann (Va) 669 Weybridge St # 5753, Middlebury, VT 05753

SONLEY, Joseph (Hai)

SONNEN, Jon Anton (Tex) 4403 Seneca St, Pasadena, TX 77504

SONNESYN, Roger Earl (Minn)

SOPER JR, Leroy Dilmore (At) 514 E. NewJersey Ave Apt. 5125, Southern Pines, NC 28387

SOPER, Robert Arthur (WTex) 300 Hollywood Dr, Edinburg, TX 78539

SORENSEN, John Thomas (Pa) 576 Concord Road, Glen Mills, PA 19342

SORENSEN, Lael (Me) St Peter's Episcopal Church, 11 White St, Rockland, ME 04841

SORENSEN, Richard Todd (Nev) 1580 G St, Sparks, NV 89431

SORENSEN, Todd (Colo) 6653 W Chatfield Ave, Littleton, CO 80128

SORENSON, James Ronald (EMich) 226 W Nicolet Blvd, Marquette, MI 49855

SOREY, Gene Christine (Fla) 4304 Redtail Hawk Dr, Jacksonville, FL 32257

SORVILLO SR, James (CFla) 9101 Palm Tree Dr., Windermere, FL 34786

SOSA, Gary Rafael (NAM) Po Box 216, Bluff, UT 84512

SO-SCHOOS, Alistair (Md) All Hallows' Parish, P.O.Box 235, Davidsonville, MD 21035

SOSNOWSKI, Frederick Skinner (SC) 2426 Sea Island Yacht Club Rd, Wadmalaw Island, SC 29487

SOSNOWSKI, John (NJ) 808 W State St, Trenton, NJ 08618

SOTELO, Fabio A (At) St Bede's Episcopal Church, 2601 Henderson Mill Rd NE, Atlanta, GA 30345

SOTELO, George Salinas (Az) 13685 N Balancing Rock Dr, Oro Valley, AZ 85755

SOTO, Luis Fernando (DR (DomRep))

SOTOMAYOR, Ricardo S (Tex)

SOUCEK, Paul (Nwk)

SOUDER, Diane J (Az) Po Box 1077, Winter Park, FL 32790

SOUGHERS, Tara Kathleen (Mass) 23 Horseshoe Dr., Plainville, MA 02762

SOUKUP, Patricia Marie (RG) 3700 Parsifal St NE, Albuquerque, NM 87111

SOULE, Judith Christine (Spok) 625 C St, Cheney, WA 99004

SOULE, Patrick Ross (Fla) 151 Kingsley Ave, Orange Park, FL 32073

SOULIS, Cameron J (WA) National Cathedral School, 3612 Woodley Rd, NW, Washington, DC 20016

SOUTH, Lynn Crisco (The Episcopal Church in Haw) 100 Kulanihakoi St, Kihei, HI 96753

SOUTHALL, Jennifer Lea (Miss) 300 Palmer Dr, Oxford, MS 38655

SOUTHERLAND, Thomas Rudolph (SO) 10555 Montgomery Rd., Apt 32, Cincinnati, OH 45242

SOUTHWICK, Susan Bowman (Ala)

SOUZA, Raymond Manuel (EC) 846 Wide Waters, Bath, NC 27808

SOWAH, Constance Kate (Minn) 4180 Lexington Ave S, Eagan, MN 55123

SOWAN, Michael George (Alb) Box 1185, Street Sacrement Lane, Bolton Landing, NY 12814

SOWARDS, William Michael (Pa) St James Episcopal Church, 3768 Germantown Pike, Collegeville, PA 19426

SOWERS, Susan R (CGC) 3200 N 12th Ave, Pensacola, FL 32503

SOWINSKI, Charles Paul (Az) 6300 N Central Ave, Phoenix, AZ 85012

SOYARS, Jonathan E (Chi) 115 W 7th St, Charlotte, NC 28202

SPACCARELLI, Cara Elizabeth (WA) 620 G St SE, Washington, DC 20003

SPAETH, Colleen Grayce (NJ) 247 Merion Ave, Haddonfield, NJ 08033

SPAFFORD, Donald Wick (Dal) 5903 Bonnard Dr, Dallas, TX 75230

SPAGNA, Amy L (Va) Christ Church, 7 Elm St, Westerly, RI 02891

SPAID, William John (WMich) 2008 Hudson Ave, Kalamazoo, MI 49008

SPAINHOUR, John Robert (Vt) 4616 McClelland Dr, Unit 203, Wilmington, NC 28405

SPALDING, Kirsten Snow (Cal) 333 Ellen Dr, San Rafael, CA 94903

SPANGENBERG, Carol (WMich) 1612 Stoney Point Dr, Lansing, MI 48917

SPANGLER, DeLiza (WNY) 128 Pearl St, Buffalo, NY 14202

SPANGLER, Haywood B (Va) 1205 Swan Lake Dr Apt 303, Charlottesville, VA 22902

SPANGLER, Robert Joseph (Okla) 7 Strathmore Dr, Arden, NC 28704

SPANN, Ron (Mich) 2971 Iroquois St, Detroit, MI 48214

SPANNAGEL JR, Lawrence Elden (NwT) 676 E Willowbrook Dr, Meridian, ID 83646

SPANNAUS, Timothy Wise (Mich) 27786 Rainbow Cir, Lathrup Village, MI 48076

✠ **SPARKS**, Doug (NI) 624 Park Ave, South Bend, IN 46616

SPARKS JR, Noy Leon (FtW) Cathedral Church of St Luke, 130 N Magnolia Ave, Orlando, FL 32801

SPARROW, Kevin H (Mass) 45 Yerxa Rd Unit 307, Cambridge, MA 02140

SPAULDING, Mark (Cal) 19179 Center St, Castro Valley, CA 94546

SPEAR, Leslie Edward (WTex) 4222 State Hwy. 7 West, Crockett, TX 75835

SPEARE-HARDY II, Benjamin (SO) 5301 Free Pike, Trotwood, OH 45426

SPEAR-JONES, Michael W (SVa) 12 Milnor Terrace, Crossville, TN 38558

SPEARS, Melanie Lea (Minn) 3543 22nd Ave S, Minneapolis, MN 55407

SPECK-EWER, Nathan Stewart (SwFla)

SPEEKS, Mark William (NY) 267 Humphrey St # 3, New Haven, CT 06511

SPEER, James D (Ct) 63 Clyde Ave, Waterbury, CT 06708

SPEER, Richard (WTex) 800 S. Inediana Ave, 800 S. Indiana Ave, Weslaco, TX 78596

SPEER, Robert Hazlett (Md) 5732 Cross Country Blvd, Baltimore, MD 21209

SPEER, William Roth (NJ) 2000 Miller Ave #12, Millville, NJ 08332

SPEIR, Edmund L (Ida)

SPEIR, Susan (Ida)

SPELLER, Lydia (EMich) Grace Church, 1213 6th St, Port Huron, MI 48060

SPELLERS, Stephanie (LI) 82 Commonwealth Ave Apt 2, Boston, MA 02116

SPELLMAN, Lynne (Ark) 1219 W Lakeridge Dr, Fayetteville, AR 72703

SPELMAN, Harold James (HB)

SPELMAN, Katherine C (Chi) 20 N American St, Philadelphia, PA 19106

SPENCER, Adam P (Chi)

SPENCER, Allison D (LI) 12706 Se Pinehurst Ct, Hobe Sound, FL 33455

SPENCER, Bonnie (Colo) 3006 S Holly Pl, Denver, CO 80222

SPENCER, Carol (Miss) 1623 Acadia Ct., Jackson, MS 39211

SPENCER, Cindy (ECR) 15163 N Cutler Dr, Tucson, AZ 85739

SPENCER, Dorothy Jane (NMich) PO Box 302, Manistique, MI 49854

SPENCER, James Scott (Cfla) 4220 Saxon Dr, New Smyrna Beach, FL 32169

SPENCER, Leon P (NC) 6005 Starboard Dr, Greensboro, NC 27410

SPENCER, Michael Edwin (NH) 325 Pleasant Street, Concord, NH 03301

SPENCER, Michael Paul (EMich) 924 N Niagara St, Saginaw, MI 48602

SPENCER, Orval James (Neb) 6700 Tamerson Ct, Raleigh, NC 27612

SPENCER, Patricia Ann (CGC) 851 Village Lake Dr S, Deland, FL 32724

SPENCER, Robert (Miss) 1623 Acadia Court, Jackson, MS 39211

SPENCER, Robert Dennis (Wyo) 4508 Cottage Ln, Cheyenne, WY 82001

SPENCER, Robert Paul (NMich) PO Box 302, Manistique, MI 49854

SPENCER, Ronald Dwight (WMo) Po Box 197, Angel Fire, NM 87710

SPENCER, Warren Dove (NJ) 68 Hull Ave, Freehold, NJ 07728

SPEROPULOS IV, Peter James (Mo)

SPERRY, Rebecca Lynne (Chi) 2056 Vermont St, Blue Island, IL 60406

SPICER JR, Clyde Allen (Md) 724 Morningside Dr, Towson, MD 21204

SPICER, John M (WMo) St. Andrews Episcopal Church, 6401 Wornall Terrace, Kansas City, MO 64113

SPICER, John Tildsley (Fla) 25 Eyrie Dr, Crawfordville, FL 32327

SPICER, Stephen L (Tex) 304 E Stockbridge St, Eagle Lake, TX 77434

SPIEGEL, Phyllis (SO) 120 Cherry Ln, Christiansburg, VA 24073

SPIERS, Linda Mitchell (Ct) 3 Whirling Dun, Canton, CT 06019

SPIGNER, Charles Bailey (Va) 10355 Spencer Trail Pl, Ashland, VA 23005

SPINA, Frank Anthony (Oly) 414 W Newell St, Seattle, WA 98119

SPINELLA, Linda Jean (NH) 270 Stark Hwy N, Dunbarton, NH 03046

SPINILLO GRZYWA, Jonathan Michael Francis (Minn) 111 3rd Ave SW, Rochester, MN 55902

SPLINTER, John Theodore (FdL) 4332 W Rotamer Rd, Janesville, WI 53546

✠ **SPONG**, John Shelby (Nwk) 24 Puddingstone Rd, Morris Plains, NJ 07950

SPOON, Bryan William (WMo)

SPORS, Daniel Paul (Mil)

SPRAGUE, James W (Los) PO Box 303, Santa Barbara, CA 93102

SPRAGUE, Minka Shura (La) 703 Audubon Trce, New Orleans, LA 70121

SPRATT, George Clifford (Kan) 828 Center St, Fulton, MO 65251

SPRICK, Lynne Ann (Minn) 110 S Oak St, Lake City, MN 55041

SPRINGER, Alice E (Dal) 1410 S Goliad St Apt 2007, Rockwall, TX 75087

SPRINGER, David R (Alb) 12 Shannon Ct, West Sand Lake, NY 12196

SPRINGER, Nancy (NwT) 4000 W Loop 250 N, Midland, TX 79707

SPRINGER, Susan W (Colo) St John's Episcopal Church, 1419 Pine St, Boulder, CO 80302

SPROAT, Jim (WTex) 2109 Sawdust Rd Apt 27102, Spring, TX 77380

SPROUL, James Renfro (EC) 881 Lakeside Dr., Lenoir City, TN 37772

SPROUSE, Herbert Warren (CPa) The Memorial Church of the Prince of Peace, 20 W. High St, Gettysburg, PA 17325

SPRUHAN, John Halsey (SD) 720 Diamond Road, Salem, VA 24153

SPRUHAN, Judy (SD) 720 Diamond Rd, Salem, VA 24153

SPRUILL, Robert Leigh (Tenn) 5825 Robert E Lee Dr, Nashville, TN 37215

SPULNIK, Frederick Joseph (RI) 4873 Collwood Blvd unit B, San Diego, CA 92115

SPURGIN, Joyce M (Okla) 516 McLish St, Ardmore, OK 73401

SPURLOCK, Michael Douglas (NY) Saint Thomas Church, 1 W. 53rd St., New York, NY 10019

SPURLOCK, Paul Allan (Colo) 10000 E Yale Ave Apt 4, 10000 E. Yale Ave Apt43, Denver, CO 80231

SQUIER, Timothy J (Ct) 500 East Depot Street, Antioch, IL 60002

SQUIRE, James Richard (Pa) Episcopal Academy, 1785 Bishop White Dr, Newtown Square, PA 19073

SQUIRE JR, Willard Searle (CFla) 748 Hammond Pl, The Villages, FL 32162

SRAMEK JR, Tom (Ore) PO Box 8834, Medford, OR 97501

SSERWADDA, Emmanuel (NY) 69 Georgia Ave, Bronxville, NY 10708

STABLER-TIPPETT, Lyn (Miss) St Stephen's Episcopal Church, 1300 Church St, Columbia, MS 39429

STACEY, Caroline (NY) 487 Hudson St, New York, NY 10014

STACK JR, Gene AJ (SO) 541 2nd Ave, Gallipolis, OH 45631

STACKHOUSE, Marcia K (Colo) 3432 Vallejo St, Denver, CO 80211

STACY, Charles Herrick (Los) 1509 Eucalyptus Dr, Solvang, CA 93463

STADEL, Jerold Russell (SwFla) 1014 Pinegrove Dr, Brandon, FL 33511

STAFFORD, Gil (Az)

STAFFORD, Robert Holmes (NY) 401 S El Cielo Rd Apt 71, Palm Springs, CA 92262

STAFFORD, William Sutherland (Fla) 4316 Hampshire Pl, San Jose, CA 95136

STAFFORD-WHITTAKER, William Paul (WA)

STAGGS, Katresia Anne (Ark) 501 S Phoenix Ave, Russellville, AR 72801

STAHL, Daryl (RI) 91 Pratt St, providence, RI 02906

STAIR, Adrian (Mass) 51 Longmeadow Dr, Amherst, MA 01002

STALEY, Mary (Va) PO Box 482, Put In Bay, OH 43456

STALLER, Margaretmary B (Cal) 4821 Wolf Way, Concord, CA 94521

STALLINGS, Buddy Monroe (NY) 435 E 52nd Street, Apt 10A2, New York, NY 10022

STAMBAUGH, Doran Bartlett (SanD) PO Box 127, Carlsbad, CA 92018

STAMBAUGH, James Ryan (Pa) 1020 Remington Rd, Wynnewood, PA 19096

STAMM, George (Eau) 13497 45th Ave, Chippewa Falls, WI 54729

ST AMOUR III, Frank (Eas) 7579 Sandy Bottom Rd, Chestertown, MD 21620

STANFORD, Bill (FtW) 3550 SW Loop 820, Fort Worth, TX 76133

STANFORD, David Dewitt (Chi) 2705 Armfield Road, Hillsborough, NC 27278

STANFORD, Donna Lynn (WMo) 100 E Red Bridge Rd, Kansas City, MO 64114

STANFORD, Iain M (Ore)

STANFORD, Virginia Francene (Md) 10901 Farrier Rd, Frederick, MD 21701

STANGER, Mark E. (Cal) 124 Panorama Dr, San Francisco, CA 94131

STANLEY, Anne Grant (Me) Po Box 63, Paris, ME 04271

STANLEY, Arthur Patrick (Ia) 9 Westbourne Court, Cooden Drive, Bexhill On Sea TN39 3AA, Great Britain (UK)

STANLEY, E Bevan (Ct) 25 South St, PO Box 248, Litchfield, CT 06759

STANLEY, Gordon John (Chi) 340 W Diversey Pkwy, Chicago, IL 60657

STANLEY, James Martin (Chi) 320 Franklin St, Geneva, IL 60134

STANLEY JR, John Hiram (FtW) 4105 Hartwood Dr, Fort Worth, TX 76109

STANLEY, Lauren Regina (SD) PO Box 256, Mission, SD 57555

STANLEY, Marjorie Jean (Spok) 255 W Shore Ln, Sandpoint, ID 83864

STANLEY, Mark (Md) Old St. Paul's Church, 309 Cathedral Street, Baltimore, MD 21201

STANLEY, Mary (Md) Old St. Paul's Church, 309 Cathedral St., Baltimore, MD 21201

STANLEY, Stephen Ranson (SwVa) St. Mark's Episcopaql Church, 111 South Roanoke St. P.O. Box 277, Fincastle, VA 24090

STANLEY, William S (Los)

STANSFIELD, Patricia Janette (Los) PO Box 152, Corona, CA 92878

STANTON JR, Barclay Reynolds (Eas) 24447 94th St S, Kent, WA 98030

STANTON, James Malcom (Ind) 321 Market St, Jeffersonville, IN 47130

✠ **STANTON**, James Monte (Dal) 1630 N Garrett Ave, Dallas, TX 75206

STANTON, John Frank (SeFla) 7900 Harbor Island Dr Apt 1501, North Bay Village, FL 33141

STANTON, John Robert (At) 4906 Sulky Dr Apt 204, Richmond, VA 23228

STANTON, Sarah Morningstar (EO) 4701 7th Ave. SW Unit 303, Olympia, WA 98502

STANTON, William B (Colo) 7157 High St, Frederick, CO 80504

STAPLES, Ann McDonald (Pgh) Po Box 1, Marion Center, PA 15759

STAPLETON JR, Jack (Colo) 4222 W. 22nd Street Road, Greeley, CO 80634

STARBUCK, Elizabeth (Ct) 88 N Main St, PO Box 983, Kent, CT 06757

STARK, Gregory (O) 105 Arizona Ave, Lorain, OH 44052

STARKES, Lionel Alfonso (Nev) Po Box 50763, Henderson, NV 89016

STARKWEATHER, Betty (ND) 679 Lehigh Dr., Merced, CA 95348

STARR, Charles Michael (Pgh) 4048 Circle Dr, Bakerstown, PA 15007

STARR, Chris (At) Church of the Atonement (Episcopal), 4945 High Point Road, Sandy Springs, GA 30342

STARR III, David H (Los) 6884 Burnside Dr, San Jose, CA 95120

STARR, Mark Lowell (CGC) 41 Olympic Blvd, Port Townsend, WA 98368

STARR, Nancy Barnard (Mil) 76 Grange Road, Mount Eden, Auckland, 1024, New Zealand (Aotearoa)

STARR, Therese Ann (Okla) PO Box 759, Eufaula, OK 74432

STASSER, Nina (U) 2225 S Jasmine St Unit 310, Denver, CO 80222

STATER, Catherine J (CFla) 319 W Wisconsin Ave, Deland, FL 32720

STATEZNI, Gregory George (Episcopal SJ) 7000 College Ave Apt 21, Bakersfield, CA 93306

STAYNER, David (Ct) 28 Myra Rd, Hamden, CT 06517

STAYNER, Sandra Hardyman (Ct) 39 Pleasant Drive, Cheshire, CT 06410

STAYTON, Darrell Lynn (Ark) PO Box 726, Stuttgart, AR 72160

ST CLAIR, Melinda Lee (Mont) Saint Luke's Church, 119 N 33rd St, Billings, MT 59101

ST CLAIRE II, Elbert Kyle (Pa) 1650 Franklin Dr, Furlong, PA 18925

STEADMAN, Darren F (Va)

STEADMAN, Larry Kenneth (WK) 705 W 31st Ave, Hutchinson, KS 67502

STEADMAN, Marguerite Alexandra (Me) 3116 O St Nw, Washington, DC 20007

STEAGALL, Patricia V (Ore) PO Box 1266, Manzanita, OR 97130

STEARNS, Fellow Clair (ECR) Po Box 2789, Saratoga, CA 95070

STEARNS, H Joanne (SO) 5380 Dovetree Blvd. Apt 10, Moraine, OH 45439

STEARNS, Samuel D (RG) 3705 Utah St Ne, Albuquerque, NM 87110

STEBBINS, Marty (NC)

STEBER, Gary David (NC) 406 Lorimer Road, Box 970, Davidson, NC 28036

STEBINGER, Peter A R (Ct) 615 Bethmour Rd, Bethany, CT 06524

STECH, Ernest William (Mich) 20500 W Old US Highway 12, Chelsea, MI 48118

STECKER IV, Rick (NH) Box 293, New London, NH 03257

STECKLINE, Donna L (Alb) P.O. Box 345, Gilbertsville, NY 13776

STEDMAN, David Algernon (WNY) Po Box 7488, St Thomas, VI 00801

STEED, Ronald Scott (Ct) 95 Route 2a, Preston, CT 06365

STEEDMAN SANBORN, Marda Leigh (Oly) Diocese of Olympia, 1551 10th Ave E, Seattle, WA 98102

STEELE, Christopher Andrew (Dal) 11122 Midway Rd, Dallas, TX 75229

STEELE, Christopher Candace (Oly) 7747 31st Ave Sw, Seattle, WA 98126

STEELE, David Regan (NY) 777 E 222nd St, Bronx, NY 10467

STEELE, Gary Ross (Ak) 2708 W 65th Ave, Anchorage, AK 99502

STEELE, James Logan (Chi) 317 Goold Park Dr, Morris, IL 60450

STEELE, Kelly Ann (Ga)

STEELE, Nancy J (EMich) PO Box 452, Chesaning, MI 48616

STEELE, Robert Emanuel (Nwk) 250 Kawaihae St Apt 1b, Honolulu, HI 96825

STEELE, Sean William (Tex) St. Isidore Episcopal, 3901 S Panther Creek Dr, The Woodlands, TX 77381

STEEN, James James (WMich) 749 Holland St, Saugatuck, MI 49453

STEEVER JR, Raymond George Edward (Los) Route 1, Box 109, Pullman, WA 99163

STEEVES, Joan Altpeter (Colo) 6337 Deframe Way, Arvada, CO 80004

STEEVES, Timothy (Pa) 409 E Lancaster Ave, Downingtown, PA 19335

STEFANIK, Alfred Thomas (Vt) 49 Raintree Circle, Palm Coast, FL 32164

STEFANOVSKY, Derek (EMich)

STEFFENHAGEN, Leverne Richard (WNY) 9705 Niagara Falls Blvd Apt 19, Niagara Falls, NY 14304

STEFFENHAGEN, Louis Keith (Pa)

STEFFENSEN, Leslie N (Va) Grace Episcopal Church, 3601 Russell Rd, Alexandria, VA 22305

STEFKO, Nadia M (Chi) 3857 N Kostner Ave, Chicago, IL 60641

STEGELMANN, Dawn M (Ct) 651 Pequot Ave, Southport, CT 06890

STEIDL, Gerald Scobie (CFla) 127 E Cottesmore Cir, Longwood, FL 32779

STEIG, George Terrance (Oly) 5241 12th Ave Ne, Seattle, WA 98105

STEILBERG, Isabel Fourqurean (SVa) 221 34th St, Newport News, VA 23607

STEIN, Edward Lee (Tex) 717 Sage Rd, Houston, TX 77056

STEINBACH, Frederick Leo (Ia) PO Box 838, Chariton, IA 50049

STEINER, Joel David (NI)

STEINER, Scott A (Mich)

STEINER IV, Skip (Md) 7474 Washington Blvd, Elkridge, MD 21075

STEINHAUER, Roger Kent (Roch) 25 Chadbourne Rd, Rochester, NY 14618

STEINHAUSER, Elizabeth (Mass) 419 Shawmut Ave., Boston, MA 02118

STELK, Lincoln Frank (NY) 241 Bluff Rd, Yarmouth, ME 04096

STELLE, Eric Arthur (Oly) 7701 Skansie Ave, Gig Harbor, WA 98335

STELLMAN, Jill (Alb) Episcopal Diocese Of Albany, 580 Burton Rd, Greenwich, NY 12834

STEN, Pamela V (WMich) 605 W 4th St Apt 2, Buchanan, MI 49107

STENNER, David Anthony (Md) 203 E Chatsworth Ave, Reisterstown, MD 21136

STENNETTE, Lloyd Roland (SeFla) PO Box 11383, Miami, FL 33101

STENNING, Gordon J (RI) 36 Brant Rd, Portsmouth, RI 02871

STEPHENS, Jeff (U) 2141 Horizon View Dr, St George, UT 84790

STEPHENS, Josh (SVa) Bruton Parish Episcopal Church, PO Box 3520, Williamsburg, VA 23187

STEPHENS, Paul Jeffery (Miss) P. O. Box 1358, Tupelo, MS 38802

STEPHENS, Stephen Daniel (RG) 400 Huning Ranch Loop W, Los Lunas, NM 87031

STEPHENS, Thomas Lee (Okla) 1560 SE Pecan Place, Bartlesville, OK 74003

STEPHENS, Wyatt E (Mil) 1538 N 58th St, Milwaukee, WI 53208

STEPHENSON, Amanda C (NC)

STEPHENSON, John William (Kan) Rr 1 Box 190, Riverton, KS 66770

STEPHENSON, Michael (Okla) 3621 24th Ave SE Apt 3, Norman, OK 73071

STEPHENSON, Randolph (WA) 4 Jeb Stuart Ct, Rockville, MD 20854

STEPHENSON-DIAZ, Lark (SanD) 1023 Iris Ct, Carlsbad, CA 92011

STEPP, Jonathan (WNC) 84 Church St, Franklin, NC 28734

STER, David (CPa) 1363 Princeton Rd, Mechanicsburg, PA 17050

STERCHI, Margaret (NJ) 11 North Ave., Wilmington, DE 19804

STERKEN, Janet Leigh (Eau) 322 N. Water St., Sparta, WI 54656

STERLING III, Edward Arthur (Oly) 3762 Palisades Pl W, University Place, WA 98466

STERLING, Franklin Mills (Cal) 1707 Gouldin Rd., Oakland, CA 94611

STERLING, Leslie (Mass) St. Bartholomew's Church, 239 Harvard Street, Cambridge, MA 02139

STERN, Linda Sue (Okla) 516 Mclish St, Ardmore, OK 73401

STERNE, Colleen Kathryn (Los) Trinity Episcopal Church, 1500 State St, Santa Barbara, CA 93101

STERNE, Martha Packer (At) 805 Mount Vernon Hwy NW, Atlanta, GA 30327

STERRY, Steven Chapin (Los) Anglican Church of the Epiphany, 5151 Cordova Rd,, La Mirada, CA 90638

STEUER, Lawrence William (Alb) 343 Pettis Rd, Gansevoort, NY 12831

STEVENS JR, Arthur Grant (WMass) 904B West Victoria St, Santa Barbara, CA 93101

STEVENS, George (Mass) St. John's Church, P.O. Box 5610, Beverly, MA 01915

STEVENS, Judy (WMass) 904B W Victoria St, Santa Barbara, CA 93101

STEVENS, Karl Peter Bush (SO)

STEVENS, Merrill Richard (EO) St Pauls Episcopal Church, 1805 Minnesota St, The Dalles, OR 97058

STEVENS, Nancy (Roch) The Church of the Epiphany, 3285 Buffalo Rd, Rochester, NY 14624

STEVENS, Patricia D (At) P.O. Box 155, Johnston, SC 29832

STEVENS JR, Rob (NH) 1113 Macon Ave, Pittsburgh, PA 15218

STEVENS, Robert Ellsworth (CFla) 2346 Colfax Ter., Evanston, IL 60201

STEVENS, Scott J (Ct) PO Box 151, Hampton, CT 06247

STEVENS III, Walter Alexander (The Episcopal Church in Haw) P.O. Box 207, Kapaau, HI 96755

STEVENS, William Clair (PR)

STEVENS-HUMMON, Rebecca M (Tenn) 2902 Overlook Dr, Nashville, TN 37212

STEVENSON, Ann (NH) P O Box 743, 18 High St, North Berwick, ME 03906

STEVENSON, Anne B (Tenn) 216 chestnut hill, Nashville, TN 37215

STEVENSON, Carolyn Eve (NH) 231 Main St, Salem, NH 03079

STEVENSON, Frank Beaumont (SO) School Lane, Stanton Saint John, Oxford, OX33 1ET, Great Britain (UK)

STEVENSON, Frederic George (CPa) 890 Mccosh St, Hanover, PA 17331

STEVENSON, Janis Jordan (Mich) 430 Nicolet St, Walled Lake, MI 48390

STEVENSON, Jeffrey Neal (Va) 6401 Wornall Ter, Kansas City, MO 64113

STEVENSON, Mark Mark (La) 7 Bruin Drive, Hamilton, NJ 08619

STEVENSON, R(Ichard) Hugh (The Episcopal NCal) 610 Los Alamos Rd, Santa Rosa, CA 95409

STEVENSON, Thomas Edward (Ore) PO Box 29, Alsea, OR 97324

STEVENS-TAYLOR, Sally Hodges (Az) PO Box 65840, Tucson, AZ 85728

STEWART, Audrey (Mass) Parish of the Epiphany, 70 Church St, Winchester, NJ 01890

STEWART, Barbara (Los) 1014 Presidio Drive, Costa Mesa, CA 92626

STEWART, Bonnie (Ore) Saint Michael And All Angels Church, 1704 NE 43rd Ave, Portland, OR 97213

STEWART, Carol Wendt (Roch) 3074 O'Donnell Rd, Wellsville, NY 14895

STEWART, Caroline (Md) 4024 Stewart Rd, Stevenson, MD 21153

STEWART, Charles Neil (CNY) PO Box 62, Skaneateles, NY 13152

STEWART, Daniel R (Oly) 322 Aoloa St Apt 1101, Kailua, HI 96734

STEWART, Duke Summerlin (Ga) 701 Gaskin Ave N, Douglas, GA 31533

STEWART, James Allen (Wyo) St Mark's Episcopal Church, 1908 Central Ave, Cheyenne, WY 82001

STEWART, James Macgregor (NC)

STEWART, Jane Louise (Ia) 912 20th Ave., Coralville, IA 52241

STEWART, John Bruce (Va) 4327 Ravensworth Rd Apt 210, Annandale, VA 22003

STEWART JR, John Plummer (Ala) St Matthias Episc Church, 2310 Skyland Blvd E, Tuscaloosa, AL 35405

STEWART, Kevin Paul (Mil) 4722 N 104th St, Wauwatosa, WI 53225

STEWART, Leslie (Dal) PO Box 292365, Lewisville, TX 75029

STEWART, Matt (Mass) 11 W. Grove St., Middleboro, MA 02346

STEWART, Natalie Ann (ECR) PO Box 515, Aromas, CA 95004

STEWART, Natasha (Mass) 407 Rochester St, Fall River, MA 02720

STEWART, Pamela Fay (Colo) 126 W 2nd Ave, Denver, CO 80223

STEWART, Ralph Roderick (Oly) 23 Turtle Rock Ct, New Paltz, NY 12561

STEWART, Sarah C (Kan)

STEWART JR, William Owen (Ga) PO Box 1171, Leesburg, GA 31763

STEWART-SICKING, Joseph (Md) 8890 McGaw Rd, Columbia, MD 21045

STEWART-SICKING, Megan Elizabeth (Md) 1509 Glencoe Rd, Glencoe, MD 21152

STEWMAN, Kerry Jo (O) Po Box 366274, Bonita Springs, FL 34136

ST GEORGE, David (Nwk) 8 Binney Rd, Old Lyme, CT 06371

ST. GERMAIN, Beverly Anne Lavallee (Vt) Three Cathedral Square 3A, Burlington, VT 05401

ST GERMAIN JR, Paul (SO) 2151 Dorset Rd, Columbus, OH 43221

ST GERMAIN-ILER III, Robert (Ala) 347 South Central Ave., Alexander City, AL 35010

STICHWEH, Michael Terry (CFla) 410 Meridian Street, Apt 604, Indianapolis, IN 46204

STICKLEY, David (Cal) 101 Gold Mine Dr, San Francisco, CA 94131

STICKNEY, Jane Burr (Ct) 14 Lone Pine Trl, Higganum, CT 06441

STICKNEY, Jim (Cal) 1324 Devonshire Ct, El Cerrito, CA 94530

STICKNEY, Joyce Erwin (Los) 28211 Pacific Coast Hwy, Malibu, CA 90265

STIEFEL, Jennifer H (NH) 30 Holiday Drive #341, Dover, NH 03820

STIEFEL, Robert (NH) 30 Holiday Dr Unit 341, Dover, NH 03820

STIEGLER, Mark A (Roch) 3835 Oneill Rd, Lima, NY 14485

STIEPER, John Richard (Chi) 7 Fernwood Dr, Barrington, IL 60010

STIFLER, Linnea (WMich) 2010 Nichols Rd, Kalamazoo, MI 49004

STILES, Katherine Mitchell (Me) 99 Brattle St, Cambridge, MA 02138

STILES-RANDAK, Susan (RI) Peace Dale Estates, 1223 Saugatucket Rd Apt A102, Peace Dale, RI 02879

STILL, Kimberly L. (Fla) 919 San Fernando St, Fernandina Beach, FL 32034

STILLINGS, Kyle David (WTenn) St. Elisabeth's Episcopal Church, 6033 Old Brownsville Rd, Memphis, TN 38135

STIMPSON, Peter K (NJ) 220 W Kilbride, Williamsburg, VA 23188

STINE, Stephen Blaine (Tex) 1220 Quirby Lane, Tyler, TX 75701

STINNETT, Roger Allen (WMo) 804 Wendy Ln, Carthage, MO 64836

STINSON, Marian (Oly) 84 Ledgewood Dr, Glastonbury, CT 06033

STINSON, Richard Lyon (Pgh) 191 Ashby Ln, Front Royal, VA 22630

STIPE, Nickie Maxine (Ak) 280 Northern Ave Apt 10-A, Avondale Estates, GA 30002

STISCIA, Alfred Ronald (CPa) 5092 Riverfront Dr, Bradenton, FL 34208

STITT, David (WLa) 713 Circle C, Hastings, NE 68901

STIVERS, Dana Morgan (Ct) PO Box 577, Ivoryton, CT 06442

STIVERS, Donald Austin (Los) 5023 Calle Tania, Santa Barbara, CA 93111

ST JOHN, Andrew Reginald (NY) 1 E 29th St, New York, NY 10016

ST JOHNS, Ernest Keys (RG) 1002 N Robert St, Ludington, MI 49431

ST LOUIS, JN Michelin (Hai)

ST LOUIS, June Allison (Ct) Virginia Theological Seminary, 3737 Seminary Road, Alexandria, VA 22304

ST LOUIS, Leslie (WA) 13106 Annapolis Rd, Bowie, MD 20720

ST LOUIS, Samuel (Hai)

STOCK, David (Okla) 4036 Neptune Dr, Oklahoma City, OK 73116

STOCKARD, Matthew (EC) Po Box 1336, Kinston, NC 28503

STOCKDALE, William Barrington (NJ)

STOCKSDALE, Robert (Ct) 183 Pin Oak Dr, Southington, CT 06489

STOCKTON, James Vernon (Tex) 16306 Ascent Cove, Pflugerville, TX 78660

STOCKTON, Marietta Grace (WK) 406 W. Kingman Ave., Lakin, KS 67860

STOCKWELL-TANGEMAN, Carolyn Lee (WMo) 5618 Wyandotte St, Kansas City, MO 64113

STODDARD, Gary David (Colo)

STODDART, David Michael (Va) Church of Our Saviour, 1165 Rio Road East, Charlottesville, VA 22901

STODGHILL, Dawnell S (WLa) St Thomas Episcopal Church, 3706 Bon Aire Drive, Monroe, LA 71203

STODGHILL, Marion (Ky) Norton Hospital, Chaplain, 200 E. Chesnut Street, Louisville, KY 40202

STODGHILL III, Thomas Whitfield (WLa) 3435 Westminster Avenue, Monroe, LA 71201

STOESSEL, Andrew James (Mass) 36 Cornell St, Roslindale, MA 02131

STOFEL, Alvin Dale (NwT)

STOFFREGEN, Diana Lynn Jacobson (Spok) 5609 S Custer Street, Spokane, WA 99223

STOFFREGEN, Megan Amy (Spok) 5609 S Custer Rd, Spokane, WA 99223

✠ **STOKES**, Chip (NJ) Episcopal Diocese Of New Jersey, 808 W State St, Trenton, NJ 08618

STOKES, Grant A (SVa) Christ and St Luke's Epis Church, 560 W Olney Rd, Norfolk, VA 23507

STOMSKI, William (Nev) 3300B S Seacrest Blvd, Boynton Beach, FL 33435

STONE, Carey Don (Ark) 112 Traveler Ln, Maumelle, AR 72113

STONE, David Lynn (HB) 940 Channing Way, Berkeley, CA 94710

STONE, Dean Putnam (Kan) 9201 West 82nd Street, Overland Park, KS 66204

STONE, John Curtis (NJ) 603 Forest Dr, Springfield, NJ 07081

STONE JR, Lewis Seymour (NH) 11 Governor Sq, Peterborough, NH 03458

STONE, Mary Ruth (NJ) 40 - B Center St, Highlands, NJ 07732

STONE, Matt (Colo) 217 W 26th St, Bryan, TX 77803

STONE, Michael D (Tex) 18300 Upper Bay Rd, Houston, TX 77058

STONE, Michael Lee (SVa) 12120 Diamond Hill Dr, Midlothian, VA 23113

STONE, Sandra Elizabeth (Lex) 3416 Crooked Creek Rd, Carlisle, KY 40311

STONE, Thomas Michael (Chi) 3601 N North St, Peoria, IL 61604

STONER, D Scott (Mil) 2017 E. Olive St., Milwaukee, WI 53211

STONER, Suzanne (Ark)

STONESIFER, John DeWitt (WA) 3603 Gleneagles Dr Apt 3c, Silver Spring, MD 20906

STOPFEL, Barry Lee (Nwk) RD1 Box 146, Mifflinburg, PA 17844

STOPPEL, Gerald Corwin (WMich) PO Box 65, Saugatuck, MI 49453

STOREY, Wayne Alton (CNY) 311 S Massey St, Watertown, NY 13601

STORM, Astrid J (NY) 19 Kent Street, Beacon, NY 12508

STORMENT, J(ohn) Douglas (WTex) 1635 Thrush Court Cir, San Antonio, TX 78248

STORMER, Eugene Allen (Spr) 825 Lorraine Ave, Springfield, IL 62704

STORY, Mark Denslow (Okla) 1701 Mission Rd, Edmond, OK 73034

STOUDEMIRE, Stewart Mcbryde (WNC) 950 - 36th Avenue Circle Northeast, Hickory, NC 28601

STOUT, Arla Jeanne (Mich) 204 Sunnyside Ave, Cameron, WI 54822

STOUT, David Alan (The Episcopal Church in Haw) St. James' Church, PO Box 278, Kamuela, HI 96743

STOUTE, Barclay Lenardo (LI) 28 Fallon Ct, Elmont, NY 11003

STOUT-KOPP, Ronnie T (Nwk) 50 Brams Hill Dr, Mahwah, NJ 07430

STOWE, Barbara E (Mass) 33 Washington St, Topsfield, MA 01983

STOWE, Howard Timothy Wheeler (NY) 79 Ne 93rd St, Miami Shores, FL 33138

STOWE, Mallene Wells (CFla)

STOWELL, Philip (NJ) 929 E Laddoos Ave, San Tan Valley, AZ 85140

ST PIERRE, Joanne Madelyn (EMich) PO Box 217, Otter Lake, MI 48464

STRADER-SASSER, James William (CPa) 120 E Market St, Danville, PA 17821

STRAHAN, Linda C (RI) 103 Kay St, Newport, RI 02840

STRALEY, Benjamin Pearce (Ct)

STRAND, Jon (Va) 543 Beulah Rd NE, Vienna, VA 22180

STRANDE, Dana (Minn) 7305 Afton Rd, Woodbury, MN 55125

STRANDLUND, Daniel P (Ala) 113 Madison Ave, Montgomery, AL 36104

STRANE, Steven Roberts (SanD) 4489 Caminito Cuarzo, San Diego, CA 92117

STRANG, Ruth Hancock (Mich) 504 Prospect St, Howell, MI 48843

STRANGE, Phillip Ross (Los) PO Box 3144, Wrightwood, CA 92397

STRASBURGER, Frank C (NJ) 27 Tidal Run Lane, Brunswick, ME 04011

STRASSER, Gabor (Va) 18525 Bear Creek Ter, Leesburg, VA 20176

STRATFORD, Jane (Cal) 66 Saint Stephens Dr, Orinda, CA 94563

STRATTON, Jonathan Robert (Mo) 1210 Locust St, Saint Louis, MO 63103

STRAUB, Gregory (Eas) 1920 S Ocean Dr Apt 1004, Fort Lauderdale, FL 33316

STRAUSS, Arlen Richard (CNY) 109 Glenside Rd, Ithaca, NY 14850

STRAVERS, Cynthia A (NY) 2 E 90th St, New York, NY 10128

STRAVERS, Richard Lee (WMich) Po Box 56, Richland, MI 49083

STRAWBRIDGE, Jennifer R (Va) Keble College, Parks Road, Oxford, OX1 3PG, Great Britain (UK)

STREEPY, Robert Shawn (Kan) 10700 W 53rd St, Shawnee, KS 66203

STREET III, Claude Parke (Colo) 35 KILDEER Rd, Hamden, CT 06517

STREET, Terry Terriell (WTenn) 210 Walnut Trace Dr, Cordova, TN 38018

STREETER, Chris (Roch) 36 S Main St, Pittsford, NY 14534

STREEVER, Hilary Brandt (Va) St. James's Episcopal Church, 1205 W. Franklin Street, Richmond, VA 23220

STREIFF, Suzanne (Oly) 305 Burma Rd, Castle Rock, WA 98611

STREIT JR, Jep (Mass) 41 Ackers Ave Apt 2, Brookline, MA 02445

STRENTH, Robert Sean (CFla) 357 Forest Park Circle, Longwood, FL 32779

STREUFERT, Nancy Stimac (The Episcopal NCal) 625 15th St, Eureka, CA 95501

STRIBLING, Anna Jones (Va) 4540 Carrington Rd, Markham, VA 22643

STRIBLING, Emily B (WA) 4621 Laverock Pl NW, WASHINGTON, DC 20007

STRIBLING JR, Jess Hawkins (Va) 1 Colley Ave Apt 600, Apt 600, Norfolk, VA 23510

STRICKLAND, Thomas James (Ga)

✠ **STRICKLAND**, Vernon Edward (WK) 665 N Desmet Ave, Buffalo, WY 82834

STRICKLAND, Virginia Lisbeth (Cal) 14 Lagunitas Rd, Ross, CA 94957

STRICKLAND JR, William Earl (Alb) 4 Avery Place, Clifton Park, NY 12065

STRICKLIN, Paul (USC) 6408 Bridgewood Rd., Columbia, SC 29206

STRID, Paul Eric (Cal) 3115 W Meadow Dr SW, Albuquerque, NM 87121

STRIDIRON, Andrea Renee (Roch) 2000 Highland Ave, Rochester, NY 14618

STRIMER, Peter (Oly) 863 E Gwinn Place, Seattle, WA 98102

STRING, Jansen Edward (Md) 2900 Dunleer Rd, Baltimore, MD 21222

STRINGER, Pam (EC) 111 N King St, Bath, NC 27808

STRINGER, Stacy (Tex) 4613 Highway 3, Dickinson, TX 77539

STRINGFELLOW III, Howard (Be) 333 Wyandotte St., Bethlehem, PA 18015

STRIZAK, Jenna (At) Holy Trinity Parish, 515 E Ponce de Leon Ave, Decatur, GA 30030

STROBEL JR, Henry Willis (Tex) 2701 Bellefontaine St Apt B32, Houston, TX 77025

STROBEL, Mark Alan (ND)

STROBEL, Pam Owen (NY) 123 Henry St, Greenwich, CT 06830

STROH, Nancy Marshall (Pa) 3440 Norwood Pl, Holland, PA 18966

STROHL, Patrick Francis (CPa) 113 S Broad St, Mechanicsburg, PA 17055

STROHM, Ralph William (WVa) 2248 Adams Ave, Huntington, WV 25704

STROHMAIER, Gretchen (Mont) Holy Spirit Episcopal Church, 130 S 6th St E, Missoula, MT 59801

STROM, Aune Juanita (Mo) St Andrew's By the Lake Episcopal, PO Box 8766, Michigan City, IN 46361

STROMBERG, Matthew Roy (Alb)

STRONG, Anne Lorraine (Az) PO Box 65840, Tucson, AZ 85728

STRONG, Daniel (WMass) 17 Exeter Dr, Auburn, MA 01501

STRONG, Elizabeth Anne (Minn) 2200 Minnehaha Ave E, Saint Paul, MN 55119

STRONG III, Maurice LeRoy (Chi) 26 E Stonegate Dr, Prospect Heights, IL 60070

STRONG, Nancy (WMass) 17 Exeter Dr, Auburn, MA 01501

STROO, Eric Edward (Oly) 111 NE 80th St, Seattle, WA 98115

STROTHEIDE, Cassandra Jo (Colo) 19210 E Stanford Dr, Aurora, CO 80015

STROUD, Daniel (Pa) PO Box 247, Ft Washington, PA 19034

STROUD, Lara (Pa) PO Box 247, Fort Washington, PA 19034

STROUD, Nancy Webb (WMass) 64 Westwood Dr, Westfield, MA 01085

STROUD, Robert L (WNC)

STROUP, Susan Louise (Oly)

STROUT, Shawn Owen (WA) 2430 K St Nw, Washington, DC 20037

STRUBEL, Gary Francis (Alb) 457 3rd St, Troy, NY 12180

STRUBLE, Kenneth C (At) 4076 Riverdale Rd., Toccoa, GA 30577

STUART, Charles Moore (EMich) 821 Adams St, Saginaw, MI 48602

STUART, Judith Lynne (Mass) PO Box 789, Chatham, MA 02633

STUART, Lawrence Earl (Mich) 3901 Cheyenne Rd, Richmond, VA 23235

STUART, Marianne D(esmarais) (Ala) 249 Arch St, Philadelphia, PA 19106

STUART, Mark (Los) 2260 N Cahuenga Blvd # 507, Los Angeles, CA 90068

STUART V, Mose Wadsworth (Ala)

STUART, Toni Freeman (The Episcopal NCal) 4881 8th St, Carpinteria, CA 93013

STUBBS, John Derek (WNY) 33 Linwood Avenue, Whitinsville, MA 01588

STUBE, Peter (Pa) 125 Timothy Circle, Wayne, PA 19087

STUBER, Richard Leonard (Wyo) 1320 Landon Ave, Yakima, WA 98902

STUCKEY, Ross W (WMo) 1654 E Cardinal St, Springfield, MO 65804

STUDDIFORD, Linton (Me) 124 Bunganuc Rd, Brunswick, ME 04011

STUDENNY, Ronald Roman (Dal) 977 W Highway 243, Canton, TX 75103

STUDLEY, Carolyn Kay Mary (Minn) 614 N Old Litchfield Rd, Litchfield Park, AZ 85340

STUDLEY, Richard E (Minn) 9817 W. Pinecrest Dr, Sun City, AZ 85351

STUDWELL, Cathleen M (Nwk)

STUERKE, Pamela Susan (Mo)

STUHLMAN, Byron David (CNY) PO Box 74, Round Pond, ME 04564

STUHLMANN, Robert (Ct) 2000 Main St, Stratford, CT 06615

STUMP, Celeste Smith (Los) 330 E 16th St, Upland, CA 91784

STUMP, Derald William (CPa) 106 S Outer Dr, State College, PA 16801

STURGEON, Mary Sue (Neb) 5176 S 149th Ct, Omaha, NE 68137

STURGEON, Stephen C (U) 85 E 100 N, Logan, UT 84321

STURGES, Harriette Horsey (WA) 3001 Wisconsin Ave NW, Washington, DC 20016

STURGES, Kathleen McAuliffe (Va) 3134 Mollifield Lane, Charlottesville, VA 22911

STURGESS, Amber D (Cal) 6208 Sutter Ave, Richmond, CA 94804

STURGIS, Janet Elizabeth (Neb) Po Box 2285, Kearney, NE 68848

STURNI, Gary Kristan (WTenn) 6922 Great Oaks Rd, Germantown, TN 38138

STURTEVANT, Henry Hobson (NY) 484 W 43rd St Apt 33-H, New York, NY 10036

STUTLER, Jamie (At) 1029 Wellesley Crest Dr, Woodstock, GA 30189

SUAREZ, Eva Noemi (WA) 335 E 116th St Apt 3, New York, NY 10029

SUAREZ ELLES, Jose Armando (Colom) Cr 3 Sur # 11-A-02, Malambo, ATLANTICO, Colombia

SUCRE-CORDOVA, Guillermo Antonio (Ve)

SUELLAU, Nancy Shebs (Fla) St Catherines Episcopal Church, 4758 Shelby Ave, Jacksonville, FL 32210

SUGENO, David Senkichi (Tex)

SUHAR, John Charles (SwFla) 771 34th Ave N, Saint Petersburg, FL 33704

SUHR, Esther Jean (Mont) 2584 Mt Hwy 284, Townsend, MT 59644

SUIT, Marvin Wilson (Lex) 440 Fountain Avenue, Flemingsburg, KY 41041

SUITTER, Andrew M (Chi) 1210 Locust St, Saint Louis, MO 63103

SULERUD, Mary (Md) 1222 Berry St, Baltimore, MD 21211

SULLIVAN, Ann Mary (The Episcopal NCal) 5850 Crestmoor Dr, Paradise, CA 95969

SULLIVAN, Bernadette Marie (LI) Po Box 243, Hampton Bays, NY 11946

SULLIVAN, Bradley Joseph (Tex) 3003 Memorial Ct Apt 2405, Houston, TX 77007

SULLIVAN, Brian Christopher (At) 3361 Clubland Drive, Marietta, GA 30068

SULLIVAN, David Andrew (Alb) P.O. Box 146, Elizabethtown, NY 12932

SULLIVAN, Elmer Lindsley (NJ) 13 Llanfair Ln, Ewing, NJ 08618

SULLIVAN, Herbert Patrick (Mich) 1400 Northwood Rd, Austin, TX 78703

SULLIVAN, John Paul (Minn)

SULLIVAN, Judith A (Pa) Philadelphia Episcopal Cathedral, 3723 Chestnut Street, Philadelphia, PA 19104

SULLIVAN, Karen Sue Racer (Ind) 1770 N. Layman Ave., Indianapolis, IN 46218

SULLIVAN, Kristin Louise (Tex)

SULLIVAN, Margaret L (SwFla) 513 Nassau St S, Venice, FL 34285

SULLIVAN, Mark Campbell (Del) 463 Nicole Ct, Smyrna, DE 19977

SULLIVAN, Mary Patricia (NMich) 201 E Ridge St, Marquette, MI 49855

SULLIVAN, Maryalice (Mass) 104 N Washington St, North Attleboro, MA 02760

SULLIVAN, Mary Bea (Ala)

SULLIVAN JR, Matthew Robert (SeFla) 8144 Bridgewater Ct Apt C, West Palm Beach, FL 33406

SULLIVAN, Michael Radford (At) 805 Mount Vernon Highway NW, Atlanta, GA 30328

SULLIVAN, Paul David (Mass) 138 Tremont St., Boston, MA 02111

SULLIVAN, Peggy (NY) P.O. Box 708, Walden, NY 12586

SULLIVAN JR, Robert Edmund (NJ) 3450 Wild Oak Bay Blvd, Apt 138, Bradenton, FL 34210

SULLIVAN, Rosemari Gaughan (Va) 402 Virginia Avenue, Alexandria, VA 22302

SULLIVAN-CLIFTON, Sonia (CFla) 5873 N Dean Rd, Orlando, FL 32817

SUMMERFIELD, Leroy James (WNC) 5365 Pine Ridge Dr, Connellys Springs, NC 28612

SUMMEROUR, Toby (WNC) 233 Deep Ford Fls, Lake Toxaway, NC 28747

SUMMERS, Joseph Holmes (Mich) 1435 South Blvd, Ann Arbor, MI 48104

SUMMERS, Ronald Wayne (Lex) 777 Liberty Ridge Ln, Lexington, KY 40509

SUMMERSON, Stephen Lyn (Me) PO Box 8, Presque Isle, ME 04769

SUMNER JR, Edwin Roberts (NJ) 8 Heath Vlg, Hackettstown, NJ 07840

✠ **SUMNER JR**, George Robinson (Dal) 20 Queens Park Crescent West, Toronto, M5S 2W2, Canada

SUMNERS III, Charles Abram (WTex) 115 Northwood Dr., Cuero, TX 77954

SUNDARA, John Deepak (Dal) 3966 Mckinney Ave, Dallas, TX 75204

SUNDERLAND, Douglas Lane (Wyo) 18 Manning Rd, Cody, WY 82414

SUNDERLAND, Edward (NY) 310 E 49th St Apt 10C, New York, NY 10017

SUNDERLAND, Melanie (O) 1103 Castleton Rd, Cleveland Heights, OH 44121

SUNDIN, Chad Ludwig (Az) 1735 S College Ave, Tempe, AZ 85281

SUPIN, Charles Robert (Nev) 554 East Landing Ridge Circle, Jefferson, NC 28640

SURGEON, Ornoldo A (SeFla) 20011 Nw 39th Ct, Miami Gardens, FL 33055

SURINER, Noreen (WMass) PO Box 464, Middlefield, MA 01243

SURUDA, Teresa Ann (NJ) 58 Ravine Dr, Matawan, NJ 07747

SUTCLIFFE, David (Alb) 75 Willett St. Apt. 41, Albany, NY 12210

SUTER, Vernon L (SanD) 30329 Keith Ave, Cathedral City, CA 92234

SUTHERLAND, Alan (Okla) 18417 Black Bear Trail, Norman, OK 73072

SUTHERLAND, Linda Ann (FtW) 830 County Road 109, Hamilton, TX 76531

SUTHERLAND, Mark (RI) St Martin of Tours, 50 Orchard Ave, Providence, RI 02906

SUTHERLAND, Melody (Eas) 219 Somerset Rd, Stevensville, MD 21666

SUTHERS, Derwent Albert (At) 1178 Circulo Canario, Rio Rico, AZ 85648

SUTOR, Jack Thomas (Va) PO Box 120, Hanover, VA 23069

SUTTERFIELD, Ragan K (Ark)

SUTTON, Christine Marie (Be) PO Box 198, Lehman, PA 18627

✠ **SUTTON**, Eugene Taylor (Md) 4 East University Parkway, Baltimore, MD 21218

SUTTON, John (Cal) 1045 Neilson St, Albany, CA 94706

SUTTON, Norma Sarah (Chi)

SUTTON, Sharon Laverne (NJ) St Stephen's Episcopal Church, 324 Bridgeboro St, Riverside, NJ 08075

SVOBODA-BARBER, Helen (NC) c/o St. Luke's Episcopal Church, 1737 Hillandale Rd, Durham, NC 27705

SWAIN, Barry Edward Bailey (NY) Church of the Resurrection, 119 East 74th Street, New York, NY 10021

SWAIN, Storm (NY)

SWAN, Clinton E (Ak) Po Box 50037, Kivalina, AK 99750

SWAN, Craig R (RI) 72 Central St, Narragansett, RI 02882

SWAN, Richard A (Spr) P.O. Box 1513, Decatur, IL 62525

SWANLUND, Callie (Pa) 8000 Saint Martins Ln, Philadelphia, PA 19118

SWANN, Albert Henry (ETenn) 4515 Glennora Drive, Walland, TN 37886

SWANN, Catherine Williams (Va) 387 Harbor Drive, Reedville, VA 22539

SWANN, Stuart Alan (Los) 1560 S Fredrica Ave, Clearwater, FL 33756

SWANSON, George Gaines (Nwk) 349 Seawall Rd, Manset, ME 04679

SWANSON, Geraldine Ann (NY) 155 Bay St Apt 6H, Staten Island, NY 10301

SWANSON, John-Julian (Mil) 450 Sunnyslope Dr Apt 305, Hartland, WI 53029

SWANSON, Karen (ECR) Saint Andrew's Episcopal Church, 1600 Santa Lucia Ave, San Bruno, CA 94066

SWANSON, Kenneth Banford (At) 1015 Old Roswell Rd, Roswell, GA 30076

SWANSON, Richard Alden (Cal) 3101 Peninsula Rd Apt 301, Oxnard, CA 93035

SWANSON, Richard Reif (Vt) PO Box 1175, Stowe, VT 05672

SWARR, J Peter (WMass) 1 Porter Rd, East Longmeadow, MA 01028

SWARTHOUT, James Edward (Chi) 10275 N. River Rd, Barrington Hills, IL 60102

SWARTSFAGER, Ames Kent (LI) 1022 Marine Dr Ne Unit 2, Olympia, WA 98501

SWARTZENTRUBER, A Orley (NJ) 309 Bridgeboro Rd Apt 22, Moorestown, NJ 08057

SWAYZE, Marie Zealor (Pa) 540 Lowell St, Wakefield, MA 01880

SWEENEY, Craig Chandler (Be) 2411 SW 35th Ter, Topeka, KS 66611

SWEENEY, David Cameron (Ore) 503 N Holladay Dr, Seaside, OR 97138

SWEENEY, Joseph Francis (NJ) 25 Quail Hollow Drive, Westampton, NJ 08060

SWEENEY, Meghan T (Mass) All Saints' Episcopal Church, 121 N Main St, Attleboro, MA 02703

SWEENEY, Sylvia A (Los) Bloy House The Episcopal Theological School At Claremont, 1325 N College Ave, Claremont, CA 91711

SWEET, Fran Maciver (Cal) Po Box 1384, Alameda, CA 94501

SWEET, Portia Ann (Tex) 1656 Blalock Rd, Houston, TX 77080

SWEIGERT, Cynthia (Pgh) 5700 Forbes Ave, Pittsburgh, PA 15217

SWENSON, Richard Clive (Minn)

SWENSON, Warren Thomas (WMo)

SWESEY, Jean Elizabeth (Minn) 1008 Transit Ave, Roseville, MN 55113

SWETMAN, Margarita O (Nwk) 2528 Palmer Ave, New Orleans, LA 70118

SWIEDLER, Anne Elizabeth (At) 5625 Mill Glen Ct, Atlanta, GA 30338

SWIFT, Daniel Willard (Los) 24874 Olive Tree Ln, Los Altos, CA 94024

SWIFT, John Kohler (WMo) 6 Hunter Dr, Guilford, CT 06437

SWIFT, Steve Albert (Md) 8403 Nunley Dr Apt E, Parkville, MD 21234

SWINDELL, Kay Howard (EC) 1514 Clifton Rd, Jacksonville, NC 28540

SWINDLE, Frank Moody (NwT) 649 Hwy 577, Pioneer, LA 71266

SWINEHART, Bruce Howard (Colo) 1404 Orchard Ave, Boulder, CO 80304

SWINEHART JR, Charles (Mich) 1615 Ridgewood Dr, East Lansing, MI 48823

✠ **SWING**, William Edwin (Cal) 105 Pepper Ave., Burlingame, CA 94010

SWINNEA, Stephanie Lavenia (Neb) 510 S 15th St, Mcalester, OK 74501

SWINSKI, Grace Elaine (RI)

SWITZ, Robert (Cal) 1189 W Park View Pl, Mount Pleasant, SC 29466

SWITZER, John B (Miss) 4412 Gautier Vancleave Rd, Gautier, MS 39553

SWONGER, Timothy Lee (Nev) 1560 Jamielinn Ln Unit 103, Las Vegas, NV 89110

SWOPE, Bob (Ak)

SWORD, Carl Richard (NY) 200 East 33rd St, Apt # 14-J, New York, NY 10016

SY, Jonathan J (Los) 21202 Spurney Ln, Huntington Beach, CA 92646

SYDNOR JR, Charles Raymond (Va) 175 Rogue Point Ln, Heathsville, VA 22473

SYEDULLAH, Masud Ibn (NY) 35 Circle Dr, Hyde Park, NY 12538

SYER, Nathan George (Nev)

SYER, Sarah Amelia (Nev) 14 Boltwood Ave, Amherst, MA 01002

SYLER, Gregory Charles (WA) St George Church, PO Box 30, Valley Lee, MD 20692

SYLVESTER, Kay (Los)

SYMINGTON, Ann Pritzlaff (Los) 4450 E Camelback Rd, Phoenix, AZ 85018

SYMINGTON, Sid (ECR) 545 Shasta Ave, Morro Bay, CA 93442

SYMONDS, John W (Pa) 321 W Chestnut St, Lancaster, PA 17603

SYMONS, Frederic Russell (The Episcopal NCal) 5301 Whitney Ave, Carmichael, CA 95608

SYNAN, Thomas (WMass) Church Of The Heavenly Rest, 2 E 90th St, New York, NY 10128

SZACHARA, Joell Beth (CNY) 3415 Havenbrook Dr Apt 104, Kingwood, TX 77339

SZARKE, Christopher J (U) 7486 Union Park Ave, Midvale, UT 84047

SZOBOTA, Nick (Va) 230 Owensville Rd, West River, MD 20778

SZOKE, Robyn J (CPa) 6 Kitszell Dr, Carlisle, PA 17015

SZOST, Lois Anne Whitcomb (NY) 57 Goodwin Rd, Stanfordville, NY 12581

SZYMANSKI, Michael Stephen (WNY) 21 Modern Ave, Lackawanna, NY 14218

SZYMANSKI, Walter (Pgh) 334 Main St, Pittsburgh, PA 15201

T

TABB, Stewart (SVa) 405 Talbot Hall Rd, Norfolk, VA 23505

TABER II, Ken (SwFla) 200 College Ave NE, Grand Rapids, MI 49503

TABER-HAMILTON, Nigel (Oly) PO Box 11, Freeland, WA 98249

TABER-HAMILTON, Rachel K (Oly) 333 High St, Freeland, WA 98249

TABOR, Henry Caleb Coleman (NC) 408 Granville St., Oxford, NC 27565

TACKKETT, Antoinette Vance (Kan) 613 Elm St, Coffeyville, KS 67337

TADKEN, Neil (Los) 122 S. California Ave., Monrovia, CA 91016

TAFLINGER, Mary (Ind) 5553 Leumas Rd, Cincinnati, OH 45239

TAFOYA, Stacey T (Colo) 315 Leyden St, Denver, CO 80220

TAFT JR, Paul Eberhart (Tex) 5504 Andover Dr, Tyler, TX 75707

TAGGART, Mary Heller (The Episcopal NCal) 209 Matheson St, Healdsburg, CA 95448

TAKACS, Erika (Pa) Saint Mark's Church, 1625 Locust St, Philadelphia, PA 19103

TAKES WAR BONNETT, Ray Lee (SD) 840 Spruce St Lot 38, Rapid City, SD 57701

TALBERT, Thomas Keith (CGC) 701 N Pine St, Foley, AL 36535

TALBIRD JR, John D (ETenn) 3184 Waterfront Drive, Chattanooga, TN 37419

TALBOT, Jarod C (SO)

TALBOTT, John Thayer (WA) 8 Ledge Road, Old Saybrook, CT 06475

TALCOTT, Barbara Geer (NH) St. Mark's School, 25 Marlboro Rd., Southborough, MA 01772

TALIAFERRO, Bob (Mo) St. Paul's Episcopal Church, 1010 N Main St, Sikeston, MO 63801

TALK IV, John Gordon (NC) 304 S Ridge St, Southern Pines, NC 28387

TALLANT, Greg (At) 3285 Kensington Road, Avondale Estates, GA 30002

TALLEVAST, William Dalton (CPa) 1501 N Campbell Ave, Dept of Pastoral Care, Tucson, AZ 85724

TALLEY, Jennie (NY) St. John's Episcopal Church, 11 Wilmot Road, New Rochelle, NY 10804

TALLMAN, Samuel Vose (WNC) St Mary of the Hills Church, PO Box 14, Blowing Rock, NC 28605

✠ **TALTON**, Chester Lovelle (Los) 1528 Oakdale Road, Modesto, CA 95355

TAMKE, Stephen Connor (LI) 325 Lattingtown Rd, Locust Valley, NY 11560

TAMMEARU, Deborah Gibson (NY) 1047 Amsterdam Avenue, New York, NY 10025

TAN, Wee Chung (Minn)

TANABE, Irene (The Episcopal Church in Haw) 1041 10th Ave, Honolulu, HI 96816

TAN CRETI, Michael J (Neb) 2051 N 94th St, Omaha, NE 68134

TANG, Chris (Md) 3118 Cape Hill Ct, Hampstead, MD 21074

TANKERSLEY, Rebecca (Dal) 9845 Mccree Rd, Dallas, TX 75238

TANNER, Michael Abbott (At)

TANTIMONACO, Dan Frank (Az) 307 N Mogollon Trail, Payson, AZ 85541

TAPLEY, William Clark (WTex) 1604 W Kansas Ave, Midland, TX 79701

TAPPE, Ibba (Fla) 2935 Tidewater St, Fernandina Beach, FL 32034

TARBOX, Janet (USC) 318 Palmer Dr, Lexington, SC 29072

TARDIFF, Dick (The Episcopal Church in Haw) PO Box 545, Kealakekua, HI 96750

TARPLEE JR, Cornelius (Nwk) 1405 Duncan St., Key West, FL 33040

TARPLEY, Kent W (SwVa) 375 East Pine St, Wytheville, VA 24382

✠ **TARRANT**, John (SD) 500 South Main Ave, Sioux Falls, SD 57104

TARRANT, Paul John (RI) 39 Jeffrey Street, Edinburgh, EH1 1DH, Great Britain (UK)

TARSIS, George Michael (O) 399 Jefferson Ave, Barberton, OH 44203

TARTT JR, Jo Cowin (WA) 2727 34th Pl Nw, Washington, DC 20007

TARVER, Brian M (WTex) 311 E Corpus Christi St, Beeville, TX 78102

TASY, Beverly Ann Moore (RG) St Christopher's Episcopal Church, 207 E Permian Dr, Hobbs, NM 88240

TATE, Donald Steven (At) 201 Ellen Ct, Warner Robins, GA 31088

TATE, Mary Katherine (Del) 18 Olive Ave, Rehoboth Beach, DE 19971

TATE, Robert Lee (Pa) 7209 Lincoln Dr., Philadelphia, PA 19119

TATE, Russell Eric (Eau) 510 S Farwell St Ste 2, Eau Claire, WI 54701

TATE, Ruth Newman (At) 201 Ellen Ct, Warner Robins, GA 31088

TATEM, Catherine Leigh (Roch) St Peter's Episcopal Church, 3825 E Henrietta Rd, Henrietta, NY 14467

TATEM, Sandra Lou (Alb) 39 Greyledge Dr, Loudonville, NY 12211

TATEM, William Arthur (Alb) 39 Graystone Rd, Loudonville, NY 12211

TATLIAN, Edward Anthony (CFla) 6400 N Socrum Loop Rd, Lakeland, FL 33809

TATLOCK, Alan Ralph (Alb) 2938 Birchton Rd, Ballston Spa, NY 12020

TATRO, Marie A (LI) St Gabriel's Episcopal Church, 331 Hawthorne St, Brooklyn, NY 11225

TATTERSALL, Elizabeth Russell (Nev) 1048 Wisteria Dr., Minden, NV 89423

TAUBE, Kimberly Lynn (WMo) 524 4th St, Boonville, MO 65233

TAUPIER, Linda (WMass)

TAVOLARO, Dante A (RI) 99 Peirce St, East Greenwich, RI 02818

TAYEBWA, Onesmus OT (Los) 5700 Rudnick Ave, Woodland Hills, CA 91367

TAYLOR, A(lice) Susan (NJ) 13 Forsythia Ct, Marlton, NJ 08053

TAYLOR, Andrea Maija (SwFla) St Davids Church, 205 Old Main St, South Yarmouth, MA 02664

TAYLOR, Anne L (Va)

TAYLOR, Arnold Godfrey (WA) 507 3rd St SE, Washington, DC 20003

TAYLOR, Barbara Brown (At) PO Box 1030, Clarkesville, GA 30523

TAYLOR, Bob (Ct) 4 Harbor View Drive, Essex, CT 06426

TAYLOR, Brenda M (CPa) 4284 Beaufort Hunt Dr, Harrisburg, PA 17110

TAYLOR, Brian (Chi) 1401 Los Arboles Avenue Northwest, Albuquerque, NM 87107

TAYLOR, Bruce W (VI) The Valley, Box 65, Virgin Gorda, VI VG1150

TAYLOR, Carlene Holder (Ga)

TAYLOR, Charles Henry (WNC) 84 Keasler Rd, Asheville, NC 28805

TAYLOR, Courtney Stacy (Miss)

TAYLOR, Cynthia nan (Ga) 973 Hunting Horn Way W, Evans, GA 30809

TAYLOR, David Edwin (SwVa) PO Box 527, Rocky Mount, VA 24151

TAYLOR, David Kenneth (Nwk) 124 Franklin Ct, Flemington, NJ 08822

TAYLOR, Dean (At) 1600 Southmont Dr, Dalton, GA 30720

TAYLOR, Edgar Garland (La) 1716 Soniat St, New Orleans, LA 70115

TAYLOR, Edward Norman (Mich) 80 Wellesley Street East #904, Toronto, M4Y 2B5, Canada

TAYLOR, George Williamson (NY) 311 Huguenot St, New Rochelle, NY 10801

TAYLOR, Gloria Atkinson (NI) 1809 Holly Ln, Munster, IN 46321

TAYLOR, Gregory Blackwell (Va) 250 Pantops Mountain Rd. Apt. 5407, Charlottesville, VA 22911

TAYLOR, James Delane (CFla) 10 Fox Cliff Way, Ormond Beach, FL 32174

TAYLOR JR, James Edward (SC) 1150 East Montague Ave., North Charleston, SC 29405

TAYLOR, James Maurice (Pa) 160 Marvin Rd, Elkins Park, PA 19027

✠ **TAYLOR**, John Harvey (Los) 1968 Paseo Luis, Yorba Linda, CA 92886

TAYLOR, Josephine A (SVa) 3100 Shore Dr Apt 625, Virginia Beach, VA 23451

TAYLOR, LeBaron (SwVa) P.O. Box 709, Covington, VA 24426

TAYLOR, Linda Sue (ECR) 1809 Palo Santo Dr, Campbell, CA 95008

TAYLOR, Lloyd (LI) 13304 109th Ave, South Ozone Park, NY 11420

TAYLOR, Margaret Anne (Ala) Po Box 361352, Birmingham, AL 35236

TAYLOR, Marjorie B (Mich) St. John's Episcopal Church, 26998 Woodward Ave, Royal Oak, MI 48067

TAYLOR, Mary Ann Demetsenaere (Me) 83 Indian Hill Ln, Frankfort, ME 04438

TAYLOR, Norman Dennis (Oly) 4218 Montgomery Place, Mount Vernon, WA 98274

TAYLOR, Patricia Lois (Oly) 75 E Lynn St Apt 104, Seattle, WA 98102

TAYLOR, Paul N. (WMass) 34 Boylston Cir., Shrewsbury, MA 01545

TAYLOR, Phyllis Gertrude (Pa) 401 Central Ave, Cheltenham, PA 19012

✠ **TAYLOR**, Porter (WNC) 44 Ravenwood Dr, Fletcher, NC 28732

TAYLOR, Ralph Douglas (Az) St Philips in the Hills, PO Box 65840, Tucson, AZ 85728

TAYLOR JR, Raymond George (NC) 461 Pemaquid Harbor Rd, Pemaquid, ME 04558

TAYLOR, Richard Louis (WLa) 108 Jason Ln, Natchitoches, LA 71457

TAYLOR, Robert (NC) 813 Darby Street, Raleigh, NC 27610

TAYLOR, Robert C (USC) 511 Roper Mtn Rd, Greenville, SC 29615

TAYLOR, Robert Stuart (SeFla) 3325 E. Community Dr., Jupiter, FL 33458

TAYLOR, Robert Vincent (Oly) 32508 W Kelly Road, Benton City, WA 99320

TAYLOR, Robin (WA) 7 Potomac Ave, Indian Head, MD 20640

TAYLOR, Ronald Brent (WNC) 7545 Sarah Dr., Denver, NC 28037

TAYLOR, Scott C (Los) 504 N Camden Dr, Beverly Hills, CA 90210

TAYLOR, Stanley Richard (HB) 157 Patrick Crescent, Essex, N8M 1X2, Canada

TAYLOR, Stefanie Elizabeth (At) 3110 Ashford Dunwoody Rd NE, Atlanta, GA 30319

TAYLOR, Susan (Me) St John's Episcopal Church, 4 Prospect Ave, Randolph, VT 05060

TAYLOR, Sylvester O'Neale (LI) 485 Linwood St, Brooklyn, NY 11208

TAYLOR, Terrence Alexander (SeFla) 20822 San Simeon Way Apt. 109, Miami, FL 33179

TAYLOR, Terry Ray (O) 1108 Secretariat Dr W, Danville, KY 40422

TAYLOR, Thomas Herbert (The Episcopal NCal) 14234 N Newcastle Dr, Sun City, AZ 85351

TAYLOR JR, Timus Gayle (Tenn) 4715 Harding Pike, Nashville, TN 37205

TAYLOR JR, Willard Seymour (EC) 245 Mcdonald Church Rd, Rockingham, NC 28379

TAYLOR JR, William Brown (SVa) 4025 Reese Dr S, Portsmouth, VA 23703

TAYLOR, Williamson Sylvanus (NY) 29 Drake St, Mount Vernon, NY 10550

TAYLOR LYMAN, Susan May (SD) 325 N Plum St, Vermillion, SD 57069

TCHAMALA, Theodore K (Md) 6515 Loch Raven Blvd., Baltimore, MD 21239

TEAGUE, Charles Steven (NC) 337 Marley Was, Fuquay Varina, NC 27526

TEASLEY, Rrobintteasley@gmail.comobin (SVa)

11406 Glenmont Road, North Chesterfield, VA 23236

TEDERSTROM, John Patton (Ky) 1007 Hess Ln, Louisville, KY 40217

TEDESCO, Robert Lincoln (Va) 407 Russell Ave Apt 605, Gaithersburg, MD 20877

TEDESCO, William Nicholas (Ct) 20 Erickson Way, South Yarmouth, MA 02664

TEED, Lee B (SanD) 4860 Circle Dr, San Diego, CA 92116

TEETS, James C (Tenn) 1140 Cason Ln, Murfreesboro, TN 37128

TEETZ, Margaret Lou-Sarah (Alb) Christ Church, 970 State St, Schenectady, NY 12307

TEMBECKJIAN, Renee Melanie (CNY) 4782 Hyde Rd, Manlius, NY 13104

TEMME, Lou (Pa) Church Of The Advent, 12 Byberry Rd, Hatboro, PA 19040

TEMPLE, Charles Sloan (NY) 1 E 29th St, New York, NY 10016

TEMPLE, Gordon Clarence (ETenn) 6808 Levi Rd, Hixson, TN 37343

TEMPLE JR, Gray (At) 10685 Bell Rd, Duluth, GA 30097

TEMPLE, Palmer Collier (At) 1883 Wycliff Rd Nw, Atlanta, GA 30309

TEMPLEMAN, Mark Alan (Mass) 60 Monument Avenue, Swampscott, MA 01907

TEMPLETON, Gary Lynn (Okla) 903 N Primrose St, Duncan, OK 73533

TEMPLETON, John (At) 274 Hershey Lane, Clayton, GA 30525

TEMPLETON, Patricia Dale (At) 4393 Garmon Road NW, Atlanta, GA 30327

TENCH, Jack Marvin (Oly) 1919 NE Ridgewood Ct, Poulsbo, WA 98370

TENDICK, James Ross (U) 1780 Plateau Cir, Moab, UT 84532

✠ **TENNIS**, Cabell (Oly) 725 9th Ave, Apt. 904, Seattle, WA 98104

TENNISON, George Nelson (La) 401 Magnolia Ln, Mandeville, LA 70471

TENNY, Claire Mary (Chi) Po Box 426, Vails Gate, NY 12584

TEPAVCHEVICH, Kathie Elaine (Chi) 6588 Shabbona Rd, Indian Head Park, IL 60525

TEPE, Donald James (EMich) 3226 Meadowview Ln, Saginaw, MI 48601

TERHUNE, Jason Scott (Tenn)

TERHUNE JR, Robert Dawbarn (Tex) 2605A Spring Ln, Austin, TX 78703

TERRILL, Bob (Kan) 3524 Sw Willow Brook Ln, Topeka, KS 66614

TERRY, Andrew (Va) 2209 E Grace St, Richmond, VA 23223

TERRY, Eleanor Applewhite (Mass) 193 Salem St, Boston, MA 02113

TERRY, Susan Preston (Kan) 3209 W 25th St, Lawrence, KS 66047

TERRY, Teresa F (Del)

TERRY, William Hutchinson (La) 626 Congress St., New Orleans, LA 70117

TERWILLIGER, David R (Ak) 257 Fawn Ct, Anchorage, AK 99515

TESCHNER, David (SVa) 31 Belmead St, Petersburg, VA 23805

TESKA, William Jay (Minn) 940 Franklin Terrace, Apt. 409, Minneapolis, MN 55406

TESS, Mike (Mil) 124 Dewey St, Sun Prairie, WI 53590

TESTA, Dennis Arthur (Md) 302 Homewood Rd, Linthicum, MD 21090

TESTER, Elizabeth B (Mil)

TESTER, Helen Whitener (Miss) 743 Milwaukee Rd, Beloit, WI 53511

TESTIN, Joan Marie (RI) Emmanuel Episcopal Church, 120 Nate Whipple Hwy, Cumberland, RI 02864

TETRAULT, David Joseph (SVa) 22501 Cypress Point Road, Williamsburg, VA 23185

TETRAULT, Joanne Russell (Md) 6400 Belair Rd, Baltimore, MD 21206

TETZLAFF, Chana (EC) Emmanuel Episcopal Church, 2410 Lexington Rd, Winchester, KY 40391

TETZLAFF, Tyler J (EC)

THABET, David George (WVa) 1305 15th St, Huntington, WV 25701

THACKER II, Bob (SwVa) 207 Lookout Point Dr., Osprey, FL 34229

THADEN, Tim Robert (Colo) 780 Devinney Ct, Golden, CO 80401

THAETE JR, William Elwood (Oly) 10239 Old Frontier Rd NW, Silverdale, WA 98383

THAMES, David Blake (Tex) 4419 Taney Ave No 202, Alexandria, VA 22304

THAO, Choua May (Minn) 2200 Minnehaha Ave E, Saint Paul, MN 55119

THAO, Thomas Zaxao (Minn)

THARAKAN, Angeline H (Ark) 501 S Phoenix Ave, Russellville, AR 72801

THARAKAN, Jos (WMo) 158 Dawn Cir., Russellville, AR 72802

THATCHER, Anne C (Pa) 8000 Saint Martins Ln, Philadelphia, PA 19118

THAYER, Andrew Richard (La) 1329 Jackson Ave, Church of the Ascension, Montgomery, AL 36104

THAYER, Evan L (Mass) 15 Elko St # 2135, Brighton, MA 02135

THAYER II, Fred (SanD) 12103 Caminito Corriente, San Diego, CA 92118

THAYER, Judith Ann (Ia) 912 20th Ave, Coralville, IA 52241

THAYER, Steven Allen (NJ) Po Box 440, Jamison, PA 18929

THEODORE, Margaret Bessie (Alb) P.O. BOX 446, Potsdam, NY 13676

THEUS SR, James Graves (WLa) 6291 Old Baton Rouge Hwy, Alexandria, LA 71302

THEW, Richard H (EO) Po Box 125, Cove, OR 97824

THEW FORRESTER, Kevin Lee (NMich) 402 Harrison St, Marquette, MI 49855

THEW FORRESTER, Rise Fay (NMich) 402 Harrison St, Marquette, MI 49855

THIBODAUX, Louise Ruprecht (Ala)

THIBODEAUX, James L (Oly) 7904 Manzanita Dr. NW, Olympia, WA 98502

THIELE, William C (Nwk) 215 Lafayette Ave., Passaic, NJ 07055

THIGPEN III, William Mccord (At) 5152 Patriot Dr, Stone Mountain, GA 30087

THIM, Paul (At) 697 Densley Dr., Decatur, GA 30033

THOBER, Ellie Thober (Neb) 4718 18th St, Columbus, NE 68601

THOENI, Thomas Andrew (SwFla) 302 Carey St, Plant City, FL 33563

THOM, Ashley Jane Squier (Chi) 3626 N. Francisco Ave., Chicago, IL 60618

✠ **THOM**, Brian (Ida) 1858 W. Judith Lane, Boise, ID 83705

THOM, Dave (Az) 540 Atchison Lane, Wickenburg, AZ 85390

THOM, Kenneth Stow (Eas) 3849 Sirman Dr, Snow Hill, MD 21863

THOMAS, Adam P (Ct) 15 Pearl St, Mystic, CT 06355

THOMAS, Allisyn (SanD) St. Paul's Cathedral, 2728 Sixth Avenue, San Diego, CA 92103

THOMAS JR, Arthur Robert (Ak) Po Box 1872, Seward, AK 99664

THOMAS JR, Benjamin A (SeFla)

THOMAS, Benjamin Randall (WK) 402 S 8th St, Salina, KS 67401

THOMAS, Bethany (Colo) 1221 Illinois St. Apt 2A, Golden, CO 80401

THOMAS, Christopher Blake (FtW) 5910 Black Oak Ln, River Oaks, TX 76114

THOMAS, Douglas Earl (WTex) 2722 Old Ranch Rd, San Antonio, TX 78217

THOMAS, Douglas Paul (NwT) 602 Meander St, Abilene, TX 79602

THOMAS, Elaine Ellis (Nwk) St. Paul's Memorial Church, 1700 University Avenue, Charlottesville, VA 22903

THOMAS, Jaime Alfredo (Dal) P.O. Box 15, Fort Ord, CA 93941

THOMAS JR, James Morris (The Episcopal NCal) 18402 Yale Court, Somoma, CA 95476

THOMAS, John (Ga) 290 Quintard Rd, Sewanee, TN 37375

THOMAS, John Alfred (Va) 3800 Powell Ln Apt 813, Falls Church, VA 22041

THOMAS, John Paul (Dal) 739 Middale Rd, Duncanville, TX 75116

THOMAS, Jonathan R (Chi) 1864 Post Rd, Darien, CT 06820

THOMAS, Joshua (Oly) 505 Alexander Ave, Durham, NC 27705

THOMAS, Kathryn Pauline (Va) 214 Church St, Madison, VA 22727

THOMAS, Kathy (NI) 10010 Aurora Pl, Fort Wayne, IN 46804

THOMAS, Keila Carpenter (Lex) 145 E 5th St, Morehead, KY 40351

THOMAS, Kenneth Dana (Ct) 5 Bassett St Apt B10, West Haven, CT 06516

THOMAS, Laughton (Fla) 516 Howard AVE, Tallahassee, FL 32310

THOMAS, Leonard Everett (EC) 916 Lord Granville Dr., Morehead City, NC 28557

THOMAS, Margaret (ECR) 1084 Paseo Guebabi, Rio Rico, AZ 85648

THOMAS, Margaret Ann (Me) 297 Wardwell Point Rd, Penobscot, ME 04476

THOMAS, Margaret Warren (Minn) 9426 Congdon Blvd, Duluth, MN 55804

THOMAS, Marilu James (Va)

THOMAS, Megan Evans (NJ) 16 All Saints Rds, Princeton, NJ 08540

THOMAS, Michael Jon (WNY) 703 W Ferry St Apt C9, Buffalo, NY 14222

THOMAS, Micki-Ann (SwFla) 7250 Quarry St, Englewood, FL 34224

THOMAS, Patricia Menne (EC) 136 Saint Andrews Cir, New Bern, NC 28562

THOMAS, Peter Glyn (Tex) 831 Walker Stone Dr Apt 104, Cary, NC 27513

THOMAS, Rachel Woodall (Ct) 155 Essex St, Deep River, CT 06417

THOMAS, Robert William (NC) 413 Dogwood Creek Pl, Fuquay Varina, NC 27526

THOMAS, Sherry (Ct) 386 N Anna Dr, Louisa, VA 23093

THOMAS, Teresa Ann Collingwood (Ak) PO Box 76, Fort Yukon, AK 99740

THOMAS, Timothy Bosworth (SeFla) 3434 N Oceanshore Blvd, Flagler Beach, FL 32136

THOMAS, Trevor Emrys George (Nwk) 90 Rossini Road, Westerly, RI 02891

THOMAS, Valerie Bricker (Fla) 244 Ashley Lake Dr, Melrose, FL 32666

THOMAS, Victor J (Tex) 3129 Southmore Blvd, Houston, TX 77004

THOMAS, Wayland Eugene (Md) 55 Brooklyn Hts Rd, Thomaston, ME 04861

THOMAS, William Carl (NJ) Christ Church, 90 Kings Hwy, Middletown, NJ 07748

THOMAS, William Steven (SeFla) 14445 Horseshoe Trce, Wellington, FL 33414

THOMASON, Clayton Leslie (Chi) 42 Ashland Ave, River Forest, IL 60305

THOMASON, Steven (Oly) 1245 10th Avenue East, Seattle, WA 98102

THOMPSON, Barkley Stuart (Tex) 1117 Texas St, Houston, TX 77002

THOMPSON, Carla Eva (Va) 322 N Alfred St, Alexandria, VA 22314

THOMPSON, Catherine M (Dal) Episcopal Church of the Annunciation, 602 N. Old Orchard Lane, Lewisville, TX 75077

THOMPSON, Chris Christopher (WVa) Church of the Holy Communion, 218 Ashley Ave, Charleston, SC 29403

THOMPSON, Danielle L (Ala) 1910 12th Ave S, Birmingham, AL 35205

THOMPSON, David Frank Ora (USC) 622 Stanton Dr, North Augusta, SC 29841

THOMPSON, David James (Dal) 417 Olive St, Texarkana, TX 75501

THOMPSON, David Joel (Colo) 360 Scrub Oak Cir, Monument, CO 80132

THOMPSON, Donald Frederick (Ct) 11 Lenox Ave, Norwalk, CT 06854

THOMPSON, Ed (Tex) 5500 St. Claude Avenue, New Orleans, LA 70119

THOMPSON, Edgar Andrew (Colo) 971 E Lone Pine Road, Pahrump, NV 89048

THOMPSON, Edward (Pa) 301 N Chester Rd, Swarthmore, PA 19081

THOMPSON, Elena M (Ga) PO Box 1167, Baxley, GA 31515

THOMPSON JR, Fred Edward (SC) 2138 Allandale Plantation Rd, Wadmalaw Island, SC 29487

THOMPSON, Fred Leonard (NC) 538 Furth Ln, Southern Pines, NC 28387

THOMPSON, Helen Plemmons (At) 91 Wylde Wood Dr, McDonough, GA 30253

THOMPSON III, Henry Lawrence (Pgh) 2310 Meadow Vue Dr, Moon Township, PA 15108

THOMPSON SR, Howard Dale (Alb) 140 Foster Rd, North Lawrence, VA 12967

THOMPSON, James Calvin (SVa) 2003 Camelia Cir, Midlothian, VA 23112

THOMPSON, James E (Episcopal SJ) 3930 SE 162nd Ave Spc 22, Portland, OR 97236

THOMPSON, Jerry A (Neb) St. Mark's on the Campus Episcopal Church, Lincoln, NE 68508

THOMPSON, John E (Roch) 21 Main Street, Geneseo, NY 14454

THOMPSON, John Francis (CFla) 90 E Jinnita St, Hernando, FL 34442

THOMPSON, John Kell (Oly) 21630 102nd Ln SW, Vashon, WA 98070

THOMPSON, John Paul (Alb) PO Box 180, Copake Falls, NY 12517

THOMPSON JR, Joseph Downing (Mo)

THOMPSON, Karen Elizabeth (EMich) 18890 Fireside Hwy, Presque Isle, MI 49777

THOMPSON, Kenneth David (Ky) 1768 Plum Ridge Rd, Taylorsville, KY 40071

THOMPSON, Kenya Angela (At)

THOMPSON, Lori Lee L (ETenn) 590 Walthour Rd, Savannah, GA 31410

THOMPSON, Marisa Tabizon (Neb) 9320 Blondo St, Omaha, NE 68134

THOMPSON, Mark (Vt) 700 Douglas Ave Apt 907, Minneapolis, MN 55403

THOMPSON, M Dion (Md) 1208 John St, Baltimore, MD 21217

THOMPSON, Michael Bruce (EC) Dashwood House, Sidgwick Avenue, Cambridge, CB3 9DA, Great Britain (UK)

THOMPSON, Michael King (NC) 103 Sheffield Rd, Williamsburg, VA 23188

✠ THOMPSON JR, Morris (La) 1623 7th Street, New Orleans, LA 70115

THOMPSON III, Morris King (Miss) 3831 35th Ave, Meridian, MS 39305

THOMPSON, Owen C (NY) Grace Church, 130 1st Ave, Nyack, NY 10960

THOMPSON, Paul Mason (Vt) 4323 Main Street, Rt 6A, Cummaquid, MA 02637

THOMPSON, Peggy Reid (ECR) 451 Vivienne Dr, Watsonville, CA 95076

THOMPSON, Peter D (Ct) 60 East Ave, Norwalk, CT 06851

THOMPSON, Richelle L. (Ala) St. Michael's Episcopal Church, 431 10th Street NW, Fayette, AL 35555

THOMPSON, Robert Gaston (Colo) 3377 Mill Vista Rd Unit 3612, Highlands Ranch, CO 80129

THOMPSON, Robert Wildan (Ky) 1206 Maple Ln, Anchorage, KY 40223

THOMPSON, Roderick James Marcellus (Cal) 601 Van Ness Ave Apt 123, San Francisco, CA 94102

THOMPSON, Scott A (Tex) Holy Cross Episc Church, 5653 W. River Park Dr., Sugar Land, TX 77479

THOMPSON SR, Stephen Lafoia (ETenn) 134 Iris Pl, Newport, TN 37821

THOMPSON, Sue (Cal) St Edmund's Episcopal Church, PO Box 688, Pacifica, CA 94044

THOMPSON, Tommy Alan (Pa) St. Andrew's Church, West Vincent, 7 Saint Andrews Ln, Glenmoore, PA 19343

THOMPSON, Wanda Jean (Me) 1375 Forest Ave. Apt. H14, Portland, ME 04103

THOMPSON, Zachary R (NY) 805 Mt Vernon Hwy NW, Atlanta, GA 30327

THOMPSON DE MEJIA, Kara Ann (Hond) Spring Garden, Islas De La Bahia, Roatan, Honduras

THOMPSON-QUARTEY, John John (NJ) 109 Brookcrest Dr, Marietta, GA 30068

THOMPSON-UBERUAGA, William (Ida) 518 N 8th St, Boise, ID 83702

THOMSEN, William Robert (WNC) 299 Locust Grove Rd, Weaverville, NC 28787

THOMSON, Jacqueline (Va) 9405 Shouse Dr, Vienna, VA 22182

THOMSON, James (Okla) 501 S Cincinnati Ave, Tulsa, OK 74103

THOMSON, Malcolm Davis (WMich)

THOMSON, Ronald Reed (RG) 733 Lakeway Dr, El Paso, TX 79932

THON, Susan Cecelia (WA) 34 Wellesley Circle, Glen Echo, MD 20812

THOR, Margaret Carlson (Minn) 60 Kent St, Saint Paul, MN 55102

THOR, Peter Chianeng (Minn) 2200 Minnehaha Ave E, Saint Paul, MN 55119

THORME, Trisha Ann (NJ) 1040 Yardville Allentown Rd, Trenton, NJ 08620

THORNBERG, Anne (EC) 3321 Rustburg Dr, Fayetteville, NC 28303

THORNBERG, Jeff (EC) 1601 Raeford Rd, Fayetteville, NC 28305

THORNE, Joyce Terrill (RI) 670 Weeden Street, Pawtucket, RI 02860

THORNELL, Kwasi (Cal) 1525 Casino Cir, Silver Spring, MD 20906

THORNLEY, Edward Charles (FtW) 9700 Saints Cir, Fort Worth, TX 76108

THORNTON, Corey Todd (The Episcopal Church in Haw) PSC 473 Box 10, FPO, AP 96349-0001, Japan

THORNTON, Daniel Ingram (Ala) 1402 Prier Dr, Marion, AL 36756

✠ **THORNTON**, John Stuart (Ida) 323 W Jefferson St Apt 204, Boise, ID 83702

THORNTON, Norman Edward (Del) Box 2805, Northfield, MA 01360

THORNTON, Theresa Joan (SO) 10345 Montgomery Rd, Cincinnati, OH 45242

THORP, Steven Tanner (Spr) 1717 Park Haven Dr, Champaign, IL 61820

THORPE, John A (Dal) 2117 North 4th Ave East, Newton, IA 50208

THORPE, Mary Brennan (Va) 110 W Franklin Street, Richmond, VA 23220

THORSTAD, Anita Fortino (SeFla) 951 De Soto Rd Apt 330, Boca Raton, FL 33432

THRALL, Barbara (WMass) 19 Hadley St Apt D12, South Hadley, MA 01075

THREADGILL, Nancy (Pgh) 335 Locust St, Johnstown, PA 15901

THROOP, John R (FdL) PO Box 29, Adams, NY 13605

THRUMSTON, Richard Emmons (SanD) 3642 Armstrong St, San Diego, CA 92111

THULLBERY, Marion (NC) Durham Va Medical Center, 508 Fulton St, Durham, NC 27705

THURBER, Lorraine Theresa (Alb)

THURSTON, Bud (Ore) 39 Greenridge Ct, Lake Oswego, OR 97035

THWEATT III, Richmond Fitzgerald (WLa) 7109 Woodridge Ave, Oklahoma City, OK 73132

THWING, Robert C (Ak) Po Box 91943, Anchorage, AK 99509

TIAPULA, Imo Siufanua (The Episcopal Church in Haw) Po Box 2030, Pago Pago, AS 96799

TIBBETTS, Catherine Johnson (Va) The Falls Chruch Episcopal, 225 E. Broad Street, Falls Church, VA 22046

TIBBETTS, Ronald Creighton (Mass) 9 Cooney Ave, Plainville, MA 02762

TICHENOR, Liz (Cal) All Souls Episcopal Parish, 2220 Cedar St, Berkeley, CA 94709

TICKNOR, Patricia Horan (WMo) 12270 N New Dawn Ave, Oro Valley, AZ 85755

TICKNOR, William Howard Correa (Md) 5757 Solomons Island Rd, Lothian, MD 20711

TIDWELL, Janet Ruth (At) 582 Walnut St, Macon, GA 31201

TIDY, John Hylton (SeFla) 4025 Pine Tree Dr, Miami Beach, FL 33140

TIEDERMAN, Nancy Jo Copass (Oly) 920 Cherry Ave NE, Bainbridge IS, WA 98110

TIEGS, Karen (Ore) All Saints' Episcopal Church, 3847 Terracina Dr., Riverside, CA 92506

TIELKING, Claudia Gould (WA) 6533 Mulroy Street, Mc Lean, VA 22101

TIERNEY, Bridget (La) 114 N Pine St, New Lenox, IL 60451

TIERNEY, Dennis Stanley (Oly) 6973 Island Center Rd NE, Bainbridge Island, WA 98110

TIERNEY III, Peter George (RI) PO Box 491, Little Compton, RI 02837

TIERNEY, Philip Joseph (RI) 1412 Providence Rd, Charlotte, NC 28207

TIERNEY, Veronica M (RI) St. George's School, PO Box 1910, Newport, RI 02840

TIFF II, Richard Olin (Los)

TIFFANY, Roger Lyman (Mich) 941 Damon Dr, Medina, OH 44256

TIFFANY, Susan Jean (O) 53720 Ironwood Rd, South Bend, IN 46635

TIGHE, Maureen (Ore) 1001 B-Ne 90th Ave, Portland, OR 97220

TILDEN, Roger (Md) 8089 Harmony Rd, Denton, MD 21629

TILING, Robert Henry (Chi) 1691 Campos Dr., The Villages, FL 32162

TILLER, Monte Jackson (SeFla) 6409 Lantana Pines Dr, Lantana, FL 33462

TILLEY, David James (La) 12636 E Robin Hood Dr, Baton Rouge, LA 70815

TILLITT, Jay Lanning (LI) 1021 N University St, Redlands, CA 92374

TILLMAN, Ann Marie (WNY) 24 Maple Rd, East Aurora, NY 14052

TILLMAN, Christine Wylie (WMich) 3828 Cook Ct. S.W., Wyoming, MI 49519

TILLMAN, Jane Guion (WMass)

TILLOTSON, Ellen (Ct) 38 Fair St, Guilford, CT 06437

TILSON, Alan Russell (Kan) 711 W 47th St, Kansas City, MO 64112

TILSON, Brent Edward (Spok) St Martin's Episcopal Church, 416 E Nelson Rd, Moses Lake, WA 98837

TILSON JR, Hugh Arval (NC) 3819 Jones Ferry Rd, Chapel Hill, NC 27516

TIMMERMAN, Melissa (SC) 484 Lymington Rd, Severna Park, MD 21146

TINDALL, Byron Cheney (SC) 102 Fir Court Unit 1260, Waleska, GA 30183

TINGLEY, Harry William (Chi)

TINNON, Becky (The Episcopal Church in Haw) 98-939 Moanalua Rd, Aiea, HI 96701

TINNON, Michael Scott (The Episcopal Church in Haw) 98-939 Moanalua Rd, Aiea, HI 96701

TINSLEY JR, Fred Haley (WLa) 3535 Santa Fe St Unit 41, Corpus Christi, TX 78411

TIPPETT, Michael R (Minn) 2202 Lexington Parkway South, Saint Paul, MN 55105

TIPTON, Harry Steadman (CGC) 129 Camellot Ct, Crestview, FL 32539

TIPTON, Tommy (USC) 1029 Old Plantation Dr, Pawleys Island, SC 29585

TIRADO, Hernan (Colom)

TIRADO, Vincent (SeFla) 18601 Sw 210th St, Miami, FL 33187

TIRRELL, Charles David (Tex) 9701 Meyer Forest Dr Apt 12112, Houston, TX 77096

TIRRELL, John Alden (Cal) Box 456, Athens, 125, Greece

TISDALE JR, William Alfred (Ct) 27 Church St, Stonington, CT 06378

TISDELLE, Celeste (Fla) St. Mary's Episcopal Church, 400 St. Johns Ave, Green Cove Springs, FL 32043

TITCOMB, Cecily Johnson (SeFla) 141 S. County rd, Palm Beach, FL 33480

TITTLE, Darlene Anne Duryea (Nwk) 11 Overhill Dr, Budd Lake, NJ 07828

TITUS, Bessie Charlotte (Ak)

TITUS, Fred David (Ia) St. Thomas' Episcopal Church, 710 N. Main St., Garden City, KS 67846

TITUS, John Clark (At) 5428 Park Cir, Stone Mountain, GA 30083

TITUS, Luke (Ak) Saint Barnabas Mission, Minto, AK 99758

TITUS, Nancy Espenshade (NC) 1739 Berwickshire Cir, Raleigh, NC 27615

TJELTVEIT, Maria Washington Eddy (Be) 124 S Madison St, Allentown, PA 18102

TJOFLAT, Marie Elizabeth (Fla) 1255 Peachtree St, Jacksonville, FL 32207

TLUCEK, Laddie (Okla) 1509 Nw 198th St, Edmond, OK 73003

TOALSTER, Rebecca D (CFla) 311 11th St, Ambridge, PA 15003

TOBER, John Milton (La) 3552 Morning Glory Ave, Baton Rouge, LA 70808

TOBERMAN, Harold Frederick (Ark) 329 Colony Green Dr, Bloomingdale, IL 60108

TOBIAS, Gwendolyn (SeFla) 3300A S. Seacrest Blvd., Boynton Beach, FL 33435

TOBIN, Barbara Kinzer (Pa) 313 Pine St, Philadelphia, PA 19106

TOBIN, Florence Lane (Roch) PO Box 304, Corning, NY 14830

Clergy List

TOBIN JR, Robert Wallace (Mass) Po Box 113, Sunset, ME 04683
TOBIN, Roger Martin (SeFla) 5690 N Kendall Dr, Miami, FL 33156
TOBOLA, Cynthia Pruet (Tex) PO Box 895, Palacios, TX 77465
TODARO, Alicia Butler (Alb) St Paul's Church, 58 3rd St, Troy, NY 12180
TODD, Charles E (Ga) St Paul Episcopal Church, 1802 Abercorn St, Savannah, GA 31401
TODD, Christopher Howard (SeFla) 30243 Coconut Hwy, Big Pine Key, FL 33043
TODD, Edward Pearson (Eur) 18 Hall Pond Lane, Copake, NY 11516-1400, Afghanistan
TODD, James Converse (NC)
TODD, Michael P (SwFla) 1620 Boathouse Cir, GR 208, Sarasota, FL 34231
TODD, Richard Alfred (Minn) 38378 Glacier Dr, North Branch, MN 55056
TODD JR, Samuel Rutherford (Tex) 2423 Mcclendon St, Houston, TX 77030
TOEBBEN, Warren B (Mil)
TOELLER-NOVAK, Thomas (WMich) 555 Michigan Ave, Holland, MI 49423
TOFANI, Ann Lael (Spr) 427 W 4th St, Mount Carmel, IL 62863
TOFFEY, Judith E (Ct) 41 Cannon Ridge Dr, Watertown, CT 06795
TOIA, Frank Phillip (Pa) 2127 Kriebel Rd, Lansdale, PA 19446
TOLA, Elaine M (NC)
TOLAND, Paula (WMass) 270 Main St, Oxford, MA 01540
TOLES, John F (Okla) 518 W Randolph Ave, Enid, OK 73701
TOLIVER, Jeffrey Thomas (RG) 1601 S Saint Francis Dr, Santa Fe, NM 87505
TOLL, Dick (Ore) 1707 Se Courtney Rd, P.O. Box 220112, Milwaukie, OR 97269
TOLLEFSON, Jane Jill Carol (Minn) 2700 Canby Ct, Northfield, MN 55057
TOLLETT, Mitchell Joseph (Tex) St. Francis Episcopal Church, 3232, Tyler, TX 75701
TOLLEY, John Charles (Cal) 594 Los Altos Drive, Chula Vista, CA 91914
TOLLISON, Ann Black (Va) PO Box 100, Gum Spring, VA 23065
TOLLISON JR, Henry Ernest (USC) 105 Freeport Dr, Greenville, SC 29615
TOLLIVER, Lisa (Ky) 7504 Westport Rd, Louisville, KY 40222
TOLLIVER, Richard (Chi) 4729 S. Drexel Blvd, Chicago, IL 60615
TOLZMANN, Lee Ann (Ct) Episcopal Church in Connecticut, 219 Pratt Street, Meriden, CT 06450
TOMAINE, Jane A (Nwk) 349 Short Dr, Mountainside, NJ 07092
TOMBAUGH, Richard Franklin (Ct) 58 Terry Rd, Hartford, CT 06105

TOMCZAK, Beth Lynn (WMich) 321 N Main St, Three Rivers, MI 49093
TOMEI, Gail R (Pa) Church Of The Ascension, 406 W 2nd Ave, Parkesburg, PA 19365
TOMLIN, Kyle R (Va) 6769 Ridge Ave # A, Philadelphia, PA 19128
TOMLINSON, Diane B (EC)
TOMLINSON, Liz (Va) 3439 Payne St, Falls Church, VA 22041
TOMLINSON, Ruth (Neb) 5704 North 159th St, Omaha, NE 68116
TOMLINSON III, Samuel Alexander (Miss) 28 Homochitto St, Natchez, MS 39120
TOMMASEO, Ellis (LI)
TOMOSO, John Hau'oli (The Episcopal Church in Haw) 51 Kuula St, Kahului, HI 96732
TOMPKIN, William Frederick (O) 307 Portage Trail East, Cuyahoga Falls, OH 44221
TOMPKINS JR, Douglas (Pa) 310 S Chester Rd, Swarthmore, PA 19081
TOMPKINS, Joyce Laura Ulrich (Pa) 310 S Chester Rd, Swarthmore, PA 19081
TOMTER, Patrick Austin (Oly) PO Box 10785, Portland, OR 97296
TONEY, Martha Ann (CFla)
TONGE, Samuel Davis (Ga) 1023 Woods Road, Waycross, GA 31501
TONGUE, Mary Jane (Md) 203 Star Pointe Ct Unit 3d, Abingdon, MD 21009
TONSMEIRE SR, Louis (At) 224 Trammell St, Calhoun, GA 30701
TONTONOZ, David Costa (Eas) 5211 Dove Point Ln, Salisbury, MD 21801
TOOF, Jan Jarred (CNY) 2006 Manchester Rd, Wheaton, IL 60187
TOOKEY, Carol (NAM) PO Box 436, Aztec, NM 87410
TOOMEY, David C (NY) 27 Harvard Ave, Brookline, MA 02446
TOONE, Susan (U) 1579 S State St, Clearfield, UT 84015
TORNQUIST, Frances C (Cal) 2748 Wemberly Dr, Belmont, CA 94002
TORO, Arthur N (Los) 135 Loden Pl, Jackson, MS 39209
TORO, Suzanne Frances Rosemary (NY) 70 Clinton St, Cornwall, NY 12518
TORRES, Julio Orlando (NY) 232 E 11th St # 3, New York, NY 10003
TORRES, Michele Angier (Mass) 103 Harvard Ave, Medford, MA 02155
TORRES, Tony (PR)
TORRES BAYAS, Javier (Cal) Guerrero #589, Tuxtepec, OAX 68313, Mexico
TORRES FUENTES, Pascual Pedro (Hond) Apdo 16, Puerto Cortes, Honduras
TORRES MARTINEZ, Wilfrido Oswaldo (EcuC) Convencion Y Solanda 056, Guaranda, Ecuador
TORREY, Bruce (Ct) 187 Dewitt Rd, Accord, NY 12404

TORREY, Dorothy Ellen (The Episcopal NCal) 901 Lincoln Rd Apt 40, Yuba City, CA 95991
TORVEND, Samuel Edward (Oly) 15 Roy St, Seattle, WA 98109
TOTHILL, Marlene Grey (NwT) 19 Winchester Ct, Midland, TX 79705
TOTMAN, Glenn Parker (CGC) 122 County Road 268, Enterprise, AL 36330
TOTTEN, Julia Kay (Spok) PO Box 15, Florence, OR 97439
TOTTEN, William (Spok) PO Box 15, Florence, OR 97439
TOTTEY JR, Alfred George (CNY) 7385 Norton Ave, Clinton, NY 13323
TOUCHSTONE, G Russell (Los) 1069 S Gramercy Pl, Los Angeles, CA 90019
TOURANGEAU, Edward J (Ind) 260 Elm Ct, Troy, VA 22974
TOURNOUX, Gregory Allen (Spr) 2056 Cherry Road, Springfield, IL 62704
TOVEN, Kenneth H (Minn) 1505 13th Street N., Princeton, MN 55371
TOWELL, Gail Richards (CFla)
TOWERS, Arlen Reginald (Cal) 43 Wildwood Pl, El Cerrito, CA 94530
TOWERS, Crystal Daphne (Md)
TOWERS, Paul (Be) St Paul's Church, 276 Church St, Montrose, PA 18801
TOWERS, Richard A (CNY) St John's Episcopal Church, 210 N Cayuga St, Ithaca, NY 14850-4333, Korea (South)
TOWLER, Lewis Wilson (Mich) 1711 Pontiac Trl, Ann Arbor, MI 48105
TOWNE, Jane Clapp (ND) 1111 N 1st St Apt 10, Bismarck, ND 58501
TOWNER, Philip Haines (NY) 552 W End Ave, New York, NY 10024
TOWNER, Robert Arthur (Mo) 38 N Fountain St, Cape Girardeau, MO 63701
TOWNSEND, Bowman (Tex) 2205 Matterhorn Ln, Austin, TX 78704
TOWNSEND, Craig D (NY) 445 Degraw St, Brooklyn, NY 11217
TOWNSEND, John Tolson (Mass) 40 Washington St, Newton, MA 02458
✠ **TOWNSEND**, Martin Gough (Eas) HC 86 Box 48 C-1, Springfield, WV 26763
TOWNSEND III, Thomas Pinckney (Ga)
TOWSON, Louis Albert (CFla) 348 Sherwood Ave, Satellite Beach, FL 32937
TOY, Fran Yee (Cal) 4151 Laguna Ave, Oakland, CA 94602
TRACHE, Robert G (SeFla) 1750 East Oakland Park Blvd, Fort Lauderdale, FL 33334
TRACHMAN, Michael David (Okla) 2213 Galaxy Dr, Altus, OK 73521
TRACY, Dick Blaylock (Kan) 3020 Oxford Cir, Lawrence, KS 66049
TRACY, Edward J. (SVa) 600 Talbot Hall Rd, Norfolk, VA 23505

TRACY, Paul John (NI) 1025 Park Pl Apt 159, Mishawaka, IN 46545

TRACY, Rita Vanessa (Kan) 3020 Oxford Cir, Lawrence, KS 66049

TRAFFORD, Edward John (RI) 45 Rotary Dr, West Warwick, RI 02893

TRAFTON, Clark Wright (Cal) 875 S Nueva Vista Dr, Palm Springs, CA 92264

TRAGER, Jane (O) 222 Eastern Heights Blvd, Elyria, OH 44035

TRAIL, Shirley Ethel (WNY) 42 Haller Ave, Buffalo, NY 14211

TRAINOR, Christine (Cal)

TRAINOR, Helen C (WA) Legal Aid & Justice Center, 1000 Preston Ave. Ste A, Charlottesville, VA 22903

TRAINOR, Jim (FdL) E942 Whispering Pines Rd, Waupaca, WI 54981

TRAINOR, Mary Patricia (Los) 10925 Valley Home Ave, Whittier, CA 90603

TRAINOR, Mary Stoddard (FdL) E942 Whispering Pines Rd, Waupaca, WI 54981

TRAKEL, Debra Lynn (Mil) N81 W13442 Golfway Drive, Menomonee Falls, WI 53051

TRAMBLEY, Adam Thomas (NwPa) 343 Forker Blvd, Sharon, PA 16146

TRAMEL, Stephanie M (Ia) 2300 Bancroft Way, Berkeley, CA 94704

TRAMMELL, Robert William (Okla) St. Augustine Of Canterbury, 14700 N. May Ave., Oklahoma City, OK 73134

TRAN, Catherine Caroline (Colo) 6556 High Dr., Morrison, CO 80465

TRAPANI, Kathleen (Cal) 30 Greenridge Pl, Danville, CA 94506

TRAPP, Grace J (SwVa) PO Box 328, Harpswell, ME 04079

TRAPP, James E (NY) PO Box 40697, Portland, OR 97240

TRAQUAIR, Megan Mcclure (Az) 10222 South 44th Lane, Laveen, AZ 85339

TRASK III, Robert Palmer (EMich) 13 Circle Ave, Wheaton, IL 60187

TRAVIS, Doug (Tex) 9701 Shadows Ct, Granbury, TX 76049

TRAVIS, Kathleen Ann (Ia) 3120 E 24th St, Des Moines, IA 50317

TRAVIS, Michelle Halsall (Mont) 1821 Westlake Dr Apt 124, Austin, TX 78746

TRAVIS, R. Carroll (CFla) 2103 Indian River Dr, Cocoa, FL 32922

TRAVIS, Robert P. (RI) 326 Kenyon Avenue, Wakefield, RI 02879

TRAVIS, Sherry (Miss) 1365 Sweetwater Dr, Brentwood, TN 37027

TRAVIS, Veronika E (Vt)

TRAYLOR, Thomas Wallace (Cal) 1801 Jackson St Apt 4, San Francisco, CA 94109

TRAYNHAM, Warner Raymond (Los) 6125 Alviso Ave, Los Angeles, CA 90043

TREADWELL III, William Charles (Tex) 11704 Via Grande Dr, Austin, TX 78739

TREANOR, Susan Mary (Be)

TREES, Thomas H (CFla) 1616 Sterns Dr, Leesburg, FL 34748

TREGO, Randall (Tex) 3106 Heritage Creek Oaks, Houston, TX 77008

TREHERNE-THOMAS, Rhoda Margaret (NY) 10 Bay Street Lndg Apt 6L, Staten Island, NY 10301

TREI, Rosemary (Dal) 5923 Royal Ln, Dallas, TX 75230

TREJO-BARAHONA, Oscar (Hond)

TRELEASE, Murray Lincoln (Oly) 343 Eagles Roost Ln, Lopez Island, WA 98261

TRELOAR-REID, Zebulun Bevans (Ia) 815 High St, Des Moines, IA 50309

TREMMEL, Marcia Ann (SwFla) 11588 57th Street Cir. E., Parrish, FL 34219

TREPPA, Joyce Lynn (Mich) 1150 Tarpon Center Dr. #503, Venice, FL 34285

TREVATHAN, W Illiam Andre (Ky) 1 Franklin Town Blvd Apt 1515, Philadelphia, PA 19103

TREVER, Stephen Cecil (Cal) 2300 Bancroft Way, Berkeley, CA 94704

TREWHELLA, Charles Keith (Ore) 19691 Nw Meadow Lake Rd, Yamhill, OR 97148

TREZEVANT, Margaret Anne (Cal) 1755 Clay St, San Francisco, CA 94109

TRIGG, Joseph (WA) Po Box 760, La Plata, MD 20646

TRIGLETH, John Paul (Mil) S3919A Highway 12, Baraboo, WI 53913

TRILLOS, Alejandra (NY) Iglesia San Andres, 22 Post St, Yonkers, NY 10705

TRIMBLE, James Armstrong (Pa) 326 S Third St, Philadelphia, PA 19106

TRIMBLE, Jim Edward (USC) 102 Monroe Rd, Spartanburg, SC 29307

TRIMBLE, Sally (Va) 3401 Chantarene Dr, Pensacola, FL 32507

TRIPLETT, Laurie Ann (RG)

TRIPP, Roy (SC) PO Box 761, Port Royal, SC 29935

TRIPP, Thomas Norman (WNY) 354 Burroughs Dr, Amherst, NY 14226-909

TRIPSES, Kathleen Ruth McDowell (Ia) 2844 NW Northcreek Circle, Ankeny, IA 50023

TRISTRAM, Geoffrey (Mass) 980 Memorial Dr, Cambridge, MA 02138

TRIVELY, Tim (SwFla) 4 Gatehouse Ct, Asheville, NC 28803

TROEGER, Thomas Henry (Colo) 56 Hickory Rd, Woodbridge, CT 06525

TROGDON, Denise (Va) 1700 Wainwright Dr, Reston, VA 20190

TRONCALE, John E (NJ) 301 Meadows Dr, Forest, VA 24551

TROTTER, Scott (Ark) 1121 W Pecan, Blytheville, AR 72315

TROUTMAN-MILLER, Jana Lee (Mil) 1840 N Prospect Ave, Milwaukee, WI 53202

TROW, Chester John (SwFla)

TROWBRIDGE, Dustin E (NY) St George's Church, 105 Grand St, Newburgh, NY 12550

TRUAX, Heidi (Ct) 31 Hilltop Rd, Sharon, CT 06069

TRUBY, Laura (Ore) 14221 Livesay Rd, Oregon City, OR 97045

TRUE, Jerry Erwin (WMass) 2612 Brightside Ct, Cape Coral, FL 33991

TRUE, Timothy E (SanD) 1550 S 14th Ave, Yuma, AZ 85364

TRUELOVE, Kenneth Elwood (WA) 508 S Mckinley Ave, Champaign, IL 61821

TRUIETT SR, Melvin Edward (Md) 2322 Ivy Ave, Baltimore, MD 21214

TRUITT, Ann Harris (Va) 1132 N Ivanhoe St, Arlington, VA 22205

TRUJILLO NIETO, Jose David (EcuC)

TRULL, Scott (NJ) 327 s juniper st, Philadelphia, PA 19107

TRUMBLE JR, John (O) 51 Walnut St, Tiffin, OH 44883

TRUMBLE, Jordan E (WVa)

TRUMBORE, Frederick Rhue (Va) xxxxxxxxxxxx, delete all of above address, Woodstock, VA 22664

TRUSCOTT, Nancy Jean Baldwin (Alb) 10 Orchard Street, Delhi, NY 13753

TRUTNER, Thomas Kirk (Cal) 22 Cedar Lane, Orinda, CA 94563

TRYGAR SR, Earl P (Be) RR 2, Box 2229, Moscow, PA 18444

TRYTTEN, Patricia Shoemaker (Oly) 310 N K St, Tacoma, WA 98403

TSAI, Ching-Yi (Tai)

TSOU, Tsai-Hsin (Tai) 1 F #5 Ln 348 Lishan St, Neihu Dist, Taipei, 11450, Taiwan

TUBBS, Adrian Quentin (Az) 168 W Arizona St, Holbrook, AZ 86025

TUBBS, James Collin (Tenn) 5256 Village Trce, Nashville, TN 37211

TUBBS, Suzanne Freeman (Tex) 604 Tryon Ct, Tyler, TX 75703

TUCHOLS, Franklin Joseph (Ct) 661 Old Post Rd, Fairfield, CT 06824

TUCK, Michael G (WMass) 114 George St, Providence, RI 02906

TUCKER, Alice Elizabeth (Tex) 2900 Bunny Run, Austin, TX 78746

TUCKER, Douglas Jon (Tex) 2 Barque Ln., Galveston, TX 77554

TUCKER, Elizabeth (CFla) 1020 Keyes Ave, Winter Park, FL 32789

TUCKER, Gene Richard (CPa) 212 Penn Street, Huntingdon, PA 16652

TUCKER, James M (NJ) 130 Prince St., Bordentown, NJ 08505

TUCKER, James Thomas (Tex) 107 Oakstone Dr., Chapel Hill, NC 27514

TUCKER, Jennifer L (U)

TUCKER, Julia (SVa) 901 Poquoson Cir, Virginia Beach, VA 23452

TUCKER, Kenneth Merrill (USC) 1502 Greenville Street, Abbeville, SC 29620

TUCKER, Martha D (Pa)

TUCKER, Tamra E (Mass)

TUCKER-GRAY, Lisa (O) 4225 Walden Dr, Ann Arbor, MI 48105

TUCKER-PARSONS, Martha L (ETenn) 8321 Georgetown Bay Dr, Ooltewah, TN 37363

TUDELA, Mary Elizabeth (Chi) 4364 Hardy Street, Lihue, HI 96766

TUDOR, Richard Beresford (Mo) 3106 Aberdeen Dr, Florissant, MO 63033

TUDOR, William Ellis (Ind) 3021 94th Ave E, Edgewood, WA 98371

TUDOR-FOLEY, Hugh (Ct) 3168 Dona Sofia Dr, Studio City, CA 91604

TUELL IV, Henry Offord (Az) PO Box 1959, Chandler, AZ 85244

TUFF, Roy Wynn (SwFla) 401 W. Henry St, Punta Gorda, FL 33950

TULIS, Edward (CNY)

TULL, Sandra Ann (Fla) 1021 Oxford Dr, Saint Augustine, FL 32084

TULLER, Stuart (Va) 2132 Owls Cove Ln, Reston, VA 20191

TULLY, Coleen Marie (Minn) 101 N 5th St, Marshall, MN 56258

TULLY, William M (NY) 1810 Loma St, Santa Barbara, CA 93103

TUMMINIO HANSEN, Danielle (Ct) 12 Quincy Ave, Quincy, MA 02169

TUNKLE, Paul Dennis (Md) 200 Common Rd, Dresden, ME 04342

TUNNELL, Janet A (SwFla) St Thomas Episcopal Church, 1200 Snell Isle Blvd NE, St Petersburg, FL 33704

TUNNEY, Liz (LI)

TUOHY, James Fidelis (Ala) 3842 11th Ave S, Birmingham, AL 35222

TURBERG, Judith Evelyn (Az) 100 S Laura Ln, Casa Grande, AZ 85194

TURBEVILLE, Keith (Dal) P.O. Box 292, Buda, TX 78610

TURCZYN, Jeffrey Robert (NY) 40 Running Hill Road, Scarborough, ME 04074

TURK, Davette Lois (Fla) 8256 Wallingford Hills Ln, Jacksonville, FL 32256

TURMO, Joel (WMich) 9798 E BC Ave, Richland, MI 49083

TURNAGE, Benjamin Whitfield (Ala) 1124 Lakeview Crescent, Birmingham, AL 35205

TURNAGE, Richard Wentworth (SC) 1920 Rimsdale Dr, Myrtle Beach, SC 29575

TURNBULL, Malcolm Edward (Va) 13342 Beachcrest Dr, Chesterfield, VA 23832

TURNER, Alice Camp (WNY) 90 South Dr, Lackawanna, NY 14218

TURNER, Alicia Beth (WNC) 900 Centre Park Dr # B, Asheville, NC 28805

TURNER, Amy (CFla) 1100 Sam Perry Blvd, Fredericksburg, VA 22401

TURNER, Anne (Va) 5814 19th St N, Arlington, VA 22205

TURNER, Arlie Raymond (RG) 397 Old Offen PO Rd, Traphill, NC 28685

TURNER, Bonnie L (NMich) 510 E Park Dr, Peshtigo, WI 54157

TURNER, Brian William (CFla) 1204 Foxridge Pl, Melbourne, FL 32940

TURNER, Carl Francis (NY) 1 W 53rd St, New York, NY 10019

TURNER, Carlton Barry (ECR) 891 Vista Del Brisa, San Luis Obispo, CA 93405

TURNER, Clay Howard (USC) 2285 Armstrong Creek Road, Marion, NC 28752

TURNER, Diana Serene (The Episcopal NCal) 605 Tahoe Island Dr., South Lake Tahoe, CA 96150

TURNER, Donald Lee (CNY) PO Box 865, Barnegat Light, NJ 08006

TURNER, Elizabeth Holder (Del) 125 Gull Pt, Millsboro, DE 19966

TURNER, Elizabeth Zarelli (Tex) 9520 Anchusa TRL, Austin, TX 78736

TURNER SR, Eric Wood (CFla) 4581 Bellaluna Dr., West Melbourne, FL 32904

TURNER, Irvin D (Minn) 37688 Tulaby Lake Rd, Waubun, MN 56589

TURNER, John Edward (The Episcopal Church in Haw) 19446 N. 110th Lane, Sun City, AZ 85373

TURNER, Linnea (Va) 5701 Hunton Wood Dr, Broad Run, VA 20137

TURNER, Maurice Edgar (Cal) 4222 Churchill Drive, Pleasanton, CA 94588

TURNER, Mollie Douglas (SVa) 77 Chestnut St Unit 201, Tryon, NC 28782

TURNER III, Philip Williams (Tex) 9520 Anchusa Trl, Austin, TX 78736

TURNER, Philippa Anne (NY) 2 E 90th St, New York, NY 10128

TURNER, Robert (NJ) 525 Pleasant Ave, Piscataway, NJ 08854

TURNER, Saundra Lee (Ga) 2104 Amberley Pass, Evans, GA 30809

TURNER, Scott Scott (Colo) St. Paul's Episcopal Church, P.O. Box 770722, Steamboat Springs, CO 80477

TURNER, Sharon Richey (Dal) 6728 Mayer Road, La Grange, TX 78945

TURNER, Shawna Kaye (Okla) 501 N Broadway Ave, Shawnee, OK 74801

TURNER, Stephen Deree (EC) 16 Gregg Way, Fort Rucker, AL 36362

TURNER III, Thomas (WTex) 200 N. Wright Streed, Alice, TX 78332

TURNER, Timothy Jay (WTex) 120 Herweck Dr, San Antonio, TX 78213

TURNER JR, William Joseph (CNY) 2 Ridgefield Pl, Biltmore Forest, NC 28803

TURNER-JONES, Nancy Marie (SO) 318 E. 4th St., Cincinnati, OH 45202

TURNER-PEREZ, Edna (CFla) 330 Bayhead Dr, Melbourne, FL 32940

TURNEY, Nancy J (O) 1632 Hilltown Pike, Hilltown, PA 18927

TURNHAM, Rena Marie (Minn) 519 Oak Grove St, Minneapolis, MN 55403

TURRELL, James Fielding (Be) School of Theology, U. of the South, 335 Tennessee Ave, Sewanee, TN 37383

TURRIE, Anne Elizabeth (RG) PO Box 2427, Mesilla Park, NM 88047

TURTON, Neil Christopher (NJ) 509 Lake Ave, Bay Head, NJ 08742

TUSKEN, Mark (Chi) 327 S 4th St, Geneva, IL 60134

TUTASIG TENORIO, Digna Mercedes (Eur)

TUTON, Dan (RG) 8409 La Ventura Ct NW, Albuquerque, NM 87120

TUTTLE, Johnny (Ga) 2425 Cherry Laurel Ln, Albany, GA 31705

TUTTLE, Margaret Constance (Nwk) 19 Oberlin St, Maplewood, NJ 07040

TUTTLE, Peggy Elaine Wills (Minn) 4603 Bontia Dr, Palm Beach Gardens, FL 33418

TUTU, Mpho A (WA) 3001 Park Center Dr Apt 1119, Alexandria, VA 22302

TUTU, Nontombi N (Tenn)

TUYISHIME, Emmanuel (SO)

TWEEDALE, David Lee (Colo) 423 E Thunderbird Dr, Fort Collins, CO 80525

TWEEDIE, William Duane (Tex) 301 E 8th St, Austin, TX 78701

TWEEDY, Jeanette Elizabeth (NY) PO Box 172, Peacham, VT 05862

TWELVES, Paul Douglass (RI) 341 Spinnaker Lane, Bristol, RI 02809

TWENTYMAN JR, Donald Graham (Ia) 107 24th St, Spirit Lake, IA 51360

TWIGGS, Frances R (Spok) 428 King St, Wenatchee, WA 98801

TWINAMAANI, Benjamin (SwFla) 9533 Pebble Glen Ave, Tampa, FL 33647

TWISS, Ian (Mich) Trinity Episcopal Church, 11575 Belleville Road, Belleville, MI 48111

TWO BEARS, Neil V (ND) Po Box 685, Fort Yates, ND 58538

TWO BULLS, Robert G (U) Po Box 168, Hermosa, SD 57744

TWO BULLS, Robert W (Los) 3317 33rd Ave S, Minneapolis, MN 55406

TWO BULLS, Twilla Ramona (SD)

TWO HAWK, Webster Aaron (SD) 604 East Missouri Avenue, Fort Pierre, SD 57532

TWOMEY, Patrick Timothy (FdL) 415 E Spring St, Appleton, WI 54911

TWYMAN, Thomas Wellwirth (CNY) 122 Metropolitan Ave, Ashland, MA 01721

TYLER, Lera Patrick (WTex) 116 US Highway 87, Comfort, TX 78013

TYLER, Pamela (Los) 1101 Witt Road, Taos, NM 87471

TYLER SMITH, Virginia Stewart (Roch) 11 Episcopal Ave, Honeoye Falls, NY 14472

TYNDALL, Constance Flanigan (WMo) 4239 E Valley Rd, Springfield, MO 65809

TYNDALL, Jeremy (Ore) The Rectory, 55 Cove Road, Farnborough Hants, GU140EX, Great Britain (UK)

TYO JR, Charles Hart (Roch) 16 Elmwood Ave, Friendship, NY 14739

TYON, Benjamin Ruben (SD) Po Box 14, Pine Ridge, SD 57770

TYREE, James Scott (Okla) 235 W Duffy St, Norman, OK 73069

TYREE-CUEVAS, Susan McCorkle (Oly) 1804 Pointe Woodworth Dr NE, Tacoma, WA 98422

TYRIVER, Marcia Rivenburg (The Episcopal NCal) 255 Ba Wood Ln, Janesville, WI 53545

TYSON, Lynda (Ct) 10 Evarts Lane, Madison, CT 06443

TYSON, Stephen Alfred (Ore) 370 Market Ave., Coos Bay, OR 97420

TZENG, Wen-Bin (Tai) No. 7 Lane 105, Section 1, Hang Chow South Road, Taipei, Taiwan

U

UBIERA, Ramon (NJ) 207 Summit Avenue Apt 1, Newark, NJ 07104

UDELL, George Morris Edson (Tex) 1436 Daventry Dr, DeSoto, TX 75115

UEDA, Ajuko Lois Kaleikea (The Episcopal Church in Haw) Rikkyo University, 1-2-26, Kitano, Niiza-shi, Saitama, Japan

UEDA, Noriaki Simon Peter (The Episcopal Church in Haw)

UFFELMAN, Stephen Paul (EO) 915 Ne Crest Dr, Prineville, OR 97754

UFFMAN, Craig David (Roch) 2000 Highland Avenue, Rochester, NY 14618

UHLIK, Charles R (Ky) 2641 E Southern Hills Blvd, Springfield, MO 65804

UITTI, Aaron (At) 124 Commercial Ave, East Palatka, FL 32131

ULLMAN, Richard L (O) 241 S 6th St Apt 2408, Philadelphia, PA 19106

ULLMANN, Clair Filbert (Eur)

ULRICH, Stephanie Lyn (Neb) 9302 Blondo St., Omaha, NE 68134

UMEOFIA, Christian Chinedu (NC) Po Box 1333, Goldsboro, NC 27533

UMPHLETT, David Alton (NC) 108 W. Farriss Ave., High Point, NC 27262

UNDEM, John (Minn)

UNDERHILL, Robin (Los) Tigh Ban, Hightae, Lockerbie, DG-11 1JN, Great Britain (UK)

UNDERHILL, Scott Andrew (Alb) 912 Route 146, Clifton Park, NY 12065

UNDERHILL, William Dudley (WA) 25 Nottingham Dr, Kingston, MA 02364

UNDERWOOD, Bonnie Gordy (At)

UNDERWOOD, Deborah Ann (Okla) 501 S. Cincinnati Ave., Tulsa, OK 74103

UPCHURCH, Stanley Ray (Okla) 617 Leaning Elm Dr, Norman, OK 73071

UPHAM, Judith Elizabeth (FtW) 9805 Livingston Rd, Fort Washington, MD 20744

UPTON, David Hugh (USC) 206 W Prentiss Ave, Greenville, SC 29605

UPTON, Thomas Lee (Neb) 14017 Washington St, Omaha, NE 68137

URANG, Gunnar (Vt) Po Box 306, Norwich, VT 05055

URBAN JR, Percy Linwood (Pa) The Quadrangle # 2301, 3300 Darby Road, Haverford, PA 19041

URBANEK, Virginia (Me) P.O. Box 455, Houlton, ME 04730

URINOSKI, Ann Kathryne (Del) PO Box 3510, Wilmington, DE 19807

URMSON-TAYLOR, Ralph (Okla) 47a Via Porta Perlici PG, Assisi, OK 06081, Italy

URQUIDI, Ashley Elizabeth (SVa) 4449 N Witchduck Rd, Virginia Beach, VA 23455

USHER JR, Guy Randolph (Eau) 303 S Hollybrook Dr, Chillicothe, IL 61523

UZOMECHINA, Gideon (NJ) 600 Cleveland Avenue, Plainfield, NJ 07060

V

VACA TAPIA, Harold Alexander (EcuC) Calle Calderon entre Argentina y Chile, Tulcan Carchi, Ecuador

VACCARO, Anthony Joseph (Chi) Church of Our Saviour, 530 W Fullerton Pkwy, Chicago, IL 60614

VADERS, Nancy Johnson (NC) St Anne's Episc Ch, 2690 Fairlawn Dr, Winston Salem, NC 27106

VAFIS, John Symon (The Episcopal NCal) PO Box 1044, Colusa, CA 95932

VAGGIONE, Richard Paul (Cal) 1601 Oxford St, Berkeley, CA 94709

VAGUENER, Martha (SwFla) 3105 Short Leaf St, Zephyrhills, FL 33543

VAIL, Jean Parker (Chi) 305 Sutherland Ct, Durham, NC 27712

VALANDRA, Linda Beth (SD) 410 University Ave, Hot Springs, SD 57747

VALANTASIS, Richard L (Mo) 17 Wildflower Way, Santa Fe, NM 87506

VALCOURT, Theodore Philippe-Francois (CGC) 401 Live Oak Ave, Pensacola, FL 32507

VALDEMA, Pierre-Henry (Hai)

VALDERRAMA SANABRIA, Juan Pablo (Colom) c/o Diocese of Colombia, Cra 6 No. 49-85 Piso 2, Bogota, BDC, Colombia

VALDES, Fernando Joaquin (Los) 514 W Adams Blvd, Los Angeles, CA 90007

VALDEZ, Pedro A (Micr) 826 Howard St, Carthage, MO 64836

VALENTINE III, A Wilson (Ak) 924 C St, Juneau, AK 99801

VALENTINE, Darcy Adrian (Minn) 615 Vermillion St, Hastings, MN 55033

VALENTINE JR, John Carney (WVa) 206 E 2nd St, Weston, WV 26452

VALENTINE, Peggy Lee (NwT) St Mark's Episcopal Church, 3150 Vogel St, Abilene, TX 79603

VALENTINE, Ronald Andrew (Chi) St James the Less Episcopal Church, 550 Sunset Ridge Rd, Northfield, IL 60093

VALENTINE DAVIS, Melinda R (Mil)

VALIATH, Abraham J (Be) 365 Lafayette Ave., Palmerton, PA 18071

VALLE, Jose Francisco (WA) 1700 Powder Mill Rd, Silver Spring, MD 20903

VALLE-PLAZA, Juan Nelson (EcuC) Casilla 0901-5250, Guayaquil, Ecuador

VALOVICH, Stephen Anthony (SeFla) 3395 Burns Rd, Palm Beach Gardens, FL 33410

VAN, Maron Ines (Ore) 4435 Fox Hollow Rd, Eugene, OR 97405

VAN ANTWERPEN, Alanna Mary (NH) 214 Main St, Nashua, NH 03060

VANAUKER, Margaret Elizabeth (Md) 225 Bowie Trl, Lusby, MD 20657

VANBAARS, Sven Layne (Va) PO Box 146, Gloucester, VA 23061

VAN BEVEREN, Eugene Charles (Neb) 3041 SW Isaac Ave, Pendleton, OR 97801

VAN BLACK, Barbara Ann (Tex)

VAN BRUNT, Thomas Harvey (SO) 534 Chapel Road, Amelia, OH 45102

VANBUREN, Andrew David (Roch) 32 East Main Street, Clifton Springs, NY 14432

VAN BUREN, Barrett (Los) 15524 Pintura Dr, Hacienda Heights, CA 91745

VANCE, Craig Douglas (The Episcopal Church in Haw) 2140 Main St, Wailuku, HI 96793

VANCE, Marcus Patrick (Ind) 2651 California St., Columubus, IN 47201

VANCE, Timothy Keith (SwVa) PO Box 344, Sewanee, TN 37375

VANCE, William Walter (CFla) 26 Willow Dr, Orlando, FL 32807

VANCOOTEN-WEBSTER, Jennifer Elizabeth (LI) 286-88 7th Ave, Brooklyn, NY 11215

VAN CULIN JR, Samuel (WA) 3900 Watson Place, NW #5D-B, Washington, DC 20016

VAN CULIN, T(homas) Andrew K. (Mich) 61 Grosse Pointe Blvd., Grosse Pointe Farms, MI 48236

VANDAGRIFF, Mary Cordelia (Ala) 220 S Wood Rd, Homewood, AL 35209

VAN DEN BLINK, Arie Johannes (Be) 315 W Washington Ave, Elmira, NY 14901

VANDERAU JR, Robert Julian (RI) 2305 Edgewater Drive, Apt 1718, Orlando, FL 32804

VANDERCOOK, Peter John (Chi) 616 8th Ave Apt 201, Monroe, WI 53566

VANDERCOOK, Ross Allan (Mich) 9900 N Meridian Rd, Pleasant Lake, MI 49272

Clergy List

VANDERCOOK, Susan Elizabeth (Mich) 9900 N Meridian Rd, Pleasant Lake, MI 49272

VAN DER HIEL, Rudolph J (CPa) 156 Jones Road, RR 1, Comp 5, Parry Sound, P2A 2W7, Canada

VANDER LEE, Jerome Neal (SD) 500 S Main Ave, Sioux Falls, SD 57104

VANDERMARK, Roy James (Alb) 825 Covered Bridge Rd, Unadilla, NY 13849

VANDERMEER, Leigh A (Chi) 19760 W Woodmere Ter, Antioch, IL 60002

VANDERSLICE, Thomas Arthur (Chi) 22 Stratham Grn, Stratham, NH 03885

VANDERVEEN, Peter Todd (Pa) 230 Pennswood Rd, Bryn Mawr, PA 19010

VAN DERVOORT, Virginia Ann (Tenn) 1106 Chickering Park Dr, Nashville, TN 37215

VANDER WEL, Brian (WA) Christ Church, 600 Farmington Rd W, Accokeek, MD 20607

VAN DE STEEG, Franklin Exford (Minn) PO Box 155, Hastings, MN 55033

VAN DEUSEN, Robert Reed (CPa) 205 King St, Northumberland, PA 17857

VAN DEUSEN, Robert Wayne (Mil) 9360 West Terra Court, Milwaukee, WI 53224

VANDEVELDER, Frank Radcliff (Va) 12191 Clipper Dr Apt 110, Woodbridge, VA 22192

VAN DEVENTER, Arthur Reed (Roch) 53 Winding Rd, Rochester, NY 14618

VANDEVENTER, Heather A (Spok) 118 N Washington St, Alexandria, VA 22314

VAN DINE JR, John Henry (Nwk) St John's Church of Boonton, 226 Cornelia St, Boonton, NJ 07005

VANDIVORT JR, Paul M (Mo) 12366 Federal Dr, Des Peres, MO 63131

VAN DOOREN, John David (NY) 5749 N Kenmore Ave, Chicago, IL 60660

VANDOREN JR, Robert Lawson (WTenn) 5097 Greenway Cv, Memphis, TN 38117

VAN DUFFELEN, Marilyn (Ia) PO Box 895, Sioux City, IA 51102

VAN DYKE, Bude (Ala) Po Box 824, Sewanee, TN 37375

VAN EENWYK, John Richter (Roch) P. O. Box 1961, Olympia, WA 98507

VAN ES, Kenneth (Eau) 2603 Yorktown Ct, Eau Claire, WI 54703

VANG, Marshall Jacob (Alb) 88 Circular St Apt1, Saratoga Springs, NY 12866

VANG, Toua (Minn) 2200 Minnehaha Ave E, Saint Paul, MN 55119

VAN GORDEN SR, Schuyler Humphrey (Eau) 120 10th Ave, Eau Claire, WI 54703

VAN GULDEN, Sarah Ann (Mass) 74 S Common St, Lynn, MA 01902

VAN HOOK, Peter (U) PO Box 17972, Salt Lake City, UT 84117

VAN HORN, Richard Scott (Los) 3050 Motor Ave, Los Angeles, CA 90064

VAN HORNE, Beverly (Mo) 11907 Bardmont Drive, Saint Louis, MO 63126

VAN HORNE, Peter (Mo) 11907 Bardmont Dr, Saint Louis, MO 63126

VAN HUSS, Teri Hewett (Episcopal SJ) PO Box 7446, Visalia, CA 93290

VANI, Benedict Sele (CFla) 2341 Port Malabar Blvd Ne, Palm Bay, FL 32905

VAN KIRK, Andrew D (Dal) 6400 McKinney Ranch Parkway, McKinney, TX 75070

VAN KIRK, Natalie Beam (Chi) 22W415 Butterfield Rd, Glen Ellyn, IL 60137

VAN KLAVEREN, Dina Els (Md) 1216 Seminole Dr, Arnold, MD 21012

VAN KOEVERING, Helen E (Lex)

✠ **VAN KOEVERING**, Mark A (Lex) 1608 Virginia St E, Charleston, WV 25311

VAN KUIKEN, Ali (NJ) 100 Sullivan Way, Trenton, NJ 08628

VAN LIEW, Christina (LI)

VANN, Deborah Louise (CFla) 380 Royal Palm Dr, Melbourne, FL 32935

VANN, Tim E (Ia) 6651 Park Crest Dr, Papillion, NE 68133

VANNIEL, Noah (Mass) 172 Main St, Hingham, MA 02043

VANO, Mary Foster (Ark) 20900 Chenal Pkwy, Little Rock, AR 72223

VAN OSS SR, Earl T (U) 737 East Center, Orem, UT 84057

VAN OSS, William Joseph (Minn) 1710 E Superior St, Duluth, MN 55812

VANOVER, Debra A (The Episcopal Church in Haw) 25 Hiatt St, Lebanon, OR 97355

VAN PARYS, Cynthia Leigh (NI) 1464 Glenlake Dr, South Bend, IN 46614

VAN PLETZEN-RANDS, Blane Frederik (WNY) Five Eighteen Belle Square, 323 State St, La Crosse, WI 54601

VAN SANT, Mark Richard (NJ) 27 Tocci Ave, Monmouth Beach, NJ 07750

VAN SANT, Paul (NJ) 38 Anne Dr, Tabernacle, NJ 08088

VAN SCOYOC, Gardner Warren (Va) 5928 Lomack Ct, Alexandria, VA 22312

VAN SICKLE, Kathleen (Cal) 555 Pierce St Apt 340e, Albany, CA 94706

VAN SICLEN, John (Me) PO Box 523, Damariscotta, ME 04543

VAN SLYKE, Charlotte Sturgis (Ala)

VANUCCI, Anthony Joseph (Pa) 9700 Entrada Pl. N.W., Albuquerque, NM 87114

VANVLIET-PULLIN, Dana Mae (SVa) St Peter's Episc Church, 224 S Military Hwy, Norfolk, VA 23502

VAN WASSENHOVE, Mark (Ind) 8755 Washington Blvd West Dr, Indianapolis, IN 46240

VAN WELY, Richard Francis (Ct) 223 Weaver St Apt 20D, Greenwich, CT 06831

VAN ZANDT, Jane Whitbeck (NH) 58 Hanson Rd, Chester, NH 03036

VAN ZANDT, Polk (Tenn) Saint Paul's Episcopal Church, 116 N Academy St, Murfreesboro, TN 37130

VAN ZANTEN JR, Peter Eric (Oly) 1111 Archwood Dr. SW #442, Olympia, WA 98502

VARAS, Dwayne Anthony (Ga) 3901 Davis Blvd, Naples, FL 34104

VARDEMANN, Brady Jodoka (Mont) 556 S Rodney St, Helena, MT 59601

VARELA SOLORZANO, Marco Antonio (Hond) Colonia La Sabana, Samparo Sula, Honduras

VARELA ZUNIGA, Nery Yolanda (Hond) Colonia Los Robles, Atlantida, Ceiba, 31105, Honduras

VARGHESE, Roy ()

VARGHESE, Winnie Sara (NY) 464 Riverside Drive. Apt. 41, New York, NY 10027

VARNER, Joshua H (Ga) Diocese of Georgia, 611 E Bay St, Savannah, GA 31401

VARNUM, Ben (Neb) 285 S 208th St, Elkhorn, NE 68022

VASQUEZ, Jaime Armando (Hond) IMS SAP Dept 215, PO Box 523900, Miami, FL 33152-3900, Honduras

VASQUEZ, Martha Sylvia Ovalle (Cal) 8002 Grissom Crst, San Antonio, TX 78251

VASQUEZ, Martir (Az) Saint Andrew's Church, 6300 W Camelback Rd, Glendale, AZ 85301

VASQUEZ, Oscar Arturo (SwFla) 2153 46th Ter SW Apt B, Naples, FL 34116

VASQUEZ, Otto Rene (Los)

VASQUEZ AVILA, Rudy Alberto (Hond) Iglesia la Resureccion, Barrio San Jose, El Paraiso, 15023, Honduras

VASQUEZ SANCHEZ, Vicente Oswaldo (Hond)

VASQUEZ-VERA, Gladys Elisa (EcuC) Ulloa 213 Y Carriba Apdo 17-02-5304, Quito, Ecuador

VATH, Jennifer Marie (Mass) 25 Central St, Andover, MA 01810

VAUGHAN, Jesse L (The Episcopal NCal) 5801 River Oak Way, Carmichael, CA 95608

VAUGHAN, John (CFla) 3295 Timucua Cir, Orlando, FL 32837

VAUGHN, Barry (Nev) Saint Alban's Church, 429 Cloudland Dr, Birmingham, AL 35226

VAUGHN, Denise C (Ga) 1512 Meadows Ln, Vidalia, GA 30474

VAUGHN, Peter Hancock (Ct) 36 Main St, Ellington, CT 06029

VAUGHN, Robert Joseph (SwFla) 327 W Hickory St, Arcadia, FL 34266

VAUGHN, S Chadwick (At) St Bede's Episcopal Church, 2601 Henderson Mill Rd NE, Atlanta, GA 30345

VAZQUEZ-GELI, Jose R (PR)

VAZQUEZ-JUAREZ, Patricia Ellen (Tex) 1534 Milam St, Columbus, TX 78934

VEACH, Deborah Joan (Ind) 215 N. 7th St., Terre Haute, IN 47807

VEAL, David (NwT) 3026 54th St Apt 410, Lubbock, TX 79413

VEALE, David Scott (Vt) 8 Bishop St, Saint Albans, VT 05478

VEALE, Donald Meier (Ore) 5346 Don Miguel Dr, Carlsbad, CA 92010

VEALE JR, Erwin Olin (Ga) 3120 Exeter Rd, Augusta, GA 30909

VEINOT, William Paul (Ct) 327 Orchard St, Rocky Hill, CT 06067

VEINTIMILLA, Carlos (EcuC) Brisas De Santay Mz G, V 30, Duran, Ecuador

VEIT JR, Rick (Wyo) 7711 Hawthorne Dr, Cheyenne, WY 82009

VELA, Debra Kay (Dal)

VELARDE, Inez Jean (NAM) St Luke's-in-the-Desert, PO Box 720, Farmington, NM 87499

VELASQUEZ BORJAS, Gladis Margarita (Hond) Aldea Santa Cruz, Tegucigalpa, Tegucigalpa M.D.C., FM 15023, Honduras

VELASQUEZ MARTINEZ, Victor Manuel (Hond) Iglesia Episcopal Manos De Dios, Detras Benefilo Cafe Rodriguez, Col. Nueva Esperanza, Danti, El Paraiso, Honduras

VELAZQUEZ-MORALES, Juan Alberto (PR)

VELEZ CASTRO, Edwin Orlando (PR)

VELEZ-RIVERA, Daniel (Va) 11625 Vantage Hill Road, Unit 11C, Reston, VA 20190

VELEZ-VELAZQUEZ, Carlos (PR)

VELLA, Joan Christine (WNC) 147 Sourwood Road, State Road, NC 28676

VELLA JR, Joseph Agius (SwFla) 125 Lamara Way Ne, Saint Petersburg, FL 33704

VELLOM, Lee Sherwin (Az) 1741 North Camino Rebecca, Nogales, AZ 85621

VELLOM, Timothy John (WTex) 15919 Colton Wl, San Antonio, TX 78247

VELTHUIZEN, Teunisje (NI) 608 Cushing St, South Bend, IN 46616

VENABLE, Charles Wallace (Ala)

VENEZIA, Deborah L (CFla) 7725 Indian Ridge Trail South, Kissimmee, FL 34747

VENKATESH, Catherine Richardson (WMass) 281 Renfrew St, Arlington, MA 02476

VENTRIS, Margaret Pyre (Los) 72348 Larrea Ave, Twentynine Palms, CA 92277

VERBECK III, Guido Fridolin (WLa) 4741 Crescent Dr, Shreveport, LA 71106

VERDI, Barry Ellis (Los) 12571 Kagel Canyon Rd, Sylmar, CA 91342

VERDON, John Thomas (Md)

VERELL, Gary Archer (SeFla) 917 E Ridge Village Dr, Miami, FL 33157

VERGARA, Winfred Bagao (LI) 40-11 68th Street #2, Woodside, NY 11377

VERGARA GRUESO, Edison (Colom) Carrera 6 No 49-85, Piso 2, Bogota, Colombia

VERHAEGHE, Ronald Edward (WMo) 4401 Wornall Rd, Kansas City, MO 64111

VERNON, Valerie Veronica (SeFla) Po Box 22462, West Palm Beach, FL 33416

VERRET, Joan Claire (CFla) 220 E Palm Dr, Lakeland, FL 33803

VERRETTE, Sallie Cheavens (Ia) St. Paul's Episcopal Church, 6th & State., Grinnell, IA 50112

VERSHURE, Claude Edward (SD) 25413 He Sapa Trail, Custer, SD 57730

VERVYNCK, Jennifer R (Oly) 290 Oak Shore Dr, Port Townsend, WA 98368

VESGA-ARDILA, Ramon (Ve)

VEST, Douglas Carter (Los) 250 Pantops Mountain Rd Apt 327, Charlottesville, VA 22911

VETINEL, Jean Marc (Hai)

VETTEL-BECKER, Richard A (Cal) 706 Tabriz Dr, Billings, MT 59105

VIA, John Albert (At) 8340 Main St., Port Republic, VA 24471

VICENS, Leigh Christiana (SD)

VICKERS, David (EMich) 8119 M 68, Indian River, MI 49749

VICKERY JR, Robby (Tex) St. Michael's Episcopal Church, 1500 N. Capital of Texas Highway, Austin, TX 78746

VIDAL, Gene Vance (Az) Po Box 13647, Phoenix, AZ 85002

VIDMAR, Mary B. (WMass) 18018 Avondale Ave, Lake Milton, OH 44429

VIE, Diane (SwVa) 3536 Willow Lawn, Lynchburg, VA 24503

VIE, Todd M (SwVa) 3536 Willow Lawn Dr, Lynchburg, VA 24503

VIECHWEG, Edrice Veronica (Ct) 503 Old Long Ridge Rd, Stamford, CT 06903

VIEL, Brian John (WK) 800 W. 32nd Ave., Hutchinson, KS 67502

VIERECK, Alexis (Mass)

VIGGIANO, Alyse Elizabeth (Pgh)

VIGGIANO, Robert Peter (Tex) 241 Yorktown Ct, Malvern, PA 19355

VIGIL, Vaughn (Md)

VIL, Jean Madoche (Hai) PO Box 407139, C/O Lynx Air, Fort Lauderdale, FL 33340-7139, Haiti

VILAR MENDEZ, Jose Francisco (PR)

VILAR-SANTIAGO, Jose E (PR) 3735 Lancewood Pl, Delray Beach, FL 33445

VILAR-SANTIAGO, Miguel E (Md) PO Box 264, Brooklanville, MD 21022

VILAS, Franklin Edward (Nwk) 18 Greylawn Dr, Lakewood, NJ 08701

VILLACIS MACIAS, Carlos Emilio (Litoral Ecu)

VILLAGOMEZA, Christian (SwFla) 1119 Dockside Dr, Lutz, FL 33559

VILLALOBOS, Fabian (Dal) Christ Episcopal Church 534 W Tenth street, Dallas, TX 75208

VILLARREAL, Arthur Wells (At)

VILLEMUER-DRENTH, Lauren Anne (NC) 321 S Cleveland Rd, Lexington, KY 40515

VILORD, Charles Louis (SwFla)

VINAL, K N (CFla) 5700 Trinity Prep Ln, Winter Park, FL 32792

VINCE, Gail Lynne (EMich) 449 Irons Park Dr, West Branch, MI 48661

VINCENT, Janet (NY) St Columba's Church, 4201 Albemarle St NW, Washington, DC 20016

VINCENT-ALEXANDER, Samantha (SVa) 431 Massachusetts Ave., Norfolk, VA 23508

VINE, Walter James (Mil) 2655 N Grant Blvd, Milwaukee, WI 53210

VINGE, Patricia Gay (WMich) 2010 Nichols Rd, Kalamazoo, MI 49004

VINSON, Donald Keith (WVa) 1701 Crestmont Dr, Huntington, WV 25701

VINSON, Richard Lee (Pa) Holy Nativity Church, 5286 Kalanianaole Highway, Honolulu, HI 96821

VIOLA JR, Carmen Joseph (NJ) 51 N Main St, Mullica Hill, NJ 08062

VIOLA, Harry Alexander (WNC) Po Box 1046, Hendersonville, NC 28793

VISCONTI, Richard Dennis (LI) 1 Dyke Rd, Setauket, NY 11733

VISGER, James Robert (Neb) 610 Sycamore Dr, Lincoln, NE 68510

VISMINAS, Christine Elizabeth (Pgh) 70 Dennison Ave, Framingham, MA 01702

VITET, Kino (LI) 1417 Union St, Brooklyn, NY 11213

VIVIAN, Tim (Episcopal SJ) 10105 Mountaingate Ln, Bakersfield, CA 93311

VIZCAINO, Roberto (EcuC) Jose Herboso 271, Cdla, La Flo, Quito, Ecuador

VOCELKA, Craig Robert (Oly) PO Box 1362, Poulsbo, WA 98370

VOELKER, Sharon L (EMich) St Alban's, 105 S Erie St, Bay City, MI 48706

VOETS, Keith A (LI) Church Of Saint Alban The Martyr, 11642 Farmers Blvd, Saint Albans, NY 11412

VOGEL, Caroline (ETenn) 425 N Cedar Bluff Rd, Knoxville, TN 37923

VOGELE, Nancy (NH) 97 Victory Cir, White River Junction, VT 05001

VOGEL-POLIZZI, Virginia Margaret (WMass)

VOIEN, Cindy (Los) 1645 W 9th St # 2, San Pedro, CA 90732

VOLKMANN, Jan Elizabeth (NY) 60 Pine Hill Park, Valatie, NY 12184

VOLLAND, Mary Catherine (RG) 1601 S Saint Francis Dr, Santa Fe, NM 87505

VOLLKOMMER, Marsha Merritt (Chi) Grace Episcopal Church, 309 Hill St, Galena, IL 61036

VOLLMAN, Michael William (Ky)

VOLPE, Gina (Chi) 9300 S. Pleasant Ave, Rectory, Chicago, IL 60643

VOLQUEZ-PEREZ, Huascar Emilio (PR) Mision Episcopal Cristo Rey, 24 Calle Palmeras, Salinas, PR 00751

VON DREELE, James Davison (Pa) 27107 Valley Run Dr., Wilmington, DE 19810

VON GONTEN, Kevin P (LI) 11571 Ruby Ct., Ellendale, DE 19941

VON GRABOW, Richard Henri (The Episcopal NCal) 580 Cooper Dr, Benicia, CA 94510

VONGSANIT, Sam Chanpheng (Episcopal SJ) 709 N Jackson Ave, Fresno, CA 93702

VON HAAREN, Barbara Elizabeth (Minn) 1862 W 6th St, Red Wing, MN 55066

VON HAAREN, Erika Shivers (Az) 6715 N Mockingbird Ln, Scottsdale, AZ 85253

✠ **VONO**, Michael (RG) Episcopal Diocese of the Rio Grande, 4304 Carlisle Blvd NE, Albuquerque, NM 87107

VON RAUTENKRANZ, Sue (WA) The Episcopal Diocese of Washington, Mount St. Alban, Washington, DC 20016

VON ROESCHLAUB, Kurt (LI) 4 Cornwall Ln, Port Washington, NY 11050

✠ **VONROSENBERG**, Charles (ETenn) 132 Beresford Creek St., Daniel Island, SC 29492

VON WRANGEL, Carola (Tenn) Church of the Advent, 5501 Franklin Pike, Nashville, TN 37220

VOORHEES, Cynthia Evans (Los) 1308 Santiago Dr, Newport Beach, CA 92660

VOORHEES, James Martin (SD) HC 30 Box 151, Belle Fourche, SD 57717

VOORHEES JR, Ted (O) 115 Washington Ave, St. Augustine, FL 32084

VORKINK II, Peter (NH) 20 Main St, Exeter, NH 03833

VOSBURGH, Linda Ann (Colo) PO Box 1023, Broomfield, CO 80038

VOTAW, Al (SC) 657 Wampler Dr, Charleston, SC 29412

VOUGA, Anne Fontaine (Ky) St Thomas Episcopal Church, 9616 Westport Road, Louisville, KY 40241

VOYLE, Rob (Ore) 24965 Nw Pederson Rd, Hillsboro, OR 97124

VOYSEY, Stephen Otte (Mass) 1 Colpitts Road, Weston, MA 02493

VROON, Daron Jon (At) 939 James Burgess Road, Suwanee, GA 30024

VRYHOF, David B (Mass) 980 Memorial Dr, Cambridge, MA 02138

VUKICH, Dawn (Los) 26391 Bodega Ln, Mission Viejo, CA 92691

VUKMANIC, Paula (Los) 2200 Via Rosa, Palos Verdes Estates, CA 90274

VUONO, Reverend Deacon Dorothy (Del) 19337 Fleatown Rd, Lincoln, DE 19960

W

WACASTER, David C (WA) 2711 Parkway Pl, Cheverly, MD 20785

WACHNER, Emily J (NY) 74 Trinity Pl, New York, NY 10006

WACOME, Karen Ann Halvorsen (Ia) 415 3rd St Nw, Orange City, IA 51041

WADDELL, Clayton Burbank (SeFla) 141 S County Rd, Palm Beach, FL 33480

WADDELL, Jonathan H (Ala) 5014 Lakeshore Dr, Pell City, AL 35128

WADDELL, Thomas Robert (Va) 5911 Edsall Rd Ph 5, Alexandria, VA 22304

WADDINGHAM, Gary Brian (Mont) 119 N 33rd St, Billings, MT 59101

WADDLE, Helen Ann (Okla) PO Box 12402, Oklahoma City, OK 73157

WADE, Carol Lynn (Lex) Christ Church Cathedral, 166 Market St, Lexington, KY 40507

WADE, Elizabeth Ann Till (WMass) 1110 Fairview St, Lee, MA 01238

WADE, Francis Howard (WA) 4800 Fillmore Ave #1452, Alexandria, VA 22311

WADE, J Merrill (Tex) 11561 Cedarcliffe Dr, Austin, TX 78750

WADE, Karin Elizabeth (Mass) Po Box 372, Rockport, MA 01966

WADE, Mary Macsherry (Miss) 2681 Lake Cir, Jackson, MS 39211

WADE, Stephen Hamel (Va) 132 N Jay St, Middleburg, VA 20117

WADE, Suzanne (Mass) 75 Cold Spring Rd, Westford, MA 01886

WADE, William St Clair (Tenn) 1 Casey Road, East Kingston, NH 03827

WAFER-CROSS, Melissa Lee (NwT) 3502 47th St, Lubbock, TX 79413

WAFF, Kay Childers (SwVa) 314 N Bridge St, Bedford, VA 24523

WAFF, William Dubard Razz (Mil) 2443 Lawson Blvd., Gurnee, IL 60031

WAFLER, Donald Samuel (Minn) 628 1st St Se, Faribault, MN 55021

WAGAMAN, Stanley Warner (Az) Episc Ch Of St Francis In The Valley, 600 S La Canada Dr, Green Valley, AZ 85614

WAGAR, Catherine (Los) The Episcopal Church of St. Philip the Evangelist, 2800 Stanford Street, South Los Angeles, CA 90011

WAGEMAN, Carole Allcroft (Vt) 173 Hollow Road, North Ferrisburgh, VT 05473

WAGENSEIL JR, Robert Arthur (SwFla) 1700 Patlin Cir S, Largo, FL 33770

WAGENSELLER, Joseph Paul (Ct) 6 Clifford Ln, Westport, CT 06880

✠ **WAGGONER JR**, James E (Spok) 8028 N Pamela St, Spokane, WA 99208

WAGGONER, Janet Cuff (FtW) 2724 Stone Oak Drive, Fort Worth, TX 76109

WAGGONER, Leigh (Colo) 110 W. North St., Cortez, CO 81321

WAGNER, Barbara Jean (WMich) 2430 Greenbriar, Harbor Springs, MI 49740

WAGNER, Beth Anne (CFla) PO Box 1115, Apo, AP 96555

WAGNER, Dan (USC)

WAGNER, David W (At) 465 Clifton Rd NE, Atlanta, GA 30307

WAGNER, John C (Be) 1070 Oakhurst Drive, Slatington, PA 18080

WAGNER, Mary M (Ia)

WAGNER, Sharon Lavonne (Cal) 1921 Hemlock Dr, Oakley, CA 94561

WAGNER, Wm Beau (Me) St Matthew's Episcopal Church, PO Box 879, Lisbon, ME 04250

WAGNER-PIZZA, Ken E (CPa) 1206 Faxon Parkway, Williamsport, PA 17701

WAGNER SHERER, Kara (Chi) 3857 N. Kostner Ave, Chicago, IL 60641

WAGNON, William S (WA) 9225 Crestview Dr, Indianapolis, IN 46240

WAHL, Eugene Richard (Colo) 4400 Wellington Rd, Boulder, CO 80301

WAHL, Hughes Edward (Md) 5010 Marina Cove Dr Apt 203, Naples, FL 34112

WAHLGREN, Matthew David (O) 206 N Park Ave, Fremont, OH 43420

WAID, Anna (Del) 301 Woodlawn Rd, Wilmington, DE 19803

WAINWRIGHT, Philip (Pgh) 326 Maple Terrace, Pittsburgh, PA 15211

WAINWRIGHT-MAKS, Laurence Christopher (Roch) 105 N Montgomery St, Starkville, MS 39759

WAIT, Curtis C (Colo) 228 S Jefferson Ave, Louisville, CO 80027

WAIT, Roger Lee (Neb) 3711 A St, Lincoln, NE 68510

WAITE, Paula Jean (Del) 307 Federal St, Milton, DE 19968

WAJDA, Kathryn (Md) 1505 Sherbrook Rd, Lutherville Timonium, MD 21093

WAJNERT, Theresa Altmix (Nwk) PO Box 37, Calistoga, CA 94515

WAKABAYASHI, Allen Mitsuo (Spr) PO Box 605, Gladstone, NJ 07934

WAKEEN, Teresa M (Mich) 4800 Woodward Ave, Detroit, MI 48201

WAKELEE-LYNCH, Julia (Cal) 1501 Washington Avenue, Albany, CA 94706

WAKELY, Nancy Kay (Okla) PO Box 2088, Norman, OK 73070

WAKEMAN, Nancy Ann (Md)

WAKITSCH, Randal John (Chi) 503 W Jackson St, Woodstock, IL 60098

WALBERG, Elsa Phyllis (Mass) PO Box 245, Danville, VT 05828

WALCOTT, Robert (O) 2173 W 7th St, Cleveland, OH 44113

WALDEN, Jan (Mass) 110 Dean St., Unit #37, Taunton, MA 02780

WALDIE, Nanette Marie (Oly) 4228 Factoria Blvd SE, Bellevue, WA 98006

WALDING, Jennifer Maureen (Minn) 4180 Lexington Ave S, Eagan, MN 55123

WALDO JR, Mark E (Ala) 311 Lindsey Road, Coosada, AL 36020

WALDO SR, Mark Edward (Ala) 2046 Hazel Hedge Ln, Montgomery, AL 36106

✠ **WALDO**, William Andrew (USC) 847 Kilbourne Rd, Columbia, SC 29205

WALDON, Mark W. (Nwk) 2 Marble Ct Apt 1, Clifton, NJ 07013

WALDON JR, Raymond J (Tex) 601 Columbus Ave, Waco, TX 76701

WALDRON, Susan G (Alb) 107 State St., Albany, NY 12207

WALDRON, Teresa Jane (Cal) 920 Oak St, Lafayette, CA 94549

WALDROP, Charlotte Macon Egerton (USC) 137 Summerwood Way, Aiken, SC 29803

WALK, Ev (SwFla) 8700 State Road 72, Sarasota, FL 34241

WALKER, Aurilla Kay (Neb)

WALKER, David Bruce (Spok) 127 E 12th Ave, Spokane, WA 99202

WALKER, David Charles (Los) 6072 Avenida De Castillo, Long Beach, CA 90803

WALKER, Edwin Montague (SwFla) 1532 Vantage Pointe, Mount Pleasant, SC 29464

WALKER, Elizabeth Ann (WVa) 3343 Davis Stuart Road, Fairlea, WV 24902

WALKER, Frederick Wyclif (SVa) 140 Tynes St, Suffolk, VA 23434

WALKER JR, Harold William (SeFla) St Thomas Episcopal Parish, 5690 N Kendall Dr, Coral Gables, FL 33156

WALKER, James Arvie (NwT)

WALKER, James Lee (Los) 4114 South Norton Ave, Los Angeles, CA 90008

WALKER, Janice Ficke (WNC) 2709 Pleasant Run Dr, Richmond, VA 23233

WALKER, Jeffrey (Ct) 4124 Berkman Dr, Austin, TX 78723

WALKER, Kathalin Ree (U) PO Box 125, Page, AZ 86040

WALKER, Kathleen Denise (SeFla) PO Box 420050, Miami, FL 33242

WALKER, Lynell Elizabeth (The Episcopal NCal) 2380 Wyda Way, Sacramento, CA 95825

WALKER, Michelle (NI) Calumet Episcopal Ministry Partnership, 1101 Park Dr, Munster, IN 46321

WALKER, Noble Ray (WTenn) 6855 Branch Rd, Olive Branch, MS 38654

WALKER, Paul Edward (Ia) 510 Columbia St, Burlington, IA 52601

WALKER, Paul Nelson (Va) 100 W Jefferson St, Charlottesville, VA 22902

WALKER, Peggy (WNC) 824 Arabella St, New Orleans, LA 70115

WALKER, Randolf D (Oly)

WALKER, Robert Lynn (NY)

WALKER, Roger D (Mich) PO Box 8101, Louisville, KY 40257

WALKER, Samuel Clevenger (WA) Zach Fowler Road, Box 8, Chaptico, MD 20621

WALKER, Scott D (CFla) 3-6-25 Shiba-Koen, Minato-ku, Tokyo, Japan 105-0011, Japan

WALKER, Seldon Matthew (Va) 118 N Washington St, Alexandria, VA 22314

WALKER, Skip (EC) 1337 Hamlet St, Fayetteville, NC 28306

WALKER, Stacy (Chi) 910 Normal Road, DeKalb, IL 60115

WALKER, Stephen Bruce (WNC) 520 Main St, Highlands, NC 28741

WALKER, Susan Kennard (WA) 1317 G St NW, Washington, DC 20005

WALKER, Terrence Alaric (SVa) PO Box 753, Lawrenceville, VA 23868

WALKER, Thomas Cecil (NC) 2933 Wycliffe Rd, Raleigh, NC 27607

WALKER, William Ray (CPa) St. Paul's Episcopal Church, P.O. Box 170, Philipsburg, PA 16866

WALKER, William Royce (Wyo) 157 Pleasant Valley Rd, Hartville, WY 82215

WALKLEY, Richard Nelson (Ga) 918 E Ridge Village Dr, Cutler Bay, FL 33157

WALL, Anne Fuller (ECR) 535 Torrey Pine Pl, Arroyo Grande, CA 93420

WALL, Daniel S (NC)

WALL, Henry Pickett (USC) 5220 Clemson Ave, Columbia, SC 29206

WALL JR, John Furman (Spr) 507 Hanover St, Fredericksburg, VA 22401

WALL, John N (NC) English Dept Of Box 8105, NC State University, Raleigh, NC 27695

WALL, Richard David (WA) 2430 K Street NW, Washington, DC 20037

WALL, Sean (Ore) 2201 SW Vermont St, Portland, OR 97219

WALLACE, Arland Lee (Kan) 8021 W 21st St N, Wichita, KS 67205

WALLACE, Gene Richard (Los) 1775 Wilson Ave, Upland, CA 91784

WALLACE, Hugh J (SC) 10172 Ocean Hwy, Pawleys Island, SC 29585

WALLACE JR, Jim (ETenn) Po Box 3073, Montgomery, AL 36109

WALLACE, John Bruce (EMich) 5845 Berry Lane, Indian River, MI 49749

WALLACE, John Robert (Pa) 736 11th Ave, Prospect Park, PA 19076

WALLACE, Kathryn McLaughlin (The Episcopal NCal) 4308 Wood St, Dunsmuir, CA 96025

WALLACE, Lance S (SwFla) 5250 Championship Cup Ln, Spring Hill, FL 34609

WALLACE, Martha Ellen (WA) 530 SW Cove Pt, Depoe Bay, OR 97341

WALLACE, Peter Marsden (At) 2920 Landrum Education Dr, Oakwood, GA 30566

WALLACE, Robert Edgar (Ky) 2140 Bonnycastle Ave Apt 9B, Louisville, KY 40205

WALLACE, Sean M (NY) 119 E 74th St, New York, NY 10021

WALLACE, Tanya (WMass) 7 Woodbridge St, South Hadley, MA 01075

WALLACE, Thomas (Tex) 407 E 22nd Ave, Belton, TX 76513

WALLACE, William Lewis (Los) 1448 15th St Ste 203, Santa Monica, CA 90404

WALLACE-WILLIAMS, Joseph A (Mo) 110 N Warson Rd, Saint Louis, MO 63124

WALLENS, Michael Gary (RG) 510 N 2nd St, Alpine, TX 79830

WALLER, Clifford Scott (WTex) Po Box 12349, San Antonio, TX 78212

WALLER, Stephen Jay (Dal) 8108 Crowberry Lane, Irving, TX 75063

WALLEY, Kent R (NJ) 182 Main St, P.O. Box 605, Gladstone, NJ 07934

WALLEY, Seth Martin (Miss) 113 S 9th St, Oxford, MS 38655

WALLING, Ann Boult (Tenn) 6501 Pennywell Dr, Nashville, TN 37205

WALLING, Carolyn M (U)

WALLING, Charles Edward (Miss) 4394 E Falcon Dr, Fayetteville, AR 72701

WALLINGFORD, Katharine Tapers (Tex) 6221 Main St, Houston, TX 77030

WALLIS, Benjamin E (Pa) Church of the Epiphany, 115 Jefferson Ave, Danville, VA 24541

WALLIS, Hugh W (Colo) 1005 S Gilpin St, Denver, CO 80209

WALLIS, James Howard (Nev) 2528 Silverton Drive, Las Vegas, NV 89134

WALLNER, Frank (Pa) 404 Levering Mill Rd., Bala Cynwyd, PA 19004

WALLNER, Ludwig John (Alb) 11631 Scenic Hills Blvd., Hudson, FL 34667

WALLS, Alfonso S (Los) 9324 Capobella, Aliso Viejo, CA 92656

WALMER, Corey Ann (Me) St Luke's Episcopal Church, PO Box 249, Farmington, ME 04938

WALMER, Tim (Me) 368 Knowlton Corner Rd, Farmington, ME 04938

WALMISLEY, Andrew John (The Episcopal Church in Haw) Po Box 625, Point Reyes Station, CA 94956

WALMSLEY, John W (CFla) 367 Jaybee Ave, Davenport, FL 33897

WALN, William W (WK)

WALPOLE, Lisa Calhoun (SC) 464 Golf Dr, Georgetown, SC 29440

WALSER, Gay Craggs (WNY) 119 N Ellicott St, Williamsville, NY 14221

WALSH, Eileen (SVa) 519 W 20th St Apt 303, Norfolk, VA 23517

Clergy List

WALSH, Lora (Ark) 617 N Mount Olive St, Siloam Springs, AR 72761

WALSH, Paul David (Ida) 1565 E 10th N, Mountain Home, ID 83647

WALSH, Peter F (Ct) 111 Oenoke Rdg, New Canaan, CT 06840

WALSH, Ruth Dimock (Va) 16640 Harwood Oaks Ct Apt 101, Dumfries, VA 22026

WALSH-MINOR, Gina (SwFla) 1A Hamilton Avenue, Cranford, NJ 07016

WALSTON, Gerald Wayne (Fla) 1718 Oakbreeze Ln, Jacksonville Beach, FL 32250

WALTER, Andrew Wallace (WA) Grace Episcopal Church, 1607 Grace Church Rd, Silver Spring, MD 20910

WALTER, Aran Evan (FdL) St Thomas Episcopal Church, 226 Washington St, Menasha, WI 54952

WALTER, Cynthia (WVa) PO Box 4063, Table Rock Lane, Wheeling, WV 26003

WALTER, Francis Xavier (Ala) 100 Rattlesnake Spring Ln, Sewanee, TN 37375

WALTER II, George Avery (Ore) 77287 S Ash Rd, Stanfield, OR 97875

WALTER, Kathy Marie (SwFla) 2638 Pinewood Dr, Dunedin, FL 34698

WALTER, Verne Leroy (FdL) 12660 Red Chestnut Ln SPC 47, Sonora, CA 95370

WALTERS, Delores Marie (ND) PO Box 214, Fort Yates, ND 58538

WALTERS, Fred Ashmore (USC) 1001 12th St, Cayce, SC 29033

WALTERS, Gloria Louise (Okla) St Mark Episcopal Church, 800 S 3rd St, Hugo, OK 74743

WALTERS, Jennifer Louise (Mich) 100 Laurel Hill Rd, Westhampton, MA 01027

WALTERS, Joshua David (Roch) Christ Church, 36 S Main St, Pittsford, NY 14534

WALTERS, Karen Graf (SVa) 150 Bella Vista Terrace, Unit D, North Venice, FL 34275

WALTERS, Larry (Mich) 11179 Delight Creek Rd, Fishers, IN 46038

WALTERS, Robert Carroll (WMass) 17 Briarwood Circle, Worcester, MA 01606

WALTERS, Roxanne S (Cal) 1217 Skycrest Dr Apt 3, Walnut Creek, CA 94595

WALTERS, Scott (WTenn)

WALTERS JR, Sumner Francis Dudley (Cal) 1217 Skycrest Dr Apt 3, Walnut Creek, CA 94595

WALTERS, William Harry (USC) 1109 W Woodmont Dr, Lancaster, SC 29720

WALTERS MALONE, Sandra A (VI) c/o St George's Episcopal Church, PO Box 28 Main St, Road Town, Tortola, British Virgin Islands VG1110, British Virgin Islands

WALTERS-PACE, Jill A (NwT) 1601 S Georgia St, Amarillo, TX 79102

WALTHALL, Chuck (Eas) 4015 W Palm Aire Dr Apt 708, Pompano Beach, FL 33069

WALTHER, Aileen Dianne Pallister (CFla) 753 Creekwater Ter Apt 101, Lake Mary, FL 32746

WALTMAN, Lynne (FtW) All Saints Episcopal Church, 5001 Crestline Rd, Fort Worth, TX 76107

WALTON, Billy R (Miss) 608 W Jefferson St, Tupelo, MS 38804

WALTON, Carol Leighann (Nev) 234 Scotgrove St, Henderson, NV 89074

WALTON JR, Harry E (Mass) 100 Park Terrace Dr Apt 143, Stoneham, MA 02180

WALTON, James Brooke (Pa) 919 Tennis Ave, Maple Glen, PA 19002

WALTON, Joy Edemy (Del) 2550 Kensington Gdns Unit 103, Ellicott City, MD 21043

WALTON, Lori Ann (Cal) 7688 Shady Hollow Dr, Newark, CA 94560

WALTON, Macon Brantley (SVa) 202 Ridgeland Dr, Smithfield, VA 23430

WALTON, Mary Fish (Md) 1810 Park Ave, Richmond, VA 23220

WALTON, Regina Laba (Mass) Parish Of The Good Shepherd, 1671 Beacon St, Waban, MA 02468

WALTON JR, Richard (WNC) PO Box 1866, Sparta, NC 28675

WALTON, Robert Harris (WMich) 2186 Tamarack Ln, Okemos, MI 48864

WALTON, Sandra Lee (Colo) 10751 W 69th Ave, Arvada, CO 80004

WALTZ, Bill (Colo) 207 Rainbow Acres Lane, PO Box 21, Gunnison, CO 81230

WALWORTH, Diana Lynn (Mich) PO Box 287, Onsted, MI 49265

WALWORTH, James Curtis (LI) 443 River Rd Ste 210, Highland Park, NJ 08904

WALWORTH, Roy Chancellor (Wyo) 216 Southridge Rd, Evanston, WY 82930

WAMSLEY, Shawn Earl (Pa) Diocese Of Pennsylvania, 3717 Chestnut St Ste 300, Philadelphia, PA 19104

WAN, Sze-Kar (Mass) 87 Herrick Rd, Newton Center, MA 02459

WANAMAKER, Katherine Elizabeth (Minn) 615 Vermillion St, Hastings, MN 55033

WAND, Thomas C (Pa) 31 Kleyona Ave, Phoenixville, PA 19460

WANDALL, Frederick Summerson (Va) Green Spring Village, 7416 Spring Village Dr Apt 116, Springfield, VA 22150

WANDREY, Bryce Philip (SC)

WANG, Kathleen Marie (Me) PO Box 158, East Waterboro, ME 04030

WANTLAND, David Cuenod (NC) 6221 Main St, Houston, TX 77030

WAPLE, Gary (WVa) RR 2 Box 243, Lewisburg, WV 24901

WARD, Barbara Pyle (Ida) 450 W Highway 30, Burley, ID 83318

WARD, Edwin Michael (Va) 8 Governors Ln, Hilton Head, SC 29928

WARD, Elizabeth Howe (Chi) 79 Meadow Hill Rd, Barrington, IL 60010

WARD, Eugene Lee (Ky) 6877 Green Meadow Cir, Louisville, KY 40207

WARD, Geoffrey F (Mil) 29 Foothills Way, Bloomfield, CT 06002

WARD JR, Herbert Arthur (Nev) 112 Wyoming St, Boulder City, NV 89005

WARD, Horace (SeFla) 18501 Nw 7th Ave, Miami, FL 33169

WARD, James (Cal) 202 El Prado Ave., San Rafael, CA 94903

WARD, Jeremiah (Tex) 43 N High Oaks Cir, Spring, TX 77380

WARD, Karen Marie (Oly) 4272 Fremont Ave N, Seattle, WA 98103

WARD, Mary Christine Mollie (Spr) 1104 N Roosevelt Ave, Bloomington, IL 61701

WARD, Meredyth W (WMass) 35 Somerset St, Worcester, MA 01609

WARD, Patrick Carroll (Mass) 147 Concord Rd, Lincoln, MA 01773

WARD JR, Patrick John (NY) 75A Prospect Ave, Ossining, NY 10562

WARD, Richard Philip (Spok) 1841 Fairmount Blvd, Eugene, OR 97403

WARD IV, Samuel Mortimer (Los) 2524 Chapala St, Santa Barbara, CA 93105

WARD, Suzanne Lynn (Episcopal SJ) 1934 S Santa Fe Ave, Visalia, CA 93292

WARD JR, Tom (Tenn) Po Box 3270, Sewanee, TN 37375

WARD, Valerie K (Las) PO Box 1868, Santa Maria, CA 93456

WARDE, Erin J (Okla) 110 E 17th St, Ada, OK 74820

WARDER, Oran (Va) 228 S Pitt St, Alexandria, VA 22314

WARE, Anita Faye (WNC) 1201 S New Hope Rd, Gastonia, NC 28054

WARE, David (Md) 5603 N Charles St, Baltimore, MD 21210

WARE, Jordan H (FtW) All Saints' Episcopal Church, 5001 Crestline Rd, Fort Worth, TX 76107

WAREHAM, George Ludwig (NwPa) 3111 Pearl Dr, New Castle, PA 16105

WAREING, Robert Edgar (Tex) 3122 Red Maple Dr, Friendswood, TX 77546

WARFEL, John (NY) 17 Crescent Pl, Middletown, NY 10940

WARFIELD, Sara Nichole (Cal)

WARING, J(ames) Donald (NY) 802 Broadway, New York, NY 10003

WARLEY, Dianne Goodwin (Ct) 73 Ayers Point Rd, Old Saybrook, CT 06475

WARNE II, William Thomas (CPa) 197 Urie Ave., Lake Winola, PA 18625

WARNE III, William Thomas (Oly) 2915 SE 173rd Ct, Vancouver, WA 98683

WARNECKE JR, Frederick John (NC) 3017 Lake Forest Dr, Greensboro, NC 27408

WARNER, Anthony Francis (Md) 2434 Cape Horn Rd, Hampstead, MD 21074

WARNER, Christopher Scott (At) 1275 Wappetaw Pl, Mount Pleasant, SC 29464

WARNER, Dale Alford (Fla) 2736 NW 77th Blvd Apt #152, Gainesville, FL 32606

WARNER, Deborah (Mass) Church of the Messiah, 13 Church St, Woods Hole, MA 02543

WARNER, Donald Emil (Neb) 422 W 2nd St # 1026, Grand Island, NE 68801

WARNER, Donald Nelson (Colo) 6961 S. Cherokee St., Littleton, CO 80120

WARNER, Janet Avery (EO) 444 NW Apollo Rd, Prineville, OR 97754

WARNER, John Seawright (Ga) 2211 Dartmouth Rd, Augusta, GA 30904

WARNER, Katherine Wakefield (SwFla) PO Box 272, Boca Grande, FL 33921

WARNER, Kevin (SwFla) 622 Tanana Fall Drive, Ruskin, FL 33570

WARNER JR, Richard Wright (EC) 835 Calabash Rd. NW, Calabash, NC 28467

WARNER, Suzanne McCarroll (Ky) 1265 Bassett Ave, Louisville, KY 40204

✠ **WARNER**, Vincent Waydell (Oly) Po Box 12126, Seattle, WA 98102

WARNKE, James William (Nwk) 680 Albin St, Teaneck, NJ 07666

WARNOCK, James Howard (NI) 2365 N Miller Ave, Marion, IN 46952

WARREN III, Allan Bevier (Mass) 30 Brimmer St, Boston, MA 02108

WARREN, Annika Laurin (Ct) 31 Woodland St, Hartford, CT 06105

WARREN, Daniel (Me) 730 Mere Point Rd, Brunswick, ME 04011

WARREN, George Henry (WMass) 12 Walnut Hill Rd, Pascoag, RI 02859

WARREN, Gregory G (Ark) 925 Mitchell St, Conway, AR 72034

WARREN JR, Hallie DeLesslin (ETenn) 1021 Meadow Lake Rd, Chattanooga, TN 37415

WARREN, Harold Robert (Colo) 6625 Holyoke Ct, Fort Collins, CO 80525

WARREN, Heather Anne (Va) 170 Reas Ford Rd, Earlysville, VA 22936

WARREN, J Lewis (Neb) 309 N 167th Plz Apt 5, Omaha, NE 68118

WARREN, John Wells (Ala) 1347 Shelton Mill Rd, Auburn, AL 36830

WARREN, Joseph Palmer (Ala) 2017 6th Ave N, Birmingham, AL 35203

WARREN, Matthew Douglas (The Episcopal NCal) Christ the King Episcopal Church, 545 Lawrence St, Quincy, CA 95971

WARREN, Penelope Sandra Muehl (Minn) 3124 Utah Ave N, Crystal, MN 55427

WARREN JR, Ralph (SeFla) 223 East Tall Oaks Circle, Palm Beach Gardens, FL 33410

WARREN, Randall Richard (WMich) 247 W Lovell St, Kalamazoo, MI 49007

WARREN, Robert James (Eur) Christ Church, 8 rue d Bon Pasteur, Clermont-Ferrand, 63000, France

WARREN, Tom (EC) 800 Rountree Ave, Kinston, NC 28501

WARREN, Victoria Daniel (Nev) 1776 Us Highway 50, Glenbrook, NV 89413

WARREN-BROWN, Judith Anne (CFla)

WARRINGTON, James Malcolm (Nwk) 2849 Meadow Ln, Falls Church, VA 22042

WARTHAN, Frank Avery (Chi) 298 S Harrison Ave, Kankakee, IL 60901

WARWICK, Charles C (Be) PO Box 406, New Milford, PA 18834

WARWICK, Eilene Robinson (Miss) 25 Twelve Oaks Dr, Madison, MS 39110

WARWICK-SABINO, Debra Ann (The Episcopal NCal) 1405 Kentucky St, Fairfield, CA 94533

WAS, Brent (Ore) 120 Main St, Amesbury, MA 01913

WASDYKE, Wesley Roger (NH) 6569 The Masters Ave, Lakewood Ranch, FL 34202

WASHAM JR, Charles W (Lex) 2734 Chancellor Drive, Suite 202, Crestview Hills, KY 41017

WASHBURN, Elizabeth Lane (WMass)

WASHINGTON, Derek Wayne (Eau) 931 Leroy Ct, River Falls, WI 54022

WASHINGTON, Lynne E (Va) 8076 Crown Colony Pkwy, Mechanicsville, VA 23116

WASHINGTON III, Vant (Minn)

WASINGER, Doug (Wyo) 513 E Hart St, Buffalo, WY 82834

WASTLER, Mark William (Md) 1415 Foxwood Ct, Annapolis, MD 21409

WASZCZAK, Brigid (Az) St Matthew's Episcopal Church, 9071 E Old Spanish Trail, Tucson, AZ 85710

WATAN, Jay Sapaen (Cal) 900 Edgewater Blvd, Foster City, CA 94404

WATERS, Elliott (Pa) 325 Cameron Station Blvd, Alexandria, VA 22304

WATERS, Margaret (Tex) 4902 Ridge Oak Dr, Austin, TX 78731

WATERS, Sonia E (Nwk) 369 Sand Shore Rd, Budd Lake, NJ 07828

WATERSONG, Auburn Lynn (Vt) Christ Episcopal Church, 64 State St, Montpelier, VT 05602

WATKINS, Gilbert Harold (WVa) 2721 Riverside Dr, Saint Albans, WV 25177

WATKINS, Jane Hill (CGC) 10100 Hillview Dr Apt 2311, Pensacola, FL 32514

WATKINS, Laurel Josephine (Okla) 210 E 9th St, Bartlesville, OK 74003

WATKINS, Leeanne Ingeborg (Minn) 1895 Laurel Ave, Saint Paul, MN 55104

WATKINS, Linda King (CPa) 407 Greenwood St, Mont Alto, PA 17237

WATKINS, LindaMay (SO) 20 W 1st St, Dayton, OH 45402

WATKINS, Lucien Alexander (SwFla) 1545 54th Ave S, Saint Petersburg, FL 33705

WATKINS, Michael Mack (Okla) 210 E 9th St, Bartlesville, OK 74003

WATKINS JR, Tommie Lee (Ala)

WATROUS, Janet Couper (NC) 415 S Boylan Ave, Raleigh, NC 27603

WATSON, Amanda Jane Price (NwT) 701 Amarillo St, Abilene, TX 79602

WATSON JR, Clyde M (Va)

WATSON, George Stennis (WTenn) 1319 Cheyenne Dr., Richardson, TX 75080

WATSON, Jack Lee (Fla) 23 Cameo Drive, Flat Rock, NC 28731

WATSON, James Darrell (Tex) 1101 Tiffany Ln, Longview, TX 75604

WATSON, Janice McKee (The Episcopal Church in Haw) Episcopal Church in Micronesia, 911 N Marine Corps Dr, Tamuning, GU 96913

WATSON JR, Joel Joel (LI) 3216 Kensington Ave, Richmond, VA 23221

WATSON, Karen (Neb) 925 S. 84th St., Omaha, NE 68114

WATSON, Margaret (SD) 503 Main St., Eagle Butte, SD 57625

WATSON, Martha (Nev) St Peter's, 3695 Rogers Ave, Ellicott City, MD 21043

WATSON, Michael Townes (NY) 85 E Main Street, Mount Kisco, NY 10549

WATSON, Richard Avery (SVa) 9 Westwood Drive, East Haddam, CT 06469

WATSON, Robert William (Ct) 52 Missionary Rd # 22, Cromwell, CT 06416

WATSON, Shayna Jamillah (CPa) 221 N Front St, Harrisburg, PA 17101

WATSON, Suzanne E (SanD) 5 Rainey Ln, Westport, CT 06880

WATSON, Wendy (The Episcopal NCal) 990 Mee Lane, St Helena, CA 94574

WATSON III, William John (SwVa) PO Box 3123, Lynchburg, VA 24503

WATSON EPTING, Susanne K (Ia) 86 Broadmoor Ln, Iowa City, IA 52245

WATT, Gilbert Merwin (Pgh) 396 Woodlands Dr, Verona, PA 15147

WATT, Jacqueline Tyndale (At) 605 Dunwoody Chace Ne, Atlanta, GA 30328

WATT, Tanya Chere (Az)

WATT, Tim (Az) 3737 Seminary Rd, Alexandria, VA 22304

WATTON, Sharon L (Mich) PoBox 80643, Rochester, MI 48308

WATTS, Charles Melvin (O) 4113 West State Street, Route 73, Wilmington, OH 45177

WATTS, Janice Diane (Az) St. Andrew's Episcopal Church, 6300 W. Camelback Rd., Glendale, AZ 85301

WATTS, Marilyn Ruth (The Episcopal Church in Haw) 1525 Wilder Ave Apt 304, Honolulu, HI 96822

WATTS, Rebecca Bridges (CFla)

WATTS, Sharon Lee Jones (Md) 4 E University Pkwy, Baltimore, MD 21218

WATTS, Timothy Joe (At)

WATTS JR, William Joseph (WMass) 19 Pleasant St, Chicopee, MA 01013

WAUTERS JR, Will (Los) 1722 Timber Oak, San Antonio, TX 78232

WAVE, John Erford (CGC) 3615 Phillips Ln, Panama City, FL 32404

WAWERU, Christine Gatheni (LI) 215 Forward Support Battalion, Battalion & 74th St, Fort Hood, TX 76544

WAWERU, David G (LI) 2142 Modoc Dr, Harker Heights, TX 76548

WAY, Edson (NwT) 2807 42nd St., Lubbock, TX 79413

WAY, Harry L (Az) 4102 W Union Hills Dr, Glendale, AZ 85308

WAY, Michael (NJ) 503 Asbury Ave, Asbury Park, NJ 07712

WAY, Russell (Mass) 6969 11 Mile Rd NE, Rockford, MI 49341

WAYLAND, David Frazee (Va) 1342 Allister Green, Charlottesville, VA 22901

WAYMAN, Eugene (EC)

WAYMAN, Teresa Lachmann (WVa) 3085 Sycamore Run Road, Glenville, WV 26351

✠ **WAYNICK**, Cate (Ind) 5537 Woodacre Ct., Indianapolis, IN 46234

WEATHERFORD, David William (SanD) 10835 Gabacho Dr, San Diego, CA 92124

WEATHERHOLT, Anne (Md) 19 West High Street, Hancock, MD 21750

WEATHERHOLT JR, Floyd Allan (Md) 2 E High Street, Hancock, MD 21750

WEATHERLY, Beverly (WA) 44078 Saint Andrews Church Rd, California, MD 20619

WEATHERLY, Joe (Tenn) 885 Spring Valley Rd, Cookeville, TN 38501

WEATHERLY, John (Va) 8441 Porter Ln, Alexandria, VA 22308

WEATHERLY, Robert H (Miss) 1414 Chambers St, Vicksburg, MS 39180

WEATHERWAX, Elizabeth May (Pgh) 402 Royal Ct, Pittsburgh, PA 15234

WEAVER III, David (Chi) 3835 Johnson Ave, Western Springs, IL 60558

WEAVER, Eric James (LI) 8 Oceanside Ct, Northport, NY 11768

WEAVER, Evelyn Jean (SD) 2018 13th Ave, Belle Fourche, SD 57717

WEAVER, Ivan Michael (SD)

WEAVER, Joshua (ETenn)

WEAVER, Lorne Edward (Los) 1725 Partridge Ave., Upland, CA 91784

WEAVER, Robert Crew (O) 2553 Derbyshire Rd, Cleveland Heights, OH 44106

WEAVER, Roger Warren (Minn) Po Box 820, Tower, MN 55790

WEAVER, Sally Sykes (Mo) 2575 Sunrise Dr, Eureka, MO 63025

WEAVER, Shahar Caren (Chi) 3801 S Wabash Ave, Chicago, IL 60653

WEBB II, Alexander Henderson (WTenn) 4645 Walnut Grove Rd, Memphis, TN 38117

WEBB, Anne Slade Newbegin (NH) 43 Thorndike Pond Rd., Jaffrey, NH 03452

WEBB, Benjamin S (Ia) 511 W 12th St, Cedar Falls, IA 50613

WEBB, Estelle C (Ct) 1651 Dickson Ave Apt 124, Scranton, PA 18509

WEBB, Fain Murphey (Nwk) P.O. Box 336, Columbia, NJ 07832

WEBB, Frieda Van Baalen (WNY) 3360 McKinley Parkway, Buffalo, NY 14219

WEBB JR, James Wilson (Miss) 309 E Parkway Dr, Indianola, MS 38751

WEBB III, Joseph (Va) 4074 Thorngate Dr, Williamsburg, VA 23188

WEBB III, Joseph Baxtar (Eau) 6101 Bannocks Dr., San Antonio, TX 78239

WEBB, Pamela Connor (Va) 8221 Old Mill Lane, Williamsburg, VA 23188

WEBB, Richard Cassius Lee (NH) 43 Thorndike Pond Rd., Jaffrey, NH 03452

WEBB, Robert Joseph (Ind) 721 W Main St, Madison, IN 47250

WEBB, Ross Allan (USC) 2534 Shiland Dr, Rock Hill, SC 29732

WEBB, William Charles (WNY) 29 Grove St, Angola, NY 14006

WEBBER, Ann (Mich) 850 Timberline Dr, Rochester Hills, MI 48309

WEBBER, Bruce Milton (NJ) 19105 35th Avenue, Apt. J, Flushing, NY 11358

WEBBER, Christopher L (Ct) 1601 19th Avenue, San Francisco, CA 94122

WEBBER, Michael Basquin (NY) Po Box 121, Paradox, NY 12858

WEBER, Claudia Jo (ECR) 443 Alberto Way Unit B221, Los Gatos, CA 95032

WEBER, Dean A (Nwk) 81 Highwood Ave, Tenafly, NJ 07670

WEBER, Lynne Bleich (Nwk) 81 Highwood Ave, Tenafly, NJ 07670

WEBER-JOHNSON, Jered Paul (Minn) 3001 Wisconsin Ave NW, Washington, DC 20016

WEBSTER, Alan K (WVa) 36 Norwood Rd, Charleston, WV 25314

WEBSTER, Alice Elizabeth (EC) 12903 Saint Georges Ln NW, Mount Savage, MD 21545

WEBSTER, Dan (Md) 5204 Downing Rd, Baltimore, MD 21212

WEBSTER, Edwin Crowe (La) 895 Will Brown Rd, Eros, LA 71238

WEBSTER, Kiah S (USC) 11540 Ferguson Rd, Dallas, TX 75228

WEBSTER, Pamela Ball (Minn) 435 Sunset Rd, Ely, MN 55731

WEBSTER II, Phillip (USC) St Mary's Church, 170 Saint Andrews Rd, Columbia, SC 29210

WEBSTER, Randy Lee (Ia) 510 Columbia St, Burlington, IA 52601

WEBSTER, Richmond Rudolphus (Ala) 202 Gordon Dr Se, Decatur, AL 35601

WEBSTER, Thomas (NC) 2906 Ridge Rd Nw, Wilson, NC 27896

WEBSTER, Valerie Minton (Mont) 311 S 3rd Ave, Bozeman, MT 59715

WEBSTER II, W Raymond (Chi) 51 Pine Grove, Amherst, MA 01002

WEDDERBURN, Derrick Hexford (NJ) Broadway & Royden, Cadmen, NJ 08104

WEDDLE, Karl G (ETenn) 313 Twinbrook Dr, Danville, KY 40422

WEDGWOOD-GREENHOW, Stephen John Francis (NwT) 15804 Alameda Dr, Bowie, MD 20716

WEEDON, Sarah Lipscomb (CPa) 150 E Lincoln St, Shamokin, PA 17872

WEEKS, Ann Gammon (ETenn)

WEEKS, Jo Ann (Los) 23446 Swan St, Moreno Valley, CA 92557

WEEKS, Lawrence Biddle (Me) 12 Catherine St, Portland, ME 04102

WEEKS, William Bradley (ETenn) Grace Episcopal Church, 20 Belvoir Ave, Chattanooga, TN 37411

WEEKS WULF, Marta Joan (SeFla) 7350 SW 162nd Street, Palmetto Bay, FL 33157

WEGER, Rohani Ann (SeFla) 1225 Texas St, Houston, TX 77002

WEGLARZ, Eileen (NY) 98 Stewart Ave, Eastchester, NY 10709

WEGMAN, Jay D (NY) Cathedral Station, Box 1111, New York, NY 10025

WEHMILLER, Paula Jean Lawrence (Pa) 612 Ogden Ave., Swarthmore, PA 19081

WEHNER, Paul (Tex) 7327 Timberlake Dr, Sugar Land, TX 774798

WEI, Fei-jan Elizabeth (Tai) 114 Fuhe Rd 6FL, Yunghe City, Taipei 23449, Taiwan

WEIDMAN, Hal (SD) 910 Soo San Dr, Rapid City, SD 57702

WEIDNER, David (Fla) 128 Bilbao Dr, Saint Augustine, FL 32086

WEIERBACH, Cornelia Miller (Va) 5613 23rd St N, Arlington, VA 22205

WEIHER, Joie Muir Clee (Va) 7057 Blackwell Rd, Warrenton, VA 20187

WEIKERT, Robert Curtis (Mich) 4212 Wylie Rd, Dexter, MI 48130

WEIL, Louis (Cal) 2451 Ridge Rd, Berkeley, CA 94709

WEILER, Matthew Gordon Beck (CFla) 3538 Lenox Rd, Birmingham, AL 35213

WEILER, William Leon (Va) 5908 9th St N, Arlington, VA 22205

WEINBERG, Richard M (WA) St. Margaret's Episcopal Church, 1830 Connecticut Ave NW, Washington, DC 20009

WEINER, Margaret Yoder (Ia) 2525 Patricia Dr, Urbandale, IA 50322

WEINER, Mary Lou (Ida) 4933 W View Dr, Meridian, ID 83642

WEINER TOMPKINS, Rebecca (NY) 145 W 46th St, New York, NY 10036

WEINREICH, Gabriel (Mich) 2116 Silver Maples Drive, Chelsea, MI 48118

WEIR, Daniel Sargent (WNY) 337 NH 16A, Intervale, NH 03845

WEIR, Silas Michael (Colo) 4009 Histead Way, Evergreen, CO 80439

WEISE, John Winfred Thorburn (WVa) Po Box 1642, Parkersburg, WV 26102

WEISER, Samuel Ivan (RG) 848 Camino De Levante, Santa Fe, NM 87501

WEISS, Chuck (Del) PO Box, Dover, DE 19903

WEISS, Edward Allen (CFla) 200 Nw 3rd St, Okeechobee, FL 34972

WEISS, James Michael Egan (Mass) Dept of Theology, Boston College, Chestnut Hill, MA 02467

WEISS, Louise Lindecamp (RG) 3900 Trinity Dr, Los Alamos, NM 87544

WEISSMAN, Stephen Edward (Mo) 434 Gorman Bridge Rd, Asheville, NC 28806

WEITZEL, Mark Augustin (Los) 1020 N. Brand Blvd., Glendale, CA 91202

WELCH, Elizabeth Jean (Cal) Sojourn Chaplain, San Fransico General Hospital, San Fransico, CA 94110

WELCH, George Truman (Mass) 1692 Beacon St, Waban, MA 02468

WELCH, Jimmy Dean (Okla) 4250 W Houston St, Broken Arrow, OK 74012

WELCH, Lauren Marie (Md) 7 Overpark Ct, Baltimore, MD 21234

WELDON JR, Jay (Mass) 4800 Old Dawson Rd, Albany, GA 31721

WELDON, Jonathan Naylor (Oly) 415 S. Garden Street, Bellingham, WA 98225

WELDY JR, Robert Lee (Cal) PO Box 430, Inverness, CA 94937

WELIN, Amy Doyle (Ct) 58 Brookfield Rd, Seymour, CT 06483

WELIN, Gregory William (Ct) 58 Brookfield Rd, Seymour, CT 06483

WELLBORN, Gay S (RG)

WELLER, Edie (Oly) 8216 14th Ave Ne, Seattle, WA 98115

WELLER, Gordon (Mich) 218 Ottawa St., Lansing, MI 48933

WELLER, Gretchen (Lex) 435 SOM Center Road, Mayfield Village, OH 44143

WELLER JR, Thomas Carroll (CGC) 2300 W Beach Dr, Panama City, FL 32401

WELLES JR, George H (Mass) 810 Monterrosa Dr., Myrtle Beach, SC 29572

WELLES, Hope Virginia (Mo) 4455 Atlantic Blvd, Jacksonville, FL 32207

WELLFORD, Eleanor (Va) 510 S Gaskins Rd, Richmond, VA 23238

WELLNER, Robert Harry (Ct) 4750 Welby Drive, P.O. Box 142, Schnecksville, PA 18078

WELLS, Ben Reid (At) St. Francis Episcopal Church, 432 Forest Hill Road, Macon, GA 31210

WELLS, Charlotte E (EO) 241 Se 2nd St, Pendleton, OR 97801

WELLS, David L (Spr) Cathedral of St. Paul the Apostle, 815 S Second Street, Springfield, IL 62704

WELLS, Della Wager (RI)

WELLS, Dorothy Sanders (WTenn) St. George's Episcopal Church, 2425 S. Germantown Road, Germantown, TN 38138

WELLS, Edgar Fisher (NY) 400 W 43rd St Apt V V, New York, NY 10036

WELLS, Jane Ely (Minn) 105 S Cedar St, Oberlin, OH 44074

WELLS, Jason (NH) 18 Kimball St, Pembroke, NH 03275

WELLS SR, John T (Tex) 14043 Horseshoe Cir, Woodway, TX 76712

WELLS, Lloyd Francis (At) 335 Forest Heights Dr, Athens, GA 30606

WELLS, Mary Beth (SeFla) 231 Spring Hill Dr, Gordonsville, VA 22942

WELLS, Robert Louis (Tex) 9302 Sunlake Dr, Pearland, TX 77584

WELLS JR, Roy Draydon (Ala) 3608 Montclair Rd, Birmingham, AL 35213

WELLS, William E (Los) 18631 Chapel Ln, Huntington Beach, CA 92646

WELLS JR, William Smith (Va) 6914 West Grace Street, Richmond, VA 23226

WELLS MILLER, Tracy (ECR) The Episcopal Church of St. John the Baptist, PO Box 188, Aptos, CA 95001

WELSAND, Randy Arthur (Minn) 1928 38th St S, St Cloud, MN 56301

WELSCH, Matthew A (Va)

WELTY III, Terrence Anthony (Tex) 106 E Crawford St, Palestine, TX 75801

WELTY, Winston W (Pa) Santa Clara #613, Riberas del Pilar, Chapala, JAL 45906, Mexico

WENDEL JR, David Deaderick (Ala) 210 Oak Ct, New Braunfels, TX 78132

WENDEL, Richard (Chi) 536 W Fullerton Pkwy, Chicago, IL 60614

WENDELL, Chris (Mass) St. Paul's Church, 100 Pine Hill Road, Bedford, MA 01730

WENDELL, Martin Paul (Alb) 405 Master St, Valley Falls, NY 12185

WENDER, Sarai Tucker (ETenn) The Episcopal Church in East Tennessee, 814 Episcopal School Way, Knoxville, TN 37932

WENDFELDT, Steve (SanD) 2728 Sixth Avenue, San Diego, CA 92103

WENGROVIUS, John H. (Colo) 1320 Arapahoe St, Golden, CO 80401

WENGROVIUS, Steve (Colo) 3712 W 99th Ave, Westminster, CO 80031

WENNER, Peter (Mass) 137 Auburndale Ave, West Newton, MA 02465

WENNER GARDNER, Rachel E (Pa) Ch Of The Ascension & Holy Trinity, 420 W 18th St, Pueblo, CO 81003

WENRICK, Heather Marie (Ore) 1444 Liberty St SE, Salem, OR 97302

WENTHE, Lanny (Me) 35 Paris St, Norway, ME 04268

WENTZIEN, Marilyn Lawrence (Ia)

WERDAL, Evelyn Paige (NY) 522 Walnut St, Mamaroneck, NY 10543

WERNER, Frederick John Emil (Mich) 13070 Independence Ave, Utica, MI 48315

WERNER, George (Pgh) 106 Sewickley Heights Dr., Sewickley, PA 15143

WERNER, Mark (USC) 2 N Hill Ct, Columbia, SC 29223

WERNICK, Mike (WMich) 1800 Bloomfield Dr. SE, Kentwood, MI 49508

WERNTZ, Pamela Louise (Mass) 120 Marshall St, Watertown, MA 02472

WESCH, Kate (Oly) 1805 38th Ave, Seattle, WA 98126

WESEN, Vicki (Oly) 1500A E College Way # 447, Mount Vernon, WA 98273

WESLEY, Carol A (Mo) 5619 Alaska Ave, Saint Louis, MO 63111

WESLEY JR, John (Fla) 338 N 10th St, Quincy, FL 32351

WESSELL, David E (FdL) 2805 Elgin St, Durham, NC 27704

WEST, Anne Kersting (Va) Blue Ridge School, 273 Mayo Dr, St George, VA 22935

WEST, Barbara Field (Ct) 7 Hillcrest Rd, Manchester, CT 06040

WEST, Clark Russell (CNY) G3 Anabel Taylor Hall, Ithaca, NY 14853

WEST, Geoffrey George (NJ) 525 Willowbrook Dr, Jeffersonville, PA 19403

WEST, Harrison Harrison (Ct) 11 Park St, Guilford, CT 06437

WEST, Hilary (EC) 411 W Bridge Ln, Nags Head, NC 27959

WEST, Hillary T (Va) 4212 Kingcrest Pkwy, Richmond, VA 23221

WEST JR, Irvin D (Ark) 401 E 10th St, Little Rock, AR 72202

WEST, Jan Hickman (Cal) 171 Prospect Ave, San Anselmo, CA 94960

WEST, Jennifer (SO) 233 S. State St., Westerville, OH 43081

WEST JR, John (Ga) 4227 Columbia Rd, Martinez, GA 30907

WEST, John Thomas (NMich) 301 N 1st St, Ishpeming, MI 49849

WEST, Philip (RG) 2243 Henry Rd Sw, Albuquerque, NM 87105

WEST, Scott (SwVa) 120 Church St NE, P.O. Box 164, Blacksburg, VA 24063

WEST, Tim (SO) 600 Dorothy Moore Avenue, Unit 10, Urbana, OH 43078

WESTBROOK, Carl (Tex)

WESTBURY JR, Rick (Fla) 15 N Wilderness Trl, Ponte Vedra Beach, FL 32082

WEST-DOOHAN, Sue (Be) HC 75 Box 32, Strange Creek, WV 25063

WESTERBERG, George Arthur (Mass) 212 North Lower Bay Road, Lovell, ME 04051

WESTERHOFF III, John Henry (At) 49 Old Ivy Sq Ne, Atlanta, GA 30342

WESTFALL, Doris Ann (Mo) 28 Whinhill Ct, Saint Peters, MO 63304

WESTHORP, Peter H (RI) 2574 Creve Coeur Mill Rd, Maryland Heights, MO 63043

WESTLING JR, Lester Leon (The Episcopal NCal) 573 Royal Oaks Dr, Redding, CA 96001

WESTON, Jane Mitchell (At) PO Box 102, Conyers, GA 30012

WESTON, Stephen Richard (Colo) 2021 South Xenia Way, Denver, CO 80231

WESTPFAHL, Carol (ETenn) 210 Redwolf Way, Lenoir City, TN 37772

WESTPHAL, Stacey Elizabeth (CFla) 522 Summerset Ct, Indian Harbour Beach, FL 32937

WETHERED, Stephanie Keith (Nwk) 224 Cornelia St, Boonton, NJ 07005

WETHERILL, Benjamin Wade (Me) P.O. Box 156, Rangeley, ME 04970

WETHERINGTON, Robert (Ark) 10 Camp Mitchell Rd, Morrilton, AR 72110

WETHERINGTON, Timothy R (CFla) Church Of The Messiah, 241 N Main St, Winter Garden, FL 34787

WETHERN, James Douglas (Ga) PO Box 20327, Saint Simons Island, GA 31522

WETMORE, Ian (Spr) St Michael's Episcopal Church, 111 Ofallon Troy Rd, O Fallon, IL 62269

WETTSTEIN, David (Ida) 6925 Copper Dr, Boise, ID 83704

WETZEL, Luke A (Ga) Trinity Episcopal Church, 1130 1st Ave, Columbus, GA 31901

WETZEL, Mary (At) P.O. Box 4548, Atlanta, GA 30302

WETZEL, Todd Harold (Dal) Po Box 429, Cedar Hill, TX 75106

WEYLS, Richard Coleman (Oly) 747 Broadway, Seattle, WA 98122

WEYMOUTH, Richard Channing (NH) RR3 Box 18, Plymouth, NH 03264

WEZA, Barbra (Oly)

WHALEN, Dena Stokes (EC) P.O. Box 490, Clarkesville, GA 30523

WHALEN, Donald (Eas) 2929 SE Ocean Blvd O-5, Stuart, FL 34996

WHALEN, Peter (Tenn) 103 Northwood Ave, Shelbyville, TN 37160

WHALEY, Stephen Foster (Tex) 605 Dulles Avenue, Stafford, TX 77477

WHALLON, Diane (Fla) 1640 NE 40th Ave Apt 106, Ocala, FL 34470

✠ **WHALON**, Pierre W (Eur) 23 Avenue George V, Paris, 75008, France

WHARTON III, George Franklin (Ia) 502 W Broadway St, Decorah, IA 52101

WHARTON, Roger (ECR) 1404 Arnold Ave, San Jose, CA 95110

WHEATLEY, Gail (Oly) St Andrew's Episcopal Church, 510 E. Park Ave, Port Angeles, WA 98362

WHEATLEY, Paul David (Dal) Church of the Incarnation, 3966 McKinney Ave, Dallas, TX 75204

WHEATLEY-JONES, Elizabeth (Miss) P.O. Box 345, Grenada, MS 38902

WHEATON, Philip Eugene (Roch) 7211 Spruce Ave, Takoma Park, MD 20912

WHEELER, Charles R (WNY) 161 E Main St, Westfield, NY 14787

WHEELER, Diana Roberta (Cal) 573 Dolores st., San Francisco, CA 94110

WHEELER, Elisa Desportes (Va) 638 Burton Point Rd, Mathews, VA 23068

WHEELER, Evelyn (Ind)

WHEELER, Frances Marie (Kan) 14301 S Blackbob Rd, Olathe, KS 66062

WHEELER, Jim (Ct) Po Box 10, Woodbury, CT 06798

WHEELER, John Bevan (Md) 2795 Topmast Ct, Annapolis, MD 21401

WHEELER, Kathryn Brown (CGC) 2002 W Lakeridge Dr, Albany, GA 31707

WHEELER JR, Louis (WA) 2001 14th St SE, Washington, DC 20020

WHEELER, Rhonda Estes (SVa) St. Andrew's Episcopal Church, 45 Main Street, Newport News, VA 23601

WHEELER, William Ramsey (Alb) Po Box 354, Boonville, NY 13309

WHEELOCK, Janet (SanD) Saint Mary's In The Valley Church, 1010 12th St, Ramona, CA 92065

WHEELOCK, Leslie Gail (RI) 8 Neptune St, Jamestown, RI 02835

WHELAN, Edgar Joseph (WMo) 13500 Rinehart Ln, Parkville, MO 64152

WHELAN, Janet Kay (WMo) 13500 Rinehart Ln, Parkville, MO 64152

WHELAN, Peter H (Ky) 1207 Meadowridge Trl, Goshen, KY 40026

WHELCHEL, Judith Hester (WNC) 67 Windsor Rd, Asheville, NC 28804

WHENAL, Barry (FdL) 6535 Oriole Road, Lake Tomahawk, WI 54539

WHENNEN, John (Chi) 2640 Park Dr, Flossmoor, IL 60422

WHETSTONE, Raymond David (Ala) Grace Episcopal Church, PO Box 1791, Anniston, AL 36202

WHIDDON, Ennis Howard (USC) 301 Piney Mountain Rd, Greenville, SC 29609

WHISENHUNT, William Allen (WNC) Trinity Episcopal Church, 60 Church St, Asheville, NC 28801

WHISTLER, Tamsen (Mo) 1020 N Duchesne Dr, Saint Charles, MO 63301

WHITAKER, Ann Latham (Miss) 806 Prairie View Road, Oxford, MS 38655

WHITAKER, Bradford G (ETenn) 305 W 7th St, Chattanooga, TN 37402

WHITAKER III, Howard Wilson (Nwk) PO Box 596, Scottsboro, AL 35768

WHITAKER, Monica (Az) 100 Arroyo Pinon Dr, Sedona, AZ 86336

WHITBECK, Marjorie Bailey Ogden (Mass) 29 Princess Rd, West Newton, MA 02465

WHITE, Andrew D'Angio (Me) Saint David's Episcopal Church, 138 York St, Kennebunk, ME 04043

WHITE JR, Arthur Bain (Colo) St Mark's Episcopal Church, PO Box 534, Craig, CO 81626

WHITE, Bruce Alan (Az) 7267 E Onda Cir, Tucson, AZ 85715

WHITE, Carolyn Connie (ECR) 5602 Dona Ana Loop NE, Rio Rancho, NM 87144

WHITE, Deborah (Cal) 130 Muir Station Rd., Martinez, CA 94553

WHITE, Dorothy (Va) 6001 Grove Ave, Richmond, VA 23226

WHITE, Harold Naylor (Va) Po Box 326, Wicomico Church, VA 22579

WHITE, Harry N (Pa) 408 Valley Ave, Atglen, PA 19310

WHITE, Helen Slingluff (Ga) 15 Willow Rd, Savannah, GA 31419

WHITE III, Hugh Couch (Va) 664 Dungeons Thicket Rd, White Stone, VA 22578

WHITE, James Lee (EMich) 39 Gainsborough Dr, Lewes, DE 19958

WHITE, Jon (CNY) St Luke's Episcopal Church, 5402 W Genesee St, Camillus, NY 13031

WHITE, K Alon (NY) 124 N Broadway, Nyack, NY 10960

WHITE, Karin Kay (ECR) 390 N Winchester Blvd Apt 9B, Santa Clara, CA 95050

WHITE, Kathryn (Chi) 3052 Jeffrey Dr, Joliet, IL 60435

WHITE, Kathryn Sawyer (WMass) 129 Roseland Park Road, Woodstock, CT 06281

WHITE, Kenneth Gordon (Mass) 11 Anita St, Sabattus, ME 04280

WHITE, Kenneth Orgill (WLa) 2320 Wooster Ln Apt 6, Sanibel, FL 33957

WHITE, Kevin Gerard (WMo) 1307 Holmes St, Kansas City, MO 64106

WHITE, Konrad Shepard (Los) 524 E Duffy St, Savannah, GA 31401

WHITE, Kristin (Ind) 1100 W 42nd St, Indianapolis, IN 46208

WHITE, Laura Dale (USC) 522 NW 8th St, Pendleton, OR 97801

WHITE, Lynn Scott (Chi) 1546 Bobolink Cir, Woodstock, IL 60098

WHITE, Mary (Alb) 10 N Main Ave, Albany, NY 12203

WHITE, Michael S (Ga) 308A Bradley Point Rd, Savannah, GA 31410

WHITE, Michelle Denise (Nwk) 707 Washington St, Hoboken, NJ 07030

WHITE, M Joanna (Md) 2125 Beach Village Court, Annapolis, MD 21403

WHITE, Nancy Anne (Md) 3267 Stepney St, Edgewater, MD 21037

WHITE, Nicholson Barney (O) 1109 Hollyheath Ln, Charlotte, NC 28209

WHITE JR, Paul Donald (WTenn) 3553 Windgarden Cv, Memphis, TN 38125

WHITE, R Scott (WNC) Trinity Church, 60 Church St, Asheville, NC 28801

WHITE, Rita Ellen (Va) 138 Pier Place, Kinsale, VA 22488

WHITE, Roger Bradley (Ct) Po Box 309, Kent, CT 06757

WHITE, Rowena Ruth (WLa) 8212 Argosy Ct, Baton Rouge, LA 70809

WHITE, Sara D (Me) 143 State St, Portland, ME 04101

WHITE, Stanley James (Ga) 101 E Central Ave Fl 3, Valdosta, GA 31601

WHITE, Stephen James (Me) 140 Bluff Road, Yarmouth, ME 04096

WHITE, Steve (NJ) 2325 Hancock Road, Williamstown, MA 01267

WHITE, Steve (CNY) 1101 N Broadway St, Knoxville, TN 37917

✠ **WHITE**, Terry Allen (Ky) 425 S Second St Suite 200, Louisville, KY 40202

WHITE, Thomas Rees (Ct) 109 Sand Hill Rd, South Windsor, CT 06074

WHITE, Warner Clock (WMich) 12 Harbor Watch Rd., Burlington, VT 05401

WHITEFORD, Cecily S (WNY) 45 S Cayuga Rd Apt G3, Williamsville, NY 14221

WHITEHAIR, Eric Ian (Md)

WHITE-HASSLER, Jane (Ct) 130 Vincent Dr, Newington, CT 06111

WHITEHEAD, Danny Ray (Ala) PO Box 756, Lytton, VOK 1Z0, Canada

WHITEHEAD, Philip Hoyle (USC) 6026 Crabtree Rd, Columbia, SC 29206

WHITE HORSE-CARDA, Patricia Ann (SD) 500 S Main Ave, Sioux Falls, SD 57104

WHITEHURST, Joseph Stewart (USC) 173 Kendallwood Ct, Aiken, SC 29803

WHITELAW, Eleanor Drake (CGC) 343 N Randolph Ave, Eufaula, AL 36027

WHITELEY, Raewynne Jean (LI) 15 Highland Ave, Saint James, NY 11780

WHITEMAN, Christopher William (Mass) PO Box 991, Groton, MA 01450

WHITESEL, Ann Brier (CPa) 12 Strawberry Dr, Carlisle, PA 17013

WHITESIDE, Henry B (EC) 7 Masonic Ave, Shelburne Falls, MA 01370

WHITFIELD, Ann (Nev) 10810 NE Sherwood Dr., Vancouver, WA 98686

WHITFIELD, Deirdre (Pa) 126 Westminster Dr, Wallingford, PA 19086

WHITFIELD, Jacqueline Rutledge (NC)

WHITFIELD, Stephen Ray (Tex) 2301 Lauren Loop, Leander, TX 78641

WHITFORD, Michele E (FdL) 1220 N 7th St, Sheboygan, WI 53081

WHITING, Raymond Arthur (Ga)

WHITING, William Richard (WMich) 2165 Chesapeake Dr Ne, Grand Rapids, MI 49505

WHITLEY, Ryan R (SwFla) 1 W Ardmore Ave, Ardmore, PA 19003

WHITLOCK III, Robin (SwFla) 949 41st Ave N, Saint Petersburg, FL 33703

WHITMAN, Frank (Minn)

WHITMAN, Marian Chandler (WTenn) 2425 S Germantown Rd, Germantown, TN 38138

WHITMER, Marlin Lee (Ia) 2602 250th St, De Witt, IA 52742

WHITMER, Ronald Delane (La) 5400 Courtyard Dr., Gonzales, LA 70737

WHITMIRE JR, Norman (LI) 8545 96th St, Woodhaven, NY 11421

WHITMORE, Bruce Gregory (Tex) 1401 Avenue O #F, Huntsville, TX 77340

WHITMORE, Chuck (WNY) 3802 James St. Unit 30, Bellingham, WA 98226

WHITMORE, Elizabeth Needham (Mass) 1391 Hyannis Barnstable Rd, Barnstable, MA 02630

✠ **WHITMORE**, Keith (Eau) 90 N National Ave, Fond Du Lac, WI 54935

WHITMORE, Paula Michele (Spok) 602 Nw 10th St, Pendleton, OR 97801

WHITNAH JR, John C (Pa) Gethsemane Cathedral, 3600 25th St S, Fargo, ND 58104

WHITNAH, Michael D (Pa)

WHITNEY, Ann Carolyn (Ak) PO Box 870995, Wasilla, AK 99687

WHITNEY, Marilla Jane (Minn) 111 N Elm St, Fairmont, MN 56031

WHITNEY, Wayne V (Az) Episcopal Church of the Nativity, 22405 N Miller Rd, Scottsdale, AZ 85255

WHITNEY-WISE, Stephen (Ore) 4033 SE Woodstock Blvd., Portland, OR 97202

WHITSITT, Helen Bonita (WMo) PO Box 57, Fayette, MO 65248

WHITTAKER, Brendan Joseph (NH) 1788 Vt Route 102, Guildhall, VT 05905

WHITTAKER JR, Richard Russell (U) 1784 Aaron Dr., Tooele, UT 84074

WHITTAKER-NAVEZ, Christine Ruth (Mass) 223 Pond St, Hopkinton, MA 01748

WHITTED, Warren Rohde (Neb) 8141 Farnam Dr Apt 328, Omaha, NE 68114

WHITTEN, James Austin (CFla) St Mary of the Angels, 6316 Matchett Rd, Orlando, FL 32809

WHITTEN, Wesley Roy (ECR) 11197 Via Vis, Nevada City, CA 95959

WHITTINGTON, Nancy Susan (WNC) 140 Chestnut Cir, Blowing Rock, NC 28605

WHITTINGTON, Richard Culbertson (Tex)

WHITTLE, Natalie Wang (Ga) 102 S Jackson Rd, Statesboro, GA 30461

WHITWORTH, Julia E (Ind) Trinity Episcopal Church, 3243 N Meridian St, Indianapolis, IN 46208

WHYTE, Horace Maxwell (NY) 170 W End Ave Apt 30-H, New York, NY 10023

WIBLE, Christina Karen Kirchner (NJ) 10 N Slope, Clinton, NJ 08809

WIBLE, Terrence Linn (Be) 57 Piper Dr, New Oxford, PA 17350

WICHAEL, Karen (Kan) 5648 W 92nd Pl, Overland Park, KS 66207

WICHELNS, Anne (CNY) Church of the Resurrecton, 120 West Fifth Street, Oswego, NY 13126

WICHELNS, Jerome Bailey (CNY) 10751 Limburg Forks Rd, Carthage, NY 13619

WICHMAN, James Henry (O) 2314 Oak Glen Ct, Akron, OH 44333

WICK, Calhoun W (Del) Po Box 3719, Wilmington, DE 19807

WICKHAM, Jonathan William (WTex) 15670 Robin Ridge, San Antonio, TX 78248

WICKHAM III, William (Del) 9410 Creek Summit Circle, Richmond, VA 23235

WICKIZER, Bob (Okla) 218 N 6th St, Muskogee, OK 74401

WIDING, Jon (Ct) 47 Fox Holw, Avon, CT 06001

WIDLAKE, Dina Elaine (Va) 6715 Georgetown Pike, McLean, VA 22101

WIECKING III, Frederick August (Ind) 4 Sunnyside Rd, Silver Spring, MD 20910

WIED, Gethin James (Los)

WIEHE, Philip (NC) 3676 Laurel Park Highway, Hendersonville, NC 28739

WIELAND, William David (Ind) (same as above), Greencastle, IN 46135

WIENK, Dennis Leslie (Roch) 1760 Blossom Rd, Rochester, NY 14610

WIENS, Dolores (NI) 315 W Harrison Ave, Wheaton, IL 60187

WIENS HEINSOHN, Lisa Marie (Minn) 2136 Carter Ave, Saint Paul, MN 55108

WIESNER, A Donald (NJ) 208 Live Oak Ln, Washington, NC 27889

WIESNER, Kurt Christopher (U) 261 S 900 E, Salt Lake City, UT 84102

WIETSTOCK, Anne Kimberley (NI) 117 N Lafayette Blvd, South Bend, IN 46601

WIGGERS, John Mark (ETenn) 1101 N Broadway St, Knoxville, TN 37917

WIGGIN-NETTLES, Duane Joseph (La) The Church Of The Annunciation, 4505 S Claiborne Ave, New Orleans, LA 70125

WIGGIN-NETTLES, Jane-Allison E (La)

WIGGINS JR, Eschol Vernon (Ga) 1009 Hillcrest Dr, Cochran, GA 31014

WIGGINS, Reese H (La) 17764 Jefferson Ridge Dr, Baton Rouge, LA 70817

WIGG-MAXWELL, Elizabeth Parker (Nwk) 44 Pittsford Way, New Providence, NJ 07974

WIGHT, Andrea (Chi) 7398 Bell Vista Terrace, Rockford, IL 61107

WIGHT, Susan (USC) 5 Blackhawk Ct, Blythewood, SC 29016

WIGHT, William Wallace (USC) 5 Blackhawk Ct, Blythewood, SC 29016

WIGLE, John Whitcombe (O) 814 Westport Dr, Youngstown, OH 44511

WIGMORE, William Joseph (Tex) 1701 Rock Creek Dr, Round Rock, TX 78681

WIGNER JR, J Douglas (Va) 1802 Dover Pointe Ct, Henrico, VA 23238

WIGODSKY, Andrea (SVa) St. Andrew's Episcopal Church, 1009 West Princess Anne Rd., Norfolk, VA 23507

WIKE, Antoinette Ray (NC) 221 Union St, Cary, NC 27511

WILBERT, Brian Kurt (O) 162 S Main St, Oberlin, OH 44074

WILBURN, James Mark (Tex) 24 McFaddan LN, Temple, TX 76502

WILBURN, Merry I (Tex) 16830 Blairstone, Houston, TX 77084

WILCOX, Diana (Nwk) St Luke's Episcopal Church, 73 S Fullerton Ave, Montclair, NJ 07042

WILCOX JR, Jack Franklyn (Okla) 101 Great Oaks Dr, Norman, OK 73071

WILCOX, John Milton (Episcopal SJ) 3909 Noel Pl, Bakersfield, CA 93306

WILCOX, Melissa (Mil) 3118 Cross St, Madison, WI 53711

WILCOXSON, Frederick Dean (CFla) 154 Terry Lane, Benton, TN 37307

WILCOXSON, JoAnn Vanessa (CFla) 154 Terry Lane, Benton, TN 37307

WILD, Geoffrey Mileham (NwPa) PO Box 287, Grove City, PA 16127

WILD, Janet (ECR) 13601 Saratoga Ave, Saratoga, CA 95070

WILD III, Philip Charles (La) 120 S New Hampshire St, Covington, LA 70433

WILDE, Gary A (SwFla) 2306 Hermitage Blvd, Venice, FL 34292

WILDE, Gregory Dean (CFla) 6164 Colfax Ln S, Minneapolis, MN 55419

WILDER, Ginny (NC) Trinity Episcopal Church, 1108 N Adams St, Wilmington, DE 19801

WILDER, Marilyn (Spok) 617 10th St, Oroville, WA 98844

WILDER III, Tracy (SwFla) 13720 Sweat Loop Rd., Wamauma, FL 33598

WILDGOOSE, Angelo (NJ) 6361 Lancaster Ave, Philadelphia, PA 19151

WILDMAN, Rachel Preston (Mass) 100 Pine Hill Rd, Bedford, MA 01730

WILE, Mary Lee (Me) 46 Willow Grove Rd, Brunswick, ME 04011

WILEMON, Zane Howard (Cal) 81 N 2nd St, San Jose, CA 95113

WILEY, George Bell (Kan) 2313 Willow Crk, Lawrence, KS 66049

WILEY, Henrietta L (Md) Cathedral of the Incarnation, 4 E University Pkwy, Baltimore, MD 21218

WILEY, Judi (SO) 234 N. High St., Hillsboro, OH 45133

WILHELM, Joseph (Los) 404 W Santa Ana St., Ojai, CA 93023

WILHELM, Quinn Jay (Colo) 2950 S University Blvd, Denver, CO 80210

WILKERSON, Bonnie Carver (Ia) St Luke's Episcopal Church, 605 Avenue E, Fort Madison, IA 52627

WILKERSON, Charles Edward (Md) St Luke's Episcopal Church, 1101 Bay Ridge Ave, Annapolis, MD 21403

WILKERSON, Christopher T (USC)

WILKES, Hugh E (Alb) 2717 2nd Ave, Watervliet, NY 12189

WILKES III, Joseph Warren (Mass) 186 Upham St, Melrose, MA 02176

WILKINS, Christopher Ian (WA) St. Philip's Episcopal Church, 13801 Baden Westwood Rd, Brandywine, MD 20613

WILKINS, Palmer Oliver (Cal) 58 Robinhood Dr, Novato, CA 94945

WILKINSON, Donald Charles (Mo) 17210 Fawn Cloud Ln, San Antonio, TX 78248

WILKINSON, Ernest Benjamin (NwT) 727 W Browning Ave, Pampa, TX 79065

WILKINSON, James Royse (Ky) 1804 Leawood Ct, Louisville, KY 40222

WILKINSON, Joyce Ann (WTex)

WILKINSON, Kirsteen (Ind) 7834 Grand Gulch Dr, Indianapolis, IN 46239

WILKINSON, Marcia Campbell (Ala) 6634 31st Pl NW, Washington, DC 20015

WILKINSON, Mark David (SVa) St. Aidan's Episc Church, 3201 Edinburgh Dr., Virginia Beach, VA 23452

WILKINSON, Mary Suzanne (NwT) 727 W Browning Ave, Pampa, TX 79065

WILKINSON, Randy (WA) Church of the Ascension, 205 S Summit Ave, Gaithersburg, MD 20877

WILKINSON, Shivaun Renee (WA) 3820 Aspen Hill Rd, Silver Spring, MD 20906

WILKINSON, Wendy (SVa) Good Samaritan Episcopal Church, 848 Baker Rd, Virginia Beach, VA 23462

WILLARD V, John Dayton (SVa) 1634 Orchard Beach Rd, Annapolis, MD 21409

WILLARD, Neil Alan (Tex) Palmer Memorial Church, 6221 Main St, Houston, TX 77030

WILLARD JR, Wilson Howard (SO) 1305 Cutter St, Cincinnati, OH 45203

WILLARD-WILLIFORD, Joy (CFla) 5625 Holy Trinity Dr, Melbourne, FL 32940

WILLCOX, Halley L (At) Charlottesville Wellness Center, 901 Preston Avenue, Charlottesville, VA 22901

WILLE, Elizabeth Suzanne (Ind) 1559 N Central Ave, Indianapolis, IN 46202

WILLEMS, James Rutherford (Los) 561 48th Street, Oakland, CA 94609

WILLERER, Rhonda (Fla) St. Patrick's Episcopal Church, 1221 State Rd 13, Saint Johns, FL 32259

WILLIAMS JR, A Lenwood (Miss) 9378 Harroway Rd, Summerville, SC 29485

WILLIAMS, Alfredo (Dal) 1516 N Leland Ave, Indianapolis, IN 46219

WILLIAMS, Alina Somodevilla (La) PO Box 126, Baton Rouge, LA 70821

WILLIAMS, Alton Paul (CPa) 5 Greenway Dr, Mechanicsburg, PA 17055

WILLIAMS, Anne Elizabeth (Ia) PO Box 33, Anamosa, IA 52205

✠ **WILLIAMS JR**, Arthur (O) 25530 Edgecliff Dr, Euclid, OH 44132

WILLIAMS, Arthur Wordsworth Lonfellow (NY) 3412 103rd St, Corona, NY 11368

WILLIAMS, Barbara Farrar (SVa) P O Box 62184, Virginia Beach, VA 23466

WILLIAMS, Brendan Ellis (Cal) 601 N Tejon St, Colorado Springs, CO 80903

WILLIAMS, Bruce McKennie (RG) 7201 San Benito St Nw, Albuquerque, NM 87120

WILLIAMS JR, Bud (Los) 1438 Coronado Ter, Los Angeles, CA 90026

WILLIAMS, Bunny Simon (Ga)

WILLIAMS, Carolynne Juanita Grant (At) 2088 Cloverdale Dr Se, Atlanta, GA 30316

WILLIAMS, Cecil David (Nwk) 515 Parker St, Newark, NJ 07104

WILLIAMS, Colin Harrington (CNY) 2850 SW Scenic Drive, Portland, OR 97225

WILLIAMS, Courtly (Chi) 425 Laurel Ave, Highland Park, IL 60035

WILLIAMS, David Anthony (SC) St. Stephen's Episcopal Church, 67 Anson St, Charleston, SC 29401

WILLIAMS, David R (NC) 1406 Victoria Ct, Elon, NC 27244

WILLIAMS, Donald B (Kan) 2510 Grand Blvd. #1103, Kansas City, MO 64108

WILLIAMS, Douglas M (Colo) 28 Cunningham Pond Rd, Peterborough, NH 03458

WILLIAMS, Edward Earl (NY)

WILLIAMS, Edward Satterfield (Ga) 353 Midway Circ, Brunswick, GA 31523

WILLIAMS, Elizabeth Ann (Los) 512 E Williams St, Barstow, CA 92311

WILLIAMS, Eric (Mich) 1948 Hunters Ridge Dr, Bloomfield Hills, MI 48304

WILLIAMS, Florence Darcy (Eas) Emmanuel Episcopal Church, PO Box 875, Chestertown, MD 21620

WILLIAMS, Francis Edward (RG) 1020 Sable Circle, Las Cruces, NM 88001

WILLIAMS, Gary Wayne (Okla) 3804 Cobble Cir, Norman, OK 73072

WILLIAMS, Glen Parker (WMich) 12057 S Elk Run, Traverse City, MI 49684

WILLIAMS, Glenn Thomas (ND) 3613 River Dr S, Fargo, ND 58104

WILLIAMS, Henrietta R (Ind) 115 Ne 66th St, Oak Island, NC 28465

WILLIAMS, Henry N (Pa) 1029 Fox Hollow Rd, Shermans Dale, PA 17090

WILLIAMS JR, Hollis (Oly) 725 9th Ave Apt 2007, Seattle, WA 98104

WILLIAMS, Howard (LI) 1102 E 73rd St Apt C, Brooklyn, NY 11234

WILLIAMS III, Hugh Elton (CFla) Po Box 91777, Lakeland, FL 33804

WILLIAMS, Jacqueline Miller (SO) 6461 Tylersville Rd, West Chester, OH 45069

WILLIAMS, James (Ala) 2130 Enon Mill Dr Sw, Atlanta, GA 30331

WILLIAMS II, James Edward (Los) 580 Hilgard Ave, Los Angeles, CA 90024

WILLIAMS JR, (Jerre) Stockton (WTex) 372 Englewood Dr, Kerrville, TX 78028

WILLIAMS, Jeryln Ann (SD) 431 Sweden St, Caribou, ME 04736

WILLIAMS, Jill Barton (SC) St Francis, 70 Highland St, Holden, MA 01520

WILLIAMS, John (Tex) PO Box 10064, College Station, TX 77842

WILLIAMS II, John F (NY) 860 Wolcott Ave, Beacon, NY 12508

WILLIAMS, Joseph Anthony (CNY) 11 Gillette Ln, Cazenovia, NY 13035

WILLIAMS, Joseph David (NwT) 1105 1/2 Madison St, Borger, TX 79007

WILLIAMS, Josie Marie (Miss) 5930 Warriors Trl, Vicksburg, MS 39180

WILLIAMS, Julie (Az) 100 Arroyo Pinon Dr, Sedona, AZ 86336

WILLIAMS, Larry C (At) Po Box 1117, Hot Springs, AR 71902

WILLIAMS, Lloyd Clyde (Ind) 702 Dr Martin Luther King Jr St, Indianapolis, IN 46202

WILLIAMS, Lois Vander Wende (Cal) 455 Fair Oaks St., San Francisco, CA 94110

WILLIAMS, Lorna H (SVa) 45 Main St, Newport News, VA 23601

WILLIAMS, Margaret A (Chi) 707 1st Ave, Sterling, IL 61081

WILLIAMS, Margaret Mary Oetjen (Tex) 18319 Otter Creek Trl, Humble, TX 77346

WILLIAMS, Mary Grace (NY) 36 New Canaan Road, Wilton, CT 06897

WILLIAMS, Melody Sue (SO) 60 S. Dorset Road, Troy, OH 45373

WILLIAMS, Michael Robert (ND) MNC-I Chaplain, Camp Victory, APO, AE 09342

WILLIAMS, Mildred (Alb) 2304 Deer Trl, Lampasas, TX 76550

WILLIAMS JR, Milton (NC) 1133 N. Lasalle Blvd., Chicago, IL 60610

WILLIAMS, Mollie (Ind) 11335 Winding Wood Ct, Indianapolis, IN 46235

WILLIAMS, Monrelle (Mass) 1073 Tremont St, Roxbury Crossing, MA 02120

WILLIAMS, Pamela Mary (Neb) 1014 N 6th St, Seward, NE 68434

WILLIAMS, Patricia S. (Mo) 336 N Lorimier St, Cape Girardeau, MO 63701

WILLIAMS, Patrick J (NY) 1047 Amsterdam Ave, New York, NY 10025

WILLIAMS, Paul Brazell (SO) 270 Blue Jacket Cir, Pickerington, OH 43147

WILLIAMS, Persis (Alb) Po Box 1662, Blue HIll, ME 04614

WILLIAMS, Peter A (CNY) PO Box 170, 13 Court Street, Cortland, NY 13045

WILLIAMS, Priscilla Mudge (Ct) 80 Lyme Rd., Apt. 212, Hanover, NH 03755

WILLIAMS, R Jane (Be) 1670 Lindberg St, Bethlehem, PA 18020

WILLIAMS, Rick (NC) PO Box 1852, Salisbury, NC 28145

WILLIAMS, Robert (Ore) 11511 SW Bull Mountain Road, Tigard, OR 97224

WILLIAMS, Robert Ernest (ECR) 231 Sunset Ave, Sunnyvale, CA 94086

WILLIAMS, Robert Harry (Oly) 1805 38th Ave, Seattle, WA 98122

WILLIAMS, Robert Lewis (Oly) 3300 Carpenter Rd SE, Electra 109, Lacey, WA 98503

WILLIAMS, R(obert) Samuel (NwPa) 22633 Phillips Dr, Pleasantville, PA 16341

WILLIAMS, Sandra Kaye (SD) 509 Jackson St, Belle Fourche, SD 57717

WILLIAMS, Sandy (Mass) 173 Georgetown Rd, Boxford, MA 01921

WILLIAMS, Scott Eugene (Miss) 1909 15th St, Gulfport, MS 39501

WILLIAMS, Sharon E (O) 2171 E 49th St, Cleveland, OH 44103

WILLIAMS, Sharon Vaughan (Tex)

WILLIAMS, Shawn M (LI) 64 Mount Misery Dr, Sag Harbor, NY 11963

WILLIAMS, Shearon Sykes (Va) 2500 Cameron Mills Rd, Alexandria, VA 22302

WILLIAMS, Stephen Junior Cherrington (RG) 49 1/2 Draper Avenue, Pittsfield, MA 01201

WILLIAMS, Stephen Lee (Los) 14252 Suffolk Street, Westminster, CA 92683

WILLIAMS, Thomas (SwFla) 9404 Oak Meadow Ct, Tampa, FL 33647

WILLIAMS, Thomas Donald (CFla) 3015 Indian River Drive, Palm Bay, FL 32905

WILLIAMS, Wendy (SeFla) 400 Seabrook Rd, Tequesta, FL 33469

WILLIAMS, Wesley Danford (Ve) Iglesia Episcopal de Venezuela, Centro Diocesano Av. Caroní No. 100, Colinas de Bello Monte Caracas 1042-A, Venezuela

WILLIAMS JR, Wesley Samuel (VI) 6501 Red Hook Plz Ste 201, St Thomas, VI 00802

WILLIAMS-DUNCAN, Stacy (WA) 372 El Camino Real, Atherton, CA 94027

WILLIAMSON, Anne (NH) 101 Chapel St, Portsmouth, NH 03801

WILLIAMSON, Barbara (Mass) 451 Concord Rd, Sudbury, MA 01776

WILLIAMSON, Emmanuel (Pa) 1101 2nd Street Pike, Southampton, PA 18966

WILLIAMSON JR, James Gray (SwFla) 8005 25th Street East, Parrish, FL 34219

WILLIAMSON, Jeremiah D (Colo) Grace and St Stephens Episcopal Church, 601 N Tejon St, Colorado Springs, CO 80903

WILLIAMSON, Randolph Lewis (Pa) 343 Michigan Ave, Swarthmore, PA 19081

WILLIAMSON, Rebecca Ann (Az) 1735 S College Ave, Tempe, AZ 85281

WILLIS, Anisa Cottrell (Lex) Cincinnati Childrens Hospital, 3333 Burnett Avenue, Cincinnati, OH 45229

WILLIS, Barbara Creighton (Va) 1905 Wildflower Terrace, Richmond, VA 23238

WILLIS JR, Frederick Webber (SVa) 5119 Blake Point Rd, Chincoteague Island, VA 23336

WILLIS, Laurie Joy (Chi) 1050 Borregas Ave SPC 103, Sunnyvale, CA 94089

WILLIS, Nancy Appleby (RI) 86 Dendron Rd, Wakefield, RI 02879

WILLIS JR, Richard Montgomery (SwVa)

WILLIS, Ronnie (Cal) 137 Caselli Ave, San Francisco, CA 94114

WILLISTON, Ashton K (Ga) 6329 Frederica Rd, Saint Simons Island, GA 31522

WILLMANN JR, Robert Everett (SO) 155 N 6th St, Zanesville, OH 43701

WILLMS, Ann (Va) P.O. Box 426, Ivy, VA 22945

WILLMS, John (Minn) 801 E 2nd St Apt 102, Duluth, MN 55805

WILLOUGHBY III, William (Ga) The Ibert, 224 E 34th Street, Savannah, GA 31401

WILLOW, Mary Margaret Gregory (SwFla) 127 Gesner St, Linden, NJ 07036

WILLS, Clark Edward (Oly) 308 - 14th Avenue East #111, Seattle, WA 98112
WILLS JR, Edwin Francis (Ark) 321 Crystal Ct, Little Rock, AR 72205
WILLS, Robert Murlin (Mich) 1506 Eagle Crest Dr, Prescott, AZ 86301
WILMER, Amelie (Va) 12291 River Rd, Richmond, VA 23238
WILMINGTON, Richard Newton (Cal) 2 Columbia Dr, Rancho Mirage, CA 92270
WILMOT, Susan Elizabeth (Az) 975 E Warner Rd, Tempe, AZ 85284
WILMOTH, Danny Stewart (Va) 3440 S Jefferson St, Falls Church, VA 22041
WILS, Duane Michael (NMich) 6971 Days River 24.5 Rd, Gladstone, MI 49837
WILSON, Anne Warrington (SO) 7730 Tecumseh Trl, Cincinnati, OH 45243
WILSON, Barbara (WMich) 9713 Oakview Dr, Portage, MI 49024
WILSON, Barrie Andrew (CFla)
WILSON JR, Charles (SO) 77 Sherman Ave, Columbus, OH 43205
WILSON JR, Charles Alexander (NwT) 1524 S. Alabama St., Amarilo, TX 79102
WILSON, Charleston D (SwFla) 222 S Palm Ave, Sarasota, FL 34236
WILSON, Charlotte Marie (Cal)
WILSON, Claudia Marie (NY) 1085 Warburton Ave Apt 326, Yonkers, NY 10701
WILSON, Clinton M (Tenn) 4715 Harding Pike, Nashville, TN 37205
WILSON, Conrad Bruce (WTex) 10 Tanglewood St, San Marcos, TX 78666
WILSON, Dana Jane Gant (FtW) 124 Oakmont Dr, Weatherford, TX 76088
WILSON, Donald Rexford (Ore) 7065 S.W. Molalla Bend Rd., Wilsonville, OR 97070
WILSON, Donald Robert (Mass) 76 Old Pine Hill Rd N, Berwick, ME 03901
WILSON, Edward Adrian (ECR) 90 Cashew Blossom Drive, San Jose, CA 95123
WILSON, Eugenia Theresa (NY) 5030 Henry Hudson Pkwy E, Bronx, NY 10471
WILSON JR, Frank E (Minn) 16376 7th Street Lane S, Lakeland, MN 55043
WILSON, Frank F(enn) (At) 803 Wilkins Dr, Monroe, GA 30655
WILSON, George Ira (Mich) 7903 Mesa Trails Cir, Austin, TX 78731
WILSON, George Steil (Oly) 3607 214th Street Southwest, Brier, WA 98036
WILSON, Greg (Pa) 246 Fox Rd, Media, PA 19063
WILSON, Harold David (CFla) 1629 Championship Blvd, Franklin, TN 37064
WILSON, Jack Fowler (EC) 4910 Crosswinds Dr., Apt. 210, Huntsville, AL 35816

WILSON II, James (Minn) 14441 92nd Avenue North, Maple Grove, MN 55369
WILSON, James Barrett (Ky) 7619 Beech Spring Ct, Louisville, KY 40241
WILSON, James G. (Ct) 54 Harbour View Place, Stratford, CT 06615
WILSON, Janey (USC) 144 Caldwell St, Rock Hill, SC 29730
WILSON, Jennifer Mccormick (SeFla)
WILSON, Kate (ECR) 611 Dellingham Dr Apt A, Indianapolis, IN 46260
WILSON, Kellie C (USC) 10 N Church St, Greenville, SC 29601
WILSON, Kenneth Wayne (CNY) 7863 Russell Ln, Manlius, NY 13104
WILSON, Linda (RG) 109 Chaparral Loop, Socorro, NM 87801
WILSON, Linda Latham (Alb) PO Box 154, 627 Roses Brook Rd, South Kortright, NY 13842
WILSON, Linda Tardy (Pgh) 215 Canterbury Ln, North Versailles, PA 15137
WILSON, Mary Elizabeth (Tex) 717 Sage Road, Houston, TX 77056
WILSON, Mauricio Jose (Cal) 114 Montecito Ave, Oakland, CA 94610
WILSON, Michael Hoover (SwFla) 5108 Plainfield Street, Midland, MI 48642
WILSON III, Morris Karl (Tenn) 3002 Westmoreland Dr, Nashville, TN 37212
WILSON, Norbert Lance Weston (Ala) 136 E Magnolia Ave, Auburn, AL 36830
WILSON, Phillip Dana (Nwk) 36 South St, Morristown, NJ 07960
WILSON, Ray Eugene (Tex) Po Box 1943, Lenox, MA 01240
WILSON, Raymond G (LI) 165 Pine St, Freeport, NY 11520
WILSON, Richard (Az)
WILSON, Richard Lawrence (CFla)
WILSON, Robert Arthur (Vt) PO Box 244, Newport, VT 05855
WILSON, Roy Dennis (Miss) 1954 Spillway Rd, Brandon, MS 39047
WILSON, Sandra Antoinette (Nwk) 116 Turrell Ave, South Orange, NJ 07079
WILSON, Stefanie G (Los) Campbell Hall School, 4533 Laurel Canyon Blvd, North Hollywood, CA 91607
WILSON, Stephen Thomas (Colo) 1530 Cherry St, Denver, CO 80220
WILSON, Steven Clark (WMo) 1213 Grand Ave, Carthage, MO 64836
WILSON, Thomas (SanD) 339 Brightwood Ave, Chula Vista, CA 91910
WILSON, Thomas Stuart (Tenn) 1000 Sunnyside Dr, Columbia, TN 38401
WILSON, Tom (EC) 101 Bear Track Ln, Kitty Hawk, NC 27949
WILSON, Tom (SC) 1853 Grovehurst Dr, Charleston, SC 29414

WILSON, William Henry (Ala) 800 Lake Colony Cir, Birmingham, AL 35242
WILSON-BARNARD, Letha (Minn) Holy Apostles, 2200 Minnehaha Ave E, Saint Paul, MN 55119
WILT, David (SeFla) 415 Duval St, Key West, FL 33040
WILTFONG, Michele (WNC)
WILTON, Glenn Warner Paul (Oly) 10 Lichfield Avenue, CANTERBURY, CT1 3YA, Great Britain (UK)
WILTSEE JR, Lamont (ECR) 138 White Oaks Lane, Carmel Valley, CA 93924
✠ **WIMBERLY**, Don Adger (Tex) 3515 Plumb St, Houston, TX 77005
WIMBUSH, Claire S (SVa) 1333 Jamestown Rd, Williamsburg, VA 23185
WIMMER, Lisa Jan (CFla) PO Box 2373, Belleview, FL 34421
WINBORN JR, James Henderson (SVa) 8880 Colonnades Ct W Apt 412, Bonita Springs, FL 34135
WINCHELL, Ron (Va) 128 Eagle Ct, Locust Grove, VA 22508
WINDAL, Claudia L (Minn) 1532 Randolph Ave, Apt. 8, St. Paul,, MN 55105
WINDEL, Marian Kathleen (Va) 1782 Yanceyville Road, Louisa, VA 23093
WINDOM, Barbara Sewell (At) 432 Forest Hill Rd, Macon, GA 31210
WINDSOR, Janice Priebe (Colo) 33741 State Highway 257, Windsor, CO 80550
WINDSOR, Robert Grover (Mass) 34 Exeter Street, West Newton, MA 02465
WINDSOR, Walter Van Zandt (Ark) PO Box 2164, Woodville, MS 39669
WINELAND, Richard Kevin (NI) 64669 Orchard Dr, Goshen, IN 46526
WING III, Arthur K (NY) 7 Van Alstine Ave, Suffern, NY 10901
WINGER, Nordon W. (Az) Good Shepherd Episcopal Church, P.O. Box 110, Cave Creek, AZ 85327
WINGERT, Anita LaVonne (NMich) 550 N Ravine St, Sault Sainte Marie, MI 49783
WINGERT JR, John Alton (CNY) 1244 Great Pond Road, Box 116, Great Pond, ME 04408
WINGFIELD, Vest Garrett (Tex) PO Box 540742, Houston, TX 77254
WINGO, Patrick J (ETenn) Diocese of Virginia, 110 W Franklin St, Richmond, VA 23220
WINGO, Sara-Scott Nelson (ETenn) 800 S Northshore Dr, Knoxville, TN 37919
WINKLER, Anne Louise (Ind) 7300 Lantern Rd, Indianapolis, IN 46256
WINKLER JR, Richard Edward (The Episcopal Church in Haw) 202 Pin Oak Dr, Harker Heights, TX 76548
WINKLER, Thomas Earl (Minn) 39259 K-C Dr, Winona, MN 55987
WINKLER JR, William Edward (NY)

WINN, John Barrington (Oly) Po Box 1961, Silverdale, WA 98383

WINNER, Lauren Frances (NC) 1737 Hillandale Rd, Durham, NC 27705

WINSETT, Steve (Chi) 2512 Bradley Ave, Louisville, KY 40217

WINSLETT JR, Hoyt (Ala) 1224 - 37th Avenue East, Tuscaloosa, AL 35404

WINSLOW, Gail George (NwPa) Church of the Ascension, 26 Chautauqua Place, Bradford, PA 16701

WINSLOW JR, K Dennis (NY) P.O. Box 93 (5023 Delaware Turnpike), RENSSELAERVILLE, NY 12147

WINSOR, Michael Michael (NY) 7602 Woodthrush Drive, Dallas, TX 75230

WINSTON, William (FtW) 3313 Minot Ave, Fort Worth, TX 76133

WINTER, Brian William (Colo) 12408 Prospect Ave. NE, Albuquerque, NM 87112

WINTER, Cheryl Ann (WVa) Po Box 424, Hurricane, WV 25526

WINTER, James L (Miss) 684 White Oak Ln, Starkville, MS 39759

WINTER, Laren Royce (RG) Po Box 2963, Ruidoso, NM 88355

WINTER JR, Lloyd H (Pa) 238 Street Rd Apt C111, Southampton, PA 18966

WINTER CHASER, Vivian Janice (Az) 725 S. Beck Ave, Tempe, AZ 85281

✠ **WINTERROWD**, William Jerry (Colo)

WINTERS JR, Charles Layfaette (WNC) 6 Timson Road, Apt B4, Asheville, NC 28803

WINTERS, Richard (Ind) 5502 Washington Blvd, Indianapolis, IN 46220

WINTERS, William Michael (Ala) PO Box 116, Guntersville, AL 35976

WINTON, Keith (Neb)

WINTON, Paul Steve (NC) Saint John's Episcopal Church, 1623 Carmel Rd, Charlotte, NC 28226

WINWARD, Mark Scott (Spr) 206 Jenkins Rd, Saco, ME 04072

WIRENIUS, John Francis (NY)

WIRES, John William (At) 4900 English Dr, Annandale, VA 22003

WIRTH, Bradley S (Mont) All Saints' Church, PO Box 1923, Whitefish, MT 59937

WISCHMEYER, Kara (NwT) 226 Chuck Wagon Rd., Lubbock, TX 79404

WISE, Christopher Matthew (WTex) 315 E Pecan St, San Antonio, TX 78205

WISE JR, Eugene Field (Tenn) Po Box 261, Murfreesboro, TN 37133

WISELEY, Jerry Lee (SC) 1746 Summit Rd, Hot Springs, SD 57747

WISEMAN, Grant Buchanan (USC) 125 Pendleton St. S.W., Aiken, SC 29801

WISEMAN, Heather Buchanan (SO) 2489 Walnutview Ct, Cincinnati, OH 45230

WISEMAN, Philip M (SO) 2489 Walnutview Ct, Cincinnati, OH 45230

WISKUS, Richard Joseph (Mo) 1151 W Columbia St, Farmington, MO 63640

WISMER, Robert D (Tex) 11310 Meadow Lake Dr, Houston, TX 77077

WISNER, Stephen Forster (NJ) 304 Woodmere Ave, Neptune, NJ 07753

WISNEWSKI JR, Robert Carew (Ala) 113 Madison Ave, Montgomery, AL 36104

WISNIEWSKI, Richard Joseph (NJ) Church Of The Holy Spirit, PO Box 174, Tuckerton, NJ 08087

WISSINK, Charles Jay (Pa) 54 Sugarplum Rd, Levittown, PA 19056

WISSLER, Kenneth John (Pa) 201 Evergreen Ave. Apt. 904, Philadelphia, PA 19118

✠ **WITCHER SR**, Robert Campbell (LI) 1934 Steele Blvd, Baton Rouge, LA 70808

WITCHGER, Anne Marie (NY) 1085 5th Ave, New York, NY 10128

WITH, David (WMo) 160 Terrace Trl W, Lake Quivira, KS 66217

WITH, Jan Louise (Neb) St Marys Episcopal Church, 212 Clark St, Bassett, NE 68714

WITHROCK JR, John William (CGC) 401 W College St, Troy, AL 36081

WITKE, E(Dward) Charles (Mich) 3000 Glazier Way, Ann Arbor, MI 48105

WITT, Anne Lane (Va) PO Box 1059, Kilmarnock, VA 22482

WITT, Bonnie Rae (WNY) Po Box 66, Gasport, NY 14067

WITT JR, Richard Cyril (NY) 16 Lawrence Rd, Accord, NY 12404

WITT JR, Robert Edward (Alb) P.O. Box 123, Morris, NY 13808

WITTIG, Nancy Constantine Hatch (Pa) 21801 Elizabeth Ave, Fairview Park, OH 44126

WITTMAYER, Kevin Edward (Tex) 906 Padon St, Longview, TX 75601

WIZOREK, Julie C (Md) 249 Double Oak Rd N, Prince Frederick, MD 20678

WLOSINSKI, Stephen Stanley (Minn) 1121 W Morgan St, Duluth, MN 55811

WODEHOUSE, Priscilla Davis (WNC)

WOEHLER, Charles (WTex) 1416 North Loop 1604 East, San Antonio, TX 78232

WOESSNER, David H (WMass) WOGGON, Harry (WNC) 5 Norwich Dr, Asheville, NC 28803

WOGGON, Karla (WA) 1048 15th Ave. N.W., Hickory, NC 28601

WOHLERS, Lee Ferry (Vt) 7297 Vt Route 14, Hardwick, VT 05843

WOHLEVER, Russell J (CFla) All Saints Church, 338 E Lyman Ave, Winter Park, FL 32789

WOJCIEHOWSKI, Arthur Anthony (Minn) 1500 Prospect Ave, Cloquet, MN 55720

WOLCOTT, Sarah Elizabeth (Neb) 512 N Oak St, Gordon, NE 69343

WOLF, David B (WA) 1516 Hamilton St NW, Washington, DC 20011

✠ **WOLF**, Gerry (RI) 275 N Main St, Providence, RI 02903

WOLF, Max J (Del) 20 Olive Ave, Rehoboth Beach, DE 19971

WOLFE, Alexander (ND) Po Box 8340, Fargo, ND 58109

✠ **WOLFE**, Dean (NY) 835 SW Polk St, Topeka, KS 66612

WOLFE, Dorothy Annabell (Neb) 603 3rd Ave, Bayard, NE 69334

WOLFE, John M (SwFla) 501 Erie Ave, Tampa, FL 33606

WOLFE, Vernon Eugene (Oly) 53565 W Ferndale Rd, Milton Freewater, OR 97862

WOLFENBARGER, Mary Suzanne (WLa) 55 Magnolia Dr, Belleville, IL 62221

WOLFF, Edda Stephanie (Eur)

WOLFF, William George (Kan) 306 W. Euclid St., Pittsburg, KS 66762

WOLFORD, Rachael Rossiter (Oly) PO Box 522, Cathlamet, WA 98612

WOLLARD, Robert Foster (Mich) 4505 Westlawn Pkwy, Waterford, MI 48328

WOLSONCROFT III, Arthur Mathew (NY) 414 E 52nd St, New York, NY 10022

WOLTER, Jack M (WNY) 668 Shadow Mountain Dr, Prescott, AZ 86301

WOLTERSTORFF, Claire Kingma (WMich) 58 Sunnybrook Ave Se, Grand Rapids, MI 49506

WOLTZ, Charles Morris (Okla) 924 N Robinson Ave, Oklahoma City, OK 73102

WOLYNIAK, Joseph Geoffrey (Pa) 53 University Pl, Princeton, NJ 08540

WOMACK JR, Egbert Morton (Colo) 7500 E Dartmouth Ave Unit 31, Denver, CO 80231

WOMACK, Lawrence (LI) 8725 Sedgeburn Drive, Charlotte, NC 28278

WOMELSDORF, Charles Stowers (CGC) 327 Honeysuckle Hill, Tallassee, AL 36078

WON, Hogil Hilary (Nwk) 403 79th St, North Bergen, NJ 07047

WON, Jonathan Sung Ho (Nwk) 16423 Maidstone Avenue, Norwalk, CA 90650

WONDRA, Ellen K (Chi) Bexley Seabury Seminary Federation, 1407 E 60th St, Chicago, IL 60637

WONG, Diane (Mass) 5B Park Terr, Arlington, MA 02474

WONG, George C (Nwk) 6030 Grosvenor Ln, Bethesda, MD 20814

WONG, Gloria Violet Lee (Mass) Po Box 825, Oak Bluffs, MA 02557

WONG, Peter Reginald (CGC) Church of the Nativity, 205 Holly Ln, Dothan, AL 36301

WONG, Philip (Oly) 62 Pine St., Rockville Centre, NY 11570

WONG, Sally (ECR)

WOO, Raymond A (The Episcopal Church in Haw) 45 N Judd St, Honolulu, HI 96817

WOOD, Ann Patricia (WMass) 13 Kelleher Dr, South Deerfield, MA 01373

WOOD, Camille Carpenter (La) 3552 Morning Glory Ave, Baton Rouge, LA 70808

WOOD, Charles Leon (Mich) 608 Lily Pl, Southern Pines, NC 28387

WOOD, Christian Michael (SwFla)

WOOD, Colette (Mass) 16 Highland Ave., Cohasset, MA 02025

WOOD, David Romaine (Colo) 1233 24th Ave. Ct., Greeley, CO 80634

WOOD, Grace Marie (EC) 198 Dogwood Trl, Elizabeth City, NC 27909

WOOD, Gretchen A (SO) 24 High Ridge Loop Apt 605, Pawleys Island, SC 29585

WOOD, Henry Palmer (CFla) 720 S Lakeshore Blvd, Lake Wales, FL 33853

WOOD, Howard Fitler (Pa) 526 Washington Ave, Hulmeville, PA 19047

WOOD, Hunter (Va) 250 Pantops Mountain Rd Apt 5126, Charlottesville, VA 22911

WOOD, Jan (O) Grace Episcopal Church, 315 Wayne Street, Sandusky, OH 44870

WOOD, Joseph A (Md) Emmanuel Church, 811 Cathedral St, Baltimore, MD 21201

WOOD, Kathrine Ringold (Ore) 437 Franklin St, Denver, CO 80218

WOOD, Linda Anne (Cal) 3080 Birdsall Ave, Oakland, CA 94619

WOOD, Mark Raymond (Ct) 89 Eddy Street, Providence, RI 02903

WOOD, Michael J (WMich)

WOOD, Nancy Currey (SVa) 1524 Southwick Rd, Virginia Beach, VA 23451

WOOD, Priscilla Peacock (Mass) 302 Linden Ponds Way Unit 512, Hingham, MA 02043

✠ **WOOD JR**, R aymond Stewart (Mich) Kendal 157, 80 Lyme Rd, Hanover, NH 03755

WOOD, Rob (WNC) 12132 Walnut Ter, Alpharetta, GA 30004

WOOD, Robert Earl (WMo) 1009 W 57th St, Kansas City, MO 64113

WOOD, Rodgers Taylor (WVa) 1223 Stanford Court, Coraopolis, PA 15108

WOOD, Roger Lee (EMich) 106 S Kennefic St, Yale, MI 48097

WOOD, Sammy (Tenn) 30 Brimmer St, Boston, MA 02108

WOOD, Sarah Anne (Va) 86 Fourth Ave., New York, NY 10003

WOOD, Stuart Clary (Va) 7120 Ore Bank Rd, Port Republic, VA 24471

WOOD III, William Hoge (Pa) 251 Montgomery Ave Unit 9, Haverford, PA 19041

WOOD, William James (Kan) 30 Spofford Lane, Trevett, ME 04571

WOOD JR, William R (WVa) 107 Elma Dr, Williamstown, WV 26187

WOODALL, Carolyn Louise (Episcopal SJ) Episcopal Church of St. Anne, 1020 W Lincoln Rd, Stockton, CA 95207

WOODALL JR, Percy J (At) 3663 SE Cambridge Drive, Stuart, FL 34997

WOODARD, Sarah Wilson (NC) 400 Moline St., Durham, NC 27707

WOODBURY, Kimberly Jean (VI) All Saints Cathedral, PO Box 1148, St Thomas, VI 00804

WOODBURY, Robert Lane (Mil) 5558 N Berkeley Blvd, Whitefish Bay, WI 53217

WOODCOCK, Bruce W (SeFla) 106 Castle Heights Ave, Nyack, NY 10960

WOODEN, Lorentho (SO) 550 E 4th St, Cincinnati, OH 45202

WOODFIN, Joseph Robert (ETenn) 305 W 7th St, Chattanooga, TN 37402

WOODHOUSE, Michelle M (Los) 4125 Creciente Dr, Santa Barbara, CA 93110

WOOD-HULL, L. D. (Ore) 6151 Willers Way, Houston, TX 77057

WOODLEY, Claire (LI) 2 Glendale Rd, Ossining, NY 10562

WOODLIEF, Vern Andrews (Az) 1069 N Paseo Iris, Green Valley, AZ 85614

WOODLIFF III, George (Miss) 712 S Montgomery St, Starkville, MS 39759

WOODLIFF, Kirk Alan (Nev) 2125 Stone View Dr, Sparks, NV 89436

WOODLIFF-STANLEY, Ruth M (Colo) 1945 Ivanhoe St, Denver, CO 80220

WOODLING, Edith (At) 25 Battle Ridge Pl Ne, Atlanta, GA 30342

WOODROOFE III, Robert (Ct) 42 Christian Street, New Preston, CT 06777

WOODRUFF, Jennifer Lynn (Lex) 449 Hackett Pike, Richmond, KY 40475

WOODRUFF, Karen (Va) Po Box 367, Lively, VA 22507

WOODRUM, Donald Lee (Fla) Po Box 1238, Live Oak, FL 32064

WOODS, Blake (Okla) 5635 E 71st St, Tulsa, OK 74136

WOODS, Harold Dean (Vt) 233 South Street, South Hero, VT 05486

WOODS JR, J (Mass) 62 Las Casas St, Malden, MA 02148

WOODS, James Christopher (Mass) 121 Freeport Boulevard, Toms River, NJ 08757

WOODS, John Michael (Dal) Rr 1 Box 253-A, Mount Vernon, TX 75457

WOODS, Joshua Wayne (CGC) 1300 Wiltshire Ave, San Antonio, TX 78209

WOODS, Michael Timothy (WTex) 3039 Ranch Road 12, San Marcos, TX 78666

WOODS, Robert Douglas (Episcopal SJ) Po Box 1837, Kernville, CA 93238

WOODS, Stephen I (NY) Above, Above, NM 87507

WOODSUM, Mark (Me) 2808 Lakemont Dr, Fallbrook, CA 92028

WOODWARD JR, Brinton Webb (NH) RR3 Box 18, Plymouth, NH 03264

WOODWARD, Deborah Marshall (Mass) 1080 Hillside St, Milton, MA 02186

WOODWARD III, George Frederick (Los) 1294 Westlyn Pl, Pasadena, CA 91104

WOODWARD, Lynn Christophersen (Okla) 4604 E 54th St Apt 203, Tulsa, OK 74135

WOODWARD, Matthew (Cal) 3900 Alameda De Las Pulgas, San Mateo, CA 94403

WOODWARD, Thomas Bullene (RG) 13 Calle Loma, Santa Fe, NM 87507

WOODWORTH, Laura T(Ufts) (NMich) 2500 South Hill Road, Gladstone, MI 49837

WOODWORTH-HILL, Nancy (Ind) 321 E Market St, Jeffersonville, IN 47130

WOODY, Robert (WTex) 13638 Liberty Oak, San Antonio, TX 78232

WOOLERY-PRICE, Edward Raymond (Tex) All Saints' Episcopal Church, 209 W 27th St, Austin, TX 78705

WOOLIVER, Tammy (Okla) 264 Woodbriar, Noble, OK 73068

WOOLLEN, Nancy Sewell (Ind)

WOOLLETT JR, Donald M (WLa)

WOOLLEY JR, Arthur Everett (Md) 13 Basswood Ct, Catonsville, MD 21228

WOOLLEY JR, Stanley Marsh (WMass) 868 Butler Drive, Livingston, SC 29107

WOOLLEY, Steven Eugene (Spok) 1803 Crestline Dr, Walla Walla, WA 99362

WOOLSEY, Deborah J (SO) St Paul's Episcopal Church, 33 W Dixon Ave, Dayton, OH 45419

WOOMER JR, Harold Gerard (Nev)

WOOTTEN, Jo Ann H (Ark) 346 Rock Springs Rd., Wake Forest, NC 27587

WOOTTEN III, Mid (Ark) 346 N Rock Springs Rd, Wake Forest, NC 27587

WORLEY, James Paul (WTex) 389 Valley View Dr, Cibolo, TX 78108

WORTH, Elsa H (NH) St James Church, 44 West St, Keene, NH 03431

WORTHINGTON, Cynthia Muirhead (RG) 6043 Royal Crk, San Antonio, TX 78239

WORTHINGTON JR, Daniel Owen (Va) P O Box 83, Gloucester, VA 23061

WORTHINGTON, William Ray (Ga) 207 Hermitage Way, Saint Simons Island, GA 31522

WORTHLEY, Christopher Thomas (Los) 2114 De La Vina St Unit 1, Santa Barbara, CA 93105

WOS, Edward John (ND)

WOSIKOWSKI, Thomas J (Mil) 4901 Hob St, Madison, WI 53716

WRAMPELMEIER, Christopher Kent (NwT) 2602 Parker St, Amarillo, TX 79109

WRATHALL, Susan L (RI) 70 Moore St., Warwick, RI 02889

WRATTEN, Kenneth Bruce (ECR) 8640 Solera Drive, San Jose, CA 95135

WREDE, Anne (NJ) 37 Northfield Rd, Millington, NJ 07946

WREDE, Richard Charles (NJ) 500 Fourth St, Riverton, NJ 08077

WREN, Dane Clark (CFla) 302 Bent Way Ln, 700 Rinehart Rd, Lake Mary, FL 32746

WRIDER, Anne Johnson (SO) 5455 N Sheridan Rd Apt 3912, Chicago, IL 60640

WRIGHT, Allan McLean (WMass) Po Box 3504, Annapolis, MD 21403

WRIGHT, Andrew Ray (FtW) 1700 N. Westmoreland Rd., Desoto, TX 75115

WRIGHT, Angus Dale (NMich) PO Box 302, Manistique, MI 49854

WRIGHT, Benjamin R (RG) 363 Park St, Beaver, PA 15009

WRIGHT, Bill (NwT) 3549 Clearview Dr, San Angelo, TX 76904

WRIGHT, Brian Theodore (Oly) 105 State St 5, Kirkland, WA 98033

✠ **WRIGHT**, Carl W (AFFM) Apo Ae 0962, PSC2 Box 9808, Ramstein, Germany

WRIGHT, Catherine Louise (Tex) 301 E 8th St, Austin, TX 78701

WRIGHT, Diana Lee (Ia)

WRIGHT, Elizabeth Louise (RI) 10 Eustis Ave, Newport, RI 02840

WRIGHT, Elton Stanley (Colo) 342 Old Cahaba Trail, Helena, AL 35080

WRIGHT, Eugene Nat (WA)

WRIGHT, Gwynne (Chi) 43 Rawcliffe Croft, York, YO305US, Great Britain (UK)

WRIGHT, Hollis E (Colo) 92-1010 Kanehoa Loop, Kapolei, HI 96707

WRIGHT, James D (Fla) 3231 Nw 47th Pl, Gainesville, FL 32605

WRIGHT, James O. Pete (Los) 1505 Monticello Ct., Redlands, CA 92373

WRIGHT, Janice Bracken (At) 7 Creek Side Way SW, Rome, GA 30165

WRIGHT, Jean Ann Frances (At) 5228 Stone Village Cir Nw, Kennesaw, GA 30152

WRIGHT, Jeannene F (SO)

WRIGHT, Jo (Okla) 821 N Foreman St Apt 118, Vinita, OK 74301

WRIGHT, John Hamil Spedden (Del) 54 Ridge Ave, Edgewater, MD 21037

WRIGHT, John Robert (NY) General Theological Seminary, 175 9th Ave, New York, NY 10011

WRIGHT, Jonathan M (SC) 1295 Abercorn Trce, Mount Pleasant, SC 29466

WRIGHT, Korey J (Tex)

WRIGHT, Lonell (La) 7696 Stevenson Way, San Diego, CA 92120- 2229

WRIGHT, Mark R (Dal) 2019 Highland Forest Dr, Highland Village, TX 75077

WRIGHT III, Martin Luther (Pgh) 1249 Main Street, PO Box 175, Shanksville, PA 15560

WRIGHT, Matthew L (NY) St Gregory's Episcopal Church, PO Box 66, Woodstock, NY 12498

WRIGHT, Michael Alfred (Oly) 1428 22nd Ave, Longview, WA 98632

WRIGHT, Milton King (Minn) 707 Saint Olaf Ave, Northfield, MN 55057

WRIGHT, Rick Lynn (At)

✠ **WRIGHT**, Robert Christopher (At) 306 Peyton Rd Sw, Atlanta, GA 30311

WRIGHT, Ross Mcgowan (SVa) 4203 Springhill Ave, Richmond, VA 23225

WRIGHT, Ryan A (SwFla) Saint Paul's, 3901 Davis Blvd, Naples, FL 34104

WRIGHT, Scot R (Oly) 650 Bellevue Way NE, Unit 2401, Bellevue, WA 98004

WRIGHT, Stanalee (Spok)

WRIGHT, Stuart Wayne (Md) 4 E. University Pkwy., Baltimore, MD 21218

✠ **WRIGHT**, Wayne (Del) 1841 North St, Philadelphia, PA 19130

WRIGHT, William J (Alb) 14 Monument St, Deposit, NY 13754

WRIGHT, Winston (SeFla) 1466 39th St, West Palm Beach, FL 33407

WU, Ming-Lung (Tai) No. 1-6 Mingxin St, Hualien City, 97050, Taiwan

WU, Peter (The Episcopal Church in Haw) 229 Queen Emma Sq, Honolulu, HI 96813

WU, Shing-Shaing (Tai) 499 Sec 4 Danjin Rd, Tamsui Dist, New Taipei City, 25135, Taiwan

WURM, Laurie J (Nwk)

WYATT, Andrea Castner (RI) 133 School St, New Bedford, MA 02740

WYATT, Benjamin Keith (Tenn)

WYATT II, Robert Odell (Chi) 110 S Marion St Unit 307, Oak Park, IL 60302

WYCKOFF, Mike (Tex) 2857 Grimes Ranch Rd, Austin, TX 78732

WYER, George William (Va) Po Box 638, Ivy, VA 22945

WYLAND, Richard Rees (Roch) 41 Great Oak Ln, Redding, CT 06896

WYLD, Kevin Andrew (CFla) 3440 N Goldenrod Rd Apt 1016, Winter Park, FL 32792

WYLIE, Craig Robert (SwVa) 170 Crestview Dr, Abingdon, VA 24210

WYLY JR, David F (SwFla)

WYMAN, Deborah Little (Mass) 986 Memorial Dr, Cambridge, MA 02138

WYMER, Seth Thomas (SO) 5101 Johnstown Rd, New Albany, OH 43054

WYNDER JR, Charles Allen (WA)

WYNDHAM, Beth Ann (WTex) St Thomas Episcopal Church, 1416 N Loop 1604 E, San Antonio, TX 78232

WYNEN, Nancy (Oly) 1399 Sw 17th St, Boca Raton, FL 33486

WYNN, James E (Pa) 520 S 61st St, Philadelphia, PA 19143

WYNN, Ronald Lloyd (Ore) 355 Stadium Dr S, Monmouth, OR 97361

WYPER, Susan (Ct) St Matthew's Episcopal Church, 382 Cantitoe st, Bedford, NY 10506

WYSOCK, Christine Phillips (Spok) 535 Shelokum Dr, Silverton, OR 97381

WYSONG, Terry Marie (Ct) PO Box 606, Marion, CT 06444

X

XIE, Songling (LI) 13532 38th Ave, Flushing, NY 11354

Y

YABROFF, Martin I Rving (Oly) 3914 136th St Ct NW, Gig Harbor, WA 98332

YAGERMAN, Steve (NY) 234 E 60th St, New York, NY 10022

YAKUBU-MADUS, Fatima Emitsela (Ind) 5625 W 30th St, Speedway, IN 46224

YALE, Elizabeth (NwPa) 1151 Buffalo St, Franklin, PA 16323

YALE, Richard Barrington (The Episcopal NCal) 4 Quista Dr., Chico, CA 95926

YAMAMOTO, Keith Akio (Los) 330 E. 16th Street, Upland, CA 91784

YANCEY, David Warren (Tenn) 1390 Jones Creek Rd, Dickson, TN 37055

YANCEY, Nancy (At) 5480 Clinchfield Trl, Norcross, GA 30092

YANCY, Stephanie Pauline (NC) 5606 Carey Pl, Durham, NC 27712

YANDELL, George Shaw (At) Church of the Holy Family, 202 Griffith Rd, Jasper, GA 30143

YANNI, Timothy John (U) 9447 S 2555 W, South Jordan, UT 84095

YAO, Ting Chang (Cal) 1111 Larch Ave, Moraga, CA 94556

YARBOROUGH, Buzz (WTex) 121 Peppertree Crossing Ave, Brunswick, GA 31525

YARBOROUGH, Clare McJimsey (Az) 5671 E. Copper Street, Tucson, AZ 85712

YARBROUGH, C Denise (Roch) St. Mark's Episcopal Church, 179 Main St., Penn Yan, NY 14527

YARBROUGH, Douglas (Ida) 1312 W Elmore Ave, Nampa, ID 83651

YARBROUGH, Eileen Elizabeth (Ida) 524 Ruth Ln, Nampa, ID 83686

YARBROUGH, Oliver Larry (Vt) 24 Oak Dr, Middlebury, VT 05753

YARBROUGH, Rebecca Ricketts (NC) P.O. Box 970, Davidson, NC 28036

YARSIAH, James (SC) 1324 Marvin Ave, Charleston, SC 29407

YATES, Adam Benjamin (Ct) 23 Parker Bridge Rd, Andover, CT 06232

YATES, Christopher Garrett () 1066 Washington Rd, Mt Lebanon, PA 15228

YATES, Dorothy Gene (Cal)

YATES, Robert Gordon (SwFla) 37505 Moore Dr, Dade City, FL 33525

YATES, William J (CFla) 3400 Wingmann Rd., Avon Park, FL 33825

YAW, Chris (Mich) St David's Episcopal Church, 16200 W 12 Mile Rd, Southfield, MI 48076

YAW, David Dixon (Ak) 3195 Jackson Heights St, Ketchikan, AK 99901

YAWN, Justin (Tex) Christ Episcopal Church, 400 San Juan Dr, Ponte Vedra Beach, FL 32082

YEAGER, Alice Elizabeth (ND) 301 Main St S, Minot, ND 58701

YEAGER, Linda (WMo) 11701 Wedd St Apt 9, Overland Park, KS 66210

YEAGER, Robert Timothy (Chi) 924 Lake Street, Oak Park, IL 60301

YEARWOOD, Kirtley (Oly) Church Of Saint Alban The Martyr, 11642 Farmers Blvd, Saint Albans, NY 11412

YEATES, Judith Ann (Neb) 6615 N 162 St, Omaha, NE 68116

YEOMAN III, Eric Burdett (Cal) 1633 Argonne Dr, Stockton, CA 95203

YEPES LOPEZ, Alvaro Nelson (DR (DomRep)) Iglesia Episcopal Dominicana, Calle Santiago No 114, Santo Domingo, 764, Dominican Republic

YERKES, Kenneth Bickford (Mo) 1 Macarthur Blvd Apt S503, Haddon Township, NJ 08108

YESKO, Francis Michael (Pgh) Episcopal Diocese Of Pittsburgh, 4099 William Penn Hwy Ste 502, Monroeville, PA 15146

YETTER, Joan (Mont) 932 Avenue F, Billings, MT 59102

YODER, Christopher W (Okla)

YODER, John Henry (Nev) 1151 Carlton Ct Apt202, Fort Pierce, FL 34949

YONKERS, Michael Allan (Chi) 920 S Aldine Ave, Park Ridge, IL 60068

YOON, Paul Hwan (Los) Box 22, Taejon, 300, Korea (South)

YOON, Young Suk (Nwk) 65 Union Ave, Little Falls, NJ 07424

YORK, Susan Spence (WMich) 2490 Basswood St, Jenison, MI 49428

YORK-SIMMONS, Noelle M (Va) 118 N Washington St, Alexandria, VA 22314

YOSHIDA, Thomas Kunio (The Episcopal Church in Haw) 1410 Makiki St, Honolulu, HI 96814

YOST, Martin C (Dal) 114 George Street, Providence, RI 02906

YOTTER, Katherine Ann (CFla) 6400 N Socrum Loop Rd, Lakeland, FL 33809

YOULL MARSHALL, Lynda Mary (Va)

YOUMANS, Timothy Sean (Okla) Casady School, 9500 N Pennsylvania Ave, Oklahoma City, OK 73120

YOUNG, Adam A (CFla) 2017 6th Ave N, Birmingham, AL 35203

YOUNG JR, Albert Leroy (Los) 1215 Del Mar Dr, Los Osos, CA 93402

YOUNG, Bernard Orson Dwight (LI) 18917 Turin Dr, Saint Albans, NY 11412

YOUNG, Bruce Alan (Mass) 46 Laurel St., Gloucester, MA 01930

YOUNG, Francene (Tex) 605 West 9th Street, Houston, TX 77007

YOUNG, Frank Whitman (Ala) 109 Hannah Lane, Oak Grove, AL 35150

YOUNG, Gary (EO) 665 Parsons Road, Hood River, OR 97031

YOUNG, Gary Reid (Neb) 17 Brentwood Ct, Scottsbluff, NE 69361

YOUNG, Gary Todd (Md) 101 S Prospect St, Hagerstown, MD 21740

✠ **YOUNG III**, George (ETenn) 814 Episcopal School Way, Knoxville, TN 37932

YOUNG, James (Minn) 2105 Ontario Lane, revjryoung@gmail.com, Northfield, MN 55057

YOUNG, James Joseph (Los) 12868 Hacienda Dr., Studio City, CA 91604

YOUNG, James Oliver (Okla) 2207 Ridgeway St, Ardmore, OK 73401

YOUNG, James Robert (The Episcopal NCal) Po Box 2334, Avila Beach, CA 93424

YOUNG, Jim (SwVa) 5260 Triad Court SE, Salem, OR 97306

YOUNG, Johanna Harriman (NH)

YOUNG, Kammy Mary (CGC) 302 N Reus St, Pensacola, FL 32501

YOUNG, Kathryn McMillan (Tenn) 704 Park Blvd, Austin, TX 78751

YOUNG, Linda M (Spok) 1410 NE Stadium Way, Pullman, WA 99163

YOUNG, Malcolm Clemens (Cal) 2674 St. Giles Lane, Mt. View, CA 94040

YOUNG, Mary Catherine (NY) Canterbury Downtown, 12 W. 11th Street, New York, NY 10011

YOUNG JR, Patterson (Dal) 617 Church St., Sulphur Springs, TX 75482

YOUNG, Ronald Bruce (Roch) Christ Episcopal Church, 26 S. Main St., Pittsford, NY 14534

YOUNG, S Matthew (Lex) 7 Court Pl, Newport, KY 41071

YOUNG, Shari Maruska (Cal) P.O. Box 872, Tiburon, CA 94920

YOUNG, Sherry Lawry (Mich) 5584 Lapeer Rd Apt 1D, Kimball, MI 48074

YOUNG, Tammy May (NJ)

YOUNG, William King (Az) 12440 W Firebird Dr, Sun City West, AZ 85375

YOUNGBLOOD, Susan Russell (Chi) 825 N Taylor Ave, Oak Park, IL 60302

YOUNGSON, Charles (Ala) 315 Devon Dr., Birmingham, AL 35209

YOUNKIN, Randy John (Pgh) 431 Alameda Ave, Youngstown, OH 44504

YOUNKIN, Ronald Willingham (Pgh)

YOUNT, Amy Clark (WA) 3801 Newark St Nw Apt E431, Washington, DC 20016

YOUSE JR, Don C (Pgh) 955 West North Avenue, Pittsburgh, PA 15233

YSKAMP, Janis (CPa) 813 Valley Rd, Mansfield, PA 16933

YUDASZ, Mitchell Victor (Mich)

YULE, Marilynn Fritz (Spok) PO Box 6318, Kennewick, WA 99336

YUNG, Bernard Yu (The Episcopal Church in Haw)

YUNKER, Judy Lee (Lex) 562 University Dr, Prestonburg, KY 41653

YUROSKO, Steven G (Mont) Saint Andrew's Episcopal Church, 110 6th Ave, Polson, MT 59860

Z

✠ **ZABALA**, Artemio M (Los) 5048 Brunswick Dr, Fontana, CA 92336

ZABRISKIE JR, Alexander Clinton (Be) 119 Northshore Dr, Burlington, VT 05408

ZABRISKIE, Marek P (Pa) 212 Washington Ln, Fort Washington, PA 19034

ZACHARIA, Manoj M (SO) 318 E 4th St, Cincinnati, OH 45202

ZACHRITZ, John Louis (RG) 13 County Road 126, Espanola, NM 87532

ZACKER, John G (NY) 64 Weir Ln, Locust Valley, NY 11560

ZADIG SR, Alfred Thomas Kurt (WMass) 12 Briarwood Cir, Worcester, MA 01606

ZAHARIA, Paul Michael (ND) 301 Main St S, Minot, ND 58701

ZAHER, Holly Ann Rankin (Tenn)

ZAHL, John A (SC)

ZAHL, Paul Francis Matthew (WA) 506 N Dillard St, Winter Garden, FL 34787

ZAHN, Marianne (Los) St Wilfred Of York, 18631 Chapel Ln, Huntington Beach, CA 92646

ZAINA, Lisa (WA) 117 Oenoke Ridge, New Canaan, CT 06840

ZAISS, John Deforest (Nev) 7832 Magnolia Glen Ave, Las Vegas, NV 89128

ZAKRZEWSKI, Joy Lael (FdL) 2336 Canterbury Ln, Sister Bay, WI 54234

ZALESAK, Richard Joseph (Tenn) 1601 Campbell Ln, Galveston, TX 77551

ZALNERAITIS JR, Herbert Benedict (Mass) 93 Main St Apt 3, Brattleboro, VT 05301

ZAMBONI, Jack (NJ) 400 New Market Road, Dunellen, NJ 08812

ZAMBRANO RECALDE, Hugo Edmundo (Colom)

ZANETTI, Diane P (Be) 4484 Heron Dr, Reading, PA 19606

ZAPATA-GARCIA, Carlos Alberto (EcuC) Calle Hernando Sarmiento, N 39-54 Y Portete, Setor El Batan Quito, Ecuador

ZAPPA, Cathy C (At) Episc Ch Of The Holy Spirit, 724 Pilgrim Mill Rd, Cumming, GA 30040

ZARTMAN, Rebecca Ann (WA)

ZAUCHA, Scott Lybrand (Chi) 503 W. Jackson St., Woodstock, IL 60098

ZAYA, Lourdes (DR (DomRep))

ZEIGLER, Luther (Mass) Episcopal Chaplaincy At Harvard, 2 Garden St, Cambridge, MA 02138

ZEILFELDER, Eugene Walter (NJ) 10913 Trestles Rd, Frisco, TX 75035

ZELLER, Maggie (ETenn) 1108 Meadow Ln, Kingsport, TN 37663

ZELLERMAYER, Charles Clayton (Mil) 400 Garland Ct, Waukesha, WI 53188

ZELLEY III, Edmund W (NJ) 11 North Monroe Ave, Wenonah, NJ 08090

ZELLEY JR, Walt (NJ) P.O. Box 2, Copake Falls, NY 12517

ZELLNER, John Clement (USC) 230 Depot St, Tryon, NC 28782

ZEMAN, Andy (Ct) 135 Ball Farm Rd, Oakville, CT 06779

ZEPEDA PADILLA, Jorge Alberto (Hond)

ZEPHIER, Richard (SD) 1410 N Kline St, Aberdeen, SD 57401

ZEREN, Corby (Md)

ZETTINGER, Bill (SanD) 1920 Hamilton Ln, Escondido, CA 92029

ZEVALLOS, Guillermina Sara (Ga)

ZIEGENFUSS, Charles William (La) 2919 Saint Charles Ave, New Orleans, LA 70115

ZIEGENHINE, Kathleen Roach (NwPa) 458 E 23rd St, Erie, PA 16503

ZIEGLER, Sally McIntosh (Colo) 2205 Paseo Del Oro, Colorado Springs, CO 80904

ZIELINSKI, Frances Gertrude (Chi) 710 S Paulina St # 904, Chicago, IL 60612

ZIEMANN, Judith Jon (The Episcopal NCal) 5905 W. 30th Ave., Wheat Ridge, CO 80214

ZIFCAK, Patricia (Mass) 2100 County St Apt 31, South Attleboro, MA 02703

ZILE, Eric Neil (Md) 4500 C Dunton Terrace, Perry Hall, MD 21128

ZIMMERMAN, Aaron M G (Tex) 305 N 30th St, Waco, TX 76710

ZIMMERMAN, Curtis Roy (Oly) 11410 NE 124 St, #624, Kirkland, WA 98034

ZIMMERMAN, Douglas Lee (SwFla) 205 S. Occident St, Tampa, FL 33609

ZIMMERMAN, Gretchen Densmore (NJ) 410 S Atlantic Ave, Beach Haven, NJ 08008

ZIMMERMAN, Janet Whaley (WMass) PO Box 114, Great Barrington, MA 01230

ZIMMERMAN, Jervis Sharp (Ct) 400 Seabury Dr Apt 1106, Bloomfield, CT 06002

ZIMMERMAN, John Paul (Alb) 6459 Vosburgh Rd, Altamont, NY 12009

ZIMMERMAN, Stephen Francis (Colo) Grace and Saint Stephen's Church, 601 North Tejon St, Colorado Springs, CO 80903

ZIMMERMANN, Matt (Kan) 214 Laura Ln, Bastrop, TX 78602

ZIMMERSCHIED, Jill Whitney (Wyo) 202 12th St, Wheatland, WY 82201

ZINK, Jesse (WMass)

ZIOBRO, Albert Fredrick (WA) 3909 Albemarle St Nw, Washington, DC 20016

ZITO, Robert John Amadeus (NY) 95 Reade St, New York, NY 10013

ZITTLE, Twyla Jeanne (Colo) 2902 Airport Rd Apt 123, Colorado Springs, CO 80910

ZIVANOV, Elizabeth Ann (The Episcopal Church in Haw) 1515 Wilder Ave, Honolulu, HI 96822

ZLATIC, Martin William (SeFla) 6321 Lansdowne Cir, Boynton Beach, FL 33472

ZOGG, Jennifer G (RI) 1336 Pawtucket Ave., Rumford, RI 02916

ZOLLER, Joan Duncan (WMo) Po Box 967, Blue Springs, MO 64013

ZOLLICKOFFER, Joseph Paul (Md)

ZOOK, Aaron Gabriel (Eau) St Alban's Episcopal Church, PO Box 281, Spooner, WI 54801

ZOOK-JONES, Jill (USC) 6148 Rutledge Hill Road, Columbia, SC 29209

ZORAWICK, Joseph Marion (NY) 40 W 67th St, New York, NY 10023

ZORRILLA-BALSEIRO, Rafael (PR) PO Box 270196, San Juan, PR 00928

ZOTALIS, James (ND) 601 N 4th St, Bismarck, ND 58501

ZSCHEILE, Dwight J (Minn) 18 Crescent Lane, North Oaks, MN 55127

ZUBIETA, Augustin Teodoro (Pgh) 5660 Lonesome Dove Ct, Clifton, VA 20124

ZUBLER, Eric John (CGC) St James Episcopal Church, 860 N Section St, Fairhope, AL 36532

ZUG, Albert Edward Roussel (Pa) 2 E Spring Oak Cir, Media, PA 19063

ZULL, Aaron Beatty (Mich) 250 E Harbortown Dr, Detroit, MI 48207

ZUMPF, Michael (NC) 600 Morgan Rd, Eden, NC 27288

ZUST, Vicki Diane (WNY) 4289 Harris Hill Rd, Buffalo, NY 14221

ZWICK, Patricia Diane (Lex) 1337 Winchester Ave, Ashland, KY 41101

ZWIFKA, David Alan (Be) St Luke's Church, 22 S 6th St, Lebanon, PA 17042

ALPHABETICAL INDEX

Alphabetical Index

Alphabetical Index

Alphabetical Index

W

Index of Advertisers

We thank you for your support.

CLASSIFIED BUYER'S GUIDE

CLASSIFIED BUYER'S GUIDE

CLASSIFIED BUYER'S GUIDE

CLASSIFIED BUYER'S GUIDE